ISSN 0360-2699

BIBLIOGRAPHIC GUIDE TO

ART AND ARCHITECTURE 1991

Volume 1
A - J

G.K. HALL & CO.
70 Lincoln Street, Boston, Massachusetts

PREFACE

G.K. Hall *Bibliographic Guides* are comprehensive annual subject bibliographies. They bring together publications cataloged by The Research Libraries of The New York Public Library and the Library of Congress for thorough subject coverage. Included are works in all languages and all forms -- non-book materials as well as books and serials.

Bibliographic Guides provide complete LC cataloging information for each title, as well as ISBN and identification of NYPL holdings. Access is by main entry (personal author, corporate body, name of conference, etc.), added entries (co-authors, editors, compilers, etc.), titles, series titles and subject headings. All entries are integrated into one alphabetical sequence. Full bibliographic information, including tracings, is given in the main entry, with abbreviated or condensed citations for secondary entries. Subject headings appear in capital letters in bold-face type. Cataloging follows the *Anglo-American Cataloging Rules*. The following is a sample entry with full bibliographic information:

(a) **Rapoport, Anatol, 1911-** (b) N-person game theory; (c) concepts and applications. (d) Ann Arbor, (e) University of Michigan Press (f) (1970) (g) 331 p. (h) illus. 22 cm. (i) (Ann Arbor science library) (j) Bibliography: p. 317-320. (k) ISBN 0-472-00117-5 (l) LC Card 79-83451 (m) DDC 512/.8 (n) 1. Games of strategy (Mathematics).
(o) I. Title.
(p) *PA27O.R34 1970*   (q) **NYPL** (r) **[JSD 72-370]**

(a) Author's name.	(i) Series.
(b) Short, or main, title	(j) Note(s).
(c) Sub-title and/or other title page information.	(k) ISBN.
	(l) LC Card number.
(d) Place of Publication.	(m) DDC number.
(e) Publisher.	(n) Subject heading.
(f) Date of Publication.	(o) Added entry.
(g) Pagination.	(p) LC Call number.
(h) Illustration statement.	(q) NYPL indicator.
	(r) NYPL Classmark.

G.K. Hall *Bibliographic Guides* offer easy, multiple access to a wealth of material in each subject area. They serve as authoritative reference sources for librarians and

Preface

scholars, valuable technical aids for library acquisition and cataloging, and useful research tools for professionals.

Bibliographic Guides for 1991 are available in twenty-three fields:

Anthropology and Archaeology
Art and Architecture
Black Studies
Business and Economics
Computer Science
Conference Publications
Dance
East Asian Studies
Education
Environment
Government Publications--Foreign
Government Publications--U.S.

Latin American Studies
Law
Maps and Atlases
Microform Publications
Middle Eastern Studies
Music
North American History
Psychology
Soviet and East European Studies
Technology
Theatre Arts

They include material cataloged between September 1, 1990 and August 31, 1991.

INTRODUCTION

The *Bibliographic Guide to Art and Architecture* lists publications cataloged during the past year by The Research Libraries of The New York Public Library and the Library of Congress. It also serves as an annual supplement to the *Dictionary Catalog of the Art and Architecture Division*, The Research Libraries of The New York Public Library (G. K. Hall & Co., 1975).

The New York Public Library's Art and Architecture Division contains one of the world's largest research collections in the fine and applied arts. The scope of the collection includes painting, drawing, sculpture, and the history of design aspects of architecture and the applied arts from the prehistoric and primitive to the latest art movements. Within these subject areas the Division aims to be comprehensive and collects intensively in all languages. All titles cataloged during the past year and held by the Art and Architecture Division are included in this *Guide*.

Entries from LC MARC tapes have been selected from the following subject areas:

- Painting (including watercolor painting, mural painting, illuminating of manuscripts and books)
- Printing (including print making and engraving, etching and aquatint, serigraphy and lithography)
- Decorative arts, Applied arts, Decoration and Ornament (including interior decorating, ceramics, pottery, costume and textile arts)
- Visual arts (including the history of art, art criticism, examination and conservation of art and public art)
- Architecture (including history, architectural design and drawing, aesthetics of cities, city planning and beautification)
- Sculpture
- Drawing, Design, Illustration (including commercial art and advertising art posters)

Selection of titles from LC MARC tapes is based on the LC Classification *X*.

A. A. S. see **Association for Asian Studies.**

A.B. Mullett . Smith, Daisy M. (Daisy Mullett)
Washington, D.C. , c1990. xii, 128 p. : ISBN
0-9611410-2-6 (hardcover) DDC 720/.92 20
NA737.M78 S65 1990

A. F. A. see **American Federation of Arts.**

A. G. M. A. N. Z. see **Art Galleries and
Museums Association of New Zealand.**

A. I. A. see **American Institute of Architects.**

A. Kertész, photographer /. Kertész, André. New
York , c1964. 63 p. : DDC 779
TR140.K4 S9
              NYPL [MFX (Kertész) 91-993]

A: le livre d'A. Pierson, Jean Marie. Metz [1977]
25 [i. e. 108] p.   *NYPL [MEMZ 91-2514]*

A. M. Adler Fine Arts Inc. Cubists in Paris
(1910-1956) . New York [1978] [8] p. :
                      NYPL [3-MAL 91-7004]

A. Marx. Marx, Antônio Augusto, 1919- Antônio
Augusto Marx, o pintor da natureza /. [Rio de
Janeiro, Brazil] , c1988. 127 p. : DDC 759.981
20
ND359.M359 A4 1988
                NYPL [3-MCZ M392 90-10880]

A Nekcsei-Biblia legszebb lapjai. Nekcsei-Lipócz
Bible. Budapest , Washington , 1988. 231 [5]
p. : ISBN 963-207-955-8
IN PROCESS (ONLINE) Rare Bk Coll
                            NYPL [JFH 91-4]

**A propos du livre d'instructions nautiques de Pīrī
Re'is [microform]** /. Soucek, Svatopluk. Paris ,
1973. p. [241]-255 ;
                      NYPL [Map Div. 87-1191]

"a.r.", mit urzeczywistniony . Płauszewski,
Andrzej. Łódź , 1989. 156 p. : ISBN
83-218-0237-0 *NYPL [3-MAM 90-11923]*

A.R. Penck, Keramik. Penck A. R., 1939- Berlin ,
c1989. 1 v. (unpaged) :
NK4210.P446 A4 1989

A.R. Penck, Venice paintings. Penck A. R., 1939-
Santa Monica , c1989. [33] p. : ISBN
0-927442-00-0
                  NYPL [3-MCK+ P41 91-7059]

A.T. Schaefer . Schaefer, Albert T., 1944-
Heidelberg , c1991. 96 p. : ISBN 3-925835-78-4
                  NYPL [MFX+ (Schaefer) 91-7672]

The A. W. Mellon lectures in the fine arts.
(1988) Shearman, John K. G. Only connect .
Princeton, N.J. , 1992. p. cm. ISBN
0-691-09972-3 (CL) : DDC 709/.45/09024 20
N6915 .S54 1992

**A.W.N. Pugin and the revival of memorial
brasses** /. Meara, David, 1947- London , New
York , 1991. p. cm. ISBN 0-7201-2070-5 : DDC
739.5/22/092 20
NK7898.P84 M43 1991

Aachen. Neue Galerie. see **Neue Galerie, Aachen.**

Aachener Kunstblätter. Kleine Reihe .
(Bd. 12) Sammlung Teo Matthéy, Aachen .
[Aachen] , c1989. 109 p.
                  NYPL [3-MAX (Matthéy) 91-3454]

AALTO, ALVAR, 1898-1976.
Pearson, Paul David, 1936- Alvar Aalto and the
International style /. London , 1989, c1978.
240 p. : ISBN 0-7134-6300-7 (pbk) DDC
720/.92/4 19
NA1455.F53A2
                  NYPL [3-MQZ+ (Aalto) 90-10795]

Schildt, Göran, 1917- [Mänskliga faktorn.
English.] Alvar Aalto, the mature years /. New
York , 1991. 328 p. : ISBN 0-8478-1329-0 DDC
720/.92 B 20
NA1455.F53 A23725 1991

Aarau, Switzerland. Aargauer Kunsthaus. see
Aargauer Kunsthaus.

Aargauer Kunsthaus. Ballmer, Karl. Karl Ballmer,
1891-1958 . Aarau , Baden , c1990. 167 p. :
ISBN 3-906700-34-8 DDC 759.9494 20
ND853.B34 A4 1990

Aaron Siskind, photographs . Siskind, Aaron.
[Milwaukee, Wis. , 1971] [28] p. :
                      NYPL [MFX (Siskind) 90-7107]

AARP, Art and archaeology research papers.
El-Khoury, Fouad. Domestic architecture in the
Lebanon /. London [1975] 25 p. :
                      NYPL [3-MRG 90-12551]

Abakanowicz, Magdalena.
Inkarnationen : [Austellung] 9. August bis 17.
September 1988 / Magdalena Abakanowicz.
Zürich : Turske & Turske, Mühle
Tiefenbrunnen, c1988. 67 p. : ill. ; 26 cm.
*1. Abakanowicz, Magdalena - Exhibitions. I. Turske &
Turske. II. Title.*
MLCM 90-03313 (N)
          NYPL [3-MGO (Abakanowicz) 90-10621]

Magdalena Abakanowicz : recent work :
October 20-November 25, 1989. New York,
N.Y. : Marlborough Gallery, c1989. 80 p. : ill. ;
30 cm. Bibliography: p. 78-80.
1. Abakanowicz, Magdalena - Exhibitions. I. Title.
              *NYPL [3-MGO+ (Abakanowicz)
                                    90-12367]*

**ABAKANOWICZ, MAGDALENA -
EXHIBITIONS.**
Abakanowicz, Magdalena. Inkarnationen .
Zürich , c1988. 67 p. :
MLCM 90-03313 (N)
          NYPL [3-MGO (Abakanowicz) 90-10621]

Abakanowicz, Magdalena. Magdalena
Abakanowicz . New York, N.Y. , c1989. 80 p. :
              *NYPL [3-MGO+ (Abakanowicz)
                                    90-12367]*

Aballéa, François. Benjamin, Isabelle. Evolution
de la professionnalité des architectes . Paris
[1990] 109 p. ; ISBN 2-11-085420-0 :
NA1996 .B46 1990

Abbate, Vincenzo.
Pittori del Seicento a Palazzo Abatellis /.
Milano , c1990. 192 p. : ISBN 88-435-3177-8
                      NYPL [3-MC 91-7058]

Il "Trionfo della morte" di Palermo . Palermo ,
c1989. 88 p., [62] p. of plates : ISBN
88-7681-040-4   *NYPL [3-MLP 90-11764]*

ABBAYE DE LIESSIES.
Etude du site de l'Abbaye de Liessies /.
[Fourmies, France] [1984] [82] leaves : DDC
726/.7/094428 19
NA5551.L4693 E88 1984
                  NYPL [3-MRBB+ 90-12771]

ABBAYE DE ROYAUMONT.
Goüin, Henry. Royaumont . [Paris] , c1990. 94
p. : ISBN 2-905674-28-3 DDC 726/.7/0944367 20
NA5551.R65 G64 1990

**ABBAYE DE SAINT-DENIS (SAINT-DENIS,
FRANCE)**
Blum, Pamela Z. Early Gothic Saint-Denis .
Berkeley , 1992. p. cm. ISBN 0-520-07371-1
(cloth) DDC 730/.944/362 20
NB1910 .B58 1992

Crosby, Sumner McK. (Sumner McKnight),
1909- The Royal Abbey of Saint-Denis . New
Haven , c1987. xxiii, 525 p., 3 folded leaves of
plates : ISBN 0-300-03143-2 (alk. paper) DDC
726/.5/0944362 19
NA5551.S214 C76 1987
                      NYPL [3-MRBB 91-6920]

**Abbaye Sainte-Croix (Les Sables-d'Olonne,
France). Musée.**
Brauner, Victor, 1903-1966. Les Victor Brauner
de la collection de l'Abbaye Sainte-Croix /. Les
Sables d'Olonne , c1991. 126 p. : ISBN
2-901432-69-7 DDC 759.4 20
ND553.B873 A4 1991

La collection d'art moderne et contemporain :
Musée de l'Abbaye Sainte-Croix, Les Sables
d'Olonne / [direction et conception du
catalogue, Didier Ottinger]. Les Sables
d'Olonne : Le Musée, c1990. 253 p. : col. ill. ;
23 cm. Includes bibliographical references (p.
251-253). ISBN 2-901432-67-0 DDC
709/.44/0744461 20
*1. Art, French - Catalogs. 2. Art, Modern - 20th
century - France - Catalogs. 3. Art - France - Les
Sables d'Olonne - Catalogs. 4. Abbaye Sainte-Croix
(Les Sables d'Olonne) Musée - Catalogs. I. Ottinger,
Didier. II. Title.*
N6848 .A58 1990

**ABBAYE SAINTE-CROIX (LES SABLES-
D'OLONNE, FRANCE). MUSÉE -
EXHIBITIONS.**
Brauner, Victor, 1903-1966. Les Victor Brauner
de la collection de l'Abbaye Sainte-Croix /. Les
Sables d'Olonne , c1991. 126 p. : ISBN
2-901432-69-7 DDC 759.4 20
ND553.B873 A4 1991

**ABBAYE SAINTE-CROIX (LES SABLES
D'OLONNE) MUSÉE - CATALOGS.**
Abbaye Sainte-Croix (Les Sables-d'Olonne,
France). Musée. La collection d'art moderne et
contemporain . Les Sables d'Olonne , c1990.
253 p. : ISBN 2-901432-67-0 DDC
709/.44/0744461 20
N6848 .A58 1990

ABBAZIA DI CASAMARI.
Farina, Federico. L'architettura cistercense e
l'Abbazia di Casamari /. Casamari , 1981,
c1978. xii, 187 p. : DDC 726/.7/0945622 19
NA5621.A22 F37 1981
                      NYPL [3-MRBD+ 90-12587]

**ABBAZIA DI S. PAOLO FUORI LE MURA
(ROME, ITALY)**
San Paolo fuori le mura a Roma /. Firenze ,
c1988. 336 p. : ISBN 88-404-1201-8
                      NYPL [3-MRBD+ 90-12663]

**ABBAZIA DI SAN MARTINO AL CIMINO -
HISTORY.**
Petrucci, Giulia. San Martino al Cimino
(Viterbo, III) /. Roma , 1987 [i.e. 1988] 73 p. :
ISBN 88-7597-033-5 (pbk.)
                      NYPL [Map Div. 88-1082]

Abbeville modern art movements.
Koplos, Janet. Contemporary Japanese sculpture
/. New York , 1991. p. cm. ISBN 1-558-59012-9
DDC 730/.952/09045 20
NB1055 .K66 1991

ABBEYS - ENGLAND - HISTORY.
Coppack, Glyn. English Heritage book of
abbeys and priories /. London , 1990. 159 p.,
[8] p. of plates : ISBN 0-7134-6308-2 (cased) :
DDC 942 20   *NYPL [3-MRBR 91-6767]*

L'abbigliamento popolare italiano / a cura di
Glauco Sanga ; [saggi di M.A. Arrigoni ... [et
al.] ; interventi di R. Bertani, P.G. Fabbri, M.
Fincardi , rasseghe di P. Clemente, G. Sanga].
Brescia : Grafo, [1986] 160 p. : ill., ports. ; 27
cm. (La ricerca folklorica : contributi allo studio della
cultura delle classi popolari, 0391-9099 . n. 14 (ottobre
1986)) Summaries in English. Includes bibliographies.
CONTENTS. - L'abbigliamento popolare italiano /
Elisabetta Silvestrini -- Costumi in cartolina / Gian
Paolo Gri -- Studiare il costume / Giuseppe Šebesta --
L'abbigliamento tradizionale femminile di Grosio /
Fabrizio Caltagirone -- La trasformazione
dell'abbigliamento rurale Cozzo Lomellina (1900-1945)
/ Maria Antonietta Arrigoni -- I colori delle vesti /
Serenella Baggio.
*1. Costume - Italy - History. I. Sanga, Glauco. II.
Silvestrini, Elisabetta. III. Arrigoni, Maria Antonietta.
IV. Bertani, Riccardo. V. Fabbri, Pier Giovanni. VI.
Clemente, Pietro. VII. Fincardi, Marco. VIII. Sanga,
Glauco. IX. Series: La Ricerca folklorica , 14.*
                      NYPL [3-MMO 90-8664]

Abbot Hall Art Gallery. 20th century Scottish
painting . [London?] , 1963. [21] p. :
                      NYPL [3-MCT 91-410]

Abbott, Berenice, 1898-
Berenice Abbott, photographer : a modern
vision : a selection of photographs and essays /
edited, with introductions and checklist by Julia
Van Haaften.1st ed. [New York] : New York
Public Library, 1989. 95 p. : ill. ; 30 cm. Catalog
of an exhibition held at the New York Public Library,
Oct. 7, 1989-Jan. 6, 1990, and at four other museums.
Includes bibliographical references (p. [92]-[94]).
ISBN 0-87104-420-X (pbk.)
*1. Abbott, Berenice, 1898- - Exhibitions. 2. New York
Public Library - Photograph collections - Exhibitions. 3.
Photography, Artistic - Exhibitions. I. Van Haaften,
Julia. II. Title.*
                  NYPL [MFX+ (Abbott) 91-3494]

ABBOTT, BERENICE, 1898- - EXHIBITIONS.
Abbott, Berenice, 1898- Berenice Abbott,
photographer . [New York] , 1989. 95 p. :
ISBN 0-87104-420-X (pbk.)
                  NYPL [MFX+ (Abbott) 91-3494]

Abbott, Berenice, 1891- New guide to better
photography / Berenice Abbott. Rev. ed. New
York : Crown, c1953. vii, 180 p., [41] leaves of
plates : ill. ; 26 cm. Includes index. Bibliography: p.
176-177.
*1. Photography - Technique. I. Title. II. Title: Better
photography.*   *NYPL [MFW 91-5017]*

Abbozzo, Edgardo. Arte orafa e iconografia
dionisiaca . [Italy , 1987] 88 p. :
                      NYPL [3-MNO+ 89-27461]

'Abd al-Jawād, Tawfīq Aḥmad. Tārīkh al-'imārah / Tawfīq Aḥmad 'Abd al-Jawād. [al-Ṭab'ah 1.]. S.l. : Jāmi'at al-Azhar, Kulliyat al-Handasah, [1968-<1969] > v. <1-2 > : ill. ; 28 cm. Includes bibliographical references. CONTENTS. - 1. al-Funūn fī al-'uṣūr al-ūlá -- 2. al-'Uṣūr al-Mutawassiṭah, al-Ūrūbbiyah wa-al-Islāmiyah.
1. Architecture - History. I. Title.
NA200 .A24

Abdallah Benanteur . Benanteur, Abdallah, 1931- [Alger] [1989] 141 p. :
NE2087.65.B45 A4 1989

ABEDIN, ZAINUL - CRITICISM AND INTERPRETATION.
Jahangir, Burhanuddin Khan. Jayanula Abedinera jijñāsā /. Ḍhākā , 1990. 82 p., [14] p. of plates :
N7310.8.B25 J344 1990

Abel, Chris. Renault centre : Swindon, 1982 : architect, Norman Foster / text, Chris Abel ; photographs, Dennis Gilbert. London : Architecture Design and Technology Press ; New York : Van Nostrand Reinhold, 1991. [60] p. : ill. (some col.), plans ; 30 cm. (Architecture in detail . 04) ISBN 1-85454-776-3 (pbk.) : DDC 720.92 20
1. Foster, Norman, 1935- - Criticism and interpretation. I. Title. II. Series.
NA997.F6
NYPL [3-MQZ+ (Foster) 91-6980]

Abel, Louis. Kembs en Sundgau rhénan : l'Eglise et l'architecte du XVIIIème siècle : François-Antoine Zeller, 1740-1816, et son activité en Haute-Alsace / par Louis Abel ; préface de Léon Hégélé ; notes de lecture de Georges Livet ; postface de Yves Ayrault et de Frédérick Luckel. [Kembs, France] : Association du souvenir de l'Eglise St-Jean-Baptiste de Kembs, c1986. 285 p. : ill. ; 24 cm. (Collection "Recherches et documents" / Société savante d'Alsace et des régions de l'Est, 0583-8836 . t. 36) Spine title: Kembs. Errata slip laid in. Includes bibliographical references and index.
1. Zeller, François-Antoine, 1740-1816 - Criticism and interpretation. 2. Church architecture - France - Kembs. 3. Architecture, German - France - Kembs. 4. Eglise St-Jean-Baptiste de Kembs (Kembs, France). 5. Kembs (France) - Buildings, structures, etc. 6. Church architecture - France - Alsace. I. Title. II. Title: Kembs. III. Series: Publications de la Société savante d'Alsace et des régions de l'Est. Collection "Recherches et documents" , t. 36.
NA1053.Z45 A83 1986

Abell, Sam. The Civil War : an aerial portrait / photography by Sam Abell ; text by Brian Pohanka. Charlottesville, Va. : Thomasson-Grant, c1990. 144 p. : ill. (some col.), ports. ; 27 x 32 cm. ISBN 0-934738-61-0 : DDC 779/.99737 20
1. United States - History - Civil War, 1861-1865 - Aerial photographs. I. Pohanka, Brian C., 1955-. II. Title.
E468.7 .A23 1990
NYPL [MFX+ (Abell) 91-2378]

Abercrombie, Douglas, 1934-
Fruit Market Gallery. Four abstract artists . Edinburgh , 1977. [14] p. : ISBN 0-902989-44-8
ND479 .F78 1977 **NYPL [3-MCT 79-734]**

ABERCROMBIE, DOUGLAS, 1934- - EXHIBITIONS.
Fruit Market Gallery. Four abstract artists . Edinburgh , 1977. [14] p. : ISBN 0-902989-44-8
ND479 .F78 1977 **NYPL [3-MCT 79-734]**

ABERCROMBIE, GERTRUDE, 1909-1977 - EXHIBITIONS.
Gertrude Abercrombie . Springfield, IL , 1991. p. cm. ISBN 0-89792-132-1 DDC 759.13 20
ND237.A235 A4 1991

Abildgaard, Nicolai, 1743-1809.
Andersen, Jørgen, 1922- De år i Rom . København , 1989. 301 p. : ISBN 87-7241-576-2 :
ND723.A2 A86 1989

ABILDGAARD, NICOLAI, 1743-1809 - FRIENDS AND ASSOCIATES.
Andersen, Jørgen, 1922- De år i Rom . København , 1989. 301 p. : ISBN 87-7241-576-2 :
ND723.A2 A86 1989

ABILDGAARD, NOCOLAI, 1743-1809 - JOURNEYS - ITALY - ROME.

Andersen, Jørgen, 1922- De år i Rom . København , 1989. 301 p. : ISBN 87-7241-576-2 :
ND723.A2 A86 1989

Abinade, José, 1922- El color humano : 20 pintores venezolanos / José Abinade. Caracas : Academia Nacional de la Historia, 1990. 170 p. ; 20 cm. (El libro menor. 167) ISBN 980-222-520-7 DDC 759.987 B 20
1. Painting, Venezuelan. 2. Painting, Modern - 20th century - Venezuela. 3. Painters - Venezuela - Biography. I. Title.
ND435 .A24 1990

Gli abiti di Carlo Crivelli . Crivelli, Carlo, 15th cent. [Ancona] [1990] 110 p. :
NYPL [3-MCF+ C93 91-5435]

Abner Cook . Hafertepe, Kenneth, 1955- Austin , c1991. p. cm. ISBN 0-87611-102-9 (cloth) DDC 720/.92 B 20
NA737.C66 H3 1991

Aboriginal art and spirituality / edited by Rosemary Crumlin ; collection curated by Rosemary Crumlin and Anthony Knight. North Blackburn, Vic. : Collins Dove, 1991. 151 p. : ill. ; 24 cm. ISBN 0-85924-998-0
1. Art, Australian (Aboriginal) - Exhibitions. I. Crumlin, Rosemary, 1932-. **NYPL [3-MADF+ 91-6923]**

ABORIGINES. see ETHNOLOGY.

Abou-El-Haj, Rifa'at Ali. The Ottoman city and its parts . New Rochelle, N.Y. , 1991. p. cm. ISBN 0-89241-473-1 DDC 307.76/09561 20
NA9229 .O87 1991

About looking /. Berger, John. New York , 1991. p. ISBN 0-679-73655-7 (pbk.) : DDC 701/.15 20
N71 .B398 1991

About two [squares]. Lissitzky, El, 1890-1941. [Suprematicheskii skaz. English.] About 2 [squares] /. Cambridge, Mass. , 1991. p. cm. ISBN 0-262-12158-1 DDC 709/.2 20
N6988.5.S9 L5713 1991

About 2 [squares] /. Lissitzky, El, 1890-1941. [Suprematicheskii skaz. English.] Cambridge, Mass. , 1991. p. cm. ISBN 0-262-12158-1 DDC 709/.2 20
N6988.5.S9 L5713 1991

Abracadabra . Charchoune, Serge, 1888-1975. [Paris , 1971] [47] p. : DDC 700/.92 20
N6853.C4715 A4 1971

Abramovič, Marina, 1946-
Marina Abramović, Ulay . Paris , c1990. 2 v. : ISBN 2-85850-550-0 (ed. complète)
NYPL [3-MCZ A161 91-7250]

ABRAMOVIČ, MARINA, 1946- - EXHIBITIONS.
Marina Abramović, Ulay . Paris , c1990. 2 v. : ISBN 2-85850-550-0 (ed. complète)
NYPL [3-MCZ A161 91-7250]

Abrams, Erika. Kupka, František, 1871-1957. La création dans les arts plastiques /. Paris , c1989. 302 p. : ISBN 2-7022-0227-6
N72.5 .K86 1989

Abrioux, Yves. Finlay, Ian Hamilton. Homage to Ian Hamilton Finlay . London [1987] 22 p., 22 p. of plates : **NYPL [MEMZ 91-2445]**

Abruzzes Molise romans / Paolo Favole, architecte ; avec la collaboration de Francesca Del Vitto ; photographies inédites de Zodiaque. La Pierre-qui-Vire (Yonne) : Zodiaque, 1990. 304 p. : ill. (some col.), plans ; 23 cm. (La Nuit des temps, 0768-0937 . 74) Includes index. ISBN 2-7369-0182-7
1. Art, Romanesque - Italy - Abruzzi. 2. Architecture, Romanesque - Italy - Abruzzi. 3. Church architecture - Italy - Abruzzi. 4. Art, Romanesque - Italy - Molise. 5. Architecture, Romanesque - Italy - Molise. 6. Church architecture - Italy - Molise. I. Favole, Paolo. II. Del Vitto, Francesca. III. Series.
NYPL [3-MQWB 91-4524]

ABSTRACT ART. see ART, ABSTRACT.

Abstract expressionism : creators and critics : an anthology / edited and with an introduction by Clifford Ross. New York : Abrams, 1990. 304 p. : ill. (some col.) ; 26 cm. Includes index. ISBN 0-8109-1908-7 : DDC 709/.73/09045 20
1. Abstract expressionism - United States. 2. Art, Modern - 20th century - United States. I. Ross, Clifford, 1952-.
N6512.5.A25 A24 1990
NYPL [3-MAMT 91-6467]

Abstract expressionism /. Anfam, David. London , c1990. 216 p. : ISBN 0-500-20243-5
NYPL [3-MAMT 91-4276]

Abstract Expressionism and the modern experience /. Polcari, Stephen. Cambridge [England] , New York , 1991. xxiii, 408 p. : ISBN 0-521-40453-3 (hardback) DDC 700/.973/0904 20
NX504 .P65 1991

ABSTRACT EXPRESSIONISM - AUSTRIA - VIENNA - EXHIBITIONS.
Der Zertrümmerte Spiegel . Klagenfurt , 1989. 392 p. : ISBN 3-85415-062-8
NYPL [3-MAL 91-7188]

ABSTRACT EXPRESSIONISM - NEW YORK (N.Y.)
Gibson, Ann Eden, 1944- Issues in abstract expressionism . Ann Arbor, Mich. , c1990. xvi, 430 p. : ISBN 0-8357-1944-8 (alk. paper) DDC 709.747/1/09044 20
N6535.N5 G53 1989
NYPL [3-MAMT 90-11594]

O'Hara, Frank. Art chronicles, 1954-1966 /. New York [1975] 165 p. : ISBN 0-8076-0755-X : DDC 709/.747/109045 20
N6535.N5 O37 1975
NYPL [MAMT 75-525]

ABSTRACT EXPRESSIONISM - NEW YORK (N.Y.) - PRIVATE COLLECTIONS - EXHIBITIONS.
The Vincent Melzac collection. Washington, D.C. [1971] 102 p. **NYPL [3-MCW 90-6402]**

ABSTRACT EXPRESSIONISM - UNITED STATES.
Abstract expressionism . New York , 1990. 304 p. : ISBN 0-8109-1908-7 : DDC 709/.73/09045 20
N6512.5.A25 A24 1990
NYPL [3-MAMT 91-6467]

Anfam, David. Abstract expressionism /. London , c1990. 216 p. : ISBN 0-500-20243-5
NYPL [3-MAMT 91-4276]

Cernuschi, Claude, 1961- Jackson Pollock . New York, NY , c1992. p. ISBN 0-06-430978-9 (cloth) : DDC 759.13 20
ND237.P73 C47 1992

Doss, Erika Lee. Benton, Pollock, and the politics of modernism . Chicago , 1991. p. cm. ISBN 0-226-15942-6 (alk. paper) DDC 759.13 20
ND237.B47 D67 1991

ABSTRACT EXPRESSONISM - UNITED STATES.
Polcari, Stephen. Abstract Expressionism and the modern experience /. Cambridge [England] , New York , 1991. xxiii, 408 p. : ISBN 0-521-40453-3 (hardback) DDC 700/.973/0904 20
NX504 .P65 1991

ABSTRACT PAINTING. see PAINTING, ABSTRACT.

ABSTRACT PHOTOGRAPHY. see PHOTOGRAPHY, ABSTRACT.

Abstraction : Art Gallery of New South Wales, 2 June-8 July 1990 / Marion Borgelt ... [et al.] ; curated by Victoria Lynn. Sydney : The Gallery, 1990. 48 p. : ill. (some col.) ; 27 cm. Includes bibliographical references. ISBN 0-7305-7696-5
1. Art, Abstract - Australia - Exhibitions. I. Borgelt, Marion, 1954-. II. Lynn, Victoria. III. Art Gallery of New South Wales. **NYPL [3-MAM 91-3723]**

Abstraction, figuration . Degand, Léon. Paris , c1988. 273 p. : ISBN 2-7022-0226-8
ND1290 .D44 1988

ABSTRACTION IN PHOTOGRAPHY. see PHOTOGRAPHY, ABSTRACT.

Abstractions. Gianella, Victor, 1918- Victor Gianella . [Ennetbaden] , c1988. 1 v. (unpaged) : ISBN 3-908028-07-3
NYPL [MFX (Gianella) 91-2650]

The absurd world of Charles Bragg /. Bragg, Charles. New York , c1991. p. cm. ISBN 1-559-70130-7 (HC) : DDC 741.5/092 20
NC1429.B733 A4 1991

ABTEI FRAUENWÖRTH.
Dannheimer, Hermann. Torhalle auf Frauenchiemsee . München , 1983, c1980. 118

p. : ISBN 3-7954-0818-0
NYPL [3-MRBB 91-6996]

ABTEI MARIA LAACH.
Dölling, Regine. Das Stiftergrabmal in Maria Laach /. Worms , c1990. 73 p. : ISBN 3-88462-069-X
NB1870 .D6 1990

Abū al-'Ulá, Muḥammad Farīd. al-Maskan al-rīfī al-Miṣrī : al-taṭawwur al-'imrānī, al-taṭawwur al-wazifī / ta'līf Muḥammad Farīd Abū al-'Ulá. al-Qāhirah : 'Alam al-Kutub, 1990. 231, 3, 11 p. : ill., maps ; 25 cm. Summary in English. Originally presented as the author's thesis (master's-- Jāmi'at al-Azhar, Cairo, 1989) under title: al-Maskan al-rīfī bayna al-taghyīr wa-al-taṭwīr. Includes bibliographical references (p. 228-231). ISBN 977-373-128-6 :
I. Title. II. Title: Maskan al-rīfī bayna al-taghyīr wa-al-taṭwīr. III. Title: Egyptian rural house.
NA7463.A1 A28 1990

ACA Galleries.
Primitive art of Papua New Guinea . New York , c1989. 31 p. : ISBN 0-925315-01-X (pbk.)
NYPL [3-MADF+ 89-20654]

Teichman, Sabina. Catalogue of an exhibition of paintings by Sabina Teichman . New York [1969] [8] p. :
NYPL [3-MCX T262 91-4230]

ACADEMIA ESPAÑOLA DE BELLAS ARTES EN ROMA.
Casado Alcalde, Esteban. Pintores de la Academia de Roma . [Madrid] , Barcelona [1990] 331 p. : ISBN 84-7782-088-0
NYPL [3-MCP+ 91-7960]

Academia Nacional de Bellas Artes (Argentina)
Academia Nacional de Bellas Artes, 1936-1986 . [Buenos Aires , 1987] 119 p. : DDC 709/.82/0748211 20
N6635 .A53 1987

Academia Nacional de Bellas Artes, 1936-1986 : catálogo de la exposición : Salas Nacionales de Exposición, Buenos Aires, junio-julio 1987. [Buenos Aires : La Academia, 1987] 119 p. : ill. (some col.) ; 23 x 26 cm. Includes bibliographies. DDC 709/.82/0748211 20
1. Art, Argentine - Exhibitions. 2. Art, Modern - 20th century - Argentina - Exhibitions. I. Academia Nacional de Bellas Artes (Argentina).
N6635 .A53 1987

Académie de Bruxelles : deux siècles d'architecture / [direction scientifique, Jean-Paul Midant ; textes, Jean-Charles Balty ... et al.]. Bruxelles : Archives d'architecture moderne, 1989. 541 p. : ill. (some col.) ; 30 cm. Includes bibliographical references. ISBN 2-87143-063-2
1. Académie royale des beaux-arts de Bruxelles. 2. Architecture - Study and teaching - Belgium - Brussels. 3. Architects - Belgium. I. Midant, Jean-Paul. II. Balty, Jean Ch. *NYPL [3-MQF+ 90-133]*

Académie de France à Rome. Braque, Georges, 1882-1963. Braque . Roma [1974] 40, [140] p. :
ND553.B86 L44
NYPL [3-MCO B821 81-286]

ACADÉMIE DES BEAUX-ARTS (FRANCE)
The French Academy . Newark : London ; 231 p. : ISBN 0-87413-343-2 (alk. paper) DDC 706/.044 19
N332.F83 P345 1990
NYPL [3-MAMI 90-11304]

Académie des Sciences Agricoles, Sofia. see Akademiiā na selskostopanskite nauki.

ACADÉMIE FRANÇAISE - HISTORY.
Hall, H. Gaston. Richelieu's Desmarets and the century of Louis XIV /. Oxford , New York , 1990. 399 p. : ISBN 0-19-815157-8 : DDC 841/.4 B 20
PQ1794.D6 H35 1990
NYPL [3-MAVZ (Hamburg) 91-3450]

ACADÉMIE ROYALE DES BEAUX-ARTS DE BRUXELLES.
Académie de Bruxelles . Bruxelles , 1989. 541 p. : ISBN 2-87143-063-2
NYPL [3-MQF+ 90-133]

Academy of Agricultural Sciences, Sofia. see Akademiiā na selskostopanskite nauki.

Academy of Sciences of the Estonian S. S. R. see Eesti NSV Teaduste Akadeemia.

Acadian hard times . Doty, C. Stewart (Charles Stewart) Orono, Me. , 1991. xiv, 184 p. : ISBN 0-89101-070-X DDC 338.1/09741/1 20
HD1775.M2 D67 1991
NYPL [MFW 91-7984]

Acanto (Madrid, Spain)
Rof Carballo, Juan. Los duendes del Prado /. Madrid [1990?] 376 p. : ISBN 84-239-5300-9 DDC 709/.4/0744641 20
N8217.F28 R64 1990

Acatos, Sylvio. Claire Nicole : passage des formes / par Sylvio Acatos. Lausanne : Editions Vie Art Cité, c1988. 88 p. : ill. (some col.) ; 27 cm. Includes bibliographical references.
1. Nicole, Claire, 1941- - Criticism and interpretation. I. Nicole, Claire, 1941-. II. Title.
NYPL [3-MCZ N642 89-27917]

Accademia Carrara /. Accademia Carrara. [Cinisello Balsamo, Milano] , c1988- v. : ISBN 88-366-0235-5 (v. 1)
NYPL [3-MAVZ (Bergamo) 90-2272]

Accademia Carrara.
Accademia Carrara / Francesco Rossi. [Cinisello Balsamo, Milano] : Silvana, c1988- v. : ill. (some col.) ; 28 cm. Cover title: Accademia Carrara, Bergamo. Includes bibliographical references and indexes. CONTENTS. - 1. Catalogo dei dipinti sec. XV-XVI -- 2. Catalogo dei dipinti sec. XVII-XVIII ISBN 88-366-0235-5 (v. 1)
1. Accademia Carrara - Catalogs. 2. Painting - Italy - Bergamo - Catalogs. I. Rossi, Francesco. II. Title. III. Title: Accademia Carrara, Bergamo.
NYPL [3-MAVZ (Bergamo) 90-2272]

Giovanni Morelli da collezionista a conoscitore . [Bergamo] , c1987. 79 p. :
NYPL [3-MAX (Morelli) 90-10868]

Accademia Carrara, Bergamo. Accademia Carrara. Accademia Carrara /. [Cinisello Balsamo, Milano] , c1988- v. : ISBN 88-366-0235-5 (v. 1)
NYPL [3-MAVZ (Bergamo) 90-2272]

ACCADEMIA CARRARA - CATALOGS.
Accademia Carrara. Accademia Carrara /. [Cinisello Balsamo, Milano] , c1988- v. : ISBN 88-366-0235-5 (v. 1)
NYPL [3-MAVZ (Bergamo) 90-2272]

Accademia di belle arti di Bologna. Crespi, Giuseppe Maria, 1665-1747. Giuseppe Maria Crespi, 1665-1747 . [Bologna] , c1990. ccxvi, 278 p. : ISBN 88-7779-148-9
NYPL [3-MCF C922 91-5467]

Accademia di Francia. see Académie de France à Rome.

Accademia di San Luca, Roma. see Accademia nazionale di San Luca.

Accademia ligustica di belle arti. Il Genio di Giovanni Benedetto Castiglione, il Grechetto /. Genova , c1990. 267 p. : ISBN 88-7058-351-1
NYPL [3-MCF C35 90-11510]

Accademia nazionale di San Luca.
I Premiati dell'Accademia, 1682-1754 /. Roma , c1989. 189 p. : ISBN 88-7140-010-0
NYPL [3-MBH 91-4486]

Prize winning drawings from the Roman Academy 1682-1754 =. Roma , c1990. 189 p. : ISBN 88-7140-013-5
NYPL [3-MBH 91-5071]

Scarpa, Carlo. Carlo Scarpa . Roma [1979] 48 p. :
MLCM 80/569 (N)
NYPL [3-MQZ (Scarpa) 90-5860]

Accademia nazionale di San Luca. Archivio Storico.
I disegni di figura nell'Archivio storico dell'Accademia di San Luca / a cura di Angela Cipriano e Enrico Valeriani ; con un saggio di Olivier Michel. Roma : Quasar, 1988- v. : ill. ; 30 cm. Includes bibliographical references. CONTENTS. - 1. Concorsi e accademie del secolo xvii -- 2. Concorsi e accademie del secolo xviii. ISBN 88-7140-011-9 (v. 2)
1. Accademia nazionale di San Luca. Archivio storico - Catalogs. 2. Drawing - 17th century - Italy - San Luca. I. Cipriani, Angela. II. Valeriani, Enrico. III. Title.
NYPL [3-MBH 90-2410]

Prize winning drawings from the Roman Academy 1682-1754 =. Roma , c1990. 189 p. : ISBN 88-7140-013-5
NYPL [3-MBH 91-5071]

ACCADEMIA NAZIONALE DI SAN LUCA. ARCHIVIO STORICO - CATALOGS.
Accademia nazionale di San Luca. Archivio Storico. I disegni di figura nell'Archivio storico dell'Accademia di San Luca /. Roma , 1988- v. : ISBN 88-7140-011-9 (v. 2)
NYPL [3-MBH 90-2410]

ACCADEMIA NAZIONALE DI SAN LUCA. ARCHIVIO STORICO - EXHIBITIONS.
I Premiati dell'Accademia, 1682-1754 /. Roma , c1989. 189 p. : ISBN 88-7140-010-0
NYPL [3-MBH 91-4486]

Prize winning drawings from the Roman Academy 1682-1754 =. Roma , c1990. 189 p. : ISBN 88-7140-013-5
NYPL [3-MBH 91-5071]

ACCADEMIA NAZIONALE DI SAN LUCA - EXHIBITIONS.
I Premiati dell'Accademia, 1682-1754 /. Roma , c1989. 189 p. : ISBN 88-7140-010-0
NYPL [3-MBH 91-4486]

Accademia romana di San Luca. see Accademia nazionale di San Luca.

Accame, Giovanni Maria. Contenir, regarder, jouer. [Paris , 1970] [58] p. :
NYPL [3-MNF 90-6809]

Accent on architecture : the American Institute of Architects honors, 1991. [Washington, D.C.] (1735 New York Ave., NW, Washington 20006) : The Institute, [c1991] 1 v. (unpaged) ; chiefly col. ill. ; 23 cm. Cover title. "The awards ... in this book were presented at the Accent on architecture gala on February 6, 1991, at the National Building Museum in Washington, D.C."--P. [2] of cover. DDC 720/.973/09045 20
1. Architecture - United States - Awards. 2. Architecture, Postmodern - United States - Awards. I. American Institute of Architects.
NA2340 .A33 1991

The Accessible housing design file / produced by Barrier Free Environments Incorporated ; with support from the National Institute on Disability and Rehabilitation Research. New York, N.Y. : Van Nostrand Reinhold, c1991. p. cm. Includes index. ISBN 0-442-00775-2 DDC 728/.042 20
1. Architecture and the physically handicapped - United States. 2. Dwellings - United States - Access for the physically handicapped. I. Barrier Free Environments, inc. II. National Institute on Disability and Rehabilitation Research (U. S.).
NA2545.P5 A34 1991

The accordion-fold book for the Umbrellas, joint project for Japan and U. S.A. /. Christo, 1935- San Francisco , c1991. p. cm. ISBN 0-938491-58-X (hardcover trade) DDC 709/.2 20
N7193.C5 A4 1991

An account of what seem'd most remarkable in the five days peregrination of the five following persons, vizt. Messieurs Tothall, Scott, Hogarth, Thornhill & Forrest, begun on Saturday, May 27th, 1723 and finished on the 31st of the same month /. Forrest, Ebenezer, fl. 1774. [Hogarth's peregrination.] Church Hanborough, Oxford , 1989 ([Didcot? England] : Didcot Press) [35] p. : DDC 760/.092 20
ND497.H7 F6 1989

Account of what seemed most remarkable in the five days peregrination ... Forrest, Ebenezer, fl. 1774. [Hogarth's peregrination.] An account of what seem'd most remarkable in the five days peregrination of the five following persons, vizt. Messieurs Tothall, Scott, Hogarth, Thornhill & Forrest, begun on Saturday, May 27th, 1723 and finished on the 31st of the same month /. Church Hanborough, Oxford , 1989 ([Didcot? England] : Didcot Press) [35] p. : DDC 760/.092 20
ND497.H7 F6 1989

Ace Gallery. An Exhibition of five recent works by Larry Bell, John McCracken, DeWain Valentine, Ron Cooper [and] Peter Alexander. Edmonton, 1971. 44 p. :
N6535.L6 E89 *NYPL [3-MAMT 81-415]*

Acervo, materpieces, Banco Chase Manhattan.
[Rio de Janeiro] : Editora Index, c1989. 118 p. : col. ill. ; 29 cm. Text in English and Portuguese. ISBN 85-7083-028-9 DDC 709/.81/0748161 20
1. Art, Brazilian - Catalogs. 2. Art, Modern - 20th

century - Brazil - Catalogs. 3. Art - Brazil - Catalogs. 4. Banco Chase Manhattan (Brazil) - Catalogs. I. Banco Chase Manhattan (Brazil).
N6655 .A24 1989

Acevedo, Myriam. Serrano, Eduardo. Andres de Santa Maria . [Bogotá] [1988] 250 p. : ISBN 958-9058-00-0
NYPL [3-MCZ+ S221 90-10769]

Achenbach, Nora von. Porzellan aus China und Japan . Berlin , c1990. 588 p. : ISBN 3-496-01070-3   DDC 738.2/0951/074434124 20
NK4565 .P64 1990

Achenbach, Sigrid, 1944- Blechen, Karl, 1798-1840. Carl Blechen . [Berlin] , München , c1990. 309 p. : ISBN 3-7913-1084-4
NYPL [3-MCK+ B6455 91-2247]

ACHILLES (GREEK MYTHOLOGY) - ART.
Kemp-Lindemann, Dagmar. Darstellungen des Achilleus in griechischer und römischer Kunst /. Bern , Frankfurt/M. , 1975. v, 287 p., [1] leaf of plates : ISBN 3-261-01770-8 :
N7760 .K45   NYPL [3-MAMZ 90-12607]

Achtzig Jahre ungarische Malerei von der Romantik bis zum Surrealismus. 80 Jahre ungarische Malerei von der Romantik bis zum Surrealismus . Mannheim [1989] 249 p. : ISBN 3-89165-063-9   DDC 759.39/074/434646 20
ND519 .A15 1989   NYPL [3-MCY 91-4203]

ACID RAIN - ENVIRONMENTAL ASPECTS - GERMANY - PICTORIAL WORKS.
Grass, Günter, 1927- Totes Holz . Göttingen , 1990. 110 p. : ISBN 3-88243-155-5
NX550.Z9 G72 1990

Acidini, Cristina.
Il Palazzo Medici Riccardi di Firenze /. Firenze , c1990. 379 p. : ISBN 88-09-20180-9   DDC 725/.17/094551 20
NA7756.F65 P35 1990

Immagini del Mugello . Firenze , c1990. 246 p. : ISBN 88-7292-117-1
NYPL [MFW+ 91-7415]

Il Palazzo Medici Riccardi di Firenze /. Florence , c1990. x, 379 p. : ISBN 88-09-20180-9
NYPL [3-MQWB+ 91-3377]

Ackerman, Phyllis, 1893- Catalogue of a loan exhibition of gothic tapestries / Phyllis Ackerman. [Chicago] : Arts Club of Chicago, 1926. 55 p. : ill. ; 31 cm. Includes bibliographical references.
1. Tapestry, Gothic - Belgium - Private collections - Exhibitions. 2. Tapestry, Gothic - Germany - Private collections - Exhibitions. 3. Tapestry, Flemish - Private collections - Exhibitions. I. Arts Club of Chicago. II. Title.   *NYPL [3-MOR+ 91-322]*

Ackermann, Max.
Max Ackermann : Klang der Farbe : Werke aus dem Nachlass : 12. Oktober bis 30. November 1989. Stuttgart : Galerie Döbele, [1989]. 61 p. : ill. ; 30 cm.
1. Ackermann, Max - Exhibitions. I. Galerie Döbele. II. Title: Klange der Farbe. III. Title: Werke aus dem Nachlass.   *NYPL [3-MCK+ A178 90-13009]*

Max Ackermann, Klang der Farbe : Werke aus dem Nachlass : 12. Oktober bis 30. November 1989, Galerie Döbele Stuttgart / [Katalog und Ausstellung, Johannes Döbele, Hedwig Döbele]. Stuttgart : Die Galerie, c1989. 61 p. : chiefly ill. (chiefly col.) ; 30 cm. Includes bibliographical references (p. 10-11).
1. Ackermann, Max - Exhibitions. I. Döbele, Johannes. II. Döbele, Hedwig. III. Galerie Döbele. IV. Title. V. Title: Klang der Farbe.
ND588.A313 A4 1989

ACKERMANN, MAX - EXHIBITIONS.
Ackermann, Max. Max Ackermann . Stuttgart [1989]. 61 p. :
NYPL [3-MCK+ A178 90-13009]

Ackermann, Max. Max Ackermann, Klang der Farbe . Stuttgart , c1989. 61 p. :
ND588.A313 A4 1989

Ackley, Clifford S. The unique print : 70s into 90s : Museum of Fine Arts, Boston, Department of Prints, Drawings, and Photographs, September 15-December 16, 1990, the Lois and Michael Torf Gallery / Clifford S. Ackley with the assistance of Anne Havinga and Judy Weinland. Boston : The Museum, c1990. 34 p. : ill. ; 28 cm. ISBN 0-87846-325-9

1. Prints - 20th century - Exhibitions. I. Havinga, Anne. II. Weinland, Judy. III. Museum of Fine Arts, Boston. Dept. of Prints, Drawings, and Photographs. IV. Title.
IN PROCESS (ONLINE)
NYPL [MDET 91-4771]

Acocella, Alfonso, 1954- Celli Tognon : opere d'architettura, 1963-1987 / Alfonso Acocella. Firenze : Alinea, c1987. 214 p. : ill. (some col.) ; 23 cm. (Cataloghi. 4) Bibliography: p. 195-199. DDC 720/.92/2 19
1. Celli Tognon - Catalogs. 2. Architecture, Modern - 20th century - Italy - Catalogs. 3. Architecture, Postmodern - Italy - Catalogs. I. Title.
NA1123.C39 A4 1987
NYPL [3-MQWB 90-3040]

Acquisitions 1955-1965. Musée d'art moderne de la ville de Paris. [Paris , 1965?] 1 v. (unpaged) :
NYPL [3-MAVZ+ (Paris) 91-229]

Acquisitions, 1964-1973 /. Musées royaux d'art et d'histoire (Belgium) Bruxelles , 1974. [106] p. :
N1835 .A516 1974

Acquisti e donazioni del Museo nazionale del Bargello, 1970-1987 /. Museo nazionale di Firenze. Firenze , c1988. xv, 158 p. : DDC 708.5/51 19
N2555 .A515 1988
NYPL [3-MAVZ (Florence) 90-11120]

ACRYLIC RESINS.
Arghir, Anca. [Transparenz als Werkstoff. English.] Transparency into art . Cologne , 1988. 218 p. :   *NYPL [3-MGD+ 89-21228]*

ACSA Technology Conference (8th : 1990 : University of Southern California) On architecture, the city, and technology /. Washington, DC , Stoneham, MA , c1990. 152 p. : ISBN 0-7506-9149-2   DDC 720/.1/05 20
NA2543.T43 O5 1990

ACT, FORGERY OF. see ART - FORGERIES.

Acta Iranica.
(v. 9) Root, Margaret Cool. The king and kingship in Achaemenid art . Leiden , 1979. xii, 357 p., lxxii p. of plates : ISBN 90-04-03902-3   DDC 709/.35 20
N5390 .R6 1979
*NYPL [*OMA 76-1696 t.19]*

(19) Root, Margaret Cool. The king and kingship in Achaemenid art . Leiden , 1979. xii, 357 p., lxxii p. of plates : ISBN 90-04-03902-3   DDC 709/.35 20
N5390 .R6 1979
*NYPL [*OMA 76-1696 t.19]*

(19) Root, Margaret Cool. The king and kingship in Achaemenid art . Leiden , 1979. xii, 357 p., lxxii p. of plates : ISBN 90-04-03902-3   DDC 709/.35 20
N5390 .R6 1979
*NYPL [*OMA 76-1696 t.19]*

Acta Universitatis Upsaliensis. Ars Suetica, 0066-7919 .
(13) Kent, Neil. Light and nature in late 19th century Nordic art and literature /. Uppsala , 1990. 92 p. : ISBN 91-554-2952-5
NYPL [3-MAM 91-6708]

Actes des colloques de la Direction du patrimoine .
(4) Les Enjeux du patrimoine architectural du XXe siècle . [Paris] [1988?] 186 p. : ISBN 2-11-085013-2
NA109.F8 E55 1988

(7) L'Ornementation architecturale en pierre dans les monuments historiques . [Paris] [1989] 280 p. : ISBN 2-11-085558-4
NA3549.A1 O76 1989

Actes sud-Papiers, 0298-0592.
Kantor, l'artiste à la fin du XXe siècle /. [Arles] [Paris] , c1990. 177 p. : ISBN 2-86943-254-2 :   DDC 700/.92 20
NX571.P64 K3635 1990

ACTING - COSTUME. see COSTUME.

Active design . Nonomura, Akira, 1934- Kyoto, Japan , c1990. 5 v. : ISBN 4-7636-8071-4 (v. 1) : DDC 746.6/2 20
NK9502.2.N65 A4 1990

The activities of Pieter Brattinga, a portrait of an era /. Brattinga, Pieter, 1931- Tokyo , The Hague , 1989. 287 p. : ISBN 90-12-06213-6
(SDU)   *NYPL [3-MDWS+ (Brattinga) 90-9941 Suppl.]*

ACTIVITY PROGRAMS IN EDUCATION - UNITED STATES.
Szeglin, Charles B. Creativities! . West Nyack, N.Y. , c1991. p. cm. ISBN 0-13-189804-3 DDC 372.5/044 20
N362 .S95 1991

Ad Reinhardt /. Reinhardt, Ad, 1913-1967. New York, N.Y. , 1991. 144 p. : ISBN 0-8478-1336-3   DDC 759.13 20
ND237.R316 A4 1991

Adair, William. The frame in America, 1700-1900 : a survey of fabrication techniques and styles / by William Adair. Washington, D.C. : American Institute of Architects Foundation, c1983. ix, 50 p. : ill. ; 28 cm. "An exhibition at The Octagon, Washington, D.C., July 19-September 11, 1983." Includes bibliographical references (p. 50).   DDC 749/.7/0973074753 20
1. Picture frames and framing - United States - Exhibitions. I. Octagon (Washington, D.C.). II. Title.
N8551.U6 A3 1983

ADALBERO, SAINT, BISHOP OF WÜRZBURG, D. 1090 - ART PATRONAGE.
Scheele, Paul-Werner. Die Herrlichkeit des Herrn . Würzburg , c1990. 136 p. : ISBN 3-429-01316-X
ND2750.L36 S34 1990

Adalbert-Stifter-Verein (Munich, Germany)
Barockmaler in Böhmen. München [1961] 36 p.
N6832.B3 H8   NYPL [3-MCY 90-5883]

Begegnungen . [Esslingen am Neckar] , c1980. 64 p. :   *NYPL [3-MAMG 90-5884]*

Adalberto Libera /. Adalberto Libera. English. New York, N.Y. , c1991. p. cm. ISBN 1-87827-114-8 :   DDC 720/.92 20
NA1123.L46 A4 1991

Adalberto Libera. English. Adalberto Libera / edited by Francesco Garofalo and Luca Veresani. New York, N.Y. : Princeton Architectural Press, c1991. p. cm. Translation of: Adalberto Libera. Includes bibliographical references. ISBN 1-87827-114-8 :   DDC 720/.92 20
1. Libera, Adalberto, 1903-1963 - Themes, motives. 2. Functionalism (Architecture) - Italy. 3. Fascism and architecture - Italy. I. Garofalo, Francesco. II. Veresani, Luca. III. Title.
NA1123.L46 A4 1991

Adam, Juliette, 1836-1936. A Vasco da Gama . Paris , 1898. 44, 16 p. :
NX549.A1 V36 1898

Adam, Peter. Art of the Third Reich / Peter Adam. New York : H.N. Abrams, 1992. p. cm. "Based on a television series Peter Adam made for the BBC in 1988"-- Includes bibliographical references and index. ISBN 0-8109-1912-5 (cloth)   DDC 709/.43/09043 20
1. National socialism and art. 2. Art, German. 3. Art, Modern - 20th century - Germany. I. Title.
N6868.5.N37 A34 1992

ADAM, SABINE, 1957-
Fassbar-anfassbar-unfassbar [Ausstellung] /. [München?] [1981?] 1 portfolio ([13] pieces) :
NYPL [3-MAL+ 82-1845]

Adams, Ansel, 1902-
The American wilderness / Ansel Adams ; edited by Andrea G. Stillman ; introduction by William A. Turnage. 1st ed. Boston : Little, Brown, c1990. 146 p. : chiefly ill. ; 33 x 41 cm. "A Bulfinch Press book." ISBN 0-8212-1799-2   DDC 779/.36/092 20
1. Adams, Ansel, 1902- - Views on nature conservation. 2. Wilderness areas - United States - Pictorial works. I. Stillman, Andrea Gray. II. Title.
TR660 .A29 1990
NYPL [MFX+ (Adams) 91-2496]

ADAMS, ANSEL, 1902- - VIEWS ON NATURE CONSERVATION.
Adams, Ansel, 1902- The American wilderness /. Boston , c1990. 146 p. : ISBN 0-8212-1799-2   DDC 779/.36/092 20
TR660 .A29 1990
NYPL [MFX+ (Adams) 91-2496]

Adams, Clinton, 1918- Printmaking in New Mexico, 1880-1990 / Clinton Adams. Albuquerque : University of New Mexico Press, c1991. p. cm. Includes bibliographical references. ISBN 0-8263-1307-8   DDC 769.9789 20
1. Prints, American - New Mexico. 2. Prints - 19th century - New Mexico. 3. Prints - 20th century - New

Mexico. I. Title.
NE535.N6 A33 1991

ADAMS COUNTY, ILL. - MAPS.
(1991) Rockford Map Publishers. Adams
County, Illinois, land atlas & plat book .
Rockford, Ill. [c1991] 1 atlas (57 p.) :
NYPL [Map Div. 91-7108]

Adams County, Illinois, land atlas & plat book .
Rockford Map Publishers. Rockford, Ill.
[c1991] 1 atlas (57 p.) :
NYPL [Map Div. 91-7108]

ADAMS COUNTY (WIS.) - MAPS.
Rockford Map Publishers. Adams County,
Wisconsin, land atlas & plat book . Rockford,
Ill. , Friendship, Wis. [c1991] 1 atlas (69 p.) :
NYPL [Map Div. 91-4407]

**Adams County, Wisconsin, land atlas & plat
book .** Rockford Map Publishers. Rockford,
Ill. , Friendship, Wis. [c1991] 1 atlas (69 p.) :
NYPL [Map Div. 91-4407]

Adams, Dennis.
Dennis Adams : the architecture of amnesia /
essay by Mary Anne Staniszewski. New York,
NY : Kent, c1990. 94 p. : ill. (some col.) ; 26
cm. "This monograph accompanies the exhibition
Dennis Adams: street vanities held at Kent Fine Art,
April 5 to May 5, 1990"--Colophon. Bibliography: p.
91-94. ISBN 1-87860-707-3
*1. Adams, Dennis - Exhibitions. I. Staniszewski, Mary
Anne. II. Kent Fine Art, Inc. III. Title. IV. Title:
Architecture of amnesia. V. Title: Dennis Adams--street
vanities.*
NYPL [3-MGO (Adams, D.) 91-4565]

ADAMS, DENNIS - EXHIBITIONS.
Adams, Dennis. Dennis Adams . New York,
NY , c1990. 94 p. : ISBN 1-87860-707-3
NYPL [3-MGO (Adams, D.) 91-4565]

Adams, Dennis, 1948- Rhetorical image . New
York , c1990. 98 p. : ISBN 0-915557-71-1
NYPL [3-MAL+ 91-5559]

Adams, Doug. Transcendence with the human
body in art : Segal, De Staebler, Johns, and
Christo / by Doug Adams. New York :
Crossroad, 1991. p. cm. Includes bibliographical
references. ISBN 0-8245-1104-2 (cloth) DDC
701/.04 20
*1. Art and religion - United States. 2. Art, Modern -
20th century - United States. 3. Figurative art - United
States. 4. Transcendence (Philosophy). I. Title.*
N6512.5.F5 A34 1991

Adams, Henry, 1949-
Nelson-Atkins Museum of Art. Handbook of
American paintings in the Nelson-Atkins
Museum of Art, Kansas City, Missouri /.
Kansas City, Mo. , 1991. p. cm. ISBN
0-942614-17-8 DDC 759.13/074/778411 20
ND205 .N34 1991

William M. Harnett /. Fort Worth : New
York : p. cm. ISBN 0-8109-3410-8 DDC 759.13
20
ND237.H315 A4 1992

Adams, John. Bermudian images : the paintings of
Bruce Stuart / text by John Adams ; foreword
by Andrew Trimingham.1st ed. Hamilton,
Bermuda : Windjammer Gallery, 1989. viii, 101
p. : col. ill. ; 29 cm. Includes bibliographical
references (p. 100-101). DDC 759.97299 20
*1. Architecture - Bermuda Island (Bermuda Islands) -
Themes, motives. I. Stuart, Bruce. II. Title.*
NA815.B47 A33 1989

Adams, John Quincy, 1767-1848. Lectures on
rhetoric and oratory : delivered to the classes of
senior and junior sophisters in Harvard
university / by John Quincy Adams.
Cambridge, Mass. : Printed by Hilliard and
Metcalf, 1810. 2 v. ; 24 cm.
I. Title.
PN175 .A4   *NYPL [3-MAL 91-5006]*

Adaptation & negation of socialist realism :
contemporary Soviet art : June 9, 1990 through
October 7, 1990 / Erik Bulatov ... [et al.].
Ridgefield, CT : Aldrich Museum of
Contemporary Art, c1990. 44 p. : ill. ; 31 cm.
*1. Art, Soviet - Exhibitions. I. Bulatov, Ėrik, 1933-. II.
Aldrich Museum of Contemporary Art (Ridgefield,
Conn.). III. Title: Adaptation and negation of socialist
realism.*   *NYPL [3-MAM+ 91-5891]*

Adaptation and negation of socialist realism.

Adaptation & negation of socialist realism .
Ridgefield, CT , c1990. 44 p. :
NYPL [3-MAM+ 91-5891]

Adaskina, N. L. (Natal'i'a Lvovna) Lioubov
Popova / par Natalia Adaskina et Dimitri
Sarabianov. Paris : P. Sers, 1989. 394 p. : ill.
(some col.) ; 32 cm. Spine title: Popova. Includes
bibliographical references. ISBN 2-904057-26-9
*1. Popova, Liubov - Criticism and interpretation. 2.
Constructivism (Art) - Russian S.F.S.R. I. Sarabʹiʹanov,
Dmitriĭ Vladimirovich. II. Title.*
NYPL [3-MCZ+ P828 90-2356]

Adaskina, N. L. (Natalʹiā Lʹvovna) Sarabʹiānov,
Dmitriĭ Vladimirovich. [Lioubov Popova.
English.] Popova /. New York , 1990. 396 p. :
ISBN 0-8109-3701-8 (soft) DDC 709/.2/4 B 19
N6999.P67 S27 1989
NYPL [3-MCZ+ P828 91-3662]

ADC (Firm) Clarke County, Va. street map.
Alexandria, Va. : ADC, c1987. 1 atlas (iii, 15
p.) : col. maps ; 36 cm. Cover title. Includes
indexes. ISBN 0-87530-029-4 : DDC 912/.75598 19
*1. Zip code - Virginia - Clarke County - Maps. 2.
Clarke County (Va.) - Maps. I. Title.*
G1293.C6 A36 1987
NYPL [Map Div. 91-2437]

Adcock, Craig E. James Turrell : the art of light
and space / Craig Adcock. Berkeley :
University of California Press, c1990. xxiv, 272
p., [32] p. of plates : ill. (some col.) ; 32 cm.
Includes bibliographical references (p. 253-266) and
index. ISBN 0-520-06728-2 (alk. paper) DDC
709/.2 20
*1. Turrell, James - Criticism and interpretation. 2.
Earthworks (Art). I. Title.*
N6537.T78 A84 1990
NYPL [3-MCX+ T941 91-5229]

Addison Gallery of American Art.
American abstraction at the Addison : April 18
through July 31, 1991 : an exhibition of
selected works from the museum's permanent
collection, including recent gifts to the Addison
Art Drive / curated by Jock Reynolds.
Andover, Mass. : Addison Gallery of American
Art, Phillips Academy, c1991. 95 p. : ill. (some
col.) ; 23 x 28 cm. Includes bibliographical
references (p. 92). ISBN 1-87988-600-6 DDC
709/.73/0747445 20
*1. Art, Abstract - United States - Exhibitions. 2. Art,
Modern - 20th century - United States - Exhibitions. 3.
Art, American - Exhibitions. 4. Addison Gallery of
American Art - Exhibitions. I. Reynolds, Jock. II. Title.*
N6512.5.A2 A33 1991

Homer, Winslow, 1836-1910. Winslow Homer
at the Addison . Andover, Mass. , 1990. 95 p. :
NYPL [3-MCX H76 90-13073]

Leaf, June, 1929- June Leaf, a survey of
paintings, sculpture, and works on paper,
1948-1991 /. Washington, D.C. , 1991. 48 p. :
ISBN 0-937237-01-9 (pbk.) DDC 709/.2 20
N6537.L398 A4 1991

**ADDISON GALLERY OF AMERICAN ART -
EXHIBITIONS.**
Addison Gallery of American Art. American
abstraction at the Addison . Andover, Mass. ,
c1991. 95 p. : ISBN 1-87988-600-6 DDC
709/.73/0747445 20
N6512.5.A2 A33 1991

Ade, Peter A. Miró, Joan, 1893- Joan Miro,
Skulpturen /. München , c1990. 246, [1] p. :
ISBN 3-7774-5300-5 DDC 730/.92 20
NB813.M5 A4 1990

Adelaide angries . Hylton, Jane. Adelaide , 1989.
80 p. : ISBN 0-7308-0772-X
NYPL [3-MCY+ 90-13322]

Adelaide Biennial of Australian Art (1990) Eagle,
Mary, 1944- 1990 Adelaide Biennial of
Australian art /. Adelaide , 1990. 113 p. :
ISBN 0-7308-0773-8
NYPL [3-MAM+ 91-5044]

Adelaide, Maria. Gharabagh /. Milano, Italia ,
1988. 107 p. : ISBN 88-85822-09-6
NYPL [3-MQW 91-4235]

Adeline, Jules, 1845-1909. La légende du violon
de faïence / Jules Adeline ; huit compositions
gravées a l'eau-forte par l'auteur. Paris : Libr. L.
Conquet, 1895 ([Paris] : A. Lahure) 46 p., [1]
leaf of plates : ill., 1 port. ; 21 cm. "Tirage unique
a 500 exemplaires (planches détruites): 1 à 150, 150 sur
papier du Japon impérial; 151 à 500, 350 sur papier

vélin du Marais à la forme"--P. [2]. LC has copy no.
398, signed by the author, bound, with original paper
wrappers. DLC LC copy has bookplate of Nicholas II,
Emperor of Russia; stamped in gold on the spine with
his cipher. DLC Source: Purchase from Israel Perlstein,
Mar. 24, 1931 (DLC #409629, 1931). DLC DDC
769.92 20
*1. Adeline, Jules, 1845-1909. 2. Champfleury,
1821-1889. Violon de faïence - Illustrations. I. Nicholas
II, Emperor of Russia, 1868-1918, former owner. II.
Title.*
NE2049.5.A34 A4 1895

ADELINE, JULES, 1845-1909.
Adeline, Jules, 1845-1909. La légende du violon
de faïence /. Paris , 1895 ([Paris] : A. Lahure)
46 p., [1] leaf of plates : DDC 769.92 20
NE2049.5.A34 A4 1895

Ades, Dawn.
Arte en Iberoamérica, 1820-1980 . [Madrid]
[1989?] xxi, 359, [3] p. : ISBN 84-7506-297-0
N6502.4 .A76 1989

The 20th-century poster : design of the
avant-garde : posters / by Dawn Ades ; with
contributions by Robert Brown ... [et al.] ;
Mildred Friedman, editor.2nd ed. Minneapolis :
Walker Art Center : New York : Abbeville
Press, [1990] 227 p. ; 26 cm. At head of title:
Posters. Includes bibliographical references (p. 218-219)
and index. ISBN 1-558-59130-3 DDC
741.6/74/0904 20
*1. Posters - History - 20th century - Themes, motives.
I. Brown, Robert K. II. Friedman, Mildred S. III.
Walker Art Center. IV. Title. V. Title:
Twentieth-century poster. VI. Title: Posters.*
NC1815 .A33 1990

ADG '86 : muestra de la Asociación de
Diseñadores Gráficos de Buenos Aires : 10-27
de abril de 1986. Buenos Aires : Municipalidad
de la Ciudad de Buenos Aires, Secretaría de
Cultura, Centro Cultural, Ciudad de Buenos
Aires, 1986. 1 v. (unpaged) : ill. ; 30 cm. Exhibit
catalog.
*1. Commercial art - Argentina - History - 20th
century - Exhibitions. 2. Logography - Exhibitions. I.
Asociación de Diseñadores Gráficos de Buenos Aires.
II. Title: Muestra de la Asociación de Diseñadores
Gráficos de Buenos Aires.*
NC1002.L63 A33 1986

Adhémar, Jean. Bibliothèque nationale (France).
Cabinet des estampes. Delacroix et la gravure
romantique. Paris , 1963. 9, [36] p. :
NYPL [MDBF 90-7193]

Adimi, Morris. Rossi, Aldo, 1931- Aldo Rossi .
New York, N.Y. , 1991. p. cm. ISBN
1-87827-115-6 (cloth) : DDC 720/.92 20
NA1123.R616 A4 1991

**ADIRONDACK MOUNTAINS (N.Y.) -
DESCRIPTION AND TRAVEL - VIEWS -
EXHIBITIONS.**
Crowley, William. Seneca Ray Stoddard . Blue
Mountain Lake, N.Y. , c1982. vii, 64 p. : ISBN
0-910020-35-3 (pbk.) DDC 770/.92/4 19
N6537.S754 A4 1982
NYPL [MFX (Stoddard) 91-8010]

ADIRONDACK MOUNTAINS (N.Y.) IN ART.
Mandel, Patricia C. F. Fair wilderness . Blue
Mountain Lake, N.Y. , 1990. 175 p. : ISBN
0-910020-40-X *NYPL [3-MCW 90-11114]*

Adirondack Museum.
Crowley, William. Seneca Ray Stoddard . Blue
Mountain Lake, N.Y. , c1982. vii, 64 p. : ISBN
0-910020-35-3 (pbk.) DDC 770/.92/4 19
N6537.S754 A4 1982
NYPL [MFX (Stoddard) 91-8010]

Mandel, Patricia C. F. Fair wilderness . Blue
Mountain Lake, N.Y. , 1990. 175 p. : ISBN
0-910020-40-X *NYPL [3-MCW 90-11114]*

ADIRONDACK MUSEUM - CATALOGS.
Mandel, Patricia C. F. Fair wilderness . Blue
Mountain Lake, N.Y. , 1990. 175 p. : ISBN
0-910020-40-X *NYPL [3-MCW 90-11114]*

Adler, Kathleen. Perspectives on Morisot . New
York , c1990. 120 p. : ISBN 1-555-95049-3 (alk.
paper) : DDC 759.4 20
ND553.M88 P47 1990
NYPL [3-MCO M86 91-4616]

Adler, Ron K. Karta (Firm) Atlas of Israel .
Tel-Aviv ; New York : [168] 80 p. : ISBN

0-02-905950-X : DDC 912/.5694 19
G2235 .K3 1985
    NYPL [*P-*PXLB++ 86-3877]

ADMONT (AUSTRIA) - BUILDINGS, STRUCTURES, ETC.
Mannewitz, Martin. Stift Admont . München , c1989. 422 p. : ISBN 3-89235-031-0 :
NA5510.A35 S755 1989

Adochi . Adochi, 1954- Berlin , c1989. 73, [2] p. :
ISBN 3-87329-934-8 DDC 759.9498 20
N7233.A36 A4 1989

Adochi, 1954-
Adochi : San Martino, Berlin, San Jose : Arbeiten 1987-1989 / [Redaktion und Gestaltung, Georg Nothelfer]. Berlin : Galerie Georg Nothelfer, c1989. 73, [2] p. : col. ill. ; 28 cm. Catalog. French and German. Includes bibliographical references (p. [74]). ISBN 3-87329-934-8 DDC 759.9498 20
1. Adochi, 1954- - Exhibitions. I. Nothelfer, Georg. II. Galerie Georg Nothelfer. III. Title.
N7233.A36 A4 1989

ADOCHI, 1954- - EXHIBITIONS.
Adochi, 1954- Adochi . Berlin , c1989. 73, [2] p. : ISBN 3-87329-934-8 DDC 759.9498 20
N7233.A36 A4 1989

Adolf Hölzel von seinen Schülern : e. Gratulationsmappe 1923 : [7. Okt.-26. Nov. 1978, Raum 1] / Galerie d. Stadt Stuttgart ; [Ausstellung u. Katalog, Eugen Keuerleber]. Stuttgart : Galerie d. Stadt Stuttgart, 1978. 61 p. : numerous ill. (some col.) ; 21 cm. Bibliography: p. 61.
1. Hölzel, Adolf, 1853-1934 - Influence - Exhibitions. 2. Art, German - Exhibitions. 3. Art, Modern - 20th century - Germany - Exhibitions. I. Hölzel, Adolf, 1853-1934. II. Kreuerleber, Eugen.
N6868 .A38   *NYPL [3-MCK H693 81-755]*

Adolf Konrad, a retrospective exhibition . Konrad, Adolf, 1915- Montclair, N.J. , c1980. 32 p. :
ND237.K598 A4 1980
    NYPL [3-MCX K823 80-2245]

Adolf Loos. Loos, Adolf, 1870-1933. [Buenos Aires] [1988?] 44 p. : DDC 720/.92 20
NA1011.5.L6 A4 1988

Adolfo-Mario Marizza . Herdies, Paul. Bruxelles [1985] 94 p. : ISBN 2-87103-011-1 DDC 759.36 20
N6811.5.M34 A4 1985

Adolfo Wildt, ein italienischer Bildhauer des Symbolismus . Wildt, Adolfo, 1868-1931. [Darmstadt] [1990] 296 p. :
    NYPL [3-MGO (Wildt) 91-5869]

Adolph Gottlieb . Gottlieb, Adolph, 1903-1974. New York , c1990. [20] p. :
    NYPL [3-MCX G686 91-3416]

Adolph, Hubert. Mittelalterliche Glasmalereien aus St. Stephan . Wien , 1990. 16 p. :
    NYPL [3-MRY 91-4404]

Adolph Menzel, 1815-1905 . Menzel, Adolph, 1815-1905. Alexandria, Va. , 1990. 235 p. :
ISBN 0-88397-096-1 DDC 741.943 20
NC251.M45 A4 1990
    NYPL [3-MCK M55 91-3333]

Adolph-Paburg, Hubert. Kurzweil, Maximilian, 1867-1916. Max Kurzweil. Wien, München [c1969] 26 p.
ND538.K87 A5
    NYPL [3-MCK K978 90-6927]

Adriana Zaefferer . Zaefferer, Adriana, 1952- New York [1990] [32] p. :
    NYPL [3-MCZ Z17 91-7031]

Adriani, Götz, 1940-
Höch, Hannah, 1889- Colagens, Hannah Höch, 1889-1978 /. Lisboa , 1989. 134 p. :
N6888.H6 A4 1989a

Kiefer, Anselm, 1945- [Anselm Kiefer Bücher, 1969-1990. English.] The books of Anselm Kiefer, 1969-1990 /. New York, N.Y. , 1991. p. cm. ISBN 0-8076-1261-8 DDC 709/.2 20
N7233.4.K54 A4 1991

Kiefer, Anselm, 1945- Anselm Kiefer, Bücher 1969-1990 . [Stuttgart] , c1990. 378 p. : ISBN 3-89322-200-6
    NYPL [MDG+ (Kiefer) 91-5802]

Adrien Dauzats. Plessier, Ghislaine. Adrien Dauzats, ou, La tentation de l'Orient .

Bordeaux , c1990. 227 p. : ISBN 2-902067-15-1 :
DDC 759.4 20
ND553.D245 A4 1990

Adrien Dauzats, ou, La tentation de l'Orient . Plessier, Ghislaine. Bordeaux , c1990. 227 p. :
ISBN 2-902067-15-1 : DDC 759.4 20
ND553.D245 A4 1990

An ADT design File.
Plans and elevations /. London , 1990. [84] p. :
ISBN 1-85454-052-1 (pbk.) : DDC 745.44941 20
NK1443   *NYPL [3-MNE 90-11636]*

The adventure of design . Vercelloni, Virgilio. [Avventura del design, Gavina. English.] New York , 1989. 220 p. : ISBN 0-8478-1039-9 DDC 749/.245 20
TS79 .V4713 1989
    NYPL [3-MNE+ 90-12985]

Adventure Publications (Firm : Cambridge, Minn.) Hanson, John M. Minnesota atlas . Cambridge, MN , 1990. 1 atlas (216 p.) : ISBN 0-934860-61-0 *NYPL [Map Div. 91-7525]*

Adventures of the symbol . Pellizzi, Francesco. New York City , 1986. 1 v. (unpaged) ; DDC 704.9/46 20
N5311 .P4 1986

ADVERTISING ART. see COMMERCIAL ART.

ADVERTISING, ART IN. see COMMERCIAL ART; ART AND INDUSTRY.

ADVERTISING, CONSUMER. see ADVERTISING.

ADVERTISING DRINKING GLASSES - COLLECTORS AND COLLECTING - UNITED STATES - CATALOGS.
Falvey, William D. The official collector's guide to Kentucky Derby mint julep glasses /. Louisville, Ky. (301 S. 30th St., Louisville 40212) , c1991. 81 p. : DDC 748.8/3/097713 20
NK5440.D75 F3 1991

ADVERTISING GLASSES - UNITED STATES - CATALOGS.
Hervey, John. Collector's guide to cartoon & promotional drinking glasses /. Gas City, IN , c1990. x, 180 p. : ISBN 0-89145-443-8 : DDC 760/.0951/07479493 20
NK5440.D75 H4 1990

ADVERTISING - JEWELRY TRADE - NEW YORK (N.Y.) - HISTORY - 20TH CENTURY.
Moore, Gene. My time at Tiffany's /. New York , c1990. 232 p. : ISBN 0-312-03473-3 DDC 659.1/57 B 20
HF5849.J6 M66 1990
    NYPL [3-MLT+ 91-3269]

ADVERTISING, PICTORIAL. see COMMERCIAL ART.

ADVERTISING - PICTORIAL WORKS.
Leitherer, Eugen. Reiz und Hülle . Basel , Boston , 1987. 301 p. : ISBN 3-7643-1827-9
    NYPL [3-MNF+ 89-24501]

ADVERTISING, RETAIL. see ADVERTISING.

ADVERTISING - RETAIL TRADE. see ADVERTISING.

ADVERTISING SPECIALITIES - UNITED STATES - CATALOGS.
Hervey, John. Collector's guide to cartoon & promotional drinking glasses /. Gas City, IN , c1990. x, 180 p. : ISBN 0-89145-443-8 : DDC 760/.0951/07479493 20
NK5440.D75 H4 1990

Advice to artists. Leonardo, da Vinci, 1452-1519. [Advice to artists.] Leonardo da Vinci's advice to artists /. Philadelphia, Pa. , c1990, 1974. 141 p. : ISBN 0-89471-834-7
    NYPL [3-MCF V7 90-11327]

Aedes Galerie für Architektur und Raum.
Eisenman, Peter, 1932- Peter Eisenman . Berlin , 1989. [46] p. :
    NYPL [3-MQZ (Eisenman) 90-12528]

Hejduk, John, 1929- John Hejduk . Berlin , c1988. [43] p. :
    NYPL [3-MCX H458 91-7235]

Ædes Hartwellianæ. Smyth, W. H. (William Henry), 1788-1865. London, 1851. vii, 414 p., 1 l.
N5245 .H4

The Aegean and the east . Crowley, Janice L.

Jonsered , 1989. xii, 507 p. : ISBN 91-86098-55-1 *NYPL [3-MAE 90-11126]*

Aegean painting in the Bronze Age /. Immerwahr, Sara Anderson, 1914- University Park , c1990. xxiv, 240 p., [45] p. of plates : ISBN 0-271-00628-5 : DDC 751.7/3/093918 19
ND2570 .I45 1990
    NYPL [3-MLP 90-10401]

Aenne Biermann . Biermann, Aenne, 1898-1933. Berlin , c1987. 141,19 p. : ISBN 3-88940-019-1
    NYPL [MFX (Biermann) 89-1352]

Aenne Biermann . Biermann, Aenne, 1898-1933. London , c1988. 141 p. : ISBN 1-85378-004-9
TR654 .B54 1988
    NYPL [MFX (Biermann) 91-8099]

AEON /. Woods, Lebbeus. [New York, N.Y.?] 1979. [4] p. : *NYPL [MEMZ 88-2418]*

AERIAL PHOTOGRAMMETRY - CONGRESSES.
Symposium on Photogrammetric Surveys and Mapping (1971 : University of Missouri, Rolla) Photogrammetric surveys and mapping. [Rolla, 1971?] iv, 59 p. *NYPL [Map Div. 90-5988]*

AERIAL PHOTOGRAPHIC SURVEYING. see AERIAL PHOTOGRAMMETRY.

AERODROMES. see AIRPORTS.

AERONAUTICS - CARICATURES AND CARTOONS.
Stevens, Bob, 1923- There I was-- 25 years /. Bonsall, CA , c1990. 597 p. ; ISBN 0-910497-03-6 DDC 741.5/973 20
NC1429.S64 A4 1990a

AEROSTATION. see AERONAUTICS.

AESTHETIC FORM. see FORM (AESTHETICS)

AESTHETICS.
Klivar, Miroslav. Estetická výchova ve společenské práci /. Praha , 1989. 122 p. :
N69.C95 K58 1989

Lloyd-Jones, Peter, 1940- Taste today . Oxford , New York , 1991. p. cm. ISBN 0-08-040251-8 : DDC 745.4/442 20
NK1520 .L46 1991

Lories, D. (Danielle) Expérience esthétique et ontologie de l'œuvre . Bruxelles [1989] 286 p. : ISBN 2-8031-0074-6 DDC 701 20
N67 .L76 1989

Ravera, Rosa María. Estética y semiótica /. [Rosario, Santa Fe, Argentina] [1988] 250 p. ;
NX180.S46 R38 1988

Thürlemann, Felix. Vom Bild zum Raum . Köln , c1990. 193 p. : ISBN 3-7701-2361-1 DDC 701 20
N68 .T54 1990

AESTHETICS, AMERICAN - HISTORY - 20TH CENTURY - EXHIBITIONS.
Aesthetics of progress . Cambridge, Mass. , c1984. 28 p. :
TS23 .A47 1984 *NYPL [3-MNE 90-10675]*

AESTHETICS, COMMUNIST. see COMMUNIST AESTHETICS.

AESTHETICS - CONGRESSES.
Kolloquium Kunst und Philosophie (1980 : Paderborn, Germany) Das Kunstwerk /. Paderborn, 1983. 379 p. : ISBN 3-506-99372-0
    NYPL [3-MAB 90-12387]

Aesthetics Cop. Shaw, Theodore L. [Hypocrisy about art. Selections.] How the Metropolitan Museum misteaches art /. [Boston, Mass.] , 195-?] 15 p. *NYPL [3-MAB 90-5666]*

AESTHETICS - EXHIBITIONS.
Michel, Régis. Le beau idéal . Paris , 1989. 176 p. : ISBN 2-7118-2317-2
    NYPL [3-MA 90-12383]

AESTHETICS, FRENCH - 17TH CENTURY.
Weyl, Martin. Passion for reason and reason of passion . New York , c1989. 314 p. ; ISBN 0-8204-0981-2 : DDC 709.44/09/032 20
N6846 .W49 1989
    NYPL [3-MAMI 91-6906]

AESTHETICS, FRENCH - 18TH CENTURY.
Saint Girons, Baldine. Esthétiques du XVIIIe siècle . Paris , c1990. 724 p. : ISBN 2-904057-31-5 *NYPL [3-MAB 91-2669]*

AESTHETICS, MODERN.
Bildfälle . Zürich , c1990. 231 p. : ISBN

3-7608-8073-8
N6350 .B547 1990

Schwarz, Hans-Günther, 1945- Orient, Okzident . München , c1990. 355 p. ; ISBN 3-89129-214-7 DDC 700 20
NX650.R83 S38 1990

AESTHETICS, MODERN - 18TH CENTURY.
Empfindung und Reflexion . Hildesheim , New York , 1986. vi, 374 p. : ISBN 3-487-07845-7
NX542 .E46 1986   *NYPL [3-MC 90-12618]*

Kohle, Hubertus. Ut pictura poesis non erit . Hildesheim , New York , 1989. 191 p. : ISBN 3-487-09096-1 : DDC 111/.85/092 20
B2018.A4 K64 1989

                    NYPL [3-MAB 91-4602]

AESTHETICS, MODERN - 20TH CENTURY.
Brock, Bazon, 1936- Die Re-Dekade . München , c1990. 298 p. : ISBN 3-7814-0288-6 :
NX550.A1 B76 1990

Discussions in contemporary culture /. Seattle , 1987- v. : ISBN 0-941920-07-0 (no. 1 : pbk.) : DDC 700/.1/03 19
N72.S6 D57 1987   *NYPL [3-MAS 88-1789]*

Untner, Alois. Das Unverständnis gegenüber moderner Malerei /. Wien , 1990. 312 p. ; ISBN 3-85369-793-3
ND195 .U58 1990

AESTHETICS, MODERN - CONGRESSES.
Fictions of culture . New York , 1991. p. cm. ISBN 0-8204-1714-9 DDC 700 20
NX449.5 .F53 1991

Aesthetics of progress : forms of the future in American design, 1930s-1980s : May 19 through June 24, 1984, Hayden Gallery, Massachusetts Institute of Technology / [organized by the MIT Committee on the Visual Arts]. Cambridge, Mass. : The Gallery, c1984. 28 p. : ill. ; 28 cm. Introductory essay by Katy Kline. "The Installation": [7] p. inserted. Bibliography: p. 26-27.
1. Design, Industrial - United States - History - Exhibitions. 2. Aesthetics, American - History - 20th century - Exhibitions. I. Kline, Katy. II. Hayden Gallery. III. MIT Committee on the Visual Arts.
TS23 .A47 1984   *NYPL [3-MNE 90-10675]*

Affiches de l'Imprimerie Bénard. Plakate aus der Druckerei Benard, Sammlung des Musée de la Vie Wallone, Lüttich =. Köln , 1980. 92 p. :
                    NYPL [3-MDW 90-4651]

Affolter, Cuno, 1958- "Mit Pikasso macht man Kasso" . Zürich , c1990. 155 p., [5] p. of plates : ISBN 3-907010-50-7
IN PROCESS (ONLINE)
                    NYPL [MDY+ 90-12785]

Affreschi decorativi di antiche case trivigiane, dal XIII al XV secolo /. Botter, Mario. Treviso , 1979 (1987 printing) 162 p. :
                    NYPL [3-MLP+ 91-4495]

AFGHANISTAN - HISTORY - SOVIET OCCUPATION, 1979-1989 - PICTORIAL WORKS.
Grazda, Ed. Afghanistan, 1980-1989 /. Zürich, Switzerland : Zürich, Switzerland ; 139 p. : ISBN 3-907509-12-9 (Parkett)
                    NYPL [MFX (Grazda) 91-3488]

Afghanistan, 1980-1989 /. Grazda, Ed. Zürich, Switzerland : Zürich, Switzerland ; 139 p. : ISBN 3-907509-12-9 (Parkett)
                    NYPL [MFX (Grazda) 91-3488]

Afluentes teórico-estéticos do neo-realismo visual português /. Alvarenga, Fernando. Porto , 1989. 209 p. : ISBN 972-360-218-0 :
N8243.S65 A43 1989

Africa. Leuzinger, Elsy. The art of Africa. New York [c1960] 247 p.
                    NYPL [MADF 90-11494]

Africa explores . Vogel, Susan. New York : Munich : 294 p. : ISBN 3-7913-1143-3 (cloth) : DDC 709/.67/07473 20
N7391.65 .V63 1991   *NYPL [Sc G 91-40]*

AFRICA, NORTH, IN ART.
Günther, Erika. Die Faszination des Fremden . Münster [1990] i, 193 p., [56] p. of plates : ISBN 3-88660-542-6
ND567 .G86 1990

AFRICAN-AMERICANS. see AFRO-AMERICANS.

African animals in Renaissance literature and art.

Lloyd, Joan Barclay. Oxford, 1971. xi, 145 p. ISBN 0-19-817180-3
NX450.5 .L5   *NYPL [Sc 704.943-L]*

AFRICAN ART. see ART, AFRICAN.

African art in Southern Africa : from tradition to township / edited by Anitra Nettleton and David Hammond-Tooke. Johannesburg : Ad. Donker, 1989. 252 p. : ill. (some col.), maps ; 28 cm. Includes bibliographical references (p. 231-252). ISBN 0-86852-158-2 DDC 704/.03968 20
1. Art, Black - South Africa. I. Nettleton, Anitra C. E. II. Hammond-Tooke, David.
N7392 .A57 1989

Afrika és Óceánia törzsi müvészete. Boglár, Lajos. Tribal art in Africa and Oceania . [Budapest] , 1971. 8, 8 p., 8, 8 p. of plates :
enghun   *NYPL [3-MADF 90-5887]*

AFRO-AMERICAN ARCHITECTS - EMPLOYMENT.
American Black architects /. New York, N.Y. , c1991. p. cm. ISBN 1-87827-138-5 : DDC 720/.89/96073 20
NA738.N5 A45 1991

AFRO-AMERICAN ART - EXHIBITIONS.
Black art . Dallas, Tex. , New York , c1989. 305 p. : ISBN 0-8109-3104-4 (Abrams) : DDC 704/.0396073/07473 20
N6538.N5 B525 1989   *NYPL [Sc G 90-16]*

AFRO-AMERICAN ART - SOUTHERN STATES - EXHIBITIONS.
Dimensions and directions . Jackson, MS , c1980. ii, 46 p. : DDC 704/.0396073075/07476251 20
N6538.N5 D47 1980

AFRO-AMERICAN ART - WASHINGTON METROPOLITAN AREA - EXHIBITIONS.
Hall, Robert L., 1950- Gathered visions . Washington, D.C. , 1991. p. ISBN 1-560-98106-7 (pbk.) : DDC 704/.042/09753074753 20
N6538.N5 H26 1991

AFRO-AMERICAN ARTISTS - BIOGRAPHY.
Schwartzman, Myron. Romare Bearden . New York , 1990. 320 p. : ISBN 0-8109-3108-7 DDC 709/.2 B 20
N6537.B4 S39 1990
                    NYPL [3-MCX B368 91-3306]

AFRO-AMERICAN ARTISTS - BIOGRAPHY - JUVENILE LITERATURE.
Everett, Gwen. Li'l Sis and Uncle Willie . Washington, DC , New York , c1991. p. cm. ISBN 0-8478-1462-9 DDC 759.13 B 20
ND237.J73 E94 1991

AFRO-AMERICAN DECORATIVE ARTS.
Vlach, John Michael, 1948- By the work of their hands . Charlottesville , c1991. p. cm. ISBN 0-8139-1366-7 (paper) DDC 745/.089/96073 20
NK839.3.A35 V54 1991a

AFRO-AMERICAN PAINTERS - ALABAMA - BIOGRAPHY.
Maresca, Frank. Bill Traylor . New York , 1991. p. ISBN 0-394-58702-2 : DDC 759.1 B 20
ND237.T617 M37 1991

AFRO-AMERICAN PAINTERS - BIOGRAPHY.
Mosby, Dewey F., 1942- Henry Ossawa Tanner . Philadelphia, PA , New York, NY , 1991. 307 p. : ISBN 0-8478-1346-0 : DDC 759.13 20
N6537.T35 A4 1991   *NYPL [Sc G 91-19]*

Powell, Richard J., 1953- Homecoming . Washington, D.C. [1991] p. ISBN 0-8478-1421-1 : DDC 759.13 20
ND237.J73 P69 1991

AFRO-AMERICAN PAINTERS - EXHIBITIONS.
Thompson, Bob, 1937-1966. Bob Thompson. [New York, 1969] 40 p. :
                    NYPL [3-MCX T468.N5]

AFRO-AMERICAN PHOTOGRAPHERS - UNITED STATES - BIOGRAPHY.
Parks, Gordon, 1912- Voices in the mirror . New York , c1990. xv, 351 p., [24] p. of plates : ISBN 0-385-26698-7 DDC 770/.92 B 20
TR140.P35 A3 1990
                    NYPL [MFX (Parks) 91-3394]

AFRO-AMERICAN QUILTS - SOUTHERN STATES - HISTORY - 19TH CENTURY.

Fry, Gladys-Marie. Stitched from the soul . New York , c1990. ix, 101 p. : ISBN 0-525-24842-0 (cloth)
                    NYPL [3-MOT 91-4318]

AFRO-AMERICAN WOMEN ARTISTS - WASHINGTON METROPOLITAN AREA - EXHIBITIONS.
Hall, Robert L., 1950- Gathered visions . Washington, D.C. , 1991. p. ISBN 1-560-98106-7 (pbk.) : DDC 704/.042/09753074753 20
N6538.N5 H26 1991

AFRO-AMERICANS - MATERIAL CULTURE.
Vlach, John Michael, 1948- By the work of their hands . Charlottesville , c1991. p. cm. ISBN 0-8139-1366-7 (paper) DDC 745/.089/96073 20
NK839.3.A35 V54 1991a

AFRO-AMERICANS - PORTRAITS.
Wheat, Ellen Harkins. Jacob Lawrence . Hampton, Va. , 1991. p. cm. ISBN 0-9616982-4-1 : DDC 759.13 20
ND237.L29 W48 1991

AFRO-AMERICANS - UNITED STATES. see AFRO-AMERICANS.

Agaleia . Löber, Karl. Köln , 1988. viii, 327 p., [4] p. of plates : ISBN 3-412-05486-0
N8012.A66 L64 1988
                    NYPL [3-MAIH+ 90-12956]

Age (Melbourne, Australia) Postle, Bruce. Images of our time . Ridgwood, Vic. Australia , 1989. 159 p. : ISBN 0-670-90229-2
                    NYPL [MFW+ 91-5034]

Age of Alexander. From Alexander to Cleopatra, Greek art of the Hellenistic Age. Astoria, NY , c1989. 1 videocassette (28 min., 30 sec.) : DDC 709.38 11
N5633

AGED - FLORIDA - MIAMI.
Scheinbaum, David, 1951- Miami Beach . Miami , Gainsville, FL , c1990. 1 v. (unpaged) : ISBN 0-8130-0933-2 (cloth) DDC 975.9/381 20
F319.M6 S34 1990
                    NYPL [MFX (Scheinbaum) 91-3587]

AGED - FLORIDA - MIAMI - PICTORIAL WORKS.
Scheinbaum, David, 1951- Miami Beach . Miami , Gainsville, FL , c1990. 1 v. (unpaged) : ISBN 0-8130-0933-2 (cloth) DDC 975.9/381 20
F319.M6 S34 1990
                    NYPL [MFX (Scheinbaum) 91-3587]

AGED - PORTRAITS - EXHIBITIONS.
Un si grand âge-- . Paris , c1986. 108 p. : ISBN 2-86754-036-4 (pbk.) DDC 779/.2/090407404361 19
TR681.A35 S5 1986   *NYPL [MFW 90-2553]*

Agee, James, 1909-1955. Southall, Thomas, 1951- Of time & place . San Francisco , Fort Worth , c1990. 88 p. : ISBN 0-933286-57-0 (cloth)
                    NYPL [MFW 91-3397]

Agee, Rufus. see Agee, James, 1909-1955.

Agee, William C. Steiner, Michael, 1945- Michael Steiner, sculpture /. New York , c1990. 113 p. :
                    NYPL [3-MGO (Steiner) 90-10796]

Agence d'urbanisme pour l'agglomération strasbourgeoise.
Le Projet d'architecture dans la ville, instrument de sa transformation . Strasbourg , 1983. 50 P. ;
NA9183 .P7 1983

Le Projet urbain dans l'histoire de Strasbourg . Paris , 1983. 110 p. ;
NA9198.S87 P7 1983

Aghasyan, A. V. (Ara V.) Hayastani eritasard nkarich'nerě /. Erevan , 1987. 166 p. :
N7292.6 .H37 1987

AGING PERSONS. see AGED.

Agnes Etherington Art Centre.
Dean, Tom, 1947- Tom Dean drawings, 1985-1990 . Kingston, Ont. [c1990] 1 v. (unpaged) . ISBN 0-88911-502-2 DDC 741.971 20
NC143.D43 A4 1990

Knox, George. 18th century Venetian art in Canadian collections =. Vancouver, B.C., Canada , c1989. 108 p. : ISBN 0-920095-81-X
IN PROCESS (ONLINE)
                    NYPL [3-MAMC+ 91-6265]

Agnes Miller Parker. Rogerson, Ian. Agnes Miller Parker, wood-engraver and book

illustrator, 1895-1980 /. Wakefield, West Yorkshire , 1990. 88 p., [6] leaves of plates : ISBN 0-948375-23-X (quarter cloth) DDC 769.92 20
NE1147.6.P37 R64 1990

Agnes Miller Parker, wood-engraver and book illustrator, 1895-1980 /. Rogerson, Ian. Wakefield, West Yorkshire , 1990. 88 p., [6] leaves of plates : ISBN 0-948375-23-X (quarter cloth) DDC 769.92 20
NE1147.6.P37 R64 1990

Agnese, Gino. Marinetti : una vita esplosiva / Gino Agnese.1. ed. Milano : Camunia, c1990. 373 p., [16] p. of plates : ill. ; 23 cm. (Storia & storie) Includes bibliographical references (p. 343-348) and index. ISBN 88-7767-094-0 :
1. Marinetti, Filippo Tommaso, 1876-1944. 2. Futurism (Art) - Italy. 3. Artists - Italy - Biography. I. Title. II. Series.
N6923.M269 A85 1990

Agosti, Giovanni. Bambaia e il classicismo lombardo / Giovanni Agosti. Torino : G. Einaudi, c1990. xix, 229 p., [128] p. of plates : ill. ; 22 cm. (Saggi. 741) Includes bibliographical references and indexes. ISBN 88-06-11778-5
1. Bambaia, 1483-1548. I. Title.
IN PROCESS (ONLINE)
    NYPL [3-MGO (Bambaia) 91-6556]

AGOSTINO DI DUCCIO, 1418-1481?
Stokes, Adrian Durham, 1902-1972. Stones of Rimini. New York [1969] 263 p. DDC 726/.59
NA5621.R5 S7 1969

Agostino Ferrari /. Caramel, Luciano. Milano , c1991. 151 p. : ISBN 88-435-3445-9
IN PROCESS (ONLINE)
    NYPL [3-MCF F366 91-7167]

AGRARIAN QUESTION. see AGRICULTURE AND STATE; AGRICULTURE - ECONOMIC ASPECTS; LAND TENURE.

Agrawal, Yashodhara. Bharat Kala Bhavan. Bhagavata Purana . Varanasi, India , c1983. 1 portfolio (6 p., 6 leaves of col. ill.) ; DDC 755/.945211 19
ND1337.I5 B488 1983
    NYPL [3-MAF+ 90-10844]

AGRIBUSINESS. see AGRICULTURE - ECONOMIC ASPECTS.

AGRICULTURAL ECONOMICS. see AGRICULTURE - ECONOMIC ASPECTS.

AGRICULTURAL INNOVATIONS - ENGLAND - HISTORY.
Fussell, G. E. (George Edwin), 1889- Landscape painting and the agricultural revolution /. London , 1984. 83 p., [16] p. of plates : ISBN 0-907132-17-0 DDC 758/.1/0942 19
ND1354.4 .F87 1984
    NYPL [3-MCT 91-5610]

AGRICULTURAL INNOVATIONS IN ART.
Fussell, G. E. (George Edwin), 1889- Landscape painting and the agricultural revolution /. London , 1984. 83 p., [16] p. of plates : ISBN 0-907132-17-0 DDC 758/.1/0942 19
ND1354.4 .F87 1984
    NYPL [3-MCT 91-5610]

AGRICULTURAL POLICY. see AGRICULTURE AND STATE.

AGRICULTURE AND STATE - MAINE - HISTORY.
Doty, C. Stewart (Charles Stewart) Acadian hard times . Orono, Me. , 1991. xiv, 184 p. : ISBN 0-89101-070-X DDC 338.1/09741/1 20
HD1775.M2 D67 1991
    NYPL [MFW 91-7984]

AGRICULTURE AND STATE - SAINT JOHN RIVER VALLEY (ME. AND N.B.) - HISTORY.
Doty, C. Stewart (Charles Stewart) Acadian hard times . Orono, Me. , 1991. xiv, 184 p. : ISBN 0-89101-070-X DDC 338.1/09741/1 20
HD1775.M2 D67 1991
    NYPL [MFW 91-7984]

AGRICULTURE - ECONOMIC ASPECTS - MAINE - HISTORY.
Doty, C. Stewart (Charles Stewart) Acadian hard times . Orono, Me. , 1991. xiv, 184 p. : ISBN 0-89101-070-X DDC 338.1/09741/1 20
HD1775.M2 D67 1991
    NYPL [MFW 91-7984]

AGRICULTURE - ECONOMIC ASPECTS - SAINT JOHN RIVER VALLEY (ME.AND N.B.) - HISTORY.
Doty, C. Stewart (Charles Stewart) Acadian hard times . Orono, Me. , 1991. xiv, 184 p. : ISBN 0-89101-070-X DDC 338.1/09741/1 20
HD1775.M2 D67 1991
    NYPL [MFW 91-7984]

AGRICULTURE - ECONOMIC ASPECTS - SOUTH AFRICA - CISKEI.
Strategy and guidelines for the physical development of the Republic of Ciskei /. [Stellenbosch] , 1982. 2 v. : ISBN 0-908422-86-5 (pbk. : set) DDC 338.9687/92 19
HC905.Z7 C578 1982
    NYPL [Map Div. 90-58]

AGRICULTURE - ECONOMIC ASPECTS - SOUTH AFRICA - CISKEI - MAPS.
Strategy and guidelines for the physical development of the Republic of Ciskei /. [Stellenbosch] , 1982. 2 v. : ISBN 0-908422-86-5 (pbk. : set) DDC 338.9687/92 19
HC905.Z7 C578 1982
    NYPL [Map Div. 90-58]

AGRICULTURE - ECONOMICS. see AGRICULTURE - ECONOMIC ASPECTS.

AGRICULTURE - ENGLAND - HISTORY.
Fussell, G. E. (George Edwin), 1889- Landscape painting and the agricultural revolution /. London , 1984. 83 p., [16] p. of plates : ISBN 0-907132-17-0 DDC 758/.1/0942 19
ND1354.4 .F87 1984
    NYPL [3-MCT 91-5610]

AGRICULTURE IN ART.
Fussell, G. E. (George Edwin), 1889- Landscape painting and the agricultural revolution /. London , 1984. 83 p., [16] p. of plates : ISBN 0-907132-17-0 DDC 758/.1/0942 19
ND1354.4 .F87 1984
    NYPL [3-MCT 91-5610]

AGRICULTURE - UKRAINE - MAPS.
Ukraïns´kyï naukovo-doslidnyï instytut hidrometeorolohiï. Agroklimaticheskiĭ atlas Ukrainskoĭ SSR /. Kiev , 1964. 1 atlas (82 p. : *G2151.C8 K5 1964 (Map)* *NYPL [*QGA+ (U. S.S.R. Glavnoye upravleniye gidrometeorologicheskoĭ sluzhby. Agroklimaticheskiĭ atlas Ukrainskoĭ SSR.)]*

AGRICULTURE - UNITED STATES - JUVENILE LITERATURE.
Ancona, George. The American family farm . San Diego , c1989. 1 v. (unpaged) : ISBN 0-15-203025-5 : DDC 630/.973 19
S519 .A53 1989
    NYPL [MFX (Ancona) 90-11254]

Agroklimaticheskiĭ atlas Ukrainskoĭ SSR /. Ukraïns´kyï naukovo-doslidnyï instytut hidrometeorolohiï. Kiev , 1964. 1 atlas (82 p. : *G2151.C8 K5 1964 (Map)* *NYPL [*QGA+ (U. S.S.R. Glavnoye upravleniye gidrometeorologicheskoĭ sluzhby. Agroklimaticheskiĭ atlas Ukrainskoĭ SSR.)]*

AGRONOMY. see AGRICULTURE.

Aguarelas do Museu de Grão Vasco /. Museu de Grão Vasco (Portugal) [Viseu] [Lisboa] , 1989. 103 p. :
    NYPL [3-MAVZ+ (Viseu) 90-13444]

Aguilar, María D. (María Dolores) Coloquio de Urbanismo Barroco (1986 : Archidona, Spain) II centenario de la Plaza Ochavada de Archidona /. [Málaga] [1989] 350 p. : ISBN 84-7496-177-7
NA1306 .C6 1986

Aguilera, Cesáreo Rodríguez. see Rodríguez Aguilera, Cesáreo.

Aguilera, Porfirio. El Quehacer de un pueblo . Morelia, Michoacán , 1986. 183, [9] p. : ISBN 968-667-045-9 DDC 745/.0972/37 20
NK845.M53 Q44 1986

Aguilo, María Paz. see Paz Aguilo, María.

Aguirre, Marco Antonio. Arquitectura, fenómeno de controversia / Marco Antonio Aguirre. [Oaxaca, Mexico? : s.n.], c1990. 61 p., [88] p. of plates : ill. ; 28 cm. Includes bibliographical references. DDC 720 20
1. Architecture. I. Title.
NA27 .A36 1990

Agustí, Anna. Tàpies, Antoni, 1923- [Works. 1989.] Tàpies . New York , 1989- v. : ISBN 0-8478-0980-3 (v. 1) DDC 709.2 20
N7113.T3 A4 1989
    NYPL [3-MCQ+ T173 90-2433]

Ahearn, John, 1951-
Zeitlin, Marilyn. South Bronx Hall of Fame . Houston, Tex. , c1991. p. cm. ISBN 0-936080-21-3 (pbk.) : DDC 730/.92 20
NB237.A35 A4 1991

AHEARN, JOHN, 1951- - EXHIBITIONS.
Zeitlin, Marilyn. South Bronx Hall of Fame . Houston, Tex. , c1991. p. cm. ISBN 0-936080-21-3 (pbk.) : DDC 730/.92 20
NB237.A35 A4 1991

Ahlberg, Nils. Scandinavian atlas of historic towns. Odense , 1977- portfolios : ISBN 87-7492-216-5 (no. 1)
    NYPL [Map Div. 82-813]

Ahlborn, Richard E. Russian copper icons and crosses from the Kunz Collection . Washington, D.C. , 1990. p. cm. DDC 730/.947 20
NK1653.S65 R8 1990

Ahlers, O. Bönitz, Helmut, 1914- Helmut Bönitz /. [Göttingen] , c1990. 119 p. :
N6888.B6165 A4 1990

Ahmad, Aijazuddin. Raza, Moonis. An atlas of tribal India . New Delhi , 1990. xxv, 472 p. : ISBN 81-7022-286-9 :
    NYPL [Map Div. 91-4975]

Ahmann, Jochem. Ganz tief unten] [Germany , 1989?] 1 v. (unpaged) :
N6868 .G34 1989

AHMANSON FOUNDATION - ART COLLECTIONS - CATALOGS.
Los Angeles County Museum of Art. The Ahmanson gifts . Los Angeles, Calif. , c1991. p. cm. ISBN 0-87587-160-7 (pbk.) DDC 759.94/074/79494 20
ND454 .L6 1991

The Ahmanson gifts . Los Angeles County Museum of Art. Los Angeles, Calif. , c1991. p. cm. ISBN 0-87587-160-7 (pbk.) DDC 759.94/074/79494 20
ND454 .L6 1991

AHRENBERG, JACOB, 1847-1914.
Lukkarinen, Ville. Classicism and history . Helsinki , 1989. 196 p. : ISBN 951-9056-90-4
    NYPL [3-MQZ+ (Ahrenberg) 91-5470]

Ahrens, Carsten. Basquiat, Jean Michel. Jean-Michel Basquiat . Hannover , 1989. [122] p. : *NYPL [3-MAW (Hanover) 73-2900 1989/4]*

Ahrens, Dieter, 1934-
Schatzkammer Simeonstift : Antike, Mittelalter, Neuzeit / Dieter Ahrens. Trier : Spee-Verlag, 1986. 164 p. : 120 ill. ; 24 cm. (Museumsdidaktische Führungstexte . Bd. 8) Bibliography of the author's works: p. 158-164. Includes bibliographical references. ISBN 3-87760-268-1 DDC 708.3/43 19
1. Städtisches Museum Trier. 2. Art - Germany, West - Trier. I. Städtisches Museum Trier. II. Title. III. Series.
N2394.5 .A94 1986
    NYPL [MAVZ (Trier) 91-6413]

Der Weg in die Abstraktion . Trier , 1986. 112 p. : ISBN 3-87760-271-1 (Deut. Bibl.) DDC 709/.04/0520740343 19
N6494.A2 W44 1986
    NYPL [MAVZ (Trier) 91-5784]

Aicher, Florian, 1954- Robert Vorhoelzer, ein Architektenleben . München , c1990. 296 p. : ISBN 3-7667-0960-7
NA1088.V67 R6 1990

Aichiken Bijutsukan. Pari no joryū gaka 6-nin ten . [Tokyo] 1983. 190 p. :
    NYPL [3-MC 90-9733]

Aida, Takefuma. Takefuma Aida : buildings and projects. New York : Princeton Architectural Press, c1990. xviii, 104 p. : ill., plans ; 26 cm. Includes bibliographical references (p. 102-104). ISBN 0-910413-65-7
1. Aida, Takefuma. 2. Architecture - Japan. I. Title.
    NYPL [3-MQZ (Aida) 90-12650]

AIDA, TAKEFUMA.
Aida, Takefuma. Takefuma Aida . New York , c1990. xviii, 104 p. : ISBN 0-910413-65-7
    NYPL [3-MQZ (Aida) 90-12650]

Aigner, Carl. Fotoseite . Salzburg , 1990. 159 p. :
ISBN 3-7013-0802-0   *NYPL [MFW+]*

Aijazuddin Ahmad. see Ahmad, Aijazuddin.

Aiken, Carol. Johnson, Dale T. American portrait
miniatures in the Manney collection /. New
York , 1990. 271 p. :   ISBN 0-87099-597-9   DDC
757/.7/09730747471 20
ND1337.U5 J64 1990
     NYPL [3-MCW 91-4980]

Air-India. Bawa, Manmohan Singh. Himalayan
trekking maps /. [Bombay?] [New Delhi,
India , 1985]. 1 atlas (unpaged) :
     NYPL [Map Div. 90-11639]

AIR NAVIGATION. see AERONAUTICS.

**AIR PILOTS, MILITARY - UNITED STATES -
BIOGRAPHY.**
Noggle, Anne, 1922- For God, country, and the
thrill of it . College Station , c1990. xi, 160 p. :
ISBN 0-89096-401-7 (alk. paper)   DDC
940.54/4973/092 B 20
D790 .N64 1990
     NYPL [MFX+ (Noggle) 91-3591]

AIR PORTS. see AIRPORTS.

AIRDROMES. see AIRPORTS.

Airport terminals . Blow, Christopher J. Oxford ,
Boston , 1991. p. cm.   ISBN 0-7506-1278-9 :
DDC 725/.39 20
NA6300 .B56 1991

AIRPORT TERMINALS.
Blow, Christopher J. Airport terminals .
Oxford , Boston , 1991. p. cm.   ISBN
0-7506-1278-9 :   DDC 725/.39 20
NA6300 .B56 1991

Jahn, Helmut, 1940- Airports /. Basel ,
Boston , c1991. p. cm.   ISBN 0-8176-2613-1 (U.
S.)   DDC 725/.39 20
NA6300 .J34 1991

Airports /. Jahn, Helmut, 1940- Basel , Boston ,
c1991. p. cm.   ISBN 0-8176-2613-1 (U. S.)   DDC
725/.39 20
NA6300 .J34 1991

**AIRPORTS - NEBRASKA - AERIAL
PHOTOGRAPHS.**
Nebraska airport directory . [Lincoln] [1985]
[110] p. :   *NYPL [Map Div. 88-2044]*

AIRPORTS - NEBRASKA - DIRECTORIES.
Nebraska airport directory . [Lincoln] [1985]
[110] p. :   *NYPL [Map Div. 88-2044]*

AIRPORTS - TERMINALS.
Jahn, Helmut, 1940- Airports /. Basel ,
Boston , c1991. p. cm.   ISBN 0-8176-2613-1 (U.
S.)   DDC 725/.39 20
NA6300 .J34 1991

Airspeed aircraft since 1931 /. Taylor, H. A.
(Harold Anthony), 1904- London , 1991. x, 206
p. :   ISBN 0-85177-848-8 :   DDC 629.133343 20
     NYPL [JSD 91-212]

AIRSPEED AIRPLANES.
Taylor, H. A. (Harold Anthony), 1904-
Airspeed aircraft since 1931 /. London , 1991.
x, 206 p. :   ISBN 0-85177-848-8 :   DDC
629.133343 20   *NYPL [JSD 91-212]*

AIRSPEED (FIRM)
Taylor, H. A. (Harold Anthony), 1904-
Airspeed aircraft since 1931 /. London , 1991.
x, 206 p. :   ISBN 0-85177-848-8 :   DDC
629.133343 20   *NYPL [JSD 91-212]*

Aitiani, Marcello. Oro d'autore . Arezzo [1989]
147 p. :   *NYPL [3-MNR 91-6510]*

Aitken, George. Epping, Ed, 1948- Ed Epping,
events echoed . New York , c1984. 16 p. :
DDC 709/.2/4 19
N6537.E66 A4 1984
     NYPL [3-MGO (Epping) 90-12638]

**AIX-EN-PROVENCE (FRANCE) -
BUILDINGS, STRUCTURES, ETC.**
Boyer, Jean, conservateur. Le patrimoine
architectural d'Aix-en-Provence, XVIe, XVIIe,
XVIIIe siècles . Aix-en-Provence , 19. 191 p. :
     NYPL [3-MQWF+ 90-11534]

Aix, France. Musée Granet. see Musée Granet.

Aizpurúa, Juan Pablo Fusi. see Fusi Aizpurúa,
Juan Pablo, 1945-

Ajaloo Instituut. see Eesti NSV Teaduste
Akadeemia. Ajaloo Instituut.

Ajello, Raffaele. Classicismo d'età Romana : la
collezione farnese / testi di Raffaele Ajello,
Francis Haskell, Carlo Gasparri ; fotografie di
Mimmo Jodice. Napoli : Guida, c1988. 203 p. :
ill. ; 30 cm. Bibliography: p. 200-201. ISBN
88-7042-955-5
1. Farnese family - Art collections - Catalogs. 2. Museo
archeologico nazionale di Napoli - Catalogs. 3.
Sculpture, Classical - Italy - Naples - Catalogs. I.
Haskell, Francis, 1928-. II. Gasparri, Carlo. III. Title.
     NYPL [3-MGH+ 90-10570]

Ajroldi, Cesare. Palermo, norma di piano e
progetto /. [Italy] , Roma , c1990. 189 p. :
DDC 720/.945/823 20
NA1121.P3 P36 1990

Akademie der bildenden Künste in Wien.
Jugendwerke vom Schillerplatz /. Wien , c1988.
280 p. :   *NYPL [3-MAMG 90-9782]*

Kunsthistorisches Museum Wien. Die Moderne
Galerie des Kunsthistorischen Museums. Wien
[1956] 24 p.
     NYPL [3-MAVZ (Vienna) 91-1153]

Österreichische Landschaftsmalerei von
Schindler bis Klimt /. Wien , 1955. 32 p., [12]
p. of plates :   *NYPL [3-MCI 90-6903]*

Sechs Architekten vom Schillerplatz. Wien ,
c1977. 78 p. :   ISBN 3-85063-072-2
     NYPL [3-MQWD 90-5756]

**AKADEMIE DER BILDENDEN KÜNSTE IN
WIEN - EXHIBITIONS.**
Jugendwerke vom Schillerplatz /. Wien , c1988.
280 p. :   *NYPL [3-MAMG 90-9782]*

Akademie der Künste (Berlin, Germany) Das
Selbstportrait im Zeitalter der Photographie .
Bern , c1985. 523 p. :
     NYPL [MFW 91-2389]

**Akademie der Landwirtschaftswissenschaften,
Sofia.** see Akademiía na selskostopanskite
nauki.

**Akademie der Wissenschaften der DDR. Institut
für Ästhetik und Kunstwissenschaften.**
Krenzlin, Ulrike. Johann Gottfried Schadow /.
Stuttgart , c1990. 197 p. :   ISBN 3-421-02997-0
DDC 730/.92 B 20
NB588.S35 K7 1990

**Akademie der Wissenschaften der Estnischen S.
S. R.** see Eesti NSV Teaduste Akadeemia.

Akademiet for de skønne kunster (Denmark)
Bramsen, Henrik Boe, 1908- Early photographs
of architecture and views in two Copenhagen
libraries. Copenhagen , 1957. 92 p. :   DDC
779.4
N4015 .B67   *NYPL [MFW 91-4572]*

**AKADEMIET FOR DE SKØNNE KUNSTER
(DENMARK) - ALUMNI -
EXHIBITIONS.**
Kongelige Kobberstiksamling (Statens museum
for kunst) Von Abildgaard bis Marstrand .
[München] , 1985. 87 p., 114 p. of plates :
DDC 741.9489/1 19
NC274.C67 K66 1985
     NYPL [3-MBH 90-12465]

Akademiía khudozhestv SSSR.
Jugend im Sozialismus . Berlin [1987] 83 p. :
N6889 .J75 1987   *NYPL [3-MAMZ 91-4201]*

Kinderbuchillustrationen aus der Sowjetunion .
Berlin [1989] 71 p. :   ISBN 3-86050-003-1   DDC
741.6/42/0947074431552 20
NC985 .K49 1989   *NYPL [MDTT 91-4009]*

Akademiía na selskostopanskite nauki.
Pochveno-klimatichno raĭonirane na glavnite
polski kulturi . [Sofia , 1969]. 45 maps :
     NYPL [Map Div. 91-1087]

Akademiía nauk Ėstonskoĭ S. S. R. see Eesti
NSV Teaduste Akadeemia.

Akademiía nauk GDR. see Akademie der
Wissenschaften der DDR.

Akademiía sel'skokhoziaĭstvennykh nauk, Sofia.
see Akademiía na selskostopanskite nauki.

Akadmie der Künste (Berlin, Germany) Zum
Umgang mit dem Gestapo-Gelände . [Berlin ,
1988] 105, 25, 73 p. :
NA1068.5.N37 Z85 1988

Akanoma, Yukimori. Higashiyama, Kaii, 1908-
Kaii Higashiyama /. Sandy Hook, Conn. , 1989.
260 p. :   ISBN 0-88185-029-2
     NYPL [3-MAG 91-3347]

Akhmetova, F. V. Iskusstvo, rozhdennoe
Oktiabrem . Kazan´ , 1989. 119 p. ;
N6999.U76 I8 1989

Akkent, Meral. Das Kopftuch : ein Stückchen
Stoff in Geschichte und Gegenwart = Başörtü :
geçmişte ve günümüzde bir parça kumaş /
Meral Akkent, Gaby Franger.1. Aufl. Frankfurt
a.M. : Dağyeli, 1987. 286 p. : ill. (some col.) ;
30 cm. German and Turkish. Includes bibliographical
references (p. 283-284). ISBN 3-924320-61-6 :
1. Kerchiefs. 2. Kerchiefs - Turkey. 3. Women,
Muslim - Turkey - Conduct of life. I. Franger, Gaby. II.
Title. III. Title: Başörtü.
GT2113 .A35 1987
     NYPL [3-MMV+ 91-4637]

Ako kopú múzy . Kamenistý, Ján. Bratislava ,
1990. 263 p. :   ISBN 80-221-0036-6 :
NX571.C92 S54 1990

Akron Art Institute. Ionescu, Alexandra.
Contemporary Romanian painting . [s.l. , 1973]
[59] p. :   DDC 759.9498/074/013
ND928 .I66   *NYPL [3-MCY 90-12375]*

Akron Art Museum. This is not a photograph .
Sarasota, Fla. , c1987. 1 v. (various pagings) :
ISBN 0-916758-23-0   DDC 779/.09/04507474 20
TR645.S372 J647 1987
     NYPL [MFW 88-3001]

Der Akt in der deutschen Renaissance .
Grewenig, Meinrad Maria, 1954- Freren , 1987.
143 p., [100] p. of plates :   ISBN 3-923641-07-9
DDC 704.9/421/0943 19
N6865 .G74 1987
     NYPL [3-MAMG 91-4610]

AKTIVISTÁK (GROUP OF ARTISTS)
Mansbach, Steven A., 1950- Standing in the
tempest . Santa Barbara, Calif. , Cambridge,
Mass. , c1991. 240 p. :   ISBN 0-262-13274-5 (MIT
Press)   DDC 709/.439/1207473 20
N6820.5.N93 M36 1991

**al-Aṭlas al-tārīkhī lil-ʻālam al-Islāmī fī al-ʻuṣūr
al-Wusṭā.** Majīd, ʻAbd al-Munʻim. [al-Qāhirah]
1967. 13, 36p.
G1786.S1 M3 1967
     NYPL [Map-Div. 85-3121]

al-Fann al-Fārisī al-qadīm /. ʻUkāshah, Tharwat.
Miṣr al-Jadīdah, al-Qāhirah , 1989. 383 p. :
ISBN 977-442-109-4 :
N5390 .U38 1989

al-Funūn al-tashkīliyah /. ʻAlī, Muḥammad Riḍā.
Ṭarābulus, al-Jamāhīriyah al-ʻArabīyah
al-Lībiyah al-Shaʻbiyah al-Ishtirākiyah [198-]
37, 39 p., 66 p. of plates :
N7389.3.A45 A4 1980z

Al Held, new paintings . Held, Al, 1928- New
York, N.Y. (41 E. 57th St., New York, N.Y.
10022) , c1989. [7] p., 11 leaves of plates (1
folded) :   *NYPL [3-MCX H645 91-4593]*

al-ʻIrāq fī al-Khawāriṭ al-qadīmah. Sousa, Ahmed.
Baghdād, 1959. 22 p.
     NYPL [Map-Div. 85-3120]

al-Maskan al-rīfī al-Miṣrī. Abū al-ʻUlá,
Muḥammad Farīd. al-Qāhirah , 1990. 231, 3,
11 p. :   ISBN 977-373-128-6 :
NA7463.A1 A28 1990

**al-Riʻāyah al-lāḥiqah lil-mufraj ʻanhum bayna
al-naẓariyah wa-al-taṭbīq.** al-Riyāḍ : Dār
al-Nashr bi-al-Markaz al-ʻArabī lil-Dirāsāt
al-Amniyah wa-al-Tadrīb bi-al-Riyāḍ, 1988. 175
p. ; 22 cm. Includes bibliographical references.
"Abḥāth al-nadwah al-ʻilmiyah al-thāminah ʻashrah
wa-allatī ʻuqidat bi-maqarr al-Markaz fī al-fatrah min
28-30 Yūliyū 1986."
1. Ex-convicts - Services for. I. Markaz al-ʻArabī
lil-Dirāsāt al-Amniyah wa-al-Tadrīb bi-al-Riyāḍ.
NV9275 .R52 1988

**Alameda & Contra Costa counties, 1987 Thomas
guide.** Thomas Bros. Maps. Alameda and Santa
Clara counties street guide & directory. [Irvine,
Calif.] [c1986] 1 atlas (1 v. (various pagings)) :
ISBN 0-88130-207-4 :
     NYPL [Map Div. 90-11938]

**Alameda and Santa Clara counties street guide &
directory.** Thomas Bros. Maps. [Irvine, Calif.]
[c1986] 1 atlas (1 v. (various pagings)) :   ISBN
0-88130-207-4 :
     NYPL [Map Div. 90-11938]

ALAMEDA COUNTY, CALIF. - MAPS.
(1986) Thomas Bros. Maps. Alameda and Santa
Clara counties street guide & directory. [Irvine,

Calif.] [c1986] 1 atlas (1 v. (various pagings)) :
ISBN 0-88130-207-4 :
NYPL [Map Div. 90-11938]

Alan Bean, art off this earth [motion picture] /
Rudy Inc. ; producer, Rudy Buttignol ; director,
Murray Battle ; writers, Rudy Buttignol and
Murray Battle. Houston, TX : Rudy Inc., 1990.
1 film reel (26 min.) : sd., col. with b&w
sequences ; 16 mm. Cataloged from contributor's
data. Narrator, Anne Medina ; music, Eugene
Martynec. A foreign film (Canada) Senior high school
through college students and adults. Issued also as
videorecording. A documentary about astronaut Alan
Bean which focuses on his paintings. DDC 759.13 11
*1. Bean, Alan, 1932- - Criticism and interpretation. I.
Rudy Inc.*
ND237

Alan Bean, art off this earth [videorecording] /
Rudy Inc. ; producer, Rudy Buttignol ; director,
Murry Battle ; writers, Rudy Buttignol and
Murray Battle. Houston, TX : Rudy Inc., 1990.
1 videocassette (26 min.) : sd., col. Cataloged
from contributor's data. Narrator, Anne Medina ;
music, Eugene Martynec. A foreign videorecording
(Canada) Senior high school through college students
and adults. Issued as U-matic 3/4 in. or Beta 1/2 in. or
VHS 1/2 in. Issued also as motion picture. A
documentary about astronaut Alan Bean which focuses
on his paintings. DDC 759.13 11
*1. Bean, Alan, 1932- - Criticism and interpretation. I.
Rudy Inc.*
ND237

Alan Sonfist, 1969-1989 . Sonfist, Alan.
Brookville, N.Y. [1990] 80 p. : ISBN
0-933699-16-6 DDC 709/.2 20
N6537.S64 A4 1990
NYPL [3-MGO (Sonfist) 91-4000]

Alanís, Judith. Gabriel Fernández Ledesma /
Judith Alanís. México : Coordinación de
Difusión Cultural, Escuela Nacional de Artes
Plásticas, Universidad Nacional Autónoma de
México, 1985. 219 p. : ill. (some col.) ; 28 cm.
(Serie antológica monográfica) Includes bibliographical
references (p. 207-212). ISBN 968-8373-78-8
*1. Fernández Ledesma, Gabriel, 1900- - Criticism and
interpretation. I. Title. II. Series.*
N6559.F46 A83 1985

Alarion Press. American art and architecture
[videorecording] /. Boulder, CO , 1990. 5
videocassettes (140 min.) : DDC 709.73 11
N6505

ALASKA - GAZETTEERS
(1991) Schorr, Alan Edward. Alaska place
names /. Juneau, Alaska , 1991. 191 p. ;
ISBN 0-938737-25-2 DDC 917.98/003 20
F902 .S36 1991 **NYPL [Map Div. 91-6451]**

Alaska place names /. Schorr, Alan Edward.
Juneau, Alaska , 1991. 191 p. ; ISBN
0-938737-25-2 DDC 917.98/003 20
F902 .S36 1991 · **NYPL [Map Div. 91-6451]**

Alastair MacLennan . MacLennan, Alastair,
1943- Bristol : Derry : 157 p. : ISBN
0-907738-20-6
NYPL [3-MCV+ M1645 90-12067]

**ALBACETE (SPAIN : PROVINCE) -
ANTIQUITIES, ROMAN.**
Mosaicos romanos de Lérida y Albacete /.
Madrid , 1989. 124 p. : **NYPL [3-MRXZ 90-12594]**

Albany County Historical Association. Bennett,
Allison P. The people's choice . [S.l.] c1980
([Albany, N.Y.] : printed by Lane Press) ix, 135
p. : DDC 709/.747/42 19
N6530.N72 A33 **NYPL [3-MAMT 81-75]**

Albany Institute of History and Art.
Albany silver, 1652-1825 : catalog of an
exhibition of Albany silver, 1652-1825, March
15-May 1, 1964 / by Norman S. Rice
[curator] ; foreword by Laurence McKinney ;
introduction by Kathryn C. Buhler ; design by
George Cole ; photographs by Helga Photo
Studio, Inc. [Albany] : Albany Institute of
History and Art, c1964. 81 p. : ill. ; 26 cm.
(Cogswell fund series . publication no. 3) Errata slip
mounted on p. [3] of cover. Bibliography: p. 78-81.
*1. Silversmithing - New York (State) - Albany. 2.
Silversmithing - Exhibitions. I. Rice, Norman S. II.
Title. III. Series.* **NYPL [JAY C-1115]**

Burchfield Center. Edwin Dickinson . [Buffalo]

[c1977] 35 p. :
ND237.D46 A4 1977
NYPL [3-MCX D563 80-2252]

Albany silver, 1652-1825 . Albany Institute of
History and Art. [Albany] , c1964. 81 p. :
NYPL [JAY C-1115]

**ALBEE, EDWARD, 1928- - ART
COLLECTIONS - EXHIBITIONS.**
Selections from the Edward Albee collection .
Reading, Penn. , 1988. 28 p. : ISBN
0-941972-07-0
NYPL [3-MAX (Albee) 90-12382]

**ALBEMARLE PARK-MANOR GROUNDS
ASSOC.**
Mathews, Jane Gianvito, 1954- The manor and
cottages . Asheville, N.C. , c1991. p. cm. ISBN
0-9630437-0-6 : DDC 728/.09756/88 20
NA9051 .M38 1991

Albergo dei poveri (Palermo, Italy) Pietro
Novelli e il suo ambiente /. Palermo , c1990.
550 p. : ISBN 88-7804-048-7
NYPL [3-MCF N9385 91-3641]

Albers, Josef.
Feeney, Kelly, 1961- Josef Albers . Alexandria,
Va. , 1991. p. cm. ISBN 0-88397-100-3 DDC
760/.092 20
NC251.A36 A4 1991

**ALBERS, JOSEF - NOTEBOOKS,
SKETCHBOOKS, ETC. - EXHIBITIONS.**
Feeney, Kelly, 1961- Josef Albers . Alexandria,
Va. , 1991. p. cm. ISBN 0-88397-100-3 DDC
760/.092 20
NC251.A36 A4 1991

Albers, Marjorie K. The Amana people and their
furniture / Marjorie K. Albers. 1st ed. Ames :
Iowa State University Press, 1990. xii, 221 p. :
ill. ; 22 cm. Includes bibliographical references (p.
205-206) and index. ISBN 0-8138-1238-0 (pbk. : alk.
paper) DDC 749.2177/653 20
*1. Amana Society. 2. Furniture, Amana. 3. Furniture -
Iowa - History. I. Title.*
NK2435.I8 A4 1990
NYPL [3-MOF 91-4695]

Albert and Vera List Visual Arts Center.
Gerlovina, Rimma. Still performances /.
Cambridge, Mass. , 1989. 39 p. : ISBN
0-938437-27-5 DDC 779/.092/2 20
NX556.Z9 G472 1989
NYPL [MFW 90-4189]

Not so simple pleasures . Cambridge, Mass. ,
1990. 32 p. : ISBN 0-938437-34-8 (pbk.) : DDC
709/.73/0747444 20
N6512 .N635 1990

Albert André, 1869-1954. Galerie Marcel Guiot.
Paris [1960] 17 p.
ND553.A5 G33 1960
NYPL [3-MCO A55 90-7046]

Albert Bierstadt . Anderson, Nancy K. New
York , c1990. 327 p. : ISBN 1-555-95059-0 :
DDC 759.13 20
ND237.B585 A4 1991
NYPL [3-MCX+ B585 91-5808]

Albert Bloch, 1882-1961 . Bloch, Albert,
1882-1961. [Utica, N.Y.] , c1974. 36 p. :
NYPL [3-MCX B643 91-6562]

Albert Coste, la musique des couleurs /.
Muntaner, Bernard, 1945- Marseille, France ,
c1990. 107 p. : ISBN 2-903963-55-X :
N6853.C728 M8 1990

Albert Coste, 1895-1985. Muntaner, Bernard,
1945- Albert Coste, la musique des couleurs /.
Marseille, France , c1990. 107 p. : ISBN
2-903963-55-X :
N6853.C728 M8 1990

Albert Durer /. Jedlicka, Gotthard, 1899-1965.
Paris , 1928. 64 p., 60 p. of plates :
NYPL [3-MCK D85 90-8674]

Albert Dürer aux Pays-Bas : son voyage
(1520-1521), son influence : [exposition], Palais
des beaux-arts, Bruxelles, 1 octobre-27
novembre 1977. Bruxelles : Palais des
beaux-arts, 1977. xxiii, 211, 144 p., [14] leaves
of plates : ill. (some col.) ; 21 x 21 cm. At head
of title: Europalia 77, Bundesrepublik Deutschland. On
spine: Dürer aux Pays-Bas. Bibliography: p. xvi-xxiii.
*1. Dürer, Albrecht, 1471-1528 - Exhibitions. 2. Dürer,
Albrecht, 1471-1528 - Influence - Exhibitions. 3. Art,
Renaissance - Germany - Exhibitions. 4. Art, Flemish -
Exhibitions. 5. Art, Renaissance - Belgium - Flanders -*

*Exhibitions. 6. Art, Dutch - Exhibitions. 7. Art,
Renaissance - Netherlands - Exhibitions. 8. Belgium in
art - Exhibitions. 9. Netherlands in art - Exhibitions. I.
Brussels. Palais des beaux arts. II. Title: Dürer aux
Pays-Bas.*
N6888.D8 A4 1977
NYPL [3-MCK D85 81-320]

Albert, Greg, 1953-
Basic drawing techniques / Greg Albert, Rachel
Wolf. 1st ed. Cincinnati, Ohio : North Light
Books, c1991. p. cm. Includes index. ISBN
0-89134-388-1 (pbk.) : DDC 741.2 20
*1. Drawing - Technique. I. Wolf, Rachel, 1951-. II.
Title.*
NC730 .A52 1991

Basic watercolor techniques /. Cincinnati,
Ohio , 1991. p. cm. ISBN 0-89134-387-3 : DDC
751.42/2 20
ND2420 .B37 1991

**ALBERT I, PRINCE OF MONACO, 1848-
1922 - ART PATRONAGE -
EXHIBITIONS.**
L'Opéra de Monte-Carlo au temps du Prince
Albert Ier de Monaco /. Paris , c1990. 72 p. :
ISBN 2-7118-2321-0
NYPL [3-MQW 91-7009]

**ALBERT, JOS, 1886-1981 - CRITICISM AND
INTERPRETATION.**
Roberts-Jones, Philippe. Jos Albert /. Bruxelles
[1986] 154 p. : DDC 759.9493 20
ND673.A35 R6 1986

Albert König . Probst, Volker G. Unterlüss ,
1990. 239 p. : ISBN 3-927399-05-1
NYPL [MDG+ (König) 91-7207]

Albert Namatjira, 1902-1959 . MacKenzie,
Andrew. Moorebank, NSW , 1989. 52 p. :
ISBN 1-86325-021-2
NYPL [3-MCZ+ N17 90-13440]

Albert Paley . Norton, Deborah. Washington,
D.C. , 1991. p. cm. ISBN 0-295-97152-5 DDC
739.27/092 20
NK7398.P35 A4 1991

Albert Pinkham Ryder /. Broun, Elizabeth.
Washington , c1989. viii, 344 p. : ISBN
0-87474-328-1 (alk. paper) DDC 759.13 19
ND237.R8 A4 1989
NYPL [3-MCX R99 90-12872]

Albert Pinkham Ryder . Corcoran Gallery of Art.
Washington, D.C. [1961] 53 p. :
NYPL [3-MCX R99 91-850]

Albert Siegenthaler, 1938-1984 /. Siegenthaler,
Albert, 1938-1984. Aarau , c1987. 119 p. :
ISBN 3-905004-03-8 DDC 730/.92 20
NB853.S46 A4 1987 **NYPL [3-MGO+
(Siegenthaler) 90-12585]**

Albert Tucker, a retrospective /. Mollison, James.
Melbourne, Vic. , 1990. 120 p. : ISBN
0-7241-0143-8
NYPL [3-MCZ+ T89 90-13380]

ALBERTI, LEON BATTISTA, 1404-1472.
Borsi, Franco. [Leon Battista Alberti. English.]
Leon Battista Alberti /. New York , c1977. 397
p. : ISBN 0-06-010411-2
NA1123.A5 .B67
NYPL [MQZ+ (Alberti) 79-1214]

Alberti, Rafael, 1902-
[Negro Motherwell. English]
El negro / lithographs by Robert
Motherwell ; poem by Rafael Alberti.
Bedford, N.Y. : Tyler Graphics, 1983. [24]
leaves (some folded) : col. ill. ; 39 cm. "A
book of nineteen original lithographs by Robert
Motherwell illuminating the poem El negro
Motherwell by Rafael Alberti. The preface was
written by Jack Flam and the English translation of
the Spanish poem by Vincente Lleó
Cañal"--Colophon. English and Spanish verses are
printed facing the illustrations. The poem and its
translation are also printed in full on leaf 4, with
caption titles: El negro Motherwell; [and]
Motherwell's black. "The edition was fifty-one, plus ten
artist proofs, one trial proof, two printer's proofs, one
right to print proof, three hors commerce and three
presentation copies. In addition, seven of the
lithographs were published individually as separately
signed and numbered editions of
ninety-eight"--Colophon. Issued in and affixed to a
fall-down-back box. LC has signed copy designated
"book number 14/51." DLC DDC 769.92 20
1. Motherwell, Robert. 2. Alberti, Rafael, 1902- Negro

Motherwell - Illustrations. I. Title. II. Title: Negro
Motherwell. III. Title: Motherwell black.
NE2312.M68 A4 1983

NEGRO MOTHERWELL - ILLUSTRATIONS.
Alberti, Rafael, 1902- [Negro Motherwell.
English.] El negro /. Bedford, N.Y. , 1983.
[24] leaves (some folded) : DDC 769.92 20
NE2312.M68 A4 1983

**Die Albertina und das Dresdner
Kupferstich-Kabinett** : Meisterzeichnungen aus
zwei alten Sammlungen : eine Ausstellung mit
der Graphischen Sammlung Albertina Wien.
Dresden : Staatliche Kunstsammlungen, 1978.
181 p. : ill. (some col.) ; 26 cm. "Ausstellung im
Albertinum 26.9.-26.11.1978." Bibliography: p. 171-180.
Includes index.
1. Drawing - Exhibitions. I. Vienna. Albertina. II.
Dresden. Kupferstichkabinett.
NC17.A8 V52   **NYPL [MBH 80-591]**

Albertina, Vienna. see Vienna. Albertina.

Albertinum (Dresden, Germany)
Hassebrauk, Ernst, 1905- Die
Wiederbegegnung . [Dresden] , c1988. 80 p. :
DDC 741.943 20
NC251.6.Z9 H372 1988
     NYPL [3-MCK H354 91-4570]

Richter, Rainer. Carl Christian Vogel von
Vogelstein, 1788-1868 . Dresden , c1988. 93,
[1] p. :
N6888.V57 A4 1988

Der silberne Boden . Stuttgart [Leipzig] ,
c1990. 510 p. : ISBN 3-421-02982-2 (Deutsche
Verlags-Anstalt)
     NYPL [3-MAMG 91-5527]

Alberto Giacometti. Giacometti, Alberto,
1901-1966. Basel , c1989. 139 p. :
    NYPL [3-MGO+ (Giacometti) 90-13215]

Alberto Giacometti . Giacometti, Alberto,
1901-1966. Basel , c1989. 139 p. : DDC 709/.2
20
N6853.G5 A4 1989

Alberto Giacometti, 10.10.1901-11.1.1966 .
Giacometti, Alberto, 1901-1966. München ,
c1989. [40] p. :
     NYPL [3-MGO (Giacometti) 91-7078]

Alberto Martini e Dante / a cura di Corrado
Gizzi. Milano : Electa, c1989. 431 p. : ill. ; 31
cm. ISBN 88-435-2984-6
1. Martini, Alberto, 1876-1954 - Exhibitions. I. Gizzi,
Corrado. II. Casa di Dante in Abruzzo.
IN PROCESS (ONLINE)
     NYPL [3-MCF+ M383 90-11582]

Alberto Savinio . Savinio, Albertó, 1891-1952.
Ferrara , 1980. ca. 250 p. :
     NYPL [3-MCF S265 90-6458]

ALBINI, FRANCO - EXHIBITIONS.
Franco Albini, architecture and design,
1934-1977 . New York, NY , c1990. 138 p. :
ISBN 0-910413-79-7 (pbk. : alk. paper) : DDC
720/.92 20
NA1123.A525 A4 1990
     NYPL [3-MQZ (Albini) 91-6735]

**Al´bom planov i diagramm, otnosīashchikhsīa k
dīelu sooruzhenīīa ēlevatorov na Kitaīskoī
Vostochnoī zh.[eleznoī] d.[oroge]** . [S.l. : s.n.,
192-?]. 6 leaves (some folded) : ill., col. maps ;
25 x 37 cm.
1. Chinese Eastern Railway. 2. Railroads -
Manchoukuo - Maps. 3. Vladivostok (R.S.F.S.R.) -
Maps. 4. Harbin (China) - Maps.
     NYPL [Map Div. 91-1086]

**ALBRECHT, BENEDIKT, CA. 1655-1730 -
CRITICISM AND INTERPRETATION.**
Seidl, Bärbel. Studien zu Johann Eustachius
Kendlbacher und Benedikt Albrecht /.
München , c1990. 133 p., 9 p. of plates : ISBN
3-88073-361-9
ND588.K442 S45 1989

Albrecht-Dürer-Gesellschaft.
Italienische Druckgraphik der Gegenwart :
Ausstellung der Albrecht Dürer Gesellschaft im
Germanischen Nationalmuseum Nürnberg vom
9.5. bis 27.6.1976 : [Katalog / Redaktion und
Gestaltung, Michael Mathias Prechtl].
Nürnberg : Albrecht Dürer Gesellschaft, [1976]
[129] p. : chiefly ill. (some col.) ; 20 x 21 cm.
(Katalog der Albrecht-Dürer Gesellschaft ; 32) Preface
also in Italian.
1. Prints, Italian - Exhibitions. I. Prechtl, Michael

Mathias. II. Nuremberg. Germanisches
Nationalmuseum. III. Series:
Albrecht-Dürer-Gesellschaft. Katalog, 32. IV. Title.
NE659 .A5 1976   **NYPL [MDBF 80-380]**

Katalog.
(32) Albrecht-Dürer-Gesellschaft. Italienische
Druckgraphik der Gegenwart . Nürnberg
[1976] [129] p. :
NE659 .A5 1976   **NYPL [MDBF 80-380]**

(36) Russische Graphik des 19. und 20.
Jahrhunderts . [Nürnberg , 1977] ca. 300 p. :
DDC 769/.074/0332 s 769.947/074/0332 19
NE1 .A48 no. 36 NE675
     NYPL [MDBF 80-378]

Russische Graphik des 19. und 20.
Jahrhunderts . [Nürnberg , 1977] ca. 300 p. :
DDC 769/.074/0332 s 769.947/074/0332 19
NE1 .A48 no. 36 NE675
     NYPL [MDBF 80-378]

**Albrecht Dürer und die Frühzeit der
Exlibriskunst** . Schutt-Kehm, Elke M., 1954-
Wiesbaden , c1990. 39 p. : ISBN 3-922835-18-X
     NYPL [MDVF 91-7231]

**Albrecht Dürer-Verein, Nuremberg. see Albrecht-
Dürer-Gesellschaft.**

**Albrecht Dürer, Verzeichnis sämtlicher
Zeichnungen** . Staatliche Museen Preussischer
Kulturbesitz. Kupferstichkabinett. [Berlin] ,
1972. 19 p., [144] p. of plates :
NC251.D8 A8   **NYPL [3-MCK D85 90-5760]**

Albrecht-Dürer-Haus. Düreriana . Nürnberg ,
c1990. 296 p. : ISBN 3-418-00349-4
N6888.D8 A4 1990
     NYPL [3-MCK+ D85 91-7549]

Albrecht Dürerhaus Stiftung.
Düreriana . Nürnberg , c1990. 296 p. : ISBN
3-418-00349-4
N6888.D8 A4 1990
     NYPL [3-MCK+ D85 91-7549]

**ALBRECHT DÜRERHAUS STIFTUNG -
EXHIBITIONS.**
Düreriana . Nürnberg , c1990. 296 p. : ISBN
3-418-00349-4
N6888.D8 A4 1990
     NYPL [3-MCK+ D85 91-7549]

Albrecht, Herbert, 1905- Leitner, Gudrun von,
1940- Gudrun von Leitner . München , c1988.
216 p. : ISBN 3-7913-0897-1 DDC 709.2 20
N6888.L365 A4 1988
     NYPL [3-MCK+ L543 90-11791]

Albright-Knox Art Gallery. Auping, Michael.
Jenny Holzer . Buffalo, N.Y. , 1991. p. cm.
ISBN 0-914782-80-0 DDC 709/.2 20
N6537.H577 A4 1991

**Albstadt, Ger. (Gemeinde) Städtische Galerie. see
Städtische Galerie Albstadt.**

Album amicorum Kenneth C. Lindsay : essays on
art and literature / edited by Susan Alyson
Stein and George D. McKee. [Binghamton,
NY] : Dept. of Art and Art History, State
University of New York at Binghamton, 1990.
xiii, 380 p. : ill. ; 24 cm. "Kenneth C. Lindsay: A
bibliography" (p. [375]-378). Includes bibliographical
references. ISBN 0-9621899-9-5 DDC 700 20
1. Art. I. Lindsay, Kenneth Clement, 1919-. II. Stein,
Susan Alyson. III. McKee, George D.
N7443.2 .A45 1990

Album das glorias . Pinheiro, Rafael Bordalo,
1846-1905. Lisboa , 1989. [42] leaves, 39 leaves
of plates :
NC1639.P56 A4 1989

**Album do nome e do renome de Diogo de
Macedo** . Macedo, Diogo de. Vila Nova de
Gaia , 1989. 127 p. : ISBN 972-95053-2-2
NB833.M16 A4 1989

**Album dos desenhos das antigualhas de Francisco
de Holanda** /. Hollanda, Francisco de,
1517-1584. Lisboa , c1989. 54, 54, 73 p., [5]
folded leaves of plates : ISBN 972-240-733-3
DDC 741.9469 20
NC290.H65 A4 1989

Album für Freunde des Bergbaues . Heuchler,
Eduard, 1801-1879. Frankfurt am Main [1977]
1 portfolio (6 p., [14] leaves of plates) :
     NYPL [MEM+ H595 89-6071]

Album (Messina, Italy) .
(1) Colonialismo e fotografia . Messina [1989?]

354 p. :
IN PROCESS (ONLINE)
     NYPL [MFW 91-8015]

The albumen & salted paper book /. Reilly,
James M., 1946- Rochester, N.Y. , 1980. 133
p. ; ISBN 0-87992-014-9 (pbk.) :
TR400 .R44   **NYPL [MFW 81-800]**

ALBUMEN PAPER.
Reilly, James M., 1946- The albumen & salted
paper book /. Rochester, N.Y. , 1980. 133 p. ;
ISBN 0-87992-014-9 (pbk.) :
TR400 .R44   **NYPL [MFW 81-800]**

Alchi . Goepper, Roger. Köln , c1982. 110 p. :
ISBN 3-7701-1479-5 DDC 755/.943/09546 19
ND2829.A415 G64 1982
     NYPL [3-MAF 90-12370]

**ALCHI GÖMPA (INDIA) - BUILDINGS,
STRUCTURES, ETC. - EXHIBITIONS.**
Goepper, Roger. Alchi . Köln , c1982. 110 p. :
ISBN 3-7701-1479-5 DDC 755/.943/09546 19
ND2829.A415 G64 1982
     NYPL [3-MAF 90-12370]

Alcide Le Beau, 1873-1943 /. Hellebranth,
Robert. [S.l.] , c1988. 73 p. :
     NYPL [3-MCO+ L442 91-5884]

Alcoa Collection of Contemporary Art. An
exhibition of works acquired from the G. David
Thompson Collection. [Pittsburgh : Alcoa,
1967?] [32] p. : ill. (some col.) ; 25 cm.
Exhibition first shown at the Carnegie Institute
Museum of Art, Pittsburgh ; circulated under the
auspices of The American Federation of Arts.
1. Thompson, G. David, d. 1965 - Art collections -
Exhibitions. 2. Alcoa Collection of Contemporary Art.
3. Painting, Modern - 20th century - Exhibitions. I.
Carnegie Institute. Museum of Art. II. Title.
     NYPL [3-MC 90-6343]

**ALCOA COLLECTION OF CONTEMPORARY
ART.**
Alcoa Collection of Contemporary Art. An
exhibition of works acquired from the G. David
Thompson Collection. [Pittsburgh , 1967?] [32]
p. :   **NYPL [3-MC 90-6343]**

**Alcolea i Blanch, Santiago, 1951-
[Museo del Prado. English]**
The Prado / by Santiago Alcolea i Blanch.
New York : Abrams, 1991. p. cm. Translation
of: Museo del Prado. Includes bibliographical
references and index. ISBN 0-8109-3715-8 DDC
759.94/074/4641 20
1. Painting - Spain - Madrid. 2. Museo del Prado. I.
Title.
N3450 .A9513 1991

Alcolea, Santiago.
Escultura catalana del segle XIX . [Barcelona]
[1989] 246 p. :   **NYPL [3-MGI+ 91-6802]**

Escultura catalana del segle XIX . Barcelona
[1989?] 246 p. : DDC 730/.946/70744672 20
NB809.C3 E83 1989

Viladomat / Santiago Alcolea i Gil, textes ;
Ramon Manent i Rodon, fotografies. Mataró :
Museu Comarcal del Maresme : Museu Arxiu
de Santa Maria, [1990?] 422 p. : ill. ; 29 cm.
1. Viladomat, Antoni, 1678-1755. I. Title.
     NYPL [3-MCQ V693 91-5242]

Alcosser, Murray, 1937- The romantic rose /
photographs by Murray Alcosser. New York :
Rizzoli, 1990. 119 p. : col. ill. ; 26 cm. ISBN
0-8478-1175-1 DDC 779/.34 20
1. Photography of plants. 2. Roses - Pictorial works. 3.
Roses - Poetry. I. Title.
TR726.R66 A43 1990
     NYPL [MFX (Alcosser) 90-11181]

Aldana, Raúl Herrera. Instituto Hidrográfico de
la Armada. Atlas hidrográfico de Chile /.
[Valparaíso] , 1974. 37, [14], [212] p. : DDC
623.89/2
G1751.C3 I5 1974
     NYPL [Map Div. 91-6470]

Aldegheri, Claudio. Immagini del post-moderno .
Venezia , c1983. 345 p. : ISBN 88-85067-09-3
DDC 724.9/1 19
NA682.P67 I48 1983
     NYPL [3-MQV 91-6389]

Aldemir Martins . Klintowitz, Jacob, 1941- [São
Paulo, Brazil?] [1989] 119 p. : ISBN
85-7087-016-7 DDC 760/.092 20
N6659.M36 A4 1989

Aldersey-Williams, Hugh.
Cranbrook design . New York , 1990. 207 p. :
ISBN 0-8478-1252-9   DDC 745.4/071/177439 20
NK1170 .C7 1990   **NYPL [3-MNF 91-4482]**

King and Miranda : the poetry of the machine
/ Hugh Aldersey-Williams. New York : Rizzoli,
1991. p. cm. (A Blueprint monograph) Includes
bibliographical references. ISBN 0-8478-1358-4 (pbk.)
DDC 745.4/4922 20
*1. King and Miranda. 2. Design - Italy - Milan -
History - 20th century. I. Title. II. Title: Poetry of the
machine. III. Series.*
NK1535.K52 A84 1991

World design : nationalism and globalism in
design / Hugh Aldersey-Williams. New York :
Rizzoli, 1992. p. cm. Includes bibliographical
references and index. ISBN 0-8478-1461-0 DDC
745.4/442 20
1. Design - History - 20th century. I. Title.
NK1390 .A43 1992

Aldin, Cecil Charles Windsor, 1870-1935. Heron,
Roy. The sporting art of Cecil Aldin /.
London , 1990. 126 p., [20] p. of plates : ISBN
0-948253-50-9 :   DDC 760.092 20
NC242.A4   **NYPL [3-MCV A36 91-5523]**

**ALDIN, CECIL CHARLES WINDSOR, 1870-
1935.**
Heron, Roy. The sporting art of Cecil Aldin /.
London , 1990. 126 p., [20] p. of plates : ISBN
0-948253-50-9 :   DDC 760.092 20
NC242.A4   **NYPL [3-MCV A36 91-5523]**

Aldo Rossi . Ferlenga, Alberto. Milano , 1990.
118 p. : ISBN 88-435-3088-7
       NYPL [3-MQZ (Rossi) 91-6524]

Aldo Rossi . Rossi, Aldo, 1931- New York ,
N.Y. , 1991. p. cm. ISBN 1-87827-115-6 (cloth) :
DDC 720/.92 20
NA1123.R616 A4 1991

Aldo Rossi, progetti e disegni, 1962-1979 =.
Rossi, Aldo, 1931- New York , 1979. 163 p. :
ISBN 0-8478-0256-6 (pbk.) :   DDC 720/.92/4
NA1123.R616 A4 1979a
       NYPL [3-MQZ (Rossi) 80-2166]

Aldo Rossi, projects and drawings, 1962-1979.
Rossi, Aldo, 1931- Aldo Rossi, progetti e
disegni, 1962-1979 =. New York , 1979. 163
p. : ISBN 0-8478-0256-6 (pbk.) :   DDC 720/.92/4
NA1123.R616 A4 1979a
       NYPL [3-MQZ (Rossi) 80-2166]

Aldous, Tony. A Prospect of Westminster .
[Westminster] , c1989. 127 p. : ISBN
0-901602-03-5
       NYPL [3-MQWK+ 90-410]

The Aldrich collection /. Aldrich, Larry. New
York , 1960. [48] p. :
       NYPL [3-MAX (Aldrich) 90-5747]

Aldrich, Larry.
The Aldrich collection / [exhibition] circulated
by the American Federation of Arts, October,
1960-April, 1962. New York : Thistle Press,
1960. [48] p. : chiefly ill., port. ; 19 x 26 cm.
Introduction by Grace L. McCann Morley.
*1. Aldrich, Larry - Art collections - Exhibitions. 2.
Art - Private collections - United States - Exhibitions. I.
Morley, Grace, 1900-. II. Title.*
       NYPL [3-MAX (Aldrich) 90-5747]

**ALDRICH, LARRY - ART COLLECTIONS -
EXHIBITIONS.**
Aldrich, Larry. The Aldrich collection /. New
York , 1960. [48] p. :
       NYPL [3-MAX (Aldrich) 90-5747]

Aldrich, Megan Brewster. The Craces .
[London] , Brighton , c1990. xiv, 202 p., [16] p.
of plates : ISBN 0-7195-4854-3 :   DDC 747.22 20
       NYPL [3-MLO 91-2246]

**Aldrich Museum of Contemporary Art
(Ridgefield, Conn.)** Adaptation & negation of
socialist realism . Ridgefield, CT , c1990. 44
p. :   **NYPL [3-MAM+ 91-5891]**

Aldridge, Peter.
New sculpture by Peter Aldridge / Steuben
Glass. New York : Steuben Glass, 1981. [24]
p. : chiefly ill. (some col.) ; 26 cm. Cover title.
*1. Aldridge, Peter - Exhibitions. 2. Glass sculpture -
Exhibitions. I. Steuben Glass. II. Title.*
    NYPL [3-MGO (Aldridge) 90-6401]

ALDRIDGE, PETER - EXHIBITIONS.
Aldridge, Peter. New sculpture by Peter
Aldridge /. New York , 1981. [24] p. :
    NYPL [3-MGO (Aldridge) 90-6401]

Alea contemporanea.
(1) Ermes Midena, architetto moderno in Friuli
/. Udine , 1988. 94 p. : ISBN 88-7772-012-3
(pbk.)
    NYPL [3-MQZ + (Midena) 90-2526]

Alechinsky, Pierre, 1927-
Pierre Alechinsky, new work : May 3 to 25,
1990, André Emmerich Gallery. New York :
The Gallery, c1990. [10] p., 15 leaves of
plates : chiefly ill. (some col.) ; 28 x 31 cm.
Includes bibliographical references (p. [8]).
*1. Alechinsky, Pierre, 1927- - Exhibitions. I. André
Emmerich Gallery. II. Title.*
    NYPL [3-MCH+ A36 91-3431]

Sicard, Michel. Alechinsky sur Rhône /. Paris ,
Arles , c1990. 123 p. : ISBN 2-86869-586-8
DDC 760/.092 20
N6973.A4 S53 1990

**ALECHINSKY, PIERRE, 1927- - CRITICISM
AND INTERPRETATION.**
Sicard, Michel. Alechinsky sur Rhône /. Paris ,
Arles , c1990. 123 p. : ISBN 2-86869-586-8
DDC 760/.092 20
N6973.A4 S53 1990

**ALECHINSKY, PIERRE, 1927- -
EXHIBITIONS.**
Alechinsky, Pierre, 1927- Pierre Alechinsky,
new work . New York , c1990. [10] p., 15
leaves of plates :
    NYPL [3-MCH+ A36 91-3431]

Alechinsky sur Rhône /. Sicard, Michel. Paris ,
Arles , c1990. 123 p. : ISBN 2-86869-586-8
DDC 760/.092 20
N6973.A4 S53 1990

Alegría, Fernando, 1918- Creadores en el mundo
hispánico / Fernando Alegría. Santiago de
Chile : Editorial Andrés Bello, [1990] 184 p. ;
23 cm. Includes bibliographical references. ISBN
956-1-30910-5
*1. Arts, Latin American. 2. Arts, Modern - 20th
century - Latin America. I. Title.*
NX501.5.A1 A43 1990

Aler, Jan. Cultural hermeneutics of modern art .
Amsterdam , Atlanta, GA , 1989. 307 p., [1] p.
of plates : ISBN 90-6203-645-7
       NYPL [3-MAS 90-10857]

ALER, JAN.
Cultural hermeneutics of modern art .
Amsterdam , Atlanta, GA , 1989. 307 p., [1] p.
of plates : ISBN 90-6203-645-7
       NYPL [3-MAS 90-10857]

**Alesio, Mateo Pérez de. see Pérez de Alesio,
Mateo, ca. 1547-ca. 1600.**

Alessandro Milesi, pittore . Milesi, Alessandro,
1856-1945. Venezia , c1989. 237 p. :
       NYPL [3-MCF+ M645 90-91]

Aletti, Vince. Hujar, Peter, 1934- Peter Hujar /.
New York, N.Y. , 1990. 95 p. : ISBN
0-934349-07-X (pbk.)
IN PROCESS (ONLINE)
       NYPL [MFX (Hujar) 91-830]

Alexander Anderson's life and engravings .
Pomeroy, Jane R. Worcester [Mass.] , 1990. p,
137-230 : ISBN 0-944026-25-7
       NYPL [MDG (Anderson) 91-4737]

Alexander Archipenko. Archipenko, Alexander,
1887-1964. Saarbrücken , 1986- 2 v. : ISBN
3-925303-31-6 (Bd. 1)
    NYPL [3-MGO (Archipenko) 87-1303]

Alexander Bodon /. Kloos, Maarten. Rotterdam ,
1990. xv, [128] p. : ISBN 90-6450-087-8
    NYPL [3-MQZ (Bodon) 91-4491]

Alexander Calder /. Marter, Joan M. Cambridge ,
New York , 1991. p. cm. ISBN 0-521-33038-6
DDC 730/.92 20
NB237.C28 M34 1991

Alexander Calder, Fernand Léger : [exhibition]
October 4-27, 1979. New York : M. Knoedler,
1979. 24 p. : ill. (8 col.) ; 26 cm. "Fernand Léger
on Alexander Calder": p. 2.
*1. Calder, Alexander, 1898-1976 - Exhibitions. 2. Léger,
Fernand, 1881-1955 - Exhibitions. I. Calder, Alexander,
1898-1976. II. Léger, Fernand, 1881-1955. III. M.
Knoedler & Co.*   **NYPL [3-MC 90-7054]**

Alexander Calder, mobiles. Calder, Alexander,
1898-1976. Alexander Calder, mobiles, Fernand
Léger, peintures. Paris , c1988. 69 p. : ISBN
2-86574-012-9
MLCM 90/03707 (N)
    NYPL [3-MGO+ (Calder) 91-3331]

**Alexander Calder, mobiles, Fernand Léger,
peintures.** Calder, Alexander, 1898-1976. Paris ,
c1988. 69 p. : ISBN 2-86574-012-9
MLCM 90/03707 (N)
    NYPL [3-MGO+ (Calder) 91-3331]

Alexander, Christopher. A foreshadowing of 21st
century art : the color and geometry of very
early Turkish carpets / Christopher Alexander.
New York : Oxford University Press, 1990. p.
cm. ISBN 0-19-520866-8 DDC 746.7/561 20
*1. Rugs - Turkey - Themes, motives. 2. Rugs, Islamic -
Turkey - Themes, motives. I. Title.*
NK2865.A1 A44 1990

Alexander, Forsyth, 1960-
Henrietta Johnston . Winston-Salem, N.C. ,
c1991. p.   DDC 741.973 20
NC139.J6 H4 1991

Museum of Early Southern Decorative Arts.
The regional arts of the early South .
Winston-Salem, N.C. , 1991. p. ISBN
0-945578-02-4 :   DDC 745/.0975/07475667 20
NK811 .M87 1991

Alexander, Kay. Discipline-based art education .
Santa Monica, Calif. , 1991. p. cm. ISBN
0-89236-171-9 :   DDC 700 20
N362 .C6 1991

Alexander, Lucy. 150 South African paintings :
past and present / Lucy Alexander, Evelyn
Cohen. Cape Town : Struikhof Publishers, 1990.
180 p. : ill. (some col.) ; 29 cm. Includes
bibliographical references and index. ISBN
0-947458-25-5 DDC 759.968 20
*1. Painting, South African - Catalogs. I. Cohen, Evelyn.
II. Title. III. Title: One hundred fifty South African
paintings.*
ND1092 .A43 1990

**ALEXANDER THE GREAT, 356-323 B. C. -
ART.**
Calcani, Giuliana. Cavalieri di bronzo . Roma ,
c1989. 182 p. : ISBN 88-7062-671-7
    NYPL [3-MGO (Lysippus) 91-5330]

Lenkey, Susan V. An unknown Leonardo
self-portrait. Stanford, Calif., 1963. 23 p.
    NYPL [3-MCF V7 91-227]

Alexej Jawlensky, vom Abbild zum Urbild .
Jawlensky, Alexej von, 1864-1941. Wasserburg
am Inn , 1979. 107 p. :
N6999.J38 A4 1979
    NYPL [3-MCZ J41 81-398]

**Alexis de Chateauneuf, ein Hamburger
Baumeister, 1799-1853 /.** Lange, Günther.
Hamburg , 1965. 147 p. :
    NYPL [3-MQZ (Chateauneuf) 91-818]

Alexis Gritchenko : sa vie, son œuvre / textes de
Raymond Charmet ... [et al.].Nouv. éd. Paris :
Editions "Quatre vents", c1964. 83 p. : ill.
(some col.), ports. ; 29 cm. French and English. "Il
a été tiré de cet ouvrage ... 280 exemplaires sur vélin
pur fil d'arches, numérotés de 26 à 305."--p. [87].
Library has no. 280.
*1. Gritchenko, Alexis, 1883-. I. Gritchenko, Alexis,
1883-. II. Charmet, Raymond.*
    NYPL [3-MCZ G874 91-903]

Alexis Smith /. Smith, Alexis, 1949- New York ,
1991. p. cm. ISBN 0-87427-076-6 DDC 700/.92
20
N6537.S58 A4 1991

Alfageme Ruano, Pedro. El romanticismo
Sevillano : Valeriano Bécquer, ilustrador / por
Pedro Alfageme Ruano ; prólogo de E.J.
Sullivan ; textos de G.A. Bécquer ... [et al.].
Sevilla : Padilla Libros, 1989. 176 p., [21] p. of
plates : ill. ; 24 cm. One col. port. inserted. Includes
bibliographical references. ISBN 84-87039-13-8
*1. Bécquer, Valeriano. 2. Art, Modern - 19th century -
Spain - Seville. 3. Illustrators - Spain - Biography. I.
Title.*   **NYPL [3-MCQ B39 91-4517]**

Alfelt, Else.
Stabell, Annette. Else Alfelt . København ,
c1990. 93 p. : ISBN 87-418-5910-3
ND723.A4 S73 1990

**ALFELT, ELSE - CRITICISM AND
INTERPRETATION.**
Stabell, Annette. Else Alfelt . København ,

c1990. 93 p. : ISBN 87-418-5910-3
ND723.A4 S73 1990

Alfred Hrdlicka. Galerie Welz Salzburg. Salzburg,
1969. 86 p.
NYPL [MDG (Hrdlicka) 91-394]

Alfred Hutty and the Charleston renaissance /.
Saunders, Boyd. Orangeburg, S.C. , c1990. 127
p. : ISBN 0-87844-089-5 DDC 769.92 B 20
NE2012.H88 S28 1990
NYPL [MDG+ (Hutty) 91-5803]

Alfred Kubin . Kubin, Alfred, 1877-1959.
München , c1990. 255 p. : ISBN 3-89409-046-4
NC245.K8 A4 1990

Alfred Kubin. Kubin, Alfred, 1877-1959.
[Stockholm] , 1990. 31, 29 p. : ISBN
91-7100-386-X
NYPL [3-MCK K95 90-11683]

Alfred Kubin 1877-1959 /. Kubin, Alfred,
1877-1959. München [1990] 400 p. : ISBN
3-88645-092-9 (Ausstellungskatalog)
IN PROCESS (ONLINE)
NYPL [3-MCK K95 91-8111]

Alfred Leslie . Stein, Judith E. St. Louis, Mo. ,
c1991. 95 p. : ISBN 0-89178-036-X
IN PROCESS (ONLINE)
NYPL [3-MCX L624 91-8119]

Alfredo Arreguín : el universo vegetal, animal y
humano de un pintor moreliano / [volumen
preparado por Enrique Arreguín V.]. [Morelia,
Mich., México] : Universidad Michoacana de
San Nicolas de Hidalgo, Centro de Estudios
sobre la Cultura Nicolaita, [1989] 214 p., [15]
leaves of plates : ill. (some col.) ; 20 cm.
(Biblioteca nicolaita de pintores michoacanos . 2)
DDC 759.972 20
1. Arreguín, Alfredo, 1935- - Criticism and
interpretation. I. Arreguín, Alfredo, 1935-. II. Arreguín
Vélez, Enrique. III. Series.
ND259.A69 A86 1989

Alfredo Jaar : geography=war / essays by W.
Avon Drake ... [et al.]. Richmond, VA :
Virginia Museum of Fine Arts : Virginia
Commonwealth University, c1991. p. cm. "An
exhibition organized jointly by the Anderson Gallery,
Virginia Commonwealth University and the Virginia
Museum of Fine Arts, Richmond, September 7-October
20, 1991." Includes bibliographical references. ISBN
0-917046-32-3 DDC 709/.2 20
1. Jaar, Alfredo - Exhibitions. 2. Installations (Art) -
United States - Exhibitions. 3. Art - Political aspects -
Exhibitions. I. Jaar, Alfredo. II. Drake, W. Avon. III.
Anderson Gallery. IV. Virginia Museum of Fine Arts.
N6537.J26 A4 1991

Alfredo Zalce /. Zalce, Alfredo, 1908- Morelia,
Michoacán , 1982. xxviii, 130 p. :
N6559.Z35 A4 1982

Algar, Ayla Esen. The Dervish lodge . Berkeley ,
c1992. p. cm. ISBN 0-520-07060-7 (alk. paper)
DDC 700/.9561 20
NX688.T9 D47 1992

**ALGIERS (ALGERIA) - BUILDINGS,
STRUCTURES, ETC.**
Golvin, Lucien. Palais et demeures d'Alger à la
période ottomane /. Aix-en-Provence [1988]
141 p., [16] p. of plates : ISBN 2-85744-307-2
NYPL [3-MQT+ 90-4959]

'Alī, Muḥammad Riḍā.
al-Funūn al-tashkīliyah / Muḥammad Riḍā 'Alī.
Ṭarābulus, al-Jamāhīriyah al-'Arabīyah
al-Lībīyah al-Sha'bīyah al-Ishtirākīyah : Jāmi'at
al-Fātiḥ, al-Idārah al-'Ammah lil-Maktabāt
wa-al-Ṭab' wa-al-Nashr, [198-] 37, 39 p., 66 p.
of plates : col. ill. ; 30 X 30 cm. Arabic and
English. Title on added t.p.: Visual arts. Includes
bibliographical references (p. 35-37 (2nd group)).
1. 'Alī, Muḥammad Riḍā - Catalogs. 2. 'Alī,
Muḥammad Riḍā - Psychology. I. Title. II. Title: Visual
arts.
N7389.3.A45 A4 1980z

'ALĪ, MUḤAMMAD RIḌĀ - CATALOGS.
'Alī, Muḥammad Riḍā. al-Funūn al-tashkīliyah
/. Ṭarābulus, al-Jamāhīriyah al-'Arabīyah
al-Lībīyah al-Sha'bīyah al-Ishtirākīyah [198-]
37, 39 p., 66 p. of plates :
N7389.3.A45 A4 1980z

'ALĪ, MUḤAMMAD RIḌĀ - PSYCHOLOGY.
'Alī, Muḥammad Riḍā. al-Funūn al-tashkīliyah
/. Ṭarābulus, al-Jamāhīriyah al-'Arabīyah
al-Lībīyah al-Sha'bīyah al-Ishtirākīyah [198-]

37, 39 p., 66 p. of plates :
N7389.3.A45 A4 1980z

Aliaga, Juan Vicente. Arte conceptual revisado
=. [Valencia] [1990?] 286 p. : ISBN
84-7721-108-6 DDC 709/.04/075 20
N6494.C63 A76 1990

Alice and beyond /. Smith, Kate, 1947- Brisbane,
Qld , 1989. 71 p. : ISBN 0-86439-089-0 DDC
759.994 20
ND1105.S65 A4 1989

Alice Trumbull Mason . Mason, Alice Trumbull,
1904-1971. New York, N.Y. , 1985. 60 p. :
ISBN 0-8008-0160-1 : DDC 769.92/4 19
NE539.M278 A4 1985
NYPL [MDG (Mason) 86-781]

**ALIENS, ILLEGAL - TEXAS - LOWER RIO
GRANDE VALLEY - PICTORIAL
WORKS.**
Anastos, Phillip. Illegal . New York , 1991. 128
p. : ISBN 0-8478-1367-3 DDC 305.9/0693 20
F392.R5 A53 1991
NYPL [MFW+ 91-6710]

**ALIKS ANDR IN A (LIBRARY) -
EXHIBITIONS.**
La Biblioteca ritrovata . Roma , 1990. 50 p. :
NYPL [3-MQWB 91-5054]

Alim Rizhinashvili. Nikonova, Nat'ela. Alim
Rižinašvili . T'bilisi , 1988. [24] p. :
NC325.G43 R592 1988

Alim Rižinašvili . Nikonova, Nat'ela. T'bilisi ,
1988. [24] p. :
NC325.G43 R592 1988

Alina [sound recording] /. Donizetti, Gaetano,
1797-1848. [Alina, regina di Golconda.]
Pontelambro, Italy , p1988. 2 sound discs (134
min.) :
Nuova era 033.6701

Alinder, James. Sexton, John, 1953- Quiet light /.
Boston , c1990. 121 p. : ISBN 0-8212-1775-5 :
DDC 779/.092 20
TR654 .S4719 1990
NYPL [MFX+ (Sexton) 90-11257]

Alisio, Giancarlo, 1930- Napoli com'era nelle
gouaches del Sette e Ottocento : le immagini
struggenti di una delle più belle e affascinanti
città-capitali d'Europa e dei suoi dintorni /
Giancarlo Alisio, Pier Andrea De Rosa, Paolo
Emilio Trastulli.1. ed. Roma : Newton
Compton, 1990. 262 p. : ill. (some col.) ; 27
cm. (Quest'Italia . 155) Includes bibliographical
references (p. 254-257). DDC 758/.994573 20
1. Watercolor painting, European - Italy - Naples -
Catalogs. 2. Watercolor painting - 18th century - Italy -
Naples - Catalogs. 3. Watercolor painting - 19th
century - Italy - Naples - Catalogs. 4. Naples (Italy) in
art - Catalogs. 5. Naples Region (Italy) in art -
Catalogs. I. De Rosa, Pier Andrea. II. Trastulli, Paolo
Emilio. III. Title. IV. Series.
ND2243.I8 A44 1990

All about creative textiles /. Holland, Stephanie
K. Oxford , 1988, c1987. 80 p. : ISBN
0-19-832737-4 (pbk) : DDC 746 19
TT699   *NYPL [3-MON 90-12316]*

All the portraits up to date. Scholte, Rob, 1958-
Rob Scholte, Amsterdam . Cologne , 1988. [48]
p. :   *NYPL [3-MCH S349 89-11,526]*

Allan D'Arcangelo . D'Arcangelo, Allan, 1930-
New York , 1971. 24 p. :
NYPL [3-MCX+ D214 91-1318]

Allan, Mea. William Robinson, 1838-1935 : father
of the English flower garden / by Mea Allan.
London : Faber and Faber, 1982. 255 p. : ill. ;
24 cm. Includes index. Bibliography: p. 238-241.
ISBN 0-571-11865-8 :
1. Robinson, W. (William), 1838-1935. 2. Gardeners -
Great Britain - Biography. I. Title.
NYPL [3-MSCC 83-2793]

**Allard Pierson Museum (Universiteit van
Amsterdam)**
Corpus vasorum antiquorum. The Netherlands.
Amsterdam, Allard Pierson Museum, University
of Amsterdam /. Amsterdam , 1988- v. : ISBN
90-71211-13-4 (v. 1)
NYPL [MPEK+ C8.A5]

**ALLARD PIERSON MUSEUM
(UNIVERSITEIT VAN AMSTERDAM) -
CATALOGS.**
Corpus vasorum antiquorum. The Netherlands.
Amsterdam, Allard Pierson Museum, University

of Amsterdam /. Amsterdam , 1988- v. : ISBN
90-71211-13-4 (v. 1)
NYPL [MPEK+ C8.A5]

Alle straten en steegjes van Brabant = Toutes
les rues et ruelles de Brabant. De Pinte : New
Always, 1985. 1 atlas (321 p.) : col. maps ; 31
cm. Instructions for use in French, Dutch, German and
English.
1. Brabant (Belgium) - Road maps. I. New Always
(Firm). II. Title: Toutes les rues et ruelles de Brabant.
NYPL [Map Div. 90-11659]

Alle straten en straatjes van Antwerpen. De
Pinte : New Always, 1985. 1 atlas (258 p.) :
col. maps ; 31 cm. Cover title: Alle straten en
straatjes van de provincie Antwerpen.
1. Antwerp (Belgium : Province) - Road maps. I. New
Always (Firm). II. Title: Alle straten en straatjes van de
provincie Antwerpen.
NYPL [Map Div. 90-11658]

**Alle straten en straatjes van de provincie
Antwerpen.** Alle straten en straatjes van
Antwerpen. De Pinte , 1985. 1 atlas (258 p.) :
NYPL [Map Div. 90-11658]

Alle straten en straatjes van Limburg. Hechtel :
Always, [1980?] 1 atlas (216 p.) : col. maps ; 31
cm.
1. Limburg (Belgium : Province) - Road maps. I.
Always (Firm).   *NYPL [Map Div. 90-11662]*

Alle straten en straatjes van Oost-Vlaanderen.
De Pinte : New Always, 1985. 1 atlas (267 p.) :
col. maps ; 31 cm.
1. East Flanders (Belgium) - Road maps. I. New
Always (Firm).   *NYPL [Map Div. 90-11660]*

Alle straten en straatjes van West-Vlaanderen.
De Pinte : New Always, 1986. 1 atlas (288 p.) :
col. maps ; 31 cm. Instructions for use in French,
Dutch, German, and English.
1. West Flanders (Belgium) - Road maps. I. New
Always (Firm).   *NYPL [Map Div. 90-11663]*

ALLEGORIES.
Hedeman, Anne Dawson. The royal image .
Berkeley , c1991. p. cm. ISBN 0-520-07069-0
DDC 745.6/7/09440902 20
ND3399.G67 H44 1991

Matthews Grieco, Sara F. Ange ou diablesse .
[Paris] , c1991. 495 p. : ISBN 2-08-211187-3
DDC 769/.424/0940931 20
NE962.W65 M38 1991

Starn, Randolph. Arts of power . Berkeley ,
c1992. p. cm. ISBN 0-520-07383-5 (cloth) DDC
725/.17/0945 20
NA6815 .S787 1992

ALLEGORIES - EXHIBITIONS.
Resplendence of the Spanish monarchy . New
York , 1991. p. cm. ISBN 0-87099-621-5 DDC
739.7/0946/0747471 20
NK3062.A1 R47 1991

**ALLEGORY (ART) see ALLEGORIES;
SYMBOLISM IN ART.**

Allen, Davis Brewster, 1916-
Slavin, Maeve. Davis Allen . New York ,
c1990. 136 p. : ISBN 0-8478-1255-3 DDC
729/.092 20
NK2004.3.A45 S5 1990
NYPL [3-MLO 91-3724]

**ALLEN, DAVIS BREWSTER, 1916- -
CRITICISM AND INTERPRETATION.**
Slavin, Maeve. Davis Allen . New York ,
c1990. 136 p. : ISBN 0-8478-1255-3 DDC
729/.092 20
NK2004.3.A45 S5 1990
NYPL [3-MLO 91-3724]

Allen, Ellen G. (Ellen Gordon), 1897- Japanese
flower arrangement : a complete primer / by
Ellen G. Allen.1st. Tuttle ed. Rutland, Vt. :
C.E. Tuttle Co., 1963, cc1962. 86 p. : ill. ; 23
cm. Includes index.
1. Flower arrangement, Japanese. I. Title.
NYPL [3-MLT 90-5857]

Allen Memorial Art Museum.
Feinberg, Larry J. From studio to studiolo .
Oberlin , Seattle , 1991. p. cm. ISBN
0-295-97145-2 : DDC 741.945/51/0903107474
20
NC256.F5 F4 1991

The Metamorphic medium . [Oberlin, Ohio] ,
c1989. ix, 46 p. :   *NYPL [MFW 90-11187]*

Russell, Margarita. Images of reality, images of
Arcadia . Winterthur [Switzerland] ,

Washington, D.C. , c1989. 131 p. : ISBN
3-907798-01-5   *NYPL [3-MCG 90-11767]*

**ALLEN MEMORIAL ART MUSEUM -
EXHIBITIONS.**
Masterworks of color and design . [Chicago]
[1991] 15 p. :   *NYPL [3-MOP 91-4288]*

Allen, Terry, 1943- De Lory, Peter. The wild and
the innocent /. Riverside, Calif. , 1987. [46] p. :
ISBN 0-9619038-2-1
NYPL [MFX (De Lory) 90-11264]

Allen, William, 1967- Interpreting contemporary
art /. London , 1991. xix, 22 p. :
0-948462-15-9 (cased) : DDC 709.047 20
N6490   *NYPL [MA 91-6285]*

Allenov, Mikhail Mikhaïlovich. Moscow,
treasures and traditions /. Washington, D.C. ,
c1990. 281 p. : ISBN 0-295-96994-6 DDC
709/.47/074753 20
N6997.M7 M65 1990
NYPL [3-MAM+ 90-11581]

Allenspach, Christoph. Bauen vor der Stadt.
English & German. Bauen vor der Stadt .
Basel , Boston , c1991. p. cm. ISBN
3-7643-2629-8 : DDC 720/.9494/33 20
NA1349.B38 B3813 1991

Allentown Art Museum. West, Benjamin,
1738-1820. The world of Benjamin West .
Allentown, Pa. , 1962. 96 p. :
ND237.W45 A65
NYPL [3-MCX W51 90-7090]

Alles Plastik . Jockel, Nils. [Hamburg] , 1985. 36
p. :   *NYPL [3-MGF 86-364]*

Allgäuer Maler. Keck, Otto, 1873-1948. Otto
Keck 1873-1948, ein Allgäuer Maler .
[Kempten (Allgäu)] , c1987. 151 p. : ISBN
3-88019-018-6 DDC 759.3 20
ND588.K36 A4 1987
NYPL [3-MCK K248 91-6957]

Allgäuer Heimatmuseum. Keck, Otto, 1873-1948.
Otto Keck 1873-1948, ein Allgäuer Maler .
[Kempten (Allgäu)] , c1987. 151 p. : ISBN
3-88019-018-6 DDC 759.3 20
ND588.K36 A4 1987
NYPL [3-MCK K248 91-6957]

Allgemeines Künstlerlexikon : die bildenden
Künstler aller Zeiten und Völker / erarbeitet,
redigiert und herausgegeben von Günter
Meissner und einem Redaktionskollektiv unter
internationaler Mitwirkung.1. Aufl. Leipzig :
E.A. Seemann, 1983- v. ; 24 cm. Includes
bibliographies. ISBN 3-363-00114-2 (v. 1) DDC
709/.2/2 B 19
*1. Artists - Biography - Dictionaries. I. Meissner,
Günter. II. E. A. Seemann Verlag.*
N40 .A63 1983   *NYPL [MAO 85-1702]*

Allibone, Jill. George Devey, architect,
1820-1886 / Jill Allibone. Cambridge, England :
Lutterworth, c1991. 189 p. : ill., plans, port. ;
27 cm. "Catalogue raisonné": p. 150-179. Includes
bibliographical references (p. 142) and index. ISBN
0-7188-2785-6 : DDC 720.92 20
*1. Devey, George, 1820-1886. 2. Architecture,
Modern - 19th century - England. 3. Vernacular
architecture - England. 4. Architecture, Domestic -
England. I. Title.*
NYPL [3-MQZ (Devey) 91-6770]

Allies : great U. S. and Russian World War II
photographs / introductions by Grigori
Chudakov and David E. Scherman ; [translation
from the Russian by Todd Bludeau]. New
York : H.L. Levin Associates : Distributed by
Macmillan, c1989. 200 p. : chiefly ill. ; 32 cm.
ISBN 0-88363-389-2 : DDC 940.53/022/2 20
1. World War, 1939-1945 - Pictorial works.
D743.2 .A45 1989 NYPL [MFW+ 91-6014]

All'ombra del Vesuvio : Napoli nella veduta
europea dal Quattrocento all'Ottocento /
[redazione, Silvia Cassani]. Napoli : Electa,
c1990. xxiv, 455 p. : ill. (some col.) ; 28 cm.
Catalog of an exhibition held at Castel Sant'Elmo,
Naples, May 12-July 29, 1990. Includes bibliographical
references (p. [445]-453). ISBN 88-435-3140-9
*1. Naples (Italy) in art - Exhibitions. 2. Naples (Italy) -
Description - Views - Exhibitions. I. Cassani, Silvia. II.
Castel Sant'Elmo (Naples, Italy).*
NYPL [3-MAMY 91-6399]

All'ombra del Vesuvio : Napoli nella veduta
europea dal Quattrocento all'Ottocento :
[mostra]. Napoli : Electa, c1990. xxiv, 455 p. :
ill. (some col.) ; 29 cm. "Napoli, Castel Sant'Elmo,

12 maggio-29 luglio 1990"--P. [vii]. Includes
bibliographical references (p. [445]-455).
*1. Naples Region (Italy) in art. 2. Art, European -
Themes, motives.*
N8214.5.I8 A35 1990

Allston, Washington, 1779-1843.
[Correspondence]
The correspondence of Washington Allston /
Nathalia Wright, editor. Lexington, Ky :
University Press of Kentucky, 1992. p. cm.
Includes bibliographical references and index. ISBN
0-8131-1708-9 : DDC 759.13 B 20
*1. Allston, Washington, 1779-1843. Correspondence. 2.
Artists - United States - Correspondence. I. Wright,
Nathalia. II. Title.*
NX512.A513 A3 1992

CORRESPONDENCE
Allston, Washington, 1779-1843.
[Correspondence.] The correspondence of
Washington Allston /. Lexington, Ky , 1992.
p. cm. ISBN 0-8131-1708-9 : DDC 759.13 B 20
NX512.A513 A3 1992

Alma Lavenson. Lavenson, Alma, 1897-
[Riverside, Calif.] , c1979. 56 p. : DDC
779/.092/4
TR647 .L38 1979
NYPL [MFX (Lavenson) 91-2392]

Alma Lavenson photographs /. Ehrens, Susan.
Berkeley, Calif. , c1990. 106 p. : ISBN
0-8263-1237-3
NYPL [MFX+ (Lavenson) 91-5848]

Alma-Tadema, Lawrence, Sir, 1836-1912.
Lovett, Jennifer Gordon. Empires restored,
Elysium revisited . Williamstown, Mass. , 1991.
p. cm. ISBN 0-931102-30-8 (pbk.) DDC 759.2 20
ND497.A4 A4 1991

SPRING.
Lippincott, Louise, 1953- Lawrence Alma
Tadema . Malibu, Calif. , 1991. p. cm. ISBN
0-89236-186-7 : DDC 759.2 20
ND497.A4 A755 1991

**ALMA-TADEMA, LAWRENCE, SIR, 1836-
1912 - EXHIBITIONS.**
Lovett, Jennifer Gordon. Empires restored,
Elysium revisited . Williamstown, Mass. , 1991.
p. cm. ISBN 0-931102-30-8 (pbk.) DDC 759.2 20
ND497.A4 A4 1991

**ALMA-TADEMA, LAWRENCE, SIR, 1836-
1912 - CATALOGUES RAISONNÉS.**
Swanson, Vern G. The biography and catalogue
raisonné of the paintings of Sir Lawrence
Alma-Tadema /. London , 1990. 511 p. : ISBN
0-906030-22-6 : DDC 759.2 20
ND497.A4   NYPL [MCV+ A44 90-12346]

Almansi, Guido, 1931- Nespolo, Ugo, 1941-
Nespolo /. Milano , c1991. 192 p. : ISBN
88-374-1163-4 : DDC 700/.92 20
NX552.Z9 N482 1991

Almaraz, Carlos.
Moonlight theater : prints and related works /
by Carlos Almaraz. Los Angeles : Grunwald
Center for the Graphic Arts, University of
California, c1991. p. cm. "This catalogue has been
published in conjunction with an exhibition held at the
Wight Art Gallery, University of California, Los
Angeles, April 9-May 19, 1991"--T.p. verso. ISBN
0-9628162-0-5 (pbk.) DDC 769.92 20
*1. Almaraz, Carlos - Exhibitions. I. Grunwald Center
for the Graphic Arts. II. Frederick S. Wight Art
Gallery. III. Title.*
NE539.A44 M66 1991

ALMARAZ, CARLOS - EXHIBITIONS.
Almaraz, Carlos. Moonlight theater . Los
Angeles , c1991. p. cm. ISBN 0-9628162-0-5
(pbk.) DDC 769.92 20
NE539.A44 M66 1991

Almasio, Gabriella. Nicaragua, una realtà delle
Americhe /. Palermo (Italia) , c1987. 206 p. :
ISBN 88-7704-010-6 :
NYPL [MFW+ 91-3429]

Almeida, Enrique. El arte genial de Víctor
Mideros : centenario de su nacimiento,
1888-1988 / Enrique Almeida. Quito : [s.n.],
1988 (Quito, Ecuador : Tall. Gráf. del Instituto
Andino de Artes Populares del Convenio
Andrés Bello) 156 p. : ill. ; 21 cm. Includes
bibliographical references. DDC 759.9866 20
*1. Mideros, Víctor, 1888-1969 - Criticism and
interpretation. I. Title.*
ND389.M5 A84 1988

ALMEIDA, ENRIQUE.
Anastasía, Luis V. Figari . Montevideo , 1976.
92 p., [15] leaves of plates :
NYPL [3-MAM 90-5569]

Alois Köchl, Stadtzeichner von Nürnberg 1984 .
Köchl, Alois, 1951- [Nürnberg] [1985] 37 p. :
MLCM 86/3093 (N)
NYPL [3-MCK K768 90-10681]

Alonso de la Sierra Fernández, Lorenzo. El
retablo neoclásico en Cádiz / Lorenzo Alonso
de la Sierra Fernández. [Cádiz] : Diputación
Provincial de Cádiz, [1989?] 177 p., [24] p. of
plates : ill. ; 22 cm. (Arte. 3) "Libros de la
Diputación de Cádiz"--P. 4 of cover. Includes
bibliographical references (p. 169-173). ISBN
84-87144-02-0
*1. Altarpieces, Spanish - Spain - Cadiz. 2.
Neoclassicism (Art) - Spain - Cadiz. I. Series. II. Series:
Arte (Cádiz (Spain : Province). Diputación Provincial) ,
3. III. Title.*
NB1910 .A48 1989

**Alonso Sánchez Coello y el retrato en la corte de
Felipe II .** Sánchez Coello, Alonso, 1531 or
2-1588. [Madrid] , c1990. 253 p. : ISBN
84-87317-03-0
NYPL [3-MCQ+ S199 91-5566]

**ALPANA (ART) - INDIA - MADHUBANI -
THEMES, MOTIVES.**
Thakur, Upendra. Madhubani painting /. New
Delhi [1981 or 1982] xii, 158 p., [36] p. of
plates : ISBN 0-391-02411-6 :
NK1476.M34 T47 1981
NYPL [3-MAF 90-5433]

Alperson, Philip. The Philosophy of the visual
arts /. New York , 1992. p. cm. ISBN
0-19-505975-1 (alk. paper) DDC 701 20
N71 .P39 1992

ALPHABET - SPECIMENS. see ALPHABETS.

**ALPHABETS - CARICATURES AND
CARTOONS.**
Earnshaw, Anthony. An eighth secret alphabet
/. Church Hanborough, Oxford , 1988
([Didcot? England] : Didcot Press) [23] p. :
DDC 741.5/942 20
NC1479.E37 A4 1988

ALPHABETS IN ART.
Hockney, David. Hockney's alphabet /. New
York, NY , c1991. p. cm. ISBN 0-679-41066-X :
DDC 741.942 20
NC242.H6 A4 1991a

Alphonse Legros, 1837-1911 . Wilcox, Timothy.
[Dijon] , 1988. 165 p., [4] p. of plates : ISBN
2-900462-27-4
N6853.L37 W55 1988
NYPL [3-MCO L519 90-11769]

Alpine Club Gallery (London, England) French
19th century paintings . London , 1977. 101
p. :   *NYPL [3-MCN 90-7134]*

Alpine Exlibris . Zebhauser, Helmuth. München ,
c1985. 192 p. : ISBN 3-7654-2043-3 DDC 769.5
19
Z994.5.A38 Z43 1985
NYPL [MDVC 91-5221]

Alpine Klassiker .
(Bd. 3) Zebhauser, Helmuth. Alpine Exlibris .
München , c1985. 192 p. : ISBN 3-7654-2043-3
DDC 769.5 19
Z994.5.A38 Z43 1985
NYPL [MDVC 91-5221]

ALPS IN BOOK-PLATES.
Zebhauser, Helmuth. Alpine Exlibris .
München , c1985. 192 p. : ISBN 3-7654-2043-3
DDC 769.5 19
Z994.5.A38 Z43 1985
NYPL [MDVC 91-5221]

Als Dada begann : Bildchronik und Erinnerungen
der Gründer / in Zusammenarbeit mit Hans
Arp, Richard Huelsenbeck, Tristan Tzara ;
herausgegeben von Peter Schifferli. [Zürich] :
Sanssouci, c1957. 92 p. : ill., ports. ; 16 cm.
(Galerie Sanssouci) German and French. "Sonderdruck
aus dem Chronik-Teil des Buches [Dada] : Die Geburt
des Dada"--T.p. verso. Spine title: Dada in Zürich.
Bibliography: p. 90-92.
*1. Dadaism - Switzerland - Zurich. 2. Art, Modern -
20th century - Switzerland - Zurich. I. Arp, Jean,
1887-1966. II. Huelsenbeck, Richard, 1892-1974. III.
Tzara, Tristan, 1896-1963. IV. Schifferli, Peter. V. Title:
Dada in Zürich.*   *NYPL [3-MAM 90-7093]*

Alšova jihočeská galerie.
Gotické umění v jižních Čechách : vybraná díla ze sbírek Alšovy jihočeské galerie : Praha-Jiřský klášter, listopad 1989-březen 1990 / [výstavu připravil, úvodní stať napsal a katalog zpracoval Hynek Rulíšek].Vyd. 1. Praha : Národní galerie v Praze, [1990] 101 p. : ill. (some col.) ; 25 cm. (Edice Výstavy . 78) Includes bibliographical references. ISBN 80-7035-013-X :
1. Art, Gothic - Czechoslovakia - Jihočeský kraj - Exhibitions. 2. Art, Czech - Czechoslovakia - Jihočeský kraj - Exhibitions. 3. Alšova jihočeská galerie - Exhibitions. I. Rulíšek, Hynek. II. Národní galerie V Praze. III. Title. IV. Series.
N6832.J53 A48 1990

Linie, barva, tvar v českém výtvarném umění třicátých let . [Prague , 1990?] 152 p. :
N6831 .L54 1990

ALŠOVA JIHOČESKÁ GALERIE - EXHIBITIONS.
Alšova jihočeská galerie. Gotické umění v jižních Cechách . Praha [1990] 101 p. : ISBN 80-7035-013-X :
N6832.J53 A48 1990

Alšova země 89 : celostátní výtvarná soutěž pro děti a mládež od tří do patnácti let v oboru kresby, malby, grafiky a trojrozměrné tvorby : 23. ročník / [úvodní text katalogu Jana Skarlantová]. V Praze : Muzeum Aloise Jiráska a Mikoláše Alše, [1989?] 44 p. : chiefly ill. ; 22 cm.
1. Children's art - Czechoslovakia - Exhibitions. I. Skarlantová, Jana. II. Muzeum Aloise Jiráska a Mikoláše Alše v Praze.
N352.2.C95 A47 1989

Alt, Otmar, 1940- Otmar Alt : ein Künstler in seiner Zeit / herausgegeben von Volker Kapp. Hamm : Artcolor Verlag, c1988. 240 p. : ill. ; 33 cm.
1. Alt, Otmar, 1940-. I. Kapp, Volker. II. Title.
NYPL [3-MCK+ A449 91-7289]

ALT, OTMAR, 1940-
Alt, Otmar, 1940- Otmar Alt . Hamm , c1988. 240 p. :   *NYPL [3-MCK+ A449 91-7289]*

Das altägyptische Wohnhaus und seine Darstellung im Flachbild /. Roik, Elke. Frankfurt am Main , New York , c1988. 2 v. : ISBN 3-8204-0163-6
NA215 .R65 1988
    NYPL [3-MQL+ 90-8068]

Die Altarbilder des Älteren Bartholomäus Bruyn . Tümmers, Horst-Johs. Köln , 1964. 235 p. :
ND588.B792 A4 1964
    NYPL [3-MCK B914 90-5875]

Altarkunst des Barock . Merk, Anton. Frankfurt am Main [197-?] 49 p. :
    NYPL [3-MRBV 90-6995]

The Altarpiece in the Renaissance / edited by Peter Humfrey and Martin Kemp. Cambridge [England] ; New York : Cambridge University Press, 1990. xiv, 273 p. : ill. (1 col.) ; 28 cm. "Based on papers given at a conference of the Society for Renaissance Studies held at the Warburg Institute and Birkbeck College in London on 20-21 March 19872--P. xiii. Essays based on papers from a conference of the Society for renaissance Studies held at the Warburg Institute and Birkbeck College in London, March 20-21, 1987. Includes bibliographical references (p. 261-264) and index. ISBN 0-521-36061-7 DDC 726/.5296 20
1. Altarpieces, Renaissance - Congresses. 2. Christian art and symbolism - Modern period, 500-1500. I. Humfrey, Peter, 1947-. II. Kemp, Martin. III. Society for Renaissance Studies (Great Britain).
N7862 .A48 1990   NYPL [3-MAIH 91-4497]

ALTARPIECES, GOTHIC - CZECHOSLOVAKIA.
Pešina, Jaroslav. [Mistr vyšebrodského cyklu. /English.] The Master of the Hohenfurth Altarpiece and Bohemian Gothic panel painting /. London , 1989. [267] p. : ISBN 0-85667-339-0
    NYPL [3-MCZ+ M665 90-788]

ALTARPIECES, GOTHIC - GERMANY (EAST) - THURINGIA.
Hintzenstern, Herbert von. Die Marienaltäre in Lippersdorf und Münchenbernsdorf /. [Berlin] , 1963. 21, [3] p., [48] p. of plates :
MLCS 87/955 (N)   NYPL [MRBV 91-277]

ALTARPIECES, RENAISSANCE - CONGRESSES.

The Altarpiece in the Renaissance /. Cambridge [England] , New York , 1990. xiv, 273 p. : ISBN 0-521-36061-7 DDC 726/.5296 20
N7862 .A48 1990   NYPL [3-MAIH 91-4497]

ALTARPIECES, SPANISH - SPAIN - CADIZ.
Alonso de la Sierra Fernández, Lorenzo. El retablo neoclásico en Cádiz /. [Cádiz] [1989?] 177 p., [24] p. of plates : ISBN 84-87144-02-0
NB1910 .A48 1989

ALTARS, BAROQUE - GERMANY - EXHIBITIONS.
Merk, Anton. Altarkunst des Barock . Frankfurt am Main [197-?] 49 p. :
    NYPL [3-MRBV 90-6995]

ALTARS, GOTHIC - GERMANY - VERDEN.
Der Antwerpener Altar in St. Georg Vreden /. Vreden , 1989. 247 p. : ISBN 3-926627-03-4
    NYPL [3-MAIH+ 91-6544]

ALTARS - ITALY - ROME.
Thelen, Heinrich. Zur Entstehungsgeschichte der Hochaltar-Architektur von St. Peter in Rom /. Berlin , c1967. 77 p., [34] p. of plates :
    NYPL [3-MRBV 90-6917]

Das alte Biel und seine Umgebung /. Propper, Emanuel Jirka. Biel (Blumenstrasse 15, 2502 Biel) , 1980. 1 portfolio (38 p., 32 leaves of plates) :   *NYPL [3-MQWD++ 88-4261]*

Alte Fächer /. Müller-Krumbach, Renate. Weimar , c1988. 87 p. : ISBN 3-7443-0066-8
    NYPL [3-MMW 90-10782]

Alte Handwerkskunst in dokumentarischen Zeichnungen. Leinweber, Ulf. Karl Rumpf (1885-1968) . [Kassel] , 1989. 621 p. : ISBN 3-87280-057-4
NK951.R86 A4 1989
    NYPL [3-MNE 91-5812]

Alte Kirchen für neue Liturgie. Widder, Erich. [Wien, c1968] 204 p.
NA4605 .W5   NYPL [3-MRB 91-852]

Alte Landkarten Sachsens und Thüringens, 16. Jahrhundert bis 1945 /. Rübesame, Otto. Halle (Saale) , 1987. 103 p. ;
Z671 .S35 no. 59 Z6027.G352S29 GA880.S29
    NYPL [Map Div. 90-11885]

Alte Meister. Rainer, Arnulf, 1929- Arnulf Rainer, "Alte Meister." Innsbruck , 1989. 124 p. :   *NYPL [3-MCK+ R155 90-340]*

Alte Nazarethkirche (Berlin, Germany) Pankok, Otto, 1893-1966. Otto Pankok . Berlin , 1989. 152 p. :
IN PROCESS (ONLINE)
    NYPL [3-MCK+ P193 91-5077]

Alte Pinakothek Munich. Alte Pinakothek (Munich, Germany) Munich , 1938. xv, 320 p., 196 p. of plates :   *NYPL [3-MAVZ (Munich) 90-7035]*

Alte Pinakothek (Munich, Germany)
Alte Pinakothek Munich. Official ed., 19th ed. Munich : [Alte Pinakothek], 1938. xv, 320 p., 196 p. of plates : ill. ; 20 cm. Title on spine: Illustrated catalogue, Alte Pinakothek Munich. Includes bibliographical references and index.
1. Alte Pinakothek (Munich, Germany) - Catalogs. 2. Painting - Germany - Munich - Catalogs. I. Title. II. Title: Illustrated catalogue, Alte Pinakothek Munich.
    NYPL [3-MAVZ (Munich) 90-7035]

ALTE PINAKOTHEK (MUNICH, GERMANY) - CATALOGS.
Alte Pinakothek (Munich, Germany) Alte Pinakothek Munich. Munich , 1938. xv, 320 p., 196 p. of plates :   *NYPL [3-MAVZ (Munich) 90-7035]*

Altea, Giuliana. Le matite di un popolo barbaro : grafici e illustratori sardi, 1905-1935 / Giuliana Altea, Marco Magnani. Cinisello Balsamo (Milano): Silvana, c1990. 190 p. : ill. (some col.) ; 31 cm. Includes bibliographical references (p. 186-190). ISBN 88-366-0285-1
1. Graphic arts - Italy - History - 20th century. 2. Sardinia (Italy) in art. I. Magnani, Marco. II. Title.
NC998.6.I8 A48 1990

Altenstein, Bernd, 1943-
Bernd Altenstein : Zeichnungen, Plastiken : [Ausstellung], Kunstverein Salzgitter 2.5.-2.6.1978 : [Katalog / Inhalt, Ekkehart Lohoff, Helmut Lingstädt]. Salzgitter : Kunstverein, 1978. 56 p. : chiefly ill. ; 21 cm.
1. Altenstein, Bernd, 1943- - Exhibitions. 2. Artists' preparatory studies - Germany, West - Exhibitions. I.

Lohoff, Ekkehart. II. Lingstädt, Helmut. III. Kunstverein Salzgitter.
NB588.A44 A4 1978
    NYPL [3-MGO (Altenstein) 81-287]

ALTENSTEIN, BERND, 1943- - EXHIBITIONS.
Altenstein, Bernd, 1943- Bernd Altenstein . Salzgitter , 1978. 56 p. :
NB588.A44 A4 1978
    NYPL [3-MGO (Altenstein) 81-287]

Alternative Museum (New York, N.Y.)
Ashes to ashes . New York, N.Y. , c1982. 16 p. :   *NYPL [3-MAMZ 90-12622]*

Chagoya, Enrique. Enrique Chagoya . New York, N.Y. , c1989. 24 p. ; ISBN 0-932075-25-8 (pbk.)   *NYPL [3-MCX C433 91-4634]*

Conwill, Houston, 1947- The Passion of St. Matthew . New York City , c1986. 16 p. : ISBN 0-932075-09-6 (pbk.) DDC 709/.2/4 19
N6537.C655 A67 1986
    NYPL [3-MGO (Conwill) 90-12371]

Dean, Peter, 1934- Peter Dean . [New York] [1990?] 16 p. : ISBN 0-932075-31-2
    NYPL [3-MCX D2785 90-13373]

Epping, Ed, 1948- Ed Epping, events echoed . New York , c1984. 16 p. : DDC 709/.2/4 19
N6537.E66 A4 1984
    NYPL [3-MGO (Epping) 90-12638]

Luminosity . New York, NY , c1986. 20 p. : ISBN 0-932075-11-8
    NYPL [3-MAL 90-10424]

Made in America . New York City , c1986. 31 p. : ISBN 0-932075-10-X (pbk.) DDC 709/.77/07401471 19
N6522 .M3 1986
    NYPL [3-MAMT 90-12369]

Occupation and resistance . New York, N.Y. , c1990. 80 p. : ISBN 0-932075-30-4
IN PROCESS (ONLINE)
    NYPL [3-MAMT 91-7487]

Rand, Harry. Emilio Cruz . New York, N.Y. , c1984. 15 p. : ISBN 0-932075-00-2 (pbk.)
MLCM 84/5528 (N)
    NYPL [3-MCX C959 90-12365]

Southern exposure . New York, NY , c1985. 55 p. : ISBN 0-932075-02-9 (pbk.) DDC 709/.75/07401471 19
N6520 .S67 1985
    NYPL [3-MAMT 90-12368]

Altes Museum (Berlin, Germany) Ruthenbeck, Reiner, 1937- Reiner Ruthenbeck /. Berlin , c1990. 23 p. : ISBN 3-88609-247-X
NB588.R86 A4 1990

Altet, Xavier Barral i. see Barral i Altet. Xavier.

Althaus, Peter F. (ed) Schweizerische National-Versicherungs-Gesellschaft. Schweizer Malerei des 20. Jahrhunderts. [Basel, 1971?] 1 v. (unpaged)
ND848 .S3   NYPL [3-MCY+ 91-1319]

Althaus, Thomas, 1941- Le Cirque à l'affiche /. Hauterive , c1989. 205 p. : ISBN 2-88256-037-0
    NYPL [3-MDW+ 91-2665]

Altmann, Beatrix. Geitlinger, Ernst, 1895-1972. Ernst Geitlinger . Ludwigshafen a. Rh. , c1989. 119 p. :   *NYPL [3-MCK+ G316 90-5281]*

Altmayer, Jay P. American presentation swords / by Jay P. Altmayer ; with an introduction by Harold L. Peterson. 1st ed. Mobile, Ala. : Rankin Press, c1958. 46 p. : ill. ; 30 cm. "A study of the design and development of presentation swords in the United States from post revolutionary times until after the close of the Spanish American War." Includes bibliographical references.
1. Presentation swords - United States - History. I. Title.   NYPL [3-MNK 90-6863]

Altner, Manfred. Dresden . Dresden , 1990. 684 p. : ISBN 3-364-00145-6
N333.G33 D744 1990

Altomonte, Martino, 1657-1745. Aurenhammer, Hans. Martino Altomonte. Wien [c1965] 206 p.
ND623.A512 A9
    NYPL [3-MCF+ A469 91-320]

ALTOMONTE, MARTINO, 1657-1745.
Aurenhammer, Hans. Martino Altomonte. Wien [c1965] 206 p.
ND623.A512 A9
    NYPL [3-MCF+ A469 91-320]

Altorfer, Esther, 1936-1988.
Esther Altorfer, 1936-1988. [Bern] :
Kunstmuseum Bern, c1989. 82 p. : ill. (some
col.), ports. ; 27 cm. Catalog of an exhibition held at
the Kunstmuseum Bern, June 9-Aug. 19, 1989. ISBN
3-907991-13-3
1. Altorfer, Esther, 1936-1988 - Exhibitions. I.
Kunstmuseum Bern. II. Title.
        NYPL [3-MCZ A469 91-6665]

**ALTORFER, ESTHER, 1936-1988 -
    EXHIBITIONS.**
Altorfer, Esther, 1936-1988. Esther Altorfer,
1936-1988. [Bern] , c1989. 82 p. : ISBN
3-907991-13-3
        NYPL [3-MCZ A469 91-6665]

Un'altra obiettività / a cura di Jean François
Chevrier, James Lingwood = Another
objectivity / curated by Jean François Chevrier,
James Lingwood. Milano : Idea Books, c1989.
253 p. : ill. (some col.) ; 27 cm. (Cataloghi. 4)
Italian and English. Catalog of an exhibition held at the
Centre national des arts plastiques, Paris, March
14-April 30, 1989 and the Museo d'arte contempoeane
Luigi Pecci, Prato, June 24-August 31, 1989. Includes
bibliographical references. ISBN 88-7017-067-5
1. Photography, Artistic - Exhibitions. I. Chevrier,
Jean-François. II. Lingwood, James. III. Centre national
des arts plastiques (France). IV. Museo d'arte
contemporanea (Prato, Italy). V. Title: Another
objectivity. VI. Series: Cataloghi (Prato, Italy) , 4.
        NYPL [MFW 90-3005]

ALUCONIDAE. see OWLS.

Alva, Luis René, 1951-
Luis Gutiérrez, Javier Cruz, Luis René Alva .
[Mexico City, Mexico] , 1988. 61 p. :
NE544 .L85 1988

ALVA, LUIS RENÉ, 1951- - CATALOGS.
Luis Gutiérrez, Javier Cruz, Luis René Alva .
[Mexico City, Mexico] , 1988. 61 p. :
NE544 .L85 1988

Alva Negri, Tomás. Julio E. Payró / Tomás Alva
Negri, Eduardo González Lanuza, José Luis
Romero. Buenos Aires : Academia Nacional de
Bellas Artes, c1976. 68 p. : ill. (some col.) ; 28
cm. (Serie Estudios) Includes bibliographical references
(p. [65]-68).
1. Payró, Julio E., 1899-1971 - Criticism and
interpretation. 2. Payró, Julio E., 1899-1971 - Catalogs.
I. González Lanuza, Eduardo, 1900- II. Romero, José
Luis, 1909- III. Series: Serie Estudios (Academia
Nacional de Bellas Artes (Argentina)). IV. Title.
N6639.P38 A94 1976

Alva, Tomás. see Alva Negri, Tomás.

Alvar Aalto and the International style /.
Pearson, Paul David, 1936- London , 1989,
c1978. 240 p. : ISBN 0-7134-6300-7 (pbk) : DDC
720/.92/4 19
NA1455.F53A2
        NYPL [3-MQZ+ (Aalto) 90-10795]

Alvar Aalto, the mature years /. Schildt, Göran,
1917- [Mänskliga faktorn. English.] New York ,
1991. 328 p. : ISBN 0-8478-1329-0 DDC 720/.92
B 20
NA1455.F53 A23725 1991

Alvarenga, Fernando. Afluentes teórico-estéticos
do neo-realismo visual português / Fernando
Alvarenga. Porto : Edições Afrontamento, 1989.
209 p. : ill. ; 24 cm. Includes bibliographical
references (p. 175-177) and index. ISBN
972-360-218-0 :
1. Social problems in art. 2. Art Portuguese. 3. Art,
Modern - 20th century - Portugal. I. Title.
N8243.S65 A43 1989

Alvarez Bravo, Manuel, 1902-
Mucho sol / Manuel Alvarez Bravo ;
presentación, Teresa del Conde. 1a ed. México :
Fondo de Cultura Económica, 1989. 94 p. :
chiefly ill. ; 22 x 28 cm. (Colección Río de luz)
Includes bibliographical references. ISBN
968-16-3242-7
1. Alvarez Bravo, Manuel, 1902-. I. Conde, Teresa del.
II. Title. III. Series.
        NYPL [MFX (Alvarez Bravo) 90-2181]

Revelaciones : the art of Manuel Alvarez
Bravo. 1st ed. San Diego, Calif. : Museum of
Photographic Arts, 1990. 134 p. : ill. ; 28 cm.
Catalog of an exhibition held at the Museum of
Photographic Arts, San Diego, Calif., July 12-Sept. 9,
1990, and at 7 other U. S. locations through Oct. 16,
1992. English and Spanish. ISBN 1-87806-200-X
1. Alvarez Bravo, Manuel, 1902- - Exhibitions. 2.

Photography, Artistic - Exhibitions. I. Museum of
Photographic Arts (San Diego, Calif.). II. Title.
        NYPL [MFX (Alvarez Bravo) 91-3500]

ALVAREZ BRAVO, MANUEL, 1902-
Alvarez Bravo, Manuel, 1902- Mucho sol /.
México , 1989. 94 p. : ISBN 968-16-3242-7
        NYPL [MFX (Alvarez Bravo) 90-2181]

**ALVAREZ BRAVO, MANUEL, 1902- -
    EXHIBITIONS.**
Alvarez Bravo, Manuel, 1902- Revelaciones .
San Diego, Calif. , 1990. 134 p. : ISBN
1-87806-200-X
        NYPL [MFX (Alvarez Bravo) 91-3500]

Alvarez Calderón, Enrique. Centenario del
nacimiento de José Sabogal, 1888-19
marzo-1988 /. Lima, Perú , 1989 (Miraflores :
Librería Editorial "Minerva") 68 p. :
N6719.S23 C46 1989

Alverà Bortolotto, Angelica. Maiolica a Venezia
nel Rinascimento / Angelica Alverà Bortolotto.
Bergamo : Bolis, c1988. 117 p. : ill. (some col.),
1 geneal. table, plans ; 29 cm. Includes index.
Illustrated lining papers. Bibliography: p. 107-109.
ISBN 88-7827-003-2
1. Majolica, Italian - Italy - Venice. 2. Majolica,
Renaissance - Italy - Venice. 3. Pottery, Italian - Italy -
Venice. 4. Pottery, Renaissance - Italy - Venice. I. Title.
        NYPL [3-MPGD 91-4946]

Alves, Armando, 1935- Resende, Júlio, 1917- Júlio
Resende /. Lisboa , 1989. 122 p. : DDC 759.69
20
ND833.R46 A4 1989

Alves, José da Felicidade. Hollanda, Francisco de,
1517-1584. Album dos desenhos das antiguailhas
de Francisco de Holanda /. Lisboa , c1989. 54,
54, 73 p., [5] folded leaves of plates : ISBN
972-240-733-3 DDC 741.9469 20
NC290.H65 A4 1989

Alvin Lucier / edited by Klaus Ottmann.
Middletown, Conn. : Ezra and Cecile Zilkha
Gallery with Davison Art Center, Wesleyan
University, c1988. 23 p. ; ill. ; 21 x 30 cm.
Catalog of exhibition held Nov. 2-23, 1988. One essay
translated from the German. ISBN 0-929687-01-9
(pbk.)
1. Lucier, Alvin - Exhibitions. 2. Installations (Art) -
United States - Exhibitions. 3. Art and music -
Exhibitions. I. Ottmann, Klaus. II. Ezra and Cecile
Zilkha Gallery. III. Davison Art Center.
        NYPL [3-MGO+ (Lucier) 89-21332]

Always (Firm)
Alle straten en straatjes van Limburg. Hechtel
[1980?] 1 atlas (216 p.) :
        NYPL [Map Div. 90-11662]
Toutes les rues et ruelles du Liège. Antwerpen ,
1982. 1 atlas (299 p.) :
        NYPL [Map Div. 90-11661]

Am Anfang, Das Junge Rheinland : zur Kunst-
und Zeitgeschichte einer Region, 1918-1945 /
herausgegeben von Ulrich Krempel. Düsseldorf :
Claassen, c1985. 351 p. : ill. (some col.) ; 30
cm. Catalog of an exhibition at Städtische Kunsthalle
Düsseldorf, Feb. 9-Apr. 8, 1985. ISBN 3-546-47771-5
DDC 700/.943/55 19
1. Junge Rheinland (Association) - Exhibitions. 2. Arts,
German - Germany (West) - Düsseldorf Region -
Exhibitions. 3. Arts, Modern - 20th century - Germany
(West) - Düsseldorf Region - Exhibitions. I. Krempel,
Ulrich.
NX550.D87 A5 1985
        NYPL [3-MAMG+ 85-2357]

Amadio, Nadine. Coburn ; John Coburn, paintings
/ Nadine Amadio. Roseville, NSW : Craftsman
House, 1988. 205 p. : ill. (chiefly col.), ports. ;
35 cm. Spine title: John Coburn, paintings. Includes
bibliographical references. ISBN 0-947131-20-5
1. Coburn, John, 1925-. I. Coburn, John, 1925-. II.
Title. III. Title: John Coburn, paintings.
        NYPL [3-MCZ+ C657 89-20391]

Amana-Gemeinde. see Amana Society.

The Amana people and their furniture /. Albers,
Marjorie K. Ames , 1990. xii, 221 p. : ISBN
0-8138-1238-0 (pbk. : alk. paper) DDC
749.2177/653 20
NK2435.I8 A4 1990
        NYPL [3-MOF 91-4695]

AMANA SOCIETY.
Albers, Marjorie K. The Amana people and
their furniture /. Ames , 1990. xii, 221 p. :
ISBN 0-8138-1238-0 (pbk. : alk. paper) DDC

749.2177/653 20
NK2435.I8 A4 1990
        NYPL [3-MOF 91-4695]

Amann, Per.
[Holzschnitt. English]
Woodcuts / Per Amann ; [translated by
Alastair Macdonald]. Avon, England : Artline
Editions, c1989. 211 p., 4 leaves of plates :
ill. (some col.) ; 23 cm. Translation of:
Holzschnitt. Includes index.
1. Wood-engraving - History. I. Title.
        NYPL [MDO+ 91-5874]

Amarante, Leonor. As bienais de São Paulo, 1951
a 1987 / Leonor Amarante. 1a. ed. São
Paulo-SP : BFB : Projeto, 1989. 407 p. : ill.
(some col.), ports. ; 27 cm. Includes bibliographical
references (p. 388-396) and indexes. ISBN
85-7165-003-9 DDC 709/.04/50748161 20
1. Bienal Internacional de São Paulo. I. Bienal
Internacional de São Paulo. II. Title.
N5030.S37 A43 1989

Amato, Pasquale. Zanotti-Bianco, Umberto. Il sud
di Umberto Zanotti Bianco . Venezia , c1981.
117 p. :
        NYPL [MFX (Zanotti-Bianco) 90-7053]

Amatörfotografklubben i Helsingfors. Carpelan,
Bo Gustaf Bertelsson, 1926- Suvihuvi =.
[Helsinki] , 1988. 80 p. : ISBN 951-9086-31-5
        NYPL [MFW 91-5797]

Amazing architecture from Japan /. Watanabe,
Hiroshi. New York , 1991. p. cm. ISBN
0-8348-0239-2 : DDC 720/.952/09048 20
NA1555 .W37 1991

**AMAZONAS (VENEZUELA : TERRITORY) -
    MAPS.**
Atlas del inventario de tierras del territorio
federal Amazonas /. Caracas, Venezuela
[1985]. 1 v. (various pagings) : ISBN
980-04-0053-2 *NYPL [Map Div. 91-7664]*

Ambert, Paul. Le Verre préromain en Europe
occidentale /. Montagnac , 1989. 191 p. :
ISBN 2-907303-00-7
        NYPL [3-MPW+ 91-7509]

Ambiente Berlin : XLIV Esposizione
internazionale d'arte, La Biennale di Venezia.
[Venezia] : Edizioni Biennale, c1990. 201 p. :
col. ill. ; 30 cm. Text in German and Italian. ISBN
88-20-80360-7 DDC 709/.431/550744531 20
1. Art, Modern - 20th century - Berlin (Germany) -
Exhibitions. 2. Art, German - Berlin (Germany) -
Exhibitions. I. Biennale di Venezia (44th : 1990).
N6885 .A46 1990

Ambrosi, Angelo. Architettura in pietra a secco .
Fasano, Br , c1990. 578 p. : ISBN
88-7514-413-3 : DDC 721/.0441 20
NA4130 .A73 1990

Ambrosi, Gustinus, 1893-1975.
Gustinus Ambrosi, Pläne und Entwürfe :
Gustinus Ambrosi-Museum, Wien, 13. Juni bis
2. September 1990 /. Wien [1990] 31 p. :
        NYPL [3-MGO (Ambrosi) 91-4660]
Schmidt, Regine. Gustinus Ambrosi, Pläne und
Entwürfe . Wien [1990] 31 p. :
N1708 .A54 nr.145 N6811.5.A48A4

**AMBROSI, GUSTINUS, 1893-1975 -
    EXHIBITIONS.**
Gustinus Ambrosi, Pläne und Entwürfe :
Gustinus Ambrosi-Museum, Wien, 13. Juni bis
2. September 1990 /. Wien [1990] 31 p. :
        NYPL [3-MGO (Ambrosi) 91-4660]
Schmidt, Regine. Gustinus Ambrosi, Pläne und
Entwürfe . Wien [1990] 31 p. :
N1708 .A54 nr.145 N6811.5.A48A4

Amedeo Modigliani . Modigliani, Amedeo,
1884-1920. Munich , New York, NY, USA ,
c1990. 227 p. : ISBN 3-7913-1095-X : DDC
709/.2 20
N6923.M55 A4 1990

Amedeo Modigliani . Schmalenbach, Werner,
1920- Munich , New York , c1990. 227
p. : ISBN 3-7913-1095-X (English ed.)
        NYPL [3-MCF+ M69 91-4500]

Amedeo Modigliani, les nus /. Ceroni, Angela.
Düdingen, Suisse , c1989. 95 p. : ISBN
3-908573-01-7
        NYPL [3-MCF+ M69 91-7282]

AMEICAN WIT AND HUMOR, PICTORIAL.
Mignery, Herb. Western horseman collection by
Mignery . Hastings, Neb. , 1991. 1 v.

(unpaged) : ISBN 0-933909-06-3 DDC 741.5/973
20
NC1429.M52 A4 1991

**AMELUNG, JOHN FREDERICK, 1741 OR 2-
1798.**
John Frederick Amelung, early American
glassmaker /. Corning : London ; 243 p., [4] p.
of plates : ISBN 0-87290-075-4 (alk. paper) DDC
748.2913 19
NK5198.A44 A4 1988
NYPL [3-MPW 91-6798]

**AMENHOTEP III, KING OF EGYPT - ART -
CONGRESSES.**
The Art of Amenhotep III . Cleveland, Ohio ,
1990. xii, 92 p., 27 p. of plates : ISBN
0-940717-01-8 DDC 732/.8 20
NB165.A44 A78 1990
NYPL [3-MAE 91-4575]

Amenoff, Gregory, 1948- Contemporary
woodblock prints . [Jersey City, N.J.], c1989.
16 p. : *NYPL [MDO 91-4747]*

America /. Rajs, Jake. New York , 1990. 256 p. :
ISBN 0-8478-1244-8 DDC 973.9/022/2 20
E169.04 .R34 1990
NYPL [MFX+ (Rajs) 91-3481]

AMERICA - ANTIQUITIES - CONGRESSES.
International Congress of Americanists, 40th,
Rome and Genoa, 1972. Atti del XL Congresso
internazionale degli americanisti. Genova
[1973-76] 4 v. *NYPL [HBC 74-2090]*

**AMERICA - DISCOVERY AND
EXPLORATION - MAPS.**
Nebenzahl, Kenneth, 1927- Atlas of Columbus
and the great discoveries /. Chicago , c1990.
viii, 168 p. : *NYPL [Map Div. 91-7246]*

America in art . Kloss, William. Santa Barbara,
Calif. , 1991. p. cm. ISBN 0-89951-083-3 DDC
759.13/074/79491 20
ND205 .K57 1991

América Latina : Lateinamerika in der bildenden
Kunst der DDR / [Verband Bildender Künstler
der DDR, Solidaritätskomitee der DDR,
Kulturzentrum "Pablo Neruda" der KP Chiles ;
Gestaltung der Katalog, László Szirmai ;
Gestaltung der Ausstellung, Dietrich
Dorfstecher]. [Berlin : Verband Bildender
Künstler der DDR, 1988?] 144 p. : chiefly ill.
(some col.) ; 23 cm. Catalog of an exhibition held at
the Ausstellungszentrum am Fernsehturm, Berlin, from
Sept. 7-28, 1988. Includes bibliographical references (p.
[140]-144).
*1. Art, German - Germany (East) - Exhibitions. 2. Art,
Modern - 20th century - Germany (East) - Exhibitions.
3. Latin America in art - Exhibitions. I. Szirmai, László.
II. Dorfstecher, Dietrich. III. Verband Bildender
Künstler der DDR. IV. Solidaritätskomitee der DDR.
V. Kulturzentrum "Pablo Neruda" (Partido Comunista
de Chile).*
N6884.5 .A44 1988
NYPL [3-MAMG 91-5083]

**AMERICAN ABORIGINES. see INDIANS;
INDIANS OF NORTH AMERICA;
INDIANS OF SOUTH AMERICA.**

American abstraction at the Addison . Addison
Gallery of American Art. Andover, Mass. ,
c1991. 95 p. : ISBN 1-87988-600-6 DDC
709/.73/0747445 20
N6512.5.A2 A33 1991

American Antiquarian Society.
Pomeroy, Jane R. Alexander Anderson's life
and engravings . Worcester [Mass.] , 1990. p,
137-230 : ISBN 0-944026-25-7
NYPL [MDG (Anderson) 91-4737]

Prints of New England . Worcester [Mass.] ,
1991. viii, 164 p. : ISBN 0-912296-92-5 DDC
769.974 19
NE510 .P74 1989 *NYPL [MDBF 91-6177]*

American architects and the mechanics of fame /.
Williamson, Roxanne, 1928- Austin , 1991. 286
p. : ISBN 0-292-75121-4 (cloth : alk. paper) DDC
720/.973 20
NA1996 W48 1990
NYPL [3-MQWO 91-5524]

American architectural classics. A Monograph of
the work of Mellor, Meigs & Howe. Boulder,
CO , c1991. 212 p. : ISBN 1-87865-001-7 DDC
720/.92/2 20
NA737.M45 A4 1991

American architectural classics series.
Mizner, Addison, 1872-1933. Florida

architecture of Addison Mizner /. Boulder,
Colo. , 1991. p. cm. ISBN 1-87865-002-5 : DDC
720/.92 20
NA737.M59 A4 1991

American architecture of the 1980s / foreword by
Donald Canty ; introduction by Andrea
Oppenheimer Dean. Washington, D.C. :
American Institute of Architects Press, 1990.
xiv, 342 p. : ill. (some col.), plans ; 31 cm.
Selection of articles from the Architecture, the monthly
magazine of the American Institute of Architects.
ISBN 1-558-35056-X : DDC 720/.973/09048 20
*1. Architecture, Modern - 20th century - United
States - Themes, motives. 2. Architecture - United
States - Themes, motives.*
NA712 .A64 1990
NYPL [MQWO+ 90-11575]

American art . H.V. Allison Galleries. New York,
N.Y. , 1985. 22 p. :
NYPL [3-MAMT 91-6712]

American art . Los Angeles County Museum of
Art. Los Angeles, Calif. , Seattle , 1991. p. cm.
ISBN 0-87587-155-0 DDC 759.13/074/79494 20
N6505 .L6 1991

AMERICAN ART. see ART, AMERICAN.

American art and architecture [videorecording] /
Alarion Press ; writers, Ann Campbell,
Erika Doss. Boulder, CO : Alarion Press, 1990.
5 videocassettes (140 min.) : sd., col. ; 1/2 in.
+ 1 teacher's guide + 1 teaching poster.
(History through art and architecture) Cataloged from
contributor's data. Graphics, Ann Campbell ; narrator,
Erik O. Furseth ; consultants, John Hoag, Robert E.
Day. VHS. Senior high school through college students
and adults. Issued also as filmstrip. Introduces basic
concepts of American history, art, and architecture to
show how art and architecture started out as survival
and have developed into sophisticated forms. DDC
709.73 19
*1. Art, American. 2. Architecture - United States. I.
Alarion Press. II. Series.*
N6505

American art around 1900 : lectures in memory
of Daniel Fraad / edited by Doreen Bolger and
Nicolai Cikovsky, Jr. Washington : National
Gallery of Art ; Hanover [N.H.] : Distributed
by the University Press of New England, 1990.
136 p. : ill. (some col.) ; 28 cm. (Studies in the
history of art, 0091-7338 . 37. 21) "Proceedings of the
symposium ... sponsored by the Center for Advanced
Study in the Visual Arts, National Gallery of Art, and
the Metropolitan Museum of Art, 4 and 18 March
1989"--T.p. verso. Includes bibliographical references.
ISBN 0-89468-143-5
*1. Art, American - Congresses. 2. Art, Modern - 19th
century - United States - Congresses. 3. Art, Modern -
20th century - United States - Congresses. 4.
Impressionism (Art) - United States - Congresses. 5.
Realism in art - United States - Congresses. I. Bolger,
Doreen, 1949-. II. Cikovsky, Nicolai. III. Center for
Advanced Study in the Visual Arts (U. S.). IV.
Metropolitan Museum of Art (New York, N.Y.). V.
Series: Studies in the history of art (Washington,
D.C.) , 37.* *NYPL [3-MAMT 91-7570]*

**American art at the nineteenth-century Paris
Salons /.** Fink, Lois Marie. Washington, D.C. :
Cambridge ; xxiv, 430 p. : ISBN 0-521-38499-0
DDC 709/.73/0903407444361 20
N6510 .F57 1990 *NYPL [3-MCW 90-11536]*

**An American art journal/Kennedy Galleries
book.**
Czestochowski, Joseph S. Arthur B. Davies .
Newark , London , c1987. 258 p., [12] p. of
plates : ISBN 0-87413-242-8 DDC 769.92/4 19
NE539.D3 A4 1987
NYPL [MDG+ (Davies) 87-4836]

American art 1960-1990. Word as image .
Milwaukee, Wis. , c1990. 171 p. :
NYPL [3-MAMT 90-12993]

American artists of the bookplate, 1970-1990 /
edited by James P. Keenan and Jacqueline E.
Davis. Cambridge, Mass. : Cambridge
Bookplate, c1990. xi, 155 p. : ill. ; 22 cm.
Includes index. ISBN 0-9627290-0-0
*1. Book-plates, American. 2. Book plate designers -
United States. I. Keenan, James P. II. Davis, Jacqueline
E.* *NYPL [MDVK 91-6220]*

American artists of the 80's. Pincus-Witten,
Robert. The last decade--American artists of the
80's . New York (130 Prince St., New York
10012) [1990] 137 p. : DDC 709/.73/0747471

20
N6512 .P492 1990

AMERICAN ARTS. see ARTS, AMERICAN.

American arts & crafts . Bowman, Leslie Greene.
Los Angeles, Calif. , Boston , c1990. 255 p. :
ISBN 0-8212-1824-7 (hardback) : DDC
745/.0973/07479494 20
NK1141 .B64 1990
NYPL [3-MNE+ 91-4630]

American arts and crafts. Bowman, Leslie
Greene. American arts & crafts . Los Angeles,
Calif. , Boston , c1990. 255 p. : ISBN
0-8212-1824-7 (hardback) : DDC
745/.0973/07479494 20
NK1141 .B64 1990
NYPL [3-MNE+ 91-4630]

American Assembly. Public money and the muse .
New York , c1991. p. cm. ISBN 0-393-03015-6
DDC 353/.0085/4 20
NX735 .P83 1991

**American Association for State and Local
History.** Clark, Ricky. Quilts in community .
Nashville, Tenn. , c1991. p. cm. ISBN
1-558-53101-7 : DDC 746.9/7/09771 20
NK9112 .C555 1991

American Black architects / Jack Travis, editor.
New York, N.Y. : Princeton Architectural
Press, c1991. p. cm. ISBN 1-87827-138-5 : DDC
720/.89/96073 20
*1. Afro-American architects - Employment. 2.
Architectural practice - United States. I. Travis, Jack,
1952-.*
NA738.N5 A45 1991

**AMERICAN BOOK-PLATES. see BOOK-
PLATES, AMERICAN.**

American capitols . Hauck, Eldon, 1914-
Jefferson, N.C. , c1991. ix, 310 p. : ISBN
0-89950-551-1 (lib bdg. : alk. paper) DDC
725/.11/0973 20
NA4411 .H38 1991

**AMERICAN CIVIL WAR. see UNITED
STATES - HISTORY - CIVIL WAR, 1861-
1865.**

AMERICAN COLONIZATION SOCIETY.
Massachusetts Colonization Society. American
Colonization Society and the colony at
Liberia/. Boston: 1832. 16 p.:
NYPL [Sc Micro R-3884 no. 7]

**American Colonization Society and the colony at
Liberia/.** Massachusetts Colonization Society.
Boston: 1832. 16 p.:
NYPL [Sc Micro R-3884 no. 7]

American cornucopia . Winterthur Library.
Winterthur, Del. , 1990. 115 p. : ISBN
0-912724-20-X DDC 026.973 20
Z733.W785 W55 1990
NYPL [3-MAVZ (Wilmington) 91-3457]

American Council for the Arts. Money for visual
artists /. New York, N.Y. , c1991. p. cm.
ISBN 0-915400-91-X DDC 707/.9/73 20
N347 .M66 1991

American country collectibles. Reno, Dawn E.
The official identification and price guide to
American country collectibles /. New York ,
1990. 521 p., [8] p. of plates : ISBN
0-87637-796-7 : DDC 745.1/0973/075 20
NK805 .R45 1990

American country flags. Mary Emmerling's
American country flags /. New York , 1991. p.
cm. ISBN 0-517-58366-6 : DDC 929.9/2/0973 20
NK839.E46 A4 1991

The American country house /. Aslet, Clive,
1955- New Haven , 1990. vii, 302 p. : ISBN
0-300-04757-6
NYPL [3-MQWO 90-12969]

**American Crafts Council. Museum of
Contemporary Crafts.** Fabric vibrations. : tie
and fold-dye wall hangings and environments :
[catalog of an exhibition] Museum of the
Contemporary Crafts of the American Crafts
Council, April 14-May 26, 1972. New York :
The Museum, 1972. [16] p. : ill. (some col.) ;
22 cm. Cover title. Bibliography: p. [5]
1. Tie-dyeing - Exhibitions. I. Title.
NYPL [3-MON 90-5448]

American design.
Gammon, Mitzi. The south /. New York ,
1991. p. cm. ISBN 0-553-07550-0 DDC

728/.37/0975 20
NA7211 .G35 1991

American drawing . Doumato, Lamia. Detroit ,
c1979. x, 246 p. ; ISBN 0-8103-1441-X : DDC
016.741/0973
Z5956.D7 D68 NC105
NYPL [3-MAC 91-7864]

American drawings : Paul Magriel collection :
[exhibition], November 8, 1979-January 31,
1980. New York : National Academy of
Design, [1979?] [40] p. : ill., ports. ; 23 cm.
Cover title: American drawings, portrait and figure
studies. Exhibition held at the National Academy of
Design, New York. Library copy imperfect: t.p. bound
at the end of book upside down.
1. Magriel, Paul David, 1906- - Art collections -
Exhibitions. 2. Portrait drawing, American - Private
collections - Exhibitions. 3. Figure drawing - Private
collections - Exhibitions. I. National Academy of
Design (U. S.). II. Title: American drawings, portrait
and figure studies.
NYPL [3-MAX (Magriel) 90-6859]

American drawings : Paul Magriel Collection :
[exhibition] November 8, 1979-January 31,
1980 : National Academy of Design, New
York. New York: The Academy, 1980. [40] p. :
ill. ; 23 cm. Text by Colin Eisler.
1. Magriel, Paul David, 1906- - Art collections -
Exhibitions. 2. Drawing, American - Private collctions -
Exhibitions. 3. Humans in art - Private collections -
Exhibitions. 4. Portrait drawing, American - Private
collections - Exhibitions. I. Eisler, Colin T. II. National
Academy of Design (U. S.).
NYPL [3-MBH 90-6350]

American drawings, portrait and figure studies.
American drawings . New York [1979?] [40]
p. : *NYPL [3-MAX (Magriel) 90-6859]*

AMERICAN ETCHINGS. see ETCHING,
AMERICAN.

The American family farm . Ancona, George. San
Diego , c1989. 1 v. (unpaged) : ISBN
0-15-203025-5 : DDC 630/.973 19
S519 .A53 1989
NYPL [MFX (Ancona) 90-11254]

American Federation of Arts. Pal, Pratapaditya.
Art of the Himalayas . New York , c1991. p.
cm. ISBN 1-555-95066-3 : DDC 709/.5496/07473
20
N7310.8.N4 P33 1991

American furniture. Swedberg, Robert W.
Collector's encyclopedia of American furniture
/. Paducah, KY , c1991- v. <1 > : ISBN
0-89145-441-1 (v. 1) : DDC 749.213/075 20
NK2405 .S894 1991

American furniture with related decorative arts,
1660-1830 /. Layton Art Collection. New
York , c1991. p. ISBN 1-555-95068-X : DDC
749.213/074/77595 20
NK2406 .L38 1991

American genre painting . Johns, Elizabeth, 1937-
New Haven , c1991. p. cm. ISBN 0-300-05019-4
DDC 754/.0973/09034 20
ND1451.5 .J64 1991

AMERICAN GENRE PAINTING. see GENRE
PAINTING, AMERICAN.

American graphic arts . Princeton University.
Library. Dept. of Rare Books and Special
Collections. Princeton, N.J. , 1990. xi, 213 p. :
ISBN 0-87811-033-X
NYPL [MDBF 90-10992]

American graphic arts . Roylance, Dale.
Princeton, N.J. , 1990. xi, 213 p. : DDC
760/.0973/07474965 20
NE954.3.U6 R68 1990

The American houses of Robert A.M. Stern /.
Stern, Robert A. M. New York , 1991. p.
ISBN 0-8478-1433-5 DDC 728/.37/092 20
NA737.S64 A4 1991

American Impressionism . Gerdts, William H.
[Lugano-Castagnola] [Einsiedeln, Switzerland] ,
c1990. 161 p. : DDC 759.13/09/03407449478 20
ND210.5.I4 G474 1990a

American imprints on art through 1865 .
Schimmelman, Janice Gayle. Boston, Mass. ,
1990. ix, 419 p. ; ISBN 0-8161-7261-7 DDC
016.7 20
Z5961.U5 S34 1990 N6505
NYPL [MAMT 91-3665]

AMERICAN INDIANS. see INDIANS;
INDIANS OF NORTH AMERICA;
INDIANS OF SOUTH AMERICA.

American infrared survey : a celebration of
infrared photography / edited by Stephen
Paternite and David Paternite. Akron, Ohio :
Photo Survey Press Pub., c1982. [82] p. :
chiefly ill. (some col.) ; 26 cm. ISBN
0-9609812-0-9 (pbk.) : DDC 779/.092/2 19
1. Infrared photography. I. Paternite, Stephen. II.
Paternite, David.
TR755 .A44 1982 ***NYPL [MFW 90-13460]***

American Institute of Architects.
Accent on architecture . [Washington, D.C.]
(1735 New York Ave., NW, Washington
20006) [c1991] 1 v. (unpaged) ; DDC
720/.973/09045 20
NA2340 .A33 1991

Making a difference : the environmental
resource guide, an introduction. Washington,
DC : American Institute of Architects, c1990.
24 p. : ill. ; 22 cm. Includes bibliographical
references (p. 24). DDC 720/.47 20
1. American Institute of Architects. Committee on the
Environment. 2. Architecture - Environmental aspects.
I. Title.
NA2542.35 .A45 1990

American Institute of Architects. Chicago
Chapter. 5 years of interior architecture
awards /. Chicago, Ill. , c1985. 104 p. : DDC
729/.09713/1109048 20
NA2850 .A14 1985

American Institute of Architects. Colorado
Chapter. Jackson, Olga.
Architecture/Colorado. [Denver, c1966] 96 p.
NYPL [3-MQWO 91-225]

AMERICAN INSTITUTE OF ARCHITECTS.
COMMITTEE ON THE ENVIRONMENT.
American Institute of Architects. Making a
difference . Washington, DC , c1990. 24 p. :
DDC 720/.47 20
NA2542.35 .A45 1990

American Institute of Architects. Kansas City
Chapter. Kansas City / The Kansas City
Chapter of the American Institute of Architects.
Kansas City, Mo. : The Chapter, c1979. 256
p. : ill., maps ; 19 cm. Writer: Joan L. Michalak.
Includes indexes.
1. Architecture - Missouri - Kansas City - Guide-books.
2. Kansas City (Mo.) - Buildings, structures, etc. -
Guide-books. I. Michalak, Joan L. II. Title.
NYPL [3-MQWO 90-6351]

American Institute of Architects. New York
Chapter. New York architecture / New York
Chapter, AIA. New York : New York
Chapter/AIA, 1988- v. : ill. ; 31 cm.
1. Architecture - New York (N.Y.). 2. Architecture,
Modern - 20th century - New York (N.Y.). 3.
Architecture - Awards. I. Title.
NYPL [MQWO+ 89-8137]

American Institute of Architects. Washington
Metropolitan Chapter. Rowan, Bob, 1944- A
capital perspective . Chatsworth, Calif. , 1991.
p. cm. ISBN 0-89781-427-4 DDC 720/.9753 20
NA735.W3 R69 1991

American Institute of Indian Studies.
Encyclopaedia of Indian temple architecture /.
New Delhi , Philadelphia , 1983- v. : ISBN
0-8122-7840-2 (U. S. : v. 1, pt. 1) DDC
726/.14/0954 19
NA6001 .E53 1983
NYPL [3-MQWS 87-1248]

American journey. Holmes, David B. (David
Bryan), 1936- David B. Holmes . New York
[1987?] 20 p. :
NYPL [3-MCZ H75 90-11603]

American kasten . Kenny, Peter (Peter M.) New
York , c1991. viii, 80 p. : ISBN 0-87099-605-3
(pbk.) DDC 749/.3 20
NK2727 .K46 1991 ***NYPL [3-MOF 91-6596]***

AMERICAN LANDSCAPE PAINTING. see
LANDSCAPE PAINTING, AMERICAN.

American landscape painting today. Harmony &
discord . Richmond , c1990. 32 p. :
MLCS 91/06468 (N)
NYPL [3-MCW 91-4406]

American light : the luminist movement,
1850-1875 : paintings, drawings, photographs /
[edited by] John Wilmerding ; with
contributions by Lisa Fellows Andrus ... [et al.].

[Laurenceville, NJ] : Princeton University
Press ; Washington, [D.C.] : National Gallery
of Art, c1989. 330 p. : ill. (some col.) ; 24 x 29
cm. Reprint. Originally published: Washington, D.C. :
National Gallery of Art, c1980; to coincide with an
exhibition, held at the National Gallery of Art Feb.
10-June 15, 1980. Includes index. Bibliography: p.
313-322. ISBN 0-691-04074-5 (alk. paper) : DDC
758/.1/09730740153 19
1. Luminism (Art) - Exhibitions. 2. Art, American -
Exhibitions. 3. Landscape in art - Exhibitions. 4. Art,
Modern - 19th century - United States - Exhibitions. 5.
Hudson River school of landscape painting -
Exhibitions. 6. Photography, Artistic - Exhibitions. I.
Wilmerding, John. II. Andrus, Lisa Fellows.
N8214.5.U6 A47 1989
NYPL [3-MAMT 90-12012]

AMERICAN LITERATURE - 20TH
CENTURY.
Hockney, David. Hockney's alphabet /. New
York, NY , c1991. p. cm. ISBN 0-679-41066-X :
DDC 741.942 20
NC242.H6 A4 1991a

AMERICAN LITERATURE - SOUTHERN
STATES - HISTORY AND CRITICISM.
Mixon, Wayne. Southern writers and the New
South movement, 1865-1913 /. Chapel Hill ,
c1980. x, 169 p. ; ISBN 0-8078-5057-8
PS261 .M5 ***NYPL [IAA 74-813 no.57]***

American Map Company, inc., New York.
Cleartype® commercial atlas of the United
States. New York : American Map Co., [198-?]
[58] leaves : 51 maps ; 56 cm. "Complete set no.
400 series state maps": county-town maps showing cities
and towns of 250 population and over (1970 census?)
Scales vary. Some maps have enlarged-scale insets of
urban areas. Issued loose-leaf. Cover title.
1. Cities and towns - United States - Maps. I. Title. II.
Title: Commercial atlas of the United States.
NYPL [Map Div. 85-883]

AMERICAN MARBLE SCULPTURE. see
MARBLE SCULPTURE, AMERICAN.

American maritime paintings of John Stobart /.
Stobart, John, 1929- New York, N.Y. , 1991. p.
cm. ISBN 0-525-93355-7 DDC 759.2 20
ND497.S797 A4 1991

American master paintings, 1768-1990 :
November 1990. New York : Kennedy
Galleries, c1990. [48] p. : ill. ; 28 cm.
1. Painting, American - Exhibitions. I. Kennedy
Galleries. ***NYPL [3-MCW 90-13371]***

American master paintings, 1768-1990 :
November 1990, Kennedy Galleries, Inc. New
York (40 W. 57th St., New York 10019) :
Kennedy Galleries, c1990. 1 v. (unpaged) : col.
ill. ; 28 cm. Includes index. DDC 759.13/074/7471
20
1. Painting, American - Exhibitions. I. Kennedy
Galleries.
ND205 .A654 1990

American masters in the West . Schriever,
George. [S.l.] , c1976. 67 p. :
NYPL [3-MCW 90-5762]

American masters of the sixties. American
masters of the 60's . New York, NY (130
Prince St., New York 10012) , c1990. 76 p. :
DDC 709/.73/0747471 20
N6512 .A6156 1990

American masters of the 60's : early & late
works : May 9 through June 23, 1990 /
curatorial advisor, Sam Hunter. New York, NY
(130 Prince St., New York 10012) : Tony
Shafrazi Gallery, c1990. 76 p. : col. ill. ; 31 cm.
Includes bibliographical references and index. DDC
709/.73/0747471 20
1. Art, American - Exhibitions. 2. Art, Modern - 20th
century - United States - Exhibitions. I. Hunter, Sam,
1923-. II. Tony Shafrazi Gallery. III. Title: American
masters of the sixties.
N6512 .A6156 1990

American miniatures. Hall, Audrey. Philadelphia,
Pa. (1806 Chestnut St., Philadelphia 19103) ,
1990. 1 v. (unpaged) : DDC
757/.7/0974090330747481 20
ND1337.U5 H34 1990

American Museum of the Moving Image. Kubota,
Shigeko, 1937- Shigeko Kubota video sculpture
/. Astoria, N.Y. , Bellevue , c1991. 96 p. :
ISBN 0-295-97131-2 DDC 700/.92 20
N7359.K83 A4 1991

American music for strings [sound recording].
Los Angeles, Calif. : Nonesuch, p1980. 1 sound
disc : analog, 33 1/3 rpm, stereo. ; 12 in. The
1st work originally for string quartet, the 3rd originally
for viola and piano, arr. by the composers. Los Angeles
Chamber Orchestra ; Gerard Schwarz, conductor.
Recorded Apr. 2, 1980, at the Ambassador Auditorium,
Pasadena, Calif. Digital recording. CONTENTS. -
Serenade for string orchestra, op. 1 / Samuel Barber
(9:19) -- Serious song / Irving Fine (8:46) -- Elegy /
Elliott Carter (4:59) -- Rounds for string orchestra /
David Diamond (13:51).
*1. String-orchestra music. 2. String-orchestra music,
Arranged. I. Fine, Irving, 1914-1962. Serious song.
1980. II. Carter, Elliott, 1908- Elegy, viola, piano; arr.
1980. III. Diamond, David, 1915- Rounds, string
orchestra. 1980.*
Nonesuch D-79002

**American naive painting of the 18th and 19th
centuries.** Garbisch, Edgar William. [New York,
1969] 159 p.   *NYPL [3-MCW 91-7028]*

American oak furniture . Swedberg, Robert W.
Radnor, Pa. , 1991. p. cm. ISBN 0-87069-621-1
(hc) : DDC 749.213/075 20
NK2405 .S89 1991b

American oak furniture . Swedberg, Robert W.
Radnor, Pa. , 1991. p. ISBN 0-87069-588-6 (pbk.)
DDC 749.213/075 20
NK2405 .S89 1991a

American oak furniture . Swedberg, Robert W.
Radnor, Pa. , c1991. ix, 195 p. : ISBN
0-87069-587-8 (pbk.) : DDC 749.213/075 20
NK2405 .S89 1991

American painter etchings, 1853-1908 .
Schneider, Rona. New York City [1989] 48
p. : ISBN 0-910672-06-7 (pbk.)
                       NYPL [MDBF 89-19631]

American painting /. Goddard, Donald Letcher.
New York , c1990. 319 p. : ISBN 0-88363-590-9
                       NYPL [MCW+ 91-2640]

**AMERICAN PAINTING. see PAINTING,
AMERICAN.**

American painting 1730-1960. Amerika kaiga
ten . [Tokyo] , c1982. [174] p. :
                       NYPL [3-MCW 90-7185]

American paintings. Hall, Audrey. Philadelphia,
PA (1806 Chestnut St., Philadelphia 19103)
[c1990] 1 v. : DDC 759.13/09/03407474811 20
ND210 .H34 1990

American paintings . Kenneth Lux Gallery. New
York, NY (1021 Madison Ave., New York
10021) [1990] 1 v. (unpaged) : DDC
759.13/074/7471 20
ND210 .K468 1990

**American paintings and sculpture at the Sterling
and Francine Clark Art Institute/.** Conrads,
Margaret C., 1955- New York , c1990. 219 p. :
ISBN 1-555-95050-7 (alk. paper) : DDC
759.13/074/7441 20
*N6505 .C645 1990   NYPL [MAVZ+
(Williamstown) 91-5440]*

**American paintings and sculpture to 1945 in the
Carnegie Museum of Art /.** Strazdes, Diana J.
New York , c1991. p. cm. ISBN 1-555-95055-8 :
DDC 759.13/074/74886 20
N6505 .S87 1991

**American paintings in the Detroit Institute of
Arts /.** Detroit. Institute of Arts. New York ,
c1991- p. ISBN 1-555-95044-2 (alk. paper) : DDC
759.13/074/77434 20
ND205 .D298 1991

**The American paintings in the Pennsylvania
Academy of the Fine Arts .** Fresella-Lee,
Nancy. Philadelphia , Seattle , c1989. xviii, 204
p. : ISBN 0-943836-11-5 : DDC 759.13/074/74811
20
*ND205 .F728 1989   NYPL [3-MAVZ
(Philadelphia) 90-13075]*

**American pastels in the Metropolitan Museum of
Art /.** Metropolitan Museum of Art (New
York, N.Y.) New York , c1989. x, 247 p. :
ISBN 0-87099-547-2 DDC 741.973/074/7471 20
NC885 .M48 1989
                       NYPL [3-MAVZ (New York) 89-27019]

American Planning Association. A Survey of
zoning definitions /. Chicago , c1989. 36 p. :
DDC 361.6/0973 361.6/03 20
NA9108 .A545 no. 421 HT169.6

**American Planning Association. Planning
Advisory Service.** A Survey of zoning
definitions /. Chicago , c1989. 36 p. : DDC
361.6/0973 361.6/03 20
NA9108 .A545 no. 421 HT169.6

American political prints, 1766-1876 . Reilly,
Bernard. Boston, MA , 1991. xxi, 638 p. :
ISBN 0-8161-0444-1   DDC 320.973/0207 20
E183.3 .R45 1991   NYPL [MDY 91-5510]

**American portrait miniatures in the Manney
collection /.** Johnson, Dale T. New York ,
1990. 271 p. : ISBN 0-87099-597-9   DDC
757/.7/09730747471 20
                       NYPL [3-MCW 91-4980]

**AMERICAN POTTERY. see POTTERY,
AMERICAN.**

American presentation swords /. Altmayer, Jay P.
Mobile, Ala. , c1958. 46 p. :
                       NYPL [3-MNK 90-6863]

American printmakers (Washington, D.C.)
Gravalos, Mary Evans O'Keefe. Bertha Lum /.
Washington, D.C. , c1991. 112 p. : ISBN
1-560-98008-7 (pbk.)   DDC 769.92 20
NE1112.L86 G73 1990
                       NYPL [MDG (Lum) 91-5860]
Mason, Tim, 1934- Helen Hyde /.
Washington , c1991. 120 p. : ISBN
1-560-98009-5 (pbk.)   DDC 769.92 20
NE539.H9 M37 1991
                       NYPL [MDG (Hyde) 91-7232]

The American quilt story . Jenkins, Susan, 1947-
Emmaus, Pa. , New York , c1991. p. cm.
ISBN 0-87857-992-3 (hardcover) : DDC 746.9/7
20
NK9112 .J4 1991

American Quilter's Society. Faoro, Victoria.
Award-winning quilts & their makers /.
Paducah, KY , c1991- v. <1 > : ISBN
0-89145-972-3 (v. 1) : DDC 746.9/7/097309048
20
NK9112 .F36 1991

American quilts /. Bowman, Doris M.
Washington, D.C. , New York, N.Y. , 1991. p.
cm. ISBN 0-517-05952-5 : DDC
746.9/7/0973074753 20
NK9112 .L4 1991

**American quilts & coverlets in the Metropolitan
Museum of Art /.** Peck, Amelia. New York ,
c1990. 262 p. : ISBN 0-87099-592-8   DDC
746.9/7/09730747471 20
NK9112 .P434 1990
                       NYPL [3-MOT 91-4453]

**American quilts and coverlets in the
Metropolitan Museum of Art.** Peck, Amelia.
American quilts & coverlets in the Metropolitan
Museum of Art /. New York , c1990. 262 p. :
ISBN 0-87099-592-8   DDC
746.9/7/09730747471 20
NK9112 .P434 1990
                       NYPL [3-MOT 91-4453]

American redware /. Ketchum, William C., 1931-
New York , c1991. x, 147 p. : ISBN
0-8050-1262-1 : DDC 738.3/0973 20
NK4283 .K4 1991   NYPL [3-MPH 91-4619]

AMERICAN REPUBLICS. see AMERICA.

American rococo, 1750-1775 . Heckscher,
Morrison H. New York : [Los Angeles] : p. cm.
ISBN 0-87099-630-4   DDC
745.4/4974/090330747471 20
NK1403.5 .H4 1992

American salons . Crunden, Robert Morse. New
York , 1992. p. cm. ISBN 0-19-506569-7 (acid-free
paper) DDC 700/.973/09034 20
NX503.7 .C78 1992

American scene painting : California, 1930s and
1940s / edited by Ruth Lilly Westphal, Janet
Blake Dominik. Irvine, Calif. : Westphal Pub.,
1991. p. cm. Includes bibliographical references and
index. ISBN 0-9610520-3-1 : DDC 758/.99794052
20
*1. Painting, American - California. 2. Painting,
Modern - 20th century - California. 3. California in art.
4. Regionalism in art. 5. Social realism - California. I.
Westphal, Ruth Lilly. II. Dominik, Janet B.*
ND230.C3 A44 1991

American Schools of Oriental Research. White,
L. Michael. Building God's house in the Roman
world . Baltimore, Md. , c1990. xv, 211 p. :

ISBN 0-8018-3906-8 (alk. paper)
NA4817 .W55 1990
                       NYPL [3-MQN 90-10439]

**AMERICAN SCULPTURE. see SCULPTURE,
AMERICAN.**

American silversmiths and their marks IV /.
Ensko, Stephen Guernsey Cook, 1896- Boston ,
1989, c1988. xiii, 477 p. : ISBN 0-87923-778-3
                       NYPL [MNP 90-11585]

American Society of Architectural Perspectivists.
Architecture in perspective . New York, N.Y. ,
c1991. p. cm. ISBN 0-442-00700-0   DDC
720/.22/27309043 20
NA2780 .A73 1991

**AMERICAN-SPANISH WAR, 1898. see
UNITED STATES - HISTORY - WAR OF
1898.**

American stoneware /. Ketchum, William C.,
1931- New York , c1991. p. cm. ISBN
0-8050-1263-X   DDC 738.3/0973 20
NK4364 .K48 1991

American studies series.
Mamiya, Christin J. Pop art and consumer
culture . Austin , 1992. p. cm. ISBN
0-292-75163-5 (alk. paper)   DDC 709/.04/071 20
N6512.5.P6 M36 1992

**American university studies. Series XX, Fine
arts .**
(vol. 16) Marc, Franz, 1880-1916. [Briefe aus
dem Feld. English.] Letters from the war /.
New York , 1992. p. cm. ISBN 0-8204-1588-X
DDC 759.3 B 20
N6888.M34 A3 1992

(vol. 17) Art and philosophy . New York ,
1991. p. cm. ISBN 0-8204-1599-5 DDC 730/.92
20
NB933.B7 A78 1991

American vernacular . Kemp, Jim. Washington,
D.C. , 1990, c1987. 256 p. : ISBN
1-558-35074-8 :
                       NYPL [3-MQWO 91-6742]

American views . Wilmerding, John. Princeton,
N.J. , 1991. p. cm. ISBN 0-691-04090-7 : DDC
759.3 20
N6505 .W57 1991

American watercolor masters. Brooklyn Museum.
Curator's choice . [Brooklyn, N.Y. , 1990] 1
folded sheet ([8] p.) :
                       NYPL [3-MCX H76 91-7969]

The American wilderness /. Adams, Ansel, 1902-
Boston , c1990. 146 p. : ISBN 0-8212-1799-2
DDC 779/.36/092 20
TR660 .A29 1990
                       NYPL [MFX+ (Adams) 91-2496]

**AMERICAN WIT AND HUMOR,
PICTORIAL.**
Baxter, Glen. Welcome to the weird world of
Glen Baxter /. New York , c1989. 185 p. :
ISBN 0-06-055167-4 : DDC 741.5/942 20
NC1429.B34 A4 1989
                       NYPL [3-MEM (Baxter) 90-10997]

Bragg, Charles. The absurd world of Charles
Bragg /. New York , c1991. p. cm. ISBN
1-559-70130-7 (HC) : DDC 741.5/092 20
NC1429.B733 A4 1991

Callahan, John. Digesting the child within /.
New York, N.Y. , 1991. p. cm. ISBN
0-688-09488-0   DDC 741.5/973 20
NC1429.C23 A4 1991

Cochran, Bruce. Bass fever . Minocqua, WI ,
c1991. p. cm. ISBN 1-559-71126-4 (hardcover) :
DDC 741.5/973 20
NC1429.C619 A4 1991

Danco, Léon A., 1923- Someday, it'll all be--
whos's? /. Cleveland , c1990. vi, 196 p. : ISBN
0-915607-09-3 (Jamieson) : DDC 741.5/973 20
NC1429.D2344 A4 1990

Dicksion, Rhonda, 1959- Lesbian survival
manual . Tallahassee, FL , 1990. 94 p. : ISBN
0-941483-71-1 DDC 741.5/973 20
NC1429.D45 A4 1990
                       NYPL [3-MEM (Dicksion) 90-13132]

Fehl, Philipp P. Birds of a feather /. Urbana ,
c1991. p. cm. ISBN 0-252-06241-8 (alk. paper)
DDC 741.973 20
NC1429.F2955 A4 1991

Friedman, Drew. Warts and all /. New York, N.Y. , 1990. [80] p. : ISBN 0-14-013086-1 (pbk.)
NYPL [3-MEM (Friedman) 90-13588]

Gately, George. [Heathcliff. Selections.] Heathcliff thinks big /. New York , 1990. 1 v. (unpaged) ISBN 0-515-10431-0 : DDC 741.5/973 20
NC1429.G3 A4 1990

Harris, Sidney. Can't you guys read? cartoons on academia /. New Brunswick , c1991. p. cm. ISBN 0-8135-1733-8 (pbk.) : DDC 741.5/973 20
NC1429.H33315 A4 1991a

Harris, Sidney. You want proof? I'll give you proof! . New York , c1991. [150] p. : ISBN 0-7167-2159-7 : DDC 741.5/973 20
NC1429.H33315 A4 1991
NYPL [3-MEM (Harris) 90-13677]

Heine, John, 1950- A good planet is hard to find /. Birmingham, Ala. , 1991. p. cm. ISBN 0-89732-108-1 DDC 741.5/973 20
NC1429.H377 A4 1991

Heller, Steven. Graphic wit . New York , 1991. p. cm. ISBN 0-8230-2161-0 : DDC 741.6 20
NC998.5.A1 H44 1991

Keane, Bil, 1922- [Family circus. Selections.] I had a frightmare! /. New York , 1990. 1 v. (unpaged) : ISBN 0-449-14615-4 : DDC 741.5/973 20
NC1429.K29 A4 1990

Ketcham, Hank, 1920- Dennis the Menace--his first 40 years /. New York , 1991. p. cm. ISBN 1-558-59157-5 DDC 741.5/973 20
NC1429.K52 A4 1991

Leake, Jerry. Far fetched /. [Boston, MA , c1986] 1 v. (unpaged) : DDC 741.5/973 20
NC1429.L373 A4 1986

McPherson, John, 1959- Life at McPherson High /. Grand Rapids, Mich. , 1991. p. cm. ISBN 0-310-71161-4 (paper) DDC 741.5/973 20
NC1429.M275 A4 1991

McPherson, John, 1959- [Marriage album.] McPherson's marriage album /. Grand Rapids, Mich. , 1991. p. cm. ISBN 0-310-53901-3 (paper) DDC 741.5/973 20
NC1429.M275 A4 1991a

Marlette, Doug, 1949- In your face . Boston , 1991. p. cm. ISBN 0-395-60236-X DDC 741.5/092 20
NC1429.M4215 A2 1991

Moore, Steve. Revolution in the bleachers . New York : Toronto : ISBN 0-02-070191-8 DDC 741.5/973 20
NC1429.M727 A4 1991

Nealy, William, 1953- Skiing tales of terror /. Birmingham, Ala. , c1990. 1 v. (unpaged) : ISBN 0-89732-106-5 DDC 741.5/973 20
NC1429.N42 A4 1990

The New breed. New York , c1990. 1 v. (unpaged) : ISBN 0-380-76071-1 : DDC 741.5/973 20
NC1426 .N49 1990

Nutzle, Futzie. Run the world--$.50 /. San Francisco , 1991. p. cm. ISBN 0-87701-842-1 : DDC 741.5/973 20
NC1429.N8 A4 1991

Olson, Eric, 1958- Horrorscope . Stamford, Conn. , 1991. p. cm. ISBN 0-681-41165-1 : DDC 741.5/973 20
NC1429.O45 A4 1991

Phillips, Steve, 1953- Farmer Johnson's psycho dairy farm for environmentally aware barnyard animals /. New York, N.Y. , 1992. p. cm. ISBN 0-385-30495-1 : DDC 741.5/973 20
NC1429.P57 A4 1992

Pope, Kevin. The dance of the seven seals, and other cartoons /. New York , 1991. p. cm. ISBN 0-312-05828-4 : DDC 741.5/973 20
NC1429.P645 A4 1991

Portlock, Rob. Climbing the church walls /. Downers Grove, Ill. , 1991. p. cm. ISBN 0-8308-1830-8 DDC 741.5/973 20
NC1429.P65 A4 1991

Rodano, Philip J. Me-ow . Lincroft, N.J. , c1990. 1 v. ; ISBN 0-9627648-1-7 DDC 741.5/973 20
NC1429.R66 A4 1990

Saget, Bob. [Tales from the crib.] Bob Saget's

Tales from the crib /. New York, NY , c1991. 95 p. : ISBN 0-399-51676-X : DDC 741.5/973 20
NC1429.S315 A4 1991

Sipress, David. It's a cat's life /. New York, N.Y., U. S. A. , c1992. p. cm. ISBN 0-453-26758-7 DDC 741.5/973 20
NC1429.S532 A4 1992

Stevens, Bob, 1923- There I was-- 25 years /. Bonsall, CA , c1990. 597 p. ; ISBN 0-910497-03-6 DDC 741.5/973 20
NC1429.S64 A4 1990a

Sumrall, Joe, 1950- Lighten up! . Santa Fe, N.M. , c1990. 95 p. : ISBN 0-939680-72-6 : DDC 741.5/973 20
NC1429.S816 A4 1990
NYPL [3-MEM (Sumrall) 91-2433]

Thaves, Bob. [Frank and Ernest. Selections.] Assemble the hyenas-- I feel a pun coming on!. New York , 1991. ca. 130 p. : ISBN 0-88687-529-3 : DDC 741.5/973 20
NC1429.T44 A4 1991

Vey, P. C. (Peter C.) If cats could talk! /. New York, N.Y., U. S. A. , c1991. 1 v. (unpaged) : ISBN 0-452-26642-4 : DDC 741.5/973 20
NC1429.V57 A4 1991

AMERICAN WIT AND HUMOR, PICTORIAL - CATALOGS.
Reilly, Bernard. American political prints, 1766-1876 . Boston, MA , 1991. xxi, 638 p. : ISBN 0-8161-0444-1 DDC 320.973/0207 20
E183.3 .R45 1991   *NYPL [MDY 91-5510]*

AMERICAN WIT AND HUMOR, PICTORIAL - JUVENILE LITERATURE.
Goldberg, Rube, 1883-1970. The best of Rube Goldberg /. Englewood Cliffs, N.J. [1979] xiii, 130 p. : ISBN 0-13-074807-2 : DDC 741.5/973
NC1429.G46 A4 1979
NYPL [3-MEM (Goldberg) 81-1046]

American women painters of the 1930s and 1940s . Henkes, Robert. Jefferson, N.C. , c1991. xv, 236 p. : ISBN 0-89950-474-4 (lib. bdg. : alk. paper) DDC 759.13/082 20
ND212 .H46 1991

American women sculptors . Rubinstein, Charlotte Streifer. Boston, MA , 1990. xv, 638 p. : ISBN 0-8161-8732-0 DDC 730/.82 20
NB236 .R8 1990   *NYPL [3-MGI 91-3389]*

AMERICANA - CATALOGS.
Ketchum, William C., 1931- The new and revised catalog of American collectibles /. New York City , 1990. 320 p. : ISBN 0-8317-6316-7
NYPL [3-MAVC 91-7510]

Americanos indianos : arquitectura i urbanisme al Garraf, Penedès i Tarragonès (Baix Gaià) : segles XVIII-XX. Vilanova i la Geltrú : Biblioteca-Museu Balaguer, 1990. 262 p. : ill. ; 22 cm.
1. Architecture - Spain - Catalonia. I. Biblioteca-Museu Víctor Balaguer.   *NYPL [3-MQWH 91-6959]*

Americans and Paris . Marlais, Michael Andrew. Waterville, Me. , c1990. 62 p. : DDC 759.13/074/7416 20
N6510 .M27 1990
NYPL [3-MAMT 90-13006]

AMERICANS - FRANCE - PARIS - EXHIBITIONS.
Americans in Paris, 1600-1900. [New York? 1972] 48 p. DDC 769/.944/07401471
NE647 .A68   *NYPL [MDE 90-7096]*

Americans in Paris, 1600-1900; one hundred and fifty works from the Print Collection of the National Library in Paris. [New York? 1972] 48 p. illus. 23 cm. Catalogue of an exhibition held in the Art Center of the New School for Social Research, February 26 through April 22, 1972. DDC 769/.944/07401471
1. Bibliothèque nationale (France). Cabinet des estampes - Exhibitions. 2. Prints, French - Exhibitions. 3. Prints, American - Exhibitions. 4. Americans - France - Paris - Exhibitions. I. New School Art Center (New York, N.Y.).
NE647 .A68   *NYPL [MDE 90-7096]*

Americas Society. Contemporary art from Chile . New York, N.Y. , c1990. 63 p. : ISBN 1-87912-802-0   *NYPL [3-MAM 91-7561]*

Amerighi, Michelangelo. see Caravaggio, Michelangelo Merisi da, 1573-1610.

Amerigi, Michelangelo. see Caravaggio, Michelangelo Merisi da, 1573-1610.

AMERIKA-GEDENKBIBLIOTHEK/BERLINER ZENTRALBIBLIOTHEK - BUILDINGS - EXHIBITIONS.
14x Amerika-Gedenkbibliothek . Berlin , c1989. 132 p. : ISBN 3-433-02288-7 (pbk.)
NYPL [3-MQWO+ 90-11060]

Amerika Haus, Berlin. 14x Amerika-Gedenkbibliothek . Berlin , c1989. 132 p. : ISBN 3-433-02288-7 (pbk.)
NYPL [3-MQWO+ 90-11060]

Amerika kaiga ten : Rokkuferā 3-sei fusai korekushon = American painting 1730-1960 : a selection from the collection of Mr. and Mrs. D. Rockefeller 3rd / [henshū Kokuritsu Seiyō Bijutsukan]. [Tokyo] : Kokuritsu Seiyō Bijutsukan, c1982. [174] p. : ill. (some col.), maps ; 24 cm. In Japanese and English. Catalog of the exhibition held at the National Museum of Western Art, Tokyo, July 27-Sept. 19, 1982. Includes bibliographical references.
1. Rockefeller, John D., 1906-1978 - Art collections - Exhibitions. 2. Rockefeller, Blanchette Hooker, 1909- - Art collections - Exhibitions. 3. Painting, American - Private collections - New York (N.Y.) - Exhibitions. I. Kokuritsu Seiyō Bijutsukan (Japan). II. Title: American painting 1730-1960.   *NYPL [3-MCW 90-7185]*

Amerikai Egyesült Allamok. see United States.

Amerikanische Zeichnungen in den achtziger Jahren : 16. Mai 1990 bis 1. Juli 1990, Graphische Sammlung Albertina, Wien, 12. September 1990 bis 4. November 1990, Museum Morsbroich, Leverkusen / zusammengestellt vom Museum Morsbroich, Leverkusen, Rolf Wedewer ; mit Fred Jahn und David Nolan ; unterstützt von Bill Goldston für die Beiträge Jasper Johns, Robert Rauschenberg und James Rosenquist ; [Übersetzung des Einleitungstextes, Benjamin Schwarz]. München : F. Jahn, c1990. 190 p. : col. ill. ; 27 cm. Exhibition catalog. German and English. DDC 741.973/09/04807443551 20
1. Drawing, American - Exhibitions. 2. Drawing - 20th century - United States - Exhibitions. I. Wedewer, Rolf. II. Jahn, Fred. III. Nolan, David. IV. Städtisches Museum Leverkusen, Schloss Morsbroich. V. Graphische Sammlung Albertina. VI. Title: Amerikanische Zeichnungen in den 80er Jahren.
NC108 .A55 1990

Amerikanische Zeichnungen in den 80er Jahren . Amerikanische Zeichnungen in den achtziger Jahren . München , c1990. 190 p. : DDC 741.973/09/04807443551 20
NC108 .A55 1990

AMERINDS. see INDIANS.

Ames, Lee J. Draw 50 creepy crawlies / Lee J. Ames with Ray Burns. 1st ed. New York : Doubleday, c1991. p. cm. Step-by-step instructions for drawing fifty different insects, spiders, and other crawling or flying creatures. ISBN 0-385-41189-8 DDC 743/.6 20
1. Insects in art - Juvenile literature. 2. Animals in art - Juvenile literature. 3. Drawing - Technique - Juvenile literature. I. Burns, Raymond, 1924-. II. Title. III. Title: Draw fifty creepy crawlies.
NC783 .A44 1991

Amiel, Alain. Guid'arts . Nice [1989] 174 p. : ISBN 2-87720-040-X :
N6485.3 .G85 1989

AMIENS (FRANCE) - BUILDINGS, STRUCTURES, ETC.
Le Nouvel Amiens /. Liège , 1989. 471 p. : ISBN 2-87009-368-3
NA9198.A42 N68 1989

Amighetti, Francisco. Francisco Amighetti / diseño y edición gráfica, Sonia Calvo. San José, Costa Rica : Editorial de la Universidad de Costa Rica, c1989. 167 p. : ill. (some col.) ; 29 cm. Spanish and English. Includes bibliographical references. ISBN 997-7671-12-5 DDC 760/.092 20
1. Amighetti, Francisco - Catalogs. I. Title.
N6575.A45 A4 1989

AMIGHETTI, FRANCISCO - CATALOGS.
Amighetti, Francisco. Francisco Amighetti /. San José, Costa Rica , c1989. 167 p. : ISBN 997-7671-12-5 DDC 760/.092 20
N6575.A45 A4 1989

Amin, Naguib. Cairo A-Z : complete Cairo street-finder / [Naguib Amin]. Zamalek, Cairo, Egypt : Palm Press, 1988. x, 151, 24, 14 p. :

col. ill., col. maps ; 24 cm. Cover title.
*1. Cairo (Egypt) - Description - Guide-books. 2. Cairo
(Egypt) - Maps. I. Title. II. Title: Cairo A to Z. III.
Title: Cairo street finder.*
IN PROCESS (ONLINE)
NYPL [Map Div. 90-11167]

The Amis collection . Amis, Kingsley.
[Selections.] London , 1990. xv, 400 p. ; ISBN
0-09-173970-5 : DDC 824.914 20
NYPL [JFE 91-1342]

Amis du Portugal. Le Bijou 1900 . Bruxelles ,
1965. 102 p., [26] p. of plates :
NYPL [3-MNR 90-6082]

Amis du Vexin français. Le Vexin français .
Pontoise [France] [196-?] 32 p. :
NYPL [3-MRGF 90-6241]

Amis, Kingsley.
[Selections]
The Amis collection : Selected Non-Fiction;
1954-1990 / Kingsley Amis with an
introduction by John McDermott. London :
Hutchinson, 1990. xv, 400 p. ; 25 cm. Includes
index. Includes bibliographical references. ISBN
0-09-173970-5 : DDC 824.914 20
I. Title. **NYPL [JFE 91-1342]**

Amish, the art of the quilt /. Hughes, Robert,
1936- New York , 1990. 207 p. : ISBN
0-394-58781-2 : DDC 746.9/708/8287 20
NK9112 .H8 1990
NYPL [3-MOT+ 90-12042]

**AMITY (ME.) - SOCIAL LIFE AND
CUSTOMS.**
Scott, Geraldine Tidd. Isaac Simpson's world .
Falmouth, Me. , c1990. xxiii, 183 p. : ISBN
0-933858-09-4 DDC 779/.99741 20
TR652 .S36 1990
NYPL [MFX (Simpson) 91-4040]

Ammann, Gustav, 1885-1955. Blühende Gärten.
Landscape gardens. Jardins en fleurs.
Erlenbach-Zürich, Verlag für Architektur
[c1955] 212 p. illus., plans. 28 cm. DDC 712
I. Title. II. Title: Landscape gardens.
SB472 .A5 **NYPL [3-MSD 90-5819]**

Ammann, Jean Christophe.
Cucchi, Enzo. Enzo Cucchi testa /. München ,
c1987. 2 v. : ISBN 3-88645-076-7 (v. 1)
NYPL [3-MCF C952 88-3505]

(comp) Von Hodler zur Antiform. Geschichte
der Kunsthalle Bern. [Von] Jean-Christophe
Ammann [und] Harald Szeemann. Bern, Benteli
[c1970] 192 p. illus. 21 cm. "Bentelireport."
*1. Kunsthalle Bern - Exhibitions - History. I. Szeemann,
Harald, joint comp. II. Title.*
N3629 .A95
NYPL [3-MAVZ (Bern) 90-7016]

Ammar Farhat et son œuvre /. El Goulli, Sophie.
Tunis , c1979. 140 p. : ISBN
NYPL [3-MCZ+ F215 90-11030]

Amon Carter Museum of Western Art.
Clift, William, 1944- Certain places . Santa Fe,
N.M. , c1987. [46] p. : ISBN 9-9618165-0-3
NYPL [MFX+ (Clift) 91-2455]

Davis, Stuart, 1892-1964. Stuart Davis . Fort
Worth, Tex. , 1986. viii, 96 p. : ISBN
0-88360-054-4 DDC 760/.092/4 19
N6537.D345 A4 1986
NYPL [MDG (Davis) 90-12799]

Kornhauser, Elizabeth Mankin, 1950- Ralph
Earl . New Haven : Yale University Press ; p.
cm. ISBN 0-300-05041-0 (cloth) DDC 759.13 20
ND1329.E23 A4 1991

McAuley, Skeet. Sign language . New York,
N.Y. , c1989. 78 p. : ISBN 0-89381-333-8 :
DDC 979.1/35 20
E99.N3 M515 1989
NYPL [MFX (McAuley) 89-26792]

Southall, Thomas, 1951- Of time & place . San
Francisco , Fort Worth , c1990. 88 p. : ISBN
0-933286-57-0 (cloth)
NYPL [MFW 91-3397]

Stella, Joseph, 1877-1946. Visual poetry .
Washington , c1990. xviii, 166 p. : ISBN
0-87474-738-4 DDC 741.973 20
N6537.S73 A4 1990
NYPL [3-MCX S82 90-11649]

Stewart, Rick, 1944- Carl Wimar . Fort Worth ,
New York , c1991. xi, 252 p. : ISBN

0-8109-3958-4
IN PROCESS (ONLINE)
NYPL [3-MCX W75 91-6150]
William M. Harnett /. Fort Worth : New
York : p. cm. ISBN 0-8109-3410-8 DDC 759.13
20
ND237.H315 A4 1992

Amor Moreno, Grato E. López-Chaves Meléndez,
Juan M. (Juan Manuel) Inventario .
[Pontevedra] , 1988- v. <1 > : ISBN
84-86845-09-02 (v. 1)
NA7775 .L6 1988

L'Amour à la carte / Pierre Ferran. Paris : P.
Horay, [c1980] ca 150 p. : chiefly ill. ; 16 x 17
cm. ISBN 2-7058-0095-6 :
*1. Love in art. 2. Postal cards - France. I. Ferran,
Pierre, fl. 1966-.*
NC1878.L68 A45 **NYPL [3-MAMZ 81-962]**

Amouric, Henri. La Faïence de Marseille au
XVIIIe siècle . [Marseille] , 1990. 311 p. :
DDC 738.3/0944/912 20
NK4210.L28 F35 1990

AMS studies in the Middle Ages .
(no. 20) Davidson, Clifford. On tradition . New
York , 1991. p. cm. ISBN 0-404-64160-1 DDC
700/.9 20
NX440 .D38 1991

Amslinger, Ingrid. Voth, Hannsjörg, 1940- Hassi
Romi /. Nürnberg , c1989. 259 p. : ISBN
3-922531-68-7
NYPL [3-MGO+ (Voth) 91-7441]

Amsterdam. Musée national Vincent van Gogh.
see **Rijksmuseum Vincent van Gogh.**

**AMSTERDAM (NETHERLANDS) -
BUILDINGS, STRUCTURES, ETC. -
CONSERVATION AND RESTORATION.**
Amsterdam (Netherlands). Gemeentelijk bureau
Monumentenzorg. Bewaard in het hart .
Amsterdam , 1965. 174 p. :
NYPL [3-MQW 90-6245]

**AMSTERDAM (NETHERLANDS) -
BUILDINGS, STRUCTURES, ETC. -
EXHIBITIONS.**
Amsterdamse school . [Amsterdam , 1975. 112
p. : **NYPL [3-MQW 90-7048]**

**AMSTERDAM (NETHERLANDS) -
DESCRIPTION - VIEWS.**
Amsterdam omstreeks 1800. Amsterdam , 1965.
227 p. : **NYPL [3-MAMY 91-295]**

Amsterdam (Netherlands). Gemeentearchief.
Dudok van Heel, Sebastien A. C. Dossier
Rembrandt . Amsterdam , 1987. 88 p. :
NYPL [3-MCH R3 91-6725]

**Amsterdam (Netherlands). Gemeentelijk bureau
Monumentenzorg.** Bewaard in het hart : een
selectie van 63 Amsterdamse mooie en
pakhuizen uit de periode van 1450 tot 1825
gekozen uit een totaal van 650 percelen die
tijdens de eerste tien jaar van het bestaan van
het gemeentelijke Bureau monumentenzorg zijn
gerestaureerd (1953-1963). Amsterdam : [s.n.],
1965. 174 p. : ill. ; 28 cm. Dutch and English.
*1. Historic buildings - Netherlands - Amsterdam -
Conservation and restoration. 2. Amsterdam
(Netherlands) - Buildings, structures, etc. - Conservation
and restoration. I. Title.*
NYPL [3-MQW 90-6245]

**AMSTERDAM (NETHERLANDS) -
HISTORY.**
Groot, Reindert. Vincent van Gogh in
Amsterdam /. Amsterdam , c1990. 128 p. :
ISBN 90-6274-045-6 :
ND653.G7 G74 1990

AMSTERDAM (NETHERLANDS) IN ART.
Amsterdam omstreeks 1800. Amsterdam , 1965.
227 p. : **NYPL [3-MAMY 91-295]**

Amsterdam (Netherlands). Stedelijk Museum.
Amsterdamse school . [Amsterdam , 1975. 112
p. : **NYPL [3-MQW 90-7048]**
Beckmann, Max, 1884-1950. Max Beckmann .
[London] , 1980. 59 p. : ISBN 0-85488-050-X
ND588.B37 A4 1980
NYPL [3-MCK B39 90-5913]

Engels, Pieter, 1938- Engels: The selfportrait of
this century. [Amsterdam, 1972] 18 p. DDC
704.94/28/074094923 s 709/.2/4
N5072.A55 A3 nr. 528 N6953.E53
NYPL [3-MCH E571 90-6259]

De Grote naïeven =. Amsterdam , 1974. [41]
p. : **NYPL [3-MCN 90-6044]**

Kramer, Friso. Friso Kramer . [Amsterdam]
1978 (Amsterdam : Stadsdrukkerij) [36] p. :
NYPL [3-MNF 90-6852]

Lucebert, 1924- Drie lagen diep. Amsterdam
[1969] [10] p.,
NC263.S95 A48
NYPL [3-MCH S961 90-6370]

50 Jahre Bauhaus . Stuttgart , 1968. 369 p. :
NYPL [3-MAL 90-6848]

Amsterdam omstreeks 1800. Amsterdam : Bezige
Bij, 1965. 227 p. : ill. ; 21 x 25 cm. Compiled by
A.M. van de Waal and Han de Vries. "100 tekeningen
van Gerrit Lamberts (1776-1850). 100 foto's van
dezelfde situaties nu, door G.L.W. Oppenheim."
Includes bibliographical references.
*1. Lamberts, Gerrit, 1776-1850. 2. Oppenheim, G. L.
W. 3. Amsterdam (Netherlands) in art. 4. Amsterdam
(Netherlands) - Description - Views. I. Lamberts,
Gerrit, 1776-1850. II. Oppenheim, G. L. W. III. Waal,
A. M. van de. IV. Vries, Han de.*
NYPL [3-MAMY 91-295]

Amsterdam. Rijksmuseum Vincent van Gogh. see
Rijksmuseum Vincent van Gogh.

AMSTERDAM. STEDELIJK MUSEUM.
Sandberg, Willem Jacob Henri Berend, 1897-
Sandberg "désigne" le Stedelijk . Paris , 1973.
[16] p. :
NYPL [3-MDWS (Sandberg) 86-3614]

Amsterdamse school : Nederlands architectur,
1910-1930 : [catalogus van der tentoonstelling
Stedelijk Museum, Amsterdam 13-9t/m9-11
1975 / voorbereiding catalogus Ellinoor
Bergvelt ... [et al.]. Amsterdam : Het Stedelijk
Museum, 1975. 112 p. : ill. ; 28 cm. Cover title.
"Catalogusnummer: 584." Bibliography: p. 109-110.
*1. Architecture - Netherlands - Amsterdam -
Exhibitions. 2. Amsterdamse school (Architecture) -
Exhibitions. 3. Amsterdam (Netherlands) - Buildings,
structures, etc. - Exhibitions. I. Bergvelt, Ellinoor. II.
Amsterdam (Netherlands). Stedelijk Museum. III. Title:
Nederlandse architectuur, 1910-1930.*
NYPL [3-MQW 90-7048]

**AMSTERDAMSE SCHOOL (ARCHITECTURE)
- EXHIBITIONS.**
Amsterdamse school . [Amsterdam , 1975. 112
p. : **NYPL [3-MQW 90-7048]**

Amt für Kulturpflege des Kantons St. Gallen.
Künstlerdokumentation des Kantons St. Gallen
/. St. Gallen , 1984. 1 v. (unpaged) :
NYPL [3-MAO+ 90-11090]

An den süssen Ufern Asiens : Ägypten, Palästina,
Osmanisches Reich : Reiseziele des 19.
Jahrhunderts in frühen Photographien : Agfa
Foto-Historama, Ausstellung im
Römisch-Germanischen Museum, Köln, 7.
Oktober bis 4. Dezember 1988 / [Bild und
Textredaktion, Bodo von Dewitz]. Köln : Agfa
Foto-Historama im
Wallraf-Richartz-Museum/Museum Ludwig,
1988. 171 p. : chiefly ill. (some col.) ; 27 cm.
Includes bibliographical references. "Panorama von
Konstantinopel um 1880" (1 folded leaf) inserted.
*1. Travel photography - Middle East - History - 19th
century - Exhibitions. I. Dewitz, Bodo von. II. Museum
Ludwig. Agfa Foto-Historama. III.
Römisch-Germanisches Museum (Cologne, Germany).*
TR790 .A5 1988   **NYPL [MFW 91-6019]**

Ana Mercedes Hoyos, de la luz al palenque /.
Hoyos, Ana Mercedes, 1942- Bogotá , 1990.
123 p. : ISBN 958-95327-0-5 DDC 759.9861 20
N6679.H6 A4 1990

Anacleto, Regina. O artista conimbricense Miguel
Costa, 1859-1914 / Regina Anacleto. Coimbra :
Faculdade de Letras, 1989. 113 p. : ill. ; 25 cm.
(Colecção Estudos . 9) Includes bibliographical
references (p. [109]-113). ISBN 972-90380-6-6 DDC
738/.092 20
*1. Costa, Miguel, 1859-1914 - Criticism and
interpretation. 2. Tiles - Portugal - Coimbra. 3.
Decoration and ornament, Architectural - Portugal -
Coimbra. I. Costa, Miguel, 1859-1914. II. Title. III.
Title: Miguel Costa, 1859-1914. IV. Series: Colecção
Estudos (Universidade de Coimbra. Faculdade de
Letras) , 9.*
NK4670.7.P63 C673 1989

Anacostia Neighborhood Museum. Hall, Robert
L., 1950- Gathered visions . Washington, D.C. ,
1991. p. ISBN 1-560-98106-7 (pbk.) : DDC

704/.042/09753074753 20
N6538.N5 H26 1991

Analecta Romana Instituti Danici. Supplementum, 0066-1406 .
(13) Mitens, Karina. Teatri greci e teatri ispirati all'architettura greca in Sicilia e nell'Italia meridionale, c. 350-50 a.C. . Roma , 1988. 176 p., [1] fold. leaf of plates :   ISBN 88-7062-660-1
NYPL [3-MQM+ 90-12635]

ANASAZI CULTURE. see PUEBLO INDIANS.

Anāshid mushammah. Ben Dhiab, Ahmed. Chants tatoués =. Rotterdam , 1987. [16], 125 p. :
ISBN 90-6330-139-1
NYPL [3-MCZ + B4495 90-8107]

Anastasía, Luis V. Figari : crónica y dibujos del caso Almeida / Luis Víctor Anastasía, Angel Kalenberg, Julio María Sanguinetti.1. ed. Montevideo : Acali Editorial, 1976. 92 p., [15] leaves of plates : ill. ; 20 cm.
1. Figari, Pedro, 1861-1938. 2. Almeida, Enrique. 3. Butler, Tomás E. 4. Artists - Uruguay - Biography. I. Figari, Pedro, 1861-1938. II. Kalenberg, Angel. III. Sanguinetti, Julio Maria, 1936-. IV. Title.
NYPL [3-MAM 90-5569]

Anastos, Phillip. Illegal : seeking the American dream / photographs and text by Phillip Anastos and Chris French. New York : Rizzoli, 1991. 128 p. : ill., map ; 31 cm.   ISBN 0-8478-1367-3   DDC 305.9/0693 20
1. Aliens, Illegal - Texas - Lower Rio Grande Valley - Pictorial works. 2. Teenage immigrants - Texas - Lower Rio Grande Valley - Pictorial works. 3. Lower Rio Grande Valley (Tex.) - Emigration and immigration - Pictorial works. I. French, Chris. II. Title.
F392.R5 A53 1991
NYPL [MFW+ 91-6710]

ANATOMY, ARTISTIC.
Brown, Clint. Drawing from life /. Fort Worth , c1992. p. cm.   ISBN 0-03-028934-3   DDC 743/.4 20
NC760 .B86 1992

Goldfinger, Eliot. A guide to human anatomy for artists . New York , 1991. p. cm.   ISBN 0-19-505206-4   DDC 702/.8 20
NC760 .G67 1991

Gordon, Louise. The figure in action . London , 1989. 128 p. :   ISBN 0-7134-5946-8   DDC 743/.49 20
NC760 .G72 1989

Jamieson, Doug. Draw from your head . New York , 1991. p. cm.   ISBN 0-8230-1374-X   DDC 743/.49 20
NC760 .J34 1991

Leonardo da Vinci, 1452-1519. Leonardo knows baseball /. San Francisco , c1991. p. cm.   ISBN 0-8118-0013-X   DDC 700/.92 20
NC257.L4 A4 1991

Parramón, José María. [Cómo dibujar la anatomía del cuerpo humano. English.] Human anatomy /. New York , 1991. p. cm.   ISBN 0-8230-2499-7 :   DDC 743/.49 20
NC760 .P3413 1991

ANATOMY FOR ARTISTS. see ANATOMY, ARTISTIC; FIGURE PAINTING; HUMAN FIGURE IN ART; FIGURE DRAWING.

Ancienne Douane, Strasbourg. see Strasbourg. Ancienne douane.

ANCIENT ART. see ART, ANCIENT.

Ancient art from the Barbier-Mueller Museum /. Musée Barbier-Müller. New York , c1991. 183 p. :   ISBN 0-8109-1904-4
NYPL [3-MAE+ 91-6535]

Ancient art in Scandinavia. Kusch, Eugen, 1905- [Alte Kunst in Skandinavien. English.] Nürnberg [1965] 83 p., 176 plates. DDC 709/.48
N7001 .K813

Ancient Chinese bronzes in the Arthur M. Sackler collections .
(v. 2) Rawson, Jessica. Western Zhou ritual bronzes from the Arthur M. Sackler collections /. Washington, D.C. : Cambridge, Mass. : 2 v. (776 p.) :   ISBN 0-674-95070-4
NYPL [3-MGR+ 91-4952]

Ancient Egypt /. Pemberton, Delia. San Francisco , 1992. p. cm.   ISBN 0-87701-847-2 (pb)   DDC 722/.2 20
NA215 .P36 1992

ANCIENT HISTORY. see HISTORY, ANCIENT.

Ancient Iranian ceramics from the Arthur M. Sackler collections /. Kawami, Trudy S., 1944- New York , 1991. p.   ISBN 0-913291-04-8   DDC 738.3/82/0935 20
NK3825 .K39 1991

Ancient mortuary traditions of China : papers on Chinese ceramic funerary sculptures / George Kuwayama, editor. Los Angeles, Calif. : Los Angeles County Museum of Art ; [Honolulu?] : Distributed by the University of Hawaii Press, c1991. p. cm. Includes bibliographical references.
ISBN 0-87587-157-7 (pbk.)   DDC 732/.71/07479494 20
1. Ming ch'i - Congresses. 2. Funeral rites and ceremonies - China - History - Congresses. I. Kuwayama, George. II. Los Angeles County Museum of Art.
NK4165 .A53 1991

Ancient painted pottery from Bulgaria. Lazarov, Mikhail, 1934- Antichna risuvana keramika v Bŭlgariia /. Sofiia , 1990. 142 p. :
NK4649 .L37 1990

Ancient sculpture copies in miniature /. Bartman, Elizabeth. Leiden , New York , 1992. p. cm.
ISBN 90-04-09532-2   DDC 733/.3 20
NB94 .B37 1992

ANCIENTS AND MODERNS, QUARREL OF.
Hall, H. Gaston. Richelieu's Desmarets and the century of Louis XIV /. Oxford , New York , 1990. 399 p. :   ISBN 0-19-815157-8 :   DDC 841/.4 B 20
PQ1794.D6 H35 1990
NYPL [3-MAVZ (Hamburg) 91-3450]

Ancona, George. The American family farm : a photo essay / by George Ancona ; text by Joan Anderson.1st ed. San Diego : Harcourt Brace Jovanovich, c1989. 1 v. (unpaged) : ill. ; 23 x 29 cm. A pictorial essay of the American family farm, focusing on the daily lives of three families in Massachusetts, Georgia, and Iowa.
0-15-203025-5 :   DDC 630/.973 19
1. Farm life - United States - Juvenile literature. 2. Family farms - United States - Juvenile literature. 3. Agriculture - United States - Juvenile literature. 4. Farm life - Pictorial works. I. Anderson, Joan. II. Title.
S519 .A53 1989
NYPL [MFX (Ancona) 90-11254]

Anda-Bührle, Hortense. The passionate eye . [Zurich?] , Zurich , c1990. 244 p. :   ISBN 0-8478-1215-4
NYPL [3-MAX (Bührle) 90-12982]

Anda, Enrique X. de. Evolución de la arquitectura en México : épocas prehispánica, virreinal, moderna y contemporánea / Enrique X. de Anda.1. ed. en español. México, D.F. : Panorama Editorial, 1987 [i.e. 1988] 235 p. : ill. ; 18 cm. (Colección Panorama) Includes bibliographical references (p. [233]-235).   ISBN 968-380-186-2   DDC 720/.972 20
1. Architecture - Mexico. I. Title.
NA750 .A49 1988

Andaloro, Maria. Matthiae, Guglielmo. Pittura romana del Medioevo /. Roma , c1987-c1988. 2 v. :   ISBN 88-7621-234-5 (v. 1)   DDC 751.7/3/09456320902 20
ND2757.R6 M34 1987
NYPL [3-MLP+ 90-12085]

De Andere fotografie : de geschiedenis van de fotomechanische reproduktie in de negentiende eeuw : tentoonstelling in het Zeeuws Museum Middelburg (1989). Vlissingen : ADZ, 1989. 44 p. ; 30 cm.   ISBN 90-72838-03-3
1. Photomechanical processes - Exhibitions. I. Zeeuws Museum (Middelburg, Netherlands).
NYPL [MFW+ 91-2393]

Andere Stadt. Scarpa, Carlo. The other city . Berlin , c1989. 397 p. :   ISBN 3-433-02097-3   DDC 720/.92 20
NA1123.S35 A4 1989

Anderegg, Jean Pierre. Die Bauernhäuser des Kantons Freiburg = La Maison paysanne fribourgeoise / Jean-Pierre Anderegg. Basel : G. Krebs, 1979-1987. 2 v. : ill. (some col.), maps ; 29 cm. (Die Bauernhäuser der Schweiz ; Bd. 7) Includes index. Errata slips inserted in both volumes. Vol. 2. has imprint: Basel : Schweizerischen Gesellschaft für Volkskunde. Includes bibliographical references.
CONTENTS. - Bd. 1. Die Bezirke Saane, See, Sense -- Bd. 2. Die Bezirke Broye, Glane, Greyerz und

Vivisbach.   DDC 728/.67/09494 s 728/.67/094945 20
1. Farmhouses - Switzerland - Fribourg (Canton). 2. Vernacular architecture - Switzerland - Fribourg (Canton). I. Title. II. Title. Title: Maison paysanne fribourgeoise. III. Series.
NA8206.S9 B38 Bd. 7, etc. NA8210
NYPL [3-MRGF 84-1334]

Andergassen, Leo, 1964- Plazer, Lukas, 1663-1723. Der barocke Franziskuszyklus von Frater Lukas Plazer in Innichen /. Innichen , 1990. 259 p. :   ISBN 88-85226-00-0
ND623.P696 A4 1990

Andernacher Beiträge .
(5) Nieuwdorp, Hans M. J. Peter Paul Rubens, Graphiken . Andernach , 1988. 60 p. :   DDC 769.92 20
NE674.R9 A4 1988
NYPL [MDG (Rubens) 90-13679]

Anders Zorn, 1860-1920 . Zorn, Anders, 1860-1920. [München] , 1989. 237 p. :   ISBN 3-923701-36-5
NYPL [3-MCZ Z89 90-11754]

Anders Zorn, 1860-1920 . Zorn, Anders, 1860-1920. [Munich] [1990?] 237 p. :   ISBN 3-923701-36-5   DDC 760/.092 20
N7093.Z6 A4 1990

Andersen, Jørgen, 1922- De år i Rom : Abildgaard, Sergel, Füssli / Jørgen Andersen.1. udg. København : Christian Ejlers' forlag, 1989. 301 p. : ill. ; 28 cm. Summary in English. Includes bibliographical references (p. 292-297) and indexes.
ISBN 87-7241-576-2 :
1. Abildgaard, Nocolai, 1743-1809 - Journeys - Italy - Rome. 2. Abildgaard, Nicolai, 1743-1809 - Friends and associates. 3. Sergel, Johan Tobias, 1740-1814 - Friends and associates. 4. Fuseli, Henry, 1741-1825 - Friends and associates. 5. Painters - Italy - Rome - Biography. 6. Rome (Italy) - Intellectual life. I. Abildgaard, Nicolai, 1743-1809. II. Sergel, Johan Tobias, 1740-1814. III. Fuseli, Henry, 1741-1825. IV. Title.
ND723.A2 A86 1989

Andersen, Kirsti. Brook Taylor's role in the history of linear perspective / Kirsti Andersen. New York : Springer-Verlag, c1991. p. cm. (Sources in the history of mathematics and physical sciences. 10) Includes Brook Taylor's Linear perspective, or, a New method of representing justly all manner of objects and his New principles of linear perspective. Includes bibliographical references and index.   ISBN 0-387-97486-5   DDC 701/.82 20
1. Perspective - Early works to 1800. I. Taylor, Brook, 1685-1731. Linear perspective. 1991. II. Taylor, Brook, 1685-1731. New principles of linear perspective. 1991. III. Title.
NC749 .A48 1991

ANDERSON, ALEXANDER, 1775-1870.
Pomeroy, Jane R. Alexander Anderson's life and engravings . Worcester [Mass.] , 1990. p, 137-230 :   ISBN 0-944026-25-7
NYPL [MDG (Anderson) 91-4737]

ANDERSON, ALEXANDER, 1775-1870 - BIBLIOGRAPHY.
Pomeroy, Jane R. Alexander Anderson's life and engravings . Worcester [Mass.] , 1990. p, 137-230 :   ISBN 0-944026-25-7
NYPL [MDG (Anderson) 91-4737]

Anderson, Frank J., 1912- A treasury of flowers : rare illustrations from the collection of the New York Botanical Garden / by Frank J. Anderson.1st ed. Boston : Little, Brown, c1990. 175 p. : col. ill. ; 37 cm. "A Bulfinch Press book." Includes index.   ISBN 0-8212-1758-5 :   DDC 582.13/022/2 20
1. New York Botanical Garden - Art collections. 2. Flower painting and illustrations. I. New York Botanical Garden. II. Title. III. Title: Flowers.
QK98.3 .A53 1990 NYPL [MDZ+ 91-6182]

Anderson, Gail, 1962- Heller, Steven. Graphic wit . New York , 1991. p. cm.   ISBN 0-8230-2161-0 :   DDC 741.6 20
NC998.5.A1 H44 1991

Anderson Gallery.
Alfredo Jaar . Richmond, VA , c1991. p. cm.   ISBN 0-917046-32-3   DDC 709/.2 20
N6537.J26 A4 1991

Gerlovina, Rimma. Still performances /. Cambridge, Mass. , 1989. 39 p. :   ISBN 0-938437-27-5   DDC 779/.092/2 20
NX556.Z9 G472 1989
NYPL [MFW 90-4189]

Anderson, Jaynie. La Pittura in Italia . 2 v. (913 p.) , 29 cm. [Milano] :
NYPL [3-MCE 90-11794]

Anderson, Jeffrey C. The New York Cruciform Lectionary / Jeffrey C. Anderson. University Park : Published for College Art Association by the Pennsylvania State University Press, 1991. p. cm. (Monographs on the fine arts . v. 48) Includes bibliographical references and index. ISBN 0-271-00743-5 DDC 745.6/7487 20
1. New York Cruciform Lectionary. 2. Evangeliaries - Illustrations. 3. Illumination of books and manuscripts, Byzantine. 4. Orthodox Eastern Church - Liturgy - Texts - Illustrations. 5. Pierpoint Morgan Library. I. College Art Association of America. II. Series: Monographs on the fine arts , 48. III. Title.
ND3359.N48 A44 1991

Anderson, Joan. Ancona, George. The American family farm . San Diego , c1989. 1 v. (unpaged) : ISBN 0-15-203025-5 : DDC 630/.973 19
S519 .A53 1989
NYPL [MFX (Ancona) 90-11254]

Anderson, Judith. Bradley, Gilbert, 1917- Derby porcelain 1750-1798 / . London , 1990. 180 p. : ISBN 0-946708-25-8 : DDC 738.207 20
NK4399.D4   *NYPL [3-MPGO 91-5746]*

Anderson, Laurie, 1947- Empty places : a performance / Laurie Anderson.1st HarperPerennial ed. New York, NY : HarperPerennial, 1991. p. cm. ISBN 0-06-096586-X (paper) DDC 700/.92 20
1. Anderson, Laurie, 1947-. 2. Performance art - United States. I. Title.
NX512.A54 A4 1991

ANDERSON, LAURIE, 1947-
Anderson, Laurie, 1947- Empty places . New York, NY , 1991. p. ISBN 0-06-096586-X (paper) : DDC 700/.92 20
NX512.A54 A4 1991

Anderson, Lisa, 1968- Minimalism and post-minimalism . Hanover, N.H. , 1990. 104 p. : ISBN 0-944722-05-9 DDC 741.973/074/7423 20
NC108 .M528 1990
NYPL [3-MBH 91-3948]

Anderson, Nancy K.
Albert Bierstadt : art & enterprise / Nancy K. Anderson, Linda S. Ferber ; with a contribution by Helena E. Wright.1st ed. New York : Hudson Hills Press in association with the Brooklyn Museum, c1990. 327 p. : ill. (some col.) ; 33 cm. "Published on the occasion of the exhibition, Albert Bierstadt: art & enterprise, organized by the Brooklyn Museum in association with the National Gallery of Art, Washington, D.C. Exhibition itinerary: the Brooklyn Museum: February 8-May 6, 1991, the Fine Arts Museums of San Francisco: June 8-September 1, 1991, National Gallery of Art, Washington, D.C.: November 3, 1991-February 17, 1992"--T.p. verso. Includes bibliographical references (p. 295-303) and index. ISBN 1-555-95059-0 : DDC 759.13 20
1. Bierstadt, Albert, 1830-1902 - Exhibitions. 2. West (U. S.) in art - Exhibitions. I. Ferber, Linda S. II. Wright, Helena, 1946-. III. Brooklyn Museum. IV. Fine Arts Museums of San Francisco. V. National Gallery of Art (U. S.). VI. Title.
ND237.B585 A4 1991
NYPL [3-MCX+ B585 91-5808]

The West as America . Washington , c1991. xiv, 389 p. : ISBN 1-560-98023-0 (h-cover : alk. paper) DDC 978/.02/074753 20
F596 .W493 1991
NYPL [3-MAMY 91-5810]

Anderson, Ross C. Thirty paintings in the Malden collection / text by Ross C. Anderson ; photography by Barney Burstein. [Malden, Mass.] : Malden Public Library, [1975?] [54] p. : ill. (some col.) ; 18 x 24 cm.
1. Malden Public Library (Mass.). 2. Painting - Massachusetts - Malden. I. Malden Public Library (Mass.). II. Title.   *NYPL [3-MAVZ (Malden, Mass.) 90-5649]*

Anderson, Sascha. Penck A. R., 1939- A.R. Penck, Keramik. Berlin , c1989. 1 v. (unpaged) :
NK4210.P446 A4 1989

Anderson, Susan M. (Susan Mary) Pursuit of the marvelous : Stanley William Hayter, Charles Howard, Gordon Onslow Ford / by Susan M.

Anderson.1st ed. Laguna Beach, Calif. : Laguna Art Museum, c1990. 64 p. : ill. (some col.) ; 31 cm. Catalog of an exhibition held at the Laguna Art Museum, OCt. 5, 1990-Jan. 13, 1991. Includes bibliographical references (p. 59-62). ISBN 0-940872-16-1 DDC 760/.09794/607479496 20
1. Hayter, Stanley William, 1901- - Exhibitions. 2. Howard, Charles, 1899-1978 - Exhibitions. 3. Onslow-Ford, Gordon - Exhibitions. 4. Surrealism - California - Exhibitions. 5. Art, Modern - 20th century - California - Exhibitions. I. Laguna Art Museum (Laguna Beach, Calif.). II. Title.
N6530.C2 A58 1990
NYPL [3-MCW+ 91-6334]

Anderson, Will, 1940- Mid-Atlantic roadside delights : roadside architecture of yesterday and today in New York, New Jersey, and Pennsylvania / by Will Anderson ; studio photography by A. & J. DuBois Commercial Photography, Lewiston, Maine ; field photography by the author. Portland, Me. : Anderson & Sons' Pub. Co., c1991. viii, 164 p. : ill. (some col.) ; 28 cm. Includes index. ISBN 0-9601056-4-6 (pbk).
1. Commercial buildings - New York (State). 2. Commercial buildings - New Jersey. 3. Commercial buildings - Pennsylvania. I. Title.
NYPL [3-MQWO 91-7968]

Andersson, Henrik O., 1939-
[Stockholms byggnader. English]
Stockholm, architecture and townscape / Henrik O. Andersson and Fredric Bedoire ; [translation by Roger Tanner and Henrik O. Andersson]. Stockholm ; Prisma, c1988. 412 p. : ill., maps ; 21 cm. Translation of: Stockholms byggnader. Includes indexes. Bibliography: p. 407-408. ISBN 91-518-1879-5
1. Architecture - Sweden - Stockholm. 2. Stockholm (Sweden) - Buildings, structures, etc. 3. Stockholm (Sweden) - Description. I. Bedoire, Fredric, 1945-. II. Title.   *NYPL [3-MQWE 89-11933]*

Andō, Tadao, 1941-
Tadao Andō. London : Academy Editions ; New York : St. Martin's Press, 1990. 128 p. : ill. (chiefly col.) ; 23 x 30 cm. (Architectural monographs. 14) Includes bibliographical references. ISBN 1-85490-010-2 (hardback : London)
1. Andō, Tadao, 1941-. 2. Architecture, Modern - 20th century - Japan. I. Series: Architectural monographs (London, England) , 14. II. Title.
NYPL [3-MQZ+ (Andō) 90-11589]

Tadao Andō : dormant lines / Darell Wayne Fields, editor. New York, N.Y. : Rizzoli, c1991. 32 p. : ill. (some col.) ; 26 cm. Published in conjunction with an exhibition of work by Ando, held at the Harvard Graduate School of Design during the spring of 1990. Architectural drawings on 16 folded leaves. ISBN 0-8478-1339-8 DDC 720/.22/22 20
1. Andō, Tadao, 1941- - Themes, motives - Exhibitions. I. Fields, Darell Wayne. II. Harvard University. Graduate School of Design. III. Title. IV. Title: Dormant lines.
NA2707.A53 A4 1991

ANDŌ, TADAO, 1941-
Andō, Tadao, 1941- Tadao Andō. London , New York , 1990. 128 p. : ISBN 1-85490-010-2 (hardback : London)
NYPL [3-MQZ+ (Andō) 90-11589]
ANDŌ, TADAO, 1941- - THEMES, MOTIVES - EXHIBITIONS.
Andō, Tadao, 1941- Tadao Ando . New York, N.Y. , c1991. 32 p. : ISBN 0-8478-1339-8 DDC 720/.22/22 20
NA2707.A53 A4 1991

ANDORRA - MAPS.
(1980) Institut d'Estudis Andorrans. Atlas d'Andorra. [Andorra] , 1980- 1 atlas : DDC 912/.4679 19
G1970 .I5 1980   *NYPL [Map Div. 90-57]*

Andrade Aguirre, David. 100 artistas del Ecuador / . Quito , 1990. 285 p. : DDC 709/.2/2866 B 20
N6985 .A15 1990

Andrade, José Manuel Pita. see Pita Andrade, José Manuel.

Andrade Ramírez, Jaime. Guerrero Romero, Javier. El Palacio Escárzaga, Durango /. Durango, Dgo., México , 1988. xii, 82 p. : ISBN 968-609-400-8
NA757.D87 G84 1986

Andral, Jean-Louis. Léger, Fernand, 1881-1955. Fernand Léger . Jérusalem , c1989. 212 p. :

ISBN 965-278-059-6 DDC 759.4 20
NC248.L43 A4 1989

André, Albert, 1869-1954.
Galerie Marcel Guiot. Albert André, 1869-1954. Paris [1960] 17 p.
ND553.A5 G33 1960
NYPL [3-MCO A55 90-7046]

ANDRÉ, ALBERT, 1869-1954 - EXHIBITIONS.
Galerie Marcel Guiot. Albert André, 1869-1954. Paris [1960] 17 p.
ND553.A5 G33 1960
NYPL [3-MCO A55 90-7046]

André Bérubé, street photographer /. Bérubé, André, 1936- Nanaimo, B.C. , c1989. [4] p., 51 leaves of plates : ISBN 0-9694007-0-5 : DDC 779/.092/4 19
NYPL [MFX (Bérubé) 91-8032]

André Brasilier. Le Pichon, Yann. André Brasilier, ses transfigurations / . Paris , c1989. 209 p. : ISBN 2-87736-064-4 DDC 759.4 20
N6853.B712 L4 1989
NYPL [3-MCO+ B824 90-7470]

André Brasilier, ses transfigurations /. Le Pichon, Yann. Paris , c1989. 209 p. : ISBN 2-87736-064-4 DDC 759.4 20
N6853.B712 L4 1989
NYPL [3-MCO+ B824 90-7470]

André Charigny /. Bichet, Pierre. Besançon , c1989. 141 p. : ISBN 2-901040-78-1
NYPL [3-MCO+ C473 89-26937]

André Emmerich Gallery.
Alechinsky, Pierre, 1927- Pierre Alechinsky, new work . New York , c1990. [10] p., 15 leaves of plates :
NYPL [3-MCH+ A36 91-3431]

Held, Al, 1928- Al Held, new paintings . New York, N.Y. (41 E. 57th St., New York, N.Y. 10022) , c1989. [7] p., 11 leaves of plates (1 folded) :   *NYPL [3-MCX H465 91-4593]*

Hockney, David. David Hockney . New York , c1990. 1 v. (unpaged)
NYPL [3-MCV H678 91-4234]

Hofmann, Hans, 1880-1966. Hans Hofmann, paintings on paper from the 1940s . New York , c1990. [21] p., 8 leaves of plates :
NYPL [3-MCK+ H71 91-6604]

Kenneth Noland, new paintings : [exhibition] December 10-January 11, 1978 / André Emmerich Gallery. New York : The Gallery, 1978. [21] p. : col. ill., port. ; 21 cm. Bibliography: p. [19-21]
1. Noland, Kenneth, 1924- - Exhibitions. I. Noland, Kenneth, 1924-. II. Title.
NYPL [3-MCX N787 90-5876]

Olitski, Jules, 1922- Jules Olitski, spray paintings of the 1960s : [exhibition] October 5-28, 1989, André Emmerich Gallery. New York, NY , c1989. [32] p. :
NYPL [3-MCX+ O47 91-5567]

Pepper, Beverly. Beverly Pepper . New York, N.Y. , c1990. 1 v. (unpaged) :
NYPL [3-MGO+ (Pepper) 91-6687]

Porter, Katherine, 1941- Katherine Porter, new paintings . New York , c1990. 1 v. (unpaged) :
NYPL [3-MCX P8397 91-6262]

André François /. François, André. Paris , c1986. 240 p. : ISBN 2-7335-0116-X
NYPL [3-MDWS (François) 91-5326]

André Kertész, photographer. Kertész, André. A. Kertész, photographer /. New York , c1964. 63 p. : DDC 779
TR140.K4 S9
NYPL [MFX (Kertész) 91-993]

André Lhote, 1885-1962. Lhote, André, 1885-1962. New York, N.Y. [1976?] 32 p. :
NYPL [3-MCO L69 90-5654]

André Masson : illustrierte Bücher, Grafikmappen, Zeichnungen. Offenbach am Main : Klingspor-Museum, 1989. 46 p. : ill. (some col.) ; 25 cm. "Ausstellung des Klingspor-Museums 15. September bis 29. Oktober 1989 in Zusammenarbeit mit dem Institut Français de Francfort mit Unterstützung des Französischen Aussenministeriums, Staatssekretariat für internationale Kulturbeziehungen." Includes bibliographical references (p. 34-36).
1. Masson, André, 1896- - Exhibitions. I.

Klingspor-Museum Offenbach.
    NYPL [3-MCO M42 91-4657]

André Masson. Masson, André 1896- [Lyon]
1967. 1 v. (unpaged)   DDC 759.4
ND553.M36 L8
    NYPL [3-MCO M42 91-1291]

Andrea del Castagno and his patrons /. Spencer,
John R. (John Richard) Durham , 1991. p. cm.
  ISBN 0-8223-1150-X   DDC 759.5 20
ND623.C47 S64 1991

Andrea del Sarto . Natali, Antonio. Firenze ,
c1989. 159 p. :   ISBN 88-7737-068-8
    NYPL [3-MCF S24 90-12007]

Andrea Gastaldi, 1826-1889 . Maggio Serra,
Rosanna. Torino , c1988. 232 p. :   ISBN
88-422-0169-3 :   DDC 759.5 20
N6923.G365 A4 1988
    NYPL [3-MCF+ G253 90-10922]

Andrea Palladio . Puppi, Lionello. [Andrea
Palladio. English.] New York , 1989, c1986.
311 p. :   ISBN 0-8478-1150-6   DDC 720/.92 20
NA1123.P2 A4 1989
    NYPL [MQZ (Palladio) 91-4643]

Andrea Palladio e la sua committenza . Zaupa,
Giovanni. Roma , c1990. 255 p. :   ISBN
88-7448-275-2 :   DDC 720/.92 20
NA1123.P2 Z34 1990

Andrea Palladio, nuovi contributi . Seminario
internazionale di storia dell'architettura (7th :
1988 Sept. 1-7 : Vicenza, Italy) Milano , c1990.
247 p. :   ISBN 88-435-3086-0
    NYPL [3-MQZ+ (Palladio) 91-4941]

Andrea rescued . Kondoleon, Harry. Montclair,
N.J. , 1987. [6], 20, [3] p. :
    NYPL [MEM (Seiffer) 88-1722]

Andreae, Stephan. Le Musée sentimental de Bâle
/ erausgegeben von Barbara Huber-Greub und
Stephen Andreae ; [Idee und künstlerische
Leitung: Daniel Spoerri]. Basel , c1989. 332 p. :
ISBN 3-85700-006-X
    NYPL [3-MAVZ (Basel) 90-13397]

Andreas, Christoph. Festschrift für Hartmut
Biermann /. Weinheim , c1990. 400 p. :   ISBN
3-527-17712-4   *NYPL [3-MAS 91-5197]*

Andreas His . His, Andreas, 1928- [Basel] ,
c1984. [65] p. :
    NYPL [3-MCZ H673 90-2126]

Andreassi, Giuseppe. Ceramica greca della
Collezione Chini nel Museo civico di Bassano
del Grappa /. Roma , c1990. 111 p. :   ISBN
88-7689-052-1   *NYPL [3-MPEK 90-12667]*

Andree, Hans, 1937- Nordlicht . Hamburg , 1989.
415 p. :   ISBN 3-88506-174-0   DDC
709/.43/51507443515 20
N332.G33 H355 1989

Andres de Santa Maria . Serrano, Eduardo.
[Bogotá] [1988] 250 p. :   ISBN 958-9058-00-0
    NYPL [3-MCZ+ S221 90-10769]

Andrés Nagel . Nagel, Andrés de, 1947- [Dallas,
Tex. , 1990] 35 p., [12] p. of plates :
MLCM 90/00934 (N)
    NYPL [3-MGO (Nagel) 91-6994]

Andresen, Hilde. Kulturens dekningsbidrag .
[Oslo] , c1991. 179 p. :   ISBN 82-02-12832-3
NX456 .K78 1991

Andreu, Paul.
La Grande Arche Tête Défense,
Paris-la-Défense : une architecture de Johan
Otto von Spreckelsen, Paul Andreu / carnet de
route par Paul Andreu & Hubert Tonka. Paris :
Editions du Demi-Cercle, c1989. 80 p. : chiefly
ill. ; 35 cm. (Etat des lieux)   ISBN 2-907757-08-3
  1. Spreckelsen, Johan-Otto von. 2. Andreu, Paul. I.
  Title.
IN PROCESS (ONLINE)   NYPL [3-MQZ+
      (Spreckelsen) 90-13216]

Paul Andreu / sous la direction de Pascale Blin.
Paris : Tempera, 1990. 1 v. (unpaged) : chiefly
ill. ; 22 cm. (Carnets de croquis ; 3)   ISBN
2-907687-06-9 :   DDC 720/.22/22 20
  1. Andreu, Paul - Themes, motives. 2. Architectural
  drawing - 20th century - France. I. Blin, Pascale. II.
  Title. III. Series.
NA2707.A55 A4 1990

ANDREU, PAUL.
Andreu, Paul. La Grande Arche Tête Défense,
Paris-la-Défense . Paris , c1989. 80 p. :   ISBN

2-907757-08-3
IN PROCESS (ONLINE)   NYPL [3-MQZ+
      (Spreckelsen) 90-13216]

ANDREU, PAUL - CRITICISM AND
INTERPRETATION.
Salat, Serge. Paul Andreu . Paris , c1990. 175
p. :   ISBN 2-86653-081-0
NA1053.A49 S25 1990

ANDREU, PAUL - THEMES, MOTIVES.
Andreu, Paul. Paul Andreu /. Paris , 1990. 1 v.
(unpaged) :   ISBN 2-907687-06-9 :   DDC
720/.22/22 20
NA2707.A55 A4 1990

Andrew Forster (1942-) . Forster, Andrew, 1942-
Halifax, N.S. , 1983. 46 p. :
    NYPL [3-MCZ F717 88-2150]

Andrews, John Harwood, 1927-
Alexander Taylor and his map of County
Kildare. 1983. Taylor, Alexander, d. 1828.
A map of the county of Kildare, 1783 /
Alex:r Taylor. Dublin , 1983. 1 atlas (1
portfolio) :   ISBN 0-901714-26-7 :   DDC
912/.4185 19
G1833.K5 T3 1983
    NYPL [Map Div. 87-747]

Andrus, Lisa Fellows. American light .
[Laurenceville, NJ] , Washington, [D.C.] ,
c1989. 330 p. :   ISBN 0-691-04074-5 (alk. paper) :
DDC 758/.1/09730740153 19
N8214.5.U6 A47 1989
    NYPL [3-MAMT 90-12012]

Andy Goldsworthy. Goldsworthy, Andy. London ,
1990. [120] p. :   ISBN 0-670-83213-8 :   DDC
709.2 20
    NYPL [3-MGO+
      (Goldsworthy) 90-11987]

Andy Warhol . Gidal, Peter. New York, N.Y.
[1991], c1971. xiii, 158 p. :   ISBN
0-306-80456-5 :   DDC 700/.92 20
NX512.W37 G5 1991

Andy Warhol . Warhol, Andy, 1928- New York ,
c1991. 1 v. (unpaged) :   ISBN 0-922678-09-X
DDC 769.92 20
NE2237.5.W37 A4 1991

Andy Warhol n'est pas un grand artiste /. Obalk,
Hector. [Paris] , c1990. 145 p. :   ISBN
2-7007-2835-1 :   DDC 700/.92 20
N6537.W28 A4 1990

Andy Warhol, photobooth pictures. Warhol,
Andy, 1928-1987. [New York , 1989] [17] p.,
196 p. of plates :
    NYPL [MFX (Warhol) 90-11260]

Andy Warhol 1928-1987 . Honnef, Klaus. Köln ,
c1989. 95 p. :   ISBN 3-8228-0255-7
    NYPL [3-MCX+ W27 91-4180]

Anecdotes of modern art . Hall, Donald, 1928-
New York , 1990. xix, 377 p. ;   ISBN
0-19-503813-4 (alk. paper) :   DDC 709.04 20
N6447 .H34 1990   *NYPL [3-MAL 90-11303]*

ANEŽSKÝ KLÁŠTER (MUSEUM)
Soukupová, Helena. Anežský klášter v Praze /.
Praha , 1989. 404 p. :   ISBN 80-207-0046-3 :
NA5533.P69 S68 1989

Anežský klášter v Praze /. Soukupová, Helena.
Praha , 1989. 404 p. :   ISBN 80-207-0046-3 :
NA5533.P69 S68 1989

Anfam, David. Abstract expressionism / David
Anfam. London : Thames and Hudson, c1990.
216 p. : ill. ; 21 cm. (World of art)   ISBN
0-500-20243-5
  1. Abstract expressionism - United States. I. Title.
    NYPL [3-MAMT 91-4276]

Ange Leccia /. Leccia, Ange, 1952- [Grenoble ,
1986?] 57 p. (1 folded) :
    NYPL [3-MGO (Leccia) 90-4535]

Ange ou diablesse . Matthews Grieco, Sara F.
[Paris] , c1991. 495 p. :   ISBN 2-08-211187-3
DDC 769/.424/0940931 20
NE962.W65 M38 1991

Angel chairs . Castle, Wendell, 1932- New York ,
1991. 111 p. :   ISBN 0-9628849-0-1   DDC 749.213
20
NK2439.C3 A4 1991

Angel Jové . Jové, Angel. [Barcelona] [1991?]
229 p. :
N7113.J68 A4 1991

Angeli, Eduard, 1942-
Eduard Angeli. Wien : Galerie Würthle, [1983?]

[21] leaves : col. ill., port. ; 28 x 31 cm. Catalog
of an exhibition held at Galerie Würthle and three
other locations.   DDC 759.36 19
  1. Angeli, Eduard, 1942- - Exhibitions. I. Galerie
  Würthle. II. Title.
ND511.5.A53 A4 1982
    NYPL [3-MCK+ A597 85-3252]

ANGELI, EDUARD, 1942- - EXHIBITIONS.
Angeli, Eduard, 1942- Eduard Angeli. Wien
[1983?] [21] leaves :   DDC 759.36 19
ND511.5.A53 A4 1982
    NYPL [3-MCK+ A597 85-3252]

Angelico, fra, ca. 1400-1455.
Didi-Huberman, Georges. Fra Angelico . Paris ,
c1990. 263 p. :   ISBN 2-08-012614-8   DDC 759.5
20
ND623.A5393 D53 1990
    NYPL [3-MCF A58 91-6120]

ANGELICO, FRA, CA. 1400-1455 -
CRITICISM AND INTERPRETATION.
Didi-Huberman, Georges. Fra Angelico . Paris ,
c1990. 263 p. :   ISBN 2-08-012614-8   DDC 759.5
20
ND623.A5393 D53 1990
    NYPL [3-MCF A58 91-6120]

Angelil, Marc M. On architecture, the city, and
technology /. Washington, DC , Stoneham,
MA , c1990. 152 p. :   ISBN 0-7506-9149-2   DDC
720/.1/05 20
NA2543.T43 O5 1990

Angelina Beloff : ilustradora y grabadora /
Consejo Nacional para la Cultura y las Artes,
Instituto Nacional de Bellas Artes, Instituto
Francés de América Latina. México, D.F. :
Museo Estudio Diego Rivera ; Guanajuato,
Gto. : Museo Casa Diego Rivera ; 95 p. : ill. (1
col.) ; 23 cm. Includes bibliographical references.
  ISBN 968-292-336-0   DDC 760/.092 20
  1. Beloff, Angelina, 1879-1969 - Exhibitions. I. Consejo
  Nacional para la Cultura y las Artes (Mexico). II.
  Instituto Nacional de Bellas Artes (Mexico). III. Institut
  français d'Amérique latine (Mexico). IV. Museo Estudio
  Diego Rivera.
N6999.B425 A4 1989

Angelina Beloff : ilustradora y grabadora /
Consejo Nacional para la Cultura y las Artes,
Instituto Nacional de Bellas Artes, Instituto
Francés de América Latina. México, D.F.,
México : Museo Estudio Diego Rivera, 1989.
95 p. : ill. (1 col.) ; 23 cm. Includes bibliographical
references. Bookplate by artist mounted on p. [2] of
cover.
  1. Beloff, Angelina, 1879-1969 - Exhibitions. I. Consejo
  Nacional para la Cultura y las Artes (Mexico).
    NYPL [MDG (Beloff) 90-11726]

Angelov, Valentin. Sŭvremenni
dekorativno-prilozhni izkustva v Bŭlgariia /.
Sofiia , 1989. 262 p. :
NK1019 .S95 1989

ANGELS IN ART.
Stuhlfauth, Georg, b. 1870. Die Engel in der
altchristlichen Kunst [microform] ... /. Freiburg
i. B. , 1896. 40 p. ;   *NYPL [*ZM-219]*

Angers (France). Musée Pincé. Miniatures
indiennes de la collection David-d'Angers .
Angers [France] [1986] 58 p. :   ISBN
2-901297-08-5
MLCS 90/02237 (N)
    NYPL [3-MAF 90-12754]

Angewandte Emblematik im Fliessensaal von
Wrisbergholzen bei Hildesheim /. Köhler,
Johannes. Hildesheim , 1988. 165 p. :   ISBN
3-7848-3757-3   *NYPL [3-MRXZ 90-13016]*

An angler's album . Traub, Charles, 1945- New
York , 1990. 215 p. :   ISBN 0-8478-1256-1   DDC
779/.979912 20
PN6071.F47 T7 1990
    NYPL [MFW 91-4963]

ANGLING. see FISHING.

Anglo-Saxon crucifixion iconography and the art
of the monastic revival /. Raw, Barbara
Catherine. Cambridge [England] , New York ,
1990. xii, 296 p., 16 p. of plates ;   ISBN
0-521-36370-5   DDC 704.9/4853/0942 20
N6763 .R38 1990
    NYPL [3-MAMZ 90-11590]

Angrill, Muntsa Calbó. Sicilia, Manel Plana.
[Cómo pintar el paisaje urbano a la acuarela.
English.] How to paint buildings /. New York ,
1991. p. cm.   ISBN 0-8230-2474-1 :   DDC

751.42/244 20
ND2310 .S513 1991

Anguiano, Raúl, 1915-
Raúl Anguiano : una vida entregada a la plástica y catálogo de la exposición de pinturas, dibujos, estampas, tapices, esculturas y cerámicas en el Instituto Cultural Cabañas, Guadalajara, Jalisco, México, del 15 de octubre al 30 de noviembre de 1985 / textos de homenaje, Emmanuel Palacios, Raúl Anguiano, Xavier Moyssén. Guadalajara : Instituto Cultural Cabañas, [1985] iii, 124 p. : ill. (some col.) ; 28 cm. (Colección Homenajes) On cover: Instituto Nacional de Bellas Artes.　DDC 709/.2 20
1. Anguiano, Raúl, 1915- Exhibitions. I. Palacios, Emmanuel. II. Moyssén Echeverría, Xavier. III. Instituto Cultural Cabañas (Guadalajara, Mexico). IV. Series: Colección Homenajes (Guadalajara, Mexico). V. Title.
N6559.A54 A4 1985

ANGUIANO, RAÚL, 1915- - EXHIBITIONS.
Anguiano, Raúl, 1915- Raúl Anguiano . Guadalajara [1985] iii, 124 p. :　DDC 709/.2 20
N6559.A54 A4 1985

Angulo, Diego [i. e. Diego Angulo Iniguez] see Angulo Iñiguez, Diego.

Angulo Iñiguez, Diego. García Sáiz, Maria Concepción. Las castas mexicanas . [S.l.] , 1989 (Milano) 253 p. :　*NYPL [3-MCY+ 91-4969]*

Anikst, Mikhail.
Chernevich, Elena, 1939- Russian graphic design /. New York, NY , 1990. 160 p. :　ISBN 1-558-59016-1 DDC 741.6/0947 20
NC998.6.R9 C47 1990
　　　　NYPL [3-MDW+ 90-11977]
Soviet commercial design of the twenties /. London , c1987. 144 p. :　ISBN 0-500-23504-X
　　　　NYPL [3-MDW+ 91-3268]

The Animal in photography, 1843-1985 / edited by Alexandra Noble. London : Photographers' Gallery, 1986. 80 p. : ill. ; 30 cm. "This catalogue is published on the occasion of The Animal in Photography 1843-1985 at The Photographers' Gallery, London from 28 June-6 September 1986"--T.p. verso.
ISBN 0-907879-09-8
I. Noble, Alexandra. II. Photographers' Gallery.
　　　　NYPL [MFW+ 90-13475]

ANIMAL KINGDOM. see ZOOLOGY.

ANIMAL PAINTERS - BELGIUM.
Eekhoud, Georges, 1854-1927. Les peintres animaliers belges. Bruxelles, 1911. 125 p.
　　　　NYPL [3-MCG 90-6348]

ANIMAL PAINTERS - CANADA.
From the wild. French. D'après nature . Saint-Laurent, Québec , c1986. 192 p. :　ISBN 2-89249-128-2 :　DDC 704.9/432/0971 19
　　　　NYPL [3-MAMZ+ 91-4177]

ANIMAL PAINTERS - UNITED STATES.
From the wild. French. D'après nature . Saint-Laurent, Québec , c1986. 192 p. :　ISBN 2-89249-128-2 :　DDC 704.9/432/0971 19
　　　　NYPL [3-MAMZ+ 91-4177]

ANIMAL SCULPTURE - FRANCE - EXHIBITIONS.
Bernard Black Gallery (New York, N.Y.) Les animaliers . New York, N.Y. [1963] [16] p. :
　　　　NYPL [3-MGI 90-5741]

ANIMALS - DICTIONARIES.
Shaw, Marvin S. A viewer's guide to art . Santa Fe, N.M. , 1991. p. cm.　ISBN 0-945465-66-1　DDC 704.9/48 20
N7760 .S4 1991

Animals in American folk art /. Lavitt, Wendy. New York , 1990. x, 244 p. :　ISBN 0-394-57156-8 :　DDC 745/.0973 20
NK805 .L38 1990
　　　　NYPL [3-MAMT 90-13276]

ANIMALS IN ART.
Czernohaus, Karola. Delphindarstellungen von der minoischen bis zur geometrischen Zeit /. Göteborg , 1988. 235, 111 p., 121 p. of plates :　ISBN 91-86098-76-4
　　　　NYPL [3-MAH 90-10819]
Eekhoud, Georges, 1854-1927. Les peintres animaliers belges. Bruxelles, 1911. 125 p.
　　　　NYPL [3-MCG 90-6348]
Eisler, Colin. Dürer's animals /. Washington , 1991. p. cm.　ISBN 0-87474-408-3 DDC 760/.092

20
N6888.D8 E57 1991

Gromme, Owen J. The world of Owen Gromme /. Minocqua, WI , 1991. p. cm.　ISBN 1-559-71130-2 :　DDC 759.13 B 20
ND237.G665 A2 1991

Landseer, Edwin Henry, Sir, 1802-1873. Landseer's animal illustrations /. Alton, Hampshire, England , 1990. 168 p. :　ISBN 1-85259-189-7
　　　　NYPL [3-MCV L26 91-4225]

Lavitt, Wendy. Animals in American folk art /. New York , 1990. x, 244 p. :　ISBN 0-394-57156-8 :　DDC 745/.0973 20
NK805 .L38 1990
　　　　NYPL [3-MAMT 90-13276]

Le Monde animal au temps de la Renaissance /. Paris , 1990. 259 p. :　ISBN 2-86433-036-9 :　DDC 700 20
NX650.A55 M66 1990

Lloyd, Joan Barclay. African animals in Renaissance literature and art. Oxford, 1971. xi, 145 p.　ISBN 0-19-817180-3
NX450.5 .L5　　　*NYPL [Sc 704.943-L]*

Parramón, José María. [Dibujando pintando apuntes. English.] Sketching people and places in all mediums /. New York , 1991. p. cm.　ISBN 0-8230-4852-7 :　DDC 741.2 20
NC730 .P28313 1991

Pinault, Madeleine. Le peintre et l'histoire naturelle /. Paris , 1990. 286 p. :
IN PROCESS (ONLINE)
　　　　NYPL [3-MAMZ+ 91-6805]

Shaw, Marvin S. A viewer's guide to art . Santa Fe, N.M. , 1991. p. cm.　ISBN 0-945465-66-1　DDC 704.9/48 20
N7760 .S4 1991

ANIMALS IN ART - CATALOGS.
Klintowitz, Jacob, 1941- Aldemir Martins . [São Paulo, Brazil?] [1989] 119 p. :　ISBN 85-7087-016-7　DDC 760/.092 20
N6659.M36 A4 1989

ANIMALS IN ART - JUVENILE LITERATURE.
Ames, Lee J. Draw 50 creepy crawlies /. New York , c1991. p. cm.　ISBN 0-385-41189-8 DDC 743/.6 20
NC783 .A44 1991
Simpson, Anne. How to draw wild animals /. Mahwah, N.J. [1991] p. cm.　ISBN 0-8167-2481-4 (lib. bdg.) :　DDC 743/.6 20
NC780 .S54 1991

ANIMALS IN LITERATURE.
Czernohaus, Karola. Delphindarstellungen von der minoischen bis zur geometrischen Zeit /. Göteborg , 1988. 235, 111 p., 121 p. of plates :　ISBN 91-86098-76-4
　　　　NYPL [3-MAH 90-10819]

ANIMALS IN POETRY. see ANIMALS IN LITERATURE.

ANIMATED FILMS - TECHNIQUE.
Thomas, Bob, 1922- Disney's Art of animation . New York , c1991. p. cm.　ISBN 1-562-82997-1 :　DDC 741.5/8/0979493 20
NC1766.U52 D568 1991

ANIMATED FILMS - TECHNIQUE - JUVENILE LITERATURE.
Jenkins, Patrick. Animation . Reading, Mass. , c1991. p. cm.　ISBN 0-201-56757-1 :　DDC 741.5/8 20
NC1765 .J46 1991

ANIMATED FILMS - UNITED STATES - HISTORY AND CRITICISM.
Lenburg, Jeff. The encyclopedia of animated cartoons /. New York , c1990. p. cm.　ISBN 0-8160-2252-6 (acid-free paper) DDC 791.43/75/0973 20
NC1766.U5 L46 1990

Animation . Jenkins, Patrick. Reading, Mass. , c1991. p. cm.　ISBN 0-201-56757-1 :　DDC 741.5/8 20
NC1765 .J46 1991

ANIMATION (CINEMATOGRAPHY) - VOCATIONAL GUIDANCE - UNITED STATES.
Gray, Milton, 1942- Cartoon animation . Northridge, CA , c1991. iv, 124 p. :　ISBN

0-9628444-5-4 :　DDC 741.5/8/02373 20
NC1765 .G7 1991

Aninger, Franz Xaver. Heilig Kreuz in Donauwörth /. Donauwörth , 1987. 203 p. :　ISBN 3-403-01848-2
　　　　NYPL [3-MRBB+ 90-2728]

Anke Holfeld . Holfeld, Anke, 1934- [Hamburg] [1980] 37 p. :
MLCS 87/3478 (N)
　　　　NYPL [3-MCK H729 90-6357]

Anna Bolena [sound recording] /. Donizetti, Gaetano, 1797-1848. Pontelambro (Como) Italy , p1988. 2 sound discs (2 hr., 12 min.) :
Nuova Era 6713-DM

Anna Eva Bergman. Bergman, Anna-Eva, 1909- Paris [1962] [33] p. :
　　　　NYPL [3-MCZ+ B495 91-4580]

Anna Peters. Peters, Anna, 1843-1926. Anna Peters, 1843-1926 . Biberach an der Riss , c1990. 55 p. :　ISBN 3-924392-13-7 DDC 759.3 20
ND588.P467 A4 1990

Anna Peters, 1843-1926 . Peters, Anna, 1843-1926. Biberach an der Riss , c1990. 55 p. :　ISBN 3-924392-13-7 DDC 759.3 20
ND588.P467 A4 1990

Annale (Università degli studi di Rome "La Sapienza." Dipartimento di progetazzione architettonia e urbana) .
(1986) Tempo e architettura /. Roma , c1987. 174 p. :　　*NYPL [3-MQD+ 90-12504]*

ANNE BOLEYN, QUEEN, CONSORT OF HENRY VIII, KING OF ENGLAND, 1507-1536 - DRAMA.
Donizetti, Gaetano, 1797-1848. Anna Bolena [sound recording] /. Pontelambro (Como) Italy , p1988. 2 sound discs (2 hr., 12 min.) :
Nuova Era 6713-DM

The Anne Burnett Tandy lectures in American civilization .
(no. 11) Kammen, Michael G. Meadows of memory . Austin , 1992. p. cm.　ISBN 0-292-75139-7 (cloth : alk. paper)　DDC 758/.9973 20
N6505 .K28 1992

Anne Rohart /. Issermann, Dominique. München , c1987. [1] p., 29 leaves of plates :　ISBN 3-88814-215-6
　　　　NYPL [MFX+ (Issermann) 91-7940]

L'année 1913. Brion-Guerry, Liliane, 1916- Paris , 1971-1973. 3 v.　　*NYPL [3-MAL 72-945]*

Les années impressionnistes, 1870-1889 /. Lévêque, Jean Jacques. Courbevoie, Paris , c1990. 660 p. :　ISBN 2-86770-042-6
IN PROCESS (ONLINE)
　　　　NYPL [3-MAMI+ 91-4871]

Les années surréalistes . Masson, André 1896- Paris , c1990. 574 p., 52 p. of plates :　ISBN 2-7377-0181-3
　　　　NYPL [3-MCO M42 90-11041]

Les Années UAM, 1929-1958 : Musée des arts décoratifs, du 27 septembre 1988 au 29 janvier 1989. Paris : Union des arts décoratifs, c1988. 268 p. : ill. (some col.) ; 27 cm. Includes bibliographical references (p. 258-263) and index.
ISBN 2-901422-11-X
1. Union des artistes modernes (Paris, France) - Exhibitions. 2. Decorative arts - France - Exhibitions. I. Musée des arts décoratifs (France). II. Union centrale des arts décoratifs (Paris, France).
　　　　NYPL [3-MLF 90-10798]

Années vingt d'Anne Bony. Les années 20 d'Anne Bony. Paris [1989] 2 v. (1275 p.) :　ISBN 2-903370-45-1 (set) DDC 700/.9/048 20
NX457 .A55 1989

Annely Juda Fine Art. Gabo, Naum, 1890- Naum Gabo, 1890-1977 . London , c1990. 127 p. :　ISBN 1-87028-022-9
　　　　NYPL [3-MGO (Gabo) 91-3725]

Annemarie Verna Galerie. Wilson, Robert, 1941- Orlando . Zürich [1989] 54 p. :
　　　　NYPL [3-MCX W7495 90-12810]

Annette Lemieux, the appearance of sound . Lemieux, Annette. Sarasota, Fla. , c1989. 16 p. :　ISBN 0-916758-27-3
　　　　NYPL [3-MCX+ L554 90-8047]

Annie, Gwen, Lilly, Pam, and Tulip /. Kincaid, Jamaica. New York , 1989. [20] p. :　ISBN

0-394-58035-4 DDC 813 20
PR9275.A585 K5633 1989
NYPL [MEMZ+ 91-3772]

Annie S. Kemerer Museum. The Strange and the sublime . Bethlehem, Pa. , c1989. 32 p. :
NYPL [MFW 91-3497]

Anotaciones de un pintor /. Gómez Jaramillo, Ignacio, 1910-1970. Medellín , 1987. 313 p. :
N7483.G64 A2 1987
NYPL [3-MCZ G632 90-12606]

Another objectivity. Un'altra obiettività /. Milano , c1989. 253 p. : ISBN 88-7017-067-5
NYPL [MFW 90-3005]

ANSCHUTZ, PHILIP - ART COLLECTIONS - EXHIBITIONS.
Schriever, George. American masters in the West . [S.l.] , c1976. 67 p. :
NYPL [3-MCW 90-5762]

Anscombe, Isabelle. Arts & crafts style / Isabelle Anscombe. New York : Rizzoli, 1991. p. cm. Includes bibliographical references and index. ISBN 0-8478-1328-2 : DDC 745.4/441 20
1. Arts and crafts movement - Great Britain. 2. Arts and crafts movement - United States. I. Title. II. Title: Arts and crafts style.
NK1142 .A52 1991

Anselm Kiefer, Bücher 1969-1990 . Kiefer, Anselm, 1945- [Stuttgart] , c1990. 378 p. : ISBN 3-89322-200-6
NYPL [MDG+ (Kiefer) 91-5802]

Ansichten eines Grenzgängers. Lichtenberg, Christian. Innere Visionen . Baden , c1988. ca. 65 p. : **NYPL [MFW 91-6669]**

Answers to fifty of the most often asked questions about watercolor glazing techniques. Rankin, Don. Answers to 50 of the most often asked questions about watercolor glazing techniques /. New York , 1991. 144 p. : ISBN 0-8230-4489-0 : DDC 751.42/2 20
ND2430 .R36 1991

Answers to 50 of the most often asked questions about watercolor glazing techniques /. Rankin, Don. New York , 1991. 144 p. : ISBN 0-8230-4489-0 : DDC 751.42/2 20
ND2430 .R36 1991

Antal, Frederick.
[Raphael between Classicism and Mannerism. German]
Raffael zwischen Klassizismus und Manierismus : eine sozialgeschichtliche Einführung in die mittelitalienische Malerei des 16. und 17. Jahrhunderts / Frederick Antal ; mit einem Vorwort herausgegeben von Nicos Hadjinicolaou ; [aus dem Englischen übertragen von Karin Stempel].1. Aufl. Giessen [Germany] : Anabas, 1980. 229 p. : ill. ; 31 cm. Translation of four lectures presented in 1934-35 at the Courtauld Institute of Art. Title of original manuscript: Raphael between Classicism and Mannerism. Includes bibliographical references. ISBN 3-87038-068-3
1. Painting, Renaissance - Italy. I. Title.
NYPL [3-MCF+ R13 85-2842]

Antebellum architecture of Kentucky /. Lancaster, Clay. Lexington, Ky. , c1991. p. cm. ISBN 0-8131-1759-3 (alk. paper) : DDC 720/.9769 20
NA730.K4 L36 1991

Antelami, Benedetto, fl. 1177-1233.
Quintavalle, Arturo Carlo. Benedetto Antelami /. Milano , c1990. 384 p. : ISBN 88-435-3176-X DDC 730/.92 20
NB623.A6 A4 1990

Quintavalle, Arturo Carlo, 1936- Benedetto Antelami /. Milano , c1990. 384 p. :
NYPL [3-MGO+ (Antelami) 90-12881]

ANTELAMI, BENEDETTO, FL. 1177-1233 - EXHIBITIONS.
Quintavalle, Arturo Carlo. Benedetto Antelami /. Milano , c1990. 384 p. : ISBN 88-435-3176-X DDC 730/.92 20
NB623.A6 A4 1990

Quintavalle, Arturo Carlo, 1936- Benedetto Antelami /. Milano , c1990. 384 p. :
NYPL [3-MGO+ (Antelami) 90-12881]

Antes del treinta y seis. Arco, Manuel del. Antes del 36. Barcelona [1966] 262 p. DDC 741.5946
NC1639.A65 A45
NYPL [MEM (Arco) 90-6369]

Antes del 36. Arco, Manuel del. Barcelona [1966] 262 p. DDC 741.5946
NC1639.A65 A45
NYPL [MEM (Arco) 90-6369]

Antes, Horst, 1936-
Horst Antes : neue Bilder 1987-1990, Kunsthalle zu Kiel der Christian-Albrechts-Universität und Schleswig-Holsteinischer Kunstverein / [herausgegeben von Jens Christian Jensen]. Kiel : Die Kunsthalle, c1990. 84 p. : ill. (some col.) ; 31 cm. Catalog of an exhibition held at the Gemäldegalerie und Graphische Sammlung Kunsthalle zu Kiel and Schleswig-Holsteinischer Kunstverein June 10-July 29, 1990, and at the Galerie Neumann, Düsseldorf, Aug. 22-Sept. 29, 1990. On cover: 10690, 29790. ISBN 3-923701-41-1
1. Antes, Horst, 1936- - Exhibitions. I. Jensen, Jens Christian, 1928-. II. Kunsthalle zu Kiel. III. Schleswig-Holsteinischer Kunstverein. IV. Galerie Michael Neumann. V. Title.
NYPL [3-MCK+ A62 91-6789]

ANTES, HORST, 1936- - EXHIBITIONS.
Antes, Horst, 1936- Horst Antes . Kiel , c1990. 84 p. : ISBN 3-923701-41-1
NYPL [3-MCK+ A62 91-6789]

Anthologie de la peinture dominicaine. Gerón, Cándido, 1950- Antología de la pintura dominicana =. [S.l.] 1990. 148 p. :
NYPL [3-MCY+ 90-13378]

Anthologie des sculpteurs et peintres burundais contemporains /. Sendegeya, Pierre-Claver, 1940- Paris , c1989. 109 p. : ISBN 2-288-82091-8
IN PROCESS (ONLINE)
NYPL [3-MADF+ 91-7959]

Anthology of Dominican painting. Gerón, Cándido, 1950- Antología de la pintura dominicana =. [Santo Domingo, Dominican Republic? , 1990] (Santo Domingo, República Dominicana : Editora Tele 3) 148 p. : DDC 759.97293 20
ND315.D6 G45 1990

Anthology of Dominican painting. Gerón, Cándido, 1950- Antología de la pintura dominicana =. [S.l.] 1990. 148 p. :
NYPL [3-MCY+ 90-13378]

Anthony d'Offay (Firm)
Gore, Spencer Frederick, 1878-1914. Spencer Frederick Gore, 1878-1914 . New York [1990] [23] p. : **NYPL [3-MCV G666 90-13021]**
Kiefer, Anselm, 1945- The high priestess /. New York , 1989. 226 p. : ISBN 0-8109-1216-3 DDC 709/.2/4 19
NB588.K43 A65 1989
NYPL [3-MGO+ (Kiefer) 89-23144]
Pollock, Jackson, 1912-1956. Jackson Pollock . London , c1989. [61] p. : ISBN 0-947564-26-8
NYPL [3-MCX P777 90-12889]

Anthony d'Offay Gallery. Baselitz, Georg, 1938- Recent paintings by Georg Baselitz /. London , c1990. 65 p. : ISBN 0-947564-30-6
NYPL [3-MCK+ B299 90-12324]

Anthony, Kathryn H. Juries on trial : the renaissance of the design studio / Kathryn H. Anthony. New York : Van Nostrand Reinhold, 1991 p. cm. Includes index. ISBN 0-442-00235-1 DDC 729/.079 20
1. Architectural design - Evaluation. 2. Architectural design - Awards. 3. Communication in architectural design. 4. Jury - Biography - History and criticism. I. Title.
NA2750 .A64 1991

Anthony Reynolds Gallery. Lawson, Thomas. Thomas Lawson. Glasgow, Scotland , 1990. 96 p. : ISBN 0-906474-96-5
NYPL [3-MCV L423 91-6447]

Anthony van Dyck /. Van Dyck, Anthony, Sir, 1599-1641. New York , 1990. 383 p. : ISBN 0-8109-3909-6
NYPL [3-MCH+ D99 91-4179]

Anti-apartheid cartoons from around the world. Selection of anti-apartheid cartoons from around the world /. New York , 1989. 84 p. ;
NYPL [3-MDY 89-18787]

Le Antiche maioliche di Castelli d'Abruzzo : [mostra] Roma, Palazzo Venezia, dicembre 1968-febbraio 1969. Roma : Officina, 1968. 50 p., [101] p. of plates : ill. (some col.) ; 23 cm. Catalogue edited by Lello Moccia. Includes

bibliographical references.
1. Majolica, Italian - Italy - Castelli - Exhibitions. I. Moccia, Lello. II. Palazzo Venezia (Rome, Italy).
NYPL [3-MPGD 90-6428]

Antichna risuvana keramika v Bŭlgariiā /. Lazarov, Mikhail, 1934- Sofiiā , 1990. 142 p. :
NK4649 .L37 1990

Antike bemalte Vasen aus Bulgarien. Lazarov, Mikhail, 1934- Antichna risuvana keramika v Bŭlgariiā /. Sofiiā , 1990. 142 p. :
NK4649 .L37 1990

Antike Kleinkunst . Pülhorn, Wolfgang. Nürnberg , 1987. 163 p. : ISBN 3-9801529-0-1 DDC 738.3/82/093807443324 20
NK3835 .P85 1987
NYPL [3-MPE 90-11122]

Die Antiken der Sammlung Werner Peek /. Stupperich, Reinhard, 1951- Münster , 1990. 77 p., [16] leaves of plates :
NYPL [3-MPEK 91-4659]

Antikensammlung . Staatliche Museen zu Berlin (Germany : East). Antikensammlung. Berlin , <1990-. v. <2 > : ISBN 3-362-00436-9 (Bd. 2) DDC 709/.38/074031552 20
N2250.P4 A52 1990

Antikensammlung Peek. Stupperich, Reinhard, 1951- Die Antiken der Sammlung Werner Peek /. Münster , 1990. 77 p., [16] leaves of plates :
NYPL [3-MPEK 91-4659]

Antiker Gold- und Silberschmuck . Museum für Kunst und Gewerbe Hamburg. Mainz am Rhein , c1968. x, 246 p. :
NK7307 .H6   **NYPL [3-MNR 90-7024]**

ANTIMENES PAINTER - CATALOGS.
Burow, Johannes. Der Antimenesmaler /. Mainz/Rhein , c1989. xii, 126 p., 160, [2] p. of plates : ISBN 3-8053-1029-3
NYPL [3-MPEK+ 90-10403]

Der Antimenesmaler /. Burow, Johannes. Mainz/Rhein , c1989. xii, 126 p., 160, [2] p. of plates : ISBN 3-8053-1029-3
NYPL [3-MPEK+ 90-10403]

Antiquaria Romana (Art gallery) Gabinetto delle stampe di Milano. Disegni di Stefano della Bella. Milano [1976?] 70 p. :
NYPL [3-MCF B367 91-1368]

Antiquarische Gesellschaft Pfäffikon. Jezler, Peter. Der spätgotische Kirchenbau in der Zürcher Landschaft . Wetzikon , c1988. 144 p. : ISBN 3-85981-150-9 : DDC 726/.5/094945707449457 20
NA5849.Z87 J49 1988
NYPL [3-MRBB 91-3251]

ANTIQUARIUM DI FERMO - CATALOGS.
Pupilli, Laura. Fermo. Bologna , c1990. v, 272 p. : ISBN 88-7019-449-3
NYPL [MAVZ (Femo, Italy) 91-5714]

Antique bamboo furniture /. Walkling, Gillian. London , 1979. 128 p., 4 p. of plates : ISBN 0-7135-1099-4 :
NK2712.6 .W34   **NYPL [MOI 81-1058]**

ANTIQUE COLLECTING. see ANTIQUES.

Antique Collectors' Club.
Gere, Charlotte. Artists' jewellery . Woodbridge [England] , c1989. 244 p. : ISBN 1-85149-024-8
NYPL [MNR 89-11557]
Hawkins, J. B. 19th century Australian silver /. Woodbridge, [England] , 1990. 2 v. : ISBN 1-85149-002-7 : DDC 739.23794 20
NYPL [3-MNO 90-12680]
Hussey, Christopher, 1899- English country houses /. London , 1988. 3 v. : ISBN 1-85149-029-9 (set : pbk.)
NYPL [3-MRG 90-12887]

Antique map prices--1983. Jolly, David C. Antique maps, sea charts, city views, celestial charts & battle plans. Brookline, Mass. , 1983. viii, 279 p. : ISBN 0-911775-00-5 DDC 912/.075 19
GA197.3 .J64 1983
NYPL [Map Div. 84-417]

Antique maps, sea charts, city views, celestial charts & battle plans . Jolly, David C. Brookline, Mass. , 1983. viii, 279 p. : ISBN 0-911775-00-5 DDC 912/.075 19
GA197.3 .J64 1983
NYPL [Map Div. 84-417]

ANTIQUES.
Peake, Jacquelyn. How to recognize and
refinish antiques for pleasure and profit /.
Chester, Conn. , c1992. p. cm.   ISBN
1-564-40020-4   DDC 745.1/028/8 20
NK1125 .P39 1992

Antiques and collectibles fix-it source book.
Kovel, Ralph M. Kovels' antiques & collectibles
fix-it source book /. New York , c1990. x, 180
p. :   ISBN 0-517-57333-4 :   DDC 745.1/028/8 20
NK1125 .K659 1990
                        NYPL [MNH 90-13220]

ANTIQUES - CATALOGS.
The Lyle price guide to collectibles and
memorabilia /. New York, NY , c1990. 512 p. :
ISBN 0-399-51515-1 (alk. paper) :   DDC
745.1/075 19
NK1125 .L79 1990   NYPL [MAVC 91-3286]
Miller, Martin. [International antiques price
guide.] Miller's International antiques price
guide /. New York, N.Y., U. S.A. , c1990. 632
p. :   *NYPL [MAVC+ 91-5384]*

ANTIQUES - COLLECTORS AND
    COLLECTING.
Curtis, Tony, 1939- There's a fortune in your
attic /. New York, NY , c1991. 512 p. :   ISBN
0-399-51677-8 (alk. paper) :   DDC 745.1/075 20
NK1125 .C8874 1991

ANTIQUES - CONSERVATION AND
    RESTORATION.
Peake, Jacquelyn. How to recognize and
refinish antiques for pleasure and profit /.
Chester, Conn. , c1992. p. cm.   ISBN
1-564-40020-4   DDC 745.1/028/8 20
NK1125 .P39 1992

ANTIQUES - CONSERVATION AND
    RESTORATION - DIRECTORIES.
Kovel, Ralph M. Kovels' antiques & collectibles
fix-it source book /. New York , c1990. x, 180
p. :   ISBN 0-517-57333-4 :   DDC 745.1/028/8 20
NK1125 .K659 1990
                        NYPL [MNH 90-13220]

ANTIQUES - HANDBOOKS, MANUALS,
    ETC.
Dunnan, Nancy. Collectibles /. Englewood
Cliffs, NJ , c1990. 128 p. :   ISBN 0-382-09918-4
DDC 745.1 20
NK1125 .D786 1990
                        NYPL [MAVC 91-5516]

ANTIQUES - HISTORY.
The Illustrated history of antiques .
Philadelphia, Pa. , 1991. p. cm.   ISBN
0-89471-888-6 :   DDC 745.1 20
NK1125 .I45 1991

ANTIQUES - INFORMATION SERVICES -
    UNITED STATES - DIRECTORIES.
Maloney, David J. Collector's information
clearinghouse antiques & collectibles resource
directory /. Radnor, Pa. , 1991. p. cm.   ISBN
0-87069-611-4 (hc) :   DDC 745.1/025/73 20
NK1127 .M34 1991

ANTIQUES - MARKETING.
Peake, Jacquelyn. How to recognize and
refinish antiques for pleasure and profit /.
Chester, Conn. , c1992. p. cm.   ISBN
1-564-40020-4   DDC 745.1/028/8 20
NK1125 .P39 1992

ANTIQUES - MICHIGAN - DEARBORN.
Popular antiques at the Henry Ford Museum.
[Westfield, N.Y.? , 1959?] 36 p. :
        NYPL [3-MAVZ+ (Dearborn, Mi.)
                                    90-5439]

ANTIQUES - PRICES.
Miller, Martin. [International antiques price
guide.] Miller's International antiques price
guide /. New York, N.Y., U. S.A. , c1990. 632
p. :   *NYPL [MAVC+ 91-5384]*
Sotheby's great sales /. London , 1989. 160 p. :
ISBN 0-7126-2137-7   DDC 707/.5 20
N8675 .S685 1989

ANTIQUES - UNITED STATES - CATALOGS.
Ketchum, William C., 1931- The new and
revised catalog of American collectibles /. New
York City , 1990. 320 p. :   ISBN 0-8317-6316-7
        NYPL [3-MAVC 91-7510]

ANTIQUES, VICTORIAN - CATALOGS.
Mace, O. Henry. Collector's guide to Victoriana
/. Radnor, Pa. , c1991. p. cm.   ISBN
0-87069-600-9 (hc)   DDC 745.1/09/034075 20
NK1378 .M3 1991

Antiquitäten Zeitung. Dokumenta .
(5) Neuwirth, Waltraud. Wiener Keramik nach
1900 . München , c1984. 2 v. :   ISBN
3-923239-16-5
                NYPL [3-MPGK+ 91-6817]

ANTIQUITIES, BUDDHIST. see BUDDHIST
    ANTIQUITIES.

ANTIQUITIES, CLASSICAL. see CLASSICAL
    ANTIQUITIES.

ANTIQUITIES, GRECIAN. see CLASSICAL
    ANTIQUITIES.

ANTIQUITIES, INDUSTRIAL. see
    INDUSTRIAL ARCHAEOLOGY.

ANTIQUITIES, PREHISTORIC. see MAN,
    PREHISTORIC; ARCHAEOLOGY.

ANTIQUITIES, ROMAN. see CLASSICAL
    ANTIQUITIES; ROME - ANTIQUITIES.

Antiquity restored . Howard, Seymour, 1928-
Vienna , 1990. 344 p. :   ISBN 3-900731-11-X
                        NYPL [3-MAH 91-4921]

Antoine Ferrari /. Di Genova, Alauzen. La
Calade, Aix-en-Provence , c1990. 136 p. :
    ISBN 2-85744-497-4   DDC 759.4 20
ND553.F44 D5 1990

Antología de la pintura dominicana =. Gerón,
Cándido, 1950- [Santo Domingo, Dominican
Republic? , 1990] (Santo Domingo, República
Dominicana : Editora Tele 3) 148 p. :   DDC
759.97293 20
ND315.D6 G45 1990

Antología de la pintura dominicana =. Gerón,
Cándido, 1950- [S.l.] 1990. 148 p. :
                NYPL [3-MCY+ 90-13378]

Antologia fotográfica .
(1) Firmo, Walter, 1937- Walter Firmo. Rio de
Janeiro , c1989. [15] p., [46] leaves of plates :
                NYPL [MFX (Firmo) 91-3319]

(2) Martins, Juca, 1949- Juca Martins. Rio de
Janeiro , c1990. [15] p., [46] leaves of plates :
ISBN 85-7222-000-11
                NYPL [MFX (Martins) 91-3427]

Antología, obras de la colección permanente.
Biblioteca Luis-Angel Arango. Bogotá, D.E. ,
1990. 88 p. :
N6670 .B5 1990

Anton Henning, new work . Henning, Anton,
1964- Norman, Okla. [1990] 1 v. (unpaged) :
                NYPL [3-MCK H5166 91-4640]

Anton Himmstedt, Skulpturen . Himmstedt, Anton,
1952- Münster , c1990. 60 p. :   ISBN
3-88789-092-2
                NYPL [3-MGO (Himmstedt) 91-6714]

Anton Wickremasinghe collection . Dharmasiri,
Albert. Modern art in Sri Lanka . Colombo, Sri
Lanka , 1988. 80 p. :   ISBN 955-9034-01-4 :
DDC 709/.5493/0745493 20
N7310.6 .D47 1988   NYPL [3-MAF 91-6910]

Antoni Clavé, exposició retrospectiva . Clavé,
Antoni, 1913- [Barcelona] , 1990. 95 p. :
IN PROCESS (ONLINE)
                NYPL [3-MCQ+ C617 91-5882]

Antonietta Raphael Mafai, Mario Mafai .
Raphaël Mafai, Antonietta, 1900-1975.
Firenze , 1971. [51] p. :
                        NYPL [3-MCE 91-1300]

Antonin Mercié, sculptor of the Lee Monument .
Knox, Joseph T. Richmond, Va. , c1990. 24 p. :
DDC 730/.92 20
NB553.M47 A4 1990

Antônio Augusto Marx, o pintor da natureza /.
Marx, Antônio Augusto, 1919- [Rio de Janeiro,
Brazil] , c1988. 127 p. :   DDC 759.981 20
ND359.M359 A4 1988
                NYPL [3-MCZ M392 90-10880]

Antonio Canova . Thorvaldsens museum.
København [1969] 54 p. :
                NYPL [3-MCF C227.B3 91-1382]

António de Macedo. Macedo, António de, 1955-
[Porto? , 1989 or 1990] (Porto : Grafislab) 58
p. :   DDC 759.69 20
ND833.M25 A4 1990

Antonio Dias . Dias, Antonio, 1944- Mülheim an
der Ruhr , 1989. 70 p. :   ISBN 3-9802023-2-1
                NYPL [3-MCX+ D525 91-4585]

Antônio Prado, cidade historica / Julio Posenato,
organizador ; Luis A. de Boni ... [et al.]. Porto

Alegre, RS : Posenato Arte & Cultura, 1989.
204 p. ; 30 cm. (Coleção Imigração italiana. 96)
*1. Architecture, Domestic - Brazil - Antônio Prado. I.
Posenato, Júlio, 1947-.*
                NYPL [3-MQWN+ 90-12545]

Antonio Ramírez /. Taracena, Bertha. México ,
1989. 38 p., [98] p. of plates :   ISBN
968-360-685-7   DDC 759.972 20
ND259.R34 A4 1989

Antonio Saura . Saura, Antonio, 1930- Paris ,
1989. 282 p. :   ISBN 2-7022-0243-8
                NYPL [3-MCQ+ S259 91-5230]

Antonio Tamburro. Tamburro, Antonio, 1948-
Milano , c1990. 143 p. :   ISBN 88-374-1110-3
IN PROCESS (ONLINE)
                NYPL [3-MCF T156 91-4049]

Antonucci, Giorgio. Dall'Albornoz all'età dei
Borgia . Todi , 1990. 385 p., [19] p. of plates :
ISBN 88-85311-01-6   DDC 709/.45/65 20
N6919.U5 D35 1990

Antunes, Alfredo da Mata. Arquitectura popular
em Portugal /. Lisboa , 1988. 3 v. :   DDC
720/.9469 20
NA1321 .A77 1988
                        NYPL [3-MQW 91-7182]

Antúnez, Nemesio.
Carta aérea / texto de Nemesio Antúnez ;
proyectó la edición, Hernán Garfias. Santiago :
Editorial Los Andes, 1988. 65 p. : ill. ; 32 cm.
1. Antúnez, Nemesio. I. Title.
                NYPL [3-MCZ+ A636 90-11576]

Carta aérea / texto de Nemesio Antúnez,
reproducción período, 1944-1988 ; proyectó la
edición, Hernán Garfias. Santiago de Chile :
Editorial Los Andes, 1988. 65 p. : ill. (some
col.) ; 32 cm.   DDC 759.983 20
*1. Antúnez, Nemesio - Catalogs. I. Garfías, Hernán. II.
Title.*
ND369.A58 A4 1988

ANTÚNEZ, NEMESIO.
Antúnez, Nemesio. Carta aérea /. Santiago ,
1988. 65 p. :
                NYPL [3-MCZ+ A636 90-11576]

ANTÚNEZ, NEMESIO - CATALOGS.
Antúnez, Nemesio. Carta aérea /. Santiago de
Chile , 1988. 65 p. :   DDC 759.983 20
ND369.A58 A4 1988

ANTWERP (BELGIUM : PROVINCE) -
    ROAD MAPS.
Alle straten en straatjes van Antwerpen. De
Pinte , 1985. 1 atlas (258 p.) :
                        NYPL [Map Div. 90-11658]

Antwerp (Belgium). Stedelijk Prentenkabinet.
Rondom Rubens : tekeningen en prenten uit
eigen verzameling / [onder redactie van
Francine de Nave ; vertaling, Altrans].
Antwerpen : Stad Antwerpen : Museum
Plantin-Moretus en het Stedelijk
Prentenkabinet, 1991. 229 p. : ill. (some col.) ;
30 cm. (Publikaties van het Musuem Plantin-Moretus
en het Stedelijk Prentenkabinet . 19) Title on t.p. verso:
Around Rubens, prints and drawings from the Stedelijk
Prentenkabinet. Exhibition catalog. Dutch and English.
Includes bibliographical references and indexes.
*1. Art, Flemish - Belgium - Antwerp - Exhibitions. 2.
Art, Modern - 17th-18th centuries - Belgium -
Antwerp - Exhibitions. 3. Rubens, Peter Paul, Sir,
1577-1640 - Influence - Exhibitions. 4. Antwerp
(Belgium). Stedelijk Prentenkabinet - Exhibitions. I.
Nave, Francine de. II. Title. III. Title: Around Rubens.
IV. Series.*
N6971.A6 A73 1991

ANTWERP (BELGIUM). STEDELIJK
    PRENTENKABINET - EXHIBITIONS.
Antwerp (Belgium). Stedelijk Prentenkabinet.
Rondom Rubens . Antwerpen , 1991. 229 p. :
N6971.A6 A73 1991

Der Antwerpener Altar in St. Georg Vreden /
mit Beiträgen von Wilhelm Elling ... [et al.].
Vreden : Heimatverein Vreden in Selbstverlag,
1989. 247 p. : ill. (some col.) ; 32 cm. Includes
bibliographical references.   ISBN 3-926627-03-4
*1. Pfarrkirche St. Georg (Verden, Germany). 2. Altars,
Gothic - Germany - Verden. 3. Church decoration and
ornament - Germany - Verden. I. Elling, Wilhelm.*
                NYPL [3-MAIH+ 91-6544]

Anupõld, Elle-Mall. Nõukogude Eesti kultuuripilt
1980 /. Tallinn , 1981. 93 p., [32] p. of plates :
NX556.A3 E755 1981

Anxious visions . Stich, Sidra. New York ,

Berkeley , 1990. 295 p. : ISBN 1-558-59109-5
DDC 709/.04/06307479467 20
N6494.S8 S75 1990
NYPL [3-MAL 90-13055]

Anzelewsky, Fedja, 1919- Staatliche Museen
Preussischer Kulturbesitz. Kupferstichkabinett.
Albrecht Dürer, Verzeichnis sämtlicher
Zeichnungen . [Berlin] , 1972. 19 p., [144] p. of
plates :
NC251.D8 A8 **NYPL [3-MCK D85 90-5760]**

**APARTHEID - CARICATURES AND
CARTOONS.**
Selection of anti-apartheid cartoons from
around the world /. New York , 1989. 84 p. ;
NYPL [3-MDY 89-18787]

APARTMENT HOUSES - BERLIN.
Meyer, Edina. Paul Mebes . Berlin , 1972. 236,
[64] p. :
NA1088. M28 M49
NYPL [3-MQZ+ (Mebes) 83-2373]

**APARTMENT HOUSES - CALIFORNIA -
LOS ANGELES - EXHIBITIONS.**
Marshall, Richard, 1947- Edward Ruscha Los
Angeles apartments, 1965 /. [New York,
N.Y.] , c1990. 63 p. : ISBN 0-87427-074-X
NYPL [3-MCX R95 90-13010]

APARTMENT HOUSES - FRANCE.
Léger, Jean-Michel. Derniers domiciles connus .
Paris , c1990. 168 p. : ISBN 2-907150-18-9 :
DDC 728/.314/0944409047 20
NA7346 .L44 1990

**APARTMENT HOUSES - SPAIN -
CATALONIA.**
Realitzacions de la Direcció General
d'Arquitectura i Habitatge i de l'Institut Català
del Sòl 1981-1987. Barcelona [1988?] 2 cases
(101 fasc.) : DDC 728/.314/0946709048 20
NA7860 .R35 1988

Aperture Foundation. Greenough, Sarah, 1951-
Paul Strand . New York, NY . 171 p. : ISBN
0-89381-442-3
NYPL [MFX+ (Strand) 91-4965]

Apollo art about .
(nr. 1) Świdziński, Jan. Quotations on
contextual art /. [Eindhoven , New York (U.
S.A.) , 1988?] 190 p. ; ISBN 90-71638-04-9
DDC 701 20
N71 .S95 1988 **NYPL [3-MA 91-4598]**

Apostolos-Cappadona, Diane. Dillenberger, Jane.
Image and spirit in sacred and secular art /.
New York , 1990. xiii, 217 p., [8] p. of plates :
ISBN 0-8245-1036-4 : DDC 701 20
N72.R4 D45 1990
NYPL [3-MAMZ 91-3989]

Apostolos Giagiannos . Stephanidès, Manos S.,
1954- Athēna , 1986. 62 p. :
NYPL [3-MCZ G43 90-8058]

**APOTHECARY JARS - ITALY - ROME -
EXHIBITIONS.**
Le Ceramiche da farmacia a Roma tra '400 e
'600 /. Viterbo [1990] 178 p. :
NYPL [3-MPGD+ 91-4305]

Appalachian Consortium. Lovingood, Paul E.
Emerging patterns in the Southern Highlands .
[Boone, N.C.] [1986?]- v. : ISBN 0-913239-36-4
(pbk.) **NYPL [Map Div. 88-2045]**

**APPALACHIAN REGION, SOUTHERN -
MAPS.**
Lovingood, Paul E. Emerging patterns in the
Southern Highlands . [Boone, N.C.] [1986?]-
v. : ISBN 0-913239-36-4 (pbk.)
NYPL [Map Div. 88-2045]

APPALACHIAN TRAIL - MAPS.
The Appalachian Trail through Kent,
Connecticut /. Kent, Conn. , 1972. 1 v.
(unpaged) : **NYPL [Map Div. 90-7145]**

The Appalachian Trail through Kent, Connecticut
/ editor, Douglas R. Olsen. Kent, Conn. : Kent
Stationery, 1972. 1 v. (unpaged) : ill. ; 22 cm.
On cover: Maps and trail guides from Dog Tail
Corners, N.Y. to Cornwall Bridge, Conn. (Dark Entry)
*1. Trails - Connecticut - Maps. 2. Appalachian Trail -
Maps. I. Olsen, Douglas R.*
NYPL [Map Div. 90-7145]

Appasamy, Jaya, 1918- (ed) 25 years of Indian
art. New Delhi [1972] 32, [8] p., [32] p. of
illus. DDC 709/.54
N7304 .T85 **NYPL [3-MAM 90-5575]**

Appearance of sound. Lemieux, Annette. Annette

Lemieux, the appearance of sound . Sarasota,
Fla. , c1989. 16 p. : ISBN 0-916758-27-3
NYPL [3-MCX+ L554 90-8047]

Appearances . Harrison, Martin, 1945- London ,
1991. 312 p. : ISBN 0-224-03067-1 (cased) :
DDC 779.93912 20
TR679 **NYPL [MFW+ 91-4961]**

Appelbaum, Stanley. The Complete "Masters of
the poster" . New York , 1990. xv, 240, [16]
p. : ISBN 0-486-26309-6 DDC 741.6/74/09034 20
NC1845.A7 C6 1990
NYPL [3-MDW+ 90-12311]

Appelhof, Ruth Ann. The Expressionist
landscape . Birmingham, Ala. , Seattle , 1988,
c1987. 216 p. : DDC 759.1 19
ND1351.6 .E97 1987
NYPL [3-MCW 88-3335]

Applebroog, Ida.
Ida Applebroog : happy families : a fifteen-year
survey / essays by Lowery S. Sims, Thomas W.
Sokolowski, Marilyn A. Zeitlin. Houston :
Contemporary Arts Museum ; Seattle, Wash. :
Distributed by University of Washington Press,
c1990. 96 p. : ill. (some col.) ; 28 cm. Published
in conjunction with the exhibition, Ida Applebroog,
happy families, 24 Feb.-20 May 1990, Contemporary
Arts Museum, Houston. Includes bibliographical
references. ISBN 0-936080-20-5 DDC 700/.92 20
*1. Applebroog, Ida - Exhibitions. I. Sims, Lowery
Stokes. II. Sokolowski, Thomas W. III. Zeitlin, Marilyn.
IV. Title: Happy families.*
ND237.A646 A4 1990
NYPL [3-MCX A649 90-12475]

APPLEBROOG, IDA - EXHIBITIONS.
Applebroog, Ida. Ida Applebroog . Houston ,
Seattle, Wash. , c1990. 96 p. : ISBN
0-936080-20-5 DDC 700/.92 20
ND237.A646 A4 1990
NYPL [3-MCX A649 90-12475]

Appleton, Honor C.
Prince, Pamela. A day spent with Josephine
and her friends /. New York, NY , 1992. p.
cm. ISBN 0-517-58303-8 : DDC 741.6/42 20
NC978.5.A67 P75 1992

**APPLETON, HONOR C. - THEMES,
MOTIVES.**
Prince, Pamela. A day spent with Josephine
and her friends /. New York, NY , 1992. p.
cm. ISBN 0-517-58303-8 : DDC 741.6/42 20
NC978.5.A67 P75 1992

**APPLIQUÉ - JAPAN - HISTORY - 20TH
CENTURY - THEMES, MOTIVES.**
Miyawaki, Ayako, 1905- Ayako Miyawaki, the
art of Japanese applique /. [Tokyo] ,
Washington D.C. , 1991. p. cm. ISBN
0-940979-17-9 DDC 746.392 20
NK9198.M59 A4 1991

**APPRECIATION OF ART. see ART
APPRECIATION.**

Appuhn-Radtke, Sibylle. Das Thesenblatt im
Hochbarock : Studien zu einer graphischen
Gattung am Beispiel der Werke Bartholomäus
Kilians / Sibylle Appuhn-Radtke. Weissenhorn :
A.H. Konrad, 1988. 307 p. : ill. ; 38 cm.
Revision of the author's thesis--Universität Freiburg im
Breisgau, 1983. Includes index. Includes bibliographical
references (p. 285-289). ISBN 3-87437-251-0
*1. Kilian, Bartholomäus, 1630-1696. 2. Kings and rulers
in art. 3. Engraving, Baroque - Germany. 4. Engraving,
German. I. Kilian, Bartholomäus, 1630-1696. II. Title.*
NYPL [MDG+ (Kilian) 90-13673]

Appunti per piazze d'Italia / a cura di Adolfo
Natalini ; i testi critici sono di Adolfo Natalini
e Vittorio Savi ; il testo relativo a Il Ferrone è
di Walter Mauri. [Milano] : Il Ferrone, c1988.
79 p. : chiefly col. ill. ; 30 cm. Caption title.
*1. Ferrone (Firm : Milan, Italy). 2. Plazas - Italy. 3.
Pavements, Brick. 4. Bricks - Italy. 5. Bricks - Germany
(West). 6. Pienza (Italy) - Buildings, structures, etc. 7.
Fidenza (Italy) - Buildings, structures, etc. I. Natalini,
Adolfo, 1941-. II. Ferrone (Firm : Milan, Italy).*
NYPL [3-MQWB+ 90-12352]

April Greiman, large scale posters. [Cullowhee,
N.C.] : Western Carolina University, c1987. v,
27 p. : chiefly col.ill. (some folded) ; 23 x 26
cm. Catalog of an exhibition held at the Art Gallery,
Belk Building, Western Carolina University, Cullowhee,
N.C., Oct. 12-Nov. 10, 1987. Includes bibliographical
references.
1. Greiman, April - Exhibitions. I. Greiman, April. II.

Belk Art Gallery.
NYPL [3-MDWS (Greiman) 90-12807]

**APT (FRANCE) - ANTIQUITIES, ROMAN -
EXHIBITIONS.**
Cavalier, Odile. Le trésor d'Apt . Avignon ,
1988. 119 p. : ISBN 2-903044-49-X
NYPL [3-MGR + 90-5010]

**Apuntes sobre el origen y evolución morfológica
de las plazas del casco histórico de Sevilla /.**
Vioque Cubero, R. (Rafael) [Seville] [1987]
225 p. : ISBN 84-505-4261-8
NA9223.S48 V56 1987

Apuntes sobre José Sabogal . Torres Bohl, José,
1946- [Lima, Peru] [1989] 154 p. : DDC
760/.092 B 20
N6719.S23 T67 1989

APURE (VENEZUELA) - MAPS.
Eje de desarrollo Orinoco-Apure atlas /.
Caracas , 1987. 1 Atlas ([16] leaves) :
NYPL [Map Div. 91-50]

Aquarelle und Grafik 1977-1987. Uccusic, Hilda,
1938- Hilda Uccusic . Oberpullendorf , c1988.
129 p. :
N6811.5.U23 A4 1988

Aquarelles et dessins impressionnistes . Mráz,
Bohumír. [Gennevilliers?] , 1987. 206 p. :
ISBN 2-86901-027-3
NYPL [3-MBH+ 89-28607]

**AQUATINT - GREAT BRITAIN - 19TH
CENTURY.**
Barr, John, 1934- Britain portrayed . London ,
1989. 126 p. : ISBN 0-7123-0174-7 :
NYPL [3-MAMY+ 91-4983]

AQUILEGIA IN ART.
Löber, Karl. Agaleia . Köln , 1988. viii, 327 p.,
[4] p. of plates : ISBN 3-412-05486-0
N8012.A66 L64 1988
NYPL [3-MAIH+ 90-12956]

**ARAB ARCHITECTURE. see
ARCHITECTURE, ISLAMIC.**

ARAB ART. see ART, ISLAMIC.

Arab Republic of Egypt. see Egypt.

Arabesques et jardins de paradis : collections
françaises d'art islamique : [exposition] Musée
du Louvre, Paris, 16 octobre 1989-15 janvier
1990. Paris : Ministère de la culture, de la
communication, des grands travaux et du
Bicentenaire, Editions de la Réunion des
musées nationaux, c1989. 334 p. : ill. (some
col.) ; 28 cm. "Le catalogue a été rédigé par Marthe
Bernus-Taylor ... [et al.]"--T.p. verso. Includes
bibliographical references (p. 313-320) and index.
ISBN 2-7118-2294-X : DDC
709/.17/67107444361 20
*1. Art, Islamic - Exhibitions. 2. Nature (Aesthetics) -
Exhibitions. 3. Arabesques - Exhibitions. 4. Art -
Collectors and collecting - France - Exhibitions. I.
Bernus-Taylor, Marthe. II. Musée du Louvre. III.
France. Ministère de la culture, de la communication,
des grands travaux et du Bicentenaire.*
N6264.F8 P317 1990

ARABESQUES - EXHIBITIONS.
Arabesques et jardins de paradis . Paris , c1989.
334 p. : ISBN 2-7118-2294-X : DDC
709/.17/67107444361 20
N6264.F8 P317 1990

**ARABS IN PALESTINE. see PALESTINIAN
ARABS.**

Aradi, Nóra. "Szabadság és a nép" . [Budapest] ,
c1981. 500 p., [116] p. of plates : ISBN
963-13-0970-3 :
N6820.5.S93 S97 1981
NYPL [3-MAMZ 91-3364]

Aragon, 1897- Lurie, Boris, 1924- NO!art .
Berlin , c1988. 135, 283, 109 p. :
NX458 .L87 1988

Aragon, Lorraine V., 1954- Taylor, Paul Michael.
Beyond the Java Sea . Washington, D.C. , New
York , 1991. p. cm. ISBN 0-8109-3112-5
(hardcover : Abrams) : DDC 709/.598 20
N7326 .T39 1991

Araguas, Philippe. Pyrénées-Atlantiques . Paris ,
1989. 719 p. : ISBN 2-11-080952-3 : DDC
709/.44/79 20
N6849.P92 P97 1989

Araldi, Giovan Francesco, 1528-1599.
Chronico della Compagnia di Giesù di Napoli.
Selections. 1990. Divenuto, Francesco.
Napoli sacra del XVI secolo : repertorio delle
fabbriche religiose napoletane nella Cronaca
del gesuita Giovan Francesco Araldo /
Francesco Divenuto. Napoli , c1990. 317 p.,
[32] p. of plates : ISBN 88-7104-562-9 : DDC
726/.5/094573 20
NA5621.N2 D58 1990

Arama-Streit, Pauline. Picture this! . [New
York] , c1990. 36 p. :
         NYPL [MDG (Daumier) 91-4770]

Arango Pérez, Débora. La Acuarela en
Antioquia . [Bogotá? , 1987] ([Bogotá] : Banco
de la República, Departamento Editorial) 59
p. : DDC 759.9861/26/07486126 20
ND1905.A58 A28 1987

Arango, Silvia, 1948-
Historia de la arquitectura colombiana / Silvia
Arango. 1a ed. Bogota : Centro Editorial y
Facultad de Artes, Universidad Nacional de
Colombia, 1989. 291 p. : ill. ; 34 cm. ISBN
958-1-70061-7
1. Architecture - Colombia - History. I. Title.
     NYPL [3-MQWN+ 90-12805]
Historia de la arquitectura en Colombia / Silvia
Arango. 1. ed. Bogotá : Centro Editorial y
Facultad de Artes, Universidad Nacional de
Colombia, 1989 [i.e. 1990] 291 p. : ill. ; 33 cm.
Includes bibliographical references (p. 287-291).
Includes index. ISBN 958-1-70061-7 DDC
720/.9861 20
1. Architecture - Colombia - History. I. Title.
NA870 .A73 1990

Arata Isozaki : architecture, 1960-1990 / preface
by Richard Koshalek ; essays by David B.
Stewart and Hajime Yatsuka. Los Angeles :
Museum of Contemporary Art ; New York :
Rizzoli, 1991. 304 p. : ill. (some col.) ; 29 cm.
Published on the occasion of an exhibition held at the
Museum of Contemporary Art, Los Angeles, Mar.
17-June 30, 1991 and elsewhere. Includes
bibliographical references (p. 296-301). ISBN
0-8478-1318-5 DDC 720/.92 20
1. Isozaki, Arata - Exhibitions. I. Isozaki, Arata. II.
Stewart, David B. III. Yatsuka, Hajime, 1948-. IV.
Museum of Contemporary Art (Los Angeles, Calif.).
NA1559.I79 A4 1991
      NYPL [3-MQZ (Isozaki) 91-7248]

Araújo, Olívio Tavares de. Bracher, Carlos, 1940-
Bracher /. São Paulo, SP, Brasil , 1989. 176 p. :
DDC 759.981 20
ND359.B69 A4 1989

Araya Iglesias, Carmen. Pérez Jiménez, José,
1887-1967. José Pérez Jiménez, 1887-1967 /.
[[Badajoz] [1989] 279 p. DDC 759.981 20
      NYPL [3-MCQ P413 90-12327]

Le arazzerie romane dal XVII al XIX secolo /.
De Strobel, Anna Maria. [Roma] , c1989. 99 p.,
[91] p. of plates : *NYPL [3-MOR 91-3766]*

**Arazzi Rubensiani e tessuti preziosi dei musei
diocesani di Ancona e Osimo :** [mostra,
Ancona, Santa Maria della Piazza, 5-28 maggio
1989 / testi, Anna Pianosi ... et al.]. Ancona :
Confartigianato Provincia di Ancona, c1989. 93
p. : col. ill. ; 30 cm. Includes bibliographical
references.
1. Rubens, Peter Paul, Sir, 1577-1640 - Exhibitions. 2.
Tapestry - Italy - Ancona - Exhibitions. 3. Church
vestments - Italy - Ancona - Exhibitions. I. Pianosi,
Anna. II. Santa Maria della Piazza (Church : Ancona,
Italy).   *NYPL [3-MOR+ 90-620]*

Arb, Giorgio von. Portraits aus Liechtenstein /
fotos von Giorgio von Arb ; mit einem essay
von Erika Billeter ; herausgegeben von Robert
Allgäuer. Bern : Benteli Verlag, c1989. 304 p. :
ill. ; 33 cm. ISBN 3-7165-0639-7
1. Portraits - Liechtenstein. I. Title.
      NYPL [MFX+ (Arb) 90-13429]

Arbeit, Wendy. Baskets in Polynesia / by Wendy
Arbeit ; with photographs by Douglas Peebles.
Honolulu : University of Hawaii Press, c1990.
x, 116 p., [8] p. of plates : ill., maps (some
col.) ; 23 cm. (A Kolowalu book) Includes
bibliographical references (p. 115-116). ISBN
0-8248-1281-6 (alk. paper) DDC 746.41/2/0996
20
1. Basket making - Polynesia. I. Title.
TT879.B3 A7 1990 NYPL [3-MNE 91-7015]

Arbeiten auf Papier. Gironcoli, Bruno, 1936-

Bruno Gironcoli, Arbeiten auf Papier . Graz
[1990] 120 p. : DDC 709/.2 20
N6811.5.G57 A4 1990

Arbeiten von 1986 bis 1990. Bönitz, Helmut,
1914- Helmut Bönitz /. [Göttingen] , c1990.
119 p. :
N6888.B6165 A4 1990

**Arbeitsbegegnung in der Druckwerkstatt
Kätelhön, Herbst 1987.** Rolf Münzner, Peter
Schnürpel, Reiner Schwarz . Hannover , c1988.
1 v. (unpaged) :
      NYPL [MDG+ (Münzner) 89-23658]

**Arbeitsgruppe Die Politische Lithographie im
Kampf um die Pariser Kommune.** Die
Politische Lithographie im Kampf um die
Pariser Kommune /. [Stuttgart , 1976. 110 p.,
[33] fold. leaves of plates :
      NYPL [MDY 90-7009]

**Arbeitsheft (Bayerisches Landesamt für
Denkmalpflege) .**
(44) Schmidt, Wolf. Das Raumbuch als
Instrument denkmalpflegerischer
Bestandsaufnahme und Sanierungsplanung /.
München , 1989. 113 p. : ISBN 3-87490-303-2
      NYPL [3-MQD+ 91-4239]
(48) Das Panorama in Altötting . München ,
1990. 112 p., 1 folded leaf of plate : ISBN
3-87490-544-6 *NYPL [3-MBO+ 91-3683]*
(48) Das Panorama in Altötting . München ,
1990. 112 p., 1 folded leaf of plate : ISBN
3-87490-544-6 *NYPL [3-MBO+ 91-3683]*

Arbeitskreis Achtundsechzig. Jawlensky, Alexej
von, 1864-1941. Alexej Jawlensky, vom Abbild
zum Urbild . Wasserburg am Inn , 1979. 107
p. :
N6999.J38 A4 1979
      NYPL [3-MCZ J41 81-398]

**Arbeitssituation und Werkprozess in der
Freskomalerei von Matthäus Günther
(1705-1788) /.** Hamacher, Bärbel, 1957-
München , c1987. ii, 198 p., [30] p. of plates :
ISBN 3-88073-277-9 (Deut. Bibl.) DDC 759.3
19
ND588.G9 H36 1987
      NYPL [3-MCK G928 91-7030]

Arbeitsstipendiaten des Landes Berlin 1984.
10X . [Berlin] [1984] 1 portfolio (10 pieces) :
      NYPL [3-MAMG+ 88-4811]

Arbeloff, Natalie d'. see D'Arbeloff, Natalie.

Arbingast, Stanley Alan, 1910-
Atlas of Texas. University of Texas. Bureau of
Business Research. 1965 industrial atlas of
Texas [by] Florence Escott, research
associate. Austin, 1965. 20, 20 p.
G1371.G1 A32 1965
      NYPL [Map Div. 90-6571]

**ARC DE TRIOMPHE DE L'ÉTOILE (PARIS,
FRANCE)**
Lafitte, Louis, 1770-1828. Description de l'arc
de triomphe de l'Étoile, et des bas-reliefs dont
ce monument est décoré. Paris, 1810. 12 p. 10
pl. *NYPL [MRI 90-12815]*

**ARCACHON (FRANCE) - BUILDINGS,
STRUCTURES, ETC.**
Arcachon, la ville d'hiver /. Liège , 1988. 238
p. : ISBN 2-87009-372-1
NA1051.A73 A73 1988

Arcachon, la ville d'hiver / Institut français
d'architecture. Liège : P. Mardaga, 1988. 238
p. : ill. (some col.), maps ; 26 cm. (Collection
Villes) Produced under the direction of Maurice Culot.
Includes bibliographical references. ISBN
2-87009-372-1
1. Architecture - France - Arcadon. 2. Health resorts,
watering places, etc. - France - Arcachon. 3. Arcachon
(France) - Buildings, structures, etc. I. Culot, Maurice.
II. Institut français d'architecture. III. Series.
NA1051.A73 A73 1988

**Arcais, Francesca d'. see Flores d'Arcais,
Francesca.**

Arcangelo Ianelli. Ianelli, Arcangelo, 1922-
Berlin , c1988. 79 p. :
ND359.I15 A4 1988

Archaeological museum S anchi /. Narendar N
ath Soz. New Delhi , c1966. 26 p., 12 p. of
plates : *NYPL [3-MAE 90-7106]*

**Archäologisches Institut des Deutschen Reichs.
see Deutsches Archäologisches Institut.**

**ARCHAEOLOGY, CLASSICAL. see
CLASSICAL ANTIQUITIES.**

ARCHAEOLOGY - MAPS.
Past worlds . Maplewood, N.J. , 1988. 319 p.:
ISBN 0-7230-0306-8 : DDC 912 19
G1046.E15 P3 1988
      NYPL [Map Div. 90-11840]

Archeogemmologia . Devoto, Guido, 1935- Roma
[1990] 247 p. : ISBN 88-7222-008-4 DDC
736/.2/093 20
NK5500 .D48 1990

**ARCHEOLOGICAL MUSEUM AT S ANCHI -
GUIDE-BOOKS.**
Narendar N ath Soz. Archaeological museum S
anchi /. New Delhi , c1966. 26 p., 12 p. of
plates /. *NYPL [3-MAE 90-7106]*

ARCHEOLOGY. see ARCHAEOLOGY.

Archer M. Huntington Art Gallery. El Taller
Torres-García . Austin , 1991. p. cm. ISBN
0-292-78121-0 DDC 709/.8/074 20
N6502.5 .T35 1991

Archer M. Huntington Gallery. Colombian
figurative graphics / Archer M. Huntington
Galleries, University Art Museum, The
University of Texas at Austin. Austin : The
University, [1976] 47 p. : ill. ; 22 cm. Exhibition
held at Archer M. Huntington Galleries, February
1-March 28, 1976. Includes biographies of the fourteen
artists exhibited.
1. Graphic arts - Colombia - 20th century - Exhibitions.
2. Printmakers - Colombia - Exhibitions. I. Title.
      NYPL [MDBF 90-5877]

**Archidona, II centenario Plaza Ochavada,
1786-1986.** Coloquio de Urbanismo Barroco
(1986 : Archidona, Spain) II centenario de la
Plaza Ochavada de Archidona /. [Málaga]
[1989] 350 p. : ISBN 84-7496-177-7
NA1306 .C6 1986

Archipenko, Alexander, 1887-1964.
Alexander Archipenko. Saarbrücken : Moderne
Galerie des Saarland-Museums, 1986- 2 v. : ill.
(some col.) ; 27 cm. Bibliography: Bd. 1, p. 238-243.
CONTENTS. - Bd. 1. Alexander Archipenko Erbe,
Werke von 1908 bis 1963 aus dem testamentarischen
Vermächtnis, Moderne Galerie des Saarland-Museums,
Saarbrücken 1986, wissenschaftlicher Katalog /
bearbeitet von Helga Schmoll gen. Eisenwerth und
Angela Heilmann. ISBN 3-925303-31-6 (Bd. 1)
1. Archipenko, Alexander, 1887-1964 - Exhibitions. I.
Schmoll gen. Eisenwerth, Helga. II. Heilmann, Angela.
III. Saarland-Museum Saarbrücken. Moderne Galerie.
IV. Title.
      NYPL [3-MGO (Archipenko) 87-1303]

**ARCHIPENKO, ALEXANDER, 1887-1964 -
EXHIBITIONS.**
Archipenko, Alexander, 1887-1964. Alexander
Archipenko. Saarbrücken , 1986- 2 v. : ISBN
3-925303-31-6 (Bd. 1)
      NYPL [3-MGO (Archipenko) 87-1303]

**ARCHITECT-DESIGNED DECORATIVE
ARTS.**
Spencer, Dorothy. Total design . San
Francisco , 1991. p. cm. ISBN 0-87701-655-8
DDC 749.2/034 20
NK2702 .S6 1991

**ARCHITECT-DESIGNED DECORATIVE
ARTS - HISTORY - 20TH CENTURY -
EXHIBITIONS.**
Il Tesoro dell'architettura . Firenze [1990] 149
p. : DDC 739.27/09/0480744551 20
NK7310 .T47 1990

ARCHITECT-DESIGNED FURNITURE.
Capella, Juli. [Diseño de arquitectos en los 80.
English.] Designed by architects in the 1980s /.
New York , 1988. 191 p. : ISBN 0-8478-0941-2 :
DDC 749.2/0498 19
NK2702 .C3713 1988
      NYPL [3-MOI 91-6559]
Spencer, Dorothy. Total design . San
Francisco , 1991. p. cm. ISBN 0-87701-655-8
DDC 749.2/034 20
NK2702 .S6 1991

**ARCHITECT-DESIGNED FURNITURE -
FRANCE.**
Vellay, Marc. Pierre Chareau, architecte,
meublier, 1883-1950 /. Paris , 1986. 111 p. :
ISBN 2-86930-026-3
      NYPL [3-MOF 90-11128]

**ARCHITECT-DESIGNED FURNITURE -
ITALY - EXHIBITIONS.**

L'Etrange univers de l'architecte Carlo
Mollino . Paris , c1989. 174 p. : ISBN
2-85850-494-6
NA1123.M65 A4 1989

ARCHITECT-DESIGNED HOUSES.
Stageberg, James. A house of one's own . New
York , c1991. vii, 200 p. : ISBN 0-517-58214-7 :
DDC 728/.37 20
NA7115 .S7 1991

**ARCHITECT-DESIGNED JEWELRY -
HISTORY - 20TH CENTURY -
EXHIBITIONS.**
Il Tesoro dell'architettura . Firenze [1990] 149
p. : DDC 739.27/09/0480744551 20
NK7310 .T47 1990

Les Architectes de la liberté, 1789-1799. Paris :
Ecole nationale supérieure des Beaux-Arts,
c1989. 396 p. : ill. (some col.), plans ; 23 cm.
Includes index. Catalog of an exhibition held at l'Ecole
nationale supérieure des Beaux-Arts, Oct. 4, 1989-Jan.
7, 1990. At head of title: Ministére de la culture et de
la Communication des grands travaux et du
Bicentenaire. Bibliography: p. 363-370. ISBN
2-903639-65-5
1. Architecture - France. 2. Architecture, Modern -
17th-18th centuries - France. 3. France - History -
Revolution, 1789-1799 - Pictorial works - Exhibitions. I.
Ecole nationale supérieure des beaux-arts (France).
NYPL [3-MQWF 90-11622]

ARCHITECTS AND COMMUNITY.
Out of site . Seattle , 1991. 251 p. : ISBN
0-941920-20-8 : DDC 720/.1/03 20
NA2543.S6 O9 1991 NYPL [JFD 91-5955]

**ARCHITECTS AND COMMUNITY -
SCOTLAND.**
Youngson, A. J. Urban development and the
Royal Fine Art Commissions / . Edinburgh ,
c1990. 186 p., [24] p. of plates : ISBN
0-7486-0114-7 DDC 711/.4/0941 20
NA9189 .Y68 1990

ARCHITECTS AND PATRONS.
Stageberg, James. A house of one's own . New
York , c1991. vii, 200 p. : ISBN 0-517-58214-7 :
DDC 728/.37 20
NA7115 .S7 1991

**ARCHITECTS AND PATRONS - ILLINOIS -
CHICAGO.**
Bluestone, Daniel M. Constructing Chicago / .
New Haven , c1991. p. cm. ISBN 0-300-04848-3
(alk. paper) DDC 711/.4/097731109034 20
NA9127.C4 B48 1991

**ARCHITECTS AND PATRONS - UNITED
STATES.**
Williamson, Roxanne, 1928- American
architects and the mechanics of fame / .
Austin , 1991. 286 p. : ISBN 0-292-75121-4
(cloth : alk. paper) DDC 720/.973 20
NA1996 W48 1990
NYPL [3-MQWO 91-5524]

ARCHITECTS - AUSTRIA - BIOGRAPHY.
Rochowanski, L. W. (Leopold Wolfgang), 1885-
Josef Hoffmann. Wien [c1950] 67 p.
NA1038.H6 R6
NYPL [3-MQZ (Hoffmann) 90-6083]

ARCHITECTS - BELGIUM.
Académie de Bruxelles . Bruxelles , 1989. 541
p. : ISBN 2-87143-063-2
NYPL [3-MQF+ 90-133]

**ARCHITECTS - BIOGRAPHY -
DICTIONARIES.**
The Illustrated encyclopedia of architects and
architecture / . New York, NY , 1991. p. cm.
ISBN 0-8230-2539-X : DDC 720/.3 20
NA40 .I45 1991

**ARCHITECTS - CZECHOSLOVAKIA -
BIOGRAPHY.**
Prušáková-Honzíková, Marie. Když hoří
obrazy . Praha , 1989. 247 p. : ISBN
80-7023-021-5 :
NA1034.5.H6 A2 1989

ARCHITECTS - FINLAND - BIOGRAPHY.
Schildt, Göran, 1917- [Mänskliga faktorn.
English.] Alvar Aalto, the mature years / . New
York , 1991. 328 p. : ISBN 0-8478-1329-0 DDC
720/.92 B 20
NA1455.F53 A23725 1991

ARCHITECTS - FRANCE - BIOGRAPHY.
McCormick, Thomas J. Charles-Louis
Clérisseau and the genesis of neo-Classicism / .
New York, N.Y. , Cambridge, Mass. , c1990.

xiv, 284 p. : ISBN 0-262-13262-1 DDC 720/.92 B
20
NA1053.C58 M38 1990
NYPL [3-MQZ (Clérisseau) 91-5011]

ARCHITECTS - GERMANY - BIOGRAPHY.
Isaacs, Reginald R., 1911- Gropius . Boston ,
c1991. xix, 344 p. : ISBN 0-8212-1753-4 : DDC
720/.92 B 20
NA1088.G85 I79 1991
NYPL [3-MQZ (Gropius) 91-5539]

Lange, Günther. Alexis de Chateauneuf, ein
Hamburger Baumeister, 1799-1853 /.
Hamburg , 1965. 147 p. :
NYPL [3-MQZ (Chateauneuf) 91-818]

**ARCHITECTS - GERMANY - BIOGRAPHY -
EXHIBITIONS.**
Robert Vorhoelzer, ein Architektenleben .
München , c1990. 296 p. : ISBN 3-7667-0960-7
NA1088.V67 R6 1990

**ARCHITECTS - GERMANY - LEIPZIG -
BIOGRAPHY.**
Hocquél, Wolfgang. Leipzig . Berlin , c1990.
284 p. : ISBN 3-350-00333-8 DDC 720/.9432/122
20
NA1086.L4 H63 1990

**ARCHITECTS - GREAT BRITAIN -
BIOGRAPHY - DICTIONARIES.**
Who's who in architecture 1914, 1923, 1926
[microform]. London , 1987. 17 microfiches ;
ISBN 1-85035-006-X : DDC 720/.92/2 19
*NA40 NYPL [*XMC-755 & *XMC-755+]*

**ARCHITECTS - GREAT BRITAIN -
CORRESPONDENCE.**
Lutyens, Edwin Landseer, Sir, 1869-1944. The
letters of Edwin Lutyens to his wife Lady
Emily /. London , 1985. 454 p. : ISBN
0-00-217063-9 : DDC 720/.92/4 B 19
NA997.L8 A3 1985
NYPL [3-MQZ (Lutyens) 90-13062]

Architect's guide to Paris /. Salvadori, Renzo.
Sevenoaks, Kent, England , 1990. 137 p. :
ISBN 0-408-50068-9 DDC 720/.944/361 20
NA1050 .S25 1990

Architect's guide to Rome /. Salvadori, Renzo.
London , Boston , 1990. 144 p. : ISBN
0-408-50054-9 DDC 720/.945/632 20
NA1120 .S27 1990

Architects in practice, New York City, 1900-1940
/. Ward, James. Union, N.J. [1989] xviii, 87
p. ; DDC 720/.25/7471 20
NA55.N5 W3 1989

ARCHITECTS - ITALY - BIOGRAPHY.
Schumacher, Thomas L. Surface & symbol .
New York, NY : London : 295 p. : ISBN
0-910413-59-2 (alk. paper) : DDC 720/.92 20
NA1123.T4 S37 1990
NYPL [3-MQZ (Terragni) 91-4868]

**ARCHITECTS - ITALY - MILAN -
BIOGRAPHY.**
Broggi, Luigi, 1851-1926. I miei ricordi,
1851-1924 . Milano, Italy , c1989. 301 p. :
ISBN 88-20-43560-8 : DDC 720/.92 B 20
NA1123.B76 A2 1989

ARCHITECTS - JAPAN - BIBLIOGRAPHY.
Noffsinger, James Philip. Lesser published
Japanese architects alphabetically arranged / .
Monticello, Ill. , 1981- v. ; DDC 016.72/092/2
19
Z5961.J3 N63 NA1558
NYPL [3-MQWS 84-2642]

**ARCHITECTS - JAPAN - PSYCHOLOGY -
EXHIBITIONS.**
Emerging Japanese architects of the 1990s / .
New York , 1991. 121 p. : DDC 720/.952/09045
20
NA1555 .E44 1991
NYPL [3-MQWS+ 91-6807]

**ARCHITECTS - MASSACHUSETTS -
BOSTON - DIRECTORIES.**
Directory of Boston architects, 1846-1970 .
Cambridge, Mass. (P.O. Box 129, Cambridge
02142) [1984]. 72 p. ; DDC 720/.25/74461 20
NA55.B67 D57 1984

**ARCHITECTS - NEW MEXICO -
BIOGRAPHY.**
Stedman, Myrtle. A house not made with hands
/. Santa Fe, N.M. , c1990. 110 p. ; ISBN
0-86534-145-1 : DDC 720/.92 B 20
NA737.S637 A2 1990
NYPL [3-MQZ (Stedman) 91-6674]

**ARCHITECTS - NEW YORK (N.Y.) -
DIRECTORIES.**
The Restoration directory . New York, NY ,
1990. 110 p. : *NYPL [MQWO 91-6663]*

Ward, James. Architects in practice, New York
City, 1900-1940 /. Union, N.J. [1989] xviii, 87
p. ; DDC 720/.25/7471 20
NA55.N5 W3 1989

**ARCHITECTS - PROFESSIONAL ETHICS -
FRANCE.**
Benjamin, Isabelle. Evolution de la
professionnalité des architectes . Paris [1990]
109 p. ; ISBN 2-11-085420-0 :
NA1996 .B46 1990

ARCHITECTS - PSYCHOLOGY.
Betsky, Aaron. Violated perfection . New
York , 1990. 208 p. : ISBN 0-8478-1269-3 DDC
724/.6 20
NA680 .B497 1990 NYPL [3-MQV 91-3682]

ARCHITECTS - SPAIN - BIOGRAPHY.
Arquitectura española contemporánea .
Barcelona , c1990. 192 p. : ISBN 84-252-1429-7
DDC 720/.946/09048 20
NA1308 .A84 1990
NYPL [3-MQWH 91-3890]

**ARCHITECTS - SPAIN - CUENCA -
BIOGRAPHY.**
Rokiski Lázaro, María Luz. Arquitectura del
siglo XVI en Cuenca . Cuenca , 1989. xxi, 464
p. : ISBN 84-505-8542-2
NA1311.C84 R66 1989

**ARCHITECTS - SPAIN - GUIPÚZCOA -
BIOGRAPHY.**
Astiazarain Achabal, María Isabel. Arquitectos
guipuzcoanos del siglo XVIII /. Guipúzcoa
[1988?-1990?] 2 v. : ISBN 84-505-7463-3
NA1109.G85 A88 1988

**ARCHITECTS - SWITZERLAND -
BIOGRAPHY.**
Hannes Meyer, 1889-1954 . Berlin , c1989. 368
p. : ISBN 3-433-02053-1 : DDC 720/.92 20
NA1353.M4 H35 1989

ARCHITECTS - TEXAS - BIOGRAPHY.
Hafertepe, Kenneth, 1955- Abner Cook .
Austin , c1991. p. cm. ISBN 0-87611-102-9
(cloth) DDC 720/.92 B 20
NA737.C66 H3 1991

**ARCHITECTS - TEXAS - HOUSTON -
BIOGRAPHY.**
Nicholson, Patrick James, 1921- William Ward
Watkin and the Rice Institute / . Houston,
Tex. , c1991. p. cm. ISBN 0-88415-012-7 DDC
727/.3/092 20
NA737.W39 N5 1991

**ARCHITECTS - UNITED STATES -
BIOGRAPHY.**
Guiton, Jacques. A life in three lands . Boston ,
c1991. 175 p. : ISBN 0-8283-1937-5 : DDC
720/.92 B 20
NA737.G8 A2 1991
NYPL [3-MQZ (Guiton) 91-5761]

Johnson, Donald Leslie. Frank Lloyd Wright
versus America . Cambridge, Mass. , c1990. xi,
436 p. : ISBN 0-262-10044-4 DDC 720/.92 B 20
NA737.W7 J6 1990
NYPL [3-MQZ (Wright) 91-4307]

West, J. (Jack) The lives of an architect / .
Sarasota, Fla. , c1988. 128 p. : ISBN
0-929464-00-1 DDC 720/.92 B 20
NA737.W47 A2 1988
NYPL [3-MQZ+ (West) 90-11082]

Wiseman, Carter. I.M. Pei . New York , 1990.
320 p. : ISBN 0-8109-3709-3 DDC 720/.92 B 20
NA737.P365 W57 1990
NYPL [3-MQZ (Pei) 90-12859]

**ARCHITECTS - UNITED STATES -
BIOGRAPHY - JUVENILE LITERATURE.**
McDonough, Yona Zeldis. Frank Lloyd Wright
/. New York , 1991. p. cm. ISBN 0-7910-1626-9
DDC 720/.92 B 20
NA737.W7 M37 1991

**ARCHITECTS - UNITED STATES -
CONGRESSES.**
Thinking the present . New York, NY , c1990.
136 p. : ISBN 0-910413-93-2
NYPL [3-MQWO 90-13419]

**ARCHITECTS - UNITED STATES -
INTERVIEWS.**
Cuff, Dana, 1953- Architecture . Cambridge,

Mass. , c1991. xi, 306 p. : ISBN 0-262-03175-2 :
DDC 720/.68 20
NA1996 .C84 1991
NYPL [3-MQWO 91-7317]

**ARCHITECTS - UNITED STATES -
SELECTION AND APPOINTMENT.**
Williamson, Roxanne, 1928- American
architects and the mechanics of fame /.
Austin , 1991. 286 p. : ISBN 0-292-75121-4
(cloth : alk. paper) DDC 720/.973 20
NA1996 W48 1990
NYPL [3-MQWO 91-5524]

**ARCHITECTS' WIVES - CZECHOSLOVAKIA -
BIOGRAPHY.**
Prušáková-Honzíková, Marie. Když hoří
obrazy . Praha , 1989. 247 p. ; ISBN
80-7023-021-5 :
NA1034.5.H6 A2 1989

**ARCHITECTS' WIVES - GREAT BRITAIN -
CORRESPONDENCE.**
Lutyens, Edwin Landseer, Sir, 1869-1944. The
letters of Edwin Lutyens to his wife Lady
Emily /. London , 1985. 454 p. : ISBN
0-00-217063-9 : DDC 720/.92/4 B 19
NA997.L8 A3 1985
NYPL [3-MQZ (Lutyens) 90-13062]

**ARCHITECTS - YUGOSLAVIA -
BIOGRAPHY.**
Karlić-Kapetanović, Jelica. Juraj Najdhart--život
i djelo /. Sarajevo , 1990. 383 p. : ISBN
86-21-00357-0
NA1453.N4 K3 1990

ARCHITECTURAL ACOUSTICS.
Kuttruff, Heinrich. Room acoustics /. London ,
New York , 1991. xiii, 329 p. : ISBN
1-85166-576-5 DDC 729/.29 20
NA2800 .K87 1991

Architectural and ornament drawings . Myers,
Mary L., 1940- New York , 1991. p. cm. ISBN
0-87099-625-8 DDC 741.944/09/0330747471 20
NC246 .M94 1991

Architectural Association (Great Britain) Wilson,
Peter, 1950- Western objects Eastern fields .
London , c1989. 64 p. : ISBN 1-87089-019-1
NYPL [3-MQZ+ (Wilson) 90-4013]

Architectural contract document production /.
Berg, Thomas, 1944- New York , 1991. p. cm.
ISBN 0-07-004857-6 DDC 720/.28/4 20
NA2584 .B47 1991

**ARCHITECTURAL CONTRACTS -
DOCUMENTATION.**
Berg, Thomas, 1944- Architectural contract
document production /. New York , 1991. p.
cm. ISBN 0-07-004857-6 DDC 720/.28/4 20
NA2584 .B47 1991

**ARCHITECTURAL CONTRACTS - UNITED
STATES - ADMINISTRATION -
HANDBOOKS, MANUALS, ETC.**
Pachner, Edmond, 1916- Handbook of
architectural contract administration /. New
York , 1992. p. cm. ISBN 0-471-55004-3 DDC
720/.68/7 20
NA1996 .P3 1992

**ARCHITECTURAL DECORATION AND
ORNAMENT. see DECORATION AND
ORNAMENT, ARCHITECTURAL.**

ARCHITECTURAL DESIGN.
Brawne, Michael. From idea to building .
Oxford , Boston , 1991. p. cm. ISBN
0-7506-1271-1 : DDC 720 20
NA2750 .B66 1991

In what style should we build? . Santa Monica,
Calif. , 1991. p. cm. ISBN 0-89236-199-9 : DDC
720/.1 20
NA2500 .I5 1991

ARCHITECTURAL DESIGN - AWARDS.
Anthony, Kathryn H. Juries on trial . New
York , 19. p. cm. ISBN 0-442-00235-1 DDC
729/.079 20
NA2750 .A64 1991

**ARCHITECTURAL DESIGN - DATA
PROCESSING.**
Buehrens, Carol. DataCAD for the architect /.
Blue Ridge Summit, PA , c1991. xxi, 450 p. :
ISBN 0-8306-3746-X (pbk.) : DDC
720/.28/402855369 20
NA2728 .B84 1991

Hersey, George L. Possible Palladian villas .
Cambridge, Mass. , c1992. p. cm. ISBN

0-262-08210-1 DDC 728.8/092 20
NA7125 .H47 1992

Jacobs, Stephen Paul. The CAD design studio .
New York , c1991. vi, 120 p. : ISBN
0-07-032227-9 DDC 721/.0285 20
NA2728 .J33 1991

Kahlen, Hans. CAD-Einsatz in der Architektur
/. Stuttgart , c1989. 200 p. : ISBN 3-17-010297-4
NA2728 .K38 1989

Löffler, Christoph, 1957- Contributions to
architectural design in digital signal processing
/. Konstanz , 1990. xiii, 277 p., [1] leaf of
plates : ISBN 3-89191-379-6 : DDC 621.382/2 20
NA2728 .L64 1990

**ARCHITECTURAL DESIGN - DATA
PROCESSING - EVALUATION.**
Evaluating and predicting design performance /.
New York, N.Y. , c1991. p. cm. ISBN
0-471-85385-2 DDC 721/.0285 20
NA2728 .E94 1991

ARCHITECTURAL DESIGN - EVALUATION.
Anthony, Kathryn H. Juries on trial . New
York , 19. p. cm. ISBN 0-442-00235-1 DDC
729/.079 20
NA2750 .A64 1991

**ARCHITECTURAL DESIGN -
FORECASTING.**
Mansfield, Howard. Cosmopolis . New
Brunswick, N.J. , c1990. vii, 165 p. : ISBN
0-88285-131-4 DDC 307.76/4 20
HT330 .M34 1990
NYPL [3-MQV 90-13391]

Architectural design profile, 0003-8504 .
(60) Fondation Le Corbusier. Drawings from
the Le Corbusier archive /. London , New
York , c1986. 88 p. : DDC 720/.22/22 20
NA2707.L4 A4 1986

**ARCHITECTURAL DESIGN - STUDY AND
TEACHING.**
Enseigner la conception /. Paris , 1986-<1989.
v. <1, 4 > :
NA2750 .E58 1986

ARCHITECTURAL DESIGN - TECHNIQUE.
Garcia, Nicolas B. Learning architectural
drafting & design /. Albany, N.Y. , c1992. p.
cm. ISBN 0-8273-4633-6 (textbook) DDC
720/.28/4 20
NA2708 .G3 1992

**ARCHITECTURAL DESIGN -
TERMINOLOGY.**
Ballast, David Kent. Architecture, design, and
construction word finder /. Englewood Cliffs,
N.J. , c1991. p. cm. ISBN 0-13-044397-2 DDC
720/.3 20
NA31 .B34 1991

**ARCHITECTURAL DESIGN - THEMES,
MOTIVES.**
Santiago Calatrava . Basel , Boston , 1991. p.
cm. ISBN 0-8176-2460-0 DDC 720/.92 20
NA1313.C35 S26 1991

**ARCHITECTURAL DESIGNS. see
ARCHITECTURE - DESIGNS AND
PLANS.**

**Architectural detailing for commercial
construction** /. Farmer, Gene (Eugene Davis)
New York , c1991. p. cm. ISBN 0-07-019983-3
DDC 725/.21/028 20
NA2718 .F37 1991

Architectural detailing in residential interiors /.
Staebler, Wendy W. New York , 1990. 247 p. :
ISBN 0-8230-0253-5 : DDC 729 20
NA2718 .S7 1990 *NYPL [3-MQG 90-10925]*

**ARCHITECTURAL DETAILS. see
ARCHITECTURE - DETAILS.**

**Architectural details from the early twentieth
century** /. Knobloch, Philip G. (Philip George),
b. 1893. [Good practice in construction].
Washington, D.C. [1991] 1 v. (unpaged) :
ISBN 1-558-35034-9 : DDC 721/.022/2 20
NA2840 .K58 1991

**ARCHITECTURAL DRAWING - 18TH
CENTURY - GERMANY.**
Schneider, Erich. Balthasar Neumann,
1687-1753 . München , c1987. 48 p. :
NYPL [3-MQZ+ (Neumann) 91-6584]

**ARCHITECTURAL DRAWING - 19TH
CENTURY - FINLAND - CATALOGS.**
Suomen Rakennustaiteen Museo. Arkisto.

Suomen Rakennustaiteen Museon Arkisto .
Helsinki [1989] 288 p. : ISBN 951-9229-60-4
NA2706.F5 S86 1989

**ARCHITECTURAL DRAWING - 19TH
CENTURY - SPAIN - BARCELONA -
CATALOGS.**
Barcelona fi de segle . Barcelona [198-] 1
portfolio ([10] leaves of plates) :
NA2706.S7 B37 1980z

**ARCHITECTURAL DRAWING - 19TH
CENTURY - UNITED STATES -
EXHIBITIONS.**
Architectural drawings of the Old Executive
Office Building, 1871-1888 . Washington, DC ,
1988. vii, 71 p. : ISBN 1-558-35012-8
NYPL [3-MQWO+ 91-4241]

**ARCHITECTURAL DRAWING - 20TH
CENTURY - ARGENTINA - BUENOS
AIRES - EXHIBITIONS.**
Glusberg, Jorge. Escuela de Buenos Aires .
Buenos Aires, Argentina [between 1984 and
1990] 31 p. :
NA2706.A7 G58 1984

**ARCHITECTURAL DRAWING - 20TH
CENTURY - EXHIBITIONS.**
Avery Library. Contemporary architectural
drawings . San Francisco , c1991. p. cm. ISBN
0-87654-767-6 : DDC 720/.22/2 20
NA2695.U6 A86 1991

**ARCHITECTURAL DRAWING - 20TH
CENTURY - FINLAND - CATALOGS.**
Suomen Rakennustaiteen Museo. Arkisto.
Suomen Rakennustaiteen Museon Arkisto .
Helsinki [1989] 288 p. : ISBN 951-9229-60-4
NA2706.F5 S86 1989

**ARCHITECTURAL DRAWING - 20TH
CENTURY - FRANCE.**
Andreu, Paul. Paul Andreu /. Paris , 1990. 1 v.
(unpaged) : ISBN 2-907687-06-9 : DDC
720/.22/22 20
NA2707.A55 A4 1990

Ripault, Jacques, 1953- Jacques Ripault /.
Paris , 1990. 1 v. (unpaged) : ISBN
2-907687-05-0 : DDC 720/.22/22 20
NA2707.R56 A4 1990

Six projets /. Paris , c1990. 509 p. :
NA2707.O34 A4 1990

**ARCHITECTURAL DRAWING - 20TH
CENTURY - FRANCE - CATALOGS.**
Fondation Le Corbusier. Drawings from the Le
Corbusier archive /. London , New York ,
c1986. 88 p. : DDC 720/.22/22 20
NA2707.L4 A4 1986

Le Corbusier, 1887-1965. The Le Corbusier
archive /. New York , Paris , 1982-1984. 32
v. : ISBN 0-8240-5050-9 (v. 1) DDC 720/.22/2 19
NA2707.L4 A4 1982d *NYPL [3-MQZ+ (Le
Corbusier) 90-10105]*

**ARCHITECTURAL DRAWING - 20TH
CENTURY - ITALY.**
Scarpa, Carlo. The other city . Berlin , c1989.
397 p. : ISBN 3-433-02097-3 DDC 720/.92 20
NA1123.S35 A4 1989

**ARCHITECTURAL DRAWING - 20TH
CENTURY - SOVIET UNION -
EXHIBITIONS.**
Architectural drawings of the Russian
avant-garde /. New York , c1990. 143 p. :
ISBN 0-87070-556-3
NYPL [3-MQG 90-11730]

**ARCHITECTURAL DRAWING - 20TH
CENTURY - THEMES, MOTIVES.**
Lacy, Bill. 100 contemporary architects . New
York , 1991. p. cm. ISBN 0-8109-3661-5 DDC
720/.22/222 20
NA2700 .L26 1991

**ARCHITECTURAL DRAWING - 20TH
CENTURY - UNITED STATES.**
Eisenman, Peter, 1932- Peter Eisenman .
Berlin , 1989. [46] p. :
NYPL [3-MQZ (Eisenman) 90-12528]

**ARCHITECTURAL DRAWING - 20TH
CENTURY - UNITED STATES -
CATALOGS.**
Kahn, Louis I., 1901-1974. The Louis I. Kahn
archive . New York , 1987. 7 v. : ISBN
0-8240-1817-6 (v. 1 : alk. paper) : DDC
720/.22/2 19
NA2707.K33 A4 1987
NYPL [MQZ+ (Kahn) 90-2931]

ARCHITECTURAL DRAWING - BIBLIOGRAPHY.
Cable, Carole. The architectural drawing, its development and history, 1300-1950 /. Monticello, Ill. , 1978. 18 p. ;
Z5943.A73 C32 NA2700
*NYPL [*XMC-357]*

ARCHITECTURAL DRAWING - DATA PROCESSING.
Buehrens, Carol. DataCAD for the architect /. Blue Ridge Summit, PA , c1991. xxi, 450 p. : ISBN 0-8306-3746-X (pbk.) : DDC 720/.28/402855369 20
NA2728 .B84 1991

Burden, Ernest E., 1934- Perspective grid sourcebook . New York , 1991. p. cm. ISBN 0-442-21132-5 DDC 720/.28/40285 20
NA2728 .B87 1991

ARCHITECTURAL DRAWING - DETAILING.
Farmer, Gene (Eugene Davis) Architectural detailing for commercial construction /. New York , c1991. p. cm. ISBN 0-07-019983-3 DDC 725/.21/028 20
NA2718 .F37 1991

Staebler, Wendy W. Architectural detailing in residential interiors /. New York , 1990. 247 p. : ISBN 0-8230-0253-5 : DDC 729 20
NA2718 .S7 1990 *NYPL [3-MQG 90-10925]*

The architectural drawing, its development and history, 1300-1950 /. Cable, Carole. Monticello, Ill. , 1978. 18 p. ;
Z5943.A73 C32 NA2700
*NYPL [*XMC-357]*

ARCHITECTURAL DRAWING - MEASURED DRAWINGS. see ARCHITECTURAL DRAWING.

ARCHITECTURAL DRAWING - RENDERING. see ARCHITECTURAL RENDERING.

ARCHITECTURAL DRAWING - TECHNIQUE.
Garcia, Nicolas B. Learning architectural drafting & design /. Albany, N.Y. , c1992. p. cm. ISBN 0-8273-4633-6 (textbook) DDC 720/.28/4 20
NA2708 .G3 1992

Schaller, Thomas W. (Thomas Wells), 1950- Architecture in watercolor /. New York, N.Y. , c1990. x, 234 p. : ISBN 0-442-23484-8 DDC 751.42/244 20
NA2726.5 .S34 1990
NYPL [3-MBO 90-11736]

Sutherland, Martha, 1927- Graphic fundamentals . New York, N.Y. , 1991. p. cm. ISBN 0-8306-3480-0 : DDC 720/.28/4 20
NA2708 .S88 1991

Architectural drawings and leisure works /. Uy, Bon-Hui. Taipei, Taiwan, ROC , Honolulu, Hawaii, U. S.A. , 1990. 159 p. : DDC 720/.22/22 20
NA2707.U9 A4 1990

Architectural drawings and watercolors by Jakob Ignaz Hittorff, 1792-1867 / [translated by Tawney Becker ... et al.]. Cologne : Wallraf-Richartz-Museum ; Washington, D.C. : Smithsonian Institution Traveling Exhibition Service, 1990. 64 p. : ill. ; 22 x 28 cm. "Published on the occasion of an exhibition on Jakob Ignaz Hittorff organized by the Smithsonian Institution Traveling Exhibition Service in collaboration with the Wallraf-Richartz-Museum in Cologne"--T.p. verso. Includes bibliographical references (p. 51). ISBN 0-86528-040-1 DDC 720/.22/22 20
1. Hittorff, Jacques Ignace, 1792-1867 - Exhibitions. I. Hittorff, Jacques Ignace, 1792-1867. II. Smithsonian Institution. Traveling Exhibition Service. III. Wallraf-Richartz-Museum.
NA2707.H58 A4 1990
NYPL [3-MQZ (Hittorff) 91-5615]

Architectural drawings of the Old Executive Office Building, 1871-1888 : creating an American masterpiece / edited by Elsa M. Santoyo ; text by Elsa M. Santoyo, Paula Mohr, Mary E. Bellor. Washington, DC : American Institute of Architects Press : American Architectural Foundation, 1988. vii, 71 p. : ill. (some col.) ; 24 x 31 cm. At head of title: Creating an American masterpiece. "Published on the occasion of the exhibition ... at the Octagon Museum, Washington, DC, May 26-June 30,

1988"--T.p. verso. Bibliography: p. 6. ISBN 1-558-35012-8
1. Mullett, A. B. (Alfred Bult), 1834-1890 - Exhibitions. 2. Von Ezdorf, Richard, 1848-1926 - Exhibitions. 3. Old Executive Office Building (Washington, D.C.) - Exhibitions. 4. Architectural drawing - 19th century - United States - Exhibitions. 5. Washington (D.C.) - Buildings, structures, etc. - Exhibitions. I. Santoyo, Elsa M. II. Mohr, Paula. III. Bellor, Mary E. IV. Octagon (Washington, D.C.). V. Title: Creating an American masterpiece. *NYPL [3-MQWO+ 91-4241]*

Architectural drawings of the Russian avant-garde / [essay by Catherine Cooke]. New York : Museum of Modern Art : Distributed by H.N. Abrams, c1990. 143 p. : ill. (some col.) ; 28 cm. Catalog of an exhibition held at the Museum of Modern Art, New York, June 21- Sept. 4, 1990. Includes bibliographical references (p. 140-141) ISBN 0-87070-556-3
1. Architectural drawing - 20th century - Soviet Union - Exhibitions. 2. Avant-garde (Aesthetics) - Soviet Union - Exhibitions. I. Cooke, Catherine. II. Museum of Modern Art (New York, N.Y.).
NYPL [3-MQG 90-11730]

ARCHITECTURAL ENGINEERING. see BUILDING; BUILDING, IRON AND STEEL.

Architectural guides for travelers.
Chan, Charis. Imperial China /. San Francisco , 1992. p. cm. ISBN 0-8118-0018-0 DDC 720/.951 20
NA1543.5 .C4 1992

McIntyre, Anthony. Medieval architecture in Tuscany and Umbria /. San Francisco , 1992. p. cm. ISBN 0-87701-846-4 DDC 720/.945/50902 20
NA1119.T8 M37 1992

Pemberton, Delia. Ancient Egypt /. San Francisco , 1992. p. cm. ISBN 0-87701-847-2 (pb) DDC 722/.2 20
NA215 .P36 1992

ARCHITECTURAL HISTORIANS - GERMANY - BIOGRAPHY.
Posener, Julius. Fast so alt wie das Jahrhundert /. Berlin , c1990. 312 p. : ISBN 3-88680-381-3 : DDC 720/.92 B 20
NA2599.8.P67 A2 1990

Architectural History Foundation (New York, N. Y.) Mead, Christopher Curtis. Charles Garnier's Paris Opéra . New York, N.Y. , Cambridge, Mass. , c1991. p. cm. ISBN 0-262-13275-3 DDC 725/.822/092 20
NA6840.F72 P379 1991

The architectural history of Glastonbury Abbey /. Willis, Robert, 1800-1875. Lampeter , 1990. x, 91 p., [6] leaves of plates : ISBN 0-947992-44-8 *NYPL [3-MRBH 91-7084]*

ARCHITECTURAL IRONWORK - EUROPE - HISTORY.
Zimelli, Umberto. [Ferro battuto. English.] Decorative ironwork /. [London , 1987. 154 p. : ISBN 0-304-32158-3 (pbk.) : DDC 739/.474 19
NK8242 *NYPL [3-MNK 91-5042]*

ARCHITECTURAL IRONWORK - FRANCE - EXHIBITIONS.
Guimard, Hector, 1867-1942. Hector Guimard . Paris , 1971. 45 p. :
NYPL [3-MRX 90-7184]

ARCHITECTURAL IRONWORK - HUNGARY.
Pereházy, Karoly. Stílus és technika a kovácsoltvas-művességben /. Budapest , 1986. 240 p. : ISBN 963-10-6741-6
NK8271.H8 P47 1986

ARCHITECTURAL IRONWORK - NEW YORK (STATE) - ALBANY.
Waite, Diana S. Ornamental ironwork . Albany, N.Y. , c1990. 141 p. : ISBN 0-9625368-0-6
NYPL [3-MRX 90-12349]

ARCHITECTURAL IRONWORK - NEW YORK (STATE) - TROY.
Waite, Diana S. Ornamental ironwork . Albany, N.Y. , c1990. 141 p. : ISBN 0-9625368-0-6
NYPL [3-MRX 90-12349]

ARCHITECTURAL IRONWORK - UNITED STATES - THEMES, MOTIVES.
Southworth, Michael. Ornamental ironwork . New York , c1991. p. cm. ISBN 0-07-159804-5 DDC 739.4/773 20
NA3503.A1 S67 1991

ARCHITECTURAL MODELS.
Schattner, Thomas G. Griechische Hausmodelle . Berlin , c1990. 229 p., [29] p. of plates : ISBN 3-7861-1585-0
NYPL [3-MQM 91-6516]

ARCHITECTURAL MODELS - SPAIN - BARCELONA.
Transformación de un frente maritimo . Barcelona , 1988. 120 p. : ISBN 84-252-1368-1
NYPL [MQWH 89-19333]

Architectural monographs (London, England) .
(13) Steele, James. Hassan Fathy /. London , New York , 1988. 149 p. : ISBN 0-312-01140-7 (U. S. : pbk.) : DDC 720/.92/4 19
NA1585.F37 S74 1988
NYPL [3-MQZ+ (Fathy) 88-4615]

(14) Andō, Tadao, 1941- Tadao Andō. London , New York , 1990. 128 p. : ISBN 1-85490-010-2 (hardback : London)
NYPL [3-MQZ+ (Andō) 90-11589]

(6) Lutyens, Edwin Landseer, Sir, 1869-1944. Edwin Lutyens. London , New York , 1986. 112 p., [7] folded leaves of plates : ISBN 0-85670-422-9 (paper) DDC 728.8/092/4 19
NA997.L8 I57 1986
NYPL [3-MQZ+ (Lutyens) 87-2200]

Richard Rogers + architects. London , New York , 1985. 160 p. : ISBN 0-312-68207-7 (St. Martin's)
NYPL [3-MQZ+ (Rogers) 86-1924]

ARCHITECTURAL PERSPECTIVE. see PERSPECTIVE.

ARCHITECTURAL PHOTOGRAPHY. see PHOTOGRAPHY, ARCHITECTURAL.

ARCHITECTURAL POLYCHROMY. see COLOR IN ARCHITECTURE.

ARCHITECTURAL PRACTICE - CANADA - CASE STUDIES.
Wilson, Forrest, 1918- Architecture . New York , c1990. xii, 243 p. : ISBN 0-442-23948-3 DDC 720/.68 20
NA1996 .W517 1990
NYPL [3-MQWM 90-10923]

ARCHITECTURAL PRACTICE - DATA PROCESSING.
Kahlen, Hans. CAD-Einsatz in der Architektur /. Stuttgart , c1989. 200 p. : ISBN 3-17-010297-4
NA2728 .K38 1989

ARCHITECTURAL PRACTICE - FRANCE.
Benjamin, Isabelle. Evolution de la professionnalité des architectes . Paris [1990] 109 p. ; ISBN 2-11-085420-0 :
NA1996 .B46 1990

ARCHITECTURAL PRACTICE, INTERNATIONAL.
Vitou, Elisabeth. Gabriel Guévrékian, 1900-1970 . Paris , c1987. 150 p. : ISBN 2-86649-003-7 : DDC 720/.92/4 19
NA1053.G77 V5 1987
NYPL [3-MQZ (Guévrékian) 91-4588]

ARCHITECTURAL PRACTICE - MANAGEMENT.
Stasiowski, Frank, 1948- Project management for the design professional /. New York , 1991. p. cm. ISBN 0-8230-4413-0 DDC 720/.68 20
NA1996 .S74 1991

ARCHITECTURAL PRACTICE - UNITED STATES.
American Black architects /. New York, N.Y. , c1991. p. cm. ISBN 1-87827-138-5 : DDC 720/.89/96073 20
NA738.N5 A45 1991

Cuff, Dana, 1953- Architecture . Cambridge, Mass. , c1991. xi, 306 p. : ISBN 0-262-03175-2 : DDC 720/.68 20
NA1996 .C84 1991
NYPL [3-MQWO 91-7317]

ARCHITECTURAL PRACTICE - UNITED STATES - MANAGEMENT.
Kaderlan, Norman S. Designing your practice . New York , c1991. xii, 191 p. : ISBN 0-07-033254-1 DDC 720/.68 20
NA1996 .K3 1991 *NYPL [JBE 91-659]*

Architectural principles in the age of historicism /. Van Pelt, Robert Jan. New Haven , 1991. p. cm. ISBN 0-300-04999-4 DDC 720/.1 20
NA2500 .V34 1991

ARCHITECTURAL RENDERING.
Forseth, Kevin. Rendering the visual field .
New York, N.Y. , c1991. p. cm.   ISBN
   0-442-20042-0   DDC 720/.28/4 20
NA2780 .F67 1991

**ARCHITECTURAL RENDERING - UNITED
STATES - AWARDS - EXHIBITIONS.**
Architecture in perspective . New York, N.Y. ,
c1991. p. cm.   ISBN 0-442-00700-0   DDC
   720/.22/27309043 20
NA2780 .A73 1991

**ARCHITECTURAL RENDERINGS. see
ARCHITECTURAL RENDERING.**

**ARCHITECTURAL SERVICES MARKETING -
CANADA - CASE STUDIES.**
Wilson, Forrest, 1918- Architecture . New
York , c1990. xii, 243 p. :   ISBN 0-442-23948-3
   DDC 720/.68 20
NA1996 .W517 1990
     NYPL [3-MQWM 90-10923]

**ARCHITECTURAL SERVICES MARKETING -
UNITED STATES.**
Pickar, Roger L. Marketing for design firms in
the 1990s /. Washington, D.C. [1991] x, 95
p. :   ISBN 1-558-35037-3 :   DDC 720/.68/8 20
NA1996 .P5 1991

Stasiowski, Frank, 1948- Staying small
successfully . New York , c1991. xv, 297 p. :
   ISBN 0-471-50652-4   DDC 720/.68 20
NA1996 .S75 1991

Williamson, Roxanne, 1928- American
architects and the mechanics of fame /.
Austin , 1991. 286 p. :   ISBN 0-292-75121-4
   (cloth : alk. paper)   DDC 720/.973 20
NA1996 W48 1990
     NYPL [3-MQWO 91-5524]

**ARCHITECTURAL SYMBOLISM. see
SYMBOLISM IN ARCHITECTURE.**

**ARCHITECTURAL WOODWORK - YEMEN -
ṢAN'A'.**
Bonnenfant, Guillemette. L'art du bois à
Sanaa . Aix-en-Provence , c1987. 208 p. :
   ISBN 2-85744-315-3
NA3573.6.Y42 S254 1987
     NYPL [3-MRX+ 91-4933]

Architecture . Cuff, Dana, 1953- Cambridge,
Mass. , c1991. xi, 306 p. :   ISBN 0-262-03175-2 :
   DDC 720/.68 20
NA1996 .C84 1991
     NYPL [3-MQWO 91-7317]

Architecture . Scully, Vincent Joseph, 1920- New
York , 1991. p. cm.   ISBN 0-312-06292-3 :   DDC
   720 20
NA2520 .S37 1991

Architecture . Spence, William Perkins, 1925-
Mission Hills, Calif. , c1991. x, 661 p. :   ISBN
   0-02-677123-3 (text)   DDC 721 20
NA2540 .S6 1991

Architecture . Wilson, Forrest, 1918- New York ,
c1990. xii, 243 p. :   ISBN 0-442-23948-3   DDC
   720/.68 20
NA1996 .W517 1990
     NYPL [3-MQWM 90-10923]

ARCHITECTURE.
Aguirre, Marco Antonio. Arquitectura,
fenómeno de controversia /. [Oaxaca,
Mexico?] c1990. 61 p., [88] p. of plates :
   DDC 720 20
NA27 .A36 1990

Benjamin, Asher, 1773-1845. The country
builder's assistant . Greenfield, Mass. , 1805.
[36] p., [1], 37 leaves of plates (2 folded) :
   DDC 720 20
NA2520 .B4 1805

Gordon, Douglas E. How architecture works /.
New York , c1991. xii, 190 p. :   ISBN
   0-442-23951-3   DDC 720 20
NA2520 .G58 1991

In what style should we build? . Santa Monica,
Calif. , 1991. p. cm.   ISBN 0-89236-199-9 :   DDC
   720/.1 20
NA2500 .I5 1991

Modiano, Ignacio, 1955- La ciudad en la obra
de Borromini y otros ensayos /. Santiago de
Chile , c1988. 107 p. :   DDC 720 20
NA27 .M62 1988

Norberg-Schulz, Christian. [Intentions in
architecture. French.] Système logique de

l'architecture /. Liège [1988] 304 p. :   ISBN
   2-87009-052-8 DDC 720/.1 20
NA2500 .N6714 1988

Reynaud, Léonce, 1803-1880. Traité
d'architecture . Paris , <1858-. v. <2 > ;
   DDC 720 20
NA2522 .R38 1858

Scully, Vincent Joseph, 1920- Architecture .
New York , 1991. p. cm.   ISBN 0-312-06292-3 :
   DDC 720 20
NA2520 .S37 1991

Vargas, Ramón. Historia de la teoría de la
arquitectura, el porfirismo /. [Mexico City] ,
1989. 221 p. :   ISBN 968-8406-73-2
NA200 .V37 1989

Architecture & ornament . White, Antony, 1941-
New York , 1991. p. cm.   ISBN 0-8306-3352-9 :
   DDC 720/.14 20
NA31 .W44 1991

ARCHITECTURE - EARLY WORKS TO 1800.
Serlio, Sebastiano, 1475-1554. [Tutte l'opere
d'architettura.] I sette libri dell'architettura .
Sala Bolognese , 1987. 2 v. :   DDC 720 19
NA2515 .S5 1978
     NYPL [3-MQD+ 90-10883]

Vitruvius Pollio. [De architectura. Spanish.] M.
Vitrvvio Pollion De architectvra /. Valencia ,
1978. 21, 178, [15] p. :   ISBN 84-7274-032-3
NA2515 .V618 1978
     NYPL [3-MQD+ 87-3849]

Architecture + recherches .
(1) Norberg-Schulz, Christian. [Intentions in
architecture. French.] Système logique de
l'architecture /. Liège [1988] 304 p. :   ISBN
   2-87009-052-8   DDC 720/.1 20
NA2500 .N6714 1988

Architecture, a modern view /. Rogers, Richard
George. [London] , c1990. 64 p. :   ISBN
   0-500-55022-0   *NYPL [3-MQ 91-6258]*

ARCHITECTURE - AESTHETICS.
Testa, Luciano, 1944- Le muse e i naufragio .
Paese (Treviso) , 1990. 111 p. :   DDC 720/.1 20
NA2500 .T48 1990

**ARCHITECTURE - AESTHETICS -
CONGRESSES.**
RIEA/Research Institute for Experimental
Architecture . New York, N.Y. , c1990. 1 v.
(unpaged) :   ISBN 1-87827-100-8
     NYPL [3-MQ 91-4439]

ARCHITECTURE - ALABAMA.
Palladio in Alabama . Montgomery, Ala. , 1991.
p. cm.   ISBN 0-89280-029-1   DDC
   720/.9761/07476147 20
NA730.A2 P3 1991

**ARCHITECTURE, AMERICAN - BERLIN
(GERMANY) - EXHIBITIONS.**
14x Amerika-Gedenkbibliothek . Berlin , c1989.
132 p. :   ISBN 3-433-02288-7 (pbk.)
     NYPL [3-MQWO+ 90-11060]

**ARCHITECTURE, AMERICAN -
CONGRESSES.**
Thinking the present . New York, NY , c1990.
136 p. :   ISBN 0-910413-93-2
     NYPL [3-MQWO 90-13419]

**ARCHITECTURE, AMERICAN - NEW YORK
(STATE) - LONG ISLAND -
EXHIBITIONS.**
Beaux Arch '89 . Sag Harbor, N.Y. , 1989. 119
p. :   ISBN 0-9623542-0-1
IN PROCESS   NYPL [3-MQWO 91-3337]

ARCHITECTURE, ANCIENT.
De Albentiis, Emidio, 1958- La casa dei
Romani /. Milano , c1990. 348 p., [8] p. of
plates :   ISBN 88-304-0930-8 :   DDC 728/.0937 20
NA324 .D44 1990   NYPL [JFD 91-5342]

ARCHITECTURE, ANCIENT - EGYPT.
Pemberton, Delia. Ancient Egypt /. San
Francisco , 1992. p. cm.   ISBN 0-87701-847-2 (pb)
   DDC 722/.2 20
NA215 .P36 1992

Roik, Elke. Das altägyptische Wohnhaus und
seine Darstellung im Flachbild /. Frankfurt am
Main , New York , c1988. 2 v. :   ISBN
   3-8204-0163-6
NA215 .R65 1988
     NYPL [3-MQL+ 90-8068]

**ARCHITECTURE, ANCIENT - RUSSIAN S.F.
S.R. - DAGESTANSKAÏA A.S.S.R.**

Drevniaia i srednevekovaia arkhitektura
Dagestana . Makhachkala , 1989. 184, [4] p. :
NA1492.8 .D7 1989

ARCHITECTURE AND COSMOLOGY.
Bonfiglioli, Sandra, 1940- L'architettura del
tempo . Napoli , 1990. 410 p. :   ISBN
   88-20-71912-6 :   DDC 720/.1 20
NA2500 .B625 1990

Architecture and design, 1934-1977. Franco
Albini, architecture and design, 1934-1977 .
New York, NY , c1990. 138 p. :   ISBN
   0-910413-79-7 (pbk. : alk. paper) :   DDC 720/.92
   20
NA1123.A525 A4 1990
     NYPL [3-MQZ (Albini) 91-6735]

**ARCHITECTURE AND ENERGY
CONSERVATION.**
Vale, Brenda. Green architecture . Boston ,
c1991. p. cm.   ISBN 0-8212-1866-2   DDC
   720/.472 20
NA2542.3 .V35 1991

ARCHITECTURE AND HISTORY.
Contancy and change in architecture /. College
Station , 1991. p. cm.   ISBN 0-89096-472-6 DDC
   720/.1 20
NA2543.H55 C67 1991

Harbison, Robert. The built, the unbuilt, and
the unbuildable . Cambridge, Mass. , 1991. 192
p. :   ISBN 0-262-08204-7 :   DDC 720/.1 20
NA2500 .H37 1991

Stone, Harris, 1934- Hands-on, hands-off . New
York , c1991. 191 p. :   ISBN 0-85345-824-3
   (pbk.) :   DDC 720/.1/04 20
NA2543.H55 S7 1991

ARCHITECTURE AND HISTORY - SPAIN.
Intervenciones en el patrimonio arquitectónico
(1980-1985) /. [Madrid] [1990] 465 p. :   ISBN
   84-7483-661-1   DDC 720/.28/8094609048 20
NA1301 .I57 1990

**Architecture and ideology in early medieval
Spain /.** Dodds, Jerrilynn D. University Park ,
c1990. xiv, 174 p., [72] p. of plates :   ISBN
   0-271-00671-4   DDC 720/.946/09021 20
NA1303 .D63 1989
     NYPL [3-MQWH 91-4942]

**ARCHITECTURE AND LITURGY. see
LITURGY AND ARCHITECTURE.**

Architecture and ornament. White, Antony, 1941-
Architecture & ornament . New York , 1991. p.
cm.   ISBN 0-8306-3352-9 :   DDC 720/.14 20
NA31 .W44 1991

**Architecture and planning of Graham, Anderson,
Probst, and White, 1912-1936 .** Chappell, Sally
Anderson. Chicago , 1991. p. cm.   ISBN
   0-226-10134-7   DDC 720/.92/2 20
NA737.G7 C48 1991

Architecture and power . Tittler, Robert. Oxford
[England] , New York , 1991. p. cm.   ISBN
   0-19-820230-X :   DDC 725/.13/0103 20
NA4435.G7 T5 1991

ARCHITECTURE AND SOCIETY.
Contancy and change in architecture /. College
Station , 1991. p. cm.   ISBN 0-89096-472-6   DDC
   720/.1 20
NA2543.H55 C67 1991

Holl, Steven. Edge of a city /. New York ,
1991. p. cm.   ISBN 1-87827-156-3 :   DDC
   711/.4/09048 20
NA9095 .H65 1991

Saldarriaga Roa, Alberto. Arquitectura para
todos los días . Bogotá , 1988. 95 p. :   ISBN
   958-1-70049-8
NA2543.S6 S23 1988

Schwarz, Alberto. Architektur und
Gesellschaft . Leipzig , c1989. 190 p. :   ISBN
   3-361-00254-0
NA2543.S6 S38 1989

**ARCHITECTURE AND SOCIETY -
ARGENTINA.**
Historia argentina de la vivienda de interés
social. Capital Federal [Argentina] [between
1986 and 1990- v. <1- > :
NA7292 .H57 1990

ARCHITECTURE AND SOCIETY - BRAZIL.
Artigas, João Batista Vilanova. A função social
do arquiteto /. São Paulo, SP , 1989. 93 p. :
   ISBN 85-21-30621-0   DDC 720/.1/0309810904

20
NA2543.S6 A76 1989

**ARCHITECTURE AND SOCIETY -
ENGLAND.**
Tittler, Robert. Architecture and power .
Oxford [England] , New York , 1991. p. cm.
   ISBN 0-19-820230-X : DDC 725/.13/0103 20
NA4435.G7 T5 1991

**ARCHITECTURE AND SOCIETY - EUROPE -
CONGRESSES.**
Le Projet d'architecture dans la ville, instrument
de sa transformation . Strasbourg , 1983. 50 P. ;
NA9183 .P7 1983

**ARCHITECTURE AND SOCIETY - FRANCE -
HISTORY - 18TH CENTURY.**
Vidler, Anthony. Claude-Nicolas Ledoux .
Cambridge, Mass. , c1990. 446 p. : ISBN
0-262-22032-6 DDC 720/.92 20
NA1053.L4 V5 1990
      NYPL [3-MQZ+ (Ledoux) 90-11790]

**ARCHITECTURE AND SOCIETY -
ILLINOIS - CHICAGO.**
Bluestone, Daniel M. Constructing Chicago /.
New Haven , c1991. p. cm. ISBN 0-300-04848-3
(alk. paper) DDC 711/.4/097731109034 20
NA9127.C4 B48 1991

ARCHITECTURE AND SOCIETY - SPAIN.
Dodds, Jerrilynn D. Architecture and ideology
in early medieval Spain /. University Park ,
c1990. xiv, 174 p., [72] p. of plates : ISBN
0-271-00671-4 DDC 720/.946/09021 20
NA1303 .D63 1989
      NYPL [3-MQWH 91-4942]

**ARCHITECTURE AND SOCIETY - UNITED
STATES.**
Cuff, Dana, 1953- Architecture . Cambridge,
Mass. , c1991. xi, 306 p. : ISBN 0-262-03175-2 :
DDC 720/.68 20
NA1996 .C84 1991
      NYPL [3-MQWO 91-7317]

**ARCHITECTURE AND SOCIOLOGY. see
ARCHITECTURE AND SOCIETY.**

ARCHITECTURE AND SOLAR RADIATION.
Yáñez Parareda, Guillermo. Arquitectura solar .
Madrid , 1988. 192 p. : ISBN 84-7433-542-6
DDC 720/.472 20
NA2542.S6 Y35 1988

**ARCHITECTURE AND SPACE. see SPACE
(ARCHITECTURE)**

**ARCHITECTURE AND STATE - BERLIN
(GERMANY)**
Balfour, Alan. Berlin . New York , 1990. 269
p. : ISBN 0-8478-1271-5 DDC 720/.1/03 20
NA9200.B4 B35 1990
      NYPL [3-MQWD 90-13618]

ARCHITECTURE AND STATE - ENGLAND.
Tittler, Robert. Architecture and power .
Oxford [England] , New York , 1991. p. cm.
   ISBN 0-19-820230-X : DDC 725/.13/0103 20
NA4435.G7 T5 1991

**ARCHITECTURE AND STATE - FRANCE -
VERSAILLES.**
Pérouse de Montclos, Jean-Marie. [Versailles.
English.] Versailles /. New York , 1991. p. cm.
   ISBN 1-558-59228-8 DDC 725/.17/0944366 20
NA7736.V5 P4713 1991

**ARCHITECTURE AND STATE - GERMANY -
HISTORY - 20TH CENTURY.**
Kunst auf Befehl? . München , c1990. 275 p. :
   ISBN 3-7814-0285-1 DDC 701/.03 20
N6868.5.N37 K85 1990

ARCHITECTURE AND STATE - ITALY.
Starn, Randolph. Arts of power . Berkeley ,
c1992. p. cm. ISBN 0-520-07383-5 (cloth) DDC
725/.17/0945 20
NA6815 .S787 1992

**ARCHITECTURE AND STATE - NEW YORK
(N.Y.)**
Urban Design Council. A report on the working
relationships of architects and the City of New
York. [New York] , 1971. 56 leaves ;
      NYPL [3-MQD 90-6629]

ARCHITECTURE AND STATE - SCOTLAND.
Youngson, A. J. Urban development and the
Royal Fine Art Commissions /. Edinburgh ,
c1990. 186 p., [24] p. of plates : ISBN
0-7486-0114-7 DDC 711/.4/0941 20
NA9189 .Y68 1990

**ARCHITECTURE AND STATE - UNITED
STATES.**
Voices in architectural education . New York ,
1991. p. cm. ISBN 0-89789-253-4 (alk. paper)
DDC 720/.7/073 20
NA2105 .V65 1991

Architecture and the after-life /. Colvin, Howard
Montagu. New Haven , 1991. p. cm. ISBN
0-300-05098-4 DDC 726/.8/094 20
NA6120 .C65 1991

ARCHITECTURE AND THE AGED.
Branson, Gary D. The complete guide to
barrier-free housing . White Hall, Va. , c1991.
176 p. : ISBN 1-558-70188-5 (pbk.) : DDC
720/.42 20
NA2545.A3 B7 1991

ARCHITECTURE AND THE HANDICAPPED.
Branson, Gary D. The complete guide to
barrier-free housing . White Hall, Va. , c1991.
176 p. : ISBN 1-558-70188-5 (pbk.) : DDC
720/.42 20
NA2545.A3 B7 1991

**ARCHITECTURE AND THE PHYSICALLY
HANDICAPPED - UNITED STATES.**
The Accessible housing design file /. New
York, N.Y. , c1991. p. cm. ISBN 0-442-00775-2
DDC 728/.042 20
NA2545.P5 A34 1991

**ARCHITECTURE AND WOMEN - GREAT
BRITAIN.**
Roberts, Marion. Living in a man-made world .
London , New York , 1991. xii, 177 p. : ISBN
0-415-05747-7 DDC 728/.0942 20
NA2543.W65 R64 1990
      NYPL [3-MQWK 91-6908]

**ARCHITECTURE AND WOMEN - UNITED
STATES.**
Weisman, Leslie. Discrimination by design .
Urbana , c1992. p. cm. ISBN 0-252-01849-4 (cl)
DDC 720/.1/03 20
NA2543.W65 W45 1992

**ARCHITECTURE, ANONYMOUS. see
VERNACULAR ARCHITECTURE.**

**ARCHITECTURE, ARAB. see
ARCHITECTURE, ISLAMIC.**

ARCHITECTURE - ARGENTINA.
Irigoyen, Adriana. Nueva arquitectura
Argentina . Bogotá, Colombia , 1990. 221 p. :
   ISBN 958-9082-52-1
IN PROCESS (ONLINE)
      NYPL [3-MQWN 91-5871]

**ARCHITECTURE - ARGENTINA -
CONGRESSES.**
Brandariz, Gustavo A. El aporte friulano a la
arquitectura argentina /. Buenos Aires , 1987.
52 leaves :
NA830 .B7 1987

**ARCHITECTURE - ARGENTINA -
MENDOZA (PROVINCE)**
Cirvini, Silvia A. La estructura profesional y
técnica en la construcción de Mendoza /.
[Mendoza, Argentina?] , 1989- v. <1 > :
NA4262.M46 C57 1989

ARCHITECTURE - ARGENTINA - ZÁRATE.
El Patrimonio arquitectónico de Zárate.
[Zárate] , 1988. 30 p. :
      NYPL [3-MQWN+ 90-4511]

**ARCHITECTURE, ARMENIAN - ARMENIAN
S.S.R.**
Cuneo, Paolo. Architettura armena dal quarto al
diciannovesimo secolo /. Roma , 1988. 2 v.
(923 p.), [1] folded leaf of plates) : ISBN
88-7813-154-7 (set)
      NYPL [3-MQW 90-12681]

**ARCHITECTURE, ARMENIAN -
AZERBAIJAN S.S.R. - NAGORNO-
KARABAKHSKAIA AVTONOMNAĬA
OBLAST'.**
Gharabagh /. Milano, Italia , 1988. 107 p. :
   ISBN 88-85822-09-6
      NYPL [3-MQW 91-4235]

ARCHITECTURE, ARMENIAN - IRAN.
Cuneo, Paolo. Architettura armena dal quarto al
diciannovesimo secolo /. Roma , 1988. 2 v.
(923 p.), [1] folded leaf of plates) : ISBN
88-7813-154-7 (set)
      NYPL [3-MQW 90-12681]

ARCHITECTURE, ARMENIAN - TURKEY.
Cuneo, Paolo. Architettura armena dal quarto al

diciannovesimo secolo /. Roma , 1988. 2 v.
(923 p.), [1] folded leaf of plates) : ISBN
88-7813-154-7 (set)
      NYPL [3-MQW 90-12681]

**ARCHITECTURE - AUSTRALIA - BRISBANE
(QLD.)**
De Gruchy, Graham. Architecture in Brisbane
/. Bowen Hills, Brisbane, Qld. , 1988. 132 p. :
   ISBN 0-86439-078-5
      NYPL [3-MQWZ+ 89-21433]

ARCHITECTURE - AUSTRALIA - HISTORY.
Freeland, J. M. (John Maxwell), 1920-
Architecture in Australia . Ringwood, Victoria,
Australia , New York, N.Y., U.S.A. , 19. 328
p. : ISBN 0-14-021152-7
NA1600 .F7 1972

**ARCHITECTURE - AUSTRIA -
EXHIBITIONS.**
Sechs Architekten vom Schillerplatz. Wien ,
c1977. 78 p. : ISBN 3-85063-072-2
      NYPL [3-MQWD 90-5756]

**ARCHITECTURE - AUSTRIA - LOWER
AUSTRIA - GUIDE-BOOKS.**
Niederösterreich . Wien , c1990. xxxviii, 1414
p., [13] leaves of plates : ISBN 3-7031-0652-2
      NYPL [3-MQWD 91-3702]

Niederösterreich nördlich der Donau /. Wien ,
c1990. xxxviii, 1414 p., 6 p. of plates : ISBN
3-7031-0652-2 DDC 720/.946/12 20
NA1009.L68 N54 1990

ARCHITECTURE - AWARDS.
American Institute of Architects. New York
Chapter. New York architecture . New York ,
1988- v. : *NYPL [MQWO+ 89-8137]*

Mies van der Rohe award for European
architecture. London , Boston , 1990. 128 p. :
   ISBN 0-408-50084-0 (pbk.) DDC 724.6 20
NA958   *NYPL [3-MQV 90-12890]*

ARCHITECTURE - BALKAN PENINSULA.
Kiel, Machiel. Studies on the Ottoman
architecture of the Balkans /. Brookfield, Vt. ,
c1990. 361 p. in various pagings : ISBN
0-86078-276-X : DDC 720/.9496 20
NA1375 .K54 1990 NYPL [3-MQT 91-3249]

**ARCHITECTURE, BAROQUE - BERLIN
REGION (GERMANY)**
Wimmer, Clemens Alexander, 1959-
Sichtachsen des Barock in Berlin und
Umgebung . Berlin, c1985. 39 p. :
      NYPL [3-MQWD 90-12627]

Wimmer, Clemens Alexander, 1959-
Sichtachsen des Barock in Berlin und
Umgebung . Berlin, c1985. 39 p. :
      NYPL [3-MQWD 90-12627]

**ARCHITECTURE, BAROQUE - BRAZIL -
MINAS GERAIS - DICTIONARIES.**
Avila, Affonso, 1928- Barroco mineiro, glossário
de arquitetura e ornamentação /. [Rio de
Janeiro?] . 220 p. :
NA3533.A3 M563 1980

ARCHITECTURE, BAROQUE - ENGLAND.
Tavernor, Robert. Palladio and Palladianism /.
New York, N.Y. , 1991. 216 p. : ISBN
0-500-20242-7
      NYPL [3-MQZ (Palladio) 91-5547]

ARCHITECTURE, BAROQUE - GERMANY.
Knapp, Ulrich, 1956- Die Wallfahrtskirche
Birnau . Friedrichshafen , c1989. 219 p. : ISBN
3-922137-58-X
NA5586.W266 K58 1989

Schneider, Erich. Balthasar Neumann,
1687-1753 . München , c1987. 48 p. :
      NYPL [3-MQZ+ (Neumann) 91-6584]

**ARCHITECTURE, BAROQUE - GERMANY -
HISTORY.**
Gerlach, Siegfried. Die deutsche Stadt des
Absolutismus im Spiegel barocker Veduten und
zeitgenössischer Pläne . Stuttgart , c1990. 80
p. : ISBN 3-515-05600-9
IN PROCESS (ONLINE)
      NYPL [3-MQWD 91-3447]

**ARCHITECTURE, BAROQUE - ITALY -
BAGHERIA.**
Tedesco, Natale. L'immago espressa, Villa
Palagonia . Siracusa , c1986. 231 p. : DDC
728.8/0945/823 20
NA7595.B298 T4 1986
      NYPL [3-MQWB+ 90-11739]

ARCHITECTURE, BAROQUE - ITALY - ROME.
Waddy, Patricia. Seventeenth-century Roman palaces . New York, N.Y. , Cambridge, Mass. , c1990. xiii, 456 p. : ISBN 0-262-23156-5 DDC 945 20
DG797.9 .W33 1990
                    NYPL [3-MQWB 91-3718]

ARCHITECTURE, BAROQUE - ITALY - VICENZA - EXHIBITIONS.
I Tiepolo e il Settecento vicentino /. Milano , c1990. 404 p. : ISBN 88-435-3180-8
                    NYPL [3-MAMC 91-5454]

ARCHITECTURE, BAROQUE - LATIN AMERICA - CONGRESSES.
Exposición barroco latinoamericano. [Buenos Aires, Argentina] [between 1983 and 1989] 116 p. : DDC 724/.16 20
NA702.2 .E97 1983

ARCHITECTURE, BAROQUE - MEXICO - MEXICO CITY.
Fernández, Martha (Fernández García) La arquitectura de la Ciudad de México en el siglo XVII /. [Mexico] , 1987. 43 p. : ISBN 968-8160-77-6 DDC 720/.972/5309032 20
NA757.M4 F46 1987

ARCHITECTURE, BAROQUE - RUSSIAN S.F. S.R. - LENINGRAD.
Ėrmitazh . Leningrad , 1989. 560 p. : ISBN 5-274-00375-3 :
N3350 .E76 1989

ARCHITECTURE, BAROQUE - SPAIN.
Bonet Correa, Antonio. Fiesta, poder y arquitectura . Madrid, España , c1990. 182 p. : ISBN 84-7600-446-6 DDC 720/.946/09033 20
NA1306 .B57 1990

ARCHITECTURE, BAROQUE - SPAIN - CONGRESSES.
Coloquio de Urbanismo Barroco (1986 : Archidona, Spain) II centenario de la Plaza Ochavada de Archidona /. [Málaga] [1989] 350 p. : ISBN 84-7496-177-7
NA1306 .C6 1986

ARCHITECTURE, BAROQUE - SPAIN - GUIPÚZCOA.
Astiazarain Achabal, María Isabel. Arquitectos guipuzcoanos del siglo XVIII /. Guipúzcoa [1988?-1990?] 2 v. : ISBN 84-505-7463-3
NA1109.G85 A88 1988

ARCHITECTURE, BAROQUE - SPAIN - LUGO.
Vila Jato, María Dolores. Lugo barroco /. Lugo (Galicia) [1989] 134 p. : ISBN 84-86824-00-1
NA5811.L79 V55 1989

ARCHITECTURE, BAROQUE - SPAIN - SANTIAGO DE COMPOSTELA.
García Iglesias, José Manuel, 1950- A Catedral de Santiago e o barroco /. Santiago de Compostela , 1990. 228 p. : ISBN 84-85665-20-1
NA5811.S46 G37 1990
                    NYPL [3-MRBN+ 91-3888]

ARCHITECTURE - BELGIUM - BRUSSELS - GUIDE-BOOKS.
Le Patrimoine monumental de la Belgique. Liège [1989- <v. 1, pt. 1 > : ISBN 2-8021-0092-0 (v. 1) DDC 720/.9493/32 20
NA1170 .P37 1989

ARCHITECTURE - BELGIUM - HERVE REGION.
Lambiet, Thomas. Le pays de Herve . [Belgium] , 1978. 343 p., [2] leaves of plates :
                    NYPL [3-MQW+ 89-10507]

ARCHITECTURE - BERLIN (GERMANY)
Klinkott, Manfred. Die Backsteinbaukunst der Berliner Schule . Berlin , c1988. 479 p., 9 leaves of plates : ISBN 3-7861-1438-2 DDC 721/.04421/094315509034 20
NA1085 .K57 1988
                    NYPL [3-MQWD 90-11025]

ARCHITECTURE - BERMUDA ISLAND (BERMUDA ISLANDS) - THEMES, MOTIVES.
Adams, John. Bermudian images . Hamilton, Bermuda , 1989. viii, 101 p. : DDC 759.97299 20
NA815.B47 A33 1989

ARCHITECTURE - BIBLIOGRAPHY.
Architektenwerkverzeichnisse /. Stuttgart [1989] 111 p. ; ISBN 3-8167-1031-X
                    NYPL [3-MQB 91-7535]

ARCHITECTURE - BIBLIOGRAPHY - INDEXES.
Vance Bibliographies (Firm) Index to Architecture series, Bibliography, no. A-1 to A-154 (June 1978-December 1979). Monticello, Ill. , 1980. 38 p. ;
Z5941 .V34 1980 NA25 ***NYPL [*XMC-359]***

ARCHITECTURE - BRAZIL.
Artigas, João Batista Vilanova. A função social do arquiteto /. São Paulo, SP , 1989. 93 p. : ISBN 85-21-30621-0 DDC 720/.1/0309810904 20
NA2543.S6 A76 1989

Segawa, Hugo M. Arquiteturas no Brasil, anos 80 /. [São Paulo] [1988?] 1 v. (various pagings) : DDC 720/.981/09048 20
NA855 .S44 1988

ARCHITECTURE - BRAZIL - GUIDE-BOOKS.
Guia dos bens tombados Brasil /. Rio de Janeiro, RJ , c1987. 512, [24] p. : DDC 720/.981 20
NA853 .G85 1987

ARCHITECTURE - BRAZIL - MINAS GERAIS - DETAILS - DICTIONARIES.
Avila, Affonso, 1928- Barroco mineiro, glossário de arquitetura e ornamentação /. [Rio de Janeiro?] . 220 p. :
NA3533.A3 M563 1980

ARCHITECTURE - BRAZIL - RIO DE JANEIRO.
Levy, Carlos Roberto Maciel, 1951- Rio imperial /. [São Paulo, Brazil?] [1988] 176 p., [2] p. of plates :
NA857.R5 L4 1988

ARCHITECTURE, BYZANTINE.
Miranda, Salvador. Etude de topographie du palais sacré de Byzance . [Paris?] 1976. 184 p., [43] p. of plates : ***NYPL [3-MQP 90-4929]***

ARCHITECTURE, BYZANTINE - GREECE - CHIOS ISLAND.
Bouras, Ch. (Charalampos) Hē Nea Monē tēs Chiou . Athēna , 1981. 212 p. :
NA5601.N4 B68 1981
                    NYPL [3-MQP+ 91-6541]

ARCHITECTURE - CALIFORNIA - LOS ANGELES.
Experimental architecture in Los Angeles /. New York , 1991. p. cm. ISBN 0-8478-1424-6 (HC) DDC 720/.9794/9409045 20
NA735.L55 E97 1991

ARCHITECTURE - CALIFORNIA - SAN FRANCISCO - DETAILS.
Delehanty, Randolph. In the Victorian style /. San Francisco , c1991. p. cm. ISBN 0-87701-750-6 (hc) : DDC 720/.9794/6109034 20
NA7238.S35 D4 1991

ARCHITECTURE - CARIBBEAN AREA - CONSERVATION AND RESTORATION.
Pérez Montas, Eugenio. Carimos . Santo Domingo, República Dominicana , 1989. 358 p. :
NA791 .P47 1989

ARCHITECTURE, CAROLINGIAN - GERMANY (WEST) - CHIEMSEE.
Dannheimer, Hermann. Torhalle auf Frauenchiemsee . München , 1983, c1980. 118 p. : ISBN 3-7954-0818-0
                    NYPL [3-MRBB 91-6996]

ARCHITECTURE, CARTHUSIAN - SPAIN - JEREZ DE LA FRONTERA - PICTORIAL WORKS.
Zubillaga, Francisco. La Cartuja de Jerez de la Frontera =. Salzburg, Austria , 1978. [97] p. :
                    NYPL [3-MRBB 90-4725]

Architecture, ceremonial, and power . Necipoğlu, Gülru. New York, N.Y. , Cambridge, Mass. , 1991. p. cm. ISBN 0-262-14050-0 DDC 725/.17/0949618 20
NA1370 .N43 1991

ARCHITECTURE - CHANNEL ISLANDS - JERSEY.
Boots, Maurice. Architecture in Jersey /. Jersey , c1986. xii, 180 p. : ISBN 0-86120-015-2 DDC 720/.9423/41 20
NA995.J47 B66 1986

ARCHITECTURE - CHILE - AWARDS.
Muñoz R., María Dolores. Premios nacionales de arquitectura, 1969-1985. [Concepción, Chile]

[1986?] 47 p. :
NA2345.C5 M85 1986

ARCHITECTURE - CHILE - COLCHAGUA.
Guarda, Gabriel. Colchagua, arquitectura tradicional /. Santiago de Chile , 1988. 177 p. : ISBN 956-1-40220-7 DDC 720/.983/33 20
NA866.C64 G83 1988

ARCHITECTURE - CHILE - SANTIAGO.
Munizaga, Gustavo. Estructura y ciudad /. Santiago de Chile , 1985. 147 p. :
NA9168.S3 M8 1985

ARCHITECTURE - CHILE - VALPARAÍSO BAY REGION - CATALOGS.
Edwards C., Hernán (Edwards Cruchaga) Monumentos nacionales y arquitectura tradicional . [Santiago, Chile] [1990?] 80 p. : DDC 720/.983/255 20
NA866.V3 E3 1990

ARCHITECTURE - CHILE - VALPARAÍSO - DESIGNS AND PLANS.
Waisberg, Myriam. Casas de Playa Ancha . Santiago [Chile] , 1988. 108 p., [1] folded leaf of plates :
NA867.V34 W34 1988

ARCHITECTURE - CHINA - MING-CH'ING DYNASTIES, 1368-1912 - GUIDE-BOOKS.
Chan, Charis. Imperial China /. San Francisco , 1992. p. cm. ISBN 0-8118-0018-0 DDC 720/.951 20
NA1543.5 .C4 1992

ARCHITECTURE - CHINA - HISTORY.
Sickman, L. C. S. (Laurence C. S.) The art and architecture of China /. Harmondsworth, Middlesex , Baltimore , 1956. xxvi, 334 p., 190 p. of plates : DDC 709.52
N7340 .S46   ***NYPL [3-MAG 90-11174]***

ARCHITECTURE, CHOLA.
Dehejia, Vidya. Art of the imperial Cholas /. New York , c1990. xviii, 148 p. : ISBN 0-231-07188-4 DDC 726/.145/09548 20
NA6007.S6 D44 1990
                    NYPL [3-MAF 90-12973]

ARCHITECTURE, CHURCH. see CHURCH ARCHITECTURE.

ARCHITECTURE, CISTERCIAN - FRANCE - CADOUIN.
Cadouin, une aventure cistercienne en Périgord /. Le Bugue [France] , 1990. 167 p. : ISBN 2-86952-017-4 DDC 726/.7/094472 20
NA5551.C28 C3 1990

ARCHITECTURE, CISTERCIAN - ITALY - LAZIO.
Farina, Federico. L'architettura cistercense e l'Abbazia di Casamari /. Casamari , 1981, c1978. xii, 187 p. : DDC 726/.7/0945622 19
NA5621.A22 F37 1981
                    NYPL [3-MRBD+ 90-12587]

ARCHITECTURE, CISTERCIAN - POLAND - SULEJÓW (PIOTRKÓW TRYBUNALSKI)
Świechowski, Zygmunt. Opactwo sulejowskie . Poznań , 1954. 69 p., 88 p. of plates (some folded) :
NA1191 .P6 t. 4, zesz. 2 NA5955.P62S92

ARCHITECTURE - COLOMBIA.
Documentos internacionales sobre patrimonio arquitectónico. [Bogotá, Colombia] [1989 or 1990] 35 p. ;
NA870 .D6 1989

ARCHITECTURE - COLOMBIA - CARTAGENA - DETAILS.
Téllez, Germán. [Repertorio formal de arquitectura doméstica, Cartagena de Indias.] Arquitectura doméstica, Cartagena de Indias /. [Bogotá] . 256 p., [1] folded leaf of plates : DDC 728/.09861/14 20
NA2840 .T45 1982b

ARCHITECTURE - COLOMBIA - HISTORY.
Arango, Silvia, 1948- Historia de la arquitectura colombiana /. Bogota , 1989. 291 p. : ISBN 958-1-70061-7
                    NYPL [3-MQWN+ 90-12805]

Arango, Silvia, 1948- Historia de la arquitectura en Colombia /. Bogotá , 1989 [i.e. 1990] 291 p. : ISBN 958-1-70061-7 DDC 720/.9861 20
NA870 .A73 1990

ARCHITECTURE - COLOMBIA - TUNJA.
Mateus Cortés, Gustavo, 1939- Nuevos apuntes para la historia del patrimonio artístico de Tunja, con el acta de fundación y el título de

ciudad /. Tunja, Boyacá, Colombia , 1989. 96
p. :
NA877.T8 M3 1989

ARCHITECTURE, COLONIAL - AUSTRALIA - SYDNEY REGION (N.S.W.)
Kingston, Daphne. Early colonial homes of the
Sydney region, 1788-1838 /. Kenthurst,
N.S.W. , 1990. 96 p. :
NYPL [3-MRG+ 91-3712]

ARCHITECTURE, COLONIAL - BRAZIL - GUIDE-BOOKS.
Guia dos bens tombados Brasil /. Rio de
Janeiro, RJ , c1987. 512, [24] p. : DDC
720/.981 20
NA853 .G85 1987

ARCHITECTURE, COLONIAL - CARIBBEAN AREA - CONSERVATION AND RESTORATION.
Pérez Montas, Eugenio. Carimos . Santo
Domingo, República Dominicana , 1989. 358
p. :
NA791 .P47 1989

ARCHITECTURE, COLONIAL - CHILE - COLCHAGUA.
Guarda, Gabriel. Colchagua, arquitectura
tradicional /. Santiago de Chile , 1988. 177 p. :
ISBN 956-1-40220-7 DDC 720/.983/33 20
NA866.C64 G83 1988

ARCHITECTURE, COLONIAL - COLOMBIA - CARTAGENA.
Téllez, Germán. [Repertorio formal de
arquitectura doméstica, Cartagena de Indias.]
Arquitectura doméstica, Cartagena de Indias /.
[Bogotá] . 256 p., [1] folded leaf of plates :
DDC 728/.09861/14 20
NA2840 .T45 1982b

ARCHITECTURE, COLONIAL - COLOMBIA - TUNJA.
Mateus Cortés, Gustavo, 1939- Nuevos apuntes
para la historia del patrimonio artístico de
Tunja, con el acta de fundación y el título de
ciudad /. Tunja, Boyacá, Colombia , 1989. 96
p. :
NA877.T8 M3 1989

ARCHITECTURE, COLONIAL - LATIN AMERICA.
Cabildos y ayuntamientos en América /. [Mar
del Plata, Argentina?] : [Azcapotzalco,
Mexico] : 134 p. : ISBN 968-636-305-X
NA4202.A1 C33 1990

ARCHITECTURE, COLONIAL - MARYLAND.
Lane, Mills. Architecture of the Old South.
1991. p. cm. ISBN 1-558-59040-4 DDC
720/.9752 20
NA730.M3 L36 1991

ARCHITECTURE, COLONIAL - MEXICO.
Mogilner, Mark. Edificaciones del Banco
Nacional de México . México , 1988. 191 p. :
ISBN 968-7009-18-7 DDC 725/.24/0972 20
NA6245.M6 M64 1988

ARCHITECTURE, COLONIAL - MEXICO - TLAXCALA DE XICOHTÉNCATL.
Palacio Legislativo del Estado de Tlaxcala,
1982. [Tlaxcala, Mexico] , 1982. 1 portfolio
(unpaged) :
NA4232.T57 P35 1982

ARCHITECTURE, COLONIAL - SOUTHERN STATES.
Forman, Henry Chandlee, 1904- The
architecture of the Old South . Cambridge ,
1948. 203 p., [7] p. of plates : DDC 720.975
NA720 .F6   *NYPL [3-MQWO 91-6780]*

ARCHITECTURE - COLOR. see COLOR IN ARCHITECTURE.

Architecture/Colorado. Jackson, Olga. [Denver,
c1966] 96 p.   *NYPL [3-MQWO 91-225]*

ARCHITECTURE - COLORADO.
Jackson, Olga. Architecture/Colorado. [Denver,
c1966] 96 p.   *NYPL [3-MQWO 91-225]*

ARCHITECTURE - COMPETITIONS - BERLIN (GERMANY) - EXHIBITIONS.
14x Amerika-Gedenkbibliothek . Berlin , c1989.
132 p. : ISBN 3-433-02288-7 (pbk.)
NYPL [3-MQWO+ 90-11060]

ARCHITECTURE - COMPETITIONS - UNITED STATES.
Bearings (Exhibition : 1988-1989 : Parsons
School of Design) Bearings. New York, N.Y. ,
1991. 79 p. : ISBN 1-87827-128-8 : DDC

720/.973/0747471 20
NA2340 .B4 1991
NYPL [3-MQAF 91-7007]

ARCHITECTURE - COMPOSITION, PROPORTION, ETC.
In what style should we build? . Santa Monica,
Calif. , 1991. p. cm. ISBN 0-89236-199-9 : DDC
720/.1 20
NA2500 .I5 1991

Schneider Berrenberg, Rüdiger. Sie bauten ein
Abbild der Seele . München , Solingen , 1988.
xii, 149 p. :
NA5586.M23 S36 1988

Tubi, Carlo. La cattedrale pitagorica . Ferrara ,
1989. 140 p. : ISBN 88-85668-47-X DDC
726/.6/094545 20
NA5621.F467 T8 1989

ARCHITECTURE - CONSERVATION AND RESTORATION - LATIN AMERICA.
Viñuales, Graciela María. Patrimonio
arquitectónico . Buenos Aires , 1990. 104 p. ;
NA702 .V5 1990

Architecture contemporaine. Cariou, Joël. Les
classiques de l'architecture contemporaine /.
Paris , c1990. 139 p. : DDC 724/.6 20
NA680 .C33 1990

ARCHITECTURE - CZECHOSLOVAKIA - BRATISLAVA.
Stavoprojekt /. Bratislava , 1989. 1 v.
(unpaged) :
NA1033.B7 S73 1989

ARCHITECTURE - CZECHOSLOVAKIA - PRAGUE.
Hrůza, Jiří. Město Praha /. Praha , 1989. 421
p. : ISBN 80-207-0065-X :
NA1033.P7 H78 1989

ARCHITECTURE - CZECHOSLOVAKIA - SLOVAK REPUBLIC.
Krivošová, Jana. Premeny súčasnej architektúry
Slovenska /. Bratislava , 1990. 198 p. : ISBN
80-05-00600-4 :
NA1032.S55 K75 1990

ARCHITECTURE - DATA PROCESSING - CONGRESSES.
Architettura & computer. [Roma, 1972] 219 p.
NA2540 .A62   *NYPL [3-MQD 90-6902]*

L'architecture de l'art nouveau / sous la direction
de Frank Russell ; traduit de l'anglais par
Florence Sébastiani. Paris : Berger-Levrault,
c1982. 332 p. : ill. (some col.), maps, plans ; 32
cm. Biographies: p. 293-313. Original title: Art
nouveau architecture (London : Academy Editions,
1979) Includes index. Bibliography: p. 316-321. ISBN
2-7013-0448-2
  1. Art nouveau. 2. Architecture, Modern - 19th
century. 3. Architecture, Modern - 20th century. I.
Russell, Frank, 1949-.
NYPL [3-MRX+ 91-7304]

ARCHITECTURE - DECORATION AND ORNAMENT. see DECORATION AND ORNAMENT, ARCHITECTURAL.

ARCHITECTURE - DENMARK.
Ilkjær, Marianne Olsson. Postmodernismen i
dansk arkitektur . [København , 1987] 104
leaves : ISBN 87-87448-52-1
NA1218 .I43 1987

ARCHITECTURE - DENMARK - NÆSTVED - CONSERVATION AND RESTORATION.
Boderne i Næstved /. [Næstved]
[Copenhagen] , 1988. 111 p. : ISBN
87-05-03735-60
NA9053.C6 B63 1988

**Architecture, design, and construction word
finder** /. Ballast, David Kent. Englewood Cliffs,
N.J. , c1991. p. cm. ISBN 0-13-044397-2 DDC
720/.3 20
NA31 .B34 1991

ARCHITECTURE - DESIGNS AND PLANS.
Lehne, Andreas. Wiener Warenhäuser,
1865-1914 /. Wien , 1990. 195 p. : ISBN
3-7005-4488-X
NA6227.D45 L44 1990

ARCHITECTURE - DESIGNS AND PLANS - PRESENTATION DRAWINGS.
Porter, Tom. Design drawing techniques . New
York : Toronto : p. cm. ISBN 0-684-19045-1
DDC 720/.28/4 20
NA2714 .P67 1991

ARCHITECTURE - DETAILS.
Congdon, Herbert Wheaton, 1876-1965. Early
American homes for today . Dublin, N.H. ,
c1985. xv, 236 p. : ISBN 0-87233-065-6 (pbk.)
DDC 728.3/7/0974 19
NA7210 .C6 1985

The Elements of style . New York , c1991. p.
cm. ISBN 0-671-73981-6 DDC 721 20
NA2850 .E44 1991

Knobloch, Philip G. (Philip George), b. 1893.
[Good practice in construction.] Architectural
details from the early twentieth century .
Washington, D.C. [1991] 1 v. (unpaged) :
ISBN 1-558-35034-9 : DDC 721/.022/2 20
NA2840 .K58 1991

ARCHITECTURE - DICTIONARIES.
Jones, Frederic H. (Frederic Hicks), 1944- A
concise dictionary of architecture /. Los Altos,
Calif. , 1991. p. cm. ISBN 1-560-52066-3 : DDC
720/.3 20
NA31 .J6 1991

Jones, Frederic H. (Frederic Hicks), 1944- A
concise dictionary of interior design /. Los
Altos, Calif. , c1990. 215 p. : ISBN
1-560-52067-1 DDC 729/.03 20
NK1704 .J6 1991

ARCHITECTURE, DOMESTIC.
Espaces des autres . [Paris] , c1987. 270 p. :
ISBN 2-903539-13-8
NA7125 .E83 1987

Shimomura, Jun'ichi, 1952- [Āru nūvō no
meitei. English.] Art nouveau architecture . San
Francisco , 1991. p. cm. ISBN 0-938491-29-6
DDC 728/.09/034 20
NA7125 .S5513 1991

ARCHITECTURE, DOMESTIC - AEGEAN SEA REGION - CONGRESSES.
L'Habitat égéen préhistorique . Athènes , Paris ,
1990. 495 p. : ISBN 2-86958-031-2
NYPL [3-MQL 91-5181]

ARCHITECTURE, DOMESTIC - ARGENTINA.
Historia argentina de la vivienda de interés
social. Capital Federal [Argentina] [between
1986 and 1990- v. <1- > :
NA7292 .H57 1990

ARCHITECTURE, DOMESTIC - AUSTRALIA - SYDNEY REGION (N.S.W.)
Kingston, Daphne. Early colonial homes of the
Sydney region, 1788-1838 /. Kenthurst,
N.S.W. , 1990. 96 p. : ISBN 0-86417-352-0
NYPL [3-MRG+ 91-3712]

ARCHITECTURE, DOMESTIC - BRAZIL - ANTÔNIO PRADO.
Antônio Prado, cidade historica /. Porto
Alegre, RS , 1989. 204 p. ;
NYPL [3-MQWN+ 90-12545]

ARCHITECTURE, DOMESTIC - CALIFORNIA - SAN FRANCISCO.
Delehanty, Randolph. In the Victorian style /.
San Francisco , c1991. p. cm. ISBN
0-87701-750-6 (hc) : DDC 720/.9794/6109034
20
NA7238.S35 D4 1991

ARCHITECTURE, DOMESTIC - COLOMBIA - CATAGENA.
Téllez, Germán. [Repertorio formal de
arquitectura doméstica, Cartagena de Indias.]
Arquitectura doméstica, Cartagena de Indias /.
[Bogotá] . 256 p., [1] folded leaf of plates :
DDC 728/.09861/14 20
NA2840 .T45 1982b

ARCHITECTURE, DOMESTIC - DATA PROCESSING.
Hersey, George L. Possible Palladian villas .
Cambridge, Mass. , c1992. p. cm. ISBN
0-262-08210-1 DDC 728.8/092 20
NA7125 .H47 1992

ARCHITECTURE, DOMESTIC - DESIGNS AND PLANS.
Israel. Misrad ha-shikun. Agaf le-tikhnun fisi.
Israel builds. [Tel Aviv, 1967?] [96] p. DDC
720/.95694
NA7419.I8 A54

ARCHITECTURE, DOMESTIC - EGYPT.
Roik, Elke. Das altägyptische Wohnhaus und
seine Darstellung im Flachbild /. Frankfurt am
Main , New York , c1988. 2 v. : ISBN

3-8204-0163-6
NA215 .R65 1988

NYPL   *[3-MQL+ 90-8068]*

ARCHITECTURE, DOMESTIC - ENGLAND.
Allibone, Jill. George Devey, architect,
1820-1886 /. Cambridge, England , c1991. 189
p. : ISBN 0-7188-2785-6 : DDC 720.92 20
NYPL   *[3-MQZ (Devey) 91-6770]*

Esher, Lionel, 1913- The glory of the English
house . Boston, Mass. , 1991. p. ISBN
0-8212-1851-4 : DDC 728/.0942 20
NA7328 .E74 1991

Lycett Green, Candida. The perfect English
country house /. New York , 1991. 175 p. :
ISBN 0-8478-1373-8 DDC 728.8/0942 20
NA7562 .L93 1991

Plaw, John, 1744 or 5-1820. Sketches for
country houses, villas and rural dwellings,
calculated for persons of moderate income and
for comfortable retirement .... Farnborough,
1972. 20 p., [42] leaves. ISBN 0-576-15175-0
DDC 728.3
NA7562 .P6 1972

NYPL   *[3-MQWK 90-5752]*

ARCHITECTURE, DOMESTIC - ENGLAND -
HAMPSHIRE.
Lewis, Elizabeth. Medieval hall houses of the
Winchester area /. [Winchester] , c1988. 128
p. : ISBN 0-86135-011-1 : DDC 728/.09422/7 19
NYPL   *[3-MQWK+ 91-4986]*

ARCHITECTURE, DOMESTIC - ENGLAND -
SUFFOLK.
Sandon, Eric. Suffolk houses . Woodbridge,
Suffolk , 1986, c1977. 344 p. : ISBN
0-902028-68-5 :
NYPL   *[3-MQWK+ 91-3318]*

ARCHITECTURE, DOMESTIC - FLORIDA -
PALM BEACH.
Schezen, Roberto. Palm Beach houses /. New
York , 1991. 324 p. : ISBN 0-8478-1313-4 DDC
728.8/09759/32 20
NA7238.P235 S34 1991

ARCHITECTURE, DOMESTIC - FLORIDA -
SAINT AUGUSTINE.
Manucy, Albert C. The houses of St. Augustine,
1565-1821 /. Jacksonville , c1992. p. cm. ISBN
0-8130-1103-5 DDC 728/.09759/18 20
NA7238.S27 M3 1992

ARCHITECTURE, DOMESTIC - FRANCE.
Léger, Jean-Michel. Derniers domiciles connus .
Paris , c1990. 168 p. : ISBN 2-907150-18-9 :
DDC 728/.314/094409047 20
NA7346 .L44 1990

ARCHITECTURE, DOMESTIC - FRANCE -
VEXIN.
Le Vexin français . Pontoise [France] [196-?]
32 p. :   *NYPL*   *[3-MRGF 90-6241]*

ARCHITECTURE, DOMESTIC - GERMANY.
Schink, Arnold. Mies van der Rohe . Stuttgart ,
c1990. 379 p. : ISBN 3-7828-4004-6
NA1088.M65 S34 1990

ARCHITECTURE, DOMESTIC - GERMANY -
AACHEN REGION.
Prokop, Eva. Bauen im Grenzland . Aachen
[1989] 227 p. : ISBN 3-89399-092-5
NA7350.A23 P76 1989

ARCHITECTURE, DOMESTIC - GERMANY -
BERLIN - GUIDE-BOOKS.
Berning, Maria. Berliner Wohnquartiere .
Berlin , c1990. xiii, 252 p. : ISBN
3-496-00382-0 :
NA7351.B65 B47 1990

ARCHITECTURE, DOMESTIC - GERMANY -
FRIESLAND.
Jessel, Hans, 1956- Friesenhaustüren /.
Hamburg , c1990. 56 p. : ISBN 3-89234-159-1
NA7350.F84 J4 1990

ARCHITECTURE, DOMESTIC - GERMANY -
RUHR RIVER VALLEY.
Wehling, Hans-Werner, 1949- Werks- und
Genossenschaftssiedlungen im Ruhrgebiet
1844-1939. Essen , 1990- v. <1 > : ISBN
3-88474-344-9 DDC 728/.0943/5509034 20
NA7553 .W44 1990

ARCHITECTURE, DOMESTIC - GERMANY -
STUTTGART.
Pommer, Richard. Weissenhof 1927 and the
modern movement in architecture /. Chicago ,
1991. xxii, 304 p., [115] p. of plates : ISBN

0-226-67515-7 (alk. paper) DDC
728/.0943/47309042 20
NA7351.S7 P6 1991

NYPL   *[3-MQWD 91-4874]*

ARCHITECTURE, DOMESTIC - GREAT
BRITAIN.
Gray, Alexander Stuart. Fanlights /. London ,
1990. 148 p. : ISBN 0-7136-3077-9 : DDC
721.823 20   *NYPL*   *[3-MRR 91-3295]*

Roberts, Marion. Living in a man-made world .
London , New York , 1991. xii, 177 p. : ISBN
0-415-05747-7 DDC 728/.0942 20
NA2543.W65 R64 1990

NYPL   *[3-MQWK 91-6908]*

ARCHITECTURE, DOMESTIC - GREAT
BRITAIN - DESIGNS AND PLANS.
Lutyens, Edwin Landseer, Sir, 1869-1944.
Edwin Lutyens. London , New York , 1986.
112 p., [7] folded leaves of plates : ISBN
0-85670-422-9 (paper) DDC 728.8/092/4 19
NA997.L8 I57 1986

NYPL   *[3-MQZ+ (Lutyens) 87-2200]*

ARCHITECTURE, DOMESTIC -
HANDBOOKS, MANUALS, ETC.
Harrison, Henry S. Houses . Chicago, IL ,
1991. p. cm. ISBN 0-7931-0332-0 (pbk.) DDC
728 20
NA7110 .H33 1991

ARCHITECTURE, DOMESTIC, IN ART.
Roik, Elke. Das altägyptische Wohnhaus und
seine Darstellung im Flachbild /. Frankfurt am
Main , New York , c1988. 2 v. : ISBN
3-8204-0163-6
NA215 .R65 1988

NYPL   *[3-MQL+ 90-8068]*

ARCHITECTURE, DOMESTIC - INDIA -
GUJARAT.
Pramar, V. S. Haveli . Middletown, NJ , 1989.
238 p. : ISBN 0-944142-15-X
NYPL   *[3-MQWS+ 90-2291]*

ARCHITECTURE, DOMESTIC - ISRAEL.
Israel. Misrad ha-shikun. Agaf le-tikhnun fisi.
Israel builds. [Tel Aviv, 1967?] [96] p. DDC
720/.95694
NA7419.I8 A54

ARCHITECTURE, DOMESTIC - ITALY.
Clarke, John R., 1945- The houses of Roman
Italy, 100 B.C.-A.D. 250 . Berkeley , c1991. p.
cm. ISBN 0-520-07267-7 (alk. paper) DDC
728/.0937 20
NA324 .C57 1991

Holberton, Paul. Palladio's villas . London ,
1990. xiii, 256 p. : ISBN 0-7195-4782-2 : DDC
720/.92/4 19
NA1123.P2

NYPL   *[3-MQZ (Palladio) 90-11020]*

ARCHITECTURE, DOMESTIC - ITALY -
FLORENCE.
Maffei, Gian Luigi. La casa fiorentina nella
storia della città dalle origini all'Ottocento /.
Venezia , 1990. 383 p. : ISBN 88-317-5346-0
NA9053.B58 M3 1990

ARCHITECTURE, DOMESTIC - ITALY -
LAZIO.
Torselli, Giorgio. Castelli e ville del Lazio /.
Roma , c1983. 284 p., [8] folded leaves of
plates :   *NYPL*   *[3-MQWB+ 90-12978]*

ARCHITECTURE, DOMESTIC - ITALY -
MILAN (PROVINCE)
Süss, Francesco. Le ville del territorio milanese.
[Milano] , 1988- v. :
NYPL   *[3-MRGF+ 90-2532]*

ARCHITECTURE, DOMESTIC - ITALY -
NAPLES.
Viggiani, Domenico. I tempi di Posillipo .
Napoli , c1989. 231 p. : ISBN 88-435-2964-1
NYPL   *[3-MQWB 91-5542]*

ARCHITECTURE, DOMESTIC - ITALY -
VARESE (PROVINCE)
Langè, Santino. Ville della provincia di Varese
/. Milano , c1984. 492 p. : DDC 728.8/0945/22
19
NA7594 .L33 1984

NYPL   *[3-MQWB+ 91-5787]*

ARCHITECTURE, DOMESTIC - ITALY -
VENETO - CATALOGS.
Battilotti, Donata. Le ville di Palladio /.
Milano , c1990. 139 p. : ISBN 88-435-3085-2

DDC 728.8/092 20
NA7594 .B34 1990

NYPL   *[3-MQZ (Palladio, A.) 91-5518]*

ARCHITECTURE, DOMESTIC - ITALY -
VENETO - GUIDE-BOOKS.
Di villa in villa . Treviso , c1990. 235 p. :
ISBN 88-85066-98-4 : DDC 728.8/0945/3 20
NA7594 .D54 1990

ARCHITECTURE, DOMESTIC - JAPAN.
Bosslet, Klaus. Asthetik und Gestaltung in der
japanischen Architektur . Düsseldorf , c1990.
viii, 154 p. : ISBN 3-8041-1247-1 :
NA7451 .B67 1990

Ueda, Atsushi, 1930- [Nihonjin to sumai.
English.] The inner harmony of the Japanese
house /. Tokyo ; New York : 199 p. : ISBN
0-87011-934-6 : DDC 728/.0952 20
NA7451 .U3313 1990

NYPL   *[3-MQWS 90-11554]*

ARCHITECTURE, DOMESTIC - LEBANON.
El-Khoury, Fouad. Domestic architecture in the
Lebanon /. London [1975] 25 p. :
NYPL   *[3-MRG 90-12551]*

Ragette, Friedrich. Architecture in Lebanon .
Beirut , 1974. xvi [i.e. viii], 214 p. : DDC
728/.095692
NA7419.L4 R33   *NYPL*   *[3-MQWS 90-5443]*

ARCHITECTURE, DOMESTIC - LOUISIANA -
NEW ORLEANS - JUVENILE
LITERATURE.
Vogt, Lloyd. A young person's guide to New
Orleans houses /. Gretna, La. , 1991. p. cm.
ISBN 0-88289-829-9 DDC 728/.09763/35 20
NA7238.N5 V65 1991

ARCHITECTURE, DOMESTIC - MEXICO.
Garrison, G. Richard (George Richard), 1898-
[Mexican houses.] Early Mexican houses .
Stamford, Conn. , 1990. xvii, 173 p. : ISBN
0-942655-03-0 : DDC 728/.0972 20
NA7244 .G3 1990

NYPL   *[3-MQWN+ 91-4465]*

ARCHITECTURE, DOMESTIC - MEXICO -
TLAXCALA (STATE)
Torre Villalpando, Guadalupe de la. Las
calpanerías de las haciendas tlaxcaltecas .
[Mexico] , 1988. 124 p. :
NA7555.M6 T67 1988

ARCHITECTURE, DOMESTIC - MIDDLE
ATLANTIC STATES - THEMES,
MOTIVES.
A Monograph of the work of Mellor, Meigs &
Howe. Boulder, CO , c1991. 212 p. : ISBN
1-87865-001-7 DDC 720/.92/2 20
NA737.M45 A4 1991

ARCHITECTURE, DOMESTIC -
NETHERLANDS - UTRECHT.
Dolfin, Marceline J. Utrecht . 's-Gravenhage ,
1989. 2 v. : ISBN 90-12-05876-7 (set)
NYPL   *[3-MRG+ 90-12086]*

ARCHITECTURE, DOMESTIC - NEW
ENGLAND.
Congdon, Herbert Wheaton, 1876-1965. Early
American homes for today . Dublin, N.H. ,
c1985. xv, 236 p. : ISBN 0-87233-065-6 (pbk.)
DDC 728.3/7/0974 19
NA7210 .C6 1985

ARCHITECTURE, DOMESTIC - NEW
ENGLAND - CONSERVATION AND
RESTORATION.
Congdon, Herbert Wheaton, 1876-1965. Early
American homes for today . Dublin, N.H. ,
c1985. xv, 236 p. : ISBN 0-87233-065-6 (pbk.)
DDC 728.3/7/0974 19
NA7210 .C6 1985

ARCHITECTURE, DOMESTIC - NEW YORK
(STATE) - SOUTHOLD - THEMES,
MOTIVES.
Langhart, Nicholas. Houses of Southold .
Southold, N.Y. , c1990. vi, 66 p. : ISBN
0-8488-0870-3 : DDC 728/.37/0974725 20
NA7238.S62 L36 1990

ARCHITECTURE, DOMESTIC - NORTH
CAROLINA - ASHEVILLE.
Mathews, Jane Gianvito, 1954- The manor and
cottages . Asheville, N.C. , c1991. p. cm. ISBN
0-9630437-0-6 : DDC 728/.09756/88 20
NA9051 .M38 1991

ARCHITECTURE, DOMESTIC -
NORTHEASTERN STATES - THEMES,
MOTIVES.

A Monograph of the work of Mellor, Meigs &
Howe. Boulder, CO , c1991. 212 p. : ISBN
1-87865-001-7 DDC 720/.92/2 20
NA737.M45 A4 1991

**ARCHITECTURE, DOMESTIC - OREGON -
PORTLAND.**
Marlitt, Richard, 1909- Matters of proportion .
[Portland, Or.] , c1989. xvii, 76 p. : ISBN
0-87595-177-5 (alk. paper) : DDC 728/.37/0922
20
NA7238.P575 M37 1989
NYPL [3-MQWO 91-5274]

**ARCHITECTURE, DOMESTIC -
PSYCHOLOGICAL ASPECTS.**
Krings-Heckemeier, Marie-Therese.
Kommunikation und gebaute Umwelt .
Witterschlick , 1990. 264 p. ; ISBN
3-925267-35-2
NA7125 .K75 1990

Rockness, Miriam Huffman, 1944- Home,
God's design . Grand Rapids, Mich. , c1990.
245 p. ; ISBN 0-310-59081-7 DDC 728/.01 20
NA7125 .R55 1990 NYPL [3-MRG 91-5022]

ARCHITECTURE, DOMESTIC - RESEARCH.
Whiteman, John E. M. Divisible by 2 /.
[Chicago] , Cambridge, Mass. , 1990. 61 p. :
ISBN 0-262-73093-6 (pbk.) DDC 728/.092 20
NA7125 .W48 1990
NYPL [3-MRG 91-6702]

ARCHITECTURE, DOMESTIC - ROME.
De Albentiis, Emidio, 1958- La casa dei
Romani /. Milano , c1990. 348 p., [8] p. of
plates : ISBN 88-304-0930-8 : DDC 728/.0937 20
NA324 .D44 1990   NYPL [JFD 91-5342]

**ARCHITECTURE, DOMESTIC - RUSSIAN S.
F.S.R. - THEMES, MOTIVES.**
Gaynor, Elizabeth, 1946- Russian houses /.
New York , 1991. p. cm. ISBN 1-556-70163-2
(cloth) : DDC 728/.0947 20
NA7367 .G3 1991

**ARCHITECTURE, DOMESTIC - SAUDI
ARABIA - MEDINA.**
Ṭāhā, Ḥātim 'Umar, 1957- Ṭaybah wa-fannuhā
al-rafi' /. [Medina] [198-] 140 p. :
NA7419.S2 T27 1980z

**ARCHITECTURE, DOMESTIC - SOUTHERN
STATES.**
Gammon, Mitzi. The south /. New York ,
1991. p. cm. ISBN 0-553-07550-0 DDC
728/.37/0975 20
NA7211 .G35 1991

**ARCHITECTURE, DOMESTIC - SPAIN -
CATALONIA.**
Realitzacions de la Direcció General
d'Arquitectura i Habitatge i de l'Institut Català
del Sòl 1981-1987. Barcelona [1988?] 2 cases
(101 fasc.) : DDC 728/.314/0946709048 20
NA7860 .R35 1988

**ARCHITECTURE, DOMESTIC - SPAIN -
IBIZA ISLAND - EXHIBITIONS.**
Maisons sur l'île d'Ibiza . Bruxelles , 1990. 127
p. : ISBN 2-87143-072-6
NA7386.I25 M35 1990

**ARCHITECTURE, DOMESTIC - UNITED
STATES.**
Craftsman-style houses. Newton, Conn. , c1991.
p. cm. ISBN 1-561-58014-7 : DDC
728/.373/09730904 20
NA7208 .C68 1991

Gillon, Edmund Vincent. Victorian houses .
New York , c1973. 1 v. (unpaged) : ISBN
0-486-22966-1 *NYPL [3-MQWO 90-7005]*

Gray, Alexander Stuart. Fanlights /. London ,
1990. 148 p. : ISBN 0-7136-3077-9 : DDC
721.823 20   *NYPL [3-MRR 91-3295]*

Gross, Steve. Old houses /. New York , 1991.
p. cm. ISBN 1-556-70184-5 : DDC 728/.0973 20
NA7205 .G764 1991

Hewitt, Mark A. The architecture of Mott B.
Schmidt /. New York , 1991. p. cm. ISBN
0-8478-1399-1 DDC 720/.92 20
NA737.S355 H4 1991

Jandl, H. Ward. Yesterday's houses of
tomorrow . Washington, DC , 1991. p. cm.
ISBN 0-89133-186-7 DDC 728/.0973/09034 20
NA7207 .J36 1991

Kemp, Jim. American vernacular . Washington,
D.C. , 1990, c1987. 256 p. : ISBN

1-558-35074-8 :
NYPL [3-MQWO 91-6742]

**ARCHITECTURE, DOMESTIC - UNITED
STATES - CONSERVATION AND
RESTORATION.**
Gross, Steve. Old houses /. New York , 1991.
p. cm. ISBN 1-556-70184-5 : DDC 728/.0973 20
NA7205 .G764 1991

Howard, Hugh, 1952- The preservationist's
progress . New York , c1991. x, 272 p. : ISBN
0-374-17303-6 : DDC 728/.028/8 20
NA7205 .H735 1991
NYPL [3-MRG 91-7075]

**ARCHITECTURE, DOMESTIC - UNITED
STATES - DESIGNS AND PLANS.**
Farmer, W. D. (William Davis) [Homes for
pleasant living.] W.D. Farmer presents homes
for pleasant living. Atlanta, Ga. (P.O. Box
450022, Atlanta 30345) , c1989. 16 p. : DDC
728/.37/0223 20
NA7205 .F37 1989

Smith, Henry Atterbury, b. 1872. [Books of a
thousand homes. Volume 1.] 500 small houses
of the twenties /. New York , 1990. 312 p. :
ISBN 0-486-26300-2 : DDC 728/.37/0222 20
NA7205 .S6525 1990
NYPL [3-MRG 91-6727]

Staebler, Wendy W. Architectural detailing in
residential interiors /. New York , 1990. 247
p. : ISBN 0-8230-0253-5 : DDC 729 20
NA2718 .S7 1990 NYPL [3-MQG 90-10925]

**ARCHITECTURE, DOMESTIC - UNITED
STATES - HISTORY - 19TH CENTURY.**
Aslet, Clive, 1955- The American country
house /. New Haven , 1990. vii, 302 p. : ISBN
0-300-04757-6
NYPL [3-MQWO 90-12969]

**ARCHITECTURE, DOMESTIC - UNITED
STATES - HISTORY - 20TH CENTURY.**
Aslet, Clive, 1955- The American country
house /. New Haven , 1990. vii, 302 p. : ISBN
0-300-04757-6
NYPL [3-MQWO 90-12969]

**ARCHITECTURE, DOMESTIC - UNITED
STATES - THEMES, MOTIVES.**
Stern, Robert A. M. The American houses of
Robert A.M. Stern /. New York , 1991. p.
ISBN 0-8478-1433-5 DDC 728/.37/092 20
NA737.S64 A4 1991

**ARCHITECTURE, DOMESTIC - YEMEN -
SAN'A'.**
Bonnenfant, Guillemette. L'art du bois à
Sanaa . Aix-en-Provence , c1987. 208 p. :
ISBN 2-85744-315-3
NA3573.6.Y42 S254 1987
NYPL [3-MRX+ 91-4933]

**ARCHITECTURE, EARLY CHRISTIAN -
EGYPT.**
Shihah, Muṣṭafá 'Abd Allāh. Dirāsāt fi
al-'imārah wa-al-funūn al-Qibṭīyah /. [Cairo]
[1988] 412 p., [1] folded leaf plates : ISBN
977-15-8516-9
NA6082 .S55 1988

ARCHITECTURE, ECCLESIASTICAL. see
CHURCH ARCHITECTURE.

ARCHITECTURE - ENGLAND.
Brunskill, R. W. Brick building in Britain /.
London , 1990. 208 p., [16] p. of plates : ISBN
0-575-04457-8 : DDC 693.210941 20
TH5501   NYPL [3-MQWK 90-11098]

Pawley, Martin. Theory and design in the
second machine age /. Oxford, UK ,
Cambridge, Mass., USA , 1990. xii, 189 p. :
ISBN 0-631-15828-6 : DDC 720/.1/05 20
NA2500 .P385 1990 NYPL [3-MQ 91-3255]

**ARCHITECTURE - ENGLAND -
CAMBRIDGESHIRE.**
Pevsner, Nikolaus, Sir,. 1902- Cambridgeshire.
Harmondsworth, 1970. 558 p. : ISBN
0-14-071010-8 DDC 914.25/9/0485
NA969.C3 P4 1970

**ARCHITECTURE - ENGLAND - DEVON -
GUIDE-BOOKS.**
Cherry, Bridget. Devon /. Harmondsworth ,
1989. 976 p., [96] p. of plates : ISBN
0-14-071050-7 :
NYPL [3-MQWK 90-12006]

ARCHITECTURE - ENGLAND - LONDON.
Byrne, Andrew. Bedford Square . London ,

Atlantic Highlands, NJ , 1990. 166 p., 8 p. of
plates : ISBN 0-485-11386-4 DDC
728/.312/0942142 20
NA970 .B9 1990
NYPL [3-MQWK+ 90-11731]

**ARCHITECTURE - ENGLAND -
SHROPSHIRE.**
Garner, Lawrence. The buildings of Shropshire
/. Shrewsbury, England , <1989-. v. <2 > :
ISBN 1-85310-091-9 (v. 2) : DDC 720/.9424/5
20
NA969.S3 G37 1989

**ARCHITECTURE - ENGLAND -
TECHNOLOGIOCAL INNOVATIONS.**
Pawley, Martin. Theory and design in the
second machine age /. Oxford, UK ,
Cambridge, Mass., USA , 1990. xii, 189 p. :
ISBN 0-631-15828-6 : DDC 720/.1/05 20
NA2500 .P385 1990 NYPL [3-MQ 91-3255]

**ARCHITECTURE, ENGLISH - ENGLAND -
LONDON.**
A Prospect of Westminster . [Westminster] ,
c1989. 127 p. : ISBN 0-901602-03-5
NYPL [3-MQWK+ 90-410]

**ARCHITECTURE - ENVIRONMENTAL
ASPECTS.**
American Institute of Architects. Making a
difference . Washington, DC , c1990. 24 p. :
DDC 720/.47 20
NA2542.35 .A45 1990

Mackenzie, Dorothy. Design for the
environment /. New York , 1991. 176 p. :
ISBN 0-8478-1390-8 DDC 720/.47 20
NA2542.35 .M34 1991

**ARCHITECTURE - ENVIRONMENTAL
ASPECTS - CONGRESSES.**
L'Architecture entre nos sens et le sens /.
Clermont-FD , 1986. 167 p. : ISBN
2-09-510800-2
NA2542.35 .A69 1986

**ARCHITECTURE - ENVIRONMENTAL
ASPECTS - GERMANY - AACHEN
REGION.**
Prokop, Eva. Bauen im Grenzland . Aachen
[1989] 227 p. : ISBN 3-89399-092-5
NA7350.A23 P76 1989

L'architecture et la géométrie. Meunié, Louis.
Paris, 1968. 93, [3] p.
NA2760 .M47   NYPL [3-MQ 90-5679]

Architecture et vie traditionnelle en Corse /.
Borel-Léandri, Jean-Marie. [Paris] , 1978. 287
p. : ISBN 2-85869-038-3
NYPL [3-MQWF 90-5907]

ARCHITECTURE - EUROPE.
Çelik, Zeynep. Displaying the Orient .
Berkeley , c1992. p. cm. ISBN 0-520-07494-7
(alk. paper) DDC 725/.91 20
NA957 .C44 1992

Festschrift für Hartmut Biermann /. Weinheim ,
c1990. 400 p. : ISBN 3-527-17712-4
NYPL [3-MAS 91-5197]

Rietzsch, Barbara. Künstliche Grotten des 16.
und 17. Jahrhunderts . München , c1987. ii,
122 p., [39] p. of plates : ISBN 3-89235-017-5
NYPL [3-MQW 91-7052]

Yarwood, Doreen. The architecture of Europe .
Chicago , c1991. vi, 170 p. : ISBN
0-929587-65-0 : DDC 724/.5 20
NA957 .Y37 1990

**ARCHITECTURE - EUROPE -
CONSERVATION AND RESTORATION -
CONGRESSES.**
Les Enjeux du patrimoine architectural du XXe
siècle . [Paris] [1988?] 186 p. : ISBN
2-11-085013-2
NA109.F8 E55 1988

**ARCHITECTURE - EUROPE - THEMES,
MOTIVES - EXHIBITIONS.**
Gianni, Benjamin, 1958- Dice thrown /. New
York, N.Y. , c1989. 56 p. : ISBN
0-910413-62-2 : DDC 728/.92/09730747468 20
NA8201 .G47 1989
NYPL [3-MQV 90-12464]

ARCHITECTURE - FATEHPUR-SIKRI.
Husain, A. B. M., 1934- Fathpur-sikri and its
architecture. Dacca [1970] x, 169 p. DDC
722/.4
NA1508.F3 H8

ARCHITECTURE - FINLAND.
Poole, Scott. The new Finnish architecture /.
New York , 1991. p. cm.   ISBN 0-8478-1316-9
(HC)   DDC 720/.94897/0904 20
NA1455.F5 P66 1991

**ARCHITECTURE - FINLAND -
EXHIBITIONS.**
Kautto, Jussi, 1942- Suomalaista
kaupunkiarkkitehtuuria =. Helsinki , 1990. 233
p. :   ISBN 951-9229-63-9
NA9241.F5 K38 1990

ARCHITECTURE - FINLAND - HELSINKI.
Pöykkö, Kalevi, 1933- Carl Ludvig Engel
1778-1840 . [Helsinki] [1990] 159 p. :   ISBN
951-772-066-1
NA1088.E6 P69 1990

**ARCHITECTURE - FINLAND - HELSINKI -
GUIDE-BOOKS.**
Helsinki, Espoo, Kauniainen, Vantaa .
Helsingissä , c1990. 195 p. :   ISBN 951-1-10582-5
NA1455.F52 H4575 1990

ARCHITECTURE - FLORIDA.
Mizner, Addison, 1872-1933. Florida
architecture of Addison Mizner /. Boulder,
Colo. , 1991. p. cm.   ISBN 1-87865-002-5 :   DDC
720/.92 20
NA737.M59 A4 1991

**ARCHITECTURE - FLORIDA - SEASIDE -
THEMES, MOTIVES - EXHIBITIONS.**
Seaside /. New York, N.Y. , c1991. p. cm.
ISBN 0-910413-26-6 (paper) :   DDC
720/.9759/41 20
NA735.S44 S43 1991

ARCHITECTURE - FRANCE.
Les Architectes de la liberté, 1789-1799. Paris ,
c1989. 396 p. :   ISBN 2-903639-65-5
NYPL [3-MQWF 90-11622]
Bibal, François. L'Institut de France /. [Paris?] ,
c1988. 164 p. :   ISBN 2-905547-05-7
NYPL [MFX+ (Bibal) 90-1062]
Le Château en France /. Paris , 1988. 448 p.,
[16] p. of plates :   ISBN 2-7013-0741-4
NYPL [3-MQWF+ 90-11996]
Vitou, Elisabeth. Gabriel Guévrékian,
1900-1970 . Paris , c1987. 150 p. :   ISBN
2-86649-003-7 :   DDC 720/.92/4 19
NYPL [3-MQZ (Guévrékian) 91-4588]

ARCHITECTURE - FRANCE - ARCADON.
Arcachon, la ville d'hiver /. Liège , 1988. 238
p. :   ISBN 2-87009-372-1
NA1051.A73 A73 1988

**ARCHITECTURE - FRANCE -
CONSERVATION AND RESTORATION -
CONGRESSES.**
Les Enjeux du patrimoine architectural du XXe
siècle . [Paris] [1988?] 186 p. :   ISBN
2-11-085013-2
NA109.F8 E55 1988

ARCHITECTURE - FRANCE - CORSICA.
Borel-Léandri, Jean-Marie. Architecture et vie
traditionnelle en Corse /. [Paris] , 1978. 287
p. :   ISBN 2-85869-038-3
NYPL [3-MQWF 90-5907]

**ARCHITECTURE - FRANCE -
EXHIBITIONS.**
40 architectes de moins de quarante ans, Paris
/. [Paris] , c1990. 311 p. :   ISBN 2-281-15116-6
NA1048 .A13 1990

ARCHITECTURE - FRANCE - LAON.
Laon, ville haute, Aisne /. Amiens , c1989. 64
p. :   ISBN 2-906340-06-5 :   DDC 720/.44/345 20
NA1051.L3 L36 1989

**ARCHITECTURE - FRANCE - MARSEILLE -
THEMES, MOTIVES.**
Architectures historiques à Marseille .
Aix-en-Provence , c1987. 141 p. :   ISBN
2-85744-290-4 :   DDC 720/.944/912 19
NA1051.M37 U73 1987
NYPL [3-MQWF+ 90-12768]

ARCHITECTURE - FRANCE - PARIS.
Parigi . Roma [1990] 242 p. :
N1050 .P27 1990

**ARCHITECTURE - FRANCE - PARIS -
EXHIBITIONS.**
Le Panthéon, symbole des révolutions .
[Montréal] : [Paris] : 339 p. :   ISBN

2-7084-0386-9 (Picard)
IN PROCESS (ONLINE)
NYPL [3-MQWF 90-10797]
Paris, la ville et ses projets . Paris , c1989. 253
p. :   ISBN 2-907742-04-3
NYPL [3-MQWF+ 90-10864]

**ARCHITECTURE - FRANCE - PARIS -
GUIDE-BOOKS.**
Martin, Hervé. Guide de l'architecture moderne
à Paris =. Paris , c1990. 318 p. :   ISBN
2-86738-483-4 :   DDC 720/.944/3610904 20
NA1050 .M35 1990
Salvadori, Renzo. Architect's guide to Paris /.
Sevenoaks, Kent, England , 1990. 137 p. :
ISBN 0-408-50068-9   DDC 720/.944/361 20
NA1050 .S25 1990

**ARCHITECTURE - FRANCE - SAINT-
VÉRAN - DETAILS.**
Perron, Claude. Saint-Véran . La Calade,
Aix-en-Provence , c1990. 159 p. :   ISBN
2-85744-465-6
NA8203 .P47 1990

**ARCHITECTURE, FRENCH - FRANCE - AIX-
EN-PROVENCE.**
Boyer, Jean, conservateur. Le patrimoine
architectural d'Aix-en-Provence, XVIe, XVIIe,
XVIIIe siècles . Aix-en-Provence , 19. 191 p. :
NYPL [3-MQWF+ 90-11534]

ARCHITECTURE, GEORGIAN - ENGLAND.
Hussey, Christopher, 1899- English country
houses /. London , 1988. 3 v. :   ISBN
1-85149-029-9 (set : pbk.)
NYPL [3-MRG 90-12887]

**ARCHITECTURE, GEORGIAN - ENGLAND -
LONDON.**
Byrne, Andrew. Bedford Square . London ,
Atlantic Highlands, NJ , 1990. 166 p., 8 p. of
plates :   ISBN 0-485-11386-4   DDC
728/.312/0942142 20
NA970 .B9 1990
NYPL [3-MQWK+ 90-11731]

**ARCHITECTURE, GEORGIAN - GREAT
BRITAIN.**
Gray, Alexander Stuart. Fanlights /. London ,
1990. 148 p. :   ISBN 0-7136-3077-9 :   DDC
721.823 20   *NYPL [3-MRR 91-3295]*

**ARCHITECTURE, GEORGIAN - UNITED
STATES.**
Gray, Alexander Stuart. Fanlights /. London ,
1990. 148 p. :   ISBN 0-7136-3077-9 :   DDC
721.823 20   *NYPL [3-MRR 91-3295]*
Hewitt, Mark A. The architecture of Mott B.
Schmidt /. New York , 1991. p. cm.   ISBN
0-8478-1399-1   DDC 720/.92 20
NA737.S355 H4 1991

**ARCHITECTURE, GERMAN - FRANCE -
KEMBS.**
Abel, Louis. Kembs en Sundgau rhénan .
[Kembs, France] , c1986. 285 p. :
NA1053.Z45 A83 1986

ARCHITECTURE - GERMANY.
Dal Co, Francesco, 1945- Figures of
architecture and thought . New York , 1990.
344 p. :   ISBN 0-8478-0654-5 (pbk.) :   DDC
720/.943 19
NA1067 .D35 1990
NYPL [3-MQWD 90-10690]
Formalhaut (Group) Formalhaut Architektur
Skulptur . Darmstadt , c1989. 54 p. :   ISBN
3-925376-40-2   *NYPL [3-MGI 91-7331]*
Kunst auf Befehl? . München , c1990. 275 p. :
ISBN 3-7814-0285-1 :   DDC 701/.03 20
N6868.5.N37 K85 1990

**ARCHITECTURE - GERMANY - BAMBERG -
CONSERVATION AND RESTORATION -
CONGRESSES.**
Denkmalkunde in Bamberg . Bamberg [1990]
77 p. :   DDC 720/.28/80943318 20
NA109.G3 D44 1990

ARCHITECTURE - GERMANY - BERLIN.
Behr, Adalbert. Bauen in Berlin, 1973 bis 1987
/. Leipzig , 1987. 199 p. :   ISBN 3-7338-0040-0
DDC 720/.9431/55 20
NA1085 .B437 1987
Zum Umgang mit dem Gestapo-Gelände .
[Berlin , 1988] 105, 25, 73 p. :
NA1068.5.N37 Z85 1988

**ARCHITECTURE - GERMANY -
BIBLIOGRAPHY.**
Bauen im Dritten Reich /. Stuttgart [1989] 73
p. ;   ISBN 3-8167-0278-3
NYPL [3-MQWD 90-10818]

**ARCHITECTURE - GERMANY -
CONSERVATION AND RESTORATION.**
Die Denkmalpflege als Plage und Frage .
München , 1989. xii, 196 p. :   ISBN
3-422-06037-5
NA109.G3 D446 1989

**ARCHITECTURE - GERMANY (EAST) -
SAXONY - CONSERVATION AND
RESTORATION.**
Magirius, Heinrich. Sachsen . Berlin , 1989. 360
p. :   ISBN 3-345-00292-2
NYPL [3-MQWD 90-2105]

**ARCHITECTURE - GERMANY -
FRIESLAND - DETAILS.**
Jessel, Hans, 1956- Friesenhaustüren /.
Hamburg , c1990. 56 p. :   ISBN 3-89234-159-1
NA7350.F84 J4 1990

ARCHITECTURE - GERMANY - HISTORY.
Festschrift für Georg Hoeltje /. Hannover ,
1988. 160 p. :
NYPL [3-MQWD+ 90-12015]

**ARCHITECTURE - GERMANY - KASSEL
(LANDKREIS)**
Kreis Kassel /. Braunschweig/Wiesbaden ,
1990- v. <1 > :   ISBN 3-528-06239-8   DDC
720/.943/412 20
NA1076.K37 K7 1990

ARCHITECTURE - GERMANY - LEIPZIG.
--Die ganze Welt im kleinen-- . Leipzig , 1989.
300 p. :   ISBN 3-363-00419-2
NYPL [MAMG 91-6223]

**ARCHITECTURE - GERMANY - LEIPZIG -
GUIDE-BOOKS.**
Hocquél, Wolfgang. Leipzig . Berlin , c1990.
284 p. :   ISBN 3-350-00333-8   DDC 720/.9432/122
20
NA1086.L4 H63 1990

**ARCHITECTURE - GERMANY - LOWER
SAXONY.**
Baudenkmale in Niedersachsen /. Hannover ,
c1990. 356 p. :   ISBN 3-87706-322-5   DDC
720/.943/59 20
NA1081 .B38 1990

**ARCHITECTURE - GERMANY -
LUDWIGSHAFEN AM RHEIN.**
Oexner, Mara. Stadt Ludwigshafen am Rhein /.
Düsseldorf , 1990. 194 p. :
NYPL [3-MQWD+ 91-4455]

**ARCHITECTURE - GERMANY - MAINZ
(RHINELAND-PALATINATE)**
Stadt Mainz /. Düsseldorf , 1986-1988. 2 v. :
ISBN 3-590-31032-4 (Bd. 1)   DDC 720/.943/43
19
NA1086.M26 S38 1986
NYPL [3-MQWD+ 90-1818]

ARCHITECTURE - GERMANY - PRUSSIA.
Buch, Felicitas. Studien zur Preussischen
Denkmalpflege am Beispiel konservatorischer
Arbeiten Ferdinand von Quasts /. Worms ,
c1990. 250 p. :   ISBN 3-88462-929-8
NA109.G3 B83 1990

**ARCHITECTURE - GERMANY - PRUSSIA -
CONSERVATION AND RESTORATION.**
Buch, Felicitas. Studien zur Preussischen
Denkmalpflege am Beispiel konservatorischer
Arbeiten Ferdinand von Quasts /. Worms ,
c1990. 250 p. :   ISBN 3-88462-929-8
NA109.G3 B83 1990

**ARCHITECTURE - GERMANY -
REGENSBURG - EXHIBITIONS.**
Architektur in Regensburg 1933-1945 /.
Regensburg , 1989. 139 p. :   ISBN 3-927730-01-7
NA1086.R4 A7 1989

**ARCHITECTURE - GERMANY - SUHL -
GUIDE-BOOKS.**
Bezirk Suhl /. Berlin , 1989. 160 p. :   ISBN
3-345-00213-2
NA1089.2.S84 B49 1989

**ARCHITECTURE - GERMANY (WEST) -
DUDERSTADT - CONSERVATION AND
RESTORATION.**
Das Rathaus in Duderstadt /. Hameln , c1989.
304 p. :   ISBN 3-87585-096-3
NYPL [3-MQWD+ 91-5449]

ARCHITECTURE - GERMANY (WEST) - HAMBURG - GUIDE-BOOKS.
Hipp, Hermann. Freie und Hansestadt Hamburg . Köln , 1990. 608 p. : ISBN 3-7701-1590-2 DDC 720/.943/515 20
NA1086.H3 H57 1990

ARCHITECTURE, GOTHIC.
Radding, Charles. Medieval architecture, medieval learning . New Haven, CT , c1991. p. cm. ISBN 0-300-04918-8 (alk. paper) DDC 723/.4 20
NA390 .R33 1991

ARCHITECTURE, GOTHIC - ENGLAND.
Kowa, Günter, 1954- Architektur der englischen Gotik /. Köln , c1990. 336 p. : ISBN 3-7701-1969-X DDC 720/.942/0902 20
NA440 .K6 1990

ARCHITECTURE, GOTHIC - EUROPE, GERMAN-SPEAKING - CONSERVATION AND RESTORATION.
Steingewordene Träume . Ulm , c1990. 111 p. :
NA5559 .S68 1990

ARCHITECTURE, GOTHIC - GERMANY - MARBURG.
Schneider Berrenberg, Rüdiger. Sie bauten ein Abbild der Seele . München , Solingen , 1988. xii, 149 p. :
NA5586.M23 S36 1988

ARCHITECTURE, GOTHIC - GERMANY - MÜNSTER IN WESTFALEN.
Böker, Hans Josef. Die Marktpfarrkirche St. Lamberti zu Münster . Bonn , 1989. 229 p. : ISBN 3-7749-2382-5
NA5586.M853 B65 1989

ARCHITECTURE, GOTHIC - ITALY - MILAN.
Pifferi, Enzo, 1940- Milano gotica /. Como , c1988. 153, [4] p. : DDC 720/.945/210902 20
NA5621.M6 P53 1988
NYPL [3-MRBD+ 91-4974]

ARCHITECTURE, GOTHIC - ITALY - VENICE.
Diruf, Hermann. Paläste Venedigs vor 1500 . München , c1990. 224 p. : ISBN 3-89235-033-7
NA7756.V4 D57 1990

ARCHITECTURE, GOTHIC - PORTUGAL.
Chicó, Mário Tavares. A arquitectura gótica em Portugal /. Lisboa , 1968. 239 p., [21] leaves of plates : DDC 726/.5/09469
NA5823 .C48 1968
NYPL [3-MQW 90-5436]

ARCHITECTURE, GOTHIC - PORTUGAL - ALENTEJO.
Silva, José Custódio Vieira da. O tardo-gótico em Portugal . Lisboa , c1989. 206 p. : ISBN 972-240-725-2 :
NA1329.A43 S55 1989

ARCHITECTURE, GOTHIC - SWITZERLAND - ZURICH (CANTON) - EXHIBITIONS.
Jezler, Peter. Der spätgotische Kirchenbau in der Zürcher Landschaft . Wetzikon , c1988. 144 p. : ISBN 3-85981-150-9 : DDC 726/.5/094945707449457 20
NA5849.Z87 J49 1988
NYPL [3-MRBB 91-3251]

ARCHITECTURE, GOTHIC - GREAT BRITAIN.
Dixon, Roger, 1935- Victorian architecture. New York , 1978. 288 p. : ISBN 0-19-520048-9 DDC 720/.941
NA967 .D59

Platt, Colin. The architecture of medieval Britain . New Haven , 1990. ix, 325 p. : ISBN 0-300-04953-6 DDC 720/.941/0902 20
NA963 .P53 1991
NYPL [3-MQWK 91-6545]

Summerson, John Newenham, Sir, 1904- The unromantic castle and other essays /. London , New York , 1990. 288 p. : ISBN 0-500-34112-5
NYPL [3-MQWK 90-10906]

ARCHITECTURE - GREAT BRITAIN - BIBLIOGRAPHY.
Harris, Eileen. British architectural books and writers, 1556-1785 /. Cambridge [England] , New York , 1990. 571 p. : ISBN 0-521-38551-2 DDC 016.72 20
NA965 .H37 1990
NYPL [MQWK 90-13195]

ARCHITECTURE - GREECE - ATHENS - EXHIBITIONS.

Athènes affaire européenne . Athènes , c1985. 2 v. :
NA1100 .A84 1985

ARCHITECTURE - GREECE - DETAILS.
Knell, Heiner. Mythos und Polis . Darmstadt , c1990. xii, 197 p. : ISBN 3-534-11025-0
NYPL [3-MGH+ 91-6124]

ARCHITECTURE, GREEK - ITALY - SICILY.
Mitens, Karina. Teatri greci e teatri ispirati all'architettura greca in Sicilia e nell'Italia meridionale, c. 350-50 a.C. . Roma , 1988. 176 p., [1] fold. leaf of plates : ISBN 88-7062-660-1
NYPL [3-MQM+ 90-12635]

ARCHITECTURE - GUIDE-BOOKS.
Wonders of the world. Chicago , Basingstoke [England] , 1991. p. cm. ISBN 0-528-83443-6 : DDC 720 20
NA200 .W66 1991

ARCHITECTURE - HANDBOOKS, MANUALS, ETC.
Notes on architecture. Los Altos, Calif. , c1990. 46 p. : ISBN 1-560-52057-4 : DDC 720 20
NA2540 .N67 1990

Spence, William Perkins, 1925- Architecture . Mission Hills, Calif. , c1991. x, 661 p. : ISBN 0-02-677123-3 (text) DDC 721 20
NA2540 .S6 1991

ARCHITECTURE, HINDU - INDIA - HAMPĪ.
Filliozat, Pierre Sylvain. Hampi-Vijayanagar . New Delhi , 1988. 1 portfolio : DDC 726/.145/095487 20
NA6008.H35 F53 1988
NYPL [3-MQWS+ 91-6052]

ARCHITECTURE - HISTORIOGRAPHY.
Van Pelt, Robert Jan. Architectural principles in the age of historicism /. New Haven , 1991. p. cm. ISBN 0-300-04999-4 DDC 720/.1 20
NA2500 .V34 1991

ARCHITECTURE - HISTORY.
'Abd al-Jawād, Tawfīq Aḥmad. Tārīkh al-'imārah /. S.l. [1968-<1969]. v. <1-2 > :
NA200 .A24

The Illustrated encyclopedia of architects and architecture /. New York, NY, 1991. p. cm. ISBN 0-8230-2539-X : DDC 720/.3 20
NA40 .I45 1991

Istoriiā arkhitektury . Moskva , 1988. 114 p. ;
NA200 .I88 1988

Lorange, Erik, 1919- Historiske byer . [Oslo] , c1990. 310 p. : ISBN 82-00-21048-0 DDC 720/.9 20
NA200 .L65 1990

Wickberg, Nils Erik, 1909- Städer, byggnader-- /. Helsingfors , c1989. 144 p. : ISBN 951-52-1262-6
NA200 .W54 1989

ARCHITECTURE - HUMAN FACTORS.
Krings-Heckemeier, Marie-Therese. Kommunikation und gebaute Umwelt . Witterschlick , 1990. 264 p. ; ISBN 3-925267-35-2
NA7125 .K75 1990

Lajcha, Ladislav. Pohyb divadla /. Bratislava , 1989. 142 p. : ISBN 80-222-0031-X :
NA6821 .L28 1989

Livingston, Rodolfo. Arquitectura y autoritarismo /. Buenos Aires [1991] 244 p. : ISBN 950-51-5038-5 DDC 720/.1/03 20
NA2542.4 .L58 1991

ARCHITECTURE - HUMAN FACTORS - CONGRESSES.
L'Architecture entre nos sens et le sens /. Clermont-FD , 1986. 167 p. : ISBN 2-09-510800-2
NA2542.35 .A69 1986

ARCHITECTURE - HUNGARY - CONGRESSES.
Magyar Építőművészek Szövetsége. Magyar Építőművészek Szövetsége IV. konferenciája és jubileumi közgyűlése . Budapest [1962] 322 p. ;
NA1012 .M33 1962

ARCHITECTURE - IDAHO.
Attebery, Jennifer Eastman, 1951- Building Idaho . Moscow, Idaho , 1991. x, 166 p. : ISBN 0-89301-139-8 DDC 720/.9796 20
NA730.I2 A88 1990
NYPL [3-MQWO 91-4971]

ARCHITECTURE - ILLINOIS - CHICAGO - CATALOGS.
Art Institute of Chicago. Fragments of Chicago's past . Chicago, IL , 1990. 180 p. : ISBN 0-86559-088-5 DDC 720/.9773/1107477311 20
NA735.C4 A77 1990
NYPL [3-MQWO 91-3419]

ARCHITECTURE - ILLINOIS - CHICAGO - HUMAN FACTORS.
Gandelsonas, Mario, 1938- The urban text /. London, England ; Boston, Mass. : p. cm. ISBN 0-262-57084-X (pbk.) DDC 711/.4/0977311 20
NA9127.C4 G36 1990

ARCHITECTURE IN ART.
Păcurariu, Dan D. Arhitectura în viziunea pictorilor /. București , 1990. 185 p., [24] p. of plates : ISBN 973-240-147-8 :
ND1410 .P25 1990

ARCHITECTURE IN ART - EXHIBITIONS.
Devlin, Harry. Portraits of American architecture, November 4th to December 2nd, 1979, Morris Museum of Arts and Sciences, Morristown, N.J. /. Morristown, N.J. , c1979. [38] p. : DDC 759.13
ND237.D43 A4 1979
NYPL [3-MCX D497 90-12735]

Dwellings . Philadelphia , c1978. 16 p. : ISBN 0-88454-050-2
N6512 .D85   *NYPL [3-MAMT+ 79-2026]*

Sironi, Mario, 1885-1961. Mario Sironi . Milano , c1990. 224 p. : ISBN 88-20-20968-3 :
N6923.S53 A4 1990

Architecture in Australia . Freeland, J. M. (John Maxwell), 1920- Ringwood, Victoria, Australia , New York, N.Y., U. S.A. , 19. 328 p. : ISBN 0-14-021152-7
NA1600 .F7 1972

Architecture in Brisbane /. De Gruchy, Graham. Bowen Hills, Brisbane, Qld. , 1988. 132 p. : ISBN 0-86439-078-5
NYPL [3-MQWZ+ 89-21433]

Architecture in detail .
(01) Jenkins, David. Mound stand, Lord's Cricket Ground, London, 1987 . London , New York , 1991. 1 v. (ca. 58 p.) : ISBN 1-85454-558-2 (pbk.) : DDC 725.827 20
NA6800
NYPL [3-MQZ+ (Hopkins) 91-6983]

(02) Manser, José. Joseph shops . London , Van Nostrand Reinhold, 1991. [60] p. : ISBN 1-85454-445-4 (pbk.) : DDC 747.8521 20
NK2195.S89   *NYPL [3-MLT+ 91-6982]*

(03) Hollamby, Edward. Red House . London , New York , 1991. [60] p. : ISBN 1-85454-704-6 (pbk.) : DDC 724.6 20
NA645.5.A
NYPL [3-MQZ+ (Webb) 91-6981]

(04) Abel, Chris. Renault centre . London , New York , 1991. [60] p. : ISBN 1-85454-776-3 (pbk.) : DDC 720.92 20
NA997.F6
NYPL [3-MQZ+ (Foster) 91-6980]

(05) Jenkins, David. Financial Times Print Works, London, 1988 . London , New York , 1991. ca. 60 p. : ISBN 1-85454-255-9 (pbk.) : DDC 725.4 20
NA6400
NYPL [3-MQZ+ (Grimshaw) 91-6989]

Architecture in Jersey /. Boots, Maurice. Jersey , c1986. xii, 180 p. : ISBN 0-86120-015-2 DDC 720/.9423/41 20
NA995.J47 B66 1986

Architecture in Lebanon . Ragette, Friedrich. Beirut , 1974. xvi [i.e. viii], 214 p. : DDC 728/.095692
NA7419.L4 R33 NYPL [3-MQWS 90-5443]

Architecture in perspective : a five-year retrospective ofaward-winning illustrations / American Society of Architectural Perspectivists. New York, N.Y. : Van Nostrand Reinhold, c1991. p. cm. Includes index. ISBN 0-442-00700-0 DDC 720/.22/27309043 20
1. Architectural rendering - United States - Awards - Exhibitions. I. American Society of Architectural Perspectivists.
NA2780 .A73 1991

Architecture in the culture of early humanism .

Smith, Christine (Christine Hunnikin) New
York , 1991. p. cm. ISBN 0-19-506128-4 (alk.
paper) DDC 724/.12 20
NA510 .S65 1991

Architecture in the Scandinavian countries /.
Donnelly, Marian C. (Marian Card) Cambridge,
Mass. , c1991. p. cm. ISBN 0-262-04118-9 DDC
720/.948 20
NA1201 .D66 1991

Architecture in watercolor /. Schaller, Thomas
W. (Thomas Wells), 1950- New York, N.Y. ,
c1990. x, 234 p. : ISBN 0-442-23484-8 DDC
751.42/244 20
NA2726.5 .S34 1990
  NYPL [3-MBO 90-11736]

ARCHITECTURE - INDIA - GOA.
Hutt, Antony. Goa . Buckhurst Hill, Essex,
England , 1988. 192 p. : ISBN 0-905906-66-7
  NYPL [3-MQWS 89-17186]

ARCHITECTURE - INDIA - HISTORY.
Tadgell, Christopher, 1939- The history of
architecture in India . London , 1990. ix, 336
p. : ISBN 1-85454-350-4 : DDC 720.95 20
NA1501 *NYPL [3-MAF 90-12863]*

ARCHITECTURE - INDIA - ORISSA.
Bose, Nirmal Kumar. Canons of Orissan
architecture /. New Delhi , 1982. vi, 211 p., 34
p. of plates : DDC 720/.954/13 20
NA1507.O7 B6 1982

ARCHITECTURE, INDIGENOUS. see
  VERNACULAR ARCHITECTURE.

ARCHITECTURE - INDONESIA -
  BANDUNG - THEMES, MOTIVES.
Dana, Djefry W. (Djefry Wahjudy) Ciri
perancangan kota Bandung /. Jakarta , 1990.
xiv, 143 p. : ISBN 979-403-916-0
NA9260.B35 D35 1990

ARCHITECTURE - INDONESIA - JAVA.
Dumarçay, Jacques. Le savoir des maîtres
d'œuvre javanais aux XIIIe et XIVe siècles /.
Paris , 1986. 122 p. : ISBN 2-85539-417-1 (pbk.)
  NYPL [3-MQWS+ 90-11045]

ARCHITECTURE, INDUSTRIAL - EUROPE.
Industriearchitektur in Europa =. Hannover ,
c1990. 128 p. : ISBN 3-87870-350-3 DDC
725/.4/09409048 20
NA6403.E85 I53 1990

ARCHITECTURE, INDUSTRIAL - SWEDEN.
When people matter /. Sweden , Solna, Sweden
[1989] 223 p. : ISBN 91-540-5059-6 DDC
725/.4/09485 20
NA6403.S8 W47 1989

Architecture intérieure et décoration en France,
des origines à 1875 /. Feray, Jean. Paris ,
c1988. 399 p. : ISBN 2-7013-0752-X DDC
729/.0944 20
NA2850 .F4 1988
  NYPL [3-MLF+ 90-12087]

ARCHITECTURE, ISLAMIC - ARAB
  COUNTRIES.
Steele, James. Hassan Fathy /. London , New
York , 1988. 149 p. : ISBN 0-312-01140-7 (U. S. :
pbk.) : DDC 720/.92/4 19
NA1585.F37 S74 1988
  NYPL [3-MQZ+ (Fathy) 88-4615]

ARCHITECTURE, ISLAMIC - BALKAN
  PENINSULA.
Kiel, Machiel. Studies on the Ottoman
architecture of the Balkans /. Brookfield, Vt. ,
c1990. 361 p. in various pagings : ISBN
0-86078-276-X : DDC 720/.9496 20
NA1375 .K54 1990 NYPL [3-MQT 91-3249]

ARCHITECTURE, ISLAMIC -
  BIBLIOGRAPHY.
Architektur und Städtebau des Islam /.
Stuttgart , 1985- v. ; ISBN 3-8167-0105-1 DDC
016.72/0917/671 19
Z5943.I84 A73 1984 NA380
  NYPL [3-MQT 91-826]

ARCHITECTURE, ISLAMIC - EUROPE.
Çelik, Zeynep. Displaying the Orient .
Berkeley , c1992. p. cm. ISBN 0-520-07494-7
(alk. paper) DDC 725/.91 20
NA957 .C44 1992

ARCHITECTURE, ISLAMIC - ITALY -
  SICILY.
Bellafiore, Giuseppe. Architettura in Sicilia nelle
età islamica e normanna . Milano , c1990. 366

p. : ISBN 88-7177-010-2 :
  NYPL [3-MQO 91-3372]
Bellafiore, Giuseppe. Architettura in Sicilia nelle
età islamica e normanna (827-1194) /.
Palermo , c1990. 366 p. : ISBN 88-7177-010-2 :
DDC 720/.945/809021 20
NA1109.S5 B4 1990

ARCHITECTURE, ISLAMIC - LEBANON.
L'Architecture libanaise du XVe au XIXe
siècle . Beyrouth, Liban [1985] 376 p., lxviii p.
of plates :
NA1476.6 .A78 1985

ARCHITECTURE, ISLAMIC - MOROCCO.
Ben el-Khadir, Mohamed. Architectures
régionales . [Morocco] 1989 (Casablanca :
Impr. Najah el Jadida) 211 p. :
NA1590 .B46 1989

ARCHITECTURE, ISLAMIC - RUSSIAN S.F.S.
  R. - DAGESTANSKAĬA A.S.S.R.
Drevniaĭa i srednevekovaĭa arkhitektura
Dagestana . Makhachkala , 1989. 184, [4] p. :
NA1492.8 .D7 1989

ARCHITECTURE, ISLAMIC - SAUDI
  ARABIA - MEDINA.
Ṭāhā, Ḥātim ‘Umar, 1957- Ṭaybah wa-fannuhā
al-rafī‘ /. [Medina] [198-] 140 p. :
NA7419.S2 T27 1980z

ARCHITECTURE, ISLAMIC - TURKEY -
  CATALOGS.
Ülgen, Ali Saim. Mimar Sinan yapıları /.
[Ankara] , 1989. 2 portfolios (266 plates) :
ISBN 975-16-0164-9
NA1373.S5 A4 1989
  *NYPL [*OPR+++ 90-6]*

ARCHITECTURE, ISLAMIC - TURKEY -
  DESIGNS AND PLANS.
Burelli, Augusto Romano, 1938- La moschea di
Sinan . Venezia , 1988. 127 p. : ISBN
88-85067-56-5 (pbk.)
  NYPL [3-MQT+ 90-10684]

ARCHITECTURE, ISLAMIC - TURKEY -
  FATIH (ISTANBUL)
Eyice, Semavi. Fotoğraflarla Fatih anıtları /.
Fatih [Istanbul, Turkey] [1989?] 126 p. :
NA1370 .E88 1989

ARCHITECTURE, ISLAMIC - TURKEY -
  ISTANBUL.
Cantay, Tanju. XVI.-XVII. yüzyıllarda
Süleymaniye Camii ve bağlı yapıları /. Beyoğlu,
İstanbul , 1989. 56, 32 p., [2] leaves of plates :
ISBN 975-7622-05-2
NA5870.S93 C36 1989

ARCHITECTURE, ISLAMIC - TURKEY -
  KONYA - THEMES, MOTIVES.
Sarre, Friedrich Paul Theodor, 1865-1945.
Konia . Berlin [1921] 30 p., 12 leaves of plates
(some folded) : DDC 720/.9564 20
NA5871.k86 S27 1921

ARCHITECTURE, ISLAMIC - UNITED
  STATES.
Çelik, Zeynep. Displaying the Orient .
Berkeley , c1992. p. cm. ISBN 0-520-07494-7
(alk. paper) DDC 725/.91 20
NA957 .C44 1992

ARCHITECTURE, ITALIAN - ITALY - BARI.
Semerari, Livia. Una vicenda urbana . Fasano
(Brindisi) , 1990. 275 p., [8] leaves of plates :
ISBN 88-7514-425-7
  NYPL [3-MQWB+ 91-5800]

ARCHITECTURE - ITALY.
Hetzer, Theodor, 1890-1946. Italienische
Architektur . Stuttgart , c1990. 472 p. : ISBN
3-87838-905-1 DDC 720/.945/09024 20
NA1115 .H48 1990

Sinisgalli, Leonardo, 1908- Promenades
architecturales /. Bergamo , c1987. 125 p. ;
ISBN 88-7766-013-9 :
NA1111 .S48 1987
  NYPL [3-MQWB 91-6903]

ARCHITECTURE - ITALY - AWARDS.
Marble Architectural Awards . [Firenze] ,
Carrara [1988?] 106 p. :
IN PROCESS (ONLINE)
  NYPL [3-MQWB 91-5870]

ARCHITECTURE - ITALY - BOLOGNA -
  HISTORY.
Palazzo Poggi da dimora aristocratica a sede
dell'Università di Bologna /. Bologna , c1988.

222 p. : ISBN 88-7779-054-7 DDC 378.45/41 20
LF3274 .P35 1988
  NYPL [3-MQWB 90-12437]

ARCHITECTURE - ITALY - DESIGNS AND
  PLANS.
Elaborati urbanistici . Milano [1987?] 10
pamphlets in portfolio :
  NYPL [3-MQWB 90-11014]

ARCHITECTURE - ITALY - FIULI-VENEZIA
  GIULIA - INFLUENCES - CONGRESSES.
Brandariz, Gustavo A. El aporte friulano a la
arquitectura argentina /. Buenos Aires , 1987.
52 leaves :
NA830 .B7 1987

ARCHITECTURE - ITALY - FLORENCE -
  DETAILS - CATALOGS.
Centro di Firenze restituito . Firenze , c1989.
614 p., 8 p. of plates :
  NYPL [3-MAVZ+ (Florence) 90-12442]

ARCHITECTURE - ITALY - GENOA -
  DETAILS.
La Scultura a Genova e in Liguria. Genova ,
c1987- v. : *NYPL [3-MGI+ 90-2770]*

ARCHITECTURE - ITALY - LIGURIA -
  DETAILS.
La Scultura a Genova e in Liguria. Genova ,
c1987- v. : *NYPL [3-MGI+ 90-2770]*

ARCHITECTURE - ITALY - LUCCA - GUIDE-
  BOOKS.
Grieco, Romy. Lucca . Bologna, Italy , Lucca
[1990?] 99 p. : DDC 709/.45/53 20
N6921.L82 G74 1990

ARCHITECTURE - ITALY - MASSA-
  CARRARA - GUIDE-BOOKS.
Giorgieri, Pietro. Itinerari apuani di architettura
moderna /. Firenze , 1989. 263 p. :
  NYPL [3-MQWB 90-11118]

ARCHITECTURE - ITALY - MODENA.
Bertuzzi, Giordano. Il rinnovamento edilizio a
Modena nella prima metà dell'Ottocento /.
Modena , 1987. 350 p. :
  NYPL [3-MQWB+ 91-6476]

ARCHITECTURE - ITALY - PALERMO.
Palermo, norma di piano e progetto /. [Italy] ,
Roma , c1990. 189 p. : DDC 720/.945/823 20
NA1121.P3 P36 1990

ARCHITECTURE - ITALY - REGGIO DI
  CALABRIA.
L'Architettura di Gino Zani per la ricostruzione
di Reggio Calabria (1909-1935) /. Roma ,
c1986. 140 p. :
  NYPL [3-MQZ (Zani) 90-12335]

ARCHITECTURE - ITALY - ROME.
D'Onofrio, Cesare, 1921- Visitiamo Roma nel
Quattrocento . Roma , 1989. 307 p. :
  NYPL [3-MQWB 91-4311]
D'Onofrio, Cesare, 1921- Visitiamo Roma nel
Quattrocento . Roma , 1989. 307 p. :
  NYPL [3-MQWB 91-4311]
Una Famiglia di architetti e costruttori a Roma,
1887-1987 /. Roma , 1987. xxiv, 75 p. : ISBN
88-7813-027-3
  NYPL [3-MQWB+ 90-9457]
Gallavotti Cavallero, Daniela. Palazzi di Roma
dal XIV al XX secolo /. Roma , c1989. 268 p. :
ISBN 88-85085-03-2
IN PROCESS (ONLINE)
  NYPL [3-MQWB+ 90-12319]

ARCHITECTURE - ITALY - ROME -
  CONSERVATION AND RESTORATION.
Santa Maria sopra Minerva /. Roma , c1990.
303 p. : ISBN 88-7060-223-0
  NYPL [3-MRBD+ 91-7451]

ARCHITECTURE - ITALY - ROME - GUIDE-
  BOOKS.
Salvadori, Renzo. Architect's guide to Rome /.
London , Boston , 1990. 144 p. : ISBN
0-408-50054-9 DDC 720/.945/632 20
NA1120 .S27 1990

ARCHITECTURE - ITALY - ROME -
  WORKING DRAWINGS.
Schumacher, Thomas L. [Danteum di Terragni.
English.] The Danteum . Princeton, NJ , c1985.
169 p. : ISBN 0-910413-09-6
NA2707.T466 S3713 1985
  NYPL [3-MQZ (Terragni) 86-3775]

ARCHITECTURE - ITALY - SICILY.
Bellafiore, Giuseppe. Architettura in Sicilia nelle

età islamica e normanna . Milano , c1990. 366
p. : ISBN 88-7177-010-2 :
NYPL [3-MQO 91-3372]

Bellafiore, Giuseppe. Architettura in Sicilia nelle
età islamica e normanna (827-1194) /.
Palermo , c1990. 366 p. : ISBN 88-7177-010-2 :
DDC 720/.945/809021 20
NA1109.S5 B4 1990

**ARCHITECTURE - ITALY - TURIN -
CONSERVATION AND RESTORATION.**
Quirico, Giambattista, 1947- Il Regio
Manicomio di Via Giulio in Torino,
1830-1985 . Torino , 1987. 117 p. :
NYPL [3-MQWB+ 90-10584]

ARCHITECTURE - ITALY - TUSCANY.
Giusti, Maria Adriana. Edilizia in Toscana dal
XV al XVII secolo /. Firenze [1990] 254 p. :
IN PROCESS (ONLINE)
NYPL [3-MQWB+ 91-6836]

McIntyre, Anthony. Medieval architecture in
Tuscany and Umbria /. San Francisco , 1992.
p. cm. ISBN 0-87701-846-4 DDC 720/.945/50902
20
NA1119.T8 M37 1992

Suppressa, Alessandro. Itinerari di architettura
moderna . Firenze [1990] 335 p. : DDC
720/.945/520904 20
NA1119.T8 S86 1990

**ARCHITECTURE - ITALY - TUSCANY -
GUIDE-BOOKS.**
Schomann, Heinz. Toskana (ohne Florenz) /.
Darmstadt , c1990. 496 p., [4] p. of plates :
ISBN 3-534-06894-7
NYPL [3-MAMC 90-11555]

ARCHITECTURE - ITALY - UMBRIA.
McIntyre, Anthony. Medieval architecture in
Tuscany and Umbria /. San Francisco , 1992.
p. cm. ISBN 0-87701-846-4 DDC 720/.945/50902
20
NA1119.T8 M37 1992

**ARCHITECTURE - ITALY - VENICE - GUIDE-
BOOKS.**
Pizzarello, Ugo, 1940- Guida alla città di
Venezia /. Venezia , 1986- v. :
NYPL [3-MQWB 91-653]

ARCHITECTURE - JAPAN.
Aida, Takefuma. Takefuma Aida . New York ,
c1990. xviii, 104 p. : ISBN 0-910413-65-7
NYPL [3-MQZ (Aida) 90-12650]

Bognár, Botond, 1944- The new Japanese
architecture /. New York , 1990. 222 p. :
ISBN 0-8478-1225-1 DDC 720/.952/09045 20
NA1555 .B54 1990
NYPL [3-MQWS 91-4685]

Watanabe, Hiroshi. Amazing architecture from
Japan /. New York , 1991. p. cm. ISBN
0-8348-0239-2 : DDC 720/.952/09048 20
NA1555 .W37 1991

ARCHITECTURE - JAPAN - EXHIBITIONS.
Architettura giapponese contemporanea.
Firenze, 1969. 282 p.
NA1555 .A8   *NYPL [3-MQWS 90-6800]*

Emerging Japanese architects of the 1990s /.
New York , 1991. 121 p. : DDC 720/.952/09045
20
NA1555 .E44 1991
NYPL [3-MQWS+ 91-6807]

**ARCHITECTURE - JAPAN - TOKYO -
EXHIBITIONS.**
Tokyo project . Bruxelles [1989] 189 p. :
NYPL [3-MQWS+ 90-11043]

**ARCHITECTURE, JESUIT - ITALY -
NAPLES.**
Divenuto, Francesco. Napoli sacra del XVI
secolo . Napoli , c1990. 317 p., [32] p. of
plates : ISBN 88-7104-562-9 : DDC
726/.5/094573 20
NA5621.N2 D58 1990

ARCHITECTURE - JUVENILE LITERATURE.
Brown, David J. The Random House book of
how things were built /. New York , 1992. p.
cm. ISBN 0-679-82044-2 (trade) DDC 720 20
NA2555 .B68 1992

ARCHITECTURE - KENTUCKY.
Lancaster, Clay. Antebellum architecture of
Kentucky /. Lexington, Ky. , c1991. p. cm.
ISBN 0-8131-1759-3 (alk. paper) : DDC
720/.9769 20
NA730.K4 L36 1991

**ARCHITECTURE - KOREA - YI DYNASTY,
1392-1910.**
Korean architecture. Seoul , 1982- v. : DDC
722/.13 19
NA1563 .K67 1982
NYPL [3-MQWS+ 87-1952]

ARCHITECTURE - LANGUAGE.
Kahn, Louis I., 1901-1974. Louis I. Kahn .
New York , 1991. p. ISBN 0-8478-1331-2 (HC)
DDC 720/.92 20
NA737.K32 A2 1991

ARCHITECTURE - LATIN AMERICA.
Viñuales, Graciela María. Patrimonio
arquitectónico . Buenos Aires , 1990. 104 p. ;
NA702 .V5 1990

**ARCHITECTURE - LATIN AMERICA -
CONGRESSES.**
Exposición barroco latinoamericano. [Buenos
Aires, Argentina] [between 1983 and 1989]
116 p. : DDC 724/.16 20
NA702.2 .E97 1983

ARCHITECTURE - LEBANON.
L'Architecture libanaise du XVe au XIXe
siècle . Beyrouth, Liban [1985] 376 p., lxviii p.
of plates :
NA1476.6 .A78 1985

ARCHITECTURE - MALTA.
Mahoney, Leonard. A history of Maltese
architecture . [Zabbar , 1988] 360 p., 120 p. of
plates : DDC 720/.9458/5 20
NA1455.M3 M3 1988

**ARCHITECTURE, MANUELINE -
PORTUGAL - LISBON.**
Carvalho, Artur Marques de. Do Mosteiro dos
Jerónimos . [Lisbon] [1990] 281 p. :
NA5830.M67 C37 1990

ARCHITECTURE - MARYLAND.
Lane, Mills. Architecture of the Old South.
1991. p. cm. ISBN 1-558-59040-4 DDC
720/.9752 20
NA730.M3 L36 1991

**ARCHITECTURE - MASSACHUSETTS -
BOSTON - HISTORY.**
Miller, Naomi. Boston architecture, 1975-1990
/. Munich , New York, NY, USA , c1990. 248
p., [1] folded leaf of plates : ISBN 3-7913-1097-6
NYPL [3-MQWO+ 91-4496]

**ARCHITECTURE, MEDIEVAL - ARMENIAN
S.S.R. - PTYKHNI.**
Gandolfo, Francesco. Ptghni/Arudch /. Milano,
Italia , 1986. 74 p. : ISBN 88-85822-03-7 DDC
720/.9566/2 s 726/.5/094792 19
NA1474 .D6 no. 16 NA5998.P84
NYPL [3-MQW 90-11667]

**ARCHITECTURE, MEDIEVAL - ARMENIAN
S.S.R. - TALISH.**
Gandolfo, Francesco. Ptghni/Arudch /. Milano,
Italia , 1986. 74 p. : ISBN 88-85822-03-7 DDC
720/.9566/2 s 726/.5/094792 19
NA1474 .D6 no. 16 NA5998.P84
NYPL [3-MQW 90-11667]

ARCHITECTURE, MEDIEVAL - EUROPE.
Medieval architecture and its intellectual
context . London , Ronceverte, WV , 1990.
xxvii, 304 p. : ISBN 1-85285-034-5 : DDC 723
20
NA350   *NYPL [3-MQO 90-11593]*

**ARCHITECTURE, MEDIEVAL - GERMANY
(WEST) - DUDERSTADT -
CONSERVATION AND RESTORATION.**
Das Rathaus in Duderstadt /. Hameln , c1989.
304 p. : ISBN 3-87585-096-3
NYPL [3-MQWD+ 91-5449]

**ARCHITECTURE, MEDIEVAL - GREAT
BRITAIN.**
Platt, Colin. The architecture of medieval
Britain . New Haven , 1990. ix, 325 p. : ISBN
0-300-04953-6 DDC 720/.941/0902 20
NA963 .P53 1991
NYPL [3-MQWK 91-6545]

**ARCHITECTURE, MEDIEVAL, IN ART -
CATALOGS.**
Der Mittelalterliche Baubetrieb Westeuropas .
Köln , 1987. 568 p. : DDC 760/.044969 19
N8217.B85 M58 1987
NYPL [3-MAMZ 91-4597]

**ARCHITECTURE, MEDIEVAL - ITALY -
SICILY.**
Bellafiore, Giuseppe. Architettura in Sicilia nelle
età islamica e normanna . Milano , c1990. 366

p. : ISBN 88-7177-010-2 :
NYPL [3-MQO 91-3372]

**ARCHITECTURE, MEDIEVAL - ITALY -
TUSCANY.**
McIntyre, Anthony. Medieval architecture in
Tuscany and Umbria /. San Francisco , 1992.
p. cm. ISBN 0-87701-846-4 DDC 720/.945/50902
20
NA1119.T8 M37 1992

Redi, Fabio. Edilizia medievale in Toscana /.
Firenze , 1989. 237 p. :
IN PROCESS (ONLINE)
NYPL [3-MQWB+ 90-11747]

**ARCHITECTURE, MEDIEVAL - ITALY -
UMBRIA.**
McIntyre, Anthony. Medieval architecture in
Tuscany and Umbria /. San Francisco , 1992.
p. cm. ISBN 0-87701-846-4 DDC 720/.945/50902
20
NA1119.T8 M37 1992

**ARCHITECTURE, MEDIEVAL - PALESTINE -
CATALOGS.**
Pringle, Denys. The churches of the Crusader
Kingdom of Jerusalem . Cambridge , New
York , 1992- p. cm. ISBN 0-521-39036-2 (v. 1)
DDC 726/.5/0956909021 20
NA5989.6 .P75 1992

ARCHITECTURE, MEDIEVAL - SPAIN.
Dodds, Jerrilynn D. Architecture and ideology
in early medieval Spain /. University Park ,
c1990. xiv, 174 p., [72] p. of plates : ISBN
0-271-00671-4 DDC 720/.946/09021 20
NA1303 .D63 1989
NYPL [3-MQWH 91-4942]

**ARCHITECTURE, MEDIEVAL - SYRIA -
CATALOGS.**
Pringle, Denys. The churches of the Crusader
Kingdom of Jerusalem . Cambridge , New
York , 1992- p. cm. ISBN 0-521-39036-2 (v. 1)
DDC 726/.5/0956909021 20
NA5989.6 .P75 1992

**ARCHITECTURE, MEDIEVAL - TURKEY -
İŞHAN.**
Kadiroğlu, Mine, 1944- The architecture of the
Georgian Church at İşhan /. Frankfurt am
Main , New York , 1991. p. cm. ISBN
3-631-42828-6 DDC 726/.5/095662 20
NA5871.I84 K33 1991

**ARCHITECTURE, MEDIEVAL -
YUGOSLAVIA - DALMATIA (CROATIA)**
Höfler, Janez. Die Kunst Dalmatiens . Graz ,
1989. 338 p. : ISBN 3-201-01466-4
NYPL [3-MAM+ 90-8024]

ARCHITECTURE - MEXICO.
Anda, Enrique X. de. Evolución de la
arquitectura en México . México, D.F. , 1987
[i.e. 1988] 235 p. : ISBN 968-380-186-2 DDC
720/.972 20
NA750 .A49 1988

Sondereguer, Pedro Conrado. Memoria y utopía
en la arquitectura mexicana /. [Azcaoitzalco] ,
México, D.F. , 1990. 101 p. : ISBN
968-636-304-1 DDC 720/.972/09045 20
NA755 .S6 1990

Vargas, Ramón. Historia de la teoría de la
arquitectura, el porfirismo /. [Mexico City] ,
1989. 221 p. : ISBN 968-8406-73-2
NA200 .V37 1989

**ARCHITECTURE - MEXICO - MEXICO
CITY.**
Fernández, Martha (Fernández García) La
arquitectura de la Ciudad de México en el siglo
XVII /. [Mexico] , 1987. 43 p. : ISBN
968-8160-77-6 DDC 720/.972/5309032 20
NA757.M4 F46 1987

**ARCHITECTURE - MISSOURI - KANSAS
CITY - GUIDE-BOOKS.**
American Institute of Architects. Kansas City
Chapter. Kansas City /. Kansas City, Mo. ,
c1979. 256 p. :   *NYPL [3-MQWO 90-6351]*

**ARCHITECTURE, MODERN - 17TH-18TH
CENTURY - BOLIVIA -
CONCERVATION AND RESTORATION.**
Conservaci'on de los monumentos virreinales de
Bolivia. La Paz , 1987. 32 p. :
NYPL [3-MQWM+ 89-26926]

**ARCHITECTURE, MODERN - 17TH-18TH
CENTURIES - FRANCE.**

Les Architectes de la liberté, 1789-1799. Paris ,
c1989. 396 p. :   ISBN 2-903639-65-5
NYPL [3-MQWF 90-11622]

**ARCHITECTURE, MODERN - 17TH-18TH
CENTURIES - FRANCE - AIX-EN-
PROVENCE.**
Boyer, Jean, conservateur. Le patrimoine
architectural d'Aix-en-Provence, XVIe, XVIIe,
XVIIIe siècles . Aix-en-Provence , 19. 191 p. :
NYPL [3-MQWF+ 90-11534]

**ARCHITECTURE, MODERN - 17TH-18TH
CENTURIES - FRANCE - EXHIBITIONS.**
Kléber, Jean-Baptiste, 1753-1800. J.B. Kléber
architecte, 1784-1793 . [Colmar, France , 1986]
96 p., xii p. of plates :
NYPL [3-MQZ (Kléber) 91-5546]
Les Architectes de la liberté, 1789-1799 .
Paris , c1989. 396 p. :   ISBN 2-903639-65-5
DDC 720/.944/07444361 20
NA1046.5.N4 A7 1989

**ARCHITECTURE, MODERN - 17TH-18TH
CENTURIES - FRANCE - PARIS -
EXHIBITIONS.**
Le Panthéon, symbole des révolutions .
[Montréal] : [Paris] : 339 p. :   ISBN
2-7084-0386-9 (Picard)
IN PROCESS (ONLINE)
NYPL [3-MQWF 90-10797]

**ARCHITECTURE, MODERN - 17TH-18TH
CENTURIES - GERMANY.**
Schneider, Erich. Balthasar Neumann,
1687-1753 . München , c1987. 48 p. :
NYPL [3-MQZ+ (Neumann) 91-6584]

**ARCHITECTURE, MODERN - 17TH-18TH
CENTURIES - GREAT BRITAIN -
BIBLIOGRAPHY.**
Harris, Eileen. British architectural books and
writers, 1556-1785 /. Cambridge [England] ,
New York , 1990. 571 p. :   ISBN 0-521-38551-2
DDC 016.72 20
NA965 .H37 1990
NYPL [MQWK 90-13195]

**ARCHITECTURE, MODERN - 17TH-18TH
CENTURIES - ITALY - BAGHERIA.**
Tedesco, Natale. L'immago espressa, Villa
Palagonia . Siracusa , c1986. 231 p. :   DDC
728.8/0945/823 20
NA7595.B298 T4 1986
NYPL [3-MQWB+ 90-11739]

**ARCHITECTURE, MODERN - 17TH-18TH
CENTURIES - KENTUCKY.**
Lancaster, Clay. Antebellum architecture of
Kentucky /. Lexington, Ky. , c1991. p. cm.
ISBN 0-8131-1759-3 (alk. paper) :   DDC
720/.9769 20
NA730.K4 L36 1991

**ARCHITECTURE, MODERN - 19TH
CENTURY.**
L'architecture de l'art nouveau /. Paris , c1982.
332 p. :   ISBN 2-7013-0448-2
NYPL [3-MRX+ 91-7304]
Buscioni, Maria Cristina. Esposizioni e "stile
nazionale" (1861-1925) . Firenze , c1990. xv,
303 p. :   DDC 725/.91 20
NA6750.A1 B8 1990
Ford, Edward R. The details of modern
architecture /. Cambridge, Mass. , c1990. ix,
371 p. :   ISBN 0-262-06121-X DDC 724/.5 20
NA2840 .F67 1989
NYPL [3-MRN 90-12073]
Hollamby, Edward. Red House . London , New
York , 1991. [60] p. :   ISBN 1-85454-704-6 (pbk.) :
DDC 724.6 20
NA645.5.A
NYPL [3-MQZ+ (Webb) 91-6981]
Reynolds, Donald M. Nineteenth-century
architecture /. Cambridge [England] , New
York , 1992. p. cm.   ISBN 0-521-35596-6
(hardcover)   DDC 724/.5 20
NA645 .R49 1992
Shimomura, Jun'ichi, 1952- [Āru nūvō no
meitei. English.] Art nouveau architecture . San
Francisco , 1991. p. cm.   ISBN 0-938491-29-6
DDC 728/.09/034 20
NA7125 .S5513 1991

**ARCHITECTURE, MODERN - 19TH
CENTURY - ALABAMA.**
Palladio in Alabama . Montgomery, Ala. , 1991.
p. cm.   ISBN 0-89280-029-1 DDC

720/.9761/07476147 20
NA730.A2 P3 1991

**ARCHITECTURE, MODERN - 19TH
CENTURY - AUSTRIA.**
Moravánszky, Ákos. Építészet az
osztrák-magyar monarchiában, 1867-1918 /.
[Budapest] , c1988. 226 p. :   ISBN 963-13-2096-0
NYPL [3-MQW 91-6539]

**ARCHITECTURE, MODERN - 19TH
CENTURY - AUSTRIA - VIENNA.**
Lehne, Andreas. Wiener Warenhäuser,
1865-1914 /. Wien , 1990. 195 p. :   ISBN
3-7005-4488-X
NA6227.D45 L44 1990

**ARCHITECTURE, MODERN - 19TH
CENTURY - BERLIN (GERMANY)**
Klinkott, Manfred. Die Backsteinbaukunst der
Berliner Schule . Berlin , c1988. 479 p., 9
leaves of plates :   ISBN 3-7861-1438-2 DDC
721/.04421/094315509034 20
NA1085 .K57 1988
NYPL [3-MQWD 90-11025]

**ARCHITECTURE, MODERN - 19TH
CENTURY - BRAZIL - ESPÍRITO
SANTO (STATE)**
Muniz, Maria Izabel Perini. Arquitetura rural
do século XIX no Espírito Santo /. Vitória-ES ,
1989 ([Vitória?] : Gráfica e Editora São José)
239 p. :
NA8210.B69 M86 1989

**ARCHITECTURE, MODERN - 19TH
CENTURY - BRAZIL - RIO DE
JANEIRO.**
Levy, Carlos Roberto Maciel, 1951- Rio
imperial /. [São Paulo, Brazil?] [1988] 176 p.,
[2] p. of plates :
NA857.R5 L4 1988

**ARCHITECTURE, MODERN - 19TH
CENTURY - CHILE - VALPARAÍSO BAY
REGION - CATALOGS.**
Edwards C., Hernán (Edwards Cruchaga)
Monumentos nacionales y arquitectura
tradicional . [Santiago, Chile] [1990?] 80 p. :
DDC 720/.983/255 20
NA866.V3 E3 1990

**ARCHITECTURE, MODERN - 19TH
CENTURY - CHILE - VALPARAÍSO -
DESIGNS AND PLANS.**
Waisberg, Myriam. Casas de Playa Ancha .
Santiago [Chile] , 1988. 108 p., [1] folded leaf
of plates :
NA867.V34 W34 1988

**ARCHITECTURE, MODERN - 19TH
CENTURY - COLOMBIA.**
Cantini Ardila, Jorge Ernesto. Pietro Cantini .
Bogotá [1990] 318 p. :   DDC 720/.92 20
NA879.C36 C3 1990

**ARCHITECTURE, MODERN - 19TH
CENTURY - CONGRESSES.**
Il Neogotico nel XIX e XX secolo /. Milano
[1990] 2 v. :   ISBN 88-20-20863-6 (set) DDC
724/.3 20
NA645.5.G68 N46 1990

**ARCHITECTURE, MODERN - 19TH
CENTURY - ENGLAND.**
Allibone, Jill. George Devey, architect,
1820-1886 /. Cambridge, England , c1991. 189
p. :   ISBN 0-7188-2785-6 :   DDC 720.92 20
NYPL [3-MQZ (Devey) 91-6770]

**ARCHITECTURE, MODERN - 19TH
CENTURY - EUROPE.**
Tahara, Keiichi, 1951- [Seikimatsu no kenchiku.
English.] Images of fin-de-siècle architecture
and interior decoration /. London , New York ,
1988. 263 p. :   ISBN 0-00-215354-8 :   DDC
724.9/1 19
NA3485
NYPL [3-MRX+ 91-3382]
Yarwood, Doreen. The architecture of Europe .
Chicago , c1991. vi, 170 p. :   ISBN
0-929587-65-0 :   DDC 724/.5 20
NA957 .Y37 1990

**ARCHITECTURE, MODERN - 19TH
CENTURY - EUROPE - THEMES,
MOTIVES.**
Mărgineanu-Cârstoiu, Monica. Romantismul în
arhitectură /. București , 1990. 261, [3] p., [48]
p. of plates :   ISBN 973-330-080-2 :
NA957 .M37 1990

**ARCHITECTURE, MODERN - 19TH
CENTURY - FINLAND - HELSINKI.**

Pöykkö, Kalevi, 1933- Carl Ludvig Engel
1778-1840 . [Helsinki] [1990] 159 p. :   ISBN
951-772-066-1
NA1088.E6 P69 1990

**ARCHITECTURE, MODERN - 19TH
CENTURY - FRANCE - PARIS.**
Mead, Christopher Curtis. Charles Garnier's
Paris Opéra . New York, N.Y. , Cambridge,
Mass. , c1991. p. cm.   ISBN 0-262-13275-3 DDC
725/.822/092 20
NA6840.F72 P379 1991

**ARCHITECTURE, MODERN - 19TH
CENTURY - FRANCE - PARIS -
EXHIBITIONS.**
Pariser Opern- und Konzerthäuser . Tübingen ,
c1989. 71 p. :   ISBN 3-8030-0149-8
NA6840.F72 P3736 1989

**ARCHITECTURE, MODERN - 19TH
CENTURY - GERMANY.**
Dal Co, Francesco, 1945- Figures of
architecture and thought . New York , 1990.
344 p. :   ISBN 0-8478-0654-5 (pbk.) :   DDC
720/.943 19
NA1067 .D35 1990
NYPL [3-MQWD 90-10690]

**ARCHITECTURE, MODERN - 19TH
CENTURY - GERMANY - RUHR RIVER
VALLEY.**
Wehling, Hans-Werner, 1949- Werks- und
Genossenschaftssiedlungen im Ruhrgebiet
1844-1939. Essen , 1990- v. <1 > :   ISBN
3-88474-344-9 DDC 728/.0943/5509034 20
NA7553 .W44 1990

**ARCHITECTURE, MODERN - 19TH
CENTURY - GERMANY (WEST) - BAD
KISSINGEN.**
Wegner, Ewald. Friedrich von Gärtner und das
Bad Kissingen /. Würzburg , 1981. v, 78 p.,
[12] p. of plates :   DDC 720/.92/4 19
NA1088.G3 W43 1981
NYPL [3-MQWD 90-5440]

**ARCHITECTURE, MODERN - 19TH
CENTURY - GERMANY (WEST) -
MUNICH - EXHIBITIONS.**
Glyptothek München, 1830-1980 . München ,
c1980. 640 p. :
NB87.M8 G55 1980
NYPL [3-MQWD 90-5627]

**ARCHITECTURE, MODERN - 19TH
CENTURY - GREAT BRITAIN.**
Curl, James Stevens, 1937- Victorian
architecture /. Newton Abbot , New York,
N.Y. , c1990. 320 p. :   ISBN 0-7153-9144-5
DDC 720/.941/09034 20
NA967 .C8 1990

**ARCHITECTURE, MODERN - 19TH
CENTURY - GREAT BRITAIN -
BIBLIOGRAPHY.**
Doumato, Lamia. Augustus Northmore Welby
Pugin, 1812-1852 [microform] /. Monticello,
Ill. , 1983. 9 p. :   ISBN 0-88066-732-X (pbk.) :
DDC 016.72/092/4 19
Z8716.2 .D68 1983 NA997.P9
*NYPL [*XMC-615]*

**ARCHITECTURE, MODERN - 19TH
CENTURY - HUNGARY.**
Moravánszky, Ákos. Építészet az
osztrák-magyar monarchiában, 1867-1918 /.
[Budapest] , c1988. 226 p. :   ISBN 963-13-2096-0
NYPL [3-MQW 91-6539]

**ARCHITECTURE, MODERN - 19TH
CENTURY - ITALY - MODENA.**
Bertuzzi, Giordano. Il rinnovamento edilizio a
Modena nella prima metà dell'Ottocento /.
Modena , 1987. 350 p. :
NYPL [3-MQWB+ 91-6476]

**ARCHITECTURE, MODERN - 19TH
CENTURY - KENTUCKY.**
Lancaster, Clay. Antebellum architecture of
Kentucky /. Lexington, Ky. , c1991. p. cm.
ISBN 0-8131-1759-3 (alk. paper) :   DDC
720/.9769 20
NA730.K4 L36 1991

**ARCHITECTURE, MODERN - 19TH
CENTURY - MAINE.**
Reed, Roger G. A delight to all who know it .
Augusta, Me. , 1990. 144 p. :   ISBN
0-935447-07-5 DDC 720/.92 20
NA7575 .R4 1990

ARCHITECTURE, MODERN - 19TH CENTURY - MARYLAND.
Lane, Mills. Architecture of the Old South. 1991. p. cm. ISBN 1-558-59040-4 DDC 720/.9752 20
NA730.M3 L36 1991

ARCHITECTURE, MODERN - 19TH CENTURY - MEXICO - DURANGO.
Guerrero Romero, Javier. El Palacio Escárzaga, Durango /. Durango, Dgo., México, 1988. xii, 82 p. : ISBN 968-609-400-8
NA757.D87 G84 1986

ARCHITECTURE, MODERN - 19TH CENTURY - MIDDLE WEST.
The Midwest in American architecture /. Urbana, c1991. xv, 259 p., [1] p. of plates : ISBN 0-252-01743-9 (alk. paper) DDC 720/.977 20
NA722 .M53 1991
NYPL [3-MQWO 91-6382]

ARCHITECTURE, MODERN - 19TH CENTURY - NETHERLANDS.
Olanda 1870-1940 . Milano , 1990, c1980. 208 p. : ISBN 88-435-3094-1
NYPL [3-MQW 91-6563]

ARCHITECTURE, MODERN - 19TH CENTURY - NETHERLANDS - ARNHEM.
Lavooij, Wim. Gebouwd in Arnhem . Zutphen , c1990. 166 p. : ISBN 90-6011-684-4 :
NA1151.A76 L38 1990

ARCHITECTURE, MODERN - 19TH CENTURY - NETHERLANDS - CATALOGS.
Polano, Sergio. [Hendrik Petrus Berlage, opera completa. English.] Hendrik Petrus Berlage, complete works /. New York , 1988. 266 p. : ISBN 0-8478-0901-3 DDC 720/.92 20
NA1153.B4 A4 1988
NYPL [3-MQZ (Berlage) 90-11983]

ARCHITECTURE, MODERN - 19TH CENTURY - PENNSYLVANIA - PHILADELPHIA - CATALOGS.
Thomas, George E. Frank Furness . New York , N.Y. , c1991. p. cm. ISBN 1-87827-104-0 : DDC 720/.92 20
NA737.F84 A4 1991

ARCHITECTURE, MODERN - 19TH CENTURY - PUERTO RICO.
Rigau, Jorge. Puerto Rico 1900 . New York , 1991. p. cm. ISBN 0-8478-1400-9 DDC 720/.97295/09041 20
NA812 .R5 1991

ARCHITECTURE, MODERN - 19TH CENTURY - RUSSIAN S.F.S.R.
Brumfield, William Craft, 1944- The origins of modernism in Russian architecture /. Berkeley , c1991. xxv, 343 p., [24] p. of plates : ISBN 0-520-06929-3 (alk. paper) DDC 720/.947/09041 20
NA1187 .B78 1991
NYPL [3-MQW 91-6488]

ARCHITECTURE, MODERN - 19TH CENTURY - SPAIN.
Arrechea, Julio I. Arquitectura y romanticismo . Valladolid, España [Salamanca] , c1989. 330 p. : ISBN 84-7762-086-5 DDC 720/.946/09034 20
NA1307 .A7 1989

ARCHITECTURE, MODERN - 19TH CENTURY - SPAIN - CATALONIA.
Gaudí i el seu temps /. Barcelona , 1990. 255 p. ; ISBN 84-7533-567-5
NA1313.G3 G39 1990

ARCHITECTURE, MODERN - 19TH CENTURY - SPAIN - CATALONIA - GUIDE-BOOKS.
Lacuesta, Raquel. Arquitectura modernista en Cataluña /. Barcelona , c1990. 213 p. : ISBN 84-252-1430-0 DDC 720/.946/70904 20
NA1309.C2 L33 1990

ARCHITECTURE, MODERN - 19TH CENTURY - UNITED STATES.
Foreman, John, 1945- The Vanderbilts and the gilded age . New York , 1991. viii, 340 p. : ISBN 0-312-05984-1 : DDC 728.8/0973 20
NA7207 .F67 1991 **NYPL [ILD 91-6528]**

Holmes, Kristin, 1955- The Victorian express /. Wilsonville, Or. , c1991. p. cm. ISBN 0-89802-568-0 : DDC 728/.37/097309034 20
NA710.5.V5 H64 1991

Jandl, H. Ward. Yesterday's houses of tomorrow . Washington, DC , 1991. p. cm. ISBN 0-89133-186-7 DDC 728/.0973/09034 20
NA7207 .J36 1991

McKim, Mead & White. [Monograph of the work of McKim, Mead & White, 1879-1915.] The architecture of McKim, Mead & White in photographs, plans, and elevations /. New York , 1990. xii, 399 p. of plates : ISBN 0-486-26556-0 (pbk.) DDC 720/.92/2 20
NA737.M4 A4 1990
NYPL [3-MQWO+ 91-4629]

Modern architecture in America . Ames , 1991. xiv, 217 p. : ISBN 0-8138-0381-0 (alk. paper) DDC 720/.973/09034 20
NA710 .M6 1991
NYPL [3-MQWO 91-6777]

O'Gorman, James F. Three American architects . Chicago , 1991. xx, 170 p. : ISBN 0-226-62071-9 DDC 720/.973/09034 20
NA710 .O35 1991
NYPL [3-MQWO 91-5189]

ARCHITECTURE, MODERN - 19TH CENTURY - UNITED STATES - CATALOGS.
Bruegmann, Robert. Holabird & Roche, Holabird & Root . New York , 1991. 3 v. : ISBN 0-8240-3974-2 : DDC 720/.92/2 20
NA737.H558 A4 1991
NYPL [MQWO+ 91-6811]

ARCHITECTURE, MODERN - 20TH CENTURY.
L'architecture de l'art nouveau /. Paris , c1982. 332 p. : ISBN 2-7013-0448-2
NYPL [3-MRX+ 91-7304]

Architektur im Wandel . Düsseldorf , c1990. 91 p. : ISBN 3-7640-0265-4
NA680 .A732 1990

Bédarida, Marc. Immeubles de bureaux /. Paris , c1991. 119 p. : ISBN 2-281-19052-8
NA6230 .B43 1991

Betsky, Aaron. Violated perfection . New York , 1990. 208 p. : ISBN 0-8478-1269-3 DDC 724/.6 20
NA680 .B497 1990 **NYPL [3-MQV 91-3682]**

Boulet, Marie-Laure. Auditoriums /. Paris , c1990. 119 p. : ISBN 2-281-19052-8 DDC 725/.81/09048 20
NA6815 .B68 1990

Buscioni, Maria Cristina. Esposizioni e "stile nazionale" (1861-1925) . Firenze , c1990. xv, 303 p. : DDC 725/.91 20
NA6750.A1 B8 1990

Busse, Hans Busso von. Wahrnehmungen . Stuttgart , c1990. 262 p. : ISBN 3-7828-1606-4
NA680 .B87 1990

Deconstruction . London , 1989. 264 p. : ISBN 0-85670-996-4 **NYPL [MQV+ 89-27959]**

Dunster, David. Key buildings of the twentieth century /. New York , c1985- v. : ISBN 0-8478-0642-1 (pbk. : v. 1) DDC 724.9/1 19
NA680 .D86 1985
NYPL [3-MQV+ 86-3952]

Ford, Edward R. The details of modern architecture /. Cambridge, Mass. , c1990. ix, 371 p. : ISBN 0-262-06121-X DDC 724/.5 20
NA2840 .F67 1989
NYPL [3-MRN 90-12073]

Glancey, Jonathan. The new moderns /. New York , c1990. 191 p. : ISBN 0-517-57662-7 : DDC 728/.09/045 20
NA680 .G57 1990
NYPL [3-MLO+ 91-4945]

Hollamby, Edward. Red House . London , New York , 1991. [60] p. : ISBN 1-85454-704-6 (pbk.) : DDC 724.6 20
NA645.5.A
NYPL [3-MQZ+ (Webb) 91-6981]

Immagini del post-moderno . Venezia , c1983. 345 p. : ISBN 88-85067-09-3 DDC 724.9/1 19
NA682.P67 I48 1983
NYPL [3-MQV 91-6389]

Jencks, Charles. The new moderns from late to neo-modernism /. London , 1990. 300 p. : ISBN 0-85670-968-9
NYPL [3-MQV+ 90-13384]

Joedicke, Jürgen. Architekturgeschichte des 20. Jahrhunderts . Stuttgart , c1990. 256 p. : ISBN

3-7828-0459-7 DDC 724/.6 20
NA680 .J574 1990

Lajcha, Ladislav. Pohyb divadla /. Bratislava , 1989. 142 p. : ISBN 80-222-0031-X :
NA6821 .L28 1989

Le Corbusier, 1887-1965. [Précision sur un état présent de l'architecture et de l'urbanisme. English.] Precisions on the present state of architecture and city planning . Cambridge, Mass. , c1991. xiii, 266 p. : ISBN 0-262-12149-2 (hc) DDC 724/.6 20
NA680 .L3613 1991
NYPL [3-MQZ (Le Corbusier) 91-5519]

Livingston, Rodolfo. Arquitectura y autoritarismo /. Buenos Aires [1991] 244 p. : ISBN 950-51-5038-5 DDC 720/.1/03 20
NA2542.4 .L58 1991

Lorenz, Clare. Women in architecture . London , 1990. 144 p. : ISBN 0-86294-106-7 : DDC 720/.88042 19
NYPL [3-MQV 91-3392]

Mendelsohn, Erich, 1887-1953. [Works. English. 1991.] Erich Mendelsohn . New York, N.Y. , 1991. p. cm. ISBN 0-910413-91-6 : DDC 720/.92 20
NA1088.M57 A4 1991

Mendelsohn, Erich, 1887-1953. Erich Mendelsohn [sound recording] . Oklahoma City [1976] 2 sound cassettes :
NA1088

Morabito, Giovanni. Forme e tecniche dell'architettura moderna /. Roma , c1990. 206 p. :
IN PROCESS (ONLINE)
NYPL [3-MQV 91-6531]

New classicism . London , 1990. 264 p. : ISBN 1-85490-028-5 (HB)
NYPL [3-MQV+ 91-3315]

OMA-Rem Koolhaas . Paris , c1990. 167 p. : ISBN 2-86653-080-2 DDC 720/.92 20
NA1153.K64 O45 1990

On rigor /. Cambridge, Mass. , c1989. 188 p. : ISBN 0-262-52138-5
NYPL [3-MQV+ 91-6328]

Panizza, Mario. Figure . Roma , 1989. 238 p. : ISBN 88-26-70066-4 :
IN PROCESS (ONLINE)
NYPL [3-MQV 90-11026]

Shimomura, Jun'ichi, 1952- [Āru nūvō no meitei. English.] Art nouveau architecture . San Francisco , 1991. p. cm. ISBN 0-938491-29-6 DDC 728/.09/034 20
NA7125 .S5513 1991

Sorkin, Michael, 1948- Exquisite corpse . London , New York , 1991. p. cm. ISBN 0-86091-323-6 DDC 724/.6 20
NA682.P67 S67 1991

Wodehouse, Lawrence. The roots of international style architecture /. West Cornwall, CT , 1991. p. cm. ISBN 0-933951-46-9 (alk. paper) : DDC 724/.6 20
NA682.I58 W6 1991

Wright, Frank Lloyd, 1867-1959. Frank Lloyd Wright in lecture delivered, May 2, 1952, at the University of Oklahoma [sound recording]. Oklahoma City [1976] 1 sound cassette :
NA737

ARCHITECTURE, MODERN - 20TH CENTURY - ALABAMA.
Palladio in Alabama . Montgomery, Ala. , 1991. p. cm. ISBN 0-89280-029-1 DDC 720/.9761/07476147 20
NA730.A2 P3 1991

ARCHITECTURE, MODERN - 20TH CENTURY - ARAB COUNTRIES.
Steele, James. Hassan Fathy /. London , New York , 1988. 149 p. : ISBN 0-312-01140-7 (U. S. : pbk.) : DDC 720/.92/4 19
NA1585.F37 S74 1988
NYPL [3-MQZ+ (Fathy) 88-4615]

ARCHITECTURE, MODERN - 20TH CENTURY - ARGENTINA.
Historia argentina de la vivienda de interés social. Capital Federal [Argentina] [between 1986 and 1990- v. <1- > :
NA7292 .H57 1990

ARCHITECTURE, MODERN - 20TH CENTURY - AUSTRALIA.

Australian architects--Australian government architects. Canberra , c1988. 111 p. : ISBN 0-644-07919-3

NYPL [3-MQWZ+ 90-10612]

ARCHITECTURE, MODERN - 20TH CENTURY - AUSTRALIA - EXHIBITIONS.
Walter Burley Griffin . Clayton, Vic. , 1988. 75 p. : ISBN 0-86746-860-2

NYPL [3-MQZ+ (Griffin) 90-2584]

ARCHITECTURE, MODERN - 20TH CENTURY - AUSTRIA.
Franz Schuster, 1892-1972 /. Wien , 1976. 136 p. : DDC 720/.92/4 19
NA1011.5.S38 A4 1976

NYPL [3-MQZ+ (Schuster) 90-12651]

Hauser, Krista. Drei Generationen Prachensky . [Austria] , 1986. 50 p. :
NYPL [3-MQWD+ 89-27463]

Moravánszky, Ákos. Epítészet az osztrák-magyar monarchiában, 1867-1918 /. [Budapest] , c1988. 226 p. : ISBN 963-13-2096-0
NYPL [3-MQW 91-6539]

ARCHITECTURE, MODERN - 20TH CENTURY - AUSTRIA - EXHIBITIONS.
Loos, Adolf, 1870-1933. Adolf Loos. [Buenos Aires] [1988?] 44 p. : DDC 720/.92 20
NA1011.5.L6 A4 1988

Sechs Architekten vom Schillerplatz. Wien , c1977. 78 p. : ISBN 3-85063-072-2
NYPL [3-MQWD 90-5756]

ARCHITECTURE, MODERN - 20TH CENTURY - AUSTRIA - STYRIA.
Moderner Holzbau in der Steiermark /. Graz/Austria [1989] 202 p. : ISBN 3-201-01504-0
NA1009.S7 M64 1989

ARCHITECTURE, MODERN - 20TH CENTURY - AUSTRIA - VIENNA.
Lehne, Andreas. Wiener Warenhäuser, 1865-1914 /. Wien , 1990. 195 p. : ISBN 3-7005-4488-X
NA6227.D45 L44 1990

ARCHITECTURE, MODERN - 20TH CENTURY - BERLIN (GERMANY)
Werner Düttmann . Basel , Boston , c1990. 322 p. : ISBN 3-7643-2413-9
NYPL [3-MQZ (Düttmann) 91-5517]

ARCHITECTURE, MODERN - 20TH CENTURY - BRAZIL.
Artigas, João Batista Vilanova. A função social do arquiteto /. São Paulo, SP , 1989. 93 p. : ISBN 85-21-30621-0 DDC 720/.1/0309810904 20
NA2543.S6 A76 1989

Harris, Elizabeth Davis, 1950- Le Corbusier . São Paulo, SP , 1987. 218 p. : ISBN 85-21-30469-2 :
NYPL [3-MQZ (Le Corbusier) 90-10663]

Segawa, Hugo M. Arquiteturas no Brasil, anos 80 /. [São Paulo] [1988?] 1 v. (various pagings) : DDC 720/.981/09048 20
NA855 .S44 1988

ARCHITECTURE, MODERN - 20TH CENTURY - CALIFORNIA - LOS ANGELES.
Breeze, Carla. L.A. deco /. New York , 1991. p. cm. ISBN 0-8478-1434-3 DDC 720/.9794/9409042 20
NA735.L55 B74 1991

Experimental architecture in Los Angeles /. New York , 1991. p. cm. ISBN 0-8478-1424-6 (HC) DDC 720/.9794/9409045 20
NA735.L55 E97 1991

ARCHITECTURE, MODERN - 20TH CENTURY - CANADA.
The Architecture of Douglas Cardinal /. Edmonton , 1989. 150 p. : ISBN 0-920897-46-0 (bound) : DDC 720/.92/4 19
NYPL [3-MQZ+ (Cardinal) 90-10573]

ARCHITECTURE, MODERN - 20TH CENTURY - CHILE - AWARDS.
Muñoz R., María Dolores. Premios nacionales de arquitectura, 1969-1985. [Concepción, Chile] [1986?] 47 p. :
NA2345.C5 M85 1986

ARCHITECTURE, MODERN - 20TH CENTURY - CHILE - CATALOGS.
Boza, Cristián. Sergio Larraín G.M. .

Bogotá-Colombia . 200, [9] p. : ISBN 958-9082-56-4
NA919.L37 A4 1990

Eliash, Humberto. Fernando Castillo . [Santiago, Chile] . 237 p. : ISBN 958-9082-44-0 (colección) DDC 720/.92 20
NA869.C37 A4 1990

ARCHITECTURE, MODERN - 20TH CENTURY - CHILE - VALPARAÍSO BAY REGION - CATALOGS.
Edwards C., Hernán (Edwards Cruchaga) Monumentos nacionales y arquitectura tradicional . [Santiago, Chile] [1990?] 80 p. : DDC 720/.983/255 20
NA866.V3 E3 1990

ARCHITECTURE, MODERN - 20TH CENTURY - CONGRESSES.
Atti del convegno di Pescara, 27-29 gennaio 1989, su il sacro, l'architettura sacra oggi /. Rimini , c1990. 319 p., [36] p. of plates :
NA4795 .A8 1990

Il Neogotico nel XIX e XX secolo /. Milano [1990] 2 v. : ISBN 88-20-20863-6 (set) DDC 724/.3 20
NA645.5.G68 N46 1990

Wars of classification . New York, N.Y. [1991] 95 p. : ISBN 0-910413-82-7 (pbk.) : DDC 724/.6 20
NA680 .W27 1991

ARCHITECTURE, MODERN - 20TH CENTURY - CZECHOSLOVAKIA - BRATISLAVA.
Stavoprojekt /. Bratislava , 1989. 1 v. (unpaged) :
NA1033.B7 S73 1989

ARCHITECTURE, MODERN - 20TH CENTURY - CZECHOSLOVAKIA - SLOVAK REPUBLIC.
Krivošová, Jana. Premeny súčasnej architektúry Slovenska /. Bratislava , 1990. 198 p. : ISBN 80-05-00600-4 :
NA1032.S55 K75 1990

ARCHITECTURE, MODERN - 20TH CENTURY - ENGLAND.
Pawley, Martin. Theory and design in the second machine age /. Oxford, UK , Cambridge, Mass., USA , 1990. xii, 189 p. : ISBN 0-631-15828-6 : DDC 720/.1/05 20
NA2500 .P385 1990   *NYPL [3-MQ 91-3255]*

ARCHITECTURE, MODERN - 20TH CENTURY - EUROPE.
Industriearchitektur in Europa =. Hannover , c1990. 128 p. : ISBN 3-87870-350-3 DDC 725/.4/09409048 20
NA6403.E85 I53 1990

Mies van der Rohe . London , New York , 1986. 112 p. : ISBN 0-85670-685-X DDC 720/.92/4 19
NA1088.M65 M54 1986   *NYPL [3-MQZ+ (Mies van der Rohe) 86-3545]*

Mies van der Rohe award for European architecture. London , Boston , 1990. 128 p. : ISBN 0-408-50084-0 (pbk.) DDC 724.6 20
NA958   *NYPL [3-MQV 90-12890]*

Richard Rogers + architects. London , New York , 1985. 160 p. : ISBN 0-312-68207-7 (St. Martin's)
NYPL [3-MQZ+ (Rogers) 86-1924]

Tahara, Keiichi, 1951- [Seikimatsu no kenchiku. English.] Images of fin-de-siècle architecture and interior decoration /. London , New York , 1988. 263 p. : ISBN 0-00-215354-8 : DDC 724.9/1 19
NA3485   *NYPL [3-MRX+ 91-3382]*

Yarwood, Doreen. The architecture of Europe . Chicago , c1991. vi, 170 p. : ISBN 0-929587-65-0 : DDC 724/.5 20
NA957 .Y37 1990

ARCHITECTURE, MODERN - 20TH CENTURY - EUROPE - CONSERVATION AND RESTORATION - CONGRESSES.
Les Enjeux du patrimoine architectural du XXe siècle . [Paris] [1988?] 186 p. : ISBN 2-11-085013-2
NA109.F8 E55 1988

ARCHITECTURE, MODERN - 20TH CENTURY - EUROPE - THEMES, MOTIVES - EXHIBITIONS.
Gianni, Benjamin, 1958- Dice thrown /. New

York, N.Y. , c1989. 56 p. : ISBN 0-910413-62-2 : DDC 728/.92/09730747468 20
NA8201 .G47 1989

NYPL [3-MQV 90-12464]

ARCHITECTURE, MODERN - 20TH CENTURY - EXHIBITIONS.
Bellini, Mario, 1935- Mario Bellini, architetture /. Milano , 1988. 115 p. : ISBN 88-435-2665-0
NYPL [3-MQZ (Bellini) 90-12540]

Biennale di Venezia (1980). Settore architettura. The presence of the past . Venice , Milan , c1980. 350 p. : ISBN 88-20-80266-X
NYPL [3-MQV 91-420]

Foster, Norman, 1935- Foster. Barcelona , c1989. 128 p. : ISBN 84-252-1385-1
NYPL [3-MQZ (Foster) 90-12468]

Klotz, Heinrich. Architektur des 20. Jahrhunderts . Frankfurt am Main , c1989. 351 p. :   *NYPL [3-MQV 90-11330]*

ARCHITECTURE, MODERN - 20TH CENTURY - FINLAND.
Poole, Scott. The new Finnish architecture /. New York , 1991. p. cm. ISBN 0-8478-1316-9 (HC) DDC 720/.94897/0904 20
NA1455.F5 P66 1991

Sirén, J. S. (Johan Sigfrid), 1889-1961. J.S. Sirén, 1889-1961, arkkitehti /. Helsinki , 1989. 108 p. : ISBN 951-9229-58-2 DDC 720/.92 20
NA1455.F53 S5537 1989

ARCHITECTURE, MODERN - 20TH CENTURY - FINLAND - EXHIBITIONS.
Kautto, Jussi, 1942- Suomalaista kaupunkiarkkitehtuuria =. Helsinki , 1990. 233 p. : ISBN 951-9229-63-9
NA9241.F5 K38 1990

ARCHITECTURE, MODERN - 20TH CENTURY - FLORIDA.
Mizner, Addison, 1872-1933. Florida architecture of Addison Mizner /. Boulder, Colo. , 1991. p. cm. ISBN 1-87865-002-5 : DDC 720/.92 20
NA737.M59 A4 1991

ARCHITECTURE, MODERN - 20TH CENTURY - FLORIDA - PALM BEACH.
Schezen, Roberto. Palm Beach houses /. New York , 1991. 324 p. : ISBN 0-8478-1313-4 DDC 728.8/09759/32 20
NA7238.P235 S34 1991

ARCHITECTURE, MODERN - 20TH CENTURY - FRANCE.
Fanelli, Giovanni. Perret e Le Corbusier . Roma , 1990. 255 p. : ISBN 88-420-3596-3 :
NA1048.5.F85 F36 1990

Léger, Jean-Michel. Derniers domiciles connus . Paris , c1990. 168 p. : ISBN 2-907150-18-9 : DDC 728/.314/094409047 20
NA7346 .L44 1990

Loyer, François. Henri Sauvage . Bruxelles , 1987. 159 p. : ISBN 2-87009-304-7 (pbk.)
NYPL [3-MQZ (Savage) 90-12030]

Salat, Serge. Paul Andreu . Paris , c1990. 175 p. : ISBN 2-86653-081-0
NA1053.A49 S25 1990

Sulle tracce di Le Corbusier. English. In the footsteps of Le Corbusier /. New York , 1991. 268 p. : ISBN 0-8478-1219-7 (pbk.) : DDC 720/.92 20
NA1053.J4 S913 1991

Vellay, Marc. Pierre Chareau, architecte, meublier, 1883-1950 /. Paris , 1986. 111 p. : ISBN 2-86930-026-3
NYPL [3-MOF 90-11128]

Vitou, Elisabeth. Gabriel Guévrékian, 1900-1970 . Paris , c1987. 150 p. : ISBN 2-86649-003-7 : DDC 720/.92/4 19
NA1053.G77 V5 1987

NYPL [3-MQZ (Guévrékian) 91-4588]

ARCHITECTURE, MODERN - 20TH CENTURY - FRANCE - CONSERVATION AND RESTORATION - CONGRESSES.
Les Enjeux du patrimoine architectural du XXe siècle . [Paris] [1988?] 186 p. : ISBN 2-11-085013-2
NA109.F8 E55 1988

ARCHITECTURE, MODERN - 20TH CENTURY - FRANCE - EXHIBITIONS.
Tony Garnier, l'œuvre complète /. Paris , c1989. 254 p. : ISBN 2-85850-527-6 DDC

720/.92 20
NA1053.G37 A4 1989

40 architectes de moins de quarante ans, Paris
/. [Paris] , c1990. 311 p. : ISBN 2-281-15116-6
NA1048 .A13 1990

**ARCHITECTURE, MODERN - 20TH
CENTURY - FRANCE - PARIS.**
Parigi . Roma [1990] 242 p. :
N1050 .P27 1990

**ARCHITECTURE, MODERN - 20TH
CENTURY - FRANCE - PARIS -
EXHIBITIONS.**
Pariser Opern- und Konzerthäuser . Tübingen ,
c1989. 71 p. : ISBN 3-8030-0149-8
NA6840.F72 P3736 1989

**ARCHITECTURE, MODERN - 20TH
CENTURY - FRANCE - PARIS - GUIDE-
BOOKS.**
Martin, Hervé. Guide de l'architecture moderne
à Paris =. Paris , c1990. 318 p. : ISBN
2-86738-483-4 : DDC 720/.944/3610904 20
NA1050 .M35 1990

**ARCHITECTURE, MODERN - 20TH
CENTURY - FRANCE - THEMES,
MOTIVES.**
Joffroy, Pascale. Claude Vasconi, 1980-1990 /.
Paris , c1990. 166 p. : ISBN 2-86653-084-5
DDC 720/.92 20
NA1053.V37 J64 1990

**ARCHITECTURE, MODERN - 20TH
CENTURY - GERMANY.**
Dal Co, Francesco, 1945- Figures of
architecture and thought . New York , 1990.
344 p. : ISBN 0-8478-0654-5 (pbk.) : DDC
720/.943 19
NA1067 .D35 1990
NYPL [3-MQWD 90-10690]

Formalhaut (Group) Formalhaut Architektur
Skulptur . Darmstadt , c1989. 54 p. : ISBN
3-925376-40-2 *NYPL [3-MGI 91-7331]*

Gärtner, Martin. Sergius Ruegenberg . Berlin ,
c1990. 115 p. : ISBN 3-7861-1581-8 DDC
720/.92 20
NA1088.R83 G37 1990

Kahle, Barbara. Deutsche Kirchenbaukunst des
20. Jahrhunderts /. Darmstadt , c1990. viii, 271
p. : ISBN 3-534-03614-X : DDC 726/.5/09430904
20
NA5568 .K35 1990

Kunst auf Befehl? . München , c1990. 275 p. :
ISBN 3-7814-0285-1 DDC 701/.03 20
N6868.5.N37 K85 1990

Schink, Arnold. Mies van der Rohe . Stuttgart ,
c1990. 379 p. : ISBN 3-7828-4004-6
NA1088.M65 S34 1990

**ARCHITECTURE, MODERN - 20TH
CENTURY - GERMANY - BERLIN.**
Behr, Adalbert. Bauen in Berlin, 1973 bis 1987
/. Leipzig , 1987. 199 p. : ISBN 3-7338-0040-0
DDC 720/.9431/55 20
NA1085 .B437 1987

Zum Umgang mit dem Gestapo-Gelände .
[Berlin , 1988] 105, 25, 73 p. :
NA1068.5.N37 Z85 1988

**ARCHITECTURE, MODERN - 20TH
CENTURY - GERMANY - BERLIN -
GUIDE-BOOKS.**
Berning, Maria. Berliner Wohnquartiere .
Berlin , c1990. xiii, 252 p. : ISBN
3-496-00382-0 :
NA7351.B65 B47 1990

**ARCHITECTURE, MODERN - 20TH
CENTURY - GERMANY -
BIBLIOGRAPHY.**
Bauen im Dritten Reich /. Stuttgart [1989] 73
p. ; ISBN 3-8167-0278-3
NYPL [3-MQWD 90-10818]

**ARCHITECTURE, MODERN - 20TH
CENTURY - GERMANY - EXHIBITIONS.**
Robert Vorhoelzer, ein Architektenleben .
München , c1990. 296 p. : ISBN 3-7667-0960-7
NA1088.V67 R6 1990

**ARCHITECTURE, MODERN - 20TH
CENTURY - GERMANY - HAMBURG-
HARBURG (HAMBURG)**
Stadtbild Hamburg. Hamburg [1990] 64 p. :
NA9053.C6 S72 1990

**ARCHITECTURE, MODERN - 20TH
CENTURY - GERMANY - MUNICH.**
Krieg, Nina A. Schon Ordnung ist Schönheit .
München , 1990. xix, 304 p. : ISBN
3-87821-286-0
NA6166 .K75 1990

**ARCHITECTURE, MODERN - 20TH
CENTURY - GERMANY - REGENSBURG -
EXHIBITIONS.**
Architektur in Regensburg 1933-1945 /.
Regensburg , 1989. 139 p. : ISBN 3-927730-01-7
NA1086.R4 A7 1989

**ARCHITECTURE, MODERN - 20TH
CENTURY - GERMANY - RUHR RIVER
VALLEY.**
Wehling, Hans-Werner, 1949- Werks- und
Genossenschaftssiedlungen im Ruhrgebiet
1844-1939. Essen , 1990- v. <1 > : ISBN
3-88474-344-9 DDC 728/.0943/5509034 20
NA7553 .W44 1990

**ARCHITECTURE, MODERN - 20TH
CENTURY - GREAT BRITAIN.**
Richard Rogers + architects. London , New
York , 1985. 160 p. : ISBN 0-312-68207-7 (St.
Martin's)
NYPL [3-MQZ+ (Rogers) 86-1924]

**ARCHITECTURE, MODERN - 20TH
CENTURY - HISTORY AND CRITICISM.**
Jimeno, Oswaldo, 1928- La magia del muro .
Lima, Peru , 1973. 151 p. :
NYPL [3-MQV 91-819]

**ARCHITECTURE, MODERN - 20TH
CENTURY - HUNGARY.**
Moravánszky, Ákos. Építészet az
osztrák-magyar monarchiában, 1867-1918 /.
[Budapest] , c1988. 226 p. : ISBN 963-13-2096-0
NYPL [3-MQW 91-6539]

**ARCHITECTURE, MODERN - 20TH
CENTURY - ILLINOIS - CHICAGO -
AWARDS.**
5 years of interior architecture awards /.
Chicago, Ill. , c1985. 104 p. : DDC
729/.09773/1109048 20
NA2850 .A14 1985

**ARCHITECTURE, MODERN - 20TH
CENTURY - INDIA.**
Curtis, William J. R. Balkrishna Doshi . New
York , 1988. 191 p. : ISBN 0-8478-0937-4 DDC
720/.92 20
NA1510.D67 C87 1988
NYPL [3-MQZ (Doshi) 89-22893]

**ARCHITECTURE, MODERN - 20TH
CENTURY - ISRAEL - EXHIBITIONS.**
Turner, Judith. White city . [Tel Aviv] , 1984.
88 p. : *NYPL [MFX (Turner) 86-728]*

**ARCHITECTURE, MODERN - 20TH
CENTURY - ITALY.**
Brunetti, Fabrizio. Momenti di architettura
italiana contemporanea /. Firenze , c1990. 204
p. : *NYPL [3-MQWB 91-7228]*

Dini, Massimo, 1946- Renzo Piano, progetti e
architetture, 1964-1983 /. Milano , c1983. 246
p. : ISBN 88-435-0921-7 : DDC 720/.92/4 19
NA1123.P47 D5 1983
NYPL [3-MQS (Piano) 90-129970]

In/progetto . Napoli , 1985. 128 p. :
NYPL [3-MQWB+ 90-10577]

Pfammatter, Ueli. Moderne und Macht .
Braunschweig , c1990. 191 p. : ISBN
3-528-08785-4
IN PROCESS (ONLINE)
NYPL [3-MQWB 91-6456]

Piano, Renzo. Renzo Piano and Building
Workshop . New York , 1989. 256 p. : ISBN
0-8478-1152-2 DDC 720/.92 20
NA1123.P47 A4 1989
NYPL [3-MQZ (Piano) 91-3402]

Savio, Giulio, 1923- Immagini di architettura e
design, 1958-1986 /. Milano , c1987. 178 p. :
ISBN 88-435-2183-7 DDC 720/.92/4 19
NA1123.S315 A4 1987
NYPL [3-MQZ (Savio) 90-13002]

Schumacher, Thomas L. Surface & symbol .
New York, NY : London : 295 p. : ISBN
0-910413-59-2 (alk. paper) : DDC 720/.92 20
NA1123.T4 S37 1990
NYPL [3-MQZ (Terragni) 91-4868]

Lo Spazio eloquente . Pordenone , c1987. 357

p. : DDC 726/.5/0945309045 20
NA5618 .S64 1987
NYPL [3-MRBD 90-12496]

Zironi, Stefano, 1948- Melchiorre Bega,
architetto /. Milano [1983] 183 p. : ISBN
88-7212-003-9 : DDC 720/.92/4 19
NA1123.B255 Z57 1983
NYPL [3-MQZ (Bega) 90-10395]

Zucchi, Benedict. The architecture of Giancarlo
De Carlo /. Oxford , Boston , 1991. p. cm.
ISBN 0-7506-1275-4 : DDC 720/.92 20
NA1123.D29 Z8 1991

**ARCHITECTURE, MODERN - 20TH
CENTURY - ITALY - CATALOGS.**
Acocella, Alfonso, 1954- Celli Tognon .
Firenze , c1987. 214 p. : DDC 720/.92/2 19
NA1123.C39 A4 1987
NYPL [3-MQWB 90-3040]

Fonatti, Franco, 1942- Architektur als
Erkenntnis =. Wien , c1989. 189 p. :
NA1123.F59 A4 1989

**ARCHITECTURE, MODERN - 20TH
CENTURY - ITALY - EXHIBITIONS.**
L'Etrange univers de l'architecte Carlo
Mollino . Paris , c1989. 174 p. : ISBN
2-85850-494-6
NA1123.M65 A4 1989

**ARCHITECTURE, MODERN - 20TH
CENTURY - ITALY - LATINA.**
Latina /. Roma , 1990. 94 p. : ISBN
88-7597-124-2 : DDC 711/.4/0945623 20
NA9204.L37 L37 1990

**ARCHITECTURE, MODERN - 20TH
CENTURY - ITALY - MASSA-CARRARA
(PROVINCE) - GUIDE-BOOKS.**
Giorgieri, Pietro. Itinerari apuani di architettura
moderna /. Firenze , 1989. 263 p. :
NYPL [3-MQWB 90-11118]

**ARCHITECTURE, MODERN - 20TH
CENTURY - ITALY - PALERMO.**
Palermo, norma di piano e progetto /. [Italy] ,
Roma , c1990. 189 p. : DDC 720/.945/823 20
NA1121.P3 P36 1990

**ARCHITECTURE, MODERN - 20TH
CENTURY - ITALY - ROME -
EXHIBITIONS.**
La Biblioteca ritrovata . Roma , 1990. 50 p. :
NYPL [3-MQWB 91-5054]

**ARCHITECTURE, MODERN - 20TH
CENTURY - ITALY - TUSCANY.**
Suppressa, Alessandro. Itinerari di architettura
moderna . Firenze [1990] 335 p. : DDC
720/.945/520904 20
NA1119.T8 S86 1990

**ARCHITECTURE, MODERN - 20TH
CENTURY - JAPAN.**
Andō, Tadao, 1941- Tadao Andō. London ,
New York , 1990. 128 p. : ISBN 1-85490-010-2
(hardback : London)
NYPL [3-MQZ+ (Andō) 90-11589]

Bognár, Botond, 1944- The new Japanese
architecture /. New York , 1990. 222 p. :
ISBN 0-8478-1225-1 DDC 720/.952/09045 20
NA1555 .B54 1990
NYPL [3-MQWS 91-4685]

Roulet, Sophie. Toyo Ito, l'architecture de
l'éphémère /. Paris , c1991. 164 p. : ISBN
2-281-15122-0 DDC 720/.92 20
NA1559.I84 R68 1991

Speidel, Manfred. Team Zoo . New York ,
1991. p. cm. ISBN 0-8478-1402-5 DDC
720/.952/09045 20
NA1559.T4 S64 1991

Takamatsu, Shin, 1948- Shin Takamatsu /.
Tokyo , c1990. 193 p. : ISBN 4-87140-415-3
NYPL [3-MQZ+ (Takamatsu) 90-11765]

Watanabe, Hiroshi. Amazing architecture from
Japan /. New York , 1991. p. cm. ISBN
0-8348-0239-2 : DDC 720/.952/09048 20
NA1555 .W37 1991

**ARCHITECTURE, MODERN - 20TH
CENTURY - JAPAN - EXHIBITIONS.**
Architettura giapponese contemporanea.
Firenze, 1969. 282 p.
NA1555 .A8 *NYPL [3-MQWS 90-6800]*

Emerging Japanese architects of the 1990s /.
New York , 1991. 121 p. : DDC 720/.952/09045

20
NA1555 .E44 1991
NYPL [3-MQWS+ 91-6807]

ARCHITECTURE, MODERN - 20TH CENTURY - MASSACHUSETTS - BOSTON.
Miller, Naomi. Boston architecture, 1975-1990 /. Munich , New York, NY, USA , c1990. 248 p., [1] folded leaf of plates : ISBN 3-7913-1097-6
NYPL [3-MQWO+ 91-4496]

ARCHITECTURE, MODERN - 20TH CENTURY - MEXICO.
The Architecture of Ricardo Legorreta /. Austin , 1990. 171 p. : ISBN 0-292-75106-0 (alk. paper) DDC 720/.92 20
NA759.L44 A87 1990 *NYPL [3-MQZ+ (Legorreta Vilchis) 91-3708]*

Sondereguer, Pedro Conrado. Memoria y utopía en la arquitectura mexicana /. [Azcaoitzalco] , México, D.F. , 1990. 101 p. : ISBN 968-636-304-1 DDC 720/.972/09045 20
NA755 .S6 1990

ARCHITECTURE, MODERN - 20TH CENTURY - MEXICO - CATALOGS.
Noelle, Louise. Ricardo Legorreta, tradición y modernidad /. México , 1989. 188 p., 12 leaves of plates : ISBN 968-361-022-6 DDC 720/.92 20
NA759.L44 A4 1989

ARCHITECTURE, MODERN - 20TH CENTURY - MIDDLE WEST.
The Midwest in American architecture /. Urbana , c1991. xv, 259 p., [1] p. of plates : ISBN 0-252-01743-9 (alk. paper) DDC 720/.977 20
NA722 .M53 1991
NYPL [3-MQWO 91-6382]

ARCHITECTURE, MODERN - 20TH CENTURY - NETHERLANDS.
Kloos, Maarten. Alexander Bodon /. Rotterdam , 1990. xv, [128] p. : ISBN 90-6450-087-8
NYPL [3-MQZ (Bodon) 91-4491]

Olanda 1870-1940 . Milano , 1990, c1980. 208 p. : ISBN 88-435-3094-1
NYPL [3-MQW 91-6563]

Taverne, Ed. Carel Weeber . Rotterdam , c1989. xv, [121] p. : ISBN 90-6450-088-6
NYPL [3-MQZ (Weeber) 90-11979]

Taverne, Ed. Carel Weeber, architect /. Rotterdam , c1989. 121 p. : ISBN 90-6450-088-6 :
NA1153.W44 T38 1989

ARCHITECTURE, MODERN - 20TH CENTURY - NETHERLANDS - ARNHEM.
Lavooij, Wim. Gebouwd in Arnhem . Zutphen , c1990. 166 p. : ISBN 90-6011-684-4 :
NA1151.A76 L38 1990

ARCHITECTURE, MODERN - 20TH CENTURY - NETHERLANDS - CATALOGS.
Polano, Sergio. [Hendrik Petrus Berlage, opera completa. English.] Hendrik Petrus Berlage, complete works /. New York , 1988. 266 p. : ISBN 0-8478-0901-3 DDC 720/.92 20
NA1153.B4 A4 1988
NYPL [3-MQZ (Berlage) 90-11983]

ARCHITECTURE, MODERN - 20TH CENTURY - NEW MEXICO.
Mead, Christopher Curtis. Houses by Bart Prince . Albuquerque , c1991. xiii, 100 p., [8] p. of col. plates : ISBN 0-8263-1254-3 DDC 728.8/092 20
NA737.P69 M4 1991
NYPL [3-MQZ (Prince) 91-6791]

ARCHITECTURE, MODERN - 20TH CENTURY - NEW YORK (N.Y.)
American Institute of Architects. New York Chapter. New York architecture /. New York , 1988- v. : *NYPL [MQWO+ 89-8137]*

ARCHITECTURE, MODERN - 20TH CENTURY - NEW YORK (N.Y.) - EXHIBITIONS.
New York Architektur, 1970-1990 /. München , c1989. 335 p., [1] leaf of plates : ISBN 3-7913-0923-4
NYPL [3-MQWO+ 89-22879]

ARCHITECTURE, MODERN - 20TH CENTURY - NEW YORK (STATE) - LONG ISLAND - EXHIBITIONS.

Beaux Arch '89 . Sag Harbor, N.Y. , 1989. 119 p. : ISBN 0-9623542-0-1
IN PROCESS NYPL [3-MQWO 91-3337]

ARCHITECTURE, MODERN - 20TH CENTURY - PENNSYLVANIA - PHILADELPHIA - CATALOGS.
Thomas, George E. Frank Furness . New York, N.Y. , c1991. p. cm. ISBN 1-87827-104-0 : DDC 720/.92 20
NA737.F84 A4 1991

ARCHITECTURE, MODERN - 20TH CENTURY - PICTORIAL WORKS.
Cariou, Joël. Les classiques de l'architecture contemporaine /. Paris , c1990. 139 p. : DDC 724/.6 20
NA680 .C33 1990

ARCHITECTURE, MODERN - 20TH CENTURY - PORTUGAL.
Taveira, Tomás. Tomás Taveira . London , New York, N.Y. , 1990. 272 p. : ISBN 1-85490-034-X
NYPL [3-MQZ+ (Taveira) 91-5456]

ARCHITECTURE, MODERN - 20TH CENTURY - PUERTO RICO.
Rigau, Jorge. Puerto Rico 1900 . New York , 1991. p. cm. ISBN 0-8478-1400-9 DDC 720/.97295/09041 20
NA812 .R5 1991

ARCHITECTURE, MODERN - 20TH CENTURY - QUÉBEC (PROVINCE) - MONTRÉAL.
Ernest Cormier et l'Université de Montréal. English. Ernest Cormier and the Université de Montréal /. Montréal , 1990. 179 p. : ISBN 0-920785-30-1
NA749.C67 E7613 1990
NYPL [3-MQZ (Cormier) 91-6585]

ARCHITECTURE, MODERN - 20TH CENTURY - RUSSIAN S.F.S.R.
Brumfield, William Craft, 1944- The origins of modernism in Russian architecture /. Berkeley , c1991. xxv, 343 p., [24] p. of plates : ISBN 0-520-06929-3 (alk. paper) DDC 720/.947/09041 20
NA1187 .B78 1991
NYPL [3-MQW 91-6488]

ARCHITECTURE, MODERN - 20TH CENTURY - RUSSIAN S.F.S.R. - MOSCOW.
Cohen, Jean-Louis. [Le Corbusier et la mystique de l'URSS. English.] Le Corbusier and the mystique of the USSR . Princeton, N.J. [1991] p. cm. ISBN 0-691-04076-1 : DDC 720/.92 20
NA1053.J4 C55 1991

ARCHITECTURE, MODERN - 20TH CENTURY - SOVIET UNION.
Natsional'noe v sovetskoĭ arkhitekture . Moskva , 1989. 127 p. : ISBN 5-274-01213-2 :
NA1188 .N27 1989

ARCHITECTURE, MODERN - 20TH CENTURY - SOVIET UNION - EXHIBITIONS.
Neuvostomaan arkkitehtuuria . [Helsinki , 1988] 81 p. : ISBN 951-9229-56-6
NA1188 .N48 1988

ARCHITECTURE, MODERN - 20TH CENTURY - SPAIN.
The Architecture of Enric Miralles and Carme Pinós /. New York, NY , c1990. 87 p. : ISBN 0-930829-14-X
NYPL [3-MQWH+ 91-6245]

Arquitectura española contemporánea . Barcelona , c1990. 192 p. : ISBN 84-252-1429-7 DDC 720/.946/09048 20
NA1308 .A84 1990
NYPL [3-MQWH 91-3890]

Levene, Richard C. Arquitectura española contemporánea, 1975/1990 =. Madrid , 1989. 2 v. (812 p.) : ISBN 84-404-5316-7 (v. 1)
NYPL [3-MQWH+ 91-6816]

ARCHITECTURE, MODERN - 20TH CENTURY - SPAIN - BARCELONA.
Bohigas, Oriol. Barcelona, city and architecture, 1980-1992 /. New York , 1991. 239 p. : ISBN 0-8478-1354-1 : DDC 720/.946/7209048 20
NA1311.B3 B64 1991

ARCHITECTURE, MODERN - 20TH CENTURY - SPAIN - CATALONIA.
Gaudí i el seu temps /. Barcelona , 1990. 255 p. ; ISBN 84-7533-567-5
NA1313.G3 G39 1990

ARCHITECTURE, MODERN - 20TH CENTURY - SPAIN - CATALONIA - EXHIBITIONS.
Arquitectura . [Barcelona?] [1988] 187 p. :
NA1309.C2 A76 1988

ARCHITECTURE, MODERN - 20TH CENTURY - SPAIN - CATALONIA - GUIDE-BOOKS.
Lacuesta, Raquel. Arquitectura modernista en Cataluña /. Barcelona , c1990. 213 p. : ISBN 84-252-1430-0 DDC 720/.946/70904 20
NA1309.C2 L33 1990

ARCHITECTURE, MODERN - 20TH CENTURY - SPAIN - MADRID.
Urrutia Núñez, Angel. Arquitectura doméstica moderna en Madrid /. Madrid [1988] 214 p. : ISBN 84-7477-173-0
NYPL [3-MRG 90-10752]

ARCHITECTURE, MODERN - 20TH CENTURY - SPAIN - PAÍS VASCO - THEMES, MOTIVES.
Mas Serra, Elías, 1945- 50 Años de arquitectura en Euskadi /. [Vitoria] , 1990. xviii, 347 p. : ISBN 84-7542-854-1 DDC 720/.946/609045 20
NA1309.P33 M37 1990

ARCHITECTURE, MODERN - 20TH CENTURY - SPAIN - VALLADOLID.
Virgili Blanquet, María Antonia. Arquitectura y urbanismo de Valladolid en el siglo XX /. Valladolid , 1988. 190 p. : ISBN 84-404-2435-3
NYPL [3-MQWH 90-9439]

ARCHITECTURE, MODERN - 20TH CENTURY - SWITZERLAND.
Glusberg, Jorge. The architecture of Mario Botta . Buenos Aires [1980] 37 p. : DDC 720/.92 20
NA1353.B67 G58 1980

Hannes Meyer, 1889-1954 . Berlin , c1989. 368 p. : ISBN 3-433-02053-1 : DDC 720/.92 20
NA1353.M4 H35 1989

Herzog & de Meuron . Cambridge, Mass. , New York , 1990. 96 p. : ISBN 0-8478-1187-5
NYPL [3-MQZ (Herzog) 90-12645]

Kieren, Martin. Hannes Meyer . Heiden , c1990. 195 p. : ISBN 3-7212-0224-4 DDC 720/.92 20
NA1353.M4 K54 1990

Vacchini, Livio, 1933- Livio Vacchini /. Berlin , c1987. 96 p. : ISBN 3-433-02275-5
NYPL [3-MQZ (Vacchini) 90-12536]

ARCHITECTURE, MODERN - 20TH CENTURY - SWITZERLAND - BASELLAND.
Bauen vor der Stadt. English & German. Bauen vor der Stadt . Basel , Boston , c1991. p. cm. ISBN 3-7643-2629-8 : DDC 720/.9494/33 20
NA1349.B38 B3813 1991

ARCHITECTURE, MODERN - 20TH CENTURY - SWITZERLAND - EXHIBITIONS.
Senn, Otto H. (Otto Heinrich), 1902- Otto Senn . Basel , c1990. 137 p. : ISBN 3-905065-12-4
NA1353.S46 A4 1990

ARCHITECTURE, MODERN - 20TH CENTURY THEMES, MOTIVES.
De Fusco, Renato, 1929- Le nuove idee di architettura . Milano , 1991. ix, 326 p. ; ISBN 88-453-0435-3
NA680 .D38 1991

ARCHITECTURE, MODERN - 20TH CENTURY - UNITED STATES.
Breeze, Carla. Pueblo deco /. New York , 1990. 112 p. : ISBN 0-8478-1177-8 (pbk.) : DDC 720/.973/09041 20
NA712.5.A7 B7 1990
NYPL [3-MQWO 90-11529]

Brownlee, David Bruce. Louis I. Kahn, architect of the American century /. New York , 1991. p. cm. ISBN 0-8478-1330-4 DDC 720/.92 20
NA737.K32 B76 1991

Chappell, Sally Anderson. Architecture and planning of Graham, Anderson, Probst, and White, 1912-1936 . Chicago , 1991. p. cm. ISBN 0-226-10134-7 DDC 720/.92/2 20
NA737.G7 C48 1991

Craftsman-style houses. Newton, Conn. , c1991. p. cm. ISBN 1-561-58014-7 : DDC

728/.373/09730904 20
NA7208 .C68 1991

Dunlop, Beth, 1947- Arquitectonica /.
Washington, D.C. , c1991. p. cm. ISBN
1-558-35043-8 : DDC 720/.92/2 20
NA737.A77 D8 1991

Hardy Holzman Pfeiffer Associates . New York
[1992] p. cm. ISBN 0-8478-1480-7 DDC
720/.92/2 20
NA737.H29 A4 1992

Jandl, H. Ward. Yesterday's houses of
tomorrow . Washington, DC , 1991. p. cm.
ISBN 0-89133-186-7 DDC 728/.0973/09034 20
NA7207 .J36 1991

McKim, Mead & White. [Monograph of the
work of McKim, Mead & White, 1879-1915.]
The architecture of McKim, Mead & White in
photographs, plans, and elevations /. New
York , 1990. xii, 399 p. of plates : ISBN
0-486-26556-0 (pbk.) DDC 720/.92/2 20
NA737.M4 A4 1990
NYPL [3-MQWO+ 91-4629]

Modern architecture in America . Ames , 1991.
xiv, 217 p. : ISBN 0-8138-0381-0 (alk. paper)
DDC 720/.973/09034 20
NA710 .M6 1991
NYPL [3-MQWO 91-6777]

Nolon, John R. Common walls/private homes .
New York , c1990. x, 196 p. : ISBN
0-07-016819-9 DDC 728/.312/0973 20
NA7520 .N6 1990
NYPL [3-MQWO 90-10404]

O'Gorman, James F. Three American
architects . Chicago , 1991. xx, 170 p. : ISBN
0-226-62071-9 DDC 720/.973/09034 20
NA710 .O35 1991
NYPL [3-MQWO 91-5189]

Penner, Richard H. Conference center planning
and design . New York , 1991. 256 p. : ISBN
0-8230-0911-4 : DDC 725/.91/097309048 20
NA6880.5.U6 P46 1991

Richard Meier. London , New York , 1990.
227 p. : ISBN 0-312-04526-3 (N.Y.)
NYPL [3-MQZ+ (Meier) 91-3359]

Tigerman, Stanley, 1930- Stanley Tigerman .
New York , 1989. 288 p. : ISBN 0-8478-1121-1 :
DDC 720/.92 20
NA737.T49 T54 1989
NYPL [3-MQZ (Tigerman) 91-4494]

**ARCHITECTURE, MODERN - 20TH
CENTURY - UNITED STATES -
AWARDS.**
5 years of interior architecture awards /.
Chicago, Ill. , c1985. 104 p. : DDC
729/.09773/1109048 20
NA2850 .A14 1985

**ARCHITECTURE, MODERN - 20TH
CENTURY - UNITED STATES -
CATALOGS.**
Bruegmann, Robert. Holabird & Roche,
Holabird & Root . New York , 1991. 3 v. :
ISBN 0-8240-3974-2 : DDC 720/.92/2 20
NA737.H558 A4 1991
NYPL [MQWO+ 91-6811]

**ARCHITECTURE, MODERN - 20TH
CENTURY - UNITED STATES -
CONGRESSES.**
Thinking the present . New York, NY , c1990.
136 p. : ISBN 0-910413-93-2
NYPL [3-MQWO 90-13419]

**ARCHITECTURE, MODERN - 20TH
CENTURY - UNITED STATES - THEMES,
MOTIVES.**
American architecture of the 1980s /.
Washington, D.C. , 1990. xiv, 342 p. : ISBN
1-558-35056-X : DDC 720/.973/09048 20
NA712 .A64 1990
NYPL [MQWO+ 90-11575]

Moss, Eric Owen, 1943- Eric Owen Moss,
buildings and projects /. New York , 1991. p.
ISBN 0-8478-1431-9 DDC 720/.92 20
NA737.M73 A4 1991

Pelli, Cesar. Cesar Pelli . New York , 1990. 288
p. : ISBN 0-8478-1262-6 DDC 720/.92 20
NA737.P39 A4 1990
NYPL [3-MQZ (Pelli) 91-5464]

Stern, Robert A. M. The American houses of
Robert A.M. Stern /. New York , 1991. p.

ISBN 0-8478-1433-5 DDC 728/.37/092 20
NA737.S64 A4 1991

**ARCHITECTURE, MODERN - 20TH
CENTURY - VENEZUELA.**
Castro, Raquel. Fruto Vivas . [Caracas] , 1989.
176 p., [16] p. of plates : ISBN 980-300-866-8
DDC 720/.92 20
NA939.V57 C37 1989

ARCHITECTURE, MODERN - HISTORY.
Strike, James. Construction into design .
Oxford , Boston , 1991. p. cm. ISBN
0-7506-1229-0 : DDC 721/.09/03 20
NA2543.T43 S7 1991

**ARCHITECTURE, MODERN - UNITED
STATES.**
Köster, Baldur. Palladio in Amerika .
München , 175 p. : ISBN 3-7913-1057-7
DDC 720/.973 20
NA705 .K63 1990

**ARCHITECTURE, MOGUL - FATEHPUR-
SIKRI.**
Husain, A. B. M., 1934- Fathpur-sikri and its
architecture. Dacca [1970] x, 169 p. DDC
722/.4
NA1508.F3 H8

**ARCHITECTURE - MONACO - MONTE-
CARLO - EXHIBITIONS.**
L'Opéra de Monte-Carlo au temps du Prince
Albert Ier de Monaco /. Paris , c1990. 72 p. :
ISBN 2-7118-2321-0
NYPL [3-MQW 91-7009]

**ARCHITECTURE, MOORISH. see
ARCHITECTURE, ISLAMIC.**

ARCHITECTURE - MOROCCO.
Ben el-Khadir, Mohamed. Architectures
régionales . [Morocco] 1989 (Casablanca :
Impr. Najah el Jadida) 211 p. :
NA1590 .B46 1989

**ARCHITECTURE, MUHAMMADAN. see
ARCHITECTURE, ISLAMIC.**

**ARCHITECTURE, MUSLIM. see
ARCHITECTURE, ISLAMIC.**

ARCHITECTURE - NETHERLANDS.
Olanda 1870-1940 . Milano , 1990, c1980. 208
p. : ISBN 88-435-3094-1
NYPL [3-MQW 91-6563]

**ARCHITECTURE - NETHERLANDS -
AMSTERDAM - EXHIBITIONS.**
Amsterdamse school . [Amsterdam , 1975. 112
p. : *NYPL [3-MQW 90-7048]*

**ARCHITECTURE - NETHERLANDS -
ARNHEM.**
Lavooij, Wim. Gebouwd in Arnhem . Zutphen ,
c1990. 166 p. : ISBN 90-6011-684-4 :
NA1151.A76 L38 1990

**ARCHITECTURE - NETHERLANDS -
HISTORY.**
Lavooij, Wim. Twee eeuwen bouwen aan
Arnhem . Zutphen , 1990. 128 p. : ISBN
90-6011-683-6 :
NA9208.A7 L38 1990

**ARCHITECTURE - NEW BRUNSWICK -
WOODSTOCK - PICTORIAL WORKS.**
Connell, Allison. A view of Woodstock .
Fredericton, N.B. , c1988. 74 p. : ISBN
0-920483-19-4 : DDC 971.5/52/0208 19
NYPL [3-MQWM 90-12592]

ARCHITECTURE - NEW YORK (N.Y.)
American Institute of Architects. New York
Chapter. New York architecture /. New York ,
1988- v. : *NYPL [MQWO+ 89-8137]*

**ARCHITECTURE - NEW YORK (N.Y.) -
EXHIBITIONS.**
New York Architektur, 1970-1990 /.
München , c1989. 335 p., [1] leaf of plates :
ISBN 3-7913-0923-4
NYPL [3-MQWO+ 89-22879]

**ARCHITECTURE - NEW YORK (N.Y.) -
THEMES, MOTIVES.**
Rencoret, Francisco Javier, 1960- New York
City . New York , 1991. p. cm. ISBN
1-87827-105-9 DDC 720/.9747/1 20
NA735.N5 R46 1991

**ARCHITECTURE - NEW YORK (STATE) -
ALBANY COUNTY.**
Bennett, Allison P. The people's choice . [S.l.]
c1980 ([Albany, N.Y.] : printed by Lane Press)

ix, 135 p. : DDC 709/.747/42 19
N6530.N72 A33 *NYPL [3-MAMT 81-75]*

**ARCHITECTURE - NEW YORK (STATE) -
PICTORIAL WORKS.**
Stewart, Milo. Main Street. [New York, c1971]
[4] p., 50 plates. DDC 779/.4/0924
NA730.N4 S83
NYPL [MFX+ (Stewart) 91-6809]

**ARCHITECTURE - NIGERIA -
EXHIBITIONS.**
Dmochowski, Z. R. (Zbigniew R.), 1906-1982.
The work of Z.R. Dmochowski . London ,
1988. 80 p. : ISBN 0-905788-90-7
NYPL [3-MQZ+ (Dmochowski) 90-95]

**ARCHITECTURE, NORMAN - ITALY -
SICILY.**
Bellafiore, Giuseppe. Architettura in Sicilia nelle
età islamica e normanna . Milano , c1990. 366
p. : ISBN 88-7177-010-2 :
NYPL [3-MQO 91-3372]

**ARCHITECTURE, NORMAN - ITALY -
SICILY - ARAB INFLUENCES.**
Bellafiore, Giuseppe. Architettura in Sicilia nelle
età islamica e normanna (827-1194) /.
Palermo , c1990. 366 p. : ISBN 88-7177-010-2 :
DDC 720/.945/809021 20
NA1109.S5 B4 1990

ARCHITECTURE - NORTH CAROLINA.
Bishir, Catherine W. North Carolina
architecture /. Chapel Hill , 1990. xiv, 514 p. :
ISBN 0-8078-1923-9 DDC 720/.9756 20
NA730.N8 B5 1990
NYPL [3-MQWO+ 91-3379]

**ARCHITECTURE - NORTH CAROLINA -
CATAWBACOUNTY.**
Catawba County . Virginia Beach, Va. , 1991. p.
cm. ISBN 0-89865-822-5 DDC 720/.9756/785 20
NA730.N82 C383 1991

ARCHITECTURE - NORWAY.
Holan, Jerri. Norwegian wood . New York ,
1990. 208 p., [16] p. of plates : ISBN
0-8478-0954-4 : DDC 721/.0448/09485 19
NA1261 .H65 1989
NYPL [3-MQWE 91-4988]

Architecture of amnesia. Adams, Dennis. Dennis
Adams . New York, NY , c1990. 94 p. : ISBN
1-87860-707-3
NYPL [3-MGO (Adams, D.) 91-4565]

**Architecture of Campbell, Zogolovitch,
Wilkinson, Gough.** Sudjic, Deyan. English
extremists . London , c1988. 112 p. : ISBN
0-947795-68-5 (pbk.)
NYPL [3-MQWK 89-4432]

The Architecture of Douglas Cardinal / Trevor
Boddy ; with essays by Douglas Cardinal.
Edmonton : NeWest Publishers, 1989. 150 p. :
ill. (some col.) ; 24 x 31 cm. Includes
bibliographical references. ISBN 0-920897-46-0
(bound) : DDC 720/.92/4 19
*1. Cardinal, Douglas. 2. Canadian Museum of
Civilization. 3. Architecture, Modern - 20th century -
Canada. 4. Métis architects - Canada - Biography. 5.
Hull (Québec) - Buildings, structures, etc. I. Boddy,
Trevor, 1953-. II. Cardinal, Douglas.*
NYPL [3-MQZ+ (Cardinal) 90-10573]

**The Architecture of Enric Miralles and Carme
Pinós** / Peter Buchanan ... [et. al.]. New York,
NY : SITES/Lumen Books, c1990. 87 p. : ill. ;
31 cm. Inlcudes bibliographical references. ISBN
0-930829-14-X
*1. Miralles, Enric. 2. Pinós, Carme. 3. Architecture,
Modern - 20th century - Spain. I. Buchanan, Peter.*
NYPL [3-MQWH+ 91-6245]

The architecture of Europe . Yarwood, Doreen.
Chicago , c1991. vi, 170 p. : ISBN
0-929587-65-0 : DDC 724/.5 20
NA957 .Y37 1990

The architecture of George Pace, 1915-75 /.
Pace, Peter G. London , 1990. 288 p. : ISBN
0-7134-6273-6 : DDC 720.92 20
NYPL [3-MQZ+ (Pace) 91-5540]

The architecture of Giancarlo De Carlo /. Zucchi,
Benedict. Oxford , Boston , 1991. p. cm. ISBN
0-7506-1275-4 : DDC 720/.92 20
NA1123.D29 Z8 1991

The Architecture of Gustav Peichl : an exhibition
of the Royal Institute of British Architects,
November 9th-November 18th, 1989.
[London] : The Institute, c1989. 32 p. : ill. ; 30
cm. Cover title: The architecture of Gustav Peichl, an

exhibition at the Royal Institute of British Architects.
*I. Peichl, Gustav, 1928- - Exhibitions. I. Royal Institute
of British Architects. II. Title: Architecture of Gustav
Peichl, an exhibition at the Royal Institute of British
Architects.*
           NYPL   [3-MQZ+ (Peichl) 90-13213]

**Architecture of Gustav Peichl, an exhibition at
the Royal Institute of British Architects.** The
Architecture of Gustav Peichl. [London] ,
c1989. 32 p. :
           NYPL   [3-MQZ+ (Peichl) 90-13213]

**The architecture of McKim, Mead & White in
photographs, plans, and elevations** /. McKim,
Mead & White. [Monograph of the work of
McKim, Mead & White, 1879-1915.] New
York , 1990. xii, 399 p. of plates : ISBN
0-486-26556-0 (pbk.)   DDC 720/.92/2 20
NA737.M4 A4 1990
              NYPL   [3-MQWO+ 91-4629]

The architecture of medieval Britain . Platt,
Colin. New Haven , 1990. ix, 325 p. : ISBN
0-300-04953-6   DDC 720/.941/0902 20
NA963 .P53 1991
              NYPL   [3-MQWK 91-6545]

The architecture of Mott B. Schmidt /. Hewitt,
Mark A. New York , 1991. p. cm.   ISBN
0-8478-1399-1   DDC 720/.92 20
NA737.S355 H4 1991

The Architecture of Ricardo Legorreta / edited
by Wayne Attoe, assisted by Sydney H.
Brisker ; commentary by Ricardo Legorreta ;
contributions by Hal Box ... [et al.] ;
photographs by Julius Shulman ... [et al.]. 1st
ed. Austin : University of Texas Press, 1990.
171 p. : ill. (some col.) ; 31 cm. Includes
bibliographical references (p. 169-170) and index.
        ISBN 0-292-75106-0 (alk. paper)   DDC 720/.92
        20
*1. Legorreta Vilchis, Ricardo. 2. Vernacular
architecture - Mexico - Influence. 3. Architecture,
Modern - 20th century - Mexico. I. Legorreta Vilchis,
Ricardo. II. Attoe, Wayne. III. Brisker, Sydney H.,
1914-. IV. Box, Hal.*
NA759.L44 A87 1990   **NYPL   [3-MQZ+
                  (Legorreta Vilchis) 91-3708]**

**The Architecture of Richard Morrison
(1767-1849) and William Vitruvius Morrison
(1794-1838).** Dublin : Irish Architectural
Archive, 1989. xiii, 189 p. : ill. ; 29 cm. Includes
bibliographical references and index.   ISBN
0-9515536-0-7
*1. Morrison, Richard, 1767-1849. 2. Morrison, William
Vitruvius, 1794-1838. I. Irish Architectural Archive.*
      NYPL   [3-MQZ (Morrison) 91-6143]

The architecture of the Georgian Church at İshan
/. Kadiroğlu, Mine, 1944- Frankfurt am Main ,
New York , 1991. p. cm.   ISBN 3-631-42828-6
DDC 726/.5/095662 20
NA5871.I84 K33 1991

Architecture of the O.M. Theatre. Nitsch,
Hermann, 1938- Die Architektur des Orgien
Mysterien Theaters =. München , c1987- v. :
            NYPL   [MDG (Nitsch) 90-11004]

The architecture of the Old South . Forman,
Henry Chandlee, 1904- Cambridge , 1948. 203
p., [7] p. of plates :   DDC 720.975
NA720 .F6   **NYPL   [3-MQWO 91-6780]**

Architecture of the Old South. Lane, Mills. 1991.
p. cm.   ISBN 1-558-59040-4   DDC 720/.9752 20
NA730.M3 L36 1991

ARCHITECTURE - OHIO - CINCINNATI.
Clubbe, John. Cincinnati observed . Columbus ,
c1991. p. cm.   ISBN 0-8142-0512-7 (cloth : alk.
paper)   DDC 720/.9771/79 20
NA735.C5 C58 1991

ARCHITECTURE, OTTOMAN.
The Dervish lodge . Berkeley , c1992. p. cm.
ISBN 0-520-07060-7 (alk. paper)   DDC
700/.9561 20
NX688.T9 D47 1992

The Ottoman city and its parts . New Rochelle,
N.Y. , 1991. p. cm.   ISBN 0-89241-473-1   DDC
307.76/09561 20
NA9229 .O87 1991

**ARCHITECTURE, OTTOMAN - ALGERIA -
     ALGIERS.**
Golvin, Lucien. Palais et demeures d'Alger à la
période ottomane /. Aix-en-Provence [1988]
141 p., [16] p. of plates : ISBN 2-85744-307-2
            NYPL   [3-MQT+ 90-4959]

**ARCHITECTURE, OTTOMAN - BALKAN
     PENINSULA.**
Kiel, Machiel. Studies on the Ottoman
architecture of the Balkans /. Brookfield, Vt. ,
c1990. 361 p. in various pagings : ISBN
0-86078-276-X :   DDC 720/.9496 20
NA1375 .K54 1990   **NYPL   [3-MQT 91-3249]**

**ARCHITECTURE, OTTOMAN - TURKEY -
     CATALOGS.**
Ülgen, Ali Saim. Mimar Sinan yapıları /.
[Ankara] , 1989. 2 portfolios (266 plates) :
        ISBN 975-16-0164-9
NA1373.S5 A4 1989
             NYPL   [*OPR+++ 90-6]

**ARCHITECTURE, OTTOMAN - TURKEY -
     ISTANBUL.**
Cantay, Tanju. XVI.-XVII. yüzyıllarda
Süleymaniye Camii ve bağlı yapıları /. Beyoğlu,
İstanbul , 1989. 56, 32 p., [2] leaves of plates :
        ISBN 975-7622-05-2
NA5870.S93 C36 1989

Necipoğlu, Gülru. Architecture, ceremonial, and
power . New York, N.Y. , Cambridge, Mass. ,
1991. p. cm.   ISBN 0-262-14050-0   DDC
725/.17/0949618 20
NA1370 .N43 1991

ARCHITECTURE - PHILOSOPHY.
Blaser, Werner, 1924- [Mies van der Rohe,
Lehre und Schule. English.] Mies van der Rohe,
continuing the Chicago school of architecture /.
Basel , Boston , 1981. 307 p. :   ISBN
3-7643-1247-5   DDC 720/.92/4 19
NA1088.M65 B5813 1981   **NYPL   [3-MQZ
                 (Mies van der Rohe) 90-10754]**

Bonfiglioli, Sandra, 1940- L'architettura del
tempo . Napoli , 1990. 410 p. :   ISBN
88-20-71912-6 :   DDC 720/.1 20
NA2500 .B625 1990

Busse, Hans Busso von. Wahrnehmungen .
Stuttgart , c1990. 262 p. :   ISBN 3-7828-1606-4
NA680 .B87 1990

Dal Co, Francesco, 1945- Figures of
architecture and thought . New York , 1990.
344 p. :   ISBN 0-8478-0654-5 (pbk.) :   DDC
720/.943 19
NA1067 .D35 1990
            NYPL   [3-MQWD 90-10690]

Drawing/building/text . New York , c1991. 175
p. :   ISBN 0-910413-71-1 :   DDC 720/.1 20
NA2500 .D7 1990

Drawing/building/text . New York, N.Y. ,
c1991. 175 p. :   ISBN 0-910413-71-1 :   DDC
720/.1 20
NA2500 .D7 1990   **NYPL   [3-MQ 91-7053]**

Harbison, Robert. The built, the unbuilt, and
the unbuildable . Cambridge, Mass. , 1991. 192
p. :   ISBN 0-262-08204-7 :   DDC 720/.1 20
NA2500 .H37 1991

Hejduk, John, 1929- Riga, Vladivostok, Lake
Baikal . New York , 1989. 272 p. :   ISBN
0-8478-1129-8 (hardbound)   DDC 700/.92 20
NA737.H36 A4 1989
            NYPL   [3-MQZ+ (Hejduk) 91-4487]

Laseau, Paul, 1937- Frank Lloyd Wright . New
York, N.Y. , c1991. p. cm.   ISBN 0-442-23478-3
DDC 720/.92 20
NA737.W7 L37 1991

Pawley, Martin. Theory and design in the
second machine age /. Oxford, UK ,
Cambridge, Mass., USA , 1990. xii, 189 p. :
        ISBN 0-631-15828-6 :   DDC 720/.1/05 20
NA2500 .P385 1990   **NYPL   [3-MQ 91-3255]**

Picon, Antoine. [Architectes et ingénieurs au
siècle des Lumières. English.] French architects
and engineers in the Age of Enlightenment /.
Cambridge , New York , 1991. p. cm.   ISBN
0-521-38253-X   DDC 720/.944/09033 20
NA1046.5.N4 P513 1991

Radding, Charles. Medieval architecture,
medieval learning . New Haven, CT , c1991. p.
cm.   ISBN 0-300-04918-8 (alk. paper)   DDC 723/.4
20
NA390 .R33 1991

Rogers, Richard George. Architecture, a
modern view /. [London] , c1990. 64 p. :
        ISBN 0-500-55022-0
            NYPL   [3-MQ 91-6258]

Strategies in architectural thinking /. Chicago,
Ill. , Cambridge, Mass. , 1991. p. cm.   ISBN

0-262-23159-X   DDC 720/.1 20
NA2500 .S83 1991

Van Pelt, Robert Jan. Architectural principles in
the age of historicism /. New Haven , 1991. p.
cm.   ISBN 0-300-04999-4   DDC 720/.1 20
NA2500 .V34 1991

**ARCHITECTURE - PICTORIAL WORKS -
     INDEXES.**
Teague, Edward H., 1952- World architecture
index . New York , 1991. xix, 447 p. ;   ISBN
0-313-22552-4 (alk. paper)   DDC 016.72 20
NA202 .T4 1991

**ARCHITECTURE - PLANS. see
     ARCHITECTURE - DESIGNS AND
     PLANS.**

ARCHITECTURE - POLITICAL ASPECTS.
Whiteman, John E. M. Divisible by 2 /.
[Chicago] , Cambridge, Mass. , 1990. 61 p. :
        ISBN 0-262-73093-6 (pbk.)   DDC 728/.092 20
NA7125 .W48 1990
              NYPL   [3-MRG 91-6702]

ARCHITECTURE - PORTUGAL - ALENTEJO.
Silva, José Custódio Vieira da. O tardo-gótico
em Portugal . Lisboa , c1989. 206 p. :   ISBN
972-240-725-2 :
NA1329.A43 S55 1989

ARCHITECTURE, POSTMODERN.
Immagini del post-moderno . Venezia , c1983.
345 p. :   ISBN 88-85067-09-3   DDC 724.9/1 19
NA682.P67 I48 1983
              NYPL   [3-MQV 91-6389]

Jencks, Charles. The language of post-modern
architecture /. New York , 1991. p. cm.   ISBN
0-8478-1359-2   DDC 724/.6 20
NA682.P67 J38 1991

New classicism . London , 1990. 264 p. :   ISBN
1-85490-028-5 (HB)
              NYPL   [3-MQV+ 91-3315]

On rigor /. Cambridge, Mass. , c1989. 188 p. :
        ISBN 0-262-52138-5
              NYPL   [3-MQV+ 91-6328]

Panizza, Mario. Figure . Roma , 1989. 238 p. :
        ISBN 88-26-70066-4 :
IN PROCESS (ONLINE)
              NYPL   [3-MQV 90-11026]

Sorkin, Michael, 1948- Exquisite corpse .
London , New York , 1991. p. cm.   ISBN
0-86091-323-6   DDC 724/.6 20
NA682.P67 S67 1991

**ARCHITECTURE, POSTMODERN -
     ARGENTINA.**
Glusberg, Jorge. Miguel Angel Roca, arquitecto
/. Buenos Aires, Argentina [between 1985 and
1990] 39 p. :   DDC 720/.92 20
NA839.R62 A4 1990

**ARCHITECTURE, POSTMODERN -
     DENMARK.**
Ilkjær, Marianne Olsson. Postmodernismen i
dansk arkitektur . [København , 1987] 104
leaves :   ISBN 87-87448-52-1
NA1218 .I43 1987

**ARCHITECTURE, POSTMODERN -
     FRANCE - PARIS.**
Portzamparc, Christian de, 1944- La Cité de la
musique . Seyssel, France [1986] 47 p. :   ISBN
2-903528-76-4 :   DDC 725/.81/0924 19
NA1053.P655 A4 1986   **NYPL   [3-MQZ+
                 (Portzamparc) 90-12557]**

**ARCHITECTURE, POSTMODERN - ITALY -
     CATALOGS.**
Acocella, Alfonso, 1954- Celli Tognon .
Firenze , c1987. 214 p. :   DDC 720/.92/2 19
NA1123.C39 A4 1987
              NYPL   [3-MQWB 90-3040]

Purini, Franco, 1941- Sette paesaggi =.
Milano , c1989. 135 p. :   ISBN 88-28-90353-8
DDC 720/.92 20
NA1123.P87 A4 1989
              NYPL   [3-MQWB 91-6918]

**ARCHITECTURE, POSTMODERN -
     PORTUGAL.**
Taveira, Tomás. Tomás Taveira . London , New
York, N.Y , 1990. 272 p. :   ISBN 1-85490-034-X
              NYPL   [3-MQZ+ (Taveira) 91-5456]

**ARCHITECTURE, POSTMODERN - THEMES,
     MOTIVES.**
Rossi, Aldo, 1931- Aldo Rossi . New York,
N.Y. , 1991. p. cm.   ISBN 1-87827-115-6 (cloth) :

DDC 720/.92 20
NA1123.R616 A4 1991

ARCHITECTURE, POSTMODERN - UNITED STATES.
Scuri, Piera. Late twentieth century skyscrapers /. New York, N.Y. , 1990. x, 158 p., [16] p. of plates : ISBN 0-442-23789-8   DDC 720/.483/097309047 20
NA6232 .S27 1990
       NYPL [3-MQWO 90-11487]

ARCHITECTURE, POSTMODERN - UNITED STATES - AWARDS.
Accent on architecture . [Washington, D.C.] (1735 New York Ave., NW, Washington 20006) [c1991] 1 v. (unpaged) ; DDC 720/.973/09045 20
NA2340 .A33 1991

Architecture, power, and national identity /.
Vale, Lawrence J., 1959- New Haven , c1992. p. cm. ISBN 0-300-04958-7 (alk. paper) DDC 725/.11 20
NA4195 .V35 1992

ARCHITECTURE, PREHISTORIC - AEGEAN SEA REGION - CONGRESSES.
L'Habitat égéen préhistorique . Athènes , Paris , 1990. 495 p. : ISBN 2-86958-031-2
       NYPL [3-MQL 91-5181]

ARCHITECTURE - PROPORTION. see **ARCHITECTURE - COMPOSITION, PROPORTION, ETC.**

ARCHITECTURE - PUERTO RICO.
Rigau, Jorge. Puerto Rico 1900 . New York , 1991. p. cm. ISBN 0-8478-1400-9 DDC 720/.97295/09041 20
NA812 .R5 1991

ARCHITECTURE - QUEBEC (PROVINCE)
Bédard, Hélène. Maisons et églises du Québec, XVIIe, XVIIIe, XIXe siècles. [Québec] 1972 [c1971] 50 p.   *NYPL [3-MQWM 90-5758]*

ARCHITECTURE - QUEBEC (PROVINCE) - MONTREAL.
Grassroots, greystones, and glass towers . Montréal , Buffalo, N.Y. , c1989. 211 p. : ISBN 1-550-65001-7 : DDC 720/.9714/28 20
NA747.M66 G7 1989

ARCHITECTURE, RENAISSANCE.
Smith, Christine (Christine Hunnikin) Architecture in the culture of early humanism . New York , 1991. p. cm. ISBN 0-19-506128-4 (alk. paper) DDC 724/.12 20
NA510 .S65 1991

ARCHITECTURE, RENAISSANCE - FRANCE - AIX-EN-PROVENCE.
Boyer, Jean, conservateur. Le patrimoine architectural d'Aix-en-Provence, XVIe, XVIIe, XVIIIe siècles . Aix-en-Provence , 19. 191 p. :
       NYPL [3-MQWF+ 90-11534]

ARCHITECTURE, RENAISSANCE - GREAT BRITAIN - BIBLIOGRAPHY.
Harris, Eileen. British architectural books and writers, 1556-1785 /. Cambridge [England] , New York , 1990. 571 p. : ISBN 0-521-38551-2 DDC 016.72 20
NA965 .H37 1990
       NYPL [MQWK 90-13195]

ARCHITECTURE, RENAISSANCE - ITALY.
Hetzer, Theodor, 1890-1946. Italienische Architektur /. Stuttgart , c1990. 472 p. : ISBN 3-87838-905-1   DDC 720/.945/09024 20
NA1115 .H48 1990

Holberton, Paul. Palladio's villas . London , 1990. xiii, 256 p. : ISBN 0-7195-4782-2 : DDC 720/.92/4 19
NA1123.P2
       NYPL [3-MQZ (Palladio) 90-11020]

Tavernor, Robert. Palladio and Palladianism /. New York, N.Y. , 1991. 216 p. : ISBN 0-500-20242-7
       NYPL [3-MQZ (Palladio) 91-5547]

ARCHITECTURE, RENAISSANCE - ITALY - BOLOGNA.
Orazi, Anna Maria. Jacopo Barozzi da Vignola, 1528-1550 . Roma , c1982. 557 p. : DDC 720/.92/4 19
NA1123.V53 O7 1982
       NYPL [3-MQZ (Vignola) 84-1736]

ARCHITECTURE, RENAISSANCE - ITALY - FLORENCE.
Il Palazzo Medici Riccardi di Firenze /.

Firenze , c1990. 379 p. : ISBN 88-09-20180-9 DDC 725/.17/094551 20
NA7756.F65 P35 1990

ARCHITECTURE, RENAISSANCE - ITALY - ROME.
Burroughs, Charles. From signs to design . Cambridge, Mass. , c1990. xii, 344 p., [54] p. of plates : ISBN 0-262-02298-2   DDC 307.76/0945/63209024 20
NA1120 .B87 1990
       NYPL [MQWB 91-4224]

ARCHITECTURE, RENAISSANCE - ITALY - VENICE.L.
Diruf, Hermann. Paläste Venedigs vor 1500 . München , c1990. 224 p. : ISBN 3-89235-033-7
NA7756.V4 D57 1990

ARCHITECTURE, RENAISSANCE - ITALY - VICENZA.
Zaupa, Giovanni. Andrea Palladio e la sua committenza . Roma , c1990. 255 p. : ISBN 88-7448-275-2 : DDC 720/.92 20
NA1123.P2 Z34 1990

ARCHITECTURE, RENAISSANCE - SPAIN.
Cámara Muñoz, Alicia. Arquitectura y sociedad en el Siglo de Oro . Madrid , c1990. 280 p., [32] p. of plates : ISBN 84-86902-07-X
       NYPL [MQWH 91-5219]

ARCHITECTURE, RENAISSANCE - YUGOSLAVIA - DALMATIA (CROATIA)
Höfler, Janez. Die Kunst Dalmatiens . Graz , 1989. 338 p. : ISBN 3-201-01466-4
       NYPL [3-MAM+ 90-8024]

ARCHITECTURE, RENZISSANCE - SPAIN - GUIPUZCOA - HISTORY.
Arrazola Echeverria, Maria Asunción. Renacimiento en Guipuzcoa /. [Guipúzcoa] [1988] 2 v. : ISBN 84-505-7460-9 (obra completa)
       NYPL [3-MQWH + 89-19331]

ARCHITECTURE - RESEARCH.
Musso, Stefano, 1952- Questioni di storia e restauro . Firenze , c1988. 216 p. ;
NA9053.C6 M87 1988
       NYPL [3-MQE 90-10753]

Recherches sur la typologie et les types architecturaux . [Paris] , c1991. 367 p. : ISBN 2-7384-0903-2
NA2000 .R38 1991

ARCHITECTURE - RESTORATION. see **ARCHITECTURE - CONSERVATION AND RESTORATION.**

ARCHITECTURE, ROCOCO - GERMANY - MUNICH.
Stalla, Robert. Die kurkölnische Bruderschafts-, Ritterordens- und Hofkirche St. Michael in Berg am Laim . Weissenhorn , c1989. 279 p. : ISBN 3-87437-271-5
NA5586.M8 S73 1989

ARCHITECTURE, ROMAN.
Scurati-Manzoni, Pietro, 1927- L'architettura romana . Milano , 1991. 504 p. : DDC 722/.7 20
NA310 .S43 1991

ARCHITECTURE, ROMAN - ITALY.
Clarke, John R., 1945- The houses of Roman Italy, 100 B.C.-A.D. 250 . Berkeley , c1991. p. cm. ISBN 0-520-07267-7 (alk. paper) DDC 728/.0937 20
NA324 .C57 1991

ARCHITECTURE, ROMANESQUE.
Radding, Charles. Medieval architecture, medieval learning . New Haven, CT , c1991. p. cm. ISBN 0-300-04918-8 (alk. paper) DDC 723/.4 20
NA390 .R33 1991

ARCHITECTURE, ROMANESQUE - ENGLAND - OXFORD.
Saint Frideswide's Monastery at Oxford . Gloucester , Wolfeboro Fall, NH , 1991. p. cm. ISBN 0-86299-773-9 : DDC 726/.7/0942574 20
NA5471.O9 S25 1991

ARCHITECTURE, ROMANESQUE - FRANCE - AIN.
Oursel, Raymond. Lyonnais, Dombes, Bugey et Savoie romans /. La Pierre-qui-Vire [France] , 1990. 387 p. : ISBN 2-7369-0177-0
       NYPL [3-MQR 91-4889]

ARCHITECTURE, ROMANESQUE - FRANCE - LYON.
Oursel, Raymond. Lyonnais, Dombes, Bugey et

Savoie romans /. La Pierre-qui-Vire [France] , 1990. 387 p. : ISBN 2-7369-0177-0
       NYPL [3-MQR 91-4889]

ARCHITECTURE, ROMANESQUE - FRANCE - SAVOIE.
Oursel, Raymond. Lyonnais, Dombes, Bugey et Savoie romans /. La Pierre-qui-Vire [France] , 1990. 387 p. : ISBN 2-7369-0177-0
       NYPL [3-MQR 91-4889]

ARCHITECTURE, ROMANESQUE - ITALY - ABRUZZI.
Abruzzes Molise romans /. La Pierre-qui-Vire (Yonne) , 1990. 304 p. : ISBN 2-7369-0182-7
       NYPL [3-MQWB 91-4524]

ARCHITECTURE, ROMANESQUE - ITALY - MOLISE.
Abruzzes Molise romans /. La Pierre-qui-Vire (Yonne) , 1990. 304 p. : ISBN 2-7369-0182-7
       NYPL [3-MQWB 91-4524]

ARCHITECTURE, ROMANESQUE - SPAIN - BURGOS (PROVINCE) - CONGRESSES.
El Románico en Silos . Burgos , 1990. 606 p. : ISBN 0-8470-0317-7 DDC 726/.7/0946353 20
NA5811.S48 R66 1990

ARCHITECTURE, ROMANESQUE - YUGOSLAVIA - SLOVENIA.
Zadnikar, Marijan. Romanika v Sloveniji . Ljubljana , 1982. 657 p. :
NA5949.S56 Z28 1982

ARCHITECTURE - ROME.
Scurati-Manzoni, Pietro, 1927- L'architettura romana . Milano , 1991. 504 p. : DDC 722/.7 20
NA310 .S43 1991

ARCHITECTURE, RURAL. see **ARCHITECTURE, DOMESTIC; FARM BUILDINGS.** .

ARCHITECTURE - RUSSIAN S.F.S.R.
Gippenreĭter, Vadim Evgen´evich. The golden ring . New York , 1991. p. cm. ISBN 1-558-59216-4 DDC 720/.947 20
NA1181 .G56 1991

ARCHITECTURE - RUSSIAN S.F.S.R. - DAGESTANSKAIA A.S.S.R.
Drevniaia i srednevekovaia arkhitektura Dagestana . Makhachkala , 1989. 184, [4] p. :
NA1492.8 .D7 1989

ARCHITECTURE - RUSSIAN S.F.S.R. - MOSCOW.
Arkhitekturnoe nasledie Moskvy . Moskva , 1988. 100 p. :
NA1197.M6 A78 1988

Berton, Kathleen. Moscow . London ; New York, NY : 256 p. : ISBN 1-85043-261-9 DDC 720/.947/312 20
NA1197.M6 B42 1990

ARCHITECTURE - RUSSIAN S.F.S.R. - MOSCOW - GUIDE-BOOKS.
Pamiatniki arkhitektury Moskvy. Moskva , 1989. 351 p. : ISBN 5-210-00253-5 :
NA1197.M6 P285 1989

ARCHITECTURE, SARACENIC. see **ARCHITECTURE, ISLAMIC.**

ARCHITECTURE - SCANDINAVIA - HISTORY.
Donnelly, Marian C. (Marian Card) Architecture in the Scandinavian countries /. Cambridge, Mass. , c1991. p. cm. ISBN 0-262-04118-9 DDC 720/.948 20
NA1201 .D66 1991

ARCHITECTURE - SCOTLAND - BRECHIN - CONSERVATION AND RESTORATION.
Brechin: a study in conservation. Edinburgh [1970] [231] p. ISBN 0-901658-08-1 DDC 711/.4 094131
NA109.G7 B7   *NYPL [3-MQWK 90-5626]*

ARCHITECTURE, SELJUK - TURKEY - KONYA - THEMES, MOTIVES.
Sarre, Friedrich Paul Theodor, 1865-1945. Konia . Berlin [1921] 30 p., 12 leaves of plates (some folded) : DDC 720/.9564 20
NA5871.k86 S27 1921

ARCHITECTURE - SLOVAK REPUBLIC - BRATISLAVA (CZECHOSLOVAKIA)
Puškárová, Blanka. Bratislava . Bratislava , 1989. 253 p. : ISBN 80-222-0024-7 :
N6833.B7 P87 1989

ARCHITECTURE - SOUTH AFRICA - THEMES, MOTIVES.
Our building heritage . [South Africa] , 1988.
iv, 312, [5] p. : ISBN 0-620-12738-4 DDC
720/.968 20
NA1592 .O94 1988

ARCHITECTURE - SOUTHERN STATES.
Forman, Henry Chandlee, 1904- The
architecture of the Old South . Cambridge ,
1948. 203 p., [7] p. of plates : DDC 720.975
NA720 .F6 ***NYPL [3-MQWO 91-6780]***

ARCHITECTURE - SOVIET UNION - EXHIBITIONS.
Neuvostomaan arkkitehtuuria . [Helsinki , 1988]
81 p. : ISBN 951-9229-56-6
NA1188 .N48 1988

ARCHITECTURE - SPAIN.
Arquitectura española contemporánea .
Barcelona , c1990. 192 p. : ISBN 84-252-1429-7
DDC 720/.946/09048 20
NA1308 .A84 1990
NYPL [3-MQWH 91-3890]

Arrechea, Julio I. Arquitectura y romanticismo .
Valladolid, España [Salamanca] , c1989. 330
p. : ISBN 84-7762-086-5 DDC 720/.946/09034 20
NA1307 .A7 1989

Bonet Correa, Antonio. Fiesta, poder y
arquitectura . Madrid, España , c1990. 182 p. :
ISBN 84-7600-446-6 DDC 720/.946/09033 20
NA1306 .B57 1990

Cámara Muñoz, Alicia. Arquitectura y sociedad
en el Siglo de Oro . Madrid , c1990. 280 p.,
[32] p. of plates : ISBN 84-86902-07-X
NYPL [MQWH 91-5219]

Dodds, Jerrilynn D. Architecture and ideology
in early medieval Spain /. University Park ,
c1990. xiv, 174 p., [72] p. of plates : ISBN
0-271-00671-4 DDC 720/.946/09021 20
NA1303 .D63 1989
NYPL [3-MQWH 91-4942]

ARCHITECTURE - SPAIN - BARCELONA.
Bohigas, Oriol. Barcelona, city and architecture,
1980-1992 /. New York , 1991. 239 p. : ISBN
0-8478-1354-1 : DDC 720/.946/7209048 20
NA1311.B3 B64 1991

ARCHITECTURE - SPAIN - BARCELONA (PROVINCE) - CONGRESSES.
Història i arquitectura . Barcelona [1986?] 260
p. : ISBN 84-505-2551-9
NA1309.B29 H57 1986
NYPL [3-MQWH+ 90-12046]

ARCHITECTURE - SPAIN - CATALONIA.
Americanos indianos . Vilanova i la Geltrú ,
1990. 262 p. : ***NYPL [3-MQWH 91-6959]***

ARCHITECTURE - SPAIN - CATALONIA - EXHIBITIONS.
Arquitectura . [Spain] [1988?] 187 p. :
NYPL [3-MQWH+ 91-6437]

ARCHITECTURE - SPAIN - CATALONIA - GUIDE-BOOKS.
Lacuesta, Raquel. Arquitectura modernista en
Cataluña /. Barcelona , c1990. 213 p. : ISBN
84-252-1430-0 DDC 720/.946/70904 20
NA1309.C2 L33 1990

ARCHITECTURE - SPAIN - CONGRESSES.
Coloquio de Urbanismo Barroco (1986 :
Archidona, Spain) II centenario de la Plaza
Ochavada de Archidona /. [Málaga] [1989]
350 p. : ISBN 84-7496-177-7
NA1306 .C6 1986

ARCHITECTURE - SPAIN - CONSERVATION AND RESTORATION.
Intervenciones en el patrimonio arquitectónico
(1980-1985) /. [Madrid] [1990] 465 p. : ISBN
84-7483-661-1 DDC 720/.28/8094609048 20
NA1301 .I57 1990

ARCHITECTURE - SPAIN - CONSERVATION AND RESTORATION - CONGRESSES.
Jornadas sobre Criterios de Intervención en el
Patrimonio Arquitectónico (1987 : Madrid,
Spain) Monumentos y proyecto . Madrid
[1990] 407 p. : ISBN 84-7483-642-5
NA109.S7 J68 1987

ARCHITECTURE - SPAIN - GUIPÚZCOA.
Astiazarain Achabal, María Isabel. Arquitectos
guipuzcoanos del siglo XVIII /. Guipúzcoa
[1988?-1990?] 2 v. : ISBN 84-505-7463-3
NA1109.G85 A88 1988

ARCHITECTURE - SPAIN - PAÍS VASCO - THEMES, MOTIVES.
Mas Serra, Elías, 1945- 50 Años de
arquitectura en Euskadi /. [Vitoria] , 1990.
xviii, 347 p. : ISBN 84-7542-854-1 DDC
720/.946/609045 20
NA1309.P33 M37 1990

ARCHITECTURE - SPAIN - SEVILLE.
Vázquez Consuegra, Guillermo. Sevilla, cien
edificios /. [Sevilla?] , 1988. 398 p. : ISBN
89-87001-08-4
NYPL [3-MQWH+ 89-25523]

ARCHITECTURE, SPANISH COLONIAL - MEXICO.
Garrison, G. Richard (George Richard), 1898-
[Mexican houses.] Early Mexican houses .
Stamford, Conn. , 1990. xvii, 173 p. : ISBN
0-942655-03-0 : DDC 728/.0972 20
NA7244 .G3 1990
NYPL [3-MQWN+ 91-4465]

ARCHITECTURE, SPANISH COLONIAL - UNITED STATES.
Newcomb, Rexford, 1886-1968.
Spanish-colonial architecture in the United
States /. New York , 1990. 39 p., 130 p. of
plates : ISBN 0-486-26263-4 : DDC 720/.973 20
NA707 .N44 1990
NYPL [3-MQWO 91-6602]

ARCHITECTURE, SPANISH - FLORIDA - INFLUENCE.
Mizner, Addison, 1872-1933. Florida
architecture of Addison Mizner /. Boulder,
Colo. , 1991. p. cm. ISBN 1-87865-002-5 : DDC
720/.92 20
NA737.M59 A4 1991

ARCHITECTURE, SPANISH - INFLUENCE.
Manucy, Albert C. The houses of St. Augustine,
1565-1821 /. Jacksonville , c1992. p. cm. ISBN
0-8130-1103-5 DDC 728/.09759/18 20
NA7238.S27 M3 1992

ARCHITECTURE - STUDY AND TEACHING - BELGIUM - BRUSSELS.
Académie de Bruxelles . Bruxelles , 1989. 541
p. : ISBN 2-87143-063-2
NYPL [3-MQF+ 90-133]

ARCHITECTURE - STUDY AND TEACHING - UNITED STATES.
Clarke, David, 1942- Frank Lloyd Wright and
the Laffer curve . Wakefield, N.H. , 1991. p.
cm. ISBN 0-89341-655-X DDC 720/.71/173 20
NA2105 .C58 1991

Voices in architectural education . New York ,
1991. p. cm. ISBN 0-89789-253-4 (alk. paper)
DDC 720/.7/073 20
NA2105 .V65 1991

ARCHITECTURE - STUDY AND TEACHING - WISCONSIN - SPRING GREEN.
Wright, Frank Lloyd, 1867-1959. "At Taliesin" .
Carbondale , c1992. p. cm. ISBN 0-8093-1709-5
DDC 720/.7/077576 20
NA2127.G74 W75 1992

ARCHITECTURE - SWEDEN - HUMAN FACTORS.
When people matter /. Sweden , Solna, Sweden
[1989] 223 p. : ISBN 91-540-5059-6 DDC
725/.4/09485 20
NA6403.S8 W47 1989

ARCHITECTURE - SWEDEN - STOCKHOLM.
Andersson, Henrik O., 1939- [Stockholms
byggnader. English.] Stockholm, architecture
and townscape /. Stockholm , c1988. 412 p. :
ISBN 91-518-1879-5
NYPL [3-MQWE 89-11933]

ARCHITECTURE - SWITZERLAND - BASELLAND.
Bauen vor der Stadt. English & German. Bauen
vor der Stadt . Basel , Boston , c1991. p. cm.
ISBN 3-7643-2629-8 : DDC 720/.9494/33 20
NA1349.B38 B3813 1991

ARCHITECTURE - SWITZERLAND - BIEL.
Propper, Emanuel Jirka. Das alte Biel und seine
Umgebung /. Biel (Blumenstrasse 15, 2502
Biel) , 1980. 1 portfolio (38 p., 32 leaves of
plates) : ***NYPL [3-MQWD++ 88-4261]***

ARCHITECTURE - SYMBOLISM. see SYMBOLISM IN ARCHITECTURE.

ARCHITECTURE - TECHNOLOGICAL INNOVATIONS.
Strike, James. Construction into design .
Oxford , Boston , 1991. p. cm. ISBN

0-7506-1229-0 : DDC 721/.09/03 20
NA2543.T43 S7 1991

ARCHITECTURE - TECHNOLOGICAL INNOVATIONS - CONGRESSES.
Building Arts Forum/New York. Symposium
(1989 : Guggenheim Museum) Bridging the
gap . New York , c1991. xv, 183 p. : ISBN
0-442-00135-5 DDC 720 20
NA2543.T43 B8 1991
NYPL [3-MQV 91-3950]

On architecture, the city, and technology /.
Washington, DC , Stoneham, MA , c1990. 152
p. : ISBN 0-7506-9149-2 DDC 720/.1/05 20
NA2543.T43 O5 1990

ARCHITECTURE - TERMINOLOGY.
Ballast, David Kent. Architecture, design, and
construction word finder /. Englewood Cliffs,
N.J. , c1991. p. cm. ISBN 0-13-044397-2 DDC
720/.3 20
NA31 .B34 1991

White, Antony, 1941- Architecture &
ornament . New York , 1991. p. cm. ISBN
0-8306-3352-9 : DDC 720/.14 20
NA31 .W44 1991

Architecture thématique, 0989-4268.
Bédarida, Marc. Immeubles de bureaux /.
Paris , c1991. 119 p. : ISBN 2-281-19052-8
NA6230 .B43 1991

Boulet, Marie-Laure. Auditoriums /. Paris ,
c1990. 119 p. : ISBN 2-281-19052-8 DDC
725/.81/09048 20
NA6815 .B68 1990

ARCHITECTURE, TROPICAL - CONGRESSES.
Arquitetura nos trópicos . Recife , 1985. 161
p. : ISBN 85-7019-095-6
NA2542.T7 A77 1985
NYPL [3-MQD 90-11121]

ARCHITECTURE - TURKEY - FATIH (ISTANBUL)
Eyice, Semavi. Fotoğraflarla Fatih anıtları /.
Fatih [Istanbul, Turkey] [1989?] 126 p. :
NA1370 .E88 1989

ARCHITECTURE, TURKISH.
Vogt-Göknil, Ulya. Osmanische Türkei /.
Fribourg , c1965. 192 p. :
NYPL [3-MQT 90-6997]

ARCHITECTURE - UKRAINE - L'VIV.
Trehubova, T. O. L'viv,
arkhitekturno-istorychnyĭ narys /. Kyïv , 1989.
270 p. : ISBN 5-7705-0178-2 :
NA1197.L85 T74 1989

ARCHITECTURE - UNITED STATES.
American art and architecture [videorecording]
/. Boulder, CO , 1990. 5 videocassettes (140
min.) : DDC 709.73 11
N6505

Çelik, Zeynep. Displaying the Orient .
Berkeley , c1992. p. cm. ISBN 0-520-07494-7
(alk. paper) DDC 725/.91 20
NA957 .C44 1992

Holmes, Kristin, 1955- The Victorian express /.
Wilsonville, Or. , c1991. p. cm. ISBN
0-89802-568-0 : DDC 728/.37/097309034 20
NA710.5.V5 H64 1991

Holmes, Kristin, 1955- The Victorian express /.
Wilsonville, Or. , c1991. p. cm. ISBN
0-89802-568-0 : DDC 728/.37/097309034 20
NA710.5.V5 H64 1991

Modern architecture in America . Ames , 1991.
xiv, 217 p. : ISBN 0-8138-0381-0 (alk. paper)
DDC 720/.973/09034 20
NA710 .M6 1991
NYPL [3-MQWO 91-6777]

O'Gorman, James F. Three American
architects . Chicago , 1991. xx, 170 p. : ISBN
0-226-62071-9 DDC 720/.973/09034 20
NA710 .O35 1991
NYPL [3-MQWO 91-5189]

ARCHITECTURE - UNITED STATES - AWARDS.
Accent on architecture . [Washington, D.C.]
(1735 New York Ave., NW, Washington
20006) [c1991] 1 v. (unpaged) ; DDC
720/.973/09045 20
NA2340 .A33 1991

ARCHITECTURE - UNITED STATES - BIBLIOGRAPHY.

Vance, Mary A. Historical society architectural publications, Georgia, Hawaii, Idaho, Illinois, and Indiana /. Monticello, Ill. , 1980. 54 p. ; Z5944.U5 V353 NA705
NYPL [3-MQWO 81-771]

ARCHITECTURE - UNITED STATES - CONSERVATION AND RESTORATION.
Smith, Daisy M. (Daisy Mullett) A.B. Mullett . Washington, D.C. , c1990. xii, 128 p. : ISBN 0-9611410-2-6 (hardcover) DDC 720/.92 20
NA737.M78 S65 1990

ARCHITECTURE - UNITED STATES - CONSERVATION AND RESTORATION - CONGRESSES.
National Trust for Historic Preservation in the United States. Historic preservation tomorrow . [Williamsburg, Va.] 1967. xi, 57 p.
NYPL [3-MQWO 90-5564]

ARCHITECTURE - UNITED STATES - CONSERVATION AND RESTORATION - STANDARDS.
The Secretary of the Interior's standards for rehabilitation and Illustrated guidelines for rehabilitating historic buildings /. Washington, D.C. , 1991. p. cm. DDC 720/.28/8021873 20
NA106 .S4 1991

ARCHITECTURE - UNITED STATES - DETAILS.
The Elements of style . New York , c1991. p. cm. ISBN 0-671-73981-6 DDC 721 20
NA2850 .E44 1991

ARCHITECTURE - UNITED STATES - GUIDE-BOOKS.
Wright sites . River Forest, Ill. , c1991. p. cm. ISBN 0-9629087-0-3 DDC 720/.92 20
NA737.W7 W75 1991

ARCHITECTURE - UNITED STATES - PICTORIAL WORKS - EXHIBITIONS.
Devlin, Harry. Portraits of American architecture, November 4th to December 2nd, 1979, Morris Museum of Arts and Sciences, Morristown, N.J. /. Morristown, N.J. , c1979. [38] p. : DDC 759.13
ND237.D43 A4 1979
NYPL [3-MCX D497 90-12735]

ARCHITECTURE - UNITED STATES - THEMES, MOTIVES.
American architecture of the 1980s /. Washington, D.C. , 1990. xiv, 342 p. : ISBN 1-558-35056-X : DDC 720/.973/09048 20
NA712 .A64 1990
NYPL [MQWO+ 90-11575]

ARCHITECTURE, VERNACULAR. see VERNACULAR ARCHITECTURE.

ARCHITECTURE, VICTORIAN - CALIFORNIA - SAN FRANCISCO.
Delehanty, Randolph. In the Victorian style /. San Francisco , c1991. p. cm. ISBN 0-87701-750-6 (hc) : DDC 720/.9794/6109034 20
NA7238.S35 D4 1991

ARCHITECTURE, VICTORIAN - GREAT BRITAIN.
Curl, James Stevens, 1937- Victorian architecture /. Newton Abbot , 1990. 320 p. : ISBN 0-7153-9144-5 : DDC 720/.941 19
NA967.5.V53   NYPL [3-MQWK 90-11107]

Curl, James Stevens, 1937- Victorian architecture /. Newton Abbot , New York, N.Y. , c1990. 320 p. : ISBN 0-7153-9144-5 DDC 720/.941/09034 20
NA967 .C8 1990

Dixon, Roger, 1935- Victorian architecture. New York , 1978. 288 p. : ISBN 0-19-520048-9 DDC 720/.941
NA967 .D59

ARCHITECTURE, VICTORIAN - ILLINOIS - CHICAGO.
Laughlin, Clarence John. Photographs of Victorian Chicago. [New York, 1968] [12] p.
TR6 .L3   NYPL [MFX (Laughlin) 90-6252]

ARCHITECTURE, VICTORIAN, IN ART.
Devlin, Harry. Portraits of American architecture . Boston , 1989. 191 p. : ISBN 0-87923-793-7 : DDC 759.13 19
ND237.D43 A4 1989
NYPL [3-MRG+ 90-2829]

ARCHITECTURE, VICTORIAN - UNITED STATES.
Devlin, Harry. Portraits of American

architecture . Boston , 1989. 191 p. : ISBN 0-87923-793-7 : DDC 759.13 19
ND237.D43 A4 1989
NYPL [3-MRG+ 90-2829]

Gillon, Edmund Vincent. Victorian houses . New York , c1973. 1 v. (unpaged) : ISBN 0-486-22966-1 NYPL [3-MQWO 90-7005]

Holmes, Kristin, 1955- The Victorian express /. Wilsonville, Or. , c1991. p. cm. ISBN 0-89802-568-0 : DDC 728/.37/097309034 20
NA710.5.V5 H64 1991

ARCHITECTURE - VIRGIN ISLANDS OF THE UNITED STATES - CHARLOTTE AMALIE.
Woods, Edith deJongh. The three quarters of the town of Charlotte Amalie . London , c1989. 158 p. : DDC 720/.97297/22 20
NA815.V5 W66 1989
NYPL [3-MQWM+ 91-6696]

ARCHITECTURE - WASHINGTON, D. C.
Rowan, Bob, 1944- A capital perspective . Chatsworth, Calif. , 1991. p. cm. ISBN 0-89781-427-4 DDC 720/.9753 20
NA735.W3 R69 1991

Architectures historiques à Marseille : éléments de l'habitat ancien. Aix-en-Provence : Edisud, c1987. 141 p. : ill., maps, plans ; 30 cm. "Rédigé par Pascal Urbain ... sous la direction de Daniel Drocourt"--P. facing t.p. At head of title: Atelier du patrimoine de la ville de Marseille. Includes bibliographical references. ISBN 2-85744-290-4 : DDC 720/.944/912 19
1. Architecture - France - Marseille - Themes, motives. 2. Decoration and ornament, Architectural - France - Marseille - Themes, motives. 3. City planning - France - Marseille - History. 4. Marseille (France) - Buildings, structures, etc. - Themes, motives. I. Urbain, Pascal. II. Drocourt, Daniel. III. Atelier du patrimoine de la ville de Marseille.
NA1051.M37 U73 1987
NYPL [3-MQWF+ 90-12768]

Architectures régionales . Ben el-Khadir, Mohamed. [Morocco] 1989 (Casablanca : Impr. Najah el Jadida) 211 p. :
NA1590 .B46 1989

Der Architekt Adolf Loos. Münz, Ludwig, 1889-1957. Wien [1964] 200 p.
NYPL [3-MQZ (Loos) 90-7197]

Architekten, Atelier 5, Bern. 1. Aufl. Stuttgart : IRB Verlag, [1988] 49 p. ; 21 cm. (IRB-Literaturauslese, 0724-5548 . Nr. 1894) "Hrsg.: Informationszentrum Raum u. Bau d. Fraunhofer-Ges. (IRB)"--T.p. verso. "Redaktionelle Bearbeitung: Klaus Kaiser"--T.p. verso. ISBN 3-8167-1816-7 (pbk.)
1. Atelier 5 (Firm) - Bibliography. I. Kaiser, Klaus, Dipl.-Ing. Arch. II. Fraunhofer-Gesellschaft. Informationszentrum Raum und Bau. III. Title: Atelier 5, Bern.   NYPL [3-MQWD 90-12512]

Architekten, Rem Koolhaas und OMA. 1. Aufl. Stuttgart : IRB, [1988] 66 p. ; 21 cm. (IRB-Literaturauslese, 0724-5548 . Nr. 1922.) "Hrsg.: Informationszentrum Raum u. Bau d. Fraunhofer-Ges. (IRB)"--T.p. verso. "Redaktionelle Bearbeitung: Klaus Kaiser"--T.p. verso. ISBN 3-8167-1844-2 (pbk.)
1. Koolhaas, Rem - Bibliography. 2. Office for Metropolitan Architecture - Bibliography. I. Kaiser, Klaus, Dipl.-Ing. Arch. II. Fraunhofer-Gesellschaft. Informationszentrum Raum und Bau. III. Title: Rem Koolhaas und OMA.
NYPL [3-MQZ (Koolhaas) 90-12511]

Architekten, Rolf Gutbrod. 1. Aufl. Stuttgart : IRB, [1988]. 51 p. ; 21 cm. (IRB-Literaturauslese, 0724-5548 . Nr. 1925) "Hrsg.: Informationszentrum Raum u. Bau d. Fraunhofer-Ges. (IRB)"--T.p. verso. "Redaktionelle Bearbeitung: Klaus Kaiser"--T.p. verso. ISBN 3-8167-1847-7 (pbk.)
1. Gutbrod, Rolf - Bibliography. I. Kaiser, Klaus, Dipl.-Ing. Arch. II. Fraunhofer-Gesellschaft. Informationszentrum Raum und Bau. III. Title: Rolf Gutbrod.
NYPL [3-MQZ (Gutbrad) 90-12742]

Architektenwerkverzeichnisse / [redaktionelle Bearbeitung, Thomas Schloz]. 2. erw. Aufl. Stuttgart : IRB Verlag, [1989] 111 p. ; 21 cm. (IRB-Literaturauslese, 0724-5548 . Nr. 1113) Includes indexes. ISBN 3-8167-1031-X
1. Architecture - Bibliography. I. Schloz, Thomas.
NYPL [3-MQB 91-7535]

Architektur als Erkenntnis =. Fonatti, Franco, 1942- Wien , c1989. 189 p. :
NA1123.F59 A4 1989

Architektur der englischen Gotik /. Kowa, Günter, 1954- Köln , c1990. 336 p. : ISBN 3-7701-1969-X DDC 720/.942/0902 20
NA440 .K6 1990

Die Architektur des Orgien Mysterien Theaters =. Nitsch, Hermann, 1938- München , c1987- v. :   NYPL [MDG (Nitsch) 90-11004]

Architektur des zwanzigsten Jahrhunderts. Klotz, Heinrich. Architektur des 20. Jahrhunderts . Frankfurt am Main , c1989. 351 p. :
NYPL [3-MQV 90-11330]

Architektur des 20. Jahrhunderts . Klotz, Heinrich. Frankfurt am Main , c1989. 351 p. :
NYPL [3-MQV 90-11330]

Architektur im Wandel : Beispiele und Meinungen / Friedbert Kind-Barkauskas (Herausgeber) ; mit Beiträgen von Hans-Busso von Busse ... [et al.]. Düsseldorf : Beton-Verlag, c1990. 91 p. : ill. (some col.) ; 28 cm. (Baumeisterforum) Includes bibliographical references and indexes. ISBN 3-7640-0265-4
1. Architecture, Modern - 20th century. I. Kind-Barkauskas, Friedbert. II. Busse, Hans Busso von. III. Series.
NA680 .A732 1990

Architektur in Regensburg 1933-1945 / Neuer Kunstverein Regensburg (Hg.) ; [redaktionelle Betreuung, Stefan Maier, Reiner R. Schmidt]. 1. Aufl. Regensburg : CH-Verlag, 1989. 139 p. : ill. ; 21 cm. (Schriftenreihe des Neuen Kunstverein Regensburg e.V. . Bd. 1) "Dieser Aufsatz erscheint aus Anlass der Ausstellung 'Architektur in Regensburg 1933-1945,' die vom Neuen Kunstverein Regensburg e.V. und dem Stadtarchiv Regensburg in der Zeit vom 10.7.1989 bis 17.9.1989 durchgeführt wird"--T.p. verso. Includes bibliographical references. ISBN 3-927730-01-7
1. Architecture - Germany - Regensburg - Exhibitions. 2. Architecture, Modern - 20th century - Germany - Regensburg - Exhibitions. 3. Regensburg (Germany) - Buildings, structures, etc. - Exhibitions. I. Maier, Stefan, 1958-. II. Schmidt, Reiner R. III. Neuer Kunstverein Regensburg. IV. Stadtarchiv Regensburg. V. Series.
NA1086.R4 A7 1989

Architektur und Gesellschaft . Schwarz, Alberto. Leipzig , c1989. 190 p. : ISBN 3-361-00254-0
NA2543.S6 S38 1989

Architektur und Städtebau des Islam / [redaktionelle Bearbeitung, Susanne Jakubowski-Zalonis]. 1. Aufl. Stuttgart : IRB Verlag, 1985- v. ; 21 cm. (IRB-Literaturauslese, 0724-5548 . Nr. 200) "Die Datenbanken des IRB"--P. 3, v. 1. "März 1985"--T.p. verso, v. 1. Includes indexes. ISBN 3-8167-0105-1 DDC 016.72/0917/671 19
1. Architecture, Islamic - Bibliography. 2. City planning - Islamic countries - Bibliography. I. Jakubowski-Zalonis, Susanne. II. Fraunhofer-Gesellschaft. Informationszentrum Raum und Bau.
Z5943.I84 A73 1984 NA380
NYPL [3-MQT 91-826]

Architektúra (Budapest, Hungary)
Bakonyi, Tibor. Magyar Ede /. Budapest , 1989. 28 p., [48] p. of plates : ISBN 963-05-4981-6 :
NA1022.5.M337 B3 1989

Kubinszky, Mihály. Otto Wagner /. Budapest , 1988. 25 p., [56] p. of plates : ISBN 963-05-4879-8 :
NA1011.5.W3 K8 1988

Architektúra, 0066-6270.
Bakonyi, Tibor. Magyar Ede /. Budapest , 1989. 28 p., [48] p. of plates : ISBN 963-05-4981-6 :
NA1022.5.M337 B3 1989

Ferkai, András. Konsztantyin Melnyikov /. Budapest , 1988. 43 p., [59] p. of plates : ISBN 963-05-4517-9
NA1199.M37 F4 1988

Kubinszky, Mihály. Otto Wagner /. Budapest , 1988. 25 p., [56] p. of plates : ISBN 963-05-4879-8 :
NA1011.5.W3 K8 1988

ARCHITEKTURBÜRO BOLLES WILSON - EXHIBITIONS.
Wilson, Peter, 1950- Western objects Eastern fields . London , c1989. 64 p. : ISBN 1-87089-019-1
NYPL [3-MQZ+ (Wilson) 90-4013]

Architekturführer DDR.
Bezirk Suhl /. Berlin , 1989. 160 p. : ISBN
3-345-00213-2
NA1089.2.S84 B49 1989

**Architekturgeschichte des zwanzigsten
Jahrhunderts.** Joedicke, Jürgen.
Architekturgeschichte des 20. Jahrhunderts .
Stuttgart , c1990. 256 p. : ISBN 3-7828-0459-7
DDC 724/.6 20
NA680 .J574 1990

Architekturgeschichte des 20. Jahrhunderts .
Joedicke, Jürgen. Stuttgart , c1990. 256 p. :
ISBN 3-7828-0459-7 DDC 724/.6 20
NA680 .J574 1990

Architekturmalerei an Fassaden . Tafelmaier,
Walter, 1935- Stuttgart , 1988. 159 p. : ISBN
3-421-02937-7 *NYPL [3-MRX 90-12633]*

Architekturmuseum in Basel. Senn, Otto H. (Otto
Heinrich), 1902- Otto Senn . Basel , c1990. 137
p. : ISBN 3-905065-12-4
NA1353.S46 A4 1990

Architettura & computer. A cura di Maria Zevi.
[Roma, Bulzoni, 1972] 219 p. illus. 23 cm.
Cover title. Half-title: Il Computer nella progettazione.
"Saggi basati sulle relazioni presentate nel corso del
Seminario tenuto nella Facoltà di architettura di Roma
nei giorni 15-20 novembre 1971." Includes
bibliographies.
*1. Architecture - Data processing - Congresses. I. Zevi,
Maria, ed. II. Title: Computer nella progettazione. III.
Title: Architettura e computer.*
NA2540 .A62   NYPL [3-MQD 90-6902]

**Architettura armena dal quarto al diciannovesimo
secolo /.** Cuneo, Paolo. Roma , 1988. 2 v. (923
p., [1] folded leaf of plates) : ISBN
88-7813-154-7 (set)
NYPL [3-MQW 90-12681]

**L'architettura cistercense e l'Abbazia di Casamari
/.** Farina, Federico. Casamari , 1981, c1978. xii,
187 p. : DDC 726/.7/0945622 19
NA5621.A22 F37 1981
NYPL [3-MRBD+ 90-12587]

Architettura come cognizione. Fonatti, Franco,
1942- Architektur als Erkenntnis = . Wien ,
c1989. 189 p. :
NA1123.F59 A4 1989

Architettura. Contemporanei.
Dini, Massimo, 1946- Renzo Piano, progetti e
architetture, 1964-1983 /. Milano , c1983. 246
p. : ISBN 88-435-0921-7 : DDC 720/.92/4 19
NA1123.P47 D5 1983
NYPL [3-MQS (Piano) 90-129970]

**L'Architettura di Gino Zani per la ricostruzione
di Reggio Calabria (1909-1935) /** a cura di
Massimo Lo Curzio ; scritti di Saverio
Liconti ... [et al.]. Roma : Gangemi, c1986. 140
p. : ill., plans ; 24 cm. Includes bibliographical
references.
*1. Zani, G. (Gino). 2. Architecture - Italy - Reggio di
Calabria. 3. Reggio di Calabria (Italy) - Buildings,
structures, etc. I. Zani, G. (Gino). II. Lo Curzio,
Massimo. III. Liconti, Saverio.*
NYPL [3-MQZ (Zani) 90-12335]

**Architettura e ambiente. Sezione Colore e arredo
urbano .**
(6) Zuccoli, Noris. Mantova . Firenze , 1986.
60 p. :   *NYPL [3-MQWB 90-12550]*

Architettura e città (Alinea editrice) .
(10) Miccini, Eugenio. Retorica della
fotografia . Firenze , c1984. 236 p. :
TR659 .M53 1984   NYPL [MFW 91-3464]

Architettura e computer. Architettura &
computer. [Roma, 1972] 219 p. :
NA2540 .A62   NYPL [3-MQD 90-6902]

Architettura, edilizia, urbanistica .
(v. 5) Elaborati urbanistici . Milano [1987?] 10
pamphlets in portfolio :
NYPL [3-MQWB 90-11014]

Architettura giapponese contemporanea. Firenze,
Orsanmichele, 15 marzo-15 aprile 1969.
Catalogo a cura di Paolo Riani. Introduzioni di
Fosco Maraini e Carlo L. Ragghianti. Firenze,
Centro Di, 1969. 282 p. illus. 28 cm. (Cataloghi.
6) Also in English; title in English: Contemporary
Japanese architecture. Bibliography: p. 23-35.
*1. Architecture - Japan - Exhibitions. 2. Architecture,
Modern - 20th century - Japan - Exhibitions. I. Riani,
Paolo. II. Title: Contemporary Japanese architecture.*
NA1555 .A8   NYPL [3-MQWS 90-6800]

Architettura in pietra a secco : atti del 1°
Seminario internazionale "Architettura in pietra
a secco" : Noci-Alberobello, 27-30 settembre
1987 / a cura di A. Ambrosi, E. Degano, C.A.
Zaccaria. Fasano, Br : Schena, c1990. 578 p. :
ill. ; 24 cm. English, French, and Italian. Includes
bibliographical references. ISBN 88-7514-413-3 :
DDC 721/.0441 20
*1. Stone buildings - Congresses. 2. Vernacular
architecture - Congresses. I. Ambrosi, Angelo. II.
Degano, E. (Enrico). III. Zaccaria, C. A. (Carlo A.).*
NA4130 .A73 1990

**Architettura in Sicilia nelle età islamica e
normanna .** Bellafiore, Giuseppe. Milano ,
c1990. 366 p. : ISBN 88-7177-010-2 :
NYPL [3-MQO 91-3372]

**Architettura in Sicilia nelle età islamica e
normanna (827-1194) /.** Bellafiore, Giuseppe.
Palermo , c1990. 366 p. : ISBN 88-7177-010-2 :
DDC 720/.945/809021 20
NA1109.S5 B4 1990

Architettura, storia e progetto .
(1) Gambardella, Carmine. Bacoli . Napoli
[1982] 70 p. :
TH7413 .G36 1982   NYPL [MQWB 91-840]

Architettura/temi.
Immagini del post-moderno . Venezia , c1983.
345 p. : ISBN 88-85067-09-3 DDC 724.9/1 19
NA682.P67 I48 1983
NYPL [3-MQV 91-6389]

A.R.C.H.I.V.E.S.
Loyer, François. Henri Sauvage . Bruxelles ,
1987. 159 p. : ISBN 2-87009-304-7 (pbk.)
NYPL [3-MQZ (Savage) 90-12030]

**Archives d'architecture moderne (Brussels,
Belgium)** Maisons sur l'île d'Ibiza .
Bruxelles , 1990. 127 p. : ISBN 2-87143-072-6
NA7386.I25 M35 1990

Archives des arts modernes .
(5-7) Devade, Marc, 1943-1983. Marc Devade .
Paris , 1989-1990. 3 v. (479 p.) ; ISBN
2-256-90867-4 DDC 701 20
N70 .D458 1989

ARCHIVES - EXHIBITIONS.
Wolff, Fritz. Karten im Archiv /. Marburg ,
1987. 64 p. : ISBN 3-923833-21-0
GA190 .W66 1987
NYPL [Map Div. 90-12429]

ARCHIVES - ITALY - LIGURIA - CATALOGS.
Documenti geocartografici nelle bibiloteche e
negli archivi privati e pubblici della Liguria.
Firenze , 1990- v. : ISBN 88-22-23788-9 (v. 1)
NYPL [Map Div. 91-69]

Archives of the Museum of Finnish Architecture.
Suomen Rakennustaiteen Museo. Arkisto.
Suomen Rakennustaiteen Museon Arkisto.
Helsinki [1989] 288 p. : ISBN 951-9229-60-4
NA2706.F5 S86 1989

Archivi dell'Ottocento.
Panzetta, Alfonso. Dizionario degli scultori
italiani dell'Ottocento /. Torino , Milano ,
c1989. 228 p. : ISBN 88-422-0224-X
NYPL [3-MGI+ 90-11558]

Panzetta, Alfonso. Dizionario degli scultori
italiani dell'Ottocento /. Torino , 19. 228 p. :
ISBN 88-422-0224-X : DDC 730/.92/245 B 20
NB622 .P36 1989

Archivi di arte antica.
Caroli, Flavio. Fede Galizia /. Torino , c1989.
102 p. : ISBN 88-422-0217-7
NYPL [3-MCF+ G155 90-12321]

Archivi di arte contemporanea.
Rama, Carol. Carol Rama /. Torino , c1989.
117 p. : ISBN 88-422-0173-1
NYPL [3-MCF+ R165 89-26726]

Archivi di arte e cultura piemontesi.
Quirico, Giambattista, 1947- Il Regio
Manicomio di Via Giulio in Torino,
1830-1985 . Torino , 1987. 117 p. :
NYPL [3-MQWB+ 90-10584]

Archivi futuristi / a cura di Mario Verdone.
Modena : Galleria Fonte d'Abisso edizioni ;
Milano : Fonte d'Abisso arte, c1990. 189 p. :
ill. (some col.) ; 30 cm. "7 aprile-14 luglio
1990"--Verso t.p. Includes bibliographical references (p.
188-189). DDC 709/.45/0744542 20
*1. Futurism (Art) - Italy - Exhibitions. 2. Art, Modern -
20th century - Italy - Exhibitions. I. Verdone, Mario. II.*

Galleria Fonte d'Abisso (Modena, Italy).
N6918.5.F8 A74 1990

Archivio del collezionismo mediceo.
Il Cardinal Leopoldo. Milano , 1987- v. :
NYPL [3-MAX (Medici) 91-6376]

Archivio Della Grazia di nuova scrittura / Paolo
Della Grazia ... [et al.]. Milano : [s.n.], 1989. 96
p., [39] p. of plates : ill. ; 31 cm. Text also in
English.
*1. Artists' books - Italy - Catalogs. 2. Artists' books -
Private collections - Italy - Milan - Catalogs. 3. Della
Grazia, Paolo - Art collections - Catalogs. I. Della
Grazia, Paolo.*
N7433.35.I8 A73 1989

**Archivio e centro studi "Giorgio Morandi"
(Bologna, Italy)** La Pittura russa nell'età
romantica /. Bologna , c1990. lx, 190 p. :
ISBN 88-7779-129-2
IN PROCESS (ONLINE)
NYPL [3-MCY 90-11768]

Archivio fotografico comunale (Rome, Italy)
Un Inglese a Roma, 1864-1877 . Roma , c1989.
239 p. :   *NYPL [MFX (Parker) 91-3346]*

**ARCHIVIO FOTOGRAFICO COMUNALE
(ROME, ITALY) - CATALOGS.**
Un Inglese a Roma, 1864-1877 . Roma , c1989.
239 p. :   *NYPL [MFX (Parker) 91-3346]*

Archivschule Marburg. Wolff, Fritz. Karten im
Archiv /. Marburg , 1987. 64 p. : ISBN
3-923833-21-0
GA190 .W66 1987
NYPL [Map Div. 90-12429]

Archuleta, Margaret, 1950- Shared visions :
native American painters and sculptors in the
twentieth century / Margaret Archuleta and
Rennard Strickland ; essays, Joy L. Gritton, W.
Jackson Rushing. Phoenix, Ariz. : Heard
Museum, 1991. 110 p. : ill. (some col.) ; 31 cm.
"Exhibition ... held at the Heard Museum, Phoenix,
Arizona from April 9 to July --, 1991 ... organized by
Margaret Archuleta, curator of Fine Art, the Heard
Museum and Dr. Rennard Strickland, director, the
Indian Law Center, University of Oklahoma, Norman,
Oklahoma"--T.p. verso. Includes bibliographical
references (p. 103-108). ISBN 0-934351-21-X :
DDC 704/.0397/0904 20
*1. Art, Indian - Exhibitions. 2. Art, Modern - 20th
century - United States - Exhibitions. 3. Indians of
North America - Art - Exhibitions. I. Strickland,
Rennard. II. Gritton, Joy L. III. Rushing, W. Jackson.
IV. Heard Museum.*
N6538.A4 A7 1991

**Arcimboldi, Giuseppe, 1527?-1593.
LIBRARIAN.**
Muench, Eugene V., 1920- Arcimboldo's
"Librarian" . Terre Haute, IN (657 Third
Ave., Terre Haute 47807) , 1990. 8 p. :
DDC 759.5 20
ND623.A5397 M84 1990

Arcimboldo's "Librarian" . Muench, Eugene V.,
1920- Terre Haute, IN (657 Third Ave., Terre
Haute 47807) , 1990. 8 p. : DDC 759.5 20
ND623.A5397 M84 1990

Arco, Manuel del. Antes del 36 [por] Del Arco.
Barcelona, Editorial AHR [1966] 262 p. illus.,
facsim. 26 cm. DDC 741.5946
*1. Arco, Manuel del. 2. Spaniards - Caricatures and
cartoons. 3. Spain - Biography. I. Title. II. Title: Antes
del treinta y seis.*
NC1639.A65 A45
NYPL [MEM (Arco) 90-6369]

ARCO, MANUEL DEL.
Arco, Manuel del. Antes del 36. Barcelona
[1966] 262 p. DDC 741.5946
NC1639.A65 A45
NYPL [MEM (Arco) 90-6369]

Arco, Maurizio Fagiolo dell'. see Fagiolo
dell'Arco, Maurizio, 1939-

Areas of communication. Espacios de
comunicación = . Barcelona , 1976. 265 p. :
ISBN 84-7031-447-5
NA2853 .E86   NYPL [3-MRN 81-422]

Arellano, Jorge Eduardo. Historia de la pintura
nicaragüense / Jorge Eduardo Arellano.
[Managua, Nicaragua : s.n.], 1990. 200 p. : ill. ;
21 cm. Cover title. Includes bibliographical references
(p. 189-200).
*1. Painting, Nicaraguan. 2. Painting, Modern - 20th
century - Nicaragua. 3. Painters - Nicaragua -*

Biography. I. Title.
ND282 .A74 1990

Arend, Henrich Conrad. Das Gedächtnis der
Ehren Albrecht Dürers / Henrich Conrad
Arend. Fotomechanischer Nachdruck der zum
200. Todestag Albrecht Dürers erschienenen
Gedenkschrift / herausgegeben und mit einem
Nachwort versehen von Matthias Mende.
Unterschneidheim : A. Uhl, 1978. [159] p. :
port. ; 18 cm. Facsim. of: Gosslar : J.C. König, 1728.
"Im Jahr der 450. Wiederkehr des Todestages Albrecht
Dürers". Includes bibliographical references.   ISBN
3-921503-53-1
I. Mende, Matthias. II. Title.
        NYPL [3-MCK D85 90-6660]

Arenkova, IŪ. I. Pami͡atniki arkhitektury Moskvy.
Moskva , 1989. 351 p. :   ISBN 5-210-00253-5 :
NA1197.M6 P285 1989

**ARETINE POTTERY. see POTTERY,
ARRETINE.**

Arez, Ilda. Vista Alegre . [Lisbon] , c1989. 267
p. :   ISBN 972-90191-9-3   DDC 738.2/09469/35 20
NK4210.F3175 V5 1989

Argan, Giulio Carlo.
Henry Moore / Giulio Carlo Argan. Milano :
Fabbri, c1987. 247 p. : ill. ; 32 cm. (Le Grandi
monografie. Scultori d'oggi)
1. Moore, Henry, 1898-. I. Series: Grandi monografie.
Scultori d'oggi. II. Title.
        NYPL [3-MGO+ (Moore) 91-6102]

Marco Aurelio . [Italy] , c1989. 277 p. :   ISBN
88-366-0280-0   *NYPL [3-MGR+ 91-5599]*

**ARGENTAN (FRANCE) - BUILDINGS,
STRUCTURES, ETC.**
Eglise Saint-Germain . [Caen, France] [1990]
16 p. :   ISBN 2-908621-00-2 :   DDC 726/.5/094423
20
NA5551.A674 E36 1990

**ARGENTINA - HISTORY - WAR OF
INDEPENDENCE, 1810-1817 - ART AND
THE WAR.**
Carril, Bonifacio del. Gericault . [Buenos
Aires?] , 1989. 27, [3] p. :   ISBN 950-0-40910-0
DDC 769.92 20
NE2349.5.G44 C37 1989
        NYPL [MDG+ (Géricault) 90-11344]

**Argentina. Ministerio de Relaciones Exteriores y
Culto.** Ideas e imágenes en la Argentina de
hoy. [Buenos Aires, Argentina] [between 1984
and 1987] 1 v. (unpaged) :   DDC
759.982/09/048074 20
ND335 .I34 1987

ARGENTINE ART. see ART, ARGENTINE.

**ARGENTINE REPUBLIC - CIVILIZATION -
AFRICAN INFLUENCES.**
Ortiz Oderigo, Néstor R., 1912- Aspectos de la
cultura africana en el Río de la Plata /. Buenos
Aires , c1974. 200 p., [8] leaves of plates :
        NYPL [HKB 77-1945]

**ARGENTINE WIT AND HUMOR,
PICTORIAL.**
Landrú, 1923- La razón de mi tía /. [Capital
Federal, Argentina] [c1990] 149 p. :   DDC
741.5/982 20
NC1460.L28 A4 1990

Arghir, Anca.
[Transparenz als Werkstoff. English]
Transparency into art : acrylic glass as a
medium / Anca Arghir ; [translated by
Jeanne Haunschild]. Cologne : Wienand,
1988. 218 p. : ill. (some col.) ; 30 cm.
Translation of: Transparenz als Werkstoff. Includes
bibliographical references.
1. Acrylic resins. 2. Plastics as art material. 3. Plexiglas.
I. Title.   *NYPL [3-MGD+ 89-21228]*

Argomenti di architettura.
Ottolini, Gianni, 1943- Storia e progetto di
arredamento =. Milano , c1989. 63 p. :   ISBN
88-7080-255-8 :
IN PROCESS (ONLINE)
        NYPL [3-MLO+ 90-11115]

Die Argonauten. Neuwirth, Markus. Graz ,
c1989. 162 p. : ISBN 3-201-01486-9
        NYPL [3-MCK K761 90-11989]

Argueta, Manlio, 1936- Kufeld, Adam. El
Salvador /. New York , c1990. 183 p. :   ISBN
0-393-02811-9 (cloth) :   DDC 972.8405/3 20
F1488.3 .K84 1990
        NYPL [MFX (Kufeld) 91-5007]

Argul, José Pedro. Prestigio del "Ottocento" : la
repuesta uruguaya : exposición / [ensayo crítico
por José Pedro Argul]. Montevideo : Instituto
Italiano di Cultura, 1969. 48 p., [4] p. of
plates : ill. (some col.) ; 26 cm. (Quaderni
dell'Istituto Italiano di Cultura) Cover title. Exhibition
held Oct.-Nov. 1969. Introductory matter in Spanish or
Italian; text in Spanish. "La Exposición de pinturas se
realiza en las salas de la Comisión Nacional de Artes
Plásticas, con los auspicios de los señores, Federico
García Capurro, Ministro de cultura ... [et al.]."
1. Painting, Uruguayan - Exhibitions. 2. Painting,
Italian - Influence - Exhibitions. 3. Painting, Modern -
19th century - Exhibitions. I. Comisión Nacional de
Artes Plásticas. II. Title.
        NYPL [3-MCY 90-7017]

Argy-Rousseau, Gabriel, 1885-1953.
Bloch-Dermant, Janine. G. Argy-Rousseau .
Paris , c1990. 229 p. :   ISBN 2-85917-105-3
DDC 748.294 20
NK5198.A74 A4 1990

**ARGY-ROUSSEAU, GABRIEL, 1885-1953 -
CATALOGUES RAISONNÉS.**
Bloch-Dermant, Janine. G. Argy-Rousseau .
Paris , c1990. 229 p. :   ISBN 2-85917-105-3
DDC 748.294 20
NK5198.A74 A4 1990

Arhitectura în viziunea pictorilor /. Păcurariu,
Dan D. Bucureşti , 1990. 185 p., [24] p. of
plates :   ISBN 973-240-147-8 :
ND1410 .P25 1990

Arikha, Avigdor, 1929-
Réflexion sur Poussin. 1989. Poussin, Nicolas,
1594?-1665. [Correspondence. Selections.]
Lettres et propos sur l'art / Nicolas Poussin ;
textes réunis et présentés par Anthony
Blunt ; avant-propos de Jacques Thuillier.
Suivi de, Réflexion sur Poussin / par Arikha.
Paris , c1989. 247 p. :   ISBN 2-7056-6105-2
ND553.P8 A3 1989

Arizona photographers : the Snell & Wilmer
collection / essay by Terence Pitts ; foreword
by Edward Jacobson. [Tucson] : Center for
Creative Photography, the University of
Arizona, c1990. 80 p. : ill. (some col.) ; 28 cm.
Catalog of an exhibition held at the Center for Creative
Photography, University of Arizona, Mar. 11 to Apr.
15, 1990, and elsewhere.   ISBN 0-938262-19-X :
DDC 779/.09791/074791 20
1. Snell & Wilmer (Firm) - Photograph collections -
Exhibitions. 2. Photography, Artistic - Exhibitions. 3.
Photographers - Arizona - Exhibitions. I. Pitts, Terence.
II. University of Arizona. Center for Creative
Photography.
TR645.T852 C463 1990
        NYPL [MFW 91-8007]

Arizona State University. Library. Collaborations
and connections . Tempe, Ariz. , c1990. viii, 36
p. :   *NYPL [MDTT 91-4768]*

**Arizona State University. University Art
Museum.** Collaborations and connections .
Tempe, Ariz. , c1990. viii, 36 p. :
        NYPL [MDTT 91-4768]

Arkansas Arts Center. Wolfe, Townsend.
National drawing invitational, March 1-April 8,
1990 /. Little Rock, Ark. (P.O. Box 2137,
Little Rock 72203) , c1990. 48 p. :   DDC
741.973/09/04807476773 20
NC108 .W65 1990

Arkansas made . Bennett, Swannee, 1949-
Fayetteville , c1990-1991. 2 v. :   ISBN
1-557-28138-6 (v. 1 : alk. paper)   DDC
709/.767/09034 20
NK835.A8 B4 1990

Arkansas Territorial Restoration (Museum)
Nineteenth century Trans-Mississippi South .
Little Rock, Ark. , 1990. vi, 33 p. :   DDC
709/.76/0903407476773 20
N6520 .N56 1990

Arkhitekturnoe nasledie Moskvy : sbornik
nauchnykh trudov / pod obshcheĭ redaktsieĭ
N.F. Guli͡anitskogo. Moskva : TSNIIP
gradostroitel'stva, 1988. 100 p. : ill. ; 22 cm. At
head of title: Gosudarstvennyĭ komitet po arkhitekture i
gradostroitel'stvu pri Gosstroe SSSR. TSentral'nyĭ
nauchno-issledovatel'skiĭ i proektnyĭ institut
gradostroitel'stva. Includes bibliographical references.
1. Architecture - Russian S.F.S.R. - Moscow. 2. City
planning - Russian S.F.S.R. - Moscow. 3. Moscow
(R.S.F.S.R.) - Buildings, structures, etc. I. Guli͡anitskiĭ,
N. F. (Nikolaĭ Feodos'evich). II. TSentral'nyĭ

nauchno-issledovatel'skiĭ i proektnyĭ institut po
gradostroitel'stvu Goskomarkhitektury (Soviet Union).
NA1197.M6 A78 1988

Arkitekten Finn Juhl . Hiort, Esbjørn.
København , 1990. 143, [1] p. :   ISBN
87-7407-093-2 :
N7023.J84 H5 1990

Arland, Marcel, 1899- Dans l'amitié de la
peinture / Marcel Arland. Paris : Luneau
Ascot, c1980. 323 p., [6] leaves of plates : ill. ;
21 cm. Errata slip inserted.   ISBN 2-903157-07-3 :
I. Title.
ND1142 .A73   *NYPL [3-MBK 81-943]*

ARLES (FRANCE) IN ART.
Dorn, Roland. Décoration . Hildesheim , New
York , 1990. xxxii, 622 p. :   ISBN 3-487-09098-8
ND653.G7 D64 1990

Arlt, Joachim. Plastik im Park . [Gera] [1984]
179 p. :
NB589.2.G32 P4 1984

Arman . Arman, 1928- New York, N.Y. , 1990.
139 p. :   *NYPL [3-MCO F363 91-4451]*

Arman, 1928-
Arman : monochrome accumulations,
1986-1989 : catalogue raisonné : [exhibition]
October 20-November 17, 1990, Vrej
Baghoomian Gallery / by Donald Kuspit. New
York, N.Y. : The Gallery, 1990. 139 p. : ill.
(chiefly col.) ; 26 cm.
1. Arman, 1928- - Exhibitions. I. Kuspit, Donald B.
(Donald Burton), 1935-. II. Vrej Baghoomian Gallery.
III. Title. IV. Title: Monochrome accumulations,
1986-1989.   *NYPL [3-MCO F363 91-4451]*

ARMAN, 1928- - EXHIBITIONS.
Arman, 1928- Arman . New York, N.Y. , 1990.
139 p. :   *NYPL [3-MCO F363 91-4451]*

Greene, Alison de Lima. Arman 1955-1991 .
Houston, Tex. , c1991. n. cm.   ISBN
0-89090-050-7 :   DDC 709/.2 20
N6853.A69 A4 1991

Arman 1955-1991 . Greene, Alison de Lima.
Houston, Tex. , c1991. n. cm.   ISBN
0-89090-050-7 :   DDC 709/.2 20
N6853.A69 A4 1991

Armand Simon . Canonne, Xavier. Bruxelles
[1987] 118 p. :   ISBN 2-87103-034-X
NC266.S54 C36 1987

Armani, Giorgio.
Giorgio Armani . Milano , c1989. 229 p. :
ISBN 88-435-2946-3
IN PROCESS (ONLINE)
        NYPL [3-MME+ 91-4011]

Martin, Richard. Giorgio Armani . New York ,
1990. 224 p. :   ISBN 0-8478-1298-7   DDC
746.9/2/092 20
TT580 .M37 1990
        NYPL [3-MME+ 91-3312]

ARMANI, GIORGIO.
Giorgio Armani . Milano , c1989. 229 p. :
ISBN 88-435-2946-3
IN PROCESS (ONLINE)
        NYPL [3-MME+ 91-4011]

ARMANI, GIORGIO - EXHIBITIONS.
Martin, Richard. Giorgio Armani . New York ,
1990. 224 p. :   ISBN 0-8478-1298-7   DDC
746.9/2/092 20
TT580 .M37 1990
        NYPL [3-MME+ 91-3312]

**The Armed Forces of the United States as seen
by the contemporary artist.** United States.
National Armed Forces Museum Advisory
Board. [Washington, 1968] vii, 64 p.   DDC
704.94/9/355000973
N6512 .A518   *NYPL [3-MAMT 90-6253]*

ARMENIA - ANTIQUITIES.
Frühe Bergvölker in Armenien und im
Kaukasus . Berlin , 1984. 84 p. :
        NYPL [3-MAE 90-10823]

Armenian alphabet. Khanjian, Grigor, 1926-
Hayots' Aybyben\u0115 /. Erevan , 1981. 1 portfolio
([4 p.], [12] leaves of plates) :
        NYPL [3-MOR 86-4591]

ARMENIAN ART. see ART, ARMENIAN.

**ARMENIAN S.S.R. - ECONOMIC
CONDITIONS - MAPS.**
Haykakan SSH Gitut'yunneri Akademia. Atlas
Armi͡anskoĭ Sovetskoĭ Sotsialisticheskoĭ
Respubliki /. Erevan , 1961. 1 atlas (viii, 111

p. :
G2157.A7 A5 1961
NYPL [Map Div. 91-1095]

ARMENIAN S.S.R. - MAPS.
Haykakan SSH Gitut'yunneri Akademia. Atlas
Armīanskoĭ Sovetskoĭ Sotsialisticheskoĭ
Respubliki /. Erevan , 1961. 1 atlas (viii, 111
p. :
G2157.A7 A5 1961
NYPL [Map Div. 91-1095]

ARMENIANS - ARGENTINA.
Binayán, Narciso. La colectividad armenia en la
Argentina /. Buenos Aires , 1974. 158 p. ;
NYPL [HKB 80-2301]

**ARMENIANS IN THE ARGENTINE
REPUBLIC.**
Binayán, Narciso. La colectividad armenia en la
Argentina /. Buenos Aires , 1974. 158 p. ;
NYPL [HKB 80-2301]

Armer, Karl Michael, 1950- Bangert, Albrecht,
1944- 80s style, designs of the decade /. New
York , 1990. 240 p. : ISBN 1-558-59117-6 DDC
745.4/442 20
NK1390 .B26 1990
NYPL [3-MNF+ 90-13410]

Armīānskiĭ alffavit. Khanjian, Grigor, 1926-
Hayots' Aybybenē /. Erevan , 1981. 1 portfolio
([4 p.], [12] leaves of plates) :
NYPL [3-MOR 86-4591]

**ARMOR, RENAISSANCE - SPAIN -
EXHIBITIONS.**
Resplendence of the Spanish monarchy . New
York , 1991. p. cm. ISBN 0-87099-621-5 DDC
739.7/0946/0747471 20
NK3062.A1 R47 1991

ARMOR - SPAIN - EXHIBITIONS.
Resplendence of the Spanish monarchy . New
York , 1991. p. cm. ISBN 0-87099-621-5 DDC
739.7/0946/0747471 20
NK3062.A1 R47 1991

**ARMS AND ARMOR - ITALY - VENICE -
CATALOGS.**
Franzoi, Umberto. L'armeria del Palazzo ducale
a Venezia /. Dosson (Treviso) [1990] 273 p. :
ISBN 88-85066-74-7
NK6702.5.I8 F7 1990

ARMS RACE.
Kidron, Michael. The new state of war and
peace . New York , c1991. 127 p. : ISBN
0-671-70521-0 : DDC 355/.009/048022 20
G1046.R1 K47 1991
NYPL [Map Div. 91-7499]

Armstrong, Anthony, 1935- Glasgow : the
paintings and drawings of Anthony Armstrong.
Glasgow : Glasgow Collection in association
with Paul Harris, 1990. 132 p. : chiefly ill.
(some col.) ; 32 cm. ISBN 0-9516481-0-1 : DDC
759.2911 20
1. Armstrong, Anthony, 1935-. I. Title.
NYPL [3-MCV+ A689 91-4953]

ARMSTRONG, ANTHONY, 1935-
Armstrong, Anthony, 1935- Glasgow .
Glasgow , 1990. 132 p. : ISBN 0-9516481-0-1 :
DDC 759.2911 20
NYPL [3-MCV+ A689 91-4953]

ARMSTRONG, ARTHUR, IRISH PAINTER.
Eight Irish paintings. [S.l. , 1985?] [11], 8 p.,
[8] leaves of plates :
NYPL [3-MCY+ 89-3282]

Armstrong, Richard.
Mind over matter : concept and object /
Richard Armstrong. New York, N.Y. : Whitney
Museum of American Art, c1990. 156 p. : ill.
(some col.) ; 25 cm. Catalog of an exhibition held at
the Whitney Museum of American Art, Oct. 3,
1990-Jan. 6, 1991. Includes bibliographical references.
ISBN 0-87427-073-1
*1. Sculpture, American - Exhibitions. 2. Sculpture,
Modern - 20th century - United States - Exhibitions. 3.
Sculptors - United States - Interviews. I. Whitney
Museum of American Art. II. Title.*
NYPL [3-MGI 91-4327]

Smith, Alexis, 1949- Alexis Smith /. New
York , 1991. p. cm. ISBN 0-87427-076-6 DDC
700/.92 20
N6537.S58 A4 1991

Arnaldo, Javier. Estilo y naturaleza : la obra de
arte en el romanticismo alemán / Javier
Arnaldo. Madrid : Visor, c1990. 284 p. : ill. ;
24 cm. (La Balsa de la Medusa . 36) Includes

bibliographical references (p. 259-269) and index.
ISBN 84-7774-536-6
*1. Romanticism in art - Germany. 2. Art, German. 3.
Art, Modern - 19th century - Germany. I. Title.*
N6867.5.R6 A76 1990

Arnaldo Pomodoro . Quintavalle, Arturo Carlo.
Milano , 1990. 163 p. : ISBN 88-435-3379-7
IN PROCESS (ONLINE)
NYPL [3-MGO+ (Pomodoro) 91-7181]

Arnason, H. Harvard. Paintings from the Joseph
H. Hirshhorn Foundation Collection : a view of
the protean century / selection of exhibition
and catalog text by H. H. Arnason ; organized
and circulated by the American Federation of
Arts, November 1962-November 1964. New
York : American Federation of Arts, c1962. 47
p. : ill. ; 21 cm. DDC 759.06/074/0153
*1. Hirshhorn, Joseph H. - Art collections. 2. Painting,
Modern - 20th century - Exhibitions. I. Title.*
ND195 .A72
NYPL [3-MAX (Hirshhorn) 85-1211]

Arnaud, Marcel, 1877-1956.
Feyt, Henri. Marcel Arnaud . Aix-en-Provence ,
c1990. 111 p. : ISBN 2-85744-463-X
NYPL [3-MCO A744 91-6751]

Feyt, Henri. Marcel Arnaud . La Calade,
Aix-en-Provence , c1990. 111 p. : ISBN
2-85744-463-X DDC 759.4 20
ND553.A589 F49 1990

ARNAUD, MARCEL, 1877-1956.
Feyt, Henri. Marcel Arnaud . Aix-en-Provence ,
c1990. 111 p. : ISBN 2-85744-463-X
NYPL [3-MCO A744 91-6751]

**ARNAUD, MARCEL, 1877-1956 - CRITICISM
AND INTERPRETATION.**
Feyt, Henri. Marcel Arnaud . La Calade,
Aix-en-Provence , c1990. 111 p. : ISBN
2-85744-463-X DDC 759.4 20
ND553.A589 F49 1990

Arne Jacobsen . Jacobsen, Arne, 1902-1971.
Paris , c1987. 79 p. : ISBN 2-901422-05-5
NYPL [3-MQZ+ (Jacobsen) 90-11627]

Arneodo, Annéto. Artigianato di tradizione nelle
Alpi occidentali italiane . Ivrea, Italy , c1990.
305 p. ; DDC 745/.0945/1 20
NK960.A536 A78 1990

Arnheim, Rudolf. To the rescue of art : twenty-six
essays / by Rudolf Arnheim. Berkeley :
University of California Press, c1992. p. cm.
Includes bibliographical references and index. ISBN
0-520-07458-0 (cloth) DDC 700 20
1. Art. I. Title.
N7425 .A64 1992

**ARNHEM (NETHERLANDS) - BUILDINGS,
STRUCTURES, ETC.**
Lavooij, Wim. Gebouwd in Arnhem . Zutphen ,
c1990. 166 p. : ISBN 90-6011-684-4 :
NA1151.A76 L38 1990

Lavooij, Wim. Twee eeuwen bouwen aan
Arnhem . Zutphen , 1990. 128 p. : ISBN
90-6011-683-6 :
NA1151.A76 L38 1990

Arnold Blanch, the years 1924-1949. University
of Minnesota. Dept. of Art. [Minneapolis, 1949]
1 v. (unpaged)
NYPL [3-MCX B637 91-1320]

Arnold, Ken. Collecting Australian found
stoneware / Ken Arnold. Maiden Gully,
Australia : Crown Castleton Publisher, c1989.
128 p. : ill. ; 28 cm. Includes bibliographical
references (p. 4) and indexes. ISBN 0-9587953-8-X
DDC 738.3/075 20
*1. Stoneware - Collectors and collecting - Australia. I.
Title.*
NK4365.A8 A76 1989

Arnold Singer, drawings and prints . Singer,
Arnold, 1920- Ithaca, N.Y. , c1974. [12] p. :
NYPL [3-MCX S599 91-7006]

Arnold, Steven. Epiphanies / [photographs by
Steven Arnold]. Pasadena, CA. : Twelvetrees
Press, 1987. [88] p. : ill. ; 27 cm. ISBN
0-942642-33-3
I. Title.
NYPL [MFX (Arnold) 90-9103]

Arnolfini Gallery.
Yeats, Jack Butler, 1871-1957. Jack B. Yeats .
Bristol : London : 111 p. : ISBN 0-907738-29-X
(Arnolfini Gallery)
NYPL [3-MCV Y41 91-6477]

Yeats, Jack Butler, 1871-1957. Jack B. Yeats .

Bristol : London : 111 p. : ISBN 0-85488-091-7
(Arnolfini) DDC 759.2/915 20
ND497.Y42 A4 1991

Arnot Art Gallery. see **Arnot Art Museum.**

Arnot Art Museum.
Sadinsky, Rachael, 1958- A collector's vision .
Elmira, N.Y. , 1989. 126 p. : ISBN
1-87788-505-3 DDC 759.94/074/74778 20
ND160 .S23 1989
NYPL [3-MAX+ (Arnot) 90-12636]

ARNOT ART MUSEUM - CATALOGS.
Sadinsky, Rachael, 1958- A collector's vision .
Elmira, N.Y. , 1989. 126 p. : ISBN
1-87788-505-3 DDC 759.94/074/74778 20
ND160 .S23 1989
NYPL [3-MAX+ (Arnot) 90-12636]

Arnot, Matthias Hollenback, 1833-1910.
Sadinsky, Rachael, 1958- A collector's vision .
Elmira, N.Y. , 1989. 126 p. : ISBN
1-87788-505-3 DDC 759.94/074/74778 20
ND160 .S23 1989
NYPL [3-MAX+ (Arnot) 90-12636]

**ARNOT, MATTHIAS HOLLENBACK, 1833-
1910 - ART COLLECTIONS - CATALOGS.**
Sadinsky, Rachael, 1958- A collector's vision .
Elmira, N.Y. , 1989. 126 p. : ISBN
1-87788-505-3 DDC 759.94/074/74778 20
ND160 .S23 1989
NYPL [3-MAX+ (Arnot) 90-12636]

Arnulf Neuwirth, Malerei und Collage.
Waissenberger, Robert. Wien, München [c1967]
102 p.
NYPL [3-MCK N498 91-1370]

Arnulf Rainer, "Alte Meister." Rainer, Arnulf,
1929- Innsbruck , 1989. 124 p. :
NYPL [3-MCK+ R155 90-340]

Arnulf Rainer, masqué-démasqué . Rainer, Arnulf,
1929- Vienne [1987] 143 p. : ISBN
3-85127-000-2
NYPL [3-MCK R155 90-12023]

Aron, Jon. Linsley, Leslie. The hooked rug . New
York , 1991. p. cm. ISBN 0-517-58102-7 : DDC
746.7/4/0973 20
NK9112 .L56 1991

Around Rubens. Antwerp (Belgium). Stedelijk
Prentenkabinet. Rondom Rubens . Antwerpen ,
1991. 229 p. :
N6971.A6 A73 1991

Arp, Jean, 1887-1966.
Als Dada begann . [Zürich] , c1957. 92 p. :
NYPL [3-MAM 90-7093]

Nevelson, Louise, 1899-1988. Nevelson /. New
York [1961?] [31] p. :
NYPL [3-MGO (Nevelson) 91-1457]

Watts, Harriett. Hans Arp und Sophie
Taeuber-Arp . Wolfenbüttel [1989] 54 p. :
ISBN 3-88373-054-8 DDC 700/.92 20
N6853.A7 A4 1989

ARP, JEAN, 1887-1966 - EXHIBITIONS.
Watts, Harriett. Hans Arp und Sophie
Taeuber-Arp . Wolfenbüttel [1989] 54 p. :
ISBN 3-88373-054-8 DDC 700/.92 20
N6853.A7 A4 1989

Arpalahti, Tomi. Suomen Rakennustaiteen Museo.
Arkisto. Suomen Rakennustaiteen Museon
Arkisto . Helsinki [1989] 288 p. : ISBN
951-9229-60-4
NA2706.F5 S86 1989

Arpilleras . Franger, Gaby. [Arpilleras : Bilder die
sprechen Organisation und Alltag der Frauen in
den Slums von Lima. Spanish.] Lima, Peru ,
1988. 110 p. : *NYPL [3-MOT 90-12715]*

Arqueros del Arte Contemporáneo. LADAC .
[Las Palmas de Gran Canarias] [1990?] 1
case : ISBN 84-87137-32-6
N7108 .L33 1990

Arquitectonica /. Dunlop, Beth, 1947-
Washington, D.C. , c1991. p. cm. ISBN
1-558-35043-8 : DDC 720/.92/2 20
NA737.A77 D8 1991

**ARQUITECTONICA (FIRM : CORAL
GABLES, FLA.)**
Dunlop, Beth, 1947- Arquitectonica /.
Washington, D.C. , c1991. p. cm. ISBN
1-558-35043-8 : DDC 720/.92/2 20
NA737.A77 D8 1991

Arquitectos guipuzcoanos del siglo XVIII /.
Astiazarain Achabal, María Isabel. Guipúzcoa

[1988?-1990?] 2 v. : ISBN 84-505-7463-3
NA1109.G85 A88 1988

Arquitectura : obra pública a Catalunya,
1980-1987 = travaux publics en Catalogne.
[Spain] : Generalitat de Catalunya,
Departament de Política Territorial i Obres
Públiques, [1988?] 187 p. : ill. ; 30 cm. Catalan
and French.
1. Architecture - Spain - Catalonia - Exhibitions. I.
Catalonia (Spain). Departament de Política Territorial i
Obres Públiques.   **NYPL [3-MQWH+ 91-6437]**

Arquitectura : obra pública a Catalunya =
travaux publics en Catalogne : 1980-1987 /
[realització del catàleg, Antoni Comas i
Baldellou]. [Barcelona?] : Generalitat de
Catalunya, Departament de Política Territorial i
Obres Públiques : Col·legi d'Arquitectes de
Catalunya, [1988] 187 p. : ill. ; 30 cm. Catalan
and French.
1. Architecture, Modern - 20th century - Spain -
Catalonia - Exhibitions. 2. Public buildings - Spain -
Catalonia - Exhibitions. I. Comas i Baldellou, Antoni.
II. Catalonia (Spain). Departament de Política
Territorial i Obres Públiques. III. Colegio Oficial de
Arquitectos de Cataluña y Baleares.
NA1309.C2 A76 1988

Arquitectura de los coros de monjas en Puebla /.
Maza, Francisco de la, 1913-1972. [Puebla]
[Mexico City] [1990] 104 p. :
NA5256.P8 M39 1990

Arquitectura del siglo dieciseis en Cuenca.
Rokiski Lázaro, María Luz. Arquitectura del
siglo XVI en Cuenca . Cuenca , 1989. xxi, 464
p. : ISBN 84-505-8542-2
NA1311.C84 R66 1989

Arquitectura del siglo XVI en Cuenca . Rokiski
Lázaro, María Luz. Cuenca , 1989. xxi, 464 p. :
ISBN 84-505-8542-2
NA1311.C84 R66 1989

Arquitectura del siglo 16 en Cuenca. Rokiski
Lázaro, María Luz. Arquitectura del siglo XVI
en Cuenca . Cuenca , 1989. xxi, 464 p. : ISBN
84-505-8542-2
NA1311.C84 R66 1989

Arquitectura doméstica, Cartagena de Indias /.
Téllez, Germán. [Repertorio formal de
arquitectura doméstica, Cartagena de Indias.]
[Bogotá] . 256 p., [1] folded leaf of plates :
DDC 728/.09861/14 20
NA2840 .T45 1982b

Arquitectura doméstica moderna en Madrid /.
Urrutia Núñez, Angel. Madrid [1988] 214 p. :
ISBN 84-7477-173-0
                    NYPL [3-MRG 90-10752]

Arquitectura española contemporánea : la década
de los 80 / introducción de Joseph Rykwert ;
Xavier Güell (ed.). Barcelona : G. Gili, c1990.
192 p. : ill. (some col. ; 27 cm. Includes
bibliographical references (p. 190-191). ISBN
84-252-1429-7 DDC 720/.946/09048 20
1. Architecture - Spain. 2. Architecture, Modern - 20th
century - Spain. 3. Architects - Spain - Biography. I.
Güell, Xavier.
NA1308 .A84 1990
                    NYPL [3-MQWH 91-3890]

Arquitectura española contemporánea, 1975/1990
=. Levene, Richard C. Madrid , 1989. 2 v.
(812 p.) : ISBN 84-404-5316-7 (v. 1)
                    NYPL [3-MQWH+ 91-6816]

Arquitectura, fenómeno de controversia /.
Aguirre, Marco Antonio. [Oaxaca, Mexico?]
c1990. 61 p., [88] p. of plates : DDC 720 20
NA27 .A36 1990

A arquitectura gótica em Portugal /. Chicó,
Mário Tavares. Lisboa , 1968. 239 p., [21]
leaves of plates : DDC 726/.5/09469
NA5823 .C48 1968
                    NYPL [3-MQW 90-5436]

Arquitectura modernista en Cataluña /. Lacuesta,
Raquel. Barcelona , c1990. 213 p. : ISBN
84-252-1430-0 DDC 720/.946/70904 20
NA1309.C2 L33 1990

Arquitectura para todos los días . Saldarriaga
Roa, Alberto. Bogotá , 1988. 95 p. : ISBN
958-1-70049-8
NA2543.S6 S23 1988

Arquitectura popular de Burgos . García Grinda,
José Luis. [Burgos] [1988] 322 p. : ISBN
84-505-7747-0
                    NYPL [3-MQWH+ 90-791]

Arquitectura popular em Portugal / [autores,
Alfredo da Mata Antunes et al. ; fotografias e
desenhos dos autores ; traduções, francês,
Maryse Bernardino, inglês, Cheilah Cardno]. 3a.
ed. Lisboa : Associação dos Arquitectos
Portugueses, 1988. 3 v. : ill. ; 29 cm. Pref. and
introd. also in English and French. CONTENTS. - 1o.
v. Zona 1, Minho. Zona 2, Trás-os-Montes -- 2o. v.
Zona 3, Beiras. Zona 4, Estremadura -- 3o. v. Zona 5,
Alentejo. Zona 6, Algarve. DDC 720/.9469 20
1. Vernacular architecture - Portugal. I. Antunes,
Alfredo da Mata. II. Associação dos Arquitectos
Portugueses.
NA1321 .A77 1988
                    NYPL [3-MQW 91-7182]

La arquitectura religiosa granadina en la crisis
del Renacimiento (1560-1650) .
Gómez-Moreno Calera, José Manuel. Granada ,
1989. 486 p. : ISBN 84-338-0944-X
IN PROCESS (ONLINE)
                    NYPL [3-MRBB 91-6097]

Arquitectura solar . Yáñez Parareda, Guillermo.
Madrid , 1988. 192 p. : ISBN 84-7433-542-6
DDC 720/.472 20
NA2542.S6 Y35 1988

Arquitectura y autoritarismo /. Livingston,
Rodolfo. Buenos Aires [1991] 244 p. : ISBN
950-51-5038-5 DDC 720/.1/03 20
NA2542.4 .L58 1991

Arquitectura y comunidad nacional.
Historia argentina de la vivienda de interés
social. Capital Federal [Argentina] [between
1986 and 1990- v. <1- > :
NA7292 .H57 1990

Arquitectura y romanticismo . Arrechea, Julio I.
Valladolid, España [Salamanca] , c1989. 330
p. : ISBN 84-7762-086-5 DDC 720/.946/09034 20
NA1307 .A7 1989

Arquitectura y sociedad en el Siglo de Oro .
Cámara Muñoz, Alicia. Madrid , c1990. 280 p.,
[32] p. of plates : ISBN 84-86902-07-X
                    NYPL [MQW 91-5219]

Arquitectura y urbanismo de Valladolid en el
siglo XX /. Virgili Blanquet, María Antonia.
Valladolid , 1988. 190 p. : ISBN 84-404-2435-3
                    NYPL [3-MQWH 90-9439]

Arquitetura nos trópicos : anais do primeiro
seminário nacional / Prefeitura da Cidade do
Recife ; Fundação Joaquim Nabuco. Recife :
Fundação Joaquim Nabuco, Editora
Massangana, 1985. 161 p. : ill. ; 24 cm. (Série
Cursos e conferências . 23) Papers from the I
Seminário Nacional sobre Arquitetura nos Trópicos,
held Sept. 18-20, 1984, and sponsored by the Fundação
Joaquim Nabuco, Recife, Brazil. ISBN 85-7019-095-6
1. Architecture, Tropical - Congresses. I. Fundação
Joaquim Nabuco. II. Seminário Nacional sobre
Arquitetura nos Trópicos (1st : 1984 : Recife, Brazil).
III. Series.
NA2542.T7 A77 1985
                    NYPL [3-MQD 90-11121]

Arquitetura rural do século XIX no Espírito
Santo /. Muniz, Maria Izabel Perini.
Vitória-ES , 1989 ([Vitória?] : Gráfica e Editora
São José] 239 p. :
NA8210.B69 M86 1989

Arquiteturas no Brasil, anos oitenta. Segawa,
Hugo M. Arquiteturas no Brasil, anos 80 /.
[São Paulo] [1988?] 1 v. (various pagings) :
DDC 720/.981/09048 20
NA855 .S44 1988

Arquiteturas no Brasil, anos 80 /. Segawa, Hugo
M. [São Paulo] [1988?] 1 v. (various pagings) :
DDC 720/.981/09048 20
NA855 .S44 1988

Arrazola Echeverria, Maria Asunción.
Renacimiento en Guipuzcoa / Ma. Asunción
Arrazola Echeverria. [Guipúzcoa] : Diputación
Foral de Guipúscoa, [1988] 2 v. : ill. ; 31 cm.
Includes bibliographical references. CONTENTS. - t.1.
Architectura -- t.2. Escultura.   ISBN 84-505-7460-9
(obra completa)
1. Architecture, Renzissance - Spain - Guipuzcoa -
History. 2. Sculpture, Renaissance - Spain -
Guipuzcoa - History. I. Title.
                    NYPL [3-MQWH + 89-19331]

Arrechea, Julio I. Arquitectura y romanticismo :
el pensamiento arquitectónico en la España del
XIX / Julio Arrechea Miguel. Valladolid,
España : Secretariado de Publicaciones,

Universidad de Valladolid ; [Salamanca] : Caja
Salamanca, c1989. 330 p. : ill. ; 24 cm. (Serie
Arquitectura y urbanismo . no. 8) Includes
bibliographical references (p. 295-328).   ISBN
84-7762-086-5 DDC 720/.946/09034 20
1. Architecture - Spain. 2. Architecture, Modern - 19th
century - Spain. 3. Eclecticism in architecture - Spain.
I. Title. II. Series.
NA1307 .A7 1989

Arredi e paramenti . Bardazzi, Silvestro. Prato ,
c1988. 318 p. :
                    NYPL [3-MRBD+ 90-11027]

Arreguín, Alfredo, 1935-
Alfredo Arreguín . [Morelia, Mich., México]
[1989] 214 p., [15] leaves of plates : DDC
759.972 20
ND259.A69 A86 1989

ARREGUÍN, ALFREDO, 1935- - CRITICISM
AND INTERPRETATION.
Alfredo Arreguín . [Morelia, Mich., México]
[1989] 214 p., [15] leaves of plates : DDC
759.972 20
ND259.A69 A86 1989

Arreguín Vélez, Enrique. Alfredo Arreguín .
[Morelia, Mich., México] [1989] 214 p., [15]
leaves of plates : DDC 759.972 20
ND259.A69 A86 1989

ARRETINE POTTERY. see POTTERY,
ARRETINE.

Arrigoni, Maria Antonietta. L'abbigliamento
popolare italiano /. Brescia [1986] 160 p. :
                    NYPL [3-MMO 90-8664]

Arrow Publishing Co. Official Arrow street map
atlas, western Massachusetts. Taunton, Mass. :
Arrow Pub. Co., c1988. 1 atlas (iii, 106 p.) :
col. maps ; 31 cm. "Including Berkshire, Franklin,
Hampden, and Hampshire counties, 102 cities and
towns," and campus maps. Includes indexes.   ISBN
0-913450-83-9
1. Cities and towns - Massachusetts - Maps. 2.
Massachusetts - Road maps. I. Title. II. Title: Street
map atlas, western Massachusetts.
                    NYPL [Map Div. 90-12431]

ARROYO, EDUARDO, 1937-
Calvo Serraller, F. (Francisco), 1948- Eduardo
Arroyo /. Madrid , 1991. 283 p. : ISBN
84-87798-00-4
                    NYPL [3-MCQ+ A778 91-5775]

Ars Helvetica : die visuelle Kultur der Schweiz /
herausgegeben von Florens Deuchler. Disentis :
Desertina, 1987- v. : ill. (some col.) ; 22 cm.
Includes bibliographical references. CONTENTS. - 1.
Kunstgeographie / Dario Gamboni -- 2. Kunstbetrieb /
Florens Deuchler -- 3. Sakrale Bauten / Heinz Horat --
4. Profane Bauten / André Meyer -- 5. Malerei des
Mittelalters / Christoph und Dorothee Eggenberger --
6. Malerei der Neuzeit / Oskar Bätschmann.   ISBN
3-85637-130-3 (set)
I. Deuchler, Florens, 1931-.
                    NYPL [3-MAM 91-6348]

Ars picturae .
(no. 1) Fleischer, Roland E. Ludolf de Jongh
(1616-1679) . Doornspijk, The Netherlands ,
c1989. 100 p., [93] p. of plates : ISBN
90-70288-53-2 DDC 759.9492 20
ND653.J4 F54 1989
                    NYPL [3-MCH J763 91-6586]

Ars, revista de arte : año IX, 1949, no. 46 :
dedicado a Federico Chopin : 1849-1949.
Buenos Aires : Ars, revista de arte, 1949. [111]
p., [1] leaf of plates : ill. (some col.) ; 32 cm.
Royes Fernandez Collection.
1. Chopin, Fryderyk Franciszek, 1810-1849 -
Anniversaries, etc., 1949.   **NYPL [JMG 84-326]**

Årsbok för statens konstmuseer .
(35) Donation Gerard Bonnier /. Stockholm
[1989] 106 p. : ISBN 91-29-59355-7
N6488.S8 S74 1989

(36) Hovstadius, Barbro, 1937- Svenskt silver .
Stockholm , c1990. 149 p., [4] leaves of plates :
ISBN 91-29-59391-3
NK7161.A1 H68 1990

Arshile Gorky . Gorky, Arshile, 1904-1948.
[Santa Fe, N.M.] , c1990. 11 p., [30] leaves of
plates : ISBN 0-935037-38-1
                    NYPL [3-MCZ G669 91-4351]

Arslan, Ermanno A.
I Longobardi /. Milano , c1990. 492 p. : ISBN
88-435-3210-3
N6919.L8 L67 1990

Il Duomo di Monza /. Milano , 1990. 2 v. :
    DDC 726/.6/09451 20
NA5621.M954 D8 1990

ART.
Album amicorum Kenneth C. Lindsay .
[Binghamton, NY] , 1990. xiii, 380 p. : ISBN
0-9621899-9-5 DDC 700 20
N7443.2 .A45 1990

Arnheim, Rudolf. To the rescue of art .
Berkeley , c1992. p. cm. ISBN 0-520-07458-0
(cloth) DDC 700 20
N7425 .A64 1992

Badii, Líbero, 1916- Frases espontáneas /.
Buenos Aires, Argentina , 1982. 47 p. : DDC
700 20
N6639.B32 A35 1982

Historia visual del arte /. Barcelona , <1989-.
v. <3-4 > : ISBN 84-316-2704-3 (v. 3)
N5300 .H58 1989

Meier-Graefe, Julius, 1867-1935.
Kunst-Schreiberei . Leipzig , 1987. 331 p. ;
    ISBN 3-378-00163-1
N7445.4 .M45 1987

Poussin, Nicolas, 1594?-1665. [Correspondence.
Selections.] Lettres et propos sur l'art /. Paris ,
c1989. 247 p. : ISBN 2-7056-6105-2
ND553.P8 A3 1989

Rafiq, Sa'īd Ahmad. Fan aur muṭāla'ah-yi fan /.
Karāci , 1988. 271 p. ;
N7425.8.U73 R34 1988

Richardson, John Adkins. Art, the way it is /.
Englewood Cliffs, N.J. , New York , 1991. p.
cm. ISBN 0-13-040437-3 (pbk.) DDC 701/.1 20
N7425 .R48 1991

Richardson, John Adkins. Art, the way it is /.
New York , 1992. p. cm. ISBN 0-8109-1911-7
(hardcover) DDC 701/.1 20
N7425 .R48 1992

Rivera, Diego, 1886-1957. Textos de arte /.
México , 1986. 430 p., [22] p. of plates : ISBN
968-8379-10-7
N6559.R58 A35 1986

Art & physics . Shlain, Leonard. New York ,
1991. p. cm. ISBN 0-688-09752-9 DDC 701 20
N70 .S48 1991

Art & war. Foot, M. R. D. (Michael Richard
Daniel), 1919- Art and war . London , 1990.
240 p. : ISBN 0-7472-0286-9 DDC 758/.994053
20
N8260 .F58 1990

ART - 16TH CENTURY - SPAIN - CUENCA.
Rokiski Lázaro, María Luz. Arquitectura del
siglo XVI en Cuenca . Cuenca , 1989. xxi, 464
p. : ISBN 84-505-8542-2
NA1311.C84 R66 1989

ART, ABSTRACT.
Boudaille, Georges. L'art abstrait /. [Paris] ,
c1990. 264, [8] p. : ISBN 2-7079-0024-9 DDC
709/.04/052 20
N6494.A2 B68 1990

**ART, ABSTRACT - AUSTRALIA -
EXHIBITIONS.**
Abstraction . Sydney , 1990. 48 p. : ISBN
0-7305-7696-5   *NYPL [3-MAM 91-3723]*

ART, ABSTRACT - AUSTRIA - VIENNA.
Secessionismus und Abstraktion =
Secessionism and abstraction . Wien , New
York , 1989. 81 p. :
            NYPL [3-MAMG+ 90-12363]

ART, ABSTRACT - EXHIBITIONS.
Arte abstracto, arte concreto . [Valencia?] ,
c1990. 439 p. : ISBN 84-7890-151-5
N6494.A2 A78 1990

A Debate on abstraction . [New York] [1988?]
79 p. :   *NYPL [3-MAL 90-12609]*

Wege zur Abstraktion /. Basel , c1989. [74] p. :
            NYPL [3-MAL+ 90-13078]

ART, ABSTRACT - ORIGIN.
Stelzer, Otto. Die Vorgeschichte der abstrakten
Kunst. München [c1964] 263 p.
N6490 .S76   *NYPL [3-MAL 90-6622]*

ART, ABSTRACT - SPAIN - EXHIBITIONS.
Arte geométrico en España, 1957-1989.
[Madrid] [1989] 320 p. : ISBN 84-7812-044-0
    DDC 709/.46/0744641 20
N7108.5.A2 A78 1989

**ART, ABSTRACT - UNITED STATES -
EXHIBITIONS.**
Addison Gallery of American Art. American
abstraction at the Addison . Andover, Mass. ,
c1991. 95 p. : ISBN 1-87988-600-6 DDC
709/.73/0747445 20
N6512.5.A2 A33 1991

ART, ACHAEMENID.
'Ukāshah, Tharwat. al-Fann al-Fārisī al-qadīm /.
Miṣr al-Jadīdah, al-Qāhirah , 1989. 383 p. :
    ISBN 977-442-109-4 :
N5390 .U38 1989

Art across America . Gerdts, William H. New
York , 1990. 3 v. : DDC 759.13 20
ND212 .G47 1990
            NYPL [MCW+ 90-11405]

ART - ADAPTATIONS - CONGRESSES.
Retaining the original . Washington , Hanover ,
c1989. 180 p. :   *NYPL [3-MAS 90-13011]*

ART - ADDRESSES, ESSAYS, LECTURES.
Winckelmann, Johann Joachim, 1717-1768.
Kleinere Schriften. Baden-Baden, 1971. 1 v.
(various pagings) ISBN 3-87320-349-9
N7445.4 .W55   *NYPL [3-MAS 81-639]*

ART, AEGEAN - INFLUENCE.
Crowley, Janice L. The Aegean and the east .
Jonsered , 1989. xii, 507 p. : ISBN
91-86098-55-1   *NYPL [3-MAE 90-11126]*

ART - AFRICA.
Ornament und Plastic fremder Völker. English.
Ornament and sculpture in primitive society.
New York [1966] [138] p. DDC 709.011
N7380 .O713 1966b
            NYPL [3-MADF 90-6405]

ART - AFRICA, CENTRAL.
Mack, John. Emil Torday and the art of the
Congo, 1900-1909 /. London , 1990. 96 :
    ISBN 0-7141-1594-0 (pbk) : DDC 709.6724 20
            NYPL [Sc E 91-236]

ART - AFRICA - HISTORY.
Leuzinger, Elsy. The art of Africa. New York
[c1960] 247 p.   *NYPL [MADF 90-11494]*

ART, AFRICAN - EXHIBITIONS.
Boglár, Lajos. Tribal art in Africa and Oceania .
[Budapest] , 1971. 8, 8 p., 8, 8 p. of plates :
enghun   *NYPL [3-MADF 90-5887]*

**ART, AFRO-AMERICAN. see AFRO-
AMERICAN ART.**

Art after philosophy and after . Kosuth, Joseph.
Cambridge, Mass. , c1991. p. cm. ISBN
0-262-11157-8 DDC 701/.17 20
N6537.K65 A35 1991

ART, AMERICAN.
American art and architecture [videorecording]
/. Boulder, CO , 1990. 5 videocassettes (140
min.) : DDC 709.73 11
N6505

Cornebise, Alfred E. Art from the trenches .
College Station , c1991. p. cm. ISBN
0-89096-349-5 (cloth) DDC 758/.99404/0973 20
N6512 .C598 1991

Fisher, Philip. Making and effacing art . New
York , 1991. p. cm. ISBN 0-19-506046-6 DDC
709/.73/0904 20
N6512. .F57 1991

Fisher, Philip. Making and effacing art . New
York , 1991. p. cm. ISBN 0-19-506046-6 DDC
709/.73/0904 20
N6512. .F57 1991

Kammen, Michael G. Meadows of memory .
Austin , 1992. p. cm. ISBN 0-292-75139-7 (cloth :
alk. paper) DDC 758/.9973 20
N6505 .K28 1992

Seitz, William Chapin. Art in the Age of
Aquarius, 1955-1970 /. Washington , 1991. p.
cm. ISBN 0-87474-868-2 DDC 709/.73/09046 20
N6512 .S335 1991

Wilmerding, John. American views . Princeton,
N.J. , 1991. p. cm. ISBN 0-691-04090-7 : DDC
759.3 20
N6505 .W57 1991

ART, AMERICAN - BIBLIOGRAPHY.
Schimmelman, Janice Gayle. American imprints
on art through 1865 . Boston, Mass. , 1990. ix,
419 p. : ISBN 0-8161-7261-7 DDC 016.7 20
Z5961.U5 S34 1990 N6505
            NYPL [MAMT 91-3665]

**ART, AMERICAN - BRANDYWINE CREEK
VALLEY (PA. AND DEL.) - CATALOGS.**
Brandywine River Museum. Catalogue of the
collection, 1969-1989 /. Chadds Ford, Pa. ,
c1991. p. DDC 709/.73/07474814 20
N6517 .B7 1991

ART, AMERICAN - CALIFORNIA.
Stofflet, Mary. California cityscapes /. New
York, NY , c1991. p. cm. ISBN 0-87663-614-8
DDC 704.9/44794/0979409048 20
N8214.5.U6 S76 1991

**ART, AMERICAN - CALIFORNIA - LOS
ANGELES - EXHIBITIONS.**
L.A. times . Boise, Idaho , c1991. p. cm. DDC
709/.794/9407479628 20
N6535.L6 L188 1991

ART, AMERICAN - CATALOGS.
Conrads, Margaret C., 1955- American
paintings and sculpture at the Sterling and
Francine Clark Art Institute/. New York ,
c1990. 219 p. : ISBN 1-555-95050-7 (alk. paper) :
DDC 759.13/074/7441 20
N6505 .C645 1990   *NYPL [MAVZ+
            (Williamstown) 91-5440]*

H.V. Allison Galleries. American art . New
York, N.Y. , 1985. 22 p. :
            NYPL [3-MAMT 91-6712]

Los Angeles County Museum of Art. American
art . Los Angeles, Calif. , Seattle , 1991. p. cm.
ISBN 0-87587-155-0 DDC 759.13/074/79494 20
N6505 .L6 1991

Strazdes, Diana J. American paintings and
sculpture to 1945 in the Carnegie Museum of
Art /. New York , c1991. p. cm. ISBN
1-555-95055-8 : DDC 759.13/074/74886 20
N6505 .S87 1991

United States. Dept. of State. Treasures of
State . New York , 1991. p. cm. ISBN
0-8109-3911-8 (cloth) DDC 709/.73/074753 20
N6505 .U48 1991

**ART, AMERICAN - COLORADO -
EXHIBITIONS.**
Colorado, 1990 . Denver, Colo. , c1990. 143
p. : ISBN 0-914738-39-9 (pbk.)
IN PROCESS (ONLIN)
            NYPL [3-MAMT 90-13383]

ART, AMERICAN - CONGRESSES.
American art around 1900 . Washington ,
Hanover [N.H.] , 1990. 136 p. : ISBN
0-89468-143-5   *NYPL [3-MAMT 91-7570]*

ART, AMERICAN - EXHIBITIONS.
Addison Gallery of American Art. American
abstraction at the Addison . Andover, Mass. ,
c1991. 95 p. : ISBN 1-87988-600-6 DDC
709/.73/0747445 20
N6512.5.A2 A33 1991

American light . [Laurenceville, NJ] ,
Washington, [D.C.] , c1989. 330 p. : ISBN
0-691-04074-5 (alk. paper) : DDC
758/.1/09730740153 19
N8214.5.U6 A47 1989
            NYPL [3-MAMT 90-12012]

American masters of the 60's . New York, NY
(130 Prince St., New York 10012) , c1990. 76
p. : DDC 709/.73/0747471 20
N6512 .A6156 1990

Art-- made in USA . [Regensburg] [1988?] 90
p. :   *NYPL [3-MAMT 89-28438]*

Art what thou eat . Mount Kisco, N.Y. , c1991.
191 p. : ISBN 1-559-21051-6 : DDC
704.9/49641/0973 20
N6512 .A763 1991
            NYPL [3-MAMZ+ 91-5410]

As seen by both sides . Boston, Mass. ,
Amersht, MA , 1991. 112 p. : ISBN
0-87023-744-6 (pbk.) : DDC
760/.04499597043/074597 20
N6512 .A788 1991

Bernard Danenberg Galleries. One hundred
recent acquisitions, by American artists. New
York, 1969. 51 p. *NYPL [3-MAMT 90-6625]*

The Charade of mastery . New York, N.Y. ,
c1990. 18 p. :   *NYPL [3-MAMT 91-4324]*

Community Arts Programs Association.
Contemporary landscape . Bayside, N.Y. ,
c1977. 28 p. :
N6512 .C5814 1977
            NYPL [3-MAMT 81-992]

Day, Holliday T. Power . Indianapolis, Ind. ,
1991. p. cm. ISBN 0-253-31658-8 DDC
709/.73/07477252 20
N72.P6 D38 1991

The Decade show . [New York] , c1990. 364
p. : ISBN 0-915557-68-1
NYPL [3-MAMT 90-12484]

Dwellings . Philadelphia , c1978. 16 p. : ISBN
0-88454-050-2
N6512 .D85   NYPL [3-MAMT+ 79-2026]

An Exhibition of five recent works by Larry
Bell, John McCracken, DeWain Valentine, Ron
Cooper [and] Peter Alexander. Edmonton,
1971. 44 p.
N6535.L6 E89   NYPL [3-MAMT 81-415]

Fekner, John. Artist as apolitical sensor .
Brookville, N.Y. , 1990. 28 p. :
NYPL [3-MAMT 91-5026]

Fink, Lois Marie. American art at the
nineteenth-century Paris Salons /. Washington,
D.C. : Cambridge ; xxiv, 430 p. : ISBN
0-521-38499-0 DDC 709/.73/0903407444361 20
N6510 .F57 1990 NYPL [3-MCW 90-11536]

Fowler, Harriet W. New Deal art .
[Lexington] , c1985. 119 p. : DDC
760/.0973/074016947 19
N8838 .F69 1985   NYPL [MDBF 87-1170]

Gelburd, Gail. The trans parent thread .
[Hempstead, N.Y.] , Philadelphia, Pa. , c1990.
124 p. : ISBN 0-8122-1376-9 (pbk.)
NYPL [3-MAMT 91-4984]

Impressionism and post impressionism .
Portland, Me. , c1991. p. cm. DDC
709/.03/4407474191 20
N6847.5.I4 I43 1991

Invisible twenty-one artists visible. Long Beach,
Calif. , 1972. 59 p. :
NYPL [3-MAMT 90-5889]

Italian-American women artists . [San
Francisco, Calif. , 1979] [19] p. :
NYPL [3-MAMT 90-12524]

Marlais, Michael Andrew. Americans and
Paris . Waterville, Me. , c1990. 62 p. : DDC
759.13/074/7416 20
N6510 .M27 1990
NYPL [3-MAMT 90-13006]

Matilsky, Barbara C. The expressionist surface .
New York , c1990. 48 p. : ISBN 0-9604514-2-0
IN PROCESS (ONLINE)
NYPL [3-MAMT+ 91-4360]

New voices in Greek-American art . Brooklyn,
N.Y. [1990] [40] p. :
NYPL [MAMT 91-6992]

Occupation and resistance . New York, N.Y. ,
c1990. 80 p. : ISBN 0-932075-30-4
IN PROCESS (ONLINE)
NYPL [3-MAMT 91-7487]

Pasadena Art Museum. A decade in the
contemporary galleries, 1949-1959. [Pasadena,
1959] 76 p.   *NYPL [3-MAMT 91-287]*

Pincus-Witten, Robert. The last
decade--American artists of the 80's . New
York (130 Prince St., New York 10012)
[1990] 137 p. : DDC 709/.73/0747471 20
N6512 .P492 1990

The Sandra Doane Turk collection of Western
art . St. Petersburg, Florida , 1985. 42 p. :
NYPL [3-MAMZ 90-11526]

Selections from the Edward Albee collection .
Reading, Penn. , 1988. 28 p. : ISBN
0-941972-07-0
NYPL [3-MAX (Albee) 90-12382]

Sport in art from American museums . New
York, NY , 1991. p. cm. ISBN 0-87663-606-7
DDC 704.9/49796/097307477252 20
N8250 .S637 1991

Stavitsky, Gail, 1954- Gertrude Stein . New
York, N.Y. , c1990. 52 p. :
NYPL [3-MAMT 91-7537]

Tate Gallery Liverpool. Minimalism. Liverpool ,
c1989. 28 p. : ISBN 1-85437-009-1
NYPL [3-MAMT 90-12390]

The Technological muse . Katonah, N.Y. ,
c1990. 96 p. : ISBN 0-915171-19-8
NYPL [3-MAMT+ 91-7609]

The (Un)making of nature. New York, N.Y. ,
c1990. 20 p. :
NYPL [3-MAMT 91-6593]

United States. National Armed Forces Museum
Advisory Board. The Armed Forces of the
United States as seen by the contemporary
artist. [Washington, 1968] vii, 64 p. DDC
704.94/9/355000973
N6512 .A518   NYPL [3-MAMT 90-6253]

Wadden, Mary Ann. The political landscape .
Brookville, N.Y. , 1990. 32 p. : ISBN
0-933699-17-4 DDC 709/.73/074747245 20
N8835 .W34 1990
NYPL [3-MAMT 91-4586]

Word as image . Milwaukee, Wis. , c1990. 171
p. :   *NYPL [3-MAMT 90-12993]*

7 artists. New York , c1970. 1 v. (unpaged) :
NYPL [3-MAMT 90-6992]

**ART, AMERICAN - GREAT LAKES REGION -
EXHIBITIONS.**
Made in America . New York City , c1986. 31
p. : ISBN 0-932075-10-X (pbk.) DDC
709/.77/07401471 19
N6522 .M3 1986
NYPL [3-MAMT 90-12369]

ART, AMERICAN - IDAHO - EXHIBITIONS.
Harthorn, Sandy, 1945- One hundred years of
Idaho art, 1850-1950 . Boise, ID , c1990. 134
p. : DDC 709/.796/07479628 20
N6530.I2 H37 1990
NYPL [3-MAMT 90-11110]

ART, AMERICAN - ILLINOIS - CHICAGO.
The old guard and the avant-garde . Chicago ,
c1990. xxiv, [16] p. of col. plates, 280 p. :
ISBN 0-226-68284-6 (alk. paper) DDC
709/.773/1109041 20
N6535.C5 O43 1990
NYPL [3-MAMT 91-5016]

**ART, AMERICAN - ILLINOIS - CHICAGO -
EXHIBITIONS.**
The Chicago show . Chicago, Ill. , c1990. 48
p. : ISBN 0-938903-09-8
N6487.C52 C6 1990
NYPL [3-MAMT 91-7597]

ART, AMERICAN - ITALIAN INFLUENCES.
The Italian presence in American art,
1860-1920 /. New York , Roma , 1991. p. cm.
ISBN 0-8232-1342-0 : DDC 709/.73/09034 20
N6510 .I8 1991

**ART, AMERICAN - ITALY - CORTONA -
EXHIBITIONS.**
City on a hill . Athens, Ga. , c1989. 1 v.
(unpaged) : ISBN 0-915977-02-8
NYPL [3-MAMT 90-11763]

**ART, AMERICAN - JAPANESE
INFLUENCES - EXHIBITIONS.**
Hosley, William. The Japan idea . Hartford,
Conn. , 1990. 211 p. : ISBN 0-918333-07-5
NYPL [3-MAMT+ 91-3289]

Meech-Pekarik, Julia. Japonisme comes to
America . New York , 1990. 256 p. : ISBN
0-8109-3501-5 DDC 760/.0973/07474942 20
N6510 .M44 1990 NYPL [MDBV 90-11897]

**ART, AMERICAN - NEW MEXICO -
CATALOGS.**
Museum of Fine Arts (Museum of New
Mexico) Artists of twentieth-century New
Mexico . Santa Fe, NM , 1992. p. cm. ISBN
0-89013-230-5 DDC 709/.789/07478956 20
N6530.N6 M87 1992

ART, AMERICAN - NEW MEXICO - TAOS.
Taggett, Sherry Clayton. Paintbrushes and
pistols . Santa Fe, N.M. , New York, N.Y. ,
1990. 271 p. [24] p. of plates : ISBN
0-945465-65-3 DDC 759.189/53 20
N6512.5.T34 T34 1990
NYPL [3-MAMT 91-4609]

ART, AMERICAN - NEW YORK (N.Y.)
O'Hara, Frank. Art chronicles, 1954-1966 /.
New York [1975] 165 p. : ISBN
0-8076-0755-X : DDC 709/.747/109045 20
N6535.N5 O37 1975
NYPL [MAMT 75-525]

**ART, AMERICAN - NEW YORK (N.Y.) -
EXHIBITIONS.**
Gober, Halley, Kessler, Wool . [Munich] ,
c1989. 89 p. : ISBN 3-923357-24-9
NYPL [3-MAMT 90-12879]

Gober, Halley, Kessler, Wool . München ,

c1989. 89 p. : ISBN 3-923357-24-9
N6535.N5 G63 1989

Living in NY . Montréal, Qc. [1988] [16] p. :
NYPL [3-MAMT 89-27022]

Painting a place in America . New York ,
Bloomington , 1991. p. cm. ISBN 0-253-33121-8
(cloth) DDC 704/.0392407471/090410747471
20
N6538.J4 P35 1991

**ART, AMERICAN - NEW YORK (STATE) -
ALBANY COUNTY.**
Bennett, Allison P. The people's choice . [S.l.]
c1980 ([Albany, N.Y.] : printed by Lane Press)
ix, 135 p. : DDC 709/.747/42 19
N6530.N72 A33   NYPL [3-MAMT 81-75]

ART, AMERICAN - OHIO - EXHIBITIONS.
Hinson, Tom E. The invitational--artists of
northeast Ohio . [Cleveland] , c1991. vii, 64 p. :
ISBN 0-940717-07-7 : DDC
709/.771/307477132 20
N6530.O3 H56 1991

Quintessence--the alternative spaces residency
program, the City Beautiful Council of Dayton,
Ohio, the Wright State University, Department
of Art. Dayton , c1978- v. : ISBN 0-9602550-0-1
(v. 2) DDC 709/.73/074017173
N6530.O3 Q56   NYPL [3-MAMT 79-2025]

**ART, AMERICAN - PENNSYLVANIA -
PITTSBURGH REGION - CATALOGS.**
Westmoreland Museum of Art. Southwestern
Pennsylvania painters . Greensburg, Pa. , 1989.
x, 138 p. : ISBN 0-931241-21-9 DDC
759.148/8/07474886 20
N6530.P42 P589 1989
NYPL [3-MCW 91-6266]

**ART, AMERICAN - SOUTH CAROLINA -
EXHIBITIONS.**
South Carolina State Museum. South Carolina
art . Columbia, S.C. [1991] 90 p. : DDC
709/.757/07475771 20
N6530.S6 S68 1991

ART, AMERICAN - SOUTHERN STATES.
Poesch, Jessie J. The art of the old South .
New York , 1983. xii, 384 p. : ISBN
0-394-40193-X : DDC 709/.75 19
N6520 .P63 1983
NYPL [3-MAMT+ 90-10836]

**ART, AMERICAN - SOUTHERN STATES -
EXHIBITIONS.**
A sense of place . Montgomery, Ala. , 1990. p.
cm. ISBN 0-89280-027-5 DDC 759.15/074/76147
20
N6520 .S46 1990

Southern exposure . New York, NY , c1985. 55
p. : ISBN 0-932075-02-9 (pbk.) DDC
709/.75/07401471 19
N6520 .S67 1985
NYPL [3-MAMT 90-12368]

**ART, AMERICAN - SOUTHWEST, OLD -
EXHIBITIONS.**
Nineteenth century Trans-Mississippi South .
Little Rock, Ark. , 1990. vi, 33 p. : DDC
709/.76/0903407476773 20
N6520 .N56 1990

**ART, AMERICAN - THEMES, MOTIVES -
EXHIBITIONS.**
Not so simple pleasures . Cambridge, Mass. ,
1990. 32 p. : ISBN 0-938437-34-8 (pbk.) : DDC
709/.73/0747444 20
N6512 .N635 1990

ART, AMERICAN - UTAH.
Swanson, Vern G. Utah art . Salt Lake City ,
1991. p. cm. ISBN 0-87905-385-2 : DDC
709/.792 20
N6530.U8 S94 1991

**ART, AMERICAN - VIRGINIA -
EXHIBITIONS.**
Un/common ground . Richmond , c1988. vii,
106 p. : ISBN 0-917046-29-3 DDC
709/.755/0740155451 19
N6530.V8 U5 1988
NYPL [3-MAMT 90-4499]

**ART, AMERICAN - WASHINGTON (STATE) -
20TH CENTURY - EXHIBITIONS.**
Northwest impressions [microform] . Seattle
[1986] [12] p. ;   *NYPL [*ZM-218 no.1]*

ART, AMERICAN - WEST (U. S.)
The Passing of the Great West . Coral Gables,

Fla. , 1975. 55 p. :
NYPL [3-MAMT 90-5902]

ART - ANALYSIS, INTERPRETATION, APPRECIATION. see AESTHETICS; ART - PHILOSOPHY; ART - STUDY AND TEACHING; PAINTING; ART CRITICISM.

ART ANATOMY. see ANATOMY, ARTISTIC.

ART, ANCIENT - ARMENIA.
Frühe Bergvölker in Armenien und im Kaukasus . Berlin , 1984. 84 p. :
NYPL [3-MAE 90-10823]

ART, ANCIENT - CATALOGS.
Musée Barbier-Müller. Ancient art from the Barbier-Mueller Museum /. New York , c1991. 183 p. : ISBN 0-8109-1904-4
NYPL [3-MAE+ 91-6535]

ART, ANCIENT - CAUCASUS.
Frühe Bergvölker in Armenien und im Kaukasus . Berlin , 1984. 84 p. :
NYPL [3-MAE 90-10823]

ART, ANCIENT - COLLECTORS AND COLLECTING - GERMANY (WEST) - KARLSRUHE.
150 Jahre Antikensammlungen in Karlsruhe . Karlsruhe , 1988. 170 p. : ISBN 3-923132-15-8
N5336.G3 K3715 1988
NYPL [3-MAE 90-12538]

ART, ANCIENT - EGYPT.
Roik, Elke. Das altägyptische Wohnhaus und seine Darstellung im Flachbild /. Frankfurt am Main , New York , c1988. 2 v. : ISBN 3-8204-0163-6
NA215 .R65 1988
NYPL [3-MQL+ 90-8068]

ART, ANCIENT - EXHIBITIONS.
Glories of the past . New York , c1990. x, 280 p. : ISBN 0-87099-593-6 DDC 709/.01 20
N5337.W47 G57 1990
NYPL [3-MAE+ 91-5037]

ART, ANCIENT - INDIA.
Soundara Rajah, K.V., 1925- Secularism in Indian art /. New Delhi , c1988. viii, 109 p. : ISBN 81-7017-245-4
NYPL [3-MAE 89-28260]

ART, ANCIENT - IRAN.
'Ukāshah, Tharwat. al-Fann al-Fārisī al-qadīm /. Miṣr al-Jadīdah, al-Qāhirah , 1989. 383 p. : ISBN 977-442-109-4 :
N5390 .U38 1989

ART, ANCIENT - MIDDLE EAST - CONGRESSES.
Investigating artistic environments in the ancient Near East /. Washington, D.C. , c1990. xii, 153 p. : ISBN 0-299-97070-1 (alk. paper) : DDC 709/.35 20
N7265 .I58 1990   *NYPL [3-MAE 90-12590]*

ART, ANCIENT - THEMES, MOTIVES.
Crowley, Janice L. The Aegean and the east . Jonsered , 1989. xii, 507 p. : ISBN 91-86098-55-1 *NYPL [3-MAE 90-11126]*
Wetzel, Christoph. Frühgeschichte und frühe Hochkulturen /. Darmstadt , c1990. 448 p. : ISBN 3-7630-1971-5
N5330 .W54 1990

Art & activities for kids.
Solga, Kim. Draw! /. Cincinnati, Ohio , c1991. p. cm. ISBN 0-89134-385-7 (paper) : DDC 741.2 20
NC730 .S66 1991

Solga, Kim. Make prints! /. Cincinnati, OH , c1991. p. cm. ISBN 0-89134-384-9 : DDC 760 20
NE855 .S5 1991

Solga, Kim. Paint! /. Cincinnati, Ohio , c1991. p. cm. ISBN 0-89134-383-0 : DDC 702/.8 20
N351 .S6 1991

The art and architecture of China /. Sickman, L. C. S. (Laurence C. S.) Harmondsworth, Middlesex , Baltimore , 1956. xxvi, 334 p., 190 p. of plates : DDC 709.52
N7340 .S46   *NYPL [3-MAG 90-11174]*

ART AND BUSINESS. see ART AND INDUSTRY.

ART AND COMMUNISM. see COMMUNISM AND ART.

Art & design. Art meets science and spirituality. London , 1990. 96 p. : ISBN 1-85490-038-2 (UK)
NYPL [3-MAL 91-8122]

Art & design profile .
(13) Italian art and the southern European tradition /. London , New York , 1989. 80 p. : ISBN 0-312-03123-8 (pbk.) :
NYPL [3-MAMC 91-6693]

(8) The New modernism . [[London] , New York , 1988. 80 p. : ISBN 0-85670-940-9
NYPL [3-MAL 90-4522]

ART AND HISTORY.
Lavin, Irving, 1927- Past-present . Berkeley , c1992. p. cm. ISBN 0-520-06816-5 (cloth) DDC 709 20
N72.H58 L38 1992

ART AND HISTORY - EXHIBITIONS.
Papyrus et pop art /. [Nivelles, Belgique , 1987] 104 p. :
N72.H58 P36 1987

Art and identity in Oceania / edited by Allan Hanson and Louise Hanson. Honolulu : University of Hawaii Press, c1990. viii, 315 p., [8] p. of plates : ill. (some col.) ; 24 cm. Selected papers of the Third International Symposium on the Art of Oceania, held in Sept. 1984 in New York; sponsored by the Pacific Art Association. Includes bibliographical references ([297]-315) ISBN 0-8248-1304-9 : DDC 700/.995 20
1. Art, Primitive - Oceania - Congresses. 2. Art - Oceania - Congresses. 3. Art and society - Oceania - Congresses. I. Hanson, F. Allan, 1939-. II. Hanson, Louise, 1940-. III. Pacific Art Association. IV. International Symposium on the Art of Oceania (3rd : 1984 : New York, N.Y.).
N7399.7 .A78 1990
NYPL [3-MADF 91-5014]

ART AND INDUSTRY.
Casciani, Stefano, 1955- Arte industriale . Milano , c1988. 194 p. : ISBN 88-85684-21-1
NYPL [3-MNE+ 90-12329]

ART AND INDUSTRY - THEMES, MOTIVES.
Leitherer, Eugen. Reiz und Hülle . Basel , Boston , 1987. 301 p. : ISBN 3-7643-1827-9
NYPL [3-MNF+ 89-24501]

ART AND INSANITY. see ART AND MENTAL ILLNESS.

Art and life in Northern Europe, 1500-1800 . Miller, Debra. St. Petersburg, Fla. , c1990. 46 p. : *NYPL [3-MAX (Gilbert) 91-5565]*

Art and life of Grandma Moses. Moses, Grandma, 1860-1961. New York, 1969. 168 p. ISBN 0-498-07437-4 DDC 759.13
ND237.M78 K3
NYPL [3-MCX M89 90-6781]

ART AND LITERATURE.
Bal, Mieke, 1946- Reading "Rembrandt". Cambridge , New York , 1991. p. cm. ISBN 0-521-39154-7 DDC 759.9492 20
ND653.R4 B18 1991

ART AND LITERATURE - EXHIBITIONS.
The Avant-garde and the text . Providence, RI , c1988. p. 306-507 : *NYPL [MDT 91-5721]*

Art and literature under the Bolsheviks /. Taylor, Brandon. Concord, MA , 1991. p. cm. ISBN 0-7453-0293-9 DDC 700/.947/09041 20
NX556.A1 T39 1991

ART AND MENTAL ILLNESS.
Thévoz, Michel. Art brut, psychose et médiumnité /. Paris , c1990. 189 p. : ISBN 2-7291-0493-3 :
IN PROCESS (ONLINE)
NYPL [3-MAL 91-7055]

ART AND MENTAL ILLNESS - EXHIBITIONS.
Open mind . Milano , c1989. 318 p. :
NYPL [3-MAMZ 90-11011]

ART AND MOTION PICTURES - EXHIBITIONS.
Von Eisenstein bis Tarkowsky . München , c1990. 159 p. : ISBN 3-7913-1068-2
NX556.A1 V6 1990

ART AND MUSIC - EXHIBITIONS.
Alvin Lucier /. Middletown, Conn. , c1988. 23 p. ; ISBN 0-929687-01-9 (pbk.)
NYPL [3-MGO+ (Lucier) 89-21332]

Art and myth in ancient Greece . Carpenter, Thomas H. London , c1991. 256 p. :
NYPL [3-MAH 91-4599]

ART AND MYTHOLOGY.
Maiorino, Giancarlo, 1943- Leonardo da Vinci . University Park, Pa. , c1992. p. cm. ISBN 0-271-00817-2 (alk. paper) DDC 709/.2 20
N6923.L33 M34 1992

ART AND NATURE. see NATURE (AESTHETICS)

ART AND NUCLEAR WARFARE - GERMANY (WEST)
Die Welt in hundert Jahren . Düsseldorf , 1985. 148 p. : ISBN 3-925282-00-9
NYPL [3-MATC+ 90-12542]

Art & patrimoine .
(4) Plault, Michel. Les lanternes des morts . Poitiers , 1988. 198 p. : ISBN 2-902170-58-0
NYPL [3-MRIF+ 89-26506]

(6) Piot, Michel. Coiffes & bonnets en Charentes, Poitou, Vendée . Poitiers , c1989. 350 p. : ISBN 2-902170-61-0
GT885.P64 P56 1989
NYPL [3-MMV+ 91-5346]

Art and philosophy : Brancusi : the courage to love / [edited by Florence M. Hetzler]. New York : P. Lang, 1991. p. cm. (American university studies. Series XX, Fine arts . vol. 17) Includes bibliographical references. ISBN 0-8204-1599-5 DDC 730/.92 20
1. Brancusi, Constantin, 1876-1957 - Criticism and interpretation. I. Hetzler, Florence M. II. Series.
NB933.B7 A78 1991

Art and physics. Shlain, Leonard. Art & physics . New York , 1991. p. cm. ISBN 0-688-09752-9 DDC 701 20
N70 .S48 1991

Art and political expression in early China /. Powers, Martin Joseph, 1949- New Haven , 1991. p. cm. ISBN 0-300-04767-3 : DDC 732/.71 20
NB1880.C6 P68 1991

ART AND PSYCHOANALYSIS. see PSYCHOANALYSIS AND ART.

ART AND RACE - EXHIBITIONS - CATALOGS.
García Sáiz, Maria Concepción. Las castas mexicanas . [S.l.] , 1989 (Milano) 253 p. :
NYPL [3-MCY+ 91-4969]

Art and recollections from eight decades. Hirschfeld, Al. Hirschfeld . New York : Toronto : p. cm. ISBN 0-684-19365-5 DDC 741.5/092 B 20
NC1429.H527 A2 1991

The art and reflections of Rupert Conrad . Conrad, Rupert, 1907-1979. New York , c1991. 205 p., [8] p. of plates : ISBN 0-8453-4824-8 (alk. paper) : DDC 709/.2 B 20
N6537.C654 A2 1990
NYPL [3-MCX C763 91-6324]

ART AND RELIGION - AUSTRIA - EXHIBITIONS.
Gott erhalte Österreich . Eisenstadt [1990] 239 p. :
N6807 .G67 1990

ART AND RELIGION - EXHIBITIONS.
Triennale internazionale d'arte sacra (1989 : Castello Trecentesco (Celano, Italy)) Triennale internazionale d'arte sacra . Bologna , c1989. 204 p. : ISBN 88-85638-84-8
IN PROCESS (ONLINE)
NYPL [3-MAW (Celano) 91-6444]

ART AND RELIGION - FRANCE.
Driskel, Michael Paul. Representing belief . University Park , c1991. p. cm. ISBN 0-271-00747-8 DDC 709/.44/09034 20
N6847 .D75 1991

ART AND RELIGION - UNITED STATES.
Adams, Doug. Transcendence with the human body in art . New York , 1991. p. cm. ISBN 0-8245-1104-2 (cloth) DDC 701/.04 20
N6512.5.F5 A34 1991

ART AND RELIGION - UNITED STATES - EXHIBITIONS.
Ceremony of memory . Santa Fe, N.M. , c1988. 48 p. : ISBN 0-929762-00-2
NYPL [3-MAMT+ 91-7407]

Contemporary Hispanic shrines . Reading, Pa. ,

c1989. 24 p. : ISBN 0-941972-09-7
IN PROCESS (ONLINE)
NYPL [3-MAMT 91-7297]

**ART AND REVOLUTIONS - EUROPE -
HISTORY - 18TH CENTURY.**
Stürmer, Michael. Scherben des Glücks .
Berlin , c1987. 99 p. : ISBN 3-88680-180-2
N6425.N4 S78 1987

ART AND REVOLUTIONS - MEXICO.
Los Zapatas de Diego Rivera /. Ciudad de
México , Cuernavaca, Morelos , 1989. 117 p.,
[2] folded leaves of plates : ISBN 968-292-333-6
DDC 760/.092 20
N6559.R58 Z37 1989
NYPL [3-MCZ R62 91-4245]

ART AND SCIENCE.
Art meets science and spirituality. London ,
1990. 96 p. : ISBN 1-85490-038-2 (UK)
NYPL [3-MAL 91-8122]

ART AND SEMIOTICS.
Thürlemann, Felix. Vom Bild zum Raum .
Köln , c1990. 193 p. : ISBN 3-7701-2361-1
DDC 701 20
N68 .T54 1990

ART AND SOCIETY - EUROPE.
Boime, Albert. Art in an age of Bonapartism,
1800-1815 /. Chicago , 1990. xxvii, 706 p. :
ISBN 0-226-06335-6 (alk. paper) : DDC
709/.03/4 20
N6757 .B56 1990 *NYPL [3-MAM 91-5522]*

Bourdieu, Pierre. [Amour de l'art. English.] The
love of art . Cambridge, UK , 1991. viii, 182
p. ; ISBN 0-7456-0598-2 : DDC 708.9/4 20
N430 .B613 1991

ART AND SOCIETY - EXHIBITIONS.
Rhetorical image . New York , c1990. 98 p. :
ISBN 0-915557-71-1
NYPL [3-MAL+ 91-5559]

Theatergarden Bestiarium . Cambridge, Mass. ,
Long Island City, N.Y. , c1990. 176 p. : ISBN
0-262-04105-7 DDC 701/.03 20
N6494.E6 T4 1990
NYPL [3-MAL+ 90-12503]

Um 1968 . Köln , c1990. 260 p. : ISBN
3-7701-2470-7
N6488.G3 D858 1990

ART AND SOCIETY - FRANCE.
Driskel, Michael Paul. Representing belief .
University Park , c1991. p. cm. ISBN
0-271-00747-8 DDC 709/.44/09034 20
N6847 .D75 1991

**ART AND SOCIETY - FRANCE - HISTORY -
17TH CENTURY.**
Weyl, Martin. Passion for reason and reason of
passion . New York , c1989. 314 p. ; ISBN
0-8204-0981-2 : DDC 709.44/09/032 20
N6846 .W49 1989
NYPL [3-MAMI 91-6906]

**ART AND SOCIETY - FRANCE - HISTORY -
20TH CENTURY.**
Moulin, Raymonde. Le marché de la peinture
en France /. Paris [1989], c1967. 613 p. :
ISBN 2-7073-0106-X
NYPL [3-MCN 90-13538]

**ART AND SOCIETY - GERMANY -
HISTORY - 20TH CENTURY.**
Weinstein, Joan. The end of expressionism .
Chicago , 1990. xiv, 332 p. : ISBN
0-226-89059-7 DDC 701/.03 19
N6868.5.E9 W45 1989
NYPL [3-MAMG 90-11096]

ART AND SOCIETY - GREAT BRITAIN.
Lang, Gladys Engel. Etched in memory .
Chapel Hill , 1990. xviii, 437 p., [46] p. of
plates : ISBN 0-8078-1908-5 (alk. paper) DDC
767/.2/094209034 20
NE2043.25 .L36 1990
NYPL [MDN 90-13667]

**ART AND SOCIETY - HISTORY - 19TH
CENTURY.**
Crary, Jonathan. Techniques of the observer .
Cambridge, Mass. , c1990. 171 p. : ISBN
0-262-03169-8 DDC 701/.15 20
N7430.5 .C7 1990 *NYPL [3-MAL 91-4620]*

ART AND SOCIETY - INDIA.
Jayakar, Pupul. The earth mother . San
Francisco, Calif. , c1990. xxx, 248 p., [32] p. of
plates : ISBN 0-06-250405-3 : DDC 700/.954 20
N8191.I4 J39 1990 *NYPL [3-MAF 91-5051]*

ART AND SOCIETY - INDIA - BENGAL.
Chatterjee, Ratnabali, 1941- From the karkhana
to the studio . New Delhi , 1990. xi, 144 p.,
[12] p. of plates : ISBN 81-85016-28-3 : DDC
701/.03/095414 20
N72.S6 C35 1990 *NYPL [3-MAF 91-6048]*

ART AND SOCIETY - ITALY - PALERMO.
Bresc-Bautier, Geneviève. Artistes, patriciens et
confréries . Roma , 1979. xviii, 315 p., [15]
leaves of plates :
N6921.P34 B73 *NYPL [3-MAMC 81-374]*

ART AND SOCIETY - LATIN AMERICA.
Morais, Frederico. [Artes plásticas na América
Latina. Spanish.] Las artes plásticas en la
América Latina . Ciudad de La Habana, Cuba ,
c1990. 121 p. ;
N72.S6 M66718 1990

ART AND SOCIETY - NETHERLANDS.
Art in history/history in art . Santa Monica,
CA [Chicago, Ill.] , 1991. p. cm. ISBN
0-89236-201-4 : DDC 701/.03/0949209032 20
N72.S6 A746 1991

ART AND SOCIETY - NEW YORK (N.Y.)
Lurie, Boris, 1924- No! art . Berlin , Köln ,
c1988. 135, 109 p., 284 p. of plates :
NYPL [3-MAMT 90-12385]

**ART AND SOCIETY - OCEANIA -
CONGRESSES.**
Art and identity in Oceania /. Honolulu ,
c1990. viii, 315 p., [8] p. of plates : ISBN
0-8248-1304-9 : DDC 700/.995 20
N7399.7 .A78 1990
NYPL [3-MADF 91-5014]

**ART AND SOCIETY - RUSSIAN S.F.S.R. -
MOSCOW - EXHIBITIONS.**
Moscow, treasures and traditions /.
Washington, D.C. , c1990. 281 p. : ISBN
0-295-96994-6 DDC 709/.47/074753 20
N6997.M7 M65 1990
NYPL [3-MAM+ 90-11581]

**ART AND SOCIETY - SPAIN - GALICIA -
HISTORY - 19TH CENTURY.**
Bozal Fernández, Valeriano. Arte y ciudad en
Galicia, siglo XIX /. Santiago de Compostela
[1990] 133 p. : ISBN 84-505-9217-8 DDC
709/.46/109034 20
N72.S6 B6 1990

ART AND SOCIETY - UNITED STATES.
Bongard, Willi. Kunst und Kommerz.
[Oldenburg, c1967] 271 p.
NYPL [3-MAMT 90-6286]

Creating a dignified past . Savage, Md. , c1991.
ix, 129 p. : ISBN 0-8476-7690-0
NYPL [3-MLF 91-6907]

Kammen, Michael G. Meadows of memory .
Austin , 1992. p. cm. ISBN 0-292-75139-7 (cloth :
alk. paper) DDC 758/.9973 20
N6505 .K28 1992

Lang, Gladys Engel. Etched in memory .
Chapel Hill , 1990. xviii, 437 p., [46] p. of
plates : ISBN 0-8078-1908-5 (alk. paper) DDC
767/.2/094209034 20
NE2043.25 .L36 1990
NYPL [MDN 90-13667]

**ART AND SOCIETY - UNITED STATES -
EXHIBITIONS.**
Day, Holliday T. Power . Indianapolis, Ind. ,
1991. p. cm. ISBN 0-253-31658-8 DDC
709/.73/07477252 20
N72.P6 D38 1991

**ART AND SOCIOLOGY. see ART AND
SOCIETY.**

**ART AND STATE - AUSTRIA -
EXHIBITIONS.**
Gott erhalte Österreich . Eisenstadt [1990] 239
p. :
N6807 .G67 1990

ART AND STATE - EGYPT.
Khiṭṭat al-nashāṭ li-'ām 1974 /. al-Qāhirah ,
1974. 9, 108 p. ;
NX750.E3 K45 1974

ART AND STATE - FINLAND.
Veikkola, Eeva-Sisko. Kulttuurin julkinen
rahoitus . Helsinki , 1989. 51 p. : ISBN
951-47-2866-1 :
NX750.F5 V45 1989

ART AND STATE - FRANCE.
Cone, Michèle S., 1932- Art, prejudice, and
persecution . Princeton, N.J. , c1992. p. cm.

ISBN 0-691-04088-5 : DDC 701/.03 20
N6848 .C66 1992

ART AND STATE - FRANCE - PARIS.
Friedrich, Otto, 1929- Olympia . New York,
NY , c1992. p. ISBN 0-06-016318-6 (cloth) :
DDC 701/.03 20
N6847 .F75 1992

**ART AND STATE - GERMANY - BADEN-
WÜRTTEMBERG.**
Kunstkonzeption des Landes
Baden-Württemberg /. Stuttgart , c1990. 391
p. : ISBN 3-923719-19-1
NX550.A3 B245 1990

**ART AND STATE - GERMANY - HISTORY -
20TH CENTURY.**
Kunst auf Befehl? . München , c1990. 275 p. :
ISBN 3-7814-0285-1 DDC 701/.03 20
N6868.5.N37 K85 1990

ART AND STATE - IRELAND.
Kennedy, Brian P. Dreams and responsibilities .
[Dublin, Ireland] [1990?] xiii, 292 p. : ISBN
0-906627-32-X DDC 700/.1/03 20
NX750.I7 K4 1990 *NYPL [JFE 91-2989]*

ART AND STATE - ITALY.
Di San Luca, Guido Clemente. Three papers /.
Napoli , c1990. 84 p. : DDC 700/.1/03 20
N8846.I8 D5 1990

ART AND STATE - LATIN AMERICA.
Morais, Frederico. [Artes plásticas na América
Latina. Spanish.] Las artes plásticas en la
América Latina . Ciudad de La Habana, Cuba ,
c1990. 121 p. ;
N72.S6 M66718 1990

ART AND STATE - QUÉBEC (PROVINCE)
Dépenses de l'administration publique
provinciale au titre de la culture, 1984-1988.
Québec, Québec [1989] 29 p. : ISBN
2-550-19744-5
NX750.C2 D47 1989

ART AND STATE - SOVIET UNION.
Taylor, Brandon. Art and literature under the
Bolsheviks /. Concord, MA , 1991. p. cm.
ISBN 0-7453-0293-9 DDC 700/.947/09041 20
NX556.A1 T39 1991

**ART AND STATE - SPAIN - NAVARRE
(KINGDOM)**
Martínez de Aguirre, Javier. Arte y monarquía
en Navarra, 1328-1425 /. Pamplona , c1987.
432 p. : ISBN 84-235-0794-7
N7109.N3 M37 1987
NYPL [3-MAML 90-12586]

ART AND STATE - TURKEY.
Żygulski, Zdzisław. Ottoman art in the service
of the empire /. New York , c1991. p. cm.
ISBN 0-8147-9671-0 : DDC 745/.09561 20
NK1011 .Z94 1991

ART AND STATE - UNITED STATES.
Public policy and the aesthetic interest .
Urbana , c1992. p. cm. ISBN 0-252-01899-0 (cl)
DDC 700/.1/03 20
NX730 .P79 1992

ART AND TECHNOLOGY.
Unger, Richard W. The Art of medieval
technology . New Brunswick , c1991. p. cm.
ISBN 0-8135-1727-3 DDC 704.9/484 20
N8180 .U54 1991

Verzeichnungen . Essen , 1989. 227 p. : ISBN
3-88474-603-0
N72.T4 V47 1989

**ART AND TECHNOLOGY - UNITED
STATES.**
Ehrlich, George, 1925- Technology and the
artist [microform] . 1960. iv, 243 leaves :
*NYPL [*ZM-231]*

**ART AND TECHNOLOGY - UNITED
STATES - EXHIBITIONS.**
Plous, Phyllis. PULSE 2 . Santa Barbara ,
Seattle , c1990. 76 p. : ISBN 0-942006-19-4
DDC 709/.73/07479491 20
N72.T4 P85 1990 *NYPL [3-MGI 91-5051]*

The Technological muse . Katonah, N.Y. ,
c1990. 96 p. : ISBN 0-915171-19-8
NYPL [3-MAMT+ 91-7609]

**ART AND THE CATHOLIC CHURCH. see
CATHOLIC CHURCH AND ART.**

**ART AND THE ORTHODOX EASTERN
CHURCH. see ORTHODOX EASTERN
CHURCH AND ART.**

ART AND THE REFORMATION. see
REFORMATION AND ART.

Art and war . Foot, M. R. D. (Michael Richard
Daniel), 1919- London , 1990. 240 p. : ISBN
0-7472-0286-9 DDC 758/.994053 20
N8260 .F58 1990

ART AND WAR.
Hale, J. R. (John Rigby), 1923- Artists and
warfare in the Renaissance /. New Haven ,
1990. ix, 278 p. : ISBN 0-300-04840-8 DDC
760/.09/024 20
N6370 .H25 1990   *NYPL [3-MAL 91-6322]*

**ART - ANECDOTES, PACETIAE, SATIRE,
ETC.**
Roessler, Arthur. Der Malkasten . Leipzig ,
1924. 134 p. ;   *NYPL [3-MAS 83-2340]*

ART, ANGLO-SAXON.
Raw, Barbara Catherine. Anglo-Saxon
crucifixion iconography and the art of the
monastic revival /. Cambridge [England] , New
York , 1990. xii, 296 p., 16 p. of plates ; ISBN
0-521-36370-5 DDC 704.9/4853/0942 20
N6763 .R38 1990
    NYPL [3-MAMZ 90-11590]

ART APPRECIATION.
Gilbert, Rita, 1942- Living with art /. New
York , c1992. p. cm. ISBN 0-07-023454-X :
DDC 701/.1 20
N7477 .G55 1992

Nemett, Barry. Images, objects, and ideas . Fort
Worth , c1991. p. cm. ISBN 0-03-021782-2
DDC 701/.1 20
N71 .N46 1991

Yenawine, Philip. How to look at modern art /.
New York , 1991. p. cm. ISBN 0-8109-2485-4
DDC 701/.1 20
N6490 .Y46 1991

ART APPRECIATION - CONGRESSES.
Nauchnaīa konferentsiīa Rol′ pamīatnikov
antichnogo iskusstva v reshenii problem
ėsticheskogo vospitaniīa naseleniīa (1988 :
Leningrad, R.S.F.S.R.) Kratkie tezisy dokladov
Nauchnoĭ konferentsii Rol′ pamīatnikov
antichnogo iskusstva v reshenii problem
ėsticheskogo vospitaniīa naseleniīa .
Leningrad , 1988. 148 p. ;
N5327 .N38 1988

ART APPRECIATION - EUROPE.
Bourdieu, Pierre. [Amour de l'art. English.] The
love of art . Cambridge, UK , 1991. viii, 182
p. ; ISBN 0-7456-0598-2 : DDC 708.9/4 20
N430 .B613 1991

ART, ARAB - JORDAN - EXHIBITIONS.
Treasures from an ancient land . Stroud,
Gloucestershire ; Wolfeboro Falls, NH : xiii,
178 p. : ISBN 0-86299-729-1 DDC
709/.5695/07442753 20
N7279.6 .T7 1991   *NYPL [*OFG 91-7466]*

ART, ARCHAEMENID.
Root, Margaret Cool. The king and kingship in
Achaemenid art . Leiden , 1979. xii, 357 p.,
lxxii p. of plates : ISBN 90-04-03902-3 DDC
709/.35 20
N5390 .R6 1979
    *NYPL [*OMA 76-1696 t.19]*

ART, ARGENTINE.
Arte argentino, siglo XX /. [Argentina] c1990
(Buenos Aires, R. Argentina [i.e. República
Argentina] : HUR) 124 p. : DDC 709/.82/0904
20
N6635 .A78 1990

ART, ARGENTINE - EXHIBITIONS.
Academia Nacional de Bellas Artes,
1936-1986 . [Buenos Aires , 1987] 119 p. :
DDC 709/.82/0748211 20
N6635 .A53 1987

**ART, ARGENTINE - HISTORY AND
CRITICISM.**
Bandin Ron, J. C. Plastica argentina . Buenos
Aires , 1978. 228, [4] p., [16] p. of plates :
    NYPL [3-MAM 90-6456]

ART, ARMENIAN.
Dézélus, Robert. L'art de Transcaucasie /.
Vienne, Autriche , c1989. 368 p. :
N7292.6 .D49 1989

ART, ARMENIAN - CATALOGS.
Hayastani eritasard nkarich‘nerĕ /. Erevan ,
1987. 166 p. :
N7292.6 .H37 1987

ART AS AN INVESTMENT.
Bernier, Georges. L'art et l'argent . Paris ,
c1990. 317 p. ; ISBN 2-85956-891-3 :
N8600 .B47 1990

Pinho, Diva Benevides. A arte como
investimento . São Paul, SP , 1989. 214 p. :
ISBN 85-21-30526-5
N8600 .P56 1989

Art-as-art . Reinhardt, Ad, 1913-1967. Berkeley ,
1991. p. cm. ISBN 0-520-07670-2 DDC 709 20
N5303 .R36 1991

ART - ASIA, CENTRAL - EXHIBITIONS.
Kreijger, Hugo. Godenbeelden uit Tibet .
['s-Gravenhage] [Amsterdam] , c1989. 129, [1]
p. : ISBN 90-12-06219-5
    NYPL [3-MAF 91-5465]

**Art Association of Indianapolis, Indiana. Herron
Museum of Art.** see **Indianapolis Museum of
Art.**

Art Association of Montreal. see **Montreal
Museum of Fine Arts.**

ART, ASSYRIAN AND BABYLONIAN. see
ART, ASSYRO-BABYLONIAN.

ART, ASSYRO-BABYLONIAN.
Wetzel, Friedrich. Assur und Babylon. Berlin
[c1949] 70 p.   *NYPL [3-MAE 90-6371]*

Art at the edge : contemporary art from Poland /
[catalogue produced and edited by Chrissie Iles,
Sarah Eckersley, Julia Elliott]. Oxford :
Museum of Modern Art, 1988. 43 p. : ill.
(some col.) ; 30 cm. Published to accompany an
exhibition of: Magdalena Abakanowicz, Jerzy Bereś
Edward Dwurnik, Izabella Gustowska, Jerzy
Nowosielski, Leon Tarasewicz at the Museum of
Modern Art, Oxford, September 18-October 30, 1988.
ISBN 0-905836-66-9 (pbk.) DDC 709/.438/074
19
*1. Art, Polish - Exhibitions. I. Iles, Chrissie. II.
Eckersley, Sarah. III. Elliott, Julia. IV. Museum of
Modern Art (Oxford, England).*
N7255.P6   *NYPL [3-MAM+ 90-4738]*

**ART - AUSTRALIA - SYDNEY (N.S.W.) -
HANDBOOKS, MANUALS, ETC.**
Menzies, Jackie. Asian collection . Sydney,
Australia , 1990. 96 p. : ISBN 0-7305-7455-5
DDC 709/.5/0749441 20
N7336 .M46 1990

ART, AUSTRALIAN (ABORIGINAL)
Layton, Robert, 1944- Historic and prehistoric
perceptions . [London] , 1990. 18 p. ; ISBN
1-85507-020-0 DDC 709/.01/130994 20
N5310.5.A83 L39 1990

**ART, AUSTRALIAN (ABORIGINAL) -
EXHIBITIONS.**
Aboriginal art and spirituality /. North
Blackburn, Vic. , 1991. 151 p. : ISBN
0-85924-998-0
    NYPL [3-MADF+ 91-6923]

Balance 1990 . South Brisbane, Qld., Australia ,
c1990. 95 p. : ISBN 0-7242-3855-7
    NYPL [3-MADF 91-7104]

Contemporary aboriginal art from the Robert
Holmes à Court Collection . Perth , 1990. 125
p. : ISBN 0-7316-8569-5
    NYPL [3-MADF+ 91-4291]

On the edge . [Perth, W.A.] , c1989. 64 p. :
ISBN 0-7309-0703-1
    NYPL [3-MADF+ 90-12876]

1990 Venice Biennale Australia . Perth, WA ,
c1990. 59 p. : ISBN 0-7309-0783-X
    NYPL [3-MCY 91-5556]

ART, AUSTRALIAN - EXHIBITIONS.
Balance 1990 . South Brisbane, Qld., Australia ,
c1990. 95 p. : ISBN 0-7242-3855-7
    NYPL [3-MADF 91-7104]

Eagle, Mary, 1944- 1990 Adelaide Biennial of
Australian art /. Adelaide , 1990. 113 p. :
ISBN 0-7308-0773-8
    NYPL [3-MAM+ 91-5044]

Edwards, Deborah. Stampede of the lower
gods . Sydney [1989] vi, 66 p. : ISBN
0-7305-6555-6 DDC 709/.94/0749441 20
N7760 .E38 1989

Hansen, David. The face of Australia . Frenchs
Forest, NSW, Australia , 1988. 127 p. : ISBN
0-86777-181-X DDC 760/.0449994 19
N7400 .H3 1988 *NYPL [3-MAM+ 91-2242]*

ART, AUSTRALIAN - HISTORY.
Smith, Bernard William. Place, taste, and
tradition . Melbourne , New York , 1979. 304
p. : ISBN 0-19-550561-1
N7400 .S55 1979   *NYPL [3-MAM 81-949]*

ART - AUSTRIA - GUIDE-BOOKS.
Müller-Dürr, Marianne. Österreich . Stuttgart ,
c1987. 600. p. : ISBN 3-17-009234-0 DDC
709/.436 20
N6801 .M85 1987

**ART - AUSTRIA - ST. PÖLTEN -
EXHIBITIONS.**
Diözesanmuseum St. Pölten (Austria) 100 Jahre
Diözesanmuseum St. Pölten, 1888-1988 . St.
Pölten, [Austria] , 1988. 96 p., [76] p. of
plates :   *NYPL [3-MAIH 91-6668]*

ART - AUSTRIA - VIENNA - EXHIBITIONS.
Kunsthistorisches Museum Wien. Die Moderne
Galerie des Kunsthistorischen Museums. Wien
[1956] 24 p.
    NYPL [3-MAVZ (Vienna) 91-1153]

**ART, AUSTRIAN - AUSTRIA - CARINTHIA -
EXHIBITIONS.**
Zaunschirm, Thomas, 1943- Fremdbild Heimat .
Wien , c1989. 101 p. : ISBN 3-900606-12-9
N6809.C3 Z36 1989

ART, AUSTRIAN - AUSTRIA - VIENNA.
Fischer, Wolfgang Georg, 1933- [Gustav Klimt
und Emilie Flöge. English.] Klimt and Emilie .
Woodstock, N.Y. , 1992. p. cm. ISBN
0-87951-451-5 : DDC 709/.2 B 20
N6811.5.K55 F513 1992

Secessionismus und Abstraktion =
Secessionism and abstraction . Wien , New
York , 1989. 81 p. :
    NYPL [3-MAMG+ 90-12363]

ART, AUSTRIAN - EXHIBITIONS.
Gott erhalte Österreich . Eisenstadt [1990] 239
p. :
N6807 .G67 1990

Jugendwerke vom Schillerplatz /. Wien , c1988.
280 p. :   *NYPL [3-MAMG 90-9782]*

Sammlung Rudi Molacek . Graz [1990] 1 v.
(unpaged) : DDC 709/.436/0744365 20
N6808 .S23 1990

Zukowsky, John, 1948- Austrian architecture
and design . Chicago , Berlin , c1991. p. cm.
ISBN 3-433-02340-9 (catalogue edition) DDC
745.4/49436/0904507477311 20
N6808 .Z8 1991

60 Tage österreichisches Museum des 21.
Jahrhunderts /. Wien , 1989. 366 p. : ISBN
3-85211-001-7
IN PROCESS (ONLINE)
    NYPL [3-MAMG+ 90-11631]

ART, AUSTRIAN - GUIDE-BOOKS.
Müller-Dürr, Marianne. Österreich . Stuttgart ,
c1987. 600 p. : ISBN 3-17-009234-0 DDC
709/.436 20
N6801 .M85 1987

ART, BALINESE - EXHIBITIONS.
Donald Friend's Bali . Sydney , 1990. 65 p. :
ISBN 0-7305-6574-2
MLCS 90/15244 (N)
    NYPL [3-MAF 91-6722]

**ART - BALTIC SEA REGION -
CONGRESSES.**
Austausch und Verbindungen in der
Kunstgeschichte des Ostseeraums. Kiel , 1988.
207 p., [8] p. of plates :
IN PROCESS (ONLINE)
    NYPL [3-MAM+ 91-4693]

ART, BAROQUE.
Studia nad sztuką renesansu i baroku /. Lublin ,
1989- v. <1 > :
N6370 .S716 1989

ART, BAROQUE - AUSTRIA - ADMONT.
Mannewitz, Martin. Stift Admont . München ,
c1989. 422 p. : ISBN 3-89235-031-0 :
NA5510.A35 S755 1989

ART, BAROQUE - EXHIBITIONS.
Národní galerie V Praze. Baroque in Bohemia.
London, 1969. 1 v. (unpaged) DDC 709/.437/1
N6818 .P7

**ART, BAROQUE - LATIN AMERICA -
THEMES, MOTIVES.**
Valbert, Christian. La iconografía simbólica en
el arte barroco de Latino América . [La Paz,

Bolivia] , 1987. 122 p. :
N7901.5 .V35 1987

**ART, BAROQUE - MEXICO - HIDALGO
(STATE)**
Vergara Vergara, José. El barroco en Hidalgo.
[Pachuca, Mexico?] , 1988. 177, [5] p. :
N7914.A3 H538 1988

ART, BAROQUE - MEXICO - QUERÉTARO.
Querétaro, ciudad barroca /. Querétaro, Qro.
[Mexico] , c1988. 228, [8] p. :   ISBN
968-614-033-6   DDC 709/.72/45 20
N6557.Q47 Q47 1988

**ART, BAROQUE - PORTUGAL -
DICTIONARIES.**
Dicionário da arte barroca em Portugal /.
Lisboa , 1989. 542 p. :   ISBN 972-231-088-7
            NYPL   [3-MAML+ 91-4315]

ART, BAROQUE - SPAIN - SEVILLE.
León, Aurora. Iconografía y fiesta durante el
lustro real, 1729-1733 /. Sevilla , 1990. 189 p. :
      ISBN 84-7798-045-4
N7111.S5 L46 1990

ART, BELGIAN - EXHIBITIONS.
L'Art en Belgique . Bruxelles , c1990. 527 p. :
      ISBN 2-87284-008-7 (Lebeer-Hossmann)
            NYPL   [3-MAME 91-4589]

La Scuola di Mons . Brescia , Milano , c1989.
103 p. :   DDC 709/.493/42 20
N6968 .S37 1989
            NYPL   [3-MAME 90-10713]

ART - BELGIUM - BRUSSELS - CATALOGS.
Le Musée d'art moderne . [Bruxelles] , c1988.
128 p. :
N6447 .M865 1988

Musées royaux d'art et d'histoire (Belgium)
Acquisitions, 1964-1973 /. Bruxelles , 1974.
[106] p. :
N1835 .A516 1974

ART, BENGALI.
Guha-Thakurta, Tapati. The making of a new
"Indian" art . Cambridge [England] , New
York , 1992. p. cm.   ISBN 0-521-39247-0   DDC
709/.54/1409034 20
N7307.B4 G84 1992

ART - BERLIN (GERMANY) - CATALOGS.
Von Caspar David Friedrich bis Adolph
Menzel . München , c1990. 283 p. :   ISBN
3-7913-1047-X   DDC 759.3/074/43613 20
N6867.5.R6 V6 1990

ART - BIBLIOGRAPHY.
Schimmelman, Janice Gayle. American imprints
on art through 1865 . Boston, Mass. , 1990. ix,
419 p. :   ISBN 0-8161-7261-7   DDC 016.7 20
Z5961.U5 S34 1990 N6505
            NYPL   [MAMT 91-3665]

The art biz . Marquis, Alice Goldfarb. Chicago ,
c1991. p. cm.   ISBN 0-8092-4283-4 (cloth) :   DDC
706/.8/8 20
N8600 .M38 1991

ART, BLACK - AFRICA. see ART, AFRICAN.

ART, BLACK - AFRICA - HISTORY.
Leuzinger, Elsy. The art of Africa. New York
[c1960] 247 p.   *NYPL   [MADF 90-11494]*

**ART, BLACK - AFRICA, SUB-SAHARAN -
EXHIBITIONS.**
Vogel, Susan. Africa explores . New York :
Munich : 294 :   ISBN 3-7913-1143-3 (cloth) :
DDC 709/.67/07473 20
N7391.65 .V63 1991   *NYPL   [Sc G 91-40]*

**ART, BLACK - CARIBBEAN AREA -
EXHIBITIONS.**
Presencia africana en el arte del Caribe .
[Puerto Rico? , 1989?] 124 p. :
N6591 .P74 1989

ART, BLACK - SOUTH AFRICA.
African art in Southern Africa . Johannesburg ,
1989. 252 p. :   ISBN 0-86852-158-2   DDC
704/.03968 20
N7392 .A57 1989

**ART, BLACK - SOUTH AFRICA -
EXHIBITIONS.**
The Neglected tradition . Johannesburg , c1988.
155 p. :   ISBN 0-620-13184-5   DDC
704/.03968/0090407468221 20
N7392 .N44 1988

**ART, BLACK - WEST INDIES -
EXHIBITIONS.**
Presencia africana en el arte del Caribe .

[Puerto Rico? , 1989?] 124 p. :
N6591 .P74 1989

ART, BOHEMIAN. see ART, CZECH.

ART, BOLIVIAN - INFLUENCE.
Gisbert, Teresa, 1926- La tradición bíblica en el
arte virreinal /. La Paz, Bolivia , 1987. viii, 33
p. :   *NYPL   [3-MAM 90-12522]*

ART - BRAZIL - CATALOGS.
Acervo, materpieces, Banco Chase Manhattan.
[Rio de Janeiro] , c1989. 118 p. :   ISBN
85-7083-028-9   DDC 709/.81/0748161 20
N6655 .A24 1989

**ART - BRAZIL - RIO DE JANEIRO -
CATALOGS.**
Senufo . [Rio de Janeiro] , 1987. [24] leaves :
NB1255.I9 S46 1987

ART - BRAZIL - SÃO PAULO - CATALOGS.
São Paulo (Brazil : State). Pinacoteca do
Estado. Pinacoteca do Estado . São Paulo ,
1988. 447 p. :   DDC 708.981/61 20
N6657.S32 S26 1988

ART, BRAZILIAN.
Battistini Filho, Duílio, 1937- Iniciação às artes
plásticas no Brasil /. Campinas, SP, Brasil
[1990] 97 p. :   ISBN 85-308-0098-2   DDC 709/.81
20
N6650 .B38 1990

Integração das artes . São Paulo , 1990. 113 p. :
N6655 .I58 1990

**ART, BRAZILIAN - BRAZIL - BAHIA
(STATE)**
Ott, Carlos. Pequena história das artes plásticas
na Bahia, entre 1550-1900 /. Bahia , 1989
(Salvador, Bahia : Revista Alfa) 63 p. :   DDC
709/.81/42 20
N6656.B2 O88 1989

**ART, BRAZILIAN - BRAZIL - MINAS
GERAIS.**
Vieira, Ivone Luzia. A Escola Guignard na
cultura modernista de Minas, 1944-1962 /.
[Pedro Leopoldo, Minas Gerais] [1988] 164
p. :   DDC 709/.81/51 20
N6656.M5 V54 1988

**ART, BRAZILIAN - BRAZIL -
PERNAMBUCO.**
Catálogo pernambucano de arte .
Recife-PE-Brasil , c1987. 1 v. (unpaged) :
DDC 709/.2/28134 B 20
N6656.P47 C38 1987

**ART, BRAZILIAN - BRAZIL - SÃO PAULO
(STATE) - CATALOGS.**
São Paulo (Brazil : State). Pinacoteca do
Estado. Pinacoteca do Estado . São Paulo ,
1988. 447 p. :   DDC 708.981/61 20
N6657.S32 S26 1988

ART, BRAZILIAN - CATALOGS.
Acervo, materpieces, Banco Chase Manhattan.
[Rio de Janeiro] , c1989. 118 p. :   ISBN
85-7083-028-9   DDC 709/.81/0748161 20
N6655 .A24 1989

ART, BRAZILIAN - THEMES, MOTIVES.
Schenberg, Mário. Pensando a arte /. São
Paulo-Brasil , 1988. 221 p. :   DDC 709/.81/0904
20
N6655 .S28 1988

ART, BRITISH.
Foot, M. R. D. (Michael Richard Daniel),
1919- Art and war . London , 1990. 240 p. :
      ISBN 0-7472-0286-9   DDC 758/.994053 20
N8260 .F58 1990

Halsby, Julian. Venice . London , 1990. 223 p.,
[32] p. of plates :   ISBN 0-7134-6606-5   DDC
758.745310922 20
            NYPL   [3-MAMY 91-4188]

ART, BRITISH - EXHIBITIONS.
The British imagination . New York . 144 p. :
      ISBN 0-915057-36-0
            NYPL   [3-MAMR 91-6691]

Igirisu bijutsu wa ima . [Tōkyō , c1990. 151 p. :
            NYPL   [3-MAMR 91-7545]

London Group. Fifty years of British art,
1914-64. [London, 1964] 1 v. (unpaged)
N6768 .L65

**ART, BRITISH - EXHIBITIONS -
DICTIONARIES.**
Royal Academy exhibitors, 1971-1989 .
Wiltshire, England , 1989. 546 p. ;   ISBN

0-904722-19-8 :   DDC 709/.047/07442132 20
N6768 .R63 1989

ART BRUT.
Thévoz, Michel. Art brut, psychose et
médiumnité /. Paris , c1990. 189 p. :   ISBN
2-7291-0493-3 :
IN PROCESS (ONLINE)
            NYPL   [3-MAL 91-7055]

ART BRUT - FRANCE.
Prévost, Claude, 1927- Les bâtisseurs de
l'imaginaire /. Jarville-La-Malgrange , c1990.
275 p. :   ISBN 2-86955-083-9 :
N7432.5.A78 P78 1990

Art brut, psychose et médiumnité /. Thévoz,
Michel. Paris , c1990. 189 p. :   ISBN
2-7291-0493-3 :
IN PROCESS (ONLINE)
            NYPL   [3-MAL 91-7055]

**ART BRUT - UNITED STATES -
EXHIBITIONS.**
Religious visionaries. Sheboygan, Wis. , 1991. p.
cm.   ISBN 0-932718-31-0   DDC
704.9/482/097307477569 20
N7904 .R44 1991

**ART, BUDDHIST - CHINA - FOREIGN
INFLUENCES.**
Rhie, Marylin M. Interrelationships between the
Buddhist art of China and the art of India and
Central Asia from 618-755 A.D. /. Napoli ,
1988. 44 p., xxxii p. of plates :   DDC
704.9/48943/095109021 20
N8193.C6 R48 1988

ART, BUDDHIST - CHINA - TIBET.
Lauf, Detlef Ingo. Eine Ikonographie des
tibetischen Buddhismus /. Graz, Austria , 1979.
204 p. :   ISBN 3-201-01092-8 :   DDC
704.9/48943923 19
N8193.T52 L38   *NYPL   [3-MAF 91-4701]*

**ART, BUDDHIST - CHINA - TIBET -
EXHIBITIONS.**
Rhie, Marylin M. Wisdom and compassion .
[San Francisco] , 1991. 406 p. :   ISBN
0-8109-3957-6   DDC
704.9/48943923/0951507473 20
N8193.T5 R47 1991
            NYPL   [3-MAF+ 91-7450]

Wellcome Institute for the History of Medicine.
Library. Catalogue of Tibetan manuscripts and
xylographs, and catalogue of thankas, banners
and other paintings and drawings in the library
of the Wellcome Institute for the History of
Medicine /. London , 1989. xiii, 112 p., [12] p.
of plates :   ISBN 0-85484-085-0   DDC 011.31
704.948943923074 20
N8193.T52   *NYPL   [3-MAF+ 90-13612]*

ART, BUDDHIST - CONGRESSES.
Buddhist iconography. New Delhi , c1989. xiii,
249 p., [48] p. of plates :   DDC 704.9/48943 20
N8193.A4 B83 1989
            NYPL   [3-MAF 91-4623]

ART, BUDDHIST - EXHIBITIONS.
Kreijger, Hugo. Godenbeelden uit Tibet .
['s-Gravenhage] [Amsterdam] , c1989. 129, [1]
p. :   ISBN 90-12-06219-5
            NYPL   [3-MAF 91-5465]

ART, BUDDHIST - JAPAN - CATALOGS.
Honolulu Academy of Arts. Visions of the
Dharma . Honolulu , 1991. p. cm.   ISBN
0-937426-14-8 (alk. paper) :   DDC
760/.048943/095207496931 20
N7352 .H66 1991

ART, BUDDHIST - JAPAN - EXHIBITIONS.
Courtly splendor . Boston [1990] 173 p. :
      ISBN 0-87846-328-3
            NYPL   [3-MAG+ 91-3336]

ART, BUDDHIST - NEPAL - EXHIBITIONS.
Pal, Pratapaditya. Art of the Himalayas . New
York , c1991. p. cm.   ISBN 1-555-95066-3 :
DDC 709/.5496/07473 20
N7310.8.N4 P33 1991

**ART, BUDDHIST - SOUTH ASIA -
EXHIBITIONS.**
Arts from the rooftop of Asia . New York
[1971] 4, [46] p. :   *NYPL   [3-MAE 91-302]*

ART, BUDDHIST - TIBET - CATALOGS.
Newark Museum. Catalogue of the Newark
Museum Tibetan collection /. Newark, N.J. ,
1983- v. :   ISBN 0-932828-12-4 (pbk.) :   DDC
709/.51/5074014932 19
N7346.T5 N48 1983   *NYPL   [MAF 91-997]*

ART, BUDDHIST - TIBET - EXHIBITIONS.
Pal, Pratapaditya. Art of the Himalayas . New
York , c1991. p. cm.   ISBN 1-555-95066-3 :
DDC 709/.5496/07473 20
N7310.8.N4 P33 1991

ART - BULGARIA - EXHIBITIONS.
Kunstschätze in bulgarischen Museen und
Klöstern . Essen [1964] 196 p., [91] p. of
plates :   *NYPL [3-MAM 91-1294]*

ART, BULGARIAN - EXHIBITIONS.
Bulgaria . [Liverpool] , 1989. 79 p. : ISBN
0-906367-38-7 (pbk.) : DDC 949.770074 20
                NYPL [3-MNE+ 90-11535]

Kunstschätze in bulgarischen Museen und
Klöstern . Essen [1964] 196 p., [91] p. of
plates :   *NYPL [3-MAM 91-1294]*

ART, BYELORUSSIAN - EXHIBITIONS.
Molodye khudozhniki Belorussii . Moskva ,
1989. 127 p. : ISBN 5-269-00285-X :
N6995.B9 M65 1989

ART, BYZANTINE.
Cantó Rubio, Juan. Arte bizantino .
Salamanca , 1989. 94 p. : ISBN 84-7299-220-9
                NYPL [3-MAK 91-3667]

Holy image, holy space--icons & frescoes from
Greece. Astoria, NY , c1988. 1 videocassette
(28 min., 30 sec.) : DDC 704.9 11
N7852.5

Revel-Neher, Elisabeth. The image of the Jew
in Byzantine art /. Oxford, England , New
York , 1991. p. cm.   ISBN 0-08-040655-6 (HC) :
DDC 704.9/499495004924 20
N6250 .R44 1991

Warland, Rainer. Das Brustbild Christi . Rom .
288 p., [46] p. of plates :
                NYPL [3-MAIH 87-2636]

ART, BYZANTINE - EXHIBITIONS.
Splendori di Bisanzio . Milano [1990] 332 p. :
N7852.5 .S66 1990

ART, BYZANTINE - GREECE -
DICTIONARIES - GERMAN.
Spitzing, Günter. Lexikon
byzantinisch-christlicher Symbole . München ,
1989. 344 p., 8 p. of plates : ISBN
3-424-00934-2 *NYPL [3-MAIH 91-4313]*

ART, BYZANTINE - ITALY - EXHIBITIONS.
Splendori di Bisanzio . Milano [1990] 332 p. :
N7852.5 .S66 1990

ART, BYZANTINE - TURKEY -
DICTIONARIES - GERMAN.
Spitzing, Günter. Lexikon
byzantinisch-christlicher Symbole . München ,
1989. 344 p., 8 p. of plates : ISBN
3-424-00934-2 *NYPL [3-MAIH 91-4313]*

ART - CALIFORNIA - LOS ANGELES -
CATALOGS.
Los Angeles County Museum of Art. American
art . Los Angeles, Calif. , Seattle , 1991. p. cm.
ISBN 0-87587-155-0 DDC 759.13/074/79494 20
N6505 .L6 1991

Museum of Contemporary Art (Los Angeles,
Calif.) The Rita and Taft Schreiber collection /.
Los Angeles, Calif. , c1991. 1 v. (unpaged) :
ISBN 0-914357-24-7 DDC 709/.04/007479494
20
N6487.L67 L677 1991

ART - CALIFORNIA - MALIBU - CATALOGS.
J. Paul Getty Museum. The J. Paul Getty
Museum handbook of the collections. Malibu,
Calif. , 1991. p. cm. ISBN 0-89236-189-1 (pbk.) :
DDC 708.194/93 20
N582.M25 A627 1991

ART - CALIFORNIA - PASADENA -
EXHIBITIONS.
Pasadena Art Museum. The Blue Four.
Pasadena [1954?] [32] p.
N6868.5.E9 P37 1954 *NYPL [3-MC 91-406]*

ART - CALIFORNIA - SAN FRANCISCO -
CATALOGS.
Asian Art Museum of San Francisco. The art of
Japan . San Francisco , c1991. p. cm. ISBN
0-8118-0055-5 (cloth) : DDC 709/.52/07479461
20
N7352 .A935 1991

ART - CALIFORNIA - SANTA BARBARA -
CATALOGS.
Santa Barbara Museum of Art. Santa Barbara
Museum of Art . Santa Barbara, Calif. [1991]

109 p. : ISBN 0-89951-078-7 : DDC 708.194/91
20
N742.S15 A195 1991

ART, CANADIAN - CATALOGS.
Burnett, David G. Masterpieces of Canadian art
from the National Gallery of Canada /.
Edmonton , 1990. x, 230 p. : ISBN
0-88830-344-0 : DDC 709/.71/07471 20
                NYPL [3-MAM+ 91-3276]

ART, CANADIAN - EXHIBITIONS.
The Canadian Art Club, 1907-1915 /.
Edmonton, Alberta, Canada [1988] 94 p. :
ISBN 0-88950-049-5 DDC 709/.71/07412334 20
N6545 .C213 1988
                NYPL [3-MAM+ 90-12373]

National Archives of Canada. A place in
history . Ottawa, Ont. , c1991. ix, 300 p. :
ISBN 0-660-13740-2 (alk. paper) DDC
760/.0449971 20
N6540 .N36 1991

ART, CANADIAN - ONTARIO -
EXHIBITIONS.
Art Gallery of Ontario. Extension Dept. The
work of art . [Toronto] [c1978] 43 p. : ISBN
0-919876-42-0
N6546.O5 A77 1978
                NYPL [3-MAM 80-2200]

ART, CANADIAN - THEMES, MOTIVES.
Moorhouse, Asheleigh. Art, sight, and
language . Kapuskasing, Ont., Canada , c1989.
173 p. : ISBN 0-921254-05-9 DDC 709/.71/09048
20
N6545 .M66 1989   *NYPL [3-MAM 91-6256]*

ART - CARICATURES AND CARTOONS -
EXHIBITIONS.
"Mit Pikasso macht man Kasso" . Zürich ,
c1990. 155 p., [5] p. of plates : ISBN
3-907010-50-7
IN PROCESS (ONLINE)
                NYPL [MDY+ 90-12785]

ART - CATALOGS.
Muze'on Yiśra'el (Jerusalem) The Sam
Weisbord Pavilion and collection /. Jerusalem ,
c1988. 21, 54, 19 p. : ISBN 965-278-062-6 DDC
708.95694/42 20
N3750.J5 A86 1988

Rowling, Nick. Art source book . Secaucus,
N.J. , c1987. 320 p. : ISBN 1-555-21031-7 DDC
704.9/4 20
N4015.G72 L67 1987

Tobey, Susan Bracaglia. The art of motherhood
/. New York , 1991. p. cm. ISBN 1-558-59105-2
DDC 704.9/493068743 20
N7630 .T63 1991

ART, CELTIC - IRELAND - EXHIBITIONS.
Frühe irische Kunst . [Germany , 1959]
(Mainz : Eggebrecht-Presse) 1 v. (unpaged) :
N6240 .F7   *NYPL [3-MAMR 91-303]*

Art Center, Milwaukee. see Milwaukee. Art
Center.

ART CENTERS - CALIFORNIA - LOS
ANGELES - DESIGNS AND PLANS.
The Getty Center . Los Angeles , 1991. p. cm.
ISBN 0-89236-210-3 (paper) : DDC 727 20
NA6813.U6 L674 1991

ART CENTERS - GREAT BRITAIN.
Arts Council of Great Britain. Housing the arts
in Great Britain. London, 1959-61. 2 v.
NA6813.G7 A77

ART, CHILEAN.
Ivelić, Milan. Intimidades . Santiago, Chile
[1989] 119 p. : ISBN 956-25-3018-2
IN PROCESS (ONLINE)
                NYPL [3-MAM+ 90-13346]

ART, CHILEAN - EXHIBITIONS.
Bienal Internacional de São Paulo (20th : 1989)
XX Bienal Internacional de São Paulo . [Chile ,
1989] 63 p. : DDC 760/.0983/090480748161 20
N6665 .B5 1989

Contemporary art from Chile . New York,
N.Y. , c1990. 63 p. : ISBN 1-87912-802-0
                NYPL [3-MAM 91-7561]

ART - CHINA - HISTORY.
Sickman, L. C. S. (Laurence C. S.) The art and
architecture of China /. Harmondsworth,
Middlesex , Baltimore , 1956. xxvi, 334 p., 190
p. of plates : DDC 709.52
N7340 .S46   *NYPL [3-MAG 90-11174]*

ART, CHINESE - TO 221 B.C.
Watson, William, 1917- [Art de l'ancienne
Chine. English.] Art of dynastic China /. New
York , 1981, c1979. 633 p. : ISBN
0-8109-0627-9 : DDC 709/.31 19
N7343.22 .W3713
                NYPL [3-MAG+ 87-1522]

ART, CHINESE - TO 221 B.C. -
CONGRESSES.
New perspectives on Chu culture during the
Eastern Zhou Period /. Washington, D.C. ,
Princeton, N.J. , c1991. p. cm. ISBN
0-691-04095-8 (Princeton Univ. Press) : DDC
700/.931 20
N7343.22 .N48 1991

ART, CHINESE - T'ANG-FIVE DYNASTIES,
618-960.
Rhie, Marylin M. Interrelationships between the
Buddhist art of China and the art of India and
Central Asia from 618-755 A.D. /. Napoli ,
1988. 44 p., xxxii p. of plates : DDC
704.9/48943/095109021 20
N8193.C6 R48 1988

ART, CHINESE - MING-CH'ING
DYNASTIES, 1368-1912 - EXHIBITIONS.
De Verboden Stad . Rotterdam , New York,
NY , c1990. 245 p. : ISBN 90-6918-065-0
                NYPL [3-MAG 91-6651]

ART, CHINESE - EXHIBITIONS.
Chinese art: symbols and images. [Wellesley,
Mass., c1967] 63 p. DDC 709/.51
N7342 .L58   *NYPL [3-MAG 90-6432]*

Freer Gallery of Art. Eugene and Agnes E.
Meyer Memorial exhibition. Washington, 1971.
77 p.   *NYPL [3-MAG 90-7182]*

Munakata, Kiyohiko, 1928- Sacred mountains
in Chinese art . Champaign, Ill. , Urbana ,
c1991. vii, 200 p. : ISBN 0-252-06188-8 (alk.
paper) DDC 704.9/436/095107477366 20
N8214.5.C6 M86 1991
                NYPL [3-MAG+ 91-5438]

Schätze Chinas in Museen der DDR . Leipzig ,
1989. 263 p. ISBN 3-363-00450-8
                NYPL [3-MAG 90-11297]

ART, CHINESE - HISTORY AND
CRITICISM.
Chinese art: symbols and images. [Wellesley,
Mass., c1967] 63 p. DDC 709/.51
N7342 .L58   *NYPL [3-MAG 90-6432]*

Art chinois : néolithique, dynastie Song :
collection Umberto Draghi /. [textes, Catherine
Noppe ... et al.]. [Morlanwelz, Belgium] :
Musée royal de Mariemont, 1990. 216 p. : col.
ill. ; 28 cm. Catalog of an exhibition held at the
Collections Baur, Geneva, begining Oct. 25, 1990.
Includes bibliographical references.   DDC
730/.0951/07449342 20
1. Pottery, Chinese - Exhibitions. 2. Porcelain,
Chinese - Sung-Yüan dynasties, 960-1368 - Exhibitions.
3. Bronzes, Chinese - To 221 B.C. - Exhibitions. 4.
Draghi, Umberto - Art collections - Exhibitions. 5.
Pottery - Private collections - Exhibitions. 6. Porcelain
- Private collections - Exhibitions. 7. Bronzes - Private
collections - Exhibitions. I. Noppe, Catherine. II. Musée
royal de Mariemont. III. Collections Baur.
NK4165 .A714 1990

ART, CHRISTIAN. see CHRISTIAN ART
AND SYMBOLISM.

ART, CHRISTIAN, EARLY. see ART, EARLY
CHRISTIAN.

Art chronicles, 1954-1966 /. O'Hara, Frank. New
York [1975] 165 p. : ISBN 0-8076-0755-X :
DDC 709/.747/109045 20
N6535.N5 O37 1975
                NYPL [MAMT 75-525]

ART, CLASSICAL.
Van Keuren, Frances Dodds, 1946- Guide to
research in classical art and mythology /.
Chicago , 1991. p. cm. ISBN 0-8389-0564-1
DDC 709/.38 20
N7760 .V3 1991

ART, CLASSICAL - ADDRESSES, ESSAYS,
LECTURES.
Studies in classical art and archaeology . Locust
Valley, N.Y. , 1979. xiv, 344 p., [45] leaves of
plates : DDC 709/.38
N5613 .S88   *NYPL [MAH 79-1946]*

ART, CLASSICAL - CATALOGS.
Staatliche Museen zu Berlin (Germany : East).
Antikensammlung. Antikensammlung . Berlin ,

<1990-. v. <2 > : ISBN 3-362-00436-9 (Bd. 2)
DDC 709/.38/074031552 20
N2250.P4 A52 1990

**ART, CLASSICAL - COLLECTORS AND
COLLECTING - GERMANY (WEST) -
KARLSRUHE.**
150 Jahre Antikensammlungen in Karlsruhe .
Karlsruhe , 1988. 170 p. : ISBN 3-923132-15-8
N5336.G3 K3715 1988
              NYPL [3-MAE 90-12538]

ART, CLASSICAL - CONGRESSES.
Nauchnaia konferentsiia Rol´ pami͡atnikov
antichnogo iskusstva v reshenii problem
èsteticheskogo vospitaniia naseleniia (1988 :
Leningrad, R.S.F.S.R.) Kratkie tezisy dokladov
Nauchnoĭ konferentsii Rol´ pami͡atnikov
antichnogo iskusstva v reshenii problem
èsteticheskogo vospitaniia naseleniia .
Leningrad , 1988. 148 p. ;
N5327 .N38 1988

ART, CLASSICAL - INDEXES.
Rochelle, Mercedes, 1955- Mythological and
classical world art index . Jefferson, N.C. ,
1991. p. cm. ISBN 0-89950-566-X (lib. bdg. : alk.
paper) DDC 704.9/47/074 20
N7760 .R63 1991

ART - COLLECTIONS. see ART MUSEUMS.

**ART - COLLECTIONS, PRIVATE. see ART -
PRIVATE COLLECTIONS.**

**ART COLLECTORS. see ART - COLLECTORS
AND COLLECTING.**

**ART - COLLECTORS AND COLLECTING -
CALIFORNIA, SOUTHERN -
EXHIBITIONS.**
Otis Art Institute. The taste of angels. [Los
Angeles, 1966] [74] p. (chiefly illus.) DDC
707/.4/019493
N5215 .L67   *NYPL [3-MAVC 90-5438]*

**ART - COLLECTORS AND COLLECTING -
FRANCE.**
Destins d'objets /. Paris , 1988. 474 p. : ISBN
2-11-002009-1 (pbk.)
              NYPL [3-MAVC 90-9455]
Distel, Anne. Les collectionneurs des
impressionnistes . [Paris] , c1989. 283 p. :
ISBN 2-85047-042-2
              NYPL [MAVC+ 91-6788]

**ART - COLLECTORS AND COLLECTING -
FRANCE - EXHIBITIONS.**
Arabesques et jardins de paradis . Paris , c1989.
334 p. : ISBN 2-7118-2294-X : DDC
709/.17/67107444361 20
N6264.F8 P317 1990

**ART - COLLECTORS AND COLLECTING -
GERMANY - LEIPZIG - EXHIBITIONS.**
Merkur & die Musen . Wien , 1989. 627 p. :
ISBN 3-900926-02-6 DDC 707/.4/43613 20
N6886.L4 M47 1989

**ART - COLLECTORS AND COLLECTING -
GREAT BRITAIN - BIOGRAPHY.**
Lowe, John, 1928- Edward James, poet, patron,
eccentric . London , 1991. xix, 262 p. : ISBN
0-00-217941-5 : DDC 700.92 20
N5247.J3
              NYPL [3-MAX (James, E.) 91-4883]

**ART - COLLECTORS AND COLLECTING -
ITALY.**
Vannugli, Antonio. La collezione Serra di
Cassano /. Salerno , c1989. 157 p., [39] p. of
plates ; ISBN 88-85651-21-6
              NYPL [3-MCE 90-5149]

**ART - COLLECTORS AND COLLECTING -
ITALY - FLORENCE - HISTORY.**
Civai, Alessandra. Dipinti e sculture in casa
Martelli . Firenze , c1990. 219 p. :
              NYPL [3-MAVC+ 91-6773]

**ART - COLLECTORS AND COLLECTING -
UNITED STATES - EXHIBITIONS.**
Impressionism and post impressionism .
Portland, Me. , c1991. p. cm. DDC
709/.03/4407474191 20
N6847.5.I4 I43 1991

Art Cologne. Kolle, Helmut, 1899-1931. Kolle .
Düsseldorf , c1988. 59 p. :
MLCM 89/07398 (N)
              NYPL [3-MCZ K799 90-10673]

ART - COLOMBIA - BOGOTÁ - CATALOGS.
Biblioteca Luis-Angel Arango. Antología, obras
de la colección permanente. Bogotá, D.E. ,

1990. 88 p. :
N6670 .B5 1990

ART, COLOMBIAN.
El Espíritu erótico /. Bogotá , 1990. 207 p. :
DDC 704.9/428/098610904 20
N8217.E6 E87 1990

Mejía de Millán, Beatriz Amelia. El arte
colombiano en el siglo XX /. Pereira,
Colombia , 1988. 155 p. : DDC 709/.861/0904
20
N6675 .M45 1988

ART, COLOMBIAN - CATALOGS.
Biblioteca Luis-Angel Arango. Antología, obras
de la colección permanente. Bogotá, D.E. ,
1990. 88 p. :
N6670 .B5 1990

ART, COLOMBIAN - COLOMBIA - TUNJA.
Mateus Cortés, Gustavo, 1939- Nuevos apuntes
para la historia del patrimonio artístico de
Tunja, con el acta de fundación y el título de
ciudad /. Tunja, Boyacá, Colombia , 1989. 96
p. :
NA877.T8 M3 1989

ART, COLOMBIAN - EXHIBITIONS.
Colombian art in Canada =. Bogotá,
Colombia , 1990. 24 p. : DDC
709/.861/07486148 20
N6675 .C65 1990

3 décadas de arte uniandino. Bogotá, Colombia
[1989] 128 p. :   *NYPL [3-MAM 91-4248]*

**ART, COLONIAL - BRAZIL - BAHIA
(STATE)**
Ott, Carlos. Pequena história das artes plásticas
na Bahia, entre 1550-1900 /. Bahia , 1989
(Salvador, Bahia : Revista Alfa) 63 p. : DDC
709/.81/42 20
N6656.B2 O88 1989

ART, COLONIAL - COLOMBIA - TUNJA.
Mateus Cortés, Gustavo, 1939- Nuevos apuntes
para la historia del patrimonio artístico de
Tunja, con el acta de fundación y el título de
ciudad /. Tunja, Boyacá, Colombia , 1989. 96
p. :
NA877.T8 M3 1989

ART, COLONIAL - ECUADOR - QUITO.
Tesoros de Quito. [Bogotá, Colombia, S.A.] ,
1990. 142 p. : ISBN 958-95232-6-9 DDC
709/.866/13 20
N6687.Q5 T47 1990

ART, COLONIAL - SOUTHERN STATES.
Poesch, Jessie J. The art of the old South .
New York , 1983. xii, 384 p. : ISBN
0-394-40193-X : DDC 709/.75 19
N6520 .P63 1983
              NYPL [3-MAMT+ 90-10836]

Art commence où finit la vie. Soutter, Louis,
1871-1942. Louis Soutter . [Marseille] : Arles :
78 p. : ISBN 2-86869-167-6 (Actes sud) :
NC293.S68 A4 1987
              NYPL [3-MCZ S728 91-6239]

**ART, COMMERCIAL. see COMMERCIAL
ART.**

**ART - COMMISSIONING - GERMANY -
NUREMBERG - HISTORY.**
Schleif, Corine. Donatio et memoria .
[München] , 1990. 288 p., [4] leaves of plates :
ISBN 3-422-06031-6
              NYPL [3-MRBB 91-7159]

ART COMMISSIONS - SCOTLAND.
Youngson, A. J. Urban development and the
Royal Fine Art Commissions /. Edinburgh ,
c1990. 186 p., [24] p. of plates : ISBN
0-7486-0114-7 DDC 711/.4/0941 20
NA9189 .Y68 1990

**ART COMMISSIONS - UNITED STATES -
DIRECTORIES.**
Directory of artist associations and exhibition
spaces, art commissions, museum curators & art
critics /. Renaissance, CA , c1990. 208 p. ;
ISBN 0-940899-14-0
              NYPL [MAV 91-6690]

**ART COMMISSIONS - UNITED STATES -
STATISTICS.**
Love, Jeffrey. Summary of state arts agencies'
grantmaking activities for fiscal year 1987 /.
Washington, D.C. (1010 Vermont Ave., N.W.,
Suite 920, Washington 20005) , c1990. vi, 211
p. : DDC 353.9/3854 20
NX398 .L6 1990

**ART - COMPOSITION. see COMPOSITION
(ART)**

ART, CONCEPTUAL. see CONCEPTUAL ART.

Art conceptuel, formes conceptuelles =.
Schlatter, Christian. Paris , 1990. 598 p. :
              NYPL [3-MAL 91-3664]

L'Art conceptuel, une perspective : 22 novembre
1989-18 février 1990 / [conception et
réalisation du catalogue, Claude Gintz, Juliette
Laffon, Angeline Scherf].2e éd. Paris : Musée
d'art moderne de la ville de Paris, c1989. 260
p. : ill. ; 28 cm. "Coédition Paris-Musée société des
amis du musée d'art moderne de la ville de
Paris"--Colophon. English and French. Includes
bibliographical references (p. 251-253).
*1. Conceptual art - Exhibitions. 2. Art, Modern - 20th
century - Exhibitions. I. Gintz, Claude. II. Laffon,
Juliette. III. Scherf, Angeline. IV. Musée d'art moderne
de la ville de Paris. Société des amis.*
              NYPL [3-MAL 90-11049]

ART - CONGRESSES.
Aspecten van vijftig jaar kunsthistorisch
onderzoek, 1938-1988 . Brussel , 1990. 137 p.,
[14] p. of plates : ISBN 90-6569-435-8
N7442.8.D8 A85 1990

**ART - CONSERVATION AND
RESTORATION - BIBLIOGRAPHY.**
Bleck, Rolf-Dieter. Pflege und Erhaltung von
Kunst- und Kulturgut . Weimar , 1984. v. ;
              NYPL [3-MAV 89-4361]

**ART - CONSERVATION AND
RESTORATION - CONGRESSES.**
Kunststoffe in der Konservierung und
Restaurierung von Kulturgütern . Bern , c1987-
v. : ISBN 3-258-03655-1 DDC 702/.8/8 19
N8560 .K79 1985
              NYPL [3-MAVC+ 88-331]

**ART - CONSERVATION AND
RESTORATION - EXHIBITIONS.**
Firenze restaura . Firenze , 1973, c1972. 154 p.,
[168] p. of plates : *NYPL [3-MBK 90-5749]*

**ART - CONSERVATION AND
RESTORATION - HANDBOOKS,
MANUALS, ETC.**
Davis, Nancy, 1959- Handling with care .
Rochester, NY , c1991. 31 p. : ISBN
0-938551-02-7 DDC 702/.8/8 20
N8585 .D38 1991

ART, COPTIC.
Du Bourguet, Pierre. Die Kopten. Baden-Baden
[1967] 237 p. DDC 709/.32
N7988 .D815   *NYPL [3-MAE 91-329]*

**ART CRITICISM - AUSTRIA - HISTORY -
19TH CENTURY.**
Olin, Margaret Rose, 1948- Forms of
representation in Alois Riegl's theory of art /.
University Park, Pa. , 1992. p. cm. ISBN
0-271-00777-X DDC 709/.2 20
N7483.R54 O35 1992

**ART CRITICISM - FRANCE - HISTORY -
19TH CENTURY.**
La Promenade du critique influent . Paris ,
c1990. 433 p. : ISBN 2-85025-225-5 DDC
701/.18/094409034 20
N7475 .P76 1990

**ART CRITICISM - FRANCE - HISTORY -
20TH CENTURY.**
Gersh-Nešić, Beth S. The early criticism of
André Salmon . New York , 1991. p. cm.
ISBN 0-8153-0115-4 (alk. paper) DDC
759.4/09/041 20
N6848.5.C82 G46 1991

**ART CRITICISM - FRANCE - PARIS -
HISTORY - 19TH CENTURY.**
Marlais, Michael Andrew. Conservative echoes
in Fin de siècle Parisian art criticism /.
University Park, Pa. , c1992. p. cm. ISBN
0-271-00773-7 (acid-free paper) DDC
701/.18/094436109034 20
N7476 .M37 1992

**ART CRITICISM - GERMANY - HISTORY -
20TH CENTURY.**
Roskill, Mark W., 1933- Klee, Kandinsky, and
the thought of their time . Urbana , c1992. p.
cm. ISBN 0-252-01857-5 (acid-free) DDC
750/.1/1894309041 20
N7475 .R67 1992

**ART CRITICISM - HISTORY - 20TH
CENTURY.**
Art theory and criticism . Jefferson, N.C. ,

c1991. xiii, 282 p. : ISBN 0-89950-595-3 (lib. bdg. : alk. paper) DDC 701 20
N71 .A7475 1991

Miller, J. Hillis (Joseph Hillis), 1928- Illustration /. Cambridge, Mass. , 1992. p. cm. ISBN 0-674-44357-8 DDC 700/.1 20
NX640 .M55 1992

Perl, Jed. Gallery going . San Diego , c1991. xxiv, 431 p., [16] p. of plates : ISBN 0-15-134260-1 : DDC 709/.04/0074 20
N6447 .P38 1991   **NYPL [3-MAV 91-7445]**

Re-visions . Englewood Cliffs, N.J. , c1991. vi, 170 p. : ISBN 0-13-779364-2 DDC 701/.18/09045 20
N7475 .R4 1991   **NYPL [3-MAS 91-4650]**

ART CRITICISM - HISTORY - 20TH CENTURY - ADDRESSES, ESSAYS, LECTURES.
Kuh, Katharine. The open eye . New York [1971] xii, 272 p. : DDC 709
N7475 .K85 1971   **NYPL [3-MAS 91-5175]**

ART CRITICISM - HISTORY - 20TH CENTURY - EXHIBITIONS.
Open mind . Milano , c1989. 318 p. :
   NYPL [3-MAMZ 90-11011]

ART CRITICISM - ITALY.
Russoli, Franco. Arte moderna cara compagna . [Milano] , c1987. 382 p. ; ISBN 88-11-59983-0
   NYPL [3-MAMC 91-4600]

ART CRITICISM - NEW YORK (N.Y.) - HISTORY - 20TH CENTURY.
Gibson, Ann Eden, 1944- Issues in abstract expressionism . Ann Arbor, Mich. , c1990. xvi, 430 p. : ISBN 0-8357-1944-8 (alk. paper) DDC 709.747/1/09044 20
N6535.N5 G53 1989
   NYPL [3-MAMT 90-11594]

ART CRITICISM - SLAVIC COUNTRIES - HISTORIOGRAPHY.
Husar, Irene. Johann Joachim Winckelmann in den ostslawischen Ländern /. Stendal , 1979. 98 p. ; DDC 709/.2/4 19
N7483.W5 H8 1979
   NYPL [3-MAB 90-12523]

ART CRITICISM - SOVIET UNION - HISTORY - 20TH CENTURY.
Puti tvorchestva i kritika . Moskva , 1990. 301 p. ; ISBN 5-85200-081-7 :
N6988 .P84 1990

ART CRITICISM - UNITED STATES - HISTORY - 20TH CENTURY.
Ashbery, John. Reported sightings . Cambridge, Mass. , 1991. xxiii, 417 p., [16] p. of col. plates : ISBN 0-674-76225-8 DDC 700 20
N7445.2 .A84 1991

Lynes, Barbara Buhler, 1942- O'Keeffe, Stieglitz, and the critics, 1916-1929 /. Chicago , 1991. x, 376 p. : ISBN 0-226-49824-7 (pbk.) DDC 759.13 20
ND237.O5 L96 1991

ART CRITICS - ITALY - BIOGRAPHY - CONGRESSES.
La Figura e l'opera di Giovanni Morelli . Bergamo , 1987. 2 v. :
   NYPL [3-MAVC 90-10867]

ART CRITICS - UNITED STATES - DIRECTORIES.
Directory of artist associations and exhibition spaces, art commissions, museum curators & art critics /. Renaissance, CA , c1990. 208 p. : ISBN 0-940899-14-0
   NYPL [MAV 91-6690]

ART CRITICSIM - COLOMBIA - HISTORY - 20TH CENTURY.
Gómez Jaramillo, Ignacio, 1910-1970. Anotaciones de un pintor /. Medellín , 1987. 313 p. :
N7483.G64 A2 1987
   NYPL [3-MCZ G632 90-12606]

ART CRITICSX - ITALY - CORRESPONDENCE.
Brandi, Cesare. Morandi /. Roma , 1990. 249 p., [37] p. of plates : ISBN 88-359-3363-3 :
N6923.M6 B7 1990

ART, CUBAN - EXHIBITIONS.
La Habana en Madrid. [Madrid] [1989?] 64 p. : DDC 709/.7291/0744641 20
N6603 .H25 1989

The Nearest edge of the world . Brookline,

MA, USA (108 Winthrop Rd., Brookline 02146) , c1990. 63, [1] p. : DDC 709/.7291/07474 20
N6603 .N4 1990

Outside Cuba . [New Brunswick, N.J.] , Miami, Fla. , 1989. 366 p. : ISBN 0-935501-13-4
   NYPL [3-MAM 90-12497]

ART, CZECH - CZECHOSLOVAKIA - JIHOČESKÝ KRAJ - EXHIBITIONS.
Alšova jihočeská galerie. Gotické umění v jižních Cechách . Praha [1990] 101 p. : ISBN 80-7035-013-X :
N6832.J53 A48 1990

ART, CZECH - CZECHOSLOVAKIA - PRAGUE.
Praha na úsvitu nových dějin . Praha , 1988. 699 p., 32 p. of plates :
N6833.P72 P68 1988

ART, CZECH - EXHIBITIONS.
Ceský neoklasicismus dvacátých let . [Prague] [1986?] 1 v. (unpaged) :
N6831.5.N46 C47 1986

Czech art in the velvet revolution . Roslyn Harbor, N.Y. , 1990. 111 p. :
N6831 .C93 1990
   NYPL [3-MAM+ 91-7464]

Devětsil . [Oxford] , London , c1990. 115 p. : ISBN 0-905836-70-7
   NYPL [3-MAM+ 90-12482]

Devětsil (Society) Devětsil . Łódź [1989]. 105 p. :
N6831.5.D48 D4 1989

Kotalík, Jiří. Kupka, Gutfreund & C. . Venezia , c1980. 114 p. : ISBN 88-20-80273-2 DDC 709/.437/0740531 19
N6831 .K67 1980   **NYPL [3-MAM 90-5445]**

Mezi klasickým řádem a selankou . [Prague] , <1990?-. v. <2> :
N6831.5.N46 M4 1990

ROH. ÚRO. Lidé, život, práce . [Prague] , 1988. 1 portfolio (unpaged) :
N6831 .R64 1988

Thomas, Karin, 1941- Tradition und Avantgarde in Prag . Köln , c1991. 220 p. : ISBN 3-7701-2842-7
   NYPL [MAM+ 91-7291]

"8" . Brno [1989?] 1 v. (unpaged) :
N6831 .A13 1989

ART, CZECH - THEMES, MOTIVES - EXHIBITIONS.
Linie, barva, tvar v českém výtvarném umění třicátých let . [Prague , 1990?] 152 p. :
N6831 .L54 1990

ART - CZECHOSLOVAKIA - BOHEMIA - EXHIBITIONS.
Gotik . [Wien , 1990] 141 p., [62] p. of plates :
N6832.B63 G68 1990

ART - CZECHOSLOVAKIA - PRAGUE.
Praha na úsvitu nových dějin . Praha , 1988. 699 p., 32 p. of plates :
N6833.P72 P68 1988

ART - CZECHOSLOVAKIA - SLOVAK REPUBLIC - GUIDE-BOOKS.
Šášky, Ladislav. Kunstdenkmäler der Slowakei . Bratislava , 1988. 613 p. :
N6832.S55 S26 1988

ART DEALERS - FRANCE.
Distel, Anne. Les collectionneurs des impressionnistes . [Paris] , c1989. 283 p. : ISBN 2-85047-042-2
   NYPL [MAVC+ 91-6788]

ART DEALERS - FRANCE - BIOGRAPHY.
Assouline, Pierre. [Homme de l'art. English.] An artful life . New York , 1990. xiii, 411 p., [16] p. of plates : ISBN 0-8021-1227-7 (alk. paper) DDC 709/.2 B 20
N8660.K3 A9513 1990
   NYPL [3-MAVC 90-12782]

Assouline, Pierre. [Homme de l'art. English.] An artful life . New York , 1991. p. cm. ISBN 0-88064-131-2 (pbk. : acid-free paper) : DDC 709/.2 B 20
N8660.K3 A9513 1991

Persin, Patrick-Gilles, 1943- Daniel-Henry Kahnweiler . Paris , c1990. 251, [5] p. : ISBN 2-907475-03-7 DDC 709/.2 B 20
N8660.K3 P46 1990

ART DEALERS - FRANCE - DIARIES.
Gimpel, René. [Journal d'un collectionneur. English.] Diary of an art dealer. New York, 1966. xii, 465 p. : DDC 706.50924
N8660.G5 A313   **NYPL [3-MAVC 91-3867]**

ART DEALERS - UNITED STATES - BIOGRAPHY.
Hall, Lee. Betty Parsons . New York , 1991. 192 p. : ISBN 0-8109-3712-3 DDC 709/.2 B 20
N8660.P37 H35 1990
   NYPL [3-MAVC 91-7302]

Art deco / consultant, Eric Knowles ; general editors, Judith and Martin Miller. New York, NY : Viking Studio Books, 1991. p. cm. (Miller's antique checklists) Includes index. ISBN 0-670-83956-6 DDC 709/.04/012075 20
1. Decoration and ornament - Art deco - Collectors and collecting - Catalogs. 2. Decorative arts - History - 20th century - Collectors and collecting - Catalogs. I. Knowles, Eric. II. Miller, Judith. III. Miller, Martin. IV. Series.
NK1396.A76 A78 1991

Art déco . Kjellberg, Pierre. [Paris] [1986] 247 p. : ISBN 2-85917-054-5 : DDC 749.24 19
NK2549 .K59 1986
   NYPL [3-MOF+ 91-5321]

ART DECO (ARCHITECTURE) - CALIFORNIA - LOS ANGELES.
Breeze, Carla. L.A. deco /. New York , 1991. p. cm. ISBN 0-8478-1434-5 DDC 720/.9794/9409042 20
NA735.L55 B74 1991

ART DECO (ARCHITECTURE) - UNITED STATES.
Breeze, Carla. Pueblo deco /. New York , 1990. 112 p. : ISBN 0-8478-1177-8 (pbk.) : DDC 720/.973/09041 20
NA712.5.A7 B7 1990
   NYPL [3-MQWO 90-11529]

Art deco Belgique, 1920-1940 : [exposition], Musée d'Ixelles, 6 octobre 1988-18 décembre 1988 / sous la direction de Pierre Loze et Dominique Vautier. [Bruxelles] : Le Musée, [1988] 307 p. : ill. (some col.) ; 21 x 23 cm. Includes index. Bibliography: p. 287-303.
1. Art deco - Belgium - Exhibitions. 2. Art, Modern - 20th century - Belgium - Exhibitions. I. Loze, Pierre. II. Vautier, Dominique. III. Musée d'Ixelles.
   NYPL [3-MAME 89-19054]

ART DECO - BELGIUM - EXHIBITIONS.
Art deco Belgique, 1920-1940 . [Bruxelles] [1988] 307 p. :   **NYPL [3-MAME 89-19054]**

Art déco en España /. Pérez Rojas, Javier. Madrid , c1990. 645 p., [32] p. of plates : ISBN 84-376-0927-5 DDC 709/.46/09042 20
N7108.5.A7 P4 1990

ART DECO - FRANCE.
Mortimer, Tony L. Lalique. . London , 1989. 128 p. : ISBN 1-87130-764-3
   NYPL [3-MNR 90-5089]

Vellay, Marc. Pierre Chareau, architecte, meublier, 1883-1950 /. Paris , 1986. 111 p. : ISBN 2-86930-026-3
   NYPL [3-MOF 90-11128]

ART DECO - SPAIN.
Pérez Rojas, Javier. Art déco en España /. Madrid , c1990. 645 p., [32] p. of plates : ISBN 84-376-0927-5 DDC 709/.46/09042 20
N7108.5.A7 P4 1990

ART DECO - UNITED STATES.
Heide, Robert, 1939- Popular art deco . New York , 1991. 228 p. : ISBN 1-558-59030-7 DDC 709/.73/09041 20
N6512.5.A7 H45 1991
   NYPL [3-MAMT 91-8075]

ART DECO - UNITED STATES - PICTORIAL WORKS.
Sideli, John. Classic plastic radios of the 1930s and 1940s . New York , c1990. 127 p. : ISBN 0-525-24608-8 (cloth)
   NYPL [3-MNF 91-6800]

Art décoratif soviétique 1917-1937 / collectif sous la direction de Vladimir Tolstoï ; mise en oeuvre, Hélène Larroche ; traduit du russe par Catherine Berendt, Véronique Fabre, Pauline de La Villejegu ; textes et iconographie établis, présentés et annotés par Isabelle d'Hauteville. Paris : Editions du Regard, c1989. 436 p. : ill. (some col.) ; 33 cm. Includes bibliographic references and index. ISBN 2-903370-46-X DDC

745/.0947/09041 20
1. Decorative arts - Soviet Union - History - 20th
century. I. Tolstoĭ, Vladimir Pavlovich. II. Larroche,
Hélène. III. Hauteville, Isabelle d'. IV. Sovetskoe
dekorativnoe iskusstvo, 1917-1945.
NK975 .A79 1989
                  NYPL [3-MLF+ 90-2331]

**ART - DEFACEMENT. see ART -
MUTILATION, DEFACEMENT, ETC.**

**ART - DENMARK - COPENHAGEN -
CATALOGS.**
Rosenborg Castle . [Copenhagen?] 1973
([Copenhagen?] : J. Jørgensen) 72 p. ;
       *NYPL [3-MAVZ (Copenhagen, Denmark)
                            90-5970]*

ART - DICTIONARIES.
Harrap's illustrated dictionary of art & artists.
Bromley, Kent , 1990. 589 p. : ISBN
0-245-54692-8   *NYPL [MAO 91-4216]*

Pierce, James Smith. From abacus to Zeus .
Englewood Cliffs, N.J. , c1991. p. cm. ISBN
0-13-338021-1 : DDC 703 20
N33 .P5 1991

ART - DICTIONARIES - GERMAN.
Haubenreisser, Wolfgang. Wörterbuch der Kunst
/. Stuttgart , c1989. ix, 932 p. : ISBN
3-520-16511-2 : DDC 703 20
N33 .H35 1989

Lexikon der Kunst . Leipzig , 1987- v. : ISBN
3-363-00286-6 (set) DDC 703/.31 19
N33 .L47 1987   *NYPL [MAO 88-2169]*

Art discourse/discourse in art /. Prinz, Jessica,
1952- New Brunswick , 1991. p. cm. ISBN
0-8135-1673-0 : DDC 700/.9/04 20
NX456.5.P66 P75 1991

ART, DOMINICAN.
Arte contemporáneo dominicano. [Santo
Domingo, Dominican Republic?] [1987?] [72]
p. ;
N6615.D6 A77 1987

L'art du bois à Sanaa . Bonnenfant, Guillemette.
Aix-en-Provence , c1987. 208 p. : ISBN
2-85744-315-3
NA3573.6.Y42 S254 1987
                  NYPL [3-MRX+ 91-4933]

Art du concept. Michel, Régis. Le beau idéal .
Paris , 1989. 176 p. : ISBN 2-7118-2317-2
                  NYPL [3-MA 90-12383]

Art du dix-neuvième siècle. L'Art du XIXe
siècle . Paris , c1990. 629 p. : ISBN
2-85088-027-2 *NYPL [3-MAL+ 91-3621]*

L'Art du XIXe siècle : 1850-1905 / sous la
direction de Françoise Cachin ; Geneviève
Lacambre ... [et al.]. Paris : Editions Citadelles,
c1990. 629 p. : ill. ; 32 cm. (L'Art et les grandes
civilisations, 0066-7951 . 20) ISBN 2-85088-027-2
1. Art, Modern - 19th century. I. Title: Art du
dix-neuvième siècle. II. Title: Art du 19e siècle.
                  NYPL [3-MAL+ 91-3621]

Art du 19e siècle. L'Art du XIXe siècle . Paris ,
c1990. 629 p. : ISBN 2-85088-027-2
                  NYPL [3-MAL+ 91-3621]

ART, DUTCH.
Herbert, Zbigniew. [Stomme van Kampen.
English.] Still life with a bridle . New York ,
c1991. p. cm. ISBN 0-88001-306-0 : DDC
709/.492/09032 20
N6946 .H4713 1991

**ART, DUTCH - 17TH CENTURY -
EXHIBITIONS.**
Miller, Debra. Art and life in Northern Europe,
1500-1800 . St. Petersburg, Fla. , c1990. 46 p. :
                  NYPL [3-MAX (Gilbert) 91-5565]

**ART, DUTCH AND FLEMISH. see ART,
DUTCH; ART, FLEMISH.**

ART, DUTCH - CATALOGS.
Museum Bredius. Museum Bredius .
['s-Gravenhage] , 1980. 176 p. :
                  NYPL [3-MAVZ (Hague) 81-647]

ART, DUTCH - EXHIBITIONS.
Albert Dürer aux Pays-Bas . Bruxelles , 1977.
xxiii, 211, 144 p., [14] leaves of plates :
N6888.D8 A4 1977
                  NYPL [3-MCK D85 81-320]

Stadscollectie 1988 . Rotterdam : Rotterdam
[1989]. 54 p. : ISBN 90-6918-041-3
                  NYPL [3-MAME 90-10813]

ART, DUTCH - JAPANESE INFLUENCES.
Imitation and inspiration . [Amsterdam] ,
c1989. 179 p. :
                  NYPL [3-MAME+ 90-11986]

**ART, DUTCH - NETHERLANDS -
AMSTERDAM - EXHIBITIONS.**
New art van Amsterdam /. Hempstead, N.Y. ,
c1990. 16 p. : *NYPL [3-MAME 91-7061]*

**ART, DUTCH - PRIVATE COLLECTIONS -
EXHIBITIONS.**
Hollandse en vlaamse kunst uit de 17e eeuw .
[Rotterdam, 1973?] 183 p. :
                  NYPL [3-MAME 90-5901]

ART, EARLY CHRISTIAN - EXHIBITIONS.
Von Constantin zu Karl dem Grossen . Mainz ,
1990. 71 p., [5] leaves of plates : ISBN
3-88467-025-5
N5760 .V57 1990

ART, EARLY CHRISTIAN - SCANDINAVIA.
Kusch, Eugen, 1905- [Alte Kunst in
Skandinavien. English.] Ancient art in
Scandinavia. Nürnberg [1965] 83 p., 176 plates.
DDC 709/.48
N7001 .K813

**ART, ECCLESIASTICAL. see CHRISTIAN
ART AND SYMBOLISM.**

**ART - ECONOMIC AND SOCIAL ASPECTS.
see ART AND SOCIETY.**

ART - ECONOMIC ASPECTS.
Grauwe, Paul de. De Nachtwacht in het
donker . Tielt [1990] 180 p. : ISBN
90-209-1766-8 :
N8600 .G73 1990

Pinho, Diva Benevides. A arte como
investimento . São Paul, SP , 1989. 214 p. :
       ISBN 85-21-30526-5
N8600 .P56 1989

ART, ECUADORIAN - CATALOGS.
100 artistas del Ecuador /. Quito , 1990. 285
p. : DDC 709/.2/2866 B 20
N6985 .A15 1990

ART, ECUADORIAN - ECUADOR - QUITO.
Tesoros de Quito. [Bogotá, Colombia, S.A.] ,
1990. 142 p. : ISBN 958-95232-6-9 DDC
709/.866/13 20
N6687.Q5 T47 1990

Art education . Bunch, Clarence. Detroit , c1978.
xv, 331 p. ; ISBN 0-8103-1272-7 DDC 016.707
Z5818.A8 B85 N85 *NYPL [3-MAC 91-7862]*

Art education . Levi, Albert William, 1911-
Urbana , c1991. p. cm. ISBN 0-252-01813-3 (cl)
       DDC 707/.073 20
N105 .L48 1991

**ART - EDUCATION. see ART - STUDY AND
TEACHING.**

ART - EGYPT - CATALOGS.
Grimm, Günter. Kunst der Ptolemäer- und
Römerzeit im Ägyptischen Museum Kairo /.
Mainz [1975] 34 p, 118 p., [6] leaves of
plates :
N5888.A1 G74   *NYPL [3-MAH 90-5474]*

ART, EGYPTIAN - EXHIBITIONS.
Beyond the pyramids . Atlanta, Ga. , c1990. 95
p. :   *NYPL [3-MAE 91-4240]*

Il Senso dell'arte nell'antico Egitto. Milano ,
c1990. 263 p. : ISBN 88-435-3157-3 DDC
709/.32/0744541 20
N5350 .S45 1990   *NYPL [3-MAE 91-5036]*

5000 Jahre Aegyptische Kunst . Zürich [1961]
141 p., [73] p. of plates (1 folded) :
                  NYPL [3-MAE 90-7095]

ART, EGYPTIAN - INFLUENCE.
Crowley, Janice L. The Aegean and the east .
Jonsered , 1989. xii, 507 p. : ISBN
91-86098-55-1 *NYPL [3-MAE 90-11126]*

ART, EGYPTIAN - NEW YORK (N.Y.)
Hayes, William Christopher, 1903-1963. The
scepter of Egypt . New York , 1990. 2 v. :
       ISBN 0-87099-572-2 (v. 1)
                  NYPL [MAE 90-12062]

ART, EGYPTIAN - THEMES, MOTIVES.
Davis, Whitney. Masking the blow . Berkeley ,
1992. p. cm. ISBN 0-520-07488-2 DDC 709/.32
20
N5310.5.E3 D38 1992

L'Art en Belgique : Flandre et Wallonie au XXe
siècle : un point de vue : Musée d'art moderne

de la ville de Paris, 13 décembre 1990-10 mars
1991. Bruxelles : Editions Lebeer-Hossmann en
coédition avec Paris-Musées et la Société des
amis du M.A.M. de la ville de Paris, c1990.
527 p. : ill. ; 27 cm. ISBN 2-87284-008-7
(Lebeer-Hossmann)
1. Art, Belgian - Exhibitions. 2. Art, Modern - 20th
century - Belgium - Exhibitions. I. Musée d'art moderne
de la ville de Paris. *NYPL [3-MAME 91-4589]*

ART - ENGLAND - EAST ANGLIA.
Collins, Ian. A broad canvas . Norwich , c1990.
144 p. : ISBN 1-87033-706-9
                  NYPL [3-MAMR 90-11517]

ART - ENGLAND - LONDON.
Ingamells, John. The Wallace Collection /.
London , 1990. 132 p. : ISBN 1-87024-843-0
                  NYPL [3-MAVZ (London) 91-6835]

ART - ENGLAND - LONDON - CATALOGS.
Courtauld Institute Galleries. The Courtauld
Institute Galleries, University of London /.
London , 1990. 128 p. : ISBN 1-87024-839-2
                  NYPL [3-MAVZ (London) 90-12082]

Smith, Lawrence. Japanese art . Bloomsbury ,
c1990. 256 p. : ISBN 0-7141-1446-4 : DDC
709/.52/074 19
N7350   *NYPL [3-MAG 90-11503]*

**ART - ENGLAND - MANCHESTER -
CATALOGS.**
Whitworth Art Gallery. The Whitworth Art
Gallery . Manchester [England] , 1989. v, 152
p. : ISBN 0-09-032612-6
                  NYPL [3-MAVZ (Manchester) 90-11602]

**ART - ENGLAND - NOTTINGHAM -
CATALOGS.**
Nottingham Castle Museum. Nottingham Castle
Museum and Art Gallery . [Nottingham]
[1988] 143 p. ; ISBN 0-905634-19-5 DDC
708.2/527 20
N1440 .A66 1988

ART, EROTIC. see EROTIC ART.

**ART, ESTONIAN - ADDRESSES, ESSAYS,
LECTURES.**
Eesti kunsti sidemeid XX sajandi algupoolelt .
Tallinn , 1978. 271 p. :
N6995.E8 E365   *NYPL [3-MAM 81-512]*

Art et pouvoirs à l'Age baroque . Poletto,
Christine, 1959- Paris , c1990. 218 p., [16] p. of
plates : ISBN 2-7384-0495-2
N7862 .P65 1990

**ART, ETRUSCAN - ITALY - VOLTERRA -
EXHIBITIONS.**
Cateni, Gabriele. Die Etrusker--Volterra .
Solingen , 1986. 90 p. :
                  NYPL [3-MAE 90-12646]

ART, ETRUSCAN - THEMES, MOTIVES.
Säflund, Gösta, 1903- Etrusker, vad menade ni
egentligen? . Partille [Sweden] , 1989. 154 p. :
       ISBN 91-86098-88-8
                  NYPL [3-MAH 91-6667]

ART - EUROPE.
Festschrift für Hartmut Biermann /. Weinheim ,
c1990. 400 p. : ISBN 3-527-17712-4
                  NYPL [3-MAS 91-5197]

**ART - EUROPE, NORTHERN -
EXHIBITIONS.**
11 steden, 11 landen . Leeuwarden, The
Netherlands , 1990. xxvii, 263 p. : ISBN
90-900348-9-7 :
N6758 .A113 1990

ART, EUROPEAN.
Ionescu, Adrian-Silvan. Artă și document .
București , 1990. 318 p., [48] p. of plates :
       ISBN 973-330-072-1 :
N8214.5.R6 155 1990

Kunst und Kunstkritik der dreissiger Jahre .
Dresden , c1990. 353 p. : ISBN 3-364-00190-1
N6868 .K7865 1990

Merkel, Kerstin. Salome . Frankfurt am Main ,
New York , c1990. 477 p. : ISBN 3-631-42540-6
N8180 .M47 1990

ART, EUROPEAN - CATALOGS.
Musée Goya (Castres, France) Le Musée
Goya . Castres , 1964. 1 v.(unpaged) :
                  *NYPL [3-MAVZ (Castres, France)
                            90-6864]*

National-Galerie (Germany) Nationalgalerie .
Berlin , c1968. 384 p. :
                  NYPL [3-MAVZ (Berlin) 90-6876]

ART, EUROPEAN - CHINESE INFLUENCES - EXHIBITIONS.
Drömmen om Kina. [Göteborg] , 1984. 55 p. :
NYPL [3-MAM 90-12530]

ART, EUROPEAN - EXHIBITIONS.
Columbus Museum of Art. Impressionism and
European modernism . Columbus, Ohio ,
Seattle , 1991. p. ISBN 0-295-97133-9 : DDC
709/.03/407477157 20
N6447 .C65 1991

Cowling, Elizabeth. On classic ground .
London , 1990. 264 p. : ISBN 1-85437-043-X
(pbk.) DDC 709/.04/107442132 20
N6758 .C68 1990

L'Europa dei razionalisti . Milano , c1989. 383
p. : ISBN 88-435-2847-5
NYPL [3-MAL 91-4900]

Europa oggi . Firenze , Milano , c1988. 253 p. :
ISBN 88-435-2560-3
NYPL [3-MAL 89-1689]

Kunst um 1800 . Magdeburg [1989] 95 p. :
DDC 709/.03/3074431822 20
N6756 .K86 1989

L'œuvre ultime de Cézanne à Dubuffet .
Saint-Paul , c1989. 269 p. : ISBN 2-900923-01-60
DDC 709/.04/007444941 20
N6757 .O43 1989

Marlborough Fine Art London (Ltd.) 19th and
20th century watercolours, drawings and
sculpture /. London, 1964. 20 p. :
NYPL [3-MAL 90-6893]

Monet to Matisse . Jerusalem , c1988. 130, [10]
p. : ISBN 965-278-085-5 (pbk)
NYPL [3-MAL + 89-6103]

Musée Fabre. Exposition des oeuvres
récemment acquises par le Musée Fabre .
[Montpellier , 1965] 40 p., [5] leaves of plates :
NYPL [3-MAVZ (Montpellier) 90-4843]

Sammlung Lenz Schönberg . Stuttgart , c1989.
262 p. : ISBN 3-89322-152-2
NYPL [3-MAX+ (Lenz) 91-2706]

Tsigakou, Fani-Maria. Through romantic eyes .
Alexandria, Va. , 1991. p. cm. ISBN
0-88397-099-6 DDC 758/.9949506 20
N8214.5.G8 T784 1991

50 Jahre Bauhaus . Stuttgart , 1968. 369 p. :
NYPL [3-MAL 90-6848]

ART, EUROPEAN - FRANCE - SEINE-ET-MARNE - EXHIBITIONS.
Trésors sacrés, trésors cachés . Melun [1988]
308 p. : ISBN 2-9503073-0-2
N7949.A3 S458 1988

ART, EUROPEAN - HISTORY AND CRITICISM.
Studien aus dem Berliner Kupferstichkabinett.
Berlin, 1966. 53 p., [20] p. of plates
NC27 .S7 *NYPL [3-MAL 90-6806]*

ART, EUROPEAN - ITALY - FLORENCE.
Civai, Alessandra. Dipinti e sculture in casa
Martelli . Firenze , c1990. 219 p. :
NYPL [3-MAVC+ 91-6773]

ART, EUROPEAN - JAPANESE INFLUENCES - EXHIBITIONS.
Verborgene Impressionen =. [Wien] , c1990.
445 p. : ISBN 3-900688-13-3 (Katalogausgabe)
NYPL [3-MAM 91-3678]

ART, EUROPEAN - THEMES, MOTIVES.
All'ombra del Vesuvio . Napoli , c1990. xxiv,
455 p. :
N8214.5.I8 A35 1990

Rof Carballo, Juan. Los duendes del Prado /.
Madrid [1990?] 376 p. : ISBN 84-239-5300-9
DDC 709/.4/0744641 20
N8217.F28 R64 1990

ART, EUROPEAN - THEMES, MOTIVES - EXHIBITIONS.
Umanesimo, disumanesimo nell'arte europea
1890/1980 . Milano , c1980. 172 p. : DDC
709/.04/00740551 19
N6757 .U42 1980 *NYPL [3-MAL 90-5471]*

ART - EXAMINATIONS, QUESTIONS, ETC.
Naar het leven? . [Zoetermeer] , 's-Gravenhage
[1990] 66 p. : ISBN 90-346-2214-2
N7432.5.R4 N33 1990

ART EXHIBITION AUDIENCES - PSYCHOLOGY.
L'Exposition imaginaire . 's-Gravenhage , 1989.

391 p. : ISBN 90-12-06105-9 :
N4396 .E96 1989 *NYPL [3-MAV 91-5887]*

ART - EXHIBITIONS.
Helfand, William H. The picture of health .
Philadelphia , c1991. p. cm. ISBN 0-8122-7962-X
(University of Pennsylvania Press) : DDC
769/.4961 20
N8223 .H44 1991

L'Exposition imaginaire . 's-Gravenhage , 1989.
391 p. : ISBN 90-12-06105-9 :
N4396 .E96 1989 *NYPL [3-MAV 91-5887]*

Museo nazionale di Firenze. Acquisti e
donazioni del Museo nazionale del Bargello,
1970-1987 /. Firenze , c1988. xv, 158 p. :
DDC 708.5/51 19
N2555 .A515 1988
NYPL [3-MAVZ (Florence) 90-11120]

Národní galerie V Praze. Sbírka Bohuslava
Duška . [Prague] [1990?] 131 p. :
N5280.C952 D876 1990

National Archives of Canada. A place in
history . Ottawa, Ont. , c1991. ix, 300 p. :
ISBN 0-660-13740-2 (alk. paper) DDC
760/.0449971 20
N6540 .N36 1991

National Gallery of Art (U. S.) Art for the
nation . Washington , c1991. xi, 528 p. : ISBN
0-89468-158-3 DDC 708.153 20
N5963.W18 N38 1991

Pan-American Exposition (1901 : Buffalo, N.Y.)
Catalogue of the exhibition of fine arts /.
Brewster, NY (Drawer 9, Brewster 10509)
[1990?] 92 p. ; DDC 707/.4/74797 20
N4485 .A66 1901

Promised gifts. Jerusalem [c1985] 1 case :
ISBN 965-278-035-9 (unb.) DDC
707/.4/0956944 19
N5085.J45 P76 1985 *NYPL [3-MAL 87-983]*

Sotheby Parke Bernet Inc. The Benjamin
Sonnenberg collection . New York , 1979. 2 v. :
NYPL [3-MAX (Sonnenberg) 90-5888]

Swann, Caroline. Paintings, drawings,
sculptures, from the collection of Caroline &
Erwin Swann. [Portland, 1964] 62 p.
N6490 .P65
NYPL [3-MAX (Swann) 85-795]

Umjetnine iz donacije dr Vinka Perčića =.
Zagreb , c1989. 144 p. :
N5280.Y8 U46 1989

ART, EXOTIC. see EXOTICISM IN ART.

ART - EXPERTISING.
Gilardoni, Arturo. X-rays in art . Mandello
Lario, Italy , 1977. 231 p. :
NYPL [3-MAS+ 90-7036]

ART, FANG (WEST AFRICAN PEOPLE) - EQUATORIAL GUINEA.
Perrois, Louis. The art of Equatorial Guinea .
New York , 1990. 177 p. : ISBN 0-8478-1275-8
DDC 730/.089/96396 20
N7399.E68 P47 1990
NYPL [3-MADF+ 91-5613]

ART, FAR EASTERN - CATALOGS.
Villa I Tatti (Florence, Italy) The Bernard
Berenson collection of oriental art at Villa I
Tatti /. New York , c1991. p. cm. ISBN
1-555-95060-4 (alk. paper) : DDC
709/.5/0744551 20
N7336 .V46 1991

ART, FAR EASTERN - HANDBOOKS, MANUALS, ETC.
Menzies, Jackie. Asian collection . Sydney,
Australia , 1990. 96 p. : ISBN 0-7305-7455-5
DDC 709/.5/0749441 20
N7336 .M46 1990

ART FESTIVALS - NORWAY.
Stenersen, Sigurd. Kultur, samhørighet .
[Harstad , 1989] 119 p. :
NX430.N8 S74 1989

ART - FINLAND - HELSINKI - GUIDE-BOOKS.
Sakari, Marja. Helsinki kuvataidekaupunkina .
Helsinki , 1991. 104 p. : ISBN 951-772-148-X
N7255.F52 H47 1991

ART, FINNISH.
Valkonen, Markku, 1946- Kultakausi /.
Porvoo , c1989. 309 p. : ISBN 951-0-15859-3 :
N7255.F5 V35 1989

ART, FINNISH - EXHIBITIONS.
Artistes finlandais en Bretagne, 1880-1890 .
Pont-Aven [1990?] 64 p. :
NYPL [3-MAM+ 90-13360]

Fabula 1 /. Helsinki [1989] 61 p. : ISBN
951-861-843-7
N7255.F5 F28 1989

ART, FLEMISH - BELGIUM - ANTWERP - EXHIBITIONS.
Antwerp (Belgium). Stedelijk Prentenkabinet.
Rondom Rubens . Antwerpen , 1991. 229 p. :
N6971.A6 A73 1991

ART, FLEMISH - CATALOGS.
Museum Bredius. Museum Bredius .
['s-Gravenhage] , 1980. 176 p. :
NYPL [3-MAVZ (Hague) 81-647]

ART, FLEMISH - EXHIBITIONS.
Albert Dürer aux Pays-Bas . Bruxelles , 1977.
xxiii, 211, 144 p., [14] leaves of plates :
N6888.D8 A4 1977
NYPL [3-MCK D85 81-320]

Rubens, Pietro Paolo Rubens (1577-1640) /.
Roma , 1990. 319 p. : ISBN 88-7813-269-1
NYPL [3-MCH+ R8 90-12995]

ART, FLEMISH - PRIVATE COLLECTIONS - EXHIBITIONS.
Hollandse en vlaamse kunst uit de 17e eeuw .
[Rotterdam, 1973?] 183 p. :
NYPL [3-MAME 90-5901]

ART, FOLK. see FOLK ART.

Art for everyday . Conway, Patricia. New York,
N.Y. , 1990. 264 p. : ISBN 0-517-57381-4 DDC
745/.0973/0904 20
NK808 .C64 1990 *NYPL [3-MLO 90-12856]*

Art for the nation . National Gallery of Art (U.
S.) Washington , c1991. xi, 528 p. : ISBN
0-89468-158-3 DDC 708.153 20
N5963.W18 N38 1991

ART - FORGERIES - EXHIBITIONS.
Fake? . London , 1990. 312 p. : ISBN
0-7141-1703-X
N8790 .F3 1990b

ART - FRANCE - CASTRES - CATALOGS.
Musée Goya (Castres, France) Le Musée
Goya . Castres , 1964. 1 v.(unpaged) :
NYPL [3-MAVZ (Castres, France) 90-6864]

ART - FRANCE - LES SABLES D'OLONNE - CATALOGS.
Abbaye Sainte-Croix (Les Sables-d'Olonne,
France). Musée. La collection d'art moderne et
contemporain . Les Sables d'Olonne , c1990.
253 p. : ISBN 2-901432-67-0 DDC
709/.44/0744461 20
N6848 .A58 1990

ART - FRANCE - MARSEILLES - CATALOGS.
Musée Borély. Donation Maurice et Pauline
Feuillet de Borsat /. Marseille, 1969. 1 v.
(unpaged)
NC27.F7 M355
NYPL [3-MAVZ (Marseilles) 91-291]

ART - FRANCE - PARIS.
Musée d'art moderne de la ville de Paris.
Acquisitions 1955-1965. [Paris , 1965?] 1 v.
(unpaged) :
NYPL [3-MAVZ+ (Paris) 91-229]

ART - FRANCE - PARIS - CATALOGS.
Musée d'Orsay. Guide to the Musée d'Orsay /.
Paris , 1987. 280 p. : ISBN 2-7118-2123-4
NYPL [3-MAVZ (Paris) 90-13020]

Musée du Louvre. [Louvre, 7 visages d'un
musée. English.] The Louvre, 7 faces of a
museum /. Paris , c1987-1989. 350 p. : ISBN
2-7119-2095-5 DDC 708.4/361 20
N2030 .M8613 1987

ART - FRANCE - PARIS - EXHIBITIONS.
La Collection A.P. de Mirimonde . Paris ,
1987. 137 p. : ISBN 2-7118-2151-X
NYPL [3-MAX (Mirimonde) 90-10806]

ART - FRANCE - PYRÉNÉES-ATLANTIQUES - CATALOGS.
Pyrénées-Atlantiques . Paris , 1989. 719 p. :
ISBN 2-11-080952-3 : DDC 709/.44/79 20
N6849.P92 P97 1989

ART - FRANCE - SIERCK-LES-BAINS (CANTON)
Canton de Sierck-les-Bains, Moselle /. [Metz] ,
c1987. 72 p. : ISBN 2-9501474-1-0 DDC

709/.44/3825 20
N6849.S53 C35 1987

ART, FRENCH.

Bernier, Rosamond. Matisse, Picasso, Miró .
New York , 1991. 69 p. :　ISBN 0-394-58670-0
　　DDC 709/.2/244 B 20
N6848 .B38 1991

Clair, Jean. Brève défense de l'art français .
[Caen] , c1989. 69 p. :　ISBN 2-905657-46-4
　　DDC 709/.44/09045 20
N6848 .C56 1989

Clayson, Hollis, 1949- Painted love . New
Haven , c1991. p. cm.　ISBN 0-300-04730-4
　　DDC 760/.0449306742/094436109034 20
N6847.5.I4 C58 1991

Driskel, Michael Paul. Representing belief .
University Park , c1991. p. cm.　ISBN
　0-271-00747-8　DDC 709/.44/09034 20
N6847 .D75 1991

Frèches-Thory, Claire. Les nabis /. Paris ,
c1990. 319 p. :　ISBN 2-08-010941-3　DDC
　709/.44/36109034 20
N6847.5.N3 F735 1990

ART, FRENCH - FRANCE - PARIS - EXHIBITIONS.

Phillips Collection. Duncan Phillips collects .
Washington, D.C. , c1991. p. cm.　ISBN
　0-943044-16-2 :　DDC 759.4/361/09041074753
　20
N6850 .P45 1991

ART, FRENCH - CATALOGS.

Abbaye Sainte-Croix (Les Sables-d'Olonne,
France). Musée. La collection d'art moderne et
contemporain . Les Sables d'Olonne , c1990.
253 p. :　ISBN 2-901432-67-0　DDC
　709/.44/0744461 20
N6848 .A58 1990

Avisseau, Jean Paul. Illustration du vieux
Bordeaux /. Avignon , c1990. 1 v. (unpaged) :
　ISBN 2-7006-0141-6
N8214.5.F8 A95 1990

ART, FRENCH - EXHIBITIONS.

Conisbee, Philip. Monet to Matisse . Los
Angeles, Calif. , c1991. 144 p. :　ISBN
　0-87587-159-3　DDC 709/.44/09034 20
N6847 .C6 1991

Diderot, Denis, 1713-1784. [Salons. Russian.]
Salony . Moskva , 1989. 2 v. :
N6846 .D4617 1989

French masters, Rococo to Romanticism . [Los
Angeles] , 1961. 72 p. :
　　　NYPL　[3-MAMI+ 90-6906]

Impressionism and post impressionism .
Portland, Me. , c1991. p. cm.　DDC
　709/.03/4407474191 20
N6847.5.I4 I43 1991

Individualités . Milano , c1984. 107 p. :
　　　NYPL　[3-MAMI 90-12643]

Kosinski, Dorothy M. Picasso, Braque, Gris,
Léger . Houston, Tex. , c1990. 67 p. :　ISBN
　0-89090-049-3 (pbk.)　DDC 759.4/074/7641411
　20
N6848.5.C82 K67 1990
　　　NYPL　[3-MCN 91-6709]

Salmon, Marie José. D'Oudry à Le Sidaner .
Beauvais , 1990. 171 p. :　ISBN 2-901290-06-X
N8214.5.F8 S25 1990

Le Style troubadour . Bourg-en-Bresse , 1971.
107 p. , 18 p. of plates :
　　　NYPL　[3-MAMI 90-7037]

Syndram, Dirk. Ruinenromantik und
Antikensehnsucht /. [Berlin] , c1986. 32 p. :
　ISBN 3-88609-199-6　DDC
　760/.0444/094074031554 19
N8237.8.R8 S96 1986
　　　NYPL　[3-MAMZ 90-9452]

Tre tendenze dell'arte francese contemporanea.
[Milano, 197-] 47 p. (chiefly illus.)
　　　NYPL　[3-MAMI 90-7183]

ART, FRENCH - FRANCE - ARLANC (CANTON)

Canton et dentelles d'Arlanc, Puy-de-Dôme /.
Clermont-Ferrand , c1989. 56 p. :　ISBN
　2-905554-03-7 :　DDC 709/.44/591 20
N6849.A69 C36 1989

ART, FRENCH - FRANCE - AUVERS-SUR-OISE - EXHIBITIONS.

Van Gogh et les peintres d'Auvers-sur-Oise .
[Paris] , 1954. xl, 100 p., xxxii p. of plates :
N6847.5.I4 V36 1954

ART, FRENCH - FRANCE - CATTENOM (CANTON)

Canton de Cattenom . [Metz] , c1988. 79 p. :
　ISBN 2-9501474-3-7　DDC 709/.44/3825 20
N6849.C36 C36 1988

ART, FRENCH - FRANCE - FALAISE.

Falaise, Calvados /. [Caen, France] [1990] 64
p. :　ISBN 2-908621-01-0 :　DDC 709/.44/22 20
N6851.F35 F35 1990

ART, FRENCH - FRANCE - LAVAL (MAYENNE)

Eraud, Dominique. Laval, Mayenne /. [Nantes]
[1990] 138 p. :　ISBN 2-906344-24-9　DDC
　709/.44/16 20
N6851.L36 E7 1990

ART, FRENCH - FRANCE - LONGUYON (CANTON)

Canton de Longuyon . [Metz] , c1988. 80 p. :
　ISBN 2-9501474-4-5　DDC 709/.44/3823 20
N6849.L74 C36 1988

ART, FRENCH - FRANCE - MARVILLE.

Marville . [Metz] , c1988. 80 p. :　ISBN
　2-9501474-5-3　DDC 709/.44/381 20
N6851.M34 M37 1988

ART, FRENCH - FRANCE - MONTREUIL-BELLAY (CANTON)

Manase, Viviane. Canton de Montreuil-Bellay /.
[Nantes] [1990] 100 p. :　ISBN 2-906344-00-00 :
　DDC 709/.44/18 20
N6849.M66 M35 1990

ART, FRENCH - FRANCE - PARIS.

Friedrich, Otto, 1929- Olympia . New York,
NY , c1992. p. cm.　ISBN 0-06-016318-6 (cloth) :
　DDC 701/.03 20
N6847 .F75 1992

ART, FRENCH - FRANCE - PYRÉNÉES-ATLANTIQUES - CATALOGS.

Pyrénées-Atlantiques . Paris , 1989. 719 p. :
　ISBN 2-11-080952-3 :　DDC 709/.44/79 20
N6849.P92 P97 1989

ART, FRENCH - FRANCE - SAINT-ETIENNE - EXHIBITIONS.

Korrespondenzen . Berlin , Saint-Etienne ,
c1989. 82 p. :
N6885 .K67 1989

ART, FRENCH - FRANCE - SEINE-ET-MARNE - EXHIBITIONS.

Trésors sacrés, trésors cachés . Melun [1988]
308 p. :　ISBN 2-9503073-0-2
N7949.A3 S458 1988

ART, FRENCH - FRANCE - SEURRE (CANTON)

Canton de Seurre . [Dijon] , c1988. 59 p. :
　ISBN 2-904727-02-7; 2-904727-02-07　DDC
　709/.44/42 20
N6849.S48 C36 1988

ART, FRENCH - FRANCE - SIERCK-LES-BAINS (CANTON)

Canton de Sierck-les-Bains, Moselle /. [Metz] ,
c1987. 72 p. :　ISBN 2-9501474-1-0　DDC
　709/.44/3825 20
N6849.S53 C35 1987

ART, FRENCH - FRANCE - TOULOUSE - EXHIBITIONS.

Toulouse et le néo-classicisme . Toulouse ,
1989. 181 p. :　　*NYPL　[3-MAMI+ 91-6672]*

ART, FRISIAN.

Fries Museum (Leeuwarden, Netherlands) Fries
Museum /. Haarlem , c1978. 110 p. :　ISBN
90-70024-07-1　　　　　　　*NYPL　[3-MAVZ
　(Leeuwarden, Netherlands) 90-5650]*

Art from Köln. [England] Liverpool : The
Gallery, 1989. 68 p. : ill. (some col.) ; 31 cm.
Catalog of an exhibition held at the Tate Gallery 20
May 1989 - 28 August 1989.　ISBN 1-85437-020-0
(pbk.)
　*1. Art, German - Exhibitions. 2. Art, Modern - 20th
century - Germany, West - Cologne - Exhibitions. I.
Tate Gallery Liverpool.*
　　　NYPL　[3-MAMG+ 90-4504]

Art from the roof of the world . Till, Barry, 1951-
Victoria , c1989. 159 p. :　ISBN 0-88885-133-2
DDC 709/.51/507471128 20
N8193.3.T36 C67 1989
　　　NYPL　[3-MAF 91-6942]

Art from the trenches . Cornebise, Alfred E.

College Station , c1991. p. cm.　ISBN
　0-89096-349-5 (cloth)　DDC 758/.99404/0973 20
N6512 .C598 1991

Art fun. Sur les murs. L'Art fun, ou, L'enfance de
l'art. Ateliers en liberté. Jouy-en-Josas [France]
[1986] 77 p. :　ISBN 2-86925-004-5
N6488.F8 J687 1986
　　　NYPL　[3-MAL+ 90-10669]

ART GALLERIES. see ART MUSEUMS.

**Art Galleries and Museums Association of New
Zealand.** No sort of iron; culture of Cook's
Polynesians. A Cook bicentenary exhibition
organized by the Art Galleries and Museums'
Association of New Zealand, 9 October 1969 to
30 June 1970. Souvenir handbook, edited by
Roger Duff. [Christchurch, 1969] 91 p. illus.
(part col.), col. map, ports. 27 cm. Bibliography:
p. 89-91.　DDC 709.01/1
　*1. Art, Primitive - Exhibitions. 2. Art, Primitive -
Polynesia. I. Duff, Roger, ed. II. Title.*
N7410 .A73

ART GALLERIES, COMMERCIAL - AUSTRALIA - DIRECTORIES.

Australian art museums and public galleries
directory. Melbourne, Vic., Clayton, Vic. ,
1990. v, 49 p. ;　ISBN 0-9595532-4-X　DDC
　708/.0025/94 20
N3910 .A93 1990

Germaine, Max, 1914- Artists & galleries of
Australia /. Roseville, NSW, Australia , c1990.
2 v. (xii, 832 p.) :　ISBN 976-8097-02-7
　　　NYPL　[MAO+ 91-2667]

ART GALLERIES, COMMERCIAL - DIRECTORIES.

Directory of galleries for the fine artist /.
Renaissance, CA , c1990. 359 p. ;　ISBN
　0-940899-08-6　　*NYPL　[MA 90-11525]*

ART GALLERIES, COMMERCIAL - EXHIBITIONS.

Perl, Jed. Gallery going . San Diego , c1991.
xxiv, 431 p., [16] p. of plates :　ISBN
　0-15-134260-1 :　DDC 709/.04/0074 20
N6447 .P38 1991　*NYPL　[3-MAV 91-7445]*

ART GALLERIES, COMMERCIAL - FINLAND - HELSINKI - DIRECTORIES.

Sakari, Marja. Helsinki kuvataidekaupunkina .
Helsinki , 1991. 104 p. :　ISBN 951-772-148-X
N7255.F52 H47 1991

ART GALLERIES, COMMERCIAL - FRANCE - PROVENCE - DIRECTORIES.

Guid'arts . Nice [1989] 174 p. :　ISBN
　2-87720-040-X ;
N6485.3 .G85 1989

ART GALLERIES, COMMERCIAL - NEW YORK (N.Y.) - GUIDE-BOOKS.

Krantz, Les. The New York art review .
Chicago, IL , c1988. 1343 p. :　ISBN
　0-913765-09-0 :　DDC 702/.5/7471 19
N600 .K7 1988　*NYPL　[MAVZ (New York,
　　　　　　　　　　N.Y.) 91-4085]*

ART GALLERIES, COMMERCIAL - SPAIN.

Catálogo nacional de arte contemporáneo.
Barcelona , c1989. 4 v. :　ISBN 84-87433-00-6
(obra completa)
N7108 .C29 1989

Art Gallery of Greater Victoria.
Scott, Susan, 1949- Susan Scott . Surrey, B.C. ,
c1984. 39 p. :　ISBN 0-920181-08-2 (pbk.)
N6549.S37 A4 1984
　　　NYPL　[3-MCZ S4192 90-12753]

Till, Barry, 1951- Art from the roof of the
world . Victoria , c1989. 159 p. :　ISBN
　0-88885-133-2　DDC 709/.51/507471128 20
N8193.3.T36 C67 1989
　　　NYPL　[3-MAF 91-6942]

**Art Gallery of New South handbook, Asian
collection.** Menzies, Jackie. Asian collection .
Sydney, Australia , 1990. 96 p. :　ISBN
　0-7305-7455-5　DDC 709/.5/0749441 20
N7336 .M46 1990

Art Gallery of New South Wales.
Abstraction . Sydney , 1990. 48 p. :　ISBN
　0-7305-7696-5　*NYPL　[3-MAM 91-3723]*

Connor, Kevin, 1932- Kevin Connor . [Sydney]
[1989] 46 p. ;　ISBN 0-7305-6366-9
　　　NYPL　[3-MCZ C744 90-12729]

Donald Friend's Bali . Sydney , 1990. 65 p. :

ISBN 0-7305-6574-2
MLCS 90/15244 (N)
       NYPL [3-MAF 91-6722]

Edwards, Deborah. Stampede of the lower gods . Sydney [1989] vi, 66 p. : ISBN 0-7305-6555-6   DDC 709/.94/0749441 20
N7760 .E38 1989

Friend, Donald. Donald Friend, 1915-1989 . Sydney , 1990. 160 p. : ISBN 0-7305-6929-2 (pbk.)   ***NYPL [3-MCZ+ F87 90-11801]***

Johnson, Michael, 1938- Michael Johnson . [Sydney] [1989?] [36] leaves :
       NYPL [3-MCZ+ J675 89-23194]

Kolenberg, Hendrik. Roger Kemp, the complete etchings /. [Sydney] , 1991. 112 p. : ISBN 0-7305-7966-2
       NYPL [MDG (kemp) 91-7000]

Menzies, Jackie. Asian collection . Sydney, Australia , 1990. 96 p. : ISBN 0-7305-7455-5 DDC 709/.5/0749441 20
N7336 .M46 1990

Mindscapes . [Sydney] [1989?] 32 p. : ISBN 0-7305-6190-9
       NYPL [3-MCY+ 89-23193]

Pearce, Barry. Donald Friend, 1915-1989 . [Sydney, N.S.W.] , 1990. 160 p. : ISBN 0-7305-6929-2 (pbk.)   DDC 709/.2 20
N7405.F7 A4 1990

Williams, John (John Frank) John Williams, photographs /. Sydney, N.S.W. , 1989. 112 p. ; ISBN 0-7305-6188-7
       NYPL [MFX (Williams) 91-2387]

ART GALLERY OF NEW SOUTH WALES.
Menzies, Jackie. Asian collection . Sydney, Australia , 1990. 96 p. : ISBN 0-7305-7455-5 DDC 709/.5/0749441 20
N7336 .M46 1990

Art Gallery of Ontario. Extension Dept.
Humorist Walter Trier . [Toronto] [c1980] 48 p. : ISBN 0-919876-56-0 (pbk.)
NC1509.T74 A4 1980
       NYPL [3-MEM (Trier) 81-644]

The work of art : six artists / organized and circulated by the Art Gallery of Ontario Extension Services, 1978-1979 ; exhibition produced by Reissa Schrager. [Toronto] : Art Gallery of Ontario, [c1978] 43 p. : ill. (some col.) ; 26 cm. ISBN 0-919876-42-0
1. Art, Canadian - Ontario - Exhibitions. 2. Artists' preparatory studies - Ontario - Exhibitions. 3. Artists - Ontario - Psychology - Exhibitions. I. Schrager, Reissa. II. Title.
N6546.O5 A77 1978
       NYPL [3-MAM 80-2200]

Art Gallery of South Australia.
Eagle, Mary, 1944- 1990 Adelaide Biennial of Australian art /. Adelaide , 1990. 113 p. : ISBN 0-7308-0773-8
       NYPL [3-MAM+ 91-5044]

Hylton, Jane. Adelaide angries . Adelaide , 1989. 80 p. : ISBN 0-7308-0772-X
       NYPL [3-MCY+ 90-13322]

Art Gallery of Vassar College. see Vassar College. Art Gallery.

Art Gallery of Windsor.
Fraser, Ted, 1946- Caven Atkins, the Winnipeg years /. Windsor, Canada , c1987. [40] p. : ISBN 0-919837-10-7
MLCM 90/03385 (N)
       NYPL [3-MCZ A865 90-8692]

M'Closkey, Kathy, 1943- Fibre . Windsor, Ont. , c1988. [56] p. : ISBN 0-919837-16-6 DDC 746.9/7 19   ***NYPL [3-MOT 90-8017]***

ART, GEORGIAN (GEORGIAN S.S.R.)
Dézélus, Robert. L'art de Transcaucasie /. Vienne, Autriche , c1989. 368 p. :
N7292.6 .D49 1989

ART, GERMAN.
Adam, Peter. Art of the Third Reich /. New York , 1992. p. cm. ISBN 0-8109-1912-5 (cloth) DDC 709/.43/09043 20
N6868.5.N37 A34 1992

Arnaldo, Javier. Estilo y naturaleza . Madrid , c1990. 284 p. : ISBN 84-7774-536-6
N6867.5.R6 A76 1990

Bushart, Magdalena. Der Geist der Gotik und die expressionistische Kunst . München , c1990.

255 p. : ISBN 3-88960-018-2 :
N6848.5.E9 B8 1990

Kunst auf Befehl? . München , c1990. 275 p. : ISBN 3-7814-0285-1   DDC 701/.03 20
N6868.5.N37 K85 1990

Kunst und Kunstkritik der dreissiger Jahre . Dresden , c1990. 353 p. : ISBN 3-364-00190-1
N6868 .K7865 1990

Meurer, Thomas. Die Eisenbahn in der deutschen Kunst . Witterschlick/Bonn , 1989. 172, [76] p. : ISBN 3-925267-28-X
N6867 .M48 1989

Oelschlegel, F. Wandel einer Sicht . Rockville, MD , 1990. 233 p. : ISBN 0-930329-38-4
N6867 .O27 1990

ART, GERMAN - 20TH CENTURY - EXHIBITIONS.
La Razón revisada = Reason revised . Madrid , c1988. 135 p. : ISBN 84-7664-183-4
       NYPL [3-MAMG 91-7022]

ART, GERMAN - BERLIN - EXHIBITIONS.
Bilder aus der grossen Stadt . Berlin-Dahlem , 1977. [96] p. :
N6885 .B55   ***NYPL [3-MAMG 81-424]***

ART, GERMAN - BERLIN (GERMANY) - EXHIBITIONS.
Ambiente Berlin . [Venezia] , c1990. 201 p. : ISBN 88-20-80360-7   DDC 709/.431/550744531 20
N6885 .A46 1990

Arte em Berlim--1900 até hoje . Lisboa , 1989. 319 p. :   DDC 709/.431/55074469425 20
N6885 .A76 1989

Das Bild der Stadt Berlin von 1945 bis zur Gegenwart . Berlin [1987] 59 p. :
       NYPL [3-MAMY 90-13015]

10X . [Berlin] [1984] 1 portfolio (10 pieces) :
       NYPL [3-MAMG+ 88-4811]

ART, GERMAN - CATALOGS.
National-Galerie (Germany) Nationalgalerie . Berlin c1968. 384 p. :
       NYPL [3-MAVZ (Berlin) 90-6876]

Staatliche Galerie Moritzburg. Staatliche Galerie Moritzburg, Halle. [Halle] 1961. 223 p. :
       NYPL [3-MAVZ (Halle) 91-563]

Von Caspar David Friedrich bis Adolph Menzel . München , c1990. 283 p. : ISBN 3-7913-1047-X   DDC 759.3/074/43613 20
N6867.5.R6 V6 1990

ART, GERMAN - EXHIBITIONS.
Adolf Hölzel von seinen Schülern . Stuttgart , 1978. 61 p. :
N6868 .A38   ***NYPL [3-MCK H693 81-755]***

Art from Köln. Liverpool , 1989. 68 p. : ISBN 1-85437-020-0 (pbk.)
       NYPL [3-MAMG+ 90-4504]

Art in Germany 1909-1936 . Munich , c1990. 271 p. : ISBN 0-944110-02-9 (pbk.) :
N6868 .F74 1990
       NYPL [3-MAMG+ 91-4806]

Asmus Jakob Carstens und Joseph Anton Koch, zwei Zeitgenossen der Französischen Revolution . Berlin [1989] 160 p. :
NC249 .A835 1989

Berlinische Galerie. Berliner Kunststücke /. Stuttgart [1990] 459 p. : ISBN 3-89322-176-X
N6868 .B44 1990

Blanchette, Manon, 1952- Blickpunkte . Montréal, Québec , c1989. 2 v. : ISBN 2-551-12161-2
N6868.5.C63 B55 1989

Degenerate art . Los Angeles, Calif. , New York , c1991. p. cm. ISBN 0-87587-158-5   DDC 709/.43/07477311 20
N6868 .D3388 1991b

Degenerate art . Los Angeles, Calif. , New York , c1991. 423 p. : ISBN 0-8109-3653-4 DDC 709/.43/07477311 20
N6868 .D3388 1991

Ganz tief unten] [Germany , 1989?] 1 v. (unpaged) :
N6868 .G314 1989

Künstlergilde. Breslauer Akademieschüler heute . Regensburg , 1979. [40] p. :
N6868 .K8 1979   ***NYPL [3-MAMG 81-1003]***

Landesmuseum für Kunst und Kulturgeschichte,

Münster. Nykysaksalaista maalaustaidetta. [Münster, 1964?] 158, [8] p.
N6868 .L3

Max und die Kunst . [Unterwellenborn] [1989] 94 p. :
N6868 .M39 1989

Meisterwerke des Expressionismus . Stuttgart , c1990. 251 p. : ISBN 3-7757-0302-0
IN PROCESS (ONLINE)
       NYPL [3-MAMG+ 91-7962]

Schlemmer, Baumeister, Krause . Wuppertal , 1979. [99] p. :
N6868 .S28   ***NYPL [3-MAMG 81-310]***

Sechzehn Künstler . Stuttgart , 1978. 101 p. :
MLCM 85/5391 (N)
       NYPL [3-MAMG+ 90-6860]

Städtisches Museum Leverkusen, Schloss Morsbroich. Graphische Sammlung . Von Arakawa bis Winzer . Leverkusen [1987?] 137 p. : ISBN 3-925520-04-X
N6868 .S765 1987

ART, GERMAN - GERMANY.
Der Kunsthund knurrt . Düsseldorf , c1983. 1 v. (unpaged) :
N6868 .K7876 1983

ART, GERMAN - GERMANY - BERLIN.
Werkstattbesuche bei Künstlern in Berlin-Wedding /. Berlin , c1989. 2 v. : ISBN 3-9801875-9-4 :
N6885 .W46 1989

ART, GERMAN - GERMANY - BERLIN - EXHIBITIONS.
Korrespondenzen . Berlin , Saint-Etienne , c1989. 82 p. :
N6885 .K67 1989

ART, GERMAN - GERMANY - DARMSTADT - EXHIBITIONS.
Quintessenz . [Darmstadt] [1989] 76 p. :
N668 .Q55 1989

ART, GERMAN - GERMANY - DRESDEN - EXHIBITIONS.
Königliches Dresden . München , c1990. 216 p. : ISBN 3-7913-1113-1
       NYPL [3-MAMG+ 91-4691]

ART, GERMAN - GERMANY, EAST.
Durch den Tag laufen . Berlin , 1989. 287 p. : ISBN 3-7303-0434-8
PT3732 .D87 1989
       NYPL [3-MAMG 90-10453]

Kunst in der DDR /. Köln , c1990. 470 p. : ISBN 3-462-02068-4   DDC 709/.431/09045 20
N6889 .K862 1990

ART, GERMAN - GERMANY (EAST) - COTTBUS - EXHIBITIONS.
Kunst in Cottbus . [Cottbus] [Cottbus] [1989] [140] p. :   ***NYPL [3-MAMG 91-6140]***

ART, GERMAN - GERMANY (EAST) - EXHIBITIONS.
América Latina . [Berlin , 1988?] 144 p. :
N6884.5 .A44 1988
       NYPL [3-MAMG 91-5083]

Jugend im Sozialismus . Berlin [1987] 83 p. :
N6889 .J75 1987   ***NYPL [3-MAMZ 91-4201]***

Skulptur, Grafik, Zeichnung aus der Deutschen Demokratischen Republik . Berlin [1984] [44] p. :
MLCM 87/97 (N)
       NYPL [3-MAMG 90-10659]

ART, GERMAN - GERMANY - MAGDEBURG (BEZIRK) - EXHIBITIONS.
Kunstausstellung des VBK-DDR, Bezirk Magdeburg anlässlich des 30. Jahrestages der DDR . Magdeburg [1979?] 96 p. :
MLCS 87/4814 (N)
       NYPL [3-MAMG 91-286]

ART, GERMAN - GERMANY - MITTELFRANKEN.
Die Kunstdenkmäler von Mittelfranken /. München , <1982-. v. <2 > : ISBN 3-486-50505-X (v. 2)
N6873 .K86 1980 vol. 5 N6876.M58

ART, GERMAN - GERMANY - NIEDERBAYERN.
Die Kunstdenkmäler von Niederbayern /. München , 1980- <1-5, 7-8, 10-18, 20-22 > : ISBN 3-486-50479-7 (v. 1)
N6873 .K86 1980 vol. 4 N6876.N54

ART, GERMAN - GERMANY - NÖRDLINGEN REGION.
Die Kunstdenkmäler von Schwaben /.
München , 1981-<1982. <v. 1-2 > : ISBN
3-486-50514-9 (v. 1)
N6873 .K86 1980 vol. 7 N6876.N58

ART, GERMAN - GERMANY - NORTH RHINE-WESTPHALIA - EXHIBITIONS.
Der Expressionismus und Westfalen /. Münster
[1990] 239 p. : ISBN 3-88789-096-5
N6879 .E97 1990

ART, GERMAN - GERMANY - OBERBAYERN.
Bezold, Gustav von. Die Kunstdenkmale des
Regierungsbezirkes Oberbayern /. München ,
1982. 10 v. : ISBN 3-486-50421-5 (v. 1)
N6873 .K86 1980 vol. 1 N6873

ART, GERMAN - GERMANY - OBERPFALZ.
Die Kunstdenkmäler von Oberpfalz &
Regensburg /. München , 1981-<1983. v.
<1-2, 4-11, 14-21 > : ISBN 3-486-50431-2 (v. 1)
N6873 .K86 1980 vol. 2 N6876.O23

ART, GERMAN - GERMANY - SAXONY - EXHIBITIONS.
Gleisberg, Dieter. Kunstschätze aus Sachsen .
Karlsruhe [1991] 399 p. : ISBN 3-7650-8091-8
NYPL [3-MAMG 91-8019]

Der silberne Boden . Stuttgart [Leipzig] ,
c1990. 510 p. : ISBN 3-421-02982-2 (Deutsche
Verlags-Anstalt)
NYPL [3-MAMG 91-5527]

ART, GERMAN - GERMANY - UNTERFRANKEN.
Die Kunstdenkmäler von Unterfranken &
Aschaffenburg /. München , 1981-<1983. v.
<1-2, 4-5, 7-8, 10, 12-18, 21-24 > : ISBN
3-486-50455-X (v. 1)
N6873 .K86 1980 vol. 3 N6882.U54

ART, GERMAN - GERMANY (WEST) - BADEN-WÜRTTEMBERG.
Jacobi, Walter. Bildersturm in der Provinz .
Freiburg , 1988. 64 p. : ISBN 3-89125-272-2
NYPL [3-MAMG 90-12384]

ART, GERMAN - GERMANY (WEST) - DURLACH.
Das Pfinzgaumuseum in Karlsruhe-Durlach .
Karlsruhe , 1976. 80 p. : ISBN 3-7880-9565-2 :
N2307.K65 P34   NYPL [3-MAMG 90-9226]

ART, GERMAN - GERMANY, WEST - EXHIBITIONS.
Banater Künstler in der Bundesrepublik
Deutschland . Berlin , 1988. 60 p. : ISBN
3-922131-57-8
N6868 .B33 1988
NYPL [3-MAMG 91-6298]

Dunkel, Trimborn, Dönselmann . [Emden,
Germany , 1988] 87 p. : ISBN 3-925564-02-0
NYPL [3-MAMG + 89-11596]

Liebe, Dokumente unserer Zeit /. [Darmstadt]
Gütersloh , 1980. 191 p. :
NYPL [3-MAMZ 90-6445]

Papierarbeiten . Bonn [1987] 155 p., [2] p. of
plates : DDC 709/.43/0740355 19
N6868 .P38 1987
NYPL [3-MAMG 91-7051]

Wolfgang Bier, Friedemann Hahn, Thomas
Kaminsky, Christiane Möbus, Wolfgang
Nestler . [Berlin] 1979. 1 case ([206] p. :
DDC 709/.43/0740341 19
N6868 .W64   NYPL [3-MAMG+ 90-7088]

Zeitbilder . Mannheim , c1989. 1 v. (unpaged) :
ISBN 3-926857-08-0
N6868 .Z437 1989

ART, GERMAN - GERMANY (WEST) - FRANCONIA - GUIDE-BOOKS.
Stolz, Georg. Franken. [München] [1989] 371
p. : ISBN 3-422-03012-3 DDC 709/.43/32 20
N6874.F7 S76 1989

ART, GERMAN - GERMANY (WEST) - KARLSRUHE.
Kunst in der Residenz . [Karlsruhe] [1990] 399
p. : ISBN 3-925835-58-X DDC
709/.43/4643074434643 20
N6886.K33 K85 1990

ART, GERMAN - GERMANY (WEST) - KARLSRUHE - EXHIBITIONS.
Kunstsituation und Künstler sein heute .

Karlsruhe , 1988. 342 p. :
N6886.K33 K88 1988
NYPL [3-MAMG 90-10706]

ART, GERMAN - GERMANY (WEST) - KEVELAER - EXHIBITIONS.
Wans, Paul. Land Stil Leben . Kleve , 1988. 7
p., 20 leaves of plates : ISBN 3-922384-08-0
NYPL [3-MCK+ W251 90-10582]

ART, GERMAN - GERMANY, WEST - RHINE VALLEY.
Rheinisches Landesmuseum Bonn .
Braunschweig , 1977. 128 p. :
N2255.R5 R46
NYPL [MAVZ (Bonn) 81-636]

ART, GERMAN - GERMANY (WEST) - STUTTGART.
Zwischen den Ruinen . Stuttgart , c1989. 143
p. : ISBN 3-87516-511-X
NYPL [3-MAMG+ 91-3257]

ART, GERMAN - GERMANY (WEST) - WESER RIVER VALLEY - EXHIBITIONS.
Renaissance im Weserraum . München , 1989.
2 v. : ISBN 3-422-06039-1 (Bd. 1)
N6882.W38 R4 1989
NYPL [3-MAMG 89-28831]

ART, GERMAN - GERMANY (WEST) - WORPSWEDE.
Boulboullé, Guido. Worpswede . Köln , c1989.
223 p. : ISBN 3-7701-1847-2
NYPL [3-MAMG 90-12605]

Worpswede . [Lilienthal] , c1989. 254 p. :
ISBN 3-922516-80-7
NYPL [3-MAMG 91-4485]

ART, GERMAN - GERMANY - WORPSWEDE.
Worpswede . [Worpswede] , c1989. 254 p. :
ISBN 3-922516-80-7 DDC 709/.43/59309034 20
N6867.5.W67 W68 1989

ART, GERMAN - GERMANY - WÜRZBURG - EXHIBITIONS.
Städtische Galerie Würzburg.
Würzburg--Künstler sehen eine Stadt .
[Würzburg] [1989?] 102 p. : ISBN
3-926916-04-4
N6886.W87 S73 1989

ART - GERMANY.
Bildende Kunst und Lebenswelten . [S.l. ,
1989?] 312 p. :   *NYPL [3-MAMG 91-5015]*

ART - GERMANY - BERLIN - CATALOGS.
National-Galerie (Germany) Nationalgalerie .
Berlin , c1968. 384 p. :
NYPL [3-MAVZ (Berlin) 90-6876]

Staatliche Museen zu Berlin (Germany : East).
Antikensammlung. Antikensammlung . Berlin ,
<1990-. v. <2 > : ISBN 3-362-00436-9 (Bd. 2)
DDC 709/.38/074031552 20
N2250.P4 A52 1990

ART - GERMANY - BERLIN - EXHIBITIONS.
Berlin, März 1990 . Berlin , Braunschweig
[1990] 88 p. :
MLCM 91/00973 (N)
NYPL [3-MAL 91-6662]

ART - GERMANY - DRESDEN - INFLUENCE - EXHIBITIONS.
Hassebrauk, Ernst, 1905- Die
Wiederbegegnung . [Dresden] , c1988. 80 p. :
DDC 741.943 20
NC251.6.Z9 H372 1988
NYPL [3-MCK H354 91-4570]

ART - GERMANY (EAST) - LEIPZIG - EXHIBITIONS.
Merkur & die Musen . [Wien] [1989] 627 p. :
ISBN 3-900926-02-6
NYPL [3-MAMG+ 90-13617]

ART - GERMANY - HALLE - CATALOGS.
Staatliche Galerie Moritzburg. Staatliche
Galerie Moritzburg, Halle. [Halle] 1961. 223 p.
NYPL [3-MAVZ (Halle) 91-563]

ART - GERMANY - LEIPZIG.
--Die ganze Welt im kleinen-- . Leipzig , 1989.
300 p. : ISBN 3-363-00419-2
NYPL [MAMG 91-6223]

ART - GERMANY - LEIPZIG - EXHIBITIONS.
Merkur & die Musen . Wien , 1989. 627 p. :
ISBN 3-900926-02-6 DDC 707/.4/43613 20
N6886.L4 M47 1989

ART - GERMANY - MAGDEBURG - EXHIBITIONS.
Kunst um 1800 . Magdeburg [1989] 95 p. :
DDC 709/.03/3074431822 20
N6756 .K86 1989

ART - GERMANY - MÖNCHENGLADBACH - CATALOGS.
Kunst der ersten Jahrhunderthälfte 1900 bis
1960 . Mönchengladbach , 1990. 425 p. : ISBN
3-924039-05-4
*IN PROCESS (ONLINE)   NYPL [MAVZ
(Mönchengladbach) 91-1142]*

ART - GERMANY - MÜHLHAUSEN (ERFURT)
Badstübner, Ernst. Das alte Mühlhausen .
Leipzig , c1989. 205 p. : ISBN 3-7338-0055-9
N6886.M78 B34 1989

ART - GERMANY (WEST) - HAMBURG - CATALOGS.
Museum für Kunst und Gewerbe Hamburg.
Kunst für Hamburg . Hamburg , c1990. 251 p. :
NYPL [3-MLF 91-6790]

ART - GERMANY (WEST) - HAMBURG - GUIDE-BOOKS.
Hipp, Hermann. Freie und Hansestadt
Hamburg . Köln , 1990. 608 p. : ISBN
3-7701-1590-2 DDC 720/.943/515 20
NA1086.H3 H57 1990

ART - GERMANY (WEST) - KREFELD - CATALOGS.
Kaiser Wilhelm Museum Krefeld. Italienische
Renaissancekunst im Kaiser Wilhelm Museum
Krefeld . [Krefeld] , 1987. 154, [2] p. : ISBN
3-926530-30-8
NYPL [3-MAVZ (Krefeld) 90-12394]

ART - GERMANY, WEST - RHINE VALLEY.
Rheinisches Landesmuseum Bonn .
Braunschweig , 1977. 128 p. :
N2255.R5 R46
NYPL [MAVZ (Bonn) 81-636]

ART - GERMANY, WEST - TRIER.
Ahrens, Dieter, 1934- Schatzkammer
Simeonstift . Trier , 1986. 164 p. : ISBN
3-87760-268-1 DDC 708.3/43 19
N2394.5 .A94 1986
NYPL [MAVZ (Trier) 91-6413]

ART GLASS - ITALY - MURANO - HISTORY - 19TH CENTURY.
Sarpellon, Giovanni. Miniature di vetro .
Venezia , c1990. 194 p. : ISBN 88-7743-080-X
DDC 748.295/31 20
NK5152.M85 S27 1990

ART GLASS - ITALY - MURANO - HISTORY - 20TH CENTURY.
Sarpellon, Giovanni. Miniature di vetro .
Venezia , c1990. 194 p. : ISBN 88-7743-080-X
DDC 748.295/31 20
NK5152.M85 S27 1990

ART, GOTHIC - HIGH GOTHIC - CZECHOSLOVAKIA - BOHEMIA - EXHIBITIONS.
Gotik . Wien [1990] 141 p. :
NYPL [3-MAM 90-11533]

ART, GOTHIC - HIGH GOTHIC - EXHIBITIONS.
Rarer gifts than gold . [Glasgow] , c1988. 69
p. : ISBN 0-85261-222-2 (pbk.)
N6318 .R374 1988
NYPL [3-MAK+ 90-12644]

ART, GOTHIC - CZECHOSLOVAKIA - BOHEMIA - EXHIBITIONS.
Gotik . [Wien , 1990] 141 p., [62] p. of plates :
N6832.B63 G68 1990

ART, GOTHIC - CZECHOSLOVAKIA - JIHOČESKÝ KRAJ - EXHIBITIONS.
Alšova jihočeská galerie. Gotické umění v
jižních Čechách . Praha [1990] 101 p. : ISBN
80-7035-013-X .
N6832.J53 A48 1990

ART, GOTHIC - INFLUENCE.
Bushart, Magdalena. Der Geist der Gotik und
die expressionistische Kunst . München , c1990.
255 p. : ISBN 3-88960-018-2 :
N6848.5.E9 B8 1990

ART, GOTHIC - ITALY.
Vasari, Giorgio, 1511-1574. [Vite de' più
eccellenti architetti, pittori et scultori italiani.
English. Selections.] Lives of the artists /.
London , New York , 1987. 2 v. ; ISBN

0-14-044500-5 (v. 1)
NYPL [3-MAMC 88-536]

ART, GOTHIC - ITALY - PALERMO.
Bresc-Bautier, Geneviève. Artistes, patriciens et confréries . Roma , 1979. xviii, 315 p., [15] leaves of plates :
N6921.P34 B73   **NYPL [3-MAMC 81-374]**

ART, GOTHIC - ITALY - UMBRIA - CONGRESSES.
Dall'Albornoz all'età dei Borgia . Todi , 1990. 385 p., [19] p. of plates : ISBN 88-85311-01-6
DDC 709/.45/65 20
N6919.U5 D35 1990

ART, GOTHIC - THEMES, MOTIVES.
Bracons i Clapés, Josep. [Claves del arte gótico. English.] The key to gothic art /. Minneapolis , 1990. 80 p. : ISBN 0-8225-2051-6 (lib. bdg.) :
DDC 709.02/2 20
N6310 .B7313 1990
NYPL [3-MAK 90-11597]

ART, GRAPHIC. see GRAPHIC ARTS.

Art graphique de la Chine . Huguette Berès (Art Gallery) Paris , 1960. [26] p. :
NYPL [MDBF 90-6890]

ART, GREEK.
Morris, Sarah P., 1954- Daidalos and the origins of Greek art /. Princeton, N.J. , 1992. p. cm. ISBN 0-691-03599-7 : DDC 700/.938 20
N5633 .M67 1992

Schefold, Karl. [Götter- und Heldensagen der Griechen in der spätarchaischen Kunst. English.] Gods and heroes in late archaic Greek art /. Cambridge , New York , 1992. p. cm.
ISBN 0-521-32718-0 DDC 704.94/7/0938 20
N7760 .S27313 1992

ART, GREEK - ISLANDS OF THE AEGEAN - EXHIBITIONS.
New York (City). Metropolitan Museum of Art. Greek art of the Aegean Islands . New York , c1979. 238 p. : ISBN 0-87099-216-3
N5640 .N48 1979   **NYPL [MAH 80-2168]**

ART, GREEK - ITALY - SICILY - EXHIBITIONS.
Lo Stile severo in Sicilia . Palermo , c1990. xxi, 380 p. : ISBN 88-373-0110-3
NYPL [3-MAH 90-11111]

ART, GREEK - SOURCES.
Pollitt, J. J. (Jerome Jordan), 1934- The art of ancient Greece . Cambridge [England] , New York , 1990. xiv, 298 p. : ISBN 0-521-25368-3
DDC 709/.38 20
N5630 .P56 1990   **NYPL [3-MAH 91-3705]**

ART, GREEK - THEMES, MOTIVES, ETC.
Carpenter, Thomas H. Art and myth in ancient Greece . London , c1991. 256 p. :
NYPL [3-MAH 91-4599]

ART, GUATEMALAN.
Lara Roche, Carlos, 1932- San José en el arte colonial guatemalteco /. Guatemala, C.A. , 1989. 161 p. :
N6576 .L37 1989

ART - HANDLING - HANDBOOKS, MANUALS, ETC.
Davis, Nancy, 1959- Handling with care . Rochester, NY , c1991. 31 p. : ISBN 0-938551-02-7 DDC 702/.8/8 20
N8585 .D38 1991

ART - HAWAII - HONOLULU - CATALOGS.
Honolulu Academy of Arts. Visions of the Dharma . Honolulu , 1991. p. cm. ISBN 0-937426-14-8 (alk. paper) : DDC 760/.048943/095207496931 20
N7352 .H66 1991

ART, HELLENISTIC.
From Alexander to Cleopatra, Greek art of the Hellenistic Age. Astoria, NY , c1989. 1 videocassette (28 min., 30 sec.) : DDC 709.38 11
N5633

ART, HELLENISTIC - CONSERVATION AND RESTORATION.
From Alexander to Cleopatra, Greek art of the Hellenistic Age. Astoria, NY , c1989. 1 videocassette (28 min., 30 sec.) : DDC 709.38 11
N5633

ART, HELLENISTIC - EGYPT - CATALOGS.
Grimm, Günter. Kunst der Ptolemäer- und Römerzeit im Ägyptischen Museum Kairo /.

Mainz [1975] 34 p, 118 p., [6] leaves of plates :
N5888.A1 G74   **NYPL [3-MAH 90-5474]**

ART, HELLENISTIC - GREECE.
Pfisterer-Haas, Susanne. Darstellungen alter Frauen in der griechischen Kunst /. Frankfurt am Main , 1989. xii, 237 p. : ISBN 3-631-41559-1   **NYPL [3-MAMZ 91-4214]**

ART, HINDU - NEPAL - EXHIBITIONS.
Pal, Pratapaditya. Art of the Himalayas . New York , c1991. p. cm. ISBN 1-555-95066-3 :
DDC 709/.5496/07473 20
N7310.8.N4 P33 1991

ART, HINDU - TIBET - EXHIBITIONS.
Pal, Pratapaditya. Art of the Himalayas . New York , c1991. p. cm. ISBN 1-555-95066-3 :
DDC 709/.5496/07473 20
N7310.8.N4 P33 1991

ART HISTORIANS - ENGLAND - BIOGRAPHY.
Pope-Hennessy, John Wyndham, Sir, 1913- Learning to look . New York , 1991. x, 336 p., [24] p. of plates : ISBN 0-385-26141-1 DDC 709/.2 B 20
N7483.P66 A3 1991   **NYPL [MA 91-5196]**

ART - HISTORIOGRAPHY.
Carrier, David, 1944- Principles of art history writing /. University Park, Pa. , c1991. xiii, 249 p. : ISBN 0-271-00711-7 (acid-free paper) DDC 707/.2 20
N380 .C37 1991   **NYPL [MAD 91-6082]**

Carter, Michael, 1944- Framing art . Sydney, NSW , c1990. 211 p. : ISBN 0-86806-354-1
NYPL [3-MAD 91-2237]

--Die ganze Welt im kleinen-- . Leipzig , 1989. 300 p. : ISBN 3-363-00419-2
NYPL [MAMG 91-6223]

ART - HISTORY.
Fichner-Rathus, Lois, 1953- Understanding art /. Englewood Cliffs, N.J. , 1992. p. cm. ISBN 0-13-932235-5 (pbk.) DDC 701/.1 20
N7430.5 .F5 1992

Gardner, Helen. [Art through the ages.] Gardner's art through the ages. San Diego , c1991. xvi, 1135 p. : ISBN 0-15-503769-2
NYPL [MAD 91-4710]

Honour, Hugh. The visual arts . New York , 1991. p. cm. ISBN 0-8109-3913-4 (cloth) DDC 709 20
N5300 .H68 1991

Janson, H. W. (Horst Woldemar), 1913- A basic history of art /. Englewood Cliffs, N.J. , New York , 1991. p. cm. ISBN 0-13-062878-6
DDC 709 20
N5300 .J29 1991

Janson, H. W. (Horst Woldemar), 1913- History of art for young people /. New York , 1992. p. cm. ISBN 0-8109-3405-1 DDC 709 20
N5300 .J33 1992

Kunst des Abendlandes /. Karlsruhe , c1960-<c1963. v. <1-3 > : DDC 709 20
N5300 .K96 1960

Nerdinger, Winfried. Perspektiven der Kunst . München , c1990. 404 p. : ISBN 3-87501-080-9
N5300 .N36 1990

Reinhardt, Ad, 1913-1967. Art-as-art . Berkeley , 1991. p. cm. ISBN 0-520-07670-2
DDC 709 20
N5303 .R36 1991

ART - HISTORY - HISTORIOGRAPHY. see ART - HISTORIOGRAPHY.

ART - HISTORY - STUDY GUIDES.
Myron, Robert. Study keys to art history /. Hauppauge, N.Y. , 1991. p. cm. ISBN 0-8120-4595-5 DDC 709 20
N5300 .M96 1991

ART, HONDURAN.
Fiallos S., Raúl (Fiallos Salgado), 1917- Datos históricos sobre la plástica hondureña /. [Tegucigalpa, Honduras?] c1989 (Tegucigalpa, Honduras, C.A. : Litografía López) 129 p. : DDC 709/.7283 20
N6579 .F5 1989

ART, HUNGARIAN - EXHIBITIONS.
Maďarská výtvarné umění XX. století (1945-1988) . V Praze , 1989. 40 p. : ISBN 80-7035-009-1 :
N6820 .M25 1989

Magyar Nemzeti Galéria. Ungarische Malerei und Bildhauerei im 19. Jahrhundert . Budapest , 1989. 47 p., [42] p. of plates :
N6819 .M28 1989

ART, HUNGARIAN - HUNGARY - BUDAPEST - EXHIBITIONS.
Hajdu, István. Les ateliers de Budapest =. Paris , c1990. 240 p. : ISBN 978-290-807-2006
NYPL [3-MAM+ 91-3623]

ART - HUNGARY - BUDAPEST - CATALOGS.
Szépművészeti Múzeum. English. The Budapest Museum of Fine Arts /. [Budapest] , c1985. 171 p. : ISBN 963-13-2297-1
NYPL [MAVZ+ (Budapest) 91-4223]

L'art hyperréaliste fantastique de Wojtek Siudmak . Siudmak, Wojtek, 1942- Paris , 1978-1989. 4 v. : ISBN 2-9500584-0-8 (album 3)
DDC 759.4
NC989.P62 S58
NYPL [3-MCZ+ S617 88-620]

ART - ILLINOIS - CHICAGO - CATALOGS.
David and Alfred Smart Museum of Art. The David and Alfred Smart Museum of Art . New York , c1990. 216 p. : ISBN 1-555-95061-2
DDC 708.173/11 20
N531.D38 D38 1990
NYPL [3-MAVZ (Chicago) 91-4808]

ART, IMMORAL. see EROTIC ART.

ART IN ADVERTISING. see COMMERCIAL ART.

Art in America in modern times. Cahill, Holger, 1887-1960. (comp) Freeport, N.Y. [1969, c1934] 110 p. : DDC 700/.973
N6505 .C3 1969

Art in an age of Bonapartism, 1800-1815 /. Boime, Albert. Chicago , 1990. xxvii, 706 p. : ISBN 0-226-06335-6 (alk. paper) : DDC 709/.03/4 20
N6757 .B56 1990   **NYPL [3-MAM 91-5522]**

Art in Australia /. Richardson, Donald. Melbourne , 1988. vii, 229 p. : ISBN 0-582-87304-5 (pbk.)
NYPL [3-MAM 89-11939]

Art in bloom /. Foshay, Ella M., 1948- New York , Oxford , 1990. 80 p. : ISBN 0-87663-603-2 (Phaidon Universe) DDC 758/.42/09 20
ND1400 .F67 1990
NYPL [3-MAMZ+ 91-4872]

Art in Germany 1909-1936 : from expressionism to resistance : the Marvin and Janet Fishman collection / Reinhold Heller ; with a foreword by Eberhard Roters ; with contributions by Stephanie D'Alessandro ... [et al.]. Munich : Prestel ;New York : Distributed in the USA and Canada by te Neues Pub. Co., c1990. 271 p. : ill. (some col.) ; 31 cm. Catalog of an exhibition entitled "From expressionism to resistance" held at the Milwaukee Art Museum, Dec. 6, 1990-Feb. 3, 1991, and at five other German and U. S. museums, Feb. 29, 1991-Aug. 30, 1992. Includes bibliographical references (p. 270). ISBN 0-944110-02-9 (pbk.) :
1. Fishman, Marvin - Art collections - Exhibitions. 2. Fishman, Janet - Art collections - Exhibitions. 3. Art, German - Exhibitions. 4. Art, Modern - 20th century - Germany - Exhibitions. I. Heller, Reinhold. II. Milwaukee Art Museum. III. Title: From expressionism to resistance.
N6868 .F74 1990
NYPL [3-MAMG+ 91-4806]

Art in history. Art in history/history in art . Santa Monica, CA [Chicago, Ill.] , 1991. p. cm. ISBN 0-89236-201-4 : DDC 701/.03/0949209032 20
N72.S6 A746 1991

Art in history/history in art : studies in seventeenth-century Dutch culture / edited by David Freedberg and Jan de Vries. Santa Monica, CA : Getty Center for the History of Art and the Humanities ; [Chicago, Ill.] : Distributed by the University of Chicago Press, 1991. p. cm. (Issues & debates) Includes bibliographical references and index. ISBN 0-89236-201-4 : DDC 701/.03/0949209032 20
1. Art and society - Netherlands. 2. Realism in art - Netherlands. 3. Painting, Dutch. 4. Painting, Modern - 17th-18th centuries - Netherlands. 5. Netherlands - Civilization - 17th century. 6. Netherlands - Intellectual life - 17th century. I. Freedberg, David. II. De Vries, Jan, 1943 Nov. 14-. III. Title: Art in history. IV. Title:

History in art. V. Series.
N72.S6 A746 1991

Art in our environment.
Lumley, Ann. Sydney's sculpture /. Melbourne,
Australia , 1990. v, 89 p. : ISBN 0-582-86820-3
    NYPL [3-MGI 90-13389]

Lumley, Ann. Sydney's sculpture /. Melbourne,
Australia , 1990. v, 89 p. : ISBN 0-582-86820-3
    DDC 730/.9944/1 20
NB1103.S93 L8 1990

Art in the Age of Aquarius, 1955-1970 /. Seitz,
William Chapin. Washington , 1991. p. cm.
    ISBN 0-87474-868-2 DDC 709/.73/09046 20
N6512 .S335 1991

Art in the Cold War . Lindey, Christine.
London , 1990. 224 p. : ISBN 1-87156-919-2 :
    DDC 709.47 709.04 20
N6981 N6490   *NYPL [3-MAL 91-3265]*

Art in the making.
Impressionism /. London , c1990. 227 p. :
    ISBN 0-300-05035-6 (cased) : DDC 759.054074
    20
ND192.I4   *NYPL [3-MCN 91-5511]*

Italian painting before 1400. [London] , c19. x,
225 p. : ISBN 0-947645-67-5 DDC
    759.5/09/02207442132 20
ND613 .I87 1989

Italian painting before 1400. London , c1989.
x, 225 p. : ISBN 0-947645-67-5 (pbk) : DDC
    759.5 19   *NYPL [3-MCE 91-3327]*

ART - INDEXES.
Rochelle, Mercedes, 1955- Historical art index,
A.D. 400-1650 . Jefferson, N.C. , c1989. v, 217
p. ; ISBN 0-89950-449-3 (lib. bdg. : alk. paper) :
    DDC 704.9/499 20
N8210 .R6 1989   *NYPL [*R-MAC 90-419]*

ART, INDIA - INDIA.
Soundara Rajah, K.V., 1925- Secularism in
Indian art /. New Delhi , c1988. viii, 109 p. :
    ISBN 81-7017-245-4
    NYPL [3-MAE 89-28260]

ART, INDIAN - EXHIBITIONS.
Archuleta, Margaret, 1950- Shared visions .
Phoenix, Ariz. , 1991. 110 p. : ISBN
    0-934351-21-X : DDC 704/.0397/0904 20
N6538.A4 A7 1991

Brach, Paul, 1924- Our land/ourselves . Albany,
N.Y. , 1991. p. ISBN 0-910763-05-4 : DDC
    760/.089/97073 20
N6538.A4 B67 1991

ART, INDIC.
Bhattacharyya, Benoytosh, 1897-1964. The
Indian Buddhist iconography. Calcutta [1968]
xxxiii, 478 p.   *NYPL [3-MAF 75-368]*

Jayakar, Pupul. The earth mother . San
Francisco, Calif. , c1990. xxx, 248 p., [32] p. of
plates : ISBN 0-06-250405-3 : DDC 700/.954 20
N8191.I4 J39 1990   *NYPL [3-MAF 91-5051]*

Srivastava, A. L., 1936- Śilpa-śrī, studies in
Indian art and culture /. Delhi , 1990. xvi, 226
p., 85 leaves of plates : ISBN 81-85067-29-5 :
    DDC 709/.54 20
N7302 .S75 1990   *NYPL [3-MAF 91-6395]*

25 years of Indian art. New Delhi [1972] 32,
[8] p., [32] p. of illus. DDC 709/.54
N7304 .T85   *NYPL [3-MAM 90-5575]*

ART, INDIC - CATALOGS.
Victoria and Albert Museum. Indian art.
London, 1952. [32] p.
    NYPL [3-MAF 90-5981]

**ART, INDIC - ENGLAND - LONDON -
CATALOGS.**
Arts of India, 1550-1900 /. London , c1990.
240 p. : ISBN 1-85177-022-4 DDC 709.54 20
N7301   *NYPL [3-MAF 91-6685]*

ART, INDIC - INDIA - ORISSA.
Arts and artisans of Orissa /. Bhubaneswar
[1981?] 106 p. ; DDC 338.4/77/095413 19
N7307.O74 A77 1981
    NYPL [3-MNE 90-5470]

ART, INDIC - INDIA - S ANCHI.
Narendar N ath Soz. Archaeological museum S
anchi /. New Delhi , c1966. 26 p., 12 p. of
plates :   *NYPL [3-MAE 90-7106]*

ART, INDONESIAN.
Hersey, Irwin. Indonesian primitive art /.
Singapore , New York , 1991. p. cm. ISBN

0-19-588553-8 : DDC 730/.089/9922 20
N7326 .H47 1991

ART, INDONESIAN - EXHIBITIONS.
Jessup, Helen Ibbitson. Court arts of Indonesia
/. New York , c1990. 288 p. : ISBN
    0-8109-3165-6
IN PROCESS (ONLINE)
    NYPL [3-MAF+ 91-6099]

**ART INDUSTRIES AND TRADE - NEW
ZEALAND - HISTORY - 20TH
CENTURY - EXHIBITIONS.**
Kahurangi . Los Angeles [1984] 63 p. : ISBN
    0-477-01518-2 (pbk.)
NK1092.A1 K35 1984
    NYPL [3-MNE 90-10614]

**ART INDUSTRIES AND TRADE - POLAND -
TORUŃ - EXHIBITIONS.**
Kunsthandwerk des 14.-19. Jahrhunderts aus
dem Bezirksmuseum Toruń. [Göttingen ,
c1982. 39 p. : DDC 745/.074/0382 19
NK1471.P62 T675 1982
    NYPL [3-MNE 84-3491]

Art Institute of Chicago.
Benezra, Neal David, 1953- Martin Puryear /.
Chicago, Ill. , New York, N.Y. , c1991. p. cm.
    ISBN 0-86559-092-3 DDC 709/.2 20
NB237.P84 A4 1991

The Chicago show . Chicago, Ill. , c1990. 48
p. : ISBN 0-938903-09-8
N6487.C52 C6 1990
    NYPL [3-MAMT 91-7597]

Clift, William, 1944- Certain places . Santa Fe,
N.M. , c1987. [46] p. : ISBN 0-9618165-0-3
    NYPL [MFX+ (Clift) 91-2455]

Degenerate art . Los Angeles, Calif. , New
York , c1991. 423 p. : ISBN 0-8109-3653-4
    DDC 709/.43/07477311 20
N6868 .D3388 1991

Degenerate art . Los Angeles, Calif. , New
York , c1991. p. cm. ISBN 0-87587-158-5 DDC
    709/.43/07477311 20
N6868 .D3388 1991b

European decorative arts in the Art Institute of
Chicago / Ian Wardropper, Lynn Springer
Roberts. Chicago, Ill. : The Institute ; New
York : Distributed by H.N. Abrams, c1991. p.
cm. ISBN 0-8109-3253-9 (Abrams : hardcover)
    DDC 745/.094/07477311 20
*1. Decorative arts - Europe - Catalogs. 2. Decorative
arts - Illinois - Chicago - Catalogs. 3. Art Institute of
Chicago - Catalogs. I. Wardropper, Ian. II. Roberts,
Lynn Springer. III. Title.*
NK925 .A78 1991

Fragments of Chicago's past : the collection of
architectural fragments at the Art Institute of
Chicago / edited by Pauline Saliga ; with essays
by Robert Bruegmann ... [et al.]. Chicago, IL :
Art Institute of Chicago, 1990. 180 p. : ill.
(some col.) ; 28 cm. Includes bibliographical
references and index. ISBN 0-86559-088-5 DDC
    720/.9773/1107477311 20
*1. Art Institute of Chicago - Catalogs. 2. Architecture -
Illinois - Chicago - Catalogs. 3. Chicago (Ill.) -
Buildings, structures, etc. - Catalogs. I. Saliga, Pauline
A. II. Bruegmann, Robert. III. Title.*
NA735.C4 A77 1990
    NYPL [3-MQWO 91-3419]

Pfahl, John, 1939- A distanced land .
[Albuquerque] , 1990. xvi, 204 p. : ISBN
    0-8263-1214-4 DDC 779/.36/092 20
TR647 .P494 1990
    NYPL [MFX (Pfahl) 91-7438]

The Radiance of jade and the clarity of water .
Chicago, IL , New York [1991] p. cm. ISBN
    0-86559-096-6 (Art Institute of Chicago) DDC
    738/.09519/07473 20
NK4168.6.A1 R34 1991

Varnedoe, Kirk, 1946- High & low . New
York , c1990. 460 p. : ISBN 0-87070-353-6
    (MoMA : hard)
    NYPL [3-MAL+ 91-3655]

Zukowsky, John, 1948- Austrian architecture
and design . Chicago , Berlin , c1991. p. cm.
    ISBN 3-433-02340-9 (catalogue edition) DDC
    745.4/49436/0904507477311 20
N6808 .Z8 1991

ART INSTITUTE OF CHICAGO.
Vinci, John. The Trading Room . Chicago, IL ,
c1989. 72 p. : ISBN 0-86559-082-6 DDC 725/.25

20
NA6253.C4 C438 1989
    NYPL [3-MQWO 90-12029]

**ART INSTITUTE OF CHICAGO -
CATALOGS.**
Art Institute of Chicago. European decorative
arts in the Art Institute of Chicago /. Chicago,
Ill. , New York , c1991. p. ISBN 0-8109-3253-9
    (Abrams : hardcover) DDC 745/.094/07477311
    20
NK925 .A78 1991

Art Institute of Chicago. Fragments of
Chicago's past . Chicago, IL , 1990. 180 p. :
    ISBN 0-86559-088-5 DDC
    720/.9773/1107477311 20
NA735.C4 A77 1990
    NYPL [3-MQWO 91-3419]

**Art Institute of Seattle. see Seattle. Art
Museum.**

Art into life : Russian Constructivism, 1914-1932
/ introduction by Richard Andrews and Milena
Kalinovska ; essays by Jaroslav Andel ... [et
al.] ; artists biographies by Owen Smith. Seattle,
Wash. : Henry Art Gallery, University of
Washington ; New York, NY : Rizzoli
International, c1990. 276 p. : ill. (some col.) ;
26 cm. Published in conjunction with the exhibition
held: Henry Art Gallery, University of Washington,
Seattle, July 4-Sept. 2, 1990; Walker Art Center,
Minneapolis, Oct. 6-Dec. 15, 1990; State Tretyakov
Gallery, Moscow, Feb.-Aug., 1991. Includes
bibliographical references. ISBN 0-935558-27-6 (pbk.)
    DDC 709/.47/074 20
*1. Constructivism (Art) - Russian S.F.S.R. - Exhibitions.
2. Art, Modern - 20th century - Russian S.F.S.R. -
Exhibitions. I. Walker Art Center. II. Gosudarstvennaia
Tret´iakovskaia galereia.*
N6988.5.C64 A68 1990
    NYPL [3-MAM 90-11568]

ART - IOWA - FORT DODGE - CATALOGS.
Blanden Memorial Art Museum. Handbook of
the collections in the Blanden Memorial Art
Museum, Fort Dodge, Iowa /. Fort Dodge,
Iowa (920 3rd Ave., South, Fort Dodge
50501) , 1989. 132 p. : DDC 708.177/51 20
N570.29 .A6 1989

ART, IRANIAN - INFLUENCE.
Daftari, Fereshteh. The influence of Persian art
on Gauguin, Matisse, and Kandinsky /. New
York , 1991. p. cm. ISBN 0-8153-0715-2 (alk.
paper) DDC 709/.2/24 20
N7280 .D34 1991

ART, IRISH.
McAvera, Brian, 1948- Art, politics, and
Ireland /. Dublin [1990?] 136 p. : ISBN
    1-87249-600-8 : DDC 701/.03 20
N8236.P5 M37 1990

ART, IRISH - EXHIBITIONS.
Frühe irische Kunst . [Germany , 1959]
(Mainz : Eggebrecht-Presse) 1 v. (unpaged) :
N6240 .F7   *NYPL [3-MAMR 91-303]*

ART, IRISH - IRELAND - EXHIBITIONS.
A new tradition . Dublin , 1990. 139 p. : ISBN
    0-907660-37-1 : DDC 709.415 20
    NYPL [3-MAMR 91-5078]

ART, ISLAMIC - CATALOGS.
Fehérvári, Géza. 1400 years of Islamic art .
London , 1984. 247 p. :
    NYPL [3-MAF+ 90-12505]

ART, ISLAMIC - EXHIBITIONS.
Arabesques et jardins de paradis . Paris , c1989.
334 p. : ISBN 2-7118-2294-X : DDC
    709/.17/67107444361 20
N6264.F8 P317 1990

Images of paradise in Islamic art /. Hanover,
N.H. , 1991. p. cm. ISBN 0-944722-07-5
    (hardcover) DDC 704.9/489723 20
N6263.D37 H664 1991

Islamic art & patronage . New York , c1990.
313 p. : ISBN 0-8478-1366-5 DDC
    709/.17/67107473 20
N6263.W3 A785 1991
    NYPL [3-MAF+ 91-5747]

ART, ISLAMIC - HISTORY.
Brend, Barbara, 1940- Islamic art /. Cambridge,
Mass. , 1991. p. cm. ISBN 0-674-46865-1: DDC
    709/.17/671 20
N6250 B76 1991

Enderlein, Volkmar. Islamische Kunst /.
Dresden , 1990. 324 p. : ISBN 3-364-00195-2

DDC 709/.17/671 20
N6260 .E64 1990

ART, ISLAMIC - JORDAN - EXHIBITIONS.
Treasures from an ancient land . Stroud,
Gloucestershire ; Wolfeboro Falls, NH : xiii,
178 p. : ISBN 0-86299-729-1 DDC
709/.5695/07442753 20
N7279.6 .T7 1991 NYPL *[*OFG 91-7466]*

ART, ISLAMIC - MOROCCO -
EXHIBITIONS.
De L'Empire romain aux villes impériales .
Paris , c1990. xxiii, 474 p. :
NYPL *[3-MAM+ 91-6786]*

ART, ISLAMIC - THEMES, MOTIVES -
CONGRESSES.
World Seminar on "Common Principles, Forms
and Themes of Islamic Art" (1983 : Istanbul,
Turkey) Islamic art . Damascus , 1989. 289,
165 p. : ISBN 92-9063-354-9
NYPL *[3-MAF 91-3423]*

ART, ITALIAN.
Robertson, Clare. Il gran cardinale . New
Haven , 1992. p. cm. ISBN 0-300-05045-3 DDC
709/.2 20
N6915 .R66 1992

Shearman, John K. G. Only connect .
Princeton, N.J. , 1992. p. cm. ISBN
0-691-09972-3 (CL) : DDC 709/.45/09024 20
N6915 .S54 1992

ART, ITALIAN - CATALOGS.
Collezione del Palazzo dei Dogi Mocenigo di S.
Samuele a Venezia di proprietž del conde
Andrea di Robilant . Firenze , 1933. 38 p., 54
leaves of plates :
NYPL *[3-MAX+ (Robilant) 87-3088]*

Stia . [Firenze] , 1990. 140 p. : DDC
709/.45/0744559 20
N6918 .S8 1990

ART, ITALIAN - EXHIBITIONS.
Artisti italiani contemporanei, 1956-1986 /.
Venezia , 1986. 61 p. : ISBN 88-7693-024-8
DDC 709/.45/0740531 19
N6918 .A819 1986
NYPL *[3-MAMC 90-12531]*

Capolavori dalle collezioni d'arte del Banco di
Napoli /. Napoli , c1989. 213 p. : ISBN
88-7042-999-7
NYPL *[3-MAVZ+ (Naples) 90-13203]*

Italy, new tendencies. New York, N.Y. [1966]
[16] p. : NYPL *[3-MAMC 90-6953]*

Syndram, Dirk. Ruinenromantik und
Antikensehnsucht /. [Berlin] , c1986. 32 p. :
ISBN 3-88609-199-6 DDC
760/.0444/094074031554 19
N8237.8.R8 S96 1986
NYPL *[3-MAMZ 90-9452]*

ART, ITALIAN - EXHIBITIONS -
CATALOGS.
Sollins, Susan. Eternal metaphors . New York,
N.Y. , c1989. 72 p. : ISBN 0-916365-28-X
NYPL *[3-MAMC 90-11056]*

ART, ITALIAN - GERMANY (WEST) -
KREFELD - CATALOGS.
Kaiser Wilhelm Museum Krefeld. Italienische
Renaissancekunst im Kaiser Wilhelm Museum
Krefeld /. [Krefeld] , 1987. 154, [2] p. : ISBN
3-926530-30-8
NYPL *[3-MAVZ (Krefeld) 90-12394]*

ART, ITALIAN - HISTORY.
La Storia dell'arte /. Busto Arsizio , 1990. 2
v. : NYPL *[3-MAMC 90-11656]*

Venturi, Adolfo, 1856-1941. Storia dell'arte
italiana /. Millwood, N.Y. , 1983. 11 v. in 25 :
NYPL *[3-MAMC 90-13336]*

ART, ITALIAN - ITALY - BERGAMO.
Mosca, Pietro. Arte e costume a Bergamo .
Bergamo , c1989-c1990. 2 v. (1020 p.) ;
IN PROCESS (ONLINE)
NYPL *[3-MAMC+ 91-5886]*

ART, ITALIAN - ITALY - FLORENCE.
Civai, Alessandra. Dipinti e sculture in casa
Martelli . Firenze , c1990. 219 p. :
NYPL *[3-MAVC+ 91-6773]*

ART, ITALIAN - ITALY - FLORENCE -
CONGRESSES.
Leonardo, Michelangelo, and Raphael in
Renaissance Florence, 1500-1508 /.
Washington, D.C. , 1991. p. cm. ISBN

0-87840-219-5 DDC 709/.2/2455109031 20
N6923.L33 L456 1991

ART, ITALIAN - ITALY - FLORENCE -
EXHIBITIONS.
L'Età di Masaccio . Milano , c1990. 265 p. :
ISBN 88-435-3211-1
NYPL *[3-MAMC 90-12878]*

Gruppo Donatello, XXVII edizione . Firenze ,
1989. 111, [34] p. :
N6921.F7 G78 1989
NYPL *[3-MAMC 90-11322]*

Iride, schedule d'arte, Firenze '82 . Firenze ,
c1982. 107 p. : NYPL *[3-MAMC+ 90-5983]*

ART, ITALIAN - ITALY - LIGURIA.
Descrizione delle pitture, scolture, e
architetture, ecc., che trovansi in alcune città,
borghi, e castelli delle due riviere dello stato
Ligure . Genova , 1780. 256, [i.e. 258], VII, [1]
p., [4] leaves of plates (1 folded) : DDC
709/.45/18 20
N6919.L54 D47 1780

ART, ITALIAN - ITALY - LOMBARDY -
EXHIBITIONS.
Settecento lombardo /. Milano , c1991. 627 p. :
ISBN 88-435-3418-1
NYPL *[3-MAMC 91-7605]*

ART, ITALIAN - ITALY - LUCCA - GUIDE-
BOOKS.
Grieco, Romy. Lucca . Bologna, Italy , Lucca
[1990?] 99 p. : DDC 709/.45/53 20
N6921.L82 G74 1990

ART, ITALIAN - ITALY - MANTUA -
THEMES, MOTIVES - EXHIBITIONS.
Giovannoni, Giannino. Mantova e i tarocchi del
Mantegna /. Mantova , Faenza [1987] 78 p. :
N6923.M249 A4 1987
NYPL *[3-MCF M29 91-7036]*

ART, ITALIAN - ITALY - MILAN.
Milan . Bologna, Italy [1990?] 157 p. : ISBN
88-7193-601-9 : DDC 709/.45/21 20
N6921.M6 M48 1990

ART, ITALIAN - ITALY - NAPLES -
SOURCES.
Ricerche sul '600 napoletano. Saggi e
documenti per la storia dell'arte. Milano , 1987.
201 p. : DDC 709/.45/7309032 20
N6921.N2 R54 1987
NYPL *[3-MAMC 90-11700]*

ART, ITALIAN - ITALY - PALERMO.
Bresc-Bautier, Geneviève. Artistes, patriciens et
confréries . Roma , 1979. xviii, 315 p., [15]
leaves of plates :
N6921.P34 B73 NYPL *[3-MAMC 81-374]*

ART, ITALIAN - ITALY - PARMA.
Fornari Schianchi, Lucia. Parma . Bologna, Italy
[1991?] 158 p. : ISBN 88-7193-650-7 DDC
709/.45/44 20
N6951.P35 F67 1991

ART, ITALIAN - ITALY - PISA.
Pisa . Bologna, Italy [Pisa] [1990?] 96 p. :
ISBN 88-7193-626-4 : DDC 709/.45/55 20
N6951.P6 P54 1990

Pisa through the centuries. Bologna, Italy ,
c1989. 93 p. : DDC 709/.45/55 20
N6921.P6 P57 1989

ART, ITALIAN - ITALY - RIVIERA.
Leonardo Massabò e l'Ottocento nella Riviera
occidentale /. Genova , c1990. 195 p., [4] p. of
plates : NYPL *[3-MCF M418 90-13278]*

ART, ITALIAN - ITALY - ROME -
CONSERVATION AND RESTORATION.
Santa Maria sopra Minerva /. Roma , c1990.
303 p. : ISBN 88-7060-223-0
NYPL *[3-MRBD+ 91-7451]*

ART, ITALIAN - ITALY - SAN VITO DEI
NORMANNI.
Chionna, Antonio. Beni culturali di San Vito
dei Normanni /. Fasano, Brindisi [1988] 471
p., [32] leaves of plates : ISBN 88-7514-253-X :
DDC 709/.45/754 20
N6921.S38 C47 1988
NYPL *[3-MAMC+ 90-10597]*

ART, ITALIAN - ITALY - SARDINIA.
Voci di Sardegna /. Siena , 1964- v. <1 > ;
N6919.S37 V6 1964

ART, ITALIAN - ITALY - TRIESTE -
EXHIBITIONS.
Neoclassico . Venezia , 1990. xix, 530 p. :

ISBN 88-317-5361-4
N6916.5.N45 N4 1990

ART, ITALIAN - ITALY - TUSCANY - GUIDE-
BOOKS.
Schomann, Heinz. Toskana (ohne Florenz) /.
Darmstadt , c1990. 496 p., [4] p. of plates :
ISBN 3-534-06894-7
NYPL *[3-MAMC 90-11555]*

ART, ITALIAN - ITALY - UMBRIA -
CONGRESSES.
Dall'Albornoz all'età dei Borgia . Todi , 1990.
385 p., [19] p. of plates : ISBN 88-85311-01-6
DDC 709/.45/65 20
N6919.U5 D35 1990

ART, ITALIAN - ITALY - VENICE.
Huse, Norbert. [Venedig, die Kunst der
Renaissance. English.] The art of Renaissance
Venice . Chicago , 1990. 382 p., [32] p. of
plates : ISBN 0-226-36107-1 (alk. paper) DDC
709/.45/3109024 20
N6921.V5 H8713 1990
NYPL *[3-MAMC 91-3259]*

ART, ITALIAN - ITALY - VENICE -
EXHIBITIONS.
Il Gioco dell'amore . Milano , 1990. 216 p. :
ISBN 88-85215-00-9
IN PROCESS (ONLINE)
NYPL *[3-MAMC 91-4481]*

Knox, George. 18th century Venetian art in
Canadian collections =. Vancouver, B.C.,
Canada , c1989. 108 p. : ISBN 0-920095-81-X
IN PROCESS (ONLINE)
NYPL *[3-MAMC+ 91-6265]*

ART, ITALIAN - ITALY - VICENZA -
EXHIBITIONS.
I Tiepolo e il Settecento vicentino /. Milano ,
c1990. 404 p. : ISBN 88-435-3180-8
NYPL *[3-MAMC 91-5454]*

ART, ITALIAN - ITALY - VICENZA
(PROVINCE) - EXHIBITIONS.
I Tiepolo e il Settecento vicentino /. Milano ,
c1990. 404 p. : ISBN 88-435-3180-8
N6923.T5 A4 1990

ART, ITALIAN - PRICES.
Enciclopedia dei pittori e scultori italiani del
Novecento . Milano [1991] 2 v. (1261 p.) :
DDC 709/.2/.2450904 B 20
N6918 .E58 1991

ART, ITALIAN - SOURCES.
Testimonianze e polemiche figurative in Italia .
Messina [1974] 507 p. ;
N6917.5.N44 B37
NYPL *[3-MAMC 90-5898]*

ART - ITALY.
I Mille musei d'Italia /. Firenze , c1988- v. :
ISBN 88-09-45125-2 (v. 1 : pbk.)
NYPL *[3-MAV 90-2271]*

ART - ITALY - FLORENCE.
Breidecker, Volker. Florenz, oder, "die Rede,
die zum Auge spricht" . München , c1990. 446
p., lvi p. of plates : ISBN 3-7705-2600-7
NYPL *[3-MAMC 91-6316]*

Mostra Medicea . [Florence] [1939] 141 p.,
[51] p. of plates : NYPL *[3-MAMC 90-7094]*

ART - ITALY - FLORENCE - CATALOGS.
Centro di Firenze restituito . Firenze , c1989.
614 p., 8 p. of plates :
NYPL *[3-MAVZ+ (Florence) 90-12442]*

Villa I Tatti (Florence, Italy) The Bernard
Berenson collection of oriental art at Villa I
Tatti /. New York , c1991. p. cm. ISBN
1-555-95060-4 (alk. paper) : DDC
709/.5/0744551 20
N7336 .V46 1991

ART - ITALY - LIGURIA.
Descrizione delle pitture, scolture, e
architetture, ecc., che trovansi in alcune città,
borghi, e castelli delle due riviere dello stato
Ligure . Genova , 1780. 256, [i.e. 258], VII, [1]
p., [4] leaves of plates (1 folded) : DDC
709/.45/18 20
N6919.L54 D47 1780

ART - ITALY - PADUA - CATALOGS.
Banzato, D. (Davide) Bronzi e placchette dei
Musei civici di Padova /. Padova , c1989. 155
p. : DDC 730/.0945/0744532 20
NK7952.A1 B36 1989
NYPL *[MGR 91-6998]*

ART - ITALY - PARMA - CATALOGS.
Fondazione Magnani Rocca. Capolavori dalle collezioni della Fondazione Magnani Rocca /. Bologna , 1990. xxxi, 131 p. : ISBN 88-7779-116-0
     NYPL [MAVZ (Parma, Italy) 91-6194]

ART - ITALY - PERUGIA - CATALOGS.
Galleria nazionale dell'Umbria. Galleria nazionale dell'Umbria /. Roma , 1969- v. :
     NYPL [MAVY (Perugia) 91-5431]

ART - ITALY - SIENA - CATALOGS.
Carli, Enzo, 1910- Il Museo dell'opera del duomo /. Siena , 1989. 63 p., [16] p. of plates :
     NYPL [3-MAVZ (Siena) 90-12388]

ART - ITALY - TUSCANY - GUIDE-BOOKS.
Schomann, Heinz. Toskana (ohne Florenz) /. Darmstadt , c1990. 496 p., [4] p. of plates : ISBN 3-534-06894-7
     NYPL [3-MAMC 90-11555]

ART - ITALY - VENICE - GUIDE-BOOKS.
Franzoi, Umberto. Il Palazzo ducale di Venezia /. Roma , 1987. 170 p., [24] p. of plates (2 folded) :   *NYPL [3-MQWB 90-10853]*

ART - ITALY - VOLTERRA - EXHIBITIONS.
Cateni, Gabriele. Die Etrusker--Volterra . Solingen , 1986. 90 p. :
     NYPL [3-MAE 90-12646]

ART, JAPANESE.
Gutiérrez, Fernando G. Japón y Occidente . Sevilla , 1990. 245 p. : ISBN 84-86080-27-4 DDC 709/.52 20
N7350 .G88 1990

ART, JAPANESE - TO 1868 - EXHIBITIONS.
Courtly splendor . [Boston, Mass.] [1990] 173 p. : ISBN 0-87846-328-3 DDC 709/.52/07474461 20
N7353 .C68 1990

Die Kunst des alten Japan . Frankfurt am Main , 1990. 199 p. : ISBN 3-89322-209-X
     NYPL [3-MAG+ 91-4469]

ART, JAPANESE - KAMAKURA-MOMOYAMA PERIODS, 1185-1600 - EXHIBITIONS.
Cunningham, Michael R. The triumph of Japanese style . [Cleveland, Ohio] , c1991. p. cm. ISBN 0-940717-12-3 DDC 709/.52/07477132 20
N7353.4 .C87 1991

Japan . New York , c1988. xi, 402 p. : ISBN 0-8076-1214-6 DDC 952/.00740153 19
DS827.D34 J37 1988
     NYPL [3-MAG+ 89-864]

ART, JAPANESE - EDO PERIOD, 1600-1868 - EXHIBITIONS.
Japan . New York , c1988. xi, 402 p. : ISBN 0-8076-1214-6 DDC 952/.00740153 19
DS827.D34 J37 1988
     NYPL [3-MAG+ 89-864]

Vos, Ken. Assignment Japan . The Hague , 1989. 107 p. : ISBN 90-12-06415-5
     NYPL [3-MAG+ 90-12025]

ART, JAPANESE - 1868- - EXHIBITIONS.
The Image of man in modern Japanese art from the Museum collection . [Tokyo] , 1988. [36] p. :   *NYPL [3-MAG 89-6015]*

ART, JAPANESE - CATALOGS.
Asian Art Museum of San Francisco. The art of Japan . San Francisco , c1991. p. cm. ISBN 0-8118-0055-5 (cloth) : DDC 709/.52/07479461 20
N7352 .A935 1991

Honolulu Academy of Arts. Visions of the Dharma . Honolulu , 1991. p. cm. ISBN 0-937426-14-8 (alk. paper) : DDC 760/.048943/095207496931 20
N7352 .H66 1991

Smith, Lawrence. Japanese art . Bloomsbury , c1990. 256 p. : ISBN 0-7141-1446-4 : DDC 709/.52/074 19
N7350   *NYPL [3-MAG 90-11503]*

ART, JAPANESE - EUROPEAN INFLUENCES.
Gutiérrez, Fernando G. Japón y Occidente . Sevilla , 1990. 245 p. : ISBN 84-86080-27-4 DDC 709/.52 20
N7350 .G88 1990

ART, JAPANESE - EXHIBITIONS.
Courtly splendor . Boston [1990] 173 p. :

ISBN 0-87846-328-3
     NYPL [3-MAG+ 91-3336]

Hosley, William. The Japan idea . Hartford, Conn. , 1990. 211 p. : ISBN 0-918333-07-5
     NYPL [3-MAMT+ 91-3289]

Metropolitan Museum of Art (New York, N.Y.) Japanese art from the Gerry collection in the Metropolitan Museum of Art /. New York , c1989. 141 p. : ISBN 0-87099-556-1 DDC 738/.0952/0747471 20
N7352 .F67 1989   *NYPL [3-MAG 89-28868]*

ART, JAPANESE - INFLUENCE.
Imitation and inspiration . [Amsterdam] , c1989. 179 p. :
     NYPL [3-MAME+ 90-11986]

ART - JERUSALEM - CATALOGS.
Muze'on Yiśra'el (Jerusalem) The Sam Weisbord Pavilion and collection /. Jerusalem , c1988. 21, 54, 19 p. : ISBN 965-278-062-6 DDC 708.95694/42 20
N3750.J5 A86 1988

ART, JEWISH.
Kampf, Avram. Chagall to Kitaj . New York , London , 1990. 206 p. : ISBN 0-275-93900-6 (alk. paper) DDC 704/.03924/0904 20
N7417 .K34 1991

ART - JORDAN - EXHIBITIONS.
Treasures from an ancient land . Stroud, Gloucestershire ; Wolfeboro Falls, NH : xiii, 178 p. : ISBN 0-86299-729-1 DDC 709/.5695/07442753 20
N7279.6 .T7 1991   *NYPL [*OFG 91-7466]*

ART - JUVENILE LITERATURE.
Isaacson, Philip M., 1924- A short walk around the Pyramids and through the world of art /. New York , 1992. p. cm. ISBN 0-679-81523-6 DDC 700 20
N7440 .I8 1992

ART, KOREAN.
The Arts of Korea. Seoul , c1979. 6 v. : DDC 709/.519
N7363 .A79   *NYPL [3-MAF+ 83-1615]*

ART, KOREAN - TO 1900.
Korean art seen through museums /. Seoul, Korea , 1979. xxi, 353 p. : DDC 709/.519/074095195 19
N7360 .K635   *NYPL [3-MAG 83-2164]*

ART, LATIN AMERICAN.
Brett, Guy. Transcontinental . London , New York , 1990. 112 p. : ISBN 0-86091-511-5 DDC 709/.8/09048 20
N6502.5 .B74 1990

ART, LATIN AMERICAN - EXHIBITIONS.
Arte en Iberoamérica, 1820-1980 . [Madrid] [1989?] xxi, 359, [3] p. : ISBN 84-7506-297-0
N6502.4 .A76 1989

Brett, Guy. Transcontinental . London ; New York : 112 p. : ISBN 0-86091-511-5
     NYPL [3-MAM 91-7008]

El Taller Torres-García . Austin , 1991. p. cm. ISBN 0-292-78121-0 DDC 709/.8/074 20
N6502.5 .T35 1991

ART, LATIN AMERICAN - HISTORY.
Castedo, Leopoldo. Historia del arte iberoamericano /. Madrid , c1988. 2 v. : ISBN 84-206-9597-1 (obra completa)
     NYPL [3-MAM 89-11457]

ART, LATIN AMERICAN - HISTORY AND CRITICISM.
Bayón, Damián Carlos. Pensar con los ojos . Bogotá, D.E. , 1982. 478 p. ;
     NYPL [3-MAM 90-6285]

ART, LATIN AMERICAN - THEMES, MOTIVES.
Valbert, Christian. La iconografía simbólica en el arte barroco de Latino América . [La Paz, Bolivia] , 1987. 122 p. :
N7901.5 .V35 1987

ART, LATIN - EXHIBITIONS.
Sussman, Elisabeth, 1939- El corazón sangrante =. Boston, Mass. , Seattle, Wash. , c1991. p. ISBN 0-910663-50-5 (paperback) DDC 704.9/46 20
N8217.H53 S87 1991

ART, LATVIAN.
Siliņš, Jānis, 1896- Latvijas māksla, 1915-1940 /. Stokholmā , 1988- v. <1 > : ISBN

91-970758-4-1 (v. 1)
N6995.L3 S582 1988

ART, LETTISH. see ART, LATVIAN.

ART, LOMBARD - ITALY - EXHIBITIONS.
I Longobardi /. Milano , c1990. 492 p. : ISBN 88-435-3210-3
N6919.L8 L67 1990

ART, LOMBARD - ITALY, NORTHERN.
Tavano, Sergio. Romani e Longobardi . Tricesimo (Ud) [1990] 183 p. :
N6913 .T38 1990

Art-- made in U. S. A. Art-- made in USA . [Regensburg] [1988?] 90 p. :
     NYPL [3-MAMT 89-28438]

Art-- made in USA : 37 Positionen Junger Kunst : 2. Dezember 1988 bis 22. Januar 1989, städtische Galerie Regensburg / [Ausstellung und Katalog, Herbert Schneidler]. [Regensburg] : Die Galerie, [1988?] 90 p. : ill. (chiefly col.) ; 22 cm. "Virginia Center for the Creative Arts (VCCA), Mt. San Angelo, Virginia. Deutsch-Amerikanisches Institut, Regensburg e.V." *1. Art, American - Exhibitions. 2. Art, Modern - 20th century - United States - Exhibitions. I. Schneidler, Herbert. II. Städtische Galerie Regensburg. III. Virginia Center for the Creative Arts. IV. Deutsch-Amerikanisches Institut. V. Title: Art-- made in U. S.A.*   *NYPL [3-MAMT 89-28438]*

ART, MALAYSIAN.
Zakaria Ali. Seni dan seniman . Kuala Lumpur , 1989. xiv, 315 p. : ISBN 983-620-896-8 :
N7325 .Z35 1989

Art Maritim '88 (1988 : Hamburg, Germany) Ostseeschiffahrt in der Kunst / Art Maritim '88 ; mit einem Beitrag von Wilhelm Treue ; [Herausgeber], Hamburg Messe. Hamburg : Hansa, c1988. 140 p. : chiefly col. ill. ; 22 cm. "Hanseboot." Exhibition was held in Hamburg, Oct. 22-30, 1988. ISBN 3-87700-058-4 DDC 758/.2/094307443515 20 *1. Marine painting, German - Exhibitions. 2. Marine painting - 19th century - Germany - Exhibitions. 3. Marine painting - 20th century - Germany - Exhibitions. 4. Baltic Sea Region in art - Exhibitions. I. Treue, Wilhelm, 1909- II. Hamburg Messe und Congress GmbH. III. Title.* *ND1373.5.G3 A78 1988*
     NYPL [3-MAMZ 91-6580]

ART - MARKETING.
Bernier, Georges. L'art et l'argent . Paris , c1990. 317 p. ; ISBN 2-85956-891-3 :
N8600 .B47 1990

Marquis, Alice Goldfarb. The art biz . Chicago , c1991. p. cm. ISBN 0-8092-4283-4 (cloth) : DDC 706/.8/8 20
N8600 .M38 1991

ART - MASSACHUSETTS - CAMBRIDGE - CATALOGS.
Fogg Art Museum. European paintings before 1900 in the Fogg Art Museum . Cambridge , c1991. p. cm. ISBN 0-916724-76-X (hardcover : acid-free paper) : DDC 759.94/074/7444 20
ND450 .F64 1991

ART - MASSACHUSETTS - WILLIAMSTOWN - CATALOGS.
Conrads, Margaret C., 1955- American paintings and sculpture at the Sterling and Francine Clark Art Institute/. New York , c1990. 219 p. : ISBN 1-555-95050-7 (alk. paper) : DDC 759.13/074/7441 20
N6505 .C645 1990   *NYPL [MAVZ+ (Williamstown) 91-5440]*

ART - MATHEMATICS.
Boles, Martha. The golden relationship . Bradford, Mass. , c1990- v. <1 > : ISBN 0-9614504-3-6 (bk. 1) DDC 701 20
N72.M3 B65 1990

ART, MEDIEVAL.
Edgerton, Samuel Y. The heritage of Giotto's geometry . Ithaca , 1991. p. cm. ISBN 0-8014-2573-5 (cloth : alk. paper) DDC 701/.8 20
N7430.5 .E34 1991

ART, MEDIEVAL - CATALOGS.
Duke University. Museum of Art. The Brummer collection of medieval art, the Duke University Museum of Art /. Durham , 1991. xix, 297 p., 16 p. of plates : ISBN 0-8223-1055-4

DDC 709/.02/074756563 20
N5963.D87 D854 1991
NYPL [3-MAK 91-5627]

Der Mittelalterliche Baubetrieb Westeuropas .
Köln , 1987. 568 p. : DDC 760/.044969 19
N8217.B85 M58 1987
NYPL [3-MAMZ 91-4597]

National Gallery of Art (U. S.) Sculpture and
decorative arts . Washington, D.C. [New
York] , 1992. p. cm. ISBN 0-89468-162-1 DDC
708.153 20
N5963.W18 N382 1992

ART, MEDIEVAL - CONGRESSES.
Artistes, artisans et production artistique au
Moyen Age . Paris , 1986-1990. 3 v. : ISBN
2-7084-0302-8 (v. 1) : DDC 338.4/77/094 19
N5961 .A78 1986   **NYPL [3-MAK 87-2303]**

ART, MEDIEVAL - EXHIBITIONS.
Moeller, Robert C. Sculpture and decorative
art. Raleigh [1967] 97 p.
NYPL [3-MAK 90-6857]

ART, MEDIEVAL - ITALY.
IL 60 . New York , c1990. xviii, 284 p. : ISBN
0-934977-18-6 : DDC 709/.45 20
N6911 .I34 1990
NYPL [3-MAMC 90-11305]

**ART, MEDIEVAL - PRIVATE
COLLECTIONS - EXHIBITIONS.**
Opus sacrum . Vienna , c1990. 399 p. : ISBN
3-900731-29-2   **NYPL [3-MAIH 91-4343]**

ART, MEDIEVAL - SCANDINAVIA.
Kusch, Eugen, 1905- [Alte Kunst in
Skandinavien. English.] Ancient art in
Scandinavia. Nürnberg [1965] 83 p., 176 plates.
DDC 709/.48
N7001 .K813

**ART, MEDIEVAL - SILESIA -
EXHIBITIONS.**
Muzeum Narodowe we Wrocławiu. Sztuka
Śląska XV-XVIII w. ze zbiorów Muzeum
Narodowego we Wrocławiu . Opole , 1990. 30
p., [20] p. of plates :
N7255.P62 S545 1990

**ART, MEDIEVAL - SPAIN - NAVARRE
(KINGDOM)**
Martínez de Aguirre, Javier. Arte y monarquía
en Navarra, 1328-1425 /. Pamplona , c1987.
432 p. : ISBN 84-235-0794-7
N7109.N3 M37 1987
NYPL [3-MAML 90-12586]

ART, MEDIEVAL - THEMES, MOTIVES.
Frugoni, Chiara, 1940- [Lontana città. English.]
A distant city . Princeton, N.J. , 1991. xv, 206
p., [80] p. of plates : ISBN 0-691-04083-4 (cloth :
alk. paper) : DDC 709/.02 20
N5975 .F7813 1991
NYPL [3-MAK 91-6315]

Iconographie médiévale . Paris , 1990. 207 p. :
ISBN 2-222-04344-1 : DDC 709/.02 20
N5970 .I26 1990

**ART, MEDIEVAL - YUGOSLAVIA -
DALMATIA (CROATIA)**
Höfler, Janez. Die Kunst Dalmatiens . Graz ,
1989. 338 p. : ISBN 3-201-01466-4
NYPL [3-MAM+ 90-8024]

**ART - MEDITERRANEAN REGION -
THEMES, MOTIVES.**
Crowley, Janice L. The Aegean and the east .
Jonsered , 1989. xii, 507 p. : ISBN
91-86098-55-1   **NYPL [3-MAE 90-11126]**

Art meets science and spirituality. London :
Academy Editions, 1990. 96 p. : ill. ; 28 cm.
(Art & design profile, 0267-3991 . 21) "Published as
part of Art & design, vol. 6, 5/6 90"--T.p. verso.
ISBN 1-85490-038-2 (UK)
1. Art and science. I. Art & design.
NYPL [3-MAL 91-8122]

**ART METAL-WORK - ENGLAND -
HISTORY - 20TH CENTURY -
EXHIBITIONS.**
Brennan, Shawn. Reflections . New York,
N.Y. , c1990. 51 p. : DDC 739/.0942/0747471 20
NK1142 .B7 1990 **NYPL [3-MNK 90-13003]**

ART METAL-WORK - FRANCE.
Faure, Philippe. Fer d'art roman /. [Dijon] ,
1988- v. <1 > : ISBN 2-86621-112-X (v. 1)
NK6449.A1 F38 1988

**ART METAL-WORK - FRANCE -
EXHIBITIONS.**

Guimard, Hector, 1867-1942. Hector Guimard .
Paris , 1971. 45 p. :
NYPL [3-MRX 90-7184]

**ART METAL-WORK - FRANCE - PARIS -
CATALOGS.**
Taburet, Elisabeth. L'orfèvrerie gothique,
XIIIe-début XVe siècle, au Musée de Cluny .
Paris , 1989. 294 p. : ISBN 2-7118-2280-X DDC
739/.094/09020744443 20
NK6408.923 .T33 1989

ART METAL-WORK, GOTHIC - CATALOGS.
Taburet, Elisabeth. L'orfèvrerie gothique,
XIIIe-début XVe siècle, au Musée de Cluny .
Paris , 1989. 294 p. : ISBN 2-7118-2280-X DDC
739/.094/09020744443 20
NK6408.923 .T33 1989

ART METAL-WORK, MEDIEVAL - EUROPE.
Haseloff, Günther. Email im frühen Mittelalter .
Marburg , c1990. 244 p. : ISBN 3-89398-020-2
NYPL [3-MNV 91-5235]

**ART METAL-WORK, ROMANESQUE -
FRANCE.**
Faure, Philippe. Fer d'art roman /. [Dijon] ,
1988- v. <1 > : ISBN 2-86621-112-X (v. 1)
NK6449.A1 F38 1988

**ART METAL-WORK - UNITED STATES -
HISTORY - 20TH CENTURY -
EXHIBITIONS.**
Brennan, Shawn. Reflections . New York,
N.Y. , c1990. 51 p. : DDC 739/.0942/0747471 20
NK1142 .B7 1990 **NYPL [3-MNK 90-13003]**

ART, MEXICAN.
Flores-Antúnez, Ignacio. Arte y artistas .
México, D.F. , 1989. 385 p. :
N6555 .F57 1989

Rivera, Diego, 1886-1957. Textos de arte /.
México , 1986. 430 p., [22] p. of plates : ISBN
968-8379-10-7
N6559.R58 A35 1986

ART, MEXICAN - EXHIBITIONS.
En tiempos de la posmodernidad. [Mexico
City] . 116 p. : ISBN 968-8405-58-2
N6555 .E5 1989

Mexico . New York , Boston , c1990. xv, 712
p. : ISBN 0-87099-595-2 DDC 709/.72/0747471 20
N6550 .M48 1990
NYPL [3-MAM+ 91-3897]

**ART, MEXICAN - MEXICO - MICHOACÁN
DE OCAMPO - CATALOGS.**
García Orozco, Aurora. Catálogo del
patrimonio artístico cultural de Michoacán /.
Morelia, Michoacán, México , 1986. 180 p. :
ISBN 968-667-047-5
N6556M5 G3 1986

ART, MEXICAN - MEXICO - QUERÉTARO.
Querétaro, ciudad barroca /. Querétaro, Qro.
[Mexico] , c1988. 228, [8] p. : ISBN
968-614-033-6 DDC 709/.72/45 20
N6557.Q47 Q47 1988

ART, MEXICAN - THEMES, MOTIVES.
Homenaje a Federico Sescosse . [Zacatecas,
Mexico] , 1990. xi, 140 p., [46] p. of plates :
DDC 709/.72 20
N6550 .H65 1990

**ART - MEXICO - GUANAJUATO -
CATALOGS.**
Museo Iconográfico del Quijote. Museo
Iconográfico del Quijote /. México, D.F. ,
1987. 103 p. : ISBN 968-7037-31-8
N910.G78 A6 1987

ART - MEXICO - JALISCO - HISTORY.
Reyes y Zavala, Ventura. Las bellas artes en
Jalisco /. Guadalajara, Jalisco, México , 1989.
xi, 44 p. ; ISBN 968-8323-84-5
NYPL [3-MAM 91-4662]

ART - MIDDLE EAST.
British Museum. Dept. of Western Asiatic
Antiquities. Fifty masterpieces of ancient Near
Eastern art in the Department of Western
Asiatic Antiquities, the British Museum.
London, 1969. 96 p. ISBN 0-7141-1069-8 DDC
732/.5
N5345 .B7 1969   **NYPL [3-MAF 90-6059]**

ART - MIDDLE EAST - CONGRESSES.
Investigating artistic environments in the
ancient Near East /. Washington, D.C. , c1990.
xii, 153 p. : ISBN 0-299-97070-1 (alk. paper) :
DDC 709/.35 20
N7265 .I58 1990 **NYPL [3-MAE 90-12590]**

ART, MINOAN - THEMES, MOTIVES.
Czernohaus, Karola. Delphindarstellungen von
der minoischen bis zur geometrischen Zeit /.
Göteborg , 1988. 235, 111 p., 121 p. of plates :
ISBN 91-86098-76-4
NYPL [3-MAH 90-10819]

Art mobil .
(Nr. 1) Spescha, Matias, 1925- Matias Spescha
/. Chur , 1987. 46 p. :
MLCS 89/21018 (N)
NYPL [3-MCZ S751 90-2847]

ART, MODERN.
Opfell, Olga S. Special visions . Jefferson,
N.C. , 1991. p. ISBN 0-89950-603-8 (lib. bdg. : alk.
paper) DDC 709/.2/2 B 20
N43 .O6 1991

ART, MODERN - 17TH-18TH CENTURIES.
Clifton-Mogg, Caroline. The neo-classical source
book /. New York , 1991. p. cm. ISBN
0-8478-1392-4 DDC 709/.03/3 20
N6425.N4 C55 1991

Herding, Klaus. Im Zeichen der Aufklärung .
Frankfurt am Main , 1989. 242, [1] p. : ISBN
3-596-23615-0   **NYPL [3-MAL 90-13019]**

**ART, MODERN - 17TH-18TH CENTURIES -
AUSTRIA - EXHIBITIONS.**
Jugendwerke vom Schillerplatz /. Wien , c1988.
280 p. :   **NYPL [3-MAMG 90-9782]**

**ART, MODERN - 17TH-18TH CENTURIES -
BELGIUM - ANTWERP - EXHIBITIONS.**
Antwerp (Belgium). Stedelijk Prentenkabinet.
Rondom Rubens . Antwerpen , 1991. 229 p. :
N6971.A6 A73 1991

**ART, MODERN - 17TH-18TH CENTURIES -
BELGIUM - CATALOGS.**
Museum Bredius. Museum Bredius .
['s-Gravenhage] , 1980. 176 p. :
NYPL [3-MAVZ (Hague) 81-647]

**ART, MODERN - 17TH-18TH CENTURIES -
ENGLAND - EXHIBITIONS.**
Brown, Walter R., 1940- The Stuart legacy .
Birmingham, Ala. , 1991. 176 p. : ISBN
0-931394-30-9 DDC 709/.42/074761781 20
N6766 .B76 1991

**ART, MODERN - 17TH-18TH CENTURIES -
EUROPE.**
Stürmer, Michael. Scherben des Glücks .
Berlin , c1987. 99 p. : ISBN 3-88680-180-2
N6425.N4 S78 1987

**ART, MODERN - 17TH-18TH CENTURIES -
EUROPE - EXHIBITIONS.**
Kunst um 1800 . Magdeburg [1989] 95 p. :
DDC 709/.03/3074431822 20
N6756 .K86 1989

**ART, MODERN - 17TH-18TH CENTURIES -
FRANCE.**
Weyl, Martin. Passion for reason and reason of
passion . New York , c1989. 314 p. : ISBN
0-8204-0981-2 : DDC 709.44/09/032 20
N6846 .W49 1989
NYPL [3-MAMI 91-6906]

**ART, MODERN - 17TH-18TH CENTURIES -
FRANCE - EXHIBITIONS.**
Diderot, Denis, 1713-1784. [Salons. Russian.]
Salony . Moskva , 1989. 2 v. :
N6846 .D4617 1989

Syndram, Dirk. Ruinenromantik und
Antikensehnsucht /. [Berlin] , c1986. 32 p. :
ISBN 3-88609-199-6 DDC
760/.0444/094074031554 19
N8237.8.R8 S96 1986
NYPL [3-MAMZ 90-9452]

**ART, MODERN - 17TH-18TH CENTURIES -
GERMANY - EXHIBITIONS.**
Asmus Jakob Carstens und Joseph Anton Koch,
zwei Zeitgenossen der Französischen
Revolution . Berlin [1989] 160 p. :
NC249 .A835 1989

**ART, MODERN - 17TH-18TH CENTURIES -
GERMANY (WEST) - KARLSRUHE -
EXHIBITIONS.**
Kunst in der Residenz . [Karlsruhe] [1990] 399
p. : ISBN 3-925835-58-X DDC
709/.43/4643074434643 20
N6886.K33 K85 1990

**ART, MODERN - 17TH-18TH CENTURIES -
GREAT BRITAIN - DICTIONARIES.**
Waterhouse, Ellis Kirkham, 1905- The
dictionary of British 18th century painters in

oils and crayons /. Woodbridge , 1981. 443 p. :
   ISBN 0-902028-93-6 :   DDC 759.2 B 19
N6766 .W29   **NYPL   [MAO 91-6317]**

**ART, MODERN - 17TH-18TH CENTURIES -
ITALY - EXHIBITIONS.**
Syndram, Dirk. Ruinenromantik und
Antikensehnsucht /. [Berlin] , c1986. 32 p. :
   ISBN 3-88609-199-6 DDC
   760/.0444/094074031554 19
N8237.8.R8 S96 1986
              NYPL   [3-MAMZ 90-9452]

**ART, MODERN - 17TH-18TH CENTURIES -
ITALY - LOMBARDY - EXHIBITIONS.**
Settecento lombardo /. Milano , c1991. 627 p. :
   ISBN 88-435-3418-1
              NYPL   [3-MAMC 91-7605]

**ART, MODERN - 17TH-18TH CENTURIES -
ITALY - NAPLES - SOURCES.**
Ricerche sul '600 napoletano. Saggi e
documenti per la storia dell'arte. Milano , 1987.
201 p. :   DDC 709/.45/7309032 20
N6921.N2 R54 1987
              NYPL   [3-MAMC 90-11700]

**ART, MODERN - 17TH-18TH CENTURIES -
ITALY - TRIESTE - EXHIBITIONS.**
Neoclassico . Venezia , 1990. xix, 530 p. :
   ISBN 88-317-5361-4
N6916.5.N45 N4 1990

**ART, MODERN - 17TH-18TH CENTURIES -
ITALY - VENICE - EXHIBITIONS.**
Knox, George. 18th century Venetian art in
Canadian collections =. Vancouver, B.C.,
Canada , c1989. 108 p. :   ISBN 0-920095-81-X
IN PROCESS (ONLINE)
              NYPL   [3-MAMC+ 91-6265]

**ART, MODERN - 17TH-18TH CENTURIES -
ITALY - VICENZA - EXHIBITIONS.**
I Tiepolo e il Settecento vicentino /. Milano ,
c1990. 404 p. :   ISBN 88-435-3180-8
              NYPL   [3-MAMC 91-5454]

**ART, MODERN - 17TH-18TH CENTURIES -
ITALY - VICENZA (PROVINCE) -
EXHIBITIONS.**
I Tiepolo e il Settecento vicentino /. Milano ,
c1990. 404 p. :   ISBN 88-435-3180-8
N6923.T5 A4 1990

**ART, MODERN - 17TH-18TH CENTURIES -
NETHERLANDS.**
Herbert, Zbigniew. [Stomme van Kampen.
English.] Still life with a bridle . New York ,
c1991. p. cm.   ISBN 0-88001-306-0 :   DDC
709/.492/09032 20
N6946 .H4713 1991

**ART, MODERN - 17TH-18TH CENTURIES -
NETHERLANDS - CATALOGS.**
Museum Bredius. Museum Bredius .
['s-Gravenhage] , 1980. 176 p. :
              NYPL   [3-MAVZ (Hague) 81-647]

**ART, MODERN - 17TH-18TH CENTURIES -
NETHERLANDS - PRIVATE
COLLECTIONS - EXHIBITIONS.**
Hollandse en vlaamse kunst uit de 17e eeuw .
[Rotterdam, 1973?] 183 p. :
              NYPL   [3-MAME 90-5901]

**ART, MODERN - 17TH-18TH CENTURIES -
SILESIA - EXHIBITIONS.**
Muzeum Narodowe we Wrocławiu. Sztuka
Śląska XV-XVIII w. ze zbiorów Muzeum
Narodowego we Wrocławiu. Opole , 1990. 30
p., [20] p. of plates :
N7255.P62 S545 1990

**ART, MODERN - 17TH-18TH CENTURIES -
SOUTHERN STATES.**
Poesch, Jessie J. The art of the old South .
New York , 1983. xii, 384 p. :   ISBN
0-394-40193-X :   DDC 709/.75 19
N6520 .P63 1983
              NYPL   [3-MAMT+ 90-10836]

**ART, MODERN - 17TH-18TH CENTURIES -
SPAIN.**
Bédat, Claude. [Académie des beaux-arts de
Madrid, 1744-1808. Spanish.] La Real
Academia de Bellas Artes de San Fernando
(1744-1808) . Madrid , 1989. 547 p. :   ISBN
84-7392-319-7
IN PROCESS (ONLINE)
              NYPL   [3-MAML 91-6080]

**ART, MODERN - 17TH-18TH CENTURIES -
SPAIN - SEVILLE.**
Serrera Contreras, Juan Miguel. Iconografía de

Sevilla, 1650-1790 /. Madrid , c1989. 292 p. :
   ISBN 84-86022-35-2
              NYPL   [3-MAML+ 91-2661]

**ART, MODERN - 17TH AND 18TH
CENTURIES - CZECHOSLOVAK
REPUBLIC.**
Národní galerie V Praze. Baroque in Bohemia.
London, 1969. 1 v. (unpaged)   DDC 709/.437/1
N6818 .P7

**ART, MODERN - 18TH CENTURY -
FRANCE - EXHIBITIONS.**
French masters, Rococo to Romanticism . [Los
Angeles] , 1961. 72 p. :
              NYPL   [3-MAMI+ 90-6906]

Le Style troubadour . Bourg-en-Bresse , 1971.
107 p., 18 p. of plates :
              NYPL   [3-MAMI 90-7037]

**ART, MODERN - 18TH CENTURY -
GERMANY - CATALOGS.**
Von Caspar David Friedrich bis Adolph
Menzel . München , c1990. 283 p. :   ISBN
3-7913-1047-X DDC 759.3/074/43613 20
N6867.5.R6 V6 1990

ART, MODERN - 19TH CENTURY.
L'Art du XIXe siècle . Paris , c1990. 629 p. :
   ISBN 2-85088-027-2
              NYPL   [3-MAL+ 91-3621]

Bourdais, Gildas, 1939- Les modernes et les
autres . Lausanne , c1990. 367 p. :   ISBN
2-88253-018-8 DDC 709/.04 20
N6447 .B67 1990

Canaday, John, 1907- Mainstreams of modern
art /. New York , c1959. xxiv, 576 p., [15]
leaves of plates /   **NYPL   [3-MAL]**

Hunter, Sam, 1923- Modern art . New York ,
1992. p. cm.   ISBN 0-8109-3609-7 DDC 709/.04
20
N6447 .H86 1992

Hunter, Sam, 1923- Modern art . Englewood
Cliffs, N.J. , New York , 1992. p. cm.   ISBN
0-13-596073-8 (pbk)   DDC 709/.04 20
N6447 .H86 1992b

James, Henry, 1843-1916. The painter's eye .
Madison, Wis. , c1989. viii, 276 p. :   ISBN
0-299-12280-8 :   DDC 759.05 20
N6450 .J36 1989   **NYPL   [3-MAL 90-10758]**

Schjeldahl, Peter. The hydrogen jukebox .
Berkeley , c1991. p. cm.   ISBN 0-520-06731-2
(alk. paper)   DDC 709/.04 20
N6447 .S345 1991

**ART, MODERN - 19TH CENTURY -
ANECDOTES.**
Hall, Donald, 1928- Anecdotes of modern art .
New York , 1990. xix, 377 p. ;   ISBN
0-19-503813-4 (alk. paper) :   DDC 709.04 20
N6447 .H34 1990   **NYPL   [3-MAL 90-11303]**

**ART, MODERN - 19TH CENTURY -
AUSTRALIA - EXHIBITIONS.**
Edwards, Deborah. Stampede of the lower
gods . Sydney [1989] vi, 66 p. :   ISBN
0-7305-6555-6 DDC 709/.94/0749441 20
N7760 .E38 1989

**ART, MODERN - 19TH CENTURY -
AUSTRIA - EXHIBITIONS.**
Gott erhalte Österreich . Eisenstadt [1990] 239
p. :
N6807 .G67 1990

Jugendwerke vom Schillerplatz /. Wien , c1988.
280 p. :   **NYPL   [3-MAMG 90-9782]**

**ART, MODERN - 19TH CENTURY -
AUSTRIA - VIENNA.**
Fischer, Wolfgang Georg, 1933- [Gustav Klimt
und Emilie Flöge. English.] Klimt and Emilie .
Woodstock, N.Y. , 1992. p. cm.   ISBN
0-87951-451-5 :   DDC 709/.2 B 20
N6811.5.K55 F513 1992

**ART, MODERN - 19TH CENTURY -
BELGIUM.**
Dictionnaire biographique illustré des artistes en
Belgique depuis 1830. [Bruxelles] , 1987. 416
p., [31] p. of plates :
              NYPL   [3-MAO 91-4886]

**ART, MODERN - 19TH CENTURY -
BRANDYWIN CREEK VALLEY (PA. AND
DEL.) - CATALOGS.**
Brandywine River Museum. Catalogue of the
collection, 1969-1989 /. Chadds Ford, Pa. ,

c1991. p.   DDC 709/.73/07474814 20
N6517 .B7 1991

**ART, MODERN - 19TH CENTURY - BRAZIL -
SÃO PAULO (STATE) - CATALOGS.**
São Paulo (Brazil : State). Pinacoteca do
Estado. Pinacoteca do Estado . São Paulo ,
1988. 447 p. :   DDC 708.981/61 20
N6657.S32 S26 1988

**ART, MODERN - 19TH CENTURY -
CATALOGS.**
Le Musée d'art moderne . [Bruxelles] , c1988.
128 p. :
N6447 .M865 1988

**ART, MODERN - 19TH CENTURY -
EUROPE.**
Artistes étrangers à Pont-Aven, Concarneau et
autres lieux de Bretagne /. [Rennes] [1989]
233 p. :   ISBN 2-86847-026-2
              NYPL   [3-MAM 91-3261]

Boime, Albert. Art in an age of Bonapartism,
1800-1815 /. Chicago , 1990. xxvii, 706 p. :
   ISBN 0-226-06335-6 (alk. paper) :   DDC
709/.03/4 20
N6757 .B56 1990   **NYPL   [3-MAM 91-5522]**

Hofmann, Werner, 1928- The earthly paradise .
New York , 1961. 436 p. :
ND457 .H613   **NYPL   [3-MAL+ 90-10772]**

Ionescu, Adrian-Silvan. Artă şi document .
Bucureşti , 1990. 318 p., [48] p. of plates :
   ISBN 973-330-072-1 :
N8214.5.R6 I55 1990

**ART, MODERN - 19TH CENTURY -
EUROPE - EXHIBITIONS.**
Impressionismo in Europa . Bologna , c1990.
170 p. :   ISBN 88-7779-126-8
              NYPL   [3-MAVZ (Prague) 91-6701]

Kunst um 1800 . Magdeburg [1989] 95 p. :
   DDC 709/.03/3074431822 20
N6756 .K86 1989

L'œuvre ultime de Cézanne à Dubuffet .
Saint-Paul , c1989. 269 p. :   ISBN 2-900923-01-60
   DDC 709/.04/007444941 20
N6757 .O43 1989

Marlborough Fine Art London (Ltd.) 19th and
20th century watercolours, drawings and
sculpture /. London, 1964. 20 p.
              NYPL   [3-MAL 90-6893]

Monet to Matisse . Jerusalem , c1988. 130, [10]
p. :   ISBN 965-278-085-5 (pbk)
              NYPL   [3-MAL + 89-6103]

Tsigakou, Fani-Maria. Through romantic eyes .
Alexandria, Va. , 1991. p. cm.   ISBN
0-88397-099-6 DDC 758/.9949506 20
N8214.5.G8 T784 1991

**ART, MODERN - 19TH CENTURY -
EUROPE - JAPANESE INFLUENCES -
EXHIBITIONS.**
Verborgene Impressionen =. [Wien] , c1990.
445 p. :   ISBN 3-900688-13-3 (Katalogausgabe)
              NYPL   [3-MAM 91-3678]

**ART, MODERN - 19TH CENTURY -
EUROPE - THEMES, MOTIVES -
EXHIBITIONS.**
Umanesimo, disumanesimo nell'arte europea
1890/1980 . Milano , c1980. 172 p. :   DDC
709/.04/00740551 19
N6757 .U42 1980   **NYPL   [3-MAL 90-5471]**

**ART, MODERN - 19TH CENTURY -
EUROPR - EXHIBITIONS.**
Columbus Museum of Art. Impressionism and
European modernism . Columbus, Ohio ,
Seattle , 1991. p.   ISBN 0-295-97133-9 :   DDC
709/.03/407477157 20
N6447 .C65 1991

**ART, MODERN - 19TH CENTURY -
EXHIBITIONS.**
Hancock, Jane H., 1949- Homecoming . St.
Paul , c1991. x, 116 p. :   ISBN 0-87351-259-6
   DDC 759.05/074/74776581 20
N6450 .H298 1991

Irises and five masterpieces. [Australia] [1989]
1 v. (unpaged)   ISBN 0-9598384-1-4
              NYPL   [MAX (Bond) 91-6719]

Perl, Jed. Gallery going . San Diego , c1991.
xxiv, 431 p., [16] p. of plates :   ISBN
0-15-134260-1 :   DDC 709/.04/0074 20
N6447 .P38 1991   **NYPL   [3-MAV 91-7445]**

Die Sammlung Woty und Theodor Werner /.
München , c1990. 131 p. : ISBN 3-7774-5460-5
NYPL [3-MAX (Werner, W.) 91-6703]

**ART, MODERN - 19TH CENTURY -
FINLAND.**
Valkonen, Markku, 1946- Kultakausi /.
Porvoo , c1989. 309 p. : ISBN 951-0-15859-3 :
N7255.F5 V35 1989

**ART, MODERN - 19TH CENTURY -
FRANCE.**
Clayson, Hollis, 1946- Painted love . New
Haven , c1991. p. cm. ISBN 0-300-04730-4
  DDC 760/.0449306742/094436109034 20
N6847.5.I4 C58 1991

Driskel, Michael Paul. Representing belief .
University Park , c1991. p. cm. ISBN
  0-271-00747-8 DDC 709/.44/09034 20
N6847 .D75 1991

Frèches-Thory, Claire. Les nabis /. Paris ,
c1990. 319 p. : ISBN 2-08-010941-3 DDC
709/.44/36109034 20
N6847.5.N3 F735 1990

Lévêque, Jean Jacques. Les années
impressionnistes, 1870-1889 /. Courbevoie,
Paris , c1990. 660 p. : ISBN 2-86770-042-6
IN PROCESS (ONLINE)
               NYPL [3-MAMI+ 91-4871]

Sefrioui, Anne. Impressionist fans /. New
York , 1991. p. cm. ISBN 0-86565-129-9 DDC
759.4/09/034 20
N6847.5.I4 S44 1991

**ART, MODERN - 19TH CENTURY -
FRANCE - ALSACE.**
Bauer, A. (Alice) Répertoire des artistes
d'Alsace des dix-neuvième et vingtième siècles .
Strasbourg , 1984-1991. 6 v. : ISBN
2-85369-036-9 (set) DDC 709/.22/2 B 19
N6849.A4 B3 1984   NYPL [MAO 86-2104]

**ART, MODERN - 19TH CENTURY -
FRANCE - AUVERS-SUR-OISE -
EXHIBITIONS.**
Van Gogh et les peintres d'Auvers-sur-Oise .
[Paris] , 1954. xl, 100 p., xxxii p. of plates :
N6847.5.I4 V36 1954

**ART, MODERN - 19TH CENTURY -
FRANCE - EXHIBITIONS.**
Conisbee, Philip. Monet to Matisse . Los
Angeles, Calif. , c1991. 144 p. : ISBN
  0-87587-159-3 DDC 709/.44/09034 20
N6847 .C6 1991

French masters, Rococo to Romanticism . [Los
Angeles] , 1961. 72 p. :
               NYPL [3-MAMI+ 90-6906]

Impressionism and post impressionism .
Portland, Me. , c1991. p. cm. DDC
709/.03/4407474191 20
N6847.5.I4 I43 1991

Le Style troubadour . Bourg-en-Bresse , 1971.
107 p., 18 p. of plates :
               NYPL [3-MAMI 90-7037]

**ART, MODERN - 19TH CENTURY -
FRANCE - PARIS.**
Friedrich, Otto, 1929- Olympia . New York,
NY , c1992. p. ISBN 0-06-016318-6 (cloth) :
  DDC 701/.03 20
N6847 .F75 1992

**ART, MODERN - 19TH CENTURY -
GERMANY.**
Arnaldo, Javier. Estilo y naturaleza . Madrid ,
c1990. 284 p. : ISBN 84-7774-536-6
N6867.5.R6 A76 1990

Meurer, Thomas. Die Eisenbahn in der
deutschen Kunst . Witterschlick/Bonn , 1989.
172, [76] p. : ISBN 3-925267-28-X
N6867 .M48 1989

Oelschlegel, F. Wandel einer Sicht . Rockville,
MD , 1990. 233 p. : ISBN 0-930329-38-4
N6867 .O27 1990

**ART, MODERN - 19TH CENTURY -
GERMANY - CATALOGS.**
Von Caspar David Friedrich bis Adolph
Menzel . München , c1990. 283 p. : ISBN
  3-7913-1047-X DDC 759.3/074/43613 20
N6867.5.R6 V6 1990

**ART, MODERN - 19TH CENTURY -
GERMANY - DARMSTADT.**
Darmstadt Künstler-Kolonie. Museum

Künstlerkolonie Darmstadt /. Darmstadt
[1989?] lv, 253 p. :   *NYPL [3-MLF 91-5455]*

**ART, MODERN - 19TH CENTURY -
GERMANY (WEST) - KARLSRUHE -
EXHIBITIONS.**
Kunst in der Residenz . [Karlsruhe] [1990] 399
p. : ISBN 3-925835-58-X DDC
  709/.43/4643074434643 20
N6886.K33 K85 1990

**ART, MODERN - 19TH CENTURY -
GERMANY (WEST) - WORPSWEDE.**
Boulboullé, Guido. Worpswede . Köln , c1989.
223 p. : ISBN 3-7701-1847-2
               NYPL [3-MAMG 90-12605]

Worpswede . [Lilienthal] , c1989. 254 p. :
  ISBN 3-922516-80-7
               NYPL [3-MAMG 91-4485]

**ART, MODERN - 19TH CENTURY -
GERMANY - WORPSWEDE.**
Worpswede . [Worpswede] , c1989. 254 p. :
  ISBN 3-922516-80-7 DDC 709/.43/59309034 20
N6867.5.W67 W68 1989

**ART, MODERN - 19TH CENTURY -
GERMANY - WÜRZBURG -
EXHIBITIONS.**
Städtische Galerie Würzburg.
Würzburg--Künstler sehen eine Stadt .
[Würzburg] [1989?] 102 p. : ISBN
  3-926916-04-4
N6886.W87 S73 1989

**ART, MODERN - 19TH CENTURY -
HUNGARY.**
Szabadi, Judit. [Magyar szecesszió művészete.
English.] Art nouveau in Hungary . [Budapest] ,
c1989. 157 p., [264] p. of plates : ISBN
  963-13-2926-7 *NYPL [3-MAM 91-3931]*

**ART, MODERN - 19TH CENTURY -
HUNGARY - EXHIBITIONS.**
Magyar Nemzeti Galéria. Ungarische Malerei
und Bildhauerei im 19. Jahrhundert . Budapest ,
1989. 47 p., [42] p. of plates :
N6819 .M28 1989

**ART, MODERN - 19TH CENTURY - IDAHO -
EXHIBITIONS.**
Harthorn, Sandy, 1945- One hundred years of
Idaho art, 1850-1950 . Boise, ID , c1990. 134
p. : DDC 709/.796/07479628 20
N6530.I2 H37 1990
               NYPL [3-MAMT 90-11110]

**ART, MODERN - 19TH CENTURY - INDIA -
BENGAL.**
Guha-Thakurta, Tapati. The making of a new
"Indian" art . Cambridge [England] , New
York , 1992. p. cm. ISBN 0-521-39247-0 DDC
  709/.54/1409034 20
N7307.B4 G84 1992

**ART, MODERN - 19TH CENTURY - ITALY -
BERGAMO.**
Mosca, Pietro. Arte e costume a Bergamo .
Bergamo , c1989-c1990. 2 v. (1020 p.) ;
IN PROCESS (ONLINE)
               NYPL [3-MAMC+ 91-5886]

**ART, MODERN - 19TH CENTURY - ITALY -
GENOA.**
Testimonianze Liberty a Genova /. Genova ,
c1986. 46 p. : ISBN 88-7058-218-3
               NYPL [3-MAMC 90-11119]

**ART, MODERN - 19TH CENTURY - ITALY -
RIVIERA.**
Leonardo Massabò e l'Ottocento nella Riviera
occidentale /. Genova , c1990. 195 p., [4] p. of
plates :   *NYPL [3-MCF M418 90-13278]*

**ART, MODERN - 19TH CENTURY - ITALY -
SOURCES.**
Testimonianze e polemiche figurative in Italia .
Messina [1974] 507 p. ;
N6917.5.N44 B37
               NYPL [3-MAMC 90-5898]

**ART, MODERN - 19TH CENTURY - ITALY -
TRIESTE - EXHIBITIONS.**
Neoclassico . Venezia , 1990. xix, 530 p. :
  ISBN 88-317-5361-4
N6916.5.N45 N4 1990

**ART, MODERN - 19TH CENTURY - LATIN
AMERICA.**
El nacionalismo en el arte. [Bogotá, Colombia]
[1984]. 90 p. ;   *NYPL [3-MAM 90-4731]*

**ART, MODERN - 19TH CENTURY - LATIN
AMERICA - EXHIBITIONS.**

Arte en Iberoamérica, 1820-1980 . [Madrid]
[1989?] xxi, 359, [3] p. : ISBN 84-7506-297-0
N6502.4 .A76 1989

**ART, MODERN - 19TH CENTURY -
NETHERLANDS.**
Visual arts in the Netherlands /. The Hague
[1989] 46 p. : DDC 709/.492 20
N6947 .V57 1989
               NYPL [3-MAME 91-5917]

**ART, MODERN - 19TH CENTURY -
NORWAY.**
Moen, Arve. Gullalderens Mestere . Olso ,
1964. 139, 165 p.
               NYPL [3-MAM+ 90-2909]

**ART, MODERN - 19TH CENTURY -
PENNSYLVANIA - PITTSBURGH
REGION - CATALOGS.**
Westmoreland Museum of Art. Southwestern
Pennsylvania painters . Greensburg, Pa. , 1989.
x, 138 p. : ISBN 0-931241-21-9 DDC
  759.148/8/07474886 20
N6530.P42 P589 1989
               NYPL [3-MCW 91-6266]

**ART, MODERN - 19TH CENTURY -
PRIVATE COLLECTIONS - UNITED
STATES - EXHIBITIONS.**
University of Kansas. Museum of Art.
Paintings, drawings, and prints of the 19th and
20th centuries. Lawrence [1960] 24 p. DDC
707.4
N5220.F56   *NYPL [3-MAL 90-6052]*

**ART, MODERN - 19TH CENTURY -
ROMANIA.**
Ionescu, Adrian-Silvan. Artă și document .
București , 1990. 318 p., [48] p. of plates :
  ISBN 973-330-072-1 :
N8214.5.R6 I55 1990

**ART, MODERN - 19TH CENTURY -
RUSSIAN S.F.S.R.**
Russkoe i sovetskoe iskusstvo . Leningrad ,
1989. 79 p. ;
N6987 .R877 1989

Sarabianov, Dimtriĭ Vladimirovich. Russian art .
London , c1990. 320 p. : ISBN 0-500-23574-0
  (bk. jkt.) :   *NYPL [3-MAM+ 90-11076]*

**ART, MODERN - 19TH CENTURY -
RUSSIAN S.F.S.R. - LENINGRAD -
EXHIBITIONS.**
St. Petersburg um 1800 . Recklinghausen ,
c1990. 568 p. : ISBN 3-7647-0401-2
N6996 .S7 1990

**ART, MODERN - 19TH CENTURY -
SCOTLAND - GLASGOW.**
Eadie, William, 1948- Movements of
modernity . London , 1990. viii, 292 p. ; ISBN
  0-415-03243-1 DDC 709/.414/4309034 20
N6781.G55 E26 1991
               NYPL [3-MAMR 90-13191]

**ART, MODERN - 19TH CENTURY -
SOUTHERN STATES.**
Poesch, Jessie J. The art of the old South .
New York , 1983. xii, 384 p. : ISBN
  0-394-40193-X : DDC 709/.75 19
N6520 .P63 1983
               NYPL [3-MAMT+ 90-10836]

**ART, MODERN - 19TH CENTURY -
SOUTHWEST, OLD - EXHIBITIONS.**
Nineteenth century Trans-Mississippi South .
Little Rock, Ark. , 1990. vi, 33 p. : DDC
  709/.76/0903407476773 20
N6520 .N56 1990

**ART, MODERN - 19TH CENTURY - SOVIET
UNION.**
Chamot, Mary, 1900- Russian painting and
sculpture /. Oxford , New York , c1963. xiii,
55 p., 36 p. of plates :
               NYPL [3-MAM 90-6295]

**ART, MODERN - 19TH CENTURY - SPAIN -
SEVILLE.**
Alfageme Ruano, Pedro. El romanticismo
Sevillano . Sevilla , 1989. 176 p., [21] p. of
plates : ISBN 84-87039-13-8
               NYPL [3-MCQ B39 91-4517]

**ART, MODERN - 19TH CENTURY -
SWITZERLAND - EXHIBITIONS.**
Das Engadin Ferdinand Hodlers und anderer
Künstler des 19. und 20. Jahrhunderts . [Chur] ,
St. Moritz , c1990. 122 p. : ISBN 3-905240-15-7
  DDC 759.9494 20
ND853.H6 A4 1990

ART, MODERN - 19TH CENTURY - THEMES, MOTIVES.

Crary, Jonathan. Techniques of the observer . Cambridge, Mass. , c1990. 171 p. : ISBN 0-262-03169-8   DDC 701/.15 20
N7430.5 .C7 1990   NYPL [3-MAL 91-4620]

Modern art and popular culture . New York , 1990. 255 p., [81] p. of plates : ISBN 0-8109-2466-8 (pbk.)   DDC 700/.9/04 20
N6447 .M63 1991   NYPL [3-MAL 91-3688]

ART, MODERN - 19TH CENTURY - THEMES, MOTIVES - EXHIBITIONS.

Varnedoe, Kirk, 1946- High & low . New York , c1990. 460 p. : ISBN 0-87070-353-6 (MoMA : hard)
NYPL [3-MAL+ 91-3655]

ART, MODERN - 19TH CENTURY - UNITED STATES.

Cock, Elizabeth M., 1925- The influence of photography on American landscape painting [microform] . 1967. 2 v. (xiii, 247 leaves) :
*NYPL [*ZM-71]*

Ehrlich, George, 1925- Technology and the artist [microform] . 1960. iv, 243 leaves :
*NYPL [*ZM-231]*

The Italian presence in American art, 1860-1920 /. New York , Roma , 1991. p. cm. ISBN 0-8232-1342-0 : DDC 709/.73/09034 20
N6510 .I8 1991

ART, MODERN - 19TH CENTURY - UNITED STATES - CONGRESSES.

American art around 1900 . Washington , Hanover [N.H.] , 1990. 136 p. : ISBN 0-89468-143-5   *NYPL [3-MAMT 91-7570]*

ART, MODERN - 19TH CENTURY - UNITED STATES - EXHIBITIONS.

American light . [Laurenceville, NJ] , Washington, [D.C.] , c1989. 330 p. : ISBN 0-691-04074-5 (alk. paper) : DDC 758/.1/09730740153 19
N8214.5.U6 A47 1989
NYPL [3-MAMT 90-12012]

Art what thou eat . Mount Kisco, N.Y. , c1991. 191 p. : ISBN 1-559-21051-6 : DDC 704.9/49641/0973 20
N6512 .A763 1991
NYPL [3-MAMZ+ 91-5410]

Bernard Danenberg Galleries. One hundred recent acquisitions, by American artists. New York, 1969. 51 p. *NYPL [3-MAMT 90-6625]*

Fink, Lois Marie. American art at the nineteenth-century Paris Salons /. Washington, D.C. : Cambridge ; xxiv, 430 p. : ISBN 0-521-38499-0   DDC 709/.73/0903407444361 20
N6510 .F57 1990   NYPL [3-MCW 90-11536]

Impressionism and post impressionism . Portland, Me. , c1991. p. cm. DDC 709/.03/4407474191 20
N6847.5.I4 143 1991

Marlais, Michael Andrew. Americans and Paris . Waterville, Me. , c1990. 62 p. : DDC 759.13/074/7416 20
N6510 .M27 1990
NYPL [3-MAMT 90-13006]

The Sandra Doane Turk collection of Western art . St. Petersburg, Florida , 1985. 42 p. :
NYPL [3-MAMZ 90-11526]

The Technological muse . Katonah, N.Y. , c1990. 96 p. : ISBN 0-915171-19-8
NYPL [3-MAMT+ 91-7609]

ART, MODERN - 19TH CENTURY - UNITED STATES - JAPANESE INFLUENCES - EXHIBITIONS.

Hosley, William. The Japan idea . Hartford, Conn. , 1990. 211 p. : ISBN 0-918333-07-5
NYPL [3-MAMT+ 91-3289]

Meech-Pekarik, Julia. Japonisme comes to America . New York , 1990. 256 p. : ISBN 0-8109-3501-5   DDC 760/.0973/07474942 20
N6510 .M44 1990   NYPL [MDBV 90-11897]

ART, MODERN - 20 CENTURY.
ART, MODERN - 20TH CENTURY.

Arte conceptual revisado =. [Valencia] [1990?] 286 p. : ISBN 84-7721-108-6 DDC 709/.04/075 20
N6494.C63 A76 1990

Boudaille, Georges. L'art abstrait /. [Paris] , c1990. 264, [8] p. : ISBN 2-7079-0024-9 DDC

709/.04/052 20
N6494.A2 B68 1990

Bourdais, Gildas, 1939- Les modernes et les autres . Lausanne , c1990. 367 p. : ISBN 2-88253-018-8 DDC 709/.04 20
N6447 .B67 1990

Donation Gerard Bonnier /. Stockholm [1989] 106 p. : ISBN 91-29-59355-7
N6488.S8 S74 1989

Fagone, Vittorio. L'immagine video . Milano , 1990. 239 p., 32 p. of plates : ISBN 88-07-10132-7 : DDC 700/.9/04 20
N6494.V53 F34 1990

Gombrich, E. H. (Ernst Hans), 1909- Topics of our time . Berkeley , 1991. p. cm. ISBN 0-520-07516-1 DDC 001.3 20
N6490 .G595 1991

Gruen, John. The artist observed . Chicago, IL , c1991. p. cm. ISBN 1-556-52103-0 : DDC 709/.2/2 B 20
N6490 .G725 1991

Heusinger von Waldegg, Joachim. Der Künstler als Märtyrer . Worms , c1989. 112 p., [48] p. of plates : ISBN 3-88462-073-8
N6490 .H468 1989

Hunter, Sam, 1923- Modern art . New York , 1992. p. cm. ISBN 0-8109-3609-7 DDC 709/.04 20
N6447 .H86 1992

Hunter, Sam, 1923- Modern art . Englewood Cliffs, N.J. , New York , 1992. p. cm. ISBN 0-13-596073-8 (pbk.)   DDC 709/.04 20
N6447 .H86 1992b

Iskusstvo i massy v sovremennom burzhuaznom obshchestve /. Moskva , 1989. 319 p. ; ISBN 5-85285-074-8 :
NX458 .I84 1989

Kampf, Avram. Chagall to Kitaj . New York , London , 1990. 206 p. : ISBN 0-275-93900-6 (alk. paper) DDC 704/.03924/0904 20
N7417 .K34 1991

Levanto, Yrjänä. Täydellinen torso . Helsinki , 1990. 239 p. : ISBN 951-37-0180-8
N6490 .L44 1990

Mascheck, Joseph. Modernities . University Park, Pa. , 1992. p. cm. ISBN 0-271-00808-3 : DDC 720/.9/04 20
N6494.M64 M37 1992

Néret, Gilles. 30 ans d'art moderne peintres et sculpteurs /. Fribourg , c1988. 248 p. : ISBN 0-209-28473-5
NYPL [3-MAL+ 90-10571]

Pavel, Amelia. Traiectorii ale privirii /. [Bucharest] , 1990. 235 p. ; ISBN 973-330-095-0 :
N6490 .P336 1990

Pellizzi, Francesco. Adventures of the symbol . New York City , 1986. 1 v. (unpaged) ; DDC 704.9/46 20
N5311 .P4 1986

Schjeldahl, Peter. The hydrogen jukebox . Berkeley , c1991. p. cm. ISBN 0-520-06731-2 (alk. paper) DDC 709/.04 20
N6447 .S345 1991

Seitz, William Chapin. Art in the Age of Aquarius, 1955-1970 /. Washington , 1991. p. cm. ISBN 0-87474-868-2 DDC 709/.73/09046 20
N6512 .S335 1991

Taboo and totem . New York , 1991. p. cm. ISBN 0-8419-1249-1 (cloth)   DDC 701/.05 20
N72.P74 T33 1991

Tilroe, Anna. De blauwe gitaar /. Amsterdam , 1990. 192 p. : ISBN 90-214-8367-X
N6490 .T556 1990

World artists 1980-1990 . New York , 1991. p. cm. ISBN 0-8242-0827-7 DDC 709/.2/2 B 20
N6489 .W67 1991

Yenawine, Philip. How to look at modern art /. New York , 1991. p. cm. ISBN 0-8109-2485-4 DDC 701/.1 20
N6490 .Y46 1991

ART, MODERN - 20TH CENTURY - ADDRESSES, ESSAYS, LECTURES.

Spies, Werner, 1937- Das Auge am Tatort . München , 1979. 347 p. : ISBN 3-7913-0484-4
N6490 .S65   NYPL [3-MAL 80-2230]

ART, MODERN - 20TH CENTURY - AFRICA, SUB-SAHARAN - EXHIBITIONS.

Vogel, Susan. Africa explores . New York : Munich : 294 p. : ISBN 3-7913-1143-3 (cloth) : DDC 709/.67/07473 20
N7391.65 .V63 1991   NYPL [Sc G 91-40]

ART, MODERN - 20TH CENTURY - ANECDOTES.

Hall, Donald, 1928- Anecdotes of modern art . New York , 1990. xix, 377 p. ; ISBN 0-19-503813-4 (alk. paper) : DDC 709.04 20
N6447 .H34 1990   NYPL [3-MAL 90-11303]

ART, MODERN - 20TH CENTURY - ARGENTINA.

Arte argentino, siglo XX /. [Argentina] c1990 (Buenos Aires, R. Argentina [i.e. República Argentina] : HUR) 124 p. : DDC 709/.82/0904 20
N6635 .A78 1990

ART, MODERN - 20TH CENTURY - ARGENTINA - EXHIBITIONS.

Academia Nacional de Bellas Artes, 1936-1986 . [Buenos Aires , 1987] 119 p. : DDC 709/.82/0748211 20
N6635 .A53 1987

ART, MODERN - 20TH CENTURY - ARGENTINA - HISTORY AND CRITITICISM.

Bandin Ron, J. C. Plastica argentina . Buenos Aires , 1978. 228, [4] p., [16] p. of plates :
NYPL [3-MAM 90-6456]

ART, MODERN - 20TH CENTURY - ARMENIAN S.S.R. - CATALOGS.

Hayastani eritasard nkarich'nerě /. Erevan , 1987. 166 p. :
N7292.6 .H37 1987

ART, MODERN - 20TH CENTURY - AUSTRALIA.

Burke, Janine. Field of vision . Ringwood, Vic., Australia , 1990. xi, 148 p., [16] p. of plates : ISBN 0-670-83586-2
NYPL [3-MAM 90-13438]

ART, MODERN - 20TH CENTUIRY - AUSTRALIA - EXHIBITIONS.
ART, MODERN - 20TH CENTURY - AUSTRALIA - EXHIBITIONS.

Balance 1990 . South Brisbane, Qld., Australia , c1990. 95 p. : ISBN 0-7242-3855-7
NYPL [3-MADF 91-7104]

Eagle, Mary, 1944- 1990 Adelaide Biennial of Australian art /. Adelaide , 1990. 113 p. : ISBN 0-7308-0773-8
NYPL [3-MAM+ 91-5044]

Edwards, Deborah. Stampede of the lower gods . Sydney [1989] vi, 66 p. : ISBN 0-7305-6555-6 DDC 709/.94/0749441 20
N7760 .E38 1989

On the edge . [Perth, W.A.] , c1989. 64 p. : ISBN 0-7309-0703-1
NYPL [3-MADF+ 90-12876]

ART, MODERN - 20TH CENTURY - AUSTRIA - CARINTHIA - EXHIBITIONS.

Zaunschirm, Thomas, 1943- Fremdbild Heimat . Wien , c1989. 101 p. : ISBN 3-900606-12-9
N6809.C3 Z36 1989

ART, MODERN - 20TH CENTURY - AUSTRIA - EXHIBITIONS.

Jugendwerke vom Schillerplatz /. Wien , c1988. 280 p. :   *NYPL [3-MAMG 90-9782]*

Neue Galerie am Landesmuseum Joanneum. Kunst der 80er Jahre . [Graz] [1990] 1 v. (unpaged) :
MLCM 91/01636 (N)
NYPL [3-MAL 91-6700]

Sammlung Rudi Molacek . Graz [1990] 1 v. (unpaged) : DDC 709/.436/0744365 20
N6808 .S23 1990

Zukowski, John, 1948- Austrian architecture and design . Chicago , Berlin , c1991. p. cm. ISBN 3-433-02340-9 (catalogue edition) DDC 745.4/49436/0904507477311 20
N6808 .Z8 1991

75 Jahre Maerz . Linz , 1988. 142 p. : ISBN 3-900762-08-2
NYPL [3-MAMG+ 90-9954]

ART, MODERN - 20TH CENTURY - AUSTRIA - VIENNA.

Fischer, Wolfgang Georg, 1933- [Gustav Klimt

und Emilie Flöge. English.] Klimt and Emilie .
Woodstock, N.Y. , 1992. p. cm.   ISBN
0-87951-451-5 :   DDC 709/.2 B 20
N6811.5.K55 F513 1992

Secessionismus und Abstraktion =
Secessionism and abstraction . Wien , New
York , 1989. 81 p. :
          NYPL [3-MAMG+ 90-12363]

**ART, MODERN - 20TH CENTURY -
AUSTRIA - VIENNA - EXHIBITIONS.**
Der Zertrümmerte Spiegel . Klagenfurt , 1989.
392 p. :   ISBN 3-85415-062-8
          NYPL [3-MAL 91-7188]

**ART, MODERN - 20TH CENTURY -
BELGIUM.**
Dictionnaire biographique illustré des artistes en
Belgique depuis 1830. [Bruxelles] , 1987. 416
p., [31] p. of plates :
          NYPL [3-MAO 91-4886]

**ART, MODERN - 20TH CENTURY -
BELGIUM - EXHIBITIONS.**
Art deco Belgique, 1920-1940 . [Bruxelles]
[1988] 307 p. :   *NYPL [3-MAME 89-19054]*

L'Art en Belgique . Bruxelles , c1990. 527 p. :
   ISBN 2-87284-008-7 (Lebeer-Hossmann)
          NYPL [3-MAME 91-4589]

La Scuola di Mons . Brescia , Milano , c1989.
103 p. :   DDC 709/.493/42 20
N6968 .S37 1989
          NYPL [3-MAME 90-10713]

**ART, MODERN - 20TH CENTURY - BERLIN -
EXHIBITIONS.**
Bilder aus der grossen Stadt . Berlin-Dahlem ,
1977. [96] p. :
N6885 .B55   *NYPL [3-MAMG 81-424]*

**ART, MODERN - 20TH CENTURY - BERLIN
(GERMANY) - CATALOGS.**
Neuer Berliner Kunstverein. 20 Jahre NBK .
Berlin [1989] 233 p. :
          NYPL [3-MAVZ (Berlin) 91-6480]

**ART, MODERN - 20TH CENTURY - BERLIN
(GERMANY) - EXHIBITIONS.**
Ambiente Berlin . [Venezia] , c1990. 201 p. :
   ISBN 88-20-80360-7 DDC 709/.431/550744531
   20
N6885 .A46 1990

Arte em Berlim--1900 até hoje . Lisboa , 1989.
319 p. :   DDC 709/.431/55074469425 20
N6885 .A76 1989

Das Bild der Stadt Berlin von 1945 bis zur
Gegenwart . Berlin [1987] 59 p. :
          NYPL [3-MAMY 90-13015]

Emotope . [Berlin] , c1988. 43 p. :   ISBN
3-923479-27-1
          NYPL [3-MAL+ 90-10665]

Junge Berliner Künstler . Ludwigshafen , c1987.
103 p. :
IN PROCESS (ONLINE)
          NYPL [3-MAMG 90-12473]

Korrespondenzen . Berlin , Saint-Etienne ,
1989. 82 p. :
          NYPL [3-MAMG 90-12480]

10X . [Berlin] [1984] 1 portfolio (10 pieces) :
          NYPL [3-MAMG+ 88-4811]

**ART, MODERN - 20TH CENTURY -
BRANDYWINE CREEK VALLEY (PA.
AND DEL.) - CATALOGS.**
Brandywine River Museum. Catalogue of the
collection, 1969-1989 /. Chadds Ford, Pa. ,
c1991. p.   DDC 709/.73/07474814 20
N6517 .B7 1991

ART, MODERN - 20TH CENTURY - BRAZIL.
Integração das artes . São Paulo , 1990. 113 p. :
N6655 .I58 1990

**ART, MODERN - 20TH CENTURY - BRAZIL -
CATALOGS.**
Acervo, materpieces, Banco Chase Manhattan.
[Rio de Janeiro] , c1989. 118 p. :   ISBN
85-7083-028-9 DDC 709/.81/0748161 20
N6655 .A24 1989

**ART, MODERN - 20TH CENTURY - BRAZIL -
MINAS GERAIS.**
Vieira, Ivone Luzia. A Escola Guignard na
cultura modernista de Minas, 1944-1962 /.
[Pedro Leopoldo, Minas Gerais] [1988] 164
p. :   DDC 709/.81/51 20
N6656.M5 V54 1988

**ART, MODERN - 20TH CENTURY - BRAZIL -
PERNAMBUCO.**
Catálogo pernambucano de arte .
Recife-PE-Brasil , c1987. 1 v. (unpaged) :
   DDC 709/.2/28134 B 20
N6656.P47 C38 1987

**ART, MODERN - 20TH CENTURY - BRAZIL -
SÃO PAULO (STATE) - CATALOGS.**
São Paulo (Brazil : State). Pinacoteca do
Estado. Pinacoteca do Estado . São Paulo ,
1988. 447 p. :   DDC 708.981/61 20
N6657.S32 S26 1988

**ART, MODERN - 20TH CENTURY - BRAZIL -
THEMES, MOTIVES.**
Schenberg, Mário. Pensando a arte /. São
Paulo-Brasil , 1988. 221 p. :   DDC 709/.81/0904
20
N6655 .S28 1988

**ART, MODERN - 20TH CENTURY -
BURUNDI.**
Sendegeya, Pierre-Claver, 1940- Anthologie des
sculpteurs et peintres burundais contemporains
/. Paris , c1989. 109 p. :   ISBN 2-288-82091-8
IN PROCESS (ONLINE)
          NYPL [3-MADF+ 91-7959]

**ART, MODERN - 20TH CENTURY -
BYELORUSSIAN S.S.R. - EXHIBITIONS.**
Molodye khudozhniki Belorussii . Moskva ,
1989. 127 p. :   ISBN 5-269-00285-X :
N6995.B9 M65 1989

**ART, MODERN - 20TH CENTURY -
CALIFORNIA.**
Stofflet, Mary. California cityscapes /. New
York, NY , c1991. p. cm.   ISBN 0-87663-614-8
   DDC 704.9/44794/0979409048 20
N8214.5.U6 S76 1991

**ART, MODERN - 20TH CENTURY -
CALIFORNIA - EXHIBITIONS.**
Anderson, Susan M. (Susan Mary) Pursuit of
the marvelous . Laguna Beach, Calif. , c1990.
64 p. :   ISBN 0-940872-16-1 DDC
760/.09794/607479496 20
N6530.C2 A58 1990
          NYPL [3-MCW+ 91-6334]

Invisible twenty-one artists visible. Long Beach,
Calif. , 1972. 59 p. :
          NYPL [3-MAMT 90-5889]

Knode, Marilu. Third Newport biennial .
Newport Beach, Calif. , 1991. p. cm.   ISBN
0-917493-19-2 DDC 709/.794/07479496 20
N6530.C2 K64 1991

**ART, MODERN - 20TH CENTURY -
CALIFORNIA - LOS ANGELES -
EXHIBITIONS.**
L.A. times . Boise, Idaho , c1991. p. cm.   DDC
709/.794/9407479628 20
N6535.L6 L188 1991

Le Démon des anges . [Barcelona] , Nantes
[1989] 245 p. :   DDC 704/.036872079494/0744672
20
N6538.M4 D46 1989

**ART, MODERN - 20TH CENTURY -
CANADA.**
Eighteen contemporary masters . [Ottawa ,
1977] 23 p. :   *NYPL [3-MAL 90-5655]*

Groh, Klaus, 1936- Der neue Dadaismus in
Nordamerika /. Augsburg , 1979. 221 p. :
   ISBN 3-87512-113-9
          NYPL [3-MAL 90-7185]

**ART, MODERN - 20TH CENTURY -
CANADA - EXHIBITIONS.**
The Canadian Art Club, 1907-1915 /.
Edmonton, Alberta, Canada [1988] 94 p. :
   ISBN 0-88950-049-5 DDC 709/.71/07412334 20
N6545 .C213 1988
          NYPL [3-MAM+ 90-12373]

**ART, MODERN - 20TH CENTURY -
CANADA - THEMES, MOTIVES.**
Moorhouse, Asheleigh. Art, sight, and
language . Kapuskasing, Ont. , c1989.
173 p. :   ISBN 0-921254-05-9 DDC 709/.71/09048
20
N6545 .M66 1989   NYPL [3-MAM 91-6256]

**ART, MODERN - 20TH CENTURY -
CATALOGS.**
The Art of Mickey Mouse /. New York ,
c1991. p. cm.   ISBN 1-562-82994-7 :   DDC
704.9/497415 20
N8224.M47 A4 1991

Kunst der ersten Jahrhunderthälfte 1900 bis
1960 . Mönchengladbach , 1990. 425 p. :   ISBN
3-924039-05-4
IN PROCESS (ONLINE)   *NYPL [MAVZ
   (Mönchengladbach) 91-1142]*

Le Musée d'art moderne . [Bruxelles] , c1988.
128 p. :
N6447 .M865 1988

Museum of Contemporary Art (Los Angeles,
Calif.) The Rita and Taft Schreiber collection /.
Los Angeles, Calif. , c1991. 1 v. (unpaged) :
   ISBN 0-914357-24-7 DDC 709/.04/007479494
20
N6487.L67 L677 1991

Trinity College (Dublin, Ireland) The modern
art collection, Trinity College Dublin /. Dublin,
Ireland , 1989. 101 p. :   ISBN 1-87140-801-6
          NYPL [3-MAVZ (Dublin) 90-11685]

**ART, MODERN - 20TH CENTURY - CHILE -
EXHIBITIONS.**
Bienal Internacional de São Paulo (20th : 1989)
XX Bienal Internacional de São Paulo . [Chile ,
1989] 63 p. :   DDC 760/.0983/090480748161 20
N6665 .B5 1989

Contemporary art from Chile . New York,
N.Y. , c1990. 63 p. :   ISBN 1-87912-802-0
          NYPL [3-MAM 91-7561]

**ART, MODERN - 20TH CENTURY -
COLOMBIA.**
El Espíritu erótico /. Bogotá , 1990. 207 p. :
   DDC 704.9/428/098610904 20
N8217.E6 E87 1990

Mejía de Millán, Beatriz Amelia. El arte
colombiano en el siglo XX /. Pereira,
Colombia , 1988. 155 p. :   DDC 709/.861/0904
20
N6675 .M45 1988

Panesso, Fausto, 1953- Arte y parte . [Bogotá,
Colombia] , 1990- v. :
          NYPL [3-MAM+ 91-3615]

Panesso, Fausto, 1953- Arte y parte . [Bogotá,
Colombia?] [1990- v. <1 > :
N6675 .P35 1990

**ART, MODERN - 20TH CENTURY -
COLOMBIA - EXHIBITIONS.**
Colombian art in Canada =. Bogotá,
Colombia , 1990. 24 p. :   DDC
   709/.861/07486148 20
N6675 .C65 1990

3 décadas de arte uniandino. Bogotá, Colombia
[1989] 128 p. :   *NYPL [3-MAM 91-4248]*

**ART, MODERN - 20TH CENTURY - CUBA -
EXHIBITIONS.**
La Habana en Madrid. [Madrid] [1989?] 64
p. :   DDC 709/.7291/0744641 20
N6603 .H25 1989

The Nearest edge of the world . Brookline,
MA, USA (108 Winthrop Rd., Brookline
02146) , c1990. 63, [1] p. :   DDC
   709/.7291/07474 20
N6603 .N4 1990

**ART, MODERN - 20TH CENTURY -
CZECHOSLOVAKIA - EXHIBITIONS.**
Český neoklasicismus dvacátých let . [Prague]
[1986?] 1 v. (unpaged) :
N6831.5.N46 C47 1986

Czech art in the velvet revolution . Roslyn
Harbor, N.Y. , 1990. 111 p. :
N6831 .C93 1990
          NYPL [3-MAM+ 91-7464]

Devětsil . [Oxford] , London , c1990. 115 p. :
   ISBN 0-905836-70-7
          NYPL [3-MAM+ 90-12482]

Devětsil (Society) Devětsil . Łódź [1989]. 105
p. :
N6831.5.D48 D4 1989

Kotalík, Jiří. Kupka, Gutfreund & C. . Venezia ,
c1980. 114 p. :   ISBN 88-20-80273-2 DDC
   709/.437/0740531 19
N6831 .K67 1980   NYPL [3-MAM 90-5445]

Mezi klasickým řádem a selankou . [Prague] ,
<1990?- v. <2 > :
N6831.5.N46 M4 1990

ROH. ÚRO. Lidé, život, práce . [Prague] ,
1988. 1 portfolio (unpaged) :
N6831 .R64 1988

Thomas, Karin, 1941- Tradition und

Avantgarde in Prag /. Köln , c1991. 220 p. :
ISBN 3-7701-2842-7
NYPL [MAM+ 91-7291]

"8" . Brno [1989?] 1 v. (unpaged) :
N6831 .A13 1989

**ART, MODERN - 20TH CENTURY -
CZECHOSLOVAKIA - THEMES,
MOTIVES - EXHIBITIONS.**
Linie, barva, tvar v českém výtvarném umění
třicátých let . [Prague , 1990?] 152 p. :
N6831 .L54 1990

**ART, MODERN - 20TH CENTURY -
DIRECTORIES.**
Guid'arts . Nice [1989] 174 p. : ISBN
2-87720-040-X :
N6485.3 .G85 1989

**ART, MODERN - 20TH CENTURY -
DOMINICAN REPUBLIC.**
Arte contemporáneo dominicano. [Santo
Domingo, Dominican Republic?] [1987?] [72]
p. ;
N6615.D6 A77 1987

**ART, MODERN - 20TH CENTURY -
ECUADOR - CATALOGS.**
100 artistas del Ecuador /. Quito , 1990. 285
p. : DDC 709/.2/2866 B 20
N6985 .A15 1990

**ART, MODERN - 20TH CENTURY -
ENGLAND - EXHIBITIONS.**
Baron, Wendy. The Camden Town Group /.
New Haven , 1980. xvi, 71 p. : ISBN
0-930606-20-5 (pbk.) DDC 759.21/42/07401468
19
N6768.5.C53 B37 1980
NYPL [3-MAMR 81-554]

**ART, MODERN - 20TH CENTURY -
ESTONIA - ADDRESSES, ESSAYS,
LECTURES.**
Eesti kunsti sidemeid XX sajandi algupoolelt .
Tallinn , 1978. 271 p. :
N6995.E8 E365   *NYPL [3-MAM 81-512]*

**ART, MODERN - 20TH CENTURY -
EUROPE.**
Artistes étrangers à Pont-Aven, Concarneau et
autres lieux de Bretagne /. [Rennes] [1989]
233 p. : ISBN 2-86847-026-2
NYPL [3-MAM 91-3261]

Kunst und Kunstkritik der dreissiger Jahre .
Dresden , c1990. 353 p. : ISBN 3-364-00190-1
N6868 .K7865 1990

**ART, MODERN - 20TH CENTURY -
EUROPE - EXHIBITIONS.**
Columbus Museum of Art. Impressionism and
European modernism . Columbus, Ohio ,
Seattle , 1991. p. ISBN 0-295-97133-9 : DDC
709/.03/407477157 20
N6447 .C65 1991

Cowling, Elizabeth. On classic ground .
London , 1990. 264 p. : ISBN 1-85437-043-X
(pbk.) DDC 709/.04/107442132 20
N6758 .C68 1990

L'Europa dei razionalisti . Milano , c1989. 383
p. : ISBN 88-435-2847-5
NYPL [3-MAL 91-4900]

Europa oggi . Firenze , Milano , c1988. 253 p. :
ISBN 88-435-2560-3
NYPL [3-MAL 89-1689]

Impressionismo in Europa . Bologna , c1990.
170 p. : ISBN 88-7779-126-8
NYPL [3-MAVZ (Prague) 91-6701]

L'œuvre ultime de Cézanne à Dubuffet .
Saint-Paul , c1989. 269 p. : ISBN 2-900923-01-60
DDC 709/.04/007444941 20
N6757 .O43 1989

Marlborough Fine Art London (Ltd.) 19th and
20th century watercolours, drawings and
sculpture /. London, 1964. 20 p.
NYPL [3-MAL 90-6893]

Mondrian e De Stijl . Milano , c1990. 273 p. :
ISBN 88-435-3172-7
NYPL [3-MCH M741 91-6318]

Monet to Matisse . Jerusalem , c1988. 130, [10]
p. : ISBN 965-278-085-5 (pbk)
NYPL [3-MAL + 89-6103]

Sammlung Lenz Schönberg . Stuttgart , c1989.
262 p. : ISBN 3-89322-152-2
NYPL [3-MAX+ (Lenz) 91-2706]

**ART, MODERN - 20TH CENTURY -
EUROPE - JAPANESE INFLUENCES -
EXHIBITIONS.**
Verborgene Impressionen =. [Wien] , c1990.
445 p. : ISBN 3-900688-13-3 (Katalogausgabe)
NYPL [3-MAM 91-3678]

**ART, MODERN - 20TH CENTURY - EUROPE,
NORTHERN - EXHIBITIONS.**
11 steden, 11 landen . Leeuwarden, The
Netherlands , 1990. xxvii, 263 p. : ISBN
90-900348-9-7 :
N6758 .A113 1990

**ART, MODERN - 20TH CENTURY -
EUROPE - THEMES, MOTIVES -
EXHIBITIONS.**
Umanesimo, disumanesimo nell'arte europea
1890/1980 . Milano , c1980. 172 p. : DDC
709/.04/00740551 19
N6757 .U42 1980   *NYPL [3-MAL 90-5471]*

**ART, MODERN - 20TH CENTURY -
EXHIBITIONS.**
L'Art conceptuel, une perspective . Paris ,
c1989. 260 p. :   *NYPL [3-MAL 90-11049]*

Arte abstracto, arte concreto . [Valencia?] ,
c1990. 439 p. : ISBN 84-7890-151-5
N6494.A2 A78 1990

Artoon . Napoli , c1989. 199 p. : ISBN
88-435-3056-9 DDC 709/.04/07107445632 20
N6494.P6 A6 1989
NYPL [3-MAL 90-12882]

Biennale di Venezia (44th : 1990) Dimensione
futuro . [Venezia] [Milano] , c1990. 348 p. :
ISBN 88-20-80356-9 DDC 709/.04/80744531 20
N6488.I8 V43 1990

Blau, Farbe der Ferne /. Heidelberg , c1990.
615 p. : ISBN 3-88423-062-X DDC
709/.04/0074434645 20
N6488.G3 H442 1990

Cobra 1948/51 . [Rotterdam , 1967?] 187 p. :
DDC 709.04
N6490 .R64   *NYPL [3-MAL 90-7044]*

A Collector's exhibition: S. B. Nitikman,
Winnipeg Art Gallery, January 6-28, 1968.
[Winnipeg? 1968?] 1 v. (unpaged) DDC
708.11/27/4
N5220 .C698
NYPL [3-MAX (Nitikman) 74-1772]

Da van Gogh a Picasso, Da Kandinsky a
Pollock . Milano , c1990. 391 p. : DDC
709/.04/10744531 20
N6488.5.T55 D3 1990

Defraoui, Silvie. Orient/occident /. Genève ,
c1989. 53 p. :
NYPL [3-MCZ + D316 89-27977]

Einleuchten . Hamburg [1989] 289 p. : ISBN
3-7672-1102-5 DDC 709/.04/507443515 20
N6488.G3 H2832 1989

Figuration critique 1990 . [Vélizy-Villacoublay]
[Séoul, Corée] [1990] 332 p. : DDC
709/.04/807444361 20
N6494.F5 F5188 1990

Forum Internationale Kunstmesse Zürich (1984)
Forum Internationale Kunstmesse Zürich =.
Zürich [1984] [124] leaves :
NYPL [3-MAL+ 90-11547]

Galerie Mathias Fels. Nouveau réalisme,
1960-1970. Paris, 1970. [34] p.
N6494.R4 G3   *NYPL [3-MAL 90-5761]*

Hajamadi, Fariba, 1957- Fariba Hajamadi .
[Philadelphia] , c1988. 1 folded sheet (7 p.) :
ISBN 0-88454-045-6
NYPL [3-MCX H152 90-12728]

Kosinski, Dorothy M. Picasso, Braque, Gris,
Léger . Houston, Tex. , c1990. 67 p. : ISBN
0-89090-049-3 (pbk.) DDC 759.4/074/7641411
20
N6848.5.C82 K67 1990
NYPL [3-MCN 91-6709]

Künstlerinnen des 20. Jahrhunderts /.
[Wiesbaden] , c1990. 399 p. : ISBN
3-89258-013-8   *NYPL [3-MAL+ 91-3896]*

Künstlerinnen des 20. Jahrhunderts .
Wiesbaden , c1990. 399 p. : ISBN 3-89258-013-8
DDC 704/.042/0904074434165 20
N6490 .K7835 1990

L'Art conceptuel, une perspective . Paris ,
c1989. 260 p. : ISBN 2-85534-607-1 DDC

709/.04/07507444361 20
N6494.C63 A75 1989

Luminosity . New York, NY , c1986. 20 p. :
ISBN 0-932075-11-8
NYPL [3-MAL 90-10424]

Magiciens de la terre . Paris , c1989. 271 p. :
ISBN 2-85850-498-9 : DDC 709/.04/007444361
20
N6488.F8 P3525 1989
NYPL [3-MAW+ (Paris) 90-2960]

Minder kan het niet . Groningen , c1989. 103
p. :   *NYPL [3-MAL 90-12610]*

Modern masterpieces from the collection of
Jacques Hachuel . [New York, N.Y.] [1990?]
123 p. : ISBN 84-86022-41-X
NYPL [3-MAX (Hachuel) 91-3852]

Mozart in art, 1900-1990 /. München , c1990.
211 p. : ISBN 3-87516-513-6 :
IN PROCESS (ONLINE)
NYPL [3-MAL+ 91-7308]

Musée d'art moderne (Musées royaux des
beaux-arts de Belgique) Collection Alla et
Bénédict Goldschmidt . Bruxelles [1990] 426
p. :   *NYPL [3-MAL 91-5716]*

A New consciousness . Yonkers, N.Y. , c1971.
[12] p. :
NYPL [3-MAX (CIBA-GEIGY) 90-7135]

L'Œil musicien . Charleroi , 1985. 106 p. :
NYPL [3-MAMZ 86-4322]

Olympiade des arts =. [Seoul] [1988] 839 p. :
DDC 709/.04/80745195 20
N6488.K6 S467 1988

Outside Cuba . [New Brunswick, N.J.] , Miami,
Fla. , 1989. 366 p. : ISBN 0-935501-13-4
NYPL [3-MAM 90-12497]

Perl, Jed. Gallery going . San Diego , c1991.
xxiv, 431 p., [16] p. of plates : ISBN
0-15-134260-1 : DDC 709/.04/0074 20
N6447 .P38 1991   *NYPL [3-MAV 91-7445]*

La Razón revisada = Reason revised . Madrid ,
c1988. 135 p. : ISBN 84-7664-183-4
NYPL [3-MAMG 91-7022]

Rhetorical image . New York , c1990. 98 p. :
ISBN 0-915557-71-1
NYPL [3-MAL+ 91-5559]

Die Sammlung Woty und Theodor Werner /.
München , c1990. 131 p. : ISBN 3-7774-5460-5
NYPL [3-MAX (Werner, W.) 91-6703]

Schlatter, Christian. Art conceptuel, formes
conceptuelles =. Paris , 1990. 598 p. :
NYPL [3-MAL 91-3664]

Schmied, Wieland, 1929- GegenwartEwigkeit .
Stuttgart , c1990. 341 p. : ISBN 3-89322-179-4 :
DDC 709/.04/5074431554 20
N6488.G3 S8565 1990

Städtisches Museum Leverkusen, Schloss
Morsbroich. Musée de Leverkusen . Lyon ,
1968. 1 v. (unpaged) :
NYPL [3-MAL 90-6993]

Stich, Sidra. Anxious visions . New York ,
Berkeley , 1990. 295 p. : ISBN 1-558-59109-5
DDC 709/.04/06307479467 20
N6494.S8 S75 1990
NYPL [3-MAL 90-13055]

Symbolism . [New York] [1989] [24] p. :
NYPL [3-MAL 91-4569]

Team spirit /. New York, N.Y. , c1990. 84 p. :
ISBN 0-916365-30-1
NYPL [3-MAL 91-6734]

Tesoros de las colecciones particulares
madrileñas . [Madrid] [1989?] 282 p. : ISBN
84-451-0090-4 DDC 759.06/074/4641 20
N6488.S7 M38 1989 *NYPL [3-MC 90-8478]*

Testuale . Milano , c1979. 255 p. : ISBN
88-20-20278-6   *NYPL [3-MAL 90-6811]*

Theatergarden Bestiarium . Cambridge, Mass. ,
Long Island City, N.Y. , c1990. 176 p. : ISBN
0-262-04105-7 DDC 701/.03 20
N6494.E6 T4 1990
NYPL [3-MAL+ 90-12503]

Tre tendenze dell'arte francese contemporanea.
[Milano, 197-] 47 p. (chiefly illus.)
NYPL [3-MAMI 90-7183]

Um 1968 . Köln , c1990. 260 p. : ISBN

3-7701-2470-7
N6488.G3 D858 1990

Von Pop zum Konzept . Aachen [1975] [64]
p., [30] leaves of plates :
N6488.G3 A28
NYPL [3-MAW+ (Aachen) 80-1119]

Wiener Diwan . Klagenfurt , c1989. 219 p. :
ISBN 3-85415-069-5 :
N6488.A9 V6 1989
NYPL [3-MAL+ 91-5876]

The 1920s . Montreal, Quebec, Canada , c1991.
638 p. : ISBN 2-89192-139-9
NYPL [3-MAL+ 91-7585]

50 Jahre Bauhaus . Stuttgart , 1968. 369 p. :
NYPL [3-MAL 90-6848]

**ART, MODERN - 20TH CENTURY -
FINLAND - EXHIBITIONS.**
Fabula 1 /. Helsinki [1989] 61 p. : ISBN
951-861-843-7
N7255.F5 F28 1989

**ART, MODERN - 20TH CENTURY -
FRANCE.**
Bernier, Rosamond. Matisse, Picasso, Miró .
New York , 1991. p. cm. ISBN 0-394-58670-0
DDC 709/.2/244 B 20
N6848 .B38 1991

Clair, Jean. Brève défense de l'art français .
[Caen] , c1989. 69 p. ; ISBN 2-905657-46-4
DDC 709/.44/09045 20
N6848 .C56 1989

Gersh-Nešić, Beth S. The early criticism of
André Salmon . New York , 1991. p. cm.
ISBN 0-8153-0115-4 (alk. paper) DDC
759.4/09/041 20
N6848.5.C82 G46 1991

**ART, MODERN - 20TH CENTURY -
FRANCE - ALSACE.**
Bauer, A. (Alice) Répertoire des artistes
d'Alsace des dix-neuvième et vingtième siècles .
Strasbourg , 1984-1991. 6 v. : ISBN
2-85369-036-9 (set) DDC 709/.2/2 B 19
N6849.A4 B3 1984 **NYPL [MAO 86-2104]**

**ART, MODERN - 20TH CENTURY -
FRANCE - CATALOGS.**
Abbaye Sainte-Croix (Les Sables-d'Olonne,
France). Musée. La collection d'art moderne et
contemporain . Les Sables d'Olonne , c1990.
253 p. : ISBN 2-901432-67-0 DDC
709/.44/0744461 20
N6848 .A58 1990

**ART, MODERN - 20TH CENTURY -
FRANCE - EXHIBITIONS.**
Conisbee, Philip. Monet to Matisse . Los
Angeles, Calif. , c1991. 144 p. : ISBN
0-87587-159-3 DDC 709/.44/09034 20
N6847 .C6 1991

Impressionism and post impressionism .
Portland, Me. , c1991. p. cm. DDC
709/.03/4407474191 20
N6847.5.I4 I43 1991

Individualités . Milano , c1984. 107 p. :
NYPL [3-MAMI 90-12643]

**ART, MODERN - 20TH CENTURY -
FRANCE - PARIS.**
Warnod, Jeanine. La Ruche & Montparnasse /.
Genève , c1978. 189 p. : ISBN 2-85889-023-4 :
N6850 .W37 **NYPL [3-MAMI 80-2220]**

**ART, MODERN - 20TH CENTURY -
FRANCE - PARIS - CONGRESSES.**
Reconstructing modernism . Cambridge, Mass. ,
1990. xvii, 418 p. : ISBN 0-262-07120-7 DDC
759.06/09/045 20
N6535.N5 R4 1990
NYPL [3-MAL 90-11100]

**ART, MODERN - 20TH CENTURY -
FRANCE - PARIS - EXHIBITIONS.**
Phillips Collection. Duncan Phillips collects .
Washington, D.C. , c1991. p. cm. ISBN
0-943044-16-2 : DDC 759.4/361/09041074753
20
N6850 .P45 1991

**ART, MODERN - 20TH CENTURY -
FRANCE - SAINT-ETIENNE -
EXHIBITIONS.**
Korrespondenzen . Berlin , Saint-Etienne ,
1989. 82 p. : **NYPL [3-MAMG 90-12480]**

Korrespondenzen . Berlin , Saint-Etienne ,

c1989. 82 p. :
N6885 .K67 1989

**ART, MODERN - 20TH CENTURY -
FRANCE - THEMES, MOTIVES.**
Le Moment extrême. Apt , Paris , 1989- v. <1
> : ISBN 2-907383-03-5 (Eraklea)
N6848.5.C66 M66 1989

**ART, MODERN - 20TH CENTURY -
GERMANY.**
Adam, Peter. Art of the Third Reich /. New
York , 1992. p. cm. ISBN 0-8109-1912-5 (cloth)
DDC 709/.43/09043 20
N6868.5.N37 A34 1992

Der Kunsthund knurrt . Düsseldorf , c1983. 1
v. (unpaged) :
N6868 .K7876 1983

The Divided heritage . Cambridge [England] ,
New York , 1991. xvi, 390 p. : ISBN
0-521-34553-7 DDC 709.43/09/04 20
N6868.5.M63 D58 1990
NYPL [3-MAMG 91-6532]

Hütt, Wolfgang. Deutsche Malerei und Graphik
im 20. Jahrhundert. Berlin, 1969. 602 p. DDC
760/.0943
N6868 .H78 **NYPL [3-MAMG 90-6799]**

Kunst auf Befehl? . München , c1990. 275 p. :
ISBN 3-7814-0285-1 DDC 701/.03 20
N6868.5.N37 K85 1990

Kunst und Kunstkritik der dreissiger Jahre .
Dresden , c1990. 353 p. : ISBN 3-364-00190-1
N6868 .K7865 1990

Meurer, Thomas. Die Eisenbahn in der
deutschen Kunst . Witterschlick/Bonn , 1989.
172, [76] p. : ISBN 3-925267-28-X
N6867 .M48 1989

Nebel, Otto, 1892-1973. Schriften zur Kunst /.
München , c1988. 379 p. : ISBN 3-88219-405-7
NYPL [3-MAL 90-12432]

**ART, MODERN - 20TH CENTURY -
GERMANY - BERLIN.**
Werkstattbesuche bei Künstlern in
Berlin-Wedding /. Berlin , c1989. 2 v. : ISBN
3-9801875-9-4 :
N6885 .W46 1989

**ART, MODERN - 20TH CENTURY -
GERMANY - BERLIN - EXHIBITIONS.**
Korrespondenzen . Berlin , Saint-Etienne ,
c1989. 82 p. :
N6885 .K67 1989

**ART, MODERN - 20TH CENTURY -
GERMANY - DARMSTADT.**
Darmstadt Künstler-Kolonie. Museum
Künstlerkolonie Darmstadt /. Darmstadt
[1989?] lv, 253 p. : **NYPL [3-MLF 91-5455]**

**ART, MODERN - 20TH CENTURY -
GERMANY - DARMSTADT -
EXHIBITIONS.**
Quintessenz . [Darmstadt] [1989] 76 p. :
N668 .Q55 1989

**ART, MODERN - 20TH CENTURY -
GERMANY, EAST.**
Durch den Tag laufen . Berlin , 1989. 287 p. :
ISBN 3-7303-0434-8
PT3732 .D87 1989
NYPL [3-MAMG 90-10453]

Germany (West). Bundesministerium für
Gesamtdeutsche Fragen. Polit-kunst in der
Sowjetischen Besatzungszone Deutschlands.
Bonn [1963?] 64 p.,
NYPL [3-MAMG 90-6808]

Kunst in der DDR /. Köln , c1990. 470 p. :
ISBN 3-462-02068-4 DDC 709/.431/09045 20
N6889 .K862 1990

**ART, MODERN - 20TH CENTURY -
GERMANY (EAST) - COTTBUS -
EXHIBITIONS.**
Kunst in Cottbus . [Cottbus] [Cottbus] [1989]
[140] p. : **NYPL [3-MAMG 91-6140]**

**ART, MODERN - 20TH CENTURY -
GERMANY (EAST) - EXHIBITIONS.**
América Latina . [Berlin , 1988?] 144 p. :
N6884.5 .A44 1988
NYPL [3-MAMG 91-5083]

Jugend im Sozialismus . Berlin [1987] 83 p. :
N6889 .J75 1987 **NYPL [3-MAMZ 91-4201]**

Skulptur, Grafik, Zeichnung aus der Deutschen
Demokratischen Republik . Berlin [1984] [44]

p. :
MLCM 87/97 (N)
NYPL [3-MAMG 90-10659]

**ART, MODERN - 20TH CENTURY -
GERMANY - EXHIBITIONS.**
Adolf Hölzel von seinen Schülern . Stuttgart ,
1978. 61 p. :
N6868 .A38 **NYPL [3-MCK H693 81-755]**

Art in Germany 1909-1936 . Munich , c1990.
271 p. : ISBN 0-944110-02-9 (pbk.) :
N6868 .F74 1990
NYPL [3-MAMG+ 91-4806]

Berlinische Galerie. Berliner Kunststücke /.
Stuttgart [1990] 459 p. : ISBN 3-89322-176-X
N6868 .B44 1990

Degenerate art . Los Angeles, Calif. , New
York , c1991. p. cm. ISBN 0-87587-158-5 DDC
709/.43/07477311 20
N6868 .D3388 1991b

Degenerate art . Los Angeles, Calif. , New
York , c1991. 423 p. : ISBN 0-8109-3653-4
DDC 709/.43/07477311 20
N6868 .D3388 1991

Ganz tief unten] [Germany , 1989?] 1 v.
(unpaged) :
N6868 .G34 1989

Max und die Kunst . [Unterwellenborn] [1989]
94 p. :
N6868 .M39 1989

Meisterwerke des Expressionismus . Stuttgart ,
c1990. 251 p. : ISBN 3-7757-0302-0
IN PROCESS (ONLINE)
NYPL [3-MAMG+ 91-7962]

Schlemmer, Baumeister, Krause . Wuppertal ,
1979. [99] p. :
N6868 .S28 **NYPL [3-MAMG 81-310]**

Städtisches Museum Leverkusen, Schloss
Morsbroich. Graphische Sammlung. Von
Arakawa bis Winzer . Leverkusen [1987?] 137
p. : ISBN 3-925520-04-X
N6868 .S765 1987

**ART, MODERN - 20TH CENTURY -
GERMANY - MAGDEBURG (BEZIRK) -
EXHIBITIONS.**
Kunstausstellung des VBK-DDR, Bezirk
Magdeburg anlässlich des 30. Jahrestages der
DDR . Magdeburg [1979?] 96 p. :
MLCS 87/4814 (N)
NYPL [3-MAMG 91-286]

**ART, MODERN - 20TH CENTURY -
GERMANY - NORTH RHINE-
WESTPHALIA - EXHIBITIONS.**
Der Expressionismus und Westfalen /. Münster
[1990] 239 p. : ISBN 3-88789-096-5
N6879 .E97 1990

**ART, MODERN - 20TH CENTURY -
GERMANY - SOCIETIES, ETC. -
EXHIBITIONS.**
Kunsthalle Bern. Chronik KGBrücke, 1913
[microform] . Bern , 1948. 32 p., [16] leaves of
plates : **NYPL [*ZM-202]**

**ART, MODERN - 20TH CENTURY -
GERMANY, WEST.**
Art today in the Federal Republic of Germany
/. Bonn , c1988. 114 p. :
NYPL [3-MAMG+ 90-12546]

The Divided heritage . Cambridge [England] ,
New York , 1991. xvi, 390 p. : ISBN
0-521-34553-7 DDC 709.43/09/04 20
N6868.5.M63 D58 1990
NYPL [3-MAMG 91-6532]

Landesmuseum für Kunst und Kulturgeschichte,
Münster. Nykysaksalaista maalaustaidetta.
[Münster, 1964?] 158, [8] p.
N6868 .L3

**ART, MODERN - 20TH CENTURY -
GERMANY, WEST - BADEN-
WÜRTTEMBERG.**
Jacobi, Walter. Bildersturm in der Provinz .
Freiburg , 1988. 64 p. : ISBN 3-89125-272-2
NYPL [3-MAMG 90-12384]

**ART, MODERN - 20TH CENTURY -
GERMANY, WEST - COLOGNE -
EXHIBITIONS.**
Art from Köln. Liverpool , 1989. 68 p. : ISBN
1-85437-020-0 (pbk.)
NYPL [3-MAMG+ 90-4504]

ART, MODERN - 20TH CENTURY - GERMANY, WEST - EXHIBITIONS.
Banater Künstler in der Bundesrepublik Deutschland . Berlin , 1988. 60 p. : ISBN 3-922131-57-8
N6868 .B33 1988
NYPL [3-MAMG 91-6298]

Dunkel, Trimborn, Dönselmann . [Emden, Germany , 1988] 87 p. : ISBN 3-925564-02-0
NYPL [3-MAMG + 89-11596]

Fassbar-anfassbar-unfassbar [Ausstellung] /. [München?] [1981?] 1 portfolio ([13] pieces) :
NYPL [3-MAL + 82-1845]

Künstlergilde. Breslauer Akademieschüler heute . Regensburg , 1979. [40] p. :
N6868 .K8 1979 NYPL [3-MAMG 81-1003]

Liebe, Dokumente unserer Zeit /. [Darmstadt] Gütersloh , 1980. 191 p. :
NYPL [3-MAMZ 90-6445]

Papierarbeiten . Bonn [1987] 155 p., [2] p. of plates : DDC 709/.43/0740355 19
N6868 .P38 1987
NYPL [3-MAMG 91-7051]

Sechzehn Künstler . Stuttgart , 1978. 101 p. :
MLCM 85/5391 (N)
NYPL [3-MAMG+ 90-6860]

Wolfgang Bier, Friedemann Hahn, Thomas Kaminsky, Christiane Möbus, Wolfgang Nestler . [Berlin] 1979. 1 case ([206] p. : DDC 709/.43/0740341 19
N6868 .W64 NYPL [3-MAMG+ 90-7088]

Zeitbilder . Mannheim , c1989. 1 v. (unpaged) : ISBN 3-926857-08-0
N6868 .Z437 1989

ART, MODERN - 20TH CENTURY - GERMANY (WEST) - FRANKFURT AM MAIN - EXHIBITIONS.
Kunst in Frankfurt 1987 . [Frankfurt am Main] [1987?] 122 p. : *NYPL [3-MCI 89-28315]*

ART, MODERN - 20TH CENTURY - GERMANY (WEST) - KARLSRUHE - EXHIBITIONS.
Kunst in der Residenz . [Karlsruhe] [1990] 399 p. : ISBN 3-925835-58-X DDC 709/.43/4643074434643 20
N6886.K33 K85 1990

Kunstsituation und Künstler sein heute . Karlsruhe , 1988. 342 p. :
N6886.K33 K88 1988
NYPL [3-MAMG 90-10706]

ART, MODERN - 20TH CENTURY - GERMANY (WEST) - KEVELAER - EXHIBITIONS.
Wans, Paul. Land Stil Leben . Kleve , 1988. 7 p., 20 leaves of plates : ISBN 3-922384-08-0
NYPL [3-MCK+ W251 90-10582]

ART, MODERN - 20TH CENTURY - GERMANY (WEST) - LÜBECK - EXHIBITIONS - CATALOG.
Ausstellungen im Museum am Dom, 1962-1983 . Lübeck , 1983. 224 p. : ISBN 3-924214-22-0
NYPL [3-MAVZ+ (Lübeck) 90-10858]

ART, MODERN - 20TH CENTURY - GERMANY (WEST) - MUNICH.
Zweite, Armin. The Blue Rider in the Lenbachhaus, Munich . Munich , 1989. 288 p. : ISBN 3-7913-0850-0
NYPL [3-MAMG+ 90-11017]

ART, MODERN - 20TH CENTURY - GERMANY (WEST) - WORPSWEDE.
Boulboullé, Guido. Worpswede . Köln , c1989. 223 p. : ISBN 3-7701-1847-2
NYPL [3-MAMG 90-12605]

Worpswede . [Lilienthal] , c1989. 254 p. : ISBN 3-922516-80-7
NYPL [3-MAMG 91-4485]

ART, MODERN - 20TH CENTURY - GERMANY - WORPSWEDE.
Worpswede . [Worpswede] , c1989. 254 p. : ISBN 3-922516-80-7 DDC 709/.43/59309034 20
N6867.5.W67 W68 1989

ART, MODERN - 20TH CENTURY - GERMANY - WÜRZBURG - EXHIBITIONS.
Städtische Galerie Würzburg. Würzburg--Künstler sehen eine Stadt . [Würzburg] [1989?] 102 p. : ISBN

3-926916-04-4
N6886.W87 S73 1989

ART, MODERN - 20TH CENTURY - GREAT BRITAIN.
Foot, M. R. D. (Michael Richard Daniel), 1919- Art and war . London , 1990. 240 p. : ISBN 0-7472-0286-9 DDC 758/.994053 20
N8260 .F58 1990

London Group. Fifty years of British art, 1914-64. [London, 1964] 1 v. (unpaged)
N6768 .L65

ART, MODERN - 20TH CENTURY - GREAT BRITAIN - EXHIBITIONS.
The British imagination . New York . 144 p. : ISBN 0-915057-36-0
NYPL [3-MAMR 91-6691]

Igirisu bijutsu wa ima . [Tōkyō , c1990. 151 p. :
NYPL [3-MAMR 91-7545]

The Independent Group . Cambridge, Mass. , c1990. 256 p. : ISBN 0-262-18139-8 DDC 709/.41/074 20
N6768.5.I53 153 1990
NYPL [3-MAMR+ 90-11745]

Royal Academy exhibitors 1971-1989 . Calne, Wiltshire, England , 1989. 546 p. ; ISBN 0-904722-19-8 *NYPL [MAO 90-9340]*

ART, MODERN - 20TH CENTURY - GREAT BRITAIN - EXHIBITIONS - DICTIONARIES.
Royal Academy exhibitors, 1971-1989 . Wiltshire, England , 1989. 546 p. ; ISBN 0-904722-19-8 : DDC 709/.047/07442132 20
N6768 .R63 1989

ART, MODERN - 20TH CENTURY - GREAT LAKES REGION - EXHIBITIONS.
Made in America . New York City , c1986. 31 p. : ISBN 0-932075-10-X (pbk.) DDC 709/.77/07401471 19
N6522 .M3 1986
NYPL [3-MAMT 90-12369]

ART, MODERN - 20TH CENTURY - HISTORY.
Livingstone, Marco. Pop art . [London] , c1990. 271 p. : ISBN 0-500-23591-0
NYPL [3-MAL 91-2611]

Rotzler, Willy. [Konstruktive Konzepte. English.] Constructive concepts . New York , 1989. 332 p. : ISBN 0-8478-1024-0 DDC 709/.04 20
N6494.C64 R6713 1989
NYPL [3-MAL 90-11560]

ART, MODERN - 20TH CENTURY - HONDURAS.
Fiallos S., Raúl (Fiallos Salgado), 1917- Datos históricos sobre la plástica hondureña /. [Tegucigalpa, Honduras?] c1989 (Tegucigalpa, Honduras, C.A. : Litografía López) 129 p. : DDC 709/.7283 20
N6579 .F5 1989

ART, MODERN - 20TH CENTURY - HUNGARY.
Mansbach, Steven A., 1950- Standing in the tempest . Santa Barbara, Calif. , Cambridge, Mass. , c1991. 240 p. : ISBN 0-262-13274-5 (MIT hbk.) DDC 709/.439/1207473 20
N6820.5.N93 M36 1991

ART, MODERN - 20TH CENTURY - HUNGARY - BUDAPEST - EXHIBITIONS.
Hajdu, István. Les ateliers de Budapest =. Paris , c1990. 240 p. : ISBN 978-290-807-2006
NYPL [3-MAM+ 91-3623]

ART, MODERN - 20TH CENTURY - HUNGARY - EXHIBITIONS.
Madarské výtvarné umění XX. století (1945-1988) . V Praze , 1989. 40 p. : ISBN 80-7035-009-1 :
N6820 .M25 1989

ART, MODERN - 20TH CENTURY - IDAHO - EXHIBITIONS.
Harthorn, Sandy, 1945- One hundred years of Idaho art, 1850-1950 . Boise, ID , c1990. 134 p. : DDC 709/.796/07479628 20
N6530.I2 H37 1990
NYPL [3-MAMT 90-11110]

ART, MODERN - 20TH CENTURY - ILLINOIS - CHICAGO.
Carroll, Patty. Spirited visions . Urbana , c1991. p. cm. ISBN 0-252-01848-6 (alk. paper) DDC

779/.2/092 20
N6535.C5 C37 1991

The old guard and the avant-garde . Chicago , c1990. xxiv, [16] p. of col. plates, 280 p. : ISBN 0-226-68284-6 (alk. paper) DDC 709/.773/1109041 20
N6535.C5 O43 1990
NYPL [3-MAMT 91-5016]

ART, MODERN - 20TH CENTURY - ILLINOIS - CHICAGO - EXHIBITIONS.
The Chicago show . Chicago, Ill. , c1990. 48 p. : ISBN 0-938903-09-8
N6487.C52 C6 1990
NYPL [3-MAMT 91-7597]

ART, MODERN - 20TH CENTURY - INDIA.
25 years of Indian art. New Delhi [1972] 32, [8] p., [32] p. of illus. DDC 709/.54
N7304 .T85 *NYPL [3-MAM 90-5575]*

ART, MODERN - 20TH CENTURY - INDIA - BENGAL.
Guha-Thakurta, Tapati. The making of a new "Indian" art . Cambridge [England] , New York , 1992. p. cm. ISBN 0-521-39247-0 DDC 709/.54/1409034 20
N7307.B4 G84 1992

ART, MODERN - 20TH CENTURY - IRELAND.
McAvera, Brian, 1948- Art, politics, and Ireland /. Dublin [1990?] 136 p. : ISBN 1-87249-600-8 : DDC 701/.03 20
N8236.P5 M37 1990

ART, MODERN - 20TH CENTURY - IRELAND - EXHIBITIONS.
A new tradition . Dublin , 1990. 139 p. : ISBN 0-907660-37-1 : DDC 709.415 20
NYPL [3-MAMR 91-5078]

ART, MODERN - 20TH CENTURY - ITALY.
Arte italiana contemporanea /. Firenze [1965?]. 11 v. : DDC 709/.2/2 19
N6918 .A788 NYPL [3-MAMC+ 88-4656]

Italian art and the southern European tradition /. London , New York , 1989. 80 p. : ISBN 0-312-03123-8 (pbk.) :
NYPL [3-MAMC 91-6693]

Russoli, Franco. Arte moderna cara compagna . [Milano] , c1987. 382 p. ; ISBN 88-11-59983-0
NYPL [3-MAMC 91-4600]

ART, MODERN - 20TH CENTURY - ITALY - BERGAMO.
Mosca, Pietro. Arte e costume a Bergamo . Bergamo , c1989-c1990. 2 v. (1020 p.) ;
IN PROCESS (ONLINE)
NYPL [3-MAMC+ 91-5886]

ART, MODERN - 20TH CENTURY - ITALY - CATALOGS.
Stia . [Firenze] , 1990. 140 p. : DDC 709/.45/0744559 20
N6918 .S8 1990

ART, MODERN - 20TH CENTURY - ITALY - CORTONA - EXHIBITIONS.
City on a hill . Athens, Ga. , c1989. 1 v. (unpaged) : ISBN 0-915977-02-8
NYPL [3-MAMT 90-11763]

ART, MODERN - 20TH CENTURY - ITALY - EXHIBITIONS.
Archivi futuristi /. Modena , Milano , c1990. 189 p. : DDC 709/.45/0744542 20
N6918.5.F8 A74 1990

Artisti italiani contemporanei, 1956-1986 /. Venezia , 1986. 61 p. : ISBN 88-7693-024-8 DDC 709/.45/0740531 19
N6918 .A819 1986
NYPL [3-MAMC 90-12531]

Italy, new tendencies. New York, N.Y. [1966] [16] p. : *NYPL [3-MAMC 90-6953]*

ART, MODERN - 20TH CENTURY - ITALY - EXHIBITIONS - CATALOGS.
Sollins, Susan. Eternal metaphors . New York, N.Y. , c1989. 72 p. : ISBN 0-916365-28-X
NYPL [3-MAMC 90-11056]

ART, MODERN - 20TH CENTURY - ITALY - FLORENCE - EXHIBITIONS.
Gruppo Donatello, XXVII edizione . Firenze , 1989. 111, [34] p. :
N6921.F7 G78 1989
NYPL [3-MAMC 90-11322]

Iride, schedule d'arte, Firenze '82 . Firenze , c1982. 107 p. : *NYPL [3-MAMC+ 90-5983]*

ART, MODERN - 20TH CENTURY - ITALY - GENOA.
Testimonianze Liberty a Genova /. Genova , c1986. 46 p. : ISBN 88-7058-218-3
NYPL [3-MAMC 90-11119]

ART, MODERN - 20TH CENTURY - ITALY - MILAN.
Vattese, Angela. Milano et mitologia . Milano [198-] 141 p. ;
IN PROCESS (ONLINE)
NYPL [3-MAMC+ 90-11588]

ART, MODERN - 20TH CENTURY - ITALY - PRICES.
Enciclopedia dei pittori e scultori italiani del Novecento . Milano [1991] 2 v. (1261 p.) :
DDC 709/.2/.2450904 B 20
N6918 .E58 1991

ART, MODERN - 20TH CENTURY - ITALY - SARDINIA.
Voci di Sardegna /. Siena , 1964- v. <1 > ;
N6919.S37 V6 1964

ART, MODERN - 20TH CENTURY - ITALY - SOURCES.
Testimonianze e polemiche figurative in Italia . Messina [1974] 507 p. ;
N6917.5.N44 B37
NYPL [3-MAMC 90-5898]

ART, MODERN - 20TH CENTURY - JAPAN - EXHIBITIONS.
The Image of man in modern Japanese art from the Museum collection . [Tokyo] , 1988. [36] p. :   *NYPL [3-MAG 89-6015]*

ART, MODERN - 20TH CENTURY - LATIN AMERICA.
Brett, Guy. Transcontinental . London , New York , 1990. 112 p. : ISBN 0-86091-511-5 DDC 709/.8/09048 20
N6502.5 .B74 1990

El nacionalismo en el arte. [Bogotá, Colombia] [1984]. 90 p. ;   *NYPL [3-MAM 90-4731]*

ART, MODERN - 20TH CENTURY - LATIN AMERICA - EXHIBITIONS.
Arte en Iberoamérica, 1820-1980 . [Madrid] [1989?] xxi, 359, [3] p. : ISBN 84-7506-297-0
N6502.4 .A76 1989

Brett, Guy. Transcontinental . London ; New York : 112 p. : ISBN 0-86091-511-5
NYPL [3-MAM 91-7008]

El Taller Torres-García . Austin , 1991. p. cm.
ISBN 0-292-78121-0 DDC 709/.8/074 20
N6502.5 .T35 1991

ART, MODERN - 20TH CENTURY - LATIN AMERICAN - EXHIBITIONS.
Sussman, Elisabeth, 1939- El corazón sangrante =. Boston, Mass. , Seattle, Wash. , c1991. p.
ISBN 0-910663-50-5 (paperback) DDC 704.9/46 20
N8217.H53 S87 1991

ART, MODERN - 20TH CENTURY - LATVIA.
Siliņš, Jānis, 1896- Latvijas māksla, 1915-1940 /. Stokholmā , 1988- v. <1 > : ISBN 91-970758-4-1 (v. 1)
N6995.L3 S582 1988

ART, MODERN - 20TH CENTURY - LOS ANGELES.
An Exhibition of five recent works by Larry Bell, John McCracken, DeWain Valentine, Ron Cooper [and] Peter Alexander. Edmonton, 1971. 44 p.
N6535.L6 E89   *NYPL [3-MAMT 81-415]*

ART, MODERN - 20TH CENTURY - MEXICO.
Flores-Antúnez, Ignacio. Arte y artistas . México, D.F. , 1989. 385 p. :
N6555 .F57 1989

Nuevos momentos del arte mexicano =. Madrid, Spain , Mexico , 1990. 212 p. : ISBN 84-7506-318-7   *NYPL [3-MAM 91-3917]*

Shapiro, Estela. Image and presence /. Mexico , 1985. 155 p. : ISBN 968-610-601-4
NYPL [3-MAM 91-4913]

ART, MODERN - 20TH CENTURY - MEXICO - EXHIBITIONS.
El Surrealismo entre Viejo y Nuevo Mundo . [Madrid] [1990] 346 p. : ISBN 84-86022-51-2
N6512.5.S87 S8 1990

En tiempos de la posmodernidad. [Mexico City] . 116 p. : ISBN 968-8405-58-2
N6555 .E5 1989

ART, MODERN - 20TH CENTURY - NETHERLANDS.
Visual arts in the Netherlands /. The Hague [1989] 46 p. : DDC 709/.492 20
N6947 .V57 1989
NYPL [3-MAME 91-5917]

ART, MODERN - 20TH CENTURY - NETHERLANDS - EXHIBITIONS.
Stadscollectie 1988, Rotterdam . Rotterdam [1989]. 54 p. : ISBN 90-6918-041-3
NYPL [3-MAME 90-10813]

ART, MODERN - 20TH CENTURY - NEW MEXICO - CATALOGS.
Museum of Fine Arts (Museum of New Mexico) Artists of twentieth-century New Mexico . Santa Fe, NM , 1992. p. cm. ISBN 0-89013-230-5 DDC 709/.789/07478956 20
N6530.N6 M87 1992

ART, MODERN - 20TH CENTURY - NEW MEXICO - TAOS.
Taggett, Sherry Clayton. Paintbrushes and pistols . Santa Fe, N.M. , New York, N.Y. , 1990. 271 p. [24] p. of plates : ISBN 0-945465-65-3 DDC 759.189/53 20
N6512.5.T34 T34 1990
NYPL [3-MAMT 91-4609]

ART, MODERN - 20TH CENTURY - NEW YORK (N.Y.)
Lurie, Boris, 1924- No! art . Berlin , Köln , c1988. 135, 109 p., 284 p. of plates :
NYPL [3-MAMT 90-12385]

O'Hara, Frank. Art chronicles, 1954-1966 /. New York [1975] 165 p. : ISBN 0-8076-0755-X : DDC 709/.747/109045 20
N6535.N5 O37 1975
NYPL [MAMT 75-525]

ART, MODERN - 20TH CENTURY - NEW YORK (N.Y.) - CONGRESSES.
Reconstructing modernism . Cambridge, Mass. , 1990. xvii, 418 p. : ISBN 0-262-07120-7 DDC 759.06/09/045 20
N6535.N5 R4 1990
NYPL [3-MAL 90-11100]

ART, MODERN - 20TH CENTURY - NEW YORK (N.Y.) - EXHIBITIONS.
Gober, Halley, Kessler, Wool . München , c1989. 89 p. : ISBN 3-923357-24-9
N6535.N5 G63 1989

Gober, Halley, Kessler, Wool . [Munich] , c1989. 89 p. : ISBN 3-923357-24-9
NYPL [3-MAMT 90-12879]

Living in NY . Montréal, Qc. [1988] [16] p. :
NYPL [3-MAMT 89-27022]

Painting a place in America . New York , Bloomington , 1991. p. cm. ISBN 0-253-33121-8 (cloth) DDC 704/.0392407471/090410747471 20
N6538.J4 P35 1991

ART, MODERN - 20TH CENTURY - NEW ZEALAND - EXHIBITIONS.
Content/context . Wellington, N.Z. , 1986. 144 p. : ISBN 0-9597785-1-9 DDC 700/.993/0904807493127 20
N7406.5 .C66 1986

ART, MODERN - 20TH CENTURY - NORWAY.
Moen, Arve. Gullalderens Mestere . Olso , 1964. 139, 165 p.
NYPL [3-MAM+ 90-2909]

ART, MODERN - 20TH CENTURY - OHIO - EXHIBITIONS.
Hinson, Tom E. The invitational--artists of northeast Ohio . [Cleveland] , c1991. vii, 64 p. : ISBN 0-940717-07-7 : DDC 709/.771/307477132 20
N6530.O3 H56 1991

Quintessence--the alternative spaces residency program, the City Beautiful Council of Dayton, Ohio, the Wright State University, Department of Art. Dayton , c1978- v. : ISBN 0-9602550-0-1 (v. 2) DDC 709/.73/074017173
N6530.O3 Q56   *NYPL [3-MAMT 79-2025]*

ART, MODERN - 20TH CENTURY - PENNSYLVANIA - PITTSBURGH REGION - CATALOGS.
Westmoreland Museum of Art. Southwestern Pennsylvania painters . Greensburg, Pa. , 1989.

x, 138 p. : ISBN 0-931241-21-9 DDC 759.148/8/07474886 20
N6530.P42 P589 1989
NYPL [3-MCW 91-6266]

ART, MODERN - 20TH CENTURY - PHILOSOPHY.
Myšlenky moderních malířů . Praha , 1989. 513 p. : ISBN 80-207-0087-0 :
N6490 .M96 1989

ART, MODERN - 20TH CENTURY - POLAND.
Płauszewski, Andrzej. "a.r.", mit urzeczywistniony . Łódź , 1989. 156 p. : ISBN 83-218-0237-0 *NYPL [3-MAM 90-11923]*

Wojciechowski, Aleksander. [Polskie malarstwo współczesne. English.] Contemporary Polish painting . Warsaw [1977] 187 p. : DDC 759.38
N7255.P6 W6213 *NYPL [3-MCY 90-12502]*

ART, MODERN - 20TH CENTURY - POLAND - EXHIBITIONS.
Den Abne dør, polsk nutidskunst, 1989 . [Copenhagen , 1989] 56 p. : ISBN 87-88944-07-7
N7255.P6 A36 1989

ART, MODERN - 20TH CENTURY - PORTUGAL.
Alvarenga, Fernando. Afluentes teórico-estéticos do neo-realismo visual português /. Porto , 1989. 209 p. : ISBN 972-360-218-0 :
N8243.S65 A43 1989

Botelho, Margarida. 75 artistas em Portugal /. Maia [Portugal] , 1989. 302 p. : ISBN 972-91572-5-1 DDC 709/.469/0904 20
N7128 .B68 1989

ART, MODERN - 20TH CENTURY - PORTUGAL - EXHIBITIONS.
Imagens do Sagrado. Lisboa , 1989. 47 p. : DDC 704.9/482/09469074469425 20
N7963.A1 I4 1989

ART, MODERN - 20TH CENTURY - PRIVATE COLLECTIONS - GERMANY - EXHIBITIONS.
Sammlung Sprengel . [Hannover , 1965] xxii, 376 p. :
N5265 .S25
NYPL [3-MAX (Sprengel) 90-6542]

ART, MODERN - 20TH CENTURY - PRIVATE COLLECTIONS - NEW JERSEY - EXHIBITIONS.
Princeton University. Art Museum. The Stanley J. Seeger Jr. Collection. [Princeton, 1961] [100] p.   *NYPL [3-MAX (Seeger) 90-7118]*

ART, MODERN - 20TH CENTURY - PRIVATE COLLECTIONS - UNITED STATES - EXHIBITIONS.
University of Kansas. Museum of Art. Paintings, drawings, and prints of the 19th and 20th centuries. Lawrence [1960] 24 p. DDC 707.4
N5220.F56   *NYPL [3-MAL 90-6052]*

ART, MODERN - 20TH CENTURY - PUERTO RICO - EXHIBITIONS.
Sturges, Hollister. New art from Puerto Rico =. Springfield, Mass. , 1990. 84 p. : ISBN 0-916746-15-1 *NYPL [3-MAM 91-6653]*

ART, MODERN - 20TH CENTURY - QUEBEC (PROVINCE)
Robert, Guy, 1933- Cent vingt du Cercle des artistes peintres du Québec /. Montréal , 1989. 255 p. : ISBN 2-920058-62-2 DDC 709/.2/2 20
N6546.Q4 R63 1989

ART, MODERN - 20TH CENTURY - QUÉBEC (PROVINCE) - MONTRÉAL - CONGRESSES.
Reconstructing modernism . Cambridge, Mass. , 1990. xvii, 418 p. : ISBN 0-262-07120-7 DDC 759.06/09/045 20
N6535.N5 R4 1990
NYPL [3-MAL 90-11100]

ART, MODERN - 20TH CENTURY - RUSSIAN S.F.S.R.
Manin, V. (Vitalii) L'art russe, 1900-1935 . Paris , c1989. 223 p. : ISBN 2-904057-37-4
NYPL [3-MAM+ 90-2663]

Russkoe i sovetskoe iskusstvo . Leningrad , 1989. 79 p. ;
N6987 .R877 1989

Sarabiānov, Dimtrii Vladimirovich. Russian art . London , c1990. 320 p. : ISBN 0-500-23574-0 (bk. jkt.) :   *NYPL [3-MAM+ 90-11076]*

**ART, MODERN - 20TH CENTURY -
RUSSIAN S.F.S.R. - EXHIBITIONS.**
Art into life . Seattle, Wash. , New York, NY ,
ç1990. 276 p. :   ISBN 0-935558-27-6 (pbk.)   DDC
709/.47/074 20
N6988.5.C64 A68 1990
             NYPL   [3-MAM 90-11568]

Artisti russi contemporanei . Prato , c1990. 208
p. :   ISBN 88-85191-01-0
             NYPL   [3-MAM 90-10469]

Jugend im Sozialismus . Berlin [1987] 83 p. :
N6889 .J75 1987   NYPL   [3-MAMZ 91-4201]

Russische Avantgarde 1910-1930 . Duisburg ,
c1990. 120 p. :   ISBN 3-923576-73-0
N6988 .R855 1990

Tradition and revolution in Russian art .
[Manchester] , 1990. 200 p. :   ISBN
0-948797-26-6   *NYPL   [3-MAM 91-5043]*

**ART, MODERN - 20TH CENTURY -
SCANDINAVIA - EXHIBITIONS.**
B., Mats, 1938- Téxun . [S.l. , 1986]
(Stockholm : Jernström Offset) [48] p. :
             NYPL   [3-MAM 90-10710]

**ART, MODERN - 20TH CENTURY -
SCOTLAND - EXHIBITIONS.**
Scatter . Glasgow , 1989. 1 v. (unpaged) :
             ISBN 0-906474-85-X
             NYPL   [3-MAMR+ 91-4062]

**ART, MODERN - 20TH CENTURY -
SCOTLAND - GLASGOW.**
Eadie, William, 1948- Movements of
modernity . London , 1990. viii, 292 p. ;   ISBN
0-415-03243-1   DDC 709/.414/4309034 20
N6781.G55 E26 1991
             NYPL   [3-MAMR 90-13191]

**ART, MODERN - 20TH CENTURY - SOUTH
AFRICA - EXHIBITIONS.**
The Neglected tradition . Johannesburg , c1988.
155 p. :   ISBN 0-620-13184-5   DDC
704/.03968/0090407468221 20
N7392 .N44 1988

**ART, MODERN - 20TH CENTURY -
SOUTHERN STATES - EXHIBITIONS.**
Dimensions and directions . Jackson, MS ,
c1980. ii, 46 p. :   DDC 704/.0396073075/07476251
20
N6538.N5 D47 1980

A sense of place . Montgomery, Ala. , 1990. p.
cm.   ISBN 0-89280-027-5   DDC 759.15/074/76147
20
N6520 .S46 1990

Southern exposure . New York, NY , c1985. 55
p. :   ISBN 0-932075-02-9 (pbk.)   DDC
709/.75/07401471 19
N6520 .S67 1985
             NYPL   [3-MAMT 90-12368]

**ART, MODERN - 20TH CENTURY - SOVIET
UNION.**
Bown, Matthew Cullerne. Art under Stalin /.
New York , c1991. p. cm.   ISBN 0-8419-1299-8
(alk. paper)   DDC 709/.47/0904 20
N6988 .B67 1991

Chamot, Mary, 1900- Russian painting and
sculpture /. Oxford , New York , c1963. xiii,
55 p., 36 p. of plates :
             NYPL   [3-MAM 90-6295]

Finizio, Luigi Paolo. L'astrattismo costruttivo .
Roma , 1990. vii, 237 p., [16] p. of plates :
             ISBN 88-420-3642-0 :   DDC 709/.47/09041 20
N6988.5.C64 F56 1990

Lissitzky, El, 1890-1941. [Suprematicheskiĭ
skaz. English.] About 2 [squares] /. Cambridge,
Mass. , 1991. p. cm.   ISBN 0-262-12158-1   DDC
709/.2 20
N6988.5.S9 L5713 1991

Russkoe i sovetskoe iskusstvo . Leningrad ,
1989. 79 p. ;
N6987 .R877 1989

**ART, MODERN - 20TH CENTURY - SOVIET
UNION - EXHIBITIONS.**
Between spring and summer . Tacoma, Wash. ,
Boston, Mass. , c1990. x, 206 p. :   ISBN
0-910663-49-1
N6988.5.C62 B48 1990
             NYPL   [3-MAM 90-12998]

Harten, Jürgen. Sowjetische Kunst um 1990 .
Köln , c1991. 299 p. :   ISBN 3-7701-2733-1
             NYPL   [3-MAM 91-8020]

**ART, MODERN - 20TH CENTURY - SOVIET
UNION - THEMES, MOTIVES.**
Puti tvorchestva i kritika . Moskva , 1990. 301
p. ;   ISBN 5-85200-081-7 :
N6988 .P84 1990

ART, MODERN - 20TH CENTURY - SPAIN.
Pérez Rojas, Javier. Art déco en España /.
Madrid , c1990. 645 p., [32] p. of plates :
             ISBN 84-376-0927-5   DDC 709/.46/09042 20
N7108.5.A7 P4 1990

**ART, MODERN - 20TH CENTURY - SPAIN -
CATALOGS.**
Catálogo nacional de arte contemporáneo.
Barcelona , c1989. 4 v. :   ISBN 84-87433-00-6
(obra completa)
N7108 .C29 1989

**ART, MODERN - 20TH CENTURY - SPAIN -
CATALONIA.**
Surrealismo en Catalunya, 1924-1936 .
Barcelona , c1988. 207 p. :   ISBN 84-343-0546-1
             NYPL   [3-MAML+ 90-10790]

**ART, MODERN - 20TH CENTURY - SPAIN -
CATALONIA - EXHIBITIONS.**
Catalan painters and sculptors . [Spain] [1990]
66 p. :   *NYPL   [3-MAML+ 91-4202]*

**ART, MODERN - 20TH CENTURY - SPAIN -
EXHIBITIONS.**
Arte geométrico en España, 1957-1989.
[Madrid] [1989] 320 p. :   ISBN 84-7812-044-0
             DDC 709/.46/0744641 20
N7108.5.A2 A78 1989

Aspetti dell'arte contemporanea spagnola.
Barcelona , c1990. 47, [1] p. :   ISBN
84-87433-11-1   DDC 709/.46/0744545 20
N7108 .A87 1990

Barnes, Lucinda. Imágenes líricas =. Long
Beach , c1990. 119 p. :   ISBN 0-936270-30-6
             NYPL   [3-MAML+ 91-5035]

Galería Barbié . Barcelona, Spain , 1975. 31 p. :
             NYPL   [3-MAML 90-7109]

LADAC . [Las Palmas de Gran Canarias]
[1990?] 1 case :   ISBN 84-87137-32-6
N7108 .L33 1990

**ART, MODERN - 20TH CENTURY - SPAIN -
GALICIA (REGION) - CATALOGS.**
Seoane, Xavier, 1954- Identidade e convulsión .
Sada, A Coruña [1990] 322 p. :   ISBN
84-7492-461-8   DDC 709/.46/109048 20
N7109.G3 S46 1990

**ART, MODERN - 20TH CENTURY - SPAIN -
LA RIOJA - CATALOGS.**
Labandíbar, José Luis. 1950-1990, cuarenta
años de artes plásticas en La Rioja /. [La Rioja]
[1989?-1990?] 2 v. :   ISBN 84-404-5495-3 (v. 1)
N7109.L3 L3 1989

**ART, MODERN - 20TH CENTURY - SRI
LANKA - CATALOGS.**
Dharmasiri, Albert. Modern art in Sri Lanka .
Colombo, Sri Lanka , 1988. 80 p. :   ISBN
955-9034-01-4 :   DDC 709/.5493/0745493 20
N7310.6 .D47 1988   NYPL   [3-MAF 91-6910]

**ART, MODERN - 20TH CENTURY -
SUBJECTS. see ART, MODERN - 20TH
CENTURY - THEMES, MOTIVES.**

**ART, MODERN - 20TH CENTURY -
SWEDEN.**
Beck & Jung. Chromo cube /. Bjärred, Sweden
(Box 123, S-237 00 Bjärred) , c1982. 49 p., [24]
leaves of plates :   ISBN 91-85752-30-4
             NYPL   [3-MAL 88-3799]

Sellem, Jean. Hardy Strid's work and Swedish
modernism in art from 1935 to 1980 /.
Munich , c1981. 224 p. :   ISBN 3-923091-00-1
             NYPL   [3-MCZ S917 85-1125]

**ART, MODERN - 20TH CENTURY -
SWEDEN - PRIVATE COLLECTIONS -
EXHIBITIONS.**
Fritz H. Erikssons samling . Stockholm , 1943.
26 p., [64] p. of plates :
             NYPL   [3-MAX (Eriksson) 90-6849]

**ART, MODERN - 20TH CENTURY -
SWITZERLAND - EXHIBITIONS.**
Das Engadin Ferdinand Hodlers und anderer
Künstler des 19. und 20. Jahrhunderts . [Chur] ,
St. Moritz , c1990. 122 p. :   ISBN 3-905240-15-7
             DDC 759.9494 20
ND853.H6 A4 1990

Defraoui, Silvie. Orient/occident /. Genève ,

c1989. 53 p. :
             NYPL   [3-MCZ + D316 89-27977]

Schweizer Kunst, 1900-1990 . [Zug] , c1990.
144 p. :   ISBN 3-908215-01-5   DDC
709/.494/074494756 20
N7148 .S253 1990

31 artistes suisses contemporains. Paris , 1972.
[72] p. :   *NYPL   [3-MAM 90-6430]*

**ART, MODERN - 20TH CENTURY -
SWITZERLAND - GRAUBÜNDEN -
EXHIBITIONS.**
Aspekte aktueller Bündner Kunst, Teil II .
Chur , 1985. 25 p. :   ISBN 3-905240-04-1
             NYPL   [3-MAM + 88-3792]

**ART, MODERN - 20TH CENTURY -
SWITZERLAND - ZURICH.**
Als Dada begann . [Zürich] , c1957. 92 p. :
             NYPL   [3-MAM 90-7093]

**ART, MODERN - 20TH CENTURY -
THEMES, MOTIVES.**
Di Piero, W. S. Out of Eden . Berkeley ,
c1991. 257 p. :   ISBN 0-520-07065-8 (cloth)   DDC
709/.04 20
N6490 .D44 1991

Groupes, mouvements, tendances de l'art
contemporain depuis 1945 /. Paris , 1990. 183
p. ;   ISBN 2-903639-61-2 :   DDC 709/.04/5 20
N6490 .G724 1990

Schwalm, Hans-Jürgen, 1955- Individuum und
Gruppe . Essen , c1990. 230 p., [36] p. of
plates :   ISBN 3-89206-329-X
N6490 .S3335 1990

**ART, MODERN - 20TH CENTURY -
THEMES, MOTIVES - EXHIBITIONS.**
Images of death in contemporary art .
Milwaukee, Wis. , c1990. 56 p. :   ISBN
0-87462-902-X   *NYPL   [3-MAMZ 91-7063]*

Not so simple pleasures . Cambridge, Mass. ,
1990. 32 p. :   ISBN 0-938437-34-8 (pbk.) :   DDC
709/.73/0747444 20
N6512 .N635 1990

Sur les murs. L'Art fun, ou, L'enfance de l'art.
Ateliers en liberté. Jouy-en-Josas [France]
[1986] 77 p. :   ISBN 2-86925-004-5
N6488.F8 J687 1986
             NYPL   [3-MAL+ 90-10669]

Varnedoe, Kirk, 1946- High & low . New
York , c1990. 460 p. :   ISBN 0-87070-353-6
(MoMA : hard)
             NYPL   [3-MAL+ 91-3655]

**ART, MODERN - 20TH CENTURY -
TURKEY.**
Tanaltay, Erdoğan. Sanat ustalarıyla-- bir gün .
Divanyolu, İstanbul [1989] 159 p. ;   ISBN
975-7704-02-4
N7168 .T36 1989

**ART, MODERN - 20TH CENTURY - UNITED
STATES.**
Abstract expressionism . New York , 1990. 304
p. :   ISBN 0-8109-1908-7 :   DDC 709/.73/09045 20
N6512.5.A25 A24 1990
             NYPL   [3-MAMT 91-6467]

Adams, Doug. Transcendence with the human
body in art . New York , 1991. p. cm.   ISBN
0-8245-1104-2 (cloth)   DDC 701/.04 20
N6512.5.F5 A34 1991

Bongard, Willi. Kunst und Kommerz.
[Oldenburg, c1967] 271 p.
             NYPL   [3-MAMT 90-6286]

Cornebise, Alfred E. Art from the trenches .
College Station , c1991. p. cm.   ISBN
0-89096-349-5 (cloth)   DDC 758/.99404/0973 20
N6512 .C598 1991

Eighteen contemporary masters . [Ottawa ,
1977] 23 p. :   *NYPL   [3-MAL 90-5655]*

Fisher, Philip. Making and effacing art . New
York , 1991. p. cm.   ISBN 0-19-506046-6   DDC
709/.73/0904 20
N6512 .F57 1991

Groh, Klaus, 1936- Der neue Dadaismus in
Nordamerika /. Augsburg , 1979. 221 p. :
             ISBN 3-87512-113-9
             NYPL   [3-MAL 90-7185]

Heide, Robert, 1939- Popular art deco . New
York , 1991. 228 p. :   ISBN 1-558-59030-7   DDC

709/.73/09041 20
N6512.5.A7 H45 1991
              NYPL [3-MAMT 91-8075]

The Italian presence in American art,
1860-1920 /. New York , Roma , 1991. p. cm.
    ISBN 0-8232-1342-0 :   DDC 709/.73/09034 20
N6510 .I8 1991

Lippard, Lucy R. Mixed blessings . New York ,
c1990. viii, 278 p., [40] p. of plates :   ISBN
0-394-57759-0; 0-06-797296-6   DDC
704/.0693/0973 20
N6537.5 .L5 1990
              NYPL [3-MAMT 91-2488]

Mamiya, Christin J. Pop art and consumer
culture . Austin , 1992. p. cm.   ISBN
0-292-77653-5 (alk. paper)   DDC 709/.04/071 20
N6512.5.P6 M36 1992

Seitz, William Chapin. Art in the Age of
Aquarius, 1955-1970 /. Washington , 1991. p.
cm.   ISBN 0-87474-868-2   DDC 709/.73/09046 20
N6512 .S335 1991

United States. National Armed Forces Museum
Advisory Board. The Armed Forces of the
United States as seen by the contemporary
artist. [Washington, 1968] vii, 64 p.   DDC
704.94/9/355000973
N6512 .A518   *NYPL [3-MAMT 90-6253]*

**ART, MODERN - 20TH CENTURY - UNITED
STATES - CONGRESSES.**
American art around 1900 . Washington ,
Hanover [N.H.] , 1990. 136 p. :   ISBN
0-89468-143-5   *NYPL [3-MAMT 91-7570]*

**ART, MODERN - 20TH CENTURY - UNITED
STATES - EXHIBITIONS.**
Addison Gallery of American Art. American
abstraction at the Addison . Andover, Mass. ,
c1991. 95 p. :   ISBN 1-87988-600-6   DDC
709/.73/0747445 20
N6512.5.A2 A33 1991

American masters of the 60's . New York, NY
(130 Prince St., New York 10012) , c1990. 76
p. :   DDC 709/.73/0747471 20
N6512 .A6156 1990

Archuleta, Margaret, 1950- Shared visions .
Phoenix, Ariz. , 1991. 110 p. :   ISBN
0-934351-21-X :   DDC 704/.0397/0904 20
N6538.A4 A7 1991

Art-- made in USA . [Regensburg] [1988?] 90
p. :   *NYPL [3-MAMT 89-28438]*

Art what thou eat . Mount Kisco, N.Y. , c1991.
191 p. :   ISBN 1-559-21051-6 :   DDC
704.9/49641/0973 20
N6512 .A763 1991
              NYPL [3-MAMZ+ 91-5410]

As seen by both sides . Boston, Mass. ,
Amersht, MA , 1991. 112 p. :   ISBN
0-87023-744-6 (pbk.) :   DDC
760/.04499597043/074597 20
N6512 .A788 1991

Bernard Danenberg Galleries. One hundred
recent acquisitions, by American artists. New
York, 1969. 51 p.   *NYPL [3-MAMT 90-6625]*

Black art . Dallas, Tex. , New York , c1989.
305 p. :   ISBN 0-8109-3104-4 (Abrams) :   DDC
704/.0396073/07473 20
N6538.N5 B525 1989   *NYPL [Sc G 90-16]*

Brach, Paul, 1924- Our land/ourselves . Albany,
N.Y. , 1991. p. :   ISBN 0-910763-05-4 :   DDC
760/.089/97073 20
N6538.A4 B67 1991

The Charade of mastery . New York, N.Y. ,
c1990. 18 p. :   *NYPL [3-MAMT 91-4324]*

Community Arts Programs Association.
Contemporary landscape . Bayside, N.Y. ,
c1977. 28 p. :
N6512 .C5814 1977
              NYPL [3-MAMT 81-992]

Day, Holliday T. Power . Indianapolis, Ind. ,
1991. p. cm.   ISBN 0-253-31658-8   DDC
709/.73/07477252 20
N72.P6 D38 1991

The Decade show . [New York] , c1990. 364
p. :   ISBN 0-915557-68-1
              NYPL [3-MAMT 90-12484]

Dwellings . Philadelphia , c1978. 16 p. :   ISBN
0-88454-050-2
N6512 .D85   *NYPL [3-MAMT+ 79-2026]*

El Surrealismo entre Viejo y Nuevo Mundo .
[Madrid] [1990] 346 p. :   ISBN 84-86022-51-2
N6512.5.S87 S8 1990

Fekner, John. Artist as apolitical sensor .
Brookville, N.Y. , 1990. 28 p. :
              NYPL [3-MAMT 91-5026]

Fowler, Harriet W. New Deal art .
[Lexington] , c1985. 119 p. :   DDC
760/.0973/074016947 19
N8838 .F69 1985   *NYPL [MDBF 87-1170]*

Gelburd, Gail. The trans parent thread .
[Hempstead, N.Y.] , Philadelphia, Pa. , c1990.
124 p. :   ISBN 0-8122-1376-9 (pbk.)
              NYPL [3-MAMT 91-4984]

Impressionism and post impressionism .
Portland, Me. , c1991. p. cm.   DDC
709/.03/4407474191 20
N6847.5.I4 I43 1991

Italian-American women artists . [San
Francisco, Calif. , 1979] [19] p. :
              NYPL [3-MAMT 90-12524]

Marlais, Michael Andrew. Americans and
Paris . Waterville, Me. , c1990. 62 p. :   DDC
759.13/074/7416 20
N6510 .M27 1990
              NYPL [3-MAMT 90-13006]

Matilsky, Barbara C. The expressionist surface .
New York , c1990. 48 p. :   ISBN 0-9604514-2-0
IN PROCESS (ONLINE)
              NYPL [3-MAMT+ 91-4360]

Montclair, N. J. Art Museum. Collage,
American masters . Montclair [c1979] [12 p.] :
N6512.5.C55 M66 1979
              NYPL [3-MAMT 80-2170]

New voices in Greek-American art . Brooklyn,
N.Y. [1990] [40] p. :
              NYPL [MAMT 91-6992]

Occupation and resistance . New York, N.Y. ,
c1990. 80 p. :   ISBN 0-932075-30-4
IN PROCESS (ONLINE)
              NYPL [3-MAMT 91-7487]

Pasadena Art Museum. A decade in the
contemporary galleries, 1949-1959. [Pasadena,
1959] 76 p.   *NYPL [3-MAMT 91-287]*

Pincus-Witten, Robert. The last
decade--American artists of the 80's . New
York (130 Prince St., New York 10012)
[1990] 137 p. :   DDC 709/.73/0747471 20
N6512 .P492 1990

The Sandra Doane Turk collection of Western
art . St. Petersburg, Florida , 1985. 42 p. :
              NYPL [3-MAMZ 90-11526]

Selections from the Edward Albee collection .
Reading, Penn. , 1988. 28 p. :   ISBN
0-941972-07-0
              NYPL [3-MAX (Albee) 90-12382]

Stavitsky, Gail, 1954- Gertrude Stein . New
York, N.Y. , c1990. 52 p. :
              NYPL [3-MAMT 91-7537]

Structure and surface . Sheboygan, Wis. ,
c1990. vii, 32 p. :   ISBN 0-932718-28-0   DDC
709/.73/07477569 20
N6512 .S78 1990
              NYPL [3-MAMT 90-13004]

Tate Gallery Liverpool. Minimalism. Liverpool ,
c1989. 28 p. :   ISBN 1-85437-009-1
              NYPL [3-MAMT 90-12390]

The Technological muse . Katonah, N.Y. ,
c1990. 96 p. :   ISBN 0-915171-19-8
              NYPL [3-MAMT+ 91-7609]

The (Un)making of nature. New York, N.Y. ,
c1990. 20 p. :   *NYPL [3-MAMT 91-6593]*

Word as image . Milwaukee, Wis. , c1990. 171
p. :   *NYPL [3-MAMT 90-12993]*

7 artists. New York , c1970. 1 v. (unpaged) :
              NYPL [3-MAMT 90-6992]

**ART, MODERN - 20TH CENTURY - UNITED
STATES - JAPANESE INFLUENCES -
EXHIBITIONS.**
Meech-Pekarik, Julia. Japonisme comes to
America . New York , 1990. 256 p. :   ISBN
0-8109-3501-5   DDC 760/.0973/07474942 20
N6510 .M44 1990   *NYPL [MDBV 90-11897]*

**ART, MODERN - 20TH CENTURY - UNITED
STATES - THEMES, MOTIVES.**
Breaking down the boundaries . Seattle, Wash. ,

c1989. 31 p. :   ISBN 0-935558-24-1   DDC 707/.5
20
N72.A77 B74 1909
              NYPL [3-MAMT+ 90-12629]

**ART, MODERN - 20TH CENTURY - UNITED
STATES - THEMES, MOTIVES -
EXHIBITIONS.**
Not so simple pleasures . Cambridge, Mass. ,
1990. 32 p. :   ISBN 0-938437-34-8 (pbk.) :   DDC
709/.73/0747444 20
N6512 .N635 1990

**ART, MODERN - 20TH CENTURY -
VENEZUELA - CARACAS -
EXHIBITIONS.**
Arte para los ochenta =. Caracas, Venezuela ,
c1980. [24] p. :   *NYPL [3-MAL 90-4430]*

**ART, MODERN - 20TH CENTURY -
VIETNAM - EXHIBITIONS.**
As seen by both sides . Boston, Mass. ,
Amersht, MA , 1991. 112 p. :   ISBN
0-87023-744-6 (pbk.) :   DDC
760/.04499597043/074597 20
N6512 .A788 1991

**ART, MODERN - 20TH CENTURY -
VIRGINIA - EXHIBITIONS.**
Un/common ground . Richmond , c1988. vii,
106 p. :   ISBN 0-917046-29-3   DDC
709/.755/0740155451 19
N6530.V8 U5 1988
              NYPL [3-MAMT 90-4499]

**ART, MODERN - 20TH CENTURY - WALES -
EXHIBITIONS.**
Jonah Jones, John Petts, Kyffin Williams .
[London, England] , 1961. 14 p., [8] p. of
plates :
MLCM 87/7416 (N)
              NYPL [3-MAMR 91-226]

ART, MODERN - CATALOGS.
Stiftung Langmatt Sidney und Jenny Brown.
Sammlungskataloge. Baden , c1990- v. :   ISBN
3-85545-044-7 (Bd. 1)
              NYPL [3-MAX+ (Brown) 91-1053]

**ART, MODERN - COLLECTORS AND
COLLECTING.**
Huer, Jon. The great art hoax . Bowling Green,
Ohio , c1990. 173 p. ;   ISBN 0-87972-491-9
              NYPL [3-MAAZ 90-12001]

ART, MODERN - EXHIBITIONS.
Düreriana . Nürnberg , c1990. 296 p. :   ISBN
3-418-00349-4
N6888.D8 A4 1990
              NYPL [3-MCK+ D85 91-7549]

Kunsthistorisches Museum Wien. Die Moderne
Galerie des Kunsthistorischen Museums. Wien
[1956] 24 p.
              NYPL [3-MAVZ (Vienna) 91-1153]

ART, MODERN - FRANCE - EXHIBITIONS.
Salmon, Marie José. D'Oudry à Le Sidaner .
Beauvais , 1990. 171 p. :   ISBN 2-901290-06-X
N8214.5.F8 S25 1990

**ART, MODERN - GERMANY - BERLIN -
EXHIBITIONS.**
Berlin, März 1990 . Berlin , Braunschweig
[1990] 88 p. :
MLCM 91/00973 (N)
              NYPL [3-MAL 91-6662]

**ART, MODERN - GERMANY -
MÜHLHAUSEN (ERFURT)**
Badstübner, Ernst. Das alte Mühlhausen .
Leipzig, c1989. 205 p. :   ISBN 3-7338-0055-9
N6886.M78 B34 1989

ART, MODERN - HISTORY.
Waller, Susan, 1948- Women artists in the
modern era . Metuchen, N.J. , 1991. xii, 392
p. ;   ISBN 0-8108-2405-1 (alk. paper)   DDC
709/.2/2 B 20
N43 .W26 1991

ART, MODERN - ITALY.
IL 60 . New York , c1990. xviii, 284 p. :   ISBN
0-934977-18-6 :   DDC 709/.45 20
N6911 .I34 1990
              NYPL [3-MAMC 90-11305]

**ART, MODERN - PRIVATE COLLECTIONS -
EXHIBITIONS.**
Opus sacrum . Vienna , c1990. 399 p. :   ISBN
3-900731-29-2   *NYPL [3-MAIH 91-4343]*

ART, MODERN - RUSSIAN S.F.S.R.
Kirichenko, Evgeniĭa Ivanovna. Russian design
and the fine arts, 1750-1917 /. New York ,

1991. p. cm.   ISBN 0-8109-3758-1   DDC 709/.47
20
N6984 .K57 1991

Voprosy izucheniiā otechestvennogo iskusstva .
Leningrad , 1989. 83 p. ;
N6984 .V6 1989

ART, MODERN - SWITZERLAND -
CATALOGS.
Museum zu Allerheiligen (Schaffhausen,
Switzerland). Kunstabteilung. Museum zu
Allerheiligen Schaffhausen . Schaffhausen ,
1989. 340 p. :   DDC 759.94/074/49458 20
N7144 .M87 1989
          NYPL   [MAVZ (Schaffhausen) 91-6567]

ART, MODERN - THEMES, MOTIVES.
Bildfälle . Zürich , c1990. 231 p. :   ISBN
3-7608-8073-8
N6350 .B547 1990

ART, MODERN - UNITED STATES -
EXHIBITIONS.
Arte minimal de la Colección Panza .
[Madrid?] , 1988. 61 p. :   ISBN 84-7750-623-18
          NYPL   [MAMT 90-5197]

ART, MODERN - 20TH CENTURY -
COLOMBIA - BOGOTA - EXHIBITIONS.
50 años, Salón Nacional de Artistas /. [Bogotá,
Colombia] , c1990. 363 p. :   ISBN 958-95220-0-9
IN PROCESS (ONLINE)
          NYPL   [3-MAM 90-13365]

ART, MODERNIST. see MODERNISM (ART)

ART, MOORISH. see ART, ISLAMIC.

ART, MOROCCAN - EXHIBITIONS.
De L'Empire romain aux villes impériales .
Paris , c1990. xxiii, 474 p. :
          NYPL   [3-MAM+ 91-6786]

ART, MUHAMMADAN. see ART, ISLAMIC.

ART MUSEUM ARCHITECTURE - UNITED
STATES - PSYCHOLOGICAL ASPECTS.
Fisher, Philip. Making and effacing art . New
York , 1991. p. cm.   ISBN 0-19-506046-6   DDC
709/.73/0904 20
N6512. .F57 1991

ART MUSEUM ARCHITECTURE -
VENEZUELA - CARACAS - DESIGNS
AND PLANS.
Proyecto nueva sede, Galería de Arte Nacional,
Caracas =. [Caracas, Venezuela] [1986] 77 p. :
    ISBN 980-603-006-0
N910.C22 P76 1986
          NYPL   [3-MQWN+ 90-11046]

Art Museum, Trivandrum.
Catalogue of selected bronzes, wood-carvings &
sculptures / Art Museum, Trivandrum.
[Trivandrum] : Dept. of Museums & Zoos,
Govt. of Kerala, 1981. [132] p. : chiefly ill.
(some col.) ; 30 cm.
    1. Art Museum, Trivandrum - Catalogs. 2. Bronzes,
Indic - India - Kerala - Catalogs. 3. Wood-carving -
India - Kerala - Catalogs. 4. Sculpture, Indic - India -
Kerala - Catalogs. I. Kerala, India (State). Museums and
Zoo Dept. II. Title.   *NYPL   [3-MGI+ 90-12595]*

ART MUSEUM, TRIVANDRUM -
CATALOGS.
Art Museum, Trivandrum. Catalogue of selected
bronzes, wood-carvings & sculptures /.
[Trivandrum] , 1981. [132] p. :
          NYPL   [3-MGI+ 90-12595]

Art Museums Association of Australia. Australian
art museums and public galleries directory.
Melbourne, Vic., Clayton, Vic. , 1990. v, 49
p. ;   ISBN 0-9595532-4-X   DDC 708/.0025/94 20
N3910 .A93 1990

ART MUSEUMS - AUSTRALIA -
DIRECTORIES.
Australian art museums and public galleries
directory. Melbourne, Vic., Clayton, Vic. ,
1990. v, 49 p. ;   ISBN 0-9595532-4-X   DDC
708/.0025/94 20
N3910 .A93 1990

Germaine, Max, 1914- Artists & galleries of
Australia /. Roseville, NSW, Australia , c1990.
2 v. (xii, 832 p.) :   ISBN 976-8097-02-7
          NYPL   [MAO+ 91-2667]

ART MUSEUMS - CONGRESSES.
Le musée et son public. [Bruxelles, 1968?] 250
p.   *NYPL   [3-MAV 90-5745]*

ART MUSEUMS - CZECHOSLOVAKIA.
Vacková, Jarmila. Nizozemské malířství 15. a

16. století . Praha , 1989. 453 p. :   ISBN
80-200-0206-5 :
ND635 .V33 1989

ART MUSEUMS - ECONOMIC ASPECTS -
UNITED STATES.
The Economics of art museums /. Chicago ,
1991. p. cm.   ISBN 0-226-24073-8 (alk. paper)
DDC 338.4/770813 20
N510 .E27 1991

ART MUSEUMS - EUROPE - VISITORS.
Bourdieu, Pierre. [Amour de l'art. English.] The
love of art . Cambridge, UK , 1991. viii, 182
p. ;   ISBN 0-7456-0598-2 :   DDC 708.9/4 20
N430 .B613 1991

ART MUSEUMS - EXHIBITIONS.
Perl, Jed. Gallery going . San Diego , c1991.
xxiv, 431 p., [16] p. of plates :   ISBN
0-15-134260-1 :   DDC 709/.04/0074 20
N6447 .P38 1991   *NYPL   [3-MAV 91-7445]*

ART MUSEUMS - FINLANF - HELSINKI -
DIRECTORIES.
Sakari, Marja. Helsinki kuvataidekaupunkina .
Helsinki , 1991. 104 p. :   ISBN 951-772-148-X
N7255.F52 H47 1991

ART MUSEUMS - FRANCE - DIRECTORIES.
Warnod, Jeanine. Le guide Warnod de la
peinture . Paris , c1990. 323 p., 32 leaves of
plates :   ISBN 2-7107-0457-9 :   DDC 750/.74/44 20
N2010 .A66 1990

ART MUSEUMS - FRANCE - PROVENCE -
DIRECTORIES.
Guid'arts . Nice [1989] 174 p. :   ISBN
2-87720-040-X :
N6485.3 .G85 1989

ART MUSEUMS - GERMANY - LEIPZIG -
EXHIBITIONS.
Merkur & die Musen . Wien , 1989. 627 p. :
    ISBN 3-900926-02-6   DDC 707/.4/43613 20
N6886.L4 M47 1989

ART MUSEUMS - GERMANY (WEST) -
EXHIBITIONS.
Russische Avantgarde 1910-1930 . Duisburg ,
c1990. 120 p. :   ISBN 3-923576-73-0
N6988 .R855 1990

ART MUSEUMS - GERMANY (WEST) -
MUNICH - EXHIBITIONS.
Glyptothek München, 1830-1980 . München ,
c1980. 640 p. :
NB87.M8 G55 1980
          NYPL   [3-MQWD 90-5627]

ART MUSEUMS - GREAT BRITAIN.
The National museums . London , 1988. 64 p. :
    ISBN 0-11-290457-2 (pbk.) :   DDC 069/.0941
708.2 19
AM41 N1020   *NYPL   [MAV 90-11367]*

ART MUSEUMS - GREAT BRITAIN -
EXHIBITIONS.
Sixty years of patronage . [London] , 1965. 29
p., 8 p. of plates :
MLCM 82/1567
          NYPL   [3-MAVZ (London) 90-5872]

ART MUSEUMS - ITALY.
Portogruaro: Museo nazionale concordiese.
[Bologna, 1973, c1971] 113 p.
N2510.P66   *NYPL   [3-MAVZ (Portogruaro,*
                                   Italy) 90-6420]

ART MUSEUMS - ITALY - DIRECTORIES.
I Mille musei d'Italia /. Firenze , c1988- v. :
    ISBN 88-09-45125-2 (v. 1 : pbk.)
          NYPL   [3-MAV 90-2271]

ART MUSEUMS - ITALY - FLORENCE -
CATALOGS.
Chiarini, Marco. I dipinti olandesi del Seicento
e del Settecento /. Roma , 1989. xxiii, 671 p. :
    ISBN 88-24-00001-0   DDC 759.9492/074/4551
20
ND646 .C48 1989

ART MUSEUMS - KOREA.
Korean art seen through museums /. Seoul,
Korea , 1979. xxi, 353 p. :   DDC
709/.519/074095195 19
N7360 .K635   *NYPL   [3-MAG 83-2164]*

ART MUSEUMS - NEW YORK (STATE) -
EXHIBITIONS.
In Medusa's gaze . Rochester, NY , c1991. p.
cm.   ISBN 0-918098-05-X :   DDC 758/.4/074747 20
ND1390 .I5 1991

ART MUSEUMS - ROMANIA.
Tzigara-Samurcaş, Al. (Alexandru), 1872-1952.

Scrieri despre arta românească /. Bucureşti ,
1987. 418 p., [12] p. of plates :
N7221 .T95 1987   *NYPL   [3-MAM 91-3417]*

ART MUSEUMS - RUSSIAN S.F.S.R. -
EXHIBITIONS.
Russische Avantgarde 1910-1930 . Duisburg ,
c1990. 120 p. :   ISBN 3-923576-73-0
N6988 .R855 1990

ART MUSEUMS - SWEDEN - CATALOGS.
Nationalmuseum (Sweden) Nationalmuseum
Stockholm . Stockholm , 1990. xxx, 479 p. :
    ISBN 91-7100-382-7
          NYPL   [3-MAVZ (Stockholm) 90-12869]

ART MUSEUMS - SWITZERLAND -
EXHIBITIONS.
Russell, Margarita. Images of reality, images of
Arcadia . Winterthur [Switzerland] ,
Washington, D.C. , c1989. 131 p. :   ISBN
3-907798-01-5   *NYPL   [3-MCG 90-11767]*

ART MUSEUMS - THAILAND.
Thailand. Krom Sinlapākōn. Kānphatthanā
phiphitthaphanthasathān læ ngān bōrānnakhadī
kh [Bangkok] , 2508 [1965] 70, [30] p., [3]
leaves of plates :
N7321 .T46 1965

ART MUSEUMS - UNITED STATES -
VISITORS.
Schuster, J. Mark Davidson, 1950- The
audience for American art museums /.
Washington , 1991. p. cm.   ISBN 0-929765-00-1 :
    DDC 708.13 20
N510 .S3 1991

ART, MUSLIM. see ART, ISLAMIC.

ART - MUTILATION, DEFACEMENT, ETC.
Freedberg, David. Iconoclasts and their motives
/. Maarssen , Montclair, N.J. , c1985. 60 p. :
    ISBN 90-6179-056-5 (pbk.)   DDC 709 19
N8557 .F74 1985   *NYPL   [3-MAS 91-5030]*

ART, MYCEANEAN - THEMES, MOTIVES.
Czernohaus, Karola. Delphindarstellungen von
der minoischen bis zur geometrischen Zeit /.
Göteborg , 1988. 235, 111 p., 121 p. of plates :
    ISBN 91-86098-76-4
          NYPL   [3-MAH 90-10819]

ART, NABATAEAN.
Patrich, J. (Joseph) The formation of Nabatean
art . Jerusalem : Leiden ; 231 p. :   ISBN
90-04-09285-4 (Brill)   DDC 709/.39/48 20
DS154.22 .P38 1990
          NYPL   [3-MAE 91-3363]

Art naïf. Tanger : Editions marocaines et
internationales, 1964. 94 p. : ill. ; 21 x 22 cm.
"Publiée à l'occasion de l'exposition circulante
'Panorama international de la peinture naïve'..." Includes
bibliographical references.
    1. Primitivism in art - History - Exhibitions. 2. Painting,
Modern - 20th century - Exhibitions. I. Panorama
international de la peinture naïve.
          NYPL   [3-MC 89-12693]

ART, NEPALI - EXHIBITIONS.
Pal, Pratapaditya. Art of the Himalayas . New
York , c1991. p. cm.   ISBN 1-555-95066-3 :
    DDC 709/.5496/07473 20
N7310.8.N4 P33 1991

ART - NETHERLANDS - HAGUE -
CATALOGS.
Museum Bredius. Museum Bredius .
['s-Gravenhage] , 1980. 176 p. :
          NYPL   [3-MAVZ (Hague) 81-647]

ART - NETHERLANDS - HISTORY.
Imitation and inspiration . [Amsterdam] ,
c1989. 179 p. :
          NYPL   [3-MAME+ 90-11986]

ART - NETHERLANDS - OTTERLO.
Kröller-Müller. English. Kröller-Müller .
Haarlem, The Netherlands , 1989. 318 p. :
    ISBN 90-70024-53-5
          NYPL   [MAVZ (Otterlo) 91-6126]

ART - NEW JERSEY - NEWARK -
CATALOGS.
Newark Museum. Catalogue of the Newark
Museum Tibetan collection /. Newark, N.J. ,
1983- v. :   ISBN 0-932828-12-4 (pbk.) :   DDC
709/.51/5074014932 19
N7346.T5 N48 1983   *NYPL   [MAF 91-997]*

ART - NEW MEXICO - SANTA FE -
CATALOGS.
Museum of Fine Arts (Museum of New
Mexico) Artists of twentieth-century New

Mexico . Santa Fe, NM , 1992. p. cm. ISBN
0-89013-230-5 DDC 709/.789/07478956 20
N6530.N6 M87 1992

**ART - NEW YORK - POUGHKEEPSIE -
CATALOGS.**
Vassar College. Art Gallery. Vassar College Art
Gallery . Poughkeepsie, N.Y. , c1967. xvi, 179
p., [7] leaves of plates : DDC 708.147/33
*N713 .A55 NYPL [3-MAVZ (Poughkeepsie)
91-1493]*

ART - NEW YORK (STATE) - EXHIBITIONS.
A New consciousness . Yonkers, N.Y., c1971.
[12] p. :
NYPL [3-MAX (CIBA-GEIGY) 90-7135]

ART, NEW ZEALAND - EXHIBITIONS.
Content/context . Wellington, N.Z. , 1986. 144
p. : ISBN 0-9597785-1-9 DDC
700/.993/0904807493127 20
N7406.5 .C66 1986

**ART - NORTH CAROLINA - DURHAM -
CATALOGS.**
Duke University. Museum of Art. The
Brummer collection of medieval art, the Duke
University Museum of Art /. Durham , 1991.
xix, 297 p., 16 p. of plates : ISBN 0-8223-1055-4
DDC 709/.02/074756563 20
N5963.D87 D854 1991
NYPL [3-MAK 91-5627]

**ART - NORTH CAROLINA - DURHAM -
EXHIBITIONS.**
Moeller, Robert C. Sculpture and decorative
art. Raleigh [1967] 97 p.
NYPL [3-MAK 90-6857]

ART, NORWEGIAN.
Moen, Arve. Gullalderens Mestere . Olso ,
1964. 139, 165 p.
NYPL [3-MAM+ 90-2909]

ART NOUVEAU.
L'architecture de l'art nouveau /. Paris , c1982.
332 p. : ISBN 2-7013-0448-2
NYPL [3-MRX+ 91-7304]
Fanelli, Giovanni. L'illustrazione Art nouveau /.
Roma , 1989. 332 p. : ISBN 88-420-3476-2
NYPL [MDTT 90-10984]
Velde, Henry van de, 1863-1957. [Essays.
Selections. 1979.] Déblaiement d'art ; suivi de,
La triple offense à la beauté ; Le nouveau ;
Max Elskamp ; La voie sacrée ; La colonne /.
Bruxelles , 1979. 198 p. ; DDC 700 19
N70 .V38 1979 NYPL [3-MAB 91-456]

Art nouveau architecture . Shimomura, Jun'ichi,
1952- [Aru nüvö no meitei. English.] San
Francisco , 1991. p. cm. ISBN 0-938491-29-6
DDC 728/.09/034 20
NA7125 .S5513 1991

ART NOUVEAU (ARCHITECTURE)
Shimomura, Jun'ichi, 1952- [Aru nüvö no
meitei. English.] Art nouveau architecture . San
Francisco , 1991. p. cm. ISBN 0-938491-29-6
DDC 728/.09/034 20
NA7125 .S5513 1991

**ART NOUVEAU (ARCHITECTURE) -
AUSTRIA - VIENNA.**
Kubinszky, Mihály. Otto Wagner /. Budapest ,
1988. 25 p., [56] p. of plates : ISBN
963-05-4879-8 :
NA1011.5.W3 K8 1988

**ART NOUVEAU (ARCHITECTURE) -
EUROPE.**
Tahara, Keiichi, 1951- [Seikimatsu no kenchiku.
English.] Images of fin-de-siècle architecture
and interior decoration /. London , New York ,
1988. 263 p. : ISBN 0-00-215354-8 : DDC
724.9/1 19
NA3485 NYPL [3-MRX+ 91-3382]

ART NOUVEAU - GERMANY.
Hollweck, Ludwig. Joseph Kaspar Sattler .
Pfaffenhofen , c1988. 156 p. : ISBN
3-7787-2090-2
IN PROCESS (ONLINE)
NYPL [MDG (Sattler) 90-5109]

ART NOUVEAU - GERMANY - DARMSTADT.
Darmstadt Künstler-Kolonie. Museum
Künstlerkolonie Darmstadt /. Darmstadt
[1989?] lv, 253 p. : *NYPL [3-MLF 91-5455]*

ART NOUVEAU - HUNGARY.
Szabadi, Judit. [Magyar szecesszió müvészete.
English.] Art nouveau in Hungary . [Budapest] ,

c1989. 157 p., [264] p. of plates : ISBN
963-13-2926-7 *NYPL [3-MAM 91-3931]*
Art nouveau in Hungary . Szabadi, Judit. [Magyar
szecesszió müvészete. English.] [Budapest] ,
c1989. 157 p., [264] p. of plates : ISBN
963-13-2926-7 *NYPL [3-MAM 91-3931]*

ART NOUVEAU - ITALY - GENOA.
Testimonianze Liberty a Genova /. Genova ,
c1986. 46 p. : ISBN 88-7058-218-3
NYPL [3-MAMC 90-11119]

ART NOUVEAU - SCOTLAND - GLASGOW.
Eadie, William, 1948- Movements of
modernity . London , 1990. viii, 292 p. ; ISBN
0-415-03243-1 DDC 709/.414/4309034 20
N6781.G55 E26 1991
NYPL [3-MAMR 90-13191]

ART, NUDE IN. see NUDE IN ART.

ART OBJECTS, ANCIENT.
Göttlicher, Arvid. Materialien für ein Corpus
der Schiffsmodelle im Altertum /. Mainz am
Rhein , c1978. 128 p., [56] p. of plates : ISBN
3-8053-0249-5 DDC 730
VM6.A1 G63 NYPL [3-MAE 90-6881]

ART OBJECTS, CHINESE - CATALOGS.
Kerr, Rose, 1953- Chinese art and design /.
Woodstock, N.Y. , 1991. p. cm. ISBN
0-87951-437-X DDC 745/.0951/07442134 20
NK1068 .K47 1991

**ART OBJECTS - CONSERVATION AND
RESTAURATION - GERMANY (EAST) -
KARL-MARX-STADT (BEZIRK) -
EXHIBITIONS.**
Restauriertes Kulturgut aus den Werkstätten des
Bezirkes Karl-Marx-Stadt . Glauchau , 1986. 68
p. ; *NYPL [3-MAW (Glauchau) 90-10827]*

ART OBJECTS, EGYPTIAN - EXHIBITIONS.
Egypt . [Bronxville, N.Y.] , c1989. 22 p. :
IN PROCESS (ONLINE)
NYPL [3-MAMY+ 90-10613]

ART OBJECTS - EUROPE - EXHIBITIONS.
Österreichisches Museum für Angewandte
Kunst. 100 Jahre Österreichisches Museum für
angewandte Kunst. [Wien, 1964] xxxxv, 109 p.
NK520.V5 V5 NYPL [3-MNC 90-6955]

**ART OBJECTS - FRANCE - PARIS -
CATALOGS.**
Musée du Louvre . Paris , 1985. 300 p. : ISBN
2-7118-2365-2
NYPL [3-MAVZ (Paris) 91-5074]

**ART OBJECTS - GERMANY - COLOGNE -
CATALOGS.**
Kunstgewerbemuseum der Stadt Köln. Cimelien
/. Köln , 1960. 96 p., 32 p. of plates :
NYPL [3-MNE 90-6793]

**ART OBJECTS - ITALY - FLORENCE -
CONSERVATION AND RESTORATION -
EXHIBITION.**
Firenze restaura . Firenze , 1973, c1972. 154 p.,
[168] p. of plates : *NYPL [3-MBK 90-5749]*

**ART OBJECTS, JADE. see JADE ART
OBJECTS.**

ART OBJECTS, KOREAN.
The Arts of Korea. Seoul , c1979. 6 v. : DDC
709/.519
N7363 .A79 NYPL [3-MAF 83-1615]

ART OBJECTS - PRIVATE COLLECTIONS.
Barlow, Sir James Alan Noel, bart., 1881-
Chinese ceramics. London [1963] 173 p. DDC
730.951
NK4165 .B3 NYPL [3-MPFF 90-11573]

**ART OBJECTS - PRIVATE COLLECTIONS -
ENGLAND - LONDON - CATALOGS.**
Kerr, Rose, 1953- Chinese art and design /.
Woodstock, N.Y. , 1991. p. cm. ISBN
0-87951-437-X : DDC 745/.0951/07442134 20
NK1068 .K47 1991

**ART OBJECTS, RUSSIAN - THEMES,
MOTIVES.**
Fabergé, Peter Carl, 1846-1920. Fabergé and
the Russian master goldsmiths /. New York ,
1991. p. cm. ISBN 0-517-02733-X DDC
739.2/092 20
NK7398.F32 A4 1991

ART, OCCIDENTAL. see ART.

ART - OCEANIA - CONGRESSES.
Art and identity in Oceania /. Honolulu ,
c1990. viii, 315 p., [8] p. of plates : ISBN

0-8248-1304-9 : DDC 700/.995 20
N7399.7 .A78 1990
NYPL [3-MADF 91-5014]

ART - OCEANIA - EXHIBITIONS.
Schnitzkunst aus der Südsee .
Erbach/Odenwald [1974] 47 p. :
NYPL [3-MADF 91-5898]

ART - OCEANICA.
Ornament und Plastic fremder Völker. English.
Ornament and sculpture in primitive society.
New York [1966] [138] p. DDC 709.011
N7380 .O713 1966b
NYPL [3-MADF 90-6405]

ART, OCEANIAN - EXHIBITIONS.
Boglár, Lajos. Tribal art in Africa and Oceania .
[Budapest] , 1971. 8, 8 p., 8, 8 p. of plates ;
enghun NYPL [3-MADF 90-5887]

The art of Africa. Leuzinger, Elsy. New York
[c1960] 247 p. *NYPL [MADF 90-11494]*

The art of Amenhotep III : art historical
analysis : papers presented at the international
symposium, held at the Cleveland Museum of
Art, Cleveland, Ohio, 20-21 November 1987 /
edited by Lawrence Michael Berman.
Cleveland, Ohio : Published by the Cleveland
Museum of Art in cooperation with Indiana
University Press, 1990. xii, 92 p., 27 p. of
plates : ill., plan ; 28 cm. English; with 1
contribution in German. Includes bibliographical
references. ISBN 0-940717-01-8 DDC 732/.8 20
*1. Amenhotep III, King of Egypt - Art - Congresses. 2.
Portrait sculpture, Egyptian - Congresses. 3. Portrait
sculpture, Ancient - Egypt - Congresses. I. Berman,
Lawrence Michael, 1952-.*
NB165.A44 A78 1990
NYPL [3-MAE 91-4575]

The art of ancient Greece . Pollitt, J. J. (Jerome
Jordan), 1934- Cambridge [England] , New
York , 1990. xiv, 298 p. : ISBN 0-521-25368-3
DDC 709/.38 20
N5630 .P56 1990 NYPL [3-MAH 91-3705]

The art of Archibald J. Motley, Jr. /.
Greenhouse, Wendy, 1955- Chicago, IL , 1991.
p. cm. ISBN 0-913820-15-6 DDC 759.13 20
ND237.M8524 A4 1991

The art of Aubrey Beardsley /. Slessor,
Catherine. London , c1989. 128 p. : ISBN
1-85076-181-7 : DDC 741.942 20
NC242.B3 NYPL [3-MCV B368 90-12980]

The art of botanical illustration . De Bray, Lys.
Bromley, Kent , c1989. 191 p. : ISBN
0-7470-0232-0 *NYPL [MDT+ 91-3771]*

Art of drawing. Kunsten å tegne . Oslo [1990]
64 p. :
N8640 .O8 nr. 532 NC95

Art of dynastic China /. Watson, William, 1917-
[Art de l'ancienne Chine. English.] New York ,
1981, c1979. 633 p. : ISBN 0-8109-0627-9 :
DDC 709/.31 19
N7343.22 .W3713
NYPL [3-MAG+ 87-1522]

The art of Equatorial Guinea . Perrois, Louis.
New York , 1990. 177 p. : ISBN 0-8478-1275-8
DDC 730/.089/96396 20
N7399.E68 P47 1990
NYPL [3-MADF+ 91-5613]

The art of Ercole de' Roberti /. Manca, Joseph,
1956- Cambridge [England] , New York , 1992.
p. cm. ISBN 0-521-39462-7 (hardback) DDC 759.5
20
ND623.R67125 M3 1992

The art of Eric Carle . Carle, Eric. Saxonville,
MA , c1991. p. cm. ISBN 0-88708-176-2 : DDC
741.6/42/092 20
NC975.5.C36 A2 1991

The art of J.M.W. Turner /. Brown, David
Blayney. London , 1990. 192 p. : ISBN
0-7472-0209-5 : DDC 760.092 20
N6797.T88 NYPL [3-MCV+ T94 91-6101]

The art of Japan . Asian Art Museum of San
Francisco. San Francisco , c1991. p. cm. ISBN
0-8118-0055-5 (cloth) : DDC 709/.52/07479461
20
N7352 .A935 1991

Art of Japanese applique. Miyawaki, Ayako,
1905- Ayako Miyawaki, the art of Japanese
applique /. [Tokyo] , Washington D.C. , 1991.
p. cm. ISBN 0-940979-17-9 DDC 746.392 20
NK9198.M59 A4 1991

The art of John Yardley /. Ranson, Ron. Newton
Abbot , New York, N.Y. , c1990. 128 p. :
ISBN 0-7153-9845-8 DDC 759.2 20
ND1942.Y37 A4 1990

The art of Kate Greenaway . Taylor, Ina. Gretna,
La. , 1991. 128 p. : ISBN 0-88289-867-1 DDC
741.6/42/092 B 20
NC978.5.G7 T37 1991

The art of Kate Greenaway . Taylor, Ina. Exeter,
Devon , 1991. 128 p. : ISBN 0-86350-397-7
NYPL [MDG (Greenaway) 91-8041]

The art of Lee Waisler /. Wendon, John.
London , 1990. 101 p. : ISBN 0-233-98612-X :
DDC 709.2 20
NYPL [3-MCX+ W143 91-6465]

The art of Louis Comfort Tiffany /. Couldrey,
Vivienne. London , 1989. 192 p. : ISBN
0-7475-0488-1
NYPL [3-MPW+ 90-11646]

The art of Louis Comfort Tiffany /. Couldrey,
Vivienne. Secaucus, N.J. , c1989. 191 p. :
ISBN 1-555-21447-9 DDC 748/.092 20
NK5198.T5 C68 1989

The Art of Mark Rothko : into an unknown
world / edited by Marc Glimcher and Mark
Pollard.1st ed. New York : Clarkson Potter :
Distributed by Crown Publishers, c1991. p. cm.
Includes index. ISBN 0-517-58148-5 : DDC 759.13
20
*1. Rothko, Mark, 1903-1970 - Criticism and
interpretation. I. Rothko, Mark, 1903-1970. II.
Glimcher, Marc. III. Pollard, Mark.*
ND237.R725 A9 1991

The Art of medieval technology . Unger, Richard
W. New Brunswick , c1991. p. cm. ISBN
0-8135-1727-3 DDC 704.9/484 20
N8180 .U54 1991

The Art of Mickey Mouse / edited by Craig Yoe
and Janet Morra-Yoe ; introduction by John
Updike. 1st ed. New York : Hyperion, c1991.
p. cm. ISBN 1-562-82994-7 : DDC 704.9/497415
20
*1. Mickey Mouse (Cartoon character) in art - Catalogs.
2. Art, American - 20th century - Catalogs. I. Yoe, Craig.
II. Morra-Yoe, Janet.*
N8224.M47 A4 1991

The art of Miles Davis /. Davis, Miles. New
York , c1991. 89 p. : ISBN 0-13-608704-3 :
DDC 759.13 B 20
ND237.D3326 A2 1991
NYPL [3-MCX+ D259 91-6131]

The Art of mosaic /. Mosaico. English. London ,
c1989. 360 p. : ISBN 0-304-31836-1
NYPL [3-MRXZ+ 91-4959]

The art of motherhood /. Tobey, Susan Bracaglia.
New York , 1991. p. cm. ISBN 1-558-59105-2
DDC 704.9/493068743 20
N7630 .T63 1991

The art of Ogata Kenzan . Wilson, Richard L.,
1949- New York , 1991. p. cm. ISBN
0-8348-0240-6 : DDC 738/.092 B 20
NK4210.O39 W55 1991

The art of pre-Columbian Mexico. Kendall,
Aubyn. Austin, 1973. x, 115 p. DDC 016.709/72
Z1208.M4 K46 *NYPL [JFD 90-11458]*

The art of Renaissance Venice. Huse, Norbert.
[Venedig, die Kunst der Renaissance. English.]
Chicago , 1990. 382 p., [32] p. of plates :
ISBN 0-226-36107-1 (alk. paper) DDC
709/.45/3109024 20
N6921.V5 H8713 1990
NYPL [3-MAMC 91-3259]

The art of sandcastling /. Siebert, Ted. Seattle,
Wash. , c1990. ix, 229 p. : ISBN 0-945265-27-1 :
DDC 736/.9 20
NB1270.S3 S54 1990

Art of sculpture by Mazzone. Mazzone,
Domenico, 1927- Domenico Mazzone, sculptor.
[New York City?] c1971. 48 p. :
NYPL [3-MGO (Mazzone) 91-874]

The art of seeing . Csikszentmihalyi, Mihaly.
Malibu, Calif. , 1990. xvii, 203 p. : ISBN
0-89236-156-5 : DDC 111/.85 20
BH301.E8 C75 1990
NYPL [3-MAB 91-6221]

The art of Shibata Zeshin . Shibata, Zeshin,
1807-1891. [London] [Honolulu] , c1979. 195

p. : ISBN 0-903697-05-X DDC 709/.2/4
N7359.S46 A4 1979
NYPL [3-MAG+ 91-6922]

The art of Simon Dinnerstein /. Dinnerstein,
Simon, 1943- Fayetteville , 1990. xii, 254 p. :
ISBN 1-557-28142-4 (alk. paper) : DDC
760/.092 20
N6537.D53 A4 1990
NYPL [3-MCX+ D587 91-3991]

The art of the Boyds . Dobrez, Patricia. Sydney ,
1990. 232 p. : ISBN 1-86256-426-4
NYPL [3-MAM+ 90-13433]

Art of the Cameroon : selections from the
Spelman College Collection of African Art /
curated by Sharon Pruitt ; organized by Donald
D. Keyes. Athens, Ga. : Georgia Museum of
Art, University of Georgia, c1990. 40 p. : ill. ;
27 cm. Catalog of an exhibition held Jan. 27-Mar. 4,
1990. Includes bibliographical references (p. 40).
ISBN 0-915977-05-2 DDC
730/.096711/0747582311 20
*1. Sculpture, Cameroon - Exhibitions. 2. Sculpture,
Primitive - Cameroon - Exhibitions. 3. Spelman
College - Art collections - Exhibitions. 4. Sculpture -
Private collections - Georgia - Atlanta - Exhibitions. I.
Pruitt, Sharon Yvette, 1953-. II. Keyes, Donald D. III.
Georgia Museum of Art.*
NB1099.C3 A7 1990

Art of the Golden West /. Axelrod, Alan, 1952-
New York , c1990. 418 p. : ISBN 1-558-59103-6
DDC 978 20
F591 .A53 1990
NYPL [3-MAMT+ 90-13272]

Art of the Himalayas . Pal, Pratapaditya. New
York , c1991. p. cm. ISBN 1-555-95066-3 :
DDC 709/.5496/07473 20
N7310.8.N4 P33 1991

Art of the imperial Cholas /. Dehejia, Vidya.
New York , c1990. xviii, 148 p. : ISBN
0-231-07188-4 DDC 726/.145/09548 20
NA6007.S6 D44 1990
NYPL [3-MAF 90-12973]

**Art of the Italian Renaissance from the Samuel
H. Kress collection.** Columbia Museum of Art.
Columbia, S.C. , 1954. 63 p. :
*NYPL [3-MAVZ (Columbia, S.C.)
90-6807]*

The art of the old South . Poesch, Jessie J. New
York , 1983. xii, 384 p. : ISBN 0-394-40193-X :
DDC 709/.75 19
N6520 .P63 1983
NYPL [3-MAMT+ 90-10836]

Art of the Third Reich /. Adam, Peter. New
York , 1992. p. cm. ISBN 0-8109-1912-5 (cloth)
DDC 709/.43/09043 20
N6868.5.N37 A34 1992

Art of the world.
Leuzinger, Elsy. The art of Africa. New York
[c1960] 247 p. *NYPL [MADF 90-11494]*

The art of Thomas Rowlandson /. Hayes, John T.
Alexandria, Va. , c1990. 196 p. : DDC 741.942
20
NC242.R66 A4 1990
NYPL [MDG+ (Rowlandson) 91-6401]

The art of vase-painting in classical Athens /.
Robertson, Martin. Cambridge , New York ,
1992. p. cm. ISBN 0-521-33010-6 DDC
738.3/82/09385 20
NK4645 .R7 1992

The art of William Morris /. Vallance, Aymer,
1862-1943. New York , 1988. xi, 167, xxx p. :
ISBN 0-486-25647-2 (pbk.) DDC 821/.8 B 19
PR5083 .V3 1988
NYPL [3-MNE+ 90-13076]

ART - OHIO - CLEVELAND.
Cleveland Museum of Art. Interpretations .
Cleveland, OH , 1991. p. cm. ISBN
0-940717-11-5 DDC 708.71/32 20
N552 .A84 1991

ART - OHIO - CLEVELAND - CATALOGS.
Cleveland Museum of Art. Handbook of the
Cleveland Museum of Art. Cleveland, Ohio ,
1991. x, 161 p. : ISBN 0-940717-00-X : DDC
708.171/32 20
N552 .A6 1991

ART, OPTICAL. see OPTICAL ART.

**ART - PAPUA NEW GUINEA -
EXHIBITIONS.**

Primitive art of Papua New Guinea . New
York , c1989. 31 p. :
NYPL [3-MADF+ 89-20654]

L'art pariétal de Rouffignac . Barrière, C. Paris ,
1982. 205 p., [4] folded leaves of plates : ISBN
2-900927-10-2 DDC 709/.01/12094472 19
GN772.22.F7 B343 1982
NYPL [3-MADF+ 91-6417]

ART, PARTHIAN.
Brentjes, Burchard. Steppenreiter und
Handelsherren . Leipzig , 1990. 132 p. : ISBN
3-363-00459-1 :
N5899.P36 B74 1990

'Ukāshah, Tharwat. al-Fann al-Fārisī al-qadīm /.
Miṣr al-Jadīdah, al-Qāhirah , 1989. 383 p. :
ISBN 977-442-109-4 :
N5390 .U38 1989

ART PATRONAGE.
Garrigou, Marcel. La culture, richesse de
l'entreprise . [Paris] , c1990. 272 p. ; ISBN
2-7007-2836-X :
NX634 .G37 1990

**ART PATRONAGE - ENGLAND -
MERSEYSIDE.**
Patronage & practice . [Liverpool] , 1989. 137
p. : ISBN 1-85437-021-9 (pbk.) : DDC 730.941 20
NB170 *NYPL [3-MGI+ 90-12483]*

ART PATRONAGE - FLANDERS.
Upton, Joel M. (Joel Morgan), 1940- Petrus
Christus . University Park , c1990. xv, 130 p.,
[62] p. of plates : ISBN 0-271-00672-2 (alk.
paper) : DDC 759.9493 20
ND673.C312 U68 1990
NYPL [3-MCH C556 91-3887]

ART PATRONAGE - FRANCE.
Garrigou, Marcel. La culture, richesse de
l'entreprise . [Paris] , c1990. 272 p. ; ISBN
2-7007-2836-X :
NX634 .G37 1990

**ART PATRONAGE - GERMANY -
NUREMBERG - HISTORY.**
Schleif, Corine. Donatio et memoria .
[München] , 1990. 288 p., [4] leaves of plates :
ISBN 3-422-06031-6
NYPL [3-MRBB 91-7159]

**ART PATRONAGE - GREAT BRITAIN -
EXHIBITIONS.**
Sixty years of patronage . [London] , 1965. 29
p., 8 p. of plates :
MLCM 82/1567
NYPL [3-MAVZ (London) 90-5872]

ART PATRONAGE - HISTORY.
Sinclair, Andrew. The need to give . London ,
c1990. 210 p. ; ISBN 1-85619-014-5 : DDC
700.79 20 *NYPL [3-MAD 91-3676]*

**ART PATRONAGE - HISTORY - 19TH
CENTURY.**
Dippie, Brian W. Catlin and his
contemporaries . Lincoln , c1990. xix, 553 p.,
[16] p. of plates : ISBN 0-8032-1683-1 (alk. paper)
DDC 759.13 20
N8835 .D57 1990
NYPL [3-MCX C36 90-10763]

ART PATRONAGE - ITALY.
Labella, Vincenzo. A season of giants . Boston ,
c1990. 240 p. : ISBN 0-316-85646-0 DDC
709/.45/09024 20
N6915 .L25 1990
NYPL [3-MAMC+ 91-3272]

ART PATRONAGE - ITALY - FLORENCE.
Spencer, John R. (John Richard) Andrea del
Castagno and his patrons /. Durham , 1991. p.
cm. ISBN 0-8223-1150-X DDC 759.5 20
ND623.C47 S64 1991

ART PATRONAGE - ITALY - PALERMO.
Bresc-Bautier, Geneviève. Artistes, patriciens et
confréries . Roma , 1979. xviii, 315 p., [15]
leaves of plates :
N6921.P34 B73 *NYPL [3-MAMC 81-374]*

ART PATRONAGE - ITALY - VICENZA.
Zaupa, Giovanni. Andrea Palladio e la sua
committenza . Roma , c1990. 255 p. : ISBN
88-7448-275-2 : DDC 720/.92 20
NA1123.P2 Z34 1990

ART PATRONAGE - RUSSIAN S.F.S.R.
Cerwinske, Laura. Russian imperial style /.
New York , c1990. 223 p. : ISBN

0-13-784810-2 :   DDC 745/.0947 20
NK975 .C45 1990
NYPL [3-MLF+ 91-3951]

ART PATRONAGE - SPAIN.
Art treasures in Spain. London, 1970. 175 p.
ISBN 0-600-03888-2 DDC 709/.46
N7101 .A83 1970

**ART PATRONAGE - SPAIN - HISTORY -
16TH CENTURY - EXHIBITIONS.**
Resplendence of the Spanish monarchy . New
York , 1991. p. cm. ISBN 0-87099-621-5 DDC
739.7/0946/0747471 20
NK3062.A1 R47 1991

**ART PATRONAGE - SPAIN - NAVARRE
(KINGDOM)**
Martínez de Aguirre, Javier. Arte y monarquía
en Navarra, 1328-1425 /. Pamplona , c1987.
432 p. : ISBN 84-235-0794-7
N7109.N3 M37 1987
NYPL [3-MAML 90-12586]

ART PATRONAGE - TURKEY.
Żygulski, Zdzisław. Ottoman art in the service
of the empire /. New York , c1991. p. cm.
ISBN 0-8147-9671-0 : DDC 745/.09561 20
NK1011 .Z94 1991

ART PATRONAGE - UNITED STATES.
Public policy and the aesthetic interest .
Urbana , c1992. p. cm. ISBN 0-252-01899-0 (cl)
DDC 700/.1/03 20
NX730 .P79 1992

ART PATRONS - BIOGRAPHY.
Prat, Véronique. Chefs-d'œuvre secrets des
grandes collections privées /. Paris , c1988. 191
p. : ISBN 2-226-03427-7 :
N5210 .P73 1988

**ART PATRONS - ENGLAND, NORTHERN -
EXHIBITIONS.**
Pre-Raphaelites . Newcastle upon Tyne,
[England] , 1989. 132 p. : ISBN 0-905974-45-X
NYPL [3-MCT 91-5066]

ART PATRONS - GERMANY - NUREMBERG.
Schleif, Corine. Donatio et memoria .
[München] , 1990. 288 p., [4] leaves of plates :
ISBN 3-422-06031-6
NYPL [3-MRBB 91-7159]

**ART PATRONS - UNITED STATES -
BIOGRAPHY.**
Mellon, Paul. Reflections in a silver spoon .
New York , 1992. p. cm. ISBN 0-688-09723-5
DDC 709/.2 B 20
N5220 .M552 1992

**ART - PENNSYLVANIA - CHADDS FORD -
CATALOGS.**
Brandywine River Museum. Catalogue of the
collection, 1969-1989 /. Chadds Ford, Pa. ,
c1991. p. DDC 709/.73/07474814 20
N6517 .B7 1991

**ART - PENNSYLVANIA - GREENSBURG -
CATALOGS.**
Westmoreland Museum of Art. Southwestern
Pennsylvania painters . Greensburg, Pa. , 1989.
x, 138 p. : ISBN 0-931241-21-9 DDC
759.148/8/07474886 20
N6530.P42 P589 1989
NYPL [3-MCW 91-6266]

**ART - PENNSYLVANIA - PITTSBURGH -
CATALOGS.**
Strazdes, Diana J. American paintings and
sculpture to 1945 in the Carnegie Museum of
Art /. New York , c1991. p. cm. ISBN
1-555-95055-8 : DDC 759.13/074/74886 20
N6505 .S87 1991

Art, perception and reality. Gombrich, E. H.
(Ernst Hans), 1909- Baltimore [1972] x, 132 p.
ISBN 0-8018-1354-9 DDC 701/.17
N71 .G64   **NYPL [3-MAB 90-5472]**

ART - PERIODICALS.
Gibson, Ann Eden, 1944- Issues in abstract
expressionism . Ann Arbor, Mich. , c1990. xvi,
430 p. : ISBN 0-8357-1944-8 (alk. paper) DDC
709.747/1/09044 20
N6535.N5 G53 1989
NYPL [3-MAMT 90-11594]

ART - PHILOSOPHY.
Art theory and criticism . Jefferson, N.C. ,
c1991. xiii, 282 p. : ISBN 0-89950-595-3 (lib.
bdg. : alk. paper) DDC 701 20
N71 .A7475 1991

Bildfälle . Zürich , c1990. 231 p. : ISBN

3-7608-8073-8
N6350 .B547 1990

Devade, Marc, 1943-1983. Marc Devade .
Paris , 1989-1990. 3 v. (479 p.) ; ISBN
2-256-90867-4 DDC 701 20
N70 .D458 1989

Die Wahrheit der Kunst . Stuttgart , c1989. 198
p. : ISBN 3-460-32881-9 DDC 701 20
N68 .W24 1989

Lories, D. (Danielle) Expérience esthétique et
ontologie de l'œuvre . Bruxelles [1989] 286 p. ;
ISBN 2-8031-0074-6 DDC 701 20
N67 .L76 1989

Nemett, Barry. Images, objects, and ideas . Fort
Worth , c1991. p. cm. ISBN 0-03-021782-2
DDC 701/.1 20
N71 .N46 1991

The Philosophy of the visual arts /. New York ,
1992. p. cm. ISBN 0-19-505975-1 (alk. paper)
DDC 701 20
N71 .P39 1992

Shlain, Leonard. Art & physics . New York ,
1991. p. cm. ISBN 0-688-09752-9 DDC 701 20
N70 .S48 1991

Thürlemann, Felix. Vom Bild zum Raum .
Köln , c1990. 193 p. : ISBN 3-7701-2361-1
DDC 701 20
N68 .T54 1990

**ART - PHILOSOPHY - COLLECTED
WORKS.**
Borduas, Paul Emile. [Selections. 1987.] Ecrits
/. Montréal, Qué., Canada , 1987- v. : ISBN
2-7606-0761-5 (v. 1)
NYPL [3-MAS 88-2798]

ART - PHILOSOPHY - EXHIBITIONS.
Michel, Régis. Le beau idéal . Paris , 1989. 176
p. : ISBN 2-7118-2317-2
NYPL [3-MA 90-12383]

ART, PHOENICIAN.
Moscati, Sabatino. L'arte dei Fenici /. Milano ,
1990. 232 p. : ISBN 88-450-3614-6 : DDC
730/.0939/44 20
N5410 .M66 1990

ART, POLISH.
Rokoko. Warszawa, 1970. 325 p.
N7255.P6 R6

ART, POLISH - EXHIBITIONS.
Art at the edge . Oxford , 1988. 43 p. : ISBN
0-905836-66-9 (pbk.) DDC 709/.438/074 19
N7255.P6   **NYPL [3-MAM+ 90-4738]**

Den Åbne dør, polsk nutidskunst, 1989 .
[Copenhagen , 1989] 56 p. : ISBN 87-88944-07-7
N7255.P6 A36 1989

Nie wieder! . [Düsseldorf] , 1989. 251 p. :
NYPL [3-MAM+ 91-6409]

ART - POLITICAL ASPECTS.
Luke, Timothy W. Shows of force . Durham ,
1992. p. cm. ISBN 0-8223-1188-7 (acid-free paper)
DDC 701/.18 20
N72.P6 L84 1992

**ART - POLITICAL ASPECTS -
EXHIBITIONS.**
Alfredo Jaar . Richmond, VA , c1991. p. cm.
ISBN 0-917046-32-3 DDC 709/.2 20
N6537.J26 A4 1991

**ART - POLITICAL ASPECTS - FRANCE -
HISTORY - 20TH CENTURY.**
Cone, Michèle S., 1932- Art, prejudice, and
persecution . Princeton, N.J. , c1992. p. cm.
ISBN 0-691-04088-5 : DDC 701/.03 20
N6848 .C66 1992

**ART - POLITICAL ASPECTS - FRANCE -
PARIS.**
Friedrich, Otto, 1929- Olympia . New York,
NY , c1992. p. ISBN 0-06-016318-6 (cloth) :
DDC 701/.03 20
N6847 .F75 1992

**ART - POLITICAL ASPECTS - GREAT
BRITAIN.**
Roberts, John, 1955- Selected errors . London ,
Concord, Mass. , 1991. p. cm. ISBN
0-7453-0498-2 DDC 701/.03 20
N72.P6 R63 1991

**ART - POLITICAL ASPECTS - SOVIET
UNION.**
Lissitzky, El, 1890-1941. [Suprematicheskiĭ
skaz. English.] About 2 [squares] /. Cambridge,

Mass. , 1991. p. cm. ISBN 0-262-12158-1 DDC
709/.2 20
N6988.5.S9 L5713 1991

**ART - POLITICAL ASPECTS - SOVIET
UNION - HISTORY - 20TH CENTURY.**
Revoliùtsiià 1905-1907 godov i izobraziteľnoe
iskusstvo . Moskva , <1989-. v. <4 > : ISBN
5-85200-180-5 (v. 4) :
N6988 .R44 1989

**ART - POLITICAL ASPECTS - UNITED
STATES.**
Roberts, John, 1955- Selected errors . London ,
Concord, Mass. , 1991. p. cm. ISBN
0-7453-0498-2 DDC 701/.03 20
N72.P6 R63 1991

**ART - POLITICAL ASPECTS - UNITED
STATES - EXHIBITIONS.**
Day, Holliday T. Power . Indianapolis, Ind. ,
1991. p. cm. ISBN 0-253-31658-8 DDC
709/.73/07477252 20
N72.P6 D38 1991

Wadden, Mary Ann. The political landscape .
Brookville, N.Y. , 1990. 32 p. : ISBN
0-933699-17-4 DDC 709/.73/074747245 20
N8835 .W34 1990
NYPL [3-MAMT 91-4586]

Art, politics, and Ireland /. McAvera, Brian,
1948- Dublin [1990?] 136 p. : ISBN
1-87249-600-8 : DDC 701/.03 20
N8236.P5 M37 1990

ART, POLYNESIAN.
Idiens, Dale. Cook Islands art /. Princes
Risborough, Buckinghamshire, UK , 1990. 64
p. : ISBN 0-7478-0061-8 (pbk.) : DDC
709.0110996 20 **NYPL [3-MADF 91-6597]**

ART, POP. see POP ART.

ART, POPULAR. see FOLK ART.

ART - PORTUGAL.
Santinho, M. Manuela (Maria Manuela) A arte
em Portugal e os Descobrimentos . Porto ,
1989. 164 p. : DDC 709/.469 20
N7121 .S27 1989

ART - PORTUGAL - DICTIONARIES.
Dicionário da arte barroca em Portugal /.
Lisboa , 1989. 542 p. : ISBN 972-231-088-7
NYPL [3-MAML+ 91-4315]

ART PORTUGUESE.
Alvarenga, Fernando. Afluentes teórico-estéticos
do neo-realismo visual português /. Porto ,
1989. 209 p. : ISBN 972-360-218-0 :
N8243.S65 A43 1989

Botelho, Margarida. 75 artistas em Portugal /.
Maia [Portugal] , 1989. 302 p. : ISBN
972-91572-5-1 DDC 709/.469/0904 20
N7128 .B68 1989

Freire, J. Moreira (José Moreira) Un problème
d'art . Lisboa , 1898. 190 p., [12] leaves of
plates : ill., ports. ; DDC 709/.469 20
N7121 .F74 1898

Gonçalves, Flávio. História da arte . [Lisbon]
[1990] 353 p. : DDC 709/.469 20
N7121 .G6 1990

ART, PORTUGUESE - EXHIBITIONS.
Imagens do Sagrado. Lisboa , 1989. 47 p. :
DDC 704.9/482/09469074469425 20
N7963.A1 I4 1989

ART, PORTUGUESE - INFLUENCE.
Freire, J. Moreira (José Moreira) Un problème
d'art . Lisboa , 1898. 190 p., [12] leaves of
plates : ill., ports. ; DDC 709/.469 20
N7121 .F74 1898

**ART, PORTUGUESE - PORTUGAL -
COIMBRA.**
Gonçalves, António Nogueira, 1901- Estudos
de história da arte da Renascença /. Aveiro
[Portugal] [between 1975 and 1987] 311 p. :
N7963.C65 G66 1975

ART, PORTUGUESE - THEMES, MOTIVES.
Marcos da arte portuguesa. Lisboa , c1986. 1 v.
(unpaged) ; DDC 709/.469 20
N7121 .M37 1986

ART POVERA. see CONCEPTUAL ART.

ART, PREHISTORIC - AUSTRALIA.
Layton, Robert, 1944- Historic and prehistoric
perceptions . [London] , 1990. 18 p. ; ISBN
1-85507-020-0 DDC 709/.01/130994 20
N5310.5.A83 L39 1990

ART, PREHISTORIC - EGYPT - THEMES, MOTIVES.
Davis, Whitney. Masking the blow . Berkeley , 1992. p. cm.   ISBN 0-520-07488-2   DDC 709/.32 20
N5310.5.E3 D38 1992

ART, PREHISTORIC - EXHIBITIONS.
Musée des antiquités nationales. Chefs d'oeuvre de l'art paléolithique. [Paris?, 1969] 96 p.
NYPL [3-MADF 90-6293]

ART, PREHISTORIC - FRANCE - EXHIBITIONS.
Musée des antiquités nationales. Chefs d'oeuvre de l'art paléolithique. [Paris?, 1969] 96 p.
NYPL [3-MADF 90-6293]

ART, PREHISTORIC - FRANCE - ROUFFIGNAC CAVE.
Barrière, C. L'art pariétal de Rouffignac . Paris , 1982. 205 p., [4] folded leaves of plates :   ISBN 2-900927-10-2   DDC 709/.01/12094472 19
GN772.22.F7 B343 1982
NYPL [3-MADF+ 91-6417]

Art, prejudice, and persecution . Cone, Michèle S., 1932- Princeton, N.J. , c1992. p. cm.   ISBN 0-691-04088-5 :   DDC 701/.03 20
N6848 .C66 1992

ART - PRICES.
Huxford's fine art value guide. Paducah, KY , <c1991-. v. <2 > :   ISBN 0-89145-427-6 (v. 2) :   DDC 707/.5 20
N8675 .H88 1991

Le Grand livre des ventes aux enchères /. Paris [1988] 288 p. :   ISBN 2-7144-2265-9 (Belfond)   DDC 707/.5 20
N8675 .G68 1988

Sotheby's great sales /. London , 1989. 160 p. :   ISBN 0-7126-2137-7   DDC 707/.5 20
N8675 .S685 1989

ART, PRIMITIVE.
Breton, André, 1896-1966. L'art magique /. [Paris] [c1991] 358 p. :   ISBN 2-85940-215-2
N8222.M3 B7 1991

ART, PRIMITIVE - CATALOGS.
Museo delle arti primitive. Museo delle arti primitive. Cinisello Balsamo [1972?] [124] p., incl. plates.
N5310.8.I8 R55   NYPL [3-MADF 90-6283]

ART, PRIMITIVE - EQUATORIAL GUINEA.
Perrois, Louis. The art of Equatorial Guinea . New York , 1990. 177 p. :   ISBN 0-8478-1275-8   DDC 730/.089/96396 20
N7399.E68 P47 1990
NYPL [3-MADF+ 91-5613]

ART, PRIMITIVE - EXHIBITIONS.
Art Galleries and Museums Association of New Zealand. No sort of iron. [Christchurch, 1969] 91 p.   DDC 709.01/1
N7410 .A73

Boglár, Lajos. Tribal art in Africa and Oceania . [Budapest] , 1971. 8, 8 p., 8, 8 p. of plates :
enghun   NYPL [3-MADF 90-5887]

ART, PRIMITIVE - INDIA.
Koppar, D. H. Forgotten art of India /. Baroda , 1989. xxiii, 266, [4] p. :   DDC 709/.54 20
N7301 .K58 1989   NYPL [3-MAF 91-6940]

ART, PRIMITIVE - INDONESIA.
Hersey, Irwin. Indonesian primitive art /. Singapore , New York , 1991. p. cm.   ISBN 0-19-588553-8 :   DDC 730/.089/9922 20
N7326 .H47 1991

ART, PRIMITIVE - INFLUENCE.
Pellizzi, Francesco. Adventures of the symbol . New York City , 1986. 1 v. (unpaged) ;   DDC 704.9/46 20
N5311 .P4 1986

ART, PRIMITIVE - OCEANIA - CONGRESSES.
Art and identity in Oceania /. Honolulu , c1990. viii, 315 p., [8] p. of plates :   ISBN 0-8248-1304-9 :   DDC 700/.995 20
N7399.7 .A78 1990
NYPL [3-MADF 91-5014]

ART, PRIMITIVE - POLYNESIA.
Art Galleries and Museums Association of New Zealand. No sort of iron. [Christchurch, 1969] 91 p.   DDC 709.01/1
N7410 .A73

ART, PRIMITIVE - SWITZERLAND - GENEVA.
Musée Barbier-Müller. [Hier, aujourd'hui, demain. English.] Yesterday, today, and tomorrow . Geneva [1987] 160 p. :   ISBN 2-88104-015-2   DDC 730/.074/49451 20
N5310.75.G46 M87613 1987

ART, PRIMITIVE - UNITED STATES - EXHIBITIONS.
Moses, Grandma, 1860-1961. Art and life of Grandma Moses. New York, 1969. 168 p.   ISBN 0-498-07437-4   DDC 759.13
ND237.M78 K3
NYPL [3-MCX M89 90-6781]

ART - PRIVATE COLLECTIONS - AUSTRALIA.
The D.R. Sheumack collection . Paddington, NSW , 1988. [153] p. :
NYPL [3-MCY 89-11925]

ART - PRIVATE COLLECTIONS - AUSTRALIA - EXHIBITIONS.
Irises and five masterpieces. [Australia] [1989] 1 v. (unpaged) :   ISBN 0-9598384-1-4
NYPL [MAX (Bond) 91-6719]

ART - PRIVATE COLLECTIONS - BELGIUM - BRUSSELS - EXHIBITIONS.
Musée d'art moderne (Musées royaux des beaux-arts de Belgique) Collection Alla et Bénédict Goldschmidt . Bruxelles [1990] 426 p. :
NYPL [3-MAL 91-5716]

ART - PRIVATE COLLECTIONS - BELGIUM - EXHIBITIONS.
Von Pop zum Konzept . Aachen [1975] [64] p., [30] leaves of plates :
N6488.G3 A28
NYPL [3-MAW+ (Aachen) 80-1119]

ART - PRIVATE COLLECTIONS - CALIFORNIA - LOS ANGELES - CATALOGS.
Museum of Contemporary Art (Los Angeles, Calif.) The Rita and Taft Schreiber collection /. Los Angeles, Calif. , c1991. 1 v. (unpaged) :   ISBN 0-914357-24-7   DDC 709/.04/007479494 20
N6487.L67 L677 1991

ART - PRIVATE COLLECTIONS - CALIFORNIA, SOUTHERN - EXHIBITIONS.
Conisbee, Philip. Monet to Matisse . Los Angeles, Calif. , c1991. 144 p. :   ISBN 0-87587-159-3   DDC 709/.44/09034 20
N6847 .C6 1991

ART - PRIVATE COLLECTIONS - CZECHOSLOVAKIA - EXHIBITIONS.
ROH. ÚRO. Lidé, život, práce . [Prague] , 1988. 1 portfolio (unpaged) :
N6831 .R64 1988

ART - PRIVATE COLLECTIONS - CZECHOSLOVAKIA - PRAGUE - EXHIBITIONS.
Národní galerie V Praze. Sbírka Bohuslava Duška . [Prague] [1990?] 131 p. :
N5280.C952 D876 1990

ART - PRIVATE COLLECTIONS - EXHIBITIONS.
Promised gifts. Jerusalem [c1985] 1 case :   ISBN 965-278-035-9 (unb.)   DDC 707/.4/0956944 19
N5085.J45 P76 1985   NYPL [3-MAL 87-983]

Rauschenberg Overseas Culture Interchange. Washington , Munich , c1991. 199 p. :   ISBN 0-89468-160-5 (softcover)   DDC 700/.92 20
N6537.R27 A4 1991
NYPL [3-MCX+ R248 91-7715]

ART - PRIVATE COLLECTIONS - FRANCE.
Destins d'objets /. Paris , 1988. 474 p. :   ISBN 2-11-002009-1 (pbk.)
NYPL [3-MAVC 90-9455]

ART - PRIVATE COLLECTIONS - FRANCE - AUVERS-SUR-OISE - EXHIBITIONS.
Van Gogh et les peintres d'Auvers-sur-Oise . [Paris] , 1954. xl, 100 p., xxxii p. of plates :
N6847.5.I4 V36 1954

ART - PRIVATE COLLECTIONS - FRANCE - EXHIBITIONS.
Galerie Charpentier. Catalogue des objets d'art et d'ameublement du XVIIIe siècle . Paris , 1935. 88 p., 44 leaves of plates :
NYPL [3-MAX+ (Saint) 91-404]

Kosinski, Dorothy M. Picasso, Braque, Gris,

Léger . Houston, Tex. , c1990. 67 p. :   ISBN 0-89090-049-3 (pbk.)   DDC 759.4/074/7641411 20
N6848.5.C82 K67 1990
NYPL [3-MCN 91-6709]

ART - PRIVATE COLLECTIONS - GERMANY - DUISBURG - CATALOGS.
Sammlung Köhler-Osbahr /. Duisburg , c1990- v. <1 > :   ISBN 3-923576-75-7
N5267.K64 S26 1990

ART - PRIVATE COLLECTIONS - GERMANY - KRANENBURG (NORTH RHINE-WESTPHALIA) - EXHIBITIONS.
Beuys, Joseph. Joseph Beuys . Hannover [1990] 267 p. :   DDC 759.3 20
N6888.B463 A4 1990

ART - PRIVATE COLLECTIONS - GERMANY - MUNICH - EXHIBITIONS.
Die Sammlung Woty und Theodor Werner . München , c1990. 131 p. :   ISBN 3-7774-5460-5
NYPL [3-MAX (Werner, W.) 91-6703]

ART - PRIVATE COLLECTIONS - GERMANY (WEST) - AACHEN - EXHIBITIONS.
Sammlung Teo Matthéy, Aachen . [Aachen] , c1989. 109 p.
NYPL [3-MAX (Matthéy) 91-3454]

ART - PRIVATE COLLECTIONS - GERMANY (WEST) - EXHIBITIONS.
Russische Avantgarde 1910-1930 . Duisburg , c1990. 120 p. :   ISBN 3-923576-73-0
N6988 .R855 1990

Sammlung Lenz Schönberg . Stuttgart , c1989. 262 p. :   ISBN 3-89322-152-2
NYPL [3-MAX+ (Lenz) 91-2706]

ART - PRIVATE COLLECTIONS - ISRAEL - EXHIBITIONS.
Grobman, Mikhail. Michail Grobman, Künstler und Sammler . Bochum [1988] 1 v. (unpaged) :   ISBN 3-8093-0123-X
N6999.G76 A4 1988

ART - PRIVATE COLLECTIONS - ITALY - CATALOGS.
Il Cardinal Leopoldo. Milano , 1987- v. :
NYPL [3-MAX (Medici) 91-6376]

ART - PRIVATE COLLECTIONS - ITALY - FLORENCE.
Civai, Alessandra. Dipinti e sculture in casa Martelli . Firenze , c1990. 219 p. :
NYPL [3-MAVC+ 91-6773]

ART - PRIVATE COLLECTIONS - ITALY - FLORENCE - CATALOGS.
Villa I Tatti (Florence, Italy) The Bernard Berenson collection of oriental art at Villa I Tatti /. New York , c1991. p. cm.   ISBN 1-555-95060-4 (alk. paper) :   DDC 709/.5/0744551 20
N7336 .V46 1991

ART - PRIVATE COLLECTIONS - ITALY - MILAN - EXHIBITIONS.
Minimal art dans la collection Panza di Biumo . Genève [1988] 1 portfolio :   ISBN 2-8306-0054-1
NYPL [3-MAL+ 90-10722]

ART - PRIVATE COLLECTIONS - ITALY - NAPLES - EXHIBITIONS.
Capolavori dalle collezioni d'arte del Banco di Napoli /. Napoli , c1989. 213 p. :   ISBN 88-7042-999-7
NYPL [3-MAVZ+ (Naples) 90-13203]

ART - PRIVATE COLLECTIONS - ITALY - PARMA - CATALOGS.
Fondazione Magnani Rocca. Capolavori dalle collezioni della Fondazione Magnani Rocca /. Bologna , 1990. xxxi, 131 p. :   ISBN 88-7779-116-0
NYPL [MAVZ (Parma, Italy) 91-6194]

ART - PRIVATE COLLECTIONS - ITALY - ROME.
Borowitz, Helen Osterman, 1929- Pawnshop and palaces . Washington , c1991. xvi, 272 p., [32] p. of plates :   ISBN 1-560-98010-9 (alk. paper)   DDC 709/.2 20
N5273.2.C36 B67 1991
NYPL [3-MAX (Campana) 91-7446]

ART - PRIVATE COLLECTIONS - KUWAIT - EXHIBITIONS.
Islamic art & patronage . New York , c1990. 313 p. :   ISBN 0-8478-1366-5   DDC 709/.17/67107473 20
N6263.W3 A785 1991
NYPL [3-MAF+ 91-5747]

ART - PRIVATE COLLECTIONS - MINNESOTA - SAINT PAUL - EXHIBITIONS.
Hancock, Jane H., 1949- Homecoming . St. Paul , c1991. x, 116 p. : ISBN 0-87351-259-6 DDC 759.05/074/74776581 20
N6450 .H298 1991

ART - PRIVATE COLLECTIONS - NETHERLANDS - EXHIBITIONS.
Kreijger, Hugo. Godenbeelden uit Tibet . ['s-Gravenhage] [Amsterdam] , c1989. 129, [1] p. : ISBN 90-12-06219-5
NYPL [3-MAF 91-5465]

ART - PRIVATE COLLECTIONS - NEW YORK (N.Y.) - EXHIBITIONS.
Da van Gogh a Picasso, Da Kandinsky a Pollock . Milano , c1990. 391 p. : DDC 709/.04/10744531 20
N6488.5.T55 D3 1990

Die Kunst des alten Japan . Frankfurt am Main , 1990. 199 p. : ISBN 3-89322-209-X
NYPL [3-MAG+ 91-4469]

Metropolitan Museum of Art (New York, N.Y.) Japanese art from the Gerry collection in the Metropolitan Museum of Art /. New York , c1989. 141 p. : ISBN 0-87099-556-1 DDC 738/.0952/0747471 20
N7352 .F67 1989 ***NYPL [3-MAG 89-28868]***

Metropolitan Museum of Art (New York, N.Y.) The lotus transcendent . New York , 1991. p. cm. ISBN 0-87099-613-4 DDC 730/.0954/0747471 20
N7300 .M47 1991

Sammlung Rudi Molacek . Graz [1990] 1 v. (unpaged) : DDC 709/.436/0744365 20
N6808 .S23 1990

ART - PRIVATE COLLECTIONS - OHIO - CLEVELAND - CATALOGS.
Dali, Salvador, 1904- Dali . Boston , c1991. 184 p. : ISBN 0-8212-1810-7 (cloth trade ed.) : DDC 759.6 20
N7113.D3 A4 1991

ART - PRIVATE COLLECTIONS - OHIO - COLUMBUS - EXHIBITIONS.
Columbus Museum of Art. Impressionism and European modernism . Columbus, Ohio , Seattle , 1991. p. ISBN 0-295-97133-9 : DDC 709/.03/407477157 20
N6447 .C65 1991

ART - PRIVATE COLLECTIONS - PENNSYLVANIA - PHILADELPHIA - EXHIBITIONS.
Helfand, William H. The picture of health . Philadelphia , c1991. p. cm. ISBN 0-8122-7962-X (University of Pennsylvania Press) : DDC 769/.4961 20
N8223 .H44 1991

ART - PRIVATE COLLECTIONS - RUSSIAN S.F.S.R. - EXHIBITIONS.
Russische Avantgarde 1910-1930 . Duisburg , c1990. 120 p. : ISBN 3-923576-73-0
N6988 .R855 1990

ART - PRIVATE COLLECTIONS - SPAIN - MADRID - EXHIBITIONS.
Tesoros de las colecciones particulares madrileñas . [Madrid] [1989?] 282 p. : ISBN 84-451-0090-4 DDC 759.06/074/4641 20
N6488.S7 M38 1989 ***NYPL [3-MC 90-8478]***

ART - PRIVATE COLLECTIONS - SRI LANKA - CATALOGS.
Dharmasiri, Albert. Modern art in Sri Lanka . Colombo, Sri Lanka , 1988. 80 p. : ISBN 955-9034-01-4 : DDC 709/.5493/074453 20
N7310.6 .D47 1988 ***NYPL [3-MAF 91-6910]***

ART - PRIVATE COLLECTIONS - SWEDEN.
Donation Gerard Bonnier /. Stockholm [1989] 106 p. : ISBN 91-29-59355-7
N6488.S8 S74 1989

ART - PRIVATE COLLECTIONS - SWITZERLAND - CATALOGS.
Landolt, Hanspeter. Gottfried Keller-Stiftung . Bern , c1990. 627 p. : ISBN 3-7165-0696-6
N5279.2.G68 L3 1990
NYPL [3-MAK 91-4989]

ART - PRIVATE COLLECTIONS - SWITZERLAND - EXHIBITIONS.
Monet to Matisse . Jerusalem , c1988. 130, [10] p. : ISBN 965-278-085-5 (pbk)
NYPL [3-MAL + 89-6103]

ART - PRIVATE COLLECTIONS - UNITED STATES - EXHIBITIONS.
Aldrich, Larry. The Aldrich collection /. New York , 1960. [48] p. :
NYPL [3-MAX (Aldrich) 90-5747]

Glories of the past . New York , c1990. x, 280 p. : ISBN 0-87099-593-6 DDC 709/.01 20
N5337.W47 G57 1990
NYPL [3-MAE+ 91-5037]

Harvard University. Art Museums. The Fredric Wertham collection . [Cambridge] , 1990. 101 p. : ISBN 0-916724-75-1
IN PROCESS (ONLINE)
NYPL [3-MAX (Wertham) 91-5499]

Impressionism and post impressionism . Portland, Me. , c1991. p. cm. DDC 709/.03/4407474191 20
N6847.5.I4 I43 1991

Pal, Pratapaditya. Art of the Himalayas . New York , c1991. p. cm. ISBN 1-555-95066-3 : DDC 709/.5496/07473 20
N7310.8.N4 P33 1991

ART - PRIVATE COLLECTIONS - WASHINGTON (D.C.) - EXHIBITIONS.
Phillips Collection. Duncan Phillips collects . Washington, D.C. , c1991. p. cm. ISBN 0-943044-16-2 : DDC 759.4/361/09041074753 20
N6850 .P45 1991

ART - PRIVATE COLLECTIONS - YUGOSLAVIA - ZAGREB (CROATIA) - EXHIBITIONS.
Umjetnine iz donacije dr Vinka Perčića =. Zagreb , c1989. 144 p. :
N5280.Y8 U46 1989

ART - PSYCHOLOGY.
Berger, John. About looking /. New York , 1991. p. ISBN 0-679-73655-7 (pbk.) : DDC 701/.15 20
N71 .B398 1991

Berger, John. Keeping a rendezvous /. New York , 1991. p. ISBN 0-679-40632-8 DDC 701/.15 20
N71 .B399 1991

Chastel, André, 1912- Fables, formes, figures /. Paris , c1978. 2 v. : DDC 701
N7560 .C46 ***NYPL [3-MA 81-444]***

Gombrich, E. H. (Ernst Hans), 1909- Art, perception and reality. Baltimore [1972] x, 132 p. ISBN 0-8018-1354-9 DDC 701/.17
N71 .G64 ***NYPL [3-MAB 90-5472]***

Huyghe, René. Psychologie de l'art . Monaco , c1991. 366 p. ; ISBN 2-268-01023-6 : DDC 701/.15 20
N71 .H79 1991

Luke, Timothy W. Shows of force . Durham , 1992. p. cm. ISBN 0-8223-1188-7 (acid-free paper) DDC 701/.18 20
N72.P6 L84 1992

Nemett, Barry. Images, objects, and ideas . Fort Worth , c1991. p. cm. ISBN 0-03-021782-2 DDC 701/.1 20
N71 .N46 1991

Pope-Hennessy, John Wyndham, Sir, 1913- Learning to look /. New York , 1991. x, 336 p., [24] p. of plates : ISBN 0-385-26141-1 DDC 709/.2 B 20
N7483.P66 A3 1991 ***NYPL [MA 91-5196]***

Untner, Alois. Das Unverständnis gegenüber moderner Malerei /. Wien , 1990. 312 p. ; ISBN 3-85369-793-3
ND195 .U58 1990

ART, PUERTO RICAN - EXHIBITIONS.
Sturges, Hollister. New art from Puerto Rico =. Springfield, Mass. , 1990. 84 p. : ISBN 0-916746-15-1 ***NYPL [3-MAM 91-6653]***

Art random .
(20) Spero, Nancy, 1926- Nancy Spero . Kyoto, Japan , c1989. 1 v. (unpaged) : ISBN 4-7636-8548-1 : DDC 760 20
N6537.S648 A4 1989

(5) Gallo, Vincent, 1961- Vincent Gallo . Kyoto, Japan , c1989. 25 leaves : ISBN 4-7636-8523-6 : DDC 709/.2 20
N6537.G35 A4 1989

Art reference collection, 0193-6867 .
(no. 12) Teague, Edward H., 1952- World architecture index . New York , 1991. xix, 447

p. ; ISBN 0-313-22552-4 (alk. paper) DDC 016.72 20
NA202 .T4 1991

ART, RENAISSANCE.
Edgerton, Samuel Y. The heritage of Giotto's geometry . Ithaca , 1991. p. cm. ISBN 0-8014-2573-5 (cloth : alk. paper) DDC 701/.8 20
N7430.5 .E34 1991

Opfell, Olga S. Special visions . Jefferson, N.C. , 1991. p. ISBN 0-89950-603-8 (lib. bdg. : alk. paper) DDC 709/.2/2 B 20
N43 .O6 1991

Studia nad sztuką renesansu i baroku /. Lublin , 1989- v. <1 > :
N6370 .S716 1989

ART, RENAISSANCE - BELGIUM - FLANDERS - EXHIBITIONS.
Albert Dürer aux Pays-Bas . Bruxelles , 1977. xxiii, 211, 144 p., [14] leaves of plates :
N6888.D8 A4 1977
NYPL [3-MCK D85 81-320]

ART, RENAISSANCE - CATALOGS.
National Gallery of Art (U. S.) Sculpture and decorative arts . Washington, D.C. [New York] , 1992. p. cm. ISBN 0-89468-162-1 DDC 708.153 20
N5963.W18 N382 1992

ART, RENAISSANCE - ENGLAND.
Renaissance bodies . London , 1990. x, 294 p. : ISBN 0-948462-09-4 (cased) : DDC 700 20
NYPL [3-MAMZ 90-11501]

ART, RENAISSANCE - EXHIBITIONS.
University of Arizona. The Samuel H. Kress collection at the University of Arizona. Tucson , c1957. [62] p. :
NYPL [3-MAVZ (Tucson) 90-5882]

ART, RENAISSANCE - GERMANY.
Grewenig, Meinrad Maria, 1954- Der Akt in der deutschen Renaissance . Freren , 1987. 143 p., [100] p. of plates : ISBN 3-923641-07-9 DDC 704.9/421/0943 19
N6865 .G74 1987
NYPL [3-MAMG 91-4610]

ART, RENAISSANCE - GERMANY - EXHIBITIONS.
Albert Dürer aux Pays-Bas . Bruxelles , 1977. xxiii, 211, 144 p., [14] leaves of plates :
N6888.D8 A4 1977
NYPL [3-MCK D85 81-320]

ART, RENAISSANCE - GERMANY (WEST) - WESER RIVER VALLEY - EXHIBITIONS.
Renaissance im Weserraum . München , 1989. 2 v. : ISBN 3-422-06039-1 (Bd. 1)
N6882.W38 R4 1989
NYPL [3-MAMG 89-28831]

ART, RENAISSANCE - HIGH RENAISSANCE - ITALY - EXHIBITIONS.
Beccafumi, Domenico, 1486-1551. Domenico Beccafumi e il suo tempo. Milano , c1990. 732 p. : ISBN 88-435-3173-5 DDC 759.5 20
ND623.B34 A4 1990

ART, RENAISSANCE - ITALY.
Barolsky, Paul, 1941- Giotto's father and the family of Vasari's lives /. University Park, PA , c1991. p. cm. ISBN 0-271-00762-1 (alk. paper) DDC 709/.2/245 B 20
N6915 .B28 1991

Barolsky, Paul, 1941- Why Mona Lisa smiles and other tales by Vasari /. University Park , c1991. xiv, 128 p. ; ISBN 0-271-00719-2 DDC 709/.2 20
N7483.V37 B36 1991
NYPL [3-MAMC 91-7319]

Labella, Vincenzo. A season of giants . Boston , c1990. 240 p. : ISBN 0-316-85646-0 DDC 709/.45/09024 20
N6915 .L25 1990
NYPL [3-MAMC+ 91-3272]

Robertson, Clare. Il gran cardinale . New Haven , 1992. p. cm. ISBN 0-300-05045-3 DDC 709/.2 20
N6915 .R66 1992

Shearman, John K. G. Only connect . Princeton, N.J. , 1992. p. cm. ISBN 0-691-09972-3 (CL) : DDC 709/.45/09024 20
N6915 .S54 1992

Vasari, Giorgio, 1511-1574. [Vite de' più eccellenti architetti, pittori et scultori italiani. English. Selections.] Lives of the artists /. London , New York , 1987. 2 v. ; ISBN 0-14-044500-5 (v. 1)
NYPL [3-MAMC 88-536]

ART, RENAISSANCE - ITALY - CATALOGS.
Kaiser Wilhelm Museum Krefeld. Italienische Renaissancekunst im Kaiser Wilhelm Museum Krefeld /. [Krefeld] , 1987. 154, [2] p. : ISBN 3-926530-30-8
NYPL [3-MAVZ (Krefeld) 90-12394]

ART, RENAISSANCE - ITALY - FLORENCE - CONGRESSES.
Leonardo, Michelangelo, and Raphael in Renaissance Florence, 1500-1508 /. Washington, D.C. , 1991. p. cm. ISBN 0-87840-219-5 DDC 709/.2/2455109031 20
N6923.L33 L456 1991

ART, RENAISSANCE - ITALY - FLORENCE - EXHIBITIONS.
L'Età di Masaccio . Milano , c1990. 265 p. : ISBN 88-435-3211-1
NYPL [3-MAMC 90-12878]

ART, RENAISSANCE - ITALY - MANTUA - THEMES, MOTIVES - EXHIBITIONS.
Giovannoni, Giannino. Mantova e i tarocchi del Mantegna /. Mantova , Faenza [1987] 78 p. :
N6923.M249 A4 1987
NYPL [3-MCF M29 91-7036]

ART, RENAISSANCE - ITALY - UMBRIA - CONGRESSES.
Dall'Albornoz all'età dei Borgia . Todi , 1990. 385 p., [19] p. of plates : ISBN 88-85311-01-6 DDC 709/.45/65 20
N6919.U5 D35 1990

ART, RENAISSANCE - ITALY - VENICE.
Huse, Norbert. [Venedig, die Kunst der Renaissance. English.] The art of Renaissance Venice . Chicago , 1990. 382 p., [32] p. of plates : ISBN 0-226-36107-1 (alk. paper) DDC 709/.45/3109024 20
N6921.V5 H8713 1990
NYPL [3-MAMC 91-3259]

ART, RENAISSANCE - JUVENILE LITERATURE.
A Renaissance Christmas /. Boston , c1991. p. ISBN 0-8212-1875-1 : DDC 704.9/4853/09409024 20
N8060 .R4 1991

ART, RENAISSANCE - NETHERLANDS - EXHIBITIONS.
Albert Dürer aux Pays-Bas . Bruxelles , 1977. xxiii, 211, 144 p., [14] leaves of plates :
N6888.D8 A4 1977
NYPL [3-MCK D85 81-320]

ART, RENAISSANCE - PORTUGAL - COIMBRA.
Gonçalves, António Nogueira, 1901- Estudos de história da arte da Renascença /. Aveiro [Portugal] [between 1975 and 1987] 311 p. :
N7963.C65 G66 1975

ART, RENAISSANCE - SILESIA - EXHIBITIONS.
Muzeum Narodowe we Wrocławiu. Sztuka Śląska XV-XVIII w. ze zbiorów Muzeum Narodowego we Wrocławiu . Opole , 1990. 30 p., [20] p. of plates :
N7255.P62 S545 1990

ART, RENAISSANCE - SPAIN.
Marías, Fernando, 1949- El largo siglo XVI . Madrid , c1989. 745 p. ; ISBN 84-306-0102-3
IN PROCESS (ONLINE)
NYPL [3-MAML 90-13399]

ART, RENAISSANCE - YUGOSLAVIA - DALMATIA (CROATIA)
Höfler, Janez. Die Kunst Dalmatiens . Graz , 1989. 338 p. : ISBN 3-201-01466-4
NYPL [3-MAM+ 90-8024]

ART - REPRODUCTIONS - CONGRESSES.
Retaining the original . Washington, Hanover , c1989. 180 p. : *NYPL [3-MAS 90-13011]*

ART, ROCOCO - ITALY - VICENZA - EXHIBITIONS.
I Tiepolo e il Settecento vicentino /. Milano , c1990. 404 p. : ISBN 88-435-3180-8
NYPL [3-MAMC 91-5454]

ART, ROCOCO - POLAND.
Rokoko. Warszawa , 1970. 325 p.
N7255.P6 R6

ART, ROMAN.
Chevrier, Jean-François. Portrait de Jurgis Baltrušaitis /. Paris , c1989. 271 p. : ISBN 2-08-012038-7
N7483.B285 C48 1989

Roman art in the private sphere . Ann Arbor , c1991. 156 p. : ISBN 0-472-10196-X (alk. paper) DDC 747.2937 20
N5760 .R66 1991

ART, ROMAN - CATALOGS.
Museo nazionale romano. Museo nazionale romano. Roma , 1979- v. in : DDC 709/.38/07405632 19
N2934 .A85
NYPL [MAVZ (Rome) 81-1402]

ART, ROMAN - EGYPT - CATALOGS.
Grimm, Günter. Kunst der Ptolemäer- und Römerzeit im Ägyptischen Museum Kairo /. Mainz [1975] 34 p, 118 p., [6] leaves of plates :
N5888.A1 G74   *NYPL [3-MAH 90-5474]*

ART, ROMAN - EXHIBITIONS.
Bellezza e seduzione nella Roma imperiale . [Roma] [c1990] 122 p. : ISBN 88-7813-283-7 :
N7629.2.I8 R663 1990

Von Constantin zu Karl dem Grossen . Mainz , 1990. 71 p., [5] leaves of plates : ISBN 3-88467-025-5
N5760 .V57 1990

ART, ROMAN, IN ART - EXHIBITIONS.
Syndram, Dirk. Ruinenromantik und Antikensehnsucht /. [Berlin] , c1986. 32 p. : ISBN 3-88609-199-6 DDC 760/.0444/094074031554 19
N8237.8.R8 S96 1986
NYPL [3-MAMZ 90-9452]

ART, ROMANESQUE - DICTIONARIES - ITALIAN.
Beigbeder, Olivier. [Lexique des symboles. Italian.] Lessico dei simboli medievali /. Milano , 1989. 304 p., [114] p. of plates : ISBN 88-16-60090-X
NYPL [3-MAMZ 91-5818]

ART, ROMANESQUE - GERMANY (WEST) - THEMES, MOTIVES.
Rudloff, Diether. Kosmische Bildwelt der Romanik . Stuttgart , 1989. 176 p. : ISBN 3-87838-592-7
NYPL [3-MAIH + 89-19334]

ART, ROMANESQUE - ITALY - ABRUZZI.
Abruzzes Molise romans /. La Pierre-qui-Vire (Yonne) , 1990. 304 p. : ISBN 2-7369-0182-7
NYPL [3-MQWB 91-4524]

ART, ROMANESQUE - ITALY - MOLISE.
Abruzzes Molise romans /. La Pierre-qui-Vire (Yonne) , 1990. 304 p. : ISBN 2-7369-0182-7
NYPL [3-MQWB 91-4524]

ART, ROMANESQUE - ITALY, NORTHERN.
Tavano, Sergio. Romani e Longobardi . Tricesimo (Ud) [1990] 183 p. :
N6913 .T38 1990

ART, ROMANIAN.
Ionescu, Adrian-Silvan. Artă și document . București , 1990. 318 p., [48] p. of plates : ISBN 973-330-072-1 :
N8214.5.R6 I55 1990

L'art russe, 1900-1935 . Manin, V. (Vitalii) Paris , c1989. 223 p. : ISBN 2-904057-37-4
NYPL [3-MAM+ 90-2663]

ART, RUSSIAN.
Finizio, Luigi Paolo. L'astrattismo costruttivo . Roma , 1990. vii, 237 p., [16] p. of plates : ISBN 88-420-3642-0 : DDC 709/.47/09041 20
N6988.5.C64 F56 1990

Kirichenko, Evgeniia Ivanovna. Russian design and the fine arts, 1750-1917 /. New York , 1991. p. cm. ISBN 0-8109-3758-1 DDC 709/.47 20
N6984 .K57 1991

Russkoe i sovetskoe iskusstvo . Leningrad , 1989. 79 p. ;
N6987 .R877 1989

Voprosy izucheniia otechestvennogo iskusstva . Leningrad , 1989. 83 p. ;
N6984 .V6 1989

ART, RUSSIAN - COLLECTORS AND COLLECTING.
Bowater, Marina. Collecting Russian art &

antiques /. New York , c1990. p. cm. ISBN 0-87052-897-1 : DDC 709/.47/075 20
N6981 .B69 1990

ART, RUSSIAN - EXHIBITIONS.
Artisti russi contemporanei . Prato , c1990. 208 p. : ISBN 88-85191-01-0
NYPL [3-MAM 90-10469]

Gosudarstvennyĭ istoricheskiĭ muzeĭ (Moscow, R.S.F.S.R.) Meraviglie sconosciute dal Museo storico di Mosca . Milano , c1989. 198 p. :
NYPL [3-MNR+ 91-4646]

Grobman, Mikhail. Michail Grobman, Künstler und Sammler . Bochum [1988] 1 v. (unpaged) : ISBN 3-8093-0123-X
N6999.G76 A4 1988

Russische Avantgarde 1910-1930 . Duisburg , c1990. 120 p. : ISBN 3-923576-73-0
N6988 .R855 1990

ART, RUSSIAN - RUSSIAN S.F.S.R.
Manin, V. (Vitalii) L'art russe, 1900-1935 . Paris , c1989. 223 p. : ISBN 2-904057-37-4
NYPL [3-MAM+ 90-2663]

ART, RUSSIAN - RUSSIAN S.F.S.R. - EXHIBITIONS.
Jugend im Sozialismus . Berlin [1987] 83 p. :
N6889 .J75 1987   *NYPL [3-MAMZ 91-4201]*

ART, RUSSIAN - RUSSIAN S.F.S.R. - LENINGRAD - EXHIBITIONS.
St. Petersburg um 1800 . Recklinghausen , c1990. 568 p. : ISBN 3-7647-0401-2
N6996 .S7 1990

ART, RUSSIAN - RUSSIAN S.F.S.R. - MOSCOW - EXHIBITIONS.
Moscow, treasures and traditions /. Washington, D.C. , c1990. 281 p. : ISBN 0-295-96994-6 DDC 709/.47/074753 20
N6997.M7 M65 1990
NYPL [3-MAM+ 90-11581]

ART - RUSSIAN S.F.S.R. - LENINGRAD - CATALOGS.
The Hermitage . New York , c1991. 164 p. : ISBN 0-385-41966-X : DDC 708.7/453 20
N3350 .H48 1991

ART, SARACENIC. see ART, ISLAMIC.

ART, SASANIAN. see ART, SASSANID.

ART, SASSANIAN. see ART, SASSANID.

ART, SASSANID.
'Ukāshah, Tharwat. al-Fann al-Fārisī al-qadīm /. Miṣr al-Jadīdah, al-Qāhirah , 1989. 383 p. : ISBN 977-442-109-4 :
N5390 .U38 1989

ART, SCANDINAVIAN - EXHIBITIONS.
B., Mats, 1938- Téxun . [S.l. , 1986] (Stockholm : Jernström Offset) [48] p. :
NYPL [3-MAM 90-10710]

ART, SCANDINAVIAN - HISTORY.
Kusch, Eugen, 1905- [Alte Kunst in Skandinavien. English.] Ancient art in Scandinavia. Nürnberg [1965] 83 p., 176 plates. DDC 709/.48
N7001 .K813

ART - SCHOLARSHIPS, FELLOWSHIPS, ETC. - BERLIN (GERMANY) - EXHIBITIONS.
10X . [Berlin] [1984] 1 portfolio (10 pieces) :
NYPL [3-MAMG+ 88-4811]

ART - SCHOLARSHIPS, FELLOWSHIPS, ETC. - UNITED STATES - DIRECTORIES.
Money for visual artists /. New York, N.Y. , c1991. p. cm. ISBN 0-915400-91-X DDC 707/.9/73 20
N347 .M66 1991

ART SCHOOLS - CANADA.
Carter, Cheryl G. North American schools of the arts . [Washington, D.C.] [c1990] vii, 172 p. : DDC 700/.71/273 20
NX303 .C37 1990

ART SCHOOLS - ESTONIA.
Nurk, Tiina. Kõrgem Kunstikool "Pallas" 1919-1940 /. Tallinn , 1977. 220 p., [86] p. of plates :
N332.E73 T376   *NYPL [3-MATA 90-6373]*

ART SCHOOLS - UNITED STATES.
Carter, Cheryl G. North American schools of the arts . [Washington, D.C.] [c1990] vii, 172

p. :   DDC 700/.71/273 20
NX303 .C37 1990

ART - SCOTLAND.
Scottish art and design . New York , 1991,
c1990. 200 p. :   ISBN 0-8109-3818-9   DDC
709/.411/07441443 20
N6772 .S37 1991
       NYPL   [3-MAMR 91-6763]

ART - SCOTLAND - EXHIBITIONS.
Rarer gifts than gold . [Glasgow] , c1988. 69
p. :   ISBN 0-85261-222-5 (pbk.)
N6318 .R374 1988
       NYPL   [3-MAK+ 90-12644]

ART, SCOTTISH.
Macmillan, Duncan. Scottish art, 1460-1990 /.
Edinburgh , 1990. 432 p. :   ISBN 1-85158-251-7
     NYPL   [3-MAMR+ 91-3719]

Scottish art and design . New York , 1991,
c1990. 200 p. :   ISBN 0-8109-3818-9   DDC
709/.411/07441443 20
N6772 .S37 1991
       NYPL   [3-MAMR 91-6763]

ART, SCOTTISH - EXHIBITIONS.
Scatter . Glasgow , 1989. 1 v. (unpaged) :
ISBN 0-906474-85-X
       NYPL   [3-MAMR+ 91-4062]

Scotland creates . London , 1990. 200 p. :
ISBN 0-297-83062-7 :   DDC 709.411 20
N6772   *NYPL   [3-MAMR 91-4385]*

**Art series (Research Centre for Islamic History,
Art and Culture)** .
(no. 5) World Seminar on "Common Principles,
Forms and Themes of Islamic Art" (1983 :
Istanbul, Turkey) Islamic art . Damascus ,
1989. 289, 165 p. :   ISBN 92-9063-354-9
       NYPL   [3-MAF 91-3423]

Art Services International.
Feeney, Kelly, 1961- Josef Albers . Alexandria,
Va. , 1991. p. cm.   ISBN 0-88397-100-3   DDC
760/.092 20
NC251.A36 A4 1991

Hayes, John T. The art of Thomas Rowlandson
/. Alexandria, Va. , c1990. 196 p. :   DDC
741.942 20
NC242.R66 A4 1990
       NYPL   [MDG+ (Rowlandson) 91-6401]

ART, SIAMESE. see ART, THAI.

ART - SIBERIA.
Ornament und Plastic fremder Völker. English.
Ornament and sculpture in primitive society.
New York [1966] [138] p.   DDC 709.011
N7380 .O713 1966b
       NYPL   [3-MADF 90-6405]

Art, sight, and language . Moorhouse, Asheleigh.
Kapuskasing, Ont., Canada , c1989. 173 p. :
ISBN 0-921254-05-9   DDC 709/.1/09048 20
N6545 .M66 1989   *NYPL   [3-MAM 91-6256]*

ART, SILESIAN - EXHIBITIONS.
Muzeum Narodowe we Wrocławiu. Sztuka
Śląska XV-XVIII w. ze zbiorów Muzeum
Narodowego we Wrocławiu . Opole , 1990. 30
p., [20] p. of plates :
N7255.P62 S545 1990

**ART - SLOVAK REPUBLIC - BRATISLAVA
(CZECHOSLOVAKIA)**
Puškárová, Blanka. Bratislava . Bratislava ,
1989. 253 p. :   ISBN 80-222-0024-7 :
N6833.B7 P87 1989

**ART, SLOVAK - SLOVAK REPUBLIC -
BRATISLAVA (CZECHOSLOVAKIA)**
Puškárová, Blanka. Bratislava . Bratislava ,
1989. 253 p. :   ISBN 80-222-0024-7 :
N6833.B7 P87 1989

**ART - SOCIAL INFLUENCE. see ART AND
SOCIETY.**

Art source book . Rowling, Nick. Secaucus, N.J. ,
c1987. 320 p. :   ISBN 1-555-21031-7   DDC
704.9/4 20
N4015.G72 L67 1987

ART, SOUTH ASIAN - EXHIBITIONS.
Metropolitan Museum of Art (New York, N.Y.)
The lotus transcendent . New York , 1991. p.
cm.   ISBN 0-87099-613-4   DDC 730/.0954/0747471
20
N7300 .M47 1991

ART, SOUTHEAST ASIAN - CATALOGS.
Villa I Tatti (Florence, Italy) The Bernard
Berenson collection of oriental art at Villa I

Tatti /. New York , c1991. p. cm.   ISBN
1-555-95060-4 (alk. paper) :   DDC
709/.5/0744551 20
N7336 .V46 1991

ART, SOUTHEAST ASIAN - EXHIBITIONS.
Metropolitan Museum of Art (New York, N.Y.)
The lotus transcendent . New York , 1991. p.
cm.   ISBN 0-87099-613-4   DDC 730/.0954/0747471
20
N7300 .M47 1991

**ART, SOUTHEAST ASIAN - HANDBOOKS,
MANUALS, ETC.**
Menzies, Jackie. Asian collection . Sydney,
Australia , 1990. 96 p. :   ISBN 0-7305-7455-5
DDC 709/.5/0749441 20
N7336 .M46 1990

ART, SOVIET.
Artaud, Evelyne. Perestroïk'art . [Paris] , c1990.
118 p. :   ISBN 2-7022-0269-1   DDC 709/.47/09048
20
N6988 .A7635 1990
       NYPL   [3-MAM 90-13376]

Bown, Matthew Cullerne. Art under Stalin /.
New York , c1991. p. cm.   ISBN 0-8419-1299-8
(alk. paper)   DDC 709/.47/0904 20
N6988 .B67 1991

In the stream of stars . New York , 1990. 183
p. :   ISBN 0-89480-705-6 (paper) :   DDC 758/.96294
20
N8234.O8 I5 1990
       NYPL   [3-MAMZ 91-5459]

Russkoe i sovetskoe iskusstvo . Leningrad ,
1989. 79 p. ;
N6987 .R877 1989

**ART, SOVIET - ENGLAND - MANCHESTER -
EXHIBITIONS.**
Tradition and revolution in Russian art .
[Manchester] , 1990. 200 p. :   ISBN
0-948797-26-6   *NYPL   [3-MAM 91-5043]*

ART, SOVIET - EXHIBITIONS.
Adaptation & negation of socialist realism .
Ridgefield, CT , c1990. 44 p. :
       NYPL   [3-MAM+ 91-5891]

Between spring and summer . Tacoma, Wash. ,
Boston, Mass. , c1990. x, 206 p. :   ISBN
0-910663-49-1
N6988.5.C62 B48 1990
       NYPL   [3-MAM 90-12998]

Harten, Jürgen. Sowjetische Kunst um 1990 .
Köln , c1991. 299 p. :   ISBN 3-7701-2733-1
       NYPL   [3-MAM 91-8020]

ART, SOVIET - THEMES, MOTIVES.
Puti tvorchestva i kritika . Moskva , 1990. 301
p. ;   ISBN 5-85200-081-7 :
N6988 .P84 1990

ART - SPAIN.
Art treasures in Spain. London, 1970. 175 p. :
ISBN 0-600-03888-2   DDC 709/.46
N7101 .A83 1970

ART - SPAIN - ANDALUSIA.
Historia del arte en Andalucía /. Sevilla
[1988]- v. :   ISBN 84-7566-015-0 (obra completa)
DDC 709/.46/8 20
N7109.A6 H57 1988
       NYPL   [3-MAML+ 91-417]

ART - SPAIN - CÁCERES (PROVINCE)
Inventario artístico de Cáceres y su provincia /.
Madrid , 1989- v. <1-2 > :   ISBN
84-7483-610-7 (obra completa)   DDC 709/.46/28
20
N7109.C15 I58 1989

ART - SPAIN - MADRID - CATALOGS.
Casal García, Raquel. Colección de glíptica del
Museo Arqueológico Nacional (serie de entalles
romanos) /. [Spain] [1990?] 2 v. :   ISBN
84-7483-657-3 (set)
NK5511.S67 M344 1990

ART - SPAIN - MÁLAGA - CATALOGS.
Romero Torres, José Luis. Museo de Bellas
Artes de Málaga /. Madrid [1989?] 79 p. :
ISBN 84-241-4945-9   DDC 709/.46/0744685 20
N7101 .R66 1989

ART, SPANISH.
Conceptos fundamentales en la historia del arte
español /. Madrid , c1989-<199. <v. 1; v. 5-6,
pt. 1; in 3 > :   ISBN 84-306-7001-7   DDC
709/.46 20
N7101 .C65 1989

Stierlin, Henri. L'essor de l'Espagne /. Paris ,
c1990. 246 p. :   ISBN 2-7003-0721-6   DDC
709/.46 20
N7101 .S74 1990

ART, SPANISH - CATALOGS.
Catálogo nacional de arte contemporáneo.
Barcelona , c1989. 4 v. :   ISBN 84-87433-00-6
(obra completa)
N7108 .C29 1989

Romero Torres, José Luis. Museo de Bellas
Artes de Málaga /. Madrid [1989?] 79 p. :
ISBN 84-241-4945-9   DDC 709/.46/0744685 20
N7101 .R66 1989

ART, SPANISH COLONIAL - GUATEMALA.
Lara Roche, Carlos, 1932- San José en el arte
colonial guatemalteco /. Guatemala, C.A. ,
1989. 161 p. :
N6576 .L37 1989

ART, SPANISH - EXHIBITIONS.
Arte geométrico en España, 1957-1989.
[Madrid] [1989] 320 p. :   ISBN 84-7812-044-0
DDC 709/.46/0744641 20
N7108.5.A2 A78 1989

Aspetti dell'arte contemporanea spagnola.
Barcelona , c1990. 47, [1] p. :   ISBN
84-87433-11-1   DDC 709/.46/0744545 20
N7108 .A87 1990

Barnes, Lucinda. Imágenes líricas =. Long
Beach , c1990. 119 p. :   ISBN 0-936270-30-6
       NYPL   [3-MAML+ 91-5035]

Galería Barbié . Barcelona, Spain , 1975. 31 p. :
       NYPL   [3-MAML 90-7109]

LADAC . [Las Palmas de Gran Canarias]
[1990?] 1 case :   ISBN 84-87137-32-6
N7108 .L33 1990

**ART, SPANISH - HISTORY AND
CRITICISM.**
Pardo, Arcadio. La visión del arte español en
los viajeros franceses del siglo XIX /.
Valladolid [1989] 672 p. ;   ISBN 84-7762-078-4
IN PROCESS (ONLINE)
       NYPL   [3-MAML 90-12090]

ART, SPANISH - SPAIN - ANDALUSIA.
Historia del arte en Andalucía /. Sevilla
[1988]- v. :   ISBN 84-7566-015-0 (obra completa)
DDC 709/.46/8 20
N7109.A6 H57 1988
       NYPL   [3-MAML+ 91-417]

**ART, SPANISH - SPAIN - CATALONIA -
EXHIBITIONS.**
Catalan painters and sculptors . [Spain] [1990]
66 p. :   *NYPL   [3-MAML+ 91-4202]*

**ART, SPANISH - SPAIN - GALICIA
(REGION) - CATALOGS.**
Seoane, Xavier, 1954- Identidade e convulsión .
Sada, A Coruña [1990] 322 p. :   ISBN
84-7492-461-8   DDC 709/.46/109048 20
N7109.G3 S46 1990

**ART, SPANISH - SPAIN - LA RIOJA -
CATALOGS.**
Labandíbar, José Luis. 1950-1990, cuarenta
años de artes plásticas en La Rioja /. [La Rioja]
[1989?-1990?] 2 v. :   ISBN 84-404-5495-3 (v. 1)
N7109.L3 L3 1989

**ART, SPANISH - SPAIN - NAVARRE
(KINGDOM)**
Martínez de Aguirre, Javier. Arte y monarquía
en Navarra, 1328-1425 /. Pamplona , c1987.
432 p. :   ISBN 84-235-0794-7
N7109.N3 M37 1987
       NYPL   [3-MAML 90-12586]

ART, SPANISH - SPAIN - SEVILLE.
León, Aurora. Iconografía y fiesta durante el
lustro real, 1729-1733 /. Sevilla , 1990. 189 p. :
ISBN 84-7798-045-4
N7111.S5 L46 1990

Serrera Contreras, Juan Miguel. Iconografía de
Sevilla, 1650-1790 /. Madrid , c1989. 292 p. :
ISBN 84-86022-35-2
       NYPL   [3-MAML+ 91-2661]

ART, SPANISH - SPAIN - TOLEDO.
Inventario artístico de Toledo /. Madrid , 1983-
v. :   ISBN 84-7483-328-0 (set)
       NYPL   [3-MAML 86-2086]

ART, SPANISH - SPAIN - VALENCIA.
Azcárraga, Adolfo de. Escritos sobre arte y
artistas valencianos /. Valencia , 1989. 330 p. :

ISBN 84-505-8230-X
NYPL [3-MAML 90-11103]

ART, SRI LANKAN - CATALOGS.
Dharmasiri, Albert. Modern art in Sri Lanka .
Colombo, Sri Lanka , 1988. 80 p. : ISBN
955-9034-01-4 : DDC 709/.5493/0745493 20
N7310.6 .D47 1988 NYPL [3-MAF 91-6910]

ART, STREET. see STREET ART.

ART, STUART - EXHIBITIONS.
Brown, Walter R., 1940- The Stuart legacy .
Birmingham, Ala. , 1991. 176 p. : ISBN
0-931394-30-9 DDC 709/.42/074761781 20
N6766 .B76 1991

ART - STUDY AND TEACHING.
Rafiq, Sa‘id Ahmad. Fan aur muṭāla‘ah-yi fan /.
Karāci , 1988. 271 p. :
N7425.8.U73 R34 1988

Röttger, Ernst. [Fläche. English.] Surfaces in
creative design. London, 1970. 119 p. (chiefly
illus. (some col.)) ISBN 0-7134-2358-7 : DDC
745
N85 .R6213 1970

Taylor, Rod. The visual arts in education /.
London , New York , 1992. p. cm. ISBN
1-85000-769-1 DDC 707/.041 20
N88 .T38 1992

**ART - STUDY AND TEACHING -
   BIBLIOGRAPHY.**
Bunch, Clarence. Art education . Detroit ,
c1978. xv, 331 p. ; ISBN 0-8103-1272-7 DDC
016.707
Z5818.A8 B85 N85 NYPL [3-MAC 91-7862]

**ART - STUDY AND TEACHING
   (ELEMENTARY)**
Souza, Alcídio Mafra de. Artes plásticas na
escola. [Rio de Janeiro, 1973, c1968] 159 p.,
[31] leaves of plates.
NYPL [3-MAT 90-5879]

**ART - STUDY AND TEACHING
   (ELEMENTARY) - UNITED STATES.**
Discipline-based art education . Santa Monica,
Calif. , 1991. p. cm. ISBN 0-89236-171-9 : DDC
700 20
N362 .C6 1991

Massey, Sue J., 1947- Learning to look .
Englewood Cliffs, N.J. , c1991. p. cm. ISBN
0-13-528795-2 DDC 701/.1/071273 20
N353 .M37 1991

Szeglin, Charles B. Creativities! . West Nyack,
N.Y. , c1991. p. cm. ISBN 0-13-189804-3 DDC
372.5/044 20
N362 .S95 1991

ART - STUDY AND TEACHING - GERMANY.
Künstlerisch handeln . Stuttgart , c1989. 170
p. : ISBN 3-7725-0914-2
N199 .K857 1989

**ART - STUDY AND TEACHING - GERMANY -
   HAMBURG - EXHIBITIONS.**
Nordlicht . Hamburg , 1989. 415 p. : ISBN
3-88506-174-0 DDC 709/.43/51507443515 20
N332.G33 H355 1989

**ART - STUDY AND TEACHING - GERMANY -
   HISTORY.**
Heller, Dieter. Die Entwicklung des Werkens
und seiner Didaktik von 1880 bis 1914 . Bad
Heilbrunn/Obb. , 1990. 322 p. : ISBN
3-7815-0652-5 :
NK249 .H44 1990

**ART - STUDY AND TEACHING - GREAT
   BRITAIN.**
Critical studies in art and design education /.
Portsmouth, NH , 1991. p. cm. ISBN
0-435-08592-1 DDC 707/.041 20
N185 .C68 1991

**ART - STUDY AND TEACHING (HIGHER) -
   GERMANY - DRESDEN.**
Dresden . Dresden , 1990. 684 p. : ISBN
3-364-00145-6
N333.G33 D744 1990

**ART - STUDY AND TEACHING
   (SECONDARY) - UNITED STATES.**
Discipline-based art education . Santa Monica,
Calif. , 1991. p. cm. ISBN 0-89236-171-9 : DDC
700 20
N362 .C6 1991

Massey, Sue J., 1947- Learning to look .
Englewood Cliffs, N.J. , c1991. p. cm. ISBN

0-13-528795-2   DDC 701/.1/071273 20
N353 .M37 1991

**ART - STUDY AND TEACHING - UNITED
   STATES.**
Levi, Albert William, 1911- Art education .
Urbana , c1991. p. cm. ISBN 0-252-01813-3 (cl)
DDC 707/.073 20
N105 .L48 1991

**ART - STUDY AND TEACHING - UNITED
   STATES - HANDBOOLS, MANUALS,
   ETC.**
Dobbs, Stephen M. The DBAE handbook .
Santa Monica, CA , 1991. p. cm. ISBN
0-89236-214-6 : DDC 707/.073 20
N105 .D63 1991

**ART - SUBJECTS. see ART - THEMES,
   MOTIVES.**

ART, SUKHOTHAI.
Subhadradis Diskul, M.C. [Namchom
Phiphitthaphanthạsathăn hæng Chăt
Rāmkhamhæng, Changwat Sukhŏthai.
English & Thai.] Namchom
Phiphitthaphanthạsathăn hæng Chăt
Rāmkhamhæng, Changwat Sukhŏthai /.
[Bangkok] [1964] 60 p., [25] p. of plates (some
folded) :
N7322.S84 S83 1964

ART, SUMERIAN.
Chevrier, Jean-François. Portrait de Jurgis
Baltrušaitis /. Paris , c1989. 271 p. : ISBN
2-08-012038-7
N7483.B285 C48 1989

**ART, SWEDISH - PRIVATE COLLECTIONS -
   EXHIBITIONS.**
Fritz H. Erikssons samling . Stockholm , 1943.
26 p., [64] p. of plates :
NYPL [3-MAX (Eriksson) 90-6849]

ART, SWISS - CATALOGS.
Museum zu Allerheiligen (Schaffhausen,
Switzerland). Kunstabteilung. Museum zu
Allerheiligen Schaffhausen . Schaffhausen ,
1989. 340 p. : DDC 759.94/074/49458 20
N7144 .M87 1989
NYPL [MAVZ (Schaffhausen) 91-6567]

ART, SWISS - EXHIBITIONS.
Das Engadin Ferdinand Hodlers und anderer
Künstler des 19. und 20. Jahrhunderts . [Chur] ,
St. Moritz , c1990. 122 p. : ISBN 3-905240-15-7
DDC 759.9494 20
ND853.H6 A4 1990

Defraoui, Silvie. Orient/occident /. Genève ,
c1989. 53 p. :
NYPL [3-MCZ + D316 89-27977]

Schweizer Kunst, 1900-1990 . [Zug] , c1990.
144 p. : ISBN 3-908215-01-5 DDC
709/.494/074494756 20
N7148 .S253 1990

31 artistes suisses contemporains. Paris , 1972.
[72] p. :   *NYPL [3-MAM 90-6430]*

**ART, SWISS - SWITZERLAND -
   GRAUBÜNDEN - EXHIBITIONS.**
Aspekte aktueller Bündner Kunst, Teil II .
Chur , 1985. 25 p. : ISBN 3-905240-04-1
NYPL [3-MAM + 88-3792]

ART - SWITZERLAND - CHUR - CATALOGS.
Meuli, Andrea. Bilder einer Sammlung .
[Switzerland] , c1989. 210 p. : ISBN
3-905241-03-X
NYPL [3-MAVZ+ (Chur) 90-8658]

**ART - SWITZERLAND - GENEVA -
   CATALOGS.**
Musée Barbier-Müller. Ancient art from the
Barbier-Mueller Museum /. New York , c1991.
183 p. : ISBN 0-8109-1904-4
NYPL [3-MAE+ 91-6535]

**ART - SWITZERLAND - SCHAFFHAUSEN -
   CATALOGS.**
Museum zu Allerheiligen (Schaffhausen,
Switzerland). Kunstabteilung. Museum zu
Allerheiligen Schaffhausen . Schaffhausen ,
1989. 340 p. : DDC 759.94/074/49458 20
N7144 .M87 1989
NYPL [MAVZ (Schaffhausen) 91-6567]

**ART - SWITZERLAND - ZÜRICH -
   CATALOGS.**
Kunsthaus Zürich. Kunsthaus Zürich . [Zürich] ,
c1959. 178 p., 12 leaves of plates :
MLCS 85/315 (N)
NYPL [3-MAVZ (Zürich) 90-6999]

**ART - SYMBOLISM. see SYMBOLISM IN
   ART.**

Art talk . Artwords 2. New York, N.Y. , 1990.
xi, 319 p. : ISBN 0-306-80414-X (pbk.) : DDC
700/.9/048 20
N6490 .A73 1990   *NYPL [3-MAL 91-6966]*

**ART, TANTRIC-BUDDHIST - CHINA -
   TIBET - EXHIBITIONS.**
Till, Barry, 1951- Art from the roof of the
world . Victoria , c1989. 159 p. : ISBN
0-88885-133-2 DDC 709/.51/507471128 20
N8193.3.T36 C67 1989
NYPL [3-MAF 91-6942]

ART - TECHNIQUE.
The Complete artist . New York, NY , 1991. p.
cm. ISBN 0-8230-0771-5 (cloth) : DDC 751.4 20
N7430 .C58 1991

Faigin, Gary, 1950- The artist's complete guide
to facial expression /. New York , 1990. 287,
[1] p. : ISBN 0-8230-1628-5 : DDC 704.9/42 20
N7573.3 .F35 1990

Klee, Paul, 1879-1940. Das bildnerische
Denken /. Basel , c1990. 555 p. : ISBN
3-7965-0889-8
N7454 .K58 Bd. 1, 1990 N6888.K55

Warner, Sally. Encouraging the artist in
yourself . New York , 1991. p. cm. ISBN
0-312-04667-7 : DDC 702/.8 20
N7430 .W37 1991

ART, THAI.
Subhadradis Diskul, M.C. Sinlapa nai Prathēt
Thai . [Bangkok] [2522 i.e. 1979] 61 p., [98] p.
of plates :
N7321 .S9◄979

ART, THAI - THAILAND - BANGKOK.
Mănit Wanliphŏdom. Sinlapa Samai ‘Ŭth
[Bangkok] [2512 i.e. 1967] 8, 105 p. [26]
leaves of plates :
N7322.P47 M3 1967

**ART, THAI - THAILAND - PHRA NAKHON
   SI AYUTTHAYA.**
Mănit Wanliphŏdom. Sinlapa Samai ‘Ŭth
[Bangkok] [2512 i.e. 1967] 8, 105 p. [26]
leaves of plates :
N7322.P47 M3 1967

Art, the way it is /. Richardson, John Adkins.
Englewood Cliffs, N.J. , New York , 1991. p.
cm. ISBN 0-13-040437-3 (pbk.) DDC 701/.1 20
N7425 .R48 1991

Art, the way it is /. Richardson, John Adkins.
New York , 1992. p. cm. ISBN 0-8109-1911-7
(hardcover) DDC 701/.1 20
N7425 .R48 1992

ART - THEMES, MOTIVES.
Ashbery, John. Reported sightings . Cambridge,
Mass. , 1991. xxiii, 417 p., [16] p. of col.
plates : ISBN 0-674-76225-8 DDC 700 20
N7445.2 .A84 1991

Die Wahrheit der Kunst . Stuttgart , c1989. 198
p. : ISBN 3-460-32881-9 DDC 701 20
N68 .W24 1989

Herzog, Karl. Die Gestalt des Menschen in der
Kunst und im Spiegel der Wissenschaft /.
Darmstadt , c1990. xii, 234 p. : ISBN
3-534-11010-2 DDC 704.9/421 20
N7572 .H47 1990

Naar het leven? . [Zoetermeer] , 's-Gravenhage
[1990] 66 p. : ISBN 90-346-2214-2
N7432.5.R4 N33 1990

Nerdinger, Winfried. Perspektiven der Kunst .
München , c1990. 404 p. : ISBN 3-87501-080-9
N5300 .N36 1990

Verzeichnungen . Essen , 1989. 227 p. : ISBN
3-88474-603-0
N72.T4 V47 1989

Wetzel, Christoph. Frühgeschichte und frühe
Hochkulturen /. Darmstadt , c1990. 448 p. :
ISBN 3-7630-1971-5
N5330 .W54 1990

Art theory and criticism : an anthology of
formalist, avant-garde, contextualist, and
post-modernist thought / edited by Sally
Everett. Jefferson, N.C. : McFarland, c1991.
xiii, 282 p. : ill. ; 24 cm. Includes bibliographical
references. ISBN 0-89950-595-3 (lib. bdg. : alk. paper)
DDC 701 20
1. Art - Philosophy. 2. Art criticism - History - 20th

century. I. Everett, Sally, 1941-.
N71 .A7475 1991

ART, TIBETAN - CATALOGS.
Newark Museum. Catalogue of the Newark
Museum Tibetan collection /. Newark, N.J. ,
1983- v. : ISBN 0-932828-12-4 (pbk.) : DDC
709/.51/5074014932 19
N7346.T5 N48 1983   **NYPL [MAF 91-997]**

ART, TIBETAN - EXHIBITIONS.
Kreijger, Hugo. Godenbeelden uit Tibet .
['s-Gravenhage] [Amsterdam] , c1989. 129, [1]
p. : ISBN 90-12-06219-5
     NYPL [3-MAF 91-5465]

Pal, Pratapaditya. Art of the Himalayas . New
York , c1991. p. cm. ISBN 1-555-95066-3 :
DDC 709/.5496/07473 20
N7310.8.N4 P33 1991
     NYPL [3-MAF 91-6942]

Till, Barry, 1951- Art from the roof of the
world . Victoria , c1989. 159 p. : ISBN
0-88885-133-2 DDC 709/.51/507471128 20
N8193.3.T36 C67 1989
     NYPL [3-MAF 91-6942]

Wellcome Institute for the History of Medicine.
Library. Catalogue of Tibetan manuscripts and
xylographs, and catalogue of thankas, banners
and other paintings and drawings in the library
of the Wellcome Institute for the History of
Medicine /. London , 1989. xiii, 112 p., [12] p.
of plates : ISBN 0-85484-085-0 DDC 011.31
704.948943923074 20
N8193.T52   **NYPL [3-MAF+ 90-13612]**

Art today in the Federal Republic of Germany /
[translation, Timothy Nevill]. Bonn : Inter
Nationes, c1988. 114 p. : ill. (some col.) ; 30
cm. Articles by Wolfgang Max Faust ... et al.
Bibliography: p. 110-112.
*1. Art, Modern - 20th century - Germany, West. I.
Faust, Wolfgang Max, 1944-. II. Inter Nationes.*
     NYPL [3-MAMG+ 90-12546]

Art treasures in Spain: monuments, masterpieces,
commissions and collections; introduction by
Juan Ainaud de Lasarte; [general editors Trewin
Copplestone, Bernard S. Myers]. London,
Hamlyn, 1970. 175 p. illus. (some col.), col.
maps (on lining papers). 29 cm. ISBN
0-600-03888-2 DDC 709/.46
*1. Art - Spain. 2. Art patronage - Spain. I. Copplestone,
Trewin, ed. II. Myers, Bernard Samuel, 1908- ed.*
N7101 .A83 1970

ART, TURKISH.
Tanaltay, Erdoğan. Sanat ustalarıyla-- bir gün .
Divanyolu, İstanbul [1989] 159 p. ; ISBN
975-7704-02-4
N7168 .T36 1989

ART, TURKISH - EXHIBITIONS.
Diplomaten und Wesire . München , 1988. 187
p., [24] p. of plates :
     NYPL [3-MAF 90-12662]

ART - UKRAINE - KHARKOV - CATALOGS.
Imperatorskiĭ khar´kovskiĭ universitet. Muzeĭ
iziāshchnykh iskusstv. [Ukazatel´ proizvedeniĭ,
khraniāshchikhsiā v Muzee iziāshchnykh
isskustv pri Imperatorskom khar´kovskom
universitete.] Ukazatel´ proizvedeniĭ,
khraniāshchikhsiā v Muzeīe iziāshchnykh
iskusstv pri Imperatorskom khar´kovskom
universitetīe. Khar´kov , 1870-1883. 3 v. ;
N3315.52 .A58 1870

Art under Stalin /. Bown, Matthew Cullerne.
New York , c1991. p. cm. ISBN 0-8419-1299-8
(alk. paper) DDC 709/.47/0904 20
N6988 .B67 1991

ART - UNITED STATES.
Cahill, Holger, 1887-1960. (comp) Art in
America in modern times. Freeport, N.Y.
[1969, c1934] 110 p. DDC 700/.973
N6505 .C3 1969

**ART - UNITED STATES - ECONOMIC
ASPECTS.**
Bongard, Willi. Kunst und Kommerz.
[Oldenburg, c1967] 271 p.
     NYPL [3-MAMT 90-6286]

ART - UNITED STATES - EXHIBITIONS.
Bernard Danenberg Galleries. One hundred
recent acquisitions, by American artists. New
York, 1969. 51 p. **NYPL [3-MAMT 90-6625]**

ART - UTAH - SPRINGVILLE.
Swanson, Vern G. Utah art . Salt Lake City ,
1991. p. cm. ISBN 0-87905-385-2 : DDC

709/.792 20
N6530.U8 S94 1991

**Art vénitien du dix-huitième siècle dans les
collections canadiennes.** Knox, George. 18th
century Venetian art in Canadian collections =.
Vancouver, B.C., Canada , c1989. 108 p. :
ISBN 0-920095-81-X
IN PROCESS (ONLINE)
     NYPL [3-MAMC+ 91-6265]

**ART, VICTORIAN - GREAT BRITAIN -
EXHIBITIONS.**
Pre-raphaelites and academics . London , 1981.
[69] p. :   **NYPL [3-MAMR 86-3397]**

**ART, VICTORIAN - UNITED STATES -
JAPANESE INFLUENCES -
EXHIBITIONS.**
Hosley, William. The Japan idea . Hartford,
Conn. , 1990. 211 p. : ISBN 0-918333-07-5
     NYPL [3-MAMT+ 91-3289]

ART, VIETNAMESE.
Nguy Vietnamese plastic arts /. Hanoi , 1987.
63 p. ;
N7314 .N46 1987

ART, VIETNAMESE - EXHIBITIONS.
As seen by both sides . Boston, Mass. ,
Amersht, MA , 1991. 112 p. : ISBN
0-87023-744-6 (pbk.) : DDC
760/.04499597043/074597 20
N6512 .A788 1991

ART, WALL. see STREET ART.

ART - WASHINGTON, D.C. - CATALOGS.
Georgetown University. Catalogue of the art
collection, Georgetown University,
Washington,D.C. Washington, D.C. , 1963. 119
p., 33 p. of plates : **NYPL [3-MAVZ
(Washington, D.C.) 91-821]**

National Gallery of Art (U. S.) Sculpture and
decorative arts . Washington, D.C. [New
York] , 1992. p. cm. ISBN 0-89468-162-1 DDC
708.153 20
N5963.W18 N382 1992

United States. Dept. of State. Treasures of
State . New York , 1991. p. cm. ISBN
0-8109-3911-8 (cloth) DDC 709/.73/074753 20
N6505 .U48 1991

**ART - WASHINGTON (STATE) - SEATTLE -
CATALOGS.**
Seattle. Art Museum. Selected works /. Seattle,
WA , c1991. p. cm. ISBN 0-932216-35-8 : DDC
708.197/772 20
N745 .A66 1991

ART, WELSH - EXHIBITIONS.
Jonah Jones, John Petts, Kyffin Williams .
[London, England] , 1961. 14 p., [8] p. of
plates :
MLCM 87/7416 (N)
     NYPL [3-MAMR 91-226]

ART - WEST (U. S.)
The Passing of the Great West . Coral Gables,
Fla. , 1975. 55 p. :
     NYPL [3-MAMT 90-5902]

Art what thou eat : images of food in American
art / by Donna Gustafson ... [et al.] ; edited by
Linda Weintraub.1st ed. Mount Kisco, N.Y. :
Moyer Bell Limited, c1991. 191 p. : ill. (some
col.) ; 32 cm. Catalog of an exhibition held at the
Edith C. Blum Art Institute, Sept. 2-Nov. 18, 1990 and
the New-York Historical Society, Dec. 18-Mar. 22,
1991. Includes bibliographical references (p. 18).
ISBN 1-559-21051-6 : DDC 704.9/49641/0973
20
*1. Art, American - Exhibitions. 2. Art, Modern - 19th
century - United States - Exhibitions. 3. Art, Modern -
20th century - United States - Exhibitions. 4. Food in
art - Exhibitions. 5. Dinners and dining in art -
Exhibitions. I. Gustafson, Donna. II. Weintraub, Linda.
III. Edith C. Blum Art Institute. IV. New York
Historical Society.*
N6512 .A763 1991
     NYPL [3-MAMZ+ 91-5410]

**ART - WISCONSIN - MADISON -
CATALOGS.**
Elvehjem Museum of Art. Handbook of the
collection /. Madison, Wis. , c1990. xvi p., 154
p. of plates : ISBN 0-932900-23-2 DDC
708.175/83 20
N582.M22 A6 1990
     NYPL [3-MAVZ (Madison) 91-4867]

Art with found materials /. Lancaster, John,
1930- New York , 1992. p. cm. ISBN

0-531-14204-3 DDC 745.5 20
N7433.7 .L36 1992

The art work of Louis C. Tiffany. Tiffany, Louis
Comfort, 1848-1933. Poughkeepsie, NY , 1987.
xxxi, 90 p., [60] p. of plates : ISBN
0-938290-06-1 DDC 709.2 20
N6537.T5 A4 1987
     NYPL [3-MPW+ 90-11567]

Art works from dr Vinko Perčić's bequest.
Umjetnine iz donacije dr Vinka Perčića =.
Zagreb , c1989. 144 p. :
N5280.Y8 U46 1989

**ART - YUGOSLAVIA - DALMATIA
(CROATIA)**
Höfler, Janez. Die Kunst Dalmatiens .
Graz/Austria , 1989. 338 p. : ISBN
3-201-01466-4 DDC 709/.497/2 20
N7249.D34 H64 1989

ART - YUGOSLAVIA - DUBROVNIK.
Beritićev zbornik . Dubrovnik , 1960. 335 p.,
[1] folded leaf of plates :
     NYPL [*QKK 83-2704]

**ART, ZAIRIAN - EXHIBITIONS - 20TH
CENTURY.**
Mack, John. Emil Torday and the art of the
Congo, 1900-1909 /. London , 1990. 96 :
ISBN 0-7141-1594-0 (pbk) DDC 709.6724 20
     NYPL [Sc E 91-236]

**ART, ZAIRIAN - PRIVATE COLLECTIONS -
LONDON.**
Mack, John. Emil Torday and the art of the
Congo, 1900-1909 /. London , 1990. 96 :
ISBN 0-7141-1594-0 (pbk) : DDC 709.6724 20
     NYPL [Sc E 91-236]

Arta fotografică in România / cuvînt introductiv
de Sylviu Comănescu = Photographic art in
Rumania / foreword by Sylviu Comănescu.
Bucureşti : Secretariatul Asociaţiei Artiştilor
Fotografi din Republica Socialistă România,
[1965?] xv p., 141 p. of plates : ill. ; 23 cm.
*1. Photography - Rumania. I. Asociaţiei Artiştilor
Fotografi din Republica Socialistă România. II. Title:
Photographic art in Rumania.*
     NYPL [MFW 91-693]

Artă şi document . Ionescu, Adrian-Silvan.
Bucureşti , 1990. 318 p., [48] p. of plates :
ISBN 973-330-072-1 :
N8214.R6 I55 1990

Artaud, Evelyne.
Gaudibert, Pierre. Ipoustéguy /. Paris , c1989.
204 p. : ISBN 2-7022-0246-2
     NYPL [3-MGO+ (Ipoustéguy) 91-3898]

Perestroïk'art : les couleurs de la transparence /
Evelyne Artaud ; Michel Chassat,
photographies. [Paris] : Editions Cercle d'art,
c1990. 118 p. : ill. (some col.) ; 24 cm. ISBN
2-7022-0269-1 DDC 709.47/09048 20
*1. Art, Soviet. 2. Avant-garde (Aesthetics) - Soviet
Union - History - 20th century. 3. Glasnost. I. Chassat,
Michel. II. Title. III. Title: Perestroïk' art.*
N6988 .A7635 1990
     NYPL [3-MAM 90-13376]

Arte.
(3) Alonso de la Sierra Fernández, Lorenzo. El
retablo neoclásico en Cádiz /. [Cádiz] [1989?]
177 p., [24] p. of plates : ISBN 84-87144-02-0
NB1910 .A48 1989

Arte abstracto, arte concreto : Cercle et carré,
Paris, 1930 : IVAM Centre Julio González, 20
septiembre/2 diciembre 1990 / [textos], Gladys
Fabre. [Valencia?] : IVAM Centre Julio
González, c1990. 439 p. : ill. (some col.) 31
cm. Spanish and English. Includes bibliographical
references. ISBN 84-7890-151-5
*1. Art, Abstract - Exhibitions. 2. Concrete art -
Exhibitions. 3. Art, Modern - 20th century -
Exhibitions. 4. Cercle et carré (Group). I. Fabre, Gladys
C. II. IVAM Centre Julio González. III. Cercle et carré.
IV. Title: Paris 1930.*
N6494.A2 A78 1990

Arte antica di Torino. Gabinetto delle stampe di
Milano. Disegni di Stefano della Bella. Milano
[1976?] 70 p. :
     NYPL [3-MCF B367 91-1368]

Arte argentino, siglo veinte. Arte argentino, siglo
XX /. [Argentina] c1990 (Buenos Aires, R.
Argentina [i.e. República Argentina] : HUR)
124 p. : DDC 709/.82/0904 20
N6635 .A78 1990

Arte argentino, siglo XX / Carlos Barbarito ... [et

al.]. [Argentina : s.n.], c1990 (Buenos Aires, R.
Argentina [i.e. República Argentina] : HUR)
124 p. : ill. ; 22 cm. Includes bibliographical
references. CONTENTS. - Acerca de las vanguardias /
Carlos Barbarito -- Alfredo Guttero y el paisaje
industrial / María Teresa Constantin -- El "objeto" en la
obra de Adolfo Nigro / Andrea Giunta -- La
petrificación, arte argentino reciente / Reinaldo
Laddaga -- Arte argentino y fin de siglo, una doble
aproximación / Héctor Ranea Sandoval.   DDC
709/.82/0904 20
   *1. Art, Argentine. 2. Art, Modern - 20th century -
Argentina. I. Barbarito, Carlos, 1955-. II. Title: Arte
argentino, siglo 20. III. Title: Arte argentino, siglo
veinte.*
N6635 .A78 1990

Arte argentino, siglo 20. Arte argentino, siglo XX
/. [Argentina] c1990 (Buenos Aires, R.
Argentina [i.e. República Argentina] : HUR)
124 p. :   DDC 709/.82/0904 20
N6635 .A78 1990

Arte bizantino . Cantó Rubio, Juan. Salamanca ,
1989. 94 p. :   ISBN 84-7299-220-9
                        NYPL [3-MAK 91-3667]

**Arte (Cádiz (Spain : Province). Diputación
   Provincial) .**
   (3) Alonso de la Sierra Fernández, Lorenzo. El
retablo neoclásico en Cádiz /. [Cádiz] [1989?]
177 p., [24] p. of plates :   ISBN 84-87144-02-0
NB1910 .A48 1989

A arte como investimento . Pinho, Diva
Benevides. São Paul, SP , 1989. 214 p. :   ISBN
85-21-30526-5
N8600 .P56 1989

Arte conceptual revisado = Conceptual art
revisited / Juan Vicente Aliaga, José Miguel G.
Cortés ; [traducción textos, Alberto Mira ... et
al.]. [Valencia] : Departamento de Escultura,
Facultad de Bellas Artes, Universidad
Politécnica de Valencia, Servicio de
Publicaciones, [1990?] 286 p. : ill. ; 21 cm.
(Documentos de escultura contemporánea) Includes
bibliographical references.   ISBN 84-7721-108-6
DDC 709/.04/075 20
   *1. Conceptual art. 2. Art, Modern - 20th century. I.
Aliaga, Juan Vicente. II. Cortés, José Miguel G. III.
Title: Conceptual art revisited. IV. Series.*
N6494.C63 A76 1990

Arte contemporanea (Editori Laterza)
Finizio, Luigi Paolo. L'astrattismo costruttivo .
Roma , 1990. vii, 237 p., [16] p. of plates :
         ISBN 88-420-3642-0 :   DDC 709/.47/09041 20
N6988.5.C64 F56 1990

Arte contemporáneo desde Chile. Contemporary
art from Chile . New York, N.Y. , c1990. 63
p. :   ISBN 1-87912-802-0
                        NYPL [3-MAM 91-7561]

Arte contemporáneo dominicano. [Santo
Domingo, Dominican Republic?] : Instituto
Dominicano de Cultura Hispánica, [1987?] [72]
p. ; 25 cm. Cover title. "Colegio Dominicano de
Artistas Plásticos del 15 al 30 de mayo 1987"--Cover.
   *1. Art, Dominican. 2. Art, Modern - 20th century -
Dominican Republic. 3. Artists - Dominican Republic -
Biography. I. Instituto Dominicano de Cultura
Hispánica. II. Colegio Dominicano de Artistas Plásticos.*
N6615.D6 A77 1987

Arte de la pintura /. Pacheco, Francisco,
1564-1644. Madrid , c1990. 782 p. :   ISBN
84-376-0871-6 DDC 750 20
ND1130 .P2 1990

Arte d'Occidente .
   (4) Vannugli, Antonio. La collezione Serra di
Cassano /. Salerno , c1989. 157 p., [39] p. of
plates ;   ISBN 88-85651-21-6
                        NYPL [3-MCE 90-5149]

Arte e costume a Bergamo . Mosca, Pietro.
Bergamo , c1989-c1990. 2 v. (1020 p.) ;
IN PROCESS (ONLINE)
                        NYPL [3-MAMC+ 91-5886]

Arte e cultura .
   (12) Bardi, P. M. (Pietro Maria), 1900- Em
torno da escultura no Brasil /. [São Paulo,
Brazil] , 1989. 119 p. :
NB350 .B37 1989

Arte em Berlim--1900 até hoje : Lisboa, 26 de
julho a 24 de setembro 1989. Lisboa : Fundação
Calouste Gulbenkian, Centro de Arte Moderna,
1989. 319 p. : ill. (some col.) ; 28 cm. Includes
bibliographical references (p. 295).   DDC

709/.431/55074469425 20
   *1. Art, German - Berlin (Germany) - Exhibitions. 2.
Art, Modern - 20th century - Berlin (Germany) -
Exhibitions. I. Centro de Arte Moderna (Fundação
Calouste Gulbenkian).*
N6885 .A76 1989

A arte em Portugal e os Descobrimentos .
Santinho, M. Manuela (Maria Manuela) Porto ,
1989. 164 p. :   DDC 709/.469 20
N7121 .S27 1989

Arte en Iberoamérica, 1820-1980 : Palacio de
Velázquez, 14 de diciembre de 1989-4 de
marzo de 1990 / Dawn Ades ; con la
colaboración de Guy Brett, Stanton Loomis
Catlin y Rosemary O'Neill. [Madrid] : Turner,
[1989?] xxi, 359, [3] p. : ill. (some col.) ; 29
cm. (Colección Encuentros. Serie Catálogos)
"Ministerio de Cultura, Centro de Arte Reina Sofía,
Centro Macional de Exposiciones." Includes
bibliographical references (p. [360]-[361]).   ISBN
84-7506-297-0
   *1. Art, Latin American - Exhibitions. 2. Art, Modern -
19th century - Latin America - Exhibitions. 3. Art,
Modern - 20th century - Latin America - Exhibitions.
4. Artists - Latin America - Biography. I. Ades, Dawn.
II. Palacio de Velázquez (Madrid, Spain). III. Series:
Colección Encuentros (Turner (Firm)). Serie Catálogs.*
N6502.4 .A76 1989

Arte funerario /. Coloquio Internacional de
Historia del Arte (1980 : Mexico City, Mexico)
México , 1987- v. :   ISBN 968-360-243-6 (set)
NB1800 .C65 1980
                        NYPL [3-MRIF 90-2698]

Arte geométrico en España, 1957-1989.
[Madrid] : Centro Cultural de la Villa, [1989]
320 p. : ill. (some col.) ; 30 cm.   ISBN
84-7812-044-0 DDC 709/.46/0744641 20
   *1. Art, Abstract - Spain - Exhibitions. 2. Art, Spanish -
Exhibitions. 3. Art, Modern - 20th century - Spain -
Exhibitions. 4. Artists - Spain - Biography. I. Centro
Cultural de la Villa de Madrid.*
N7108.5.A2 A78 1989

Arte. Grandes temas.
Pacheco, Francisco, 1564-1644. Arte de la
pintura /. Madrid , c1990. 782 p. :   ISBN
84-376-0871-6 DDC 750 20
ND1130 .P2 1990

Arte industriale . Casciani, Stefano, 1955-
Milano , c1988. 194 p. :   ISBN 88-85684-21-1
                        NYPL [3-MNE+ 90-12329]

Arte italiana contemporanea / [introduzione,
Luciano Budigna ; testi critici, L.V. Masini ... et
al. ; traduzioni, G. Elliot ... et al.]. Firenze : La
ginestra, [1965?]. 11 v. : ill. (some col.), ports. ;
31 cm. Introductions also in English, French, and
German. Editors and contributors vary. CONTENTS. -
1. Emilia, Liguria, Toscana, Veneto.--2. Artisti italiani
contemporanei del centro e settentrione.--3. Lombardia,
Alto Veneto, Liguria, Toscana, Lazio.--4. [Without
special title].--5. Sicilia, Umbria.--v. 6. Introduzione e
selezione artistica del Lazio e Abruzzo.--v. 7. Marche,
Abruzzo.--v. 8. Marche, Puglia.--v. 9. Calabria
completamento Marche, Puglie, Sicilia.--v. 10.
Piemonte, Liguria.--v. 11. Lombardia.   DDC 709/.2/2
19
   *1. Art, Modern - 20th century - Italy. 2. Artists -
Italy - Biography. I. Budigna, Luciano.*
N6918 .A788   *NYPL [3-MAMC+ 88-4656]*

Arte Madí /. Kosice, Gyula, 1924- Buenos Aires,
Argentina , c1982. 198 p. :   ISBN 950-0-00418-6
DDC 700/.982/074098211 19
NX531.A1 K67 1982
                        NYPL [3-MAM 85-1850]

Arte minimal de la Colección Panza :
[exposición] : Centro de Arte Reina Sofía, 24
de marzo-31 de diciembre, 1988. [Madrid?] :
Ministerio de Cultura, Dirección General de
Bellas Artes y Archivos : Centro Nacional de
Exposiciónes, 1988. 61 p. : col. ill. ; 28 cm.
Cover title: Colección Panza. Includes bibliographical
references.   ISBN 84-7750-623-18
   *1. Panza, Guisseppe - Art collections - Exhibitions. 2.
Minimal art - United States - Exhibitions. 3. Minimal
sculpture - United States - Exhibitions. 4. Art,
Modern - United States - Exhibitions. I. Centro de Arte
Reina Sofiá. II. Title: Colección Panza.*
                        NYPL [MAMT 90-5197]

Arte moderna cara compagna . Russoli, Franco.
[Milano] , c1987. 382 p. ;   ISBN 88-11-59983-0
                        NYPL [3-MAMC 91-4600]

Arte orafa e iconografia dionisiaca : Torgiano,

4-12 novembre 1987 / [testi di Abbozzo,
edgardo ... et al.]. [Italy : s.n., 1987] 88 p. : ill.
(some col.) ; 31 cm. Cover title. Italian and English.
At head of title: Dionysos 1987. Exhibition held in
conjunction with the seventh Banco d'assaggio dei vini
d'Italia. Includes bibliographical references.
   *1. Dionysus (Greek deity) - Art - Exhibitions. 2.
Goldwork - Themes, motives - Exhibitions. I. Abbozzo,
Edgardo. II. Banco d'assaggio dei vini d'Italia (7th :
1987 : Torgiano, Italy). III. Title: Dionysos 1987.*
                        NYPL [3-MNO+ 89-27461]

Arte para los ochenta = Art for the eighties /
Galería Durbán, Caracas ; [exhibición
organizada por Roberto White y Scott Crook ;
en colaboración con César Segnini]. Caracas,
Venezuela : La Galería, c1980. [24] p. : ill. ; 23
cm. Spanish and English. "Inauguración, miércoles, 3
de septiembre, 1980."
   *1. Art, Modern - 20th century - Venezuela - Caracas -
Exhibitions. I. Galería Durbán.*
                        NYPL [3-MAL 90-4430]

**L'Arte per i papi e per i principi nella campagna
   romana :** grande pittura del '600 e del '700 :
Roma, Museo nazionale del Palazzo di Venezia,
8 marzo-13 maggio 1990. Roma : Quasar,
c1990. 2 v. : ill. (some col.) ; 28 cm. At head of
title: Ministero per i beni culturali e ambientali,
Soprintendenza per i beni artistici e storici di Roma.
Includes bibliographical references and indexes.
CONTENTS. - v. 1. Schede -- v. 2. Saggi.   ISBN
88-7140-015-1 (v. 1) :
   *1. Painting, Italian - Italy - Campagna di Roma -
Exhibitions. 2. Painting, Modern - 17th-18th centuries -
Italy - Campagna di Roma - Exhibitions. 3.
Counter-Reformation in art - Exhibitions. I. Italy.
Soprintendenza per i beni artistici e storici di Roma. II.
Museo di Palazzo Venezia (Rome, Italy).*
ND1432.I8 A77 1990
                        NYPL [3-MCE 91-3418]

Arte popular chileno /. Lago, Tomás. Santiago de
Chile [1985] 136 p. :
NK901 .L33 1985

ARTE POVERA. see CONCEPTUAL ART.

Arte sacra di Palazzo : la Cappella reale di
Napoli e i suoi arredi : un patrimonio di arti
decorative / a cura di Annalisa Porzio. Napoli :
Arte tipografica, 1989. 263 p. : ill. (some col.) ;
24 cm. Includes bibliographical references (p. 253-258)
and index.   DDC 704.9/482/09450744573 20
   *1. Cappella reale di Napoli (Palazzo reale) - Catalogs. 2.
Christian art and symbolism - Modern period, 1500-
Italy - Naples - Catalogs. 3. Church decoration and
ornament - Italy - Naples - Catalogs. I. Porzio,
Annalisa.*
N7952.N36 A74 1989
                        NYPL [3-MAIH 91-4840]

Arte y artistas . Flores-Antúnez, Ignacio. México,
D.F. , 1989. 385 p. :
N6555 .F57 1989

Arte y artistas valencianos. Azcárraga, Adolfo de.
Escritos sobre arte y artistas valencianos /.
Valencia , 1989. 330 p. :   ISBN 84-505-8230-X
                        NYPL [3-MAML 90-11103]

Arte y ciudad en Galicia, siglo XIX /. Bozal
Fernández, Valeriano. Santiago de Compostela
[1990] 133 p. :   ISBN 84-505-9217-8 DDC
709/.46/109034 20
N72.S6 B6 1990

Arte y estética .
   (22) Bonet Correa, Antonio. Fiesta, poder y
arquitectura . Madrid, España , c1990. 182 p. :
         ISBN 84-7600-446-6 DDC 720/.946/09033 20
NA1306 .B57 1990

Arte y monarquía en Navarra, 1328-1425 /.
Martínez de Aguirre, Javier. Pamplona , c1987.
432 p. :   ISBN 84-235-0794-7
N7109.N3 M37 1987
                        NYPL [3-MAML 90-12586]

Arte y parte . Panesso, Fausto, 1953- [Bogotá,
Colombia?] [1990- v. <1 > :
N6675 .P35 1990

Arte y parte . Panesso, Fausto, 1953- [Bogotá,
Colombia] , 1990- v. :
                        NYPL [3-MAM+ 91-3615]

Artes decorativas modernas del Japón :
[exposición] / Instituto Nacional de Bellas
Artes, Embajada del Japón en México.
México : Departamento de Artes Plásticas,
1964. [14] p. : ill. ; 23 cm.
   1. Decoration and ornament - Japan - Exhibitions. I.

Instituto Nacional de Bellas Artes (Mexico).
Depardamento de Artes Plásticas.
NYPL [3-MNE 91-833]

Artes e estilos .
(1) Benini, Mirella. [Ceramica del
Rinascimento. Portuguese.] Cerâmica do
Renascimento /. Lisboa , 1989. 82 p. :
NK4103 .B416 1989

Artes plásticas na escola. Souza, Alcídio Mafra
de. [Rio de Janeiro, 1973, c1968] 159 p., [31]
leaves of plates.   NYPL [3-MAT 90-5879]

Artesanato da região norte : catálogo =
Traditional and contemporary crafts in northern
Portugal : catalogue. Porto : Instituto do
Emprego e Formação Profissional, Delegação
Regional do Norte, Núcleo de Apoio ao
Artesanato, 1989. 406 p. : col. ill. ; 29 cm.
English and Portuguese. "Colaboração, Centro Regional
de Artes Tradicionais." ISBN 972-90030-0-9 DDC
745/.09469 20
1. Decorative arts - Portugal. 2. Handicraft - Portugal.
I. Instituto do Emprego e Formação Profissional
(Portugal). Delegação Regional do Norte. Núcleo de
Apoio ao Artesanato. II. Centro Regional de Artes
Tradicionais (Portugal). III. Title: Traditional and
contemporary crafts in northern Portugal.
NK1003 .A83 1989

Artesanía dominicana /. Castillo, José del, 1947-
Santo Domingo, República Dominicana , 1989.
125 p. : DDC 745/.097293 20
NK886.D65 C38 1989

An artful life . Assouline, Pierre. [Homme de
l'art. English.] New York , 1990. xiii, 411 p.,
[16] p. of plates : ISBN 0-8021-1227-7 (alk. paper)
DDC 709/.2 B 20
N8660.K3 A9513 1990
                NYPL [3-MAVC 90-12782]

An artful life . Assouline, Pierre. [Homme de
l'art. English.] New York , 1991. p. cm. ISBN
0-88064-131-2 (pbk. : acid-free paper) : DDC
709/.2 B 20
N8660.K3 A9513 1991

Arthaud, Christian. Musée Matisse. Henri
Matisse . Nice , 1988. 366 p. : ISBN
2-86941-071-9
                NYPL [3-MCO+ M43 91-5314]

Arthur A. Houghton Jr. Gallery. Symbolism .
[New York] [1989] [24] p. :
                NYPL [3-MAL 91-4569]

Arthur B. Davies . Czestochowski, Joseph S.
Newark , London , c1987. 258 p., [12] p. of
plates : ISBN 0-87413-242-8 DDC 769.92/4 19
NE539.D3 A4 1987
                NYPL [MDG+ (Davies) 87-4836]

Arthur B. Davies . M. Knoedler & Co. New
York , c1975. 55 p. :
                NYPL [3-MCX D25 91-905]

**Arthur, King - Romances. see Arthurian
romances.**

Arthur M. Sackler collections. Rawson, Jessica.
Western Zhou ritual bronzes from the Arthur
M. Sackler collections /. Washington, D.C. :
Cambridge, Mass. : 2 v. (776 p.) : ISBN
0-674-95070-4   NYPL [3-MGR+ 91-4952]

Arthur M. Sackler Foundation. Rawson, Jessica.
Western Zhou ritual bronzes from the Arthur
M. Sackler collections /. Washington, D.C. :
Cambridge, Mass. : 2 v. (776 p.) : ISBN
0-674-95070-4   NYPL [3-MGR+ 91-4952]

**Arthur M. Sackler Gallery (Smithsonian
Institution)**
Fu, Shen, 1937- Challenging the past .
Washington, D.C. , Seattle , c1991. p. cm.
ISBN 0-295-97124-X (cloth : alk. paper) DDC
759.951 20
ND1049.C4523 A4 1991

Investigating artistic environments in the
ancient Near East /. Washington, D.C. , c1990.
xii, 153 p. : ISBN 0-299-97070-1 (alk. paper) :
DDC 709/.35 20
N7265 .I58 1990   NYPL [3-MAE 90-12590]

Kawami, Trudy S., 1944- Ancient Iranian
ceramics from the Arthur M. Sackler
collections /. New York , 1991. p. ISBN
0-913291-04-8 DDC 738.3/82/0935 20
NK3825 .K39 1991

New perspectives on Chu culture during the
Eastern Zhou Period /. Washington, D.C. ,
Princeton, N.J. , c1991. p. cm. ISBN

0-691-04095-8 (Princeton Univ. Press) : DDC
700/.931 20
N7343.22 .N48 1991

Yonemura, Ann, 1947- Yokohama .
Washington, D.C. , 1990. 198 p. : ISBN
0-87474-993-X (alk. paper) DDC
769/.499521364031 20
NE1321.8 .Y64 1990
                NYPL [MDBV+ 90-11723]

**ARTHUR M. SACKLER GALLERY
(SMITHSONIAN INSTITUTION) -
CATALOGS.**
Kawami, Trudy S., 1944- Ancient Iranian
ceramics from the Arthur M. Sackler
collections /. New York , 1991. p. ISBN
0-913291-04-8 DDC 738.3/82/0935 20
NK3825 .K39 1991

Arthur M. Sackler Museum.
Harvard University. Art Museums. The Fredric
Wertham collection . [Cambridge] , 1990. 101
p. : ISBN 0-916724-75-1
IN PROCESS (ONLINE)
                NYPL [3-MAX (Wertham) 91-5499]

Rawson, Jessica. Western Zhou ritual bronzes
from the Arthur M. Sackler collections /.
Washington, D.C. : Cambridge, Mass. : 2 v.
(776 p.) : ISBN 0-674-95070-4
                NYPL [3-MGR+ 91-4952]

**ARTHUR M. SACKLER MUSEUM -
CATALOGS.**
Rawson, Jessica. Western Zhou ritual bronzes
from the Arthur M. Sackler collections /.
Washington, D.C. : Cambridge, Mass. : 2 v.
(776 p.) : ISBN 0-674-95070-4
                NYPL [3-MGR+ 91-4952]

Arthur Tooth & Sons. 6 American abstract
painters . London , 1961. [20] p. :
                NYPL [3-MCW 90-6267]

Arthur Watson Sparks, American impressionist .
Sparks, Arthur Watson, 1871?-1919.
Greensburg, Pa. [1963] [19] p. :
                NYPL [3-MCX S736 91-5548]

Arthur Weyhe--sculpture, 1972-1989 /. Weyhe,
Arthur. Brookville, N.Y. , c1990. 48 p. : ISBN
0-933699-19-0 DDC 709/.2 20
NB237.W443 A4 1990

**ARTHURIAN LEGENDS. see ARTHURIAN
ROMANCES.**

**ARTHURIAN ROMANCES -
ILLUSTRATIONS.**
Woods-Marsden, Joanna, 1936- The Gonzaga of
Mantua and Pisanello's Arthurian frescoes /.
Princeton, N.J. , 1988. xxv, 274 p., [129] p. of
plates : ISBN 0-691-04048-6 (alk. paper) : DDC
758/.980880351/094528 19
N6923.P497 W66 1988
                NYPL [3-MCF P67 91-4621]

Articles of faith /. Clark, Douglas. Toronto ,
c1990. 18 [i.e. 46] p. : ISBN 0-88910-343-7 :
DDC 709/.2 20
                NYPL [MEMZ+ 91-7485]

Artigas, João Batista Vilanova. A função social
do arquiteto / Vilanova Artigas. São Paulo, SP :
Nobel, 1989. 93 p. : ill. ; 21 cm. (Cidade aberta)
"Concurso do Prof. Arq. João B. Vilanova Artigas para
professor titular da disciplina de projeto da Faculdade
de Arquitetura e Urbanismo da Universidade de São
Paulo realizado em junho de 1984." Includes
bibliographical references. ISBN 85-21-30621-0
DDC 720/.1/0309810904 20
1. Architecture and society - Brazil. 2. Architecture -
Brazil. 3. Architecture, Modern - 20th century - Brazil.
I. Title.
NA2543.S6 A76 1989

ARTIGAS, JOSÉ GERVASIO, 1764-1850.
Uruguay. Comisión Nacional Archivo Artigas.
Archivo Artigas. Montevideo, 1950- v.
                NYPL [HGB+ (Uruguay. Archivo
                Artigas, Com. Nac. Archivo Artigas)]

**Artigianato di tradizione nelle Alpi occidentali
italiane :** significato, arte, cultura / testi e
ricerca di Annéto Arneodo ... [et al.]. Ivrea,
Italy : Priuli & Verlucca, c1990. 305 p. : ill.
(some col.) ; 34 cm. French and Italian. Title on
added t.p.: Artisanat traditionnel des Alpes occidentales
italiennes. At head of title: 203o Distretto del Rotary
International.   DDC 745/.0945/1 20
1. Decorative arts - Italy - Alps, Italian - History - 20th
century. 2. Handicraft - Italy - Alps, Italian - History -
20th century. I. Arneodo, Annéto. II. Rotary

International. 203o Distretto. III. Title: Artisanat
traditionnel des Alpes occidentales italiannes.
NK960.A536 A78 1990

**Artisanat traditionnel des Alpes occidentales
italiennes.** Artigianato di tradizione nelle Alpi
occidentali italiane . Ivrea, Italy , c1990. 305
p. : DDC 745/.0945/1 20
NK960.A536 A78 1990

**ARTISANS - ECONOMIC CONDITIONS -
CONGRESSES.**
Artistes, artisans et production artistique au
Moyen Age . Paris , 1986-1990. 3 v. : ISBN
2-7084-0302-8 (v. 1) : DDC 338.4/77/094 19
N5961 .A78 1986   NYPL [3-MAK 87-2303]

ARTISANS - HEALTH AND HYGIENE.
Rossol, Monona. The artist's complete health
and safety guide /. New York , Cincinnati,
OH , c1990. 328 p. : ISBN 0-927629-10-0
                NYPL [MBN 91-4596]

**ARTISANS - INDIA - ORISSA - ECONOMIC
CONDITIONS.**
Arts and artisans of Orissa /. Bhubaneswar
[1981?] 106 p. ; DDC 338.4/77/095413 19
N7307.O74 A77 1981
                NYPL [3-MNE 90-5470]

**ARTISANS - INDIA - ORISSA - SOCIAL
CONDITIONS.**
Arts and artisans of Orissa /. Bhubaneswar
[1981?] 106 p. ; DDC 338.4/77/095413 19
N7307.O74 A77 1981
                NYPL [3-MNE 90-5470]

**ARTISANS - NEW YORK (N.Y.) -
DIRECTORIES.**
The Restoration directory . New York, NY ,
1990. 110 p. :   NYPL [MQWO 91-6663]

Artist as apolitical sensor . Fekner, John.
Brookville, N.Y. , 1990. 28 p. :
                NYPL [3-MAMT 91-5026]

**Artist associations and exhibition spaces, art
commissions, museum curators & art critics.**
Directory of artist associations and exhibition
spaces, art commissions, museum curators & art
critics /. Renaissance, CA , c1990. 208 p. ;
ISBN 0-940899-14-0
                NYPL [MAV 91-6690]

**ARTIST COLONIES - FRANCE - AUVERS-
SUR-OISE - EXHIBITIONS.**
Van Gogh et les peintres d'Auvers-sur-Oise .
[Paris] , 1954. xl, 100 p., xxxii p. of plates :
N6847.5.I4 V36 1954

**ARTIST COLONIES - ITALY -
CASTIGLIONCELLO.**
Dini, Piero. I macchiaioli e la scuola di
Castiglioncello /. [Rosignano Marittimo]
[1990] 217 p. :
ND617.5.M3 D57 1990

ARTIST - IRAN - BIOGRAPHY.
Yädmän-i Suhräb Sipihri /. [Tehran] , 1367
[1989] 399 p. :
N7289.S5 Y36 1989

The artist observed . Gruen, John. Chicago, IL ,
c1991. p. cm. ISBN 1-556-52103-0 : DDC
709/.2/2 B 20
N6490 .G725 1991

**Artist-Run Galleries, Association of. see
Association of Artist-Run Galleries.**

Un Artista etrusco e il suo mondo : il pittore di
Micali / [catalogo a cura di Maria Antonitta
Rizzo ; testi di M. Cristofani ... et al. ;
traduzioni dall'inglese, F. Gilotta]. Roma : De
Luca, 1988. 112 p., [8] p. of plates : ill. (some
col.) ; 27 cm. (Studi di archeologia . 5) Catalog of an
exhibition held at the Museo nazionale etrusco di Villa
Giulia, Mar. 22-June 30, 1988; and the Civiche raccolte
archeologiche e numismatiche, Dec. 1988. At head of
title: Soprintendenza archeologica per l'Etruria
meridionale, British School at Rome. Preface in English.
Includes bibliographical references. ISBN
88-7813-131-8
1. Micali Painter - Exhibitions. 2. Vases, Black-figured -
Italy - Etruria - Exhibitions. 3. Vase-painting,
Etruscan - Italy - Exhibitions. 4. Vases, Etruscan -
Italy - Exhibitions. I. Rizzo, Maria Antonietta. II.
Civiche raccolte numismatiche di Milano. III. Italy.
Soprintendenza archeologica per l'Etruria meridionale.
IV. Museo nazionale di Villa Giulia. V. British School
at Rome. VI. Series. VII. Series: Studi di archeologia
(Italy. Soprintendenza archeologica per l'Etruria
meridionale) , 5.   NYPL [3-MPEK 90-12767]

Un artista ferrarese del legno, Ernesto Maldarelli (1850-1930) /. Maldarelli, Ernesto, 1850-1930. Ferrara , c1989. 107 p. :
NYPL [3-MOC 90-12376]

Artistas de Guanajuato.
Gallardo, Jesús, 1931- Cuaderno de dibujos /. Guanajuato, Gto. [i.e. Guanajuato, Mexico] , 1989. 112 p. :   ISBN 968-617-017-0   DDC 741.972 20
NC146.G35 A4 1989

L'artiste /. Bertrand, Pierre. Montréal, Québec , c1985. 193 p. ;   ISBN 2-89006-233-3   DDC 701 19
N70 .B466 1985   *NYPL [3-MAS 90-12750]*

Artistes, artisans et production artistique au Moyen Age : colloque international, Centre national de la recherche scientifique, Université de Rennes II, Haute-Bretagne, 2-6 mai 1983 / organisé et édité par Xavier Barral i Altet. Paris : Picard, 1986-1990. 3 v. : ill. ; 24 cm. French, English, Spanish, and Catalan. Includes index (v. 3). Includes bibliographical references. CONTENTS. - v. 1. Les hommes -- v. 2. Commande et travail -- v. 3. Fabrication et comsummation de l'œuvre.   ISBN 2-7084-0302-8 (v. 1) :   DDC 338.4/77/094 19
1. Art, Medieval - Congresses. 2. Artists - Economic conditions - Congresses. 3. Artisans - Economic conditions - Congresses. I. Barral i Altet. Xavier.
N5961 .A78 1986   *NYPL [3-MAK 87-2303]*

Artistes au service de la patrie en danger. L'Enrôlement des volontaires de 1792 . Beauvais [1989] 258 p. :   ISBN 2-901290-05-1
NYPL [3-MCO C87 91-5550]

Artistes étrangers à Pont-Aven, Concarneau et autres lieux de Bretagne / cet ouvrage collectif a été réalisé sous la direction de Denise Delouche. [Rennes] : Presses universitaires de Rennes 2, [1989] 233 p. : ill. (some col.), map ; 22 x 25 cm. (Arts de l'Ouest, 0220-2220) Includes bibliographical references and indexes.   ISBN 2-86847-026-2
1. Art, Modern - 19th century - Europe. 2. Art, Modern - 20th century - Europe. 3. Artists - Europe. 4. Artists - France - Brittany. I. Delouche, Denise. II. Series.   *NYPL [3-MAM 91-3261]*

Artistes finlandais en Bretagne, 1880-1890 : Musée de Pont-Aven, 1er juillet-26 septembre 1990, Institut finlandais, Paris, 11 octobre-11 novembre 1990. Pont-Aven : Le Musée, [1990?] 64 p. : ill. ; 30 cm.
1. Art, Finnish - Exhibitions. I. Musée de Pont-Aven.
NYPL [3-MAM+ 90-13360]

Artistes, patriciens et confréries . Bresc-Bautier, Geneviève. Roma , 1979. xviii, 315 p., [15] leaves of plates :
N6921.P34 B73   *NYPL [3-MAMC 81-374]*

Artisti italiani contemporanei, 1956-1986 / [mostra a cura di Francesca Barnabò e Paolo Sprovieri]. 1a ed. Venezia : Cataloghi Marsilio, 1986. 61 p. : ill. (some col.) ; 24 cm.   ISBN 88-7693-024-8   DDC 709/.45/0740531 19
1. Art, Italian - Exhibitions. 2. Art, Modern - 20th century - Italy - Exhibitions. I. Barnabò, Francesca. II. Sprovieri, Paolo.
N6918 .A819 1986
NYPL [3-MAMC 90-12531]

Artisti russi contemporanei : Erik Bulatov ... [et al.] / mostra e catalogo, Amnon Barzel, Claudia Jolles = Contemporary Russian artists : Erik Bulatov ... [et al.] / exhibition and catalog, Amnon Barzel, Claudia Jolles. Prato : Centro per l'arte contemporanea Luigi Pecci, Museo d'arte contemporanea, c1990. 208 p. : ill. (some col.), ports. ; 27 cm. (Catalogo . 6) English and Italian. Catalog of an exhibition held Feb. 10-May 14, 1990 at the Museo d'arte contemporanea Luigi Pecci, Prato. Includes writings by the artists. Includes bibliographical references (p. 208)   ISBN 88-85191-01-0
1. Art, Russian - Exhibitions. 2. Art, Modern - 20th century - Russian S.F.S.R. - Exhibitions. I. Bulatov, Érik, 1933-. II. Barzel, Amnon. III. Jolles, Claudia. IV. Museo d'arte contemporanea Prato. V. Title. VI. Title: Contemporary Russian artists. VII. Series: Cataloghi (Prato, Italy) , 6.   *NYPL [3-MAM 90-10469]*

Artisti subalpini in Roma nei secoli XV, XVI e XVII. Bertolotti, Antonino, 1836-1893. Bologna [1965] 284 p.   *NYPL [3-MAMC 91-304]*

ARTISTIC ANATOMY. see ANATOMY, ARTISTIC.

Artistic and monumental guide-book. Pisa through the centuries. Bologna, Italy , c1989. 93 p. :   DDC 709/.45/55 20
N6921.P6 P57 1989

ARTISTIC PHOTOGRAPHY. see PHOTOGRAPHY, ARTISTIC.

ARTISTS.
D'Arcy Galleries (New York, N.Y.) Surrealist intrusion in the enchanters' domain. New York, [1960] 124 p.   DDC 759.06
ND1265 .D353   *NYPL [3-MAL 90-7006]*

ARTISTS, AFRO-AMERICAN. see AFRO-AMERICAN ARTISTS.

Artists & galleries of Australia /. Germaine, Max, 1914- Roseville, NSW, Australia , c1990. 2 v. (xii, 832 p.) :   ISBN 976-8097-02-7
NYPL [MAO+ 91-2667]

Artists and galleries of Australia. Germaine, Max, 1914- Artists & galleries of Australia /. Roseville, NSW, Australia , c1990. 2 v. (xii, 832 p.) :   ISBN 976-8097-02-7
NYPL [MAO+ 91-2667]

ARTISTS AND MUSEUMS - EXHIBITIONS.
Theatergarden Bestiarium . Cambridge, Mass. , Long Island City, N.Y. , c1990. 176 p. :   ISBN 0-262-04105-7   DDC 701/.03 20
N6494.E6 T4 1990
NYPL [3-MAL+ 90-12503]

ARTISTS AND MUSEUMS - UNITED STATES.
Breaking down the boundaries . Seattle, Wash. , c1989. 31 p. :   ISBN 0-935558-24-1   DDC 707/.5 20
N72.A77 B74 1909
NYPL [3-MAMT+ 90-12629]

ARTISTS AND PATRONS - GREAT BRITAIN.
Lang, Gladys Engel. Etched in memory . Chapel Hill , 1990. xviii, 437 p., [46] p. of plates :   ISBN 0-8078-1908-5 (alk. paper)   DDC 767/.2/094209034 20
NE2043.25 .L36 1990
NYPL [MDN 90-13667]

ARTISTS AND PATRONS - INDIA - BENGAL.
Chatterjee, Ratnabali, 1941- From the karkhana to the studio . New Delhi , 1990. xi, 144 p., [12] p. of plates :   ISBN 81-85016-28-3 :   DDC 701/.03/095414 20
N72.S6 C35 1990   *NYPL [3-MAF 91-6048]*

ARTISTS AND PATRONS - ITALY - FLORENCE.
Spencer, John R. (John Richard) Andrea del Castagno and his patrons /. Durham , 1991. p. cm.   ISBN 0-8223-1150-X   DDC 759.5 20
ND623.C47 S64 1991

ARTISTS AND PATRONS - UNITED STATES.
Breaking down the boundaries . Seattle, Wash. , c1989. 31 p. :   ISBN 0-935558-24-1   DDC 707/.5 20
N72.A77 B74 1909
NYPL [3-MAMT+ 90-12629]

Lang, Gladys Engel. Etched in memory . Chapel Hill , 1990. xviii, 437 p., [46] p. of plates :   ISBN 0-8078-1908-5 (alk. paper)   DDC 767/.2/094209034 20
NE2043.25 .L36 1990
NYPL [MDN 90-13667]

Artists and warfare in the Renaissance /. Hale, J. R. (John Rigby), 1923- New Haven , 1990. ix, 278 p. :   ISBN 0-300-04840-8   DDC 760/.09/024 20
N6370 .H25 1990   *NYPL [3-MAL 91-6322]*

ARTISTS - ANECDOTES.
Connor, Alexandra. Rembrandt's monkey and other tales from the secret lives of the great artists /. New York , 1991. p. cm.   ISBN 0-312-06004-1   DDC 709/.2/2 20
N7460 .C66 1991

Hall, Donald, 1928- Anecdotes of modern art . New York , 1990. xix, 377 p. ;   ISBN 0-19-503813-4 (alk. paper) :   DDC 709.04 20
N6447 .H34 1990   *NYPL [3-MAL 90-11303]*

ARTISTS - ARMENIAN S.S.R. - CATALOGS.
Hayastani eritasard nkarich'nerĕ . Erevan , 1987. 166 p. :
N7292.6 .H37 1987

ARTISTS AS AUTHORS - AUSTRIA.
Van Zon, Gabriele, 1937- Word and picture . New York , 1991. p. cm.   ISBN 0-8204-1475-1   DDC 700/.92 20
NX548.Z9 K838 1991

ARTISTS AS TEACHERS - MINNESOTA - MINNEAPOLIS.
Petheo, Bela, 1934- Mission and commissions . Collegeville, Minn. , 1991. p. cm.   DDC 759.36 20
ND511.5.K6 P48 1991

ARTISTS - AUSTRALIA - BIOGRAPHY.
Germaine, Max, 1914- Artists & galleries of Australia /. Roseville, NSW, Australia , c1990. 2 v. (xii, 832 p.) :   ISBN 976-8097-02-7
NYPL [MAO+ 91-2667]

ARTISTS - AUSTRIA - BIOGRAPHY.
Kallir, Jane. Egon Schiele, the complete works . New York , 1990. 687 p. :   ISBN 0-8109-3802-2   DDC 709/.2 B 20
N6811.5.S34 K35 1990
NYPL [MCK+ S332 91-5491]

Schweiger, Werner J., 1949- Der junge Kokoschka . Wien , c1983. 272 p. :   ISBN 3-85447-035-5   DDC 760/.092/4 B 19
N6811.5.K56 S39 1983
NYPL [3-MCZ+ K79 91-4016]

Seibert, Ingrit. Die Schwierigen . Wien , c1986. 199 p. :   ISBN 3-7046-0053-9
NX548.Z8 S45 1986

ARTISTS - AUSTRIA - VIENNA - BIOGRAPHY.
Fischer, Wolfgang Georg, 1933- [Gustav Klimt und Emilie Flöge. English.] Klimt and Emilie . Woodstock, N.Y. , 1992. p. cm.   ISBN 0-87951-451-5 :   DDC 709/.2 B 20
N6811.5.K55 F513 1992

ARTISTS - BANAT - BIOGRAPHY.
Banater Künstler in der Bundesrepublik Deutschland . Berlin , 1988. 60 p. :   ISBN 3-922131-57-8
N6868 .B33 1988
NYPL [3-MAMG 91-6298]

ARTISTS - BELGIUM.
Bertrand, Olivier. Belgian artists in the world's salerooms, 1988-1989 /. Brussels , 1989. xxxv, 334 p. :   *NYPL [3-MAZ 91-5792]*

ARTISTS - BELGIUM - BIOGRAPHY - DICTIONARIES.
Dictionnaire biographique illustré des artistes en Belgique depuis 1830. [Bruxelles] , 1987. 416 p., [31] p. of plates :
NYPL [3-MAO 91-4886]

ARTISTS - BIOGRAPHY.
Connor, Alexandra. The wrong side of the canvas /. London , 1989. 200 p. :   ISBN 0-86051-587-7 :   DDC 759 B 20
N40 .C65 1989   *NYPL [MC 90-4306]*

World artists 1980-1990 . New York , 1991. p. cm.   ISBN 0-8242-0827-7   DDC 709/.2/2 B 20
N6489 .W67 1991

ARTISTS - BIOGRAPHY - DICTIONARIES.
Allgemeines Künstlerlexikon . Leipzig , 1983- v. ;   ISBN 3-363-00114-2 (v. 1)   DDC 709/.2/2 B 19
N40 .A63 1983   *NYPL [MAO 85-1702]*

Cortanze, Gérard de. Le monde du surréalisme /. Paris , c1991. 182 p. :   ISBN 2-85199-550-2   DDC 700 20
NX456.5.S8 C67 1991

De Piro, Nicholas, 1941- The international dictionary of artists who painted Malta /. Valletta, Malta , 1988. 207 p. :   ISBN 1-87168-400-5   DDC 758/.994585 20
N8213 .D4 1988

Harrap's illustrated dictionary of art & artists. Bromley, Kent , 1990. 589 p. :   ISBN 0-245-54692-8   *NYPL [MAO 91-4216]*

International dictionary of art and artists /. Chicago , c1990. 2 v. :   ISBN 1-558-62000-1 (v. [1])   *NYPL [MAO 90-11519]*

ARTISTS - BIOGRAPHY - HISTORY AND CRITICISM.
Hughes, Robert, 1936- Nothing if not critical . New York , 1990. xii, 429 p. ;   ISBN 0-394-58026-5 :   DDC 709 20
N7445.2 .H83 1990
NYPL [3-MAN 90-13402]

Taboo and totem . New York , 1991. p. cm.
ISBN 0-8419-1249-1 (cloth)   DDC 701/.05 20
N72.P74 T33 1991

ARTISTS - BIOGRAPHY - INDEXES.
Gorenflo, Roger M. Verzeichnis der bildenden
Künstler von 1880 bis heute . Rüsselsheim ,
1988. 3 v. (989 p.) ;   ISBN 3-926759-00-3 (set)
NYPL [3-MAO 90-10802]

**ARTISTS, BLACK - BIOGRAPHY -
JUVENILE LITERATURE.**
Historic Blacks in the arts /. Chicago, IL ,
c1990. p. cm.   ISBN 0-922162-58-1 :   DDC
700/.92/2 B 20
NX164.B55 H57 1990

Artists' books : a critical anthology and
sourcebook / edited by Joan Lyons. Rochester,
N.Y. : Visual Studies Workshop Press ; Layton,
Utah : Distributed by G.M. Smith, Peregrine
Smith Books, 1985. 269 p. : ill. ; 24 cm. Includes
bibliographies and index. ISBN 0-89822-041-6 DDC
700/.9/04 19
I. Lyons, Joan, 1937-.
N7433.3 .A75 1985   ***NYPL [MDTT 85-2116]***

ARTISTS' BOOKS - AUSTRIA.
Strobl, Ingeborg, 1949- Ingeborg Strobl, oder,
Mit den kleinen Wölfen heulen. St. Gallen ,
1989. 1 v. (unpaged) :   ISBN 3-909090-01-X
NYPL [MEMZ 91-3982]

ARTISTS' BOOKS - CANADA.
Clark, Douglas. Articles of faith /. Toronto ,
c1990. 18 [i.e. 46] p. :   ISBN 0-88910-343-7 :
DDC 709/.2 20
NYPL [MEMZ+ 91-7485]

Artists' Books Collection (Library of Congress)
Cortot, Jean. Morand--memorandum /. 1989.
[13] p. :   DDC 700/.92 20
N7433.4.C66 A4 1989

ARTISTS' BOOKS - ENGLAND.
D'Arbeloff, Natalie. Pater Noster. [London] ,
1988. [12] leaves ;   DDC 700/.92 20
N7433.4.D35 A4 1988

ARTISTS' BOOKS - EXHIBITIONS.
Artists of the book 1988 . Boston, Mass. ,
c1988. 40 p. :   ISBN 0-934552-53-3
NYPL [MDTT 91-4772]

Collaborations and connections . Tempe, Ariz. ,
c1990. viii, 36 p. :   ***NYPL [MDTT 91-4768]***

Mœglin-Delcroix, Anne. Livres d'artistes /.
Paris , c1985. 159 p. :   ISBN 2-7335-0085-6
NYPL [MDT 86-3500]

Stein, Donna. Contemporary illustrated books .
New York, N.Y. , c1989. 72 p. :   ISBN
0-916365-00-X   ***NYPL [MDTT+ 91-6216]***

Volùmina /. [Senigallia] , 1990. 45 p. :
NYPL [MDTT 91-7590]

ARTISTS' BOOKS - FRANCE.
Cortot, Jean. Morand--memorandum /. 1989.
[13] p. :   DDC 700/.92 20
N7433.4.C66 A4 1989

Moucha, Miloslav, 1942- Journal impersonal,
1968-1972 /. Paris [between 1972 and 1974] 1
v. (unpaged) :   ***NYPL [MEMZ 91-567]***

Parant, Jean Luc, 1944- Le bouleversement /.
Paris , c1990. 111 p. :   ISBN 2-7291-0537-9 :
DDC 700/.92 20
N7433.4.P32 A4 1990

ARTISTS' BOOKS - GERMANY.
Kiefer, Anselm, 1945- [Anselm Kiefer Bücher,
1969-1990. English.] The books of Anselm
Kiefer, 1969-1990 /. New York, N.Y. , 1991. p.
cm. ISBN 0-8076-1261-8 DDC 709/.2 20
N7333.4.K54 A4 1991

**ARTIST'S BOOKS - GERMANY -
EXHIBITIONS.**
Kiefer, Anselm, 1945- Anselm Kiefer, Bücher
1969-1990 . [Stuttgart] , c1990. 378 p. :   ISBN
3-89322-200-6
NYPL [MDG+ (Kiefer) 91-5802]

ARTISTS' BOOKS - ITALY - CATALOGS.
Archivio Della Grazia di nuova scrittura /.
Milano , 1989. 96 p., [39] p. of plates :
N7433.35.I8 A73 1989

**ARTISTS' BOOKS - PRIVATE
COLLECTIONS - ITALY - MILAN -
CATALOGS.**
Archivio Della Grazia di nuova scrittura /.
Milano , 1989. 96 p., [39] p. of plates :
N7433.35.I8 A73 1989

**ARTISTS' BOOKS - QUÉBEC (PROVINCE) -
MONTRÉAL.**
De humani corporis fabrica. Montréal, Québec,
Canada , 1988, c1985-c1986. 3 v. in 1 case :
DDC 700/.92/271428 20
N7433.35.C2 D4 1988
NYPL [MEMZ 90-11163]

ARTISTS' BOOKS - SPECIMENS.
Woods, Lebbeus. AEON /. [New York, N.Y.?]
1979. [4] p. :   ***NYPL [MEMZ 88-2418]***

Woods, Lebbeus. Odysseus wall drawing /.
New York City , c1979. [16] p. :
NYPL [MEMZ 88-2417]

ARTISTS' BOOKS - UNITED STATES.
Beard, Mark. Utah reader /. New York , 1986.
[34] leaves :   DDC 700/.92 20
N7433.4.B4 A4 1986b

De Lory, Peter. The wild and the innocent /.
Riverside, Calif. , 1987. [46] p. :   ISBN
0-9619038-2-1
NYPL [MFX (De Lory) 90-11264]

Ely, Timothy. Totem /. 1989. [24] p. :   DDC
700/.92 20
N7433.4.E35 A4 1989

Horton, David. Luminous perceptions /. [New
Milford, N.Y.] [1988] 1 strip ;   DDC 709/.2 20
N7433.4.H658 A4 1988

Lovett, Ann. Palimpsest /. Rochester, NY ,
1990. [47] p. :   ISBN 0-89822-064-5
NYPL [MEMZ 91-3507]

Osborn, Kevin, 1951- Vector rev /. [Arlington,
Va. , 1983] [288] p. ;   DDC 709/.2 20
N7433.4.O83 A4 1983

Porter, Bern, 1911- Sweet end /. Brunswick,
Me. , c1989. 1 v. (unpaged) :   ISBN
0-937966-27-4 (pbk.)
NYPL [MEMZ 89-27403]

Scholder, Fritz, 1937- Tarot /. Tempe, Ariz. ,
c1987. 6 cards :   DDC 709/.2 20
N7433.4.S36 A4 1987

Small, Deborah, 1948- 1492 . New York,
N.Y. , 1991. p. cm.   ISBN 0-85345-836-7 :   DDC
700/.92 20
N7433.4.S43 A4 1991

Walker, Anne. On Cape Ann. [Paris , 1989] 1
strip :   DDC 700/.92 20
N7433.4.W33 A4 1989

Wallenstein, Ellen. A game of chess /. [S.l.] ,
c1986. 1 folded sheet ([12] p.) :
NYPL [MEMZ 91-3563]

**ARTISTS' BOOKS - UNITED STATES -
EXHIBITIONS.**
Gerstler, Amy. Past lives /. Santa Monica,
Calif. , c1989. 40 p. :   ISBN 0-929335-01-5 DDC
700/.92 20
N7433.4.G45 A4 1989

ARTISTS - BRAZIL - BIOGRAPHY.
Oswald, Carlos, 1882-1971. Como me tornei
pintor . Petrópolis, R.J. , 1957. 254 p. :
N6659.O85 A2 1957

**ARTISTS - BRAZIL - PERNAMBUCO -
BIOGRAPHY.**
Catálogo pernambucano de arte .
Recife-PE-Brasil , c1987. 1 v. (unpaged) :
DDC 709/.2/28134 B 20
N6656.P47 C38 1987

ARTISTS, BRITISH - BIOGRAPHY.
Berlin, Sven. Pride of the peacock. London,
1972. 255 p., leaf.   ISBN 0-8021-1675-8 DDC
759.2
NX93.B4 A36
NYPL [3-MCV B515 90-6356]

**ARTISTS - BULGARIA - KIŪSTENDIL -
BIOGRAPHY.**
30 godini Druzhestvo na
khudozhnitsite--Kiūstendil, 1959-1989 /. [S.l. ,
1989] (Sofiia : Ofsetgrafik) 47 p. :
N7191.K58 A15 1989

ARTISTS - BURUNDI - BIOGRAPHY.
Sendegeya, Pierre-Claver, 1940- Anthologie des
sculpteurs et peintres burundais contemporains
/. Paris , c1989. 109 p. :   ISBN 2-288-82091-8
IN PROCESS (ONLINE)
NYPL [3-MADF+ 91-7959]

ARTISTS - CALIFORNIA.
Coran, James L. If pictures could talk .
Oakland, Calif. , c1989. 382 p. :   ISBN

0-938842-07-2
NYPL [3-MCW+ 90-12851]

**ARTISTS - CALIFORNIA - LOS ANGELES -
BIOGRAPHY.**
L.A. times . Boise, Idaho , c1991. p. cm.   DDC
709/.794/9407479628 20
N6535.L6 L188 1991

ARTISTS - COLOMBIA - BIOGRAPHY.
Mejía de Millán, Beatriz Amelia. El arte
colombiano en el siglo XX /. Pereira,
Colombia , 1988. 155 p. :   DDC 709/.861/0904
20
N6675 .M45 1988

Panesso, Fausto, 1953- Arte y parte . [Bogotá,
Colombia?] [1990- v. <1 > :
N6675 .P35 1990

The artist's complete guide to facial expression /.
Faigin, Gary, 1950- New York , 1990. 287, [1]
p. :   ISBN 0-8230-1628-5 :   DDC 704.9/42 20
N7573.3 .F35 1990

The artist's complete health and safety guide /.
Rossol, Monona. New York , Cincinnati, OH ,
c1990. 328 p. :   ISBN 0-927629-10-0
NYPL [MBN 91-4596]

ARTISTS' CONTRACTS - UNITED STATES.
The Artist's friendly legal guide /. Cincinnati,
Ohio , c1991. 142 p. :   ISBN 0-89134-365-2
(pbk.) :   DDC 346.7304/82 347.306482 20
KF390.A7 A785 1991   ***NYPL [MA 91-7466]***

**ARTISTS - CZECHOSLOVAKIA - SLOVAK
REPUBLIC - BIOGRAPHY.**
Kamenistý, Ján. Ako kopú múzy . Bratislava ,
1990. 263 p. :   ISBN 80-221-0036-6 :
NX571.C92 S54 1990

**ARTISTS - CZECHOSLOVAKIA - SLOVAK
REPUBLIC - INTERVIEWS.**
Kamenistý, Ján. Ako kopú múzy . Bratislava ,
1990. 263 p. :   ISBN 80-221-0036-6 :
NX571.C92 S54 1990

ARTISTS - DENMARK - BIOGRAPHY.
Hiort, Esbjørn. Arkitekten Finn Juhl .
København , 1990. 143, [1] p. :   ISBN
87-7407-093-2 :
N7023.J84 H5 1990

**ARTISTS - DOMINICAN REPUBLIC -
BIOGRAPHY.**
Arte contemporáneo dominicano. [Santo
Domingo, Dominican Republic?] [1987?] [72]
p. ;
N6615.D6 A77 1987

**ARTISTS - ECONOMIC CONDITIONS -
CONGRESSES.**
Artistes, artisans et production artistique au
Moyen Age . Paris , 1986-1990. 3 v. :   ISBN
2-7084-0302-8 (v. 1)   DDC 338.4/77/094 19
N5961 .A78 1986   ***NYPL [3-MAK 87-2303]***

ARTISTS - ECUADOR - BIOGRAPHY.
100 artistas del Ecuador /. Quito , 1990. 285
p. :   DDC 709/.2/2866 B 20
N6985 .A15 1990

ARTISTS - ENGLAND - BIOGRAPHY.
Delaney, J. G. Paul. Charles Ricketts . Oxford,
England , New York, NY , 1990. xxiii, 429 p. :
ISBN 0-19-817212-5 :   DDC 709/.2/4 B 19
N6797.R5 D45 1989
NYPL [3-MCV R55 90-11599]

Heron, Roy. The sporting art of Cecil Aldin /.
London , 1990. 126 p., [20] p. of plates :   ISBN
0-948253-50-9 :   DDC 760.092 20
NC242.A4   ***NYPL [3-MCV A36 91-5523]***

Paulson, Ronald. Hogarth /. New Brunswick ,
c1991- v. <1- > :   ISBN 0-8135-1694-3 (v. 1)
DDC 760/.092 B 20
N6797.H6 P38 1991

Poulson, Christine. William Morris /. London ,
c1989. 128 p. :   ISBN 1-85076-183-3 :   DDC 709.2
20
PR5083   ***NYPL [3-MLH 90-11508]***

**ARTISTS - ENGLAND - PSYCHOLOGY -
CONGRESSES.**
L'Artiste, témoin de son temps (?) .
Aix-en-Provence , 1990. xiv, 168 p. ;   ISBN
2-85399-238-1 :   DDC 700/.942 20
NX543 .A83 1990

**ARTISTS - ENGLAND - SUTTON (LONDON)
- BIOGRAPHY - DICTIONARIES.**
Beasley, Maureen. Five centuries of artists in
Sutton . Sutton, Surrey , 1989. 144 p. :   ISBN

0-907335-19-5　DDC 709/.2/242192 B 20
N6770 .B43 1989

ARTISTS - ESTONIA - BIOGRAPHY.
Kirme, Kaalu. Jaan Koorti päevaraamat /.
Tallinn , 1989. 320 p., [48] p. of plates :
N6999.K588 K5 1989

Peil, Voldemar. Lavakujunduse sünd /. Tallinn ,
1989. 96 p., [64] p. of plates :
N6999.P4 A2 1989

ARTISTS - EUROPE.
Artistes étrangers à Pont-Aven, Concarneau et
autres lieux de Bretagne /. [Rennes] [1989]
233 p. :　ISBN 2-86847-026-2
　　　　　　NYPL [3-MAM 91-3261]

**ARTISTS - EUROPE - JUVENILE
LITERATURE.**
Giants of the arts . New York , 1991. p. cm.
　ISBN 1-85435-414-0 :　DDC 700/.92/24 20
NX633 .G53 1991

**ARTISTS, EXPATRIATE - BERLIN
(GERMANY)**
Russen in Berlin . Leipzig , 1990. xv, 614 p. :
　ISBN 3-379-00119-8
NX556.A1 R86 1990

**ARTISTS, EXPATRIATE - SOUTHERN
STATES - EXHIBITIONS.**
Southern exposure . New York, NY , c1985. 55
p. :　ISBN 0-932075-02-9 (pbk.)　DDC
　709/.75/07401471 19
N6520 .S67 1985
　　　　　　NYPL [3-MAMT 90-12368]

The artist's eye /. Shorr, Harriet. New York ,
1990. 144 p. :　ISBN 0-8230-0299-3 :　DDC 751.45
　20
ND1500 .S49 1990
　　　　　　NYPL [3-MCX S559 90-12495]

The artist's eye, Victor Pasmore . Pasmore,
Victor, 1908- London , 1990. 56 p. ;　ISBN
　0-947645-76-4　DDC 759.94/074/42132 20
ND454 .P37 1990

**ARTISTS - FRANCE - ALSACE -
BIOGRAPHY - DICTIONARIES.**
Bauer, A. (Alice) Répertoire des artistes
d'Alsace des dix-neuvième et vingtième siècles .
Strasbourg , 1984-1991. 6 v. :　ISBN
　2-85369-036-9 (set)　DDC 709/.2/2 B 19
N6849.A4 B3 1984　　*NYPL [MAO 86-2104]*

ARTISTS - FRANCE - BIOGRAPHY.
Bernier, Rosamond. Matisse, Picasso, Miró .
New York , 1991. p. cm.　ISBN 0-394-58670-0
　DDC 709/.2/244 B 20
N6848 .B38 1991

Daix, Pierre. Picasso /. [Paris] , c1990. 159, [1]
p. :　ISBN 2-85108-654-5 :　DDC 709/.2 B 20
N6853.P5 D26 1990

Franzke, Andreas. Dubuffet /. Köln , c1990.
207 p. :　ISBN 3-7701-2523-1　DDC 709/.2 20
N6853.D78 F72 1990

Hahn, Otto. Daniel Spoerri /. Paris , c1990.
190 p. :　ISBN 2-08-012140-5 :　DDC 709/.2 20
N6853.S6 H34 1990

Higonnet, Anne, 1959- Berthe Morisot, une
biographie /] Paris , c1989. 236 p., [16] p. of
plates :　ISBN 2-87660-048-7 (cover):
　　　　　　NYPL [3-MCO M86 90-13217]

Richardson, John. A life of Picasso /. New
York , c1991- v. :　ISBN 0-394-53192-2 (v. 1) :
　DDC 709/.2 B 20
N6853.P5 R56 1990
　　　　　　NYPL [3-MCQ P58 91-667]

**ARTISTS - FRANCE - BIOGRAPHY -
JUVENILE LITERATURE.**
Beardsley, John. Pablo Picasso /. New York ,
1991. p. cm.　ISBN 0-8109-3713-1　DDC 709/.2 B
　20
N6853.P5 B43 1991

Rodari, Florian. [Dimanche avec Picasso.
English.] A weekend with Picasso /. New
York , 1991. p. cm.　ISBN 0-8478-1437-8　DDC
　709/.2 20
N6853.P3 R5713 1991

ARTISTS - FRANCE - BRITTANY.
Artistes étrangers à Pont-Aven, Concarneau et
autres lieux de Bretagne /. [Rennes] [1989]
233 p. :　ISBN 2-86847-026-2
　　　　　　NYPL [3-MAM 91-3261]

ARTISTS - FRANCE - CORRESPONDENCE.
Masson, André 1896- Les années surréalistes .

Paris , c1990. 574 p., 52 p. of plates :　ISBN
　2-7377-0181-3
　　　　　　NYPL [3-MCO M42 90-11041]

Toulouse-Lautrec, Henri de, 1864-1901.
[Correspondence. English.] The letters of Henri
de Toulouse-Lautrec /. Oxford [England] , New
York , c1990. p. cm.　ISBN 0-19-817214-1 :
　DDC 760/.092 B 20
N6853.T6 A3 1990

ARTISTS - FRANCE - INTERVIEWS.
Lamarche-Vadel, Bernard, 1949- Villeglé .
Paris , c1990. 137 p. :　ISBN 2-86234-056-1
　DDC 760 20
N6853.V493 A35 1990

Parant, Jean Luc, 1944- Le bouleversement /.
Paris , c1990. 111 p. :　ISBN 2-7291-0537-9 :
　DDC 700/.92 20
N7433.4.P32 A4 1990

**ARTISTS - FRANCE - PARIS -
EXHIBITIONS.**
Marlais, Michael Andrew. Americans and
Paris . Waterville, Me. , c1990. 62 p. :　DDC
　759.13/074/7416 20
N6510 .M27 1990
　　　　　　NYPL [3-MAMT 90-13006]

The Artist's friendly legal guide / Floyd
Conner ... [et al.]. Rev. and updated ed.
Cincinnati, Ohio : North Light Books, c1991.
142 p. : forms ; 26 cm. (Artist's market business
series) Includes index.　ISBN 0-89134-365-2 (pbk.) :
　DDC 346.7304/82 347.306482 20
*1. Artists' contracts - United States. 2. Copyright -
Art - United States. 3. Copyright - Moral rights -
United States. 4. Artists - Taxation - Law and
legislation - United States. I. Conner, Floyd, 1951-. II.
Series.*
KF390.A7 A785 1991　　NYPL [MA 91-7466]

**ARTISTS - GERMANY - BERLIN -
BIOGRAPHY.**
Werkstattbesuche bei Künstlern in
Berlin-Wedding /. Berlin , c1989. 2 v. :　ISBN
　3-9801875-9-4 :
N6885 .W46 1989

ARTISTS - GERMANY - BIOGRAPHY.
Bauernfeind, Gustav, 1848-1904. Der
Orientmaler Gustav Bauernfeind, 1848-1904 .
Stuttgart , 1990. xi, 368 p. :　ISBN 3-7762-0319-6
　　　　　　NYPL [3-MCK+ B3385 91-7206]

Corinth, Lovis, 1858-1925. Das Leben Walter
Leistikows . Berlin , 1910. 129 p., [2] leaves of
plates :　DDC 709/.2 B 20
N6888.L362 C67 1910

Johannes-Wüsten-Symposium (1976 : Görlitz,
Dresden, Germany) Protokollband
Johannes-Wüsten-Symposium, Görlitz, 1976, 2.
Oktober /. Görlitz , 1978. 109 p. :
NX550.Z9 W875 1976
　　　　　　NYPL [3-MCK W953 90-13398]

Kleine, Gisela, 1926- Gabriele Münter und
Wassily Kandinsky . Frankfurt am Main , 1990.
813 p., 16 p. of plates :　ISBN 3-458-16090-6
ND588.M83 K5 1990

Mohr, Arno, 1910- Zeit der Kindheit /. Berlin ,
1987. 23 p. :　ISBN 3-358-00754-5　DDC 769.92 B
　20
NE2050.5.M58 A2 1987

Pese, Claus. Franz Marc . Stuttgart , c1989.
224 p. :　ISBN 3-7630-1968-5
　　　　　　NYPL [3-MCK+ M31 91-6787]

Stachelhaus, Heiner. [Joseph Beuys. English.]
Joseph Beuys /. New York , 1991. 223 p. :
　ISBN 1-558-59107-9　DDC 709/.2 B 20
N6888.B463 S7413 1991
　　　　　　NYPL [3-MCK B569 91-6313]

**ARTISTS - GERMANY - BIOGRAPHY -
EXHIBITIONS.**
Nuremberg. Germanisches Nationalmuseum.
Archiv für Bildende Kunst. Dokumente zu
Leben und Werk des Malers Otto Dix .
Nürnberg , 1977. 80 p. :
N6888.D5 A4 1977
　　　　　　NYPL [3-MCK D619 81-446]

**ARTISTS - GERMANY -
CORRESPONDENCE.**
Kirchner, Ernst Ludwig, 1880-1938. Ernst
Ludwig Kirchner . Bern , 1989. 147 p. :　ISBN
　3-85773-022-6
N6888.K45 A3 1989
　　　　　　NYPL [3-MCK K58 90-11101]

Marc, Franz, 1880-1916. [Briefe aus dem Feld.
English.] Letters from the war /. New York ,
1992. p. cm.　ISBN 0-8204-1588-X　DDC 759.3 B
　20
N6888.M34 A3 1992

**ARTISTS - GERMANY - DRESDEN -
BIOGRAPHY.**
Dresden . Dresden , 1990. 684 p. :　ISBN
　3-364-00145-6
N333.G33 D744 1990

**ARTISTS - GERMANY - SOCIETIES, ETC. -
EXHIBITIONS.**
Kunsthalle Bern. Chronik KGBrücke, 1913
[microform] . Bern , 1948. 32 p., [16] leaves of
plates :　　　　　*NYPL [*ZM-202]*

ARTISTS - GERMANY, WEST - BIOGRAPHY.
Franken, Franz Hermann. Hans Meid .
Stuttgart-Bad Cannstatt , c1987. 462 p. :　ISBN
　3-922608-58-2
　　　　　　NYPL [3-MCK+ M4978 90-11755]
Röttger, Friedhelm. Volker Böhringer /.
Stuttgart , c1987. 200 p. :　ISBN 3-608-76244-2
　DDC 759.3 19
N6888.B597 R6 1987
　　　　　　NYPL [3-MCK B6712 88-1458]

**ARTISTS - GERMANY (WEST) -
CORRESPONDENCE.**
Marcks, Gerhard. The letters of Gerhard
Marcks & Marguerite Wildenhain, 1970-1981 .
Ames, Decorah, Iowa , 1991. p. cm.　ISBN
　0-8138-0504-X　DDC 730/.92 B 20
N6888.M344 A3 1991

**ARTISTS - GERMANY (WEST) -
INTERVIEWS.**
Trülzsch, Holger. Le garage de Hegel /.
[Paris] , c1989. 108 p. :　ISBN 2-86234-050-2
　DDC 709/.2 20
N6888.T697 A4 1989

**ARTISTS - GERMANY (WEST) -
WORPSWEDE.**
Boulboullé, Guido. Worpswede . Köln , c1989.
223 p. :　ISBN 3-7701-1847-2
　　　　　　NYPL [3-MAMG 90-12605]
Worpswede . [Lilienthal] , c1989. 254 p. :
　ISBN 3-922516-80-7
　　　　　　NYPL [3-MAMG 91-4485]

**ARTISTS - GERMANY - WORPSWEDE -
BIOGRAPHY.**
Worpswede . [Worpswede] , c1989. 254 p. :
　ISBN 3-922516-80-7　DDC 709/.43/59309034 20
N6867.5.W67 W68 1989

ARTISTS - GREAT BRITAIN - BIOGRAPHY.
Vallance, Aymer, 1862-1943. The art of
William Morris /. New York , 1988. xi, 167,
xxx p. :　ISBN 0-486-25647-2 (pbk.)　DDC 821/.8 B
　19
PR5083 .V3 1988
　　　　　　NYPL [3-MNE+ 90-13076]
Victoria and Albert Museum. Catalogue of
British oil paintings, 1820-1860 /. London ,
1990. xx, 314 p. :　ISBN 0-11-290463-7 :　DDC
　759.2/074 19
　　　　　　NYPL [3-MAVZ+ (London) 90-10927]

**ARTISTS - GREAT BRITAIN - BIOGRAPHY -
DICTIONARIES.**
Waterhouse, Ellis Kirkham, 1905- The
dictionary of British 18th century painters in
oils and crayons /. Woodbridge , 1981. 443 p. :
　ISBN 0-902028-93-6 :　DDC 759.2 B 19
N6766 .W29　　*NYPL [MAO 91-6317]*

**ARTISTS - GREAT BRITAIN -
DICTIONARIES.**
Royal Academy exhibitors 1971-1989 . Calne,
Wiltshire, England , 1989. 546 p. :　ISBN
　0-904722-19-8　　*NYPL [MAO 90-9340]*

**ARTISTS - GREAT BRITAIN -
EXHIBITIONS - DICTIONARIES.**
Royal Academy exhibitors, 1971-1989 .
Wiltshire, England , 1989. 546 p. ;　ISBN
　0-904722-19-8 :　DDC 709/.047/07442132 20
N6768 .R63 1989

ARTISTS - GREECE - INTERVIEWS.
Kallia, Helenē. Thelō na mathō perissotera gia
sas . Athēna [1989?] 445 p. :　ISBN
　960-02-0821-2
NX551.Z8 K34 1989

The artist's guide to using color . Blake, Wendon.
[Color book.] Cincinnati, Ohio , c1992. p. cm.
　ISBN 0-89134-378-4 (hard cover) :　DDC 751.4

20
ND1488 .B55 1992

The artist's handbook of materials and techniques. Mayer, Ralph, 1895- New York [1970] xv, 750 p. ISBN 0-670-13665-4 DDC 751.4
ND1500 .M3 1970   *NYPL [MBN 71-210]*

ARTISTS - HEALTH AND HYGIENE.
Rossol, Monona. The artist's complete health and safety guide /. New York , Cincinnati, OH , c1990. 328 p. : ISBN 0-89134-00-X
   NYPL [MBN 91-4596]

ARTISTS - HONDURAS - BIOGRAPHY.
Fiallos S., Raúl (Fiallos Salgado), 1917- Datos históricos sobre la plástica hondureña /. [Tegucigalpa, Honduras?] c1989 (Tegucigalpa, Honduras, C.A. : Litografía López) 129 p. : DDC 709/.7283 20
N6579 .F5 1989

ARTISTS - HOUSING - UNITED STATES.
Kartes, Cheryl. Creating space . New York, N.Y. , 1991. p. cm. ISBN 0-915400-92-8 DDC 700/.68/2 20
N8520 .K37 1991

ARTISTS - ILLINOIS - CHICAGO - PORTRAITS.
Carroll, Patty. Spirited visions . Urbana , c1991. p. cm. ISBN 0-252-01848-6 (alk. paper) DDC 779/.2/092 20
N6535.C5 C37 1991

ARTISTS' ILLUSTRATED BOOKS.
Iliazd, 1894-1975. Rogelio Lacourière pêcheur de cuivres /. [Paris] , c1968. [46] leaves : DDC 769.9/04 20
NE890 .I45 1968

ARTISTS' ILLUSTRATED BOOKS - EXHIBITIONS.
Das Buch des Künstlers . [Hannover] [1989] 179 p. : DDC 708.3/5954 s 769.9/04/074435954 20
N5070.H3 K4 1989/3 NE890
   NYPL [3-MAW (Hannover) 73-2900 1989/3]

Stein, Donna. Contemporary illustrated books . New York, N.Y. , c1989. 72 p. : ISBN 0-916365-00-X   *NYPL [MDTT+ 91-6216]*

ARTISTS' ILLUSTRATED BOOKS - SPAIN.
Caballero, José, 1916- José Caballero . [Sevilla] [1988?] 1 v. (unpaged) : DDC 769.92 20
NE702.C3 A4 1988

Artists in Snowdonia /. Bogle, James. Talybont , 1990. 84 p. : ISBN 0-86243-222-7 (pbk.)
   NYPL [3-MCT 91-6967]

ARTISTS - INDIA - BIOGRAPHY.
Hore, Somnath, 1921- Tebhaga . Calcutta , 1990. xiii, 61 p. : ISBN 81-7046-078-6
   NYPL [3-MCZ H792 91-4053]

ARTISTS - INDIA - KARNATAKA - BIOGRAPHY.
Veṅkaṭappa, Ke., 1887-1967. K. Venkatappa, 1886-1965. [Bangalore , 1988?] 72 p. :
   NYPL [3-MAF+ 90-10767]

ARTISTS - INDIA - ORISSA - ECONOMIC CONDITIONS.
Arts and artisans of Orissa /. Bhubaneswar [1981?] 106 p. ; DDC 338.4/77/095413 19
N7307.O74 A77 1981
   NYPL [3-MNE 90-5470]

ARTISTS - INDIA - ORISSA - SOCIAL CONDITIONS.
Arts and artisans of Orissa /. Bhubaneswar [1981?] 106 p. ; DDC 338.4/77/095413 19
N7307.O74 A77 1981
   NYPL [3-MNE 90-5470]

ARTISTS - INDONESIA - BIOGRAPHY.
33 profil budayawan Indonesia /. [Jakarta] [1990] vii, 208 p. :
NX579.A1 A13 1990

ARTISTS - INFORMATION SERVICES - UNITED STATES.
Information on artists . New York, NY , c1989. 2 v. (various pagings) ; DDC 331.7/617/00973 20
N58 .I54 1989

ARTISTS, INSANE. see ART AND MENTAL ILLNESS.

ARTISTS - INTERVIEWS.
Bomb . San Francisco , 1992. p. cm. ISBN 0-87286-261-5 ; DDC 700/.9/04 20
NX458 .B66 1992

Gruen, John. The artist observed . Chicago, IL , c1991. p. cm. ISBN 1-556-52103-0 : DDC 709/.2/2 B 20
N6490 .G725 1991

Rhetorical image . New York , c1990. 98 p. : ISBN 0-915557-71-1
   NYPL [3-MAL+ 91-5559]

ARTISTS - ITALY - BIOGRAPHY.
Agnese, Gino. Marinetti . Milano , c1990. 373 p., [16] p. of plates : ISBN 88-7767-094-0 :
N6923.M269 A85 1990

Arte italiana contemporanea /. Firenze [1965?]. 11 v. : DDC 709/.2/2 19
N6918 .A788   *NYPL [3-MAMC+ 88-4656]*

Barolsky, Paul, 1941- Giotto's father and the family of Vasari's lives /. University Park, PA , c1991. p. cm. ISBN 0-271-00762-1 (alk. paper) DDC 709/.2/245 B 20
N6915 .B28 1991

Bramly, Serge, 1949- [Léonard de Vinci. English.] Leonardo . New York , c1991. p. cm. ISBN 0-06-016065-9 : DDC 709/.2 B 20
N6923.L33 B7313 1991

Della Torre, Renato. Vita di Michelangelo . Firenze , 1990. v, 341 p., 16 p. of plates : DDC 700/.92 B 20
N6923.B9 D36 1990
   NYPL [3-MCF B9 91-4624]

Gazzera, Romano, 1906-1985. La rosa di Clarissa /. Milano , c1990. 279 p., [16] p. of plates : ISBN 88-7712-078-9 :
N6923.G394 A2 1990
   NYPL [3-MCF G284 91-5003]

Scribner, Charles. Gianlorenzo Bernini /. New York , 1991. 128 p. : ISBN 0-8109-3111-7 DDC 709/.2 20
N6923.B5 S37 1991
   NYPL [3-MGO+ (Bernini) 91-7243]

Vasari, Giorgio, 1511-1574. [Vite de' più eccellenti architetti, pittori et scultori italiani. English. Selections.] Lives of the artists /. London , New York , 1987. 2 v. ; ISBN 0-14-044500-5 (v. 1)
   NYPL [3-MAMC 88-536]

Vasari, Giorgio, 1511-1574. [Vite de' più eccellenti architetti, pittori et scultori italiani. English. Selections.] The lives of the artists /. Oxford , New York , 1991. p. cm. ISBN 0-19-281754-X : DDC 709/.2/245 B 20
N6922 .V2213 1991

ARTISTS - ITALY - BIOGRAPHY - DICTIONARIES.
Enciclopedia dei pittori e scultori italiani del Novecento . Milano [1991] 2 v. (1261 p.) : DDC 709/.2/.2450904 B 20
N6918 .E58 1991

ARTISTS - ITALY - BIOGRAPHY - JUVENILE LITERATURE.
Richmond, Robin. Introducing Michelangelo /. Boston , 1992. p. cm. ISBN 0-316-74440-9 : DDC 709/.2 B 20
N6923.B9 R52 1992

Skira-Venturi, Rosabianca. [Dimanche avec Leonardo da Vinci. English.] A weekend with Leonardo da Vinci /. New York , 1992. p. cm. ISBN 0-8478-1440-8 DDC 709/.2 20
N6923.L33 S5813 1992

Venezia, Mike. Michelangelo /. Chicago , 1991. p. cm. ISBN 0-516-02293-8 DDC 700/.92 B 20
N6923.B9 V44 1991

ARTISTS - ITALY - BOLOGNA - CORRESPONDENCE.
Gli Scritti dei Carracci . Bologna , 1990. 202 p. ; ISBN 88-7779-139-X
   NYPL [3-MCF C32 91-5526]

ARTISTS - ITALY - CORRESPONDENCE.
Brandi, Cesare. Morandi /. Roma , 1990. 249 p., [37] p. of plates : ISBN 88-359-3363-3 :
N6923.M6 B7 1990

ARTISTS - ITALY - FAMILY RELATIONSHIPS.
Barolsky, Paul, 1941- Giotto's father and the family of Vasari's lives /. University Park, PA , c1991. p. cm. ISBN 0-271-00762-1 (alk. paper) DDC 709/.2/245 B 20
N6915 .B28 1991

ARTISTS - ITALY - INTERVIEWS.
Grisi, Laura. Laura Grisi . New York , 1990.

---

276 p. : ISBN 0-8478-1222-7 DDC 709/.2 20
N6923.G73 A35 1990
   NYPL [3-MGO+ (Grisi) 91-3273]

ARTISTS - ITALY - PALERMO - EXHIBITIONS.
Pietro Novelli e il suo ambiente /. Palermo , c1990. 550 p. : ISBN 88-7804-048-7
   NYPL [3-MCF N9385 91-3641]

ARTISTS - ITALY - PUGLIA - BIOGRAPHY - DICTIONARIES.
Sorrenti, Pasquale. Pittori, scultori, architetti e artigiani pugliesi dall'antichità ai nostri giorni /. Bari , c1990. 500 p. ;
   NYPL [3-MAMC 91-4052]

ARTISTS - ITALY - PUGLIA - REGISTERS.
Sorrenti, Pasquale. Pittori, scultori, architetti e artigiani pugliesi dall'antichità ai nostri giorni /. Bari , c1990. 500 p. ; DDC 709/.2/24575 b 20
N6921.P86 S67 1990

ARTISTS - ITALY - ROME.
Bertolotti, Antonino, 1836-1893. Artisti subalpini in Roma nei secoli XV, XVI e XVII. Bologna [1965] 284 p.
   NYPL [3-MAMC 91-304]

ARTISTS - ITALY - SARDINIA - BIOGRAPHY.
Voci di Sardegna /. Siena , 1964- v. <1 > ;
N6919.S37 V6 1964

Artists' jewellery . Gere, Charlotte. Woodbridge [England] , c1989. 244 p. : ISBN 1-85149-024-8
   NYPL [MNR 89-11557]

ARTISTS, JEWISH - GERMANY - BIOGRAPHY.
Nussbaum, Felix, 1904-1944. Felix Nussbaum . Bramsche , c1990. 440 p. : ISBN 3-922469-46-9 DDC 759.3 20
ND588.N8 A4 1990

ARTISTS, JEWISH - NEW YORK (N.Y.) - EXHIBITIONS.
Painting a place in America . New York , Bloomington , 1991. p. cm. ISBN 0-253-33121-8 (cloth) DDC 704/.0392407471/090410747471 20
N6538.J4 P35 1991

ARTISTS - LATIN AMERICA - BIOGRAPHY.
Arte en Iberoamérica, 1820-1980 . [Madrid] [1989?] xxi, 359, [3] p. : ISBN 84-7506-297-0
N6502.4 .A76 1989

ARTISTS - LATVIA - BIOGRAPHY.
Lāce, Rasma. Arvīds Egle /. Riga , 1985. 108 p. :   *NYPL [3-MCZ E299 90-11091]*

ARTISTS - LEGAL STATUS, LAWS, ETC. - UNITED STATES.
Graphic Artists Guild (U. S.) Graphic Artists Guild handbook . New York, NY , Cincinnatti, OH , c1991. 235 p. ; ISBN 0-932102-07-7
   NYPL [3-MDW+ 91-5861]

Artist's market business series.
The Artist's friendly legal guide /. Cincinnati, Ohio , c1991. 142 p. : ISBN 0-89134-365-2 (pbk.) DDC 346.7304/82 347.306482 20
KF390.A7 A785 1991   *NYPL [MA 91-7466]*

Davis, Sally Prince, 1942- The graphic artist's guide to marketing and self-promotion /. Cincinnati, Ohio , 1991. p. cm. ISBN 0-89134-416-0 : DDC 741.6/068/8 20
NC1001.6 .D38 1991

Stewart, Joyce M., 1962- How to make your design business profitable /. Cincinnati, Ohio , c1992. p. cm. ISBN 0-89134-391-1 (paper) : DDC 745.4/068 20
NK1403 .S74 1992

ARTIST'S MARKS - BELGIUM - DICTIONARIES.
Piron, Paul-L. Belgian artists' signatures /. [Brussels] [1989] 544 p. :
   NYPL [3-MAME 91-5520]

ARTISTS' MARKS - DIRECTORIES.
Castagno, John, 1930- Artists' monograms and indiscernible signatures . Metuchen, N.J. , 1991. p. cm. ISBN 0-8108-2415-9 DDC 702/.78 20
N45 .C374 1991

ARTISTS' MARKS - UNITED STATES - DICTIONARIES.
Falk, Peter H. Dictionary of signatures & monograms of American artists . Madison, Conn. , Land O'Lakes, FL , 1988. 556 p., [1] leaf of plates : ISBN 0-932087-04-3 (alk. paper) :

DDC 702/.78 20
N45 .F35 1988   *NYPL [MAO 90-11577]*

**ARTISTS - MASSACHUSETTS - NEW
BEDFORD - BIOGRAPHY -
DICTIONARIES.**
Blasdale, Mary Jean. Artists of New Bedford .
New Bedford, Mass. , 1990. xiii, 220 p. :
IN PROCESS (ONLINE)
NYPL [3-MAO 91-6926]

ARTISTS' MATERIALS.
Creevy, Bill. The pastel book . New York ,
1991. 175 p. : ISBN 0-8230-3902-1 : DDC
741.2/35 20
NC880 .C74 1991

Mertz, Werner. Watercolor paper handbook /.
New York , 1991. 111 p. : ISBN 0-8230-5678-3
DDC 751.42/2 20
ND2422 .M47 1991

Sánchez Sánchez, Isidro. [Yo dibujo, yo pinto
acuarela. English.] Water color . New York ,
c1991. p. cm. ISBN 0-8120-4717-6 DDC
751.42/2 20
ND2420 .S2613 1991

ARTISTS' MATERIALS - EXHIBITIONS.
Impressionism /. London , c1990. 227 p. :
ISBN 0-300-05035-6 (cased) : DDC 759.054074
20
ND192.I4   *NYPL [3-MCN 91-5511]*
Italian painting before 1400 . London , c1989.
x, 225 p. : ISBN 0-947645-67-5 (pbk) : DDC
759.5 19   *NYPL [3-MCE 91-3327]*

**ARTISTS' MATERIALS - SAFETY
MEASURES.**
Rossol, Monona. The artist's complete health
and safety guide /. New York , Cincinnati,
OH , c1990. 328 p. : ISBN 0-927629-10-0
NYPL [MBN 91-4596]

ARTISTS' MATERIALS - TOXICOLOGY.
Rossol, Monona. The artist's complete health
and safety guide /. New York , Cincinnati,
OH , c1990. 328 p. : ISBN 0-927629-10-0
NYPL [MBN 91-4596]

ARTISTS, MEXICAN.
Martorrev. Estructuralismo plástico mexicano .
Guadalajara, Jalisco, México , 1987. 120, [3]
p. :   *NYPL [3-MCY 89-11595]*

ARTISTS - MEXICO - AUTOGRAPHS.
Catálogo de artistas y artesanos de México /.
México, D.F. , 1986 [i.e. 1987] 292 p. : ISBN
968-603-853-1
N6547.M56 C37 1986

ARTISTS - MEXICO - BIOGRAPHY.
Cajigas R., María de los Angeles. El mundo
desconocido de José Luis Cuevas /. México ,
c1990. 154 p. : ISBN 968-409-526-0 DDC
760/.092 B 20
N6559.C8 C34 1990

Cuevas, José Luis, 1934- Historias del viajero /.
México, D.F. , 1987. 78 p. : ISBN 968-434-446-5
DDC 760/.092/4 B 19
N6559.C8 A2 1987
NYPL [3-MCZ C955 90-12616]

Cuevas, José Luis, 1934- Historias para una
exposición /. Tlahuapan, Puebla [Mexico] ,
1988. 95 p. : DDC 760/.092 B 20
N6559.C8 A2 1988
NYPL [3-MCZ C955 91-5025]

Drucker, Malka. Frida Kahlo . New York ,
1991. p. cm. ISBN 0-553-07165-3 DDC 759.972
B 92 20
N6559.K34 D7 1991

Rivera Marín, Guadalupe, 1924- Un río, dos
Riveras . [Mexico] , México, D.F. , c1989. 211
p. : ISBN 968-390-325-8 DDC 759.972 B 20
N6559.R586 R5 1989

ARTISTS - MEXICO - INTERVIEWS.
Peden, Margaret Sayers. Out of the volcano .
Washington, D.C. , 1991. p. cm. ISBN
1-560-98060-5 DDC 700/.92/272 B 20
NX514.A1 P4 1991

**ARTISTS - MEXICO - JALISCO -
BIOGRAPHY.**
Farías, Ixca. Pintores jaliscienses /. Guadalajara,
Jalisco, México , 1969. 93 p. ;
N6556.J3 F37 1969

Reyes y Zavala, Ventura. Las bellas artes en

Jalisco /. Guadalajara, Jalisco, México , 1989.
xi, 44 p. ; ISBN 968-8323-84-5
NYPL [3-MAM 91-4662]

ARTISTS - MEXICO - REGISTERS.
Catálogo de artistas y artesanos de México /.
México, D.F. , 1986 [i.e. 1987] 292 p. : ISBN
968-603-853-1
N6547.M56 C37 1986

ARTISTS - MISCELLANEA.
Connor, Alexandra. Rembrandt's monkey and
other tales from the secret lives of the great
artists /. New York , 1991. p. cm. ISBN
0-312-06004-1 DDC 709/.2/2 20
N7460 .C66 1991

ARTISTS - MISSOURI - BIOGRAPHY.
Kellner, Bruce. The last dandy, Ralph Barton .
Columbia , c1991. p. cm. ISBN 0-8262-0774-X
DDC 741.6/092 B 20
NC139.B36 K45 1991

Artists' monograms and indiscernible signatures .
Castagno, John, 1930- Metuchen, N.J. , 1991.
p. cm. ISBN 0-8108-2415-9 DDC 702/.78 20
N45 .C374 1991

ARTISTS - NETHERLANDS - BIOGRAPHY.
Cremer . Amsterdam , 's-Gravenhage , c1990.
191 p. : ISBN 90-12-06739-1
NX554.Z9 C7434 1990

Descargues, Pierre. Rembrandt /. [Paris] ,
c1990. 304 p., [8] p. of plates : DDC 759.9492 B
20
ND653.R4 D39 1990

Dorn, Roland. Décoration . Hildesheim , New
York , 1990. xxxii, 622 p. : ISBN 3-487-09098-8
ND653.G7 D64 1990

Groot, Irene de. Maritime prints by the Dutch
Masters /. London , 1980. 284 p. : ISBN
0-86092-052-6
NYPL [MDBF+ 90-12796]

Groot, Reindert. Vincent van Gogh in
Amsterdam /. Amsterdam , c1990. 128 p. :
ISBN 90-6274-045-6 :
ND653.G7 G74 1990

Wilkie, Kenneth, 1942- [Van Gogh assignment.]
In search of van Gogh /. Rocklin, CA , 1991.
p. cm. ISBN 1-559-58101-8 : DDC 759.9492 B 20
ND653.G7 W54 1991

**ARTISTS - NETHERLANDS - BIOGRAPHY -
JUVENILE LITERATURE.**
Schwartz, Gary, 1940- Rembrandt /. New
York, N.Y. , 1992. p. cm. ISBN 0-8109-3760-3
DDC 759.9492 B 20
N6953.R4 S437 1992

**ARTISTS - NEW MEXICO - SANTA FE -
BIOGRAPHY.**
Dispenza, Joseph, 1942- Will Shuster . Santa
Fe, N.M. , c1989. xvi, 135 p., [32] p. of plates :
ISBN 0-89013-198-8 DDC 759.13 B 19
N6537.S537 D57 1989
NYPL [3-MCX S566 90-12340]

ARTISTS - NORWAY - BIOGRAPHY.
Eggum, Arne. Edvard Munch . [Oslo] , c1990.
303 p. : ISBN 82-7201-164-6
N7073.M8 E34 1990

Finne, Ferdinand, 1910- Vandrer mot en annen
strand . Oslo , c1990. 187 p. : ISBN
82-09-10612-0
N7073.F56 A2 1990

Paulsen, Åshild. Magnus Berg, 1666-1739 .
Oslo , c1989. 348 p. : ISBN 82-09-10580-9 :
NK5998.B47 P38 1989

Portrett av jeg /. Oslo , c1990. 131 p. : ISBN
82-504-1793-3
N7073.E36 P67 1990

Artists of books for children : a primer for peace.
Milwaukee, Wis. : Milwaukee Art Museum,
c1987. 56 p. : ill. ; 26 cm. Cover title. "Exhibition
dates: March 22-May 24, 1987"--P. [2]
*1. Illustration of books - 20th century - Exhibitions. 2.
Illustrated books, Children's - Exhibitions. 3. Peace in
art - Exhibitions. I. Milwaukee Art Museum. II. Title:
Primer for peace.*   *NYPL [MDTT 91-2512]*

Artists of New Bedford . Blasdale, Mary Jean.
New Bedford, Mass. , 1990. xiii, 220 p. :
IN PROCESS (ONLINE)
NYPL [3-MAO 91-6926]

Artists of the book 1988 : a facet of modernism /
introduction by Peter A. Wick. Boston, Mass. :
Boston Athenæum, c1988. 40 p. : ill. ; 28 cm.

"The catalogue of an exhibition held at the Boston
Athenæum, June 15 through August 19, 1988." "A
traveling exhibition of the New England Foundation for
the Arts." ISBN 0-934552-53-3
*1. Bibliographical exhibitions - Massachusetts - Boston.
2. Bookbinding - Exhibitions. 3. Artists' books -
Exhibitions. 4. Illustrated books - Exhibitions. 5.
Printing - Exhibitions. I. Wick, Peter A. II. Boston
Athenæum. III. New England Foundation for the Arts.*
NYPL [MDTT 91-4772]

Artists of twentieth-century New Mexico .
Museum of Fine Arts (Museum of New
Mexico) Santa Fe, NM , 1992. p. cm. ISBN
0-89013-230-5 DDC 709/.789/07478956 20
N6530.N6 M87 1992

**ARTISTS - ONTARIO - PSYCHOLOGY -
EXHIBITIONS.**
Art Gallery of Ontario. Extension Dept. The
work of art . [Toronto] [c1978] 43 p. : ISBN
0-919876-42-0
N6546.O5 A77 1978
NYPL [3-MAM 80-2200]

**ARTISTS - ONTARIO - TORONTO -
BIOGRAPHY.**
Society of Estonian Artists in Toronto. EKKT
1956-1990 art album /. [Toronto] [1990] 180
p. : DDC 709/.2/2713541 B 20
N6547.T67 S65 1990

ARTISTS - PERU - BIOGRAPHY.
Torres Bohl, José, 1946- Apuntes sobre José
Sabogal . [Lima, Peru] [1989] 154 p. : DDC
760/.092 B 20
N6719.S23 T67 1989

ARTISTS - PERU - INTERVIEWS.
Martínez, Cesáreo. Desde la vigilia . [Peru?]
1989. 212 p. ;
N6718 .M37 1989

ARTISTS - PHILOSOPHY.
Bertrand, Pierre. L'artiste /. Montréal, Québec ,
c1985. 193 p. ; ISBN 2-89006-233-3 DDC 701
19
N70 .B466 1985   *NYPL [3-MAS 90-12750]*

ARTISTS - PORTRAITS - EXHIBITIONS.
Das Selbstportrait im Zeitalter der
Photographie . Bern , c1985. 523 p. :
NYPL [MFW 91-2389]

Moral, Jean-Marie del, 1952- Les temps du
peintre . Niort [1987] 99 p. :
TR681.A7 M68 1987
NYPL [3-MAN 90-10272]

**ARTISTS - PORTUGAL - BIOGRAPHY -
DICTIONARIES.**
Dicionário da arte barroca em Portugal /.
Lisboa , 1989. 542 p. : ISBN 972-231-088-7
NYPL [3-MAML+ 91-4315]

ARTISTS' PREPARATORY STUDIES.
Christo, 1935- The accordion-fold book for the
Umbrellas, joint project for Japan and U. S.A.
/. San Francisco , c1991. p. cm. ISBN
0-938491-58-X (hardcover trade) DDC 709/.2
20
N7193.C5 A4 1991

Studien zur Künstlerzeichnung . Stuttgart ,
c1990. 334 p. : ISBN 3-7757-0306-3
NC40 .S78 1990

**ARTISTS' PREPARATORY STUDIES -
ENGLAND - CATALOGS.**
Essick, Robert N. William Blake's commercial
book illustrations . Oxford [England] , New
York , 1991. p. cm. ISBN 0-19-817390-3 : DDC
769.92 20
NE2047.6.B55 A4 1991

**ARTISTS' PREPARATORY STUDIES -
EXHIBITIONS.**
Moore, Henry, 1898- Henry Moore . London ,
1990. 32 p. : ISBN 1-85332-055-2
NYPL [3-MGO+ (Moore) 91-6697]

Schmaltz, K. L., 1932- K-L Schmaltz . [Kiel ,
1979] [33] leaves :
N6888.S366 A4 1979
NYPL [3-MGO (Schmaltz) 81-963]

**ARTISTS' PREPARATORY STUDIES -
FRANCE.**
Schönwald, Peter. Cathelin . Paris , c1990. 109
p. : DDC 746.392 20
NK3049.A3 C372 1990

**ARTISTS' PREPARATORY STUDIES -
FRANCE - EXHIBITIONS.**

L'Enrôlement des volontaires de 1792 .
Beauvais [1989] 258 p. : ISBN 2-901290-05-1
NYPL [3-MCO C87 91-5550]

**ARTISTS' PREPARATORY STUDIES -
GERMANY (WEST) - CATALOGS.**
Szymanski, Rolf. Rolf Szymanski . Stuttgart ,
c1989. 175 p. : ISBN 3-7757-0266-0 DDC
730/.92 20
NB588.S98 A4 1989
NYPL [3-MGO+ (Szymanski) 91-6925]

**ARTISTS' PREPARATORY STUDIES -
GERMANY, WEST - EXHIBITIONS.**
Altenstein, Bernd, 1943- Bernd Altenstein .
Salzgitter , 1978. 56 p. :
NB588.A44 A4 1978
NYPL [3-MGO (Altenstein) 81-287]

**ARTISTS' PREPARATORY STUDIES -
GREECE.**
Sperantzas, V. (Vasilēs) V. Sperantzas /. Kea
Kykladōn [1990] 143 p. :
N6903.S64 A4 1990

**ARTISTS' PREPARATORY STUDIES -
ITALY.**
Barbera, Gioacchino. I bozzetti di Sartorio per
il Duomo di Messina /. Palermo, c1989. 158
p. : ISBN 88-7681-048-X :
NC257.S2685 B37 1989

**ARTISTS' PREPARATORY STUDIES -
ITALY - CATALOGS.**
Ferrari, Oreste. Bozzetti italiani dal manierismo
al barocco /. Napoli, c1990. 285 p. :
ND615 .F47 1990 *NYPL [3-MCE 91-4960]*

**ARTISTS' PREPARATORY STUDIES -
ITALY - EMILIA-ROMAGNA.**
Disegni emiliani del Sei-Settecento . [Cinisello
Balsamo, Milano] [1990] 318 p. : ISBN
88-366-0306-8 *NYPL [3-MLP+ 91-7177]*

**ARTISTS' PREPARATORY STUDIES -
ONTARIO - EXHIBITIONS.**
Art Gallery of Ontario. Extension Dept. The
work of art . [Toronto] [c1978] 43 p. : ISBN
0-919876-42-0
N6546.O5 A77 1978
NYPL [3-MAM 80-2200]

**ARTISTS' PREPARATORY STUDIES -
UNITED STATES - EXHIBITIONS.**
Carter, Curtis L. Richard Lippold, sculpture /.
Milwaukee, Wis. [c1990] 64 p. : DDC 730/.92
20
N6537.L56 A4 1990

**ARTISTS' PREPARATORY STUDIES -
UNITED STATES - THEMES, MOTIVES.**
Barker, Clive, 1952- Clive Barker, illustrator /.
Forestville, Calif. , c1990. iv, 124 p., [18] p. of
plates : ISBN 1-560-60026-8 (limited signed
clothbound) : DDC 741/.092 20
NC139.B33 A4 1990

**ARTISTS - PROFESSIONAL ETHICS -
UNITED STATES.**
Graphic Artists Guild (U. S.) Graphic Artists
Guild handbook . New York, NY , Cincinnatti,
OH , c1991. 235 p. ; ISBN 0-932102-07-7
NYPL [3-MDW+ 91-5861]

**ARTISTS - PSYCHOLOGICAL ASPECTS -
EXHIBITIONS.**
Open mind . Milano , c1989. 318 p. :
NYPL [3-MAMZ 90-11011]

ARTISTS - PSYCHOLOGY.
Bertrand, Pierre. L'artiste /. Montréal, Québec ,
c1985. 193 p. ; ISBN 2-89006-233-3 DDC 701
19
N70 .B466 1985 *NYPL [3-MAS 90-12750]*

Borrell, Joan. L'artiste-roi . [Paris] , c1990. 398
p. ; ISBN 2-7007-3473-4 : DDC 700/.1 20
NX454 .B63 1990

Clébert, Jean Paul. Femmes d'artistes . Paris ,
c1989. 415 p. : ISBN 2-85616-499-4 :
NX165 .C6 1989

**ARTISTS - QUÉBEC (PROVINCE) -
BIOGRAPHY.**
Robert, Guy, 1933- Cent vingt du Cercle des
artistes peintres du Québec /. Montréal , 1989.
255 p. : ISBN 2-920058-62-2 DDC 709/.2/2 20
N6546.Q4 R63 1989

**ARTISTS - QUÉBEC (PROVINCE) -
ECONOMIC CONDITIONS.**
Lacroix, Jean-Guy, 1945- La condition
d'artiste. Outremont, Québec , Ville
Saint-Laurent, Québec , c1990. 249 p. ; ISBN

2-89005-389-X DDC 338.4/77/00971409048 20
NX513.A3 Q35 1990

**ARTISTS - QUÉBEC (PROVINCE) - SOCIAL
CONDITIONS.**
Lacroix, Jean-Guy, 1945- La condition
d'artiste. Outremont, Québec , Ville
Saint-Laurent, Québec , c1990. 249 p. ; ISBN
2-89005-389-X DDC 338.4/77/00971409048 20
NX513.A3 Q35 1990

ARTISTS - REGISTERS.
McConkey, Wilfred J. Klee as in clay .
Lanham, Md. , 1991. p. cm. ISBN 0-8191-8247-8
(pbk. : alk. paper) DDC 700/.92/2 20
NX163 .M3 1991

ARTISTS - RELATIONSHIP WITH WOMEN.
Clébert, Jean Paul. Femmes d'artistes /. Paris ,
c1989. 415 p. ; ISBN 2-85616-499-4 :
NX165 .C6 1989

ARTISTS - RUSSIAN S.F.S.R. - BIOGRAPHY.
Kleine, Gisela, 1926- Gabriele Münter und
Wassily Kandinsky . Frankfurt am Main , 1990.
813 p., 16 p. of plates : ISBN 3-458-16090-6
ND588.M83 K5 1990

Sarab´ i̇̄anov, Dmitriĭ Vladimirovich. [Lioubov
Popova. English.] Popova /. New York , 1990.
396 p. : ISBN 0-8109-3701-8 (soft) DDC 709/.2/4
B 19
N6999.P67 S27 1989
NYPL [3-MCZ+ P828 91-3662]

**ARTISTS - RUSSIAN S.F.S.R. - BIOGRAPHY -
JUVENILE LITERATURE.**
Bober, Natalie. Marc Chagall . Philadelphia ,
1991. p. cm. ISBN 0-8276-0379-7 DDC 759.7 B
20
N6999.C46 B6 1991

ARTISTS - SOUTH AFRICA - BIOGRAPHY.
Reynolds, Marjorie, 1914- Everything you do is
a portrait of yourself . Rosebank, S.A. , 1989.
xiii, 490 p. : ISBN 0-620-12883-6 DDC 760/.092
B 20
N7396.K38 R48 1989

ARTISTS - SPAIN - BIOGRAPHY.
Arte geométrico en España, 1957-1989.
[Madrid] [1989] 320 p. : ISBN 84-7812-044-0
DDC 709/.46/0744641 20
N7108.5.A2 A78 1989

Carol, Márius. Dalí . Esplugues de Llobregat,
Barcelona , 1990. 204 p., [16] p. of plates :
ISBN 84-01-35171-5 DDC 759.6 B 20
N7113.D3 C36 1990

Catálogo nacional de arte contemporáneo.
Barcelona , c1989. 4 v. : ISBN 84-87433-00-6
(obra completa)
N7108 .C29 1989

Gassier, Pierre. [Goya. English.] Goya /. New
York , 1989. 129 p. : ISBN 0-8478-1108-5 DDC
760/.092 B 20
N7113.G68 G3713 1989
NYPL [3-MCQ 91-2506]

Montagud, Bernardo. José Segrelles Albert .
Alzira , 1985. 239 p. : ISBN 84-398-3281-8
ND813.S388 M65 1985

Seghers, Pierre. Clavé /. Paris , 1989. 423 p. :
ISBN 2-7022-0239-X DDC 709/.2 B 20
N7113.C57 S4 1989

ARTISTS - SPAIN - CORRESPONDENCE.
Gris, Juan, 1887-1927. Juan Gris /. [Valencia,
Spain] [Paris, France] [1990] 150 p. : ISBN
2-85850-595-0
NC287.G76 A4 1990

**ARTISTS - SPAIN - GALICIA (REGION) -
CATALOGS.**
Seoane, Xavier, 1954- Identidade e convulsión .
Sada, A Coruña [1990] 322 p. : ISBN
84-7492-461-8 DDC 709/.46/109048 20
N7109.G3 S46 1990

ARTISTS - SPAIN - INTERVIEWS.
Barnes, Lucinda. Imágenes líricas =. Long
Beach , c1990. 119 p. : ISBN 0-936270-30-6
NYPL [3-MAML+ 91-5035]

**ARTISTS - SPAIN - LA RIOJA -
BIOGRAPHY.**
Labandíbar, José Luis. 1950-1990, cuarenta
años de artes plásticas en La Rioja /. [La Rioja]
[1989?-1990?] 2 v. : ISBN 84-404-5495-3 (v. 1)
N7109.L3 L3 1989

ARTISTS - SPAIN - VALENCIA.
Azcárraga, Adolfo de. Escritos sobre arte y

artistas valencianos /. Valencia , 1989. 330 p. :
ISBN 84-505-8230-X
NYPL [3-MAML 90-11103]

ARTISTS - SPAINT - BIOGRAPHY.
Perez Sanchez, Alfonso E. [Goya. English.]
Goya /. London , 1990. 160 p. : ISBN
0-7126-3926-8 : DDC 759.6 20
ND813.G7 NYPL [3-MCQ+ G72 90-11752]

ARTISTS - SRI LANKA - BIOGRAPHY.
Dharmasiri, Albert. Modern art in Sri Lanka .
Colombo, Sri Lanka , 1988. 80 p. : ISBN
955-9034-01-4 : DDC 709/.5493/0745493 20
N7310.6 .D47 1988 NYPL [3-MAF 91-6910]

ARTISTS' STUDIOS - ENGLAND.
Bewick, Thomas, 1753-1828. The watercolours
and drawings of Thomas Bewick and his
workshop apprentices /. Stocksfield,
Northumberland : Winchester : 2 v. : ISBN
0-906795-85-0 (set) DDC 769.92 20
N6797.B48 A4 1989
NYPL [3-MCV B5722 91-3680]

ARTISTS' STUDIOS - GERMANY - BERLIN.
Werkstattbesuche bei Künstlern in
Berlin-Wedding /. Berlin , c1989. 2 v. : ISBN
3-9801875-9-4 :
N6885 .W46 1989

ARTISTS' STUDIOS - UNITED STATES.
Kartes, Cheryl. Creating space . New York,
N.Y. , 1991. p. cm. ISBN 0-915400-92-8 DDC
700/.68/2 20
N8520 .K37 1991

ARTISTS - SWITZERLAND.
31 artistes suisses contemporains. Paris , 1972.
[72] p. : *NYPL [3-MAM 90-6430]*

ARTISTS - SWITZERLAND - BIOGRAPHY.
Honegger, Karl Lukas, 1902- Mein Leben und
Werk . Stein am Rhein , 1990. 528 p. : ISBN
3-7171-0934-0 DDC 709/.2 B 20
N7153.H654 A2 1990

Schweizerisches Künstler-Lexikon /. Nendeln ,
1982. 4 v. ; *NYPL [MAO 90-2421]*

Studer-Geisser, Isabella. Augustin Meinrad
Bächtiger, 1888-1971 /. St. Gallen , 1988. 95
p. : ISBN 3-85603-003-4
N7153.B23 S78 1988
NYPL [3-MCZ B1345 90-10412]

**ARTISTS - SWITZERLAND - SAINT GALL
(CANTON) - BIOGRAPHY.**
Künstlerdokumentation des Kantons St. Gallen
/. St. Gallen , 1984. 1 v. (unpaged) :
NYPL [3-MAO+ 90-11090]

**ARTISTS - TAXATION - LAW AND
LEGISLATION - UNITED STATES.**
The Artist's friendly legal guide /. Cincinnati,
Ohio , c1991. 142 p. : ISBN 0-89134-365-2
(pbk.) : DDC 346.7304/82 347.306482 20
KF390.A7 A785 1991 NYPL [MA 91-7466]

ARTISTS - THAILAND - BIOGRAPHY.
Phon Trawēn. Sinlapin 'ek hǣng Krung
Rattanakōsin /. [Bangkok] [24]94 [1951] 6,
385 ;
NX578.7.A1 P47 1951

ARTISTS - TURKEY - INTERVIEWS.
Tanaltay, Erdoğan. Sanat ustalarıyla-- bir gün .
Divanyolu, İstanbul [1989] 159 p. ; ISBN
975-7704-02-4
N7168 .T36 1989

ARTISTS - UKRAINE - BIOGRAPHY.
Werner, Xenia. Wassili Masjutin in Riga,
Moskau und Berlin . Berlin , 1989. 107 p. :
NYPL [MDG+ (Masjutin) 90-834]

ARTISTS - UNITED STATES - BIOGRAPHY.
Baldwin, Neil, 1947- Man Ray, American artist
/. New York [1991], c1988. xii, 449 p. : ISBN
0-306-80423-9 : DDC 709/.2 B 20
N6537.R3 B3 1991

Christie, Victor J. W. Bessie Pease Gutmann .
Radnor, Pa. , c1990. xv, 199 p. : ISBN
0-87069-561-4 : DDC 741.6/092 B 20
N6537.G88 C4 1990 *NYPL [3-MCX G983 91-3649]*

Conrad, Rupert, 1907-1979. The art and
reflections of Rupert Conrad . New York ,
c1991. 205 p., [8] p. of plates : ISBN
0-8453-4824-8 (alk. paper) : DDC 709/.2 B 20
N6537.C654 A2 1990
NYPL [3-MCX C763 91-6324]

Failing, Patricia. Doris Chase, artist in motion .

Seattle , c1991. p. cm.   ISBN 0-295-97112-6
DDC 700/.92 B 20
N6537.C4638 F35 1991

Fleming, Gordon H., 1920- Whistler . New
York , 1991. p. cm.   ISBN 0-312-05995-7 :   DDC
760/.092 B 20
N6537.W4 F57 1991

Koch, Stephen. Stargazer . New York , 1991. p.
cm.   ISBN 0-7145-2920-6 :   DDC 791.43/0233/092
20
NX512.W37 K6 1991

Kotz, Mary Lynn. Rauschenberg, art and life /.
New York , 1990. 320 p. :   ISBN 0-8109-3752-2
DDC 700/.92 B 20
N6537.R27 K67 1990
NYPL   [3-MCX R248 91-3365]

Peters, Sarah Whitaker. Becoming O'Keeffe .
New York , 1991. p. cm.   ISBN 0-89659-907-8
DDC 759.13 B 20
N6537.O39 P48 1991

Spencer, Robin. Whistler . New York , 1991. p.
cm.   ISBN 0-517-05773-5   DDC 760/.092 B 20
N6537.W4 S6 1991

**ARTISTS - UNITED STATES -
    CORRESPONDENCE.**
Allston, Washington, 1779-1843.
[Correspondence.] The correspondence of
Washington Allston /. Lexington, Ky , 1992. p.
cm.   ISBN 0-8131-1708-9 :   DDC 759.13 B 20
NX512.A513 A3 1992

O'Keeffe, Georgia, 1887-1986. Lovingly,
Georgia . New York , c1990. xxvii, 365 p. :
ISBN 0-671-69236-4 (hardcover) :   DDC 759.13
B 20
N6537.O39 A3 1990
NYPL   [3-MCX O41 90-11778]

ARTISTS - UNITED STATES - DIARIES.
Townsend, Harry Everett. War diary of a
combat artist /. Niwot, Colo. , c1991. xiv, 284
p. :   ISBN 0-87081-231-9   DDC 740/.92 B 20
N6537.T66 A2 1991

**ARTISTS - UNITED STATES -
    EXHIBITIONS.**
Marlais, Michael Andrew. Americans and
Paris . Waterville, Me. , c1990. 62 p. :   DDC
759.13/074/7416 20
N6510 .M27 1990
NYPL   [3-MAMT 90-13006]

ARTISTS - UNITED STATES - INTERVIEWS.
Bomb . San Francisco , 1992. p. cm.   ISBN
0-87286-261-5 :   DDC 700/.9/04 20
NX458 .B66 1992

In the Vernacular . Jefferson, N.C. , 1991. p.
ISBN 0-89950-645-3 (lib. bdg. : alk. paper)   DDC
700/.92/273 20
NX504 .I526 1991

Newman, Barnett, 1905-1970. Barnett
Newman . New York , 1990, c1989. xxxi, 331
p., [16] p. of plates :   ISBN 0-394-58038-9 :
DDC 709.2 20
ND237.N475 B37 1990
NYPL   [MCX N55 91-3262]

ARTISTS - URUGUAY - BIOGRAPHY.
Anastasía, Luis V. Figari . Montevideo , 1976.
92 p., [15] leaves of plates :
NYPL   [3-MAM 90-5569]

ARTISTS - VENEZUELA - BIOGRAPHY.
Banco Industrial de Venezuela. Arturo
Michelena . [Caracas, Venezuela] [1989?] 183
p. :   DDC 759.987 20
N6739.M53 B36 1989

**ARTISTS' WIVES - CARICATURES AND
    CARTOONS.**
Swain, Sally. Great housewives of art revisited
/. New York , 1992. p. cm.   ISBN
0-14-015837-5 :   DDC 741.5/994 20
NC1759.S93 A4 1992

ARTISTS' WIVES - PSYCHOLOGY.
Clébert, Jean Paul. Femmes d'artistes /. Paris ,
c1989. 415 p. ;   ISBN 2-85616-499-4 :
NX165 .C6 1989

ARTISTS - YUGOSLAVIA - BIOGRAPHY.
Jagodič, Stane. Stane Jagodič /. Zagreb , 1989.
399 p. ;   ISBN 86-343-0514-7
NYPL   [3-MCZ+ J247 90-11068]

Artoon : l'influenza del fumetto nelle arti visive
del XX secolo. Napoli : Electa, c1989. 199 p. :
ill. (some col.) ; 29 cm. Italian and English. Catalog

---

of an exhibition held in Rome at the Palazzo civiltà del
lavoro, 11-25-89/1-15-90.   ISBN 88-435-3056-9
DDC 709/.04/07107445632 20
*1. Pop art - Exhibitions. 2. Art, Modern - 20th
century - Exhibitions.*
N6494.P6 A6 1989
NYPL   [3-MAL 90-12882]

The Arts : a history of expression in the 20th
century / edited by Ronald Tamplin. Oxford ;
New York : Oxford University Press, 1991. 256
p. : ill. (some col.) ; 29 cm. "An Equinox
book"--T.p. verso. Includes bibliographical references (p.
251) and index.   ISBN 0-19-520852-8   DDC
700/.9/04 20
*1. Arts, Modern - 20th century - History. I. Tamplin,
Ronald.*
NX456 .A76 1991

ARTS.
Barthes, Roland. [Obvie et l'obtus. English.]
The responsibility of forms . Berkeley , 1991. p.
cm.   ISBN 0-520-07238-3 (pbk.)   DDC 700 20
NX65 .B37513 1991

Clébert, Jean Paul. Femmes d'artistes /. Paris ,
c1989. 415 p. ;   ISBN 2-85616-499-4 :
NX165 .C6 1989

Kulturens dekningsbidrag . [Oslo] , c1991. 179
p. ;   ISBN 82-02-12832-3
NX456 .K78 1991

La Tauromachie, art et littérature /. Paris ,
c1990. 151 p. ;   ISBN 2-7384-0685-8   DDC 700
20
NX650.B84 T38 1990

Miller, J. Hillis (Joseph Hillis), 1928-
Illustration /. Cambridge, Mass. , 1992. p. cm.
ISBN 0-674-44357-8   DDC 700/.1 20
NX640 .M55 1992

Passmore, John Arthur. Serious art /. La Salle,
Ill. , 1991. p. cm.   ISBN 0-8126-9181-4 (cloth)
DDC 700/.1 20
NX620 .P37 1991

Sporre, Dennis J. Reality through the arts /.
Englewood Cliffs, N.J. , c1991. 352 p. :   ISBN
0-13-764119-2   DDC 700 20
NX600.R4 S73 1991

Voprosy metodologii i sotsiologii iskusstva .
Leningrad , 1988. 175 p. :
NX160 .V66 1988

Arts & crafts /. Haslam, Malcolm. London ,
1988. 168 p. :   ISBN 0-356-15633-8 :   DDC
745/.0941/075 20
NK1142 .H38 1988

Arts & crafts carpets /. Haslam, Malcolm. New
York , 1991. p. cm.   ISBN 0-8478-1388-6   DDC
746.7/2 20
NK2843 .H37 1991

Arts & crafts style /. Anscombe, Isabelle. New
York , 1991. p.   ISBN 0-8478-1328-2 :   DDC
745.4/441 20
NK1142 .A52 1991

**ARTS ADMINISTRATORS - TRAINING OF -
    UNITED STATES.**
Survey of arts administration training, 1991-92
/. New York, N.Y. , c1991. p. cm.   ISBN
0-915400-90-1 (PBK)   DDC 700/.68 20
NX765 .S842 1991

ARTS, AMERICAN.
Crunden, Robert Morse. American salons .
New York , 1992. p. cm.   ISBN 0-19-506569-7
(acid-free paper)   DDC 700/.973/09034 20
NX503.7 .C78 1992

Honour, Hugh. The Venetian hours of Henry
James, Whistler, Sargent /. Boston , c1991. p.
ISBN 0-8212-1861-1   DDC 700 20
NX653.V46 H66 1991

ARTS, AMERICAN - SOUTH DAKOTA.
Huseboe, Arthur R., 1931- An illustrated
history of the arts in South Dakota /. Sioux
Falls, S.D. , 1989. xiii, 396 p. :   ISBN
0-931170-44-3 :   DDC 700/.9783 20
NX510.S8 H87 1989

Arts & architecture the Entenza years / edited
by Barbara Goldstein ; essay by Esther McCoy.
Cambridge, Mass. : MIT Press, c1990. 248 p. :
ill. ; 34 cm.   ISBN 0-262-07131-2 :   DDC
700/.9/04 20
*1. Arts, Modern - 20th century. I. Entenza, John,
1903-. II. Goldstein, Barbara. III. McCoy, Esther. IV.*

Arts & architecture.
NX456.5.M64 A7 1990
NYPL   [3-MAL+ 91-3679]

Arts & architecture. Arts & architecture .
Cambridge, Mass. , c1990. 248 p. :   ISBN
0-262-07131-2 :   DDC 700/.9/04 20
NX456.5.M64 A7 1990
NYPL   [3-MAL+ 91-3679]

Arts and artisans of Orissa / edited by Basudeb
Sahoo. Bhubaneswar , [1981?] 106
p. ; 26 cm. Bibliography: p. 106.   DDC
338.4/77/095413 19
*1. Handicrafts - India - Orissa. 2. Art, Indic - India -
Orissa. 3. Artists - India - Orissa - Economic
conditions. 4. Artisans - India - Orissa - Economic
conditions. 5. Artists - India - Orissa - Social
conditions. 6. Artisans - India - Orissa - Social
conditions. I. Sahoo, Basudeb, 1933-.*
N7307.O74 A77 1981
NYPL   [3-MNE 90-5470]

**ARTS AND BUSINESS. see ART AND
    INDUSTRY.**

Arts and crafts. Haslam, Malcolm. Arts & crafts
/. London , 1988. 168 p. :   ISBN 0-356-15633-8 :
DDC 745/.0941/075 20
NK1142 .H38 1988

Arts and crafts carpets. Haslam, Malcolm. Arts &
crafts carpets /. New York , 1991. p. cm.
ISBN 0-8478-1388-6   DDC 746.7/2 20
NK2843 .H37 1991

Arts & crafts for home decorating.
Bedroom decorating. Minnetonka, MN , 1991.
p. cm.   ISBN 0-86573-351-1 :   DDC 747.7/7 20
NK2117.B4 B424 1991

**ARTS AND CRAFTS MOVEMENT -
    ENGLAND.**
Haslam, Malcolm. Arts & crafts carpets /. New
York , 1991. p. cm.   ISBN 0-8478-1388-6   DDC
746.7/2 20
NK2843 .H37 1991

**ARTS AND CRAFTS MOVEMENT -
    ENGLAND - EXHIBITIONS.**
Brennan, Shawn. Reflections . New York,
N.Y. , c1990. 51 p. :   DDC 739/.0942/0747471 20
NK1142 .B7 1990   ***NYPL   [3-MNK 90-13003]***

**ARTS AND CRAFTS MOVEMENT - GREAT
    BRITAIN.**
Anscombe, Isabelle. Arts & crafts style /. New
York , 1991. p.   ISBN 0-8478-1328-2 :   DDC
745.4/441 20
NK1142 .A52 1991

Haslam, Malcolm. Arts & crafts /. London ,
1988. 168 p. :   ISBN 0-356-15633-8 :   DDC
745/.0941/075 20
NK1142 .H38 1988

Wilhide, Elizabeth. William Morris . New
York , 1991. p. cm.   ISBN 0-8109-3623-2 (cloth)
DDC 745.4/492 20
NK2043.Z9 M648 1991

**ARTS AND CRAFTS MOVEMENT -
    INFLUENCE.**
Tahara, Keiichi, 1951- [Seikimatsu no kenchiku.
English.] Images of fin-de-siècle architecture
and interior decoration /. London , New York ,
1988. 263 p. :   ISBN 0-00-215354-8 :   DDC
724.9/1 19
NA3485   ***NYPL   [3-MRX+ 91-3382]***

**ARTS AND CRAFTS MOVEMENT - UNITED
    STATES.**
Anscombe, Isabelle. Arts & crafts style /. New
York , 1991. p.   ISBN 0-8478-1328-2 :   DDC
745.4/441 20
NK1142 .A52 1991

**ARTS AND CRAFTS MOVEMENT - UNITED
    STATES - EXHIBITIONS.**
Bowman, Leslie Greene. American arts &
crafts . Los Angeles, Calif. , Boston , c1990.
255 p. :   ISBN 0-8212-1824-7 (hardback) :   DDC
745/.0973/07479494 20
NK1141 .B64 1990
NYPL   [3-MNE+ 91-4630]

**ARTS AND CRAFTS MOVEMENT - UNITED
    STATES - INFLUENCE.**
Craftsman-style houses. Newton, Conn. , c1991.
p. cm.   ISBN 1-561-58014-7 :   DDC
728/.373/09730904 20
NA7208 .C68 1991

**ARTS AND CRAFTS MOVEMENTS -
    UNITED STATES - EXHIBITIONS.**

Brennan, Shawn. Reflections . New York,
N.Y. , c1990. 51 p. :   DDC 739/.0942/0747471 20
NK1142 .B7 1990   **NYPL [3-MNK 90-13003]**

Arts and crafts of Mexico /. Sayer, Chloë.
London , 1990. 160 p. :   ISBN 0-87701-781-6 :
NYPL [3-MNE 91-4573]

The arts and crafts of the Swat Valley. Kalter,
Johannes. New York, NY , 1991. 180 p. :
ISBN 0-500-97384-9
NYPL [3-MNE 91-7551]

Arts and crafts style. Anscombe, Isabelle. Arts &
crafts style /. New York , 1991. p.   ISBN
0-8478-1328-2 :   DDC 745.4/441 20
NK1142 .A52 1991

Arts & Decoration Book Society. Bowman,
Irving. A portfolio of interiors . [New York]
[1941?] 17, 17 leaves :
NYPL [3-MLO+ 90-2451]

**ARTS AND FEMINISM. see FEMINISM
AND THE ARTS.**

ARTS AND SOCIETY.
Cultural literacy & arts education /. Urbana ,
c19. :xvi, 171 p. :   ISBN 0-252-01845-1 (alk. paper)
DDC 700/.1/03 20
NX294 .C85 1992

Kulturanalyse /. [Oslo] , c1990. 236 p. ;   ISBN
82-05-18967-6
NX456 .K77 1990

ARTS AND SOCIETY - AUSTRALIA.
Cultivating the country. Oxford [England] ,
New York , 1988. 118 p. :   ISBN 0-19-554944-9
(pbk.)   **NYPL [3-MAM 89-17144]**

ARTS AND SOCIETY - CONGRESSES.
Symposium on Research and Marketing for the
Arts (1990 : Florence, Italy) Symposium on
Research and Marketing for the Arts .
Amsterdam, The Netherlands [1990] v, 249
p. :   ISBN 92-831-1160-5   DDC 700/.1/03 20
NX180.S6 S9 1990

ARTS AND SOCIETY - ENGLAND.
Renaissance bodies . London , 1990. x, 294 p. :
ISBN 0-948462-09-4   DDC 700 20
NX650.F45 R46 1990

**ARTS AND SOCIETY - ENGLAND -
CONGRESSES.**
L'Artiste, témoin de son temps (?) .
Aix-en-Provence , 1990. xiv, 168 p. ;   ISBN
2-85399-238-1 :   DDC 700/.942 20
NX543 .A83 1990

**ARTS AND SOCIETY - FRANCE - HISTORY -
20TH CENTURY.**
Rigby, Brian. Popular culture in modern
France . London , New York , 1992. p. cm.
ISBN 0-415-01246-5   DDC 700/.1/0309440904
20
NX180.S6 R54 1992

**ARTS AND SOCIETY - HISTORY - 19TH
CENTURY.**
Borrell, Joan. L'artiste-roi . [Paris] , c1990. 398
p. ;   ISBN 2-7007-3473-4 :   DDC 700/.1 20
NX454 .B63 1990

**ARTS AND SOCIETY - HISTORY - 20TH
CENTURY.**
Out there . New York, N.Y. , Cambridge,
Mass. , c1990. 446 p. :   ISBN 0-262-06132-5
DDC 700/.1/0308693 20
NX180.S6 O97 1990   **NYPL [3-MA 91-3296]**

ARTS AND SOCIETY - SCANDINAVIA.
Kulturanalyse /. [Oslo] , c1990. 236 p. ;   ISBN
82-05-18967-6
NX456 .K77 1990

ARTS AND SOCIETY - SPAIN - HISTORY.
Cámara Muñoz, Alicia. Arquitectura y sociedad
en el Siglo de Oro . Madrid , c1990. 280 p.,
[32] p. of plates :   ISBN 84-86902-07-X
NYPL [MQWH 91-5219]

ARTS AND SOCIETY - UNITED STATES.
Berger, Maurice. Labyrinths . New York ,
c1989. xvi, 175 p. :   ISBN 0-06-430384-5 :   DDC
700/.92/4 19
NX512.M67 B47 1989
NYPL [3-MGO (Morris) 90-11779]

Trend, David. Cultural pedagogy . New York ,
1992. p. cm.   ISBN 0-89789-256-9   DDC
700/.1/03 20
NX180.S6 T7 1992

**ARTS AND SOCIETY - UNITED STATES -
HISTORY - 20TH CENTURY.**

Berger, Maurice. How art becomes history .
New York, N.Y. , c1992. p.   ISBN
0-06-430385-3 :   DDC 700/.1/03 20
NX180.S6 B47 1992

Watson, Steven. Strange bedfellows . New
York , c1991. 439 p. :   ISBN 0-89659-934-5 :
DDC 700/.973/09041 20
NX504 .W38 1991   **NYPL [MAMT 91-5715]**

**ARTS AND SOCIOLOGY. see ARTS AND
SOCIETY.**

**ARTS AND TECHNOLOGY. see
TECHNOLOGY AND THE ARTS.**

ARTS AND THE AGED - UNITED STATES.
Clark, Patch. Intergenerational arts in the
nursing home . New York , 1991. p. cm.   ISBN
0-313-25965-8 (alk. paper)   DDC 362.1/6 20
NX180.A35 C5 1991

Hoffman, Donald H. Arts for older adults .
Englewood Cliffs, N.J. , 1992. p. cm.   ISBN
0-13-048182-3   DDC 700/.1/03 20
NX180.A35 H64 1992

ARTS, AUSTRIAN.
Seibert, Ingrit. Die Schwierigen . Wien , c1986.
199 p. :   ISBN 3-7046-0053-9
NX548.Z8 S45 1986

Van Zon, Gabriele, 1937- Word and picture .
New York , 1991. p. cm.   ISBN 0-8204-1475-1
DDC 700/.92 20
NX548.Z9 K838 1991

**ARTS, AUSTRIAN - AUSTRIA - VIENNA -
EXHIBITIONS.**
Biedermeier in Wien 1815-1848 . Mainz ,
c1990. 251 p. :   ISBN 3-8053-1128-1
NX548.V53 B54 1990

ARTS, BAROQUE.
Maiorino, Giancarlo, 1943- The cornucopian
mind and the baroque unity of the arts /.
University Park , c1990. x, 210 p. :   ISBN
0-271-00679-X .   DDC 700/.1 20
NX451.5.B3 M35 1990
NYPL [3-MAK 90-10647]

ARTS - BRAZIL.
Teles, Fídias. Os malabaristas da vida . Recife,
Pernambuco , 1989. 398 p. :
NX533.A1 T45 1989

ARTS, BRITISH.
Sillars, Stuart, 1951- British romantic art and
the Second World War /. New York , 1991. p.
cm.   ISBN 0-312-06719-4   DDC 700 20
NX543 .S52 1991

ARTS, BYZANTINE - CONGRESSES.
The Twilight of Byzantium . Princeton, N.J. ,
c1991. p. cm.   ISBN 0-691-04091-5 (alk. paper) :
DDC 700/.9495 20
NX449 .T85 1991

Arts Club of Chicago.
Ackerman, Phyllis, 1893- Catalogue of a loan
exhibition of gothic tapestries /. [Chicago] ,
1926. 55 p. :   **NYPL [3-MOR+ 91-322]**

Folon, Jean Michel. Folon and Topor.
[Chicago?, 1972] [16] p.
NYPL [3-MCN 90-6752]

González, Julio, 1876-1942. Sculpture,
drawings, collages. [Chicago 1969] 1
v.(unpaged)
NYPL [3-MGO (González) 90-6908]

Masterworks of color and design . [Chicago]
[1991] 15 p. :   **NYPL [3-MOP 91-4288]**

**ARTS, COLOMBIAN - COLOMBIA -
BOGOTÁ.**
Cronología de la cultura, 1950-1990 /. [Bogotá,
Colombia] , 1990. 524 p. :   ISBN 958-9138-62-4
DDC 700/.9/045 20
NX535.B64 C76 1990

Arts Council Gallery (London, England) Sixty
years of patronage . [London] , 1965. 29 p., 8
p. of plates :
MLCM 82/1567
NYPL [3-MAVZ (London) 90-5872]

Arts Council of Great Britain.
Housing the arts in Great Britain; report.
London, [s.n.], 1959-61. 2 v. illus. 25 cm.
CONTENTS. - --pt. 1. London, Scotland, Wales.--pt. 2.
The needs of the English provinces.
1. Art centers - Great Britain. 2. The arts - Great
Britain. I. Title.
NA6813.G7 A77

London Group. Fifty years of British art,
1914-64. [London, 1964] 1 v. (unpaged)
N6768 .L65

Národní galerie V Praze. Baroque in Bohemia.
London, 1969. 1 v. (unpaged)   DDC 709/.437/1
N6818 .P7

Arts Council of Great Britain. Welsh Committee.
Jonah Jones, John Petts, Kyffin Williams .
[London, England] , 1961. 14 p., [8] p. of
plates :
MLCM 87/7416 (N)
NYPL [3-MAMR 91-226]

ARTS, CUBAN - THEMES, MOTIVES.
Barnet, Miguel, 1940- Autógrafos cubanos /.
Ciudad de La Habana , c1990. 151 p. :   DDC
700/.97291/0904 20
NX525.A1 B37 1990

ARTS, CZECH - CONGRESSES.
Proudy české umělecké tvorby 19. století .
Praha , 1990. 262 p. :
NX650.I34 P76 1990

**ARTS - CZECHOSLOVAKIA - SLOVAK
REPUBLIC.**
Kamenistý, Ján. Ako kopú múzy . Bratislava ,
1990. 263 p. :   ISBN 80-221-0036-6 :
NX571.C92 S54 1990

ARTS, DANISH - EXHIBITIONS.
Kitsch & konkret . København , 1990. 95 p. :
ISBN 87-89556-00-3 :
NX558.A1 K58 1990

Arts de bâtir traditionnels . Coignet, Jean.
Aix-en-Provence , c1987. 130 p. :   ISBN
2-85744-252-1   **NYPL [3-MQD+ 91-4827]**

Arts de l'Ouest, 0220-2220.
Artistes étrangers à Pont-Aven, Concarneau et
autres lieux de Bretagne /. [Rennes] [1989]
233 p. :   ISBN 2-86847-026-2
NYPL [3-MAM 91-3261]

**ARTS, DECORATIVE. see DECORATION
AND ORNAMENT; INTERIOR
DECORATION; ARTS AND CRAFTS
MOVEMENT.**

ARTS - ECONOMIC ASPECTS.
Garrigou, Marcel. La culture, richesse de
l'entreprise . [Paris] , c1990. 272 p. ;   ISBN
2-7007-2836-X :
NX634 .G37 1990

ARTS - ECONOMIC ASPECTS - FRANCE.
Garrigou, Marcel. La culture, richesse de
l'entreprise . [Paris] , c1990. 272 p. ;   ISBN
2-7007-2836-X :
NX634 .G37 1990

ARTS, ENGLISH.
Renaissance bodies . London , 1990. x, 294 p. :
ISBN 0-948462-09-4   DDC 700 20
NX650.F45 R46 1990

ARTS, ENGLISH - CONGRESSES.
L'Artiste, témoin de son temps (?) .
Aix-en-Provence , 1990. xiv, 168 p. ;   ISBN
2-85399-238-1 :   DDC 700/.942 20
NX543 .A83 1990

ARTS, ESTONIAN.
Nõukogude Eesti kultuuripilt 1980 /. Tallinn ,
1981. 93 p., [32] p. of plates ;
NX556.A3 E755 1981

ARTS, ESTONIAN - ESTONIA - TARTU.
Tartu ja kultuur /. Tallinn , 1990. 215 p. :
NX556.T37 T37 1990

ARTS, ETHNIC. see ETHNIC ARTS.

ARTS, EUROPEAN.
Barkan, Leonard. Transuming passion .
Stanford, Calif. , 1991. 147 p. :   ISBN
0-8047-1851-2 (cloth : acid-free paper) :   DDC
700 20
NX652.G35 B37 1991
NYPL [3-MAMZ 91-6123]

Empfindung und Reflexion . Hildesheim, New
York , 1986. vi, 374 p. :   ISBN 3-487-07845-7
NX542 .E46 1986   **NYPL [3-MC 90-12618]**

**ARTS FACILITIES - UNITED STATES -
DIRECTORIES.**
Directory of artist associations and exhibition
spaces, art commissions, museum curators & art
critics /. Renaissance, CA , c1990. 208 p. ;
ISBN 0-940899-14-0
NYPL [MAV 91-6690]

ARTS, FINE. see ART; ARTS.

ARTS - FINLAND - FINANCE.
Veikkola, Eeva-Sisko. Kulttuurin julkinen
rahoitus . Helsinki , 1989. 51 p. : ISBN
951-47-2866-1 :
NX750.F5 V45 1989

Arts for older adults . Hoffman, Donald H.
Englewood Cliffs, N.J. , 1992. p. cm. ISBN
0-13-048182-3 DDC 700/.1/03 20
NX180.A35 H64 1992

ARTS, FRENCH.
Entre deux guerres . Paris , c1990. 631 p. ;
ISBN 2-87686-057-0 : DDC 700/.944/09041 20
NX549.A1 E5 1990

A Vasco da Gama . Paris , 1898. 44, 16 p. :
NX549.A1 V36 1898

**ARTS, FRENCH - RUSSIAN INFLUENCES -
EXHIBITIONS.**
Paris-Moscou, 1900-1930. Paris , 1979. 580 p. :
ISBN 2-85850-002-9 :
NX549.A1 P373   *NYPL [MAL+ 80-2210]*

Arts from the rooftop of Asia : Tibet, Nepal,
Kashmir : [exhibition] / [text by Fong Chow].
New York : Metropolitan Museum of Art,
[1971] 4, [46] p. : ill. ; 26 cm. Cover title.
*1. Art, Buddhist - South Asia - Exhibitions. 2.
Decorative arts, Buddhist - South Asia - Exhibitions. I.
Chow, Fong. II. Metropolitan Museum of Art (New
York, N.Y.). Dept. of Far Eastern Art.*
NYPL [3-MAE 91-302]

ARTS, GERMAN.
Brock, Bazon, 1936- Die Re-Dekade .
München , c1990. 298 p. : ISBN 3-7814-0288-6 :
NX550.A1 B76 1990

**ARTS, GERMAN - GERMANY - BADEN-
WÜRTTEMBERG.**
Kunstkonzeption des Landes
Baden-Württemberg /. Stuttgart , c1990. 391
p. : ISBN 3-923719-19-1
NX550.A3 B245 1990

**ARTS, GERMAN - GERMANY (WEST) -
BAVARIA - EXHIBITIONS.**
Begegnungen . [Esslingen am Neckar] , c1980.
64 p. :   *NYPL [3-MAMG 90-5884]*

**ARTS, GERMAN - GERMANY (WEST) -
DÜSSELDORF REGION -
EXHIBITIONS.**
Am Anfang, Das Junge Rheinland .
Düsseldorf , c1985. 351 p. : ISBN 3-546-47771-5
DDC 700/.943/55 19
NX550.D87 A5 1985
NYPL [3-MAMG+ 85-2357]

**ARTS, GERMAN - GERMANY, WEST -
MUNICH - EXHIBITIONS.**
Die Zwanziger Jahre in München . München ,
1979. xxiii, 768 p. :
NX550.M86 Z9   *NYPL [3-MAMG 81-913]*

**ARTS, GERMAN - GERMANY (WEST) -
STUTTGART.**
Stuttgart, Kunst & Kultur . Stuttgart , 1988.
480 p. : ISBN 3-925860-08-8 DDC
700/.943/47109048 20
NX550.S77 S77 1988

**ARTS - GERMANY - BERLIN - GUIDE-
BOOKS.**
Gerber, Bärbel. Kultur und Kunst in Berlin .
Berlin , 1988. 248 p. : ISBN 3-7442-0022-1
NX550.B4 G4 1988

**ARTS - GERMANY (EAST) - LEIPZIG -
EXHIBITIONS.**
Merkur & die Musen . [Wien] [1989] 627 p. :
ISBN 3-900926-02-6
NYPL [3-MAMG+ 90-13617]

ARTS - GERMANY - LEIPZIG.
--Die ganze Welt im kleinen-- . Leipzig , 1989.
300 p. : ISBN 3-363-00419-2
NYPL [MAMG 91-6223]

ARTS, GRAPHIC. see GRAPHIC ARTS.

ARTS - HISTORY.
Chesnais, Robert. Les racines de l'audio-visuel .
Paris , c1990. 285 p. ; ISBN 2-7178-1862-6 :
NX440 .C536 1990

Davidson, Clifford. On tradition . New York ,
1991. p. cm. ISBN 0-404-64160-1 DDC 700/.9 20
NX440 .D38 1991

**Arts in Education Special Projects Handbook
update, 1986-1990** / edited by Georgia Hornsey
Voils, Teresa Goettsch Wingert. Washington,
DC : National Endowment for the Arts, 1991.

p. cm. Includes index. DDC 700/.7/073 20
*1. Federal aid to the arts - United States. 2. Arts -
Study and teaching (Elementary) - United States. 3.
Arts - Study and teaching (Secondary) - United States.
I. Voils, Georgia Hornsey, 1947-. II. Wingert, Teresa
Goettsch, 1959-. III. National Endowment for the Arts.
Arts in Education.*
NX398 .A82 1991

**ARTS IN SCHOOLS BASIC EDUCATION
GRANTS PROGRAM (U. S.)**
Stevens, Louise K., 1953- Planning to make the
arts basic . Washington, D.C. , 1991. p. cm.
DDC 700/.71/273 20
NX303 .S74 1991

ARTS, INDIC.
Jayakar, Pupul. The earth mother /. New
Delhi, India , New York, N.Y., U. S.A. , 1989.
229 p., [32] p. of plates : ISBN 0-14-012352-0 :
DDC 704.9/4894/0954 20
NX576.A1 J38 1989
NYPL [3-MAF 91-3706]

ARTS - IRELAND.
Kennedy, Brian P. Dreams and responsibilities .
[Dublin, Ireland] [1990?] xiii, 292 p. : ISBN
0-906627-32-X DDC 700/.1/03 20
NX750.I7 K4 1990   *NYPL [JFE 91-2989]*

ARTS, IRISH.
Kennedy, Brian P. Dreams and responsibilities .
[Dublin, Ireland] [1990?] xiii, 292 p. : ISBN
0-906627-32-X DDC 700/.1/03 20
NX750.I7 K4 1990   *NYPL [JFE 91-2989]*

ARTS, ISLAMIC - TURKEY.
The Dervish lodge . Berkeley , c1992. p. cm.
ISBN 0-520-07060-7 (alk. paper) DDC
700/.9561 20
NX688.T9 D47 1992

ARTS, ITALIAN - EXHIBITIONS.
L'Età del divisionismo /. Milano , c1990. 295
p., [2] p. of plates : ISBN 88-435-3179-4 DDC
700 20
NX552.A1 E78 1990
NYPL [3-MAMC 91-4384]

ARTS - JUVENILE LITERATURE.
Historic Blacks in the arts /. Chicago, IL ,
c1990. p. cm. ISBN 0-922162-58-1 : DDC
700/.92/2 B 20
NX164.B55 H57 1990

ARTS, LATIN AMERICAN.
Alegría, Fernando, 1918- Creadores en el
mundo hispánico /. Santiago de Chile [1990]
184 p. ; ISBN 956-1-30910-5
NX501.5.A1 A43 1990

ARTS, LATVIAN.
Veronika Strēlerte . [Stockholm] , c1982. 128
p. :
NX556.Z9 S778 1982

ARTS - MARKETING - CONGRESSES.
Symposium on Research and Marketing for the
Arts (1990 : Florence, Italy) Symposium on
Research and Marketing for the Arts .
Amsterdam, The Netherlands [1990] v, 249
p. : ISBN 92-831-1160-5 DDC 700/.1/03 20
NX180.S6 S9 1990

**ARTS, MEDIEVAL - SWITZERLAND - ST.
GALL.**
Die Kultur der Abtei Sankt Gallen /. Zürich ,
c1990. 223 p. : ISBN 3-7630-1220-6
NX663.S9 K84 1990

ARTS, MEXICAN.
Peden, Margaret Sayers. Out of the volcano .
Washington, D.C. , 1991. p. cm. ISBN
1-560-98060-5 DDC 700/.92/272 B 20
NX514.A1 P4 1991

ARTS, MODERN.
Schwarz, Hans-Günther, 1945- Orient,
Okzident . München , c1990. 355 p. ; ISBN
3-89129-214-7 DDC 700 20
NX650.R83 S38 1990

ARTS, MODERN - 18TH CENTURY.
Park, William, 1930- The idea of Rococo /.
Newark , 1992. p. cm. ISBN 0-87413-434-X
DDC 700/.9/033 20
NX452.5.R6 P37 1992

**ARTS, MODERN - 18TH CENTURY -
EUROPE.**
Empfindung und Reflexion . Hildesheim , New
York , 1986. vi, 374 p. : ISBN 3-487-07845-7
NX542 .E46 1986   *NYPL [3-MC 90-12618]*

ARTS, MODERN - 19TH CENTURY.
Ashton, Dore. A fable of modern art /.
Berkeley , c1991. p. cm. ISBN 0-520-07301-0
DDC 700/.9/04 20
NX454 .A8 1991

Borrell, Joan. L'artiste-roi . [Paris] , c1990. 398
p. ; ISBN 2-7007-3473-4 : DDC 700/.1 20
NX454 .B63 1990

Kroeber, Karl, 1926- Retelling/rereading . New
Brunswick , c1992. p. cm. ISBN 0-8135-1765-6 :
DDC 700 20
NX650.N37 K76 1992

**ARTS, MODERN - 19TH CENTURY -
AUSTRIA.**
Sterk, Harald. Biedermeier . Wien , c1988. 124
p. ; ISBN 3-85128-010-5
NX549.6 .S73 1988

**ARTS, MODERN - 19TH CENTURY -
AUSTRIA - VIENNA - EXHIBITIONS.**
Biedermeier in Wien 1815-1848 . Mainz ,
c1990. 251 p. : ISBN 3-8053-1128-1
NX548.V53 B54 1990

**ARTS, MODERN - 19TH CENTURY -
FRANCE.**
A Vasco da Gama . Paris , 1898. 44, 16 p. :
NX549.A1 V36 1898

**ARTS, MODERN - 19TH CENTURY -
GERMANY.**
Sterk, Harald. Biedermeier . Wien , c1988. 124
p. ; ISBN 3-85128-010-5
NX549.6 .S73 1988

**ARTS, MODERN - 19TH CENTURY - ITALY -
EXHIBITIONS.**
L'Età del divisionismo /. Milano , c1990. 295
p., [2] p. of plates : ISBN 88-435-3179-4 DDC
700 20
NX552.A1 E78 1990
NYPL [3-MAMC 91-4384]

**ARTS, MODERN - 19TH CENTURY -
RUSSIAN S.F.S.R. - LENINGRAD -
EXHIBITIONS.**
St. Petersburg um 1800 . Recklinghausen ,
c1990. 568 p. : ISBN 3-7647-0401-2
NYPL [3-MAVZ (Leningrad) 90-13200]

**ARTS, MODERN - 19TH CENTURY -
UNITED STATES.**
Crunden, Robert Morse. American salons .
New York , 1992. p. cm. ISBN 0-19-506569-7
(acid-free paper) DDC 700/.973/09034 20
NX503.7 .C78 1992

ARTS, MODERN - 20TH CENTURY.
Arts & architecture . Cambridge, Mass. , c1990.
248 p. : ISBN 0-262-07131-2 : DDC 700/.9/04 20
NX456.5.M64 A7 1990
NYPL [3-MAL+ 91-3679]

Ashton, Dore. A fable of modern art /.
Berkeley , c1991. p. cm. ISBN 0-520-07301-0
DDC 700/.9/04 20
NX454 .A8 1991

Bomb . San Francisco , 1992. p. cm. ISBN
0-87286-261-5 : DDC 700/.9/04 20
NX458 .B66 1992

Cronología de la cultura, 1950-1990 /. [Bogotá,
Colombia] , 1990. 524 p. : ISBN 958-9138-62-4
DDC 700/.9/045 20
NX535.B64 C76 1990

Dachy, Marc. [Journal du mouvement Dada.
English.] The Dada movement, 1915-1923 /.
Geneva , New York , 1990. 230 p. : ISBN
0-8478-1110-7 DDC 700/.9/04 20
NX456.5.D3 D32513 1990
NYPL [3-MAL+ 91-2295]

The Helicon nine reader . Kansas City , c1990.
512 p. : ISBN 0-9627460-0-2 DDC 700/.82 20
NX180.F4 H44 1990

Huelsenbeck, Richard, 1892-1974. Memoirs of a
Dada drummer /. Berkeley , 1991. liv, 202 p.,
[12] p. of plates : ISBN 0-520-07370-3 (pbk.)
DDC 700 20
NX600.D3 H79 1991   *NYPL [MAL 91-7694]*

Kirstein, Lincoln, 1907- By with to & from .
New York , 1991. p. cm. ISBN 0-374-18765-7 :
DDC 700/.9/04 20
NX456 .K56 1991

Kroeber, Karl, 1926- Retelling/rereading . New
Brunswick , c1992. p. cm. ISBN 0-8135-1765-6 :
DDC 700 20
NX650.N37 K76 1992

Kulturanalyse /. [Oslo] , c1990. 236 p. ;　ISBN
82-05-18967-6
NX456 .K77 1990

Kulturens dekningsbidrag . [Oslo] , c1991. 179
p. :　ISBN 82-02-12832-3
NX456 .K78 1991

Les années 20 d'Anne Bony. Paris　[1989] 2 v.
(1275 p.) :　ISBN 2-903370-45-1 (set)　DDC
700/.9/048 20
NX457 .A55 1989

Lurie, Boris, 1924- NO!art . Berlin , c1988.
135, 283, 109 p. :
NX458 .L87 1988

Moholy-Nagy . New York, N.Y.　[1991]. xviii,
238 p. :　ISBN 0-306-80455-7 :　DDC 700/.9/04 20
NX65 .M64 1991

Prinz, Jessica, 1952- Art discourse/discourse in
art /. New Brunswick , 1991. p. cm.　ISBN
0-8135-1673-0 :　DDC 700/.9/04 20
NX456.5.P66 P75 1991

Scarpetta, Guy, 1946- L'artifice /. Paris ,
c1988. 314 p. ;　ISBN 2-246-40581-5
NX456 .S3 1988

Silva, José Antônio, 1951- A impressão da
cultura /. Porto Alegre-RS , c1990. 104 p. :
ISBN 85-20-50026-9
NX456 .S53 1990

Sontag, Susan, 1933- Under the sign of Saturn
/. New York , 1991. 203 p. ;　ISBN
0-385-26712-6　DDC 700/.9/04 20
NX456 .S58 1991

Surrealism and women /. Cambridge, Mass. ,
1991. 240 p. :　ISBN 0-262-53098-8 :　DDC 700
20
NX456.5.S8 S87 1991

View . New York , Emeryville, CA , c1991. p.
cm.　ISBN 1-560-25013-5 :　DDC 700/.9/04 20
NX456 .V49 1991

Werckmeister, O. K. (Otto Karl), 1934-
[Zitadellenkultur. English.] Citadel culture /.
Chicago , 1991. 210 p. ;　ISBN 0-226-89361-8
(alk. paper) :　DDC 700/.9/048 20
NX456.5.P66 W4713 1991

**ARTS, MODERN - 20TH CENTURY -
ADDRESSES, ESSAYS, LECTURES.**
Time and space concepts in art /. New York ,
1980. viii, 157 p., 4 leaves of plates :
NX650.S8 T55　　*NYPL [3-MAMZ 80-2228]*

**ARTS, MODERN - 20TH CENTURY -
ARGENTINE REPUBLIC.**
Kosice, Gyula, 1924- Arte Madí /. Buenos
Aires, Argentina , c1982. 198 p. :　ISBN
950-0-00418-6　DDC 700/.982/074098211 19
NX531.A1 K67 1982
　　　　　　　NYPL [3-MAM 85-1850]

**ARTS, MODERN - 20TH CENTURY -
AUSTRIA.**
Seibert, Ingrit. Die Schwierigen . Wien , c1986.
199 p. :　ISBN 3-7046-0053-9
NX548.Z8 S45 1986

Van Zon, Gabriele, 1937- Word and picture .
New York , 1991. p. cm.　ISBN 0-8204-1475-1
DDC 700/.92 20
NX548.Z9 K838 1991

**ARTS, MODERN - 20TH CENTURY -
BRAZIL.**
Teles, Fídias. Os malabaristas da vida . Recife,
Pernambuco , 1989. 398 p. :
NX533.A1 T45 1989

**ARTS, MODERN - 20TH CENTURY -
COLOMBIA - BOGOTÁ.**
Cronología de la cultura, 1950-1990 /. [Bogotá,
Colombia] , 1990. 524 p. :　ISBN 958-9138-62-4
DDC 700/.9/045 20
NX535.B64 C76 1990

**ARTS, MODERN - 20TH CENTURY - CUBA -
THEMES, MOTIVES.**
Barnet, Miguel, 1940- Autógrafos cubanos /.
Ciudad de La Habana , c1990. 151 p. :　DDC
700/.97291/0904 20
NX525.A1 B37 1990

**ARTS, MODERN - 20TH CENTURY -
CZECHOSLOVAKIA - CONGRESSES.**
Proudy české umělecké tvorby 19. století .
Praha , 1990. 262 p. :
NX650.I34 P76 1990

**ARTS, MODERN - 20TH CENTURY -
DENMARK - EXHIBITIONS.**
Kitsch & konkret . København , 1990. 95 p. :
ISBN 87-89556-00-3 :
NX558.A1 K58 1990

**ARTS, MODERN - 20TH CENTURY -
DICTIONARIES.**
Brownstone, David M. 20th century culture .
[New York?] , 1991. p. cm.　ISBN
0-13-210519-5 :　DDC 700/.9/04 20
NX456 .B76 1991

Cortanze, Gérard de. Le monde du surréalisme
/. Paris , c1991. 182 p. :　ISBN 2-85199-550-2
DDC 700 20
NX456.5.S8 C67 1991

**ARTS, MODERN - 20TH CENTURY -
ENGLAND.**
Bloomsbury . Boston , c1990. 328 p. :　ISBN
0-8212-1768-2 :　DDC 700/.942 20
NX543 .B58 1990
　　　　　　NYPL [3-MAMR+ 91-3278]

**ARTS, MODERN - 20TH CENTURY -
ESTONIA.**
Nõukogude Eesti kultuuripilt 1980 /. Tallinn ,
1981. 93 p., [32] p. of plates ;
NX556.A3 E755 1981

**ARTS, MODERN - 20TH CENTURY -
EUROPE.**
Ohrt, Roberto. Phantom Avantgarde . Hamburg
[München] , 1990. 333 p., [16] p. of plates :
ISBN 3-89401-168-8
NX542 .O38 1990

Plant, Sadie, 1964- The most radical gesture .
London , New York, NY , 1992. p. cm.　ISBN
0-415-06221-7　DDC 700/.1/03 20
NX542 .P5 1992

**ARTS, MODERN - 20TH CENTURY -
EUROPE - ADDRESSES, ESSAYS,
LECTURES.**
Collage et montage au théâtre et dans les autres
arts durant les années vingt /. Lausanne , cop.
1978. 296 p., [32] p. of plates :　DDC 700/.94 19
NX542 .C64　　　　*NYPL [JFE 81-222]*

**ARTS, MODERN - 20TH CENTURY -
EXHIBITIONS.**
The Avant-garde and the text . Providence, RI ,
c1988. p. 306-507 :　　*NYPL [MDT 91-5721]*

Buchstäblich Nürnberger wörtliche Tage .
[Nürnberg] , c1990. 80 p. :　ISBN 3-922531-77-6
NX458 .B83 1990

A Debate on abstraction . [New York]　[1988?]
79 p. :　　　　*NYPL [3-MAL 90-12609]*

**ARTS, MODERN - 20TH CENTURY -
FRANCE.**
Delons, André, 1909-1940. Au carrefour du
Grand jeu et du surréalisme /. [Mortemart,
Mézière-sur-Issoire]　[1988] 201 p. ;
NX549.A1 D45 1988
　　　　　　NYPL [3-MAMI 90-11123]

Entre deux guerres . Paris , c1990. 631 p. ;
ISBN 2-87686-057-0 :　DDC 700/.944/09041 20
NX549.A1 E5 1990

**ARTS, MODERN - 20TH CENTURY -
FRANCE - EXHIBITIONS.**
Paris-Moscou, 1900-1930. Paris , 1979. 580 p. :
ISBN 2-85850-002-9 :
NX549.A1 P373　　*NYPL [MAL+ 80-2210]*

**ARTS, MODERN - 20TH CENTURY -
GERMANY.**
Brock, Bazon, 1936- Die Re-Dekade .
München , c1990. 298 p. :　ISBN 3-7814-0288-6 :
NX550.A1 B76 1990

The Ideological crisis of expressionism .
Columbia, S.C. , c1990. 299 p. :　ISBN
0-938100-77-7 (alk. paper)　DDC 700 20
NX550.A1 I33 1990
　　　　　　NYPL [3-MAMG 90-11742]

Taylor, Seth, 1955- Left-wing Nietzscheans .
Berlin , New York , 1990. x, 254 p. ;　ISBN
0-89925-695-3 (U. S.) :　DDC 700/.944/09041
20
NX550.A1 T39 1990
　　　　　　NYPL [3-MAMG 91-3362]

**ARTS, MODERN - 20TH CENTURY -
GERMANY (WEST) - BAVARIA -
EXHIBITIONS.**
Begegnungen . [Esslingen am Neckar] , c1980.
64 p. :　　　　*NYPL [3-MAMG 90-5884]*

**ARTS, MODERN - 20TH CENTURY -
GERMANY (WEST) - DÜSSELDORF
REGION - EXHIBITIONS.**
Am Anfang, Das Junge Rheinland .
Düsseldorf , c1985. 351 p. :　ISBN 3-546-47771-5
DDC 700/.943/55 19
NX550.D87 A5 1985
　　　　　　NYPL [3-MAMG+ 85-2357]

**ARTS, MODERN - 20TH CENTURY -
GERMANY, WEST - MUNICH -
EXHIBITIONS.**
Die Zwanziger Jahre in München . München ,
1979. xxiii, 768 p. :
NX550.M86 Z9　　*NYPL [3-MAMG 81-913]*

**ARTS, MODERN - 20TH CENTURY -
GERMANY (WEST) - STUTTGART.**
Stuttgart, Kunst & Kultur . Stuttgart , 1988.
480 p. :　ISBN 3-925860-08-8　DDC
700/.943/47109048 20
NX550.S77 S77 1988

**ARTS, MODERN - 20TH CENTURY - GREAT
BRITAIN.**
Sillars, Stuart, 1951- British romantic art and
the Second World War /. New York , 1991. p.
cm.　ISBN 0-312-06719-4　DDC 700 20
NX543 .S52 1991

**ARTS, MODERN - 20TH CENTURY -
HISTORY.**
The Arts . Oxford , New York , 1991. 256 p. :
ISBN 0-19-520852-8　DDC 700/.9/04 20
NX456 .A76 1991

**ARTS, MODERN - 20TH CENTURY -
HISTORY AND CRITICISM.**
Brion-Guerry, Liliane, 1916- L'année 1913.
Paris, 1971-1973. 3 v.
　　　　　　NYPL [3-MAL 72-945]

**ARTS, MODERN - 20TH CENTURY -
INDONESIA.**
33 profil budayawan Indonesia /. [Jakarta]
[1990] vii, 208 p. :
NX579.A1 A13 1990

**ARTS, MODERN - 20TH CENTURY - ITALY -
EXHIBITIONS.**
L'Età del divisionismo /. Milano , c1990. 295
p., [2] p. of plates :　ISBN 88-435-3179-4　DDC
700 20
NX552.A1 E78 1990
　　　　　　NYPL [3-MAMC 91-4384]

**ARTS, MODERN - 20TH CENTURY - LATIN
AMERICA.**
Alegría, Fernando, 1918- Creadores en el
mundo hispánico /. Santiago de Chile [1990]
184 p. ;　ISBN 956-1-30910-5
NX501.5.A1 A43 1990

**ARTS, MODERN - 20TH CENTURY -
MEXICO.**
Peden, Margaret Sayers. Out of the volcano .
Washington, D.C. , 1991. p. cm.　ISBN
1-560-98060-5　DDC 700/.92/272 B 20
NX514.A1 P4 1991

**ARTS, MODERN - 20TH CENTURY -
NORWAY.**
Stenersen, Sigurd. Kultur, samhørighet .
[Harstad , 1989] 119 p. :
NX430.N8 S74 1989

ARTS, MODERN - 20TH CENTURY - PERU.
Martínez, Cesáreo. Desde la vigilia . [Peru?]
1989. 212 p. ;
N6718 .M37 1989

**ARTS, MODERN - 20TH CENTURY -
RUSSIA - EXHIBITIONS.**
Paris-Moscou, 1900-1930. Paris , 1979. 580 p. :
ISBN 2-85850-002-9 :
NX549.A1 P373　*NYPL [MAL+ 80-2210]*

**ARTS, MODERN - 20TH CENTURY -
RUSSIAN S.F.S.R. - EXHIBITIONS.**
Von Eisenstein bis Tarkowsky . München ,
c1990. 159 p. :　ISBN 3-7913-1068-2
NX556.A1 V6 1990

**ARTS, MODERN - 20TH CENTURY -
SCANDINAVIA.**
Kulturanalyse /. [Oslo] , c1990. 236 p. ;　ISBN
82-05-18967-6
NX456 .K77 1990

**ARTS, MODERN - 20TH CENTURY -
SOVIET UNION.**
Taylor, Brandon. Art and literature under the
Bolsheviks /. Concord, MA , 1991. p. cm.
ISBN 0-7453-0293-9　DDC 700/.947/09041 20
NX556.A1 T39 1991

ARTS, MODERN - 20TH CENTURY - SOVIET UNION - CONGRESSES.
The Revolution and the avant-garde . Seattle , 1991. p. ISBN 0-935558-30-6 DDC 700/.947/09041 20
NX556.A1 R48 1991

ARTS, MODERN - 20TH CENTURY - SPAIN.
Coad, Emma Dent. Spanish design and architecture /. London , 1990. 208 p. : ISBN 0-289-80030-7
NYPL [3-MAML 90-11570]

ARTS, MODERN - 20TH CENTURY - UNITED STATES.
Bomb . San Francisco , 1992. p. cm. ISBN 0-87286-261-5 : DDC 700/.9/04 20
NX458 .B66 1992

Crunden, Robert Morse. American salons . New York , 1992. p. cm. ISBN 0-19-506569-7 (acid-free paper) DDC 700/.973/09034 20
NX503.7 .C78 1992

In the Vernacular . Jefferson, N.C. , 1991. p. ISBN 0-89950-645-3 (lib. bdg. : alk. paper) DDC 700/.92/273 20
NX504 .I526 1991

Polcari, Stephen. Abstract Expressionism and the modern experience /. Cambridge [England] , New York , 1991. xxiii, 408 p. : ISBN 0-521-40453-3 (hardback) DDC 700/.973/0904 20
NX504 .P65 1991

ARTS, MODERN - 20TH CENTURY - VENEZUELA.
La Flor imaginaria . Caracas , 1989. 160 p. : ISBN 980-255-018-3 DDC 700 20
NX650.F57 F58 1989

ARTS, MODERN - CONGRESSES.
Fictions of culture . New York , 1991. p. cm. ISBN 0-8204-1714-9 DDC 700 20
NX449.5 .F53 1991

ARTS, NORWEGIAN.
Stenersen, Sigurd. Kultur, samhørighet . [Harstad , 1989] 119 p. :
NX430.N8 S74 1989

Arts of India, 1550-1900 / edited by John Guy and Deborah Swallow ; [contributions by] Rosemary Crill ... [et al.] London : Victoria & Albert Museum, c1990. 240 p. : ill. (some col.) ; 28 cm. Half title: Arts of India, 1550-1900, the Nehru Gallery of Indian Art. Includes bibliographical references (p. 230-237) and index. ISBN 1-85177-022-4 DDC 709.54 20
1. Art, Indic - England - London - Catalogs. I. Guy, John, 1949-. II. Swallow, D. A. III. Crill, Rosemary. IV. Nehru Gallery of Indian Art. V. Title: Arts of India 1550-1900, the Nehru Gallery of Indian Art.
N7301   NYPL [3-MAF 91-6685]

Arts of India 1550-1900, the Nehru Gallery of Indian Art. Arts of India, 1550-1900 /. London , c1990. 240 p. : ISBN 1-85177-022-4 DDC 709.54 20
N7301   NYPL [3-MAF 91-6685]

The Arts of Korea. Seoul : Dong Hwa Pub. Co., c1979. 6 v. : ill. (some col.), maps ; 31 cm. Based on the series Han'guk misul chŏnjip. CONTENTS. - 1. Kim, W. Y., Han, B. S., Chin, H. S. Ancient art.--2. Kim, W. Y., Choi, S. U., Im, C. S. Paintings.--3. Hwang, S. Y. Buddhist art.--4. Choi, S. U., Chung, Y. M. Ceramics.--5. Chin, H. S., Choi, S. U., Chung, Y. M. Handicrafts.--6. Kim, C. K., Hwang, S. Y., Chung, Y. H. Architecture. DDC 709/.519
1. Art, Korean. 2. Art objects, Korean. I. Tonghwa Ch'ulp'ansa. II. Han'guk misul Chŏnjip.
N7363 .A79   NYPL [3-MAF+ 83-1615]

Arts of power . Starn, Randolph. Berkeley , c1992. p. cm. ISBN 0-520-07383-5 (cloth) DDC 725/.17/0945 20
NA6815 .S787 1992

ARTS - PHILOSOPHY.
Cultural hermeneutics of modern art . Amsterdam , Atlanta, GA , 1989. 307 p., [1] p. of plates : ISBN 90-6203-645-7
NYPL [3-MAS 90-10857]

ARTS, POLISH.
Helman, Włodzimierz. Wkład Polaków i Polonii do światowej sztuki /. Warszawa , 1988. 70 p. ;
NX571.P6 H45 1988

ARTS - POLITICAL ASPECTS - UNITED STATES.
Trend, David. Cultural pedagogy . New York , 1992. p. cm. ISBN 0-89789-256-9 DDC

700/.1/03 20
NX180.S6 T7 1992

ARTS - QUÉBEC (PROVINCE)
Lacroix, Jean-Guy, 1945- La condition d'artiste . Outremont, Québec , Ville Saint-Laurent, Québec , c1990. 249 p. ; ISBN 2-89005-389-X DDC 338.4/77/00971409048 20
NX513.A3 Q35 1990

ARTS - QUÉBEC (PROVINCE) - FINANCE - STATISTICS.
Dépenses de l'administration publique provinciale au titre de la culture, 1984-1988. Québec, Québec [1989] 29 p. : ISBN 2-550-19744-5
NX750.C2 D47 1989

ARTS - QUÉBEC (PROVINCE) - PUBLIC OPINION.
Pronovost, Gilles. Les comportements des Québécois en matière d'activités culturelles de loisir . Québec [1990] 94 p. ; ISBN 2-551-14099-4 DDC 700/.9714 20
NX513.A3 Q368 1990

ARTS, RENAISSANCE.
Le Monde animal au temps de la Renaissance /. Paris , 1990. 259 p. : ISBN 2-86433-036-9 : DDC 700 20
NX650.A55 M66 1990

ARTS, RENAISSANCE - ENGLAND.
Renaissance bodies . London , 1990. x, 294 p. : ISBN 0-948462-09-4 DDC 700 20
NX650.F45 R46 1990

ARTS, RENAISSANCE - ITALY.
Barolsky, Paul, 1941- Michelangelo's nose . University Park , c1990. xx, 169 p. : ISBN 0-271-00695-1 : DDC 700/.92 20
NX552.Z9 M533 1990
NYPL [3-MCF B9 91-2293]

ARTS, ROCOCO.
Park, William, 1930- The idea of Rococo /. Newark , 1992. p. cm. ISBN 0-87413-434-X DDC 700/.9/033 20
NX452.5.R6 P37 1992

ARTS, RUSSIAN - FRENCH INFLUENCES - EXHIBITIONS.
Paris-Moscou, 1900-1930. Paris , 1979. 580 p. : ISBN 2-85850-002-9 :
NX549.A1 P373   NYPL [MAL+ 80-2210]

ARTS, RUSSIAN - RUSSIAN S.F.S.R.
Russen in Berlin . Leipzig , 1990. xv, 614 p. : ISBN 3-379-00119-8
NX556.A1 R86 1990

ARTS, RUSSIAN - RUSSIAN S.F.S.R. - EXHIBITIONS.
Von Eisenstein bis Tarkowsky . München , c1990. 129 p. ; ISBN 3-7913-1068-2
NX556.A1 V6 1990

ARTS - RUSSIAN S.F.S.R. - LENINGRAD - EXHIBITIONS.
St. Petersburg um 1800 . Recklinghausen , c1990. 568 p. : ISBN 3-7647-0401-2
NYPL [3-MAVZ (Leningrad) 90-13200]

ARTS - SCHOLARSHIPS, FELLOWSHIPS, ETC. - UNITED STATES.
Public policy and the aesthetic interest . Urbana , c1992. p. cm. ISBN 0-252-01899-0 (cl) DDC 700/.1/03 20
NX730 .P79 1992

ARTS - SCHOLARSHIPS, FELLOWSHIPS, ETC. - UNITED STATES - DIRECTORIES.
Blum, Laurie. Free money for people in the arts /. New York , Toronto , 1991. p. cm. ISBN 0-02-028175-7 DDC 700/.79/73 20
NX398 .B58 1991

ARTS - SCHOLARSHIPS, FELLOWSHIPS, ETC. - UNITED STATES - STATISTICS.
Love, Jeffrey. Summary of state arts agencies' grantmaking activities for fiscal year 1987 /. Washington, D.C. (1010 Vermont Ave., N.W., Suite 920, Washington 20005) , c1990. vi, 211 p. : DDC 353.9/3854 20
NX398 .L6 1990

ARTS - SOCIAL ASPECTS. see ARTS AND SOCIETY.

ARTS - SOUTH CAROLINA - CHARLESTON.
Saunders, Boyd. Alfred Hutty and the Charleston renaissance /. Orangeburg, S.C. , c1990. 127 p. : ISBN 0-87844-089-5 DDC 769.92

B 20
NE2012.H88 S28 1990
NYPL [MDG+ (Hutty) 91-5803]

ARTS, SOVIET.
Taylor, Brandon. Art and literature under the Bolsheviks /. Concord, MA , 1991. p. cm. ISBN 0-7453-0293-9 DDC 700/.947/09041 20
NX556.A1 T39 1991

ARTS, SPANISH.
Gaya, Ramón. [Works. 1990.] Obra completa /. Valencia , c1990- v. <1 > ; ISBN 84-87101-33-X (obra completa)
NX440 .G3 1990

ARTS - STUDY AND TEACHING.
Cultural literacy & arts education /. Urbana , c19. :xvi, 171 p. : ISBN 0-252-01845-1 (alk. paper) DDC 700/.1/03 20
NX294 .C85 1992

ARTS - STUDY AND TEACHING (ELEMENTARY) - CALIFORNIA.
Visual and performing arts framework . Sacramento , 1982. x, 166 p. : DDC 700/.71/2794 20
NX310.C2 V5 1982

Visual and performing arts framework . Sacramento , 1989. xiv, 167 p. : ISBN 0-8011-0805-5 : DDC 700/.71/2794 20
NX310.C2 V5 1989

ARTS - STUDY AND TEACHING (ELEMENTARY) - CANADA.
Carter, Cheryl G. North American schools of the arts . [Washington, D.C.] [c1990] vii, 172 p. : DDC 700/.71/273 20
NX303 .C37 1990

ARTS - STUDY AND TEACHING (ELEMENTARY) - NEW JERSEY.
Literacy in the Arts Task Force (New Jersey) Literacy in the arts . Trenton, N.J. [1989] 52 p. ; DDC 700/.71/2749 20
NX310.N3 L58 1989

ARTS - STUDY AND TEACHING (ELEMENTARY) - UNITED STATES.
Arts in Education Special Projects Handbook update, 1986-1990 /. Washington, DC , 1991. p. cm. DDC 700/.7/073 20
NX398 .A82 1991

Carter, Cheryl G. North American schools of the arts . [Washington, D.C.] [c1990] vii, 172 p. : DDC 700/.71/273 20
NX303 .C37 1990

ARTS - STUDY AND TEACHING (HIGHER) - NETHERLANDS.
Velden, R. K. W. van der. Letteren en arbeidsmarkt /. Groningen , 's-Gravenhage [1989] 129 p. ;
NX554.A1 V4 1989

ARTS - STUDY AND TEACHING (SECONDARY) - CALIFORNIA.
Visual and performing arts framework . Sacramento , 1982. x, 166 p. : DDC 700/.71/2794 20
NX310.C2 V5 1982

Visual and performing arts framework . Sacramento , 1989. xiv, 167 p. : ISBN 0-8011-0805-5 : DDC 700/.71/2794 20
NX310.C2 V5 1989

ARTS - STUDY AND TEACHING (SECONDARY) - CANADA.
Carter, Cheryl G. North American schools of the arts . [Washington, D.C.] [c1990] vii, 172 p. : DDC 700/.71/273 20
NX303 .C37 1990

ARTS - STUDY AND TEACHING (SECONDARY) - NEW JERSEY.
Literacy in the Arts Task Force (New Jersey) Literacy in the arts . Trenton, N.J. [1989] 52 p. ; DDC 700/.71/2749 20
NX310.N3 L58 1989

ARTS - STUDY AND TEACHING (SECONDARY) - UNITED STATES.
Arts in Education Special Projects Handbook update, 1986-1990 /. Washington, DC , 1991. p. cm. DDC 700/.7/073 20
NX398 .A82 1991

Carter, Cheryl G. North American schools of the arts . [Washington, D.C.] [c1990] vii, 172 p. : DDC 700/.71/273 20
NX303 .C37 1990

ARTS - STUDY AND TEACHING - UNITED STATES.
Swanger, David. Essays in aesthetic education. San Francisco , 1991. p. cm. ISBN 0-7734-9900-8 DDC 700/.7/073 20
NX303 .S94 1991

ARTS SURVEYS - QUÉBEC (PROVINCE)
Pronovost, Gilles. Les comportements des Québécois en matière d'activités culturelles de loisir . Québec [1990] 94 p. ; ISBN 2-551-14099-4 DDC 700/.9714 20
NX513.A3 Q368 1990

ARTS, SWISS - SWITZERLAND - BASEL - EXHIBITIONS.
Le Musée sentimental de Bâle / erausgegeben von Barbara Huber-Greub und Stephen Andreae ; [Idee und künstlerische Leitung: Daniel Spoerri]. Basel , c1989. 332 p. : ISBN 3-85700-006-X
NYPL [3-MAVZ (Basel) 90-13397]

ARTS - SWITZERLAND - BASEL - EXHIBITIONS.
Le Musée sentimental de Bâle / erausgegeben von Barbara Huber-Greub und Stephen Andreae ; [Idee und künstlerische Leitung: Daniel Spoerri]. Basel , c1989. 332 p. : ISBN 3-85700-006-X
NYPL [3-MAVZ (Basel) 90-13397]

ARTS - THAILAND.
Phon Trawën. Sinlapin 'ek hæng Krung Rattanakōsin /. [Bangkok] [24]94 [1951] 6, 385 ;
NX578.7.A1 P47 1951

ARTS, TURKISH.
The Dervish lodge . Berkeley , c1992. p. cm. ISBN 0-520-07060-7 (alk. paper) DDC 700/.9561 20
NX688.T9 D47 1992
Türkali, Vedat, 1919- Savunmalar . [İstanbul] [1989] 192 p. ; ISBN 975-406-087-8
NX565.A1 T86 1989

ARTS, TURKISH - CYPRUS.
Gökçeoğlu, M. (Mustafa), 1942- Tezler ve sözler /. [Cyprus] [1985?]- v. < 1 > :
NX573.6.C9 G64 1985

ARTS, UDMURT - SOURCES.
Istoki iskusstva Udmurtii . Izhevsk , 1989. 116 p., [8] p. of plates :
NX556.A3 U3538 1989

ARTS, VENEZUELAN.
La Flor imaginaria . Caracas , 1989. 160 p. : ISBN 980-255-018-3 DDC 700 20
NX650.F57 F58 1989

ARTS - VOCATIONAL GUIDANCE - NETHERLANDS.
Velden, R. K. W. van der. Letteren en arbeidsmarkt /. Groningen , 's-Gravenhage [1989] 129 p. ;
NX554.A1 V4 1989

Artscan Datamap (Firm) Canadian atlas of F.S.A. postal areas. Scarborough, ON , c1990. 1 atlas (v, 69 [i.e. 138], 69 p.) : DDC 383/.145 20
NYPL [Map Div. 91-8103]

Arturo Michelena . Banco Industrial de Venezuela. [Caracas, Venezuela] [1989?] 183 p. : DDC 759.987 20
N6739.M53 B36 1989

Artwalks in New York . Harrison, Marina, 1939- New York , 1991. p. cm. ISBN 0-935576-40-1 DDC 709/.747/1 20
N8845.N7 H3 1991

Artwords 2. Art talk : the early 80s / edited by Jeanne Siegel. New York, N.Y. : Da Capo Press, 1990. xi, 319 p. : ill., ports. ; 23. (A Da Capo paperback) Reprint. Originally published: Artwords 2. Ann Arbor, Mich. : UMI Research Press, c1988. Includes index. ISBN 0-306-80414-X (pbk.) : DDC 700/.9/048 20
I. Siegel, Jeanne. II. Title.
N6490 .A73 1990 NYPL [3-MAL 91-6966]

Arudch/Ptghni. Gandolfo, Francesco. Ptghni/Arudch /. Milano, Italia , 1986. 74 p. : ISBN 88-85822-03-7 DDC 720/.9566/2 s 726/.5/094792 19
NA1474 .D6 no. 16 NA5998.P84
NYPL [3-MQW 90-11667]

Arutiūnĭan, Aramais Bagrotovich. Haykakan SSH Gitut'yunneri Akademia. Atlas Armĭanskoĭ Sovetskoĭ Sotsialisticheskoĭ Respubliki /.

Erevan , 1961. 1 atlas (viii, 111 p. :
G2157.A7 A5 1961
NYPL [Map Div. 91-1095]

Arvada Center for the Arts and Humanities. As seen by both sides . Boston, Mass. , Amersht, MA , 1991. 112 p. : ISBN 0-87023-744-6 (pbk.) : DDC 760/.04499597043/074597 20
N6512 .A788 1991

Arvīds Egle /. Lāce, Rasma. Rīga , 1985. 108 p. :
NYPL [3-MCZ E299 90-11091]

Ary, Henry, 1807-1859.
Piwonka, Ruth. Mount Merino . Kinderhook, N.Y. , c1978. [44] p. :
NYPL [3-MCW+ 90-7105]

ARY, HENRY, 1807-1859 - EXHIBITIONS.
Piwonka, Ruth. Mount Merino . Kinderhook, N.Y. , c1978. [44] p. :
NYPL [3-MCW+ 90-7105]

Arya, R. P. Tamilnad Printers & Traders Private Ltd. The city atlas of India . Madras, India , 1985. 1 atlas (232 p.) : DDC 912/.54 19
G2284.A1 T3 1985
NYPL [Map Div. 91-6606]

As bienais de São Paulo, 1951 a 1987 /.
Amarante, Leonor. São Paulo-SP , 1989. 407 p. : ISBN 85-7165-003-9 DDC 709/.04/50748161 20
N5030.S37 A43 1989

As Maine goes. Bowdoin College. Museum of Art. Brunswick, Maine, 1966. 1 v. (unpaged)
NYPL [MFX (McKee) 90-5881]

As seen by both sides : American and Vietnamese artists look at the war / edited by C. David Thomas. Boston, Mass. : Indochina Arts Project, William Joiner Foundation ; Amersht, MA : Distributed by the University of Massachusetts Press, 1991. 112 p. : ill. (some col.) ; 28 cm. Catalog of an exhibition held at the Arvada Center for the Arts and Humanities, Arvada, Colo., May 11-June 6, 1990, and other museums. Includes bibliographical references (p. 31). ISBN 0-87023-744-6 (pbk.) : DDC 760/.04499597043/074597 20
1. Art, American - Exhibitions. 2. Art, Modern - 20th century - United States - Exhibitions. 3. Art, Vietnamese - Exhibitions. 4. Art, Modern - 20th century - Vietnam - Exhibitions. 5. Vietnamese Conflict, 1961-1975 - Art and the conflict - Exhibitiopns. I. Thomas, C. David. II. Arvada Center for the Arts and Humanities.
N6512 .A788 1991

Ašarina, Nina. Gosudarstvennyĭ istoricheskiĭ muzeĭ (Moscow, R.S.F.S.R.) Meraviglie sconosciute dal Museo storico di Mosca . Milano , c1989. 198 p. :
NYPL [3-MNR+ 91-4646]

Ascani Orsini, Riccardo, 1940- Gilardoni, Arturo. X-rays in art . Mandello Lario, Italy , 1977. 231 p. : *NYPL [3-MAS+ 90-7036]*

Aschengreen, Cristina Piacenti. see Piacenti Aschengreen, Cristina.

Aschoff, Jürgen C. Magie der Pflanzen : visuelle Streifzug durch Gewächshäuser botanischer Gärten = The magic of plants : visual perambulations through the greenhouses of botanical gardens / Jürgen C. Aschoff. München : MC Verlag, J. Knips, 1987. 79 p. : ill. ; 22 x 30 cm. ISBN 3-923558-12-0
1. Aschoff, Jürgen C. 2. Botanical gardens - Pictorial works. I. Title.
NYPL [MFX+ (Aschoff) 89-20434]

ASCHOFF, JÜRGEN C.
Aschoff, Jürgen C. Magie der Pflanzen . München , 1987. 79 p. : ISBN 3-923558-12-0
NYPL [MFX+ (Aschoff) 89-20434]

Asharina, N. A. (Nina Aleksandrovna) Russian glass of the 17th-20th centuries / Nina Asharina, Tamara Malinina, Liudmila Kazakova. Corning, N.Y. : Corning Museum of Glass, c1990. 191 p. : ill. (some col.) ; 28 cm. Exhibition at the Corning Museum of Glass, April 22-October 14, 1990. Biographical sketches: p. 174-189. Includes bibliographical references (p. 190-191) ISBN 0-87290-123-8
1. Glassware, Russian - Exhibitions. 2. Glass art - Soviet Union - Exhibitions. I. Malinina, T. II. Kazakova, Lĭudmila. III. Corning Museum of Glass. IV. Title. V. Title: Russian glass of the seventeenth to twentieth centuries.
NYPL [3-MPW 90-11677]

Ashbery, John. Reported sightings : art chronicles, 1957-1987 / John Ashbery ; edited by David Bergman.1st Harvard University Press pbk. ed. Cambridge, Mass. : Harvard University Press, 1991. xxiii, 417 p., [16] p. of col. plates : ill. ; 24 cm. Reprint. Originally published: New York : Knopf, 1989. Includes bibliographical references and index. ISBN 0-674-76225-8 DDC 700 20
1. Art - Themes, motives. 2. Art criticism - United States - History - 20th century. I. Bergman, David, 1950-. II. Title.
N7445.2 .A84 1991

Ashburnham-Morgan Beatus (Manuscript) Maius, fl. 926-968. A Spanish Apocalypse . New York , 1991. p. cm. ISBN 0-8076-1262-6 : DDC 745.6/7/092 20
ND3361.R52 B436 1991

Ashes to ashes : visions of death : March 5th-April 9th, 1983 / Toby Buonagurio ... [et al.] ; curator, Geno Rodriguez. New York, N.Y. : Alternative Museum, c1982. 16 p. : ill. ; 22 x 28 cm.
1. Death in art - Exhibitions. I. Buonagurio, Toby, 1947-. II. Alternative Museum (New York, N.Y.).
NYPL [3-MAMZ 90-12622]

ASHEVILLE (N.C.) - BUILDINGS, STRUCTURES, ETC.
Mathews, Jane Gianvito, 1954- The manor and cottages . Asheville, N.C. , c1991. p. cm. ISBN 0-9630437-0-6 : DDC 728/.09756/88 20
NA9051 .M38 1991

Ashmolean Museum.
Buckland Wright, John, 1897-1954. The engravings of John Buckland Wright /. Aldershot, Hants , 1990. 160 p. : ISBN 0-85967-850-4 : DDC 769.92 20
NE642.B8 A4 1990 NYPL [MDG (Buckland Wright) 91-7278]

Kakiemon porcelain from the English country house . London , 1989. 64 p. : ISBN 0-903432-35-8 *NYPL [3-MPFK 91-4566]*

Rossetti, Dante Gabriel, 1828-1882. [Portrait drawings of Elizabeth Siddall.] Rossetti's portrait drawings of Elizabeth Siddall . Brookfield, Vt. , 1991. p. cm. ISBN 1-85967-885-7 DDC 741.942 20
NC242.R646 A4 1991

Whistler, Catherine. Impressionist and modern . Oxford , 1990. 128 p. : ISBN 0-907849-97-0 (pbk.) *NYPL [3-MAX (Gross) 90-11583]*

Ashton, Dore.
A critical study of Philip Guston / by Dore Ashton. Berkeley : University of California Press, [1990], c1976. xvii, 216 p., 15 p. of plates : ill. (some col.) ; 26 cm. Previously published as: Yes but--. New York : Viking Press, 1976. With additional material. Includes bibliographical references (p. 201-206) and index. ISBN 0-520-06931-5 (alk. paper) DDC 759.13 20
1. Guston, Philip, 1913- - Criticism and interpretation. I. Ashton, Dore. Yes, but--. II. Title.
ND237.G8 A82 1990
NYPL [3-MCX G982 91-5624]

A fable of modern art / Dore Ashton. Berkeley : University of California Press, c1991. p. cm. Originally published: New York : Thames and Hudson, 1980. Includes bibliographical references and index. ISBN 0-520-07301-0 DDC 700/.9/04 20
1. Art, Modern - 19th century. 2. Art, Modern - 20th century. 3. Nature (Aesthetics). 4. Balzac, Honoré de, 1799-1850. Le chef-d'œuvre inconnu - Influence. I. Title.
NX454 .A8 1991

Hadzi, Dimitri, 1921- Dimitri Hadzi /. New York, N.Y. , 1989. 23 p. :
NYPL [3-MGO (Hadzi) 91-5082]

Noguchi east and west / Dore Ashton ; with special photographs by Denise Browne Hare. New York : Knopf, 1992. p. cm. Includes bibliographical references and index. ISBN 0-394-58804-5 DDC 709/.2 B 20
1. Noguchi, Isamu, 1904-. 2. Japanese American sculptors - Biography. I. Title.
NB237.N6 A8 1992

Yes, but-- Ashton, Dore. A critical study of Philip Guston / by Dore Ashton. Berkeley [1990], c1976. xvii, 216 p., 15 p. of plates : ISBN 0-520-06931-5 (alk. paper) DDC 759.13 20
ND237.G8 A82 1990
NYPL [3-MCX G982 91-5624]

The Asia collection.
Hersey, Irwin. Indonesian primitive art /.
Singapore , New York , 1991. p. cm. ISBN
0-19-588553-8 :   DDC 730/.089/9922 20
N7326 .H47 1991

Khoo, Joo Ee, 1940- Kendi . Singapore , New
York , 1991. p. cm. ISBN 0-19-588939-8 : DDC
738/.095/0745951 20
NK4163 .K48 1991

**Asia in maps from ancient times to the mid 19th
century.** Asien auf Karten . Weinheim , c1989.
xviii p. :   *NYPL [Map Div. 90-11078]*

ASIA - MAPS.
(1989) Asien auf Karten . Weinheim , c1989.
xviii p. :   *NYPL [Map Div. 90-11078]*

Asia Society.
Fu, Shen, 1937- Challenging the past .
Washington, D.C. , Seattle , c1991. p. cm.
ISBN 0-295-97124-X (cloth : alk. paper) DDC
759.951 20
ND1049.C4523 A4 1991

Images of paradise in Islamic art /. Hanover,
N.H. , 1991. p. cm. ISBN 0-944722-07-5
(hardcover) DDC 704.9/489723 20
N6263.D37 H664 1991

Asia Society. Galleries. Jessup, Helen Ibbitson.
Court arts of Indonesia /. New York , c1990.
288 p. : ISBN 0-8109-3165-6
IN PROCESS (ONLINE)
          NYPL [3-MAF+ 91-6099]

Asian Art Museum of San Francisco.
The art of Japan : masterworks in the Asian
Art Museum of San Francisco / Yoshiko
Kakudo. San Francisco : Chronicle Books,
c1991. p. cm. Includes bibliographical references
(p.). ISBN 0-8118-0055-5 (cloth) : DDC
709/.52/07479461 20
*1. Art, Japanese - Catalogs. 2. Art - California - San
Francisco - Catalogs. 3. Asian Art Museum of San
Francisco - Catalogs. I. Kakudo, Yoshiko. II. Title.*
N7352 .A935 1991

The Radiance of jade and the clarity of water .
Chicago, IL , New York [1991] p. cm. ISBN
0-86559-096-6 (Art Institute of Chicago) DDC
738/.09519/07473 20
NK4168.6.A1 R34 1991

**ASIAN ART MUSEUM OF SAN
FRANCISCO - CATALOGS.**
Asian Art Museum of San Francisco. The art of
Japan . San Francisco , c1991. p. cm. ISBN
0-8118-0055-5 (cloth) :   DDC 709/.52/07479461
20
N7352 .A935 1991

Asian collection . Menzies, Jackie. Sydney,
Australia , 1990. 96 p. : ISBN 0-7305-7455-5
DDC 709/.5/0749441 20
N7336 .M46 1990

Asien auf Karten : von der Autike bis zur Mitte
des 19. Jahrhunderts = Asia in maps from
ancient times to the mid-19th century /
herausgegeben und erläutert von Egon Klemp ;
[translated from the German by Alison and
Alistair Wightman]. Weinheim : VCH, c1989.
xviii p. : 75 maps (some col., some folded) ; 52
cm. (Acta humaniora) Includes 13 folded maps in
pocket. In German with parallel translation in English.
Includes bibliographical references.
*1. Cartography - Asia - History. 2. Maps, Early. 3.
Asia - Maps. I. Klemp, Egon. II. Title: Asia in maps
from ancient times to the mid 19th century.*
          NYPL [Map Div. 90-11078]

Aslan, Carlo, 1953- Dru, Line, 1957- [Cafés.
English.] Cafes /. New York, NY , c1989. 118
p. : ISBN 0-910413-66-5
          NYPL [3-MLO 90-10718]

Aslet, Clive, 1955- The American country house
/ Clive Aslet. New Haven : Yale University
Press, 1990. vii, 302 p. : ill. (some col.), plans ;
27 cm. Includes bibliographical references and index.
ISBN 0-300-04757-6
*1. Mansions - United States - History. 2. Country
homes - United States - History. 3. Architecture,
Domestic - United States - History - 19th century. 4.
Architecture, Domestic - United States - History - 20th
century. 5. United States - Social life and customs -
1865-1918. I. Title.*
          NYPL [3-MQWO 90-12969]

Asmus, Gesine. Rom in frühen Photographien
1846-1878 aus römischen und dänischen
Sammlungen /. München [1988] 231 p. :

ISBN 3-88814-282-2
          NYPL [MFW 91-2610]

Asmus Jakob Carstens, Joseph Anton Koch.
Asmus Jakob Carstens und Joseph Anton Koch,
zwei Zeitgenossen der Französischen
Revolution . Berlin [1989] 160 p. :
NC249 .A835 1989

**Asmus Jakob Carstens und Joseph Anton Koch,
zwei Zeitgenossen der Französischen
Revolution** : Zeichnungen : Staatliche Museen
zu Berlin, Nationalgalerie, Ausstellung in der
Nationalgalerie vom 14. Dezember 1989 bis 25.
Februar 1990 [Konzeption, Aufbau,
Katalogredaktion, Claude Keisch ; Textbeiträge
von Hilmar Frank ... et al.]. Berlin : Die
Nationalgalerie, [1989] 160 p. : ill. (some col.) ;
27 cm. Cover title: Asmus Jakob Carstens, Joseph
Anton Koch. Includes bibliographical references (p.
[157]-160).
*1. Art, German - Exhibitions. 2. Art, Modern -
17th-18th centuries - Germany - Exhibitions. 3.
Carstens, Asmus Jakob, 1754-1798 - Exhibitions. 4.
Koch, Joseph Anton, 1768-1839 - Exhibitions. I.
Carstens, Asmus Jakob, 1754-1798. II. Koch, Joseph
Anton, 1768-1839. III. Keisch, Claude. IV. Frank,
Hilmar. V. Nationalgalerie (Germany : East). VI. Title:
Asmus Jakob Carstens, Joseph Anton Koch.*
NC249 .A835 1989

**ASOCIACIÓN DE ARTE CONSTRUCTIVO -
EXHIBITIONS.**
El Taller Torres-García . Austin , 1991. p. cm.
ISBN 0-292-78121-0 DDC 709/.8/074 20
N6502.5 .T35 1991

Asociación de Artistas Plásticos de México.
Cabrera, Geles, 1930- Imaginación de la
materia . [Mexico] [1988] 1 v. (unpaged) :
DDC 730/.92 20
NB249.C33 A4 1988

**Asociación de Diseñadores Gráficos de Buenos
Aires.** ADG '86 . Buenos Aires , 1986. 1 v.
(unpaged) :
NC1002.L63 A33 1986

**Asociación de Reporteros Gráficos de la
República Argentina.** Periodismo gráfico
argentino . [Buenos Aires] [1986] 88 p. :
          NYPL [MFW 90-623]

**Asociaţiei Artiştilor Fotografi din Republica
Socialistă România.** Arta fotografică in
România /. Bucureşti [1965?] xv p., 141 p. of
plates :   *NYPL [MFW 91-693]*

**ASOR library of biblical and Near Eastern
archaeology.**
White, L. Michael. Building God's house in the
Roman world . Baltimore, Md. , c1990. xv, 211
p. : ISBN 0-8018-3906-8 (alk. paper)
NA4817 .W55 1990
          NYPL [3-MQN 90-10439]

Asp, Hjalmar, 1879-1940.
Litografier, Hjalmar Asp. [Malmö] : Malmö
museum, 1984. 1 v. (unpaged) : ill. ; 8 x 11 cm.
(Katalog . nr. 352)
*1. Asp, Hjalmar, 1879-1940 - Exhibitions. I. Malmö
museum. II. Series: Katalog (Malmö museum) , nr. 352.
III. Title.*   *NYPL [MDG (Asp) 91-3644]*

ASP, HJALMAR, 1879-1940 - EXHIBITIONS.
Asp, Hjalmar, 1879-1940. Litografier, Hjalmar
Asp. [Malmö] , 1984. 1 v. (unpaged) :
          NYPL [MDG (Asp) 91-3644]

**Aspecten van vijftig jaar kunsthistorisch
onderzoek, 1938-1988** : colloquium
georganiseerd ter gelegenheid van vijftig jaar
zelfstandigheid der Koninklijke Academie voor
Wetenschappen, Letteren en Schone Kunsten
van België, Brussel, 3-4 november, 1988.
Brussel : AWLSK, 1990. 137 p., [14] p. of
plates : ill. ; 24 cm. Dutch, French, and German.
Includes bibliographical references. ISBN
90-6569-435-8
*1. Art - Congresses. 2. Koninklijke Academie voor
Wetenschappen, Letteren en Schone Kunsten van
België - Congresses. I. Koninklijke Academie voor
Wetenschappen, Letteren en Schone Kunsten van
België.*
N7442.8.D8 A85 1990

**Aspectos de la cultura africana en el Río de la
Plata** . Ortiz Oderigo, Néstor R., 1912-
Buenos Aires , c1974. 200 p., [8] leaves of
plates :   *NYPL [HKB 77-1945]*

Aspectos del arte contemporáneo español. Aspetti
dell'arte contemporanea spagnola. Barcelona ,

c1990. 47, [1] p. : ISBN 84-87433-11-1 DDC
709/.46/0744545 20
N7108 .A87 1990

Aspects of modern art : an anthology of writings
on modern art from L'Œil, the European art
magazine / edited by Georges and Rosamond
Bernier. Paris : G. & R. Bernier ; New York :
Reynal, [1957] 188 p. : ill. (some col.), ports. ;
32 cm. (The selective eye . 3)
*I. Bernier, Georges. II. Bernier, Rosamond. III. L'Œil.
IV. Series.*   *NYPL [3-MAL+ 90-11498]*

"Aspects of slavery" . Bahamas. Public Records
Office. Nassau , 1974. 28 p. :
HT1119.B34 B36 1974
          NYPL [HRG 78-1237]

Aspekte aktueller Bündner Kunst, Teil II :
Katalog zur Ausstellung ..., 4. Mai bis 9. Juni
1985 / Redaktion, Beat Stutzer. Chur : Bündner
Kunstmuseum, 1985. 25 p. : ill. (some col.) ; 30
cm. Caption title. Includes bibliographical references.
ISBN 3-905240-04-1
*1. Art, Swiss - Switzerland - Graubünden - Exhibitions.
2. Art, Modern - 20th century - Switzerland -
Graubünden - Exhibitions.*
          NYPL [3-MAM + 88-3792]

Aspenström, Werner, 1918- Donation Gerard
Bonnier /. Stockholm [1989] 106 p. : ISBN
91-29-59355-7
N6488.S8 S74 1989

Aspetti dell'arte contemporanea spagnola.
Barcelona : Edizioni d'arte iberico 2mil, c1990.
47, [1] p. : col. ill. ; 27 cm. Italian and Spanish.
"Aspectos del arte contemporáneo español"--P. [6].
"Comune di Ferrara, Assessorato istituzioni culturali,
Galleria civica d'arte moderna, Palazzo dei
Diamanti"--p. "Editado in occasione della
esposizione ... dal 27 ottobre 1990 al 5 gennaio
1991"--P. [48]. Issued in a slipcase with: Rafael
Canogar. ISBN 84-87433-11-1 DDC
709/.46/0744545 20
*1. Art, Spanish - Exhibitions. 2. Art, Modern - 20th
century - Spain - Exhibitions. I. Ferrara (Italy).
Assessorato alle istituzioni culturali. II. Ferrara (Italy).
Galleria civica d'arte moderna. III. Title: Aspectos del
arte contemporáneo español.*
N7108 .A87 1990

Aspin, Roy. Lewis Carroll and his camera / by
Roy Aspin. Clayhall, Ilford, Essex : Brent
Publications in association with Robert
Odcombe Associates, c1989. 55, [2] p., [36]
leaves of plates : ill. ; 30 cm. Includes
bibliographical references (p. [57]). ISBN
0-948706-04-X (pbk.)
*1. Carroll, Lewis, 1832-1898. 2. Photography - Portraits.
3. Photography of children. I. Carroll, Lewis,
1832-1898. II. Title.*
          NYPL [MFX+ (Carroll) 91-7443]

**ASSEMBLAGE (ART) - CALIFORNIA - LOS
ANGELES.**
Whiteson, Leon, 1930- The Watts Towers /.
Oakville, Ont. , 1989. 96 p. : ISBN
0-88962-394-5 (bound) : DDC 725/.97/0979494
19   *NYPL [3-MQWO 91-6779]*

ASSEMBLAGE (ART) - FRANCE.
Lamarche-Vadel, Bernard, 1949- Villeglé .
Paris , c1990. 137 p. : ISBN 2-86234-056-1
DDC 760 20
N6853.V493 A35 1990

Assemble the hyenas-- I feel a pun coming on! .
Thaves, Bob. [Frank and Ernest. Selections.]
New York , 1991. ca. 130 p. : ISBN
0-88687-529-3 : DDC 741.5/973 20
NC1429.T44 A4 1991

Assignment Japan . Vos, Ken. The Hague , 1989.
107 p. : ISBN 90-12-06415-5
          NYPL [3-MAG+ 90-12025]

Associação dos Arquitectos Portugueses.
Arquitectura popular em Portugal /. Lisboa ,
1988. 3 v. : DDC 720/.9469 20
NA1321 .A77 1988
          NYPL [3-MQW 91-7182]

Associação dos Ilustradores do Rio de Janeiro.
Mostra de Ilustrações para Crianças (1987 : Rio
de Janeiro, Brazil) Mostra de Ilustrações para
Crianças, Rio 87 /. Rio de Janeiro [1987] 87
p. : DDC 741.6/42/09810748153 20
NC976.B6 M6 1987

Associação Portuguesa de Arqueologia Industrial.
O Vidro em Portugal . [Lisbon] [1989] 75 p. :

DDC 748.2969/074469425 20
NK5143.A1 V5 1989

Association culturelle du Département de Maine et Loire. Autour de la Nativité dans la peinture des collections angevines . [Angers] [1989] 200 p. :   ISBN 2-905608-01-3 :
ND1432.F8 A98 1989

Association for Asian Studies. Reference series.
A historical atlas of South Asia; /. Chicago , 1978. xxxix, 352 p.   ISBN 0-226-74221-0
G2661.S1 H5 1978   **NYPL   [Map Div. 79-12]**

Association française d'action artistique.
Raynaud, Jean Pierre, 1939- Jean-Pierre Raynaud . Houston, Tex. , c1991. 135 p. :   ISBN 0-939594-23-4 :   DDC 709/.2 20
N6853.R33 A4 1991
NYPL   [3-MGO (Raynaud) 91-7980]

Association of Artist-Run Galleries. Time and space concepts in art /. New York , 1980. viii, 157 p., 4 leaves of plates :
NX650.S8 T55   **NYPL   [3-MAMZ 80-2228]**

Association of Collegiate Schools of Architecture.
On architecture, the city, and technology /. Washington, DC , Stoneham, MA , c1990. 152 p. :   ISBN 0-7506-9149-2   DDC 720/.1/05 20
NA2543.T43 O5 1990

Association of Hispanic Arts (New York, N.Y.)
Folklore! . New York, N.Y. [1988?] 31 p. :
NYPL   [3-MNE 90-11620]

Quaderni di Brera. see Quaderni di Brera.

Associazione culturale Le tarot (Faenza, Italy)
Giovannoni, Giannino. Mantova e i tarocchi del Mantegna /. Mantova , Faenza [1987] 78 p. :
N6923.M249 A4 1987
NYPL   [3-MCF M29 91-7036]

Associazione italiana cultura sport.
Zanotti-Bianco, Umberto. Il sud di Umberto Zanotti Bianco . Venezia , c1981. 117 p. :
NYPL   [MFX (Zanotti-Bianco) 90-7053]

Associazione nazionale per gli interessi del Mezzogiorno d'Italia. Zanotti-Bianco, Umberto. Il sud di Umberto Zanotti Bianco . Venezia , c1981. 117 p. :
NYPL   [MFX (Zanotti-Bianco) 90-7053]

Assopiastrelle. Tunick, Susan. Ceramic ornament in the New York subway system /. New York, N.Y. , Italy [1989?] [14] p. :
NYPL   [3-MRXZ+ 90-10715]

Assouline, Pierre.
[Homme de l'art. English]
An artful life : a biography of D.H. Kahnweiler, 1884-1979 / Pierre Assouline ; translated from the French by Charles Ruas.1st American ed. New York : G. Weidenfeld, 1990. xiii, 411 p., [16] p. of plates : ill. :; 25 cm. Translation of: L'homme de l'art. Includes index. Includes bibliographical references (p. 389-396).   ISBN 0-8021-1227-7 (alk. paper)   DDC 709/.2 B 20
1. Art dealers - France - Biography. I. Title.
N8660.K3 A9513 1990
NYPL   [3-MAVC 90-12782]
An artful life : a biography of D.H. Kahnweiler, 1884-1979 / Pierre Assouline ; translated from the French by Charles Ruas.1st pbk. ed. New York : Fromm International Pub. Corp., c1991. p. cm. Translation of: L'homme de l'art. Includes bibliographical references (p.) and index.   ISBN 0-88064-131-2 (pbk. : acid-free paper) :   DDC 709/.2 B 20
1. Kahnweiler, Daniel Henry, 1884-. 2. Art dealers - France - Biography. I. Title.
N8660.K3 A9513 1991

Assur und Babylon. Wetzel, Friedrich. Berlin [c1949] 70 p.   **NYPL   [3-MAE 90-6371]**

ASSYRO-BABYLONIAN ART. see ART, ASSYRO-BABYLONIAN.

Astala, Lauri. Fabula 1 /. Helsinki [1989] 61 p. :   ISBN 951-861-843-7
N7255.F5 F28 1989

Astbury, Leigh, 1950- Sunlight and shadow : Australian impressionist painters, 1880-1900 / Leigh Astbury ; general editor, Jennifer Phipps. Sydney : Bay Books, 1989. 232 p. : col. ill. ; 33 cm. Includes index. Bibliography: p. 220-222.   ISBN 1-86256-295-4

1. Impressionism (Art) - Australia. 2. Painting, Modern - 19th century - Australia. I. Title.
NYPL   [3-MCY+ 90-882]

Ästhetik und Gestaltung in der japanischen Architektur . Bosslet, Klaus. Düsseldorf , c1990. viii, 154 p. :   ISBN 3-8041-1247-1 :
NA7451 .B67 1990

Astiazarain Achabal, María Isabel. Arquitectos guipuzcoanos del siglo XVIII / Ma. Isabel Astiazarain. Guipúzcoa : Diputación Foral de Guipúzcoa, Departamento de Cultura, [1988?-1990?] 2 v. : ill. ; 30 cm. Includes bibliographical references and indexes. CONTENTS. - [1] Martín de Zaldúa, José de Lizardi, Sebastián de Lecuona -- [2] Ignacio de Ibero, Francisco de Ibero.   ISBN 84-505-7463-3
1. Architecture - Spain - Guipúzcoa. 2. Architecture, Baroque - Spain - Guipúzcoa. 3. Architects - Spain - Guipúzcoa - Biography. I. Title.
NA1109.G85 A88 1988

ASTROLOGY AND ARCHITECTURE - INDIA - ORISSA.
Bose, Nirmal Kumar. Canons of Orissan architecture /. New Delhi , 1982. vi, 211 p., 34 p. of plates :   DDC 720/.954/13 20
NA1507.O7 B6 1982

Astrua, Paola. Pinacoteca di Brera . Milano , c1989. 457 p. :   ISBN 88-435-3080-1
NYPL   [3-MCE 91-5231]

Åstvedt, Marit. Kulturens dekningsbidrag . [Oslo] , c1991. 179 p. :   ISBN 82-02-12832-3
NX456 .K78 1991

Asvarishch, B. (Boris) Nemetskaia i avstriiskaia zhivopis' XIX-XX veka : katalog / avtor-sostavitel' B.I. Asvarishch. Leningrad : "Iskusstvo", 1988. 370 p. : ill. ; 34 cm. (Sobranie zapadnoevropeiskoi zhivopisi / Gosudarstvennyi Ermitazh . 15) Includes bibliographical references and indexes.
1. Painting, German - Catalogs. 2. Painting, Modern - 19th century - Germany - Catalogs. 3. Painting, Modern - 20th centuryt - Germany - Catalogs. 4. Painting, Austrian - Catalogs. 5. Painting, Modern - 19th century - Austria - Catalogs. 6. Painting, Modern - 20th century - Austria - Catalogs. 7. Painting - Russian S.F.S.R. - Leningrad - Catalogs. 8. Gosudarstvennyi Ermitazh (Soviet Union) - Catalogs. I. Title. II. Title: Nemetskaia i avstriiskaia zhivopis' 19.-20. veka. III. Title: Nemetskaia i avstriiskaia zhivopis' deviatnadtsatogo-dvadtsatogo veka. IV. Series: Gosudarstvennyi Ermitazh (Soviet Union). Sobranie zapadnoevropeiskoi zhivopisi , 15.
ND450 .G67 1983 vol. 15 ND567

"At Taliesin" . Wright, Frank Lloyd, 1867-1959. Carbondale , c1992. p. cm.   ISBN 0-8093-1709-5   DDC 720/.7/077576 20
NA2127.G74 W75 1992

At work & play . Davies, Alan, 1946- [Sydney] , 1989. 128 p. :   ISBN 0-7305-6293-X
NYPL   [MFW+ 90-1035]

Ataíde, José. Bajado, 1912- Bajado, um artista de Olinda /. Olinda [Brasil] , 1985. 48 p. :   DDC 759.981 19
ND359.B34 A35 1985
NYPL   [3-MCZ B1583 90-9450]

ATAKA SANGYŌ KABUSHIKI KAISHA - ART COLLECTIONS.
The Radiance of jade and the clarity of water . Chicago, IL , New York [New York?] 1991. p. cm.   ISBN 0-86559-096-6 (Art Institute of Chicago)   DDC 738/.09519/07473 20
NK4168.6.A1 R34 1991

Atamanov, M. G. Istoki iskusstva Udmurtii . Izhevsk , 1989. 116 p., [8] p. of plates :
NX556.A3 U3538 1989

ATCHINSON, TOPEKA, AND SANTA FE RAILWAY COMPANY.
D'Emilio, Sandra, 1939- Visions and visionaries . Salt Lake City , 1991. p. cm.   ISBN 0-87905-383-6 :   DDC 758/.9978 20
N8214.5.U6 D46 1991

ATCHITECTURE, ISLAMIC - TURKEY.
Vogt-Göknil, Ulya. Osmanische Türkei /. Fribourg , c1965. 192 p. :
NYPL   [3-MQT 90-6997]

[Atelier, che cosa, con che cosa .
(12)] Galli, Giovanna. Il mosaico . Torino , 1989. 115 p. :   ISBN 88-414-2039-2
NYPL   [3-MRXZ 91-7273]

Atelier du patrimoine de la ville de Marseille.
Architectures historiques à Marseille . Aix-en-Provence , c1987. 141 p. :   ISBN 2-85744-290-4 :   DDC 720/.944/912 19
NA1051.M37 U73 1987
NYPL   [3-MQWF+ 90-12768]

Atelier 3. Schönwald, Peter. Cathelin . Paris , c1990. 109 p. :   DDC 746.392 20
NK3049.A3 C372 1990

ATELIER 3.
Schönwald, Peter. Cathelin . Paris , c1990. 109 p. :   DDC 746.392 20
NK3049.A3 C372 1990

Atelier 5, Bern. Architekten, Atelier 5, Bern. Stuttgart [1988] 49 p. ;   ISBN 3-8167-1816-7 (pbk.)   **NYPL   [3-MQWD 90-12512]**

ATELIER 5 (FIRM) - BIBLIOGRAPHY.
Architekten, Atelier 5, Bern. Stuttgart [1988] 49 p. ;   ISBN 3-8167-1816-7 (pbk.)
NYPL   [3-MQWD 90-12512]

Les ateliers de Budapest =. Hajdu, István. Paris , c1990. 240 p. :   ISBN 978-290-807-2006
NYPL   [3-MAM+ 91-3623]

Les ateliers de Soulages /. Ragon, Michel. Paris , c1990. 156 p. :   ISBN 2-226-04871-5
NYPL   [3-MCO+ S722 91-5846]

Ateliers en liberté. Sur les murs. L'Art fun, ou, L'enfance de l'art. Ateliers en liberté. Jouy-en-Josas [France] [1986] 77 p. :   ISBN 2-86925-004-5
N6488.F8 J687 1986
NYPL   [3-MAL+ 90-10669]

Ateliers in Budapest. Hajdu, István. Les ateliers de Budapest =. Paris , c1990. 240 p. :   ISBN 978-290-807-2006
NYPL   [3-MAM+ 91-3623]

Ateneo Científico, Literario y Artístico de Madrid. Masats, Ramón. Masats . [Madrid? , 1961] 1 v. (unpaged) :
NYPL   [MFX (Masats) 90-7136]

Ateneo de Caracas. La Flor imaginaria . Caracas , 1989. 160 p. :   ISBN 980-255-018-3   DDC 700 20
NX650.F57 F58 1989

Ateneo de Madrid. see Ateneo Científico, Literario y Artístico de Madrid.

Athanassoglou-Kallmyer, Nina M., 1945- Eugène Delacroix : prints, politics, and satire (1814-1822) / Nina Maria Athanassoglou-Kallmyer. New Haven, CT : Yale University Press, 1991. p. cm. Includes bibliographical references and index.   ISBN 0-300-04931-5   DDC 741.5/092 20
1. Delacroix, Eugène, 1798-1863 - Political and social views. 2. French wit and humor, Pictorial - History - 19th century. 3. France - History - Restoration, 1814-1830 - Caricatures and cartoons. I. Title.
NC1499.D36 A9 1991

Athènes affaire européenne : du 12 octobre au 2 décembre 1985 au Zappeion Megaron à Athènes. Athènes : Ministère de la culture, c1985. 2 v. : ill. (some col.) ; 28 cm. "Athènes capitale culturelle de l'Europe 1985." CONTENTS. - 1. [Without special title] -- 2. Athènes, ville capitale / sous la direction de Yannis Tsiomis.
1. Architecture - Greece - Athens - Exhibitions. 2. Athens (Greece) - Buildings, structures, etc. - Exhibitions. I. Greece. Hypourgeio Politismou.
NA1100 .A84 1985

ATHENS (GREECE) - BUILDINGS, STRUCTURES, ETC. - EXHIBITIONS.
Athènes affaire européenne . Athènes , c1985. 2 v. :
NA1100 .A84 1985

ATHLETES IN ART.
Kozar, Andrew J. The sport sculpture of R. Tait McKenzie /. Champaign, IL , c1992. p. cm.   ISBN 0-87329-336-5 (hard cover)   DDC 730/.92 20
NB237.M277 K69 1992

Atıl, Esin. Islamic art & patronage . New York , c1990. 313 p. :   ISBN 0-8478-1366-5   DDC 709/.17/67107473 20
N6263.W3 A785 1991
NYPL   [3-MAF+ 91-5747]

Atkins, Caven.
Fraser, Ted, 1946- Caven Atkins, the Winnipeg years /. Windsor, Canada , c1987. [40] p. :

ISBN 0-919837-10-7
MLCM 90/03385 (N)
NYPL [3-MCZ A865 90-8692]

ATKINS, CAVEN - EXHIBITIONS.
Fraser, Ted, 1946- Caven Atkins, the Winnipeg
years /. Windsor, Canada , c1987. [40] p. :
ISBN 0-919837-10-7
MLCM 90/03385 (N)
NYPL [3-MCZ A865 90-8692]

Atkinson, D. Scott, 1953- Homer, Winslow,
1836-1910. Winslow Homer in Gloucester /.
Chicago, Ill. , c1990. 112 p. : ISBN
0-8478-1315-0
NYPL [3-MCX+ H76 91-5348]

Atl, Dr., 1875-1964.
Dr. Atl : pinturas y dibujos / prólogo de Carlos
Pellicer.1. ed. México : Fondo Editorial de las
Plástica Mexicana, 1974. 137 p. : ill. (some
col.) ; 45 cm. DDC 759.972 20
1. Atl, Dr., 1875-1964 - Catalogs. I. Title. II. Title:
Doctor Atl.
N6559.A85 A4 1974

ATL, DR., 1875-1964 - CATALOGS.
Atl, Dr., 1875-1964. Dr. Atl . México , 1974.
137 p. : DDC 759.972 20
N6559.A85 A4 1974

Atlanta. High Museum of Art. see High Museum
of Art.

Atlante della Svizzera. Atlas der Schweiz =.
Wabern-Bern , 1981- v. :
NYPL [Map Div. 87-2890]

Atlante enciclopedico Touring. Volume 2, Europa
/. Touring club italiano. Servizio cartografico.
Milano , c1987. 1 atlas (xi, 180 p.) : ISBN
88-365-0299-7 DDC 912/.4 19
G1797.2 .T64 1987
NYPL [Map Div. 90-10885]

Atlante enciclopedico Touring. Volume 4, Storia
antica e medievale /. Touring club italiano.
Servizio cartografico. Milano , c1987. 1 atlas
(143 p.) : ISBN 88-365-0301-2
NYPL [Map Div. 91-7773]

Atlante storico delle città italiane. Lazio .
(2) Petrucci, Giulia. San Martino al Cimino
(Viterbo, III) /. Roma , 1987 [i.e. 1988] 73 p. :
ISBN 88-7597-033-5 (pbk.)
NYPL [Map Div. 88-1082]

(5) Latina /. Roma , 1990. 94 p. : ISBN
88-7597-124-2 : DDC 711/.4/0945623 20
NA9204.L37 L37 1990

(5) Latina /. Roma , 1990. 94 p. :
NYPL [Map Div. 91-5807]

Atlante Touring. 2, Europa. Touring club italiano.
Servizio cartografico. Atlante enciclopedico
Touring. Volume 2, Europa /. Milano , c1987.
1 atlas (xi, 180 p.) : ISBN 88-365-0299-7 DDC
912/.4 19
G1797.2 .T64 1987
NYPL [Map Div. 90-10885]

Atlante Touring. 4, Storia antica e medievale.
Touring club italiano. Servizio cartografico.
Atlante enciclopedico Touring. Volume 4, Storia
antica e medievale /. Milano , c1987. 1 atlas
(143 p.) : ISBN 88-365-0301-2
NYPL [Map Div. 91-7773]

ATLANTIC OCEAN - MAPS.
Blaeu, Willem Janszoon, 1571-1638. The light
of navigation. [Amsterdam, c1964] xiii, [60],
114, 118 p.
G1793 .B52 1964 (Map)
NYPL [Map Div. 84-1067]

Atlantide.
Zaupa, Giovanni. Andrea Palladio e la sua
committenza . Roma , c1990. 255 p. : ISBN
88-7448-275-2 : DDC 720/.92 20
NA1123.P2 Z34 1990

Aṭlas al-ṣuwar al-fadạ̈'iyah li-Dawlat Qaṭar min
al-qamar al-ṣinā'ī "Landsāt" /. Yaḥyá,
Muḥammad 'Adil Aḥmad. al-Dawḥah , 1983. 1
atlas (vii, 166 p.) : DDC 912/.5363 19
G2249.81.C2 Y2 1983
NYPL [Map Div. 91-2599]

Atlas Armi̇ānskoĭ Sovetskoĭ Sotsialisticheskoĭ
Respubliki /. Haykakan SSH Gitut'yunneri
Akademia. Erevan , 1961. 1 atlas (viii, 111 p. :
G2157.A7 A5 1961
NYPL [Map Div. 91-1095]

Atlas básico de Colombia /. Instituto Geográfico

"Agustín Codazzi." Subdirección de
Investigación y Divulgación Geográfica.
[Bogotá] , 1986. 1 atlas (217 p. (some folded)) :
DDC 912/.861 19
G1730 .I53 1986   *NYPL [Map Div. 87-697]*

Atlas básico de Colombia /. Instituto Geográfico
"Agustín Codazzi." Subdirección de
Investigación y Divulgación Geográfica.
[Bogotá] , 1989. 1 atlas (446 p. (some folded)) :
NYPL [Map Div. 91-6225]

Atlas d'Andorra. Institut d'Estudis Andorrans.
[Andorra] , 1980- 1 atlas :   DDC 912/.4679 19
G1970 .I5 1980   *NYPL [Map Div. 90-57]*

Atlas de historia universal /. Vallés Perdrix,
Edmundo. Barcelona , c1973. [86] p. :
NYPL [Map Div. 81-234]

Atlas de la médina de Fès : action intégrée 35.
Toulouse : Presses universitaires du Mirail,
1990. 1 atlas (46 p.) : maps (some col.) ; 45 x
59 cm. At head of title: Université Toulouse-Le Mirail,
Institut de géographie, Centre interdisciplinaire d'études
urbaines; Faculté des lettres de Fès, Département de
géographie. Project coordinator: Jean-Paul Laborie.
Includes bibliographical references.   ISBN
2-85816-137-2
1. Fès (Morocco) - Population - Maps. 2. Fès
(Morocco) - Industries - Maps. 3. Fès (Morocco) -
Maps. I. Laborie, Jean Paul. II. Université de
Toulouse-Le Mirail. Centre interdisciplinaire d'études
urbaines. III. Faculté des lettres de Fès. Département
de géographie. IV. Université de Toulouse-Le Mirail.
Institut de géographie.
NYPL [Map Div. 91-161]

Atlas de la República Mexicana. García Cubas,
Antonio, 1832-1912. Atlas geográfico,
estadístico e histórico de la República Mexicana
/. Mexico , 1989, c1988. 1 atlas (various
pagings) :   ISBN 968-8421-57-X
NYPL [Map Div. 91-131]

Atlas de la República Oriental del Uruguay /.
Daroczi, Isabel. Montevideo , 1990. 1 atlas
(109 p.) :   *NYPL [Map Div. 90-13118]*

Atlas de la Suisse. Atlas der Schweiz =.
Wabern-Bern , 1981- v. :
NYPL [Map Div. 87-2890]

Atlas de Portugal . Selecções do Reader's Digest
(Firm) Lisboa , 1988. 1 atlas (159 p.) :   DDC
912.469 20
G1975 .S4 1988   *NYPL [Map Div. 91-80]*

Atlas del inventario de tierras del territorio
federal Amazonas / [República de Venezuela,
Ministerio del Ambiente y de los Recursos
Naturales Renovables, Dirección General
Sectorial de Información e Investigación del
Ambiente, Dirección de Suelos, Vegetación y
Fauna ; Office de la Recherche Scientifique et
Technique Outre Mer, France]. Caracas,
Venezuela : La Dirección, [1985]. 1 v. (various
pagings) : ill., maps ; 59 cm. Cover title.   ISBN
980-04-0053-2
1. Natural resources - Venezuela - Amazonas - Maps. 2.
Amazonas (Venezuela : Territory) - Maps. I. Venezuela.
Dirección de Suelos, Vegetación y Fauna. II. France.
Office de la recherche scientifique et technique
outre-mer.   NYPL [Map Div. 91-7664]

Atlas der Donauländer. Atlas of the Danubian
countries. Atlas des pays danubiens. [Atlas
dunaĭskikh stran] Hrsg.: Österr. Ost- u.
Südosteuropainst. Red.: Josef Breu. Wien,
Deuticke in Komm., 1970- v. (loose-leaf) fold.
col. maps 69 cm. + Register. Issued in parts. Text
in English, French, German, and Russian. Includes
indexes. DDC 912/.496 19
1. Danube River Valley - Maps. 2. Danube River
Valley - Description and travel. I. Breu, Josef. II.
Österreichisches Ost- und Südosteuropa-Institut. III.
Title: Atlas of the Danubian countries.
G1882.D3 A8 1970
NYPL [Map Div. 72-267]

Atlas der Schweiz = Atlas de la Suisse =
Atlante della Svizzera / herausgegeben im
Auftrage des Schweizerischen Bundesrates ;
Gesamtleitung und Präsident der
Redaktionskommission (seit 1978), Ernst
Spiess ; Mitglieder der Redaktionskommission,
Ernst Huber ... [et al.].2., erneuerte Ausg.
Wabern-Bern : Verlag des Bundesamtes für
Landestopographie, 1981- v. : ill., col. maps ;
52 cm. Cover title. Issued in fascicles, beginning with
v. 10; previous vols. (1. Ausg.) cataloged separately (id
744727249b) under: Switzerland. Landestopographie.

Scale of principal maps 1 : 500,000. German, French
and Italian. First ed. entered under Switzerland.
Landestopographie. Includes bibliographical references.
1. Switzerland - Maps. 2. Switzerland - Economic
conditions - Maps. I. Spiess, Ernst. II. Switzerland.
Bundesamt für Landestopographie. III. Title: Atlas de la
Suisse. IV. Title: Atlante della Svizzera.
NYPL [Map Div. 87-2890]

Atlas des cultures vivrières. Atlas of food crops.
Par Jacques Bertin [et al.] Cartes de
Marie-Claude Lapeyre, Nancy François [et]
Monique Veerkamp. Paris, Mouton [1971] 41 p.
18 col. maps. 42 cm. (Inventaire géographique et
chronologique pour un atlas d'histoire mondiale) Issued
in a case. Geographical and chronological survey for an
atlas of world history. Scale of maps 1:55,000,000.
Bibliography: p. 19-41.
1. Field crops - Maps. I. Bertin, Jacques. II. Title. III.
Title: Atlas of food crops.
NYPL [Map Div. 73-116]

Atlas didáctico de Costa Rica. [1a ed.]. [San
José : Jiménez & Tanzi, 1990. 37 p. : maps (1
col., folded) ; 22 x 33 cm. ISBN 997-7911-31-2
1. Costa Rica - Maps.
NYPL [Map Div. 90-11874]

Atlas eje de desarrollo Orinoco-Apure. Eje de
desarrollo Orinoco-Apure atlas /. Caracas ,
1987. 1 Atlas ([16] leaves) :
NYPL [Map Div. 91-50]

Atlas geográfico, estadístico e histórico de la
República Mexicana /. García Cubas, Antonio,
1832-1912. Mexico , 1989, c1988. 1 atlas
(various pagings) :   ISBN 968-8421-57-X
NYPL [Map Div. 91-131]

Atlas geograficzny /. Państwowe Przedsiębiorstwo
Wydawnictw Kartograficznych im. Eugeniusza
Romera. Warszawa , 1987. 1 atlas (120, 32 p.) :
ISBN 83-7000-011-8 : DDC 912 20
G1021 .P222 1987
NYPL [Map Div. 90-11797]

Atlas hidrográfico de Chile /. Instituto
Hidrográfico de la Armada. [Valparaíso] , 1974.
37, [14], [212] p. :   DDC 623.89/2
G1751.C3 I5 1974
NYPL [Map Div. 91-6470]

Atlas histórico cartográfico do Recife / José Luiz
Mota Menezes (org.) ; apresentação de Jaime
de Azevêdo Gusmão Filho ; prefácio de José
Antônio Gonsalves de Mello. Recife :
Massangana, 1988. 1 atlas (114, [10] p.) :
ill.(some col.), maps ; 32x47 cm. (Série Obras de
consultas . 9) Includes bibliographical references.
ISBN 85-7019-172-3
1. Cartography - Brazil - Recife - History. 2. Recife
(Brazil) - Maps. I. Menezes, José Luiz da Mota. II.
Fundação Joaquim Nabuco. III. Series.
NYPL [Map Div. 91-7611]

Atlas Kalininskoĭ oblasti /. Soviet Union.
Glavnoe upravlenie geodezii i kartografii.
Moskva , 1964. 1 atlas ([8] p., 34 p. :
NYPL [Map Div. 91-1093]

Atlas mundial escolar : Puerto Rico y el mundo
en due vivimos. San Juan de P.R. : Editorial
Cordillera, c1981. 1 atlas (28 p.) : col. ill.,
maps ; 30 cm. ISBN 84-373-0004-5
1. Puerto Rico - Maps.   NYPL [Map Div. 86-32]

Atlas of Australian resources. Australia. Division
of National Mapping. Canberra , 1980- 1 atlas
(v.) :   ISBN 0-642-51458-5 (set)   DDC
912/.13337/0994 19
G2751.G3 A4 1980
NYPL [Map Div. 81-377]

Atlas of Bergen County, New Jersey . Bromley,
George W. Philadelphia, Pa. , 1912-1913. 2
atlases :   *NYPL [Map Div. 91-4094]*

Atlas of classical history / edited by Richard J.A.
Talbert. London ; New York : Routledge,
c1985, 1988. 1 atlas (217 p.) : ill., maps ; 26
cm. Bibliography: p. 179-189.   ISBN 0-415-03463-9
(pbk.)
1. Classical geography - Maps. 2. Geography,
Historical - Maps. 3. History, Ancient. I. Talbert,
Richard J. A., 1947-.
NYPL [Map Div. 91-5122]

Atlas of Columbus and the great discoveries /.
Nebenzahl, Kenneth, 1927- Chicago , c1990.
viii, 168 p. :   *NYPL [Map Div. 91-7246]*

Atlas of F.S.A. postal areas. Canadian atlas of

F.S.A. postal areas. Scarborough, ON , c1990. 1 atlas (v, 69 [i.e. 138], 69 p.) : DDC 383/.145 20
NYPL [*Map Div. 91-8103*]

Atlas of Fairfield County, Connecticut. Hagstrom Company, inc., New York. Hagstrom's atlas of Fairfield County, Conneticut. New York, 1966. 70 p. :
G1243.F3 H3 1966 NYPL [*Map Div. 90-61*]

Atlas of food crops. Atlas des cultures vivrières. Paris [1971] 41 p. *NYPL* [*Map Div. 73-116*]

Atlas of Hudson County, New Jersey. Philadelphia, Pa. : G.M. Hopkins Co., 1908-1909. 2 atlases : col. maps ; 59 x 44 cm. Includes indexes.
1. Hudson County, N. J. - Maps. 2. Jersey City (N.J.) - Maps. I. G.M. Hopkins Company. II. Title.
NYPL [*Map Div. 91-4092*]

Atlas of Israel . Karṭa (Firm) Tel-Aviv ; New York : [168] 80 p. : ISBN 0-02-905950-X : DDC 912/.5694 19
G2235 .K3 1985
NYPL [**P-*PXLB++ 86-3877*]

Atlas of major Texas gas reservoirs / Elisabeth C. Kosters ... [et al.] ; Robert J. Finley, project director ; assisted by Nancy J. Banta ... [et al.]. Chicago, Ill. : Gas Research Institute ; Austin, Tex. : Bureau of Economic Geology, University of Texas at Austin, 1989. 1 atlas (ix, 161 p.) : ill., maps (some col.) ; 44 x 56 cm. "[The Atlas] contains information on more than 1,828 reservoirs with emphasis on 868 reservoirs having cumulative production greater than 30 billion cubic feet of natural gas" -- Foreword. A companion volume to the Atlas of major Texas oil reservoirs (1983). Plates 1-4 have been folded and placed in a pocket. Includes bibliographical references and index.
1. Gas reservoirs - Texas - Maps. 2. Gas fields - Texas - Maps. 3. Geology, Structural - Maps. I. Kosters, Elisabeth C. II. Finley, Robert J. III. Gas Research Institute. IV. University of Texas at Austin. Bureau of Economic Geology.
NYPL [*Map Div. 90-11657*]

Atlas of National Wetlands Inventory maps for New Jersey / Ralph W. Tiner, Jr., Regional Wetland Coordinator ... . Newton Corner, Mass. : United States Department of the Interior, Fish and Wildlife Service, Region Five, Habitat Resources, 1984. 1 atlas (10, [175] p.) : maps ; "February 1984."
1. Wetlands - New Jersey - Maps. 2. Wetland ecology - New Jersey - Maps. I. Tiner, Ralph W. II. National Wetlands Inventory (U. S.).
NYPL [*Map Div. 88-2052*]

The atlas of Nepal in the modern world /. Sill, Michael. London , 1991. 1 atlas (159 p.) :
ISBN 1-85383-032-1 (hbk): DDC 912/.549/6 19 *NYPL* [*Map Div. 91-5868*]

Atlas of Qatar from Landsat images. Yaḥyá, Muḥammad 'Adil Aḥmad. Aṭlas al-ṣuwar al-faḍā'iyah li-Dawlat Qaṭar min al-qamar al-ṣinā'i "Landsāt" /. al-Dawḥah , 1983. 1 atlas (vii, 166 p.) : DDC 912/.5363 19
G2249.81.C2 Y2 1983
NYPL [*Map Div. 91-2599*]

An atlas of Roman Britain /. Jones, Barri. Oxford , Cambridge, Mass., USA , 1990. vii, 341 p. : ISBN 0-631-13791-2 : DDC 911.41 20
NYPL [*Map Div. 90-10987*]

Atlas of the city of New York--borough of the Bronx . Bromley, firm, publishers. Philadelphia , 1923-1924 [i.e. 1963-1978]. 2 v. :
NYPL [*Map Div. 83-39*]

The Atlas of the Crusades / edited by Jonathan Riley-Smith. New York : Facts on File, 1991, c1990. 192 p. : col. ill., maps ; 29 cm. Includes index. Includes bibliographical references (p. 173).
ISBN 0-8160-2186-4 DDC 911 20
1. Crusades - Maps. 2. Geography, Medieval - Maps. I. Riley-Smith, Jonathan Simon Christopher, 1938-.
G1034 .R5 1990 NYPL [*Map Div. 91-4709*]

Atlas of the Danubian countries. Atlas der Donauländer. Wien, 1970- v. (loose-leaf) DDC 912/.496 19
G1882.D3 A8 1970
NYPL [*Map Div. 72-267*]

Atlas of the kingdom of Saudi Arabia. National guide & atlas of the kingdom of Saudi Arabia. [Jeddah, Saudi Arabia , 1989] 1 v. (various pagings) : *NYPL* [*Map Div. 91-5950*]

Atlas of the Oranges Essex County, N.J. .

Robinson, E. (Elisha) Philadelphia, Pa. , 1904. 1 atlas ([4] leaves of plates, 26 double leaves of plates) : *NYPL* [*Map Div. 91-4093*]

Atlas of the world. The Times atlas of the world /. New York , c1990. xlvii, 225 p., [123] p. of plates : ISBN 0-8129-1874-6
NYPL [*Map Div. 90-11947*]

An atlas of tribal India . Raza, Moonis. New Delhi , 1990. xxv, 472 p. : ISBN 81-7022-286-9 :
NYPL [*Map Div. 91-4975*]

An atlas of Venice : the form of the city on a 1:1000 scale photomap and line map / edited by Edoardo Salzano.3rd ed. [Venezia] : Comune di Venezia ;London : Architecture Design and Technology, 1990. 1 atlas (44 p., 186 [i.e. 372] p. of plates) : chiefly col. ill., maps ; 30 cm. Translated from the Italian. Includes bibliographical references. ISBN 1-85454-003-3 : DDC 912.4531 20
1. Venice (Italy) - Maps. 2. Venice (Italy) - Photo maps. I. Salzano, Edoardo, 1930-.
NYPL [*Map Div. 91-8140*]

Atlas routier. Karṭa (Firm) Carta's Israel motor atlas =. Jerusalem , c1980. 1 atlas (73 [i.e. 78] p.) : ISBN 965-220-011-5 DDC 912/.5694 19
G2236.P2 K3 1980
NYPL [*Map Div. 90-9721*]

Atlas Smolenskoĭ oblasti /. Soviet Union. Glavnoe upravlenie geodezii i kartografii. Moskva , 1964. 1 atlas (v, 31 p. :
NYPL [*Map Div. 91-1094*]

Atlas transcanadien /. Deschênes-Damian, Luce. Montréal , c1988. 1 atlas (145 p.) : ISBN 2-7601-1923-8 : DDC 912/.71 19
NYPL [*Map Div. 91-7753*]

Atlas urbano de la ciudad del Cusco / Werner Will [editor]. Cusco, Perú : Centro de Estudios Rurales Andinos "Bartolomé de las Casas, 1989. 1 atlas ([54] folded leaves) : col. maps ; 35 x 51 cm.
1. Cuzco (Peru) - Maps. I. Will, Werner.
NYPL [*Map Div. 91-6021*]

Atlas Weltmeer. Hermann Haack Geographisch-Kartographische Anstalt Gotha. Haack Atlas Weltmeer /. Gotha [1989] 1 atlas (viii, 136 p.) : ISBN 3-7301-0010-6
NYPL [*Map Div. 91-7352*]

Atlas zarubezhnykh stran dlīa sredneĭ shkoly . Soviet Union. Glavnoe upravlenie geodezii i kartografii. [Moskva , 1964). 1 atlas (40 p. :
NYPL [*Map Div. 91-1092*]

ATLASES - EARLY WORKS TO 1800.
Blaeu, Willem Janszoon, 1571-1638. The light of navigation. [Amsterdam, c1964] xiii, [60], 114, 118 p.
G1793 .B52 1964 (Map)
NYPL [*Map Div. 84-1067*]

ATLASES, AMERICAN. see ATLASES.

ATLASES, AUSTRALIAN.
(1990) The Macmillan Australian atlas /. South Melbourne , 1990. 1 atlas (134 p.) : ISBN 0-7329-0192-8
NYPL [*Map Div. 90-12898*]

ATLASES, BRITISH.
(1968) Reader's Digest Association (Great Britain) The Reader's Digest great world atlas. London, Sydney [etc.] 1968. 179 p. DDC 912
G1019 .R555 1968
NYPL [*Map Div. 90-12412*]

(1988) Longman new secondary atlas for Tanzania. Burnt Mill, Harlow, Essex , 1988. 152 p. : ISBN 0-582-03507-4 (pbk) DDC 912 19
G1021   *NYPL* [*Map Div. 91-7427*]

ATLASES, BULGARIAN.
Bulgaria. Upravlenie po geodeziia i kartografiia. Geografski atlas =. Sofiia , 1969. 1 atlas (65 p.) :
NYPL [*Map Div. 91-1090*]

ATLASES, CANADIAN.
(1988) Deschênes-Damian, Luce. Atlas transcanadien /. Montréal , c1988. 1 atlas (145 p.) : ISBN 2-7601-1923-8 : DDC 912/.71 19
NYPL [*Map Div. 91-7753*]

ATLASES - CONGRESSES.
The Purpose and use of national and regional atlases . Toronto, Canada , 1979. vii, 100 p. : ISBN 0-919870-23-6 (pbk).
GA101.2 .P87 NYPL [*Map Div. 81-199*]

ATLASES, FRENCH.
(1950) Larousse, firm, publishers, Paris. Atlas

international Larousse. Paris [1950] xix, [144], 42, 41 p. *NYPL* [*Map Div. 90-64*]

(1987) Prévot, Victor. Géopolitique transparente . [Paris] , 1987. 1 atlas (255 p.) : ISBN 2-210-98004-6 :
NYPL [*Map Div. 91-6046*]

ATLASES, GERMAN.
(1989) Meyers neuer weltatlas /. Mannheim , 1989. 321 p. : ISBN 3-411-02354-6
NYPL [*Map Div. 90-11958*]

(1990) Meyers Universal Atlas . Mannheim , c1990. 1 atlas (224 p.) : ISBN 3-411-07285-7
NYPL [*Map Div. 91-7165*]

ATLASES, HISTORICAL. see GEOGRAPHY, HISTORICAL - MAPS.

ATLASES, POLISH.
(1987) Państwowe Przedsiębiorstwo Wydawnictw Kartograficznych im. Eugeniusza Romera. Atlas geograficzny /. Warszawa , 1987. 1 atlas (120, 32 p.) : ISBN 83-7000-011-8 : DDC 912 20
G1021 .P222 1987
NYPL [*Map Div. 90-11797*]

ATLASES, RUSSIAN.
(1964) Soviet Union. Glavnoe upravlenie geodezii i kartografii. Atlas zarubezhnykh stran dlīa sredneĭ shkoly . [Moskva , 1964]. 1 atlas (40 p. : *NYPL* [*Map Div. 91-1092*]

ATLASES, SWEDISH.
(1978) Reader's Digest Association (Great Britain) [Reader's digest great world atlas. Swedish.] Det Bästas stora världsatlas. Stockholm , c1978. 1 atlas (215 p.) : ISBN 91-7030-070-4 *NYPL* [*Map Div. 91-7523*]

Atroshenko, V. I. Mediterranean vernacular : a vanishing architectural tradition / Viacheslav I. Atroshenko and Milton Grundy ; contributing editor, Neil Parkyn. New York : Rizzoli, 1991. p. cm. Includes bibliographical references and index. ISBN 0-8478-1386-X DDC 720/.9182/2 20
1. Vernacular architecture - Mediterranean Region. I. Grundy, Milton. II. Parkyn, Neil, 1943-. III. Title.
NA1458 .A87 1991

Attebery, Jennifer Eastman, 1951- Building Idaho : an architectural history / Jennifer Eastman Attebery. Moscow, Idaho : University of Idaho Press, 1991. x, 166 p. : ill. ; 29 cm. Includes bibliographical references (p. 149-155) and index. ISBN 0-89301-139-8 DDC 720/.9796 20
1. Architecture - Idaho. I. Title.
NA730.I2 A88 1990
NYPL [*3-MQWO 91-4971*]

Attems, Franz, 1926- Kirchen und Stifte der Steiermark / Text von Franz Attems und Johannes Koren ; Fotos von Lothar Beckel ... [et al.]. Innsbruck : Pinguin-Verlag, c1988. 163 p. : col. ill. ; 25 cm. Includes bibliographical references (p. 162-163). ISBN 3-7016-2296-5 DDC 726/.5/094365 20
1. Church architecture - Austria - Styria. 2. Styria (Austria) - Church history. I. Koren, Johannes. II. Beckel, Lothar. III. Title.
NA5509.S8 A88 1988
NYPL [*3-MRBB 90-11074*]

Atterbury, Paul.
The dictionary of Minton / Paul Atterbury and Maureen Batkin ; historical introduction by Terence A. Lockett. Woodbridge, Suffolk, England : Antique Collectors' Club, 1990. 370 p. : ill. (some col.), geneal. table, ports. ; 28 cm. Includes bibliographical references (p. 367-368). ISBN 1-85149-073-6 : DDC 738/.0942 19
1. Minton Ltd. - Dictionaries. 2. Pottery, English - Dictionaries. I. Batkin, Maureen. II. Title. III. Title: Minton.   *NYPL* [*3-MPGO 90-10594*]

The Parian phenomenon . Shepton Beauchamp, Somerset, Eng. , 1989. 268 p. : ISBN 0-903685-22-1
NYPL [*3-MPGO+ 90-2731*]

Attersee . Baumer, Dorothea. München [1987?] 26 leaves :
MLCM 88/01498 (N)
NYPL [*3-MCK+ A88 90-9373*]

ATTERSEE, CHRISTIAN LUDWIG, 1941- - EXHIBITIONS.
Baumer, Dorothea. Attersee . München [1987?] 26 leaves :
MLCM 88/01498 (N)
NYPL [*3-MCK+ A88 90-9373*]

Atti del convegno di Pescara, 27-29 gennaio 1989, su il sacro, l'architettura sacra oggi / [Adriano Di Bonaventura, organizzatore]. Rimini : Il Cerchio, c1990. 319 p., [36] p. of plates : ill. (some col.) ; 24 cm. Cover title: Il sacro, l'architettura sacra oggi. Cover has subtitle: Atti del congresso internazionale di Pescara, gennaio 1989. Includes bibliographical references.
1. Church architecture - Congresses. 2. Architecture, Modern - 20th century - Congresses. I. Di Bonaventura, Adriano. II. Title: Sacro, l'architettura sacra oggi.
NA4795 .A8 1990

Atti del XL Congresso internazionale degli americanisti. International Congress of Americanists, 40th, Rome and Genoa, 1972. Genova [1973-76] 4 v.
NYPL [HBC 74-2090]

Attie, Dottie. Symbolism . [New York] [1989]
[24] p. : *NYPL [3-MAL 91-4569]*

Attoe, Wayne. The Architecture of Ricardo Legorreta /. Austin , 1990. 171 p. : ISBN 0-292-75106-0 (alk. paper) DDC 720/.92 20
NA759.L44 A87 1990 *NYPL [3-MQZ+ (Legorreta Vilchis) 91-3708]*

Attwood, Philip. Wilcox, Timothy. Alphonse Legros, 1837-1911 . [Dijon] , 1988. 165 p., [4] p. of plates : ISBN 2-900462-27-4
N6853.L37 W55 1988
NYPL [3-MCO L519 90-11769]

Au carrefour du Grand jeu et du surréalisme /. Delons, André, 1909-1940. [Mortemart, Mézière-sur-Issoire] [1988] 201 p. ;
NX549.A1 D45 1988
NYPL [3-MAMI 90-11123]

Aubert, Hans Joachim. Weber, Hans, 1938- Marokko . Köln , c1989. 56 p., [176] p. of plates : ISBN 3-7701-2305-0
NYPL [MFX+ (Weber) 90-1054]

Aubert-Yong, Joëlle. Khan-Magomedov, S. O. (Selim Omarovich) Vhutemas . Paris , c1990. 2 v. (880 p.) : ISBN 2-903370-55-9 (set) DDC 707/.1/147312 20
N332.S65 M675 1990

Auburtin, Jean-Francis, 1866-1930.
Jean-Francis Auburtin, 1866-1930 : le symboliste de la mer / présenté par la Délégation à l'action artistique de la ville de Paris ; sous la direction de Christian Briend ; préface de Jacques Foucart ; avec la participation de Béatrice de Andia, Francine Quentin, Joyce Henri Robinson. Paris : La Délégation, [1990?] 158 p. : ill. (some col.) ; 29 cm. Exhibition catalog. Includes bibliographical references (p. 153-156). ISBN 2-905118-27-X
1. Auburtin, Jean-Francis, 1866-1930 - Exhibitions. I. Briend, Christian. II. Délégation à l'action artistique de la ville de Paris. III. Title.
NYPL [3-MCO A897 91-7473]

AUBURTIN, JEAN-FRANCIS, 1866-1930 - EXHIBITIONS.
Auburtin, Jean-Francis, 1866-1930. Jean-Francis Auburtin, 1866-1930 . Paris [1990?] 158 p. : ISBN 2-905118-27-X
NYPL [3-MCO A897 91-7473]

Auch kleine Dinge : Dürer and the decorative tradition / catalogue and exhibition by R. Bruce Livie. [Cambridge] : Busch-Reisinger Museum, Harvard University, [1971] [174] p. : ill. ; 18 cm. Exhibition dates: Mar. 4 - Apr. 3, 1971. Bibliography: p. [169-174]
1. Dürer, Albrecht, 1471-1528 - Influence - Exhibitions. 2. Decoration and ornament, Renaissance - Exhibitions. I. Livie, R. Bruce. II. Busch-Reisinger Museum.
NYPL [3-MNC 90-5886]

Auckland City Art Gallery.
Blackley, Roger, 1953- Two centuries of New Zealand landscape art /. Auckland, N.Z. , c1990. 128 p. : ISBN 0-86463-179-0
NYPL [3-MAMY 91-5463]

Hundertwasser, 1928- Hundertwasser. Glarus, Switzerland, c1973. 97 p.
NYPL [3-MCK H933 90-5895]

McCahon, Colin. Colin McCahon . Auckland, New Zealand , c1988. 157 p. : ISBN 0-86463-165-0
NYPL [3-MCZ+ M116 91-6649]

The audience for American art museums /. Schuster, J. Mark Davidson, 1950- Washington , 1991. p. cm. ISBN 0-929765-00-1 :

DDC 708.13 20
N510 .S3 1991

AUDIENCES - PSYCHOLOGY.
Shearman, John K. G. Only connect . Princeton, N.J. , 1992. p. cm. ISBN 0-691-09972-3 (CL) : DDC 709/.45/09024 20
N6915 .S54 1992

Auditoriums /. Boulet, Marie-Laure. Paris , c1990. 119 p. : ISBN 2-281-19052-8 DDC 725/.81/09048 20
NA6815 .B68 1990

AUDITORIUMS.
Boulet, Marie-Laure. Auditoriums /. Paris , c1990. 119 p. : ISBN 2-281-19052-8 DDC 725/.81/09048 20
NA6815 .B68 1990

Audsley, George Ashdown, 1838-1925. Audsley, W. (William), b. 1833. [Polychromatic decoration as applied to buildings in the mediaeval styles.] Victorian sourcebook of medieval decoration /. New York , 1991. p. cm. ISBN 0-486-26834-9 (pbk.) DDC 729/.4 20
NK1548 .A84 1991

Audsley, W. (William), b. 1833.
[Polychromatic decoration as applied to buildings in the mediaeval styles]
Victorian sourcebook of medieval decoration / W. & G. Audsley. New York : Dover Publications, 1991. p. cm. (Dover pictorial archive series) Reprint. Originally published: Polychromatic decoration as applied to buildings in the mediaeval styles. London : H. Sotheran & Co., 1882. ISBN 0-486-26834-9 (pbk.) DDC 729/.4 20
1. Color decoration and ornament. 2. Decoration and ornament, Medieval. 3. Decoration and ornament, Architectural. I. Audsley, George Ashdown, 1838-1925. II. Title.
NK1548 .A84 1991

Auer, Michael. Jandl, H. Ward. Yesterday's houses of tomorrow . Washington, DC , 1991. p. cm. ISBN 0-89133-186-7 DDC 728/.0973/09034 20
NA7207 .J36 1991

Auer, Michel. 150 ans d'appareils photographiques : à travers la collection Michel Auer = 150 years of cameras : trough [sic] the Michel Auer collection / Michel Auer. Hermance : Editions Camera obscura, [1989] 1 v. (unpaged) : ill. (some col.) ; 29 cm. French and English. Includes index. ISBN 2-903671-07-9
1. Cameras - Collectors and collecting. I. Title. II. Title: Cent cinquante ans d'appareils photographiques. III. Title: 150 years of cameras. IV. Title: One hundred fifty years of cameras. *NYPL [MFW 91-4967]*

Auf dem Balkon . Polgar, Alfred, 1875-1955. Reinbek bei Hamburg , 1989 (Neu-Isenburg : Druck der Edition Tiessen) 33 p. : ISBN 3-920947-89-4
NYPL [MEM+ E735 90-2434]

Auf den Spuren der Kartoffel in Kunst und Literatur. Völksen, Wilhelm. Hildesheim [1965] 64 p.
N8236.P6 V6 *NYPL [3-MAMZ 91-519]*

Auffarth, Sid, 1938- Festschrift für Georg Hoeltje /. Hannover , 1988. 160 p. :
NYPL [3-MQWD+ 90-12015]

Das Auge am Tatort . Spies, Werner, 1937- München , 1979. 347 p. : ISBN 3-7913-0484-4
N6490 .S65 *NYPL [3-MAL 80-2230]*

August Macke . Moeller, Magdalena M. München , c1989. 128 p. : ISBN 3-7913-0990-0
NYPL [3-MCK+ M15 90-415]

August Macke . Moeller, Magdalena M. [Auguste Macke. French.] [Paris] , c1990. 128 p. : ISBN 2-85025-219-7
NYPL [3-MCK+ M15 90-13092]

Auguste Rodin . Goldscheider, Cécile. Paris , Lausanne , c1989- v. : ISBN 2-908063-03-4 (set) DDC 730/.92 20
NB553.R7 A4 1989
NYPL [3-MGO+ (Rodin) 91-391]

Augustin Lesage : 1876-1954 / par Annick Notter ... [et al.] ; préface de Olivier Chevrillon ; photographies de Claude Thériez. Paris : P. Sers, 1989. 222 p. : ill. (some col.), facsims., ports. ; 31 cm. Issued in conjunction with a retrospective of the artist's work held in Arras, Béthune, Lausanne, Florence and Cairo from October 15, 1988 to autumn, 1989. Catalogue raisonné: p. 207-214. Bibliography: p. 215-221.

1. Lesage, Augustin, 1876-1954 - Catalogues raisonnés. 2. Spiritualism in art. I. Lesage, Augustin, 1876-1954. II. Notter, Annick.
NYPL [3-MCO+ L618 90-10803]

Augustin Meinrad Bächtiger, 1888-1971 /. Studer-Geisser, Isabella. St. Gallen , 1988. 95 p. : ISBN 3-85603-003-4
N7153.B23 S78 1988
NYPL [3-MCZ B1345 90-10412]

Augustinermuseum (Freiburg im Breisgau, Germany) Thoma, Hans, 1839-1924. Hans Thoma, Lebensbilder . Königstein im Taunus , c1989. 336 p. : ISBN 3-7845-7870-X DDC 759.3 20
ND588.T4 A4 1989

Augustus Northmore Welby Pugin, 1812-1852 [microform] /. Doumato, Lamia. Monticello, Ill. , 1983. 9 p. ; ISBN 0-88066-732-X (pbk.) : DDC 016.72/092/4 19
Z8716.2 .D68 1983 NA997.P9
*NYPL [*XMC-615]*

Auke de Vries . Vries, Auke de, 1937- [Wiesbaden] , c1990. 117 p. : ISBN 3-89258-008-1
IN PROCESS (ONLINE)
NYPL [3-MGO+ (Vries) 91-4353]

Auping, Michael. Jenny Holzer : the Venice installation / [Michael Auping] Buffalo, N.Y. : Albright-Knox Art Gallery, 1991. p. cm. Includes bibliographical references. ISBN 0-914782-80-0 DDC 709/.2 20
1. Holzer, Jenny, 1950- - Exhibitions. 2. Installations (Art) - United States - Exhibitions. I. Albright-Knox Art Gallery. II. Title.
N6537.H577 A4 1991

Aurélie Nemours /. Lemoine, Serge. Zürich , Reutlingen , c1989. 254 p. : ISBN 3-908080-28-2
NYPL [3-MCO N436 90-8474]

Aurenhammer, Gertrude. Aurenhammer, Hans. Martino Altomonte. Wien [c1965] 206 p.
ND623.A512 A9
NYPL [3-MCF+ A469 91-320]

Aurenhammer, Hans.
J. B. Fischer von Erlach. Cambridge, Mass., Harvard University Press, 1973. 193 p. illus. 26 cm. Includes bibliographical references. ISBN 0-674-46988-7 DDC 720/.92/4
1. Fischer von Erlach, Johann Bernhard, 1656-1723. I. Fischer von Erlach, Johann Bernhard, 1656-1723.
NA1011.5.F57 A94 1973b *NYPL [3-MQZ (Fischer von Erlach) 90-5573]*

Martino Altomonte. Mit einem Beitrag "Martino Altomonte als Zeichner und Graphiker" von Gertrude Aurenhammer. Wien, Herold [c1965] 206 p. illus., plates (part col.) port. 30 cm. (Veröffentlichung der Österreichischen Galerie in Wien) Includes bibliographical references.
1. Altomonte, Martino, 1657-1745. 2. Painters - Italy - Biography. I. Altomonte, Martino, 1657-1745. II. Aurenhammer, Gertrude. III. Title.
ND623.A512 A9
NYPL [3-MCF+ A469 91-320]

Aurier, Gabriel-Albert, 1865-1892. Le symbolisme en peinture : Van Gogh, Gauguin et quelques autres / G.-Albert Aurier ; textes réunis et présentés par Pierre-Louis Mathieu. [Caen] : L'Echoppe, c1991. 87 p. ; 22 cm. Includes bibliographical references (p. 83) and index. ISBN 2-905657-77-4
1. Symbolism (Art movement) - France. 2. Painting, French. 3. Painting, Modern - 19th century - France. I. Mathieu, Pierre-Louis. II. Title.
ND547.5.N3 A93 1991

Aus Archiv und Chronik der Stadt Villingen-Schwenningen.
Villingen-Schwenningen und Umgebung in alten Karten und Plänen . Villingen-Schwenningen , 1987- v. : ISBN 3-87450-014-4 (Bd. 1)
GA875.V55 V54 1987
NYPL [Map Div. 91-63]

Aus dem Schweizerischen Landesmuseum.
Schneider, Jenny, 1924- Kabinettscheiben des 16. und 17. Jahrhunderts /. Bern , c1986. 12 p., [16] p. of plates : *NYPL [3-MRY 91-521]*

Aus der Werkstatt des Künstlers : [Austellung] , veranstaltet vom Verein für Originalradierung, München e. V. , Farbwerke Hoechst Frankfurt, Jahrhunderthalle, 16. Dezember 1969 bis 10. Januar 1970 ... [et al. : Katalog / Redaktion, Adolf Brunner] [S.l. : s.n., 1969?] (München :

R. Koehler) ca. 100 p. : chiefly ill., ports. ; 23 cm.
1. Prints, German - Exhibitions. 2. Prints - 20th century - Germany (West) - Exhibitions. I. Brunner, Adolf, 1905-. II. Verein für Originalradierung München. III. Höchst (Frankfurt am Main, Germany) Jahrhunderthalle.   **NYPL [MDBF 90-5879]**

Aus-Druck . Furtwängler, Felix Martin, 1954- Frankfurt am Main [1989] 112 p. : ISBN 3-88270-048-3 DDC 769.92 20
NE654.F84 A4 1989
            NYPL [MDG (Furtwängler) 90-13668]

Aus einem Guss : Eisenguss in Kunst und Technik / mit Beiträgen von Jörg Schmalfuss ... [et al.]. Berlin : Nicolaische Verlagsbuchhandlung, c1988. 248 p. : ill. ; 26 cm. (Berliner Beiträge zur Technikgeschichte und Industriekultur . Bd. 9) Catalog of an exhibition organized by the Museum für Verkehr und Technik Berlin. Includes bibliographical references (p. 244-247). ISBN 3-87584-203-0 DDC 730/.0943/074431554 20
1. Barth, Ewald, 1898-1968 - Art collections - Exhibitions. 2. Fischer, Frank - Art collections - Exhibitions. 3. Ironwork - Prussia (Germany) - History - 19th century - Exhibitions. 4. Ironwork - Private collections - Berlin (Germany) - Exhibitions. I. Schmalfuss, Jörg, 1954-. II. Museum für Verkehr und Technik Berlin. III. Series.
NK8250.A3 P784 1988
            NYPL [3-MNK 91-3716]

Aus Erde geformt : Lehmbauten in West- und Nordafrika / mit Beiträgen von Annemarie Fiedermutz-Laun ... [et al.]. Mainz : P. von Zabern, [1990] 171 p. : 214 ill. (48 col.), 1 map ; 29 cm. At head of title: Frobenius-Institut. Includes bibliographical references. ISBN 3-8053-1107-9 :
1. Building, Clay - Africa, North. 2. Vernacular architecture - Africa, North. 3. Building, Clay - Africa, West. 4. Vernacular architecture - Africa, West. I. Fiedermutz-Laun, Annemarie. II. Universität Frankfurt am Main. Frobenius-Institut.
NA1588 .A97 1990   **NYPL [Sc F 91-122]**

Aus westfälischen Bildsammlungen . (Bd. 1) Jakob, Volker. Menschen im Silberspiegel . Greven , 1989. 168 p. : ISBN 3-923166-30-3
IN PROCESS (ONLINE)
            NYPL [MFW 91-2653]

Ausbeute : Bergbau und Bergarbeit in der Fotografie : eine Ausstellung des Ruhrlandmuseums der Stadt Essen / [herausgegeben vom Ruhrlandmuseum der Stadt Essen]. Essen : Das Museum, c1989. 182 p. : ill. (some col.) ; 30 cm. Includes bibliographical references (p. 178-179). ISBN 3-87034-045-2 DDC 779/.96 20
1. Photography, Industrial - Exhibitions. 2. Photography of coal mines - Exhibitions. I. Ruhrlandmuseum Essen. II. Title: Bergbau und Bergarbeit in der Fotografie.
TR706 .A95 1989   **NYPL [MFW+ 91-7294]**

Ausdruck. Furtwängler, Felix Martin, 1954- Aus-Druck . Frankfurt am Main [1989] 112 p. : ISBN 3-88270-048-3 DDC 769.92 20
NE654.F84 A4 1989
            NYPL [MDG (Furtwängler) 90-13668]

Ausgeblendete Realität : Modefotos aus der DDR : Institut für Kostümkunde, Hochschule für angewandte Kunst in Wien, Mai-Juni 1989 / [Zusammenstellung der Fotos, Thea Melis ; Katalogredaktion, Gerda Buxbaum ; Ausstellung, Oswald Oberhuber, Gerda Buxbaum]. Wien : Die Hochschule, 1989. 95 p. : ill. ; 30 cm. Includes bibliographical references.
1. Fashion photography - Germany (East) - Exhibitions. I. Melis, Thea. II. Buxbaum, Gerda, 1949-. III. Oberhuber, Oswald. IV. Hochschule für Angewandte Kunst (Vienna, Austria). Institut für Kostümkunde.
            NYPL [MFW+ 90-11185]

Ausstellung Joel Fisher. Fisher, Joel. Ein unwiderruflicher Schritt =. [s.l. , 1975?] (Mönchengladbach : H. Schlechtriem] 48 p. :
N6537.F48 A58
            NYPL [3-MCX F532 81-643]

Ausstellungen im Museum am Dom, 1962-1983 : Dokumentation / bearbeitet von Elisabeth Spies-Hankammer. Lübeck : [Das Museum?], 1983. 224 p. : ill. ; 30 cm. (Veröffentlichungen des Senats der Hansestadt Lübeck, Amt für Kultur. Reihe B . Heft 1) ISBN 3-924214-22-0
1. Art, Modern - 20th century - Germany (West) -

Lübeck - Exhibitions - Catalog. I. Spies-Hankammer, Elisabeth. II. Museum am Dom (Lübeck, Germany).
            NYPL [3-MAVZ+ (Lübeck) 90-10858]

Ausstellungshallen Mathildenhöhe Darmstadt. Wildt, Adolfo, 1868-1931. Adolfo Wildt, ein italienischer Bildhauer des Symbolismus . [Darmstadt] [1990] 296 p. :
            NYPL [3-MGO (Wildt) 91-5869]

Ausstellungskatalog des Germanischen Nationalmuseums Nürnberg. Sitz-Gelegenheiten . Nürnberg , c1989. 263 p. : ISBN 3-926982-13-6
IN PROCESS (ONLINE)
            NYPL [3-MOF 91-6263]

Werner, Martina, 1929- Der graue Fetisch . Nürnberg , c1987. 44 p. :
MLCS 88/03971 (N)
            NYPL [3-MGO (Werner) 90-13400]

Ausstellungskatalog (Galerie Wolfgang Ketterer . (140) Rauh, Caspar Walter, 1912-1983. Caspar Walter Rauh, 1912-1983 . München [1987] 16 p. :   **NYPL [MDG (Rauh) 90-11352]**

Ausstellungskatalog (Stadtgeschichtliche Museen Nürnberg) . (Nr. 17) Kunsthandwerk im Stadtmuseum . [Nürnberg] [1987] 55 p. : DDC 730/.0943/320740332 19
NK952.M58 K86 1987
            NYPL [3-MLF 90-12631]

Ausstellungsserie Fotografie in Deutschland von 1850 bis heute. Subjektive Fotografie . Stuttgart , c1989. 131 p. :
IN PROCESS (ONLINE)
            NYPL [MFW+ 90-10203]

Austausch und Verbindungen in der Kunstgeschichte des Ostseeraums : Homburger Gespräche 9, 22.-25.11.1987, Christian-Albrechts-Universität, Kiel / herausgegeben von Lars Olof Larsson, Jan von Bonsdorff. Kiel : Martin-Carl-Adolf-Böckler-Stiftung, 1988. 207 p., [8] p. of plates : ill. ; 30 cm.
1. Art - Baltic Sea Region - Congresses. I. Homburger Gespräche (9th : 1987 : Kiel, Germany).
IN PROCESS (ONLINE)
            NYPL [3-MAM+ 91-4693]

AUSTIN, JAMES BLISS, 1904- - ART COLLECTIONS - EXHIBITIONS. Eight hundred years of Japanese printmaking . Pittsburgh , c1976. 126 p. :
            NYPL [MDBV 90-6041]

Austin, Tex. University. see Texas. University at Austin.

Austin/Desmond Fine Art. Ayrton, Michael, 1921-1975. Michael Ayrton . London , c1990. 44 p. : ISBN 1-87292-608-8
            NYPL [3-MGO (Ayrton) 91-6889]

Australia Council. 1990 Venice Biennale Australia . Perth, WA , c1990. 59 p. : ISBN 0-7309-0783-X   **NYPL [3-MCY 91-5556]**

AUSTRALIA - CULTURAL POLICY. Cultivating the country . Oxford [England] , New York , 1988. 118 p. : ISBN 0-19-554944-9 (pbk.)   **NYPL [3-MAM 89-17144]**

Australia. Dept. of National Development. Division of National Mapping. see Australia. Division of National Mapping.

Australia. Dept. of National Development. Geographic Section. Atlas of Australian resources. 2nd series. Australia. Division of National Mapping. Atlas of Australian resources. 3rd series. Canberra , 1980- 1 atlas (v.) : ISBN 0-642-51458-5 (set) DDC 912/.13337/0994 19
G2751.G3 A4 1980
            NYPL [Map Div. 81-377]

Australia. Director of National Mapping. see Australia. Division of National Mapping.

AUSTRALIA - DISCOVERY AND EXPLORATION. Baudin in Australian waters . Melbourne , 1988. 347 p. : ISBN 0-19-554787-X
            NYPL [3-MAMY+ 90-10770]

Australia. Division of National Mapping. Atlas of Australian resources. 3rd series. Canberra : Division of National Mapping, 1980- 1 atlas (v.) : col. maps (some folded) ; 44 cm. Rev. ed. of: Atlas of Australian resources. 2nd series. 1962.

Principal maps 1:5,000,000; supplementary maps at various scales. Principal maps also published separately in the "Australia 1:5,000,000 map series"--Preface. Two folded col. maps inserted in v. 6. Includes bibliographical references. CONTENTS. - v. 1. Soils and land use -- v. 2. Population -- v. 3. Agriculture -- v. 4. Climate -- v. 6. Vegetation. ISBN 0-642-51458-5 (set) DDC 912/.13337/0994 19
1. Natural resources - Australia - Maps. 2. Australia - Economic conditions - Maps. I. Australia. Dept. of National Development. Geographic Section. Atlas of Australian resources. 2nd series. II. Title.
G2751.G3 A4 1980
            NYPL [Map Div. 81-377]

AUSTRALIA - ECONOMIC CONDITIONS - MAPS. Australia. Division of National Mapping. Atlas of Australian resources. Canberra , 1980- 1 atlas (v.) : ISBN 0-642-51458-5 (set) DDC 912/.13337/0994 19
G2751.G3 A4 1980
            NYPL [Map Div. 81-377]

AUSTRALIA - HISTORY - 20TH CENTURY - PICTORIAL WORKS. Postle, Bruce. Images of our time . Ridgwood, Vic. Australia , 1989. 159 p. : ISBN 0-670-90229-2   **NYPL [MFW+ 91-5034]**

AUSTRALIA IN ART. Baudin in Australian waters . Melbourne , 1988. 347 p. : ISBN 0-19-554787-X
            NYPL [3-MAMY+ 90-10770]

Smith, Kate, 1947- Alice and beyond /. Brisbane, Qld , 1989. 71 p. : ISBN 0-86439-089-0 DDC 759.994 20
ND1105.S65 A4 1989

AUSTRALIA IN ART - EXHIBITIONS. Hansen, David. The face of Australia . Frenchs Forest, NSW, Australia , 1988. 127 p. : ISBN 0-86777-181-X DDC 760/.0449994 19
N7400 .H3 1988   **NYPL [3-MAM+ 91-2242]**

Australia. National Mapping, Division of. see Australia. Division of National Mapping.

AUSTRALIA - SOCIAL LIFE AND CUSTOMS - PICTORIAL WORKS. Davies, Alan, 1946- At work & play . [Sydney] , 1989. 128 p. : ISBN 0-7305-6293-X
            NYPL [MFW+ 90-1035]

AUSTRALIAN ABORIGINES - ART. see ART, AUSTRALIAN (ABORIGINAL)

Australian architects . (4) Australian architects--Australian government architects. Canberra , c1988. 111 p. : ISBN 0-644-07919-3
            NYPL [3-MQWZ+ 90-10612]

Australian architects--Australian government architects. Canberra : [Australian Government Publishing Service], c1988. 111 p. : ill. (some col.) ; 30 cm. (Australian architects. 4) "Editor: Roger Pegrum"--P. 2 of cover. "An AGPS Press Publication"--P. 2 of cover. ISBN 0-644-07919-3
1. Architecture, Modern - 20th century - Australia. I. Pegrum, Roger. II. Title: Australian government architects. III. Series.
            NYPL [3-MQWZ+ 90-10612]

AUSTRALIAN ART. see ART, AUSTRALIAN.

Australian art museums and public galleries directory. Melbourne, Vic.: Art Museums Association of Australia ; Clayton, Vic. : National Centre for Research and Development in Australian Studies, Monash University, 1990. v, 49 p. ; 30 cm. ISBN 0-9595532-4-X DDC 708/.0025/94 20
1. Art museums - Australia - Directories. 2. Art galleries, Commercial - Australia - Directories. I. Art Museums Association of Australia. II. National Centre for Research and Development in AustralianStudies.
N3910 .A93 1990

Australian atlas. The Macmillan Australian atlas /. South Melbourne , 1990. 1 atlas (134 p.) : ISBN 0-7329-0192-8
            NYPL [Map Div. 90-12898]

Australian bark painting from the Collection of Dr. Edward L. Ruhe . Ruhe, Edward Lehman, 1923- Rochester, Mich. [1975] [32] p. : DDC 750/.899915094295 19
ND1101 .R79   **NYPL [3-MADF 81-343]**

Australian Bicentennial Authority. Hansen, David. The face of Australia . Frenchs Forest, NSW, Australia , 1988. 127 p. : ISBN

0-86777-181-X   DDC 760/.0449994 19
N7400 .H3 1988   NYPL [3-MAM+ 91-2242]

Australian country furniture /. Hooper, Toby.
South Yarra, Vic., Australia , 1988. 138 p., [24]
p. of plates :   ISBN 0-670-90074-5
NYPL [3-MOF+ 91-7961]

Australian drawings and watercolours . Australian
National Gallery. Canberra , c1988. 64 p. :
ISBN 0-642-13032-9
NYPL [3-MBH+ 90-10417]

Australian fashion : the contemporary art :
Twentieth Century Gallery, Victoria & Albert
Museum, London, 7 June - 13 August 1989 and
Powerhouse Museum of Applied Arts and
Sciences, Sydney, 4 October 1989 - 24
February 1990 / an exhibition curated by Jane
de Teliga for the Museum of Applied Arts and
Sciences, Sydney in association with the
Australian Council. Sydney : The Museum,
1989. 64 p. : ill. (some col.) ; 29 cm. ISBN
1-86317-002-2
1. Costume design - Australia. 2. Fashion - Australia. I.
Powerhouse Museum of Applied Arts and Sciences
(Australia). II. Victoria and Albert Museum.
NYPL [3-MME+ 91-6591]

Australian government architects. Australian
architects--Australian government architects.
Canberra , c1988. 111 p. :   ISBN 0-644-07919-3
NYPL [3-MQWZ+ 90-10612]

AUSTRALIAN LANDSCAPE PAINTING. see
LANDSCAPE PAINTING, AUSTRALIAN.

Australian modern painting . Eagle, Mary, 1944-
Sydney , 1990. 216 p. :   ISBN 1-86256-427-2
NYPL [3-MCY+ 90-13348]

Australian National Gallery.
Australian drawings and watercolours : a
souvenir book from the Australian National
Gallery / Andrew Sayers. Canberra : The
Gallery, c1988. 64 p. : col. ill., ports. ; 30 cm.
Includes drawings from the National Library of
Australia--Cf. introduction.   ISBN 0-642-13032-9
1. Australian National Gallery - Catalogs. 2. Drawing,
Australian - Catalogs. 3. Drawing - Australia - Canberra
(A.C.T.) - Catalogs. 4. Watercolor painting, Australian -
Catalogs. 5. Watercolor painting - Australia - Canberra
(A.C.T.) - Catalogs. I. Sayers, Andrew. II. National
Library of Australia. III. Title.
NYPL [3-MBH+ 90-10417]

Irises and five masterpieces. [Australia] [1989]
1 v. (unpaged) :   ISBN 0-9598384-1-4
NYPL [MAX (Bond) 91-6719]

Maxwell, Robyn J. Textiles of Southeast Asia .
[Canberra] : Melbourne ; 432 p. :   ISBN
0-19-553186-8   *NYPL [3-MON 91-3305]*

AUSTRALIAN NATIONAL GALLERY -
CATALOGS.
Australian National Gallery. Australian
drawings and watercolours . Canberra , c1988.
64 p. : ISBN 0-642-13032-9
NYPL [3-MBH+ 90-10417]

Maxwell, Robyn J. Textiles of Southeast Asia .
[Canberra] : Melbourne ; 432 p. :   ISBN
0-19-553186-8   *NYPL [3-MON 91-3305]*

AUSTRALIAN PAINTING. see PAINTING,
AUSTRALIAN.

AUSTRALIAN POTTERY. see POTTERY,
AUSTRALIAN.

Australian watercolour painters, 1780 to present
day /. Campbell, Jean, 1913- Roseville, N.S.W.,
Australia , 1989. 394 p. :   ISBN 0-947131-28-0
NYPL [3-MCY+ 90-5307]

AUSTRALIAN WIT AND HUMOR,
PICTORIAL.
Swain, Sally. Great housewives of art revisited
/. New York , 1992. p. cm.   ISBN
0-14-015837-5 :   DDC 741.5/994 20
NC1759.S93 A4 1992

Australian Wool Corporation. Wool quilts old and
new . North Melbourne, Vic. , 1985. 25 p. :
ISBN 0-642-07720-7   DDC 746.9/7/0994074945
20
NK9190.A1 W67 1985

Australians at home . Lane, Terence, 1946-
Melbourne , New York , 1990. xiii, 449 p. :
ISBN 0-19-553128-0   DDC 747.2994 20
NK2090.A1 L36 1990

AUSTRIA - BIOGRAPHY - CARICATURES
AND CARTOONS.

Esterle, Max von, 1870-1947. Karikaturen und
Kritiken /. Salzburg , c1971. 237 p. :   ISBN
3-7013-0455-6
NC1489.E85 A4 1971
NYPL [MEM (Esterle) 90-6541]

Austria. Bundesministerium für Unterricht.
Sotriffer, Kristian, 1932- Contemporary graphic
art from Austria. [Vienna, 1969?] 47, [5] p.
DDC 760
NE643.4 .S6   *NYPL [MDBF 90-6251]*

AUSTRIA - DESCRIPTION AND TRAVEL -
1981- - GUIDE-BOOKS.
Müller-Dürr, Marianne. Österreich . Stuttgart ,
c1987. 600 p. :   ISBN 3-17-009234-0   DDC
709/.436 20
N6801 .M85 1987

Austria - Government. see Austria - Politics and
government.

AUSTRIA - POLITICS AND GOVERNMENT -
20TH CENTURY - CARICATURES AND
CARTOONS.
Die Muskete . Wien , c1983. 235 p. :   ISBN
3-85063-137-0
DB30 .M87x 1983   *NYPL [MDY 87-1108]*

AUSTRIA - SOCIAL LIFE AND CUSTOMS -
CARICATURES AND CARTOONS.
Die Muskete . Wien , c1983. 235 p. :   ISBN
3-85063-137-0
DB30 .M87x 1983   *NYPL [MDY 87-1108]*

Austria. Unterricht, Bundesministerium für. see
Austria. Bundesministerium für Unterricht.

AUSTRIAN ARTS. see ARTS, AUSTRIAN.

AUSTRIAN SATIRE. see SATIRE,
AUSTRIAN.

AUSTRIAN WIT AND HUMOR, PICTORIAL.
Esterle, Max von, 1870-1947. Karikaturen und
Kritiken /. Salzburg , c1971. 237 p. :   ISBN
3-7013-0455-6
NC1489.E85 A4 1971
NYPL [MEM (Esterle) 90-6541]

AUSTRO-SARDINIAN WAR, 1848-1849 -
CARICATURES AND CARTOONS.
Chiappori, Alfredo, 1943- Storie d'Italia .
Milano , 1978. 174 p. :   DDC 945.081/02/07
DG552 .C47
NYPL [3-MEM (Chiappori) 90-4348]

AUTHORS AS ARTISTS - AUSTRIA.
Van Zon, Gabriele, 1937- Word and picture .
New York , 1991. p. cm.   ISBN 0-8204-1475-1
DDC 700/.92 20
NX548.Z9 K838 1991

AUTHORS AS ARTISTS - GREAT BRITAIN -
EXHIBITIONS.
Berg Collection. Pen & brush . [New York] ,
c1969 (Lunenburg, Vt. : Stinehour Press) 59 p. :
ISBN 0-87104-142-1   DDC 741.942
NC15.N43 N47   *NYPL [MAMZ 75-566]*

AUTHORS AS ARTISTS - UNITED STATES -
EXHIBITIONS.
Berg Collection. Pen & brush . [New York] ,
c1969 (Lunenburg, Vt. : Stinehour Press) 59 p. :
ISBN 0-87104-142-1   DDC 741.942
NC15.N43 N47   *NYPL [MAMZ 75-566]*

AUTHORS, ENGLISH - 19TH CENTURY -
BIOGRAPHY.
Poulson, Christine. William Morris /. London ,
c1989. 128 p. :   ISBN 1-85076-183-3 :   DDC 709.2
20
PR5083   *NYPL [3-MLH 90-11508]*

Vallance, Aymer, 1862-1943. The art of
William Morris /. New York , 1988. xi, 167,
xxx p. :   ISBN 0-486-25647-2 (pbk.)   DDC 821/.8 B
19
PR5083 .V3 1988
NYPL [3-MNE+ 90-13076]

AUTHORS, ENGLISH - 20TH CENTURY -
BIOGRAPHY.
Kennedy, Richard, 1910- A boy at the Hogarth
Press /. London , 1972. x, 85 p., [1] folded leaf
of plates :   ISBN 0-435-18510-1
NYPL [3-MEM (Kennedy) 90-11892]

AUTHORS, FRENCH - 17TH CENTURY -
BIOGRAPHY.
Hall, H. Gaston. Richelieu's Desmarets and the
century of Louis XIV /. Oxford , New York ,
1990. 399 p. :   ISBN 0-19-815157-8 :   DDC 841/.4
B 20
PQ1794.D6 H35 1990
NYPL [3-MAVZ (Hamburg) 91-3450]

AUTHORS, GERMAN - 19TH CENTURY -
BIOGRAPHY.
Wilhelm Busch und seine Freunde in Frankfurt
und Kronberg /. Frankfurt am Main , c1984.
104 p. :   ISBN 3-7829-0289-0 :   DDC 831/.8 19
PT2603.U8 Z895 1984
NYPL [3-MCK B97 86-1055]

AUTHORS, PERUVIAN - 20TH CENTURY -
INTERVIEWS.
Martínez, Cesáreo. Desde la vigilia . [Peru?]
1989. 212 p. ;
N6718 .M37 1989

Autógrafos cubanos /. Barnet, Miguel, 1940-
Ciudad de La Habana , c1990. 151 p. :   DDC
700/.97291/0904 20
NX525.A1 B37 1990

AUTOGRAPHS - DIRECTORIES.
Castagno, John, 1930- Artists' monograms and
indiscernible signatures . Metuchen, N.J. , 1991.
p. cm.   ISBN 0-8108-2415-9   DDC 702/.78 20
N45 .C374 1991

AUTOGRAPHS - UNITED STATES -
DICTIONARIES.
Falk, Peter H. Dictionary of signatures &
monograms of American artists . Madison,
Conn. , Land O'Lakes, FL , 1988. 556 p., [1]
leaf of plates :   ISBN 0-932087-04-3 (alk. paper) :
DDC 702/.78 20
N45 .F35 1988   *NYPL [MAO 90-11577]*

AUTOMATIC DRAFTING. see COMPUTER
GRAPHICS.

Automne, hiver de l'homme du fer /. Bonnet,
Serge, 1924- [Nancy] [Metz] , c1986. 102 p. :
ISBN 2-86480-255-4
HD8039.I52 F823 1986
NYPL [MFW+ 89-20431]

AUTOMOBILE GRAVEYARDS - UNITED
STATES.
Kytola, Pat, 1951- Diamonds in the rust .
Osceola, WI , 1989. 128 p. :   ISBN
0-87938-368-2   DDC 779/.9629222 20
TD795.4 .K98 1989
NYPL [MFX (Kytola, L.) 91-2394]

AUTOMOBILES IN ART.
Zolomij, John J. The motor car in art .
Kutztown, Pa. , c1990. 300 p. :   ISBN
0-915038-95-1
IN PROCESS (ONLINE)
NYPL [3-MAMZ 91-5234]

AUTONOMY (PSYCHOLOGY)
Herding, Klaus. Courbet . New Haven , 1991.
p. cm.   ISBN 0-300-03744-9   DDC 759.4 20
ND553.C9 H47 1991

Autoportrait à l'âge de la photographie. Das
Selbstportrait im Zeitalter der Photographie .
Bern , c1985. 523 p. :
NYPL [MFW 91-2389]

Autour de la Nativité dans la peinture des
collections angevines : Angers, Hôtel du
Département ... 5 décembre 1989-25 février
1990 / [organisée par l'Association culturelle du
Département de Maine-et-Loire ; catalogue
rédigé par Guy Le Goff ... et al.]. [Angers] :
L'Association culturelle, [1989] 200 p. : ill.
(some col.) ; 28 cm. Exhibition catalog. Includes
bibliographical references (p. 190-193) and index.
ISBN 2-905608-01-3 :
1. Jesus Christ - Nativity - Art - Exhibitions. 2. Mary,
Blessed Virgin, Saint - Art - Exhibitions. 3. Painting,
European - Exhibitions. I. Le Goff, Guy. II. Association
culturelle du Département de Maine et Loire.
ND1432.F8 A98 1989

AUVERS-SUR-OISE (FRANCE) IN ART -
EXHIBITIONS.
Van Gogh et les peintres d'Auvers-sur-Oise .
[Paris] , 1954. xl, 100 p., xxxii p. of plates :
N6847.5.I4 V36 1954

Aux quatre coins de la pièce. Iliazd, 1894-1975.
Rogelio Lacourière pêcheur de cuivres /.
[Paris] , c1968. [46] leaves :   DDC 769.9/04 20
NE890 .I45 1968

Avagnina, M. Elisa. Sansovino, Iacopo,
1486-1570. Jacopo Sansovino a Vittorio
Veneto . [Treviso] , 1989. 67 p. :   ISBN
88-85066-55-0
NYPL [3-MGO (Sansovino) 91-3693]

Avagnina, Maria Elisa. Tiepolo, le ville vicentine
/ Maria Elisa Avagnina, Fernando Rigon, Remo
Schiavo. Milano : Electa, c1990. 94 p. : ill.
(some col.) ; 24 cm. Includes index. Bibliography: p.

93-94. ISBN 88-435-3102-6
1. Portraits, Italian - Exhibitions. 2. Portrait painting -
18th century - Italy - Exhibitions. I. Rignon, Fernando.
II. Schiavo, Remo. III. Title.
NYPL [3-MAMC 91-7054]

**AVALLE, FILIPPO, 1947- - CRITICISM AND
INTERPRETATION.**
Monteforte, Franco. Filippo Avalle /. Milano ,
1990. 124 p. : ISBN 88-444-1147-4 : DDC 709/.2
20
N6923.A89 M66 1990

**AVANT-GARDE (AESTHETICA) -
CALIFORNIA - LOS ANGELES -
HISTORY - 20TH CENTURY.**
Experimental architecture in Los Angeles /.
New York , 1991. p. cm. ISBN 0-8478-1424-6
(HC) DDC 720/.9794/9409045 20
NA735.L55 E97 1991

AVANT-GARDE (AESTHETICS)
Von Pop zum Konzept . Aachen [1975] [64]
p., [30] leaves of plates :
N6488.G3 A28
NYPL [3-MAW+ (Aachen) 80-1119]

**AVANT-GARDE (AESTHETICS) - 20TH
CENTURY - GREAT BRITAIN.**
Goldsworthy, Andy. Andy Goldsworthy.
London , 1990. [120] p. : ISBN 0-670-83213-8 :
DDC 709.2 20   **NYPL [3-MGO+
(Goldsworthy) 90-11987]**

**AVANT-GARDE (AESTHETICS) - AUSTRIA -
VIENNA - HISTORY - 20TH CENTURY -
EXHIBITIONS.**
Der Zertrümmerte Spiegel . Klagenfurt , 1989.
392 p. : ISBN 3-85415-062-8
NYPL [3-MAL 91-7188]

**AVANT-GARDE (AESTHETICS) - BRAZIL -
HISTORY - 20TH CENTURY.**
Teles, Fídias. Os malabaristas da vida . Recife,
Pernambuco , 1989. 398 p. :
NX533.A1 T45 1989

**AVANT-GARDE (AESTHETICS) - CHINA -
HISTORY - 20TH CENTURY -
EXHIBITIONS.**
I don't want to play cards with Cézanne, and
other works . Pasadena, Calif. , 1991. xii, 104
p. : ISBN 1-87792-105-X DDC
760/.0951/07479493 20
ND1045 .I16 1991

**AVANT-GARDE (AESTHETICS) -
CZECHOSLOVAKIA - HISTORY - 20TH
CENTURY - EXHIBITIONS.**
Devětsil . [Oxford] , London , c1990. 115 p. :
ISBN 0-905836-70-7
NYPL [3-MAM+ 90-12482]

Devětsil (Society) Devětsil . Łódź [1989]. 105
p. :
N6831.5.D48 D4 1989

**AVANT-GARDE (AESTHETICS) - EUROPE -
HISTORY - 20TH CENTURY.**
Ohrt, Roberto. Phantom Avantgarde . Hamburg
[München] , 1990. 333 p., [16] p. of plates :
ISBN 3-89401-168-8
NX542 .O38 1990

Plant, Sadie, 1964- The most radical gesture .
London , New York, NY , 1992. p. cm. ISBN
0-415-06221-7 DDC 700/.1/03 20
NX542 .P5 1992

Prušáková-Honzíková, Marie. Když hoří
obrazy . Praha , 1989. 247 p. ; ISBN
80-7023-021-5 :
NA1034.5.H6 A2 1989

**AVANT-GARDE (AESTHETICS) -
EXHIBITIONS.**
The Avant-garde and the text . Providence, RI ,
c1988. p. 306-507 :   **NYPL [MDT 91-5721]**

**AVANT-GARDE (AESTHETICS) - GERMANY -
HISTORY - 20TH CENTURY.**
Weinstein, Joan. The end of expressionism .
Chicago , 1990. xiv, 332 p. : ISBN
0-226-89059-7 DDC 701/.03 19
N6868.5.E9 W45 1990
NYPL [3-MAMG 90-11096]

**AVANT-GARDE (AESTHETICS) - HISTORY -
20TH CENTURY.**
Marcadé, Jean-Claude. Malévitch /. Paris
[1990] 279 p. : ISBN 2-7079-0025-7 DDC 709/.2
20
N6999.M34 M37 1990

Seitz, William Chapin. Art in the Age of

Aquarius, 1955-1970 /. Washington , 1991. p.
cm. ISBN 0-87474-868-2 DDC 709/.73/09046 20
N6512 .S335 1991

View . New York , Emeryville, CA , c1991. p.
cm. ISBN 1-560-25013-5 : DDC 700/.9/04 20
NX456 .V49 1991

**AVANT-GARDE (AESTHETICS) - HISTORY -
20TH CENTURY - THEMES, MOTIVES.**
New art /. New York , 1990. 205 p. : ISBN
0-8109-2443-9 DDC 709/.04 20
N6493 1980 .N48 1990
NYPL [3-MAL+ 90-11610]

**AVANT-GARDE (AESTHETICS) - HUNGARY -
HISTORY - 20TH CENTURY.**
Mansbach, Steven A., 1950- Standing in the
tempest . Santa Barbara, Calif. , Cambridge,
Mass. , c1991. 240 p. : ISBN 0-262-13274-5 (MIT
hbk.) DDC 709/.439/1207473 20
N6820.5.N93 M36 1991

**AVANT-GARDE (AESTHETICS) - HUNGARY -
HISTORY - 20TH CENTURY -
EXHIBITIONS.**
Ungarische Avantgarde in der Malerei der
achtziger Jahre . [Mannheim] [Budapest] ,
c1989. 55 p. : ISBN 3-927224-01-4
ND520 .U54 1989

**AVANT-GARDE (AESTHETICS) - MEXICO -
HISTORY - 20TH CENTURY -
EXHIBITIONS.**
El Surrealismo entre Viejo y Nuevo Mundo .
[Madrid] [1990] 346 p. : ISBN 84-86022-51-2
N6512.5.S87 S8 1990

**AVANT-GARDE (AESTHETICS) - RUSSIAN S.
F.S.R. - HISTORY - 20TH CENTURY.**
I͡Ablonskai͡a, M. (Mi͡uda) Women artists of
Russia's new age, 1900-1935 /. London ,
c1990. 248 p. : ISBN 0-500-23559-7
NYPL [3-MAM 90-12322]

Russen in Berlin . Leipzig , 1990. xv, 614 p. :
ISBN 3-379-00119-8
NX556.A1 R86 1990

**AVANT-GARDE (AESTHETICS) - RUSSIAN S.
F.S.R. - HISTORY - 20TH CENTURY -
EXHIBITIONS.**
The Russian and Soviet avant-garde . Montreal,
Quebec, Canada , 1989. 175 p. : ISBN
2-89192-108-9 DDC 759.7/074/71428 20
ND688.5.A24 R87 1989
NYPL [3-MCY+ 91-3731]

Russische Avantgarde 1910-1930 . Duisburg ,
c1990. 120 p. : ISBN 3-923576-73-0
N6988 .R855 1990

**AVANT-GARDE (AESTHETICS) - SOVIET
UNION - EXHIBITIONS.**
Architectural drawings of the Russian
avant-garde /. New York , c1990. 143 p. :
ISBN 0-87070-556-3
NYPL [3-MQG 90-11730]

**AVANT-GARDE (AESTHETICS) - SOVIET
UNION - HISTORY - 20TH CENTURY.**
Artaud, Evelyne. Perestroïk'art . [Paris] , c1990.
118 p. : ISBN 2-7022-0269-1 DDC 700/.47/09048
20
N6988 .A7635 1990
NYPL [3-MAM 90-13376]

**AVANT-GARDE (AESTHETICS) - SOVIET
UNION - HISTORY - 20TH CENTURY -
CONGRESSES.**
The Revolution and the avant-garde . Seattle ,
1991. p. ISBN 0-935558-30-6 DDC
700/.947/09041 20
NX556.A1 R48 1991

**AVANT-GARDE (AESTHETICS) - SOVIET
UNION - HISTORY - 20TH CENTURY -
EXHIBITIONS.**
Das Leben zur Kunst machen . Zürich , c1989.
151 p. : ISBN 3-906396-02-9
NYPL [3-MAM+ 91-6598]

**AVANT-GARDE (AESTHETICS) - UNITED
STATES - HISTORY - 20TH CENTURY.**
Seitz, William Chapin. Art in the Age of
Aquarius, 1955-1970 /. Washington , 1991. p.
cm. ISBN 0-87474-868-2 DDC 709/.73/09046 20
N6512 .S335 1991

Watson, Steven. Strange bedfellows . New
York , c1991. 439 p. : ISBN 0-89659-934-5 :
DDC 700/.973/09041 20
NX504 .W38 1991 **NYPL [MAMT 91-5715]**

**AVANT-GARDE (AESTHETICS) - UNITED
STATES - HISTORY - 20TH CENTURY -
EXHIBITIONS.**
El Surrealismo entre Viejo y Nuevo Mundo .
[Madrid] [1990] 346 p. : ISBN 84-86022-51-2
N6512.5.S87 S8 1990

The Avant-garde and the text : exhibition
catalogue. Providence, RI : Visible Language,
c1988. p. 306-507 : ill. ; 23 cm. (Visible language,
0022-2224 . v. 21, no. 3/4 (summer/autumn 1987))
"This volume has a dual function. On one side,
consecutive right-reading pages present critical analyses
of the Avant-Garde text, forming the Summer/Autumn
issue of the journal Visible language--while on the other
side, consecutive left-reading pages running in the
opposite direction form the catalogue for a traveling
exhibition"--P. 502. Exhibition held Sept. 9-Oct. 14,
1988 at the Visual Studies Workshop, Rochester, N.Y.,
and at 5 other locations through March 11, 1990.
"Guest editors, Stephen Foster, Estera Milman"--Label
mounted on special issue t.p. Includes bibliographical
references. Library's copy lacks label listing guest
editors.
1. Kleinschmidt, Hans J. - Art collections - Exhibitions.
2. Avant-garde (Aesthetics) - Exhibitions. 3. Art and
literature - Exhibitions. 4. Words in art - Exhibitions. 5.
Dadaism - Exhibitions. 6. Arts, Modern - 20th
century - Exhibitions. I. Foster, Stephen C. II. Milman,
Estera. III. Visual Studies Workshop. IV. Series: Visible
language , v. 21, no. 3/4. **NYPL [MDT 91-5721]**

Avery Library.
Contemporary architetural drawings : donations
to the Avery Library centennial drawings
archive / Janet Parks, editor.1st ed. San
Francisco : Pomegranate Artbooks, c1991. p.
cm. Catalog of an exhibition of drawings by American
and international architects that was on display at
Columbia University, Apr. 3-May 4, 1991. ISBN
0-87654-767-6 : DDC 720/.22/2 20
1. Architectural drawing - 20th century - Exhibitions. 2.
Avery Library - Exhibitions. I. Parks, Janet. II. Title.
NA2695.U6 A86 1991

AVERY LIBRARY - EXHIBITIONS.
Avery Library. Contemporary architetural
drawings . San Francisco , c1991. p. cm. ISBN
0-87654-767-6 : DDC 720/.22/2 20
NA2695.U6 A86 1991

Avery, Milton, 1885-1965.
Kramer, Linda Konheim. Milton Avery in black
and white . Brooklyn, N.Y. , c1990. 96 p. :
ISBN 0-87273-127-8 DDC 741.973 20
NC139.A93 A4 1990
NYPL [3-MCX A95 91-4649]

Milton Avery, works from the 1950s : in the
collection of the Modern Art Museum of Fort
Worth. [Fort Worth, Tex.] : Modern Art
Museum of Fort Worth, 1990. viii, 48 p. : ill.
(some col.) ; 28 cm. Includes bibliographical
references (p. 27) ISBN 0-929865-05-7 DDC
760/.092 20
1. Avery, Milton, 1885-1965 - Catalogs. 2. Modern Art
Museum of Fort Worth - Catalogs. I. Modern Art
Museum of Fort Worth. II. Title.
NC139.A93 A4 1990a
NYPL [3-MCX A95 91-3915]

AVERY, MILTON, 1885-1965 - CATALOGS.
Avery, Milton, 1885-1965. Milton Avery, works
from the 1950s . [Fort Worth, Tex.] , 1990. viii,
48 p. : ISBN 0-929865-05-7 DDC 760/.092 20
NC139.A93 A4 1990a
NYPL [3-MCX A95 91-3915]

**AVERY, MILTON, 1885-1965 -
EXHIBITIONS.**
Kramer, Linda Konheim. Milton Avery in black
and white . Brooklyn, N.Y. , c1990. 96 p. :
ISBN 0-87273-127-8 DDC 741.973 20
NC139.A93 A4 1990
NYPL [3-MCX A95 91-4649]

AVERY, SAMUEL PUTNAM, 1822-1904.
Editorials and resolutions in memory of Samuel
Putnam Avery. New York, 1905. 3 p.l., 3-81,
[1] p., 1 l.
N8384 .A8   **NYPL [3-MAS 91-331]**

Avery, Sid. Hollywood at home : a family album,
1950-1965 / photographs by Sid Avery ; text
by Richard Schickel.1st ed. New York : Crown
Publishers, c1990. 144 p. : ill. ; 29 cm. ISBN
0-517-57696-1 :
1. Motion picture actors and actresses - United States -
Portraits. 2. Television personalities - United States -
Portraits. 3. Entertainers - United States - Portraits. I.

Schickel, Richard. II. Title.
PN1998.2 .A85 1990
              NYPL [MFX (Avery) 91-5134]

AVIATION. see AERONAUTICS.

Avila A., Jorge (Avila Ayala) Vergara Vergara, José. El barroco en Hidalgo. [Pachuca, Mexico?] , 1988. 177, [5] p. :
N7914.A3 H538 1988

Avila, Affonso, 1928- Barroco mineiro, glossário de arquitetura e ornamentação / Affonso Avila, João Marcos Machado Gontijo, Reinaldo Guedes Machado. [Rio de Janeiro?] : Fundação João Pinheiro : Fundação Roberto Marinho : 220 p. : ill. (some col.) ; 27 cm. Includes bibliographical references (p. 217-220).
1. Decoration and ornament, Architectural - Brazil - Minas Gerais - Dictionaries. 2. Architecture, Baroque - Brazil - Minas Gerais - Dictionaries. 3. Architecture - Brazil - Minas Gerais - Details - Dictionaries. I. Gontijo, João Marcos Machado. II. Machado, Reinaldo Guedes. III. Title.
NA3533.A3 M563 1980

Avila, Alin Alexis. Bernard Buffet / texte de Alin Alexis Avila. [Paris] : Nouvelles éditions françaises / Casterman, 1989. 251 p. : ill. (some col.), ports. ; 33 cm. Includes bibliographical references. ISBN 2-7079-0021-4
1. Buffet, Bernard, 1928- - Criticism and interpretation. I. Buffet, Bernard, 1928-. II. Title.
       NYPL [3-MCO+ B929 89-24429]

Ávila, Fernando Bastos de.
O Clero no Parlamento brasileiro /. Brasília , Rio de Janeiro , 1978-79. 2 v. : ISBN 85-7004-002-4
JL2454 .C53   *NYPL [HFE 80-1465]*

O Clero no Parlamento brasileiro /. Brasília , Rio de Janeiro , 1978- v. : ISBN 85-7004-002-4
JL2454 .C53   *NYPL [HFE 80-1378]*

Avisseau, Jean Paul. Illustration du vieux Bordeaux / Jean-Paul Avisseau et Jean-Pierre Poussou. Avignon : Aubanel, c1990. 1 v. (unpaged) : ill. (some col.) ; 22 x 28 cm. "Index des noms de personnes et des lieux" ([11] p.) inserted. ISBN 2-7006-0141-6
1. Bordeaux (France) in art - Catalogs. 2. Art, French - Catalogs. I. Poussou, Jean Pierre. II. Title.
N8214.5.F8 A95 1990

Avitabile, Gunhild.
Chao Shao-an : ein Meister der südchinesischen Lingnan-Schule / Gunhild Avitabile ; [Mitarbeit am Katalog und Übersetzung der chinesischen Aufschriften, Rainald Simon ; herausgegeben im Auftrag des Dezernats Kultur und Freizeit Frankfurt am Main und Roemer-Museum, Hildesheim]. Frankfurt am Main : Museum für Kunsthandwerk, c1988. 58 p. : chiefly ill. ; 30 cm. Catalog of an exhibition held at the Museum für Kunsthandwerk, Frankfurt am Main; Übersee-Museum, Bremen; Roemer-Museum, Hildesheim; Museum der Stadt Ettlingen und Künstlerhaus e.V. in Göttingen. Bibliography: p. 17. ISBN 3-88270-046-7 DDC 759.951 20
1. Chao, Shao-ang, 1905- - Exhibitions. 2. Ling-nan school of painting - Exhibitions. I. Chao, Shao-ang, 1905-. II. Simon, Rainald, 1951-. III. Museum für Kunsthandwerk Frankfurt am Main. IV. Frankfurt am Main (Germany). Dezernat Kultur und Freizeit. V. Roemer-Museum. VI. Title.
ND1049.C4527 A4 1988
               NYPL [3-MAG+ 91-6442]

Die Kunst des alten Japan . Frankfurt am Main , 1990. 199 p. : ISBN 3-89322-209-X
               NYPL [3-MAG+ 91-4469]

Award-winning quilts and their makers. Faoro, Victoria. Award-winning quilts & their makers /. Paducah, KY , c1991- v. <1 > : ISBN 0-89145-972-3 (v. 1) : DDC 746.9/7/097309048 20
NK9112 .F36 1991

Axel Kasseböhmer . Kasseböhmer, Axel, 1952- Münster , c1989. 84 p. :
               NYPL [3-MCK K183 91-6475]

Axelrod, Alan, 1952- Art of the Golden West / Alan Axelrod. 1st ed. New York : Abbeville Press, c1990. 418 p. : ill. (some col.) ; 34 cm. Includes bibliographical references (p. 403-405) and index. ISBN 1-558-59103-6 DDC 978 20
1. West (U. S.) in art. 2. West (U. S.) - History. I. Title.
F591 .A53 1990
             NYPL [3-MAMT+ 90-13272]

Ayako Miyawaki, the art of Japanese applique /. Miyawaki, Ayako, 1905- [Tokyo] , Washington D.C. , 1991. p. cm. ISBN 0-940979-17-9 DDC 746.392 20
NK9198.M59 A4 1991

Ayars, Walter. Larkin Co. Larkin China . Summerdale, PA , c1990. 178 p. : DDC 738/.09/041 20
NK3930 .L38 1990

Aycock, Alice.
Complex visions : sculpture and drawings by Alice Aycock : May 21-October 31, 1990 / [interview and essay, Jonathan Fineberg]. Mountainville, N.Y. : Storm King Art Center, c1990. 47, [1] p. : ill. ; 23 cm. Includes bibliographical references (p. [48]).
1. Aycock, Alice - Exhibitions. 2. Aycock, Alice - Interviews. I. Fineberg, Jonathan David. II. Title.
        NYPL [3-MGO (Aycock) 91-7401]

AYCOCK, ALICE - EXHIBITIONS.
Aycock, Alice. Complex visions .
Mountainville, N.Y. , c1990. 47, [1] p. :
        NYPL [3-MGO (Aycock) 91-7401]

AYCOCK, ALICE - INTERVIEWS.
Aycock, Alice. Complex visions .
Mountainville, N.Y. , c1990. 47, [1] p. :
        NYPL [3-MGO (Aycock) 91-7401]

Ayers, John. Porcelain for palaces : the fashion for Japan in Europe, 1650-1750 / John Ayers, Oliver Impey and J.V.G. Mallet ; with contributions by Anthony du Boulay and Lawrence Smith. [London] : Oriental Ceramic Society, c1990. 328 p. : ill. (some col.) ; 30 cm. "An exhibition organised jointly with the British Museum in the new Japanese galleries, 6th July to 4th November 1990." Includes index. Bibliography: p. 304-309. ISBN 0-903421-24-0
1. Porcelain, Japanese - Edo period, 1600-1868 - Exhibitions. 2. Porcelain, European - Foreign influences - Exhibitions. I. Impey, O. R. (Oliver R.). II. Mallet, J. V. G. III. Oriental Ceramic Society. IV. Title.
               NYPL [3-MPFK 91-7595]

AYME, ALBERT - CRITICISM AND INTERPRETATION.
Bosseur, Jean-Yves. Le paradigme musical d'Albert Ayme /. Paris , Malakoff , c1986. 73, [2] p. : ISBN 2-903551-00-6 (pbk.) : DDC 759.4 19
ND553.A95 B67 1986
             NYPL [3-MCO B744 90-12648]

Ayres, Anne, 1936- Knode, Marilu. Third Newport biennial . Newport Beach, Calif. , 1991. p. cm. ISBN 0-917493-19-2 DDC 709/.794/07479496 20
N6530.C2 K64 1991

Ayres, Julia. Monotype : mediums and methods for painterly printmaking / Julia Ayres. New York : Watson-Guptill Publications, 1991. 144 p. : ill. (some col.) ; 29 cm. Includes index. ISBN 0-8230-3129-2 : DDC 760 20
1. Monotype (Engraving) - Technique. I. Title.
NE2242 .A95 1991

Ayrton, Michael, 1921-1975.
Michael Ayrton : sculpture, paintings, drawings, prints. London : Austin/Desmond Fine Art, c1990. 44 p. : ill. ; 24 cm. ISBN 1-87292-608-8
1. Ayrton, Michael, 1921-1975 - Exhibitions. I. Austin/Desmond Fine Art. II. Title.
        NYPL [3-MGO (Ayrton) 91-6889]

AYRTON, MICHAEL, 1921-1975 - EXHIBITIONS.
Ayrton, Michael, 1921-1975. Michael Ayrton . London , c1990. 44 p. : ISBN 1-87292-608-8
        NYPL [3-MGO (Ayrton) 91-6889]

Ayvazian, Marian. Shishmanian, Ṛafayel Martirosi. Ṛafayel Shishmanian . Erevan , 1985. [32]p., 86p. of plates :
        NYPL [3-MCZ S557 87-4695]

AZ Geographers' London atlas / Geographers' A-Z Map Company. Ed. 11. Sevenoaks : Geographers' A-Z Map Company, 1991. 259 p. : chiefly col. maps ; 26 cm. 11th ed published 1990. Includes index. ISBN 0-85039-000-1
1. London (England) - Maps. I. Geographers' Map Company, Ltd.   *NYPL [Map Div. 90-17553]*

AZ Newcastle-upon-Tyne. Geographers' A-Z Map Company. Newcastle-upon-Tyne, Sunderland, City of Durham . Sevenoaks, Kent , c1988. 1 atlas (144, [86] p.) :
            NYPL [Map Div. 90-13146]

AZ Sheffield. Geographers' A-Z Map Company. Sheffield . Sevenoaks, Kent , c1988. 1 atlas (200 p.) : ISBN 0-85039-212-8 :
            NYPL [Map Div. 90-13147]

AZ street atlas, Newcastle-Upon-Tyne. Geographers' A-Z Map Company. Newcastle-upon-Tyne, Sunderland, City of Durham . Sevenoaks, Kent , c1988. 1 atlas (144, [86] p.) : *NYPL [Map Div. 90-13146]*

A'zamī, Walīd. Jamharat al-khaṭṭāṭīn al-Baghdādiyīn : mundhu ta'sīs Baghdād ḥattā nihāyat al-qarn al-rābi' 'ashar al-Hijrī / Walīd al-A'zamī.al-Ṭab'ah 1. A'zamīyah, Baghdād, al-'Irāq : Dār al-Shu'ūn al-Thaqāfīyah al-'Ammah "Āfāq 'Arabīyah", 1989. 2 v. (800 p.) : ill. ; 24 cm. "Yataḍammanu al-kitāb sittin wa-arba'umi'at tarjamah." Includes bibliographical references (v. 2, p. 768-784).
1. Calligraphers - Iraq - Baghdad - Biography. 2. Baghdad (Iraq) - Biography. I. Title.
NK3630.6.I72 A93 1989

Azcárraga, Adolfo de. Escritos sobre arte y artistas valencianos / Adolfo de Azcárraga. 1a ed. Valencia : Caja de Valencia, 1989. 330 p. : ill. (some col.) ; 24 cm. Includes index. ISBN 84-505-8230-X
1. Artists - Spain - Valencia. 2. Art, Spanish - Spain - Valencia. I. Title. II. Title: Arte y artistas valencianos.
               NYPL [3-MAML 90-11103]

Aziz Efendi, 1871 or 2-1934. Hattat Aziz Efendi / [hazırlayan] Muhittin Serin. İstanbul : Kubbealtı Akademisi Kültür ve San'at Vakfı, 1988. 119 p. : ill. (chiefly col.) ; 33 cm. (Türk hat üstadları . 1) "Kubbealtı Neşriyatı no. 22"--T.p. verso. Summary in English. Includes bibliographical references (p. 46).
1. Aziz Efendi, 1871 or 2-1934. 2. Calligraphers - Turkey - Biography. 3. Calligraphy, Islamic - Turkey. I. Serin, Muhiddin. II. Title. III. Series.
NK3636.5.A95 A2 1988

AZIZ EFENDI, 1871 OR 2-1934.
Aziz Efendi, 1871 or 2-1934. Hattat Aziz Efendi / . İstanbul , 1988. 119 p. :
NK3636.5.A95 A2 1988

Azpeitia, Rafael Carrillo. see Carrillo Azpeitia, Rafael.

AZTEC LANGUAGE - DIALECTS - PUEBLA (STATE)
Marschall, Wolfgang. Beiträge zur Ethnographie der Sierra-Totonaken. Wiesbaden, 1972. 112 p.:
               NYPL [HTC 74-1117 Bd. 4]

AZTEC LANGUAGE - DIALECTS - TLAXCALA (STATE)
Marschall, Wolfgang. Beiträge zur Ethnographie der Sierra-Totonaken. Wiesbaden, 1972. 112 p.:
               NYPL [HTC 74-1117 Bd. 4]

Azulejaria em Portugal nos séculos XV e XVI . Simões, J. M. dos Santos (João Miguel dos Santos), 1907-1972. Lisboa , 1990. 197 p. : DDC 738.6/09469/09024 20
NK4670.7.P6 S57 1990

Azulejaria em Portugal, sécs. XV e XVI. Simões, J. M. dos Santos (João Miguel dos Santos), 1907-1972. Azulejaria em Portugal nos séculos XV e XVI . Lisboa , 1990. 197 p. : DDC 738.6/09469/09024 20
NK4670.7.P6 S57 1990

B.C.L.I.K. Domenig, Gerald, 1953- BCLIK /. [S.l.] , c1988. 1 v. (unpaged) :
               NYPL [MFX+ (Domenig) 91-2386]

B., Mats, 1938- Téxun : la Biennale di Venezia, 1986 : Finlandia, Norvegia, Svezia / [curatore della mostra e del catalogo: Mats B.]. [S.l. : s.n., 1986] (Stockholm : Jernström Offset) [48] p. : ill. (some col.) ; 21 cm. Italian and English. Includes bibliographical references.
1. Art, Scandinavian - Exhibitions. 2. Art, Modern - 20th century - Scandinavia - Exhibitions. I. Biennale di Venezia (42nd : 1986). II. Title.
               NYPL [3-MAM 90-10710]

Baal, Frédéric. Reinhoud / Frédéric Baal. Anvers : Fonds Mercator ; Paris : A. Michel, c1989. 1 v. (unpaged) : ill. (some col.) ; 40 cm. ISBN 90-6153-197-7 (Fonds Mercator) DDC 730/.92 20
1. Reinhoud - Criticism and interpretation. I. Reinhoud. II. Title.
NB673.R44 B33 1989<fol.>

Baard, H. P. (Henricus Petrus), 1906-
[Frans Hals en het Haarlemse groepportret in het Gemeentemuseum 1528-1737. English]
Frans Hals and the groupportraits at Harlem, 1528-1737 / H.P. Baard ; [translated by Mrs. C. D. te Winkel]. 2nd ed. Harlem : Erven F. Bohn, 1952. 72 p. : ill. ; 16 cm. Translation of Frans Hals en het Haarlemse groepportret in het Gemeentemuseum 1528-1737.
1. Hals, Frans, 1584-1666. 2. Frans Halsmuseum. 3. Portraits, Group - Netherlands - Haarlem. I. Title.
NYPL [3-MCH H2 90-5924]

Babelon, Jean Pierre. Le Château en France /. Paris , 1988. 448 p., [16] p. of plates : ISBN 2-7013-0741-4
NYPL [3-MQWF+ 90-11996]

Bablet, Denis. Collage et montage au théâtre et dans les autres arts durant les années vingt /. Lausanne , cop. 1978. 296 p., [32] p. of plates :
DDC 700/.94 19
NX542 .C64   **NYPL [JFE 81-222]**

Baboni, Andrea. Mario Puccini : per un catalogo dell'opera / Andrea Baboni ; prefazione di Raffaele De Grada ; contributi iconografici, biografici e bibliografici dalla tesi di laurea di Daniela Leonardini Bruzzone. Firenze : Pananti, c1989. xiv, 480 p. : ill. (some col.), facsims., ports. ; 30 cm. Includes bibliographical references (p. 473-480).
1. Puccini, Mario, 1869-1920 - Catalogues raisonnés. I. Puccini, Mario, 1869-1920. II. Leonardini Bruzzone, Daniela. III. Title.
NYPL [3-MCF+ P17 90-12977]

Baburina, N. I. (Nina Ivanovna)
Chernevich, Elena, 1939- Russian graphic design /. New York, NY , 1990. 160 p. : ISBN 1-558-59016-1   DDC 741.6/0947 20
NC998.6.R9 C47 1990
NYPL [3-MDW+ 90-11977]

Sovetskiĭ zrelishchnyĭ plakat. English. The Soviet arts poster . London, England , New York, N.Y., USA , 1990. 207 p. : ISBN 0-14-012018-1:   DDC 741.6/74/09470904 20
NC1807.S65 S6613 1990

Baccarat . Compagnie des cristalleries de Baccarat. [Baccarat, France] : Paris ; 222 p. : ISBN 2-906309-00-1 :   DDC 748.8/2/09443823 19
NK5205.C65 A4 1986
NYPL [3-MPW 90-10581]

Bacchi, Andrea. Imago lignea . Trento , c1989. 287 p. : ISBN 88-85114-07-5
NYPL [3-MGI+ 91-4470]

Bach, Elvira, 1951-
Elvira Bach / herausgegeben von Margarethe Jochimsen ; mit Beiträgen von Klaus Gallwitz ... [et al.] München : Prestel, c1990. 103 p. : ill. (some col.) ; 31 cm. Catalogue published on the occasion of the exhibition at the Kunstverein Mannheim, Jun. 10-July 8, 1990; the Kunsthalle der Stadt Wilhelmshaven, Mar. 7-Apr. 7, 1991; and the Neue Galerie am Landesmuseum Joanneum, Graz, Apr.-May 1991. Includes bibliographical references (p. 103)   ISBN 3-7913-1093-3
1. Bach, Elvira, 1951- - Exhibitions. I. Jochimsen, Margarethe. II. Mannheimer Kunstverein. III. Neue Galerie am Landesmuseum Joanneum. IV. Title.
NYPL [3-MCK+ B118 91-3385]

BACH, ELVIRA, 1951- - EXHIBITIONS.
Bach, Elvira, 1951- Elvira Bach /. München , c1990. 103 p. : ISBN 3-7913-1093-3
NYPL [3-MCK+ B118 91-3385]

Bach, Otto Karl. German expressionist paintings . [S.l. , 196-] [60] p. :   **NYPL [3-MCI 90-5896]**

Bachellerie, Frédérique. Schönwald, Peter. Cathelin . Paris , c1990. 109 p. :   DDC 746.392 20
NK3049.A3 C372 1990

Bacherich, Martine. Je regarde Manet / Martine Bacherich. Paris : A. Biro, c1990. 160 p. : ill. ; 22 cm. (Collection Essais) Includes bibliographical references (p. 153-[158]).   ISBN 2-87660-074-9 :   DDC 759.4 20
1. Manet, Edouard, 1832-1883 - Psychology. 2. Painting - Appreciation. I. Series: Collection "Essais" (Adam Biro (Firm)). II. Title.
ND553.M3 B24 1990

BACHKOVSKI MANASTIR - CATALOGS.
Santova, Mila. 24 zlatarski tvorbi ot

Bachkovskiĭa manastir /. Sofiĭa , 1990. 47 p. :
NK7215 .S34 1990

Bachman, Ben. Benson, Robert. The Connecticut River /. Boston , c1989. 125 p. : ISBN 0-8212-1730-5
NYPL [MFX+ (Benson) 89-28166]

Bachmann, Manfred, 1928-
Hassebrauk, Ernst, 1905- Die Wiederbegegnung . [Dresden] , c1988. 80 p. :
DDC 741.943 20
NC251.6.Z9 H372 1988
NYPL [3-MCK H354 91-4570]

Der silberne Boden . Stuttgart [Leipzig] , c1990. 510 p. :   ISBN 3-421-02982-2 (Deutsche Verlags-Anstalt)
NYPL [3-MAMG 91-5527]

Bachmayer, Hans Matthäus.
Hans Matthäus Bachmayer. München : Galerie van de Loo, 1988. 51 p. : ill. (some col.) ; 32 cm. Catalog of an exhibition at the Galerie van de Loo, Munich, April 1988. "Auflage 300 Exemplare." Library's copy is no. 142.
1. Bachmayer, Hans Matthäus - Exhibitions. I. Title.
NYPL [3-MCK+ B126 89-28417]

BACHMAYER, HANS MATTHÄUS - EXHIBITIONS.
Bachmayer, Hans Matthäus. Hans Matthäus Bachmayer. München , 1988. 51 p. :
NYPL [3-MCK+ B126 89-28417]

Bach's Goldberg variations. Presser, Elena, 1940- Elena Presser, Bach's Goldberg variations . Miami , c1985. [28] p. :   ISBN 0-916203-09-3
NYPL [3-MDG (Presser) 88-4568]

Bächtiger, Augustin Meinrad, 1888-1971.
Studer-Geisser, Isabella. Augustin Meinrad Bächtiger, 1888-1971 /. St. Gallen , 1988. 95 p. : ISBN 3-85603-003-4
N7153.B23 S78 1988
NYPL [3-MCZ B1345 90-10412]

BÄCHTIGER, AUGUSTIN MEINRAD, 1888-1971.
Studer-Geisser, Isabella. Augustin Meinrad Bächtiger, 1888-1971 /. St. Gallen , 1988. 95 p. : ISBN 3-85603-003-4
N7153.B23 S78 1988
NYPL [3-MCZ B1345 90-10412]

Backer-Grøndahl, Agathe, 1847-1907.
[Selections]
Piano pieces ; Songs [sound recording] / Agathe Backer Grøndahl. Oslo : Norsk kulturråds klassikerserie, p1988. 1 sound disc : digital, stereo. ; 4 3/4 in. Songs for soprano and piano; sung in Norwegian and German. Kari Frisell, soprano ; Liv Glaser, piano. Compact disc. Biographical and program notes in Norwegian with English and German translations (15 p.) inserted in container. Previously released as NKF 30008 (tracks 1-13) and NKF 30007 (tracks 14-30).
1. Piano music. 2. Songs (High voice) with piano. I. Backer-Grøndahl, Agathe, 1847-1907. Songs. Selections. 1988.
Norsk kulturråds klassikerserie NKFCD 50019-2

Songs. Selections. 1988. Backer-Grøndahl, Agathe, 1847-1907. [Selections.] Piano pieces ; Songs [sound recording] / Agathe Backer Grøndahl. Oslo , p1988. 1 sound disc :
Norsk kulturråds klassikerserie NKFCD 50019-2

Die Backsteinbaukunst der Berliner Schule . Klinkott, Manfred. Berlin , c1988. 479 p., 9 leaves of plates : ISBN 3-7861-1438-2   DDC 721/.04421/094315509034 20
NA1085 .K57 1988
NYPL [3-MQWD 90-11025]

Bäckström, Holger. Beck & Jung. Chromo cube /. Bjärred, Sweden (Box 123, S-237 00 Bjärred) , c1982. 49 p., [24] leaves of plates : ISBN 91-85752-30-4
NYPL [3-MAL 88-3799]

Bacoli . Gambardella, Carmine. Napoli [1982] 70 p. :
TH7413 .G36 1982   **NYPL [MQWB 91-840]**

Bacon, Richard M. Wall stenciling / by Richard M. Bacon. Camden, Me. : Yankee Books, 1991. p. cm. (The Forgotten arts) Includes bibliographical references and index.   ISBN 0-89909-326-4 :   DDC 745.7/3 20

1. Stencilwork - United States. I. Title. II. Series.
NK8662 .B3 1991

Bacou, Roseline. Musée du Louvre. Cabinet des dessins. Dessins de Taddeo et Federico Zuccaro. Paris, 1969. 79 p.
NYPL [3-MBH 91-1497]

Badaloni, Pier Giorgio. Tempo e architettura /. Roma , c1987. 174 p. :
NYPL [3-MQD+ 90-12504]

Baden-Württemberg (Germany)
Kunstkonzeption des Landes Baden-Württemberg /. Stuttgart , c1990. 391 p. :   ISBN 3-923719-19-1
NX550.A3 B245 1990

BADEN-WÜRTTEMBERG (GERMANY) - CULTURAL POLICY.
Kunstkonzeption des Landes Baden-Württemberg /. Stuttgart , c1990. 391 p. :   ISBN 3-923719-19-1
NX550.A3 B245 1990

Bader, Alfred, Mrs. The Detective's eye . [Milwaukee] , c1989. 124 p. :
NYPL [MCG 89-19048]

Bader, Alfred, 1924- The Detective's eye . [Milwaukee] , c1989. 124 p. :
NYPL [MCG 89-19048]

Badii, Líbero, 1916- Frases espontáneas / Líbero Badii. 2. ed. Buenos Aires, Argentina : Ediciones de Arte Gaglianone, 1982. 47 p. : ill. ; 23 cm.   DDC 700 20
1. Art. I. Title.
N6639.B32 A35 1982

Badischer Kunstverein. Odenbach, Marcel, 1953- Marcel Odenbach . Karlsruhe , c1988. 100 p. : ISBN 3-922531-57-1
N6888.O237 A4 1988
NYPL [3-MCK 0245 90-11059]

Badisches Landesmuseum Karlsruhe.
Corpus vasorum antiquorum. Deutschland. Karlsruhe--Badisches Landesmuseum. München, 1951-1952. v.
NK4640.C6 G4 Bd. 7-8
NYPL [MPEK+ C8.K2]

Planstädte der Neuzeit, vom 16. bis zum 18. Jahrhundert . Karlsruhe , c1990. 381 p. :   ISBN 3-7650-9026-3
NA9094.3 .P53 1990

150 Jahre Antikensammlungen in Karlsruhe . Karlsruhe , 1988. 170 p. :   ISBN 3-923132-15-8
N5336.G3 K3715 1988
NYPL [3-MAE 90-12538]

BADISCHES LANDESMUSEUM KARLSRUHE.
150 Jahre Antikensammlungen in Karlsruhe . Karlsruhe , 1988. 170 p. :   ISBN 3-923132-15-8
N5336.G3 K3715 1988
NYPL [3-MAE 90-12538]

BADISCHES LANDESMUSEUM KARLSRUHE - CATALOGS.
Corpus vasorum antiquorum. Deutschland. Karlsruhe--Badisches Landesmuseum. München, 1951-1952. v.
NK4640.C6 G4 Bd. 7-8
NYPL [MPEK+ C8.K2]

Badstübner, Ernst. Das alte Mühlhausen : Kunstgeschichte einer mittelalterlichen Stadt / Ernst Badstübner ; mit Aufnahmen von Constantin Beyer.1. Aufl. Leipzig : Koehler & Amelang, c1989. 205 p. : ill. (some col.) ; 22 cm. Includes bibliographical references (p. 196-201) and index.   ISBN 3-7338-0055-9
1. Art - Germany - Mühlhausen (Erfurt). 2. Art, Modern - Germany - Mühlhausen (Erfurt). I. Beyer, Constantin. II. Title.
N6886.M78 B34 1989

Baehr, Ulrich, 1938-
Ulrich Baehr 1964-1988 : [Ausstellung] Staatliche Kunsthalle Berlin, 17. Oktober bis 16. November 1988. 1. Aufl. [Berlin] : Die Kunsthalle, c1988. 160 p. : ill. (some col.) ; 28 cm. Includes bibliographical references (p. 146).
1. Baehr, Ulrich, 1938- - Exhibitions. II. Title.
NYPL [3-MCK B1395 90-8491]

BAEHR, ULRICH, 1938- - EXHIBITIONS.
Baehr, Ulrich, 1938- Ulrich Baehr 1964-1988 . [Berlin] , c1988. 160 p. :
NYPL [3-MCK B1395 90-8491]

Baekeland, Frederick. Images of America : the painter's eye, 1833-1925 / by Frederick

Baekeland. Birmingham, Ala. : Birmingham Museum of Art, 1991. p. cm. Exhibition held at the Spencer Museum of Art, University of Kansas, Lawrence, Kan., August 25-October 13, 1991 ... [et al.]. Includes bibliographical references and index. ISBN 0-931394-31-7 : DDC 759.13/09/03407473 20
1. Painting, American - Exhibitions. 2. Painting, Modern - 19th century - United States - Exhibitions. 3. Painting, Modern - 20th century - United States - Exhibitions. 4. United States in art - Exhibitions. I. Birmingham Museum of Art (Birmingham, Ala.). II. Helen Foresman Spencer Museum of Art. III. Title.
ND1460.U54 B34 1991

Bærtling. Brunius, Teddy, 1922- [Stockholm] , 1990. 157 p. :
NYPL [3-MCZ B135 91-6323]

Bærtling, Olle, 1911- Brunius, Teddy, 1922- Bærtling . [Stockholm] , 1990. 157 p. :
NYPL [3-MCZ B135 91-6323]

BÆRTLING, OLLE, 1911-
Brunius, Teddy, 1922- Bærtling . [Stockholm] , 1990. 157 p. :
NYPL [3-MCZ B135 91-6323]

Baetcke, Christine. Junge Berliner Künstler . Ludwigshafen , c1987. 103 p. :
IN PROCESS (ONLINE)
NYPL [3-MAMG 90-12473]

Bäuerliche russische Holzskulptur. Chekalov, A. K. (Aleksandr Kalimovich), 1928-1970. Dresden [c1967] 110 p.
NK9756.A1 C4515 ***NYPL [3-MOC 90-5991]***

Bagatti Valsecchi, Pier Fausto. Süss, Francesco. Le ville del territorio milanese. [Milano] , 1988- v. : ***NYPL [3-MRGF+ 90-2532]***

BAGHDAD (IRAQ) - BIOGRAPHY.
A'zamī, Walīd. Jamharat al-khaṭṭāṭīn al-Baghdādīyīn . A'zamīyah, Baghdād, al-'Irāq , 1989. 2 v. (800 p.) :
NK3630.6.I72 A93 1989

BAGHDAD (IRAQ) - BUILDINGS, STRUCTURES, ETC.
Khalil, Samir. The monument . Berkeley , c1991. xv, 153 p. : ISBN 0-520-07375-4 (alk. paper) DDC 725/.96/0956747 20
NA9380.B34 K43 1991
NYPL [3-MRI 91-7589]

BAGHERIA (ITALY) - BUILDINGS, STRUCTURES, ETC.
Tedesco, Natale. L'immago espressa, Villa Palagonia . Siracusa , c1986. 231 p. : DDC 728.8/0945/823 20
NA7595.B298 T4 1986
NYPL [3-MQWB+ 90-11739]

Bagnoli, Alessandro. La Pittura in Italia . [Milano , 1989, c1988. 2 v. (967 p.) :
NYPL [3-MCE 90-11795]

BAHAMAS - HISTORY - SOURCES - BIBLIOGRAPHY.
Saunders, D. Gail. Guide to the records of the Bahamas /. [Nassau , 1973] xvi, 109, 28 p. ;
CD3882 .S27 ***NYPL [HRG 76-607]***

Bahamas. Public Records Office. "Aspects of slavery" : a booklet of the exhibition of historical documents held at the Public Records Office, Mackey St., 12-16 February 1974. Nassau : The Office, 1974. 28 p. : ill. ; 28 cm.
1. Slavery in the Bahamas - Exhibitions. I. Title.
HT1119.B34 B36 1974
NYPL [HRG 78-1237]

Bähler, Arnold. Propper, Emanuel Jirka. Das alte Biel und seine Umgebung /. Biel (Blumenstrasse 15, 2502 Biel) , 1980. 1 portfolio (38 p., 32 leaves of plates) :
NYPL [3-MQWD++ 88-4261]

Bahr, Hans-Dieter.
Machinationen : Fährtenwechsel zwischen Philosophie und Kunst / Hans-Dieter Bahr, Michael Schulze. Tübingen : C. Gehrke, [1987?] 117 p. : ill. ; 21 cm. ISBN 3-88769-028-1
1. Schulze, Michael, 1952-. I. Schulze, Michael, 1952-. II. Title. ***NYPL [3-MGO (Schulze) 91-3798]***
Verzeichnungen . Essen , 1989. 227 p. : ISBN 3-88474-603-0
N72.T4 V47 1989

BAIER, FRED.
Houston, John. Fred Baier . London , 1990. 64 p. : ISBN 0-947792-46-5 (pbk.) : DDC 749.22 20
NYPL [3-MOF 90-11124]

Baile de Laperriere, Charles.
Royal Academy exhibitors 1971-1989 . Calne, Wiltshire, England , 1989. 546 p. ; ISBN 0-904722-19-8 ***NYPL [MAO 90-9340]***
Royal Academy exhibitors, 1971-1989 . Wiltshire, England , 1989. 546 p. ; ISBN 0-904722-19-8 : DDC 709/.047/07442132 20
N6768 .R63 1989

Bailey, Colin J. Leighton, John. Caspar David Friedrich . London , 1990. 72 p. : ISBN 0-947645-75-6 (pbk)
NYPL [3-MCK F91 90-12688]

Bailey, Frederick Augustus Washington. see Douglass, Frederick, 1817-1895.

Bailey, Martin, 1947- Gogh, Vincent van, 1853-1890. [Correspondence. English. Selections.] Van Gogh, letters from Provence /. New York , c1990. 160 p. : ISBN 0-517-58144-2 : DDC 759.9492 B 20
ND653.G7 A3 1990
NYPL [3-MCH G61 91-2645]

BAILEY, WILLIAM, 1930- - CATALOGS.
Briganti, Giuliano. William Bailey /. New York , 1991. 195 p. : ISBN 0-8478-1345-2 : DDC 759.13 20
N6537.B16 A4 1991

Bailly, Patricia. Buffet-Challié, Laurence. Manolo Ruiz Pipó /. Paris, France [1990] 174 p. : ISBN 2-908517-12-4 DDC 759.6 20
N7113.R86 A4 1990

Bain, Iain. Bewick, Thomas, 1753-1828. The watercolours and drawings of Thomas Bewick and his workshop apprentices /. Stocksfield, Northumberland : Winchester : 2 v. : ISBN 0-906795-85-0 (set) DDC 769.92 20
N6797.B48 A4 1989
NYPL [3-MCV B5722 91-3680]

Bairati, Eleonora. Ferrari, Roberto. Gio Batta Ferrari, 1829-1906 /. Brescia , 1990. 110 p. : ISBN 88-7385-059-6
NYPL [3-MCF F372 91-5212]

Baj, Enrico, 1924-
Baudrillard, Jean. Enrico Baj . Paris , c1990. 55 p. : ISBN 2-7291-0617-0 : DDC 759.5 20
ND623.B17 B38 1990

BAJ, ENRICO, 1924- - CRITICISM AND INTERPRETATION.
Baudrillard, Jean. Enrico Baj . Paris , c1990. 55 p. : ISBN 2-7291-0617-0 : DDC 759.5 20
ND623.B17 B38 1990

Bajado, um artista de Olinda /. Bajado, 1912- Olinda [Brasil] , 1985. 48 p. : DDC 759.981 19
ND359.B34 A35 1985
NYPL [3-MCZ B1583 90-9450]

Bajado, 1912- Bajado, um artista de Olinda / [organizado por, Juliana Cuentro ; apresentação do Prefeito de Olinda, José Arnaold Amaral ; depoimentos de João Câmara Filho ... et al. ; entrevista a José Ataíde e Juliana Cuentro]. Olinda [Brasil] : Fundação Centro de Preservação dos Sítios de Olinda, 1985. 48 p. : ill. ; 22 cm. (Gente de Olinda . 1) DDC 759.981 19
1. Bajado, 1912-. 2. Painters - Brazil - Interviews. 3. Primitivism in art - Brazil. I. Cuentro, Juliana. II. Ataíde, José. III. Fundação Centro de Preservação dos Sítios Históricos de Olinda. IV. Title. V. Series.
ND359.B34 A35 1985
NYPL [3-MCZ B1583 90-9450]

BAJADO, 1912-
Bajado, 1912- Bajado, um artista de Olinda /. Olinda [Brasil] , 1985. 48 p. : DDC 759.981 19
ND359.B34 A35 1985
NYPL [3-MCZ B1583 90-9450]

Bajpai, Shiva Gopal. A historical atlas of South Asia; /. Chicago , 1978. xxxix, 352 p. ISBN 0-226-74221-0
G2661.S1 H5 1978 ***NYPL [Map Div. 79-12]***

Bakalova, Elka. Rozhenskiíat manastir / Elka Bakalova. 1. izd. Sofiía : Dŭrzhavno izd-vo "Septemvri", 1990. 107 p. : ill. (some col.) ; 19 x 21 cm.
1. Mural painting and decoration, Bulgarian - Bulgaria - Melnik. 2. Icons, Bulgarian - Bulgaria - Melnik. 3. Rozhenski manastir (Melnik, Bulgaria). I. Title.
ND2802.M45 B3 1990

Baker, Eric, 1949- Trademarks of the 40's and 50's / by Eric Baker & Tyler Blik ; introduction by Steven Heller. San Francisco : Chronicle Books, c1988. 156 p. : ill. (some col.) ; 21 x 23 cm. Spine title: Trademarks of the 40's & 50's. ISBN 0-87701-485-X : DDC 741.6 19
1. Commercial art - United States - Themes, motives. 2. Trademarks - United States - History - 20th century - Themes, motives. 3. Decoration and ornament - United States - Art deco - Themes, motives. I. Blik, Tyler. II. Title. III. Title: Trademarks of the forties and fifties.
NC998.5.A1 B36 1988
NYPL [MNF 88-3842]

Baker, Geoffrey H. (Geoffrey Howard) Le Corbusier, early works by Charles-Edouard Jeanneret-Gris /. London , New York , 1987. 136 p. : ISBN 0-312-47583-7 (paper)
NYPL [3-MQZ+ (Le Corbusier) 87-3750]

Baker, Kenneth, 1946-
Objectives . Newport Beach, Calif. , c1990. 1 v. (unpaged) : ISBN 0-8478-1207-3 (Rizzoli) DDC 730/.9/04807479496 20
NB198 .O25 1990
NYPL [3-MGI+ 90-11029]
Roth, Sanford, 1906-1962. Italy '50s . San Francisco , St. Paul, Minn. , 1990. xii, 138 p. : ISBN 0-916515-72-9 : DDC 779/.092 20
TR654 .R6794 1990
NYPL [MFX (ROTH) 91-3432]

Bakonyi, Tibor. Magyar Ede / írta, Bakonyi Tibor ; sajtó alá rendezte, Kubinszky Mihály. Budapest : Akadémiai Kiadó, 1989. 28 p., [48] p. of plates : ill. ; 23 cm. (Architektúra, 0066-6270) Includes bibliographical references (p. 25-27). ISBN 963-05-4991-6 :
1. Magyar, Ede, 1877-1912 - Criticism and interpretation. 2. Eclecticism in architecture - Hungary. I. Magyar, Ede, 1877-1912. II. Series. III. Series: Architektúra (Budapest, Hungary). IV. Title.
NA1022.5.M337 B3 1989

Bakos, Katalin. A Változás jelei . Budapest [1990?] 64 p. :
NC1807.H8 V34 1990

Bakrač, Ivanka. Narodna nošnja Kupinca : priručnik za rekonstrukciju nošnje / Ivanka Bakrač. Zagreb : Kulturno-prosvjetni sabor Hrvatske, 1986. 69 p., [28] p. of plates : ill. (some col.) ; 24 cm. (Biblioteka "Narodne nošnje Hrvatske") In Serbo-Croatian (roman), English, French, and German. ISBN 86-80825-06-9
1. Costume - Yugoslavia - Kupinec (Croatia). 2. Folklore - Yugoslavia - Kupinec (Croatia). I. Title. II. Series.
NK4771.Y82 K863 1986

Bal, Mieke, 1946- Reading "Rembrandt" : beyond the word-image opposition : the Northrop Frye lectures in literary theory / Mieke Bal. Cambridge ; New York : Cambridge University Press, 1991. p. cm. (Cambridge new art history and criticism) Includes bibliographical references and index. ISBN 0-521-39154-7 DDC 759.9492 20
1. Rembrandt Harmenszoon van Rijn, 1606-1669 - Criticism and interpretation. 2. Women in art. 3. Ut pictura poesis (Aesthetics). 4. Art and literature. I. Title. II. Title: Northrop Frye lectures in literary theory. III. Series.
ND653.R4 B18 1991

Balance 1990: views, visions, influences / [editor, Janet Hogan]. South Brisbane, Qld., Australia : Queensland Art Gallery, c1990. 95 p. : ill. ; 27 cm. Exhibition catalog. ISBN 0-7242-3855-7
1. Art, Australian (Aboriginal) - Exhibitions. 2. Art, Australian - Exhibitions. 3. Art, Modern - 20th century - Australia - Exhibitions. I. Hogan, Janet, 1941-. II. Queensland Art Gallery.
NYPL [3-MADF 91-7104]

Balassa, M. Iván. A parasztház évszázadai : a magyar lakóház középkori fejlődésének vázlata / Balassa M. Iván. Békéscsaba : Tevan Andor Nyomdaipari Szakközép- és Szakmunkásképző Iskola, 1985. 188 p. : ill. ; 24 cm. Summary in German. Bibliography: p. 166-[175] ISBN 963-01-6472-8
1. Farmhouses - Hungary. 2. Vernacular architecture - Hungary. I. Title.
NA8210.H9 B35 1985
NYPL [3-MRGF 90-12492]

Balboa, Calif. Newport Harbor Art Museum. see Newport Harbor Art Museum.

Baldani, Claudio. Il Vittoriano . Roma, Italy , c1986. 188 p. : ISBN 88-7621-298-1 : DDC 725/.94/0945632 20
NA9355.R7 V5 1986
NYPL [3-MQWB 90-13008]

Baldass, Ludwig, 1887-1963. Jan van Eyck / by
Ludwig Baldass. New York : Phaidon :
distributed by Garden City Books, 1952. 297
p. : ill. (some col.) ; 31 cm. Includes bibliographical
references and index.   DDC 927.5
1. Eyck, Jan van, 1390-1440.
ND673.E9 B33 1952a
NYPL [3-MCH+ E97 91-4308]

Balder, A. P.
Mariner's atlas. Long Island Sound & the South
Shore / A.P. Balder. 2nd ed. [Baltimore, Md. :
Chartcrafters, c1989] 1 atlas (80 p) : ill., col.
maps ; 36 cm. Cover title.   ISBN 0-930151-07-0 :
*1. Nautical charts - Northeastern States. 2. Boats and
boating - Northeastern States - Maps. I. Title. II. Title:
Long Island Sound & South Shore. III. Title: Mariner's
atlas, Long Island Sound & South Shore.*
NYPL [Map Div. 90-11550]

Mariner's atlas. New England / A.P. Balder.
2nd ed. Baltimore, Md. : Chartcrafters, c1989.
1 atlas ([112] p.) : ill. (some col.), col. maps ;
36 cm. Cover title.   ISBN 0-930151-08-9 :
*1. Nautical charts - New England. 2. Boats and
boating - New England - Maps. I. Title. II. Title: New
England. III. Title: Mariner's atlas, New England.*
NYPL [Map Div. 90-11551]

Mariner's atlas. Southern California / A.P.
Balder. Houston, Tex. : Gulf Pub. Co., c1989. 1
atlas (112 p.) : ill. (some col.), col. maps ; 36
cm. Cover title. "NOAA charts from Monterey Bay to
Cabo Punta Banda, Baja California." "Not for
navigation"--Verso t.p.   ISBN 0-87201-466-5 (pbk.):
$39.95   DDC 623.89/297949 20
*1. Nautical charts - California, Southern. 2. Boats and
boating - California, Southern - Maps. I. Title. II. Title:
Southern California. III. Title: Mariner's atlas, Southern
California.*
G1526.P5 B3 1989
NYPL [Map Div. 90-11549]

Baldessari, John, 1931-
Bruggen, Coosje van. John Baldessari /. New
York , 1990. 256 p. :   ISBN 0-8478-1182-4 :
DDC 709/.2 20
N6537.B17 B78 1990
NYPL [3-MCX+ B176 90-11225]

Discourses . Cambridge, Mass. , New York,
N.Y. , 1990. 471 p. :   ISBN 0-262-06125-2   DDC
700/.9/048 20
NX456.5.P66 D57 1990
NYPL [3-MAL 91-3360]

Ingres and other parables. [London, Studio
International Publications] 1971 [i.e. 1972] 22
p. illus. 31 cm. English, French, German and Italian.
ISBN 0-902063-10-3
1. Baldessari, John, 1931-. I. Title.
N6512 .B26   NYPL [3-MCX+ B176 81-385]

Nipor ésas = Not even so / John Baldessari.
[Madrid] : Ministerio de Cultura, Dirección
General de Bellas Artes y Archivos, Centro
Nacional de Exposiciones, [1989] 92 p. : ill.
(some col.) ; 28cm. Catalog of an exhibition held at
Centro de Arte Reina Sofia, Madrid, 11 enero 20
febrero, 1989; CAPC, Mus'ee d'Art Contemporain,
Burdeos, 10 marzo-23 abril, 1989; IVAM, Instituto
Valenciamo de Arte Moderno, Valencia, Centre Julio
Gonz'alez, 15 mayo-15 julio, 1989. Captions in English
and Spanish. Includes bibliographical references.   ISBN
84-7506-254-7 (pbk.)
*1. Baldessari, John, 1931- - Exhibitions. 2. Photography,
Artistic - Exhibitions. I. Centro de Arte Reina Sofiá. II.
Musée d'Art Contemporain de Bordeaux. III. IVAM
Centre Julio González. IV. Title. V. Title: Not even so.*
NYPL [MFX (Baldessari) 89-28407]

BALDESSARI, JOHN, 1931-
Baldessari, John, 1931- Ingres and other
parables. [London] 1971 [i.e. 1972] 22 p.   ISBN
0-902063-10-3
N6512 .B26   NYPL [3-MCX+ B176 81-385]

BALDESSARI, JOHN, 1931- - EXHIBITIONS.
Baldessari, John, 1931- Nipor ésas =. [Madrid]
[1989] 92 p. :   ISBN 84-7506-254-7 (pbk.)
NYPL (MFX (Baldessari) 89-28407]

Bruggen, Coosje van. John Baldessari /. New
York , 1990. 256 p. :   ISBN 0-8478-1182-4 :
DDC 709/.2 20
N6537.B17 B78 1990
NYPL [3-MCX+ B176 90-11225]

**Baldessari, R. M. (Roberto Marcello), 1894-
1965.**
Scudiero, Maurizio. R.M. Baldessari, opere
futuriste /. [Roma] , 1989. 231 p. :   ISBN

88-7165-004-2 :   DDC 709/.2 20
N6923.B257 A4 1989

**BALDESSARI, R. M. (ROBERTO
MARCELLO), 1894-1965 - CATALOGS.**
Scudiero, Maurizio. R.M. Baldessari, opere
futuriste /. [Roma] , 1989. 231 p. :   ISBN
88-7165-004-2 :   DDC 709/.2 20
N6923.B257 A4 1989

Baldini, Umberto. La Cappella Brancacci /
Umberto Baldini, Ornella Casazza. Milano :
Olivetti : Electa, c1990. 377 p. : ill. (some
col.) ; 29 cm. Includes bibliographical references (p.
365-373) and index.   ISBN 88-435-3199-9
*1. Cappella Brancacci (Santa Maria del Carmine
(Church : Florence, Italy). 2. Mural painting and
decoration, Italian - Italy - Florence. 3. Mural painting
and decoration, Renaissance - Italy - Florence. I.
Casazza, Ornella. II. Title.*
ND2757.F5 B3 1990
NYPL [3-MLP 91-7284]

Baldini, Umberto, 1893- Firenze restaura .
Firenze , 1973, c1972. 154 p., [168] p. of
plates :   *NYPL [3-MBK 90-5749]*

Baldwin, Gordon.
Gordon Baldwin : mysterieuze volumes =
mysterious volumes : 1/7-20/8, 89, Museum
Boymans-Van Beuningen, Rotterdam / [redactie
catalogus, Dorris U. Kuyken-Schneider, Th. de
Duits]. Rotterdam : Museum Boymans-Van
Beuningen, [1989] 39 p. : ill. (some col.) ; 27
cm. Dutch and English. Includes bibliographical
references (p. 39).   ISBN 90-6918-044-8
*1. Baldwin, Gordon - Exhibitions. 2. Ceramic
sculpture - 20th century - Great Britain - Exhibitions. I.
Kuyken-Schneider, D. U. II. Duits, Thimo te. III.
Museum Boymans-Van Beuningen. IV. Title.*
NK4210.B33 A4 1989

BALDWIN, GORDON - EXHIBITIONS.
Baldwin, Gordon. Gordon Baldwin . Rotterdam
[1989] 39 p. :   ISBN 90-6918-044-8
NK4210.B33 A4 1989

Baldwin, Helen. Children of the dreamtime /
Helen Baldwin ; edited by Laura Murray. 1st
ed. Frenchs Forest, NSW, Australia : Child &
Associates, 1989. 103 p. : ill. ; 30 cm.   ISBN
0-86777-278-6
1. Baldwin, Helen. I. Title.
NYPL [3-MCX+ B181 90-12952]

BALDWIN, HELEN.
Baldwin, Helen. Children of the dreamtime /.
Frenchs Forest, NSW, Australia , 1989. 103 p. :
ISBN 0-86777-278-6
NYPL [3-MCX+ B181 90-12952]

Baldwin, Neil, 1947- Man Ray, American artist /
by Neil Baldwin. New York : Da Capo Press,
[1991], c1988. xii, 449 p. : ill. ; 24 cm. (A Da
Capo paperback) Includes bibliographical references (p.
415-431) and index.   ISBN 0-306-80423-9 :   DDC
709/.2 B 20
*1. Ray, Man, 1890-1976. 2. Artists - United States -
Biography. I. Title.*
N6537.R3 B3 1991

Balfour, Alan. Berlin : the politics of order,
1737-1989 / Alan Balfour. New York : Rizzoli,
1990. 269 p. : ill., maps ; 27 cm. Includes index.
Includes bibliographical references (p. 262).   ISBN
0-8478-1271-5   DDC 720/.1/03 20
*1. City planning - Berlin (Germany). 2. Architecture
and state - Berlin (Germany). 3. Neoclassicism
(Architecture) - Berlin (Germany). I. Title.*
NA9200.B4 B35 1990
NYPL [3-MQWD 90-13618]

BALINESE ART. see ART, BALINESE.

Balis, Arnout. La Peinture flamande au Prado /.
Anvers , Paris , c1989. 318 p. :   ISBN
90-6153-199-3 (Fonds Mercator)   DDC
759.9493/1/0744641 20
ND669.F5 P43 1989

Balkenhol, Stephan, 1957- Dorothea von
Stetten-Kunstpreis 1988 . Bonn , 1988. 126 p. :
DDC 730/.943/074435518 20
NB568 .D74 1988   NYPL [3-MGI 91-7194]

Balkrishna Doshi . Curtis, William J. R. New
York , 1988. 191 p. :   ISBN 0-8478-0937-4   DDC
720/.92 20
NA1510.D67 C87 1988
NYPL [3-MQZ (Doshi) 89-22893]

Ball, Joanne Dubbs. Jewelry of the stars :
creations from Joseff of Hollywood / Joanne
Dubbs Ball. West Chester, Pa. : Schiffer Pub.,

c1991. 192 p. : ill. (some col.) ; 29 cm.
Filmography: p. 188-190. Includes bibliographical
references (p. 187) and index.   ISBN 0-88740-294-1
DDC 739.27/092 20
*1. Joseff, Eugene, 1905-1948 - Themes, motives. 2.
Costume jewelry - United States. 3. Motion picture
industry - United States. I. Title.*
NK7398.J67 B35 1991

Ballagna, Francis. Garrigou, Marcel. La culture,
richesse de l'entreprise . [Paris] , c1990. 272
p. ;   ISBN 2-7007-2836-X :
NX634 .G37 1990

Ballast, David Kent. Architecture, design, and
construction word finder / David Kent Ballast.
Englewood Cliffs, N.J. : Prentice-Hall, c1991. p.
cm.   ISBN 0-13-044397-2   DDC 720/.3 20
*1. Architecture - Terminology. 2. Architectural design -
Terminology. 3. Building - Terminology. I. Title.*
NA31 .B34 1991

BALLET - HISTORY.
Starr, Sandra Leonard. Joseph Cornell and the
ballet /. New York , c1983. viii, 87 p. :   DDC
709/.2/4 19
N6537.C66 A4 1983
NYPL [MCX C795 84-702]

BALLET IN ART - EXHIBITIONS.
Starr, Sandra Leonard. Joseph Cornell and the
ballet /. New York , c1983. viii, 87 p. :   DDC
709/.2/4 19
N6537.C66 A4 1983
NYPL [MCX C795 84-702]

Ballmer, Karl.
Karl Ballmer, 1891-1958 : der Maler /
[verantwortlich für Ausstellung und Katalog,
Beat Wismer]. Aarau : Aargauer Kunsthaus ;
Baden : L. Müller [distributor], c1990. 167 p. :
ill. (some col.) ; 31 cm. Catalog of the exhibition of
the same name held May 27-Aug. 12, 1990, at the
Aargauer Kunsthaus Aarau, Sept. 14-Oct. 31, 1990, at
the Richard-Haizmann-Museum Niebüll, and to be held
at the Kunstmuseum des Kantons Thurgau, May-June
1991. Includes bibliographical references (p. 167).
ISBN 3-906700-34-8   DDC 759.9494 20
*1. Ballmer, Karl - Exhibitions. I. Wismer, Beat. II.
Aargauer Kunsthaus. III. Richard-Haizmann-Museum
Niebüll. IV. Kunstmuseum des Kantons Thurgau. V.
Title.*
ND853.B34 A4 1990

BALLMER, KARL - EXHIBITIONS.
Ballmer, Karl. Karl Ballmer, 1891-1958 .
Aarau , Baden , c1990. 167 p. :   ISBN
3-906700-34-8   DDC 759.9494 20
ND853.B34 A4 1990

Balmori, Santos.
Homenaje a Santos 90 Balmori en su
nonagésimo aniversario : exposición
retrospectiva. [Mexico] : Consejo Nacional para
la Cultura y las Artes : Instituto Nacional de
Bellas Artes, [1989] 1 v. (unpaged) : ill. (some
col.) ; 28 cm. Cover title. Catalog of an exhibition
held at Museo del Palacio de Bellas Artes in 1989.
Includes bibliographical references.   DDC 709/.2 20
*1. Balmori, Santos - Exhibitions. I. Museo del Palacio
de Bellas Artes (Mexico). II. Title. III. Title: Homenaje
a Santos Balmori en su nonagésimo aniversario.*
N6559.B35 A4 1989
NYPL [3-MCZ B193 91-5072]

BALMORI, SANTOS - EXHIBITIONS.
Balmori, Santos. Homenaje a Santos 90 Balmori
en su nonagésimo aniversario . [Mexico]
[1989] 1 v. (unpaged) :   DDC 709/.2 20
N6559.B35 A4 1989
NYPL [3-MCZ B193 91-5072]

Balog, James. Survivors : a new vision of
endangered wildlife / photographs & text by
James Balog. New York : H.N. Abrams, 1990.
144 p. : col. ill. ; 24 cm.   ISBN 0-8109-3908-8
DDC 779/.32/092 20
*1. Balog, James. 2. Endangered species - Pictorial
works. I. Title.*
TR727 .B25 1990
NYPL [MFX+ (Balog) 91-5850]

BALOG, JAMES.
Balog, James. Survivors . New York , 1990. 144
p. :   ISBN 0-8109-3908-8   DDC 779/.32/092 20
TR727 .B25 1990
NYPL [MFX+ (Balog) 91-5850]

Baloghné Horváth, Terézia.
[Népi ékszerek. English]
Hungarian folk jewelry / Terézia
Balogh-Horváth ; [translated by Zsuzsa

Béres ; translation revised by Joyce Winkel].
Budapest : Corvina Kiadó : Kultura,
[distributor], 1983. 66 p., [56] p. of plates :
ill. (some col.) ; 19 cm. (Hungarian folk art,
0324-7996) Translation of: Népi ékszerek.
Bibliography: p. 57-[60] ISBN 963-13-1762-5
DDC 739.27/09439 19
*1. Jewelry - Hungary. I. Series: Magyar népművészet.
English. II. Title.*
GT2252.H9 B3513 1983
NYPL [3-MNR 90-11105]

Balté, Teresa. Semke, Hein, 1899- Hein Semke .
Lisboa [1989] 153 p. :
NB833.S46 S46 1989

Balthasar Burkhard. Burkhard, Balthasar. [Bern] ,
1988. 94 p. :
NYPL [MFX (Burkhard) 91-2391]

Balthasar Neumann, 1687-1753 . Schneider,
Erich. München , c1987. 48 p. :
NYPL [3-MQZ+ (Neumann) 91-6584]

Balthus /. Leymarie, Jean. Geneva , New York ,
1990. 1 v. (unpaged) : ISBN 0-8478-0188-8
NYPL [3-MCO+ B197 90-11466]

**BALTHUS, 1908- - CRITICISM AND
INTERPRETATION.**
García Ponce, Juan. Una lectura pseudognóstica
de la pintura de Balthus /. México , 1987. 39
p. :
ND553.B23 G37 1987

**BALTIC SEA REGION IN ART -
EXHIBITIONS.**
Art Maritim '88 (1988 : Hamburg, Germany)
Ostseeschiffahrt in der Kunst /. Hamburg ,
c1988. 140 p. : ISBN 3-87700-058-4 DDC
758/.2/094307443515 20
ND1373.5.G3 A78 1988
NYPL [3-MAMZ 91-6580]

Baltimore. Museum of Art.
Segal, George, 1924- George Segal .
Philadelphia [1976] 39 p. : ISBN 0-88454-019-7
NB237.S44 A4 1976
NYPL [3-MGO (Segal) 81-782]

Shapiro, Joel. Joel Shapiro . Des Moines, Ia. ,
1990. 80 p. : ISBN 1-87900-300-7
NYPL [3-MGO (Shapiro) 91-7050]

**Baltrušaitis, Jurgis, 1903-
Art sumérien, art roman. 1989.** Chevrier,
Jean-François. Portrait de Jurgis Baltrušaitis /
Jean-François Chevrier. & Art sumérien, art
roman / par Jurgis Baltrušaitis. Paris , c1989.
271 p. : ISBN 2-08-012038-7
N7483.B285 C48 1989

**BALTRUŠAITIS, JURGIS, 1903- -
CRITICISM AND INTERPRETATION.**
Chevrier, Jean-François. Portrait de Jurgis
Baltrušaitis /. Paris , c1989. 271 p. : ISBN
2-08-012038-7
N7483.B285 C48 1989

Balty, Jean Ch. Académie de Bruxelles .
Bruxelles , 1989. 541 p. : ISBN 2-87143-063-2
NYPL [3-MQF+ 90-133]

**Balzac, Honoré de, 1799-1850.
LE CHEF-D'ŒUVRE INCONNU -
INFLUENCE.**
Ashton, Dore. A fable of modern art /.
Berkeley , c1991. p. cm. ISBN 0-520-07301-0
DDC 700/.9/04 20
NX454 .A8 1991

BAMBAIA, 1483-1548.
Agosti, Giovanni. Bambaia e il classicismo
lombardo /. Torino , c1990. xix, 229 p., [128]
p. of plates : ISBN 88-06-11778-5
IN PROCESS (ONLINE)
NYPL [3-MGO (Bambaia) 91-6556]

Bambaia e il classicismo lombardo /. Agosti,
Giovanni. Torino , c1990. xix, 229 p., [128] p.
of plates : ISBN 88-06-11778-5
IN PROCESS (ONLINE)
NYPL [3-MGO (Bambaia) 91-6556]

Bamber, Judie.
L.A. times . Boise, Idaho , c1991. p. cm. DDC
709/.794/9407479628 20
N6535.L6 L188 1991

Not so simple pleasures . Cambridge, Mass. ,
1990. 32 p. : ISBN 0-938437-34-8 (pbk.) : DDC
709/.73/0747444 20
N6512 .N635 1990

**BAMBERG (GERMANY) - BUILDINGS,
STRUCTURES, ETC. - CONGRESSES.**

Denkmalkunde in Bamberg . Bamberg [1990]
77 p. : DDC 720/.28/80943318 20
NA109.G3 D44 1990

BAMBOO FURNITURE.
Ottillinger, Eva. Korbmöbel /. Salzburg , c1990.
191 p. : ISBN 3-7017-0633-6 DDC 749 20
NK2712.7 .O87 1990

BAMBOO FURNITURE - HISTORY.
Walkling, Gillian. Antique bamboo furniture /.
London , 1979. 128 p., 4 p. of plates : ISBN
0-7135-1099-4 :
NK2712.6 .W34   **NYPL [MOI 81-1058]**

Bamgboye, Oladele Ajiboye, 1963- Through
photography /. Glasgow , 1989. 1 v.
(unpaged) : ISBN 0-906474-86-8
NYPL [MFW+ 91-7478]

Banares Hindu University. Bharat Kala Bhavan.
see **Bharat Kala Bhavan.**

Banares Hindu University. Museum. see **Bharat
Kala Bhavan.**

**Banater Künstler in der Bundesrepublik
Deutschland :** Landestreffen der Banater
Schwaben, Nürnberger Kultur- und Heimattage
Mai 1988, Ehrenhalle im Alten Rathaus
Nürnberg / [herausgegeben von der
Landsmannschaft der Banater Schwaben aus
Rumänien in der Bundesrepublik Deutschland
e.V. ; mit einem Vorwort von Franz Heinz ;
Gestaltung des Katalogs, Ingo Glass, Manfred
Engelmann].1. Aufl. Berlin : Westkreuz-Verlag,
1988. 60 p. : chiefly ill. (some col.) ; 24 cm.
Exhibition catalog. ISBN 3-922131-57-8
*1. Art, German - Germany, West - Exhibitions. 2. Art,
Modern - 20th century - Germany, West - Exhibitions.
3. Artists - Banat - Biography. I. Glass, Ingo, 1941-. II.
Engelmann, Manfred, 1956-. III. Landsmannschaft der
Banater Schwaben aus Rumänien in Deutschland.*
N6868 .B33 1988
NYPL [3-MAMG 91-6298]

Banchieri Vitone, Orietta. Testimonianze Liberty
a Genova /. Genova , c1986. 46 p. : ISBN
88-7058-218-3
NYPL [3-MAMC 90-11119]

Banco Chase Manhattan (Brazil)
Acervo, materpieces, Banco Chase Manhattan.
[Rio de Janeiro] , c1989. 118 p. : ISBN
85-7083-028-9 DDC 709/.81/0748161 20
N6655 .A24 1989

**BANCO CHASE MANHATTAN (BRAZIL) -
CATALOGS.**
Acervo, materpieces, Banco Chase Manhattan.
[Rio de Janeiro] , c1989. 118 p. : ISBN
85-7083-028-9 DDC 709/.81/0748161 20
N6655 .A24 1989

**Banco d'assaggio dei vini d'Italia (7th : 1987 :
Torgiano, Italy)** Arte orafa e iconografia
dionisiaca . [Italy , 1987] 88 p. :
NYPL [3-MNO+ 89-27461]

Banco de la República (Colombia)
Bogotá en caricatura. [Bogotá] [1988] 235 p. :
DDC 986.1/48 20
F2291.B62 B64 1988
NYPL [3-MDY+ 91-6190]

La Acuarela en Antioquia . [Bogotá? , 1987]
([Bogotá] : Banco de la República,
Departamento Editorial) 59 p. : DDC
759.9861/26/07486126 20
ND1905.A58 A28 1987

Merino, Hernán, 1922-1973. Hernán Merino .
Bogotá [1986?] 107 p. :
NC1460.M47 A4 1986

**BANCO DE LA REPÚBLICA (COLOMBIA) -
CATALOGS.**
Biblioteca Luis-Angel Arango. Antología, obras
de la colección permanente. Bogotá, D.E. ,
1990. 88 p. :
N6670 .B5 1990

Banco di Napoli.
Capolavori dalle collezioni d'arte del Banco di
Napoli /. Napoli , c1989. 213 p. : ISBN
88-7042-999-7
NYPL [3-MAVZ+ (Naples) 90-13203]

**BANCO DI NAPOLI - ART COLLECTIONS -
CATALOGS.**
Capolavori dalle collezioni d'arte del Banco di
Napoli /. Napoli , c1989. 213 p. : ISBN
88-7042-999-7
NYPL [3-MAVZ+ (Naples) 90-13203]

Banco Exterior de España. Varo, Remedios,
1908-1963. Remedios Varo . Madrid , c1988.
167 p. : ISBN 84-86884-57-8
NYPL [3-MCQ + V323 89-18083]

Banco Hipotecario Nacional (La Paz, Bolivia)
Pintura boliviana del siglo XX /. La Paz,
Bolivia , 1989. 317 p. : DDC 759.984/074 20
ND345 .P56 1989

Banco Industrial de Venezuela. Arturo
Michelena : su obra y su tiempo, 1863-1898 /
[María Cristina Capriles ... et al.]. [Caracas,
Venezuela] : Banco Industrial de Venezuela,
[1989?] 183 p. : ill. (some col.) ; 32 cm.
(Colección Banco Industrial de Venezuela) Includes
bibliographical references (p. 178-179). Spanish with
parallel English and French translations. DDC
759.987 20
*1. Michelena, Arturo, 1863-1898. 2. Artists -
Venezuela - Biography. I. Michelena, Arturo,
1863-1898. II. Capriles, María Cristina. III. Title. IV.
Series.*
N6739.M53 B36 1989

**BANCO NACIONAL DE MÉXICO -
BUILDINGS.**
Mogilner, Mark. Edificaciones del Banco
Nacional de México . México , 1988. 191 p. :
ISBN 968-7009-18-7 DDC 725/.24/0972 20
NA6245.M6 M64 1988

Bandaranayake, Senake. The rock and wall
paintings of Sri Lanka / Senake
Bandaranayake ; photographs by Gamini
Jayasinghe. Colombo : Lake House Bookshop,
c1986. 300 p. : chiefly col. ill., maps ; 31 cm.
Includes index. Bibliography : p. 281-288. ISBN
955-9029-00-2 : DDC 751.7/3/095493 19
*1. Rock paintings - Sri Lanka. 2. Mural painting and
decoration, Sri Lankan. I. Jayasinghe, Gamini, 1940-. II.
Title.*
ND2830.A1 B36 1986
NYPL [3-MAF+ 90-11751]

Bandin Ron, J. C. Plastica argentina : reportaje a
los años 70 / Bandin Ron.1. ed. Buenos Aires :
Corregidor, 1978. 228, [4] p., [16] p. of plates :
ill. ; 20 cm. (Serie mayor. M-1240)
*1. Art, Argentine - History and criticism. 2. Art,
Modern - 20th century - Argentina - History and
crititicism. I. Title.*   **NYPL [3-MAM 90-6456]**

Banegas, Angel Darío. Y reír es de sabios /
Angel Darío Benegas. Tegucigalpa, Honduras :
Ediciones Librería Paradiso, 1989. 1 v.
(unpaged) : chiefly ill. ; 17 x 22 cm.
1. Honduras - Caricatures and cartoons. I. Title.
NYPL [3-MDY 90-11033]

Bänfer, Carl. (ed) Landesmuseum für Kunst und
Kulturgeschichte, Münster. Nykysaksalaista
maalaustaidetta. [Münster, 1964?] 158, [8] p.
N6868 .L3

Bang, Molly. Picture this : shapes on a rectangle
/ Molly Bang ; foreword by Rudolf
Arnheim.1st ed. Boston : Little, Brown, 1991.
p. cm. "A Bulfinch Press book." ISBN 0-8212-1855-7
DDC 741.6 20
*1. Visual perception. 2. Design. 3. Little Red Riding
Hood - Illustrations. I. Title.*
NK1510 .B258 1991

Bangert, Albrecht, 1944- 80s style, designs of the
decade / by Albrecht Bangert and Karl Michael
Armer ; foreword by Ettore Sottsass. 1st ed.
New York : Abbeville Press, 1990. 240 p. : col.
ill. ; 30 cm. Includes index. ISBN 1-558-59117-6
DDC 745.4/442 20
*1. Design - History - 20th century - Themes, motives.
I. Armer, Karl Michael, 1950-. II. Title. III. Title:
Eighties style, designs of the decade.*
NK1390 .B26 1990
NYPL [3-MNF+ 90-13410]

Bangkok guide and street directory. Thailand.
Krom Phænthi Thahän. Bangkok [1966] 245 p.
G2379.B3 T4 1966
NYPL [Map Div. 91-220]

**BANGKOK, THAILAND - DESCRIPTION -
GUIDE-BOOKS.**
Thailand. Krom Phænthi Thahän. Bangkok
guide and street directory. Bangkok [1966] 245
p.
G2379.B3 T4 1966
NYPL [Map Div. 91-220]

BANGKOK (THAILAND) - MAPS.
Thailand. Krom Phænthi Thahän. Bangkok
guide and street directory. Bangkok [1966] 245

p.
G2379.B3 T4 1966
NYPL *[Map Div. 91-220]*

Banik-Schweitzer, Renate, 1939- Historischer
Atlas von Wien /. Wien , 1981- 1 atlas (v.
(loose-leaf)) : ISBN 3-7141-6044-2 (1. Lfg.) DDC
911/.43613 19
G1939.V4S1 H5 1981
NYPL *[Map Div. 90-56]*

BANK BUILDINGS - MEXICO.
Mogilner, Mark. Edificaciones del Banco
Nacional de México . México , 1988. 191 p. :
ISBN 968-7009-18-7 DDC 725/.24/0972 20
NA6245.M6 M64 1988

BANK OF ENGLAND - BUILDINGS.
Schumann-Bacia, Eva, 1950- [Bank von
England und ihr Architekt John Soane.
English.] John Soane and the Bank of England
/. New York , 1991. p. cm. ISBN
1-87827-131-8 : DDC 725/.24/092 20
NA6245.G72 L63713 1991

Banka, Lawrence. Bukovnik, Gary, 1947-
Flowers . New York , 1990. 119 p. : ISBN
0-8109-3105-2 DDC 760/.092 20
N6537.B835 A4 1990
NYPL *[3-MCX B924 90-11081]*

Banks, William Nathaniel. Keyes, Donald D.
George Cooke, 1793-1849 /. [Athens, Ga.] ,
1991. 104 p. : ISBN 0-915977-07-9 DDC 759.13
20
ND237.C6785 A4 1991

Bann, Stephen.
Interpreting contemporary art /. London , 1991.
xix, 22 p. : ISBN 0-948462-15-9 (cased) : DDC
709.047 20
N6490
NYPL *[MA 91-6285]*
Lebrun, Christopher. Fifty etchings /. London ,
1991. 123 p. : ISBN 0-904866-88-2
NYPL *[MDG+ (Lebrun) 91-8018]*

Bannā, 'Alī. Majīd, 'Abd al-Mun'im. al-Aṭlas
al-tārikhī lil-'ālam al-Islāmī fī al-'uṣūr al-Wustá.
[al-Qāhirah] 1967. 13, 36p.
G1786.S1 M3 1967
NYPL *[Map-Div. 85-3121]*

Banque Bruxelles Lambert. Opalescence .
Bruxelles , 1986. 1 v. (unpaged) :
NYPL *[3-MPW+ 90-4506]*

BANQUETS. see DINNERS AND DINING.

A Bantam-Barnard biography.
Drucker, Malka. Frida Kahlo . New York ,
1991. p. cm. ISBN 0-553-07165-3 DDC 759.972
B 92 20
N6559.K34 D7 1991

Bantens, Robert James. Eugène Carrière : the
symbol of creation / by Robert James Bantens ;
with an introduction by Robert Rosenblum.
New York : Kent, c1990. 131 p. : ill. (some
col.) ; 27 cm. Includes bibliographical references (p.
128-129). ISBN 1-87860-708-1
*1. Carrière, Eugène, 1849-1906. I. Carrière, Eugène,
1849-1906. II. Title.*
NYPL *[3-MCO C31 90-11584]*

Banu, Georges.
Garnier, Charles, 1825-1898. Le théâtre /.
Arles , c1990. 254 p. ; ISBN 2-86869-530-2
DDC 725/.822 20
NA6821 .G3 1990
Kantor, l'artiste à la fin du XXe siècle /.
[Arles] [Paris] , c1990. 177 p. : ISBN
2-86943-254-2 : DDC 700/.92 20
NX571.P64 K3635 1990

Banzato, D. (Davide) Bronzi e placchette dei
Musei civici di Padova / Davide Banzato,
Franca Pellegrini. Padova : Editoriale
Programma, c1989. 155 p. : ill. (some col.) ; 28
cm. Includes bibliographical references (p. 149-154).
DDC 730/.0945/0744532 20
*1. Musei civici agli Eremitani - Catalogs. 2. Bronze
figurines, Italian - Catalogs. 3. Plaques, plaquettes -
Italy - Catalogs. 4. Plaques, plaquettes, Renaissance -
Italy - Catalogs. 5. Plaques, plaquettes, Baroque - Italy -
Catalogs. 6. Art - Italy - Padua - Catalogs. I. Pellegrini,
Franca. II. Musei civici agli Eremitani. III. Title.*
NK7952.A1 B36 1989
NYPL *[MGR 91-6998]*

Báo chí văn ngh Đ Hà N 1989. 35 p. ;
NX180.M3 D6 1989

Baran, Ludvík. Johnová, Helena, 1884-1962.
Lidový malovaný nábytek v českých zemích . V

Praze , 1989. 196 p. : ISBN 80-7038-034-9 :
NK2635.C9 J64 1989

BARANYA MEGYE (HUNGARY) IN ART.
Martyn, Ferenc, 1899- Baranyai képek /.
Budapest , c1979. 102 p. : ISBN 963-336-196-6 :
NC312.H83 M332 1979
NYPL *[3-MCZ M388 90-6921]*

BARANYA MEGYE (HUNGARY) - POETRY.
Martyn, Ferenc, 1899- Baranyai képek /.
Budapest , c1979. 102 p. : ISBN 963-336-196-6 :
NC312.H83 M332 1979
NYPL *[3-MCZ M388 90-6921]*

Baranyai képek /. Martyn, Ferenc, 1899-
Budapest , c1979. 102 p. : ISBN 963-336-196-6 :
NC312.H83 M332 1979
NYPL *[3-MCZ M388 90-6921]*

Barbados Museum and Historical Society. White,
Golde, 1890-1977. Sunlight & shadow .
[Barbados] [198-] 12 p. :
NYPL *[3-MCZ W584 91-5909]*

Barbara Kruger . Kruger, Barbara, 1945-
Wellington, N.Z. , c1988. 73 p. : ISBN
0-9597785-5-1
NYPL *[3-MCX+ K935 90-10674]*

Barbara Kruger . Kruger, Barbara, 1945- New
York, N.Y. , 1991. p. cm. ISBN 0-941863-19-0
DDC 700/.92 20
N7433.4.K78 A4 1991

Barbarito, Carlos, 1955- Arte argentino, siglo XX
/. [Argentina] c1990 (Buenos Aires, R.
Argentina [i.e. República Argentina) : HUR)
124 p. : DDC 709/.82/0904 20
N6635 .A78 1990

BARBEAU, MARCEL, 1925-
Gagnon, Carolle. Marcel Barbeau . [Canada] ,
c1990. 243 p. : ISBN 2-9802034-5-9 (prestige ed.)
NYPL *[3-MCZ+ B233 91-7596]*

Barbecue strut [sound recording].
Chantenay-Villedieu : NATO, p1986. 1 sound
disc : analog, 33 1/3 rpm, stereo. ; 12 in. Brief
record. CONTENTS. - Highly perpendicular --
Nylon? -- Big tensions -- Chinchon -- Jour de fête --
Glances exchanged between nurses -- Cote a ouvrir --
Hawaiian gravity -- Pearl dropper -- Deterred man.
1. Jazz.
NATO 907

Barbera, Gioacchino. I bozzetti di Sartorio per il
Duomo di Messina / Gioacchino Barbera, Anna
Maria Damigella ; introduzione di Rossana
Bossaglia ; appendice documentaria a cura di
Giovanni Molonia. Palermo : Sellerio, c1989.
158 p. : ill. (some col.) ; 34 cm. (I Cristalli)
Includes bibliographical references. ISBN
88-7681-048-X :
*1. Sartorio, Giulio Aristide, 1860-1932 - Criticism and
interpretation. 2. Artists' preparatory studies - Italy. 3.
Duomo di Messina. I. Damigella, Anna Maria. II. Title.*
NC257.S2685 B37 1989

BARBERINI FAMILY.
Waddy, Patricia. Seventeenth-century Roman
palaces . New York, N.Y. , Cambridge, Mass. ,
c1990. xiii, 456 p. : ISBN 0-262-23156-5 DDC
945 20
DG797.9 .W33 1990
NYPL *[3-MQWB 91-3718]*

BARBIANI, BARTOLOMEO, D. 1645.
Pittura del Seicento in Umbria . Todi , 1990.
351 p., [20] p. of plates :
NYPL *[3-MCE+ 91-4970]*

Barbican Art Gallery.
Kampf, Avram. Chagall to Kitaj . New York ,
London , 1990. 206 p. : ISBN 0-275-93900-6 (alk.
paper) DDC 704/.03924/0904 20
N7417 .K34 1991
Ławniczakowa, Agnieszka. Malczewski, a vision
of Poland . London , 1990. 136 p. : ISBN
0-946372-19-5 DDC 759.38 20
ND955.P6 M3435 1990
Malczewski, Jacek, 1854-1929. Malczewski .
London , 1990. 136 p. : ISBN 0-946372-19-5
NYPL *[3-MCZ m243 90-13532]*
The pursuit of the real . London , c1990. 127
p. : ISBN 0-85331-571-X (pbk.)
NYPL *[3-MCT 90-11527]*
Smith, Matthew, 1879-1959. Matthew Smith .
London , c1983. 79 p. : ISBN 0-946372-04-7
(pbk.) : DDC 759.2 19
ND497.S57 A4 1983
NYPL *[3-MCV S65 85-2305]*

BARBIE DOLLS - CLOTHING - CATALOGS.
Eames, Sarah Sink. Barbie fashion /. Paducah,
Ky. , c1990- v. <1- > : ISBN 0-89145-418-7 (v.
1) : DDC 688.7/221/0979493075 20
NK4894.3.B37 E17 1990

Barbie fashion /. Eames, Sarah Sink. Paducah,
Ky. , c1990- v. <1- > : ISBN 0-89145-418-7 (v.
1) : DDC 688.7/221/0979493075 20
NK4894.3.B37 E17 1990

Barbier, Nicole. Claudel, Camille, 1864-1943. C.
Claudel . Martigny, Suisse , c1990. 167 p. :
DDC 730/.92 20
NB553.C44 A4 1990b

Barbknecht, Monika. Der Mittelalterliche
Baubetrieb Westeuropas . Köln , 1987. 568 p. :
DDC 760/.044969 19
N8217.B85 M58 1987
NYPL *[3-MAMZ 91-4597]*

Barbosa, Marcos. Mosteiro de São Bento / texto
de Marcos Barbosa ; fotos de Hugo Leal. Rio
de Janeiro Brasil : Edições "Lumen Christi,"
1984. [8] p., xviii leaves of plates : ill. ; 38 cm.
Issued in portfolio. Portuguese and English
*1. Mosterio de São Bento do Rio de Janeiro - Pictorial
works. I. Leal, Hugo. II. Title.*
NYPL *[3-MRBB + 88-775]*

Barbour, David. The landscape : eight Canadian
photographers = Le paysage : huit
photographes canadiens / David Barbour.
[Kleinburg, Ont.] : McMichael Canadian Art
Collection, c1990. 63 p. : ill. (some col.) ; 25 x
29 cm. English and French. "Catalogue to accompany
an exhibition held at McMichael Canadian Art
Collection from August 19 to December 2, 1990"--T.p.
verso. Includes bibliographical references. ISBN
0-7729-7293-1 DDC 779/.3671 20
*1. Photography - Landscapes - Exhibitions. 2.
Photographers - Canada - Biography. I. McMichael
Canadian Collection. II. Title. III. Title: Paysage : huit
photographes canadiens.* **NYPL** *[MFW 91-6157]*

Barceló, Miquel, 1957- Moral, Jean-Marie del,
1952- Les temps du peintre . Niort [1987] 99
p. :
TR681.A7 M68 1987
NYPL *[3-MAN 90-10272]*

Barcelona, city and architecture, 1980-1992 /.
Bohigas, Oriol. New York , 1991. 239 p. :
ISBN 0-8478-1354-1 : DDC 720/.946/7209048
20
NA1311.B3 B64 1991

**Barcelona. Colegio Oficial de Arquitectos de
Cataluña y Baleares.** see Colegio Oficial de
Arquitectos de Cataluña y Baleares.

Barcelona fi de segle : façanes i monuments.
Barcelona : GEA Edicions, [198-] 1 portfolio
([10] leaves of plates) : ill. ; 36 x 43 cm. Title
from portfolio.
*1. Façades - Spain - Barcelona - Catalogs. 2.
Monuments - Spain - Barcelona - Catalogs. 3.
Architectural drawing - 19th century - Spain -
Barcelona - Catalogs. 4. Barcelona (Spain) - Buildings,
structures, etc. - Catalogs.*
NA2706.S7 B37 1980z

Barcelona. Sala Gaspar. see Sala Gaspar.

**Barcelona (Spain : Province). Servei de
Catalogació i Conservació de Monuments.**
Història i arquitectura . Barcelona [1986?] 260
p. : ISBN 84-505-2551-9
NA1309.B29 H57 1986
NYPL *[3-MQWH+ 90-12046]*

**BARCELONA (SPAIN) - BUILDINGS,
STRUCTURES, ETC.**
Bohigas, Oriol. Barcelona, city and architecture,
1980-1992 /. New York , 1991. 239 p. : ISBN
0-8478-1354-1 : DDC 720/.946/7209048 20
NA1311.B3 B64 1991

**BARCELONA (SPAIN) - BUILDINGS,
STRUCTURES, ETC. - CATALOGS.**
Barcelona fi de segle . Barcelona [198-] 1
portfolio ([10] leaves of plates) :
NA2706.S7 B37 1980z

Barcelona (Spain). Museo de Arte Moderno.
Hugué, Manuel, 1872-1945. Manolo Hugué .
[Catalunya] [Barcelona] [1990?] 269 p. :
ISBN 84-7609-342-X
IN PROCESS (ONLINE)
NYPL *[3-MGO (Hugué) 91-6103]*

Barche, Gisela, 1949- Bellotto, Bernardo,
1721-1780. Bernardo Bellotto . Milano , c1990.

172 p. : ISBN 88-435-3242-1
ND623.B43 A4 1990

Bardasano, José. Mi patria sangra : estampas de
la independencia de España / por Bardasano.
[Barcelona] : Publicaciones Antifeixistes de
Catalunya, [193-] [3] p., 13 leaves of plates : ill.
(some col.) ; 35 cm. Cover title.
*1. Bardasano, José. 2. Spain - History - Civil War,
1936-1939 - Posters. I. Title.*
                    NYPL [3-MCQ+ B24 90-8712]

BARDASANO, JOSÉ.
Bardasano, José. Mi patria sangra . [Barcelona]
[193-] [3] p., 13 leaves of plates :
                    NYPL [3-MCQ+ B24 90-8712]

Bardazzi, Silvestro. Arredi e paramenti : S.
Vincenzo, S. Niccolò, S. Clemente in Prato /
[testi di] Silvestro Bardazzi [ed] Eugenio
Castellani ; [fotografie di Eugenio e Marcello
Castellani]. Prato : Edizioni del Palazzo, c1988.
318 p. : chiefly ill. (chiefly col.) ; 33 cm.
Includes index. Bibliography: p. 305-306.
*1. Monastero di S. Clemente (Prato, Italy). 2. San
Niccolo (Church : Prato, Italy). 3. S. Vincenzo in Prato
(Church : Milan, Italy). 4. Church decoration and
ornament - Italy - Prato. 5. Church vestments - Italy -
Prato. 6. Church furniture - Italy - Prato. I. Castellani,
Eugenio. II. Title.*
                    NYPL [3-MRBD+ 90-11027]

Bardey, Jeanne, 1872-1954. Thiolier, Hubert.
Jeanne Bardey et Rodin /. [Bron, France]
[1990] 270 p. : ISBN 2-9504835-3-4 DDC 709/.2
B 20
NB553.B23 T48 1990

BARDEY, JEANNE, 1872-1954.
Thiolier, Hubert. Jeanne Bardey et Rodin /.
[Bron, France] [1990] 270 p. : ISBN
2-9504835-3-4 DDC 709/.2 B 20
NB553.B23 T48 1990

Bardi, P. M. (Pietro Maria), 1900- Em torno da
escultura no Brasil / P.M. Bardi. [São Paulo,
Brazil] : Banco Sudameris Brasil, 1989. 119 p. :
ill. (some col.) ; 31 cm. (Arte e cultura . 12)
1. Sculpture, Brazilian. I. Title. II. Series.
NB350 .B37 1989

Bardon, Annie. Partenheimer, Jürgen. Jürgen
Partenheimer, Linolschnitte und Bücher .
Reutlingen , 1988. 139 p. : ISBN 90-71584-09-7
DDC 769.92 20
NE1336.P36 A4 1988
                    NYPL [MDG (Partenheimer) 90-13141]

Bareau, Juliet Wilson.
Manet, Édouard, 1832-1883. Manet by
himself . Boston , c1991. 320 p. : ISBN
0-8212-1842-5 : DDC 759.4 B 20
ND553.M3 A3 1991

Wivel, Mikael. Manet . København , 1989. 173
p. : ISBN 87-88692-04-3
ND553.M3 A4 1989

Barfod, Jörn. Lankau, Hans-Helmut. Eduard
Bischoff, 1890-1974 . Husum , c1990. 96 p. :
ISBN 3-88042-460-8 DDC 759.3 20
ND588.B5 A4 1990

Bargellini, Clara. Homenaje a Federico Sescosse .
[Zacatecas, Mexico] , 1990. xi, 140 p., [46] p.
of plates : DDC 709/.72 20
N6550 .H65 1990

Bargellini, Piero, 1897- Santa Reparata : la
cattedrale risorta / Piero Bargellini, Guido
Morozzi, Giorgio Batini. Firenze : Bonechi,
c1970. 127 p. : ill. ; 27 cm. (Italia artistica)
*1. Santa Maria del Fiore (Florence, Italy). 2. Church
architecture - Conservation and restoration. I. Morozzi,
Guido. II. Batini, Giorgio. III. Title.*
                    NYPL [3-MRBN 90-6794]

Bargheer, Eduard, 1901-1979.
Eduard Bargheer, 1901-1979, Ölbilder,
Aquarelle, Graphik : [Ausstellung]. Düsseldorf :
Galerie Vömel, 1982. [16] p. : chiefly ill. (some
col.) ; 21 cm.
*1. Bargheer, Eduard, 1901-1979 - Exhibitions. I. Galerie
Vömel.*   *NYPL [3-MCK B245 90-10707]*

**BARGHEER, EDUARD, 1901-1979 -
EXHIBITIONS.**
Bargheer, Eduard, 1901-1979. Eduard Bargheer,
1901-1979, Ölbilder, Aquarelle, Graphik .
Düsseldorf , 1982. [16] p. :
                    NYPL [3-MCK B245 90-10707]

Bari (Italy : Province). Pinacoteca provinciale.
De Nittis, Giuseppe, 1846-1884. Giuseppe De

Nittis, dipinti 1864-1884 /. [Firenze , 1990. 205
p. :   *NYPL [3-MCF N73 91-6553]*

Barilli, Renato.
Iride, schedule d'arte, Firenze '82 . Firenze ,
c1982. 107 p. : *NYPL [3-MAMC+ 90-5983]*

Levini, Felice, 1956- Felice Levini . Milano ,
1988. 77 p. :
N6923.L345 A4 1988
                    NYPL [3-MCF L665 90-12541]

Barkan, Leonard. Transuming passion :
Ganymede and the erotics of humanism /
Leonard Barkan. Stanford, Calif. : Stanford
University Press, 1991. 147 p. : ill. ; 24 cm.
Includes bibliographical references (p. [117]-141) and
index. ISBN 0-8047-1851-2 (cloth : acid-free paper) :
DDC 700 20
*1. Ganymede (Greek mythology) - Art. 2.
Homosexuality in art. 3. Arts, European. I. Title.*
NX652.G35 B37 1991
                    NYPL [3-MAMZ 91-6123]

Barker, Clive, 1952-
Clive Barker, illustrator / edited by Steve
Niles ; text by Fred Burke. Forestville, Calif. :
Arcane/Eclipse Books, c1990. iv, 124 p., [18] p.
of plates : ill. (some col.) ; 31 cm. ISBN
1-560-60026-8 (limited signed clothbound) :
DDC 741/.092 20
*1. Barker, Clive, 1952- - Themes, motives. 2. Artists'
preparatory studies - United States - Themes, motives.
I. Niles, Steve. II. Burke, Fred, 1965-. III. Title.*
NC139.B33 A4 1990

**BARKER, CLIVE, 1952- - THEMES,
MOTIVES.**
Barker, Clive, 1952- Clive Barker, illustrator /.
Forestville, Calif. , c1990. iv, 124 p., [18] p. of
plates : ISBN 1-560-60026-8 (limited signed
clothbound) : DDC 741/.092 20
NC139.B33 A4 1990

Barker, Lizzie. Kendall, Richard. Van Gogh to
Picasso . London , 1991. 209 p. : ISBN
0-947645-83-7 (hardback) DDC 709.0346 20
N6754 *NYPL [3-MAX (Berggruen) 91-8105]*

Barker, Nicolas. Fake? . London , 1990. 312 p. :
ISBN 0-7141-1703-X
N8790 .F3 1990b

Barkhouse, Joyce C. The Lorenzen collection /
by Joyce Barkhouse ; with illustrations by
Dinamarca Lorenzen-King. Halifax, N.S. :
Maritime Flavour Gallery (MCS Ventures),
1985. 58 p. : col. ill. ; 22 cm. ISBN
0-9692387-0-3 : DDC 738.0922 19
*1. Lorenzen, Alma. 2. Lorenzen, Ernst. 3. Pottery,
Canadian - Nova Scotia - Catalogs. 4. Ceramic
sculpture - 20th century - Nova Scotia - Catalogs. 5.
Mushrooms - Nova Scotia - Models - Pictorial works.
6. Mushrooms - Nova Scotia - Identification. I.
Lorenzen-King, Dinamarca. II. Title.*
                    NYPL [MPH 91-3761]

Barkla, Robin. Bradley, Gilbert, 1917- Derby
porcelain 1750-1798 /. London , 1990. 180 p. :
ISBN 0-946708-25-8 : DDC 738.207 20
NK4399.D4   *NYPL [3-MPGO 91-5746]*

Barkóczi, István. Szépművészeti Múzeum.
English. The Budapest Museum of Fine Arts /.
[Budapest] , c1985. 171 p. : ISBN 963-13-2297-1
                    NYPL [MAVZ+ (Budapest) 91-4223]

Barlach, Ernst, 1870-1938.
Paris. Musée d'Orsay. Un Sculpteur-écrivain
Ernst Barlach . Paris , 1988. 64 p. : ISBN
2-7118-2181-1 :
                    NYPL [3-MGO (Barlach) 90-4429]

BARLACH, ERNST, 1870-1938.
Reiser, Katharyn D. Ernst Barlach: 1870-1938.
[n.p., 1970] 1 v. (unpaged)
N6888.B35 R4

**BARLACH, ERNST, 1870-1938 -
EXHIBITIONS.**
Paris. Musée d'Orsay. Un Sculpteur-écrivain
Ernst Barlach . Paris , 1988. 64 p. : ISBN
2-7118-2181-1 :
                    NYPL [3-MGO (Barlach) 90-4429]

Barletta, Riccardo. Laura Fiume : affabulazioni
ironiche e altre storie / Riccardo Barletta.
Bologna : Bora, [1989] 1 v. (unpaged) : ill.
(some col.) ; 23 cm. (Collana polivalente . 21)
Italian and English. ISBN 88-85638-89-9 DDC
759.5 20
*1. Fiume, Laura, 1953- - Criticism and interpretation. 2.
Primitivism in art - Italy. I. Fiume, Laura, 1953-. II.*

Title.
ND623.F558 B37 1989

Barletti, Emanuele. Il Palazzo arcivescovile di
Firenze : vicende architettoniche dal 1533 al
1895 / Emanuele Barletti ; prefazione di
Silvano Piovanelli ; introduzione di Carlo C.
Calzolai. Firenze : [s.n.], 1989 (Firenze : Arti
grafiche "Il Torchio") 209 p. : ill. ; 30 cm.
1. Palazzo arcivescovile di Firenze. I. Title.
IN PROCESS (ONLINE)
                    NYPL [3-MQWB+ 90-12719]

Barlow, H. B. (Horace Basil) Rank Prize Funds'
International Symposium (1986 : Royal Society)
Images and understanding . Cambridge , New
York , 1990. xiii, 401 p. : ISBN 0-521-34177-9
DDC 152.1/4 19
QP474 .R36 1986   *NYPL [JFF 90-2299]*

Barlow, Raymond E.
Glass industry in Sandwich. Barlow, Raymond
E. A guide to Sandwich glass : whale oil
lamps and accessories / Raymond E. Barlow,
Joan E. Kaiser ; photographs by Forward's
Color Productions, Inc., Len Lorette, Hugo
G. Poisson ; edited by Lloyd C.
Nickerson.1st ed. West Chester, PA ,
Windham, NH , c1989. 1 v. (unpaged) :
ISBN 0-88740-171-6 DDC 749/.63 20
NK5112 .B335 1989
                    NYPL [3-MPW+ 90-10804]

A guide to Sandwich glass : whale oil lamps
and accessories / Raymond E. Barlow, Joan E.
Kaiser ; photographs by Forward's Color
Productions, Inc., Len Lorette, Hugo G.
Poisson ; edited by Lloyd C. Nickerson.1st ed.
West Chester, PA : Schiffer Pub. ; Windham,
NH : Barlow-Kaiser Pub. Co., c1989. 1 v.
(unpaged) : ill. (some col.) ; 31 cm. Guide book
with photos from v. 2 of the author's The glass industry
in Sandwich. Includes bibliographical references. ISBN
0-88740-171-6 DDC 749/.63 20
*1. Glassware - Massachusetts - Sandwich - Catalogs. 2.
Lamps - Massachusetts - Sandwich - Catalogs. 3.
Lampshades, Glass - Massachusetts - Sandwich -
Catalogs. I. Kaiser, Joan E. II. Nickerson, Lloyd C. III.
Barlow, Raymond E. Glass industry in Sandwich. IV.
Title.*
NK5112 .B335 1989
                    NYPL [3-MPW+ 90-10804]

Barlow, Sir James Alan Noel, bart., 1881-
Chinese ceramics, bronzes and jades in the
collection of Sir Alan and Lady Barlow, by
Michael Sullivan. London, Faber and Faber
[1963] 173 p. plates (part col.) maps. 29 cm.
Bibliography: p. 165-170. DDC 730.951
*1. Art objects - Private collections. I. Sullivan, Michael,
1916-. II. Title.*
NK4165 .B3   *NYPL [3-MPFF 90-11573]*

Barnabò, Francesca. Artisti italiani
contemporanei, 1956-1986 /. Venezia , 1986.
61 p. : ISBN 88-7693-024-8 DDC
709/.45/0740531 19
N6918 .A819 1986
                    NYPL [3-MAMC 90-12531]

Barnard, George N., 1819-1902. Davis, Keith F.,
1952- George N. Barnard, photographer of
Sherman's campaign /. Kansas City, Mo. ,
Albuquerque, N.M. , c1990. 232 p. : ISBN
0-87529-627-0
IN PROCESS (ONLINE)
                    NYPL [MFX+ (Barnard) 91-6015]

BARNARD, GEORGE N., 1819-1902.
Davis, Keith F., 1952- George N. Barnard,
photographer of Sherman's campaign /. Kansas
City, Mo. , Albuquerque, N.M. , c1990. 232
p. : ISBN 0-87529-627-0
IN PROCESS (ONLINE)
                    NYPL [MFX+ (Barnard) 91-6015]

Barnard, Nicholas.
Gillow, John. Traditional Indian textiles /.
London , c1991. 160 p. : ISBN 0-500-01491-4
                    NYPL [3-MON+ 91-5640]

Living with decorative textiles : tribal art from
Africa, Asia and the Americas / Nicholas
Barnard ; photographs by James Merrell.
London : Thames and Hudson, c1989. 192 p. :
ill. (some col.), maps ; 27 cm. Col. ill. on lining
papers. Includes bibliographical references. ISBN
0-500-01471-X
*1. Textile fabrics in interior decoration. I. Merrell,
James. II. Title.* *NYPL [3-MON 89-25866]*

Living with folk art : ethnic styles from around

the world / Nicholas Barnard ; photographs by
James Merrell.1st U. S. ed. Boston : Little,
Brown, 1991. p. cm. "A Bulfinch Press book."
Includes index.   ISBN 0-8212-1840-9   DDC 745/.089
20
  1. Folk art. 2. Ethnic art. I. Title.
N5313 .B37 1991

Barnes, Bernadine Ann. Russell, H. Diane (Helen
Diane) Eva/Ave . Washington : New York,
N.Y. : 238 p. :   ISBN 0-89468-157-5 (pbk.) :
  DDC 769/.424/094074753 20
NE962.W65 R87 1990
                            NYPL [MDZ 91-4755]

Barnes, Gina Lee. The Rise of a great tradition .
New York [1990?] 112 p. : ISBN 0-913304-30-1
                NYPL [3-MPFK+ 91-5067]

Barnes, Lucinda.
  Cragg, Tony, 1949- Tony Cragg, sculpture
1975-1990 /. London , New York , 1991. 177
p. :   *NYPL [3-MGO+ (Cragg) 91-4461]*
  Imágenes líricas = New Spanish visions / by
Lucinda Barnes ; edited by Lucinda Barnes and
Constance Glenn ; an exhibition organized by
the University Art Museum, California State
University, Long Beach ; co-sponsored and
circulated by Independent Curators
Incorporated, New York. Long Beach : The
Museum, c1990. 119 p. : ill (some col.) ; 30
cm. English and Spanish. Catalog of an exhibition held
at the Albright-Knox Art Gallery, Buffalo, May 12-July
1, 1990, and elsewhere through Mar. 15, 1992. Includes
interviews with the artists. Includes bibliographical
references (p. 117).   ISBN 0-936270-30-6
  1. Art, Spanish - Exhibitions. 2. Art, Modern - 20th
century - Spain - Exhibitions. 3. Artists - Spain -
Interviews. I. Glenn, Constance. II. California State
University, Long Beach. University Art Museum. III.
Independent Curators Incorporated. IV. Title. V. Title:
New Spanish visions.
                NYPL [3-MAML+ 91-5035]
  Ray, Charles, 1953- Charles Ray /. Newport
Beach, Calif. , c1990. 44 p. : ISBN
0-917493-16-8 DDC 730/.92 20
NB237.R35 A4 1990
                    NYPL [3-MGO (Ray) 91-3921]

Barnet, Miguel, 1940- Autógrafos cubanos /
Miguel Barnet. Ciudad de La Habana :
Ediciones Unión, c1990. 151 p. : ill. ; 23 cm.
  DDC 700/.97291/0904 20
  1. Arts, Cuban - Themes, motives. 2. Arts, Modern -
20th century - Cuba - Themes, motives. I. Title.
NX525.A1 B37 1990

Barnet-Sánchez, Holly. Signs from the heart .
Venice, Calif. , c1990. 105 p. :   ISBN
0-9626419-0-1   *NYPL [3-MCW 90-12027]*

Barnett Newman . Newman, Barnett, 1905-1970.
New York , 1990, c1989. xxxi, 331 p., [16] p.
of plates : ISBN 0-394-58038-9 : DDC 709.2 20
ND237.N475 B37 1990
                        NYPL [MCX N55 91-3262]

Barnett, Pennina. Embroidery in women's lives,
1300-1900. Women and textiles today /.
[Manchester, England]s , 1988. 64 p. :   ISBN
0-903261-24-3 (pbk.)
                    NYPL [3-MOT+ 89-23508]

Barnett, Richard David, 1909- British Museum.
Dept. of Western Asiatic Antiquities. Fifty
masterpieces of ancient Near Eastern art in the
Department of Western Asiatic Antiquities, the
British Museum. London, 1969. 96 p   ISBN
0-7141-1069-8 DDC 732/.5
N5345 .B7 1969   *NYPL [3-MAF 90-6059]*

Barnett, Vivian Endicott. Kandinsky
watercolours : catalogue raisonné / Vivian
Endicott Barnett. Ithaca, N.Y. : Cornell
University Press, 1992- p. cm. Includes
bibliographical references and index. CONTENTS. - v.
1. 1900-1921.   ISBN 0-8014-2690-1 DDC 759.7 20
  1. Kandinsky, Wassily, 1866-1944 - Catalogues
raisonnés. I. Title.
ND1978.K3 A4 1992

Barnhart, Richard M., 1934- Wang, Fang-yü,
1913- Master of the lotus garden . New
Haven , c1990. 299 p. : ISBN 0-89467-054-9
                        NYPL [3-MAG+ 91-3672]

Barnhart, Tim. The Helicon nine reader . Kansas
City , c1990. 512 p. : ISBN 0-9627460-0-2 DDC
700/.82 20
NX180.F4 H44 1990

Barnhill, Georgia Brady, 1944- Prints of New
England /. Worcester [Mass.] , 1991. viii, 164
p. : ISBN 0-912296-92-5 DDC 769.974 19
NE510 .P74 1989   *NYPL [MDBF 91-6177]*

Barnouw-De Ranitz, Louise. Museum Bredius.
Museum Bredius . ['s-Gravenhage] , 1980. 176
p. :   *NYPL [3-MAVZ (Hague) 81-647]*

Barocchi, Paola. Testimonianze e polemiche
figurative in Italia . Messina [1974] 507 p. ;
N6917.5.N44 B37
                            NYPL [3-MAMC 90-5898]

Barocco mediterraneo : Genova Napoli Venezia
nei musei di Francia / coordinamento della
mostra, Brigitte Daprà, Mariella Utili. [Naples] :
Electa Napoli, c1989. 245 p. : ill. (some col.),
maps, ports. ; 28 cm. Catalog of an exhibition held
in Naples at the Museo di Capodimonte, March
18-May 21, 1989. The paintings in this exhibition, and
others, were shown at the Musée des beaux-arts in
Marseilles, Oct. 8, 1988-Jan. 15, 1989, in the exhibition
entitled "Escales du Baroque." Bibliography: p. 237-242.
  ISBN 88-435-2807-6
  1. Painting, Baroque - Italy - Exhibitions. 2. Painting,
Baroque - France - Exhibitions. 3. Painting, Italian -
Italy - Genoa - Exhibitions. 4. Painting, Italian - Italy -
Naples - Exhibitions. 5. Painting, Italian - Italy -
Venice - Exhibitions. I. Daprà, Brigitte. II. Utili,
Mariella. III. Musée des beaux-arts de Marseille. IV.
Museo e gallerie nazionali di Capodimonte. V. Title:
Escales du Baroque.   *NYPL [3-MCE 91-3396]*

Barockmaler in Böhmen; Ausstellung des
Adalbert Stifter Vereins./ [Text; Erich Hubala]
München, Prestel Verlag [1961] 36 p. illus.,
plates 28 cm. Catalog of the exhibition held
May-Nov. 1961 at the Wallraf-Richartz-Museum,
Cologne, Prinz-Carl-Palais, Munich, and Germanisches
National-museum, Nuremberg.
  1. Drawing, Baroque - Czechoslovakia - Bohemia -
Exhibitions. 2. Painting, Baroque - Czechoslovakia -
Bohemia - Exhibitions. I. Hubala, Erich, 1920-. II.
Adalbert-Stifter-Verein (Munich, Germany). III.
Wallraf-Richartz-Museum. IV. Prinz-Carl-Palais
(Munich, Germany). V. Germanisches Nationalmuseum
Nürnberg. VI. Title.
N6832.B3 H8   *NYPL [3-MCY 90-5883]*

Barockskulptur : im Westfälischen Landesmuseum
für Kunst und Kulturgeschichte Münster / Géza
Jászai. Münster : Landschaftsverband
Westfalen-Lippe, 1979. 163 p. : chiefly ill. ; 23
cm. (Bildhefte des Westfälischen Landesmuseums für
Kunst und Kulturgeschichte Münster) Bibliography: p.
159-163.
  1. Westfälisches Landesmuseum für Kunst und
Kulturgeschichte Münster - Catalogs. 2. Sculpture,
Baroque - Catalogs. 3. Sculpture - Germany, West -
Münster - Catalogs. I. Jászai, Géza, 1931-. II. Series.
NB193 .B37   *NYPL [3-MGI 81-434]*

**Baroda State Museum and Picture Gallery
  (India)** Sculptures from Sāmalāji and Roḍā,
North Gujarat : in the Baroda Museum / by
Umakant P. Shah. Baroda : Published by V.L.
Devkar for the Museum and Picture Gallery,
Baroda, [1960?] vii, 136 p. : ill. (part col.) ; 28
cm. "Reprinted from the Bulletin of the Baroda
Museum and Picture Gallery"--Front cover. Illustrated
cover. Includes bibliographical references.
  1. Baroda State Museum and Picture Gallery (India). 2.
Sculpture, Hindu - India - Gujarat. I. Shah, Umakant
Premanand, 1915-. II. Title.
                        NYPL [3-MGI 90-6404]

**BARODA STATE MUSEUM AND PICTURE
  GALLERY (INDIA)**
  Baroda State Museum and Picture Gallery
(India) Sculptures from Sāmalāji and Roḍā,
North Gujarat . Baroda [1960?] vii, 136 p. :
                        NYPL [3-MGI 90-6404]

Barokní zátiší . Machytka, Lubor. Pardubice ,
1988. 37 p. :
ND182.B3 M3 1988

Barolsky, Paul, 1941-
  Giotto's father and the family of Vasari's lives /
Paul Barolsky. University Park, PA :
Pennsylvania State University Press, c1991. p.
cm. Includes bibliographical references and index.
  ISBN 0-271-00762-1 (alk. paper)   DDC
709/.2/245 B 20
  1. Artists - Italy - Family relationships. 2. Artists -
Italy - Biography. 3. Art, Renaissance - Italy. 4. Vasari,
Giorgio, 1511-1574, Vite di più eccellenti architetti,
pittori et scultori italiani. I. Title.
N6915 .B28 1991
  Michelangelo's nose : a myth and its maker /

Paul Barolsky. University Park : Pennsylvania
State University Press, c1990. xx, 169 p. : ill. ;
24 cm. Includes index. Bibliography: p. [163]-166.
  ISBN 0-271-00695-1 : DDC 700/.92 20
  1. Michelangelo Buonarroti, 1475-1564 - Criticism and
interpretation. 2. Michelangelo Buonarroti, 1475-1564 -
Psychology. 3. Arts, Renaissance - Italy. I. Title.
NX552.Z9 M533 1990
                        NYPL [3-MCF B9 91-2293]
  Why Mona Lisa smiles and other tales by
Vasari / Paul Barolsky. University Park :
Pennsylvania State University Press, c1991. xiv,
128 p. ; 24 cm. Includes bibliographical references
and index.   ISBN 0-271-00719-2 DDC 709/.2 20
  1. Vasari, Giorgio, 1511-1574 - Criticism and
interpretation. 2. Art, Renaissance - Italy. I. Vasari,
Giorgio, 1511-1574. Vite de' più eccellenti pittori. II.
Title.
N7483.V37 B36 1991
                            NYPL [3-MAMC 91-7319]

Barón, Francisco, 1931-
  Ortega Coca, María Teresa. Francisco Barón /.
[Valladolid] [1989?] 60 p., [64] p. of plates :
    ISBN 84-7852-010-4 DDC 730/.92 20
NB813.B29 A4 1989
                    NYPL [3-MGO (Barón) 91-6088]

BARÓN, FRANCISCO, 1931- - CATALOGS.
  Ortega Coca, María Teresa. Francisco Barón /.
[Valladolid] [1989?] 60 p., [64] p. of plates :
    ISBN 84-7852-010-4 DDC 730/.92 20
NB813.B29 A4 1989
                    NYPL [3-MGO (Barón) 91-6088]

Baron, Stanley. Herbert, Susan, 1945- Diary of a
Victorian cat . Boston , c1991. p. cm. ISBN
0-8212-1865-4 DDC 759.2 20
ND497.H49 A4 1991

Baron, Wendy. The Camden Town Group / by
Wendy Baron and Malcolm Cormack. New
Haven : Yale Center for British Art, 1980. xvi,
71 p. : ill. ; 28 cm. Catalog published on the
occasion of an exhibition held at the Yale Center for
British Art, New Haven, Conn., April 16-June 29,
1980. Bibliography: p. xv. ISBN 0-930606-20-5 (pbk.)
  DDC 759.21/42/07401468 19
  1. Camden Town Group - Exhibitions. 2. Art, Modern -
20th century - England - Exhibitions. I. Cormack,
Malcolm. II. Title.
N6768.5.C53 B37 1980
                            NYPL [3-MAMR 81-554]

BAROQUE ART. see ART, BAROQUE.

BAROQUE ARTS. see ARTS, BAROQUE.

Baroque in Bohemia. Národní galerie V Praze.
London, 1969. 1 v. (unpaged) DDC 709/.437/1
N6818 .P7

**BAROQUE PAINTING. see PAINTING,
  BAROQUE.**

Barotte, René. Ismaël de la Serna, silent builder--
/ René Barotte. [New York, N.Y. : Hammer
Galleries, 196-?] 31 p. : ill. ; 22 cm. In English
and French.
  1. Serna, Ismael de la, 1897?-1968. I. Serna, Ismael de
la, 1897?-1968. II. Title.
                        NYPL [3-MCQ L111 90-6381]

Barovier Mentasti, Rosa. Il vetro veneziano : dal
Medioevo al movecento / Rosa Barovier
Mentasti. Milano : Electa, 1988, c1982. 346 p. :
ill. (some col.) ; 29 cm. Includes index.
Bibliography: p. 327-330.
  1. Glassware - Italy - Venice - History. I. Title.
                        NYPL [3-MPW 90-11729]

Barr, Alfred Hamilton, 1902- (joint comp) Cahill,
Holger, 1887-1960. (comp) Art in America in
modern times. Freeport, N.Y. [1969, c1934]
110 p. DDC 700/.973
N6505 .C3 1969

Barr, John, 1934- Britain portrayed : a Regency
album, 1780-1830 / John Barr. London : British
Library, 1989. 126 p. : ill. (some col.) ; 22 x 31
cm. Includes bibliographies. ISBN 0-7123-0174-7 :
  1. Aquatint - Great Britain - 19th century. 2. Great
Britain in art. 3. Great Britain - Civilization - 19th
century - Pictorial works. I. Title.
                        NYPL [3-MAMY+ 91-4983]

Barradas, Efraín. Sturges, Hollister. New art from
Puerto Rico =. Springfield, Mass. , 1990. 84
p. : ISBN 0-916746-15-1
                        NYPL [3-MAM 91-6653]

Barral i Altet. Xavier.
  Artistes, artisans et production artistique au
Moyen Age . Paris , 1986-1990. 3 v. : ISBN

2-7084-0302-8 (v. 1) : DDC 338.4/77/094 19
N5961 .A78 1986   **NYPL** *[3-MAK 87-2303]*

Duby, Georges. [Sculpture. English.] Sculpture .
New York , 1990. 318 p. : ISBN 0-8478-1285-5
DDC 734 20
NB170 .D813 1990
         NYPL *[3-MGF+ 91-3656]*

Mosaico. English. The Art of mosaic /.
London , c1989. 360 p. : ISBN 0-304-31836-1
         NYPL *[3-MRXZ+ 91-4959]*

Barral, Xavier. see Barral i Altet. Xavier.

Barré-Despond, Arlette. Khan-Magomedov, S. O.
(Selim Omarovich) Vhutemas . Paris , c1990. 2
v. (880 p.) : ISBN 2-903370-55-9 (set) DDC
707/.1/147312 20
N332.S65 M675 1990

Barrena, Clemente. Estampas, 1984-1985 .
Madrid , 1988. 331 p. : ISBN 84-600-5307-5
         NYPL *[MDBF 91-5842]*

Barrera, Francesco. Il Piemonte nella cartografia
degli Stati Sardi tra restaurazione e unità
d'Italia / Francesco Barrera. [Torino] : Camera
di commercio, industria, artigianato e
agricoltura di Torino : Società degli ingegneri e
degli architetti in Torino, [1989?] 105 p. : maps
(some col.) ; 30 cm.
   1. Cartography - Italy - Piemonte - History. 2.
Cartography - Italy - Sardinia - History. I. Title.
         NYPL *[Map Div. 91-136]*

Barrett, Nancy.
Davis, Keith F., 1952- Clarence John Laughlin .
Kansas City, Mo. , c1990. 166 p. : ISBN
0-87529-629-7
        NYPL *[MFX+ (Laughlin) 91-7437]*

Parallels & contrasts. Beverly Hills, Calif. ,
Albuquerque, N.M. , c1988. 140 p. : ISBN
0-09-668081-0 DDC 779/.074 20
TR646.U62 N497 1988
         NYPL *[MFW 91-8027]*

Barrett, Terry Michael, 1945- Criticizing
photographs : an introduction to understanding
images / Terry Barrett. Mountain View, Calif. :
Mayfield Pub. Co., c1990. xii, 180 p. : ill. ; 24
cm. Includes bibliographical references (p. 158-167)
and index. ISBN 0-87484-906-3 DDC 770/.1 20
   I. Title.
TR642 .B365 1990   **NYPL** *[MFW 91-5783]*

Barrié, Roger. Châteaux de Haut-Léon .
Saint-Brice-en Coglès , c1987. 32 p. : ISBN
2-86934-006-0
         NYPL *[3-MQWF+ 90-5362]*

Barrier Free Environments, inc. The Accessible
housing design file / New York, N.Y. , c1991.
p. cm. ISBN 0-442-00775-2 DDC 728/.042 20
NA2545.P5 A34 1991

Barrière, C. L'art pariétal de Rouffignac : la
grotte aux cent mammouths / Claude Barrière.
Paris : Picard, 1982. 205 p., [4] folded leaves of
plates : ill. (some col.) ; 34 cm. (Mémoire no IV
de l'Institut d'art préhistorique de Toulouse) Spine title:
Rouffignac. At head of title: Fondation Singer-Polignac.
Includes bibliographical references. ISBN
2-900927-10-2 DDC 709/.01/12094472 19
   1. Art, Prehistoric - France - Rouffignac Cave. 2.
Cave-drawings - France - Rouffignac Cave. 3.
Rouffignac Cave (France). I. Fondation Singer-Polignac.
II. Title. III. Title: Rouffignac. IV. Series: Mémoire ...
de l'Institut d'art préhistorique de Toulouse , no 4.
GN772.22.F7 B343 1982
         NYPL *[3-MADF+ 91-6417]*

Barringer, J. C. Faden, William, 1750?-1836.
Faden's map of Norfolk /. Dereham, Norfolk ,
1989. 11 p., [97] p. of plates : ISBN
0-948400-09-9 (pbk.) : DDC 911/.426/1 19
         NYPL *[Map Div. 91-8124]*

Barroco mineiro, glossário de arquitetura e
ornamentação /. Avila, Affonso, 1928- [Rio de
Janeiro?] . 220 p. :
NA3533.A3 M563 1980

Barron, Roderick. Decorative maps / Roderick
Barron. London : Studio Editions, 1990,c1989.
8 p., 40 leaves of plates : col. maps ; 38 cm.
(Poster art series) ISBN 1-85170-298-9
   1. Cartography - History. 2. Maps, Early. I. Title. II.
Series.   **NYPL** *[Map Div. 91-4236]*

Barron, Stephanie.
Degenerate art . Los Angeles, Calif. , New
York , c1991. p. cm. ISBN 0-87587-158-5 DDC

709/.43/07477311 20
N6868 .D3388 1991b

Degenerate art . Los Angeles, Calif. , New
York , c1991. 423 p. : ISBN 0-8109-3653-4
DDC 709/.43/07477311 20
N6868 .D3388 1991

Robert Gore Rifkind Center for German
Expressionism Studies. German expressionist
prints and drawings . Los Angeles, Calif. :
Munich, Federal Republic of Germany : 2 v. :
   ISBN 3-7913-0959-5 (Prestel Verlag : set) DDC
760/.0943 19
N6868.5.E9 R6 1989
         NYPL *[MDE+ 91-5830]*

Barron's study keys.
Myron, Robert. Study keys to art history /.
Hauppauge, N.Y. , 1991. p. cm. ISBN
0-8120-4595-5 DDC 709 20
N5300 .M96 1991

Barros de Estremoz . Vermelho, Joaquim.
[Portugal] , 1990. 145 p. : DDC 738.8/2/0946952
20
NK4660 .V47 1990

Barrot, Olivier. Entre deux guerres . Paris ,
c1990. 631 p. ; ISBN 2-87686-057-0 : DDC
700/.944/09041 20
NX549.A1 E5 1990

BARRY COUNTY (MICH.) - MAPS.
Rockford Map Publishers. Barry County,
Michigan, land atlas & plat book . Rockford,
Ill. , Hastings, Mich. , c1990. 1 atlas (49 p.) :
         NYPL *[Map Div. 90-12842]*

Barry County, Michigan, land atlas & plat book .
Rockford Map Publishers. Rockford, Ill. ,
Hastings, Mich. , c1990. 1 atlas (49 p.) :
         NYPL *[Map Div. 90-12842]*

Barryte, Bernard. In Medusa's gaze . Rochester,
NY , c1991. p. cm. ISBN 0-918098-05-X : DDC
758/.4/074747 20
ND1390 .I5 1991

BARS - CARICATURES AND CARTOONS.
Nani, 1951- Nani em 51ns [i.e. cinquenta e
uns] cartuns de bar. [Brazil , 198-] 1 v.
(unpaged) : DDC 741.5/981 20
NC1460.N356 A4 1980z

Bartelink, Nicolette. Minder kan het niet .
Groningen , c1989. 103 p. :
         NYPL *[3-MAL 90-12610]*

BARTH, EWALD, 1898-1968 - ART
COLLECTIONS - EXHIBITIONS.
Aus einem Guss . Berlin , c1988. 248 p. :
   ISBN 3-87584-203-0 DDC
730/.0943/074431554 20
NK8250.A3 P784 1988
         NYPL *[3-MNK 91-3716]*

Barth, Gerda. Slama, Victor Th., 1890-1973. Von
der Sinnlichkeit der roten Farbe . [Wien]
[1990?] 112 p. :
NC1850.S56 A4 1990

Barth, Peter.
Conrad Felixmüller, die Dresdner Jahre
1913-1933 / Text, Peter Barth. Düsseldorf :
Galerie Remmert und Barth, 1987. 128 p. : ill.,
parts. ; 24 cm. (Die Zwanziger Jahre in Dresden . T.
1) Exhibition held at the Galerie Remmert und Barth,
Düsseldorf, from May 9th to Aug. 1st, 1987. Includes
index.
   1. Felixmüller, Conrad, 1897-1977 - Exhibitions. I.
Felixmüller, Conrad, 1897-1977. II. Galerie Remmert
und Barth. III. Title.
         NYPL *[3-MCK F316 89-18042]*

Rathke, Christian. Conrad Felixmüller .
[Schleswig] [1990] 282 p. :
         NYPL *[3-MCK F316 91-7198]*

Barth, Wolfgang. Pariser Opern- und
Konzerthäuser . Tübingen , c1989. 71 p. :
   ISBN 3-8030-0149-8
NA6840.F72 P3736 1989

Barthel Gilles, 1891-1977 . Oellers, Adam C.
Recklinghausen , c1987. 326 p. : ISBN
3-7647-0387-3
ND588.G46 O45 1987
         NYPL *[3-MCK G475 91-4613]*

Barthes, Roland.
[Obvie et l'obtus. English]
   The responsibility of forms : critical essays on
music, art, and representation / Roland
Barthes ; translated from the French by
Richard Howard. Berkeley : University of

California Press, 1991. p. cm. Translation of:
L'obvie et l'obtus. Reprint. Originally published: New
York : Hill and Wang, 1985. ISBN 0-520-07238-3
(pbk.) DDC 700 20
   1. Arts. I. Title.
NX65 .B37513 1991

Bartholdy, Felix Mendelssohn- see Mendelssohn-
Bartholdy, Felix, 1809-1847.

Bartholomäus-Schmucker-Heimatmuseum
Ruhpolding /. Paukner, Josef. München ,
c1987. 64 p. : ISBN 3-7954-0755-9
NK480.R84 P38 1987
         NYPL *[3-MNE 91-3452]*

Bartholomäi, Reinhart Chr. Internationaler
Kongress Europäisches Kunsthandwerk (1988 :
Stuttgart, Germany) Internationaler Kongress
Europäisches Kunsthandwerk 1988, Stuttgart .
Frankfurt , 1988. 56 p. ; ISBN 3-87864-176-1
         NYPL *[3-MNC+ 90-12554]*

Bartholomäus-Schmucker-Heimatmuseum
Ruhpolding. Paukner, Josef.
Bartholomäus-Schmucker-Heimatmuseum
Ruhpolding /. München , c1987. 64 p. : ISBN
3-7954-0755-9
NK480.R84 P38 1987
         NYPL *[3-MNE 91-3452]*

BARTHOLOMÄUS-SCHMUCKER-
HEIMATMUSEUM RUHPOLDING.
Paukner, Josef.
Bartholomäus-Schmucker-Heimatmuseum
Ruhpolding /. München , c1987. 64 p. : ISBN
3-7954-0755-9
NK480.R84 P38 1987
         NYPL *[3-MNE 91-3452]*

Bartlett, Bo, 1955-
Bo Bartlett : paintings and drawings : Jan.
5-Jan. 26, 1991. NYC : P.P.O.W., [1991?] 55
p. : col. ill. ; 30 cm. Bibliography: p. 53.
   1. Bartlett, Bo, 1955- - Exhibitions. I. P.P.O.W.
(Gallery). II. Title.
         NYPL *[3-MCX+ B288 91-4352]*

BARTLETT, BO, 1955- - EXHIBITIONS.
Bartlett, Bo, 1955- Bo Bartlett . NYC [1991?]
55 p. :   **NYPL** *[3-MCX+ B288 91-4352]*

Bartman, Elizabeth. Ancient sculpture copies in
miniature / by Elizabeth Bartman. Leiden ;
New York : E.J. Brill, 1992. p. cm. (Columbia
studies in the classical tradition, 0166-1302 . v. 19)
Includes bibliographical references and index. ISBN
90-04-09532-2 DDC 733/.3 20
   1. Sculpture, Greek - Copying. 2. Figurines. I. Title. II.
Series.
NB94 .B37 1992

Bartolini, Anna Maria. Effleurage / etchings by
Anna Maria Bartolini ; introduction by Mario
Graziano Parri. [Leeds, Mass.] : Gehenna Press,
1989. [13] p., [26] leaves of plates : ill. ; 36 cm.
"Thirty-eight copies of Effleurage have been printed by
the Gehenna press during the early winter of 1989. The
etchings by Anna Maria Bartolini were printed at
Florence, Italy"--Colophon. Issued in a case. LC has
copy no. 12. DLC Source: Purchase, Aug. 8, 1990.
DLC DDC 769.92 20
   1. Bartolini, Anna Maria. I. Parri, Mario Graziano,
1936-. II. Title.
NE2052.5.B364 A4 1989

BARTOLINI, ANNA MARIA.
Bartolini, Anna Maria. Effleurage /. [Leeds,
Mass.] , 1989. [13] p., [26] leaves of plates :
   DDC 769.92 20
NE2052.5.B364 A4 1989

Bartolini, Elio, 1922- Neorealismo e fotografia .
Udine , 1987. 186 p. : ISBN 88-85893-01-5
         NYPL *[MFW+ 91-4966]*

Bartolini, Luigi, 1892-1963.
Luigi Bartolini, 1892-1965 [sic] : l'uomo,
l'artista, lo scrittore. Roma : De Luca, c1989.
203 p. : ill. (some col.) ; 27 cm. Catalog of an
exhibition held at Palazzo Ricci, Macerata,
6-17/9-30/1989. Includes bibliographical references (p.
191-203). ISBN 88-7813-222-5 : DDC 760/.092 20
   1. Bartolini, Luigi, 1892-1963 - Exhibitions. I. Title.
N6923.B29 A4 1989
         NYPL *[3-MCF B28 91-4632]*

BARTOLINI, LUIGI, 1892-1963 -
EXHIBITIONS.
Bartolini, Luigi, 1892-1963. Luigi Bartolini,
1892-1965 [sic] . Roma , c1989. 203 p. : ISBN

88-7813-222-5 :   DDC 760/.092 20
N6923.B29 A4 1989
            NYPL [3-MCF B28 91-4632]

BARTOLOMEO, FRA, 1472-1517 -
CATALOGS.
Fischer, Chris. Fra Bartolommeo . Rotterdam ,
Seattle , c1990. 415 p. :   ISBN 90-6918-070-7
DDC 741.945 20
NC257.B3418 A4 1990

Barton, Carol June. Books & bookends . [S.l.] ,
c1990. 73 p. :
IN PROCESS (ONLINE)
            NYPL   [MDTT 91-6180]

Barton, Jane. Wada, Yoshiko. Shibori . Tokyo ;
New York : 303 p. :   ISBN 0-87011-559-6 (U. S.) :
DDC 746.6/64/0952 19
NK9505.5 .W3 1983
            NYPL   [3-MON+ 91-5786]

BARTON, RALPH, 1891-1931.
Kellner, Bruce. The last dandy, Ralph Barton .
Columbia , c1991. p. cm.   ISBN 0-8262-0774-X
DDC 741.6/092 B 20
NC139.B36 K45 1991

Bartoszyńska-Potemska, Albina. Wyczółkowski,
Leon, 1852-1936. Leon Wyczółkowski,
1852-1936. [Wilhelmshaven] , c1989. 77 p. :
N7255.P63 W892 1989
            NYPL   [3-MCZ+ W97 91-7562]

Bartsch, Adam von, 1757-1821.
[Peintre graveur. English]
The illustrated Bartsch / [general editor,
Walter L. Strauss]. New York : Abaris Books,
1978- v. : ill. ; 32 cm. Captions in English and
French. Originally published under title: Le
peintre graveur. Some vols. have companion vols. with
subtitle: Commentary. Includes bibliographies and
indexes.   ISBN 0-89835-000-X   DDC 760/.074
1. Engraving - Catalogs. I. Strauss, Walter L. II. Title.
NE90 .B213   NYPL [MDD+ 80-258]

Bartsch, Johann Adam Bernhard von. see
Bartsch, Adam von, 1757-1821.

Baruch College Gallery. Catalan painters and
sculptors . [Spain] [1990] 66 p. :
            NYPL   [3-MAML+ 91-4202]

BARUCHELLO, GIANFRANCO - CRITICISM
AND INTERPRETATION.
Huber, Hans Dieter, 1953- System und
Wirkung . München , c1989. 191 p., 29 p. of
plates :   ISBN 3-7705-2504-3
N6490 .H796 1989   NYPL [3-MAL 91-4622]

Baruffi, Andrea. (ill) Geringer, Laura. Yours 'til
the ice cracks . New York , 1992. p. cm.   ISBN
0-06-020399-4   DDC 741.6/84 20
NC1860 .G47 1992

Barwick, JoAnn. Scandinavian country / by
JoAnn Barwick and the editors of House
beautiful ; text by Norma Skurka. 1st ed. New
York : Clarkson Potter Publishers, c1991. p.
cm. Includes index.   ISBN 0-517-57661-9 :   DDC
745.4/4948 20
1. Decoration and ornament, Rustic - Scandinavia. 2.
Country furniture - Scandinavia. I. Skurka, Norma. II.
House beautiful. III. Title.
NK1457 .B37 1991

Barye, Antoine Louis, 1796-1875.
Pivar, Stuart. The Barye bronzes . Woodbridge,
Suffolk c1974. 307 p., [16] p. of plates :
ISBN 1-85149-142-2
            NYPL   [MGO (Barye) 91-5162]

BARYE, ANTOINE-LOUIS, 1796-1875 -
CATALOGUES RAISONNÉS.
Pivar, Stuart. The Barye bronzes . Woodbridge,
Suffolk , c1974. 307 p., [16] p. of plates :
ISBN 1-85149-142-2
            NYPL   [MGO (Barye) 91-5162]

The Barye bronzes . Pivar, Stuart. Woodbridge,
Suffolk , c1974. 307 p., [16] p. of plates :
ISBN 1-85149-142-2
            NYPL   [MGO (Barye) 91-5162]

Barzel, Amnon.
Artisti russi contemporanei . Prato , c1990. 208
p. :   ISBN 88-85191-01-0
            NYPL   [3-MAM 90-10469]

Europa oggi . Firenze , Milano , c1988. 253 p. :
ISBN 88-435-2560-3
            NYPL   [3-MAL 89-1689]

Schnabel, Julian, 1951- Julian Schnabel /.
Prato , c1989. 159 p. :   ISBN 88-85191-00-2
            NYPL   [3-MCX S358 90-4741]

BAS-RELIEF.
Nehru, Lolita. Origins of the Gandhāran style .
Delhi , 1989. xxii, 230 p. :   ISBN 0-19-562472-6
            NYPL   [3-MGI 90-11988]

Basaldúa. Whitelow, Guillermo. Héctor Basaldúa
/. [Buenos Aires, Argentina] [1980] 65 p. :
DDC 759.982 20
ND339.B3 A4 1980

Basaldúa, Héctor.
Whitelow, Guillermo. Héctor Basaldúa /.
[Buenos Aires, Argentina] [1980] 65 p. :   DDC
759.982 20
ND339.B3 A4 1980

BASALDÚA, HÉCTOR - CATALOGS.
Whitelow, Guillermo. Héctor Basaldúa /.
[Buenos Aires, Argentina] [1980] 65 p. :   DDC
759.982 20
ND339.B3 A4 1980

BASEL (SWITZERLAND) - HISTORY -
EXHIBITIONS.
Le Musée sentimental de Bâle / erausgegeben
von Barbara Huber-Greub und Stephen
Andreae ; [Idee und künstlerische Leitung:
Daniel Spoerri]. Basel , c1989. 332 p. :   ISBN
3-85700-006-X
            NYPL   [3-MAVZ (Basel) 90-13397]

Baselitz. Baselitz, Georg, 1938- [Dresdner
Frauen. English.] The women of Dresden . New
York , c1990. 43 p., 1 folded sheet of plates
(20 leaves) :   ISBN 1-87828-311-1   DDC 730/.92
20
NB588.B358 A4 1990

Baselitz, Georg, 1938-
[Dresdner Frauen. English]
The women of Dresden : October
19-November 24, 1990 ; 45 : October
19-December 1, 1990 / Georg Baselitz. New
York : Pace Gallery, c1990. 43 p., 1 folded
sheet of plates (20 leaves) : ill. (some col.) ;
31 cm. Translation of: Die Dresdner Frauen. Cover
title: Baselitz. No collective t.p.; titles transcribed
from individual title pages. Text by Thomas
McEvilley.   ISBN 1-87828-311-1   DDC 730/.92 20
1. Baselitz, Georg, 1938- - Exhibitions. I. McEvilley,
Thomas, 1939-. II. Baselitz, Georg, 1938- 45. 1990. III.
Pace Gallery. IV. Title. V. Title: Baselitz. VI. Title: 45.
VII. Title: Forty-five.
NB588.B358 A4 1990

Georg Baselitz : hero paintings. New York :
Michael Werner, [1990?] 9 p., [11] leaves of
plates : ill. ; 19 cm.
1. Baselitz, Georg, 1938- - Exhibitions. I. Michael
Werner Gallery. II. Title.
            NYPL   [3-MCK B299 91-3832]

Georg Baselitz : Druckgraphik 1985-1990 :
Ausstellung der Bayerischen Vereinsbank im
Palais Preysing, München, vom 13. März bis 4.
Mai 1991. München : Bayerische Vereinsbank,
c1991. 111 p. : ill. ; 30 cm.
1. Baselitz, Georg, 1938- - Exhibitions. I. Bayerische
Vereinsbank. II. Title.
            NYPL   [MDG+ (Baselitz) 91-8026]

Georg Baselitz, Bilder aus Berliner Privatbesitz :
Staatliche Museen zu Berlin, Nationalgalerie,
Altes Museum, 4. April-4. Juni 1990 /
[Katalog, Hartmut Ackermeier ; Mitarbeit, Tina
Aujesky, Brigitte Crockett, H.U. Davitt ;
Herausgeber, Hartmut Ackermeier]. Berlin
(West) : Nicolaische Verlagsbuchh., c1990. 94
p. : ill. ; 30 cm.   ISBN 3-87584-312-6
1. Baselitz, Georg, 1938- - Exhibitions. I.
Nationalgalerie (Germany : East). II. Title.
            NYPL   [3-MCK+ B299 90-11612]

Recent paintings by Georg Baselitz / with an
essay by Norman Rosenthal. London : Anthony
d'Offay Gallery, c1990. 65 p. : col. ill., port. ;
31 cm. Catalog of an exhibition held at the Anthony
d'Offay Gallery, Apr. 11-May 15, 1990. English, with
foreword also in German. Includes bibliographical
references.   ISBN 0-947564-30-6
1. Baselitz, Georg, 1938- - Exhibitions. I. Rosenthal,
Norman. II. Anthony d'Offay Gallery. III. Title.
            NYPL   [3-MCK+ B299 90-12324]

45. 1990. Baselitz, Georg, 1938- [Dresdner
Frauen. English.] The women of Dresden :
October 19-November 24, 1990 ; 45 :
October 19-December 1, 1990 / Georg
Baselitz. New York , c1990. 43 p., 1 folded
sheet of plates (20 leaves) :   ISBN
1-87828-311-1   DDC 730/.92 20
NB588.B358 A4 1990

BASELITZ, GEORG, 1938- - EXHIBITIONS.
Baselitz, Georg, 1938- [Dresdner Frauen.
English.] The women of Dresden . New York ,
c1990. 43 p., 1 folded sheet of plates (20
leaves) :   ISBN 1-87828-311-1   DDC 730/.92 20
NB588.B358 A4 1990

Baselitz, Georg, 1938- Georg Baselitz . New
York [1990?] 9 p., [11] leaves of plates :
            NYPL   [3-MCK B299 91-3832]

Baselitz, Georg, 1938- Georg Baselitz .
München , c1991. 111 p. :
            NYPL   [MDG+ (Baselitz) 91-8026]

Baselitz, Georg, 1938- Georg Baselitz, Bilder
aus Berliner Privatbesitz . Berlin (West) ,
c1990. 94 p. :   ISBN 3-87584-312-6
            NYPL   [3-MCK+ B299 90-11612]

Baselitz, Georg, 1938- Recent paintings by
Georg Baselitz /. London , c1990. 65 p. :
ISBN 0-947564-30-6
            NYPL   [3-MCK+ B299 90-12324]

BASF Aktiengesellschaft.
Compton, Susan P. [Marc Chagall. English.]
Marc Chagall . Munich, Federal Republic of
Germany , New York, NY, USA , c1990. 268
p. :   ISBN 3-7913-1064-X   DDC 760/.092 20
N6999.C46 A4 1990

Compton, Susan P. [Marc Chagall. English.]
Marc Chagall . Munich , New York, NY,
USA , c1990. 268 p. :   ISBN 3-7913-1064-X
            NYPL   [3-MCZ+ C43 90-13436]

Basic drawing techniques /. Albert, Greg, 1953-
Cincinnati, Ohio , c1991. p. cm.   ISBN
0-89134-388-1 (pbk.) :   DDC 741.2 20
NC730 .A52 1991

A basic history of art /. Janson, H. W. (Horst
Woldemar), 1913- Englewood Cliffs, N.J. , New
York , 1991. p. cm.   ISBN 0-13-062878-6   DDC
709 20
N5300 .J29 1991

Basic principles & language of fine art /. Cortel,
Tine. Newton Abbot , New York, N.Y. , 1989.
116 p. :   ISBN 0-7153-9475-4   DDC 750/.18 20
ND1500 .C67 1989

Basic principles and language of fine art. Cortel,
Tine. Basic principles & language of fine art /.
Newton Abbot , New York, N.Y. , 1989. 116
p. :   ISBN 0-7153-9475-4   DDC 750/.18 20
ND1500 .C67 1989

Basic watercolor techniques / edited by Greg
Albert and Rachel Wolf. 1st ed. Cincinnati,
Ohio : North Light Books, 1991. p. cm. Includes
index.   ISBN 0-89134-387-3 :   DDC 751.42/2 20
1. Watercolor painting - Technique. I. Albert, Greg,
1953-. II. Wolf, Rachel, 1951-.
ND2420 .B37 1991

Basile, E. I. (Elisabetta Ingrid) I Supporti nelle
arti pittoriche . Milano , c1990. 2 v. :   DDC
702/.8/8 20
ND1640 .S89 1990

BASILICA DI SAN MARCO (VENICE,
ITALY)
Butor, Michel. Description de San Marco /.
[Paris] [1989], c1963. 111 p., [1] folded leaf of
plates :   ISBN 2-07-021099-5
            NYPL   [3-MRBN 91-4656]

BASILICA DI SAN PIETRO IN VATICANO.
Thelen, Heinrich. Zur Entstehungsgeschichte
der Hochaltar-Architektur von St. Peter in Rom
/. Berlin , c1967. 77 p., [34] p. of plates :
            NYPL   [3-MRBV 90-6917]

Basilica di Sant'Antonio (Padua, Italy)
Donatello, 1386?-1466. Donatello . Padova ,
c1989. 185 p. (some folded) :   ISBN
88-7026-883-7
            NYPL   [3-MGO+ (Donatello) 91-3657]

BASILICA DI SANT'ANTONIO (PADUA,
ITALY)
Donatello, 1386?-1466. Donatello . Padova ,
c1989. 185 p. (some folded) :   ISBN
88-7026-883-7
            NYPL   [3-MGO+ (Donatello) 91-3657]

Basilica palladiana (Vicenza, Italy) I Tiepolo e il
Settecento vicentino /. Milano , c1990. 404 p. :
ISBN 88-435-3180-8
            NYPL   [3-MAMC 91-5454]

BASILICAS.
White, L. Michael. Building God's house in the
Roman world . Baltimore, Md. , c1990. xv, 211

p. : ISBN 0-8018-3906-8 (alk. paper)
NA4817 .W55 1990
NYPL [3-MQN 90-10439]

Basis katalogus van de Belgische postkaarten.
Esteveny, François. Catalogue de base des
cartes postales belges =. [Bruxelles] [1987]
269, [2] p. :
NC1878.7.B4 E88 1987

BASKET MAKING - PENNSYLVANIA.
Lasansky, Jeannette. Willow, oak & rye .
University Park, Pa. , c1979. 60 p. : ISBN
0-271-00229-8 DDC 746.4/1
TT879.B3 L37 **NYPL [3-MNE 81-851]**

BASKET MAKING - POLYNESIA.
Arbeit, Wendy. Baskets in Polynesia /.
Honolulu , c1990. x, 116 p., [8] p. of plates :
ISBN 0-8248-1281-6 (alk. paper) DDC
746.41/2/0996 20
TT879.B3 A7 1990 **NYPL [3-MNE 91-7015]**

**BASKET MAKING - UNITED STATES -
HISTORY - 20TH CENTURY -
EXHIBITIONS.**
McQueen, John, 1943- John McQueen .
Washington, D.C. , 1991. p. ISBN 0-295-97153-3
DDC 746.41/2/092 20
NK3649.55.U64 M372 1991

Baskets in Polynesia /. Arbeit, Wendy.
Honolulu , c1990. x, 116 p., [8] p. of plates :
ISBN 0-8248-1281-6 (alk. paper) DDC
746.41/2/0996 20
TT879.B3 A7 1990 **NYPL [3-MNE 91-7015]**

Baskett, John. Mellon, Paul. Reflections in a
silver spoon . New York , 1992. p. cm. ISBN
0-688-09723-5 DDC 709/.2 B 20
N5220 .M552 1992

BASKETWORK - PHILIPPINES.
Lane, Robert F. Philippine basketry . Makati,
Metro Manila, Philippines , c1986. x, 220, [1]
p. : ISBN 971-13-4014-3 DDC 746.41/2/09599 19
NK3649.5 .L36 1986
NYPL [3-MNE 90-13051]

Baskin, Leonard, 1922- Gunn, Thom. Mandrakes
/. [London] , c1973. 33, [3] p. : DDC 821/.9/14
PR6013.U65 M3
NYPL [*KP+ (Rampant) 76-52]

Başörtü. Akkent, Meral. Das Kopftuch .
Frankfurt a.M. , 1987. 286 p. : ISBN
3-924320-61-6 :
GT2113 .A35 1987
NYPL [3-MMV+ 91-4637]

BASQUES IN ART.
Fornells Angelats, Montserrat, 1953- Los
lienzos de José María Sert en la Iglesia de San
Telmo, de José de San Sebastián /. San Sebastián ,
1985. 206, [12] p. :
ND813.S47 F67 1985
NYPL [3-MCQ S49 90-13288]

Basquiat, Jean Michel.
Jean-Michel Basquiat : das zeichnerische Werk
/ herausgegeben von Carl Haenlein ; mit
Texten von Carsten Ahrens, Demosthenes
Davvetas, Carl Haenlein und Keith Haring.
Hannover : Kestner-Gesellschaft, 1989. [122]
p. : ill. (chiefly col.), port. ; 30 cm. (Katalog .
4/1989) Catalog of an exhibition held at
Kestner-Gesellschaft, Hannover, Sept. 15-Oct. 22, 1989.
Includes bibliographical references.
*1. Basquiat, Jean Michel - Exhibitions. I. Haenlein, Carl
Albrecht. II. Ahrens, Carsten. III. Series:
Kestner-Gesellschaft. Katalog, 1989/4. IV. Title.*
**NYPL [3-MAW (Hanover) 73-2900
1989/4]**

Jean-Michel Basquiat : 21 October to 25
November 1989. New York, NY : Vrej
Baghoomian, c1989. 153 p. : chiefly col. ill. ; 31
cm. Includes bibliographical references (p. 152-153).
ISBN 0-922678-03-0 DDC 760/.092 20
*1. Basquiat, Jean Michel - Exhibitions. I. Vrej
Baghoomian Gallery. II. Title.*
N6608.B276 A4 1989
NYPL [3-MCX+ B317 91-3366]

Jean Michel Basquiat drawings / edited by
John Cheim ; introduction by Robert Storr. 1st
paperback ed. Boston : Little, Brown, c1990. p.
cm. Catalog of an exhibition held at the Robert Miller
Gallery, New York in Nov. 1990. "A Bulfinch Press
book." Includes bibliographical references. ISBN
0-8212-1887-5 : DDC 741.973 20
1. Basquiat, Jean Michel - Exhibitions. I. Cheim, John.

II. Robert Miller Gallery (New York, N.Y.). III. Title.
NC179.B37 A4 1990

**BASQUIAT, JEAN MICHEL -
EXHIBITIONS.**
Basquiat, Jean Michel. Jean-Michel Basquiat .
Hannover , 1989. [122] p. : **NYPL [3-MAW
(Hanover) 73-2900 1989/4]**

Basquiat, Jean Michel. Jean-Michel Basquiat .
New York, NY , c1989. 153 p. : ISBN
0-922678-03-0 DDC 760/.092 20
N6608.B276 A4 1989
NYPL [3-MCX+ B317 91-3366]

Basquiat, Jean Michel. Jean Michel Basquiat
drawings /. Boston , c1990. p. ISBN
0-8212-1887-5 : DDC 741.973 20
NC179.B37 A4 1990

Basquin, Kit. Images of death in contemporary
art . Milwaukee, Wis. , c1990. 56 p. : ISBN
0-87462-902-X **NYPL [3-MAMZ 91-7063]**

Bass fever . Cochran, Bruce. Minocqua, WI ,
c1991. p. cm. ISBN 1-559-71126-4 (hardcover) :
DDC 741.5/973 20
NC1429.C619 A4 1991

Basseches, Joshua T., 1962- The scrimshaw of
Manuel Cunha, late work from Madeira
revealed / Joshua T. Basseches. Sharon, Mass.,
USA : Kendall Whaling Museum, 1988. 19 p. :
ill. ; 28 cm. (Kendall Whaling Museum monograph
series . no. 2) Includes bibliographical references.
ISBN 0-937854-26-3 DDC 736/.62 20
*1. Cunha, Manuel de Paiva e, 1910-1987 - Themes,
motives. 2. Scrimshaws - Madeira (Madeira Islands) -
Themes, motives. I. Title. II. Series.*
NK6022 .B38 1988

Bassegoda i Hugas, Bonaventura. Pacheco,
Francisco, 1564-1644. Arte de la pintura /.
Madrid , c1990. 782 p. : ISBN 84-376-0871-6
DDC 750 20
ND1130 .P2 1990

Bassi, Elena. Milesi, Alessandro, 1856-1945.
Alessandro Milesi, pittore . Venezia , c1989.
237 p. : **NYPL [3-MCF+ M645 90-91]**

BASSUS, JUNIUS - TOMB.
Malbon, Elizabeth Struthers. The iconography
of the sarcophagus of Junius Bassus /.
Princeton, N.J. , c1990. xix, 256 p., [22] p. of
plates : ISBN 0-691-07355-4 (alk. paper) : DDC
733/.5/09376 20
NB1810 .M26 1990
NYPL [3-MGH 91-4522]

Det Bästas stora världsatlas. Reader's Digest
Association (Great Britain) [Reader's digest
great world atlas. Swedish.] Stockholm , c1978.
1 atlas (215 p.) : ISBN 91-7030-070-4
NYPL [Map Div. 91-7523]

Bastert, Nicolaas, 1854-1939. Jonge, Lia de.
Nicolaas Bastert . Alphen aan den Rijn , 1990.
120 p. : ISBN 90-6471-238-7 :
ND653.B36 J66 1990

BASTERT, NICOLAAS, 1854-1939.
Jonge, Lia de. Nicolaas Bastert . Alphen aan
den Rijn , 1990. 120 p. : ISBN 90-6471-238-7 :
ND653.B36 J66 1990

Bastian, Jacques. Musée de l'hôtel Sandelin.
Chefs-d'œuvre de la faïence du Musée de
Saint-Omer . Saint-Omer , c1988. 245 p. : DDC
738.3/7/0940744427 20
NK4305 .M78 1988
NYPL [3-MPGG+ 90-12652]

Bastin, Christine. Watelet, Jacques Grégoire,
1917- Serrurier-Bovy . Paris [1989, c1987] 134
p. : **NYPL [MOF 91-6858]**

Bastos de Ávila, Fernando. see Ávila, Fernando
Bastos de.

Basu, Bishnu. Sukumāra Rāya, śilpa o sāhitya /.
Kalakātā , 1989. 216 p. :
NX576.Z9 R388 1989

Bateau-Lavoir (Gallery : Paris, France) Redon,
Odilon, 1840-1916. Odilon Redon; dessins,
eaux-fortes, lithographies. Paris , 1969. [33] p. :
NE650 .R4 A47
NYPL [MDG (Redon) 90-6457]

Bates, David, 1952-
David Bates : November 6-24, 1990. New
York, NY : Charles Cowles Gallery, c1990.
[42] p. : col. ill. ; 26 cm. Text by Ronny Cohen.

*1. Bates, David, 1952- - Exhibitions. I. Cohen, Ronny.
II. Charles Cowles Gallery. III. Title.*
NYPL [3-MCX B329 91-4403]

BATES, DAVID, 1952- - EXHIBITIONS.
Bates, David, 1952- David Bates . New York,
NY , c1990. [42] p. :
NYPL [3-MCX B329 91-4403]

Bateson, Margaret. Lellie, Herman. A Victorian
dollhouse /. New York , 1991. p. cm. ISBN
0-312-06228-1 : DDC 688.7/23 20
NK4893 .L39 1991

Bath, Eng. Holburne of Menstrie Museum. see
Holburne of Menstrie Museum.

Batini, Giorgio. Bargellini, Piero, 1897- Santa
Reparata . Firenze , c1970. 127 p. :
NYPL [3-MRBN 90-6794]

Batkin, Maureen.
Atterbury, Paul. The dictionary of Minton /.
Woodbridge, Suffolk, England , 1990. 370 p. :
ISBN 1-85149-073-6 : DDC 738/.0942 19
NYPL [3-MPGO 90-10594]

The Parian phenomenon . Shepton Beauchamp,
Somerset, Eng. , 1989. 268 p. : ISBN
0-903685-22-1
NYPL [3-MPGO+ 90-2731]

Batkin, Norton. Photography and philosophy /
Norton Batkin. New York : Garland Pub.,
1990, c1981. xiii, 219 p. : ill. ; 25 cm. (Harvard
dissertations in philosophy) Thesis (Ph. D.)--Harvard
University, 1981. Includes bibliographical references (p.
216-219). ISBN 0-8240-3389-2 (alk. paper) : DDC
770/.1 20
1. Photography - Philosophy. I. Title. II. Series.
TR183 .B27 1990 **NYPL [MFW 91-3465]**

Batlle, Manuel Arturo Peña. see Peña Batlle,
Manuel Arturo.

Bätschmann, Oskar, 1943-
**Dialektik der Malerei von Nicolas Poussin.
English. 1990.** Bätschmann, Oskar, 1943-
Nicolas Poussin, dialectics of painting /
Oskar Bätschmann. London , 1990. viii, 163
p. : ISBN 0-948462-10-8
NYPL [3-MCO P87 91-6812]

Nicolas Poussin, dialectics of painting / Oskar
Bätschmann. London : Reaktion Books, 1990.
viii, 163 p. : ill. (some col.) ; 29 cm. "Part I was
first published in German in 1982 as Dialektik der
Malerei von Nicolas Poussin by the Schweizerisches
Institut für Kunstwissenschaft, Zürich"--T.p. verso.
Includes index. Bibliography: p. 150-155. ISBN
0-948462-10-8
*1. Poussin, Nicolas, 1594?-1665. I. Poussin, Nicolas,
1594?-1665. II. Bätschmann, Oskar, 1943- Dialektik der
Malerei von Nicolas Poussin. English. 1990. III. Title.*
NYPL [3-MCO P87 91-6812]

Batsford vocational handbooks.
Gatrell, Anthony. Dictionary of floristry and
flower arranging /. London , 1988. 184 p., [2]
p. of plates : ISBN 0-7134-5904-2 :
NYPL [MLT 90-12341]

Battersea Arts Centre. Lawson, Thomas. Thomas
Lawson. Glasgow, Scotland , 1990. 96 p. :
ISBN 0-906474-96-5
NYPL [3-MCV L423 91-6447]

Battie, David.
Sotheby's concise encyclopedia of glass /.
Boston , c1991. p. ISBN 0-316-08374-7 : DDC
748.29 20
NK5104 .S66 1991

Sotheby's concise encyclopedia of porcelain /.
London , 1990. 208 p. : ISBN 1-85029-251-5 :
DDC 738.209 20
NK4370 **NYPL [MPC 91-3277]**

Battilotti, Donata. Le ville di Palladio / Donata
Battilotti. Milano : Electa, c1990. 139 p. : ill.
(some col.) ; 24 cm. (Guide artistiche Electa)
Includes bibliographical references (p. 135-139). ISBN
88-435-3085-2 DDC 728.8/092 20
*1. Palladio, Andrea, 1508-1580 - Catalogs. 2.
Architecture, Domestic - Italy - Veneto - Catalogs. I.
Title. II. Series.*
NA7594 .B34 1990
NYPL [3-MQZ (Palladio, A.) 91-5518]

Battistoni Filho, Duílio, 1937- Iniciação às artes
plásticas no Brasil / Duílio Battistoni Filho.
Campinas, SP, Brasil : Papirus Editora, [1990]
97 p. : ill. ; 21 cm. Includes bibliographical
references (p. 95-97). ISBN 85-308-0098-2 DDC
709/.81 20

1. Art, Brazilian. I. Title.
N6650 .B38 1990

Batty, J. (Joseph) Landseer, Edwin Henry, Sir, 1802-1873. Landseer's animal illustrations /. Alton, Hampshire, England , 1990. 168 p. :
ISBN 1-85259-189-7
    NYPL [3-MCV L26 91-4225]

Batz, Eugen, 1905-
Eugen Batz : vom Bauhaus bis zur Gegenwart : Bilder aus dem Gesamtwerk : 25. Februar-12. April 1989, Galerie Hedwig Döbele, Ravensburg / [Autor, Rainer Wick]. Ravensburg : Die Galerie, c1989. 65 p. : chiefly col. ill. ; 20 cm. Price list inserted. Includes bibliographical references.
1. Batz, Eugen, 1905- - Exhibitions. I. Wick, Rainer. II. Galerie Döbele. III. Title.
    NYPL [3-MCK B3365 90-262]

BATZ, EUGEN, 1905- - EXHIBITIONS.
Batz, Eugen, 1905- Eugen Batz . Ravensburg , c1989. 65 p. :
    NYPL [3-MCK B3365 90-262]

BAUDE, HENRI, 15TH CENTURY - CRITICISM AND INTERPRETATION.
Baude, Henri, 15th century. Dictz moraulx pour faire tapisserie /. Paris , 1988. 89 p. : ISBN 2-903920-04-4
    NYPL [3-MCO B328 89-89984]

Baudelaire and caricature . Hannoosh, Michele, 1954- University Park, Pa. , c1992. p. cm.
ISBN 0-271-00804-0 (acid-free paper) : DDC 741.5/09 20
NC1325 .H36 1992

Baudelaire, Charles, 1821-1867.
BAUDELAIRE, CHARLES, 1821-1867 - PHILOSOPHY.
Hannoosh, Michele, 1954- Baudelaire and caricature . University Park, Pa. , c1992. p. cm.
ISBN 0-271-00804-0 (acid-free paper) : DDC 741.5/09 20
NC1325 .H36 1992

FLEURS DU MAL. ENGLISH. SELECTIONS - ILLUSTRATIONS.
Blasphemies, ecstasies, cries . [London] , 1989. 71 p. : ISBN 1-87081-425-8
    NYPL [3-MAL 90-11604]

Baudenkmale in Niedersachsen / herausgegeben vom Niedersächsischen Ministerium für Wissenschaft und Kunst ; [bearbeitet von Dirk Jonkanski, mit Beiträgen von Kathrin Dittmer und Angelika Meyer ; Einführung, Hans-Herbert Möller]. Hannover : Schlütersche, c1990. 356 p. : col. ill., col. map ; 30 cm. Includes bibliographical references (p. 353) and index.
ISBN 3-87706-322-5 DDC 720/.943/59 20
1. Architecture - Germany - Lower Saxony. I. Jonkanski, Dirk. II. Dittmer, Kathrin. III. Meyer, Angelika. IV. Lower Saxony (Germany). Ministerium für Wissenschaft und Kunst.
NA1081 .B38 1990

Baudin in Australian waters : the artwork of the French voyage of discovery to the Southern lands 1800-1804 : with a complete descriptive catalogue of drawings and paintings of Australian subjects by C.-A. Lesueur and N.-M. Petit from the Lesueur Collection in the Muséum d'Histoire Naturelle, Le Havre, France / edited by Jacqueline Bonnemains, Elliott Forsyth and Bernard Smith. Melbourne : Oxford University Press in association with the Australian Academy of the Humanities, 1988. 347 p. : ill. (some col.), maps ; 36 cm. Maps also on endpapers. Includes indexes. Bibliography: p. 341-344. ISBN 0-19-554787-X
1. Baudin, Nicolas, 1754-1803. 2. Australia in art. 3. Australia - Discovery and exploration. I. Lesueur, Charles Alexandre, 1778-1846. II. Petit, Nicolas-Martin. III. Bonnemains, Jacqueline. IV. Forsyth, Elliot William. V. Smith, Bernard. VI. Muséum d'histoire naturelle du Havre.   *NYPL [3-MAMY+ 90-10770]*

BAUDIN, NICOLAS, 1754-1803.
Baudin in Australian waters . Melbourne , 1988. 347 p. : ISBN 0-19-554787-X
    NYPL [3-MAMY+ 90-10770]

Baudoin, Jacques. Les croix du Massif central / Jacques Baudoin. Nonette [France] : Créer, [1989] 346 p., [36] p. of plates : ill. (some col.) ; 32 cm. Includes index. Includes bibliographical references (p. 199-201). ISBN 2-902894-64-3 DDC 730/.944/59 20
1. Crosses - France - Massif Central Region - Themes,

motives. 2. Sculpture, French - France - Massif Central Region - Themes, motives. 3. Crosses - France - Massif Central Region - Cultus. I. Title.
CC321.M37 B38 1989
    NYPL [3-MAIH+ 90-8320]

Baudot, François. Les assises du siècle / François Baudot ; photographies, François Boissonnet. Paris : Éditions Du May, c1990. 116 p. : col. ill. ; 26 cm. ISBN 2-906450-46-4 DDC 749/.32/0904 20
1. Chairs - History - 19th century. 2. Chairs - History - 20th century. I. Title.
NK2715 .B3 1990

Baudouin, Piet. Vlaamse kunst van de oorsprong tot heden. Italian. L'Arte fiamminga dalle origini ai giorni nostri /. Milano , 1988. 589 p. [1] folded leaf of plates :
    NYPL [3-MAME+ 91-5411]

Baudrillard, Jean.
Enrico Baj : transparence du kitsch / Enrico Baj. Paris : Éditions de la Différence : Galerie Beaubourg, c1990. 55 p. : col. ill. ; 40 cm. (L'Autre musée. Grandes monographies) ISBN 2-7291-0617-0 : DDC 759.5 20
1. Baj, Enrico, 1924- - Criticism and interpretation. I. Baj, Enrico, 1924-. II. Title. III. Series.
ND623.B17 B38 1990

Please follow me. 1983. Calle, Sophie. [Suite venitienne.] Suite venitienne / Sophie Calle. Please follow me / Jean Baudrillard. [Paris] , 1983. 93 p. : ISBN 2-86642-005-5
    NYPL [MFX (Calle) 90-11190]

Baudson, Françoise, 1913- Le Style troubadour . Bourg-en-Bresse , 1971. 107 p., 18 p. of plates :
    NYPL [3-MAMI 90-7037]

Bauen im Dritten Reich / [Herausgeber, Informationszentrum Raum und Bau der Fraunhofer-Gesellschaft ; redaktionelle Bearbeitung, Folker Frank]. 3. erw. Aufl. Stuttgart : IRB Verlag, [1989] 73 p. ; 21 cm. (IRB-Literaturauslese, 0724-5548 . Nr. 371) Includes indexes. ISBN 3-8167-0278-3
1. National socialism and architecture - Bibliography. 2. Architecture - Germany - Bibliography. 3. Architecture, Modern - 20th century - Germany - Bibliography. I. Frank, Folker. II. Fraunhofer-Gesellschaft. Informationszentrum Raum und Bau.
    NYPL [3-MQWD 90-10818]

Bauen im Grenzland . Prokop, Eva. Aachen [1989] 227 p. : ISBN 3-89399-092-5
NA7350.A23 P76 1989

Bauen in Berlin, 1973 bis 1987 /. Behr, Adalbert. Leipzig , 1987. 199 p. : ISBN 3-7338-0040-0 DDC 720/.9431/55 20
NA1085 .B437 1987

Bauen vor der Stadt . Bauen vor der Stadt. English & German. Basel , c1991. p. cm. ISBN 3-7643-2629-8 : DDC 720/.9494/33 20
NA1349.B38 B3813 1991

Bauen vor der Stadt. English & German. Bauen vor der Stadt : Beispiel, Kanton Basel-Landschaft / herausgegeben von Dieter Wronsky und Werner Blaser = Suburban building : example, Basel-Country / edited by Dieter Wronsky and Werner Blaser ; with contributions by Christoph Allenspach, Hans Rudolf Heyer, and Dieter Wronsky ; [Übersetzung ins Englische, D.Q. Stephenson]. Basel ; Boston : Birkhäuser Verlag, c1991. p. cm. ISBN 3-7643-2629-8 : DDC 720/.9494/33 20
1. Architecture - Switzerland - Baselland. 2. Architecture, Modern - 20th century - Switzerland - Baselland. 3. Suburbs - Switzerland - Baselland. I. Wronsky, Dieter, 1934-. II. Blaser, Werner, 1924-. III. Allenspach, Christoph. IV. Heyer, Hans Rudolf. V. Title.
NA1349.B38 B3813 1991

Bauer, A. (Alice) Répertoire des artistes d'Alsace des dix-neuvième et vingtième siècles : peintres, sculpteurs, graveurs, dessinateurs / A. Bauer et J. Carpentier. Strasbourg : Editions Oberlin, 1984-1991. 6 v. : ill. (some col.) ; 23-24 cm. Includes bibliographies. CONTENTS. - [1] A-D -- [2] E-H -- [3] H-L -- [5] S-U -- [6] V-Z. ISBN 2-85369-036-9 (set) DDC 709/.2/2 B 19
1. Artists - France - Alsace - Biography - Dictionaries. 2. Art, Modern - 19th century - France - Alsace. 3. Art, Modern - 20th century - France - Alsace. I. Carpentier, J. (Janine). II. Title.
N6849.A4 B3 1984   *NYPL [MAO 86-2104]*

Bauer, Hermann, 1929- Corpus der barocken Deckenmalerei in Deutschland / Hermann Bauer, Bernhard Rupprecht ; wissenschaftl. Texte, Anna Bauer-Wild ... [et al.] ; photogr. Aufnahmen, Wolf-Christian von der Mülbe. München : Süddeutscher Verlag, 1976- v. : numerous ill. (some col.), maps ; 34 cm. Includes bibliographical references and indexes. CONTENTS. - Bd. 1. Freistaat Bayern, Regierungsbezirk Oberbayern, die Landkreise Landsberg am Lech, Starnberg, Weilheim-Schongau.--Bd. 2. Freistaat Bayern, Regierungsbezirk Oberbayern, die Landkreise Bad Tölz-Wolfratshausen, Garmisch-Partenkirchen, Miesbach.--Bd. 3. Freistaat Bayern, Regierungsbezirk Oberbayern, Stadt und Landkreis München. T. 1. Sakralbauten. ISBN 3-7991-5737-9 (v. 1) :
1. Mural painting and decoration, Baroque - Germany. 2. Ceilings - Germany. I. Rupprecht, Bernhard. II. Title.
ND2749 .B37   *NYPL [MLP+ 78-312]*

Bauerle, Dorothée. Steingewordene Träume . Ulm , c1990. 111 p. :
NA5559 .S68 1990

Bauernfeind, Gustav, 1848-1904. Der Orientmaler Gustav Bauernfeind, 1848-1904 : Leben und Werk : das Leben Gustav Bauernfeinds : eine historische Einführung / von Alex Carmel ; das künstlerische Werk gesammelt und vorgestellt von Hugo Schmid = The life and work of Gustav Bauernfeind : orientalist painter, 1848-1904: the life of Gustav Bauernfeind : a historical introduction / by Alex Carmel ; translated from the German by Ted Gorelick ; the artistic work compiled and presented by Hugo Schmid. Stuttgart : E. Hauswedell, 1990. xi, 368 p. : ill. ; 31 cm. Text in English and German. ISBN 3-7762-0319-6
1. Bauernfeind, Gustav, 1848-1904. 2. Artists - Germany - Biography. I. Carmel, Alex. II. Title. III. Title: Life and work of Gustav Bauernfeind, orientalist painter, 1848-1904. IV. Title: Life of Gustav Bauernfeind, a historical introduction. V. Title: Leben Gustav Bauernfeinds, eine historische Einführung.
    NYPL [3-MCK+ B3385 91-7206]

BAUERNFEIND, GUSTAV, 1848-1904.
Bauernfeind, Gustav, 1848-1904. Der Orientmaler Gustav Bauernfeind, 1848-1904 . Stuttgart , 1990. xi, 368 p. : ISBN 3-7762-0319-6
    NYPL [3-MCK+ B3385 91-7206]

Bauernhäuser der Schweiz =. Gschwend, Max. Blauen , c1988. 306 p. : ISBN 3-907080-07-6
    NYPL [3-MRGF+ 89-25516]

Die Bauernhäuser des Kantons Freiburg =. Anderegg, Jean Pierre. Basel , 1979-1987. 2 v. : DDC 728/.67/09494 s 728/.67/094945
NA8206.S9 B38 Bd. 7, etc. NA8210
    NYPL [3-MRGF 84-1334]

BAUHAUS.
Schädlich, Christian. Bauhaus Weimar 1919-1925 /. [Weimar] , 1989. 96 p. : ISBN 3-910053-09-2
    NYPL [3-MAMG 90-12699]

Bauhaus Archiv, Museum für Gestaltung.
Hannes Meyer, 1889-1954 . Berlin , c1989. 368 p. : ISBN 3-433-02053-1 : DDC 720/.92 20
NA1353.M4 H35 1989

Keramik und Bauhaus . Berlin [1989] 286 p. :
ISBN 3-89181-404-6
NK4099 .K446 1989

BAUHAUS - EXHIBITIONS.
Fotografie am Bauhaus. English. Photography at the Bauhaus /. Cambridge, Mass. , 1990. 362 p. : ISBN 0-262-06126-0 DDC 779/.09431/84 20
TR653 .F66513 1990
    NYPL [MFW+ 91-189]

Keramik und Bauhaus /. Berlin [1989] 286 p. :
ISBN 3-89181-404-6
    NYPL [3-MPGK 90-11031]

Keramik und Bauhaus . Berlin [1989] 286 p. :
ISBN 3-89181-404-6
NK4099 .K446 1989

50 Jahre Bauhaus . Stuttgart , 1968. 369 p. :
    NYPL [3-MAL 90-6848]

BAUHAUS - INFLUENCE - EXHIBITIONS.
Röhl, Karl Peter, 1890-1975. Karl Peter Röhl, Bauhausjahre . Köln , c1990. 109 p. :
NC251.R62 A4 1990

Bauhaus Weimar 1919-1925 /. Schädlich, Christian. [Weimar] , 1989. 96 p. : ISBN 3-910053-09-2
    NYPL [3-MAMG 90-12699]

Bauhausjahre. Röhl, Karl Peter, 1890-1975. Karl Peter Röhl, Bauhausjahre . Köln , c1990. 109 p. :
NC251.R62 A4 1990

Baukhage, Gerd, 1911-
Gerd Baukhage : Bilder :
Josef-Haubrich-Kunsthalle Köln, 18. August bis 1. Oktober 1989, Städtische Kunsthalle Recklinghausen, 21. Januar bis 25. Februar 1990 / [Redaktion, Klaus Flemming]. [Köln] : Stadt Köln, [1989] 114 p. : chiefly ill. (some col.) ; 28 cm. Bibliography: p. 113.
1. Baukhage, Gerd, 1911- - Exhibitions. I. Flemming, Klaus. II. Josef-Haubrich-Kunsthalle Köln. III. Städtische Kunsthalle Recklinghausen. IV. Title.
MLCM 90/03723 (N)
              NYPL [3-MCK B339 91-2508]

BAUKHAGE, GERD, 1911- - EXHIBITIONS.
Baukhage, Gerd, 1911- Gerd Baukhage . [Köln] [1989] 114 p. :
MLCM 90/03723 (N)
              NYPL [3-MCK B339 91-2508]

Baukunst (Art Gallery : Cologne, Germany)
Surrealismus in Europa. Köln, 1969. 137 p.
              NYPL [3-MC 90-5909]

Baum, Paul, 1859-1932.
Paul Baum 1859-1932 : Staatliche Kunstsammlungen Kassel / [Katalog, Andrea Linnebach, Angela Stief ; Redaktion, Andrea Linnebach]. [Kassel] : Die Kunstsammlungen, [1990] 72 p. : ill. (some col.) ; 25 cm. (Staatliche Kunstsammlungen Kassel : 1) Catalog of an exhibition held at the Neue Galerie, May 13-Aug. 19, 1990. Includes bibliographical references (p. 70-72). ISBN 3-923461-03-8 DDC 760/.092 20
1. Baum, Paul, 1859-1932 - Exhibitions. I. Linnebach, Andrea. II. Stief, Angela, 1953-. III. Staatliche Kunstsammlungen Kassel. Neue Galerie. IV. Series: Staatliche Kunstsammlungen Kassel (Series) , 1. V. Title.
N6888.B38175 A4 1990

BAUM, PAUL, 1859-1932 - EXHIBITIONS.
Baum, Paul, 1859-1932. Paul Baum 1859-1932 . [Kassel] [1990] 72 p. : ISBN 3-923461-03-8 DDC 760/.092 20
N6888.B38175 A4 1990

Baum, Peter. 75 Jahre Maerz . Linz , 1988. 142 p. : ISBN 3-900762-08-2
              NYPL [3-MAMG+ 90-9954]

Baum, Peter, 1939-
Das Bildhauersymposion . Stuttgart , c1988. 163 p. : ISBN 3-7757-0263-6
              NYPL [3-MGI 90-11129]

Kubin, Alfred, 1877-1959. Alfred Kubin 1877-1959 /. München [1990] 400 p. : ISBN 3-88645-092-9 (Ausstellungskatalog)
IN PROCESS (ONLINE)
              NYPL [3-MCK K95 91-8111]

Baum, Timothy. Kaplan, Gilbert E. The graphic work of René Magritte /. New York, N.Y. , c1982. [50] p. : DDC 769.92/4 19
NE2049.5.M29 A4 1982
              NYPL [MDG (Magritte) 83-207]

BAUMANN, H. TH.
Kapp, Volker. H.Th. Baumann . Marburg , c1989. 228 p. : ISBN 3-89398-004-0
IN PROCESS (ONLINE)
              NYPL [3-MNF+ 90-11083]

Baumberger, Otto, 1889-1961.
Otto Baumberger, 1889-1961 : [Ausstellung], Museum für Gestaltung Zürich, 26. Mai bis 17. Juli 1988, Gewerbemuseum Basel, Museum für Gestaltung, 6. August bis 9. Oktober 1988, Deutsches Plakat-Museum Essen, 20. November 1988 bis 22. Januar 1989 / [Redaktion, Martin Heller, Christina Reble, Polly Bertram und Daniel Volkart]. Zürich : Schule und Museum für Gestaltung, c1988. 127 p. : ill. (some col.) ; 20 cm. (Wegleitung. 365) Reihe Schweizer Plakatgestalter ; 4 Exhibition catalog. Includes bibliographical references. ISBN 3-907065-27-1 DDC 741.6/74/092 20
1. Baumberger, Otto, 1889-1961 - Exhibitions. I. Heller, Martin. II. Reble, Christina. III. Museum für Gestaltung Zürich. IV. Gewerbemuseum Basel. V. Deutsches Plakat Museum Essen. VI. Title.
NC1850.B38 A4 1988
              NYPL [3-MDW 90-13136]

BAUMBERGER, OTTO, 1889-1961 - EXHIBITIONS.
Baumberger, Otto, 1889-1961. Otto Baumberger, 1889-1961 . Zürich , c1988. 127 p. : ISBN 3-907065-27-1 DDC 741.6/74/092 20
NC1850.B38 A4 1988
              NYPL [3-MDW 90-13136]

Baumeister, Willi, 1889-1955.
Kermer, Wolfgang, 1935- Willi Baumeister . Stuttgart [1989] 350 p. : ISBN 3-89322-145-X
              NYPL [3-MCK+ B35 90-12548]

Schlemmer, Baumeister, Krause . Wuppertal , 1979. [99] p. :
N6868 .S28
              NYPL [3-MAMG 81-310]

UNBEKANNTE IN DER KUNST.
Hirner-Schüssele, René. Von der Anschauung zur Formerfindung . Worms , c1990. 283 p. ; ISBN 3-88462-931-X
N68.B323 H57 1990

Willi Baumeister : Zeichnungen, Goachen, Collagen : eine Ausstellung zum 100. Geburtstag des Künstlers : Staatsgalerie Stuttgart, 9. April-25. Juni 1899, Museum Fridericianum Kassel, 9. Juli-17. September 1989, Kunstmuseum Bern, 2. Februar-1. April 1990. / [Ausstellung und Catalog, Ulrike Gauss]. Stuttgart : Cantz, [1989?] 275 p. : ill. (chiefly col.) ; 31 cm. one essay in english. Includes bibliographical references. ISBN 3-89322-130-1
1. Baumeister, Willi, 1889-1955 - Exhibitions. I. Gauss, Ulrike. II. Staatsgalerie Stuttgart. III. Museum Fridericianum Kassel. IV. Kunstmuseum Bern. V. Title.
              NYPL [3-MCK+ B35 89-21287]

BAUMEISTER, WILLI, 1889-1955 - CRITICISM AND INTERPRETATION.
Bott, Gudrun, 1957- Figuration und Bildformat . Frankfurt am Main , New York , c1990. 208 p. ; ISBN 3-631-42715-8 DDC 759.3 20
ND588.B35 B6 1990

BAUMEISTER, WILLI, 1889-1955 - EXHIBITIONS.
Baumeister, Willi, 1889-1955. Willi Baumeister . Stuttgart [1989?] 275 p. : ISBN 3-89322-130-1
              NYPL [3-MCK+ B35 89-21287]

Kermer, Wolfgang, 1935- Willi Baumeister . Stuttgart [1989] 350 p. : ISBN 3-89322-145-X
              NYPL [3-MCK+ B35 90-12548]

Schlemmer, Baumeister, Krause . Wuppertal , 1979. [99] p. :
N6868 .S28
              NYPL [3-MAMG 81-310]

Baumeisterforum.
Architektur im Wandel . Düsseldorf , c1990. 91 p. : ISBN 3-7640-0265-4
NA680 .A732 1990

Bäumer, Angelica. Josef Bramer / Angelica Bäumer ; herausgegeben von Ernst Hilger. [Wien] : Europaverlag, [1990] 89 p. : chiefly ill. (chiefly col.) ; 28 cm. ISBN 3-203-51094-4 DDC 759.36 20
1. Bramer, Josef, 1948- - Catalogs. I. Bramer, Josef, 1948-. II. Hilger, Ernst. III. Title.
ND511.5.B69 A4 1990

Baumer, Dorothea. Attersee : frühe Bilder 1964-1974 : 24. September-21. November 1987, Galerie Klewan, München / Dorothea Baumer ; [Katalog, Dorothee Siegelin]. München : Die Galerie : Vertrieb, Autorenbuchhandlung, [1987?] 26 leaves : chiefly ill. (chiefly col.) ; 30 cm.
1. Attersee, Christian Ludwig, 1941- - Exhibitions. I. Galerie Klewan. II. Title.
MLCM 88/01498 (N)
              NYPL [3-MCK+ A88 90-9373]

Baumgärtner, Sabine. Bremer Landesmuseum für Kunst- und Kulturgeschichte. Glaskunst vom Empire bis zum Historismus . Bremen , 1988. 214 p. :
              NYPL [3-MPW 91-4604]

Baumgart, Fritz Erwin, 1902- Kuhn, Hans, 1905- Hans Kuhn. Köln [1968] 105, [6] p. DDC 759.3
ND588.K88 B3
              NYPL [3-MCK K956 91-880]

Baumgartner, Hans Michael, 1933- Kolloquium Kunst und Philosophie (1980 : Paderborn, Germany) Das Kunstwerk / . Paderborn , 1983. 379 p. ; ISBN 3-506-99372-0
              NYPL [3-MAB 90-12387]

Bauquier, Georges.
Léger, Fernand, 1881-1955. Fernand Léger . [Paris] , c1990- v. : ISBN 2-86941-098-0 (v. 1) DDC 759.4 20
ND553.L58 A4 1990a
              NYPL [MCO L512 91-826]

Léger, Fernand, 1881-1955. Fernand Léger . Köln , c1990. 102 p. :
ND553.L58 A4 1990

Bautier, Geneviève Bresc- see **Bresc-Bautier, Geneviève.**

Bauwelt Fundamente, 0522-5094 .
(85) Pfammatter, Ueli. Moderne und Macht . Braunschweig , c1990. 191 p. : ISBN 3-528-08785-4
IN PROCESS (ONLINE)
              NYPL [3-MQWB 91-6456]

BAVARIA - ANTIQUITIES.
Dannheimer, Hermann. Keramik des Mittelalters aus Bayern. Kallmünz (Opf.) , 1973. 74, 55 p. :   *NYPL [L-11 3436 Nr. 15]*

Bavaria - Archaeology. see **Bavaria - Antiquities.**

Bavaria. Bayerische Staatsgemäldesammlungen.
Gulbransson, Olaf, 1873-1958. Olaf Gulbransson . Hannover , c1979. 72 p. : ISBN 3-921752-08-6
NC1619.G85 A4 1979
              NYPL [3-MCZ G971 81-538]

Jawlensky, Alexej von, 1864-1941. Alexej Jawlensky, vom Abbild zum Urbild . Wasserburg am Inn , 1979. 107 p. :
N6999.J38 A4 1979
              NYPL [3-MCZ J41 81-398]

BAVARIA (GERMANY) - HISTORICAL GEOGRAPHY - MAPS.
Historischer Atlas von Bayerisch-Schwaben /. Augsburg , Weissenhorn , 1982- 1 atlas (1 v. (loose-leaf)) : ISBN 3-922518-96-6 DDC 911/.433 19
G1923.B3 H35 1982
              NYPL [Map Div. 84-179]

BAVARIA (GERMANY) - HISTORY.
Historischer Atlas von Bayerisch-Schwaben /. Augsburg , Weissenhorn , 1982- 1 atlas (1 v. (loose-leaf)) : ISBN 3-922518-96-6 DDC 911/.433 19
G1923.B3 H35 1982
              NYPL [Map Div. 84-179]

Bavaria. Staatsgemäldesammlungen. see **Bavaria. Bayerische Staatsgemäldesammlungen.**

Bawa, Manmohan Singh. Himalayan trekking maps / [compiled and drawn by Manmohan Singh Bawa]. [Bombay?] : Air-India ; [New Delhi, India : Distributed by] Himalayan Books, [1985]. 1 atlas (unpaged) : col. maps ; 38 x 49 cm. Cover title. "Based upon the Survey of India map with the permission of the Surveyor General of India"--Maps. "Department of Tourism, Government of India."
1. Trails - Himalaya Mountains - Maps. 2. Hiking - Himalaya Mountains - Maps. 3. Mountaineering - Himalaya Mountains - Maps. 4. Himalaya Mountains - Maps. I. Air-India. II. India. Dept. of Tourism. III. Survey of India. IV. Title.
              NYPL [Map Div. 90-11639]

Baxter, Glen. Welcome to the weird world of Glen Baxter / Glen Baxter. 1st ed. New York : Perennial Library, c1989. 185 p. : chiefly ill. ; 28 cm. ISBN 0-06-055167-4 : DDC 741.5/942 20
1. American wit and humor, Pictorial. I. Title.
NC1429.B34 A4 1989
              NYPL [3-MEM (Baxter) 90-10997]

Bayer, Patricia.
The jewelry design source book /. New York , c1989. 191 p. : ISBN 0-442-23828-2 :
              NYPL [3-MNR 91-4492]

Utt, Mary Lou. Lalique perfume bottles /. New York, N.Y. , 1990. xiii, 160 p. : ISBN 0-517-57191-9 : DDC 748.8/2/0924 19
NK5198.L44 A4 1989
              NYPL [3-MPW 91-4987]

Bayerische Akademie der Wissenschaften. Kommission für Bayerische Landesgeschichte. Historischer Atlas von Bayerisch-Schwaben /. Augsburg , Weissenhorn , 1982- 1 atlas (1 v. (loose-leaf)) : ISBN 3-922518-96-6 DDC 911/.433 19
G1923.B3 H35 1982
              NYPL [Map Div. 84-179]

Bayerische Gesellschaft zur Förderung der Beziehungen Zwischen der Bundesrepublik Deutschland und der Sowjetunion. Russische Graphik des 19. und 20. Jahrhunderts . [Nürnberg , 1977] ca. 300 p. : DDC

769/.074/0332 s 769.947/074/0332 19
NE1 .A48 no. 36 NE675
NYPL [MDBF 80-378]

Das bayerische Glas des Historismus dargestellt an der Hütte Theresienthal . Gropplero di Troppenburg, Elianna. München , c1988. 285 p., [32] p. of plates : ISBN 3-88073-275-2 DDC 338.7/6661/094336 19
NK5198.H78 G76 1988
NYPL [3-MPW 91-5027]

Bayerische Museen .
(Bd. 5) Paukner, Josef. Bartholomäus-Schmucker-Heimatmuseum Ruhpolding /. München , c1987. 64 p. : ISBN 3-7954-0755-9
NK480.R84 P38 1987
NYPL [3-MNE 91-3452]

Bayerische Staatsbibliothek. Die Graphiksammlung des Humanisten Hartmann Schedel /. München , c1990. 336 p. : ISBN 3-7913-1083-6 DDC 769.94/09/02407443364 20
NE59.G4 S324 1990 **NYPL [MDE 91-7276]**

Bayerische Staatsgemäldesammlung. Della Torre, Enrico, 1931- Enrico della Torre . München , c1987. 64 p. :
NYPL [3-MCF+ D343 90-5284]

Bayerische Staatsgemäldesammlungen.
Die Sammlung Woty und Theodor Werner /. München , c1990. 131 p. : ISBN 3-7774-5460-5
NYPL [3-MAX (Werner, W.) 91-6703]

BAYERISCHE STAATSGEMÄLDESAMMLUNGEN - EXHIBITIONS.
Die Sammlung Woty und Theodor Werner /. München , c1990. 131 p. : ISBN 3-7774-5460-5
NYPL [3-MAX (Werner, W.) 91-6703]

Bayerische Vereinsbank.
Baselitz, Georg, 1938- Georg Baselitz . München , c1991. 111 p. :
NYPL [MDG+ (Baselitz) 91-8026]

Mozart in art, 1900-1990 /. München , c1990. 211 p. : ISBN 3-87516-513-6 :
IN PROCESS (ONLINE)
NYPL [3-MAL+ 91-7308]

Bayerisches Landesamt für Denkmalpflege.
Denkmalkunde in Bamberg . Bamberg [1990] 77 p. : DDC 720/.28/80943318 20
NA109.G3 D44 1990

Die Kunstdenkmäler von Mittelfranken /. München , <1982-. v. <2 > : ISBN 3-486-50505-X (v. 2)
N6873 .K86 1980 vol. 5 N6876.M58

Bayerisches Nationalmuseum. Frühe irische Kunst . [Germany , 1959] (Mainz : Eggebrecht-Presse) 1 v. (unpaged) :
N6240 .F7 **NYPL [3-MAMR 91-303]**

Baynes-Cope, A.D. The study and conservation of globes / by A.D. Baynes-Cope. Wien : Internationale Coronelli-Gesellschaft, 1985. 80 p., [15] p. of plates : ill. ; 21 cm. Preface and glossary in English and German.
1. Globes - Conservation and restoration. I. Title.
NYPL [Map Div. 86-526]

Bayón, Damián. La peinture de l'Amérique latine au XXe siècle : identité et modernité / Damián Bayón, Roberto Pontual. Paris : Mengès, c1990. 224 p. : ill. (some col.) ; 25 cm. bibliographical references (p. 218-219) and index. ISBN 2-85620-302-7 DDC 759.98/09/04 20
1. Painting, Latin American. 2. Painting, Modern - 20th century - Latin America. I. Pontual, Roberto. II. Title.
ND202 .B39 1990

Bayón, Damián Carlos. Pensar con los ojos : ensayos de arte latinoamericano / Damián Bayón.1a. ed. Bogotá, D.E. : Procultura, 1982. 478 p. ; 21 cm. (Colección Temas latinoamericanos . 3) Includes bibliographical references.
1. Art, Latin American - History and criticism. I. Series: Temas latinoamericanos , 3. II. Title.
NYPL [3-MAM 90-6285]

Bayside, N. Y. Queensborough Community College. see Queensborough Community College.

Bazaine /. Bazaine, Jean, 1904- Genève , Paris , c1990. 178 p. : ISBN 2-605-00162-8 DDC 759.4 20
ND553.B42 A4 1990

Bazaine, Jean, 1904-
Bazaine / [exposition, Galeries nationales du

Grand Palais, Paris, du 20 mars au 28 mai 1990 / conception du catalogue, Jean de Bengy et Jean-Luc Daval]. Genève : Skira ; Paris : Centre national des arts plastiques, c1990. 178 p. : ill. (some col.) ; 29 cm. "Écrits et propos de Jean Bazaine": p. 164-166; "Bibliographie critique": p. 166-170. ISBN 2-605-00162-8 DDC 759.4 20
1. Bazaine, Jean, 1904- - Exhibitions. I. Bengy, Jean de. II. Daval, Jean Luc. III. Galeries nationales du Grand Palais (France). IV. Title.
ND553.B42 A4 1990

Bazaine. Paris : Skira : Centre national des arts plastiques, c1990. 178 p. : ill. (some col.) ; 28 cm. Catalog of an exhibition held at the Galeries nationales du Grand Palais, Mar. 30-May 28, 1990. Includes essays by Bernard Ceysson, Daniel Dobbels, Pierre Cabanne, and Jean-Pierre Greff. Bibliography: p. 166-170. ISBN 2-605-00162-8
1. Bazaine, Jean, 1904- - Exhibitions. I. Ceysson, Bernard. II. Dobbels, Daniel. III. Cabanne, Pierre. IV. Greff, Jean-Pierre. V. Galeries nationales du Grand Palais (France). VI. Centre national des arts plastiques (France). **NYPL [3-MCO B35 90-12858]**

BAZAINE, JEAN, 1904- - EXHIBITIONS.
Bazaine, Jean, 1904- Bazaine /. Genève , Paris , c1990. 178 p. : ISBN 2-605-00162-8 DDC 759.4 20
ND553.B42 A4 1990

Bazaine, Jean, 1904- Bazaine. Paris , c1990. 178 p. : ISBN 2-605-00162-8
NYPL [3-MCO B35 90-12858]

Bažant, Jan, PhDr. Corpus vasorum antiquorum. Tchécoslovaquie. Prague--Musée national. Prague , 1990- v. : ISBN 80-200-0115-8 (fasc. 1) : DDC 738.3/82/0938074 s 738.3/82/093807443712 20
NK4640.C6 C95 fasc. 2, etc.,
NYPL [MPEK+ C8.P82]

Bazin, Germain.
La peinture au Louvre / par Germain Bazin. Paris : Somogy, 1990, c1957. 277 p. : col. ill. ; 23 cm. Includes indexes. ISBN 2-85056-192-4
1. Musée du Louvre - Catalogs. 2. Painting - France - Paris - Catalogs. I. Title.
NYPL [3-MAVZ (Paris) 90-13647]

Théodore Géricault : étude critique, documents et catalogue raisonné / Germain Bazin. Paris : Bibliothèque des arts, c1987-c1990. 4 v. : ill. (some col.) ; 33 cm. Includes bibliographical references and indexes. CONTENTS. - t. 1. L'homme : biographie, témoignages et documents -- t. 2. L'œuvre, période de formation: étude critique et catalogue raissoné -- t. 3. La gloire de l'empire et la première restauration: étude critique et catalogue raisonné -- t. 4. Le voyage en Italie: étude critique et catalogue raisonné. ISBN 2-85047-016-3 (t. 1) DDC 759.4 20
1. Géricault, Théodore, 1791-1824 - Criticism and interpretation. 2. Géricault, Théodore, 1791-1824 - Catalogues raisonnés. I. Géricault, Théodore, 1791-1824. II. Title.
N6853.G355 B39 1987
NYPL [MCO+ G36 89-6652]

Van Gogh et les peintres d'Auvers-sur-Oise . [Paris] , 1954. xl, 100 p., xxxii p. of plates :
N6847.5.I4 V36 1954

Bazzana, Andrés. La céramique islamique du Musée archéologique provincial de Jaén (Espagne) / par André Bazzana et Yves Montmessin, avec la collaboration de Patrice Cressier et Anne Duluc ; avant-propos par Juan González Navarrete. Madrid : Casa de Velázquez ; Paris : Diffusion De Boccard, 1985. 78 p. : ill. ; 30 cm. (Publications de la Casa de Velázquez. Série Etudes et documents, 0213-1803 . 1) Bibliography: p. [77]-78. DDC 738.3/0946/83 20
1. Museo Provincial de Jaén - Catalogs. 2. Pottery, Islamic - Spain - Jaén (Province). 3. Jaén (Spain : Province) - Antiquities - Catalogs. I. Montmessin, Yves. II. Cressier, Patrice. III. Duluc, Anne. IV. Title. V. Series.
DP302.J1 B38 1985
NYPL [3-MPG+ 91-5911]

BCLIK /. Domenig, Gerald, 1953- [S.l.] , c1988. 1 v. (unpaged) :
NYPL [MFX+ (Domenig) 91-2386]

BE BOP MUSIC. see JAZZ MUSIC.

BEADS IN ART - EXHIBITIONS.
Structure and surface . Sheboygan, Wis. , c1990. vii, 32 p. : ISBN 0-932718-28-0 DDC

709/.73/07477569 20
N6512 .S78 1990
NYPL [3-MAMT 90-13004]

BEADWORK - GERMANY (WEST) - EXHIBITIONS.
Dittler, Ingeborg. Seligenstädter Perlenstickerei . Seligenstadt , 1981. 87 p. :
NYPL [3-MOT 89-27386]

Beal, Graham William John. Segal, George, 1924- George Segal, sculptures /. Minneapolis , c1978. 99 p. : DDC 730/.92/4
NB237.S44 A4 1978
NYPL [3-MGO (Segal) 91-5273]

Beall, Karen F. Graphic excursions--American prints in black and white, 1900-1950 . Boston, Mass. , 1991. 155 p. : ISBN 0-87923-902-6 DDC 769.973/074/73 20
NE508 .G74 1991 **NYPL [MDE 91-5862]**

Beam, Philip C. Winslow Homer in the 1890s . New York , c1990. 154 p. : ISBN 1-555-95042-6 (alk. paper) : DDC 759.13 20
ND237.H7 A4 1990b
NYPL [3-MCX H76 90-13349]

BEAN, ALAN, 1932- - CRITICISM AND INTERPRETATION.
Alan Bean, art off this earth [motion picture] /. Houston, TX , 1990. 1 film reel (26 min.) : DDC 759.13 11
ND237

Alan Bean, art off this earth [videorecording] /. Houston, TX , 1990. 1 videocassette (26 min.) : DDC 759.13 11
ND237

Bean, Jacob. Metropolitan Museum of Art (New York, N.Y.) 18th century Italian drawings in the Metropolitan Museum of Art /. New York , 1990. 288 p. : ISBN 0-87099-585-5 DDC 741.945/074/7471 20
NC255 .M4 1990
NYPL [3-MAVZ (New York) 91-3640]

Bear, Joy. Langhart, Nicholas. Houses of Southold . Southold, N.Y. , c1990. vi, 66 p. : ISBN 0-8488-0870-3 : DDC 728/.37/0974725 20
NA7238.S62 L36 1990

Bear pond /. Weber, Bruce, 1946- [Boston] , c1990. 1 v. (unpaged) : ISBN 0-8212-1831-X : DDC 779/.23/092 20
TR675 .W43 1990
NYPL [MFX (Weber) 91-7434]

Beard, Mark.
Points along the Côte d'Azur triangle /. New York , c1985. 36 p. : ISBN 0-935581-00-6
NYPL [3-MAMT 90-4521]

Utah reader / Mark Beard. New York : Vincent Fitz Gerald, 1986. [34] leaves : col. ill. ; 30 x 39 cm. Mounted illustrations (predominantly linocuts; some folded or with flaps) with descriptive text reproduced from manuscript. Limited ed. of 40 copies. LC has copy no. 34. DLC Source: Purchase, Mar. 4, 1990. DLC DDC 700/.92 20
1. Beard, Mark. 2. Artists' books - United States. I. Title.
N7433.4.B4 A4 1986b

BEARD, MARK.
Beard, Mark. Utah reader /. New York , 1986. [34] leaves : DDC 700/.92 20
N7433.4.B4 A4 1986b

Bearden, Romare, 1911-1988.
Memory and metaphor : the art of Romare Bearden, 1940-1987 / introduction by Kinshasha Holman Conwill ; essays by Mary Schmidt Campbell and Sharon F. Patton. New York : Studio Museum in Harlem : Oxford University Press, 1991. xiv, 128 p. : ill. (some col.) ; 26 cm. Catalog of an exhibition to be held at the Studio Museum in Harlem and in five other cities. Includes bibliographical references (p. 111-112) and index. ISBN 0-19-506347-3 (cl : alk. paper) DDC 709/.2 20
1. Bearden, Romare, 1911-1988 - Exhibitions. I. Campbell, Mary Schmidt. II. Patton, Sharon F. III. Studio Museum in Harlem. IV. Title.
N6537.B4 A4 1991 **NYPL [Sc F 91-121]**

BEARDEN, ROMARE, 1911-1988 - EXHIBITIONS.
Bearden, Romare, 1911-1988. Memory and metaphor . New York , 1991. xiv, 128 p. : ISBN 0-19-506347-3 (cl : alk. paper) DDC

709/.2 20
N6537.B4 A4 1991   *NYPL [Sc F 91-121]*

Bearden, Romare, 1914- Schwartzman, Myron.
Romare Bearden . New York , 1990. 320 p. :
ISBN 0-8109-3108-7 DDC 709/.2 B 20
N6537.B4 S39 1990
     NYPL [3-MCX B368 91-3306]

BEARDEN, ROMARE, 1914-
Schwartzman, Myron. Romare Bearden . New
York , 1990. 320 p. : ISBN 0-8109-3108-7 DDC
709/.2 B 20
N6537.B4 S39 1990
     NYPL [3-MCX B368 91-3306]

Beardsley, Aubrey, 1872-1898. Slessor, Catherine.
The art of Aubrey Beardsley /. London ,
c1989. 128 p. : ISBN 1-85076-181-7 : DDC
741.942 20
NC242.B3   *NYPL [3-MCV B368 90-12980]*

BEARDSLEY, AUBREY, 1872-1898.
Reade, Brian. Beardsley re-mounted /. London ,
1989. 39 p. : ISBN 0-905744-14-4 : DDC 741.942
20
NC242.B3
     NYPL [MDG+ (Beardsley) 91-6490]

Slessor, Catherine. The art of Aubrey Beardsley
/. London , c1989. 128 p. : ISBN
1-85076-181-7 : DDC 741.942 20
NC242.B3   *NYPL [3-MCV B368 90-12980]*

Beardsley, John. Pablo Picasso / John Beardsley.
New York : H.N. Abrams, 1991. p. cm. (First
impressions) Includes index. Examines the life and
work of Picasso, discussing how and why his art looks
the way it does and how it relates to the artist.   ISBN
0-8109-3713-1 DDC 709/.2 B 20
*1. Picasso, Pablo, 1881-1973 - Juvenile literature. 2.
Artists - France - Biography - Juvenile literature. I.
Series: First impressions (New York, N.Y.). II. Title.*
N6853.P5 B43 1991

Beardsley re-mounted /. Reade, Brian. London ,
1989. 39 p. : ISBN 0-905744-14-4 : DDC 741.942
20
NC242.B3
     NYPL [MDG+ (Beardsley) 91-6490]

Bearings. Bearings (Exhibition : 1988-1989 :
Parsons School of Design) New York, N.Y. ,
1991. 79 p. : ISBN 1-87827-128-8 : DDC
720/.973/0747471 20
NA2340 .B4 1991
     NYPL [3-MQAF 91-7007]

**Bearings (Exhibition : 1988-1989 : Parsons
School of Design)** Bearings. New York,
N.Y. : Princeton Architectural Press : Parsons
School of Design, 1991. 79 p. : ill., plans ; 22
cm. Catalog of exhibitions held Dec. 7, 1988-Jan. 7,
1989, and Jan. 16-Feb. 8, 1991, at the Parsons
Exhibition Center.   ISBN 1-87827-128-8 : DDC
720/.973/0747471 20
*1. Schools of architecture - United States - Faculty -
Exhibitions. 2. Architecture - Competitions - United
States. I. Parsons School of Design. II. Bearings
(Exhibition : 1991 : Parsons School of Design). III.
Title.*
NA2340 .B4 1991
     NYPL [3-MQAF 91-7007]

**Bearings (Exhibition : 1991 : Parsons School of
Design)** Bearings (Exhibition : 1988-1989 :
Parsons School of Design) Bearings. New York,
N.Y. , 1991. 79 p. : ISBN 1-87827-128-8 : DDC
720/.973/0747471 20
NA2340 .B4 1991
     NYPL [3-MQAF 91-7007]

Bears for all seasons . Volpp, Rosemary.
Cumberland, Md. , c1989. 96 p. : ISBN
0-87588-348-6 : DDC 688.7/24 20
NK8740 .V64 1989

Beasley, Maureen. Five centuries of artists in
Sutton : a biographical dictionary of artists
associated with Sutton, London / Maureen
Beasley. Sutton, Surrey : Sutton Libraries and
Arts Services, 1989. 144 p. : ill. (some col.) ;
29 cm. Includes bibliographical references.   ISBN
0-907335-19-5 DDC 709/.2/242192 B 20
*1. Artists - England - Sutton (London) - Biography -
Dictionaries. I. Title. II. Title: 5 centuries of artists in
Sutton.*
N6770 .B43 1989

BEASTS. see ZOOLOGY.

Beate Kuhn, Keramik, 1953-1989 . Kuhn, Beate,
1927- Frankfurt am Main , C1989. 128 p. :

ISBN 3-88270-047-5
     NYPL [3-MPGK 90-12032]

Beatrice Wood . Wood, Beatrice. Phoenix, Ariz. ,
c1973. [16] p. :   DDC 738/.092/4
NK4210.W63 P56   *NYPL [3-MPH 91-6661]*

Beatus, Saint, presbyter of Liebana, d. 798.
In Apocalipsin. Maius, fl. 926-968. A Spanish
Apocalypse : the Morgan Beatus manuscript
/ introduction and plate commentaries by
John Williams ; codicological analysis by
Barbara A. Shailor. New York , 1991. p. cm.
ISBN 0-8076-1262-6 :   DDC 745.6/7/092 20
ND3361.R52 B436 1991

IN APOCALIPSIN - ILLUSTRATIONS.
Maius, fl. 926-968. A Spanish Apocalypse .
New York , 1991. p. cm.   ISBN
0-8076-1262-6 :   DDC 745.6/7/092 20
ND3361.R52 B436 1991

Le beau idéal . Michel, Régis. Paris , 1989. 176
p. :   ISBN 2-7118-2317-2
     NYPL [3-MA 90-12383]

Beaute, Georges. Toulouse-Lautrec vu par les
photographes ; suivi de, Témoignages inédits /
Georges Beaute. Lausanne : Edita, c1988. 148
p. : ill., ports. ; 30 cm. (Archives photographiques)
ISBN 2-88001-241-4
*1. Toulouse-Lautrec, Henri de, 1864-1901 - Portraits. 2.
Toulouse-Lautrec, Henri de, 1864-1901. I. Title. II.
Title: Témoignages inédits.*
     NYPL [3-MCO+ T72 90-335]

La beauté nue . Metzger, A. [Paris] , c1984. 251
p. :   ISBN 2-85940-053-2 DDC 738.3/82/0938 19
NK4645 .M48 1984
     NYPL [3-MPEK+ 90-12508]

**BEAUTIFICATION OF CITIES AND TOWNS.
see URBAN BEAUTIFICATION.**

**BEAUTIFUL, THE. see AESTHETICS; ART -
PHILOSOPHY.**

**BEAUTY. see AESTHETICS; ART -
PHILOSOPHY.**

Beauty and the beast : a study in contrasts :
[exhibition], 4 November to 31 December 1976
/ [essays by Suzanne Preston Blier]. New York
City : L. Kahan Gallery, [1976] 14 p. : ill. ; 16
x 23 cm. Imprint from label mounted on t.p.
Bibliography: p. 14.
*1. Masks (Sculpture) - Nigeria - Exhibitions. 2.
Sculpture, Nigerian - Exhibitions. 3. Rites and
ceremonies - Nigeria. I. Blier, Suzanne Preston. II. L.
Kahan Gallery.*   *NYPL [3-MADF 90-7112]*

Beauty of bit & byte. Computerkultur, oder, "The
Beauty of bit & byte" /. Bremen , 1989. 223
p. :   ISBN 3-924252-06-8
     NYPL [3-MAL+ 91-5883]

Beauty of bit and byte. Computerkultur, oder,
"The Beauty of bit & byte" /. Bremen , 1989.
223 p. :   ISBN 3-924252-06-8
     NYPL [3-MAL+ 91-5883]

The Beauty of Japan. Tokyo, Japan : Tokyo
Metropolitan Culture Foundation, c1987. [12],
118 p. : ill. ; 28 cm. (Tokyo Metropolitan Teien Art
Museum catalogue . no. 11) English and Japanese.
Catalog of an exhibition of photographs by Ihē Kimura,
Yoshio Watanabe,, Ken Domon and Hiroshi Hamaya
held at the Tōkyō-to Teien Bijutsukan, May 23-June
30, 1987.
*1. Kimura, Ihē, 1901-1974 - Exhibitions. 2. Watanabe,
Yoshio, 1907- - Exhibitions. 3. Domon, Ken, 1909- -
Exhibitions. 4. Hamaya, Hiroshi, 1915- - Exhibitions. I.
Tōkyō-to Teien Bijutsukan. II. Series: Tōkyō-to Teien
Bijutsukan shiryō , dai 11-shū.*
     NYPL [MFW 91-3529]

The beauty of stained glass /. Reyntiens, Patrick.
London , 1990. 224 p. :   ISBN 1-87156-925-7 :
DDC 748.59 20
NK5306   *NYPL [3-MRY 91-3631]*

**Beauvais. Musée départemental de l'Oise. see
Musée départemental de l'Oise.**

Beaux Arch '89 : an exposition of recent
architecture on Long Island / Alastair Gordon,
editor. Sag Harbor, N.Y. : Hampton Day
School, 1989. 119 p. : chiefly ill. (some col.) ;
28 cm.   ISBN 0-9623542-0-1
*1. Architecture, American - New York (State) - Long
Island - Exhibitions. 2. Architecture, Modern - 20th
century - New York (State) - Long Island - Exhibitions.
I. Gordon, Alastair.*
IN PROCESS   *NYPL [3-MQWO 91-3337]*

Beazley, Elisabeth.
**Design and detail of the space between
buildings.** Pinder, Angi. Beazley's Design
and detail of the space between buildings /
Angi and Alan Pinder. London , 1990. xii,
289 p. :   ISBN 0-419-13620-7
     NYPL [MRA 91-6548]

Beazley, J. D. (John Davidson), 1885-1970.
Some Attic vases in the Cyprus Museum / by
J.D. Beazley ; edited by Donna Carol Kurtz.
[Oxford, England] : Oxford University
Committee for Archaeology, 1989. 46 p., 19 p.
of plates : ill. ; 25 cm. (Oxford University
Committee for Archaeology. Monograph . no. 27)
Includes bibliographical references.   ISBN
0-947816-27-5 (pbk)
*1. Vases, Greek. I. Kurtz, Donna C. II. Kypriakon
Mouseion (Cyprus). III. Title.*
     NYPL [3-MPEK 91-3456]

**Beazley's Design and detail of the space between
buildings /.** Pinder, Angi. London , 1990. xii,
289 p. :   ISBN 0-419-13620-7
     NYPL [MRA 91-6548]

BEBOP MUSIC. see JAZZ MUSIC.

Beccafumi, Domenico, 1486-1551.
Domenico Beccafumi e il suo tempo. Milano :
Electa, c1990. 732 p. : ill. (some col.) ; 28 cm.
Catalog of an exhibition held in Siena at the Chiesa di
Sant'Agostino and elsewhere ("Sezione dipinti e
affreschi"), June 16-Nov. 4, 1990, and at the Pinacoteca
nazionale di Siena ("Sezione grafica"), June 16-Sept. 16,
1990. Includes bibliographical references (p. 716-730)
and index.   ISBN 88-435-3173-5 DDC 759.5 20
*1. Beccafumi, Domenico, 1486-1551 - Exhibitions. 2.
Art, Renaissance - High Renaissance - Italy -
Exhibitions. 3. Mannerism (Art) - Italy - Exhibitions. I.
Chiesa di Sant'Agostino (Siena, Italy). II. Pinacoteca
nazionale di Siena. III. Title.*
ND623.B34 A4 1990

**BECCAFUMI, DOMENICO, 1486-1551 -
EXHIBITIONS.**
Beccafumi, Domenico, 1486-1551. Domenico
Beccafumi e il suo tempo. Milano , c1990. 732
p. :   ISBN 88-435-3173-5 DDC 759.5 20
ND623.B34 A4 1990

Domenico Beccafumi e il suo tempo. Milano ,
c1990. 732 p. :   ISBN 88-435-3173-5
     NYPL [3-MCF B365 91-2303]

Becchetti, Piero. Giacomo Caneva e la scuola
fotografica romana (1847/1855) / di Piero
Becchetti. Firenze : Alinari, c1989. 197 p. : ill. ;
30 cm. (Programma arte e cultura 1988-1989, Palazzo
Rondanini alla Rotonda-Roma . 3) Includes index.
Catalog of an exhibition held at the Palazzo Rondanini
alla Rotonda Roma from May 10 to June 24, 1989. At
head of title: Regione Lazio. Includes bibliographical
references.   ISBN 88-7292-106-8
*1. Caneva, Giacomo, 1810-1890 - Exhibitions. I.
Palazzo Rondanini (Rome, Italy). II. Lazio (Italy).
Assessorato alla cultura. III. Title. IV. Series.*
     NYPL [MFX+ (Caneva) 91-6016]

Beceyro, Raúl. Ensayos sobre fotografía / Raúl
Beceyro. 1. ed. México : Editorial Arte y
Libros, 1978. 91 p., [7] leaves of plates : ill. ;
20 cm.
1. Photography - Addresses, essays, lectures. I. Title.
TR185 .B35   *NYPL [MFW 81-439]*

Becher, Bernd, 1931-
Hochöfen / Bernd und Hilla Becher. München :
Schirmer/Mosel, c1990. 15 p., 223 p. of plates :
ill. ; 30 cm. ISBN 3-88814-352-7
*1. Blast-furnaces - Pictorial works. I. Becher, Hilla. II.
Title.*   *NYPL [MFX+ (Becher) 91-7985]*

[Hochöfen. English]
Blast furnaces / Bernd and Hilla Becher.
Cambridge, Mass. : MIT Press, c1990. 15 p.,
223 p. of plates : chiefly ill. ; 30 cm.
Translation of: Hochöfen.   ISBN 0-262-02311-3
(hc.) DDC 669/.1413 20
*1. Blast-furnaces - Pictorial works. I. Becher, Hilla. II.
Title.*
TN677 .B38513 1990
     NYPL [MFX+ (Becher) 91-195]

Becher, Hilla.
Becher, Bernd, 1931- Hochöfen /. München ,
c1990. 15 p., 223 p. of plates :   ISBN
3-88814-352-7
     NYPL [MFX+ (Becher) 91-7985]

Becher, Bernd, 1931- [Hochöfen. English.] Blast
furnaces /. Cambridge, Mass. , c1990. 15 p.,
223 p. of plates :   ISBN 0-262-02311-3 (hc.) DDC

669/.1413 20
TN677 .B38513 1990
NYPL [MFX+ (Becher) 91-195]

Becher, Ulrich, 1910- Grosz, George, 1893-1959. George Grosz, Deutschland über Alles . Roma , 1963. 19 p., [84] leaves of plates :
NYPL [3-MCK G879 91-1374]

Bechert, Tilmann. Töpferstempel aus Südgallien / T. Bechert, M. Vanderhoeven. Duisburg : Niederrheinisches Museum der Stadt Duisburg : Naturfreunde Duisburg, 1988. 102 p. : ill. ; 30 cm. (Funde aus Asciburgium . Heft 9)
1. Pottery - Marks. I. Title. II. Series.
IN PROCESS (ONLINE)
NYPL [3-MPK+ 91-4448]

Beck & Jung. Chromo cube / Beck & Jung ; [texts, Leif Eriksson ... et al. ; translation from French by Jacqueline Lindenfeld ; translations from Swedish by Lars-Håkan Svensson]. Bjärred, Sweden (Box 123, S-237 00 Bjärred) : Wedgepress & Cheese, c1982. 49 p., [24] leaves of plates : ill. (some col.) ; 21 cm. English, French, and Swedish. ISBN 91-85752-30-4
1. Beck & Jung. 2. Art, Modern - 20th century - Sweden. I. Eriksson, Leif. II. Bäckström, Holger. III. Ljungberg, Bo. IV. Title.
NYPL [3-MAL 88-3799]

BECK & JUNG.
Beck & Jung. Chromo cube /. Bjärred, Sweden (Box 123, S-237 00 Bjärred) , c1982. 49 p., [24] leaves of plates : ISBN 91-85752-30-4
NYPL [3-MAL 88-3799]

Beck, Gerlinde, 1930- Gerlinde Beck : Zeichen im Raum / Einführung von Günther Wirth. Stuttgart : J. Hoffmann, c1990. 120 p. : ill. ; 30 cm. In German; introd. also in English and French. ISBN 3-87346-093-9
1. Beck, Gerlinde, 1930-. I. Title.
NYPL [3-MGO+ (Beck) 91-5636]

BECK, GERLINDE, 1930-
Beck, Gerlinde, 1930- Gerlinde Beck . Stuttgart , c1990. 120 p. : ISBN 3-87346-093-9
NYPL [3-MGO+ (Beck) 91-5636]

Beck, Herbert, 1941- Polyklet . Mainz am Rhein , c1990. 678 p., 8 p. of plates : ISBN 3-8053-1175-3 DDC 730/.92 20
NB101 .P65 1990

Beck, Herbert, 1920-
Herbert Beck : German expressionism, second generation : watercolors : October 20-November 25, 1989. New York, NY (33 East 74th Street, New York 10021) : Leonard Hutton Galleries, c1989. 32 p. : ill. (some col.) ; 31 cm.
1. Beck, Herbert, 1920- - Exhibitions. I. Leonard Hutton Galleries. II. Title.
MLCL 89/00926 (N)
NYPL [3-MCK+ B3862 91-4293]

BECK, HERBERT, 1920- - EXHIBITIONS.
Beck, Herbert, 1920- Herbert Beck . New York, NY (33 East 74th Street, New York 10021) , c1989. 32 p. :
MLCL 89/00926 (N)
NYPL [3-MCK+ B3862 91-4293]

Beck, James H. Jacopo della Quercia / James Beck. New York : Columbia University Press, 1991. p. cm. Includes bibliographical references and index. ISBN 0-231-07200-7 DDC 730/.92 B 20
1. Jacopo, della Quercia, 1372?-1436. 2. Sculptors - Italy - Biography. 3. Jacopo, della Quercia, 1372?-1436 - Catalogues raisonnés. I. Title.
NB623.O4 B39 1991

Beck, Jerry. I tawt I taw a puddy tat : Tweety and Sylvester's golden jubilee / Jerry Beck.1st American ed. New York : H. Holt, c1991. p. cm. ISBN 0-8050-1644-9 DDC 741.5/09794/03 20
1. Tweety Pie (Fictitious character). 2. Sylvester (Fictitious character). 3. Warner Bros. Cartoons - History. I. Title.
NC1766.U52 W37334 1991

Beck, Rainer, 1947- Odious . [München , 1988] 245 p. : ISBN 3-923244-05-3
NYPL [3-MGI 89-28056]

Beckel, Lothar. Attems, Franz, 1926- Kirchen und Stifte der Steiermark / . Innsbruck , c1988. 163 p. : ISBN 3-7016-2296-5 DDC 726/.5/094365 20
NA5509.S8 A88 1988
NYPL [3-MRBB 90-11074]

Becker, Ingeborg, 1947- Schmuckkunst im Jugendstil / Ingeborg Becker. Buchhandelsausg.

Berlin : D. Reimer, c1988. 95 p. : ill. ; 24 cm. (Veröffentlichungen des Bröhan-Museums . Nr. 4) ISBN 3-496-01064-9
1. Jewelry - Europe - History - 19th century - Exhibitions. 2. Jewelry - Europe - History - 20th century - Exhibitions. I. Bröhan-Museum Berlin. II. Series: Veröffentlichung des Bröhan-Museums , Nr. 4. III. Title.
NYPL [3-MNR 90-12395]

Becker, Jack. Eirich, E. C. (Edward Conrad), 1877-1929. E.C. Eirich (1877-1929) . [Philadelphia, Pa.] , c1991. 48 p. :
NYPL [3-MCX E35 91-7603]

Becker, Vivienne, 1953- Rough diamonds : the Butler & Wilson collection / Vivienne Becker ; foreword by Ali MacGraw. London : Pavilion, 1990. 175 p. : ill. (some col.) ports. ; 31 cm. Includes index. ISBN 1-85145-521-3 : DDC 739.27 20
1. Butler & Wilson (Firm). 2. Costume jewelry - England - History - 20th century. I. Title.
NK7304
NYPL [MNR+ 91-3889]

Becker, Wm. B. (William B.)
Cameron, John B. Photography's beginnings . Rochester, Mich. , Albuquerque , c1989. 176 p. : ISBN 0-925859-00-1 (softbound) DDC 770/.9 20
TR15 .C36 1989
NYPL [MFW 91-6729]

BECKER, WM. B. (WILLIAM B.) - PHOTOGRAPH COLLECTIONS - EXHIBITIONS.
Cameron, John B. Photography's beginnings . Rochester, Mich. , Albuquerque , c1989. 176 p. : ISBN 0-925859-00-1 (softbound) DDC 770/.9 20
TR15 .C36 1989
NYPL [MFW 91-6729]

Becker, Wolfgang. Von Pop zum Konzept . Aachen [1975] [64] p., [30] leaves of plates :
N6488.G3 A28
NYPL [3-MAW+ (Aachen) 80-1119]

Beckers, Christiane. Papyrus et pop art /. [Nivelles, Belgique , 1987] 104 p. :
N72.H58 P36 1987

Beckett, Samuel, 1906- Yeats, Jack Butler, 1871-1957. Jack B. Yeats . Bristol : London : 111 p. : ISBN 0-907738-29-X (Arnolfini Gallery)
NYPL [3-MCV Y41 91-6477]

BECKMAN, PAUL - EXHIBITIONS.
Stadscollectie 1988, Rotterdam . Rotterdam [1989]. 54 p. : ISBN 90-6918-041-3
NYPL [3-MAME 90-10813]

Beckmann als Landschaftsmaler /. Rother, Susanne. München , c1990. 212 p. : ISBN 3-89235-034-5 :
ND588.B37 R67 1990

Beckmann, Max, 1884-1950.
Hofmaier, James. Max Beckmann . Bern , c1990. 2 v. (894 p.) : ISBN 3-85773-024-2
NYPL [MDG+ (Beckmann) 90-11722]

Max Beckmann : the triptychs : an exhibition organised by the Whitechapel Art Gallery in association with the Arts Council of Great Britain, 13 November 1980-11 January 1981 / [edited by Nicholas Serota]. [London] : Published by the Trustees of the Whitechapel Art Gallery, 1980. 59 p. : ill. (some col.) ; 21 x 27 cm. Exhibition also held at Stedelijk Museum, Amsterdam, Jan. 22-Mar. 8, 1981. Bibliography: p. 58-59. ISBN 0-85488-050-X
1. Beckmann, Max, 1884-1950 - Exhibitions. 2. Beckmann, Max, 1884-1950 - Criticism and interpretation. 3. Triptychs - Germany - Themes, motives - Exhibitions. I. Serota, Nicholas. II. Whitechapel Art Gallery. III. Amsterdam (Netherlands). Stedelijk Museum. IV. Title.
ND588.B37 A4 1980
NYPL [3-MCK B39 90-5913]

Max Beckmann : opere grafiche, 1911-1925 : Città di Castello, Pinacoteca comunale, Palazzo Vitelli alla Cannoniera, 22 agosto-15 settembre 1985 / a cura di Eugen Blume ; introduzione di Mario De Micheli. [Italy] : Vangelista, [1985] 141 p. : ill. ; 22 cm. Catalog of an exhibition. Bibliography: p. [139] DDC 769.92/4 19
1. Beckmann, Max, 1884-1950 - Exhibitions. 2. Beckmann, Max, 1884-1950 - Criticism and interpretation. 3. Expressionism (Art) - Germany - Exhibitions. I. Blume, Eugen. II. Città di Castello (Italy). Pinacoteca comunale. III. Title.
NE654.B37 A4 1985
NYPL [MDG (Beckmann) 86-4332]

Max Beckmann : Gemälde 1905-1950 / Herausgeber, Klaus Gallwitz. Stuttgart : G. Hatje, c1990. 258 p. : ill. (some col.) ; 29 cm. "Dieses Katalogbuch erscheint anlässlich der Ausstellungen in Leipzig, Museum der bildenden Künste, 21.7.-23.9.1990, Frankfurt am Main, Städelsches Kunstinstitut, 10.10.1990-13.1.1991"--Colophon. Includes bibliographical references (p. 256-257). ISBN 3-7757-0314-4
1. Beckmann, Max, 1884-1950 - Exhibitions. I. Gallwitz, Klaus. II. Museum der Bildenden Künste (Leipzig, Germany). III. Städtische Galerie im Städelschen Kunstinstitut Frankfurt am Main. IV. Title.
NYPL [3-MCK B39 91-7591]

Die Realität der Träume in den Bildern : Schriften und Gespräche 1911 bis 1950 / Mac Beckmann ; herausgegeben und mit einem Nachwort versehen von Rudolf Pillep. München : Piper, c1990. 147 p. ; 19 cm. (Serie Piper. 814) Includes bibliographical references. ISBN 3-492-10814-8
1. Beckmann, Max, 1884-1950 - Written works (p. 136-[148]). I. Pillep, Rudolf. II. Title.
NYPL [3-MCK B39 91-7029]

"Die Synagoge" von Max Beckmann : Wirklichkeit und Sinnbild : eine Kabinettausstellung des Pädagogischen Dienstes im Städel zum 50. Jahrestag der Pogromnacht, 11. November bis 30. Dezember 1988, Städtische Galerie im Städelschen Kunstinstitut Frankfurt am Main. Frankfurt am Main : Die Galerie, c1988. 53 p. : ill. ; 24 cm. Includes bibliographical references (p. 52-53)
1. Beckmann, Max, 1884-1950 - Exhibitions. I. Städtische Galerie im Städelschen Kunstinstitut Frankfurt am Main. II. Title.
NYPL [3-MCK B39 90-12466]

BECKMANN, MAX, 1884-1950 - CRITICISM AND INTERPRETATION.
Beckmann, Max, 1884-1950. Max Beckmann . [London] , 1980. 59 p. : ISBN 0-85488-050-X
ND588.B37 A4 1980
NYPL [3-MCK B39 90-5913]

Beckmann, Max, 1884-1950. Max Beckmann . [Italy] [1985] 141 p. : DDC 769.92/4 19
NE654.B37 A4 1985
NYPL [MDG (Beckmann) 86-4332]

Lackner, Stephen. Max Beckmann /. New York , 1991. 126 p. : ISBN 0-8109-3109-5 DDC 759.3 20
ND588.B37 L298 1991
NYPL [3-MCK+ B39 91-7174]

Rother, Susanne. Beckmann als Landschaftsmaler /. München , c1990. 212 p. : ISBN 3-89235-034-5 :
ND588.B37 R67 1990

BECKMANN, MAX, 1884-1950 - EXHIBITIONS.
Beckmann, Max, 1884-1950. Max Beckmann . [London] , 1980. 59 p. : ISBN 0-85488-050-X
ND588.B37 A4 1980
NYPL [3-MCK B39 90-5913]

Beckmann, Max, 1884-1950. Max Beckmann . [Italy] [1985] 141 p. : DDC 769.92/4 19
NE654.B37 A4 1985
NYPL [MDG (Beckmann) 86-4332]

Beckmann, Max, 1884-1950. Max Beckmann . Stuttgart , c1990. 258 p. : ISBN 3-7757-0314-4
NYPL [3-MCK B39 91-7591]

Beckmann, Max, 1884-1950. "Die Synagoge" von Max Beckmann . Frankfurt am Main , c1988. 53 p. :
NYPL [3-MCK B39 90-12466]

BECKMANN, MAX, 1884-1950 - CATALOGUES RAISONNÉS.
Hofmaier, James. Max Beckmann . Bern , c1990. 2 v. (894 p.) : ISBN 3-85773-024-2
NYPL [MDG+ (Beckmann) 90-11722]

BECKMANN, MAX, 1884-1950 - WRITTEN WORKS (P. 136-[148])
Beckmann, Max, 1884-1950. Die Realität der Träume in den Bildern . München , c1990. 147 p. ; ISBN 3-492-10814-8
NYPL [3-MCK B39 91-7029]

Beckner, Ross.
Ross Bleckner : 6 April to 27 April 1991. New York, N.Y. : Mary Boone Gallery, 1991. p. cm. Includes bibliographical references. ISBN 0-941863-18-2 DDC 759.13 20

1. Beckner, Ross - Exhibitions. I. Mary Boone Gallery (New York, N.Y.). II. Title.
ND237.B38 A4 1991

BECKNER, ROSS - EXHIBITIONS.
Beckner, Ross. Ross Bleckner . New York,
N.Y. , 1991. p. cm. ISBN 0-941863-18-2 DDC
759.13 20
ND237.B38 A4 1991

Beck's archäologische Bibliothek.
Müller-Wiener, Wolfgang. Griechisches
Bauwesen in der Antike /. München , c1988.
221 p. : ISBN 3-406-32993-4
NYPL [3-MQM 90-12379]

Becoming O'Keeffe . Peters, Sarah Whitaker. New
York , 1991. p. cm. ISBN 0-89659-907-8 DDC
759.13 B 20
N6537.O39 P48 1991

BÉCQUER, VALERIANO.
Alfageme Ruano, Pedro. El romanticismo
Sevillano . Sevilla , 1989. 176 p., [21] p. of
plates : ISBN 84-87039-13-8
NYPL [3-MCQ B39 91-4517]

Bédard, Hélène. Maisons et églises du Québec,
XVIIe, XVIIIe, XIXe siècles; étude commandée
par le Musée du Québec. 2e éd. rev. et corr.
[Québec, Ministère des Affaires Culturelles]
1972 [c1971] 50 p. illus. 18 cm. (Civilisation du
Québec. 1. Série Architecture) Bibliography: p. 49-50.
1. Architecture - Quebec (Province). 2. Quebec
(Province) - Historic buildings. I. Title.
NYPL [3-MQWM 90-5758]

Bédarida, Marc. Immeubles de bureaux / Marc
Bédarida, Milka Milatović. Paris : Editions du
Moniteur, c1991. 119 p. : ill. (some col.) ; 28
cm. (Architecture thématique, 0989-4265) Includes
bibliographical references (p. 118). ISBN
2-281-19052-8
1. Office buildings. 2. Architecture, Modern - 20th
century. I. Milatović, Milka, 1950-. II. Title. III. Series.
NA6230 .B43 1991

Bédat, Claude.
[Académie des beaux-arts de Madrid, 1744-
1808. Spanish]
La Real Academia de Bellas Artes de San
Fernando (1744-1808) : contribución al
estudio de las influencias estilísticas y de la
mentalidad artística en la España del siglo
XVIII / Claude Bédat ; prólogo por Enrique
Lafuente Ferrari. Madrid : Fundación
Universitaria Española : Real Academia de
Bellas Artes de San Fernando, 1989. 547 p. :
ill. ; 24 cm. (Publicaciones de la Fundación
Universitaria Española. Bellas artes . 8) Translation
of: Académie des beaux-arts de Madrid, 1744-1808.
Includes bibliographical references (p. [455]-462) and
index. ISBN 84-7392-319-7
1. Real Academia de Bellas Artes de San Fernando. 2.
Art, Modern - 17th-18th centuries - Spain. I. Lafuente
Ferrari, Enrique. II. Real Academia de Bellas Artes de
San Fernando. III. Title. IV. Series.
IN PROCESS (ONLINE)
NYPL [3-MAML 91-6080]

Bedford Square . Byrne, Andrew. London ,
Atlantic Highlands, NJ , 1990. 166 p., 8 p. of
plates : ISBN 0-485-11386-4 DDC
728/.312/0942142 20
NA970 .B9 1990
NYPL [3-MQWK+ 90-11731]

BEDFORD SQUARE (LONDON, ENGLAND)
Byrne, Andrew. Bedford Square . London ,
Atlantic Highlands, NJ , 1990. 166 p., 8 p. of
plates : ISBN 0-485-11386-4 DDC
728/.312/0942142 20
NA970 .B9 1990
NYPL [3-MQWK+ 90-11731]

BEDFORD SQUARE (LONDON, ENGLAND) -
BUILDINGS, STRUCTURES, ETC.
Byrne, Andrew. Bedford Square . London ,
Atlantic Highlands, NJ , 1990. 166 p., 8 p. of
plates : ISBN 0-485-11386-4 DDC
728/.312/0942142 20
NA970 .B9 1990
NYPL [3-MQWK+ 90-11731]

Bedoire, Fredric, 1945- Andersson, Henrik O.,
1939- [Stockholms byggnader. English.]
Stockholm, architecture and townscape /.
Stockholm , c1988. 412 p. : ISBN 91-518-1879-5
NYPL [3-MQWE 89-11933]

Bedroom decorating. Minnetonka, MN : C.
DeCosse Inc., 1991. p. cm. (Arts & crafts for home
decorating) Includes index. ISBN 0-86573-351-1 :

DDC 747.7/7 20
1. Bedrooms. 2. Interior decoration. I. Cy DeCosse
Incorporated. II. Series.
NK2117.B4 B424 1991

BEDROOMS.
Bedroom decorating. Minnetonka, MN , 1991.
p. cm. ISBN 0-86573-351-1 : DDC 747.7/7 20
NK2117.B4 B424 1991

BEDROOMS - FRANCE - HISTORY.
Ladd, Mary-Sargent. The Frenchwoman's
bedroom /. New York , c1991. p. cm. ISBN
0-385-26558-1 : DDC 747.7/7 20
NK2117.B4 L33 1991

Beeh-Lustenberger, Suzanne. Hindorf, Heinz.
Heinz Hindorf, Glasfenster /. Freiburg , c1989.
176 p. : ISBN 3-451-21540-3 : DDC 748.593 20
NK5398.H56 A4 1989

Beeldenstorm . Davidson, Steef, 1943-
Amsterdam , 1978. 176 p. : ISBN
90-6012-315-8 :
PN6714 .D3 *NYPL [3-MDY+ 90-4753]*

Beeld/spraak .
(3) Popelier, Bert, 1945- Roel D'Haese . Gent
[1987] 63 p. :
NB673.H3 P67 1987

Beer, Alice Baldwin. Trade goods; a study of
Indian chintz in the Collection of the
Cooper-Hewitt Museum of Decorative Arts and
Design, Smithsonian Institution. Washington,
Smithsonian Institution Press; [for sale by the
Supt. of Docs., U. S. Govt. Print. Off.] 1970.
133 p. illus. (part col.), maps. 26 cm.
Bibliography: p. 125-129. DDC 746.6
1. Cooper-Hewitt Museum - Catalogs. 2. Chintz -
India - Catalogs. 3. Textile fabrics, India - Catalogs. I.
Cooper-Hewitt Museum. II. Title.
NK8876.A2 B4 *NYPL [3-MON 91-994]*

Beer, Evelyn. L'Exposition imaginaire .
's-Gravenhage , 1989. 391 p. : ISBN
90-12-06105-9 :
N4396 .E96 1989 *NYPL [3-MAV 91-5887]*

Beeren, W. A. L. (Willem A. L.) Cremer .
Amsterdam , 's-Gravenhage , c1990. 191 p. :
ISBN 90-12-06739-1
NX554.Z9 C7434 1990

Beesch, Ruth K. (Ruth Konnan), 1958- Florida
visionaries, 1870-1930 . Gainesville, Fla. ,
c1989. 80 p. : ISBN 0-8130-0929-4 (pbk.)
NYPL [3-MAMY 90-12386]

Beethoven, Ludwig van, 1770-1827.
[Sonatas, piano]
Piano sonatas [sound recording] / Beethoven.
Monmouth, England : Nimbus ; Foster City,
Calif. : Distributed by Audio Source,
p1979-p1980. 17 sound discs : analog, 33 1/3
rpm, stereo. ; 12 in. Nimbus: DC901--DC904.
Distributor from label mounted on v. 1 container.
Bernard Roberts, piano. Recorded 1978-1979,
Nimbus Records Studio, Wyastone Leys. In 4
containers. Direct to disc recording. Program notes
by Roger Nichols (7 p. : ill. ; 29 cm.) laid in
containers. CONTENTS. - v. 1. No. 1-7 -- v. 2. No.
8-15 -- v. 3. No. 16-25 -- v. 4. No. 23-32.
1. Sonatas (Piano).
Nimbus DC901--DC904

BEETHOVEN, LUDWIG VON, 1770-1827 -
CRITICISM AND INTERPRETATION -
JUVENILE LITERATURE.
Giants of the arts . New York , 1991. p. cm.
ISBN 1-85435-414-0 : DDC 700/.92/24 20
NX633 .G53 1991

Beethovenhouse, Villingen-Schwenningen. see
Villingen-Schwenningen, Ger. Beethovenhaus.

BEGA, MELCHIORRE, 1898-
Zironi, Stefano, 1948- Melchiorre Bega,
architetto /. Milano [1983] 183 p. : ISBN
88-7212-003-9 : DDC 720/.92/4 19
NA1123.B255 Z57 1983
NYPL [3-MQZ (Bega) 90-10395]

Begegnung mit der Stile = Face au silence :
Aquarelle von Zoran Music ... [et al
Ausstellung], Galerie Vita, Bern, 8. April-15.
Mai 1988. Bern : Galerie Vita, 1988. [35]
leaves : col. ill. ; 30 cm. Cover title. German or
French.
1. Painting, Modern - 20th century - Exhibitions. 2.
Painting, Swiss - Exhibitions. I. Galerie Vita. II. Title:
Face au silence. *NYPL [3-MAL 89-11598]*

Begegnungen : 30 Jahre in Bayern : [Ausstellung]
Ostdeutsche Galerie Regensburg, 26. September

bis 9. November 1980 / Landesverband Bayern
der Künstlergilde in Zusammenarbeit mit dem
Adalbert Stifter Verein München ;
[verantwortlich, Rudolf Mayer-Freiwaldau].
[Esslingen am Neckar] : Der Landesverband,
c1980. 64 p. : ill. : music ; 27 cm.
1. Künstlergilde. 2. Arts, German - Germany (West) -
Bavaria - Exhibitions. 3. Arts, Modern - 20th century -
Germany (West) - Bavaria - Exhibitions. I.
Mayer-Freiwaldau, Rudolf. II. Künstlergilde. III.
Adalbert-Stifter-Verein (Munich, Germany). IV.
Ostdeutsche Galerie Regensburg.
NYPL [3-MAMG 90-5884]

Begegnungen. Clausen, Rosemarie. Köln, c1967.
21 leaves of plates :
NB1310 .C58
NYPL [3-MGO (Clausen) 90-6801]

Beginner's guide to brass rubbing. Busby, Richard
J. London, 1969. 128 p. ISBN 0-7207-0244-5 :
DDC 739.5/22
NC915.R8 B8

Behind the facade . Roland, Henry, 1907-
London , 1991. 138 p., [8] p. of plates : ISBN
0-297-81161-4 *NYPL [3-MA 91-4833]*

Behl, Ulrich.
Ulrich Behl : Objekte, Zeichnungen, Graphik :
Ausstellung 25. Oktober-22. November,
Kunsthalle zu Kiel
(Christian-Albrechts-Universität) und
Schleswig-Holsteinischer Kunstverein :
Werkverzeichnis der Druckgraphik, 1967-1987
/ [Katalog und Ausstellung, Johann Schlick und
Ulrich Behl]. [Kiel] : Die Kunsthalle, [1987]
[97] p. : ill. (some col.), ports. ; 30 cm. Includes
bibliographical references. ISBN 3-923701-24-1
1. Behl, Ulrich - Exhibitions. 2. Behl, Ulrich - Catalogs.
I. Schlick, Johann. II. Kunsthalle zu Kiel. III.
Schleswig-Holsteinischer Kunstverein. IV. Title.
NYPL [3-MGO+ (Behl) 90-812]

BEHL, ULRICH - CATALOGS.
Behl, Ulrich. Ulrich Behl . [Kiel] [1987] [97]
p. : ISBN 3-923701-24-1
NYPL [3-MGO+ (Behl) 90-812]

BEHL, ULRICH - EXHIBITIONS.
Behl, Ulrich. Ulrich Behl . [Kiel] [1987] [97]
p. : ISBN 3-923701-24-1
NYPL [3-MGO+ (Behl) 90-812]

Behling, Heinz. Null Problemo . [Berlin] ,
Berlin , 1990. 1 v. (unpaged) : ISBN
3-88520-332-4
NYPL [3-MDY+ 90-13163]

Behling, Holger. Hans Gudewerdt der jüngere
(um 1600-1671) : Bildschnitzer zu Eckernförde
/ Holger Behling. Neumünster : K. Wachholtz,
1990. 375 p. : ill. ; 30 cm. (Studien zur
schleswig-holsteinischen Kunstgeschichte. Bd. 16)
Includes bibliographical references (p.355-374). ISBN
3-529-02515-1
1. Gudewerdt, Hans, ca. 1600-1671. 2. Wood-carving -
Germany - 17th century. I. Title. II. Series.
NYPL [3-MGO+ (Gudewerdt) 91-6536]

Behr, Adalbert. Bauen in Berlin, 1973 bis 1987 /
Adalbert Behr ; herausgegeben von Ehrhardt
Gisske. 1. Aufl. Leipzig : Koehler & Amelang,
1987. 199 p. : ill. (some col.) ; 28 cm. Includes
bibliographical references (p. 195-198). ISBN
3-7338-0040-0 DDC 720/.9431/55 20
1. Architecture - Germany - Berlin. 2. Architecture,
Modern - 20th century - Germany - Berlin. 3. Berlin
(Germany) - Buildings, structures, etc. I. Gisske,
Ehrhardt. II. Title.
NA1085 .B437 1987

BEHRENS, PETER, 1868-1940 -
EXHIBITIONS.
Peter Behrens . Düsseldorf , c1990. 182 p. :
ISBN 3-7640-0278-6
NYPL [3-MQZ+ (Behrens) 91-6522]

Beigbeder, Olivier.
[Lexique des symboles. Italian]
Lessico dei simboli medievali / testo di
Olivier Beigbeder ; fotografie di Zodiaque ;
[traduzione, Elio Robberto]. Milano : Jaca
Book, 1989. 304 p., [114] p. of
plates : ill. (some col.) ; 23 cm. (Già e non
ancora. Arte . 90) Translation of: Lexique des
symboles. ISBN 88-16-60090-X
1. Symbolism in art - Dictionaries - Italian. 2. Art,
Romanesque - Dictionaries - Italian. I. Title. II. Series.
NYPL [3-MAMZ 91-5818]

Beineke, D. (Dieter) Brenta-Monographie .
München [1987] 187 p. :
GA895.B73 B74 1987
NYPL [Map Div. 91-4143]

Beiträge zur Ethnographie der Sierra-Totonaken.
Marschall, Wolfgang. Wiesbaden, 1972. 112 p.:
NYPL [HTC 74-1117 Bd. 4]

Beiträge der Winckelmann-Gesellschaft .
(Bd. 9) Husar, Irene. Johann Joachim
Winckelmann in den ostslawischen Ländern /.
Stendal , 1979. 98 p. ;   DDC 709/.2/4 19
N7483.W5 H8 1979
NYPL [3-MAB 90-12523]

**Beiträge zu der internationalen Wirkung Johann
Joachim Winckelmanns .**
(T. 2/3) Husar, Irene. Johann Joachim
Winckelmann in den ostslawischen Ländern /.
Stendal , 1979. 98 p. ;   DDC 709/.2/4 19
N7483.W5 H8 1979
NYPL [3-MAB 90-12523]

**Beiträge zu Wirtschafts- und
Sozialwissenschaften .**
(Bd. 11) Krings-Heckemeier, Marie-Therese.
Kommunikation und gebaute Umwelt .
Witterschlick , 1990. 264 p. ;   ISBN
3-925267-35-2
NA7125 .K75 1990

**Beiträge zur Denkmal- und Stadtbildpflege des
Wuppertals .**
(Bd. 5) Wuppertal wiederentdeckt . Wuppertal ,
1986. 248 p. :   *NYPL [3-MQWD 91-5872]*

**Beiträge zur Erschliessung hellenistischer und
kaiserzeitlicher Skulptur und Architektur .**
(Bd. 11) Bergemann, Johannes. Römische
Reiterstatuen . Mainz am Rhein , c1990. xii,
196 p., 96 p. of plates :   ISBN 3-8053-1149-4
NYPL [3-MGH+ 91-5688]

Beiträge zur historischen Bildungsforschung .
(Bd. 7) Köhler, Johannes. Angewandte
Emblematik im Fliesensaal von Wrisbergholzen
bei Hildesheim /. Hildesheim , 1988. 165 p. :
ISBN 3-7848-3757-3
NYPL [3-MRXZ 90-13016]

**Beiträge zur Kunstgeschichte (Witterschlick,
Germany) .**
(Bd. 3) Meurer, Thomas. Die Eisenbahn in der
deutschen Kunst . Witterschlick/Bonn , 1989.
172, [76] p. :   ISBN 3-925267-28-X
N6867 .M48 1989

(Bd. 4) Hampel, Frithjof Detlev Paul. Schinkels
Möbelwerk und seine Voraussetzungen /.
Witterschlick/Bonn , 1989. 255 p., [8] p. of
plates :   ISBN 3-925267-29-8
NK2554.S35 H35 1989

Beiträge zur Kunstwissenschaft, 0175-7202 .
(Bd. 7) Rietzsch, Barbara. Künstliche Grotten
des 16. und 17. Jahrhunderts . München ,
c1987. ii, 122 p., [39] p. of plates :   ISBN
3-89235-017-5   *NYPL [3-MQW 91-7052]*

(Bd. 31) Mannewitz, Martin. Stift Admont .
München , c1989. 422 p. :   ISBN 3-89235-031-0 :
NA5510.A35 S755 1989

(Bd. 33) Diruf, Hermann. Paläste Venedigs vor
1500 . München , c1990. 224 p. :   ISBN
3-89235-033-7
NA7756.V4 D57 1990

(Bd. 34) Rother, Susanne. Beckmann als
Landschaftsmaler /. München , c1990. 212 p. :
ISBN 3-89235-034-5 :
ND588.B37 R67 1990

Beke, Laszló. 80 Jahre ungarische Malerei von
der Romantik bis zum Surrealismus . Mannheim
[1989] 249 p. :   ISBN 3-89165-063-9 DDC
759.39/074/434646 20
ND519 .A15 1989   *NYPL [3-MCY 91-4203]*

Bekker, Gerrit, 1943-
Gerrit M. Bekker, Gemälde : Katalog zu einer
Ausstellung im Museum für Hamburgische
Geschichte vom 29. April bis zum 2. August
1987 / Vorwort und Katalog, Jörgen Bracker.
Hamburg : Das Museum, [1987] 56 p. : col.
ill. ; 34 cm. Includes bibliographical references.
1. Bekker, Gerrit, 1943- - Exhibitions. I. Bracker,
Jörgen. II. Museum für Hamburgische Geschichte.
NYPL [3-MCK+ B424 91-6718]

BEKKER, GERRIT, 1943- - EXHIBITIONS.
Bekker, Gerrit, 1943- Gerrit M. Bekker,
Gemälde . Hamburg [1987] 56 p. :
NYPL [3-MCK+ B424 91-6718]

Belamri, Rabah, 1946- Benanteur, Abdallah,
1931- Abdallah Benanteur . [Alger] [1989] 141
p. :
NE2087.65.B45 A4 1989

Beldescu, Alexandra. Manuscrise persane în
colecţii din România / Alexandra Beldescu.
Bucureşti : Editura Meridiane, 1987. 77 p., 40
leaves of plates : col. ill. ; 25 cm. (Manuscris)
Summary in English. Includes bibliographical references
(p. 66-[69]). Includes index.
1. Illumination of books and manuscripts, Iranian -
Catalogs. 2. Illumination of books and manuscripts -
Romania - Catalogs. I. Title.
ND3241 .B353 1987

**Beleidsgerichte studies hoger onderwijs en
wetenschappelijk onderzoek .**
(20) Velden, R. K. W. van der. Letteren en
arbeidsmarkt /. Groningen , 's-Gravenhage
[1989] 129 p. ;
NX554.A1 V4 1989

Belford, Marilyn. Time and space concepts in art
/. New York , 1980. viii, 157 p., 4 leaves of
plates :
NX650.S8 T55   *NYPL [3-MAMZ 80-2228]*

Belfort (France : Territory). Conseil général.
Billot, Renée. Léon Delarbre, le peintre
déporté . Jarville-La Malgrange [1989] 125 p. :
ISBN 2-86955-088-X
NYPL [3-MCO+ D339 91-6125]

BELFRIES. see TOWERS.

**Belgian artists in the world's salerooms,
1988-1989 /.** Bertrand, Olivier. Brussels , 1989.
xxxv, 334 p. :   *NYPL [3-MAZ 91-5792]*

Belgian artists' signatures /. Piron, Paul-L.
[Brussels] [1989] 544 p. :
NYPL [3-MAME 91-5520]

**BELGIOIOSO (ITALY) - BUILDINGS,
STRUCTURES, ETC.**
Castello di Belgioioso . Milano , 1987. 15 p. :
ISBN 88-7111-010-2
NYPL [MDG+ (Dal Re) 90-10839]

Belgische Boerenbond. Schilders van het
landelijke leven in België . Tielt , 1990. 173 p. :
ISBN 90-209-1787-0 :
ND469.F5 S35 1990

Belgisches Haus (Cologne, Germany) Plakate aus
der Druckerei Benard, Sammlung des Musée de
la Vie Wallone, Lüttich =. Köln , 1980. 92 p. :
NYPL [3-MDW 90-4651]

Belgisches Haus (Gallery) Maréchal, François,
1861- François Maréchal, 1861-1945 . Köln ,
1979. [74] p. :
NE2055.5.M37 A4 1979
NYPL [MDG (Maréchal) 81-1028]

Belgium. Administration du patrimoine culturel.
Le Patrimoine monumental de la Belgique.
Liège [1989- <v. 1, pt. 1 > :   ISBN
2-8021-0092-0 (v. 1)   DDC 720/.9493/32 20
NA1170 .P37 1989

**Belgium. Bestuur voor Monumenten en
Landschappen.** Le Patrimoine monumental de
la Belgique. Liège [1989- <v. 1, pt. 1 > :
ISBN 2-8021-0092-0 (v. 1)   DDC 720/.9493/32
20
NA1170 .P37 1989

BELGIUM - BIOGRAPHY - DICTIONARIES.
Dictionnaire biographique illustré des artistes en
Belgique depuis 1830. [Bruxelles] , 1987. 416
p., [31] p. of plates :
NYPL [3-MAO 91-4886]

**Belgium. Culture française, Ministère de la. see
Belgium. Ministère de la culture française.**

**BELGIUM - DESCRIPTION AND TRAVEL -
1971- - GUIDE-BOOKS.**
Remoortere, Julien van. Ippa's kastelengids voor
België /. Tielt , 1988. 431 p. :   ISBN
90-209-1647-5
NA7725 .R46 1988

**Belgium. Diffusion des arts, Service de la. see
Belgium. Service de la diffusion des arts.**

**BELGIUM - HISTORY - GERMAN
OCCUPATION, 1914-1918.**
The Ideological crisis of expressionism .
Columbia, S.C. , c1990. 299 p. :   ISBN
0-938100-77-7 (alk. paper)   DDC 700 20
NX550.A1 I33 1990
NYPL [3-MAMG 90-11742]

BELGIUM IN ART - EXHIBITIONS.
Albert Dürer aux Pays-Bas . Bruxelles , 1977.
xxiii, 211, 144 p., [14] leaves of plates :
N6888.D8 A4 1977
NYPL [3-MCK D85 81-320]

**Belgium. Ministère de la communauté française.
Commissariat général aux relations
internationales.** La Scuola di Mons . Brescia ,
Milano , c1989. 103 p. :   DDC 709/.493/42 20
N6968 .S37 1989
NYPL [3-MAME 90-10713]

Belgium. Ministère de la culture française.
Félicien Rops, 1833-1898 . Brüssel , 1979. 88
p. :
N6973.R67 A4 1979
NYPL [3-MCH R78 81-420]

**Belgium. Ministère de la culture française.
Service de la diffusion des arts. see Belgium.
Service de la diffusion des arts.**

**Belgium. Ministerie van de Vlaamse
Gemeenschap.** Open mind . Milano , c1989.
318 p. :   *NYPL [3-MAMZ 90-11011]*

Belgium. Service de la diffusion des arts. Félicien
Rops, 1833-1898 . Brüssel , 1979. 88 p. :
N6973.R67 A4 1979
NYPL [3-MCH R78 81-420]

**Belgrad. Muzej savremene umetnosti. see Muzej
savremene umetnosti.**

Beliaeva, L. I. Soviet Union. Glavnoe upravlenie
geodezii i kartografii. Atlas zarubezhnykh stran
dlia srednei shkoly . [Moskva , 1964]. 1 atlas
(40 p. :   *NYPL [Map Div. 91-1092]*

Believers, United Society of. see Shakers.

Belk Art Gallery. April Greiman, large scale
posters. [Cullowhee, N.C.] , c1987. v, 27 p. :
NYPL [3-MDWS (Greiman) 90-12807]

Belkin, Arnold.
Arnold Belkin : 33 años de producción
artística : Museo del Palacio de Bellas Artes,
julio-agosto, México, D.F. 1989. 1a ed. [Mexico
City] : Instituto Nacional de Bellas Artes,
c1989. 206 p., [8] folded leaves of plates : ill.
(some col.) ; 27 cm. Includes bibliographical
references (186-194). ISBN 968-292-434-0
1. Belkin, Arnold - Exhibitions. I. Palacio de Bellas
Artes (Mexico City, Mexico). II. Instituto Nacional de
Bellas Artes (Mexico).
NYPL [3-MCZ B432 91-4574]

BELKIN, ARNOLD - EXHIBITIONS.
Belkin, Arnold. Arnold Belkin . [Mexico City] ,
c1989. 206 p., [8] folded leaves of plates :
ISBN 968-292-434-0
NYPL [3-MCZ B432 91-4574]

Bell, Charles, 1935-
Geldzahler, Henry. Charles Bell . New York ,
1991. p. cm.   ISBN 0-8109-3114-1 (cloth)   DDC
759.13 20
N6537.B447 A4 1991

BELL, CHARLES, 1935- - CATALOGS.
Geldzahler, Henry. Charles Bell . New York ,
1991. p. cm.   ISBN 0-8109-3114-1 (cloth)   DDC
759.13 20
N6537.B447 A4 1991

Bell, Daniel. Immagini del post-moderno .
Venezia , c1983. 345 p. :   ISBN 88-85067-09-3
DDC 724.9/1 19
NA682.P67 I48 1983
NYPL [3-MQV 91-6389]

Bellabarba, Marco.
Imago lignea . Trento , c1989. 287 p. :   ISBN
88-85114-07-5   *NYPL [3-MGI+ 91-4470]*

Imago lignea . Trento, Italia , c1989. 287 p. :
ISBN 88-85114-07-5 :   DDC 730/.945/38 20
NB1255.I8 I45 1989

Bellafiore, Giuseppe.
Architettura in Sicilia nelle età islamica e
normanna : (827-1194) / Giuseppe Bellafiore.
Milano : A. Lombardi, c1990. 366 p. : ill.,
plans ; 28 cm. (Civiltà siciliana . 1) Includes index.
Includes bibliographical references (p. 195-212). ISBN
88-7177-010-2 :
1. Architecture, Medieval - Italy - Sicily. 2.
Architecture - Italy - Sicily. 3. Architecture, Islamic -
Italy - Sicily. 4. Architecture, Norman - Italy - Sicily. I.
Title. II. Series.   *NYPL [3-MQO 91-3372]*

Architettura in Sicilia nelle età islamica e
normanna (827-1194) / Giuseppe Bellafiore.
Palermo : A. Lombardi, c1990. 366 p. : ill. ; 28

Las bellas artes en Jalisco /.

cm. (La Civiltà siciliana . 1) Includes bibliographical references (p. 195-212) and indexes. ISBN 88-7177-010-2 : DDC 720/.945/809021 20
1. Architecture, Islamic - Italy - Sicily. 2. Architecture, Norman - Italy - Sicily - Arab influences. 3. Architecture - Italy - Sicily. I. Title. II. Series.
NA1109.S5 B4 1990

Las bellas artes en Jalisco /. Reyes y Zavala, Ventura. Guadalajara, Jalisco, México , 1989. xi, 44 p. ; ISBN 968-8323-84-5
NYPL [3-MAM 91-4662]

Bellati, Nally. New Italian design / Nally Bellati ; introduction by Alberto Alessi. New York : Rizzoli, c1990. 203 p. : ill. (some col.) ; 26 cm. Includes index. ISBN 0-8478-1258-8 DDC 745.4/4945/09048 20
1. Design - Italy - History - 20th century. I. Title.
NK1452.A1 B4 1990
NYPL [3-MNE 91-4847]

Bellec, François. Sillages néerlandais : la vie maritime dans l'art des Pays-Bas = Kunst in het kielzog : het maritieme leven in de Nederlandse kunst / F. Bellec, Ph. Bosscher, A. Erftemeijer. Zutphen : De Walburg Pers, c1989. 172 p. : ill. (some col.), maps ; 28 cm. French and Dutch. Issued in conjunction with an exhibition held in the Musée de la marine, Paris, Oct. 1989-Jan. 1990. Includes bibliographical references (p. [155]-159) and index. ISBN 90-6011-657-7
1. Marine art - Netherlands - Exhibitions. 2. Marine painting - Netherlands - Exhibitions. 3. Navigation - Netherlands - History - Exhibitions. I. Bosscher, Ph. M. II. Erftemeijer, A. (Antoon). III. Musée de la marine (Paris, France). IV. Title. V. Title: Kunst in het kielzog.
NYPL [3-MAME 91-6109]

Belleroche, Albert de. Exposition de l'oeuvre lithographique d'Albert de Belleroche : Bruxelles, 12 janvier-12 mars, 1933 / Bibliothèque Royal de Belgique. Bruxelles : La Bibliothèque, 1933 (Renaix : J. Leherte-Courtin) [37] p., [8] leaves of plates : ill., port. ; 24 cm.
1. Belleroche, Albert de - Exhibitions. I. Bibliothèque royale de Belgique. II. Title.
NYPL [MDG (Belleroche) 90-5547]

BELLEROCHE, ALBERT DE - EXHIBITIONS.
Belleroche, Albert de. Exposition de l'oeuvre lithographique d'Albert de Belleroche . Bruxelles , 1933 (Renaix : J. Leherte-Courtin) [37] p., [8] leaves of plates :
NYPL [MDG (Belleroche) 90-5547]

Belles endormies. Monod-Fontaine, Isabelle. Matisse, Le rêve, ou les belles endormies /. Paris , c1989. 63 p., [1] folded leaf of plates : ISBN 0-287-66005-1
NYPL [3-MCO M43 91-3726]

BELLES-LETTRES. see LITERATURE.

Bellevue Art Museum (Wash.) Kingsbury, Martha, 1941- George Tsutakawa /. Seattle , Bellevue, Wash. , c1990. 156 p. : ISBN 0-295-97020-0 (alk. paper) DDC 709/.2 20
N6537.T74 A4 1990
NYPL [3-MGO (Tsutakawa) 91-6230]

Bellezza e seduzione nella Roma imperiale : Roma, Palazzo dei Conservatori, 11 giugno-31 luglio 1990. [Roma] : De Luca edizioni d'arte, [c1990] 122 p. : ill. (some col.) ; 32 cm. At head of title: Comune di Roma, Assessorato alla cultura. "La mostra è stata realizzata dall'Assessorato alla cultura del comune di Roma, in collaborazione con Laura Biagiotti"--P. [6]. Includes bibliographical references (p. 119-122). ISBN 88-7813-283-7 :
1. Feminine beauty (Aesthetics) - Rome - Exhibitions. 2. Art, Roman - Exhibitions. 3. Women in art - Exhibitions. I. Biagiotti, Laura, 1943-. II. Palazzo dei Conservatori (Rome, Italy). III. Rome (Italy). Assessorato alla cultura.
N7629.2.I8 R663 1990

Belli Barsali, Isa.
[Smalto in Europa. English]
European enamels / Isa Belli Barsali ; [translated by Raymond Rudorff]. London : Cassell, 1988. 157 p. : col. ill. ; 19 cm. (Cassell's styles in art) Translation of: Lo smalto in Europa. ISBN 0-304-32179-6 (pbk) DDC 738.4/094 19
1. Enamel and enameling - Europe. I. Title. II. Series.
NYPL [3-MNV 90-9465]

Belli, Gabriella.
Divisionismo italiano /. [Milano , c1990. 480

p. : ISBN 88-435-3178-6
NYPL [3-MCE 90-12999]

L'Età del divisionismo /. Milano , c1990. 295 p., [2] p. of plates : ISBN 88-435-3179-4 DDC 700 20
NX552.A1 E78 1990
NYPL [3-MAMC 91-4384]

Bellingham, Wash. Western Washington University. see Western Washington University.

Bellini, Giovanni, d. 1516.
FEAST OF THE GODS.
Bull, David, 1934- The Feast of the gods . Washington , Hanover, N.H. , 1990. 106 p. : ISBN 0-89468-144-3 DDC 709 s 759.5 20
N386.U5 S78 vol. 40 ND623.B39
NYPL [3-MCF B39 90-8050]

Bellini, Mario, 1935-
Mario Bellini, architetture / a cura di Ermanno Ranzani. Milano : Electa, 1988. 115 p. : ill. (some col.) ; 24 cm. Catalog of an exhibition at the Galleria Antonia Jannone, Milan, Oct. 1988. ISBN 88-435-2665-0
1. Bellini, Mario, 1935- - Exhibitions. 2. Architecture, Modern - 20th century - Exhibitions. I. Ranzani, Ermanno. II. Galleria A. Jannone. III. Title.
NYPL [3-MQZ (Bellini) 90-12540]

BELLINI, MARIO, 1935- - EXHIBITIONS.
Bellini, Mario, 1935- Mario Bellini, architetture /. Milano , 1988. 115 p. : ISBN 88-435-2665-0
NYPL [3-MQZ (Bellini) 90-12540]

Belliston, Larry, 1949-
Hanks, Kurt, 1947- Draw! . Los Altos, Calif. , 1990. p. cm. ISBN 1-560-52054-X : DDC 741.2 20
NC730 .H27 1990

Hanks, Kurt, 1947- Rapid viz . Los Altos, CA , c1990. 149 p. : ISBN 1-560-52055-8 (pbk.). : DDC 741.6 20
NC877.8 .H36 1990

Bellonci, Maria. Mantegna, Andrea, 1431-1506. L'opera completa del Mantegna. Milano, 1967. 128 p. :
ND623.M3 B42
NYPL [3-MCF+ M29 91-5642]

Bellonzi, Fortunato.
(ed) Cagli, Corrado, 1910- Cagli . Firenze , 1974. [8] leaves, [47] leaves of plates :
NC257.C23 B44
NYPL [3-MCF C125 91-472]

Scultura figurativa italiana del XX secolo / Fortunato Bellonzi Roma : De Luca edizioni d'arte c1989. 167 p. : chiefly ill. ; 22 cm. Includes index. ISBN 88-7813-240-3 : DDC 730/.945/0904 20
1. Sculpture, Modern - 20th century - Italy. I. Title.
NB1930 .B45 1989 *NYPL [3-MGI 91-6913]*

Bellor, Mary E. Architectural drawings of the Old Executive Office Building, 1871-1888 . Washington, DC , 1988. vii, 71 p. : ISBN 1-558-35012-8
NYPL [3-MQWO+ 91-4241]

Bellotto, Bernardo, 1721-1780.
Bernardo Bellotto : Verona e le città europee / a cura di Sergio Marinelli ; scritti di Gisela Barche ... [et al.]. Milano : Electa, c1990. 172 p. : ill. (some col.) ; 28 cm. Catalog of an exhibition held in Verona, at the Museo di Castelvecchio, June 15-Sept. 16, 1990, in collaboration with the Istituto di storia dell'arte della Fondazione Giorgio Cini di Venezia. Includes bibliographical references (p. 171-172). ISBN 88-435-3242-1
1. Bellotto, Bernardo, 1721-1780 - Exhibitions. 2. Europe in art - Exhibitions. I. Marinelli, Sergio. II. Barche, Gisela, 1949-. III. Museo di Castelvecchio (Verona, Italy). IV. Istituto di storia dell'arte (Fondazione "Giorgio Cini"). V. Title.
ND623.B43 A4 1990

BELLOTTO, BERNARDO, 1721-1780 - EXHIBITIONS.
Bellotto, Bernardo, 1721-1780. Bernardo Bellotto . Milano , c1990. 172 p. : ISBN 88-435-3242-1
ND623.B43 A4 1990

BELLOWS, GEORGE, 1882-1925 - CRITICISM AND INTERPRETATION.
Doezema, Marianne, 1950- George Bellows and urban America . New Haven, CT , c1991. p. cm. ISBN 0-300-05043-7 DDC 759.13 20
ND237.B45 D6 1991

BELLOWS, GEORGE, 1882-1925 - EXHIBITIONS.
Bellows, George, 1882-1925. George Bellows (1882-1925) . New York, N.Y. [1984] 30 p. :
NYPL [3-MCX B44 91-6268]

George Bellows . Fort Worth, Tex. : Los Angeles, Calif. : p. cm. ISBN 0-8109-3119-2 DDC 759.13 20
ND237.B45 A4 1992

Bellows, George, 1882-1925. George Bellows (1882-1925) : paintings, drawings and lithographs : October 26-December 21, 1984. New York, N.Y. : H.V. Allison Galleries, [1984] 30 p. : ill. ; 23 cm. "An exhibition in memory of Gordon K. Allison (1904-1984)."
1. Bellows, George, 1882-1925 - Exhibitions. I. H.V. Allison Galleries. II. Title.
NYPL [3-MCX B44 91-6268]

BELOFF, ANGELINA, 1879-1969 - EXHIBITIONS.
Angelina Beloff . México, D.F. , México , 1989. 95 p. : *NYPL [MDG (Beloff) 90-11726]*

Angelina Beloff . México, D.F. : Guanajuato, Gto. : 95 p. : ISBN 968-292-336-0 DDC 760/.092 20
N6999.B425 A4 1989

Belting, Hans, 1935- Bild und Kult : eine Geschichte des Bildes vor dem Zeitalter der Kunst / Hans Belting. München : C.H. Beck, c1990. 700 p. : ill. (some col.) ; 25 cm. Includes bibliographical references (p. 667-676) and index. ISBN 3-406-34367-8
1. Christian art and symbolism - Medieval, 500-1500 - Europe. 2. Icons - Cult. I. Title.
NYPL [3-MAIH 90-12870]

Beltrame, Aldo, 1932- La fotografia antagonista / Aldo Beltrame ; prefazione di Gianna Ciao Pointer. Piombino : TraceEdizioni, 1989. 67 p., [6] leaves of plates : ill. ; 24 cm. (Studi di difesa sociale . 2) DDC 770 20
1. Photography. I. Title. II. Series.
TR185 .B42 1989 *NYPL [MFW 91-3721]*

Beltrame Quattrocchi, Enrichetta. Gabinetto nazionale delle stampe. Disegni toscani e umbri del primo Rinascimento . Roma [1979] 183 p. :
NC256.T8 G32 1979
NYPL [3-MBH 81-532]

Beltrán, Antonio [i. e. Antonio Beltrán Martínez] see **Beltrán Martínez, Antonio, 1916-**

Beltrán Lloris, Miguel. Guía de la cerámica romana / Miguel Beltrán Lloris. Zaragoza : Libros Pórtico, 1990. 373 p. : ill. ; 31 cm. ISBN 84-85264-80-5
I. Title.
IN PROCESS (ONLINE)
NYPL [3-MPEK+ 91-2666]

Beltrán Martínez, Antonio, 1916- Ensayo sobre el rigen y significación del arte prehistórico / Antonio Beltrán Martínez. 1a ed. Zaragoza, España : Prensas Universitarias Zaragoza, 1989. 199 p. ; 22 cm. (Ciencias sociales. 12) ISBN 84-7733-136-7
I. Series: Ciencias sociales (Zaragoza, Spain) , 12. II. Title.
IN PROCESS (ONLINE)
NYPL [3-MADF 91-4516]

BELTSCHEW, KOITSCHO - ART COLLECTIONS - EXHIBITIONS.
Russische Ikonen 1400-1700. [Hamburg] [1990] 74, [2] p. : DDC 704.9/482 20
N8189.S62 R9757 1990

Belvedere designbook.
(v. 26) Textile patternbook . Rome, Italy , 1989. xxi, 79, 79, 79 p. : ISBN 88-7070-076-3
NYPL [3-MON+ 91-4270]

Ben and Abby Grey Foundation. Mairs, Clara, 1878-1963. Clara . St. Paul, Minn. , c1976. 47 p. : *NYPL [MDG (Mairs) 90-5656]*

Ben Cunningham--a life with color /. Nemser, Cindy. Post, Tex. , c1989. 91 p. : ISBN 0-9622235-0-6 DDC 759.13 B 20
ND237.C8496 N46 1989
NYPL [3-MCX C973 91-6760]

Ben Dhiab, Ahmed. Chants tatoués = Tattooed songs / Ahmed Ben Dhiab. Rotterdam : Hiwar, 1987. [16], 125 p. : ill. ; 30 cm. Title on added t.p.: Anāshid mūshammah. Errata slip inserted. French with English and Arabic translation. ISBN

90-6330-139-1
I. Title. II. Title: Tattooed songs. III. Title: Anāshīd mushammah.
NYPL [3-MCZ + B4495 90-8107]

Ben el-Khadir, Mohamed. Architectures régionales : un parcours à travers le nord marocain / Mohamed Ben el-Khadir, Abderrafih Lahbabi.1re éd. [Morocco : s.n.], 1989 (Casablanca : Impr. Najah el Jadida) 211 p. : ill. ; 28 cm. Includes bibliographical references (p. 208-211).
1. Regionalism in architecture - Morocco. 2. Architecture, Islamic - Morocco. 3. Architecture - Morocco. I. Lahbabi, Abderrafih. II. Title.
NA1590 .B46 1989

Ben Kelly Design. Plans and elevations /. London , 1990. [84] p. : ISBN 1-85454-052-1 (pbk.) : DDC 745.44941 20
NK1443   **NYPL   [3-MNE 90-11636]**

Ben Nicholson /. Lewison, Jeremy. New York , c1991. p. cm. ISBN 0-8478-1395-9 DDC 759.2 20
ND497.N58 A4 1991

Ben Nicholson . Nicholson, Ben, 1894-
Hannover , c1967. 25 p., [32] p. of plates :
NYPL [3-MCV N619 90-7121]

Ben Nicholson, recent oil-wash drawings.
Nicholson, Ben, 1894- Ben Nicholson .
Hannover , c1967. 25 p., [32] p. of plates —
NYPL [3-MCV N619 90-7121]

Ben Tré, Howard, 1949-
Johnson, Linda L., 1961- Howard Ben Tré .
Washington, D.C. , 1989. 48 p. : ISBN 0-943044-14-6 : DDC 730/.92 20
NB237.B434 J64 1989
NYPL [3-MGO (Ben Tré) 91-6438]

BEN TRÉ, HOWARD, 1949- - EXHIBITIONS.
Johnson, Linda L., 1961- Howard Ben Tré .
Washington, D.C. , 1989. 48 p. : ISBN 0-943044-14-6 : DDC 730/.92 20
NB237.B434 J64 1989
NYPL [3-MGO (Ben Tré) 91-6438]

Ben Yosef, Ute. The graven image : the life and work of Moses Kottler / by Ute Ben Yosef. Cape Town : Perskor, c1989. 128 p. : ill. ; 21 cm. Includes bibliographical references (p. 126-128). ISBN 0-628-03407-5 DDC 730/.92 B 20
1. Kottler, Moses, 1896-1977. 2. Sculptors - South Africa - Biography. I. Title.
NB1096.K67 B46 1989

Ben-Zion.
Ben-Zion 1933-1959 : a retrospect / [text by Stephen S. Kayser]. New York : The Jewish Museum, [1959] xxxii p. : ill. ; 22 cm. Cover title. An exhibition held at the Jewish Museum, New York on Sept. 17-Oct. 28, 1959.
1. Ben-Zion - Exhibitions. I. Kayser, Stephen S., 1900-. II. Jewish Theological Seminary of America. Jewish Museum. III. Title.
NYPL [3-MCZ B470 90-12696]

BEN-ZION - EXHIBITIONS.
Ben-Zion. Ben-Zion 1933-1959 . New York [1959] xxxii p. :
NYPL [3-MCZ B470 90-12696]

Ben-Zion 1933-1959 . Ben-Zion. New York [1959] xxxii p. :
NYPL [3-MCZ B470 90-12696]

Benanteur, Abdallah, 1931-
Abdallah Benanteur : gravures / textes de Rabah Belamri ... [et al.]. [Alger] : ENAG : Editions-AEFAB, [1989] 141 p. : col. ill. ; 34 cm. Includes bibliographical references (p. 31-33).
1. Benanteur, Abdallah, 1931- - Catalogs. I. Belamri, Rabah, 1946-. II. Title.
NE2087.65.B45 A4 1989

BENANTEUR, ABDALLAH, 1931- - CATALOGS.
Benanteur, Abdallah, 1931- Abdallah Benanteur . [Alger] [1989] 141 p. :
NE2087.65.B45 A4 1989

Bénard, Auguste, 1854-1907.
Plakate aus der Druckerei Benard, Sammlung des Musée de la Vie Wallone, Lüttich =.
Köln , 1980. 92 p. :
NYPL [3-MDW 90-4651]

BÉNARD, AUGUSTE, 1854-1907 - EXHIBITIONS.
Plakate aus der Druckerei Benard, Sammlung des Musée de la Vie Wallone, Lüttich =.

Köln , 1980. 92 p. :
NYPL [3-MDW 90-4651]

Bendavid-Val, Leah. Changing reality : recent Soviet photography / by Leah Bendavid-Val. [Washington, D.C.] : Starwood Pub. in association with the Corcoran Gallery of Art and Art Services International, c1991. 132 p. : ill. ; 26 cm. ISBN 0-912347-76-7
1. Photography - Soviet Union - Exhibitions. 2. Soviet Union - Social life and customs - 1970- - Pictorial works - Exhibitions. I. Corcoran Gallery of Art. II. Title.
NYPL [MFW 91-6156]

Bendicht Friedli. Killer, Peter, 1945- Bendicht Friedli, oder, Der Weg entsteht im Gehen /. Bern , c1989. 112 p. : ISBN 3-258-04138-5 DDC 759.9494 20
ND853.F69 A4 1989
NYPL [3-MCZ F869 91-4185]

Bendicht Friedli, oder, Der Weg entsteht im Gehen /. Killer, Peter, 1945- Bern , c1989. 112 p. : ISBN 3-258-04138-5 DDC 759.9494 20
ND853.F69 A4 1989
NYPL [3-MCZ F869 91-4185]

Benedetto Antelami /. Quintavalle, Arturo Carlo.
Milano , c1990. 384 p. : ISBN 88-435-3176-X DDC 730/.92 20
NB623.A6 A4 1990

Benedetto Antelami /. Quintavalle, Arturo Carlo, 1936- Milano , c1990. 384 p. :
NYPL [3-MGO+ (Antelami) 90-12881]

Benedict, Brad. Dyer, Rod. Coast to coast . New York , 1991. p. cm. ISBN 1-558-59156-7 DDC 741.6/92/0973 20
NC1002.L3 D94 1991

Benedict, E. Sozialistische Staaten Mittel- und Südosteuropas /. Gotha , 1986. 1 atlas (190 p.) : ISBN 3-7301-0032-7
NYPL [Map Div. 91-3783]

BENEDIKTINERKLOSTER HEILIG KREUZ ZU DONAUWÖRTH.
Heilig Kreuz in Donauwörth /. Donauwörth , 1987. 203 p. : ISBN 3-403-01848-2
NYPL [3-MRBB+ 90-2728]

BENEDIKTINERSTIFT LAMBACH.
Scheele, Paul-Werner. Die Herrlichkeit des Herrn . Würzburg , c1990. 136 p. : ISBN 3-429-01316-X
ND2750.L36 S34 1990

Benedito. Benedito, Concha. Concha Benedito. Paris [1989] 120 p. : ISBN 2-906905-26-7
MLCM 90/06996 (N)
NYPL [3-MCQ+ B458 91-4061]

Benedito, Concha. Concha Benedito. Paris : Area, [1989] 120 p. : ill. (some col.) ; 29 cm. Cover title: Benedito. ISBN 2-906905-26-7
1. Benedito, Concha. I. Title. II. Title: Benedito.
MLCM 90/06996 (N)
NYPL [3-MCQ+ B458 91-4061]

BENEDITO, CONCHA.
Benedito, Concha. Concha Benedito. Paris [1989] 120 p. : ISBN 2-906905-26-7
MLCM 90/06996 (N)
NYPL [3-MCQ+ B458 91-4061]

BENENSON, EDWARD H. - ART COLLECTIONS - EXHIBITIONS.
Duke University, Durham, N. C. Art Museum. Selected works from the Benenson Collection . Durham, N.C. , 1976. [24] p. : DDC 750/.74/0156563 19
ND189 .D84 1976 **NYPL [3-MAL 81-352]**

BENENSON, GLADYS - ART COLLECTIONS - EXHIBITIONS.
Duke University, Durham, N. C. Art Museum. Selected works from the Benenson Collection . Durham, N.C. , 1976. [24] p. : DDC 750/.74/0156563 19
ND189 .D84 1976 **NYPL [3-MAL 81-352]**

Benesch, Evelyn.
Niederösterreich . Wien , c1990. xxxviii, 1414 p., [13] leaves of plates : ISBN 3-7031-0652-2
NYPL [3-MQWD 91-3702]

Niederösterreich nördlich der Donau /. Wien , c1990. xxxviii, 1414 p., 6 p. of plates : ISBN 3-7031-0652-2 DDC 720/.946/12 20
NA1009.L68 N54 1990

Bénévent L'Abbaye /. Conquet, Jean. Guéret, Creuse , c1988. 126 p. : ISBN 2-903870-28-4
NA5551.B514 C6 1988

BÈNÈVENT-L'ABBAYE (FRANCE) - HISTORY.
Conquet, Jean. Bénévent L'Abbaye /. Guéret, Creuse , c1988. 126 p. : ISBN 2-903870-28-4
NA5551.B514 C6 1988

Benevides Pinho, Diva. see Pinho, Diva Benevides.

Benezra, Neal David, 1953- Martin Puryear / by Neal Benezra ; with an essay by Robert Storr. Chicago, Ill. : Art Institute of Chicago ; New York, N.Y. : Thames and Hudson, c1991. p. cm. Prepared on the occasion of the exhibition organized by the Art Institute of Chicago. Exhibition held at the Art Institute of Chicago, Nov. 2, 1991-Jan. 5, 1992; Hirshhorn Museum and Sculpture Garden, Smithsonian Institution, Washington, D.C., Feb. 5-May 10, 1992; The Museum of Contemporary Art, Los Angeles, July 26-Oct. 4, 1992; Philadelphia Museum of Art, Nov. 8, 1992-Jan. 3, 1993. Includes bibliographical references. ISBN 0-86559-092-3 DDC 709/.2 20
1. Puryear, Martin, 1941- - Exhibitions. I. Puryear, Martin, 1941-. II. Art Institute of Chicago. III. Title.
NB237.P84 A4 1991

BENGALI ART. see ART, BENGALI.

Bengy, Jean de. Bazaine, Jean, 1904- Bazaine /. Genève , Paris , c1990. 178 p. : ISBN 2-605-00162-8 DDC 759.4 20
ND553.B42 A4 1990

Beni culturali di San Vito dei Normanni /. Chionna, Antonio. Fasano, Brindisi [1988] 471 p., [32] leaves of plates : ISBN 88-7514-253-X : DDC 709/.45/754 20
N6921.S38 C47 1988
NYPL [3-MAMC+ 90-10597]

Benić, Slavomir. Beritićev zbornik . Dubrovnik , 1960. 335 p., [1] folded leaf of plates :
NYPL [*QKK 83-2704]

Benini, Mirella.
[Ceramica del Rinascimento. Portuguese]
Cerâmica do Renascimento / Mirella Benini. 1a. ed. Lisboa : Editorial Presença, 1989. 82 p. : ill. (some col.) ; 24 cm. (Artes e estilos . 1) Translation of: Ceramica del Rinascimento. Includes bibliographical references (p. 82).
1. Pottery, Italian. 2. Pottery, Renaissance - Italy. 3. Pottery, European. 4. Pottery, Renaissance - Europe. I. Title. II. Series.
NK4103 .B416 1989

Benito Messeguer en Chiapas /. López Moreno, Roberto, 1942- [Tuxtla Gutiérrez, Chiapas] [1989] 69 p. : DDC 759.972 20
ND813.M475 A4 1989

Benjamin, Andrew E. Deconstruction . London , 1989. 264 p. : ISBN 0-85670-996-4
NYPL [MQV+ 89-27959]

Benjamin, Asher, 1773-1845. The country builder's assistant : fully explaining, the best methods for striking regular and quirked mouldings ... correctly engraved on thirty-seven copperplates with a printed explanation to each / by Asher Benjamin. Greenfield, Mass. : J. Denio, 1805. [36] p., [1], 37 leaves of plates (2 folded) : ill., plans ; 20 cm. NUC pre-1956, NB 0310865 Shaw & Shoemaker 7974 Source: Exchange with Charles B. Wood III, Nov. 26, 1990. DLC DDC 720 20
1. Architecture. 2. Carpentry. I. Title.
NA2520 .B4 1805

Benjamin, Isabelle. Evolution de la professionnalité des architectes : diversification des pratiques, actualisation de la qualification / Isabelle Benjamin, François Aballéa. Paris : Fondation pour la recherche sociale, [1990] 109 p. ; 22 cm. (Recherches, 0249-8804) At head of title: Ministère de l'équipement, du logement, des transports et de la mer, Plan Construction et architecture. "Mai 1990." Includes bibliographical references. ISBN 2-11-085420-0 :
1. Architectural practice - France. 2. Architects - Professional ethics - France. 3. Public relations - France - Architects. I. Aballéa, François. II. Series: Recherches (Plan Construction et architecture (France)). III. Title.
NA1996 .B46 1990

The Benjamin Sonnenberg collection . Sotheby Parke Bernet Inc. New York , 1979. 2 v. :
NYPL [3-MAX (Sonnenberg) 90-5888]

Benjamin, Tritobia H. Lois Mailou Jones . Washington, DC [1988?] 29 p. : DDC 759.13

20
N6537.J68 A4 1988

Benjamin West and his American students /.
Evans, Dorinda. Washington, D.C. , 1980. 203
p. : ill. ; ISBN 0-87474-418-0 DDC 759.13/074/0153
ND207 .E94   *NYPL [3-MCW 91-6652]*

Benje, Peter. Die Produktionsleitlinie / Peter
Benje. Bremen : P. Benje, 1989. 63 leaves ; 30
cm. "Rohfassung." Title on added t.p.: The guide of
production. Title on added t.p.: Le guide de production.
*1. Furniture design - History - 20th century. I. Title. II.
Title: Guide of production. III. Title: Guide de
production.*   *NYPL [3-MOF+ 91-4271]*

Bennett, Allison P. The people's choice : a
history of Albany County in art and
architecture / by Allison P. Bennett ; sponsored
by the Albany County Historical Association.
[S.l. : s.n.], c1980 ([Albany, N.Y.] : printed by
Lane Press) ix, 135 p. : ill. ; 29 cm. Bibliography:
p. 133-135. DDC 709/.747/42 19
*1. Art, American - New york (State) - Albany County.
2. Architecture - New York (State) - Albany County. I.
Albany County Historical Association. II. Title.*
N6530.N72 A33   *NYPL [3-MAMT 81-75]*

Bennett, Clifford A. Conrad, Rupert, 1907-1979.
The art and reflections of Rupert Conrad . New
York , c1991. 205 p., [8] p of plates : ISBN
0-8453-4824-8 (alk. paper) : DDC 709/.2 B 20
N6537.C654 A2 1990
    NYPL [3-MCX C763 91-6324]

Bennett, David. Understanding jewellery / David
Bennett & Daniela Mascetti. Woodbridge :
Antique Collectors' Club, c1989. 386 p. : ill.
(some col.), ports. (some col.) ; 28 cm. Includes
index. Bibliography: p. 377. ISBN 1-85149-075-2 :
DDC 739.2709 20
*1. Jewelry - History. I. Mascetti, Daniela. II. Title. III.
Title: Understanding jewelry.*
NK7306   *NYPL [MNR 90-11502]*

Bennett, H. H. (Henry Hamilton), 1843-1908.
Henry Hamilton Bennett 1843-1908. New
York : Witkin Gallery, c1978. [12] p. : ill.,
port. ; 28 cm. Cover title. Exhibition held at the
Witkin Gallery, Mar. 8 - Apr. 8, 1978. Bibliography : p.
4 of cover.
*1. Bennett, Henry Hamilton, 1843-1908 - Exhibitions.
2. Photography, Stereoscopic - Exhibitions. I. Witkin
Gallery. II. Title.*
    NYPL [MFX (Bennett) 90-5652]

**BENNETT, HENRY HAMILTON, 1843-1908 -
EXHIBITIONS.**
Bennett, H. H. (Henry Hamilton), 1843-1908.
Henry Hamilton Bennett 1843-1908. New
York , c1978. [12] p. :
    NYPL [MFX (Bennett) 90-5652]

Bennett, Swannee, 1949- Arkansas made : a
survey of the decorative, mechanical, and fine
arts produced in Arkansas, 1819-1870 /
Swannee Bennett & William B. Worthen.
Fayetteville : University of Arkansas Press,
c1990-1991. 2 v. : ill. (some col.), map ; 32 cm.
Includes bibliographical references. CONTENTS. - v. 1.
Furniture, quilts, silver, pottery, firearms -- v. 2.
Photography, art. ISBN 1-557-28138-6 (v. 1 : alk.
paper) DDC 709/.767/09034 20
*1. Decorative arts - Arkansas - History - 19th century.
2. Folk art - Arkansas - History - 19th century. I.
Worthen, William B., 1947-. II. Title.*
NK835.A8 B4 1990

Bennett, William, 1948- Un/common ground .
Richmond , c1988. vii, 106 p. : ISBN
0-917046-29-3 DDC 709/.755/0740155451 19
N6530.V8 U5 1988
    NYPL [3-MAMT 90-4499]

Benning, A. H. Community industries of the
Shakers . [Colonie, N.Y.] , c1983. 48 p. : DDC
338/.008288 19
BX9784 .C66 1983
    NYPL [3-MNE 90-12552]

Benoytosh Bhattacharyya. see **Bhattacharyya,
Benoytosh, 1897-1964.**

Benozzo, di Lese, 1420-1497. Padoa Rizzo, Anna.
Benozzo Gozzoli, pittore fiorentino. Firenze
[1972] 178 p.
ND623.G8 P32   *NYPL [3-MCF G72 91-763]*

BENOZZO, DI LESE, 1420-1497.
Padoa Rizzo, Anna. Benozzo Gozzoli, pittore
fiorentino. Firenze [1972] 178 p.
ND623.G8 P32   *NYPL [3-MCF G72 91-763]*

Benozzo Gozzoli, pittore fiorentino. Padoa Rizzo,

Anna. Firenze [1972] 178 p.
ND623.G8 P32   *NYPL [3-MCF G72 91-763]*

Benson, Harry. Harry Benson's people.
Edinburgh : Mainstream, 1990. 167 p. : ports.
(some col.) ; 30 cm. Includes index. ISBN
1-85158-322-X (cased) :   DDC 779.2 20
1. Benson, Harry. 2. Photography - Portraits. I. Title.
    NYPL [MFX+ (Benson) 91-8014]

BENSON, HARRY.
Benson, Harry. Harry Benson's people.
Edinburgh , 1990. 167 p. : ISBN 1-85158-322-X
(cased) : DDC 779.2 20
    NYPL [MFX+ (Benson) 91-8014]

Benson, Richard, 1943- Lay this laurel : an album
on the Saint-Gaudens memorial on Boston
Common, honoring Black and white men
together, who served the Union cause with
Robert Gould Shaw and died with him July 18,
1863 / with photographs by Richard Benson
and an essay by Lincoln Kirstein. New York :
Eakins Press, c1973. [83] p. : ill. ; 24 cm.
Simmonds, H. Kirstein, 225. "Typography ... by C.
Freeman Keith ... text ... printed by The Stinehour
Press [Lunenburg, Vt.]"--P. [83]. Bibliography: p.
[81-82]. ISBN 0-87130-036-2 DDC 973.7/4/44
*1. Shaw, Robert Gould, 1837-1863. 2. Boston. Shaw
Monument. 3. Massachusetts Infantry. 54th Regt.,
1863-1865. 4. United States - History - Civil War,
1861-1865 - Regimental histories - Massachusetts
Infantry. I. Kirstein, Lincoln, 1907-. II. Saint-Gaudens,
Augustus, 1848-1907. III. Title.*
F73.64.S53 B46
    NYPL [IKG (Mass., 54th Regt.) 75-116]

Benson, Robert. The Connecticut River /
photographs by Robert Benson ; essay by Ben
Bachman. 1st ed. Boston : Bulfinch Press :
Little, Brown and Co., c1989. 125 p. : ill.
(chiefly col.), map ; 30 cm. ISBN 0-8212-1730-5
*1. Connecticut River - Description and travel - Views.
2. Connecticut River Valley - Description and travel -
Views. I. Bachman, Ben. II. Title.*
    NYPL [MFX+ (Benson) 89-28166]

Bentini, Jadranka. Disegni emiliani del
Sei-Settecento . [Cinisello Balsamo, Milano]
[1990] 318 p. : ISBN 88-366-0306-8
    NYPL [3-MLP+ 91-7177]

Bentivoglio, Mirella, 1922- Volùmina /.
[Senigallia] , 1990. 45 p. :
    NYPL [MDTT 91-7590]

Bentley, Nicolas, 1907- Nicolas Bentley drew the
pictures / edited with an introduction and
bibliography by Ruari McLean. Aldershot,
Hants, England ; Brookfield, Vt., USA : Scolar
Press, 1990. xxvi, 133 p. : ill. ; 24 cm. Includes
bibliographical references (p. 115-132) and index.
ISBN 0-85967-843-1 DDC 741.5/942 20
*1. English wit and humor, Pictorial. I. McLean, Ruari.
II. Title.*
NC1479.B485 A4 1990

Benton, Pollock, and the politics of modernism .
Doss, Erika Lee. Chicago , 1991. p. cm. ISBN
0-226-15942-6 (alk. paper) DDC 759.13 20
ND237.B47 D67 1991

Benton, Thomas Hart, 1889-1975.
Benton's America : works on paper and
selected paintings : January 19 to March 2,
1991 / introduction by Douglas Dreishpoon.
New York, N.Y. : Hirschl & Adler Galleries,
c1991. 63 p. : ill. (some col.) ; 26 cm. Includes
bibliographical references. ISBN 0-915057-39-5
*1. Benton, Thomas Hart, 1889-1975 - Exhibitions. I.
Dreishpoon, Douglas. II. Title.*
    NYPL [3-MCX B47 91-6240]

**BENTON, THOMAS HART, 1889-1975 -
CRITICISM AND INTERPRETATION.**
Doss, Erika Lee. Benton, Pollock, and the
politics of modernism . Chicago , 1991. p. cm.
ISBN 0-226-15942-6 (alk. paper) DDC 759.13
20
ND237.B47 D67 1991

**BENTON, THOMAS HART, 1889-1975 -
EXHIBITIONS.**
Benton, Thomas Hart, 1889-1975. Benton's
America . New York, N.Y. , c1991. 63 p. :
ISBN 0-915057-39-5
    NYPL [3-MCX B47 91-6240]

MISSOURI MURAL.
Priddy, Bob. Only the rivers are peaceful .
Independence, Mo. , c1989. 282 p., [8] p. of

plates :   ISBN 0-8309-0534-0 :   DDC 759.13 19
ND237.B47 A73 1989
    NYPL [3-MCX B47 90-13013]

Benton's America . Benton, Thomas Hart,
1889-1975. New York, N.Y. , c1991. 63 p. :
ISBN 0-915057-39-5
    NYPL [3-MCX B47 91-6240]

**Berbagai pola kain tenun dan kehidupan
pengrajinnya /.** Marah, Soerisman. [Jakarta]
[1989?] v, 68 p. :
NK8980.A1 M37 1989

Bercht, Fatima. Contemporary art from Chile .
New York, N.Y. , c1990. 63 p. : ISBN
1-87912-802-0   *NYPL [3-MAM 91-7561]*

Berenice Abbott, photographer . Abbott,
Berenice, 1898- [New York] , 1989. 95 p. :
ISBN 0-87104-420-X (pbk.)
    NYPL [MFX+ (Abbott) 91-3494]

**BERENSON, BERNARD, 1865-1959 - ART
COLLECTIONS - CATALOGS.**
Villa I Tatti (Florence, Italy) The Bernard
Berenson collection of oriental art at Villa I
Tatti /. New York , c1991. p. cm. ISBN
1-555-95060-4 (alk. paper) :   DDC
709/.5/0744551 20
N7336 .V46 1991

Berg Collection. Pen & brush : the author as
artist : an exhibition in the Berg Collection of
English and American Literature / Lola L.
Szladits and Harvey Simmonds. [New York] :
New York Public Library, Astor, Lenox and
Tilden Foundations, c1969 (Lunenburg, Vt. :
Stinehour Press) 59 p. : ill. ; 27 cm. One of 2000
copies printed. Includes index. CONTENTS. - William
Makepeace Thackeray -- William Blake to Denton
Welch. ISBN 0-87104-142-1 DDC 741.942
*1. Thackeray, William Makepeace, 1811-1863 -
Exhibitions. 2. Illustration of books - Great Britain -
Exhibitions. 3. Illustration of books - United States -
Exhibitions. 4. Authors as artists - Great Britain -
Exhibitions. 5. Authors as artists - United States -
Exhibitions. I. Szladits, Lola L. II. Simmonds, Harvey.
III. Title. IV. Title: Pen and brush.*
NC15.N43 N47   *NYPL [MAMZ 75-566]*

Berg, Knut, 1925- Portrett av jeg /. Oslo , c1990.
131 p. : ISBN 82-504-1793-3
N7073.E36 P67 1990

Berg, Magnus, 1666-1739. Paulsen, Åshild.
Magnus Berg, 1666-1739 . Oslo , c1989. 348
p. : ISBN 82-09-10580-9 :
NK5998.B47 P38 1989

BERG, MAGNUS, 1666-1739.
Paulsen, Åshild. Magnus Berg, 1666-1739 .
Oslo , c1989. 348 p. : ISBN 82-09-10580-9 :
NK5998.B47 P38 1989

Berg, Thomas, 1944- Architectural contract
document production / Thomas Berg. New
York : McGraw-Hill, 1991. p. cm. ISBN
0-07-004857-6 DDC 720/.28/4 20
*1. Architectural contracts - Documentation. 2.
Communication in architectural design. I. Title.*
NA2584 .B47 1991

Bergamini, Giuseppe. Il Castello di Udine /
Giuseppe Bergamini, Maurizio Buora. [Udine] :
Comune di Udine, [1990] vii, 273 p. : ill. ; 31
cm.
1. Castello di Udine. I. Title.
    NYPL [3-MQWB+ 91-3865]

Bergbau und Bergarbeit in der Fotografie.
Ausbeute . Essen , c1989. 182 p. : ISBN
3-87034-045-2 DDC 779/.96 20
TR706 .A95 1989   *NYPL [MFW+ 91-7294]*

Bergbau und Kunst in Sachsen. Der silberne
Boden . Stuttgart [Leipzig] , c1990. 510 p. :
ISBN 3-421-02982-2 (Deutsche Verlags-Anstalt)
    NYPL [3-MAMG 91-5527]

Berge-Gerbaud, Mària van.
Fondation Custodia. Le héraut du dix-septième
siècle . Paris , 1985. xi, 153 p., 80 p. of plates :
NE670.G74 A4 1985

Quimper, France. Musée des beaux-arts.
Tableaux flamands et hollandais du Musée des
beaux-arts de Quimper. Paris , Quimper , 1987.
xxxiv, 101 p. : ISBN 2-906739-10-3 DDC
759.9492/074/44361 20
ND636 .Q5 1987

Berge, Mària van. Wenzel Hollar, 1607-1677 :
dessins, gravures, cuivres : [exposition, 11
janvier-25 février 1979], Institut néerlandais,

Paris : [catalogue / établi par Mària van Berge].
Paris : L'Institut, 1979. 77 p., [15] leaves of
plates : ill. ; 26 cm. Bibliography: p. 75-77.
*1. Hollar, Wenceslaus, 1607-1677 - Exhibitions. I.
Hollar, Wenceslaus, 1607-1677. II. Institut néerlandais,
Paris.*
NE642.H7 A4 1979
NYPL   [3-MCZ H737 81-151]

Bergemann, Johannes. Römische Reiterstatuen :
Ehrendenkmäler im öffentlichen Bereich /
Johannes Bergemann. Mainz am Rhein : P. von
Zabern, c1990. xii, 196 p., 96 p. of plates : ill. ;
32 cm. (Beiträge zur Erschliessung hellenistischer und
kaiserzeitlicher Skulptur und Architektur . Bd. 11)
ISBN 3-8053-1149-4
1. Equestrian statues - Rome. I. Title. II. Series.
NYPL   [3-MGH+ 91-5688]

BERGEN COUNTY, N. J. - MAPS.
(1912) Bromley, George W. Atlas of Bergen
County, New Jersey . Philadelphia, Pa. ,
1912-1913. 2 atlases :
NYPL   [Map Div. 91-4094]

(1936) Property atlas of Bergen County, N. J. .
Philadelphia, Pa. , 1936- 4 v. :
NYPL   [Map Div. 91-4090]

Bergen, Jeffrey B. Primitive art of Papua New
Guinea . New York , c1989. 31 p. : ISBN
0-925315-01-X (pbk.)
NYPL   [3-MADF+ 89-20654]

Bergens billedgalleri. Catalog over det Bergenske
Museums Malerisamling, 1840. [Bergen] :
Universitetet i Bergen, 1961. 32 p. : ill. ; 21
cm. (Norges eldste kunstsamling . 19) Includes
bibliographical references.
*1. Bergens billedgalleri. 2. Painting - Norway - Bergen -
Catalogs. I. Title.* **NYPL   [3-MAVZ (Bergen,**
Norway) 90-5454]

BERGENS BILLEDGALLERI.
Bergens billedgalleri. Catalog over det
Bergenske Museums Malerisamling, 1840.
[Bergen] , 1961. 32 p. :   **NYPL   [3-MAVZ**
(Bergen, Norway) 90-5454]

Berger, Eva. Nussbaum, Felix, 1904-1944. Felix
Nussbaum . Bramsche , c1990. 440 p. : ISBN
3-922469-46-9   DDC 759.3 20
ND588.N8 A4 1990

Berger, John.
About looking / John Berger. 1st Vintage
international ed. New York : Vintage Books,
1991. p. cm. Originally published: New York :
Pantheon Books, c1980. ISBN 0-679-73655-7 (pbk.) :
DDC 701/.15 20
*1. Art - Psychology. 2. Visual perception. 3. Meaning
(Psychology). I. Title.*
N71 .B398 1991

Keeping a rendezvous / by John Berger. New
York : Pantheon Books, 1991. p. cm. ISBN
0-679-40632-8   DDC 701/.15 20
1. Art - Psychology. I. Title.
N71 .B399 1991

The success and failure of Picasso / John
Berger ; updated and with a new preface by the
author. Rev. ed. New York : Pantheon Books,
c1989. xviii, 220 p. : ill. ; 21 cm.   ISBN
0-679-72272-6 :   DDC 759.4 19
*1. Picasso, Pablo, 1881-1973 - Criticism and
interpretation. I. Title.*
ND553.P5 B45 1989
NYPL   [3-MCQ P58 91-3796]

Berger, Maurice.
A Debate on abstraction . [New York] [1988?]
79 p. :   **NYPL   [3-MAL 90-12609]**

How art becomes history : essays on art,
society, and culture in post-New Deal America
/ Maurice Berger. New York, N.Y. : Icon
Editions, c1992. p. cm.   ISBN 0-06-430385-3 :
DDC 700/.1/03 20
*1. Arts and society - United States - History - 20th
century. 2. United States - Civilization - 20th century.
I. Title.*
NX180.S6 B47 1992

Labyrinths : Robert Morris, minimalism, and
the 1960s / Maurice Berger.1st ed. New York :
Harper & Row, c1989. xvi, 175 p. : ill. ; 25 cm.
(Icon editions) Includes bibliographical references.
ISBN 0-06-430384-5 :   DDC 700/.92/4 19
*1. Morris, Robert, 1931- - Criticism and interpretation.
2. Minimal art - United States. 3. Arts and society -*

United States. I. Title.
NX512.M67 B47 1989
NYPL   [3-MGO (Morris) 90-11779]

Berger, Ursel. Georg Kolbe, Leben und Werk :
mit dem Katalog der Kolbe-Plastiken im
Georg-Kolbe-Museum / Ursel Berger. Berlin :
Mann-Verlag, 1990. 429 p. : ill. ; 26 cm.
Includes bibliographical references (p. 395-419) and
index. ISBN 3-7861-1589-3   DDC 730/.92 20
*1. Kolbe, Georg, 1877-1947. 2. Kolbe, Georg,
1877-1947 - Catalogues raisonnés. 3.
Georg-Kolbe-Museum Berlin - Catalogs. 4. Sculptors -
Germany - Biography. I. Kolbe, Georg, 1877-1947. II.
Georg-Kolbe-Museum Berlin. III. Title.*
NB588.K6 B38 1990
NYPL   [MGO (Kolbe) 91-5528]

Bergevin, Al. Drugstore tins & their prices / Al
Bergevin. Radnor, Pa. : Wallace-Homestead
Book Co., c1990. 282 p., [10] p. of plates : ill.
(some col.) ; 23 cm. ISBN 0-87069-568-1 :   DDC
741.6/7/0973075 20
*1. Tin containers - Collectors and collecting - Catalogs.
I. Title. II. Title: Drugstore tins and their prices.*
NK8425 .B45 1990
NYPL   [3-MNH 91-3998]

BERGGRUEN, HEINZ - ART
COLLECTIONS - EXHIBITIONS.
Kendall, Richard. Van Gogh to Picasso .
London , 1991. 209 p. : ISBN 0-947645-83-7
(hardback)   DDC 709.0346 20
N6754 **NYPL   [3-MAX (Berggruen) 91-8105]**

Bergheim, Laura, 1962- The Map catalog . New
York , c1990. 364 p. : ISBN 0-394-58326-4 :
DDC 912/.0294 20
Z6028 .M23 1990 GA105.3
NYPL   [Map Div. 91-7838]

Bergisches Museum Schloss Burg an der
Wupper. Cateni, Gabriele. Die
Etrusker--Volterra . Solingen , 1986. 90 p. :
NYPL   [3-MAE 90-12646]

Bergman, Anna-Eva, 1909-
Anna Eva Bergman. Paris : Galerie de France,
[1962] [33] p. : ill. (some col.) ; 24 cm.
"Cette plaquette a été éditée à l'occasion de l'exposition
des œuvres récentes d'Anna Eva Bergman (30 mars-29
avril 1962) à la Galerie de France"--P. [33]
*1. Bergman, Anna-Eva, 1909- - Exhibitions. I. Galerie
de France (Paris, France). II. Title.*
NYPL   [3-MCZ+ B495 91-4580]

BERGMAN, ANNA-EVA, 1909- -
EXHIBITIONS.
Bergman, Anna-Eva, 1909- Anna Eva Bergman.
Paris [1962] [33] p. :
NYPL   [3-MCZ+ B495 91-4580]

Bergman, David, 1950- Ashbery, John. Reported
sightings . Cambridge, Mass. , 1991. xxiii, 417
p., [16] p. of col. plates : ISBN 0-674-76225-8
DDC 700 20
N7445.2 .A84 1991

Bergmann, Ulrike. Schnütgen-Museum. Die
Holzskulpturen des Mittelalters (1000-1400) /.
Köln , 1989. 381 p. :
NYPL   [3-MGI 91-4187]

Bergstrom-Mahler Museum.
Glass paperweights of the Bergstrom-Mahler
Museum / introduction and cameo incrustations
by Geraldine J. Casper. Richmond, Va. : United
States Historical Society Press ; New York :
Distributed by Harry N. Abrams, c1989. xxxv,
112, [16] p. : ill. (some col.) ; 29 cm. Spine title:
Glass paperweights. ISBN 0-927997-00-2 DDC
748.8/4/07477564 20
*1. Bergstrom-Mahler Museum - Catalogs. 2.
Paperweights - Wisconsin - Neenah - Catalogs. I.
Casper, Geraldine J. II. Title: Glass paperweights.*
NK5440.P3 B44 1989
NYPL   [3-MPW 91-6422]

BERGSTROM-MAHLER MUSEUM -
CATALOGS.
Bergstrom-Mahler Museum. Glass paperweights
of the Bergstrom-Mahler Museum /. Richmond,
Va. , New York , c1989. xxxv, 112, [16] p. :
ISBN 0-927997-00-2 DDC 748.8/4/07477564 20
NK5440.P3 B44 1989
NYPL   [3-MPW 91-6422]

Bergvelt, Ellinoor.
Amsterdamse school . [Amsterdam , 1975. 112
p. :   **NYPL   [3-MQW 90-7048]**

Glas in lood in Nederland, 1817-1968 /.
's-Gravenhage [1990?] 414 p. : ISBN

90-12-06146-6
NK5354.A1 G57 1990

Berichte über begonnene und geplante Arbeiten.
Im Auftrag des Mexiko- Arbeitskreises
zusammengestellt von Franz Tichy. Wiesbaden,
F. Steiner, 1968. 210 p. illus., maps (2 fold. col.
in pocket) 29 cm. (Mexiko-Projekt der Deutschen
Forschungsgemeinschaft . Bd. 1) Added t. p.: Informe
sobre los trabajos iniciados y proyectados. Summaries in
Spanish. Includes bibliographies.
*1. Indians of Mexico - History. I. Tichy, Franz, comp.
II. Mexiko-Arbeitskreis. III. Title: Informe sobre los
trabajos iniciados y proyectados. IV. Series.*
NYPL   [HTC 74-1117 Bd. 1]

Berio, Marina. Schnabel, Julian, 1951- Julian
Schnabel /. Prato , c1989. 159 p. : ISBN
88-85191-00-2
NYPL   [3-MCX S358 90-4741]

Beritić, Lukša. Beritićev zbornik . Dubrovnik ,
1960. 335 p., [1] folded leaf of plates :
NYPL   [*QKK 83-2704]

BERITIĆ, LUKŠA.
Beritićev zbornik . Dubrovnik , 1960. 335 p.,
[1] folded leaf of plates :
NYPL   [*QKK 83-2704]

Beritićev zbornik : bornik radova iz dubrovačke
povijesti u počast sedamdesetogodišnjice
dubrovačkog konzervatora Lukše Beritića :
melanges de travaux sur le passé de Dubrovnik
a Lukša Beritić, conservateur des monuments
historiques de Dubrovnik a l'occasion de la 70e
année de sa vie / redakcioni odbor : Slavomir
Benić ... [et al.] Dubrovnik : Društvo prijatelja
dubrovačke starine, 1960. 335 p., [1] folded leaf
of plates : ill., folded map, port. ; 24 cm. Text in
Serbo-Croatian, subtitle and table of contents in
Serbo-Croatian and French, summaries in French.
Bibliography of Beritić' works: p. 13-15.
*1. Beritić, Lukša. 2. Art - Yugoslavia - Dubrovnik. 3.
Dubrovnik, Yugoslavia - History. I. Benić, Slavomir. II.
Beritić, Lukša.* **NYPL   [*QKK 83-2704]**

Berkel, Sabri, 1907-
Sabri Berkel / metin yazarı, Jale Erzen ; [çeviri,
Fred Stark]. [Turkey] : Arçelik A.Ş., [1988] 167
p. : ill. (some col.) ; 31 cm. English and Turkish.
Includes bibliographical references (p. 161-162). DDC
760/.092 20
*1. Berkel, Sabri, 1907- - Themes, motives. 2. Berkel,
Sabri, 1907- - Criticism and interpretation. I. Erzen,
Jale N. II. Title.*
ND873.B47 A4 1988

BERKEL, SABRI, 1907- - CRITICISM AND
INTERPRETATION.
Berkel, Sabri, 1907- Sabri Berkel /. [Turkey]
[1988] 167 p. :   DDC 760/.092 20
ND873.B47 A4 1988

BERKEL, SABRI, 1907- - THEMES,
MOTIVES.
Berkel, Sabri, 1907- Sabri Berkel /. [Turkey]
[1988] 167 p. :   DDC 760/.092 20
ND873.B47 A4 1988

Berko, P. Fernand Toussaint : 1873-1956 /
Patrick et Viviane Berko, Stéphane Rey ;
préface de Gérald Schurr. [Knokke-Heist,
Belgium : Berko, 1986] 112 p. : ill. (some col.) ;
29 cm. (Collection Berko) French and English. ISBN
90-70481-94-4   DDC 759.9493 20
*1. Toussaint, Fernand, 1873-1956? - Catalogs. 2.
Toussaint, Fernand, 1873-1956? - Criticism and
interpretation. I. Berko, V. II. Rey, Stéphane. III.
Toussaint, Fernand, 1873-1956?. IV. Title.*
ND673.T68 A4 1986
NYPL   [3-MCH T725 90-10766]

Berko, Patrick. Paul Mathieu, 1872-1932 /
Patrick et Viviane Berko, Stéphane Rey ;
préface de Marcel Croës. [Knokke-Zoute,
Belgium] : Berko Editions, [1989] 161, [2] p. :
col. ill. ; 29 cm. (Collection Berko) French and
English. Bibliography: p. [163]. ISBN 90-70481-80-4
*1. Mathieu, Paul, 1872-1932. I. Berko, V. II. Rey,
Stéphane. III. Title.*
NYPL   [3-MCH M435 90-12987]

Berko, V.
Berko, P. Fernand Toussaint . [Knokke-Heist,
Belgium , 1986] 112 p. : ISBN 90-70481-94-4
DDC 759.9493 20
ND673.T68 A4 1986
NYPL   [3-MCH T725 90-10766]

Berko, Patrick. Paul Mathieu, 1872-1932 /.
[Knokke-Zoute, Belgium] [1989] 161, [2] p. :

ISBN 90-70481-80-4
NYPL [3-MCH M435 90-12987]

Berkson, Bill.
Ronald Bladen : early and late, San Francisco
Museum of Modern Art, May 30-August 18,
1991 / Bill Berkson. San Francisco : San
Francisco Museum of Modern Art, c1991. p.
cm. Includes bibliographical references. ISBN
0-918471-19-2 DDC 759.13 20
*1. Bladen, Ronald, 1918-1988 - Exhibitions. I. Bladen,
Ronald, 1918-1988. II. San Francisco. Museum of
Modern Art. III. Title.*
N6537.B554 A4 1991

Thiebaud, Wayne. Ties, pies, cities, and other
things /. San Francisco , c1991. p. cm. ISBN
0-938491-56-3 (paper) : DDC 769.92 20
NE539.T5 A4 1991

Berlage, Hendrik Petrus, 1856-1934.
Polano, Sergio. [Hendrik Petrus Berlage, opera
completa. English.] Hendrik Petrus Berlage,
complete works /. New York , 1988. 266 p. :
ISBN 0-8478-0901-3 DDC 720/.92 20
NA1153.B4 A4 1988
NYPL [3-MQZ (Berlage) 90-11983]

**BERLAGE, HENDRIK PETRUS, 1856-1934 -
CATALOGUES RAISONNÉS.**
Polano, Sergio. [Hendrik Petrus Berlage, opera
completa. English.] Hendrik Petrus Berlage,
complete works /. New York , 1988. 266 p. :
ISBN 0-8478-0901-3 DDC 720/.92 20
NA1153.B4 A4 1988
NYPL [3-MQZ (Berlage) 90-11983]

Berlin . Balfour, Alan. New York , 1990. 269 p. :
ISBN 0-8478-1271-5 DDC 720/.1/03 20
NA9200.B4 B35 1990
NYPL [3-MQWD 90-13618]

Berlin . Jahn, Hans, 1884- [Berlin] [1920?] 25
p. : *NYPL [Map Div. 91-6615]*

Berlin. Akademie der Wissenschaften der DDR.
see Akademie der Wissenschaften der DDR.

Berlin. Amerika Haus. see Amerika Haus, Berlin.

**Berlin. Archäologisches Institut des Deutschen
Reichs.** see Deutsches Archäologisches
Institut.

Berlin. Berlin Museum. Jacob, Julius, 1842-1929.
Der Berliner Maler Julius Jacob . [Berlin]
[1979] 16, [40] p. :
ND588.J27 A4 1979
NYPL [3-MCK J158 81-436]

Berlin. Berlinische Galerie. see Berlinische
Galerie.

Berlin. Brücke-Museum. see Brücke-Museum.

Berlin. Deutsches Archäologisches Institut. see
Deutsches Archäologisches Institut.

Berlin. Galerie Georg Nothelfer. see Galerie
Georg Nothelfer.

Berlin. Galerie Pels-Leusden. see Galerie Pels-
Leusden.

Berlin. Galerie Springer. see Galerie Springer,
Berlin.

**Berlin (Germany : West). Senator für Bau- und
Wohnungswesen.** 14x
Amerika-Gedenkbibliothek . Berlin , c1989. 132
p. : ISBN 3-433-02288-7 (pbk.)
NYPL [3-MQWO+ 90-11060]

**Berlin (Germany : West). Senatsverwaltung für
Stadtentwicklung.** Peter Joseph Lenné .
Berlin , c1989. 315 p. : ISBN 3-87584-277-4
NYPL [3-MSCC 91-2632]

**BERLIN (GERMANY) - BIOGRAPHY -
PORTRAITS.**
Kelm, Ursula. Berliner Porträts . Berlin , c1990.
167 p. : ISBN 3-87024-158-6
NYPL [MFW (Kelm) 91-6829]

**BERLIN (GERMANY) - BUILDINGS,
STRUCTURES, ETC.**
Behr, Adalbert. Bauen in Berlin, 1973 bis 1987
/. Leipzig , 1987. 199 p. : ISBN 3-7338-0040-0
DDC 720/.9431/55 20
NA1085 .B437 1987

Klinkott, Manfred. Die Backsteinbaukunst der
Berliner Schule . Berlin , c1988. 479 p., 9
leaves of plates : ISBN 3-7861-1438-2 DDC
721/.04421/094315509034 20
NA1085 .K57 1988
NYPL [3-MQWD 90-11025]

Rietdorf, Werner. Stadterneuerung . Berlin ,

1989. 256 p. : ISBN 3-345-00282-5
NA9200.B4 R54 1989

Waldenburg, Hermann, 1940- The Berlin Wall
book /. London , 1990. 119 p. : ISBN
0-500-97385-7 *NYPL [3-MLP 90-12020]*

Werner Düttmann . Basel , Boston , c1990. 322
p. : ISBN 3-7643-2413-9
NYPL [3-MQZ (Düttmann) 91-5517]

Wiesinger, Liselotte, 1917- Das Berliner
Schloss . Darmstadt , c1989. viii, 237 p. :
ISBN 3-534-09234-1
NYPL [3-MQWD 90-5266]

Zum Umgang mit dem Gestapo-Gelände .
[Berlin , 1988] 105, 25, 73 p. :
NA1068.5.N37 Z85 1988

**BERLIN (GERMANY) - BUILDINGS,
STRUCTURES, ETC. - COMPETITIONS -
EXHIBITIONS.**
14x Amerika-Gedenkbibliothek . Berlin , c1989.
132 p. : ISBN 3-433-02288-7 (pbk.)
NYPL [3-MQWO+ 90-11060]

**BERLIN (GERMANY) - BUILDINGS,
STRUCTURES, ETC. - GUIDE-BOOKS.**
Berning, Maria. Berliner Wohnquartiere .
Berlin , c1990. xiii, 252 p. : ISBN
3-496-00382-0 :
NA7351.B65 B47 1990

BERLIN (GERMANY) - DESCRIPTION.
Rathenow, Lutz, 1952- Berlin-Ost . Berlin ,
c1990. 133 p. : ISBN 3-86163-006-0
NYPL [MFX (Rathenow) 91-6720]

**BERLIN (GERMANY) - DESCRIPTION -
VIEWS.**
Rathenow, Lutz, 1952- Berlin-Ost . Berlin ,
c1990. 133 p. : ISBN 3-86163-006-0
NYPL [MFX (Rathenow) 91-6720]

**BERLIN (GERMANY) - HISTORICAL
GEOGRAPHY - MAPS.**
Jahn, Hans, 1884- Berlin . [Berlin] [1920?] 25
p. : *NYPL [Map Div. 91-6615]*

BERLIN (GERMANY) - HISTORY.
Jahn, Hans, 1884- Berlin . [Berlin] [1920?] 25
p. : *NYPL [Map Div. 91-6615]*

**BERLIN (GERMANY) - HISTORY -
PICTORIAL WORKS.**
Vier Tage im November /. Hamburg , 1990,
c1989. 160 p. : ISBN 3-570-00876-2
NYPL [MFW+ 91-2376]

**BERLIN (GERMANY) IN ART -
EXHIBITIONS.**
Das Bild der Stadt Berlin von 1945 bis zur
Gegenwart . Berlin [1987] 59 p. :
NYPL [3-MAMY 90-13015]

**BERLIN (GERMANY) - INTELLECTUAL
LIFE - GUIDE-BOOKS.**
Gerber, Bärbel. Kultur und Kunst in Berlin .
Berlin , 1988. 248 p. : ISBN 3-7442-0022-1
NX550.B4 G4 1988

BERLIN IN ART - EXHIBITIONS.
Berliner Pressezeichner der Zwanziger Jahre .
Berlin , 1977. [68] p. :
NC970 .B47 *NYPL [3-MAMG 81-294]*

Bilder aus der grossen Stadt . Berlin-Dahlem ,
1977. [96] p. :
N6885 .B55 *NYPL [3-MAMG 81-424]*

Jacob, Julius, 1842-1929. Der Berliner Maler
Julius Jacob . [Berlin] [1979] 16, [40] p. :
ND588.J27 A4 1979
NYPL [3-MCK J158 81-436]

Berlin-Information. Gerber, Bärbel. Kultur und
Kunst in Berlin . Berlin , 1988. 248 p. : ISBN
3-7442-0022-1
NX550.B4 G4 1988

Berlin. Künstlerhaus Bethanien. see Künstlerhaus
Bethanien.

Berlin. Kupferstichkabinett (West Berlin) Bilder
aus der grossen Stadt . Berlin-Dahlem , 1977.
[96] p. :
N6885 .B55 *NYPL [3-MAMG 81-424]*

BERLIN - LITERARY COLLECTIONS.
Bilder aus der grossen Stadt . Berlin-Dahlem ,
1977. [96] p. :
N6885 .B55 *NYPL [3-MAMG 81-424]*

Berlin, März neunzehnhundertneunzig. Berlin,
März 1990 . Berlin , Braunschweig [1990] 88

p. :
MLCM 91/00973 (N)
NYPL [3-MAL 91-6662]

Berlin, März 1990 : 6. Mai-10. Juni 1990,
Wiensowski & Harbord, Berlin, 5. Juli-2.
September 1990, Kunstverein Braunschweig :
[Ausstellungskatalog / Autoren, Wulf
Herzogenrath ... et al.]. Berlin : Wiensowski &
Harbord ; Braunschweig : Kunstverein
Braunschweig, [1990] 88 p. : col. ill. ; 27 cm. In
German; one essay in English and German.
*1. Art, Modern - Germany - Berlin - Exhibitions. 2.
Art - Germany - Berlin - Exhibitions. I. Herzogenrath,
Wulf. II. Wiensowski & Harbord. III. Title: Berlin,
März neunzehnhundertneunzig.*
MLCM 91/00973 (N)
NYPL [3-MAL 91-6662]

Berlin Museum. Berliner Pressezeichner der
Zwanziger Jahre . Berlin , 1977. [68] p. :
NC970 .B47 *NYPL [3-MAMG 81-294]*

Berlin. Neue Berliner Galerie. see Neue Berliner
Galerie.

Berlin. Neuer Berliner Kunstverein. see Neuer
Berliner Kunstverein.

Berlin-Ost . Rathenow, Lutz, 1952- Berlin ,
c1990. 133 p. : ISBN 3-86163-006-0
NYPL [MFX (Rathenow) 91-6720]

Berlin. Print Room (West Berlin) see Berlin.
Kupferstichkabinett (West Berlin)

**Berlin Society for Anthropology, Ethnology and
Prehistory.** see Berliner Gesellschaft für
Anthropologie, Ethnologie und Urgeschichte.

Berlin. Staatliche Kunsthalle. see Staatliche
Kunsthalle Berlin.

**Berlin. Staatliche Museen (West Berlin).
Kupferstichkabinett.** see Berlin.
Kupferstichkabinett (West Berlin)

**Berlin. Staatliche Museen (West Berlin). Print
Room.** see Berlin. Kupferstichkabinett (West
Berlin)

**Berlin. Staatsbibliothek der Stiftung Preussischer
Kulturbesitz.** see Staatsbibliothek
Preussischer Kulturbesitz.

Berlin, Sven. Pride of the peacock: the evolution
of an artist. London, Collins, 1972. 255 p., leaf.
port. 22 cm. ISBN 0-8021-1675-8 DDC 759.2
1. Berlin, Sven. 2. Artists, British - Biography. I. Title.
NX93.B4 A36
NYPL [3-MCV B515 90-6356]

BERLIN, SVEN.
Berlin, Sven. Pride of the peacock. London,
1972. 255 p., leaf. ISBN 0-8021-1675-8 DDC
759.2
NX93.B4 A36
NYPL [3-MCV B515 90-6356]

Berlin. Verein Berlinische Galerie. see
Berlinische Galerie.

**BERLIN WALL, BERLIN, GERMANY, 1961-
1989 - PICTORIAL WORKS -
EXHIBITIONS.**
Hildebrandt, Rainer, 1914- Die Mauer . Berlin ,
1989. 52 p. : ISBN 3-922484-22-0
IN PROCESS (ONLINE)
NYPL [MFW+ 91-7248]

The Berlin Wall book /. Waldenburg, Hermann,
1940- London , 1990. 119 p. : ISBN
0-500-97385-7 *NYPL [3-MLP 90-12020]*

BERLIN WALL (1961-)
Tillman, Terry. The writings on the wall . Santa
Monica, Calif. , Emeryville, Calif. , c1990. 152
p. : ISBN 0-9626551-0-4
NYPL [MFX (Tillman) 91-2668]

Vier Tage im November /. Hamburg , 1990,
c1989. 160 p. : ISBN 3-570-00876-2
NYPL [MFW+ 91-2376]

Waldenburg, Hermann, 1940- The Berlin Wall
book /. London , 1990. 119 p. :
0-500-97385-7 *NYPL [3-MLP 90-12020]*

Berlin (West). Senat. Schmied, Wieland, 1929-
GegenwartEwigkeit . Stuttgart , c1990. 341 p. :
ISBN 3-89322-179-4 : DDC
709/.04/5074431554 20
N6488.G3 S8565 1990

**Berliner Beiträge zur Technikgeschichte und
Industriekultur .**
(Bd. 9) Aus einem Guss . Berlin , c1988. 248
p. : ISBN 3-87584-203-0 DDC

730/.0943/074431554 20
NK8250.A3 P784 1988
                    NYPL [3-MNK 91-3716]

**Berliner Gesellschaft für Anthropologie,
Ethnologie und Urgeschichte.** Frühe
Bergvölker in Armenien und im Kaukasus .
Berlin , 1984. 84 p. :
                    NYPL [3-MAE 90-10823]

Berliner Hefte, 0177-7742 .
(2) Wimmer, Clemens Alexander, 1959-
Sichtachsen des Barock in Berlin und
Umgebung . Berlin, c1985. 39 p. :
                    NYPL [3-MQWD 90-12627]

Berliner Kunststücke /. Berlinische Galerie.
Stuttgart [1990] 459 p. : ISBN 3-89322-176-X
N6868 .B44 1990

Der Berliner Maler Julius Jacob . Jacob, Julius,
1842-1929. [Berlin] [1979] 16, [40] p. :
ND588.J27 A4 1979
                    NYPL [3-MCK J158 81-436]

Berliner Porträts . Kelm, Ursula. Berlin , c1990.
167 p. : ISBN 3-87024-158-6
                    NYPL [MFW (Kelm) 91-6829]

Berliner Pressezeichner der Zwanziger Jahre : e.
Kaleidoskop Berliner Lebens : Orig.-Zeichn. u.
Drucke : Berlin-Museum, Ausstellung vom 27.
August-20. November 1977 / [im Rahmen d.
15. Europ. Kunstausstellung Berlin 1977,
Tendenzen d. Zwanziger Jahre ; Bildh., Irmgard
Wirth]. Berlin : Berlin-Museum, 1977. [68] p. :
chiefly ill. ; 24 cm.
*1. Newspapers - Illustrations - Exhibitions. 2. German
newspapers - Berlin - History - Exhibitions. 3. Berlin in
art - Exhibitions. 4. Germany in art - Exhibitions. 5.
Germany - History - 20th century - Exhibitions. I.
Wirth, Irmgard. II. Berlin Museum.*
NC970 .B47   *NYPL [3-MAMG 81-294]*

Das Berliner Schloss . Wiesinger, Liselotte, 1917-
Darmstadt , c1989. viii, 237 p. : ISBN
3-534-09234-1 *NYPL [3-MQWD 90-5266]*

BERLINER SECESSION.
Laux, Walter Stephan. Waldemar Rösler .
Worms , c1989. iii, 436 p., [20] p. of plates :
ISBN 3-88462-923-9
ND588.R594 L38 1989

Berliner Sezession. see Berliner Secession.

Berliner Wohnquartiere . Berning, Maria. Berlin ,
c1990. xiii, 252 p. : ISBN 3-496-00382-0 :
NA7351.B65 B47 1990

Berlinische Galerie.
Berliner Kunststücke / [Herausgeber],
Berlinische Galerie, [in Zusammenarbeit mit
dem Museumspädagogischen Dienst Berlin].
Stuttgart : Edition Cantz, [1990] 459 p. : ill.
(some col.) ; 25 cm. (Gegenwart Museum . [13])
"Die Sammlung der Berlinischen Galerie zu Gast im
Museum der Bildenden Künste Leipzig, 19. Mai bis 8.
Juli 1990, [und] in der Neuen Berliner Galerie des
Zentrums für Kunstausstellungen der DDR im Alten
Museum Berlin, 13. September bis 7. Oktober 1990"--P.
facing t.p. Includes bibliographical references (p.
448-451) and index. ISBN 3-89322-176-X
*1. Art, German - Exhibitions. 2. Art, Modern - 20th
century - Germany - Exhibitions. 3. Berlinische
Galerie - Exhibitions. I. Museumspädagogischer Dienst
Berlin (Germany). II. Museum der Bildenden Künste
(Leipzig, Germany). III. Neue Berliner Galerie. IV.
Title. V. Series.*
N6868 .B44 1990

Korrespondenzen . Berlin , Saint-Etienne ,
c1989. 82 p. :
N6885 .K67 1989

BERLINISCHE GALERIE - EXHIBITIONS.
Berlinische Galerie. Berliner Kunststücke /.
Stuttgart [1990] 459 p. : ISBN 3-89322-176-X
N6868 .B44 1990

Berlinsche Galerie. Loewig, Roger, 1930- Roger
Loewig, Zeichnungen und Lithographien /.
Berlin [1988] 134 p. :
                    NYPL [MDG (Loewig) 90-10854]

Berman, Esmé. The story of South African
painting / Esmé Berman.-- 1st ed. Cape Town :
A.A. Balkema, 1975, c1974. xv, 256 p. : ill.
(some col.) ; 29 cm. Includes index. ISBN
0-86961-067-8
1. Painting, South African - History. I. Title.
                    NYPL [3-MCY 91-3274]

Berman, Lawrence Michael, 1952- The Art of
Amenhotep III . Cleveland, Ohio , 1990. xii, 92

p., 27 p. of plates : ISBN 0-940717-01-8 DDC
732/.8 20
NB165.A44 A78 1990
                    NYPL [3-MAE 91-4575]

Berman, Marietta, 1917-
Calzadilla, Juan. Marietta Berman . Caracas,
Venezuela [1990] 138, [6] p. : ISBN
980-216-065-2 DDC 759.987 20
N6834.5.B48 A4 1990

BERMAN, MARIETTA, 1917- - CATALOGS.
Calzadilla, Juan. Marietta Berman . Caracas,
Venezuela [1990] 138, [6] p. : ISBN
980-216-065-2 DDC 759.987 20
N6834.5.B48 A4 1990

Berman, Ronald. Public policy and the aesthetic
interest. Urbana , c1992. p. cm. ISBN
0-252-01899-0 (cl) DDC 700/.1/03 20
NX730 .P79 1992

Bermúdez, Egberto. El nacionalismo en el arte.
[Bogotá, Colombia] [1984]. 90 p. ;
                    NYPL [3-MAM 90-4731]

Bermudian images . Adams, John. Hamilton,
Bermuda , 1989. viii, 101 p. : DDC 759.97299
20
NA815.B47 A33 1989

Bernac, Jean.
Caillebotte bequest to the Luxembourg. 1966.
Wildenstein & Co. (London, England)
Gustave Caillebotte, 1848-1894 : a loan
exhibition in aid of the Hertford British
Hospital in Paris, 15th June-16th July, 1966.
[London, 1966] 35 p. :
                    NYPL [3-MCO C134 91-1182]

**The Bernard Berenson collection of oriental art
at Villa I Tatti** /. Villa I Tatti (Florence, Italy)
New York , c1991. p. cm. ISBN 1-555-95060-4
(alk. paper) DDC 709/.5/0744551 20
N7336 .V46 1991

Bernard Black Gallery (New York, N.Y.) Les
animaliers : French animal sculpture of the
nineteenth century : exhibition, February
26-March 30, 1963, Bernard Black Gallery of
Paintings, Sculpture and Antiques. New York,
N.Y. : The Gallery, [1963] [16] p. : ill. ; 23 cm.
*1. Animal sculpture - France - Exhibitions. 2. Bronzes,
French - Exhibitions. 3. Bronzes - 19th century -
France - Exhibitions. I. Title.*
                    NYPL [3-MGI 90-5741]

Bernard Buffet /. Avila, Alin Alexis. [Paris] ,
1989. 251 p. : ISBN 2-7079-0021-4
                    NYPL [3-MCO+ B929 89-24429]

Bernard Danenberg Galleries. One hundred
recent acquisitions, by American artists.
[Exhibition] Spring-Summer, 1969. New York,
1969. 51 p. chiefly illus. 28 cm.
*1. Art, American - Exhibitions. 2. Art, Modern - 20th
century - United States - Exhibitions. 3. Art, Modern -
19th century - United States - Exhibitions. 4. Art -
United States - Exhibitions. I. Title.*
                    NYPL [3-MAMT 90-6625]

Bernard, Émile, 1868-1941.
Emile Bernard, 1868-1941 : a pioneer of
modern art / catalogue, MaryAnne Stevens ...
[et al.] ; exhibition, MaryAnne Stevens ... [et
al.] ; [translation, Connie Homburg ... et al.] =
Emile Bernard, 1868-1941 : ein Wegbereiter der
Moderne / katalog, MaryAnne Stevens ...[et
al.] ; ausstellung, MaryAnne Stevens ... [et al.] ;
[übersetzung, Connie Homburg ... et al.].
Mannheim : Städtische Kunsthalle ;
Amsterdam : Van Gogh Museum ; 384 p. : ill.
(some col.) ; 29 cm. English and German.
"Accompanies the exhibition of the works of Emile
Bernard in the Städtische Kunsthalle Mannheim from
12 May to 5 August 1990 and in the Rijksmuseum
Vincent van Gogh in Amsterdam from 24 August to 4
November 1990"--Colophon. Includes bibliographical
references (p. 368-372). ISBN 90-6630-151-1 (glued)
DDC 760/.092 20
*1. Bernard, Emile, 1868-1941 - Exhibitions. I. Stevens,
Mary Anne. II. Städtische Kunsthalle Mannheim. III.
Rijksmuseum Vincent van Gogh. IV. Title.*
N6853.B386 A4 1990

**BERNARD, EMILE, 1868-1941 -
EXHIBITIONS.**
Bernard, Émile, 1868-1941. Emile Bernard,
1868-1941 . Mannheim : Amsterdam : 384 p. :
ill. (some col.) ; ISBN 90-6630-151-1 (glued)
DDC 760/.092 20
N6853.B386 A4 1990

**BERNARD, JOSEPH, 1866-1931 -
EXHIBITIONS.**
Rinuy, Paul-Louis. Pierres et marbres de Joseph
Bernard /. Saint-Rémy-lès-Chevreuse , 1989. 95
p. : ISBN 2-908115-04-2
                    NYPL [3-MGO (Bernard) 91-5897]

Bernard Quentin . Lambert, Jean Clarence.
Paris , c1991. 215 p. : DDC 709/.2 20
N6853.Q46 A4 1991

Bernard Stern /. Restany, Pierre. London , New
York , 1990. 199 p. : ISBN 1-85490-022-6 (UK)
                    NYPL [3-MCV+ S828 90-12079]

BERNARDI, GIOVANNI, 1494-1553.
Donati, Valentino. Pietre dure e medaglie del
Rinascimento . Ferrara [1989]. 291 p. :
                    NYPL [3-MGW+ 91-7173]

Bernardo Bellotto . Bellotto, Bernardo,
1721-1780. Milano , c1990. 172 p. : ISBN
88-435-3242-1
ND623.B43 A4 1990

Bernd Klötzer, Zeichnungen /. Klötzer, Bernd,
1941- Nürnberg , c1988. 152 p. : ISBN
3-922531-60-1
                    NYPL [3-MGO+ (Klötzer) 90-8494]

Bernhard, Betz, 1952- Yard art . Boise, Idaho ,
c1991. 1 v. (unpaged) : DDC
745/.0979/07479628 20
NK824 .Y37 1991

Bernhard Heiliger . Heiliger, Bernhard, 1915-
Berlin , 1987. 48 p. :
                    NYPL [3-MGO+ (Heiliger) 90-254]

Bernhard Heiliger /. Salzmann, Siegfried. Berlin ,
c1989. 356 p. : ISBN 3-549-05308-8
                    NYPL [3-MGO+ (Heiliger) 91-5239]

Bernhard Luginbühl, Figuren 1947-1989 /.
Luginbühl, Bernhard, 1929- Bern , c1989. 511
p. : ISBN 3-7165-0692-3 DDC 730/.92 20
NB853.L8 A4 1989
                    NYPL [3-MGO+ (Luginbühl) 91-5929]

Bernhard Luginbühl im Städel . Luginbühl,
Bernhard, 1929- Frankfurt am Main [1979]
[68] p. :
N7153.T56 A4 1979   *NYPL [3-MGO
                    (Luginbühl) 80-865 [pt. 1]]*

Bernier, Georges.
Aspects of modern art . Paris , New York
[1957] 188 p. : *NYPL [3-MAL+ 90-11498]*

L'art et l'argent : le marché de l'art à la fin du
XXe siècle / Georges Bernier. Paris : Ramsay,
c1990. 317 p. ; 24 cm. Includes bibliographical
references (p. 298-[300]) and index. ISBN
2-85956-891-3 :
1. Art - Marketing. 2. Art as an investment. I. Title.
N8600 .B47 1990

The Selective eye . Paris , New York [1955]
193 p. :   *NYPL [3-MA+ 91-4266]*

Bernier, Rosamond.
Aspects of modern art . Paris , New York
[1957] 188 p. : *NYPL [3-MAL+ 90-11498]*

Matisse, Picasso, Miró : as I knew them / by
Rosamond Bernier ; foreword by John
Russell.1st ed. New York : Alfred A. Knopf ;
Distributed by Random House, 1991. p. cm.
Includes index. ISBN 0-394-58670-0 DDC
709/.2/244 B 20
*1. Matisse, Henri, 1869-1954. 2. Miró, Joan, 1893-. 3.
Picasso, Pablo, 1881-1973. 4. Artists - France -
Biography. 5. Art, French. 6. Art, Modern - 20th
century - France. 7. Bernier, Rosamond - Friends and
associates. I. Title.*
N6848 .B38 1991

The Selective eye . Paris , New York [1955]
193 p. :   *NYPL [3-MA+ 91-4266]*

**BERNIER, ROSAMOND - FRIENDS AND
ASSOCIATES.**
Bernier, Rosamond. Matisse, Picasso, Miró .
New York , 1991. p. cm. ISBN 0-394-58670-0
DDC 709/.2/244 B 20
N6848 .B38 1991

Berning, Maria. Berliner Wohnquartiere : ein
Führer durch 40 Siedlungen / von Maria
Berning, Michael Braum und Engelbert
Lütke-Daldrup ; mit einem Vorwort von Harald
Bodenschatz. Berlin : Reimer, c1990. xiii, 252
p. : ill. ; 25 cm. Includes bibliographical references
(p. 225-248). ISBN 3-496-00382-0 :
*1. Architecture, Domestic - Germany - Berlin -
Guide-books. 2. Architecture, Modern - 20th century -*

Germany - Berlin - Guide-books. 3. Planned
communities - Germany - Berlin - Guide-books. 4.
Berlin (Germany) - Buildings, structures, etc. -
Guide-books. I. Braum, Michael. II. Lütke-Daldrup,
Engelbert. III. Title.
NA7351.B65 B47 1990

**BERNINGHAUSEN, ALICE Z. - ART
COLLECTIONS - EXHIBITIONS.**
Cahill, James, 1926- New dimensions in
Chinese ink painting . Middlebury, Vt. , c1991.
p. cm. ISBN 0-9625262-3-1 DDC
759.951/074/7435 20
ND2068 .C33 1991

**BERNINGHAUSEN, JOHN DAVID - ART
COLLECTIONS - EXHIBITIONS.**
Cahill, James, 1926- New dimensions in
Chinese ink painting . Middlebury, Vt. , c1991.
p. cm. ISBN 0-9625262-3-1 DDC
759.951/074/7435 20
ND2068 .C33 1991

Bernini and the idealization of death . Perlove,
Shelley Karen. University Park , c1990. xiv, 95
p., [40] p. of plates : ISBN 0-271-00684-6 :
DDC 730/.92 20
NB623.B5 A65 1990
NYPL [3-MGO (Bernini) 91-3371]

Bernini, Dante. Il restauro della Città ideale di
Urbino . [Urbino , 1978] 39 p. :
NYPL [3-MBK 90-5658]

Bernini, Gian Lorenzo, 1598-1680.
BLESSED LUDOVICA ALBERTONI.
Perlove, Shelley Karen. Bernini and the
idealization of death . University Park ,
c1990. xiv, 95 p., [40] p. of plates : ISBN
0-271-00684-6 : DDC 730/.92 20
NB623.B5 A65 1990
NYPL [3-MGO (Bernini) 91-3371]

BERNINI, GIAN LORENZO, 1598-1680.
Scribner, Charles. Gianlorenzo Bernini /. New
York , 1991. 128 p. : ISBN 0-8109-3111-7 DDC
709/.2 20
N6923.B5 S37 1991
NYPL [3-MGO+ (Bernini) 91-7243]

Bernini Pezzini, Grazia. Il restauro della Città
ideale di Urbino . [Urbino , 1978] 39 p. :
NYPL [3-MBK 90-5658]

Bernstein, Riva. Figueiredo, Guilherme.
Patrimônio histórico do Rio de Janeiro /. [Rio
de Janeiro] , c1988. 1 portfolio :
NYPL [3-MQWN++ 89-26567]

Bernstein, Theresa.
Echoes of New York : the paintings of Theresa
Bernstein. New York, NY : Museum of the
City of New York, [1990?] [16] p. : ill. ; 22 cm.
Cover title. Catalog of an exhibition held at the
Museum of the City of New York, Nov. 20, 1990-Mar.
31, 1991.
*1. Bernstein, Theresa - Exhibitions. I. Museum of the
City of New York. II. Title.*
NYPL [3-MCX B531 91-3442]

BERNSTEIN, THERESA - EXHIBITIONS.
Bernstein, Theresa. Echoes of New York . New
York, NY [1990?] [16] p. :
NYPL [3-MCX B531 91-3442]

Bernus-Taylor, Marthe. Arabesques et jardins de
paradis . Paris , c1989. 334 p. : ISBN
2-7118-2294-X : DDC 709/.17/67107444361 20
N6264.F8 P317 1990

Beroepsvereniging Nederlandse Ontwerpers.
Ontwerpen in opdracht . Amsterdam , 1990. 2
v. : ISBN 90-72007-04-2 (set) :
NC999.6.N4 O57 1990

Berroeta, Pedro. Las Mismas manos /. [Caracas?]
[198-?] 57 p. : ISBN 980-606-316-3 DDC
751.7/3/098709048 20
ND2722 .M57 1980z

Berry, Claude. The racehorse in twentieth century
art / Claude Berry ; foreword by the Earl of
Halifax. London : Sportsman's Press, 1989. 128
p., 22 p. of plates : ill. (some col.) ; 29 cm.
Includes index. Includes bibliographical references (p.
123). ISBN 0-948253-34-7 : DDC 704.9/432 19
1. Race horses in art. I. Title.
NYPL [3-MAMZ 90-11561]

Berry-Hill Galleries.
Frieseke, Frederick C. (Frederick Carl),
1874-1939. Frederick C. Frieseke . New York,
N.Y. (11 E. 70th St., New York 10021) ,

c1990. 47 p. :
IN PROCESS (ONLINE)
NYPL [3-MCX F916 91-6495]
Harvey, Bunny, 1946- Bunny Harvey . New
York, N.Y. , c1990. 32 p. :
NYPL [3-MCX H341 90-13537]

Berry, Wendell, 1934- Harlan Hubbard : life and
work / Wendell Berry. New York : Pantheon
Books, 1992. p. cm. Originally published:
Lexington : University of Kentucky Press, 1990.
Includes bibliographical references and index. ISBN
0-679-73858-4 (pbk.) : DDC 759.13 B 20
*1. Hubbard, Harlan - Criticism and interpretation. I.
Title.*
NX512.H82 B47 1992

Berryman, Gregg, 1942- Notes on graphic design
and visual communication / Gregg Berryman.
Rev. ed. Los Altos, Calif. : Crisp Publications,
1990. p. cm. Includes bibliographical references.
ISBN 1-560-52044-2 DDC 741.6 20
1. Graphic arts. 2. Visual communication. I. Title.
NC997 .B43 1990

Bersi, Paolo. Klusemann, Georg, 1942- Georg
Klusemann, La meccanica della illusione.
Milano , c1988. 77 p. : ISBN 88-85684-22-X
NYPL [3-MCK+ K658 89-25779]

Bert, Lore, 1936-
Lore Bert : 2. Februar-12. März 1989,
Gutenberg-Museum Mainz / [Texte, Eva-Maria
Hanebutt-Benz, Lothar Romain ;
Übersetzungen, Elisabeth Cabell]. [Mainz] : Das
Museum, c1989. 40 p. : ill. (some col.) ; 29 cm.
German and English.
*1. Bert, Lore, 1936- - Exhibitions. I.
Gutenberg-Museum Mainz. II. Title.*
MLCM 89/00848 (N)
NYPL [3-MCK B536 91-5899]

BERT, LORE, 1936- - EXHIBITIONS.
Bert, Lore, 1936- Lore Bert . [Mainz] , c1989.
40 p. :
MLCM 89/00848 (N)
NYPL [3-MCK B536 91-5899]

Bertani, Licia. La Compagnia della Santissima
Annunziata . Firenze , c1989. 61 p. : ISBN
88-7038-178-1 ***NYPL [3-MLP 90-10711]***

Bertani, Riccardo. L'abbigliamento popolare
italiano /. Brescia [1986] 160 p. :
NYPL [3-MMO 90-8664]

**Bertelà, Giovanna Gaeta. see Gaeta Bertelà,
Giovanna.**

Bertelli, Carlo. Mosaico. English. The Art of
mosaic /. London , c1989. 360 p. : ISBN
0-304-31836-1
NYPL [3-MRXZ+ 91-4959]

Bertha Lum /. Gravalos, Mary Evans O'Keefe.
Washington, D.C. , c1991. 112 p. : ISBN
1-560-98008-7 (pbk.) DDC 769.92 20
NE1112.L86 G73 1990
NYPL [MDG (Lum) 91-5860]

Berthe Morisot, une biographie /. Higonnet,
Anne, 1959- Paris , c1989. 236 p., [16] p. of
plates : ISBN 2-87660-048-7 (cover):
NYPL [3-MCO M86 90-13217]

Berthe Morisot's images of women /. Higonnet,
Anne, 1959- Cambridge, Mass. , 1992. p. cm.
ISBN 0-674-06798-3 (acid-free) DDC 759.4 20
ND553.M88 H53 1992

Bertheux, Wil. Kramer, Friso. Friso Kramer .
[Amsterdam] 1978 (Amsterdam :
Stadsdrukkerij) [36] p. :
NYPL [3-MNF 90-6852]

Berthold Schepers . Schepers, Berthold, 1952-
Berlin , 1988. 53 p. : ISBN 3-926639-10-5 (pbk.)
NYPL [MFX+ (Schepers) 89-21476]

Berthon, Simon. The shape of the World /
[Simon Berthon, Andrew Robinson ; host,
Patrick Stewart]. Chicago : Rand McNally,
1991. 192 p. : ill., maps ; 28 cm. Includes index.
Includes bibliographical references (p. 189). ISBN
0-528-83419-3
*1. Cartography - History. I. Robinson, Andrew. II.
Stewart, Patrick. III. Title.*
NYPL [Map Div. 91-5306]

Berti, Luciano.
L'Età di Masaccio . Milano , c1990. 265 p. :
ISBN 88-435-3211-1
NYPL [3-MAMC 90-12878]
Masaccio : catalogo completo dei dipinti /

Luciano Berti, Rossella Foggi. Firenze : Cantini,
c1989. 159 p. : ill. (some col.) ; 21 cm. (I Gigli
dell'arte . 7) Includes bibliographical references (p.
[150]-159) and index. ISBN 88-7737-059-9
*1. Masaccio, 1401-1428?. - Catalogues raisonnés. I.
Masaccio, 1401-1428?. II. Foggi, Rossella. III. Title. IV.
Series.* ***NYPL [MCF M39 90-13563]***

**BERTILLON, ALPHONSE, 1853-1914 -
HUMOR.**
Lemant, Albert. Les carnets épatants et patents
d'Alphonse Célestin Bertillon . Paris , 1988.
[16] p. : ISBN 2-86234-016-2
NYPL [3-MEM+ (Lemant) 89-27091]

Bertin, Jacques. Atlas des cultures vivrières. Paris
[1971] 41 p. ***NYPL [Map Div. 73-116]***

Bertini, Chiara. Gentili, Augusto. Sebastiano del
Piombo . Venezia , 1985. 32 p., [16] p. of
plates : ***NYPL [3-MCF P66 90-12518]***

Bertolotti, Antonino, 1836-1893. Artisti subalpini
in Roma nei secoli XV, XVI e XVII; ricerche e
studi negli archivi romani. Bologna, A. Forni
[1965] 284 p. 24 cm. Reprint of the 1884 Mantova
ed. Limited ed. of 200 copies.
1. Artists - Italy - Rome. I. Title.
NYPL [3-MAMC 91-304]

BERTOLOTTO, CATERINA.
Luminosity . New York, NY , c1986. 20 p. :
ISBN 0-932075-11-8
NYPL [3-MAL 90-10424]

Berton, Kathleen. Moscow : an architectural
history / Kathleen Berton. London ; New York,
NY : I.B. Tauris , 256 p. : ill., maps ; 26 cm.
Originally published: London : Studio Vista ; New
York : Macmillan, 1977. Includes bibliographical
references (p. 248-251) and index. ISBN
1-85043-261-9 DDC 720/.947/312 20
*1. Architecture - Russian S.F.S.R. - Moscow. 2.
Moscow (R.S.F.S.R.) - Buildings, structures, etc. I.
Title.*
NA1197.M6 B42 1990

Bertrand Lavier . Lavier, Bertrand, 1949- Paris ,
c1991. 127 p. : ISBN 2-85850-598-5 :
IN PROCESS (ONLINE)
NYPL [3-MGO (Lavier) 91-8115]

Bertrand, Olivier. Belgian artists in the world's
salerooms, 1988-1989 / Olivier Bertrand.
Brussels : Arts Antiques Auctions, 1989. xxxv,
334 p. : ill. ; 24 cm. Cover title. French and
Flemish.
1. Artists - Belgium. I. Title.
NYPL [3-MAZ 91-5792]

Bertrand, Pierre. L'artiste / Pierre Bertrand.
Montréal, Québec : L'Hexagone, c1985. 193
p. ; 23 cm. (Collection Positions philosophiques)
ISBN 2-89006-233-3 DDC 701 19
*1. Artists - Philosophy. 2. Artists - Psychology. I. Title.
II. Series.*
N70 .B466 1985 ***NYPL [3-MAS 90-12750]***

Bertuzzi, Giordano. Il rinnovamento edilizio a
Modena nella prima metà dell'Ottocento /
Giordano Bertuzzi. Modena : Aedes
Muratoriana, 1987. 350 p. : ill., plans ; 31 cm.
(Biblioteca. Serie speciale / Deputazione di storia patria
per le antiche provincie modenesi . n. 12) One folded
plan inserted. Includes bibliographical references and
index.
*1. Architecture - Italy - Modena. 2. Architecture,
Modern - 19th century - Italy - Modena. 3. Modena
(Italy) - Buildings, structures, etc. I. Series: Biblioteca
(Deputazione di storia patria per le antiche provincie
modenesi). Serie speciale , n. 12. II. Title.*
NYPL [3-MQWB+ 91-6476]

Bérubé, André, 1936- André Bérubé, street
photographer / introduction by Mark
Kaarremaa. Nanaimo, B.C. : Champlain
Publisher, c1989. [4] p., 51 leaves of plates :
ill. ; 19 cm. ISBN 0-9694007-0-5 : DDC
779/.092/4 19
1. Bérubé, André, 1936-. I. Title.
NYPL [MFX (Bérubé) 91-8032]

BÉRUBÉ, ANDRÉ, 1936-
Bérubé, André, 1936- André Bérubé, street
photographer /. Nanaimo, B.C. , c1989. [4] p.,
51 leaves of plates : ISBN 0-9694007-0-5 : DDC
779/.092/4 19
NYPL [MFX (Bérubé) 91-8032]

Besancenot, Jean.
[Costumes du Maroc. English]
Costumes of Morocco / Jean Besancenot ;
preface by James Bynon ; translated from the

French by Caroline Stone. London ; New
York : Kegan Paul International ; 204 p. : ill.
(60 col.), map ; 37 cm. Translation of: Costumes
du Maroc. ISBN 0-7103-0359-9 DDC 391/.00964
20
1. Costume - Morocco - History - 20th century. I. Title.
GT1582 .B4713 1990
            NYPL [3-MMR+ 91-7287]

Bescós, Jean, 1950- Saura, Antonio, 1930-
Antonio Saura . Paris , 1989. 282 p. : ISBN
2-7022-0243-8
            NYPL [3-MCQ+ S259 91-5230]

Besouchet, Lídia. Carybé, 1911- Carybé /.
[Salvador] , 1989. 452 p. : DDC 709/.2 20
N6659.C39 A4 1989

Bess, Forrest, 1911-1977.
Forrest Bess (1911-1977) : here is a sign :
[exhibition] Museum Ludwig Köln,
28.1.-27.3.1989. Köln : Das Museum, c1989.
151 p. : ill. (some col.), ports. ; 28 cm. English
and German. Bibliography: p. 147.
1. Bess, Forrest, 1911-1977 - Exhibitions.
            NYPL [3-MCX B549 90-13382]

BESS, FORREST, 1911-1977 - EXHIBITIONS.
Bess, Forrest, 1911-1977. Forrest Bess
(1911-1977) . Köln , c1989. 151 p. :
            NYPL [3-MCX B549 90-13382]

Bessie Pease Gutmann . Christie, Victor J. W.
Radnor, Pa. , c1990. xv, 199 p. : ISBN
0-87069-561-4 : DDC 741.6/092 B 20
N6537.G88 C4 1990
            NYPL [3-MCX G983 91-3649]

Besson, George. Galerie Marcel Guiot. Albert
André, 1869-1954. Paris [1960] 17 p.
ND553.A5 G33 1960
            NYPL [3-MCO A55 90-7046]

Best, Carsten. Einleuchten . Hamburg [1989]
289 p. : ISBN 3-7672-1102-5 DDC
709/.04/507443515 20
N6488.G3 H2832 1989

The Best in international textile design.
Japanese style. Kyoto, Japan , Tokyo, Japan ,
c1989. 2 v. in 6 : ISBN 4-7636-8059-5 (v. 1)
DDC 745.4/4952 20
NK8984.A1 J37 1989

The best of Rube Goldberg /. Goldberg, Rube,
1883-1970. Englewood Cliffs, N.J. [1979] xiii,
130 p. : ISBN 0-13-074807-2 : DDC 741.5/973
NC1429.G46 A4 1979
            NYPL [3-MEM (Goldberg) 81-1046]

Bestandsaufnahme, Kunsthandwerk.
Internationaler Kongress Europäisches
Kunsthandwerk (1988 : Stuttgart, Germany)
Internationaler Kongress Europäisches
Kunsthandwerk 1988, Stuttgart . Frankfurt ,
1988. 56 p. ; ISBN 3-87864-176-1
            NYPL [3-MNC+ 90-12554]

Bestandskatalog ... der Graphischen Sammlung .
(1) Städtisches Museum Leverkusen, Schloss
Morsbroich. Graphische Sammlung. Von
Arakawa bis Winzer . Leverkusen [1987?] 137
p. : ISBN 3-925520-04-X
N6868 .S765 1987

**Bestandskatalog (Kaiser Wilhelm Museum
Krefeld) .**
(Nr. 10) Kaiser Wilhelm Museum Krefeld.
Italienische Renaissancekunst im Kaiser
Wilhelm Museum Krefeld /. [Krefeld] , 1987.
154, [2] p. : ISBN 3-926530-30-8
            NYPL [3-MAVZ (Krefeld) 90-12394]

**BET HA-HOLIM "HADASAH" (JERUSALEM).
SYNAGOGUE.**
Chagall, Marc, 1887- [Vitraux pour Jerusalem.
German.] Glasmalereien für Jerusalem /. Monte
Carlo , c1962. 211 p. :
            NYPL [3-MCZ+ C43 91-7160]

Bethusy-Huc, Reinhold, Graf. Kokoschka, Oskar,
1886- Das Konzert . Salzburg , c1988. 67 p. :
            NYPL [3-MCZ K79 89-4191]

Betonamu dōko zuroku. Dong son drums in Viet
Nam /. Tōkyō , 1990. 282 p. : ISBN
4-8453-3038-5 :
NK7978.6.V5 D66 1990

Betonamu Kōko Kenkyūjo. Dong son drums in
Viet Nam /. Tōkyō , 1990. 282 p. : ISBN
4-8453-3038-5 :
NK7978.6.V5 D66 1990

**Betonamu Shakai Kagaku Iinkai. Kokusai
Kyōryokubu.** Dong son drums in Viet Nam /.
Tōkyō , 1990. 282 p. : ISBN 4-8453-3038-5 :
NK7978.6.V5 D66 1990

Betsky, Aaron.
Experimental architecture in Los Angeles /.
New York , 1991. p. cm. ISBN 0-8478-1424-6
(HC) DDC 720/.9794/9409045 20
NA735.L55 E97 1991

Violated perfection : architecture and the
fragmentation of the modern / Aaron Betsky ;
concept developed by Paul Florian, Stephen
Wierzbowski and Aaron Betsky ; with a
violation by Paul Florian and Stephen
Wierzbowski. New York : Rizzoli International,
1990. 208 p. : ill. (some col.) ; 29 cm. Includes
bibliographical references and index. ISBN
0-8478-1269-3 DDC 724/.6 20
*1. Architecture, Modern - 20th century. 2. Architects -
Psychology. I. Florian, Paul. II. Wierzbowski, Stephen.
III. Title.*
NA680 .B497 1990 ***NYPL [3-MQV 91-3682]***

Better photography. Abbott, Berenice, 1891- New
guide to better photography /. New York ,
c1953. vii, 180 p., [41] leaves of plates :
            NYPL [MFW 91-5017]

Betthausen, Peter.
Menzel, Adolph, 1815-1905. Adolph Menzel,
1815-1905 . Alexandria, Va. , 1990. 235 p. :
ISBN 0-88397-096-1 DDC 741.943 20
NC251.M45 A4 1990
            NYPL [3-MCK M55 91-3333]

Nationalgalerie (Germany : East) Von Caspar
David Friedrich bis Adolph Menzel .
München , 1990. 283 p. : ISBN 3-7913-1047-X
            NYPL [3-MCI+ 91-3367]

Von Caspar David Friedrich bis Adolph
Menzel . München , c1990. 283 p. : ISBN
3-7913-1047-X DDC 759.3/074/43613 20
N6867.5.R6 V6 1990

Betti, Claudia. Drawing : a contemporary
approach / Claudia Betti, Teel Sale.3rd ed. Fort
Worth, TX : Holt, Rinehart, and Winston,
1991. p. cm. Includes bibliographical references and
index. ISBN 0-03-053147-0 DDC 741.2 20
1. Drawing - Technique. I. Sale, Teel. II. Title.
NC730 .B43 1991

Bettis, Kathleen, 1947- Harthorn, Sandy, 1945-
One hundred years of Idaho art, 1850-1950 .
Boise, ID , c1990. 134 p. : DDC
709/.796/07479628 20
N6530.I2 H37 1990
            NYPL [3-MAMT 90-11110]

Betty Parsons . Hall, Lee. New York , 1991. 192
p. : ISBN 0-8109-3712-3 DDC 709/.2 B 20
N8660.P37 H35 1990
            NYPL [3-MAVC 91-7302]

Between ourselves. Garrard, Rose. Rose Garrard .
Birmingham [England] [1983?] 32 p. :
N6797.G37 I5 1983
            NYPL [3-MGO (Garrard) 90-10680]

Between spring and summer : Soviet conceptual
art in the era of late communism. Tacoma,
Wash. : Tacoma Art Museum ; Boston, Mass. :
Institute of Contemporary Art, c1990. x, 206
p. : ill. (some col.) ; 26 cm. Catalog of an
exhibition held June 15-Sept. 9, 1990 at the Tacoma
Art Museum; Nov. 1, 1990-Jan. 6, 1991 at the Institute
of Contemporary Art, Boston; Feb. 16-Mar. 31, 1991 at
the Des Moines Art Center. Includes essays translated
from the Russian. Includes bibliographical references (p.
[201]-202) ISBN 0-910663-49-1
*1. Conceptual art - Soviet Union - Exhibitions. 2. Art,
Soviet - Exhibitions. 3. Art, Modern - 20th century -
Soviet Union - Exhibitions. I. Tacoma. Art Museum. II.
Institute of Contemporary Art (Boston, Mass.). III. Des
Moines Art Center.*
N6988.5.C62 B48 1990
            NYPL [3-MAM 90-12998]

Between the rivers. Heslip, Colleen Cowles.
Williamstown, Mass. , c1990. 95 p. : ISBN
0-931102-28-6 : DDC 759.14/074/744 20
ND215 .H47 1990 ***NYPL [3-MCW 91-4583]***

Between worlds : contemporary Mexican
photography / [editor, Trisha Ziff.]. New York :
New Amsterdam Books, 1990. 144 p. : ill.
(some col.) ; 26 cm. ISBN 1-561-31003-4
1. Photography - Mexico. I. Ziff, Trisha.
            NYPL [MFW 90-13455]

Beurden, Leontien van. Mode in de 20ste eeuw /
Leontien van Beurden. Nijmegen : SUN, c1988.
143 p. (some col.) ; 23 cm. Includes index.
Includes bibliographical references (p. 142). ISBN
90-6168-291-6 :
*1. Fashion - History - 20th century. I. Title. II. Title:
Mode in de twintigste eeuw.*
GT596 .B48 1988 ***NYPL [3-MME 90-10712]***

**BEUREN (ESSLINGEN, GERMANY) -
BUILDINGS, STRUCTURES, ETC.**
Braun, Dietrich. Nikolauskirche Beuren .
Villingen , c1988. 96 p. : ISBN 3-7883-1904-6
NA5586.B4395 B73 1988

Beuttenmüller, Alberto, 1935- Volpi, Ianelli,
Aldir : 3 coloristas / Alberto Beuttenmüller.
[São Paulo : Grupo IOB, 1989] 1 v. (unpaged) :
col. ill. ; 29 cm. Cover title. Includes bibliographical
references.
*1. Painting, Brazilian - Themes, motives. 2. Painting,
Modern - 20th century - Brazil - Themes, motives. 3.
Color in art. 4. Volpi, Alfredo, 1896- - Themes,
motives. 5. Ianelli, Arcangelo, 1922- - Themes, motives.
6. Souza, Aldir Mendes de, 1941- - Themes, motives. I.
Volpi, Alfredo, 1896-. II. Ianelli, Arcangelo, 1922-. III.
Souza, Aldir Mendes de, 1941-. IV. Title.*
ND355 .B48 1989

Beuys. Beuys, Joseph. Joseph Beuys im Gespräch
mit Knut Fischer und Walter Smerling. Köln ,
c1989. 75 p. : ISBN 3-462-01970-8
            NYPL [3-MGO (Beuys) 90-2524]

Beuys, Joseph.
Joseph Beuys . Darmstadt , c1989. 179 p. :
ISBN 3-925376-30-5 (trade ed.)
            NYPL [3-MGO (Beuys) 91-6704]

Joseph Beuys : a private collection : 22.
Februar bis 29. April 1990, A11 Artforum,
München. München : Das Artforum, c1990.
228 p. : chiefly ill. (some col.) ; 29 cm. German
and English.
1. Beuys, Joseph - Exhibitions. I. Title.
MLCM 91/01681 (N)
            NYPL [3-MCK+ B569 91-6473]

Joseph Beuys : plastische Bilder 1947-1970 /
mit Textbeiträgen von Franz Joseph van der
Grinten ... [et al.]. Stuttgart : G. Hatje, c1990.
135 p. : ill. ; 30 cm. ISBN 3-7757-0313-6
*1. Beuys, Joseph - Exhibitions. I. Galerie der Stadt
Kornwestheim. II. Title.*
            NYPL [3-MCK+ B569 91-3920]

Joseph Beuys : eine innere Mongolei :
Dschingis Khan, Schamanen, Aktricen :
Ölfarben, Wasserfarben und Bleistiftzeichnungen
aus der Sammlung van der Grinten /
herausgegeben von Carl Haenlein. Hannover :
Kestner-Gesellschaft, [1990] 267 p. : chiefly ill.
(chiefly col.) ; 33 cm. Catalog of an exhibition of
the Kestner-Gesellschaft and the Stiftung
Niedersachsen, July 20-Sept. 16, 1990. Includes
bibliographical references (p. 261-267). DDC 759.3 20
*1. Beuys, Joseph - Exhibitions. 2. Grinten, Joseph van
der - Art collections - Exhibitions. 3. Art - Private
collections - Germany - Kranenburg (North
Rhine-Westphalia) - Exhibitions. I. Haenlein, Carl
Albrecht. II. Kestner-Gesellschaft. III. Stiftung
Niedersachsen. IV. Title. V. Title: Innere Mongolei.*
N6888.B463 A4 1990

Joseph Beuys im Gespräch mit Knut Fischer
und Walter Smerling. Köln : Kiepenheuer &
Witsch, c1989. 75 p. : ill. ; 24 cm. (Kunst heute ;
Nr. 1) Cover title: Beuys. ISBN 3-462-01970-8
*1. Beuys, Joseph - Interviews. I. Fischer, Knut. II.
Smerling, Walter. III. Title. IV. Title: Beuys. V. Series.*
            NYPL [3-MGO (Beuys) 90-2524]

BEUYS, JOSEPH.
Joseph Beuys . Darmstadt , c1989. 179 p. :
ISBN 3-925376-30-5 (trade ed.)
            NYPL [3-MGO (Beuys) 91-6704]

Stachelhaus, Heiner. [Joseph Beuys. English.]
Joseph Beuys /. New York , 1991. 223 p. :
ISBN 1-558-59107-9 DDC 709/.2 B 20
N6888.B463 S7413 1991
            NYPL [3-MCK B569 91-6313]

BEUYS, JOSEPH - CATALOGS.
Joseph Beuys . Darmstadt , c1989. 179 p. :
ISBN 3-925376-30-5 (trade ed.)
            NYPL [3-MGO (Beuys) 91-6704]

**BEUYS, JOSEPH - CRITICISM AND
INTERPRETATION.**
Nolte, Jost, 1927- Kollaps der Moderne .
Hamburg , c1989. 239 p. : ISBN 3-89136-234-X
            NYPL [3-MAL 90-12617]

BEUYS, JOSEPH - EXHIBITIONS.
Beuys, Joseph. Joseph Beuys . München ,
c1990. 228 p. :
MLCM 91/01681 (N)
NYPL [3-MCK+ B569 91-6473]

Beuys, Joseph. Joseph Beuys . Stuttgart , c1990.
135 p. :   ISBN 3-7757-0313-6
NYPL [3-MCK+ B569 91-3920]

Beuys, Joseph. Joseph Beuys . Hannover
[1990] 267 p. :   DDC 759.3 20
N6888.B463 A4 1990

BEUYS, JOSEPH - INTERVIEWS.
Beuys, Joseph. Joseph Beuys im Gespräch mit
Knut Fischer und Walter Smerling. Köln ,
c1989. 75 p. :   ISBN 3-462-01970-8
NYPL [3-MGO (Beuys) 90-2524]

Bever, Suzy van. Suzynisme : Suzy van Bever :
de vrouw achter een stijlbegrip / [auteurs,
Rooske Brems ... et al.]. Nieuwrode :
VriendenKring Suzy van Bever, 1985. [103] p. :
ill. (some col.), ports. ; 30 cm.   ISBN
90-900087-1-3
1. Bever, Suzy van. I. Brems, Rooske. II. Title.
NYPL [3-MCH+ B569 90-2141]

BEVER, SUZY VAN.
Bever, Suzy van. Suzynisme . Nieuwrode ,
1985. [103] p. :   ISBN 90-900087-1-3
NYPL [3-MCH+ B569 90-2141]

Beverley R. Robinson Collection.
Naval prints from the Beverley R. Robinson
Collection / compiled and edited bt Sigrid
Trumpy, curator, and Sari Hornstein.
Annapolis, Md. : Beverley R. Robinson
Collection, United States Naval Academy
Museum, 1991- p. cm. Includes bibliographical
references and indexes. CONTENTS. - v. 1. 1514-1791
ISBN 0-9628260-0-6 (hardcover)   DDC
769/.493594/07475256 20
*1. Naval prints - Catalogs. 2. Naval battles in art -
Catalogs. 3. Beverley R. Robinson Collection - Catalogs.
a. 4. Naval prints - Private collections - Maryland -
Annapolis - Catalogs. 5. Naval prints - Maryland -
Annapolis - Catalogs. 6. United States Naval Academy.
Museum - Catalogs. I. Trumpy, Sigrid, 1946-. II.
Hornstein, Sari R., 1955-. III. Title.*
NE957 .B48 1991

BEVERLEY R. ROBINSON COLLECTION - CATALOGS. A.
Beverley R. Robinson Collection. Naval prints
from the Beverley R. Robinson Collection /.
Annapolis, Md. , 1991- p.   ISBN 0-9628260-0-6
(hardcover)   DDC 769/.493594/07475256 20
NE957 .B48 1991

Beverly Pepper . Pepper, Beverly. New York,
N.Y. , c1990. 1 v. (unpaged) :
NYPL [3-MGO+ (Pepper) 91-6687]

Bevers, Holm. Niederländische Zeichnungen des
16. Jahrhunderts in der Staatlichen Graphischen
Sammlung München . München , 1989. 219 p. :
ISBN 3-927803-00-6
NYPL [3-MBH 91-4571]

Bewaard in het hart . Amsterdam (Netherlands).
Gemeentelijk bureau Monumentenzorg.
Amsterdam , 1965. 174 p. :
NYPL [3-MQW 90-6245]

Bewick, Pauline, 1935-
Pauline Bewick's Ireland : an artist's year.
London : Methuen, 1990. 192 p. : col. ill. ; 25
cm.   ISBN 0-413-64320-4 (cased) :   DDC
914.1504824 20
*1. Bewick, Pauline, 1935- - Notebooks, sketchbooks,
etc. 2. Ireland - Description and travel - 1981-. 3.
Ireland - Description and travel - 1981- Views. I. Title.
II. Title: Ireland, and artist's year.*
DA978   **NYPL [3-MCV B572 91-4511]**

BEWICK, PAULINE, 1935- - NOTEBOOKS, SKETCHBOOKS, ETC.
Bewick, Pauline, 1935- Pauline Bewick's
Ireland . London , 1990. 192 p. :   ISBN
0-413-64320-4 (cased) :   DDC 914.1504824 20
DA978   **NYPL [3-MCV B572 91-4511]**

Bewick, Thomas, 1753-1828. The watercolours
and drawings of Thomas Bewick and his
workshop apprentices / Introduced and with
editorial notes by Iain Bain. Stocksfield,
Northumberland : Thomas Bewick Birthplace
Trust ; Winchester : in association with St
Paul's Bibliographies ; 2 v. : ill. (some col.) ; 23
x 26 cm. "First published by the Gordon Fraser
Gallery Ltd, London and Bedford"--T.p. verso, v. 2.

Includes bibliographical references and index.   ISBN
0-906795-85-0 (set)   DDC 769.92 20
*1. Bewick, Thomas, 1753-1828. 2. Artists' studios -
England. I. Bain, Iain. II. Title.*
N6797.B48 A4 1989
NYPL [3-MCV B5722 91-3680]

BEWICK, THOMAS, 1753-1828.
Bewick, Thomas, 1753-1828. The watercolours
and drawings of Thomas Bewick and his
workshop apprentices /. Stocksfield,
Northumberland : Winchester : 2 v. :   ISBN
0-906795-85-0 (set)   DDC 769.92 20
N6797.B48 A4 1989
NYPL [3-MCV B5722 91-3680]

Beyer, Constantin. Badstübner, Ernst. Das alte
Mühlhausen . Leipzig , c1989. 205 p. :   ISBN
3-7338-0055-9
N6886.M78 B34 1989

Beyer, Victor. Les vitraux des musées de
Strasbourg / catalogue par Victor Beyer ;
avant-propos de Hans Haug. Strasbourg :
Edition des musées de la ville, 1965. 2 v. in 1 :
ill. (some col.) ; 19 cm. "Artistes contemporains
residant en Alsace": [2] p., inserted. Cover title:
Exposition Mille ans d'art du vitrail à l'ancienne
douane, du 5 juin au 31 août 1965, Strasbourg. Includes
bibliographical references.
*1. Glass painting and staining - France - Strasbourg -
Exhibitions. I. Strasbourg. Ancienne douane. II. Title.
III. Title: Exposition Mille ans d'art du vitrail.*
NYPL [3-MRY 85-4411]

Beyond the Java Sea . Taylor, Paul Michael.
Washington, D.C. , New York , 1991. p. cm.
ISBN 0-8109-3112-5 (hardcover : Abrams) :
DDC 709/.598 20
N7326 .T39 1991

Beyond the pyramids : Egyptian regional art from
the Museo egizio, Turin / edited by Gay
Robins ; with contributions by Elvira
D'Amicone ... [et al.]. Atlanta, Ga. : Emory
University Museum of Art and Archaeology,
c1990. 95 p. : ill. (some col.) ; 27 cm. Errata slip
inserted. Catalog of an exhibition held at Emory
University Museum of Art and Archaeology, Atlanta,
Oct. 24, 1990-Mar. 10, 1991. At head of title: Emory
University Museum of Art and Archaeology, Atlanta,
Museo egizio di Torino. Includes bibliographical
references.
*1. Museo egizio di Torino - Exhibitions. 2. Art,
Egyptian - Exhibitions. 3. Egypt - Antiquities -
Exhibitions. I. Robins, Gay. II. D'Amicone, Elvira. III.
Emory University. Museum of Art and Archaeology.*
NYPL [3-MAE 91-4240]

Bezirk Suhl / Rudolf Ziessler ... [et al.]. 1. Aufl.
Berlin : VEB Verlag für Bauwesen, 1989. 160
p. : ill., maps ; 19 cm. (Architekturführer DDR)
Includes bibliographical references (p. 147-150).
Includes indexes.   ISBN 3-345-00213-2
*1. Architecture - Germany - Suhl - Guide-books. 2.
Suhl (Germany) - Description and travel - Guide-books.
I. Ziessler, Rudolf. II. Series.*
NA1089.2.S84 B49 1989

**Bezirksverband Bildender Künstler (Karlsruhe,
Germany)** Kunstsituation und Künstler sein
heute . Karlsruhe , 1988. 342 p. :
N6886.K33 K88 1988
NYPL [3-MAMG 90-10706]

Bezold, Gustav von. Die Kunstdenkmale des
Regierungsbezirkes Oberbayern / bearbeitet von
Gustav von Bezold und Berthold Riehl ; unter
Mitwirkung anderer Gelehrter und Künstler.
München : R. Oldenbourg, 1982. 10 v. : ill. ;
26 cm. (Die Kunstdenkmäler von Bayern ; 1) Cover
title: Oberbayern. Vols. 4-10 also prepared by G. Hager.
Reprint. Originally published: München : R.
Oldenbourg, 1895-1905. (Die Kunstdenkmale des
Königreiches Bayern ; 1. Bd.) Includes bibliographical
references. Vol. 10: Index to vols. 1-9.   ISBN
3-486-50421-5 (v. 1)
*1. Art, German - Germany - Oberbayern. 2.
Oberbayern (Germany) - Description and travel. I.
Riehl, Berthold. II. Hager, Georg, b. 1863. III. Title.
IV. Title: Oberbayern. V. Series.*
N6873 .K86 1980 vol. 1 N6873

Bhagavata Purana . Bharat Kala Bhavan.
Varanasi, India , c1983. 1 portfolio (6 p., 6
leaves of col. ill.) ;   DDC 755/.945211 19
ND1337.I5 B488 1983
NYPL [3-MAF+ 90-10844]

Bhāgavatapurāṇa. see Puranas. Bhāgavatapurāṇa.

Bharat Kala Bhavan.
Bhagavata Purana : Krishna lila / text & notes
by Yashodhara Agrawal. Varanasi, India :
Banaras Hindu University, c1983. 1 portfolio (6
p., 6 leaves of col. ill.) ; 32 cm. (Treasures of
Indian art in Bharat Kala Bhavan. ser. 4) Title from
portfolio.   DDC 755/.945211 19
*1. Bharat Kala Bhavan - Catalogs. 2. Puranas.
Bhāgavatapurāṇa - Illustrations - Catalogs. 3. Miniature
painting, Indic - Catalogs. 4. Krishna (Hindu deity) -
Art - Catalogs. I. Agrawal, Yashodhara. II. Series:
Bharat Kala Bhavan. Treasures of Indian art in Bharat
Kala Bavan , ser. 4. III. Title.*
ND1337.I5 B488 1983
NYPL [3-MAF+ 90-10844]

BHARAT KALA BHAVAN - CATALOGS.
Bharat Kala Bhavan. Bhagavata Purana .
Varanasi, India , c1983. 1 portfolio (6 p., 6
leaves of col. ill.) ;   DDC 755/.945211 19
ND1337.I5 B488 1983
NYPL [3-MAF+ 90-10844]

**Bharat Kala Bhavan. Treasures of Indian art in
Bharat Kala Bavan .**
(ser. 4) Bharat Kala Bhavan. Bhagavata
Purana . Varanasi, India , c1983. 1 portfolio (6
p., 6 leaves of col. ill.) ;   DDC 755/.945211 19
ND1337.I5 B488 1983
NYPL [3-MAF+ 90-10844]

**Bhārata kī janagaṇanā, 1981. Śṛṅkhalā 1,
Bhārata.** Census of India, 1981. Series 1, India.
Delhi , 1983- v. in :   DDC 304.6/0954/021 19
HA4581.5 1981g
NYPL [JLM 88-578 & Map Div. 90-54]

Bhatia, Usha. Indian miniature painting series 2.
New Delhi , 1986. 1 portfolio ([4] p., 8 leaves
of col. ; 11.);   **NYPL [3-MAF+ 87-3545]**

Bhattacharyya, Benoytosh, 1897-1964. The
Indian Buddhist iconography, mainly based on
the Sādhanamālā and Cognate tāntric texts and
rituals. [2nd ed., rev. and enl.] Calcutta, Firma
K. L. Mukhopadhyay [1968] xxxiii, 478 p. illus.
25 cm. "Select bibliography": p. [xxx]-xxxiii.
*1. Gautama Buddha - Iconography. 2. Art, Indic. 3.
India - Antiquities. I. Sādhanamālā. II. Title.*
NYPL [3-MAF 75-368]

Biadene, Susanna. Tiziano. Venezia , 1990. xv,
432 p. :   ISBN 88-317-5330-4   DDC 759.5 20
ND623.T7 A4 1990
NYPL [3-MCF+ T63 91-4869]

Biagiotti, Laura, 1943- Bellezza e seduzione nella
Roma imperiale . [Roma] [c1990] 122 p. :
ISBN 88-7813-283-7 :
N7629.2.I8 R663 1990

Bialopetravičienė, Laima. Čiurlionis und die
litauische Malerei, 1900-1940 : 2. Juli-3.
September 1989, Wilhelm-Lehmbruck-Museum
der Stadt Duisburg / [Ausstellung und Katalog,
Laima Bialopetravičienė, Oswaldas Daugelis,
Renate Heidt Heller]. Duisburg : Das Museum,
c1989. 105 p. : ill. (some col.) ; 27 cm.
Bibliography: p. 102-105.   ISBN 3-923576-57-9
*1. Čiurlionis, Mikalojus Konstantinas, 1875-1911 -
Exhibitions. 2. Painting, Lithuanian - Exhibitions. 3.
Painting, Modern - 20th century - Lithuania -
Exhibitions. I. Čiurlionis, Mikalojus Konstantinas,
1875-1911. II. Daugelis, Oswaldas. III. Heidt, Renate.
IV. Title.*   **NYPL [3-MCY 90-10676]**

Bianchi, Domenico, 1955-
Domenico Bianchi : Castello di Rivoli, 6
ottobre-3 dicembre 1989 / a cura di Rudi
Fuchs, Johannes Gachnang, Cristina Mundici.
[Turin] : Castello di Rivoli, museo d'arte
contemporanea, [1989] 1 v. (unpaged) : chiefly
col. ill. ; 23 cm. Text also in English. Includes
bibliographical references.
*1. Bianchi, Domenico, 1955- - Exhibitions. I. Castello
di Rivoli (Museum : Turin, Italy). II. Title.*
N6923.B557 A4 1989

BIANCHI, DOMENICO, 1955- - EXHIBITIONS.
Bianchi, Domenico, 1955- Domenico Bianchi .
[Turin] [1989] 1 v. (unpaged) :
N6923.B557 A4 1989

Bianchino, Gloria. Quintavalle, Arturo Carlo.
Arnaldo Pomodoro . Milano , 1990. 163 p. :
ISBN 88-435-3379-7
IN PROCESS (ONLINE)
NYPL [3-MGO+ (Pomodoro) 91-7181]

**Bianco, Umberto Zanotti- see Zanotti-Bianco,
Umberto.**

Biāshimova, N. S. (Nurgozel´ Saryevna)
Polivnaīa keramika IUzhnogo Turkmenistana,
IX-XIV vv. / N.S. Biāshimova ; otvetstvennyĭ
redaktor G.A. Pugachenkova. Ashkhabad :
"Ylym", 1989. 222, [2] p. ; 20 cm. At head of
title: Akademiīa nauk SSSR. Institut istorii im. Sh.
Batyrova. Includes bibliographical references (p.
209-[223]).   ISBN 5-8338-0278-4 :
1. Luster-ware, Islamic - Turkmen S.S.R. 2.
Luster-ware - Turkmen S.S.R. I. Pugachenkova, Galina
Anatol´evna. II. Title. III. Title: Polivnaīa keramika
IUzhnogo Turkmenistana, 9.-14. vv. IV. Title: Polivnaīa
keramika IUzhnogo Turkmenistana,
deviātogo-chetyrnadtsatogo vekov.
NK4399.L9 B5 1989

Bibal, François. L'Institut de France /
photographies de François Bibal. [Paris?] :
François Bibel, c1988. 164 p. : ill. (chiefly col.),
ports. ; 31 cm. Ill. on lining papers   ISBN
2-905547-05-7
1. Institut de France - Pictorial works. 2. Architecture -
France. I. Title.
    NYPL   [MFX+   (Bibal) 90-1062]

Biberstein, Michael, 1948-
Michael Biberstein : 'Über die Apotheose des
menschlichen Geistes im Sehen der Landschaft'
'On the apotheosis of the human spirit through
the seeing of landscape.' Düsseldorf :
Kunstverein für die Rheinlande und Westfalen,
1989. 2 v. : chiefly ill. (some col., some
folded) ; 28 cm. Catalog of an exhibition held at the
Kunstverein für die Rheinlande und Westfalen,
Düsseldorf, Apr. 29-May 28, 1989. German and
English. Includes bibliographical references.
CONTENTS. - [Bd. 1] Bilder -- [Bd. 2] Zeichnungen
und Aquarelle.   ISBN 3-925974-08-3
1. Biberstein, Michael, 1948- - Exhibitions. I.
Kunstverein für die Rheinlande und Westfalen. II. Title.
III. Title: Über die Apotheose des menschlichen Geistes
im Sehen der Landschaft. IV. Title: On the apotheosis
of the human spirit through the seeing of landscape.
    NYPL   [3-MCZ B5765 90-781]

BIBERSTEIN, MICHAEL, 1948- -
   EXHIBITIONS.
Biberstein, Michael, 1948- Michael Biberstein .
Düsseldorf , 1989. 2 v. :   ISBN 3-925974-08-3
    NYPL   [3-MCZ B5765 90-781]

Bible - Atlases. see Bible - Geography - Maps.

BIBLE - BOLIVIA - INFLUENCE.
Gisbert, Teresa, 1926- La tradición bíblica en el
arte virreinal /. La Paz, Bolivia , 1987. viii, 33
p. :   *NYPL   [3-MAM 90-12522]*

BIBLE - DICTIONARIES.
Duchet-Suchaux, Gaston. La Bible et les
saints . Paris , c1990. 319 p., xxxii p. of plates :
   ISBN 2-08-011725-4
    NYPL   [3-MAIH 91-6578]

La Bible et les saints . Duchet-Suchaux, Gaston.
Paris , c1990. 319 p., xxxii p. of plates :   ISBN
2-08-011725-4   *NYPL   [3-MAIH 91-6578]*

BIBLE - GEOGRAPHY - MAPS.
Karṭa (Firm) Grosser Bibelstudien Atlas.
Stuttgart , 1987. 1 atlas (17 p.) :   ISBN
3-7675-7760-7   *NYPL   [Map Div. 90-9723]*

BIBLE - ILLUSTRATIONS.
Duchet-Suchaux, Gaston. La Bible et les
saints . Paris , c1990. 319 p., xxxii p. of plates :
   ISBN 2-08-011725-4
    NYPL   [3-MAIH 91-6578]

Rembrandt Harmenzoon van Rijn, 1606-1669.
Rembrandt legt die Bibel aus . Berlin , 1970.
[387] p. :
NC263.R4 T8
    NYPL   [MDG (Rembrandt) 90-7045]

Bible. Latin. Nekcsei-Lipócz Bible. ca. 1335.
Nekcsei-Lipócz Bible. A Nekcsei-Biblia legszebb
lapjai. Budapest , Washington , 1988. 231 [5]
p. :   ISBN 963-207-955-8
IN PROCESS (ONLINE) Rare Bk Coll
    NYPL   [JFH 91-4]

Bible. Latin. Vulgate. ca. 1335. Nekcsei-Lipócz
Bible. A Nekcsei-Biblia legszebb lapjai.
Budapest , Washington , 1988. 231 [5] p. :
   ISBN 963-207-955-8
IN PROCESS (ONLINE) Rare Bk Coll
    NYPL   [JFH 91-4]

Bible - Maps. see Bible - Geography - Maps.

BIBLE. N.T. MATTHEW - ILLUSTRATIONS.
New light on Michelangelo in the Sistine
Chapel. German. Der neue Michelangelo .

Luzern, Schweiz , c1989-c1991. 3 v. :   ISBN
3-85672-033-2 (set)
    NYPL   [MCF++ B9 91-6340]

BIBLE. O.T. EXODUS - ILLUSTRATIONS.
Mayer, Klaus. Ich bin mit dir . Würzburg ,
1989. 115 p. :   ISBN 3-429-01137-3
    NYPL   [MDG+ (Chagall) 89-18773]

BIBLE. O.T. OCTATEUCH -
   ILLUSTRATIONS.
Lowden, John. The Octateuches . University
Park, Pa. , c1992. p. cm.   ISBN 0-271-00771-0
   DDC 745.6/7487 20
ND3358.O27 L68 1992

Bible - Pictures, illustrations, etc. see Bible -
   Illustrations.

BIBLIOGRAPHICAL EXHIBITIONS -
   MASSACHUSETTS - BOSTON.
Artists of the book 1988 . Boston, Mass. ,
c1988. 40 p. :   ISBN 0-934552-53-3
    NYPL   [MDTT 91-4772]

BIBLIOGRAPHY - EARLY PRINTED
   BOOKS - 15TH CENTURY. see
   INCUNABULA.

BIBLIOGRAPHY - EXHIBITIONS. see
   BIBLIOGRAPHICAL EXHIBITIONS.

Bibliography of map projections /. Snyder, John
Parr, 1926- Washington, D.C. , Denver, CO ,
1989. xii, 110 p. ;   DDC 557.3 s 016.5268 19
QE75 .B9 no. 1856 Z6021 GA110
    NYPL   [Map Div. 90-11485]

BIBLIOPHILY. see BOOK COLLECTING.

Biblioteca apostolica vaticana.
Michelangelo e la Sistina . Roma , 1990. 306
p. :   ISBN 88-7621-595-6
    NYPL   [3-MCF+ B9 90-12802]

Morello, Giovanni. Libri d'ore della Biblioteca
apostolica vaticana /. Zürich , c1988. 143 p. :
   DDC 745.6/7/09407445634 20
ND2899.V36 M6 1988

BIBLIOTECA APOSTOLICA VATICANA -
   EXHIBITIONS.
Morello, Giovanni. Libri d'ore della Biblioteca
apostolica vaticana /. Zürich , c1988. 143 p. :
   DDC 745.6/7/09407445634 20
ND2899.V36 M6 1988

Biblioteca comunale classense (Ravenna, Italy)
Fifteenth century Italian woodcuts from the
Biblioteca Classense in Ravenna. Ravenna ,
c1989. 13 p., [46] p. of plates :
    NYPL   [MDOH 90-11354]

BIBLIOTECA COMUNALE CLASSENSE
   (RAVENNA, ITALY) - CATALOGS.
Fifteenth century Italian woodcuts from the
Biblioteca Classense in Ravenna. Ravenna ,
c1989. 13 p., [46] p. of plates :
    NYPL   [MDOH 90-11354]

Biblioteca comunale di Fidenza (Italy)
Emanuelli, Oreste. Oreste Emanuelli . Parma ,
c1985. 124 p. :   *NYPL   [3-MCF E53 91-6419]*

Biblioteca de arheologie.
(25) Busuioc, Elena. Ceramica de uz comun
nesmălțuită din Moldova . București , 1975. 87
p., [25] leaves of plates :
TP803.R6 B86   *NYPL   [3-MPG 90-5750]*

Biblioteca de artă. Biografii, memorii, eseuri.
Tzigara-Samurcaș, Al. (Alexandru), 1872-1952.
Scrieri despre arta românească /. București ,
1987. 418 p., [12] p. of plates :
N7221 .T95 1987   *NYPL   [3-MAM 91-3417]*

Biblioteca de autores y temas almerienses. Serie
   mayor .
(16) Fernández Martínez, Carlos María.
Trinidad Cuartara Cassinello, arquitecto .
Almería , 1989. 392 p. :   ISBN 84-85219-75-9
    NYPL   [MQZ (Cuartara Cassinello)
    91-5988]

Biblioteca de Castilla y León. Serie Arte .
(no. 1) Pardo, Arcadio. La visión del arte
español en los viajeros franceses del siglo XIX
/. Valladolid [1989] 672 p. ;   ISBN
84-7762-078-4
IN PROCESS (ONLINE)
    NYPL   [3-MAML 90-12090]

Biblioteca (Deputazione di storia patria per le
   antiche provincie modenesi). Serie speciale .
(n. 12) Bertuzzi, Giordano. Il rinnovamento

---

edilizio a Modena nella prima metà
dell'Ottocento /. Modena , 1987. 350 p. :
    NYPL   [3-MQWB+ 91-6476]

Biblioteca di archeologia (Milan, Italy) .
(v. 13) De Albentiis, Emidio, 1958- La casa dei
Romani /. Milano , c1990. 348 p., [8] p. of
plates :   ISBN 88-304-0930-8 :   DDC 728/.0937 20
NA324 .D44 1990   *NYPL   [JFD 91-5342]*

Biblioteca di architettura urbanistica, teoria e
   storia .
(3) Serlio, Sebastiano, 1475-1554. [Tutte l'opere
d'architettura.] I sette libri dell'architettura .
Sala Bolognese , 1987. 2 v. :   DDC 720 19
NA2515 .S5 1978
    NYPL   [3-MQD+ 90-10883]

Biblioteca di cultura moderna (Editori Laterza) .
(985) Fanelli, Giovanni. Perret e Le Corbusier .
Roma , 1990. 255 p. :   ISBN 88-420-3596-3 :
NA1048.5.F85 F36 1990

Biblioteca di disegni. Firenze, Istituto Alinari
1976-1981. 29 v. chiefly col. illus. 53 cm. Cover
title. Issued in portfolio. English, some introductory
material also in Italian. The text was set and printed
under the supervision of Giovanni and Martino
Mardersteig at the Stamperia Valdonega of Verona in
325 numbered copies. This is number 48." Includes
index. Includes bibliographical references.
CONTENTS. - 1. Maestri lombardi e lombardo-veneti
del Rinascimento.--2. Maestri lombardi del
Seicento.--3-4. Maestri Veneti del Quattrocento.--5-6.
Maestri veneti del Cinquecento.--7. Maestri veneti del
Seicento.--8-9. Maestri veneti del Settecento.--10.
Maestri genovesi dal Cinque al Settecento.--11. Maestri
emiliani del Quattro e Cinquecento.--12. Maestri
emiliani del secondo Cinquecento.--13. Maestri emiliani
del Sei e Settecento.--14. Maestri senesi e marchigiani
del Cinquecento.--15. Maestri umbri del Quattro e
Cinquecento.--16. Maestri a Roma nel
Cinquecento.--17-18. Maestri toscani del
Quattrocento.--19. Maestri toscani del quattro e del
primo Cinquecento.--20-22. Maestri toscani del
Cinquecento.--23. Maestri toscani del secondo
Cinquecento.--24. Maestri del Sei e Settecento
toscano.--25. Maestri romani del Sei e Settecento.--26.
Maestri napoletani del Sei e Settecento.--27. Maestri
della caricatura.--28. Maestri della decorazione e del
teatro.--[29] General index.
I. Mardersteig, Hans, 1892-1977.
    NYPL   [MBH++ 78-481]

Biblioteca di S.M. il re (Turin, Italy)
Da Leonardo a Rembrandt. English. From
Leonardo to Rembrandt . Torino , c1990. 409
p. :   ISBN 88-422-0260-6
    NYPL   [3-MBH+ 91-5774]

BIBLIOTECA DI S.M. IL RE (TURIN, ITALY)
   - EXHIBITIONS.
Da Leonardo a Rembrandt. English. From
Leonardo to Rembrandt . Torino , c1990. 409
p. :   ISBN 88-422-0260-6
    NYPL   [3-MBH+ 91-5774]

Biblioteca Grandes humoristas argentinos.
Landrú, 1923- La razón de mi tía /. [Capital
Federal, Argentina] [c1990] 149 p. :   DDC
741.5/982 20
NC1460.L28 A4 1990

Biblioteca Luis-Angel Arango.
Antología, obras de la colección permanente.
Bogotá, D.E. : Banco de la República,
Biblioteca Luis-Angel Arango, 1990. 88 p. : ill.
(some col.) ; 28 cm.
1. Art, Colombian - Catalogs. 2. Art - Colombia -
Bogotá - Catalogs. 3. Banco de la República
(Colombia) - Catalogs. I. Title.
N6670 .B5 1990

Bogotá en caricatura . [Bogotá] [1988] 235 p. :
   DDC 986.1/48 20
F2291.B62 B64 1988
    NYPL   [3-MDY+ 91-6190]

Degas, Edgar, 1834-1917. Edgar Degas .
Bogotá, D.E., Colombia [1990] 1 v.
(unpaged) :   DDC 730/.92 20
NB553.D4 A4 1990

La Acuarela en Antioquia . [Bogotá? , 1987]
([Bogotá] : Banco de la República,
Departamento Editorial) 59 p. :   DDC
759.9861/26/07486126 20
ND1905.A58 A28 1987

Merino, Hernán, 1922-1973. Hernán Merino .
Bogotá [1986?] 107 p. :
NC1460.M47 A4 1986

Biblioteca Luis-Angel Arango. (cont.)

3 décadas de arte uniandino. Bogotá, Colombia [1989] 128 p. : **NYPL [3-MAM 91-4248]**

4 maestros latinoamericanos . [Bogotá, Colombia] [1987] 71 p. : ND202.5 .A14 1987

Biblioteca-Museu Víctor Balaguer. Americanos indianos . Vilanova i la Geltrú , 1990. 262 p. : **NYPL [3-MQWH 91-6959]**

Biblioteca nicolaita de pintores michoacanos . (2) Alfredo Arreguín . [Morelia, Mich., México] [1989] 214 p., [15] leaves of plates : DDC 759.972 20 ND259.A69 A86 1989

Biblioteca pública de Nueva York. see New York Public Library.

La Biblioteca ritrovata : il contributo romano al concorso internazionale per la nuova biblioteca di Alessandria d'Egitto / a cura di Giuseppe Strappa ; progetti di Massimiliano Fuksas ... [et al.]. Roma : Edizioni Carte segrete, 1990. 50 p. : ill. (some col.), plans ; 28 cm. "La mostra è stato organizzata dal dipartimento di Architettura e Analisi della Città dell'Università di Roma diretto dal Prof. Claudio Dall'Olio e si è svolta nella sede della Facoltà di Architettura di via Gramsci nei giorni 4-16 dicembre 1989"--Prelim. p. At head of title: Facoltà di architettura di Roma, Dipartimento di architettura e analisi della città.
1. Aliks andr in a (Library) - Exhibitions. 2. Library architecture - Competitions - Egypt - Alexandria - Exhibitions. 3. Architecture, Modern - 20th century - Italy - Rome - Exhibitions. I. Strappa, Giuseppe. II. Fuksas, Massimiliano, 1944-. III. Università degli studi did Roma "La Sapienza". Dipartimento di architettura e analisi della città. **NYPL [3-MQWB 91-5054]**

Biblioteka Likovne monografije.
Bužančić, Vlado. Ivica Propadalo . Zagreb , 1990. 151 p. : ISBN 86-343-0618-6 NC312.Y83 P762 1990

Biblioteka "Narodne nošnje Hrvatske" Bakrač, Ivanka. Narodna nošnja Kupinca . Zagreb , 1986. 69 p., [28] p. of plates : ISBN 86-80825-06-9 NK4771.Y82 K863 1986

Bibliotheca artibus et historiae.
Howard, Seymour, 1928- Antiquity restored . Vienna , 1990. 344 p. : ISBN 3-900731-11-X **NYPL [3-MAH 91-4921]**

Bibliotheca oecumenica Salmanticensis .
(15) Cantó Rubio, Juan. Arte bizantino . Salamanca , 1989. 94 p. : ISBN 84-7299-220-9 **NYPL [3-MAK 91-3667]**

Bibliothèque de l'Institut des hautes études chinoises .
(v. 16) Mi, Fu, 1051-1107. [Hua shih. French.] Le Houa-che de Mi Fou (1051-1107), ou, Le carnet d'un connaisseur à l'époque des Song du nord / . Paris , 1964. xxiv, 193 p. : ND1043.3 .M513 1964

Bibliothèque du Collège international de philosophie.
Borrell, Joan. L'artiste-roi . [Paris] , c1990. 398 p. ; ISBN 2-7007-3473-4 : DDC 700/.1 20 NX454 .B63 1990

Bibliothèque Forney. 2000 ans de peinture décorative . [Dourdan] [1990] 104 p. : ISBN 2-85101-024-7 DDC 751.7/3/094407444361 20 ND2550 .A17 1990

Bibliothèque nationale (France)
Mœglin-Delcroix, Anne. Livres d'artistes / . Paris , c1985. 159 p. : ISBN 2-7335-0085-6 **NYPL [MDT 86-3500]**

Le Notre et l'art des jardins. Paris : Bibliothèque nationale, 1964. 62 p. : ill., plans ; 21 x 27 cm. "Cet album est publié ... à l'occasion de l'exposition 'Le Notre et l'art des jardins'." Exhibition held Dec. 1964-Jan. 1965. Text signed: Louis Hautecoeur. "Catalogue sommaire de l'exposition" (19 p.) inserted.
1. Le Notre, André, 1613-1700 - Exhibitions. 2. Gardens - France - Design - History - 17th century - Exhibitons. I. Hautecoeur, Louis, 1884-. II. Title. **NYPL [3-MSCC 91-517]**

Bibliothèque nationale (France). Cabinet des estampes.
Delacroix et la gravure romantique. Paris : La Bibliothèque, 1963. 9, [36] p. : ill. ; 21 cm. Catalog of an exhibition held 1963 at the Bibliothèque nationale. "Catalogue rédigé par Jacques Lethève et Jean Adhémar"--P. 11. Includes bibliographical

references.
1. Delacroix, Eugène, 1798-1863 - Exhibitions. 2. Bibliothèque nationale (France). Cabinet des estampes. 3. Prints - 19th century - France - Exhibitions. 4. Prints, French - Exhibitions. I. Lethève, Jacques. II. Adhémar, Jean. III. Title. **NYPL [MDBF 90-7193]**

BIBLIOTHÈQUE NATIONALE (FRANCE). CABINET DES ESTAMPES.
Bibliothèque nationale (France). Cabinet des estampes. Delacroix et la gravure romantique. Paris , 1963. 9, [36] p. : **NYPL [MDBF 90-7193]**

BIBLIOTHÈQUE NATIONALE (FRANCE). CABINET DES ESTAMPES - EXHIBITIONS.
Americans in Paris, 1600-1900. [New York? 1972] 48 p. DDC 769/.944/07401471 NE647 .A68 **NYPL [MDE 90-7096]**

Fossier, François. Il fiore dell'impressionismo =. Milano , c1990. 388 p. : NE647.6.I4 F67 1990

Bibliothèque royale de Belgique. Belleroche, Albert de. Exposition de l'oeuvre lithographique d'Albert de Belleroche . Bruxelles , 1933 (Renaix : J. Leherte-Courtin) [37] p., [8] leaves of plates : **NYPL [MDG (Belleroche) 90-5547]**

Bicentenaire de la Révolution française (Apt, France)
Le Moment extrême. Apt , Paris , 1989- v. <1 > : ISBN 2-907383-03-5 (Eraklea) N6848.5.C66 M66 1989

Bichet, Pierre. André Charigny / Pierre Bichet, Roland Bouhéret. Besançon : Cêtre, c1989. 141 p. : ill. (some col.), ports. ; 31 cm. "Une leçon d'harmonie, par Roland Bouhéret. Souvenirs, par Pierre Bichet. Étude biographique." ISBN 2-901040-78-1
1. Charigny, André - Criticism and interpretation. I. Bouhéret, Roland, 1930-. II. Charigny, André. III. Title. **NYPL [3-MCO+ C473 89-26937]**

Bidlo, Mike.
Mike Bidlo, masterpieces. Zurich/Switzerland : Edition Bischofberger, c1989. 1 v. (unpaged) : ill. ; 30 cm. ISBN 3-905173-26-3
1. Bidlo, Mike - Exhibitions. I. Galerie Bruno Bischofberger. II. Title. **NYPL [3-MCX+ B582 90-11086]**

BIDLO, MIKE - EXHIBITIONS.
Bidlo, Mike. Mike Bidlo, masterpieces. Zurich/Switzerland , c1989. 1 v. (unpaged) : ISBN 3-905173-26-3 **NYPL [3-MCX+ B582 90-11086]**

Bidó, Cándido, 1936-
Tolentino, Marianne de. Cándido Bidó . Santo Domingo, República Dominicana , 1989-1990. 2 v. : DDC 759.97293 20 ND315.D6 T565 1989

BIDÓ, CÁNDIDO, 1936- - CATALOGS.
Tolentino, Marianne de. Cándido Bidó . Santo Domingo, República Dominicana , 1989-1990. 2 v. : DDC 759.97293 20 ND315.D6 T565 1989

BIDÓ, CÁNDIDO, 1936- - CRITICISM AND INTERPRETATION.
Tolentino, Marianne de. Cándido Bidó . Santo Domingo, República Dominicana , 1989-1990. 2 v. : DDC 759.97293 20 ND315.D6 T565 1989

Biedermeier . Sterk, Harald. Wien , c1988. 124 p. : ISBN 3-85128-010-5 NX549.6 .S73 1988

BIEDERMEIER (ART) - AUSTRIA.
Sterk, Harald. Biedermeier . Wien , c1988. 124 p. ; ISBN 3-85128-010-5 NX549.6 .S73 1988

BIEDERMEIER (ART) - AUSTRIA - VIENNA - EXHIBITIONS.
Biedermeier in Wien 1815-1848 . Mainz , c1990. 251 p. : ISBN 3-8053-1128-1 NX548.V53 B54 1990

BIEDERMEIER (ART) - GERMANY.
Sterk, Harald. Biedermeier . Wien , c1988. 124 p. ; ISBN 3-85128-010-5 NX549.6 .S73 1988

BIEDERMEIER (ART) - GERMANY, WEST - WÜRTTEMBERG - EXHIBITIONS.
Doerr, Carl, 1777-1842. Biedermeierliches

Württemberg . Heilbronn , c1979. 94 p. : N6888.D63 A4 1979 **NYPL [3-MCK D672 81-1042]**

Biedermeier in Wien 1815-1848 : Sein und Schein einer Bürgeridylle. Mainz : Ph. von Zabern, c1990. 251 p. : 288 ill. (47 col.) ; 28 cm. At head of title: Internationale Tage Ingelheim. Catalog of an exhibition of the Historisches Museum der Stadt Wien held in conjunction with the Internationale Tage Ingelheim at the Museum-Altes-Rathaus, Ingelheim am Rhein, Apr. 29-June 24, 1990. Includes bibliographical references (p. 249-250) and index. ISBN 3-8053-1128-1
1. Biedermeier (Art) - Austria - Vienna - Exhibitions. 2. Arts, Austrian - Austria - Vienna - Exhibitions. 3. Arts, Modern - 19th century - Austria - Vienna - Exhibitions. 4. Vienna (Austria) - Social life and customs - Exhibitions. I. Internationale Tage [1990 : Ingelheim am Rhein, Germany]. II. Historisches Museum der Stadt Wien. III. Museum Altes Rathaus (Ingelheim am Rhein, Germany). NX548.V53 B54 1990

Biedermeierliches Württemberg . Doerr, Carl, 1777-1842. Heilbronn , c1979. 94 p. : N6888.D63 A4 1979 **NYPL [3-MCK D672 81-1042]**

BIEL (SWITZERLAND) - DESCRIPTION - VIEWS.
Propper, Emanuel Jirka. Das alte Biel und seine Umgebung /. Biel (Blumenstrasse 15, 2502 Biel) , 1980. 1 portfolio (38 p., 32 leaves of plates) : **NYPL [3-MQWD++ 88-4261]**

Bielefeld. Kunsthalle. see Richard Kaselowsky Haus, Kunsthalle der Stadt Bielefeld.

Bielefeld. Richard Kaselowsky Haus. see Richard Kaselowsky Haus, Kunsthalle der Stadt Bielefeld.

Bielefeld. Richard Kaselowsky Haus, Kunsthalle. see Richard Kaselowsky Haus, Kunsthalle der Stadt Bielefeld.

Bielefeld. Städtisches Museum. Kunsthalle Richard Kaselowsky Haus. see Richard Kaselowsky Haus, Kunsthalle der Stadt Bielefeld.

Bielefelder Kunstverein. Näher, Christa, 1947- Christa Näher . [Bielefeld] [Leverkusen] , 1987. 70 p. : MLCM 88/00380 (N) **NYPL [3-MCK N1385 91-7515]**

Bieli, Toni, 1936- Toni Bieli : Serigraphie, Serigrafie-Unikate. Basel : Wiese, c1989. 156 p., [4] plates : ill. (chiefly col.) ; 25 cm. German, English, French and Italian. Text by Werner G. Christen. Four plates inserted in pocket. ISBN 3-909158-27-7
1. Bieli, Toni, 1936-. I. Christen, Werner G. II. Title. **NYPL [MDG (Bieli) 90-12800]**

BIELI, TONI, 1936-
Bieli, Toni, 1936- Toni Bieli . Basel , c1989. 156 p., [4] plates : ISBN 3-909158-27-7 **NYPL [MDG (Bieli) 90-12800]**

Biella (Italy). Museo civico. Premio internazionale Biella per l'incisione 1971. [Biella, 1971] xxv, 116 p. **NYPL [MDB 90-6615]**

Bienal Internacional de São Paulo. Amarante, Leonor. As bienais de São Paulo, 1951 a 1987 /. São Paulo-SP , 1989. 407 p. : ISBN 85-7165-003-9 DDC 709/.04/50748161 20 N5030.S37 A43 1989

BIENAL INTERNACIONAL DE SÃO PAULO.
Amarante, Leonor. As bienais de São Paulo, 1951 a 1987 /. São Paulo-SP , 1989. 407 p. : ISBN 85-7165-003-9 DDC 709/.04/50748161 20 N5030.S37 A43 1989

Bienal Internacional de São Paulo (20th : 1989)
Brecheret, Victor, 1894-1955. Brecheret /. São Paulo, SP , 1989. 79 p. : ISBN 85-85118-05-9 **NYPL [3-MGO+ (Brecheret) 90-8597]**

Figge, Eddie, 1904- Eddie Figge /. Stockholm, Sweden [1989?] 1 v. (unpaged) : ISBN 91-86164-10-4 DDC 709/.2 20 N7093.F54 A4 1989

Goodwin, Betty, 1923- Betty Goodwin, steel notes . [Ottawa] , c1989. 151 p. : ISBN 0-88884-602-9 **NYPL [3-MCZ G658 91-6759]**

XX Bienal Internacional de São Paulo : Chile / Bernardita Vattier ... [et al.]. [Chile : s.n., 1989]

63 p. : ill. (some col.) ; 27 cm. DDC
760/.0983/090480748161 20
1. Art, Chilean - Exhibitions. 2. Art, Modern - 20th
century - Chile - Exhibitions. I. Vattier, Bernardita,
1944-. II. Title. III. Title: 20. Bienal Internacional de
São Paulo.
N6665 .B5 1989

Bienkowski, Piotr. Treasures from an ancient
land . Stroud, Gloucestershire ; Wolfeboro Falls,
NH : xiii, 178 p. : ISBN 0-86299-729-1 DDC
709/.5695/07442753 20
N7279.6 .T7 1991   *NYPL   [*OFG 91-7466]*

**Biennale de la gravure européenne. see Biennial
of European Graphic Arts, 1st, Heidelberg,
1979.**

Biennale di Venezia (1980) Kotalík, Jiří. Kupka,
Gutfreund & C. . Venezia , c1980. 114 p. :
   ISBN 88-20-80273-2 DDC 709/.437/0740519 19
N6831 .K67 1980   *NYPL   [3-MAM 90-5445]*

Biennale di Venezia (1980). Settore architettura.
The presence of the past : First International
Exhibition of Architecture : the Corderia of the
Arsenale / La Biennale di Venezia,
Architectural Section ; [translations, Thomas
Becker ... et al. ; editor, Gabriella Borsano].
Venice : Edizioni La Biennale di Venezia ;
Milan : Electa, c1980. 350 p. : ill. (some col.),
facsims., plans ; 24 cm. Includes bibliographical
references and index. ISBN 88-20-80266-X
1. Architecture, Modern - 20th century - Exhibitions. I.
Borsano, Gabriella. II. Title. III. Title: First
International Exhibition of Architecture.
           NYPL   [3-MQV 91-420]

Biennale di Venezia (42nd : 1986) B., Mats,
1938- Téxun . [S.l. , 1986] (Stockholm :
Jernström Offset) [48] p. :
      NYPL   [3-MAM 90-10710]

Biennale di Venezia (44th : 1990)
Ambiente Berlin . [Venezia] , c1990. 201 p. :
   ISBN 88-20-80360-7 DDC 709/.431/550744531
20
N6885 .A46 1990

Chillida, Eduardo, 1924- Eduardo Chillida .
[Venezia] [1990] 199 p. : ISBN 88-20-80358-5
   DDC 709/.2 20
N7113.C555 A4 1990

Dimensione futuro : l'artista e lo spazio :
catalogo general 1990 : XLIV Esposizione
internazionale d'arte, La Biennale di Venezia. 1.
ed : Edizioni Biennale ; [Milano] :
Realizzazione Fabbri editori, c1990. 348 p. : ill.
(some col.) ; 30 cm. Spine title: Catalogo generale
1990. "Catalogo a cura di Marie-George Gervasoni"--P.
[8]. Issued in a slipcase. Includes indexes. ISBN
88-20-80356-9 DDC 709/.04/80744531 20
1. Art, Modern - 20th century - Exhibitions. I.
Gervasoni, Marie-George. II. Title. III. Title: Catalogo
generale 1990. IV. Title: XLIV Esposizione
internazionale d'arte, La Biennale di Venezia. V. Title:
44o Esposizione internazionale d'arte, La Biennale di
Venezia.
N6488.I8 V43 1990

1990 Venice Biennale Australia . Perth, WA ,
c1990. 59 p. : ISBN 0-7309-0783-X
           NYPL   [3-MCY 91-5556]

**Biennial of European Graphic Arts, 1st,
Heidelberg, 1979.** 1. Biennale der
Europäischen Grafik= 1st biennial of European
graphic arts = 1ère biennale de la gravure
européenne: Heidelberg, August 5th - October
7th 1979. Heidelberg : Biennial Society, 1979.
462 p. : ill. ; 29 cm. German, French, English.
Includes bibliographical references and index.
1. Prints, European - Germany, West - Heidelberg -
Exhibitions. 2. Prints - 20th century - Germany, West -
Heidelberg - Exhibitions. II. Title: 1st biennial
of European graphic arts. III. Title: 1ère biennale de la
gravure européenne.   *NYPL   [MDET 80-2314]*

Bier, Wolfgang, 1943-
Wolfgang Bier, Friedemann Hahn, Thomas
Kaminsky, Christiane Möbus, Wolfgang
Nestler . [Berlin] 1979. 1 case ([206] p. :
   DDC 709/.43/0740341 19
N6868 .W64   *NYPL   [3-MAMG+ 90-7088]*

BIER, WOLFGANG, 1943- - EXHIBITIONS.
Wolfgang Bier, Friedemann Hahn, Thomas
Kaminsky, Christiane Möbus, Wolfgang
Nestler . [Berlin] 1979. 1 case ([206] p. :
   DDC 709/.43/0740341 19
N6868 .W64   *NYPL   [3-MAMG+ 90-7088]*

Bierman, Irene A. The Ottoman city and its
parts . New Rochelle, N.Y. , 1991. p. cm.
   ISBN 0-89241-473-1 DDC 307.76/09561 20
NA9229 .O87 1991

Biermann, Aenne, 1898-1933.
Aenne Biermann : Fotografien 1925-33. Berlin :
Nishen, c1987. 141,19 p. : ill. ; 28 cm. (Serie
Folkwang) Bibliography: p. 119-121. ISBN
3-88940-019-1
1. Biermann, Aenne, 1898-1933. I. Title. II. Series.
      NYPL   [MFX (Biermann) 89-1352]

Aenne Biermann : photographs, 1925-33 /
translated by Iain Boyd Whyte. London :
Nishen, c1988. 141 p. : ill. ; 28 cm. (Folkwang
series) Includes bibliographical references. ISBN
1-85378-004-9
1. Biermann, Aenne, 1898-1933. I. Title. II. Series.
TR654 .B54 1988
      NYPL   [MFX (Biermann) 91-8099]

BIERMANN, AENNE, 1898-1933.
Biermann, Aenne, 1898-1933. Aenne
Biermann . Berlin , c1987. 141,19 p. : ISBN
3-88940-019-1
      NYPL   [MFX (Biermann) 89-1352]

Biermann, Aenne, 1898-1933. Aenne
Biermann . London , c1988. 141 p. : ISBN
1-85378-004-9
TR654 .B54 1988
      NYPL   [MFX (Biermann) 91-8099]

Biermann, Hartmut, 1925- Festschrift für
Hartmut Biermann /. Weinheim , c1990. 400
p. : ISBN 3-527-17712-4
           NYPL   [3-MAS 91-5197]

BIERMANN, HARTMUT, 1925-
Festschrift für Hartmut Biermann /. Weinheim ,
c1990. 400 p. : ISBN 3-527-17712-4
           NYPL   [3-MAS 91-5197]

**BIERSTADT, ALBERT, 1830-1902 -
EXHIBITIONS.**
Anderson, Nancy K. Albert Bierstadt . New
York , c1990. 327 p. : ISBN 1-555-95059-0 :
   DDC 759.13 20
ND237.B585 A4 1991
      NYPL   [3-MCX+ B585 91-5808]

Biesboer, P. Hals, Frans, 1584-1666. Frans Hals
/. Munich , New York, NY, USA , c1989. 437
p. : ISBN 3-7913-1032-1 DDC 759.9492 20
ND1329.H33 A4 1989

Biese, Karl, 1863-1926. Die Grötzinger
Malerkolonie . Karlsruhe / c1975. 239 p. :
N6867.5.G7 G76   *NYPL   [3-MCI 90-7040]*

Biesty, Stephen.
The incredible cross-section book / Stephen
Biesty. New York : Knopf, 1992. p. cm. Includes
index. Cross-sectional illustrations present an inside
view of such structures as a medieval castle, factory,
and subway station. ISBN 0-679-81411-6 DDC
741.6/42/092 20
1. Biesty, Stephen - Themes, motives - Juvenile
literature. 2. Interior architecture - Juvenile literature. I.
Title.
NC975.5.B5 A4 1992

**BIESTY, STEPHEN - THEMES, MOTIVES -
JUVENILE LITERATURE.**
Biesty, Stephen. The incredible cross-section
book /. New York , 1992. p. cm. ISBN
0-679-81411-6 DDC 741.6/42/092 20
NC975.5.B5 A4 1992

**Bièvres, France (Essonne). Musée français de la
photographie. see Musée français de la
photographie.**

BIG BAND MUSIC.
Flash [sound recording]. Stockholm , p1984. 1
sound disc :
Nostalgia NOST 7655

The big book of painting nature in oil /.
Schaeffer, S. Allyn, 1935- [Selections. 1991.]
New York , 1991. 399 p. : ISBN 0-8230-0503-8 :
   DDC 751.45/436 20
ND1500 .S2425 1991

Biggs, Lewis. Minimalism /. Liverpool , c1989.
28 p. :   *NYPL   [3-MGI 91-7014]*

Biggs, Melissa E., 1967- In the Vernacular .
Jefferson, N.C. , 1991. p. ISBN 0-89950-645-3
(lib. bdg. : alk. paper) DDC 700/.92/273 20
NX504 .I526 1991

Bigley, Sandra. Love, Jeffrey. Summary of state
arts agencies' grantmaking activities for fiscal
year 1987 /. Washington, D.C. (1010 Vermont

Ave., N.W., Suite 920, Washington 20005) ,
c1990. vi, 211 p. : DDC 353.9/3854 20
NX398 .L6 1990

Bijou mille neuf cent. Le Bijou 1900 . Bruxelles ,
1965. 102 p., [26] p. of plates :
           NYPL   [3-MNR 90-6082]

Bikāsū, Bāblū. see Picasso, Pablo, 1881-1973.

**Das Bild der Stadt Berlin von 1945 bis zur
Gegenwart :** Mai-August 1987, Märkisches
Museum / Berlin : Das
Museum, [1987] 59 p. : chiefly ill. (some col.) ;
15 x 20 cm. Bibliography: p. 12.
1. Art, German - Berlin (Germany) - Exhibitions. 2.
Art, Modern - 20th century - Berlin (Germany) -
Exhibitions. 3. Berlin (Germany) in art - Exhibitions. I.
Märkisches Museum.
           NYPL   [3-MAMY 90-13015]

Bild, Schema, Konstruktion . Gerhardus,
Dietfried. St. Ingbert , 1989. 72 p. : ISBN
3-924555-33-8
IN PROCESS (ONLINE)
           NYPL   [3-MGO (Koch) 91-7233]

Bild und Kult . Belting, Hans, 1935- München ,
c1990. 700 p. : ISBN 3-406-34367-8
           NYPL   [3-MAIH 90-12870]

Bildannoncen aus der Jahrhundertwende .
Schwarz, Jürgen. Frankfurt [am Main] , 1990.
224 p. : ISBN 3-923813-06-6 :
NC998.6.G4 S38 1990

Bildende Kunst und Lebenswelten : Festschrift
für Hans Wille / herausgegeben von Ursula
Schumacher. [S.l. : s.n., 1989?] 312 p. : ill.
(some col.) ; 23 cm. Includes bibliographical
references.
1. Art - Germany. I. Wille, Hans. II. Schumacher,
Ursula.   *NYPL   [3-MAMG 91-5015]*

**Bilder, Aquarelle, Zeichnungen, Photographien,
Druckgraphik.** Wols, 1913-1951. Wols .
[Zürich] , c1989. 407 p. : DDC 760/.092 20
N6888.W68 A4 1989
           NYPL   [3-MCK W867 91-4027]

Bilder aus dem alten Köln /. Rüdell, Carl. Köln ,
1988. 110 p. : ISBN 3-7743-0237-5
           NYPL   [3-MCK+ R895 89-17168]

Bilder aus dem altjüdischen Familienleben /.
Oppenheim, Moritz, d. 1882. Frankfurt am
Main [188-?] Portfolio ([14] leaves of plates) :
           *NYPL   [*PVP 84-1266]*

Bilder aus der Bundesrepublik : eine Ausstellung
zum 10-jährigen Bestehen der Spectrum
Photogalerie : Spectrum Photogalerie im
Kunstmuseum Hannover mit Sammlung
Sprengel, 19. Dezember 1982-23. Januar 1983 /
[Katalogbearbeitung und Konzeption, Peter
Gauditz, Heinrich Riebesehl]. Hannover :
Spectrum Photogalerie, c1982. [92] p. : ill. ; 25
cm.
1. Spectrum Photogalerie - Exhibitions. 2.
Photography - Germany (West) - Exhibitions. 3.
Germany (West) - Description and travel - Views -
Exhibitions. I. Gauditz, Peter. II. Riebesehl, Heinrich.
III. Spectrum Photogalerie.
           NYPL   [MFW 84-1657]

Bilder aus der grossen Stadt : e. Reportage von
Gross-Berlin : Druckgraphik u. Handzeichn. :
Staatl. Museen Preuss. Kulturbesitz,
Kupferstichkabinett, Berlin-Dahlem,
23.9-4.12.1977 / Ausstellung und Katalog
Alexander Dückers. Berlin-Dahlem :
Kupferstichkabinett, 1977. [96] p. : chiefly ill. ;
26 cm. Bibliography: p. [84]
1. Art, German - Berlin - Exhibitions. 2. Art, Modern -
20th century - Berlin - Exhibitions. 3. Berlin in art -
Exhibitions. 4. Berlin - Literary collections. I. Dückers,
Alexander, 1939-. II. Berlin. Kupferstichkabinett (West
Berlin).
N6885 .B55   *NYPL   [3-MAMG 81-424]*

Bilder einer Sammlung . Meuli, Andrea.
[Switzerland] , c1989. 210 p. : ISBN
3-905241-03-X
           NYPL   [3-MAVZ+ (Chur) 90-8658]

Bilder, Skulpturen, Zeichnungen, 1965-1990.
Mätzig, Konrad, 1940- Konrad Mätzig .
Göttingen , c1990. 82 p. :
N6888.M368 A4 1990

Bilder vom Bodensee : die Darstellung einer
Landschaft von der Buchmalerei bis zur
Postkarte / [zusammengestellt von] Erich
Hofmann ; Texte von Andrea Hofmann.1. Aufl.
Konstanz : Bahn, 1987. 192 p. : chiefly ill.

(chiefly col.) ; 29 cm. "Beilagen: farbige Sonderdrucke aus dem Bildband 'Bilder vom Bodensee'" (4 in envelope) laid in. Includes index. Bibliography: p. 192. ISBN 3-7621-8000-8 DDC 943/.462 20
1. Constance, Lake of, in art. 2. Constance, Lake of, Region - Description and travel - Views. I. Hofmann, Erich, 1924-. II. Hofmann, Andrea, 1956-.
DD801.C74 B5 1987
NYPL [3-MAMY 90-11013]

Bilder von Sergio Emery in der Galerie Medici, 27. August bis 14. Oktober 1989 /. Emery, Sergio, 1928- Solothurn [1989] 1 v. (unpaged) :
MLCM 90/03081 (N)
NYPL [3-MCZ+ E515 91-5903]

Bilder zum Lesen . Lauter, Marlene. Köln , 1990. 424 p. : ISBN 3-412-18089-0
N6888.U96 L38 1990

Bilderhefte der Hamburger Kunsthalle . (11) Friedrich, Caspar David, 1774-1840. Caspar David Friedrich . [Hamburg] [1990] 35 p. :
NC251.F66 A4 1990

Bilderhefte der Staatlichen Museen Berlin, Stiftung Preussischer Kulturbesitz . (Heft 60/61) Schlegel, Ursula. Italienische Skulpturen . Berlin , c1989. 27 p., [52] p. of plates : ISBN 3-7861-1579-6
NYPL [3-MGI 90-12655]

Bilderlust : erotische Photographien aus der Sammlung Uwe Scheid / herausgegeben von Ulrich Domröse ... [et al.].1. Aufl. Heidelberg : Edition Braus, 1991. 200 p. : ill. ; 30 cm. Exhibition catalog. ISBN 3-925835-74-1
1. Scheid, Uwe - Photograph collections - Exhibitions. 2. Photography, Erotic - Exhibitions. I. Domröse, Ulrich. **NYPL [MFW+ 91-6341]**

Bildersturm in der Provinz . Jacobi, Walter. Freiburg , 1988. 64 p. : ISBN 3-89125-272-2
NYPL [3-MAMG 90-12384]

Bilderwelten . (1) Französische Illustrationen des 18. und 19. Jahrhunderts . Dortmund , 1985. 267 p. : ISBN 3-924302-16-2 DDC 741.64/074/0356 s 741.64/0944/0740356 19
NC980 .B54 1985 vol. 1
NYPL [MDT 91-2511]

Bildfälle : die Moderne im Zwielicht / herausgegeben von Beat Wyss. Zürich : Verlag für Architektur Artemis, c1990. 231 p. : ill. ; 25 cm. Includes bibliographical references. ISBN 3-7608-8073-8
1. Art, Modern - Themes, motives. 2. Art - Philosophy. 3. Aesthetics, Modern. I. Wyss, Beat, 1947-.
N6350 .B547 1990

Bildfolgen. Pfahler, Georg Karl, 1926- Georg Karl Pfahler . Stuttgart , c1990. 126 p. : ISBN 3-89322-180-8
ND588.P523 A4 1990

Der Bildhauer Martin Mayer /. Haftmann, Werner. München , c1988. 269 p. : ISBN 3-7667-0900-3 DDC 730/.92 20
NB588.M384 A4 1988
NYPL [3-MGO+ (Mayer) 90-10579]

Die Bildhauerin Anna Mahler /. Mahler, Anna. Salzburg , 1989, c1988. 140 p. : ISBN 3-85349-127-8
NYPL [3-MGO+ (Mahler) 89-25676]

Das Bildhauersymposion : Entstehung und Entwicklung einer neuen Form kollektiver und künstlerischer Arbeit / [herausgegeben von] Wolfgang Hartmann, Werner Pokorny ; mit Beiträgen von Peter Baum ... [et al.]. Stuttgart : G. Hatje, c1988. 163 p. : ill. ; 21 cm. Includes index. Includes bibliographical references. ISBN 3-7757-0263-6
1. Sculpture, Modern - History - 20th century - Congresses. 2. Sculpture, Modern - Congresses. I. Hartmann, Wolfgang, 1938-. II. Pokorny, Werner. III. Baum, Peter, 1939-. **NYPL [3-MGI 90-11129]**

Bildhefte des Westfälischen Landesmuseums für Kunst und Kulturgeschichte . (Nr. 27) Kessemeier, Siegfried. Köpfe der französischen Revolution . Münster , 1989. 121 p. : ISBN 3-88789-088-4
NYPL [MDZ 91-5816]

(Nr. 28) Jászai, Géza, 1931- Das Werk des Bildhauers Gerhard Gröninger, 1582-1652 /. Münster , 1989. 207 p. : ISBN 3-88789-090-6
NYPL [3-MGO (Gröninger) 91-6968]

Bildhefte des Westfälischen Landesmuseums für Kunst und Kulturgeschichte Münster. Barockskulptur . Münster , 1979. 163 p. :
NB193 .B37 **NYPL [3-MGI 81-434]**

Bilhetes postais de boas festas, cartões de boas festas. Ferreira, Jaime M. M. Bilhetes postais e cartões de boas festas /. Lisboa , 1989- v. <1 > : DDC 741.6/83/09469075 20
NC1878.7.P8 F4 1989

Bilhetes postais e cartões de boas festas /. Ferreira, Jaime M. M. Lisboa , 1989- v. <1 > : DDC 741.6/83/09469075 20
NC1878.7.P8 F4 1989

Bill, Max, 1908- Kunstverein Winterthur: Max Bill : Ausstellung im Kunstmuseum Winterthur, 3. April-22. Mai 1960. Winterthur : Das Kunstmuseum, 1960. 27 p. : ill. ; 21 cm.
1. Bill, Max, 1908- - Exhibitions. I. Kunstverein, Winterthur. II. Kunstmuseum Winterthur. III. Title.
NYPL [3-MCZ B587 91-1157]

BILL, MAX, 1908-
Seckendorff, Eva von. Die Hochschule für Gestaltung in Ulm . Marburg , c1989. 184 p. : ISBN 3-922561-81-0 :
N332.G33 U467 1989

BILL, MAX, 1908- - EXHIBITIONS.
Bill, Max, 1908- Kunstverein Winterthur: Max Bill . Winterthur , 1960. 27 p. :
NYPL [3-MCZ B587 91-1157]

Bill Traylor . Maresca, Frank. New York , 1991. p. ISBN 0-394-58702-2 : DDC 759.1 B 20
ND237.T617 M37 1991

Bill Viola, The city of man. Viola, Bill, 1951- Brockton, Mass. , 1989. [8] p. : ISBN 0-934358-24-9 **NYPL [3-MAL 89-25255]**

Billedkunst . Fogh, Dorte. Copenhagen , 1990. 231 p. : ISBN 87-00-48782-1 :
ND717 .F69 1990

Billeter, Erika, 1927-
Collage et montage au théâtre et dans les autres arts durant les années vingt /. Lausanne , cop. 1978. 296 p., [32] p. of plates : DDC 700/.94 19
NX542 .C64 **NYPL [JFE 81-222]**

Das Selbstportrait im Zeitalter der Photographie . Bern , c1985. 523 p. :
NYPL [MFW 91-2389]

Grösse--klein . Bern , c1989. 292 p. :
NYPL [3-MGI 91-5536]

Iseli, Rolf, 1934- Rolf Iseli /. Bern , c1990. 178 p. : **NYPL [3-MCZ I78 91-6919]**

Kunstgewerbemuseum Zürich. Glas aus der Sammlung des Kunstgewerbemuseums Zürich. Zürich , c1969. 239 p. :
NYPL [3-MPW 90-6938]

Billot, Renée.
Léon Delarbre, le peintre déporté : croquis d'Auschwitz, Buchenwald et Dora / par Renée Billot ; avec la collaboration du Conseil général, territoire de Belfort, de la ville de Belfort et de l'Association Musée-Beaux-Arts. Jarville-La Malgrange : Editions de l'Est, [1989] 125 p. : ill. (some col.) ; 31 cm. ISBN 2-86955-088-X
1. Delarbre, Léon, 1889-. I. Delarbre, Léon, 1889-. II. Belfort (France : Territory). Conseil général. III. Title.
NYPL [3-MCO+ D339 91-6125]

Léon Delarbre, le peintre déporté : croquis d'Auschwitz, Buchenwald et Dora / par Renée Billot. Jarville-La Malgrange : Editions de l'Est, [1989] 125 p. : ill. (some col.) ; 31 cm. (Collection Prestiges de l'Est) ISBN 2-86955-088-X
1. Delarbre, Léon, 1889-1974 - Appreciation. 2. Prisoners of war as artists - France. 3. Concentration camps in art. I. Delarbre, Léon, 1889-1974. II. Title. III. Title: Léon Delarbre. IV. Series.
N6853.D3385 B55 1989

Billy Morrow Jackson . Wooden, Howard E. Urbana , c1990. 147 p. : ISBN 0-252-01735-8 (alk. paper) DDC 760/.092 20
N6537.J29 W6 1990
NYPL [3-MCX+ J129 91-3992]

Binaghi Olivari, Maria Teresa.
(joint author) Romano, Giovanni. Il Maestro della Pala Sforzesca /. Firenze , 1978. 48 p. :
ND623.M174 R65 **NYPL [3-MCE 81-524]**

Süss, Francesco. Le ville del territorio milanese. [Milano] , 1988- v. : **NYPL [3-MRGF+ 90-2532]**

Binationale, Israel-UdSSR. Harten, Jürgen. Sowjetische Kunst um 1990 . Köln , c1991. 299 p. : ISBN 3-7701-2733-1
NYPL [3-MAM 91-8020]

Binationale, Yiśra'el-SSSR. Harten, Jürgen. Sowjetische Kunst um 1990 . Köln , c1991. 299 p. : ISBN 3-7701-2733-1
NYPL [3-MAM 91-8020]

Binayán, Narciso. La colectividad armenia en la Argentina / Narciso Binayán. Buenos Aires : Alzamor Editores, 1974. 158 p. ; 22 cm. (Colección del sol. 3) Includes bibliography.
1. Armenians - Argentina. 2. Armenians in the Argentine Republic. I. Title.
NYPL [HKB 80-2301]

Binder, Walter, 1931- Französische Photographie, 1840-1871 . [Zürich] [1987] 104 p. :
TR71 .F675 1987 **NYPL [MFW 91-2388]**

Binding, Günther. Der Mittelalterliche Baubetrieb Westeuropas . Köln , 1987. 568 p. : DDC 760/.044969 19
N8217.B85 M58 1987
NYPL [3-MAMZ 91-4597]

Binding, Günter. Fachterminologie für den historischen Holzbau . Köln , 1990. 49 p. :
NA4115 .F34 1990

BINDING OF BOOKS. see BOOKBINDING.

Bindis, Ricardo. Rugendas en Chile / Ricardo Bindis. Santiago de Chile : Editorial Los Andes, 1989. 111 p. : ill. (some col.) ; 31 pm. Previously published: Ediciones Barcelona, 1973. Includes bibliographical references (p. 111). DDC 759.3 B 20
1. Rugendas, Johann Moritz, 1802-1858. 2. Chile in art. I. Rugendas, Johann Moritz, 1802-1858. II. Title.
ND588.R8 A4 1989

Binet, Jacques-Louis. Trémois : peintures, gravures, sculptures / textes de Jacques-Louis Binet. Paris : Editions du Rocher, [1991] 232 p. : ill. (some col.) ; 35 cm. Includes bibliographical references (p. 206-232). ISBN 2-268-01147-X : DDC 709/.2 20
1. Trémois, Pierre Yves, 1921- - Catalogs. I. Trémois, Pierre Yves, 1921-. II. Title.
N6853.T68 A4 1991

BINGHAM, GEORGE CALEB, 1811-1879 - CRITICISM AND INTERPRETATION.
Rash, Nancy, 1940- The painting and politics of George Caleb Bingham /. New Haven , c1991. x, 286 p. : ISBN 0-300-04731-2 (alk. paper) DDC 759.13 20
ND237.B59 R37 1991
NYPL [3-MCX B61 91-6961]

BINGHAM, GEORGE CALEB, 1811-1879 - POLITICAL AND SOCIAL VIEWS.
Rash, Nancy, 1940- The painting and politics of George Caleb Bingham /. New Haven , c1991. x, 286 p. : ISBN 0-300-04731-2 (alk. paper) DDC 759.13 20
ND237.B59 R37 1991
NYPL [3-MCX B61 91-6961]

Binkley, Timothy, 1943- Symmetry studio : creative computer resources for two dimensional design / by Timothy Binkley ; with software for Macintosh computers by Timothy Binkley and John F. Simon, Jr. ; illustrations by Vibeke Riisberg and New York, N.Y. : Van Nostrand Reinhold, c1991. p. cm. Includes bibliographical references and index. ISBN 0-442-00911-9 DDC 745.4 20
1. Repetitive patterns (Decorative arts) - Data processing. I. Simon, John F. II. Title.
NK1570 .B64 1991

Binns, Betty, 1929- Designing with two colors / Betty Binns with Sue Heinemann. New York : Watson-Guptill Publications, 1991. 127 p. : ill. (some col.) ; maps (some col.) ; 25 cm. "A Roundtable Press book." Includes bibliographical references (p. 126) and index. ISBN 0-8230-1334-0 : DDC 741.6 20
1. Color in design. I. Heinemann, Sue, 1948-. II. Title. III. Title: Designing with 2 colors.
NK1548 .B56 1991

Binsfeld, Wolfgang. Von Constantin zu Karl dem Grossen . Mainz , 1990. 71 p., [5] leaves of plates : ISBN 3-88467-025-5
N5760 .V57 1990

Binyon, Laurence, 1869-1943. Painting in the Far East; an introduction to the history of pictorial art in Asia, especially China and Japan. 4th ed., rev. throughout. New York, Dover Publications

[1969] xvi, 302 p. illus. 24 cm.　ISBN
0-486-20520-7 :　DDC 759.951
1. Painting, Chinese - History. 2. Painting, Japanese -
History. I. Title.
ND1037 .B6 1969

Biografía de pintores jaliscienses. Farías, Ixca.
Pintores jaliscienses /. Guadalajara, Jalisco,
México , 1969. 93 p. ;
N6556.J3 F37 1969

Biografías de pintores jaliscienses. Farías, Ixca.
Pintores jaliscienses /. Guadalajara, Jalisco,
México , 1969. 93 p. ;
N6556.J3 F37 1969

Biografías y memorias.
Carol, Márius. Dalí . Esplugues de Llobregat,
Barcelona , 1990. 204 p., [16] p. of plates :
ISBN 84-01-35171-5　DDC 759.6 B 20
N7113.D3 C36 1990

**The biography and catalogue raisonné of the
paintings of Sir Lawrence Alma-Tadema /.**
Swanson, Vern G. London , 1990. 511 p. :
ISBN 0-906030-22-6 :　DDC 759.2 20
ND497.A4　　**NYPL [MCV+ A44 90-12346]**

Biomechanics. Giger, H. R. (Hansruedi), 1940-
[Biomechanics. English.] H.R. Giger's
Biomechanics /. Beverly Hills, CA , 1990. 95
p. : ISBN 0-9623447-1-0　DDC 709/.2 20
N7153.G48 A4 1990

Biomechanics. Giger, H. R. (Hansruedi), 1940-
H.R. Giger's Biomechanics. Zug, Switzerland ,
1988. 95 p. :　ISBN 3-89082-527-3
NYPL [3-MCZ++ G455 89-25898]

Birch, Dinah.
Ruskin on Turner / Dinah Birch. London :
Cassell, 1990. 144 p. : ill. (some col.) ; 28 cm.
Includes bibliographical references (p. 142-144).　ISBN
0-304-31845-0 :　DDC 759.2 20
1. Turner, J. M. (Joseph Mallord William), 1775-1851 -
Criticism and interpretation. I. Ruskin, John,
1819-1900. II. Turner, J. M. W. (Joseph Mallord
William), 1775-1851. III. Title.
ND497.T8 B57 1990

Ruskin on Turner / Dinah Birch. London :
Cassell, 1990. 144 p. : ill. (some col.), port. ; 28
cm. "An Albion book"--T.p. verso. Includes
bibliographical references (p. 144).　ISBN
0-304-31845-0 :　DDC 759.2 20
1. Turner, J. M. W. (Joseph Mallord William),
1775-1851. 2. Ruskin, John, 1819-1900. I. Turner, J. M.
W. (Joseph Mallord William), 1775-1851. II. Title.
ND497.T　　**NYPL [3-MCV T94 91-7162]**

Bird etchings . Jackson, Christine E. (Christine
Elisabeth), 1936- Ithaca , 1985. 292 p., [4]
leaves of plates :　ISBN 0-8014-1695-7 (alk paper)
DDC 598/.022/2 19
NE2043 .J33 1985　　**NYPL [MDZ 85-4087]**

Bird stencil designs /. Bush, Robert G. New
York , 1991. 60 p. of plates :　ISBN
0-486-26704-0 (pbk.)　DDC 745.4 20
NK8655 .B87 1991

Birds. Hosking, Eric John. Eric Hosking's birds .
London , 1979. 224 p. :　ISBN 0-7207-1163-0 :
TR729.B5 H67 1979b
NYPL [MFX (Hosking) 81-890]

Birds. Lifton, Robert Jay, 1926- New York
[1969] [95] p.　DDC 741.5973
NC1429.L537 A42
NYPL [3-MEM (Lifton) 91-6205]

BIRDS.
Hosking, Eric John. Eric Hosking's birds .
London , 1979. 224 p. :　ISBN 0-7207-1163-0 :
TR729.B5 H67 1979b
NYPL [MFX (Hosking) 81-890]

BIRDS IN ART.
Bush, Robert G. Bird stencil designs /. New
York , 1991. 60 p. of plates :　ISBN
0-486-26704-0 (pbk.)　DDC 745.4 20
NK8655 .B87 1991

Gromme, Owen J. The world of Owen
Gromme /. Minocqua, WI , 1991. p. cm.　ISBN
1-559-71130-2 :　DDC 759.13 B 20
ND237.G665 A2 1991

Jackson, Christine E. (Christine Elisabeth),
1936- Bird etchings . Ithaca , 1985. 292 p., [4]
leaves of plates :　ISBN 0-8014-1695-7 (alk paper)
DDC 598/.022/2 19
NE2043 .J33 1985　　**NYPL [MDZ 85-4087]**

Mohrhardt, David. Songbird painting projects /.
Harrisburg, PA , c1992. p. cm.　ISBN

0-8117-3012-3 (pbk.) :　DDC 751.42/2 20
ND1380 .M65 1992

Birds of a feather /. Fehl, Philipp P. Urbana ,
c1991. p. cm.　ISBN 0-252-06241-8 (alk. paper)
DDC 741.973 20
NC1429.F2955 A4 1991

Birkhäuser, Peter.
Light from the darkness : the paintings of Peter
Birkhäuser = Licht aus dem Dunkel : die
Malerei von Peter Birkhäuser. Basel ; Boston :
Birkhäuser Verlag, 1991. p. cm. Text in English
and German.　ISBN 3-7643-1190-8 :　DDC 759.9494
20
1. Birkhäuser, Peter - Themes, motives. 2.
Psychoanalysis and art. I. Title. II. Title: Licht aus dem
Dunkel.
ND853.B525 A4 1991

**BIRKHÄUSER, PETER - THEMES,
MOTIVES.**
Birkhäuser, Peter. Light from the darkness .
Basel , Boston , 1991. p. cm.　ISBN
3-7643-1190-8 :　DDC 759.9494 20
ND853.B525 A4 1991

Birks-Hay, Tony. Gray, Alexander Stuart.
Fanlights /. London , 1990. 148 p. :　ISBN
0-7136-3077-9 :　DDC 721.823 20
NYPL [3-MRR 91-3295]

Birmingham City Museum and Art Gallery.
Národní galerie V Praze. Baroque in Bohemia.
London, 1969. 1 v. (unpaged)　DDC 709/.437/1
N6818 .P7

**Birmingham, Eng. Birmingham Museums and Art
Gallery. see Birmingham Museums and Art
Gallery.**

**Birmingham, Eng. City Museum and Art Gallery.
see Birmingham Museums and Art Gallery.**

Birmingham Museum and Art Gallery. Rossetti,
Dante Gabriel, 1828-1882. [Portrait drawings of
Elizabeth Siddall.] Rossetti's portrait drawings
of Elizabeth Siddall . Brookfield, Vt. , 1991. p.
cm.　ISBN 1-85967-885-7　DDC 741.942 20
NC242.R646 A4 1991

Birmingham Museum of Art. The Expressionist
landscape . Birmingham, Ala. , Seattle , 1988,
c1987. 216 p. :　DDC 759.1 19
ND1351.6 .E97 1987
NYPL [3-MCW 88-3335]

Birmingham Museum of Art (Birmingham, Ala.)
Baekeland, Frederick. Images of America .
Birmingham, Ala. , 1991. p. cm.　ISBN
0-931394-31-7 :　DDC 759.13/09/03407473 20
ND1460.U54 B34 1991

Brown, Walter R., 1940- The Stuart legacy .
Birmingham, Ala. , 1991. 176 p. :　ISBN
0-931394-30-9　DDC 709/.42/074761781 20
N6766 .B76 1991

Birmingham Museums and Art Gallery.
Catalogue of paintings. Birmingham [England] :
City Museum and Art Gallery, [1960?] 172 p. :
plates ; 22 cm.
1. Birmingham Museums and Art Gallery - Catalogs. 2.
Painting, European - Catalogs. 3. Painting - England -
Birmingham - Catalogs. I. Title.　**NYPL [3-MAVZ
(Birmingham, England) 90-6875]**

**BIRMINGHAM MUSEUMS AND ART
GALLERY - CATALOGS.**
Birmingham Museums and Art Gallery.
Catalogue of paintings. Birmingham [England]
[1960?] 172 p. :　　**NYPL [3-MAVZ
(Birmingham, England) 90-6875]**

Birney, Earle, 1904- Nexus & Earle Birney.
Album III [sound recording]. Norland, Ont.,
Canada : Nexus, [1982] 1 sound disc (49 min.,
25 sec.) : analog, 33 1/3 rpm, stereo. ; 12 in.
Poetry reading and music. Written and read by Earl
Birney ; music by the ensemble Nexus. Recorded at
McClear Place Studios Ltd., Toronto, Apr. 9-11, 1982.
CONTENTS. - War & peace: Each lie. Billboards build
freedom of choice. Prosperity in Poza Rica. Letter to a
conceivable great-grandson. For Steve. The ebb begins
from dream. Irapuato. I accuse us -- Transcontinental:
Copernican fix. Maritime faces. Appeal to a lady with a
diaper. Mammorial stunzas Aimee Simple McFarcin.
Prairie counterpoint. The monarch of the id. Canada,
case history 1945. Canada, case history 1973. First
flight. Trawna tuh Bellvul by Knayjin Psifik.
I. Title.
Nexus NE 04

Biroli Stefanelli, Lucia Pirzio. Il Bronzo dei
Romani . Roma , c1990. 298 p. :　ISBN

88-7062-675-X
IN PROCESS (ONLINE)
NYPL [3-MGR 91-3253]

Birrer, Patrik. Senn, Otto H. (Otto Heinrich),
1902- Otto Senn . Basel , c1990. 137 p. :　ISBN
3-905065-12-4
NA1353.S46 A4 1990

BIRTH-RATE. see POPULATION.

Bisacca, George. Newbery, Timothy J. The Italian
Renaissance frames /. New York , c1990. 111
p. :　ISBN 0-87099-587-1　DDC
749/.7/09450747471 20
NK9752.A1 N49 1990
NYPL [3-MNE 90-11624]

Bisanz, Hans, 1929- Schiele, Egon, 1890-1918.
Egon Schiele . [Wien] [1990?] 104 p. :　DDC
709/.2 20
N6811.5.S34 A4 1990
NYPL [3-MCK S332 91-5564]

Bischof, Hans. Geissberger, Hans. Übergänge .
Stuttgart , c1990. 135 p. :　ISBN 3-87838-641-9
NYPL [3-MCZ G314 91-4261]

Bischof, Marco, 1947- Werner Bischof,
1916-1954 : his life and work : a book / by
Marco Bischof and René Burri ; introduction by
Hugo Loetscher ; text by Marco Bischof and
Guido Magnaguagno. London : Thames and
Hudson, 1990. 255 p. : ill. ; 31 cm. "This
publication accompanies the travelling exhibition
'Werner Bischof, 1916-1954' which is supported by Pro
Helvetia, Arts Council of Switzerland"--T.p. verso.
ISBN 0-500-09215-X
1. Bischof, Werner Adalbert, 1916-1954 - Exhibitions. I.
Title.　　**NYPL [MFX+ (Bischof) 91-11187]**

**BISCHOF, WERNER ADALBERT, 1916-1954 -
EXHIBITIONS.**
Bischof, Marco, 1947- Werner Bischof,
1916-1954 . London , 1990. 255 p. :　ISBN
0-500-09215-X
NYPL [MFX+ (Bischof) 91-11187]

**BISCHOFF, EDUARD, 1890-1974 -
EXHIBITIONS.**
Lankau, Hans-Helmut. Eduard Bischoff,
1890-1974 . Husum , c1990. 96 p. :　ISBN
3-88042-460-8　DDC 759.3 20
ND588.B5 A4 1990

Bischoff, Hans-Helmut, 1890-1974. Lankau,
Hans-Helmut. Eduard Bischoff, 1890-1974 .
Husum , c1990. 96 p. :　ISBN 3-88042-460-8
DDC 759.3 20
ND588.B5 A4 1990

Bischöfliches Dom- und Diözesanmuseum Trier.
Das neue Bischöfliche Dom- und
Diözesanmuseum : Bildband zur
Wiedereröffnung / [Autoren der Bildtexte, Gerd
Martin Forneck ... et al.]. Trier : Das Museum,
1988. 123 p. : ill. (some col.) ; 25 cm.
Bibliography: p. 112-118.
1. Bischöfliches Dom- und Diözesanmuseum Trier. 2.
Christian art and symbolism - Medieval, 500-1500 -
Germany (West) - Trier. 3. Christian art and
symbolism - Modern period, 1500 - Germany (West) -
Trier. I. Forneck, Gerd Martin. II. Title.
NYPL [3-MAIH 90-10260]

**BISCHÖFLICHES DOM- UND
DIÖZESANMUSEUM TRIER.**
Bischöfliches Dom- und Diözesanmuseum Trier.
Das neue Bischöfliche Dom- und
Diözesanmuseum . Trier , 1988. 123 p. :
NYPL [3-MAIH 90-10260]

Bishir, Catherine W. North Carolina architecture
/ Catherine W. Bishir ; photography by Tim
Buchman. Chapel Hill : University of North
Carolina Press for the Historic Preservation
Foundation of North Carolina, c1990. xiv, 514
p. : ill. (some col.) ; 37 cm. Includes bibliographical
references (p. 493-500) and index.　ISBN
0-8078-1923-9　DDC 720/.9756 20
1. Architecture - North Carolina. I. Title.
NA730.N8 B5 1990
NYPL [3-MQWO+ 91-3379]

Bishop, Isabel, 1902- Isabel Bishop, etchings and
aquatints : a catalogue raisonné / compiled and
edited by Susan Pirpiris Teller ; foreword by
Robert P. Conway.2nd ed. New York, NY (20
W. 57th St., New York 10019) : Associated
American Artists, 1985. 60 p. : ill. ; 23 cm.
Includes index. Bibliography: p. 57.　DDC 769.92/4 19
1. Bishop, Isabel - Catalogues raisonnés. I. Teller,

Susan. II. Title.
NE2012.B55 A4 1985
          NYPL   [MDG (Bishop) 90-12809]

BISHOP, ISABEL - CATALOGUES RAISONNÉS.
Bishop, Isabel, 1902- Isabel Bishop, etchings and aquatints . New York, NY (20 W. 57th St., New York 10019) , 1985. 60 p. :   DDC 769.92/4 19
NE2012.B55 A4 1985
          NYPL   [MDG (Bishop) 90-12809]

Bishop Museum Press miscellaneous publication . (34) Motteler, Lee S. Pacific Island names . Honolulu , 1986. 91 p. :   ISBN 0-930897-12-9 (pbk.)   DDC 912/.9 19
DU18 .M68 1986   **NYPL   [Map Div. 88-67]**

Bishop, Philippa. Gainsborough in Bath . Bath [England] [1988] 40 p. :   ISBN 0-86197-081-0 (pbk.)   **NYPL   [3-MCV+ G14 89-28866]**

Bishop's moose and the pinkerton men. Durham, Jimmie. Jimmie Durham . New York , c1990. 37 p. :   **NYPL   [3-MGO (Durham) 90-10679]**

Bister, Donna, 1951- Cleveland, Richard L. Plain and fancy . San Francisco , 1991. p. cm.   ISBN 0-913327-30-1 (ppr)   DDC 746.9/7/09743 20
NK9112 .C57 1991

Bitossi, Carlo. Fiasella, Domenico, 1589-1669. Domenico Fiasella /. Genova , c1990. 287 p. :
          NYPL   [3-MCF F464 90-13082]

Bits and pieces . Lasansky, Jeannette. Lewisburg, Pa. , c1991. 120 p. :   ISBN 0-917127-06-4 :   DDC 746.9/7/0973 20
NK9112 .L33 1991

Bivins, John, 1940- Museum of Early Southern Decorative Arts. The regional arts of the early South . Winston-Salem, N.C. , 1991. p.   ISBN 0-945578-02-4 :   DDC 745/.0975/07475667 20
NK811 .M87 1991

Bizzarri, Giulio. La Coppia =. Milano , c1989. 205 p. :   DDC 745.4/442 20
NK1390 .C66 1989
          NYPL   [3-MNF 90-11125]

Björn Hultén . Hultén, Björn. [S.l. , 1988?] [24] p. :   ISBN 91-7360-161-6
IN PROCESS (ONLINE)
          NYPL   [3-MOF 91-7025]

BJÖRNSON-GULBRANSSON, DAGNY - ART COLLECTIONS - EXHIBITIONS.
Gulbransson, Olaf, 1873-1958. Olaf Gulbransson . Hannover , c1979. 72 p. :   ISBN 3-921752-08-6
NC1619.G85 A4 1979
          NYPL   [3-MCZ G971 81-538]

Blaauw, Willem Janszoon. see **Blaeu, Willem Janszoon, 1571-1638.**

Blaauwen, A. L. den. Nederlands zilver =. 's-Gravenhage , 1979. L, 390 p. :   ISBN 90-12-02571-0 (pbk.)   DDC 739.2/37492/074
NK7154.A1 N42   **NYPL   [MNO 80-2184]**

BLACK AMERICANS. see **AFRO-AMERICANS.**

Black and white /. Knott, Herbie. London , 1990. 128 p. :   ISBN 1-85283-283-5 :   DDC 779.0942 20
          NYPL   [MFX (Knott) 91-3406]

Black art : ancestral legacy : the African impulse in African-American art. Dallas, Tex. : Dallas Museum of Art ; New York : H.N. Abrams, c1989. 305 p. : ill. (some col.) ; 32 cm. "Exhibition itinerary: Dallas Museum of Art, Dallas, Texas, December 3, 1989-February 25, 1990; High Museum of Art, Atlanta, Georgia, May 22-August 5, 1990; Milwaukee Art Museum, Milwaukee, Wisconsin, September 14-November 18, 1990; Virginia Museum of Art, Richmond, Virginia, January 28, 1991-March 24, 1991"--T.p. verso. Includes bibliographical references (p. 299-301)   ISBN 0-8109-3104-4 (Abrams) :   DDC 704/.0396073/07473 20
1. Afro-American art - Exhibitions. 2. Art, Modern - 20th century - United States - Exhibitions. I. Dallas Museum of Art.
N6538.N5 B525 1989   **NYPL   [Sc G 90-16]**

BLACK ARTISTS. see **ARTISTS, BLACK.**

Black artists of the South. Dimensions and directions . Jackson, MS , c1980. ii, 46 p. :   DDC 704/.0396073075/07476251 20
N6538.N5 D47 1980

Black history publications series . (v. 8) Historic Blacks in the arts /. Chicago,

IL , c1990. p. cm.   ISBN 0-922162-58-1 :   DDC 700/.92/2 B 20
NX164.B55 H57 1990

BLACK IN ART.
An Exhibition of five recent works by Larry Bell, John McCracken, DeWain Valentine, Ron Cooper [and] Peter Alexander. Edmonton, 1971. 44 p.
N6535.L6 E89   **NYPL   [3-MAMT 81-415]**

Black, Mary (Mary C.) Detroit. Institute of Arts. American paintings in the Detroit Institute of Arts /. New York , c1991- p.   ISBN 1-555-95044-2 (alk. paper) :   DDC 759.13/074/77434 20
ND205 .D298 1991

Black, Max, 1909- Gombrich, E. H. (Ernst Hans), 1909- Art, perception and reality. Baltimore [1972] x, 132 p.   ISBN 0-8018-1354-9   DDC 701/.17
N71 .G64   **NYPL   [3-MAB 90-5472]**

BLACK PEOPLE (U. S.) see **AFRO-AMERICANS.**

Black, Wendell H., d. 1972.
Sayre, Henry M., 1948- The lost prints of Wendell H. Black /. Corvallis, Or. , c1990. 1 v. (various pagings) :   ISBN 0-87071-364-7   DDC 769.92 20
NE539.B57 S28 1990

BLACK, WENDELL H., D. 1972 - CATALOGS.
Sayre, Henry M., 1948- The lost prints of Wendell H. Black /. Corvallis, Or. , c1990. 1 v. (various pagings) :   ISBN 0-87071-364-7   DDC 769.92 20
NE539.B57 S28 1990

BLACK, WENDELL H., D. 1972 - CRITICISM AND INTERPRETATION.
Sayre, Henry M., 1948- The lost prints of Wendell H. Black /. Corvallis, Or. , c1990. 1 v. (various pagings) :   ISBN 0-87071-364-7   DDC 769.92 20
NE539.B57 S28 1990

Black, white & color. Skrebneski, Victor. Skrebneski . Boston , c1989. [188] p. :   ISBN 0-8212-1748-8
          NYPL   [MFX+ (Skrebneski) 89-26820]

Black, white and color. Skrebneski, Victor. Skrebneski . Boston , c1989. [188] p. :   ISBN 0-8212-1748-8
          NYPL   [MFX+ (Skrebneski) 89-26820]

Blackbridge, Persimmon, 1951- Still sane / Persimmon Blackbridge and Sheila Gilhooly ; photography by Kiku Hawkes. Vancouver, B.C., Canada : Press Gang Publishers, 1985. 101 p. : ill. (some col.) ; 22 x 24 cm. Bibliography: p. 95-99.   ISBN 0-88974-028-3 :   DDC 730/.971 19
1. Blackbridge, Persimmon, 1951-. 2. Gilhooly, Sheila, 1951-. 3. Psychotherapy patients in art. 4. Psychotherapy patients - Abuse of - Art. 5. Women in art. 6. Lesbianism. I. Gilhooly, Sheila, 1951-. II. Title.
          NYPL   [3-MGO (Blackbridge) 90-12979]

BLACKBRIDGE, PERSIMMON, 1951-
Blackbridge, Persimmon, 1951- Still sane /. Vancouver, B.C., Canada , 1985. 101 p. :   ISBN 0-88974-028-3 :   DDC 730/.971 19
          NYPL   [3-MGO (Blackbridge) 90-12979]

Blackburn, Jemima, 1823-1909. Jemima : the paintings and memoirs of a Victorian lady / edited with an introduction by Robert Fairley. Edinburgh : Canongate, 1988. 207 p. : ill. (some col.) ; 27 cm.   ISBN 0-86241-186-6
1. Blackburn, Jemima, 1823-1909. 2. Women artists - Scotland - Biography. 3. Watercolorists - Scotland - Biography. I. Fairley, Robert. II. Title.
          NYPL   [3-MCV B628 90-12435]

BLACKBURN, JEMIMA, 1823-1909.
Blackburn, Jemima, 1823-1909. Jemima . Edinburgh , 1988. 207 p. :   ISBN 0-86241-186-6
          NYPL   [3-MCV B628 90-12435]

Blackburne, Harry William, 1878- The romance of St George's Chapel, Windsor Castle / by Harry W. Blackburne and Maurice F. Bond ; foreword by E.K.C. Hamilton. 5th ed. Windsor : Oxley, 1958. vi, 90 p., [49] p. of plates : ill., plan ; 19 cm. Bibliography: p. 87-88.
1. Windsor Castle. St. George's Chapel. I. Bond, Maurice Francis. II. Title. III. Title: Romance of Saint George's Chapel, Windsor Castle.
NA5471.W73 B6 1958
          NYPL   [3-MRBH 83-2146]

Blackley, Roger, 1953- Two centuries of New Zealand landscape art / Roger Blackley. Rev. ed. Auckland, N.Z. : Auckland City Art Gallery, c1990. 128 p. : col. ill. ; 21 x 27 cm. Published in conjunction with an exhibition at the Auckland City Art Gallery from Feb. 2-Apr. 22, 1990. Includes index. Bibliography: p. 113-125.   ISBN 0-86463-179-0
1. Landscape in art - Exhibitions. 2. Landscape painting, New Zealand - Exhibitions. 3. New Zealand in art - Exhibitions. I. Auckland City Art Gallery. II. Title.   **NYPL   [3-MAMY 91-5463]**

BLACKS - BIOGRAPHY.
Historic Blacks in the arts /. Chicago, IL , c1990. p. cm.   ISBN 0-922162-58-1 :   DDC 700/.92/2 B 20
NX164.B55 H57 1990

BLACKS - BRAZIL - SALVADOR.
Verger, Pierre. Centro histórico de Salvador . São Paulo , 1989. 1 v. (unpaged)
          NYPL   [MFX+ (Verger) 90-13439]

BLACKS IN ART - EXHIBITIONS.
The Neglected tradition . Johannesburg , c1988. 155 p. :   ISBN 0-620-13184-5   DDC 704/.03968/0090407468221 20
N7392 .N44 1988

BLACKS - WEST INDIES - SONGS AND MUSIC - HISTORY AND CRITICISM.
Gilbert, Will G. Rumbamuziek [microform]. s-Gravenhage [1947?] 119 p.
          NYPL   [Sc Micro R-5903 no.2]

Blackwell, Lewis. International interiors 2 : offices, studios, shops, restaurants, bars, clubs, hotels, cultural and public buildings / Lewis Blackwell with 356 colour illustrations, architects' drawings and plans. London : Thames and Hudson, c1990. 256 p. : ill. (chiefly col.) ; 30 cm. Includes bibliographical references.   ISBN 1-558-59013-7
1. Interior architecture. I. Title. II. Title: International interiors two.   **NYPL   [3-MLO+ 90-12789]**

Blackwood, John. London's immortals : the complete outdoor commemorative statues / John Blackwood ; photographs by Caroline Irwin, Richard Cheatle and Philip Ward-Jackson. Highgate, London : Savoy Press, 1989. 380 p. : ill. (some col.) ; 30 cm. Includes bibliographical references.   ISBN 0-9514296-0-4
1. Statues - England - London. 2. Outdoor sculpture - England - London. I. Title.
          NYPL   [3-MGI+ 90-2430]

Bladen, Ronald, 1918-1988.
Berkson, Bill. Ronald Bladen . San Francisco , c1991. p. cm.   ISBN 0-918471-19-2   DDC 759.13 20
N6537.B554 A4 1991

BLADEN, RONALD, 1918-1988 - EXHIBITIONS.
Berkson, Bill. Ronald Bladen . San Francisco , c1991. p. cm.   ISBN 0-918471-19-2   DDC 759.13 20
N6537.B554 A4 1991

Bladon, Patricia P., 1946- Callicott, Burton, 1907- Burton Callicott . Memphis, Tenn. , c1991. 56 p. :   DDC 759.13 20
ND237.C195 A4 1991

Blaeser, Norbert. Pillhofer, Josef, 1921- Josef Pillhofer. Düsseldorf [1989?] [76] p. :
NB511.5.P5 A4 1989

Blaeu, Guiljelmus. see **Blaeu, Willem Janszoon, 1571-1638.**

Blaeu, Jan. see **Blaeu, Willem Janszoon, 1571-1638.**

Blaeu, Willem Janszoon, 1571-1638. The light of navigation. Amsterdam 1612. [by] Willem Jansz Blaeu (William Iohnson). With an introd. by R.A. Skelton. [Amsterdam, N. Israel, c1964] xiii, [60], 114, 118 p. Illus., maps (41 fold.), port. 27x31 cm. (Theatrum orbis terrarum; a series of atlases in facsimile. 1st series, v.6) Facsmile of the British Museum copy.
1. Atlases - Early works to 1800. 2. Navigation - Early works to 1800. 3. Nautical charts - Europe. 4. Pilot guides - Europe. 5. Atlantic Ocean - Maps. I. Skelton, R. A. (Raleigh Ashlin), 1906-1970. II. Title.
G1793 .B52 1964 (Map)
          NYPL   [Map Div. 84-1067]

Blaeuw, Willem. see **Blaeu, Willem Janszoon, 1571-1638.**

Blair, John (W. John) Saint Frideswide's Monastery at Oxford . Gloucester , Wolfeboro Fall, NH , 1991. p. cm. ISBN 0-86299-773-9 : DDC 726/.7/0942574 20
NA5471.O9 S25 1991

Blair, Sheila S. Images of paradise in Islamic art /. Hanover, N.H. , 1991. p. cm. ISBN 0-944722-07-5 (hardcover) DDC 704.9/489723 20
N6263.D37 H664 1991

Blake, Sylvia Dugger. Flow blue. [Des Moines, Wallace-Homestead Book Co., c1971] v, [48] p. col. illus. 23 cm. Cover title. DDC 738.2
1. Blue and white transfer ware - Collectors and collecting. 2. Porcelain, English - Collectors and collecting. 3. Porcelain - Collectors and collecting. I. Title.   ***NYPL [3-MPGO 90-6862]***

Blake, Wendon.
[Color book]
The artist's guide to using color : a complete step-by-step guide in watercolor, acrylic, and oil / by Wendon Blake ; paintings by Ferdinand Petrie and other artists where credited. Cincinnati, Ohio : North Light Books, c1992. p. cm. Originally published as: The Color book. Includes bibliographical references and index. ISBN 0-89134-378-4 (hard cover) : DDC 751.4 20
1. Color in art. 2. Color guides. 3. Painting - Technique. I. Petrie, Ferdinand, 1925-. II. Title.
ND1488 .B55 1992

Getting started in drawing / Wendon Blake ; with drawings by Ferdinand Petrie. 1st ed. Cincinnati, Ohio : North Light Books, c1991. vi, 137 p. : ill. ; 29 cm. Includes index. ISBN 0-89134-343-X (hrdcvr.) : DDC 741.2 20
1. Drawing - Technique. I. Petrie, Ferdinand, 1925-. II. Title.
NC730 .B535 1991

Blake, William, 1757-1827.
Essick, Robert N. William Blake's commercial book illustrations . Oxford [England] , New York , 1991. p. cm. ISBN 0-19-817390-3 : DDC 769.92 20
NE2047.6.B55 A4 1991

Norvig, Gerda S. Dark figures in the desired country . Berkeley , c1992. p. cm. ISBN 0-520-04471-1 (alk. paper) DDC 759.2 20
NC978.5.B55 N67 1992

BLAKE, WILLIAM, 1757-1827 - CATALOGS.
Essick, Robert N. William Blake's commercial book illustrations . Oxford [England] , New York , 1991. p. cm. ISBN 0-19-817390-3 : DDC 769.92 20
NE2047.6.B55 A4 1991

BLAKE, WILLIAM, 1757-1827 - CRITICISM AND INTERPRETATION.
Essick, Robert N. William Blake's commercial book illustrations . Oxford [England] , New York , 1991. p. cm. ISBN 0-19-817390-3 : DDC 769.92 20
NE2047.6.B55 A4 1991

Norvig, Gerda S. Dark figures in the desired country . Berkeley , c1992. p. cm. ISBN 0-520-04471-1 (alk. paper) DDC 759.2 20
NC978.5.B55 N67 1992

Blakemore, Colin. Rank Prize Funds' International Symposium (1986 : Royal Society) Images and understanding . Cambridge , New York , 1990. xiii, 401 p. : ISBN 0-521-34177-9 DDC 152.1/4 19
QP474 .R36 1986   ***NYPL [JFF 90-2299]***

Blanch, Arnold, 1896-1968.
University of Minnesota. Dept. of Art. Arnold Blanch, the years 1924-1949. [Minneapolis, 1949] 1 v. (unpaged)
NYPL [3-MCX B637 91-1320]

BLANCH, ARNOLD, 1896-1968 - EXHIBITIONS.
University of Minnesota. Dept. of Art. Arnold Blanch, the years 1924-1949. [Minneapolis, 1949] 1 v. (unpaged)
NYPL [3-MCX B637 91-1320]

Blanchette, Manon, 1952- Blickpunkte : [exposition] 13 septembre 1989-14 janvier 1990, Musée d'art contemporain de Montréal / [catalogue] Manon Blanchette, Wolfgang Max Faust. Montréal, Québec : Le Musée, c1989. 2 v. : ill. (some col.) ; 30 cm. French and English. Vol. 2 published by Goethe-Institut Montréal.

"Biobibliographies"--V. 1, p. 133-182. ISBN 2-551-12161-2
1. Art, German - Exhibitions. 2. Conceptual art - Germany (West) - Exhibitions. 3. Postmodernism - Germany (West) - EXhibitions. 4. Performing arts - Germany, West. I. Faust, Wolfgang Max, 1944-. II. Musée d'art contemporain de Montréal. III. Goethe-Institut Montréal. IV. Title.
N6868.5.C63 B55 1989

Blanckenhagen, Peter Heinrich von. Studies in classical art and archaeology . Locust Valley, N.Y. , 1979. xiv, 344 p., [45] leaves of plates : DDC 709/.38
N5613 .S88   ***NYPL [MAH 79-1946]***

BLANCKENHAGEN, PETER HEINRICH VON.
Studies in classical art and archaeology . Locust Valley, N.Y. , 1979. xiv, 344 p., [45] leaves of plates : DDC 709/.38
N5613 .S88   ***NYPL [MAH 79-1946]***

Blanco, Alberto. Toledo, Francisco, 1940- Canto a la sombra de los animales /. [Mexico?] , 1988. 88 p. :
IN PROCESS (ONLINE)
NYPL [JFD 91-2852]

Blanco, Venancio, 1923-
Ortega Coca, María Teresa. Venancio Blanco /. [Valladolid] [1989?] 57 p., [46] p. of plates : ISBN 84-7852-008-2 DDC 730/.92 20
NB813.B52 A4 1989
NYPL [3-MGO (Blanco) 91-6429]

BLANCO, VENANCIO, 1923- - CATALOGS.
Ortega Coca, María Teresa. Venancio Blanco /. [Valladolid] [1989?] 57 p., [46] p. of plates : ISBN 84-7852-008-2 DDC 730/.92 20
NB813.B52 A4 1989
NYPL [3-MGO (Blanco) 91-6429]

Blanden Memorial Art Museum.
Handbook of the collections in the Blanden Memorial Art Museum, Fort Dodge, Iowa / compiled and edited by Margaret Carney Xie. 1st ed. Fort Dodge, Iowa (920 3rd Ave., South, Fort Dodge 50501) : Blanden Charitable Foundation, 1989. 132 p. : ill. (some col.) ; 28 cm. DDC 708.177/51 20
1. Art - Iowa - Fort Dodge - Catalogs. 2. Blanden Memorial Art Museum - Catalogs. I. Xie, Margaret Carney. II. Title.
N570.29 .A6 1989

BLANDEN MEMORIAL ART MUSEUM - CATALOGS.
Blanden Memorial Art Museum. Handbook of the collections in the Blanden Memorial Art Museum, Fort Dodge, Iowa /. Fort Dodge, Iowa (920 3rd Ave., South, Fort Dodge 50501) , 1989. 132 p. : DDC 708.177/51 20
N570.29 .A6 1989

Blandi, Gaetano. Sculture di Messina / Gaetano Blandi. [Italy] : Edizioni AERRE, 1990. 263 p. : ill. ; 35 cm.
1. Sculpture, Italian - Italy - Messina. I. Title.
NYPL [3-MGI+ 91-5806]

Blankert, Albert. Museum Bredius. Museum Bredius . ['s-Gravenhage] , 1980. 176 p. :
NYPL [3-MAVZ (Hague) 81-647]

Blanket statement. Duffek, Karen, 1956- Bob Boyer . [Vancouver] , c1988. 1 folded sheet (8) p. ; ISBN 0-88865-111-2 (pbk.)
NYPL [3-MON 89-19266]

Blaschko, Horst. Schilling, Heinz. Urbane Zeiten . Frankfurt [am Main] [1990] 371 p. : ISBN 3-923992-32-7
NA9199 .S37 1990

Blasco Carrascosa, Juan Angel. Mestre Sancho, Juan Antonio. Juego y deporte en la pintura de Goya /. [Valencia] [1990?] 294 p. : ISBN 84-7890-087-X DDC 760/.092 20
N7113.G68 A4 1990a

Blasdale, Mary Jean. Artists of New Bedford : a biographical dictionary / Mary Jean Blasdale. New Bedford, Mass. : Old Dartmouth Historical Society, 1990. xiii, 220 p. : ill. (some col.) ; 23 x 29 cm. Includes bibliographical references.
1. Artists - Massachusetts - New Bedford - Biography - Dictionaries. 2. New Bedford (Mass.) - Biography - Dictionaries. I. Title.
IN PROCESS (ONLINE)
NYPL [3-MAO 91-6926]

Blaser, Werner, 1924-
Bauen vor der Stadt. English & German. Bauen vor der Stadt . Basel , Boston , c1991. p. cm. ISBN 3-7643-2629-8 : DDC 720/.9494/33 20
NA1349.B38 B3813 1991

Foster, Norman, 1935- [Norman Foster. German & English.] Norman Foster . Basel , Boston , c1992. p. cm. ISBN 3-7643-2546-1 : DDC 720/.22/22 20
NA2707.F67 A4 1992

Jahn, Helmut, 1940- Airports /. Basel , Boston , c1991. p. cm. ISBN 0-8176-2613-1 (U. S.) DDC 725/.39 20
NA6300 .J34 1991

Santiago Calatrava . Basel , Boston , 1991. p. cm. ISBN 0-8176-2460-0 DDC 720/.92 20
NA1313.C35 S26 1991

[Mies van der Rohe, Lehre und Schule. English]
Mies van der Rohe, continuing the Chicago school of architecture / Werner Blaser. 2nd ed. Basel ; Boston : Birkhäuser Verlag, 1981. 307 p. : ill. (some col.) ; 25 cm. Expanded translation of: Mies van der Rohe, Lehre und Schule. Includes bibliographies and index. ISBN 3-7643-1247-5 DDC 720/.92/4 19
1. Architecture - Philosophy. I. Title.
NA1088.M65 B5813 1981   ***NYPL [3-MQZ (Mies van der Rohe) 90-10754]***

Blasphemies, ecstasies, cries : [exhibition] / [curated by Andrew Brighton ; organized by Andrea Schlieker]. [London] : Serpentine Gallery, 1989. 71 p. : ill., (some col.) ; 21 cm. "Essay by Andrew Brighton, introduction by Andrew Brighton and Andrea Schlieker"--Colophon. "Quotations on p. 2, 3, and 16-69 are taken from: Charles Baudelaire, Les Fleurs du Mal, translated by Richard Howard, Picador Classics, 1987." Exhibition at Serpentine Gallery 18 Jan.-26 Feb. 1989, Norwich School of Art Gallery, 17 Apr.-13 May 1989, and Mostyn Gallery, Llandudno, 10 June-8 July 1989. Includes index. ISBN 1-87081-425-8
1. Baudelaire, Charles, 1821-1867 Fleurs du Mal. English. Selections - Illustrations. 2. Art, Modern - 19th century - Exhibitions. 3. Art, Modern - 20th century - Exhibitions. I. Brighton, Andrew. II. Schlieker, Andrea. III. Serpentine Gallery. IV. Norwich School of Art. Gallery. V. Mostyn Gallery.
NYPL [3-MAL 90-11604]

Blasse-Hegeman, H. Nederlandse portretten . 's-Gravenhage , 1990. 388 p. : ISBN 90-12-06435-X   ***NYPL [3-MCG 91-3264]***

Blast furnaces /. Becher, Bernd, 1931- [Hochöfen. English.] Cambridge, Mass. , c1990. 15 p., 223 p. of plates : ISBN 0-262-02311-3 (hc.) DDC 669/.1413 20
TN677 .B38513 1990
NYPL [MFX+ (Becher) 91-195]

BLAST-FURNACES - PICTORIAL WORKS.
Becher, Bernd, 1931- Hochöfen /. München , c1990. 15 p., 223 p. of plates : ISBN 3-88814-352-7
NYPL [MFX+ (Becher) 91-7985]

Becher, Bernd, 1931- [Hochöfen. English.] Blast furnaces /. Cambridge, Mass. , c1990. 15 p., 223 p. of plates : ISBN 0-262-02311-3 (hc.) DDC 669/.1413 20
TN677 .B38513 1990
NYPL [MFX+ (Becher) 91-195]

Blau, Farbe der Ferne / Hans Gercke, Herausgeber ; [Redaktion des Katalogs, Sigrid Niederhausen]. Heidelberg : Wunderhorn, c1990. 615 p. : ill. (chiefly col.) ; 31 cm. "Eine Ausstellung des Heidelberger Kunstvereins ... vom 2. März bis zum 13. Mai 1990"--P. facing t.p. Includes bibliographical references and index. ISBN 3-88423-062-X DDC 709/.04/0074434645 20
1. Art, Modern - 20th century - Exhibitions. 2. Blue in art - Exhibitions. I. Gercke, Hans, 1941-. II. Niederhausen, Sigrid. III. Heidelberger Kunstverein.
N6488.G3 H442 1990

Blau-Gelbe Galerie der NÖ Kulturabteilung.
Denk, Wolfgang, 1947- Wolfgang Denk . Wien , Rastenfeld , 1986. 1 v. (unpaged) : *AM101 .V5344 n.F., Nr. 175 ND511.5.D45*
NYPL [3-MCK D396 91-5501]

Hammerstiel, Robert F., 1957- Stand-Orte /. [Wien] , c1988. 1 v. (unpaged) : ISBN 3-900464-91-1
NYPL [MFX (Hammerstiel) 90-13462]

BLAUE REITER (GROUP OF ARTISTS)
Zweite, Armin. The Blue Rider in the
Lenbachhaus, Munich . Munich , 1989. 288 p. :
ISBN 3-7913-0850-0
NYPL [3-MAMG+ 90-11017]

**BLAUE REITER (GROUP OF ARTISTS) -
EXHIBITIONS.**
Edinburgh Festival Society. The Blue Rider
group. Edinburgh, 1960. 32 p.
ND586.M9 E3   NYPL [3-MC 91-285]

Pasadena Art Museum. The Blue Four.
Pasadena [1954?] [32] p.
N6868.5.E9 P37 1954   NYPL [3-MC 91-406]

Blauth, Rudolf. Schichtwechsel . [Ahlen] [1988?]
94 p. :
IN PROCESS (ONLINE)
NYPL [3-MAMZ 91-7103]

Blazhev, Svilen. 30 godini Druzhestvo na
khudozhnitsite--Kiustendil, 1959-1989 /. [S.l. ,
1989] (Sofiia : Ofsetgrafik) 47 p. :
N7191.K58 A15 1989

Blázquez, José María. Mosaicos romanos de
Lérida y Albacete /. Madrid , 1989. 124 p. :
ISBN 84-00-06983-8
NYPL [3-MRXZ 90-12594]

Blechen, Karl, 1798-1840.
Carl Blechen : zwischen Romantik und
Realismus / herausgegeben von Peter-Klaus
Schuster ; mit Beiträgen von Sigrid
Achenbach ... [et al.]. [Berlin] : Nationalgalerie
Berlin ; München : Prestel-Verlag, c1990. 309
p. : ill. (some col.) ; 31 cm. Catalog of an
exhibition held at the Nationalgalerie Berlin, Aug.
31-Nov. 4, 1990. Includes bibliographical references (p.
300-307) and index.   ISBN 3-7913-1084-4
*1. Blechen, Karl, 1798-1840 - Exhibitions. 2.
Romanticism in art - Europe - Exhibitions. 3. Realism
in art - Europe - Exhibitions. 4. Painting, Modern -
19th century - Europe - Exhibitions. I. Schuster,
Peter-Klaus. II. Achenbach, Sigrid, 1944-. III.
Nationalgalerie (Germany : West). IV. Title.*
NYPL [3-MCK+ B6455 91-2247]

**BLECHEN, KARL, 1798-1840 -
EXHIBITIONS.**
Blechen, Karl, 1798-1840. Carl Blechen .
[Berlin] , München , c1990. 309 p. :   ISBN
3-7913-1084-4
NYPL [3-MCK+ B6455 91-2247]

Bleck, Rolf-Dieter. Pflege und Erhaltung von
Kunst- und Kulturgut : Bibliographie /
Rolf-Dieter Bleck. Weimar : Museum für Ur-
und Frühgeschichte Thüringens, 1984. v. ; 30
cm. (Restaurierung und Museumstechnik, 0232-2609 .
5)
*1. Art - Conservation and restoration - Bibliography. I.
Title. II. Series.   NYPL [3-MAV 89-4361]*

Bleeding heart. Sussman, Elisabeth, 1939- El
corazón sangrante =. Boston, Mass. , Seattle,
Wash. , c1991. p.   ISBN 0-910663-50-5 (paperback)
DDC 704.9/46 20
N8217.H53 S87 1991

Blende auf-- Klick : Bochum in
Momentaufnahmen : Fotojournalisten sehen
ihre Stadt : Ausstellung vom 30.5. bis 27.6.1989
im Informationszentrum Bochum, Rathaus.
[Bochum] : Stadt Bochum, Der
Oberstadtdirektor, Presse- und Informationsamt,
[1989] 58 p. : ill. ; 30 cm.
1. Photojournalism - Germany - Bochum - Exhibitions.
NYPL [MFW+ 91-7688]

Bleyl, Matthias.
Essentielle Malerei in Deutschland : Wege zur
Kunst nach 1945 / Matthias Bleyl. Nürnberg :
Verlag für moderne Kunst, c1988. 252 p. : ill.
(some col.) ; 24 cm. Includes index. Includes
bibliographical references (p. 241-247)   ISBN
3-922531-56-3
*1. Painting, Modern - 20th century - Germany, West. I.
Title.   NYPL [3-MCI 90-12463]*

Essentielle Malerei in Deutschland : Wege zur
Kunst nach 1945 / Matthias Bleyl. Nürnberg :
Verlag für Moderne Kunst, c1988. 252 p. : ill.
(some col.) ; 24 cm. Includes bibliographical
references (p. 241-247). Includes index.   ISBN
3-922531-56-3
*1. Painting, Abstract - Germany - Exhibitions. 2.
Painting, German - Exhibitions. 3. Painting, Modern -
20th century - Germany - Exhibitions. I. Title.*
ND568.5.A14 B57 1988

Joseph Beuys . Darmstadt , c1989. 179 p. :
ISBN 3-925376-30-5 (trade ed.)
NYPL [3-MGO (Beuys) 91-6704]

Blickpunkte . Blanchette, Manon, 1952-
Montréal, Québec , c1989. 2 v. :   ISBN
2-551-12161-2
N6868.5.C63 B55 1989

Blier, Suzanne Preston. Beauty and the beast .
New York City [1976] 14 p. :
NYPL [3-MADF 90-7112]

Blik, Tyler. Baker, Eric, 1949- Trademarks of the
40's and 50's /. San Francisco , c1988. 156 p. :
ISBN 0-87701-485-X :   DDC 741.6 19
NC998.5.A1 B36 1988
NYPL [MNF 88-3842]

Blimlinger, Eva. Hrdlička, Alfred, 1928- Das
Frauenbild /. Wien [198-?] 131 p. :   ISBN
3-900318-48-4
NYPL [3-MCK+ H857 90-5270]

Blin, Pascale.
Andreu, Paul. Paul Andreu /. Paris , 1990. 1 v.
(unpaged) : ISBN 2-907687-06-9 :   DDC
720/.22/22 20
NA2707.A55 A4 1990

Ripault, Jacques, 1953- Jacques Ripault /.
Paris , 1990. 1 v. (unpaged) :   ISBN
2-907687-05-0 :   DDC 720/.22/22 20
NA2707.R56 A4 1990

Blind knot =. Rayo, Omar, 1928- [S.l. , 1972?] 1
v. (unpaged) :
NE606.R38 A4 1972

The blitz . Rodger, George. London , 1990. 176
p. :   ISBN 0-14-014513-3   DDC 940.54212 20
D787   NYPL [MFX (Rodger) 91-3486]

Blix, Ragnvald, 1882-
Ragnvald Blix, 1882-1958 : [utställning].
[Stockholm : Nationalmuseum, 1977] [13] p. :
ill. ; 22 cm. (Nationalmusei utställningskatalog . nr.
406) Cover title.   ISBN 91-7100-124-7
*1. Blix, Ragnvald, 1882- - Exhibitions. I.
Nationalmuseum (Sweden). II. Title.*
NYPL [MEM (Blix) 90-5759]

BLIX, RAGNVALD, 1882- - EXHIBITIONS.
Blix, Ragnvald, 1882- Ragnvald Blix,
1882-1958 . [Stockholm , 1977] [13] p. :   ISBN
91-7100-124-7
NYPL [MEM (Blix) 90-5759]

Blizzard, Gladys S. Come look with me :
enjoying art with children / Gladys S. Blizzard.
Charlottesville, Va. : Thomasson-Grant, c1990.
p. cm. Presents twelve color reproductions of paintings
by artists from Holbein to Picasso, with questions to
stimulate discussion and background information on
each artist and painting.   ISBN 0-934738-76-9   DDC
750/.1/1 20
1. Painting - Appreciation - Juvenile literature. I. Title.
ND1143 .B53 1990

Bloch, Albert, 1882-1961.
Albert Bloch, 1882-1961 : an American
expressionist : paintings, drawings, prints :
February 3 through March 3, 1974, shown
concurrently, paintings, Museum of Art,
Munson-Williams-Proctor Institute, Utica, New
York : drawings and prints, The Edward W.
Root Art Center, Hamilton College, Clinton,
New York. [Utica, N.Y.] :
Munson-Williams-Proctor Institute, c1974. 36
p. : ill. (1 col.), port. ; 24 cm. Foreword by James
Penney.
*1. Bloch, Albert, 1882-1961 - Exhibitions. I. Penney,
James. II. Munson-Williams-Proctor Institute. Museum
of Art. III. Edward W. Root Art Center. IV. Title.*
NYPL [3-MCX B643 91-6562]

**BLOCH, ALBERT, 1882-1961 -
EXHIBITIONS.**
Bloch, Albert, 1882-1961. Albert Bloch,
1882-1961 . [Utica, N.Y.] , c1974. 36 p. :
NYPL [3-MCX B643 91-6562]

Bloch, Augustyn. Schleswig-Holstein, Ingeborg zu.
Weg ins Licht . Hamburg , c1988. 78 p. :
ISBN 3-7672-1062-2
ND588.S2819 A4 1988
NYPL [3-MCK+ S343 90-10580]

Bloch-Dermant, Janine. G. Argy-Rousseau : les
pâtes de verre : catalogue raisonné / Janine
Bloch-Dermant ; préface et catalogue raisonné
par Yves Delaborde. Paris : Editions de
l'Amateur, c1990. 229 p. : ill. (some col.) ; 29
cm. Includes bibliographical references (p. 227).
ISBN 2-85917-105-3   DDC 748.294 20

*1. Argy-Rousseau, Gabriel, 1885-1953 - Catalogues
raisonnés. 2. Pâte de verre - France - Catalogs. I.
Argy-Rousseau, Gabriel, 1885-1953. II. Delaborde,
Yves. III. Title. IV. Title: Pâtes de verre.*
NK5198.A74 A4 1990

Bloch, E. Maurice. Focusing on nature :
landscape drawings from the collection of E.
Maurice Bloch / by E. Maurice Bloch. San
Marino, Calif. : Huntington Library and Art
Gallery, c1991. p. cm. "An exhibition in the
Virginia Steele Scott Gallery, the Huntington Library
and Art Gallery, May through August, 1991." Includes
index.   ISBN 0-87328-133-0 :   DDC
741.973/074/79493 20
*1. Landscape drawing, American - Exhibitions. 2.
mioch, E. Maurice - Art collections - Exhibitions. 3.
Drawing - Private collections - California - San
Marino - Exhibitions. 4. Henry E. Huntington Library
and Art Gallery - Exhibitions. I. Virginia Steele Scott
Gallery. II. Henry E. Huntington Library and Art
Gallery. III. Title.*
NC790 .B58 1991

Bloch, Georges. Pablo Picasso / Georges Bloch.
4e éd. Berne : Kornfeld et Cie, c1984. 4 v. : ill.
(some col.) ; 30 cm. French, English and German;
catalog in French. Errata slip inserted in v. 1. Vol. 2:
2nd ed.; published by Kornfeld et Klipstein, 1977. Vol.
4, published by Kornfeld et Klipstein, 1979.
CONTENTS. - t. 1. Catalogue de l'œuvre gravé et
lithographié, 1904-1967 -- t. 2. Catalogue de l'œuvre
gravé et lithographié, 1966-1969 -- t. 3. Catalogue de
l'œuvre gravé céramique, 1949-1971 -- t. 4. Catalogue
de l'œuvre gravé et lithographié, 1970-1972.
Suppléments t. 1-2.
*1. Picasso, Pablo, 1881-1973 - Catalogues raisonnés. I.
Title.   NYPL [MDG+ (Picasso) 91-6149]*

Bloch, Peter, 1925-
Ethos und Pathos . Berlin , c1990. 419 p. :
ISBN 3-7861-1597-4
NYPL [3-MGI 90-12677]

Festschrift für Peter Bloch zum 11. Juli 1990 /.
Mainz am Rhein , c1990. xviii, 420 p. :   ISBN
3-8053-1120-6   *NYPL [3-MAS+ 91-4807]*

BLOCH, PETER, 1925-
Festschrift für Peter Bloch zum 11. Juli 1990 /.
Mainz am Rhein , c1990. xviii, 420 p. :   ISBN
3-8053-1120-6   *NYPL [3-MAS+ 91-4807]*

Blochet, Edgar, 1870- Catalogue of an exhibition
of Persian paintings from the XIIth to the
XVIIIth cent. : formerly from the collections of
the shahs of Persia and of the great moguls :
held at the galleries of Demotte Inc., New York
City / compiled by E. Blochet. [s.l. : s.n.,
1930?]. 79 p. : ill. ; 22 cm.
*1. Painting, Iranian - Exhibitions. I. Demotte Inc. II.
Title.   NYPL [3-MAF 83-2314]*

Block and lot maps. New York (N.Y.). Dept. of
City Planning. Block & lot maps-- Brooklyn
Community District ... atlas /. New York,
N.Y. , c1990. 18 v. :
NYPL [Map Div. 91-6366]

**Block & lot maps-- Bronx Community District ...
atlas /.** New York (N.Y.). Dept. of City
Planning. New York, N.Y. , c1990. 12 v. :
NYPL [Map Div. 91-7471]

**Block and Lot maps-- Bronx Community
District ... atlas.** New York (N.Y.). Dept. of
City Planning. Block & lot maps-- Bronx
Community District ... atlas /. New York,
N.Y. , c1990. 12 v. :
NYPL [Map Div. 91-7471]

**Block & lot maps-- Brooklyn Community
District ... atlas /.** New York (N.Y.). Dept. of
City Planning. New York, N.Y. , c1990. 18 v. :
NYPL [Map Div. 91-6366]

**Block & lot maps-- Manhattan Community
District ... atlas /.** New York (N.Y.). Dept. of
City Planning. New York, N.Y. , c1989. 12 v. :
NYPL [Map Div. 91-7469]

**Block and lot maps-- Manhattan Community
District ... atlas.** New York (N.Y.). Dept. of
City Planning. Block & lot maps-- Manhattan
Community District ... atlas /. New York,
N.Y. , c1989. 12 v. :
NYPL [Map Div. 91-7469]

**Block & lot maps-- Queens Community
District ... atlas /.** New York (N.Y.). Dept. of
City Planning. New York, N.Y. , c1991- v. :
NYPL [Map Div. 91-7475]

Block and lot maps-- Queens Community District ... atlas. New York (N.Y.). Dept. of City Planning. Block & lot maps-- Queens Community District ... atlas /. New York, N.Y. , c1991- v. :
NYPL [Map Div. 91-7475]

BLOCK-BOOKS.
Vanderwielen, Betty. An index of woodcuts and engravings in incunabula and early printed books (to 1600) in the Library of the Institute of Cistercian Studies /. Kalamazoo, Mich. , 1988. viii, 284 leaves ; ISBN 0-918720-92-3 DDC 769.94/09/03107477417 20
NE1052 .V36 1988

BLOCK PRINTING. see BLOCK-BOOKS.

Block, René.
KP Brehmer, KH Hödicke, Sigmar Polke, Gerhard Richter, Wolf Vostell : Werkverzeichnisse der Druckgrafik : Band II, September 1971 bis Mai 1976 / bearbeitet von René Block. Berlin : Edition R. Block, 1976. p. 200-266 : ill. ; 21 x 24 cm. "Band I mit dem Titel 'Grafik des Kapitalistischen Realismus' herausgegeben von René Block unter Mitarbeit von Carl Vogel, Berlin, 1971, enthält die Verzeichnisse 1960-1971."
I. Grafik des Kapitalistischen Realismus. II. Title.
NYPL [MDBF (Block, R. Grafik)]

Torres, Francesc, 1948- Francesc Torres, Plus ultra /. Berlin , c1988. 60, [4] p. : ISBN 3-89357-010-1
NYPL [3-MGO (Torres) 90-13375]

BLOCKS (CITY PLANNING) - ITALY - FLORENCE.
Maffei, Gian Luigi. La casa fiorentina nella storia della città dalle origini all'Ottocento /. Venezia , 1990. 383 p. : ISBN 88-317-5346-0
NA9053.B58 M3 1990

Bloem, Marja. De Grote naïeven =. Amsterdam , 1974. [41] p. :
NYPL [3-MCN 90-6044]

Blomfield, John. Colman Foods. The Colman Collection of silver mustard pots /. Norwich , 1979. 143 p. : ISBN 0-9506456-0-5 (pbk.) :
NK7236.M88 C64 1979
NYPL [MNO 81-450]

Blomstedt, Severi. Neuvostomaan arkkitehtuuria. [Helsinki , 1988] 81 p. : ISBN 951-9229-56-6
NA1188 .N48 1988

Sirén, J. S. (Johan Sigfrid), 1889-1961. J.S. Sirén, 1889-1961, arkkitehti /. Helsinki , 1989. 108 p. : ISBN 951-9229-58-2 DDC 720/.92 20
NA1455.F53 S5537 1989

Blondel, Alain. Guimard, Hector, 1867-1942. Hector Guimard . Paris , 1971. 45 p. :
NYPL [3-MRX 90-7184]

BLONDEL, ANDRÉ.
Henry-Thiébaut, Pierre. Blues /. Paris , 1949. [14] p. : *NYPL [MEM B658 89-4051]*

Bloom, Barbara.
The reign of narcissism : guide book = Führer / Barbara Bloom. Stuttgart : Württembergischer Kunstverein ; Zürich : Kunsthalle Zürich ; 219, [43] p. : ill. (some col.) ; 21 cm. Issued in conjunction with an exhibition/installation at the Württembergischer Kunstverein, Stuttgart, 8 Feb.-11 Mar. 1990; Kunsthalle Zürich, 31 Mar.-27 May 1990; Serpentine Gallery, London, 1 Aug.-9 Sept. 1990. English and German.
1. Bloom, Barbara - Exhibitions. 2. Narcissism - Exhibitions. I. Württembergischer Kunstverein. II. Kunsthalle Zürich. III. Serpentine Gallery. IV. Title.
NYPL [3-MGO (Bloom) 91-5281]

BLOOM, BARBARA - EXHIBITIONS.
Bloom, Barbara. The reign of narcissism . Stuttgart : Zürich : 219, [43] p. :
NYPL [3-MGO (Bloom) 91-5281]

Bloom, Jonathan (Jonathan M.)
Images of paradise in Islamic art /. Hanover, N.H. , 1991. p. cm. ISBN 0-944722-07-5 (hardcover) DDC 704.9/489723 20
N6263.D37 H664 1991

Minaret, symbol of Islam / Jonathan Bloom. Oxford [England] : Published by Oxford University Press for the Board of the Faculty of Oriental Studies, University of Oxford, c1989. 216 p. : ill. ; 26 cm. (Oxford studies in Islamic art . 7) Includes index. Includes bibliographical references (p. 195-207). ISBN 0-19-728013-7 DDC 726/.2 20
1. Minarets. 2. Islamic art and symbolism. I. Title. II.

Series.
NA4670 .B55 1989
NYPL [3-MQT 90-12010]

Bloomsbury : its artists, authors, and designers / edited by Gillian Naylor.1st U. S. ed. Boston : Little, Brown, c1990. 328 p. : ill. (some col.) ; 32 cm. "A Bulfinch Press book." Includes bibliographical references (p. 325) and index. ISBN 0-8212-1768-2 : DDC 700/.942 20
1. Arts, Modern - 20th century - England. I. Naylor, Gillian.
NX543 .B58 1990
NYPL [3-MAMR+ 91-3278]

Blow, Christopher J. Airport terminals : Christopher J. Blow. Oxford ; Boston : Butterworth Architecture, 1991. p. cm. (Butterworth Architecture library of planning and design) Includes bibliographical references and index. ISBN 0-7506-1278-9 : DDC 725/.39 20
1. Airport terminals. I. Title. II. Series.
NA6300 .B56 1991

BLUE AND WHITE TRANSFER WARE - COLLECTORS AND COLLECTING.
Blake, Sylvia Dugger. Flow blue. [Des Moines, c1971] v, [48] p. DDC 738.2
NYPL [3-MPGO 90-6862]

The Blue Four. Pasadena Art Museum. Pasadena [1954?] [32] p.
N6868.5.E9 P37 1954 *NYPL [3-MC 91-406]*

BLUE IN ART - EXHIBITIONS.
Blau, Farbe der Ferne /. Heidelberg , c1990. 615 p. : ISBN 3-88423-062-X DDC 709/.04/0074434645 20
N6488.G3 H442 1990

BLUE MOUNTAINS (N.S.W.) - MAPS.
H.E.C. Robinson Pty. Ltd. Robinson's official Blue Mountains (N.S.W.) street directory and tourist guide . Sydney, Australia [196-?] 64 p. :
NYPL [Map Div. 90-6266]

Blue note : the album cover art / edited by Graham Marsh, Glyn Callingham, and Felix Cromey ; foreword by Horace Silver. San Francisco : Chronicle Books, 1991. p. cm. Includes index. ISBN 0-8118-0036-9 DDC 741.6/6 20
1. Sound recordings - Album covers - United States - Catalogs. 2. Blue Note - Catalogs. I. Marsh, Graham. II. Callingham, Glyn. III. Cromey, Felix.
NC1883.U6 B58 1991

Blue note. Korf, Anthony. [Symphonies, no. 2.] Symphony no. 2 . New York, NY , p1989. 1 sound disc :
New World Records NW 383-2

BLUE NOTE - CATALOGS.
Blue note . San Francisco , 1991. p. cm. ISBN 0-8118-0036-9 DDC 741.6/6 20
NC1883.U6 B58 1991

The Blue Rider group. Edinburgh Festival Society. Edinburgh, 1960. 32 p.
ND586.M9 E3 *NYPL [3-MC 91-285]*

The Blue Rider in the Lenbachhaus, Munich . Zweite, Armin. Munich , 1989. 288 p. : ISBN 3-7913-0850-0
NYPL [3-MAMG+ 90-11017]

Blue up . Schäfer, Peter Maria, 1961- Berlin , c1989. 70 p. : ISBN 3-924040-39-7
NYPL [MFX+ (Schäfer) 91-7467]

Blue willow /. Gaston, Mary Frank. Paducah, Ky. , c1990. 191 p. : ISBN 0-89145-396-2 : DDC 738 20
NK4277 .G37 1990
NYPL [3-MPK 90-12474]

Blühende Gärten. Ammann, Gustav, 1885-1955. Erlenbach-Zürich [c1955] 212 p. DDC 712
SB472 .A5 *NYPL [3-MSD 90-5819]*

A Blueprint monograph. Aldersey-Williams, Hugh. King and Miranda . New York , 1991. p. ISBN 0-8478-1358-4 (pbk.) DDC 745.4/4922 20
NK1535.K52 A84 1991

Blues /. Henry-Thiébaut, Pierre. Paris , 1949. [14] p. : *NYPL [MEM B658 89-4051]*

Bluestone, Daniel M. Constructing Chicago / Daniel Bluestone. New Haven : Yale University Press, c1991. p. cm. Includes bibliographical references (p.) and index. ISBN 0-300-04848-3 (alk. paper) DDC 711/.4/097731109034 20
1. City planning - Illinois - Chicago - History - 19th century. 2. Urban beautification - Illinois - Chicago -

History - 19th century. 3. Architects and patrons - Illinois - Chicago. 4. Architecture and society - Illinois - Chicago. 5. Chicago (Ill.) - Buildings, structures, etc. I. Title.
NA9127.C4 B48 1991

Blum, Laurie. Free money for people in the arts / Laurie Blum. New York : Macmillan ; Toronto : Collier Macmillan Canada, 1991. p. cm. Includes bibliographical references and index. ISBN 0-02-028175-7 DDC 700/.79/73 20
1. Arts - Scholarships, fellowships, etc. - United States - Directories. I. Title.
NX398 .B58 1991

Blum, Pamela Z.
Crosby, Sumner McK. (Sumner McKnight), 1909- The Royal Abbey of Saint-Denis . New Haven , c1987. xxiii, 525 p., 3 folded leaves of plates : ISBN 0-300-03143-2 (alk. paper) DDC 726/.5/0944362 19
NA5551.S214 C76 1987
NYPL [3-MRBB 91-6920]

Early Gothic Saint-Denis : restorations and survivals / Pamela Z. Blum. Berkeley : University of California Press, 1992. p. cm. Includes bibliographical references and index. ISBN 0-520-07371-1 (cloth) DDC 730/.944/362 20
1. Sculpture, Gothic - Conservation and restoration - France - Saint-Denis. 2. Sculpture, French - Conservation and restoration - France - Saint-Denis. 3. Christian art and symbolism - Medieval, 500-1500 - Conservation and restoration - France - Saint-Denis. 4. Abbaye de Saint-Denis (Saint-Denis, France). I. Title.
NB1910 .B58 1992

Blume, Dieter.
Schumacher, Emil, 1912- Emil Schumacher . Braunschweig [1978] 204 p. :
N6888.S412 A4 1978
NYPL [3-MCK S389 81-546]

Uecker, Günther, 1930- Uecker . Braunschweig , 1979. 145 p. :
N6888.U37 A4 1979
NYPL [3-MCK U125 86-2625]

Blume, Eugen.
Beckmann, Max, 1884-1950. Max Beckmann . [Italy] [1985] 141 p. : DDC 769.92/4 19
NE654.B37 A4 1985
NYPL [MDG (Beckmann) 86-4332]

Schimansky, Hanns, 1949- Hanns Schimansky, Zeichnungen /. Berlin , c1990. 24 p. : ISBN 3-88609-248-8
NC251.S3277 A4 1990

Blunt, Anthony, 1907-1983.
Poussin, Nicolas, 1594?-1665. [Correspondence. Selections.] Lettres et propos sur l'art /. Paris , c1989. 247 p. : ISBN 2-7056-6105-2
ND553.P8 A3 1989

The Roman drawings of the XVII & XVIII centuries in the collection of Her Majesty the Queen at Windsor Castle / by Anthony Blunt and Hereward Lester Cooke. London : Phaidon Press, c1960. 197 p. : ill. ; 30 cm. Cover title: Roman drawings at Windsor Castle. Includes bibliographical references and index. DDC 741.945/632/093207442296 20
1. Drawing, Italian - Italy - Rome - Catalogs. 2. Drawing - 17th century - Italy - Rome - Catalogs. 3. Drawing - 18th century - Italy - Rome - Catalogs. 4. Elizabeth, II, Queen of Great Britain, 1926- - Art collections - Catalogs. 5. Drawing - Private collections - England - Windsor (Berkshire) - Catalogs. 6. Windsor Castle. Royal Library - Catalogs. I. Cooke, Hereward Lester. II. Windsor Castle. Royal Library. III. Title. IV. Title: Roman drawings of the seventeenth & eighteenth centuries in the collection of Her Majesty the Queen at Windsor Castle. V. Title: Roman drawings of the 17th & 18th centuries in the collection of Her Majesty the Queen at Windsor Castle. VI. Title: Roman drawings at Windsor Castle.
NC256.R6 B4 1960

bMuseo Espanol de Arte Contemporáneo. El simbolismo en la pintura francesa. octubre - noviembre, 1972. Madrid [1972] 244 p. illus. 26 cm. At head of title: Comisaría de Exposiciones. Dirección General de Bellas Artes. Ministerio de Educación y Ciencia, con la colaboración de los Ministerios de Negocios Extranjeros y Asuntos Culturales de Francia. Bibliography: p. 223-238.
1. Symbolism in art - France. 2. Painting, French - Exhibitions. 3. Painting, Modern - 19th century - France - Exhibitions. I. Spain. Dirección General de Bellas Artes. II. Title. *NYPL [3-MCN 90-5447]*

BNMAU-yn Shinzhlĕkh Ukhaany Akademi.
Mongolia. Gosudarstvennoe upravlenie geodezii
i kartografii. Mongol'skaĭa Narodnaĭa
Respublika . Ulan-Bator , Moskva , 1990. 1
atlas (144 p.) :   *NYPL [Map Div. 91-7231]*

Bo Bartlett . Bartlett, Bo, 1955- NYC [1991?]
55 p. :   *NYPL [3-MCX+ B288 91-4352]*

**BOATS AND BOATING - CALIFORNIA,
SOUTHERN - MAPS.**
Balder, A. P. Mariner's atlas. Southern
California /. Houston, Tex. , c1989. 1 atlas
(112 p.) :   ISBN 0-87201-466-5 (pbk.): $39.95
DDC 623.89/297949 20
G1526.P5 B3 1989
      NYPL [Map Div. 90-11549]

**BOATS AND BOATING - NEW ENGLAND -
MAPS.**
Balder, A. P. Mariner's atlas. New England /.
Baltimore, Md. , c1989. 1 atlas ([112] p.) :
  ISBN 0-930151-08-9 :
      NYPL [Map Div. 90-11551]

**BOATS AND BOATING - NORTHEASTERN
STATES - MAPS.**
Balder, A. P. Mariner's atlas. Long Island
Sound & the South Shore /. [Baltimore, Md. ,
c1989] 1 atlas (80 p) :   ISBN 0-930151-07-0 :
      NYPL [Map Div. 90-11550]

Bob Boyer . Duffek, Karen, 1956- [Vancouver] ,
c1988. 1 folded sheet (8) p. ;   ISBN
0-88865-111-2 (pbk.)
      NYPL [3-MON 89-19266]

Bob Saget's Tales from the crib /. Saget, Bob.
[Tales from the crib.] New York, NY , c1991.
95 p. :   ISBN 0-399-51676-X :   DDC 741.5/973 20
NC1429.S315 A4 1991

Bober, Natalie. Marc Chagall : painter of dreams
/ Natalie S. Bober ; illustrated by Vera
Rosenberry.1st ed. Philadelphia : Jewish
Publication Society, 1991. p. cm. Includes index.
Traces the life of the noted painter, from his birth in
Russia to his death in France, with an emphasis on his
Jewish background.   ISBN 0-8276-0379-7   DDC
759.7 B 20
*1. Chagall, Marc, 1887- - Childhood and youth -
Juvenile literature. 2. Artists - Russian S.F.S.R. -
Biography - Juvenile literature. 3. Jews, Russian - Social
life and customs - Juvenile literature. I. Rosenberry,
Vera, ill.*
N6999.C46 B6 1991

Boberg, Jørgen.
Bogen om Bellis : en billedroman / Jørgen
Boberg. København Valby : Borgen, c1990. 71
p. : col. ill. ; 28 cm.   ISBN 87-418-5903-0
1. Boberg, Jørgen - Exhibitions. I. Title.
ND723.B59 A4 1990

BOBERG, JØRGEN - EXHIBITIONS.
Boberg, Jørgen. Bogen om Bellis . København
Valby , c1990. 71 p. :   ISBN 87-418-5903-0
ND723.B59 A4 1990

Bobrinskoĭ, Aleksei Alekseevich, graf. Narodnyĭa
russkiĭa derevi͡annyĭa izdi͡elii͡a predmety
domashni͡ago, khozi͡aĭstvennago i otchasti
tserkovnago obikhoda /A.A. Bobrinskoĭ.
Moskva : T-vo skoropech. A.A. Levenson,
1910. 7, 18, 7, 5, 6, 5, 5, 7, 163 leaves of
plates : ill. (some col.) ; 42 cm. "13 fototip. tabl. iz
nikh odna tsvenaĭa rab. fot. P.P. Pavlova".
*1. Folk art - Soviet Union. 2. Wood-carving - Soviet
Union. 3. Building, Wooden - Soviet Union. I. Title.*
*NYPL [Slav. Reserve 90-4456 no. 37
(Bates)]*

Boccioni . Verzotti, Giorgio. Firenze , c1989. 159
p. :   ISBN 88-7737-055-6
      NYPL [3-MCF B665 90-12871]

Boccioni, Umberto, 1882-1916.
Verzotti, Giorgio. Boccioni . Firenze , c1989.
159 p. :   ISBN 88-7737-055-6
      NYPL [3-MCF B665 90-12871]

**BOCCIONI, UMBERTO, 1882-1916 -
CATALOGUES RAISONNÉS.**
Verzotti, Giorgio. Boccioni . Firenze , c1989.
159 p. :   ISBN 88-7737-055-6
      NYPL [3-MCF B665 90-12871]

**Bochumer Schriften zur Kunstgeschichte, 0722-
2564** .
(Bd. 16) Bott, Gudrun, 1957- Figuration und
Bildformat . Frankfurt am Main , New York ,
c1990. 208 p. ;   ISBN 3-631-42715-8   DDC 759.3
20
ND588.B35 B6 1990

Bock, Ulrich. Ikonen und ostkirchliches Kultgerät
aus rheinischem Privatbesitz . Köln , 1990. 205
p. :   DDC 704.9/482 20
N8186.G3 C655 1990

Böckstiegel, Peter August, 1889-1951.
P.A. Böckstiegel / herausgegeben von
Ernst-Gerhard Güse ; mit Beiträgen von Peter
August Böckstiegel ... [et al.]. [Münster] :
Westfälisches Landesmuseum für Kunst und
Kulturgeschichte Münster, Landschaftsverband
Westfalen-Lippe, 1989. 237 p. : ill. (some col.) ;
28 cm. "Peter August Böckstiegel, Retrospektive zum
100. Geburtstag; Westfälisches Landesmuseum für
Kunst und Kulturgeschichte Münster,
Landschaftsverband Westfalen-Lippe, 5. März bis 7.
Mai 1989"--P. 1. Includes index. Includes
bibliographical references (p. 231-235).   ISBN
3-7757-0236-9   DDC 760/.092 20
*1. Böckstiegel, Peter August, 1889-1951 - Exhibitions. I.
Güse, Ernst-Gerhard. II. Title.*
N6888.B58 A4 1989
      NYPL [3-MCK B663 90-10619]

**BÖCKSTIEGEL, PETER AUGUST, 1889-1951 -
EXHIBITIONS.**
Böckstiegel, Peter August, 1889-1951. P.A.
Böckstiegel /. [Münster] , 1989. 237 p. :   ISBN
3-7757-0236-9   DDC 760/.092 20
N6888.B58 A4 1989
      NYPL [3-MCK B663 90-10619]

Bodart, Didier. Rubens, Pietro Paolo Rubens
(1577-1640) /. Roma , 1990. 319 p. :   ISBN
88-7813-269-1
      NYPL [3-MCH+ R8 90-12995]

Boddy, Trevor, 1953- The Architecture of
Douglas Cardinal /. Edmonton , 1989. 150 p. :
  ISBN 0-920897-46-0 (bound) :   DDC 720/.92/4
19
      NYPL [3-MQZ+ (Cardinal) 90-10573]

Bode, Ursula. Botero, Fernando, 1932- Botero,
der Maler . Berlin , 1991. 72 p. :   ISBN
3-87972-071-1
      NYPL [3-MCZ+ B74 91-7449]

Boderne i Næstved / [udgivet ... ved Kurt
Rosenkrans Høyer]. [Næstved] : Næstved
kommune [Copenhagen] : Miljøministeriet,
Planstyrelsen, 1988. 111 p. : ill. (some col.) ; 30
cm. Includes bibliographical references.   ISBN
87-05-03735-60
*1. Architecture - Denmark - Næstved - Conservation
and restoration. 2. Næstved (Denmark) - Buildings,
structures, etc. I. Høyer, Kurt Rosenkrans. II. Næstved
kommune (Denmark). III. Denmark. Planstyrelsen.*
NA9053.C6 B63 1988

BODON, ALEXANDER.
Kloos, Maarten. Alexander Bodon /.
Rotterdam , 1990. xv, [128] p. :   ISBN
90-6450-087-8
      NYPL [3-MQZ (Bodon) 91-4491]

BODY, HUMAN.
Herzog, Karl. Die Gestalt des Menschen in der
Kunst und im Spiegel der Wissenschaft /.
Darmstadt , c1990. xii, 234 p. :   ISBN
3-534-11010-2   DDC 704.9/421 20
N7572 .H47 1990

Boeckl, Matthias. Wiener Diwan . Klagenfurt ,
c1989. 219 p. :   ISBN 3-85415-069-5 :
N6488.A9 V6 1989
      NYPL [3-MAL+ 91-5876]

Boehm, Gottfried, 1942- Klee, Paul, 1879-1940.
Paul Klee . Essen , 1989. 163 p. :
      NYPL [3-MCZ+ K63 90-12860]

Boehme, Sarah E. Rendezvous to roundup : the
first 100 years of art in Wyoming / by Sarah E.
Boehme. Cody, Wyo. : Buffalo Bill Historical
Center, c1990. vi, 49 p. : ill. ; 26 cm.   ISBN
0-931618-30-4
1. Wyoming in art - Exhibitions. I. Title.
      NYPL [3-MAMY 90-13300]

Böhmer, Gunter, 1911-
Gespräch : Zeichnungen / Gunter Böhmer.
[Memmingen] : Edition C. Visel, 1989. 1 v.
(unpaged) : ill. ; 32 cm. Limited ed. of 500 copies.
Library's copy is no. 123.   ISBN 3-922406-43-2
1. Böhmer, Gunter, 1911-. I. Title.
      NYPL [3-MCK+ B671 91-5538]

Gunter Böhmer : die Stiftung Gunter Böhmer
in der Städtischen Galerie Albstadt /
[herausgegeben von Alfred Hagenlocher].
Albstadt : Städtische Galerie Albstadt, 1980.
220 p. : ill. (some col.) ; 24 cm.

(Veröffentlichungen der Städtischen Galerie Albstadt.
21) Catalog of an exhibition held Dec. 7, 1980-Feb. 15,
1981. Includes bibliographical references.
*1. Böhmer, Gunter, 1911- - Exhibitions. 2. Städtische
Galerie Albstadt - Exhibitions. I. Hagenlocher, Alfred.
II. Städtische Galerie Albstadt.*
      NYPL [3-MCK B671 91-1151]

BÖHMER, GUNTER, 1911-
Böhmer, Gunter, 1911- Gespräch .
[Memmingen] , 1989. 1 v. (unpaged) :   ISBN
3-922406-43-2
      NYPL [3-MCK+ B671 91-5538]

Böhmisches Glas 1880-1940. Lötz . München ,
c1989. 2 v. :   ISBN 3-7913-0984-6 (Bd.1)
      NYPL [3-MPW+ 90-13666]

Boerderijen van het Noordererf /. Molen, S. J.
van der. Zutphen , c1979. 159 p. :   ISBN
90-6011-065-X :
NA8206.N4 M597   *NYPL [3-MRGF 81-908]*

Boerenbond belge. see **Belgische Boerenbond.**

Het boerenhuis in Nederland /. Post, Kees.
S'Gravenhage , c1975. 119 p. :   ISBN
90-239-2895-4   *NYPL [3-MRGF 90-5859]*

Boestin-Stengel, Albert. Zeichnungen des 16. bis
18. Jahrhunderts . [Stuttgart , 1989?] 207 p. :
IN PROCESS (ONLINE)
      NYPL [3-MBH 90-12017]

Bogart, Bram, 1921-
Paquet, Marcel. Bram Bogart /. Paris [1990]
335 p. :   ISBN 2-7291-0586-7   DDC 709/.2 20
N6953.B636 A4 1990

BOGART, BRAM, 1921- - CATALOGS.
Paquet, Marcel. Bram Bogart /. Paris [1990]
335 p. :   ISBN 2-7291-0586-7   DDC 709/.2 20
N6953.B636 A4 1990

Bogdanowitsch, Cheryl, 1945- Southern
exposure . New York, NY , c1985. 55 p. :
  ISBN 0-932075-02-9 (pbk.)   DDC
709/.75/07401471 19
N6520 .S67 1985
      NYPL [3-MAMT 90-12368]

Bogen om Bellis . Boberg, Jørgen. København
Valby , c1990. 71 p. :   ISBN 87-418-5903-0
ND723.B59 A4 1990

Boggess, Bill. Identifying American brillant cut
glass / Bill and Louise Boggess. Rev. & enl. ed.
West Chester, Pa. : Schiffer, c1991. x, 283 p. :
ill. (some col.) ; 23 cm. Includes bibliographical
references (p. 261-264) and index.   ISBN
0-88740-296-8   DDC 748.2913/075 20
*1. Cut glass - United States - History. I. Boggess,
Louise. II. Title.*
NK5203 .B64 1991

Boggess, Louise. Boggess, Bill. Identifying
American brillant cut glass /. West Chester,
Pa. , c1991. x, 283 p. :   ISBN 0-88740-296-8
  DDC 748.2913/075 20
NK5203 .B64 1991

Boggs, Jean Sutherland. Degas, Edgar,
1834-1917. Degas . New York , Ottawa , 1988.
640 p. :   ISBN 0-87099-519-7   DDC 709.2 19
N6853.D33 A4 1988
      NYPL [3-MCO+ D31 90-12588]

Boglár, Lajos. Tribal art in Africa and Oceania :
exhibition of the Ethnographical Museum in the
Museum of Fine Arts = Afrika és Óceánia
törzsi müvészete : a Néprajzi Múzeum kiállítása
a Szépmüvészeti Múzeumban / [catalogue
composed by Lajos Boglár and Csaba Ecsedy].
[Budapest] : Népüvelési Propaganda Iroda,
1971. 8, 8 p., 8, 8 p. of plates : ill. ; 21 cm.
Hungarian and English. Parts devoted to Africa and
Oceania, each with general t.p., inverted with respect to
one another. Includes bibliographies.
*1. Art, African - Exhibitions. 2. Art, Oceanian -
Exhibitions. 3. Art, Primitive - Exhibitions. I. Ecsedy,
Csaba. II. Néprajzi Múzeum (Hungary). III.
Szépmüvészeti Múzeum (Hungary). IV. Title. V. Title:
Afrika és Óceánia törzsi müvészete.*
enghun   *NYPL [3-MADF 90-5887]*

Bogle, James. Artists in Snowdonia / James
Bogle. Talybont : Y Lolfa, 1990. 84 p. : col.
ill. ; 15 x 21 cm.   ISBN 0-86243-222-7 (pbk.)
*1. Landscape painting - Wales - Gwynedd. 2.
Snowdonia (Wales) - Description and travel - Views. I.
Title.*   *NYPL [3-MCT 91-6967]*

Bogle, Michael. Modern Australian furniture :
profiles of contemporary designer-makers /
Michael Bogle and Peta Landman. Roseville,

NSW, Australia : Craftsman House, 1989. 144 p. : col. ill. ; 31 cm. Includes index. ISBN 0-947131-26-4 DDC 749.2994/09048 20
1. Furniture - Australia - History - 20th century. 2. Furniture designers - Australia - Biography. 3. Cabinetmakers - Australia - Biography. I. Landman, Peta. II. Title.
NK2689 .B64 1989
           NYPL [3-MOF+ 90-8166]

Bognár, Botond, 1944- The new Japanese architecture / Botond Bognár ; introduction by John Morris Dixon ; essays by Hajime Yatsuka and Lynne Breslin. New York : Rizzoli, 1990. 222 p. : ill. (some col.) ; 29 cm. Includes bibliographical references. ISBN 0-8478-1225-1 DDC 720/.952/09045 20
1. Architecture, Modern - 20th century - Japan. 2. Architecture - Japan. I. Title.
NA1555 .B54 1990
           NYPL [3-MQWS 91-4685]

BOGOTÁ (COLOMBIA) IN ART - CATALOGS.
Núñez Borda, Luis, 1872-1970. L. Núñez Borda, el pintor de Bogotá /. [Bogotá, Colombia?] 1988 (Bogotá, Colombia : Litográficos de Escala) 116 p. : ISBN 958-9082-41-6 DDC 759.9861 20
ND379.N85 A4 1988

BOGOTÁ (COLOMBIA) - POLITICS AND GOVERNMENT - CARICATURES AND CARTOONS - EXHIBITIONS.
Bogotá en caricatura . [Bogotá] [1988] 235 p. : DDC 986.1/48 20
F2291.B62 B64 1988
           NYPL [3-MDY+ 91-6190]

BOGOTÁ (COLOMBIA) - SOCIAL CONDITIONS - CARICATURES AND CARTOONS - EXHIBITIONS.
Bogotá en caricatura . [Bogotá] [1988] 235 p. : DDC 986.1/48 20
F2291.B62 B64 1988
           NYPL [3-MDY+ 91-6190]

BOGOTÁ (COLOMBIA) - SOCIAL LIFE AND CUSTOMS - CARICATURES AND CARTOONS - EXHIBITIONS.
Bogotá en caricatura . [Bogotá] [1988] 235 p. : DDC 986.1/48 20
F2291.B62 B64 1988
           NYPL [3-MDY+ 91-6190]

Bogotá en caricatura : Biblioteca Luis-Angel Arango, Bogotá, agosto-octubre 1988. [Bogotá] : Banco de la República, [1988] 235 p. : ill. (some col.) ; 30 cm. (Historia de la caricatura en Colombia . 5) Catalog of an exhibition. Includes bibliographical references. DDC 986.1/48 20
1. Colombian wit and humor, Pictorial - Exhibitions. 2. Bogotá (Colombia) - Social life and customs - Caricatures and cartoons - Exhibitions. 3. Bogotá (Colombia) - Politics and government - Caricatures and cartoons - Exhibitions. 4. Bogotá (Colombia) - Social conditions - Caricatures and cartoons - Exhibitions. I. Banco de la República (Colombia). II. Biblioteca Luis-Angel Arango. III. Series.
F2291.B62 B64 1988
           NYPL [3-MDY+ 91-6190]

Bohe, Walter Meyer- . see **Meyer-Bohe, Walter.**

BOHEMIAN ART. see ART, CZECH.

BOHEMIAN SCHOOL OF ART - EXHIBITIONS.
Gotik . Wien [1990] 141 p. :
           NYPL [3-MAM 90-11533]

Bohigas, Oriol. Barcelona, city and architecture, 1980-1992 / Oriol Bohigas, Peter Buchanan, Vittorio Magnago Lampugnani. New York : Rizzoli, 1991. 239 p. : ill. (some col.) ; cm. ISBN 0-8478-1354-1 : DDC 720/.946/7209048 20
1. Architecture, Modern - 20th century - Spain - Barcelona. 2. Architecture - Spain - Barcelona. 3. Barcelona (Spain) - Buildings, structures, etc. I. Buchanan, Peter. II. Magnano Lampugnani, Vittorio, 1951-. III. Title.
NA1311.B3 B64 1991

Böhler, Hans, 1884-1961.
Breicha, Otto. Hans Böhler, Gemälde und Graphik /. Salzburg , c1981. 119 p. of plates : ISBN 3-85349-084-0 : DDC 741.9436 19
N6811.5.B64 A4 1981
           NYPL [3-MCK B68 91-5395]

BÖHLER, HANS, 1884-1961 - CATALOGS.
Breicha, Otto. Hans Böhler, Gemälde und

Graphik /. Salzburg , c1981. 119 p. of plates : ISBN 3-85349-084-0 : DDC 741.9436 19
N6811.5.B64 A4 1981
           NYPL [3-MCK B68 91-5395]

Bohm-Duchen, Monica.
Thomas Lowinsky / Monica Bohm-Duchen. London : Tate Gallery, 1990. 72 p. : ill. (some col.) ; 27 cm. Catalogue of an exhibition held at the Tate Gallery, Feb. 28-April 16, 1990, and then toured by the South Bank Centre to The Mead Gallery Arts Centre, Coventry, April 23-June 2, 1990, and Graves Art Gallery, Sheffield, June 9-July 22, 1990. Includes bibliographical references (p. 71). ISBN 1-85437-040-5
1. Lowinsky, Thomas, 1892-1974 - Exhibitions. I. Tate Gallery. II. South Bank Centre. III. Title.
           NYPL [3-MCV L842 90-10812]

Thomas Lowinsky / Monica Bohm-Duchen. London : Tate Gallery, c1990. 72 p. : ill. (some col.) ; 27 cm. Catalogue of an exhibition. Includes bibliographical references (p. 71). ISBN 1-85437-040-5 DDC 760/.092 20
1. Lowinsky, Thomas - Exhibitions. I. Lowinsky, Thomas. II. Tate Gallery. III. Title.
N6797.L67 A4 1990

BÖHMER, GUNTER, 1911- - EXHIBITIONS.
Böhmer, Gunter, 1911- Gunter Böhmer . Albstadt , 1980. 220 p. :
           NYPL [3-MCK B671 91-1151]

Böhmer, Sylvia. Sammlung Teo Matthéy, Aachen . [Aachen] , c1989. 109 p.
           NYPL [3-MAX (Matthéy) 91-3454]

Böhringer, Volker, 1912-1961.
Röttger, Friedhelm. Volker Böhringer /. Stuttgart , c1987. 200 p. : ISBN 3-608-76244-2 DDC 759.3 19
N6888.B597 R6 1987
           NYPL [3-MCK B6712 88-1458]

BÖHRINGER, VOLKER, 1912-1961.
Röttger, Friedhelm. Volker Böhringer /. Stuttgart , c1987. 200 p. : ISBN 3-608-76244-2 DDC 759.3 19
N6888.B597 R6 1987
           NYPL [3-MCK B6712 88-1458]

BÖHRINGER, VOLKER, 1912-1961 - CATALOGS.
Röttger, Friedhelm. Volker Böhringer /. Stuttgart , c1987. 200 p. : ISBN 3-608-76244-2 DDC 759.3 19
N6888.B597 R6 1987
           NYPL [3-MCK B6712 88-1458]

Bohunovsky, Irmgard. Zaunschirm, Thomas, 1943- Fremdbild Heimat . Wien , c1989. 101 p. : ISBN 3-900606-12-9
N6809.C3 Z36 1989

Boichard, Jean. Prévot, Victor. Géopolitique transparente . [Paris] , 1987. 1 atlas (255 p.) : ISBN 2-210-98004-6
           NYPL [Map Div. 91-6046]

Boime, Albert.
Art in an age of Bonapartism, 1800-1815 / Albert Boime. Chicago : University of Chicago Press, 1990. xxvii, 706 p. : ill. ; 24 cm. (A Social history of modern art . v. 2) Includes bibliographical references (p. 657-688) and index. ISBN 0-226-06335-6 (alk. paper) : DDC 709/.03/4 20
1. Napoleon I, Emperor of the French, 1769-1821 - Influence. 2. Art, Modern - 19th century - Europe. 3. Romanticism in art - Europe. 4. Art and society - Europe. I. Series: Boime, Albert. Social history of modern art , v. 2. II. Title.
N6757 .B56 1990   **NYPL [3-MAM 91-5522]**

The magisterial gaze : manifest destiny and the American landscape painting, c. 1830-1865 / by Albert Boime. Washington, D.C. : Smithsonian Institution, 1991. p. cm. (New directions) Includes bibliographical references and index. ISBN 1-560-98095-8 DDC 758/.1/097309034 20
1. Landscape painting, American. 2. Landscape painting - 19th century - United States. 3. Messianism, Political - United States - Influence. I. Series: New directions (Smithsonian Institution). II. Title.
ND1351.5 .B65 1991

Social history of modern art .
(v. 2) Boime, Albert. Art in an age of Bonapartism, 1800-1815 /. Chicago , 1990. xxvii, 706 p. : ISBN 0-226-06335-6 (alk. paper) : DDC 709/.03/4 20
N6757 .B56 1990   **NYPL [3-MAM 91-5522]**

Bois, Yve-Alain. Painting as model / Yve-Alain Bois. Cambridge, Mass. : MIT Press, c1990.

xxx, 327 p. : ill. ; 24 cm. "An October book." Includes bibliographical references and index. ISBN 0-262-02306-7 DDC 750/.1 20
I. Title.
ND1140 .B59 1990   **NYPL [3-MBK 91-5521]**

Boise Art Museum.
Harthorn, Sandy, 1945- One hundred years of Idaho art, 1850-1950 . Boise, ID , c1990. 134 p. : DDC 709/.796/07479628 20
N6530.I2 H37 1990
           NYPL [3-MAMT 90-11110]

L.A. times . Boise, Idaho , c1991. p. cm. DDC 709/.794/9407479628 20
N6535.L6 L188 1991

Yard art . Boise, Idaho , c1991. 1 v. (unpaged) : DDC 745/.0979/07479628 20
NK824 .Y37 1991

Boisléve, Jacques, 1943- Les vitraux vendéens et les maîtres verriers angevins / texte et photos de Jacques Boisléve ; préface du cardinal Paul Poupard. [Maulevrier, France] : Herault, c1987. 110 p. : ill. (some col.) ; 23 cm. DDC 748.594/18 19
1. Glass painting and staining - France - Angers - History - 19th century. 2. Glass painting and staining - France - Angers - History - 20th century. 3. Vendean War, 1793-1800, in art. I. Title.
NK5349.A54 B65 1987
           NYPL [3-MRY 90-12359]

Boisselier, Jean.
[Tendances de l'art khmèr. English]
Trends in Khmer art / Jean Boisselier ; edited by Natasha Eilenberg ; translated by Natasha Eilenberg and Melvin Elliott. Ithaca, N.Y. : Southeast Asia Program, Cornell University, 1989. 118 p. : ill. ; 26 cm. (Studies on Southeast Asia) Rev. translation of: Tendances de l'art khmèr. Includes bibliographical references (p. [117]-118). ISBN 0-87727-705-2 DDC 730/.9596/074596 20
1. Musee national du Cambodge - Catalogs. 2. Sculpture, Khmer - Catalogs. 3. Sculpture - Cambodia - Phnom Penh - Catalogs. I. Eilenberg, Natasha. II. Title. III. Series.
NB1015 .B6213 1989
           NYPL [3-MAF 91-3339]

Boissieu, Jean.
Latour, Marielle. Marseille et les peintres /. [Paris?] , 1990. 127 p. : ISBN 2-86276-207-5
           NYPL [3-MC+ 91-6764]

Latour, Marielle. Marseille et les peintres /. [Marseille] , c1990. 127 p. : ISBN 2-86276-207-5 :
ND551.M37 L38 1990

Bojani, Gian Carlo. Ceramica toscana dal medioevo al XVIII secolo /. Monte S. Savino [1990] 472 p. : DDC 738/.0945/50744559 20
NK4104.T9 C4 1990

Bok, Marten Jan. Schwartz, Gary, 1940- Pieter Saenredam . London , 1990. 356 p. : ISBN 0-500-23586-4
           NYPL [3-MCH S12 90-11511]

Böker, Hans Josef. Die Marktpfarrkirche St. Lamberti zu Münster : die Bau- und Restaurierungsgeschichte einer spätgotischen Stadtkirche / Hans Josef Böker. Bonn : R. Habelt, 1989. 229 p. : ill. ; 31 cm. (Denkmalpflege und Forschung in Westfalen . Bd. 18) Originally presented as the author's Habilitationsschrift, Universität Hannover, 1987. Includes bibliographical references (p. 171-173). ISBN 3-7749-2382-5
1. Lambertikirche (Münster in Westfalen, Germany). 2. Architecture, Gothic - Germany - Münster in Westfalen. 3. Church architecture - Germany - Münster in Westfalen. 4. Münster in Westfalen (Germany) - Buildings, structures, etc. I. Title. II. Title: Marktpfarrkirche Sankt Lamberti zu Münster. III. Series.
NA5586.M853 B65 1989

Bol, Peter. Polyklet . Mainz am Rhein , c1990. 678 p., 8 p. of plates : ISBN 3-8053-1175-3 DDC 730/.92 20
NB101 .P65 1990

Bold romantic gardens . Oehme, Wolfgang, 1930- Reston, Va. , 1990. 310 p. : ISBN 0-87491-950-9 : DDC 712/.0973 20
SB473 .O44 1990   **NYPL [3-MSK+ 91-4459]**

Boles, Martha. The golden relationship : art, math & nature / by Martha Boles & Rochelle Newman ; design & illustrations by Sylvia T.

Burnside.Rev. ed. Bradford, Mass. :
Pythagorean Press, c1990- v. <1 > : ill. ; 28
cm. Includes bibliographical references (bk. 1, p.
208-209) and index. CONTENTS. - bk. 1. Universal
patterns. ISBN 0-9614504-3-6 (bk. 1) DDC 701 20
*1. Art - Mathematics. 2. Nature (Aesthetics). 3.
Composition (Art). I. Newman, Rochelle. II. Title.*
N72.M3 B65 1990

Bolger, Doreen. Metropolitan Museum of Art
(New York, N.Y.) American pastels in the
Metropolitan Museum of Art /. New York ,
c1989. x, 247 p. : ISBN 0-87099-547-2 DDC
741.973/074/7471 20
NC885 .M48 1989
　　　　　NYPL [3-MAVZ (New York) 89-27019]

Bolger, Doreen, 1949-
American art around 1900 . Washington ,
Hanover [N.H.] , 1990. 136 p. : ISBN
0-89468-143-5 *NYPL [3-MAMT 91-7570]*

William M. Harnett /. Fort Worth : New
York : p. cm. ISBN 0-8109-3410-8 DDC 759.13
20
ND237.H315 A4 1992

Bollati, Renato. L'organismo architettonico :
metodo grafico di lettura / Renato Bollati,
Sergio Bollati, Giuseppe Lonetti ; contributi di
Salvatore Contrafatto, Roberto Maccarrone,
Salvatore Rapisarda. Firenze : Alinea, c1990.
173 p. : ill., plans ; 22 cm. (Studi e documenti di
architettura. Nuova serie . n. 18 (nov. 1990)) Includes
bibliographical references.
*I. Lonetti, Giuseppe. II. Series: Studi e documenti di
architettura. Nuova serie , n. 18. III. Title.*
　　　　NYPL [MGA 74-741 nuova ser., n.18]

BOLOGNA (ITALY) - CORRESPONDENCE.
Gli Scritti dei Carracci . Bologna , 1990. 202
p. ; ISBN 88-7779-139-X
　　　　　　NYPL [3-MCF C32 91-5526]

Bologna (Italy). Galleria d'arte moderna.
Morandi, Giorgio, 1890-1964. Giorgio Morandi,
1890-1990 /. Milano , c1990. 419 p. : ISBN
88-435-3185-9
　　　　NYPL [3-MCF M82 90-12991]

Bolon, Carol R. Forms of the Goddess Lajjā
Gaurī in Indian art / Carol Radcliffe Bolon.
University Park, PA : Published for College Art
Association by Pennsylvania State University
Press, 1991. p. cm. (Monographs on the fine arts .
v. 49) Includes bibliographical references and index.
ISBN 0-271-00761-3 DDC 730/.954 20
*1. Lajjā Gaurī (Hindu deity) - Art. 2. Sculpture, Indic.
I. Series: Monographs on the fine arts , 49. II. Title.*
NB1912.L34 .B65 1991

BOLSHEVISM. see COMMUNISM.

**Bolton Eng. (Lancashire). Museum and Art
Gallery. see Bolton Museum and Art
Gallery.**

Bolton Museum and Art Gallery. Folly & vice .
London , c1989. 63 p. : ISBN 1-85332-053-6
DDC 741.5/94/07442 20
NC1312.G7 B664 1989

**BOLTON, WILLIAM JAY, 1816?-1884 -
CRITICISM AND INTERPRETATION.**
Clark, Willene B. The stained glass art of
William Jay Bolton /. Syracuse, N.Y. , 1992. p.
cm. ISBN 0-8156-2553-7 DDC 748.5913 20
NK5398.B65 C53 1992

Bomb : interviews / edited by Betsy Sussler. San
Francisco : City Lights Books, 1992. p. cm.
ISBN 0-87286-261-5 : DDC 700/.9/04 20
*1. Artists - Interviews. 2. Arts, Modern - 20th century.
3. Artists - United States - Interviews. 4. Arts,
Modern - 20th century - United States. 5. Bomb (New
York, N.Y.). I. Sussler, Betsy. II. Bomb (New York,
N.Y.).*
NX458 .B66 1992

Bomb (New York, N.Y.) Bomb . San Francisco ,
1992. p. cm. ISBN 0-87286-261-5 : DDC
700/.9/04 20
NX458 .B66 1992

BOMB (NEW YORK, N.Y.)
Bomb . San Francisco , 1992. p. cm. ISBN
0-87286-261-5 : DDC 700/.9/04 20
NX458 .B66 1992

Bomchil, Sara. El mueble colonial de las
Américas y su circunstancia histórica / Sara
Bomchil, Virginia Carreño. Buenos Aires :
Editorial Sudamericana, c1987. 919 p., [24] p.
of plates : ill. ; 23 cm. Bibliography: p. 899-908.
ISBN 950-0-70386-6 DDC 749.297 19

*1. Furniture - South America - History. 2. Furniture -
North America - History. I. Carreño, Virginia. II. Title.*
NK2401.A1 B66 1987
　　　　　　　　NYPL [3-MOF 91-2686]

Bomford, David.
Impressionism /. London , c1990. 227 p. :
ISBN 0-300-05035-6 (cased) : DDC 759.054074
20
ND192.I4　　　　*NYPL [3-MCN 91-5511]*

Italian painting before 1400 . [London] , c19. x,
225 p. : ISBN 0-947645-67-5 DDC
759.5/09/02207442132 20
ND613 .I87 1989

Italian painting before 1400 . London , c1989.
x, 225 p. : ISBN 0-947645-67-5 (pbk) DDC
759.5 19　　　*NYPL [3-MCE 91-3327]*

Bon, Caterina. Il Collegio del Cambio / di
Caterina Bon Valsassina. Roma : F.lli Palombi,
1987. 61 p., [8] p. of plates : ill. (some col.),
facsim., map ; 24 cm. (Itinerari d'arte e di cultura.
Musei) Bibliography: p. 60-61.
1. Collegio del cambio (Museum). I. Title. II. Series.
　　　NYPL [3-MAVZ (Perugia) 90-12513]

Bona Castellotti, Marco. Scritti in onore di
Giuliano Briganti. Milano , c1990. 344 p., [4]
leaves of plates : ISBN 88-304-0921-9
　　　　　　　NYPL [3-MAS 91-5232]

Bonafoux, Pascal. Van Gogh / Pascal Bonafoux ;
translated from the French by Alexandra
Campbell. London : Barrie & Jenkins, 1990.
160 p. : ill. (some col.) ; 32 cm. (Profiles in art)
Includes index. Includes bibliographical references (p.
160). ISBN 0-7126-3828-8 : DDC 759.9492 19
*1. Painters - Netherlands - Biography. I. Title. II.
Series.*
ND653.G7 *NYPL [3-MCH+ G61 90-11080]*

**Bonaparte, Napoleon. see Napoléon I, Emperor
of the French, 1769-1821.**

**BOND, ALAN - ART COLLECTIONS -
EXHIBITIONS.**
Irises and five masterpieces. [Australia] [1989]
1 v. (unpaged) : ISBN 0-9598384-1-4
　　　　　　NYPL [MAX (Bond) 91-6719]

Bond, Maurice Francis. Blackburne, Harry
William, 1878- The romance of St George's
Chapel, Windsor Castle /. Windsor , 1958. vi,
90 p., [49] p. of plates :
NA5471.W73 B6 1958
　　　　　　　NYPL [3-MRBH 83-2146]

Bondanella, Julia Conaway. Vasari, Giorgio,
1511-1574. [Vite de' più eccellenti architetti,
pittori et scultori italiani. English. Selections.]
The lives of the artists /. Oxford , New York ,
1991. p. cm. ISBN 0-19-281754-X : DDC
709/.2/245 B 20
N6922 .V2213 1991

Bondanella, Peter E., 1943- Vasari, Giorgio,
1511-1574. [Vite de' più eccellenti architetti,
pittori et scultori italiani. English. Selections.]
The lives of the artists /. Oxford , New York ,
1991. p. cm. ISBN 0-19-281754-X : DDC
709/.2/245 B 20
N6922 .V2213 1991

BONE CARVING.
Krzyszkowska, O. (Olga) Ivory and related
materials . London , 1990. xv, 109 p., [70] p. of
plates : ISBN 0-900587-62-8
　　　　　　NYPL [3-MNW 91-7005]

Bonera, Franco.
[Maiale. English]
Pigs : art, legend, history / Franco Bonera ;
[English translation by John Gilbert].1st U. S.
ed. Boston : Little, Brown, 1991. p. cm. (The
Bulfinch library of collectibles) Translation of: Il
maiale. ISBN 0-8212-1873-5 DDC 704.9/432 20
*1. Swine in art. 2. Swine - Collectibles. 3. Swine -
Legends. 4. Swine - History. I. Title. II. Series.*
N7668.S95 M3513 1991

**Bonet, Antonio [i.e. Antonio Bonet Correa] see
Bonet Correa, Antonio.**

Bonet Correa, Antonio.
Bozal Fernández, Valeriano. Arte y ciudad en
Galicia, siglo XIX /. Santiago de Compostela
[1990] 133 p. : ISBN 84-505-9217-8 DDC
709/.46/109034 20
N72.S6 B6 1990

Fiesta, poder y arquitectura : aproximaciones al
barroco español / Antonio Bonet Correa.
Madrid, España : Akal, c1990. 182 p. : ill. ; 24

cm. (Arte y estética . 22) Includes bibliographical
references and index. ISBN 84-7600-446-6 DDC
720/.946/09033 20
*1. Architecture, Baroque - Spain. 2. Architecture -
Spain. I. Title. II. Series.*
NA1306 .B57 1990

Bonfand, Alain. Rose, Barbara. Jean-Pierre
Pincemin /. [Aubusson] [Paris] [1986] 79 p. :
ISBN 2-7291-0207-4 :
MLCM 89/01361 (N)
　　　　　　　NYPL [3-MCO P643 90-12613]

Bonfanti, Arturo, 1905- Bonfanti, 1905-1978 :
saggio storico critico / di Willy Rotzler ; e
contributi bibliografici. Milano : Alfieri, [1979]
237 p. : ill. ; 29 cm. English, German, French, or
Italian.
1. Bonfanti, Arturo, 1905-. I. Rotzler, Willy.
N6923.B5933 A4 1979
　　　　　　NYPL [3-MCF B703 90-5870]

BONFANTI, ARTURO, 1905-
Bonfanti, Arturo, 1905- Bonfanti, 1905-1978 .
Milano [1979] 237 p. :
N6923.B5933 A4 1979
　　　　　　NYPL [3-MCF B703 90-5870]

Bonfiglioli, Sandra, 1940- L'architettura del
tempo : la città multimediale / Sandra
Bonfiglioli.1. ed. Napoli : Liguori, 1990. 410
p. : ill. ; 22 cm. (Strumenti) Includes bibliographical
references (p. [383]-404) and index. ISBN
88-20-71912-6 : DDC 720/.1 20
*1. Architecture - Philosophy. 2. Architecture and
cosmology. I. Title.*
NA2500 .B625 1990

Bongard, Willi. Kunst und Kommerz; zwischen
Passion und Spekulation. [Oldenburg] G.
Stalling [c1967] 271 p. plates. 24 cm.
*1. Art and society - United States. 2. Art, Modern -
20th century - United States. 3. Art - United States -
Economic aspects. I. Title.*
　　　　　　　NYPL [3-MAMT 90-6286]

Bonheur de peindre. Cruysmans, Philippe, 1925-
Lise Brachet, ou, Le bonheur de peindre /.
Bruxelles [1985] 127 p. : ISBN 2-87103-014-6
DDC 759.9493 20
ND673.B5438 A35 1985

Bonhommes de neige /. Samivel, 1907- [Paris] ,
1987. 95 p. : ISBN 2-905292-13-X
　　　NYPL [3-MEM+ (Samivel) 90-2327]

Boni, Paolo, 1926-
Boni - Comune di Ferrara, Galleria civica d'arte
moderna, Palazzo dei Diamanti, Centro attività
visive, 10 settembre-10 ottobre 1977. Roma :
Edizione della Stamperia Il Cigno, [1977] [70]
p. : ill. (some col.) ; 21 cm. Text in English,
French, or Italian. Bibliography: p. [65]-[69]
*1. Boni, Paolo, 1926- - Exhibitions. I. Galleria civica
d'arte moderna, Ferrara. II. Centro attività visive.*
ND623.B5688 A4 1977
　　　　　　NYPL [3-MCF B704 81-336]

Paolo Boni, peintures, reliefs sur métaux,
sculptures et gravures : [exposition] juillet-août
1965. Antibes : Musée Grimaldi, 1965. [20] p. :
ill. (1 col.) ; 21 cm.
*1. Boni, Paolo, 1926- - Exhibitions. I. Musée Picasso
(Antibes, France). II. Title.*
　　　　　　NYPL [3-MCF B704 90-6795]

BONI, PAOLO, 1926- - EXHIBITIONS.
Boni, Paolo, 1926- Boni . Roma [1977] [70]
p. :
ND623.B5688 A4 1977
　　　　　　NYPL [3-MCF B704 81-336]

Boni, Paolo, 1926- Paolo Boni, peintures, reliefs
sur métaux, sculptures et gravures . Antibes ,
1965. [20] p. :
　　　　　　NYPL [3-MCF B704 90-6795]

Boni, Zé de. Paisagem mágica : fotografias da
Chapada Diamantina / Zé de Boni ; texto,
Walfrido Moraes. [São Paulo] : Empresa das
Artes, [1990?] [128] p. : ill. (some col.) ; 27 x
30 cm.
*1. Chapada Diamantina (Brazil) - Description and
travel - Views. I. Title.*
　　　　　　NYPL [MFX (Boni) 91-3410]

Bonito Fanelli, Rosalia. Il Piviale duecentesco di
Ascoli Piceno . Firenze , 1991. 180 p. : ISBN
88-7737-143-9 :
NK9310 .P58 1991

Bonito Oliva, Achille. Plessi, Fabrizio, 1940-
Plessi /. Treviso , c1990. 175 p. : ISBN

88-85066-70-4   DDC 700/.92 20
N6923.P55 A4 1990
    NYPL [3-MGO+ (Plessi) 91-5437]

Bönitz, Helmut, 1914-
Helmut Bönitz / [Organisation und Realisation,
Reinhard Irmscher ; Katalogredaktion und
Ausstellungsorganisation, O. Ahlers, Helmut
Bönitz, Reinhard Irmscher]. [Göttingen] :
Städtisches Museum Göttingen : Kulturamt der
Stadt Göttingen, c1990. 119 p. : ill. (chiefly
col.) ; 22 cm. Catalog of an exhibition at the
Städtisches Museum Göttingen, organized by the
Kulturamt. Spine title: Arbeiten von 1986 bis 1990.
*1. Bönitz, Helmut, 1914- - Exhibitions. I. Irmscher,
Reinhard. II. Ahlers, O. III. Städtisches Museum
Göttingen. IV. Kulturamt der Stadt Göttingen. V. Title.
VI. Title: Arbeiten von 1986 bis 1990.*
N6888.B6165 A4 1990

BÖNITZ, HELMUT, 1914- - EXHIBITIONS.
Bönitz, Helmut, 1914- Helmut Bönitz /.
[Göttingen] , c1990. 119 p. :
N6888.B6165 A4 1990

Bonn. Galerie Hennemann. see **Galerie
Hennemann.**

Bonn. Kunstverein. see **Bonner Kunstverein.**

Bonn. Provinzialmuseum. see **Bonn. Rheinisches
Landesmuseum.**

BONN. RHEINISCHES LANDESMUSEUM.
Rheinisches Landesmuseum Bonn .
Braunschweig , 1977. 128 p. :
N2255.R5 R46
        NYPL [MAVZ (Bonn) 81-636]

Bonn. Städtisches Kunstmuseum. see **Städtisches
Kunstmuseum Bonn.**

Bonnard, Olivier. Et la lumière fut! :
photographies d'Olivier Bonnard / préface de
Jacques Neirynck.1re éd. Lausanne, Suisse :
Presses polytechniques romandes, c1989. 1 v.
(unpaged) : ill. ; 31 cm. ISBN 2-88074-166-1
1. Bonnard, Olivier. I. Title.
        NYPL [MFX+ (Bonnard) 91-5994]

BONNARD, OLIVIER.
Bonnard, Olivier. Et la lumière fut! . Lausanne,
Suisse , c1989. 1 v. (unpaged) : ISBN
2-88074-166-1
        NYPL [MFX+ (Bonnard) 91-5994]

Bonnard, Pierre, 1867-1947.
An exhibition of works by Pierre Bonnard :
15th June-29th July, 1978. London : Lefevre
Gallery, [1978] 30 p. : col. ill. ; 28 cm.
1. Bonnard, Pierre, 1867-1947 - Exhibitions. I. Title.
        NYPL [3-MCO B716 90-6128]

Heilbrun, Françoise. Pierre Bonnard
photographe /. Paris , 1987. 148 p. : ISBN
2-904057-24-2   DDC 779/.092 20
TR647 .B647 1987
        NYPL [MFX+ (Bonnard) 91-2568]

Heilbrun, Françoise. [Pierre Bonnard
photographe. English.] Pierre Bonnard . New
York , c1988. 148 p. : ISBN 0-89381-322-2 :
        DDC 779/.092/4 19
TR647 .B64713 1988
        NYPL [MFX+ (Bonnard) 89-17895]

Pierre Bonnard, 1867-1947 : drawings,
1906-1936. Los Angeles, Calif. : Marilyn Pink,
c1979. 28 p. : ill. ; 19 x 22 cm. Exhibition held
Aug. 6-Oct. 6, 1979. "Ex-collection The Terrasse
Family"--P. 2 of cover. Price list ([1] leaf) inserted.
*1. Bonnard, Pierre, 1867-1947 - Exhibitions. 2. Terrasse
family - Art collections - Exhibitions. I. Pink, Marilyn.
II. Title.*   ***NYPL [3-MCO B716 90-5653]***

**BONNARD, PIERRE, 1867-1947 -
    EXHIBITIONS.**
Bonnard, Pierre, 1867-1947. An exhibition of
works by Pierre Bonnard . London [1978] 30
p. :   ***NYPL [3-MCO B716 90-6128]***

Bonnard, Pierre, 1867-1947. Pierre Bonnard,
1867-1947 . Los Angeles, Calif. , c1979. 28 p. :
        NYPL [3-MCO B716 90-5653]

Heilbrun, Françoise. Pierre Bonnard
photographe /. Paris , 1987. 148 p. : ISBN
2-904057-24-2   DDC 779/.092 20
TR647 .B647 1987
        NYPL [MFX+ (Bonnard) 91-2568]

Heilbrun, Françoise. [Pierre Bonnard
photographe. English.] Pierre Bonnard . New
York , c1988. 148 p. : ISBN 0-89381-322-2 :

DDC 779/.092/4 19
TR647 .B64713 1988
        NYPL [MFX+ (Bonnard) 89-17895]

Bonnemains, Jacqueline. Baudin in Australian
waters . Melbourne , 1988. 347 p. : ISBN
0-19-554787-X
        NYPL [3-MAMY+ 90-10770]

Bonnenfant, Guillemette. L'art du bois à Sanaa :
architecture domestique / Guillemette et Paul
Bonnenfant ; 411 dessins de Guillemette
Bonnenfant ; 178 photos de Paul Bonnenfant.
Aix-en-Provence : Edisud, c1987. 208 p. : ill.
(some col.) ; 31 cm. (Recherche pluridisciplinaire
sur les architectures domestiques d'Arabie . v. 1)
"Appareil critique" (p. 193-208) in pocket inside p. [3]
of cover. Includes indexes. Bibliography: p. 204-206.
    ISBN 2-85744-315-3
*1. Architectural woodwork - Yemen - Ṣanʿāʾ. 2.
Decoration and ornament, Architectural - Yemen -
Ṣanʿāʾ. 3. Architecture, Domestic - Yemen - Ṣanʿāʾ. 4.
Decoration and ornament, Islamic - Yemen - Ṣanʿāʾ. I.
Bonnenfant, Paul. II. Title. III. Series.*
NA3573.6.Y42 S254 1987
        NYPL [3-MRX+ 91-4933]

Bonnenfant, Paul. Bonnenfant, Guillemette. L'art
du bois à Sanaa . Aix-en-Provence , c1987. 208
p. : ISBN 2-85744-315-3
NA3573.6.Y42 S254 1987
        NYPL [3-MRX+ 91-4933]

Bonner Kunstverein. Sander, Ernemann F., 1925-
Ernemann F. Sander, Skulpturen und
Zeichnungen . Bonn , c1985. 76 p. :
MLCM 87/63 (N)
        NYPL [3-MGO (Sander) 90-10662]

Die Bonnerinnen : Szenarien aus Geschichte und
Zeitgenössischer Kunst / [Herausgeberinnen,
Frauen Museum, Frauen former ihre Stadt
e.V. ; Katalog, K. Eberlein...[et al.]. Bonn : Das
Museum, 1988. 333 p. : ill. (some col.) ; 31 cm.
Catalog of an exhibition.
*1. Women artists - Germany (West) - Bonn -
Exhibitions. 2. Women - Germany (West) - Bonn -
History - Exhibitions. I. Eberlein, K. II. Frauenmuseum
Bonn (Germany).*
        NYPL [3-MAMG+ 89-25284]

Bonnet, Jacqueline. Les Bronzes antiques de Paris
/. Paris , 1989. 512 p. : ISBN 2-901414-34-6
    DDC 730/.09364 20
NK7949.P2 B7 1989

Bonnet, Serge, 1924- Automne, hiver de l'homme
du fer / Serge Bonnet ; photographies de
Robert Doisneau ... [et al.]. [Nancy] : Presses
universitaires de Nancy ; [Metz] : Editions
Serpenoise, c1986. 102 p. : chiefly ill. ; 30 cm.
Includes bibliographical references.   ISBN
2-86480-255-4
*1. Iron and steel workers - France - Pictorial works. 2.
Iron miners - France - Pictorial works. I. Doisneau,
Robert. II. Title.*
HD8039.I52 F823 1986
        NYPL [MFW+ 89-20431]

Bonnici, Claude-Jeanne.
Paul Guigou : 1834-1871 / Claude-Jeanne
Bonnici ; préface de Jean-Roger Soubiran. La
Calade, Aix-en-Provence : Edisud, c1989. 235
p. : ill. (some col.) ; 33 cm. Includes bibliographical
references (p. 122-128).   ISBN 2-85744-436-2 DDC
759.4 B 20
*1. Guigou, Paul, 1834-1871. 2. Painters - France -
Biography. 3. Guigou, Paul, 1834-1871 - Catalogues
raisonnés. I. Guigou, Paul, 1834-1871. II. Title.*
ND553.G893 B66 1989

Paul Guigou, 1834-1871 / Claude-Jeanne
Bonnici ; préface de Jean-Roger Soubiran ; avec
le concours de Artemis Group et William
Beadleston, Inc. Aix-en-Provence [France] :
Edisud, c1989. 235 p. : ill. (some col.) ; 33 cm.
Bibliography: p. 122-128.   ISBN 2-85744-436-2
*1. Guigou, Paul, 1834-1871 - Catalogues raisonnés. I.
Guigou, Paul, 1834-1871. II. Title.*
        NYPL [3-MCO+ G945 91-3279]

Bonnier, Gerard, 1917-
Donation Gerard Bonnier /. Stockholm [1989]
106 p. : ISBN 91-29-59355-7
N6488.S8 S74 1989 .

**BONNIER, GERARD, 1917- - ART
    COLLECTIONS.**
Donation Gerard Bonnier . Stockholm [1989]
106 p. : ISBN 91-29-59355-7
N6488.S8 S74 1989

Bonset, I. K. pseud. see **Doesburg, Theo van,
1883-1931.**

Bony, Anne.
Goguel, Solange. René Herbst /. Paris , c1990.
363 p. : ISBN 2-903370-56-7
        NYPL [3-MLH+ 91-5789]

Les années 20 d'Anne Bony. Paris [1989] 2 v.
(1275 p.) : ISBN 2-903370-45-1 (set)   DDC
700/.9/048 20
NX457 .A55 1989

BOOK ART. see **ARTISTS' BOOKS.**

**BOOK COLLECTING - TERMINOLOGY -
    CARICATURES AND CARTOONS.**
Searle, Ronald, 1920- Slightly foxed-- but still
desirable . London , 1989. 124 p. : ISBN
0-285-62945-X
        NYPL [3-MEM + (Searle) 89-28590]

BOOK DESIGN.
Children's book illustration and design /. New
York , 1991. p. cm. ISBN 0-86636-147-2   DDC
741.6/42/09048 20
NC965 .C43 1991

BOOK DESIGN - ARMENIAN S.S.R.
Kojoyan, Hakob, 1883-1959. Hakob Kojoyan.
Erevan , 1983. 215 p. :
        NYPL [3-MCZ K784 89-27414]

BOOK DESIGN - EXHIBITIONS.
Collaborations and connections . Tempe, Ariz. ,
c1990. viii, 36 p. :   ***NYPL [MDTT 91-4768]***

**BOOK DESIGN - RUSSIAN S.F.S.R. -
    HISTORY - 19TH CENTURY.**
Chernevich, Elena, 1939- Russian graphic
design /. New York, NY , 1990. 160 p. : ISBN
1-558-59016-1   DDC 741.6/0947 20
NC998.6.R9 C47 1990
        NYPL [3-MDW+ 90-11977]

BOOK ILLUSTRATION. see **ILLUSTRATION
OF BOOKS.**

Book illustrations and title-pages /. Judson, J.
Richard (Jay Richard) Brussels , Philadelphia,
PA , 1977. 2 v. (552 p., unpaged p. of plates) :
ISBN 2-8005-0124-3
ND673.R9 C63 pt. 21 1977 NC984.5.R8

**Book illustrations from six centuries in the
Library of the Sterling & Francine Clark Art
Institute /.** Sterling and Francine Clark Art
Institute. Library. Williamstown, Mass. , 1990.
116 p. : ISBN 0-931102-29-4 (paper)   DDC
741.6/4/0747441 20
NC961.W55 S747 1990
        NYPL [MDT 91-2365]

BOOK INDUSTRIES. see **BOOK
INDUSTRIES AND TRADE.**

**BOOK INDUSTRIES AND TRADE -
    GERMANY (EAST) - LEIPZIG -
    EXHIBITIONS.**
Merkur & die Musen . [Wien] [1989] 627 p. :
ISBN 3-900926-02-6
        NYPL [3-MAMG+ 90-13617]

Book of abbeys and priories. Coppack, Glyn.
English Heritage book of abbeys and priories /.
London , 1990. 159 p., [8] p. of plates : ISBN
0-7134-6308-2 (cased) :   DDC 942 20
        NYPL [3-MRBR 91-6767]

Book of living rooms. Harling, Robert. The
House & garden book of living rooms /. New
York , 1991. p. cm. ISBN 0-86565-125-6 DDC
747.7/5 20
NK2117.L5 H37 1991

BOOK-PLATE DESIGNERS - EXHIBITIONS.
Nechwatal, Norbert. Richard Wagner im
Exlibris . Wiesbaden , c1988. 124 p. : ISBN
3-922835-11-2   ***NYPL [MDVF 90-10990]***

**BOOK PLATE DESIGNERS - UNITED
    STATES.**
American artists of the bookplate, 1970-1990 /.
Cambridge, Mass. , c1990. xi, 155 p. : ISBN
0-9627290-0-0   ***NYPL [MDVK 91-6220]***

BOOK-PLATES, AMERICAN.
American artists of the bookplate, 1970-1990 /.
Cambridge, Mass. , c1990. xi, 155 p. : ISBN
0-9627290-0-0   ***NYPL [MDVK 91-6220]***

BOOK-PLATES, ENGLISH.
Butler, W. E. Modern British bookplates /.
Cambridge [Eng.] , 1990. 58 p. :
        NYPL [MDVK 90-12776]

Book-plates, European.

BOOK-PLATES, EUROPEAN.
Severin, Mark. Engraved bookplates. Pinner,
1972. 176 p. (chiefly facsims.) ISBN
0-900002-91-3 *NYPL [MDVC 90-7007]*

BOOK-PLATES - EXHIBITIONS.
Nechwatal, Norbert. Richard Wagner im
Exlibris . Wiesbaden , c1988. 124 p. : ISBN
3-922835-11-2 *NYPL [MDVF 90-10990]*

BOOK-PLATES, GERMAN.
Zebhauser, Helmuth. Alpine Exlibris .
München , c1985. 192 p. : ISBN 3-7654-2043-3
DDC 769.5 19
Z994.5.A38 Z43 1985
NYPL [MDVC 91-5221]

BOOK-PLATES, GERMAN - CATALOGS.
Witte, Klaus. Georg Broel, 1884-1940 .
Frederikshavn , 1984. 86 p. : ISBN
87-7317-116-6
NYPL [MDVK (bBroel) 90-13584]
Witte, Klaus. Martin E. Philipp, 1881-1978 .
Frederikshavn , 1984. [73] p. :
NYPL [MDVK (Philipp) 90-13583]

**BOOK-PLATES, GERMAN - GERMANY
(WEST)**
Rother, Richard. Richard Rother und sein
Werk . Würzburg , c1987. 88 p. : ISBN
3-429-01100-0 DDC 769.5 19
Z996 .R65 1987
NYPL [MDVK (Rother) 89-26556]

BOOK-PLATES, SWISS.
Zebhauser, Helmuth. Alpine Exlibris .
München , c1985. 192 p. : ISBN 3-7654-2043-3
DDC 769.5 19
Z994.5.A38 Z43 1985
NYPL [MDVC 91-5221]

**BOOK TRADE. see BOOK INDUSTRIES
AND TRADE.**

BOOKBINDING.
Wolfe, Richard J. Marbled paper .
Philadelphia , c1990. xvi, 245 p., [38] p. of
plates : ISBN 0-8122-8188-8 DDC 686.3/6 20
Z271 .W638 1990 NYPL [MDZ+ 91-2284]

BOOKBINDING - EXHIBITIONS.
Artists of the book 1988 . Boston, Mass. ,
c1988. 40 p. : ISBN 0-934552-53-3
NYPL [MDTT 91-4772]

**BOOKBINDING - MARBLING. see
MARBLING (BOOKBINDING)**

**BOOKPLATES - HISTORY - 20TH
CENTURY - CONGRESSES.**
Thoms, Klaus. Das Exlibris von heute
1988-1990 . Wiesbaden , c1990. 286 p. : ISBN
3-922835-20-1 *NYPL [MDVF 91-7229]*

**BOOKPLATES - HISTORY - 20TH
CENTURY - EXHIBITIONS.**
Thoms, Klaus. Das Exlibris von heute
1988-1990 . Wiesbaden , c1990. 286 p. : ISBN
3-922835-20-1 *NYPL [MDVF 91-7229]*

BOOKPLATES - HISTORY - CONGRESSES.
Schutt-Kehm, Elke M., 1954- Albrecht Dürer
und die Frühzeit der Exlibriskunst .
Wiesbaden , c1990. 39 p. : ISBN 3-922835-18-X
NYPL [MDVF 91-7231]

BOOKPLATES - HISTORY - EXHIBITIONS.
Schutt-Kehm, Elke M., 1954- Albrecht Dürer
und die Frühzeit der Exlibriskunst .
Wiesbaden , c1990. 39 p. : ISBN 3-922835-18-X
NYPL [MDVF 91-7231]

Books & bookends : sculptural approaches :
1989-1991 traveling exhibition / curated by
Carol Barton and Henry Barrow. [S.l.] : Popular
Kinetics Press, c1990. 73 p. : ill. ; 16 cm.
I. Barton, Carol June. II. Title: Books and bookends.
IN PROCESS (ONLINE)
NYPL [MDTT 91-6180]

Books and bookends. Books & bookends . [S.l.] ,
c1990. 73 p. :
IN PROCESS (ONLINE)
NYPL [MDTT 91-6180]

BOOKS, ARTISTS'. see ARTISTS' BOOKS.

**BOOKS - EXHIBITIONS. see
BIBLIOGRAPHICAL EXHIBITIONS.**

**BOOKS FOR CHILDREN. see CHILDREN'S
LITERATURE.**

**BOOKS, ILLUSTRATED. see ILLUSTRATION
OF BOOKS.**

The books of Anselm Kiefer, 1969-1990 /. Kiefer,

Anselm, 1945- [Anselm Kiefer Bücher,
1969-1990. English.] New York, N.Y. , 1991. p.
cm. ISBN 0-8076-1261-8 DDC 709/.2 20
N7333.4.K54 A4 1991

Bool, Flip. Broos, C. De nieuwe fotografie in
Nederland /. Amsterdam , c1989. 143 p. :
ISBN 90-6579-019-5 :
IN PROCESS (ONLINE)
NYPL [MFW 91-5142]

Boom, Mattie. Foto in omslag . Amsterdam ,
1989. 143 p. : ISBN 90-6579-033-0 (pbk.)
NYPL [MFW+ 91-3603]

Booth-Clibborn, Edward. Myerson, Jeremy.
Design . London , c1990. 255 p. :
0-904866-77-7 *NYPL [3-MNF 91-6321]*

Booth, Mark Haworth- see **Haworth-Booth,
Mark.**

Boots, Maurice. Architecture in Jersey / by
Maurice Boots. Jersey : La Haule Books, c1986.
xii, 180 p. : ill. ; 25 cm. ISBN 0-86120-015-2
DDC 720/.9423/41 20
1. Architecture - Channel Islands - Jersey. I. Title.
NA995.J47 B66 1986

Borchert, Christian, 1942- Christian Borchert,
Gruppenbilder und Künstlerporträts. [Cottbus] :
Die Galerie, 1980. 41 p. : ill. ; 21 cm. Exhibition
held in the Galerie Kunstsammlung Cottbus from
March 29th to June 1st, 1980. Bibliography: p. 39.
1. Borchert, Christian, 1942-.
NYPL [MFX (Borchert) 88-1743]

BORCHERT, CHRISTIAN, 1942-
Borchert, Christian, 1942- Christian Borchert,
Gruppenbilder und Künstlerporträts. [Cottbus] ,
1980. 41 p. :
NYPL [MFX (Borchert) 88-1743]

Bordeaux, cité médiévale /. Gardelles, Jacques.
Bordeaux , c1989. 221 p. : ISBN 2-907202-13-8
N7949.B67 G37 1989

**BORDEAUX (FRANCE) IN ART -
CATALOGS.**
Avisseau, Jean Paul. Illustration du vieux
Bordeaux /. Avignon , c1990. 1 v. (unpaged) :
ISBN 2-7006-0141-6
N8214.5.F8 A95 1990

Bordeaux (France). Musée des arts décoratifs. La
Manufacture des Terres de Bordes en Paludate .
Bordeaux , 1989. 102 p. :
NYPL [3-MPGG 90-4725]

Bordeaux (France). Musée des beaux-arts.
L'or & l'ombre : catalogue critique et raisonné
des peintures hollandaises du dix-septième et du
dix-huitième siècles, conservées au Musée des
beaux-arts de Bordeaux / par Olivier Le Bihan ;
avant-propos de Philippe Le Leyzour ; préface
de Jacques Foucart. [Bordeaux] : Le Musée :
William Blake and Co., c1990. 459 p., xxxii p.
of plates : ill. (some col.) ; 29 cm. Includes
bibliographical references (p. 425-442) and index.
ISBN 2-902067-14-3
1. Bordeaux, France. Musée des beaux-arts - Catalogs.
2. Painting, Dutch - Catalogs. 3. Painting, Modern -
17th-18th centuries - Netherlands - Catalogs. 4.
Painting - France - Bordeaux - Catalogs. I. Le Bihan,
Olivier. II. Title. III. Title: Or et l'ombre.
NYPL [MAVZ (Bordeaux) 91-5492]

Plessier, Ghislaine. Adrien Dauzats, ou, La
tentation de l'Orient . Bordeaux , c1990. 227
p. : ISBN 2-902067-15-1 : DDC 759.4 20
ND553.D245 A4 1990

**BORDEAUX (FRANCE). MUSÉE DES
BEAUX-ARTS - CATALOGS.**
Bordeaux (France). Musée des beaux-arts.
L'or & l'ombre . [Bordeaux] , c1990. 459 p.,
xxxii p. of plates : ISBN 2-902067-14-3
NYPL [MAVZ (Bordeaux) 91-5492]

Bordenache Battaglia, Gabriella. Le Ciste
prenestine /. [Roma] , 1979- v. :
DG70.P33 C57 1979
NYPL [3-MGR+ 83-2202]

**BORDERS, ORNAMENTAL (DECORATIVE
ARTS)**
Hornung, Clarence Pearson. Geometrix . New
York , c1991. vii, 115 p. : ISBN 0-486-26674-5 :
DDC 745.4 20
NK1570 .H595 1991

Bordignon Elestici, Letizia. Gli ombrelli =
Umbrellas / Letizia Bordignon Elestici.1a ed.
Milano : BE-MA editrice, 1990. 143 p. : col.
ill. ; 17 cm. (Itinerari d'immagini . 32) Italian and

English. ISBN 88-7143-093-X
1. Umbrellas and parasols. I. Title. II. Title: Umbrellas.
III. Series. NYPL [3-MMW 91-4277]

**Borduas et les automatistes, Montréal,
1942-1955.** Québec (Province). Musée d'art
contemporain. [Montréal] [1971] 154 p.
ND246.Q4 M88 NYPL [3-MCY 90-5662]

**Borduas, Paul Émile.
[Selections. 1987]**
Ecrits / Paul-Emile Borduas ; édition critique
par André-G. Bourassa, Jean Fisette, et Gilles
Lapointe. Montréal, Qué., Canada : Presses
de l'Université de Montréal, 1987- v. : ill. ;
22 cm. (Bibliothèque du nouveau monde) Includes
editorial matter in English. Includes index.
Bibliography: p. [677]-694. ISBN 2-7606-0761-5 (v.
1)
*1. Borduas, Paul Émile. 2. Art - Philosophy - Collected
works. I. Bourassa, André-G., 1936-. II. Fisette, Jean.
III. Lapointe, Gilles. IV. Title.*
NYPL [3-MAS 88-2798]

BORDUAS, PAUL ÉMILE.
Borduas, Paul Emile. [Selections. 1987.] Ecrits
/. Montréal, Qué., Canada , 1987- v. : ISBN
2-7606-0761-5 (v. 1)
NYPL [3-MAS 88-2798]

**BORDUAS, PAUL-EMILE, 1905-1960 -
EXHIBITIONS.**
Québec (Province). Musée d'art contemporain.
Borduas et les automatistes, Montréal,
1942-1955. [Montréal] [1971] 154 p.
ND246.Q4 M88 NYPL [3-MCY 90-5662]

Boreas (Münster, Germany). Beiheft.
(5) Hübner, Birgitta. Ikonographische
Untersuchung zum Motivschatz der
stadtrömischen mythologischen Sarkophage des
2. Jhs. n. Chr. /. Münster , 1990. 217 p. :
NYPL [3-MGH 91-5059]

(6) Stupperich, Reinhard, 1951- Die Antiken
der Sammlung Werner Peek /. Münster , 1990.
77 p., [16] leaves of plates :
NYPL [3-MPEK 91-4659]

Borein, Edward, 1872-1945.
Davidson, Harold G., 1912- Edward Borein, the
update . Santa Barbara, Calif. , 1991. 219 p. :
ISBN 0-9627674-0-9 : DDC 760/.092 20
N6537.B63 D39 1991

**BOREIN, EDWARD, 1872-1945 - CRITICISM
AND INTERPRETATION.**
Davidson, Harold G., 1912- Edward Borein, the
update . Santa Barbara, Calif. , 1991. 219 p. :
ISBN 0-9627674-0-9 : DDC 760/.092 20
N6537.B63 D39 1991

Borel-Léandri, Jean-Marie. Architecture et vie
traditionnelle en Corse / Jean-Marie
Borel-Léandri. [Paris] : SERG, 1978. 287 p. :
ill. (part col.) ; 28 cm. Errata page inserted.
Bibliography: p. 287. ISBN 2-85869-038-3
*1. Architecture - France - Corsica. 2. Corsica (France) -
Civilization. I. Title. NYPL [3-MQWF 90-5907]*

Borgelt, Marion, 1954- Abstraction . Sydney ,
1990. 48 p. : ISBN 0-7305-7696-5
NYPL [3-MAM 91-3723]

Borges, Jorge Luis, 1899- Toledo, Francisco,
1940- Zoología fantástica . México , 1989. 58
p. : *NYPL [3-MCY T649 91-6144]*

Borghi & Co. Solotareff, Boris, 1889-1966. Boris
Solotareff, 1889-1966 . New York, NY [1990]
viii, 86 p. : *NYPL [3-MCZ S685 91-3922]*

Boris Solotareff, 1889-1966 . Solotareff, Boris,
1889-1966. New York, NY [1990] viii, 86 p. :
NYPL [3-MCZ S685 91-3922]

Börje Veslen. Kubin, Alfred, 1877-1959. Alfred
Kubin. [Stockholm] , 1990. 31, 29 p. : ISBN
91-7100-386-X
NYPL [3-MCK K95 90-11683]

Born, Richard A. David and Alfred Smart
Museum of Art. The David and Alfred Smart
Museum of Art . New York , c1990. 216 p. :
ISBN 1-555-95061-2 DDC 708.173/11 20
N531.D38 D38 1990
NYPL [3-MAVZ (Chicago) 91-4808]

Bornay, Erika. Las hijas de Lilith / Erika Bornay.
Madrid : Cátedra, c1990. 404 p. : ill. ; 21 cm.
(Ensayos arte) Includes bibliographical references (p.
395-404). ISBN 84-376-0868-6
*1. Femmes fatales in art. 2. Women in art. 3. Sexism in
art. 4. Feminism and the arts. I. Series: Ensayos arte*

Cátedra. II. Title.
NX652.F45 B6 1990

Bornstein, Christine Verzár. Portals and politics
in the early Italian city-state : the sculpture of
Nicholaus in context / Christine Verzár
Bornstein. [Parma] : Università degli Studi di
Parma, Istituto di storia dell'arte, Centro di
studi medievali, [1988] 175 p. : ill. ; 35 cm.
(Civiltà medievale) Summary in Italian. Added t.p. title
in Italian: Portali e politica alle origini dei comuni
italiani, la scultura di Nicholaus. "Published with the
assistance of the J. Paul Getty Trust." Bibliography: p.
166-172.
*1. Niccolò da Ficarolo, 12th cent. 2. Church doorways -
Italy. 3. Sculpture, Romanesque - Italy - Themes,
motives. I. Niccolò da Ficarolo, 12th cent. II. Title. III.
Title: Portali e politica alle origini dei comuni italiani.
IV. Series.*
            NYPL [3-MGO+ (Niccoló) 90-10768]

Borobudur /. Dumarçay, Jacques. Singapore ,
New York , 1992. p. cm. ISBN 0-19-588550-3 :
            DDC 726/.143/095982 20
NA6026.6.B6 D8513 1992

**BOROBUDUR (TEMPLE : MAGELANG,
     INDONESIA)**
Dumarçay, Jacques. Borobudur /. Singapore ,
New York , 1992. p. cm. ISBN 0-19-588550-3 :
            DDC 726/.143/095982 20
NA6026.6.B6 D8513 1992

Boross, Géza, 1908-1971. Pénzes, Éva N. Boross
Géza emlékkiállítása . [Budapest] , 1975. [42]
p., [9] leaves of plates :
N6822.5.B62 P46
            NYPL [3-MCZ B733 79-2198]

BOROSS, GÉZA, 1908-1971.
Pénzes, Éva N. Boross Géza emlékkiállítása .
[Budapest] , 1975. [42] p., [9] leaves of plates :
N6822.5.B62 P46
            NYPL [3-MCZ B733 79-2198]

Borough of Pompton Lakes. Roome & Lamscha
Surveyors. Butler, N.J. , 1910. 1 atlas (10
leaves) :   *NYPL [Map Div. 91-4091]*

Borowitz, Albert, 1930- Borowitz, Helen
Osterman, 1929- Pawnshop and palaces .
Washington , c1991. xvi, 272 p., [32] p. of
plates : ISBN 1-560-98010-9 (alk. paper) DDC
            709/.2 20
N5273.2.C36 B67 1991
            NYPL [3-MAX (Campana) 91-7446]

Borowitz, Helen Osterman, 1929- Pawnshop and
palaces : the fall and rise of the Campana art
museum / Helen and Albert Borowitz.
Washington : Smithsonian Institution Press,
c1991. xvi, 272 p., [32] p. of plates : ill. ; 24
cm. Includes bibliographical references (p. 255-261)
and index. ISBN 1-560-98010-9 (alk. paper) DDC
709/.2 20
*1. Campana, Giampietro, marchese di Cavelli,
1808-1880 - Art collections. 2. Campana, Giampietro,
marchese di Cavelli, 1808-1880 - Art patronage. 3.
Art - Private collections - Italy - Rome. I. Borowitz,
Albert, 1930-. II. Title.*
N5273.2.C36 B67 1991
            NYPL [3-MAX (Campana) 91-7446]

Bórquez, María Angélica, 1958-
Ma. Angélica Bórquez. 1. ed. [Santiago,
Chile?] : Fundación Andes, 1988. 1 portfolio
([8] leaves of plates) : col. ill. ; 24 cm. Cover
title: María Angélica Bórquez. DDC 709/.2 20
*1. Bórquez, María Angélica, 1958- - Catalogs. I. Title.
II. Title: María Angélica Bórquez.*
N6669.B67 A4 1988

**BÓRQUEZ, MARÍA ANGÉLICA, 1958- -
     CATALOGS.**
Bórquez, María Angélica, 1958- Ma. Angélica
Bórquez. [Santiago, Chile?] , 1988. 1 portfolio
([8] leaves of plates) : DDC 709/.2 20
N6669.B67 A4 1988

Borràs, Maria Lluïsa. Picabia / Maria Lluïsa
Borràs. New York : Rizzoli, 1985. 549 p. : ill.
(some col.) ; 30 cm. Bibliography: p. 547-548.
     ISBN 0-8478-0603-0 : DDC 759.4 B 19
*1. Picabia, Francis, 1879-1953. 2. Painters - France -
Biography. I. Picabia, Francis, 1879-1953. II. Title.*
ND553.P47 B67 1985
            NYPL [3-MCO+ P58 86-1244]

Borrell, Joan. L'artiste-roi : essais sur les
représentations / Joan Borrell. [Paris] : Aubier,
c1990. 398 p. ; 22 cm. (Bibliothèque du Collège
international de philosophie) Includes bibliographical
references (p. [389]-398). ISBN 2-7007-3473-4 :

DDC 700/.1 20
*1. Arts, Modern - 19th century. 2. Arts and society -
History - 19th century. 3. Artists - Psychology. I. Title.
II. Series.*
NX454 .B63 1990

Borremans, Guglielmo, 1670-1744.
Siracusano, Citti, 1948- Guglielmo Borremans
tra Napoli e Sicilia /. Palermo , c1990. 186 p. :
     ISBN 88-7177-009-9 : DDC 759.5 20
ND623.B684 A4 1990

**BORREMANS, GUGLIELMO, 1670-1744 -
     CATALOGS.**
Siracusano, Citti, 1948- Guglielmo Borremans
tra Napoli e Sicilia /. Palermo , c1990. 186 p. :
     ISBN 88-7177-009-9 : DDC 759.5 20
ND623.B684 A4 1990

Borroni, Laura. Tempo e architettura /. Roma ,
c1987. 174 p. :   *NYPL [3-MQD+ 90-12504]*

Borsano, Gabriella. Biennale di Venezia (1980).
Settore architettura. The presence of the past .
Venice , Milan , c1980. 350 p. : ISBN
     88-20-80266-X   *NYPL [3-MQV 91-420]*

Borshchevskiĭ, M. V. Sotsial'nye problemy
arkhitekturno-gradostroitel'nogo razvitiia
Moskvy . Moskva , 1988. 103 p. ;
NA9212.M6 S67 1988

Borsi, Franco.
Dall'art déco al Novecento / Franco Borsi ; a
cura di Corinna Vasić Vatovec ; contributi di
Luciana Capaccioli ... [et al.]. Firenze : Alinea,
c1983. 250 p., [4] p. of plates : ill. ; 24 cm.
(Saggi e documenti di storia dell'architettura . 3)
Bibliography: p. 147-149. DDC 709/.04/012 19
*I. Vasić Vatovec, Corinna, 1949-. II. Capaccioli,
Luciana. III. Title. IV. Series.*
N6494.A7 B67 1983
            NYPL [3-MAL 91-4191]

Finsterlin, Hermann, 1887-1973. [Selections.
Italian & German. 1969.] Hermann Finsterlin .
Firenze , 1969, c1968. 382 p. :
            NYPL [3-MQZ (Finsterlin) 90-5737]

[Leon Battista Alberti. English]
Leon Battista Alberti / Franco Borsi. 1st U.
S. ed. New York : Harper & Row, c1977.
397 p. : ill. ; 29 cm. Translation of: Leon Battista
Alberti. Includes index. Bibliography: p. 377-387.
     ISBN 0-06-010411-2
1. Alberti, Leon Battista, 1404-1472. I. Title.
NA1123.A5 .B67
            NYPL [MQZ+ (Alberti) 79-1214]

Palazzo Cenci / testi di Franco Borsi,
Francesco Quinterio, Giuseppina Magnanimi ;
presentazione di Giovanni Spadolini. Roma :
Editalia, c1989. 119 p. : ill. (some col.) ; 33 cm.
(I Palazzi del Senato) Includes bibliographical
references. ISBN 88-7060-222-2
*1. Palazzo Cenci (Rome, Italy). I. Quinterio, Francesco.
II. Magnanimi, Giuseppina. III. Title. IV. Series.*
IN PROCESS (ONLINE)
            NYPL [3-MQWB+ 91-4178]

Santa Maria sopra Minerva /. Roma , c1990.
303 p. : ISBN 88-7060-223-0
            NYPL [3-MRBD+ 91-7451]

Borsook, Eve. Messages in mosaic : the royal
programmes of Norman Sicily, 1130-1187 /
Eve Borsook. Oxford [Oxfordshire] : Clarendon
Press ; New York : Oxford University Press,
1990. xxiv, 112 p., [126] p. of plates : ill. (some
col.), plans ; 29 cm. (Clarendon studies in the
history of art) Errata slip inserted. Includes index.
Bibliography: p. [87]-101. ISBN 0-19-817504-3 :
     DDC 729/.7/09458 19
*1. Mosaics, Norman - Italy - Sicily - Themes, motives.
2. Normans - Italy - Sicily. I. Title. II. Series.*
NA3792.N67 B67 1988
            NYPL [3-MRXZ 90-11788]

Bortone, Sandro. Camusso, Lorenzo. Ceramics of
the world . New York, N.Y. , 1992. p. cm.
     ISBN 0-8109-3175-3 DDC 738/.09 20
NK3780 .C37 1992

Börtz-Laine, Agneta. Nicodemus Tessin d.y.
1654-1728 : Tessinska palatset, Slottsbacken,
Stockholm, 27 maj- 16 juni 1978 / en
utställning anordnad av Nationalmuseum ;
[katalogredaktor, Agneta Börtz-Laine och Börje
Magnusson]. Stockholm : Nationalmuseum,
1978. 15 p. : ill. ; 22 cm. (Nationalmusei
utställningskatalog . 412) ISBN 91-7100-139-5
*1. Tessin, Nicodemus, 1654-1728 - Exhibitions. 2.
Tessinska palatset (Stockholm, Sweden). I. Magnusson,*

*Börje, 1943-. II. Tessinska palatset (Stockholm,
Sweden). III. Sweden. Nationalmuseum. IV. Title.*
            NYPL [3-MQZ (Tessin) 90-6256]

Bosch /. Delevoy, Robert L. [Bosch. English.]
Geneva , New York , 1990. 139 p. : ISBN
     0-8478-1348-7 DDC 759.9492 20
ND653.B65 D353 1991

Bosch. Linfert, Carl, 1900- [Hieronymus Bosch.
English.] Hieronyus Bosch /. New York , 1989.
126 p. : ISBN 0-8109-0719-4 DDC 759.9492 19
ND653.B65 L513 1989
            NYPL [MCH+ B74 89-26502]

Bosch, Hieronymus, d. 1516.
Delevoy, Robert L. [Bosch. English.] Bosch /.
Geneva , New York , 1990. 139 p. : ISBN
     0-8478-1348-7 DDC 759.9492 20
ND653.B65 D353 1991

Linfert, Carl, 1900- [Hieronymus Bosch.
English.] Hieronyus Bosch /. New York , 1989.
126 p. : ISBN 0-8109-0719-4 DDC 759.9492 19
ND653.B65 L513 1989
            NYPL [MCH+ B74 89-26502]

L'opera completa di Bosch / presentazione di
Dino Buzzati ; apparati critici e filologici di
Mia Cinotti. 1a ed. Milano : Rizzoli, 1966. 119
p. : ill. (some col.) ; 32 cm. (Classici dell'arte. 2)
Includes indexes. Bibliography: p. 82.
*1. Bosch, Hieronymus, d. 1516. I. Buzzati, Dino,
1906-1972. II. Cinotti, Mia. III. Title.*
            NYPL [3-MCH+ B74 91-5658]

BOSCH, HIERONYMUS, D. 1516.
Bosch, Hieronymus, d. 1516. L'opera completa
di Bosch /. Milano , 1966. 119 p. :
            NYPL [3-MCH+ B74 91-5658]

Delevoy, Robert L. [Bosch. English.] Bosch /.
Geneva , New York , 1990. 139 p. : ISBN
     0-8478-1348-7 DDC 759.9492 20
ND653.B65 D353 1991

**BOSCH, HIERONYMUS, D. 1516 -
     CRITICISM AND INTERPRETATION.**
Linfert, Carl, 1900- [Hieronymus Bosch.
English.] Hieronyus Bosch /. New York , 1989.
126 p. : ISBN 0-8109-0719-4 DDC 759.9492 19
ND653.B65 L513 1989
            NYPL [MCH+ B74 89-26502]

Bosch i Planas, Joan, 1951- Ricard Clausells, el
pintor i el poeta, 1864-1939 / Joan Bosch i
Planas. 1a ed. Vilafranca del Penedès : J. Bosch
i Planas, 1990. 141 p. : ill. ; 25 cm. (Col·lecció
Vilatana . núm. 1)
1. Clausells, Ricard, 1864-1939. I. Title. II. Series.
IN PROCESS (ONLINE)
            NYPL [3-MCQ C616 91-4303]

Boschloo, Anton W. A. (Anton Willem Adriaan)
Crespi, Giuseppe Maria, 1665-1747. Giuseppe
Maria Crespi, 1665-1747 . Bologna , c1990.
xxcvi, 278 p. : ISBN 88-7779-148-9 DDC 759.5
     20
ND623.C8 A4 1990

Boschloo, Anton W. A. (Anton Willem Andriaan)
Crespi, Giuseppe Maria, 1665-1747. Giuseppe
Maria Crespi, 1665-1747 . [Bologna] , c1990.
ccxvi, 278 p. : ISBN 88-7779-148-9
            NYPL [3-MCF C922 91-5467]

Bose, Nirmal Kumar. Canons of Orissan
architecture / Nirmal Kumar Bose. New Delhi :
Cosmo, 1982. vi, 211 p., 34 p. of plates : ill. ;
25 cm. English, Oriya (Devanagari), and Sanskrit.
Reprint. Originally published: Calcutta : R. Chatterjee,
1932. Includes index. DDC 720/.954/13 20
*1. Architecture - India - Orissa. 2. Temples - India -
Orissa. 3. Astrology and architecture - India - Orissa. I.
Title.*
NA1507.O7 B6 1982

Bosi, Enrico. Di castello in castello : il Chianti /
Enrico Bosi, Gianluigi Scarfiotti. Milano : I
Libri del Bargello, c1990. 279 p. : ill. ; 26 cm.
(La Pietra) ISBN 88-85271-02-2
*1. Castles - Italy - Chianti Mountains. I. Title. II.
Series.*
IN PROCESS (ONLINE)
            NYPL [3-MQWB 91-7180]

Bosio, Luciano. Carta archeologica del Veneto /.
Modena [1988]- 4 v. :
            NYPL [Map Div. 90-2171]

Boskovits, Miklós. The Thyssen-Bornemisza
Collection : early Italian painting, 1290-1470 /
Miklós Boskovits ; in collaboration with Serena
Padovani ; translated from the Italian by
Françoise Pouncey Chiarini. London : Sotheby's

Bosqued Lacambra, Pilar.
Publications ; New York, N.Y., U. S.A. : distributed in the USA and Canada by Rizzoli International, 1990. 226 p. : ill. (some col.) ; 30 cm. Catalog of a number of internationally held exhibitions. Includes bibliographical references and index. ISBN 0-85667-381-1
1. Thyssen-Bornemisza, Heinrich, Baron - Art collections - Catalogs. 2. Thyssen-Bornemisza, Hans Heinrich, Baron - Art collections - Catalogs. 3. Sammlung Thyssen-Bornemisza. 4. Painting, Italian - History - Catalogs. 5. Painting, Medieval - Italy - Catalogs. I. Padovani, Serena. II. Sammlung Thyssen-Bornemisza. III. Title. IV. Title: Early Italian painting, 1290-1470. **NYPL [3-MCE+ 91-7306]**

Bosqued Lacambra, Pilar. Flora y vegetación en los tapices de La Seo / Pilar Bosqued Lacambra. Zaragoza : Caja de Ahorros de la Inmaculada, Aragón, 1989. 123 p. ; 31 cm. ISBN 84-505-8690-9
1. Tapestry, Flemish. I. Title.
IN PROCESS (ONLINE)
NYPL [3-MOR+ 90-12501]

Bosquet, Alain, 1919- La Fantastique contemporain . Paris , 1972. [126] p. :
NYPL [3-MAL 91-288]

Bossaglia, Rossana.
Catalogo generale dei dipinti di Giuseppe Cesetti / testi di Rossana Bossaglia e Paolo Levi. Milano : G. Mondadori, c1989- v. : ill. ; 33 cm. CONTENTS. - 1. Repertorio (1923-1989) ISBN 88-374-1088-3 (v. 1)
1. Cesetti, Giuseppe, 1902- - Catalogues raisonnés. I. Title. **NYPL [3-MCF+ C42 90-10852]**

De Nittis, Giuseppe, 1846-1884. Giuseppe De Nittis, dipinti 1864-1884 / . [Firenze , 1990. 205 p. : **NYPL [3-MCF N73 91-6553]**

Il Neogotico nel XIX e XX secolo /. Milano [1990] 2 v. : ISBN 88-20-20863-6 (set) DDC 724/.3 20
NA645.5.G68 N46 1990

Settecento lombardo /. Milano , c1991. 627 p. : ISBN 88-435-3418-1
NYPL [3-MAMC 91-7605]

La Storia dell'arte /. Busto Arsizio , 1990. 2 v. : **NYPL [3-MAMC 90-11656]**

BOSSANYI, ERVIN, 1891-1975 - CRITICISM AND INTERPRETATION.
Hayes, Dagmar. Ervin Bossanyi. [Canterbury] 1965. 37 p. **NYPL [3-MRY 90-7119]**

Bosscher, Ph. M. Bellec, François. Sillages néerlandais . Zutphen , c1989. 172 p. : ISBN 90-6011-657-7 **NYPL [3-MAME 91-6109]**

BOSSCKE, LODEW, 1900-1980 - APPRECIATION.
Herdies, Paul. Lodew Bosscke . Bruxelles [1985] 120 p. : ISBN 2-87103-016-2 DDC 759.9493 20
ND673.B5393 A4 1985

BOSSCKE, LODEW, 1900-1980 - CATALOGS.
Herdies, Paul. Lodew Bosscke . Bruxelles [1985] 120 p. : ISBN 2-87103-016-2 DDC 759.9493 20
ND673.B5393 A4 1985

Bossert, Helmuth Theodor, 1889-1961.
[Ornamente der Völker. English]
Folk art of primitive peoples : six hundred decorative motifs in color, forming a survey of the applied art of Africa, Asia, Australia and Oceania, North, Central and South America / Helmuth Th. Bossert. New York : Praeger, [1955] 15 p., 40 leaves of plates : col. ill. ; 35 cm. (Books that matter) Translation of: Ornamente der Völker. Includes index. DDC 745
1. Decoration and ornament, Primitive. I. Title.
NK1177 .B612 **NYPL [3-MNE+ 91-5923]**

Bosseur, Jean-Yves. Le paradigme musical d'Albert Ayme / Jean-Yves Bosseur. Paris : Traversière ; Malakoff : Distribution, Distique, c1986. 73, [2] p. : ill. (some col., 1 folded) ; 22 cm. Bibliography: p. [74] ISBN 2-903551-00-6 (pbk.) : DDC 759.4 19
1. Ayme, Albert - Criticism and interpretation. 2. Painting, Abstract - France. 3. Painting, Modern - 20th century - France. 4. Music, Influence of. I. Title.
ND553.A95 B67 1986
NYPL [3-MCO B744 90-12648]

Bosslet, Klaus. Ästhetik und Gestaltung in der japanischen Architektur : das traditionelle Wohnhaus / Klaus Bosslet, Sabine Schneider.1.

Aufl. Düsseldorf : Werner-Verlag, c1990. viii, 154 p. : ill. ; 24 cm. Includes bibliographical references (p. 150-152). ISBN 3-8041-1247-1 :
1. Architecture, Domestic - Japan. 2. Room layout (Dwellings) - Japan. 3. Japan - Social life and customs. I. Schneider, Sabine, 1960-. II. Title.
NA7451 .B67 1990

Boston architecture, 1975-1990 /. Miller, Naomi. Munich , New York, NY, USA , c1990. 248 p., [1] folded leaf of plates : ISBN 3-7913-1097-6
NYPL [3-MQWO+ 91-4496]

Boston Athenaeum. Artists of the book 1988 . Boston, Mass. , c1988. 40 p. : ISBN 0-934552-53-3 **NYPL [MDTT 91-4772]**

Boston College. Museum of Art. Wolf, Reva, 1956- Goya and the satirical print in England and on the Continent, 1730 to 1850 /. Boston , c1991. viii, 109 p. : ISBN 0-87923-897-6 (hardcover : acid-free) DDC 769.92 20
NC1639.G6 A4 1991

Boston Harbor tidal current charts. Tidal current charts, Boston Harbor. Rockville, Md. , 1974. [31] p. : **NYPL [JSH 84-1]**

BOSTON (MASS.) - BUILDINGS, STRUCTURES, ETC.
Miller, Naomi. Boston architecture, 1975-1990 /. Munich , New York, NY, USA , c1990. 248 p., [1] folded leaf of plates : ISBN 3-7913-1097-6
NYPL [3-MQWO+ 91-4496]

BOSTON. SHAW MONUMENT.
Benson, Richard, 1943- Lay this laurel . New York , c1973. [83] p. : ISBN 0-87130-036-2 DDC 973.7/4/44
F73.64.S53 B46
NYPL [IKG (Mass., 54th Regt.) 75-116]

Boswell, Thom. The Costumemaker's art . Asheville, N.C. , 1992. p. ISBN 0-937274-58-5 : DDC 746.9/2/0973 20
NK4860.5.U6 C6 1992

BOTANIC GARDENS. see BOTANICAL GARDENS.

BOTANICAL GARDENS - PICTORIAL WORKS.
Aschoff, Jürgen C. Magie der Pflanzen . München , 1987. 79 p. : ISBN 3-923558-12-0
NYPL [MFX+ (Aschoff) 89-20434]

BOTANICAL ILLUSTRATION - HISTORY.
De Bray, Lys. The art of botanical illustration . Bromley, Kent , c1989. 191 p. : ISBN 0-7470-0232-0 **NYPL [MDT+ 91-3771]**

Botelho, Margarida. 75 artistas em Portugal / Margarida Botelho. Maia [Portugal] : Castoliva Editora, 1989. 302 p. : ill. (chiefly col.) ; 30 cm. "A razão deste livro aí está. Textos, que não são críticas; repositório, que não é exaustivo; referências, sobre o que foi mostrado." ISBN 972-91572-5-1 DDC 709/.469/0904 20
1. Art Portuguese. 2. Art, Modern - 20th century - Portugal. I. Title. II. Title: Setenta e cinco artistas em Portugal.
N7128 .B68 1989

Botero . Botero, Fernando, 1932- Martigny , c1990. 139 p. :
NYPL [3-MCZ B74 91-4899]

Botero. Soavi, Giorgio, 1923- Fernando Botero /. Milano , c1988. 275 p. :
ND379.B6 S63 1988
NYPL [3-MCZ+ B74 90-12665]

Botero, Fernando, 1932-
Botero = Fondation Pierre Gianadda, Martigny, 6 avril au 10 juin 1990. 2e éd. Martigny : La Fondation, c1990. 139 p. : ill. ; 24 cm.
1. Botero, Fernando, 1932- - Exhibitions. I. Fondation Pierre-Gianadda. II. Title.
NYPL [3-MCZ B74 91-4899]

Botero, der Maler : Bilder und Zeichnungen aus 30 Jahren / herausgegeben von Dieter Brusberg ; Texte von Ursula Bode und Octavio Paz ; mit einem Interview von Ernst Beyeler mit Fernando Botero. Berlin : Edition Brusberg, 1991. 72 p. : ill. (some col.), ports. ; 34 cm. (Brusberg Dokumente . 26) Catalog of an exhibition held at the Galerie Brusberg, Mar. 16-May 11, 1991. ISBN 3-87972-071-1
1. Botero, Fernando, 1932- - Exhibitions. I. Bode, Ursula. II. Paz, Octavio, 1914-. III. Brusberg, Dieter. IV. Galerie Brusberg. V. Series.
NYPL [3-MCZ+ B74 91-7449]

Cau, Jean, 1925- Fernando Botero . Paris ,

c1990. 161 p. : ISBN 2-85047-159-3 DDC 759.9861 20
N6679.B6 A4 1990b

Soavi, Giorgio, 1923- Fernando Botero /. Milano , c1988. 275 p. :
ND379.B6 S63 1988
NYPL [3-MCZ+ B74 90-12665]

BOTERO, FERNANDO, 1932- - CATALOGS.
Cau, Jean, 1925- Fernando Botero . Paris , c1990. 161 p. : ISBN 2-85047-159-3 DDC 759.9861 20
N6679.B6 A4 1990b

Soavi, Giorgio, 1923- Fernando Botero /. Milano , c1988. 275 p. :
ND379.B6 S63 1988
NYPL [3-MCZ+ B74 90-12665]

BOTERO, FERNANDO, 1932- - EXHIBITIONS.
Botero, Fernando, 1932- Botero . Martigny , c1990. 139 p. :
NYPL [3-MCZ B74 91-4899]

Botero, Fernando, 1932- Botero, der Maler . Berlin , 1991. 72 p. : ISBN 3-87972-071-1
NYPL [3-MCZ+ B74 91-7449]

Bothwell, Dorr. Notan : the dark-light principle of design / Dorr Bothwell and Marlys Mayfield. New York : Dover Publications, 1991. p. cm. Reprint. Originally published: New York : Reinhold Book Corp., 1968. ISBN 0-486-26856-X (pbk.) DDC 745.4 20
1. Design. 2. Composition (Art). I. Mayfield, Marlys, 1931-. II. Title.
NK1510 .B67 1991

Botí, Rafael, 1900- Rafael Botí /. Madrid , c1989. 135 p. : ISBN 84-86938-14-7 (rústica)
NYPL [3-MCQ+ B748 91-6320]

BOTÍ, RAFAEL, 1900-
Rafael Botí /. Madrid , c1989. 135 p. : ISBN 84-86938-14-7 (rústica)
NYPL [3-MCQ+ B748 91-6320]

Botschaft der Taube . Wirth, Günther. Stuttgart , c1989. 327 p. : ISBN 3-7831-1004-1
NYPL [3-MCK+ O279 89-28163]

BOTSWANA - MAPS.
(1988) The Botswana Society social studies atlas /. Stockholm , 1988. 1 atlas (48 [i.e. 50] p.) : ISBN 999-12-6003-X DDC 912.6883 20
G2579.7 B6 1988
NYPL [Map Div. 91-7948]

Botswana Society. The Botswana Society social studies atlas /. Stockholm , 1988. 1 atlas (48 [i.e. 50] p.) : ISBN 999-12-6003-X DDC 912.6883 20
G2579.7 B6 1988
NYPL [Map Div. 91-7948]

The Botswana Society social studies atlas / general editor, Q.N. Parsons ; Botswana cartographer, B. Makwiti ; compiled by the Botswana Society, Gaborone in collaboration with the Government of Botswana and Esselte Map Service. Stockholm : Esselte Map Service, 1988. 1 atlas (48 [i.e. 50] p.) : col. ill., col. maps ; 33 cm. Caption title p. 2 of cover. Includes index. ISBN 999-12-6003-X DDC 912.6883 20
1. Botswana - Maps. I. Parsons, Q. N. II. Makwiti, B. III. Botswana Society. IV. Esselte Map Service. V. Title: Social studies atlas.
G2579.7 B6 1988
NYPL [Map Div. 91-7948]

BOTT, FRANCIS, 1904- - CATALOGUE RAISONNÉ.
Henze, Wolfgang, 1944- Francis Bott, das Gesamtwerk /. Stuttgart , Zürich , c1988. 395 p. : ISBN 3-7630-2062-4
NYPL [3-MCK+ B7895 90-11079]

Bott, Gudrun, 1957- Figuration und Bildformat : zur Auflösung des Bildbegriffs in der Malerei Willi Baumeisters / Gudrun Bott. Frankfurt am Main ; New York : P. Lang, c1990. 208 p. ; 21 cm. (Bochumer Schriften zur Kunstgeschichte, 0722-2564 . Bd. 16) ISBN 3-631-42715-8 DDC 759.3 20
1. Baumeister, Willi, 1889-1955 - Criticism and interpretation. I. Title. II. Series.
ND588.B35 B6 1990

BOTTA, MARIO, 1943- - CRITICISM AND INTERPRETATION.
Glusberg, Jorge. The architecture of Mario Botta . Buenos Aires [1980] 37 p. : DDC

720/.92 20
NA1353.B67 G58 1980

Bottaro, Silvia. Intarsiatori savonesi dell'Ottocento / Silvia Bottaro ; presentazione di Francesco Surdich. 1a ed. Savona : M. Sabatelli, c1989. 181 p. : ill. (some col.) ; 25 cm. (Collana Arte e artisti liguri) Includes bibliographical references (p. 171-177).   DDC 745.51 20
1. Marquetry - Italy - Savona - History - 19th century. I. Title. II. Series.
NK9924.18 B67 1989
NYPL [3-MOC 90-13408]

Botter, Mario. Affreschi decorativi di antiche case trivigiane, dal XIII al XV secolo / Mario Botter ; testi di Giovanni Comisso, Bepi Mazzotti e Memi Botter. 1a ed. Treviso : Edizioni Canova, 1979 (1987 printing) 162 p. : ill. (some col.) ; 35 cm. Includes bibliographical references.
1. Mural painting and decoration - Italy - Treviso. 2. Decoration and ornament, Architectural - Italy - Treviso. 3. Decoration and ornament - Italy - Treviso. I. Title.
NYPL [3-MLP+ 91-4495]

Böttger, Tete. Rodchenko, Aleksandr Mikhaĭlovich, 1891-1956. Rodtschenko, Fotograf, 1891-1956 . Göttingen , 1989. 157 p. :   ISBN 3-923257-08-2
NYPL [MFX+ (Rodchenko) 91-6659]

Botticelli . Pons, Nicoletta. Milano , 1989. 117 p. :   ISBN 88-17-25702-8
NYPL [MCF+ B75 90-12664]

Botticelli e Dante / a cura di Corrado Gizzi. Milano : Electa, c1990. 361 p. : ill. (some col.) ; 31 cm. "Casa di Dante in Abruzzo, 20 ottobre"--T.p. verso ISBN 88-435-3329-0
1. Botticelli, Sandro, 1444 or 5-1510 - Criticism and interpretation. 2. Dante Alighieri, 1265-1321 - Influence. 3. Dante Alighieri, 1265-1321. Divina commedia - Illustrations. I. Gizzi, Corrado. II. Casa di Dante in Abruzzo.
N6923.B67 A4 1990
NYPL [3-MCF+ B75 91-5452]

Botticelli, Sandro, 1444 or 5-1510. L'incoronazione della Vergine del Botticelli : restauro e ricerche : Firenze, Galleria degli Uffizi, dall'11 gennaio 1990 / a cura di Marco Ciatti. Firenze : Edifir, 1990. 141 p. : ill. ; 28 cm.
1. Botticelli, Sandro, 1444 or 5-1510. Coronation of the Virgin - Exhibitions. I. Galleria degli Uffizi. II. Title.
IN PROCESS (ONLINE)
NYPL [3-MCF B75 90-11619]

Pons, Nicoletta. Botticelli . Milano , 1989. 117 p. :   ISBN 88-17-25702-8
NYPL [MCF+ B75 90-12664]

BOTTICELLI, SANDRO, 1444 OR 5-1510. Lightbown, R. W. Sandro Botticelli . New York , c1989. 336 p. :   ISBN 0-89659-931-0 DDC 759.5 B 20
ND623.B7 L53 1989
NYPL [MCF+ B75 90-4403]

BOTTICELLI, SANDRO, 1444 OR 5-1510 - CRITICISM AND INTERPRETATION. Botticelli e Dante /. Milano , c1990. 361 p. :   ISBN 88-435-3329-0
N6923.B67 A4 1990
NYPL [3-MCF+ B75 91-5452]

BOTTICELLI, SANDRO, 1444 OR 5-1510 - CRITICISM AND INTERPRETATION - JUVENILE LITERATURE. Venezia, Mike. Sandro Botticelli /. Chicago , 1991. p. cm. ISBN 0-516-02291-1 DDC 759.5 B 92 20
ND623.B7 V37 1991

CORONATION OF THE VIRGIN - EXHIBITIONS. Botticelli, Sandro, 1444 or 5-1510. L'incoronazione della Vergine del Botticelli . Firenze , 1990. 141 p. :
IN PROCESS (ONLINE)
NYPL [3-MCF B75 90-11619]

BOTTICELLI, SANDRO, 1444 OR 5-1510 - CATALOGUES RAISONNÉS. Pons, Nicoletta. Botticelli . Milano , 1989. 117 p. :   ISBN 88-17-25702-8
NYPL [MCF+ B75 90-12664]

Bottineau, Yves. Versailles : miroir des princes / Yves Bottineau. Paris : Arthaud, c1989. 198 p. : ill. (some col.) ; 32 cm. Includes bibliographical

references (p. 192-195).   ISBN 2-7003-0747-X
1. Château de Versailles (Versailles, France). I. Title.
NYPL [3-MQWF+ 90-2605]

Bottle & label design / [art direction and design] Hideo Saitoh ; photography, Sasaki Studio, Chikao Todoroki, Izuru Yoshikawa. Tokyo : Bijutsu Shuppan-sha, 1990. 219 p. : chiefly col. ill. ; 31 cm. Text in English and Japanese. ISBN 4-568-50104-0
1. Bottles - Japan - Catalogs. 2. Labels - Japan - Catalogs. 3. Design - Japan - History - 20th century - Catalogs. I. Saitō, Hideo, 1939-. II. Todoroki, Chikao. III. Yoshikawa, Izuru. IV. Sasaki Studio (Tokyo, Japan). V. Title: Bottle and label design.
NK5440.B6 B578 1990

Bottle and label design. Bottle & label design /. Tokyo , 1990. 219 p. :   ISBN 4-568-50104-0
NK5440.B6 B578 1990

BOTTLES - JAPAN - CATALOGS. Bottle & label design /. Tokyo , 1990. 219 p. :   ISBN 4-568-50104-0
NK5440.B6 B578 1990

Botto, Lisa C., 1965- (ill) Simpson, Anne. How to draw wild animals /. Mahwah, N.J. [1991] p. cm. ISBN 0-8167-2481-4 (lib. bdg.) :   DDC 743/.6 20
NC780 .S54 1991

Boucheix, F. (François) Le rêve et la lumière : 1960-1990 / F. Boucheix ; [texte, Bernard Gauthron]. Craponne-sur-Arzon, France : Editions Battistella, [1991?] 207 p. : ill. (some col.) ; 34 cm. ISBN 2-907858-00-9 DDC 759.4 20
1. Boucheix, F. (François) - Catalogs. 2. Surrealism - France - Catalogs. I. Gauthron, Bernard. II. Title.
ND553.B698 A4 1991

BOUCHEIX, F. (FRANÇOIS) - CATALOGS. Boucheix, F. (François) Le rêve et la lumière . Craponne-sur-Arzon, France [1991?] 207 p. :   ISBN 2-907858-00-9 DDC 759.4 20
ND553.B698 A4 1991

Boucher, Bruce. The sculpture of Jacopo Sansovino / Bruce Boucher. New Haven, Conn. : Yale University Press, 1991. p. cm. Includes bibliographical references and index. ISBN 0-300-04759-2 DDC 730/.92 20
1. Sansovino, Iacopo, 1488-1570 - Criticism and interpretation. 2. Sculpture, Renaissance - Italy. I. Sansovino, Iacopo, 1486-1570. II. Title.
NB623.S3514 B6 1991

Boucher, François, b. 1885. Paris miroir de la mode : crinolines et calèches, 1855-1867 / texte par François Boucher. Paris : Editions Rombaldi, [1959] xi p., 24 leaves of plates : col. ill. ; 40 cm. (Costumes et modes d'autrefois . 7) Issued in portfolio.
1. Costume - France - Paris - History - 19th century. I. Title. II. Series.
GT875 .B6 1959 **NYPL [3-MML+ 91-7290]**

Boucher, Philip P., 1944- Les nouvelles Frances : France in America, 1500-1815, an imperial perspective / by Philip P. Boucher. Providence, RI : The John Carter Brown Library, 1989. xxi, 122 p. : ill., maps ; 26 cm. "This exhibition catalogue was published on occasion of the opening of the Library's exhibition, 'Les Nouvelles Frances,' in the spring of 1989." Includes indexes. Errata slip inserted. Bibliography: p. 113-115. Library's copy lacks errata slip. ISBN 0-916617-32-7
1. France - Colonies - North America. I. Title.
NYPL [Map Div. 90-11548]

Bouchery /. Rollin, Jean. Paris , c1989. 137 p. :
NYPL [3-MCO+ B7537 90-13204]

BOUCHERY, MICHEL, 1929- Rollin, Jean. Bouchery /. Paris , c1989. 137 p. :
NYPL [3-MCO+ B7537 90-13204]

Boudaille, Georges. L'art abstrait / textes de Georges Boudaille, Patrick Javault. [Paris] : Nouvelles Editions françaises : Casterman, c1990. 264, [8] p. : ill. (some col.) ; 33 cm. "ISSN 0338-6287"--Verso t.p. Includes bibliographical references (p. 263-[265]) and index. ISBN 2-7079-0024-9 DDC 701/.04/052 20
1. Art, Abstract. 2. Art, Modern - 20th century. I. Javault, Patrick. II. Title.
N6494.A2 B68 1990

Boudin . Boudin, Eugène, 1824-1898. Salem, Mass. , 1991. p. DDC 759.4 20
ND553.B73 A4 1991

Boudin, Eugène, 1824-1898. Boudin : impressionist marine paintings / Peter C. Sutton with an historical essay by Daniel Finamore. Salem, Mass. : Peabody Museum of Salem, 1991. p. cm. Includes bibliographical references.   DDC 759.4 20
1. Boudin, Eugène, 1824-1898 - Exhibitions. 2. Impressionism (Art) - France - Exhibitions. 3. Normandy (France) in art - Exhibitions. 4. Sea in art - Exhibitions. 5. Ships in art - Exhibitions. I. Sutton, Peter C. II. Finamore, Daniel. III. Peabody Museum of Salem. IV. Title.
ND553.B73 A4 1991

Louis Eugène Boudin : precursor of Impressionism : an exhibition / organized by Mahonri Sharp Young and Katherine Wallace Paris. Santa Barbara : Santa Barbara Museum of Art, c1976. ca. 50 p. : chiefly ill. ; 21 x 25 cm. Travelling exhibition held Oct. 8-Nov. 21, 1976 at Santa Barbara Museum of Art and four other institutions. Includes bibliography.
1. Boudin, Eugène, 1824-1898 - Exhibitions. I. Young, Mahonri Sharp, 1911-. II. Paris, Katherine Wallace. III. Santa Barbara Museum of Art. IV. Title.
NYPL [3-MCO B756 91-405]

BOUDIN, EUGÈNE, 1824-1898 - EXHIBITIONS. Boudin, Eugène, 1824-1898. Boudin . Salem, Mass. , 1991. p. DDC 759.4 20
ND553.B73 A4 1991

Boudin, Eugène, 1824-1898. Louis Eugène Boudin . Santa Barbara , c1976. ca. 50 p. :
NYPL [3-MCO B756 91-405]

Boudon, Philippe. Enseigner la conception /. Paris , 1986-<1989.> v. <1, 4 > :
NA2750 .E58 1986

Sur l'espace architectural : essai d'epistémologie de l'architecture / Philippe Boudon ; préface de Antoine Haumont. Paris : Dunod, 1971. 138 p. : ill., plans ; 22 cm. (Collection Aspects de l'urbanisme) Bibliography: p. [107]-108. ISBN 2-04-000446-7
I. Title.
NA2765 .B6   **NYPL [3-MQ 90-6535]**

Bougoux, Christian. De l'origine des lanternes des morts / Christian Bougoux. Bordeaux : Bellus, c1989. 151 p. : ill. ; 21 cm. Cover title. Includes bibliographical references (p. 148) and index. ISBN 2-9503805-0-6
1. Lanterns of the dead. 2. Sepulchral monuments - France. 3. Sepulchral monuments, Medieval - France. 4. France - Religious life and customs. I. Title.
NA6165 .B68 1989

Bouhéret, Roland, 1930- Bichet, Pierre. André Charigny /. Besançon , c1989. 141 p. :   ISBN 2-901040-78-1
NYPL [3-MCO+ C473 89-26937]

Bouillon, François, 1944- François Bouillon : Abbaye Saint-André, Centre d'art contemporain, Meymac, Centre régional d'art contemporain Midi-Pyrénées, Labège Innopole, Toulouse [et] Institut français de Zagreb [et] FRAC Champagne-Ardenne, Reims, 1990-1991. [Labège, France : Editions ARPAD, 1990] 160 p. : ill. (some col.) ; 29 cm. Includes bibliographical references (p. 158-159). ISBN 2-905992-32-8 DDC 709/.2 20
1. Bouillon, François, 1944- - Exhibitions. I. Centre d'art contemporain (Abbaye Saint-André (Meymac, France)). II. Title.
N6853.B588 A4 1990

BOUILLON, FRANÇOIS, 1944- - EXHIBITIONS. Bouillon, François, 1944- François Bouillon . [Labège, France , 1990] 160 p. :   ISBN 2-905992-32-8 DDC 709/.2 20
N6853.B588 A4 1990

Bouillon, Jean Paul. La Promenade du critique influent . Paris , c1990. 433 p. :   ISBN 2-85025-225-5 DDC 701/.18/094409034 20
N7475 .P76 1990

Bouillot, Roger. Setsuko Migishi : a retrospective / Roger Bouillot, Yasuto Ota, Hideo Takumi. [Tokyo] : Asahi Shimbun ; Washington, D.C. : National Museum of Women in the Arts, 1991. p. cm. Includes bibliographical references. ISBN 0-940979-16-0 DDC 759.952 20
1. Migishi, Setsuko, 1905- - Exhibitions. I. Ota, Yasuto. II. Takumi, Hideo, 1924-. III. Migishi, Setsuko, 1905-.

IV. Title.
ND1059.M472 A4 1991

Boulboullé, Guido. Worpswede : Kulturgeschichte eines Künstlerdorfes / Guido Boulboullé, Michael Zeiss ; unter Mitarbeit von Renate Harden ... [et al]. Köln : DuMont, c1989. 223 p. : ill. (some col.), [2] folded col. maps ; 21 cm. (DuMont Dokumente) "Kurzbiographien Worpsweder Künstlerinnen und Künstler": p. 195-200. Includes index. Maps on p. 2 and p. 3 of cover. Bibliography: p. 213-215. ISBN 3-7701-1847-2
1. Worpsweder Künstlervereinigung. 2. Art, German - Germany (West) - Worpswede. 3. Art, Modern - 19th century - Germany (West) - Worpswede. 4. Art, Modern - 20th century - Germany (West) - Worpswede. 5. Artists - Germany (West) - Worpswede. 6. Worpswede (Germany). I. Zeiss, Michael. II. Harden, Renate. III. Title. **NYPL [3-MAMG 90-12605]**

Boulet, Marie-Laure. Auditoriums / Marie-Laure Boulet, Christine Moissinac, Françoise Soulignac. Paris : Editions du Moniteur, c1990. 119 p. : ill. (some col.) ; 28 cm. (Architecture thématique, 0989-4268) Includes bibliographical references (p. 113). ISBN 2-281-19052-8 DDC 725/.81/09048 20
1. Auditoriums. 2. Architecture, Modern - 20th century. I. Moissinac, Christine. II. Soulignac, Françoise. III. Title. IV. Series.
NA6815 .B68 1990

Boulot, Catherine. Robert, Hubert, 1733-1808. Hubert Robert et la Révolution /. Valence , 1989. 179 p. :
NYPL [3-MCO R641 90-11133]

Boundaries of the self . Vinograd, Richard Ellis. Cambridge [England] , New York , 1992. p. cm. ISBN 0-521-38548-2 DDC 757/.0951 20
ND1326 .V56 1992

Bouras, Ch. (Charalampos) Hē Nea Monē tēs Chiou : historia kai architektonikē / Charalampou Boura. Athēna : Ekdosē Emporikēs Trapezēs tēs Hellados, 1981. 212 p. : ill., plans ; 30 cm. (Seira 4.--Vyzantina mnēmeia) Includes bibliographical references and indexes.
1. Nea Monē tēs Chiou. 2. Architecture, Byzantine - Greece - Chios Island. I. Title. II. Series.
NA5601.N4 B68 1981
NYPL [3-MQP+ 91-6541]

Bourassa, André-G., 1936- Borduas, Paul Emile. [Selections. 1987.] Ecrits /. Montréal, Qué., Canada , 1987- v. : ISBN 2-7606-0761-5 (v. 1)
NYPL [3-MAS 88-2798]

Bourcier, Paul G. Dolls and duty--Martha Chase and the progressive agenda, 1889-1925 /. Providence, R.I. (110 Benevolent St., Providence 02906) , 1989. 48 p. : DDC 688.7/221/097451 20
NK4894.2.C43 A4 1989

Bourdais, Gildas, 1939- Les modernes et les autres : cent ans d'art moderne dans le monde / Gildas Bourdais. Lausanne : Livre total, c1990. 367 p. : col. ill. ; 34 cm. Includes bibliographical references (p. 355-357) and index. ISBN 2-88253-018-8 DDC 709/.04 20
1. Art, Modern - 19th century. 2. Art, Modern - 20th century. I. Title.
N6447 .B67 1990

Bourdieu, Pierre.
[Amour de l'art. English]
The love of art : European art museums and their public / Pierre Bourdieu and Alain Darbel with Dominique Schnapper ; translated by Caroline Beattie and Nick Merriman. Cambridge, UK : Polity Press, 1991. viii, 182 p. ; 24 cm. Translation of: L'Amour de l'art. Includes bibliographical references (p. [174]-176) and index. ISBN 0-7456-0598-2 : DDC 708.9/4 20
1. Art museums - Europe - Visitors. 2. Art appreciation - Europe. 3. Art and society - Europe. I. Darbel, Alain. II. Schnapper, Dominique. III. Title.
N430 .B613 1991

Bouret, Jean.
Degas / par Jean Bouret. Paris : A. Somogy, c1987. 223 p. : ill. (some col.) ; 22 cm. Includes index. ISBN 2-85056-186-X :
1. Degas, Edgar, 1834-1917 - Criticism and interpretation. I. Degas, Edgar, 1834-1917. II. Title.
NYPL [3-MCO D31 90-13587]

Dufresne, Charles, 1876-1936. Charles Dufresne (1876-1936) New York, 1971. [18] p.
NYPL [3-MCO D846 91-890]

Bourgeois, Louise, 1911- Louise Bourgeois : [Ausstellung], Frankfurter Kunstverein, Steinernes Haus am Römerberg, Frankfurt am Main, 13.12.1989-28.1.1990 / [Katalogredaktion, Peter Weiermair, unter Mitarbeit von Cornelia Walter]. Frankfurt : Der Kunstverein ; Schaffhausen : Edition Stemmle, c1989. 194 p. : ill. (some col.) ; 23 cm. Includes bibliographical references (p. 173-183). ISBN 3-7231-0401-0 DDC 730/.92 20
1. Bourgeois, Louise - Exhibitions. I. Weiermair, Peter. II. Walter, Cornelia. III. Frankfurter Kunstverein. IV. Title.
NB237.B65 A4 1989

BOURGEOIS, LOUISE - EXHIBITIONS.
Bourgeois, Louise, 1911- Louise Bourgeois . Frankfurt , Schaffhausen , c1989. 194 p. : ISBN 3-7231-0401-0 DDC 730/.92 20
NB237.B65 A4 1989

BOURGES (FRANCE) - BUILDINGS, STRUCTURES, ETC.
Muté, S. Cathédrale de Bourges. Bourges, Cher [1923?-<1925?. v. <1-3 > (<72 > leaves of plates) DDC 726/.6/0944552 20
NA5551.B7 M87 1923

Bourgin, Pierre. Garneret, Jean. La maison du montagnon /. Besançon , 1981. 557 p., [2] p. of plates : DDC 728/.67/094445 s 728/.67/094445 19
NA8208.52.F8 M34 1981, t. 1
NYPL [3-MQWF 90-5444]

Bourguet, Pierre du. see Du Bourguet, Pierre.

Bourlard-Collin, Simone. Musée Borély. Donation Maurice et Pauline Feuillet de Borsat /. Marseille, 1969. 1 v. (unpaged)
NC27.F7 M355
NYPL [3-MAVZ (Marseilles) 91-291]

Bourniquel, Camille. Cathelin : peintures : 1982-1990 / Camille Bourniquel. [Paris] : Editions M. Trinckvel, c1991. 233 p. : ill. (some col.) ; 33 cm. Text in French, English, and Japanese. DDC 759.4 20
1. Cathelin, Bernard - Catalogs. I. Cathelin, Bernard. II. Title.
ND553.C316 A4 1991

Bourrié, André, 1936-
Dessins-pastels, peintures, lithographies / André Bourrié ; préface Henri Queffélec. Paris : Libr. Séguier, c1990. 163 p. : ill. (some col.) ; 31 cm. ISBN 2-87736-085-7 DDC 760/.092 20
1. Bourrié, André, 1936- - Catalogs. I. Title.
N6853.B625 A4 1990
NYPL [3-MCO+ B774 90-13050]

BOURRIÉ, ANDRÉ, 1936- - CATALOGS.
Bourrié, André, 1936- Dessins-pastels, peintures, lithographies /. Paris , c1990. 163 p. : ISBN 2-87736-085-7 DDC 760/.092 20
N6853.B625 A4 1990
NYPL [3-MCO+ B774 90-13050]

Boven, Margriet van. Noordbrabants Museum. Noordbrabants Museum /. Haarlem , c1979. 92 p. : ISBN 90-70024-17-9 DDC 069/.9492/4 19
AM101.H134 A49 1979 **NYPL [3-MAVZ (Hertogenbosch, Netherlands) 90-5574]**

Bovy, Gustave Serrurier- see Serrurier-Bovy, Gustave, 1858-1910.

Bowater, Marina. Collecting Russian art & antiques / Marina Bowater. New York : Hippocrene Books, c1990. p. cm. Includes bibliographical references. ISBN 0-87052-897-1 : DDC 709/.47/075 20
1. Art, Russian - Collectors and collecting. I. Title. II. Title: Collecting Russian art and antiques.
N6981 .B69 1990

Bowdoin College. Museum of Art.
As Maine goes, photographs by John McKee, introduction by William O. Douglas. Brunswick, Maine, Bowdoin College Museum of Art, 1966. 1 v. (unpaged) illus. 29 cm.
1. Douglas, William O. (William Orville), 1898-. 2. Photography, Artistic - Exhibitions. 3. Maine - Description and travel - Views. I. McKee, John, 1936-. II. Bowdoin College. Museum of Art. III. Title.
NYPL [MFX (McKee) 90-5881]

Bowdoin College. Museum of Art. As Maine goes. Brunswick, Maine, 1966. 1 v. (unpaged)
NYPL [MFX (McKee) 90-5881]

Bowdoin College. Museum of Fine Arts. see Bowdoin College. Museum of Art.

Bowdoin Museum of Fine Arts. see Bowdoin College. Museum of Art.

Bowers, Susan. Sexuality, the female gaze, and the arts . Selinsgrove [N.J.] , London , 1992. p. cm. ISBN 0-945636-32-6 (alk. paper) DDC 700/.1/03 20
NX180.F4 S49 1992

Bowles, Edmund A. (Edmund Addison), 1925- Musical ensembles in festival books, 1500-1800 : an iconographical & documentary survey / by Edmund A. Bowles. Ann Arbor, Mich. : UMI Research Press, c1989. xxii, 583 p. : ill. ; 23 x 29 cm. (Studies in music. no. 103) Includes index. "Annotated bibliography": p. 547-571. ISBN 0-8357-1872-7 (alk. paper) DDC 704.9/49785 19
1. Musical instruments in art. 2. Festivals in art. I. Series. II. Series: Studies in music (Ann Arbor, Mich.) , no. 103. III. Title.
ML85 .B66 1989 **NYPL [JMD 89-232]**

Bowlt, John E. The Quest for self-expression . Columbus, Ohio , Seattle , 1990. 191 p. : ISBN 0-295-97061-8 : DDC 759.7/312/07474 20
ND697.M6 Q4 1990
NYPL [3-MCY+ 91-5070]

Bowman, Doris M. American quilts / Doris M. Bowman ; analysis of the quilts by Joan Stephens. Washington, D.C. : Smithsonian Institution Press ; New York, N.Y. : Distributed by Outlet Book Co., 1991. p. cm. (The Smithsonian treasury) "A Gramercy book." ISBN 0-517-05952-5 : DDC 746.9/7/0973074753 20
1. Quilts - United States - Catalogs. 2. Quilts - Washington (D.C.) - Catalogs. 3. National Museum of American History - Catalogs. I. Stephens, Joan. Analysis of the Quilts. II. Title. III. Series.
NK9112 .L4 1991

Bowman, Irving. A portfolio of interiors : series II / designs by Irving Bowman ; color schemes by Ina M. Germaine. [New York] : Arts & Decoration Book Society, [1941?] 17, 17 leaves : ill. ; 39 cm.
1. Interior decoration - United States. I. Germaine, Ina M. (Ina May). II. Arts & Decoration Book Society. III. Title. **NYPL [3-MLO+ 90-2451]**

Bowman, Leslie Greene.
American arts & crafts : virtue in design / Leslie Greene Bowman.1st ed. Los Angeles, Calif. : Los Angeles County Museum of Art ; Boston : Bulfinch Press/Little, Brown, c1990. 255 p. : ill. (some col.) ; 32 cm. "A catalogue of the Palevsky/Evans Collection and related works at the Los Angeles County Museum of Art." Includes bibliographical references (p. 251-252) and index. ISBN 0-8212-1824-7 (hardback) : DDC 745/.0973/07479494 20
1. Palevsky, Max - Art collections - Exhibitions. 2. Evans, Jodie - Art collections - Exhibitions. 3. Los Angeles County Museum of Art - Exhibitions. 4. Arts and crafts movement - United States - Exhibitions. 5. Decorative arts - United States - History - 19th century - Exhibitions. 6. Decorative arts - United States - History - 20th century - Exhibitions. 7. Decorative arts - Private collections - California - Los Angeles - Exhibitions. I. Los Angeles County Museum of Art. II. Title. III. Title: American arts and crafts.
NK1141 .B64 1990
NYPL [3-MNE+ 91-4630]

Heckscher, Morrison H. American rococo, 1750-1775 . New York : [Los Angeles] : p. cm. ISBN 0-87099-630-4 DDC 745.4/4974/090330747471 20
NK1403.5 .H4 1992

Bown, Matthew Cullerne. Art under Stalin / Matthew Cullerne Bown. New York : Holmes & Meier, c1991. p. cm. Includes bibliographical references and index. ISBN 0-8419-1299-8 (alk. paper) DDC 709/.47/0904 20
1. Art, Soviet. 2. Socialist realism in art - Soviet Union. 3. Art, Modern - 20th century - Soviet Union. I. Title.
N6988 .B67 1991

Bown-Taevernier, Sabine. Hoozee, Robert. [James Ensor, tekeningen en prenten. French.] James Ensor, dessins et estampes /. Antwerpen , Paris , c1987. 271 p. : ISBN 90-6153-177-2 (Fonds Mercator) DDC 760/.092 20
N6973.E5 A4 1987

Bowness, Alan. Pollock, Jackson, 1912-1956. Jackson Pollock . London , c1989. [61] p. : ISBN 0-947564-26-8
NYPL [3-MCX P777 90-12889]

Bowron, Edgar Peters. Fogg Art Museum. European paintings before 1900 in the Fogg Art Museum . Cambridge , c1991. p. cm. ISBN 0-916724-76-X (hardcover : acid-free paper) : DDC 759.94/074/7444 20
ND450 .F64 1991

Box, Hal. The Architecture of Ricardo Legorreta /. Austin , 1990. 171 p. : ISBN 0-292-75106-0 (alk. paper) DDC 720/.92 20
NA759.L44 A87 1990   NYPL [3-MQZ+ (Legorreta Vilchis) 91-3708]

Boxer, David, 1946- Edna Manley, sculptor / David Boxer ; with a tribute by Rex Nettleford. [Kingston] : National Gallery of Jamaica, c1990. 204 p. : ill. ; 29 x 32 cm. "Published on the occasion of the Edna Manley retrospective exhibition held at the National Gallery of Jamaica in 1990"--P. [6] ISBN 0-9623836-2-7
1. Manley, Edna - Exhibitions. I. Manley, Edna. II. National Gallery of Jamaica. III. Title.
NYPL [3-MGO+ (Manley) 91-7698]

A boy at the Hogarth Press /. Kennedy, Richard, 1910- London , 1972. x, 85 p., [1] folded leaf of plates : ISBN 0-435-18510-1
NYPL [3-MEM (Kennedy) 90-11892]

Boyanoski, Christine, 1955- The 1950s : works on paper / Christine Boyanoski. Toronto, Canada : Art Gallery of Ontario, 1988. iii, 48 p. : ill. ; 26 cm. "Organized and circulated by the Art Gallery of Ontario." Catalogue of an exhibition held at the Laurentian University Museum and Arts Centre, Sudbury, Oct. 13-Nov. 13, 1988, and elsewhere. Bibliography: p. 22. ISBN 0-919777-65-1 DDC 741.971/074/0113541 19
1. Drawing, Canadian - Exhibitions. 2. Watercolor painting, Canadian - Exhibitions. 3. Prints, Canadian - Exhibitions. 4. Drawing - 20th century - Canada - Exhibitions. 5. Watercolor painting - 20th century - Canada - Exhibitions. 6. Prints - 20th century - Canada - Exhibitions. I. Laurentian University Museum and Arts Centre. II. Title. III. Title: Nineteen fifties.
NYPL [3-MCY 90-12731]

BOYD FAMILY.
Dobrez, Patricia. The art of the Boyds . Sydney , 1990. 232 p. : ISBN 1-86256-426-4
NYPL [3-MAM+ 90-13433]

Boyer, Bob, 1948-
Duffek, Karen, 1956- Bob Boyer . [Vancouver] , c1988. 1 folded sheet (8) p. ; ISBN 0-88865-111-2 (pbk.)
NYPL [3-MON 89-19266]

BOYER, BOB, 1948- - EXHIBITIONS.
Duffek, Karen, 1956- Bob Boyer . [Vancouver] , c1988. 1 folded sheet (8) p. ; ISBN 0-88865-111-2 (pbk.)
NYPL [3-MON 89-19266]

Boyer, Jean, conservateur. Le patrimoine architectural d'Aix-en-Provence, XVIe, XVIIe, XVIIIe siècles : recueil d'études historiques et architecturales / Jean Boyer. Aix-en-Provence : Roubaud, 1985 191 p. : ill., plans ; 30 cm. One folded leaf of plans inserted. Includes bibliographical references.
1. Architecture, French - France - Aix-en-Provence. 2. Architecture, Renaissance - France - Aix-en-Provence. 3. Architecture, Modern - 17th-18th centuries - France - Aix-en-Provence. 4. Aix-en-Provence (France) - Buildings, structures, etc. I. Title.
NYPL [3-MQWF+ 90-11534]

Boyer, Patricia Eckert. Helfand, William H. The picture of health . Philadelphia , c1991. p. cm. ISBN 0-8122-7962-X (University of Pennsylvania Press) : DDC 769/.4961 20
N8223 .H44 1991

Boyle, Richard. Kaelin, Charles Salis, 1858-1929. Dialogues with nature . New York , c1990. 41 p., [30] p. of plates : ISBN 0-945936-09-5
NYPL [3-MCX K118 90-13101]

Boyle-Turner, Caroline. Jan Verkade, Hollandse volgeling van Gauguin / Caroline Boyle-Turner ; met bijdragen van Adolf Smitmans, J.A. van Beers en Tim Huisman. Zwolle : Waanders ; Amsterdam : Rijksmuseum Vincent van Gogh, c1989. 190 p. : ill. (some col.), ports. ; 30 cm. "Deze publicatie vergezelt de gelijknamige tentoonstelling in het Rijksmuseum Vincent van Gogh te Amsterdam van 11 maart t/m 21

mei 1989"--P. 190. Includes bibliographical references. ISBN 90-6630-171-6
1. Verkade, Jan, 1868-1946 - Exhibitions. I. Smitmans, Adolf. II. Verkade, Jan, 1868-1946. III. Title.
NYPL [3-MCH+ V52 89-28467]

Boz, pseud. see Dickens, Charles, 1812-1870.

Boza, Cristián. Sergio Larraín G.M. : la vanguardia como propósito / Cristián Boza Díaz. Bogotá-Colombia : Facultad de Arquitectura, Universidad Católica de Chile : Revista Ars-Chile : 200, [9] p. : ill. (some col.) ; 23 x 24 cm. (Colección SomoSur . t. 9) Includes bibliographical references (p. [205]-[206]). ISBN 958-9082-56-4
1. Larraín García Moreno, Sergio, 1905- - Catalogs. 2. Architecture, Modern - 20th century - Chile - Catalogs. I. Title.
NA919.L37 A4 1990

Bozzetti italiani dal manierismo al barocco /. Ferrari, Oreste. Napoli , c1990. 285 p. :
ND615 .F47 1990   NYPL [3-MCE 91-4960]

Bozzolini . Bozzolini, Silvano, 1911- Paris [1971?] 64 p. :
NYPL [3-MCF B785 90-6085]

Bozzolini, Silvano, 1911-
Bozzolini : [exposition]. Paris : Galerie de Seine, [1971?] 64 p. : ill. ; 21 cm. Exhibition held Apr. 21-May 15, 1971. Library's copy imperfect. T.p. mutilated, with imprint area cut out.
1. Bozzolini, Silvano, 1911- - Exhibitions. I. Galerie de Seine. II. Title.   NYPL [3-MCF B785 90-6085]

BOZZOLINI, SILVANO, 1911- - EXHIBITIONS.
Bozzolini, Silvano, 1911- Bozzolini . Paris [1971?] 64 p. :
NYPL [3-MCF B785 90-6085]

BRABANT (BELGIUM) - ROAD MAPS.
Alle straten en steegjes van Brabant =. De Pinte , 1985. 1 atlas (321 p.) :
NYPL [Map Div. 90-11659]

Braccelli, Giovanni Battista, fl. 1624-1649.
Bracelli, gravures / présentation et catalogue de l'œuvre, Maxime Préaud ; propos sur Giovanni Battista Braccelli, Tristan Tzara. Paris : Chêne, 1975. 103 p. : ill. ; 27 cm. (Dossiers graphiques du Chêne 0335-8089) ISBN 2-85108-043-1 : DDC 769/.92/4
1. Braccelli, Giovanni Battista, fl. 1624-1649. I. Préaud, Maxime. II. Title.
NE2052.5.B72 P73
NYPL [MDG (Bracelli) 90-4378]

BRACCELLI, GIOVANNI BATTISTA, FL. 1624-1649.
Braccelli, Giovanni Battista, fl. 1624-1649. Bracelli, gravures /. Paris , 1975. 103 p. : ISBN 2-85108-043-1 : DDC 769/.92/4
NE2052.5.B72 P73
NYPL [MDG (Bracelli) 90-4378]

Bracelli, gravures /. Braccelli, Giovanni Battista, fl. 1624-1649. Paris , 1975. 103 p. : ISBN 2-85108-043-1 : DDC 769/.92/4
NE2052.5.B72 P73
NYPL [MDG (Bracelli) 90-4378]

Brach, Paul, 1924-
Kacere / préface de Jean Louis Ferrier ; texte de Paul Brach. [Paris] : Lavignes-Bastille : Filipacchi, c1989. 169 p. : ill. (some col.), ports. ; 31 cm. "Ce livre a été réalisé à l'occasion de l'exposition John Kacere à la Galerie Lavignes-Bastille du 12 septembre au 15 octobre 1989"--P. 168. Ill. on lining papers. Spine title: John Kacere. Includes bibliographical references. ISBN 2-85018-313-X
1. Kacere, John - Exhibitions. I. Kacere, John. II. Galerie Lavignes-Bastille. III. Title. IV. Title: John Kacere.   NYPL [3-MCX+ K115 90-2574]

Our land/ourselves : American Indian contemporary artists : an exhibition organized by the University Art Gallery, University at Albany, State University of New York / Jaune Quick-to-See Smith, guest curator ; essays by Paul Brach, Rick Hill, Lucy R. Lippard. Albany, N.Y. : University Art Gallery, University at Albany, State University of New York, 1991. p. cm. notes Includes bibliographical references. ISBN 0-910763-05-4 : DDC 760/.089/97073 20
1. Art, Indian - Exhibitions. 2. Art, Modern - 20th century - United States - Exhibitions. I. Hill, Rick (Richard). II. Lippard, Lucy R. III. State University of New York at Albany. Art Gallery. IV. Title.
N6538.A4 B67 1991

Bracher /. Bracher, Carlos, 1940- São Paulo, SP, Brasil , 1989. 176 p. :
ND359.B69 A4 1989

Bracher, Carlos, 1940-
Bracher / textos, Moacyr Laterza, Ferreira Gullar, Olívio Tavares de Araújo ; poemas, Affonso Romano de Sant'Anna, Haroldo de Campos ; citações de poemas e textos de Carlos Drummond de Andrade, Carlos Bracher ; editor, Olívio Tavares de Araújo = Bracher / texts by Moacyr Laterza, Ferreira Gullar, Olívio Tavares de Araújo ; poems by Affonso Romano de Sant'Anna, Haroldo de Campos ; citation of poems and texts by Carlos Drummond de Andrade, Carlos Bracher ; editor, Olívio Tavares de Araújo. São Paulo, SP, Brasil : Métron, 1989. 176 p. : ill. (some col.) ; 31 cm. Texts in Portuguese and English. DDC 759.981 20
1. Bracher, Carlos, 1940- - Catalogs. I. Laterza, Moacyr. II. Araújo, Olívio Tavares de. III. Title.
ND359.B69 A4 1989

BRACHER, CARLOS, 1940- - CATALOGS.
Bracher, Carlos, 1940- Bracher /. São Paulo, SP, Brasil , 1989. 176 p. : DDC 759.981 20
ND359.B69 A4 1989

BRACHET, LISE - CATALOGS.
Cruysmans, Philippe, 1925- Lise Brachet, ou, Le bonheur de peindre /. Bruxelles [1985] 127 p. : ISBN 2-87103-014-6 DDC 759.9493 20
ND673.B5438 A35 1985

BRACHET, LISE - INTERVIEWS.
Cruysmans, Philippe, 1925- Lise Brachet, ou, Le bonheur de peindre /. Bruxelles [1985] 127 p. : ISBN 2-87103-014-6 DDC 759.9493 20
ND673.B5438 A35 1985

Bracker, Jörgen. Bekker, Gerrit, 1943- Gerrit M. Bekker, Gemälde . Hamburg [1987] 56 p. :
NYPL [3-MCK+ B424 91-6718]

Bracons i Clapés, Josep.
[Claves del arte gótico. English]
The key to gothic art / José Bracons. Minneapolis : Lerner Publications Co., 1990. 80 p. : col. ill. ; 22 cm. (The Key to art) Translation of: Las claves del arte gótico. "A David Bateman book"--T.p. verso. Includes index. Discusses the history and characteristics of Gothic art, as represented in architecture, illuminated manuscripts, painting, stained glass, and sculpture. ISBN 0-8225-2051-6 (lib. bdg.) : DDC 709.02/2 20
1. Art, Gothic - Themes, motives. I. Title. II. Title: Gothic art. III. Series.
N6310 .B7313 1990   NYPL [3-MAK 90-11597]

Bradfield, Geoffrey. Spectre, Jay. Point of view . Boston , c1991. p. cm. ISBN 0-8212-1849-2 : DDC 729/.092 20
NK2004.3.S68 A4 1991

Bradford Art Galleries and Museums.
Wadsworth, Edward, 1889-1949. A genius of industrial England . [Bradford] , c1990. 128 p. : ISBN 0-9505532-7-1
NYPL [3-MCV W12 91-6333]

Wadsworth, Edward, 1889-1949. A genius of industrial England . [London] : [Bradford] : 128 p. : ISBN 0-9505532-7-1 DDC 760/.092 20
N6797.W26 A4 1990

Bradford, William. Courtauld Institute Galleries. The Courtauld Institute Galleries, University of London /. London , 1990. 128 p. : ISBN 1-87024-839-2
NYPL [3-MAVZ (London) 90-12082]

Bradley, Gilbert, 1917- Derby porcelain 1750-1798 / Gilbert Bradley with Judith Anderson and Robin Barkla ; foreword by J.V.G. Mallet. London : T. Heneage, 1990. 180 p. : ill. (some col.) ; 28 cm. Includes bibliographical references and index. ISBN 0-946708-25-8 : DDC 738.207 20
1. Derby porcelain. I. Anderson, Judith. II. Barkla, Robin. III. Title.
NK4399.D4   NYPL [3-MPGO 91-5746]

Bradley, Josephine. In pursuit of the unicorn / Josephine Bradley. Corte Madera, Calif. : Pomegranate Artbooks, 1980. [111]p. : ill. (some col.) ; 28 cm. ISBN 0-917556-06-2
1. Unicorns. 2. Unicorns in art. I. Title.
NYPL [3-MAMZ 91-6657]

Bradshaw, Peter, 1922- Derby porcelain figures 1750-1848 / Peter Bradshaw. London ; Boston :

Faber and Faber, 1990. xxvii, 484 p., [16] p. of plates : ill. (some col.) ; 25 cm. (The Faber monographs on pottery and porcelain) Includes bibliographical references (p. 466-469) and index. ISBN 0-571-15332-1 : DDC 738.8/2/0942517 20
1. Derby porcelain. 2. Porcelain figures - England. I. Title.
NK4399.D4 B74 1990
NYPL [3-MPGO 91-2617]

Brady, Carolyn.
McManus, Irene, 1951- The watercolors of Carolyn Brady ; including a catalogue raisonné, 1972-1990 /. New York , 1991. p. cm. ISBN 1-555-95048-5 (alk. paper) : DDC 759.13 20
ND1839.B69 A4 1991

BRADY, CAROLYN - CATALOGUES RAISONNÉS.
McManus, Irene, 1951- The watercolors of Carolyn Brady ; including a catalogue raisonné, 1972-1990 /. New York , 1991. p. cm. ISBN 1-555-95048-5 (alk. paper) : DDC 759.13 20
ND1839.B69 A4 1991

Brady, Mathew B., 1823 (ca.)-1896.
Civil War photographs [microform] . [Washington, D.C. , 1961] 5 v. :
NYPL [*ZM-232]
House of Representatives of the United States [microform] : 1864 / by M. B. Brady. [New York : Brady's National Photographic Portrait Galleries, 1864] 1 album (193 carte-de-visite photoprints) : ports. ; 29x23 cm. Cover title. Microfilm. Washington, D.C. : Library of Congress Photoduplication Service, 1981. 1 microfilm reel ; 35 mm.
1. United States. Congress. House - Photograph collections. I. Title. **NYPL [*ZM-233]**

Bragança, João de Orleans e. Levy, Carlos Roberto Maciel, 1951- Rio imperial /. [São Paulo, Brazil?] [1988] 176 p., [2] p. of plates :
NA857.R5 L4 1988

Bragg, Charles. The absurd world of Charles Bragg / text by Geoffrey Taylor. Rev. ed. New York : Arcade Pub., c1991. p. cm. ISBN 1-559-70130-7 (HC) : DDC 741.5/092 20
1. American wit and humor, Pictorial. I. Taylor, Geoffrey, 1950-. II. Title.
NC1429.B733 A4 1991

Braham, Helen.
Courtauld Institute Galleries. The Courtauld Institute Galleries, University of London /. London , 1990. 128 p. : ISBN 1-87024-839-2
NYPL [3-MAVZ (London) 90-12082]
Rubens : paintings, drawings, prints in the Princes Gate Collection / Helen Braham. London : The Trustees of The Home House Society for the Courtauld Institute of Art, University of London, c1988. 58, [2] p. : ill. ; 30 cm. Catalog of an exhibition held at the Courtauld Institute Galleries, University of London, Oct. 6, 1988-Jan. 8, 1989. Bibliography: p. [59] ISBN 0-7187-0878-4
1. Rubens, Peter Paul, Sir, 1577-1640 - Exhibitions. 2. Rubens, Peter Paul, Sir, 1577-1640 - Catalogs. 3. Courtauld Institute of Art - Catalogs. 4. Courtauld Institute of Art - Exhibitions. I. Courtauld Institute Galleries. II. Title: Princes Gate Collection.
NYPL [3-MCH+ R8 91-6137]

Brahms, Johannes, 1833-1897.
Choralvorspiele, op. 122. Selections; arr. 1980.
The Organ chorale preludes of Bach and Brahms as transcribed for piano by Ferruccio Busoni [sound recording]. Los Angeles, Calif. , p1980. 1 sound disc :
Nonesuch H-71375

[Sonatas, violin & piano]
The complete sonatas for violin and piano [sound recording] / Johannes Brahms. Los Angeles, Calif. : Nonesuch, [1982], p1977. 2 sound discs : analog, 33 1/3 rpm, stereo. ; 12 in. Toshiya Eto, violin ; William Masselos, piano. Recorded Jan. 1977, Iruma City Public Hall, Japan. CONTENTS. - No. 1 in G major, op. 78 (24:06) -- No. 2 in A major, op. 100 (18:21) -- No. 3 in D minor, op. 108 (19:03) -- F.A.E. sonata : in A minor / Albert Dietrich, Robert Schumann, Brahms (22:14).
1. Sonatas (Violin and piano). I. Schumann, Robert, 1810-1856.
Nonesuch HB-73034

Bram Bogart /. Paquet, Marcel. Paris [1990] 335

p. : ISBN 2-7291-0586-7 DDC 709/.2 20
N6953.B636 A4 1990

Bramer, Josef, 1948-
Bäumer, Angelica. Josef Bramer /. [Wien] [1990] 89 p. : ISBN 3-203-51094-4 DDC 759.36 20
ND511.5.B69 A4 1990

BRAMER, JOSEF, 1948- - CATALOGS.
Bäumer, Angelica. Josef Bramer /. [Wien] [1990] 89 p. : ISBN 3-203-51094-4 DDC 759.36 20
ND511.5.B69 A4 1990

Bramly, Serge, 1949-
[Léonard de Vinci. English]
Leonardo : discovering the life of Leonardo da Vinci / Serge Bramly ; translated by Siân Reynolds.1st U. S. ed. New York : HarperCollinsPublishers, c1991. p. cm. Translation of: Léonard de Vinci. Includes bibliographical references and index. ISBN 0-06-016065-9 : DDC 709/.2 B 20
1. Leonardo da Vinci, 1452-1519. 2. Artists - Italy - Biography. I. Title.
N6923.L33 B7313 1991

Bramsen, Henrik Boe, 1908- Early photographs of architecture and views in two Copenhagen libraries, by Henrik Bramsen, Marianne Brøns [and] Bjørn Ochsner. Copenhagen : Thaning & Appel, 1957. 92 p. : illus. ; 27 cm. Bibliography: p. 4. DDC 779.4
1. Photograph collections - Denmark - Copenhagen - Catalogs. I. Brons, Marianne. II. Ochsner, Bjørn. III. Akademiet for de skønne kunster (Denmark). IV. Kongelige Bibliotek (Denmark). V. Title.
N4015 .B67 **NYPL [MFW 91-4572]**

BRANCUSI, CONSTANTIN, 1876-1957 - CRITICISM AND INTERPRETATION.
Art and philosophy . New York , 1991. p. cm. ISBN 0-8204-1599-5 DDC 730/.92 20
NB933.B7 A78 1991

Brandariz, Gustavo A. El aporte friulano a la arquitectura argentina / por Gustavo A. Brandariz (parte general) y Cecilia Padilla (colonias). Buenos Aires : [s.n.], 1987. 52 leaves : ill. ; 21 cm. "Trabajo presentado al Primer Congreso Internacional "Presencia Italiana en la Argentina," Tucumán, Argentina, septiembre-octubre de 1987." Includes bibliographical references (leaves 51-52).
1. Architecture - Argentina - Congresses. 2. Architecture - Italy - Fiuli-Venezia Giulia - Influences - Congresses. I. Padilla, Cecilia. II. Congreso Internacional "Presencia Italiana en la Argentina" (1st : 1987 : San Miguel de Tucumán, Argentina). III. Title.
NA830 .B7 1987

Brandenburger, Gerlinde. Kunst in der Residenz . [Karlsruhe] [1990] 399 p. : ISBN 3-925835-58-X DDC 709/.43/4643074434643 20
N6886.K33 K85 1990

Brandi, Cesare.
Morandi / Cesare Brandi ; introduzione di Vittorio Rubiu ; con il carteggio Brandi-Morandi, 1938-1963 ; a cura di Marilena Pasquali. 1. ed. Roma : Editori riuniti, 1990. 249 p., [37] p. of plates : col. ill. ; 22 cm. (I Grandi) ISBN 88-359-3363-3 :
1. Morandi, Giorgio, 1890-1964 - Criticism and interpretation. 2. Morandi, Giorgio, 1890-1964 - Correspondence. 3. Brandi, Cesare - Correspondence. 4. Artists - Italy - Correspondence. 5. Art criticsx - Italy - Correspondence. I. Morandi, Giorgio, 1890-1964. II. Pasquali, Marilena. III. Title. IV. Series.
N6923.M6 B7 1990

BRANDI, CESARE - CORRESPONDENCE.
Brandi, Cesare. Morandi /. Roma , 1990. 249 p., [37] p. of plates : ISBN 88-359-3363-3 :
N6923.M6 B7 1990

Brandimarte, Cynthia. Inside Texas : culture, houses, and identity, 1878-1920 / by Cynthia Brandimarte. Ft. Worth, Tex. : Texas Christian University Press, 1991. p. cm. Includes bibliographical references and index. ISBN 0-87565-092-9 DDC 747.2164 20
1. Interior decoration - Texas - History - 19th century. 2. Interior decoration - Texas - History - 20th century. 3. Interior decoration - Texas - Human factors. I. Title.
NK2003.5 .B7 1991

BRANDL, HERBERT - EXHIBITIONS.
Oberhuber, Konrad. Herbert Brandl, Josef Danner, Otto Zitko /. Wien , 1988. 4 v. in 1 :
NYPL [3-MCK B818 90-8683]

Brandon, Reiko Mochinaga. Textile art of Okinawa / Reiko Mochinaga Brandon and Barbara B. Stephan. Honolulu : Honolulu Academy of Arts, 1990. viii, 46 p. : ill. (some col.), map ; 28 cm. Catalog of the exhibition at the Honolulu Academy of Arts, May 24-July 1, 1990. Includes bibliographical references (p. 46). ISBN 0-937426-12-1 DDC 746.9/2/09522907496931 20
1. Textile fabrics - Japan - Okinawa-ken - History - 19th century - Exhibitions. 2. Textile fabrics - Japan - Okinawa-ken - History - 20th century - Exhibitions. 3. Textile design - Japan - Okinawa-ken - History - 19th century - Exhibitions. 4. Textile design - Japan - Okinawa-ken - History - 20th century - Exhibitions. I. Stephan, Barbara B. II. Honolulu Academy of Arts. III. Title.
NK8984.A3 O383 1990
NYPL [3-MON 91-3749]

Brandstätter, Karl, 1946-
Graphisches Werk 1965-1990 = Œuvre gravé 1965-1990 = Graphic works 1965-1990 / Karl Brandstätter ; mit einem Vorwort von Bertram Karl Steiner ; [translated by Susanne Brandstätter-Waldman ; traduction de Bertram Karl Steiner]. Klagenfurt : Galerie B, c1989. 1 v. (unpaged) : 242 ill. (chiefly col.) ; 28 cm. Text in German, English, and French. ISBN 3-85391-088-2 DDC 769.92 20
1. Brandstätter, Karl, 1946- - Catalogs. I. Title. II. Title: Œuvre gravé 1965-1990. III. Title: Graphic works 1965-1990.
NE646.B7 A4 1989

BRANDSTÄTTER, KARL, 1946- - CATALOGS.
Brandstätter, Karl, 1946- Graphisches Werk 1965-1990 =. Klagenfurt , c1989. 1 v. (unpaged) : ISBN 3-85391-088-2 DDC 769.92 20
NE646.B7 A4 1989

Brandt, C. F. (Christian Friedrich), 1823-1891.
C.F. Brandt : der St. Victors-Dom zu Xanten 1868 in Photographien / herausgegeben von Gerhard Kaldewei und Rolf Sachsse ; mit einem Beitrag von Wilhelm Müllers. Kleve : Boss-Verlag, c1991. 122 p. : ill. ; 30 cm. "Begleitveröffentlichung zur gleichnamigen Ausstellung im Städtischen Museum Kalkar vom 1. April bis 28. April 1991"--T.p. verso. ISBN 3-89413-192-6
1. Brandt, C. F. (Christian Friedrich), 1823-1891 - Exhibitions. 2. Dom zu Xanten - Exhibitions. I. Städtisches Museum Kalkar. II. Title. III. Title: St. Victors-Dom zu Xanten 1868 in Photographien.
NYPL [MFX+ (Brandt) 91-7695]

BRANDT, C. F. (CHRISTIAN FRIEDRICH), 1823-1891 - EXHIBITIONS.
Brandt, C. F. (Christian Friedrich), 1823-1891. C.F. Brandt . Kleve , c1991. 122 p. : ISBN 3-89413-192-6
NYPL [MFX+ (Brandt) 91-7695]

Brandt, Klaus Joachim. Linden-Museum Stuttgart. Chinesische Lackarbeiten /. Stuttgart , c1988. 159 p. :
NYPL [3-MNX+ 90-10961]

Brandt, M. Kirchenkunst des Mittelalters . Hildesheim, c1989. 275 p. : ISBN 3-87065-528-3
NYPL [3-MAIH 90-12031]

Brandt, Michael, Dr. Kirchenkunst des Mittelalters, erhalten und erforschen . Hildesheim, 1989. 275 p. : ISBN 3-87065-528-3 DDC 704.9/482/0907435958 20
N7850 .K57 1989

BRANDYWINE CREEK VALLEY (PA. AND DEL.) IN ART - CATALOGS.
Brandywine River Museum. Catalogue of the collection, 1969-1989 /. Chadds Ford, Pa. , c1991. p. DDC 709/.73/07474814 20
N6517 .B7 1991

Brandywine River Museum.
Catalogue of the collection, 1969-1989 / Brandywine River Museum. Chadds Ford, Pa. : Brandywine Conservancy, c1991. p. cm. Includes bibliographical references and index. DDC 709/.73/07474814 20
1. Art, American - Brandywine Creek Valley (Pa. and Del.) - Catalogs. 2. Art, Modern - 19th century - Brandywin Creek Valley (Pa. and Del.) - Catalogs. 3. Art, Modern - 20th century - Brandywine Creek Valley (Pa. and Del.) - Catalogs. 4. Brandywine Creek Valley (Pa. and Del.) in art - Catalogs. 5. Art - Pennsylvania - Chadds Ford - Catalogs. 6. Brandywine River Museum - Catalogs. I. Title.
N6517 .B7 1991

BRANDYWINE RIVER MUSEUM - CATALOGS.
Brandywine River Museum. Catalogue of the collection, 1969-1989 /. Chadds Ford, Pa. , c1991. p.   DDC 709/.73/07474814 20
N6517 .B7 1991

Branom, Frederick Kenneth, 1891- New international atlas of the world /. Chicago , c1943. 224, lxiv p. :
NYPL [Map Div. 91-4958]

Branson, Gary D. The complete guide to barrier-free housing : convenient living for the elderly and physically handicapped / Gary D. Branson ; Hilary W. Swinson, contributing editor. White Hall, Va. : Betterway Publications, c1991. 176 p. : ill. ; 28 cm. Includes bibliographical references (p. 163-168) and index.   ISBN 1-558-70188-5 (pbk.) :   DDC 720/.42 20
1. Architecture and the aged. 2. Architecture and the handicapped. I. Swinson, Hilary W. II. Title.
NA2545.A3 B7 1991

Braque . Braque, Georges, 1882-1963. London , 1990. 71 p. :   ISBN 1-85332-060-9
NYPL [3-MCO B821 91-4401]

Braque, Georges, 1882-1963.
Braque : Accademia di Francia, Villa Medici, Roma 15 novembre 1974-20 gennaio 1975 / [Catalogo a cura di Jean Leymarie]. Roma : De Luca, [1974] 40, [140] p. : ill. (some col.) ; 24 cm. Bibliography: p. 37-40.
1. Braque, Georges, 1882-1963. I. Leymarie, Jean. II. Académie de France à Rome.
ND553.B86 L44
NYPL [3-MCO B821 81-286]

Braque : still lifes and interiors. London : South Bank Centre, 1990. 71 p. : ill. (some col.) ; 22 x 25 cm. Catalog of an exhibition held at the Walker Art Gallery, Liverpool, Sept. 7-Oct. 21, 1990 and the Bristol Museum & Art Gallery, Oct. 27-Dec. 9, 1990. "A South Bank Centre touring exhibition 1990." Includes bibliographical references.   ISBN 1-85332-060-9
1. Braque, Georges, 1882-1963 - Exhibitions. I. Walker Art Gallery. II. City of Bristol Museum and Art Gallery. III. South Bank Centre. IV. Title.
NYPL [3-MCO B821 91-4401]

Wilkin, Karen. Georges Braque /. New York , 1991. p. cm.   ISBN 0-89659-944-2 (cloth)   DDC 759.4 20
N6853.B7 W53 1991

BRAQUE, GEORGES, 1882-1963.
Braque, Georges, 1882-1963. Braque . Roma [1974] 40, [140] p. :
ND553.B86 L44
NYPL [3-MCO B821 81-286]

BRAQUE, GEORGES, 1882-1963 - CRITICISM AND INTERPRETATION.
Wilkin, Karen. Georges Braque /. New York , 1991. p. cm.   ISBN 0-89659-944-2 (cloth)   DDC 759.4 20
N6853.B7 W53 1991

BRAQUE, GEORGES, 1882-1963 - EXHIBITIONS.
Braque, Georges, 1882-1963. Braque . London , 1990. 71 p. :   ISBN 1-85332-060-9
NYPL [3-MCO B821 91-4401]

Brasil =. Villar Guanaes, Lúcia. [Paris] , c1988. [118] p. :   ISBN 2-86234-020-0
NYPL [MFX (Villar Guanaes) 91-3501]

Brasil. see Brazil.

Brasilier, André, 1929-
Le Pichon, Yann. André Brasilier, ses transfigurations /. Paris , c1989. 209 p. :   ISBN 2-87736-064-4   DDC 759.4 20
N6853.B712 L4 1989
NYPL [3-MCO+ B824 90-7470]

BRASILIER, ANDRÉ, 1929- - THEMES, MOTIVES.
Le Pichon, Yann. André Brasilier, ses transfigurations /. Paris , c1989. 209 p. :   ISBN 2-87736-064-4   DDC 759.4 20
N6853.B712 L4 1989
NYPL [3-MCO+ B824 90-7470]

Braslina, Aija. Latvijas PSR Valsts Mākslas akadēmija /. Rīga , c1989. 279 p. :
N332.L33 R57 1989

BRASS RUBBING.
Busby, Richard J. Beginner's guide to brass rubbing. London, 1969. 128 p.   ISBN

0-7207-0244-5 :   DDC 739.5/22
NC915.R8 B8

BRASSES - ENGLAND - HISTORY - 19TH CENTURY.
Meara, David, 1947- A.W.N. Pugin and the revival of memorial brasses /. London , New York , 1991. p. cm.   ISBN 0-7201-2070-5 :   DDC 739.5/22/092 20
NK7898.P84 M43 1991

BRASSWORK - INDIA - JAIPUR.
Government Central Museum (Jaipur, India) Jaipur brassware in Government Central Museum, Jaipur. Jaipur , 1955. 61 p. :
NYPL [3-MNK 90-7182]

Brater, Michael. Künstlerisch handeln . Stuttgart , c1989. 170 p. :   ISBN 3-7725-0914-2
N199 .K857 1989

Bratislava . Puškárová, Blanka. Bratislava , 1989. 253 p. :   ISBN 80-222-0024-7 :
N6833.B7 P87 1989

BRATISLAVA (CZECHOSLOVAKIA) - BUILDINGS, STRUCTURES, ETC.
Puškárová, Blanka. Bratislava . Bratislava , 1989. 253 p. :   ISBN 80-222-0024-7 :
N6833.B7 P87 1989

Stavoprojekt /. Bratislava , 1989. 1 v. (unpaged) :
NA1033.B7 S73 1989

Bratke, Elke.
Dorothea von Stetten-Kunstpreis 1988 . Bonn , 1988. 126 p. :   DDC 730/.943/074435518 20
NB568 .D74 1988   *NYPL [3-MGI 91-7194]*

Papierarbeiten . Bonn [1987] 155 p., [2] p. of plates :   DDC 709/.43/0740355 19
N6868 .P38 1987
NYPL [3-MAMG 91-7051]

Brattinga, Pieter, 1931- The activities of Pieter Brattinga, a portrait of an era / compiled and written by Geneviève Waldemann = De activiteiten van Pieter Brattinga, een tijdsbeeld / verzameld, geverifieerd en verwerkt door Geneviève Waldmann. 1st ed. Tokyo : Kodansha ; The Hague : SDU, 1989. 287 p. : ill. (some col.), ports. ; 31 cm. + 1 booklet. English, Dutch and Japanese. Accompanied by a separately-bound booklet (69 p.) in Japanese. Title in Japanese: Pītā Burattinga sakuhinshū. Includes bibliographical references.   ISBN 90-12-06213-6 (SDU)
1. Brattinga, Pieter, 1931-. 2. Graphic arts - Netherlands. I. Waldemann, Geneviève. II. Title. III. Title: Pītā Burattinga sakuhinshū.
NYPL [3-MDWS+ (Brattinga) 90-9941 Suppl.]

BRATTINGA, PIETER, 1931-
Brattinga, Pieter, 1931- The activities of Pieter Brattinga, a portrait of an era /. Tokyo , The Hague , 1989. 287 p. :   ISBN 90-12-06213-6 (SDU)   *NYPL [3-MDWS+ (Brattinga) 90-9941 Suppl.]*

Brauer. Brauer, Erich, 1929- München [1968] c1963. 59 p.   DDC 759.36
ND588.B72 F55
NYPL [3-MCK B823 91-396]

Brauer, Amy. Harvard University. Art Museums. Stone sculptures . Cambridge [Mass.] , 1990. 184 p. :   ISBN 0-916724-70-0   DDC 733/.074/7444 20
NB87 .H37 1990   *NYPL [3-MGH 91-3444]*

Brauer bunte Mauer =. Brauer, Erich, 1929- München [c1975] 89 p. :   ISBN 3-7654-1632-0   DDC 759.36
ND511.5.B72 L47
NYPL [3-MCK B823 90-6049]

Brauer, Erich, 1929-
Brauer; Malerei des phantastischen Realismus. Hrsg. von Herbert Fleissner; mit Beiträgen von Erich Brauer, Pierre Restany und Alfred Schmeller. München, Langen-Müller [1968] c1963. 59 p. illus., facsims., 28 col. plates, group port. 22 x 23 cm. CONTENTS. - Der Letzte der Gerechten, von P. Restany.--Das realistische und das phantastische Leben, von E. Brauer.--Sieben Briefe über Erich Brauer, von A. Schmeller.--Vollständiges Verzeichnis aller Ölbilder und Aquarelle bis Sommer 1968.   DDC 759.36
1. Brauer, Erich, 1929-. I. Fleissner, Herbert, ed. II. Restany, Pierre. III. Schmeller, Alfred. IV. Title.
ND588.B72 F55
NYPL [3-MCK B823 91-396]

Brauer bunte Mauer = varicoloured wall = Le

mur de couleurs : in Bildern / von Erich Lessing. München : F. Bruckmann, [c1975] 89 p. : ill. (some col.) ; 25 cm. English, French, and German.   ISBN 3-7654-1632-0   DDC 759.36
1. Brauer, Erich, 1929-. I. Lessing, Erich. II. Title. III. Title: Bunte Mauer. IV. Title: Varicoloured wall.
ND511.5.B72 L47
NYPL [3-MCK B823 90-6049]

BRAUER, ERICH, 1929-
Brauer, Erich, 1929- Brauer. München [1968] c1963. 59 p.   DDC 759.36
ND588.B72 F55
NYPL [3-MCK B823 91-396]

Brauer, Erich, 1929- Brauer bunte Mauer =. München [c1975] 89 p. :   ISBN 3-7654-1632-0   DDC 759.36
ND511.5.B72 L47
NYPL [3-MCK B823 90-6049]

Braum, Michael. Berning, Maria. Berliner Wohnquartiere . Berlin , c1990. xiii, 252 p. :   ISBN 3-496-00382-0 :
NA7351.B65 B47 1990

Braun, Dietrich. Nikolauskirche Beuren : 800 Jahre erlebte Geschichte / Dietrich Braun ; [Redaktion und Gestaltung, H.G. Giehler].[Neuaufl.]. Villingen : Neckar-Verlag, c1988. 96 p. : ill. (some col.) ; 22 cm. (Schriftenreihe "Beuren" . Bd. 1) Includes bibliographical references (p. 96).   ISBN 3-7883-1904-6
1. Nikolauskirche Beuren (Beuren, Esslingen, Germany). 2. Church architecture - Germany - Beuren (Esslingen). 3. Beuren (Esslingen, Germany) - Buildings, structures, etc. I. Giehler, H. G. (Hans-Georg). II. Title. III. Series.
NA5586.B4395 B73 1988

Braun, Emanuel. Kreis Kassel /. Braunschweig/Wiesbaden , 1990- v. <1 > :   ISBN 3-528-06239-8   DDC 720/.943/412 20
NA1076.K37 K7 1990

Braun, Karin. Studien zur klassischen Archäologie . Saarbrücken , Amsterdam , 1986. 219 p. :   ISBN 3-925384-00-6
NYPL [3-MAH 90-12469]

Braun-Munk, Eugène Clarence. Le Théâtre de la Mode /. Paris , c1990. 166 p. :   ISBN 2-906450-41-3
NYPL [3-MME+ 90-13056]

Brauner, Victor, 1903-1966.
Les Victor Brauner de la collection de l'Abbaye Sainte-Croix / [direction et conception du catalogue, Didier Ottinger]. Les Sables d'Olonne : Musée des Sables d'Olonne, c1991. 126 p. : ill. (some col.) ; 24 cm. Spine title: Collection d'art moderne et contemporain. Includes bibliographical references (p. 124-125).   ISBN 2-901432-69-7   DDC 759.4 20
1. Brauner, Victor, 1903-1966 - Exhibitions. 2. Abbaye Sainte-Croix (Les Sables-d'Olonne, France). Musée - Exhibitions. I. Ottinger, Didier. II. Abbaye Sainte-Croix (Les Sables-d'Olonne, France). Musée. III. Title. IV. Title: Collection d'art moderne et contemporain.
ND553.B873 A4 1991

BRAUNER, VICTOR, 1903-1966 - EXHIBITIONS.
Brauner, Victor, 1903-1966. Les Victor Brauner de la collection de l'Abbaye Sainte-Croix /. Les Sables d'Olonne , c1991. 126 p. :   ISBN 2-901432-69-7   DDC 759.4 20
ND553.B873 A4 1991

Braunschweigische Wissenschaftliche Gesellschaft. Kommission für Niedersächsische Bau- und Kunstgeschichte. Der Magdeburger Dom . Leipzig , 1989. 229 p., [120] p. of plates :   ISBN 3-363-00425-7   DDC 726/.6/09431822 20
NA5586.M15 M34 1989

Braunschweigisches Landesmuseum für Geschichte und Volkstum. Idee . [Braunschweig] , 1988. 169 p. :   ISBN 3-88895-025-2
IN PROCESS (ONLINE)
NYPL [3-MDW 91-6406]

Bräutigam, Herbert. Schätze Chinas in Museen der DDR . Leipzig , 1989. 263 p.   ISBN 3-363-00450-8   *NYPL [3-MAG 90-11297]*

Brawne, Michael. From idea to building : issues in architecture / Michael Brawne. Oxford ; Boston : Butterworth Architecture, 1991. p. cm. Includes bibliographical references and index.   ISBN 0-7506-1271-1 :   DDC 720 20

1. Architectural design. I. Title.
NA2750 .B66 1991

Brayer, Hermione, 1921- Un passé si présent :
mémoires / Hermione Brayer ; préface de Célia
Bertin. Paris : Libr. Séguier, c1990. 417 p., [8]
p. of plates : ill. ; 21 cm.   ISBN 2-87736-048-2 :
DDC 759.4 B 20
1. Brayer, Hermione, 1921-. 2. Painters' wives -
France - Biography. 3. Brayer, Yves, 1907-. 4.
Painters - France - Biography. I. Title.
ND553.B874 A2 1990

BRAYER, HERMIONE, 1921-
Brayer, Hermione, 1921- Un passé si présent .
Paris , c1990. 417 p., [8] p. of plates :   ISBN
2-87736-048-2 :   DDC 759.4 B 20
ND553.B874 A2 1990

Brayer, Yves, 1907- Giono, Jean, 1895-1970.
Yves Brayer /. Paris , c1990. 171 p. :   ISBN
2-85047-154-2   DDC 759.4 20
ND553.B875 G48 1990

BRAYER, YVES, 1907-
Brayer, Hermione, 1921- Un passé si présent .
Paris , c1990. 417 p., [8] p. of plates :   ISBN
2-87736-048-2 :   DDC 759.4 B 20
ND553.B874 A2 1990

Giono, Jean, 1895-1970. Yves Brayer /. Paris ,
c1990. 171 p. :   ISBN 2-85047-154-2   DDC 759.4
20
ND553.B875 G48 1990

Braynard, Frank Osborn, 1916- A picture
postcard history of U. S. steamships / by Frank
O. Braynard ; introduction by Walter Cronkite.
1st ed. Vestal, N.Y. : Almar Press, c1991. p.
cm. Includes bibliographical references and index.
ISBN 0-930256-15-8   DDC 741.6/83/0973 20
1. Steamboats in art. 2. Postcards - United States. 3.
Steamboats - United States - History. I. Title.
NC1878.S4 B73 1991

Brazil. Congress. Cámara dos Deputados.
Documentaçã e Informação, Centro de. see
Brazil. Congresso. Câmara dos Deputados.
Centro de Documentação e Informação.

Brazil. Congresso. Câmara dos Deputados.
Documentos parlamentares.
(124 124) O Clero no Parlamento brasileiro
/. Brasília , Rio de Janeiro , 1978- v. :   ISBN
85-7004-002-4
JL2454 .C53 　　　*NYPL [HFE 80-1378]*

(124/A-B 124) O Clero no Parlamento
brasileiro /. Brasília , Rio de Janeiro ,
1978-79. 2 v. :   ISBN 85-7004-002-4
JL2454 .C53 　　　*NYPL [HFE 80-1465]*

Brazil. Congresso. Câmara dos Deputados.
Centro de Documentação e Informação.
O Clero no Parlamento brasileiro /. Brasília ,
Rio de Janeiro , 1978-79. 2 v. :   ISBN
85-7004-002-4
JL2454 .C53 　　　*NYPL [HFE 80-1465]*

O Clero no Parlamento brasileiro /. Brasília ,
Rio de Janeiro , 1978- v. :   ISBN 85-7004-002-4
JL2454 .C53 　　　*NYPL [HFE 80-1378]*

Brazil. Congresso. Centro de Documentação e
Informação. see **Brazil. Congresso. Câmara**
dos Deputados. Centro de Documentação e
Informação.

BRAZIL. CONGRESSO - HISTORY.
O Clero no Parlamento brasileiro /. Brasília ,
Rio de Janeiro , 1978-79. 2 v. :   ISBN
85-7004-002-4
JL2454 .C53 　　　*NYPL [HFE 80-1465]*

O Clero no Parlamento brasileiro /. Brasília ,
Rio de Janeiro , 1978- v. :   ISBN 85-7004-002-4
JL2454 .C53 　　　*NYPL [HFE 80-1378]*

BRAZIL - DESCRIPTION AND TRAVEL -
1981- - VIEWS.
Villar Guanaes, Lúcia. Brasil =. [Paris] , c1988.
[118] p. :   ISBN 2-86234-020-0
NYPL [MFX (Villar Guanaes) 91-3501]

BRAZIL IN ART.
Peixoto, Maria Elizabete Santos. Pintores
alemães no Brasil durante o século XIX =. Rio
de Janeiro , 1989. 244 p. :   ISBN 85-7191-001-4
NYPL [3-MCI+ 90-8914]

BRAZIL IN ART - EXHIBITIONS.
Post, Frans, 1612 (ca.)-1680. Frans Post,
1612-1680 /. [Basel] [Tübingen] , 1990. 99 p. :
DDC 759.9492 20
ND653.P6 A4 1990

Brazil. Ministério da Educação e Cultura.
Fundação Casa de Rui Barbosa. see
Fundação Casa de Rui Barbosa.

BRAZILIAN ART. see **ART, BRAZILIAN.**

Brazilian drawing. Margutti, Mário. Desenho
brasileiro . Rio de Janeiro , 1988. 136 p. :
DDC 741.981 20
NC198 .M37 1988

BRAZILIAN WIT AND HUMOR,
PICTORIAL.
Nani, 1951- Nani em 51ns [i.e. cinquenta e
uns] cartuns de bar. [Brazil , 198-] 1 v.
(unpaged) :   DDC 741.5/981 20
NC1460.N356 A4 1980z

BRAZILIAN WIT AND HUMOR,
PICTORIAL - CATALOGS.
Loredano, Cássio. Guevara e Figueroa . Rio de
Janeiro, RJ , 1988. 131 p. :
NC1460.G84 A4 1988

Breaking down the boundaries : artists and
museums - / Chris Bruce ... [et al.]. Seattle,
Wash. : Henry Art Gallery, University of
Washington, c1989. 31 p. : ill. ; 30 cm.   ISBN
0-935558-24-1   DDC 707/.5 20
1. Artists and museums - United States. 2. Artists and
patrons - United States. 3. Art, Modern - 20th
century - United States - Themes, motives. 4. Public
art - United States - Themes, motives. 5. Conceptual
art - United States - Themes, motives. I. Bruce, Chris.
N72.A77 B74 1909
NYPL [3-MAMT+ 90-12629]

Breccia Fratadocchi, Tommaso. Cuneo, Paolo.
Architettura armena dal quarto al
diciannovesimo secolo /. Roma , 1988. 2 v.
(923 p., [1] folded leaf of plates) :   ISBN
88-7813-154-7 (set)
NYPL [3-MQW 90-12681]

Brecheret /. Brecheret, Victor, 1894-1955. São
Paulo, SP , 1989. 79 p. :   ISBN 85-85118-05-9
NYPL [3-MGO+ (Brecheret) 90-8597]

Brecheret, Victor, 1894-1955.
Brecheret / [organizado por Cesar Luis Piers de
Mello]. São Paulo, SP : Marca d'Água, 1989.
79 p. : chiefly ill. (chiefly col.) ; 32 cm.
Portuguese and English. "Edição comemorativa." "20a
Bienal de São Paulo"--P. [15] Includes index.   ISBN
85-85118-05-9
1. Brecheret, Victor, 1894-1955 - Exhibitions. I. Mello,
Cesar Luis Pires de. II. Bienal Internacional de São
Paulo (20th : 1989). III. Title.
NYPL [3-MGO+ (Brecheret) 90-8597]

BRECHERET, VICTOR, 1894-1955 -
EXHIBITIONS.
Brecheret, Victor, 1894-1955. Brecheret /. São
Paulo, SP , 1989. 79 p. :   ISBN 85-85118-05-9
NYPL [3-MGO+ (Brecheret) 90-8597]

Brecheret, Vítor, 1894-1955.
Victor Brecheret, 1894-1955 / textos, Sandra
Brecheret Pellegrini, Fábio Magalhães. [Rio de
Janeiro] : Editora Revan, 1989. 108 p. : ill.
(some col.) ; 23 x 32 cm. English and Portuguese.
ISBN 85-7106-017-7   DDC 730/.92 20
1. Brecheret, Vítor 1894-1955 - Catalogs. I. Pellegrini,
Sandra Brecheret. II. Magalhães, Fábio. III. Title.
NB359.B73 A4 1989

BRECHERET, VÍTOR 1894-1955 - CATALOGS.
Brecheret, Vítor, 1894-1955. Victor Brecheret,
1894-1955 /. [Rio de Janeiro] , 1989. 108 p. :
ISBN 85-7106-017-7   DDC 730/.92 20
NB359.B73 A4 1989

Brechin: a study in conservation. by W. Edwin
Bulley [and others]. Edinburgh, Joint
Department of Architecture, Heriot-Watt
University and Edinburgh College of Art [1970]
[231] p. illus., maps (some col.), plans. 30 cm.
ISBN 0-901658-08-1   DDC 711/.4 094131
1. Architecture - Scotland - Brechin - Conservation and
restoration. I. Bulley, W. Edwin.
NA109.G7 B7 　　　*NYPL [3-MQWK 90-5626]*

Brédif, Josette.
[Toiles de Jouy. English]
Printed French fabrics = Toiles de Jouy /
Josette Brédif. New York : Rizzoli, 1989. 184
p. : ill. (some col.) ; 32 cm. Translation of:
Toiles de Jouy. Published in London by Thames &
Hudson with the title: Classic printed textiles from
France, 1760-1843. Includes bibliographical
references (p. 178-180).   ISBN 0-8478-1135-2
DDC 746.6/2/0944366 20
1. Calico-printing - France. I. Title. II. Title: Toiles de

Jouy.
TP930 .B6413 1989
NYPL [3-MON+ 91-3401]

BREDIUS, ABRAHAM, 1850-1946.
Museum Bredius. Museum Bredius .
['s-Gravenhage] , 1980. 176 p. :
NYPL [3-MAVZ (Hague) 81-647]

Breedam, Camiel van, 1936-
Hasior, Władysław, 1928- Władysław Hasior,
Camiel Van Breedam . Bruxelles , c1989. 287
p. :   ISBN 90-71386-13-9
NYPL [3-MGO+ (Hasior) 91-6879]

BREEDAM, CAMIEL VAN, 1936- -
EXHIBITIONS.
Hasior, Władysław, 1928- Władysław Hasior,
Camiel Van Breedam . Bruxelles , c1989. 287
p. :   ISBN 90-71386-13-9
NYPL [3-MGO+ (Hasior) 91-6879]

Breer, Robert.
Robert Breer : a painter in Paris, 1949-1959 :
exhibition, September 11-29, 1990 / text by
Billy Klüver and Julie Martin. Paris : Galerie
1900-2000, c1990. 28 p. : col. ill. ; 24 x 30 cm.
Bibliography: p. 28.
1. Breer, Robert - Exhibitions. I. Klüver, Billy, 1927-.
II. Martin, Julie. III. Galerie 1900-2000 (Paris, France).
IV. Title. 　　　*NYPL [3-MCX+ B832 91-7234]*

BREER, ROBERT - EXHIBITIONS.
Breer, Robert. Robert Breer . Paris , c1990. 28
p. : 	*NYPL [3-MCX+ B832 91-7234]*

Bréerette, Geneviève. Individualités . Milano ,
c1984. 107 p. :   *NYPL [3-MAMI 90-12643]*

Breeskin, Adelyn Dohme, 1896- Mary Cassatt : a
catalogue raisonné of the oils, pastels,
watercolors, and drawings / Adelyn Dohme
Breeskin. Washington, D.C. : Smithsonian
Institution Press, 1991. p. cm. Includes
bibliographical references and index.   ISBN
0-87474-100-9   DDC 759.13 20
1. Cassatt, Mary, 1844-1926 - Catalogues raisonnés. I.
Title.
N6537.C35 A4 1991

Breeze, Carla.
L.A. deco / Carla Breeze ; introduction by
David Gebhard. New York : Rizzoli, 1991. p.
cm. Includes bibliographical references.   ISBN
0-8478-1434-3   DDC 720/.9794/9409042 20
1. Art deco (Architecture) - California - Los Angeles. 2.
Architecture, Modern - 20th century - California - Los
Angeles. 3. Decoration and ornament, Architectural -
California - Los Angeles. 4. Los Angeles (California) -
Buildings, structures, etc. I. Title.
NA735.L55 B74 1991

Pueblo deco / photographs and text by Carla
Breeze. New York : Rizzoli International
Publications, 1990. 112 p. : col. ill. ; 22 x 24
cm. Includes bibliographical references (p. 110-111).
ISBN 0-8478-1177-8 (pbk.) :   DDC
720/.973/09041 20
1. Art deco (Architecture) - United States. 2.
Architecture, Modern - 20th century - United States. 3.
Pueblos - Southwest, New - Influence. I. Title.
NA712.5.A7 B7 1990
NYPL [3-MQWO 90-11529]

Bregler, Charles.
Foster, Kathleen A. Writing about Eakins .
Philadelphia , c1989. xiv, 411 p. :   ISBN
0-8122-8107-1   DDC 016.7/092 20
Z6616.E23 F67 1989 ND237.E15
NYPL [3-MCX E12 90-10747]

BREGLER, CHARLES.
Foster, Kathleen A. Writing about Eakins .
Philadelphia , c1989. xiv, 411 p. :   ISBN
0-8122-8107-1   DDC 016.7/092 20
Z6616.E23 F67 1989 ND237.E15
NYPL [3-MCX E12 90-10747]

BREGLER, CHARLES - LIBRARY -
CATALOGS.
Foster, Kathleen A. Writing about Eakins .
Philadelphia , c1989. xiv, 411 p. :   ISBN
0-8122-8107-1   DDC 016.7/092 20
Z6616.E23 F67 1989 ND237.E15
NYPL [3-MCX E12 90-10747]

BREGNO, GIOVANNI BATTISTA, D. 1523 -
CRITICISM AND INTERPRETATION.
Schulz, Anne Markham, 1938- Giambattista
and Lorenzo Bregno . Cambridge [England] ,
New York , 1991. xi, 564 p. :   ISBN
0-521-38406-0   DDC 730/.92 20
NB623.B746 S38 1991

BREGNO, LORENZO, D. 1524 OR 5 - CRITICISM AND INTERPRETATION.
Schulz, Anne Markham, 1938- Giambattista and Lorenzo Bregno . Cambridge [England] , New York , 1991. xi, 564 p. : ISBN 0-521-38406-0 DDC 730/.92 20
NB623.B746 S38 1991

Breicha, Otto.
Giacometti, Alberto, 1901-1966. Alberto Giacometti, 10.10.1901-11.1.1966 . München , c1989. [40] p. :
NYPL [3-MGO (Giacometti) 91-7078]

Hans Böhler, Gemälde und Graphik / Otto Breicha ; [Herausgeber, Österreichische Galerie]. Salzburg : Verlag Galerie Welz, c1981. 119 p. of plates : 75 ill. (some col.) ; 18 cm.
ISBN 3-85349-084-0 : DDC 741.9436 19
1. Böhler, Hans, 1884-1961 - Catalogs. I. Böhler, Hans, 1884-1961. II. Österreichische Galerie. III. Title.
N6811.5.B64 A4 1981
NYPL [3-MCK B68 91-5395]

Rainer, Arnulf, 1929- Arnulf Rainer, masqué-démasqué . Vienne [1987] 143 p. :
ISBN 3-85127-000-2
NYPL [3-MCK R155 90-12023]

Breidecker, Volker. Florenz, oder, "die Rede, die zum Auge spricht" : Kunst, Fest und Macht im Ambiente der Stadt / Volker Breidecker. München : W. Fink, c1990. 446 p., lvi p. of plates : ill. ; 25 cm. Includes bibliographical references (p. [422]-434) and indexes ISBN 3-7705-2600-7
1. Art - Italy - Florence. 2. Florence (Italy) - History. 3. Florence (Italy) - Intellectual life. 4. Florence (Italy) - Social life and customs. I. Title. II. Title: Rede, die zum Auge spricht.
NYPL [3-MAMC 91-6316]

Breitenbach, Josef, 1896-1984.
Die Sammlung Josef Breitenbach zur Geschichte der Photographie . [München] , c1979. 177 p. : ***NYPL [MFW 91-6018]***

BREITENBACH, JOSEF, 1896-1984 - PHOTOGRAPH COLLECTIONS - EXHIBITIONS.
Die Sammlung Josef Breitenbach zur Geschichte der Photographie . [München] , c1979. 177 p. : ***NYPL [MFW 91-6018]***

Breitling, Gisela.
Gisela Breitling / [Gestaltung, Regelindis Westphal]. Stuttgart : Parkland, c1987. 95 p. : ill. (some col.) ; 27 cm. Bibliography: p. 93-95.
ISBN 3-88059-280-2 DDC 759.3 20
1. Breitling, Gisela - Catalogs. I. Westphal, Regelindis. II. Title.
ND588.B757 A4 1987
NYPL [3-MCK B835 90-12642]

Der verborgene Eros : Weiblichkeit und Männlichkeit im Zerrspiegel der Künste : Aufsätze / Gisela Breitling.[Originalausg.] Frankfurt am Main : Fischer Taschenbuch Verlag, 1990. 242 p. : ill. ; 19 cm. (Frau in der Gesellschaft) Includes bibliographical references.
ISBN 3-596-24740-3
1. Women in art. 2. Men in art. 3. Women artists. I. Title. II. Series. ***NYPL [3-MAMZ 90-11131]***

BREITLING, GISELA - CATALOGS.
Breitling, Gisela. Gisela Breitling /. Stuttgart , c1987. 95 p. : ISBN 3-88059-280-2 DDC 759.3 20
ND588.B757 A4 1987
NYPL [3-MCK B835 90-12642]

Breitman, Marc, 1949- Le Nouvel Amiens /. Liège , 1989. 471 p. : ISBN 2-87009-368-3
NA9198.A42 N68 1989

BREITNER, GEORGE HENDRIK, 1857-1923 - EXHIBITIONS.
Hefting, Paul. De foto's van Breitner /. 's-Gravenhage , 1989. 142 p. : ISBN 90-12-06046-X (pbk.)
NYPL [MFX (Hefting) 91-2475]

Brejon de Lavergnée, Barbara. Renaissance et baroque . Milano , c1989. 159 p. : ISBN 2-902092-10-5 ***NYPL [3-MBH+ 91-6534]***

Brekke, Nils Georg, 1938- Lærum, O. D. Røykstova . [Oslo] , c1990. 143 p. : ISBN 82-00-21044-8
NA7566.N8 L3 1990

Bremen. Graphisches Kabinett Kunsthandel Wolfgang Werner. see Graphisches Kabinett Kunsthandel Wolfgang Werner.

Bremen. Kunsthalle. Greune, Karl Heinrich, 1933- Karl Heinrich Greune . Bremen [1979] [80] p. :
N6888.G733 A4 1979
NYPL [3-MCK G837 81-784]

Bremer Landesmuseum für Kunst- und Kulturgeschichte.
Glaskunst vom Empire bis zum Historismus : Bremen Landesmuseum/Focke-Museum : Bestandskatalog 1988 / Bearbeitung, Sabine Baumgärtner ; [Redaktion, Rosemarie Pohl-Weber]. Bremen : Das Landesmuseum, 1988. 214 p. : chiefly ill. (some col.) ; 22 cm. (Hefte des Focke-Museums . Nr. 77) Includes bibliographical references (p. 210-214)
1. Bremer Landesmuseum für Kunst- und Kulturgeschichte - Catalogs. 2. Glassware - Catalogs. 3. Glassware - Germany (West) - Bremen - Catalogs. I. Baumgärtner, Sabine. II. Pohl-Weber, Rosemarie. III. Title. IV. Series. ***NYPL [3-MPW 91-4604]***

BREMER LANDESMUSEUM FÜR KUNST- UND KULTURGESCHICHTE - CATALOGS.
Bremer Landesmuseum für Kunst- und Kulturgeschichte. Glaskunst vom Empire bis zum Historismus . Bremen , 1988. 214 p. :
NYPL [3-MPW 91-4604]

Bremer, Rosemarie. Neuer Berliner Kunstverein. 20 Jahre NBK . Berlin [1989] 233 p. :
NYPL [3-MAVZ (Berlin) 91-6480]

Bremerhaven, Ger. Kunsthalle. see Kunsthalle Bremerhaven.

Bremerhaven, Ger. Kunstverein. see Kunstverein Bremerhaven.

Brems, Rooske. Bever, Suzy van. Suzynisme . Nieuwrode , 1985. [103] p. : ISBN 90-900087-1-3
NYPL [3-MCH+ B569 90-2141]

Breña, Gabriel. Calderwood, Michael. Mexico, a higher vision . La Jolla, Calif. , c1990. 192 p. :
ISBN 0-9625399-5-3
NYPL [MFX+ (Calderwood) 91-3343]

Brend, Barbara, 1940- Islamic art / Barbara Brend. Cambridge, Mass. : Harvard University Press, 1991. p. cm. Includes bibliographical references and index. ISBN 0-674-46865-1: DDC 709/.17/671 20
1. Art, Islamic - History. I. Title.
N6250 B76 1991

Brennan, Fanny.
Skyshades : sixty small paintings / by Fanny Brennan ; foreword by Calvin Tomkins.1st ed. New York, N.Y. : C.N. Potter, c1990. 80 p. : chiefly col. ill. ; 16 cm. "A Panache Press book."
ISBN 0-517-57671-6 : DDC 759.13 20
1. Brennan, Fanny - Catalogs. I. Title.
ND237.B835 A4 1989
NYPL [3-MCX B832 91-6902]

BRENNAN, FANNY - CATALOGS.
Brennan, Fanny. Skyshades . New York, N.Y. , c1990. 80 p. : ISBN 0-517-57671-6 : DDC 759.13 20
ND237.B835 A4 1989
NYPL [3-MCX B832 91-6902]

Brennan, Shawn. Reflections : arts & crafts metalwork in England and the United States / foreword, Catherine Kurland and Lori Zabar ; introduction, Barry Harwood ; catalog text, Shawn Brennan. New York, N.Y. : Kurland-Zabar, c1990. 51 p. : ill. (some col.) ; 23 x 28 cm. Catalog of an exhibition held May 15 through June 23, 1990 at Kurland-Zabar, New York. DDC 739/.0942/0747471 20
1. Art metal-work - England - History - 20th century - Exhibitions. 2. Arts and crafts movement - England - Exhibitions. 3. Art metal-work - United States - History - 20th century - Exhibitions. 4. Arts and crafts movements - United States - Exhibitions. I. Kurland-Zabar (Art gallery). II. Title.
NK1142 .B7 1990 **NYPL [3-MNK 90-13003]**

Brenner-Studien. Sonderreihe .
(Bd. 1) Esterle, Max von, 1870-1947. Karikaturen und Kritiken /. Salzburg , c1971. 237 p. : ISBN 3-7013-0455-6
NC1489.E85 A4 1971
NYPL [MEM (Esterle) 90-6541]

Brent, Isabelle. Cameo cats / illustrated by Isabelle Brent. 1st U. S. ed. Boston : Little, Brown, 1992. p. cm. ISBN 0-316-10836-7 : DDC 745.6/7/092 20

1. Brent, Isabelle. 2. Cats in art. I. Title.
ND3410.B74 A4 1992

BRENT, ISABELLE.
Brent, Isabelle. Cameo cats /. Boston , 1992. p. cm. ISBN 0-316-10836-7 : DDC 745.6/7/092 20
ND3410.B74 A4 1992

Brenta-Monographie : Grundlagenforschung auf dem Gebiet der Hochgebirgskartographie / mit Beiträgen von D. Beineke ... [et al.] ; herausgegeben von G. Neugebauer. München : Studiengang Vermessungswesen, Universität der Bundeswehr München, [1987] 187 p. : ill. (some folded), maps (some col.) ; 30 cm. (Schriftenreihe / Studiengang Vermessungswesen, Universität der Bundeswehr München, 0173-1009 . Heft 24) "August 1987." Includes bibliographies.
1. Cartography - Italy - Brenta Mountains. 2. Brenta Mountains (Italy) - Maps. I. Beineke, D. (Dieter). II. Neugebauer, Gustav, 1922-. III. Université der Bundeswehr München. Studiengang Vermessungswesen. IV. Series: Schriftenreihe (Universität der Bundeswehr München. Studiengang Vermessungswesen) , Heft 24.
GA895.B73 B74 1987
NYPL [Map Div. 91-4143]

BRENTA MOUNTAINS (ITALY) - MAPS.
Brenta-Monographie . München [1987] 187 p. :
GA895.B73 B74 1987
NYPL [Map Div. 91-4143]

Brentjens, Yvonne. Delaunay, Sonia. Sonia Delaunay, dessins /. Tilburg , 1988. 96 p. :
ISBN 90-70962-03-9 (pbk.)
NYPL [3-MCO+ D344 90-10425]

Brentjes, Burchard. Steppenreiter und Handelsherren : die Kunst der Partherzeit in Vorderasien / Burchard Brentjes. Leipzig : E.A. Seemann, 1990. 132 p. : ill. ; 20 cm. (Seeman-Beiträge zur Kunstwissenschaft) Includes bibliographical references (p. 120-121). Includes index.
ISBN 3-363-00459-1 :
1. Art, Parthian. 2. Iran - Antiquities. I. Title. II. Series.
N5899.P36 B74 1990

Bréon, Emmanuel. Sabbagh, Georges, 1887-1951. Georges Sabbagh . Thonon-les-Bains, Haute-Savoie , c1990. 141 p. : ISBN 2-908528-09-6 : DDC 759.4 20
ND553.S23 A4 1990

Bresc-Bautier, Geneviève. Artistes, patriciens et confréries : production et consommation de l'œuvre d'art à Palerme et en Sicile occidentale (1348-1460) / Geneviève Bresc-Bautier. Roma : École française de Rome, 1979. xviii, 315 p., [15] leaves of plates : ill. ; 25 cm. (Collection de l'École française de Rome . 40) Bibliography: p. [xi]-xv.
1. Art, Italian - Italy - Palermo. 2. Art, Gothic - Italy - Palermo. 3. Art patronage - Italy - Palermo. 4. Art and society - Italy - Palermo. I. Title.
N6921.P34 B73 **NYPL [3-MAMC 81-374]**

Brescia (Italy : Province). Assessorato alla cultura. La Scuola di Mons . Brescia , Milano , c1989. 103 p. : DDC 709/.493/42 20
N6968 .S37 1989
NYPL [3-MAME 90-10713]

Brescia (Italy). Assessorato alla cultura. La Scuola di Mons . Brescia , Milano , c1989. 103 p. : DDC 709/.493/42 20
N6968 .S37 1989
NYPL [3-MAME 90-10713]

BRESCIA (ITALY) - BUILDINGS, STRUCTURES, ETC.
Terraroli, Valerio. I chiostri di Brescia . [Brescia] [1989] 171 p. : ISBN 88-7385-052-9
NYPL [3-MRBD+ 91-3675]

Terraroli, Valerio. I chiostri di Brescia . [Brescia] [1989] 171 p. : ISBN 88-7385-052-9 DDC 726/.7/094526 20
NA5621.B8 T47 1989

BRESCIA (ITALY) - CHURCH HISTORY.
Terraroli, Valerio. I chiostri di Brescia . [Brescia] [1989] 171 p. : ISBN 88-7385-052-9 DDC 726/.7/094526 20
NA5621.B8 T47 1989

Bresenhan, Karoline Patterson. Lone stars : a legacy of Texas quilts, 1836-1936 / by Karoline Patterson Bresenhan and Nancy O'Bryant Puentes ; foreword by Jonathan Holstein. Austin : University of Texas Press, c1986-1990. 2 v. : col. ill. ; 31 cm.m. Volume 2: 1st ed. Exhibition catalog. Bibliography: 154-156. ISBN 0-292-74641-5 (v. 1) DDC

746.9/7/097640740164 19
1. Quilts - Texas - History - 19th century - Exhibitions.
2. Quilts - Texas - History - 20th century - Exhibitions.
I. Puentes, Nancy O'Bryant. II. Title.
NK9112 .B68 1986
NYPL [3-MOT+ 86-3404]

Brésil. Villar Guanaes, Lúcia. Brasil =. [Paris] ,
c1988. [118] p. :   ISBN 2-86234-020-0
NYPL [MFX (Villar Guanaes) 91-3501]

Breslauer Akademieschüler heute . Künstlergilde.
Regensburg , 1979. [40] p. :
N6868 .K8 1979   **NYPL [3-MAMG 81-1003]**

Breslauer, Jan, 1961- Knode, Marilu. Third
Newport biennial . Newport Beach, Calif. ,
1991. p. cm.   ISBN 0-917493-19-2   DDC
709/.794/07479496 20
N6530.C2 K64 1991

Breton, André, 1896-1966. L'art magique / André
Breton ; avec le concours de Gérard Legrand.
[Paris] : A. Biro : Phébus, [c1991] 358 p. : ill.
(some col.) ; 31 cm.   ISBN 2-85940-215-2
1. Magic in art. 2. Art, Primitive. 3. Fantasy in art. 4.
Grotesque in art. I. Title.
N8222.M3 B7 1991

Brett, Guy.
Transcontinental : an investigation of reality :
nine Latin American artists : Waltercio
Caldas ... [et al.] / Guy Brett ; with texts by
the artists, Lu Menezes and Paulo Venancio
Filho. London ; New York : Verso : 112 p. : ill.
(some col.) ; 27 cm. Catalog of an exhibition held
Mar. 24-Apr. 28, 1990. Includes bibliographical
references.   ISBN 0-86091-511-5
1. Art, Latin American - Exhibitions. 2. Art, Modern -
20th century - Latin America - Exhibitions. I. Caldas
Júnior, Waltercio, 1946-. II. Menezes, Lu. III. Venancio
Filho, Paulo. IV. Ikon Gallery. V. Cornerhouse
(Gallery : Manchester, England). VI. Title.
NYPL [3-MAM 91-7008]

Transcontinental : an investigation of reality :
nine Latin American artists, Waltercio Caldas ...
/ Guy Brett ; with texts by the artists, Lu
Menezes and Paulo Venancio Filho. London ;
New York : Verso, 1990. 112 p. : ill. ; 27 cm.
    ISBN 0-86091-511-5   DDC 709/.8/09048 20
1. Art, Latin American. 2. Art, Modern - 20th
century - Latin America. I. Title.
N6502.5 .B74 1990

Brettell, Richard R.
Columbus Museum of Art. Impressionism and
European modernism . Columbus, Ohio ,
Seattle , 1991. p.   ISBN 0-295-97133-9 :   DDC
709/.03/407477157 20
N6447 .C65 1991

Pissarro and Pontoise : the painter in a
landscape / Richard R. Brettell ; with assistance
from Joachim Pissarro. New Haven : Yale
University Press, 1990. xi, 227 p. : ill. (some
col.) ; 29 cm. Includes bibliographical references (p.
218-223) and index.   ISBN 0-300-04336-8   DDC
760/.92 20
1. Pissarro, Camille, 1830-1903 - Criticism and
interpretation. 2. Pontoise (France) in art. 3. Pontoise,
France - History. I. Title.
N6853.P57 B74 1990
NYPL [3-MCO P67 90-12984]

Breu, Josef. Atlas der Donauländer. Wien, 1970-
v. (loose-leaf)   DDC 912/.496 19
G1882.D3 A8 1970
NYPL [Map Div. 72-267]

Breuer, Tilmann. Denkmalkunde in Bamberg .
Bamberg [1990] 77 p. :   DDC 720/.28/80943318
20
NA109.G3 D44 1990

Breuille, Jean-Philippe. Dictionnaire de la
peinture allemande et d'Europe centrale /.
Paris , c1990. 415 p. :   ISBN 2-03-740017-9
DDC 759.3/03 20
ND561 .D53 1990   **NYPL [3-MAO 91-7701]**

Breule, l'aimée verte. Jaffrennou, Michel. Vaduz,
1968. 1 v. (unpaged)
NYPL [MDG (Jaffrennou) 91-1292]

Brève défense de l'art français . Clair, Jean.
[Caen] , c1989. 69 p. ;   ISBN 2-905657-46-4
DDC 709/.44/09045 20
N6848 .C56 1989

**BREWSTER, DAVID, SIR, 1781-1868 -
PHOTOGRAPH COLLECTIONS -
CATALOGS.**
Smith, Graham, 1942- Disciples of light .

Malibu [Calif.] , 1990. 170 p. :   ISBN
0-89236-158-1   DDC 779/.074 20
TR654 .S555 1990   **NYPL [MFW 91-3475]**

Brezeanu, Barbu, 1909- N.N. Tonitza / Barbu
Brezianu ; [translated from the Romanian by
Andrei Bantas]. [Bucharest] : Meridiane Pub.
House, 1986. 31, [1] p., [64] p. of plates : ill.
(some col.) ; 33 cm. Cover title: Tonitza.
Bibliography: p. 29-[32]
1. Tonitza, Nicolae N., 1886-1940. 2. Painters -
Romania - Biography. I. Tonitza, Nicolae N.,
1886-1940. II. Title. III. Title: Tonitza.
NYPL [3-MCZ+ T665 90-12666]

Brianchon, Maurice, 1899-1979.
Maurice Brianchon, 1899-1979 : Fondation de
l'Hermitage, Lausanne, du 13 octobre 1989 au
28 janvier 1990. Lausanne : La Fondation,
c1989. 201 p. : ill. ; 28 cm.
1. Brianchon, Maurice, 1899-1979 - Exhibitions. I.
Fondation de l'Hermitage. II. Title.
IN PROCESS (ONLINE)
NYPL [3-MCO B85 91-4217]

**BRIANCHON, MAURICE, 1899-1979 -
EXHIBITIONS.**
Brianchon, Maurice, 1899-1979. Maurice
Brianchon, 1899-1979 . Lausanne , c1989. 201
p. :
IN PROCESS (ONLINE)
NYPL [3-MCO B85 91-4217]

Brice Marden . Marden, Brice, 1938- New York ,
c1991. 63 p. :   ISBN 0-9624347-6-0
NYPL [3-MCX+ M315 91-6583]

Brick building in Britain /. Brunskill, R. W.
London , 1990. 208 p., [16] p. of plates :   ISBN
0-575-04457-8 :   DDC 693.210941 20
TH5501   **NYPL [3-MQWK 90-11098]**

**BRICK PAVEMENTS. see PAVEMENTS,
BRICK.**

BRICKS - ENGLAND.
Brunskill, R. W. Brick building in Britain /.
London , 1990. 208 p., [16] p. of plates :   ISBN
0-575-04457-8 :   DDC 693.210941 20
TH5501   **NYPL [3-MQWK 90-11098]**

BRICKS - GERMANY (WEST)
Appunti per piazze d'Italia /. [Milano] , c1988.
79 p. :   **NYPL [3-MQWB+ 90-12352]**

BRICKS - ITALY.
Appunti per piazze d'Italia /. [Milano] , c1988.
79 p. :   **NYPL [3-MQWB+ 90-12352]**

Bridgeman Art Library.
Rowling, Nick. Art source book . Secaucus,
N.J. , c1987. 320 p. :   ISBN 1-555-21031-7   DDC
704.9/4 20
N4015.G72 L67 1987

BRIDGEMAN ART LIBRARY - CATALOGS.
Rowling, Nick. Art source book . Secaucus,
N.J. , c1987. 320 p. :   ISBN 1-555-21031-7   DDC
704.9/4 20
N4015.G72 L67 1987

Bridges, John. Harling, Robert. The House &
garden book of living rooms /. New York ,
1991. p. cm.   ISBN 0-86565-125-6   DDC 747.7/5
20
NK2117.L5 H37 1991

Bridget Riley. Riley, Bridget, 1931- New York ,
1990. 152 p. :   **NYPL [3-MCV R57 91-6698]**

Bridging the gap . Building Arts Forum/New
York. Symposium (1989 : Guggenheim
Museum) New York , c1991. xv, 183 p. :
    ISBN 0-442-00135-5   DDC 720 20
NA2543.T43 B8 1991
NYPL [3-MQV 91-3950]

**Briefwechsel mit einem jungen Ehepaar,
1927-1937.** Kirchner, Ernst Ludwig, 1880-1938.
Ernst Ludwig Kirchner . Bern , 1989. 147 p. :
    ISBN 3-85773-022-6
N6888.K45 A3 1989
NYPL [3-MCK K58 90-11101]

Briend, Christian. Auburtin, Jean-Francis,
1866-1930. Jean-Francis Auburtin, 1866-1930 .
Paris [1990?] 158 p. :   ISBN 2-905118-27-X
NYPL [3-MCO A897 91-7473]

Briessen, Fritz van. The way of the brush :
painting techniques of China and Japan / by
Fritz van Briessen. Rutland, Vermont : C. E.
Tuttle, 1962. 329 p. : ill. [some col.] ; 28 cm.
Includes index. Bibliography: p. 323-324.   ISBN
0-8048-0625-X   DDC 759.95

1. Painting - Technique. I. Title.
ND1040 .B69 1962   NYPL [3-MAG 91-3352]

Briganti, Giuliano.
La Pittura in Italia . 2 v. (913 p.) , 29 cm.
[Milano] :   **NYPL [3-MCE 90-11794]**

William Bailey / Giuliano Briganti, John
Hollander. New York : Rizzoli, 1991. 195 p. :
ill. (some col.) ; 32 cm. Includes bibliographical
references (p. 192-195).   ISBN 0-8478-1345-2 :   DDC
759.13 20
1. Bailey, William, 1930- - Catalogs. I. Hollander, John.
II. Title.
N6537.B16 A4 1991

BRIGANTI, GIULIANO.
Scritti in onore di Giuliano Briganti. Milano ,
c1990. 344 p., [4] leaves of plates :   ISBN
88-304-0921-9   **NYPL [3-MAS 91-5232]**

Briggs, Martin S. (Martin Shaw), b. 1882- A
pictorial guide to cathedral architecture : with a
glossary of architectural terms / by Martin S.
Briggs. [London : Pitkin Pictorials], 1964. 24
p. : ill., plans ; 23 cm. (Pitkin "Pride of Britain"
books) Cover title.
1. Cathedrals - England. 2. Church architecture -
England. I. Title. II. Title: Cathedral architecture.
NYPL [3-MRBR 90-6038]

**BRIGHT CHILDREN. see GIFTED
CHILDREN.**

Brighton, Andrew. Blasphemies, ecstasies, cries .
[London] , 1989. 71 p. :   ISBN 1-87081-425-8
NYPL [3-MAL 90-11604]

**Brighton Art Gallery and Museum. see Royal
Pavilion, Art Gallery and Museums.**

**Brighton, Eng. Royal Pavillion, Art Gallery and
Museums. see Royal Pavilion, Art Gallery
and Museums.**

Brilliant, Richard. Portraiture / by Richard
Brilliant. Cambridge ; Mass. : Harvard
University Press, 1991. p. cm. Includes
bibliographical references.   ISBN 0-674-69175-X
DDC 704.9/42 20
1. Portraits - History. I. Title.
N7575 .B75 1991

Brill's studies in intellectual history, 0920-8607 .
(v. 25) Farago, Claire J. Leonardo da Vinci's
Paragone . Leiden, The Netherlands , New
York , 1991. p. cm.   ISBN 90-04-09415-6 (cloth)
DDC 750 20
ND1140 .F35 1991

Brink, G. J. M. van den (Gabriël J. M.) De
Wevers en Vincent van Gogh /. Zwolle ,
c1990. 127 p. :   ISBN 90-6630-222-4 :
N6953.G63 D4 1990

Brinkmann, Jens-Uwe, 1944- Stein, Gottfried,
1915- Gottfried Stein zum 75. Geburtstag .
[Göttingen] , c1990. 31 p. :   DDC 759.3 20
ND588.S67 A4 1990

**BRION CEMETERY (TREVISO, ITALY :
PROVINCE)**
Scarpa, Carlo. The other city . Berlin , c1989.
397 p. :   ISBN 3-433-02097-3   DDC 720/.92 20
NA1123.S35 A4 1989

Brion-Guerry, Liliane, 1916- L'année 1913; les
formes esthétiques de l'œuvre d'art à la veille
de la Première Guerre mondiale. Travaux et
documents inédits réunis sous la direction de L.
Brion-Guerry. Paris, Klincksieck, 1971-1973. 3
v. illus. 23 cm. (Collection d'esthétique. 9, 17)
Includes bibliographies.
1. Arts, Modern - 20th century - History and criticism.
I. Title.   **NYPL [3-MAL 72-945]**

**BRISBANE (QLD.) - BUILDINGS,
STRUCTURES, ETC.**
De Gruchy, Graham. Architecture in Brisbane
/. Bowen Hills, Brisbane, Qld. , 1988. 132 p. :
    ISBN 0-86439-078-5
NYPL [3-MQWZ+ 89-21433]

Brisker, Sydney H., 1914- The Architecture of
Ricardo Legorreta /. Austin , 1990. 171 p. :
    ISBN 0-292-75106-0 (alk. paper)   DDC 720/.92
20
NA759.L44 A87 1990   **NYPL [3-MQZ+
(Legorreta Vilchis) 91-3708]**

Bristol City Art Gallery. Jones, David Michael,
1895-1974. David Jones . London , c1989. 48
p. :   ISBN 1-85332-040-4 (pbk.)
NYPL [3-MCV+ J765 89-19109]

BRISTOL (ENGLAND) - DESCRIPTION - VIEWS.
Winstone, Reece. Bristol's earliest photographs /. Bristol , 1970. 80 p. :
NYPL [MFW 90-6062]

Bristol's earliest photographs /. Winstone, Reece. Bristol , 1970. 80 p. :
NYPL [MFW 90-6062]

Bristow, Nicholas. Screen printing : design & technique / Nicholas Bristow. London : B. Batsford, 1990. 160 p. : ill. (some col.) ; 30 cm. Includes index. ISBN 0-7134-5812-7 DDC 764/.8 20
1. Serigraphy - Technique. I. Title.
NE2236 .B75 1990 *NYPL [MDL+ 91-6945]*

Britain portrayed. Barr, John, 1934- London , 1989. 126 p. : ISBN 0-7123-0174-7 :
NYPL [3-MAMY+ 91-4983]

Brite, Jane Fassett. Rossbach, Ed. Ed Rossbach . Asheville, N.C. , Washington, D.C. , 1990. 164 p. : ISBN 0-937274-52-6 : DDC 746/.092 20
NK8998.R68 A4 1990
NYPL [3-MON 90-11617]

British architectural books and writers, 1556-1785 /. Harris, Eileen. Cambridge [England] , New York , 1990. 571 p. : ISBN 0-521-38551-2 DDC 016.72 20
NA965 .H37 1990
NYPL [MQWK 90-13195]

British art now. Igirisu bijutsu wa ima . [Tōkyō , c1990. 151 p. : *NYPL [3-MAMR 91-7545]*

BRITISH ARTS. see **ARTS, BRITISH.**

British craftsmanship in wood /. Norbury, Betty. London , 1990. [192] p. : ISBN 0-85442-043-6 : DDC 684.08 20
TT180   *NYPL [3-MOC 91-6457]*

BRITISH ETCHING. see **ETCHING, BRITISH.**

The British imagination : twentieth-century paintings, sculpture, and drawings : November 10, 1990 to January 12, 1991, Hirschl & Adler Galleries / introduction by Edward Lucie-Smith. New York : Hirschl & Adler, cc1990. 144 p. : chiefly col. ill. ; 26 cm. Editor, Sheila Schwartz. Includes bibliographical references (p. 143) and index. ISBN 0-915057-36-0
1. Art, British - Exhibitions. 2. Art, Modern - 20th century - Great Britain - Exhibitions. I. Schwartz, Sheila. *NYPL [3-MAMR 91-6691]*

BRITISH LANDSCAPE PAINTING. see **LANDSCAPE PAINTING, BRITISH.**

BRITISH LITERATURE. see **ENGLISH LITERATURE.**

British Museum.
Fake? . London , 1990. 312 p. : ISBN 0-7141-1703-X
N8790 .F3 1990b

Jewelry, 7000 years . New York [1991] p. cm. ISBN 0-8109-8103-3 DDC 739.27/09 20
NK7306 .J494 1991

BRITISH MUSEUM.
Jewelry, 7000 years . New York [1991] p. cm. ISBN 0-8109-8103-3 DDC 739.27/09 20
NK7306 .J494 1991

BRITISH MUSEUM - CATALOGS.
A Checklist of Canadian copyright deposits in the British Museum, 1895-1923 /. Halifax, N.S., Canada , 1984- v. ; ISBN 0-7703-0179-7 (pbk.: v. 1) : DDC 015.71 19
Z1365 .C48 1984 *NYPL [Map Div. 85-549]*

Smith, Lawrence. Japanese art . Bloomsbury , c1990. 256 p. : ISBN 0-7141-1446-4 : DDC 709/.52/074 19
N7350   *NYPL [3-MAG 90-11503]*

British Museum. Dept. of Prints and Drawings.
Rowlandson, Thomas, 1756-1827. The rumbustious world of Thomas Rowlandson . London , 1989. 16 p. :
NYPL [MDG+ (Rowlandson) 90-13687]

BRITISH MUSEUM. DEPT. OF PRINTS AND DRAWINGS - EXHIBITIONS.
Rowlandson, Thomas, 1756-1827. The rumbustious world of Thomas Rowlandson . London , 1989. 16 p. ;
NYPL [MDG+ (Rowlandson) 90-13687]

British Museum. Dept. of Western Asiatic Antiquities. Fifty masterpieces of ancient Near Eastern art in the Department of Western Asiatic Antiquities, the British Museum, by R. D. Barnett & D. J. Wiseman. [2nd ed.] London, British Museum, 1969. 96 p. illus. (some col.) 22 cm. ISBN 0-7141-1069-8 DDC 732/.5
1. British Museum. Dept. of Western Asiatic Antiquities. 2. Art - Middle East. I. Barnett, Richard David, 1909-. II. Wiseman, D. J. (Donald John). III. Title.
N5345 .B7 1969   *NYPL [3-MAF 90-6059]*

BRITISH MUSEUM. DEPT. OF WESTERN ASIATIC ANTIQUITIES.
British Museum. Dept. of Western Asiatic Antiquities. Fifty masterpieces of ancient Near Eastern art in the Department of Western Asiatic Antiquities, the British Museum. London, 1969. 96 p. ISBN 0-7141-1069-8 DDC 732/.5
N5345 .B7 1969   *NYPL [3-MAF 90-6059]*

BRITISH MUSEUM - EXHIBITIONS.
Stainton, Lindsay. Nature into art . London [1991] 75 p., 100 p. of plates : ISBN 0-7141-1649-1 (pbk) DDC 759.2074 20
ND1928   *NYPL [3-MCT 91-6694]*

British Museum. Prints and Drawings, Dept. of. see **British Museum. Dept. of Prints and Drawings.**

British Museum. Trustees. Mack, John. Emil Torday and the art of the Congo, 1900-1909 /. London , 1990. 96 : ISBN 0-7141-1594-0 (pbk.) : DDC 709.6724 20   *NYPL [Sc E 91-236]*

British Museum. Western Asiatic Antiquities, Dept. of. see **British Museum. Dept. of Western Asiatic Antiquities.**

British oil paintings, 1820-1860. Victoria and Albert Museum. Catalogue of British oil paintings, 1820-1860 /. London , 1990. xx, 314 p. : ISBN 0-11-290463-7 : DDC 759.2/074 19
NYPL [3-MAVZ+ (London) 90-10927]

British paintings of the sixteenth through nineteenth centuries /. National Gallery of Art (U. S.) Washington, D.C. [New York] , 1991. p. cm. ISBN 0-89468-156-7 DDC 759.2/074/753 20
ND464 .N38 1991

British paintings of the 16th through 19th centuries. National Gallery of Art (U. S.) British paintings of the sixteenth through nineteenth centuries /. Washington, D.C. [New York] , 1991. p. cm. ISBN 0-89468-156-7 DDC 759.2/074/753 20
ND464 .N38 1991

BRITISH PERIODICALS - BIBLIOGRAPHY - CATALOGS.
Jolly, David C. Maps in British periodicals /. Brookline, Mass. , 1990-1991. 2 v. : ISBN 0-911775-51-X (v. 1) DDC 016.912 20
Z6028 .J64 1990 GA300
NYPL [Map Div. 90-47]

The British photographer abroad : the first thirty years / [compiled by] Robert Hershkowitz. London : Hershkowitz, 1980. 95 p. : chiefly ill. ; 25 x 29 cm. Bibliography: p. 90. ISBN 0-9507057-0-5 :
1. Travel photography - History. 2. Photography - Great Britain - History. I. Hershkowitz, Robert.
TR790 .B74   *NYPL [MFW 81-889]*

BRITISH PORTRAITS. see **PORTRAITS, BRITISH.**

BRITISH POSTERS. see **POSTERS, BRITISH.**

BRITISH PRINTS. see **PRINTS, BRITISH.**

British racing prints, 1700-1940 /. Lane, Charles. London , 1990. 200 p., 16 p. of plates : ISBN 0-948253-45-2 : DDC 769/.432 20
NE960.3.G7 L26 1990

British romantic art and the Second World War /. Sillars, Stuart, 1951- New York , 1991. p. cm. ISBN 0-312-06719-4 DDC 700 20
NX543 .S52 1991

British School at Rome. Un Artista etrusco e il suo mondo . Roma , 1988. 112 p., [8] p. of plates : ISBN 88-7813-131-8
NYPL [3-MPEK 90-12767]

British Society of Master Glass Painters.
Thomas, Brian. Directory of master glass-painters. Newcastle upon Tyne, 1972. [6],

122 p. ISBN 0-85362-147-0 DDC 748.5/92
NK5300.7 .T48   *NYPL [3-MRY 90-5473]*

British studio pottery . Watson, Oliver. Oxford , 1990. 287 p. : ISBN 0-7148-8067-1
NYPL [3-MPGO 91-5198]

British wallpapers 1930-1960. A popular art . London [1989?] 72 p. : ISBN 0-904804-98-3
NYPL [3-MLP 91-6600]

BRITISH WOOD-ENGRAVING. see **WOOD-ENGRAVING, BRITISH.**

Britt, John. Heart of American Carnival Glass Association. [Buckner, MO] : The Association, [c1990] 150 p. : ill. ; 22 cm. (Educational series. 1) Cover title. Written by John & Lucile Britt. DDC 748.2913/09/041 20
1. Carnival glass - United States. I. Britt, Lucile. II. Series: Educational series (Buckner, Mo.) , 1. III. Title.
NK5439.C35 B75 1990

Britt, Lucile. Britt, John. Heart of American Carnival Glass Association. [Buckner, MO] [c1990] 150 p. : DDC 748.2913/09/041 20
NK5439.C35 B75 1990

BRITTANY (FRANCE) IN ART.
Delouche, Denise. Les peintres et le paysan breton /. Baillé , 1988. xii, 216 p. : ISBN 2-86934-011-7 *NYPL [3-MAMY 91-7021]*

BRITTANY IN ART - CATALOGS.
Gamet, Pierre. Henri Rivière . Douarnenez , 1989. 40 p., 48 leaves of plates : ISBN 2-903708-20-7 DDC 769.92 20
N6853.R5 A4 1989

A broad canvas . Collins, Ian. Norwich , c1990. 144 p. : ISBN 1-87033-706-9
NYPL [3-MAMR 90-11517]

Broadbent, Geoffrey. Taveira, Tomás. Tomás Taveira . London , New York, N.Y , 1990. 272 p. : ISBN 1-85490-034-X
NYPL [3-MQZ+ (Taveira) 91-5456]

Broaddus, John Eric, 1943-
Spin 1/2 : books, paintings, and memorabilia by John Eric Broaddus, June 7-August 31, 1990, Center for Book Arts. New York, N.Y. (626 Broadway, New York 10012) : The Center, c1990 ([New York] : Lower East Side Printshop) 15 p. : col. ill. ; 16 cm. "Catalog ... produced under the direction of Ruth Antrich Ely"--P. 12. Introd. by Jan van der Wateren. "Printed in an edition of 400"--P. 12. LC has copy no. 293. DLC Source: Gift of Tony Zwicker, Dec. 10, 1990. DLC DDC 709/.2 20
1. Broaddus, John Eric, 1943- - Exhibitions. I. Center for Book Arts (New York, N.Y.). II. Title. III. Title: Spin one/two.
N6537.B7 A4 1990

BROADDUS, JOHN ERIC, 1943- - EXHIBITIONS.
Broaddus, John Eric, 1943- Spin 1/2 . New York, N.Y. (626 Broadway, New York 10012) , c1990 ([New York] : Lower East Side Printshop) 15 p. : DDC 709/.2 20
N6537.B7 A4 1990

Broadgate . Mason, Robert, 1946- [London] , 1990. 63 p. : ISBN 1-87317-500-0
NYPL [3-MCV+ M397 90-12886]

BROADGATE (LONDON, ENGLAND) IN ART - EXHIBITIONS.
Mason, Robert, 1946- Broadgate . [London] , 1990. 63 p. : ISBN 1-87317-500-0
NYPL [3-MCV+ M397 90-12886]

Broadhead, Caroline. Houston, John, 1935- Caroline Broadhead . London , 1990. 64 p. : ISBN 0-947792-48-1 (pbk.) : DDC 739.27092 20
NYPL [3-MNR 90-12744]

BROADHEAD, CAROLINE.
Houston, John, 1935- Caroline Broadhead . London , 1990. 64 p. : ISBN 0-947792-48-1 (pbk.) : DDC 739.27092 20
NYPL [3-MNR 90-12744]

Brochado, Alexandrino. O Porto e suas igrejas azulejadas / Alexandrino Brochado. Porto : Banco Comercial Português, 1990. 102 p. : col. ill. ; 28 cm. Includes bibliographical references (p. 102).
1. Tiles - Portugal - Porto. 2. Church decoration and ornament - Portugal - Porto. 3. Façades - Portugal - Porto. I. Title.
NK4670.7.P62 P673 1990

Brock, Astrid. Von Pop zum Konzept . Aachen
[1975] [64] p., [30] leaves of plates :
N6488.G3 A28
    NYPL [3-MAW+ (Aachen) 80-1119]

Brock, Bazon, 1936-
Die Re-Dekade : Kunst und Kultur der 80er
Jahre / Bazon Brock. München : Klinkhardt &
Biermann, c1990. 298 p. : ill. (some col.) ; 24
cm. (Zeit, Zeuge, Kunst) ISBN 3-7814-0288-6 :
    *1. Arts, German. 2. Arts, Modern - 20th century -
Germany. 3. Germany - Cultural policy - History - 20th
century. 4. Aesthetics, Modern - 20th century. I. Title.
II. Title: Kunst und Kultur der 80er Jahre. III. Series.*
NX550.A1 B76 1990

Kunst auf Befehl? . München , c1990. 275 p. :
    ISBN 3-7814-0285-1   DDC 701/.03 20
N6868.5.N37 K85 1990

Brockhaus, Christoph, fl. 1975- Russische
Avantgarde 1910-1930 . Duisburg , c1990. 120
p. :   ISBN 3-923576-73-0
N6988 .R855 1990

Brockmann, Gottfried, 1903-
Gottfried Brockmann, drawings 1921-1931 :
November 8 through December 6, 1975.
Birmingham, Mich. : Donald Morris Gallery,
c1975. [32] p. : ill. ; 22 cm. Catalog by Joseph
Downing.
    *1. Brockmann, Gottfried, 1903- - Exhibitions. I.
Downing, Joseph. II. Donald Morris Gallery. III. Title.*
    NYPL [3-MCK B862 91-1178]

**BROCKMANN, GOTTFRIED, 1903- -
EXHIBITIONS.**
Brockmann, Gottfried, 1903- Gottfried
Brockmann, drawings 1921-1931 . Birmingham,
Mich. , c1975. [32] p. :
    NYPL [3-MCK B862 91-1178]

Brockmann, Josef Müller- see Müller-Brockmann,
Josef, 1914-

Brockton Art Museum. Viola, Bill, 1951- Bill
Viola, The city of man. Brockton, Mass. , 1989.
[8] p. :   ISBN 0-934358-24-9
    NYPL [3-MAL 89-25255]

Brod Gallery (London, England) Jan Brueghel the
elder : a loan exhibition of paintings, 21
June-20 July, 1979. London : Brod Gallery,
c1979. 122 p. : ill. (some col.) ; 30 cm.
Bibliography: p. 35-38.   DDC 759.9493 19
    *1. Bruegel, Jan, 1568-1625 - Exhibitions. I. Bruegel,
Jan, 1568-1625. II. Title.*
ND673.B72 A4 1979
    NYPL [3-MCH+ B88-90-12668]

Broders, Roger, 1883-1953.
Montry, Annie de. Voyages, avec Roger
Broders . Paris , c1991. 117 p. :   ISBN
2-86738-595-4
NC1850.B76 A4 1991

BRODERS, ROGER, 1883-1953 - CATALOGS.
Montry, Annie de. Voyages, avec Roger
Broders . Paris , c1991. 117 p. :   ISBN
2-86738-595-4
NC1850.B76 A4 1991

Brodhead, Michael J. Long, Walter S. (Walter
Sully), 1842-1907. Brushwork diary . Reno ,
1991. p. cm.   ISBN 0-87417-174-1 (alk. paper)
    DDC 759.13 20
ND1837.L66 A4 1991

Brodsky & Utkin / Lois Nesbitt, editor. New
York : Princeton Architectural Press : R.
Feldman Fine Arts, c1990. p. cm. Includes
bibliographical references.   ISBN 1-87827-113-X :
    DDC 769.92/2 20
    *1. Brodsky, Alexander, 1955- - Catalogs. 2. Utkin,
Alexander, 1955- - Catalogs. 3. Buildings in art -
Catalogs. I. Brodsky, Alexander, 1955-. II. Utkin, Ilya,
1955-. III. Nesbitt, Lois Ellen. IV. Title: Brodsky and
Utkin.*
NE2056.5.B76 A4 1990

Brodsky, Alexander, 1955-
Brodsky & Utkin /. New York , c1990. p. cm.
    ISBN 1-87827-113-X :   DDC 769.92/2 20
NE2056.5.B76 A4 1990

BRODSKY, ALEXANDER, 1955- - CATALOGS.
Brodsky & Utkin /. New York , c1990. p. cm.
    ISBN 1-87827-113-X :   DDC 769.92/2 20
NE2056.5.B76 A4 1990

Brodsky and Utkin. Brodsky & Utkin /. New
York , c1990. p. cm.   ISBN 1-87827-113-X :
    DDC 769.92/2 20
NE2056.5.B76 A4 1990

Brody, Annemarie. Contemporary aboriginal art
from the Robert Holmes à Court Collection .
Perth , 1990. 125 p. :   ISBN 0-7316-8569-5
    NYPL [3-MADF+ 91-4291]

Broekel, Ray. Maps and globes / by Ray Broekel.
Chicago : Childrens Press, c1983. 45 p. : col.
ill. ; 22 cm. (A New true book) Includes index.
Briefly discusses different types of maps and globes and
explains such map-related terms as symbol, key,
direction, and scale.   ISBN 0-516-01695-4   DDC 912
19
    *1. Maps - Juvenile literature. 2. Globes - Juvenile
literature. I. Title.*
GA105.6 .B76 1983
    NYPL [Map Div. 91-2532]

BROEL, GEORG, 1884-1940.
Witte, Klaus. Georg Broel, 1884-1940 .
Frederikshavn , 1984. 86 p. :   ISBN
87-7317-116-6
    NYPL [MDVK (bBroel) 90-13584]

Broggi, Luigi, 1851-1926. I miei ricordi,
1851-1924 : settant'anni di vita italiana nelle
memorie di un architetto milanese / Luigi
Broggi ; a cura di Maria Canella. Milano, Italy :
F. Angeli, c1989. 301 p. : ill. ; 23 cm. (Quaderni
di storia in Lombardia . 3) Includes bibliographical
references and index.   ISBN 88-20-43560-8 :   DDC
720/.92 B 20
    *1. Broggi, Luigi, 1851-1926. 2. Architects - Italy -
Milan - Biography. 3. Milan (Italy) - Biography. I.
Canella, Maria. II. Title. III. Series.*
NA1123.B76 A2 1989

BROGGI, LUIGI, 1851-1926.
Broggi, Luigi, 1851-1926. I miei ricordi,
1851-1924 . Milano, Italy , c1989. 301 p. :
    ISBN 88-20-43560-8 :   DDC 720/.92 B 20
NA1123.B76 A2 1989

Bröhan-Museum Berlin. Becker, Ingeborg, 1947-
Schmuckkunst im Jugendstil /. Berlin , c1988.
95 p. :   ISBN 3-496-01064-9
    NYPL [3-MNR 90-12395]

Broido, Lucy. The posters of Jules Chéret : 46
full-color plates & an illustrated catalogue
raisonné / by Lucy Broido.2nd, rev. & enl. ed.
New York : Dover, 1991. p. cm. Includes
bibliographical references and index.   ISBN
0-486-26966-3 (pbk.)   DDC 741.6/74/092 20
    *1. Chéret, Jules, 1836-1932 - Catalogues raisonnés. I.
Chéret, Jules, 1836-1932. II. Title.*
NC1850.C47 A4 1991

Bromhead, Peter, 1933- The king and the
dragon : [an adult fairy-tale] / [written and
illustrated by Bromhead]. [Auckland : Hodder
and Stoughton], 1978. [63] p. : ill. ; 20 cm.
Political satire of New Zealand leadership in cartoons
and captions.   ISBN 0-340-23143-2 :
    I. Title.
PZ4.B86816 Ki PR9639.3.B69
    NYPL [3-MEM (Bromhead) 80-379]

Bromley, firm, publishers.
Atlas of the city of New York--borough of the
Bronx : from actual surveys and official plans /
by George W. and Walter S. Bromley.
Philadelphia : G.W. Bromley, 1923-1924 [i.e.
1963-1978]. 2 v. : col. maps ; 59 cm. Corrections
pasted on original maps. Label mounted on imprint of
v. 1 reads: Sanborn Map Co., Pelham, N.Y. Includes
index. CONTENTS. - v. 1. South of 172nd Street.
Correction no. 243 (1978) -- v. 2. North of 172nd
Street. Correction no. 215 (1963).
    *1. Real property - New York (State) - Bronx
(Borough) - Maps. 2. Bronx (Borough) - Maps. I.
Bromley, George Washington. II. Bromley, Walter
Scott. III. Title.*   *NYPL [Map Div. 83-39]*

Bronx land book of the city of New York.
Desk and library ed. [vol. 3, rev. 1979] New
York, c1960- v. maps. 28 x 45 cm. Scale of most
sectional maps: 1:1,920; 160 feet to the inch. Ms. rev.
note on t.p.
    *1. Real property - New York (State) - Bronx (Borough).
2. Bronx (Borough) - Maps. I. Title.*   *NYPL [Map
Div. (Bromley, G.W., & Company. Bronx
land book of the city of New York)]*

Bromley, G. W., & Company. see Bromley, firm,
publishers.

Bromley, George W. Atlas of Bergen County,
New Jersey : from actual surveys and official
plans / by George W. and Walter S. Bromley.
Philadelphia, Pa. : G.W. Bromley and Co.,
1912-1913. 2 atlases : col. maps ; 57 cm.
CONTENTS. - v.1. Properties lying between the

Hudson River and Hackensack River -- v.2. Properties
lying west of the Hackensack River.
    *1. Bergen County, N. J. - Maps. I. Bromley, Walter S.
II. Title.*   *NYPL [Map Div. 91-4094]*

Bromley, George Washington. Bromley, firm,
publishers. Atlas of the city of New
York--borough of the Bronx . Philadelphia ,
1923-1924 [i.e. 1963-1978]. 2 v. :
    NYPL [Map Div. 83-39]

Bromley, Walter S. Bromley, George W. Atlas of
Bergen County, New Jersey . Philadelphia, Pa. ,
1912-1913. 2 atlases :
    NYPL [Map Div. 91-4094]

Bromley, Walter Scott. Bromley, firm, publishers.
Atlas of the city of New York--borough of the
Bronx . Philadelphia , 1923-1924 [i.e.
1963-1978]. 2 v. :   *NYPL [Map Div. 83-39]*

Brommer, Frank. Vasenlisten zur griechischen
Heldensage / von Frank Brommer. 3., erw.
Aufl. Marburg : Elwert, 1973. xii, 646 p. ; 22
cm. Bibliography: p. ix-x.   ISBN 3-7708-0468-6
    *1. Vase-painting, Greek - Indexes. 2. Mythology,
Greek - Illustrations - Indexes. I. Title.*
    NYPL [3-MPEK 91-995]

Bronkhorst, Hans.
Vincent van Gogh : zijn leven, zijn werk /
Hans Bronkhorst. Weert : MP, c1990. 200 p. :
ill. (some col.) ; 31 cm. Includes bibliographical
references (p. 196-197) and index.   ISBN
90-6590-394-1 :   DDC 759.9492 B 20
    *1. Gogh, Vincent van, 1853-1890. 2. Painters -
Netherlands - Biography. I. Gogh, Vincent van,
1853-1890. II. Title.*
ND653.G7 B724 1990

Vincent Van Gogh / Hans Bronkhorst.
London : Weidenfeld and Nicolson, 1990. 200
p. : col. ill. ; 31 cm. "Translated from the Dutch by
Tony Langham and Plym Peters"--T.p. verso. Includes
index. Bibliography: p. 196-197.
    NYPL [3-MCH+ G61 91-6423]

Brons, Marianne. Bramsen, Henrik Boe, 1908-
Early photographs of architecture and views in
two Copenhagen libraries. Copenhagen , 1957.
92 p. :   DDC 779.4
N4015 .B67   *NYPL [MFW 91-4572]*

BRONX (BOROUGH) - MAPS.
(1923) Bromley, firm, publishers. Atlas of the
city of New York--borough of the Bronx .
Philadelphia , 1923-1924 [i.e. 1963-1978]. 2 v. :
    NYPL [Map Div. 83-39]

(1960) Bromley, firm, publishers. Bronx land
book of the city of New York. New York,
c1960- v.   *NYPL [Map Div. (Bromley,
G.W., & Company. Bronx land book of the
city of New York)]*

Bronx (Borough). Museum of the Arts. see
Bronx Museum of the Arts.

Bronx Community District ... atlas. New York
(N.Y.). Dept. of City Planning. Block & lot
maps-- Bronx Community District ... atlas /.
New York, N.Y. , c1990. 12 v. :
    NYPL [Map Div. 91-7471]

Bronx land book of the city of New York.
Bromley, firm, publishers. New York, c1960- v.
    *NYPL [Map Div. (Bromley, G.W., &
Company. Bronx land book of the city of
New York)]*

Bronx Museum of the Arts. Franta, 1930- Franta.
Bronx, N.Y. , 1989. [32] p. :
    NYPL [3-MCZ+ F836 91-5469]

BRONX (NEW YORK, N.Y.) - MAPS.
New York (N.Y.). Dept. of City Planning.
Block & lot maps-- Bronx Community
District ... atlas /. New York, N.Y. , c1990. 12
v. :   *NYPL [Map Div. 91-7471]*

BRONZE AGE - ARMENIA.
Frühe Bergvölker in Armenien und im
Kaukasus . Berlin , 1984. 84 p. :
    NYPL [3-MAE 90-10823]

BRONZE AGE - CAUCASUS.
Frühe Bergvölker in Armenien und im
Kaukasus . Berlin , 1984. 84 p. :
    NYPL [3-MAE 90-10823]

BRONZE AGE - ITALY, SOUTHERN.
Yntema, Douwe Geert. The matt-painted
pottery of Southern Italy . Galatina , 1990. 370
p. :   ISBN 88-7786-428-0
    NYPL [3-MPGD 91-5545]

BRONZE FIGURINES, ANCIENT.
Small bronze sculpture from the ancient world .
Malibu, Calif. , 1990. 284 p. :   ISBN
0-89236-176-X (paper) :   DDC 730/.093 20
NK7907 .S63 1990   **NYPL [3-MGR 91-6336]**

**BRONZE FIGURINES, BUDDHIST -
THAILAND .**
Känsäng Phraphutthawachiramongkut .
[Bangkok] [2511 i.e. 1968] 44 p. :
NK7978.7.A1 K36 1968

**BRONZE FIGURINES, ITALIAN -
CATALOGS.**
Banzato, D. (Davide) Bronzi e placchette dei
Musei civici di Padova /. Padova , c1989. 155
p. :   DDC 730/.0945/0744532 20
NK7952.A1 B36 1989
                    NYPL [MGR 91-6998]

BRONZE FIGURINES - THAILAND.
Känsäng Phraphutthawachiramongkut .
[Bangkok] [2511 i.e. 1968] 44 p. :
NK7978.7.A1 K36 1968

**BRONZE FOUNDING - THAILAND -
BANGKOK.**
Känsäng Phraphutthawachiramongkut .
[Bangkok] [2511 i.e. 1968] 44 p. :
NK7978.7.A1 K36 1968

**BRONZE IMPLEMENTS - FRANCE - APT -
EXHIBITIONS.**
Cavalier, Odile. Le trésor d'Apt . Avignon ,
1988. 119 p. :   ISBN 2-903044-49-X
                    NYPL [3-MGR + 90-5010]

BRONZE IMPLEMENTS IN ART.
Riz, Anna Elisabeth. Bronzegefässe in der
römisch-pompejanischen Wandmalerei /. Mainz
am Rhein , 1990. xvii, 115 p. , 63 p. of
plates :ill. (chiefly col.) ;   ISBN 3-8053-1121-4 :
DDC 758/.9739512/09377 20
ND2575 .R58 1990

BRONZE IMPLEMENTS - ROME.
Il Bronzo dei Romani . Roma , c1990. 298 p. :
ISBN 88-7062-675-X
IN PROCESS (ONLINE)
                    NYPL [3-MGR 91-3253]

**BRONZE SCULPTURE - CONSERVATION
AND RESTORATION - ITALY - ROME.**
Marco Aurelio . [Italy] , c1989. 277 p. :   ISBN
88-366-0280-0   **NYPL [3-MGR+ 91-5599]**

**BRONZE SCULPTURE - CONSERVATION
AND RESTORATION - ITALY - VENICE.**
The Lion of Venice . Munich , 1990. 234 p. :
                    NYPL [3-MGR 91-7309]

BRONZE SCULPTURE - ROME.
Il Bronzo dei Romani . Roma , c1990. 298 p. :
ISBN 88-7062-675-X
IN PROCESS (ONLINE)
                    NYPL [3-MGR 91-3253]

**Bronzegefässe in der römisch-pompejanischen
Wandmalerei /.** Riz, Anna Elisabeth. Mainz am
Rhein , 1990. xvii, 115 p. , 63 p. of plates :ill.
(chiefly col.) ;   ISBN 3-8053-1121-4 :   DDC
758/.9739512/09377 20
ND2575 .R58 1990

**BRONZES - 19TH CENTURY - FRANCE -
EXHIBITIONS.**
Bernard Black Gallery (New York, N.Y.) Les
animaliers . New York, N.Y. [1963] [16] p. :
                    NYPL [3-MGI 90-5741]

BRONZES, AMERICAN - EXHIBITIONS.
Chiriacka, Ernest, 1920- Ernest Chiriacka.
New York, N.Y. , 1976. [17] p. :
                    NYPL [3-MCX C541 90-5910]

BRONZES, ANCIENT - CHINA - CATALOGS.
Rawson, Jessica. Western Zhou ritual bronzes
from the Arthur M. Sackler collections /.
Washington, D.C. : Cambridge, Mass. : 2 v.
(776 p.) :   ISBN 0-674-95070-4
                    NYPL [3-MGR+ 91-4952]

**BRONZES, ANCIENT - FRANCE - PARIS -
CATALOGS.**
Les Bronzes antiques de Paris /. Paris , 1989.
512 p. :   ISBN 2-901414-34-6   DDC 730/.09364 20
NK7949.P2 B7 1989

**BRONZES, CHINESE - TO 221 B.C. -
CATALOGS.**
Rawson, Jessica. Western Zhou ritual bronzes
from the Arthur M. Sackler collections /.
Washington, D.C. : Cambridge, Mass. : 2 v.
(776 p.) :   ISBN 0-674-95070-4
                    NYPL [3-MGR+ 91-4952]

**BRONZES, CHINESE - TO 221 B.C. -
EXHIBITIONS.**
Art chinois . [Morlanwelz, Belgium] , 1990. 216
p. :   DDC 730/.0951/07449342 20
NK4165 .A714 1990

BRONZES, CLASSICAL - EXHIBITIONS.
Herrscher, Krieger und Geliebte . Innsbruck ,
c1989. 95 p., [6] p. of plates :
                    NYPL [3-MGR 91-3460]

BRONZES, CLASSICAL - ITALY - VENICE.
The Lion of Venice . Munich , 1990. 234 p. :
                    NYPL [3-MGR 91-7309]

**BRONZES, ETRUSCAN - ITALY -
PALESTRINA - CATALOGS.**
Le Ciste prenestine /. [Roma] , 1979- v. :
DG70.P33 C57 1979
                    NYPL [3-MGR+ 83-2202]

BRONZES - FRANCE - PARIS - CATALOGS.
Les Bronzes antiques de Paris /. Paris , 1989.
512 p. :   ISBN 2-901414-34-6   DDC 730/.09364 20
NK7949.P2 B7 1989

BRONZES, FRENCH - EXHIBITIONS.
Bernard Black Gallery (New York, N.Y.) Les
animaliers . New York, N.Y. [1963] [16] p. :
                    NYPL [3-MGI 90-5741]

**BRONZES, GALLO-ROMAN - FRANCE -
APT - EXHIBITIONS.**
Cavalier, Odile. Le trésor d'Apt . Avignon ,
1988. 119 p. :   ISBN 2-903044-49-X
                    NYPL [3-MGR + 90-5010]

**BRONZES - GERMANY - FRANKFURT AM
MAIN - CATALOGS.**
Kohlert-Németh, Maria. Römische Bronzen .
Frankfurt am Main , c1988- v. <1 > :   ISBN
3-88270-311-3 (v. 1)   DDC
739.5/12/0937074434164 20
NK7907.3 .K6 1988

BRONZES, GREEK.
Calcani, Giuliana. Cavalieri di bronzo . Roma ,
c1989. 182 p. :   ISBN 88-7062-671-7
                    NYPL [3-MGO (Lysippus) 91-5330]

BRONZES, IBERIAN - CATALOGS.
Nicolini, Gérard. Die iberischen Bronzevotive.
Kallmünz/Opf., 1967. 49 p. with illus.
                    NYPL [L-11 3436 Nr. 10]

**BRONZES, INDIC - INDIA - KERALA -
CATALOGS.**
Art Museum, Trivandrum. Catalogue of selected
bronzes, wood-carvings & sculptures /.
[Trivandrum] , 1981. [132] p. :
                    NYPL [3-MGI+ 90-12595]

BRONZES, JAPANESE.
Fattorini, Tommaso. I meravigliosi bronzi del
Giappone . Milano , c1990. 147 p. :
                    NYPL [3-MAG 91-7721]

**BRONZES - MASSACHUSETTS -
CAMBRIDGE - CATALOGS.**
Rawson, Jessica. Western Zhou ritual bronzes
from the Arthur M. Sackler collections /.
Washington, D.C. : Cambridge, Mass. : 2 v.
(776 p.) :   ISBN 0-674-95070-4
                    NYPL [3-MGR+ 91-4952]

**BRONZES - PRIVATE COLLECTIONS -
EXHIBITIONS.**
Art chinois . [Morlanwelz, Belgium] , 1990. 216
p. :   DDC 730/.0951/07449342 20
NK4165 .A714 1990

BRONZES, ROMAN - CATALOGS.
Kohlert-Németh, Maria. Römische Bronzen .
Frankfurt am Main , c1988- v. <1 > :   ISBN
3-88270-311-3 (v. 1)   DDC
739.5/12/0937074434164 20
NK7907.3 .K6 1988

**BRONZES, ROMAN - CONSERVATION AND
RESTORATION - ITALY - ROME.**
Marco Aurelio . [Italy] , c1989. 277 p. :   ISBN
88-366-0280-0   **NYPL [3-MGR+ 91-5599]**

BRONZES, ROMAN - EXHIBITIONS.
Los Bronces romanos en España . [Madrid]
[1990?] 358 p. :   ISBN 84-7483-623-9   DDC
739.5/12/093660744641 20
NK7907.3 .B76 1990

BRONZES - ROME.
Il Bronzo dei Romani . Roma , c1990. 298 p. :
ISBN 88-7062-675-X
IN PROCESS (ONLINE)
                    NYPL [3-MGR 91-3253]

BRONZES - ROME - CATALOGS.
Zahlhaas, Gisela. Römische Reliefspiegel /.
Kallmünz/Opf. , 1975. 79, 31 p. :   ISBN
3-7847-5117-2 :
NK7907.3 .Z34   **NYPL [L-11 3436 Nr. 17]**

BRONZES, VIETNAMESE - CATALOGS.
Dong son drums in Viet Nam /. Tōkyō , 1990.
282 p. :   ISBN 4-8453-3038-5 :
NK7978.6.V5 D66 1990

Bronzi e placchette dei Musei civici di Padova /.
Banzato, D. (Davide) Padova , c1989. 155 p. :
DDC 730/.0945/0744532 20
NK7952.A1 B36 1989
                    NYPL [MGR 91-6998]

Il Bronzo dei Romani : arredo e suppellettile / a
cura di Lucia Pirzio Biroli Stefanelli ; testi di
Maddalena Cima Di Puolo ... [et al.]. Roma :
"L'Erma" di Bretschneider, c1990. 298 p. : ill.
(some col.), maps ; 28 cm. Includes index. Includes
bibliographical references (p. [290]-296).   ISBN
88-7062-675-X
*1. Bronzes - Rome. 2. Bronze sculpture - Rome. 3.
Bronze implements - Rome. I. Cima, Maddalena. II.
Biroli Stefanelli, Lucia Pirzio.*
IN PROCESS (ONLINE)
                    NYPL [3-MGR 91-3253]

**Brook Taylor's role in the history of linear
perspective /.** Andersen, Kirsti. New York ,
c1991. p. cm.   ISBN 0-387-97486-5   DDC 701/.82
20
NC749 .A48 1991

Brooke, Janet M. Discerning tastes : Montreal
collectors 1880-1920 / by Janet M. Brooke.
Montréal, Québec, Canada : Montreal Museum
of Fine Arts, c1989. 254 p. : ill. (some col.),
ports. ; 28 cm. Catalog of an exhibition held at the
Musée des beaux-arts de Montréal, Dec. 8, 1989-Feb.
15, 1990. Includes index. Bibliography: p. 250-253.
ISBN 2-89192-123-2
*1. Collectors and collecting - Québec (Province) -
Montréal - Exhibitions. I. Title.*
                    NYPL [3-MAVC 90-12883]

Brooke, Xanthe, 1960- Murillo in focus : 16
November 1990-13 January 1991, Walker Art
Gallery, Liverpool / exhibition researched and
organised by Xanthe Brooke. [Liverpool] :
National Museums and Galleries on
Merseyside, [1990] 48 p. : ill. (2 col.) ; 26 cm.
Correction slip inserted. Bibliography: p. 46-47.
Library's copy lacks correction slip.   ISBN
0-906367-44-1
*1. Murillo, Bartolomé Esteban, 1617-1682 - Exhibitions.
I. Walker Art Gallery. II. Title.*
                    NYPL [3-MCQ M97 91-5562]

Brookes, Mona, 1937- Drawing for older
children, teens, and adult beginners / Mona
Brookes. 1st ed. Los Angeles : J.P. Tarcher ;
New York : Distributed by St. Martin's Press,
c1991. p. cm. Includes bibliographical references and
index.   ISBN 0-87477-660-0 :   DDC 741.2 20
1. Drawing - Technique. I. Title.
NC730 .B657 1991

Brooking, Charles.
[Map of the city and suburbs of Dublin]
The city of Dublin, 1728 / Charles
Brooking ; with introduction and notes by
Maurice Craig. Dublin : Irish Architectural
Archive : Friends of the Library, Trinity
College, Dublin, 1983. 1 portfolio : ill. ; 30
cm. "Reproduced from A map of the city and
suburbs of Dublin... by Charles Brooking, London,
1728."   ISBN 0-904720-14-4 :   DDC 941.8/35 19
*1. Dublin (Dublin) - Description - Views. 2. Dublin
(Dublin) - Maps. I. Craig, Maurice James. II. Title.*
DA995.D8 B76 1983
                    NYPL [Map Div. 87-655]

Brooklyn Community District ... atlas. New York
(N.Y.). Dept. of City Planning. Block & lot
maps-- Brooklyn Community District ... atlas /.
New York, N.Y. , c1990. 18 v. :
                    NYPL [Map Div. 91-6366]

Brooklyn Museum.
Anderson, Nancy K. Albert Bierstadt . New
York , c1990. 327 p. :   ISBN 1-555-95059-0 :
DDC 759.13 20
ND237.B585 A4 1991
                    NYPL [3-MCX+ B585 91-5808]

Broun, Elizabeth. Albert Pinkham Ryder /.
Washington , c1989. viii, 344 p. :   ISBN

Brooklyn Museum. (cont.)

0-87474-328-1 (alk. paper)   DDC 759.13 19
ND237.R8 A4 1989
    NYPL [3-MCX R99 90-12872]

Curator's choice : American watercolor
masters : Winslow Homer and John Singer
Sargent : the Brooklyn Museum, July 7 to
September 2, 1990. [Brooklyn, N.Y. : The
Museum, 1990] 1 folded sheet ([8] p.) : ill. ; 25
cm. Cover title. Essay by Barbara Dayer Gallati.
*1. Homer, Winslow, 1836-1910 - Exhibitions. 2.
Sargent, John Singer, 1856-1925 - Exhibitions. 3.
Brooklyn Museum - Exhibitions. 4. Watercolor painting,
American - Exhibitions. I. Gallati, Barbara Dayer. II.
Title. III. Title: American watercolor masters.*
    NYPL [3-MCX H76 91-7969]

Greene, Alison de Lima. Arman 1955-1991 .
Houston, Tex. , c1991. p. cm.   ISBN
0-89090-050-7 :   DDC 709/.2 20
N6853.A69 A4 1991

Kramer, Linda Konheim. Milton Avery in black
and white . Brooklyn, N.Y. , c1990. 96 p. :
    ISBN 0-87273-127-8 DDC 741.973 20
NC139.A93 A4 1990
    NYPL [3-MCX A95 91-4649]

BROOKLYN MUSEUM - EXHIBITIONS.
Brooklyn Museum. Curator's choice .
[Brooklyn, N.Y. , 1990] 1 folded sheet ([8] p.) :
    NYPL [3-MCX H76 91-7969]

BROOKLYN (NEW YORK, N.Y.) - MAPS.
Dripps, Matthew. Map of the city of Brooklyn .
New York , 1869. 1 atlas (8 leaves) :
    NYPL [Map Div. 87-470]

New York (N.Y.). Dept. of City Planning.
Block & lot maps-- Brooklyn Community
District ... atlas /. New York, N.Y. , c1990. 18
v. :   **NYPL [Map Div. 91-6366]**

Brookman, Philip. Leaf, June, 1929- June Leaf, a
survey of paintings, sculpture, and works on
paper, 1948-1991 /. Washington, D.C. , 1991.
48 p. :   ISBN 0-937237-01-9 (pbk.) DDC 709/.2 20
N6537.L398 A4 1991

Brooks, George R., 1929- Smith, Jedediah Strong,
1799-1831. The Southwest expedition of
Jedediah S. Smith . Glendale, Calif. , 1977. 259
p. :   ISBN 0-87062-123-8
F800 .S55 1977   **NYPL [IW 80-2691]**

Brooks, H. Allen (Harold Allen), 1925- Le
Corbusier, 1887-1965. The Le Corbusier archive
/. New York , Paris , 1982-1984. 32 v. :   ISBN
0-8240-5050-9 (v. 1)   DDC 720/.22/2 19
NA2707.L4 A4 1982d **NYPL [3-MQZ+ (Le
                Corbusier) 90-10105]**

Brooks, James, 1906-
James Brooks, Giorgio Cavallon . New York ,
1979. 24 p. :   **NYPL [3-MCW 91-284]**

BROOKS, JAMES, 1906- - EXHIBITIONS.
James Brooks, Giorgio Cavallon . New York ,
1979. 24 p. :   **NYPL [3-MCW 91-284]**

Broos, B. P. J. Great Dutch paintings from
America : Mauritshuis, The Hague, 28
September 1990-13 January 1991 ; The Fine
Arts Museums of San Francisco, 16 February
1991-5 May 1991 / catalogue by Ben Broos ;
with contributions by Edwin Buijsen ... [et al.] ;
final editing by Rieke van Leeuwen ; exhibition
organized by Hans R. Hoetink. The Hague :
Mauritshuis ; Zwolle : Waanders Publishers,
c1990. 561 p. : ill. (some col.) ; 29 cm. Includes
index. Includes bibliographical references (p. 499-542).
    ISBN 90-6630-253-4 (paperback)
*1. Painting, Dutch - Exhibitions. I. Buijsen, Edwin. II.
Leeuwen, Rieke van. III. Hoetink, Hans. IV.
Mauritshuis (Hague, Netherlands). V. Fine Arts
Museums of San Francisco. VI. Title.*
    NYPL [3-MCG 91-5531]

Broos, C. De nieuwe fotografie in Nederland /
Kees Broos en Flip Bool. Amsterdam :
Fragment, c1989. 143 p. : ill. (some col.) ; 27
cm. Includes bibliographical references.   ISBN
90-6579-019-5 :
*1. Photography - Netherlands. 2. Photographers -
Netherlands. I. Bool, Flip. II. Title.*
IN PROCESS (ONLINE)
    NYPL [MFW 91-5142]

Bröstler, Horst. Gradl, Hermann, 1883-1964.
Hermann Gradl . Marktheidenfeld am Main ,
1989. 190 p. :   ISBN 3-927439-06-1
    NYPL [3-MCK+ G73 91-5156]

Broude, Norma.
Impressionism : a feminist reading : the

gendering of art, science, and nature in the
nineteenth century / by Norma Broude. New
York : Rizzoli, 1991. p. cm. Includes
bibliographical references.   ISBN 0-8478-1397-5
    DDC 759.05/4 20
*1. Impressionism (Art) - France. 2. Painting, Modern -
19th century - France. 3. Feminism and art - France. I.
Title.*
ND547.5.I4 B76 1991

World Impressionism . New York , 1990. 424
p. :   ISBN 0-8109-1774-2   DDC 759.05/4 20
ND192.I4 W67 1990
    NYPL [3-MC+ 90-13049]

Broun, Elizabeth. Albert Pinkham Ryder /
Elizabeth Broun ; with catalogue by Eleanor L.
Jones ... [et al.]. Washington : Published for the
National Museum of American Art by the
Smithsonian Institution Press, c1989. viii, 344
p. : ill. (some col.) ; 29 cm. Catalogue of the
exhibition held at National Museum of American Art,
Apr. 6-July 29, 1990; Brooklyn Museum, Sept. 14,
1990-Jan. 8, 1991. Includes index. Bibliography: p.
329-335.   ISBN 0-87474-328-1 (alk. paper) DDC
759.13 19
*1. Ryder, Albert Pinkham, 1847-1917 - Exhibitions. I.
Ryder, Albert Pinkham, 1847-1917. II. Jones, Eleanor
L. III. National Museum of American Art (U. S.). IV.
Brooklyn Museum. V. Title.*
ND237.R8 A4 1989
    NYPL [3-MCX R99 90-12872]

Brouwer, Mariane. Theatergarden Bestiarium .
Cambridge, Mass. , Long Island City, N.Y. ,
c1990. 176 p. :   ISBN 0-262-04105-7 DDC
701/.03 20
N6494.E6 T4 1990
    NYPL [3-MAL+ 90-12503]

Brower, Kenneth, 1944- One earth : portrait of a
fragile planet : photographed by more than 80
of the world's best photojournalists / written by
Kenneth Brower ; introduction by Michael
Tobias. San Francisco : Collins Publishers,
1990. 192 p. : chiefly ill. ; 30 cm.   ISBN
0-00-215730-6 :   DDC 363.73/022/2 20
*1. Pollution - Pictorial works. 2. Man - Influence on
nature - Pictorial works. I. Title.*
TD174 .B76 1990   **NYPL [MFW+ 91-3904]**

Brown book. Landmark yellow pages .
Washington, D.C. , 1990. 319 p. :   ISBN
0-89133-154-9   DDC 363.6/9/0973 20
E159 .L28 1990
    NYPL [Desk-USLHG 90-10086]

Brown, Christopher, 1948-
The drawings of Anthony van Dyck /
Christopher Brown. New York : Pierpont
Morgan Library, 1991. 294 p. : ill. (some col.) ;
33 cm. Catalog of an exhibition held at the Pierpont
Morgan Library, Feb. 15-Apr. 21, 1991, and the
Kimbell Art Museum, June 1-Aug. 11, 1991. Includes
index. Bibliography: p. 284-289.   ISBN 0-87598-091-0
*1. Van Dyck, Anthony, Sir, 1599-1641 - Exhibitions. I.
Van Dyck, Anthony, Sir, 1599-1641. II. Pierpont
Morgan Library. III. Kimbell Art Museum. IV. Title.*
    NYPL [3-MCH+ D99 91-5935]

Second sight . London , 1980. 24 p. :
    NYPL [3-MCH R3 86-3872]

Brown, Clint. Drawing from life / Clint Brown,
Cheryl McLean. Fort Worth : Harcourt Brace
Jovanovich College Publishers, c1992. p. cm.
Includes bibliographical references and index.   ISBN
0-03-028934-3   DDC 743/.4 20
*1. Anatomy, Artistic. 2. Drawing - Technique. I.
McLean, Cheryl, 1957-. II. Title.*
NC760 .B86 1992

Brown, David Blayney. The art of J.M.W. Turner
/ David Blayney Brown. London : Headline,
1990. 192 p. : ill. (some col.) ; 34 cm. "A Quarto
book"--T.p. verso. Includes index.   ISBN
0-7472-0209-5 :   DDC 760.092 20
*1. Turner, J. M. W. (Joseph Mallord William),
1775-1851. I. Title.*
N6797.T88   **NYPL [3-MCV+ T94 91-6101]**

Brown, David J. The Random House book of
how things were built / David J. Brown. New
York : Random House, 1992. p. cm. Includes
index. An illustrated history of more than sixty notable
structures of the ancient and modern world. Includes
detailed diagrams and a glossary of architectural terms.
    ISBN 0-679-82044-2 (trade)   DDC 720 20
*1. Architecture - Juvenile literature. I. Title. II. Title:
How things were built.*
NA2555 .B68 1992

Brown, Harrison B. The Land and the sea of five
Maine artists . [Waterville, Maine , 1965] [31]
p. :   **NYPL [3-MCW 90-5878]**

BROWN, HARRISON B.
The Land and the sea of five Maine artists .
[Waterville, Maine , 1965] [31] p. :
    NYPL [3-MCW 90-5878]

Brown, James.
James Brown : Stabat mater. Paris : Galerie
Lelong, 1989. 32 p. : Chiefly ill. ; 32 cm.
(Repères : cahiers dárt contemporain, 0751-4241 . no
58)   ISBN 2-85587-173-5
*1. Brown, James - Exhibitions. I. Galerie Lelong (Paris,
France). II. Title. III. Title: Stabat mater. IV. Series:
Repères (Paris, France) , no 58.*
    NYPL [3-MGO+ (Brown) 90-10558]

BROWN, JAMES - EXHIBITIONS.
Brown, James. James Brown . Paris , 1989. 32
p. :   ISBN 2-85587-173-5
    NYPL [3-MGO+ (Brown) 90-10558]

Brown, James, 1951- James Brown : salt /
préface de Jean Frémon. Paris : Galerie Lelong,
c1990. 42 p. : chiefly col. ill. ; 32 cm. (Repères,
0751-4241 . no 67)   ISBN 2-85587-184-0
*1. Brown, James, 1951-. I. Frémon, Jean, 1946-. II.
Galerie Lelong (Paris, France). III. Title. IV. Title: Salt.
V. Series: Repères (Paris, France) , no 67.*
    NYPL [3-MCX+ B8765 90-13074]

BROWN, JAMES, 1951-
Brown, James, 1951- James Brown . Paris ,
c1990. 42 p. :   ISBN 2-85587-184-0
    NYPL [3-MCX+ B8765 90-13074]

Brown, Jane. Sissinghurst : portrait of a garden /
Jane Brown ; photographs by John Miller.
London : Weidenfeld & Nicolson, 1990. 136
p. : col. ill. ; 27 cm. Includes index. "Published in
association with the National Trust." Includes
bibliographical references.   ISBN 0-297-83043-0
*1. Gardens - England - Kent. 2. Sissinghurst Garden
(England). I. Miller, John. II. Gift of the Morgan
Guaranty Trust Endowment for the Economics and
Public Affairs Division. III. Title.*
    NYPL [3-MSK 90-11984]

Brown, Jonathan, 1939-
Francisco de Zurbarán / text by Jonathan
Brown. New York : H.N. Abrams, [1991] p.
cm. (Masters of art) Includes bibliographical
references.   ISBN 0-8109-3962-2   DDC 759.6 20
*1. Zurbarán, Francisco, 1598-1664 - Criticism and
interpretation. 2. Painting, Baroque - Spain. I. Series:
Masters of art (Harry N. Abrams, Inc.). II. Title.*
ND813.Z85 B76 1991

The Golden Age of painting in Spain /
Jonathan Brown. New Haven : Yale University
Press, 1991. ix, 330 p. : ill. (some col.) ; 29 cm.
Includes index. Includes bibliographical references (p.
319-323).   ISBN 0-300-04760-6   DDC 759.6/09/03
20
1. Painting, Modern - Spain. I. Title.
ND804 .B74 1991
    NYPL [3-MCP+ 91-4955]

Brown, Joseph, 1802-1874. Deas, Malcolm D.,
1941- Tipos y costumbres de la Nueva
Granada . Bogotá , 1989. 229 p. :   ISBN
958-9144-25-X
IN PROCESS (ONLINE)
    NYPL [3-MCV+ B8785 90-13354]

BROWN, JOSEPH, 1802-1874.
Deas, Malcolm D., 1941- Tipos y costumbres
de la Nueva Granada . Bogotá , 1989. 229 p. :
    ISBN 958-9144-25-X
IN PROCESS (ONLINE)
    NYPL [3-MCV+ B8785 90-13354]

Brown, Robert K. Ades, Dawn. The 20th-century
poster . Minneapolis , New York [1990] 227
p. ;   ISBN 1-558-59130-3   DDC 741.6/74/0904 20
NC1815 .A33 1990

Brown, Susan M. (Susan Mattseld), 1944-
Nordfeldt, Bror Julius Olsson, 1878-1955. The
woodblock prints of B.J.O. Nordfeldt .
Minneapolis , c1991. 72 p. :   ISBN 0-938713-08-6
    DDC 769.92 20
NE1300.6.N6 A4 1991

Brown, Walter R., 1940- The Stuart legacy :
English art, 1603-1714 / Walter R. Brown ;
with contributions by E. Bryding Adams ... [et
al.]. Birmingham, Ala. : Birmingham Museum of
Art in association with the University of
Washington Press, 1991. 176 p. : ill. (some
col.) ; 28 cm. "Birmingham Museum of Art, March

24-May 7, 1991; Memphis Brooks Museum of Art, August 11-September 22, 1991"--T.p. verso. Includes bibliographical references (p. 174-175). ISBN 0-931394-30-9 DDC 709/.42/074761781 20
1. Art, Stuart - Exhibitions. 2. Art, Modern - 17th-18th centuries - England - Exhibitions. I. Birmingham Museum of Art (Birmingham, Ala.). II. Memphis Brooks Museum of Art. III. Title.
N6766 .B76 1991

Brown, Will. United States. Dept. of State. Treasures of State . New York , 1991. p. cm. ISBN 0-8109-3911-8 (cloth) DDC 709/.73/074753 20
N6505 .U48 1991

Brownell, Charles De Wolf, 1822-1909. Charles De Wolf Brownell (1822-1909) : explorer of the American landscape : March 1991. New York : Kennedy Galleries, c1991. [68] p. : ill. ; 28 cm.
1. Brownell, Charles De Wolf, 1822-1909 - Exhibitions. I. Kennedy Galleries. II. Title.
     NYPL [3-MCX B884 91-4294]

BROWNELL, CHARLES DE WOLF, 1822-1909 - EXHIBITIONS. Brownell, Charles De Wolf, 1822-1909. Charles De Wolf Brownell (1822-1909) . New York , c1991. [68] p. :
     NYPL [3-MCX B884 91-4294]

Brownlee, David Bruce. Louis I. Kahn, architect of the American century / by David B. Brownlee and David G. De Long ; preface by Vincent Scully. New York : Rizzoli, 1991. p. cm. Includes bibliographical references and index. ISBN 0-8478-1330-4 DDC 720/.92 20
1. Kahn, Louis I., 1901-1974 - Criticism and interpretation. 2. Architecture, Modern - 20th century - United States. I. De Long, David Gilson, 1939-. II. Title.
NA737.K32 B76 1991

Brownstone, David M. 20th century culture : a dictionary of the arts and literature of our time / David Brownstone, Irene Franck.1st ed. [New York?] : Prentice Hall Press, 1991. p. cm. Includes index. ISBN 0-13-210519-5 : DDC 700/.9/04 20
1. Arts, Modern - 20th century - Dictionaries. I. Franck, Irene M. II. Title. III. Title: Twentieth century culture.
NX456 .B76 1991

Browse, Lillian. Sickert / Lillian Browse. London : Hart-Davis, 1960. 124 p., [118] p. of plates : ill. (some col.) ; 30 cm. Includes indexes. Bibliography: p. 54. DDC 759.2
1. Sickert, Walter, 1860-1942. I. Title.
ND497.S48 B7
     NYPL [3-MCV+ S56 90-11556]

Bruce, Chris. Breaking down the boundaries . Seattle, Wash. , c1989. 31 p. : ISBN 0-935558-24-1 DDC 707/.5 20
N72.A77 B74 1909
     NYPL [3-MAMT+ 90-12629]

Bruce Museum. Cummings, Hildegard. J. Alden Weir . Storrs , c1991. p. cm. ISBN 0-918386-43-8 DDC 759.13 20
ND237.W4 A4 1991

Bruce Parsons, United Technologies and gardens . Parsons, Bruce. Montréal [1986] 55 p. : DDC 709/.2/4 19
     NYPL [3-MCZ P267 90-10791]

Bruce, Susan. A treasury of Australian bush painting / notes on the painters by Susan Bruce. Ringwood, Vic., Australia ; New York, N.Y., U. S. A. : Viking O'Neil, 1987. 72 p. : col. ill. ; 30 cm. Includes index. ISBN 0-670-90021-4 DDC 758/.194/0994 20
1. Landscape painting, Australian. 2. Landscape painting - 19th century - Australia. 3. Landscape painting - 20th century - Australia. I. Title.
ND1367.A85 B78 1987

Brücke (Artists' group) Kunsthalle Bern. Chronik KGBrücke, 1913 [microform] . Bern , 1948. 32 p., [16] leaves of plates :   *NYPL [*ZM-202]*

BRÜCKE (ARTISTS' GROUP) Kunsthalle Bern. Chronik KGBrücke, 1913 [microform] . Bern , 1948. 32 p., [16] leaves of plates :   *NYPL [*ZM-202]*

BRÜCKE (ARTISTS' GROUP) - EXHIBITIONS. Meisterwerke des Expressionismus . Stuttgart ,

c1990. 251 p. : ISBN 3-7757-0302-0
IN PROCESS (ONLINE)
     NYPL [3-MAMG+ 91-7962]

BRÜCKE-MUSEUM - EXHIBITIONS. Meisterwerke des Expressionismus . Stuttgart , c1990. 251 p. : ISBN 3-7757-0302-0
IN PROCESS (ONLINE)
     NYPL [3-MAMG+ 91-7962]

Brücke. Kunsthalle Bern. Chronik KGBrücke, 1913 [microform] . Bern , 1948. 32 p., [16] leaves of plates :   *NYPL [*ZM-202]*

Brücke-Museum. Meisterwerke des Expressionismus . Stuttgart , c1990. 251 p. : ISBN 3-7757-0302-0
IN PROCESS (ONLINE)
     NYPL [3-MAMG+ 91-7962]

Bruegel /. Delevoy, Robert L. [Brueghel. English.] New York , 1990. 138 p. : ISBN 0-8478-1349-5 (pbk.) DDC 760/.092 20
ND673.B73 D6613 1991

Bruegel. Marijnissen, Roger H. Bruegel, tout l'œuvre peint et dessiné /. [Anvers] , Paris , c1988. 419 p. : ISBN 90-6153-191-8 DDC 760/.092 20
N6973.B68 A4 1988

Bruegel and Netherlandish landscape painting from the National Gallery Prague / [organized by the National Museum of Western Art, Tokyo ... et al.] ; edited by Akira Kofuku, Toshiharu Nakamura]. [Tokyo?] : Asahi Shimbun, c1990. 193 p. : ill. (some col.) ; 23 x 28 cm. Catalog of an exhibition held at the National Museum of Western Art, Tokyo, 20 March-27 May 1990, and the National Museum of Modern Art, Kyoto, 10 July-16 Sept., 1990. Includes bibliographical references (p. 189-193).
1. Bruegel, Pieter, ca. 1525-1569 - Influence - Exhibitions. 2. Patinir, Joachim, ca. 1485-1524 - Influence - Exhibitions. 3. Národní galerie V Praze. 4. Landscape painting - 16th century - Netherlands - Exhibitions. 5. Landscape painting - 17th century - Netherlands - Exhibitions. 6. Landscape painting, Dutch - Exhibitions. I. Kofuku, Akira. II. Nakamura, Toshiharu. III. Kokuritsu Seiyō Bijutsukan. IV. Kyōto Kokuritsu Kindai Bijutsukan.
     NYPL [3-MCG 91-4592]

Bruegel, Jan, 1568-1625. Brod Gallery (London, England) Jan Brueghel the elder . London , c1979. 122 p. : DDC 759.9493 19
ND673.B72 A4 1979
     NYPL [3-MCH+ B88-90-12668]

BRUEGEL, JAN, 1568-1625 - EXHIBITIONS. Brod Gallery (London, England) Jan Brueghel the elder . London , c1979. 122 p. : DDC 759.9493 19
ND673.B72 A4 1979
     NYPL [3-MCH+ B88-90-12668]

Bruegel, or, The workshop of dreams /. Rocquet, Claude Henri. [Bruegel, ou L'atelier des songes. English.] Chicago , c1991. p. cm. ISBN 0-226-72342-9 (alk. paper) DDC 760/.092 B 20
ND673.B73 R6413 1991

Bruegel, Pieter, ca. 1525-1569. FALL OF ICARUS. Wyss, Beat, 1947- Pieter Bruegel . Frankfurt am Main , c1990. 80, [1] p. : ISBN 3-596-23962-1 : DDC 759.9493 20
ND673.B73 A65 1990

Marijnissen, Roger H. Bruegel, tout l'œuvre peint et dessiné /. [Anvers] , Paris , c1988. 419 p. : ISBN 90-6153-191-8 DDC 760/.092 20
N6973.B68 A4 1988

Pieter Bruegel the Elder / text by Wolfgang Stechow. New York : H.N. Abrams, 1990. 126 p. : ill. ; 31 cm. "... concise ed. of Wolfgang Stechow's Bruegel, originally published in 1970"-- T.p. verso. ISBN 0-8109-3103-6 : DDC 759.9493 20
1. Bruegel, Pieter, ca. 1525-1569. I. Stechow, Wolfgang, 1896-1974. II. Title.
ND673.B73 A4 1990
     NYPL [3-MCH+ B89 90-11789]

BRUEGEL, PIETER, CA. 1525-1569. Bruegel, Pieter, ca. 1525-1569. Pieter Bruegel the Elder /. New York , 1990. 126 p. : ISBN 0-8109-3103-6 : DDC 759.9493 20
ND673.B73 A4 1990
     NYPL [3-MCH+ B89 90-11789]

Rocquet, Claude Henri. [Bruegel, ou L'atelier des songes. English.] Bruegel, or, The workshop

of dreams /. Chicago , c1991. p. cm. ISBN 0-226-72342-9 (alk. paper) DDC 760/.092 B 20
ND673.B73 R6413 1991

BRUEGEL, PIETER, CA. 1525-1569 - CATALOGUES RAISONNÉS. Marijnissen, Roger H. Bruegel, tout l'œuvre peint et dessiné /. [Anvers] , Paris , c1988. 419 p. : ISBN 90-6153-191-8 DDC 760/.092 20
N6973.B68 A4 1988

BRUEGEL, PIETER, CA. 1525-1569 - CRITICISM AND INTERPRETATION. Delevoy, Robert L. [Brueghel. English.] Bruegel /. New York , 1990. 138 p. : ISBN 0-8478-1349-5 (pbk.) DDC 760/.092 20
ND673.B73 D6613 1991

BRUEGEL, PIETER, CA. 1525-1569 - INFLUENCE - EXHIBITIONS. Bruegel and Netherlandish landscape painting from the National Gallery Prague /. [Tokyo?] , c1990. 193 p. :   *NYPL [3-MCG 91-4592]*

Bruegel, Pieter, 1564-1638. Galerie Robert Finck présente l'exposition de trente-trois tableaux de Pierre Breughel le jeune dans les collections privées belges. Bruxelles : La Galerie, 1969. 1 v. (unpaged) : ill. ; 22 x 28 cm. Exhibition: Apr. 19-Mai 18, 1969.
1. Bruegel, Pieter, 1564-1638 - Exhibitions. 2. Painting - Private collections - Belgium - Exhibitions. I. Galerie Robert Finck. II. Title. III. Title: Trente-trois tableaux de Pierre Breughel le jeune dans les collections privées belges.   *NYPL [3-MCH B891 91-305]*

BRUEGEL, PIETER, 1564-1638 - EXHIBITIONS. Bruegel, Pieter, 1564-1638. Galerie Robert Finck présente l'exposition de trente-trois tableaux de Pierre Breughel le jeune dans les collections privées belges. Bruxelles , 1969. 1 v. (unpaged) :   *NYPL [3-MCH B891 91-305]*

Bruegel, tout l'œuvre peint et dessiné /. Marijnissen, Roger H. [Anvers] , Paris , c1988. 419 p. : ISBN 90-6153-191-8 DDC 760/.092 20
N6973.B68 A4 1988

Bruegmann, Robert. Art Institute of Chicago. Fragments of Chicago's past . Chicago, IL , 1990. 180 p. : ISBN 0-86559-088-5 DDC 720/.9773/1107477311 20
NA735.C4 A77 1990
     NYPL [3-MQWO 91-3419]

Holabird & Roche, Holabird & Root : an illustrated catalog of works / by Robert Bruegmann. New York : Garland, 1991. 3 v. : ill., maps ; 32 cm. "In cooperation with the Chicago Historical Society." Includes bibliographical references (v. 1, p. xxv-xxvi) and indexes. CONTENTS. - v. 1. 1880-1911 -- v. 2. 1911-1927 -- v. 3. 1927-1940. ISBN 0-8240-3974-2 : DDC 720/.92/2 20
1. Holabird & Roche (Chicago, Ill.) - Catalogs. 2. Holabird & Root (Chicago, Ill.) - Catalogs. 3. Architecture, Modern - 19th century - United States - Catalogs. 4. Architecture, Modern - 20th century - United States - Catalogs. I. Holabird & Roche (Chicago, Ill.). II. Holabird & Root (Chicago, Ill.). III. Chicago Historical Society. IV. Title. V. Title: Holabird and Roche, Holabird and Root.
NA737.H558 A4 1991
     NYPL [MQWO+ 91-6811]

Brugerolles, Emmanuelle. Les Dessins vénitiens des collections de l'École des beaux-arts . Paris , c1990. xlii, 257 p. : ISBN 2-903639-68-X
     NYPL [3-MBH+ 90-12996]

Brugge Concertgebouw. Retrospectieve tentoonstelling War van Overstraeten . Brugge , c1979. 57 p. : *NYPL [3-MCH 096 87-3370]*

Brüggemann, W. (Werner) Schneider, Gerd. Pflanzliche Bauornamente der Seldschuken in Kleinasien /. Wiesbaden , c1989. 278 p. : ISBN 3-88226-472-1
NA3565.A1 S36X1989

Bruggen, Coosje van. John Baldessari / Coosje van Bruggen. New York : Rizzoli International Publications, 1990. 256 p. : ill. (some col.) ; 31 cm. Catalog of an exhibition at the Museum of Contemporary Art, Los Angeles, Mar. 25-June 17, 1990, and 5 other museums through Feb. 1992. Includes index. Bibliography: p. 243-249. ISBN 0-8478-1182-4 : DDC 709/.2 20
1. Baldessari, John, 1931- - Exhibitions. 2. Conceptual art - United States. I. Baldessari, John, 1931-. II. Museum of Contemporary Art (Los Angeles, Calif.). III.

Title.
N6537.B17 B78 1990
      NYPL [3-MCX+ B176 90-11225]

Oldenburg, Claes, 1929- Claes Oldenburg, large-scale projects, 1977-1980 . New York , 1980. 100 p. : ISBN 0-8478-0351-1 (pbk.)
NB237.O42 A4 1980
      NYPL [MGO (Oldenburg) 81-267]

Bruggen-Oldenburg, Coosje van. see **Bruggen, Coosje van.**

Brugger, Ingried. Modefotografie . Wien , c1990. 240 p. :   *NYPL [MFW 91-4480]*

Brugger, V. G. Soviet Union. Glavnoe upravlenie geodezii i kartografii. Atlas zarubezhnykh stran dlīā sredneĭ shkoly. [Moskva , 1964]. 1 atlas (40 p.) :   *NYPL [Map Div. 91-1092]*

Brühl, Georg, 1931- Porzellanfiguren : Zierde des bürgerlichen Salons / Georg Brühl ; [Fotografien von Wolfgang G. Schröter]. München : Callwey, 1989. 156 p. : ill. (some col.) ; 23 cm. Includes index. Illustrated lining papers. Also published by Edition Leipzig as: Vertikoporzellan 1860-1920. Includes bibliographical references. ISBN 3-7667-0929-1
1. Porcelain, European - History - 19th century. 2. Porcelain industry - Europe - History - 19th century. 3. Porcelain figures - Europe - History - 19th century. 4. Kitsch - Europe - History - 19th century. I. Title. II. Title: Vertikoporzellan 1860-1920. III. Title: Zierde des bürgerlichen Salons. NYPL [3-MPG 91-6257]

Bruhn, Roger, 1941- Dreams in dry places / Roger Bruhn ; foreword by Ted Kooser ; notes by Edward F. Zimmer. Lincoln : University of Nebraska Press, c1990. xix, 143 p. : chiefly ill. ; 25 cm. (The Great plains photography series) Includes bibliographical references and index. ISBN 0-8032-1214-3 : DDC 779/.4782/092 20
1. Bruhn, Roger, 1941-. 2. Nebraska - Description and travel - 1981- - Views. I. Title. II. Series.
TR660 .B784 1990
      NYPL [MFX (Bruhn) 91-3589]

BRUHN, ROGER, 1941-
Bruhn, Roger, 1941- Dreams in dry places /. Lincoln , c1990. xix, 143 p. : ISBN 0-8032-1214-3 : DDC 779/.4782/092 20
TR660 .B784 1990
      NYPL [MFX (Bruhn) 91-3589]

Bruhns, Maike. Volker Meier, ein Maler in Hamburg : Arbeiten von 1955-1987 / Maike Bruhns. Hamburg : Sautter + Lackmann, c1989. 183 p. : ill. (some col.) ; 32 cm. Includes bibliographical references. ISBN 3-88920-009-5
1. Meier, Volker - Catalogues raisonnés. I. Meier, Volker. II. Title.
      NYPL [3-MCK+ M4997 90-8746]

Brumfield, William Craft, 1944- The origins of modernism in Russian architecture / William Craft Brumfield. Berkeley : University of California Press, c1991. xxv, 343 p., [24] p. of plates : ill. (some col.) ; 29 cm. Includes bibliographical references (p. 323-327) and index. ISBN 0-520-06929-3 (alk. paper) DDC 720/.947/09041 20
1. Nationalism and architecture - Russian S.F.S.R. 2. Architecture, Modern - 19th century - Russian S.F.S.R. 3. Architecture, Modern - 20th century - Russian S.F.S.R. 4. Eclecticism in architecture - Russian S.F.S.R. I. Title.
NA1187 .B78 1991
      NYPL [3-MQW 91-6488]

The Brummer collection of medieval art, the Duke University Museum of Art /. Duke University. Museum of Art. Durham , 1991. xix, 297 p., 16 p. of plates : ISBN 0-8223-1055-4 DDC 709/.02/074756563 20
N5963.D87 D854 1991
      NYPL [3-MAK 91-5627]

BRUMMER, ERNEST - ART COLLECTIONS.
Moeller, Robert C. Sculpture and decorative art. Raleigh [1967] 97 p.
      NYPL [3-MAK 90-6857]

BRUMMER, ERNEST - ART COLLECTIONS - CATALOGS.
Duke University. Museum of Art. The Brummer collection of medieval art, the Duke University Museum of Art /. Durham , 1991. xix, 297 p., 16 p. of plates : ISBN 0-8223-1055-4 DDC 709/.02/074756563 20
N5963.D87 D854 1991
      NYPL [3-MAK 91-5627]

Brun, Carl. Schweizerisches Künstler-Lexikon /. Nendeln , 1982. 4 v. ;
      NYPL [MAO 90-2421]

Brun, Hans-Jakob. Widerberg, Frans, 1934- Frans Widerberg . Oslo, Norway , c1990. 248 p. : ISBN 82-7393-008-4 DDC 769.92 20
NE694.W55 A4 1990

Brundage, Frances, 1854-1937.
Budd, Ellen H. Frances Brundage post cards . [Cincinnati, OH] (6910 Tenderfoot La., Cincinnati 45249) [1990] 140 p. : DDC 741.6/83/092 20
NC1879.B76 A4 1990

BRUNDAGE, FRANCES, 1854-1937 - CATALOGS.
Budd, Ellen H. Frances Brundage post cards . [Cincinnati, OH] (6910 Tenderfoot La., Cincinnati 45249) [1990] 140 p. : DDC 741.6/83/092 20
NC1879.B76 A4 1990

Brunelleschi, Filippo, 1377-1446.
Klotz, Heinrich. Filippo Brunelleschi . London , 1990. 175 p. : ISBN 0-85670-986-7
      NYPL [3-MQZ (Brunelleschi) 90-11571]

BRUNELLESCHI, FILIPPO, 1377-1446 - CRITICISM AND INTERPRETATION.
Klotz, Heinrich. Filippo Brunelleschi . London , 1990. 175 p. : ISBN 0-85670-986-7
      NYPL [3-MQZ (Brunelleschi) 90-11571]

Brunetti, Fabrizio. Momenti di architettura italiana contemporanea / Fabrizio Brunetti ; a cura di Paola Signori. Firenze : Alinea, c1990. 204 p. : ill. ; 24 cm. (Saggi e documenti di storia dell'architettura . 8)
1. Architecture, Modern - 20th century - Italy. I. Title. II. Series. NYPL [3-MQWB 91-7228]

Brunhammer, Yvonne.
[Artistes décorateurs. English]
The decorative arts in France, 1900-1942 : la Société des artistes décorateurs / Yvonne Brunhammer and Suzanne Tise. New York : Rizzoli, 1990. 288 p. : ill. (some col.) ; 32 cm. Translation of: Les artistes décorateurs. Includes bibliographical references (p. 263-268) and index. ISBN 0-8478-1251-0 DDC 745/.0944/09041 20
1. Société des artistes décorateurs (France). 2. Decorative arts - France - History - 20th century. I. Tise, Suzanne. II. Title.
NK1396.S63 A7813 1990
      NYPL [3-MNE+ 91-3934]

Brüning, Peter. Deutsches Informel . Düsseldorf [1987] 39 p. :   *NYPL [3-MCI+ 91-4284]*

Brunius, Jan Axel Teodor. see **Brunius, Teddy, 1922-**

Brunius, Teddy, 1922- Bærtling : mannen, verket / Teddy Brunius. [Stockholm] : Sveriges allmänna konstförening, 1990. 157 p. : ill. (some col.), ports. ; 26 cm. (Publikation / Sveriges allmänna konstförening . 99)
1. Bærtling, Olle, 1911-. I. Bærtling, Olle, 1911-. II. Series: Publikation / Sveriges allmänna konstförening , 99. III. Title. NYPL [3-MCZ B135 91-6323]

Brunk, Karsten. Kartographische Arbeiten und deutsche Namengebung in Neuschwabenland, Antarktis : bisherige Arbeiten, Rekonstruktion der Flugwege der Deutschen Antarktischen Expedition 1938/39 und Neubearbeitung des deutschen Namengutes in Neuschwabenland / Karsten Brunk. Frankfurt am Main : Verlag des Instituts für Angewandte Geodäsie, 1986. 2 v. : ill., maps ; 32 cm. (Reihe E--Geschichte und Entwicklung der Geodäsie . Heft Nr. 24) Mitteilung Nr. 175 des Instituts für Angewandte Geodäsie (Abt. II des Deutschen Geodätischen Forschungsinstituts), 0071-9196 Summary in English, French, German, and Spanish. Vol. 2 issued in portfolio. Includes bibliographies. DDC 912/.989 19
1. Cartography - Antarctic regions - New Schwabenland. 2. Names, Geographical - Antarctic regions - New Schwabenland. I. Series. II. Series: Mitteilung des Instituts für Angewandte Geodäsie , Nr. 175. III. Title.
GA357 .B78 1986
      NYPL [Map Div. 91-4127]

Die Brunnen in Weimar . Hemmann, Paul, 1895-1977. Weimar , 1990. 96 p. : ISBN 3-910053-43-0 *NYPL [3-MRK 91-7023]*

Brunner, Adolf, 1905- Aus der Werkstatt des Künstlers . [S.l. , 1969?] (München : R.

Koehler) ca. 100 p. :
      NYPL [MDBF 90-5879]

Brunner, Fritz, 1908- Fritz Brunner, geboren am 24. April 1908 in Glarus. Glarus : Buchh. Baeschlin, c1989. 131 p. : ill. ; 26 cm. ISBN 3-85546-040-X
1. Brunner, Fritz, 1908-. I. Title.
IN PROCESS (ONLINE)
      NYPL [3-MCZ B8975 91-2454]

BRUNNER, FRITZ, 1908-
Brunner, Fritz, 1908- Fritz Brunner, geboren am 24. April 1908 in Glarus. Glarus , c1989. 131 p. : ISBN 3-85546-040-X
IN PROCESS (ONLINE)
      NYPL [3-MCZ B8975 91-2454]

Bruno Gironcoli, Arbeiten auf Papier . Gironcoli, Bruno, 1936- Graz [1990] 120 p. : DDC 709/.2 20
N6811.5.G57 A4 1990

Bruno Innocenti . Cappugi, Luana. Firenze , 1991. 79 p., [51] p. of plates : ISBN 88-22-23837-0
      NYPL [3-MCF I57 91-5735]

BRUNSCHWILER, LEO, 1955- - EXHIBITIONS.
Installation, Klangraum, Musik . [St. Gallen] [1983] [29] p. :   *NYPL [3-MAL 90-12516]*

Brunskill, R. W. Brick building in Britain / R.W. Brunskill. London : Gollancz, 1990. 208 p., [16] p. of plates : ill. (some col.) ; 26 cm. Includes index. Includes bibliographical references (p. [202]-204). ISBN 0-575-04457-8 : DDC 693.210941 20
1. Building, Brick - England - History. 2. Architecture - England. 3. Bricks - England. I. Title.
TH5501   *NYPL [3-MQWK 90-11098]*

Brus, Günter.
Günter Brus : Zeichnungen und Schriften. [Bern] : Kunsthalle Bern, c1976. [36] p. : col. ill. ; 27 cm. Catalog of an exhibition in Kunsthalle Bern, Oct. 24-Nov. 28, 1976. Includes bibliographical references.
1. Brus, Günter - Exhibitions. I. Kunsthalle Bern. II. Title.   *NYPL [3-MCK B895 91-1317]*
Der Zertrümmerte Spiegel . Klagenfurt , 1989. 392 p. : ISBN 3-85415-062-8
      NYPL [3-MAL 91-7188]

BRUS, GÜNTER - EXHIBITIONS.
Brus, Günter. Günter Brus . [Bern] , c1976. [36] p. :   *NYPL [3-MCK B895 91-1317]*

Brusberg, Dieter. Botero, Fernando, 1932- Botero, der Maler . Berlin , 1991. 72 p. : ISBN 3-87972-071-1
      NYPL [3-MCZ+ B74 91-7449]

Brusberg Dokumente .
(26) Botero, Fernando, 1932- Botero, der Maler . Berlin , 1991. 72 p. : ISBN 3-87972-071-1
      NYPL [3-MCZ+ B74 91-7449]

'The brush dances & the ink sings' . Farrer, Anne. London , c1990. 143 p. : ISBN 1-85332-058-7 *NYPL [3-MAG 91-6891]*

Brush dances and the ink sings. Farrer, Anne. 'The brush dances & the ink sings' . London , c1990. 143 p. : ISBN 1-85332-058-7
      NYPL [3-MAG 91-6891]

BRUSH DRAWING - TECHNIQUE.
Wang, Chi-yüan, 1895- Oriental brushwork /. New York , c1964. 46 p. :
ND1260 .W24   *NYPL [3-MAF 90-5665]*

Brushes with power . Kraus, Richard Curt. Berkeley , c1991. xii, 208 p. : ISBN 0-520-07285-5 (cloth : alk. paper) DDC 745.6/19951 20
NK3634.A2 K73 1991

Brushwork diary . Long, Walter S. (Walter Sully), 1842-1907. Reno , 1991. p. cm. ISBN 0-87417-174-1 (alk. paper) DDC 759.13 20
ND1837.L66 A4 1991

BRUSSELS (BELGIUM) - BUILDINGS, STRUCTURES, ETC.
Le Patrimoine monumental de la Belgique. Liège [1989- <v. 1, pt. 1 > : ISBN 2-8021-0092-0 (v. 1) DDC 720/.9493/32 20
NA1170 .P37 1989

Brussels. Crédit communal de Belgique. see **Crédit communal de Belgique.**

Brussels. Galerie Robert Finck. see **Galerie Robert Finck.**

Brussels. Koninklijke museums voor schoone kunsten van België. see **Brussels. Musées royaux des beaux-arts de Belgique.**

Brussels. Musée royal des beaux-arts de Belgique. see **Brussels. Musées royaux des beaux-arts de Belgique.**

Brussels. Musées royaux de peinture et de sculpture de Belgique. see **Brussels. Musées royaux des beaux-arts de Belgique.**

Brussels. Musées royaux des beaux-arts de Belgique. Hommage à Paul Delvaux . Bruxelles, [r. du Musée 9] [1977] [68] p. :
N6973.D44 A4 1977
NYPL [3-MCH D32 81-766]

Brussels. Palais des beaux arts. Albert Dürer aux Pays-Bas . Bruxelles , 1977. xxiii, 211, 144 p., [14] leaves of plates :
N6888.D8 A4 1977
NYPL [3-MCK D85 81-320]

Brussels. Paleis voor schone Kunsten. see **Brussels. Palais des beaux arts.**

Das Brustbild Christi . Warland, Rainer. Rom . 288 p., [46] p. of plates :
NYPL [3-MAIH 87-2636]

BRUTALISM (ARCHITECTURE) - HONG KONG.
Williams, Stephanie. Hongkong Bank . Boston , c1989. 302 p. : ISBN 0-316-94238-3 : DDC 725/.24/095125 20
NA6245.C62 H668 1989
NYPL [3-MQZ (Foster) 91-4484]

Brutvan, Cheryl A. Pfahl, John, 1939- A distanced land . [Albuquerque] , 1990. xvi, 204 p. : ISBN 0-8263-1214-4 DDC 779/.36/092 20
TR647 .P494 1990
NYPL [MFX (Pfahl) 91-7438]

Bruyn, Bartholomäus, 1493-1555.
Tümmers, Horst-Johs. Die Altarbilder des Älteren Bartholomäus Bruyn . Köln , 1964. 235 p. :
ND588.B792 A4 1964
NYPL [3-MCK B914 90-5875]

BRUYN, BARTHOLOMÄUS, 1493-1555 - CATALOGUES RAISONNÉS.
Tümmers, Horst-Johs. Die Altarbilder des Älteren Bartholomäus Bruyn . Köln , 1964. 235 p. :
ND588.B792 A4 1964
NYPL [3-MCK B914 90-5875]

BRUYN, BARTHOLOMÄUS, 1493-1555 - CRITICISM AND INTERPRETATION.
Tümmers, Horst-Johs. Die Altarbilder des Älteren Bartholomäus Bruyn . Köln , 1964. 235 p. :
ND588.B792 A4 1964
NYPL [3-MCK B914 90-5875]

Bruzelius, Caroline Astrid. Duke University. Museum of Art. The Brummer collection of medieval art, the Duke University Museum of Art /. Durham , 1991. xix, 297 p., 16 p. of plates : ISBN 0-8223-1055-4 DDC 709/.02/074756563 20
N5963.D87 D854 1991
NYPL [3-MAK 91-5627]

Bryan, E. H. (Edwin Horace), 1898-
Guide to islands in the tropical Pacific.
Motteler, Lee S. Pacific Island names : a map and name guide to the new Pacific / Lee S. Motteler. Honolulu , 1986. 91 p. : ISBN 0-930897-12-9 (pbk.) DDC 912/.9 19
DU18 .M68 1986   ***NYPL [Map Div. 88-67]***

Bryan, Michael, 1757-1821. Bryan's dictionary of painters and engravers. New ed., rev. and enl. / under the supervision of George C. Williamson. New York : Macmillan ; London : George Bell and Sons, 1903-1905. 5 v. : ill., ports. ; 28 cm.
First ed. published in 1816 under title: A biographical and critical dictionary of painters and engravers.
Library's copy lacks plates.
1. Painters - Dictionaries. 2. Engravers - Dictionaries. I. Williamson, George Charles, 1858-1943. II. Title. III. Title: Dictionary of painters and engravers.
NYPL [MCA 91-4552]

Bryan's dictionary of painters and engravers.
Bryan, Michael, 1757-1821. New York , London , 1903-1905. 5 v. :
NYPL [MCA 91-4552]

Bryant, Julius. The Iveagh Bequest, Kenwood / Julius Bryant. [London] : London Historic

House Museum Trust, 1990. 84 p. : ill. (some col.) ; 26 cm. Includes bibliographical references (p. 84). ISBN 1-85074-278-2
1. Iveagh Bequest, Kenwood (London, England). 2. London (England) - Buildings, structures, etc. I. Title. II. Title: Kenwood.
NYPL [3-MQWK 90-11057]

Bryant, Richard. Glancey, Jonathan. The new moderns /. New York , c1990. 191 p. : ISBN 0-517-57662-7 : DDC 728/.09/045 20
NA680 .G57 1990
NYPL [3-MLO+ 91-4945]

Bryson, Norman, 1949-
In Medusa's gaze . Rochester, NY , c1991. p. cm. ISBN 0-918098-05-X : DDC 758/.4/074747 20
ND1390 .I5 1991

Looking at the overlooked : four essays on still life painting / Norman Bryson. Cambridge, Mass. : Harvard University Press, 1990. 192 p. : ill. (some col.) ; 24 cm. Includes bibliographical references. ISBN 0-674-53905-2 DDC 758/.4 20
I. Title.
ND1390 .B8 1990   ***NYPL [3-MBT 90-10759]***

BSA/arkitektur, 0109-6885 .
(6) Ilkjær, Marianne Olsson. Postmodernismen i dansk arkitektur . [København , 1987] 104 leaves : ISBN 87-87448-52-1
NA1218 .I43 1987

Bubennikova, L. K. Iskusstvo v khudozhestvennoǐ zhizni sotsialisticheskogo obshchestva /. Moskva , 1990. 173 p. ; ISBN 5-02-012744-2 :
NX556.A1 I85 1990

BUBONIDAE. see **OWLS.**

**Das Buch des Künstlers : die schönsten Malerbücher aus der Sammlung der Herzog August Bibliothek, Wolfenbüttel, ausgestellt in Buchhäusern von Walter Pichler : 18. April bis 16. Juli 1989, Kestner-Gesellschaft Hannover / kommentierende Texte von Harriett Watts ; herausgegeben von Carl Haenlein. [Hannover] : Die Gesellschaft, [1989] 179 p. : ill. (some col.) ; 24 cm. (Katalog (Kestner-Gesellschaft) . 3/1989) DDC 708.3/5954 s 769.9/04/074435954 20
1. Herzog August Bibliothek - Exhibitions. 2. Artists' illustrated books - Exhibitions. 3. Illustrated books - 20th century - Exhibitions. I. Pichler, Walter, 1936-. II. Watts, Harriet. III. Haenlein, Carl Albrecht. IV. Herzog August Bibliothek. V. Series. VI. Series: Kestner-Gesellschaft. Katalog, 1989/3.
N5070.H3 K4 1989/3 NE890
NYPL [3-MAW (Hanover) 73-2900 1989/3]

Buch, Felicitas. Studien zur Preussischen Denkmalpflege am Beispiel konservatorischer Arbeiten Ferdinand von Quasts / Felicitas Buch. Worms : Wernersche Verlagsgesellschaft, c1990. 250 p. : ill. ; 24 cm. (Manuskripte zur Kunstwissenschaft in der Wernerschen Verlagsgesellschaft . Bd. 30) Revision of the author's thesis (doctoral)--Technische Hochschule Darmstadt, 1989. Spine title: Ferdinand von Quast. Includes bibliographical references (p.241-250). ISBN 3-88462-929-8
1. Architecture - Germany - Prussia - Conservation and restoration. 2. Architecture - Germany - Prussia. 3. Quast, Ferdinand von, 1807-1877. I. Title. II. Title: Ferdinand von Quast. III. Series.
NA109.G3 B83 1990

Buchanan, Peter.
The Architecture of Enric Miralles and Carme Pinós /. New York, NY , c1990. 87 p. : ISBN 0-930829-14-X
NYPL [3-MQWH+ 91-6245]
Bohigas, Oriol. Barcelona, city and architecture, 1980-1992 /. New York , 1991. 239 p. : ISBN 0-8478-1354-1 : DDC 720/.946/7209048 20
NA1311.B3 B64 1991

BUCHAREST - MAPS.
(1982) Ionescu, Alexandru. Bucuresti, ghidul străzilor . [Bucharest] , 1982. 1 atlas (132, 138 p.) : DDC 912/.4982 19
G2039 .B816 1982
NYPL [Map Div. 84-1514]

Bucharest. Muzeul de Artă al Republicii Socialiste România. see **Muzeul de Artă al Republicii Socialiste România.**

Buchheister, Carl, 1890-1964.
Carl Buchheister, 1890-1964, Werkverzeichnis der gegenständlichen Arbeiten : Gemälde, Gouachen, Aquarelle, Zeichnungen,

typographische Arbeiten, Druckgraphik / bearbeitet von Elisabeth Buchheister und Willi Kemp ; mit einer Einführung von Claus Pese. Nürnberg : Germanisches Nationalmuseum, c1986. 367 p. : chiefly ill. (some col.) ; 27 cm. (Wissenschaftliche Beibände zum Anzeiger des Germanischen Nationalmuseums . Bd. 5) Includes bibliographical references. DDC 760/.092/4 19
1. Buchheister, Carl, 1890-1964 - Catalogs. I. Buchheister, Elisabeth. II. Kemp, Willi. III. Title. IV. Series.
N6888.B753 A4 1986
NYPL [3-MCK B919 90-12854]

BUCHHEISTER, CARL, 1890-1964 - CATALOGS.
Buchheister, Carl, 1890-1964. Carl Buchheister, 1890-1964, Werkverzeichnis der gegenständlichen Arbeiten . Nürnberg , c1986. 367 p. : DDC 760/.092/4 19
N6888.B753 A4 1986
NYPL [3-MCK B919 90-12854]

Buchheister, Elisabeth. Buchheister, Carl, 1890-1964. Carl Buchheister, 1890-1964, Werkverzeichnis der gegenständlichen Arbeiten . Nürnberg , c1986. 367 p. : DDC 760/.092/4 19
N6888.B753 A4 1986
NYPL [3-MCK B919 90-12854]

Buchholz, Wolff, 1935-
Werkverzeichnis der Druckgraphik 1957-1971. [Bearbeitung des Katalogs: W. Buchholz und Rolf Pyroth. Hamburg] Verlag Artoma-Galerie T. Levy [1971] 170 p. (chiefly illus.(part col.)) 27 cm. Includes bibliographical references.
1. Buchholz, Wolff, 1935- - Catalogs. I. Pyroth, Rolf. II. Title.
NE2350.5.B82 P96
NYPL [MDG (Buchholz) 90-5452]

BUCHHOLZ, WOLFF, 1935- - CATALOGS.
Buchholz, Wolff, 1935- Werkverzeichnis der Druckgraphik 1957-1971. [Hamburg, 1971] 170 p.
NE2350.5.B82 P96
NYPL [MDG (Buchholz) 90-5452]

Buchmann, Felix. Katz, Benjamin, 1939- Vier Künstler . [Stuttgart] , c1990. 167 p. : ISBN 3-89322-178-6 DDC 730/.943/09048 20
NB568 .K38 1990

Buchser, Frank, 1828-1890.
Frank Buchser 1828-1890 : Kunstmuseum Solothurn, 9. Juni-16. September 1990 / mit Essays von Roman Hollenstein und Petra ten-Doesschate Chu. Einsiedeln : Eidolon, c1990. 284 p. : ill. (some col.) ; 29 cm. Includes bibliographical references (p. 281-283).
1. Buchser, Frank, 1828-1890 - Exhibitions. I. Hollenstein, Roman. II. Chu, Petra ten-Doesschate. III. Kunstmuseum Solothurn. IV. Title.
NYPL [3-MCZ+ B92 91-8120]

BUCHSER, FRANK, 1828-1890 - EXHIBITIONS.
Buchser, Frank, 1828-1890. Frank Buchser 1828-1890 . Einsiedeln , c1990. 284 p. :
NYPL [3-MCZ+ B92 91-8120]

Buchstäblich Nürnberger wörtliche Tage : Dokumentation von Aktionen und Vorträgen, anlässlich der Ausstellung "buchstäblich wörtlich-wörtlich buchstäblich" in der Kunsthalle Nürnberg im Juni und Juli 1989 / herausgegeben von Michael Glasmeier und Lucius Grisebach ; künstlerische Beiträge von Frieder Butzmann ... [et al.] ; Vorträge von Michael Glasmeier ... [et al.] ; beigelegt eine Schalplatte mit Beiträgen von Frieder Butzmann ... [et al.]. [Nürnberg] : Verlag für moderne Kunst Nürnberg, c1990. 80 p. : ill. ; 27 cm. + 1 sound disc in pocket. ISBN 3-922531-77-6
1. Arts, Modern - 20th century - Exhibitions. I. Glasmeier, Michael, 1951-. II. Griesebach, Lucius. III. Butzmann, Frieder. IV. Kunsthalle Nürnberg.
NX458 .B83 1990

Buchsteiner, Thomas. Bush, Martin H. Duane Hanson, Skulpturen . [Stuttgart] , c1990. 111 p. : ISBN 3-89322-205-7
NYPL [3-MGO (Hanson) 91-7453]

Buck, Louisa. Relative values, or What's art worth? / Louisa Buck and Philip Dodd. London : BBC Books, 1991. 176 p. : ill. ; 23 cm. Includes bibliographical references (p. 165-168) and index. ISBN 0-563-36118-2 (cased) : DDC 700.1 20

I. Dodd, Philip. II. Title.
N7425   *NYPL [MA 91-5744]*

Bucki, Krzysztof, 1936-1983.
Kowal-Moik, Katarzyna. "Maluję dla ludzi
czujących--" . Opole , 1990. 75 p., [28] p. of
plates :
ND955.P63 B385 1990

**BUCKI, KRZYSZTOF, 1936-1983 -
CRITICISM AND INTERPRETATION.**
Kowal-Moik, Katarzyna. "Maluję dla ludzi
czujących--" . Opole , 1990. 75 p., [28] p. of
plates :
ND955.P63 B385 1990

Buckland Wright, Christopher. Buckland Wright,
John, 1897-1954. The engravings of John
Buckland Wright /. Aldershot, Hants , 1990.
160 p. : ISBN 0-85967-850-4 : DDC 769.92 20
*NE642.B8 A4 1990   NYPL [MDG (Buckland
Wright) 91-7278]*

Buckland Wright, John, 1897-1954.
The engravings of John Buckland Wright /
edited and with an introduction by Christopher
Buckland Wright. Aldershot, Hants : Ashgate
Editions, 1990. 160 p. : ill. (some col.) ; 28 cm.
Published on the occasion of an exhibition held at the
Ashmolean Museum, Oxford, Oct. 23-Dec. 2, 1990.
Includes bibliographical references (p. [159]-160).
    ISBN 0-85967-850-4 : DDC 769.92 20
1. Buckland Wright, John, 1897-1954 - Exhibitions. 2.
Buckland Wright, John, 1897-1954 - Catalogs. I.
Buckland Wright, Christopher. II. Ashmolean Museum.
III. Title.
*NE642.B8 A4 1990   NYPL [MDG (Buckland
Wright) 91-7278]*

**BUCKLAND WRIGHT, JOHN, 1897-1954 -
CATALOGS.**
Buckland Wright, John, 1897-1954. The
engravings of John Buckland Wright /.
Aldershot, Hants , 1990. 160 p. : ISBN
0-85967-850-4 : DDC 769.92 20
*NE642.B8 A4 1990   NYPL [MDG (Buckland
Wright) 91-7278]*

**BUCKLAND WRIGHT, JOHN, 1897-1954 -
EXHIBITIONS.**
Buckland Wright, John, 1897-1954. The
engravings of John Buckland Wright /.
Aldershot, Hants , 1990. 160 p. : ISBN
0-85967-850-4 : DDC 769.92 20
*NE642.B8 A4 1990   NYPL [MDG (Buckland
Wright) 91-7278]*

Bückling, Maraike.
Festschrift für Hartmut Biermann /. Weinheim ,
c1990. 400 p. : ISBN 3-527-17712-4
                    NYPL [3-MAS 91-5197]
Polyklet . Mainz am Rhein , c1990. 678 p., 8 p.
of plates : ISBN 3-8053-1175-3 DDC 730/.92 20
NB101 .P65 1990

Bucuresti, ghidul străzilor /. Ionescu, Alexandru.
[Bucharest] , 1982. 1 atlas (132, 138 p.) : DDC
912/.4982 19
G2039 .B816 1982
                    NYPL [Map Div. 84-1514]

**Budapest. Galerie nationale hongroise. see
Budapest. Magyar Nemzeti Galéria.**

Budapest. Magyar Nemzeti Galéria. Pénzes, Éva
N. Boross Géza emlékkiállítása . [Budapest] ,
1975. [42] p., [9] leaves of plates :
N6822.5.B62 P46
                    NYPL [3-MCZ B733 79-2198]

**Budapest. Nemzeti Galéria. see Budapest.
Magyar Nemzeti Galéria.**

Budapesti műtermek. Hajdu, István. Les ateliers
de Budapest =. Paris , c1990. 240 p. : ISBN
978-290-807-2006
                    NYPL [3-MAM+ 91-3623]

Budd, Ellen H. Frances Brundage post cards : an
illustrated reference guide / Ellen H. Budd.[1st
ed.] [Cincinnati, OH] (6910 Tenderfoot La.,
Cincinnati 45249) : E.H. Budd, [1990] 140 p. :
ill. ; 28 cm. DDC 741.6/83/092 20
1. Brundage, Frances, 1854-1937 - Catalogs. I.
Brundage, Frances, 1854-1937. II. Title.
NC1879.B76 A4 1990

Buddha, Gautama. see Gautama Buddha.

**BUDDHIST ANTIQUITIES - INDIA - S
ANCHI.**
Narendar N ath Soz. Archaeological museum S
anchi /. New Delhi , c1966. 26 p., 12 p. of
plates :   *NYPL [3-MAE 90-7106]*

BUDDHIST ART. see ART, BUDDHIST.

**BUDDHIST ART AND SYMBOLISM -
CHINA - TIBET.**
Lauf, Detlef Ingo. Eine Ikonographie des
tibetischen Buddhismus /. Graz, Austria , 1979.
204 p. : ISBN 3-201-01092-8 : DDC
704.9/48943923 19
N8193.T52 L38   *NYPL [3-MAF 91-4701]*
Vitali, Roberto. Early temples of central Tibet
/. London , 1990. 150 p. : ISBN 0-906026-25-3 :
    DDC 951.5 20   *NYPL [3-MAF+ 91-4702]*

**BUDDHIST ART AND SYMBOLISM -
CHINA - TIBET - EXHIBITIONS.**
Rhie, Marylin M. Wisdom and compassion .
[San Francisco] , 1991. 406 p. : ISBN
0-8109-3957-6 DDC
704.9/48943923/0951507473 20
N8193.T5 R47 1991
                    NYPL [3-MAF+ 91-7450]

**BUDDHIST ART AND SYMBOLISM -
INDIA.**
Symbols in art and religion . London , Glenn
Dale, MD , 1990. xiii, 221 p. : ISBN
0-913215-69-4 DDC 704.94894 20
N7301   *NYPL [3-MAF 91-6383]*

Buddhist iconography. New Delhi : Tibet House,
c1989. xiii, 249 p., [48] p. of plates : ill. ; 23
cm. (Sambhota series . 2) Papers presented at an
international seminar organized by Tibet House.
Includes bibliographical references. DDC 704.9/48943
20
1. Art, Buddhist - Congresses. I. Tibet House
(Organization : New Delhi, India). II. Series.
N8193.A4 B83 1989
                    NYPL [3-MAF 91-4623]

Budigna, Luciano. Arte italiana contemporanea /.
Firenze [1965?]. 11 v. : DDC 709/.2/2 19
N6918 .A788   *NYPL [3-MAMC+ 88-4656]*

Büchner, Joachim.
Kunstmuseum Hannover mit Sammlung
Sprengel /. Braunschweig , 1979. 128 p. :
N6488.G3 H345
                    NYPL [MAVZ (Hannover) 81-536]
Kunstsammlung Nordrhein-Westfalen
(Germany) Malerei des zwanzigsten
Jahrhunderts. [Düsseldorf, c1965] 279 p.
                    NYPL [3-MAVZ (Dusseldorf) 90-6621]

Bühler, Hans-Peter. Heinrich Bürkel : mit
Werkverzeichnis der Gemälde / Hans-Peter
Bühler, Albrecht Krückl. München :
Bruckmann, c1989. 343 p. : ill. ; 28 cm. ISBN
3-7654-2232-0
1. Bürkel, Heinrich, 1802-1869. I. Title.
                    NYPL [3-MCK B928 90-13435]

Buehrens, Carol. DataCAD for the architect /
Carol Buehrens. 2nd ed. Blue Ridge Summit,
PA : McGraw Hill, c1991. xxi, 450 p. : ill. ; 24
cm. (Computer graphics technology and management
series) Includes index. ISBN 0-8306-3746-X (pbk.) :
DDC 720/.28/402855369 20
1. DataCAD (Computer program). 2. Architectural
design - Data processing. 3. Architectural drawing -
Data processing. I. Title. II. Series.
NA2728 .B84 1991

Buenos Aires. Museo Nacional de Bellas Artes.
150 años de pintura chilena; [exposición] del 20
setiembre al 22 de ottubre, 1972. Buenos Aires
[1972?] 31 p. illus. 26 cm.
1. Painting, Chilean - Exhibitions. 2. Painting, Modern -
19th century - Chile - Exhibitions. 3. Painting Modern -
20th century - Chile - Exhibitions. I. Title. II. Title:
Ciento cincuenta años de pintura chilena.
ND364.B83   *NYPL [3-MCY 83-2303]*

**Buffalo. Albright-Knox Art Gallery. see Albright-
Knox Art Gallery.**

Buffalo Bill Historical Center. Shapiro, Michael
Edward. Frederic Remington . New York
[1991] p. cm. ISBN 0-8109-8104-1 DDC 709/.2
20
N6537.R4 S5 1991

Buffet, Bernard, 1928-
Avila, Alin Alexis. Bernard Buffet /. [Paris] ,
1989. 251 p. : ISBN 2-7079-0021-4
                    NYPL [3-MCO+ B929 89-24429]

**BUFFET, BERNARD, 1928- - CRITICISM
AND INTERPRETATION.**
Avila, Alin Alexis. Bernard Buffet /. [Paris] ,
1989. 251 p. : ISBN 2-7079-0021-4
                    NYPL [3-MCO+ B929 89-24429]

Buffet-Challié, Laurence. Manolo Ruiz Pipó /
Laurence Buffet-Challié, Patricia Bailly ;
traducción, Rafael y David Conte. Paris,
France : C. y A. Bailly, [1990] 174 p. : chiefly
ill. (some col.) ; 33 cm. Text in Spanish;
introduction in French. Title on cover: Ruiz Pipó.
    ISBN 2-908517-12-4 DDC 759.6 20
1. Ruiz Pipó, Manolo, 1929- - Catalogs. I. Ruiz Pipó,
Manolo, 1929-. II. Bailly, Patricia. III. Title. IV. Title:
Ruiz Pipó.
N7113.R86 A4 1990

**Buford, Harry T. see Velazquez, Loreta Janeta,
1842-**

Bügel, Martina. Kunstsituation und Künstler sein
heute . Karlsruhe , 1988. 342 p. :
N6886.K33 K88 1988
                    NYPL [3-MAMG 90-10706]

Buhagiar, Mario, 1945- The iconography of the
Maltese Islands, 1400-1900 : painting / Mario
Buhagiar ; [organized by] World Confederation
of Salesian Past Pupils of Don Bosco, [and]
Lions Club (Malta). Valletta, Malta : Progress
Press Co., 1988. 202 p. : col. ill. ; 31 cm.
Includes bibliographical references and index. DDC
759.58/5 20
1. Painting, Maltese. 2. Painting, Italian. I. World
Confederation of Salesian Past Pupils of Don Bosco. II.
Lions Club (Malta). III. Title.
ND955.M3 B84 1988

**BÜHRLE, EMIL GEORG, 1890-1956 - ART
COLLECTIONS - EXHIBITIONS.**
The passionate eye . [Zurich?] , Zurich , c1990.
244 p. : ISBN 0-8478-1215-4
                    NYPL [3-MAX (Bührle) 90-12982]

Buijsen, Edwin. Broos, B. P. J. Great Dutch
paintings from America . The Hague , Zwolle ,
c1990. 561 p. : ISBN 90-6630-253-4 (paperback)
                    NYPL [3-MCG 91-5531]

Building Arts Forum/New York.
Building Arts Forum/New York. Symposium
(1989 : Guggenheim Museum) Bridging the
gap . New York , c1991. xv, 183 p. : ISBN
0-442-00135-5 DDC 720 20
NA2543.T43 B8 1991
                    NYPL [3-MQV 91-3950]

**Building Arts Forum/New York. Symposium
(1989 : Guggenheim Museum)** Bridging the
gap : rethinking the relationship of architect
and engineer : the proceedings of the Building
Arts Forum/New York Symposium, held in
April of 1989 at the Guggenheim Museum /
Building Arts Forum/New York. New York :
Van Nostrand Reinhold, c1991. xv, 183 p. :
ill. ; 24 cm. Includes bibliographical references (p.
172-178) and index. ISBN 0-442-00135-5 DDC 720
20
1. Architecture - Technological innovations -
Congresses. 2. Group work in architecture - Congresses.
I. Building Arts Forum/New York. II. Title.
NA2543.T43 B8 1991
                    NYPL [3-MQV 91-3950]

BUILDING, BRICK - BERLIN (GERMANY)
Klinkott, Manfred. Die Backsteinbaukunst der
Berliner Schule . Berlin , c1988. 479 p., 9
leaves of plates : ISBN 3-7861-1438-2 DDC
721/.04421/094315509034 20
NA1085 .K57 1988
                    NYPL [3-MQWD 90-11025]

BUILDING, BRICK - ENGLAND - HISTORY.
Brunskill, R. W. Brick building in Britain /.
London , 1990. 208 p., [16] p. of plates : ISBN
0-575-04457-8 : DDC 693.210941 20
TH5501   *NYPL [3-MQWK 90-11098]*

BUILDING, CLAY - AFRICA, NORTH.
Aus Erde geformt . Mainz [1990] 171 p. :
    ISBN 3-8053-1107-9 :
NA1588 .A97 1990   NYPL [Sc F 91-122]

BUILDING, CLAY - AFRICA, WEST.
Aus Erde geformt . Mainz [1990] 171 p. :
    ISBN 3-8053-1107-9 :
NA1588 .A97 1990   NYPL [Sc F 91-122]

BUILDING DESIGN. see ARCHITECTURE.

**BUILDING - EUROPE - HISTORY -
SOURCES - CATALOGS.**
Der Mittelalterliche Baubetrieb Westeuropas .
Köln , 1987. 568 p. : DDC 760/.044969 19
N8217.B85 M58 1987
                    NYPL [3-MAMZ 91-4597]

Building God's house in the Roman world .
White, L. Michael. Baltimore, Md. , c1990. xv,

211 p. :   ISBN 0-8018-3906-8 (alk. paper)
NA4817 .W55 1990
NYPL [3-MQN 90-10439]

BUILDING - HUNGARY - CONGRESSES.
Magyar Épitőművészek Szövetsége. Magyar
Épitőművészek Szövetsége IV. konferenciája és
jubileumi közgyűlése . Budapest [1962] 322 p. ;
NA1012 .M33 1962

Building Idaho . Attebery, Jennifer Eastman,
1951- Moscow, Idaho , 1991. x, 166 p. :   ISBN
0-89301-139-8   DDC 720/.9796 20
NA730.I2 A88 1990
NYPL [3-MQWO 91-4971]

BUILDING IN ART - CATALOGS.
Der Mittelalterliche Baubetrieb Westeuropas .
Köln , 1987. 568 p. :   DDC 760/.044969 19
N8217.B85 M58 1987
NYPL [3-MAMZ 91-4597]

**BUILDING INDUSTRY. see
CONSTRUCTION INDUSTRY.**

**BUILDING, IRON AND STEEL - FRANCE -
PARIS - EXHIBITIONS.**
Marrey, Bernard. Le fer à Paris . [Paris] , 1989.
209 p., [1] leaf of plates :   ISBN 2-7084-0379-6
NYPL [3-MQWF+ 90-243]

**BUILDING MATERIALS - HANDBOOKS,
MANUALS, ETC.**
Harrison, Henry S. Houses . Chicago, IL ,
1991. p. cm.   ISBN 0-7931-0332-0 (pbk.)   DDC
728 20
NA7110 .H33 1991

BUILDING - TERMINOLOGY.
Ballast, David Kent. Architecture, design, and
construction word finder /. Englewood Cliffs,
N.J. , c1991. p. cm.   ISBN 0-13-044397-2   DDC
720/.3 20
NA31 .B34 1991

BUILDING, WOODEN - AUSTRIA - STYRIA.
Moderner Holzbau in der Steiermark /.
Graz/Austria [1989] 202 p. :   ISBN
3-201-01504-0
NA1009.S7 M64 1989

BUILDING, WOODEN - NORWAY.
Holan, Jerri. Norwegian wood . New York ,
1990. 208 p., [16] p. of plates :   ISBN
0-8478-0954-4 :   DDC 721/.0448/09485 19
NA1261 .H65 1989
NYPL [3-MQWE 91-4988]

BUILDING, WOODEN - SOVIET UNION.
Bobrinskoĭ, Alekseĭ Alekseevich, graf.
Narodnyia russkiia dereviannyia izdieliia
predmety domashniago, khoziaĭstvennago i
otchasti tserkovnago obikhoda. Moskva , 1910.
7, 18, 7, 5, 6, 5, 5, 7, 163 leaves of plates :
*NYPL [Slav. Reserve 90-4456 no. 37
(Bates)]*

**BUILDINGS - ACOUSTICS. see
ARCHITECTURAL ACOUSTICS.**

**BUILDINGS - BOLIVIA - CONSERVATION
AND RESTORATION.**
Conservaci´on de los monumentos virreinales de
Bolivia. La Paz , 1987. 32 p. :
NYPL [3-MQWM+ 89-26926]

**BUILDINGS - COLOR. see COLOR IN
ARCHITECTURE.**

**BUILDINGS, COMMERCIAL. see OFFICE
BUILDINGS.**

**BUILDINGS - CONSERVATION AND
RESTORATION.**
Smeallie, Peter H. New construction for older
buildings . New York , c1990. xi, 211 p., [8] p.
of plates :   ISBN 0-471-83134-4   DDC 720/.28/6
20
NA2793 .S58 1990   *NYPL [MQD 91-2642]*

BUILDINGS - DESIGNS AND PLANS.
Dunster, David. Key buildings of the twentieth
century /. New York , c1985- v. :   ISBN
0-8478-0642-1 (pbk. : v. 1) :   DDC 724.9/1 19
NA680 .D86 1985
NYPL [3-MQV+ 86-3952]

**BUILDINGS - DETAILS. see
ARCHITECTURE - DETAILS.**

**BUILDINGS - EARTHQUAKE EFFECTS -
ITALY - PALAZZOLO ACREIDE -
EXHIBITIONS.**
Palazzolo Acreide . Siracusa , Palermo , c1989.
xv, 140, [3] p. :
NYPL [3-MQWB+ 91-5408]

BUILDINGS, FARM. see FARM BUILDINGS.

BUILDINGS - GREECE.
Müller-Wiener, Wolfgang. Griechisches
Bauwesen in der Antike /. München , c1988.
221 p. :   ISBN 3-406-32993-4
NYPL [3-MQM 90-12379]

BUILDINGS IN ART.
Parramón, José María. Painting buildings in oil
/. New York [1991] p. cm.   ISBN
0-8230-3582-4 :   DDC 751.45/44 20
ND1410 .P3 1991

Sicilia, Manel Plana. [Cómo pintar el paisaja
urbano a la acuarela. English.] How to paint
buildings /. New York , 1991. p. cm.   ISBN
0-8230-2474-1 :   DDC 751.42/244 20
ND2310 .S513 1991

Taylor, Richard S. Buildings in watercolour /.
London , 1989. 126 p. :   ISBN 0-7134-6178-0
DDC 751.42/244 20
ND2310 .T38 1989

BUILDINGS IN ART - CATALOGS.
Brodsky & Utkin /. New York , c1990. p. cm.
ISBN 1-87827-113-X :   DDC 769.92/2 20
NE2056.5.B76 A4 1990

Buildings in watercolour /. Taylor, Richard S.
London , 1989. 126 p. :   ISBN 0-7134-6178-0
DDC 751.42/244 20
ND2310 .T38 1989

**BUILDINGS, LIBRARY. see LIBRARY
ARCHITECTURE.**

**BUILDINGS - MATERIALS. see BUILDING
MATERIALS.**

**BUILDINGS - MODELS. see
ARCHITECTURAL MODELS.**

Buildings of England.
Cherry, Bridget. Devon /. Harmondsworth ,
1989. 976 p., [96] p. of plates :   ISBN
0-14-071050-7 :
NYPL [3-MQWK 90-12006]

Buildings of Mimar Sinan. Ülgen, Ali Saim.
Mimar Sinan yapıları /. [Ankara] , 1989. 2
portfolios (266 plates) :   ISBN 975-16-0164-9
NA1373.S5 A4 1989
*NYPL [*OPR+++ 90-6]*

The buildings of Shropshire /. Garner, Lawrence.
Shrewsbury, England , <1989-. v. <2> :
ISBN 1-85310-091-9 (v. 2) :   DDC 720/.9424/5
20
NA969.S3 G37 1989

**BUILDINGS, OFFICE. see OFFICE
BUILDINGS.**

**BUILDINGS, PREFABRICATED - HONG
KONG.**
Williams, Stephanie. Hongkong Bank . Boston ,
c1989. 302 p. :   ISBN 0-316-94238-3 :   DDC
725/.24/095125 20
NA6245.C62 H668 1989
NYPL [3-MQZ (Foster) 91-4484]

**BUILDINGS, PUBLIC. see PUBLIC
BUILDINGS.**

**BUILDINGS, RESTORATION OF. see
ARCHITECTURE - CONSERVATION
AND RESTORATION.**

**BUILDINGS - ROME - REMODELING FOR
OTHER USE.**
White, L. Michael. Building God's house in the
Roman world . Baltimore, Md. , c1990. xv, 211
p. :   ISBN 0-8018-3906-8 (alk. paper)
NA4817 .W55 1990
NYPL [3-MQN 90-10439]

**BUILDINGS - SPAIN - REMODELING FOR
OTHER USE.**
Intervenciones en el patrimonio arquitectónico
(1980-1985) /. [Madrid] [1990] 465 p. :   ISBN
84-7483-661-1   DDC 720/.28/8094609048 20
NA1301 .I57 1990

**BUILDINGS - SPAIN - SEVILLE -
REMODELLING FOR OTHER USE.**
Vázquez Consuegra, Guillermo. Sevilla, cien
edificios /. [Sevilla?] , 1988. 398 p. :   ISBN
89-87001-08-4
NYPL [3-MQWH+ 89-25523]

**BUILDINGS - UNITED STATES -
REMODELING FOR OTHER USE -
CASESTUDIES.**
Croft, Virginia. Recycled as restaurants . New
York , 1991. 223 p. :   ISBN 0-8230-4513-7 :

DDC 725/.71/0973 20
NA2500 .C76 1991

The built, the unbuilt, and the unbuildable .
Harbison, Robert. Cambridge, Mass. , 1991. 192
p. :   ISBN 0-262-08204-7 :   DDC 720/.1 20
NA2500 .H37 1991

Buisseret, David.
From sea charts to satellite images . Chicago ,
1990. xvi, 324 p., [8] p. of plates :   ISBN
0-226-07991-0 (alk. paper)   DDC 973/.022/3 20
E179 .F84 1990   *NYPL [Map Div. 90-12430]*

Rural images : the estate plan in the old and
new worlds / catalog prepared by David
Buisseret. Chicago : Newberry Library, 1988.
vi, 37 p. : ill. ; 18 x 23 cm. (Kenneth Nebenzahl,
Jr., lectures in the history of cartography) "A
cartographic exhibit at the Newberry Library on the
occasion of the ninth series of Kenneth Nebenzahl, Jr.,
lectures in the history of cartography."   ISBN
0-911028-40-4   DDC 333.3/022/3 20
1. Real property - Maps - Exhibitions. I. Newberry
Library. II. Title. III. Series.
GA109.5 .B85 1988
NYPL [Map Div. 91-2536]

Bujold, Françoise, 1933-1981.
Françoise Bujold : une exposition / organisée
par le Service d'animation et d'éducation.
[Québec] : Ministère des affaires culturelles,
c1982. 55 p. : ill. ; 21 cm. Exhibition held June
10-July 4, 1982, Musée d'art contemporain, Montréal.
ISBN 2-550-02474-5
1. Bujold, Françoise, 1933-1981 - Exhibitions. I. Québec
(Province). Musée d'art contemporain. II. Title.
MLCS 82/8466
NYPL [MDG (Bujold) 91-891]

**BUJOLD, FRANÇOISE, 1933-1981 -
EXHIBITIONS.**
Bujold, Françoise, 1933-1981. Françoise
Bujold . [Québec] , c1982. 55 p. :   ISBN
2-550-02474-5
MLCS 82/8466
NYPL [MDG (Bujold) 91-891]

Bukovnik, Gary, 1947- Flowers : Gary Bukovnik
watercolors & monotypes / foreword by James
J. White ; conversation with Robert Flynn
Johnson ; essay by Judith Gordon ; [compiled
and organized ... by Lawrence Banka]. New
York : Abrams, 1990. 119 p. : chiefly col. ill. ;
22 x 28 cm. Includes bibliographical references (p.
118).   ISBN 0-8109-3105-2   DDC 760/.092 20
1. Bukovnik, Gary, 1947-. I. Gordon, Judith. II.
Johnson, Robert Flynn. III. Banka, Lawrence. IV. Title.
V. Title: Gary Bukovnik watercolors & monotypes.
N6537.B835 A4 1990
NYPL [3-MCX B924 90-11081]

BUKOVNIK, GARY, 1947-
Bukovnik, Gary, 1947- Flowers . New York ,
1990. 119 p. :   ISBN 0-8109-3105-2   DDC
760/.092 20
N6537.B835 A4 1990
NYPL [3-MCX B924 90-11081]

Bulaka, Mečislovas, 1907-
Vilnius senamiestis : 24 sangvino piešiniai /
Mečislovas Bulaka.2. leidimas. Vilnius : Vaga,
1987. 1 portfolio : 24 ill. ; 42 cm. Lithuanian,
English, and Russian. Title from t.p. verso: Vil′niūs,
staryĭ gorod.
1. Bulaka, Mečislovas, 1907- - Catalogs. 2. Vilnus
(Lithuania) in art - Catalogs. I. Title. II. Title: Vil′niūs,
staryĭ gorod.
NC269.B85 A4 1987

BULAKA, MEČISLOVAS, 1907- - CATALOGS.
Bulaka, Mečislovas, 1907- Vilnius senamiestis .
Vilnius , 1987. 1 portfolio :
NC269.B85 A4 1987

Bulatov, Ėrik, 1933-
Adaptation & negation of socialist realism .
Ridgefield, CT , c1990. 44 p. :
NYPL [3-MAM+ 91-5891]

Artisti russi contemporanei . Prato , c1990. 208
p. :   ISBN 88-85191-01-0
NYPL [3-MAM 90-10469]

The Bulfinch library of collectibles.
Bonera, Franco. [Maiale. English.] Pigs .
Boston , 1991. p. cm.   ISBN 0-8212-1873-5   DDC
704.9/432 20
N7668.S95 M3513 1991

Cenzato, Elena. [Gufi & civette. English.]
Owls . Boston , c1991. p.   ISBN 0-8212-1879-4 :

DDC 704.9/432 20
N7666.O94 C4613 1991

Ribuoli, Patrizia. [Rana. English.] Frogs .
Boston , c1991. p. ISBN 0-8212-1876-X : DDC
704.9/432 20
N7668.F76 R3613 1991

Bulgaria : tradition & beauty / edited by
Elizabeth I. Kwasnik. [Liverpool] : National
Museums & Galleries on Merseyside, 1989. 79
p. : col. ill. ; 30 cm. Published to accompany an
exhibition at Liverpool Museum, 1989. Includes
bibliographical references. ISBN 0-906367-38-7
(pbk.) : DDC 949.770074 20
*1. Folk art - Bulgaria - Exhibitions. 2. Decoration and
ornament - Bulgaria - Exhibitions. 3. Art, Bulgarian -
Exhibitions. I. Kwasnik, Elizabeth I. II. National
Museums and Galleries on Merseyside. III. Liverpool
Museum (Liverpool, England). IV. Title: Bulgaria,
tradition and beauty.*
NYPL [3-MNE+ 90-11535]

BULGARIA - CLIMATE - MAPS.
Pochveno-klimatychno raĭonirane na glavnite
polski kulturi . [Sofia , 1969]. 45 maps :
NYPL [Map Div. 91-1087]

Bulgaria. Komitet za kultura. Traci . Milano ,
c1989. 347 p. :
NK1000.T48 T73 1989
NYPL [3-MAE+ 91-6582]

BULGARIA - MAPS.
(1961) Bulgaria. Upravlenie Geodeziiā i
kartografiiā. Geografski atlas . Sofiiā , 1961. 1
atlas (14 p. : *NYPL [Map Div. 91-1091]*

(1969) Pochveno-klimatychno raĭonirane na
glavnite polski kulturi . [Sofia , 1969]. 45
maps : *NYPL [Map Div. 91-1087]*

Bulgaria, tradition and beauty. Bulgaria .
[Liverpool] , 1989. 79 p. : ISBN 0-906367-38-7
(pbk.) : DDC 949.770074 20
NYPL [3-MNE+ 90-11535]

Bulgaria. Upravlenie Geodeziiā i kartografiiā.
Geografski atlas : za chetvŭrti klas / [redaktor
M. Kirilov]. Sofiiā : Upravlenie Geodeziiā i
kartografiiā, 1961. 1 atlas (14 p. : ill., col.
maps) ; 24 cm. Cover title.
1. Bulgaria - Maps. I. Kirilov, M. II. Title.
NYPL [Map Div. 91-1091]

Bulgaria. Upravlenie po geodeziiā i kartografiiā.
Geografski atlas : za osmi klas i pŭrvi kurs na
tekhnikumite / [redaktsionna kolegiiā Ivan
Dragomirov (otg. redaktor) ... et al.].6-o popr.
izd. Sofiiā : Glavno upravlenie po geodeziiā i
kartografiiā, 1969. 1 atlas (65 p. : ill., col.
maps) ; 32 cm. Cover title.
1. Atlases, Bulgarian. I. Dragomirov, Ivan. II. Title.
NYPL [Map Div. 91-1090]

BULGARIAN ART. see ART, BULGARIAN.

Bull, David, 1934- The Feast of the gods :
conservation, examination, and interpretation /
David Bull, Joyce Plesters. Washington :
National Gallery of Art ; Hanover, N.H. :
Distributed by the University Press of New
England, 1990. 106 p. : ill. (some col.) ; 28 cm.
(Studies in the history of art, 0091-7338 . v. 40. 2)
Includes bibliographical references (p. 105-106). ISBN
0-89468-144-3 DDC 709 s 759.5 20
*1. Bellini, Giovanni, d. 1516. Feast of the gods. 2.
Bellini, Giovanni, d. 1516 - Criticism and interpretation.
3. Titian, ca. 1488-1576 - Criticism and interpretation.
4. National Gallery of Art (U. S.). 5. Painting, Italian -
Expertising. 6. Painting, Italian - Conservation and
restoration. I. Plesters, Joyce. II. Series: Studies in the
history of art (Washington, D.C.) . v. 40. III. Title.*
N386.U5 S78 vol. 40 ND623.B39
NYPL [3-MCF B39 90-8050]

Bull, George Anthony. Vasari, Giorgio,
1511-1574. [Vite de' più eccellenti architetti,
pittori et scultori italiani. English. Selections.]
Lives of the artists /. London , New York ,
1987. 2 v. ; ISBN 0-14-044500-5 (v. 1)
NYPL [3-MAMC 88-536]

Bulletin de correspondance hellénique.
Supplément.
(19) L'Habitat égéen préhistorique . Athènes ,
Paris , 1990. 495 p. : ISBN 2-86958-031-2
NYPL [3-MQL 91-5181]

Bulletin supplement (University of London.
Institute of Classical Studies) .
(no. 59) Krzyszkowska, O. (Olga) Ivory and

related materials . London , 1990. xv, 109 p.,
[70] p. of plates : ISBN 0-900587-62-8
NYPL [3-MNW 91-7005]

Bulley, W. Edwin. Brechin: a study in
conservation. Edinburgh [1970] [231] p. ISBN
0-901658-08-1 DDC 711/.4 094131
NA109.G7 B7 *NYPL [3-MQWK 90-5626]*

BULLFIGHTS IN ART.
La Tauromachie, art et littérature /. Paris ,
c1990. 151 p. ; ISBN 2-7384-0685-8 DDC 700
20
NX650.B84 T38 1990

Zaldívar, Rafael. El cartel taurino . Madrid ,
1990. 370 p. : ISBN 84-239-5426-9 DDC
741.6/74/0946 20
NC1849.B84 Z35 1990

BULLFIGHTS IN ART - CATALOGS.
Cau, Jean, 1925- Fernando Botero . Paris ,
c1990. 161 p. : ISBN 2-85047-159-3 DDC
759.9861 20
N6679.B6 A4 1990b

BULLFIGHTS IN ART - EXHIBITIONS.
Goya, Francisco, 1746-1828. Goya . [Madrid] ,
c1990. 161 p. : ISBN 84-7483-633-6
NYPL [3-MCQ G72 91-3635]

BULLFIGHTS - MEXICO - TIJUANA -
PICTORIAL WORKS.
Wiener, Leigh. Tijuana Sunday /. [Los Angeles,
Calif.] , c1989. 265 p. : ISBN 0-9619146-1-0
NYPL [MFX (Wiener) 91-5840]

Bullivant, Lucy. International interior design /
Lucy Bullivant ; coordinating researcher
Jennifer Hudson. New York : Abbeville Press,
1991. p. cm. Includes index. ISBN 1-558-59235-0
DDC 725/.09/048 20
*1. Interior decoration - History - 20th century -
Themes, motives. I. Hudson, Jennifer. II. Title.*
NK1980 .B84 1991

BULLS AND BEARS. see STOCK-
EXCHANGE.

Buluță, Gheorghe. Manuscrise miniate și ornate
românești în colecții din Austria / Gheorghe
Buluță. București : Editura Meridiane, 1990.
142 p. : ill. (some col.) ; 25 cm. (Manuscris)
Summary and table of contents in German. Includes
bibliographical references (p. 30-[55]). ISBN
973-330-070-5 :
*1. Illumination of books andmanuscrpts, Romanian -
Catalogs. 2. Illumination of books and manuscripts -
Austria - Catalogs. I. Title.*
ND3227 .B84 1990

Bumpus, Judith. Impressionist gardens / Judith
Bumpus. Oxford : Phaidon, 1990. 80 p. : ill.
(some col.) ; 32 cm. Illustrations on lining papers.
Includes bibliographical references. ISBN
0-7148-2660-X : DDC 759.054 20
*1. Impressionism (Art) - France. 2. Painting, Modern -
19th century - France. 3. Gardens in art. I. Title.*
ND192.I4 *NYPL [3-MCN+ 90-13280]*

Bunch, Clarence. Art education : a guide to
information sources / Clarence Bunch. Detroit :
Gale Research Co., c1978. xv, 331 p. ; 23 cm.
(Art and architecture information guide series. v. 6)
Includes indexes. ISBN 0-8103-1272-7 DDC
016.707
1. Art - Study and teaching - Bibliography. I. Title.
Z5818.A8 B85 N85 NYPL [3-MAC 91-7862]

Bündner Kunstmuseum Chur.
Das Engadin Ferdinand Hodlers und anderer
Künstler des 19. und 20. Jahrhunderts . [Chur]
St. Moritz , c1990. 122 p. : ISBN 3-905240-15-7
DDC 759.9494 20
ND853.H6 A4 1990

Meuli, Andrea. Bilder einer Sammlung .
[Switzerland] , c1989. 210 p. : ISBN
3-905241-03-X
NYPL [3-MAVZ+ (Chur) 90-8658]

Spescha, Matias, 1925- Matias Spescha /.
Chur , 1987. 46 p. :
MLCS 89/21018 (N)
NYPL [3-MCZ S751 90-2847]

BÜNDNER KUNSTMUSEUM CHUR -
CATALOGS.
Meuli, Andrea. Bilder einer Sammlung .
[Switzerland] , c1989. 210 p. : ISBN
3-905241-03-X
NYPL [3-MAVZ+ (Chur) 90-8658]

Bungalows, camps, and mountain houses /.
Comstock, William Phillips. Washington, D.C. ,

c1990. xxvi, 125 p. : ISBN 1-558-35063-2 :
DDC 728/.373 20
NA7571 .C7 1990
NYPL [3-MRGG 91-3451]

BUNGALOWS - UNITED STATES.
Comstock, William Phillips. Bungalows, camps,
and mountain houses /. Washington, D.C. ,
c1990. xxvi, 125 p. : ISBN 1-558-35063-2 :
DDC 728/.373 20
NA7571 .C7 1990
NYPL [3-MRGG 91-3451]

Bunnell, Peter C. A Photographic vision . Salt
Lake City , 1980. viii, 212 p. : ISBN
0-87905-059-4 DDC 770 19
TR642 .P45 *NYPL [MFW 91-4692]*

Bunny Harvey . Harvey, Bunny, 1946- New
York, N.Y. , c1990. 32 p. :
NYPL [3-MCX H341 90-13537]

Bunte Mauer. Brauer, Erich, 1929- Brauer bunte
Mauer =. München [c1975] 89 p. : ISBN
3-7654-1632-0 DDC 759.36
ND511.5.B72 L47
NYPL [3-MCK B823 90-6049]

Bunyan, John, 1628-1688.
PILGRIM'S PROGRESS -
ILLUSTRATIONS.
Norvig, Gerda S. Dark figures in the desired
country . Berkeley , c1992. p. cm. ISBN
0-520-04471-1 (alk. paper) DDC 759.2 20
NC978.5.B55 N67 1992

Buonagurio, Toby, 1947- Ashes to ashes . New
York, N.Y. , c1982. 16 p. :
NYPL [3-MAMZ 90-12622]

Buoninsegna, Duccio di. see Duccio di
Buoninsegna, d. 1319.

Burāne, Ingrīda. Latvijas PSR Valsts Mākslas
akadēmija /. Riga , c1989. 279 p. :
N332.L33 R57 1989

Burant, James. National Archives of Canada. A
place in history . Ottawa, Ont. , c1991. ix, 300
p. : ISBN 0-660-13740-2 (alk. paper) DDC
760/.0449971 20
N6540 .N36 1991

Burchfield Center. Edwin Dickinson : tribute
exhibition : Burchfield Center, State University
College at Buffalo, September 18 to November
6, 1977, Herbert F. Johnson Museum of Art,
Cornell University, November 16 to December
23, 1977, Albany Institute of History and Art,
January 14 to February 19, 1978 / [organized
by the Burchfield Center, State University
College at Buffalo] [Buffalo] : The Center,
[c1977] 35 p. : ill. ; 23 cm.
*1. Dickinson, Edwin Walter, 1891- - Exhibitions. I.
Albany Institute of History and Art.*
ND237.D46 A4 1977
NYPL [3-MCX D563 80-2252]

Burchfield, Charles Ephraim, 1893-1967.
Charles Burchfield's journals : the poetry of
place / edited by J. Benjamin Townsend.
Albany, N.Y. : State University of New York
Press, 1992. p. cm. Includes bibliographical
references and index. ISBN 0-7914-0991-0 (CH :
acid-free) DDC 759.13 b 20
*1. Burchfield, Charles Ephraim, 1893-1967 - Diaries. 2.
Painters - United States - Diaries. I. Townsend, J.
Benjamin. II. Title.*
ND237.B89 A2 1992

BURCHFIELD, CHARLES EPHRAIM, 1893-
1967 - DIARIES.
Burchfield, Charles Ephraim, 1893-1967.
Charles Burchfield's journals . Albany, N.Y. ,
1992. p. cm. ISBN 0-7914-0991-0 (CH : acid-free)
DDC 759.13 b 20
ND237.B89 A2 1992

Burden, Ernest E., 1934- Perspective grid
sourcebook : photographic and computer
generated tracing grids for architectural and
interior design drawings / Ernest Burden. New
York : Van Nostrand Reinhold, 1991. p. cm.
Includes index. ISBN 0-442-21132-5 DDC
720/.28/40285 20
*1. Architectural drawing - Data processing. 2. Interior
decoration - Data processing. 3. Perspective - Data
processing. I. Title.*
NA2728 .B87 1991

Burden Gallery. McAuley, Skeet. Sign language .
New York, N.Y. , c1989. 78 p. : ISBN

0-89381-333-8 :   DDC 979.1/35 20
E99.N3 M515 1989
NYPL [MFX (McAuley) 89-26792]

Burdett, Richard. On rigor /. Cambridge, Mass. ,
c1989. 188 p. :   ISBN 0-262-52138-5
NYPL [3-MQV+ 91-6328]

Burdett, Richard (Richard M.) Strategies in
architectural thinking /. Chicago, Ill. ,
Cambridge, Mass. , 1991. p. cm.   ISBN
0-262-23159-X   DDC 720/.1 20
NA2500 .S83 1991

Bure, Gilles de. Gruau, René, 1909- Gruau /.
Paris , c1989. 191 p. :   ISBN 2-7335-0172-0
DDC 741.6/092 20
TT509 .G77 1989
NYPL [3-MME+ 91-5612]

Bureau de la statistique du Québec. Dépenses de
l'administration publique provinciale au titre de
la culture, 1984-1988. Québec, Québec [1989]
29 p. :   ISBN 2-550-19744-5
NX750.C2 D47 1989

Bureau, Pierre, 1937- Témoignage sur Marcel
Leprin, mon ami / par Pierre Bureau. Paris :
Editions Mayer, [1984] 113 p., [46] p. of
plates : ill. (some col.) ; 25 cm. Title on added
t.p.: Marcel Leprin, 1891-1933.   DDC 759.4 B 19
*1. Leprin, Marcel, 1891-1933. 2. Painters - France -
Biography. I. Title. II. Title: Marcel Leprin, 1891-1933.*
ND553.L8335 B87 1984
NYPL [3-MCO L599 91-6390]

Burelli, Augusto Romano, 1938- La moschea di
Sinan : i disegni dello studio Burelli e Gennaro
= Sinan's mosque : drawings by Burelli and
Gennaro / Augusto Romano Burelli.1a ed.
Venezia : Cluva Editrice, 1988. 127 p. : ill.
(chiefly col.), plans ; 33 cm. (Architettura
fondamenti . [1] = [1]) Bibliography: p. 122.   ISBN
88-85067-56-5 (pbk.)
*1. Sinan, Mimar, 1489 or 90-1588. 2. Mosques -
Turkey - Designs and plans. 3. Architecture, Islamic -
Turkey - Designs and plans. I. Gennaro, Paola. II. Title.
III. Title: Sinan's mosque. IV. Series: Architettura
fondamenti .*   **NYPL [3-MQT+ 90-10684]**

Buren, Daniel.
Daniel Buren : [Ausstellungskatalog] :
Staatsgalerie Stuttgart, 30. Juni bis 9. September
1990. Stuttgart : Die Staatsgalerie, c1990. 408
p. : ill. (some col.) ; 24 cm. Includes bibliographical
references (p. 405-408).
*1. Buren, Daniel - Exhibitions. I. Staatsgalerie Stuttgart.
II. Title.*
ND553.B984 A4 1990
NYPL [3-MCO B952 91-6020]

BUREN, DANIEL - EXHIBITIONS.
Buren, Daniel. Daniel Buren . Stuttgart , c1990.
408 p. :
ND553.B984 A4 1990
NYPL [3-MCO B952 91-6020]

Burgard, Timothy Anglin, 1963- Foshay, Ella M.,
1948- Mr. Luman Reed's picture gallery . New
York , 1990. 228 p. :   ISBN 0-8109-3751-4   DDC
759.14/074/7471 20
ND210 .F65 1990
NYPL [3-MCW 90-12446]

Burgenländische Landesgalerie.
Novoszel, Erich, 1955- Novoszel Erich .
Eisenstadt [1989] 1 v. (unpaged) :
NYPL [3-MCK N945 91-7966]

Uccusic, Hilda, 1938- Hilda Uccusic .
Oberpullendorf , c1988. 129 p. :
N6811.5.U23 A4 1988

Burger, Angelika. Muche, Georg, 1895- Georg
Muche--Leise sagen . Kassel , 19. 143 p. :
NYPL [3-MCK MGO 88-2455]

Burgmann, Sigrid. Kunst um 1800 . Magdeburg
[1989] 95 p. :   DDC 709/.03/3074431822 20
N6756 .K86 1989

BURGOS, SPAIN - HISTORY.
Ibáñez Pérez, Alberto C. Historia de la Casa
del Cordón de Burgos /. [Burgos] , 1987. 359
p. :   ISBN 84-505-5944-8
NYPL [3-MQWH 91-7280]

Burijisoton. Bijutsukan, Tokyo. La peinture
française de Corot à Brague dans la Collection
Ishibâshi de Tokyo . [Paris] . 76 p. :
NYPL [3-MAW (Paris) 86-3731]

Burke, Fred, 1965- Barker, Clive, 1952- Clive
Barker, illustrator /. Forestville, Calif. , c1990.
iv, 124 p., [18] p. of plates :   ISBN 1-560-60026-8

(limited signed clothbound) :   DDC 741/.092 20
NC139.B33 A4 1990

**BURKE, JACKSON, 1908-1975 - ART
COLLECTIONS - EXHIBITIONS.**
Die Kunst des alten Japan . Frankfurt am
Main , 1990. 199 p. :   ISBN 3-89322-209-X
NYPL [3-MAG+ 91-4469]

Burke, Janine. Field of vision : a decade of
change : women's art in the seventies / Janine
Burke. Ringwood, Vic., Australia : Viking, 1990.
xi, 148 p., [16] p. of plates : ill. (some col.) ; 29
cm. Includes bibliographical references and index.
ISBN 0-670-83586-2
*1. Art, Modern - 20th century - Australia. 2. Women
artists - Australia - Biography. I. Title.*
NYPL [3-MAM 90-13438]

**BURKE, MARY - ART COLLECTIONS -
EXHIBITIONS.**
Die Kunst des alten Japan . Frankfurt am
Main , 1990. 199 p. :   ISBN 3-89322-209-X
NYPL [3-MAG+ 91-4469]

BÜRKEL, HEINRICH, 1802-1869.
Bühler, Hans-Peter. Heinrich Bürkel .
München , c1989. 343 p. :   ISBN 3-7654-2232-0
NYPL [3-MCK B928 90-13435]

Burkhard, Balthasar.
Balthasar Burkhard. [Bern] : Kunsthalle Bern,
1988. 94 p. : ill. (some col.) ; 27 cm. German
and French. Catalog of an exhibition held at the
Kunsthalle Bern, Oct. 1-Nov. 13, 1988, the Kunsthalle
St. Gallen, Jan. 14-Feb. 25, 1989, and the Musée de La
Roche-sur-Yon, Apr. 15-June 11, 1989.
*1. Burkhard, Balthasar - Exhibitions. I. Kunsthalle Bern.
II. Kunsthalle St. Gallen. III. La Roche-sur-Yon
(France). Musée municipal. IV. Title.*
NYPL [MFX (Burkhard) 91-2391]

BURKHARD, BALTHASAR - EXHIBITIONS.
Burkhard, Balthasar. Balthasar Burkhard.
[Bern] , 1988. 94 p. :
NYPL [MFX (Burkhard) 91-2391]

Burkhardt, Hans Gustav, 1904-
Catastrophe according to Hans Burkhardt /
text, Donald Kuspit ; introduction, Dorothy
White. Allentown : Muhlenberg College, 1990.
1 v. (unpaged) : col. ill. ; 28 cm. Catalog of an
exhibition held at the Muhlenberg College, Jan. 26-Mar.
6, 1990. Includes bibliographical references.   ISBN
0-9625911-0-6
*1. Burkhardt, Hans Gustav, 1904- - Exhibitions. I.
Kuspit, Donald B. (Donald Burton), 1935-. II. White,
Dorothy. III. Muhlenberg College. IV. Title.*
NYPL [3-MCX B953 90-10666]

Hans Burkhardt : retrospective exhibition,
1950-1972 : Long Beach Museum of Art, July
16-September 24, 1972. Long Beach, Calif. :
The Museum, [1972] [20] p. : ill. (1 col.) ; 22 x
28 cm. Includes bibliographical references.   DDC
759.13
*1. Burkhardt, Hans Gustav, 1904- - Exhibitions. I. Long
Beach Museum of Art. II. Title.*
ND237.B896 L66
NYPL [3-MCX B953.L849]

**BURKHARDT, HANS GUSTAV, 1904- -
EXHIBITIONS.**
Burkhardt, Hans Gustav, 1904- Catastrophe
according to Hans Burkhardt /. Allentown ,
1990. 1 v. (unpaged) :   ISBN 0-9625911-0-6
NYPL [3-MCX B953 90-10666]

Burkhardt, Hans Gustav, 1904- Hans
Burkhardt . Long Beach, Calif. [1972] [20] p. :
DDC 759.13
ND237.B896 L66
NYPL [3-MCX B953.L849]

Burkom, Frans van.
Foto in omslag . Amsterdam , 1989. 143 p. :
ISBN 90-6579-033-0 (pbk.)
NYPL [MFW+ 91-3603]

Glas in lood in Nederland, 1817-1968 /.
's-Gravenhage [1990?] 414 p. :   ISBN
90-12-06146-6
NK5354.A1 G57 1990

Burks, John (John H.) Hull, Joan Gray. Hull, the
heavenly pottery /. Huron, SD (1376 Nevada
SW, Huron 57350) , c1990. 128 p. :   DDC
738.3/09771/59 20
NK4210.H84 A4 1990

BURLE MARX, ROBERTO, 1909-
Eliovson, Sima. The gardens of Roberto Burle
Marx /. New York , c1991. 237 p. :   ISBN

0-8109-3357-8   DDC 712/.092 B 20
SB470.B87 E45 1991
NYPL [3-MSCC 91-6489]

Burliŭk, David, 1882-1967. David Burliuk: 55
years of painting. Long Beach, N.Y. Lido
Galleries [c1962] 12, [20] p. illus. 27 cm.
Includes "Burliuk, a fable" by Elizabeth McCausland.
*1. Burliŭk, David, 1882-1967. I. McCausland, Elizabeth,
1899-1965. Burliuk, a fable. 1962. II. Title.*
NYPL [3-MCZ B95 90-7138]

BURLIŬK, DAVID, 1882-1967.
Burliŭk, David, 1882-1967. David Burliuk. Long
Beach, N.Y [c1962] 12, [20] p.
NYPL [3-MCZ B95 90-7138]

Burmeister, Katalin. Iride, schedule d'arte,
Firenze '82 . Firenze , c1982. 107 p. :
NYPL [3-MAMC+ 90-5983]

BURNETT COUNTY, WIS. - MAPS.
(1991) Burnett County, Wisconsin, land atlas &
plat book . Rockford, Ill. , Siren, Wis. , c1991.
1 atlas (100 p.) :   **NYPL [Map Div. 91-8055]**

**Burnett County, Wisconsin, land atlas & plat
book :** 1991. 14th ed. Rockford, Ill. : Rockford
Map Publishers ; Siren, Wis. : Distributed by
Burnett County 4-H Leaders Association,
c1991. 1 atlas (100 p.) : maps ; 28 cm. Cover
title. Includes indexes.
*1. Real property - Wisconsin - Burnett County - Maps.
2. Burnett County, Wis. - Maps. I. Rockford Map
Publishers. II. Title: Land atlas & plat book, Burnett
County, Wisconsin. III. Title: Land atlas and plat book,
burnett County, Wisconsin.*
NYPL [Map Div. 91-8055]

Burnett, David G. Masterpieces of Canadian art
from the National Gallery of Canada / David
Burnett ; foreword by Shirley L.Thomson.
Edmonton : Hurtig, 1990. x, 230 p. : ill. (some
col.) ; 32 cm. Includes index. Includes bibliographical
references.   ISBN 0-88830-344-0 :   DDC
709/.71/07471 20
*1. National Gallery of Canada - Catalogs. 2. Art,
Canadian - Catalogs. I. Title.*
NYPL [3-MAM+ 91-3276]

Burnham, Jack, 1931- Carter, Curtis L. Richard
Lippold, sculpture /. Milwaukee, Wis. [c1990]
64 p. :   DDC 730/.92 20
N6537.L56 A4 1990

Burns, Carol. Thinking the present . New York,
NY , c1990. 136 p. :   ISBN 0-910413-93-2
NYPL [3-MQWO 90-13419]

Burns, Edward. Stein, Gertrude, 1874-1946.
Gertrude Stein on Picasso. New York [1970]
122, [16] p. :   ISBN 0-87140-513-X   DDC 759.6
ND553.P5 S76
NYPL [3-MCQ P58 90-11647]

Burns, John A. Jandl, H. Ward. Yesterday's
houses of tomorrow . Washington, DC , 1991.
p. cm.   ISBN 0-89133-186-7   DDC
728/.0973/09034 20
NA7207 .J36 1991

Burns, Raymond, 1924- Ames, Lee J. Draw 50
creepy crawlies /. New York , c1991. p. cm.
ISBN 0-385-41189-8   DDC 743/.6 20
NC783 .A44 1991

Burns, Stanley B. Sleeping beauty : memorial
photography in America / Stanley B. Burns.1st
ed. Altadena, Calif. : Twelvetrees Press, 1990. 1
v. (unpaged) : ill. (some col.) ; 32 cm. (The
Burns archive) Photocopy of relevant Ann Landers
column inserted. Includes bibliographical references.
ISBN 0-942642-32-5
*1. Dead - Portraits - History - 19th century. 2.
Mourning customs - United States - History - 19th
century. 3. Portraits - Portraits - History - 19th
century. 4. Photography - United States - History -
19th century. 5. Photography, Medical - United States -
History - 19th century. I. Title.*
NYPL [MFW+ 91-6778]

Burnside, Madeleine. Tucker, Toba. Toba
Tucker . East Hampton, N.Y. , c1987. 23 p. :
ISBN 0-933793-07-3   DDC 779/.2/092 20
E99.S38 T83 1987   **NYPL [MFW 91-6717]**

Burow, Johannes. Der Antimenesmaler /
Johannes Burow. Mainz/Rhein : P. von Zabern,
c1989. xii, 126 p., 160, [2] p. of plates : ill. (2
col.) ; 32 cm. (Forschungen zur antiken Keramik. II.
Reihe, Kerameus . Bd. 7) Revised version of the
author's thesis (doctoral--Eberhard-Karls-Universität
Tübingen, 1982). Revision of the author's thesis
(doctoral)--Eberhard-Karls-Universität Tübingen, 1982.

Includes bibliographical references (p. xi-xii).   ISBN
3-8053-1029-3
1. Antimenes Painter - Catalogs. 2. Vases,
Black-figured - Greece - Catalogs. 3. Vase-painting,
Greek. I. Title.   **NYPL [3-MPEK+ 90-10403]**

Burrell Collection. Rarer gifts than gold .
[Glasgow] , c1988. 69 p. :   ISBN 0-85261-222-2
(pbk.)
N6318 .R374 1988
                        NYPL   [3-MAK+ 90-12644]

Burrett, Tony. How to use oil paints . Newton
Abbot , New York, N.Y. , 1989. 116 p. :   ISBN
0-7153-9474-6   DDC 751.45 20
ND1500 .H67 1989

Burroughs, Charles. From signs to design :
environmental process and reform in early
Renaissance Rome / Charles Burroughs.
Cambridge, Mass. : MIT Press, c1990. xii, 344
p., [54] p. of plates : ill., maps ; 27 cm. Includes
bibliographical references (p. 302-327) and index.
ISBN 0-262-02298-2   DDC
307.76/0945/63209024 20
1. Architecture, Renaissance - Italy - Rome. 2. City
planning - Italy - Rome - History - 15th century. 3.
Urbanization - Italy - Rome - History. 4. Rome (Italy) -
Buildings, structures, etc. I. Title.
NA1120 .B87 1990
                        NYPL [MQWB 91-4224]

Burrows, Tracy, 1962- A Survey of zoning
definitions /. Chicago , c1989. 36 p. :   DDC
361.6/0973 361.6/03 20
NA9108 .A545 no. 421 HT169.6

Burstein, David, 1947- Project management for the design professional
/. New York , 1991. p. cm.   ISBN 0-8230-4413-0
DDC 720/.68 20
NA1996 .S74 1991

Burt Lancaster . Crowther, Bruce, 1933-
London , 1991. 192 p., [16] p. of plates :   ISBN
0-7090-4349-X   DDC 791.43092 12A
                        NYPL [MES (Lancaster, B.)]

Burton Callicott . Callicott, Burton, 1907-
Memphis, Tenn. , c1991. 56 p. :   DDC 759.13 20
ND237.C195 A4 1991

Bury, Pol, 1922-
Les petits moutons blancs qui sortent en rang
du lavoir / Pol Bury. [Montpellier] : Fata
Morgana, c1976. 49 p. : ill. ; 23 cm. Includes
951.05/092/4 B
1. Mao, Tse-tung, 1893-1976 - Humor. I. Title.
DS778.M3 B88   **NYPL [MEMZ 91-2515]**

Pol Bury : sculptures, cinétisations 1953-1988 :
[exposition] Galerie Renée Ziegler, Zürich.
Zürich : Le Galerie, [1989] 54 p. : ill. (some
col.) ; 26 cm.
1. Bury, Pol, 1922- - Exhibitions. I. Galerie Renée
Ziegler. II. Title.
                  NYPL [3-MGO (Bury) 90-12639]

BURY, POL, 1922- - EXHIBITIONS.
Bury, Pol, 1922- Pol Bury . Zürich [1989] 54
p. :   **NYPL [3-MGO (Bury) 90-12639]**

Busby, Richard J. Beginner's guide to brass
rubbing [by] Richard J. Busby. London, Pelham,
1969. 128 p. 16 plates illus., form. 23 cm.
Includes bibliographies.   ISBN 0-7207-0244-5 :   DDC
739.5/22
1. Brass rubbing. I. Title.
NC915.R8 B8

Busch, Günter. Modersohn-Becker, Paula,
1876-1907. [Paula Modersohn-Becker in Briefen
und Tagebüchern. English.] Paula
Modersohn-Becker, the letters and journals /.
Evanston, Ill. , 1990. ix, 576 p., [22] p. of
plates :   ISBN 0-8101-0902-6   DDC 739.3 B 20
ND588.M58 A3 1990
                  NYPL [3-MCK M68 90-12461]

Busch, Ralf. Jaeger, Heino, 1938- Heino Jaeger .
Hamburg , 1988. 99 p. :   ISBN 3-7672-1072-X
DDC 760/.092 20
NC251.J265 A4 1988
                  NYPL [3-MCK+ J221 91-4186]

Busch-Reisinger Museum.
Auch kleine Dinge . [Cambridge] [1971] [174]
p. :   **NYPL [3-MNC 90-5886]**

Fogg Art Museum. European paintings before
1900 in the Fogg Art Museum . Cambridge ,
c1991. p. cm.   ISBN 0-916724-76-X (hardcover :
acid-free paper) :   DDC 759.94/074/7444 20
ND450 .F64 1991

Harvard University. Art Museums. The Fredric
Wertham collection . [Cambridge] , 1990. 101
p. :   ISBN 0-916724-75-1
IN PROCESS (ONLINE)
                  NYPL [3-MAX (Wertham) 91-5499]

Reiser, Katharyn D. Ernst Barlach: 1870-1938.
[n.p., 1970] 1 v. (unpaged)
N6888.B35 R4

The Walter Gropius Archive : an illustrated
catalogue of the drawings, prints, and
photographs in the Walter Gropius Archive at
the Busch-Reisinger Museum, Harvard
University / edited by Winfried Nerdinger.
New York : Garland Pub. ; Cambridge, Mass. :
Harvard University, 1990. 3 v. : ill., plans ; 31
cm. (Garland architectural archives) Includes index.
ISBN 0-8240-3340-X (v. 1) :   DDC 720/.22/2 20
1. Gropius, Walter, 1883-1969 - Archives - Catalogs. 2.
Busch-Reisinger Museum - Catalogs. I. Nerdinger,
Winfried. II. Title.
NA1088.G85 A4 1990
                  NYPL [3-MQZ+ (Gropius) 90-12990]

BUSCH-REISINGER MUSEUM - CATALOGS.
Busch-Reisinger Museum. The Walter Gropius
Archive . New York , Cambridge, Mass. , 1990.
3 v. :   ISBN 0-8240-3340-X (v. 1) :   DDC
720/.22/2 20
NA1088.G85 A4 1990
                  NYPL [3-MQZ+ (Gropius) 90-12990]

Fogg Art Museum. European paintings before
1900 in the Fogg Art Museum . Cambridge ,
c1991. p. cm.   ISBN 0-916724-76-X (hardcover :
acid-free paper) :   DDC 759.94/074/7444 20
ND450 .F64 1991

Busch, Wilhelm, 1832-1908.
Gesammelte Werke / Wilhelm Busch.
München : Braun & Schneider, c1959. 996 p. :
ill. ; 22 cm. "Alles was Busch bekannt und berühmt
gemacht hat."
1. German wit and humor, Pictorial. I. Title.
                  NYPL [3-MEM (Busch) 91-6173]

Wilhelm Busch : Malerei / herausgegeben von
Jochen Poetter. Stuttgart : G. Hatje, c1990. 199
p. : chiefly ill. (chiefly col.) ; 32 cm. Includes
bibliographical references.   ISBN 3-7757-0308-X
DDC 759.3 20
1. Busch, Wilhelm, 1832-1908 - Catalogs. I. Poetter,
Jochen. II. Title. III. Title: Malerei.
ND588.B86 A4 1990

Wilhelm Busch und seine Freunde in Frankfurt
und Kronberg /. Frankfurt am Main , c1984.
104 p. :   ISBN 3-7829-0289-0 :   DDC 831/.8 19
PT2603.U8 Z895 1984
                  NYPL [3-MCK B97 86-1055]

BUSCH, WILHELM, 1832-1908 - CATALOGS.
Busch, Wilhelm, 1832-1908. Wilhelm Busch .
Stuttgart , c1990. 199 p. :   ISBN 3-7757-0308-X
DDC 759.3 20
ND588.B86 A4 1990

Busch, Wilhelm M. (Wilhelm Martin), 1908-
Küster, Bernd, 1952- Wilh. M. Busch .
Marburg , c1990. 174 p. :   ISBN 3-89398-037-7
                  NYPL [3-MCK+ B973 91-4048]

**BUSCH, WILHELM M. (WILHELM
MARTIN), 1908-**
Küster, Bernd, 1952- Wilh. M. Busch .
Marburg , c1990. 174 p. :   ISBN 3-89398-037-7
                  NYPL [3-MCK+ B973 91-4048]

**BUSCH, WILHELM, 1832-1908 - FRIENDS
AND ASSOCIATES.**
Wilhelm Busch und seine Freunde in Frankfurt
und Kronberg /. Frankfurt am Main , c1984.
104 p. :   ISBN 3-7829-0289-0 :   DDC 831/.8 19
PT2603.U8 Z895 1984
                  NYPL [3-MCK B97 86-1055]

**BUSCH, WILHELM, 1832-1908 - HOMES
AND HAUNTS - GERMANY (WEST) -
FRANKFURT AM MAIN.**
Wilhelm Busch und seine Freunde in Frankfurt
und Kronberg /. Frankfurt am Main , c1984.
104 p. :   ISBN 3-7829-0289-0 :   DDC 831/.8 19
PT2603.U8 Z895 1984
                  NYPL [3-MCK B97 86-1055]

**BUSCH, WILHELM, 1832-1908 - HOMES
AND HAUNTS - GERMANY (WEST) -
KRONBERG IM TAUNUS.**
Wilhelm Busch und seine Freunde in Frankfurt
und Kronberg /. Frankfurt am Main , c1984.

104 p. :   ISBN 3-7829-0289-0 :   DDC 831/.8 19
PT2603.U8 Z895 1984
                  NYPL [3-MCK B97 86-1055]

Buschlen-Mowatt Gallery. Frankenthaler, Helen,
1928- Helen Frankenthaler, works on paper .
Vancouver , c1989. 43 p. :   ISBN 0-9693328-7-4 :
DDC 759.13 20
                  NYPL [3-MCX F825 91-3252]

Buscioni, Maria Cristina. Esposizioni e "stile
nazionale" (1861-1925) : il linguaggio
dell'architettura nei padiglioni italiani delle
grandi kermesses nazionali ed internazionali /
Maria Cristina Buscioni. Firenze : Alinea
editrice, c1990. xv, 303 p. : ill. ; 28 cm. (Saggi e
documenti di storia dell'architettura . 16) Includes
bibliographical references (p. 287-303).   DDC 725/.91
20
1. Exhibition buildings. 2. Architecture, Modern - 19th
century. 3. Architecture, Modern - 20th century. I.
Title. II. Series.
NA6750.A1 B8 1990

Busetto, Giorgio. I Querini Stampalia . Venezia ,
1987. 255 p. :   **NYPL [3-MAX+ (Querini
Stampalia) 90-12441]**

BUSH, JACK, 1909-
Jack Bush [motion picture] /. New York, NY ,
1979. 1 film reel (56 min., 50 sec.) :   DDC
759.971 11
ND249

Jack Bush [videorecording] /. New York, NY ,
1979. 1 videocassette (56 min., 50 sec.) :   DDC
759.971 11
ND249

Bush, Martin H. Duane Hanson, Skulpturen /
Martin H. Bush, Thomas Buchsteiner.
[Stuttgart] : Edition Cantz, c1990. 111 p. : ill.
(some col.) ; 26 cm. Catalog of an exhibition held at
the Kunsthalle Tübingen/Kunstverein Tübingen, Nov.
24, 1990-Feb. 10, 1991, and at 5 other locations
through Apr. 1992. Includes bibliographical references.
ISBN 3-89322-205-7
1. Hanson, Duane - Exhibitions. I. Hanson, Duane. II.
Buchsteiner, Thomas. III. Kunstverein Tübingen. IV.
Title.   **NYPL [3-MGO (Hanson) 91-7453]**

Bush, Martin H., 1930- see **Bush, Martin H.**

Bush, Robert G. Bird stencil designs / Robert G.
Bush. New York : Dover Publications, 1991. 60
p. of plates : all ill. ; 28 cm. (Dover pictorial
archive series)   ISBN 0-486-26704-0 (pbk.) :   DDC
745.4 20
1. Stencil work - Themes, motives. 2. Birds in art. I.
Title.
NK8655 .B87 1991

Bushart, Magdalena. Der Geist der Gotik und die
expressionistische Kunst : Kunstgeschichte und
Kunsttheorie 1911-1925 / Magdalena Bushart.
München : S. Schreiber, c1990. 255 p. : ill. ; 21
cm. Originally presented as the author's thesis
(doctoral--Freie Universität Berlin, 1989). Includes
bibliographical references (p. 233-247). Includes index.
ISBN 3-88960-018-2 :
1. Expressionism (Art) - Germany. 2. Art, German. 3.
Art, Gothic - Influence. I. Title.
N6848.5.E9 B8 1990

Busi, Aldo, 1948- Pâté d'homme : tragoedia
peninsulare in tre atti, uno strappo, due
estrazioni e taglio finale / Aldo Busi ; disegni
di Dario Cioli ; adattamento di Carmen
Covito.1a ed. Milano : A. Mondadori, 1989.
158 p. : chiefly col. ill. ; 34 cm. A comic strip
version of the play followed by its text.   ISBN
88-04-32902-5
I. Cioli, Dario, 1959-. II. Title.
                  NYPL [3-MEM+ (Cioli) 90-11342]

BUSINESS AND ART. see **ART AND
INDUSTRY.**

BUSINESS PATRONAGE OF THE ARTS. see
ART PATRONAGE.

Busse, Hans Busso von.
Architektur im Wandel . Düsseldorf , c1990. 91
p. :   ISBN 3-7640-0265-4
NA680 .A732 1990

Wahrnehmungen : Standpunkte zur Architektur
/ Hans Busso von Busse. Stuttgart : K. Krämer,
c1990. 262 p. : ill. (some col.) ; 26 cm. Includes
bibliographical references (p. 246-255).   ISBN
3-7828-1606-4
1. Architecture, Modern - 20th century. 2.
Architecture - Philosophy. I. Title.
NA680 .B87 1990

Busuioc, Elena. Ceramica de uz comun
nesmălțuită din Moldova : secolul al XIV-lea
pînă la mijlocul secolului al XVI-lea / Elena
Busuioc. București : Editura Academiei
Republicii Socialiste România, 1975. 87 p., [25]
leaves of plates : ill. ; 27 cm. (Biblioteca de
arheologie. 25) At head of title: Academia de Științe
Sociale și Politice a Republicii Socialiste România.
Institutul de Arheologie. Summary in French.
Explanatory matter in Romanian and French. Includes
bibliographical references.
1. Pottery - Romania - Moldavia - History. I. Title. II.
Series.
TP803.R6 B86   **NYPL [3-MPG 90-5750]**

Buti, Remo. Oro d'autore . [Arezzo] [1988] 135
p. :   **NYPL [3-MNR 91-6356]**

Butler, A. S. G. (Arthur Stanley George), 1888-
1965.
[Architecture of Sir Edwin Luytens. Vol. 1]
The domestic architecture of Sir Edwin
Lutyens / A.S.G. Butler ; with the
collaboration of George Stewart &
Christopher Hussey. Woodbridge, Suffolk :
Antique Collectors' Club, 1989. 61 p., 110,
[120] p. of plates : ill., plans ; 42 cm. "A
reprint of the Country-Houses volume from the three
volume Lutyens Memorial set 'The architecture of
Sir Edwin Lutyens.'" Reprint. Originally published:
Country Life. London ; New York : Scribner, 1950.
Includes index. ISBN 1-85149-100-7
1. Lutyens, Edwin Landseer, Sir, 1869-1944. 2. Country
homes - England - Designs and plans. I. Stewart,
George. II. Hussey, Christopher, 1899-1970. III. Title.
    NYPL [3-MQZ++ (Lutyens) 90-12076]

BUTLER & WILSON (FIRM)
Becker, Vivienne, 1953- Rough diamonds .
London , 1990. 175 p. : ISBN 1-85145-521-3 :
DDC 739.27 20
NK7304   **NYPL [MNR+ 91-3889]**

BUTLER COUNTY (PA.) - MAPS.
Rockford Map Publishers. Land atlas & plat
book Butler County . Rockford, Ill. , c1991. 1
atlas (99 p.) :   **NYPL [Map Div. 91-7772]**

Butler, D. J. Butler, W. E. Modern British
bookplates /. Cambridge [Eng.] , 1990. 58 p. :
       NYPL [MDVK 90-12776]

Butler Institute of American Art. Wegman,
William. The history of travel . Cincinnati,
Ohio , Youngstown, Ohio [1990] 36 p. : ISBN
0-915577-19-4
    NYPL [3-MCX W411 91-3443]

BUTLER, TOMÁS E.
Anastasía, Luis V. Figari . Montevideo , 1976.
92 p., [15] leaves of plates :
       NYPL [3-MAM 90-5569]

Butler, W. E. Modern British bookplates / W.E.
and D.J. Butler. Cambridge [Eng.] : Silent
Books, 1990. 58 p. : ill. ; 21 cm.
1. Book-plates, English. I. Butler, D. J. II. Title.
    NYPL [MDVK 90-12776]

Butman, John. Car wars : how General Motors
Europe built 'the car of the future' / John
Butman. London : Grafton Books, 1991. 236 p.,
[16] p. of plates : ill. ; 25 cm. Includes index.
Includes bibliographical references (p. [225]-229).
ISBN 0-246-13541-7 : DDC 338.76292202094
1. General Motors Corporation - History. I. Title.
TL240   **NYPL [JBE 91-1425]**

Butor, Michel.
Description de San Marco / par Michel Butor.
[Paris] : Gallimard, [1989], c1963. 111 p., [1]
folded leaf of plates : plan ; 24 cm. ISBN
2-07-021099-5
1. Basilica di San Marco (Venice, Italy). I. Title.
    NYPL [3-MRBN 91-4656]

Prêtre, Jean Claude, 1942- Suzanne, le procès
du modèle /. Paris [1990] 421 p. : ISBN
2-85047-174-7 DDC 755/.4 20
ND1430 .P74 1990

Therrien, Robert, 1947- 7 & 6 /. Albuquerque,
N.M. , c1988. [136] p. : DDC 709/.2 20
N6537.T473 A4 1988

BUTÔT, F. C. - ART COLLECTIONS -
EXHIBITIONS.
Hollandse en vlaamse kunst uit de 17e eeuw .
[Rotterdam, 1973?] 183 p. :
       NYPL [3-MAME 90-5901]

Butterfield, Deborah, 1949-
Horses : the sculpture of Deborah Butterfield /
essay by Donald Kuspit ; interview by Marcia

Tucker. Coral Gables, Fla. : Lowe Art Museum,
University of Miami ; San Francisco : Chronicle
Books, 1992. p. cm. Includes bibliographical
references. ISBN 0-8118-0137-3 (hard) : DDC
730/.92 20
1. Butterfield, Deborah, 1949- - Exhibitions. 2. Horses
in art - Exhibitions. I. Kuspit, Donald B. (Donald
Burton), 1935-. II. Tucker, Marcia. III. Lowe Art
Museum. IV. Title.
NB237.B87 A4 1992

BUTTERFIELD, DEBORAH, 1949- -
EXHIBITIONS.
Butterfield, Deborah, 1949- Horses . Coral
Gables, Fla. , San Francisco , 1992. p. cm.
ISBN 0-8118-0137-3 (hard) : DDC 730/.92 20
NB237.B87 A4 1992

Butterworth Architecture architect's guides.
Salvadori, Renzo. Architect's guide to Paris /.
Sevenoaks, Kent, England , 1990. 137 p. :
    ISBN 0-408-50068-9 DDC 720/.944/361 20
NA1050 .S25 1990

Salvadori, Renzo. Architect's guide to Rome /.
London , Boston , 1990. 144 p. : ISBN
0-408-50054-9 DDC 720/.945/632 20
NA1120 .S27 1990

Butterworth Architecture library of planning and
design.
Blow, Christopher J. Airport terminals .
Oxford , Boston , 1991. p. cm. ISBN
0-7506-1278-9 : DDC 725/.39 20
NA6300 .B56 1991

Buttlar, Florian von. Peter Joseph Lenné .
Berlin , c1989. 315 p. : ISBN 3-87584-277-4
       NYPL [3-MSCC 91-2632]

The button lover's book /. Green, Marilyn V.
Radnor, Pa. , c1991. p. ISBN 0-8019-8184-0
(hc) : DDC 646/.19 20
NK3668.5 .G7 1991

Buttons /. Epstein, Diana. New York , 1991. p.
cm. ISBN 0-8109-3113-3 : DDC 646/.19 20
NK3668.5 .E665 1991

Buttons. Epstein, Diana. The collector's guide to
buttons /. New York , 1990. 84 p. : ISBN
0-8027-7342-7 : DDC 646/.19 20
NK3668.5 .E67 1990
    NYPL [3-MNH 91-6705]

BUTTONS.
Wilzbach, Annette. Knopfdesign /. Frankfurt
am Main , c1990. 131 p. : ISBN 3-87150-315-0
    NYPL [3-MMW+ 91-8095]

BUTTONS - CATALOGS.
Epstein, Diana. Buttons /. New York , 1991. p.
cm. ISBN 0-8109-3113-3 : DDC 646/.19 20
NK3668.5 .E665 1991

BUTTONS - COLLECTORS AND
COLLECTING.
Epstein, Diana. The collector's guide to buttons
/. New York , 1990. 84 p. : ISBN
0-8027-7342-7 : DDC 646/.19 20
NK3668.5 .E67 1990
    NYPL [3-MNH 91-6705]

Green, Marilyn V. The button lover's book /.
Radnor, Pa. , c1991. p. ISBN 0-8019-8184-0
(hc) : DDC 646/.19 20
NK3668.5 .G7 1991

BUTTONS - HISTORY.
Green, Marilyn V. The button lover's book /.
Radnor, Pa. , c1991. p. ISBN 0-8019-8184-0
(hc) : DDC 646/.19 20
NK3668.5 .G7 1991

BUTTONS - PRIVATE COLLECTIONS - NEW
YORK (N.Y.) - CATALOGS.
Epstein, Diana. Buttons /. New York , 1991. p.
cm. ISBN 0-8109-3113-3 : DDC 646/.19 20
NK3668.5 .E665 1991

Butzmann, Frieder. Buchstäblich Nürnberger
wörtliche Tage . [Nürnberg] , c1990. 80 p. :
ISBN 3-922531-77-6
NX458 .B83 1990

Buxbaum, Gerda, 1949- Ausgeblendete Realität .
Wien , 1989. 95 p. :
       NYPL [MFW+ 90-11185]

Buxbaum, Tim. Scottish garden buildings : from
food to folly / Tim Buxbaum. Edinburgh :
Mainstream, 1988. 192 p. : ill., (some col.),
plans ; 25 cm. Includes bibliographical references.
ISBN 1-85158-113-8 : DDC 717 19
1. Gardens - Scotland. 2. Garden structures - Scotland.
I. Title.   **NYPL [3-MSK 90-11993]**

Buyck, Jean. Joostens, Paul, 1889-1960. Paul
Joostens . [Brussel] [1986] 59 p. :
       NYPL [3-MCH J815 90-8180]

Buysse, Chr. Retrospectieve tentoonstelling War
van Overstraeten . Brugge , c1979. 57 p. :
       NYPL [3-MCH 096 87-3370]

Buyssens, Danièlle. Geneva (Switzerland). Musée
d'art et d'histoire. Peintures et pastels de
l'ancienne école genevoise . Genève , 1988. 270
p., [83] p. of plates : ISBN 2-8306-0056-8
ND851.G4 G45 1988

Bužančić, Vlado. Ivica Propadalo : monografija
crteža = a monograph of drawings / Vlado
Bužančić. Zagreb : Globus, 1990. 151 p. : ill.
(some col.) ; 31 cm. (Biblioteka Likovne
monografije) English and Serbo-Croatian (roman).
Includes bibliographical references (p. 149-151). ISBN
86-343-0618-6
1. Propadalo, Ivica, 1950- - Catalogs. I. Propadalo,
Ivica, 1950-. II. Title. III. Series.
NC312.Y83 P762 1990

Buzurgmihr, Nāṣir. Yādmān-i Suhrāb Sipihrī /.
[Tehran] , 1367 [1989] 399 p. :
N7289.S5 Y36 1989

Buzzati, Dino, 1906-1972. Bosch, Hieronymus, d.
1516. L'opera completa di Bosch /. Milano ,
1966. 119 p. :   **NYPL [3-MCH+ B74 91-5658]**

By og bygd i Buskerud. Drammens museum.
[Drammen] [1990] 36 p. :
NK992.B8 D73 1990

By Shaker hands . Sprigg, June. Hanover, N.H. ,
c1990. xi, 212, vii p. : ISBN 0-87451-542-4 (alk.
paper) DDC 289/.8 20
BX9771 .S67 1990
       NYPL [3-MNE+ 91-3949]

By the work of their hands . Vlach, John
Michael, 1948- Charlottesville , c1991. p. cm.
ISBN 0-8139-1366-7 (paper) DDC
745/.089/96073 20
NK839.3.A35 V54 1991a

By with & from . Kirstein, Lincoln, 1907- New
York , 1991. p. cm. ISBN 0-374-18765-7 : DDC
700/.9/04 20
NX456 .K56 1991

By with to and from. Kirstein, Lincoln, 1907- By
with to & from . New York , 1991. p. cm.
ISBN 0-374-18765-7 : DDC 700/.9/04 20
NX456 .K56 1991

Byars, James Lee.
Elliott, James. The perfect thought . Berkeley,
Calif. , 1990. 154 p. :
       NYPL [3-MGO (Byars) 91-6418]

BYARS, JAMES LEE - EXHIBITIONS.
Elliott, James. The perfect thought . Berkeley,
Calif. , 1990. 154 p. :
       NYPL [3-MGO (Byars) 91-6418]

Byrne, Andrew. Bedford Square : an architectural
study / Andrew Byrne. London ; Atlantic
Highlands, NJ : Athlone Press, 1990. 166 p., 8
p. of plates : ill. (some col.) ; 31 cm. Includes
indexes. Includes bibliographical references (p. [159]).
ISBN 0-485-11386-4 DDC 728/.312/0942142 20
1. Architecture - England - London. 2. Architecture,
Georgian - England - London. 3. Bedford Square
(London, England). 4. London (England) - Buildings,
structures, etc. 5. Bedford Square (London, England) -
Buildings, structures, etc. I. Title.
NA970 .B9 1990
       NYPL [3-MQWK+ 90-11731]

Byrne, Janet S. Renaissance ornament prints and
drawings / Janet S. Byrne. New York :
Metropolitan Museum of Art, c1981. 143 p. :
ill. ; 27 cm. "Published in connection with an
exhibition at the Metropolitan Museum of Art, New
York, from December 11, 1981 to February 14,
1982"--Verso t.p. Includes index. ISBN 0-87099-288-0
DDC 760/.094/07401471 19
1. Prints, Renaissance - Exhibitions. 2. Drawing,
Renaissance - Exhibitions. 3. Decoration and ornament,
Renaissance - Exhibitions. I. Metropolitan Museum of
Art (New York, N.Y.) II. Title.
NE441 .B97   **NYPL [MDB 83-1989]**

BYZANTINE ARCHITECTURE. see
ARCHITECTURE, BYZANTINE.

BYZANTINE EMPIRE - CIVILIZATION.
Cantó Rubio, Juan. Arte bizantino .
Salamanca , 1989. 94 p. : ISBN 84-7299-220-9
       NYPL [3-MAK 91-3667]

BYZANTINE EMPIRE - CIVILIZATION - CONGRESSES.
The Twilight of Byzantium . Princeton, N.J. , c1991. p. cm.   ISBN 0-691-04091-5 (alk. paper) :   DDC 700/.9495 20
NX449 .T85 1991

BYZANTINE ICONS. see ICONS, BYZANTINE.

BYZANTINE ILLUMINATIONS OF BOOKS AND MANUSCRIPTS. see ILLUMINATION OF BOOKS AND MANUSCRIPTS, BYZANTINE.

A Byzantine masterpiece recovered . Carr, Annemarie Weyl. Austin , c1991. p. cm.   ISBN 0-292-78117-2 :   DDC 751.7/3/095645 20
ND2819.C92 L974 1991

C. C. I. see Centre de création industrielle.

C. Claudel . Claudel, Camille, 1864-1943. Martigny, Suisse , c1990. 167 p. :   DDC 730/.92 20
NB553.C44 A4 1990b

C. Claudel . Claudel, Camille, 1864-1943. Martigny, Suisse , c1990. 167 p. :
NYPL [3-MGO (Claudel) 91-7335]

C.F. Brandt . Brandt, C. F. (Christian Friedrich), 1823-1891. Kleve , c1991. 122 p. :   ISBN 3-89413-192-6
NYPL [MFX+ (Brandt) 91-7695]

C. I. A. see United States. Central Intelligence Agency.

C. N. A. C. see Centre national d'art contemporain.

C.T.P. Corpus Topographicum Pompeianum. Rome , 1977- (Rome, Italy : Edizioni dell'Elefante) v. ;   ISBN 0-930084-06-3 (set)   DDC 937/.7 19
DG70.P7 C629 1977   NYPL [JFM 82-182 & Map Div. 86-1278]

Ca' Vendramin Calergi /. Gemin, Massimo. Milano , c1990. 147 p. :   ISBN 88-85215-01-7
NYPL [3-MQWB 90-13059]

Ca' Vendramin Calergi (Venice, Italy)
Il Gioco dell'amore . Milano , 1990. 216 p. :   ISBN 88-85215-00-9
IN PROCESS (ONLINE)
NYPL [3-MAMC 91-4481]

CA' VENDRAMIN CALERGI (VENICE, ITALY) - HISTORY.
Gemin, Massimo. Ca' Vendramin Calergi /. Milano , c1990. 147 p. :   ISBN 88-85215-01-7
NYPL [3-MQWB 90-13059]

Caballero, José, 1916- José Caballero : obra gráfica para Bibliofilia, 1971-1987. [Sevilla] : Junta de Andalucía, Consejería de Cultura, [1988?] 1 v. (unpaged) : ill. (some col.) ; 32 cm. "En los libros: 'Oceana' con poemas de Pablo Neruda, 'Al toro' con poemas de José Bergamín, 'Marismaire' con poemas de Abelardo Rodríguez, 'La suerte o la muerte' con poemas de Gerardo Diego." DDC 769.92 20
1. Caballero, José, 1916-. 2. Artists' illustrated books - Spain. I. Title.
NE702.C3 A4 1988

CABALLERO, JOSÉ, 1916-
Caballero, José, 1916- José Caballero . [Sevilla] [1988?] 1 v. (unpaged) :   DDC 769.92 20
NE702.C3 A4 1988

Cabanne, Pierre.
Bazaine, Jean, 1904- Bazaine. Paris , c1990. 178 p. :   ISBN 2-605-00162-8
NYPL [3-MCO B35 90-12858]

Clavé / Pierre Cabanne. Paris : Editions de la Différence, [1990] 381 p. : chiefly ill. (some col.) ; 28 x 30 cm. (Mains et merveilles, 0989-3857) Filmography: p. 367. Includes bibliographical references (p. 368-373).   ISBN 2-7291-0602-2   DDC 709/.2 20
1. Clavé, Antoni, 1913- - Catalogs. I. Clavé, Antoni, 1913-. II. Title. III. Series.
N7113.C57 A4 1990

Jean Fautrier / Pierre Cabanne. Paris : Editions de la Différence, c1988. 167 p. : ill. (some col.) ; 24 cm. (Classiques du XXIe siècle . 1) Include bibliographical references.   DDC 759.4 20
1. Fautrier, Jean, 1898-1964 - Catalogs. 2. Fautrier, Jean, 1898-1964 - Criticism and interpretation. I. Fautrier, Jean, 1898-1964. II. Title. III. Series.
ND553.F36 A4 1988

Seghers, Pierre. Clavé /. Paris , 1989. 423 p. :   ISBN 2-7022-0239-X   DDC 709/.2 B 20
N7113.C57 S4 1989

Cabanne, Pierre, 1921- Rohner / Pierre Cabanne. Paris : Les Éditions de l'Amateur, 1989. 207 p. : ill. (part col.) ; 32 cm. Includes bibliographical references (p. 152-154)   ISBN 2-85917-091-X
1. Rohner, Georges, 1913- - Catalogs. I. Rohner, Georges, 1913-. II. Title.
NYPL [3-MCO+ R73 90-8588]

CABARETS. see MUSIC-HALLS (VARIETY THEATERS, CABARETS, ETC.)

Cabarga, Leslie, 1954- Trademark designs of the twenties / by Leslie Cabarga and Marcie Cabarga. New York : Dover Publications, 1991. p. cm.   ISBN 0-486-26858-6 (pbk.)   DDC 741.6 20
1. Trademarks - United States - Themes, motives. 2. Design - United States - History - 20th century - Themes, motives. I. Cabarga, Marcie. II. Title.
NC998.5.A1 C33 1991

Cabarga, Marcie. Cabarga, Leslie, 1954- Trademark designs of the twenties /. New York , 1991. p. cm.   ISBN 0-486-26858-6 (pbk.)   DDC 741.6 20
NC998.5.A1 C33 1991

Cabildos y ayuntamientos en América / Ramón Gutiérrez ... [et al.]. 1a ed. [Mar del Plata, Argentina?] : IAIHAU ; [Azcapotzalco, Mexico] : Universidad Autónoma Metropolitana-Azcapotzalco ; 134 p. : ill. ; 28 cm. Includes bibliographical references.   ISBN 968-636-305-X
1. Public buildings - Latin America. 2. Church architecture. - Latin America. 3. Architecture, Colonial - Latin America. I. Gutiérrez, Ramón.
NA4202.A1 C33 1990

CABINET-MAKERS - FRANCE - BIOGRAPHY.
Kjellberg, Pierre. Le mobilier français du XVIIIe siècle . Paris , c1989. 887 p. :   ISBN 2-85917-087-1   *NYPL [3-MOF 90-11781]*

CABINET-WORK - FRANCE.
Janneau, Guillaume, 1887- Le meuble d'ebénisterie /. Paris , c1989. 236 p. :   ISBN 2-85917-083-9   *NYPL [3-MOI 91-6666]*

CABINET-WORKERS - FRANCE - BIOGRAPHY - DICTIONARIES.
Kjellberg, Pierre. Art déco . [Paris] [1986] 247 p. :   ISBN 2-85917-054-5 :   DDC 749.24 19
NK2549 .K59 1986
NYPL [3-MOF+ 91-5321]

CABINET-WORKERS - FRANCE - PARIS - BIOGRAPHY.
Ledoux-Lebard, Denise. Le mobilier français du XIXe siècle . Paris , c1989. 700 p., xxxii p. of plates :   *NYPL [3-MOF 90-11782]*

CABINETMAKERS - AUSTRALIA - BIOGRAPHY.
Bogle, Michael. Modern Australian furniture . Roseville, NSW, Australia , 1989. 144 p. :   ISBN 0-947131-26-4   DDC 749.2994/09048 20
NK2689 .B64 1989
NYPL [3-MOF+ 90-8166]

Cable, Carole. The architectural drawing, its development and history, 1300-1950 / Carole Cable. Monticello, Ill. : Vance Bibliographies, 1978. 18 p. ; 28 cm. (Architecture series: Bibliography. A-16) Microfiche (neg.) 1 sheet. 11 x 15 cm. (NYPL FSN 36,154)
1. Architectural drawing - Bibliography. I. Title.
Z5943.A73 C32 NA2700
*NYPL [*XMC-357]*

Cabrera, Geles, 1930-
Imaginación de la materia : Geles Cabrera. [Mexico] : Asociación de Artistas Plásticos de México, Comité Nacional Mexicano de la Association internationale des arts plastiques, AIAP, UNESCO, [1988] 1 v. (unpaged) : chiefly ill. ; 27 cm. Includes bibliographical references.   DDC 730/.92 20
1. Cabrera, Geles, 1930- - Catalogs. I. Asociación de Artistas Plásticos de México. II. Title.
NB249.C33 A4 1988

CABRERA, GELES, 1930- - CATALOGS.
Cabrera, Geles, 1930- Imaginación de la materia . [Mexico] [1988] 1 v. (unpaged) :   DDC 730/.92 20
NB249.C33 A4 1988

Cabu. Le gros blond avec sa chemise noire / [Cabu]. Paris : A. Michel, c1987. 1 v.

(unpaged) : all ill. ; 30 cm.   ISBN 2-226-03167-7
1. Le Pen, Jean-Marie, 1928- - Caricatures and cartoons. 2. Front national (France: 1972-) - Caricatures and cartoons. 3. France - Politics and government - 1981- - Caricatures and cartoons. I. Title.
NYPL [3-MEM+ (Cabu) 89-27328]

Cabutti, Lucido. Nespolo, Ugo, 1941- Nespolo /. Milano , c1991. 192 p. :   ISBN 88-374-1163-4 :   DDC 700/.92 20
NX552.Z9 N482 1991

CÁCERES (SPAIN : PROVINCE) - ANTIQUITIES.
Inventario artístico de Cáceres y su provincia /. Madrid , 1989- v. <1-2 > :   ISBN 84-7483-610-7 (obra completa)   DDC 709/.46/28 20
N7109.C15 I58 1989

Cachin, Françoise. Manet / Françoise Cachin. [Paris] : Chêne, [c1990] 155, [5] p. : ill. (some col.) ; 33 cm. (Profils de l'art) Includes bibliographical references (p. [160]).   ISBN 2-85108-640-5 :   DDC 759.4 B 20
1. Manet, Édouard, 1832-1883. 2. Painters - France - Biography. I. Manet, Édouard, 1832-1883. II. Title. III. Series.
ND553.M3 C3 1990

Cachin-Nora, Françoise. see Cachin, Françoise.

The CAD design studio . Jacobs, Stephen Paul. New York , c1991. vi, 120 p. :   ISBN 0-07-032227-9   DDC 721/.0285 20
NA2728 .J33 1991

CAD-Einsatz in der Architektur /. Kahlen, Hans. Stuttgart , c1989. 200 p. :   ISBN 3-17-010297-4
NA2728 .K38 1989

CADASTRAL SURVEYS. see REAL PROPERTY.

Cadieux, Geneviève. Emotope . [Berlin] , c1988. 43 p. :   ISBN 3-923479-27-1
NYPL [3-MAL+ 90-10665]

Cadior ak Amary N'Goné Sobel /. Samb, Kany. Dakar [1968?] 78 leaves ;
NLCM 91/09260 (D)

Cadouin, Cadouin, une aventure cistercienne en Périgord /. Le Bugue [France] , 1990. 167 p. :   ISBN 2-86952-017-4   DDC 726/.7/094472 20
NA5551.C28 C3 1990

CADOUIN (ABBEY)
Cadouin, une aventure cistercienne en Périgord /. Le Bugue [France] , 1990. 167 p. :   ISBN 2-86952-017-4   DDC 726/.7/094472 20
NA5551.C28 C3 1990

CADOUIN (FRANCE) - BUILDINGS, STRUCTURES, ETC.
Cadouin, une aventure cistercienne en Périgord /. Le Bugue [France] , 1990. 167 p. :   ISBN 2-86952-017-4   DDC 726/.7/094472 20
NA5551.C28 C3 1990

Cadouin, une aventure cistercienne en Périgord / Brigitte Delluc ... [et al.], avec la collaboration du père Albert C. de Veer, de Guy Ponceau et de Marcel Berthier ; préfaces du président Pierre Merlhiot et de Jean Briquet. Nouv. éd. rev. et augm. Le Bugue [France] : PLB, 1990. 167 p. : ill. (some col.) ; 23 cm. (Collection Fleur de lys, 0989-6406) Updated ed. of: Cadouin, une aventure cistercienne en Périgord / Gilles Delluc, Jean Secret. 1965. Includes bibliographical references (p. 159-164).   ISBN 2-86952-017-4   DDC 726/.7/094472 20
1. Cadouin (Abbey). 2. Architecture, Cistercian - France - Cadouin. 3. Cadouin (France) - Buildings, structures, etc. I. Delluc, Brigitte. II. Delluc, Gilles. Cadouin, une aventure cistercienne en Périgord. III. Title: Cadouin. IV. Series: Collection Fleur de lys (Le Bugue, France).
NA5551.C28 C3 1990

CAFÉ THEATER. see MUSIC-HALLS (VARIETY THEATERS, CABARETS, ETC.)

Cafes /. Dru, Line, 1957- [Cafés. English.] New York, NY , c1989. 118 p. :   ISBN 0-910413-66-5
NYPL [3-MLO 90-10718]

Cafferty, James H., 1819-1869.
James Henry Cafferty, N.A. (1819-1869) / by David Stewart Hull ; with preface by James B. Bell. New York : New-York Historical Society, c1986. 55 p. : ill., ports. ; 28 cm. Catalogue of an exhibition held at the New-York Historical Society, New York City, May 22-Aug. 24, 1986. "Catalogue

raisonné": p. 45-54. Additional exhibition records of paintings with dates, 2 leaves, inserted. Bibliography: p. 55.
1. Cafferty, James H., 1819-1869 - Exhibitions. I. Hull, David Stewart. II. New York Historical Society. III. Title.   *NYPL [3-MCX C129 91-6656]*

CAFFERTY, JAMES H., 1819-1869 - EXHIBITIONS.
Cafferty, James H., 1819-1869. James Henry Cafferty, N.A. (1819-1869) /. New York , c1986. 55 p. :   *NYPL [3-MCX C129 91-6656]*

Cage, John.
The New River watercolors / John Cage. Richmond : Va. Museum of Fine Arts, 1988. v, 22 p. : ill. (some col.), ports. ; 19 x 22 cm. Catalogue of an exhibition held at the Virginia Museum of Fine Arts, the Flossie Martin Art Gallery, Roanoke Museum of Fine Arts, and the Phillips Collection. Bibliography: p. 20-21. ISBN 0-917046-30-7 DDC 759.13 19
1. Cage, John - Exhibitions. I. Virginia Museum of Fine Arts. II. Title.
ND1839.C28 A4 1988
    NYPL [3-MCX C131 90-12510]

CAGE, JOHN - EXHIBITIONS.
Cage, John. The New River watercolors /. Richmond , 1988. v, 22 p. : ISBN 0-917046-30-7 DDC 759.13 19
ND1839.C28 A4 1988
    NYPL [3-MCX C131 90-12510]

Cagli . Cagli, Corrado, 1910- Firenze , 1974. [8] leaves, [47] leaves of plates :
NC257.C23 B44
    NYPL [3-MCF C125 91-472]

Cagli, Corrado, 1910-
Cagli : cinquanta disegni / [a cura di] Fortunato Bellonzi. Firenze : La Gradiva, 1974. [8] leaves, [47] leaves of plates : ill. ; 30 cm. Published on the occasion of the exhibition held in Florence in 1974.
1. Cagli, Corrado, 1910-. I. Bellonzi, Fortunato, ed. II. Title.
NC257.C23 B44
    NYPL [3-MCF C125 91-472]

La Fondazione Cagli per Firenze : mostra, Palazzo Strozzi, Firenze, 28 aprile-30 giugno 1979 / Comune di Firenze, Provincia di Firenze, Azienda autonoma di turismo ; [catalogo, Raffaele Monti]. [Florence] : Vallecchi, 1979. 77 p., [183] p. of plates : ill. (some col.) ; 24 cm. Bibliography: p. 33.
1. Cagli, Corrado, 1910- - Exhibitions. 2. Fondazione Cagli - Exhibitions. I. Monti, Raffaele. II. Fondazione Cagli. III. Palazzo Strozzi. IV. Fondazione Cagli. V. Title.   *NYPL [3-MCF C125 90-5873]*

CAGLI, CORRADO, 1910-
Cagli, Corrado, 1910- Cagli . Firenze , 1974. [8] leaves, [47] leaves of plates :
NC257.C23 B44
    NYPL [3-MCF C125 91-472]

CAGLI, CORRADO, 1910- - EXHIBITIONS.
Cagli, Corrado, 1910- La Fondazione Cagli per Firenze . [Florence] , c1979. 77 p., [183] p. of plates :   *NYPL [3-MCF C125 90-5873]*

Cagliaritano, Ubaldo. Voci di Sardegna /. Siena , 1964- v. <1> ;
N6919.S37 V6 1964

Cahiers de l'inventaire .
(cahier no 18) Orfèvrerie nantaise . Paris , 1989. xlviii, 395 p. : ISBN 2-11-081040-8 DDC 739.2/0944/14 20
NK7210 .O74 1989
    NYPL [3-MNP 91-3349]

Cahiers du Léopard d'or .
(1) Le Vêtement . Paris , c1989. 332 p. : ISBN 2-86377-089-6 :
GT575 .V48 1989   *NYPL [3-MMG 91-6577]*

Cahiers Henri Matisse .
(3) Matisse, Henri, 1869-1954. Henri Matisse, l'art du livre. Nice , 1989. 143 p. : ISBN 2-901412-05-X
    NYPL [MDG (Matisse) 91-6192]

(6) Musée Matisse. Henri Matisse . Nice , 1988. 366 p. : ISBN 2-86941-071-9
    NYPL [3-MCO+ M43 91-5314]

Cahill, Holger, 1887-1960. (comp) Art in America in modern times. Edited by Holger Cahill and Alfred H. Barr, Jr. Freeport, N.Y., Books for Libraries Press [1969, c1934] 110 p. illus. (part. col.); 32 cm. (Essay index reprint series) The material in this book formed the basis of a national radio

broadcast over NBC from Oct. 6, 1934 through Jan. 26, 1935. The present volume, and the broadcasts, were prepared with the cooperation of the Museum of Moder Art. Includes bibliographies. DDC 700/.973
1. Art - United States. I. Barr, Alfred Hamilton, 1902- joint comp. II. Museum of Modern Art (New York, N.Y.). III. Title.
N6505 .C3 1969

Cahill, James, 1926- New dimensions in Chinese ink painting : works from the collection of John and Alice Z. Berninghausen / essay by James Cahill ; introduction by Jen-mei Ma. Middlebury, Vt. : Christian A. Johnson Memorial Gallery, Middlebury College, c1991. p. cm. "Published on the occasion of an exhibition at the Christian A. Johnson Memorial Gallery, Middlebury College, Middlebury, Vermont, 28 July = 13 October 1991"--T.p. verso. Includes bibliographical references. ISBN 0-9625262-3-1 DDC 759.951/074/7435 20
1. Ink painting, Chinese - 20th century - Exhibitions. 2. Berninghausen, John David - Art collections - Exhibitions. 3. Berninghausen, Alice Z. - Art collections - Exhibitions. 4. Ink painting - Private collections - United States - Exhibitions. I. Christian A. Johnson Memorial Gallery. II. Title.
ND2068 .C33 1991

Cahill, Joanne. Masterpieces of Australian photography . Paddington, Sydney, Australia , c1989. 200 p. :   *NYPL [MFW+ 91-3430]*

Cahn, Laurent. Vierges et saints : les statuettes en faïence de Quimper / Laurent Cahn. [Quimper] : L. Cahn, [1990] 159 p. : ill. (some col.) ; 29 cm. Includes bibliographical references (p. 158).
1. Faïenceries de Quimper - Catalogs. 2. Mary, Blessed Virgin, Saint - Art - Catalogs. 3. Christian saints in art - Catalogs. I. Title.
NK4210.F345 C35 1990

Caiger-Smith, Martin. Mahr, Mari. Isolated incidents /. London , c1989. [8] p., [27] p. of plates : ISBN 0-907879-21-7
    NYPL [MFX+ (Mahr) 89-21465]

Caillebotte and the garden at Yerres /. Wittmer, Pierre. [Caillebotte au jardin. English.] New York , 1991. p. cm. ISBN 0-8109-3167-2 (cloth) DDC 759.4 20
ND553.C243 W5813 1991

Caillebotte au jardin . Wittmer, Pierre. Saint-Rémy-en-l'Eau , c1990. 344 p. : ISBN 2-903824-15-0 DDC 759.4 20
ND553.C243 W58 1990

Caillebotte, Gustave, 1848-1894.
Les dessins de Caillebotte / [présentés par] Jean Chardeau. Paris : Hermé, c1989. 127 p. : chiefly ill. (some col.) ; 30 cm. ISBN 2-86665-084-0 DDC 759.4 20
1. Caillebotte, Gustave, 1848-1894 - Catalogs. I. Chardeau, Jean. II. Title.
NC248.C27 A4 1989
    NYPL [3-MCO+ C134 91-3741]

Wildenstein & Co. (London, England) Gustave Caillebotte, 1848-1894 . [London, 1966] 35 p. :
    NYPL [3-MCO C134 91-1182]

Wittmer, Pierre. Caillebotte au jardin . Saint-Rémy-en-l'Eau , c1990. 344 p. : ISBN 2-903824-15-0 DDC 759.4 20
ND553.C243 W58 1990

Wittmer, Pierre. [Caillebotte au jardin. English.] Caillebotte and the garden at Yerres /. New York , 1991. p. cm. ISBN 0-8109-3167-2 (cloth) DDC 759.4 20
ND553.C243 W5813 1991

CAILLEBOTTE, GUSTAVE, 1848-1894 - HOMES AND HAUNTS - FRANCE - YERRES.
Wittmer, Pierre. Caillebotte au jardin . Saint-Rémy-en-l'Eau , c1990. 344 p. : ISBN 2-903824-15-0 DDC 759.4 20
ND553.C243 W58 1990

Wittmer, Pierre. [Caillebotte au jardin. English.] Caillebotte and the garden at Yerres /. New York , 1991. p. cm. ISBN 0-8109-3167-2 (cloth) DDC 759.4 20
ND553.C243 W5813 1991

CAILLEBOTTE, GUSTAVE, 1848-1894 - CATALOGS.
Caillebotte, Gustave, 1848-1894. Les dessins de Caillebotte /. Paris , c1989. 127 p. : ISBN

2-86665-084-0 DDC 759.4 20
NC248.C27 A4 1989
    NYPL [3-MCO+ C134 91-3741]

CAILLEBOTTE, GUSTAVE, 1848-1894 - EXHIBITIONS.
Wildenstein & Co. (London, England) Gustave Caillebotte, 1848-1894 . [London, 1966] 35 p. :
    NYPL [3-MCO C134 91-1182]

Cailles, Françoise. Le prix des bijoux, 1986, 1987, 1988 / Françoise Cailles ; avec la collaboration de Jean-Norbert Salit. Courbevoie, Paris : ACR, c1989. 373 p. : ill. ; 30 cm. ISBN 2-86770-035-3
1. Jewelry - Prices. I. Title.
    NYPL [3-MNR+ 91-8]

Caillet, Gérard, 1920- Foucart, Bruno. Landowski /. Paris , c1989. 111 p. : ISBN 2-85299-009-1 DDC 730/.92 20
NB553.L25 F6 1989
    NYPL [3-MGO+ (Landowski) 91-3328]

Cairo A to Z. Amin, Naguib. Cairo A-Z . Zamalek, Cairo, Egypt , 1988. x, 151, 24, 14 p. :
IN PROCESS (ONLINE)
    NYPL [Map Div. 90-11167]

Cairo A-Z . Amin, Naguib. Zamalek, Cairo, Egypt , 1988. x, 151, 24, 14 p. :
IN PROCESS (ONLINE)
    NYPL [Map Div. 90-11167]

CAIRO (EGYPT) - DESCRIPTION - GUIDE-BOOKS.
Amin, Naguib. Cairo A-Z . Zamalek, Cairo, Egypt , 1988. x, 151, 24, 14 p. :
IN PROCESS (ONLINE)
    NYPL [Map Div. 90-11167]

CAIRO (EGYPT) - MAPS.
Amin, Naguib. Cairo A-Z . Zamalek, Cairo, Egypt , 1988. x, 151, 24, 14 p. :
IN PROCESS (ONLINE)
    NYPL [Map Div. 90-11167]

Cairo street finder. Amin, Naguib. Cairo A-Z . Zamalek, Cairo, Egypt , 1988. x, 151, 24, 14 p. :
IN PROCESS (ONLINE)
    NYPL [Map Div. 90-11167]

Caisse nationale des monuments historiques et des sites (France)
Le Château en France /. Paris , 1988. 448 p., [16] p. of plates : ISBN 2-7013-0741-4
    NYPL [3-MQWF+ 90-11996]

Feray, Jean. Architecture intérieure et décoration en France, des origines à 1875 /. Paris , c1988. 399 p. : ISBN 2-7013-0752-X DDC 729/.0944 20
NA2850 .F4 1988
    NYPL [3-MLF+ 90-12087]

Caja de Ahorros y Monte de Piedad de Madrid. Escuela de Madrid . [Madrid] [1990?] 293 p. : ISBN 84-505-9356-5 DDC 759.6/41/090450744641 20
ND808.5.M28 E83 1990

Cajani, Franco, 1943- Harry Rosenthal, scultore / Franco Cajani, Emile Noël Laurent. [Italy] : Besana Brianza, c1988. 223 p. : chiefly ill. (some col.) ; 25 cm. "1988, Cernobbio (Co), Villa Erba, mostra personale"--P. 216. DDC 730/.92 20
1. Rosenthal, Harry, 1922- - Exhibitions. I. Rosenthal, Harry, 1922-. II. Laurent, Emile Noël. III. Title.
NB979.R67 A4 1988

Cajigas, María de los Angeles. El mundo desconocido de José Luis Cuevas / María de los Angeles Cajigas. México EDAMEX, c1990. 154 p. : ill. ; 21 cm.
1. Cuevas, José Luis, 1934- - Criticism and interpretation. I. Title.
    NYPL [3-MCZ C955 91-4665]

Cajigas R., María de los Angeles. El mundo desconocido de José Luis Cuevas / María de los Angeles Cajigas R. México : EDAMEX, c1990. 154 p. : ill. ; 22 cm. ISBN 968-409-526-0 DDC 760/.092 B 20
1. Cuevas, José Luis, 1934-. 2. Cuevas, José Luis, 1934- - Relations with women. 3. Artists - Mexico - Biography. I. Title.
N6559.C8 C34 1990

Calabrese, Mattia. see Preti, Mattia.

Calabrese, Omar. Plessi, Fabrizio, 1940- Plessi /. Treviso , c1990. 175 p. : ISBN 88-85066-70-4

DDC 700/.92 20
N6923.P55 A4 1990
    NYPL [3-MGO+ (Plessi) 91-5437]

Calatrava, Santiago, 1951-
Santiago Calatrava . Basel , Boston , 1991. p.
cm. ISBN 0-8176-2460-0 DDC 720/.92 20
NA1313.C35 S26 1991

**CALATRAVA, SANTIAGO, 1951- -
   CRITICISM AND INTERPRETATION.**
Santiago Calatrava . Basel , Boston , 1991. p.
cm. ISBN 0-8176-2460-0 DDC 720/.92 20
NA1313.C35 S26 1991

**CALATRAVA, SANTIAGO, 1951- -
   EXHIBITIONS.**
Santiago Calatrava . València , 1986. 103 p. :
   ISBN 84-7579-104-2
     NYPL [3-MQZ (Calatrava) 91-6420]

Calcani, Giuliana. Cavalieri di bronzo : la torma
di Alessandro opera di Lisippo / Giuliana
Calcani. Roma : "L'Erma" di Bretschneider,
c1989. 182 p. : ill. ; 25 cm. (Studia archaeologica.
53) Includes bibliographical references (p. 163-175) and
index. ISBN 88-7062-671-7
*1. Alexander the Great, 356-323 B. C. - Art. 2.
Lysippus - Criticism and interpretation. 3. Equestrian
statues. 4. Horsemen and horsewomen in art. 5.
Bronzes, Greek. I. Series. II. Series: Studia
archaeologica ("Erma" di Bretschneider) , 53. III. Title.*
    NYPL [3-MGO (Lysippus) 91-5330]

Calcografía Nacional (Spain)
Estampas, 1984-1985 . Madrid , 1988. 331 p. :
   ISBN 84-600-5307-5
     NYPL [MDBF 91-5842]

Ribera, José de, 1588?-1652. Jusepe de Ribera,
grabador, 1591-1652 . [Valencia] , c1989. 113
p. : ISBN 84-7664-196-6 DDC 769.92 20
NE2062.5.R52 A4 1989
     NYPL [MDG (Ribera) 91-3604]

Calcografia nazionale (Italy) La Linea astratta
dell'incisione italiana . Milano , c1989. 209 p. :
   ISBN 88-435-3024-0 :
IN PROCESS (ONLINE)
     NYPL [MDBF 90-13122]

Caldas Júnior, Waltercio, 1946- Brett, Guy.
Transcontinental . London ; New York : 112
p. : ISBN 0-86091-511-5
     NYPL [3-MAM 91-7008]

Calder, Alexander, 1898-1976.
Alexander Calder, Fernand Léger . New York ,
1979. 24 p. :   *NYPL [3-MC 90-7054]*

Alexander Calder, mobiles, Fernand Léger,
peintures. Paris : L. Carré, c1988. 69 p. : ill.
(some col.) ; 30 cm. "Cet ouvrage est publié à
l'occasion de l'exposition Calder/Léger présentée à la
Galerie Louis Carré & Cie du 13 octobre au 26
novembre 1988"--P. facing t.p. Essay by André
Parinaud in French and English Includes bibliographical
references (p. 67-68). ISBN 2-86574-012-9
*1. Calder, Alexander, 1898-1976 - Exhibitions. 2. Léger,
Fernand, 1881-1955 - Exhibitions. I. Léger, Fernand,
1881-1955. II. Galerie Louis Carré. III. Title. IV. Title:
Alexander Calder, mobiles.*
MLCM 90/03707 (N)
     NYPL [3-MGO+ (Calder) 91-3331]

[Calder. English]
  Calder : 1898-1976 retrospective, December
  1987-January 1988, Linssen Gallery /
  [redaktion und Gestaltung, Werner Linssen].
  Köln : The Gallery, c1987. 120 p. : ill. (some
  col.) ; 32 cm. Translation of: Calder. Catalog of an
  exhibition. Summary in German. ISBN
  3-926835-03-6 DDC 709/.2 20
*1. Calder, Alexander, 1898-1976 - Exhibitions. I.
Linssen, Werner. II. Galerie Linssen.*
N6537.C33 A4 1987

Marter, Joan M. Alexander Calder /.
Cambridge , New York , 1991. p. cm. ISBN
0-521-33038-6 DDC 730/.92 20
NB237.C28 M34 1991

**CALDER, ALEXANDER, 1898-1976 -
   CRITICISM AND INTERPRETATION.**
Marter, Joan M. Alexander Calder /.
Cambridge , New York , 1991. p. cm. ISBN
0-521-33038-6 DDC 730/.92 20
NB237.C28 M34 1991

**CALDER, ALEXANDER, 1898-1976 -
   EXHIBITIONS.**
Alexander Calder, Fernand Léger . New York ,
1979. 24 p. : *NYPL [3-MC 90-7054]*

Calder, Alexander, 1898-1976. Alexander

Calder, mobiles, Fernand Léger, peintures.
Paris , c1988. 69 p. : ISBN 2-86574-012-9
MLCM 90/03707 (N)
     NYPL [3-MGO+ (Calder) 91-3331]

Calder, Alexander, 1898-1976. [Calder.
English.] Calder . Köln , c1987. 120 p. : ISBN
3-926835-03-6 DDC 709/.2 20
N6537.C33 A4 1987

Calderón Schrader, Camilo. 50 años, Salón
Nacional de Artistas /. [Bogotá, Colombia] ,
c1990. 363 p. : ISBN 958-95220-0-9
IN PROCESS (ONLINE)
     NYPL [3-MAM 90-13365]

Calderwood, Michael. Mexico, a higher vision :
an aerial journey from past to present / Carlos
Fuentes, introduction ; Michael Calderwood,
aerial photography ; Michael Calderwood,
Gabriel Breña, text. La Jolla, Calif. : Alti
Publishing, c1990. 192 p. : chiefly col. ill. ; 32
cm. ISBN 0-9625399-5-3
*1. Mexico - Aerial photographs. 2. Mexico -
Description and travel - 1981- - Views. I. Fuentes,
Carlos. II. Breña, Gabriel. III. Title.*
     NYPL [MFX+ (Calderwood) 91-3343]

CALICO-PRINTING - FRANCE.
Brédif, Josette. [Toiles de Jouy. English.]
Printed French fabrics =. New York , 1989.
184 p. : ISBN 0-8478-1135-2 DDC
746.6/2/0944366 20
TP930 .B6413 1989
     NYPL [3-MON+ 91-3401]

**California. Board of Education. see California.
   State Board of Education.**

California cityscapes /. Stofflet, Mary. New York,
NY , c1991. p. cm. ISBN 0-87663-614-8 DDC
704.9/44794/0979409048 20
N8214.5.U6 S76 1991

**California. Curriculum Development and
   Supplemental Materials Commission.**
Visual and performing arts framework .
Sacramento , 1982. x, 166 p. : DDC
700/.71/2794 20
NX310.C2 V5 1982

Visual and performing arts framework .
Sacramento , 1989. xiv, 167 p. : ISBN
0-8011-0805-5 : DDC 700/.71/2794 20
NX310.C2 V5 1989

**CALIFORNIA - DESCRIPTION AND
   TRAVEL - TO 1848.**
Smith, Jedediah Strong, 1799-1831. The
Southwest expedition of Jedediah S. Smith .
Glendale, Calif. , 1977. 259 p. : ISBN
0-87062-123-8
F800 .S55 1977   *NYPL [IW 80-2691]*

**CALIFORNIA - DESCRIPTION AND
   TRAVEL - 1981- - GUIDE-BOOKS.**
Gousha California road atlas and visitor's guide.
San Jose, Calif. , c1991. 56 p. : ISBN
0-13-110891-3 :
     NYPL [Map Div. 90-13143]

**CALIFORNIA - DESCRIPTION AND
   TRAVEL - VIEWS - EXHIBITIONS.**
J.J. Reilly . Yuba City, Calif. , 1989. 48 p. :
     NYPL [MFX (Reilly) 91-3601]

**California. Education, State Board of. see
   California. State Board of Education.**

CALIFORNIA IN ART.
American scene painting . Irvine, Calif. , 1991.
p. ISBN 0-9610520-3-1 : DDC 758/.99794052 20
ND230.C3 A44 1991

Coran, James L. If pictures could talk .
Oakland, Calif. , c1989. 382 p. : ISBN
0-938842-07-2
     NYPL [3-MCW+ 90-12851]

Stofflet, Mary. California cityscapes /. New
York, NY , c1991. p. cm. ISBN 0-87663-614-8
DDC 704.9/44794/0979409048 20
N8214.5.U6 S76 1991

CALIFORNIA IN ART - EXHIBITIONS.
Oakland Museum. A time and place . Oakland,
Calif. , c1990. iv, 175 p. :
     NYPL [3-MCW+ 91-7175]

California masters series .
(no. 10) Emboden, William A. Jean Cocteau
and the illustrated book /. [Northridge, Calif.] ,
1990. 29 p. :
     NYPL [MDG+ (Cocteau) 90-11895]

California Museum of Photography.
De Lory, Peter. The wild and the innocent /.
Riverside, Calif. , 1987. [46] p. : ISBN
0-9619038-2-1
     NYPL [MFX (De Lory) 90-11264]

Lavenson, Alma, 1897- Alma Lavenson.
[Riverside, Calif.] , c1979. 56 p. : DDC
779/.092/4
TR647 .L38 1979
     NYPL [MFX (Lavenson) 91-2392]

California Palace of the Legion of Honor. M. H.
De Young Memorial Museum. Man: glory, jest,
and riddle. San Francisco, 1964. 1 v. (unpaged)
     NYPL [3-MAMZ 90-7043]

California road atlas and visitor's guide. Gousha
California road atlas and visitor's guide. San
Jose, Calif. , c1991. 56 p. : ISBN 0-13-110891-3 :
     NYPL [Map Div. 90-13143]

CALIFORNIA - ROAD MAPS.
Gousha California road atlas and visitor's guide.
San Jose, Calif. , c1991. 56 p. : ISBN
0-13-110891-3 :
     NYPL [Map Div. 90-13143]

California. State Board of Education.
Visual and performing arts framework .
Sacramento , 1982. x, 166 p. : DDC
700/.71/2794 20
NX310.C2 V5 1982

Visual and performing arts framework .
Sacramento , 1989. xiv, 167 p. : ISBN
0-8011-0805-5 : DDC 700/.71/2794 20
NX310.C2 V5 1989

**CALIFORNIA STATE PRISON AT
   VACAVILLE.**
Camhi, Morrie, 1928- The prison experience /.
Rutland, Vt. , Tokyo, Japan , 1989. 140 p. :
   ISBN 0-8048-1632-8   *NYPL [Sc F 90-73]*

**California State University, Long Beach.
   University Art Museum.**
Barnes, Lucinda. Imágenes líricas =. Long
Beach , c1990. 119 p. : ISBN 0-936270-30-6
     NYPL [3-MAML+ 91-5035]

Levinthal, David. Centric 35 /. Long Beach ,
c1989. [20] p. :
     NYPL [MFX (Levinthal) 90-11261]

California studies in the history of art. Discovery
series .
(1) Mellinkoff, Ruth. The devil at Isenheim .
Berkeley , c1988. xv, 109 p. : ISBN
0-520-06204-3 (alk. paper) DDC 759.3 19
ND588.G7 A645 1988
     NYPL [3-MCK+ G88 90-10399]

(2) Horn, Walter William, 1908- The forgotten
hermitage of Skellig Michael /. Berkeley ,
c1990. xi, 111 p. : ISBN 0-520-06410-0 (alk.
paper) DDC 941.9/6 19
BX2602.S54 H67 1989
     NYPL [3-MRBB+ 91-3376]

**California. University. University at Los Angeles.
   Frederick S. Wight Art Gallery. see
   Frederick S. Wight Art Gallery.**

**California. University. University at Los Angeles.
   Grunwald Center for the Graphic Arts. see
   Grunwald Center for the Graphic Arts.**

**California. Visual and Performing Arts
   Curriculum Framework and Criteria
   Committee.**
Visual and performing arts framework .
Sacramento , 1982. x, 166 p. : DDC
700/.71/2794 20
NX310.C2 V5 1982

Visual and performing arts framework .
Sacramento , 1989. xiv, 167 p. : ISBN
0-8011-0805-5 : DDC 700/.71/2794 20
NX310.C2 V5 1989

Callahan, John. Digesting the child within / by
John Callahan. New York, N.Y. : W. Morrow,
1991. p. cm. ISBN 0-688-09488-0 DDC
741.5/973 20
*1. Life - Caricatures and cartoons. 2. American wit and
humor, Pictorial. I. Title.*
NC1429.C23 A4 1991

**Callaway County, Missouri, land atlas & plat
   book .** Rockford Map Publishers. Rockford,
Ill. , Fulton, Mo. , c1990. 1 atlas (55 p.) :
     NYPL [Map Div. 90-12836]

CALLAWAY COUNTY, MO. - MAPS.
Rockford Map Publishers. Callaway County,

Missouri, land atlas & plat book . Rockford, Ill. , Fulton, Mo. , c1990. 1 atlas (55 p.) :
NYPL [Map Div. 90-12836]

Calle, Sophie.
[Suite venitienne]
Suite venitienne / Sophie Calle. Please follow me / Jean Baudrillard. [Paris] : Editions de l'Etoile, 1983. 93 p. : ill. ; 21 cm. (Ecrit sur l'image) ISBN 2-86642-005-5
1. Calle, Sophie. I. Baudrillard, Jean. Please follow me. 1983. II. Title. *NYPL [MFX (Calle) 90-11190]*

CALLE, SOPHIE.
Calle, Sophie. [Suite venitienne.] Suite venitienne /. [Paris] , 1983. 93 p. : ISBN 2-86642-005-5
NYPL [MFX (Calle) 90-11190]

Callegari, Paola. Dipinti dei musei e gallerie di Roma. Roma , 1978- v. ;
N4035.G33 D56 1981
NYPL [MAVZ+ (Rome) 91-6377]

Callicott, Burton, 1907-
Burton Callicott : a retrospective / organized by Patricia P. Bladon ; with an essay by Ray Kass. Memphis, Tenn. : Memphis Brooks Museum of Art, c1991. 56 p. : ill. (some col.) ; 31 cm. Catalog of an exhibition held at the Memphis Brooks Museum of Art, Feb. 24-Mar. 31, 1991, and at the Tennessee State Museum, Nashville, May 16-June 30, 1991. DDC 759.13 20
1. Callicott, Burton, 1907- - Exhibitions. I. Bladon, Patricia P., 1946-. II. Kass, Ray. III. Memphis Brooks Museum of Art. IV. Tennessee State Museum. V. Title.
ND237.C195 A4 1991

CALLICOTT, BURTON, 1907- - EXHIBITIONS.
Callicott, Burton, 1907- Burton Callicott . Memphis, Tenn. , c1991. 56 p. : DDC 759.13 20
ND237.C195 A4 1991

CALLIGRAPHERS - IRAQ - BAGHDAD - BIOGRAPHY.
A'zamī, Walīd. Jamharat al-khaṭṭāṭīn al-Baghdādīyīn . A'ẓamīyah, Baghdād, al-'Irāq , 1989. 2 v. (800 p.) :
NK3630.6.I72 A93 1989

CALLIGRAPHERS - TURKEY - BIOGRAPHY.
Aziz Efendi, 1871 or 2-1934. Hattat Aziz Efendi /. İstanbul , 1988. 119 p. :
NK3636.5.A95 A2 1988

CALLIGRAPHY, ARABIC - CATALOGS.
Zahāwī, Khalīl. Tashkīlāt al-khaṭṭ al-'Arabī /. [Beirut] , 1986. 150 leaves :
NK3633.Z24 A4 1986

CALLIGRAPHY, CHINESE - CONGRESSES.
Words and images . New York , 1991. p. cm.
ISBN 0-87099-604-5 DDC 745.6/19951 20
NK3634.A2 W67 1991

CALLIGRAPHY, CHINESE - POLITICAL ASPECTS.
Kraus, Richard Curt. Brushes with power . Berkeley , c1991. xii, 208 p. : ISBN 0-520-07285-5 (cloth : alk. paper) DDC 745.6/19951 20
NK3634.A2 K73 1991

CALLIGRAPHY, ISLAMIC - CATALOGS.
Zahāwī, Khalīl. Tashkīlāt al-khaṭṭ al-'Arabī /. [Beirut] , 1986. 150 leaves :
NK3633.Z24 A4 1986

CALLIGRAPHY, ISLAMIC - TURKEY.
Aziz Efendi, 1871 or 2-1934. Hattat Aziz Efendi /. İstanbul , 1988. 119 p. :
NK3636.5.A95 A2 1988

CALLIGRAPHY, JAPANESE - HISTORY - 20TH CENTURY - EXHIBITIONS.
Immagini scritte . [Tokyo] , c1984. 171 p. :
DDC 745.6/19956/074 20
NK3637.A2 I46 1984

Worte in Bewegung . [Tokyo] , c1984. 187 p. :
DDC 745.6/19956/074 20
NK3637.A2 W67 1984

CALLIGRAPHY, ZEN - EXHIBITIONS.
Zenga . New Orleans, LA , 1990. 197 p. :
ISBN 0-89494-032-5
NYPL [3-MAG+ 91-2672]

Callingham, Glyn. Blue note . San Francisco , 1991. p. cm. ISBN 0-8118-0036-9 DDC 741.6/6 20
NC1883.U6 B58 1991

Callot, Jacques, 1592-1635.
Fatal consequences . Hanover, N.H. , 1990. 92

p. : ISBN 0-944722-04-0 DDC 769.92 20
NE2149.W37 F38 1990
NYPL [MDG+ (Callot) 91-4763]

MISERIES OF WAR - EXHIBITIONS.
Fatal consequences . Hanover, N.H. , 1990. 92 p. : ISBN 0-944722-04-0 DDC 769.92 20
NE2149.W37 F38 1990
NYPL [MDG+ (Callot) 91-4763]

Callow, Philip. Vincent Van Gogh : a life / Philip Callow. London : Allison & Busby, 1990. xviii, 295 p., [8] leaves of plates : ill. ; 24 cm. Includes index. Bibliography: p. 287-288. ISBN 0-85031-866-1
1. Painters - Netherlands - Biography. I. Title.
NYPL [MCH G61 90-11595]

Calloway, Stephen.
The Elements of style . New York , c1991. p. cm. ISBN 0-671-73981-6 DDC 721 20
NA2850 .E44 1991

Royal style : five centuries of influence and fashion / Stephen Calloway and Stephen Jones. Boston : Little, Brown, 1991. p. cm. Includes bibliographical references and index. ISBN 0-316-12509-1 : DDC 745/.094 20
1. Decorative arts - Europe - History. 2. Interior decoration - Europe - History. 3. Europe - Kings and rulers - Art patronage. I. Jones, Stephen, 1954-. II. Title.
NK925 .C35 1991

CALO, CAROLE GOLD.
Impressionism and post impressionism . Portland, Me. , c1991. p. cm. DDC 709/.03/4407474191 20
N6847.5.I4 I43 1991

Cals, Joseph, 1949- New art van Amsterdam /. Hempstead, N.Y. , c1990. 16 p. :
NYPL [3-MAME 91-7061]

CALVARIES. see CROSSES.

Calvesi, Maurizio. L'Ultimo Caravaggio . Siracusa , c1987. 376 p. :
NYPL [3-MCF C26 90-9486]

Calvo Serraller, F. (Francisco), 1948-
Conceptos fundamentales en la historia del arte español /. Madrid , c1989-<199. <v. 1; v. 5-6, pt. 1; in 3 > : ISBN 84-306-7001-7 DDC 709/.46 20
N7101 .C65 1989

Eduardo Arroyo / texto, F. Calvo Serraller. Madrid : Ediarte, 1991. 283 p. : ill. ; 33 cm. ISBN 84-87798-00-4
1. Arroyo, Eduardo, 1937-. I. Title.
NYPL [3-MCQ+ A778 91-5775]

Pintores españoles entre dos fines de siglo (1880-1990) / Francisco Calvo Serraller ; de Eduardo Rosales a Miquel Barceló. Madrid : Alianza, c1990. 367 p. : ill. ; 23 cm. (Alianza forma. 99) Includes bibliographical references. ISBN 84-206-7099-5 DDC 759.6/09/04 20
1. Painting, Spanish - Themes, motives. 2. Painting, Modern - 19th century - Spain - Themes, motives. 3. Painting, Modern - 20th century - Spain - Themes, motives. I. Title.
ND807 .C35 1990

Calza, Gian Carlo. Japanische Plakate heute . Mailand , c1979. 165 p. :
NYPL [3-MDW 90-4437]

Calzadilla, Juan. Marietta Berman : cosmovisión / [textos de] Juan Calzadilla, María Elena Ramos. Caracas, Venezuela : Armitano, [1990] 138, [6] p. : ill. (some col.) ; 27 cm. Includes bibliographical references (p. [139]-[140]). ISBN 980-216-065-2 DDC 759.987 20
1. Berman, Marietta, 1917- - Catalogs. I. Berman, Marietta, 1917-. II. Ramos, María Elena, 1947-. III. Title. IV. Title: Cosmovisión.
N6834.5.B48 A4 1990

Calzavara Capuis, Loredana. Carta archeologica del Veneto /. Modena [1988]- 4 v. :
NYPL [Map Div. 90-2171]

Calzona, Arturo.
Quintavalle, Arturo Carlo. Benedetto Antelami /. Milano , c1990. 384 p. : ISBN 88-435-3176-X DDC 730/.92 20
NB2826.A6 A4 1990

Quintavalle, Arturo Carlo, 1936- Benedetto Antelami /. Milano , c1990. 384 p. :
NYPL [3-MGO+ (Antelami) 90-12881]

Câmara, Filho, João, 1944-
João Câmara. [Berlin] : Staatliche Kunsthalle Berlin, 1988. 78 p. : ill. ; 32 cm. German and

Portuguese.
1. Câmara Filho, João, 1944- - Exhibitions. I. Title.
NYPL [3-MCZ+ C171 90-13212]

CÂMARA FILHO, JOÃO, 1944- - EXHIBITIONS.
Câmara Filho, João, 1944- João Câmara. [Berlin] , 1988. 78 p. :
NYPL [3-MCZ+ C171 90-13212]

Camara, Fodé, 1958-
Revolution française sous les tropiques . [Paris , 1989] 74 p. : *NYPL [3-MCY 91-5057]*

CAMARA, FODÉ, 1958- - EXHIBITIONS.
Revolution française sous les tropiques . [Paris , 1989] 74 p. : *NYPL [3-MCY 91-5057]*

Cámara Muñoz, Alicia. Arquitectura y sociedad en el Siglo de Oro : idea, traza y edificio / Alicia Cámara Muñoz. Madrid : Ediciones El Arquero, c1990. 280 p., [32] p. of plates : ill. ; 22 cm. (Textos universitarios) Includes bibliographical references (p. 251-277) ISBN 84-86902-07-X
1. Architecture, Renaissance - Spain. 2. Architecture - Spain. 3. Arts and society - Spain - History. 4. Spain - Civilization - 1516-1700. I. Series: Textos universitarios (Ediciones El Arquero). II. Title.
NYPL [MQWH 91-5219]

Camargo, Iberê, 1914- No andar do tempo : 9 contos e um esboço autobiográfico / Iberê Camargo. Porto Alegre, RS : L&PM Editores, c1988. 101 p. : ill. ; 21 cm. ISBN 85-25-40197-8
1. Camargo, Iberê, 1914-. 2. Painters - Brazil - Biography. I. Title.
NYPL [3-MCZ C172 90-12392]

CAMARGO, IBERÊ, 1914-
Camargo, Iberê, 1914- No andar do tempo . Porto Alegre, RS , c1988. 101 p. : ISBN 85-25-40197-8
NYPL [3-MCZ C172 90-12392]

CAMBRIDGE (CAMBRIDGESHIRE) - DESCRIPTION - VIEWS.
Le Keux, John, 1783-1846. [Engravings of Victorian Cambridge.] Le Keux's Engravings of Victorian Cambridge. Cambridge , New York , 1985. 135 p. : ISBN 0-521-30350-8 DDC 914.26/59/00222 19
DA690.C2 L45 1985
NYPL [MDG (Le Keux) 87-4848]

CAMBRIDGE (ENGLAND) - SOCIAL LIFE AND CUSTOMS.
Raverat, Gwen, 1885-1957. Period piece /. Ann Arbor , 1991. p. cm. ISBN 0-472-09475-0 (cloth : alk. paper) DDC 769.92 B 20
NE1147.6.R28 A2 1991

Cambridge, Mass. Gropper Art Gallery. see Gropper Art Gallery.

Cambridge, Mass. Harvard University. see Harvard University.

Cambridge, Mass. Hayden Gallery. see Hayden Gallery.

Cambridge monographs on American artists.
Staiti, Paul J. Samuel F.B. Morse /. Cambridge , New York , 1989. xxii, 298 p., 16 p. of plates : ISBN 0-521-32218-9 DDC 759.13 19
N6537.M66 A4 1989
NYPL [3-MCX M88 90-4481]

Webster, Sally. William Morris Hunt, 1824-1879 /. Cambridge , New York , 1991. p. cm. ISBN 0-521-34583-9 DDC 759.13 B 20
ND237.H9 W4 1991

Cambridge new art history and criticism.
Bal, Mieke, 1946- Reading "Rembrandt" . Cambridge , New York , 1991. p. cm. ISBN 0-521-39154-7 DDC 759.9492 20
ND653.R4 B18 1991

Cheetham, Mark A. (Mark Arthur), 1954- The rhetoric of purity . Cambridge , New York , 1991. xx, 194 p. : ISBN 0-521-38546-6 DDC 750/.1 20
ND196.A2 C4 1991 *NYPL [3-MC 91-5174]*

Pointon, Marcia R. Naked authority . Cambridge , New York , 1990. xi, 160 p. : ISBN 0-521-38528-8 DDC 757/.09/034 20
ND1290 .P6 1991
NYPL [3-MAMZ 90-13556]

Cambridge studies in Anglo-Saxon England .
(1) Raw, Barbara Catherine. Anglo-Saxon crucifixion iconography and the art of the monastic revival /. Cambridge [England] , New York , 1990. xii, 296 p., 16 p. of plates ; ISBN

0-521-36370-5   DDC 704.9/4853/0942 20
N6763 .R38 1990
NYPL [3-MAMZ 90-11590]

Cambridge studies in the history of architecture.
Picon, Antoine. [Architectes et ingénieurs au
siècle des Lumières. English.] French architects
and engineers in the Age of Enlightenment /.
Cambridge , New York , 1991. p. cm.   ISBN
0-521-38253-X   DDC 720/.944/09033 20
NA1046.5.N4 P513 1991

Cambridge studies in the history of art.
Miller, Dwight C. (Dwight Cameron), 1923-
Marcantonio Franceschini and the
Liechtensteins . Cambridge , New York , 1991.
xx, 296 p., [16] p. of plates :   ISBN
0-521-36503-1   DDC 759.5 B 20
ND623.F78125 A3 1990
NYPL [3-MCF F813 91-7475]

Cambridgeshire. Pevsner, Nikolaus, Sir, 1902-
Harmondsworth, 1970. 558 p.,   ISBN
0-14-071010-8   DDC 914.25/9/0485
NA969.C3 P4 1970

Camden Arts Centre. Hayman, Patrick, 1915-
Patrick Hayman, a voyage of discovery .
London , c1990. 60 p. :   ISBN 1-85332-056-0
NYPL [3-MCV H4155 91-5046]

The Camden Town Group /. Baron, Wendy. New
Haven , 1980. xvi, 71 p. :   ISBN 0-930606-20-5
(pbk.)   DDC 759.21/42/07401468 19
N6768.5.C53 B37 1980
NYPL [3-MAMR 81-554]

CAMDEN TOWN GROUP - EXHIBITIONS.
Baron, Wendy. The Camden Town Group /.
New Haven , 1980. xvi, 71 p. :   ISBN
0-930606-20-5 (pbk.)   DDC 759.21/42/07401468
19
N6768.5.C53 B37 1980
NYPL [3-MAMR 81-554]

Cameirana, Arrigo. Ceramica in banca . Albisola
Superiore , 1989. 78 p. :
NYPL [3-MPGD 91-6609]

Camelot world.
Werner, Vivian L. Dolls . New York, NY ,
c1991. 120 p. :   ISBN 0-380-76044-4 :   DDC
688.7/221/09 20
NK4894.A2 W43 1991

CAMENZIND, BALZ, 1907-
Fassbind, Franz. Balz Camenzind . [Schwyz] ,
1982. 32 p. :   **NYPL [3-MCZ C178 88-4435]**

Cameo cats /. Brent, Isabelle. Boston , 1992. p.
cm.   ISBN 0-316-10836-7 :   DDC 745.6/7/092 20
ND3410.B74 A4 1992

CAMEOS.
Miller, Anna M., 1933- Cameos old & new /.
New York, N.Y. , c1991. xiv, 216 p. :   ISBN
0-442-00278-5   DDC 736/.222 20
NK5720 .M55 1991

Cameos old & new /. Miller, Anna M., 1933-
New York, N.Y. , c1991. xiv, 216 p. :   ISBN
0-442-00278-5   DDC 736/.222 20
NK5720 .M55 1991

Cameos old and new. Miller, Anna M., 1933-
Cameos old & new /. New York, N.Y. , c1991.
xiv, 216 p. :   ISBN 0-442-00278-5   DDC 736/.222
20
NK5720 .M55 1991

**CAMERA INDUSTRY - UNITED STATES -
HISTORY.**
Collins, Douglas, 1945- The story of Kodak /.
New York , 1990. 392 p. :   ISBN 0-8109-1222-8
DDC 338.7/681418/0973 20
HD9708.U64 E273 1990
NYPL [MFW+ 91-5847]

Camera portraits . National Portrait Gallery
(Great Britain) New York , 1990. 320 p. :
ISBN 0-19-520858-7   DDC 779/.2/07442132 20
TR680 .N34 1990 **NYPL [MFW+ 91-5845]**

**CAMERAS - COLLECTORS AND
COLLECTING.**
Auer, Michel. 150 ans d'appareils
photographiques . Hermance [1989] 1 v.
(unpaged) :   ISBN 2-903671-07-9
NYPL [MFW 91-4967]

Cameron, Dan. Ferran García Sevilla : Sama /
text by Dan Cameron. New York : Galerie
Lelong, c1990. [24] p. : ill. ; 31 cm.
*1. García Sevilla, Ferran, 1949- - Exhibitions. I. Galerie
Lelong (New York, N.Y.). II. Title.*
NYPL [3-MCQ+ G236 91-4299]

Cameron, Eric, 1935-
Divine comedy : installation and essay / Eric
Cameron. Ottawa : National Gallery of Canada,
1990. 75 p., 27 p. of plates : ill. ; 21 x 26 cm.
Catalog for an exhibition which opened at the National
Gallery of Canada, Jan. 5, 1990 and traveled to the
Winnipeg Art Gallery, Mar. 17, 1990. Includes
bibliographical references.   ISBN 0-88884-594-4
DDC 709/.2 20
*1. Cameron, Eric, 1935- - Exhibitions. I. Winnipeg Art
Gallery. II. Title.*
N6549.C35 A4 1990
NYPL [3-MGO (Cameron)]

CAMERON, ERIC, 1935- - EXHIBITIONS.
Cameron, Eric, 1935- Divine comedy . Ottawa ,
1990. 75 p., 27 p. of plates :   ISBN
0-88884-594-4   DDC 709/.2 20
N6549.C35 A4 1990
NYPL [3-MGO (Cameron)]

CAMERON, EVELYN, D. 1928.
Lucey, Donna M., 1951- Photographing
Montana, 1894-1928 . New York , 1990. xvii,
250 p. :   ISBN 0-394-54036-0   DDC 770/.92 B 20
TR140.C26 L83 1990
NYPL [MFX (Cameron) 91-3595]

Cameron, John B. Photography's beginnings : a
visual history : featuring the collection of Wm.
B. Becker / John B. Cameron, Wm. B. Becker ;
introduction by H.K. Henisch ; [photography,
R.H. Hensleigh]. Rochester, Mich. : Oakland
University, Meadow Brook Art Gallery ;
Albuquerque : Distributed by University of
New Mexico Press, c1989. 176 p. : ill. (some
col.) ; 23 x 27 cm. "Published in conjunction with an
exhibition presented at the Meadow Brook Art Gallery
of Oakland University and the Grand Rapids Art
Museum"--T.p. verso. Includes bibliographical references
(p. 17).   ISBN 0-925859-00-1 (softbound)   DDC
770/.9 20
*1. Becker, Wm. B. (William B.) - Photograph
collections - Exhibitions. 2. Photography - History -
Exhibitions. I. Becker, Wm. B. (William B.). II.
Meadow Brook Art Gallery. III. Grand Rapids Art
Museum. IV. Title.*
TR15 .C36 1989   **NYPL [MFW 91-6729]**

Camfield, William A. Tabu Dada . Bern , c1983.
139 p. :   DDC 709/.04/062074094945 19
N6853.C86 A4 1983
NYPL [3-MCZ C946 83-2831]

Camhi, Morrie, 1928- The prison experience /
photography, Morrie Camhi. 1st ed. Rutland,
Vt. : Tuttle ; Tokyo, Japan : IPC, 1989. 140 p. :
ill. ; 27 cm.   ISBN 0-8048-1632-8
*1. California State Prison at Vacaville. 2. Prisoners -
California - Vacaville - Pictorial works. I. Title.*
NYPL [Sc F 90-73]

El camilismo en la América Latina. López Oliva,
Enrique, 1936- (comp) [La Habana] 1970. 97 p.
NYPL [Sc S261.7-L]

Camille Pissarro . Pissarro, Camille, 1830-1903.
Bremen, Deutschland [1990] 111 p. :
NYPL [MCO P67 91-5995]

Camille Pissarro and his friends. South Yarra,
Vic., Australia : Tolarno Galleries, [1986?] 1 v.
(unpaged) : chiefly ill. (some col.) ; 22 cm. Title
from cover.
*1. Pissarro, Camille, 1830-1903 - Exhibitions. I. Tolarno
Galleries.*
MLCS 89/19072 (N)
NYPL [3-MCO P67 90-11528]

**Caminando en mis sueños pos la estela de los
caballos blancos de Picasso .** Vindel, Pedro.
[Madrid] [1990?] 109 p. ;   ISBN 84-404-6676-5
N7113.P514 V56 1990

Camp, Liselotte. Neue Pinakothek, Staatsgalerie
moderner Kunst München /. Braunschweig
[1978?] 128 p. :
N2330 .N48
NYPL [3-MAVY (Munich) 81-632]

**CAMP SITES, FACILITIES, ETC. - UNITED
STATES.**
Comstock, William Phillips. Bungalows, camps,
and mountain houses /. Washington, D.C. ,
c1990. xxvi, 125 p. :   ISBN 1-558-35063-2 :
DDC 728/.373 20
NA7571 .C7 1990
NYPL [3-MRGG 91-3451]

**CAMPAGNA DI ROMA (ITALY) -
DESCRIPTION AND TRAVEL - VIEWS -
EXHIBITIONS.**
Graphische Sammlung Albertina. Claude

Lorrain und die Meister der römischen
Landschaft im XVII Jahrhundert . [Wien, 1965]
xv, 187 p. :   **NYPL [3-MBH 91-1175]**

**CAMPAIGNS, PRESIDENTIAL. see
PRESIDENTS - UNITED STATES -
ELECTION.**

**CAMPANA, GIAMPIETRO, MARCHESE DI
CAVELLI, 1808-1880 - ART
COLLECTIONS.**
Borowitz, Helen Osterman, 1929- Pawnshop
and palaces . Washington , c1991. xvi, 272 p.,
[32] p. of plates :   ISBN 1-560-98010-9 (alk. paper)
DDC 709/.2 20
N5273.2.C36 B67 1991
NYPL [3-MAX (Campana) 91-7446]

**CAMPANA, GIAMPIETRO, MARCHESE DI
CAVELLI, 1808-1880 - ART PATRONAGE.**
Borowitz, Helen Osterman, 1929- Pawnshop
and palaces . Washington , c1991. xvi, 272 p.,
[32] p. of plates :   ISBN 1-560-98010-9 (alk. paper)
DDC 709/.2 20
N5273.2.C36 B67 1991
NYPL [3-MAX (Campana) 91-7446]

Campano, Miguel Angel, 1948- Moral, Jean-Marie
del, 1952- Les temps du peintre . Niort [1987]
99 p. :
TR681.A7 M68 1987
NYPL [3-MAN 90-10272]

Campbell, James D., 1956- Thinking the body :
Ron Martin / James D. Campbell. Toronto :
Carmen Lamanna Gallery, [1989] 43 p. : ill. ;
25 cm. Poems. Includes bibliographical references (p.
21).   ISBN 0-9693914-0-4 :   DDC 759.11 19
I. Title. **NYPL [3-MGO (Martin) 90-10793]**

**Campbell, James Graham- see Graham-Campbell,
James.**

Campbell, Jean, 1913- Australian watercolour
painters, 1780 to present day / Jean Campbell.
Roseville, N.S.W., Australia : Craftsman House,
1989. 394 p. : ill. (some col.) ; 30 cm. Includes
index. Includes bibliographical references (p. 387-390).
ISBN 0-947131-28-0
*1. Watercolor painting, Australian. 2. Watercolorists -
Australia - Biography. I. Title.*
NYPL [3-MCY+ 90-5307]

Campbell, Julian. Frank O'Meara, 1853-1888 /
Julian Campbell ; with additional research by
Mary Stratton ; exhibition organised by Barbara
Dawson ; catalogue edited by Kim-Maï Mooney
and Barbara Dawson. Dublin : Dublin Corp. for
the Hugh Lane Municipal Gallery of Modern
Art, c1989. xii, 90 p., [6] p. of plates : ill.
(some col.), ports. ; 20 x 22 cm. Catalog of an
exhibition held at the Hugh Lane Municipal Gallery of
Modern Art, and at other locations in Ireland. Includes
index. Cover title: Frank O'Meara and his
contemporaries. Includes bibliograpical references
(79-83).   ISBN 0-9514246-0-2 (pbk.)   DDC
709/.415/074 19
*1. O'Meara, Frank, 1853-1888 - Exhibitions. I. Hugh
Lane Municipal Gallery of Modern Art. II. Title. III.
Title: Frank O'Meara and his contemporaries.*
N6789   **NYPL [3-MCZ O54 91-4562]**

Campbell, Mary Schmidt. Bearden, Romare,
1911-1988. Memory and metaphor . New
York , 1991. xiv, 128 p. :   ISBN 0-19-506347-3
(cl : alk. paper)   DDC 709/.2 20
N6537.B4 A4 1991   **NYPL [Sc F 91-121]**

Campbell, Suzan. D'Emilio, Sandra, 1939- Visions
and visionaries . Salt Lake City , 1991. p. cm.
ISBN 0-87905-383-6 :   DDC 758/.9978 20
N8214.5.U6 D46 1991

Campbell, Tony. Hodson, Yolande. Ordnance
surveyors' drawings, 1789-c.1840 . Reading,
England , 1989. 154 p. :   ISBN 0-86257-101-4
DDC 016.91242 20
Z6027.G7 H66 1989 GA791
NYPL [Map Div. 91-169]

Campeggi, Silvano.
Il Cinema nei manifesti di Silvano Campeggi
Nano, 1945-1969 . Firenze [1988] 158 p. :
DDC 741.6/74/092 20
NC1850.C36 A4 1988

CAMPEGGI, SILVANO - EXHIBITIONS.
Il Cinema nei manifesti di Silvano Campeggi
Nano, 1945-1969 . Firenze [1988] 158 p. :
DDC 741.6/74/092 20
NC1850.C36 A4 1988

Campendonk, Heinrich, 1889-1957.
Heinrich Campendonk : ein Maler des Blauen

Reiter : Kaiser Wilhelm Museum Krefeld,
Städtische Galerie im Lenbachhaus München /
[Ausstellung und Katalog, Sabine Röder].
Krefeld : Krefelder Kunstmuseen, c1989. 159
p. : ill. (chiefly col.) ; 29 cm. Catalog of an
exhibition held at the Kaiser Wilhelm Museum Krefeld
9/24-11/26/1989 and at the Städtische Galerie im
Lenbachhaus München 12/13/1989-2/4/1990. Includes
bibliographical references. ISBN 3-926530-38-3
*1. Campendonk, Heinrich, 1889-1957 - Exhibitions. I.
Röder, Sabine. II. Kaiser Wilhelm Museum Krefeld. III.
Städtische Galerie im Lenbachhaus München. IV. Title.*
N6888.C35 A4 1989

**CAMPENDONK, HEINRICH, 1889-1957 -
EXHIBITIONS.**
Campendonk, Heinrich, 1889-1957. Heinrich
Campendonk . Krefeld , c1989. 159 p. : ISBN
3-926530-38-3
N6888.C35 A4 1989

Campigli. Campigli, Massimo, 1895-1971.
Massimo Campigli . Ferrara , 1979. 1 v.
(unpaged) :   ***NYPL [3-MCF C19 90-5911]***

Campigli, Massimo, 1895-1971.
Massimo Campigli : [mostra] Comune di
Ferrara, Galleria civica d'arte moderna, Palazzo
dei Diamanti, 30 giugno 7 ottobre 1979.
Ferrara : La Galleria, 1979. 1 v. (unpaged) : ill.
(some col.) ; 22 cm. Cover title: Campigli. Includes
bibliographical references.
*1. Campigli, Massimo, 1895-1971 - Exhibitions. 2.
Campigli, Massimo, 1895-1971 - Criticism and
interpretation. I. Ferrara (Italy). Galleria civica d'arte
moderna. II. Title. III. Title: Campigli.*
NYPL [3-MCF C19 90-5911]

**CAMPIGLI, MASSIMO, 1895-1971 -
CRITICISM AND INTERPRETATION.**
Campigli, Massimo, 1895-1971. Massimo
Campigli . Ferrara , 1979. 1 v. (unpaged) :
NYPL [3-MCF C19 90-5911]

**CAMPIGLI, MASSIMO, 1895-1971 -
EXHIBITIONS.**
Campigli, Massimo, 1895-1971. Massimo
Campigli . Ferrara , 1979. 1 v. (unpaged) :
NYPL [3-MCF C19 90-5911]

Campione, Adele. Il cappello da donna =
Women's hats / Adele Campione.1a ed.
Milano : BE-MA editrice, 1989. 143 p. : col.
ill. ; 17 cm. (Itinerari d'immagini . 30) Italian and
English. ISBN 88-7143-086-7
1. Hats. I. Title. II. Title: Women's hats. III. Series.
NYPL [3-MMV 91-7599]

Campoy, Antonio Manuel. Rafael Botí /.
Madrid , c1989. 135 p. : ISBN 84-86938-14-7
(rústica)
NYPL [3-MCQ+ B748 91-6320]

**CAMPUS DISORDERS. see STUDENT
MOVEMENTS.**

Camusso, Lorenzo. Ceramics of the world : from
4000 B.C. to the present / Lorenzo Camusso,
Sandro Bortone. New York, N.Y. : H.N.
Abrams, Inc., 1992. p. cm. Includes bibliographical
references and index. ISBN 0-8109-3175-3 DDC
738/.09 20
*1. Pottery - History. 2. Porcelain - History. I. Bortone,
Sandro. II. Title.*
NK3780 .C37 1992

**Canada. Film board. see National Film Board of
Canada.**

**CANADA - HISTORICAL GEOGRAPHY -
MAPS.**
Historical atlas of Canada. Toronto , Buffalo
[1987]- v. : ISBN 0-8020-2495-5 (v. 1)
NYPL [Map Div. 87-990]

Ruggles, Richard I., 1923- A country so
interesting . Montreal , Buffalo , c1991. xix,
300 p. : ISBN 0-7735-0679-9 : DDC 912.71 20
NYPL [Map Div. 91-6178]

**CANADA - HISTORICAL GEOGRAPHY -
MAPS - CATALOGS.**
Ruggles, Richard I., 1923- A country so
interesting . Montreal , Buffalo , c1991. xix,
300 p. : ISBN 0-7735-0679-9 : DDC 912.71 20
NYPL [Map Div. 91-6178]

**Canada - History - Atlases. see Canada -
Historical geography - Maps.**

CANADA - IMPRINTS - CATALOGS.
A Checklist of Canadian copyright deposits in
the British Museum, 1895-1923 /. Halifax,
N.S., Canada , 1984- v. ; ISBN 0-7703-0179-7

(pbk. : v. 1) : DDC 015.71 19
Z1365 .C48 1984   ***NYPL [Map Div. 85-549]***

CANADA - MAPS.
(1988) Deschênes-Damian, Luce. Atlas
transcanadien /. Montréal , c1988. 1 atlas (145
p.) : ISBN 2-7601-1923-8 : DDC 912/.71 19
NYPL [Map Div. 91-7753]

**Canada. National Film Board. see National Film
Board of Canada.**

**Canada. Office national du film. see National
Film Board of Canada.**

CANADA - ROAD MAPS.
(1989) Mobil road atlas and trip planning
guide . New York, N.Y. , 1989. 1 atlas (144
p.) : ISBN 0-13-586025-3 (pbk.)
NYPL [Map Div. 89-100]

(1990) H.M. Gousha Company. Pocket road
atlas, United States, Canada, Mexico. San Jose,
CA , 1990, c1989. 1 atlas (64 p.) : ISBN
0-13-622465-2
NYPL [Map Div. 90-12566]

(1991) United States, Canada, Mexico road
atlas. San Jose, (A , 1991. 1 atlas (80 p.) :
ISBN 0-13-471731-7
NYPL [Map Div. 91-2415]

CANADA - SOCIAL CONDITIONS - TO 1763.
De Marly, Diana. Dress in North America /.
New York , 1990- v. : ISBN 0-8419-1199-1
DDC 391/.0097 20
GT603 .D4 1990   ***NYPL [3-MMP 91-3984]***

Canaday, John, 1907- Mainstreams of modern art
/ John Canaday. New York : Simon and
Schuster, c1959. xxiv, 576 p., [15] leaves of
plates : ill. (some col.) ; 26 cm. Includes index.
1. Art, Modern - 19th century. I. Title.
NYPL [3-MAL]

CANADIAN ART. see ART, CANADIAN.

**CANADIAN ART CLUB (TORONTO, ONT.) -
EXHIBITIONS.**
The Canadian Art Club, 1907-1915 /.
Edmonton, Alberta, Canada [1988] 94 p. :
ISBN 0-88950-049-5 DDC 709/.71/07412334 20
N6545 .C213 1988
NYPL [3-MAM+ 90-12373]

The Canadian Art Club, 1907-1915 / [exhibition
organized by Robert J. Lamb for the Edmonton
Art Gallery]. Edmonton, Alberta, Canada :
Edmonton Art Gallery, [1988] 94 p. : ill. (some
col.) ; 31 cm. English and French. Bibliography: p.
82-85. ISBN 0-88950-049-5 DDC
709/.71/07412334 20
*1. Canadian Art Club (Toronto, Ont.) - Exhibitions. 2.
Art, Canadian - Exhibitions. 3. Nationalism and art -
Canada - Exhibitions. 4. Art, Modern - 20th century -
Canada - Exhibitions. I. Lamb, Robert J.*
N6545 .C213 1988
NYPL [3-MAM+ 90-12373]

Canadian artists series (Toronto, Ont.)
Lind, Jane. Gathie Falk /. Vancouver , c1989.
40 p. : ISBN 0-88894-815-8 : DDC 709.2 20
NYPL [3-MAL 90-12811]

Canadian atlas of F.S.A. postal areas.
Scarborough, ON : Artscan Datamap, c1990. 1
atlas (v, 69 [i.e. 138], 69 p.) : maps (some
folded) ; 28 x 30 cm. Co-published by Financial
Post Information Service and COMPUSEARCH.
Includes index. DDC 383/.145 20
*1. Zip code - Canada - Maps. I. Artscan Datamap
(Firm). II. Title: Atlas of F.S.A. postal areas.*
NYPL [Map Div. 91-8103]

Canadian cartographer. The Purpose and use of
national and regional atlases . Toronto,
Canada , 1979. vii, 100 p. : ISBN 0-919870-23-6
(pbk.)
GA101.2 .P87   ***NYPL [Map Div. 81-199]***

CANADIAN (EXPRESS TRAIN)
Courtemanche, Gil. Trente artistes dans un
train /. Montréal , c1989. 153 p. : ISBN
2-920718-29-0 : DDC 751.7/3/0971 20
NYPL [3-MLP 91-6235]

Canadian lives (Markham, Ont.)
Taylor, Kate. Painters /. Markham, Ont. , 1989.
64 p. : ISBN 0-88902-853-2 : DDC j759.11 19
NYPL [3-MCY 91-4450]

CANADIAN MUSEUM OF CIVILIZATION.
The Architecture of Douglas Cardinal /.
Edmonton , 1989. 150 p. : ISBN 0-920897-46-0
(bound) : DDC 720/.92/4 19
NYPL [3-MQZ+ (Cardinal) 90-10573]

The Canadian Pacific Rockies . Harmon, Byron,
1876-1934. Banff [Alta.] [1928?] 24 leaves of
plates :   ***NYPL [MFX+ (Harmon) 87-132]***

**CANADIAN ROCKIES (B.C. AND ALTA.) -
DESCRIPTION AND TRAVEL - VIEWS.**
Harmon, Byron, 1876-1934. The Canadian
Pacific Rockies . Banff [Alta.] [1928?] 24
leaves of plates :
NYPL [MFX+ (Harmon) 87-132]

Canadian studies (Lewiston, N.Y.) .
(v. 14) Pomedli, Michael. William Kurelek's
Huronia mission paintings /. Lewiston, N.Y. ,
1991. p. cm. ISBN 0-7734-9731-5 DDC 759.11 20
ND249.K85 P66 1991

ÇANAKKALE POTTERY.
Öney, Gönül. Türk devri Çanakkale seramikleri.
[Ankara, 1971] vi, 79 p.
NYPL [3-MPF 90-5450]

Canaletto, 1697-1768.
Canaletto drawings : 47 works / by Canaletto.
New York : Dover, 1991. 44 p. : chiefly ill. ;
29 cm. (Dover art library) ISBN 0-486-26647-8
(pbk.) : DDC 741.945 20
1. Canaletto, 1697-1768 - Catalogs. I. Title. II. Series.
NC257.C27 A4 1991

CANALETTO, 1697-1768 - CATALOGS.
Canaletto, 1697-1768. Canaletto drawings .
New York , 1991. 44 p. : ISBN 0-486-26647-8
(pbk.) : DDC 741.945 20
NC257.C27 A4 1991

Parker, K. T. (Karl Theodore), 1895- The
drawings of Antonio Canaletto in the collection
of Her Majesty the Queen at Windsor Castle /.
Bologna, Italy , 1990. 174 p. : ISBN
88-7779-105-5
NYPL [3-MCF+ C21 91-5238]

Canaletto drawings . Canaletto, 1697-1768. New
York , 1991. 44 p. : ISBN 0-486-26647-8 (pbk.) :
DDC 741.945 20
NC257.C27 A4 1991

CANALS - GREAT BRITAIN - MAPS.
Crowther, G. L. National atlas showing canals,
navigable rivers, mineral tramroads, railways,
and street tramways /. Preston, Lancs. , 1985-
1 atlas (v.) : ISBN 0-948850-50-7 (lib. ed. : v. 1)
DDC 912/.41 19
G1812.21.P1 C7 1985
NYPL [Map Div. 90-2]

**Canary Islands. Viceconsejería de Cultura y
Deportes.**
LADAC . [Las Palmas de Gran Canarias]
[1990?] 1 case : ISBN 84-87137-32-6
N7108 .L33 1990

Millares, Manolo, 1926-1972. Millares . [Canary
Islands] [1989] 146 p. : ISBN 84-87137-24-5
MLCM 90/05881 (N)
NYPL [3-MCQ M645 91-2648]

Canby, Sheila R. Persian masters . Bombay ,
c1990. viii, 144 p. : ISBN 81-85026-10-6 :
IN PROCESS (ONLINE)
NYPL [3-MAF+ 91-8109]

Cándido Bidó . Tolentino, Marianne de. Santo
Domingo, República Dominicana , 1989-1990. 2
v. : DDC 759.97293 20
ND315.D6 T565 1989

CANDLESTICKS - POLAND - HISTORY.
Hołubiec, Jerzy. Polskie lampy i świeczniki /.
Wrocław , 1990. 176 p., [190] p. of plates :
ISBN 83-04-02227-3
NK6196 .H65 1990

Canella, Maria. Broggi, Luigi, 1851-1926. I miei
ricordi, 1851-1924 . Milano, Italy , c1989. 301
p. : ISBN 88-20-43560-8 : DDC 720/.92 B 20
NA1123.B76 A2 1989

**CANEVA, GIACOMO, 1810-1890 -
EXHIBITIONS.**
Becchetti, Piero. Giacomo Caneva e la scuola
fotografica romana (1847/1855) /. Firenze ,
c1989. 197 p. : ISBN 88-7292-106-8
NYPL [MFX+ (Caneva) 91-6016]

Canevari, D. Russian futurism, 1910-1916 : poetry
and manifestoes / [D. Canevari]. Cambridge,
[Cambridgeshire] Eng. : Chadwyck-Healey,
[1977?] 18 leaves : facsims. ; 28 cm. Caption title.
Introduction and "Finding list" to microfiche set:
Russian futurism, 1910-1916 (located in: *XMS-1,000)
*1. Futurism (Literary movement) - Russia. 2. Futurism
(Art) - Russia. I. Russian futurism, 1910-1916. II. Title.*
NYPL [Desk-Slav. Div. 85-672]

Caniggia, Gianfranco. Maffei, Gian Luigi. La casa fiorentina nella storia della città dalle origini all'Ottocento /. Venezia , 1990. 383 p. : ISBN 88-317-5346-0
NA9053.B58 M3 1990

Canogar. Rubio, Miguel. Rafael Canogar /. Barcelona , c1990. 47, [1] p. : ISBN 84-87433-10-3
N6913.C36 A4 1990

Canogar, Rafael, 1935-
Rubio, Miguel. Rafael Canogar /. Barcelona , c1990. 47, [1] p. : ISBN 84-87433-10-3
N6913.C36 A4 1990

CANOGAR, RAFAEL, 1935- - EXHIBITIONS.
Rubio, Miguel. Rafael Canogar /. Barcelona , c1990. 47, [1] p. : ISBN 84-87433-10-3
N6913.C36 A4 1990

Canonne, Xavier. Armand Simon : de l'autre côté du miroir / Xavier Canonne. Bruxelles : Editeurs d'art associés, [1987] 118 p. : ill. (some col.) ; 28 cm. (Collection "La Mémoire de l'art") Includes bibliographical references (p. 112-116). ISBN 2-87103-034-X
1. Simon, Armand, 1906-1981 - Criticism and interpretation. 2. Surrealism - Belgium. I. Title. II. Series.
NC266.S54 C36 1987

Canons of Orissan architecture /. Bose, Nirmal Kumar. New Delhi , 1982. vi, 211 p., 34 p. of plates : DDC 720/.954/13 20
NA1507.O7 B6 1982

Canova, Antonio.
Di villa in villa . Treviso , c1990. 235 p. : ISBN 88-85066-98-4
NYPL   [3-MQWB 91-4915]
Di villa in villa . Treviso , c1990. 235 p. : ISBN 88-85066-98-4 : DDC 728.8/0945/3 20
NA7594 .D54 1990

Canova, Antonio, 1757-1822.
Stefani, Ottorino, 1928- I rilievi del Canova . Milano , c1990. 179 p. :
NYPL   [3-MGO (Canova) 91-6792]

CANOVA, ANTONIO, 1757-1822.
Stefani, Ottorino, 1928- I rilievi del Canova . Milano , c1990. 179 p. :
NYPL   [3-MGO (Canova) 91-6792]

CANOVA, ANTONIO, 1757-1822 - EXHIBITIONS.
Thorvaldsens museum. Antonio Canova . København [1969] 54 p. :
NYPL   [3-MCF C227.B3 91-1382]

Can't you guys read? cartoons on academia /. Harris, Sidney. New Brunswick , c1991. p. cm. ISBN 0-8135-1733-8 (pbk.) : DDC 741.5/973 20
NC1429.H33315 A4 1991a

Cantay, Tanju. XVI.-XVII. yüzyıllarda Süleymaniye Camii ve bağlı yapıları / Tanju Cantay. 1. baskı. Beyoğlu, İstanbul : Eren Yayıncılık ve Kitapçılık, 1989. 56, 32 p., [2] leaves of plates : ill. (some col.) ; 25 cm. "89.34.Y.70.0009." Cover title: Süleymaniye Camii. Includes bibliographical references (p. 55-56). ISBN 975-7622-05-2
1. Süleymaniye Camii (Istanbul, Turkey). 2. Architecture, Ottoman - Turkey - Istanbul. 3. Architecture, Islamic - Turkey - Istanbul. 4. Istanbul (Turkey) - Buildings, structures, etc. I. Title. II. Title: Süleymaniye Camii. III. Title: 16.-17. yüzyıllarda Süleymaniye Camii ve bağlı yapıları.
NA5870.S93 C36 1989

Cantini Ardila, Jorge Ernesto. Pietro Cantini : semblanza de un arquitecto / Jorge Ernesto Cantini Ardila. Bogotá : Corporación La Candelaria, [1990] 318 p. : ill. (some col.) ; 30 cm. (Colección Corporación La Candelaria, Alcaldía Mayor de Bogotá) Includes bibliographical references. DDC 720/.92 20
1. Cantini, Pietro, 1847-1929 - Criticism and interpretation. 2. Architecture, Modern - 19th century - Colombia. I. Title. II. Series.
NA879.C36 C3 1990

CANTINI, PIETRO, 1847-1929 - CRITICISM AND INTERPRETATION.
Cantini Ardila, Jorge Ernesto. Pietro Cantini . Bogotá [1990] 318 p. : DDC 720/.92 20
NA879.C36 C3 1990

Cantisán, Regla Merchán. see **Merchán Cantisán, Regla.**

Canto a la sombra de los animales /. Toledo, Francisco, 1940- [Mexico?] , 1988. 88 p. :
IN PROCESS (ONLINE)
NYPL   [JFD 91-2852]

Il canto dei nuovi emigranti /. Costabile, Franco, 1924-1965. Vibo Valentia, CZ , Milano , 1989. 64 p., [62] p. of plates : ISBN 88-16-64013-8 DDC 851/.914 20
PQ4863.O767 C36 1989
NYPL   [MFX+ (Giacomelli) 91-3400]

Cantó Rubio, Juan. Arte bizantino : el cielo / Juan Cantó Rubio. Salamanca : Centro de Estudios Orientales y Ecumenicos "Juan XXIII." Universidad Pontificia Salamanca, 1989. 94 p. : ill. ; 22 cm. (Bibliotheca oecumenica Salmanticensis . 15) Bibliography: p. 91. ISBN 84-7299-220-9
1. Art, Byzantine. 2. Christian art and symbolism - Medieval, 500-1500 - Byzantine Empire. 3. Byzantine Empire - Civilization. I. Title. II. Series.
NYPL   [3-MAK 91-3667]

Canton de Cattenom : Moselle / Ministère de la culture, Inventaire général des monuments et des richesses artistiques de la France, Région de Lorraine. [Metz] : Éditions Serpenoise, c1988. 79 p. : ill. (some col.) ; 30 cm. (Images du patrimoine . no 49) Cover title. ISBN 2-9501474-3-7 DDC 709/.44/3825 20
1. Art, French - France - Cattenom (Canton). I. Inventaire général des monuments et des richesses artistiques de la France. Région de Lorraine. II. Series.
N6849.C36 C36 1988

Canton de Longuyon : Meurthe-et-Moselle / Ministère de la culture, Inventaire général des monuments et des richesses artistiques de la France, Région de Lorraine. [Metz] : Éditions Serpenoise, c1988. 80 p. : ill. ; 30 cm. (Images du patrimoine . no 50) Cover title. ISBN 2-9501474-4-5 DDC 709/.44/3823 20
1. Art, French - France - Longuyon (Canton). I. Inventaire général des monuments et des richesses artistiques de la France. Région de Lorraine. II. Series.
N6849.L74 C36 1988

Canton de Montreuil-Bellay /. Manase, Viviane. [Nantes] [1990] 100 p. : ISBN 2-906344-00-00 : DDC 709/.44/18 20
N6849.M66 M35 1990

Canton de Seurre : Côte-d'Or / Ministère de la culture et de la communication, Inventaire général des monuments et des richesses artistiques de la France, Région de Bourgogne. [Dijon] : Association pour la connaissance du patrimoine de Bourgogne, c1988. 59 p. : ill. (some col.) ; 30 cm. (Images du patrimoine . no 54) Cover title. ISBN 2-904727-02-7; 2-904727-02-07 DDC 709/.44/42 20
1. Art, French - France - Seurre (Canton). I. Inventaire général des monuments et des richesses artistiques de la France. Région de Bourgogne. II. Series.
N6849.S48 C36 1988

Canton de Sierck-les-Bains, Moselle / Ministère de la culture, Inventaire général des monuments et des richesses artistiques de la France, Région de Lorraine. [Metz] : Éditions Serpenoise, c1987. 72 p. : ill. (some col.) ; 30 cm. (Images du patrimoine . no 26) Cover title. ISBN 2-9501474-1-0 DDC 709/.44/3825 20
1. Art, French - France - Sierck-les-Bains (Canton). I. Art - France - Sierck-les-Bains (Canton). I. Inventaire général des monuments et des richesses artistiques de la France. Région de Lorraine. II. Series.
N6849.S53 C35 1987

Canton et dentelles d'Arlanc, Puy-de-Dôme / [réalisé par] Ministère de la culture et de la communication, Inventaire général des monuments et des richesses artistiques de la France, Région d'Auvergne. Clermont-Ferrand : Inventaire général Auvergne, c1989. 56 p. : ill. (some col.), map ; 30 cm. (Images du patrimoine . no 58) Cover title. ISBN 2-905554-03-7 : DDC 709/.44/591 20
1. Art, French - France - Arlanc (Canton). 2. Vernacular architecture - France - Arlanc (Canton). 3. Lace and lace making - France - Arlanc (Canton). I. Inventaire général des monuments et des richesses artistiques de la France. Région d'Auvergne. II. Series.
N6849.A69 C36 1989

Cantor, Laurel Masten. The Sculpture of Princeton University . [Princeton, N.J. , c1982] [32] p. :
NYPL   [3-MGI 91-4577]

CANVAS EMBROIDERY - PERU - LIMA.
Franger, Gaby. [Arpilleras : Bilder die sprechen Organisation und Alltag der Frauen in den Slums von Lima. Spanish.] Arpilleras . Lima,

Peru , 1988. 110 p. :
NYPL   [3-MOT 90-12715]

Capacci, Alberto. Documenti geocartografici nelle bibiloteche e negli archivi privati e pubblici della Liguria. Firenze , 1990- v. : ISBN 88-22-23788-9 (v. 1)
NYPL   [Map Div. 91-69]

Capaccioli, Luciana. Borsi, Franco. Dall'art déco al Novecento /. Firenze , c1983. 250 p., [4] p. of plates : DDC 709/.04/012 19
N6494.A7 B67 1983
NYPL   [3-MAL 91-4191]

Cape, Stephen. Lilly Library (Indiana University, Bloomington) Changing images . Bloomington, Ind. , 1991. 62 p. : ISBN 1-87959-800-0 DDC 741.6/4/09034074772255 20
NC978 .L55 1991

Capel Margarito, Manuel.
Corpus de las artes suntuarias de Granada . (v. 1-2) Capel Margarito, Manuel. Orfebrería religiosa de Granada /. [Granada] , 1983-1986. 2 v. : ISBN 84-500-8997-2 (set) DDC 739.2/0946/82 19
NK7215 .C36 1983   NYPL   [3-MNP 88-3107]
Orfebrería religiosa de Granada / Manuel Capel Margarito. [Granada] : Publicaciones de la Diputación Provincial de Granada, 1983-1986. 2 v. : ill. ; 28 cm. (Corpus de las artes suntuarias de Granada Manuel Capel Margarito . v. 1-2) Includes bibliographies and indexes. ISBN 84-500-8997-2 (set) DDC 739.2/0946/82 19
1. Church plate - Spain - Granada. 2. Silversmiths - Spain - Granada - Biography. I. Series: Capel Margarito, Manuel. Corpus de las artes suntuarias de Granada . v. 1-2. II. Title.
NK7215 .C36 1983   NYPL   [3-MNP 88-3107]

Capella, Juli.
[Diseño de arquitectos en los 80. English]
Designed by architects in the 1980s / Juli Capella and Quim Larrea. New York : Rizzoli, 1988. 191 p. : chiefly ill. (some col.) ; 27 cm. Translation of: Diseño de arquitectos en los 80. Bibliography: p. 188-189. ISBN 0-8478-0941-2 : DDC 749.2/0498 19
1. Architect-designed furniture. 2. Furniture - History - 20th century. 3. Decorative arts - History - 20th century. 4. Design - History - 20th century. I. Larrea, Quim. II. Title.
NK2702 .C3713 1988
NYPL   [3-MOI 91-6559]

Capiscar la fior de la mà morta. Jové, Angel. Angel Jové . [Barcelona] [1991?] 229 p. :
N7113.J68 A4 1991

Capitaine, Jean-Louis. Le Peintre et l'affiche . Paris , c1988. 133, [3] p. : ISBN 2-86941-062-X
NC1806.8 .P4 1988

Capitanio, Ester. Pizzarello, Ugo, 1940- Guida alla città di Venezia /. Venezia , 1986- v. :
NYPL   [3-MQWB 91-653]

Capitol, Rome. see **Rome (City). Capitol.**

CAPITOLS.
Vale, Lawrence J., 1959- Architecture, power, and national identity /. New Haven , c1992. p. cm. ISBN 0-300-04958-7 (alk. paper) DDC 725/.11 20
NA4195 .V35 1992

Capolavori dalle collezioni d'arte del Banco di Napoli / a cura di Nicola Spinosa. Napoli : Guida editori, c1989. 213 p. : ill. (chiefly col.), ports. ; 30 cm. Catalogue of an exhibition held at Museo Diego Aragona Pignatelli Cortes, Naples, Sept. 21-Nov. 19, 1989. "Le schede delle tavole e le biografie sono state curate da Luisa Martorelli ... [et al.]"--T.p. verso. Includes bibliographical references (p. 205-207). ISBN 88-7042-999-7
1. Banco di Napoli - Art collections - Catalogs. 2. Art - Private collections - Italy - Naples - Exhibitions. 3. Art, Italian - Exhibitions. I. Spinosa, Nicola, 1943-. II. Martorelli, Luisa. III. Museo principe Diego Aragona Pignatelli Cortes. IV. Banco di Napoli.
NYPL   [3-MAVZ+ (Naples) 90-13203]

Capolavori dalle collezioni della Fondazione Magnani Rocca /. Fondazione Magnani Rocca. Bologna , 1990. xxxi, 131 p. : 88-7779-116-0
NYPL   [MAVZ (Parma, Italy) 91-6194]

Capp, Al, 1909- My well-balanced life on a wooden leg / Al Capp. Santa Barbara, CA : John Daniel, 1991. p. cm. ISBN 0-936784-93-8 : DDC 741.5/092 B 20

1. Capp, Al, 1909-. 2. Cartoonists - United States - Biography. I. Title.
NC1429.C295 A2 1991

CAPP, AL, 1909-
Capp, Al, 1909- My well-balanced life on a wooden leg /. Santa Barbara, CA , 1991. p. cm.
ISBN 0-936784-93-8 :   DDC 741.5/092 B 20
NC1429.C295 A2 1991

La Cappella Brancacci /. Baldini, Umberto.
Milano , c1990. 377 p. :   ISBN 88-435-3199-9
ND2757.F5 B3 1990
NYPL   [3-MLP 91-7284]

La Cappella Brancacci . Casazza, Ornella.
Modena [1989] 108 p. :   ISBN 88-7686-147-5
IN PROCESS (ONLINE)
NYPL   [3-MLP+ 91-4774]

CAPPELLA BRANCACCI (SANTA MARIA DEL CARMINE (CHURCH : FLORENCE, ITALY)
Baldini, Umberto. La Cappella Brancacci /.
Milano , c1990. 377 p. :   ISBN 88-435-3199-9
ND2757.F5 B3 1990
NYPL   [3-MLP 91-7284]

Casazza, Ornella. La Cappella Brancacci .
Modena [1989] 108 p. :   ISBN 88-7686-147-5
IN PROCESS (ONLINE)
NYPL   [3-MLP+ 91-4774]

CAPPELLA REALE DI NAPOLI (PALAZZO REALE) - CATALOGS.
Arte sacra di Palazzo . Napoli , 1989. 263 p. :
DDC 704.9/482/09450744573 20
N7952.N36 A74 1989
NYPL   [3-MAIH 91-4840]

Il cappello da donna =. Campione, Adele.
Milano , 1989. 143 p. :   ISBN 88-7143-086-7
NYPL   [3-MMV 91-7599]

Cappugi, Luana. Bruno Innocenti : disegni giovanili (1921-1928) / catalogo di Luana Cappugi ; con una nota introduttiva di Carlo Del Bravo. Firenze : L.S. Olschki, 1991. 79 p., [51] p. of plates : ill. ; 23 cm. (Gabinetto disegni e stampe degli Uffizi (Series) . 73) Bibliography: p. 75-77.
ISBN 88-22-23837-0
1. Innocenti, Bruno, 1906-1986 - Catalogs. 2. Gabinetto disegni e stampe degli Uffizi - Catalogs. I. Gabinetto disegni e stampe degli Uffizi. II. Series: Cataloghi (Gabinetto disegni e stampe degli Uffizi) , 73. III. Title.
NYPL   [3-MCF I57 91-5735]

Los Caprichos de Francisco de Goya y Lucientes /. Cela, Camilo José, 1916- [Madrid] , c1989.
172 p. :   ISBN 84-7737-018-4
NYPL   [MDG (Goya) 90-10979]

Capriles, María Cristina. Banco Industrial de Venezuela. Arturo Michelena . [Caracas, Venezuela] [1989?] 183 p. :   DDC 759.987 20
N6739.M53 B36 1989

Capturing light and color with pastel /. Dawson, Doug, 1944- Cincinnati, Ohio , c1991. p. cm.
ISBN 0-89134-376-8 (hrdcvr) :   DDC 741.2/35 20
NC880 .D35 1991

Caputo, Fulvio, 1953- Neoclassico . Venezia , 1990. xix, 530 p. :   ISBN 88-317-5361-4
N6916.5.N45 N4 1990

Car wars . Butman, John. London , 1991. 236 p., [16] p. of plates :   ISBN 0-246-13541-7 :   DDC 338.76292222094
TL240
NYPL   [JBE 91-1425]

CARA National Advisory Committee. Chicano art . Los Angeles , 1991. p. cm.   ISBN 0-943739-16-0 :   DDC 704/.0368/7207307479494 20
N6538.M4 C45 1991

CARA (Series) .
(11) L'Artiste, témoin de son temps (?) .
Aix-en-Provence , 1990. xiv, 168 p. ;   ISBN 2-85399-238-1 :   DDC 700/.942 20
NX543 .A83 1990

CARACAS (VENEZUELA) - BUILDINGS, STRUCTURES, ETC.
Proyecto nueva sede, Galería de Arte Nacional, Caracas =. [Caracas, Venezuela] [1986] 77 p. :
ISBN 980-603-006-0
N910.C22 P76 1986
NYPL   [3-MQWN+ 90-11046]

Caracci, Annibale. see Carracci, Annibale, 1560-1609.

Caramel, Luciano.
Agostino Ferrari / Luciano Caramel. Milano : Electa, c1991. 151 p. : ill. (some col.) ; 29 cm.
Italian and English. Includes bibliographical references.
ISBN 88-435-3445-9
1. Ferrari, Agostino, 1938-. I. Title.
IN PROCESS (ONLINE)
NYPL   [3-MCF F366 91-7167]

L'Europa dei razionalisti . Milano , c1989. 383 p. :   ISBN 88-435-2847-5
NYPL   [3-MAL 91-4900]

Testuale . Milano , c1979. 255 p. :   ISBN 88-20-20278-6   *NYPL   [3-MAL 90-6811]*

Veronesi, Luigi, 1908- Luigi Veronesi . Milano , c1989. 191 p. :   ISBN 88-20-20924-1 :
IN PROCESS (ONLINE)
NYPL   [3-MCF V543 91-6523]

CARAVAGGIO, MICHELANGELO MERISI DA, 1573-1610.
L'Ultimo Caravaggio . Siracusa , c1987. 376 p. :
NYPL   [3-MCF C26 90-9486]

Carballo Juan Rof. see Rof Carballo, Juan.

CARCATURES AND CARTOONS - HISTORY - 20TH CENTURY - CATALOGS.
Ralin, Radoĭ, 1923- Svetŭt e otseli͡al, zashtoto se e smi͡al =. Sofii͡a , 1989. 239 p. :
NC1355 .R34 1989

Carco, Francis, 1886-1958. Le nu dans la peinture moderne, 1863-1920 / Francis Carco. Paris : G. Crès, 1924. iv, 162 p., [33] leaves of plates : ill. ; 26 cm. Includes bibliographical references.
DDC 757/.4/09034 20
1. Nude in art. 2. Women in art. 3. Painting, Modern - 19th century. 4. Painting, Modern - 20th century. I. Title.
ND1290.7 .C37 1924

Carcopino, Francis. see Carco, Francis, 1886-1958.

Cardinal, Douglas. The Architecture of Douglas Cardinal /. Edmonton , 1989. 150 p. :   ISBN 0-920897-46-0 (bound) :   DDC 720/.92/4 19
NYPL   [3-MQZ+ (Cardinal) 90-10573]

CARDINAL, DOUGLAS.
The Architecture of Douglas Cardinal /.
Edmonton , 1989. 150 p. :   ISBN 0-920897-46-0 (bound) :   DDC 720/.92/4 19
NYPL   [3-MQZ+ (Cardinal) 90-10573]

Il Cardinal Leopoldo . Milano : R. Ricciardi, 1987- v. : ill. (some col.) ; 25 cm. (Archivio del collezionismo mediceo) Includes bibliographical references and indexes. CONTENTS. - v. 1. Rapporti con il mercato veneto. t. 1. Archivio elettronico del carteggio / a cura di Miriam Fileti Mazza -- t. 2. Catalogo storico dei disegni / a cura di Giovanna Gaeta Bertelà.
1. Medici, Leopoldo de', 1617-1675 - Art collections - Catalogs. 2. Art - Private collections - Italy - Catalogs. I. Series.   *NYPL   [3-MAX (Medici) 91-6376]*

Cardinali, Ferdinando. Le chiese minori delle colline bolognesi : passeggiata guidata sui primi colli bolognesi / Ferdinando Cardinali. Bologna : Ponte Nuovo, 1986. 58 p. : ill. (some col.) ; 28 cm. Ill. on lining papers. Bibliography: p. 58.
1. Church architecture - Italy - Bologna (Province). 2. Churches - Italy - Bologna (Province). I. Title.
NYPL   [3-MRBD 90-13374]

Cardona-Hine, Alvaro. Patten, Christine Taylor, 1940- Miss O'Keeffe /. Alburquerque , c1992. p. cm.   ISBN 0-8263-1322-1   DDC 759.13 B 20
ND237.O5 P37 1992

Cardoso, Homem. Vista Alegre . [Lisbon] , c1989. 267 p. :   ISBN 972-90191-9-3   DDC 738.2/09469/35 20
NK4210.F3175 V5 1989

Cardoso, Miguel Esteves. Cutileiro, João, 1937- Lorelei /. Porto, Portugal [1989] 1 v. (unpaged) :   DDC 730/.92 20
NB833.C88 A4 1989

CARDS, GREETING. see GREETING CARDS.

Carducci, Alberto. La Cripta della Cattedrale di Taranto /. Taranto [1986] 98 p. :
NYPL   [3-MRBN+ 90-10741]

Cardyn-Oomen, Dorine. Joostens, Paul, 1889-1960. Paul Joostens . [Brussel] [1986] 59 p. :   *NYPL   [3-MCH J815 90-8180]*

Carel Visser . Visser, Carel, 1928- [Hannover] ,

c1990. 78 p. :   ISBN 3-89169-053-3
IN PROCESS (ONLINE)
NYPL   [3-MGO (Visser) 90-13386]

Carel Weeber . Taverne, Ed. Rotterdam , c1989. xv, [121] p. :   ISBN 90-6450-088-6
NYPL   [3-MQZ (Weeber) 90-11979]

Carel Weeber, architect /. Taverne, Ed. Rotterdam , c1989. 121 p. :   ISBN 90-6450-088-6 :
NA1153.W44 T38 1989

Ca'Rezzonico. Mariacher, Giovanni. Venezia [1967] 38 p.   *NYPL   [3-MAVZ 90-6429]*

CARICATURE.
Staake, Bob, 1957- The complete book of caricature /. Cincinnati, Ohio , c1991. 134 p. :
ISBN 0-89134-367-9 :   DDC 741.5 20
NC1320 .S75 1991

CARICATURE AND COMIC ART. see CARICATURE; CARICATURES AND CARTOONS.

CARICATURE - HISTORY.
Hannoosh, Michele, 1954- Baudelaire and caricature . University Park, Pa. , c1992. p. cm.
ISBN 0-271-00804-0 (acid-free paper) :   DDC 741.5/09 20
NC1325 .H36 1992

CARICATURE - MARKETING.
Staake, Bob, 1957- The complete book of caricature /. Cincinnati, Ohio , c1991. 134 p. :
ISBN 0-89134-367-9 :   DDC 741.5 20
NC1320 .S75 1991

CARICATURES AND CARTOONS - GERMANY.
Haese, Klaus. Frau Republik geht pleite . Berlin , c1990. 144 p. :   ISBN 3-361-00251-6 :
IN PROCESS (ONLINE)
NYPL   [MDY 91-3467]

CARICATURES AND CARTOONS - GERMANY, EAST.
Null Problemo . [Berlin] , Berlin , 1990. 1 v. (unpaged) :   ISBN 3-88520-332-4
NYPL   [3-MDY+ 90-13163]

CARICATURES AND CARTOONS - GERMANY (WEST) - EXHIBITIONS.
Papan. Karikaturen . [Mannheim] , 1988. [50] p. :   ISBN 3-926857-01-3
NYPL   [3-MEM+ (Papan) 89-11634]

CARICATURES AND CARTOONS - JAPAN - HISTORY - 20TH CENTURY - EXHIBITIONS.
Tezuka, Osamu, 1926- Osamu Tezuku =. [Tōkyō] 1990. 348 p. :
NYPL   [3-MDG+ (Tezuka) 91-5811]

CARICATURES AND CARTOONS - UNITED STATES - HISTORY - 20TH CENTURY.
Ketcham, Hank, 1920- Dennis the Menace--his first 40 years /. New York , 1991. p. cm.
ISBN 1-558-59157-5   DDC 741.5/973 20
NC1429.K52 A4 1991

Carimos . Pérez Montas, Eugenio. Santo Domingo, República Dominicana , 1989. 358 p. :
NA791 .P47 1989

Cariou, Joël. Les classiques de l'architecture contemporaine / Joël Cariou. Paris : Editions Syros-Alternatives, c1990. 139 p. : col. ill. ; 29 cm.   DDC 724/.6 20
1. Architecture, Modern - 20th century - Pictorial works. I. Title. II. Title: Architecture contemporaine.
NA680 .C33 1990

Carl Blechen . Blechen, Karl, 1798-1840. [Berlin] , München , c1990. 309 p. :   ISBN 3-7913-1084-4
NYPL   [3-MCK+ B6455 91-2247]

Carl Buchheister, 1890-1964, Werkverzeichnis der gegenständlichen Arbeiten . Buchheister, Carl, 1890-1964. Nürnberg , c1986. 367 p. :
DDC 760/.092/4 19
N6888.B753 A4 1986
NYPL   [3-MCK B919 90-12854]

Carl Christian Vogel von Vogelstein, 1788-1868 . Richter, Rainer. Dresden , c1988. 93, [1] p. :
N6888.V57 A4 1988

Carl Croll /. Vlk, Miloslav. [Ústí nad Labem] , 1989. 131 p. :   ISBN 80-7047-018-6 :
ND534.5.C76 V58 1989

Carl Larsson, 1853-1919 . Larsson, Carl, 1853-1919. [Modum] , 1989. 152 p. :   ISBN

82-907340-3-4
ND793.L26 A4 1989

Carl Ludvig Engel 1778-1840 . Pöykkö, Kalevi,
1933- [Helsinki] [1990] 159 p. : ISBN
951-772-066-1
NA1088.E6 P69 1990

Carl Otto Czeschka . Fanelli, Giovanni. Firenze
[1990?] 127 p. : ISBN 88-7737-079-3
NYPL [MDG (Czeschka) 91-3839]

Carl Timner . Timner, Carl, 1933- Berlin , 1988.
109 p. : DDC 760/.092 20
N6888.T55 A4 1988
NYPL [3-MCK T578 91-6122]

Carl Unger . Sotriffer, Kristian, 1932- München ,
c1990. 115 p. :
NYPL [3-MCK U488 91-3256]

Carl Wagner 1796-1867. König, Oskar Alfred.
Der romantische Landschaftsmaler und
Meininger Hofmaler Carl Wagner 1796-1867 /.
Crailsheim , c1990. 199 p. : ISBN 3-9802532-0-1
NYPL [3-MCK W1323 91-5341]

Carl Wimar . Stewart, Rick, 1944- Fort Worth ,
New York , c1991. xi, 252 p. : ISBN
0-8109-3958-4
IN PROCESS (ONLINE)
NYPL [3-MCX W75 91-6150]

Carle, Eric.
The art of Eric Carle : with an autobiography
of the artist. Saxonville, MA : Picture Book
Studio, c1991. p. cm. Includes bibliographical
references. The noted author-illustrator discusses his life
and art. ISBN 0-88708-176-2 : DDC 741.6/42/092
20
1. Carle, Eric - Juvenile literature. 2. Illustrators -
United States - Biography - Juvenile literature. I. Title.
NC975.5.C36 A2 1991

CARLE, ERIC - JUVENILE LITERATURE.
Carle, Eric. The art of Eric Carle . Saxonville,
MA , c1991. p. cm. ISBN 0-88708-176-2 : DDC
741.6/42/092 20
NC975.5.C36 A2 1991

Carli, Enzo, 1910-
Il Duomo di Pisa . Firenze , c1989. 236 p. :
ISBN 88-404-1204-2 DDC 726/.6/094555 20
NA5621.P713 D86 1989
NYPL [3-MRBN+ 90-10929]

La scultura italiana : da Wiligelmo al
Novecento / Enzo Carli. Milano : Martello,
c1990. 584 p. : col. ill. ; 22 cm. DDC 730/.945
20
1. Sculpture, Italian. I. Title.
NB611 .C37 1990

Il Museo dell'opera del duomo / Enzo Carli.
Siena : Ente provinciale per il turismo di Siena,
1989. 63 p., [16] p. of plates : ill. (some col.) ;
24 cm. Cover title: Il Museo dell'opera del duomo di
Siena. At head of title: Opera della metropolitana di
Siena.
1. Museo dell'opera del duomo (Siena, Italy). 2.
Christian art and symbolism - Italy - Siena - Catalogs.
3. Art - Italy - Siena - Catalogs. I. Duomo di Siena. II.
Title. III. Title: Museo dell'opera del duomo di Siena.
NYPL [3-MAVZ (Siena) 90-12388]

Carlo Marcellini, accademico "spiantato" nella
cultura fiorentina tardo-barocca /. Visonà,
Mara. Ospedaletto, Pisa , c1990. 166 p., [79] p.
of plates : ISBN 88-7781-006-8
NYPL [3-MGO (Marcellini) 91-6515]

Carlo Scarpa . Scarpa, Carlo. Roma [1979] 48
p. :
MLCM 80/569 (N)
NYPL [3-MQZ (Scarpa) 90-5860]

Carlos Relvas, fotógrafo, 1838-1894 . Vicente,
Antonio Pedro. [Portugal] [1984] 99, [8] p. :
MLCM 85/4105 (N)
NYPL [MFX (Relvas) 91-3323]

CARLTON COUNTY, MINN. - MAPS.
(1990) Rockford Map Publishers. Carlton
County, Minnesota, land atlas & plat book .
Rockford, Ill. , c1990. 1 atlas (57 p.) :
NYPL [Map Div. 90-12844]

Carlton County, Minnesota, land atlas & plat
book . Rockford Map Publishers. Rockford,
Ill. , c1990. 1 atlas (57 p.) :
NYPL [Map Div. 90-12844]

Carmassi, Arturo, 1925-
Carmassi, Graphik 1963-1980 : Universität
Innsbruck, 14. Mai-18. Juni 1982, Foyer des
Opernhauses, Köln, 10. Juni-4. Juli 1982 /

[Redaktion und Übersetzung, Marise Carmassi
Druart, Hans T. Siepe, Barbara Schulz]. [S.l. :
s.n., 1982] 1 v. (unpaged) : ill. ; 29 cm.
1. Carmassi, Arturo, 1925- - Exhibitions. I. Universität
Innsbruck. II. Title.
NYPL [MDG (Carmassi) 90-10999]

CARMASSI, ARTURO, 1925- -
EXHIBITIONS.
Carmassi, Arturo, 1925- Carmassi, Graphik
1963-1980 . [S.l. , 1982] 1 v. (unpaged) :
NYPL [MDG (Carmassi) 90-10999]

Carmassi, **Graphik 1963-1980** . Carmassi, Arturo,
1925- [S.l. , 1982] 1 v. (unpaged) :
NYPL [MDG (Carmassi) 90-10999]

Carmel, Alex. Bauernfeind, Gustav, 1848-1904.
Der Orientmaler Gustav Bauernfeind,
1848-1904 . Stuttgart , 1990. xi, 368 p. : ISBN
3-7762-0319-6
NYPL [3-MCK+ B3385 91-7206]

Carmel, Gérard Titus- see **Titus-Carmel, Gérard,**
1942-

Carmen sings Monk [sound recording]. New
York : Novus, p1990. 1 sound disc : digital,
stereo. ; 4 3/4 in. Brief record. CONTENTS. - Get
it straight -- Ruby, my dear -- Well you needn't --
Monkery's the blues -- I mean you -- Little butterfly --
Listen to Monk -- How I wish -- Man, that was a
dream -- 'Round midnight -- Still we dream -- In
walked Bud -- Looking back -- In walked Bud -- Get it
straight.
1. Jazz vocals.
Novus 3086-2-N

Carmignani, Marina. 'Imparaticci' =. [Firenze] ,
c1986. 78, [1] p. : ISBN 88-7038-120-X
NK9109 .I663 1986
NYPL [3-MOT 90-10855]

Cârneci, Magda. Lucian Grigorescu / Magda
Cârneci. [Bucharest] : Meridiane, 1989. 77 p.,
[64] p. of plates : ill. (some col.) ; 33 cm.
Summaries in English and French. Includes
bibliographical references.
1. Grigorescu, Lucian, 1894- - Criticism and
interpretation. I. Title.
NYPL [3-MCZ+ G849 89-24509]

Carnegie Institute. Museum of Art.
Alcoa Collection of Contemporary Art. An
exhibition of works acquired from the G. David
Thompson Collection. [Pittsburgh , 1967?] [32]
p. : *NYPL [3-MC 90-6343]*
Eight hundred years of Japanese printmaking .
Pittsburgh , c1976. 126 p. :
NYPL [MDBV 90-6041]

Carnegie Museum of Art.
Mellon Bank. In the watercolor tradition .
Pittsburgh, Pa. , 1990. 78 p. : ISBN
0-88039-046-8 : DDC 759.2/074/74886 20
ND1928 .M45 1990
NYPL [3-MBO 91-6675]

Strazdes, Diana J. American paintings and
sculpture to 1945 in the Carnegie Museum of
Art /. New York , c1991. p. cm. ISBN
1-555-95055-8 : DDC 759.13/074/74886 20
N6505 .S87 1991

CARNEGIE MUSEUM OF ART - CATALOGS.
Strazdes, Diana J. American paintings and
sculpture to 1945 in the Carnegie Museum of
Art /. New York , c1991. p. cm. ISBN
1-555-95055-8 : DDC 759.13/074/74886 20
N6505 .S87 1991

Carnet d'un connaisseur à l'époque des Song du
nord. Mi, Fu, 1051-1107. [Hua shih. French.]
Le Houa-che de Mi Fou (1051-1107), ou, Le
carnet d'un connaisseur à l'époque des Song du
nord /. Paris , 1964. xxiv, 193 p. :
ND1043.3 .M513 1964

Carnets de croquis .
(2) Ripault, Jacques, 1953- Jacques Ripault /.
Paris , 1990. 1 v. (unpaged) : ISBN
2-907687-05-0 : DDC 720/.22/22 20
NA2707.R56 A4 1990

(3) Andreu, Paul. Paul Andreu /. Paris , 1990.
1 v. (unpaged) : ISBN 2-907687-06-9 : DDC
720/.22/22 20
NA2707.A55 A4 1990

Les carnets épatants et patents d'Alphonse
Célestin Bertillon . Lemant, Albert. Paris ,
1988. [16] p. : ISBN 2-86234-016-2
NYPL [3-MEM+ (Lemant) 89-27091]

Carnets (Plon (Firm))
Titus-Carmel, Gérard, 1942- Notes d'atelier &
autres textes de la contre-allée /. [Paris] ,
c1990. 214 p. ; ISBN 2-259-02380-0 :
N6853.T58 A2 1990

CARNIVAL GLASS - UNITED STATES.
Britt, John. Heart of American Carnival Glass
Association. [Buckner, MO] [c1990] 150 p. :
DDC 748.2913/09/041 20
NK5439.C35 B75 1990

CARÖE, WILLIAM DOUGLAS, 1857-1938 -
CRITICISM AND INTERPRETATION.
Freeman, Jennifer. W.D. Caröe, RStO, FSA .
Manchester, UK ; New York, NY, USA : xiii,
258 p., [4] p. of plates : ISBN 0-7190-2449-8
DDC 720/.92 20
NA997.C325 F7 1990
NYPL [3-MQZ (Caröe) 91-4076]

Carol, Màrius. Dalí : el final oculto de un
exhibicionista / Màrius Carol.1. ed. Esplugues
de Llobregat, Barcelona : Plaza & Janés, 1990.
204 p., [16] p. of plates : ill. ; 22 cm. (Biografías
y memorias) Includes bibliographical references (p.
[201]-204) and index. ISBN 84-01-35171-5 DDC
759.6 B 20
1. Dalí, Salvador, 1904-. 2. Artists - Spain - Biography.
I. Title. II. Series.
N7113.D3 C36 1990

Carol Rama /. Rama, Carol. Torino , c1989. 117
p. : ISBN 88-422-0173-1
NYPL [3-MCF+ R165 89-26726]

Caroli, Flavio.
Fede Galizia / Flavio Caroli. Torino : U.
Allemandi, c1989. 102 p. : ill. (some col.) ; 32
cm. (Archivi di arte antica) Includes bibliographical
references (p. [97]-102). ISBN 88-422-0217-7
1. Galizia, Fede, 1578-1630 - Catalogs. I. Galizia, Fede,
1578-1630. II. Series.
NYPL [3-MCF+ G155 90-12321]

Testuale . Milano , c1979. 255 p. : ISBN
88-20-20278-6 *NYPL [3-MAL 90-6811]*

Vago, Valentino, 1931- Valentino Vago /.
Milano [1975] [48] p. :
NYPL [3-MCF+ V126 91-6299]

Carolinas road atlas and recreation directory.
Rand McNally and Company. Rand McNally
Carolinas road atlas and recreation directory.
Chicago , c1990. 1 atlas (112 p.) : ISBN
0-528-90230-X
IN PROCESS (ONLINE)
NYPL [Map Div. 90-13046]

Carolinas road atlas and travel guide. Rand
McNally and Company. Rand McNally
Carolinas road atlas and travel guide. Boston ,
c1990. 1 atlas (112 p.) : ISBN 0-528-90288-1
NYPL [Map Div. 91-71]

Caroline Broadhead . Houston, John, 1935-
London , 1990. 64 p. : ISBN 0-947792-48-1
(pbk.) : DDC 739.27092 20
NYPL [3-MNR 90-12744]

Caroutch, Yvonne. Le livre de la licorne :
symboles, mythes et réalités / Yvonne
Caroutch. Puiseaux : Pardès, c1989. 243 p. : ill.
(some col.) ; 30 cm. Includes bibliographical
references (p. 235-239). ISBN 2-86714-066-8
1. Unicorns. 2. Unicorns in art. I. Title.
NYPL [3-MAMZ+ 90-8348]

Carpeggiani, Paolo. Sant'Andrea in Mantova : un
tempio per la città del principe / Paolo
Carpeggiani, Chiara Tellini Perina ; prefazione
di Lionello Puppi. Mantova : Publi-Paolini,
c1987. 182 p. : ill. (some col.), plans ; 32 cm.
Includes index. Bibliography: p. 169-173.
1. Sant'Andrea in Mantova (Church). 2. Church
architecture - Italy - Mantua. 3. Church decoration and
ornament - Italy - Mantua. 4. Mantua (Italy) -
Buildings, structures, etc. I. Tellini Perina, Chiara,
1937-. II. Title. *NYPL [3-MRBD+ 91-4615]*

Carpelan, Bo Gustaf Bertelsson, 1926- Suvihuvi
= Sommarnöje / teksti: Bo Carpelan ; kuvat:
Amatörfotografklubben i Helsingfors.
[Helsinki] : Suomen Valokuvataiteen Museo,
1988. 80 p. : chiefly ill., ports. ; 28 cm. Text in
Finnish and Swedish; summary in English. ISBN
951-9086-31-5
1. Photography - Finland. I. Amatörfotografklubben i
Helsingfors. II. Title. *NYPL [MFW 91-5797]*

Carpenter Center for Visual Arts.
Contemporary aboriginal art from the Robert
Holmes à Court Collection . Perth , 1990. 125

p. :   ISBN 0-7316-8569-5
NYPL [3-MADF+ 91-4291]

Le Corbusier, 1887-1965. Le Corbusier . New York, NY , c1990. 37 p. :   ISBN 1-87827-122-9
NYPL [3-MCO J42 91-4349]

Carpenter, Thomas H. Art and myth in ancient Greece : a handbook / Thomas H. Carpenter. London : Thames and Hudson, 1991. 256 p. : ill. ; 22 cm. (World of art) Includes indexes. Includes bibliographical references (p. 247-249).
    1. Art, Greek - Themes, motives, etc. 2. Mythology, Greek, in art. I. Title.   **NYPL [3-MAH 91-4599]**

CARPENTERS - SPAIN - CUENCA - BIOGRAPHY.
Rokiski Lázaro, María Luz. Arquitectura del siglo XVI en Cuenca . Cuenca , 1989. xxi, 464 p. :   ISBN 84-505-8542-2
NA1311.C84 R66 1989

Carpentier, J. (Janine) Bauer, A. (Alice) Répertoire des artistes d'Alsace des dix-neuvième et vingtième siècles . Strasbourg , 1984-1991. 6 v. :   ISBN 2-85369-036-9 (set)   DDC 709/.2/2 B 19
N6849.A4 B3 1984   **NYPL [MAO 86-2104]**

CARPENTRY.
Benjamin, Asher, 1773-1845. The country builder's assistant . Greenfield, Mass. , 1805. [36] p., [1], 37 leaves of plates (2 folded) :   DDC 720 20
NA2520 .B4 1805

CARPETS AND RUGS. see RUGS.

CARPETS - ENGLAND - HISTORY - 19TH CENTURY.
Haslam, Malcolm. Arts & crafts carpets /. New York , 1991. p. cm. ISBN 0-8478-1388-6 DDC 746.7/2 20
NK2843 .H37 1991

CARPETS - ENGLAND - HISTORY - 20TH CENTURY.
Haslam, Malcolm. Arts & crafts carpets /. New York , 1991. p. cm. ISBN 0-8478-1388-6 DDC 746.7/2 20
NK2843 .H37 1991

CARPETS - EUROPE.
Faraday, Cornelia Bateman. European and American carpets and rugs /. Woodbridge, Suffolk, England , c1990. 484 p. :   ISBN 1-85149-092-2 : DDC 746.7 19
NK2795   **NYPL [3-MOP 90-11733]**

CARPETS - UNITED STATES.
Faraday, Cornelia Bateman. European and American carpets and rugs /. Woodbridge, Suffolk, England , c1990. 484 p. :   ISBN 1-85149-092-2 : DDC 746.7 19
NK2795   **NYPL [3-MOP 90-11733]**

Carr, Annemarie Weyl. A Byzantine masterpiece recovered : the thirteenth-century murals of Lysi, Cyprus / Annemarie Weyl Carr, Laurence J. Morrocco ; introduction by Bertrand Davezac. Austin : University of Texas Press : Published in association with the Menil Foundation, c1991. p. cm. ISBN 0-292-78117-2 :   DDC 751.7/3/095645 20
    1. Mural painting and decoration, Byzantine - Cyprus - Lysi. 2. Mural painting and decoration, Byzantine - Conservation and restoration - Cyprus - Lysi. 3. Mural painting and decoration - Conservation and restoration - Technique. I. Morrocco, Laurence J., 1947-. II. Title.
ND2819.C92 L974 1991

Carr, Dawson W. (Dawson William), 1951-
Looking at paintings : a guide to technical terms / Dawson W. Carr and Mark Leonard. Malibu, Calif. : J. Paul Getty Museum in association with British Museum Publications, c1992. p. cm. Includes bibliographical references. ISBN 0-89236-213-8 DDC 750/.3 20
    1. Painting - Dictionaries. I. Leonard, Mark, 1954-. II. Title.
ND31 .C37 1992

Carr, Emily, 1871-1945.
CARR, EMILY, 1871-1945.
Shadbolt, Doris. Emily Carr /. Vancouver , Seattle , c1990. 240 p. :   ISBN 0-295-97003-0 (University of Washington Press) : DDC 759.11 B 20
ND249.C3 S54 1990
    NYPL [3-MCZ C28 90-13014]

[Correspondence]
    Dear Nan : letters of Emily Carr, Nan Cheney, and Humphrey Toms / edited by

---

Doreen Walker. Vancouver : University of British Columbia Press, 1990. xlvi, 436 p., [24] p. of plates : ill., ports. ; 24 cm. Includes index. Includes bibliographical references. ISBN 0-7748-0348-7 (cloth)
    1. Carr, Emily, 1871-1945. Correspondence. 2. Cheney, Nan, 1887-1985 - Correspondence. 3. Toms, Humphrey N. W. - Correspondence. 4. Painters - Canada - Correspondence. I. Cheney, Nan, 1887-1985. II. Toms, Humphrey N. W. III. Walker, Doreen, 1920-. IV. Title.
    NYPL [3-MCZ c28 91-7320]

CORRESPONDENCE
Carr, Emily, 1871-1945. [Correspondence.] Dear Nan . Vancouver , 1990. xlvi, 436 p., [24] p. of plates :   ISBN 0-7748-0348-7 (cloth)
    NYPL [3-MCZ c28 91-7320]

Carr, Tom, 1956-
Tom Carr. Hamburg : Galerie Hans Barlach, 1987. 33 p. : ill. ; 25 cm. German and English. ISBN 3-89018-029-9
    1. Carr, Tom, 1956- - Exhibitions. I. Galerie Barlach. II. Title.   **NYPL [3-MGO (Carr) 91-4300]**

CARR, TOM, 1956- - EXHIBITIONS.
Carr, Tom, 1956- Tom Carr. Hamburg , 1987. 33 p. :   ISBN 3-89018-029-9
    NYPL [3-MGO (Carr) 91-4300]

CARRACCI, AGOSTINO, 1557-1602.
Gli Scritti dei Carracci . Bologna , 1990. 202 p. ;   ISBN 88-7779-139-X
    NYPL [3-MCF C32 91-5526]

CARRACCI, ANNIBALE, 1560-1609.
Gli Scritti dei Carracci . Bologna , 1990. 202 p. ;   ISBN 88-7779-139-X
    NYPL [3-MCF C32 91-5526]

CARRACCI, LODOVICO, 1555-1619.
Gli Scritti dei Carracci . Bologna , 1990. 202 p. ;   ISBN 88-7779-139-X
    NYPL [3-MCF C32 91-5526]

Carrache, Annibal. see Carracci, Annibale, 1560-1609.

Carrazzoni, Maria Elisa. Guia dos bens tombados Brasil /. Rio de Janeiro, RJ , c1987. 512, [24] p. :   DDC 720/.981 20
NA853 .G85 1987

Carreño Corbella, Pilar. LADAC . [Las Palmas de Gran Canarias] [1990?] 1 case :   ISBN 84-87137-32-6
N7108 .L33 1990

Carreño, Virginia. Bomchil, Sara. El mueble colonial de las Américas y su circunstancia histórica /. Buenos Aires , c1987. 919 p., [24] p. of plates :   ISBN 950-0-70386-6 DDC 749.297 19
NK2401.A1 B66 1987
    NYPL [3-MOF 91-2686]

Carrete Parrondo, Juan. Madrid (Spain). Museo Municipal. Gabinete de Estampas. Catálogo del Gabinete de Estampas del Museo Municipal de Madrid /. [Madrid] , 1985- v. in :   ISBN 84-398-4272-4 (set) DDC 769.946/074/0641 19
NE699 .M33 1985   **NYPL [MDE 91-282]**

Carrier, David, 1944-
Poussin's paintings / David Carrier. University Park, Pa. : Pennsylvania State University Press, c1992. p. cm. Includes bibliographical references (p.) and index. ISBN 0-271-00816-4 DDC 759.4 20
    1. Poussin, Nicolas, 1594?-1665 - Criticism and interpretation. 2. Classicism in art - France. I. Poussin, Nicolas, 1594?-1665. II. Title.
ND553.P8 C35 1992

Principles of art history writing / David Carrier. University Park, Pa. : Pennsylvania State University Press, c1991. xiii, 249 p. : ill. ; 24 cm. Includes bibliographical references and index. ISBN 0-271-00711-7 (acid-free paper) DDC 707/.2 20
    1. Art - Historiography. I. Title.
N380 .C37 1991   **NYPL [MAD 91-6082]**

Carrière, Eugène, 1849-1906. Bantens, Robert James. Eugène Carrière . New York , c1990. 131 p. :   ISBN 1-87860-708-1
    NYPL [3-MCO C31 90-11584]

CARRIÈRE, EUGÈNE, 1849-1906.
Bantens, Robert James. Eugène Carrière . New York , c1990. 131 p. :   ISBN 1-87860-708-1
    NYPL [3-MCO C31 90-11584]

Carril, Bonifacio del. Gericault : las litografías argentinas / Bonifacio del Carril. [Buenos Aires?] : Emecé Editores, 1989. 27, [3] p. : ill.

(some col.) ; 35 cm. Includes bibliographical references (p. [28]). ISBN 950-0-40910-0 DDC 769.92 20
    1. Géricault, Théodore, 1791-1824 - Criticism and interpretation. 2. Argentina - History - War of Independence, 1810-1817 - Art and the war. I. Title.
NE2349.5.G44 C37 1989
    NYPL [MDG+ (Géricault) 90-11344]

Carrillo Azpeitia, Rafael. Pellicer, Carlos, 1897?-1977. [Pintura mural de la revolución mexicana. English.] Mural painting of the Mexican revolution /. México , 1985. 316 p. :   ISBN 968-665-804-1 (English ed.) DDC 758/.9972816 20
ND2644 .P4513 1985

Carrillo, Rafael. see Carrillo Azpeitia, Rafael.

Carrington, Fitz Roy, 1869-1954. Engravers and etchers; six lectures delivered on the Scammon Foundation at the Art Institute of Chicago, March 1916, by Fitzroy Carrington ... with 133 illustrations. [Chicago] The Art Institute of Chicago, 1917. 9 p. L., 13-278 p. incl. front., plates, ports. 25 cm. Bibliography at end of each lecture. CONTENTS. - German engraving: from the beginnings to Martin Schongauer.--Italian engraving: the Florentines.--German engraving: the master of the Amsterdam cabinet and Albrecht Dürer.--Italian engraving: Mantegna to Marcantonio Raimondi.--Some masters of portraiture.--Landscape etching.
    1. Engraving - History. 2. Etching - History. I. Title.
NE400 .C3   **NYPL [MDB 91-7805]**

Carroll, Lewis, 1832-1898. Aspin, Roy. Lewis Carroll and his camera /. Clayhall, Ilford, Essex , c1989. 55, [2] p., [36] leaves of plates :   ISBN 0-948706-04-X (pbk.)
    NYPL [MFX+ (Carroll) 91-7443]

CARROLL, LEWIS, 1832-1898.
Aspin, Roy. Lewis Carroll and his camera /. Clayhall, Ilford, Essex , c1989. 55, [2] p., [36] leaves of plates :   ISBN 0-948706-04-X (pbk.)
    NYPL [MFX+ (Carroll) 91-7443]

Carroll, Patty. Spirited visions : portraits of Chicago artists / by Patty Carroll ; text by James Yood ; foreword by Neal Benezra ; introduction by Debora Duez Donato. Urbana : University of Illinois Press, c1991. p. cm. (Visions of Illinois) ISBN 0-252-01848-6 (alk. paper) DDC 779/.2/092 20
    1. Artists - Illinois - Chicago - Portraits. 2. Art, Modern - 20th century - Illinois - Chicago. I. Yood, James. II. Title. III. Series.
N6535.C5 C37 1991

Carson, Edward. (joint author) Saunders, D. Gail. Guide to the records of the Bahamas /. [Nassau , 1973] xvi, 109, 28 p. ;
CD3882 .S27   **NYPL [HRG 76-607]**

Carstens, Asmus Jakob, 1754-1798.
Asmus Jakob Carstens und Joseph Anton Koch, zwei Zeitgenossen der Französischen Revolution . Berlin [1989] 160 p. :
NC249 .A835 1989

Neuwirth, Markus. Die Argonauten . Graz , c1989. 162 p. :   ISBN 3-201-01486-9
    NYPL [3-MCK K761 90-11989]

CARSTENS, ASMUS JAKOB, 1754-1798 - EXHIBITIONS.
Asmus Jakob Carstens und Joseph Anton Koch, zwei Zeitgenossen der Französischen Revolution . Berlin [1989] 160 p. :
NC249 .A835 1989

Carta aérea /. Antúnez, Nemesio. Santiago de Chile , 1988. 65 p. :   DDC 759.983 20
ND369.A58 A4 1988

Carta aérea /. Antúnez, Nemesio. Santiago , 1988. 65 p. :
    NYPL [3-MCZ+ A636 90-11576]

Carta archeologica del Veneto / a cura di Loredana Capuis ... [et al.] ; coordinamento scientifico, Luciano Bosio. Modena : Panini, [1988]- 4 v. : col. ill., maps (some col.) ; 25 cm. At head of title: Regione del Veneto, Giunta Regionale, Segreteria Regionale per il Territorio. Includes bibliographical references. CONTENTS. - v. 1. Carta d'Italia IGM 1:100.000, Fogli 11-12-13-22-23-36-37-38-39-40 -- v. 2. Carta d'Italia IGM 1:100.000, Fogli 35-48-49-62-63-75.
    1. Man, Prehistoric - Italy - Veneto. 2. Veneto, Italy - Antiquities. 3. Veneto (Italy) - Antiquities - Maps. 4. Italy - Antiquities. I. Calzavara Capuis, Loredana. II.

Bosio, Luciano. III. Veneto (Italy). Segreteria regionale
per il territorio.   **NYPL [Map Div. 90-2171]**

Carta's Israel motor atlas =. Karṭa (Firm)
Jerusalem , c1980. 1 atlas (73 [i.e. 78] p.) :
    ISBN 965-220-011-5 DDC 912/.5694 19
G2236.P2 K3 1980
              NYPL [Map Div. 90-9721]

Carter, Cheryl G. North American schools of the
arts : a profile of arts schools K-12 : a project
of the Network of Performing and Visual Arts
Schools / by Cheryl G. Carter and Suzy Logan
Jenkins. [Washington, D.C.] : The Network,
[c1990] vii, 172 p. : ill. ; 28 cm. DDC
    700/.71/273 20
1. Art schools - United States. 2. Arts - Study and
teaching (Elementary) - United States. 3. Arts - Study
and teaching (Secondary) - United States. 4. Art
schools - Canada. 5. Arts - Study and teaching
(Elementary) - Canada. 6. Arts - Study and teaching
(Secondary) - Canada. I. Jenkins, Suzy Logan. II.
Network of Performing and Visual Arts Schools. III.
Title.
NX303 .C37 1990

Carter, Curtis L.
Images of death in contemporary art .
Milwaukee, Wis. , c1990. 56 p. : ISBN
0-87462-902-X **NYPL [3-MAMZ 91-7063]**

Richard Lippold, sculpture / by Curtis L.
Carter, Jack W. Burnham, Edward Lucie-Smith.
Milwaukee, Wis. : Patrick and Beatrice
Haggerty Museum of Art, Marquette
University, [c1990] 64 p. : ill. (some col.) ; 27
cm. "Exhibition November 30, 1990-February 17,
1991." Includes bibliographical references. DDC
    730/.92 20
1. Lippold, Richard, 1915- - Exhibitions. 2. Artists'
preparatory studies - United States - Exhibitions. I.
Lippold, Richard, 1915-. II. Burnham, Jack, 1931-. III.
Lucie-Smith, Edward. IV. Patrick and Beatrice Haggerty
Museum of Art. V. Title.
N6537.L56 A4 1990

Carter, David E. International corporate design
systems /. New York , 1989- 127 p. : ISBN
0-88108-069-1 **NYPL [3-MDW 91-1143]**

Carter, Elliott, 1908-
Elegy, viola, piano; arr. 1980. American music
for strings [sound recording]. Los Angeles,
Calif. , p1990. 1 sound disc :
Nonesuch D-79002

Carter, Michael, 1944- Framing art : introducing
theory and the visual image / Michael Carter.
Sydney, NSW : Hale & Iremonger, c1990. 211
p. : ill. ; 23 cm. (Transvisual studies) ISBN
0-86806-354-1
1. Art - Historiography. I. Title.
              NYPL [3-MAD 91-2237]

Cartier (Firm)
L'Art de Cartier . [Paris] , 1989. 177 p. : ISBN
2-905028-27-0 DDC 739.27/092/2 20
NK7398.C37 A4 1989

CARTIER (FIRM) - EXHIBITIONS.
L'Art de Cartier . [Paris] , 1989. 177 p. : ISBN
2-905028-27-0 DDC 739.27/092/2 20
NK7398.C37 A4 1989

A cartobibliography of separately published U. S.
Geological Survey special maps and river
surveys /. Stark, Peter L. (Peter LeRoy), 1953-
Santa Cruz, Calif. , 1989. xxii, 336 p. : ISBN
0-939112-14-0 DDC 016.91273 20
Z6027.U5 S7 1989 GA405
              NYPL [Map Div. 90-11842]

La cartografía de la Península Ibèrica i la seva
extensió al continent americà . Cicle de
Conferències sobre Història de Cartografia
(1991 : Barcelona, Spain) Barcelona , 1991. 279
p. : ISBN 84-393-1670-4
              NYPL [Map Div. 91-7426]

Cartographica monograph.
(no. 23) The Purpose and use of national and
regional atlases . Toronto, Canada , 1979. vii,
100 p. : ISBN 0-919870-23-6 (pbk.)
GA101.2 .P87   **NYPL [Map Div. 81-199]**

Cartography and remote sensing imagery.
Ehrenberg, Ralph E., 1937- Scholars' guide to
Washington, D.C., for cartography and remote
sensing imagery . Washington, D.C. , 1987. xx,
385 p. : ISBN 0-87474-406-7 DDC
    026/.912/025753 19
GA193.U5 E37 1987
              NYPL [Map Div. 87-819]

CARTOGRAPHY - ANTARCTIC REGIONS -
    NEW SCHWABENLAND.
Brunk, Karsten. Kartographische Arbeiten und
deutsche Namengebung in Neuschwabenland,
Antarktis . Frankfurt am Main , 1986. 2 v. :
    DDC 912/.989 19
GA357 .B78 1986
              NYPL [Map Div. 91-4127]

CARTOGRAPHY - ASIA - HISTORY.
Asien auf Karten . Weinheim , c1989. xviii p. :
              NYPL [Map Div. 90-11078]

CARTOGRAPHY - BIBLIOGRAPHY.
Information sources in cartography /. London
[England] , New York , c1990. xiii, 540 p. ;
    ISBN 0-408-02458-5 (U. S.) DDC 016.526 20
Z6021 .I53 1990 GA105.3
              NYPL [Map Div. 91-2555]

CARTOGRAPHY - BRAZIL - RECIFE -
    HISTORY.
Atlas histórico cartográfico do Recife /. Recife ,
1988. 1 atlas (114, [10] p.) : ISBN 85-7019-172-3
              NYPL [Map Div. 91-7611]

CARTOGRAPHY - CONGRESSES.
Kartographenkongress (1989 : Vienna, Austria)
Kartographenkongress Wien 1989 . [Wien] ,
c1990. 288 p. : ISBN 3-900830-04-5
              NYPL [Map Div. 91-5664]

CARTOGRAPHY - CYPRUS - HISTORY.
Cyprus . Nicosia , 1986. 12 p., [1] folded leaf
of plates :   **NYPL [Map Div. 90-11332]**

CARTOGRAPHY - GERMANY - HISTORY.
Bucker, Johann. Johann Bucker Karte des
Rheins von Duisburg bis Arnheim aus dem
Jahre 1713 . Düsseldorf , 1984. 1 atlas (14
leaves) : DDC 912/.43 19
G1797.22.R5 B7 1984
              NYPL [Map Div. 90-1]

Jolig, K. Niederlandische Einflüsse in der
deutschen Kartographie besonders des 18.
Jahrhunderts /. Amsterdam , 1980. 82 p. ;
    ISBN 90-6041-143-9
              NYPL [Map Div. 90-7139]

Quad, Matthias, 1557-1613. Einzelkarten des
Matthias Quad (1557-1613) /.
Mönchengladbach , 1984. 1 atlas (1 portfolio
([10] folded leaves of plates)) : DDC 911/.43 19
G1912.2 .Q8 1984 **NYPL [Map Div. 87-177]**

CARTOGRAPHY - GERMANY, WEST -
    FRIESLAND - HISTORY.
Lang, Arend W. Kleine Kartengeschichte
Frieslands zwischen Ems und Jade . Norden ,
1985. 111 p., [16] p. of plates : ISBN
3-922365-56-6 **NYPL [Map Div. 87-222]**

CARTOGRAPHY - GREECE - HISTORY -
    CONGRESSES.
Chartographēsē tou Hellēnikou paraliou kai
nēsiōtikou chōrou . [Athēna] , c1989. 84 p. :
GA881 .C43 1989
              NYPL [Map Div. 91-3879]

CARTOGRAPHY - HISTORY.
Barron, Roderick. Decorative maps /. London ,
1990,c1989. 8 p., 40 leaves of plates : ISBN
1-85170-298-9 **NYPL [Map Div. 91-4236]**

Berthon, Simon. The shape of the World /.
Chicago , 1991. 192 p. : ISBN 0-528-83419-3
              NYPL [Map Div. 91-5306]

From sea charts to satellite images . Chicago ,
1990. xvi, 324 p., [8] p. of plates : ISBN
0-226-07991-0 (alk. paper) DDC 973/.022/3 20
E179 .F84 1990 **NYPL [Map Div. 90-12430]**

R. V. Tooley Ltd. An introduction to the
history of maps and mapmaking. London ,
1980. 68 p. :   **NYPL [Map Div. 91-4077]**

What use is a map?. London , 1989. 40 p. :
    ISBN 0-7123-0197-6 (pbk) DDC 912/.09 19
              NYPL [Map Div. 90-11277]

CARTOGRAPHY - IRAQ - HISTORY.
Sousa, Ahmed. al-'Irāq fī al-Khawāriṭ
al-qadīmah. Baghdād, 1959. 22 p. :
              NYPL [Map-Div. 85-3120]

CARTOGRAPHY - IRELAND - KILDARE
    (COUNTY) - HISTORY.
Taylor, Alexander, d. 1828. A map of the
county of Kildare, 1783 /. Dublin , 1983. 1
atlas (1 portfolio) : ISBN 0-901714-26-7 : DDC
912/.4185 19
G1833.K5 T3 1983
              NYPL [Map Div. 87-747]

CARTOGRAPHY - ISRAEL.
Karṭa (Firm) Atlas of Israel . Tel-Aviv ; New
York : [168] 80 p. : ISBN 0-02-905950-X : DDC
912/.5694 19
G2235 .K3 1985
              NYPL [*P-*PXLB++ 86-3877]

CARTOGRAPHY - ITALY - BRENTA
    MOUNTAINS.
Brenta-Monographie . München [1987] 187
p. :
GA895.B73 B74 1987
              NYPL [Map Div. 91-4143]

CARTOGRAPHY - ITALY - HISTORY.
Ventura, António. Gli stati italiani di Piri
Re'is . [Cavallino] [1991?] 1 atlas ([15] p., 13
leaves of plates) : **NYPL [Map Div. 91-6616]**

CARTOGRAPHY - ITALY - PIEMONTE -
    HISTORY.
Barrera, Francesco. Il Piemonte nella cartografia
degli Stati Sardi tra restaurazione e unità
d'Italia /. [Torino] [1989?] 105 p. :
              NYPL [Map Div. 91-136]

CARTOGRAPHY - ITALY - SARDINIA -
    HISTORY.
Barrera, Francesco. Il Piemonte nella cartografia
degli Stati Sardi tra restaurazione e unità
d'Italia /. [Torino] [1989?] 105 p. :
              NYPL [Map Div. 91-136]

CARTOGRAPHY - NETHERLANDS -
    HISTORY - EXHIBITIONS.
Die Niederlande im Bild alter Karten und
Ansichten . Münster , 1989. 94 p. : ISBN
3-9801781-0-2
              NYPL [Map Div. 90-11773]

CARTOGRAPHY - NOVA SCOTIA -
    HISTORY.
Dawson, Joan, 1932- The mapmaker's eye .
Halifax, N.S. , 1988. x, 156 p. : ISBN
0-921054-12-2
              NYPL [Map Div. 90-11404]

Cartography of the shores and islands of Greece.
Chartographēsē tou Hellēnikou paraliou kai
nēsiōtikou chōrou . [Athēna] , c1989. 84 p. :
GA881 .C43 1989
              NYPL [Map Div. 91-3879]

CARTOGRAPHY - ROMANIA -
    TRANSYLVANIA - HISTORY.
Erdély és a Részek térképe és helységnévtára .
Szeged , 1987 ([Budapest] : Franklin Nyomda)
1 atlas (41, 214 p., [9] p. of plates) : ISBN
963-481-771-8 : DDC 912/.4984 19
G2037.T7 E7 1987
              NYPL [Map Div. 91-145]

CARTOGRAPHY - SPAIN - CONGRESSES.
Cicle de Conferències sobre Història de
Cartografia (1991 : Barcelona, Spain) La
cartografía de la Península Ibèrica i la seva
extensió al continent americà . Barcelona ,
1991. 279 p. : ISBN 84-393-1670-4
              NYPL [Map Div. 91-7426]

CARTOGRAPHY - TURKEY - HISTORY.
Ventura, António. Gli stati italiani di Piri
Re'is . [Cavallino] [1991?] 1 atlas ([15] p., 13
leaves of plates) : **NYPL [Map Div. 91-6616]**

Cartoon & promotional drinking glasses. Hervey,
John. Collector's guide to cartoon &
promotional drinking glasses /. Gas City, IN ,
c1990. x, 180 p. : ISBN 0-89145-443-8 : DDC
    760/.0951/07479493 20
NK5440.D75 H4 1990

Cartoon and promotional drinking glasses.
Hervey, John. Collector's guide to cartoon &
promotional drinking glasses /. Gas City, IN ,
c1990. x, 180 p. : ISBN 0-89145-443-8 : DDC
    760/.0951/07479493 20
NK5440.D75 H4 1990

Cartoon animation . Gray, Milton, 1942-
Northridge, CA , c1991. iv, 124 p. : ISBN
0-9628444-5-4 : DDC 741.5/8/02373 20
NC1765 .G7 1991

CARTOON CHARACTERS - UNITED
    STATES.
Rovin, Jeff. The illustrated encyclopedia of
cartoon animals /. New York , 1991. p. cm.
    ISBN 0-13-275561-0 DDC 741.5/0973 20
NC1766.U5 R6 1991

Cartooning /. Keener, Polly, 1946- Englewood
Cliffs, N.J. , 1991. 191 p. cm. ISBN 0-13-117912-8
    DDC 741.5 20
NC1320 .K44 1991

CARTOONING - SOUTH AFRICA - HISTORY - 20TH CENTURY.
Schoonraad, Murray. Companion to South African cartoonists /. Houghton, Johannesburg , 1989. 398 p. : ISBN 0-86852-114-0 DDC 741.5/092/268 B 20
NC1740.S6 S36 1989

CARTOONING - TECHNIQUE.
Hamm, Jack. Drawing and cartooning 1,001 faces, places, and things /. New York, NY , c1991. p. cm. ISBN 0-399-51687-5 (alk. paper) DDC 741.2 20
NC730 .H25 1991

Keener, Polly, 1946- Cartooning /. Englewood Cliffs, N.J. , 1991. p. cm. ISBN 0-13-117912-8 DDC 741.5 20
NC1320 .K44 1991

CARTOONISTS - BIOGRAPHY.
Muster, Hans Peter. Who's who in satire and humour . Basel , 1989- v. : ISBN 3-909158-25-0 (v. 1) : DDC 741.5/092/2 B 20
NC1305 .M88 1989
NYPL [MDY+ 91-2375]

CARTOONISTS - FRANCE - BIOGRAPHY.
Charpin, Catherine. Les arts incohérents (1882-1893) /. Paris , c1990. 128 p. : ISBN 2-86738-465-6 : DDC 741.5/0944/09034 20
NC1495 .C58 1990

CARTOONISTS - SOUTH AFRICA - BIOGRAPHY.
Schoonraad, Murray. Companion to South African cartoonists /. Houghton, Johannesburg , 1989. 398 p. : ISBN 0-86852-114-0 DDC 741.5/092/268 B 20
NC1740.S6 S36 1989

CARTOONISTS - UNITED STATES - BIOGRAPHY.
Capp, Al, 1909- My well-balanced life on a wooden leg /. Santa Barbara, CA , 1991. p. cm. ISBN 0-936784-93-8 : DDC 741.5/092 B 20
NC1429.C295 A2 1991

Hirschfeld, Al. Hirschfeld . New York : Toronto : p. cm. ISBN 0-684-19365-5 DDC 741.5/092 B 20
NC1429.H527 A2 1991

CARTOONS. see CARICATURES AND CARTOONS.

CARTUJA DE CAZALLA DE LA SIERRA.
Zubillaga, Francisco. Las cartujas de las Cuevas, Cazalla de la Sierra y Granada =. Salzburg , 1979. [109] p. : DDC 726/.7/094682
NA5811.S4876 Z8
NYPL [3-MRBB+ 81-645]

CARTUJA DE GRANADA.
Zubillaga, Francisco. Las cartujas de las Cuevas, Cazalla de la Sierra y Granada =. Salzburg , 1979. [109] p. : DDC 726/.7/094682
NA5811.S4876 Z8
NYPL [3-MRBB+ 81-645]

La Cartuja de Jerez de la Frontera =. Zubillaga, Francisco. Salzburg, Austria , 1978. [97] p. :
NYPL [3-MRBB 90-4725]

CARTUJA DE JEREZ DE LA FRONTERA.
Zubillaga, Francisco. La Cartuja de Jerez de la Frontera =. Salzburg, Austria , 1978. [97] p. :
NYPL [3-MRBB 90-4725]

CARTUJA DE SANTA MARÍA DE LAS CUEVAS (SEVILLE, SPAIN)
Zubillaga, Francisco. Las cartujas de las Cuevas, Cazalla de la Sierra y Granada =. Salzburg , 1979. [109] p. : DDC 726/.7/094682
NA5811.S4876 Z8
NYPL [3-MRBB+ 81-645]

Las cartujas de las Cuevas, Cazalla de la Sierra y Granada =. Zubillaga, Francisco. Salzburg , 1979. [109] p. : DDC 726/.7/094682
NA5811.S4876 Z8
NYPL [3-MRBB+ 81-645]

Carvalhais, Stuart, b. 1887.
Vida e obra de Stuart Carvalhais / [catálogo de Paulo Madeira Rodrigues]. Lisboa : Serviços Culturais da Câmara Municipal de Lisboa, 1982. 244 p., [54] p. of plates : ill. (some col.) ; 24 cm. Spine title: Exposição vida e obra de Stuart, 1982. Catalog of exhibition held May/June 1982 at the Palácio dos Coruchéus, Lisbon, and sponsored by the Câmara Municipal de Lisboa. Includes bibliographical references (p. 247-248).
1. Carvalhais, Stuart, b. 1887 - Exhibitions. I. Rodrigues, Paulo Madeira. II. Lisbon (Portugal).

Câmara Municipal. III. Centro de Artes Plásticas dos Coruchéus. IV. Title. V. Title: Exposição vida e obra de Stuart, 1982.
N7133.C34 A4 1982

CARVALHAIS, STUART, B. 1887 - EXHIBITIONS.
Carvalhais, Stuart, b. 1887. Vida e obra de Stuart Carvalhais /. Lisboa , 1982. 244 p., [54] p. of plates :
N7133.C34 A4 1982

Carvalho, Artur Marques de. Do Mosteiro dos Jerónimos : de Belém, termo de Lisboa / Artur Marques de Carvalho. [Lisbon] : Impr. Nacional-Casa da Moeda, [1990] 281 p. : ill. (some col.) ; 28 cm. (Colecção Presenças da imagem) Originally presented as the author's thesis (mestrado), Universidade Nova de Lisboa, 1984. Includes bibliographical references (p. 273-277).
1. Mosteiro dos Jerónimos (Lisbon, Portugal). 2. Architecture, Manueline - Portugal - Lisbon. 3. Lisbon (Portugal) - Buildings, structures, etc. I. Title. II. Series.
NA5830.M65 C37 1990

CARVING (DECORATIVE ARTS)
Krzyszkowska, O. (Olga) Ivory and related materials . London , 1990. xv, 109 p., [70] p. of plates : ISBN 0-900587-62-8
NYPL [3-MNW 91-7005]

CARVING (DECORATIVE ARTS) - ITALY - EXHIBITIONS.
Maldarelli, Ernesto, 1850-1930. Un artista ferrarese del legno, Ernesto Maldarelli (1850-1930) /. Ferrara , c1989. 107 p. :
NYPL [3-MOC 90-12376]

Carybé /. Carybé, 1911- [Salvador] , 1989. 452 p. : DDC 709/.2 20
N6659.C39 A4 1989

Carybé, 1911-
Carybé / Bruno Furrer ; Apresentação na sobrecapa, Antônio Celestino ; Introdução, Jorge Amado ; Textos, Carybé, Lídia Besouchet, José Cláudio da Silva ; Pesquisa e biografia, Gardênia Melo = Carybé / Bruno Furrer ; Presentation on the dust jacket, Antônio Celestino ; Introduction, Jorge Amado ; Texts, Carybé, Lídia Besouchet, José Cláudio da Silva ; Research and biography, Gardênia Melo. [Salvador] : Odebrecht, 1989. 452 p. : ill. (chiefly col.) ; 33 cm. Portuguese and English. DDC 709/.2 20
1. Carybé, 1911- - Catalogs. I. Furrer, Bruno, 1929-. II. Besouchet, Lídia. III. Silva, José Cláudio da. IV. Title.
N6659.C39 A4 1989

CARYBÉ, 1911- - CATALOGS.
Carybé, 1911- Carybé /. [Salvador] , 1989. 452 p. : DDC 709/.2 20
N6659.C39 A4 1989

Carzou . Carzou, Jean, 1907- Tokyo , c1980. 126 p. :
NYPL [3-MCO C333 91-4298]

Carzou, Jean, 1907-
Carzou : Tokyo, Galerie Mikimoto, 9 octobre-28 octobre 1980. Tokyo : La Galerie, c1980. 126 p. : ill. ; 24 cm. French and Japanese. Added t.p. in Japanese.
1. Carzou, Jean, 1907- - Exhibitions. I. Title.
NYPL [3-MCO C333 91-4298]

CARZOU, JEAN, 1907- - EXHIBITIONS.
Carzou, Jean, 1907- Carzou . Tokyo , c1980. 126 p. : *NYPL [3-MCO C333 91-4298]*

Casa de la Cultura Franz Tamayo. Imaná, Gil, 1933- Gil Imaná . [La Paz, Bolivia , 1989?] 1 v. (unpaged) : DDC 759.984 20
ND349.I43 A4 1989

Casa de las Artesanías del Estado de Michoacán.
El Quehacer de un pueblo . Morelia, Michoacán , 1986. 183, [9] p. : ISBN 968-667-045-9 DDC 745/.0972/37 20
NK845.M53 Q44 1986

CASA DE LOS AZULEJOS (MEXICO CITY, MEXICO)
Rangel, Magdalena E. de. La Casa de los Azulejos . [Mexico] , 1986. 131 p., [10] p. of plates :
NA3511.M65 R35 1986

La casa dei Romani /. De Albentiis, Emidio, 1958- Milano , c1990. 348 p., [8] p. of plates : ISBN 88-304-0930-8 : DDC 728/.0937 20
NA324 .D44 1990   *NYPL [JFD 91-5342]*

CASA DEL CORDÓN (BURGOS, SPAIN)
Ibáñez Pérez, Alberto C. Historia de la Casa del Cordón de Burgos /. [Burgos] , 1987. 359

p. : ISBN 84-505-5944-8
NYPL [3-MQWH 91-7280]

Casa del Mantegna. Giovannoni, Giannino. Mantova e i tarocchi del Mantegna /. Mantova , Faenza [1987] 78 p. :
N6923.M249 A4 1987
NYPL [3-MCF M29 91-7036]

Casa di Dante in Abruzzo.
Alberto Martini e Dante /. Milano , c1989. 431 p. : ISBN 88-435-2984-6
IN PROCESS (ONLINE)
NYPL [3-MCF+ M383 90-11582]

Botticelli e Dante /. Milano , c1990. 361 p. : ISBN 88-435-3329-0
N6923.B67 A4 1990
NYPL [3-MCF+ B75 91-5452]

Casa fiorentina. Maffei, Gian Luigi. La casa fiorentina nella storia della città dalle origini all'Ottocento /. Venezia , 1990. 383 p. : ISBN 88-317-5346-0
NA9053.B58 M3 1990

Casa Llotja de Mar (Barcelona, Spain) Escultura catalana del segle XIX . [Barcelona] [1989] 246 p. : *NYPL [3-MGI+ 91-6802]*

Casado Alcalde, Esteban. Pintores de la Academia de Roma : la primera promoción / Esteban Casado Alcalde. [Madrid] : Ministerio de Asuntos Exteriores, Secretaría de Estado para la Cooperación Internacional y para Iberoamérica, Dirección General de Relaciones Culturales y Científicas ; Barcelona : Lunwerg Editores, [1990] 331 p. : ill. ; 32 cm. Spanish and English. ISBN 84-7782-088-0
1. Academia Española de Bellas Artes en Roma. I. Title. *NYPL [3-MCP+ 91-7960]*

Casal García, Raquel. Colección de glíptica del Museo Arqueológico Nacional (serie de entalles romanos) / Raquel Casal García. [Spain] : Ministerio de Cultura, Dirección General de Bellas Artes y Archivos, Dirección General de los Museos Estatales, [1990?] 2 v. : ill. ; 29 cm. Includes bibliographical references and indexes. ISBN 84-7483-657-3 (set)
1. Gems - Catalogs. 2. Art - Spain - Madrid - Catalogs. 3. Museo Arqueológico Nacional (Spain) - Catalogs. I. Title.
NK5511.S67 M344 1990

Casale, Gerardo.
I Premiati dell'Accademia, 1682-1754 /. Roma , c1989. 189 p. : ISBN 88-7140-010-0
NYPL [3-MBH 91-4486]

Prize winning drawings from the Roman Academy 1682-1754 =. Roma , c1990. 189 p. : ISBN 88-7140-013-5
NYPL [3-MBH 91-5071]

Casanave, Martha. Past lives / photographs by Martha Casanave with essays by Ted Orland and Lyn Hejinian. 1st ed. Boston : David R. Godine, 1991. 55 p. : ill. (some col.) ; 32 cm. ISBN 0-87923-872-0
I. Title. *NYPL [MFX+ (Casanave) 91-4962]*

Casas de Playa Ancha . Waisberg, Myriam. Santiago [Chile] , 1988. 108 p., [1] folded leaf of plates :
NA867.V34 W34 1988

Casas en la isla de Ibiza. Maisons sur l'île d'Ibiza. Bruxelles , 1990. 127 p. : ISBN 2-87143-072-6
NA7386.I25 M35 1990

Casas Reales.
(2. etapa, no. 20) Pérez Montas, Eugenio. Carimos . Santo Domingo, República Dominicana , 1989. 358 p. :
NA791 .P47 1989

Casazza, Ornella.
Baldini, Umberto. La Cappella Brancacci /. Milano , 1990. 377 p. : ISBN 88-435-3199-9
ND2757.F5 B3 1990
NYPL [3-MLP 91-7284]

La Cappella Brancacci : conservazione e restauro nei documenti della grafica antica / Ornella Casazza, Paola Cassinelli Lazzeri. Modena : Panini, [1989] 108 p. : ill. (some col.) ; 31 cm. Includes bibliographical references. ISBN 88-7686-147-5
1. Cappella Brancacci (Santa Maria del Carmine (Church : Florence, Italy). I. Cassinelli Lazzeri, Paola. II. Title.
IN PROCESS (ONLINE)
NYPL [3-MLP+ 91-4774]

Casciani, Stefano, 1955- Arte industriale : gioco, oggetto, pensiero Danese e la sua produzione / Stefano Casciani ; contributo di Bruno Munari ; postfazione di Renato Pedio. Milano : Arcadia, c1988. 194 p. : ill. (some col.), ports. ; 31 cm. (Dal progetto al produtto . 5) Includes index. Bibliography: p. 189-190. ISBN 88-85684-21-1
1. Danese (Firm). 2. Design, Industrial - Italy. 3. Art and industry. I. Munari, Bruno. II. Pedio, Renato, 1929-. III. Title. IV. Series.
NYPL [3-MNE+ 90-12329]

Case rurali in Svizzera. Gschwend, Max. Bauernhäuser der Schweiz =. Blauen , c1988. 306 p. : ISBN 3-907080-07-6
NYPL [3-MRGF+ 89-25516]

Casorati . Casorati, Felice, 1883-1963. Milano , 1989. 171 p. : ISBN 88-435-3139-5
NYPL [3-MCF C338 90-13079]

Casorati, Felice, 1883-1963. Casorati : [mostra antologica : Milano, Palazzo Reale, 17 marzo-20 maggio 1990 / mostra a cura di Claudia Gian Ferrari ; catalogo a cura di Maria Mimita Lamberti]. Milano : Electa, 1989. 171 p. : ill. (chiefly col.) ; 28 cm. Includes bibliographical references (p. 168). ISBN 88-435-3139-5
1. Casorati, Felice, 1883-1963 - Exhibitions. I. Lamberti, Maria Mimita. II. Gian Ferrari, Claudia. III. Palazzo reale di Milano. IV. Title.
NYPL [3-MCF C338 90-13079]

CASORATI, FELICE, 1883-1963 - EXHIBITIONS. Casorati, Felice, 1883-1963. Casorati . Milano , 1989. 171 p. : ISBN 88-435-3139-5
NYPL [3-MCF C338 90-13079]

Caspar David Friedrich . Friedrich, Caspar David, 1774-1840. [Hamburg] [1990] 35 p. :
NC251.F66 A4 1990

Caspar David Friedrich and the subject of landscape /. Koerner, Joseph Leo. London , 1990. 256 p. : ISBN 0-948462-13-2 : DDC 759.3 20
ND588.F   NYPL [3-MCK F91 91-4267]

Caspar David Friedrich and the subject of landscape /. Koerner, Joseph Leo. New Haven , 1990. 256 p. : ISBN 0-300-04926-9 DDC 759.3 20
ND588.F75 K64 1990
NYPL [3-MCK F91 91-7554]

Caspar Walter Rauh, 1912-1983 . Rauh, Caspar Walter, 1912-1983. München [1987] 16 p. :
NYPL [MDG (Rauh) 90-11352]

Casper, Geraldine J. Bergstrom-Mahler Museum. Glass paperweights of the Bergstrom-Mahler Museum /. Richmond, Va. , New York , c1989. xxxv, 112, [16] p. : ISBN 0-927997-00-2 DDC 748.8/4/07477564 20
NK5440.P3 B44 1989
NYPL [3-MPW 91-6422]

Cass, Bill. Environmental figuration . Springfield, Ill. , c1990. 31 p. : ISBN 0-89792-130-5 DDC 757/.09773/1107477325 20
ND1292 .E59 1990

Cassa di risparmio di Genova e Imperia. Ceramica in banca . Albisola Superiore , 1989. 78 p. : *NYPL [3-MPGD 91-6609]*

CASSA DI RISPARMIO DI GENOVA E IMPERIA - ART COLLECTIONS - EXHIBITIONS. Ceramica in banca . Albisola Superiore , 1989. 78 p. : *NYPL [3-MPGD 91-6609]*

Cassani, Silvia. All'ombra del Vesuvio . Napoli , c1990. xxiv, 455 p. : ISBN 88-435-3140-9
NYPL [3-MAMY 91-6399]

CASSATT, MARY, 1844-1926 - CATALOGUES RAISONNÉS. Breeskin, Adelyn Dohme, 1896- Mary Cassatt . Washington, D.C. , 1991. p. cm. ISBN 0-87474-100-9 DDC 759.13 20
N6537.C35 A4 1991

CASSATT, MARY, 1844-1926 - JUVENILE LITERATURE. Turner, Robyn. Mary Cassatt /. Boston , 1992. p. cm. ISBN 0-316-85650-9 : DDC 759.13 B 20
ND237.C3 T87 1992

CASSATT, MARY, 1845-1926 - EXHIBITIONS. Pari no joryü gaka 6-nin ten . [Tokyo] 1983. 190 p. : *NYPL [3-MC 90-9733]*

Cassell's styles in art. Belli Barsali, Isa. [Smalto in Europa. English.] European enamels /. London , 1988. 157 p. : ISBN 0-304-32179-6 (pbk) DDC 738.4/094 19
NYPL [3-MNV 90-9465]

Zimelli, Umberto. [Ferro battuto. English.] Decorative ironwork /. [London , 1987. 154 p. : ISBN 0-304-32158-3 (pbk.) : DDC 739/.474 19
NK8242   NYPL [3-MNK 91-5042]

Cassiano dal Pozzo : atti del Seminario internazionale di studi / a cura di Francesco Solinas. Roma : De Luca, c1989. 260 p. : ill., facsims. ; 24 cm. Italian, English, and French. "Seminario su Cassiano dal Pozzo svoltosi a Napoli all'Istituto Universitario "Suor Orsola Benincasa" il 18 e 19 dicembre 1987"--T.p. verso. At head of title: Istituto universitario "Suor Orsola Benincasa", Napoli. Progretto di Ateneo: Le Corrispondenze letterarie, scientifiche ed erudite dal Rinascimento all'età moderna, Università di Roma "La Sapienza." Includes bibliographical references.
1. Dal Pozzo, Cassiano, 1588-1657 - Art collections - Congresses. I. Solinas, Francesco. II. Istituto universitario di magistero "Suor Orsola Benincasa". III. Università degli studi di Roma "La Sapienza.".
NYPL [3-MAVC 90-12003]

Cassinelli Lazzeri, Paola. Casazza, Ornella. La Cappella Brancacci . Modena [1989] 108 p. : ISBN 88-7686-147-5
IN PROCESS (ONLINE)
NYPL [3-MLP+ 91-4774]

CASTAGNO, ANDREA DEL, 1423-1457 - CRITICISM AND INTERPRETATION. Spencer, John R. (John Richard) Andrea del Castagno and his patrons /. Durham , 1991. p. cm. ISBN 0-8223-1150-X DDC 759.5 20
ND623.C47 S64 1991

Castagno, John, 1930- Artists' monograms and indiscernible signatures : an international directory, 1800-1991 / by John Castagno. Metuchen, N.J. : Scarecrow Press, 1991. p. cm. Includes index. ISBN 0-8108-2415-9 DDC 702/.78 20
1. Artists' marks - Directories. 2. Monograms - Directories. 3. Autographs - Directories. I. Title.
N45 .C374 1991

Castaño Castillo, Alvaro, 1920- Cronología de la cultura, 1950-1990 /. [Bogotá, Colombia] , 1990. 524 p. : ISBN 958-9138-62-4 DDC 700/.9/045 20
NX535.B64 C76 1990

Las castas mexicanas . García Sáiz, Maria Concepción. [S.l.] , 1989 (Milano) 253 p. :
NYPL [3-MCY+ 91-4969]

Castedo, Leopoldo. Historia del arte iberoamericano / Leopoldo Castedo. Madrid : Alianza Editorial, c1988. 2 v. : ill. ; 26 cm. Includes bibliographies and indexes. CONTENTS. - 1. Precolombino. El arte colonial -- 2. Siglo XIX. Siglo XX. ISBN 84-206-9597-1 (obra completa)
1. Art, Latin American - History. I. Title.
NYPL [3-MAM 89-11457]

Castel Sant'Elmo (Naples, Italy) All'ombra del Vesuvio . Napoli , c1990. xxiv, 455 p. : ISBN 88-435-3140-9
NYPL [3-MAMY 91-6399]

La Pittura russa nell'età romantica . Bologna , c1990. lx, 190 p. : ISBN 88-7779-129-2
IN PROCESS (ONLINE)
NYPL [3-MCY 90-11768]

Castelao . Castelao, 1886-1950. Sada, A Coruña , 1982. 183 p. : ISBN 84-7492-114-7
NYPL [3-MEM (Castelao) 90-5990]

Castelao, 1886-1950. Castelao : escolma / edición de Clodio González Pérez. Sada, A Coruña : Edicións do Castro, 1982. 183 p. : ill. ; 18 cm. (Os Nosos humoristas . 1) Bibliography: p. 28-30. ISBN 84-7492-114-7
1. Spanish wit and humor, Pictorial. I. González Pérez, Clodio. II. Title. III. Series.
NYPL [3-MEM (Castelao) 90-5990]

Castellani, Eugenio. Bardazzi, Silvestro. Arredi e paramenti . Prato , c1988. 318 p. :
NYPL [3-MRBD+ 90-11027]

Castelli e ville del Lazio /. Torselli, Giorgio. Roma , c1983. 284 p., [8] folded leaves of plates : *NYPL [3-MQWB+ 90-12978]*

Castelli, Feigen, Corcoran. Starr, Sandra Leonard. Joseph Cornell and the ballet /. New York ,

c1983. viii, 87 p. : DDC 709/.2/4 19
N6537.C66 A4 1983
NYPL [MCX C795 84-702]

Castello di Belgioioso : "descrizione della Villa di Belgioioso" con le incisioni di Marc'Antonio Dal Re / a cura di Saverio Lomartire. Milano : Edizioni Targa Italiana, 1987. 15 p. : ill. ; 32 cm. + [31] folded leaves of plates. Issued in portfolio. Includes bibliographical references (p. 15). ISBN 88-7111-010-2
1. Castello di Belgioioso (Belgioioso, Italy). 2. Belgioioso (Italy) - Buildings, structures, etc. I. Del Re, Marc'Antonio, 1697-1766. II. Lomartire, Saverio. III. Centro arte e cultura Castello di Belgioioso.
NYPL [MDG+ (Dal Re) 90-10839]

CASTELLO DI BELGIOIOSO (BELGIOIOSO, ITALY) Castello di Belgioioso . Milano , 1987. 15 p. : ISBN 88-7111-010-2
NYPL [MDG+ (Dal Re) 90-10839]

Castello di Rivoli (Museum : Turin, Italy) Bianchi, Domenico, 1955- Domenico Bianchi . [Turin] [1989] 1 v. (unpaged) :
N6923.B557 A4 1989

Charlton, Alan. Alan Charlton . [Turin] [1989] 1 v. (unpaged) : DDC 759.2 20
ND497.C5455 A4 1989

Fabro, Luciano, 1936- Luciano Fabro . Bompiani [Turin] , c1989. 254 p. ::
NYPL [3-MGO (Fabro) 90-11538]

Förg, Günther, 1952- Günther Förg . [Turin] [1989] 1 v. (unpaged) : DDC 709/.2 20
N6888.F62 A4 1989a

Verhoef, Toon, 1946- Toon Verhoef . [Turin] [1989] 1 v. (unpaged) : DDC 759.9492 20
ND653.V453 A4 1989

Il Castello di Udine /. Bergamini, Guiseppe. [Udine] [1990] vii, 273 p. :
NYPL [3-MQWB+ 91-3865]

CASTELLO DI UDINE. Bergamini, Guiseppe. Il Castello di Udine /. [Udine] [1990] vii, 273 p. :
NYPL [3-MQWB+ 91-3865]

Castello Trecentesco (Celano, Italy) Triennale internazionale d'arte sacra (1989 : Castello Trecentesco (Celano, Italy)) Triennale internazionale d'arte sacra . Bologna , c1989. 204 p. : ISBN 88-85638-84-8
IN PROCESS (ONLINE)
NYPL [3-MAW (Celano) 91-6444]

Castelnuovo, Enrico. Imago lignea . Trento, c1989. 287 p. : ISBN 88-85114-07-5 *NYPL [3-MGI+ 91-4470]*

Imago lignea . Trento, Italia , c1989. 287 p. : ISBN 88-85114-07-5 : DDC 730/.945/38 20
NB1255.I8 I45 1989

Petit Larousse de la peinture. Italian. Dizionario della pittura e dei pittori /. Torino , c1989- v. : ISBN 88-06-11573-1 (v. 1)
NYPL [MAO 90-2147]

Castelo, Hernán Rodríguez. see Rodríguez Castelo, Hernán, 1933-

Castes, a genre of Mexican painting. García Sáiz, Maria Concepción. Las castas mexicanas . [S.l.] , 1989 (Milano) 253 p. :
NYPL [3-MCY+ 91-4969]

Castiglione, Giovanni Benedetto, 1610?-1670? Il Genio di Giovanni Benedetto Castiglione, il Grechetto /. Genova , c1990. 267 p. : ISBN 88-7058-351-1
NYPL [3-MCF C35 90-11510]

CASTIGLIONE, GIOVANNI BENEDETTO, 1610?-1670? - EXHIBITIONS. Il Genio di Giovanni Benedetto Castiglione, il Grechetto /. Genova , c1990. 267 p. : ISBN 88-7058-351-1
NYPL [3-MCF C35 90-11510]

Castillo, José del, 1947- Artesanía dominicana / José del Castillo, Manuel A. García Arévalo. Santo Domingo, República Dominicana : Consorcio Financiero Bantillano, 1989. 125 p. : col. ill. ; 26 cm. Spanish and English. Includes bibliographical references (p. 96-97). DDC 745/.097293 20
1. Decorative arts - Dominican Republic. 2. Handicraft - Dominican Republic. 3. Folk art - Dominican Republic. I. García Arévalo, Manuel

195

ART & ARCHITECTURE: 1991
Cataloghi (Vatican City. Direzione generale dei monumenti, musei

Antonio. II. Title.
NK886.D65 C38 1989

Castillo, Richard Griswold del. see **Griswold del Castillo, Richard.**

CASTILLO VELASCO, FERNANDO, 1918- - CATALOGS.
Eliash, Humberto. Fernando Castillo .
[Santiago, Chile] . 237 p. : ISBN 958-9082-44-0
(colección) DDC 720/.92 20
NA869.C37 A4 1990

Castillos /. Cooper, Jason, 1942- [Castles.
Spanish.] Vero Beach, Fla. , 1991. p. cm. ISBN
0-86592-937-8 DDC 728.8/1/094 20
NA7710 .C6918 1991

CASTLE - FRANCE - HAUT-LÉON.
Châteaux de Haut-Léon . Saint-Brice-en
Coglès , c1987. 32 p. : ISBN 2-86934-006-0
NYPL [3-MQWF+ 90-5362]

Castle, Frederick Ted, 1938- Ouattara. Ouattara.
New York, N.Y. , 1990. [47] p. : ISBN
0-922678-07-3 DDC 759.96668 20
N7399.I83 O922 1990
NYPL [3-MCZ+ O877 91-3374]

Castle, Wendell, 1932-
Angel chairs : new works by Wendell Castle /
essays by Arthur C. Danto, Peter T. Joseph,
and Emma T. Cobb. New York : Peter Joseph
Gallery, 1991. 111 p. : ill. (some col.) ; 28 cm.
Catalog of an exhibition held at the Peter Joseph
Gallery. Includes bibliographical references (p. 111).
ISBN 0-9628849-0-1 DDC 749.213 20
1. Castle, Wendell, 1932- - Exhibitions. 2. Furniture -
United States - History - 20th century - Exhibitions. I.
Danto, Arthur Coleman, 1924-. II. Joseph, Peter T.
(Peter Thomas), 1950-. III. Cobb, Emma T. IV. Peter
Joseph Gallery. V. Title.
NK2439.C3 A4 1991

CASTLE, WENDELL, 1932- - EXHIBITIONS.
Castle, Wendell, 1932- Angel chairs . New
York , 1991. 111 p. : ISBN 0-9628849-0-1 DDC
749.213 20
NK2439.C3 A4 1991

Castles /. Cooper, Jason, 1942- Vero Beach, Fla. ,
1991. p. cm. ISBN 0-86592-629-8 DDC
728.8/1/094 20
NA7710 .C69 1991

CASTLES - BELGIUM - GUIDE-BOOKS.
Remoortere, Julien van. Ippa's kastelengids voor
België /. Tielt , 1988. 431 p. : ISBN
90-209-1647-5
NA7725 .R46 1988

CASTLES - CZECHOSLOVAKIA.
Hrady a zámky v Československu . Praha ,
Martin , 1990. 383 p. : ISBN 80-7038-100-0 :
NA7720 .H73 1990

CASTLES - CZECHOSLOVAKIA - EXHIBITIONS.
Machytka, Lubor. Barokní zátiší . Pardubice ,
1988. 37 p. :
ND182.B3 M3 1988

CASTLES - CZECHOSLOVAKIA - MAPS.
Mapa hradů a zámků Československé republiky
/. [Praha] , 1959. 80 p., [16] p. of plates :
NYPL [Map Div. 88-934]

CASTLES - FRANCE.
Le Château en France /. Paris , 1988. 448 p.,
[16] p. of plates : ISBN 2-7013-0741-4
NYPL [3-MQWF+ 90-11996]

CASTLES - FRANCE - DESIGN AND CONSTRUCTION.
Le Château en France /. Paris , 1988. 448 p.,
[16] p. of plates : ISBN 2-7013-0741-4
NYPL [3-MQWF+ 90-11996]

CASTLES - FRANCE - HISTORY.
Le Château en France /. Paris , 1988. 448 p.,
[16] p. of plates : ISBN 2-7013-0741-4
NYPL [3-MQWF+ 90-11996]

CASTLES - FRANCE - LOIRE VALLEY.
Nagel Publishers. Châteaux of the Loire.
Geneva ; New York [c1971] 192, 10 p.
NYPL [JFB 90-371]

CASTLES - FRANCE - MAINCY.
France, Anatole, 1844-1924. Le château de
Vaux-le-Vicomte /. Etrépilly , 1988. v, 212 p.,
[8] p. of plates : ISBN 2-905563-19-2
NYPL [3-MQWF 90-12695]

CASTLES - ITALY - CHIANTI MOUNTAINS.
Bosi, Enrico. Di castello in castello . Milano ,

c1990. 279 p. : ISBN 88-85271-02-2
IN PROCESS (ONLINE)
NYPL [3-MQWB 91-7180]

CASTLES - ITALY - LAZIO.
Torselli, Giorgio. Castelli e ville del Lazio /.
Roma , c1983. 284 p., [8] folded leaves of
plates : *NYPL [3-MQWB+ 90-12978]*

CASTLES - ITALY - PESARO.
L'Isauro e la foglia . Provincia di Pesaro e
Urbino :bAmministrazione Provinciale di Pesaro
e Urbino, 1986. 428 p. :
NYPL [3-MCF L782 90-10784]

CASTLES - JUVENILE LITERATURE.
Cooper, Jason, 1942- Castles /. Vero Beach,
Fla. , 1991. p. cm. ISBN 0-86592-629-8 DDC
728.8/1/094 20
NA7710 .C69 1991

Cooper, Jason, 1942- [Castles. Spanish.]
Castillos /. Vero Beach, Fla. , 1991. p. cm.
ISBN 0-86592-937-8 DDC 728.8/1/094 20
NA7710 .C6918 1991

CASTLES - NETHERLANDS.
Guillermo, Jorge. Dutch houses and castles /.
London , New York, N.Y. , c1990. 208 p. :
ISBN 1-85043-237-6 DDC 720.9492 20
NYPL [3-MQW+ 91-3636]

Castleton, Kenneth Bitner, 1903- Petroglyphs and
pictographs of Utah / Kenneth B. Castleton.
Salt Lake City : Utah Museum of Natural
History, 1978-1979. 2 v. : ill. ; 28 cm. Includes
indexes. Bibliography: v. 1, p. 211-214; v. 2, p. 335-339.
CONTENTS. - v. 1. The east and northwest.--v. 2. The
south, central, west, and northwest. DDC
709/.01/1309792 19
1. Indians of North America - Utah - Art. 2. Indians of
North America - Utah - Antiquities. 3. Rock paintings -
Utah. 4. Petroglyphs - Utah. 5. Utah - Antiquities. I.
Title.
E78.U55 C37 *NYPL [HBC 81-457]*

Castri, Serenella. Imago lignea . Trento , c1989.
287 p. : ISBN 88-85114-07-5
NYPL [3-MGI+ 91-4470]

Castriota, David, 1950- Riegl, Alois, 1858-1905.
[Stilfragen. English.] Problems of style .
Princeton, NJ , 1993. p. cm. ISBN
0-8071-1706-4 : DDC 745.4/4 20
NK1175 .R513 1993

Castro, Laura. Resende, Júlio, 1917- Júlio
Resende /. Lisboa , 1989. 122 p. : DDC 759.69
20
ND833.R46 A4 1990

Castro, Maria de Lourdes de Mello e, 1903-
Maria de Lourdes de Mello e Castro / [texto
de Maria Matilde Tomaz do Couto ; texto de
apresentação de João Pinharanda ; coordenação,
João Manuel P. Vargas Moniz]. Tomar
[Portugal] : Fábricas Mendes Godinho, 1989.
99 p. : chiefly col. ill. ; 31 cm.
1. Castro, Maria de Lourdes de Mello e, 1903- -
Catalogs. I. Couto, Maria Matilde Tomaz do. II. Title.
NYPL [3-MCQ+ C355 90-12670]

**CASTRO, MARIA DE LOURDES DE MELLO
E, 1903- - CATALOGS.**
Castro, Maria de Lourdes de Mello e, 1903-
Maria de Lourdes de Mello e Castro /. Tomar
[Portugal] , 1989. 99 p. :
NYPL [3-MCQ+ C355 90-12670]

Castro, Raquel. Fruto Vivas : del barro al metal /
Raquel Castro. [Caracas] : CVG Siderúrgica del
Orinoco, 1989. 176 p., [16] p. of plates : ill.
(some col.) ; 23 x 30 cm. Includes bibliographical
references (p. 171-175). ISBN 980-300-866-8 DDC
720/.92 20
1. Vivas, Fruto, 1928-. 2. Architecture, Modern - 20th
century - Venezuela. I. Title. II. Title: Del barro al
metal.
NA939.V57 C37 1989

CASTRUCCI, ANDREW - EXHIBITIONS.
Fekner, John. Artist as apolitical sensor .
Brookville, N.Y. , 1990. 28 p. :
NYPL [3-MAMT 91-5026]

Cat. (Centro Di)
(169, etc) La Galleria del Costume. Firenze ,
c1983- v. : ISBN 88-7038-077-7 (v. 1)
NYPL [3-MME 84-2509]

(203) 'Imparaticci' =. [Firenze] , c1986. 78, [1]
p. : ISBN 88-7038-120-X
NK9109 .I663 1986
NYPL [3-MOT 90-10855]

(226) Europa oggi . Firenze , Milano , c1988.
253 p. : ISBN 88-435-2560-3
NYPL [3-MAL 89-1689]

(239) Visser Travagli, Anna Maria. Ceramiche a
Ferrara in età estense dalla collezione Pasetti .
Firenze , c1989. 81 p. : ISBN 88-7038-175-7
NYPL [3-MPGD 90-10656]

The cat in photography /. Eauclaire, Sally.
Boston , c1990. 198 p. : ISBN 0-8212-1782-8
DDC 779/.092 20
TR729.C3 E28 1990 *NYPL [MFW 91-2489]*

CATACOMBS - ITALY - ROME.
Wronikowska, Bożena. Picturae sacrae . Lublin ,
1990. 228 p. : ISBN 83-228-0163-7
ND2757.R6 W7 1990

Catalá, Francesc. see **Català Roca, Francesc.**

Català Roca, Francesc. Permanyer, L. Clavé,
escultor /. Barcelona, España , c1989. 286 p. :
ISBN 84-343-0557-7
NYPL [3-MGO+ (Clavé) 90-605]

Catalan painters and sculptors : the second
vanguard : the Baruch College Gallery, Baruch
College of the City University of New York,
February 9 to March 7. [Spain] : Generalitat de
Catalunya, [1990] 66 p. : col. ill. ; 30 cm.
1. Art, Spanish - Spain - Catalonia - Exhibitions. 2. Art,
Modern - 20th century - Spain - Catalonia -
Exhibitions. I. Baruch College Gallery.
NYPL [3-MAML+ 91-4202]

Catàleg del Museu de les Arts Gràfiques .
(2) Obiols i Palau, Josep, 1894-1967. Xilografies
de Josep Obiols . [Barcelona] [1990?] 125 p. :
ISBN 84-7609-364-0
NE1162.5.O25 A4 1990

Catalog of American collectibles. Ketchum,
William C., 1931- The new and revised catalog
of American collectibles /. New York City ,
1990. 320 p. : ISBN 0-8317-6316-7
NYPL [3-MAVC 91-7510]

Catalog of International Silver Co. International
Silver Company. Catalogue of International
Silver Co. . New York, U. S. A. [1915?] 160
p. :
NK7241.5.I58 A4 1915

Catalog of the exhibition of fine arts.
Pan-American Exposition (1901 : Buffalo, N.Y.)
Catalogue of the exhibition of fine arts / .
Brewster, NY (Drawer 9, Brewster 10509)
[1990?] 92 p. ; DDC 707/.4/74797 20
N4485 .A66 1901

**Catalog over det Bergenske Museums
Malerisamling, 1840.** Bergens billedgalleri.
[Bergen] , 1961. 32 p. : *NYPL [3-MAVZ
(Bergen, Norway) 90-5454]*

Cataloghi d'arte (Treviso, Italy)
Plessi, Fabrizio, 1940- Plessi /. Treviso , c1990.
175 p. : ISBN 88-85066-70-4 DDC 700/.92 20
N6923.P55 A4 1990
NYPL [3-MGO+ (Plessi) 91-5437]

Cataloghi dei Civici musei di Reggio nell'Emilia .
(10) Civica galleria "Anna e Luigi Parmeggiani."
Dipinti della Civica galleria "Anna e Luigi
Parmeggiani." Reggio Emilia [Italy] , 1988- v. :
NYPL [3-MCE 91-6861]

**Cataloghi (Gabinetto disegni e stampe degli
Uffizi) .**
(73) Cappugi, Luana. Bruno Innocenti .
Firenze , 1991. 79 p., [51] p. of plates : ISBN
88-22-23837-0
NYPL [3-MCF I57 91-5735]

Cataloghi (Prato, Italy) .
(4) Un'altra obiettività /. Milano , c1989. 253
p. : ISBN 88-7017-067-5
NYPL [MFW 90-3005]

(5) Schnabel, Julian, 1951- Julian Schnabel /.
Prato , c1989. 159 p. : ISBN 88-85191-00-2
NYPL [3-MCX S358 90-4741]

(6) Artisti russi contemporanei . Prato , c1990.
208 p. : ISBN 88-85191-01-0
NYPL [3-MAM 90-10469]

**Cataloghi (Vatican City. Direzione generale dei
monumenti, musei e gallerie pontificie.
Reparto per l'arte bizantina, medioevale e
moderna)**
(1) Vatican. Pinacoteca. I dipinti dal X secolo
fino a Giotto /. [Città del Vaticano] , 1979. 66
p., [71] p. of plates : ISBN 88-20-90009-2
NYPL [MAVZ (Vatican) 82-938]

BIBLIOGRAPHIC GUIDE

Cataloghi (Vatican City. Direzione generale dei monumenti, musei

196

Pinacoteca vaticana. Il Trecento, Firenze e
Siena /. Città del Vaticano , 1987. 84 p., [109]
p. of plates : ISBN 88-20-91673-8
    NYPL [MAVZ+ (Vatican) 89-3559]

CATALOGING OF GRAPHIC MATERIALS.
LC thesaurus for graphic materials .
Washington, D.C. , 1987. xxvi, 591 p. ; DDC
025.3/47 19
Z695.718 .L37 1987   NYPL [MFW 88-830]

CATALOGING OF PICTURES.
LC thesaurus for graphic materials .
Washington, D.C. , 1987. xxvi, 591 p. ; DDC
025.3/47 19
Z695.718 .L37 1987   NYPL [MFW 88-830]

**Catálogo / Sala de Exposiciones de la Dirección
General de Bellas Artes .**
(no. 72) XIV Salón de Grabado, diciembre de
1964 . [Madrid] [1964] [64] p. :
MLCS 83/618 (N)   NYPL [MDBF 90-5976]

Catálogo de artistas y artesanos de México /
Glorinela González Franco ... [et al.]. 1. ed.
México, D.F. : Instituto Nacional de
Antropologia e Historia, 1986 [i.e. 1987] 292
p. : facsims. ; 27 cm. (Colección Fuentes) Lists
artists and artisans of Mexico City (1554-1869) and
elsewhere in Mexico (1645-1866). Includes
bibliographical references (p. [127]-129) and indexes.
ISBN 968-603-853-1
*1. Artists - Mexico - Registers. 2. Artists - Mexico -
Autographs. I. González Franco, Glorinela. II. Series.*
N6547.M56 C37 1986

Catálogo de las pinturas. Madrid (Spain). Museo
Municipal. Madrid , 1990. xiv, 385 p. : ISBN
84-505-9855-9 DDC 759.6/074/4641 20
ND801 .M25 1990

**Catálogo de porcelana y cerámica española del
Patrimonio Nacional en los palacios reales /.**
Sánchez Hernández, María Leticia. Madrid ,
1989- v. : ISBN 84-7120-133-X
IN PROCESS (ONLINE)
    NYPL [3-MPG+ 91-3398]

Catalogo dei disegni antichi /. Gallerie
dell'Accademia di Venezia. Milano , c1982- v. :
  ISBN 88-435-0801-6 (v. 1) DDC
741.94/074/0531 19
NC255 .G35 1982   NYPL [3-MBH 85-260]

**Catálogo del Gabinete de Estampas del Museo
Municipal de Madrid /.** Madrid (Spain). Museo
Municipal. Gabinete de Estampas. [Madrid] ,
1985- v. in : ISBN 84-398-4272-4 (set) DDC
769.946/074/0641 19
NE699 .M33 1985   NYPL [MDE 91-282]

**Catálogo del Museo Episcopal y Capitular de
Huesca /.** Museo Episcopal y Capitular de
Huesca (Spain) Zaragoza [1984?] 223 p., [6] p.
of plates : ISBN 84-7611-002-2
N7823.S7 H846 1984
    NYPL [3-MAIH 87-353]

**Catálogo del patrimonio artístico cultural de
Michoacán /.** García Orozco, Aurora. Morelia,
Michoacán, México , 1986. 180 p. : ISBN
968-667-047-5
N6556M5 G3 1986

Catalogo della mostra. Magagnato, Licisco.
Verona, 1971. 147 p.
    NYPL [3-MCE 90-6447]

Catalogo della Pinacoteca Vaticana .
(v. 1 1) Vatican. Pinacoteca. I dipinti dal X
secolo fino a Giotto /. [Città del Vaticano] ,
1979. 66 p., [71] p. of plates : ISBN
88-20-90009-2
    NYPL [MAVZ (Vatican) 82-938]
(v. 2) Pinacoteca vaticana. Il Trecento, Firenze
e Siena /. Città del Vaticano , 1987. 84 p.,
[109] p. of plates : ISBN 88-20-91673-8
    NYPL [MAVZ+ (Vatican) 89-3559]

Catalogo della pittura italiana del '600 e '700.
Pittura italiana del '600 e '700 . Milano ,
c1990. 263 p. : ISBN 88-374-1141-3 DDC
759.5/09/032 20
ND616 .P576 1990

Catálogo do Museu de Martins Sarmento .
Museu de Martins Sarmento. Guimarães , 1967.
23 p., [19] p. of plates : *NYPL [3-MAVZ
(Guimarães, Portugal) 90-6061]*

Catalogo generale dei dipinti di Giuseppe Cesetti
/. Bossaglia, Rossana. Milano , c1989- v. :
  ISBN 88-374-1088-3 (v. 1)
    NYPL [3-MCF+ C42 90-10852]

Catalogo generale 1990. Biennale di Venezia
(44th : 1990) Dimensione futuro . [Venezia]
[Milano] , c1990. 348 p. : ISBN 88-20-80356-9
DDC 709/.04/80744531 20
N6488.I8 V43 1990

**Catálogo (Museo de Arte Contemporáneo de
Caracas) .**
(no. 80) Picasso, Pablo, 1881-1973. Picasso .
[Caracas] [1987] 133 p. : ISBN 980-272-025-9
DDC 769.92 20
NE650.P62 A4 1987

Catálogo nacional de arte contemporáneo. Ed.
89/90. Barcelona : Ibérico 2Mil, c1989. 4 v. :
ill. (some col.) ; 28 cm. "Han colaborado en la
elaboración de este catálogo: María Luisa Galanti ... [et
al.]"--V. 1, p. opp. t.p. Issued in a slipcase. Includes
bibliographical references and indexes. CONTENTS. -
v. 1. Artistas -- v. 2. Galerías de arte -- v. 3.
Seleccionados -- v. 4. Joaquim Chancho. Premio Ibérico
2Mil 1989/90. ISBN 84-87433-00-6 (obra completa)
*1. Art, Spanish - Catalogs. 2. Art, Modern - 20th
century - Spain - Catalogs. 3. Artists - Spain -
Biography. 4. Art galleries, Commercial - Spain. I.
Galanti, María Luisa. II. Chancho, Joaquim, 1943-.*
N7108 .C29 1989

Catálogo pernambucano de arte : 1987. 1a. ed.
Recife-PE-Brasil : Grupo X Promoções e
Empreendimentos Artísticos, c1987. 1 v.
(unpaged) : col. ill. ; 30 cm. DDC 709/.2/28134
B 20
*1. Art, Brazilian - Brazil - Pernambuco. 2. Art,
Modern - 20th century - Brazil - Pernambuco. 3.
Artists - Brazil - Pernambuco - Biography. I. Grupo X
Promoções e Empreendimentos Artísticos.*
N6656.P47 C38 1987

Catalogos de arquitectura contemporanea.
Linazasoro, José Ignacio. J. I. Linazasoro /.
Barcelona , c1989. 96 p. : ISBN 84-252-1388-6
    NYPL [3-MQZ (Linazasoro) 90-11075]
Vacchini, Livio, 1933- Livio Vacchini /. Berlin ,
c1987. 96 p. : ISBN 3-433-02275-5
    NYPL [3-MQZ (Vacchini) 90-12536]

Catalogue. Frost & Reed. Bristol [England] ,
1913. 92 p. :   *NYPL [MDF 89-12517]*

**Catalogue complet de l'œuvre de Jean-Emile
Laboureur /.** Laboureur, Sylvain. Neuchâtel,
Suisse , c1989-c1990. 2 v. : ISBN 2-8258-0026-0
(v. 1)
    NYPL [MDG (Laboureur) 90-1276]

Catalogue de base des cartes postales belges =.
Esteveny, François. [Bruxelles] [1987] 269, [2]
p. :
NC1878.7.B4 E88 1987

**Catalogue de la collection de feu Cloud Massot
comprenant--Faïences et porcelaines
anciennes ... :** dont la vente aux enchères aura
lieu à Marseilles ... les 12, 13 mars 1929 ....
[Marseille] : Commissaires-Priseurs de
Marseille, [1929] 34 p., xxxii leaves of plates :
ill. ; 29 cm. Cover title: Collection de feu Cloud
Massot.
*1. - Massot, Cloud - Art collections. I. Title: Collection
de feu Cloud Massot.*
    NYPL [3-MAX (Massot) 86-3753]

Catalogue de l'école française XIX siècle.
Museum Mesdag. Catalogue des collections du
Musée Mesdag XIX siècle . La Haye [1964]
158 p. : *NYPL [3-MAVZ (Hague) 90-7104]*

**Catalogue des collections du Musée Mesdag XIX
siècle .** Museum Mesdag. La Haye [1964] 158
p. :   *NYPL [3-MAVZ (Hague) 90-7104]*

**Catalogue des estampes des trois écoles,
portraits, catafalques, pompes funèbres, plans,
cartes géographiques, etc., qui se trouvent à
Paris, au Musée central des arts .** Muséum
central des arts et de la République (Paris,
France) Paris , an 9 [1801] (Paris : Impr. des
sciences et arts) iv, 40 p. ;
N2030 .R63 1803 .F7

**Catalogue des objets d'art et d'ameublement du
XVIIIe siècle .** Galerie Charpentier. Paris ,
1935. 88 p., 44 leaves of plates :
    NYPL [3-MAX+ (Saint) 91-404]

**Catalogue des peintures du Musée des beaux-arts
de Rouen.** Rouen (France). Musée des beaux
arts. Paris [1967] 156 p.
    NYPL [3-MAVZ (Rouen) 90-6400]

Catalogue des tapisseries. Musées royaux d'art et
d'histoire (Belgium) [Bruxelles, 1956] 94 p.
NK2985.B7 B7   NYPL [3-MOR 91-326]

**Catalogue of a loan exhibition of gothic
tapestries /.** Ackerman, Phyllis, 1893-
[Chicago] , 1926. 55 p. :
    NYPL [3-MOR+ 91-322]

**Catalogue of an exhibition of paintings by Sabina
Teichman .** Teichman, Sabina. New York
[1969] [8] p. :
    NYPL [3-MCX T262 91-4230]

**Catalogue of an exhibition of Persian paintings
from the XIIth to the XVIIIth cent. .** Blochet,
Edgar, 1870- [s.l. , 1930?]. 79 p. :
    NYPL [3-MAF 83-2314]

Catalogue of British oil paintings, 1820-1860 /.
Victoria and Albert Museum. London , 1990.
xx, 314 p. : ISBN 0-11-290463-7 : DDC
759.2/074 19
    NYPL [3-MAVZ+ (London) 90-10927]

**Catalogue of etchings, engravings and color
prints.** Frost & Reed. Catalogue. Bristol
[England] , 1913. 92 p. :
    NYPL [MDF 89-12517]

**Catalogue of furniture in the exhibition of
embroidered quilts from the Museu de Arte
Antiga, Lisboa .** Museu Nacional de Arte
Antiga (Portugal) London , 1978. 1 v.
(unpaged) :   *NYPL [3-MOF 91-296]*

Catalogue of International Silver Co. .
International Silver Company. New York, U.
S.A. [1915?] 160 p. :
NK7241.5.I58 A4 1915

Catalogue of International Silver Company.
International Silver Company. Catalogue of
International Silver Co. . New York, U. S.A.
[1915?] 160 p. :
NK7241.5.I58 A4 1915

Catalogue of maps (June 1971). Nigeria. Survey
Division. Lagos, 1971. 110 p. DDC 016.912/669
Z6027.N55 N54 1971a GA1588
    NYPL [Map Div. 91-1163]

Catalogue of paintings. Birmingham Museums
and Art Gallery. Birmingham [England]
[1960?] 172 p. :   *NYPL [3-MAVZ
(Birmingham, England) 90-6875]*

**Catalogue of selected bronzes, wood-carvings &
sculptures /.** Art Museum, Trivandrum.
[Trivandrum] , 1981. [132] p. :
    NYPL [3-MGI+ 90-12595]

**Catalogue of the art collection, Georgetown
University, Washington,D.C.** Georgetown
University. Washington, D.C. , 1963. 119 p., 33
p. of plates : *NYPL [3-MAVZ (Washington,
D.C.) 91-821]*

Catalogue of the collection, 1969-1990 /.
Brandywine River Museum. Chadds Ford, Pa. ,
c1991. p. DDC 709/.73/07474814 20
N6517 .B7 1991

**Catalogue of the etchings and dry-points of
Childe Hassam, N.A., of the American
Academy of Arts and Letters /.** Hassam,
Childe, 1859-1935. San Francisco , 1989. 224
p. : ISBN 1-556-60029-1
    NYPL [MDG+ (Hassam) 89-27271]

Catalogue of the exhibition of fine arts /.
Pan-American Exposition (1901 : Buffalo, N.Y.)
Brewster, NY (Drawer 9, Brewster 10509)
[1990?] 92 p. ; DDC 707/.4/74797 20
N4485 .A66 1901

**Catalogue of the National Museum of Modern
Art, Tokyo 1964.** Kokuritsu Kindai Bijutsukan
(Japan) Kokuritsu Kindai Bijutsukan shozōhin
mokuroku 1964 =. Tōkyō , Shōwa 39 [1964]
220 p. : *NYPL [3-MAVZ (Tokyo) 90-6959]*

**Catalogue of the Newark Museum Tibetan
collection /.** Newark Museum. Newark, N.J. ,
1983- v. : ISBN 0-932828-12-4 (pbk.) : DDC
709/.51/5074014932 19
N7346.T5 N48 1983   NYPL [MAF 91-997]

**Catalogue of Tibetan manuscripts and xylographs,
and catalogue of thankas, banners and other
paintings and drawings in the library of the
Wellcome Institute for the History of
Medicine /.** Wellcome Institute for the History
of Medicine. Library. London , 1989. xiii, 112
p., [12] p. of plates : ISBN 0-85484-085-0 DDC
011.31 704.948943923074 20
N8193.T52   NYPL [3-MAF+ 90-13612]

**The catalogue raisonné of the prints of Charles
Meryon /.** Schneiderman, Richard S. London ,

1990. 216 p., [1] folded leaf of plates : ISBN
0-906030-23-4 : DDC 769.92 20
NYPL [MDG+ (Meryon) 90-12795]

Catalogue sommaire illustré des peintures /.
Musée d'Orsay. [Paris] , c1990. 2 v. (521 p.) :
ISBN 2-7118-2255-9 (éd. complète)
NYPL [3-MAVZ (Paris) 90-11545]

Catalonia (Spain). Departament de Política
Territorial i Obres Públiques.
Arquitectura . [Spain] [1988?] 187 p. :
NYPL [3-MQWH+ 91-6437]

Arquitectura . [Barcelona?] [1988] 187 p. :
NA1309.C2 A76 1988

Catalonia (Spain). Direcció General
d'Arquitectura i Habitatge. Realitzacions de
la Direcció General d'Arquitectura i Habitatge i
de l'Institut Català del Sòl 1981-1987.
Barcelona [1988?] 2 cases (101 fasc.) : DDC
728/.314/0946709048 20
NA7860 .R35 1988

Catalonia (Spain). Direcció General de Promoció
Cultural. Arts Plàstiques. Jové, Angel. Angel
Jové . [Barcelona] [1991?] 229 p. :
N7113.J68 A4 1991

CATALONIA (SPAIN) - INTELLECTUAL
LIFE - 19TH CENTURY.
Gaudí i el seu temps /. Barcelona , 1990. 255
p. ; ISBN 84-7533-567-5
NA1313.G3 G39 1990

CATALONIA (SPAIN) - INTELLECTUAL
LIFE - 20TH CENTURY.
Gaudí i el seu temps /. Barcelona , 1990. 255
p. ; ISBN 84-7533-567-5
NA1313.G3 G39 1990

CATASTRAL SURVEYS. see REAL
PROPERTY.

Catastrophe according to Hans Burkhardt /.
Burkhardt, Hans Gustav, 1904- Allentown ,
1990. 1 v. (unpaged)
NYPL [3-MCX B953 90-10666]

Catawba County : an architectural history / by
the Catawba County Historical Association.
Virginia Beach, Va. : Donning Co./Publishers,
1991. p. cm. Includes index. ISBN 0-89865-822-5
DDC 720/.9756/785 20
*1. Architecture - North Carolina - CatawbaCounty. I.
Catawba County Historical Association.*
NA730.N82 C383 1991

Catawba County Historical Association. Catawba
County . Virginia Beach, Va. , 1991. p. cm.
ISBN 0-89865-822-5 DDC 720/.9756/785 20
NA730.N82 C383 1991

CATEDRAL DE SANTIAGO DE
COMPOSTELA.
García Iglesias, José Manuel, 1950- A Catedral
de Santiago e o barroco /. Santiago de
Compostela , 1990. 228 p. : ISBN 84-85665-20-1
NA5811.S46 G37 1990
NYPL [3-MRBN+ 91-3888]

A Catedral de Santiago e o barroco /. García
Iglesias, José Manuel, 1950- Santiago de
Compostela , 1990. 228 p. : ISBN 84-85665-20-1
NA5811.S46 G37 1990
NYPL [3-MRBN+ 91-3888]

Cateni, Gabriele. Die Etrusker--Volterra : Kunst,
Kultur, Geschichte : archäologische
Kostbarkeiten aus dem Museum Guarnacci,
Volterra : Ausstellung, Bergisches Museum
Schloss Burg an der Wupper, 25. Mai bis 24.
August 1986 / [Katalogtexte, Gabriele Cateni,
Dirk Soechting]. Solingen : Bergisches Museum,
1986. 90 p. : ill. (some col.), map ; 21 cm.
Includes bibliographical references.
*1. Museo Guarnacci - Exhibitions. 2. Art, Etruscan -
Italy - Volterra - Exhibitions. 3. Art - Italy - Volterra -
Exhibitions. 4. Volterra (Italy) - Antiquities -
Exhibitions. 5. Italy - Antiquities - Exhibitions. I.
Soechting, Dirk. II. Bergisches Museum Schloss Burg
an der Wupper. III. Title.*
NYPL [3-MAE 90-12646]

Cathedral architecture. Briggs, Martin S. (Martin
Shaw), b. 1882- A pictorial guide to cathedral
architecture . [London] 1964. 24 p. :
NYPL [3-MRBR 90-6038]

The cathedral builders /. Perdrizet, Marie-Pierre.
[Bâtisseurs de cathédrales. English.] Brookfield,
Conn. [1992] p. cm. ISBN 1-562-94162-3 DDC
726/.6/0940902 20
NA4830 .P3713 1992

Cathédrale de Bourges. Muté, S. Bourges, Cher
[1923?-<1925?>. v. <1-3 > (<72 > leaves of
plates) : DDC 726/.6/0944552 20
NA5551.B7 M87 1923

Cathédrale Notre-Dame de Tournai. La Croix
byzantine du Trésor de la Cathédrale de
Tournai /. Louvain-la-Neuve , 1987. 88 p. :
NYPL [3-MAIH 89-28301]

CATHÉDRALE NOTRE-DAME (ROUEN,
FRANCE) IN ART.
Pissarro, Joachim. Monet's cathedral . New
York , 1990. 96 p. : ISBN 0-394-58871-1 : DDC
759.4 20
ND553.M7 P56 1990
NYPL [3-MCO+ M74 91-3378]

CATHÉDRALE SAINT-ETIENNE DE
BOURGES - PICTORIAL WORKS.
Muté, S. Cathédrale de Bourges. Bourges, Cher
[1923?-<1925?. v. <1-3 > (<72 > leaves of
plates) : DDC 726/.6/0944552 20
NA5551.B7 M87 1923

CATHEDRALS - ENGLAND.
Briggs, Martin S. (Martin Shaw), b. 1882- A
pictorial guide to cathedral architecture .
[London] 1964. 24 p. :
NYPL [3-MRBR 90-6038]

CATHEDRALS - GERMANY - MAGDEBURG -
CONGRESSES.
Der Magdeburger Dom . Leipzig , 1989. 229 p.,
[120] p. of plates : ISBN 3-363-00425-7 DDC
726/.6/09431822 20
NA5586.M15 M34 1989

CATHEDRALS - JUVENILE LITERATURE.
Macdonald, Fiona. A medieval cathedral /.
New York , 1991. p. cm. ISBN 0-87226-350-9
DDC 726/.6/0940902 20
NA4830 .M34 1991

Perdrizet, Marie-Pierre. [Bâtisseurs de
cathédrales. English.] The cathedral builders /.
Brookfield, Conn. [1992] p. cm. ISBN
1-562-94162-3 DDC 726/.6/0940902 20
NA4830 .P3713 1992

Cathelin . Bourniquel, Camille. [Paris] , c1991.
233 p. : DDC 759.4 20
ND553.C316 A4 1991

Cathelin . Schönwald, Peter. Paris , c1990. 109
p. : DDC 746.392 20
NK3049.A3 C372 1990

Cathelin, Bernard.
Bourniquel, Camille. Cathelin . [Paris] , c1991.
233 p. : DDC 759.4 20
ND553.C316 A4 1991

Cathelin, lithographe / préface de Roger
Passeron. Monte-Carlo : Editions A. Sauret,
c1990. 2 v. : ill. ; 33 cm. French and English;
preface also in Japanese. CONTENTS. - 1.
1957-1982 -- 2. 1983-1989.
1. Cathelin, Bernard - Catalogs. I. Title.
NYPL [MDG+ (Cathelin) 90-13575]

Schönwald, Peter. Cathelin . Paris , c1990. 109
p. : DDC 746.392 20
NK3049.A3 C372 1990

CATHELIN, BERNARD - CATALOGS.
Bourniquel, Camille. Cathelin . [Paris] , c1991.
233 p. : DDC 759.4 20
ND553.C316 A4 1991

Cathelin, Bernard. Cathelin, lithographe /.
Monte-Carlo , c1990. 2 v. :
NYPL [MDG+ (Cathelin) 90-13575]

CATHELIN, BERNARD - THEMES,
MOTIVES.
Schönwald, Peter. Cathelin . Paris , c1990. 109
p. : DDC 746.392 20
NK3049.A3 C372 1990

Cathelin, lithographe /. Cathelin, Bernard.
Monte-Carlo , c1990. 2 v. :
NYPL [MDG+ (Cathelin) 90-13575]

Cather, Sharon.
The Conservation of wall paintings . Marina del
Rey, CA , 1991. p. cm. ISBN 0-89236-162-X
(pbk.) : DDC 751.6/2 20
ND2552 .C64 1991

Early medieval wall painting and painted
sculpture in England . Oxford, England , 1990.
xxii, 262 p. ; ISBN 0-86054-719-1
NYPL [3-MAMR+ 91-3440]

CATHOLIC CHURCH AND
ARCHITECTURE - ITALY.

Lo Spazio eloquente . Pordenone , c1987. 357
p. : DDC 726/.5/0945309045 20
NA5618 .S64 1987
NYPL [3-MRBD 90-12496]

CATHOLIC CHURCH AND ART.
Lewine, Carol F. The Sistine Chapel walls and
the Roman liturgy /. University Park, Pa. ,
c1992. p. cm. ISBN 0-271-00792-3 DDC
755/.2/0945634 20
ND2757.V35 L48 1992

Toubert, Hélène. Un art dirigé . Paris , 1990.
495 p. : ISBN 2-204-04105-X :
N7850 .T68 1990

CATHOLIC CHURCH AND ART -
CATALOGS.
Morales y Marín, José Luis, 1946- Goya, pintor
religioso /. [Zaragoza] [1990] 354 p. : ISBN
84-7753-132-3 DDC 759.6 20
ND813.G7 A4 1990

CATHOLIC CHURCH - DOCTRINES.
Toubert, Hélène. Un art dirigé . Paris , 1990.
495 p. : ISBN 2-204-04105-X :
N7850 .T68 1990

CATHOLIC CHURCH - LITURGY.
Widder, Erich. Alte Kirchen für neue Liturgie.
[Wien, c1968] 204 p.
NA4605 .W5   *NYPL [3-MRB 91-852]*

CATHOLIC CHURCH - LITURGY - TEXTS -
ILLUSTRATIONS.
Lewine, Carol F. The Sistine Chapel walls and
the Roman liturgy /. University Park, Pa. ,
c1992. p. cm. ISBN 0-271-00792-3 DDC
755/.2/0945634 20
ND2757.V35 L48 1992

Catholic Church, Roman. see Catholic Church.

Catlin and his contemporaries . Dippie, Brian W.
Lincoln , c1990. xix, 553 p., [16] p. of plates :
ISBN 0-8032-1683-1 (alk. paper) DDC 759.13
20
N8835 .D57 1990
NYPL [3-MCX C36 90-10763]

CATLIN, GEORGE, 1796-1872.
Sufrin, Mark. George Catlin . New York :
Toronto : p. cm. ISBN 0-689-31608-9 DDC
759.13 B 92 20
ND237.C35 S8 1991

CATLIN, GEORGE, 1796-1872 - JUVENILE
LITERATURE.
Sufrin, Mark. George Catlin . New York :
Toronto : p. cm. ISBN 0-689-31608-9 DDC
759.13 B 92 20
ND237.C35 S8 1991

CATLIN, GEORGE, 1796-1872 - FINANCE,
PERSONAL.
Dippie, Brian W. Catlin and his
contemporaries . Lincoln , c1990. xix, 553 p.,
[16] p. of plates : ISBN 0-8032-1683-1 (alk. paper)
DDC 759.13 20
N8835 .D57 1990
NYPL [3-MCX C36 90-10763]

CATS - CARICATURES AND CARTOONS.
Rodano, Philip J. Me-ow . Lincroft, N.J. ,
c1990. 1 v. ; ISBN 0-9627648-1-7 DDC
741.5/973 20
NC1429.R66 A4 1990

Sipress, David. It's a cat's life /. New York,
N.Y., U. S. A. , c1992. p. cm. ISBN
0-453-26758-7 DDC 741.5/973 20
NC1429.S532 A4 1992

Vey, P. C. (Peter C.) If cats could talk! /. New
York, N.Y., U. S. A. , c1991. 1 v. (unpaged) :
ISBN 0-452-26642-4 : DDC 741.5/973 20
NC1429.V57 A4 1991

CATS IN ADVERTISING.
Montry, Annie de. Chat pub . Paris , c1988.
191 p. : ISBN 2-7007-2814-9
NYPL [3-MDW+ 89-25688]

CATS IN ART.
Brent, Isabelle. Cameo cats /. Boston , 1992. p.
cm. ISBN 0-316-10836-7 : DDC 745.6/7/092 20
ND3410.B74 A4 1992

Herbert, Susan, 1945- Diary of a Victorian cat .
Boston, c1991. p. cm. ISBN 0-8212-1865-4
DDC 759.2 20
ND497.H49 A4 1991

Ivory, Lesley Anne. Christmas cats /. New
York , 1991. p. cm. ISBN 0-517-58549-9 : DDC

Cats in art. (cont.)

759.13 20
ND237.I94 A4 1991

Ivory, Lesley Anne. Glorious cats . New York ,
1992. p. cm. ISBN 0-517-58692-4 : DDC 759.13
20
ND237.I94 A4 1992

Leman, Martin. Martin Leman's painted cats.
London, England , New York, N.Y., USA , 19.
1 v. : ISBN 0-7207-1808-2 DDC 759.2 20
ND497.L67 A4 1988b

Lohan, Frank. Sketching cats . Chicago , c1991.
p. cm. ISBN 0-8092-4059-9 : DDC 743/.6974428
20
NC783.8.C36 L64 1991

CATS IN LITERATURE.
Leman, Martin. Martin Leman's painted cats.
London, England , New York, N.Y., USA , 19.
1 v. : ISBN 0-7207-1808-2 DDC 759.2 20
ND497.L67 A4 1988b

Cattaui, Jean-Louis, 1931-1968. Jean-Louis
Cattaui [di] Franco Passoni. Milano, Edizioni
Galleria Cortina [1970] 56 p. plates, part col.,
port. 22 x 24 cm. Italian, French, and English.
Errata slip inserted.
1. Cattaui, Jean-Louis, 1931-1968. I. Passoni, Franco.
ND237.C37 P3
      NYPL [3-MCO C368 90-6360]

CATTAUI, JEAN-LOUIS, 1931-1968.
Cattaui, Jean-Louis, 1931-1968. Jean-Louis
Cattaui. Milano [1970] 56 p.
ND237.C37 P3
      NYPL [3-MCO C368 90-6360]

CATTEDRALE DI FERRARA.
Tubi, Carlo. La cattedrale pitagorica . Ferrara ,
c1989. 140 p., [23] leaves of plates ;
      NYPL [3-MRBN 91-3263]

Tubi, Carlo. La cattedrale pitagorica . Ferrara ,
1989. 140 p. : ISBN 88-85668-47-X DDC
726/.6/094545 20
NA5621.F467 T8 1989

CATTEDRALE DI TARANTO (ITALY)
La Cripta della Cattedrale di Taranto /. Taranto
[1986] 98 p. : **NYPL [3-MRBN+ 90-10741]**

La cattedrale pitagorica . Tubi, Carlo. Ferrara ,
c1989. 140 p., [23] leaves of plates ;
      NYPL [3-MRBN 91-3263]

Cau, Jean, 1925- Fernando Botero : la corrida /
Jean Cau. Paris : Bibliothèque des arts, c1990.
161 p. : ill. (some col.) ; 36 cm. ISBN
2-85047-159-3 DDC 759.9861 20
1. Botero, Fernando, 1932- - Catalogs. 2. Bullfights in
art - Catalogs. I. Botero, Fernando, 1932-. II. Title. III.
Title: Corrida.
N6679.B6 A4 1990b

CAUCASUS - ANTIQUITIES.
Frühe Bergvölker in Armenien und im
Kaukasus . Berlin , 1984. 84 p. :
      NYPL [3-MAE 90-10823]

Causey, Andrew.
Wadsworth, Edward, 1889-1949. A genius of
industrial England . [Bradford] , c1990. 128 p. :
ISBN 0-9505532-7-1
      NYPL [3-MCV W12 91-6333]

Wadsworth, Edward, 1889-1949. A genius of
industrial England . [London] : [Bradford] : 128
p. : ill. ISBN 0-9505532-7-1 DDC 760/.092 20
N6797.W26 A4 1990

Causey, Susan. Tradition and revolution in
Russian art . [Manchester] , 1990. 200 p. :
ISBN 0-948797-26-6
      NYPL [3-MAM 91-5043]

Cavaglieri, Mario, 1887-1969.
Monti, Raffaele. Mario Cavaglieri /. Roma ,
c1988. 179 p. : ISBN 88-7813-011-7
ND623.C489 A4 1988
      NYPL [3-MCF+ C3595 90-12679]

**CAVAGLIERI, MARIO, 1887-1969 -
CATALOGS.**
Monti, Raffaele. Mario Cavaglieri /. Roma ,
c1988. 179 p. : ISBN 88-7813-011-7
ND623.C489 A4 1988
      NYPL [3-MCF+ C3595 90-12679]

Cavalier, Odile. Le trésor d'Apt : un ensemble de
vaisselle métallique gallo-romaine / par Odile
Cavalier ; dessins, Marie-Noëlle Baudrand.
Avignon : La Fondation du Muséum Calvet,
1988. 119 p. : ill. (some col.) ; 30 cm. "Édité à
l'occasion de l'exposition 'Le Trésor d'Apt. Un

ensemble de vaisselle gallo-romaine' (14 octobre
1988-15 décembre 1988) organisée par la Ville
d'Avignon au Musée Lapidaire"--P. 116. Includes
bibliographical references. ISBN 2-903044-49-X
1. Bronze implements - France - Apt - Exhibitions. 2.
Bronzes, Gallo-Roman - France - Apt - Exhibitions. 3.
Apt (France) - Antiquities, Roman - Exhibitions. I.
Musée lapidaire (Avignon, France). II. Title.
      NYPL [3-MGR + 90-5010]

Cavalieri di bronzo . Calcani, Giuliana. Roma ,
c1989. 182 p. : ISBN 88-7062-671-7
      NYPL [3-MGO (Lysippus) 91-5330]

Cavallo, Luigi.
Crippa / Luigi Cavallo ; testi di Giampiero
Giani ... [et al.]. Firenze : Centro Tornabuoni,
1990. 111 p. : ill. ; 24 cm. (Arte contemporanea)
1. Crippa, Roberto, 1921-1972. I. Title.
      NYPL [3-MCF C927 90-13555]

Russoli, Franco. Arte moderna cara compagna .
[Milano] , c1987. 382 p. ; ISBN 88-11-59983-0
      NYPL [3-MAMC 91-4600]

Cavallon, Giorgio, 1904-
James Brooks, Giorgio Cavallon . New York ,
1979. 24 p. :   **NYPL [3-MCW 91-284]**

**CAVALLON, GIORGIO, 1904- -
EXHIBITIONS.**
James Brooks, Giorgio Cavallon . New York ,
1979. 24 p. :   **NYPL [3-MCW 91-284]**

CAVE ARCHITECTURE.
Rietzsch, Barbara. Künstliche Grotten des 16.
und 17. Jahrhunderts . München , c1987. ii,
122 p., [39] p. of plates : ISBN 3-89235-017-5
      NYPL [3-MQW 91-7052]

**CAVE DRAWINGS AND PAINTINGS. see
CAVE-DRAWINGS.**

**CAVE-DRAWINGS - FRANCE -
ROUFFIGNAC CAVE.**
Barrière, C. L'art pariétal de Rouffignac .
Paris , 1982. 205 p., [4] folded leaves of plates :
ISBN 2-900927-10-2 DDC 709/.01/12094472 19
GN772.22.F7 B343 1982
      NYPL [3-MADF+ 91-6417]

Caven Atkins, the Winnipeg years /. Fraser, Ted,
1946- Windsor, Canada , c1987. [40] p. : ISBN
0-919837-10-7
MLCM 90/03385 (N)
      NYPL [3-MCZ A865 90-8692]

Cavina, Anna Ottani. see Ottani Cavina, Anna.

Caviness, Madeline Harrison, 1938- Sumptuous
arts at the royal abbeys in Reims and Braine :
ornatus elegantiae, varietate stupendes /
Madeline Harrison Caviness. Princeton, N.J. :
Princeton University Press, 1990. xxv, 401 p. :
ill. (some col.) ; 31 cm. Includes bibliographical
references (p. 157-162) and indexes. ISBN
0-691-04058-3 : DDC 748.594/32 20
1. Saint-Nicaise de Reims (Abbey). 2. Saint-Yved
(Church : Braine, France). 3. Glass painting and
staining, Romanesque - France - Reims. 4. Glass
painting and staining - France - Reims. 5. Glass
painting and staining, Romanesque - France - Braine. 6.
Glass painting and staining - France - Braine. I. Title.
NK5349.R3 C38 1990
      NYPL [3-MRY+ 91-4463]

Caws, Mary Ann. Surrealism and women /.
Cambridge, Mass. , 1991. 240 p. : ISBN
0-262-53098-8 : DDC 700 20
NX456.5.S8 S87 1991

Cayeux, Jean de. Robert, Hubert, 1733-1808.
Hubert Robert et la Révolution /. Valence ,
1989. 179 p. :
      NYPL [3-MCO R641 90-11133]

Cazalet, Camilla. Kendall, Richard. Van Gogh to
Picasso . London , 1991. 209 p. : ISBN
0-947645-83-7 (hardback) DDC 709.0346 20
N6754 **NYPL [3-MAX (Berggruen) 91-8105]**

Cazalla de la Sierra. La Cartuja. see Cartuja de
Cazalla de la Sierra.

**CAZENOVE, YOLAND, 19124- -
EXHIBITIONS.**
Cazenove, Yoland, 1914- Yoland Cazenove .
[Orléans, France , 1988. 79 p. :
MLCS 90/01954 (N)
      NYPL [3-MPGG 90-10600]

Cazenove, Yoland, 1914- Yoland Cazenove :
céramiste : rétrospective 1950-1986 : Musée des
beaux-arts d'Orléans, 8 juillet-23 octobre 1988.
[Orléans, France : Le Musée, 1988. 79 p. : ill.
(some col.) ; 20 cm. Includes bibliographical

references.
1. Cazenove, Yoland, 19124- - Exhibitions. I. Musée
des beaux-arts d'Orléans. II. Title.
MLCS 90/01954 (N)
      NYPL [3-MPGG 90-10600]

Cecchi, Alessandro. Natali, Antonio. Andrea del
Sarto . Firenze , c1989. 159 p. : ISBN
88-7737-068-8
      NYPL [3-MCF S24 90-12007]

Cecchi, Dante. Il Piviale duecentesco di Ascoli
Piceno . Firenze , 1991. 180 p. : ISBN
88-7737-143-9 :
NK9310 .P58 1991

Cécile Wick . Wick, Cécile, 1954- Kartause
Ittingen , c1990. 1 v. (unpaged) :
IN PROCESS (ONLINE)
      NYPL [MFX+ (Wick) 91-7678]

Cécile Wick, Fotoarbeiten. Wick, Cécile, 1954-
Cécile Wick . Kartause Ittingen , c1990. 1 v.
(unpaged) :
IN PROCESS (ONLINE)
      NYPL [MFX+ (Wick) 91-7678]

Cedar Rapids Art Association. Czestochowski,
Joseph S. Grant Wood . Cedar Rapids, Iowa ,
c1991. p. cm. ISBN 0-942982-10-X DDC
760/.092 20
NE2312.W66 A4 1991

Cederwall, Sandraline. Spratling silver /
Sandraline Cederwall and Hal Riney ; with
Barnaby Conrad ; stamp chronology by Edward
Forcum. San Francisco : Chronicle Books,
c1990. 128 p. : ill. ; 32 cm. Includes bibliographical
references (p. 127-128). ISBN 0-87701-845-6 DDC
739.2/372 20
1. Spratling, William, 1900-1967 - Exhibitions. 2.
Silverwork - Mexico - Taxco de Alarcón - History -
20th century - Exhibitions. I. Riney, Hal. II. Title.
NK7198.S67 A4 1990
      NYPL [3-MNO+ 91-7670]

**CEILINGS - FRANCE - DESIGNS AND
PLANS.**
Profils de corniches de plafonds /. [Paris] ,
1990- v. < 1 > : ISBN 2-11-086067-7
NA2960 .P76 1990

CEILINGS - GERMANY.
Bauer, Hermann, 1929- Corpus der barocken
Deckenmalerei in Deutschland /. München ,
1976- v. : ISBN 3-7991-5737-9 (v. 1) :
ND2749 .B37   **NYPL [MLP+ 78-312]**

CEILINGS - ITALY - BOLOGNA.
Feinblatt, Ebria. Seventeenth-century Bolognese
ceiling decorators /. Santa Barbara, Calif. ,
1991. p. cm. ISBN 0-931832-89-6 : DDC
729/.4/09454109032 20
ND2757.B54 F45 1991

Cela, Camilo José, 1916- Los Caprichos de
Francisco de Goya y Lucientes / Camilo José
Cela. [Madrid] : Sílex, c1989. 172 p. : 80 ill. ;
24 cm. (Sílex literatura) ISBN 84-7737-018-4
1. Goya, Francisco, 1746-1828. Caprichos. 2. Spanish
wit and humor. I. Goya, Francisco, 1746-1828.
Caprichos. 1989. II. Title.
      NYPL [MDG (Goya) 90-10979]

Celant, German. Da van Gogh a Picasso, Da
Kandinsky a Pollock . Milano , c1990. 391 p. :
DDC 709/.04/10744531 20
N6488.5.T55 D3 1990

Celant, Germano.
Grisi, Laura. Laura Grisi . New York , 1990.
276 p. : ISBN 0-8478-1222-7 DDC 709/.2 20
N6923.G73 A35 1990
      NYPL [3-MGO+ (Grisi) 91-3273]

Mondrian e De Stijl . Milano , c1990. 273 p. :
ISBN 88-435-3172-7
      NYPL [3-MCH M741 91-6318]

Celebrating the stitch . Smith, Barbara Lee.
Newtown, CT , c1991. p. cm. ISBN
0-942391-39-X : DDC 746.44/0973/09045 20
NK9212 .S64 1991

Celebration . Sarah Scaife Gallery. Pittsburgh
[1974] ca. 150 p. : DDC 759.94/074/014886
ND189 .S27 1974 **NYPL [3-MC 91-1192]**

A Celebration of hand-hooked rugs / the staff of
Rug hooking magazine. Harrisburg, PA : Rug
Hooking Magazine : Stackpole Books, c1991. p.
cm. Includes index. ISBN 0-8117-1867-0 DDC
746.7/4/0922 20
1. Rugs, Hooked. I. Rug hooking.
NK9105 .C45 1991

CELEBRITIES - PORTUGAL - CARICATURES AND CARTOONS.
Pinheiro, Rafael Bordalo, 1846-1905. Album das glorias . Lisboa , 1989. [42] leaves, 39 leaves of plates :
NC1639.P56 A4 1989

Çelik, Zeynep. Displaying the Orient : architecture of Islam at nineteenth-century world's fairs / Zeynep Çelik. Berkeley : University of California Press, c1992. p. cm. (Comparative studies on Muslim societies . 12) Includes bibliographical references (p.) and index. ISBN 0-520-07494-7 (alk. paper) DDC 725/.91 20
1. Architecture, Islamic - Europe. 2. Architecture - Europe. 3. Exhibition buildings - Europe - History - 19th century. 4. Architecture, Islamic - United States. 5. Architecture - United States. 6. Exhibition buildings - United States - History - 19th century. 7. Exoticism in architecture - Europe. 8. Exoticism in architecture - United States. I. Title. II. Series.
NA957 .C44 1992

Celli Tognon . Acocella, Alfonso, 1954- Firenze , c1987. 214 p. : DDC 720/.92/2 19
NA1123.C39 A4 1987
NYPL [3-MQWB 90-3040]

CELLI TOGNON - CATALOGS.
Acocella, Alfonso, 1954- Celli Tognon . Firenze , c1987. 214 p. : DDC 720/.92/2 19
NA1123.C39 A4 1987
NYPL [3-MQWB 90-3040]

Cellini, Benvenuto, 1500-1571.
CELLINI, BENVENUTO, 1500-1571.
Cellini, Benvenuto, 1500-1571. [Vita. English.] The life of Benvenuto Cellini /. London , 1949. xiv, 498 p. : DDC 927.3
NB623.C3 S45 1949
NYPL [3-MGO (Cellini) 91-6392]

[Vita. English]
The life of Benvenuto Cellini / [Translated by John Addington Symonds. Introduced and illustrated by John Pope Hennessy] London : Phaidon Press, 1949. xiv, 498 p. : plates, ports. ; 19 cm. Translation of: Vita. "Written by himself." Includes index. "Bibliographical note": p. [469]-470. DDC 927.3
1. Cellini, Benvenuto, 1500-1571. 2. Sculptors - Italy - Biography. I. Symonds, John Addington, 1840-1893. II. Title.
NB623.C3 S45 1949
NYPL [3-MGO (Cellini) 91-6392]

CELTIC ART. see ART, CELTIC.

Celtic designs and motifs /. Davis, Courtney, 1946- New York , 1991. 44 p. : ISBN 0-486-26718-0 (pbk.) : DDC 745.4/41/09364 20
NK1264 .D38 1991

Cem pintores portugueses do século XX.
Gonçalves, Rui Mário. 100 pintores portugueses do século XX /. Lisboa , c1986. 268 p. :
ND828 .G66 1986

CEMETERIES - GERMANY - MUNICH.
Krieg, Nina A. Schon Ordnung ist Schönheit . München , 1990. xix, 304 p. : ISBN 3-87821-286-0
NA6166 .K75 1990

Cendo, Nicolas. Soutter, Louis, 1871-1942. Louis Soutter . [Marseille] : Arles : 78 p. : ISBN 2-86869-167-6 (Actes sud) :
NC293.S68 A4 1987
NYPL [3-MCZ S728 91-6239]

Census of India, 1981. Series 1, India. Delhi : Controller of Publications, 1983- v. in : ill., maps (some col., some folded) ; 30-52 cm. Some vols. have text in English and Hindi. Some vols. have title also in Hindi: Bhārata kī janagaṇanā, 1981. Śṛṅkhalā 1, Bhārata. Issued by P. Padmanabha, Registrar General & Census Commissioner for India. CONTENTS. -- pt. 2 special. Report & tables based on 5 per cent sample data -- pt. 2A. General population tables. (2 v.) -- pt. 2B. Primary census abstract. (i) General population. (ii-iii) Scheduled castes. (3 v.) -- pt. 3A-B. General economic tables. (8 v.) -- pt. 4A-B. Social and cultural tables. (6 v. in 5) -- pt. 5A-B. Migration tables. (8 v.) -- pt. 6A-B. Fertility tables -- pt. 7A. Uses to which census houses are put -- pt. 7B. The physically handicapped. Report and tables -- pt. 8A-B. Household tables. (7 v.) -- pt. 10A. Town directory. (2 v.) -- pt. 12. Census atlas. National vol. DDC 304.6/0954/021 19
1. India - Census, 1981. I. India. Office of the Registrar General. II. India. Census Commissioner. III. Title:

Bhārata kī janagaṇanā, 1981. Śṛṅkhalā 1, Bhārata.
HA4581.5 1981g
NYPL [JLM 88-578 & Map Div. 90-54]

Cent cinquante ans d'appareils photographiques.
Auer, Michel. 150 ans d'appareils photographiques . Hermance [1989] 1 v. (unpaged) : ISBN 2-903671-07-9
NYPL [MFW 91-4967]

Cent dessins d'Helmut Kolle . Kolle, Helmut, 1899-1931. [France? :s.n.], 1972 (Saint-Omer : Société Norimprim) [46] p. :
NYPL [MCZ K799 90-6271]

Cent dessins du Musée Kröller-Müller.
Rijksmuseum Kröller-Müller. Bruxelles, c1971. [viii], 100, [xvi] p. DDC 741.9/074/04582
NC17.N4 O8773 *NYPL [3-MBH 90-6298]*

Cent-onze dessins du Québec : [exposition] Musée d'art Contemporain, Montréal, 1er avril au 9 mai, 1976. [Québec, Québec] : Ministère des Affaires Culturelles, c1976. 54 p. : chiefly ill. ; 23 x 31 cm.
1. Drawing, Canadian - Québec (Province) - Exhibitions. 2. Drawing - 20th century - Québec (Province) - Exhibitions. I. Québec (Province). Musée d'art contemporain. *NYPL [3-MBH+ 90-6892]*

Cent tableaux du Musée Condé . Musée Condé. [France] [19--] (Paris : Sté St-Quentinoise) [10] p., 100 p. of plates :
NYPL [3-MCN 90-7039]

Cent vingt du Cercle. Robert, Guy, 1933- Cent vingt du Cercle des artistes peintres du Québec /. Montréal , 1989. 255 p. : ISBN 2-920058-62-2 DDC 709/.2/2 20
N6546.Q4 R63 1989

Cent vingt du Cercle des artistes peintres du Québec /. Robert, Guy, 1933- Montréal , 1989. 255 p. : ISBN 2-920058-62-2 DDC 709/.2/2 20
N6546.Q4 R63 1989

Centauro, Giuseppe.
Dipinti murali di Piero della Francesca : la basilica di S. Francesco ad Arezzo : indagini su sette secoli / Giuseppe Centauro. Milano : Electa, c1990. 317 p. : ill. (some col.), plans, maps ; 28 cm. "Comitato Nazionale per il Quinto Centenario della morte di Piero della Francesca ; Ministero per i Beni Culturali e Ambientali, Soprintendenza ai Beni Ambientali, Architettonici, Artistici, e Storici di Arezzo"-P. [4] Includes bibliographical references (p. 294-298) and index. ISBN 88-435-3147-6
1. Piero, della Francesca, 1416?-1492. 2. San Francesco (Church : Arezzo, Italy). 3. Mural painting and decoration, Italian - Italy - Arezzo. 4. Mural painting and decoration, Renaissance - Italy - Arezzo. I. Comitato nazionale per il quinto centenario della morte di Piero della Francesca (Italy). II. Italy. Soprintendenza per i beni ambientali, architettonici, artistici, e storici di Arezzo. III. Title.
NYPL [3-MCF F81 91-7303]

Dipinti murali di Piero della Francesca : la basilica di S. Francesco ad Arezzo : indagini su sette secoli / Giuseppe Centauro. Milano : Electa, c1990. 317 p. : ill. (some col.) ; 28 cm. "Piero, 500 anni, 1492-1992"--Cover. Includes bibliographical references (p. 294-298) and index. ISBN 88-435-3147-6 DDC 759.5 20
1. Piero, della Francesca, 1416?-1492 - Criticism and interpretation. I. Piero, della Francesca, 1416?-1492. II. San Francesco (Church : Arezzo, Italy). III. Title.
ND623.P548 C45 1990

Centenario del nacimiento de José Sabogal, 1888-19 marzo-1988 / presentes, Ernesto [i.e. Enrique] Alvarez Calderón ... [et al. ; compilación, revisión y edición por Jorge Falcón]. Ed. de homenaje, Ed. del año del centenario de su nacimiento. Lima, Perú : [s.n.], 1989 (Miraflores : Librería Editorial "Minerva") 68 p. : ill. ; 24 cm. Cover title: José Sabogal, 1888-marzo-1988. At head of title: Instituto Sabogal de Arte, Comisión Centenario José Sabogal, Jorge Falcón, Banco Continental, Museo de Arte.
1. Sabogal Diéguez, José, 1888-1956 - Appreciation. I. Sabogal Diéguez, José, 1888-1956. II. Alvarez Calderón, Enrique. III. Falcón, Jorge, 1908-. IV. Instituto Sabogal de Arte. V. Title: José Sabogal, 1888-marzo-1988.
N6719.S23 C46 1989

Center for Advanced Study in the Visual Arts (U. S.)
American art around 19 . Washington , Hanover [N.H.] , 1990. 136 p. : ISBN 0-89468-143-5 *NYPL [3-MAMT 91-7570]*

Retaining the original . Washington , Hanover , c1989. 180 p. : *NYPL [3-MAS 90-13011]*
Winslow Homer . Washington , Hanover , N.H. , 1990. 156 p. : ISBN 0-89468-132-X DDC 759.13 20
ND237.H7 W56 1990

Center for African Art (New York, N.Y.) Vogel, Susan. Africa explores . New York : Munich : 294 p. : ISBN 3-7913-1143-3 (cloth) : DDC 709/.67/07473 20
N7391.65 .V63 1991 *NYPL [Sc G 91-40]*

Center for Book Arts (New York, N.Y.)
Broaddus, John Eric, 1943- Spin 1/2 . New York, N.Y. (626 Broadway, New York 10012) , c1990 ([New York] : Lower East Side Printshop) 15 p. : DDC 709/.2 20
N6537.B7 A4 1990

Center for Inter-American Relations. Art Gallery. Poleo, Héctor. Héctor Poleo, a retrospective exhibition . New York [1974?] [44] p. : *NYPL [3-MCZ P756 91-871]*

Center for the Fine Arts (Miami, Fla.) Shapiro, Joel. Joel Shapiro . Des Moines, Ia. , 1990. 80 p. : ISBN 1-87900-300-7
NYPL [3-MGO (Shapiro) 91-7050]

Cento anni di fotografia in Sicilia .
(3) Scianna, Ferdinando. Città del mondo /. Milano , c1988. 95 p. :
NYPL [MFX (Scianna) 91-5705]

Le cento immagini di Andy Warhol . Warhol, Andy, 1928- Milano , c1989. 116 p. : ISBN 88-20-20906-3
NYPL [3-MCX W27 90-11112]

CENTRAL AMERICA - ANTIQUITIES - PICTORIAL WORKS.
Schezen, Roberto. Visions of ancient America /. New York , 1990. 216 p. : ISBN 0-8478-1178-6 : DDC 709/.997201 20
F1219 .S38 1990
NYPL [MFX (Schezen) 91-3399]

Central America - Archaeology. see Central America - Antiquities.

CENTRAL EUROPE - ROAD MAPS.
Continental Gummi-Werke AG. Continental Atlas für Mittel-Europa. Hannover [1924] viii, 65 (i.e. 66) fold. col. maps.
G1881.P2 C6 1924
NYPL [Map Div. 83-672]

Central Intelligence Agency (U. S.) see United States. Central Intelligence Agency.

Central Pennsylvania redware pottery, 1780-1904 /. Lasansky, Jeannette. Lewisburg, Pa. , c1979. 60 p. : DDC 738.3/09748
NK4025.P4 L36 *NYPL [3-MPH 81-850]*

Centre aixois de recherches anglaises. L'Artiste, témoin de son temps (?) . Aix-en-Provence , 1990. xiv, 168 p. ; ISBN 2-85399-238-1 : DDC 700/.942 20
NX543 .A83 1990

Centre canadien d'architecture.
Emerging Japanese architects of the 1990s /. New York , 1991. 121 p. : DDC 720/.952/09045 20
NA1555 .E44 1991
NYPL [3-MQWS+ 91-6807]

Le Panthéon, symbole des révolutions . [Montréal] : [Paris] : 339 p. : ISBN 2-7084-0386-9 (Picard)
IN PROCESS (ONLINE)
NYPL [3-MQWF 90-10797]

Centre Cultural de la Caixa d'Estalvis de Valencia. Santiago Calatrava . València , 1986. 103 p. : ISBN 84-7579-104-2
NYPL [3-MQZ (Calatrava) 91-6420]

Centre Cultural del Palau de la Virreina (Barcelona, Spain) Oppenheim, Meret, 1913- Meret Oppenheim . Londres [Barcelona] [1990] 95 p. : ISBN 84-7609-343-8
IN PROCESS (ONLINE)
NYPL [3-MCZ 062 91-6503]

Centre d'art contemporain (Abbaye Saint-André (Meymac, France)) Bouillon, François, 1944- François Bouillon . [Labège, France , 1990] 160 p. : ISBN 2-905992-32-8 : DDC 709/.2 20
N6853.B588 A4 1990

Centre d'Art Santa Mònica (Barcelona, Spain)
Jové, Angel. Angel Jové . [Barcelona] [1991?]

229 p. :
N7113.J68 A4 1991

Le Démon des anges . [Barcelona] , Nantes
[1989] 245 p. :   DDC 704/.036872079494/0744672
20
N6538.M4 D46 1989

Centre de création contemporaihe (Tours,
France) Defraoui, Silvie. Orient/occident /.
Genève , c1989. 53 p. :
NYPL [3-MCZ + D316 89-27977]

Centre de création industrielle.
L'Etrange univers de l'architecte Carlo
Mollino . Paris , c1989. 174 p. :   ISBN
2-85850-494-6
NA1123.M65 A4 1989

Tony Garnier, l'œuvre complète /. Paris ,
c1989. 254 p. :   ISBN 2-85850-527-6   DDC
720/.92 20
NA1053.G37 A4 1989

Centre de documentation égyptologique. see
Markaz Tasjīl al-Āthār al-Miṣrīyah.

Centre de documentation et d'étude sur
l'ancienne Egypte. see Markaz Tasjīl al-
Āthār al-Miṣrīyah.

Centre de documentation et d'études sur l'Égypte
ancienne. see Markaz Tasjīl al-Āthār al-
Miṣrīyah.

Centre de documentation et d'études sur l'histoire
de l'art et de la civilisation de l'ancienne
Égypte. see Markaz Tasjīl al-Āthār al-
Miṣrīyah.

Centre de recherche sur l'habitat (France)
Recherches sur la typologie et les types
architecturaux . [Paris] , c1991. 367 p. :   ISBN
2-7384-0903-2
NA2000 .R38 1991

Centre de recherches sur la Renaissance (Series)
.
(15) Le Monde animal au temps de la
Renaissance /. Paris , 1990. 259 p. :   ISBN
2-86433-036-9 :   DDC 700 20
NX650.A55 M66 1990

Centre de recherches sur les monuments
historiques (France) Profils de corniches de
plafonds /. [Paris] , 1990- v. <1 > :   ISBN
2-11-086067-7
NA2960 .P76 1990

Centre Gallery (Surfers Paradise, Qld.) Larner,
Bronwyn. A complementary caste . Surfers
Paradise [1988] 230 p. :   ISBN 0-7316-4346-1
IN PROCESS (ONLINE)
NYPL [3-MAMM+ 90-13299]

Centre Georges Pompidou.
L'Etrange univers de l'architecte Carlo
Mollino . Paris . c1989. 174 p. :   ISBN
2-85850-494-6
NA1123.M65 A4 1989

Centre Georges Pompidou. Bibliothèque publique
d'information. Mœglin-Delcroix, Anne. Livres
d'artistes /. Paris , c1985. 159 p. :   ISBN
2-7335-0085-6   NYPL [MDT 86-3500]

Centre international d'art contemporain de
Montréal. Raynaud, Jean Pierre, 1939-
Jean-Pierre Raynaud . Houston, Tex. , c1991.
135 p. :   ISBN 0-939594-23-4 :   DDC 709/.2 20
N6853.R33 A4 1991
NYPL [3-MGO (Raynaud) 91-7980]

Centre national d'art contemporain. Courtin,
Pierre, 1921- Pierre Courtin, gouaches et
peintures /. Paris , 1976. 90 p. :   ISBN
2-7004-0015-1 :
ND553.C918 C46
NYPL [3-MCO C864 80-2164]

Centre national d'art et de culture Georges
Pompidou. see Centre Georges Pompidou.

Centre national de la photographie (France) Un
si grand âge-- . Paris , c1986. 108 p. :   ISBN
2-86754-036-4 (pbk.)   DDC
779/.2/090407404361 19
TR681.A35 S5 1986   NYPL [MFW 90-2553]

Centre national de la recherche scientifique
(France)
Collage et montage au théâtre et dans les autres
arts durant les années vingt /. Lausanne , cop.
1978. 296 p., [32] p. of plates :   DDC 700/.94 19
NX542 .C64   NYPL [JFE 81-222]

Salomé, Marie Rose. Code pour l'analyse des

représentations figurées sur les vases grecs /.
Paris , 1980. 161 p. :   ISBN 2-222-02677-6
NYPL [3-MPR 90-5663]

Centre national des arts plastiques (France)
Un'altra obiettività /. Milano , c1989. 253 p. :
ISBN 88-7017-067-5
NYPL [MFW 90-3005]

Bazaine, Jean, 1904- Bazaine. Paris , c1990.
178 p. :   ISBN 2-605-00162-8
NYPL [3-MCO B35 90-12858]

Centre socialiste d'éducation permanente.
Papyrus et pop art /. [Nivelles, Belgique , 1987]
104 p. :
N72.H58 P36 1987

Centric 35 /. Levinthal, David. Long Beach ,
c1989. [20] p. :
NYPL [MFX (Levinthal) 90-11261]

Centro arte e cultura Castello di Belgioioso.
Castello di Belgioioso . Milano , 1987. 15 p. :
ISBN 88-7111-010-2
NYPL [MDG+ (Dal Re) 90-10839]

Centro attività visive. Boni, Paolo, 1926- Boni .
Roma [1977] [70] p. :
ND623.B5688 A4 1977
NYPL [3-MCF B704 81-336]

Centro Cultural de la Villa de Madrid.
Arte geométrico en España, 1957-1989.
[Madrid] [1989] 320 p. :   ISBN 84-7812-044-0
DDC 709/.46/0744641 20
N7108.5.A2 A78 1989

La Habana en Madrid. [Madrid] [1989?] 64
p. :   DDC 709/.7291/0744641 20
N6603 .H25 1989

Centro Cultural Dr. Alberto Rouges. Ezequiel
Linares . San Miguel de Tucumán, Argentina
[1990] 1 v. (unpaged) :
ND339.L5 A4 1990

Centro Cultural/Arte Contemporáneo (Mexico)
El Arte de la platería mexicana, 500 años .
[Mexico] [c1989] 595 p. :   ISBN 968-619-120-8
DDC 739.2/3772 20
NK7114.A1 A73 1989

Izquierdo, María, 1906- Maria Izquierdo.
Mexico , 1988. 415 p. :   ISBN 968-619-110-0
NYPL [3-MCZ I99 90-12875]

Martín Ramírez, pintor mexicano (1885-1960).
[Mexico City] , 1989. 198 p. :   ISBN
968-619-113-5   DDC 760 20
NC146.R36 A4 1989

Centro culturale città di Ferrara. Maldarelli,
Ernesto, 1850-1930. Un artista ferrarese del
legno, Ernesto Maldarelli (1850-1930) /.
Ferrara , c1989. 107 p. :
NYPL [3-MOC 90-12376]

Centro de Arte Moderna (Fundação Calouste
Gulbenkian)
Arte em Berlim--1900 até hoje . Lisboa , 1989.
319 p. :   DDC 709/.431/55074469425 20
N6885 .A76 1989

Imagens do Sagrado. Lisboa , 1989. 47 p. :
DDC 704.9/482/09469074469425 20
N7963.A1 I4 1989

Resende, Júlio, 1917- Júlio Resende /. Lisboa ,
1989. 122 p. :   DDC 759.69 20
ND833.R46 A4 1989

Centro de Arte Reina Sofiá.
Arte minimal de la Colección Panza .
[Madrid?] , 1988. 61 p. :   ISBN 84-7750-623-18
NYPL [MAMT 90-5197]

Baldessari, John, 1931- Nipor ésas =. [Madrid]
[1989] 92 p. :   ISBN 84-7506-254-7 (pbk.)
NYPL [MFX (Baldessari) 89-28407]

Centro de Artes Plásticas dos Coruchéus.
Carvalhais, Stuart, b. 1887. Vida e obra de
Stuart Carvalhais . Lisboa , 1982. 244 p., [54]
p. of plates :
N7133.C34 A4 1982

Centro di Firenze restituito : affreschi e
frammenti lapidei nel Museo di San Marco / a
cura di Maria Sframeli. Firenze : A. Bruschi,
c1989. 614 p., 8 p. of plates : ill. (some col.),
plans ; 30 cm. Includes bibliographical references (p.
583-593).
1. Museo di San Marco - Catalogs. 2. Art - Italy -
Florence - Catalogs. 3. Mural painting and decoration,
Italian - Italy - Florence - Catalogs. 4. Architecture -
Italy - Florence - Details - Catalogs. 5. Florence

(Italy) - Antiquities - Catalogs. 6. Florence (Italy) -
Buildings, structures, etc. - History. I. Sframeli, Maria.
NYPL [3-MAVZ+ (Florence) 90-12442]

Centro di studio per l'archeologia etrusco-italica.
Le Ciste prenestine /. [Roma] , 1979- v. :
DG70.P33 C57 1979
NYPL [3-MGR+ 83-2202]

Centro Habitat de Colombia. El nacionalismo en
el arte. [Bogotá, Colombia] [1984]. 90 p. ;
NYPL [3-MAM 90-4731]

Centro histórico de Salvador . Verger, Pierre. São
Paulo , 1989. 1 v. (unpaged) :
NYPL [MFX+ (Verger) 90-13439]

Centro internazionale di studi di architettura
"Andrea Palladio" di Vicenza. Seminario
internazionale di storia dell'architettura (7th :
1988 Sept. 1-7 : Vicenza, Italy) Andrea
Palladio, nuovi contributi . Milano , c1990. 247
p. :   ISBN 88-435-3086-0
NYPL [3-MQZ+ (Palladio) 91-4941]

Centro internazionale di studi sul barocco in
Sicilia.
Palazzolo Acreide . Siracusa , Palermo , c1989.
xv, 140, [3] p. :
NYPL [3-MQWB+ 91-5408]

L'Ultimo Caravaggio . Siracusa , c1987. 376 p. :
NYPL [3-MCF C26 90-9486]

Centro João Vinte e Três.
O Clero no Parlamento brasileiro /. Brasília ,
Rio de Janeiro , 1978-79. 2 v. :   ISBN
85-7004-002-4
JL2454 .C53   NYPL [HFE 80-1465]

O Clero no Parlamento brasileiro /. Brasília ,
Rio de Janeiro , 1978- v. :   ISBN 85-7004-002-4
JL2454 .C53   NYPL [HFE 80-1378]

Centro Nacional de Exposiciones (Spain) Los
Bronces romanos en España . [Madrid] [1990?]
358 p. :   ISBN 84-7483-623-9   DDC
739.5/12/093660744641 20
NK7907.3 .B76 1990

Centro per la promozione della cultura molisana,
Università degli studi di Molise (Series) .
(1) Trombetta, Ada. Mondo contadino d'altri
tempi . Napoli , c1989. 333 p. :   ISBN
88-7104-150-X
NYPL [3-MMO+ 91-3733]

Centro per l'arte contemporanea Luigi Pecci.
Schnabel, Julian, 1951- Julian Schnabel /.
Prato , c1989. 159 p. :   ISBN 88-85191-00-2
NYPL [3-MCX S358 90-4741]

Centro Regional de Artes Tradicionais (Portugal)
Artesanato da região norte . Porto , 1989. 406
p. :   ISBN 972-90030-0-9   DDC 745/.09469 20
NK1003 .A83 1989

Centro studi Gianni Bosio. Zanotti-Bianco,
Umberto. Il sud di Umberto Zanotti Bianco .
Venezia , c1981. 117 p. :
NYPL [MFX (Zanotti-Bianco) 90-7053]

Centuries of darkness : a challenge to the
conventional chronology of Old World
archaeology / Peter James, in collaboration
with I.J. Thorpe ... [et al.] ; foreword by Colin
Renfrew. London : J. Cape, 1991. xxii, 434 p.,
[8] p. of plates : ill. ; 24 cm. Maps on lining
papers. Includes index. Includes bibliographical
references (p. 395)-426) and index. Includes
bibliographical references (p. 395)-426).   ISBN
0-224-02647-X :   DDC 930 20
1. Civilization, Ancient - Chronology. 2. Chronology,
Egyptian. I. James, Peter. II. Thorpe, I. J.
CB311   NYPL [JFE 91-4489]

A century of Alexandria, District of Columbia &
Georgetown silver . Corcoran Gallery of Art.
[Washington , 1966] 28 p. :
NK7112 .C67 1966
NYPL [3-MNO 90-5570]

A Century of Philadelphia artists. Philadelphia :
Frank S. Schwarz & Son, 1988. 64 p. : ill.
(some col.) ; 25 cm. (Philadelphia collection. 37,
summer 1988) Catalog of an exhibition held summer
1988. "Audrey Hall ... organized the catalogue and
researched and wrote the majority of the entries"--p.
[4]. Includes bibliographical references and index.
1. Painting, American - Pennsylvania - Philadelphia -
Exhibitions. 2. Painting, Modern - 19th century -
Pennsylvania - Philadelphia - Exhibitions. 3. Painters -
Pennsylvania - Philadelphia - Biography. I. Hall,
Audrey. II. Frank S. Schwarz & Son.
NYPL [3-MCW 90-13578]

The Century of Tung Ch'i-ch'ang / Wai-kam Ho, editor ; contributors to the catalogue, Wai-kam Ho ... [et al.]. Kansas City, Mo. : Nelson-Atkins Museum of Art, 1992. p. cm. Catalogue of exhibition organized by the Nelson-Atkins Museum of Art, Kansas City, Mo. Includes bibliographical references and indexes. ISBN 0-295-97157-6 DDC 759.951 20
1. Tung, Ch'i-ch'ang, 1555-1636 - Exhibitions. I. Ho, Wai-kam. II. Nelson-Atkins Museum of Art.
N7349.T86 A4 1992

Cenzato, Elena.
  [Gufi & civette. English]
  Owls : art, legend, history / Elena Cenzato, Fabio Santopietro ; [English translation by Graham Fawcett and John Gilbert]1st U. S. ed. Boston : Little, Brown, c1991. p. cm. (The Bulfinch library of collectibles) Translation of: Gufi & civette "A Bulfinch Press book." ISBN 0-8212-1879-4 : DDC 704.9/432 20
  1. Owls in art. 2. Owls - Collectibles. 3. Owls - Legends. I. Santopietro, Fabio. II. Title. III. Series.
  N7666.O94 C4613 1991

Cërabregu, Muharem. Kosova në hartat e vjetra : kontribut gjeografisë historike të Kosovës / Muharem Cërabregu. Prishtinë : Universiteti, Fakulteti Matematik-Natyror, 1977. 301 p. : maps ; 25 cm. Originally presented as the author's thesis, Zagreb, 1972. Summary in English and Serbo-Croatian. Bibliography: p. 241-247. DDC 911/.4971 19
  1. Kosovo (Serbia) - Historical geography. I. Title.
  DR701.K7 C47 1977
                    NYPL [Map Div. 91-5727]

The Ceramic art of China : a symposium / George Kuwayama, editor. Los Angeles, Calif. : Los Angeles County Museum of Art ; [Honolulu?] : Distributed by the University of Hawaii Press, c1991. p. cm. Includes bibliographical references. ISBN 0-87587-156-9 (pbk.) DDC 738/.0951 20
  1. Pottery, Chinese - Congresses. 2. Porcelain, Chinese - Congresses. I. Kuwayama, George. II. Los Angeles County Museum of Art.
  NK4165 .C44 1991

Ceramic ornament in the New York subway system /. Tunick, Susan. New York, N.Y. , Italy [1989?] [14] p. :
                    NYPL [3-MRXZ+ 90-10715]

CERAMIC SCULPTURE - 20TH CENTURY - ENGLAND - CATALOGS.
Los Angeles County Museum of Art. Clay today . Los Angeles, Calif. , San Francisco, Calif. , c1990. 239 p. : ISBN 0-87701-756-5 (Chronicle Books) : DDC 730/.0973/07479494 20
NK4008 .L67 1990
                    NYPL [3-MPH+ 90-11630]

CERAMIC SCULPTURE - 20TH CENTURY - GERMANY (EAST) - EXHIBITIONS.
Möhwald, Gertraud, 1929- Gertraud Möhwald . Halle , 1989. 182 p. : ISBN 3-86105-026-9 DDC 730/.092 20
NK4210.M585 A4 1989
                    NYPL [3-MPGK 91-5045]

CERAMIC SCULPTURE - 20TH CENTURY - GREAT BRITAIN - EXHIBITIONS.
Baldwin, Gordon. Gordon Baldwin . Rotterdam [1989] 39 p. : ISBN 90-6918-044-8
NK4210.B33 A4 1989

CERAMIC SCULPTURE - 20TH CENTURY - NORWAY.
Gaustad, Randi, 1942- Samtidskeramikk . Oslo , c1990. 127 p. : ISBN 82-09-10613-9
NK4119 .G38 1990

CERAMIC SCULPTURE - 20TH CENTURY - NOVA SCOTIA - CATALOGS.
Barkhouse, Joyce C. The Lorenzen collection /. Halifax, N.S. , 1985. 58 p. : ISBN 0-9692387-0-3 : DDC 738.0922 19
                    NYPL [MPH 91-3761]

CERAMIC SCULPTURE - 20TH CENTURY - UNITED STATES - CATALOGS.
Los Angeles County Museum of Art. Clay today . Los Angeles, Calif. , San Francisco, Calif. , c1990. 239 p. : ISBN 0-87701-756-5 (Chronicle Books) : DDC 730/.0973/07479494 20
NK4008 .L67 1990
                    NYPL [3-MPH+ 90-11630]

CERAMIC SCULPTURE - ENGLAND - 20TH CENTURY.
Houston, John. Richard Slee . London , 1990. 64 p. : ISBN 0-947792-47-3 (pbk.) : DDC 738.092 20
                    NYPL [3-MPGO 90-12737]

CERAMIC SCULPTURE - PRIVATE COLLECTIONS - CALIFORNIA - LOS ANGELES - CATALOGS.
Los Angeles County Museum of Art. Clay today . Los Angeles, Calif. , San Francisco, Calif. , c1990. 239 p. : ISBN 0-87701-756-5 (Chronicle Books) : DDC 730/.0973/07479494 20
NK4008 .L67 1990
                    NYPL [3-MPH+ 90-11630]

CERAMIC TABLEWARE - CANADA - CATALOGS.
Luckin, Richard W. Dining on rails . Golden, CO (621 Cascade Ct., Golden 80403-1581) , 1990- v. <1- > : DDC 738/.0973/075 20
NK4005 .L83 1990

McIntyre, Douglas W. The official guide to railroad dining car china /. Lockport, NY (20 Cleveland Pl., Lockport 14094) , c1990 (Marceline, MO : Walsworth Press Co. Inc., Commercial Book Division) 204 p. : DDC 738/.0973/075 20
NK4005 .M37 1990

CERAMIC TABLEWARE - GERMANY.
Reinheckel, Günter. Meissener Prunkservice /. Stuttgart , 1990. 239 p. : ISBN 3-421-02960-1 DDC 738.2/09432 14 20
NK4380 .R45 1990

CERAMIC TABLEWARE - UNITED STATES - CATALOGS.
Luckin, Richard W. Dining on rails . Golden, CO (621 Cascade Ct., Golden 80403-1581) , 1990- v. <1- > : DDC 738/.0973/075 20
NK4005 .L83 1990

McIntyre, Douglas W. The official guide to railroad dining car china /. Lockport, NY (20 Cleveland Pl., Lockport 14094) , c1990 (Marceline, MO : Walsworth Press Co. Inc., Commercial Book Division) 204 p. : DDC 738/.0973/075 20
NK4005 .M37 1990

CERAMIC TABLEWARE - UNITED STATES - HISTORY - 20TH CENTURY - CATALOGS.
Kovel, Ralph M. [Depression glass & American dinnerware price list.] Kovels' depression glass & American dinnerware price list /. New York , c1991. 250 p. : ISBN 0-517-58444-1 : DDC 738/.0973/075 20
NK5439.D44 K67 1991

CERAMIC TEAPOTS - CALIFORNIA - HISTORY - 20TH CENTURY.
Shire, Peter. Tempest in a teapot . New York , 1991. 144 p. : ISBN 0-8478-1322-3 DDC 738/.092 20
NK4210.S534 D76 1991

Cerámica de Tonalá, Jalisco . López Cervantes, Gonzalo. México, D.F. , 1990. 146 p. : ISBN 968-606-895-3 DDC 738.3/0972/35 20
NK4032.T66 L66 1990

Ceramica de uz comun nesmălțuită din Moldova . Busuioc, Elena. București , 1975. 87 p., [25] leaves of plates :
                    NYPL [3-MPG 90-5750]

Cerâmica do Renascimento /. Benini, Mirella. [Ceramica del Rinascimento. Portuguese.] Lisboa , 1989. 82 p. :
NK4103 .B416 1989

Ceramica greca della Collezione Chini nel Museo civico di Bassano del Grappa / Giuseppe Andreassi ... [et al.]. Roma : G. Bretschneider, c1990. 111 p. : ill. ; 29 cm. (Collezioni e musei archeologici del Veneto. [33]) ISBN 88-7689-052-1
  1. Pottery, Greek - Catalogs. I. Andreassi, Giuseppe.
                    NYPL [3-MPEK 90-12667]

Ceramica in banca : 50 maioliche liguri della Cassa di Risparmio di Genova e Imperia / a cura di Arrigo Cameirana. Albisola Superiore : Museo della ceramica "Manlio Trucco", 1989. 78 p. : ill. (some col.), 1 port. ; 27 cm. Catalog of the inaugural exhibition of the Museo della ceramica "Manlio Trucco", Albisola Superiore, May 21-Aug. 27, 1989. Includes bibliographical references (p. 66-70).
  1. Cassa di risparmio di Genova e Imperia - Art collections - Exhibitions. 2. Majolica, Italian - Italy -

Liguria - Exhibitions. I. Cameirana, Arrigo. II. Museo della ceramica "Manlio Trucco.". III. Cassa di risparmio di Genova e Imperia. IV. Title: 50 maioliche liguri della Cassa di Risparmio di Genova e Imperia. V. Title: Cinquanta maioliche liguri della Cassa di Risparmio di Genova e Imperia.   *NYPL [3-MPGD 91-6609]*

Ceramica toscana dal medioevo al XVIII secolo / a cura di Gian Carlo Bojani. Monte S. Savino : Banca toscana, [1990] 472 p. : ill. (some col.) ; 22 cm. "Monte S. Savino-Il Cassero, 2 giugno-26 agosto 1990"--T.p. verso. Includes bibliographical references (p. 436-458). DDC 738/.0945/50744559 20
  1. Pottery, Italian - Italy - Tuscany - Exhibitions. 2. Pottery - Italy - Tuscany - Exhibitions. I. Bojani, Gian Carlo.
  NK4104.T9 C4 1990

Ceramiche a Ferrara in età estense dalla collezione Pasetti /. Visser Travagli, Anna Maria. Firenze , c1989. 81 p. : ISBN 88-7038-175-7 *NYPL [3-MPGD 90-10656]*

Le Ceramiche da farmacia a Roma tra '400 e '600 / a cura di Otto Mazzucato. Viterbo : Faul, [1990] 178 p. : ill. (some col.) ; 31 cm. Catalogue of an exhibition supported by Wellcome Italia at the Palazzo Braschi, Mar. 30-May 6, 1990. Includes bibliographical references (p. 120-122).
  1. Apothecary jars - Italy - Rome - Exhibitions. I. Mazzucato, Otto. II. Wellcome Italia. III. Palazzo Braschi.   *NYPL [3-MPGD+ 91-4305]*

Le ceramiche di Antonio Manzi /. Riccomini, Franco. [S.l.] 1986. 222 p. :
                    NYPL [3-MPGD+ 90-11513]

Ceramics : artists, galleries / editor, Janet Mansfield. Sydney : Potters' Society of Australia, 1990. 120 p. : ill. ; 27 cm.
  1. Pottery, Australian. 2. Pottery - 20th century - Australia. 3. Potters - Australia - Biography. I. Mansfield, Janet.   *NYPL [3-MPC 91-5319]*

Ceramics in studio. Houston, John. Richard Slee . London , 1990. 64 p. : ISBN 0-947792-47-3 (pbk.) : DDC 738.092 20
                    NYPL [3-MPGO 90-12737]

Ceramics of the world . Camusso, Lorenzo. New York, N.Y. , 1992. p. cm. ISBN 0-8109-3175-3 DDC 738/.09 20
NK3780 .C37 1992

La céramique art déco /. Pelichet, Edgar. Lausanne , Paris , c1988. 199 p. : ISBN 2-88148-007-1 DDC 738/.09/041 20
NK3930.3.A77 P4 1988
                    NYPL [3-MPC+ 90-11744]

La céramique islamique du Musée archéologique provincial de Jaén (Espagne) /. Bazzana, Andrés. Madrid , Paris , 1985. 78 p. : DDC 738.3/0946/83 20
DP302.J1 B38 1985
                    NYPL [3-MPG+ 91-5911]

Céramique lorraine : chefs-d'œuvre des XVIIIe & XIXe siècles = French ceramics : 18th and 19th century masterpieces from Lorraine. Nancy : Presses universitaires de Nancy ; Metz : Editions Serpenoise, c1990. 367 p. : ill. (some col.), maps ; 27 cm. English and French. Exhibition held at the High Museum of Art, Atlanta, Ga. Includes bibliographical references (p. 359-160) and index. ISBN 2-86480-458-1
  1. Pottery, French - France - Lorraine - Exhibitions. 2. Pottery - 18th century - France - Lorraine - Exhibitions. 3. Pottery - 19th century - France - Lorraine - Exhibitions. 4. Potters - France - Lorraine. I. High Museum of Art. II. French ceramics : 18th and 19th century masterpieces from Lorraine.
                    NYPL [3-MPGG 91-7166]

Céramique lorraine : chefs-d'œuvre des XVIIIe & XIXe siècles = French ceramics : 18th and 19th Century masterpieces from Lorraine. Nancy : Presses universitaires de Nancy ; Metz : Editions Serpenoise, c1990. 367 p. : ill. (some col.) ; 27 cm. "Maître d'ouvrage ... Conseil régional de Lorraine ... Commissariat de l'exposition ... Emile Decker"--P. 8. French and English. Includes bibliographical references (p. 359-360). ISBN 2-86480-458-1 : DDC 738/.0944/38074758231 20
  1. Pottery, French - France - Lorraine - Exhibitions. 2. Pottery - 18th century - France - Lorrainr - Exhibitions. 3. Pottery - 19th century - France - Lorraine - Exhibitions. I. Decker, Emile. II. Conseil régional de Lorraine. III. Title: French ceramics.
  NK4098.L67 C47 1990

Céramiques grecques de Marseille. Musée Borély. Marseille [1970] [42] p.
NB91.M35 M8   ***NYPL [3-MPE 90-6994]***

Cercle d'art contemporain. Lambert, Jean Clarence. Bernard Quentin . Paris , c1991. 215 p. :   DDC 709/.2 20
N6853.Q46 A4 1991

Cercle d'art contemporain. Seghers, Pierre. Clavé /. Paris , 1989. 423 p. :   ISBN 2-7022-0239-X   DDC 709/.2 B 20
N7113.C57 S4 1989

Cercle des artistes peintres du Québec. Robert, Guy, 1933- Cent vingt du Cercle des artistes peintres du Québec /. Montréal , 1989. 255 p. :   ISBN 2-920058-62-2   DDC 709/.2/2 20
N6546.Q4 R63 1989

CERCLE DES ARTISTES PEINTRES DU QUÉBEC - MEMBERSHIP. Robert, Guy, 1933- Cent vingt du Cercle des artistes peintres du Québec /. Montréal , 1989. 255 p. :   ISBN 2-920058-62-2   DDC 709/.2/2 20
N6546.Q4 R63 1989

Cercle et carré. Arte abstracto, arte concreto . [Valencia?] , c1990. 439 p. :   ISBN 84-7890-151-5
N6494.A2 A78 1990

CERCLE ET CARRÉ (GROUP) Arte abstracto, arte concreto . [Valencia?] , c1990. 439 p. :   ISBN 84-7890-151-5
N6494.A2 A78 1990

CEREMONIES. see RITES AND CEREMONIES.

Ceremony of memory : new expressions in spirituality among contemporary Hispanic artists / curated by Amalia Mesa-Bains. Santa Fe, N.M. : Center for Contemporary Arts of Santa Fe, c1988. 48 p. : col. ill. ; 31 cm. Catalog of a exhibition held at the Lannan Museum, Lake Worth, Fla., Jan. 28-Mar. 4, 1989 and at 9 other U. S. locations through Mar. 6, 1991. Includes bibliographical references (p. 48).   ISBN 0-929762-00-2
1. Art and religion - United States - Exhibitions. 2. Hispanic American art - Exhibitions. I. Mesa-Bains, Amalia.   ***NYPL [3-MAMT+ 91-7407]***

CERESA, CARLO, 1609-1679. Milesi, Silvana. Fra Galgario tra Seicento e Settecento . Bergamo , c1990. 206 p. :
NYPL [3-MCF+ G43 91-5343]

CERESA, CARLO, 1609-1679 - CATALOGS. Milesi, Silvana. Fra Galgario tra Seicento e Settecento . Bergamo , c1990. 206 p. :
ND1318.3 .M5 1990

Cernuschi, Claude, 1961- Jackson Pollock : meaning and significance / by Claude Cernuschi.1st ed. New York, NY : Icon Editions, c1992. p. cm. Includes bibliographical references and index.   ISBN 0-06-430978-9 (cloth) :   DDC 759.13 20
1. Pollock, Jackson, 1912-1956. 2. Painters - United States - Biography. 3. Abstract expressionism - United States. I. Pollock, Jackson, 1912-1956. II. Title.
ND237.P73 C47 1992

Ceroni, Angela. Amedeo Modigliani, les nus / Angela Ceroni. Düdingen, Suisse : Trio, c1989. 95 p. : ill. ; 29 x 31 cm.   ISBN 3-908573-01-7
1. Modigliani, Amedeo, 1884-1920. 2. Women in art. I. Title.   ***NYPL [3-MCF+ M69 91-7282]***

Certain places . Clift, William, 1944- Santa Fe, N.M. , c1987. [46] p. :   ISBN 0-9618165-0-3
NYPL [MFX+ (Clift) 91-2455]

CERUTI, GIACOMO, D. 1768. Milesi, Silvana. Fra Galgario tra Seicento e Settecento . Bergamo , c1990. 206 p. :
NYPL [3-MCF+ G43 91-5343]

CERUTI, GIACOMO, D. 1768 - CATALOGS. Milesi, Silvana. Fra Galgario tra Seicento e Settecento . Bergamo , c1990. 206 p. :
ND1318.3 .M5 1990

Cervantes, Gonzalo López. see López Cervantes, Gonzalo.

Cervantes, Miguel de. see Cervantes Saavedra, Miguel de, 1547-1616.

CERVANTES SAAVEDRA, MIGUEL DE, 1547-1616 - CHARACTERS - DON QUIXOTE - CATALOGS. Museo Iconográfico del Quijote. Museo Iconográfico del Quijote /. México, D.F. , 1987. 103 p. :   ISBN 968-7037-31-8
N910.G78 A6 1987

CERVETERI (ITALY) - ANTIQUITIES - EXHIBITIONS. Civiche raccolte numismatiche di Milano. Gli Etruschi e Cerveteri . Milano , c1980. 267 p. :   DDC 937/.5 19
DG70.C12 E88 1980
NYPL [3-MPEK 89-13643]

Cerveteri, Italy - Archaeology. see Cerveteri, Italy - Antiquities.

Cerwinske, Laura. Russian imperial style / Laura Cerwinske ; with the cooperation of A La Vieille Russie ; with photography by Anthony Johnson. 1st ed. New York : Prentice Hall Editions, c1990. 223 p. : col. ill. ; 32 cm. Includes bibliographical references (p. 220) and index.   ISBN 0-13-784810-2 :   DDC 745/.0947 20
1. Decorative arts - Russian S.F.S.R. 2. Art patronage - Russian S.F.S.R. 3. Russian S.F.S.R. - Social life and customs. I. Johnson, Anthony. II. Title.
NK975 .C45 1990
NYPL [3-MLF+ 91-3951]

Ces tableaux qui ont une histoire. Warnod, Jeanine. Le guide Warnod de la peinture . Paris , c1990. 323 p., 32 leaves of plates :   ISBN 2-7107-0457-9 :   DDC 750/.74/44 20
N2010 .A66 1990

César Manrique, Maler & Bildhauer & Architekt /. Sack, Manfred, 1928- Heidelberg , 1987. 1 v. (unpaged) :   ISBN 3-921524-93-8
NYPL [3-MCQ M285 91-5008]

César Manrique, Maler und Bildhauer und Architekt. Sack, Manfred, 1928- César Manrique, Maler & Bildhauer & Architekt /. Heidelberg , 1987. 1 v. (unpaged) :   ISBN 3-921524-93-8
NYPL [3-MCQ M285 91-5008]

César, ou, Les métamorphoses d'un grand art /. Hachet, Jean-Charles. Paris , 1989. 92 p. :
IN PROCESS (ONLINE)
NYPL [3-MGO+ (Baldaccini) 90-11990]

Cesar Pelli . Pelli, Cesar. New York , 1990. 288 p. :   ISBN 0-8478-1262-6   DDC 720/.92 20
NA737.P39 A4 1990
NYPL [3-MQZ (Pelli) 91-5464]

César Valverde /. Valverde, César. San José, Costa Rica , 1986. 264 p. :   DDC 759.97286 20
ND275.V34 A4 1986

CESETTI, GIUSEPPE, 1902- - CATALOGUES RAISONNÉS. Bossaglia, Rossana. Catalogo generale dei dipinti di Giuseppe Cesetti /. Milano , c1989-v. :   ISBN 88-374-1088-3 (v. 1)
NYPL [3-MCF+ C42 90-10852]

Česká legie. see Legie česká.

České iluminované rukopisy třináctého/šestnáctého století. Krása, Josef. České iluminované rukopisy 13./16. století /. Praha , 1990. 455 p. :   ISBN 80-207-0114-1 :   DDC 745.6/7/094370902 20
ND3235.C9 K69 1990

České iluminované rukopisy 13./16. století /. Krása, Josef. Praha , 1990. 455 p. :   ISBN 80-207-0114-1 :   DDC 745.6/7/094370902 20
ND3235.C9 K69 1990

Československá legie ve Francii. see Legie česká.

Československá vědeckotechnická společnost. "8" . Brno [1989?] 1 v. (unpaged) :
N6831 .A13 1989

Československé legie. see Legie česká.

Český neoklasicismus dvacátých let : první část, Malba-kresba = [výběr vystavených děl, koncepce výstavy a text katalogu Hana Rousová]. [Prague] : Galerie hlavního města Prahy, [1986?] 1 v. (unpaged) : ill. (some col.) ; 27 cm. Includes bibliographical references.
1. Neoclassicism (Art) - Czechoslovakia - Exhibitions. 2. Art, Czech - Exhibitions. 3. Art, Modern - 20th century - Czechoslovakia - Exhibitions. 4. Women in art - Exhibitions. 5. Nude in art - Exhibitions. I. Rousová, Hana. II. Galerie hlavního města Prahy.
N6831.5.N46 C47 1986

Cessi, Francesco. Vincenzo e Gian Gerolamo Grandi, scultori (secolo XVI) / a cura di Francesco Cessi. 1a ed. Trento : CAT, 1967. 116 p. : ill. ; 18 cm. (Collana Artisti trentini. 51) Bibliography: p. 78-81
1. Grandi, Vincenzo. 2. Grandi, Gian Gerolamo.
NYPL [3-MGO (Grandi) 90-6345]

Čeští ilustrátoři v současné knize pro děti a mládež /. Holešovský, František. Praha , 1989. 455 p. :
NC989.C9 H62 1989

Cevese, Renato. Seminario internazionale di storia dell'architettura (7th : 1988 Sept. 1-7 : Vicenza, Italy) Andrea Palladio, nuovi contributi . Milano , c1990. 247 p. :   ISBN 88-435-3086-0
NYPL [3-MQZ+ (Palladio) 91-4941]

Ceysson, Bernard. Bazaine, Jean, 1904- Bazaine. Paris , c1990. 178 p. :   ISBN 2-605-00162-8
NYPL [3-MCO B35 90-12858]

Cézanne /. Coutagne, Denis. Paris , c1990. 240 p. :   ISBN 2-903702-27-6 :   DDC 759.4 20
ND553.C33 C68 1990

Cézanne. Wadley, Nicholas. The paintings of Cézanne /. London , 1989. 128 p. :   ISBN 0-600-56504-1 :   DDC 759.4 19
ND553.C33   ***NYPL [3-MCO C42 90-12444]***

Cézanne and Poussin . Verdi, Richard. Edinburgh , London , 1990. [202] p. :   ISBN 0-85331-569-8 (pbk.) :   DDC 759.4 759.4 20
ND553.P8   ***NYPL [3-MCO P87 90-12306]***

Cézanne and Poussin . Verdi, Richard. London , c1990. 202 p. :   ISBN 0-85331-569-8   DDC 759.4 20
N6853.P66 A4 1990

Cézanne, Paul, 1839-1906. Sainte-Victoire, Cézanne, 1990. Paris : Reunion des musées nationaux ; Aix-en-Provence : Musée Granet, c1990. 358 p. : ill. (some col.) ; 28 cm. Catalog of an exhibition held at the Musée Granet, June 16-Sept. 2, 1990. Includes bibliographical references.   ISBN 2-7118-2366-0 (pbk.)
1. Cézanne, Paul, 1839-1906 - Exhibitions. I. Musée Granet. II. Title.
NYPL [3-MCO C42 90-12981]

Verdi, Richard. Cézanne and Poussin . London , c1990. 202 p. :   ISBN 0-85331-569-8   DDC 759.4 20
N6853.P66 A4 1990

Wadley, Nicholas. The paintings of Cézanne /. London , 1989. 128 p. :   ISBN 0-600-56504-1 :   DDC 759.4 19
ND553.C33   ***NYPL [3-MCO C42 90-12444]***

CÉZANNE, PAUL, 1839-1906. Verdi, Richard. Cézanne and Poussin . Edinburgh , London , 1990. [202] p. :   ISBN 0-85331-569-8 (pbk.) :   DDC 759.4 759.4 20
ND553.P8   ***NYPL [3-MCO P87 90-12306]***

Wadley, Nicholas. The paintings of Cézanne /. London , 1989. 128 p. :   ISBN 0-600-56504-1 :   DDC 759.4 19
ND553.C33   ***NYPL [3-MCO C42 90-12444]***

CÉZANNE, PAUL, 1839-1906 - CRITICISM AND INTERPRETATION. Coutagne, Denis. Cézanne /. Paris , c1990. 240 p. :   ISBN 2-903702-27-6 :   DDC 759.4 20
ND553.C33 C68 1990

CÉZANNE, PAUL, 1839-1906 - EXHIBITIONS. Cézanne, Paul, 1839-1906. Sainte-Victoire, Cézanne, 1990. Paris , Aix-en-Provence , c1990. 358 p. :   ISBN 2-7118-2366-0 (pbk.)
NYPL [3-MCO C42 90-12981]

Verdi, Richard. Cézanne and Poussin . London , c1990. 202 p. :   ISBN 0-85331-569-8   DDC 759.4 20
N6853.P66 A4 1990

Ch. Cottet /. Cottet, Charles, 1924- Bulle , c1988. 157 p. :   ISBN 2-88039-010-9
NYPL [3-MCZ C847 90-2627]

Chabot, Hendrik, 1894-1949. Hendrik Chabot : schilderijen en beeldhouwwerken = paintings and sculptures : 11 maart t-m 22 april 1990, Rotterdam, Museum Boymans-van Beuningen. Rotterdam : Het Museum, [1990] 24 p. : ill. (some col.) ; 27 cm. Dutch and English. Includes bibliographical references (p. 21).   ISBN 90-6918-057-X
1. Chabot, Hendrik, 1894-1949 - Exhibitions. I. Museum Boymans-Van Beuningen. II. Title.
NYPL [3-MCH C42 91-7291]

CHABOT, HENDRIK, 1894-1949 - EXHIBITIONS. Chabot, Hendrik, 1894-1949. Hendrik Chabot . Rotterdam [1990] 24 p. :   ISBN 90-6918-057-X
NYPL [3-MCH C42 91-7291]

Chaco body /. Gittings, Kirk. Albuquerque,
N.M. , 1991. 85 p. :   ISBN 0-8263-1277-2
     NYPL [MFX (Gittings) 91-6549]

**CHACO CANYON (N.M.) - DESCRIPTION
AND TRAVEL - VIEWS.**
Gittings, Kirk. Chaco body /. Albuquerque,
N.M. , 1991. 85 p. :   ISBN 0-8263-1277-2
     NYPL [MFX (Gittings) 91-6549]

Chadds Ford, Pa. Brandywine River Museum. see
Brandywine River Museum.

Chadwick, Eva. Farr, Dennis, 1929- Lynn
Chadwick sculptor . Oxford [England] , New
York , 1990. 347 p., [12] p. of plates :   ISBN
0-19-817213-3 :   DDC 730/.92 20
NB497.C45 A4 1990
     NYPL [3-MGO (Chadwick) 91-4618]

**CHADWICK, LYNN, 1914- - CATALOGUES
RAISONNÉS.**
Farr, Dennis, 1929- Lynn Chadwick sculptor .
Oxford [England] , New York , 1990. 347 p.,
[12] p. of plates :   ISBN 0-19-817213-3 :   DDC
730/.92 20
NB497.C45 A4 1990
     NYPL [3-MGO (Chadwick) 91-4618]

Chagall e la ceramica /. Forestier, Sylvie.
Milano , 1990. 187 p. :   ISBN 88-16-60103-5
     NYPL [3-MCZ+ C43]

Chagall, Marc, 1887-
Compton, Susan P. [Marc Chagall. English.]
Marc Chagall . Munich, Federal Republic of
Germany , New York, NY, USA , c1990. 268
p. :   ISBN 3-7913-1064-X   DDC 760/.092 20
N6999.C46 A4 1990

Die 100 Radierungen zu den Fabeln von La
Fontaine / Marc Chagall ; mit einer Einführung
von Otto Breicha. Salzburg : [Salzburger
Landessammlungen Rupertinum, 1989] 223 p. :
ill. ; 29 cm. (Eine Publikation in der Schriftenreihe
der Salzburger Landessammlungen Rupertinum)
Includes fables by J.d. La Fontaine in German.   DDC
769.92 20
*1. Chagall, Marc, 1887-. 2. La Fontaine, Jean de,
1621-1695. Fables - Illustrations. I. La Fontaine, Jean
de, 1621-1695. Fables. German. Selections. 1989. II.
Title. III. Title: Hundert Radierungen zu den Fabeln
von La Fontaine. IV. Series: Publikation in der Reihe
der Schriften der Salzburger Landessammlungen
Rupertinum.*
NE2056.5.C45 A4 1989

Noir et blanc : lavis et sculptures / Marc
Chagall. Paris : Galerie Enrico Navarra, c1990.
94 p. : ill. (some col.) ; 30 cm.   DDC 709/.2 20
1. Chagall, Marc, 1887- - Exhibitions. I. Title.
N6999.C46 A4 1990a

CHAGALL, MARC, 1887-
Chagall, Marc, 1887- Die 100 Radierungen zu
den Fabeln von La Fontaine /. Salzburg [1989]
223 p. :   DDC 769.92 20
NE2056.5.C45 A4 1989

CHAGALL, MARC, 1887- - CATALOGS.
Compton, Susan P. [Marc Chagall. English.]
Marc Chagall . Munich, Federal Republic of
Germany , New York, NY, USA , c1990. 268
p. :   ISBN 3-7913-1064-X   DDC 760/.092 20
N6999.C46 A4 1990

**CHAGALL, MARC, 1887- - CHILDHOOD
AND YOUTH - JUVENILE
LITERATURE.**
Bober, Natalie. Marc Chagall . Philadelphia ,
1991. p. cm.   ISBN 0-8276-0379-7   DDC 759.7 B
20
N6999.C46 B6 1991

CHAGALL, MARC, 1887- - EXHIBITIONS.
Chagall, Marc, 1887- Noir et blanc . Paris ,
c1990. 94 p. :   DDC 709/.2 20
N6999.C46 A4 1990a

Compton, Susan P. [Marc Chagall. English.]
Marc Chagall . Munich , New York, NY,
USA , c1990. 268 p. :   ISBN 3-7913-1064-X
     NYPL [3-MCZ+ C43 90-13436]

[Vitraux pour Jerusalem. German]
Glasmalereien für Jerusalem / Marc Chagall ;
Text von Jean Leymarie ; [aus dem
Französischen übersetzt von U.R.
Hemmerich]. Monte Carlo : A. Sauret, c1962.
211 p. : ill. (some col.) ; 34 cm. "Marc Chagall
hat für dieses Buch eigens zwei Originallithographien
geschaffen"--P. [3] Translation of Vitraux pour
Jerusalem.
1. Bet ha-ḥolim "Hadasah" (Jerusalem). Synagogue. 2.

*Glass painting and staining - Jerusalem - History - 20th
century. I. Leymarie, Jean. II. Title. III. Title: Marc
Chagall, Glasmalereien für Jerusalem.*
     NYPL [3-MCZ+ C43 91-7160]

CHAGALL, MARE, 1887-
Mayer, Klaus. Ich bin mit dir . Würzburg ,
1989. 115 p. :   ISBN 3-429-01137-3
     NYPL [MDG+ (Chagall) 89-18773]

Chagall to Kitaj . Kampf, Avram. New York ,
London , 1990. 206 p. :   ISBN 0-275-93900-6 (alk.
paper)   DDC 704/.03924/0904 20
N7417 .K34 1991

Chagoya, Enrique.
Enrique Chagoya : when paradise arrived :
[exhibition] Alternative Museum, March
11-April 29, 1989. New York, N.Y. : The
Museum, c1989. 24 p. ; ill., port. ; 28 cm.
Includes an interview with the artist by Moira Roth.
     ISBN 0-932075-25-8 (pbk.)
*1. Chagoya, Enrique - Exhibitions. I. Roth, Moira. II.
Alternative Museum (New York, N.Y.). III. Title. IV.
Title: When paradise arrived.*
     NYPL [3-MCX C433 91-4634]

CHAGOYA, ENRIQUE - EXHIBITIONS.
Chagoya, Enrique. Enrique Chagoya . New
York, N.Y. , c1989. 24 p. ;   ISBN 0-932075-25-8
(pbk.)   *NYPL [3-MCX C433 91-4634]*

Chaillot, Babina. Defraoui, Silvie. Orient/occident
/. Genève , c1989. 53 p. :
     NYPL [3-MCZ + D316 89-27977]

Chaimowicz, Georg, 1929-
Georg Chaimowicz : Ersichtliches : Städtische
Galerie Lüdenscheid, 22. Januar-21. Februar
1988 / [Herausgeber, Städtische Galerie
Lüdenscheid] ; in Zusammenarbeit mit dem
Kultursekretariat Gütersloh, gefördert durch den
Kultusminister des Landes
Nordrhein-Westfalen ; [Katalogredaktion
und -gestaltung, Uwe Obier]. Lüdenscheid : Die
Galerie, c1988. 100 p. : chiefly ill. ; 21 x 30
cm.
*1. Chaimowicz, Georg, 1929- - Exhibitions. I.
Städtische Galerie Lüdenscheid. II. Title. III. Title:
Ersichtliches.*
MLCS 88/02633 (N)
     NYPL [3-MCK+ C434 91-5888]

**CHAIMOWICZ, GEORG, 1929- -
EXHIBITIONS.**
Chaimowicz, Georg, 1929- Georg Chaimowicz .
Lüdenscheid , c1988. 100 p. :
MLCS 88/02633 (N)
     NYPL [3-MCK+ C434 91-5888]

CHAIRS - HISTORY - 19TH CENTURY.
Baudot, François. Les assises du siècle /. Paris ,
c1990. 116 p. :   ISBN 2-906450-46-4   DDC
749/.32/0904 20
NK2715 .B3 1990

CHAIRS - HISTORY - 20TH CENTURY.
Baudot, François. Les assises du siècle /. Paris ,
c1990. 116 p. :   ISBN 2-906450-46-4   DDC
749/.32/0904 20
NK2715 .B3 1990

**CHAIRS - MASSACHUSETTS - CONCORD -
EXHIBITIONS.**
Haines, Carol L. "Forms to sett on" . Concord,
Mass. [1984?] 36 p. :
NK2715 .H35 1984
     NYPL [3-MOF 90-12018]

Chakra, Narisa. Terence Cuneo, railway painter
of the century / Narisa Chakra. 1st ed.
London : New Cavendish Books, 1990. 160 p. :
ill. ; 28 x 34 cm.   ISBN 0-904568-74-1
1. Cuneo, Terence. I. Title.
     NYPL [3-MCV+ C972 90-11746]

CHALEPAS, GIANNOULĒS, 1851-1938.
Kairophylas, Giannēs, 1927- Giannoulēs
Chalepas . Athēna , 1986. 79 p. :
     NYPL [3-MGO (Chalepas) 90-4715]

Challenging the past . Fu, Shen, 1937-
Washington, D.C. , Seattle , c1991. p. cm.
     ISBN 0-295-97124-X (cloth : alk. paper)   DDC
759.951 20
ND1049.C4523 A4 1991

Challié, Laurence Buffet- see **Buffet-Challié,
Laurence.**

Cham sculpture album. T Hà N 1988. 232 p., [1]
leaf of plates :
NB1910 .T36 1988

Cham, 1819-1879. Croquis Parisiens / par Cham.
Paris : Au Bureau du journal le Charivari,
c[18--] [15] leaves : all ill. ; 24 cm. On cover:
Album.
1. French wit and humor, Pictorial. I. Title.
     NYPL [3-MEM (Cham) 88-3113]

Chamay, Jacques. Sculptures en pierre du Musée
de Genève /. Mainz am Rhein , c1989- v. :
     ISBN 3-8053-1130-3 (t. 1)
     NYPL [MGH+ 89-24649]

Chamberlain, David, 1949-
Melodic forms : the sculpture of David
Chamberlain / [editor, Pamela Wolfson].1st ed.
Boston : D.R. Godine : Pucker Safrai Gallery,
1990. [67] p. : chiefly col. ill. ; 29 cm.   ISBN
0-87923-854-2   DDC 730/.92 20
*1. Chamberlain, David, 1949- - Themes, motives. I.
Wolfson, Pamela. II. Pucker-Safrai Gallery. III. Title.*
NB237.C425 A4 1991
     NYPL [3-MGO (Chamberlain) 91-6227]

**CHAMBERLAIN, DAVID, 1949- - THEMES,
MOTIVES.**
Chamberlain, David, 1949- Melodic forms .
Boston , 1990. [67] p. :   ISBN 0-87923-854-2
DDC 730/.92 20
NB237.C425 A4 1991
     NYPL [3-MGO (Chamberlain) 91-6227]

Chamberlain, John, 1927-
John Chamberlain, new sculpture : March
8-April 13, 1991. New York : Pace Gallery,
c1991. 17 p., [15] leaves of plates : ill. (some
col.) ; 23 cm. Text by Julie Sylvester. Errata slip
inserted. ISBN 1-87828-314-6
*1. Chamberlain, John, 1927- - Exhibitions. I. Sylvester,
Julie, 1954-. II. Title.*
     NYPL [MGO (Chamberlain) 91-5999]

**CHAMBERLAIN, JOHN, 1927- -
EXHIBITIONS.**
Chamberlain, John, 1927- John Chamberlain,
new sculpture . New York , c1991. 17 p., [15]
leaves of plates :   ISBN 1-87828-314-6
     NYPL [MGO (Chamberlain) 91-5999]

Chambers, Karen S. Trompe l'oeil at home : faux
finishes and fantasy settings / Karen S.
Chambers. New York : Rizzoli, c1991. p. cm.
Includes bibliographical references and index.   ISBN
0-8478-1420-3   DDC 751.7/3 20
*1. Visual perception. 2. Trompe l'œil painting. 3.
Optical illusions. 4. Illusion in art. 5. Interior
decoration. I. Title.*
N7430.5 .C48 1991

Chambers, Marlene. Colorado, 1990 . Denver,
Colo. , c1990. 143 p. :   ISBN 0-914738-39-9 (pbk.)
IN PROCESS (ONLIN)
     NYPL [3-MAMT 90-13383]

Chambord . Cloulas, Ivan. Paris , c1989. 143 p. :
     ISBN 2-09-241001-6
     NYPL [3-MQWF+ 90-2437]

Chameleon with a camera . Darling, Dennis
Carlyle. Wimberley, Tex. , c1989. 91 p. :   ISBN
0-945618-02-6 (sbk.)   *NYPL [MFW 90-643]*

**CHAMORRO, KOLDO, 1949- -
EXHIBITIONS.**
Pitts, Terence. 4 Spanish photographers .
[Tucson, Ariz.] , c1988. 23 p. :
     NYPL [MFW+ 89-1448]

Chamot, Mary, 1900- Russian painting and
sculpture / by Mary Chamot. Oxford :
Pergamon Press ; New York : Macmillan,
c1963. xiii, 55 p., 36 p. of plates : ill. (The
Commonwealth and international library of science,
technology, engineering and liberal studies. 147)
Pergamon Oxford Russian studies. Background books ;
2 Includes index. Bibliography: p. 50-51.
*1. Art, Modern - 19th century - Soviet Union. 2. Art,
Modern - 20th century - Soviet Union. I. Title.*
     NYPL [3-MAM 90-6295]

Champa, Kermit Swiler. The rise of landscape
painting in France : Corot to Monet / Kermit
S. Champa ; with contributions by Fronia E.
Wissman and Deborah Johnson ; with an
introduction by Richard R. Brettell.
Manchester, N.H. : Currier Gallery of Art ;
New York : Distributed by H.N. Abrams,
c1991. 231 p. : ill. ; 28 cm.   ISBN 0-929710-06-1
(Currier : pbk.)
*1. Landscape painting, French - Exhibitions. 2.
Landscape painting - 19th century - France -
Exhibitions. I. Currier Gallery of Art. II. Title.*
     NYPL [3-MCN 91-4059]

CHAMPAIGN COUNTY, ILL. - MAPS.
(1990) Rockford Map Publishers. Champaign
County, Illinois, land atlas & plat book .
Rockford, Ill. [c1990] 1 atlas (65 p.) :
    NYPL [Map Div. 90-11380]

**Champaign County, Illinois, land atlas & plat
book** . Rockford Map Publishers. Rockford, Ill.
[c1990] 1 atlas (65 p.) :
    NYPL [Map Div. 90-11380]

**Champfleury, 1821-1889.
VIOLON DE FAÏENCE - ILLUSTRATIONS.**
Adeline, Jules, 1845-1909. La légende du
violon de faïence /. Paris , 1895 ([Paris] : A.
Lahure) 46 p., [1] leaf of plates : DDC 769.92
20
NE2049.5.A34 A4 1895

CHAMPLEVÉ, MEDIEVAL - EUROPE.
Haseloff, Günther. Email im frühen Mittelalter .
Marburg , c1990. 244 p. : ISBN 3-89398-020-2
    NYPL [3-MNV 91-5235]

**Champs de bataille des légions chécoslovaques en
France.** Nejedlý, Otakar, 1883-1957.
Francouzská bojiště československých legií .
Praze [1920?] [4] p., [8] leaves of plates :
    NYPL [3-MAMY+++ 83-2786]

Chamu chōkoku. T Hà N 1988. 232 p., [1] leaf of
plates :
NB1910 .T36 1988

CH'AN BUDDHISM. see ZEN BUDDHISM.

Chan, Charis. Imperial China / Charis Chan. San
Francisco : Chronicle Books, 1992. p. cm.
(Architectural guides for travelers) Includes
bibliographical references (p.) and index. ISBN
0-8118-0018-0 DDC 720/.951 20
*1. Architecture - China - Ming-Ch'ing dynasties,
1368-1912 - Guide-books. 2. China - Royal household -
Dwellings - Guide-books. 3. Palaces - China -
Guide-books. 4. China - Description and travel -
1976- - Guide-books. I. Title. II. Series.*
NA1543.5 .C4 1992

**CHANCELLORSVILLE, BATTLE OF, 1863 -
MAPS.**
Wilshin, Francis F. Tour of the battlefields of
Fredericksburg, Chancellorsville, Wilderness,
Spotsylvania C.H. . [Fredericksburg, Va.]
[1955?] [17] leaves :
    NYPL [Map Div. 90-949]

Chancho, Joaquim, 1943- Catálogo nacional de
arte contemporáneo. Barcelona , c1989. 4 v. :
ISBN 84-87433-00-6 (obra completa)
N7108 .C29 1989

Chanel . Madsen, Axel. New York , c1990. x,
388 p., [16] leaves of plates : ISBN
0-8050-0961-2 : DDC 746.9/2/092 B 20
TT505.C45 M33 1990
    NYPL [3-MME 90-11139]

CHANEL, COCO, 1883-1971.
Madsen, Axel. Chanel . New York , c1990. x,
388 p., [16] leaves of plates : ISBN
0-8050-0961-2 : DDC 746.9/2/092 B 20
TT505.C45 M33 1990
    NYPL [3-MME 90-11139]

Chanel, Gabrielle. see Chanel, Coco, 1883-1971.

Chang, Phil Inje. Gosney, Michael, 1954- The
Verbum book of scanned imagery /. Redwood
City, CA , 1990. p. cm. ISBN 1-558-51091-5 :
DDC 760 20
N7433 .G68 1990

**Chang sha Ma wang dui yi hao han mu.
Selections. English.** The Lacquers of the
Mawangdui tomb / translated by Joanna
Waley-Cohen from the sections dealing with the
lacquer finds in Changsha Mawangdui yihao
Han mu (Beijing, 1973). [Great Britain] :
Oriental Ceramic Society, [1984?] (Hong
Kong : Millennia) 43 p. : ill. ; 29 cm. (Oriental
Ceramic Society translations . no. 11) Translation of:
selections from Chang sha Ma wang dui yi hao han mu.
DDC 745.7/2/0931 19
*1. Lacquer and lacquering - China - Ch'ang-sha shih. 2.
Ch'ang-sha shih (China) - Antiquities. 3. Ch'ang-sha
shih (China) - Tombs. I. Waley-Cohen, Joanna. II.
Oriental Ceramic Society. III. Title. IV. Series.*
    NYPL [3-MNX+ 89-25211]

**CH'ANG-SHA SHIH (CHINA) -
ANTIQUITIES.**
Chang sha Ma wang dui yi hao han mu.
Selections. English. The Lacquers of the
Mawangdui tomb /. [Great Britain] [1984?]
(Hong Kong : Millennia) 43 p. : DDC

745.7/2/0931 19
    NYPL [3-MNX+ 89-25211]

CH'ANG-SHA SHIH (CHINA) - TOMBS.
Chang sha Ma wang dui yi hao han mu.
Selections. English. The Lacquers of the
Mawangdui tomb /. [Great Britain] [1984?]
(Hong Kong : Millennia) 43 p. : DDC
745.7/2/0931 19
    NYPL [3-MNX+ 89-25211]

Chang, Ta-ch'ien, 1899-
Fu, Shen, 1937- Challenging the past .
Washington, D.C. , Seattle , c1991. p. cm.
    ISBN 0-295-97124-X (cloth : alk. paper) DDC
759.951 20
ND1049.C4523 A4 1991

**CHANG, TA-CH'IEN, 1899- - CRITICISM
AND INTERPRETATION.**
Fu, Shen, 1937- Challenging the past .
Washington, D.C. , Seattle , c1991. p. cm.
    ISBN 0-295-97124-X (cloth : alk. paper) DDC
759.951 20
ND1049.C4523 A4 1991

CHANG, TA-CH'IEN, 1899- - EXHIBITIONS.
Fu, Shen, 1937- Challenging the past .
Washington, D.C. , Seattle , c1991. p. cm.
    ISBN 0-295-97124-X (cloth : alk. paper) DDC
759.951 20
ND1049.C4523 A4 1991

Changements /. Michals, Duane. Paris , c1981. 1
v. (unpaged) : ISBN 2-7335-0019-8
    NYPL [MFX (Michals) 91-7988]

Changing images . Lilly Library (Indiana
University, Bloomington) Bloomington, Ind. ,
1991. 62 p. : ISBN 1-87959-800-0 DDC
741.6/4/09034074772255 20
NC978 .L55 1991

Changing images of pictorial space . Dunning,
William, 1933- Syracuse , 1991. xi, 254 p. :
    ISBN 0-8156-2505-7 (cloth : alk. paper) DDC
750/.1/8 20
ND1475 .D86 1991   *NYPL [3-MC 91-5767]*

Changing reality . Bendavid-Val, Leah.
[Washington, D.C.] , c1991. 132 p. : ISBN
0-912347-76-7   *NYPL [MFW 91-6156]*

Chanin, Eileen. Contemporary Australian painting
/. Roseville, NSW, Australia , c1990. 192 p. :
ISBN 0-947131-25-6
    NYPL [3-MCY+ 90-13279]

Chants tatoués =. Ben Dhiab, Ahmed.
Rotterdam , 1987. [16], 125 p. : ISBN
90-6330-139-1
    NYPL [3-MCZ + B4495 90-8107]

Chao Shao-an . Avitabile, Gunhild. Frankfurt am
Main , c1988. 58 p. : ISBN 3-88270-046-7 DDC
759.951 20
ND1049.C4527 A4 1988
    NYPL [3-MAG+ 91-6442]

Chao, Shao-ang, 1905-
Avitabile, Gunhild. Chao Shao-an . Frankfurt
am Main , c1988. 58 p. : ISBN 3-88270-046-7
DDC 759.951 20
ND1049.C4527 A4 1988
    NYPL [3-MAG+ 91-6442]

CHAO, SHAO-ANG, 1905- - EXHIBITIONS.
Avitabile, Gunhild. Chao Shao-an . Frankfurt
am Main , c1988. 58 p. : ISBN 3-88270-046-7
DDC 759.951 20
ND1049.C4527 A4 1988
    NYPL [3-MAG+ 91-6442]

Chao, Wu-chi. see Zao, Wou-ki, 1921-

CHAOTIC BEHAVIOR IN SYSTEMS.
Porter, Eliot, 1901- Nature's chaos /. New
York, N.Y., U. S. A. , 1990. 125, [1] p. : ISBN
0-670-83532-3 : DDC 779/.3 20
TR721 .G58 1990
    NYPL [MFX+ (Porter) 91-6781]

**CHAPADA DIAMANTINA (BRAZIL) -
DESCRIPTION AND TRAVEL - VIEWS.**
Boni, Zé de. Paisagem mágica . [São Paulo]
[1990?] [128] p. :
    NYPL [MFX (Boni) 91-3410]

Chapellier Galleries (New York, N.Y.)
Chase, William Merritt, 1849-1916. William
Merritt Chase, 1849-1916 ... . New York
[1969] [32] p. :
    NYPL [3-MCX C49 90-6403]

Wiles, Irving Ramsay, 1861-1948. Irving
Ramsey Wiles, 1861-1948 . [New York] ,

c1967. ca. 50 p. :
    NYPL [3-MCX W669 91-879]

Chapin Library. Rubens and the book .
[Williamstown, Mass.] [c1977] ix, 307 p. :
    DDC 741.64/092/4
NC984.5.R8 A4 1977a
    NYPL [MDG (Rubens) 86-4489]

Chaplin, Patrice. Into the darkness laughing : the
story of Modigliani's last mistress, Jeanne
Hébuterne / Patrice Chaplin. London : Virago,
1990. 151 p., [8] p. of plates : ill., ports. ; 24
cm. ISBN 1-85381-235-8
*1. Hébuterne, Jeanne. 2. Modigliani, Amadeo,
1884-1920 - Relations with women - Jeanne Hébuterne.
3. Painters - France - Biography. I. Title. II. Title: Story
of Modigliani's last mistress, Jeanne Hébuterne.*
    NYPL [3-MCF M69 91-4515]

Chappell, Sally Anderson. Architecture and
planning of Graham, Anderson, Probst, and
White, 1912-1936 : transforming tradition /
Sally A. Kitt Chappell. Chicago : University of
Chicago Press, 1991. p. cm. (Chicago architecture
and urbanism) Includes bibliographical references and
index. ISBN 0-226-10134-7 DDC 720/.92/2 20
*1. Graham, Anderson, Probst, White. 2. Architecture,
Modern - 20th century - United States. I. Title. II.
Series.*
NA737.G7 C48 1991

The Charade of mastery : deciphering modernism
in contemporary art : Whitney Museum of
American Art, Downtown at Federal Reserve
Plaza, October 31, 1990-January 11, 1991. New
York, N.Y. : Whitney Museum of American
Art, c1990. 18 p. : ill. ; 23 cm. Cover title.
*1. Art, American - Exhibitions. 2. Art, Modern - 20th
century - United States - Exhibitions. I. Whitney
Museum of American Art. II. Whitney Museum of
American Art, Downtown at Federal Reserve Plaza.*
    NYPL [3-MAMT 91-4324]

Charchoune. Creuze, Raymond. Charchouniana /.
Paris , c1989. 119 p. : ISBN 2-905037-06-7
    DDC 759.4 20
ND553.S52 A4 1989

Charchoune, Serge, 1888-1975.
Abracadabra : de signes, lettres, billets, triangles
magiques, messages musicaux, écritures
imaginaires, sphynx et serpents graphiques,
silhouettes et signatures du peintre Serge
Charchoune, adressés à Pierre Lecuire. [Paris :
Editions des livres de Pierre Lecuire, 1971] [47]
p. : ill. (some col.) ; 24 x 39 cm. The letters and
other examples of the artist's writing are reproduced in
facsimile. Issued in loose sections in a decorated paper
cover, in a case. "Il a été tiré de cette édition ... 12
exemplaires numérotés de 1 à 12 sur Japon Hosho, avec
une suite sur Chine des 6 bois du livre et 1 bois
supplémentaire; 54 exemplaires numérotés de 13 à 66
sur grand vélin d'Arches; 10 exemplaires, marqués de A
à J, réservés aux collaborateurs"--P. [45].
"Poème-portrait du peintre Serge Charchoune par Pierre
Lecuire": p. [37]. LC has copy no. 27. DLC Source:
Purchase from Pierre Lecuire, Aug. 18, 1987. DLC
    DDC 700/.92 20
*1. Charchoune, Serge, 1888-1975. I. Lecuire, Pierre,
1922-. II. Title.*
N6853.C4715 A4 1971

Creuze, Raymond. Charchouniana /. Paris ,
c1989. 119 p. : ISBN 2-905037-06-7 DDC 759.4
20
ND553.S52 A4 1989

CHARCHOUNE, SERGE, 1888-1975.
Charchoune, Serge, 1888-1975. Abracadabra .
[Paris , 1971] [47] p. : DDC 700/.92 20
N6853.C4715 A4 1971

**CHARCHOUNE, SERGE, 1888-1975 -
CATALOGS.**
Creuze, Raymond. Charchouniana /. Paris ,
c1989. 119 p. : ISBN 2-905037-06-7 DDC 759.4
20
ND553.S52 A4 1989

Charchouniana /. Creuze, Raymond. Paris ,
c1989. 119 p. : ISBN 2-905037-06-7 DDC 759.4
20
ND553.S52 A4 1989

Charcot, deux concepts de nature. De humani
corporis fabrica. Montréal, Québec, Canada ,
1988, c1985-c1986. 3 v. in 1 case : DDC
700/.92/271428 20
N7433.35.C2 D4 1988
    NYPL [MEMZ 90-11163]

Chardeau, Jean. Caillebotte, Gustave, 1848-1894. Les dessins de Caillebotte /. Paris , c1989. 127 p. : ISBN 2-86665-084-0 DDC 759.4 20
NC248.C27 A4 1989
NYPL [3-MCO+ C134 91-3741]

Chardin /. Rosenberg, Pierre. [Chardin. English.] Geneva , New York , 1991. 117 p. : ISBN 0-8478-1350-9 (pbk.) DDC 759.4 20
ND553.C4 R5813 1991

Chardin, Jean Baptiste Siméon, 1699-1779. Conisbee, Philip. Soap bubbles by Jean-Siméon Chardin /. Los Angeles, Calif. , c1990. 25 p. : ISBN 0-87587-154-2
NYPL [3-MCO C47 91-6592]

CHARDIN, JEAN BAPTISTE SIMÉON, 1699-1779. Kohle, Hubertus. Ut pictura poesis non erit . Hildesheim , New York , 1989. 191 p. : ISBN 3-487-09096-1 : DDC 111/.85/092 20
B2018.A4 K64 1989
NYPL [3-MAB 91-4602]

Rosenberg, Pierre. [Chardin. English.] Chardin /. Geneva , New York , 1991. 117 p. : ISBN 0-8478-1350-9 (pbk.) DDC 759.4 20
ND553.C4 R5813 1991

SOAP BUBBLES - EXHIBITIONS. Conisbee, Philip. Soap bubbles by Jean-Siméon Chardin /. Los Angeles, Calif. , c1990. 25 p. : ISBN 0-87587-154-2
NYPL [3-MCO C47 91-6592]

Chardonnet, Jean, 1913- (ed) Larousse, firm, publishers, Paris. Atlas international Larousse. Paris [1950] xix, [144], 42, 41 p.
NYPL [Map Div. 90-64]

CHAREAU, PIERRE. Vellay, Marc. Pierre Chareau, architecte, meublier, 1883-1950 /. Paris , 1986. 111 p. : ISBN 2-86930-026-3
NYPL [3-MOF 90-11128]

Chargesheimer 1924-1972 . Chargesheimer, 1924-1972. [München] [1983] 24 p. :
NYPL [MFX (Chargesheimer) 90-13458]

Chargesheimer, 1924-1972. Chargesheimer 1924-1972 : Fotografien = Chargesheimer, 1924-1972 : photographs / [Konzept der Ausstellung und Texte, Evelyn Weiss]. [München] : Goethe-Institut, [1983] 24 p. : ill. ; 27 cm. German and English. 1. Chargesheimer, 1924-1972 - Exhibitions. I. Goethe-Institut (Munich, Germany). II. Title. III. Title: Chargesheimer, 1924-1972 : photographs.
NYPL [MFX (Chargesheimer) 90-13458]

CHARGESHEIMER, 1924-1972 - EXHIBITIONS. Chargesheimer, 1924-1972. Chargesheimer 1924-1972 . [München] [1983] 24 p. :
NYPL [MFX (Chargesheimer) 90-13458]

Chargesheimer, 1924-1972 : photographs. Chargesheimer, 1924-1972. Chargesheimer 1924-1972 . [München] [1983] 24 p. :
NYPL [MFX (Chargesheimer) 90-13458]

Charigny, André. Bichet, Pierre. André Charigny /. Besançon , c1989. 141 p. : ISBN 2-901040-78-1
NYPL [3-MCO+ C473 89-26937]

CHARIGNY, ANDRÉ - CRITICISM AND INTERPRETATION. Bichet, Pierre. André Charigny /. Besançon , c1989. 141 p. : ISBN 2-901040-78-1
NYPL [3-MCO+ C473 89-26937]

The Charles and Elizabeth Prothro Texas photography series . (no. 1) Noggle, Anne, 1922- For God, country, and the thrill of it . College Station , c1990. xi, 160 p. : ISBN 0-89096-401-7 (alk. paper) DDC 940.54/4973/092 B 20
D790 .N64 1990
NYPL [MFX+ (Noggle) 91-3591]

The Charles and Emma Frye Art Museum . Charles and Emma Frye Art Museum. Seattle, Wash., U. S. A. (704 Terry Ave., Seattle 98122) , c1989. 128 p. : DDC 750/.74/797772 20
N745.5 .A54 1989
NYPL [3-MAVZ (Seattle) 91-3459]

Charles and Emma Frye Art Museum. The Charles and Emma Frye Art Museum : a handbook of the collection. Seattle, Wash., U. S.A. (704 Terry Ave., Seattle 98122) : The Museum, c1989. 128 p. : col. ill. ; 24 cm.

Includes index. DDC 750/.74/797772 20 1. Charles and Emma Frye Art Museum - Catalogs. 2. Painting - Washington (State) - Seattle - Catalogs. I. Title.
N745.5 .A54 1989
NYPL [3-MAVZ (Seattle) 91-3459]

CHARLES AND EMMA FRYE ART MUSEUM - CATALOGS. Charles and Emma Frye Art Museum. The Charles and Emma Frye Art Museum . Seattle, Wash., U. S. A. (704 Terry Ave., Seattle 98122) , c1989. 128 p. : DDC 750/.74/797772 20
N745.5 .A54 1989
NYPL [3-MAVZ (Seattle) 91-3459]

Charles Bell . Geldzahler, Henry. New York , 1991. p. cm. ISBN 0-8109-3114-1 (cloth) DDC 759.13 20
N6537.B447 A4 1991

Charles Burchfield's journals . Burchfield, Charles Ephraim, 1893-1967. Albany, N.Y. , 1992. p. cm. ISBN 0-7914-0991-0 (CH : acid-free) DDC 759.13 b 20
ND237.B89 A2 1992

Charles Conder, Robert Henri, James Morrice, Maurice Prendergast : the formative years, Paris 1890's : [exhibition] May 13-May 31, 1975. New York : Davis & Long Company, [1975] [54] p. : ill. ; 23 cm. 1. Conder, Charles, 1868-1909 - Exhibitions. 2. Henri, Robert, 1865-1929 - Exhibitions. 3. Morrice, James Wilson, 1865-1924 - Exhibitions. 4. Prendergast, Maurice Brazil, 1859-1924 - Exhibitions. 5. Painting, Modern - 19th century - France - Paris - Exhibitions. I. Davis & Long Company. **NYPL [3-MC 90-5453]**

Charles Cowles Gallery. Bates, David, 1952- David Bates . New York, NY , c1990. [42] p. :
NYPL [3-MCX B329 91-4403]

Charles De Wolf Brownell (1822-1909) . Brownell, Charles De Wolf, 1822-1909. New York , c1991. [68] p. :
NYPL [3-MCX B884 91-4294]

Charles Dufresne (1876-1936) Dufresne, Charles, 1876-1936. New York, 1971. [18] p
NYPL [3-MCO D846 91-890]

Charles Garnier's Paris Opéra . Mead, Christopher Curtis. New York, N.Y. , Cambridge, Mass. , c1991. p. cm. ISBN 0-262-13275-3 DDC 725/.822/092 20
NA6840.F72 P379 1991

Charles Hepburn Scott . Scott, Charles Hepburn, 1886-1964. Vancouver, B.C. , c1989. 28 p. : ISBN 0-920095-75-5
MLCM 89/07144 (N)
NYPL [3-MCZ S418 90-12641]

Charles, Jacques. De Versailles à Paris . Paris , 1989. 288 p., [38] p. of plates : ISBN 2-9504070-0-5
NYPL [3-MAWC (Paris) 90-12345]

Charles Lapicque . Lapicque, Charles, 1898- Paris , c1989. 85 p. : ISBN 2-86574-014-5
NYPL [3-MCO+ L305 91-3426]

Charles Le Brun, 1619-1690, célébration du tricentenaire de la mort de l'artiste : le décor de l'escalier des Ambassadeurs à Versailles : Musée national du château de Versailles, 19 novembre 1990-10 février 1991. Paris : Réunion des musées nationaux, c1990. 102 p. : ill. (some col.) ; 24 cm. Exhibition organized by the Musée national of Versailles. Preface signed Jacques Thuillier. Includes bibliographical references (p. 101). ISBN 2-7118-2393-8 1. Le Brun, Charles, 1619-1690 - Exhibitions. 2. Decoration and ornament - France - Versailles - Exhibitions. 3. Mural painting and decoration - France - Versailles - Exhibitions. I. Le Brun, Charles, 1619-1690. II. Thuillier, Jacques. III. Musée national de Versailles.
NYPL [3-MCO L454 91-5557]

Charles-Louis Clérisseau and the genesis of neo-Classicism /. McCormick, Thomas J. New York, N.Y. , Cambridge, Mass. , c1990. xiv, 284 p. : ISBN 0-262-13262-1 DDC 720/.92 B 20
NA1053.C58 M38 1990
NYPL [3-MQZ (Clérisseau) 91-5011]

Charles, Prince of Wales, 1948- HRH the Prince of Wales watercolours. 1st ed. Boston : Little, Brown, 1991. p. cm. "A Bulfinch Press book." ISBN 0-8212-1881-6 : DDC 759.2 20 1. Charles, Prince of Wales, 1948- - Contributions to landscape painting. I. Title.
ND1942.C46 A4 1991

CHARLES, PRINCE OF WALES, 1948- - CONTRIBUTIONS TO LANDSCAPE PAINTING. Charles, Prince of Wales, 1948- HRH the Prince of Wales watercolours. Boston , 1991. p. ISBN 0-8212-1881-6 : DDC 759.2 20
ND1942.C46 A4 1991

Charles Ray /. Ray, Charles, 1953- Newport Beach, Calif. , c1990. 44 p. : ISBN 0-917493-16-8 DDC 730/.92 20
NB237.R35 A4 1990
NYPL [3-MGO (Ray) 91-3921]

Charles Ricketts . Delaney, J. G. Paul. Oxford, England , New York, NY , 1990. xxiii, 429 p. : ISBN 0-19-817212-5 : DDC 709/.2/4 B 19
N6797.R5 D45 1989
NYPL [3-MCV R55 90-11599]

Charles-Roux, Edmonde. Le Théâtre de la Mode /. Paris , c1990. 166 p. : ISBN 2-906450-41-3
NYPL [3-MME+ 90-13056]

Charles Russell /. Russell, Charles M. (Charles Marion), 1864-1926. New York , 1989. 112 p. : ISBN 0-517-67598-6 DDC 709/.2/4 19
N6537.R88 A4 1989
NYPL [3-MCX+ R96 90-11089]

Charles Sheeler and the cult of the machine /. Lucic, Karen, 1950- Cambridge, Mass. , 1991. p. cm. ISBN 0-674-11110-9 (alk. paper) DDC 759.13 20
ND237.S47 L8 1991

Charles Sheeler and the cult of the machine /. Lucic, Karen, 1950- London , 1991. 167 p. : ISBN 0-948462-17-5 (pbk.) : DDC 709.2 20
NYPL [3-MCX S541 91-6965]

Charleston, R. J. (Robert Jesse), 1916- Masterpieces of glass : a world history from the Corning Museum of Glass / Robert J. Charleston ; with contributions by David B. Whitehouse and Susanne K. Frantz.Expanded ed. New York : H.N. Abrams, 1990. 256 p. : ill. (some col.) ; 31 cm. (A Corning Museum of Glass monograph) Includes index. Bibliography: p. 245-248. ISBN 0-8109-3607-0 1. Corning Museum of Glass. 2. Glassware - History. 3. Glassware - New York (State) - Corning. I. Whitehouse, David. II. Frantz, Susanne K. III. Corning Museum of Glass. IV. Series: Corning Museum of Glass monographs. V. Title.
NYPL [3-MPW+ 91-5598]

CHARLESTON (S.C.) IN ART. Saunders, Boyd. Alfred Hutty and the Charleston renaissance /. Orangeburg, S.C. , c1990. 127 p. : ISBN 0-87844-089-5 DDC 769.92 B 20
NE2012.H88 S28 1990
NYPL [MDG+ (Hutty) 91-5803]

Charlesworth, Sarah. Taking the picture . New York, N.Y. [1990?] 1 v. (unpaged) :
NYPL [MFW 91-4296]

Charlot, Jean, 1898- Jean Charlot : a retrospective : The University of Hawaii Art Gallery, Honolulu, Hawaii / [organized by the University of Hawaii Art Gallery ; sponsored by the University of Hawaii Department of Art]. Honolulu, Hawaii : University of Hawaii Art Gallery, 1991. p. cm. "March 18 to April 29, 1990." Includes bibliographical references. DDC 760/.092 20 1. Charlot, Jean, 1898- - Exhibitions. I. University of Hawaii at Manoa. Art Gallery. II. University of Hawaii at Manoa. Dept. of Art. III. Title.
N6853.C4733 A4 1991

CHARLOT, JEAN, 1898- - EXHIBITIONS. Charlot, Jean, 1898- Jean Charlot . Honolulu, Hawaii , 1991. p. cm. DDC 760/.092 20
N6853.C4733 A4 1991

CHARLOTTE AMALIE (V.I.) - BUILDINGS, STRUCTURES, ETC. Woods, Edith deJongh. The three quarters of the town of Charlotte Amalie . London , c1989. 158 p. : DDC 720/.97297/22 20
NA815.V5 W66 1989
NYPL [3-MQWM+ 91-6696]

Charlton, Alan. Alan Charlton : Castello di Rivoli, 6 ottobre-3 dicembre 1989 / a cura di Rudi Fuchs, Johannes Gachnang, Cristina Mundici. [Turin] : Castello di Rivoli, museo d'arte contemporanea, [1989] 1 v. (unpaged) : chiefly ill. ; 17 x 23 cm. Text also in English. Includes bibliographical references.

DDC 759.2 20
1. Charlton, Alan - Exhibitions. I. Castello di Rivoli (Museum : Turin, Italy).
ND497.C5455 A4 1989

CHARLTON, ALAN - EXHIBITIONS.
Charlton, Alan. Alan Charlton . [Turin] [1989]
1 v. (unpaged) : DDC 759.2 20
ND497.C5455 A4 1989

The charm of Turner /. Mason, James. London
[1911?] 47 p., [4] leaves of plates :
NYPL [MCV T94 91-5635]

Charmet, Raymond. Alexis Gritchenko . Paris ,
c1964. 83 p. : **NYPL [3-MCZ G874 91-903]**

Charpin, Catherine. Les arts incohérents
(1882-1893) / Catherine Charpin ; préface de
François Caradec. Paris : Syros/Alternatives,
c1990. 128 p. : ill. ; 22 cm. (Zigzags) Includes
bibliographical references (p. 122-124). ISBN
2-86738-465-6 : DDC 741.5/0944/09034 20
1. French wit and humor, Pictorial - Exhibitions. 2.
Cartoonists - France - Biography. I. Title. II. Series.
NC1495 .C58 1990

Charre, Alain. Raynaud, Patrick. Patrick
Raynaud . Paris , c1989. 165 p. : ISBN
2-904632-20-4
NYPL [3-MGO+ (Raynaud) 91-3659]

Charrière, Gérard, 1935- Points along the Côte
d'Azur triangle /. New York , c1985. 36 p. :
ISBN 0-935581-00-6
NYPL [3-MAMT 90-4521]

CHARRIERE, GERARD, 1935-
Points along the Côte d'Azur triangle /. New
York , c1985. 36 p. : ISBN 0-935581-00-6
NYPL [3-MAMT 90-4521]

CHARROS IN ART - EXHIBTIONS.
Icaza, Ernesto. Un charro pintor . [Monterrey,
Mexico] [1986] 1 v. (unpaged) : DDC 759.972
20
ND259.I28 A4 1986

Charterhouse of Jerez de la Frontera. Zubillaga,
Francisco. La Cartuja de Jerez de la Frontera
=. Salzburg, Austria , 1978. [97] p. :
NYPL [3-MRBB 90-4725]

**Charterhouses of Las Cuevas, Cazalla de la
Sierra and Granada.** Zubillaga, Francisco. Las
cartujas de las Cuevas, Cazalla de la Sierra y
Granada =. Salzburg , 1979. [109] p. : DDC
726/.7/094682
NA5811.S4876 Z8
NYPL [3-MRBB+ 81-645]

**Chartographēsē tou Hellēnikou paraliou kai
nēsiōtikou chōrou :** Hellēnikē Hetaireia
Chartographias, 7o Diethnes Symposio 1989,
Athēna, Ethnikē Pinakothēkē, 12 Septemvriou-8
Oktōvriou 1989 / [Anglikē metaphrasē,
Leonora Navarē ; epimeleia keimenou, Diana
Zapheiropoulou] = Cartography of the shores
and islands of Greece : Society for Hellenic
Cartography, 7th International Symposium
1989, Athens, National Gallery, 12 September-8
October 1989 / [English translation, Leonora
Navari ; editorial advisor, Diana Zafiropoulou].
[Athēna] : Hellēnikē Hetaireia Chartographias,
c1989. 84 p. : maps (some col.) ; 23 x 24 cm.
Greek and English. At head of title: IMCoS. Includes
bibliographical references (p. 78-84).
1. Cartography - Greece - History - Congresses. I.
Zapheiropoulou, Diana. II. IMCoS. III. Hellēnikē
Hetaireia Chartographias. IV. Ethnikē Pinakothēkē,
Mouseion Alexandrou Soutsou. V. Title: Cartography of
the shores and islands of Greece.
GA881 .C43 1989
NYPL [Map Div. 91-3879]

CHARTOGRAPHY. see CARTOGRAPHY.

CHARTRAND, ESTEBAN, 1840-1883.
Ruiz, Raúl R. Esteban Chartrand . La Habana,
Cuba , 1987. 85 p. :
NYPL [3-MCZ C486 89-26612]

**CHARTS, NAUTICAL. see NAUTICAL
CHARTS.**

Chase, Aaron. Falvey, William D. The official
collector's guide to Kentucky Derby mint julep
glasses /. Louisville, Ky. (301 S. 30th St.,
Louisville 40212) , c1991. 81 p. : DDC
748.8/3/097713 20
NK5440.D75 F3 1991

CHASE, DORIS, 1923-
Failing, Patricia. Doris Chase, artist in motion .
Seattle , c1991. p. cm. ISBN 0-295-97112-6

DDC 700/.92 B 20
N6537.C4638 F35 1991

Chase, John, 1953- Experimental architecture in
Los Angeles /. New York , 1991. p. cm. ISBN
0-8478-1424-6 (HC) DDC 720/.9794/9409045
20
NA735.L55 E97 1991

Chase, Linda. In the romantic style : creating
intimacy, fantasy and charm in the
contemporary home / by Linda Chase and
Laura Cerwinske. New York, N.Y. : Thames
and Hudson, 1990. 160 p. : ill. ; 26 cm. ISBN
0-500-23592-9
I. Title. **NYPL [3-MLO 90-11995]**

Chase, Martha Jenks, 1851-1925.
Dolls and duty--Martha Chase and the
progressive agenda, 1889-1925 /. Providence,
R.I. (110 Benevolent St., Providence 02906) ,
1989. 48 p. : DDC 688.7/221/097451 20
NK4894.2.C43 A4 1989

**CHASE, MARTHA JENKS, 1851-1925 -
EXHIBITIONS.**
Dolls and duty--Martha Chase and the
progressive agenda, 1889-1925 /. Providence,
R.I. (110 Benevolent St., Providence 02906) ,
1989. 48 p. : DDC 688.7/221/097451 20
NK4894.2.C43 A4 1989

Chase, William Merritt, 1849-1916.
William Merritt Chase, 1849-1916 ... : [catalog
of an exhibition] April, 1969. New York :
Chapellier Galleries, [1969] [32] p. : chiefly ill.
(3 col.), ports. ; 26 cm. Exhibition held April 1969
at Chapellier Galleries.
1. Chase, William Merritt, 1849-1916 - Exhibitions. I.
Chapellier Galleries (New York, N.Y.). II. Title.
NYPL [3-MCX C49 90-6403]

**CHASE, WILLIAM MERRITT, 1849-1916 -
EXHIBITIONS.**
Chase, William Merritt, 1849-1916. William
Merritt Chase, 1849-1916 ... . New York
[1969] [32] p. :
NYPL [3-MCX C49 90-6403]

Chassat, Michel.
Artaud, Evelyne. Perestroïk'art . [Paris] , c1990.
118 p. : ISBN 2-7022-0269-1 DDC 709/.47/09048
20
N6988 .A7635 1990
NYPL [3-MAM 90-13376]

Gaudibert, Pierre. Ipoustéguy /. Paris , c1989.
204 p. : ISBN 2-7022-0246-2
NYPL [3-MGO+ (Ipoustéguy) 91-3898]

Chastel, André, 1912-
Fables, formes, figures / André Chastel. Paris :
Flammarion, c1978. 2 v. : ill. (some col.) ; 24
cm. (Idées et recherches) Includes bibliographical
references and index. DDC 701
1. Art - Psychology. I. Title.
N7560 .C46 **NYPL [3-MA 81-444]**

Seminario internazionale di storia
dell'architettura (7th : 1988 Sept. 1-7 : Vicenza,
Italy) Andrea Palladio, nuovi contributi .
Milano , c1990. 247 p. : ISBN 88-435-3086-0
NYPL [3-MQZ+ (Palladio) 91-4941]

Chat pub . Montry, Annie de. Paris , c1988. 191
p. : ISBN 2-7007-2814-9
NYPL [3-MDW+ 89-25688]

**CHÂTEAU DE CHAMBORD (CHAMBORD,
LOIR-ET-CHER, FRANCE)**
Cloulas, Ivan. Chambord . Paris , c1989. 143
p. : ISBN 2-09-241001-6
NYPL [3-MQWF+ 90-2437]

Le château de Vaux-le-Vicomte /. France,
Anatole, 1844-1924. Etrépilly , c1987. v, 212
p., [8] p. of plates : ISBN 2-905563-19-2
NYPL [3-MQWF 90-12695]

**CHÂTEAU DE VAUX-LE-VICOMTE MAINCY,
FRANCE)**
France, Anatole, 1844-1924. Le château de
Vaux-le-Vicomte /. Etrépilly , c1987. v, 212 p.,
[8] p. of plates : ISBN 2-905563-19-2
NYPL [3-MQWF 90-12695]

**CHÂTEAU DE VERSAILLES (VERSAILLES,
FRANCE)**
Bottineau, Yves. Versailles . Paris , c1989. 198
p. : ISBN 2-7003-0747-X
NYPL [3-MQWF+ 90-2605]

**CHÂTEAU DE VERSAILLES (VERSAILLES,
FRANCE) - HISTORY.**
Pérouse de Montclos, Jean-Marie. [Versailles.

English.] Versailles /. New York , 1991. p. cm.
ISBN 1-558-59228-8 DDC 725/.17/0944366 20
NA7736.V5 P4713 1991

**CHÂTEAU DE VILLANDRY (VILLANDRY,
FRANCE)**
Fleurent, Maurice. Villandry . Paris , c1989.
105 p. : ISBN 2-85889-052-1
NYPL [3-MSK 91-3221]

Le Château en France / sous la direction de
Jean-Pierre Babelon. 2e tirage rev. et corr. et
augm. d'un index. Paris : Berger-Levrault :
Caisse nationale des monuments historiques et
des sites, 1988. 448 p., [16] p. of plates : ill.
(some col.) ; 31 cm. Includes indexes. Includes
bibliographical references (p. 405-420) and index.
ISBN 2-7013-0741-4
1. Castles - France. 2. Castles - France - History. 3.
Castles - France - Design and construction. 4.
Architecture - France. 5. France - Description and
travel - 1975- - Views. I. Babelon, Jean Pierre. II.
Caisse nationale des monuments historiques et des sites
(France). **NYPL [3-MQWF+ 90-11996]**

CHATEAUNEUF, ALEXIS DE, 1799-1853.
Lange, Günther. Alexis de Chateauneuf, ein
Hamburger Baumeister, 1799-1853 /.
Hamburg , 1965. 147 p. :
NYPL [3-MQZ (Chateauneuf) 91-818]

CHÂTEAUX. see CASTLES.

Châteaux de Haut-Léon : Finistère / [conception
et rédaction, Christel Douard ; avec la
collaboration de Roger Barrié ... et al.].
Saint-Brice-en-Coglès : URSA, c1987. 32 p. :
ill. (some col.) ; 30 cm. (Images du patrimoine . no
34) Cover title. Maps on p. [4] of cover. ISBN
2-86934-006-0
1. Castle - France - Haut-Léon. I. Douard, Christel. II.
Barrié, Roger. III. Series.
NYPL [3-MQWF+ 90-5362]

Châteaux of the Loire. Nagel Publishers.
Geneva ; New York [c1971] 192, 10 p. :
NYPL [JFB 90-371]

Châtelet, Albert. Van Gogh et les peintres
d'Auvers-sur-Oise . [Paris] , 1954. xl, 100 p.,
xxxii p. of plates :
N6847.5.I4 V36 1954

Chatterjee, Ratnabali, 1941- From the karkhana
to the studio : a study in the changing social
roles of patron and artist in Bengal / Ratnabali
Chatterjee. New Delhi : Books & Books, 1990.
xi, 144 p., [12] p. of plates : ill. (some col.) ; 25
cm. Includes bibliographical references (p. [138]-144).
ISBN 81-85016-28-3 : DDC 701/.03/095414 20
1. Art and society - India - Bengal. 2. Artists and
patrons - India - Bengal. I. Title. II. Title: Study in the
changing social roles of patron and artist in Bengal.
N72.S6 C35 1990 **NYPL [3-MAF 91-6048]**

Chatto curiosities of the British street.
Stamp, Gavin. Telephone boxes /. London ,
1989. 106 p. : ISBN 0-7011-3366-X (pbk.) DDC
363.6/9 19 **NYPL [3-MQWK 90-12389]**

Chaval. see Le Louarn, Yvan Francis, 1915-1968.

Chaval's Fotoschule . Le Louarn, Yvan Francis,
1915-1968. Zürich , 1975. 45 p. : ISBN
3-257-00788-4
NYPL [3-MEM (Le Louarn) 84-2309]

Chaves, Alvaro. El Espíritu erótico /. Bogotá ,
1990. 207 p. : DDC 704.9/428/098610904 20
N8217.E6 E87 1990

Chaves, Joaquim Matos. Santa Rita, vida e obra :
precisões e considerações / Joaquim Matos
Chaves. Lisboa : Quimera, c1989. 106 p. : ill.
(some col.) ; 29 cm. ISBN 972-589-019-1 : DDC
759.69 20
1. Santa Rita, Guilherme, 1889-1918. I. Title.
ND833.S19 A4 1989

Chávez Morado, José, 1909- José Chávez
Morado : su tiempo, su país, obra plástica. 1a
ed. Guanajuato, Gto. : Gobierno del Estado de
Guanajuato, 1988. 215 p. : ill. (some col.) ; 27
cm. ISBN 968-617-012-X
1. Chávez Morado, José, 1909-. I. Guanajuato, Mexico
(State). II. Title.
NYPL [3-MCZ C51 90-11331]

CHÁVEZ MORADO, JOSÉ, 1909-
Chávez Morado, José, 1909- José Chávez
Morado . Guanajuato, Gto. , 1988. 215 p. :
ISBN 968-617-012-X
NYPL [3-MCZ C51 90-11331]

Chazal, Gilles. L'Art de Cartier . [Paris] , 1989.
177 p. :   ISBN 2-905028-27-0   DDC 739.27/092/2
20
NK7398.C37 A4 1989

**CHEB (CZECHOSLOVAKIA) - SOCIAL LIFE
AND CUSTOMS.**
Eger und das Egerland . München , c1988. 671
p. :   ISBN 3-7844-2178-4
NYPL [3-MNE+ 90-597]

**CHEB REGION (CZECHOSLOVAKIA) -
SOCIAL LIFE AND CUSTOMS.**
Eger und das Egerland . München , c1988. 671
p. :   ISBN 3-7844-2178-4
NYPL [3-MNE+ 90-597]

**A Checklist of Canadian copyright deposits in
the British Museum, 1895-1923** / edited by
John R.T. Ettlinger and Patrick B. O'Neill.
Halifax, N.S., Canada : Dalhousie University,
School of Library Service, 1984- v. ; 22 cm.
Includes bibliographical references and index.
CONTENTS. - v. 1. Maps -- v. 2. Insurance plans -- v.
3, pt. 1. City and area directories -- v. 4. Sheet music --
v. 5. Photographs.   ISBN 0-7703-0179-7 (pbk. : v. 1) :
DDC 015.71 19
*1. British Museum - Catalogs. 2. Canada - Imprints -
Catalogs. I. Ettlinger, John R. T. II. O'Neill, Patrick B.
III. Dalhousie University. School of Library Service.*
Z1365 .C48 1984   NYPL [Map Div. 85-549]

Cheek, Richard. Reed, Roger G. A delight to all
who know it . Augusta, Me. , 1990. 144 p. :
ISBN 0-935447-07-5   DDC 720/.92 20
NA7575 .R4 1990

Cheetham, Mark A. (Mark Arthur), 1954- The
rhetoric of purity : essentialist theory and the
advent of abstract painting / Mark A.
Cheetham. Cambridge ; New York : Cambridge
University Press, 1991. xx, 194 p. : ill. ; 26 cm.
(Cambridge new art history and criticism) Includes
index. Bibliography: p. 181-190.   ISBN 0-521-38546-6
DDC 750/.1 20
*1. Painting, Abstract - Philosophy. 2. Purity
(Philosophy). I. Title. II. Series.*
ND196.A2 C4 1991   NYPL [3-MC 91-5174]

**Chefs-d'œuvre de la faïence du Musée de
Saint-Omer.** Musée de l'hôtel Sandelin.
Saint-Omer , c1988. 245 p. :   DDC
738.3/7/0940744427 20
NK4305 .M78 1988
NYPL [3-MPGG+ 90-12652]

Chefs d'oeuvre de l'art paléolithique. Musée des
antiquités nationales. [Paris?, 1969] 96 p.
NYPL [3-MADF 90-6293]

Chefs-d'œuvre secrets. Prat, Véronique.
Chefs-d'œuvre secrets des grandes collections
privées /. Paris , c1988. 191 p. :   ISBN
2-226-03427-7 :
N5210 .P73 1988

**Chefs-d'œuvre secrets des grandes collections
privées /.** Prat, Véronique. Paris , c1988. 191
p. :   ISBN 2-226-03427-7 :
N5210 .P73 1988

Cheim, John. Basquiat, Jean Michel. Jean Michel
Basquiat drawings /. Boston , c1990. p.   ISBN
0-8212-1887-5 :   DDC 741.973 20
NC179.B37 A4 1990

**Chekalov, A. K. (Aleksandr Kalimovich), 1928-
1970.** Bäuerliche russische Holzskulptur.
[Von] Alexander K. Tschekalow. [Aus dem
russischen Manuskript übertragen von Helmut
Barth] Dresden, Verlag der Kunst [c1967] 110
p. illus.(some col.) 20 cm. Bibliography: p. 109-110.
*1. Folk art - Soviet Union. 2. Wood-carving - Soviet
Union. I. Title.*
NK9756.A1 C4515   NYPL [3-MOC 90-5991]

The Chelsea House library of biography.
McDonough, Yona Zeldis. Frank Lloyd Wright
/. New York , 1991. p. cm.   ISBN 0-7910-1626-9
DDC 720/.92 B 20
NA737.W7 M37 1991

Chelten Art Gallery and Museums. Scott, Peter,
Sir, 1909- Sir Peter Scott at 80 . Gloucester ,
Wolfeboro, N.H., USA , 1989. xxvi, 146 p.,
[12] p. of plates :   ISBN 0-86299-651-1 (pbk)
DDC 598.092 20
SK17.S27   NYPL [3-MCV S429 90-4753]

Chemelli, Aldo. Trento illustrata : la città e il
territorio in piante e vedute dal XVI al XX
secolo / Aldo Chemelli, Carlo e Marcus Perini.
Padova : Editoriale programma, c1991. 213 p. :
ill. (some col.) ; 34 cm. "Le città illustrate,

3"--Jacket. Includes bibliographical references (p. 213).
ISBN 88-7123-110-4   DDC 769/.4445385/094 20
*1. Trento (Italy) in art - Catalogs. 2. Prints, European -
Catalogs. I. Perini, Carlo. II. Perini, Marcus. III. Title.
IV. Title: Città illustrate.*
NE954.3.I8 C44 1991

Chemiakin, Mihail. see **Shemīakin, Mikhail,
1943-**

**CHEMNITZ (GERMANY) - DESCRIPTION -
VIEWS.**
Voigt, May. Historische Photographie in
Chemnitz /. [Karl-Marx-Stadt] , 1988. 96 p. :
NYPL [MFW 91-6682]

Chenard. Chenard, Christian, 1918- Christian
Chenard . Paris , c1989. 110 p. :   ISBN
2-905037-04-0   DDC 759.4 20
ND553.C479 A4 1989

Chenard, Christian, 1918-
Christian Chenard : Chartres (Eure-et-Loir) 24
novembre 1918. Paris : R. Creuze, c1989. 110
p. : col. ill. ; 31 cm. Cover title: Chenard.   ISBN
2-905037-04-0   DDC 759.4 20
*1. Chenard, Christian, 1918- - Themes, motives. 2.
Painting, Abstract - France. I. Title. II. Title: Chenard.*
ND553.C479 A4 1989

**CHENARD, CHRISTIAN, 1918- - THEMES,
MOTIVES.**
Chenard, Christian, 1918- Christian Chenard .
Paris , c1989. 110 p. :   ISBN 2-905037-04-0
DDC 759.4 20
ND553.C479 A4 1989

Chenevière, Antoine.
[Russian furniture. French]
Splendeurs du mobilier russe, 1780-1840 /
Antoine Chenevière ; avec la collaboration
d'Emmanuel Ducamp. Paris : Flammarion,
c1989. 312 p. : ill. ; 30 cm. Translation of:
Russian furniture : the golden age, 1780-1840.
ISBN 2-08-010916-2
*1. Furniture - Soviet Union - History - 18th century. 2.
Furniture - Soviet Union - History - 19th century. I.
Title.*   *NYPL [3-MOF+ 91-6353]*

Cheney, Nan, 1887-1985.
Carr, Emily, 1871-1945. [Correspondence.]
Dear Nan . Vancouver , 1990. xlvi, 436 p., [24]
p. of plates :   ISBN 0-7748-0348-7 (cloth)
NYPL [3-MCZ c28 91-7320]

**CHENEY, NAN, 1887-1985 -
CORRESPONDENCE.**
Carr, Emily, 1871-1945. [Correspondence.]
Dear Nan . Vancouver , 1990. xlvi, 436 p., [24]
p. of plates :   ISBN 0-7748-0348-7 (cloth)
NYPL [3-MCZ c28 91-7320]

Cheng, Chen-Sun. A young painter : the life and
paintings of Wang Yani-- China's extraordinary
young artist / by Zheng Zhensun and Alice
Low. New York : Scholastic, Inc., 1991. p. cm.
Examines the life and works of the young Chinese girl
who started painting animals at the age of three and in
her teens became the youngest artist to have a
one-person show at the Smithsonian Institution.   ISBN
0-590-44906-0 :   DDC 759.951 B 92 20
*1. Wang, Ya-ni, 1975- - Criticism and interpretation -
Juvenile literature. I. Low, Alice. II. Title.*
ND1049.W3435 C4 1991

Chéret, Jules, 1836-1932.
Broido, Lucy. The posters of Jules Chéret .
New York , 1991. p. cm   ISBN 0-486-26966-3
(pbk.)   DDC 741.6/74/092 20
NC1850.C47 A4 1991

**CHÉRET, JULES, 1836-1932 - CATALOGUES
RAISONNÉS.**
Broido, Lucy. The posters of Jules Chéret .
New York , 1991. p. cm   ISBN 0-486-26966-3
(pbk.)   DDC 741.6/74/092 20
NC1850.C47 A4 1991

Cherkasova, N. V. Razina, T. M. (Tat´īana
Mikhaĭlovna) Folk art in the Soviet Union /.
New York , Leningrad , 1990. 459 p. :   ISBN
0-8109-0944-8   DDC 745/.0947 19
NK975 .R35 1991   NYPL [3-MNE 90-11088]

Chermayeff, Ivan. Ivan Chermayeff : collages /
with texts by Emilio Ambasz ... [et al.]. New
York : H.N. Abrams, 1991. 64 p. : ill. ; 41 cm.
ISBN 0-8109-2476-5
1. Chermayeff, Ivan. I. Title.
NYPL [3-MCX++ C517 91-5325]

CHERMAYEFF, IVAN.
Chermayeff, Ivan. Ivan Chermayeff . New
York , 1991. 64 p. :   ISBN 0-8109-2476-5
NYPL [3-MCX++ C517 91-5325]

Chernevich, Elena. Soviet commercial design of
the twenties /. London , c1987. 144 p. :   ISBN
0-500-23504-X
NYPL [3-MDW+ 91-3268]

Chernevich, Elena, 1939- Russian graphic design
/ text by Elena Chernevich ; compiled by
Mikhail Anikst & Nina Baburina ; designed by
Mikhail Anikst. New York, NY : Abbeville
Press, 1990. 160 p. : col. ill. ; 31 cm. Cover title:
Russian graphic design, 1880-1917.   ISBN
1-558-59016-1   DDC 741.6/0947 20
*1. Commercial art - Russian S.F.S.R. - History - 19th
century. 2. Graphic arts - Russian S.F.S.R. - History -
19th century. 3. Book design - Russian S.F.S.R. -
History - 19th century. I. Anikst, Mikhail. II. Baburina,
N. I. (Nina Ivanovna). III. Title. IV. Title: Russian
graphic design, 1880-1917.*
NC998.6.R9 C47 1990
NYPL [3-MDW+ 90-11977]

Cherney, Marvin, 1925-1967.
Marvin Cherney. [New York] : Kennedy
Galleries, c1980. [16] p. : chiefly ill. ; 28 cm.
Cover title. Catalog of the exhibition held Feb. 20-Mar.
8, 1980 at Kennedy Galleries,New York. Includes
index.
*1. Cherney, Marvin, 1925-1967 - Exhibitions. I.
Kennedy Galleries, inc., New York.*
ND237.C4914 A4 1980
NYPL [3-MCX C518 80-2193]

**CHERNEY, MARVIN, 1925-1967 -
EXHIBITIONS.**
Cherney, Marvin, 1925-1967. Marvin Cherney.
[New York] , c1980. [16] p. :
ND237.C4914 A4 1980
NYPL [3-MCX C518 80-2193]

Cherry, Bridget. Devon / by Bridget Cherry and
Nikolaus Pevsner. 2nd ed., extensively revised.
Harmondsworth : Penguin, 1989. 976 p., [96] p.
of plates : ill., maps ; 23 cm. (Buildings of
England) Previous edition published in 2 v. in 1952 as
North Devon and South Devon by Nikolaus Pevsner.
Includes indexes. Includes bibliographical references.
ISBN 0-14-071050-7 :
*1. Architecture - England - Devon - Guide-books. I.
Pevsner, Nikolaus, 1902-1983. II. Title. III. Series.*
NYPL [3-MQWK 90-12006]

Cherubini, Giovanni.
Il Palazzo Medici Riccardi di Firenze /.
Firenze , c1990. 379 p. :   ISBN 88-09-20180-9
DDC 725/.17/094551 20
NA7756.F65 P35 1990

Il Palazzo Medici Riccardi di Firenze /.
Florence , c1990. x, 379 p. :   ISBN
88-09-20180-9
NYPL [3-MQWB+ 91-3377]

Cherubini, Luigi, 1760-1842. Lodoïska [sound
recording] / Cherubini. Pontelambro, Italy :
Nuova era ; N[ew] Y[ork] : Dist. by Qualiton
Imports, p1989. 2 sound discs (132 min., 38
sec.) : digital, stereo. ; 4 3/4 in. (Rediscovered
opera) Reprints Nuova era: 2236--2237. Opera in 3
acts. Sung in Italian. Libretto by Claude François
Fillette-Loraux. Ilva Ligabue, soprano ; Renata Mattioli,
mezzo-soprano ; Giacinto Prandelli, tenor ; Sesto
Bruscantini, bass ; other soloists ; Orchestra sinfonica e
Coro di Roma della RAI ; Oliviero De Fabritiis,
conductor. Recorded live July 4, 1965, Rome, Italy.
Distributor from label on container. Compact discs.
Analog recording. Program notes by Roberto Di Perna
in Italian and English translation and Italian libretto (56
p.) included.
1. Operas. I. Title. II. Series.
Nuova era 2236--2237

Cherubini, Maria Luigi Carlo Zenobio Salvatore.
see **Cherubini, Luigi, 1760-1842.**

Chesnais, Robert. Les racines de l'audio-visuel :
esquisse d'une histoire de la figuration et de la
représentation en Occident / Robert Chesnais ;
préface de Jean-François Lacan. Paris :
Anthropos : Diffusion, Economica, c1990. 285
p. ; 24 cm. (Collection "Culture et communication")
Includes bibliographical references (p. [249]-278) and
index.   ISBN 2-7178-1862-6 :
*1. Arts - History. 2. Visual communication. I. Title. II.
Series.*
NX440 .C536 1990

Chester, Catherine. Sotheby's great sales /.
London , 1989. 160 p. :   ISBN 0-7126-2137-7
DDC 707/.5 20
N8675 .S685 1989

Chevalier, Denys.
[Picasso, époques bleue et rose. English]
Picasso, the blue and rose periods / by
Denys Chevalier. New York : Crown
Publishers, 1991. p. cm. (Crown art library)
Translation of: Picasso, époques bleue et rose.
Includes bibliographical references.   ISBN
0-517-00904-8 :   DDC 759.4 20
*1. Picasso, Pablo, 1881-1973 - Criticism and
interpretation. 2. Red 2 FC09. I. Title. II. Series.*
ND553.P5 C4853 1991

Chevlowe, Susan. Painting a place in America .
New York , Bloomington , 1991. p. cm.   ISBN
0-253-33121-8 (cloth)   DDC
704/.0392407471/090410747471 20
N6538.J4 P35 1991

Chevolleau /. Chevolleau, Jean.
Fontenay-le-Comte [1989?] 293 p. :
                          NYPL [3-MCO C5285 91-6928]

Chevolleau, Jean. Chevolleau / Gilbert
Prouteau ... [et al.]. Fontenay-le-Comte :
Editions L.B., [1989?] 293 p. : ill. ; 29 cm.
French and English.
1. Chevolleau, Jean. I. Prouteau, Gilbert. II. Title.
                          NYPL [3-MCO C5285 91-6928]

CHEVOLLEAU, JEAN.
Chevolleau, Jean. Chevolleau /.
Fontenay-le-Comte [1989?] 293 p. :
                          NYPL [3-MCO C5285 91-6928]

Chevrier, Jean-François.
Un'altra obiettività /. Milano , c1989. 253 p. :
ISBN 88-7017-067-5
                          NYPL [MFW 90-3005]

Portrait de Jurgis Baltrušaitis / Jean-François
Chevrier. & Art sumérien, art roman / par
Jurgis Baltrušaitis. Paris : Flammarion, c1989.
271 p. : ill. ; 24 cm. "Bibliographie de Jurgis
Baltrušaitis": p. 270-271.   ISBN 2-08-012038-7
*1. Baltrušaitis, Jurgis, 1903- - Criticism and
interpretation. 2. Art, Sumerian. 3. Art, Roman. I.
Baltrušaitis, Jurgis, 1903- Art sumérien, art roman.
1989. II. Title.*
N7483.B285 C48 1989

Chew, Paul A. Westmoreland Museum of Art.
Southwestern Pennsylvania painters .
Greensburg, Pa. , 1989. x, 138 p. :   ISBN
0-931241-21-9 DDC 759.148/8/07474886 20
N6530.P42 P589 1989
                          NYPL [3-MCW 91-6266]

Ch'i, Pai-shih, 1863-1957.
Malerei von Qi Baishi : aus dem Besitz der
Ostasiatischen Sammlung der Staatlichen
Museen zu Berlin : Sonderausstellung vom 5.
Oktober bis 31. Dezember 1988 im
Pergamonmuseum / [Auswahl und
wissenschaftliche Bearbeitung sowie
Titelkalligraphie, Yang Enlin]. Berlin : Die
Sammlung, c1988. 95, [1] p. : chiefly ill. (some
col.) ; 26 cm. Includes bibliographical references (p.
[96]).   DDC 759.951 20
*1. Ch'i, Pai-shih, 1863-1957 - Exhibitions. I. Yang,
Enlin. II. Staatliche Museen zu Berlin (Germany :
East). Ostasiatische Sammlung. III. Staatliche Museen
zu Berlin (Germany : East). Antikensammlung. IV.
Title.*
ND1049.C5 A4 1988
                          NYPL [3-MAG 91-4576]

CH'I, PAI-SHIH, 1863-1957 - EXHIBITIONS.
Ch'i, Pai-shih, 1863-1957. Malerei von Qi
Baishi . Berlin , c1988. 95, [1] p. :   DDC
759.951 20
ND1049.C5 A4 1988
                          NYPL [3-MAG 91-4576]

Chia, Sandro, 1946-
Sandro Chia : novanta spine al vento : 1989,
Museum Moderner Kunst, Wien, ICC
Antwerpen, La Biennale di Venezia, Schloss
Rheda-Wiedenbrück, Museo de Arte
Contemporaneo Internacional Ruffino Tamayo,
Ciudad de Mexico, Museo de Monterrey.
Salzburg : T. Ropac, c1989. 211 p. : ill. (chiefly
col.) ; 28 cm. English, German, Italian, and Spanish.
Issued in conjunction with an exhibition.
*1. Chia, Sandro, 1946- - Exhibitions. I. Museum
Moderner Kunst (Austria). II. Title.*
                          NYPL [3-MCF C525 91-4644]

CHIA, SANDRO, 1946- - EXHIBITIONS.
Chia, Sandro, 1946- Sandro Chia . Salzburg ,
c1989. 211 p. :
                          NYPL [3-MCF C525 91-4644]

Chiang, I. see Chiang, Yee, 1903-

Chiang, Yee, 1903- The Chinese eye; an
interpretation of Chinese painting. With a pref.
by S.I. Hsiung.[4th ed.] London, Methuen
[1960] xvi, 239 p. illus. 19 cm.
I. Title.   *NYPL [3-MAG 90-10781]*

Chiappori, Alfredo, 1943- Storie d'Italia : il
Quarantotto (1846-1860) / [di] Chiappori ; con
un commento di Franco Della Peruta.1. ed.
Milano : Feltrinelli, 1978. 174 p. : col. ill. ; 28
cm.   DDC 945.081/02/07
*1. Austro-Sardinian War, 1848-1849 - Caricatures and
cartoons. 2. Italian wit and humor, Pictorial. 3. Italy -
History - 1849-1870 - Caricatures and cartoons. I. Della
Peruta, Franco, 1924-. II. Title.*
DG552 .C47
                          NYPL [3-MEM (Chiappori) 90-4348]

Chiari, Giovanni, 18th cent. Statue di Firenze. In
Fir[enz]e [17--?] 3 v. :   DDC 730/.945/51 20
NB621.F6 S73 1700z

Chiari Moretto Wiel, M. Agnese (Maria Agnese)
Tiziano : corpus dei disegni autografi / M.
Agnese Chiari Moretto Wiel. Milano : Berenice,
c1989. 111, [1] p. : ill. (some col.) ; 34 cm. (Le
Raccolte di disegni dei grandi pittori) Includes
bibliographical references (p. 99-[112])   ISBN
88-85880-22-3
*1. Titian, ca. 1488-1576 - Catalogues raisonnés. I.
Titian, ca. 1488-1576. II. Title. III. Series.*
                          NYPL [3-MCF+ T63 90-10931]

Chiarini, Marco.
I dipinti olandesi del Seicento e del Settecento
/ Marco Chiarini. Roma : Gallerie e musei
statali di Firenze, 1989. xxiii, 671 p. : ill. (some
col.) ; 27 cm. (Cataloghi dei musei e gallerie d'Italia.
nuova ser., n. 1) Includes bibliographical references (p.
653-662) and index.   ISBN 88-24-00001-0   DDC
759.9492/074/4551 20
*1. Painting, Dutch - Catalogs. 2. Painting, Modern -
17th-18th centuries - Netherlands - Catalogs. 3.
Painting - Italy - Florence - Catalogs. 4. Art museums -
Italy - Florence - Catalogs. I. Title.*
ND646 .C48 1989

Tableaux italiens : catalogue raisonné de la
collection de peinture italienne XIVe-XIXe
siècles : Grenoble, Musée de peinture et de
sculpture / Marco Chiarini. Grenoble : Le
Musée, 1988. 175 p. : ill. (some col.) ; 27 cm.
Includes index. Bibliography: p. 168-171.
*1. Musée de Grenoble - Catalogs. 2. Painting, Italian -
Catalogs. 3. Painting - France - Grenoble - Catalogs. I.
Musée de Grenoble. II. Title.*
                          NYPL [3-MAVZ (Grenoble) 90-10794]

Le chic et le look . Delbourg-Delphis, Marylène.
[Paris] , c1981. 279 p., [8] p. of plates :   ISBN
2-01-008276-1 :   DDC 391/.2/0944 19
GT853 .D37 1981   *NYPL [3-MME 90-6057]*

Chicago architecture and urbanism.
Chappell, Sally Anderson. Architecture and
planning of Graham, Anderson, Probst, and
White, 1912-1936 . Chicago , 1991. p. cm.
ISBN 0-226-10134-7 DDC 720/.92/2 20
NA737.G7 C48 1991

Chicago. Art Institute. German expressionist
paintings . [S.l. , 196-] [60] p. :
                          NYPL [3-MCI 90-5896]

Chicago. Arts Club. see Arts Club of Chicago.

Chicago Historical Society.
Bruegmann, Robert. Holabird & Roche,
Holabird & Root . New York , 1991. 3 v. :
ISBN 0-8240-3974-2 :   DDC 720/.92/2 20
NA737.H558 A4 1991
                          NYPL [MQWO+ 91-6811]

Greenhouse, Wendy, 1955- The art of
Archibald J. Motley, Jr. /. Chicago, IL , 1991.
p. cm.   ISBN 0-913820-15-6 :   DDC 759.13 20
ND237.M8524 A4 1991

**CHICAGO (ILL.) - BUILDINGS,
STRUCTURES, ETC.**
Bluestone, Daniel M. Constructing Chicago /.
New Haven , c1991. p. cm.   ISBN 0-300-04848-3
(alk. paper) DDC 711/.4/097731109034 20
NA9127.C4 B48 1991

Vinci, John. The Trading Room . Chicago, IL ,
c1989. 72 p. :   ISBN 0-86559-082-6 DDC 725/.25

20
NA6253.C4 C438 1989
                          NYPL [3-MQWO 90-12029]

**CHICAGO (ILL.) - BUILDINGS,
STRUCTURES, ETC. - CATALOGS.**
Art Institute of Chicago. Fragments of
Chicago's past . Chicago, IL , 1990. 180 p. :
ISBN 0-86559-088-5 DDC
720/.9773/1107477311 20
NA735.C4 A77 1990
                          NYPL [3-MQWO 91-3419]

Chicago (Ill.). Dept. of Cultural Affairs. The
Chicago show . Chicago, Ill. , c1990. 48 p. :
ISBN 0-938903-09-8
N6487.C52 C6 1990
                          NYPL [3-MAMT 91-7597]

**CHICAGO (ILL.) - DESCRIPTION - 1951-
1980 - VIEWS.**
Laughlin, Clarence John. Photographs of
Victorian Chicago. [New York, 1968] [12] p.
TR6 .L3   *NYPL [MFX (Laughlin) 90-6252]*

Chicago Institute for Architecture and Urbanism.
Strategies in architectural thinking /. Chicago,
Ill. , Cambridge, Mass. , 1991. p. cm.   ISBN
0-262-23159-X DDC 720/.1 20
NA2500 .S83 1991

Whiteman, John E. M. Divisible by 2 /.
[Chicago] , Cambridge, Mass. , 1990. 61 p. :
ISBN 0-262-73093-6 (pbk.) DDC 728/.092 20
NA7125 .W48 1990
                          NYPL [3-MRG 91-6702]

Chicago Public Library. Cultural Center. The
Chicago show . Chicago, Ill. , c1990. 48 p. :
ISBN 0-938903-09-8
N6487.C52 C6 1990
                          NYPL [3-MAMT 91-7597]

**CHICAGO SCHOOL OF ARCHITECTURE
(MOVEMENT)**
The Midwest in American architecture /.
Urbana , c1991. xv, 259 p., [1] p. of plates :
ISBN 0-252-01743-9 (alk. paper) DDC 720/.977
20
NA722 .M53 1991
                          NYPL [3-MQWO 91-6382]

The Chicago show : May 5 through July 3, 1990 :
an exhibition presented at the Chicago Public
Library Cultural Center / co-organized by City
of Chicago, Department of Cultural Affairs, the
Art Institute of Chicago, Museum of
Contemporary Art. Chicago, Ill. : City of
Chicago, Dept. of Cultural Affairs, c1990. 48
p. : chiefly ill. (some col.) ; 28 cm.   ISBN
0-938903-09-8
*1. Art, American - Illinois - Chicago - Exhibitions. 2.
Art, Modern - 20th century - Illinois - Chicago -
Exhibitions. I. Chicago (Ill.). Dept. of Cultural Affairs.
II. Art Institute of Chicago. III. Museum of
Contemporary Art (Chicago, Ill.). IV. Chicago Public
Library. Cultural Center.*
N6487.C52 C6 1990
                          NYPL [3-MAMT 91-7597]

Chicano art : resistance and affirmation,
1965-1985 / edited by Richard Griswold del
Castillo, Teresa McKenna, and Yvonne
Yarbro-Bejarano. Los Angeles : Wight Art
Gallery, University of California, 1991. p. cm.
Published in conjunction with the exhibition organized
by the UCLA Wight Art Gallery and the CARA
National Advisory Committee." Includes bibliographical
references and index.   ISBN 0-943739-16-0 :   DDC
704/.0368/7207307479494 20
*1. Mexican American art - Exhibitions. 2. Politics in
art - Exhibitions. 3. Mexican Americans - Civil rights.
I. Griswold del Castillo, Richard. II. Mckenna, Teresa.
III. Yarbro-Bejarano, Yvonne. IV. Frederick S. Wight
Art Gallery. V. CARA National Advisory Committee.*
N6538.M4 C45 1991

CHICANOS. see **MEXICAN AMERICANS.**

CHICHIMECS.
Reyes García, Luis. Cuauhtinchan del siglo XII
[doce] al XVI [dieciséis] . Wiesbaden , 1977.
xviii, 127 p., [21] leaves of plates (1 fold.) :
ISBN 3-515-02572-3
F1203 .D46 vol. 10 F1219
                          NYPL [HTC 74-1117 [Bd.] 10]

Chicó, Mário Tavares. A arquitectura gótica em
Portugal / Mário Tavares Chicó. 2. ed. Lisboa :
Livros Horizonte, 1968. 239 p., [21] leaves of
plates : ill. ; 24 cm. Includes index. Bibliography: p.
220-222. DDC 726/.5/09469
1. Church architecture - Portugal. 2. Architecture,

Gothic - Portugal. I. Title.
NA5823 .C48 1968
NYPL [3-MQW 90-5436]

Chiego, William J. (William Joseph) Portland
Art Museum (Or.) Master prints from the
Gilkey collection . [Portland, Or.] , c1980. [35]
p. :   **NYPL [MDE 91-5247]**

Chiesa del Carmine (Taormina, Italy) Santomaso,
Giuseppe. Giuseppe Santomaso . Torino ,
c1988. 101 p. :   ISBN 88-381-0057-8
NYPL [3-MCF S235 90-234]

Chiesa dell'Incoronata (Lodi, Italy) Sciolla,
Gianni Carlo. I Piazza da Lodi . Milano ,
c1989. 406 p. :   ISBN 88-435-3015-1
NYPL [3-MCE 90-11748]

La chiesa dello "spedaletto" in Venezia /. Pilo,
Giuseppe Maria. [Venezia] [Udine] [198-] xii,
271 p., [29] p. of plates :
NYPL [3-MCE+ 90-11574]

**CHIESA DI S. MARIA RIPA (EMPOLI,
ITALY)**
Pagni, Lucia. La chiesa e il convento di S.
Maria a Ripa . Tirrenia (Pisa) , 1988. 238 p. :
NYPL [MRBD 91-3395]

**CHIESA DI S. MARIA RIPA (EMPOLI,
ITALY) - HISTORY - SOURCES.**
Pagni, Lucia. La chiesa e il convento di S.
Maria a Ripa . Tirrenia (Pisa) , 1988. 238 p. :
NYPL [MRBD 91-3395]

**CHIESA DI S. MARIA SOPRA MINERVA
(ROME, ITALY)**
Palmerio, Giancarlo. Storia edilizia di S. Maria
sopra Minerva in Roma, 1275-1870 /. Roma ,
1989. 317 p., [25] leaves of plates (some
folded) :   ISBN 88-85669-19-0
NYPL [3-MRBD 91-6771]

Santa Maria sopra Minerva /. Roma , c1990.
303 p. :   ISBN 88-7060-223-0
NYPL [3-MRBD+ 91-7451]

Chiesa di San Cristoforo (Lodi, Italy) Sciolla,
Gianni Carlo. I Piazza da Lodi . Milano ,
c1989. 406 p. :   ISBN 88-435-3015-1
NYPL [3-MCE 90-11748]

**CHIESA DI SAN MARCO (FLORENCE,
ITALY)**
La Chiesa e il Convento di San Marco a
Firenze. [Firenze?] , c1989- v. :
NYPL [3-MRBD+ 90-2804]

**CHIESA DI SANTA MARIA DEI DERELITTI
(VENICE, ITALY)**
Pilo, Giuseppe Maria. La chiesa dello
"spedaletto" in Venezia /. [Venezia] [Udine]
[198-] xii, 271 p., [29] p. of plates :
NYPL [3-MCE+ 90-11574]

Chiesa di Sant'Agostino (Siena, Italy) Beccafumi,
Domenico, 1486-1551. Domenico Beccafumi e
il suo tempo. Milano , c1990. 732 p. :   ISBN
88-435-3173-5   DDC 759.5 20
ND623.B34 A4 1990

**CHIESA DI SANT'ANDREA (VOLTERRA,
ITALY)**
Sant'Andrea degli Olivetani . Volterra [1989]
74 p. :   **NYPL [3-MRBD 91-6542]**

La chiesa e il convento di S. Maria a Ripa .
Pagni, Lucia. Tirrenia (Pisa) , 1988. 238 p. :
NYPL [MRBD 91-3395]

La Chiesa e il Convento di San Marco a Firenze.
[Firenze?] : Giunti, c1989- v. : ill. (some col.),
plans ; 34 cm. Includes bibliographical references.
1. Chiesa di San Marco (Florence, Italy). 2. Convento
di San Marco (Florence, Italy). 3. Florence (Italy) -
Buildings, structures, etc.
NYPL [3-MRBD+ 90-2804]

Chiese di Lecce /. Paone, Michele. Galatina ,
1978-1979. 2 v. :
NA5619.L42 P36   **NYPL [3-MRBD 80-2560]**

Chiese in Liguria /. Pazzini Paglieri, Nadia.
Genova , 1990. 214 p. :   ISBN 88-7058-361-9 :
DDC 726./5/094518 20
NA5619.L5 P39 1990

Le chiese minori delle colline bolognesi .
Cardinali, Ferdinando. Bologna , 1986. 58 p. :
NYPL [3-MRBD 90-13374]

Chiese monumentali d'Italia.
Il Duomo di Pisa . Firenze , c1989. 236 p. :
ISBN 88-404-1204-2   DDC 726./6/094555 20
NA5621.P713 D86 1989
NYPL [3-MRBN+ 90-10929]

San Paolo fuori le mura a Roma /. Firenze ,
c1988. 336 p. :   ISBN 88-404-1201-8
NYPL [3-MRBD+ 90-12663]

Le Chiese rurali del territorio di Ostuni / a cura
di Giuseppe Palasciano ; censimento eseguito da
Pasqua M. Colucci ... [et al.] ; fotografie di
Francesco Semeraro. [Fasano di Brindisi] :
Schena, [1990] 94 p. : ill. (some col.) ; 30
cm.+ 1 folded map. Folded map in back pocket.
ISBN 88-7514-395-1
1. Churches - Italy - Ostuni. 2. Christian art and
symbolism - Italy - Ostuni. I. Palasciano, Giuseppe.
NYPL [3-MRBD+ 91-3446]

Chihuly, Dale, 1941-
Venetians / Dale Chihuly. 1st ed. Altadena,
Calif. : Twin Palms Publishers, 1989. 1 v. : col.
ill. ; 37 cm.   ISBN 0-944092-08-X   DDC 730/.92
20
1. Chihuly, Dale, 1941- - Themes, motives. 2. Glass
art - United States - History - 20th century - Themes,
motives. I. Title.
NK5198.C43 A4 1989

**CHIHULY, DALE, 1941- - THEMES,
MOTIVES.**
Chihuly, Dale, 1941- Venetians /. Altadena,
Calif. , 1989. 1 v. :   ISBN 0-944092-08-X   DDC
730/.92 20
NK5198.C43 A4 1989

Chikan embroidery . Paine, Sheila. Aylesbury,
Bucks, UK , 1989. 60 p. :   ISBN 0-7478-0009-X :
DDC 746.44 20
NK9276.A1 P35 1989

**CHILD AND MOTHER. see MOTHER AND
CHILD.**

Childe Hassam: etchings & dry-points. Hassam,
Childe, 1859-1935. Catalogue of the etchings
and dry-points of Childe Hassam, N.A., of the
American Academy of Arts and Letters /. San
Francisco , 1989. 224 p. :   ISBN 1-556-60029-1
NYPL [MDG+ (Hassam) 89-27271]

CHILDREN AS ARTISTS.
Gray, Donna B., 1944- A parent's guide to
teaching art . White Hall, Va. , c1991. p. cm.
ISBN 1-558-70202-4 (pbk.) :   DDC 700 20
N351 .G73 1991

Souza, Alcídio Mafra de. Artes plásticas na
escola. [Rio de Janeiro, 1973, c1968] 159 p.,
[31] leaves of plates.
NYPL [3-MAT 90-5879]

**CHILDREN AS ARTISTS - JUVENILE
LITERATURE.**
Solga, Kim. Paint! /. Cincinnati, Ohio , c1991.
p. cm.   ISBN 0-89134-383-0 :   DDC 702/.8 20
N351 .S6 1991

**CHILDREN - CARICATURES AND
CARTOONS.**
Saget, Bob. [Tales from the crib.] Bob Saget's
Tales from the crib /. New York, NY , c1991.
95 p. :   ISBN 0-399-51676-X :   DDC 741.5/973 20
NC1429.S315 A4 1991

**CHILDREN, GIFTED. see GIFTED
CHILDREN.**

**CHILDREN - GREAT BRITAIN - BOOKS
AND READING - HISTORY - 19TH
CENTURY.**
Vries, Leonard de. A treasury of illustrated
children's books . New York , 1989. 285 p. :
ISBN 0-89659-939-6   DDC 011/.62 19
Z1037 .V75 1989 PN1009.A1
NYPL [MDTO+ 90-9497]

Children of the dreamtime /. Baldwin, Helen.
Frenchs Forest, NSW, Australia , 1989. 103 p. :
ISBN 0-86777-278-6
NYPL [3-MCX+ B181 90-12952]

**CHILDREN - PHOTOGRAPHY. see
PHOTOGRAPHY OF CHILDREN.**

CHILDREN - PORTRAITS.
McKenzie, Joseph, 1929- Gorbals children .
Glasgow , 1990. [128] p. :   ISBN 0-86267-269-4
(pbk) :   DDC 779/.092/4 19
NYPL [MFX (McKensie) 90-11268]

**CHILDREN - UNITED STATES - PICTORIAL
WORKS.**
Young America . New York , 1990. 144 p. :
ISBN 0-8264-0479-0 :   DDC 779/.2/097307473
20
TR681.F28 Y68 1990
NYPL [MFW 91-3590]

**CHILDREN'S ART - CZECHOSLOVAKIA -
EXHIBITIONS.**
Alšova země 89 . V Praze [1989?] 44 p. :
N352.2.C95 A47 1989

**CHILDREN'S ART - EUROPE -
EXHIBITIONS.**
'Imparaticci' =. [Firenze] , c1986. 78, [1] p. :
ISBN 88-7038-120-X
NK9109 .I663 1986
NYPL [3-MOT 90-10855]

CHILDREN'S ART - GERMANY (WEST)
Die Welt in hundert Jahren . Düsseldorf , 1985.
148 p. :   ISBN 3-925282-00-9
NYPL [3-MATC+ 90-12542]

**CHILDREN'S ART - UNITED STATES -
EXHIBITIONS.**
'Imparaticci' =. [Firenze] , c1986. 78, [1] p. :
ISBN 88-7038-120-X
NK9109 .I663 1986
NYPL [3-MOT 90-10855]

Children's book illustration and design / edited
by Julie Cummins. New York : Library of
Applied Design, PBC International, 1991. p.
cm. Includes indexes.   ISBN 0-86636-147-2   DDC
741.6/42/09048 20
1. Illustrated books, Children's. 2. Illustration of books -
20th century. 3. Illustrators - Biography. 4. Book
design. I. Cummins, Julie.
NC965 .C43 1991

**CHILDREN'S BOOKS. see ILLUSTRATED
BOOKS, CHILDREN'S; CHILDREN'S
LITERATURE.**

CHILDREN'S DRAWINGS.
Jugendliche im Gefängnis . Köln , 1987. 95 p. :
ISBN 3-7701-2138-4
NYPL [3-MATC+ 89-25803]

**CHILDREN'S ILLUSTRATED BOOKS. see
ILLUSTRATED BOOKS, CHILDREN'S.**

**CHILDREN'S LITERATURE, ARABIC -
ILLUSTRATIONS - THEMES, MOTIVES.**
Malaṣ, Muḥammad. Kutub al-aṭfāl
al-muṣawwarah . 'Ammān, al-Mamlakah
al-Urdunīyah al-Hāshimīyah , 1989. 90 p. ;
NC965 .M33 1989

**CHILDREN'S LITERATURE, CZECH -
ILLUSTRATIONS.**
Holešovský, František. Čeští ilustrátoři v
současné knize pro děti a mládež /. Praha ,
1989. 455 p. :
NC989.C9 H62 1989

**CHILDREN'S LITERATURE, ENGLISH -
BIBLIOGRAPHY.**
Vries, Leonard de. A treasury of illustrated
children's books . New York , 1989. 285 p. :
ISBN 0-89659-939-6   DDC 011/.62 19
Z1037 .V75 1989 PN1009.A1
NYPL [MDTO+ 90-9497]

**CHILDREN'S LITERATURE - PICTURE
BOOKS. see ILLUSTRATED BOOKS,
CHILDREN'S.**

**CHILDREN'S LITERATURE - PUBLISHING -
GREAT BRITAIN - HISTORY - 19TH
CENTURY.**
Vries, Leonard de. A treasury of illustrated
children's books . New York , 1989. 285 p. :
ISBN 0-89659-939-6   DDC 011/.62 19
Z1037 .V75 1989 PN1009.A1
NYPL [MDTO+ 90-9497]

Childs, Elizabeth C. Femmes d'esprit .
Middlebury, Vt. , Hanover , c1990. 146 p. :
ISBN 0-9625262-0-7   DDC 741.5/944 20
NC1499.D3 A4 1990
NYPL [MDG (Daumier) 90-11002]

Chile. Chile from within, 1973-1988 /. New
York , 1990. 143 p. :   ISBN 0-393-02817-8 (cl.)
DDC 983.06/5 20
F3100 .F4722 1990   **NYPL [MFW 91-4452]**

CHILE - BIOGRAPHY.
Tupper, Patricio, 1945- Somerscales, con el
catálogo de su obra /. [Santiago, Chile] [1979]
175 p. :   DDC 759.2 B 19
ND497.S73 T86 1979
NYPL [3-MCV S705 90-12589]

Chile from within, 1973-1988 / photographs by
Paz Errázuriz ... [et al.] ; texts by Marco
Antonio de la Parra, Ariel Dorfman ; edited
with Susan Meiselas. New York : W.W.
Norton, 1990. 143 p. : ill. ; 22x26 cm.
CONTENTS. - Fragments of a self-portrait / Marco

Antonio de la Parra, translated by Marcelo
Montealegre -- Memories of hope / Ariel Dorfman.
ISBN 0-393-02817-8 (cl.)   DDC 983.06/5 20
*1. Violence - Chile - History - 20th century - Pictorial
works. 2. Photography, Documentary - Chile. 3. Chile -
Politics and government - 1973- - Pictorial works. I.
Errázuriz, Paz. II. Parra, Marco Antonio de la. III.
Dorfman, Ariel. IV. Meiselas, Susan. V. Title: Chile.*
F3100 .F4722 1990   **NYPL** *[MFW 91-4452]*

**Chile - Government. see Chile - Politics and
government.**

CHILE IN ART.
Bindis, Ricardo. Rugendas en Chile /. Santiago
de Chile , 1989. 111 p. :   DDC 759.3 B 20
ND588.R8 A4 1989

**CHILE - POLITICS AND GOVERNMENT -
1970- - ADDRESSES, ESSAYS,
LECTURES.**
Chile 1973: ni reforma, ni revolución! Medellín
[1973] 1 v.   **NYPL** *[HIO 75-1240]*

**CHILE - POLITICS AND GOVERNMENT -
1973- - PICTORIAL WORKS.**
Chile from within, 1973-1988 /. New York ,
1990. 143 p. :   ISBN 0-393-02817-8 (cl.)   DDC
983.06/5 20
F3100 .F4722 1990   **NYPL** *[MFW 91-4452]*

Chile 1973: ni reforma, ni revolución! Selección
de documentos para el análisis histórico.
Medellín, Colombia, Editorial La Pulga [1973]
1 v. 17 cm. "Una serie de artículos tomados de los
órganos de difusión de los partidos de izquierda más
representativos."
*1. Chile - Politics and government - 1970- - Addresses,
essays, lectures. I. Editorial La Pulga.*
     NYPL *[HIO 75-1240]*

Chillida /. Chillida, Eduardo, 1924- [Stuttgart] ,
c1991. 183 p. :   ISBN 3-7757-0321-7
     NYPL *[3-MGO+ (Chillida) 96-629]*

Chillida. Chillida, Eduardo, 1924- Eduardo
Chillida, Zeichnung als Skulptur 1948-1989 .
Bonn , Münster , c1989. 161 p. :   DDC 709/.2
20
N6913 .C48 1989
     NYPL *[3-MGO+ (Chillida) 90-12885]*

Chillida, Eduardo, 1924-
Chillida / Beiträge von Eduardo Chillida ... [et
al.]. [Stuttgart] : G. Hatje, c1991. 183 p. : ill. ;
31 cm. Summary in English.   ISBN 3-7757-0321-7
1. Chillida, Eduardo, 1924-. I. Title.
     NYPL *[3-MGO+ (Chillida) 96-629]*

Eduardo Chillida : XLIV Esposizione
internazionale d'arte, La Biennale di Venezia.
[Venezia] : Edizioni Biennale, [1990] 199 p. :
ill. (some col.) ; 30 cm. Includes bibliographical
references (p. [192]-195.   ISBN 88-20-80358-5   DDC
709/.2 20
*1. Chillida, Eduardo, 1924- - Exhibitions. I. Biennale di
Venezia (44th : 1990). II. Title.*
N7113.C555 A4 1990

Eduardo Chillida, Zeichnung als Skulptur
1948-1989 : [Ausstellung], Städtisches
Kunstmuseum Bonn, 20. Juni bis 6. August
1989, Westfälisches Landesmuseum Münster,
24. September bis 26. November 1989 /
[Redaktion, Katharina Schmidt, Mario-Andreas
von Lüttichau]. Bonn : Das Museum ;
Münster : Das Museum, c1989. 161 p. : ill.
(some col.) ; 31 cm. Cover title: Chillida. Includes
bibliographical references (p. 160).   DDC 709/.2 20
*1. Chillida, Eduardo, 1924- - Exhibitions. I. Schmidt,
Katharina, Dr. II. Lüttichau, Mario-Andreas von. III.
Städtisches Kunstmuseum Bonn. IV. Title. V. Title:
Zeichnung als Skulptur 1948-1989. VI. Title: Chillida.*
N6913 .C48 1989
     NYPL *[3-MGO+ (Chillida) 90-12885]*

CHILLIDA, EDUARDO, 1924-
Chillida, Eduardo, 1924- Chillida /. [Stuttgart] ,
c1991. 183 p. :   ISBN 3-7757-0321-7
     NYPL *[3-MGO+ (Chillida) 96-629]*

**CHILLIDA, EDUARDO, 1924- -
EXHIBITIONS.**
Chillida, Eduardo, 1924- Eduardo Chillida .
[Venezia] [1990] 199 p. :   ISBN 88-20-80358-5
DDC 709/.2 20
N7113.C555 A4 1990

Chillida, Eduardo, 1924- Eduardo Chillida,
Zeichnung als Skulptur 1948-1989 . Bonn ,
Münster , c1989. 161 p. :   DDC 709/.2 20
N6913 .C48 1989
     NYPL *[3-MGO+ (Chillida) 90-12885]*

CHINA - ANTIQUITIES - CONGRESSES.
New perspectives on Chu culture during the
Eastern Zhou Period /. Washington, D.C. ,
Princeton, N.J. , c1991. p. cm.   ISBN
0-691-04095-8 (Princeton Univ. Press) :   DDC
700/.931 20
N7343.22 .N48 1991

CHINA - ANTIQUITIES - EXHIBITIONS.
Magic, art and order . Palm Springs, Calif. ,
c1990. 155 p. :   **NYPL** *[3-MNW+ 90-13208]*

China - Archaeology. see China - Antiquities.

CHINA - CIVILIZATION.
Dexel, Thomas, 1890- Frühe Keramik in China.
Braunschweig [c1973] 84, [48] p.
GN799.P6 D49   **NYPL** *[3-MPFF 90-6053]*

**CHINA - CIVILIZATION - TO 221 B.C. -
CONGRESSES.**
New perspectives on Chu culture during the
Eastern Zhou Period /. Washington, D.C. ,
Princeton, N.J. , c1991. p. cm.   ISBN
0-691-04095-8 (Princeton Univ. Press) :   DDC
700/.931 20
N7343.22 .N48 1991

**CHINA - COURT AND COURTIERS -
PICTORIAL WORKS.**
Dickinson, Gary. Imperial wardrobe /.
London , 1990. 203 p. :   ISBN 1-87007-607-9 :
DDC 391.0220951 20
     NYPL *[3-MMR+ 91-4972]*

CHINA - CULTURAL POLICY.
Kraus, Richard Curt. Brushes with power .
Berkeley , c1991. xii, 208 p. :   ISBN
0-520-07285-5 (cloth : alk. paper)   DDC
745.6/19951 20
NK3634.A2 K73 1991

**CHINA - DESCRIPTION AND TRAVEL -
1976- - GUIDE-BOOKS.**
Chan, Charis. Imperial China /. San Francisco ,
1992. p. cm.   ISBN 0-8118-0018-0   DDC 720/.951
20
NA1543.5 .C4 1992

**CHINA - DESCRIPTION AND TRAVEL -
1976- - VIEWS.**
A Day in the life of China /. San Francisco ,
1989. 220 p. :   ISBN 0-00-215321-1 (returnable
ed.) :   DDC 951.05/8/0222 20
DS712 .D39 1989
     NYPL *[MFW+ 90-11175]*

China House Gallery. Giacalone, Vito. The
Eccentric painters of Yangzhou /. New York
City , 1990. 92 p. :   ISBN 0-295-97087-1
     NYPL *[3-MAG 91-6594]*

China Institute in America. Giacalone, Vito. The
Eccentric painters of Yangzhou /. New York
City , 1990. 92 p. :   ISBN 0-295-97087-1
     NYPL *[3-MAG 91-6594]*

China Institute in America. China House Gallery.
see **China House Gallery.**

**CHINA - KINGS AND RULERS -
PICTORIAL WORKS.**
Dickinson, Gary. Imperial wardrobe /.
London , 1990. 203 p. :   ISBN 1-87007-607-9 :
DDC 391.0220951 20
     NYPL *[3-MMR+ 91-4972]*

CHINA PAINTING.
Tailor, Heather. Lustre for china painters and
potters /. Kenthurst , 1990. 47 p. :   ISBN
0-86417-294-X   DDC 738.1/5 20
NK4605 .T25 1990

CHINA PAINTING - THEMES, MOTIVES.
Harle, Lesley. Designer china . New York ,
1991. p. cm.   ISBN 0-688-10923-3   DDC 738.1/5
20
NK4605 .H36 1991

**CHINA - ROYAL HOUSEHOLD -
DWELLINGS - GUIDE-BOOKS.**
Chan, Charis. Imperial China /. San Francisco ,
1992. p. cm.   ISBN 0-8118-0018-0   DDC 720/.951
20
NA1543.5 .C4 1992

China - Rulers. see China - Kings and rulers.

**CHINA - SOCIAL LIFE AND CUSTOMS -
1976- - PICTORIAL WORKS.**
A Day in the life of China /. San Francisco ,
1989. 220 p. :   ISBN 0-00-215321-1 (returnable
ed.) :   DDC 951.05/8/0222 20
DS712 .D39 1989
     NYPL *[MFW+ 90-11175]*

CHINA TRADE PORCELAIN - CATALOGS.
Sargent, William R. (William Robert), 1945-
The Copeland collection . Salem, Mass. , c1991.
p. cm.   ISBN 0-87577-157-2 (cloth : acid free) :
DDC 738.8/2/095107473 20
NK4565.5 .S26 1991

**CHINA TRADE PORCELAIN -
EXHIBITIONS.**
Chinese export porcelain . Hong Kong , 1989.
303 p. :   ISBN 962-215-094-2
     NYPL *[3-MPFF 91-5164]*

Crossman, Carl L. A design catalogue of
Chinese export porcelain for the American
market /. Salem, Mass. , 1969. 48 p. :   ISBN
0-87577-019-3   **NYPL** *[3-MPFF 90-6436]*

CHINAWARE. see POTTERY.

**CHINESE AMERICAN ARTISTS -
BIOGRAPHY.**
Kingman, Dong, 1911- Paint the yellow tiger /.
New York , 1991. 128 p. :   ISBN 0-8069-8316-7 :
DDC 759.13 B 20
N6537.K522 A2 1991

CHINESE ART. see ART, CHINESE.

Chinese art and design /. Kerr, Rose, 1953-
Woodstock, N.Y. , 1991. p. cm.   ISBN
0-87951-437-X :   DDC 745/.0951/07442134 20
NK1068 .K47 1991

**CHINESE ART OBJECTS. see ART OBJECTS,
CHINESE.**

Chinese art: symbols and images. [Wellesley,
Mass., Wellesley College, c1967] 63 p. illus. 26
cm. Catalogue of an exhibition held at Wellesley
College, Jewett Arts Center, April 16-June 6, 1967,
sponsored by the Mayling Soong Foundation.
Introduction by Max Loehr. Includes bibliographical
references.   DDC 709/.51
*1. Art, Chinese - Exhibitions. 2. Art, Chinese - History
and criticism. I. Loehr, Max. II. Jewett Arts Center
(Wellesley, Mass.). III. Mayling Soong Foundation
(Wellesley, Mass.).*
N7342 .L58   **NYPL** *[3-MAG 90-6432]*

**CHINESE BRONZES. see BRONZES,
CHINESE.**

**CHINESE CALLIGRAPHY. see
CALLIGRAPHY, CHINESE.**

Chinese ceramics. Barlow, Sir James Alan Noel,
bart., 1881- London [1963] 173 p.   DDC
730.951
NK4165 .B3   **NYPL** *[3-MPFF 90-11573]*

Chinese earth-sheltered dwellings . Golany,
Gideon. Honolulu , c1992. p. cm.   ISBN
0-8248-1369-3   DDC 728/.0473/0951 20
NA7448 .G6 1992

CHINESE EASTERN RAILWAY.
Al'bom planov i diagramm, otnosi͡ashchikhsi͡a k
di͡elu sooruzheni͡ia ͡elevatorov na Kitaĭskoĭ
Vostochnoĭ zh.[eleznoĭ] d.[oroge]. [S.l. , 192-?].
6 leaves (some folded) /.
     NYPL *[Map Div. 91-1086]*

Chinese export porcelain : chine de commande
from the Royal Museums of Art and History in
Brussels : 30.11.89-27.2.90, Flagstaff House
Museum of Tea Ware ... / organized by the
Royal Museums of Art and History in
Brussels ; catalogue by C.J.A. Jörg. Hong
Kong : Urban Council, 1989. 303 p. : ill. ; 29
cm. English and Chinese. "Jointly presented by the
Urban Council, Hong Kong and the Belgium-Hong
Kong Society with the assistance of the Belgian
Consulate General in Hong Kong and the Commissariat
General for the International Cooperation of the
Flemish Community."   ISBN 962-215-094-2
*1. Musées royaux d'art et d'histoire (Belgium) -
Exhibitions. 2. China trade porcelain - Exhibitions. I.
Jörg, C. J. A. II. Flagstaff House Museum of Tea Ware
(Hong Kong).*   **NYPL** *[3-MPFF 91-5164]*

The Chinese eye. Chiang, Yee, 1903- London
[1960] xvi, 239 p.   **NYPL** *[3-MAG 90-10781]*

**CHINESE LANDSCAPE PAINTING. see
LANDSCAPE PAINTING, CHINESE.**

**CHINESE LANGUAGE - ORTHOGRAPHY
AND SPELLING. see CHINESE
LANGUAGE - TRANSLITERATION.**

**CHINESE LANGUAGE -
TRANSLITERATION.**
A Perspective on the Pinyin romanization of
Chinese characters . Washington, D.C. , 1981.

iv, 101 p., :   DDC 495.1/11 19
PL1185 .P45   **NYPL [Map Div. 86-743]**

Chinese painters; a critical study. Petrucci, Raphaël, 1872-1917. [Peintres chinois. English.] Freeport, N.Y. [1969] 155 p. ISBN 0-8369-5138-7 DDC 759.951
ND1040 .P413 1969

Chinese painting /. Ting, Francisca. New York , 1991. 128 p. : ISBN 0-486-26785-7 : DDC 751.4/251 20
ND1040 .T56 1991

CHINESE PAINTING. see PAINTING, CHINESE.

Chinese paintings. Fang, Chün-pi, 1898- Fang Chün-pi kuo hua chi /. [S.l. , 1938] 2 v., [32] p. of plates :   **NYPL [3-MAG 90-6901]**

Chinese paintings in the Palace Museum, Beijing, 4th-14th century /. Hall, Dickson. Hong Kong , 1989. viii, 175 p., [12] p. of plates : ISBN 962-04-0691-5 : DDC 759.951/074/51156 20
ND2068 .H35 1989
                    NYPL [3-MAG 91-5448]

CHINESE POETRY - HISTORY AND CRITICISM - CONGRESSES.
Words and images . New York , 1991. p. cm. ISBN 0-87099-604-5 DDC 745.6/19951 20
NK3634.A2 W67 1991

CHINESE PORCELAIN. see PORCELAIN, CHINESE.

CHINESE POTTERY. see POTTERY, CHINESE.

Chinese pottery and porcelain /. Vainker, S. J. New York , 1991. p. cm. ISBN 0-8076-1260-X DDC 738/.0951 20
NK4165 .V3 1991

Chinesische Lackarbeiten /. Linden-Museum Stuttgart. Stuttgart , c1988. 159 p. :
                    NYPL [3-MNX+ 90-10961]

CHINTZ - INDIA - CATALOGS.
Beer, Alice Baldwin. Trade goods. Washington, 1970. 133 p. DDC 746.6
NK8876.A2 B4   **NYPL [3-MON 91-994]**

Chionna, Antonio. Beni culturali di San Vito dei Normanni / Antonio Chionna. Fasano, Brindisi : Schena, [1988] 471 p., [32] leaves of plates : ill. (some col.) ; 31 cm. Includes bibliographical references (p. 435-437). ISBN 88-7514-253-X : DDC 709/.45/754 20
1. Art, Italian - Italy - San Vito dei Normanni. 2. Christian art and symbolism - Italy - San Vito dei Normanni. I. Title.
N6921.S38 C47 1988
                    NYPL [3-MAMC+ 90-10597]

I chiostri di Brescia . Terraroli, Valerio. [Brescia] [1989] 171 p. : ISBN 88-7385-052-9
                    NYPL [3-MRBD+ 91-3675]

Chips from the quarries /. Williamson, Harry Albro, 1875- New York, 1971. 407 ft. of microfilm. **NYPL [Sc Micro R-1295-1299]**

Chiriacka, Ernest, 1920-
Ernest Chiriacka : the old West in painting and bronzes : exhibition, December 1-30 [held at] Kennedy Galleries. New York, N.Y. : The Galleries, 1976. [17] p. : chiefly ill. (some col.) ; 26 cm. Cover title.
1. Chiriacka, Ernest, 1920- - Exhibitions. 2. Painting, American - Exhibitions. 3. Painting, Modern - 20th century - United States - Exhibitions. 4. Bronzes, American - Exhibitions. 5. West (U. S.) in art - Exhibitions. I. Kennedy Galleries, inc., New York. II. Title: Old West in paintings and bronzes.
                    NYPL [3-MCX C541 90-5910]

CHIRIACKA, ERNEST, 1920- - EXHIBITIONS.
Chiriacka, Ernest, 1920- Ernest Chiriacka . New York, N.Y. , 1976. [17] p. :
                    NYPL [3-MCX C541 90-5910]

Chirico, Giorgio, 1888- Mémoires / traduction de l'italien par Marin Tassilit revue par l'auteur ; préface de Pierre Mazars. Paris : La Table Ronde, 1965. 307 p. ; 21 cm. Includes bibliographical references (p. [303]-307).
1. De Chirico, Giorgio, 1888-. 2. Painters - Italy - Biography. I. Title.
                    NYPL [3-MCF C535 91-6673]

Chisholm, George Goudie, 1850-193. Longmans' new school atlas / edited by Geo. G. Chisholm

and C.H. Leete. New York : Longmans, Green, 1904. iv, 31 p. : 40 col. maps. ; 29 cm.
I. Lette, Charles Henry, 1857-. II. Title. III. Title: New school atlas.   **NYPL [Map Div. 90-12773]**

Chistes VIII /. Mingote, Angel Antonio, 1919- Madrid , 1965. 181 p. :
                    NYPL [MEM (Mingote) 91-1189]

Chistes 8. Mingote, Angel Antonio, 1919- Chistes VIII /. Madrid , 1965. 181 p. :
                    NYPL [MEM (Mingote) 91-1189]

CHOIR-STALLS, BAROQUE - MEXICO - PUEBLA (STATE)
Maza, Francisco de la, 1913-1972. Arquitectura de los coros de monjas en Puebla /. [Puebla] [Mexico City] [1990] 104 p. :
NA5256.P8 M39 1990

CHOIR-STALLS - ENGLAND.
Tracy, Charles, 1938- English Gothic choir-stalls, 1400-1540 /. Woodbridge, Suffolk [England] , Rochester, NY, USA , 1990. xx, 75 p., [112] p. of plates : ISBN 0-85115-272-4 (hardback : acid-free paper) : DDC 726/.5293 20
NA5463 .T74 1990
                    NYPL [3-MRBV+ 91-4462]

CHOIR-STALLS, GOTHIC - ENGLAND.
Tracy, Charles, 1938- English Gothic choir-stalls, 1400-1540 /. Woodbridge, Suffolk [England] , Rochester, NY, USA , 1990. xx, 75 p., [112] p. of plates : ISBN 0-85115-272-4 (hardback : acid-free paper) : DDC 726/.5293 20
NA5463 .T74 1990
                    NYPL [3-MRBV+ 91-4462]

CHOIR-STALLS - MEXICO - PUEBLA (STATE)
Maza, Francisco de la, 1913-1972. Arquitectura de los coros de monjas en Puebla /. [Puebla] [Mexico City] [1990] 104 p. :
NA5256.P8 M39 1990

Chōkoku no Mori Bijutsukan.
Hunter, Sam, 1923- In the mountains of Japan . New York, NY [1988?] 288 p. : ISBN 0-89659-949-3 DDC 735/.23/00740952136 19
NB198 .H86 1988
                    NYPL [3-MGI+ 90-11775]

CHŌKOKU NO MORI BIJUTSUKAN - CATALOGS.
Hunter, Sam, 1923- In the mountains of Japan . New York, NY [1988?] 288 p. : ISBN 0-89659-949-3 DDC 735/.23/00740952136 19
NB198 .H86 1988
                    NYPL [3-MGI+ 90-11775]

CHOLA ARCHITECTURE. see ARCHITECTURE, CHOLA.

Choose me . Grace, Arthur. [Waltham, Mass.] Hanover, NH , c1989. 127 p. : ISBN 0-87451-491-6
                    NYPL [MFX (Grace) 89-28159]

CHOPIN, FRYDERYK FRANCISZEK, 1810-1849 - ANNIVERSARIES, ETC., 1949.
Ars, revista de arte . Buenos Aires , 1949. [111] p., [1] leaf of plates : **NYPL [JMG 84-326]**

CHORAL SYMPHONIES. see SYMPHONIES.

Die Chorkrypta des romanischen Domes in Salzburg . Fuhrmann, Franz. Salzburg , 1962. 32 p. :   **NYPL [3-MRIF 90-4729]**

Chorkrypta des romanischen Domes zu Salzburg.
Fuhrmann, Franz. Die Chorkrypta des romanischen Domes in Salzburg . Salzburg , 1962. 32 p. : **NYPL [3-MRIF 90-4729]**

Chou, Shih-hsin. Chung-kuo hua hui hua chi ch'u = The fundamentals of Chinese floral painting / Chou Shih-hsin pien hui. [Taipei?] : Art Book Co., [1976?] 263 p. : col. ill. ; 29 cm. Chinese and English.
1. Painting, Chinese - Technique. I. Title. II. Title: Mei lan chu chü p'u. III. Title: Fundamentals of Chinese floral painting.   **NYPL [3-MAF+ 90-6353]**

Choung-Fux, Eva. "Haut und Hülle" . Wien [1989?] 82 p. : **NYPL [MFW+ 91-2502]**

Chountas, Giōrgos. Sperantzas V. (Vasilēs) V. Sperantzas /. Kea Kykladōn [1990] 143 p. :
N6903.S64 A4 1990

Chow, Fong. Arts from the rooftop of Asia . New York [1971] 4, [46] p. :
                    NYPL [3-MAE 91-302]

Chrēstou, Chrysanthos, 1922- Hē Eurōpaikē zōgraphikē tou 17ou aiōna : to Barok / Chrysanthou Chrēstou. Thessalonikē : Ekdoseis

Vanias, 1989. 516 p. : ill. ; 24 cm. Includes bibliographical references.
1. Painting, European. 2. Painting, Baroque. 3. Painting, Modern - 17th-18th centuries - Europe. I. Title. II. Title: Eurōpaikē zōgraphikē tou dekatou hevdomou aiōna.
ND456 .C47 1989

Christa Näher . Näher, Christa, 1947- [Bielefeld] [Leverkusen] , 1987. 70 p. :
MLCM 88/00380 (N)
                    NYPL [3-MCK N1385 91-7515]

Christa Näher. Näher, Christa, 1947- Münster , c1988. 51 p. : ISBN 3-925047-06-9
                    NYPL [3-MCK+ N1385 89-25682]

Christen, Werner G. Bieli, Toni, 1936- Toni Bieli . Basel , c1989. 156 p., [4] plates : ISBN 3-909158-27-7
                    NYPL [MDG (Bieli) 90-12800]

CHRISTENBERRY, WILLIAM, 1936-
Southall, Thomas, 1951- Of time & place . San Francisco , Fort Worth , c1990. 88 p. : ISBN 0-933286-57-0 (cloth)
                    NYPL [MFW 91-3397]

Christian A. Johnson Memorial Gallery.
Cahill, James, 1926- New dimensions in Chinese ink painting . Middlebury, Vt. , c1991. p. cm. ISBN 0-9625262-3-1 DDC 759.951/074/7435 20
ND2068 .C33 1991

Femmes d'esprit . Middlebury, Vt. , Hanover , c1990. 146 p. : ISBN 0-9625262-0-7 DDC 741.5/944 20
NC1499.D3 A4 1990
                    NYPL [MDG (Daumier) 90-11002]

CHRISTIAN ANTIQUITIES - ENGLAND - OXFORD.
Saint Frideswide's Monastery at Oxford . Gloucester , Wolfeboro Fall, NH , 1991. p. cm. ISBN 0-86299-773-9 : DDC 726/.7/0942574 20
NA5471.O9 S25 1991

CHRISTIAN ANTIQUITIES - IRELAND - GREAT SKELLIG ISLAND.
Horn, Walter William, 1908- The forgotten hermitage of Skellig Michael . Berkeley , c1990. xi, 111 p. : ISBN 0-520-06410-0 (alk. paper) DDC 941.9/6 19
BX2602.S54 H67 1989
                    NYPL [3-MRBB+ 91-3376]

CHRISTIAN ART AND SYBOLISM - SPAIN - TOLEDO.
Inventario artístico de Toledo /. Madrid , 1983-v. : ISBN 84-7483-328-0 (set)
                    NYPL [3-MAML 86-2086]

CHRISTIAN ART AND SYMBOLISM.
Christus in der bildenden Kunst . München , c1989. 150 p. : ISBN 3-466-36334-9
N8050 .C44 1989

Taverna Irigoyen, J. M. Del arte religioso a lo religioso del arte /. Rosario [Argentina] , 1990. 111 p. :
N7790 .T3 1990

CHRISTIAN ART AND SYMBOLISM - MODERN PERIOD, 500-1500.
CHRISTIAN ART AND SYMBOLISM - MEDIEVAL, 500-1500.
The Altarpiece in the Renaissance /. Cambridge [England] , New York , 1990. xiv, 273 p. : ISBN 0-521-36061-7 DDC 726 20
N7862 .A48 1990 **NYPL [3-MAIH 91-4497]**

Holy image, holy space--icons & frescoes from Greece. Astoria, NY , c1988. 1 videocassette (28 min., 30 sec.) : DDC 704.9 11
N7852.5

Radler, Gudrun. Die Schreinmadonna "Vierge ouvrante" . Frankfurt am Main , 1990. 366 p., [184] p. of plates : ISBN 3-923813-05-8 :
NB1912.M37 R33 1990

Toubert, Hélène. Un art dirigé . Paris , 1990. 495 p. : ISBN 2-204-04105-X :
N7850 .T68 1990

Unger, Richard W. The Art of medieval technology . New Brunswick , c1991. p. cm. ISBN 0-8135-1727-3 DDC 704.9/484 20
N8180 .U54 1991

CHRISTIAN ART AND SYMBOLISM - MEDIEVAL, 500-1500 - AUSTRIA - EXHIBITIONS.

Salzburger Domkepitel. Schöne Madonnen,
1350-1450. [Salzburg, c1965] 126 p.
NYPL [3-MAI 90-7120]

**CHRISTIAN ART AND SYMBOLISM -
MEDIEVAL, 500-1500 - BYZANTINE
EMPIRE.**
Cantó Rubio, Juan. Arte bizantino .
Salamanca , 1989. 94 p. : ISBN 84-7299-220-9
NYPL [3-MAK 91-3667]

**CHRISTIAN ART AND SYMBOLISM -
MEDIEVAL, 500-1500 - BYZANTINE
EMPIRE - EXHIBITIONS.**
Splendori di Bisanzio . Milano [1990] 332 p. :
N7852.5 .S66 1990

**CHRISTIAN ART AND SYMBOLISM -
MEDIEVAL, 500-1500 - CONSERVATION
AND RESTORATION - FRANCE - SAINT-
DENIS.**
Blum, Pamela Z. Early Gothic Saint-Denis .
Berkeley , 1992. p. cm. ISBN 0-520-07371-1
(cloth) DDC 730/.944/362 20
NB1910 .B58 1992

**CHRISTIAN ART AND SYMBOLISM -
MEDIEVAL, 500-1500 - ENGLAND -
CATALOGS.**
Sheingorn, Pamela. The Easter sepulchre in
England /. Kalamazoo, MI , 1987. 426 p., [36]
p. of plates : ISBN 0-918720-79-6 (hardbound)
DDC 730/.942/0902 20
NB1912.J47 S48 1987

**CHRISTIAN ART AND SYMBOLISM -
MEDIEVAL, 500-1500 - ENGLAND -
WEST RIDING OF YORKSHIRE -
THEMES, MOTIVES.**
Palmer, Barbara D. The early art of the West
Riding of Yorkshire . Kalamazoo, Mich. , 1990.
xxii, 363 p., [44] p. of plates : ISBN
0-918720-32-X (case) DDC
704.9/482/0942810902 20
N7944.W47 P35 1990

**CHRISTIAN ART AND SYMBOLISM -
MEDIEVAL, 500-1500 - EUROPE.**
Belting, Hans, 1935- Bild und Kult . München ,
c1990. 700 p. : ISBN 3-406-34367-8
NYPL [3-MAIH 90-12870]

Haseloff, Günther. Email im frühen Mittelalter .
Marburg , c1990. 244 p. : ISBN 3-89398-020-2
NYPL [3-MNV 91-5235]

**CHRISTIAN ART AND SYMBOLISM -
MEDIEVAL, 500-1500 - EXHIBITIONS.**
Kirchenkunst des Mittelalters, erhalten und
erforschen . Hildesheim , 1989. 275 p. : ISBN
3-87065-528-3 DDC 704.9/482/0907435958 20
N7850 .K57 1989

Opus sacrum . Vienna , c1990. 399 p. : ISBN
3-900731-29-2 *NYPL [3-MAIH 91-4343]*

**CHRISTIAN ART AND SYMBOLISM -
MEDIEVAL, 500-1500 - FRANCE - AIN.**
Oursel, Raymond. Lyonnais, Dombes, Bugey et
Savoie romans /. La Pierre-qui-Vire [France] ,
1990. 387 p. : ISBN 2-7369-0177-0
NYPL [3-MQR 91-4889]

**CHRISTIAN ART AND SYMBOLISM -
MEDIEVAL, 500-1500 - FRANCE -
BORDEAUX.**
Gardelles, Jacques. Bordeaux, cité médiévale /.
Bordeaux , c1989. 221 p. : ISBN 2-907202-13-8
N7949.B67 G37 1989

**CHRISTIAN ART AND SYMBOLISM -
MEDIEVAL, 500-1500 - FRANCE - LYON.**
Oursel, Raymond. Lyonnais, Dombes, Bugey et
Savoie romans /. La Pierre-qui-Vire [France] ,
1990. 387 p. : ISBN 2-7369-0177-0
NYPL [3-MQR 91-4889]

**CHRISTIAN ART AND SYMBOLISM -
MEDIEVAL, 500-1500 - FRANCE -
SAVOIE.**
Oursel, Raymond. Lyonnais, Dombes, Bugey et
Savoie romans /. La Pierre-qui-Vire [France] ,
1990. 387 p. : ISBN 2-7369-0177-0
NYPL [3-MQR 91-4889]

**CHRISTIAN ART AND SYMBOLISM -
MEDIEVAL, 500-1500 - GERMANY
(WEST) - HILDESHEIM -
EXHIBITIONS.**
Kirchenkunst des Mittelalters . Hildesheim ,
c1989. 275 p. : ISBN 3-87065-528-3
NYPL [3-MAIH 90-12031]

**CHRISTIAN ART AND SYMBOLISM -
MEDIEVAL, 500-1500 - GERMANY**

(WEST) - TRIER.
Bischöfliches Dom- und Diözesanmuseum Trier.
Das neue Bischöfliche Dom- und
Diözesanmuseum . Trier , 1988. 123 p. :
NYPL [3-MAIH 90-10260]

**CHRISTIAN ART AND SYMBOLISM -
MEDIEVAL, 500-1500 - ITALY - PISA.**
Il Duomo di Pisa . Firenze , c1989. 236 p. :
ISBN 88-404-1204-2 DDC 726/.6/094555 20
NA5621.P713 D86 1989
NYPL [3-MRBN+ 90-10929]

**CHRISTIAN ART AND SYMBOLISM -
MEDIEVAL, 500-1500 - ITALY - ROME.**
Nordhagen, Per Jonas. Studies in Byzantine and
early medieval painting /. London , 1990. 493
p. : ISBN 0-907132-47-2
NYPL [3-MRXZ 91-3778]

**CHRISTIAN ART AND SYMBOLISM -
MEDIEVAL, 500-1500 - ITALY -
TRENTINO-ALTO ADIGE.**
Imago lignea . Trento, c1989. 287 p. : ISBN
88-85114-07-5 *NYPL [3-MGI+ 91-4470]*

Imago lignea . Trento, Italia , c1989. 287 p. :
ISBN 88-85114-07-5 : DDC 730/.945/38 20
NB1255.I8 I45 1989

**CHRISTIAN ART AND SYMBOLISM -
MEDIEVAL, 500-1500 - JUVENILE
LITERATURE.**
Perdrizet, Marie-Pierre. [Bâtisseurs de
cathédrales. English.] The cathedral builders /.
Brookfield, Conn. [1992] p. cm. ISBN
1-562-94162-3 DDC 726/.6/0940902 20
NA4830 .P3713 1992

**CHRISTIAN ART AND SYMBOLISM -
MEDIEVAL, 500-1500 - SPAIN - BURGOS
(PROVINCE) - CONGRESSES.**
El Románico en Silos . Burgos , 1990. 606 p. :
ISBN 0-8470-0317-7 DDC 726/.7/0946353 20
NA5811.S48 R66 1990

**CHRISTIAN ART AND SYMBOLISM -
MEDIEVAL, 500-1500 - SWITZERLAND -
ST. GALL.**
Die Kultur der Abtei Sankt Gallen /. Zürich ,
c1990. 223 p. : ISBN 3-7630-1220-6
NX663.S9 K84 1990

**CHRISTIAN ART AND SYMBOLISM -
MEDIEVAL, 1050-1500.**
Löber, Karl. Agaleia . Köln , 1988. viii, 327 p.,
[4] p. of plates : ISBN 3-412-05486-0
N8012.A66 L64 1988
NYPL [3-MAIH+ 90-12956]

**CHRISTIAN ART AND SYMBOLISM -
RENAISSANCE, 1450-1600 - ITALY -
COMO, LAKE, REGION.**
Rossi, Marco. Pittura in Alto Lario tra Quattro
e Cinquecento /. Milano [1988] xv, 261 p. :
ISBN 88-85858-03-1
NYPL [3-MCE+ 91-7283]

**CHRISTIAN ART AND SYMBOLISM -
RENAISSANCE, 1450-1600 - PORTUGAL -
COIMBRA.**
Gonçalves, António Nogueira, 1901- Estudos
de história da arte da Renascença /. Aveiro
[Portugal] [between 1975 and 1987] 311 p. :
N7963.C65 G66 1975

**CHRISTIAN ART AND SYMBOLISM -
MODERN PERIOD, 1500-**
Löber, Karl. Agaleia . Köln , 1988. viii, 327 p.,
[4] p. of plates : ISBN 3-412-05486-0
N8012.A66 L64 1988
NYPL [3-MAIH+ 90-12956]

Poletto, Christine, 1959- Art et pouvoirs à
l'Age baroque . Paris , c1990. 218 p., [16] p. of
plates : ISBN 2-7384-0495-2
N7862 .P65 1990

**CHRISTIAN ART AND SYMBOLISM -
MODERN PERIOD, 1500- -
EXHIBITIONS.**
Opus sacrum . Vienna , c1990. 399 p. : ISBN
3-900731-29-2 *NYPL [3-MAIH 91-4343]*

**CHRISTIAN ART AND SYMBOLISM -
MODERN PERIOD, 1500- - GERMANY.**
Gross, Friedrich. Jesus, Luther und der Papst
im Bilderkampf 1871 bis 1918 . Marburg ,
c1989. 588 p. : ISBN 3-922561-37-3
ND566 .G75 1989

**CHRISTIAN ART AND SYMBOLISM -
MODERN PERIOD, 1500- - GERMANY
(WEST) - TRIER.**
Bischöfliches Dom- und Diözesanmuseum Trier.

Das neue Bischöfliche Dom- und
Diözesanmuseum . Trier , 1988. 123 p. :
NYPL [3-MAIH 90-10260]

**CHRISTIAN ART AND SYMBOLISM -
MODERN PERIOD, 1500- - GERMANY -
WIEDENBRÜCK.**
Grosse Hovest, Benedikt. Die Wiedenbrücker
Schule . Paderborn , c1991. 124 p. : ISBN
3-87088-662-5 *NYPL [3-MAIH 91-7956]*

**CHRISTIAN ART AND SYMBOLISM -
MODERN PERIOD, 1500- - ITALY -
NAPLES - CATALOGS.**
Arte sacra di Palazzo . Napoli , 1989. 263 p. :
DDC 704.9/482/09450744573 20
N7952.N36 A74 1989
NYPL [3-MAIH 91-4840]

**CHRISTIAN ART AND SYMBOLISM -
MODERN PERIOD, 1500- - ITALY -
VOLTERRA.**
Sant'Andrea degli Olivetani . Volterra [1989]
74 p. : *NYPL [3-MRBD 91-6542]*

**CHRISTIAN ART AND SYMBOLISM -
MODERN PERIOD, 1500- - LATIN
AMERICA - THEMES, MOTIVES.**
Valbert, Christian. La iconografía simbólica en
el arte barroco de Latino América . [La Paz,
Bolivia] , 1987. 122 p. :
N7901.5 .V35 1987

**CHRISTIAN ART AND SYMBOLISM -
MODERN PERIOD, 1500- - MEXICO -
HIDALGO (STATE)**
Vergara Vergara, José. El barroco en Hidalgo.
[Pachuca, Mexico?] , 1988. 177, [5] p. :
N7914.A3 H538 1988

**CHRISTIAN ART AND SYMBOLISM -
MODERN PERIOD, 1500- - MEXICO -
PUEBLA (STATE)**
Monterrosa Prado, Mariano. La pintura mural
de los conventos franciscanos en Puebla .
[Mexico] [1990] 1 v. (unpaged) :
ND2645.P84 M66 1990

**CHRISTIAN ART AND SYMBOLISM -
MODERN PERIOD, 1500- - PORTUGAL -
ALGARVE.**
Lameira, Francisco I. C. Inventário artístico do
Algarve . Faro , 1989-<1990. v. <1-3 > :
NB1255.P8 L3 1989

**CHRISTIAN ART AND SYMBOLISM -
MODERN PERIOD, 1500- - PORTUGAL -
EXHIBITIONS.**
Imagens do Sagrado. Lisboa , 1989. 47 p. :
DDC 704.9/482/09469074469425 20
N7963.A1 I4 1989

**CHRISTIAN ART AND SYMBOLISM -
MODERN PERIOD, 1500- - RUSSIAN S.
F.S.R.**
Russian copper icons and crosses from the
Kunz Collection . Washington, D.C. , 1990. p.
cm. DDC 730/.947 20
NK1653.S65 R8 1990

**CHRISTIAN ART AND SYMBOLISM -
MODERN PERIOD, 1500- - SPAIN -
SEGOVIA (PROVINCE)**
Collar de Cáceres, Fernando. Pintura en la
antigua Diócesis de Segovia (1500-1631) /.
[Segovia] , 1989. 2 v. (799 p.) : ISBN
84-86789-23-0 (set) DDC
755/.2/09463570903107446357 20
ND809.S44 C65 1989

**CHRISTIAN ART AND SYMBOLISM -
MODERN PERIOD - UNITED STATES -
EXHIBITIONS.**
Religious visionaries. Sheboygan, Wis. , 1991. p.
cm. ISBN 0-932718-31-0 DDC
704.9/482/097307477569 20
N7904 .R44 1991

**CHRISTIAN ART AND SYMBOLISM -
AUSTRIA - EXHIBITIONS.**
Diözesanmuseum St. Pölten (Austria) 100 Jahre
Diözesanmuseum St. Pölten, 1888-1988 . St.
Pölten, [Austria] , 1988. 96 p., [76] p. of
plates : *NYPL [3-MAIH 91-6668]*

**CHRISTIAN ART AND SYMBOLISM -
AUSTRIA - ST. PÖLTEN -
EXHIBITIONS.**
Diözesanmuseum St. Pölten (Austria) 100 Jahre
Diözesanmuseum St. Pölten, 1888-1988 . St.
Pölten, [Austria] , 1988. 96 p., [76] p. of
plates : *NYPL [3-MAIH 91-6668]*

CHRISTIAN ART AND SYMBOLISM - DICTIONARIES.
Duchet-Suchaux, Gaston. La Bible et les saints . Paris , c1990. 319 p., xxxii p. of plates :
ISBN 2-08-011725-4
NYPL [3-MAIH 91-6578]

CHRISTIAN ART AND SYMBOLISM - EUROPE.
Merkel, Kerstin. Salome . Frankfurt am Main , New York , c1990. 477 p. : ISBN 3-631-42540-6
N8180 .M47 1990

CHRISTIAN ART AND SYMBOLISM - FRANCE - SEINE-ET-MARNE - EXHIBITIONS.
Trésors sacrés, trésors cachés . Melun [1988] 308 p. : ISBN 2-9503073-0-2
N7949.A3 S458 1988

CHRISTIAN ART AND SYMBOLISM - GERMANY - EXHIBITIONS.
Diözesanmuseum St. Pölten (Austria) 100 Jahre Diözesanmuseum St. Pölten, 1888-1988 . St. Pölten, [Austria] , 1988. 96 p., [76] p. of plates : *NYPL [3-MAIH 91-6668]*
Religiöse Graphik aus der Zeit des Kölner Dombaus 1842-1880 . Köln [1980] 63 p. , [52] p. of plates : *NYPL [MDET 91-1492]*

CHRISTIAN ART AND SYMBOLISM - GERMANY - NUREMBERG.
Schleif, Corine. Donatio et memoria . [München] , 1990. 288 p., [4] leaves of plates : ISBN 3-422-06031-6
NYPL [3-MRBB 91-7159]

CHRISTIAN ART AND SYMBOLISM - GREECE - DICTIONARIES - GERMAN.
Spitzing, Günter. Lexikon byzantinisch-christlicher Symbole . München , 1989. 344 p., 8 p. of plates : ISBN 3-424-00934-2 *NYPL [3-MAIH 91-4313]*

CHRISTIAN ART AND SYMBOLISM - GREECE - THESSALONIKE.
Tsigaridas, Euth. N. Latomou monastery . Thessaloniki , 1988. 89 p., 32 p. of plates :
NYPL [3-MRBN 89-25752]

CHRISTIAN ART AND SYMBOLISM - ITALY.
Mazzoni, Piero. La leggenda della Croce nell'arte italiana / . Firenze [1914]. 182 p., [13] leaves of plates : *NYPL [3-MAI 90-5667]*

CHRISTIAN ART AND SYMBOLISM - ITALY - MONZA.
Il Duomo di Monza / . Milano , 1990. 2 v. : DDC 726/.6/09451 20
NA5621.M954 D8 1990

CHRISTIAN ART AND SYMBOLISM - ITALY - ORVIETO - CONSERVATION ANDRESTORATION.
Testa, Giusi. La Cattedrale di Orvieto . [Roma] , c1990. 249, [2] p. : ISBN 88-24-00040-1 DDC 726/.6/0945652 20
NA5621.O426 T4 1990

CHRISTIAN ART AND SYMBOLISM - ITALY - OSTUNI.
Le Chiese rurali del territorio di Ostuni / . [Fasano di Brindisi] [1990] 94 p. : ISBN 88-7514-395-1
NYPL [3-MRBD+ 91-3446]

CHRISTIAN ART AND SYMBOLISM - ITALY - ROME.
San Paolo fuori le mura a Roma / . Firenze , c1988. 336 p. : ISBN 88-404-1201-8
NYPL [3-MRBD+ 90-12663]

CHRISTIAN ART AND SYMBOLISM - ITALY - SAN VITO DEI NORMANNI.
Chionna, Antonio. Beni culturali di San Vito dei Normanni / . Fasano, Brindisi [1988] 471 p., [32] leaves of plates : ISBN 88-7514-253-X : DDC 709/.45/754 20
N6921.S38 C47 1988
NYPL [3-MAMC+ 90-10597]

CHRISTIAN ART AND SYMBOLISM - ITALY - SIENA - CATALOGS.
Carli, Enzo, 1910- Il Museo dell'opera del duomo / . Siena , 1989. 63 p., [16] p. of plates :
NYPL [3-MAVZ (Siena) 90-12388]

CHRISTIAN ART AND SYMBOLISM - ITALY - TOLMEZZO.
Marcolini, Silvia. Il duomo di Tolmezzo . Udine , c1990. 137, [4] p. :
IN PROCESS (ONLINE)
NYPL [3-MRBD+ 91-6937]

CHRISTIAN ART AND SYMBOLISM - ITALY - TRENTINO-ALTO ADIGE.
Giatti, Natalia. Iconografia mariana nei masi dell'Alto Adige / . Calliano [Trento] , c1990. 256 p. : ISBN 88-7024-408-3
NYPL [3-MAIH+ 91-4956]

CHRISTIAN ART AND SYMBOLISM - POLAND - CZĘSTOCHOWA.
Pasierb, Janusz St. The Shrine of the Black Madonna at Częstochowa / . Warsaw [1989] 223, [1] p. : ISBN 83-223-2501-0
NYPL [3-MAIH+ 90-12436]

CHRISTIAN ART AND SYMBOLISM - RUSSIAN S.F.S.R. - EXHIBITIONS.
Icônes et merveilles . Paris , c[1988] [116] p. : ISBN 2-905197-10-2
NYPL [3-MAIH 91-5048]

CHRISTIAN ART AND SYMBOLISM - SPAIN.
Navascués Palacio, Pedro. Monasterios de España / . Madrid , 1985- v. : ISBN 84-239-5271-1 DDC 726/.7/0946 19
NA5801 .N383 1985
NYPL [3-MRBB+ 85-3759]

CHRISTIAN ART AND SYMBOLISM - SPAIN - HUESCA - CATALOGS.
Museo Episcopal y Capitular de Huesca (Spain) Catálogo del Museo Episcopal y Capitular de Huesca / . Zaragoza [1984?] 223 p., [6] p. of plates : ISBN 84-7611-002-2
N7823.S7 H846 1984
NYPL [3-MAIH 87-353]

CHRISTIAN ART AND SYMBOLISM - SPAIN - SANTA CANDIA.
Església de Santa Càndia d'Orpí / . [Barcelona] , c1989. 64 p. : ISBN 84-7794-049-5
NA5821.S26 E8 1989

CHRISTIAN ART AND SYMBOLISM - SPAIN - SORIA (PROVINCE)
Manrique Mayor, María Angeles. Inventario artístico de Soria y su provincia / . Madrid , 1989. 2 v. : ISBN 84-7483-539-9 (obra completa)
NYPL [3-MAI 90-13098]

CHRISTIAN ART AND SYMBOLISM - SWITZERLAND - ZILLIS.
Rudloff, Diether. Kosmische Bildwelt der Romanik . Stuttgart , 1989. 176 p. : ISBN 3-87838-592-7
NYPL [3-MAIH + 89-19334]

CHRISTIAN ART AND SYMBOLISM - TURKEY - DICTIONARIES - GERMAN.
Spitzing, Günter. Lexikon byzantinisch-christlicher Symbole . München , 1989. 344 p., 8 p. of plates : ISBN 3-424-00934-2 *NYPL [3-MAIH 91-4313]*

Christian Chenard . Chenard, Christian, 1918- Paris , c1989. 110 p. : ISBN 2-905037-04-0 DDC 759.4 20
ND553.C479 A4 1989

Christian Dior /. De Marly, Diana. New York , 1990. 96 p., [8] p. of plates : ISBN 0-8419-1260-2 : DDC 746.9/2/092 20
TT507 .D47 1990 NYPL [3-MME 90-12028]

CHRISTIAN LIFE - CARICATURES AND CARTOONS.
Portlock, Rob. Climbing the church walls / . Downers Grove, Ill. , 1991. p. cm. ISBN 0-8308-1830-8 DDC 741.5/973 20
NC1429.P65 A4 1991

Christian Peltenburg-Brechneff .
Peltenburg-Brechneff, Christian, 1950- Basel, Schweiz , c1988. [52] p. :
NYPL [3-MCZ P393 90-13412]

CHRISTIAN PILGRIMS AND PILGRIMAGES - SPAIN - SANTIAGO DE COMPOSTELA.
Durliat, Marcel. La sculpture romane de la route de Saint-Jacques . Mont-de-Marsan , c1990. 508 p. : ISBN 2-9501584-1-2 :
NB549.S7 D87 1990

Christian Rohlfs zum einhundertvierzigsten Geburtstag . Rohlfs, Christian, 1849-1938. Berlin , 1989. 72 p. :
NYPL [3-MCK+ R738 91-4220]

Christian Rohlfs zum 140. Geburtstag. Rohlfs, Christian, 1849-1938. Christian Rohlfs zum einhundertvierzigsten Geburtstag . Berlin , 1989. 72 p. :
NYPL [3-MCK+ R738 91-4220]

CHRISTIAN SAINTS - ART. see CHRISTIAN SAINTS IN ART.

CHRISTIAN SAINTS - ICONOGRAPHY. see CHRISTIAN SAINTS IN ART.

CHRISTIAN SAINTS IN ART.
Four Byzantine and Russian icons in the Menil Collection / . Houston, Tex. , c1991. p. cm. ISBN 0-939594-21-8 DDC 704.9/482 20
N8186.U6 M474 1991

CHRISTIAN SAINTS IN ART - CATALOGS.
Cahn, Laurent. Vierges et saints . [Quimper] [1990] 159 p. :
NK4210.F345 C35 1990

CHRISTIAN SHRINES - EUROPE.
Radler, Gudrun. Die Schreinmadonna "Vierge ouvrante" . Frankfurt am Main , 1990. 366 p., [184] p. of plates : ISBN 3-923813-05-8 :
NB1912.M37 R33 1990

CHRISTIAN SYMBOLISM. see CHRISTIAN ART AND SYMBOLISM.

Christian Vogt . Vogt, Christian, 1946- Basel , c1988. 123 p. :
NYPL [MFX+ (Vogt) 89-28354]

Christiane Kubrick paintings /. Kubrick, Christiane, 1932- New York, NY , c1990. 12 p., [70] leaves of plates : ISBN 0-446-51583-3 DDC 759.13 20
ND237.K755 A4 1990
NYPL [3-MCK+ K9531 91-4954]

Christie, Håkon, 1922- Nes stavkirke = The stave church of Nes / Hakön Christie ; utgitt av Riksantikvariatet ; [engelsk oversettelse ved Patrick N. Chaffey]. [Oslo] : Fabritius, c1979. 111 p. : ill., plans ; 30 cm. (Riksantikvarens skrifter. Nr. 3 = no. 3) Norwegian and English. Includes bibliographical references. ISBN 82-07-00487-8
1. Stave churches - Norway - Nes. I. Title. II. Title: Stave church of Nes. NYPL [3-MRBB 90-6045]

Christie, Manson & Woods. Kakiemon porcelain from the English country house . London , 1989. 64 p. : ISBN 0-903432-35-8
NYPL [3-MPFK 91-4566]

Christie, Robyn.
Cultivating the country . Oxford [England] , New York , 1988. 118 p. : ISBN 0-19-554944-9 (pbk.) *NYPL [3-MAM 89-17144]*
The D.R. Sheumack collection . Paddington, NSW , 1988. [153] p. :
NYPL [3-MCY 89-11925]

Christie, Victor J. W. Bessie Pease Gutmann : her life and works / Victor J.W. Christie. Radnor, Pa. : Wallace-Homestead Book Co., c1990. xv, 199 p. : ill. (some col.) ; 26 cm. Includes indexes. Bibliography: p. 189-190. ISBN 0-87069-561-4 : DDC 741.6/092 B 20
1. Gutmann, Bessie Pease. 2. Artists - United States - Biography. I. Title.
N6537.G88 C4 1990
NYPL [3-MCX G983 91-3649]

CHRISTIE'S INTERNATIONAL GROUP.
Herbert, John, 1924- Inside Christie's / . London , 1990. 407 p., [16] p. of plates : ISBN 0-340-43043-5 : DDC 381/.1 19
NYPL [3-MAZ 90-10748]

CHRISTMAS BOOKS. see CHRISTMAS.

Christmas cats /. Ivory, Lesley Anne. New York , 1991. ISBN 0-517-58549-9 : DDC 759.13 20
ND237.I94 A4 1991

CHRISTMAS IN ART.
Ivory, Lesley Anne. Christmas cats /. New York , 1991. p. cm. ISBN 0-517-58549-9 : DDC 759.13 20
ND237.I94 A4 1991

CHRISTMAS IN ART - JUVENILE LITERATURE.
A Renaissance Christmas /. Boston , c1991. p. ISBN 0-8212-1875-1 : DDC 704.9/4853/09409024 20
N8060 .R4 1991

CHRISTMAS - JUVENILE LITERATURE.
A Renaissance Christmas /. Boston , c1991. p. ISBN 0-8212-1875-1 : DDC 704.9/4853/09409024 20
N8060 .R4 1991

CHRISTMAS - NEW YORK (N.Y.) - PICTORIAL WORKS.

BIBLIOGRAPHIC GUIDE

Christmas - New York (N.Y.) - Pictorial works. (cont.)

214

Gambee, Robert. Wall Street Christmas /. New York , c1990. 272 p. : ISBN 0-393-02835-6
DDC 394.2/68282/097471 20
GT4986.A2 N484 1990
NYPL [MFX (Gambee) 91-3471]

Christo /. Vaizey, Marina. New York , 1990. 128 p. : ISBN 0-8478-1239-1 DDC 709/.2 20
N7193.C5 V35 1990
NYPL [3-MGO+ (Christo) 91-4614]

Christo, 1935-
The accordion-fold book for the Umbrellas, joint project for Japan and U. S.A. / Christo ; foreword and interview by Masahiko Yanagi. 1st ed. San Francisco : Bedford Arts, c1991. p. cm. ISBN 0-938491-58-X (hardcover trade) DDC 709/.2 20
1. Christo, 1935-. 2. Artists' preparatory studies. I. Yanagi, Masahiko, 1957-. II. Title.
N7193.C5 A4 1991

CHRISTO, 1935-
Christo, 1935- The accordion-fold book for the Umbrellas, joint project for Japan and U. S.A. /. San Francisco , c1991. p. cm. ISBN 0-938491-58-X (hardcover trade) DDC 709/.2 20
N7193.C5 A4 1991

CHRISTO, 1935- - CRITICISM AND INTERPRETATION.
Vaizey, Marina. Christo /. New York , 1990. 128 p. : ISBN 0-8478-1239-1 DDC 709/.2 20
N7193.C5 V35 1990
NYPL [3-MGO+ (Christo) 91-4614]

Christoph M. Dornier. Kluckert, Ehrenfried. Von der Kunst die Phantasie zu leben . Stuttgart , c1989. 93 p. : ISBN 3-89322-172-7 DDC 709/.2 20
N6888.D665 K58 1989

Christopher Dresser /. Halén, Widar. Oxford , 1990. 208 p. : ISBN 0-07-148008-5 DDC 745.20924 20 *NYPL [3-MNE 91-3313]*

Christopher Wilmarth, drawings 1963-1987 . Wilmarth, Christopher. New York [1989] 48 p. : ISBN 0-942051-17-3
NYPL [3-MCX W735 90-12637]

Christopher Wood Gallery. Pre-raphaelites and academics . London , 1981. [69] p. :
NYPL [3-MAMR 86-3397]

Christus Dominator . Pattis, Erich. Innsbruck [1964] 287 p. :
MLCM 87/381 (N) *NYPL [3-MAI 91-292]*

Christus in der bildenden Kunst : von den Anfängen bis zur Gegenwart : eine Einführung / Katharina Winnekes (Hrsg.) ; mit Beiträgen von August Heuser, Friedhelm Mennekes und Giovanna Pisacane-Rudorf und einem Vorwort von Günter Rombold. München : Kösel, c1989. 150 p. : ill. (some col.) ; 25 cm. Text by the editor and three other authors. Includes bibliographical references. ISBN 3-466-36334-9
1. Jesus Christ - Art. 2. Christian art and symbolism. I. Winnekes, Katharina, 1951-. II. Heuser, August, 1949-.
N8050 .C44 1989

CHRISTUS, PETRUS, CA. 1410-1472 OR 3 - CRITICISM AND INTERPRETATION.
Upton, Joel M. (Joel Morgan), 1940- Petrus Christus . University Park , c1990. xv, 130 p., [62] p. of plates : ISBN 0-271-00672-2 (alk. paper) : DDC 759.9493 20
ND673.C312 U68 1990
NYPL [3-MCH C556 91-3887]

CHROMATIC VISION. see COLOR VISION.

CHROMATICS. see COLOR.

Chromo cube /. Beck & Jung. Bjärred, Sweden (Box 123, S-237 00 Bjärred) , c1982. 49 p., [24] leaves of plates : ISBN 91-85752-30-4
NYPL [3-MAL 88-3799]

CHROMOPHOTOGRAPHY. see COLOR PHOTOGRAPHY.

The chronicle of western costume . Peacock, John. London , c1991. 224 p. : ISBN 0-500-01490-6 *NYPL [3-MMC 91-5165]*

Chronik KGBrücke, 1913 [microform] . Kunsthalle Bern. Bern , 1948. 32 p., [16] leaves of plates : *NYPL [*ZM-202]*

CHRONOLOGY, EGYPTIAN.
Centuries of darkness . London , 1991. xxii, 434 p., [8] p. of plates : ISBN 0-224-02647-X :

DDC 930 20
CB311 *NYPL [JFE 91-4489]*

Chrysler Museum. This is not a photograph . Sarasota, Fla. , c1987. 1 v. (various pagings) : ISBN 0-916758-23-0 DDC 779/.09/04507474 20
TR645.S372 J647 1987
NYPL [MFW 88-3001]

Chu, Chia-shu. Ch'üan kuo hai pao ta chan chuan chi /. Hsin-chu shih , min kuo 74 [1985] 217 p. : DDC 769.5/074/0951249 19
NC1807.T28 C4 1985
NYPL [3-MDW+ 89-16256]

Chu, Myŏng-dŏk, 1940- Korean architecture. Seoul , 1982- v. : DDC 722/.13 19
NA1563 .K67 1982
NYPL [3-MQWS+ 87-1952]

Chu, Petra ten-Doesschate.
Buchser, Frank, 1828-1890. Frank Buchser 1828-1890 . Einsiedeln , c1990. 284 p. :
NYPL [3-MCZ+ B92 91-8120]

Courbet, Gustave, 1819-1877. [Correspondence. English. Selections.] Letters of Gustave Courbet /. Chicago , 1992. p. cm. ISBN 0-226-11653-0 (cloth) DDC 759.4 B 20
ND553.C9 A3 1992

Chu, Ta, 1626-ca. 1705.
Wang, Fang-yü, 1913- Master of the lotus garden . New Haven , c1990. 299 p. : ISBN 0-89467-054-9 *NYPL [3-MAG+ 91-3672]*

CHU, TA, 1626-CA. 1705 - EXHIBITIONS.
Wang, Fang-yü, 1913- Master of the lotus garden . New Haven , c1990. 299 p. : ISBN 0-89467-054-9 *NYPL [3-MAG+ 91-3672]*

Ch'üan kuo hai pao ta chan chuan chi / pien chi Chu Chia-shu ... [et al.] = National Poster Exhibition of the Republic of China / editors, Chu Chia Su ... [et al.] ; sponsor, Taiwan Provincial Hsinchu Social Education Center. Hsin-chu shih : T'ai-wan sheng li Hsin-chu she hui chiao yü kuan, min kuo 74 [1985] 217 p. : chiefly ill. (some col.) ; 31 cm. Chinese and English. Colophon title. DDC 769.5/074/0951249 19
1. T'ai-wan sheng li Hsin-chu she hui chiao yü kuan - Exhibitions. 2. Posters, Chinese - Taiwan - Exhibitions. 3. Posters, Chinese - 20th century - Exhibitions. I. Chu, Chia-shu. II. T'ai-wan sheng li Hsin-chu she hui chiao yü kuan. III. Title: National Poster Exhibition of the Republic of China.
NC1807.T28 C4 1985
NYPL [3-MDW+ 89-16256]

Chumbley, Ann. Turner and the human figure : studies of contemporary life / Ann Chumbley & Ian Warrell. London : Tate Gallery, 1989. 63 p. : ill. (some col.) ; 27 cm. Catalog for the exhibition of April 5-July 2, 1989, at the Tate Gallery. Bibliography: p. 62. ISBN 1-85437-011-1
1. Turner, J. M. W. (Joseph Mallord William), 1775-1851 - Exhibitions. I. Turner, J. M. W. (Joseph Mallord William), 1775-1851. II. Warrell, Ian. III. Tate Gallery. IV. Title.
NYPL [3-MCV T94 90-12021]

Chung-kuo hua hui hua ch'u =. Chou, Shih-hsin. [Taipei?] [1976?] 263 p. :
NYPL [3-MAF+ 90-6353]

CHURCH AND STATE IN BRAZIL.
O Clero no Parlamento brasileiro /. Brasília , Rio de Janeiro , 1978- v. : ISBN 85-7004-002-4
JL2454 .C53 *NYPL [HFE 80-1378]*

O Clero no Parlamento brasileiro /. Brasília , Rio de Janeiro , 1978-79. 2 v. : ISBN 85-7004-002-4
JL2454 .C53 *NYPL [HFE 80-1465]*

CHURCH ARCHITECTURE.
Colvin, Howard Montagu. Architecture and the after-life /. New Haven , 1991. p. cm. ISBN 0-300-05098-4 DDC 726/.8/094 20
NA6120 .C65 1991

Nyman, Helge Johannes, 1910- Kyrkorum, kyrkosång, kyrkobruk /. [Vasa] [1989] 187 p. : ISBN 951-550-388-4
NA4829.L8 N9 1989

CHURCH ARCHITECTURE - AUSTRIA - LAMBACH (UPPER AUSTRIA) - EXHIBITIONS.
Oberösterreichische Landesausstellung (1989 : Benediktinerstift Lambach) 900 Jahre Klosterkirche Lambach . Linz , 1989. 231 p. :
NA5510.L355 O23 1989
NYPL [3-MRBB 91-7295]

CHURCH ARCHITECTURE - AUSTRIA - STYRIA.
Attems, Franz, 1926- Kirchen und Stifte der Steiermark /. Innsbruck , c1988. 163 p. : ISBN 3-7016-2296-5 DDC 726/.5/094365 20
NA5509.S8 A88 1988
NYPL [3-MRBB 90-11074]

CHURCH ARCHITECTURE - AZERBAIJAN S.S.R. - NAGORNO-KARABAKHSKAĬA AVTONOMNAĬA OBLAST'.
Gharabagh /. Milano, Italia , 1988. 107 p. : ISBN 88-85822-09-6
NYPL [3-MQW 91-4235]

CHURCH ARCHITECTURE - CONGRESSES.
Atti del convegno di Pescara, 27-29 gennaio 1989, su il sacro, l'architettura sacra oggi /. Rimini , c1990. 319 p., [36] p. of plates :
NA4795 .A8 1990

CHURCH ARCHITECTURE - CONSERVATION AND RESTORATION.
Bargellini, Piero, 1897- Santa Reparata . Firenze , c1970. 127 p. :
NYPL [3-MRBN 90-6794]

CHURCH ARCHITECTURE - CZECHOSLOVAKIA - PRAGUE.
Soukupová, Helena. Anežský klášter v Praze /. Praha , 1989. 404 p. : ISBN 80-207-0046-3 :
NA5533.P69 S68 1989

CHURCH ARCHITECTURE - ENGLAND.
Briggs, Martin S. (Martin Shaw), b. 1882- A pictorial guide to cathedral architecture . [London] 1964. 24 p. :
NYPL [3-MRBR 90-6038]

Coppack, Glyn. English Heritage book of abbeys and priories /. London , 1990. 159 p., [8] p. of plates : ISBN 0-7134-6308-2 (cased) : DDC 942 20 *NYPL [3-MRBR 91-6767]*

Kowa, Günter, 1954- Architektur der englischen Gotik /. Köln , c1990. 336 p. : ISBN 3-7701-1969-X DDC 720/.942/0902 20
NA440 .K6 1990

CHURCH ARCHITECTURE - EUROPE.
Widder, Erich. Alte Kirchen für neue Liturgie. [Wien, c1968] 204 p.
NA4605 .W5 *NYPL [3-MRB 91-852]*

CHURCH ARCHITECTURE - EUROPE, GERMAN-SPEAKING - CONSERVATION AND RESTORATION.
Steingewordene Träume . Ulm , c1990. 111 p. :
NA5559 .S68 1990

CHURCH ARCHITECTURE - FINLAND.
Pettersson, Lars. Suomalainen puukirkko =. Helsinki , c1989. 160 p. : ISBN 951-9229-59-0
NA5955.F5 P48 1989

CHURCH ARCHITECTURE - FRANCE - ALSACE.
Abel, Louis. Kembs en Sundgau rhénan . [Kembs, France] , c1986. 285 p. :
NA1053.Z45 A83 1986

CHURCH ARCHITECTURE - FRANCE - KEMBS.
Abel, Louis. Kembs en Sundgau rhénan . [Kembs, France] , c1986. 285 p. :
NA1053.Z45 A83 1986

CHURCH ARCHITECTURE - FRANCE - LIESSIES - EXPERTISING.
Etude du site de l'Abbaye de Liessies /. [Fourmies, France] [1984] [82] leaves : DDC 726/.7/094428 19
NA5551.L4693 E88 1984
NYPL [3-MRBB+ 90-12771]

CHURCH ARCHITECTURE - GERMANY.
Kahle, Barbara. Deutsche Kirchenbaukunst des 20. Jahrhunderts /. Darmstadt , c1990. viii, 271 p. : ISBN 3-534-03614-X : DDC 726/.5/09430904 20
NA5568 .K35 1990

CHURCH ARCHITECTURE - GERMANY - BEUREN (ESSLINGEN)
Braun, Dietrich. Nikolauskirche Beuren . Villingen , c1988. 96 p. : ISBN 3-7883-1904-6
NA5586.B4395 B73 1988

CHURCH ARCHITECTURE - GERMANY - MÜNSTER IN WESTFALEN.
Böker, Hans Josef. Die Marktpfarrkirche St. Lamberti zu Münster . Bonn , 1989. 229 p. : ISBN 3-7749-2382-5
NA5586.M853 B65 1989

CHURCH ARCHITECTURE - GERMANY - NUREMBERG.
Schleif, Corine. Donatio et memoria .
[München] , 1990. 288 p., [4] leaves of plates :
ISBN 3-422-06031-6
NYPL [3-MRBB 91-7159]

CHURCH ARCHITECTURE - GERMANY - ZWIEFALTEN.
900 Jahre Benediktinerabtei Zwiefalten /. Ulm ,
1990. 564 p., [80] p. of plates : ISBN
3-88294-119-7   *NYPL [MRBN 91-7665]*

CHURCH ARCHITECTURE - GREAT BRITAIN.
Pace, Peter G. The architecture of George
Pace, 1915-75 /. London , 1990. 288 p. : ISBN
0-7134-6273-6 : DDC 720.92 20
NYPL [3-MQZ+ (Pace) 91-5540]

CHURCH ARCHITECTURE - GREECE - THESSALONIKE.
Tsigaridas, Euth. N. Latomou monastery .
Thessaloniki , 1988. 89 p., 32 p. of plates :
NYPL [3-MRBN 89-25752]

CHURCH ARCHITECTURE - HISTORY.
Norman, Edward R. The house of God . New
York, N.Y. , 1990. 312 p. : ISBN
0-500-25108-8 : DDC 726/.5/09 20
NA4800 .N587 1990
NYPL [3-MRB+ 91-3658]

CHURCH ARCHITECTURE - ITALY.
Lo Spazio eloquente . Pordenone , c1987. 357
p. : DDC 726/.5/0945309045 20
NA5618 .S64 1987
NYPL [3-MRBD 90-12496]

CHURCH ARCHITECTURE - ITALY - ABRUZZI.
Abruzzes Molise romans /. La Pierre-qui-Vire
(Yonne) , 1990. 304 p. : ISBN 2-7369-0182-7
NYPL [3-MQWB 91-4524]

CHURCH ARCHITECTURE - ITALY - BOLOGNA (PROVINCE)
Cardinali, Ferdinando. Le chiese minori delle
colline bolognesi . Bologna , 1986. 58 p. :
NYPL [3-MRBD 90-13374]

CHURCH ARCHITECTURE - ITALY - LIGURIA - GUIDE-BOOKS.
Pazzini Paglieri, Nadia. Chiese in Liguria /.
Genova , 1990. 214 p. : ISBN 88-7058-361-9 :
DDC 726/.5/094518 20
NA5619.L5 P39 1990

CHURCH ARCHITECTURE - ITALY - MANTUA.
Carpeggiani, Paolo. Sant'Andrea in Mantova .
Mantova , c1987. 182 p. :
NYPL [3-MRBD+ 91-4615]

CHURCH ARCHITECTURE - ITALY - MILAN.
Pifferi, Enzo, 1940- Milano gotica /. Como ,
c1988. 153, [4] p. : DDC 720/.945/210902 20
NA5621.M6 P53 1988
NYPL [3-MRBD+ 91-4974]

CHURCH ARCHITECTURE - ITALY - MOLISE.
Abruzzes Molise romans /. La Pierre-qui-Vire
(Yonne) , 1990. 304 p. : ISBN 2-7369-0182-7
NYPL [3-MQWB 91-4524]

CHURCH ARCHITECTURE - ITALY - NAPLES.
Divenuto, Francesco. Napoli sacra del XVI
secolo . Napoli , c1990. 317 p., [32] p. of
plates : ISBN 88-7104-562-9 : DDC
726/.5/094573 20
NA5621.N2 D58 1990

CHURCH ARCHITECTURE - ITALY - VENICE.
Pilo, Giuseppe Maria. La chiesa dello
"spedaletto" in Venezia /. [Venezia] [Udine]
[198-] xii, 271 p., [29] p. of plates :
NYPL [3-MCE+ 90-11574]

CHURCH ARCHITECTURE. - LATIN AMERICA.
Cabildos y ayuntamientos en América /. [Mar
del Plata, Argentina?] : [Azcapotzalco,
Mexico] : 134 p. : ISBN 968-636-305-X
NA4202.A1 C33 1990

CHURCH ARCHITECTURE - NEW MEXICO.
Kubler, George, 1912- The religious
architecture of New Mexico in the colonial
period and since the American occupation /.
Albuquerque , 1990. xxxv, 232 p. : ISBN

0-8263-1210-1   DDC 726/.5/09789 20
NA5230.N6 K8 1990
NYPL [3-MRBB+ 91-4591]

CHURCH ARCHITECTURE - PORTUGAL.
Chicó, Mário Tavares. A arquitectura gótica em
Portugal /. Lisboa , 1968. 239 p., [21] leaves of
plates : DDC 726/.5/09469
NA5823 .C48 1968
NYPL [3-MQW 90-5436]

CHURCH ARCHITECTURE - RESTORATION. see CHURCH ARCHITECTURE - CONSERVATION AND RESTORATION.

CHURCH ARCHITECTURE - RUSSIAN S.F.S.R.
Gippenreĭter, Vadim Evgen´evich. The golden
ring . New York , 1991. p. cm. ISBN
1-558-59216-4   DDC 720/.947 20
NA1181 .G56 1991

CHURCH ARCHITECTURE - SPAIN.
Navascués Palacio, Pedro. Monasterios de
España /. Madrid , 1985- v. :
84-239-5271-1   DDC 726/.7/0946 19
NA5801 .N383 1985
NYPL [3-MRBB+ 85-3759]

CHURCH ARCHITECTURE - SPAIN - GRANADA (PROVINCE)
Gómez-Moreno Calera, José Manuel. La
arquitectura religiosa granadina en la crisis del
Renacimiento (1560-1650) . Granada , 1989.
486 p. : ISBN 84-338-0944-X
IN PROCESS (ONLINE)
NYPL [3-MRBB 91-6097]

CHURCH ARCHITECTURE - SPAIN - JEREZ DE LA FRONTERA - PICTORIAL WORKS.
Zubillaga, Francisco. La Cartuja de Jerez de la
Frontera =. Salzburg, Austria , 1978. [97] p. :
NYPL [3-MRBB 90-4725]

CHURCH ARCHITECTURE - SPAIN - LUGO.
Vila Jato, María Dolores. Lugo barroco /. Lugo
(Galicia) [1989] 134 p. : ISBN 84-86824-00-1
NA5811.L79 V55 1989

CHURCH ARCHITECTURE - SWITZERLAND - ZURICH (CANTON) - EXHIBITIONS.
Jezler, Peter. Der spätgotische Kirchenbau in
der Zürcher Landschaft . Wetzikon , c1988.
144 p. : ISBN 3-85981-150-9 : DDC
726/.5/094945707449457 20
NA5849.Z87 J49 1988
NYPL [3-MRBB 91-3251]

CHURCH ARCHITECTURE - TURKEY - IŞHAN - EXPERTISING.
Kadiroğlu, Mine, 1944- The architecture of the
Georgian Church at İşhan /. Frankfurt am
Main , New York , 1991. p. cm. ISBN
3-631-42828-6   DDC 726/.5/095662 20
NA5871.I84 K33 1991

CHURCH ARCHITECTURE - YUGOSLAVIA - SLOVENIA.
Zadnikar, Marijan. Romanika v Sloveniji .
Ljubljana , 1982. 657 p. :
NA5949.S56 Z28 1982

CHURCH BUILDINGS. see CHURCHES.

CHURCH DECORATION AND ORNAMENT - AUSTRIA - ADMONT.
Mannewitz, Martin. Stift Admont . München ,
c1989. 422 p. : ISBN 3-89235-031-0 :
NA5510.A35 S755 1989

CHURCH DECORATION AND ORNAMENT - AUSTRIA - LAMBACH (UPPER AUSTRIA) - EXHIBITIONS.
Oberösterreichische Landesausstellung (1989 :
Benediktinerstift Lambach) 900 Jahre
Klosterkirche Lambach . Linz , 1989. 231 p. :
NA5510.L355 O23 1989
NYPL [3-MRBB 91-7295]

CHURCH DECORATION AND ORNAMENT - EUROPE.
Feuchtmayr, Andrea. Kulissenheiliggräber im
Barock . München , c1989. 139, [26] p. of
plates : ISBN 3-88073-309-0
ND2725 .F48 1989

CHURCH DECORATION AND ORNAMENT - GERMANY.
Knapp, Ulrich, 1956- Die Wallfahrtskirche
Birnau . Friedrichshafen , c1989. 219 p. : ISBN
3-922137-58-X
NA5586.W266 K58 1989

CHURCH DECORATION AND ORNAMENT - GERMANY - CHIEMSEE.
Dannheimer, Hermann. Torhalle auf
Frauenchiemsee . München , 1983, c1980. 118
p. : ISBN 3-7954-0818-0
NYPL [3-MRBB 91-6996]

CHURCH DECORATION AND ORNAMENT - GERMANY - VERDEN.
Der Antwerpener Altar in St. Georg Vreden /.
Vreden , 1989. 247 p. : ISBN 3-926627-03-4
NYPL [3-MAIH+ 91-6544]

CHURCH DECORATION AND ORNAMENT - GERMANY (WEST) - MÜNSTER.
Jászai, Géza, 1931- Das Werk des Bildhauers
Gerhard Gröninger, 1582-1652 /. Münster ,
1989. 207 p. : ISBN 3-88789-090-6
NYPL [3-MGO (Gröninger) 91-6968]

CHURCH DECORATION AND ORNAMENT - ITALY - MANTUA.
Carpeggiani, Paolo. Sant'Andrea in Mantova .
Mantova , c1987. 182 p. :
NYPL [3-MRBD+ 91-4615]

CHURCH DECORATION AND ORNAMENT - ITALY - MONZA.
Il Duomo di Monza /. Milano , 1990. 2 v. :
DDC 726/.6/09451 20
NA5621.M954 D8 1990

CHURCH DECORATION AND ORNAMENT - ITALY - NAPLES - CATALOGS.
Arte sacra di Palazzo . Napoli , 1989. 263 p. :
DDC 704.9/482/09450744573 20
N7952.N36 A74 1989
NYPL [3-MAIH 91-4840]

CHURCH DECORATION AND ORNAMENT - ITALY - ORVIETO - CONSERVATION AND RESTORATION.
Testa, Giusi. La Cattedrale di Orvieto .
[Roma] , c1990. 249, [2] p. : ISBN
88-24-00040-1   DDC 726/.6/0945652 20
NA5621.O426 T4 1990

CHURCH DECORATION AND ORNAMENT - ITALY - PRATO.
Bardazzi, Silvestro. Arredi e paramenti . Prato ,
c1988. 318 p. :
NYPL [3-MRBD+ 90-11027]

CHURCH DECORATION AND ORNAMENT - ITALY - ROME.
De Strobel, Anna Maria. Le arazzerie romane
dal XVII al XIX secolo /. [Roma] , c1989. 99
p., [91] p. of plates :
NYPL [3-MOR 91-3766]

San Paolo fuori le mura /. Firenze ,
c1988. 336 p. : ISBN 88-404-1201-8
NYPL [3-MRBD+ 90-12663]

CHURCH DECORATION AND ORNAMENT - ITALY - VENICE.
Pilo, Giuseppe Maria. La chiesa dello
"spedaletto" in Venezia /. [Venezia] [Udine]
[198-] xii, 271 p., [29] p. of plates :
NYPL [3-MCE+ 90-11574]

CHURCH DECORATION AND ORNAMENT - MEXICO - HIDALGO (STATE)
Vergara Vergara, José. El barroco en Hidalgo.
[Pachuca, Mexico?] , 1988. 177, [5] p. :
N7914.A3 H538 1988

CHURCH DECORATION AND ORNAMENT - PORTUGAL - PORTO.
Brochado, Alexandrino. O Porto e suas igrejas
azulejadas /. Porto , 1990. 102 p. :
NK4670.7.P62 P673 1990

CHURCH DECORATION AND ORNAMENT - SPAIN - SANTIAGO DE COMPOSTELA.
García Iglesias, José Manuel, 1950- A Catedral
de Santiago o o barroco /. Santiago de
Compostela , 1990. 228 p. : ISBN 84-85665-20-1
NA5811.S46 G37 1990
NYPL [3-MRBN+ 91-3888]

CHURCH DECORATION AND ORNAMENT - SWITZERLAND - ZILLIS.
Rudloff, Diether. Kosmische Bildwelt der
Romanik . Stuttgart , 1989. 176 p. : ISBN
3-87838-592-7
NYPL [3-MAIH + 89-19334]

CHURCH DOORWAYS - GERMANY - REGENSBURG.
Fuchs, Friedrich. Das Hauptportal des
Regensburger Domes . München , c1990. 175
p. : ISBN 3-7954-0652-8
NA5586.R385 F8 1990

CHURCH DOORWAYS - ITALY.
Bornstein, Christine Verzár. Portals and politics in the early Italian city-state . [Parma] [1988] 175 p. :
    NYPL [3-MGO+ (Niccoló) 90-10768]

CHURCH EMBROIDERY. see ECCLESIASTICAL EMBROIDERY.

Church, Frederick Edwin, 1826-1900.
Kelly, Franklin. Frederic Edwin Church /. Washington , c1989. 211 p. : ISBN 0-89468-136-2 DDC 759.13 20
ND237.C52 A4 1989
    NYPL [3-MCX C56 90-10398]

CHURCH, FREDERICK EDWIN, 1826-1900 - EXHIBITIONS.
Kelly, Franklin. Frederic Edwin Church /. Washington , c1989. 211 p. : ISBN 0-89468-136-2 DDC 759.13 20
ND237.C52 A4 1989
    NYPL [3-MCX C56 90-10398]

CHURCH FURNITURE - ITALY - PRATO.
Bardazzi, Silvestro. Arredi e paramenti . Prato , c1988. 318 p. :
    NYPL [3-MRBD+ 90-11027]

CHURCH MUSICIANS - GERMANY - BIOGRAPHY.
Herrmann, Ursula. Eberhard Wenzel . Berlin , c1989. 210 p. ; ISBN 3-374-00804-6 DDC 780/.92 B 20
NK410.W464 H5 1989

CHURCH PLATE - BULGARIA - BACHKOVO - CATALOGS.
Santova, Mila. 24 zlatarski tvorbi ot Bachkovskiĭa manastir /. Sofiĭa , 1990. 47 p. :
NK7215 .S34 1990

CHURCH PLATE - COLOMBIA - EXHIBITIONS.
Oribes y plateros en la Nueva Granada . [Bogotá, Colombia , 1990] 91 p. :
NK7215 .O76 1990

CHURCH PLATE, COLONIAL - COLOMBIA - EXHIBITIONS.
Oribes y plateros en la Nueva Granada . [Bogotá, Colombia , 1990] 91 p. :
NK7215 .O76 1990

CHURCH PLATE - SPAIN - GRANADA.
Capel Margarito, Manuel. Orfebrería religiosa de Granada /. [Granada] , 1983-1986. 2 v. :
    ISBN 84-500-8997-2 (set) DDC 739.2/0946/82 19
NK7215 .C36 1983 NYPL [3-MNP 88-3107]

CHURCH PLATE - VENEZUELA.
Duarte, Carlos F. El arte de la platería en Venezuela . Caracas, Venezuela , 1988. 438 p. :
    ISBN 980-300-084-5 DDC 739.2/3787 20
NK7141.A1 D8 1988

CHURCH TOWERS. see TOWERS.

CHURCH VESTMENTS - ITALY - ANCONA - EXHIBITIONS.
Arazzi Rubensiani e tessuti preziosi dei musei diocesani di Ancona e Osimo . Ancona , c1989. 93 p. :   *NYPL [3-MOR+ 90-620]*

CHURCH VESTMENTS - ITALY - PRATO.
Bardazzi, Silvestro. Arredi e paramenti . Prato , c1988. 318 p. :
    NYPL [3-MRBD+ 90-11027]

CHURCHES - BRAZIL - MINAS GERAIS.
Negro, Carlos del. Escultura ornamental barrôca do Brasil. [Belo Horizonte, 1967] 2 v.,
NB1285 .N4   *NYPL [3-MRX 91-6337]*

CHURCHES IN ART.
Schwartz, Gary, 1940- Pieter Saenredam . London , 1990. 356 p. : ISBN 0-500-23586-4
    NYPL [3-MCH S12 90-11511]

Churches in the prefecture of Pella /.
Moutsopoulos, Nikolaos K., 1927- Thessaloniki , 1973. xi, 504 p., [1] folded leaf of plates :
NA5599.M34 M6 1973

CHURCHES - ITALY.
Portogruaro: Museo nazionale concordiese. [Bologna, 1973, c1971] 113 p.
N2510.P66   *NYPL [3-MAVZ (Portogruaro, Italy) 90-6420]*

CHURCHES - ITALY - BOLOGNA (PROVINCE)
Cardinali, Ferdinando. Le chiese minori delle colline bolognesi . Bologna , 1986. 58 p. :
    NYPL [3-MRBD 90-13374]

CHURCHES - ITALY - OSTUNI.
Le Chiese rurali del territorio di Ostuni /. [Fasano di Brindisi] [1990] 94 p. : ISBN 88-7514-395-1
    NYPL [3-MRBD+ 91-3446]

CHURCHES - ITALY - TOLMEZZO - CONSERVATION AND RESTORATION.
Marcolini, Silvia. Il duomo di Tolmezzo . Udine , c1990. 137, [4] p. :
IN PROCESS (ONLINE)
    NYPL [3-MRBD+ 91-6937]

CHURCHES, LUTHERAN.
Nyman, Helge Johannes, 1910- Kyrkorum, kyrkosång, kyrkobruk /. [Vasa] [1989] 187 p. : ISBN 951-550-388-4
NA4829.L8 N9 1989

CHURCHES - NEW MEXICO.
Kubler, George, 1912- The religious architecture of New Mexico in the colonial period and since the American occupation /. Albuquerque , 1990. xxxv, 232 p. : ISBN 0-8263-1210-1 DDC 726/.5/09789 20
NA5230.N6 K8 1990
    NYPL [3-MRBB+ 91-4591]

The churches of the Crusader Kingdom of Jerusalem . Pringle, Denys. Cambridge , New York , 1992- p. cm. ISBN 0-521-39036-2 (v. 1) DDC 726/.5/0956909021 20
NA5989.6 .P75 1992

CHURCHES, ORTHODOX EASTERN - GREECE - MACEDONIA.
Moutsopoulos, Nikolaos K., 1927- Churches in the prefecture of Pella /. Thessaloniki , 1973. xi, 504 p., [1] folded leaf of plates :
NA5599.M34 M6 1973

CHURCHES - PALESTINE - CATALOGS.
Pringle, Denys. The churches of the Crusader Kingdom of Jerusalem . Cambridge , New York , 1992- p. cm. ISBN 0-521-39036-2 (v. 1) DDC 726/.5/0956909021 20
NA5989.6 .P75 1992

CHURCHES - SYRIA - CATALOGS.
Pringle, Denys. The churches of the Crusader Kingdom of Jerusalem . Cambridge , New York , 1992- p. cm. ISBN 0-521-39036-2 (v. 1) DDC 726/.5/0956909021 20
NA5989.6 .P75 1992

CHURCHILL, WINSTON, SIR, 1874-1965.
Soames, Mary. Winston Churchill . London , 1990. 224 p. : ISBN 0-00-217868-0
ND497.C548 S63 1990b

CHURCHILL, WINSTON S., SIR, 1874-1965.
Soames, Mary. Winston Churchill . London , 1990. 224 p. : ISBN 0-00-217868-0 : DDC 941.082092 20
DA566.9.C5 NYPL [3-MCV C563 90-13282]

Ciardi, Roberto Paolo. Sant'Andrea degli Olivetani . Volterra [1989] 74 p. :
    NYPL [3-MRBD 91-6542]

Ciba-Geigy Corporation.
Texas. University at Austin. Art Museum. Visual r & d: a corporation collects. [Austin, 1973] [24] p.
ND212 .T42 1973 NYPL [3-MCW 79-2127]

CIBA-GEIGY CORPORATION - ART COLLECTIONS.
Texas. University at Austin. Art Museum. Visual r & d: a corporation collects. [Austin, 1973] [24] p.
ND212 .T42 1973 NYPL [3-MCW 79-2127]

CIBA-GEIGY CORPORATION - ART COLLECTIONS - EXHIBITIONS.
A New consciousness . Yonkers, N.Y. , c1971. [12] p. :
    NYPL [3-MAX (CIBA-GEIGY) 90-7135]

Cicatelli, Amelia. Maldarelli, Ernesto, 1850-1900. Un artista ferrarese del legno, Ernesto Maldarelli (1850-1930) /. Ferrara , c1989. 107 p. :   *NYPL [3-MOC 90-12376]*

Cichorius, Conrad, 1863- Trajan's Column : a new edition of the Cichorius plates / introduction, commentary, and notes by Frank Lepper and Sheppard Frere. Gloucester, UK ; Wolfboro, N.H., USA : Alan Sutton, 1988. xviii, 339 p. [94] p. of plates : ill. ; 26 cm. Includes index. Bibliography: p. xiii-xviii. ISBN 0-86299-467-5 :

DDC 937/.07 19
1. Trajan, Emperor of Rome, 53-117 - Monuments - Italy - Rome. 2. Dacian War, 1st, 101-102. 3. Dacian War, 2nd, 105-106. 4. Trajan's Column (Rome, Italy). 5. Rome (Italy) - Antiquities. 6. Italy - Antiquities. I. Lepper, F. A. II. Frere, Sheppard Sunderland. III. Title.
DG59.D3 C63 1988
    NYPL [3-MGH 91-6949]

Cicinelli, Aldo. Dipinti dei musei e gallerie di Roma. Roma , 1978- v. ;
N4035.G33 D56 1981
    NYPL [MAVZ+ (Rome) 91-6377]

Cicle de Conferències sobre Història de Cartografia (1991 : Barcelona, Spain) La cartografia de la Península Ibèrica i la seva extensió al continent americà : 2on curs : 11,12,13 i 14 de febrer de 1991 / organitzat per l'Institut Cartogràfic de Catalunya i el Departament de Geografia de la Universitat Autònoma de Barcelona.1a ed. Barcelona : Institut Cartogràfic de Catalunya, 1991. 279 p. : ill. ; 25 cm. (Col·lecció Monografies) ISBN 84-393-1670-4
1. Cartography - Spain - Congresses. I. Title.
    NYPL [Map Div. 91-7426]

Cien años de la pintura dominicana. 100 años de la pintura dominicana /. [Santo Domingo, Dominican Republic] , 1989. 291 p. : ISBN 84-89532-00-5 DDC 759.97293/074/729375 20
ND315.D6 A15 1989

Cien edificios de Sevilla. Vázquez Consuegra, Guillermo. Sevilla, cien edificios /. [Sevilla?] , 1988. 398 p. : ISBN 89-87001-08-4
    NYPL [3-MQWH+ 89-25523]

Ciencias sociales (Zaragoza, Spain)
(12) Beltrán Martínez, Antonio, 1916- Ensayo sobre el rigen y significación del arte prehistórico /. Zaragoza, España , 1989. 199 p. ; ISBN 84-7733-136-7
IN PROCESS (ONLINE)
    NYPL [3-MADF 91-4516]

Ciento artistas del Ecuador. 100 artistas del Ecuador /. Quito , 1990. 285 p. : DDC 709/.2/2866 B 20
N6985 .A15 1990

Ciento cincuenta años de pintura chilena. Buenos Aires. Museo Nacional de Bellas Artes. 150 años de pintura chilena. Buenos Aires [1972?] 31 p.
ND364.B83   *NYPL [3-MCY 83-2303]*

Cieri Via, Claudia. Andrea Mantegna : pala di San Zeno / Claudia Cieri Via. Venezia : Arsenale editrice, 1985. 32 p., [16] p. of plates : 15 cm. (Hermia . 7) Bibliography: p. 30-32.
1. Mantegna, Andrea, 1431-1506. Pala di San Zeno.
    NYPL [3-MCF M29 90-12520]

ČIKIRIZ, RADOSAV, CA. 1823-1864?
Nikolić, Radojko. Kamenorezac Radosav Čikiriz /. Gornji Milanovac , 1989. 147 p. : ISBN 86-367-0306-9
NB953.C54 N54 1989

Cikovsky, Nicolai.
American art around 1900 . Washington , Hanover [N.H.] , 1990. 136 p. : ISBN 0-89468-143-5   *NYPL [3-MAMT 91-7570]*

Winslow Homer / Nicolai Cikovsky, Jr. New York : Abrams, 1990. 156 p. : ill. (some col.) ; 32 cm. (Library of American art) "In association with the National Museum of American Art, Smithsonian Institution." Includes bibliographical references (p. 148-150) and index. ISBN 0-8109-1193-0 DDC 759.13 B 20
1. Homer, Winslow, 1836-1910. 2. Painters - United States - Biography. I. National Museum of American Art (U. S.). II. Series: Library of American art (Harry N. Abrams, Inc.). III. Title.
ND237.H7 C54 1990
    NYPL [3-MCX+ H76 91-6394]

Winslow Homer . Washington , Hanover, N.H. , 1990. 156 p. : ISBN 0-89468-132-X DDC 759.13 20
ND237.H7 W56 1990

Cima, Maddalena. Il Bronzo dei Romani . Roma , c1990. 298 p. : ISBN 88-7062-675-X
IN PROCESS (ONLINE)
    NYPL [3-MGR 91-3253]

Cimelien /. Kunstgewerbemuseum der Stadt Köln. Köln , 1960. 96 p., 32 p. of plates :
    NYPL [3-MNE 90-6793]

Cincinnati. Art Museum. The Fine art of folk art /. [Cincinnati] , c1990. 43 p. : ISBN 0-931537-12-6 DDC 709/.73/07477178 20
NK806 .F56 1990

Cincinnati Museum. see **Cincinnati. Art Museum.**

Cincinnati Museum Association. Art Museum. see **Cincinnati. Art Museum.**

Cincinnati observed . Clubbe, John. Columbus , c1991. p. cm. ISBN 0-8142-0512-7 (cloth : alk. paper) DDC 720/.9771/79 20
NA735.C5 C58 1991

CINCINNATI (OHIO) - BUILDINGS, STRUCTURES, ETC.
Clubbe, John. Cincinnati observed . Columbus , c1991. p. cm. ISBN 0-8142-0512-7 (cloth : alk. paper) DDC 720/.9771/79 20
NA735.C5 C58 1991

Cinco grandes de la pintura mexicana. México : Promexa, c1980. 143 p., [80] p. of plates : ill. (some col.) ; 36 cm. (Los Grandes maestros de la pintura universal ; [v. 12]) CONTENTS. - Velasco / por Víctor M. Reyes -- Orozco / por Antonio del Guercio -- Rivera / por Enrique F. Gual -- Siqueiros / por Mario de Micheli -- Tamayo / por Xavier Moyssén. ISBN 968-340-118-X
1. Painting, Mexican - Catalogs. 2. Painting, Modern - 20th century - Mexico - Catalogs. I. Series.
ND255 .C56 1980

Cincuenta años de arquitectura en Euskadi. Mas Serra, Elías, 1945- 50 Años de arquitectura en Euskadi /. [Vitoria] , 1990. xviii, 347 p. : ISBN 84-7542-854-1 DDC 720/.946/609045 20
NA1309.P33 M37 1990

Cincuenta años, Salón Nacional de Artistas. 50 años, Salón Nacional de Artistas /. [Bogotá, Colombia] , c1990. 363 p. : ISBN 958-95220-0-9
IN PROCESS (ONLINE)
   NYPL [3-MAM 90-13365]

Cindy Sherman . Sherman, Cindy. New York , 1990. 14 p., 40 leaves of plates : ISBN 0-8478-1274-X DDC 779/.24/092 20
TR654 .S478 1990
   NYPL [MFX+ (Sherman) 91-3482]

Cinema in Iran, 1900-1979 /. Issari, Mohammad Ali. Metuchen, N.J. , 1989. ix, 446 : ISBN 0-8108-2142-7 DDC 791.43/0955 19
PN1993.5.I846 I87 1989
   NYPL [MLF 90-12713]

Cinema Ireland 1896-1950 . O'Leary, Liam. [Dublin] , 1990. 35 p. : ISBN 0-907328-17-2 (pbk.) : DDC 791.4309415 20
   NYPL [MFLE 91-4433]

Cinema Productions (Firm)
Jack Bush [motion picture] /. New York, NY , 1979. 1 film reel (56 min., 50 sec.) : DDC 759.971 11
ND249

Jack Bush [videorecording] /. New York, NY , 1979. 1 videocassette (56 min., 50 sec.) : DDC 759.971 11
ND249

Cinotti, Mia. Bosch, Hieronymus, d. 1516. L'opera completa di Bosch /. Milano , 1966. 119 p. :   *NYPL [3-MCH+ B74 91-5658]*

Cinq milles musées en France. Morley-Schaeffer, Alain. 5000 musées en France . Paris , c1989. 349 p. : ISBN 2-86274-134-5
   NYPL [MAVZ (France) 90-631]

Cinqualbre, Olivier. Tony Garnier, l'œuvre complète /. Paris , c1989. 254 p. : ISBN 2-85850-527-6 DDC 720/.92 20
NA1053.G37 A4 1989

Cinquanta maioliche liguri della Cassa di Risparmio di Genova e Imperia. Ceramica in banca . Albisola Superiore , 1989. 78 p. :
   NYPL [3-MPGD 91-6609]

Cinquecento. La Pittura in Italia . 2 v. (913 p.) , 29 cm. [Milano] :   *NYPL [3-MCE 90-11794]*

Nani em 51ns [i.e. cinquenta e uns] cartuns de bar. Nani, 1951- [Brazil , 198-] 1 v. (unpaged) : DDC 741.5/981 20
NC1460.N356 A4 1980z

Ciol, Elio. Donatello, 1386?-1466. Donatello . Padova , c1989. 185 p. (some folded) : ISBN 88-7026-883-7
   NYPL [3-MGO+ (Donatello) 91-3657]

Cioli, Dario, 1959- Busi, Aldo, 1948- Pâté d'homme . Milano , 1989. 158 p. : ISBN 88-04-32902-5
   NYPL [3-MEM+ (Cioli) 90-11342]

CIPHERS (LETTERING) see **MONOGRAMS.**

Cipriani, Angela.
Accademia nazionale di San Luca. Archivio Storico. I disegni di figura nell'Archivio storico dell'Accademia di San Luca /. Roma , 1988- v. : ISBN 88-7140-011-9 (v. 2)
   NYPL [3-MBH 90-2410]

I Premiati dell'Accademia, 1682-1754 /. Roma , c1989. 189 p. : ISBN 88-7140-010-0
   NYPL [3-MBH 91-4486]

Prize winning drawings from the Roman Academy 1682-1754 =. Roma , c1990. 189 p. : ISBN 88-7140-013-5
   NYPL [3-MBH 91-5071]

Circolo degli artisti (Biella, Italy) Premio internazionale Biella per l'incisione 1971. [Biella, 1971] xxv, 116 p.
NE491 .P73   *NYPL [MDB 90-6615]*

Circolo degli artisti (Turin, Italy) Rama, Carol. Carol Rama /. Torino , c1989. 117 p. : ISBN 88-422-0173-1
   NYPL [3-MCF+ R165 89-26726]

CIRCUITS, INTEGRATED. see **INTEGRATED CIRCUITS.**

CIRCUS - POSTERS.
Le Cirque à l'affiche /. Hauterive , c1989. 205 p. : ISBN 2-88256-037-0
   NYPL [3-MDW+ 91-2665]

Ciri perancangan kota Bandung /. Dana, Djefry W. (Djefry Wahjudy) Jakarta , 1990. xiv, 143 p. : ISBN 979-403-916-0
NA9260.B35 D35 1990

Cirlot, Lourdes. Subirachs / Lourdes Cirlot ; pròleg de J. Corredor-Matheos. [Barcelona?] : A. Ramon, [1990?] 219 p. : ill. ; 30 cm. ISBN 84-404-7513-6
1. Subirachs, José María, 1927-. I. Title.
   NYPL [3-MGO+ (Subirachs) 91-5342]

Le Cirque à l'affiche / préface de S.A.S. le Prince Rainier III de Monaco ; textes de Thomas Althaus ... [et al.]. Hauterive : Editions G. Attinger, c1989. 205 p. : ill. ; 33 cm. French and German. "Affiches reproduites de la collection privée d'Hubert Tièche." ISBN 2-88256-037-0
1. Tièche, Hubert - Poster collections. 2. Circus - Posters. I. Althaus, Thomas, 1941-.
   NYPL [3-MDW+ 91-2665]

Cirvini, Silvia A. La estructura profesional y técnica en la construcción de Mendoza / Silvia A. Cirvini. [Mendoza, Argentina?] : Instituto Argentino de Investigaciones de Historia de la Arquitectura y del Urbanismo, 1989- v. <1 > : ill. ; 21 x 24 cm. Includes bibliographical references (v. 1, p. 181-184). CONTENTS. - t. 1. Los agrimensores
1. Architecture - Argentina - Mendoza (Province). 2. Public buildings - Argentina - Mendoza (Province). I. Title.
NA4262.M46 C57 1989

CISKEI (SOUTH AFRICA) - ECONOMIC CONDITIONS.
Strategy and guidelines for the physical development of the Republic of Ciskei /. [Stellenbosch] , 1982. 2 v. : ISBN 0-908422-86-5 (pbk. : set) DDC 338.9687/92 19
HC905.Z7 C578 1982
   NYPL [Map Div. 90-58]

CISKEI (SOUTH AFRICA) - ECONOMIC CONDITIONS - MAPS.
Strategy and guidelines for the physical development of the Republic of Ciskei /. [Stellenbosch] , 1982. 2 v. : ISBN 0-908422-86-5 (pbk. : set) DDC 338.9687/92 19
HC905.Z7 C578 1982
   NYPL [Map Div. 90-58]

Le Ciste prenestine /. Consiglio nazionale delle ricerche, Centro di studio per l'archeologia etrusco-italica. [Roma] : Consiglio nazionale delle ricerche, 1979- v. : ill. ; 30 cm. Vol. 2 in German. Includes bibliographical references. CONTENTS. - 1. Corpus, [pt.] 1. A, 1-2, numeri I-XX. B, numeri 1-56 / Gabriella Bordenache Battaglia, con la collaborazione di Adriana Emiliozzi (2 v.). [pt.] 2. [without special title] / Gabriella Bordenache Battaglia, Adriana Emiliozzi (2 v.) -- 2. Studi e contributi, [pt.] 1. "Cistenfüsse" etruskische und praenestiner

Bronzewerkstätten / Fritzi Jurgeit.
1. Cists (Boxes) - Italy - Palestrina - Catalogs. 2. Bronzes, Etruscan - Italy - Palestrina - Catalogs. 3. Etruscans - Italy - Palestrina - Catalogs. 4. Palestrina (Italy) - Antiquities - Catalogs. 5. Italy - Antiquities - Catalogs. I. Bordenache Battaglia, Gabriella. II. Emiliozzi, Adriana. III. Jurgeit, Fritzi. IV. Centro di studio per l'archeologia etrusco-italica.
DG70.P33 C57 1979
   NYPL [3-MGR+ 83-2202]

CISTS (BOXES) - ITALY - PALESTRINA - CATALOGS.
Le Ciste prenestine /. [Roma] , 1979- v. :
DG70.P33 C57 1979
   NYPL [3-MGR+ 83-2202]

Citadel culture /. Werckmeister, O. K. (Otto Karl), 1934- [Zitadellenkultur. English.] Chicago , 1991. 210 p. ; ISBN 0-226-89361-8 (alk. paper) DDC 700/.9/048 20
NX456.5.P66 W4713 1991

La Cité de la musique . Portzamparc, Christian de, 1944- Seyssel, France [1986] 47 p. : ISBN 2-903528-76-4 DDC 725/.81/0924 19
NA1053.P655 A4 1986   *NYPL [3-MQZ+ (Portzamparc) 90-12557]*

CITÉ DE LA MUSIQUE (PARIS, FRANCE)
Portzamparc, Christian de, 1944- La Cité de la musique . Seyssel, France [1986] 47 p. : ISBN 2-903528-76-4 DDC 725/.81/0924 19
NA1053.P655 A4 1986   *NYPL [3-MQZ+ (Portzamparc) 90-12557]*

Cities : statistical, administrative and graphical information on the major urban areas of the world / sponsored by United Nations Population Fund, Ministerio de Obras Públicas y Urbanismo, España, Corporació Metropolitana de Barcelona ; with the collaboration of Ministerio de Asuntos Exteriores, España ... [et al.]. [Barcelona] : Institut d'Estudis Metropolitans de Barcelona, 1988. 5 v. (xxix, 1673 p.) : ill. (some col.), maps ; 30 cm. Spine title: Cities of the world. Vol. 1: errata (4 p.) for vols. 1-5 inserted. Vol. 1: 1 folded map inserted. ISBN 84-404-2436-1 (set)
1. Cities and towns - Statistics. 2. Metropolitan areas - Statistics. 3. Municipal government - Statistics. I. United Nations Population Fund. II. Spain. Ministerio de Obras Públicas y Urbanismo. III. Corporació Metropolitana de Barcelona. IV. Spain. Ministerio de Asuntos Exteriores. V. Institut d'Estudis Metropolitans de Barcelona. VI. Title: Cities of the world.
   NYPL [Map Div. 91-162]

CITIES AND TOWNS - BEAUTIFICATION. see **URBAN BEAUTIFICATION.**

CITIES AND TOWNS - CONSERVATION AND RESTORATION.
Hlobil, Ivo. Teorie městských památkových rezervací, 1900-1975 /. Praha , 1985. 123 p. ;
NA9050 .H58 1985

CITIES AND TOWNS - ENGLAND - DORSET - MAPS.
Estate Publications (Firm) Estate Publications Dorset . Tenterden, Kent [1980?] 1 atlas (34, [6] p.) : ISBN 0-86084-108-1
   NYPL [Map Div. 91-1161]

CITIES AND TOWNS - EUROPE - VIEWS - CATALOGS.
Kunstverlag Möller. Original-Radierungen mit Motiven europäischer Städte /. Lübeck [198-?] 80 p. :   *NYPL [MDZ + 90-1093]*

CITIES AND TOWNS - GERMANY - HISTORY.
Gerlach, Siegfried. Die deutsche Stadt des Absolutismus im Spiegel barocker Veduten und zeitgenössischer Pläne . Stuttgart , c1990. 80 p. : ISBN 3-515-05600-9
IN PROCESS (ONLINE)
   NYPL [3-MQWD 91-3447]

CITIES AND TOWNS - GERMANY, WEST - MAPS.
Mairs Geographischer Verlag. Der Grosse Shell Atlas. Stuttgart , c1965-1966. viii, 283, [166], x-xxii p. :   *NYPL [Map Div. 90-5904]*

CITIES AND TOWNS IN ART.
Doezema, Marianne, 1950- George Bellows and urban America /. New Haven, CT , c1991. p. cm. ISBN 0-300-05043-7 DDC 759.13 20
ND237.B45 D6 1991

CITIES AND TOWNS IN ART - CATALOGS.
Spanish cities of the golden age . Berkeley ,

c1989. 415 p. : ISBN 0-520-05610-8 (alk. paper)
DDC 741.9493 19
NC266.W96 A4 1989
              NYPL [3-MCH+ W962 90-11753]

CITIES AND TOWNS - INDIA - MAPS.
Tamilnad Printers & Traders Private Ltd. The
city atlas of India . Madras, India , 1985. 1
atlas (232 p.) : DDC 912/.54 19
G2284.A1 T3 1985
              NYPL [Map Div. 91-6606]

**CITIES AND TOWNS, ISLAMIC - TURKEY -
HISTORY.**
The Ottoman city and its parts . New Rochelle,
N.Y. , 1991. p. cm. ISBN 0-89241-473-1 DDC
307.76/09561 20
NA9229 .O87 1991

CITIES AND TOWNS - ITALY - VITERBO.
Petrucci, Giulia. San Martino al Cimino
(Viterbo, III) /. Roma , 1987 [i.e. 1988] 73 p. :
ISBN 88-7597-033-5 (pbk.)
              NYPL [Map Div. 88-1082]

**CITIES AND TOWNS - MASSACHUSETTS -
MAPS.**
Arrow Publishing Co. Official Arrow street map
atlas, western Massachusetts. Taunton, Mass. ,
c1988. 1 atlas (iii, 106 p.) : ISBN 0-913450-83-9
              NYPL [Map Div. 90-12431]

CITIES AND TOWNS, MEDIEVAL.
Scandinavian atlas of historic towns. Odense ,
1977- portfolios : ISBN 87-7492-216-5 (no. 1)
              NYPL [Map Div. 82-813]

CITIES AND TOWNS, MOVEMENT TO. see
URBANIZATION.

CITIES AND TOWNS, MUSLIM. see **CITIES
AND TOWNS, ISLAMIC.**

CITIES AND TOWNS - PLANNING. see **CITY
PLANNING.**

**CITIES AND TOWNS - SCANDINAVIA -
HISTORY.**
Scandinavian atlas of historic towns. Odense ,
1977- portfolios : ISBN 87-7492-216-5 (no. 1)
              NYPL [Map Div. 82-813]

**CITIES AND TOWNS - SCANDINAVIA -
MAPS.**
Scandinavian atlas of historic towns. Odense ,
1977- portfolios : ISBN 87-7492-216-5 (no. 1)
              NYPL [Map Div. 82-813]

**CITIES AND TOWNS - SPAIN - HISTORY -
16TH CENTURY - PICTORIAL WORKS -
CATALOGS.**
Spanish cities of the golden age . Berkeley ,
c1989. 415 p. : ISBN 0-520-05610-8 (alk. paper)
DDC 741.9493 19
NC266.W96 A4 1989
              NYPL [3-MCH+ W962 90-11753]

CITIES AND TOWNS - STATISTICS.
Cities . [Barcelona] , 1988. 5 v. (xxix, 1673 p.) :
ISBN 84-404-2436-1 (set)
              NYPL [Map Div. 91-162]

**CITIES AND TOWNS - SWITZERLAND -
MAPS.**
Kümmerly + Frey. Schweiz . [Bern] , 1989. 1
atlas (92 p.) : ISBN 3-259-01521-3
              NYPL [Map Div. 90-13241]

**CITIES AND TOWNS - UNITED STATES -
DIRECTORIES.**
The Instant national locator guide. San
Francisco, Calif. , c1991. 1 v. (various
pagings) :   ***NYPL [Map Div. 91-7663]***

**CITIES AND TOWNS - UNITED STATES -
MAPS.**
American Map Company, inc., New York.
Cleartype® commercial atlas of the United
States. New York [198-?] [58] leaves :
              NYPL [Map Div. 85-883]

The Instant national locator guide. San
Francisco, Calif. , c1991. 1 v. (various
pagings):   ***NYPL [Map Div. 91-7663]***

Cities of the world. Cities . [Barcelona] , 1988. 5
v. (xxix, 1673 p.) : ISBN 84-404-2436-1 (set)
              NYPL [Map Div. 91-162]

Cito Filomarino, Anna Maria. L'ottocento: i
mobili del tempo dei nonni. Dall'impero al
liberty. [Milano] Görlich [c1969]. 255 p. illus.
28 cm. Errata slip inserted.
1. Furniture - Italy - History - 19th century. I. Title.
NK2561 .C58   ***NYPL [3-MOF 90-6347]***

Città del mondo /. Scianna, Ferdinando. Milano ,

c1988. 95 p. :
              NYPL [MFX (Scianna) 91-5705]

Città di Castello (Italy). Pinacoteca comunale.
Beckmann, Max, 1884-1950. Max Beckmann .
[Italy] [1985] 141 p. : DDC 769.92/4 19
NE654.B37 A4 1985
              NYPL [MDG (Beckmann) 86-4332]

**CITTÀ IDEALE (PAINTING) -
EXHIBITIONS.**
Il restauro della Città ideale di Urbino .
[Urbino , 1978] 39 p. :
              NYPL [3-MBK 90-5658]

Città illustrate. Chemelli, Aldo. Trento illustrata .
Padova , c1991. 213 p. : ISBN 88-7123-110-4
DDC 769/.4445385/094 20
NE954.3.I8 C44 1991

La Città ritrovata : interventi di recupero urbano
a Novara. [Novara] : Commune di Novara,
[1988] 414 p. ; 31 cm.
*1. Novara (Italy) - Buildings, structures, etc. -
Conservation and restoration. I. Novara (Italy).*
              NYPL [3-MQWB+ 90-10357]

CITY AND TOWN LIFE - GERMANY.
Schilling, Heinz. Urbane Zeiten . Frankfurt [am
Main] [1990] 371 p. : ISBN 3-923992-32-7
NA9199 .S37 1990

CITY AND TOWN LIFE IN ART.
Hemingway, Andrew. Naturalism and
modernity . Cambridge [England] , New York ,
1992. p. cm. ISBN 0-521-39118-0 (hardback)
DDC 758/.1/41094109034 20
ND1354.5 .H46 1992

The city atlas of India . Tamilnad Printers &
Traders Private Ltd. Madras, India , 1985. 1
atlas (232 p.) : DDC 912/.54 19
G2284.A1 T3 1985
              NYPL [Map Div. 91-6606]

CITY BEAUTIFICATION. see **URBAN
BEAUTIFICATION.**

City Beautiful Council of Dayton, Ohio.
Quintessence--the alternative spaces residency
program, the City Beautiful Council of Dayton,
Ohio, the Wright State University, Department
of Art. Dayton , c1978- v. : ISBN 0-9602550-0-1
(v. 2) DDC 709/.73/074017173
N6530.O3 Q56   ***NYPL [3-MAMT 79-2025]***

CITY GOVERNMENT. see **MUNICIPAL
GOVERNMENT.**

CITY HALLS - ENGLAND.
Tittler, Robert. Architecture and power .
Oxford [England] , New York , 1991. p. cm.
ISBN 0-19-820230-X : DDC 725/.13/0103 20
NA4435.G7 T5 1991

CITY HALLS - GREECE.
Gneisz, Doris. Das antike Rathaus . Wien ,
1990. viii, 369 p. : ISBN 3-85369-786-0 DDC
725/.13/0938 20
NA278.P6 G58 1990

CITY HALLS - ROME.
Gneisz, Doris. Das antike Rathaus . Wien ,
1990. viii, 369 p. : ISBN 3-85369-786-0 DDC
725/.13/0938 20
NA278.P6 G58 1990

City impressions . Stoddard, Sheena. Bristol ,
1990. 120 p. : ISBN 1-87297-120-2 (pbk.) : DDC
758.9942393 20
ND1354.4   ***NYPL [MDNH 91-4822]***

CITY LIFE. see **CITY AND TOWN LIFE.**

City Museum and Art Gallery, Birmingham. see
Birmingham Museums and Art Gallery.

City of Bristol Museum and Art Gallery. Braque,
Georges, 1882-1963. Braque . London , 1990.
71 p. : ISBN 1-85332-060-9
              NYPL [3-MCO B821 91-4401]

The city of Dublin, 1728 /. Brooking, Charles.
[Map of the city and suburbs of Dublin.]
Dublin , 1983. 1 portfolio : ISBN 0-904720-14-4 :
DDC 941.8/35 19
DA995.D8 B76 1983
              NYPL [Map Div. 87-655]

City of man. Viola, Bill, 1951- Bill Viola, The city
of man. Brockton, Mass. , 1989. [8] p. : ISBN
0-934358-24-9 ***NYPL [3-MAL 89-25255]***

City on a hill : twenty years of artists at Cortona.
Athens, Ga. : Georgia Museum of Art,
University of Georgia, c1989. 1 v. (unpaged) :
ill. ; 26 cm. Catalogue of an exhibition held at the

Georgia Museum of Art, The University of Georgia,
March 25-May 7, 1989. ISBN 0-915977-02-8
*1. University of Georgia. Studies Abroad Program. 2.
Art, American - Italy - Cortona - Exhibitions. 3. Art,
Modern - 20th century - Italy - Cortona - Exhibitions.*
              NYPL [3-MAMT 90-11763]

CITY PLANNING.
Coppa, Mario. Piccola storia dell'urbanistica /.
Torino , c1990. 5 v. : ISBN 88-7750-097-2 (v. 1) :
NA9090 .C67 1990

**CITY PLANNING - ADDRESSES, ESSAYS,
LECTURES.**
Informazioni di base . Roma [1978?] 99 p.,
[1] :
HT166 .I545   ***NYPL [JLL 80-69 n.4]***

CITY PLANNING - BERLIN (GERMANY)
Balfour, Alan. Berlin . New York , 1990. 269
p. : ISBN 0-8478-1271-5 DDC 720/.1/03 20
NA9200.B4 B35 1990
              NYPL [3-MQWD 90-13618]

**CITY PLANNING - BERLIN REGION
(GERMANY) - HISTORY - 17TH
CENTURY.**
Wimmer, Clemens Alexander, 1959-
Sichtachsen des Barock in Berlin und
Umgebung . Berlin, c1985. 39 p. :
              NYPL [3-MQWD 90-12627]

**CITY PLANNING - BERLIN REGION
(GERMANY) - HISTORY - 18TH
CENTURY.**
Wimmer, Clemens Alexander, 1959-
Sichtachsen des Barock in Berlin und
Umgebung . Berlin, c1985. 39 p. :
              NYPL [3-MQWD 90-12627]

CITY PLANNING - CHILE - SANTIAGO.
Munizaga, Gustavo. Estructura y ciudad /.
Santiago de Chile , 1985. 147 p. :
NA9168.S3 M8 1985

**CITY PLANNING - CZECHOSLOVAKIA -
PRAGUE - HISTORY.**
Hrůza, Jiří. Město Praha /. Praha , 1989. 421
p. : ISBN 80-207-0065-X :
NA1033.P7 H78 1989

**CITY PLANNING - EUROPE - HISTORY -
20TH CENTURY - CONGRESSES.**
Le Projet d'architecture dans la ville, instrument
de sa transformation . Strasbourg , 1983. 50 P. ;
NA9183 .P7 1983

Le Projet urbain et la construction de la cité .
Strasbourg , 1983. 96 p. ;
NA9095 .P76 1983

**CITY PLANNING - FINLAND - HISTORY -
20TH CENTURY - EXHIBITIONS.**
Kautto, Jussi, 1942- Suomalaista
kaupunkiarkkitehtuuria =. Helsinki , 1990. 233
p. : ISBN 951-9229-63-9
NA9241.F5 K38 1990

CITY PLANNING - FORECASTING.
Mansfield, Howard. Cosmopolis . New
Brunswick, N.J. , c1990. vii, 165 p. : ISBN
0-88285-131-4 DDC 307.76/4 20
HT330 .M34 1990
              NYPL [3-MQV 90-13391]

**CITY PLANNING - FRANCE - AMIENS -
HISTORY - 20TH CENTURY.**
Le Nouvel Amiens /. Liège , 1989. 471 p. :
ISBN 2-87009-368-3
NA9198.A42 N68 1989

**CITY PLANNING - FRANCE - MARSEILLE -
HISTORY.**
Architectures historiques à Marseille .
Aix-en-Provence , c1987. 141 p. : ISBN
2-85744-290-4 : DDC 720/.944/912 19
NA1051.M37 U73 1987
              NYPL [3-MQWF+ 90-12768]

**CITY PLANNING - FRANCE - PARIS -
EXHIBITIONS.**
Paris, la ville et ses projets . Paris , c1989. 253
p. : ISBN 2-907742-04-3
              NYPL [3-MQWF+ 90-10864]

CITY PLANNING - GERMANY.
Schilling, Heinz. Urbane Zeiten . Frankfurt [am
Main] [1990] 371 p. : ISBN 3-923992-32-7
NA9199 .S37 1990

**CITY PLANNING - GERMANY - BERLIN -
HISTORY - 20TH CENTURY.**
Rietdorf, Werner. Stadterneuerung . Berlin ,
1989. 256 p. : ISBN 3-345-00282-5
NA9200.B4 R54 1989

CITY PLANNING - GERMANY (EAST) - HISTORY - 20TH CENTURY.
Rietdorf, Werner. Stadterneuerung . Berlin , 1989. 256 p. : ISBN 3-345-00282-5
NA9200.B4 R54 1989

CITY PLANNING - GERMANY - EXHIBITIONS.
Peter Joseph Lenné . Berlin , c1989. 315 p. : ISBN 3-87584-277-4
NYPL [3-MSCC 91-2632]

CITY PLANNING - GERMANY - HAMBURG-HARBURG (HAMBURG) - HISTORY - 20TH CENTURY.
Stadtbild Hamburg. Hamburg [1990] 64 p. :
NA9053.C6 S72 1990

CITY PLANNING - GERMANY - HISTORY - 16TH CENTURY.
Stubenvoll, Willi. Die deutschen Hugenottenstädte /. Frankfurt am Main , c1990. 208 p. : ISBN 3-524-69093-9
NA9199 .S78 1990

CITY PLANNING - GERMANY - HISTORY - 17TH CENTURY.
Stubenvoll, Willi. Die deutschen Hugenottenstädte /. Frankfurt am Main , c1990. 208 p. : ISBN 3-524-69093-9
NA9199 .S78 1990

CITY PLANNING - GLOSSARIES, VOCABULARIES, ETC.
A Survey of zoning definitions /. Chicago , c1989. 36 p. : DDC 361.6/0973 361.6/03 20
NA9108 .A545 no. 421 HT169.6

CITY PLANNING - HISTORY - 16TH CENTURY - EXHIBITIONS.
Planstädte der Neuzeit, vom 16. bis zum 18. Jahrhundert . Karlsruhe , c1990. 381 p. : ISBN 3-7650-9026-3
NA9094.3 .P53 1990

CITY PLANNING - HISTORY - 17TH CENTURY - EXHIBITIONS.
Planstädte der Neuzeit, vom 16. bis zum 18. Jahrhundert . Karlsruhe , c1990. 381 p. : ISBN 3-7650-9026-3
NA9094.3 .P53 1990

CITY PLANNING - HISTORY - 18TH CENTURY - EXHIBITIONS.
Planstädte der Neuzeit, vom 16. bis zum 18. Jahrhundert . Karlsruhe , c1990. 381 p. : ISBN 3-7650-9026-3
NA9094.3 .P53 1990

CITY PLANNING - HISTORY - 20TH CENTURY.
Holl, Steven. Edge of a city /. New York , 1991. p. cm. ISBN 1-87827-156-3 : DDC 711/.4/09048 20
NA9095 .H65 1991

Le Corbusier, 1887-1965. [Précision sur un état présent de l'architecture et de l'urbanisme. English.] Precisions on the present state of architecture and city planning . Cambridge, Mass. , c1991. xiii, 266 p. : ISBN 0-262-12149-2 (hc) : DDC 724/.6 20
NA680 .L3613 1991
NYPL [3-MQZ (Le Corbusier) 91-5519]

CITY PLANNING - ILLINOIS - CHICAGO.
Gandelsonas, Mario, 1938- The urban text /. London, England ; Boston, Mass. : p. cm. ISBN 0-262-57084-X (pbk.) DDC 711/.4/0977311 20
NA9127.C4 G36 1990

CITY PLANNING - ILLINOIS - CHICAGO - HISTORY - 19TH CENTURY.
Bluestone, Daniel M. Constructing Chicago /. New Haven , c1991. p. cm. ISBN 0-300-04848-3 (alk. paper) DDC 711/.4/097731109034 20
NA9127.C4 B48 1991

CITY PLANNING - INDONESIA - BANDUNG.
Dana, Djefry W. (Djefry Wahjudy) Ciri perancangan kota Bandung /. Jakarta , 1990. xiv, 143 p. : ISBN 979-403-916-0
NA9260.B35 D35 1990

CITY PLANNING - ISLAMIC COUNTRIES - BIBLIOGRAPHY.
Architektur und Städtebau des Islam /. Stuttgart , 1985- v. ; ISBN 3-8167-0105-1 DDC 016.72/0917/671 19
Z5943.I84 A73 1984 NA380
NYPL [3-MQT 91-826]

CITY PLANNING - ISRAEL - HISTORY - 20TH CENTURY.
Israel builds. [Jerusalem , 1964] 1 v. (unpaged) :
NA9051 .I77 1964

CITY PLANNING - ITALY.
Elaborati urbanistici . Milano [1987?] 10 pamphlets in portfolio :
NYPL [3-MQWB 90-11014]

CITY PLANNING - ITALY - ADDRESSES, ESSAYS, LECTURES.
Informazioni di base . Roma [1978?] 99 p., [1] :
HT166 .I545 NYPL [JLL 80-69 n.4]

CITY PLANNING - ITALY - LATINA.
Latina /. Roma , 1990. 94 p. : ISBN 88-7597-124-2 : DDC 711/.4/0945623 20
NA9204.L37 L37 1990

CITY PLANNING - ITALY - LATINA (PROVINCE)
Latina /. Roma , 1990. 94 p. :
NYPL [Map Div. 91-5807]

CITY PLANNING - ITALY - MASSA-CARRARA - HISTORY.
Giorgieri, Pietro. Itinerari apuani di architettura moderna /. Firenze , 1989. 263 p. :
NYPL [3-MQWB 90-11118]

CITY PLANNING - ITALY - PALERMO - HISTORY - 20TH CENTURY.
Palermo, norma di piano e progetto /. [Italy] , Roma , c1990. 189 p. : DDC 720/.945/823 20
NA1121.P3 P36 1990

CITY PLANNING - ITALY - ROME - HISTORY - 15TH CENTURY.
Burroughs, Charles. From signs to design . Cambridge, Mass. , c1990. xii, 344 p., [54] p. of plates : ISBN 0-262-02298-2 DDC 307.76/0945/63209024 20
NA1120 .B87 1990
NYPL [MQWB 91-4224]

CITY PLANNING - ITALY - VITERBO.
Petrucci, Giulia. San Martino al Cimino (Viterbo, III) /. Roma , 1987 [i.e. 1988] 73 p. : ISBN 88-7597-033-5 (pbk.)
NYPL [Map Div. 88-1082]

CITY PLANNING - NETHERLANDS.
Olanda 1870-1940 . Milano , 1990, c1980. 208 p. : ISBN 88-435-3094-1
NYPL [3-MQW 91-6563]

Taverne, Ed. Carel Weeber . Rotterdam , c1989. xv, [121] p. : ISBN 90-6450-088-6
NYPL [3-MQZ (Weeber) 90-11979]

CITY PLANNING - NETHERLANDS - ARNHEM - HISTORY.
Lavooij, Wim. Twee eeuwen bouwen aan Arnhem . Zutphen , 1990. 128 p. : ISBN 90-6011-683-6 :
NA9208.A7 L38 1990

CITY PLANNING - NEW YORK (STATE)
New York (City). City Planning Commission. Plan for New York City, 1969. Cambridge, Mass. [c1969] 6 v. ISBN 0-262-64004-X (v. 1) varies
HT168.N5 A5 NYPL [Map Div. 80-680]

New York (N.Y.). Dept. of City Planning. Block & lot maps-- Bronx Community District ... atlas /. New York, N.Y. , c1990. 12 v. : *NYPL [Map Div. 91-7471]*

New York (N.Y.). Dept. of City Planning. Block & lot maps-- Brooklyn Community District ... atlas /. New York, N.Y. , c1990. 18 v. : *NYPL [Map Div. 91-6366]*

New York (N.Y.). Dept. of City Planning. Block & lot maps-- Manhattan Community District ... atlas /. New York, N.Y. , c1989. 12 v. : *NYPL [Map Div. 91-7469]*

New York (N.Y.). Dept. of City Planning. Block & lot maps-- Queens Community District ... atlas /. New York, N.Y. , c1991- v. : *NYPL [Map Div. 91-7475]*

CITY PLANNING - PUERTO RICO - HISTORY - 19TH CENTURY.
Rigau, Jorge. Puerto Rico 1900 . New York , 1991. p. cm. ISBN 0-8478-1400-9 DDC 720/.97295/09041 20
NA812 .R5 1991

CITY PLANNING - PUERTO RICO - HISTORY - 20TH CENTURY.

CITY PLANNING - PUERTO RICO - (continued)
Rigau, Jorge. Puerto Rico 1900 . New York , 1991. p. cm. ISBN 0-8478-1400-9 DDC 720/.97295/09041 20
NA812 .R5 1991

CITY PLANNING - RUSSIAN S.F.S.R. - HISTORY.
Gippenreĭter, Vadim Evgen'evich. The golden ring . New York , 1991. p. cm. ISBN 1-558-59216-4 DDC 720/.947 20
NA1181 .G56 1991

CITY PLANNING - RUSSIAN S.F.S.R. - MOSCOW.
Arkhitekturnoe nasledie Moskvy . Moskva , 1988. 100 p. :
NA1197.M6 A78 1988

CITY PLANNING - RUSSIAN S.F.S.R. - MOSCOW - HISTORY - 20TH CENTURY.
Sotsial'nye problemy arkhitekturno-gradostroitel'nogo razvitiia Moskvy . Moskva , 1988. 103 p. ;
NA9212.M6 S67 1988

CITY PLANNING - SCOTLAND - HISTORY - 20TH CENTURY.
Youngson, A. J. Urban development and the Royal Fine Art Commissions /. Edinburgh , c1990. 186 p., [24] p. of plates : ISBN 0-7486-0114-7 DDC 711/.4/0941 20
NA9189 .Y68 1990

CITY PLANNING - SPAIN - BARCELONA.
Transformación de un frente maritimo . Barcelona , 1988. 120 p. : ISBN 84-252-1368-1
NYPL [MQWH 89-19333]

CITY PLANNING - SPAIN - CONGRESSES.
Coloquio de Urbanismo Barroco (1986 : Archidona, Spain) II centenario de la Plaza Ochavada de Archidona /. [Málaga] [1989] 350 p. : ISBN 84-7496-177-7
NA1306 .C6 1986

CITY PLANNING - SPAIN - SEVILLE - HISTORY.
Vioque Cubero, R. (Rafael) Apuntes sobre el origen y evolución morfológica de las plazas del casco histórico de Sevilla /. [Seville] [1987] 225 p. : ISBN 84-505-4261-8
NA9223.S48 V56 1987

CITY PLANNING - SPAIN - VALLADOLID - HISTORY.
Virgili Blanquet, María Antonia. Arquitectura y urbanismo de Valladolid en el siglo XX /. Valladolid , 1988. 190 p. : ISBN 84-404-2435-3
NYPL [3-MQWH 90-9439]

CITY PLANNING - TENNESSEE - JONESBORO.
Tennessee State Planning Commission. Upper East Tennessee Office. Historic district plan, Jonesborough, Tennessee /. Johnson City, Tenn. , Springfield, Va. , 1972. 115 p. :
NYPL [3-MQWO 90-6607]

CITY PLANNING - TURKEY - HISTORY.
The Ottoman city and its parts . New Rochelle, N.Y. , 1991. p. cm. ISBN 0-89241-473-1 DDC 307.76/09561 20
NA9229 .O87 1991

CITY PLANNING - UKRAINE - L'VIV.
Trehubova, T. O. L'viv, arkhitekturno-istorychnyĭ narys /. Kyïv , 1989. 270 p. : ISBN 5-7705-0178-2 :
NA1197.L85 T74 1989

CITY PLANNING - UNITED STATES - HISTORY - 20TH CENTURY.
People places . New York, N.Y. , 1990. xvii, 295 p. : ISBN 0-442-31929-0 : DDC 711/.4 20
NA9070 .P45 1990
NYPL [3-MQWO 90-11592]

CITY PLANNING - ZONE SYSTEM. see ZONING.

City University of New York. Fellowship Fund in Art History. Ten American painters /. New York , c1990. 187 p. : ISBN 0-945936-07-9
NYPL [3-MCW 90-11805]

CITY WALLS - ITALY - MILAN - HISTORY.
Pifferi, Enzo, 1940- Milano, le porte : la storia di Milano attraverso le porte /. Como , c1989. 137 p. : DDC 945/.21 20
DG664 .P54 1989
NYPL [3-MQWB+ 91-4912]

CityPlace Gallery (Boston, Mass.) Duarte, Carlota. Odella . Albuquerque, N.M. , c1990.

[56] p. :   ISBN 0-9624109-0-X
NYPL [MFX (Duarte) 90-13481]

Cityviews. Goldsmith, Lloyd, 1945- Lloyd
Goldsmith, cityviews . New York, N.Y. [1982]
[16] p. :   *NYPL [3-MAMY 91-1159]*

CIUDAD UNIVERSITARIA (MEXICO)
Linares, Mercedes. Murales. [Mexico, 1967] 38
p.   *NYPL [3-MLP 90-6889]*

Ciudad y cultura .
(2) Fernández, Martha (Fernández García) La
arquitectura de la Ciudad de México en el siglo
XVII /. [Mexico] , 1987. 43 p. :   ISBN
968-8160-77-6   DDC 720/.972/5309032 20
NA757.M4 F46 1987

Čiurlionis, Mikalojus Konstantinus, 1875-1911.
Bialopetravičienė, Laima. Čiurlionis und die
litauische Malerei, 1900-1940 . Duisburg ,
c1989. 105 p. :   ISBN 3-923576-57-9
NYPL [3-MCY 90-10676]

**ČIURLIONIS, MIKALOJUS
KONSTANTINUS, 1875-1911 -
EXHIBITIONS.**
Bialopetravičienė, Laima. Čiurlionis und die
litauische Malerei, 1900-1940 . Duisburg ,
c1989. 105 p. :   ISBN 3-923576-57-9
NYPL [3-MCY 90-10676]

Čiurlionis und die litauische Malerei, 1900-1940 .
Bialopetravičienė, Laima. Duisburg , c1989. 105
p. :   ISBN 3-923576-57-9
NYPL [3-MCY 90-10676]

Civai, Alessandra. Dipinti e sculture in casa
Martelli : storia di una collezione patrizia
fiorentina dal Quattrocento all'Ottocento /
Allesandra Civai. Firenze : Opus Libri, c1990.
219 p. : ill. (some col.) ; 30 cm. Includes index.
Includes bibliographical references (p. 187-209).
1. Palazzo Martelli (Florence, Italy). 2. Art - Collectors
and collecting - Italy - Florence - History. 3. Art -
Private collections - Italy - Florence. 4. Art, European -
Italy - Florence. 5. Art, Italian - Italy - Florence. I.
Title.   *NYPL [3-MAVC+ 91-6773]*

CIVIC PLANNING. see CITY PLANNING.

Civica galleria "Anna e Luigi Parmeggiani."
Dipinti della Civica galleria "Anna e Luigi
Parmeggiani." Reggio Emilia [Italy] : Grafis,
1988- v. : ill. (some col.), ports. ; 29 cm.
(Cataloghi dei Civici musei di Reggio nell'Emilia . 10)
Vol. 1 introduction in Spanish. Bibliography: v. 1, p. 10.
CONTENTS. - 1. I dipinti spagnoli / Alfonso E. Pérez
Sánchez.
1. Civica galleria "Anna e Luigi Parmeggiani" -
Catalogs. 2. Painting - Italy - Reggio Emilia - Catalogs.
I. Title. II. Series.   *NYPL [3-MCE 91-6861]*

**CIVICA GALLERIA "ANNA E LUIGI
PARMEGGIANI" - CATALOGS.**
Civica galleria "Anna e Luigi Parmeggiani."
Dipinti della Civica galleria "Anna e Luigi
Parmeggiani." Reggio Emilia [Italy] , 1988- v. :
NYPL [3-MCE 91-6861]

Civiche raccolte numismatiche di Milano.
Un Artista etrusco e il suo mondo . Roma ,
1988. 112 p., [8] p. of plates :   ISBN
88-7813-131-8   *NYPL [3-MPEK 90-12767]*
Gli Etruschi e Cerveteri : nuove acquisizioni
delle Civiche raccolte archeologiche : la
prospezione archeologica nell'attività della
Fondazione Lerici : Milano, Palazzo reale,
settembre 1980-gennaio 1981. Milano : Electa,
c1980. 267 p. : ill. (some col.) ; 25 cm. Includes
bibliographical references.
1. Fondazione Lerici. 2. Civiche raccolte numismatiche
di Milano. 3. Vases, Etruscan - Italy - Cerveteri -
Exhibitions. 4. Etruscans - Italy - Cerveteri -
Exhibitions. 5. Vases, Greek - Italy - Cerveteri -
Exhibitions. 6. Cerveteri (Italy) - Antiquities -
Exhibitions. 7. Italy - Antiquities - Exhibitions. I.
Fondazione Lerici. II. Palazzo reale di Milano. III.
Title.
DG70.C12 E88 1980
NYPL [3-MPEK 89-13643]

**CIVICHE RACCOLTE NUMISMATICHE DI
MILANO.**
Civiche raccolte numismatiche di Milano. Gli
Etruschi e Cerveteri . Milano , c1980. 267 p. :
DDC 937/.5 19
DG70.C12 E88 1980
NYPL [3-MPEK 89-13643]

Civici musei di Reggio Emilia (Italy) Plessi,
Fabrizio, 1940- Plessi /. Treviso , c1990. 175

p. :   ISBN 88-85066-70-4   DDC 700/.92 20
N6923.P55 A4 1990
NYPL [3-MGO+ (Plessi) 91-5437]

Civico museo del castello (Gorizia, Italy) Trionfo
barocco . [Monfalcone] [1990] 265 p. :   ISBN
88-85296-00-9   DDC 759.04/6/07445392 20
ND182.B3 T75 1990

**CIVIL ENGINEERING - MANAGEMENT. see
ENGINEERING - MANAGEMENT.**

The Civil War . Abell, Sam. Charlottesville, Va. ,
c1990. 144 p. :   ISBN 0-934738-61-0 :   DDC
779/.99737 20
E468.7 .A23 1990
NYPL [MFX+ (Abell) 91-2378]

The Civil War in motion pictures. United States.
Library of Congress. Stack and Reader
Division. Washington, 1961. vi, 109 p.
NYPL [IK 74-921]

Civil War photographs [microform] : a selection
from negatives in the Mathew B. Brady
Collection in the Prints and Photographs
Division of the Library of Congress.
[Washington, D.C. : Library of Congress, 1961]
5 v. : chiefly ill., ports. Microfilm. Washington,
D.C. : Library of Congress Photoduplication Service,
1961. 2 microfilm reels ; 35 mm. CONTENTS. - pt. 1.
The main Eastern Theater of War -- pt. 2. The Federal
Navy, and seaborne expeditions against the Atlantic
coastline of the Confederacy -- pt. 3. The war in the
West -- pt. 4. Washington, 1863-1865 -- pt. 5. Portraits.
1. United States - History - Civil War, 1861-1865 -
Pictorial works. I. Brady, Mathew B., 1823 (ca.)-1896.
II. Library of Congress. Prints and Photographs
Division.   *NYPL [*ZM-232]*

**CIVIL WAR - UNITED STATES. see UNITED
STATES - HISTORY - CIVIL WAR, 1861-
1865.**

Civiltà medievale.
Quintavalle, Arturo Carlo, 1936- Benedetto
Antelami /. Milano , c1990. 384 p. :
NYPL [3-MGO+ (Antelami) 90-12881]

**Civilization, American. see United States -
Civilization.**

CIVILIZATION, ANCIENT - CHRONOLOGY.
Centuries of darkness . London , 1991. xxii,
434 p., [8] p. of plates :   ISBN 0-224-02647-X :
DDC 930 20
CB311   *NYPL [JFE 91-4489]*

**CIVILIZATION, ESTRUSCAN. see
ETRUSCANS.**

**CIVILIZATION, SPANISH. see SPAIN -
CIVILIZATION.**

Civiltà medievale.
Bornstein, Christine Verzár. Portals and politics
in the early Italian city-state . [Parma] [1988]
175 p. :
NYPL [3-MGO+ (Niccoló) 90-10768]
Quintavalle, Arturo Carlo. Benedetto Antelami
/. Milano , c1990. 384 p. :   ISBN 88-435-3176-X
DDC 730/.92 20
NB623.A6 A4 1990

Civiltà siciliana.
(1) Bellafiore, Giuseppe. Architettura in Sicilia
nelle età islamica e normanna . Milano , c1990.
366 p. :   ISBN 88-7177-010-2 :
NYPL [3-MQO 91-3372]

Cladders, Johannes.
Ettl, Georg, 1940- Georg Ettl, Arbeiten
1968-1989 =. Düsseldorf , 1990. 102 p. :
ISBN 3-925974-14-8
NYPL [3-MGO (ETTL) 91-4445]
Fisher, Joel. Ein unwiderruflicher Schritt =.
[s.l. , 1975?] (Mönchengladbach : H.
Schlechtriem) 48 p. :
N6537.F48 A58
NYPL [3-MCX F532 81-643]

Claer, Vera von. Museum für Kunst und Gewerbe
Hamburg. Antiker Gold- und Silberschmuck .
Mainz am Rhein , c1968. x, 246 p. :
NK7307 .H6   *NYPL [3-MNR 90-7024]*

Claes Oldenburg . Oldenburg, Claes, 1929- New
York , 1991. p.   ISBN 0-8478-1335-5   DDC 709/.2
20
NB237.O42 A4 1991

**Claes Oldenburg, large-scale projects,
1977-1980** . Oldenburg, Claes, 1929- New

York , 1980. 100 p. :   ISBN 0-8478-0351-1 (pbk.)
NB237.O42 A4 1980
NYPL [MGO (Oldenburg) 81-267]

Clair, Jean. Brève défense de l'art français :
1945-1968 / Jean Clair. [Caen] : l'Echoppe,
c1989. 69 p. ; 19 cm.   ISBN 2-905657-46-4   DDC
709/.44/09045 20
1. Art, French. 2. Art, Modern - 20th century - France.
I. Title.
N6848 .C56 1989

Clair, Jean, 1940- The 1920s . Montreal, Quebec,
Canada , c1991. 638 p. :   ISBN 2-89192-139-9
NYPL [3-MAL+ 91-7585]

Claire Nicole . Acatos, Sylvio. Lausanne , c1988.
88 p. :   *NYPL [3-MCZ N642 89-27917]*

Claisse, Geneviève, 1935-
Geneviève Claisse : parcours 1960-1989 :
Musée Matisse, Le Cateau-Cambrésis,
exposition, 22 avril-18 juin 1989. Le
Cateau-Cambrésis : Le Musée, [1989] 95 p. : ill.
(some col.) ; 27 cm.   ISBN 2-907545-08-6
1. Claisse, Geneviève, 1935- - Exhibitions. I. Musée
Matisse (Le Cateau-Cambrésis, France). II. Title.
MLCM 90/03414 (N)
NYPL [3-MCO C585 91-7060]

**CLAISSE, GENEVIÈVE, 1935- -
EXHIBITIONS.**
Claisse, Geneviève, 1935- Geneviève Claisse .
Le Cateau-Cambrésis [1989] 95 p. :   ISBN
2-907545-08-6
MLCM 90/03414 (N)
NYPL [3-MCO C585 91-7060]

Clancy, Judith S.
Judith Clancy : Paris vivant, le point de vue
d'une Américaine : dessins et collages : Musée
Carnavalet, 25 avril-6 juillet 1986. [Paris] :
Musées de la ville de Paris, c1986. 71 p. : ill.
(some col.) ; 24 cm. French and English.   ISBN
2-901414-19-2
1. Clancy, Judith S. - Exhibitions. 2. Paris (France) in
art - Exhibitions. I. Musée Carnavalet. II. Title.
NYPL [3-MCX C587 88-2596]

CLANCY, JUDITH S. - EXHIBITIONS.
Clancy, Judith S. Judith Clancy . [Paris] ,
c1986. 71 p. :   ISBN 2-901414-19-2
NYPL [3-MCX C587 88-2596]

Clapp, James A. Stofflet, Mary. California
cityscapes /. New York, NY , c1991. p. cm.
ISBN 0-87663-614-8   DDC
704.9/44794/0979409048 20
N8214.5.U6 S76 1991

Clara . Mairs, Clara, 1878-1963. St. Paul, Minn. ,
c1976. 47 p. :
NYPL [MDG (Mairs) 90-5656]

Clare, John, 1793-1864. Hanscomb, Brian. Sun,
sea & earth /. Andoversford, Gloucestershire ,
1989. [21] p. :   ISBN 1-85428-004-X   DDC 769.92
20
NE642.H34 A4 1989

Clarence John Laughlin . Davis, Keith F., 1952-
Kansas City, Mo. , c1990. 166 p. :   ISBN
0-87529-629-7
NYPL [MFX+ (Laughlin) 91-7437]

Clarendon studies in the history of art.
Borsook, Eve. Messages in mosaic . Oxford
[Oxfordshire] , New York , 1990. xxiv, 112 p.,
[126] p. of plates :   ISBN 0-19-817504-3 :   DDC
729/.7/09458 19
NA3792.N67 B67 1988
NYPL [3-MRXZ 90-11788]

Clarice Smith . Smith, Clarice, 1933- New York,
NY , c1991. 1 v. (unpaged) :
NYPL [3-MCX s643 91-5152]

Clark, Carol, 1947- Prendergast, Maurice Brazil,
1858-1924. Maurice Brazil Prendergast, Charles
Prendergast . Williamstown, MA , Munich,
Germany , 1990. 811 p. :   ISBN 3-7913-0965-X
(Prestel)   DDC 760/.092 20
N6537.P68 A4 1989a
NYPL [MCX+ P92 90-10787]

CLARK COUNTY (ILL.) - MAPS.
Rockford Map Publishers. Clark County,
Illinois, land atlas & plat book . Rockford, Ill. ,
Marshall, Ill. [c1991] 1 atlas (34 p.) :
NYPL [Map Div. 91-4674]

Clark County, Illinois, land atlas & plat book .
Rockford Map Publishers. Rockford, Ill. ,
Marshall, Ill. [c1991] 1 atlas (34 p.) :
NYPL [Map Div. 91-4674]

Clark, Douglas. Articles of faith / Douglas Clark. Toronto : Coach House Press, c1990. 18 [i.e. 46] p. : col. ill. ; 32 x 11 cm. ISBN 0-88910-343-7 : DDC 709/.2 20
1. Clark, Douglas. 2. Artists' books - Canada. I. Title.
NYPL [MEMZ+ 91-7485]

CLARK, DOUGLAS.
Clark, Douglas. Articles of faith /. Toronto , c1990. 18 [i.e. 46] p. : ISBN 0-88910-343-7 : DDC 709/.2 20
NYPL [MEMZ+ 91-7485]

Clark, Eliot Candee, 1883-
Eliot Clark (1883-1980) . New York, N.Y. [1990] 53 p. :
MLCM 90/01921 (N)
NYPL [3-MCX C592 91-7404]

CLARK, ELIOT CANDEE, 1883- - EXHIBITIONS.
Eliot Clark (1883-1980) . New York, N.Y. [1990] 53 p. :
MLCM 90/01921 (N)
NYPL [3-MCX C592 91-7404]

Clark, Janet E. Frances Anne Hopkins, 1838-1919 : Canadian scenery = le paysage canadien / by Janet E. Clark, Robert H. Stacey. Thunder Bay, Ont. : Thunder Bay Art Gallery, 1989. 112 p. : ill., (some col.) ; 28 cm. Catalogue of an exhibition held at the Thunder Bay Art Gallery, 27 January-18 March 1990, and travelling to other galleries. Text in English and French. Includes bibliographical references (p. 108-110). ISBN 0-920539-30-0 : DDC 759.11 20
1. Hopkins, Frances Anne, 1838-1919 - Exhibitions. I. Stacey, R. H. (Robert H.). II. Hopkins, Frances Anne, 1838-1919. III. Thunder Bay Art Gallery. IV. Title.
NYPL [3-MCV H762 90-10799]

Clark, Kenneth, 1903-
National Gallery (Great Britain) 100 details from pictures in the National Gallery /. London , Cambridge, Mass. , 1990. ix, 109 p. : ISBN 0-674-63862-X (cloth) : DDC 759.94 20
ND1143 .N37 1991

National Gallery (Great Britain) 100 details from pictures in the National Gallery /. London , Cambridge, Mass. , 1990. ix, 109 p. : ISBN 0-674-63862-X (cloth) : DDC 759.94 20
ND1143 .N37 1991
NYPL [MAVZ (London) 91-5241]

Clark, Patch. Intergenerational arts in the nursing home : a handbook / Patch Clark. New York : Greenwood Press, 1991. p. cm. Includes bibliographical references and index. ISBN 0-313-25965-8 (alk. paper) DDC 362.1/6 20
1. Arts and the aged - United States. 2. Nursing homes - United States - Recreational activities. I. Title.
NX180.A35 C5 1991

Clark, Phillip Evans. Nazor, Maria. Maria Nazor . New York (155 Spring St., New York, 10012) , c1989. 1 v. (unpaged) :
NYPL [3-MCX N295 90-12014]

Clark, Ricky. Quilts in community : Ohio's traditions / Ricky Clark, George W. Knepper, and Ellice Ronsheim ; edited by Ricky Clark ; with the support of American Association for State and Local History ... [et al.]. Nashville, Tenn. : Rutledge Hill Press, c1991. p. cm. Includes bibliographical references and index. ISBN 1-558-53101-7 : DDC 746.9/7/09771 20
1. Quilts - Ohio - History. 2. Quiltmakers - Ohio - Biography. I. Knepper, George W., 1926-. II. Ronsheim, Ellice, 1951-. III. American Association for State and Local History. IV. Title.
NK9112 .C555 1991

CLARK, ROLAND, 1874-1957.
Ordeman, John T. To keep a tryst with the dawn . Henderson, N.C. , 1989. 118 p. : ISBN 0-9610638-3-1 (regular ed.)
NYPL [MDG (Clark) 90-11343]

Clark, Timothy. Smith, Lawrence. Japanese art . Bloomsbury , c1990. 256 p. : ISBN 0-7141-1446-4 : DDC 709/.52/074 19
N7350
NYPL [3-MAG 90-11503]

Clark, Willene B. The stained glass art of William Jay Bolton / Willene B. Clark ; photographs by Leland A. Cook. 1st ed. Syracuse, N.Y. : Syracuse University Press, 1992. p. cm. Includes bibliographical references and index. ISBN 0-8156-2553-7 DDC 748.5913 20
1. Bolton, William Jay, 1816?-1884 - Criticism and interpretation. 2. Glass painting and staining - United

States - History - 19th century. I. Title.
NK5398.B65 C53 1992

Clark, William W., 1940-
Herschman, Joel, 1936- Un voyage héliographique à faire . [S.l. , 1981] 37 p. : DDC 779/.4/0740147243 19
DC20 .H47
NYPL [MFW 91-8054]

Radding, Charles. Medieval architecture, medieval learning . New Haven, CT , c1991. p. cm. ISBN 0-300-04918-8 (alk. paper) DDC 723/.4 20
NA390 .R33 1991

Clark, C. Michael. Whitworth Art Gallery. Pollaiuolo to Picasso . Manchester [1980] [1], 36 p., [38] p. of plates : ISBN 0-903261-13-8 (pbk.)
NE45.G7 M348
NYPL [MDET 81-1029]

CLARKE COUNTY (VA.) - MAPS.
ADC (Firm) Clarke County, Va. street map. Alexandria, Va. , c1987. 1 atlas (iii, 15 p.) : ISBN 0-87530-029-4 : DDC 912/.75598 19
G1293.C6 A36 1987
NYPL [Map Div. 91-2437]

Clarke County, Va. street map. ADC (Firm) Alexandria, Va. , c1987. 1 atlas (iii, 15 p.) : ISBN 0-87530-029-4 : DDC 912/.75598 19
G1293.C6 A36 1987
NYPL [Map Div. 91-2437]

Clarke, David, 1942- Frank Lloyd Wright and the Laffer curve : essays on architecture and education / by David S. Clarke. Wakefield, N.H. : Longwood Academic, 1991. p. cm. ISBN 0-89341-655-X DDC 720/.71/173 20
1. Architecture - Study and teaching - United States. 2. Educational evaluation - United States. I. Title.
NA2105 .C58 1991

Clarke, Ethne. The gardens of Tuscany / text by Ethne Clarke ; photographs by Raffaello Bencini. London : Weidenfeld & Nicolson, 1990. 160 p. : col. ill. ; 20 x 26 cm. Includes bibliographical references (p. 157) and index. ISBN 0-297-83044-9 :
1. Gardens - Tuscany Region. 2. Gardens - Tuscany Region - History. I. Title.
NYPL [3-MSK 91-3390]

Clarke, John R., 1945- The houses of Roman Italy, 100 B.C.-A.D. 250 : ritual, space, and decoration / John R. Clarke. Berkeley : University of California Press, c1991. p. cm. Includes bibliographical references and index. ISBN 0-520-07267-7 (alk. paper) DDC 728/.0937 20
1. Architecture, Roman - Italy. 2. Architecture, Domestic - Italy. 3. Mural painting and decoration, Roman - Italy. 4. Mural painting and decoration - Italy. 5. Mosaics, Roman - Italy. 6. Mosaics - Italy. I. Title.
NA324 .C57 1991

Clarke, Michael, 1952- Corot and the art of landscape / Michael Clarke. 1st American ed. New York : Cross River Press, c1991. p. cm. Includes bibliographical references and index. ISBN 1-558-59223-7 DDC 759.4 20
1. Corot, Jean-Baptiste Camille, 1796-1875 - Criticism and interpretation. I. Title.
ND553.C8 C5 1991

Classic plastic : a look at design, 1950-1974 : 17 November-21 December 1989. London : Fischer Fine Art, [1989] 36 p. : ill. ; 20 x 22 cm. Essay by Nigel Whiteley. Bibliography: p. 35.
1. Plastics - Exhibitions. 2. Design - History - 20th century - Exhibitions. I. Whiteley, Nigel. II. Fischer Fine Art Limited.
NYPL [3-MNF 91-7530]

Classic plastic radios of the 1930s and 1940s . Sideli, John. New York , c1990. 127 p. : ISBN 0-525-24608-8 (cloth)
NYPL [3-MNF 91-6800]

CLASSICAL ANTIQUITIES.
De Carolis, Ernesto. Lucerne greche e romane /. Roma , 1982. 84 p. : DDC 738.8 19
DE61.L34 D43 1982
NYPL [3-MNHL 90-6882]

CLASSICAL ANTIQUITIES - ADDRESSES, ESSAYS, LECTURES.
Studies in classical art and archaeology . Locust Valley, N.Y. , 1979. xiv, 344 p., [45] leaves of plates : DDC 709/.38
N5613 .S88
NYPL [MAH 79-1946]

CLASSICAL ARCHAEOLOGY. see CLASSICAL ANTIQUITIES.

CLASSICAL ART. see ART, CLASSICAL.

CLASSICAL GEOGRAPHY - MAPS.
Atlas of classical history /. London , New York , c1985, 1988. 1 atlas (217 p.) : ISBN 0-415-03463-9 (pbk.)
NYPL [Map Div. 91-5122]

Classical handbook .
(3) Krzyszkowska, O. (Olga) Ivory and related materials . London , 1990. xv, 109 p., [70] p. of plates : ISBN 0-900587-62-8
NYPL [3-MNW 91-7005]

CLASSICAL MARBLE SCULPTURE. see MARBLE SCULPTURE, CLASSICAL.

Classicism and history . Lukkarinen, Ville. Helsinki , 1989. 196 p. : ISBN 951-9056-90-4
NYPL [3-MQZ+ (Ahrenberg) 91-5470]

CLASSICISM IN ARCHITECTURE.
New classicism . London , 1990. 264 p. : ISBN 1-85490-028-5 (HB)
NYPL [3-MQV+ 91-3315]

CLASSICISM IN ARCHITECTURE - ALABAMA.
Palladio in Alabama . Montgomery, Ala. , 1991. p. cm. ISBN 0-89280-029-1 DDC 720/.9761/07476147 20
NA730.A2 P3 1991

CLASSICISM IN ART.
Howard, Seymour, 1928- Antiquity restored . Vienna , 1990. 344 p. : ISBN 3-900731-11-X
NYPL [3-MAH 91-4921]

CLASSICISM IN ART - CATALOGS.
Hollanda, Francisco de, 1517-1584. Album dos desenhos das antigualhas de Francisco de Holanda /. Lisboa , c1989. 54, 54, 73 p., [5] folded leaves of plates : ISBN 972-240-733-3 DDC 741.9469 20
NC290.H65 A4 1989

CLASSICISM IN ART - EXHIBITIONS.
Winner, Matthias, 1931- Zeichner sehen die Antike. Berlin-Dahlem [1967] 134 p. DDC 741/.094
NC225 .W5
NYPL [3-MBH 91-1293]

CLASSICISM IN ART - FRANCE.
Carrier, David, 1944- Poussin's paintings /. University Park, Pa. , c1992. p. cm. ISBN 0-271-00816-4 DDC 759.4 20
ND553.P8 C35 1992

The French Academy . Newark : London ; 231 p. : ISBN 0-87413-343-2 (alk. paper) DDC 706/.044 19
N332.F83 P345 1990
NYPL [3-MAMI 90-11304]

Lichtenstein, Jacqueline. [Couleur éloquente. English.] The eloquence of color . Berkeley , 1992. p. cm. ISBN 0-520-06907-2 DDC 759.4/09/032 20
ND546 .L6613 1992

Mérot, Alain. Poussin /. Paris , c1990. 330 p. : ISBN 2-85025-220-4 DDC 759.4 B 20
ND553.P8 M44 1990

Weyl, Martin. Passion for reason and reason of passion . New York , c1989. 314 p. ; ISBN 0-8204-0981-2 : DDC 709.44/09/032 20
N6846 .W49 1989
NYPL [3-MAMI 91-6906]

CLASSICISM IN ART - FRANCE - EXHIBITIONS.
Syndram, Dirk. Ruinenromantik und Antikensehnsucht /. [Berlin] , c1986. 32 p. : ISBN 3-88609-199-6 DDC 760/.0444/094074031554 19
N8237.8.R8 S96 1986
NYPL [3-MAMZ 90-9452]

Verdi, Richard. Cézanne and Poussin . London , c1990. 202 p. : ISBN 0-85331-569-8 DDC 759.4 20
N6853.P66 A4 1990

CLASSICISM IN ART - FRANCE - LANGRES.
Ronot, Henry. Richard et Jean Tassel . Paris , 1990. xv, 367 p., [103] p. of plates : ISBN 2-7233-0409-2
ND553.T32 R66 1990

CLASSICISM IN ART - FRANCE - VERSAILLES.
Pérouse de Montclos, Jean-Marie. [Versailles. English.] Versailles /. New York , 1991. p. cm. ISBN 1-558-59228-8 DDC 725/.17/0944366 20
NA7736.V5 P4713 1991

CLASSICISM IN ART - GERMANY.
Hampel, Frithjof Detlev Paul. Schinkels
Möbelwerk und seine Voraussetzungen /.
Witterschlick/Bonn , 1989. 255 p., [8] p. of
plates : ISBN 3-925267-29-8
NK2554.S35 H35 1989

**CLASSICISM IN ART - ITALY -
EXHIBITIONS.**
Syndram, Dirk. Ruinenromantik und
Antikensehnsucht /. [Berlin] , c1986. 32 p. :
ISBN 3-88609-199-6 DDC
760/.0444/094074031554 19
N8237.8.R8 S96 1986
        NYPL [3-MAMZ 90-9452]

Classicismo d'età Romana . Ajello, Raffaele.
Napoli , c1988. 203 p. : ISBN 88-7042-955-5
        NYPL [3-MGH+ 90-10570]

Classiques de la Manufacture.
Masson, André 1896- Les années surréalistes .
Paris , c1990. 574 p., [52] p. of plates (some
col.) : ISBN 2-7377-0181-3 : DDC 759.4 B 20
ND553.M36 A3 1990

**Classiques du XXe siècle (Musée national d'art
moderne (France))**
Magnelli, Alberto, 1888-1971. Magnelli /.
Paris , c1989. 290 p. ; ISBN 2-85850-539-X
(reliée)   *NYPL [3-MCF M225 90-12855]*

[Classiques du XXe siècle], 0760-5153.
Magnelli, Alberto, 1888-1971. Magnelli . Paris ,
c1989. 290 p. : ISBN 2-85850-539-X DDC
709/.2 20
N6923.M235 A4 1989

Classiques du XXIe siècle .
(1) Cabanne, Pierre. Jean Fautrier /. Paris ,
c1988. 167 p. : ISBN 2-7291-0346-5 DDC 759.4
20
ND553.F36 A4 1988

Claude Bernard Gallery. Kupka, František,
1871-1957. Kupka . New York , c1990. 63 p. :
ISBN 0-936827-19-X
IN PROCESS (ONLINE)
        NYPL [3-MCZ K965 91-6305]

**Claude Lorrain und die Meister der römischen
Landschaft im XVII Jahrhundert .** Graphische
Sammlung Albertina. [Wien, 1965] xv, 187 p. :
        NYPL [3-MBH 91-1175]

Claude Monet /. Waldron, Ann. New York ,
1991. p. cm. ISBN 0-8109-3620-8 (cloth) DDC
759.4 B 20
ND553.M7 W24 1991

Claude Monet-Auguste Rodin : centenaire de
l'exposition de 1889 : [exposition] 14 novembre
1989-21 janvier 1990. Paris : Musée Rodin,
[1989] 241 p. : ill. (some col.) ; 28 cm. Includes
bibliographical references. ISBN 2-901428-25-8
*1. Monet, Claude, 1840-1926 - Exhibitions. 2. Rodin,
Auguste, 1840-1917 - Exhibitions. I. Monet, Claude,
1840-1926. II. Musée Rodin.*
        NYPL [3-MCO M74 90-11787]

Claude-Nicolas Ledoux . Vidler, Anthony.
Cambridge, Mass. , c1990. 446 p. : ISBN
0-262-22032-6 DDC 720/.92 20
NA1053.L4 V5 1990
        NYPL [3-MQZ+ (Ledoux) 90-11790]

Claude to Corot : the development of landscape
painting in France / edited by Alan
Wintermute ; essays by Michael Kitson ... [et
al.]. New York : Colnaghi ; Seattle : In
association with the University of Washington
Press, c1990. 289 p. : ill. (some col.) ; 24 x 27
cm. "Catalogue accompanies an exhibition held at
Colnaghi from November 1 through December 15,
1990"--T.p. verso. Includes bibliographical references
and index. ISBN 0-295-97086-3 DDC
758/.1/09440747471 20
*1. Landscape painting, French - Exhibitions. 2.
Landscape painting - 17th century - France -
Exhibitions. 3. Landscape painting - 18th century -
France - Exhibitions. 4. Landscape painting - 19th
century - France - Exhibitions. I. Wintermute, Alan. II.
Kitson, Michael. III. Colnaghi (Gallery).*
ND1356.3 .C58 1990
        NYPL [3-MCN 91-5076]

Claude Vasconi, 1980-1990 /. Joffroy, Pascale.
Paris , c1990. 166 p. : ISBN 2-86653-084-5
DDC 720/.92 20
NA1053.V37 J64 1990

Claudel, Camille, 1864-1943.
C. Claudel : Fondation Pierre Gianadda,
Martigny, Suisse, 16 novembre 1990-24 février

1991 / commissaire de l'exposition, Nicole
Barbier.3e éd. Martigny, Suisse : La Fondation,
c1990. 167 p. : ill. ; 24 cm.
*1. Claudel, Camille, 1864-1943 - Exhibitions. I.
Fondation Pierre-Gianadda. II. Title.*
        NYPL [3-MGO (Claudel) 91-7335]

C. Claudel : Fondation Pierre Gianadda,
Martigny, Suisse : 16 novembre 1990-24 février
1991 / commissaire de l'exposition, Nicole
Barbier.3e éd. Martigny, Suisse : La Fondation,
c1990. 167 p. : ill. (some col.) ; 24 cm. Includes
bibliographical references (p. 158). DDC 730/.92 20
*1. Claudel, Camille, 1864-1943 - Exhibitions. I. Barbier,
Nicole. II. Fondation Pierre-Gianadda. III. Title.*
NB553.C44 A4 1990b

Paris, Reine-Marie. L'œuvre de Camille
Claudel . Paris , c1990. 303 p. : ISBN
2-87660-088-9 DDC 709/.2 20
NB553.C44 A4 1990

Paris, Reine-Marie. L'œuvre de Camille
Claudel . Paris , c1991. 303 p. : ISBN
2-87660-088-9
        NYPL [3-MGO+ (Claudel) 91-5643]

**CLAUDEL, CAMILLE, 1864-1943 -
CATALOGUES RAISONNÉS.**
Paris, Reine-Marie. L'œuvre de Camille
Claudel . Paris , c1990. 303 p. : ISBN
2-87660-088-9 DDC 709/.2 20
NB553.C44 A4 1990

Paris, Reine-Marie. L'œuvre de Camille
Claudel . Paris , c1991. 303 p. : ISBN
2-87660-088-9
        NYPL [3-MGO+ (Claudel) 91-5643]

**CLAUDEL, CAMILLE, 1864-1943 -
EXHIBITIONS.**
Claudel, Camille, 1864-1943. C. Claudel .
Martigny, Suisse , c1990. 167 p. :
        NYPL [3-MGO (Claudel) 91-7335]

Claudel, Camille, 1864-1943. C. Claudel .
Martigny, Suisse , c1990. 167 p. : DDC 730/.92
20
NB553.C44 A4 1990b

Cláudio, Mário. Emerenciano, ou, O teor das
actas / Mário Cláudio. Lisboa : Impr.
Nacional-Casa da Moeda, 1989. 115 p. : ill.
(some col.) ; 24 cm. (Colecção Arte e artistas)
Includes bibliographical references (p. 109-115).
*1. Rodrigues, Emerenciano da Silva, 1946- - Catalogs. I.
Rodrigues, Emerenciano da Silva, 1946-. II. Title. III.
Series.*
ND833.R63 A4 1989

Claus Sluter, artist at the Court of Burgundy /.
Morand, Kathleen. Austin , 1991. 399 p., 8 p.
of plates : ISBN 0-292-71117-4
        NYPL [3-MGO (Sluter) 91-6518]

Claus Weidensdorfer . Weidensdorfer, Claus,
1931- [Leipzig] [1989?] 95 p. : ISBN
3-86060-007-9 DDC 769.92 20
NE654.W39 A4 1989

CLAUSELLS, RICARD, 1864-1939.
Bosch i Planas, Joan, 1951- Ricard Clausells, el
pintor i el poeta, 1864-1939 /. Vilafranca del
Penedès , 1990. 141 p. :
IN PROCESS (ONLINE)
        NYPL [3-MCQ C616 91-4303]

Clausen, Rosemarie. Begegnungen. 21 Fotos nach
Totenmasken. Köln, Du Mont Schauberg c1967.
21 leaves of plates illus. 31 cm. Issued in case.
1. Clausen, Rosemarie. 2. Masks (Sculpture). I. Title.
NB1310 .C58
        NYPL [3-MGO (Clausen) 90-6801]

CLAUSEN, ROSEMARIE.
Clausen, Rosemarie. Begegnungen. Köln, c1967.
21 leaves of plates
NB1310 .C58
        NYPL [3-MGO (Clausen) 90-6801]

Clavé /. Cabanne, Pierre. Paris [1990] 381 p. :
ISBN 2-7291-0602-2 DDC 709/.2 20
N7113.C57 A4 1990

Clavé /. Seghers, Pierre. Paris , 1989. 423 p. :
ISBN 2-7022-0239-X DDC 709/.2 B 20
N7113.C57 S4 1989

Clavé, Antoni, 1913-
Antoni Clavé, exposició retrospectiva : Palau
Robert, Passeig de Gràcia, 107, del 18 de gener
al 28 de febrer, Barcelona 1989. 1a ed.
[Barcelona] : Generalitat de Catalunya,
Departament de Cultura, 1990. 95 p. : ill. ; 30
cm.

*1. Clavé, Antoni, 1913- - Exhibitions. I. Palau Robert
(Barcelona, Spain). II. Title.*
IN PROCESS (ONLINE)
        NYPL [3-MCQ+ C617 91-5882]

Cabanne, Pierre. Clavé /. Paris [1990] 381 p. :
ISBN 2-7291-0602-2 DDC 709/.2 20
N7113.C57 A4 1990

Permanyer, L. Clavé, escultor /. Barcelona,
España , c1989. 286 p. : ISBN 84-343-0557-7
        NYPL [3-MGO+ (Clavé) 90-605]

Seghers, Pierre. Clavé /. Paris , 1989. 423 p. :
ISBN 2-7022-0239-X DDC 709/.2 B 20
N7113.C57 S4 1989

CLAVÉ, ANTONI, 1913-
Seghers, Pierre. Clavé /. Paris , 1989. 423 p. :
ISBN 2-7022-0239-X DDC 709/.2 B 20
N7113.C57 S4 1989

CLAVÉ, ANTONI, 1913- - CATALOGS.
Cabanne, Pierre. Clavé /. Paris [1990] 381 p. :
ISBN 2-7291-0602-2 DDC 709/.2 20
N7113.C57 A4 1990

**CLAVÉ, ANTONI, 1913- - CRITICISM AND
INTERPRETATION.**
Permanyer, L. Clavé, escultor /. Barcelona,
España , c1989. 286 p. : ISBN 84-343-0557-7
        NYPL [3-MGO+ (Clavé) 90-605]

CLAVÉ, ANTONI, 1913- - EXHIBITIONS.
Clavé, Antoni, 1913- Antoni Clavé, exposició
retrospectiva . [Barcelona] , 1990. 95 p. :
IN PROCESS (ONLINE)
        NYPL [3-MCQ+ C617 91-5882]

Clavé, escultor /. Permanyer, L. Barcelona,
España , c1989. 286 p. : ISBN 84-343-0557-7
        NYPL [3-MGO+ (Clavé) 90-605]

Clay, Steve. (ill) Historic Blacks in the arts /.
Chicago, IL , c1990. p. cm. ISBN
0-922162-58-1 : DDC 700/.92/2 B 20
NX164.B55 H57 1990

Clay today . Los Angeles County Museum of Art.
Los Angeles, Calif. , San Francisco, Calif. ,
c1990. 239 p. : ISBN 0-87701-756-5 (Chronicle
Books) : DDC 730/.0973/07479494 20
NK4008 .L67 1990
        NYPL [3-MPH+ 90-11630]

Clayson, Hollis, 1946- Painted love : prostitution
in French art of the impressionist era / Hollis
Clayson. New Haven : Yale University Press,
c1991. p. cm. Includes bibliographical references and
index. ISBN 0-300-04730-4 DDC
760/.0449306742/094436109034 20
*1. Impressionism (Art) - France. 2. Prostitution in art.
3. Art, French. 4. Art, Modern - 19th century - France.
I. Title.*
N6847.5.I4 C58 1991

**Cleartype® commercial atlas of the United
States.** American Map Company, inc., New
York. New York. New York [198-?] [58] leaves :
        NYPL [Map Div. 85-883]

CLEARWATER COUNTY, MINN. - MAPS.
(1990) Rockford Map Publishers. Clearwater
County, Minnesota, land atlas & plat book .
Rockford, Ill. , Bagley, Minn. [c1990] 1 atlas
(51 p.) :   *NYPL [Map Div. 90-11387]*

**Clearwater County, Minnesota, land atlas & plat
book .** Rockford Map Publishers. Rockford,
Ill. , Bagley, Minn. [c1990] 1 atlas (51 p.) :
        NYPL [Map Div. 90-11387]

Clébert, Jean Paul. Femmes d'artistes / Jean-Paul
Clébert. Paris : Presses de la Renaissance,
c1989. 415 p. ; 23 cm. Includes bibliographical
references and index. ISBN 2-85616-499-4 :
*1. Artists - Relationship with women. 2. Artists -
Psychology. 3. Artists' wives - Psychology. 4. Arts. I.
Title.*
NX165 .C6 1989

Clegg & Guttmann : corporate landscapes.
[Bremerhaven] : Kunstverein Bremerhaven ;
Velbert-Neviges : Museum Schloss Hardenberg,
1989. 73 p. : ill. ; 29 cm. Exhibition catalog.
English and German. ISBN 3-926133-17-1
*1. Clegg, Michael, 1957- - Exhibitions. 2. Guttmann,
Martin, 1957- - Exhibitions. 3. Photography -
Landscapes - Exhibitions. I. Kunstverein Bremerhaven.
II. Städtische Museen Schloss Hardenberg.*
        NYPL [MFW+ 91-2570]

CLEGG, MICHAEL, 1957- - EXHIBITIONS.
Clegg & Guttmann . [Bremerhaven] ,
Velbert-Neviges , 1989. 73 p. : ISBN
3-926133-17-1   *NYPL [MFW+ 91-2570]*

Clemens-Sels-Museum. Neuhaus, Josef, 1923-
Josef Neuhaus, Plastiken und Reliefs . Neuss ,
1988. 77 p. :
NYPL [3-MGO (Neuhaus) 89-25259]

Clemente, Francesco, 1952-
Francesco Clemente : Testa coda / introduction
by Dieter Koepplin ; essay and interview by
Michael McClure. New York : Gagosian
Gallery in association with Rizzoli, 1991. p. cm.
Includes bibliographical references. ISBN
0-8478-1469-6 DDC 759.5 20
*1. Clemente, Francesco, 1952- - Themes, motives. I.
McClure, Michael. II. Gagosian Gallery. III. Title. IV.
Title: Testa coda.*
ND1962.C58 A4 1991

Percy, Ann. Francesco Clemente . Philadelphia,
Pa. , New York , 1990. 184, [1] p. : ISBN
0-87633-084-7 (Philadelphia Museum) DDC
709/.2 20
NC257.C575 A4 1990
NYPL [3-MCF+ C621 91-3673]

**CLEMENTE, FRANCESCO, 1952- - THEMES,
MOTIVES.**
Clemente, Francesco, 1952- Francesco
Clemente . New York , 1991. p. cm. ISBN
0-8478-1469-6 DDC 759.5 20
ND1962.C58 A4 1991

**CLEMENTE, FRANCESCO, 1952- -
EXHIBITIONS.**
Percy, Ann. Francesco Clemente . Philadelphia,
Pa. , New York , 1990. 184, [1] p. : ISBN
0-87633-084-7 (Philadelphia Museum) DDC
709/.2 20
NC257.C575 A4 1990
NYPL [3-MCF+ C621 91-3673]

Clemente Ochoa, escultor /. Clemente Ochoa,
Manuel. Barcelona , 1990. 156 p. : ISBN
84-7665-654-8 *NYPL [3-MGO (Clemente
Ochoa) 91-5687]*

Clemente Ochoa, Manuel. Clemente Ochoa,
escultor / introducció de José Luis Aranguren ;
i textos de Ángel Aguirre Baztán. 1. ed.
Barcelona : PPU, 1990. 156 p. : ill. ; 29 cm.
Catalan, English, French and Spanish. ISBN
84-7665-654-8
1. Clemente Ochoa, Manuel. I. Title.
*NYPL [3-MGO (Clemente Ochoa)
91-5687]*

CLEMENTE OCHOA, MANUEL.
Clemente Ochoa, Manuel. Clemente Ochoa,
escultor /. Barcelona , 1990. 156 p. : ISBN
84-7665-654-8 *NYPL [3-MGO (Clemente
Ochoa) 91-5687]*

Clemente, Pietro. L'abbigliamento popolare
italiano /. Brescia [1986] 160 p. :
NYPL [3-MMO 90-8664]

Clercq, M. de (Louis), 1836-1901. Louis de
Clercq : "Voyage en Orient" / herausgegeben
von Rolf Mayer ; [Übersetzung
Englisch-Französisch durch Geneviève Chapuis,
Isabelle Seguela und Elisabeth Galloy ;
Übersetzung Englisch-Deutsch durch Katharina
Feil, Gabriele Glöckler und Astrid
Rotzler-Lung]. Stuttgart-Bad Cannstatt : Edition
Cantz, c1989. 111 p. : ill. ; 25 x 32 cm. German,
English and French. ISBN 3-89322-163-8
*1. Middle East - Description and travel - Views. I.
Title. II. Title: Voyage en Orient.*
IN PROCESS (ONLINE)
NYPL [MFX+ (Clercq) 91-2371]

CLERGY - POLITICAL ACTIVITY.
O Clero no Parlamento brasileiro /. Brasília ,
Rio de Janeiro , 1978-79. 2 v. : ISBN
85-7004-002-4
JL2454 .C53 *NYPL [HFE 80-1465]*

Clerici, Fabrizio, 1913-
Fabrizio Clerici / a cura di Bruno Mantura.
Roma : De Luca Edizioni d'Arte, 1990. 260 p. :
ill. (some col.), ports. ; 27 cm. Catalog of an
exhibition held at the Galleria Nazionale d'Arte
Moderna, Rome, Apr. 20-Sept. 16, 1990. Includes
bibliographical references (p. 253-260). ISBN
88-7813-268-3
*1. Clerici, Fabrizio, 1913- - Exhibitions. I. Mantura,
Bruno. II. Galleria nazionale d'arte moderna (Italy). III.
Title.* *NYPL [3-MCF C625 91-5535]*

CLERICI, FABRIZIO, 1913- - EXHIBITIONS.
Clerici, Fabrizio, 1913- Fabrizio Clerici /.
Roma , 1990. 260 p. : ISBN 88-7813-268-3
NYPL [3-MCF C625 91-5535]

CLÉRISSEAU, CHARLES-LOUIS, 1721-1820.
McCormick, Thomas J. Charles-Louis
Clérisseau and the genesis of neo-Classicism /.
New York, N.Y. , Cambridge, Mass. , c1990.
xiv, 284 p. : ISBN 0-262-13262-1 DDC 720/.92 B
20
NA1053.C58 M38 1990
NYPL [3-MQZ (Clérisseau) 91-5011]

O Clero no Parlamento brasileiro / [colaboraram
na preparação deste trabalho, organização geral
do plano, Fernando Bastos de Avila ;
coordinação, Américo Jacobina Lacombe].
Brasília : Câmara dos Deputados, Centro de
Documentação e Informação, Coordenação de
Publicações ; Rio de Janeiro : Centro João
XXIII (IBRADES) : Fundação Casa de Rui
Barbosa, Centro de Estudos Históricos,
1978-79. 2 v. : ill. ; 25 cm. (Brazil. Congresso.
Câmara dos Deputados. Documentos parlamentares.
124/A-B 124) Includes bibliographical references.
CONTENTS. - - v. 2. Câmara dos deputados
(1826-1829). v. 3. Câmara dos deputados (1830-1842).
ISBN 85-7004-002-4
*1. Brazil. Congresso - History. 2. Church and state in
Brazil. 3. Clergy - Political activity. I. Ávila, Fernando
Bastos de. II. Lacombe, Américo Jacobina, 1909-. III.
Brazil. Congresso. Câmara dos Deputados. Centro de
Documentação e Informação. IV. Centro João Vinte e
Três. V. Fundação Casa de Rui Barbosa. Centro de
Estudos Históricos. VI. Series.*
JL2454 .C53 *NYPL [HFE 80-1465]*

O Clero no Parlamento brasileiro / [colaboraram
na preparação deste trabalho, organização geral
do plano, Fernando Bastos de Avila ;
coordinação, Américo Jacobina Lacombe].
Brasília : Câmara dos Deputados, Centro de
Documentação e Informação, Coordenação de
Publicações ; Rio de Janeiro : Centro João
XXIII (IBRADES) : Fundação Casa de Rui
Barbosa, Centro de Estudos Históricos, 1978-
v. : ill. ; 25 cm. (Brazil. Congresso. Câmara dos
Deputados. Documentos parlamentares. 124 124)
Includes bibliographical references. CONTENTS. - - v.
4. Câ,ra dos Deputados (1843-1862) ISBN
85-7004-002-4
*1. Brazil. Congresso - History. 2. Church and state in
Brazil. I. Ávila, Fernando Bastos de. II. Lacombe,
Américo Jacobina, 1909-. III. Brazil. Congresso. Câmara
dos Deputados. Centro de Documentação e Informação.
IV. Centro João Vinte e Três. V. Fundação Casa de Rui
Barbosa. Centro de Estudos Históricos. VI. Series.*
JL2454 .C53 *NYPL [HFE 80-1378]*

Cleveland builds an art museum . Leedy, Walter
C. Cleveland , 1991. ix, 94 p. : ISBN
0-940717-09-3 DDC 708.171/32 20
N552 .L44 1991

Cleveland Museum of Art.
Handbook of the Cleveland Museum of Art.
Cleveland, Ohio : The Museum, 1991. x, 161
p. : ill. ; 23 x 28 cm. Includes index. ISBN
0-940717-00-X : DDC 708.171/32 20
*1. Art - Ohio - Cleveland - Catalogs. 2. Cleveland
Museum of Art - Catalogs. I. Title.*
N552 .A6 1991

Hinson, Tom E. The invitational--artists of
northeast Ohio . [Cleveland] , c1991. vii, 64 p. :
ISBN 0-940717-07-7 : DDC
709/.771/307477132 20
N6530.O3 H56 1991

Interpretations : sixty-five works in the
Cleveland Museum of Art. Cleveland, OH :
Cleveland Museum of Art, 1991. p. cm. ISBN
0-940717-11-5 DDC 708.71/32 20
*1. Art - Ohio - Cleveland. 2. Cleveland Museum of Art.
I. Title.*
N552 .A84 1991

Object lessons . Cleveland , 1991. ix, 203 p. :
ISBN 0-940717-08-5 DDC 708.171/32 20
N552 .O25 1991

CLEVELAND MUSEUM OF ART.
Cleveland Museum of Art. Interpretations .
Cleveland, OH , 1991. p. cm. ISBN
0-940717-11-5 DDC 708.71/32 20
N552 .A84 1991

Leedy, Walter C. Cleveland builds an art
museum . Cleveland , 1991. ix, 94 p. : ISBN
0-940717-09-3 DDC 708.171/32 20
N552 .L44 1991

**CLEVELAND MUSEUM OF ART -
CATALOGS.**
Cleveland Museum of Art. Handbook of the
Cleveland Museum of Art. Cleveland, Ohio ,

1991. x, 161 p. : ISBN 0-940717-00-X : DDC
708.171/32 20
N552 .A6 1991

CLEVELAND MUSEUM OF ART - HISTORY.
Object lessons . Cleveland , 1991. ix, 203 p. :
ISBN 0-940717-08-5 DDC 708.171/32 20
N552 .O25 1991

Cleveland, Richard L. Plain and fancy :
Vermont's people and their quilts as a reflection
of America / Richard L. Cleveland and Donna
Bister. San Francisco : Quilt Digest Press, 1991.
p. cm. Includes bibliographical references. ISBN
0-913327-30-1 (ppr) : DDC 746.9/7/09743 20
*1. Quilts - Vermont - History. 2. Quiltmakers -
Vermont - Biography. 3. Vermont - History. I. Bister,
Donna, 1951-. II. Title.*
NK9112 .C57 1991

Cleveland. Salvador Dali Museum. see Salvador
Dali Museum.

Click one. Click 1 . Cincinnati, Ohio , c1990. 149
p. : ISBN 0-89134-348-2 : DDC 700 20
N7433.8 .C55 1990
NYPL [3-MAL+ 91-4501]

Click 1 : the brightest in computer-generated
design and illustration / project editor, J. Ellen
Gerken ; with a foreword by Primo Angeli.1st
ed. Cincinnati, Ohio : North Light Books,
c1990. 149 p. : ill. (some col.) ; 31 cm. ISBN
0-89134-348-2 : DDC 700 20
*1. Computer art - Themes, motives. I. Gerken, J. Ellen.
II. Title: Click one.*
N7433.8 .C55 1990
NYPL [3-MAL+ 91-4501]

**Clifford Last sculpture, a retrospective
exhibition .** Edwards, Geoffrey. Melbourne ,
1989. 71 p. :
NYPL [3-MGO+ (Last) 91-4348]

Clift, William, 1944-
Certain places : photographs / by William Clift.
Santa Fe, N.M. : William Clift Editions, c1987.
[46] p. : chiefly ill. ; 29 x 31 cm. Published on the
occasion of an exhibition held at the Art Institute of
Chicago, Apr. 25-June 21, 1987 and at the Amon
Carter Museum, July 11-Sept. 6, 1987. ISBN
0-9618165-0-3
*1. Clift, William, 1944- - 4Exhibitions. 2. Photography,
Artistic - Exhibitions. I. Art Institute of Chicago. II.
Amon Carter Museum of Western Art. III. Title.*
NYPL [MFX+ (Clift) 91-2455]

CLIFT, WILLIAM, 1944- - 4EXHIBITIONS.
Clift, William, 1944- Certain places . Santa Fe,
N.M. , c1987. [46] p. : ISBN 0-9618165-0-3
NYPL [MFX+ (Clift) 91-2455]

Clifton-Mogg, Caroline. The neo-classical source
book / Caroline Clifton-Mogg. New York :
Rizzoli, 1991. p. cm. Includes bibliographical
references. ISBN 0-8478-1392-4 DDC 709/.03/3 20
*1. Neoclassicism (Art). 2. Art, Modern - 17th-18th
centuries. I. Title.*
N6425.N4 C55 1991

Climbing the church walls /. Portlock, Rob.
Downers Grove, Ill. , 1991. p. cm. ISBN
0-8308-1830-8 DDC 741.5/973 20
NC1429.P65 A4 1991

CLINTON COUNTY, ILL. - MAPS.
(1991) Rockford Map Publishers. Clinton
County, Illinois, land atlas & plat book .
Rockford, Ill. [c1991] 1 atlas (39 p.) :
NYPL [Map Div. 91-4408]

Clinton County, Illinois, land atlas & plat book .
Rockford Map Publishers. Rockford, Ill.
[c1991] 1 atlas (39 p.) :
NYPL [Map Div. 91-4408]

Clive Barker, illustrator /. Barker, Clive, 1952-
Forestville, Calif. , c1990. iv, 124 p., [18] p. of
plates : ISBN 1-560-60026-8 (limited signed
clothbound) : DDC 741/.092 20
NC139.B33 A4 1990

CLOCK-TOWERS. see TOWERS.

Clocktower Gallery. Rhodes, Rod, 1944- Rod
Rhodes . New York , c1989. 64 p. :
NYPL [3-MGO (Rhodes) 91-6397]

CLOISONNÉ, MEDIEVAL - EUROPE.
Haseloff, Günther. Email im frühen Mittelalter .
Marburg , c1990. 244 p. : ISBN 3-89398-020-2
NYPL [3-MNV 91-5235]

Clore Gallery.
Lyles, Anne. Young Turner . London , 1989.
43 p. : ISBN 1-85437-026-X (pbk.)
NYPL [3-MCV T94 90-11675]

Turner, J. M. W. (Joseph Mallord William),
1775-1851. [Turner watercolours in the Clore
Gallery. French.] Turner, aquarelles . Paris ,
c1987. 148 p. : ISBN 2-87660-002-1
NYPL [3-MCV+ T94 90-1063]

CLOSE RANGE PHOTOGRAPHY. see
PHOTOGRAPHY, CLOSE-UP.

Close up /. Klein, William. London , 1989. 175
p. : ISBN 0-500-54159-0
NYPL [MFX+ (Klein) 90-1009]

Close-up. Klein, William. Close up /. London ,
1989. 175 p. : ISBN 0-500-54159-0
NYPL [MFX+ (Klein) 90-1009]

CLOSE-UP PHOTOGRAPHY. see
PHOTOGRAPHY, CLOSE-UP.

CLOTH. see **TEXTILE FABRICS.**

Cloulas, Ivan. Chambord : rêve des rois / Ivan
Cloulas ; photographies, Daniel Philippe. Paris :
Nathan : CNMHS, c1989. 143 p. : ill. (chiefly
col.), 29 x 31 cm. Includes bibliographical references
(p. 139-143). ISBN 2-09-241001-6
1. Château de Chambord (Chambord, Loir-et-Cher,
France). I. Title. *NYPL [3-MQWF+ 90-2437]*

**CLOWNS IN ART - JUVENILE
LITERATURE.**
Soloff-Levy, Barbara. How to draw clowns /.
Mahwah, N.J. , c1992. p. cm. ISBN
0-8167-2477-6 (lib. bdg.) : DDC 743/.8979133
20
NC765 .S65 1992

Clubbe, John. Cincinnati observed : architecture
and history / John Clubbe. Columbus : Ohio
State University Press, c1991. p. cm. (Urban life
and urban landscape series) "A Sandstone book."
Includes bibliographical references and index. ISBN
0-8142-0512-7 (cloth : alk. paper) DDC
720/.9771/79 20
1. Architecture - Ohio - Cincinnati. 2. Cincinnati
(Ohio) - Buildings, structures, etc. I. Title. II. Series.
NA735.C5 C58 1991

Clues to American furniture /. Federico, Jean
Taylor, 1940. Washington DC , 1991. p. cm.
ISBN 0-913515-75-2 : DDC 749.213/075 20
NK2405 .F43 1991

Clunas, Craig. Kerr, Rose, 1953- Chinese art and
design /. Woodstock, N.Y. , 1991. p. cm.
ISBN 0-87951-437-X : DDC
745/.0951/07442134 20
NK1068 .K47 1991

CMP bulletin. De Lory, Peter. The wild and the
innocent /. Riverside, Calif. , 1987. [46] p. :
ISBN 0-9619038-2-1
NYPL [MFX (De Lory) 90-11264]

Cnodder, Remi de.
Cruysmans, Philippe, 1925- Linou Truffino, ou,
Les voix de la mer /. Bruxelles [1986] 127 p. :
ISBN 2-87103-024-8 DDC 759.9493 20
ND673.T75 A4 1986

Cruysmans, Philippe, 1925- Lise Durez peint
Victor Hugo /. Bruxelles [1986] 183 p. : ISBN
2-87103-023-5
N6973.D85 C7 1986

Co, Francesco dal. see **Dal Co, Francesco, 1945-**

Coad, Emma Dent. Spanish design and
architecture / Emma Dent Coad. London :
Studio Vista, 1990. 208 p. : col. ill. ; 27 cm.
Includes index. Includes bibliographical references (p.
204). ISBN 0-289-80030-7
1. Arts, Modern - 20th century - Spain. I. Title.
NYPL [3-MAML 90-11570]

**COAL MINES AND MINING IN ART -
EXHIBITIONS.**
Schichtwechsel . [Ahlen] [1988?] 94 p. :
IN PROCESS (ONLINE)
NYPL [3-MAMZ 91-7103]

COAL-OIL. see **PETROLEUM.**

COAST-PILOT GUIDES. see **PILOT GUIDES.**

Coast to coast . Dyer, Rod. New York , 1991. p.
cm. ISBN 1-558-59156-7 DDC 741.6/92/0973 20
NC1002.L3 D94 1991

COASTS - QATAR - MAPS.
Yaḥyá, Muḥammad ʿAdil Aḥmad. Aṭlas
al-ṣuwar al-faḍāʾiyah li-Dawlat Qaṭar min

al-qamar al-ṣināʿī "Landsāt" /. al-Dawḥah ,
1983. 1 atlas (vii, 166 p.) : DDC 912/.5363 19
G2249.81.C2 Y2 1983
NYPL [Map Div. 91-2599]

Cobb, Emma T. Castle, Wendell, 1932- Angel
chairs . New York , 1991. 111 p. : ISBN
0-9628849-0-1 DDC 749.213 20
NK2439.C3 A4 1991

COBRA (ASSOCIATION) - EXHIBITIONS.
Cobra 1948/51 . [Rotterdam , 1967?] 187 p. :
DDC 709.04
N6490 .R64 *NYPL [3-MAL 90-7044]*

Cobra 1948/51 : Museum Boymans-Van
Beuningen, Rotterdam, 20 mei/17 juli.
[Rotterdam : Museum Boymans-Van Beuningen,
1967?] 187 p. : ill. (some col.) ; 25 cm.
Bibliography: p. 173-184. DDC 709.04
1. Cobra (Association) - Exhibitions. 2. Art, Modern -
20th century - Exhibitions. I. Museum Boymans-Van
Beuningen.
N6490 .R64 *NYPL [3-MAL 90-7044]*

Coburn . Amadio, Nadine. Roseville, NSW ,
1988. 205 p. : ISBN 0-947131-20-5
NYPL [3-MCZ+ C657 89-20391]

Coburn, John, 1925- Amadio, Nadine. Coburn .
Roseville, NSW , 1988. 205 p. : ISBN
0-947131-20-5
NYPL [3-MCZ+ C657 89-20391]

COBURN, JOHN, 1925-
Amadio, Nadine. Coburn . Roseville, NSW ,
1988. 205 p. : ISBN 0-947131-20-5
NYPL [3-MCZ+ C657 89-20391]

Cocconi, Corrado. Una Famiglia di architetti e
costruttori a Roma, 1887-1987 /. Roma , 1987.
xxiv, 75 p. : ISBN 88-7813-027-3
NYPL [3-MQWB+ 90-9457]

Cochran, Bruce. Bass fever : fishing cartoons / by
Bruce Cochran. Minocqua, WI : Willow Creek
Press, c1991. p. cm. ISBN 1-55971126-4
(hardcover) : DDC 741.5/973 20
1. Fishing - Caricatures and cartoons. 2. American wit
and humor, Pictorial. I. Title.
NC1429.C619 A4 1991

Cock, Elizabeth M., 1925- The influence of
photography on American landscape painting
[microform] : 1839-1880 / by Elizabeth M.
Cock. 1967. 2 v. (xiii, 247 leaves) : ill. Thesis
(Ph.D.)--New York University, 1967. Bibliography: v. 1,
leaves 179-196. Microfilm. Ann Arbor, Mich. : Xerox
University Microfilms, 1970. 1 microfilm reel ; 35 mm.
CONTENTS. - v. 1. Text -- v. 2. Illustrations.
1. Art, Modern - 19th century - United States. I. Title.
*NYPL [*ZM-71]*

Cockcroft, Eva Sperling. Signs from the heart .
Venice, Calif. , c1990. 105 p. : ISBN
0-9626419-0-1 *NYPL [3-MCW 90-12027]*

Cockcroft, James D. Diego Rivera / James
Cockcroft. New York : Chelsea House, c1991.
119 p., [8] p. of col. plates : ill. ; 25 cm.
(Hispanics of achievement) Includes bibliographical
references and index. Examines the life and times of
the noted Mexican muralist, discussing his art and
politics. ISBN 0-7910-1252-2 : DDC 759.972 B 92
20
1. Rivera, Diego, 1886-1957. 2. Painters - Mexico -
Biography. I. Title. II. Series.
ND259.R5 C57 1991

Cockrill, Pauline. The ultimate teddy bear book /
Pauline Cockrill ; introduction by Paul and
Rosemary Volpp ; photography by Roland
Kemp. 1st American ed. New York : Dorling
Kindersley, 1991. p. cm. ISBN
1-87943-106-8 : DDC 688.7/24 20
1. Teddy bears - Collectors and collecting. I. Title.
NK8740 .C6 1991

Cocteau, Jean, 1889-1963.
Jean Cocteau : Gemälde, Zeichnungen,
Keramik, Tapisserien, Literatur, Theater, Film,
Ballett / herausgegeben von Jochen Poetter ;
unter Mitarbeit von Dirk Teuber ;
Gastkuratorin, Geneviève Albrechtskirchinger.
Köln : DuMont, c1989. 418 p. : ill. (some
col.) ; 30 cm. Anlässlich einer Ausstellung der
Staatlichen Kunsthalle Baden-Baden, die [...] vom 5.
Mai bis 30. Juli 1989 stattfand"--T.p. verso. Includes
bibliographical references. ISBN 3-7701-2380-8
1. Cocteau, Jean 1889-1963 - Exhibitions. 2. Cocteau,
Jean 1889-1963 - Catalogues raisonnés. I. Poetter,
Jochen. II. Teuber, Dirk. III. Staatliche Kunsthalle

Baden-Baden. IV. Title.
NYPL [3-MCO C66 89-21295]

COCTEAU, JEAN, 1889-1963.
Emboden, William A. Jean Cocteau and the
illustrated book /. [Northridge, Calif.] , 1990.
29 p. : *NYPL [MDG+ (Cocteau) 90-11895]*

**COCTEAU, JEAN 1889-1963 - CATALOGUES
RAISONNÉS.**
Cocteau, Jean, 1889-1963. Jean Cocteau .
Köln , c1989. 418 p. : ISBN 3-7701-2380-8
NYPL [3-MCO C66 89-21295]

COCTEAU, JEAN 1889-1963 - EXHIBITIONS.
Cocteau, Jean, 1889-1963. Jean Cocteau .
Köln , c1989. 418 p. : ISBN 3-7701-2380-8
NYPL [3-MCO C66 89-21295]

Les cocus du vieil art moderne /. Dali, Salvador,
1904- Paris [1989], c1956. 115 p. : ISBN
2-246-42142-X
NYPL [3-MCQ D14 91-5414]

**Code pour l'analyse des représentations figurées
sur les vases grecs** /. Salomé, Marie Rose.
Paris , 1980. 161 p. : ISBN 2-222-02677-6
NYPL [3-MPR 90-5663]

CODESIDO, JULIA, 1883-1979 - CATALOGS.
Moll, Eduardo, 1929- Julia Codesido,
1883-1979 /. [Lima, Peru?] 1990 (Lima :
Editorial Navarrete) 127 p. : DDC 759.985 20
ND419.C62 A4 1990

CODEX VATICANUS URBINAS 1270.
Farago, Claire J. Leonardo da Vinci's
Paragone . Leiden, The Netherlands , New
York , 1991. p. cm. ISBN 90-04-09415-6 (cloth)
DDC 750 20
ND1140 .F35 1991

Codognato, Attilio. Warhol, Andy, 1928- Le
cento immagini di Andy Warhol . Milano ,
c1989. 116 p. : ISBN 88-20-20906-3
NYPL [3-MCX W27 90-11112]

Codrington, Stephen B., 1953- The Macmillan
Australian atlas /. South Melbourne , 1990. 1
atlas (134 p.) : ISBN 0-7329-0192-8
NYPL [Map Div. 90-12898]

Cody, Wyo. Buffalo Bill Historical Center. see
Buffalo Bill Historical Center.

Coe Kerr Gallery. Wyeth, James, 1946- James
Wyeth . [Omaha?] c1975 (Omaha : Barnhart
Press) [64] p. :
NYPL [3-MCX W980 90-7181]

Coe, Sue, 1951- Paintings and drawings / by Sue
Coe ; foreword by Marshall Arisman ;
introduction by Russell Mills. Metuchen, N.J. :
Scarecrow Press, 1985. x, 150 p. : chiefly ill. ;
29 cm. (Drawings and graphics) ISBN
0-8108-1782-9 DDC 759.2 19
1. Coe, Sue, 1951-. I. Title. II. Series.
N6797.C55 A4 1985
NYPL [3-MCV C672 91-6814]

COE, SUE, 1951-
Coe, Sue, 1951- Paintings and drawings /.
Metuchen, N.J. , 1985. x, 150 p. : ISBN
0-8108-1782-9 DDC 759.2 19
N6797.C55 A4 1985 *NYPL [3-MCV C672 91-6814]*

Cogeval, Guy. Vuillard, Édouard, 1868-1940.
Vuillard . Paris , c1990. 237 p. : ISBN
2-08-011730-0 DDC 760/.092 20
N6853.V85 A4 1990

Cogniet, Attilio.
Léon Cogniet, 1794-1880.
Léon Cogniet, 1794-1880 : Musée des
beaux-arts d'Orléans, 14 juin-10 septembre 1990
/ [exposition organisée par David Ojalvo avec
le concours de Françoise Demange et Catherine
Moindreau]. Orléans : Le Musée, [1990] 197
p. : ill. (some col.) ; 23 cm. Bibliography: p.
193-194.
1. Cogniet, Léon, 1794-1880 - Exhibitions. I. Ojalvo,
David. II. Demange, F. III. Moindreau, Catherine. IV.
Musée des beaux-arts d'Orléans. V. Title.
NYPL [3-MCO C676 91-6494]

**COGNIET, LÉON, 1794-1880 -
EXHIBITIONS.**
Cogniet, Léon, 1794-1880. Léon Cogniet,
1794-1880 . Orléans [1990] 197 p. :
NYPL [3-MCO C676 91-6494]

Cogswell fund series .
(publication no. 3) Albany Institute of History
and Art. Albany silver, 1652-1825 . [Albany] ,
c1964. 81 p. : *NYPL [JAY C-1115]*

Cohen, David, 1955- A Day in the life of China /. San Francisco , 1989. 220 p. : ISBN 0-00-215321-1 (returnable ed.) : DDC 951.05/8/0222 20
DS712 .D39 1989
NYPL [MFW+ 90-11175]

Cohen, Evelyn. Alexander, Lucy. 150 South African paintings . Cape Town , 1990. 180 p. : ISBN 0-947458-25-5 DDC 759.968 20
ND1092 .A43 1990

Cohen, Jean-Louis.
[Le Corbusier et la mystique de l'URSS. English]
Le Corbusier and the mystique of the USSR : theories and projects for Moscow, 1928-1936 / Jean-Louis Cohen. Princeton, N.J. : Princeton University Press, [1991] p. cm.
Translation of: Le Corbusier et la mystique de l'URSS. Includes indexes. ISBN 0-691-04076-1 : DDC 720/.92 20
1. Le Corbusier, 1887-1965 - Criticism and interpretation. 2. Functionalism (Architecture) - Russian S.F.S.R. - Moscow. 3. Architecture, Modern - 20th century - Russian S.F.S.R. - Moscow. 4. Moscow (R.S.F.S.R.) - Buildings, structures, etc. I. Title.
NA1053.J4 C55 1991

Paris, la ville et ses projets . Paris , c1989. 253 p. : ISBN 2-907742-04-3
NYPL [3-MQWF+ 90-10864]

Cohen, Jeffrey A., 1952- Thomas, George E. Frank Furness . New York, N.Y. , c1991. p. cm. ISBN 1-87827-104-0 : DDC 720/.92 20
NA737.F84 A4 1991

Cohen, Mildred Thaler. Eliot Clark (1883-1980) . New York, N.Y. [1990] 53 p. :
MLCM 90/01921 (N)
NYPL [3-MCX C592 91-7404]

Cohen, Ronny. Bates, David, 1952- David Bates . New York, NY , c1990. [42] p. :
NYPL [3-MCX B329 91-4403]

Cohn, Don J. Vignettes from the Chinese . Hong Kong , c1987. vi, 105 p. : ISBN 962-7255-01-7
NYPL [MDZ 90-13685]

Cohn, Marjorie B. Wash and gouache : a study of the development of the materials of watercolor / by Marjorie B. Cohn ; catalogue of the exhibition by Rachel Rosenfield. [Cambridge, Mass.] : Center for Conservation and Technical Studies, Fogg Art Museum, c1977. 116 p. : ill. (some col.) ; 21 x 26 cm.
Exhibition held at the Fogg Art Museum, May 12-June 22, 1977. Includes index. Bibliography: p. 84-86. ISBN 0-916724-06-9 DDC 751.4/22
1. Watercolor painting - Technique - Exhibitions. I. Rosenfield, Rachel, 1951-. II. Fogg Art Museum. III. Title.
ND2430 .C63
NYPL [MBO 79-96]

Coiffes & bonnets en Charentes, Poitou, Vendée . Piot, Michel. Poitiers , c1989. 350 p. : ISBN 2-902170-61-0
GT885.P64 P56 1989
NYPL [3-MMV+ 91-5346]

Coiffes et bonnets en Charentes, Poitou, Vendée. Piot, Michel. Coiffes & bonnets en Charentes, Poitou, Vendée . Poitiers , c1989. 350 p. : ISBN 2-902170-61-0
GT885.P64 P56 1989
NYPL [3-MMV+ 91-5346]

COIFFURE. see HAIRDRESSING.

Coignet, Jean. Arts de bâtir traditionnels : connaissance et techniques de réhabilitation / Jean Coignet. Aix-en-Provence : Edisud, c1987. 130 p. : ill. ; 30 cm. Cover title: Réhabilitation : arts de bâtir traditionnels, connaissance et techniques. Bibliography: p. 130. ISBN 2-85744-252-1
I. Title. *NYPL [3-MQD+ 91-4827]*

COIN BANKS - COLLECTORS AND COLLECTING - CATALOGS.
McCumber, Robert L. Registering banks . Glastonbury, CT (201 Carriage Dr., Glastonbury 06033) , 1990. 159 p. : DDC 688.7/28 20
NK4698 .M37 1990

COINS - EXHIBITIONS.
Il Tesoro di via Alessandrina /. [S.l.] , Cinisello Balsamo, Milano , c1990. 115 p. :
NYPL [3-MAX (Martinetti) 91-5544]

Colaço, Madeleine.
Madeleine Colaço / apresentações, Dilys Blum ... [et al] ; introdução, Antônio Houaiss ;

vida e obra de Madeleine, na cadência do "samba bordado," Eduardo Kac, Antonio Fernandes Fagundes = Madeleine Colaço / presentations, Dilys Blum ... [et al.] ; introduction, Antônio Houaiss ; the life and art of Madeleine, the thythm of the "embroired samba," Eduardo Kac, Antonio Fernandes Fagundes. Rio de Janeiro, RJ : Caixa Econômica Federal : Editora Index, 1988. 1 v. (unpaged) : ill. (chiefly col.) ; 32 cm. English and Portuguese. Includes bibliographical references. ISBN 85-7083-020-3 DDC 746.392 20
1. Colaço, Madeleine - Catalogs. 2. Tapestry - Brazil - History - 20th century - Catalogs. I. Title.
NK3033.A3 C65 1988

COLAÇO, MADELEINE - CATALOGS.
Colaço, Madeleine. Madeleine Colaço /. Rio de Janeiro, RJ , 1988. 1 v. (unpaged) : ISBN 85-7083-020-3 DDC 746.392 20
NK3033.A3 C65 1988

Colagens, Hannah Höch, 1889-1978 /. Höch, Hannah, 1889- Lisboa , 1989. 134 p. :
N6888.H6 A4 1989a

Colalucci, Gianluigi. New light on Michelangelo in the Sistine Chapel. German. Der neue Michelangelo . Luzern, Schweiz , c1989-c1991. 3 v. : ISBN 3-85672-033-2 (set)
NYPL [MCF++ B9 91-6340]

Colani, Luigi. Luigi Colani = Design 1. Zofingen : Inova-Verlag, c1986. 1 v. (unpaged) : ill. ; 24 cm. Title from spine. Addenda (7 p.) inserted. ISBN 3-906460-01-2
1. Colani, Luigi. I. Title. II. Title: Design 1.
NYPL [3-MNF 91-6398]

COLANI, LUIGI.
Colani, Luigi. Luigi Colani . Zofingen , c1986. 1 v. (unpaged) : ISBN 3-906460-01-2
NYPL [3-MNF 91-6398]

Colas-Adler, Marie-Hélène. Groupes, mouvements, tendances de l'art contemporain depuis 1945 /. Paris , 1990. 183 p. ; ISBN 2-903639-61-2 : DDC 709/.04/5 20
N6490 .G724 1990

Colby College. Museum of Art.
The Land and the sea of five Maine artists . [Waterville, Maine , 1965] [31] p. :
NYPL [3-MCW 90-5878]

Marlais, Michael Andrew. Americans and Paris . Waterville, Me. , c1990. 62 p. : DDC 759.13/074/7416 20
N6510 .M27 1990
NYPL [3-MAMT 90-13006]

Colchagua, arquitectura tradicional /. Guarda, Gabriel. Santiago de Chile , 1988. 177 p. : ISBN 956-1-40220-7 DDC 720/.983/33 20
NA866.C64 G83 1988

Cole, Barbie Campbell. Richard Rogers + architects. London , New York , 1985. 160 p. : ISBN 0-312-68207-7 (St. Martin's)
NYPL [3-MQZ+ (Rogers) 86-1924]

Cole, Sylvan. Davis, Stuart, 1892-1964. Stuart Davis . Fort Worth, Tex. , 1986. viii, 96 p. : ISBN 0-88360-054-4 DDC 760/.092/4 19
N6537.D345 A4 1986
NYPL [MDG (Davis) 90-12799]

COLE, THOMAS, 1801-1848 - CRITICISM AND INTERPRETATION.
Powell, Earl A. Thomas Cole /. New York , 1990. 144 p. (some col.) ; ISBN 0-8109-3158-3 DDC 759.13 20
ND237.C6 A4 1990
NYPL [3-MCX C68 90-12862]

Coleção Estudos (São Paulo, Brazil) .
(112) Fabris, Annateresa. Portinari, pintor social /. São Paulo, SP, Brasil . xvi, 147 p. : ISBN 85-27-30027-3 DDC 759.981 20
ND359.P6 F3 1990

Colecção Arte e artistas.
Cláudio, Mário. Emerenciano, ou, O teor das actas /. Lisboa , 1989. 115 p. :
ND833.R63 A4 1989

Gastão, Marques, 1914- Encontros com António Duarte /. [Lisbon, Portugal] [1989] 128 p. : DDC 730/.92 20
NB833.D8 G37 1989

Gonçalves, Flávio. História da arte . [Lisbon] [1990] 353 p. : DDC 709/.469 20
N7121 .G6 1990

Oliveira, Emídio Rosa de. A pintura de

Noronha da Costa /. Lisboa [1989] 115 p., [36] p. of plates : DDC 759.69 20
ND833.C63 O45 1989

Semke, Hein, 1899- Hein Semke . Lisboa [1989] 153 p. :
NB833.S46 S46 1989

Vicente, Antonio Pedro. Carlos Relvas, fotógrafo, 1838-1894 . [Portugal] [1984] 99, [8] p. :
MLCM 85/4105 (N)
NYPL [MFX (Relvas) 91-3323]

Colecção Artes/história.
Pacheco, Jorge, 1954- A divina arte negra e o livro português . Lisboa [1988?] 282 p. :
NE1163 .P33 1988
NYPL [MDOH 90-12803]

Colecção Escola de Gaia .
(no. 2) Macedo, Diogo de. Album do nome e do renome de Diogo de Macedo . Vila Nova de Gaia , 1989. 127 p. : ISBN 972-95053-2-2
NB833.M16 A4 1989

Colecção Estudos de arte .
(9) Silva, José Custódio Vieira da. O tardo-gótico em Portugal . Lisboa , c1989. 206 p. : ISBN 972-240-725-2 :
NA1329.A43 S55 1989

Colecção Estudos (Universidade de Coimbra. Faculdade de Letras) .
(9) Anacleto, Regina. O artista conimbricense Miguel Costa, 1859-1914 /. Coimbra , 1989. 113 p. : ISBN 972-90380-6-6 DDC 738/.092 20
NK4670.7.P63 C673 1989

Colecção História da arte.
Pinto, M. H. Mendes (Maria Helena Mendes) Lacas namban em Portugal . [Portugal] , c1990. 127 p. : ISBN 972-90192-3-1 DDC 745.7/26/0952074469 20
NK9900.7.J3 P56 1990

Vista Alegre . [Lisbon] , c1989. 267 p. : ISBN 972-90191-9-3 DDC 738.2/09469/35 20
NK4210.F3175 V5 1989

Colecção Paisagem-arte .
(4) Gonçalves, António Nogueira, 1901- Estudos de história da arte da Renascença /. Aveiro [Portugal] [between 1975 and 1987] 311 p. :
N7963.C65 G66 1975

Colecção Presenças da imagem.
Carvalho, Artur Marques de. Do Mosteiro dos Jerónimos . [Lisbon] [1990] 281 p. :
NA5830.M67 C37 1990

Colecção universitária.
Serrão, Vítor, 1952- Estudos de pintura maneirista e barroca /. Lisboa , c1989. 416 p., [32] p. of plates : ISBN 972-210-454-3 : DDC 759.69/09/031 20
ND825 .S47 1989

Colección "Antologías" (San Sebastián, Spain) .
(38) Jiménez, María Paz, 1909-1975. María Paz Jiménez (1909-1975). [San Sebastián] , 1989. 181 p. : ISBN 84-7173-143-6
MLCM 90/01366 (N)
NYPL [3-MCQ J58 91-5339]

Colección Autores antioqueños .
(v. 39) Gómez Jaramillo, Ignacio, 1910-1970. Anotaciones de un pintor /. Medellín , 1987. 313 p. :
N7483.G64 A2 1987
NYPL [3-MCZ G632 90-12606]

Colección Banco Industrial de Venezuela.
Banco Industrial de Venezuela. Arturo Michelena . [Caracas, Venezuela] [1989?] 183 p. : DDC 759.987 20
N6739.M53 B36 1989

Colección científica (Instituto Nacional de Antropología e Historia (Mexico)) .
(206) Ortiz Angulo, Ana. Definición y clasificación del arte popular /. México, D.F. , 1990. 150 p. : ISBN 968-606-893-7 DDC 709/.72 20
NK844 .O78 1990

Colección Corporación La Candelaria, Alcaldía Mayor de Bogotá.
Cantini Ardila, Jorge Ernesto. Pietro Cantini . Bogotá [1990] 318 p. : DDC 720/.92 20
NA879.C36 C3 1990

Colección de arte (Universidad Nacional Autónoma de México. Coordinación de Humanidades) .

(41) Noelle, Louise. Ricardo Legorreta, tradición y modernidad /. México , 1989. 188 p., 12 leaves of plates : ISBN 968-361-022-6 DDC 720/.92 20
NA759.L44 A4 1989

Colección de bolsillo (Universidad Autónoma de Madrid) .
(15) Urrutia Núñez, Angel. Arquitectura doméstica moderna en Madrid /. Madrid [1988] 214 p. : ISBN 84-7477-173-0
NYPL   [3-MRG 90-10752]

Colección de glíptica del Museo Arqueológico Nacional (serie de entalles romanos) /. Casal García, Raquel. [Spain] [1990?] 2 v. : ISBN 84-7483-657-3 (set)
NK5511.S67 M344 1990

Colección Divulgación.
(9) Hernández Guardiola, Lorenzo, 1953- Pintura decorativa barroca en la provincia de Alicante /. Alicante [1990- v. : ISBN 84-7784-037-7   *NYPL   [3-MCP 91-858]*

Colección Encuentros (Turner (Firm)). Serie Catálogos.
El Surrealismo entre Viejo y Nuevo Mundo . [Madrid] [1990] 346 p. : ISBN 84-86022-51-2
N6512.5.S87 S8 1990

Colección Encuentros (Turner (Firm)). Serie Catálogs.
Arte en Iberoamérica, 1820-1980 . [Madrid] [1989?] xxi, 359, [3] p. : ISBN 84-7506-297-0
N6502.4 .A76 1989

Colección Ensayos (Universidad Autónoma Metropolitana. Unidad Xochimilco)
Vargas, Ramón. Historia de la teoría de la arquitectura, el porfirismo /. [Mexico City] , 1989. 221 p. : ISBN 968-8406-73-2
NA200 .V37 1989

Colección Estudios y monografías (Zaragoza, Spain) .
(12) Morales y Marín, José Luis, 1946- Goya, pintor religioso /. [Zaragoza] [1990] 354 p. : ISBN 84-7753-132-3 DDC 759.6 20
ND813.G7 A4 1990

Colección Fuentes.
Catálogo de artistas y artesanos de México /. México, D.F. , 1986 [i.e. 1987] 292 p. : ISBN 968-603-853-1
N6547.M56 C37 1986

López Cervantes, Gonzalo. Cerámica de Tonalá, Jalisco . México, D.F. , 1990. 146 p. : ISBN 968-606-895-3 DDC 738.3/0972/35 20
NK4032.T66 L66 1990

Colección Homenajes (Guadalajara, Mexico)
Anguiano, Raúl, 1915- Raúl Anguiano . Guadalajara [1985] iii, 124 p. : DDC 709/.2 20
N6559.A54 A4 1985

Colección ibérica (Editorial Everest)
Romero Torres, José Luis. Museo de Bellas Artes de Málaga /. Madrid [1989?] 79 p. : ISBN 84-241-4945-9 DDC 709/.46/0744685 20
N7101 .R66 1989

Colección La Tauromaquia .
(26) Zaldívar, Rafael. El cartel taurino . Madrid , 1990. 370 p. : ISBN 84-239-5426-9 DDC 741.6/74/0946 20
NC1849.B84 Z35 1990

Colección Nuestros países. Serie Estudios.
Morais, Frederico. [Artes plásticas na América Latina. Spanish.] Las artes plásticas en la América Latina . Ciudad de La Habana, Cuba , c1990. 121 p. ;
N72.S6 M66718 1990

Colección Panza. Arte minimal de la Colección Panza . [Madrid?] , 1988. 61 p. : ISBN 84-7750-623-18   *NYPL   [MAMT 90-5197]*

Colección Patrimonio arquitectónico colombiano .
(1) Documentos internacionales sobre patrimonio arquitectónico. [Bogotá, Colombia] [1989 or 1990] 35 p. ;
NA870 .D6 1989

Colección Rajuela.
Gómez Arriola, Ignacio. Comala . Colima, Col. [Mexico] [1985] 75 p. :
NA757.C66 G66 1985

Colección Río de luz.
Alvarez Bravo, Manuel, 1902- Mucho sol /. México , 1989. 94 p. : ISBN 968-16-3242-7
NYPL   [MFX (Alvarez Bravo) 90-2181]

Colección Universidad Tecnológica de Pereira. Serie Humanística .
(no. 1) Mejía de Millán, Beatriz Amelia. El arte colombiano en el siglo XX /. Pereira, Colombia , 1988. 155 p. : DDC 709/.861/0904 20
N6675 .M45 1988

La colectividad armenia en la Argentina /. Binayán, Narciso. Buenos Aires , 1974. 158 p. ;
NYPL   [HKB 80-2301]

Colegio de Arquitectos de Cataluña y Baleares. see Colegio Oficial de Arquitectos de Cataluña y Baleares.

Colegio Dominicano de Artistas Plásticos. Arte contemporáneo dominicano. [Santo Domingo, Dominican Republic?] [1987?] [72] p. ;
N6615.D6 A77 1987

Colegio Oficial de Arquitectos de Cataluña y Baleares.
Arquitectura . [Barcelona?] [1988] 187 p. :
NA1309.C2 A76 1988

Colegio Oficial de Arquitectos de Cataluña y Baleares. Delegación de Barcelona. Comisión de Defensa del Patrimonio Arquitectónico.
Història i arquitectura . Barcelona [1986?] 260 p. : ISBN 84-505-2551-9
NA1309.B29 H57 1986
NYPL   [3-MQWH+ 90-12046]

Colin, Christine. Starck / Christine Colin. Liège : P. Mardaga, [1988?] 348 p. : ill. (some col.) ; 31 cm. Includes bibliographical references. ISBN 2-87009-332-2
1. Starck, Philippe. 2. Design - France - History - 20th century. I. Starck, Philippe. II. Title.
NYPL   [3-MLO + 90-2824]

Colin McCahon . McCahon, Colin. Auckland, New Zealand , c1988. 157 p. : ISBN 0-86463-165-0
NYPL   [3-MCZ+ M116 91-6649]

Coll Bardolet /. Manzano, Rafael, 1917- Barcelona [1977?] 119 p. : ISBN 84-85321-52-1 DDC 759.6 20
ND813.C59 A4 1977

Coll Bardolet /. Rodríguez Aguilera, Cesáreo. Barcelona , c1980. 207 p. : ISBN 84-300-2270-8 DDC 759.6 20
ND813.C59 A4 1980

Coll Bardolet, Josep.
Manzano, Rafael, 1917- Coll Bardolet /. Barcelona [1977?] 119 p. : ISBN 84-85321-52-1 DDC 759.6 20
ND813.C59 A4 1977

COLL BARDOLET, JOSEP - CATALOGS.
Manzano, Rafael, 1917- Coll Bardolet /. Barcelona [1977?] 119 p. : ISBN 84-85321-52-1 DDC 759.6 20
ND813.C59 A4 1977

Rodríguez Aguilera, Cesáreo. Coll Bardolet /. Barcelona , c1980. 207 p. : ISBN 84-300-2270-8 DDC 759.6 20
ND813.C59 A4 1980

Collaborations and connections : 20th century collaborative bookworks : February 11-March 25, 1990, University Art Museum and Hayden Library, Arizona State University, Tempe, Arizona / [general editor, Lucinda H. Gedeon]. Tempe, Ariz. : The Museum, c1990. viii, 36 p. : ill. ; 28 cm. Bibliography: p. 35-36.
1. Book design - Exhibitions. 2. Graphic arts - Exhibitions. 3. Artists' books - Exhibitions. 4. Printing - History - 20th century - Exhibitions. I. Gedeon, Lucinda H. II. Arizona State University. University Art Museum. III. Arizona State University. Library.
NYPL   [MDTT 91-4768]

COLLAGE.
Scott, Margaret Kennedy. Pressed flowers and flower pictures /. London , 1988. 118 p. : ISBN 0-7134-5245-5 DDC 745.92/8 19
SB449.3.P7 S362 1988
NYPL   [3-MLT 90-10805]

COLLAGE, AMERICAN - EXHIBITIONS.
Montclair, N. J. Art Museum. Collage, American masters . Montclair [c1979] [12 p.] :
N6512.5.C55 M66 1979
NYPL   [3-MAMT 80-2170]

Collage, American masters . Montclair, N. J. Art Museum. Montclair [c1979] [12 p.] :
N6512.5.C55 M66 1979
NYPL   [3-MAMT 80-2170]

COLLAGE, AUSTRALIAN.
McIntyre, Arthur, 1945- Contemporary Australian collage and its origins /. Roseville, NSW, Australia , 1990. 224 p. : ISBN 0-947131-31-0
NYPL   [3-MAM+ 90-13198]

Collage et montage au théâtre et dans les autres arts durant les années vingt / Table ronde internationale du Centre national de la recherche scientifique ; communications de E[rika] Billeter ... [et al.], présentées par D[enis] Bablet. Lausanne : La Cité : L'Age d'Homme, cop. 1978. 296 p., [32] p. of plates : ill. ; 24 cm. (Théâtre années vingt: Études) Includes bibliographical references. DDC 700/.94 19
1. Arts, Modern - 20th century - Europe - Addresses, essays, lectures. 2. Collage - Europe - Addresses, essays, lectures. 3. Photography, Composite - Addresses, essays, lectures. I. Billeter, Erika, 1927-. II. Bablet, Denis. III. Centre national de la recherche scientifique (France).
NX542 .C64   *NYPL   [JFE 81-222]*

COLLAGE - EUROPE - ADDRESSES, ESSAYS, LECTURES.
Collage et montage au théâtre et dans les autres arts durant les années vingt /. Lausanne , cop. 1978. 296 p., [32] p. of plates : DDC 700/.94 19
NX542 .C64   *NYPL   [JFE 81-222]*

COLLAGE - SPAIN - EXHIBITIONS.
El "Collage" surrealista en España . Teruel [1989] 99 p. : ISBN 84-87183-06-9
MLCM 90/01381 (N)
NYPL   [3-MAML 91-6796]

El "Collage" surrealista en España : 21 septiembre-22 octubre 1989 / [textos, Rafael Santos Torroella, Francesc Rodon, Manuel Pérez-Lizano]. Teruel : Museo de Teruel, Diputación Provincial de Teruel, [1989] 99 p. : ill. (some col.) ; 29 cm. ISBN 84-87183-06-9
1. Collage - Spain - Exhibitions. 2. Surrealism - Spain - Exhibitions. I. Santos Torroella, Rafael.
MLCM 90/01381 (N)
NYPL   [3-MAML 91-6796]

Collana Arte, cultura, artigianato dell'Irpinia .
(1) I Dipinti dei Guarino e le arti decorative nella Collegiata di Solofra /. Napoli , c1987. 205 p. :
ND616 .D5 1987
NYPL   [3-MCF+ G924 90-12954]

Collana Arte e artisti liguri.
Bottaro, Silvia. Intarsiatori savonesi dell'Ottocento /. Savona , c1989. 181 p. : DDC 745.51 20
NK9924.I8 B67 1989
NYPL   [3-MOC 90-13408]

Collana del Dipartimento .
(4) Yntema, Douwe Geert. The matt-painted pottery of Southern Italy . Galatina , 1990. 370 p. : ISBN 88-7786-428-0
NYPL   [3-MPGD 91-5545]

Collana di arte moderna.
Scudiero, Maurizio. R.M. Baldessari, opere futuriste /. [Roma] , 1989. 231 p. : ISBN 88-7165-004-2 : DDC 709/.2 20
N6923.B257 A4 1989

Collana di estetica .
(2) Testa, Luciano, 1944- Le muse e il naufragio . Paese (Treviso) , 1990. 111 p. : DDC 720/.1 20
NA2500 .T48 1990

Collana Queriniana .
(10) Fotografie di Ikona Gallery . Venezia , 1989. 54 p. :   *NYPL   [3-MFW+ 91-7282]*
(2) Davanzo Poli, Doretta. Tessuti . Venezia , 1987. [30] p. :   *NYPL   [3-MON+ 90-10944]*
(3) I Querini Stampalia . Venezia , 1987. 255 p. :   *NYPL   [3-MAX+ (Querini Stampalia) 90-12441]*

Collar de Cáceres, Fernando. Pintura en la antigua Diócesis de Segovia (1500-1631) / Fernando Collar de Cáceres. [Segovia] : Diputación Provincial de Segovia, 1989. 2 v. (799 p.) : ill. (some col.) ; 25 cm. Revision of an appendix to the author's thesis (doctoral--Universidad Autónoma de Madrid). "Vol. segundo, Láminas"--V. 2, t.p. Includes bibliographical references (v. 1, p. 453-480) and indexes. ISBN 84-86789-23-0 (set) DDC 755/.2/09463570903107446357 20
1. Painting, Spanish - Spain - Segovia (Province) - Catalogs. 2. Painting - 16th century - Spain - Segovia (Province) - Catalogs. 3. Painting, Modern - 17th-18th

centuries - Spain - Segovia (Province) - Catalogs. 4.
Christian art and symbolism - Modern period, 1500- -
Spain - Segovia (Province). I. Title.
ND809.S44 C65 1989

Colle, Enrico. Maldarelli, Ernesto, 1850-1930. Un
artista ferrarese del legno, Ernesto Maldarelli
(1850-1930) /. Ferrara , c1989. 107 p. :
NYPL [3-MOC 90-12376]

Col·lecció universitària. Geografia e historia .
(16) Gasco Sidro, Antonio J. (Antonio José) El
escultor Ortells . [Castelló] , 1989. 191 p. :
ISBN 84-86895-11-1 DDC 730/.92 B 20
NB813.O697 G37 1989

Col·lecció Vilatana.
(núm. 1) Bosch i Planas, Joan, 1951- Ricard
Clausells, el pintor i el poeta, 1864-1939 /.
Vilafranca del Penedès , 1990. 141 p. :
IN PROCESS (ONLINE)
NYPL [3-MCQ C616 91-4303]

Collected essays, 1981-1987 /. Halley, Peter
[Essays. Selections.] New York , Venice, CA ,
1989, c1988. 302 p. : ISBN 3-905173-24-2
NYPL [3-MC 89-19486]

Collectibles /. Dunnan, Nancy. Englewood Cliffs,
NJ , c1990. 128 p. : ISBN 0-382-09918-4 DDC
745.1 20
NK1125 .D786 1990
NYPL [MAVC 91-5516]

COLLECTIBLES.
Curtis, Tony, 1939- There's a fortune in your
attic /. New York, NY , c1991. 512 p. : ISBN
0-399-51677-8 (alk. paper) DDC 745.1/075 20
NK1125 .C8874 1991

**COLLECTIBLES - CONSERVATION AND
RESTORATION - DIRECTORIES.**
Kovel, Ralph M. Kovels' antiques & collectibles
fix-it source book /. New York , c1990. x, 180
p. : ISBN 0-517-57333-4 : DDC 745.1/028/8 20
NK1125 .K659 1990
NYPL [MNH 90-13220]

Collecting antique linens, lace, and needlework /.
Johnson, Frances. Radnor, Pa. , c1991. p. cm.
ISBN 0-87069-634-3 (hc) : DDC 746/.075 20
NK8904 .J64 1991

Collecting Australian found stoneware /. Arnold,
Ken. Maiden Gully, Australia , c1989. 128 p. :
ISBN 0-9587953-8-X DDC 738.3/075 20
NK4365.A8 A76 1989

Collecting political Americana /. Sullivan,
Edmund B. Hanover, MA , c1991. vii, 248 p.,
[40] leaves of plates : ISBN 0-8158-0462-8 DDC
745 20
NK805 .S9 1991

Collecting Russian art & antiques /. Bowater,
Marina. New York , c1990. p. cm. ISBN
0-87052-897-1 : DDC 709/.47/075 20
N6981 .B69 1990

Collecting Russian art and antiques. Bowater,
Marina. Collecting Russian art & antiques /.
New York , c1990. p. cm. ISBN 0-87052-897-1 :
DDC 709/.47/075 20
N6981 .B69 1990

Collecting toys . O'Brien, Richard, 1934-
Florence, AL , c1990. iv, 494 p., [16] p. of
plates : ISBN 0-89689-073-2 : DDC
688.7/2/0973075 20
NK9509.65.U6 O25 1990

Collecting Victorian Staffordshire pottery figures
/. Kies, Kenyon Charles. [Marietta, OH]
c1989. 54 p. : ISBN 0-915410-66-4 DDC
738.8/2/09424630 20
NK4087.S6 K5 1989

La Collection A.P. de Mirimonde : legs aux
musées de Gray et de Tours / sous la direction
d'Elisabeth Foucart-Walter ; avant-propos de
Hubert Landais ; introduction de Raoul
Ergmann ; [catalogue rédigé par Pierre
Rosenberg]. Paris : Ministère de la culture et de
la communication, Editions de la Réunion des
musées nationaux, 1987. 137 p. : ill.
(some
col.) ; 27 cm. Catalog of an exhibition held at the
Musée du Louvre, Pavillon de Flore, Nov. 27,
1987-Apr. 25, 1988. At head of title: Musée du Louvre.
Includes index. Bibliography: p. 135-136. ISBN
2-7118-2151-X
*1. Mirimonde, Albert P. de - Art collections. 2. Art -
France - Paris - Exhibitions. I. Foucart-Walter,
Elisabeth. II. Rosenberg, Pierre. III. Musée du Louvre.
IV. Musée Baron Martin. V. Musée des beaux-arts de*
Tours.
NYPL [3-MAX (Mirimonde) 90-10806]

Collection Alla et Bénédict Goldschmidt . Musée
d'art moderne (Musées royaux des beaux-arts
de Belgique) Bruxelles [1990] 426 p. :
NYPL [3-MAL 91-5716]

Collection Archives (Casablanca, Morocco)
Terrasse, Henri, 1895-1971. Les arts décoratifs
au Maroc /. Casablanca , c1988. 198 p. :
NK1487.75.A1 T47 1988

Collection Avant/après.
Coutagne, Denis. Cézanne /. Paris , c1990. 240
p. : ISBN 2-903702-27-6 : DDC 759.4 20
ND553.C33 C68 1990

Collection "Biographie" (Edita (Firm))
Ducrey, Marina. Félix Vallotton . Lausanne ,
c1989. 163 p. : ISBN 2-88001-248-1 DDC
759.9494 20
ND853.V3 D8 1989
NYPL [3-MCZ+ V19 90-11783]

Collection Chemins de la mémoire .
Poletto, Christine, 1959- Art et pouvoirs à
l'Age baroque . Paris , c1990. 218 p., [16] p. of
plates : ISBN 2-7384-0495-2
N7862 .P65 1990

Collection "Culture et communication"
Chesnais, Robert. Les racines de l'audio-visuel .
Paris , c1990. 285 p. : ISBN 2-7178-1862-6 :
NX440 .C536 1990

Collection d'art moderne et contemporain.
Brauner, Victor, 1903-1966. Les Victor Brauner
de la collection de l'Abbaye Sainte-Croix /. Les
Sables d'Olonne , c1991. 126 p. : ISBN
2-901432-69-7 DDC 759.4 20
ND553.B873 A4 1991

Collection de feu Cloud Massot. Catalogue de la
collection de feu Cloud Massot
comprenant--Faïences et porcelaines
anciennes ... . [Marseille] [1929] 34 p., xxxii
leaves of plates :
NYPL [3-MAX (Massot) 86-3753]

Collection de l'École française de Rome .
(40) Bresc-Bautier, Geneviève. Artistes,
patriciens et confréries . Roma , 1979. xviii,
315 p., [15] leaves of plates :
N6921.P34 B73 *NYPL [3-MAMC 81-374]*

Collection Découverte (Nice, France)
Guid'arts . Nice [1989] 174 p. : ISBN
2-87720-040-X
N6485.3 .G85 1989

Collection "Essais" (Adam Biro (Firm))
Bacherich, Martine. Je regarde Manet . Paris ,
c1990. 160 p. : ISBN 2-87660-074-9 : DDC 759.4
20
ND553.M3 B24 1990

Collection études et travaux .
(no 1) Destins d'objets /. Paris , 1988. 474 p. :
ISBN 2-11-002009-1 (pbk.)
NYPL [3-MAVC 90-9455]

Collection Fleur de lys (Le Bugue, France)
Cadouin, une aventure cistercienne en Périgord
/. Le Bugue [France] , 1990. 167 p. : ISBN
2-86952-017-4 DDC 726/.7/094472 20
NA5551.C28 C3 1990

**Collection France (Institut français
d'architecture). Panoramique .**
(1) 40 architectes de moins de quarante ans,
Paris /. [Paris] , c1990. 311 p. : ISBN
2-281-15116-6
NA1048 .A13 1990

Collection H2A.
(1) La Promenade du critique influent . Paris ,
c1990. 433 p. : ISBN 2-85025-225-5 DDC
701/.9/094409034 20
N7475 .P76 1990

Collection "La Mémoire de l'art"
Canonne, Xavier. Armand Simon . Bruxelles
[1987] 118 p. : ISBN 2-87103-034-X
NC266.S54 C36 1987

Cruysmans, Philippe, 1925- Linou Truffino, ou,
Les voix de la mer . Bruxelles [1986] 127 p. :
ISBN 2-87103-024-8 DDC 759.9493 20
ND673.T75 A4 1986

Cruysmans, Philippe, 1925- Lise Brachet, ou,
Le bonheur de peindre . Bruxelles [1985] 127
p. : ISBN 2-87103-014-6 DDC 759.9493 20
ND673.B5438 A35 1985

Cruysmans, Philippe, 1925- Lise Durez peint

Victor Hugo /. Bruxelles [1986] 183 p. : ISBN
2-87103-023-5
N6973.D85 C7 1986

Herdies, Paul. Adolfo-Mario Marizza . Bruxelles
[1985] 94 p. : ISBN 2-87103-011-1 DDC 759.36
20
N6811.5.M34 A4 1985

Herdies, Paul. Lodew Bosscke . Bruxelles
[1985] 120 p. : ISBN 2-87103-016-2 DDC
759.9493 20
ND673.B5393 A4 1985

Collection Le Canada et ses trésors.
Courtemanche, Gil. Trente artistes dans un
train /. Montréal , c1989. 153 p. : ISBN
2-920718-29-0 : DDC 751.7/3/0971 20
NYPL [3-MLP 91-6235]

Collection "Les Grands sculpteurs contemporains"
Hachet, Jean-Charles. César, ou, Les
métamorphoses d'un grand art /. Paris , 1989.
92 p. :
IN PROCESS (ONLINE)
NYPL [3-MGO+ (Baldaccini) 90-11990]

Collection L'esprit des lieux.
Fleurent, Maurice. Villandry . Paris , c1989.
105 p. : ISBN 2-85889-052-1
NYPL [3-MSK 91-3221]

Collection Monographie, 0988-033X.
L'Etrange univers de l'architecte Carlo
Mollino . Paris , c1989. 174 p. : ISBN
2-85850-494-6
NA1123.M65 A4 1989

Tony Garnier, l'œuvre complète /. Paris ,
c1989. 254 p. : ISBN 2-85850-527-6 DDC
720/.92 20
NA1053.G37 A4 1989

Collection of architectural designs . Schinkel,
Karl Friedrich, 1781-1841. [Sammlung
Architektonischer Entwürfe. English.] New
York , 1989. 54, 11 p., 174 p. of plates : ISBN
0-910413-56-8 DDC 720/.92/4 19
NA1088.S3 A4 1989
NYPL [3-MQZ (Schinkel) 91-6053]

Collection of sculptures. Pramūan phāp pratimā
=. [Bangkok , 2508 i.e. 1965] 4, 43, 3, 42 p.,
100 leaves of plates :
NB1912.G38 P7 1965

Collection "Photographes"
Trülzsch, Holger. Le garage de Hegel /.
[Paris] , c1989. 108 p. : ISBN 2-86234-050-2
DDC 709/.2 20
N6888.T697 A4 1989

Collection Positions philosophiques.
Bertrand, Pierre. L'artiste /. Montréal, Québec ,
c1985. 193 p. ; ISBN 2-89006-233-3 DDC 701
19
N70 .B466 1985 *NYPL [3-MAS 90-12750]*

Collection Prestiges de l'Est.
Billot, Renée. Léon Delarbre, le peintre
déporté . Jarville-La Malgrange [1989] 125 p. :
ISBN 2-86955-088-X :
N6853.D3385 B55 1989

Collection Récifs.
La Tauromachie, art et littérature /. Paris ,
c1990. 151 p. ; ISBN 2-7384-0685-8 DDC 700
20
NX650.B84 T38 1990

**Collection scientifique (Markaz Tasjīl al-Āthār al-
Miṣrīyah)**
Desroches-Noblecourt, Christiane, 1913- Grand
temple d'Abou Simbel . Le Caire , 1971. vi, 65
leaves, xlii leaves of plates :
ND2865.A2 D4 1971

Collection Sémaphore.
Mœglin-Delcroix, Anne. Livres d'artistes .
Paris , c1985. 159 p. : ISBN 2-7335-0085-6
NYPL [MDT 86-3500]

Collection "un sur un"
Monod-Fontaine, Isabelle. Matisse, Le rêve, ou,
les belles endormies /. Paris , c1989. 63 p., [1]
folded leaf of plates : ISBN 0-287-66005-1
NYPL [3-MCO M43 91-3726]

Collection Villes.
Arcachon, la ville d'hiver /. Liège , 1988. 238
p. : ISBN 2-87009-372-1
NA1051.A73 A73 1988

Le Nouvel Amiens /. Liège , 1989. 471 p. :
ISBN 2-87009-368-3
NA9198.A42 N68 1989

Collection Voie d'accès.
Prévost, Claude, 1927- Les bâtisseurs de
l'imaginaire /. Jarville-La-Malgrange , c1990.
275 p. : ISBN 2-86955-083-9 :
N7432.5.A78 P78 1990

Collection "XIXe siècle / Photographie" .
(1) Heilbrun, Françoise. Les paysages des
impressionnistes /. Paris , c1986. 95 p. : ISBN
2-85025-116-X   *NYPL [MFW 90-11191]*

Les collectionneurs des impressionnistes . Distel,
Anne. [Paris] , c1989. 283 p. : ISBN
2-85047-042-2   *NYPL [MAVC+ 91-6788]*

Collections Baur. Art chinois . [Morlanwelz,
Belgium] , 1990. 216 p. : DDC
730/.0951/07449342 20
NK4165 .A714 1990

Collections du Musée Carnavalet.
Les Bronzes antiques de Paris /. Paris , 1989.
512 p. : ISBN 2-901414-34-6 DDC 730/.09364 20
NK7949.P2 B7 1989

**Collections flamandes et hollandaises des musées
de province.** Quimper, France. Musée des
beaux-arts. Tableaux flamands et hollandais du
Musée des beaux-arts de Quimper. Paris ,
Quimper , 1987. xxxiv, 101 p. : ISBN
2-906739-10-3 DDC 759.9492/074/44361 20
ND636 .Q5 1987

Collector Books. Huxford's fine art value guide.
Paducah, KY , <c1991-. v. <2 > : ISBN
0-89145-427-6 (v. 2) : DDC 707/.5 20
N8675 .H88 1991

Collector prints, old and new. Luckey, Carl F.
Florence, Ala. , c1982. vii, 350 p., [16] p. of
plates : ISBN 0-89689-025-2
     NYPL [3-MAYZ 90-12763]

**COLLECTORS AND COLLECTING -
HANDBOOKS, MANUALS, ETC.**
Dunnan, Nancy. Collectibles . Englewood
Cliffs, NJ , c1990. 128 p. : ISBN 0-382-09918-4
DDC 745.1 20
NK1125 .D786 1990
     NYPL [MAVC 91-5516]

**COLLECTORS AND COLLECTING -
QUÉBEC (PROVINCE) - MONTRÉAL -
EXHIBITIONS.**
Brooke, Janet M. Discerning tastes . Montréal,
Québec, Canada , c1989. 254 p. : ISBN
2-89192-123-2   *NYPL [3-MAVC 90-12883]*

Collector's encyclopedia of American furniture /.
Swedberg, Robert W. Paducah, KY , c1991- v.
<1 > : ISBN 0-89145-441-1 (v. 1) : DDC
749.213/075 20
NK2405 .S894 1991

**The collector's encyclopedia of Gaudy Dutch and
Welsh /.** Shuman, John A. [Paducah, KY]
(P.O. Box 300, Paducah 42002-3009) [c1991]
175 p. : DDC 738.3/0942/0973 20
NK4340.G38 S5 1991

**The collector's encyclopedia of Occupied Japan
collectibles** . Florence, Gene, 1944- Paducah,
KY , c1990. 127 p. : ISBN 0-89145-401-2 :
DDC 738/.0952/075 20
NK1071 .F583 1990

**The collector's encyclopedia of Russel Wright
designs /.** Kerr, Ann, 1921- Paducah, KY ,
c1990. 189 p. : ISBN 0-89145-423-3 : DDC
745.4/492 20
NK839.W75 K47 1990

**A Collector's exhibition: S. B. Nitikman,
Winnipeg Art Gallery, January 6-28, 1968.**
[Winnipeg? 1968?] 1 v. (unpaged) illus. 21 cm.
DDC 708.11/27/4
1. Nitikman, Sam B. - Art collections. 2. Art, Modern -
20th century - Exhibitions. I. Winnipeg Art Gallery.
N5220 .C698
     NYPL [3-MAX (Nitikman) 74-1772]

The collector's guide to buttons /. Epstein,
Diana. New York , 1990. 84 p. : ISBN
0-8027-7342-7 : DDC 646/.19 20
NK3668.5 .E67 1990
     NYPL [3-MNH 91-6705]

**Collector's guide to cartoon & promotional
drinking glasses /.** Hervey, John. Gas City,
IN , c1990. x, 180 p. : ISBN 0-89145-443-8 :
DDC 760/.0951/07479493 20
NK5440.D75 H4 1990

**Collector's guide to cartoon and promotional
drinking glasses.** Hervey, John. Collector's
guide to cartoon & promotional drinking glasses

/. Gas City, IN , c1990. x, 180 p. : ISBN
0-89145-443-8 : DDC 760/.0951/07479493 20
NK5440.D75 H4 1990

A collector's guide to magazine paper dolls /.
Young, Mary, 1933- Paducah, KY , c1990. 278
p. : ISBN 0-89145-424-1 : DDC 769.5/3/0973075
20
NK4894.U6 Y66 1990

Collector's guide to Victoriana /. Mace, O.
Henry. Radnor, Pa. , c1991. p. cm. ISBN
0-87069-600-9 (hc) : DDC 745.1/09/034075 20
NK1378 .M3 1991

**Collector's information clearinghouse antiques &
collectibles resource directory /.** Maloney,
David J. Radnor, Pa. , 1991. p. cm. ISBN
0-87069-611-4 (hc) : DDC 745.1/025/73 20
NK1127 .M34 1991

**Collector's information clearinghouse antiques
and collectibles resource directory.** Maloney,
David J. Collector's information clearinghouse
antiques & collectibles resource directory /.
Radnor, Pa. , 1991. p. cm. ISBN 0-87069-611-4
(hc) : DDC 745.1/025/73 20
NK1127 .M34 1991

A collector's vision . Sadinsky, Rachael, 1958-
Elmira, N.Y. , 1989. 126 p. : ISBN
1-87788-505-3 DDC 759.94/074/74778 20
ND160 .S23 1989
   NYPL [3-MAX+ (Arnot) 90-12636]

College Art Association of America. Anderson,
Jeffrey C. The New York Cruciform Lectionary
/. University Park , 1991. p. cm. ISBN
0-271-00743-5 DDC 745.6/7487 20
ND3359.N48 A44 1991

Collège de France. Huyghe, René. Psychologie de
l'art . Monaco , c1991. 366 p. ; ISBN
2-268-01023-6 : DDC 701/.15 20
N71 .H79 1991

**COLLEGE GRADUATES - EMPLOYMENT -
NETHERLANDS.**
Velden, R. K. W. van der. Letteren en
arbeidsmarkt /. Groningen , 's-Gravenhage
[1989] 129 p. ;
NX554.A1 V4 1989

**Col·legi Oficial d'Arquitectes de la Comunitat
Valenciana.** Santiago Calatrava . València ,
1986. 103 p. : ISBN 84-7579-104-2
     NYPL [3-MQZ (Calatrava) 91-6420]

**COLLEGIATA DI SAN MICHELE (SOLOFRA,
ITALY)**
I Dipinti dei Guarino e le arti decorative nella
Collegiata di Solofra /. Napoli , c1987. 205 p. :
ND616 .D5 1987
    NYPL [3-MCF+ G924 90-12954]

Il Collegio del Cambio /. Bon, Caterina. Roma ,
1987. 61 p., [8] p. of plates :
    NYPL [3-MAVZ (Perugia) 90-12513]

COLLEGIO DEL CAMBIO (MUSEUM)
Bon, Caterina. Il Collegio del Cambio /. Roma ,
1987. 61 p., [8] p. of plates :
    NYPL [3-MAVZ (Perugia) 90-12513]

Collegium Historiae Urbanae. see International
Commission for the History of Towns.

Collezione Basilea. Biografie .
(4) Lamacchia, Giovanni. Giuseppe De Nittis,
capolista degli impressionisti /. Firenze [1990]
257 p., [39] p. of plates : DDC 759.5 B 20
ND623.D417 L5 1990

(4) Lamacchia, Giovanni. Giuseppe De Nittis .
Firenze [1990] 257 p., [9] leaves, [23] p. of
plates :   *NYPL [3-MCF N73 90-12002]*

**Collezione del Palazzo dei Dogi Mocenigo di S.
Samuele a Venezia di proprietà del conde
Andrea di Robilant :** esposizione dal 17 al 21
maggio, vendita dal 22 al 27 maggio. Firenze ,
Galleria Bellini, 1933. 38 p., 54 leaves of
plates : ill. ; 32 cm.
1. Robilant, Andrea, conte - Art collections - Catalogs.
2. Art, Italian - Catalogs. I. Galleria Bellini (Florence,
Italy).   *NYPL [3-MAX+ (Robilant) 87-3088]*

La collezione Serra di Cassano /. Vannugli,
Antonio. Salerno , c1989. 157 p., [39] p. of
plates ; ISBN 88-85651-21-6
     NYPL [3-MCE 90-5149]

Collier, Caroline. Jones, David Michael,
1895-1974. David Jones . London , c1989. 48
p. : ISBN 1-85332-040-4 (pbk.)
    NYPL [3-MCV+ J765 89-19109]

Collier, John, 1913- Doty, C. Stewart (Charles
Stewart) Acadian hard times . Orono, Me. ,
1991. xiv, 184 p. : ISBN 0-89101-070-X DDC
338.1/09741/1 20
HD1775.M2 D67 1991
     NYPL [MFW 91-7984]

Collin, Simone Bourlard- see **Bourlard-Collin,
Simone.**

Collins, Douglas, 1945- The story of Kodak /
Douglas Collins. New York : H.N. Abrams,
1990. 392 p. : ill. (some col.) ; 29 cm. Includes
index. ISBN 0-8109-1222-8 DDC
338.7/681418/0973 20
1. Eastman Kodak Company - History. 2. Photographic
industry - United States - History. 3. Photographic film
industry - United States - History. 4. Camera industry -
United States - History. I. Title.
HD9708.U64 E273 1990
     NYPL [MFW+ 91-5847]

Collins, Ian. A broad canvas : art in East Anglia
since 1880 / Ian Collins. Norwich : Parke
Sutton, c1990. 144 p. : ill. ; 29 cm. ISBN
1-87033-706-9
1. Art - England - East Anglia. I. Title.
     NYPL [3-MAMR 90-11517]

Collins, Max Allan. Dick Tracy (Comic strip).
Selections. 1990. The Dick Tracy casebook .
New York , 1990. x, 273 p. : ISBN
0-312-04461-5 (deluxe) : DDC 741.5/0973 20
PN6728.D53 D534 1990
    NYPL [3-MEM (Gould) 90-10998]

Collins Publishers San Francisco. A Day in the
life of Italy /. San Francisco, Calif. , 1990. 220
p. : ISBN 0-00-215729-2 : DDC 945/.0022/2 20
DG420 .D35 1990   *NYPL [MFW+ 91-3408]*

Collins road atlas, Britain. William Collins Sons
and Co. Road atlas, Britain. Glasgow , c1986. 1
atlas (129 p.) :   *NYPL [Map Div. 91-5505]*

Collins road atlas Italy /. William Collins Sons
and Co. Glasgow , 1990, c1989. 1 atlas (128
p.) :   *NYPL [Map Div. 91-2596]*

Collins, Tricia. Pincus-Witten, Robert. The last
decade--American artists of the 80's . New
York (130 Prince St., New York 10012)
[1990] 137 p. : DDC 709/.73/0747471 20
N6512 .P492 1990

Collischan, Judy.
Cotter, Holland, 1947- Kay WalkingStick .
Brookville, NY , 1991. p. cm. ISBN
0-933699-20-4 : DDC 759.13 20
ND237.W316 A4 1991

Weyhe, Arthur. Arthur Weyhe--sculpture,
1972-1989 /. Brookville, N.Y. , c1990. 48 p. :
ISBN 0-933699-19-0 DDC 709/.2 20
NB237.W443 A4 1990

Collobi, Licia Ragghianti. see **Ragghianti Collobi,
Licia.**

Collura, Domenico. (joint author) Romano,
Giovanni. Il Maestro della Pala Sforzesca /.
Firenze , 1978. 48 p. :
ND623.M174 R65   *NYPL [3-MCE 81-524]*

The Colman Collection of silver mustard pots /.
Colman Foods. Norwich , 1979. 143 p. : ISBN
0-9506456-0-5 (pbk.)
NK7236.M88 C64 1979
     NYPL [MNO 81-450]

Colman Foods.
The Colman Collection of silver mustard pots /
[photographed by John Blomfield ; researched
by Honor Godfrey]. Norwich : Colman Foods,
1979. 143 p. : ill. ; 20 cm. Includes index. ISBN
0-9506456-0-5 (pbk.) :
1. Colman Foods - Art collections - Catalogs. 2.
Mustard pots - Great Britain - Catalogs. 3. Silverwork -
Great Britain - Catalogs. 4. Hall-marks. I. Blomfield,
John. II. Godfrey, Honor. III. Title.
NK7236.M88 C64 1979
     NYPL [MNO 81-450]

**COLMAN FOODS - ART COLLECTIONS -
CATALOGS.**
Colman Foods. The Colman Collection of silver
mustard pots /. Norwich , 1979. 143 p. : ISBN
0-9506456-0-5 (pbk.)
NK7236.M88 C64 1979
     NYPL [MNO 81-450]

Colnaghi (Gallery) Claude to Corot . New York ,
Seattle , c1990. 289 p. : ISBN 0-295-97086-3

DDC 758/.1/09440747471 20
ND1356.3 .C58 1990
        NYPL [3-MCN 91-5076]

Colo, 1946- Durham, Jimmie. Jimmie Durham .
New York , c1990. 37 p. :
        NYPL [3-MGO (Durham) 90-10679]

Cologne. Galerie Gmurzynska-Bargera. see
Galerie Gmurzynska-Bargera.

**COLOGNE (GERMANY) - BUILDINGS,
    STRUCTURES, ETC.**
Heinen, Werner. Köln . Köln , 1988. 327 p. :
    ISBN 3-7616-0929-9
        NYPL [3-MQWD 91-5588]

**COLOGNE (GERMANY) - DESCRIPTION -
    VIEWS.**
Rüdell, Carl. Bilder aus dem alten Köln /.
Köln , 1988. 110 p. : ISBN 3-7743-0237-5
        NYPL [3-MCK+ R895 89-17168]

COLOGNE (GERMANY) IN ART.
Rüdell, Carl. Bilder aus dem alten Köln /.
Köln , 1988. 110 p. : ISBN 3-7743-0237-5
        NYPL [3-MCK+ R895 89-17168]

Cologne. Josef-Haubrich-Kunsthalle. see **Cologne.
Kunsthalle.**

Cologne. Kunsthalle. In unnachahmlicher Treue .
Köln , 1979. 370 p. :
TR6.G3 C644   *NYPL [MFW 81-577]*

Cologne. Museum Ludwig. see **Museum Ludwig.**

**Cologne. Wallraf-Richartz-Museum. Museum
Ludwig.** see **Museum Ludwig.**

**COLOMBIA - ECONOMIC CONDITIONS -
    1971- - MAPS.**
Instituto Geográfico "Agustín Codazzi."
Subdirección de Investigación y Divulgación
Geográfica. Atlas básico de Colombia /.
[Bogotá] , 1986. 1 atlas (217 p. (some folded)) :
    DDC 912/.861 19
G1730 .I53 1986   *NYPL [Map Div. 87-697]*

Instituto Geográfico "Agustín Codazzi."
Subdirección de Investigación y Divulgación
Geográfica. Atlas básico de Colombia /.
[Bogotá] , 1989. 1 atlas (446 p. (some folded)) :
        NYPL [Map Div. 91-6225]

Colombia en Canada. Colombian art in Canada
= . Bogotá, Colombia , 1990. 24 p. : DDC
709/.861/07486148 20
N6675 .C65 1990

COLOMBIA - MAPS.
(1986) Instituto Geográfico "Agustín Codazzi."
Subdirección de Investigación y Divulgación
Geográfica. Atlas básico de Colombia /.
[Bogotá] , 1986. 1 atlas (217 p. (some folded)) :
    DDC 912/.861 19
G1730 .I53 1986   *NYPL [Map Div. 87-697]*

(1988) Instituto Geográfico "Agustín Codazzi."
Subdirección Agrológica. Suelos y bosques de
Colombia. Bogotá , 1988. 1 atlas (133 p.) :
        NYPL [Map Div. 91-13234]

(1989) Instituto Geográfico "Agustín Codazzi."
Subdirección de Investigación y Divulgación
Geográfica. Atlas básico de Colombia /.
[Bogotá] , 1989. 1 atlas (446 p. (some folded)) :
        NYPL [Map Div. 91-6225]

Colombia. Ministerio de Relaciones Exteriores.
Colombian art in Canada = . Bogotá,
Colombia , 1990. 24 p. : DDC
709/.861/07486148 20
N6675 .C65 1990

Integración latinoamericana, 1986-1987 .
[Bogotá, Colombia] [Roldanillo, Colombia]
[between 1986 and 1990] 57 p. :
NE502 .I58 1986

Colombia. Relaciones Exteriores, Ministerio de.
see **Colombia. Ministerio de Relaciones
Exteriores.**

**COLOMBIA - SOCIAL CONDITIONS -
    MAPS.**
Instituto Geográfico "Agustín Codazzi."
Subdirección de Investigación y Divulgación
Geográfica. Atlas básico de Colombia /.
[Bogotá] , 1986. 1 atlas (217 p. (some folded)) :
    DDC 912/.861 19
G1730 .I53 1986   *NYPL [Map Div. 87-697]*

Instituto Geográfico "Agustín Codazzi."
Subdirección de Investigación y Divulgación

Geográfica. Atlas básico de Colombia /.
[Bogotá] , 1989. 1 atlas (446 p. (some folded)) :
        NYPL [Map Div. 91-6225]

COLOMBIAN ART. see **ART, COLOMBIAN.**

**Colombian art in Canada = Colombia en
Canada.** Bogotá, Colombia : Ministerio de
Relaciones Exteriores, 1990. 24 p. : ill. (some
col.) ; 22 x 25 cm. DDC 709/.861/07486148 20
*1. Art, Colombian - Exhibitions. 2. Art, Modern - 20th
century - Colombia - Exhibitions. 3. Folk art -
Colombia - Exhibitions. I. Colombia. Ministerio de
Relaciones Exteriores. II. Title: Colombia en Canada.*
N6675 .C65 1990

Colombian figurative graphics /. Archer M.
Huntington Gallery. Austin [1976] 47 p. :
        NYPL [MDBF 90-5877]

**COLOMBIAN WIT AND HUMOR,
    PICTORIAL - EXHIBITIONS.**
Bogotá en caricatura . [Bogotá] [1988] 235 p. :
    DDC 986.1/48 20
F2291.B62 B64 1988
        NYPL [3-MDY+ 91-6190]

Merino, Hernán, 1922-1973. Hernán Merino .
Bogotá [1986?] 107 p. :
NC1460.M47 A4 1986

Colonial furniture in New Zealand.
Northcote-Bade, Stanley. Wellington [1971] 164
p. ISBN 0-589-00683-5 DDC 749.2/9931
NK2692.A1 N67   *NYPL [3-MOF 90-5434]*

**COLONIAL REVIVAL (ART) - UNITED
    STATES.**
Creating a dignified past . Savage, Md. , c1991.
ix, 129 p. : ISBN 0-8476-7690-0
        NYPL [3-MLF 91-6907]

Colonial Williamsburg, inc. National Trust for
Historic Preservation in the United States.
Historic preservation tomorrow . [Williamsburg,
Va.] 1967. xi, 57 p.
        NYPL [3-MQWO 90-5564]

Colonialismo e fotografia : il caso italiano /
[curatore, Luigi Goglia]. Messina : Sicania,
[1989?] 354 p. : ill. ; 23 x 25 cm. (L'Album . 1)
Catalog of an exhibition held at the Teatro Vittorio
Emanuele, Messina, Oct. 25-Nov. 11, 1989. Includes
bibliographical references (p. 353-354).
*1. Italy - Colonies - History - Pictorial works. I. Goglia,
Luigi, 1943-. II. Series: Album (Messina, Italy) , 1.*
IN PROCESS (ONLINE)
        NYPL [MFW 91-8015]

**Coloquio de Urbanismo Barroco (1986 :
    Archidona, Spain)** II centenario de la Plaza
Ochavada de Archidona / actas del Coloquio
de Urbanismo Barroco, Archidona, 1986 ;
coordina la edición, M. Dolores Aguilar García.
[Málaga] : Universidad de Málaga, [1989] 350
p. : ill., maps ; 22 cm. Cover title: Archidona, II
centenario Plaza Ochavada, 1786-1986. Includes
bibliographical references. ISBN 84-7496-177-7
*1. Architecture - Spain - Congresses. 2. Architecture,
Baroque - Spain - Congresses. 3. City planning - Spain -
Congresses. I. Aguilar, María D. (María Dolores). II.
Title. III. Title: Segundo centenario de la Plaza
Ochavada de Archidona. IV. Title: 2o centenario de la
Plaza Ochavada de Archidona. V. Title: Archidona, II
centenario Plaza Ochavada, 1786-1986.*
NA1306 .C6 1986

**Coloquio Internacional de Historia del Arte
    (1980 : Mexico City, Mexico)** Arte funerario
/ Coloquio Internacional de Historia del Arte ;
coordinado por Beatriz de la Fuente ; edición a
cargo de Louise Noelle. 1a ed. México :
Universidad Nacional Autónoma de México,
1987- v. : ill. ; 23 cm. (Cuadernos de historia del
arte . 41) Spanish, English, and French. Includes
bibliographical references. ISBN 968-360-243-6 (set)
*1. Sepulchral monuments - History - Congresses. I.
Fuente, Beatriz de la. II. Noelle, Louise. III. Series:
Cuadernos de historia del arte (Universidad Nacional
Autónoma de México. Instituto de Investigaciones
Estéticas) , 41. IV. Title.*
NB1800 .C65 1980
        NYPL [3-MRIF 90-2698]

Color and meaning . Hall, Marcia B. Cambridge ,
New York , 1991. p. cm. ISBN 0-521-39222-5
    DDC 759.03 20
ND170 .H3 1991

Color atmospheres . Kaufman, Donald. New
York , 1991. p. cm. ISBN 0-517-57660-0 : DDC
728 20
NK2115.5.C6 K38 1991

COLOR DECORATION AND ORNAMENT.
Audsley, W. (William), b. 1833. [Polychromatic
decoration as applied to buildings in the
mediaeval styles.] Victorian sourcebook of
medieval decoration /. New York , 1991. p.
cm. ISBN 0-486-26834-9 (pbk.) DDC 729/.4 20
NK1548 .A84 1991

Marx, Ina Brosseau, 1929- Professional painted
finishes . New York , 1991. p. cm. ISBN
0-8230-4418-1 : DDC 667/.9 20
NK2175 .M37 1991

COLOR DISCRIMINATION. see **COLOR
VISION.**

COLOR DRAWING - TECHNIQUE.
Lorenz, Albert, 1941- Drawing in color . New
York , 1991. p. cm. ISBN 0-8230-1384-7 DDC
741.2 20
NC758 .L67 1991

**COLOR-FIELD PAINTING - WASHINGTON
    (D.C.) - PRIVATE COLLECIONS -
    EXHIBITIONS.**
The Vincent Melzac collection. Washington,
D.C. [1971] 102 p. *NYPL [3-MCW 90-6402]*

COLOR - GREECE - HISTORY - TO 146 B.C.
Stulz, Heinke. Die Farbe Purpur im frühen
Griechentum . Stuttgart , 1990. 205 p. ; ISBN
3-519-07455-9   *NYPL [3-MBM 91-4521]*

COLOR GUIDES.
Blake, Wendon. [Color book.] The artist's guide
to using color . Cincinnati, Ohio , c1992. p. cm.
    ISBN 0-89134-378-4 (hard cover) : DDC 751.4
    20
ND1488 .B55 1992

COLOR IN ARCHITECTURE.
Limkilde, Svend. Noget om farver og arkitektur
/. [Copenhagen] , 1991. 47 p. :
NA2795 .L49 1991

Nemcsics, Antal. Színdinamika . Budapest ,
1990. 351 p., [32] p. of plates : ISBN
963-05-4602-7 :
ND1488 .N46 1990

**COLOR IN ARCHITECTURE - FRANCE -
    MOSELLE.**
Massel, Christiane, 1953- Couleurs &
architecture . [Sarreguemines] , c1989. 157 p. :
    ISBN 2-7085-0075-9 DDC 728/.0944/3825 20
NA3549.A3 M676 1989

**COLOR IN ARCHITECTURE - ITALY -
    MANTUA.**
Zuccoli, Noris. Mantova . Firenze , 1986. 60
p. :   *NYPL [3-MQWB 90-12550]*

**COLOR IN ARCHITECTURE - ITALY -
    SANTA MARIA CAPUA VETERE.**
Vargas, Davide. Colore e arredo urbano .
Napoli [Santa Maria Capua Vetere] [1990]
154 p. :
NA3552.S27 V3 1990

COLOR IN ART.
Beuttenmüller, Alberto, 1935- Volpi, Ianelli,
Aldir . [São Paulo , 1989] 1 v. (unpaged) :
ND355 .B48 1989

Blake, Wendon. [Color book.] The artist's guide
to using color . Cincinnati, Ohio , c1992. p. cm.
    ISBN 0-89134-378-4 (hard cover) : DDC 751.4
    20
ND1488 .B55 1992

Cortel, Tine. Basic principles & language of fine
art /. Newton Abbot , New York, N.Y. , 1989.
116 p. : ISBN 0-7153-9475-4 DDC 750/.18 20
ND1500 .C67 1989

Gerstner, Karl. The forms of color . Cambridge,
Mass. , c1986. 179 p. : ISBN 0-262-07100-2
    DDC 701/.8 19
ND1489 .G4713 1986
        NYPL [3-MAMZ 91-6985]

Le Clair, Charles. Color in contemporary
painting /. New York , 1991. p. cm. ISBN
0-8230-0738-3 DDC 752 20
ND1489 .L4 1991

Nemcsics, Antal. Színdinamika . Budapest ,
1990. 351 p., [32] p. of plates : ISBN
963-05-4602-7 :
ND1488 .N46 1990

Nemser, Cindy. Ben Cunningham--a life with
color /. Post, Tex. , c1989. 91 p. : ISBN
0-9622235-0-6 DDC 759.13 B 20
ND237.C8496 N46 1989
        NYPL [3-MCX C973 91-6760]

COLOR IN ART - EXHIBITIONS.
Colorists 1950-1965 . [San Francisco , 1965]
[66] p. :   *NYPL [3-MC 83-2195]*

**COLOR IN BUILDING. see COLOR IN
ARCHITECTURE.**

Color in contemporary painting /. Le Clair,
Charles. New York , 1991. p. cm. ISBN
   0-8230-0738-3 DDC 752 20
ND1489 .L4 1991

COLOR IN DESIGN.
Binns, Betty, 1929- Designing with two colors
/. New York , 1991. 127 p. : ISBN
   0-8230-1334-0 : DDC 741.6 20
NK1548 .B56 1991

COLOR IN INTERIOR DECORATION.
Kaufman, Donald. Color atmospheres . New
York , 1991. p. cm. ISBN 0-517-57660-0 : DDC
   728 20
NK2115.5.C6 K38 1991

COLOR IN LIGHT.
Dawson, Doug, 1944- Capturing light and color
with pastel /. Cincinnati, Ohio , c1991. p. cm.
   ISBN 0-89134-376-8 (hrdcvr) : DDC 741.2/35
   20
NC880 .D35 1991

COLOR PERCEPTION. see COLOR VISION.

COLOR (PHILOSOPHY)
Stulz, Heinke. Die Farbe Purpur im frühen
Griechentum . Stuttgart , 1990. 205 p. ; ISBN
   3-519-07455-9 *NYPL [3-MBM 91-4521]*

COLOR PHOTOGRAPHY - EXHIBITIONS.
Spectrum . Honolulu, Hawaii , c1979. [32] p. :
               NYPL [MFW 91-1278]

COLOR PRINTS - 20TH CENTURY - JAPAN.
Merritt, Helen. Modern Japanese woodblock
prints . Honolulu, HI , c1990. x, 324 p., [16] p.
of plates : ISBN 0-8248-1200-X DDC
   769.952/09/041 20
NE1323 .M47 1990

               NYPL [MDBV 90-11891]

**COLOR PRINTS, JAPANESE - EDO PERIOD,
1600-1868 - EXHIBITIONS.**
Yonemura, Ann, 1947- Yokohama .
Washington, D.C. , 1990. 198 p. : ISBN
   0-87474-993-X (alk. paper) DDC
   769/.499521364031 20
NE1321.8 .Y64 1990

               NYPL [MDBV+ 90-11723]

**COLOR PRINTS, JAPANESE - MEIJI
PERIOD, 1868-1912 - CATALOGS.**
Elvehjem Museum of Art. The Edward Burr
Van Vleck collection of Japanese prints.
Madison , 1990. vi, 352 p. : ISBN
   0-932900-24-0 : DDC 769.952/074/77583 20
NE1321.8 .E48 1990

**COLOR PRINTS, JAPANESE - MEIJI
PERIOD, 1868-1912 - EXHIBITIONS.**
Yonemura, Ann, 1947- Yokohama .
Washington, D.C. , 1990. 198 p. : ISBN
   0-87474-993-X (alk. paper) DDC
   769/.499521364031 20
NE1321.8 .Y64 1990

               NYPL [MDBV+ 90-11723]

**COLOR PRINTS - PRIVATE COLLECTIONS -
WASHINGTON (D.C.) - EXHIBITIONS.**
Yonemura, Ann, 1947- Yokohama .
Washington, D.C. , 1990. 198 p. : ISBN
   0-87474-993-X (alk. paper) DDC
   769/.499521364031 20
NE1321.8 .Y64 1990

               NYPL [MDBV+ 90-11723]

**COLOR PRINTS - PRIVATE COLLECTIONS -
WISCONSIN - MADISON - CATALOGS.**
Elvehjem Museum of Art. The Edward Burr
Van Vleck collection of Japanese prints.
Madison , 1990. vi, 352 p. : ISBN
   0-932900-24-0 : DDC 769.952/074/77583 20
NE1321.8 .E48 1990

**COLOR PRINTS - WISCONSIN - MADISON -
CATALOGS.**
Elvehjem Museum of Art. The Edward Burr
Van Vleck collection of Japanese prints.
Madison , 1990. vi, 352 p. : ISBN
   0-932900-24-0 : DDC 769.952/074/77583 20
NE1321.8 .E48 1990

COLOR SENSE. see COLOR VISION.

COLOR VISION.
Nemcsics, Antal. Színdinamika . Budapest ,
1990. 351 p., [32] p. of plates : ISBN

   963-05-4602-7 :
ND1488 .N46 1990

Colorado road atlas. H.M. Gousha Company.
Gousha Colorado road atlas and visitor's guide
/. New York, NY , c1991. 1 atlas (56 p.) :
   ISBN 0-13-151275-7
               NYPL [Map Div. 90-11950]

COLORADO - ROAD MAPS.
H.M. Gousha Company. Gousha Colorado road
atlas and visitor's guide /. New York, NY ,
c1991. 1 atlas (56 p.) : ISBN 0-13-151275-7
               NYPL [Map Div. 90-11950]

Colorado, 1990 : Denver Art Museum, April
28-June 24, 1990 / [editor, Marlene Chambers].
Denver, Colo. : The Museum, c1990. 143 p. :
ill. (some col.) ; 28 cm. ISBN 0-914738-39-9
(pbk.)
   *1. Art, American - Colorado - Exhibitions. I. Chambers,
   Marlene. II. Denver. Art Museum.*
IN PROCESS (ONLIN)
               NYPL [3-MAMT 90-13383]

Colore e arredo urbano . Vargas, Davide. Napoli
[Santa Maria Capua Vetere] [1990] 154 p. :
NA3552.S27 V3 1990

**COLORED PENCIL DRAWING -
TECHNIQUE.**
Sánchez Sánchez, Isidro. [Yo dibujo, yo pinto
lápices de colores. English.] Colored pencils .
New York , c1991. p. cm. ISBN 0-8120-4719-2
   DDC 741.2/4 20
NC892 .S2613 1991

Colored pencils . Sánchez Sánchez, Isidro. [Yo
dibujo, yo pinto lápices de colores. English.]
New York , c1991. p. cm. ISBN 0-8120-4719-2
   DDC 741.2/4 20
NC892 .S2613 1991

COLORED PENCILS.
Sánchez Sánchez, Isidro. [Yo dibujo, yo pinto
lápices de colores. English.] Colored pencils .
New York , c1991. p. cm. ISBN 0-8120-4719-2
   DDC 741.2/4 20
NC892 .S2613 1991

**COLORED PEOPLE (UNITED STATES) see
AFRO-AMERICANS.**

Colorists nineteen fifty nineteen sixty-five.
Colorists 1950-1965 . [San Francisco , 1965]
[66] p. :   *NYPL [3-MC 83-2195]*

Colorists 1950-1965 : [exhibition] San Francisco
Museum of Art, October 15-November 21,
1965. [San Francisco : The Museum, 1965] [66]
p. : ill. (some col.) ; 23 cm. Includes bibliographical
references.
   *1. Painting, Modern - 20th century - Exhibitions. 2.
   Color in art - Exhibitions. I. San Francisco. Museum of
   Art. II. Title: Colorists nineteen fifty nineteen sixty-five.*
               NYPL [3-MC 83-2195]

**COLOT PRINTS, JAPANESE - EDO PERIOD,
1600-1868 - CATALOGS.**
Elvehjem Museum of Art. The Edward Burr
Van Vleck collection of Japanese prints.
Madison , 1990. vi, 352 p. : ISBN
   0-932900-24-0 : DDC 769.952/074/77583 20
NE1321.8 .E48 1990

Colpaart, Adri. Wingen, Ed. Wolvecamp /. Venlo,
Nederland , c1990. 168 p. : ISBN
   90-6216-215-0 :
ND653.W64 W55 1990

**Columbia College, New York. see Columbia
University.**

Columbia County Historical Society (N.Y.)
Piwonka, Ruth. Mount Merino . Kinderhook,
N.Y. , c1978. [44] p. :
               NYPL [3-MCW+ 90-7105]

**COLUMBIA COUNTY (N.Y.) IN ART -
EXHIBITIONS.**
Piwonka, Ruth. Mount Merino . Kinderhook,
N.Y. , c1978. [44] p. :
               NYPL [3-MCW+ 90-7105]

Columbia Museum of Art. Art of the Italian
Renaissance from the Samuel H. Kress
collection. Columbia, S.C. : The Museum, 1954.
63 p. : ill. ; 28 cm. The Kress collection is part of
the collection of the Columbia Museum of Art.
   *1. Kress, Samuel Henry, 1863-1955 - Art collections -
   Exhibitions. 2. Columbia Museum of Art. 3. Painting,
   Renaissance - Italy. 4. Painting - South Carolina -
   Columbia. I. Title.* *NYPL [3-MAVZ (Columbia,
                              S.C.) 90-6807]*

COLUMBIA MUSEUM OF ART.
Columbia Museum of Art. Art of the Italian
Renaissance from the Samuel H. Kress
collection. Columbia, S.C. , 1954. 63 p. :
   *NYPL [3-MAVZ (Columbia, S.C.)
                        90-6807]*

**Columbia studies in the classical tradition, 0166-
1302 .**
(v. 19) Bartman, Elizabeth. Ancient sculpture
copies in miniature /. Leiden , New York ,
1992. p. cm. ISBN 90-04-09532-2 DDC 733/.3 20
NB94 .B37 1992

Columbia studies on art .
(no. 3) Emerging Japanese architects of the
1990s /. New York , 1991. 121 p. : DDC
   720/.952/09045 20
NA1555 .E44 1991
               NYPL [3-MQWS+ 91-6807]

(no. 4) Tsai, Eugenie. Robert Smithson
unearthed . New York , c1991. p. cm. ISBN
   0-231-07258-9 DDC 700/.92 20
N6537.S6184 A4 1991

**Columbia University. Graduate School of
Business. American Assembly. see American
Assembly.**

**Columbia University. Research Center for Arts
and Culture.** Information on artists . New
York, NY , c1989. 2 v. (various pagings) ;
   DDC 331.7/617/00973 20
N58 .I54 1989

Columbus Museum (Columbus, Ga.)
Pousette-Dart, Richard, 1916- Richard
Pousette-Dart /. Indianapolis, Ind. , c1990. 195
p. : ISBN 0-936260-51-3
               NYPL [3-MCX+ P878 91-3358]

Columbus Museum of Art.
Hawkins, William, 1895-1990. Popular images,
personal visions . [Columbus] , c1990. 32 p. :
   ISBN 0-918881-23-4
               NYPL [3-MCX H424 90-13390]

Impressionism and European modernism : the
Sirak collection / with essays by Richard
Brettell and Peter Selz ; catalogue entries by
Richard Brettell ... [et al.] ; research and
documentation by Leslie Stewart Curtis ; edited
by Norma Roberts. Columbus, Ohio : Columbus
Museum of Art ; Seattle : Distributed by
University of Washington Press, 1991. p. cm.
Includes bibliographical references. ISBN
0-295-97133-9 : DDC 709/.03/407477157 20
   *1. Art, European - Exhibitions. 2. Modernism (Art) -
   Europe - Exhibitions. 3. Art, Modern - 19th century -
   Europr - Exhibitions. 4. Art, Modern - 20th century -
   Europe - Exhibitions. 5. Sirak, Howard D. - Art
   collections - Exhibitions. 6. Sirak, Babette L. - Art
   collections - Exhibitions. 7. Art - Private collections -
   Ohio - Columbus - Exhibitions. 8. Columbus Museum
   of Art - Exhibitions. I. Brettell, Richard R. II. Selz,
   Peter Howard, 1919-. III. Roberts, Norma J. IV. Title.*
N6447 .C65 1991

The Quest for self-expression . Columbus,
Ohio , Seattle , 1990. 191 p. : ISBN
   0-295-97061-8 : DDC 759.7/312/07474 20
ND697.M6 Q4 1990
               NYPL [3-MCY+ 91-5070]

Robertson, Bruce, 1955- Reckoning with
Winslow Homer . Cleveland, Ohio , 1990. xvi,
196 p. : ISBN 0-940717-02-6 DDC 759.13 20
ND237.H7 A4 1990
               NYPL [3-MCX H76 91-3391]

**COLUMBUS MUSEUM OF ART -
EXHIBITIONS.**
Columbus Museum of Art. Impressionism and
European modernism . Columbus, Ohio ,
Seattle , 1991. p. ISBN 0-295-97133-9 : DDC
   709/.03/407477157 20
N6447 .C65 1991

Colvin, Howard Montagu. Architecture and the
after-life / Howard Colvin. New Haven : Yale
University Press, 1991. p. cm. Includes
bibliographical references and index. ISBN
0-300-05098-4 DDC 726/.8/094 20
   *1. Mausoleums. 2. Martyria. 3. Sepulchral monuments.
   4. Church architecture. I. Title.*
NA6120 .C65 1991

Comala . Gómez Arriola, Ignacio. Colima, Col.
[Mexico] [1985] 75 p. :
NA757.C66 G66 1985

**COMALA (MEXICO) - BUILDINGS,
STRUCTURES, ETC.**

COMMERCIAL BUILDINGS - NEW JERSEY.
Anderson, Will, 1940- Mid-Atlantic roadside
delights . Portland, Me. , c1991. viii, 164 p. :
ISBN 0-9601056-4-6 (pbk.)
　　　　　NYPL [3-MQWO 91-7968]

**COMMERCIAL BUILDINGS - NEW YORK
(STATE)**
Anderson, Will, 1940- Mid-Atlantic roadside
delights . Portland, Me. , c1991. viii, 164 p. :
ISBN 0-9601056-4-6 (pbk.)
　　　　　NYPL [3-MQWO 91-7968]

**COMMERCIAL BUILDINGS -
PENNSYLVANIA.**
Anderson, Will, 1940- Mid-Atlantic roadside
delights . Portland, Me. , c1991. viii, 164 p. :
ISBN 0-9601056-4-6 (pbk.)
　　　　　NYPL [3-MQWO 91-7968]

COMMERCIAL CORNERS. see **STOCK-
EXCHANGE.**

COMMERCIAL DESIGN. see **COMMERCIAL
ART.**

**Commission international pour l'histoire des
villes.** see **International Commission for the
History of Towns.**

Committee for Simon Rodia's Towers in Watts.
Rosen, Seymour. Simon Rodia's towers in
Watts. [Los Angeles] 1962. 48 p.
NA2930 .R67
　　　　　NYPL [3-MGO (Rodia) 90-7105]

**Committee for the Preservation of Architectural
Records.** Ward, James. Architects in practice,
New York City, 1900-1940 /. Union, N.J.
[1989] xviii, 87 p. ;　DDC 720/.25/7471 20
NA55.N5 W3 1989

Common market countries. see **European
Economic Community countries.**

Common walls/private homes . Nolon, John R.
New York , c1990. x, 196 p. :　ISBN
0-07-016819-9　DDC 728/.312/0973 20
NA7520 .N6 1990
　　　　　NYPL [3-MQWO 90-10404]

COMMUNICATION.
Krings-Heckemeier, Marie-Therese.
Kommunikation und gebaute Umwelt .
Witterschlick , 1990. 264 p. ;　ISBN
3-925267-35-2
NA7125 .K75 1990

**COMMUNICATION IN ARCHITECTURAL
DESIGN.**
Anthony, Kathryn H. Juries on trial . New
York , 19. p. cm.　ISBN 0-442-00235-1　DDC
729/079 20
NA2750 .A64 1991

Berg, Thomas, 1944- Architectural contract
document production /. New York , 1991. p.
cm.　ISBN 0-07-004857-6　DDC 720/.28/4 20
NA2584 .B47 1991

Krings-Heckemeier, Marie-Therese.
Kommunikation und gebaute Umwelt .
Witterschlick , 1990. 264 p. ;　ISBN
3-925267-35-2
NA7125 .K75 1990

COMMUNICATION IN ART.
Świdziński, Jan. Quotations on contextual art /.
[Eindhoven , New York (U. S.A.) , 1988?] 190
p. ;　ISBN 90-71638-04-9　DDC 701 20
N71 .S95 1988　　　*NYPL [3-MA 91-4598]*

COMMUNICATION, INTERCULTURAL. see
INTERCULTURAL COMMUNICATION.

COMMUNISM AND ART - CUBA.
Marinello, Juan, 1898-1977. Conversación con
nuestros pintores abstractos. Habana [1961] 111
p.　　　　*NYPL [3-MC 90-6744]*

**COMMUNISM AND ART - RUSSIAN S.F.S.R.
- MOSCOW.**
Khan-Magomedov, S. O. (Selim Omarovich)
Vhutemas . Paris , c1990. 2 v. (880 p.) :　ISBN
2-903370-55-9 (set)　DDC 707/.1/147312 20
N332.S65 M675 1990

COMMUNISM - CUBA.
Movimiento Unidad Revolucionaria. Conozca lo
que le ocurrirá a usted y a su país si el
comunismo logra adueñarse del poder. [Coral
Gables, Fla., 1963] 46 p.
　　　　　*NYPL [*XMB-2143]*

COMMUNIST AESTHETICS.
Voprosy metodologii i sotsiologii iskusstva .

Leningrad , 1988. 175 p. :
NX160 .V66 1988

Community Arts Programs Association.
Contemporary landscape : image and idea :
Burko, Feigenbaum, Hendricks, Resnick,
Richards : an exhibition : April 13-May 12,
1977 ... Queensborough Community College,
the City University of New York, Bayside, New
York / organized by CAPA (Community Arts
Programs Association). Bayside, N.Y. : CAPA,
c1977. 28 p. : ill. ; 22 cm. Includes bibliographies.
*1. Art, American - Exhibitions. 2. Art, Modern - 20th
century - United States - Exhibitions. 3. Landscape in
art - Exhibitions. I. Queensborough Community
College. II. Title.*
N6512 .C5814 1977
　　　　　NYPL [3-MAMT 81-992]

Community industries of the Shakers : a new
look : a catalog of highlights of an exhibition at
the New York State Museum, 1983-84 /
prepared by the staff of the New York State
Museum ; edited for the Shaker Heritage
Society by A.D. Emerich and A.H. Benning.
[Colonie, N.Y.] : Shaker Heritage Society at
Watervliet, c1983. 48 p. : ill. ; 28 cm.　DDC
338/.008288 19
*1. Shakers - Industries - Exhibitions. 2. Furniture,
Shaker - Exhibitions. I. Emerich, A. D. II. Benning, A.
H. III. New York State Museum. IV. Shaker Heritage
Society.*
BX9784 .C66 1983
　　　　　NYPL [3-MNE 90-12552]

**Community Memorial Museum (Yuba City,
Calif.)** J.J. Reilly . Yuba City, Calif. , 1989.
48 p. :　　　*NYPL [MFX (Reilly) 91-3601]*

Community of True Inspiration at Ebenezer. see
Amana Society.

Como me tornei pintor . Oswald, Carlos,
1882-1971. Petrópolis, R.J. , 1957. 254 p. :
N6659.O85 A2 1957

La Compagnia della Santissima Annunziata :
restauro e restituzione degli affreschi del
chiostro / a cura dell'Ufficio Restauri della
Soprintendenza per i Beni Artistici e Storici di
Firenze e Pistoia ; [testi di Licia Bertani ... et
al.]. Firenze : Centro Di, c1989. 61 p. : ill.
(some col.), 1 plan ; 24 cm. (Quaderni dell'ufficio
restauri della soprintendenza per i beni artistici e storici
di Firenze e Pistoia . 1) Cover title reads: La
Compagnia della Santissima Annunziata a Firenze: gli
affreschi del chiostro. Includes bibliographical
references.　ISBN 88-7038-178-1
*1. SS. Annunziata (Church : Florence, Italy) -
Conservation and restoration. 2. Mural painting and
decoration - Conservation and restoration - Italy -
Florence. I. Bertani, Licia. II. Italy. Soprintendenza ai
beni artistici e storici per le province di Firenze e
Pistoia. Ufficio restauri. III. Title: Restauro e
restituzione degli affreschi del chiostro. IV. Title:
Compagnia della Santissima Annunziata a Firenze : gli
affreschi del chiostro. V. Series.*
　　　　　NYPL [3-MLP 90-10711]

**Compagnia della Santissima Annunziata a
Firenze : gli affreschi del chiostro.** La
Compagnia della Santissima Annunziata .
Firenze , c1989. 61 p. :　ISBN 88-7038-178-1
　　　　　NYPL [3-MLP 90-10711]

Compagnie des cristalleries de Baccarat.
Baccarat : les flacons à parfum = the perfume
bottles. [Baccarat, France] : Compagnie des
cristalleries de Baccarat ; Paris ; 222 p. : ill.
(some col.) ; 29 cm. French and English.　ISBN
2-906309-00-1 :　DDC 748.8/2/09443823 19
*1. Compagnie des cristalleries de Baccarat. 2. Crystal
glass - France - History - 19th century. 3. Crystal
glass - France - History - 20th century. 4. Perfume
bottles - France. I. Title.*
NK5205.C65 A4 1986
　　　　　NYPL [3-MPW 90-10581]

**COMPAGNIE DES CRISTALLERIES DE
BACCARAT.**
Compagnie des cristalleries de Baccarat.
Baccarat . [Baccarat, France] : Paris ; 222 p. :
ISBN 2-906309-00-1 :　DDC 748.8/2/09443823
19
NK5205.C65 A4 1986
　　　　　NYPL [3-MPW 90-10581]

**COMPAGNIE DES PROPRIÉTAIRES DE
L'ENTREPRISE DE LA GRAVURE DU
MUSÉE CENTRAL DES ARTS (PARIS,
FRANCE) - BY-LAWS.**
Compagnie des propriétaires de l'entreprise de

la gravure du Musée central des arts (Paris,
France) Projet d'association pour l'entreprise de
la gravure des tableaux et monuments d'arts,
composant le Musée central des arts. [Paris]
[1800] 20 p. ;
N2030 .R63 1803 NE60

**Compagnie des propriétaires de l'entreprise de la
gravure du Musée central des arts (Paris,
France)**
Projet d'association pour l'entreprise de la
gravure des tableaux et monumens d'arts,
composant le Musée central des arts. [Paris] :
De l'imprimerie de Porthmann, successeur du
cit. Desenne ., [1800] 20 p. ; 25 cm. (4to)
Articles of association, by the engraver Pierre Laurent
and others, for the proposed organization: Compagnie
des propriétaires de l'entreprise de la gravure du Musée
central des arts. Caption title. "Enregistré à Paris ...
vendémiaire an 9 de la République [i.e. Sept./Oct.
1800]"--P. 20. Signatures: A-B⁴ C². With: Prospectus.
[Paris : Robillard-Péronville et Laurent, 1803?]. Bound
together subsequent to publication. DLC
*1. Compagnie des propriétaires de l'entreprise de la
gravure du Musée central des arts (Paris, France) -
By-laws. I. Laurent, Pierre, 1739-1809. II. Muséum
central des arts et de la République (Paris, France). III.
Title.*
N2030 .R63 1803 NE60

Companion to South African cartoonists /.
Schoonraad, Murray. Houghton, Johannesburg ,
1989. 398 p. :　ISBN 0-86852-114-0　DDC
741.5/092/268 B 20
NC1740.S6 S36 1989

**Company of Adventurers of England Trading
with Hudson's Bay.** see **Hudson's Bay
Company.**

Comparative studies on Muslim societies .
(12) Çelik, Zeynep. Displaying the Orient .
Berkeley , c1992. p. cm.　ISBN 0-520-07494-7
(alk. paper)　DDC 725/.91 20
NA957 .C44 1992

The Dervish lodge . Berkeley , c1992. p. cm.
ISBN 0-520-07060-7 (alk. paper)　DDC
700/.9561 20
NX688.T9 D47 1992

A complementary caste . Larner, Bronwyn.
Surfers Paradise [1988] 230 p. :　ISBN
0-7316-4346-1
IN PROCESS (ONLINE)
　　　　　NYPL [3-MAMM+ 90-13299]

The Complete artist : painting and drawing better
landscapes, still lifes, figures, and portraits /
edited by Ken Howard. New York, NY :
Watson-Guptill Publications, 1991. p. cm.
ISBN 0-8230-0771-5 (cloth)　DDC 751.4 20
1. Art - Technique. I. Howard, Ken, 1932-.
N7430 .C58 1991

The complete book of caricature /. Staake, Bob,
1957- Cincinnati, Ohio , c1991. 134 p. :　ISBN
0-89134-367-9 :　DDC 741.5 20
NC1320 .S75 1991

**The Complete book of covers from The New
Yorker, 1925-1989 /** with a foreword by John
Updike. 1st ed. New York : A.A. Knopf, 1989.
vii, 391 p. : chiefly col. ill. ; 31 cm. "Compiled by
the editors of The New Yorker."--Book jacket.　ISBN
0-394-57841-4
*1. New Yorker (New York, N.Y. : 1925). 2. Magazine
covers - New York (N.Y.). I. New Yorker (New York,
N.Y. : 1925).*　　　*NYPL [MDY+ 90-2826]*

The complete "Chinese ornament" . Jones, Owen,
1809-1874. New York , 1990. 100 p. of plates :
ISBN 0-486-26259-6 :　DDC 745.4/4951 20
NK1483.A1 J64 1990
　　　　　NYPL [3-MLF+ 91-3685]

A complete dictionary of furniture /. Gloag,
John, 1896- Woodstock, N.Y. , 1991. 828 p. :
ISBN 0-87951-414-0　DDC 749 20
NK2205 .G54 1991　*NYPL [MOF 91-6208]*

The complete guide to barrier-free housing .
Branson, Gary D. White Hall, Va. , c1991. 176
p. :　ISBN 1-558-70188-5 (pbk.) :　DDC 720/.42 20
NA2545.A3 B7 1991

**A complete guide to public lands and water
accesses.** Hanson, John M. Minnesota atlas .
Cambridge, MN , 1990. 1 atlas (216 p.) :　ISBN
0-934860-61-0　*NYPL [Map Div. 91-7525]*

The complete letters of Vincent van Gogh .
Gogh, Vincent van, 1853-1890 -

Correspondence. Greenwich, Conn. , 1958. 3
v. :   *NYPL [3-MCH G61 90-11512]*

The Complete "Masters of the poster" : all 256
color plates from "Les maîtres de l'affiche" /
edited by Stanley Appelbaum. New York :
Dover, 1990. xv, 240, [16] p. : col. ill. ; 31 cm.
    ISBN 0-486-26309-6   DDC 741.6/74/09034 20
*1. Posters - 19th century - Catalogs. 2. Decoration and
ornament - Art nouveau - Catalogs. I. Appelbaum,
Stanley. II. Maîtres de l'affiche.*
NC1845.A7 C6 1990
    NYPL [3-MDW+ 90-12311]

The Complete potter.
Phillips, Anthony. Slips and slipware /.
London , 1990. 96 p. :   ISBN 0-7134-6187-X :
    DDC 738.15 20
NK4285   *NYPL [3-MPR 91-6795]*

Complex visions . Aycock, Alice. Mountainville,
N.Y. , c1990. 47, [1] p. :
    NYPL [3-MGO (Aycock) 91-7401]

COMPOSERS - GERMANY - BIOGRAPHY.
Herrmann, Ursula. Eberhard Wenzel . Berlin ,
c1989. 210 p. ;   ISBN 3-374-00804-6   DDC
780/.92 B 20
NK410.W464 H5 1989

COMPOSITION (ART)
Boles, Martha. The golden relationship .
Bradford, Mass. , c1990- v. <1 > :   ISBN
0-9614504-3-6 (bk. 1)   DDC 701 20
N72.M3 B65 1990

Bothwell, Dorr. Notan . New York , 1991. p.
cm.   ISBN 0-486-26856-X (pbk.)   DDC 745.4 20
NK1510 .B67 1991

Fichner-Rathus, Lois, 1953- Understanding art
/. Englewood Cliffs, N.J. , 1992. p. cm.   ISBN
0-13-932235-5 (pbk.)   DDC 701/.1 20
N7430.5 .F5 1992

**A comprehensive exhibition of bronze sculpture
by Gerhard Marcks.** Marcks, Gerhard. New
York, N.Y. [1967] 28 p. :
    NYPL [3-MGO (Marcks) 90-6998]

Compton, Susan P.
[Marc Chagall. English]
Marc Chagall : my life, my dream : Berlin
and Paris, 1922-1940 / Susan Compton.
Munich, Federal Republic of Germany :
Prestel ; New York, NY, USA : Distributed
in the USA and Canada by te Neues Pub.,
c1990. 268 p. : ill. (some col.) ; 31 cm. "This
book originally appeared in German as the catalogue
to the exhibition "Marc Chagall: Mein Leben-Mein
Traum, Berlin und Paris 1922-1940," organized by
the City of Ludwigshafen am Rhein and the BASF
Aktiengesellschaft and held at the
Wilhelm-Hack-Museum, Ludwigshafen am Rhein, 7
April-3 June 1990"--Verso of t.p. Includes
bibliographical references (p. 268).   ISBN
3-7913-1064-X   DDC 760/.092 20
*1. Chagall, Marc, 1887- - Catalogs. I. Chagall, Marc,
1887-. II. Ludwigshafen am Rhein (Germany). III.
BASF Aktiengesellschaft. IV. Wilhelm-Hack-Museum.
V. Title.*
N6999.C46 A4 1990

Marc Chagall : my life, my dream : Berlin
and Paris, 1922-1940 / Susan Compton.
Munich : Prestel ; New York, NY, USA :
Distributed in the USA and Canada by te
Neues, c1990. 268 p. : ill. (some col.) ; 31
cm. "This book originally appeared in German as the
catalogue to the exhibition 'Marc Chagall : mein
Leben, mein Traum : Berlin und Paris, 1922-1940,'
organized by the City of Ludwigshafen am Rhein and
the BASF Aktiengesellschaft and held at the
Wilhelm-Hack-Museum, Ludwigshafen am Rhein, 7
April-3 June 1990"--T.p. verso. Bibliography: p. 268.
    ISBN 3-7913-1064-X
*1. Chagall, Marc, 1887- - Exhibitions. I. BASF
Aktiengesellschaft. II. Wilhelm-Hack-Museum. III. Title.*
    NYPL [3-MCZ+ C43 90-13436]

COMPUTER AIDED DESIGN.
Jacobs, Stephen Paul. The CAD design studio .
New York , c1991. vi, 120 p. :   ISBN
0-07-032227-9   DDC 721/.0285 20
NA2728 .J33 1991

Kahlen, Hans. CAD-Einsatz in der Architektur
/. Stuttgart , c1989. 200 p. :   ISBN 3-17-010297-4
NA2728 .K38 1989

Stasiowski, Frank, 1948- Project management
for the design professional /. New York , 1991.

p. cm.   ISBN 0-8230-4413-0   DDC 720/.68 20
NA1996 .S74 1991

**COMPUTER-AIDED DESIGN -
EVALUATION.**
Evaluating and predicting design performance /.
New York, N.Y. , c1991. p. cm.   ISBN
0-471-85385-2   DDC 721/.0285 20
NA2728 .E94 1991

COMPUTER ART.
Computerkultur, oder, "The Beauty of bit &
byte" /. Bremen , 1989. 223 p. :   ISBN
3-924252-06-8   *NYPL [3-MAL+ 91-5883]*

COMPUTER ART - STUDY AND TEACHING.
Gosney, Michael, 1954- The Verbum book of
scanned imagery /. Redwood City, CA , 1990.
p. cm.   ISBN 1-558-51091-5 :   DDC 760 20
N7433 .G68 1990

COMPUTER ART - TECHNIQUE.
Gosney, Michael, 1954- The Verbum book of
digital painting /. Redwood City, Calif. , 1990.
ix, 211 p. :   ISBN 1-558-51090-7   DDC 760 20
N7433.8 .G68 1990

COMPUTER ART - THEMES, MOTIVES.
Click 1 . Cincinnati, Ohio , c1990. 149 p. :
    ISBN 0-89134-348-2 :   DDC 700 20
N7433.8 .C55 1990
    NYPL [3-MAL+ 91-4501]

**COMPUTER ART - UNITED STATES -
THEMES, MOTIVES.**
Greiman, April. Hybrid imagery . New York ,
1990. 158 p. :   ISBN 0-8230-2518-7 :   DDC 741.6
20
NC998.5.A1 G75 1990
    NYPL [3-MDW 90-10910]

COMPUTER GRAPHICS - TECHNIQUE.
Hiebert, Kenneth J. Graphic design processes .
New York , c1992. 208 p. :   ISBN 0-442-00839-2
    DDC 741.6 20
NC1000 .H54 1991

**Computer graphics technology and management
series.**
Buehrens, Carol. DataCAD for the architect /.
Blue Ridge Summit, PA , c1991. xxi, 450 p. :
    ISBN 0-8306-3746-X (pbk.) :   DDC
720/.28/402855369 20
NA2728 .B84 1991

Computer nella progettazione. Architettura &
computer. [Roma, 1972] 219 p.
NA2540 .A62   *NYPL [3-MQD 90-6902]*

Computerkultur, oder, "The Beauty of bit & byte"
/ Michael Weisser (Hrsg.). Bremen : TMS,
1989. 223 p. : ill. ; 31 cm. + compact disc.
Library's copy lacks compact disc.   ISBN
3-924252-06-8
*1. Computer art. I. Weisser, Michael. II. Title: Beauty
of bit & byte. III. Title: Beauty of bit and byte.*
    NYPL [3-MAL+ 91-5883]

Comstock, William Phillips. Bungalows, camps,
and mountain houses / William Phillips
Comstock and Clarence Eaton Schermerhorn ;
with an introduction by Tony P. Wrenn.
Washington, D.C. : American Institute of
Architects Press, c1990. xxvi, 125 p. : ill.,
plans ; 26 cm. Reprint, with new introd. Originally
published: Washington, D.C. : W.T. Comstock, Co.
1915. "80 designs by American architects"--Cover.
Includes bibliographical references.   ISBN
1-558-35063-2 :   DDC 728/.373 20
*1. Bungalows - United States. 2. Camp sites, facilities,
etc. - United States. 3. Log cabins - United States. I.
Schermerhorn, Clarence Eaton, 1872-1925. II. Title.*
NA7571 .C7 1990
    NYPL [3-MRGG 91-3451]

Comte, Philippe.
[Klee. English]
Paul Klee / Philippe Comte ; translated from
the French by Carol Marshall. Woodstock,
N.Y. : Overlook Press, 1991. p. cm.
Translation of: Klee.   ISBN 0-87951-438-8 :   DDC
760/.092 20
*1. Klee, Paul, 1879-1940 - Criticism and interpretation.
I. Title.*
N6888.K55 C6613 1991

Con cariño, el arte folklórico mexicano. San
Antonio Museum Association. Con cariño,
Mexican folk art. [San Antonio] [1986] 69 p. :
    DDC 745/.0972/0740164351 19
NK844 .S26 1986   *NYPL [3-MNE 88-2957]*

Con cariño, Mexican folk art . San Antonio
Museum Association. [San Antonio] [1986] 69

p. :   DDC 745/.0972/0740164351 19
NK844 .S26 1986   *NYPL [3-MNE 88-2957]*

Conaway, Judith, 1948- Historic Blacks in the
arts /. Chicago, IL , c1990. p. cm.   ISBN
0-922162-58-1 :   DDC 700/.92/2 B 20
NX164.B55 H57 1990

CONCENTRATION CAMPS IN ART.
Billot, Renée. Léon Delarbre, le peintre
déporté . Jarville-La Malgrange [1989] 125 p. :
    ISBN 2-86955-088-X :
N6853.D3385 B55 1989

CONCEPT ART. see CONCEPTUAL ART.

Concept conceptruimte /. Penck A. R., 1939-
Rotterdam [1979] 83 p. :
ND588.P46 A4 1979
    NYPL [3-MCK+ P41 81-481]

**Conceptos fundamentales en la historia del arte
español** / director, Francisco Calvo Serraller.
Madrid : Taurus, c1989-<1990> <v. 1; v. 5-6,
pt. 1; in 3 > : ill. ; 21 cm. Includes bibliographical
references and indexes. CONTENTS. - 1. El arte
medieval hasta el año mil / Fernando de Olaguer-Feliú
Alonso -- 5. El largo siglo XVI / Fernando Marías -- 6.
El arte del barroco. 1, Arquitectura y escultura /
Virginia Tovar, Juan José Martín González.   ISBN
84-306-7001-7   DDC 709/.46 20
*1. Art, Spanish. I. Calvo Serraller, F. (Francisco),
1948-.*
N7101 .C65 1989

**Conceptos fundamentales en la historia del arte
español** .
(5) Marías, Fernando, 1949- El largo siglo
XVI . Madrid , c1989. 745 p. ;   ISBN
84-306-0102-3
IN PROCESS (ONLINE)
    NYPL [3-MAML 90-13399]

CONCEPTUAL ART.
Arte conceptual revisado =. [Valencia] [1990?]
286 p. :   ISBN 84-7721-108-6   DDC 709/.04/075
20
N6494.C63 A76 1990

Conceptual art, conceptual forms. Schlatter,
Christian. Art conceptuel, formes conceptuelles
=. Paris , 1990. 598 p. :
    NYPL [3-MAL 91-3664]

**CONCEPTUAL ART - CZECHOSLOVAKIA -
EXHIBITIONS.**
Knížák, Milan. Milan Knížák . [Brno , 1990?] 1
v. (unpaged) :
N6834.5.K56 A4 1990

**CONCEPTUAL ART - EUROPE -
EXHIBITIONS.**
De Europa . New York [1972] [52] p. :
    NYPL [3-MAL 91-639]

CONCEPTUAL ART - EXHIBITIONS.
L'Art conceptuel, une perspective . Paris ,
c1989. 260 p. :   *NYPL [3-MAL 90-11049]*

In other words . [Stuttgart] [1989] 107 p. :
    ISBN 3-89322-159-X
    NYPL [3-MAL 90-8164]

L'Art conceptuel, une perspective . Paris ,
c1989. 260 p. :   ISBN 2-85534-607-1   DDC
709/.04/07507444361 20
N6494.C63 A75 1989

Schlatter, Christian. Art conceptuel, formes
conceptuelles =. Paris , 1990. 598 p. :
    NYPL [3-MAL 91-3664]

Wodiczko, Krzysztof. Krzysztof Wodiczko .
New York [1990?] 46 p. :   ISBN 0-913263-29-X :
    DDC 709/.2 20
N7255.P63 W642 1990
    NYPL [MFX (Wodiczko) 91-4633]

CONCEPTUAL ART - FRANCE.
Hahn, Otto. Daniel Spoerri /. Paris , c1990.
190 p. :   ISBN 2-08-012140-5
    NYPL [3-MGO (Spoerri) 90-13083]

**CONCEPTUAL ART - FRANCE -
EXHIBITIONS.**
Les Immatériaux. Paris , c1985. 2 v. :   ISBN
2-85850-299-4 (Epreuves d'écriture)
    NYPL [3-MAL+ 86-2657]

**CONCEPTUAL ART - FRANCE - THEMES,
MOTIVES.**
Le Moment extrême. Apt , Paris , 1989- v. <1
> :   ISBN 2-907383-03-5 (Eraklea)
N6848.5.C66 M66 1989

**CONCEPTUAL ART - GERMANY (WEST) -
EXHIBITIONS.**

Blanchette, Manon, 1952- Blickpunkte .
Montréal, Québec , c1989. 2 v. : ISBN
2-551-12161-2
N6868.5.C63 B55 1989

CONCEPTUAL ART - ITALY.
Fabio Sargentini. Milano , c1990. 125 p. :
ISBN 88-7816-032-6
IN PROCESS (ONLINE)
NYPL [MWES (Sargentini, F.) 91-4430]

**CONCEPTUAL ART - ITALY -
EXHIBITIONS.**
Merz, Mario. Mario Merz at MOCA. [Milan]
[c1989] 126 p. : ISBN 0-914357-17-4 (Museum of
Contemporary Art) DDC 709/.2 20
N6923.M43 A4 1989
NYPL [3-MGO (Merz) 91-6017]

Plessi, Fabrizio, 1940- Plessi /. Treviso , c1990.
175 p. : ISBN 88-85066-70-4 DDC 700/.92 20
N6923.P55 A4 1990
NYPL [3-MGO+ (Plessi) 91-5437]

Conceptual art revisited. Arte conceptual revisado
=. [Valencia] [1990?] 286 p. : ISBN
84-7721-108-6 DDC 709/.04/075 20
N6494.C63 A76 1990

**CONCEPTUAL ART - RUSSIAN S.F.S.R. -
EXHIBITIONS.**
Gerlovina, Rimma. Still performances /.
Cambridge, Mass. , 1989. 39 p. : ISBN
0-938437-27-5 DDC 779/.092/2 20
NX556.Z9 G472 1989
NYPL [MFW 90-4189]

**CONCEPTUAL ART - SOVIET UNION -
EXHIBITIONS.**
Between spring and summer . Tacoma, Wash. ,
Boston, Mass. , c1990. x, 206 p. : ISBN
0-910663-49-1
N6988.5.C62 B48 1990
NYPL [3-MAM 90-12998]

CONCEPTUAL ART - UNITED STATES.
Bruggen, Coosje van. John Baldessari /. New
York , 1990. 256 p. : ISBN 0-8478-1182-4 :
DDC 709/.2 20
N6537.B17 B78 1990
NYPL [3-MCX+ B176 90-11225]

Horn, Roni, 1955- To place . New York , 1991-
p. cm. ISBN 0-941863-21-2 DDC 709.2 20
N6537.H644 A4 1991

Kosuth, Joseph. Art after philosophy and after .
Cambridge, Mass. , c1991. p. cm. ISBN
0-262-11157-8 DDC 701/.17 20
N6537.K65 A35 1991

**CONCEPTUAL ART - UNITED STATES -
EXHIBITIONS.**
Ferguson, Bruce. Sherrie Levine--Fountain .
New York , 1991. p. cm. ISBN 0-941863-20-4
DDC 709/.2 20
N6537.L453 A4 1991

**CONCEPTUAL ART - UNITED STATES -
THEMES, MOTIVES.**
Breaking down the boundaries . Seattle, Wash. ,
c1989. 31 p. : ISBN 0-935558-24-1 DDC 707/.5
20
N72.A77 B74 1909
NYPL [3-MAMT+ 90-12629]

CONCERTOS (VIOLIN)
Nielsen, Carl, 1865-1931. [Concertos, violin,
orchestra, op. 33.] Concerto for violin &
orchestra, op. 33 ; Symphony no. 4, op. 29 .
Oslo, Norway , p1989. 1 sound disc :
Norsk IDCD 5

**CONCERTOS (VIOLIN AND PIANO WITH
STRING ORCHESTRA)**
Mendelssohn-Bartholdy, Felix, 1809-1847.
[Concertos, violin, piano, string orchestra, D
minor.] Konzert für Violine und Klavier =.
Pontelambro (Co), Italy , p1987. 1 sound disc :
Nuova era 033.6704

Concha Benedito. Benedito, Concha. Paris [1989]
120 p. : ISBN 2-906905-26-7
MLCM 90/06996 (N)
NYPL [3-MCQ+ B458 91-4061]

**Conciliul Culturii și Educației Socialiste. Oficiul
pentru Organizarea Expozițiilor.** Ionescu,
Alexandra. Contemporary Romanian painting .
[s.l. , 1973] [59] p. : DDC 759.9498/074/013
ND928 .I66   *NYPL [3-MCY 90-12375]*

**The concise catalogue of the Scottish National
Portrait Gallery /.** Scottish National Portrait
Gallery. Edinburgh , 1990. 414 p. : ISBN

0-903148-93-5
NYPL [3-MAVZ (Edinburgh) 90-13640]

A concise dictionary of architecture /. Jones,
Frederic H. (Frederic Hicks), 1944- Los Altos,
Calif. , 1991. p. cm. ISBN 1-560-52066-3 : DDC
720/.3 20
NA31 .J6 1991

A concise dictionary of interior design /. Jones,
Frederic H. (Frederic Hicks), 1944- Los Altos,
Calif. , c1990. 215 p. ; ISBN 1-560-52067-1
DDC 729/.03 20
NK1704 .J6 1991

The Concise dictionary series.
Jones, Frederic H. (Frederic Hicks), 1944- A
concise dictionary of architecture /. Los Altos,
Calif. , 1991. p. cm. ISBN 1-560-52066-3 : DDC
720/.3 20
NA31 .J6 1991

Jones, Frederic H. (Frederic Hicks), 1944- A
concise dictionary of interior design /. Los
Altos, Calif. , c1990. 215 p. ; ISBN
1-560-52067-1 DDC 729/.03 20
NK1704 .J6 1991

Concise encyclopedia of porcelain. Sotheby's
concise encyclopedia of porcelain /. London ,
1990. 208 p. : ISBN 1-85029-251-5 : DDC
738.209 20
NK4370   *NYPL [MPC 91-3277]*

**The concise guide to British pottery and
porcelain /.** Godden, Geoffrey A. London ,
1990. 224 p. : ISBN 0-7126-3600-5 DDC
738/.0941/075 20
NK4085 .G62 1990

Concord Antiquarian Society. Museum. Haines,
Carol L. "Forms to sett on" . Concord, Mass.
[1984?] 36 p. :
NK2715 .H35 1984
NYPL [3-MOF 90-12018]

Concord seating furniture. Haines, Carol L.
"Forms to sett on" . Concord, Mass. [1984?] 36
p. :
NK2715 .H35 1984
NYPL [3-MOF 90-12018]

**Concorso pianistico internazionale "Busoni"
[sound recording]** = Internationaler Pianisten
Wettweberb "Busoni". Pontelambro (Co), Italy :
Nuova era, p1988. 6 sound discs : digital,
stereo. ; 4 3/4 in. Nuova era: 6716-DM--6721-DM.
Titles on containers: Concorso pianistico internazionale
"Ferruccio Busoni" Bolzano : 30 anni di storia pianistica
= Internationaler Pianisten Wettweberb "Ferruccio
Busoni" Bozen : 30 Jahre Klaviergeschichte.
Performances by prize winners of the Busoni
Competition. Recorded 1956-1986 by RAI from the
festival site in Bolzano. Compact discs. CONTENTS. -
v. 1. Jörg Demus. Martha Argerich. Michael Ponti.
François-Joel Thiollier -- v. 2. Garrick Ohlsson. Richard
Goode. Mark Szeltzer. Vladimir Selivochin -- v. 3.
Annamaria Cigoli. Ursula Oppens. Pascal Devoyon.
Robert Benz. Terence Judd -- v. 4. Daniel Rivera.
Roberto Cappello. Boris Bloch. Catherine Vickers.
Margarita Höhenrieder. Lev Natochenny -- v. 5. Hung
Kuan Chen. Louis Lortie. José Carlos Cocarelli. Liliya
Zilberstein -- v. 6. Garrick Ohlsson. Richard Goode.
*1. Piano music. I. F. Busoni International Piano
Competition. II. Title: Internationaler Pianisten
Wettweberb "Busoni". III. Title: Concorso pianistico
internazionale "Ferruccio Busoni" Bolzano. IV. Title:
Internationaler Pianisten Wettweberb "Ferruccio Busoni"
Bozen.*
Nuova era 6716-DM--6721 DM

**Concorso pianistico internazionale "Ferruccio
Busoni" Bolzano.** Concorso pianistico
internazionale "Ferruccio Busoni" [sound recording] =.
Pontelambro (Co), Italy , p1988. 6 sound discs :
Nuova era 6716-DM--6721 DM

CONCRETE ART - EXHIBITIONS.
Arte abstracto, arte concreto . [Valencia?] ,
c1990. 439 p. : ISBN 84-7890-151-5
N6494.A2 A78 1990

Conde, Teresa del. Alvarez Bravo, Manuel, 1902-
Mucho sol /. México , 1989. 94 p. : ISBN
968-16-3242-7
NYPL [MFX (Alvarez Bravo) 90-2181]

**CONDER, CHARLES, 1868-1909 -
EXHIBITIONS.**
Charles Conder, Robert Henri, James Morrice,
Maurice Prendergast . New York [1975] [54]
p. :   *NYPL [3-MC 90-5453]*

Cone, Michèle S., 1932- Art, prejudice, and
persecution : Vichy, France, 1940-1944 /
Michèle C. Cone. Princeton, N.J. : Princeton
University Press, c1992. p. cm. Includes
bibliographical references and index. ISBN
0-691-04088-5 : DDC 701/.03 20
*1. Art and state - France. 2. Art - Political aspects -
France - History - 20th century. 3. France - History -
German occupation, 1940-1945. I. Title.*
N6848 .C66 1992

Confederación Granadina. see Colombia.

**Confederate States of America - Regimental
histories. see United States - History - Civil
War, 1861-1865 - Regimental histories.**

Confederation Centre Art Gallery and Museum.
Laurette, Patrick Condon. John O'Brien,
1831-1891 /. Halifax, N.S. , c1984. 128 p. :
ND249.O37 L38 1984
NYPL [3-MCZ+ O128 90-9675]

Confédération suisse. see Switzerland.

Conference center planning and design . Penner,
Richard H. New York , 1991. 256 p. : ISBN
0-8230-0911-4 : DDC 725/.91/097309048 20
NA6880.5.U6 P46 1991

**Conference of Historical Societies. see American
Association for State and Local History.**

**Conference on Women, the Arts, and Society
(1988 : Susquehanna University)** Sexuality,
the female gaze, and the arts . Selinsgrove
[N.J.] , London , 1992. p. cm. ISBN
0-945636-32-6 (alk. paper) DDC 700/.1/03 20
NX180.F4 S49 1992

**Conference report (National Bureau of Economic
Research)**
The Economics of art museums /. Chicago ,
1991. p. cm. ISBN 0-226-24073-8 (alk. paper)
DDC 338.4/770813 20
N510 .E27 1991

Confronting the uncomfortable : questioning truth
and power. [New Haven, Ct.] : Yale University
Art Gallery, c1989. 36 p. : ill. ; 28 cm. Cover
title. Preface: Mary E. Law. "This publication
accompanies an exhibition at the Yale University Art
Gallery 2 September-22 October 1989"--P. 18. Includes
bibliographical references. ISBN 0-89467-052-2
*1. Photography of women - Exhibitions. 2. Photography
of the nude - Exhibitions. I. Law, Mary E. II. Yale
University. Art Gallery.*
NYPL [MFW 90-11183]

Congdon, Herbert Wheaton, 1876-1965. Early
American homes for today : a treasury of
decorative details and restoration procedures /
Herbert Wheaton Congdon. Dublin, N.H. :
W.L. Bauhan, c1985. xv, 236 p. : ill. ; 25 cm.
Originally published: Rutland, Vt. : C.D. Tuttle Co.,
1963. "New introduction by William Morgan." Includes
index. ISBN 0-87233-065-6 (pbk.) DDC
728.3/7/0974 19
*1. Architecture, Domestic - New England. 2.
Architecture, Domestic - New England - Conservation
and restoration. 3. Architecture - Details. I. Morgan,
William, 1944-. II. Title.*
NA7210 .C6 1985

Conger, Clement E. United States. Dept. of State.
Treasures of State . New York , 1991. p. cm.
ISBN 0-8109-3911-8 (cloth) DDC
709/.73/074753 20
N6505 .U48 1991

Congrat-Butlar, Stefan. Russian revolutionary
posters, 1917-1929 /. New York , c1967. [14]
p. :   *NYPL [3-MDW 90-4813]*

**Congreso Internacional "Presencia Italiana en la
Argentina" (1st : 1987 : San Miguel de
Tucumán, Argentina)** Brandariz, Gustavo A.
El aporte friulano a la arquitectura argentina /.
Buenos Aires , 1987. 52 leaves :
NA830 .B7 1987

**Congresso Internazionale degli Americanisti. see
International Congress of Americanists, 40th,
Rome and Genoa, 1972.**

Conil-Lacoste, Michel. Tinguely, l' énergétique de
l'insolence / Michel Conil Lacoste. Paris :
Editions de la Différence, [1989?] 2 v. : ill.
(some col.) ; 28 cm. (La Vue, le texte, 0989-3733 ;
6) Includes bibliographical references. CONTENTS. -
1. [without special title] -- 2. œuvres. ISBN
2-7291-0389-9 (set)
*1. Tinguely, Jean, 1925- - Criticism and interpretation.
I. Tinguely, Jean, 1925-. II. Title. III. Title: Energétique*

235

de l'insolence. *NYPL [3-MGO (Tinguely) 90-266]*

Conisbee, Philip.
Los Angeles County Museum of Art. The
Ahmanson gifts . Los Angeles, Calif. , c1991. p.
cm. ISBN 0-87587-160-7 (pbk.) DDC
759.94/074/79494 20
ND454 .L6 1991

Monet to Matisse : French art in Southern
California collections / Philip Conisbee, Judi
Freeman, Richard Rand. Los Angeles, Calif. :
Los Angeles County Museum of Art, c1991.
144 p. : ill. (some col.) ; 28 cm. Catalogue of an
exhibition held at the Los Angeles County Museum of
Art, June 9-Aug. 11, 1991. Includes bibliographical
references (p. 17) and index. ISBN 0-87587-159-3
DDC 709/.44/09034 20
*1. Art, French - Exhibitions. 2. Art, Modern - 19th
century - France - Exhibitions. 3. Art, Modern - 20th
century - France - Exhibitions. 4. Art - Private
collections - California, Southern - Exhibitions. I.
Freeman, Judi. II. Rand, Richard. III. Los Angeles
County Museum of Art. IV. Title.*
N6847 .C6 1991

Soap bubbles by Jean-Siméon Chardin / essay
by Philip Conisbee ; with a note on materials
and techniques by Joseph Fronek. Los Angeles,
Calif. : Los Angeles County Museum of Art,
c1990. 25 p. : ill (some col., 1 folded) ; 23 cm.
(Masterpiece in focus) Catalog prepared in conjunction
with the exhibition, Masterpiece in Focus: "Soap
Bubbles" by Jean-Siméon Chardin, October 18,
1990-January 20, 1991. Bibliography: p. [29]. ISBN
0-87587-154-2
*1. Chardin, Jean Baptiste Siméon, 1699-1779. Soap
bubbles - Exhibitions. 2. Los Angeles County Museum
of Art - Exhibitions. I. Chardin, Jean Baptiste Siméon,
1699-1779. II. Los Angeles County Museum of Art. III.
Title. IV. Series.* *NYPL [3-MCO C47 91-6592]*

Connaway, Jay Hall, 1893-1970.
Jay Connaway, fifty years of his works,
1919-1969; a retrospective exhibition, October
19-November 16, 1969, University Art Gallery,
State University of New York at Binghamton.
[Binghamton, c1969] 60 p. illus. (part col.),
port. 22 x 28 cm. Label mounted on t.p.: Supplied
by Worldwide Books, Boston. Bibliography: p. 15-16.
DDC 759.13
*1. Connaway, Jay Hall, 1893-1970 - Exhibitions. I.
State University of New York at Binghamton.
University Art Gallery. II. Title.*
ND237.C677 A47 *NYPL [3-MCX C752.N5]*

**CONNAWAY, JAY HALL, 1893-1970 -
EXHIBITIONS.**
Connaway, Jay Hall, 1893-1970. Jay Connaway,
fifty years of his works, 1919-1969.
[Binghamton, c1969] 60 p. DDC 759.13
ND237.C677 A47 *NYPL [3-MCX C752.N5]*

The Connecticut atlas /. Sherer, Thomas E. West
Hartford, Conn. , c1990. v, 102 p. :
NYPL [Map Div. 90-12951]

CONNECTICUT - MAPS.
(1990) Sherer, Thomas E. The Connecticut
atlas /. West Hartford, Conn. , c1990. v, 102
p. : *NYPL [Map Div. 90-12951]*

The Connecticut River /. Benson, Robert.
Boston , c1989. 125 p. : ISBN 0-8212-1730-5
NYPL [MFX+ (Benson) 89-28166]

**CONNECTICUT RIVER - DESCRIPTION
AND TRAVEL - VIEWS.**
Benson, Robert. The Connecticut River /.
Boston , c1989. 125 p. : ISBN 0-8212-1730-5
NYPL [MFX+ (Benson) 89-28166]

**CONNECTICUT RIVER VALLEY -
DESCRIPTION AND TRAVEL - VIEWS.**
Benson, Robert. The Connecticut River /.
Boston , c1989. 125 p. : ISBN 0-8212-1730-5
NYPL [MFX+ (Benson) 89-28166]

Connecticut. University. Museum of Art. see
William Benton Museum of Art.

**Connecticut. University. William Benton Museum
of Art.** see **William Benton Museum of Art.**

Connell, Allison. A view of Woodstock : historic
homes of the nineteenth century / text by
Allison Connell. Fredericton, N.B. : New
Ireland Press, c1988. 74 p. : ill. ; 22 x 27 cm.
Bibliography: p. 73-74. ISBN 0-920483-19-4 : DDC
971.5/52/0208 19
*1. Historic buildings - New Brunswick - Woodstock -
Pictorial works. 2. Architecture - New Brunswick -*

*Woodstock - Pictorial works. 3. Woodstock (N.B.) -
Buildings, structures, etc. - Pictorial works. 4.
Woodstock (N.B.) - Description - Views. I. Title.*
NYPL [3-MQWM 90-12592]

Conner, Floyd, 1951- The Artist's friendly legal
guide / . Cincinnati, Ohio , c1991. 142 p. :
ISBN 0-89134-365-2 (pbk.) : DDC 346.7304/82
347.306482 20
KF390.A7 A785 1991 *NYPL [MA 91-7466]*

Connoisseurship of Chinese furniture . Wang,
Shih-hsiang, 1914- [Ming shih chia chü yen
chiu. English.] Chicago, Ill. , 1990. 2 v. : ISBN
1-87852-901-3 *NYPL [3-MOF+ 91-4916]*

Connor, Alexandra.
Rembrandt's monkey and other tales from the
secret lives of the great artists / Alexandra
Connor. New York : St. Martin's Press, 1991.
p. cm. ISBN 0-312-06004-1 DDC 709/.2/2 20
1. Artists - Anecdotes. 2. Artists - Miscellanea. I. Title.
N7460 .C66 1991

The wrong side of the canvas / Alexandra
Connor. London : Robson Books, 1989. 200 p. :
ill. ; 23 cm. Includes bibliographical references (p.
199-200). ISBN 0-86051-587-7 : DDC 759 B 20
1. Artists - Biography. I. Title.
N40 .C65 1989 *NYPL [MC 90-4306]*

Connor, Kevin, 1932-
Kevin Connor : paintings and drawings
1947-88 : Art Gallery of New South Wales,
Sydney, 1 September-15 October 1989 : Heide
Park and Art Gallery, Melbourne, 21
November-19 December 1989 : Tasmanian
Museum and Art Gallery, Hobart, 17
January-18 February 1990. [Sydney] : Art
Gallery of New South Wales, [1989] 46 p. ; 21
x 22 cm. ISBN 0-7305-6366-9
*1. Connor, Kevin, 1932- - Exhibitions. I. Art Gallery of
New South Wales. II. Title.*
NYPL [3-MCZ C744 90-12729]

CONNOR, KEVIN, 1932- - EXHIBITIONS.
Connor, Kevin, 1932- Kevin Connor. [Sydney]
[1989] 46 p. ;
NYPL [3-MCZ C744 90-12729]

Connor, Linda, 1944-
Spiral journey : photographs 1967-1990 / Linda
Connor ; preface by Denise Miller-Clark ;
introduction by Rebecca Solnit. Chicago :
Museum of Contemporary Photography,
Columbia College Chicago, c1990. 18 p., 49 p.
of plates (unpaged) : ill. ; 31 cm. Catalog of an
exhibition held Apr. 13-May 30, 1990. Includes
bibliographical references. ISBN 0-932026-21-4
*1. Connor, Linda, 1944- - Exhibitions. 2. Photography,
Artistic - Exhibitions. I. Miller-Clark, Denise. II. Solnit,
Rebecca. III. Museum of Contemporary Photography
(Columbia College (Chicago, Ill.)). IV. Title.*
NYPL [MFX+ (Connor) 91-6726]

CONNOR, LINDA, 1944- - EXHIBITIONS.
Connor, Linda, 1944- Spiral journey . Chicago ,
c1990. 18 p., 49 p. of plates (unpaged) : ISBN
0-932026-21-4
NYPL [MFX+ (Connor) 91-6726]

**Conozca lo que le ocurrirá a usted y a su país si
el comunismo logra adueñarse del poder.**
Movimiento Unidad Revolucionaria. [Coral
Gables, Fla., 1963] 46 p.
*NYPL [*XMB-2143]*

Conquet, Jean. Bénévent L'Abbaye / Jean
Conquet. Guéret, Creuse : Editions Verso,
c1988. 126 p. : ill. ; 21 cm. (Dernières parutions)
Includes bibliographical references (p. 125). ISBN
2-903870-28-4
*1. Bènèvent-L'Abbaye (France) - History. I. Title. II.
Series.*
NA5551.B514 C6 1988

Conrad Felixmüller . Rathke, Christian.
[Schleswig] [1990] 282 p. :
NYPL [3-MCK F316 91-7198]

Conrad Felixmüller, 1897-1977 . Felixmüller,
Conrad, 1897-1977. Dusseldorf [1982?] [38]
p. : *NYPL [3-MCK F316 91-868]*

Conrad Geiger . Schneider, Erich, Dr. Nürnberg ,
1990. 213 p. : ISBN 3-924461-09-0 : DDC 759.3
20
ND588.G33 A4 1990

Conrad, Rupert, 1907-1979. The art and
reflections of Rupert Conrad : the naked dawn
/ completed by Ruth Conrad ; edited by
Clifford A. Bennett. New York : Cornwall
Books, c1991. 205 p., [8] p. of plates : ill.

(some col.) ; 29 cm. ISBN 0-8453-4824-8 (alk.
paper) : DDC 709/.2 B 20
*1. Conrad, Rupert, 1907-1979. 2. Artists - United
States - Biography. I. Conrad, Ruth, 1917-. II. Bennett,
Clifford A. III. Title.*
N6537.C654 A2 1990
NYPL [3-MCX C763 91-6324]

CONRAD, RUPERT, 1907-1979.
Conrad, Rupert, 1907-1979. The art and
reflections of Rupert Conrad . New York ,
c1991. 205 p., [8] p. of plates : ISBN
0-8453-4824-8 (alk. paper) : DDC 709/.2 B 20
N6537.C654 A2 1990
NYPL [3-MCX C763 91-6324]

Conrad, Ruth, 1917- Conrad, Rupert, 1907-1979.
The art and reflections of Rupert Conrad . New
York , c1991. 205 p., [8] p. of plates : ISBN
0-8453-4824-8 (alk. paper) : DDC 709/.2 B 20
N6537.C654 A2 1990
NYPL [3-MCX C763 91-6324]

Conrad Waider . Spanner, Heinrich, 1922-
Bozen , 1990. 96 p. : ISBN 88-7014-574-3 DDC
759.3 20
ND588.W25 S66 1990

Conrads, Margaret C., 1955- American paintings
and sculpture at the Sterling and Francine
Clark Art Institute/ Margaret C. Conrads. 1st
ed. New York : Hudson Hills Press :
Distributed in the U. S. by Rizzoli International
Publications, c1990. 219 p. : ill. (chiefly col.) ;
31 cm. Includes bibliographical references and index.
ISBN 1-555-95050-7 (alk. paper) : DDC
759.13/074/7441 20
*1. Sterling and Francine Clark Art Institute - Catalogs.
2. Art, American - Catalogs. 3. Art - Massachusetts -
Williamstown - Catalogs. I. Sterling and Francine Clark
Art Institute. II. Title.*
N6505 .C645 1990 *NYPL [MAVZ+
(Williamstown) 91-5440]*

Conseil de l'Europe. see **Council of Europe.**

Conseil international des musées. see
International Council of Museums.

Conseil régional de Lorraine. Céramique
lorraine . Nancy , Metz , c1990. 367 p. : ISBN
2-86480-458-1 : DDC 738/.0944/38074758231
20
NK4098.L67 C47 1990

Consejo de Europa. see **Council of Europe.**

**Consejo Nacional para la Cultura y las Artes
(Mexico)**
Angelina Beloff . México, D.F. : Guanajuato,
Gto. : 95 p. : ISBN 968-292-336-0 DDC 760/.092
20
N6999.B425 A4 1989

Angelina Beloff . México, D.F., México , 1989.
95 p. : *NYPL [MDG (Beloff) 90-11726]*

**Conservaci'on de los monumentos virreinales de
Bolivia.** La Paz : Instituto Boliviano de
Cultura : Embajada de España en Bolivia, 1987.
32 p. : ill. ; 30 cm.
*1. Buildings - Bolivia - Conservation and restoration. 2.
Architecture, Modern - 17th-18th century - Bolivia -
Concervation and restoration. I. Instituto Boliviano de
Cultura.* *NYPL [3-MQWM+ 89-26926]*

CONSERVATION OF BUILDINGS. see
**ARCHITECTURE - CONSERVATION
AND RESTORATION.**

CONSERVATION OF PAINTINGS. see
**PAINTING - CONSERVATION AND
RESTORATION.**

**The Conservation of the Orpheus Mosaic at
Paphos, Cyprus.** Marinadel Rey, CA : Getty
Conservation Institute, 1991. p. cm. ISBN
0-89236-188-3 (paperback) : DDC 738.5/2 20
*1. Orpheus mosaic (New Paphos). 2. Orpheus (Greek
mythology) - Art. 3. Mosaics, Roman - Conservation
and restoration - Cyprus - New Paphos (Ancient city).
4. Pavements, Mosaic - Conservation and restoration -
Cyprus - New Paphos (Ancient city). I. Getty
Conservation Institute.*
NA3770 .C65 1991

The Conservation of wall paintings : proceedings
of a symposium organized by the Courtauld
Institute of Art and the Getty Conservation
Institute, London, July 13-16, 1987 / Sharon
Cather, editor. Marina del Rey, CA : Getty
Conservation Institute, 1991. p. cm. Includes
bibliographical references. ISBN 0-89236-162-X
(pbk.) : DDC 751.6/2 20
1. Mural painting and decoration - Conservation and

restoration - Congresses. I. Cather, Sharon. II.
Courtauld Institute of Art. III. Getty Conservation
Institute.
ND2552 .C64 1991

**CONSERVATION OF WATER-COLORS. see
PAINTING - CONSERVATION AND
RESTORATION.**

**Conservative echoes in Fin de siècle Parisian art
criticism** /. Marlais, Michael Andrew.
University Park, Pa. , c1992. p. cm. ISBN
  0-271-00773-7 (acid-free paper) DDC
  701/.18/094436109034 20
N7476 .M37 1992

Conservatoire François Joseph Gossec. Faïences
et objets révolutionnaires . Gagny , 1989. 150
p. :   *NYPL [3-MPGG+ 90-252]*

Consiglio dell'Europa. see Council of Europe.

**Consociazione turistica italiana. see Touring club
italiano.**

**Conspectus formarum terrae sigillatae Italico
modo confectae** / Elisabeth Ettlinger ... [et al.].
Bonn : Habelt, 1990. ix, 213 p. : ill. (some
folded) ; 31 cm. (Materialien zur
römisch-germanischen Keramik . Heft 10) At head of
title: Römisch-Germanische Kommission des Deutschen
Archäologischen Instituts zu Frankfurt A.M. English,
German, and Italian. Includes bibliographical references.
  ISBN 3-7749-2456-2
*1. Pottery, Arretine. I. Ettlinger, Elisabeth. II.
Deutsches Archäologisches Institut.
Römisch-Germanische Kommission. III. Series.*
    *NYPL [3-MPA+ (Materialien zur
römisch-germanischen Keramik. Heft 10)]*

Constable and his drawings /. Fleming-Williams,
Ian. London , 1990. 328 p. : ISBN
  0-85667-380-3 (cased) : DDC 741.942 20
NC242.C5   *NYPL [3-MCV+ C75 91-3316]*

Constable and the critics, 1802-1837 /. Ivy, Judy
Crosby, 1945- Woodbridge, Suffolk , Rochester,
NY, USA , 1991. xv, 255 p. : ISBN
  0-85115-293-7 (acid-free paper) : DDC 759.2 20
ND497.C7 I9 1991

Constable, John, 1776-1837.
Fleming-Williams, Ian. Constable and his
drawings /. London , 1990. 328 p. : ISBN
  0-85667-380-3 (cased) : DDC 741.942 20
NC242.C5   *NYPL [3-MCV+ C75 91-3316]*

John Constable, R.A (1776-1837) : an
exhibition : paintings, drawings, watercolors,
mezzotints. New York, NY : Salander-O'Reilly
Galleries, [1988] 201 p. : ill. (some color) ; 27
cm. Essays by Graham Reynolds, Charles Rhyne, and
Julius Meier-Graefe. Includes bibliographical references
and indexes. DDC 760/.092 20
*1. Constable, John, 1776-1837 - Exhibitions. I.
Reynolds, Graham. II. Rhyne, Charles. III.
Salander-O'Reilly Galleries. IV. Title.*
N6797.C63 A4 1988
    NYPL [3-MCV C75 90-13632]

CONSTABLE, JOHN, 1776-1837.
Fleming-Williams, Ian. Constable and his
drawings /. London , 1990. 328 p. : ISBN
  0-85667-380-3 (cased) : DDC 741.942 20
NC242.C5   *NYPL [3-MCV+ C75 91-3316]*

CONSTABLE, JOHN, 1776-1837 - CATALOGS.
Ivy, Judy Crosby, 1945- Constable and the
critics, 1802-1837 /. Woodbridge, Suffolk ,
Rochester, NY, USA , 1991. xv, 255 p. : ISBN
  0-85115-293-7 (acid-free paper) : DDC 759.2 20
ND497.C7 I9 1991

**CONSTABLE, JOHN, 1776-1837 - CRITICISM
AND INTERPRETATION.**
Ivy, Judy Crosby, 1945- Constable and the
critics, 1802-1837 /. Woodbridge, Suffolk ,
Rochester, NY, USA , 1991. xv, 255 p. : ISBN
  0-85115-293-7 (acid-free paper) : DDC 759.2 20
ND497.C7 I9 1991

Walker, John, 1906 Dec. 24- John Constable /.
New York , 1991. p. cm. ISBN 0-8109-3171-0
(cloth) DDC 759.2 20
ND497.C7 W34 1991

**CONSTABLE, JOHN, 1776-1837 -
CHRONOLOGY.**
Rhyne, Charles. John Constable . Portland,
Oregon , 1990. xi, 206 p. ; ISBN 0-9627197-0-6
    NYPL [3-MCV C75 90-11734]

**CONSTABLE, JOHN, 1776-1837 -
EXHIBITIONS.**
Constable, John, 1776-1837. John Constable,

R.A (1776-1837) . New York, NY [1988] 201
p. : DDC 760/.092 20
N6797.C63 A4 1988
    NYPL [3-MCV C75 90-13632]

CONSTANCE, LAKE OF, IN ART.
Bilder vom Bodensee . Konstanz , 1987. 192
p. : ISBN 3-7621-8000-8 DDC 943/.462 20
DD801.C74 B5 1987
    NYPL [3-MAMY 90-11013]

**CONSTANCE, LAKE OF, REGION -
DESCRIPTION AND TRAVEL - VIEWS.**
Bilder vom Bodensee . Konstanz , 1987. 192
p. : ISBN 3-7621-8000-8 DDC 943/.462 20
DD801.C74 B5 1987
    NYPL [3-MAMY 90-11013]

Construcciones, seis escultores. Konstruktioner,
seks skulptører . København , 1989. 1 v.
(unpaged) :
NB808 .K66 1989

Constructa-Preis '90. Industriearchitektur in
Europa =. Hannover , c1990. 128 p. : ISBN
  3-87870-350-3 DDC 725/.4/09409048 20
NA6403.E85 I53 1990

Constructing Chicago /. Bluestone, Daniel M.
New Haven , c1991. p. cm. ISBN 0-300-04848-3
(alk. paper) DDC 711/.4/097731109034 20
NA9127.C4 B48 1991

**CONSTRUCTION. see ARCHITECTURE;
BUILDING; ENGINEERING.**

Construction economics and building design .
Turner, R. Gregory, 1952- New York , c1986.
136 p. : ISBN 0-442-28309-1 DDC 692/.5 19
TH435 .T88 1986   *NYPL [JLE 86-2742]*

**CONSTRUCTION INDUSTRY -
TECHNOLOGICAL INNOVATIONS -
INFLUENCE.**
Strike, James. Construction into design .
Oxford , Boston , 1991. p. cm. ISBN
  0-7506-1229-0 : DDC 721/.09/03 20
NA2543.T43 S7 1991

Construction into design . Strike, James. Oxford ,
Boston , 1991. p. cm. ISBN 0-7506-1229-0 :
DDC 721/.09/03 20
NA2543.T43 S7 1991

Constructive concepts . Rotzler, Willy.
[Konstruktive Konzepte. English.] New York ,
1989. 332 p. : ISBN 0-8478-1024-0 DDC 709/.04
  20
N6494.C64 R6713 1989
    NYPL [3-MAL 90-11560]

**CONSTRUCTIVISM (ARCHITECTURE) -
RUSSIAN S.F.S.R.**
Ferkai, András. Konsztantyin Melnyikov /.
Budapest , 1988. 43 p., [59] p. of plates : ISBN
  963-05-4517-9
NA1199.M37 F4 1988

CONSTRUCTIVISM (ART) - HISTORY.
Rotzler, Willy. [Konstruktive Konzepte.
English.] Constructive concepts . New York ,
1989. 332 p. : ISBN 0-8478-1024-0 DDC 709/.04
  20
N6494.C64 R6713 1989
    NYPL [3-MAL 90-11560]

**CONSTRUCTIVISM (ART) - RUSSIAN S.F.S.
R.**
Adaskina, N. L. (Natal'i'a Lʹvovna) Lioubov
Popova /. Paris , 1989. 394 p. : ISBN
  2-904057-26-9
    NYPL [3-MCZ+ P828 90-2356]

IAblonskaīa, M. (Mīuda) Women artists of
Russia's new age, 1900-1935 /. London ,
c1990. 248 p. : ISBN 0-500-23559-7
    NYPL [3-MAM 90-12322]

Sarabʹīanov, Dmitriī Vladimirovich. [Lioubov
Popova. English.] Popova /. New York , 1990.
396 p. : ISBN 0-8109-3701-8 (soft) DDC 709/.2/4
B 19
N6999.P67 S27 1989
    NYPL [3-MCZ+ P828 91-3662]

**CONSTRUCTIVISM (ART) - RUSSIAN S.F.S.
R. - EXHIBITIONS.**
Art into life . Seattle, Wash. , New York, NY ,
c1990. 276 p. : ISBN 0-935558-27-6 (pbk.) DDC
  709/.47/074 20
N6988.5.C64 A68 1990
    NYPL [3-MAM 90-11568]

**CONSTRUCTIVISM (ART) - RUSSIAN S.F.S.
R. - MOSCOW.**
Khan-Magomedov, S. O. (Selim Omarovich)

Vhutemas . Paris , c1990. 2 v. (880 p.) : ISBN
  2-903370-55-9 (set) DDC 707/.1/147312 20
N332.S65 M675 1990

**CONSTRUCTIVISM (ART) - SOVIET
UNION - CONGRESSES.**
The Revolution and the avant-garde . Seattle ,
1991. p. ISBN 0-935558-30-6 DDC
  700/.947/09041 20
NX556.A1 R48 1991

**CONSTRUCTIVISM (ART) - SOVIET
UNION - INFLUENCE - CONGRESSES.**
The Revolution and the avant-garde . Seattle ,
1991. p. ISBN 0-935558-30-6 DDC
  700/.947/09041 20
NX556.A1 R48 1991

CONSTRUCTIVISM - SOVIET UNION.
Finizio, Luigi Paolo. L'astrattismo costruttivo .
Roma , 1990. vii, 237 p., [16] p. of plates :
  ISBN 88-420-3642-0 : DDC 709/.47/09041 20
N6988.5.C64 F56 1990

**CONSUMER ADVERTISING. see
ADVERTISING.**

CONSUMER PROTECTION - LABELING.
Ryan, Joseph P. Design of warning labels and
instructions /. New York , c1991. xiv, 201 p. :
  ISBN 0-442-31953-3 DDC 741.6/92 20
NC1002.L3 R94 1990

CONSUMERS - PSYCHOLOGY.
Lloyd-Jones, Peter, 1940- Taste today .
Oxford , New York , 1991. p. cm. ISBN
  0-08-040251-8 : DDC 745.4/442 20
NK1520 .L46 1991

**CONTAMINATION OF ENVIRONMENT. see
POLLUTION.**

Contancy and change in architecture / edited by
Malcolm Quantrill and Bruce Webb. 1st ed.
College Station : Texas A&M University Press,
1991. p. cm. (Studies in architecture and culture . no.
1) Includes index. ISBN 0-89096-472-6 DDC
  720/.1 20
*1. Architecture and history. 2. Architecture and society.
I. Quantrill, Malcolm, 1931-. II. Webb, Bruce, 1941-.
III. Series.*
NA2543.H55 C67 1991

**Contemporains (Musée national d'art moderne
(France))** .
(16) Lavier, Bertrand, 1949- Bertrand Lavier .
Paris , c1991. 127 p. : ISBN 2-85850-598-5 :
IN PROCESS (ONLINE)
    NYPL [3-MGO (Lavier) 91-8115]

**Contemporary aboriginal art from the Robert
Holmes à Court Collection** : Carpenter Center
for the Visual Arts, Harvard University, 22
February-25 March, James Ford Bell Museum,
University of Minnesota, 20 April-2 June,
Lakewood Center for the Arts, Lake Oswego,
15 June-19 July / [introduction, Anne Marie
Brody]. Perth : Heytesbury Holdings, 1990. 125
p. : ill. ; 31 cm. ISBN 0-7316-8569-5
*1. Holmes à Court, Robert - Art collections -
Exhibitions. 2. Art, Australian (Aboriginal) -
Exhibitions. I. Brody, Annemarie. II. Carpenter Center
for Visual Arts.*   *NYPL [3-MADF+ 91-4291]*

Contemporary architetural drawings . Avery
Library. San Francisco , c1991. p. cm. ISBN
  0-87654-767-6 : DDC 720/.22/2 20
NA2695.U6 A86 1991

**CONTEMPORARY ART. see ART, MODERN -
20TH CENTURY.**

Contemporary art from Chile : February 7-April
28, 1991 / organized by the Americas Society,
New York ; curated by Fatima Bercht = Arte
contemporáneo desde Chile : 7 de febrero-28 de
abril, 1991 / organizada por Americas Society,
Nueva York ; curadora, Fatima Bercht. New
York, N.Y. : The Society, c1990. 63 p. : ill. ;
28 cm. English and Spanish. ISBN 1-87912-802-0
*1. Art, Chilean - Exhibitions. 2. Art, Modern - 20th
century - Chile - Exhibitions. I. Bercht, Fatima. II.
Americas Society. III. Title: Arte contemporáneo desde
Chile.*   *NYPL [3-MAM 91-7561]*

Contemporary artists of Orissa series .
(2) Debo, Sarat Chandra, 1911-1973. Sarat
Chandra Debo /. Bhubaneswar , 1987. [22] p.,
[21] p. of plates : DDC 759.954 20
ND2049.D36 A4 1987
    NYPL [3-MAF 91-4520]

Contemporary Arts Museum. Zeitlin, Marilyn.
South Bronx Hall of Fame . Houston, Tex. ,
c1991. p. cm. ISBN 0-936080-21-3 (pbk.) : DDC

730/.92 20
NB237.A35 A4 1991

Contemporary arts series (Chicago, Ill.)
Contemporary designers /. Chicago , 1990. x,
[6], 641 p. :   ISBN 0-912289-69-4
NYPL [MNF+ 91-4858]

Contemporary Australian collage and its origins
/. McIntyre, Arthur, 1945- Roseville, NSW,
Australia , 1990. 224 p. :   ISBN 0-947131-31-0
NYPL [3-MAM+ 90-13198]

Contemporary Australian painting / edited by
Eileen Chanin. Roseville, NSW, Australia :
Craftsman House, c1990. 192 p. : ill. ; 34 cm.
ISBN 0-947131-25-6
I. Chanin, Eileen. **NYPL [3-MCY+ 90-13279]**

Contemporary Australian sculpture /. Sturgeon,
Graeme, 1936- Roseville, NSW, Australia ,
c1991. xxiii, 127 p. :   ISBN 976-8097-10-8
NYPL [3-MGI+ 91-6519]

Contemporary Danish furniture design . Sieck,
Frederik, 1916- [Nutidig dansk møbeldesign.
English.] [Copenhagen] , c1990. 231 p. :   ISBN
87-17-06121-0 (pbk.) :   DDC 749.289/09/045 20
NK2585 .S513 1990

Contemporary designers / editor, Colin Naylor.
2nd ed. Chicago : St. James Press, 1990. x, [6],
641 p. : ill. ; 32 cm. (Contemporary arts series)
Includes bibliographical references.   ISBN
0-912289-69-4
*1. Designers - Biography - Dictionaries. 2. Design -
History - 20th century - Dictionaries. I. Naylor, Colin.
II. Series: Contemporary arts series (Chicago, Ill.).*
NYPL [MNF+ 91-4858]

Contemporary graphic art from Austria. Sotriffer,
Kristian, 1932- [Vienna, 1969?] 47, [5] p.   DDC
760
NE643.4 .S6   *NYPL [MDBF 90-6251]*

Contemporary graphic design /. Labuz, Ronald,
1953- New York , c1991. xi, 156 p. :   ISBN
0-442-31887-1   DDC 741.6/09/048 20
NK1505 .L24 1991
NYPL [3-MDW 91-4184]

Contemporary Hispanic shrines : October
17-November 19, 1989, Freedman Gallery,
Albright College, Reading, Pennsylvania.
Reading, Pa. : The Gallery, c1989. 24 p. : col.
ill. ; 26 cm. English and Spanish. Includes
bibliographical references (p. 20).   ISBN 0-941972-09-7
*1. Art and religion - United States - Exhibitions. 2.
Hispanic American art - Exhibitions. I. Freedman
Gallery (Reading, Pa.).*
IN PROCESS (ONLINE)
NYPL [3-MAMT 91-7297]

Contemporary illustrated books . Stein, Donna.
New York, N.Y. , c1989. 72 p. :   ISBN
0-916365-00-X   *NYPL [MDTT+ 91-6216]*

Contemporary Japanese architecture. Architettura
giapponese contemporanea. Firenze, 1969. 282
p.
NA1555 .A8   *NYPL [3-MQWS 90-6800]*

Contemporary Japanese sculpture /. Koplos,
Janet. New York , 1991. p. cm.   ISBN
1-558-59012-9   DDC 730/.952/09045 20
NB1055 .K66 1991

Contemporary landscape . Community Arts
Programs Association. Bayside, N.Y. , c1977.
28 p. :
N6512 .C5814 1977
NYPL [3-MAMT 81-992]

**CONTEMPORARY PAINTING. see
PAINTING, MODERN - 20TH CENTURY.**

Contemporary Polish painting . Wojciechowski,
Aleksander. [Polskie malarstwo współczesne.
English.] Warsaw [1977] 187 p. :   DDC 759.38
N7255.P6 W6213   *NYPL [3-MCY 90-12502]*

Contemporary public sculpture . Senie, Harriet.
New York , 1992. p. cm.   ISBN 0-19-507318-5
DDC 735/.235 20
NB198 .S355 1992

Contemporary Romanian painting . Ionescu,
Alexandra. [s.l. , 1973] [59] p. :   DDC
759.9498/074/013
ND928 .I66   *NYPL [3-MCY 90-12375]*

Contemporary Russian artists. Artisti russi
contemporanei . Prato , c1990. 208 p. :   ISBN
88-85191-01-0   *NYPL [3-MAM 90-10469]*

**CONTEMPORARY SCULPTURE. see
SCULPTURE, MODERN - 20TH**

CENTURY.

Contemporary woodblock prints : Jersey City
Museum, December 6, 1989-March 3, 1990 /
Gregory Amenoff ... [et al.]. [Jersey City,
N.J.] : The Museum, c1989. 16 p. : ill. ; 26 cm.
*1. Wood-engraving - 20th century - Exhibitions. I.
Amenoff, Gregory, 1948-. II. Jersey City Museum.*
NYPL [MDO 91-4747]

Contenir, regarder, jouer : 14 janvier-9 mars
1970, Musée des arts décoratifs, Palais du
Louvre, Pavillon de Marsan : exposition des
Productions et Editions de Danese / cette
exposition est organisée avec le concours du
Centre de création industrielle. [Paris : Le
Musée,] [58] p. : ill. ; 16 cm. "Texts of the
catalogue" in English inserted at end. Introduction by
Giovanni Maria Accame. Bibliography: p. [54-56]
*1. Design, Industrial - Italy - Exhibitions. I. Accame,
Giovanni Maria. II. Musée des arts décoratifs (France).*
NYPL [3-MNF 90-6809]

Content/context : a survey of recent New
Zealand art 1986. Wellington, N.Z. : National
Art Gallery, New Zealand, 1986. 144 p. : ill. ;
28 cm. Catalogue of an exhibition. Includes
bibliographical references.   ISBN 0-9597785-1-9
DDC 700/.993/0904807493127 20
*1. Art, New Zealand - Exhibitions. 2. Art, Modern -
20th century - New Zealand - Exhibitions. I. National
Art Gallery (N.Z.).*
N7406.5 .C66 1986

Contes de la ville quotidienne /. Interfoto
(Agency) Genève , c1987. 123 p. :
NYPL [MFW 90-13469]

Conti, Raúl, 1931-
Raúl Conti. Buenos Aires : Museo Eduardo
Sívori, 1988. 64 p. : ill. (some col.) ; 21 x 24
cm. Catalogue of an exhibition. "Raúl Conti, pintor y
escultor, Buenos Aires--New York, 1970-1988"--P. [5].
Includes bibliographical references.
*1. Conti, Raúl, 1931- - Catalogs. I. Museo Municipal de
Artes Plásticas Eduardo Sívori. II. Title.*
NC290.C6 A4 1988
NYPL [3-MCZ C758 91-6588]

CONTI, RAÚL, 1931- - CATALOGS.
Conti, Raúl, 1931- Raúl Conti. Buenos Aires ,
1988. 64 p. :
NC290.C6 A4 1988
NYPL [3-MCZ C758 91-6588]

Conti, Roberto. Il Duomo di Monza /. Milano ,
1990. 2 v. :   DDC 726/.6/09451 20
NA5621.M954 D8 1990

Continent Kirkeby /. Lamarche-Vadel, Bernard,
1949- [Labège, France] [1987] 64 p. :   ISBN
2-905992-16-6 (jacket)   DDC 759.89 20
N7023.K53 A4 1987

Continental Atlas für Mittel-Europa. Continental
Gummi-Werke AG. Hannover [1924] viii, 65
(i.e. 66) fold. col. maps.
G1881.P2 C6 1924
NYPL [Map Div. 83-672]

**Continental Caoutchouc- und Gutta-Percha-
Compagnie. see Continental Gummi-Werke
AG.**

**Continental Caoutchouc-Compagnie G. m. b. H.
see Continental Gummi-Werke AG.**

Continental Gummi-Werke AG. Continental Atlas
für Mittel-Europa. 8. verb. Aufl. Hannover
[1924] viii, 65 (i.e. 66) fold. col. maps. 21 cm.
Running title. Continental Landstrassen-Atlas. Published
by the firm under its earlier name: Continental
Caoutchouc-und Gutta-Percha-Compagnie. First
published in 1907 under title: Continental
Landstrassen-Atlas für Mittel-Europa. Scale of maps
1:1,000,000 or 1:300
*1. Central Europe - Road maps. 2. Germany - Road
maps. I. Title.*
G1881.P2 C6 1924
NYPL [Map Div. 83-672]

Contini, Maria Teresa. Strumenti fotografici
1845-1950 / Maria Teresa Contini. Roma :
NER, c1990. 172 p. : ill. ; 31 cm.   ISBN
88-85085-07-5
I. Title.   *NYPL [MFW+ 91-5139]*

Contos crioulos da Bahia /. Santos, Deoscoredes
Maximiliano dos. Petrópolis , 1976, c1974. 73
p. ;
GR133.B6 S32 1976
NYPL [HAER 79-3109]

**CONTRACTS, GOVERNMENT. see PUBLIC
CONTRACTS.**

**CONTRACTS, PUBLIC. see PUBLIC
CONTRACTS.**

**Contradicciones en las distintas alternativas
políticas de Puerto Rico y Los costos de la
estadidad** /. Sánchez Tarniella, Andrés. Río
Piedras, P.R. , 1979. 133 p. ;
JL1056 .S26   *NYPL [HPR 81-345]*

Contreras, Jesús F. (Jesús Fructuoso), 1866-1902.
Jesús F. Contreras, 1866-1902 : escultor
finisecular : [exposición] Consejo Nacional para
la Cultura y las Artes, Instituto Nacional de
Bellas Artes, Museo Nacional de Arte,
mayo-julio, 1990, México, D.F. [Mexico City] :
El Museo, c1990. 129 p. : ill. (some col.) ; 28
cm. Includes bibliographical references (p. 123-124).
DDC 730/.92 20
*1. Contreras, Jesús F. (Jesús Fructuoso), 1866-1902 -
Exhibitions. I. Museo Nacional de Arte (Mexico). II.
Title.*
NB259.C65 A4 1990

**CONTRERAS, JESÚS F. (JESÚS
FRUCTUOSO), 1866-1902 -
EXHIBITIONS.**
Contreras, Jesús F. (Jesús Fructuoso),
1866-1902. Jesús F. Contreras, 1866-1902 .
[Mexico City] , c1990. 129 p. :   DDC 730/.92 20
NB259.C65 A4 1990

**Contributions to architectural design in digital
signal processing** /. Löffler, Christoph, 1957-
Konstanz , 1990. xiii, 277 p., [1] leaf of plates :
ISBN 3-89191-379-6 :   DDC 621.382/2 20
NA2728 .L64 1990

**CONURBATIONS. see METROPOLITAN
AREAS.**

**Convegno Internazionale di Studi su Paolo
Veronese (1988 : Università di Venezia)**
Nuovi studi su Paolo Veronese /. Venezia ,
c1990. xi, 422 p. :   ISBN 88-7743-056-7
NYPL [3-MCF V54 91-3715]

**Convegno internazionale su "Il neogotico nel XIX
e XX secolo (1985 : Pavia, Italy)** Il
Neogotico nel XIX e XX secolo /. Milano
[1990] 2 v. :   ISBN 88-20-20863-6 (set)   DDC
724/.3 20
NA645.5.G68 N46 1990

**Convegno su Giovanni Morelli e la cultura dei
conoscitori (1987 : Bergamo, Italy)**
La Figura e l'opera di Giovanni Morelli.
Bergamo , 1987. 2 v. :
NYPL [3-MAVC 90-10867]

Giovanni Morelli da collezionista a
conoscitore. [Bergamo] , c1987. 79 p. :
NYPL [3-MAX (Morelli) 90-10868]

**CONVENTION FACILITIES - UNITED
STATES.**
Penner, Richard H. Conference center planning
and design . New York , 1991. 256 p. :   ISBN
0-8230-0911-4 :   DDC 725/.91/097309048 20
NA6880.5.U6 P46 1991

**CONVENTO DI S. MARIA RIPA (EMPOLI,
ITALY)**
Pagni, Lucia. La chiesa e il convento di S.
Maria a Ripa . Tirrenia (Pisa) , 1988. 238 p. :
NYPL [MRBD 91-3395]

**CONVENTO DI S. MARIA RIPA (EMPOLI,
ITALY) - HISTORY - SOURCES.**
Pagni, Lucia. La chiesa e il convento di S.
Maria a Ripa . Tirrenia (Pisa) , 1988. 238 p. :
NYPL [MRBD 91-3395]

**CONVENTO DI SAN MARCO (FLORENCE,
ITALY)**
La Chiesa e il Convento di San Marco a
Firenze. [Firenze?] , c1989- v. :
NYPL [3-MRBD+ 90-2804]

**CONVENTS AND NUNNERIES - ITALY -
BRESCIA.**
Terraroli, Valerio. I chiostri di Brescia .
[Brescia] [1989] 171 p. :   ISBN 88-7385-052-9
NYPL [3-MRBD+ 91-3675]

CONVENTS - ITALY - BRESCIA.
Terraroli, Valerio. I chiostri di Brescia .
[Brescia] [1989] 171 p. :   ISBN 88-7385-052-9
DDC 726/.7/094526 20
NA5621.B8 T47 1989

Conversación con nuestros pintores abstractos.
Marinello, Juan, 1898-1977. Habana [1961] 111
p.   *NYPL [3-MC 90-6744]*

CONVICTS. see EX-CONVICTS; PRISONERS.

Conway, Patricia. Art for everyday : the new craft movement / by Patricia Conway.1st ed. New York, N.Y. : Clarkson Potter Publishers, 1990. 264 p. : ill. (some col.) ; 26 cm. ISBN 0-517-57381-4 DDC 745/.0973/0904 20
1. Decorative arts - United States - History - 20th century. 2. Design - United States - History - 20th century. I. Title.
NK808 .C64 1990 **NYPL** *[3-MLO 90-12856]*

Conwill, Houston, 1947-
The Passion of St. Matthew : paintings and sculpture : [exhibition] May 3-May 31, 1986 / Houston Conwill. New York City : Alternative Museum, c1986. 16 p. : ill. ; 28 cm. Catalog of an exhibition held at the Alternative Museum, May 3-31, 1986. Bibliography: p. 16. ISBN 0-932075-09-6 (pbk.) DDC 709/.2/4 19
1. Conwill, Houston, 1947- Passion of St. Matthew. 2. Installations (Art) - New York (N.Y.) - Exhibitions. I. Alternative Museum (New York, N.Y.). II. Title. III. Title: Passion of Saint Matthew.
N6537.C655 A67 1986
NYPL *[3-MGO (Conwill) 90-12371]*

PASSION OF ST. MATTHEW.
Conwill, Houston, 1947- The Passion of St. Matthew . New York City , c1986. 16 p. : ISBN 0-932075-09-6 (pbk.) DDC 709/.2/4 19
N6537.C655 A67 1986
NYPL *[3-MGO (Conwill) 90-12371]*

COOK, ABNER, 1814-1884.
Hafertepe, Kenneth, 1955- Abner Cook . Austin , c1991. p. cm. ISBN 0-87611-102-9 (cloth) DDC 720/.92 B 20
NA737.C66 H3 1991

Cook, Andrew S. Survey of the shores and islands of the Persian Gulf, 1820-1829 / prepared for publication and with an introduction by Andrew S. Cook. [Farnham Common] : Archive Editions, 1989. 5 v. : maps (some col.) ; 24 cm. CONTENTS. - v. 1. [Text] -- v. 2-5. [Maps] ISBN 1-85207-190-7
1. Persian Gulf - Maps. I. Title.
NYPL *[Map Div. 91-7527]*

Cook Islands art /. Idiens, Dale. Princes Risborough, Buckinghamshire, UK , 1990. 64 p. : ISBN 0-7478-0061-8 (pbk.) : DDC 709.0110996 20 **NYPL** *[3-MADF 91-6597]*

Cook, Peter, 1936- Sudjic, Deyan. English extremists . London , c1988. 112 p. : ISBN 0-947795-68-5 (pbk.)
NYPL *[3-MQWK 89-4432]*

Cooke, Catherine.
Architectural drawings of the Russian avant-garde /. New York , c1990. 143 p. : ISBN 0-87070-556-3
NYPL *[3-MQG 90-11730]*

Deconstruction . London , 1989. 264 p. : ISBN 0-85670-996-4 **NYPL** *[MQV+ 89-27959]*

Soviet commercial design of the twenties /. London , c1987. 144 p. : ISBN 0-500-23504-X
NYPL *[3-MDW+ 91-3268]*

Cooke, G. (George), 1793-1849.
Keyes, Donald D. George Cooke, 1793-1849 /. [Athens, Ga.] , 1991. 104 p. : ISBN 0-915977-07-9 DDC 759.13 20
ND237.C6785 A4 1991

COOKE, G. (GEORGE), 1793-1849 - EXHIBITIONS.
Keyes, Donald D. George Cooke, 1793-1849 /. [Athens, Ga.] , 1991. 104 p. : ISBN 0-915977-07-9 DDC 759.13 20
ND237.C6785 A4 1991

Cooke, Hereward Lester. Blunt, Anthony, 1907-1983. The Roman drawings of the XVII & XVIII centuries in the collection of Her Majesty the Queen at Windsor Castle /. London , c1960. 197 p. : DDC 741.945/632/093207442296 20
NC256.R6 B4 1960

Cooke, Lynne. McKeever, Ian, 1946- Ian McKeever, a history of rocks, 1986-1988 /. München [1990] 49 p. : DDC 759.2 20
ND497.M5 A4 1990

Cooke, Susette. Masterpieces of Australian photography . Paddington, Sydney, Australia , c1989. 200 p. : **NYPL** *[MFW+ 91-3430]*

COOLING.
Yáñez Parareda, Guillermo. Arquitectura solar . Madrid , 1988. 192 p. : ISBN 84-7433-542-6

DDC 720/.472 20
NA2542.S6 Y35 1988

Cooper, Dennis, 1953- Ray, Charles, 1953- Charles Ray /. Newport Beach, Calif. , c1990. 44 p. : ISBN 0-917493-16-8 DDC 730/.92 20
NB237.R35 A4 1990
NYPL *[3-MGO (Ray) 91-3921]*

COOPER, DOUGLAS, 1911- - ART COLLECTIONS - EXHIBITIONS.
Kosinski, Dorothy M. Picasso, Braque, Gris, Léger . Houston, Tex. , c1990. 67 p. : ISBN 0-89090-049-3 (pbk.) DDC 759.4/074/7641411 20
N6848.5.C82 K67 1990
NYPL *[3-MCN 91-6709]*

COOPER, DOUGLAS, 1911- - ART PATRONAGE - EXHIBITIONS.
Kosinski, Dorothy M. Picasso, Braque, Gris, Léger . Houston, Tex. , c1990. 67 p. : ISBN 0-89090-049-3 (pbk.) DDC 759.4/074/7641411 20
N6848.5.C82 K67 1990
NYPL *[3-MCN 91-6709]*

Cooper-Hewitt Museum.
Beer, Alice Baldwin. Trade goods. Washington, 1970. 133 p. DDC 746.6
NK8876.A2 B4 **NYPL** *[3-MON 91-994]*

COOPER-HEWITT MUSEUM - CATALOGS.
Beer, Alice Baldwin. Trade goods. Washington, 1970. 133 p. DDC 746.6
NK8876.A2 B4 **NYPL** *[3-MON 91-994]*

Cooper, Jason, 1942-
Castles / by Jason Cooper. Vero Beach, Fla. : Rourke Enterprises, 1991. p. cm. (Man made wonders) Includes index. Discusses the history, purpose, and construction of different types of castles. ISBN 0-86592-629-8 DDC 728.8/1/094 20
1. Castles - Juvenile literature. I. Title. II. Series.
NA7710 .C69 1991

[Castles. Spanish]
Castillos / por Jason Cooper ; versión en español de Aída E. Marcuse. Vero Beach, Fla. : Rourke Enterprises, 1991. p. cm. (Maravillas de la humanidad) Translation of: Castles. Includes index. Discusses the history, purpose, and construction of different types of castles. ISBN 0-86592-937-8 DDC 728.8/1/094 20
1. Castles - Juvenile literature. I. Series: Cooper, Jason, 1942- Maravillas de la humanidad. II. Title.
NA7710 .C6918 1991

Man made wonders.
Cooper, Jason, 1942- Skyscrapers /. Vero Beach, Fla. , 1991. p. cm. ISBN 0-86592-637-9 DDC 720/.483 20
NA6232 .C66 1991

Maravillas de la humanidad.
Cooper, Jason, 1942- [Castles. Spanish.] Castillos /. Vero Beach, Fla. , 1991. p. cm. ISBN 0-86592-937-8 DDC 728.8/1/094 20
NA7710 .C6918 1991

Cooper, Jason, 1942- [Skyscrapers. Spanish.] Rascacielos /. Vero Beach, Fla. , 1991. p. cm. ISBN 0-86592-935-1 DDC 720/.483 20
NA6236 .C6618 1991

Skyscrapers / by Jason Cooper. Vero Beach, Fla. : Rourke Enterprises, 1991. p. cm. (Man made wonders) Includes bibliographical references and index. Discusses the nature, history, and building of skyscrapers. ISBN 0-86592-637-9 DDC 720/.483 20
1. Skyscrapers - United States - Juvenile literature. I. Series. II. Series: Cooper, Jason, 1942- Man made wonders. III. Title.
NA6232 .C66 1991

[Skyscrapers. Spanish]
Rascacielos / por Jason Cooper ; versión en español de Aída E. Marcuse. Vero Beach, Fla. : Rourke Enterprises, 1991. p. cm. (Maravillas de la humanidad) Translation of: Skyscrapers. Includes index. Discusses the nature, history, and building of skyscrapers. ISBN 0-86592-935-1 DDC 720/.483 20
1. Skyscrapers - United States - Juvenile literature. I. Series: Cooper, Jason, 1942- Maravillas de la humanidad. II. Title.
NA6236 .C6618 1991

Cooper, Nancy Kelly. The development of roof revetment in the Peloponnese / by Nancy Kelly Cooper. Jonsered [Sweden] : P. Aström, 1989. v, 135 p., 57 p. of plates (1 folded) : ill. ; 21 cm. (Studies in Mediterranean archaeology and

literature. Pocket-book . 88) Originally presented as the author's thesis (Ph.D.)--University of Minnesota, 1983. Includes bibliographical references (p. 119-135). ISBN 91-85058-44-0
1. Tiles, Roofing - Greece. I. Title. II. Series.
NYPL *[3-MLEC 90-11039]*

Cooper Union for the Advancement of Science and Art.
Symbolism . [New York] [1989] [24] p. :
NYPL *[3-MAL 91-4569]*

Cooper Union for the Advancement of Science and Art. School of Art. New voices in Greek-American art . Brooklyn, N.Y. [1990] [40] p. : **NYPL** *[MAMT 91-6992]*

Coopey, Judith Redline. Gromme, Owen J. The world of Owen Gromme /. Minocqua, WI , 1991. p. cm. ISBN 1-559-71130-2 : DDC 759.13 B 20
ND237.G665 A2 1991

COORDINATES.
Sutherland, Martha, 1927- Graphic fundamentals . New York, N.Y. , 1991. p. cm. ISBN 0-8306-3480-0 : DDC 720/.28/4 20
NA2708 .S88 1991

COORDINATION OF INDUSTRIAL DESIGNS. see INDUSTRIAL DESIGN COORDINATION.

The Copeland collection . Sargent, William R. (William Robert), 1945- Salem, Mass. , c1991. p. cm. ISBN 0-87577-157-2 (cloth : acid free) : DDC 738.8/2/095107473 20
NK4565.5 .S26 1991

COPELAND, LAMMOT DU PONT, MRS. - ART COLLECTIONS - CATALOGS.
Sargent, William R. (William Robert), 1945- The Copeland collection . Salem, Mass. , c1991. p. cm. ISBN 0-87577-157-2 (cloth : acid free) : DDC 738.8/2/095107473 20
NK4565.5 .S26 1991

Coplans, John.
Hand : self portraits / by John Coplans. New York : Galerie Lelong, c1988. 1 v. (unpaged) : chiefly ill. ; 23 cm. Catalog of an exhibition held Jan. 12-Feb. 11, 1989 at Galerie Lelong, N.Y.
1. Coplans, John - Self-portraits - Exhibitions. 2. Photography, Artistic - Exhibitions. 3. Photography of hands - Exhibitions. I. Galerie Maeght Lelong (New York, N.Y.). II. Title.
NYPL *[MFX (Coplans) 91-4595]*

John Coplans : Frankfurter Kunstverein, Steinernes Haus am Römerberg, 2. Juni-8. Juli 1990, Frankfurt am Main / [herausgegeben von Peter Weiermair]. Frankfurt am Main : Der Kunstverein, [1990] 60 p. : chiefly ill. ; 24 cm. Includes bibliographical references (p. 57-58).
1. Coplans, John - Self-portraits - Exhibitions. 2. Photography, Artistic - Exhibitions. I. Weiermair, Peter. II. Frankfurter Kunstverein. III. Title.
NYPL *[MFX (Coplans) 91-7947]*

Weegee, 1899-1968. Weegee . München [1984] 18 p., 84 p. of plates : ISBN 3-88814-136-2
NYPL *[MFX (Weegee) 91-3437]*

COPLANS, JOHN - SELF-PORTRAITS - EXHIBITIONS.
Coplans, John. Hand . New York , c1988. 1 v. (unpaged) : **NYPL** *[MFX (Coplans) 91-4595]*

Coplans, John. John Coplans . Frankfurt am Main [1990] 60 p. :
NYPL *[MFX (Coplans) 91-7947]*

Coppa, Luigi, 1934-
Steinböck, Wilhelm. Luigi Coppa /. Graz, Austria , c1990. 149 p. : ISBN 3-201-01502-4 DDC 759.5 20
ND623.C694 A4 1990

COPPA, LUIGI, 1934- - CATALOGS.
Steinböck, Wilhelm. Luigi Coppa /. Graz, Austria , c1990. 149 p. : ISBN 3-201-01502-4 DDC 759.5 20
ND623.C694 A4 1990

Coppa, Mario. Piccola storia dell'urbanistica / Mario Coppa. Torino : UTET-Libreria, c1990. 5 v. : ill. ; 21 cm. Includes bibliographical references. CONTENTS. - 1. Abitazione e habitat -- 2. Paesaggio e ambiente -- 3. Sviluppi urbani -- 4. Edifici pubblici e servizi -- 5. Economia e società. ISBN 88-7750-097-2 (v. 1)
1. City planning. I. Title.
NA9090 .C67 1990

Coppack, Glyn. English Heritage book of abbeys and priories / Glyn Coppack. London : Batsford/English Heritage, 1990. 159 p., [8] p. of plates : ill. (some col.), plans (some col.) ; 26 cm. Includes index. Includes bibliographical references. ISBN 0-7134-6308-2 (cased) : DDC 942 20
1. Abbeys - England - History. 2. Priories - England - History. 3. Church architecture - England. I. Title. II. Title: Book of abbeys and priories.
         NYPL [3-MRBR 91-6767]

COPPERWORK - RUSSIAN S.F.S.R.
Russian copper icons and crosses from the Kunz Collection . Washington, D.C. , 1990. p. cm. DDC 730/.947 20
NK1653.S65 R8 1990

La Coppia = The Couple / [catalogo a cura di Giulio Bizzarri ; traduzioni, Ilaria Magnani, Jannina Veit Teuten]. Milano : Edizioni Lybra immagine, c1989. 205 p. : col. ill. ; 24 cm. Italian and English in parallel columns. At head of title: Italia's cup, young designers new ideas and projects. Triennale di Milano. Third Italia's Cup exhibition organized by Società Italia's, held at the Palazzo dell'arte, June 1989, Milan. DDC 745.4/442 20
1. Design - History - 20th century - Exhibitions. 2. Industrial design - History - 20th century - Exhibitions. I. Bizzarri, Giulio. II. Società Italia's. III. Palazzo dell'arte (Milan, Italy). IV. Italia's Cup (3rd : 1989 : Milan, Italy). V. Triennale di Milano (17th : 1989). VI. Title: Couple.
NK1390 .C66 1989
         NYPL [3-MNF 90-11125]

Copplestone, Trewin. (ed) Art treasures in Spain. London, 1970. 175 p. ISBN 0-600-03888-2 DDC 709/.46
N7101 .A83 1970

Coppola, Maria Rosaria. Terracina : il foro emiliano : Terracina, luglio-ottobre 1986 / catalogo di Maria Rosaria Coppola. Roma : Quasar, 1986. 42 p. : ill., maps, plans ; 25 cm. At head of title: Comune di Terracina, Assessorato alla cultura. Bibliography: p. 41-42. ISBN 88-85020-74-7
1. Forums, Roman - Italy - Terracina - Exhibitions. 2. Excavations (Archaeology) - Italy - Terracina - Exhibitions. 3. Foro emiliano (Terracina, Italy) - Exhibitions. 4. Terracina (Italy) - Antiquities, Roman - Exhibitions. I. Terracina (Italy). Assessorato alla cultura. II. Title.   *NYPL [3-MQM 90-13012]*

COPTIC ART. see ART, COPTIC.

Coptic fabrics /. Rutschowscaya, Marie-Hélène. Paris, France , c1990. 159 p. : ISBN 2-87660-084-6 DDC 746/.089/932 20
NK8988.3 .R8 1990

COPYRIGHT - ART - UNITED STATES.
The Artist's friendly legal guide /. Cincinnati, Ohio , c1991. 142 p. : ISBN 0-89134-365-2 (pbk.) : DDC 346.7304/82 347.306482 20
KF390.A7 A785 1991   *NYPL [MA 91-7466]*

COPYRIGHT - MORAL RIGHTS - UNITED STATES.
The Artist's friendly legal guide /. Cincinnati, Ohio , c1991. 142 p. : ISBN 0-89134-365-2 (pbk.) : DDC 346.7304/82 347.306482 20
KF390.A7 A785 1991   *NYPL [MA 91-7466]*

Corà, Bruno. Merz, Mario. Mario Merz at MOCA. [Milan] [c1989] 126 p. : ISBN 0-914357-17-4 (Museum of Contemporary Art) DDC 709/.2 20
N6923.M43 A4 1989
         NYPL [3-MGO (Merz) 91-6017]

Corace, Erminia. Mattia Preti /. Roma , c1989. 188 p.: ISBN 88-7621-387-2 :
IN PROCESS (ONLINE)
         NYPL [3-MCF+ P93 91-7171]

Coracle Press.
Finlay, Ian Hamilton. Homage to Ian Hamilton Finlay . London [1987] 22 p., 22 p. of plates :
         NYPL [MEMZ 91-2445]

Lincoln, Paul. In tribute to Madame de Pompadour and the court of Louis XV /. Cambridge , 1985. 1 v. (unpaged) :
         NYPL [MEMZ 91-2442]

Coral Gables, Fla. Lowe Art Museum. see Lowe Art Museum.

CORALS.
Liverino, Basilio, 1917- [Corallo, esperienze e ricordi di un corallaro. English.] Red coral . Bologna, Italy , 1990. 208 p. ;
         NYPL [3-MNR 91-7237]

CORALS IN ART.
Liverino, Basilio, 1917- [Corallo, esperienze e ricordi di un corallaro. English.] Red coral . Bologna, Italy , 1990. 208 p. ;
         NYPL [3-MNR 91-7237]

Coran, James L. If pictures could talk : stories about California paintings in our collection / by James L. Coran and Walter A. Nelson-Rees. Oakland, Calif. : WIM, c1989. 382 p. : chiefly col. ill. ; 36 cm. Includes bibliographical references (p. 367-372) and index. CONTENTS. - "The art temperaments of Northern and Southern California compared" by Arthur Millier -- "Collecting California art: an interpretive essay" by Joseph Armstrong Baird, Jr. -- "California art, North and South" by Nancy Dustin Wall Moure. ISBN 0-938842-07-2
1. Painting, American - California. 2. Artists - California. 3. California in art. 4. Landscape painters - California. 5. Landscape painting, American - California. I. Nelson, Rees, Walter A. II. Title.
         NYPL [3-MCW+ 90-12851]

Corbierre, Pascal.
Eglise Saint-Germain . [Caen, France] [1990] 16 p. : ISBN 2-908621-00-2 : DDC 726/.5/094423 20
NA5551.A674 E36 1990

Falaise, Calvados /. [Caen, France] [1990] 64 p. : ISBN 2-908621-01-0 : DDC 709/44/22 20
N6851.F35 F35 1990

Corbijn, Anton. Famouz : Anton Corbijn photographs, 1976-88. München : Schirmer/Mosel, c1989. [146] p. : chiefly ill., ports. ; 36 cm. ISBN 3-88814-313-6
1. Corbijn, Anton. 2. Musicians - Portraits. 3. Photography - Portraits. I. Title.
         NYPL [MFX+ (Corbijn) 89-28153]

CORBIJN, ANTON.
Corbijn, Anton. Famouz . München , c1989. [146] p. : ISBN 3-88814-313-6
         NYPL [MFX+ (Corbijn) 89-28153]

Corbusier. Harris, Elizabeth Davis, 1950- Le Corbusier . São Paulo, SP , 1987. 218 p. : ISBN 85-21-30469-2 :
         NYPL [3-MQZ (Le Corbusier) 90-10663]

Le Corbusier e L'Esprit nouveau /. Gabetti, Roberto. [Torino] [c1975] x, 273 p., [12] p. of plates :
NA1053.J4 G22
         NYPL [3-MCO J42 90-6619]

Corbusier Fondation. see Fondation Le Corbusier.

Corcoran Gallery of Art.
Albert Pinkham Ryder : [exhibition] April 8-May 12, 1961, The Corcoran Gallery of Art, Washington, D. C. Washington, D.C. : The Gallery, [1961] 53 p. : ill. (som col.) ; 28 cm. "The essay on the artist ... [was] prepared for this catalogue [by Lloyd Goodrich]"--p. 5.
1. Ryder, Albert Pinkham, 1847-1917 - Exhibitions. I. Goodrich, Lloyd, 1897-. II. Ryder, Albert Pinkham, 1847-1917. III. Title.
         NYPL [3-MCX R99 91-850]

Bendavid-Val, Leah. Changing reality . [Washington, D.C.] , c1991. 132 p. : ISBN 0-912347-76-7   *NYPL [MFW 91-6156]*

A century of Alexandria, District of Columbia & Georgetown silver : a loan exhibition / organized by the Associates of the Corcoran Gallery of Art, February 4-March 6, 1966. [Washington : Corcoran Gallery of Art, 1966] 28 p. : ill. ; 22 cm.
1. Silverwork - Washington Metropolitan Area - Exhibitions. 2. Silversmiths - Washington Metropolitan Area. I. Title.
NK7112 .C67 1966
         NYPL [3-MNO 90-5570]

Haden, Whistler, and Pennell : three master printmakers in the Corcoran Gallery of Art / Linda Crocker Simmons with the assistance of Emily J. Nash. Washington, D.C. : The Gallery, c1990. [18] p., [18] leaves of plates : ill. ; 31 cm. Issued in portfolio. Includes catalog of the exhibition held Sept. 7-Dec. 2, 1990. Title from catalog cover. Includes bibliographical references. ISBN 0-88675-035-0 DDC 769.92/2/074753 20
1. Haden, Francis Seymour, Sir, 1818-1910 - Exhibitions. 2. Whistler, James McNeill, 1834-1903 - Exhibitions. 3. Pennell, Joseph, 1857-1926 - Exhibitions. 4. Corcoran Gallery of Art - Exhibitions. I. Haden, Francis Seymour, Sir 1818-1910. II. Whistler, James McNeill, 1834-1903. III. Pennell, Joseph, 1857-1926. IV. Simmons, Linda Crocker, 1948-. V.

Nash, Emily, 1968-. VI. Title.
NE2043.25 .C67 1990
         NYPL [MDE+ 91-4773]

Ionescu, Alexandra. Contemporary Romanian painting . [s.l. , 1973] [59] p. : DDC 759.9498/074/013
ND928 .I66   *NYPL [3-MCY 90-12375]*

Laughlin, Clarence John. Photographs of Victorian Chicago. [New York, 1968] [12] p.
TR6 .L3   *NYPL [MFX (Laughlin) 90-6252]*

Livingston, Jane. Odyssey . Charlottesville, Va. , c1988. 363 p. : ISBN 0-934738-45-9 : DDC 779/.074/0153 19
TR790 .L58 1988   *NYPL [MFW+ 90-556]*

Robertson, Bruce, 1955- Reckoning with Winslow Homer . Cleveland, Ohio , 1990. xvi, 196 p. : ISBN 0-940717-02-6 DDC 759.13 20
ND237.H7 A4 1990
         NYPL [3-MCX H76 91-3391]

Sultan, Terrie, 1952- Inability to endure or deny the world . Washington, D.C. , c1990. 65 p. : ISBN 0-88675-036-9 : DDC 760/.092 20
ND237.M74 A4 1990
         NYPL [3-MCX+ M877 91-4930]

Terra sancta . Washington, D.C. , c1990. [32] p. : ISBN 0-88675-034-2
         NYPL [MFW 91-4044]

The Vincent Melzac collection. Washington, D.C. [1971] 102 p. *NYPL [3-MCW 90-6402]*

Wiley, William T., 1937- William T. Wiley : struck! sure? sound/unsound /. Washington, D.C. , c1991. p. cm. ISBN 0-88675-037-7 DDC 709/.2 20
N6537.W47 A4 1991

CORCORAN GALLERY OF ART - EXHIBITIONS.
Corcoran Gallery of Art. Haden, Whistler, and Pennell . Washington, D.C. , c1990. [18] p., [18] leaves of plates : ISBN 0-88675-035-0 DDC 769.92/2/074753 20
NE2043.25 .C67 1990
         NYPL [MDE+ 91-4773]

Cordaro, Michele. Il "Trionfo della morte" di Palermo . Palermo , c1989. 88 p., [62] p. of plates : ISBN 88-7681-040-4
         NYPL [3-MLP 90-11764]

Cordey, Jean. France, Anatole, 1844-1924. Le château de Vaux-le-Vicomte /. Etrépilly , c1987. v, 212 p., [8] p. of plates : ISBN 2-905563-19-2
         NYPL [3-MQWF 90-12695]

Corgnati, Maurizio, 1917- Il Lauro e il bronzo . [Italy , 1990] 182 p. ; DDC 730/.945/0744512 20
NB617 .L3 1990

Corinth, Lovis, 1858-1925.
Das Leben Walter Leistikows : ein Stück Berliner Kulturgeschichte / von Lovis Corinth ; mit zwei Originalradierungen und zahlreichen Abbildungen im Text. Berlin : Paul Cassirer, 1910. 129 p., [2] leaves of plates : ill. (2 col.), facsims., ports. ; 24 cm. "Von diesem Buche wurden 100 Exemplare auf echtes Büttenpapier abgezogen. Die Originalradierungen von Walter Leistikow, die diesen 100 Exemplaren beigeheftet sind, wurden ... auf Kaiserliches Japan gedruckt. Die Exemplare sind in der Presse numeriert, und von Lovis Corinth handschriftlich signiert worden"--P. [2]. Much of the illustrative matter is mounted. LC has copy of the unnumbered trade issue. LC Source: Purchase, Jan. 14, 1991. DLC DDC 709/.2 B 20
1. Leistikow, Walter, 1865-1908. 2. Artists - Germany - Biography. I. Title.
N6888.L362 C67 1910

Das Erlernen der Malerei : ein Handbuch / von Lovis Corinth ; mit einer Originallithographie von Lovis Corinth.3. Aufl. Berlin : P. Cassirer, c1920. 205 p. : ill. ; 24 cm.
1. Painting - Technique. I. Title.
         NYPL [MEM C798 91-5924]

Corlett, Mary Lee. National Gallery of Art (U. S.) Graphicstudio . Washington , 1991. p. cm. ISBN 0-89468-164-8 DDC 769.9759/65/074753 20
NE538.T35 N37 1991

Cormack, Malcolm.
Baron, Wendy. The Camden Town Group /. New Haven , 1980. xvi, 71 p. : ISBN 0-930606-20-5 (pbk.) DDC 759.21/42/07401468

19
N6768.5.C53 B37 1980
NYPL [3-MAMR 81-554]

The paintings of Thomas Gainsborough /
Malcolm Cormack. Cambridge ; New York :
Cambridge University Press, 1991. p. cm. ISBN
0-521-38241-6 DDC 759.2 20
1. Gainsborough, Thomas, 1727-1788 - Catalogs. I.
Title.
ND497.G2 A4 1991

**CORMIER, ERNEST - CRITICISM AND
INTERPRETATION.**
Ernest Cormier et l'Université de Montréal.
English. Ernest Cormier and the Université de
Montréal /. Montréal , 1990. 179 p. : ISBN
0-920785-30-1
NA749.C67 E7613 1990
NYPL [3-MQZ (Cormier) 91-6585]

Corna Pellegrini, Alessandra.
Terraroli, Valerio. I chiostri di Brescia .
[Brescia] [1989] 171 p. : ISBN 88-7385-052-9
NYPL [3-MRBD+ 91-3675]

Terraroli, Valerio. I chiostri di Brescia .
[Brescia] [1989] 171 p. : ISBN 88-7385-052-9
DDC 726/.7/094526 20
NA5621.B8 T47 1989

Cornebise, Alfred E.
Art from the trenches : America's uniformed
artists in World War I / by Alfred Emile
Cornebise.1st ed. College Station : Texas A&M
University Press, c1991. p. cm. (Texas A & M
University military history series . no. 20) Includes
bibliographical references (p.) and index. ISBN
0-89096-349-5 (cloth) DDC 758/.99404/0973 20
1. Art, American. 2. Art, Modern - 20th century -
United States. 3. World War, 1914-1918 - Art and the
war. I. Series. II. Series: Texas A & M University
military history series , 20. III. Title.
N6512 .C598 1991

Townsend, Harry Everett. War diary of a
combat artist /. Niwot, Colo. , c1991. xiv, 284
p. : ISBN 0-87081-231-9 DDC 740/.92 B 20
N6537.T66 A2 1991

Corneille . Paquet, Marcel. Paris [1988] 137 p.,
leaves of plates : ISBN 2-906510-01-7
NYPL [3-MCH C813 91-6813]

Corneille, 1922-
Paquet, Marcel. Corneille . Paris [1988] 137 p.,
leaves of plates : ISBN 2-906510-01-7
NYPL [3-MCH C813 91-6813]

**CORNEILLE, 1922- - CRITICISM AND
INTERPRETATION.**
Paquet, Marcel. Corneille . Paris [1988] 137 p.,
leaves of plates : ISBN 2-906510-01-7
NYPL [3-MCH C813 91-6813]

Cornelis Zitman . Zitman, Cornelis, 1926- Berne
[Switzerland] , c1989. 85 p. : ISBN
3-7165-0670-2
MLCM 90/04069 (N)
NYPL [3-MGO (Zitman) 91-3522]

Cornell, Joseph.
Jaguer, Edouard. Joseph Cornell /. [Paris] ,
c1989. 93 p. : ISBN 2-85018-249-4
NYPL [3-MCX+ C795 90-11997]

Seven boxes by Joseph Cornell. [Tokyo] ,
c1978. 41 p. :
NYPL [3-MGO (Cornell) 88-4763]

CORNELL, JOSEPH.
Jaguer, Edouard. Joseph Cornell /. [Paris] ,
c1989. 93 p. : ISBN 2-85018-249-4
NYPL [3-MCX+ C795 90-11997]

CORNELL, JOSEPH - EXHIBITIONS.
Seven boxes by Joseph Cornell. [Tokyo] ,
c1978. 41 p. :
NYPL [3-MGO (Cornell) 88-4763]

Starr, Sandra Leonard. Joseph Cornell and the
ballet /. New York , c1983. viii, 87 p. : DDC
709/.2/4 19
N6537.C66 A4 1983
NYPL [MCX C795 84-702]

Cornerhouse (Gallery : Manchester, England)
Brett, Guy. Transcontinental . London ; New
York : 112 p. : ISBN 0-86091-511-5
NYPL [3-MAM 91-7008]

Embroidery in women's lives, 1300-1900.
Women and textiles today /. [Manchester,
England]s , 1988. 64 p. : ISBN 0-903261-24-3
(pbk.) NYPL [3-MOT+ 89-23508]

Tradition and revolution in Russian art .
[Manchester] , 1990. 200 p. : ISBN
0-948797-26-6 NYPL [3-MAM 91-5043]

**CORNERS, COMMERCIAL. see STOCK-
EXCHANGE.**

CORNICES - DESIGNS AND PLANS.
Profils de corniches de plafonds /. [Paris] ,
1990- v. <1 > : ISBN 2-11-086067-7
NA2960 .P76 1990

Corning Museum of Glass.
Asharina, N. A. (Nina Aleksandrovna) Russian
glass of the 17th-20th centuries /. Corning,
N.Y. , c1990. 191 p. : ISBN 0-87290-123-8
NYPL [3-MPW 90-11677]

Charleston, R. J. (Robert Jesse), 1916-
Masterpieces of glass . New York , 1990. 256
p. : ISBN 0-8109-3607-0
NYPL [3-MPW+ 91-5598]

John Frederick Amelung, early American
glassmaker /. Corning : London ; 243 p., [4] p.
of plates : ISBN 0-87290-075-4 (alk. paper) DDC
748.2913 19
NK5198.A44 A4 1988
NYPL [3-MPW 91-6798]

CORNING MUSEUM OF GLASS.
Charleston, R. J. (Robert Jesse), 1916-
Masterpieces of glass . New York , 1990. 256
p. : ISBN 0-8109-3607-0
NYPL [3-MPW+ 91-5598]

Corning Museum of Glass monographs.
Charleston, R. J. (Robert Jesse), 1916-
Masterpieces of glass . New York , 1990. 256
p. : ISBN 0-8109-3607-0
NYPL [3-MPW+ 91-5598]

Cornips, Marie Hélène. Minder kan het niet .
Groningen , c1989. 103 p. :
NYPL [3-MAL 90-12610]

Cornu, Renate. Einleuchten . Hamburg [1989]
289 p. : ISBN 3-7672-1102-5 DDC
709/.04/507443515 20
N6488.G3 H2832 1989

**The cornucopian mind and the baroque unity of
the arts /.** Maiorino, Giancarlo, 1943-
University Park , c1990. x, 210 p. : ISBN
0-271-00679-X : DDC 700/.1 20
NX451.5.B3 M35 1990
NYPL [3-MAK 90-10647]

CORONATIONS - FRANCE - HISTORY.
Morel, Bernard. The French crown jewels .
Antwerp [1988] 417 p. : ISBN 90-6153-188-8
DDC 739.27/0944 20
NK7415.F8 M67 1988

Corot /. Taillandier, Yvon. Paris , 1990. 93, [1]
p. : ISBN 2-08-011554-5
NYPL [3-MCO C82 91-4944]

Corot and the art of landscape /. Clarke,
Michael, 1952- New York , c1991. p. cm.
ISBN 1-558-59223-7 DDC 759.4 20
ND553.C8 C5 1991

Corot in Italy . Galassi, Peter. New Haven,
Conn. , c1991. viii, 258 p. : ISBN 0-300-04957-9
DDC 759.4 20
ND553.C8 G245 1991
NYPL [3-MCO+ C82 91-7307]

**COROT, JEAN-BAPTISTE CAMILLE, 1796-
1875.**
Taillandier, Yvon. Corot /. Paris , 1990. 93, [1]
p. : ISBN 2-08-011554-5
NYPL [3-MCO C82 91-4944]

**COROT, JEAN-BAPTISTE CAMILLE, 1796-
1875 - CRITICISM AND
INTERPRETATION.**
Clarke, Michael, 1952- Corot and the art of
landscape /. New York , c1991. p. cm. ISBN
1-558-59223-7 DDC 759.4 20
ND553.C8 C5 1991

Galassi, Peter. Corot in Italy . New Haven,
Conn. , c1991. viii, 258 p. : ISBN 0-300-04957-9
DDC 759.4 20
ND553.C8 G245 1991
NYPL [3-MCO+ C82 91-7307]

**COROT, JEAN-BAPTISTE-CAMILLE, 1796-
1875 - JOURNEYS - ITALY.**
Galassi, Peter. Corot in Italy . New Haven,
Conn. , c1991. viii, 258 p. : ISBN 0-300-04957-9
DDC 759.4 20
ND553.C8 G245 1991
NYPL [3-MCO+ C82 91-7307]

Corporación Metropolitana de Barcelona. Cities .
[Barcelona] , 1988. 5 v. (xxix, 1673 p.) : ISBN
84-404-2436-1 (set)
NYPL [Map Div. 91-162]

**CORPORATE DESIGN COORDINATION. see
INDUSTRIAL DESIGN
COORDINATION.**

CORPORATE IMAGE.
International corporate design systems /. New
York , 1989- 127 p. : ISBN 0-88108-069-1
NYPL [3-MDW 91-1143]

**CORPORATE IMAGE AND DESIGN. see
INDUSTRIAL DESIGN
COORDINATION.**

**CORPORATE STYLE. see INDUSTRIAL
DESIGN COORDINATION.**

Corpus architectonicum .
(1) Palazzolo Acreide . Siracusa , Palermo ,
c1989. xv, 140, [3] p. :
NYPL [3-MQWB+ 91-5408]

Corpus de mosaicos de España .
(fasc. 8) Mosaicos romanos de Lérida y
Albacete /. Madrid , 1989. 124 p. : ISBN
84-00-06983-8 NYPL [3-MRXZ 90-12594]

**Corpus der barocken Deckenmalerei in
Deutschland /.** Bauer, Hermann, 1929-
München , 1976- v. : ISBN 3-7991-5737-9 (v. 1) :
ND2749 .B37 NYPL [MLP+ 78-312]

Corpus Rubenianum Ludwig Burchard .
(pt. 21) Judson, J. Richard (Jay Richard) Book
illustrations and title-pages /. Brussels ,
Philadelphia, PA , 1977. 2 v. (552 p., unpaged
p. of plates) : ISBN 2-8005-0124-3
ND673.R9 C63 pt. 21 1977 NC984.5.R8

Corpus speculorum Etruscorum. Denmark.
[Odense] : Odense University Press, 1981- v. 1,
fasc. 1 : ill. ; 32 cm. Fasc. 1 by Helle Salskov
Roberts. Includes bibliographical references.
CONTENTS. - 1. Copenhagen--The Danish National
Museum, the Ny Carlsberg Glyptothek. fasc. 1. ISBN
87-7492-323-4 DDC 739/.512/09375074089 19
1. Nationalmuseet (Denmark) - Catalogs. 2. Ny
Carlsberg glyptotek - Catalogs. 3. Mirrors, Etruscan -
Denmark - Catalogs. I. Salskov Roberts, Helle.
DG223.7.M55 C666 1981
NYPL [3-MAE+ 91-1339]

Corpus speculorum Etruscorum. France. Roma :
"L'Erma" di Bretschneider, c1988- v. : ill. ; 33
cm. Includes bibliographical references. CONTENTS. -
1. Fasc. 1-2. Paris, Musée du Louvre / par Denise
Emmanuel-Rebuffat. ISBN 88-7062-645-8
1. Mirrors, Etruscan - France - Catalogs. 2. Mirrors -
France - Catalogs. 3. Italy - Antiquities - Catalogs. I.
Emmanuel-Rebuffat, Denise.
NYPL [3-MAE+ 89-23865]

Corpus Topographicum Pompeianum. Rome : H.
Van der Poel, 1977- (Rome, Italy : Edizioni
dell'Elefante) v. ; 29 cm. "The University of Texas
at Austin"--P. i. Ill. on lining papers. On spine: CTP.
Includes bibliographical references. CONTENTS. - pt.
2. Toponomy.--pt. 3. The RICA maps of Pompeii.--pt. 3
A. The insulae of regions I-V.--pt. 4. Bibliography / by
Halsted B. Van der Poel.--pt. 5. Cartography. ISBN
0-930084-06-3 (set) DDC 937/.7 19
1. Pompeii - Collected works. 2. Pompeii - Maps. I.
Van der Poel, Halsted B. II. Title: RICA maps of
Pompeii. III. Title: CTP. IV. Title: C.T.P.
DG70.P7 C629 1977 NYPL [JFM 82-182 &
Map Div. 86-1278]

Corpus vasorum antiquorum. Deutschland.
(Bd. 55) Corpus vasorum antiquorum.
Deutschland. Kiel. Kunsthalle,
Antikensammlung. München , c1988- v. :
ISBN 3-406-32830-X
NYPL [MPEK+ C8.K54]

(Bd. 55) Corpus vasorum antiquorum.
Deutschland. Kiel. Kunsthalle,
Antikensammlung. München , c1988- v. :
ISBN 3-406-32830-X
NYPL [MPEK+ C8.K54]

(Bd. 7-8, 60) Corpus vasorum antiquorum.
Deutschland. Karlsruhe--Badisches
Landesmuseum. München , 1951-1952. v.
NK4640.C6 G4 Bd. 7-8
NYPL [MPEK+ C8.K2]

**Corpus vasorum antiquorum. Deutschland.
Karlsruhe--Badisches Landesmuseum.** München,
C. H. Beck, 1951-1952. v. illus., plates. 33 cm.
(Corpus vasorum antiquorum. Deutschland. Bd. 7-8, 60)
Veröffentlichungen des Badischen Landesmuseums, Bd.

3-4 At head of title: Union académique internationale.
Edited by G. Hafner; v. 3 compiled by Carina Weiss.
Issued in portfolios. Includes bibliographical references.
1. Badisches Landesmuseum Karlsruhe - Catalogs. 2.
Vases, Ancient - Germany (West) - Karlsruhe -
Catalogs. 3. Vases - Germany (West) - Karlsruhe -
Catalogs. I. Hafner, German. II. Weiss, Carina. III.
Badisches Landesmuseum Karlsruhe. IV. Series. V.
Series: Karlsruhe. Badisches Landesmuseum.
Veröffentlichungen, Bd. 3-4.
NK4640.C6 G4 Bd. 7-8
          NYPL [MPEK+ C8.K2]

Corpus vasorum antiquorum. Deutschland. Kiel.
Kunsthalle, Antikensammlung. München :
Beck, c1988- v. : ill. ; 33 cm. (Corpus vasorum
antiquorum. Deutschland. Bd. 55) At head of title:
Union académique internationale. Vol. 1 edited by
Brigitte Freyer-Schauenburg. Issued in portfolios.
Includes bibliographical references and indexes.   ISBN
3-406-32830-X
1. Kunsthalle zu Kiel - Catalogs. 2. Vases, Ancient -
Germany (West) - Kiel - Catalogs. 3. Vases, Greek -
Germany (West) - Kiel - Catalogs. I.
Freyer-Schauenburg, Brigitte. II. Kunsthalle zu Kiel. III.
Union académique internationale. IV. Series. V. Series:
Corpus vasorum antiquorum. Deutschland, Bd. 55.
          NYPL [MPEK+ C8.K54]

Corpus vasorum antiquorum. Pays - Bas. see
    Corpus vasorum antiquorum. The
    Netherlands.

Corpus vasorum antiquorum. Tchécoslovaquie.
(fasc. 2-) Corpus vasorum antiquorum.
Tchécoslovaquie. Prague--Musée national.
Prague , 1990- v. :   ISBN 80-200-0115-8 (fasc. 1) :
DDC 738.3/82/0938074 s
738.3/82/093807443712 20
NK4640.C6 C95 fasc. 2, etc.,
          NYPL [MPEK+ C8.P82]

(fasc. 2, etc) Corpus vasorum antiquorum.
Tchécoslovaquie. Prague--Musée national.
Prague , 1990- v. :   ISBN 80-200-0115-8 (fasc. 1) :
DDC 738.3/82/0938074 s
738.3/82/093807443712 20
NK4640.C6 C95 fasc. 2, etc.,
          NYPL [MPEK+ C8.P82]

Corpus vasorum antiquorum. Tchécoslovaquie.
Prague--Musée national. Vyd. 1. Prague :
Academia, 1990- v. : ill. ; 32 cm. (Corpus
vasorum antiquorum. Tchécoslovaquie. fasc. 2-) At
head of title: Union académique internationale. Edited
by Jan Bažant, et al. Issued in portfolios. Includes
bibliographical references and indexes.   ISBN
80-200-0115-8 (fasc. 1) :   DDC
738.3/82/0938074 s 738.3/82/093807443712 20
1. Národní muzeum v Praze - Catalogs. 2. Vases,
Ancient - Czechoslovakia - Prague - Catalogs. 3.
Vases - Czechoslovakia - Prague - Catalogs. I. Bažant,
Jan, PhDr. II. Národní muzeum v Praze. III. Series. IV.
Series: Corpus vasorum antiquorum. Tchécoslovaquie,
fasc. 2, etc.
NK4640.C6 C95 fasc. 2, etc.,
          NYPL [MPEK+ C8.P82]

Corpus vasorum antiquorum. The Netherlands.
(fasc. 6) Corpus vasorum antiquorum. The
Netherlands. Amsterdam, Allard Pierson
Museum, University of Amsterdam /.
Amsterdam , 1988- v. :   ISBN 90-71211-13-4 (v.
1)   **NYPL [MPEK+ C8.A5]**

(fasc. 6, etc) Corpus vasorum antiquorum. The
Netherlands. Amsterdam, Allard Pierson
Museum, University of Amsterdam /.
Amsterdam , 1988- v. :   ISBN 90-71211-13-4 (v.
1)   **NYPL [MPEK+ C8.A5]**

Corpus vasorum antiquorum. The Netherlands.
Amsterdam, Allard Pierson Museum,
University of Amsterdam / by J.M. Hemelrijk.
Amsterdam : The Museum, 1988- v. : ill. ; 33
cm. (Corpus vasorum antiquorum. The Netherlands.
fasc. 6) At head of title: Union académique
internationale. Includes bibliographies and indexes.
ISBN 90-71211-13-4 (v. 1)
1. Allard Pierson Museum (Universiteit van
Amsterdam) - Catalogs. 2. Vases, Greek - Catalogs. 3.
Vases - Netherlands - Amsterdam - Catalogs. I.
Hemelrijk, Jaap M. II. Allard Pierson Museum
(Universiteit van Amsterdam). III. Union académique
internationale. IV. Series. V. Series: Corpus vasorum
antiquorum. The Netherlands, fasc. 6, etc.
          NYPL [MPEK+ C8.A5]

Corpus vitrearum Medii Aevi: Deutsche
    Demokratische Republik.
(Bd. 1, T. 1-2) Drachenberg, Erhard. Die

mittelalterliche Glasmalerei in Erfurt. Berlin,
Wien, 1976- v in.   ISBN 3-205-00581-3 (v. 2, pt. 1)
    NYPL [MRY+ 77-1943 Bd.1, T.1-2]

Correa, Antonio Bonet. see Bonet Correa,
    Antonio.

Correct distance /. Tabrizian, Mitra. Manchester ,
1990. 1 v. (unpaged) :   ISBN 0-948797-16-9
    NYPL [MFX (Tabrizian) 91-7452]

Correia, Alberto. Museu de Grão Vasco
(Portugal) Aguarelas do Museu de Grão Vasco
/. [Viseu] [Lisboa] , 1989. 103 p. :
    NYPL [3-MAVZ+ (Viseu) 90-13444]

Correspondance. Korrespondenzen . Berlin ,
Saint-Etienne , c1989. 82 p. :
N6885 .K67 1989

Correspondence. Korrespondenzen . Berlin ,
Saint-Etienne , 1989. 82 p. :
    NYPL [3-MAMG 90-12480]

The correspondence of Washington Allston /.
Allston, Washington, 1779-1843.
[Correspondence.] Lexington, Ky , 1992. p. cm.
ISBN 0-8131-1708-9 :   DDC 759.13 B 20
NX512.A513 A3 1992

Corrida. Cau, Jean, 1925- Fernando Botero .
Paris , c1990. 161 p. :   ISBN 2-85047-159-3
DDC 759.9861 20
N6679.B6 A4 1990b

CORSICA (FRANCE) - CIVILIZATION.
Borel-Léandri, Jean-Marie. Architecture et vie
traditionnelle en Corse /. [Paris] , 1978. 287
p. :   ISBN 2-85869-038-3
    NYPL [3-MQWF 90-5907]

Cort, Louise Allison, 1944- Seto and Mino
ceramics / Louise Allison Cort. Washington,
D.C. : Freer Gallery of Art, Smithsonian
Institution ; Honolulu, Hawaii : Distributed by
University Press of Hawaii, 1992. p. cm.
(Japanese collections in the Freer Gallery of Art)
Includes bibliographical references and index.   ISBN
0-08-248143-1 :   DDC 738/.0952/16 20
1. Seto pottery - Catalogs. 2. Mino pottery - Catalogs.
3. Pottery - Washington (D.C.) - Catalogs. 4. Freer
Gallery of Art - Catalogs. I. Title. II. Series.
NK4168.S4 C67 1992

Cortanze, Gérard de. Le monde du surréalisme /
Gérard de Cortanze ; lettrines originales de
Santiago Arranz. Paris : H. Veyrier, c1991. 182
p. : ill. ; 28 cm. (Les Plumes du temps ; 41e)
Includes bibliographical references (p. 173-175) and
index.   ISBN 2-85199-550-2   DDC 700 20
1. Surrealism - Dictionaries. 2. Arts, Modern - 20th
century - Dictionaries. 3. Artists - Biography -
Dictionaries. I. Series: Plumes du temps ; 41. II. Title.
NX456.5.S8 C67 1991

Cortel, Tine. Basic principles & language of fine
art / [research and text, Tine Cortel and Theo
Stevens ; translation by Tony Burrett and Carla
van Splunteren]. Newton Abbot : David &
Charles ; New York, N.Y. : Distributed by
Sterling Pub. Co., 1989. 116 p. : ill. (some
col.) ; 27 cm. (The Fine arts series : theory and
practice) Distributor from label mounted on t.p.   ISBN
0-7153-9475-4   DDC 750/.18 20
1. Painting - Technique. 2. Color in art. I. Stevens,
Theo. II. Title. III. Title: Basic principles and language
of fine art. IV. Series: Fine arts series (Newton Abbot,
England).
ND1500 .C67 1989

Cortenova, Giorgio. Picasso in Italia /. Milano ,
c1990. 215 p. :   ISBN 88-20-20953-5 :   DDC
709/.2 20
N6853.P5 A4 1990

Cort´es Guti´errez, Laura.
Cortés Gutiérrez, Laura.
Rivera, Diego, 1886-1957. Diego Rivera .
[M´exico, D.F.] , 1988. 339 p. :   ISBN
968-290-640-7 (pbk.)
    NYPL [3-MCZ R62 90-12543]

Rivera, Diego, 1886-1957. Diego Rivera .
[Mexico City, Mexico] , 1988. 387 p. :   ISBN
968-292-277-1   DDC 759.972 20
ND259.R5 A4 1988

Rivera, Diego, 1887-1957. Diego Rivera .
[Mexico City, Mexico] , 1989. 339 p. :   ISBN
968-290-640-7   DDC 760/.092 20
N6559.R55 A4 1989

Cortés, José Miguel G. Arte conceptual revisado
=. [Valencia] [1990?] 286 p. :   ISBN

84-7721-108-6   DDC 709/.04/075 20
N6494.C63 A76 1990

Cortigiane di Venezia dal Trecento al Settecento.
Il Gioco dell'amore . Milano , 1990. 216 p. :
ISBN 88-85215-00-9
IN PROCESS (ONLINE)
    NYPL [3-MAMC 91-4481]

Cortina Portilla, Manuel. Seis charlas sobre
costumbres en México / Manuel Cortina
Portilla. Ciudad de México : [s.n.], 1989. 55 p.,
[1] leaf of plates : col. ill. ; 30 x 40 cm. "Edición
fuera de comercio destinada a los amigos del Grupo
CONSA, distribuidores de los productos Ford"--P.
opposite t.p.
1. Painting, Mexican. 2. Painting, Modern - 19th
century - Mexico. 3. Painting, Modern - 20th century -
Nexico. 4. Mexico - Social life and customs. I. Title.
ND254 .C67 1989

Cortissoz, Royal, 1869-1948. Hassam, Childe,
1859-1935. Catalogue of the etchings and
dry-points of Childe Hassam, N.A., of the
American Academy of Arts and Letters /. San
Francisco , 1989. 224 p. :   ISBN 1-556-60029-1
    NYPL [MDG+ (Hassam) 89-27271]

Cortot, Jean. Morand--memorandum / Jean
Cortot, Dorny. 1989. [13] p. : col. ill. ; 19 cm.
Artist's book consisting of hand-drawn French text and
collages. Colophon: 3/7. Paris, juin 1989. Dorny, Jean
Cortot. Purchase, July 31, 1990. On double leaves.
DDC 700/.92 20
1. Cortot, Jean. 2. Artists' books - France. I. Dorny,
Bertrand, 1931-. II. Artists' Books Collection (Library
of Congress). III. Title.
N7433.4.C66 A4 1989

CORTOT, JEAN.
Cortot, Jean. Morand--memorandum /. 1989.
[13] p. :   DDC 700/.92 20
N7433.4.C66 A4 1989

Corzas, Francisco, 1936- Francisco
Corzas. México, D.F. [1985] 137 p. :   ISBN
968-8400-43-2
N6559.C65 A4 1985

Corzas, Francisco, 1936-
Francisco Corzas. 1. ed. México, D.F. :
Universidad Autónoma Metropolitana, [1985]
137 p. : ill. (some col.) ; 29 cm. Cover title:
Corzas. Includes bibliographical references (p. 131-137).
ISBN 968-8400-43-2
1. Corzas, Francisco, 1936- - Catalogs. I. Title. II. Title:
Corzas.
N6559.C65 A4 1985

CORZAS, FRANCISCO, 1936- - CATALOGS.
Corzas, Francisco, 1936- Francisco Corzas.
México, D.F. [1985] 137 p. :   ISBN
968-8400-43-2
N6559.C65 A4 1985

Cosentino /. Cosentino, Gino, 1916- Teufen
[Switzerland] [1975?] 59 p. :
    NYPL [3-MGO (Cosentino) 90-6543]

Cosentino, Gino, 1916- Cosentino / prefazione
Hans Neuburg ; introduzione Gillo Dorfles.
Teufen [Switzerland] : A. Niggli, [1975?] 59 p. :
ill., port. ; 20 x 23 cm. Italian, German and
English.
1. Cosentino, Gino, 1916-. I. Title.
    NYPL [3-MGO (Cosentino) 90-6543]

COSENTINO, GINO, 1916-
Cosentino, Gino, 1916- Cosentino /. Teufen
[Switzerland] [1975?] 59 p. :
    NYPL [3-MGO (Cosentino) 90-6543]

Cosmopolis . Mansfield, Howard. New Brunswick,
N.J. , c1990. vii, 165 p. :   ISBN 0-88285-131-4
DDC 307.76/4 20
HT330 .M34 1990
          NYPL [3-MQV 90-13391]

Cosmovisión. Calzadilla, Juan. Marietta Berman .
Caracas, Venezuela [1990] 138, [6] p. :   ISBN
980-216-065-2   DDC 759.987 20
N6834.5.B48 A4 1990

Costa, Luís Mário Azevedo Noronha da, 1942-
Oliveira, Emídio Rosa de. A pintura de
Noronha da Costa /. Lisboa [1989] 115 p.,
[36] p. of plates :   DDC 759.69 20
ND833.C63 O45 1989

COSTA, LUÍS MÁRIO AZEVEDO
    NORONHA DA, 1942- - CRITICISM AND
    INTERPRETATION.
Oliveira, Emídio Rosa de. A pintura de
Noronha da Costa /. Lisboa [1989] 115 p.,

[36] p. of plates : DDC 759.69 20
ND833.C63 O45 1989

Costa, Miguel, 1859-1914.
Anacleto, Regina. O artista conimbricense
Miguel Costa, 1859-1914 /. Coimbra , 1989.
113 p. : ISBN 972-90380-6-6 DDC 738/.092 20
NK4670.7.P63 C673 1989

**COSTA, MIGUEL, 1859-1914 - CRITICISM
AND INTERPRETATION.**
Anacleto, Regina. O artista conimbricense
Miguel Costa, 1859-1914 /. Coimbra , 1989.
113 p. : ISBN 972-90380-6-6 DDC 738/.092 20
NK4670.7.P63 C673 1989

COSTA RICA - MAPS.
(1990) Atlas didáctico de Costa Rica. [San
José , 1990. 37 p. : ISBN 997-7911-31-2
NYPL [Map Div. 90-11874]

Costabile, Franco, 1924-1965.
Il canto dei nuovi emigranti / Franco
Costabile ; foto di Mario Giacomelli ; a cura di
Goffredo Plastino ; testi di Francesco Adornato,
Luigi M. Lombardi Satriani, Goffredo Plastino ;
presentazione di Leopoldo Chieffallo ; selezione
delle immagini di Teresa Bova e Goffredo
Plastino. 1a ed. italiana. Vibo Valentia, CZ :
Qualecultura ; Milano : Jaca book, 1989. 64 p.,
[62] p. of plates : ill. ; 24 x 31 cm. (Punto e
virgola) Includes bibliographical references. ISBN
88-16-64013-8 DDC 851/.914 20
*1. Costabile, Franco, 1924-1965. Canto dei nuovi
emigranti. 2. Photography, Documentary - Italy -
Calabria. 3. Calabria (Italy) - Social life and customs -
Pictorial works. I. Giacomelli, Mario. II. Plastino,
Goffredo. III. Title. IV. Series.*
PQ4863.O767 C36 1989
NYPL [MFX+ (Giacomelli) 91-3400]

CANTO DEI NUOVI EMIGRANTI.
Costabile, Franco, 1924-1965. Il canto dei
nuovi emigranti /. Vibo Valentia, CZ ,
Milano , 1989. 64 p., [62] p. of plates :
ISBN 88-16-64013-8 DDC 851/.914 20
PQ4863.O767 C36 1989
NYPL [MFX+ (Giacomelli) 91-3400]

Costakis, Georgi.
The Russian and Soviet avant-garde . Montreal,
Quebec, Canada , 1989. 175 p. : ISBN
2-89192-108-9 DDC 759.7/074/71428 20
ND688.5.A24 R87 1989
NYPL [3-MCY+ 91-3731]

**COSTAKIS, GEORGI - ART COLLECTIONS -
EXHIBITIONS.**
The Russian and Soviet avant-garde . Montreal,
Quebec, Canada , 1989. 175 p. : ISBN
2-89192-108-9 DDC 759.7/074/71428 20
ND688.5.A24 R87 1989
NYPL [3-MCY+ 91-3731]

Costantini, Paolo, 1929- Neorealismo e
fotografia . Udine , 1987. 186 p. : ISBN
88-85893-01-5 *NYPL [MFW+ 91-4966]*

Costantini, Paolo, 1959- L'Insistenza dello
sguardo . Firenze , c1989. 316 p. : ISBN
88-7292-141-4
IN PROCESS NYPL [MFW+ 91-7442]

Costanzi, Costanza. Pupilli, Laura. Fermo .
Bologna , c1990. v, 272 p. : ISBN 88-7019-449-3
NYPL [MAVZ (Femo, Italy) 91-5714]

Coste, Albert, 1895-1985.
Muntaner, Bernard, 1945- Albert Coste, la
musique des couleurs /. Marseille, France ,
c1990. 107 p. : ISBN 2-903963-55-X :
N6853.C728 M8 1990

**COSTE, ALBERT, 1895-1985 - CRITICISM
AND INTERPRETATION.**
Muntaner, Bernard, 1945- Albert Coste, la
musique des couleurs /. Marseille, France ,
c1990. 107 p. : ISBN 2-903963-55-X :
N6853.C728 M8 1990

COSTUME - AUSTRIA - EXHIBITIONS.
Groth-Schmachtenberger, Erika. Volks-trachten
aus Oberbayern, Österreich, Ungarn,
Jugoslawien, mit den Donauschwaben,
Rumänien, mit den Siebenbürger Sachsen /.
[München?] , 1980. 181 p., 6 leaves of plates :
NYPL [3-MMM 90-10816]

**COSTUME - AUSTRIA - VIENNA -
HISTORY - 19TH CENTURY -
EXHIBITIONS.**
Historisches Museum der Stadt Wien. Modes
romantiques viennoises, 1800-1860 . Paris ,

1970. [28] p., 16 p. of plates :
GT821.V5 P3 NYPL [3-MMM 91-516]

**COSTUME - AUSTRIA - VIENNA -
HISTORY - EXHIBITIONS.**
Historiches Museum der Stadt Wien. 200 Jahre
Mode in Wien . Wien , 1976. 120 p., [34]
leaves of plates : *NYPL [3-MMM 90-6048]*

COSTUME - BIBLIOGRAPHY.
Mode, Tracht, Kostüm . [Ober-Ramstadt]
[1988?] vii, 259 p. :
NYPL [3-MMB+ 91-5900]

COSTUME - CANADA - HISTORY.
De Marly, Diana. Dress in North America /.
New York , 1990- v. : ISBN 0-8419-1199-1
DDC 391/.0097 20
GT603 .D4 1990 NYPL [3-MMP 91-3984]

**COSTUME - CHINA - HISTORY - MING-
CH'ING DYNASTIES, 1368-1912.**
Dickinson, Gary. Imperial wardrobe /.
London , 1990. 203 p. : ISBN 1-87007-607-9 :
DDC 391.0220951 20
NYPL [3-MMR+ 91-4972]

**COSTUME - CHINA - HISTORY - MING-
CH'ING DYNASTIES, 1368-1912 -
EXHIBITIONS.**
De Verboden Stad . Rotterdam , New York,
NY , c1990. 245 p. : ISBN 90-6918-065-0
NYPL [3-MAG 91-6651]

**COSTUME - CHINA - PEKING -
EXHIBITIONS.**
De Verboden Stad . Rotterdam , New York,
NY , c1990. 245 p. : ISBN 90-6918-065-0
NYPL [3-MAG 91-6651]

**COSTUME - CZECHOSLOVAKIA - CHEB
REGION.**
Egerländer Trachtenfibel /. Frankfurt / M. ,
1986. 136 p. : *NYPL [3-MMM+ 89-25288]*

Costume de Nazaré. Silva, Abílio Leal de Mattos
e. O trajo da Nazaré. Lisboa, 1970. 77 p.
GT1232.N3 S5 NYPL [3-MMO 90-6242]

**COSTUME DESIGN - ARGENTINA -
HISTORY.**
Saulquin, Susana. La moda en la Argentina /.
Buenos Aires, Argentina , c1990. 284 p., [26] p.
of plates : ISBN 950-0-41007-9
TT504.6.A7 S38 1990
NYPL [3-MMP 91-6766]

COSTUME DESIGN - AUSTRALIA.
Australian fashion . Sydney , 1989. 64 p. :
ISBN 1-86317-002-2
NYPL [3-MME+ 91-6591]

**COSTUME DESIGN - FRANCE - PARIS -
HISTORY - 20TH CENTURY.**
De Marly, Diana. Christian Dior /. New York ,
1990. 96 p., [8] p. of plates : ISBN
0-8419-1260-2 : DDC 746.9/2/092 20
TT507 .D47 1990 NYPL [3-MME 90-12028]

COSTUME DESIGN - UNITED STATES.
Daria, Irene. The fashion cycle . New York ,
c1990. 240 p., [16] p. of plates : ISBN
0-671-66729-7 DDC 746.9/2/092273 20
TT507 .D345 1990 NYPL [3-MMP 91-3812]

**COSTUME DESIGNERS - ENGLAND -
BIOGRAPHY.**
De Marly, Diana. Worth . New York , 1990.
xv, 238 p. : ISBN 0-8419-1242-4 (pbk. : alk. paper)
DDC 746.9/2/092 B 20
TT505.W58 D42 1990
NYPL [3-MME 91-3977]

**COSTUME DESIGNERS - FRANCE -
BIOGRAPHY.**
De Marly, Diana. Worth . New York , 1990.
xv, 238 p. : ISBN 0-8419-1242-4 (pbk. : alk. paper)
DDC 746.9/2/092 B 20
TT505.W58 D42 1990
NYPL [3-MME 91-3977]

Madsen, Axel. Chanel . New York , c1990. x,
388 p., [16] leaves of plates : ISBN
0-8050-0961-2 : DDC 746.9/2/092 B 20
TT505.C45 M33 1990
NYPL [3-MME 90-11139]

COSTUME DESIGNERS - FRANCE - PARIS.
De Marly, Diana. Christian Dior /. New York ,
1990. 96 p., [8] p. of plates : ISBN
0-8419-1260-2 : DDC 746.9/2/092 20
TT507 .D47 1990 NYPL [3-MME 90-12028]

COSTUME DESIGNERS - NETHERLANDS.
Meij, Letse. Frans Molenaar . De Bilt , c1986.
176 p. : ISBN 90-213-0378-7 (speciale luxe ed.)
NYPL [3-MMO 89-19034]

COSTUME DESIGNERS - UNITED STATES.
Daria, Irene. The fashion cycle . New York ,
c1990. 240 p., [16] p. of plates : ISBN
0-671-66729-7 DDC 746.9/2/092273 20
TT507 .D345 1990 NYPL [3-MMP 91-3812]

COSTUME - EUROPE - CATALOGS.
La Galleria del Costume. Firenze , c1983- v. :
ISBN 88-7038-077-7 (v. 1)
NYPL [3-MME 84-2509]

**COSTUME - FRANCE - HISTORY - 20TH
CENTURY - EXHIBITIONS.**
Musée des arts de la mode (France) Histoires
de mode d'hier et d'aujourd'hui . Paris , c1988.
55 p. : ISBN 2-901422-13-6 :
NYPL [3-MME+ 91-5058]

**COSTUME - FRANCE - PARIS - HISTORY -
19TH CENTURY.**
Boucher, François, b. 1885. Paris miroir de la
mode . Paris [1959] xi p., 24 leaves of plates :
GT875 .B6 1959 NYPL [3-MML+ 91-7290]

**COSTUME - FRANCE - PARIS - HISTORY -
20TH CENTURY.**
Le Théâtre de la Mode /. Paris , c1990. 166
p. : ISBN 2-906450-41-3
NYPL [3-MME+ 90-13056]

**COSTUME - FRANCE - PARIS - HISTORY -
COLLECTED WORKS.**
Parisian fashion, from the "Journal des dames et
des modes," vol. 1, 1912-1913 /. New York ,
c1979. [12] p., [93] p. of plates : ISBN
0-8478-0253-1 : DDC 391/.2/0944361
GT887 .P3 NYPL [MML 81-188]

**COSTUME - GERMANY, (WEST) -
OBERBAYERN - EXHIBITIONS.**
Groth-Schmachtenberger, Erika. Volks-trachten
aus Oberbayern, Österreich, Ungarn,
Jugoslawien, mit den Donauschwaben,
Rumänien, mit den Siebenbürger Sachsen /.
[München?] , 1980. 181 p., 6 leaves of plates :
NYPL [3-MMM 90-10816]

COSTUME - HISTORY.
Peacock, John. The chronicle of western
costume . London , c1991. 224 p. : ISBN
0-500-01490-6 *NYPL [3-MMC 91-5165]*

**COSTUME - HISTORY - MEDIEVAL, 500-
1500.**
Le Vêtement . Paris , c1989. 332 p. : ISBN
2-86377-089-6 :
GT575 .V48 1989 NYPL [3-MMG 91-6577]

**COSTUME - HISTORY - 15TH CENTURY -
EXHIBITIONS.**
Crivelli, Carlo, 15th cent. Gli abiti di Carlo
Crivelli . [Ancona] [1990] 110 p. :
NYPL [3-MCF+ C93 91-5435]

COSTUME - HISTORY - 19TH CENTURY.
Kunciov, Robert. Mr. Godey's ladies. Princeton
[N.J.] 1971. viii, 183 p. ISBN 0-87861-009-X
DDC 391/.07/20973
GT610 .K8 NYPL [3-MMP 90-5497]

COSTUME - HUNGARY - EXHIBITIONS.
Groth-Schmachtenberger, Erika. Volks-trachten
aus Oberbayern, Österreich, Ungarn,
Jugoslawien, mit den Donauschwaben,
Rumänien, mit den Siebenbürger Sachsen /.
[München?] , 1980. 181 p., 6 leaves of plates :
NYPL [3-MMM 90-10816]

COSTUME - ITALY - CATALOGS.
La Galleria del Costume. Firenze , c1983- v. :
ISBN 88-7038-077-7 (v. 1)
NYPL [3-MME 84-2509]

COSTUME - ITALY - EXHIBITIONS.
Crivelli, Carlo, 15th cent. Gli abiti di Carlo
Crivelli . [Ancona] [1990] 110 p. :
NYPL [3-MCF+ C93 91-5435]

**COSTUME - ITALY - FLORENCE -
CATALOGS.**
La Galleria del costume /. Firenze , 1988. 93
p. : ISBN 88-7038-145-5
NYPL [3-MMO 88-4827]

COSTUME - ITALY - HISTORY.
L'abbigliamento popolare italiano /. Brescia
[1986] 160 p. : *NYPL [3-MMO 90-8664]*

**COSTUME - ITALY - HISTORY - 18TH
CENTURY - EXHIBITIONS.**
Museo nazionale delle arti e tradizioni popolari

(Italy) Oreficeria popolare italiana e costumi regionali del '700 . Lugano , 1978. 57 p., 36 leaves of plates :   *NYPL [3-MNR 90-5751]*

COSTUME - ITALY - MOLISE - HISTORY.
Trombetta, Ada. Mondo contadino d'altri tempi . Napoli , c1989. 333 p. :   ISBN 88-7104-150-X
    NYPL [3-MMO+ 91-3733]

COSTUME - JAPAN - HISTORY.
Kennedy, Alan. Japanese costume . Paris, France , New York, N.Y. , 1990. 153, [3] p. : ISBN 2-87660-083-8   DDC 391/.00952 20
GT1560 .K42 1990
    NYPL [3-MMR+ 91-4466]

COSTUME JEWELRY.
Greindl, Gabriele. [Strass. English.] Gems of costume jewelry /. New York , 1991. p. cm.
   ISBN 1-558-59207-5   DDC 391/.7 20
NK4890.C67 G7413 1991

COSTUME JEWELRY - ENGLAND - HISTORY - 20TH CENTURY.
Becker, Vivienne, 1953- Rough diamonds . London , 1990. 175 p. :   ISBN 1-85145-521-3 : DDC 739.27 20
NK7304   *NYPL [MNR+ 91-3889]*

COSTUME JEWELRY - UNITED STATES.
Ball, Joanne Dubbs. Jewelry of the stars . West Chester, Pa. , c1991. 192 p. :   ISBN 0-88740-294-1   DDC 739.27/092 20
NK7398.J67 B35 1991

COSTUME, MEDIEVAL. see COSTUME - HISTORY - MEDIEVAL, 500-1500.

COSTUME - MEXICO - HISTORY.
Sayer, Chloë. Mexican textiles /. London , 1990, c1985. 240 p. :   ISBN 0-7141-2501-6 (pbk.) : DDC 391.00972 20
GT625   *NYPL [3-MMP 91-5065]*

COSTUME - MOROCCO - HISTORY - 20TH CENTURY.
Besancenot, Jean. [Costumes du Maroc. English.] Costumes of Morocco /. London ; New York : 204 p. :   ISBN 0-7103-0359-9 DDC 391/.00964 20
GT1582 .B4713 1990
    NYPL [3-MMR+ 91-7287]

Costume of Nazaré. Silva, Abílio Leal de Mattos e. O trajo da Nazaré. Lisboa, 1970. 77 p.
GT1232.N3 S5   *NYPL [3-MMO 90-6242]*

COSTUME - PORTUGAL - NAZARÉ.
Silva, Abílio Leal de Mattos e. O trajo da Nazaré. Lisboa, 1970. 77 p.
GT1232.N3 S5   *NYPL [3-MMO 90-6242]*

COSTUME - ROMANIA - EXHIBITIONS.
Groth-Schmachtenberger, Erika. Volks-trachten aus Oberbayern, Österreich, Ungarn, Jugoslawien, mit den Donauschwaben, Rumänien, mit den Siebenbürger Sachsen /. [München?] , 1980. 181 p., 6 leaves of plates :
    NYPL [3-MMM 90-10816]

COSTUME - SOVIET UNION - HISTORY - EXHIBITIONS.
Les Costumes historiques russes du Musée de l'Ermitage de Léningrad . [Paris?] [1989] 78 p. :   *NYPL [3-MMO 89-8777]*

COSTUME, THEATRICAL. see COSTUME.

COSTUME - TURKEY.
Historical costumes of Turkish women. Istanbul, Turkey , 1986. 175 p. :
    NYPL [3-MMR + 89-19091]

COSTUME - TURKEY - ISTANBUL - CATALOGS.
Topkapı Sarayı. Costumes et tissus brodés /. Paris , 1987. 235 p. :   ISBN 2-86950-035-3
    NYPL [3-MON+ 90-12899]

COSTUME - UNITED STATES - HISTORY.
De Marly, Diana. Dress in North America /. New York , 1990- v. :   ISBN 0-8419-1199-1 DDC 391/.0097 20
GT603 .D4 1990   *NYPL [3-MMP 91-3984]*

Kunciov, Robert. Mr. Godey's ladies. Princeton [N.J.] 1971. viii, 183 p.   ISBN 0-87861-009-X DDC 391/.07/20973
GT610 .K8   *NYPL [3-MMP 90-5497]*

COSTUME - UNITED STATES - HISTORY - 20TH CENTURY - THEMES, MOTIVES.
The Costumemaker's art . Asheville, N.C. , 1992. p.   ISBN 0-937274-58-5 : DDC

746.9/2/0973 20
NK4860.5.U6 C6 1992

COSTUME - YUGOSLAVIA - EXHIBITIONS.
Groth-Schmachtenberger, Erika. Volks-trachten aus Oberbayern, Österreich, Ungarn, Jugoslawien, mit den Donauschwaben, Rumänien, mit den Siebenbürger Sachsen /. [München?] , 1980. 181 p., 6 leaves of plates :
    NYPL [3-MMM 90-10816]

COSTUME - YUGOSLAVIA - KUPINEC (CROATIA)
Bakrač, Ivanka. Narodna nošnja Kupinca . Zagreb , 1986. 69 p., [28] p. of plates : ISBN 86-80825-06-9
NK4771.Y82 K863 1986

The Costumemaker's art : cloaks of fantasy, masks of revelation / edited by Thom Boswell. Asheville, N.C. : Lark Books, 1992. p. cm. Includes index.   ISBN 0-937274-58-5 :   DDC 746.9/2/0973 20
1. Wearable art - United States - Themes, motives. 2. Costume - United States - History - 20th century - Themes, motives. I. Boswell, Thom. II. Lark Books.
NK4860.5.U6 C6 1992

Costumes des femmes françaises du XIIe au XVIIIe siècle /. La Mésangère, Pierre de, 1761-1831. Paris , 1900. [5] leaves, [70] col. leaves of plates :   *NYPL [3-MML+ 84-1125]*

Costumes et modes d'autrefois .
(7) Boucher, François, b. 1885. Paris miroir de la mode . Paris [1959] xi p., 24 leaves of plates :
GT875 .B6 1959   *NYPL [3-MML+ 91-7290]*

Les Costumes historiques russes du Musée de l'Ermitage de Léningrad : Le bal costume de l'Ermitage, février 1903: [Exposition] la salle de la Mascarade au Musée Jacquemart-André, Paris du 1er mars au 31 mai 1989 / [texte, Elise de Moncan ; photographies originales du bal de l'Ermitage ... New York Public Library, Slavonic Division]. [Paris?] : Mécène, [1989] 78 p. : ill. ; 19 cm. At head of title: Yves Saint Laurent présente ...
1. Costume - Soviet Union - History - Exhibitions. I. Moncan, Elise de. II. Saint-Laurent, Yves. III. Gosudarstvennyĭ Ermitazh (Soviet Union). IV. Musée Jacquemart-André. V. New York Public Library. Slavonic Division.   *NYPL [3-MMO 89-8777]*

Costumes of Morocco /. Besancenot, Jean. [Costumes du Maroc. English.] London ; New York : 204 p. :   ISBN 0-7103-0359-9   DDC 391/.00964 20
GT1582 .B4713 1990
    NYPL [3-MMR+ 91-7287]

COTMAN, JOHN SELL, 1782-1842 - EXHIBITIONS.
The Norwich school . Manchester [England] [1961] 44 p. :   *NYPL [3-MCT 91-402]*

Cotosman, Roman.
Cotosman, Valenta / [Text, Roman Cotosman, Jan Kotik, Diet Sayler]. Nürnberg : Galerie Johanna Ricard, c1981. [25] p. : ill. ; 15 x 22 cm. Cover title. Catalog of an exhibition held at the Galerie Johanna Ricard in 1981. Bibliography: p. [8]
1. Cotosman, Roman - Exhibitions. 2. Valenta, Rudolf - Exhibitions. I. Valenta, Rudolf. II. Kotik, Jan, 1916--. III. Sayler, Diet. IV. Galerie Johanna Ricard. V. Title.
    NYPL [3-MGO (Cotosman) 90-2044]

COTOSMAN, ROMAN - EXHIBITIONS.
Cotosman, Roman. Cotosman, Valenta /. Nürnberg , c1981. [25] p. :
    NYPL [3-MGO (Cotosman) 90-2044]

Cotosman, Valenta /. Cotosman, Roman. Nürnberg , c1981. [25] p. :
    NYPL [3-MGO (Cotosman) 90-2044]

COTSWOLD HILLS (ENGLAND) - DESCRIPTION AND TRAVEL.
Tookey, John. The Cotswolds . London , 1990. 60 p. :   ISBN 0-233-98554-9 :   DDC 759.2 20
ND1942.T66 A4 1990

COTSWOLD HILLS (ENGLAND) IN ART.
Tookey, John. The Cotswolds . London , 1990. 60 p. :   ISBN 0-233-98554-9 :   DDC 759.2 20
ND1942.T66 A4 1990

The Cotswolds . Tookey, John. London , 1990. 60 p. :   ISBN 0-233-98554-9 :   DDC 759.2 20
ND1942.T66 A4 1990

COTTAGES - ENGLAND.
Elsam, Richard, Esq. An essay on rural architecture. Farnborough, 1972. [5], v, 54 p.,

---

[31] leaves. ISBN 0-576-15164-5   DDC 728.6
NA7562 .E73 1803a
    NYPL [3-MQZ (Elsam) 90-6797]

COTTAGES - ENGLAND - CUMBERLAND.
Ramm, Herman Gabriel. Shielings and bastles. London, 1970. xv, 104 p., 41 plates (2 fold.).
   ISBN 0-11-700468-5   DDC 914.28
GT287.C8 R3   *NYPL [3-MRGF 90-6851]*

COTTAGES - GREAT BRITAIN.
Rice, Matthew. Traditional houses of rural Britain /. New York , 1992. p. cm.   ISBN 1-558-59338-1   DDC 728/.0941 20
NA8210.G67 R5 1992

Wood, John. A series of plans for cottages or habitations of the labourer. Farnborough, 1972. 31 p.   ISBN 0-576-15177-7   DDC 728.6/4
NA7562 .W6 1972
    NYPL [3-MQZ (Wood, J.) 90-6796]

COTTAGES - MICHIGAN.
Northup, A. Dale, 1941- Frank Lloyd Wright in Michigan /. Algonac, Mich. , 1991. 100 p. :   ISBN 0-917256-51-4   DDC 728/.373/092 20
NA737.W7 N6 1991

COTTAGES - NORWAY.
Lærum, O. D. Røykstova. [Oslo] , c1990. 143 p. :   ISBN 82-00-21044-8
NA7566.N8 L3 1990

Cottbus (Germany : Bezirk). Rat. Kunst in Cottbus . [Cottbus] [Cottbus] [1989] [140] p. :
    NYPL [3-MAMG 91-6140]

Cotter, Holland. Steir, Pat, 1940- Pat Steir . New York , 1990. 1 v. (unpaged) :   ISBN 0-944680-10-0
    NYPL [3-MCX S814 91-5079]

Cotter, Holland, 1947- Kay WalkingStick : paintings, 1974-1990 / [text by] Holland Cotter and Thomas W. Leavitt ; curator, Judy Collischan. Brookville, NY : Long Island University, 1991. p. cm. "March 13-April 28, 1991, Hillwood Art Museum, Long Island University; August 31-November 17, 1991, Heard Museum, Phoenix, Arizona." Includes bibliographical references. ISBN 0-933699-20-4 :   DDC 759.13 20
1. WalkingStick, Kay - Exhibitions. I. WalkingStick, Kay. II. Leavitt, Thomas W. III. Collischan, Judy. IV. Hillwood Art Museum. V. Heard Museum. VI. Title.
ND237.W316 A4 1991

Cottet, Charles, 1924-
Ch. Cottet / préface de Bernard Blatter ; "Propos et divagations sur les peintures de Charles Cottet" par Frédéric Wandelère ; textes de Charles Cottet. Bulle : Editions Bim, c1988. 157 p. : ill. (some col.), ports. ; 27 cm. French and German.   ISBN 2-88039-010-9
1. Cottet, Charles, 1924- - Criticism and interpretation. I. Wandelère, Frédéric. II. Title.
    NYPL [3-MCZ C847 90-2627]

COTTET, CHARLES, 1924- - CRITICISM AND INTERPRETATION.
Cottet, Charles, 1924- Ch. Cottet /. Bulle , c1988. 157 p. :   ISBN 2-88039-010-9
    NYPL [3-MCZ C847 90-2627]

Cottle, Simon. Sotheby's concise encyclopedia of glass /. Boston , c1991. p.   ISBN 0-316-08374-7 : DDC 748.29 20
NK5104 .S66 1991

Couch, Tony. Watercolor techniques / Tony Couch. 1st ed. Cincinnati, Ohio : North Light Books, c1991. p. cm. Includes index. ISBN 0-89134-389-X   DDC 751.42/2 20
1. Watercolor painting - Technique. I. Title.
ND2420 .C68 1991

Couldrey, Vivienne.
The art of Louis Comfort Tiffany / Vivienne Couldrey. London : Bloomsbury, 1989. 192 p. : ill. (some col.) ; 34 cm. "A Quarto book"--T.p. verso. Includes index. Bibliography: p. 192. ISBN 0-7475-0488-1
1. Tiffany, Louis Comfort, 1848-1933. I. Title.
    NYPL [3-MPW+ 90-11646]

The art of Louis Comfort Tiffany / Vivienne Couldrey. Secaucus, N.J. : Wellfleet Press, c1989. 191 p. : ill. (some col.) ; 34 cm. "A Quarto book." Includes bibliographical references and index. ISBN 1-555-21447-9   DDC 748/.092 20
1. Tiffany, Louis Comfort, 1848-1933 - Criticism and interpretation. 2. Glassware - United States - History - 19th century. 3. Glassware - United States - History - 20th century. I. Title.
NK5198.T5 C68 1989

Couleurs & architecture . Massel, Christiane, 1953- [Sarreguemines] , c1989. 157 p. : ISBN 2-7085-0075-9 DDC 728/.0944/3825 20
NA3549.A3 M676 1989

Couleurs du noir . Guillerm, Jean-Pierre. [Lille] , c1990. 197 p. : ISBN 2-85939-379-X : DDC 759.4 20
ND553.D33 A2 1990

Couleurs et architecture. Massel, Christiane, 1953- Couleurs & architecture .
[Sarreguemines] , c1989. 157 p. : ISBN 2-7085-0075-9 DDC 728/.0944/3825 20
NA3549.A3 M676 1989

Coulter, Lane, 1944- New Mexican tinwork, 1840-1940 / Lane Coulter, Maurice Dixon, Jr. ; foreword by Ward Alan Minge. 1st ed. Albuquerque : University of New Mexico Press, c1990. xxii, 189 p. : ill. (some col.) ; 21 x 26 cm. Includes index. Includes bibliographical references (p. 175-181). ISBN 0-8263-1180-6 DDC 739.5/32/09789 20
1. Tinsmithing - New Mexico - History. 2. Tinsmiths - New Mexico - History. 3. Tinware, American - New Mexico. 4. New Mexico - Industries. I. Dixon, Maurice, 1947-. II. Title. III. Title: Tinwork.
TS600 .C68 1990   **NYPL [3-MNK 90-11509]**

Council of Europe. Comité pour la Campagne européenne pour la renaissance de la cité.
Le Projet d'architecture dans la ville, instrument de sa transformation . Strasbourg , 1983. 50 P. ;
NA9183 .P7 1983

Le Projet urbain dans l'histoire de Strasbourg . Paris , 1983. 110 p. ;
NA9198.S87 P7 1983

Le Projet urbain et la construction de la cité . Strasbourg , 1983. 96 p. ;
NA9095 .P76 1983

COUNTER-REFORMATION AND ART.
Poletto, Christine, 1959- Art et pouvoirs à l'Age baroque . Paris , c1990. 218 p., [16] p. of plates : ISBN 2-7384-0495-2
N7862 .P65 1990

COUNTER-REFORMATION IN ART.
Moroni in Val Seriana /. Brescia , 1978. 69 p. :
ND623.M76 M67
     NYPL [3-MCF M86 81-635]

COUNTER-REFORMATION IN ART - EXHIBITIONS.
L'Arte per i papi e per i principi nella campagna romana . Roma , c1990. 2 v. : ISBN 88-7140-015-1 (v. 1) :
ND1432.I8 A77 1990
     NYPL [3-MCE 91-3418]

Restauro delle tele dei miracoli alla Basilica della Ghiara . [Reggio Emilia] [1976?] 51 p. :
ND1651.I8 R437   **NYPL [3-MCE 79-2043]**

The country builder's assistant . Benjamin, Asher, 1773-1845. Greenfield, Mass. , 1805. [36] p., [1], 37 leaves of plates (2 folded) : DDC 720 20
NA2520 .B4 1805

COUNTRY FURNITURE - AUSTRALIA.
Hooper, Toby. Australian country furniture /. South Yarra, Vic., Australia , 1988. 138 p., [24] p. of plates : ISBN 0-670-90074-5
     NYPL [3-MOF+ 91-7961]

COUNTRY FURNITURE - SCANDINAVIA.
Barwick, JoAnn. Scandinavian country /. New York , c1991. p. cm. ISBN 0-517-57661-9 : DDC 745.4/4948 20
NK1457 .B37 1991

COUNTRY HOMES - ENGLAND.
Elsam, Richard, Esq. An essay on rural architecture. Farnborough, 1972. [5], v, 54 p., [31] leaves. ISBN 0-576-15164-5 DDC 728.6
NA7562 .E73 1803a
     NYPL [3-MQZ (Elsam) 90-6797]

Hussey, Christopher, 1899- English country houses /. London , 1988. 3 v. : ISBN 1-85149-029-9 (set : pbk.)
     NYPL [3-MRG 90-12887]

Jackson-Stops, Gervase. The country house in perspective /. London , 1990. 160 p. : ISBN 1-85145-383-0 : DDC 728.8 20
NA7620   **NYPL [3-MRGF+ 91-6514]**

Lycett Green, Candida. The perfect English country house /. New York , 1991. 175 p. : ISBN 0-8478-1373-8 DDC 728.8/0942 20
NA7562 .L93 1991

COUNTRY HOMES - ENGLAND - CONGRESSES.
The Fashioning and functioning of the British country house /. Washington, D.C. , Hanover [N.H.] , 1989. 417 p. : ISBN 0-89468-128-1
     NYPL [3-MRG 90-12992]

COUNTRY HOMES - ENGLAND - DESIGNS AND PLANS.
Butler, A. S. G. (Arthur Stanley George), 1888-1965. [Architecture of Sir Edwin Luytens. Vol. 1.] The domestic architecture of Sir Edwin Lutyens /. Woodbridge, Suffolk , 1989. 61 p., 110, [120] p. of plates : ISBN 1-85149-100-7
   NYPL [3-MQZ++ (Lutyens) 90-12076]

Plaw, John, 1744 or 5-1820. Sketches for country houses, villas and rural dwellings, calculated for persons of moderate income and for comfortable retirement .... Farnborough, 1972. 20 p., [42] leaves. ISBN 0-576-15175-0 DDC 728.3
NA7562 .P6 1972
     NYPL [3-MQWK 90-5752]

COUNTRY HOMES - FRANCE - VEXIN.
Le Vexin français . Pontoise [France] [196-?] 32 p. :   **NYPL [3-MRGF 90-6241]**

COUNTRY HOMES - IRELAND.
FitzGerald, Desmond. Vanishing country houses of Ireland /. [Dublin] [Leixlip] , 1988. vi, 161 p. : ISBN 0-948018-04-6
     NYPL [3-MRGF 89-17124]

COUNTRY HOMES - ITALY - LAZIO.
Torselli, Giorgio. Castelli e ville del Lazio /. Roma , c1983. 284 p., [8] folded leaves of plates :   **NYPL [3-MQWB+ 90-12978]**

COUNTRY HOMES - ITALY - TURIN (PROVINCE)
Roggero Bardelli, Costanza. Ville Sabaude /. Milano , 1990. 529 p. : ISBN 88-18-32007-6
     NYPL [3-MRGF+ 91-5349]

COUNTRY HOMES - ITALY - VENETO.
Di villa in villa . Treviso , c1990. 235 p. : ISBN 88-85066-98-4
     NYPL [3-MQWB 91-4915]

COUNTRY HOMES - NETHERLANDS.
Guillermo, Jorge. Dutch houses and castles /. London , New York, N.Y. , c1990. 208 p. : ISBN 1-85043-237-6 DDC 720.9492 20
     NYPL [3-MQW+ 91-3636]

COUNTRY HOMES - UNITED STATES - HISTORY.
Aslet, Clive, 1955- The American country house /. New Haven , 1990. vii, 302 p. : ISBN 0-300-04757-6
     NYPL [3-MQWO 90-12969]

The country house in perspective /. Jackson-Stops, Gervase. London , 1990. 160 p. : ISBN 1-85145-383-0 : DDC 728.8 20
NA7620   **NYPL [3-MRGF+ 91-6514]**

COUNTRY LIFE - ENGLAND - CONGRESSES.
The Fashioning and functioning of the British country house /. Washington, D.C. , Hanover [N.H.] , 1989. 417 p. : ISBN 0-89468-128-1
     NYPL [3-MRG 90-12992]

COUNTRY LIFE IN ART.
Schilders van het landelijke leven in België . Tielt , 1990. 173 p. : ISBN 90-209-1787-0 :
ND469.F5 S35 1990

COUNTRY LIFE - UNITED STATES - COLLECTIBLES - CATALOGS.
Reno, Dawn E. The official identification and price guide to American country collectibles /. New York , 1990. 521 p., [8] p. of plates : ISBN 0-87637-796-7 : DDC 745.1/0973/075 20
NK805 .R45 1990

COUNTRY LIFE - UNITED STATES - PICTORIAL WORKS.
Country USA /. Champaign, Ill. , 1989. 187 p. : ISBN 0-9624617-0-9
IN PROCESS (ONLINE)
     NYPL [MFW+ 91-7456]

COUNTRY PAINTED FURNITURE - CZECHOSLOVAKIA - THEMES, MOTIVES.
Johnová, Helena, 1884-1962. Lidový malovaný nábytek v českých zemích . V Praze , 1989. 196 p. : ISBN 80-7038-034-9 :
NK2635.C9 J64 1989

A country so interesting . Ruggles, Richard I.,

1923- Montreal , Buffalo , c1991. xix, 300 p. : ISBN 0-7735-0679-9 : DDC 912.71 20
     NYPL [Map Div. 91-6178]

Country USA / photographed by 102 of America's best photographers. 1st ed. Champaign, Ill. : Silver Image, 1989. 187 p. : col. ill. ; 24 x 30 cm. ISBN 0-9624617-0-9
1. Country life - United States - Pictorial works. 2. United States - Description and travel - 1981- - Views.
IN PROCESS (ONLINE)
     NYPL [MFW+ 91-7456]

County maps of Wisconsin /. Wisconsin. State Highway Commission. [Madison, Wis. , 1966] 1 atlas (unpaged) :   **NYPL [Map Div. 91-1140]**

Couple. La Coppia =. Milano , c1989. 205 p. : DDC 745.4/442 20
NK1390 .C66 1989
     NYPL [3-MNF 90-11125]

Courbet . Herding, Klaus. New Haven , 1991. p. cm. ISBN 0-300-03744-9 DDC 759.4 20
ND553.C9 H47 1991

Courbet et Ornans /. Fernier, Jean-Jacques. Paris , 1989. 126 p. : ISBN 2-7335-0170-4
     NYPL [3-MCO C858 91-5529]

Courbet, Gustave, 1819-1877. [Correspondence. English. Selections]
Letters of Gustave Courbet / edited and translated by Petra ten-Doesschate Chu. Chicago : University of Chicago Press, 1992. p. cm. Translated from the French. Includes bibliographical references and index. ISBN 0-226-11653-0 (cloth) DDC 759.4 B 20
1. Courbet, Gustave, 1819-1877 - Correspondence. 2. Painters - France - Correspondence. I. Chu, Petra ten-Doesschate. II. Title.
ND553.C9 A3 1992

COURBET, GUSTAVE, 1819-1877 - CORRESPONDENCE.
Courbet, Gustave, 1819-1877. [Correspondence. English. Selections.] Letters of Gustave Courbet /. Chicago , 1992. p. cm. ISBN 0-226-11653-0 (cloth) DDC 759.4 B 20
ND553.C9 A3 1992

COURBET, GUSTAVE, 1819-1877 - PSYCHOLOGY.
Herding, Klaus. Courbet . New Haven , 1991. p. cm. ISBN 0-300-03744-9 DDC 759.4 20
ND553.C9 H47 1991

Courbet, Jean Désiré Gustave. see Courbet, Gustave, 1819-1877.

Court arts of Indonesia /. Jessup, Helen Ibbitson. New York , c1990. 288 p. : ISBN 0-8109-3165-6
IN PROCESS (ONLINE)
     NYPL [3-MAF+ 91-6099]

Courtauld Institute Galleries.
Braham, Helen. Rubens . London , c1988. 58, [2] p. : ISBN 0-7187-0878-4
     NYPL [3-MCH+ R8 91-6137]

The Courtauld Institute Galleries, University of London / Dennis Farr, William Bradford, Helen Braham. London : Scala, 1990. 128 p. : col. ill. ; 28 cm. Includes index. ISBN 1-87024-839-2
1. Courtauld Institute Galleries - Catalogs. 2. Art - England - London - Catalogs. I. Farr, Dennis, 1929-. II. Bradford, William. III. Braham, Helen. IV. Title.
     NYPL [3-MAVZ (London) 90-12082]

COURTAULD INSTITUTE GALLERIES - CATALOGS.
Courtauld Institute Galleries. The Courtauld Institute Galleries, University of London /. London , 1990. 128 p. : ISBN 1-87024-839-2
     NYPL [3-MAVZ (London) 90-12082]

The Courtauld Institute Galleries, University of London /. Courtauld Institute Galleries. London , 1990. 128 p. : ISBN 1-87024-839-2
     NYPL [3-MAVZ (London) 90-12082]

Courtauld Institute of Art.
The Conservation of wall paintings . Marina del Rey, CA , 1991. p. cm. ISBN 0-89236-162-X (pbk.) : DDC 751.6/2 20
ND2552 .C64 1991

COURTAULD INSTITUTE OF ART - CATALOGS.
Braham, Helen. Rubens . London , c1988. 58, [2] p. : ISBN 0-7187-0878-4
     NYPL [3-MCH+ R8 91-6137]

COURTAULD INSTITUTE OF ART - EXHIBITIONS.
Braham, Helen. Rubens . London , c1988. 58,

[2] p. : ISBN 0-7187-0878-4
NYPL [3-MCH+ R8 91-6137]

Courtemanche, Gil. Trente artistes dans un train /
Gil Courtemanche ; [réalisé avec la
collaboration de Via Rail Canada]. Montréal :
Art Global, c1989. 153 p. : col. ill. ; 27 cm.
(Collection Le Canada et ses trésors) ISBN
2-920718-29-0 : DDC 751.7/3/0971 20
*1. Mural painting and decoration - 20th century -
Canada. 2. Mural painting and decoration, Canadian. 3.
Painting, Modern -20th century - Canada. 4. Painters -
Canada. 5. Railroads - Canada - Trains - History. 6.
Canadian (Express train). I. VIA Rail Canada. II. Title.
III. Title: 30 artistes dans un train. IV. Series.*
NYPL [3-MLP 91-6235]

COURTESANS IN ART - EXHIBITIONS.
Il Gioco dell'amore . Milano , 1990. 216 p. :
ISBN 88-85215-00-9
IN PROCESS (ONLINE)
NYPL [3-MAMC 91-4481]

**COURTESANS - ITALY - VENICE -
EXHIBITIONS.**
Il Gioco dell'amore . Milano , 1990. 216 p. :
ISBN 88-85215-00-9
IN PROCESS (ONLINE)
NYPL [3-MAMC 91-4481]

A Courthouse conservation handbook.
Washington : Preservation Press, National Trust
for Historic Preservation, 1976. 75 p. : ill. ; 27
cm. A project of the National Trust for Historic
Preservation in cooperation with the National
Clearinghouse for Criminal Justice Planning and
Architecture; prepared for use at the National
Conference on Historic Courthouses held March
31-April 2, 1976, St. Louis, Mo. Bibliography: p. 71-72.
ISBN 0-89133-036-4 DDC 725/.15
*1. Courthouses - United States - Conservation and
restoration. I. National Trust for Historic Preservation
in the United States. II. National Clearinghouse for
Criminal Justice Planning and Architecture. III.
National Conference on Historic Courthouses (1976 :
St. Louis, Mo.).*
NA4471 .C68 NYPL [3-MQWO 90-6344]

**COURTHOUSES - UNITED STATES -
CONSERVATION AND RESTORATION.**
A Courthouse conservation handbook.
Washington , 1976. 75 p. : ISBN 0-89133-036-4
DDC 725/.15
NA4471 .C68 NYPL [3-MQWO 90-6344]

Courtin, Pierre, 1921- Pierre Courtin, gouaches et
peintures / [préface par Jacques Demougin].
Paris : Y. Rivière : Arts et métiers graphiques,
1976. 90 p. : ill. (some col.) ; 28 cm. "Ouvrage ...
publié ... à l'occasion de l'Exposition Pierre Courtin,
organisée par le Centre national d'art et de culture
Georges Pompidou, Musée national d'art moderne, du
24 février au 29 mars 1976, au Centre national d'art
contemporain ... Paris." Includes index. ISBN
2-7004-0015-1 :
*1. Courtin, Pierre, 1921-. I. Centre national d'art
contemporain. II. Paris. Musée national d'art moderne.
III. Title.*
ND553.C918 C46
NYPL [3-MCO C864 80-2164]

COURTIN, PIERRE, 1921-
Courtin, Pierre, 1921- Pierre Courtin, gouaches
et peintures . Paris , 1976. 90 p. : ISBN
2-7004-0015-1 :
ND553.C918 C46
NYPL [3-MCO C864 80-2164]

Courtly splendor : twelve centuries of treasures
from Japan = Ōchō kizoku no bijutsu. [Boston,
Mass.] : Museum of Fine Arts, Boston, [1990]
173 p. : col. ill. ; 30 cm. "Exhibition dates, Museum
of Fine Arts, Boston, October 17 to November 25,
1990"--T.p. verso. ISBN 0-87846-328-3 DDC
709/.52/07474461 20
*1. Art, Japanese - To 1868 - Exhibitions. I. Museum of
Fine Arts, Boston. II. Title: Ōchō kizoku no bijutsu.*
N7353 .C68 1990

Courtly splendor : twelve centuries of treasures
from Japan. Boston : Museum of Fine Arts,
[1990] 173 p. : col. ill. ; 30 cm. Catalog of an
exhibition held at the Museum of Fine Arts, Boston,
Oct. 17-Nov. 25, 1990. "The exhibition is organized to
honor the enthronement of Emperor Akihito of Japan,
and to celebrate the centennial of the Department of
Asiatic Art, Museum of Fine Arts, Boston"--P. [5].
English and Japanese. "The entry explanations in the
catalogue were written by the staff of the Arts and
Crafts Section, Agency for Cultural Affairs, Japan"--P.
[4]. ISBN 0-87846-328-3

---

*1. Museum of Fine Arts, Boston. Dept. of Asiatic Art -
Anniversaries, etc. 2. Art, Japanese - Exhibitions. 3.
Art, Buddhist - Japan - Exhibitions. 4. Japan - Kings
and rulers - Art patronage - Exhibitions. I. Museum of
Fine Arts, Boston. II. Title: Twelve centuries of
treasures from Japan. III. Title: 12 centuries of treasures
from Japan.* ***NYPL [3-MAG+ 91-3336]***

Cousinou, Olivier. Deux, Fred, 1924- Fred Deux .
Marseille [France] [Arles] , c1989. 103 p. :
ISBN 2-86869-298-2 :
MLCS 90/03392 (N)
NYPL [MDG (Deux) 90-11000]

Coutagne, Denis. Cézanne / Denis Coutagne.
Paris : Critérion, c1990. 240 p. : ill. ; 21 cm.
(Collection Avant/après) Includes bibliographical
references (p. [235]-237). ISBN 2-903702-27-6 :
DDC 759.4 20
*1. Cézanne, Paul, 1839-1906 - Criticism and
interpretation. I. Title. II. Series.*
ND553.C33 C68 1990

Coutaud, Lucien, 1904-1977.
Lucien Coutaud : gravures et dessins dans les
collections des musées de la Ville de Nîmes :
Musée du vieux Nîmes, 7 mars-30 juin 1989.
Nîmes : Le Musée, 1989. 162 p. : chiefly ill. ;
27 cm. ISBN 2-902309-54-6 DDC 760/.092 20
*1. Coutaud, Lucien, 1904-1977 - Exhibitions. 2. Musée
du vieux Nîmes - Exhibitions. I. Musée du vieux
Nîmes. II. Title.*
N6853.C756 A4 1989

**COUTAUD, LUCIEN, 1904-1977 -
EXHIBITIONS.**
Coutaud, Lucien, 1904-1977. Lucien Coutaud .
Nîmes , 1989. 162 p. : ISBN 2-902309-54-6
DDC 760/.092 20
N6853.C756 A4 1989

Coutinho, Wilson. Gerchman, Rubens, 1942-
Gerchman. [Rio de Janeiro-RJ] [c1989] 208
p. : DDC 759.981 20
ND359.G47 A4 1989

Couto, Maria Matilde Tomaz do.
Castro, Maria de Lourdes de Mello e, 1903-
Maria de Lourdes de Mello e Castro /. Tomar
[Portugal] , 1989. 99 p. :
NYPL [3-MCQ+ C355 90-12670]

Mello e Castro, Maria de Lourdes de, 1903-
Maria de Lourdes de Mello e Castro /. Tomar
[Portugal] , 1989. 99 p. : DDC 759.69 20
ND833.M426 A4 1989

Couturier, Elisabeth. Pignon Ernest, Ernest.
Ernest Pignon Ernest /. [Paris] , c1990. 157,
[3] p. : ISBN 2-7335-0160-7 DDC 709/.2 20
N6853.P53 A4 1990

Couvrat Desvergnes, Thierry, 1945- Paul
Dupré-Lafon, décorateur des millionnaires / par
Thierry Couvrat Desvergnes. Paris, France :
Richer : Editions de l'Amateur, c1990. 206, [2]
p. : chiefly ill. (some col.) ; 32 cm. Cover title:
Dupré Lafon, décorateur des millionnaires. Spine title:
Dupré-Lafon. Includes bibliographical references (p.
[207]). ISBN 2-901151-45-0 (Editions de l'Amateur)
DDC 747.24 20
*1. Dupré-Lafon, Paul, 1900-1971 - Criticism and
interpretation. 2. Interior decoration - France -
History - 20th century. I. Dupré-Lafon, Paul,
1900-1971. II. Title. III. Title: Dupré Lafon, décorateur
des millionnaires. IV. Title: Dupré-Lafon.*
NK2049.Z9 D8633 1990

Coventry Mead Gallery. Moore, Henry, 1898-
Henry Moore . London , 1990. 32 p. : ISBN
1-85332-055-2
NYPL [3-MGO+ (Moore) 91-6697]

**COVERED BRIDGES - PENNSYLVANIA -
MAPS.**
Pennsylvania county maps . [Lyndon Station,
WI , 1986 or 1987]. 1 atlas 147 p. :
NYPL [Map Div. 90-63]

**COVERLETS - NEW YORK (N.Y.) -
CATALOGS.**
Peck, Amelia. American quilts & coverlets in
the Metropolitan Museum of Art /. New
York , c1990. 262 p. : ISBN 0-87099-592-8
DDC 746.9/7/09730747471 20
NK9112 .P434 1990
NYPL [3-MOT 91-4453]

**COVERLETS - ONTARIO SOUTHERN -
EXHIBITIONS.**
M'Closkey, Kathy, 1943- Fibre . Windsor,
Ont. , c1988. [56] p. : ISBN 0-919837-16-6
DDC 746.9/7 19 *NYPL [3-MOT 90-8017]*

**COVERLETS - UNITED STATES -
CATALOGS.**
Peck, Amelia. American quilts & coverlets in
the Metropolitan Museum of Art /. New
York , c1990. 262 p. : ISBN 0-87099-592-8
DDC 746.9/7/09730747471 20
NK9112 .P434 1990
NYPL [3-MOT 91-4453]

**COVERLETS - UNITED STATES -
EXHIBITIONS.**
Fox, Sandi. Wrapped in glory . New York , Los
Angeles , c1990. 167 p. : ISBN 0-500-01499-X
DDC 746.9/7/097307479494 20
NK9112 .F698 1990
NYPL [3-MOT 91-3344]

Covre, Jolanda Nigro. see Nigro Covre, Jolanda.

Cowling, Elizabeth. On classic ground : Picasso,
Léger, de Chirico, and the new classicism,
1910-1930 / Elizabeth Cowling, Jennifer
Mundy. London : Tate Gallery, 1990. 264 p. :
col. ill. ; 30 cm. "Published ... on the occasion of the
exhibition at the Tate Gallery, 6 June-2 September
1990"--T.p. verso. Includes index. ISBN
1-85437-043-X (pbk.) DDC 709/.04/107442132
20
*1. Neoclassicism (Art) - Europe - Exhibitions. 2. Art,
European - Exhibitions. 3. Art, Modern - 20th
century - Europe - Exhibitions. I. Mundy, Jennifer. II.
Tate Gallery. III. Title.*
N6758 .C68 1990

COWS IN ART.
Spuren, die ins Freie führen . [Kiesen,
Switzerland] , 1986. 40 p. :
NYPL [3-MAMZ 90-10960]

CRACE FAMILY - EXHIBITIONS.
The Craces . [London] , Brighton , c1990. xiv,
202 p., [16] p. of plates : ISBN 0-7195-4854-3 :
DDC 747.22 20 *NYPL [3-MLO 91-2246]*

The Craces : royal decorators, 1768-1899 / edited
by Megan Aldrich. [London] : J. Murray ;
Brighton : Royal Pavilion, Art Gallery and
Museums, c1990. xiv, 202 p., [16] p. of plates :
ill. (some col.) ; 28 cm. "Published to accompany
the exhibition ... at the Royal Pavilion, Art Gallery &
Museums, 9 October-30 December 1990"--T.p. verso.
Includes bibliographical references and index. ISBN
0-7195-4854-3 : DDC 747.22 20
*1. Crace family - Exhibitions. I. Aldrich, Megan
Brewster. II. Royal Pavilion, Art Gallery and Museums.*
NYPL [3-MLO 91-2246]

Craddock, Paul. Fake? . London , 1990. 312 p. :
ISBN 0-7141-1703-X
N8790 .F3 1990b

Cradock, H. C., Mrs. Prince, Pamela. A day
spent with Josephine and her friends /. New
York, NY , 1992. p. cm. ISBN 0-517-58303-8 :
DDC 741.6/42 20
NC978.5.A67 P75 1992

Craft and Folk Art Museum. Folk Art Council.
Kalb, Laurie Beth. Santos statues & sculpture .
Los Angeles , c1988. [24] p., [2] leaves of
plates (some folded) : DDC 704.9/482 19
NK9712 .K35 1988
NYPL [3-MNE 90-12649]

Craft in studio.
Houston, John. Fred Baier . London , 1990. 64
p. : ISBN 0-947792-46-5 (pbk.) : DDC 749.22 20
NYPL [3-MOF 90-11124]

Houston, John, 1935- Caroline Broadhead .
London , 1990. 64 p. : ISBN 0-947792-48-1
(pbk.) : DDC 739.27092 20
NYPL [3-MNR 90-12744]

Crafts Council of New Zealand. Mau mahara .
Auckland, N.Z. , 1990. 130 p. : ISBN
1-86941-093-9 *NYPL [3-MNE 91-5081]*

**CRAFTS (HANDICRAFTS) see
HANDICRAFT.**

Craftsman-style houses. Newton, Conn. : Taunton
Press, c1991. p. cm. "Fine homebuilding--great
houses." "Collection of articles from the first ten years
of Fine hombuilding"--Introd. Includes index. ISBN
1-561-58014-7 : DDC 728/.373/09730904 20
*1. Small houses - United States. 2. Architecture,
Domestic - United States. 3. Arts and crafts
movement - United States - Influence. 4. Architecture,
Modern - 20th century - United States. I. Fine
homebuilding.*
NA7208 .C68 1991

Cragg, Tony, 1949-
Tony Cragg / [Konzeption der Ausstellung,

Tony Cragg, Maria Müller ; Katalogredaktion, Maria Müller ; Bibliographie und Verzeichnis der Ausstellungen, Bernd Finkeldey]. Düsseldorf : Kunstsammlung Nordrhein-Westfalen, c1989. 51 p. : ill. (some col.) ; 29 cm. Includes bibliographical references (p. 50-51). ISBN 3-926154-07-1
1. Cragg, Tony, 1949- - Exhibitions. I. Müller, Maria, 1956-. II. Kunstsammlung Nordrhein-Westfalen (Germany). III. Title.
NYPL [3-MGO (Cragg) 90-12497]

Tony Cragg, sculpture 1975-1990 / exhibition organized by Paul Schimmel, guest curator and Marilu Knode, assistant curator ; text by Lucinda Barnes ... [et al.]. London ; New York : Thames and Hudson in association with Newport Harbor Art Museum, 1991. 177 p. : ill. (some col.) ; 32 cm. Exhibition held at the Newport Harbor Art Museum from 14 Oct. to 30 Dec. 1990 and at three other museums through Feb. 1992. Includes bibliographical references (p. 169-175).
1. Cragg, Tony, 1949- - Exhibitions. I. Schimmel, Paul. II. Knode, Marilu. III. Barnes, Lucinda. IV. Title.
NYPL [3-MGO+ (Cragg) 91-4461]

CRAGG, TONY, 1949- - EXHIBITIONS.
Cragg, Tony, 1949- Tony Cragg /. Düsseldorf, c1989. 51 p. : ISBN 3-926154-07-1
NYPL [3-MGO (Cragg) 90-12497]

Cragg, Tony, 1949- Tony Cragg, sculpture 1975-1990 /. London, New York, 1991. 177 p. : **NYPL [3-MGO+ (Cragg) 91-4461]**

Craig-Martin, Michael, 1941-
Michael Craig-Martin : a retrospective 1968-1989 London : Whitechapel, c1989. 128 p. : ill. (some col.) ; 28 cm. "The exhibition has been organised by the Whitechapel Art Gallery and will be shown from 10 November 1989 - 7 January 1990." -- t. p. verso. ISBN 0-85488-086-0
1. Craig-Martin, Michael, 1941- - Exhibitions. I. Whitechapel Art Gallery. II. Title.
NYPL [3-MGO (Craig-Martin) 90-10427]

Tate Gallery Liverpool. Minimalism. Liverpool, c1989. 28 p. : ISBN 1-85437-009-1
NYPL [3-MAMT 90-12390]

CRAIG-MARTIN, MICHAEL, 1941- - EXHIBITIONS.
Craig-Martin, Michael, 1941- Michael Craig-Martin. London, c1989. 128 p. : ISBN 0-85488-086-0
NYPL [3-MGO (Craig-Martin) 90-10427]

Craig, Maurice James. Brooking, Charles. [Map of the city and suburbs of Dublin.] The city of Dublin, 1728 /. Dublin, 1983. 1 portfolio : ISBN 0-904720-14-4 : DDC 941.8/35 19
DA995.D8 B76 1983
NYPL [Map Div. 87-655]

CRANBROOK ACADEMY OF ART - CURRICULA.
Cranbrook design. New York, 1990. 207 p. : ISBN 0-8478-1252-9 DDC 745.4/071/177439 20
NK1170 .C7 1990 **NYPL [3-MNF 91-4482]**

Cranbrook design : the new discourse / Hugh Aldersey-Williams ... [et al.]. New York : Rizzoli, 1990. 207 p. : ill. (some col.) ; 29 cm. Includes index. ISBN 0-8478-1252-9 DDC 745.4/071/177439 20
1. Cranbrook Academy of Art - Curricula. 2. Design - Study and teaching - Michigan - Bloomfield Hills. I. Aldersey-Williams, Hugh.
NK1170 .C7 1990 **NYPL [3-MNF 91-4482]**

Crane, Sylvia E. White silence : Greenough, Powers, and Crawford, American sculptors in nineteenth-century Italy [by] Sylvia E. Crane. Coral Gables [Fla.] University of Miami Press [1972] xviii, 499 p. : illus. ; 27 cm. Bibliography: p. [459]-489. ISBN 0-87024-199-0 DDC 730/.973
1. Greenough, Horatio, 1805-1852. 2. Powers, Hiram, 1805-1873. 3. Crawford, Thomas, 1813-1857. I. Title.
NB236 .C72 **NYPL [3-MGI 90-11552]**

Crary, Jonathan. Techniques of the observer : on vision and modernity in the nineteenth century / Jonathan Crary. Cambridge, Mass. : MIT Press, c1990. 171 p. : ill. ; 24 cm. "An October book." Includes bibliographical references (p. [151]-162) and index. ISBN 0-262-03169-8 DDC 701/.15 20
1. Visual perception. 2. Art, Modern - 19th century - Themes, motives. 3. Art and society - History - 19th century. I. Title.
N7430.5 .C7 1990 **NYPL [3-MAL 91-4620]**

Craven, Wayne. Foshay, Ella M., 1948- Mr. Luman Reed's picture gallery. New York,

1990. 228 p. : ISBN 0-8109-3751-4 DDC 759.14/074/7471 20
ND210 .F65 1990
NYPL [3-MCW 90-12446]

CRAWFORD COUNTY, WIS. - MAPS.
(1990) Rockford Map Publishers. Crawford County, Wisconsin, land atlas & plat book. Rockford, Ill., c1990. 1 atlas (47 p.) :
NYPL [Map Div. 90-12839]

Crawford County, Wisconsin, land atlas & plat book. Rockford Map Publishers. Rockford, Ill., c1990. 1 atlas (47 p.) :
NYPL [Map Div. 90-12839]

Crawford, Ralston, 1906-
Ralston Crawford : Milwaukee Art Center, February 6-March 9, 1958. Milwaukee : Hammersmith-Kortmeyer Co., [1958?] 47 p. : ill. ; 28 cm.
1. Crawford, Ralston, 1906- - Exhibitions. I. Milwaukee. Art Center. II. Title.
MLCM 87/7408 (N)
NYPL [3-MCX C92 90-5854]

CRAWFORD, RALSTON, 1906- - EXHIBITIONS.
Crawford, Ralston, 1906- Ralston Crawford. Milwaukee [1958?] 47 p. :
MLCM 87/7408 (N)
NYPL [3-MCX C92 90-5854]

CRAWFORD, THOMAS, 1813-1857.
Crane, Sylvia E. White silence. Coral Gables [Fla., 1972] xviii, 499 p. : ISBN 0-87024-199-0 DDC 730/.973
NB236 .C72 **NYPL [3-MGI 90-11552]**

Crawhall, Joseph, 1861-1913.
Hamilton, Vivien. Joseph Crawhall, 1861-1913. London, 1990. xiii, 177 p. : ISBN 0-7195-4827-6 : DDC 759.2/911 20
ND1942.C89 A4 1990

CRAWHALL, JOSEPH, 1861-1913 - CRITICISM AND INTERPRETATION.
Hamilton, Vivien. Joseph Crawhall, 1861-1913. London, 1990. xiii, 177 p. : ISBN 0-7195-4827-6 : DDC 759.2/911 20
ND1942.C89 A4 1990

CRAWHALL, JOSEPH, 1861-1913 - EXHIBITIONS.
Hamilton, Vivien. Joseph Crawhall, 1861-1913. London, 1990. xiii, 177 p. : ISBN 0-7195-4827-6 : DDC 759.2/911 20
ND1942.C89 A4 1990

CRAYON DRAWING - TECHNIQUE.
Rouira, Albert. [Yo dibujo, yo pinto ceras. English.] Wax crayons. New York, c1991. p. cm. ISBN 0-8120-4718-4 DDC 741.2/3 20
NC870 .R6813 1991

CRAYONS.
Rouira, Albert. [Yo dibujo, yo pinto ceras. English.] Wax crayons. New York, c1991. p. cm. ISBN 0-8120-4718-4 DDC 741.2/3 20
NC870 .R6813 1991

Craze, Sophia. Russell, Charles M. (Charles Marion), 1864-1926. Charles Russell /. New York, 1989. 112 p. : ISBN 0-517-67598-6 DDC 709/.2/4 19
N6537.R88 A4 1989
NYPL [3-MCX+ R96 90-11089]

Creadores en el mundo hispánico /. Alegría, Fernando, 1918- Santiago de Chile [1990] 184 p. ; ISBN 956-1-30910-5
NX501.5.A1 A43 1990

Creating a dignified past : museums and the colonial revival / Geoffrey L. Rossano, editor. Savage, Md. : Rowman & LIttlefield in association with Historic Cherry Hill, c1991. ix, 129 p. : ill. ; 24 cm. Papers from a symposium sponsored by Historic Cherry Hill, Albany, N.Y., Oct. 24-25, 1987. Includes bibliographical references. ISBN 0-8476-7690-0
1. Interior decoration - United States - History - 19th century. 2. Decoration and ornament, Victorian - United States. 3. Colonial revival (Art) - United States. 4. Art and society - United States. 5. Historical museums - United States. 6. United States - Civilization - 1865-1918. I. Rossano, Geoffrey Louis. II. Historic Cherry Hill (Corporation).
NYPL [3-MLF 91-6907]

Creating a sense of place. Kinsey, Joni. Washington, 1992. p. cm. ISBN 1-560-98117-2 (alk. paper) DDC 759.13 20
ND237.M715 K56 1992

Creating a sense of place. Meyerowitz, Joel, 1938- Washington, c1990. 63 p. : ISBN 1-560-98004-4 DDC 770/.92 20
TR654 .M46373 1990
NYPL [MFX (Meyerowitz) 91-3489]

Creating an American masterpiece. Architectural drawings of the Old Executive Office Building, 1871-1888. Washington, DC, 1988. vii, 71 p. : ISBN 1-558-35012-8
NYPL [3-MQWO+ 91-4241]

Creating space. Kartes, Cheryl. New York, N.Y., 1991. p. cm. ISBN 0-915400-92-8 DDC 700/.68/2 20
N8520 .K37 1991

Creating textures in watercolor. Johnson, Cathy (Cathy A.) Cincinnati, Ohio, c1992. p. cm. ISBN 0-89134-417-9 (hrdcvr) : DDC 751.42/2 20
ND2422 .J64 1992

Creation & craft : three centuries of American prints : October 2 to November 3, 1990. New York, N.Y. : Hirschl & Adler Galleries, c1990. 135 p. : ill. (some col.) ; 26 cm. Includes index. Bibliography: p. 130-133. ISBN 0-915057-37-9
1. Prints, American - Exhibitions. I. Title: Creation and craft.
IN PROCESS (ONLINE)
NYPL [MDF 91-3722]

Creation and craft. Creation & craft. New York, N.Y., c1990. 135 p. : ISBN 0-915057-37-9
IN PROCESS (ONLINE)
NYPL [MDF 91-3722]

Création contemporaine.
Hahn, Otto. Daniel Spoerri /. Paris, c1990. 190 p. : ISBN 2-08-012140-5
NYPL [3-MGO (Spoerri) 90-13083]

CREATION (LITERARY, ARTISTIC, ETC.)
Künstlerisch handeln. Stuttgart, c1989. 170 p. : ISBN 3-7725-0914-2
N199 .K857 1989

CREATION (LITERARY, ARTISTIC, ETC.) - PSYCHOLOGICAL ASPECTS - EXHIBITIONS.
Open mind. Milano, c1989. 318 p. :
NYPL [3-MAMZ 90-11011]

CREATIVE ABILITY IN CHILDREN.
Lynch-Fraser, Diane. Playdancing. Pennington, NJ, c1991. xi, 122 p. : ISBN 0-87127-152-4 (pbk.) : DDC 372.86 20
GV452 .L97 1990 **NYPL [MGSB 91-722]**

Creative cards. Kitagawa, Yoshiko. New York, 1987. 88 p. : ISBN 0-87011-818-8 DDC 745.594 19
TT872 .K58 1987 **NYPL [3-MNH 90-12489]**

Creative machine arts series.
Green, Marilyn V. The button lover's book /. Radnor, Pa., c1991. p. ISBN 0-8019-8184-0 (hc) : DDC 646/.19 20
NK3668.5 .G7 1991

Creative origami /. Kasahara, Kunihiko, 1941- Tokyo, 1977, c1967. 176 p. : ISBN 0-87040-411-3 **NYPL [3-MNH+ 81-761]**

CREATIVE THINKING.
Künstlerisch handeln. Stuttgart, c1989. 170 p. : ISBN 3-7725-0914-2
N199 .K857 1989

CREATIVENESS. see CREATION (LITERARY, ARTISTIC, ETC.)

Creativities! Szeglin, Charles B. West Nyack, N.Y., c1991. p. cm. ISBN 0-13-189804-3 DDC 372.5/044 20
N362 .S95 1991

CREATIVITY. see CREATION (LITERARY, ARTISTIC, ETC.)

CREATIVITY IN ART.
Voprosy metodologii i sotsiologii iskusstva. Leningrad, 1988. 175 p. :
NX160 .V66 1988

Crédit communal de Belgique. Marbres helleniques. Brussels, 1987. 191 p. : ISBN 2-87193-050-3
NYPL [3-MGH+ 90-12355]

Creeley, Robert, 1926-
Therrien, Robert, 1947- 7 & 6 /. Albuquerque,

N.M. , c1988. [136] p. :   DDC 709/.2 20
N6537.T473 A4 1988

Waterworks . New York, N.Y. , 1990. [20] p. :
NYPL [3-MCW 91-7056]

Creese, Walter L. The Midwest in American
architecture /. Urbana , c1991. xv, 259 p., [1]
p. of plates :   ISBN 0-252-01743-9 (alk. paper)
DDC 720/.977 20
NA722 .M53 1991
NYPL [3-MQWO 91-6382]

CREESE, WALTER L.
The Midwest in American architecture /.
Urbana , c1991. xv, 259 p., [1] p. of plates :
ISBN 0-252-01743-9 (alk. paper) DDC 720/.977
20
NA722 .M53 1991
NYPL [3-MQWO 91-6382]

Creevy, Bill. The pastel book : materials and
techniques for today's artist / Bill Creevy. New
York : Watson-Guptill Publications, 1991. 175
p. : col. ill. ; 28 cm. Includes index.   ISBN
0-8230-3902-1 :   DDC 741.2/35 20
*1. Pastel drawing - Technique. 2. Artists' materials. I.
Title.*
NC880 .C74 1991

Cremer : festo és íro / W.A.L. Beeren es masok
= Cremer : schilder, schrijver / W.A.L. Beeren
en anderen. Amsterdam : Jaski Art Gallery ,
's-Gravenhage : SDU, c1990. 191 p. : ill. (some
col.) ; 31 cm. Dutch and Hungarian. Includes
bibliographical references (p. 189).   ISBN
90-12-06739-1
*1. Cremer, Jan. 2. Artists - Netherlands - Biography. I.
Cremer, Jan. II. Beeren, W. A. L. (Willem A. L.).*
NX554.Z9 C7434 1990

Cremer, Jan. Cremer . Amsterdam ,
's-Gravenhage , c1990. 191 p. :   ISBN
90-12-06739-1
NX554.Z9 C7434 1990

CREMER, JAN.
Cremer . Amsterdam , 's-Gravenhage , c1990.
191 p. :   ISBN 90-12-06739-1
NX554.Z9 C7434 1990

Cremer, Susannah. Kunstmuseum Düsseldorf.
Akademiesammlung. Facetten des Barock .
Düsseldorf , 1990. 295 p. :   DDC
741.94/09/032074435534 20
NC225 .K87 1990

Crespi, Giuseppe Maria, 1665-1747.
Giuseppe Maria Crespi, 1665-1747 : Pinacoteca
nazionale di Bologna, Staatsgalerie Stuttgart,
Puskin Museum, Mosca : Bologna, Pinacoteca
nazionale e accademia di belle arti, Palazzo
Pepoli Campogrande : 7 settembre-11 novembre
1990 / a cura di Andrea Emiliani e August B.
Rave ; con scritti di Anton A.W. Boschloo ...
[et al.] ; introduzione di Andrea Emiliani.
Bologna : Nuova alfa, c1990. xxcvi, 278 p. :
chiefly col. ill. ; 28 cm. Includes bibliographical
references (p. 267-278).   ISBN 88-7779-148-9   DDC
759.5 20
*1. Crespi, Giuseppe Maria, 1665-1747 - Exhibitions. I.
Emiliani, Andrea. II. Rave, August. III. Boschloo,
Anton W. A. (Anton Willem Adriaan). IV. Pinacoteca
nazionale (Bologna, Italy). V. Staatsgalerie Stuttgart. VI.
Gosudarstvennyï muzeï izobrazitel'nykh iskussty imeni
A.S. Pushkina. VII. Palazzo PepoliCampogrande.*
ND623.C8 A4 1990

Giuseppe Maria Crespi, 1665-1747 : Bologna,
Pinacoteca nazionale e Accademia di belle arti,
Palazzo Pepoli Campogrande, 7 settembre-11
novembre 1990 / Pinacoteca nazionale di
Bologna, Staatsgalerie, Stuttgart, Puskin
Museum, Mosca ; a cura di Andrea Emiliani e
August B. Rave ; con scritti di Anton A.W.
Boschloo ... [et al.]. [Bologna] : Nuovo Alfa,
c1990. ccxvi,
278 p. : ill. (some col.) ; 28 cm. Catalog by Silvia
Evangelisti and others. Includes bibliographical
references (p. 267-278).   ISBN 88-7779-148-9
*1. Crespi, Giuseppe Maria, 1665-1747 - Exhibitions. I.
Emiliani, Andrea. II. Rave, August. III. Boschloo,
Anton W. A. (Anton Willem Andriaan). IV. Evangelisti,
Silvia. V. Accademia di belle arti di Bologna. VI.
Palazzo Pepoli Campogrande. VII. Staatsgalerie
Stuttgart. VIII. Gosudarstvennyï muzeï izobrazitel'nykh
iskusstv imeni A.S. Pushkina. IX. Pinacoteca nazionale
(Bologna, Italy). X. Title.*
NYPL [3-MCF C922 91-5467]

**CRESPI, GIUSEPPE MARIA, 1665-1747 -
EXHIBITIONS.**

Crespi, Giuseppe Maria, 1665-1747. Giuseppe
Maria Crespi, 1665-1747 . Bologna , c1990.
xxcvi, 278 p. :   ISBN 88-7779-148-9   DDC 759.5
20
ND623.C8 A4 1990

Crespi, Giuseppe Maria, 1665-1747. Giuseppe
Maria Crespi, 1665-1747 . [Bologna] , c1990.
ccxvi, 278 p. :   ISBN 88-7779-148-9
NYPL [3-MCF C922 91-5467]

Crespo, Francesc.
[Cómo pintar marinas. English]
How to paint seascapes / Francesc Crespo.
New York : Watson-Guptill Publications,
1991. 96 p. : ill. (some col.) ; 25 cm.
(Watson-Guptill artists library) Translation of: Cómo
pintar marinas.   ISBN 0-8230-2472-5 :   DDC
751.42/2437 20
1. Marine painting - Technique. I. Title. II. Series.
ND1370 .C7413 1991

Crespo, Soledad. Dahm, Jorge. Jorge Dahm .
[Santiago, Chile] [1990?] 1 v. (unpaged) :
DDC 759.983 20
ND369.D35 A4 1990

Cress, George.
George Cress : 50 years of painting / edited by
Ellen Simak ; essay by E. Alan White ;
organized by the Hunter Museum of Art,
Chattanooga, Tennessee. Chattanooga, Tenn. :
The Museum, c1990. 56 p. : ill. ; 22 x 28 cm.
*1. Cress, George - Exhibitions. I. Hunter Museum of
Art. II. Title.*   **NYPL [3-MCX C922 91-7066]**

CRESS, GEORGE - EXHIBITIONS.
Cress, George. George Cress . Chattanooga,
Tenn. , c1990. 56 p. :
NYPL [3-MCX C922 91-7066]

Cressier, Patrice. Bazzana, Andrés. La céramique
islamique du Musée archéologique provincial de
Jaén (Espagne) /. Madrid , Paris , 1985. 78 p. :
DDC 738.3/0946/83 20
DP302.J1 B38 1985
NYPL [3-MPG+ 91-5911]

Cresswell, Donald H. Lane, Christopher W.
Prints of Philadelphia at the Philadelphia Print
Shop . Philadelphia , 1990. 128 p. :
NYPL [MDZ 91-3491]

CRESTS - ROMANIA - TRANSYLVANIA.
Erdély és a Részek térképe és helységnévtára .
Szeged , 1987 ([Budapest] : Franklin Nyomda)
1 atlas (41, 214 p., [9] p. of plates) :   ISBN
963-481-771-8 :   DDC 912/.4984 19
G2037.T7 E7 1987
NYPL [Map Div. 91-145]

**Creswell, K. A. C. (Keppel Archibald Cameron),
Sir, b. 1879.** A short account of early
Muslim architecture / K.A.C. Creswell.
Harmondsworth, Middlesex ; Baltimore, Md. :
Penguin Books, 1958. 330 p., 72 p. of plates :
ill. ; 17 cm. (Pelican . A407) Bibliography: p.
323-324.
I. Title.   **NYPL [3-MQT 90-5435]**

Creuze, Raymond. Charchouniana / Raymond
Creuze. Paris : R. Creuze, c1989. 119 p. : ill.
(some col.) ; 31 cm. On cover: Charchoune.   ISBN
2-905037-06-7   DDC 759.4 20
*1. Charchoune, Serge, 1888-1975 - Catalogs. 2.
Painting, Abstract - France - Catalogs. I. Charchoune,
Serge, 1888-1975. II. Title. III. Title: Charchoune.*
ND553.S52 A4 1989

Crick-Kuntziger, Marthe. Musées royaux d'art et
d'histoire (Belgium) Catalogue des tapisseries.
[Bruxelles, 1956] 94 p.
NK2825.B7 B7   **NYPL [3-MOR 91-326]**

Crill, Rosemary. Arts of India, 1550-1900 /.
London , c1990. 240 p. :   ISBN 1-85177-022-4
DDC 709.54 20
N7301   **NYPL [3-MAF 91-6685]**

Criollos for export : 12 dibujantes en busca de un
texto. Buenos Aires, Argentina : Sociedad
Argentina de Artistas Plásticos, Departamento
de Dibujo, [1990] 149 p., [5] p. of plates : ill. ;
28 cm.
*1. Illustrators - Argentina - Biography. I. Sociedad
Argentina de Artistas Plásticos. Departamento de
Dibujo.*
NC976.A7 C75 1990

Crippa /. Cavallo, Luigi. Firenze , 1990. 111 p.
NYPL [3-MCF C927 90-13555]

CRIPPA, ROBERTO, 1921-1972.
Cavallo, Luigi. Crippa /. Firenze , 1990. 111
p. :   **NYPL [3-MCF C927 90-13555]**

La Cripta della Cattedrale di Taranto / a cura di
Cosimo D'Angela ; contributi di Alberto
Carducci ... [et al.]. Taranto : Scorpione, [1986]
98 p. : ill. (some col.), plans ; 31 cm. (Il
Meridione nell'arte . 2) Includes bibliographical
references.
*1. Cattedrale di Taranto (Italy). 2. Mural painting and
decoration, Italian - Italy - Taranto. 3. Crypts - Italy -
Taranto. I. D'Angela, Cosimo. II. Carducci, Alberto. III.
Series.*   **NYPL [3-MRBN+ 90-10741]**

Crispolti, Enrico.
Guttuso, il testamento / testi di Enrico
Crispolti ; interventi di Lia Pasqualino Noto,
Antonio Pasqualino, Roberto Ando. [Roma] :
Rotundo, [1987] 97 p. : ill. (some col.) ; 28 cm.
+ 1 poster. Cover title. Bibliography: p. 30. Library's
copy lacks poster.
*1. Guttuso, Renato, 1912-. I. Guttuso, Renato, 1912-.
II. Title.*
ND623.G97 C65 1987
NYPL [3-MCF G985 90-12762]

Trubbiani / Enrico Crispolti ; introduzione e
diario critico di Giuseppe Marchiori. Bologna :
Edizioni Bora, c1990. 2 v. (665 p.) : ill. (some
col.) ; 31 cm. Includes bibliographical references.
ISBN 88-85638-93-7 :   DDC 730/.92 20
*1. Trubbiani, Valeriano, 1937- - Catalogs. I. Marchiori,
Giuseppe. II. Title.*
NB623.T77 A4 1990

Crist, Jacqueline S., 1949- L.A. times . Boise,
Idaho , c1991. p. cm.   DDC 709/.794/9407479628
20
N6535.L6 L188 1991

CRISTALLERIE DAUM.
Pétry-Parisot, Claude. Daum dans les musées de
Nancy /. [Nancy , 1989] 183 p. :   ISBN
2-901408-03-6   **NYPL [3-MPW 91-6650]**

Critical studies in art and design education /
edited by David Thistlewood ; with a foreword
by Al Hurwitz. Portsmouth, NH : Heinemann,
1991. p. cm. "First published in 1989 by Longman
Group UK Limited, in association with the National
Society for Education in Art and Design"--T.p. verso.
Includes index.   ISBN 0-435-08592-1   DDC 707/.041
20
*1. Art - Study and teaching - Great Britain. 2. Design -
Study and teaching - Great Britain. I. Thistlewood,
David.*
N185 .C68 1991

Critical studies in education & culture.
Trend, David. Cultural pedagogy . New York ,
1992. p. cm.   ISBN 0-89789-256-9   DDC
700/.1/03 20
NX180.S6 T7 1992

Voices in architectural education . New York ,
1991. p. cm.   ISBN 0-89789-253-4 (alk. paper)
DDC 720/.7/073 20
NA2105 .V65 1991

A critical study of Philip Guston /. Ashton,
Dore. Berkeley [1990], c1976. xvii, 216 p., 15
p. of plates :   ISBN 0-520-06931-5 (alk. paper)
DDC 759.13 20
ND237.G8 A82 1990
NYPL [3-MCX G982 91-5624]

Critical views.
Renaissance bodies . London , 1990. x, 294 p. :
ISBN 0-948462-09-4   DDC 700 20
NX650.F45 R46 1990

Criticizing photographs . Barrett, Terry Michael,
1945- Mountain View, Calif. , c1990. xii, 180
p. :   ISBN 0-87484-906-3   DDC 770/.1 20
TR642 .B365 1990   **NYPL [MFW 91-5783]**

The Critics debate.
Reid, Su. To the lighthouse /. Houndmills,
Basingstoke, Hampshire , 1991. 116 p. ;   ISBN
0-333-47386-8 (cased)   DDC 823.912 20
PR6045.O72Z   **NYPL [JFD 91-4651]**

Crivelli, Carlo, 15th cent.
Gli abiti di Carlo Crivelli : Ancona, 9 giugno-28
ottobre 1990 / a cura di Michele Polverari.
[Ancona] : Comune di Ancona, Assessorato ai
beni, attività culturali e P.I., Pinacoteca
comunale "Francesco Podesti," [1990] 110 p. :
ill. (some col.) ; 29 cm. Includes bibliographical
references.
*1. Crivelli, Carlo, 15th cent. - Exhibitions. 2. Costume -
History - 15th century - Exhibitions. 3. Costume -
Italy - Exhibitions. I. Polverari, Michele, 1950-. II.
Pinacoteca comunale "Francesco Podesti.". III. Title.*
NYPL [3-MCF+ C93 91-5435]

**CRIVELLI, CARLO, 15TH CENT. -
EXHIBITIONS.**
Crivelli, Carlo, 15th cent. Gli abiti di Carlo
Crivelli . [Ancona] [1990] 110 p. :
NYPL [3-MCF+ C93 91-5435]

CROCHETING - HISTORY.
Potter, Annie Louise. A living mystery .
[United States?] , c1990. 160 p. : ISBN
1-87940-900-3 DDC 746.43/4/09 20
NK9106 .P67 1990

CROCKERY. see POTTERY.

Croës, Catherine de, 1941- Félicien Rops,
1833-1898 . Brüssel , 1979. 88 p. :
N6973.R67 A4 1979
NYPL [3-MCH R78 81-420]

Croft, Virginia. Recycled as restaurants : case
studies in adaptive reuse / Virginia Croft. New
York : Whitney Library of Design, 1991. 223
p. : ill. (some col.) ; 29 cm. Includes bibliographic
references (p. 214, 216-217) and index. ISBN
0-8230-4513-7 : DDC 725/.71/0973 20
*1. Restaurants, lunch rooms, etc. - United States -
Decoration - Case studies. 2. Buildings - United States -
Remodeling for other use - Casestudies. I. Title.*
NA7856 .C76 1991

Croissant, Hermann, 1897-1963. Diehl, Wolfgang.
Hermann Croissant . Landau/Pfalz , c1987. 200
p. : ISBN 3-87629-120-8 DDC 759.3 B 20
ND588.C85 D53 1987
NYPL [3-MCK C942 90-10583]

CROISSANT, HERMANN, 1897-1963.
Diehl, Wolfgang. Hermann Croissant .
Landau/Pfalz , c1987. 200 p. : ISBN
3-87629-120-8 DDC 759.3 B 20
ND588.C85 D53 1987
NYPL [3-MCK C942 90-10583]

Croissant, Michael, 1928-
Michael Croissant : Retrospektive 1958-1989 :
Frankfurter Kunstverein, Steinernes Haus am
Römerberg, Frankfurt am Main,
17.2.-25.3.1990. Frankfurt am Main : Der
Kunstverein, [1990] 121 p. : ill. ; 23 cm.
Includes bibliographical references (p. 113-115).
*1. Croissant, Michael, 1928- - Exhibitions. I.
Frankfurter Kunstverein. II. Title.*
NYPL [3-MGO (Croissant) 91-4350]

**CROISSANT, MICHAEL, 1928- -
EXHIBITIONS.**
Croissant, Michael, 1928- Michael Croissant .
Frankfurt am Main [1990] 121 p. :
NYPL [3-MGO (Croissant) 91-4350]

**La Croix byzantine du Trésor de la Cathédrale
de Tournai** / par Frédérique de Cuyper ... [et
al.]. Louvain-la-Neuve : Institut Supérieur
d'archéologie et d'histoire de l'art, Université
Catholique de Louvain, 1987. 88 p. : ill. (some
col.) ; 26 cm. (Tornacum . 1) Publications d'histoire
de l'art et d'archéologie de l'Université Catholique de
Louvain ; 52. Includes bibliographical references.
*I. Cuyper, Frédérique de. II. Cathédrale Notre-Dame de
Tournai. III. Series. IV. Series: Publications d'histoire
de l'artet d'archéologie de l'Université catholique de
Louvain. Aurifex , 7.*
NYPL [3-MAIH 89-28301]

Les croix du Massif central /. Baudoin, Jacques.
Nonette [France] [1989] 346 p., [36] p. of
plates : ISBN 2-902894-64-3 DDC 730/.944/59 20
CC321.M37 B38 1989
NYPL [3-MAIH+ 90-8320]

Croizé, Jean Claude. Recherches sur la typologie
et les types architecturaux . [Paris] , c1991. 367
p. : ISBN 2-7384-0903-2
NA2000 .R38 1991

**CROLL, CARL, 1800-1863 - CRITICISM AND
INTERPRETATION.**
Vlk, Miloslav. Carl Croll /. [Ústí nad Labem] ,
1989. 131 p. : ISBN 80-7047-018-6 :
ND534.5.C76 V58 1989

Crombie, Isobel. A picturesque sensibility .
[Melbourne] , 1989. [12] p. :
NYPL [MFW+ 90-1079]

CROME, JOHN, 1768-1821 - EXHIBITIONS.
The Norwich school . Manchester [England]
[1961] 44 p. : *NYPL [3-MCT 91-402]*

Cromey, Felix. Blue note . San Francisco , 1991.
p. cm. ISBN 0-8118-0036-9 DDC 741.6/6 20
NC1883.U6 B58 1991

Cromley, Elizabeth C. The Elements of style .
New York , c1991. p. cm. ISBN 0-671-73981-6

DDC 721 20
NA2850 .E44 1991

Crone, Rainer, 1942-
Kazimir Malevich : the climax of disclosure /
Rainer Crone and David Moos. Chicago :
University of Chicago Press, 1991. p. cm.
Includes bibliographical references and index. ISBN
0-226-12093-7 (alk. paper) DDC 759.7 20
*1. Malevich, Kazimir Severinovich, 1878-1935 -
Criticism and interpretation. I. Moos, David. II. Title.*
N6999.M34 C7 1991

Paul Klee : legends of the sign / Rainer Crone
and Joseph Leo Koerner. New York : Columbia
University Press, c1991. p. cm. (Interpretations in
art) Includes bibliographical references and index.
ISBN 0-231-07034-6 (alk. paper) : DDC
759.9494 20
*1. Klee, Paul, 1879-1940 - Criticism and interpretation.
2. Signs and symbols in art. I. Koerner, Joseph Leo. II.
Title. III. Series.*
ND588.K5 C76 1991

Croner, Ted. Meller, Susan. Textile designs . New
York , 1991. p. cm. ISBN 0-8109-3853-7 DDC
746.6/2041 20
NK9500 .M45 1991

Cronkite, Walter. Ellis, Ray G. Westwind /.
Birmingham, Ala. , c1990. 125 p. : ISBN
0-8487-0763-X
NYPL [3-MCX+ E473 91-3383]

Cronología de la cultura, 1950-1990 / director de
la obra, Alvaro Castaño Castillo ; asesores,
Gonzalo Rueda Caro, Gonzalo Mallarino
Botero, Gloria Valencia de Castaño ; editor,
Benjamín Villegas Jiménez. 1. ed. [Bogotá,
Colombia] : Villegas Editores, 1990. 524 p. :
ill. ; 24 cm. + 6 sound cassettes (88 min.
each : analog) On spine: HJCK. "Edición
conmemorativa de los 40 años de la Emisora H.J.C.K.,
El Mundo en Bogotá"--P. [2]. Includes
index. ISBN 958-9138-62-4 DDC 700/.9/045 20
*1. Arts, Colombian - Colombia - Bogotá. 2. Arts,
Modern - 20th century - Colombia - Bogotá. 3. Arts,
Modern - 20th century. 4. Radio programs - Colombia.
5. Emisora H.J.C.K. (Bogotá, Colombia). I. Castaño
Castillo, Alvaro, 1920-. II. Villegas Jiménez, Benjamín.
III. Emisora H.J.C.K. (Bogotá, Colombia).*
NX535.B64 C76 1990

Crookshank, Anne. Trinity College (Dublin,
Ireland) Paintings and sculptures in Trinity
College Dublin . Dublin , 1990. 205 p. : ISBN
1-87140-803-2 DDC 709/.94/07441835 20
N7621.2.I73 D838 1990

Croom, C.H. (ed) Symposium on Photogrammetric
Surveys and Mapping (1971 : University of
Missouri, Rolla) Photogrammetric surveys and
mapping. [Rolla, 1971?] iv, 59 p.
NYPL [Map Div. 90-5988]

Croquis Parisiens /. Cham, 1819-1879. Paris ,
c[18--] [15] leaves :
NYPL [3-MEM (Cham) 88-3113]

**Crosby, Sumner McK. (Sumner McKnight),
1909-** The Royal Abbey of Saint-Denis : from
its beginnings to the death of Suger, 475-1151 /
Sumner McKnight Crosby ; edited and
completed by Pamela Z. Blum. New Haven :
Yale University Press, c1987. xxiii, 525 p., 3
folded leaves of plates : ill. ; 29 cm. (Yale
publications in the history of art. 37) Includes index.
Bibliography: p. 503-515. ISBN 0-300-03143-2 (alk.
paper) DDC 726/.5/0944362 19
*1. Suger, Abbot of Saint Denis, 1081-1151 -
Contributions in church architecture. 2. Abbaye de
Saint-Denis (Saint-Denis, France). 3. Eglise abbatiale de
Saint-Denis. 4. Saint-Denis (France) - Buildings,
structures, etc. I. Blum, Pamela Z. II. Title. III. Series.*
NA5551.S214 C76 1987
NYPL [3-MRBB 91-6920]

CROSSES - FRANCE - BRITTANY.
Royer, Eugène. Nouveau guide des calvaires
bretons /. Rennes , c1985. 233 p. : ISBN
2-85882-905-5 DDC 914.4/104838 19
CC321.B7 R68 1985
NYPL [3-MAIH 90-11102]

**CROSSES - FRANCE - MASSIF CENTRAL
REGION - CULTUS.**
Baudoin, Jacques. Les croix du Massif central /.
Nonette [France] [1989] 346 p., [36] p. of
plates : ISBN 2-902894-64-3 DDC 730/.944/59 20
CC321.M37 B38 1989
NYPL [3-MAIH+ 90-8320]

**CROSSES - FRANCE - MASSIF CENTRAL
REGION - THEMES, MOTIVES.**
Baudoin, Jacques. Les croix du Massif central /.
Nonette [France] [1989] 346 p., [36] p. of
plates : ISBN 2-902894-64-3 DDC 730/.944/59 20
CC321.M37 B38 1989
NYPL [3-MAIH+ 90-8320]

CROSSES - RUSSIAN S.F.S.R.
Russian copper icons and crosses from the
Kunz Collection . Washington, D.C. , 1990. p.
cm. DDC 730/.947 20
NK1653.S65 R8 1990

CROSSES - WASHINGTON (D.C.)
Russian copper icons and crosses from the
Kunz Collection . Washington, D.C. , 1990. p.
cm. DDC 730/.947 20
NK1653.S65 R8 1990

Crossley, Paul. Medieval architecture and its
intellectual context . London , Ronceverte,
WV , 1990. xxvii, 304 p. : ISBN 1-85285-034-5 :
DDC 723 20
NA350 *NYPL [3-MQO 90-11593]*

Crossman, Carl L. A design catalogue of Chinese
export porcelain for the American market / by
Carl L. Crossman. Salem, Mass. : Peabody
Museum, 1969. 48 p. : ill. ; 22 cm. ISBN
0-87577-019-3
*1. China trade porcelain - Exhibitions. I. Peabody
Museum of Salem. II. Title.*
NYPL [3-MPFF 90-6436]

Crossroads of clay : the southern alkaline-glazed
stoneware tradition / edited by Catherine
Wilson Horne. Columbia, S.C. : McKissick
Museum, University of South Carolina, 1990.
xi, 129 p. : ill. (some col.) ; 28 cm. Includes
bibliographical references (p. 125-129). ISBN
0-938983-08-3 : DDC 738.3/0975/07475771 20
*1. Stoneware - Southern States. I. Horne, Catherine
Wilson, 1957-. II. McKissick Museum.*
NK3634 .C76 1990
NYPL [3-MPH 90-11055]

Crotti, Jean, 1878-1958.
Tabu Dada . Bern , c1983. 139 p. : DDC
709/.04/062074094945 19
N6853.C86 A4 1983
NYPL [3-MCZ C946 83-2831]

CROTTI, JEAN, 1878-1958 - EXHIBITIONS.
Tabu Dada . Bern , c1983. 139 p. : DDC
709/.04/062074094945 19
N6853.C86 A4 1983
NYPL [3-MCZ C946 83-2831]

Crouch, Elizabeth G., 1942- Showcase of interior
design / Elizabeth G. Crouch, Madja Kallab ;
with an introduction by Mary Jane Pool.
Eastern ed. Grand Rapids, Mich. : Vitae Pub.,
1991. p. cm. Includes index. ISBN 0-9624596-2-3:
DDC 729/.025/74 20
*1. Interor decoration firms - East (U. S.). 2. Interior
decoration - East (U. S.) - History - 20th century. I.
Kallab, Madja. II. Title.*
NK2004 .C76 1991

Crowe, J. A. (Joseph Archer), 1825-1896. Kugler,
Franz, 1808-1858. Handbook of painting.
London, 1898. St. Clair Shores, Mich., 1972. 2
v. (xi, 586 p.) ISBN 0-403-01059-4 DDC 759.3
ND625 .K8 1972

Crowley, Janice L. The Aegean and the east : an
investigation into the transference of artistic
motifs between the Aegean, Egypt, and the
Near East in the Bronze Age / by Janice L.
Crowley. Jonsered : P. Aströms forlag, 1989.
xii, 507 p. : ill. ; 21 cm. (Studies in Mediterranean
archaeology and literature. Pocket-book . 51) Includes
index. Bibliography: p. 301-334. ISBN 91-86098-55-1
*1. Symbolism in art - Mediterranean region. 2. Art,
Ancient - Themes, motives. 3. Art, Egyptian -
Influence. 4. Art, Aegean - Influence. 5. Art -
Mediterranean region - Themes, motives. I. Title. II.
Series.* *NYPL [3-MAE 90-11126]*

Crowley, William. Seneca Ray Stoddard :
Adirondack illustrator : an exhibition at the
Adirondack Museum, Blue Mountain Lake,
New York, June 15 to October 15, 1981 &
1982 / by William Crowley. Blue Mountain
Lake, N.Y. : The Museum, c1982. vii, 64 p. :
ill. ; 21 x 26 cm. Includes bibliographical references.
ISBN 0-910020-35-3 (pbk.) DDC 770/.92/4 19
*1. Stoddard, Seneca Ray, 1844-1917 - Exhibitions. 2.
Adirondack Mountains (N.Y.) - Description and travel -
Views - Exhibitions. I. Stoddard, Seneca Ray,*

1844-1917. II. Adirondack Museum. III. Title.
N6537.S754 A4 1982
NYPL [MFX (Stoddard) 91-8010]

Crown art library.
Chevalier, Denys. [Picasso, époques bleue et
rose. English.] Picasso, the blue and rose
periods /. New York , 1991. p. cm. ISBN
0-517-00904-8 : DDC 759.4 20
ND553.P5 C4853 1991

Janssens, Jacques. [James Ensor. English.]
Ensor /. New York , c1990. p. cm. ISBN
0-517-53284-0 : DDC 760/.092 20
N6973.E5 J3613 1990

Julien, Edouard. [Lautrec. English.]
Toulouse-Lautrec /. New York , 1991. p. cm.
ISBN 0-517-03718-1 : DDC 759.4 20
ND553.T7 J8413 1991

Selz, Jean. Turner /. New York , 1991. p. cm.
ISBN 0-517-52361-2 DDC 759.2 20
ND497.T8 S44 1991

Vallier, Dora. [Henri Rousseau. English.] Henri
Rousseau /. New York , c1990. 95 p. : ISBN
0-517-53697-8 : DDC 759.4 20
ND553.R67 V33 1991

**The Crown House collection of textile
documents.** Whaley Bridge, Derbyshire,
England : Crown House Pub., c1990- v. :
chiefly col. ill. ; 36 cm. CONTENTS: -- v. 1. The
printed calicos of Manchester, circa 1900 -- v. 2. Fleurs
de France : weaves, prints and original designs,
1850-1905 ISBN 1-87266-900-X (v. 1)
1. Textile design. I. Crown House Publishing.
NYPL [MON+ 91-5785]

Crown House Publishing. The Crown House
collection of textile documents. Whaley Bridge,
Derbyshire, England , c1990- v. : ISBN
1-87266-900-X (v. 1)
NYPL [MON+ 91-5785]

CROWN JEWELS - FRANCE - HISTORY.
Morel, Bernard. The French crown jewels .
Antwerp [1988] 417 p. ; ISBN 90-6153-188-8
DDC 739.27/0944 20
NK7415.F8 M67 1988

Crowther, Bruce, 1933- Burt Lancaster : a life in
films / Bruce Crowther. London : Robert Hale,
1991. 192 p., [16] p. of plates : ill. ; 23 cm.
Includes bibliographical references (p. 169) and index.
Filmography: p. 170-187. ISBN 0-7090-4349-X :
DDC 791.43092 12A
1. Lancaster, Burt, 1913-. 2. Motion picture actors and
actresses - United States - Biography. I. Title.
NYPL [MES (Lancaster, B.)]

Crowther, G. L. National atlas showing canals,
navigable rivers, mineral tramroads, railways,
and street tramways / G.L. Crowther. Eds.
vary. Preston, Lancs. : G.L. Crowther, 1985- 1
atlas (v.) : all maps ; 30 cm. Cover title. Spine
title: Water, tram & rail atlas. CONTENTS. - v. 1.
Scotland (2 v.) -- v. 2. North West of England (5 v.) --
v. 3. North East (2 v.) -- v. 4. Wales and the Welsh
marshes (2 v.) -- v. 5. Midlands (2 v.)-- v. 6.
Lincolnshire and East Anglia -- v. 7. South West (2
v.) -- v. 8, pt. 1-4. [London]. -- v. 8a. Home counties --
v. 8b. London & the Thames estuary -- v. 9. Ireland (2
v.). ISBN 0-948850-50-7 (lib. ed. : v. 1) DDC
912/.41 19
1. Canals - Great Britain - Maps. 2. Horse railroads -
Great Britain - Maps. 3. Railroads - Great Britain -
Maps. 4. Rivers - Great Britain - Maps. I. Title. II.
Title: Water, tram & rail atlas. III. Title: Water, tram
and rail atlas.
G1812.21.P1 C7 1985
NYPL [Map Div. 90-2]

Croy, Otto R., 1902- Das Porträt : eine neue
Kamera-Schule / Otto Croy. Seebruck am
Chiemsee : Heering, c1951. 208 p. : ill. ; 22
cm.
1. Photography - Portraits - Lighting and posing. I.
Title. **NYPL [MFW 91-391]**

**Crucifixion of Christ. see Jesus Christ -
Crucifixion.**

**Crude oil pipeline atlas of the United States and
Canada.** PennWell Publishing Company. Crude
oil pipelines atlas of the United States and
Canada . Tulsa, Okla. , c1990. 1 atlas (44 p.) :
NYPL [Map Div. 91-3505]

**Crude oil pipelines atlas of the United States
and Canada .** PennWell Publishing Company.
Tulsa, Okla. , c1990. 1 atlas (44 p.) :
NYPL [Map Div. 91-3505]

Crum, Robin Eadie. Westmoreland Museum of
Art. Southwestern Pennsylvania painters .
Greensburg, Pa. , 1989. x, 138 p. : ISBN
0-931241-21-9 DDC 759.148/8/07474886 20
N6530.P42 P589 1989
NYPL [3-MCW 91-6266]

Crumbiegel, Dieter, 1938-
Dieter Crumbiegel : Arbeiten von 1961 bis
heute : Keramikmuseum Westerwald, Deutsche
Sammlung für Historische und Zeitgenössische
Keramik, Höhr-Grenzhausen, Ausstellung vom
21. Februar bis 3. April 1988 : Forum Form
Clemenswerth im Emslandmuseum Schloss
Clemenswerth, Sögel, Ausstellung vom 14. Mai
bis 26. Juni 1988 / [Herausgeber des Kataloges,
Kreisverwaltung des Westerwaldkreises in
Montabaur, in Verbindung mit dem
Keramikmuseum Westerwald ; Autoren, Dieter
Crumbiegel, Harald Reinhold, Eckard Wagner].
Montabaur : Verlagsabteilung des
Westerwaldkreises, c1988. 107 p. : chiefly ill.
(some col.) ; 27 cm. ISBN 3-921548-39-X
1. Crumbiegel, Dieter, 1938- - Exhibitions. I. Reinhold,
Harald. II. Wagner, Eckard. III. Keramikmuseum
Westerwald. IV. Emslandmuseum. V. Title.
MLCM 89/07955 (N)
NYPL [3-MPGK 90-8715]

**CRUMBIEGEL, DIETER, 1938- -
EXHIBITIONS.**
Crumbiegel, Dieter, 1938- Dieter Crumbiegel .
Montabaur , c1988. 107 p. : ISBN
3-921548-39-X
MLCM 89/07955 (N)
NYPL [3-MPGK 90-8715]

Crumlin, Rosemary, 1932- Aboriginal art and
spirituality /. North Blackburn, Vic. , 1991. 151
p. : ISBN 0-85924-998-0
NYPL [3-MADF+ 91-6923]

Crunden, Robert Morse. American salons : how
the Steins, the Arensbergs, Alfred Steiglitz, and
their friends encountered European modernism,
1885-1917 / Robert M. Crunden. New York :
Oxford University Press, 1992. p. cm. Includes
bibliographical references and index.
0-19-506569-7 (acid-free paper) DDC
700/.973/09034 20
1. Modernism (Art) - United States. 2. Arts, American.
3. Arts, Modern - 19th century - United States. 4. Arts,
Modern - 20th century - United States. I. Title.
NX503.7 .C78 1992

CRUSADES - MAPS.
The Atlas of the Crusades /. New York , 1991,
c1990. 192 p. : ISBN 0-8160-2186-4 DDC 911
20
G1034 .R5 1990 **NYPL [Map Div. 91-4709]**

Cruysmans, Philippe, 1925-
Linou Truffino, ou, Les voix de la mer /
Philippe Cruysmans, Remi de Cnodder ; préface
de Paul Caso. Bruxelles : Editeurs d'art
associés, [1986] 127 p. : ill. (some col.) ; 33 cm.
(Collection "La Mémoire de l'art") French and Dutch;
summaries in English and German. ISBN
2-87103-024-8 DDC 759.9493 20
1. Truffino, Linou - Catalogs. 2. Sea in art - Catalogs. I.
Cnodder, Remi de. II. Title. III. Title: Linou Truffino.
IV. Title: Voix de la mer. V. Series.
ND673.T75 A4 1986

Lise Brachet, ou, Le bonheur de peindre /
Philippe Cruysmans. Bruxelles : Editeurs d'art
associés, [1985] 127 p. : ill. (some col.) ; 28 cm.
(Collection "La Mémoire de l'art") Summaries in Dutch,
English, German, and Japanese. Includes bibliographical
references. ISBN 2-87103-014-6 DDC 759.9493 20
1. Brachet, Lise - Interviews. 2. Painters - Belgium -
Interviews. 3. Brachet, Lise - Catalogs. 4. Primitivism in
art - Belgium. I. Title. II. Title: Lise Brachet. III. Title:
Bonheur de peindre. IV. Series.
ND673.B5438 A35 1985

Lise Durez peint Victor Hugo / Philippe
Cruysmans, Remi de Cnodder, Lucien de
Meyer ; préface de Paul Caso. Bruxelles :
Editeurs d'art associés, [1986] 183 p. : ill.
(some col.) ; 32 cm. (Collection "La Mémoire de
l'art") French and Dutch with summaries in English
and German. ISBN 2-87103-023-5
1. Durez, Lise - Criticism and interpretation. 2. Women
in art. 3. Romanticism in art - Belgium. 4. Hugo,
Victor, 1802-1885 - Influence. I. Cnodder, Remi de. II.
Meyer, Lucien de. III. Title. IV. Title: Lise Durez. V.
Series.
N6973.D85 C7 1986

Cruz, Emilio, 1938-
Rand, Harry. Emilio Cruz . New York, N.Y. ,
c1984. 15 p. : ISBN 0-932075-00-2 (pbk.)
MLCM 84/5528 (N)
NYPL [3-MCX C959 90-12365]

CRUZ, EMILIO, 1938- - EXHIBITIONS.
Rand, Harry. Emilio Cruz . New York, N.Y. ,
c1984. 15 p. : ISBN 0-932075-00-2 (pbk.)
MLCM 84/5528 (N)
NYPL [3-MCX C959 90-12365]

Cruz, Javier, 1952-
Luis Gutiérrez, Javier Cruz, Luis René Alva .
[Mexico City, Mexico] , 1988. 61 p. :
NE544 .L85 1988

CRUZ, JAVIER, 1952- - CATALOGS.
Luis Gutiérrez, Javier Cruz, Luis René Alva .
[Mexico City, Mexico] , 1988. 61 p. :
NE544 .L85 1988

Cruz-Taura, Graciella. Outside Cuba . [New
Brunswick, N.J.] , Miami, Fla. , 1989. 366 p. :
ISBN 0-935501-13-4
NYPL [3-MAM 90-12497]

CRYPTS - AUSTRIA - SALZBURG.
Fuhrmann, Franz. Die Chorkrypta des
romanischen Domes in Salzburg . Salzburg ,
1962. 32 p. : **NYPL [3-MRIF 90-4729]**

CRYPTS - ITALY - TARANTO.
La Cripta della Cattedrale di Taranto /. Taranto
[1986] 98 p. : **NYPL [3-MRBN+ 90-10741]**

**CRYSTAL GLASS - FRANCE - HISTORY -
19TH CENTURY.**
Compagnie des cristalleries de Baccarat.
Baccarat . [Baccarat, France] : Paris ; 222 p. :
ISBN 2-906309-00-1 : DDC 748.8/2/09443823
19
NK5205.C65 A4 1986
NYPL [3-MPW 90-10581]

**CRYSTAL GLASS - FRANCE - HISTORY -
20TH CENTURY.**
Compagnie des cristalleries de Baccarat.
Baccarat . [Baccarat, France] : Paris ; 222 p. :
ISBN 2-906309-00-1 : DDC 748.8/2/09443823
19
NK5205.C65 A4 1986
NYPL [3-MPW 90-10581]

Csap, Erzsébet. Tar, István. Tar István
(1910-1971) bemlékkiállítása . Budapest , 1972.
[96] p. : **NYPL [3-MGO (Tar) 90-6462]**

Csikszentmihalyi, Mihaly. The art of seeing : an
interpretation of the aesthetic encounter /
Mihaly Csikszentmihalyi, Rick E. Robinson.
Malibu, Calif. : J.P. Getty Museum ; Getty
Center for Education in the Arts, 1990. xvii,
203 p. : ill. ; 23 cm. Includes bibliographical
references. ISBN 0-89236-156-5 : DDC 111/.85 20
1. Experience. I. Robinson, Rick Emery, 1958-. II.
Title.
BH301.E8 C75 1990
NYPL [3-MAB 91-6221]

Csorba, Géza. Magyar Nemzeti Galéria.
Ungarische Malerei und Bildhauerei im 19.
Jahrhundert . Budapest , 1989. 47 p., [42] p. of
plates :
N6819 .M28 1989

CTP. Corpus Topographicum Pompeianum.
Rome , 1977- (Rome, Italy : Edizioni
dell'Elefante) v. ; ISBN 0-930084-06-3 (set) DDC
937/.7 19
DG70.P7 C629 1977 **NYPL [JFM 82-182 &
Map Div. 86-1278]**

Cuaderno de dibujos /. Gallardo, Jesús, 1931-
Guanajuato, Gto. [i.e. Guanajuato, Mexico] ,
1989. 112 p. : ISBN 968-617-017-0 DDC 741.972
20
NC146.G35 A4 1989

Cuadernos Arte Cátedra .
(22) Paz Aguilo, María. El mueble clásico
español /. Madrid , 1987. 237 p. : ISBN
84-376-0679-9 DDC 749.26 19
NK2599 .P38 1987 **NYPL [3-MOF 91-6670]**

(26) Reyero, Carlos. La pintura de historia en
España . Madrid , c1989. 230 p. : ISBN
84-376-0867-8 **NYPL [3-MCP 90-11005]**

(27) Pérez Rojas, Javier. Art déco en España /.
Madrid , c1990. 645 p., [32] p. of plates :
ISBN 84-376-0927-5 DDC 709/.46/09042 20
N7108.5.A7 P4 1990

**Cuadernos de arquitectura de la Unión
Internacional de Arquitectos.**

Cuadernos de arquitectura de la Unión Internacional de

Glusberg, Jorge. Escuela de Buenos Aires .
Buenos Aires, Argentina [between 1984 and
1990] 31 p. :
NA2706.A7 G58 1984

Glusberg, Jorge. Miguel Angel Roca, arquitecto
/. Buenos Aires, Argentina [between 1985 and
1990] 39 p. : DDC 720/.92 20
NA839.R62 A4 1990

Cuadernos de historia del arte (Universidad
Nacional Autónoma de México. Instituto de
Investigaciones Estéticas) .
(41) Coloquio Internacional de Historia del
Arte (1980 : Mexico City, Mexico) Arte
funerario /. México , 1987- v. : ISBN
968-360-243-6 (set)
NB1800 .C65 1980
        NYPL [3-MRIF 90-2698]

Cuadra, Francisco de la Maza y de la. see Maza,
Francisco de la, 1913-1972.

Cuadros que hablan vida cotidiana y organización
de mujeres. Franger, Gaby. [Arpilleras : Bilder
die sprechen Organisation und Alltag der
Frauen in den Slums von Lima. Spanish.]
Arpilleras . Lima, Peru , 1988. 110 p. :
        NYPL [3-MOT 90-12715]

Cuarenta años de artes plásticas en La Rioja.
Labandíbar, José Luis. 1950-1990, cuarenta
años de artes plásticas en La Rioja /. [La Rioja]
[1989?-1990?] 2 v. : ISBN 84-404-5495-3 (v. 1)
N7109.L3 L3 1989

Cuarenta maestros del arte de los argentinos.
Squirru, Rafael F. 40 maestros del arte de los
argentinos /. Buenos Aires , 1990. 297 p. :
        ISBN 950-99493-1-0 DDC 759.982 B 20
ND335 .S63 1990   NYPL [3-MCY 91-5611]

CUARTARA CASSINELLO, TRINIDAD, 1847-
1912.
Fernández Martínez, Carlos María. Trinidad
Cuartara Cassinello, arquitecto . Almería , 1989.
392 p. : ISBN 84-85219-75-9   *NYPL [MQZ*
        (Cuartara Cassinello) 91-5988]

Cuatro maestros latinoamericanos. 4 maestros
latinoamericanos . [Bogotá, Colombia] [1987]
71 p. :
ND202.5 .A14 1987

Cuauhtinchan del siglo XII [doce] al XVI
[dieciséis] . Reyes García, Luis. Wiesbaden ,
1977. xviii, 127 p., [21] leaves of plates (1
fold.) : ISBN 3-515-02572-3
F1203 .D46 vol. 10 F1219
        NYPL [HTC 74-1117 [Bd.] 10]

Cuauhtinchan, Mexico. see Quauhtinchan,
Mexico.

CUBA - DESCRIPTION AND TRAVEL.
Levine, Robert M. Cuba in the 1850s . Tampa ,
c1990. xv, 86 p. : ISBN 0-8130-1010-1 (alk. paper)
DDC 779/.99729105 20
F1763 .L65 1990
        NYPL [MFX (Fredricks) 91-3474]

Wurdemann, John George F., 1810-1849. Notes
on Cuba. New York, 1971. x, 359 p. ISBN
0-405-01720-0
F1763 .W96 1971   *NYPL [HOY 72-590]*

CUBA - DESCRIPTION AND TRAVEL -
VIEWS.
Levine, Robert M. Cuba in the 1850s . Tampa ,
c1990. xv, 86 p. : ISBN 0-8130-1010-1 (alk. paper)
DDC 779/.99729105 20
F1763 .L65 1990
        NYPL [MFX (Fredricks) 91-3474]

Salon and picturesque photography in Cuba,
1860-1920 . Daytona Beach, Fla. , c1988. 44
p. : ISBN 0-933053-02-9
        NYPL [MFW 90-13474]

CUBA - HISTORY - 1810-1899.
Levine, Robert M. Cuba in the 1850s . Tampa ,
c1990. xv, 86 p. : ISBN 0-8130-1010-1 (alk. paper)
DDC 779/.99729105 20
F1763 .L65 1990
        NYPL [MFX (Fredricks) 91-3474]

CUBA - HISTORY - 1810-1899 - PICTORIAL
WORKS.
Levine, Robert M. Cuba in the 1850s . Tampa ,
c1990. xv, 86 p. : ISBN 0-8130-1010-1 (alk. paper)
DDC 779/.99729105 20
F1763 .L65 1990
        NYPL [MFX (Fredricks) 91-3474]

Cuba in the 1850s . Levine, Robert M. Tampa ,
c1990. xv, 86 p. : ISBN 0-8130-1010-1 (alk. paper)

DDC 779/.99729105 20
F1763 .L65 1990
        NYPL [MFX (Fredricks) 91-3474]

CUBA - POLITICS AND GOVERNMENT -
1959-
Movimiento Unidad Revolucionaria. Conozca lo
que le ocurrirá a usted y a su país si el
comunismo logra adueñarse del poder. [Coral
Gables, Fla., 1963] 46 p.
        *NYPL [*XMB-2143]*

Cubas, Antonio García. see García Cubas,
Antonio, 1832-1912.

CUBISM - EXHIBITIONS.
Kosinski, Dorothy M. Picasso, Braque, Gris,
Léger . Houston, Tex. , c1990. 67 p. : ISBN
0-89090-049-3 (pbk.) DDC 759.4/074/7641411
20
N6848.5.C82 K67 1990
        NYPL [3-MCN 91-6709]

Kotalík, Jiří. Kupka, Gutfreund & C . Venezia ,
c1980. 114 p. : ISBN 88-20-80273-2 DDC
709/.437/0740531 19
N6831 .K67 1980   NYPL [3-MAM 90-5445]

Lhote, André, 1885-1962. André Lhote,
1885-1962 . New York, N.Y. [1976?] 32 p. :
        NYPL [3-MCO L69 90-5654]

CUBISM - FRANCE.
Gersh-Nešić, Beth S. The early criticism of
André Salmon . New York , 1991. p. cm.
        ISBN 0-8153-0115-4 (alk. paper) DDC
759.4/09/041 20
N6848.5.C82 G46 1991

Palau i Fabre, Josep, 1917- [Picasso cubisme
(1907-1917). English.] Picasso cubism
(1907-1917) /. New York , 1990. 529 p. :
        ISBN 0-8478-1238-3 DDC 759.4 20
ND553.P5 P282713 1990
        NYPL [MCQ P58 91-2638]

CUBISM - FRANCE - PARIS -
EXHIBITIONS.
Cubists in Paris (1910-1956) . New York
[1978] [8] p. :   *NYPL [3-MAL 91-7004]*

Cubists in Paris (1910-1956) : a selection of fine
paintings by the Cubist artists working in Paris
in the first half of this century, at A.M. Adler
Fine Arts, May 18th-June 10th, 1978. New
York : A.M. Adler Fine Arts, [1978] [8] p. :
ill. ; 21 cm.
        1. Cubism - France - Paris - Exhibitions. I. A. M. Adler
        Fine Arts Inc.   *NYPL [3-MAL 91-7004]*

Čubrda, Zdeněk. ROH. ÚRO. Lidé, život, práce .
[Prague] , 1988. 1 portfolio (unpaged) :
N6831 .R64 1988

Cucchi, Enzo.
Enzo Cucchi, etchings and lithographs,
1979-1985. Munich : Edition Schellmann,
c1985. 1 v. (unpaged) : ill. ; 27 cm. ISBN
3-921629-12-8
        1. Cucchi, Enzo - Catalogs. I. Title.
        NYPL [MDG (Cucchi) 90-11907]

Enzo Cucchi testa / herausgegeben von Helmut
Friedel ; [Katalog und Ausstellung, Helmut
Friedel ; Texte von Jean-Christophe
Ammann ... et al.] München : Lenbachhaus,
c1987. 2 v. : ill. (some col.) ; 22 cm. Catalog of
an exhibition held at the Städtische Galerie im
Lenbachhaus, Munich, July 1-Sept. 13, 1987, the
Fruitmarket Gallery, Edinburgh, Oct. 3-Nov. 15, 1987,
and the Musée de la Ville de Nice, Dec. 4, 1987-Jan.
31, 1988. CONTENTS. - [1] Katalog -- [2]
Dokumentation der Ausstellung. ISBN 3-88645-076-7
(v. 1)
        1. Cucchi, Enzo - Exhibitions. I. Friedel, Helmut. II.
        Ammann, Jean Christophe. III. Städtische Galerie im
        Lenbachhaus München. IV. Fruitmarket Gallery. V.
        Musée de la Ville de Nice. VI. Title. VII. Title: Testa.
        NYPL [3-MCF C952 88-3505]

CUCCHI, ENZO - CATALOGS.
Cucchi, Enzo. Enzo Cucchi, etchings and
lithographs, 1979-1985. Munich , c1985. 1 v.
(unpaged) : ISBN 3-921629-12-8
        NYPL [MDG (Cucchi) 90-11907]

CUCCHI, ENZO - EXHIBITIONS.
Cucchi, Enzo. Enzo Cucchi testa /. München ,
c1987. 2 v. : ISBN 3-88645-076-7 (v. 1)
        NYPL [3-MCF C952 88-3505]

CUENCA (SPAIN) - BIOGRAPHY.
Rokiski Lázaro, María Luz. Arquitectura del
siglo XVI en Cuenca . Cuenca , 1989. xxi, 464

p. : ISBN 84-505-8542-2
NA1311.C84 R66 1989

Cuentro, Juliana. Bajado, 1912- Bajado, um
artista de Olinda /. Olinda [Brasil] , 1985. 48
p. : DDC 759.981 19
ND359.B34 A35 1985
        NYPL [3-MCZ B1583 90-9450]

Cuernica-bra, el drama que nunca existió. Vindel,
Pedro. Caminando en mis sueños pos la estela
de los caballos blancos de Picasso . [Madrid]
[1990?] 109 p. ; ISBN 84-404-6676-5
N7113.P514 V56 1990

Cuevas, José Luis, 1934-
Historias del viajero / José Luis Cuevas. 1a ed.
México, D.F. : Premià, 1987. 78 p. : ill. ; 21
cm. (La Red de Jonás. Literatura mexicana . 42)
        ISBN 968-434-446-5 DDC 760/.092/4 B 19
        1. Cuevas, José Luis, 1934-. 2. Artists - Mexico -
        Biography. I. Title. II. Series.
N6559.C8 A2 1987
        NYPL [3-MCZ C955 90-12616]

Historias para una exposición / José Luis
Cuevas. 1 ed. Tlahuapan, Puebla [Mexico] :
Premià, 1988. 95 p. : ill. ; 21 cm. (La Red de
Jonás. Literatura mexicana . 45) DDC 760/.092 B 20
        1. Cuevas, José Luis, 1934-. 2. Artists - Mexico -
        Biography. I. Title. II. Series.
N6559.C8 A2 1988
        NYPL [3-MCZ C955 91-5025]

CUEVAS, JOSÉ LUIS, 1934-
Cajigas R., María de los Angeles. El mundo
desconocido de José Luis Cuevas /. México ,
c1990. 154 p. : ISBN 968-409-526-0 DDC
760/.092 B 20
N6559.C8 C34 1990

Cuevas, José Luis, 1934- Historias del viajero /.
México, D.F. , 1987. 78 p. : ISBN 968-434-446-5
DDC 760/.092/4 B 19
N6559.C8 A2 1987   *NYPL [3-MCZ C955 90-12616]*

Cuevas, José Luis, 1934- Historias para una
exposición /. Tlahuapan, Puebla [Mexico] ,
1988. 95 p. : DDC 760/.092 B 20
N6559.C8 A2 1988
        NYPL [3-MCZ C955 91-5025]

CUEVAS, JOSÉ LUIS, 1934- - RELATIONS
WITH WOMEN.
Cajigas R., María de los Angeles. El mundo
desconocido de José Luis Cuevas /. México ,
c1990. 154 p. : ISBN 968-409-526-0 DDC
760/.092 B 20
N6559.C8 C34 1990

CUEVAS, JOSÉ LUIS, 1934- - CRITICISM
AND INTERPRETATION.
Cajigas, María de los Angeles. El mundo
desconocido de José Luis Cuevas /. México,
c1990. 154 p. :
        NYPL [3-MCZ C955 91-4665]

Cuff, Dana, 1953- Architecture : the story of
practice / Dana Cuff. Cambridge, Mass. : MIT
Press, c1991. xi, 306 p. : ill. ; 26 cm. Includes
bibliographical references (p. [287]-298) and index.
        ISBN 0-262-03175-2 : DDC 720/.68 20
        1. Architectural practice - United States. 2. Architects -
        United States - Interviews. 3. Architecture and society -
        United States. I. Title.
NA1996 .C84 1991
        NYPL [3-MQWO 91-7317]

Cuisenier, Jean, 1927- Destins d'objets /. Paris ,
1988. 474 p. : ISBN 2-11-002009-1 (pbk.)
        NYPL [3-MAVC 90-9455]

Culot, Maurice. Arcachon, la ville d'hiver /.
Liège , 1988. 238 p. : ISBN 2-87009-372-1
NA1051.A73 A73 1988

Cult objects . Sudjic, Deyan. London , 1985. 159
p. : ISBN 0-586-08483-5 (pbk.) DDC 745.2/09/04
19
NK1390 .S83 1985   NYPL [3-MNF 91-5813]

Cultivating the country : living with the arts in
regional Australia / edited by Peter Timms and
Robyn Christie ; photographs by Gerrit
Fokkema. Oxford [England] ; New York :
Oxford University Press Australia, 1988. 118
p. : ill., ports. ; 29 cm. Includes bibliographical
references. ISBN 0-19-554944-9 (pbk.)
        1. Arts and society - Australia. 2. Australia - Cultural
        policy. I. Timms, Peter. II. Christie, Robyn.
        NYPL [3-MAM 89-17144]

CULTURAL ANTHROPOLOGY. see
ETHNOLOGY.

Cultural Center of the Philippines. Museo ng
Kalinangang Pilipino . Maynila, Pilipinas , 1989.
190, [1] p. :
NX581.A1 M88 1989

Cultural hermeneutics of modern art : essays in
honor of Jan Aler / edited by Hubert Dethier,
Eldert Willems. Amsterdam ; Atlanta, GA :
Rodopi, 1989. 307 p., [1] p. of plates : port. ;
22 cm. (Lier & Boog studies . v. 4) English, French
and German. Includes bibliographical references.
ISBN 90-6203-645-7
*1. Aler, Jan. 2. Arts - Philosophy. I. Aler, Jan. II.
Dethier, Hubert. III. Willems, Eldert. IV. Series.*
NYPL [3-MAS 90-10857]

Cultural literacy & arts education / edited by
Ralph A. Smith. Urbana : University of Illinois
Press, c1991 :xvi, 171 p. : ill. ; 23 cm. "The
essays in this book originally appeared in the Journal of
aesthetic education, volume 24, number 1 (1990)"--T.p.
verso. "An Illini book from the University of Illinois
Press"--P. [4] of cover. Includes bibliographical
references and index. ISBN 0-252-01845-1 (alk.
paper)   DDC 700/.1/03 20
*1. Arts - Study and teaching. 2. Arts and society. I.
Smith, Ralph Alexander. II. Title: Cultural literacy and
arts education.*
NX294 .C85 1992

Cultural literacy and arts education. Cultural
literacy & arts education /. Urbana , c19. :xvi,
171 p. :   ISBN 0-252-01845-1 (alk. paper)   DDC
700/.1/03 20
NX294 .C85 1992

Cultural pedagogy . Trend, David. New York ,
1992. p. cm.   ISBN 0-89789-256-9   DDC
700/.1/03 20
NX180.S6 T7 1992

**CULTURAL PROPERTY, PROTECTION OF -
FRANCE.**
Destins d'objets /. Paris , 1988. 474 p. :   ISBN
2-11-002009-1 (pbk.)
NYPL [3-MAVC 90-9455]

**CULTURAL PROPERTY, PROTECTION OF -
UNITED STATES - BIBLIOGRAPHY.**
Landmark yellow pages . Washington, D.C. ,
1990. 319 p. :   ISBN 0-89133-154-9   DDC
363.6/9/0973 20
E159 .L28 1990
NYPL [Desk-USLHG 90-10086]

**CULTURAL PROPERTY, PROTECTION OF -
UNITED STATES - HANDBOOKS,
MANUALS, ETC.**
Landmark yellow pages . Washington, D.C. ,
1990. 319 p. :   ISBN 0-89133-154-9   DDC
363.6/9/0973 20
E159 .L28 1990
NYPL [Desk-USLHG 90-10086]

**CULTURAL PROPERTY, PROTECTION OF -
UNITED STATES - SOCIETIES, ETC. -
DIRECTORIES.**
Landmark yellow pages . Washington, D.C. ,
1990. 319 p. :   ISBN 0-89133-154-9   DDC
363.6/9/0973 20
E159 .L28 1990
NYPL [Desk-USLHG 90-10086]

CULTURAL RELATIVISM.
Gombrich, E. H. (Ernst Hans), 1909- Topics of
our time . Berkeley , 1991. p. cm.   ISBN
0-520-07516-1   DDC 001.3 20
N6490 .G595 1991

Cultural tourism . McCarthy, Bridget Beattie.
Santa Fe, N.M. , 1991. p. cm.   ISBN
0-9611710-5-7 :   DDC 338.4/7917304928 20
NX180.T67 M35 1991

**CULTURE, POPULAR. see POPULAR
CULTURE.**

Cumming, Robert, 1943-
Discovering Turner / Robert Cumming.
London : Tate Gallery, 1990. 72 p. : ill. (some
col.) ; 21 cm.   ISBN 1-85437-039-1
*1. Turner, J. M. W. (Joseph Mallord William),
1775-1851 - Criticism and interpretation. I. Turner, J.
M. W. (Joseph Mallord William), 1775-1851. II. Tate
Gallery. III. Title.*
NYPL [3-MCV T94 91-6306]

Guide Christie's du collectionneur /. Paris ,
c1986. 223 p. :   ISBN 2-7000-2140-1
NYPL [3-MAVC 89-25308]

Cumming, William Patterson, 1900- North
Carolina in maps, by William P. Cumming.
Raleigh, State Dept. of Archives and History,

1966. vii, 36 p. maps. 28 cm. Includes
bibliographical references.   DDC G3900s var.C8
*1. Maps, Early - Facsimiles. 2. North Carolina - Maps.
I. Title.*
G1300 .C8 1966   NYPL [Map Div. 90-5905]

Cummings, Hildegard. J. Alden Weir : a place of
his own / Hildegard Cummings, Helen K.
Fusscas, Susan G. Larkin. Storrs : William
Benton Museum of Art, University of
Connecticut, c1991. p. cm. "The William Benton
Museum of Art, Storrs, 4 June-18 August 1991. The
Bruce Museum, Greenwich, 15 September-3 November
1991"--T.p. verso. Includes bibliographical references.
ISBN 0-918386-43-8   DDC 759.13 20
*1. Weir, Julian Alden, 1852-1919 - Exhibitions. I.
Fusscas, Helen K., 1943-. II. Larkin, Susan G., 1943-.
III. William Benton Museum of Art. IV. Bruce
Museum. V. Title.*
ND237.W4 A4 1991

Cummings, Pat. Talking with artists . New York :
Toronto : p. cm.   ISBN 0-02-724245-5   DDC
741.6/42/092273 B 20
NC975 .T34 1991

Cummins, Julie. Children's book illustration and
design /. New York , 1991. p. cm.   ISBN
0-86636-147-2   DDC 741.6/42/09048 20
NC965 .C43 1991

Cúneo, José, 1887-1977. Pereda, Raquel. José
Cúneo . Montevideo [1988] xiii, 196 p. :   DDC
759.9895 B 20
ND429.C8 P47 1988

CÚNEO, JOSÉ, 1887-1977.
Pereda, Raquel. José Cúneo . Montevideo
[1988] xiii, 196 p. :   DDC 759.9895 B 20
ND429.C8 P47 1988

Cuneo, Paolo. Architettura armena dal quarto al
diciannovesimo secolo / Paolo Cuneo ; con
testi e contributi di Tommaso Breccia
Fratadocchi ... [et al.]. Roma : De Luca, 1988.
2 v. (923 p., [1] folded leaf of plates) : ill., map,
plans ; 25 cm. Includes bibliographical references (p.
873-908) and indexes. CONTENTS. - t. 1. Testi
introduttivi e schede degli edifici -- t. 2. Tavole
sinottiche e apparati di consultazione.   ISBN
88-7813-154-7 (set)
*1. Architecture, Armenian - Armenian S.S.R. 2.
Architecture, Armenian - Turkey. 3. Architecture,
Armenian - Iran. I. Breccia Fratadocchi, Tommaso. II.
Title.*   *NYPL [3-MQW 90-12681]*

CUNEO, TERENCE.
Chakra, Narisa. Terence Cuneo, railway painter
of the century /. London , 1990. 160 p. :   ISBN
0-904568-74-1
NYPL [3-MCV+ C972 90-11746]

**CUNHA, MANUEL DE PAIVA E, 1910-1987 -
THEMES, MOTIVES.**
Basseches, Joshua T., 1962- The scrimshaw of
Manuel Cunha, late work from Madeira
revealed /. Sharon, Mass., USA , 1988. 19 p. :
ISBN 0-937854-26-3   DDC 736/.62 20
NK6022 .B38 1988

Cunning, Robert. Picture framing / Robert
Cunning. 1st paperback ed. London : Ward
Lock ; New York, N.Y. : Distributed by
Sterling Pub., 1990. 80 p. : ill. (some col.) ; 21
cm. (Living style) "First published in Great Britain in
1986 by Ward Lock"--Verso of t.p. Distributor from
label on t.p. verso. Includes bibliographical references
(p. 75-79) and index.   ISBN 0-7063-6913-0   DDC
749/.7 20
*1. Pictures frames and framing. I. Series: Living style
(London, England). II. Title.*
N8550 .C86 1990

CUNNINGHAM, BEN, 1904-1975.
Nemser, Cindy. Ben Cunningham--a life with
color /. Post, Tex. , c1989. 91 p. :   ISBN
0-9622235-0-6   DDC 759.13 B 20
ND237.C8496 N46 1989
NYPL [3-MCX C973 91-6760]

Cunningham, Joe. Marston, Gwen. Mary Schafer
and her quilts /. East Lansing, Mich. , c1990.
58 p. :   ISBN 0-944311-04-0   DDC 746.9/7/092 20
NK9198.S33 M37 1990

Cunningham, Michael R. The triumph of
Japanese style : 16th-century art in Japan / by
Michael R. Cunningham, with contributions by
Suzuki Norio, Miyajima Shin'ichi, and Saito
Takamasa. [Cleveland, Ohio] : Cleveland
Museum of Art, c1991. p. cm. Catalog of an
exhibition held at the Cleveland Museum of Art, Oct.
19-Dec. 1, 1991. Includes bibliographical references.

ISBN 0-940717-12-3   DDC 709/.52/07477132 20
*1. Art, Japanese - Kamakura-Momoyama periods,
1185-1600 - Exhibitions. I. Title.*
N7353.4 .C87 1991

Cuomo, Alberto. In/progetto . Napoli , 1985. 128
p. :   *NYPL [3-MQWB+ 90-10577]*

**CUPBOARDS - NEW JERSEY - HISTORY -
17TH CENTURY - EXHIBITIONS.**
Kenny, Peter (Peter M.) American kasten .
New York , c1991. viii, 80 p. :   ISBN
0-87099-605-3 (pbk.)   DDC 749/.3 20
NK2727 .K46 1991   NYPL [3-MOF 91-6596]

**CUPBOARDS - NEW JERSEY - HISTORY -
18TH CENTURY - EXHIBITIONS.**
Kenny, Peter (Peter M.) American kasten .
New York , c1991. viii, 80 p. :   ISBN
0-87099-605-3 (pbk.)   DDC 749/.3 20
NK2727 .K46 1991   NYPL [3-MOF 91-6596]

**CUPBOARDS - NEW YORK (STATE) -
HISTORY - 17TH CENTURY -
EXHIBITIONS.**
Kenny, Peter (Peter M.) American kasten .
New York , c1991. viii, 80 p. :   ISBN
0-87099-605-3 (pbk.)   DDC 749/.3 20
NK2727 .K46 1991   NYPL [3-MOF 91-6596]

**CUPBOARDS - NEW YORK (STATE) -
HISTORY - 18TH CENTURY -
EXHIBITIONS.**
Kenny, Peter (Peter M.) American kasten .
New York , c1991. viii, 80 p. :   ISBN
0-87099-605-3 (pbk.)   DDC 749/.3 20
NK2727 .K46 1991   NYPL [3-MOF 91-6596]

Curator's choice . Brooklyn Museum. [Brooklyn,
N.Y. , 1990] 1 folded sheet ([8] p.) :
NYPL [3-MCX H76 91-7969]

Ćurčić, Slobodan. The Twilight of Byzantium .
Princeton, N.J. , c1991. p. cm.   ISBN
0-691-04091-5 (alk. paper) :   DDC 700/.9495 20
NX449 .T85 1991

Curcio, Judith. Federico, Jean Taylor, 1940. Clues
to American furniture /. Washington DC ,
1991. p. cm.   ISBN 0-913515-75-2 :   DDC
749.213/075 20
NK2405 .F43 1991

Curdes, Gerhard, 1933- Prokop, Eva. Bauen im
Grenzland . Aachen [1989] 227 p. :   ISBN
3-89399-092-5
NA7350.A23 P76 1989

Curl, James Stevens, 1937-
Victorian architecture / James Stevens Curl.
Newton Abbot : David & Charles, 1990. 320
p. : ill. ; 24 cm. Includes index. Includes
bibliographical references (p. 305-313).   ISBN
0-7153-9144-5 :   DDC 720/.941 19
1. Architecture, Victorian - Great Britain. I. Title.
NA967.5.V53   NYPL [3-MQWK 90-11107]

Victorian architecture / James Stevens Curl.
Newton Abbot : David & Charles ; New York,
N.Y. : Distributed by Sterling Pub. Co., c1990.
320 p. : ill. ; 24 cm. Distributor from label on t.p.
Includes bibliographical references (p. 305-303) and
index.   ISBN 0-7153-9144-5   DDC 720/.941/09034
20
*1. Architecture, Victorian - Great Britain. 2.
Architecture, Modern - 19th century - Great Britain. I.
Title.*
NA967 .C8 1990

Currier Gallery of Art.
Champa, Kermit Swiler. The rise of landscape
painting in France . Manchester, N.H. , New
York , c1991. 231 p. :   ISBN 0-929710-06-1
(Currier : pbk.)   *NYPL [3-MCN 91-4059]*

Heirlooms [microform] . Manchester, N.H.
[1985] [5] leaves :   *NYPL [*ZM-218 no.2]*

Curtis, Penelope.
Minimalism /. Liverpool , c1989. 28 p. :
NYPL [3-MGI 91-7014]

Patronage & practice . [Liverpool] , 1989. 137
p. :   ISBN 1-85437-021-9 (pbk.)   DDC 730.941 20
NB170   NYPL [3-MGI+ 90-12483]

Curtis, Tony, 1939-
The Lyle price guide to collectibles and
memorabilia /. New York, NY , c1990. 512 p. :
ISBN 0-399-51515-1 (alk. paper) :   DDC
745.1/075 19
NK1125 .L79 1990   NYPL [MAVC 91-3286]

There's a fortune in your attic / by Anthony
Curtis. New York, NY : Perigee Books, c1991.
512 p. : ill. ; 22 cm. Title on cover: Lyle, there's a

fortune in your attic. ISBN 0-399-51677-8 (alk.
paper) : DDC 745.1/075 20
*1. Antiques - Collectors and collecting. 2. Collectibles.
I. Title. II. Title: Lyle, there's a fortune in your attic.*
NK1125 .C8874 1991

Curtis, William J. R. Balkrishna Doshi : an
architecture for India / William J.R. Curtis ;
[editor, Carmen Kagal]. New York : Rizzoli,
1988. 191 p. : ill. (some col.) ; 23 x 29 cm.
Bibliography: p. 175-179. ISBN 0-8478-0937-4 DDC
720/.92 20
1. Doshi, Balkrishna V. - Criticism and interpretation.
2. Architecture, Modern - 20th century - India. I. Title.
NA1510.D67 C87 1988
NYPL [3-MQZ (Doshi) 89-22893]

Curto, Silvio. Storia del Museo egizio di Torino /
Silvio Curto. 3a ed. riv. e aggiornata. Torino :
Centro studi piemontesi, 1990. vi, 149 p., [64]
p. of plates : ill. ; 28 cm. Includes index. Includes
bibliographical references.
1. Museo egizio di Torino. I. Title.
NYPL [3-MAVZ (Turin) 91-4943]

Cusco Peru tourist guide. Tourist guide of Cusco
and surrounding area. Lima, Peru , 1988. 32
p. : *NYPL [Map Div. 91-3642]*

CUT GLASS - CONNECTICUT - CATALOGS.
International Silver Company. Catalogue of
International Silver Co. . New York, U. S.A.
[1915?] 160 p. :
NK7241.5.I58 A4 1915

CUT GLASS - UNITED STATES - HISTORY.
Boggess, Bill. Identifying American brillant cut
glass /. West Chester, Pa. , c1991. x, 283 p. :
ISBN 0-88740-296-8 DDC 748.2913/075 20
NK5203 .B64 1991

Cutileiro, João, 1937-
Lorelei : esculturas de João Cutileiro /
fotografias de Gérard Castello Lopes ; textos de
Miguel Esteves Cardoso. Porto : Porto Editora,
1989. 1 v. (unpaged) : chiefly ill. ; 31 cm.
1. Cutileiro, João, 1937- - Criticism and interpretation.
2. Women in art. I. Lopes, Gérard Castello. II. Title.
NYPL [3-MGO+ (Cutileiro) 90-12676]

Lorelei / esculturas de João Cutileiro /
fotografias de Gérard Castello Lopes ; textos de
Miguel Esteves Cardoso. Porto, Portugal : Porto
Editora, [1989] 1 v. (unpaged) : ill. ; 30 cm.
DDC 730/.92 20
1. Cutileiro, João, 1937- - Themes, motives. 2. Nude in
art. I. Lopes, Gérard Castello. II. Cardoso, Miguel
Esteves. III. Title.
NB833.C88 A4 1989

CUTILEIRO, JOÃO, 1937- - THEMES,
MOTIVES.
Cutileiro, João, 1937- Lorelei /. Porto, Portugal
[1989] 1 v. (unpaged) : DDC 730/.92 20
NB833.C88 A4 1989

CUTILEIRO, JOÃO, 1937- - CRITICISM AND
INTERPRETATION.
Cutileiro, João, 1937- Lorelei . Porto , 1989. 1
v. (unpaged) :
NYPL [3-MGO+ (Cutileiro) 90-12676]

Cutul, Ann-Marie. Twentieth-century European
painting : a guide to information sources /
Ann-Marie Cutul. Detroit, Mich. : Gale
Research Co., c1980. xv, 520 p. ; 23 cm. (Art
and architecture information guide series. v. 9) Gale
information guide to library Includes indexes. ISBN
0-8103-1438-X DDC 016.75994
1. Painting, European - Bibliography. 2. Painting,
Modern - 20th century - Europe - Bibliography. I. Title.
Z5949.E9 C87 ND458
NYPL [3-MAC 91-7865]

Cuyper, Frédérique de. La Croix byzantine du
Trésor de la Cathédrale de Tournai /.
Louvain-la-Neuve , 1987. 88 p. :
NYPL [3-MAIH 89-28301]

CUZCO (PERU) - DESCRIPTION - GUIDE-
BOOKS.
Tourist guide of Cusco and surrounding area.
Lima, Peru , 1988. 32 p. :
NYPL [Map Div. 91-3642]

CUZCO (PERU) - MAPS.
Atlas urbano de la ciudad del Cusco /. Cusco,
Peru , 1989. 1 atlas ([54] folded leaves) :
NYPL [Map Div. 91-6021]

Cuzin, Jean Pierre.
Laclotte, Michel. The Louvre . Paris , c1989.
vii, 287 p. : DDC 759.94/074/44361 20
N2030 .A62 1989

Petit Larousse de la peinture. Italian. Dizionario
della pittura e dei pittori /. Torino , c1989- v. :
ISBN 88-06-11573-1 (v. 1)
NYPL [MAO 90-2147]

Cy DeCosse Incorporated. Bedroom decorating.
Minnetonka, MN , 1991. p. cm. ISBN
0-86573-351-1 : DDC 747.7/7 20
NK2117.B4 B424 1991

Cy Twombly. Twombly, Cy, 1928- Houston, TX ,
1990. 129 p. : ISBN 0-939594-22-6 DDC 709/.2
20
N6537.T96 A4 1990
NYPL [3-MCX T965 90-11580]

The Cycladic spirit . Renfrew, Colin, 1937- New
York , 1991. p. cm. ISBN 0-8109-3169-9 DDC
732/.3/093915 20
NB130.C78 R4 1991

CYCLISTS - COSTUME - HISTORY -
EXHIBITIONS.
Fiets en mode . [Netherlands] 1966
(Ijsselstein : Drukkerij De Kroon) 1 v.
(unpaged) : *NYPL [3-MMED 91-294]*

Cygnaeuksen galleria. Löfgren, Erik Johan,
1825-1884. Erik Johan Löfgren . Helsinki ,
1989. 1 v. (unpaged) : ISBN 951-9075-31-3
ND955.F53 L642 1989

Cyphers, Peggy, 1954-
Peggy Cyphers : new paintings : April 1990 /
essays by Robert C. Morgan and Duncan
Smith. New York : E.M. Donahue Gallery,
[1990] [12] p. : ill. ; 23 cm.
1. Cyphers, Peggy, 1954- - Exhibitions. I. E. M.
Donahue Gallery. II. Title.
NYPL [3-MCX C996 91-6446]

CYPHERS, PEGGY, 1954- - EXHIBITIONS.
Cyphers, Peggy, 1954- Peggy Cyphers . New
York [1990] [12] p. :
NYPL [3-MCX C996 91-6446]

CYPRIOTE POTTERY. see POTTERY,
CYPRIOTE.

Cyprus : 2500 years of cartography. Nicosia :
Bank of Cyprus Cultural Foundation, 1986. 12
p., [1] folded leaf of plates : col. maps ; 30 cm.
Cover title. Maps selected from the collections of the
Bank of Cyprus Cultural Foundation, and text written
by A.J. Hadjipaschalis. Includes bibliographical
references.
1. Trapeza Kyprou. Politistiko Hidryma - Catalogs. 2.
Cartography - Cyprus - History. 3. Cyprus - Maps -
History. I. Hadjipaschalis, A. J.
NYPL [Map Div. 90-11332]

CYPRUS - MAPS - HISTORY.
Cyprus . Nicosia , 1986. 12 p., [1] folded leaf
of plates : *NYPL [Map Div. 90-11332]*

Cytherea studiosorum. Rollos, Peter, 17th cent.
Vita Corneliana, sive Cytherea studiosorum .
[S.l.] 1639. [4] p., 58 [i.e. 59] leaves of plates :
NE654.R57 A4 1639

Czartoryska, Urszula. Devětsil (Society)
Devětsil . Łódź [1989]. 105 p. :
N6831.5.D48 D4 1989

CZECH ART. see ART, CZECH.

Czech art in the velvet revolution : December 15,
1990-April 7, 1991. Roslyn Harbor, N.Y. :
Nassau County Museum of Art, 1990. 111 p. :
ill. (some col.) ; 31 cm. Errata slip inserted.
1. Art, Czech - Exhibitions. 2. Art, Modern - 20th
century - Czechoslovakia - Exhibitions. I. Nassau
County Museum of Art.
N6831 .C93 1990
NYPL [3-MAM+ 91-7464]

Czech avant-garde of the 1920s and 30s.
Devětsil . [Oxford] , London , c1990. 115 p. :
ISBN 0-905836-70-7
NYPL [3-MAM+ 90-12482]

CZECH CHILDREN'S LITERATURE. see
CHILDREN'S LITERATURE, CZECH.

CZECH ILLUMINATION OF BOOKS AND
MANUSCRIPTS. see ILLUMINATION
OF BOOKS AND MANUSCRIPTS,
CZECH.

CZECH SCULPTURE. see SCULPTURE,
CZECH.

Czech Socialist Republic (Czechoslovakia).
Ministerstvo kultury. Maďarské výtvarné
umění XX. století (1945-1988) . V Praze ,
1989. 40 p. : ISBN 80-7035-009-1 :
N6820 .M25 1989

Czecho-Slovak Expeditionary Force. see Legie
česká.

Czechoslovak legions. see Legie česká.

CZECHOSLOVAKIA - DESCRIPTION AND
TRAVEL - GUIDE-BOOKS.
Mapa hradů a zámků Československé republiky
/. [Praha] , 1959. 80 p., [16] p. of plates :
NYPL [Map Div. 88-934]

CZECHOSLOVAKIA IN ART,
Vlk, Miloslav. Carl Croll /. [Ústí nad Labem] ,
1989. 131 p. : ISBN 80-7047-018-6 :
ND534.5.C76 V58 1989

Czechoslovakia. Ústřední správa geodésie a
kartografie. Mapa hradů a zámků
Československé republiky /. [Praha] , 1959. 80
p., [16] p. of plates : *NYPL [Map Div. 88-934]*

Czechoslovakian perfume bottles and boudoir
accessories /. North, Jacquelyne Y. Jones.
Marietta, Ohio , c1990. 128 p. : ISBN
0-915410-65-6 (hardbound) DDC
748.8/2/09437090407520
NK5440.B65 N67 1990

Czeike, Felix. Historischer Atlas von Wien /.
Wien , 1981- 1 atlas (v. (loose-leaf) : ISBN
3-7141-6044-2 (1. Lfg.) DDC 911/.43613 19
G1939.V4S1 H5 1981
NYPL [Map Div. 90-56]

Czernin, Franz Josef.
Herbert Brandl. 1988. Oberhuber, Konrad.
Herbert Brandl, Josef Danner, Otto Zitko /
Konrad Oberhuber. Wien , 1988. 4 v. in 1 :
NYPL [3-MCK B818 90-8683]

Czernohaus, Karola. Delphindarstellungen von der
minoischen bis zur geometrischen Zeit / von
Karola Czernohaus. Göteborg : P. Aström,
1988. 235, 111 p., 121 p. of plates : ill. ; 21 cm.
(Studies in Mediterranean archaeology and literature.
Pocket-book . 67) Bibliography: p. 220-235. ISBN
91-86098-76-4
1. Art, Minoan - Themes, motives. 2. Art, Myceanean -
Themes, motives. 3. Dolphins. 4. Animals in art. 5.
Animals in literature. 6. Dolphins - Folklore. I. Title. II.
Series. NYPL [3-MAH 90-10819]

Czernovsky, Michaela. Sammlung Rudi Molacek .
Graz [1990] 1 v. (unpaged) : DDC
709/.436/0744365 20
N6808 .S23 1990

Czeschka, Carl Otto, 1878-1960.
Fanelli, Giovanni. Carl Otto Czeschka . Firenze
[1990?] 127 p. : ISBN 88-7737-079-3
NYPL [MDG (Czeschka) 91-3839]

CZESCHKA, CARL OTTO, 1878-1960 -
CATALOGS.
Fanelli, Giovanni. Carl Otto Czeschka . Firenze
[1990?] 127 p. : ISBN 88-7737-079-3
NYPL [MDG (Czeschka) 91-3839]

Czestochowski, Joseph S.
Arthur B. Davies : a catalogue raisonné of the
prints / Joseph S. Czestochowski. Newark :
University of Delaware Press ; London :
Associated University Presses, c1987. 258 p.,
[12] p. of plates : ill. (some col.) ; 32 cm. (An
American art journal/Kennedy Galleries book) Includes
index. Bibliography: p. 251-254. ISBN 0-87413-242-8
DDC 769.92/4 19
1. Davies, Arthur B. (Arthur Bowen), 1862-1928 -
Catalogues raisonnés. I. Title. II. Series.
NE539.D3 A4 1987
NYPL [MDG+ (Davies) 87-4836]

Grant Wood : prints and drawings / Joseph S.
Czestochowski. Cedar Rapids, Iowa : Cedar
Rapids Museum of Art, c1991. p. cm. Includes
bibliographical references and index. ISBN
0-942982-10-X DDC 760/.092 20
1. Wood, Grant 1892-1942 - Catalogues raisonnés. I.
Cedar Rapids Art Association. II. Title.
NE2312.W66 A4 1991

Czóbel, Béla, 1883-
Homage to Béla Czóbel, 1883-1976 : paintings,
watercolors, drawings. Chicago, Ill. : R.S.
Johnson Fine Art, 1990. 64 p. : ill. ; 25 cm.
1. Czóbel, Béla, 1883- - Exhibitions. I. R. S. Johnson
Fine Art. II. Title.
NYPL [3-MCZ C998 91-6706]

CZÓBEL, BÉLA, 1883- - EXHIBITIONS.
Czóbel, Béla, 1883- Homage to Béla Czóbel,
1883-1976 . Chicago, Ill. , 1990. 64 p. :
NYPL [3-MCZ C998 91-6706]

CZWG (FIRM) - EXHIBITIONS.
Sudjic, Deyan. English extremists . London ,
c1988. 112 p. : ISBN 0-947795-68-5 (pbk.)
     NYPL [3-MQWK 89-4432]

Czymmek, Götz. Landschaft im Licht . Köln ,
Zürich , c1990. 519 p. : DDC
     759.05/4/074435514 20
ND192.I4 L27 1990
     NYPL [3-MC+ 91-5272]

Đ Báo chí văn ngh Đ Hà N S 1989. 35 p. ; 19
cm. Includes bibliographical references.
   1. Mass media and the arts - Vietnam. I. Title.
NX180.M3 D6 1989

D. A. A. D. see Deutscher Akademischer
Austauschdienst.

Đ Motifs d'art décoratif lao. [Vientiane] : Kasüang
Sinlapäk [1959?] [100] p. : chiefly ill. ; 28 cm.
Captions and preface in French and Lao. Cover title.
At head of title: Pharätsa'änächak Läo. Illustrations of
principal decorative motifs used in Lao architecture.
   1. Decoration and ornament, Architectural - Laos -
Themes, motives. I. Laos. Ministère des beaux-arts. II.
Title: Motifs d'art décoratif lao.
NA3578.6.L3 D64 1959

The D.R. Sheumack collection : eighty years of
Australian painting / compiled by Robyn
Christie and Justin Miller. Paddington, NSW :
Sotheby's Australia, 1988. [153] p. : col. ill.,
ports. ; 28 cm. Ill. on lining papers. Includes index.
   1. Sheumack, Donald R. - Art collections. 2. Art -
Private collections - Australia. I. Christie, Robyn. II.
Miller, Justin. III. Sotheby & Co. (Australia). IV. Title:
Eighty years of Australian painting.
     NYPL [3-MCY 89-11925]

Da Ficarolo, Niccolò. see Niccolò da Ficarolo,
12th cent.

Da Leonardo a Rembrandt. English. From
Leonardo to Rembrandt : drawings from the
Royal Library of Turin / [edited] by Gianni
Carlo Sciolla. Torino : U. Allemandi, c1990.
409 p. : ill. (some col.) ; 35 cm. Translation of:
Da Leonardo a Rembrandt : disegni della Biblioteca
reale di Torino. Exhibition catalog. Includes
bibliographical references (p. 389-408) and index.
   ISBN 88-422-0260-6
   1. Biblioteca di S.M. il re (Turin, Italy) - Exhibitions. 2.
Drawing, European - Exhibitions. 3. Drawing - Italy -
Turin - Exhibitions. I. Sciolla, Gianni Carlo. II.
Biblioteca di S.M. il re (Turin, Italy).
     NYPL [3-MBH+ 91-5774]

Da van Gogh a Picasso, Da Kandinsky a
Pollock : il percorso dell'arte moderna / a cura
di Thomas Krens, con Germano Celant, Lisa
Dennison. Milano : Bompiani, c1990. 391 p. :
ill. (some col.) ; 29 cm. At head of title: Solomon
R. Guggenheim Museum, New York, Thannhauser
Collection. Catalog of an exhibition held at the Palazzo
Grassi, Venice. Includes bibiliographical references and
index. DDC 709/.04/10744531 20
   1. Art, Modern - 20th century - Exhibitions. 2.
Thannhauser, Justin, 1892-1976 - Art collections -
Exhibitions. 3. Art - Private collections - New York
(N.Y.) - Exhibitions. 4. Solomon R. Guggenheim
Museum - Exhibitions. I. Krens, Thomas. II. Celant,
German. III. Dennison, Lisa. IV. Solomon R.
Guggenheim Museum. V. Palazzo Grassi.
N6488.5.T55 D3 1990

Daad. see Deutscher Akademischer
Austauschdienst.

Dabrowski, Magdalena. Liubov Popova /
Magdalena Dabrowski. New York : Museum of
Modern Art : distributed by H.N. Abrams,
c1991. 135 p. : ill. (some col.) ; 31 cm. Catalog
of an exhibition held at the Museum of Modern Art,
Feb. 13-Apr. 23, 1991, and at three other museums
through Feb. 16, 1992. Includes bibliographical
references (p. 125). ISBN 0-87070-567-9 (MoMA :
hard)
   1. Popova, Liubov - Exhibitions. I. Popova, Liubov. II.
Museum of Modern Art (New York, N.Y.).
     NYPL [3-MCZ+ P828 91-5571]

Dachy, Marc.
   [Journal du mouvement Dada. English]
     The Dada movement, 1915-1923 / by Marc
Dachy. Geneva : Skira ; New York : Rizzoli,
1990. 230 p. : ill. (some col.) ; 36 cm.
Translation of: Journal du mouvement Dada. Includes
bibliographical references (p. 217-222) and index.
ISBN 0-8478-1110-7 DDC 700/.9/04 20

   1. Dadaism. 2. Arts, Modern - 20th century. I. Title.
NX456.5.D3 D32513 1990
     NYPL [3-MAL+ 91-2295]

DACIAN WAR, 1ST, 101-102.
Cichorius, Conrad, 1863- Trajan's Column .
Gloucester, UK , Wolfboro, N.H., USA , 1988.
xviii, 339 p. [94] p. of plates : ISBN
   0-86299-467-5 : DDC 937/.07 19
DG59.D3 C63 1988
     NYPL [3-MGH 91-6949]

DACIAN WAR, 2ND, 105-106.
Cichorius, Conrad, 1863- Trajan's Column .
Gloucester, UK , Wolfboro, N.H., USA , 1988.
xviii, 339 p. [94] p. of plates : ISBN
   0-86299-467-5 : DDC 937/.07 19
DG59.D3 C63 1988
     NYPL [3-MGH 91-6949]

Dada in Zürich. Als Dada begann . [Zürich] ,
c1957. 92 p. :   *NYPL [3-MAM 90-7093]*

The Dada movement, 1915-1923 /. Dachy, Marc.
[Journal du mouvement Dada. English.]
Geneva , New York , 1990. 230 p. : ISBN
   0-8478-1110-7 DDC 700/.9/04 20
NX456.5.D3 D32513 1990
     NYPL [3-MAL+ 91-2295]

DADAISM.
Dachy, Marc. [Journal du mouvement Dada.
English.] The Dada movement, 1915-1923 /.
Geneva , New York , 1990. 230 p. : ISBN
   0-8478-1110-7 DDC 700/.9/04 20
NX456.5.D3 D32513 1990
     NYPL [3-MAL+ 91-2295]

Huelsenbeck, Richard, 1892-1974. Memoirs of a
Dada drummer /. Berkeley , 1991. liv, 202 p.,
[12] p. of plates : ISBN 0-520-07370-3 (pbk.)
   DDC 700 20
NX600.D3 H79 1991   *NYPL [MAL 91-7694]*

DADAISM - CANADA.
Groh, Klaus, 1936- Der neue Dadaismus in
Nordamerika /. Augsburg , 1979. 221 p. :
   ISBN 3-87512-113-9
     NYPL [3-MAL 90-7185]

DADAISM - EXHIBITIONS.
The Avant-garde and the text . Providence, RI ,
c1988. p. 306-507 :   *NYPL [MDT 91-5721]*

Tabu Dada . Bern , c1983. 139 p. : DDC
   709/.04/062074094945 19
N6853.C86 A4 1983
     NYPL [3-MCZ C946 83-2831]

DADAISM - GERMANY - EXHIBITIONS.
Höch, Hannah, 1889- Hannah Höch
1889-1978 . [Berlin] , 1989. 223, [24] p. :
   ISBN 3-87024-156-X (Argon)
     NYPL [3-MCK H691 90-12356]

DADAISM - SWITZERLAND - ZURICH.
Als Dada begann . [Zürich] , c1957. 92 p. :
     NYPL [3-MAM 90-7093]

DADAISM - UNITED STATES.
Groh, Klaus, 1936- Der neue Dadaismus in
Nordamerika /. Augsburg , 1979. 221 p. :
   ISBN 3-87512-113-9
     NYPL [3-MAL 90-7185]

DADE COUNTY, FLA. - MAPS.
(1991) Dolph's street atlas of Dade County,
Florida. Fort Lauderdale, Florida , 1991. 141
p. :   *NYPL [Map Div. 91-7313]*

DAEDALUS (GREEK MYTHOLOGY) -
   INFLUENCE.
Morris, Sarah P., 1954- Daidalos and the
origins of Greek art /. Princeton, N.J. , 1992.
p. cm. ISBN 0-691-03599-7 : DDC 700/.938 20
N5633 .M67 1992

Daftari, Fereshteh. The influence of Persian art
on Gauguin, Matisse, and Kandinsky /
Fereshteh Daftari. New York : Garland Pub.,
1991. p. cm. (Garland publications in the fine arts)
Thesis (Ph.D.)--Columbia University, 1988. Includes
bibliographical references. ISBN 0-8153-0715-2 (alk.
paper) DDC 709/.2/24 20
   1. Art, Iranian - Influence. 2. Exoticism in art - Europe.
3. Gauguin, Paul, 1848-1903 - Criticism and
interpretation. 4. Matisse, Henri, 1869-1954 - Criticism
and interpretation. 5. Kandinsky, Wassily, 1866-1944 -
Criticism and interpretation. I. Title. II. Series.
N7280 .D34 1991

D'Agapeyeff, A. (Alexander) Maps / Alexander
D'Agapeyeff and E. C. R. Hadfield. 2d ed.
London : Geoffrey Cumberlege, Oxford
University Press, 1950 (1953 printing) 199 p.,

[8] leaves of plates : ill. ; 20 cm. (Compass books.
no.3) Bibliography: p.195.
   I. Hadfield, Charles, 1909-. II. Title.
     NYPL [Map Div. 91-1013]

Dagens billeder, et panorama /. Nielsen, Palle,
1920- [Copenhagen] , c1990. ca. 150 p. of
plates : ISBN 87-7385-166-3
NC275.N5 A4 1990

DAGUERREOTYPE - MARYLAND -
   BALTIMORE - HISTORY.
Kelbaugh, Ross J. Supplemental directory of
Baltimore daguerreotypists /. Baltimore, Md. ,
1989. vii p., 43 leaves ; ISBN 0-914931-01-6
     NYPL [3-MFW 91-7016]

Dahl, Bjørn Westerbeek. Kongelige
Kobberstiksamling (Statens museum for kunst)
Von Abildgaard bis Marstrand . [München] ,
1985. 87 p., 114 p. of plates : DDC 741.9489/1
   19
NC274.C67 K66 1985
     NYPL [3-MBH 90-12465]

Dahl, Taffy. Kaufman, Donald. Color
atmospheres . New York , 1991. p. cm. ISBN
0-517-57660-0 : DDC 728 20
NK2115.5.C6 K38 1991

Dahm, Jorge.
Jorge Dahm : retrospectiva : óleos, dibujos,
collage : un homenaje de ICP, Instituto
Cultural, I. Municipalidad de Providencia /
[redacción, Soledad Crespo]. [Santiago, Chile] :
El Instituto, [1990?] 1 v. (unpaged) : ill. (some
col.) ; 17 x 21 cm. Catalog of an exhibit, Nov. 6-30,
[1990?]. Includes bibliographical references. DDC
759.983 20
   1. Dahm, Jorge - Exhibitions. I. Crespo, Soledad. II.
Providencia (Santiago, Chile). Instituto Cultural. III.
Title.
ND369.D35 A4 1990

DAHM, JORGE - EXHIBITIONS.
Dahm, Jorge. Jorge Dahm . [Santiago, Chile]
[1990?] 1 v. (unpaged) : DDC 759.983 20
ND369.D35 A4 1990

Dahn, Walter, 1954-
Walter Dahn : Kunstverein München, 1989.
München : Der Kunstverein, c1989. 8, [44] p. :
ill. ; 30 cm. Exhibition held June 15-July 16, 1989.
ISBN 3-923357-25-7
   1. Dahn, Walter, 1954- - Exhibitions. I. Kunstverein
München. II. Title.
IN PROCESS (ONLINE)
     NYPL [3-MCK+ D132 91-7406]

DAHN, WALTER, 1954- - EXHIBITIONS.
Dahn, Walter, 1954- Walter Dahn . München ,
c1989. 8, [44] p. : ISBN 3-923357-25-7
IN PROCESS (ONLINE)
     NYPL [3-MCK+ D132 91-7406]

Daidalos and the origins of Greek art /. Morris,
Sarah P., 1954- Princeton, N.J. , 1992. p. cm.
   ISBN 0-691-03599-7 : DDC 700/.938 20
N5633 .M67 1992

DAIMYO - EXHIBITIONS.
Japan . New York , c1988. xi, 402 p. : ISBN
0-8076-1214-6 DDC 952/.00740153 19
DS827.D34 J37 1988
     NYPL [3-MAG+ 89-864]

Dairy Barn Quilt National. The New quilt 1 .
Newtown, CT , c1991. p. cm. ISBN
   0-942391-99-3 : DDC 746.9/7/0904807477197
   20
NK9110 .N4 1991

Dairy Barn Southeastern Ohio Cultural Arts
   Center. The New quilt 1 . Newtown, CT ,
c1991. p. cm. ISBN 0-942391-99-3 : DDC
   746.9/7/0904807477197 20
NK9110 .N4 1991

Daix, Pierre. Picasso / Pierre Daix. [Paris] :
Chêne, c1990. 159, [1] p. : ill. (some col.) ; 33
cm. (Profils de l'art) Includes bibliographical references
(p. [160]) and index. ISBN 2-85108-654-5 : DDC
709/.2 B 20
   1. Picasso, Pablo, 1881-1973. 2. Artists - France -
Biography. I. Picasso, Pablo, 1881-1973. II. Title. III.
Series.
N6853.P5 D26 1990

DAKOTA INDIANS - ARTS.
Huseboe, Arthur R., 1931- An illustrated
history of the arts in South Dakota /. Sioux
Falls, S.D. , 1989. xiii, 396 p. : ISBN
   0-931170-44-3 : DDC 700/.9783 20
NX510.S8 H87 1989

Dakshiṇa Kosala kī kalā .

Dakshiṇa Kosala kī kalā . Yadu, Hemūlāla, 1953- Naī Dillī , 1990. xiv, 200 p., [29] p. of plates :
NB1912.H55 Y33 1990

Dal Co, Francesco, 1945- Figures of architecture and thought : German architectural culture 1890-1920 / Francesco Dal Co. New York : Rizzoli, 1990. 344 p. : ill. ; 23 cm. (Rizzoli Essays on architecture . 2) "Chapters 1-4 translated from the Itatian by Stephen Sartarelli"--t.p. verso.
ISBN 0-8478-0654-5 (pbk.) : DDC 720/.943 19
1. Architecture - Germany. 2. Architecture, Modern - 19th century - Germany. 3. Architecture, Modern - 20th century - Germany. 4. Modernism (Art) - Influence. 5. Architecture - Philosophy. I. Title. II. Series.
NA1067 .D35 1990
      NYPL [3-MQWD 90-10690]

Dal Fabbro, Armando. La Geometria in funzione nell'architettura e nella costruzione della città /. Venezia , c1985. 157 p. : ISBN 88-85067-29-8
NA2760 .G38 1985
      NYPL [3-MQD+ 90-12625]

Dal monastero di S. Ambrogio all'Università Cattolica / a cura di Maria Luisa Gatti Perer. Milano : Vita e pensiero, 1990. 301 p. : ill. ; 32 cm. ISBN 88-343-3007-2
1. Monastero di S. Ambrogio (Milan, Italy). I. Gatti Perer, Maria Luisa.
IN PROCESS (ONLINE)
      NYPL [3-MRBD+ 91-5237]

Dal Poggetto, Paolo. Firenze restaura . Firenze , 1973, c1972. 154 p., [168] p. of plates :
      NYPL [3-MBK 90-5749]

DAL POZZO, CASSIANO, 1588-1657 - ART COLLECTIONS - CONGRESSES.
Cassiano dal Pozzo . Roma , c1989. 260 p. :
      NYPL [3-MAVC 90-12003]

Dal progetto al produtto .
(5) Casciani, Stefano, 1955- Arte industriale . Milano , c1988. 194 p. : ISBN 88-85684-21-1
      NYPL [3-MNE+ 90-12329]

Dalaretos, Nikos M. Sperantzas, V. (Vasilēs) V. Sperantzas /. Kea Kykladōn [1990] 143 p. :
N6903.S64 A4 1990

Daley, Susan, 1953- Gross, Steve. Old houses /. New York , 1991. n. cm. ISBN 1-556-70184-5 :
DDC 728/.0973 20
NA7205 .G764 1991

Dalhousie University. School of Library Service. A Checklist of Canadian copyright deposits in the British Museum, 1895-1923 /. Halifax, N.S., Canada , 1984- v. : ISBN 0-7703-0179-7
(pbk. - v. 1) : DDC 015.71 19
Z1365 .C48 1984   **NYPL [Map Div. 85-549]**

Dali . Carol, Márius. Esplugues de Llobregat, Barcelona , 1990. 204 p., [16] p. of plates :
ISBN 84-01-35171-5 DDC 759.6 B 20
N7113.D3 C36 1990

Dali . Dali, Salvador, 1904- Boston , c1991. 184 p. : ISBN 0-8212-1810-7 (cloth trade ed.) : DDC 759.6 20
N7113.D3 A4 1991

Dali, Salvador, 1904-
Les cocus du vieil art moderne / Salvador Dalí. Paris : B. Grasset, [1989], c1956. 115 p. : ill. ; 19 cm. (Les Cahiers rouges, 0756-7170 . 107) ISBN 2-246-42142-X :
I. Title.   **NYPL [3-MCQ D14 91-5414]**

Dali : the Salvador Dali Museum collection / foreword by A. Reynolds Morse ; introduction by Robert S. Lubar.1st ed. Boston : Little, Brown, c1991. 184 p. : chiefly ill. (some col.) ; 24 x 29 cm. "A Bulfinch Press book." Includes bibliographical references (p. 17-18). ISBN 0-8212-1810-7 (cloth trade ed.) : DDC 759.6 20
1. Dali, Salvador, 1904- - Catalogs. 2. Morse, Albert Reynolds, 1914- - Art collections - Catalogs. 3. Art - Private collections - Ohio - Cleveland - Catalogs. 4. Salvador Dali Museum - Catalogs. I. Salvador Dali Museum. II. Title.
N7113.D3 A4 1991

Dedicatòries / Salvador Dalí. Barcelona : Editorial Mediterrània, [1990] 223 p. : chiefly ill. (some col.) ; 22 cm. (Col·lecció Portlligat . 3) Introductory matter also in English. ISBN 84-85984-55-2
1. Dalí, Salvador, 1904- - Autographs. I. Title.
NC287.D3 A4 1990
      NYPL [3-MCQ D14 91-4506]

Maur, Karin von, 1938- Salvador Dali,

1904-1989 /. Stuttgart , c1989. xxxix, 519 p. :
ISBN 3-7757-0275-X
      NYPL [3-MCQ+ D14 89-22881]

Salvador Dali. Montreal, Quebec, Canada : Montreal Museum of Fine Arts, c1990. 223 p. : ill. (some col.) ; 32 cm. Catalogue of an exhibition held 04/27-07/29/90 at the Montreal Museum of Fine Arts. Includes bibliographical references (p. 209-212) and index. ISBN 2-89192-129-1 : DDC 709/.2 20
1. Dalí, Salvador, 1904- - Exhibitions. I. Montreal Museum of Fine Arts. II. Title.
N7113.D3 A4 1990

Salvador Dali / [exhibition ... organized by Pierre Théberge]. Montreal : The Montreal Museum of Fine Arts, c1990. 223 p. : ill. (some col.) ; 32 cm. Published on the occasion of an exhibition held at the Montreal Museum of Fine Arts, Apr. 27-July 29, 1990. Bibliography: p. 211-212.
ISBN 2-89192-129-1
1. Dalí, Salvador, 1904- - Exhibitions. I. Théberge, Pierre.   **NYPL [3-MCQ+ D14 91-6776]**

DALI, SALVADOR, 1904-
Carol, Márius. Dalí . Esplugues de Llobregat, Barcelona , 1990. 204 p., [16] p. of plates :
ISBN 84-01-35171-5 DDC 759.6 B 20
N7113.D3 C36 1990

DALI, SALVADOR, 1904- - CATALOGS.
Dali, Salvador, 1904- Dali . Boston , c1991. 184 p. : ISBN 0-8212-1810-7 (cloth trade ed.) : DDC 759.6 20
N7113.D3 A4 1991

DALÍ, SALVADOR, 1904- - EXHIBITIONS.
Dali, Salvador, 1904- Salvador Dali. Montreal, Quebec, Canada , c1990. 223 p. : ISBN 2-89192-129-1 : DDC 709/.2 20
N7113.D3 A4 1990

Dali, Salvador, 1904- Salvador Dali /. Montreal , c1990. 223 p. : ISBN 2-89192-129-1
      NYPL [3-MCQ+ D14 91-6776]

Maur, Karin von, 1938- Salvador Dali, 1904-1989 /. Stuttgart , c1989. xxxix, 519 p. :
ISBN 3-7757-0275-X
      NYPL [3-MCQ+ D14 89-22881]

DALÍ, SALVADOR, 1904- - AUTOGRAPHS.
Dali, Salvador, 1904- Dedicatòries /. Barcelona [1990] 223 p. : ISBN 84-85984-55-2
NC287.D3 A4 1990
      NYPL [3-MCQ D14 91-4506]

Dalla Chiesa, Giovanna. De Chirico scultore / a cura di Giovanna dalla Chiesa. Milano : G. Mondadori, c1988. 111 p. : ill. (some col.), ports. ; 30 cm. Includes bibliographical references.
ISBN 88-374-1036-0
1. De Chirico, Giorgio, 1888-. I. De Chirico, Giorgio, 1888-. II. Title.
      NYPL [3-MGO+ (De Chirico) 91-6552]

Dalla pittura al pittore . Ragghianti, Carlo Ludovico. Milano , c1987. 166 p. :
      NYPL [3-MCF+ F211 90-12787]

Dallal, Alberto. Zalce, Alfredo, 1908- Alfredo Zalce /. Morelia, Michoacán , 1982. xxviii, 130 p. :
N6559.Z35 A4 1982

Dall'Albornoz all'età dei Borgia : questioni di cultura figurativa nell'Umbria meridionale : atti del convegno di studi, Amelia, Teatro Sociale, 1-2-3 ottobre 1987 / contributi di Federico Zeri ... [et al.] ; [cura del volume e coordinamento redazionale, Giorgio Antonucci].2. ed. Todi : Ediart, 1990. 385 p., [19] p. of plates : ill. (some col.) ; 30 cm. Includes bibliographical references and index. ISBN 88-85311-01-6 DDC 709/.45/65 20
1. Art, Italian - Italy - Umbria - Congresses. 2. Art, Gothic - Italy - Umbria - Congresses. 3. Art, Renaissance - Italy - Umbria - Congresses. I. Zeri, Federico. II. Antonucci, Giorgio. III. Teatro sociale (Amelia, Italy).
N6919.U5 D35 1990

Dall'art déco al Novecento /. Borsi, Franco. Firenze , c1983. 250 p., [4] p. of plates : DDC 709/.04/012 19
N6494.A7 B67 1983
      NYPL [3-MAL 91-4191]

Dallas Museum of Art. Black art . Dallas, Tex. , New York , c1989. 305 p. : ISBN 0-8109-3104-4 (Abrams) : DDC 704/.0396073/07473 20
N6538.N5 B525 1989   **NYPL [Sc G 90-16]**

Dallas. Southern Methodist University. Meadows Museum. see Meadows Museum.

Dallas. Valley House Gallery. see Valley House Gallery.

DALMATIA (CROATIA) - ART.
Höfler, Janez. Die Kunst Dalmatiens . Graz , 1989. 338 p. : ISBN 3-201-01466-4
      NYPL [3-MAM+ 90-8024]

Damgård-Sørensen, Henning. Den Åbne dør, polsk nutidskunst, 1989 . [Copenhagen , 1989] 56 p. : ISBN 87-88944-07-7
N7255.P6 A36 1989

Damian, Raymond. Deschênes-Damian, Luce. Atlas transcanadien /. Montréal , c1988. 1 atlas (145 p.) : ISBN 2-7601-1923-8 :
      NYPL [Map Div. 91-7753]

Damiani, Sandro. Mostra di stampe italiane del Seicento . [Brescia , 1972] 144 p. :
      NYPL [MDBF 91-820]

D'Amicone, Elvira. Beyond the pyramids . Atlanta, Ga. , c1990. 95 p. :
      NYPL [3-MAE 91-4240]

Damigella, Anna Maria. Barbera, Gioacchino. I bozzetti di Sartorio per il Duomo di Messina /. Palermo , c1989. 158 p. : ISBN 88-7681-048-X :
NC257.S2685 B37 1989

Damm, Hans. Ornament und Plastic fremder Völker. English. Ornament and sculpture in primitive society. New York [1966] [138] p. :
DDC 709.011
N7380 .O713 1966b
      NYPL [3-MADF 90-6405]

Dammé, Claude Jacques. Goüin, Henry. Royaumont . [Paris] , c1990. 94 p. : ISBN 2-905674-28-3 DDC 726/.7/0944367 20
NA5551.R65 G64 1990

Dampierre, Florence de. The decorator / Florence de Dampierre ; principal photography by Antoine Bootz. New York : Rizzoli, 1989. 255 p. : chiefly ill. (some col.) ; 32 cm. ISBN 0-08-478118-2 DDC 729/.092/2 B 20
1. Interior decorators - Biography. 2. Interior decoration - History - 20th century. I. Title.
NK2115.8 .D36 1989
      NYPL [3-MLO+ 91-3369]

Damsch-Wiehager, Renate. Henderikse, Jan, 1937- Modern times . Kiel , c1990. 65 p. :
      NYPL [MFX (Henderikse) 91-4590]

Dan Fern. Fern, Dan, 1945- London , 1990. 108 p. : ISBN 1-85454-149-8 (pbk.) DDC 760.092 20
      NYPL [3-MDWS (Fern) 91-6335]

Dana, Djefry W. (Djefry Wahjudy) Ciri perancangan kota Bandung / Djefry W. Dana. Jakarta : Gramedia Pustaka Utama, 1990. xiv, 143 p. : ill., maps ; 21 cm. Includes bibliographical references (p. 135-136). Includes index. Characteristic of architectural planning in Bandung city. ISBN 979-403-916-0
1. City planning - Indonesia - Bandung. 2. Architecture - Indonesia - Bandung - Themes, motives. I. Title.
NA9260.B35 D35 1990

Danbolt, Gunnar. Gaustad, Randi, 1942- Samtidskeramikk . Oslo , c1990. 127 p. : ISBN 82-09-10613-9
NK4119 .G38 1990

DANCE BAND MUSIC. see BIG BAND MUSIC.

DANCE IN ART.
Nitschke, August, 1926- Körper in Bewegung . Stuttgart , c1989. 399 p. : ISBN 3-7831-0955-8 DDC 704.9/42 20
N7625.5 .N58 1989

DANCE OF DEATH.
Der Totentanz auf der Spreuerbrücke in Luzern =. Luzern [195-?] [64] p. :
      NYPL [3-MBO 89-20195]

DANCE OF DEATH - EXHIBITIONS.
Totentanzfolgen . Braunschweig , 1989. 98 p. ;
ISBN 3-927288-04-7
IN PROCESS (ONLINE)
      NYPL [3-MAMZ 90-12755]

The dance of the seven seals, and other cartoons /. Pope, Kevin. New York , 1991. n. cm. ISBN 0-312-05828-4 : DDC 741.5/973 20
NC1429.P645 A4 1991

DANCING FOR CHILDREN - STUDY AND TEACHING (ELEMENTARY)
Lynch-Fraser, Diane. Playdancing . Pennington, NJ , c1991. xi, 122 p. : ISBN 0-87127-152-4

(pbk.) : DDC 372.86 20
GV452 .L97 1990   **NYPL [MGSB 91-722]**

DANCING FOR CHILDREN - STUDY AND
TEACHING (PRESCHOOL)
Lynch-Fraser, Diane. Playdancing . Pennington,
NJ , c1991. xi, 122 p. : ISBN 0-87127-152-4
(pbk.) : DDC 372.86 20
GV452 .L97 1990   **NYPL [MGSB 91-722]**

The dancing goddess . Göttner-Abendroth, Heide,
1941- [Tanzende Göttin. English.] Boston ,
c1991. p. cm. ISBN 0-8070-6753-9 (alk.) DDC
700/.1/03 20
NX180.F4 G613 1991

DANCING IN ART.
La Danza en la escultura de la India. Buenos
Aires , 1947. 9 p., 20 p. of plates :
                        NYPL [3-MGI 91-663]

Danco, Léon A., 1923- Someday, it'll all be--
whos's? / Léon Danco, Donald J. Jonovic.
Cleveland : Center for Family Business ; Family
Business Management Services, c1990. vi, 196
p. : ill. ; 24 cm. "Joint publication of the University
Press ... Cleveland, Ohio and Jamieson Press ...
Cleveland, Ohio"--T.p. verso ISBN 0-915607-09-3
(Jamieson) : DDC 741.5/973 20
1. Family-owned business enterprises - Caricatures and
cartoons. 2. American wit and humor, Pictorial. I.
Jonovic, Donald J., 1943-. II. Title.
NC1429.D2344 A4 1990

Danenberg Galleries. see Bernard Danenberg
Galleries.

DANESE (FIRM)
Casciani, Stefano, 1955- Arte industriale .
Milano , c1988. 194 p. : ISBN 88-85684-21-1
                    NYPL [3-MNE+ 90-12329]

DANESE (FIRM) - EXHIBITIONS.
Design, Kunst, Spiele . Geisenheim , 1989. 96
p. : ISBN 3-9802208-0-X
                        NYPL [MNE 91-3753]

Danese Milano 1957 bis heute. Design, Kunst,
Spiele . Geisenheim , 1989. 96 p. : ISBN
3-9802208-0-X   **NYPL [MNE 91-3753]**

D'Angela, Cosimo. La Cripta della Cattedrale di
Taranto /. Taranto [1986] 98 p. :
                    NYPL [3-MRBN+ 90-10741]

Daniel Buren . Buren, Daniel. Stuttgart , c1990.
408 p. :
ND553.B984 A4 1990
                    NYPL [3-MCO B952 91-6020]

Daniel-Henry Kahnweiler . Persin, Patrick-Gilles,
1943- Paris , c1990. 251, [5] p. : ISBN
2-907475-03-7 DDC 709/.2 B 20
N8660.K3 P46 1990

Daniel Spoerri /. Hahn, Otto. Paris , c1990. 190
p. : ISBN 2-08-012140-5
                    NYPL [3-MGO (Spoerri) 90-13083]

Daniel Spoerri /. Hahn, Otto. Paris , c1990. 190
p. : ISBN 2-08-012140-5 DDC 709/.2 20
N6853.S6 H34 1990

Danish Committee for Urban History.
Scandinavian atlas of historic towns. Odense ,
1977- portfolios : ISBN 87-7492-216-5 (no. 1)
                    NYPL [Map Div. 82-813]

Danish jewelry. Thage, Jacob. Danske smykker
=. [Copenhagen] , 1990. 191 p. : ISBN
87-7512-366-5 :
NK7358.A1 T48 1990

DANISH PAINTING. see PAINTING,
DANISH.

Danly, Susan.
Pennsylvania Academy of the Fine Arts. Light,
air, and color . Philadelphia, Pa. , c1990. 91 p. :
ISBN 0-943836-13-1 DDC 759.13/074/74811 20
ND212.5.I45 P4 1990
                        NYPL [3-MCW 91-7196]

Pennsylvania Academy of the Fine Arts. Telling
tales . New York, N.Y. , c1991. p. cm. ISBN
0-917418-94-8 DDC 759.13/074/74811 20
ND1451.5 .P46 1991

Danmark. see Denmark.

DANNER, JOSEF - EXHIBITIONS.
Oberhuber, Konrad. Herbert Brandl, Josef
Danner, Otto Zitko /. Wien , 1988. 4 v. in 1 :
                    NYPL [3-MCK B818 90-8683]

Dannheimer, Hermann.
Keramik des Mittelalters aus Bayern: e.
Katalog/ Hermann Dannheimer. Prähistorische

Staatssammlung München. [Zeichn.: I. Mohr u.
a. Fotos: L. Ohlenroth; S. Mulzer]. - Kallmünz
(Opf.) : Lassleben, 1973. 74, 55 p. : numerous
ill., maps, 1 fold. (in pocket) 24 cm. (Kataloge
der Prähistorischen Staatssammlung . Nr. 15) "Beiträge
zur Volkstumsforschung; Bd. 21." At head of title:
Prähistorische Staatssammlung München. Bibliography:
p. 74.
1. Pottery - Germany, West - Bavaria. 2. Bavaria -
Antiquities. I. Title. II. Series.
                        NYPL [L-11 3436 Nr. 15]

Torhalle auf Frauenchiemsee : Zeugnisse zur
Frühgeschichte des Klosters Frauenwörth :
romanische Fresken aus dem Sanktuarium des
Münsters von Frauenwörth : Denkmäler
bayerischer Frömmigkeit aus der Zeit der
Agilolfinger und Karolinger / Hermann
Dannheimer.3., erw. Aufl. München : Schnell &
Steiner, 1983, c1980. 118 p. : ill. (some col.),
geneal. tables, plans ; 24 cm. (Grosse Kunstführer.
83) Grosse Ausstellungsführer ; Bd. 2 Summaries in
English and French. Genealogical tables inserted in rear
pocket. Includes bibliographical references. ISBN
3-7954-0818-0
1. Abtei Frauenwörth. 2. Architecture, Carolingian -
Germany (West) - Chiemsee. 3. Mural painting and
decoration, German - Germany - Chiemsee. 4. Mural
painting and decoration, Romanesque - Germany -
Chiemsee. 5. Decorative arts, Medieval - Germany -
Chiemsee. 6. Church decoration and ornament -
Germany - Chiemsee. I. Series: Grosse
Ausstellungsführer (Prähistorische Staatssamlung
(Bavaria, Germany)) ; Bd. 2. II. Title.
                        NYPL [3-MRBB 91-6996]

Danoff, I. Michael.
Fernand Léger, study for three portraits,
1910-11 / [text by I. Michael Danoff].
[Milwaukee] : Milwaukee Art Center, c1977. 17
p. : ill. ; 28 cm. Cover title. Includes bibliographical
references.
1. Léger, Fernand, 1881-1955 - Criticism and
interpretation. 2. Léger, Fernand, 1881-1955. Essai pour
trois portraits. 3. Milwaukee. Art Center. I. Léger,
Fernand, 1881-1955. II. Title.
                    NYPL [3-MCO L512 90-7194]

Joan Miró / [essay by I. Michael Danoff].
[Milwaukee] : Milwaukee Art Center, 1977. 15
p. : ill. ; 28 cm. Cover title. Includes bibliographical
references.
1. Miró, Joan, 1893-- Criticism and interpretation. 2.
Milwaukee. Art Center. I. Miró, Joan, 1893-. II. Title.
                    NYPL [3-MCQ M67 91-401]

Dans l'amitié de la peinture /. Arland, Marcel,
1899- Paris , c1980. 323 p., [6] leaves of
plates : ISBN 2-903157-07-3 :
ND1142 .A73   **NYPL [3-MBK 81-943]**

Danse macabre. see Dance of death.

Dansk møbelkunst i det tyvende århundrede.
Karlsen, Arne. Dansk møbelkunst i det 20.
århundrede /. København , 1990- v. <1 > :
ISBN 87-7241-677-7 (set)
NK2585 .K37 1990

Dansk møbelkunst i det 20. århundrede /.
Karlsen, Arne. København , 1990- v. <1 > :
ISBN 87-7241-677-7 (set)
NK2585 .K37 1990

Dansk 50-tal : Scandinavian design : [utställning]
7/10-29/11 1981, Nationalmuseum, Stockholm.
Stockholm : Nationalmuseum, 1981. 36, [1] p. :
ill. ; 21 cm. (Nationalmusei utställningskatalog . nr
448) Cover title. Bibliography: p. [37] ISBN
91-7100-198-0
1. Design, Decorative - Denmark - Exhibitions. 2.
Design, Industrial - Denmark - Exhibitions. I.
Nationalmuseum (Sweden).
                        NYPL [3-MNE 90-5648]

Danske kongers kronologiske samling.
Rosenborg Castle . [Copenhagen?] 1973
([Copenhagen?] : J. Jørgensen) 72 p. ;
        NYPL [3-MAVZ (Copenhagen, Denmark)
                                    90-5970]

DANSKE KONGERS KRONOLOGISKE
SAMLING - CATALOGS.
Rosenborg Castle . [Copenhagen?] 1973
([Copenhagen?] : J. Jørgensen) 72 p. ;
        NYPL [3-MAVZ (Copenhagen, Denmark)
                                    90-5970]

Danske kunstindustrimuseum. Salto, Axel,
1889-1961. Det brændende nu, Axel Salto .
[Copenhagen] [1989] 78 p. : ISBN

87-87075-60-1
N7023.S25 A4 1989

Danske smykker =. Thage, Jacob.
[Copenhagen] , 1990. 191 p. : ISBN
87-7512-366-5 :
NK7358.A1 T48 1990

Dante Alighieri, 1265-1321.
DIVINA COMMEDIA - ILLUSTRATIONS.
Botticelli e Dante /. Milano , c1990. 361 p. :
ISBN 88-435-3329-0
N6923.B67 A4 1990
                    NYPL [3-MCF+ B75 91-5452]

DANTE ALIGHIERI, 1265-1321 -
INFLUENCE.
Botticelli e Dante /. Milano , c1990. 361 p. :
ISBN 88-435-3329-0
N6923.B67 A4 1990
                    NYPL [3-MCF+ B75 91-5452]

Schumacher, Thomas L. [Danteum di Terragni.
English.] The Danteum . Princeton, NJ , c1985.
169 p. : ISBN 0-910413-09-6
NA2707.T466 S3713 1985
                    NYPL [3-MQZ (Terragni) 86-3775]

The Danteum . Schumacher, Thomas L.
[Danteum di Terragni. English.] Princeton, NJ ,
c1985. 169 p. : ISBN 0-910413-09-6
NA2707.T466 S3713 1985
                    NYPL [3-MQZ (Terragni) 86-3775]

DANTEUM (ROME, ITALY)
Schumacher, Thomas L. [Danteum di Terragni.
English.] The Danteum . Princeton, NJ , c1985.
169 p. : ISBN 0-910413-09-6
NA2707.T466 S3713 1985
                    NYPL [3-MQZ (Terragni) 86-3775]

Danto, Arthur Coleman, 1924-
Castle, Wendell, 1932- Angel chairs . New
York , 1991. 111 p. : ISBN 0-9628849-0-1 DDC
749.213 20
NK2439.C3 A4 1991

Encounters & reflections : art in the historical
present / Arthur C. Danto.1st ed. New York :
Farrar, Straus, Giroux, 1990. 355 p. ; 24 cm.
Includes index. ISBN 0-374-14819-8 DDC 709/.04
20
I. Title. II. Title: Encounters and reflections.
N6490 .D237 1990
                        NYPL [3-MAL 90-11092]

Mark Tansey : visions and revisions / Arthur
C. Canto ; Christopher Sweet, editor. New
York : Abrams, 1992. p. cm. Includes
bibliographical references. ISBN 0-8109-3912-6
DDC 759.13 20
1. Tansey, Mark, 1949-- Criticism and interpretation. I.
Sweet, Christopher. II. Title.
ND237.T346 D3 1992

D'Antonio, Nino. De Stefano . [Napoli] [1989] 1
v. (unpaged) :
N6923.D395 D4 1989
                    NYPL [3-MCF+ D476 90-11563]

Dantraique, Pierre. La peinture vénitienne /
Pierre Dantraique. Neuchâtel : Ides et
Calendes, c1989. 338 p. : ill. (some col.) ; 31
cm. Includes bibliographical references (p. 337-338)
and indexes. ISBN 2-8258-0027-9 DDC 759.5/31
20
1. Painting, Italian - Italy - Venice. 2. Painting - 15th
century - Italy - Venice. 3. Painting - 16th century -
Italy - Venice. 4. Painting, Modern - 17th-18th
centuries - Italy - Venice. I. Title.
ND621.V5 D28 1989

DANUBE RIVER VALLEY - DESCRIPTION
AND TRAVEL.
Atlas der Donauländer. Wien, 1970- v.
(loose-leaf) DDC 912/.496 19
G1882.D3 D8 1970
                        NYPL [Map Div. 72-267]

DANUBE RIVER VALLEY - MAPS.
Atlas der Donauländer. Wien, 1970- v.
(loose-leaf) DDC 912/.496 19
G1882.D3 A8 1970
                        NYPL [Map Div. 72-267]

Danuser, Hans, 1953- In vivo / Hans Danuser.
Baden : Verlag Lars Müller, c1989. 1 v. : all
ill. ; 38 cm. English and German. "93 photographs in
seven series." Includes "List of captions", 1 sheet,
inserted. ISBN 3-906700-19-4
I. Title.   **NYPL [MFX+ (Danuser) 91-4457]**

Daprà, Brigitte. Barocco mediterraneo .
[Naples] , c1989. 245 p. : ISBN 88-435-2807-6
                        NYPL [3-MCE 91-3396]

Darbel, Alain. Bourdieu, Pierre. [Amour de l'art. English.] The love of art . Cambridge, UK , 1991. viii, 182 p. ;   ISBN 0-7456-0598-2 :   DDC 708.9/4 20
N430 .B613 1991

D'Arbeloff, Natalie. Pater Noster. [London] : Natalie dArbeloff, 1988. [12] leaves ; 26 cm. An original art work, with the Pater Noster blind-stamped on leaves of varying size. These leaves may be turned in the usual way or they may be pulled into a pyramid/altar configuration. The text is drawn twice on the pyramidal steps in such a manner that it may then be read from 2 angles. Title on flap attached to cover. Issued in a painted paper-on-cotton wrapper, in a muslin bag. "Edition of 5 similar but not identical copies on Fabriano Satinata, hand-coloured. This is no. 4. [Signed:] Natalie dArbeloff July 1988"--Ms. label. Accompanied by a sheet of ms. instructions for displaying the work. Source: Purchase, July 17, 1990. DLC DDC 700/.92 20
1. D'Arbeloff, Natalie. 2. Artists' books - England. I. Title.
N7433.4.D35 A4 1988

D'ARBELOFF, NATALIE. D'Arbeloff, Natalie. Pater Noster. [London] , 1988. [12] leaves ;   DDC 700/.92 20
N7433.4.D35 A4 1988

D'Arcangelo, Allan, 1930- Allan D'Arcangelo : recent work. New York : Marlborough Gallery, 1971. 24 p. : ill. (some col.), port. ; 30 cm. Catalog of an exhibition held at Marlborough Gallery, New York, Nov. 1971.
1. D'Arcangelo, Allan, 1930- - Exhibitions. I. Title.
NYPL [3-MCX+ D214 91-1318]

D'ARCANGELO, ALLAN, 1930- - EXHIBITIONS. D'Arcangelo, Allan, 1930- Allan D'Arcangelo . New York , 1971. 24 p. :
NYPL [3-MCX+ D214 91-1318]

Darcque, Pascal. L'Habitat égéen préhistorique . Athènes , Paris , 1990. 495 p. :   ISBN 2-86958-031-2   *NYPL [3-MQL 91-5181]*

D'Arcy Galleries (New York, N.Y.) Surrealist intrusion in the enchanters' domain. New York, [1960] 124 p. illus. 18 cm. Essays and biographies, translated from the French by Julien Levy and Claud Tarnaud. DDC 759.06
1. Surrealism - Exhibitions. 2. Surrealism - Sources. 3. Artists. I. Title.
ND1265 .D353   *NYPL [3-MAL 90-7006]*

Daria, Irene. The fashion cycle : a behind-the-scenes look at a year with Bill Blass, Liz Claiborne, Donna Karan, Arnold Scaasi, and Adrienne Vittadini / Irene Daria. New York : Simon and Schuster, c1990. 240 p., [16] p. of plates : ill. ; 25 cm. ISBN 0-671-66729-7 DDC 746.9/2/092273 20
1. Costume design - United States. 2. Costume designers - United States. I. Title.
TT507 .D345 1990 NYPL [3-MMP 91-3812]

DARK AGES. see MIDDLE AGES.

Dark figures in the desired country . Norvig, Gerda S. Berkeley , c1992. p. cm. ISBN 0-520-04471-1 (alk. paper) DDC 759.2 20
NC978.5.B55 N67 1992

Darling, Dennis Carlyle. Chameleon with a camera : a unique primer on travel photography and how to survive the trip / Dennis Carlyle Darling.1st ed. Wimberley, Tex. : Dorsoduro Press, c1989. 91 p. : ill. ; 14 x 21 cm. ISBN 0-945618-02-6 (sbk.)
1. Photography - Handbooks, manuals, etc. 2. Travel photography - Handbooks, manuals, etc. I. Title.
NYPL [MFW 90-643]

Darling, Jay N. (Jay Norwood), 1876-1962. Worthen, Amy N. The prints of J.N. Darling /. Ames, Iowa , 1991. 126 p. :   ISBN 0-8138-1996-2
IN PROCESS (ONLINE)
NYPL [MDG (Darling) 91-6947]

DARLING, JAY N. (JAY NORWOOD), 1876-1962 - CATALOGS. Worthen, Amy N. The prints of J.N. Darling /. Ames, Iowa , 1991. 126 p. :   ISBN 0-8138-1996-2
IN PROCESS (ONLINE)
NYPL [MDG (Darling) 91-6947]

Darmstadt. Kunsthalle. see Kunsthalle Darmstadt.

Darmstadt Künstler-Kolonie. Museum Künstlerkolonie Darmstadt / [Katalogbearbeitung, Renate Ulmer].

Darmstadt : Das Museum, [1989?] lv, 253 p. : ill. (some col.) ; 29 cm. Title on prelim. t.p.: Museum Künstlerkolonie Darmstadt, Katalog. Includes bibliographical references (p. 249-253).
1. Darmstadt Künstler-Kolonie - History. 2. Decoration and ornament - Germany - Darmstadt. 3. Art Nouveau - Germany - Darmstadt. 4. Art, Modern - 19th century - Germany - Darmstadt. 5. Art, Modern - 20th century - Germany - Darmstadt. I. Ulmer, Renate. II. Title. III. Title: Museum Künstlerkolonie Darmstadt, Katalog. IV. Title: Katalog, Museum Künstlerkolonie Darmstadt.   *NYPL [3-MLF 91-5455]*

DARMSTADT KÜNSTLER-KOLONIE - HISTORY. Darmstadt Künstler-Kolonie. Museum Künstlerkolonie Darmstadt /. Darmstadt [1989?] lv, 253 p. :   *NYPL [3-MLF 91-5455]*

Darmstadt. Mathildenhöhe. Voigt, Reinhard, 1940- Reinhard Voigt . [s.l.] 1979 (Darmstadt : Roether-Druck) [37] p. :
N6888.V63 A4 1979
NYPL [3-MCK+ V895 81-1497]

Wolfgang Bier, Friedemann Hahn, Thomas Kaminsky, Christiane Möbus, Wolfgang Nestler . [Berlin] 1979. 1 case ([206] p. :   DDC 709/.43/0740341 19
N6868 .W64   *NYPL [3-MAMG+ 90-7088]*

Daroczi, Isabel. Atlas de la República Oriental del Uruguay / Isabel Daroczi, Elena García, Miguel Ligüera. 2a ed. actualizada. Montevideo : Amauta, 1990. 1 atlas (109 p.) : col. ill. ; 31 cm. Includes indexes.
1. Uruguay - Maps. 2. Uruguay - Statistics. 3. Uruguay - Description and travel - Views. I. García, Elena. II. Liguera, Miguel. III. Title.
NYPL [Map Div. 90-13118]

Darovannaĭa krasota. Zaremba, Volodymyr. Podarovana krasa . Dnipropetrovs´k , 1990. 284 p., [16] p. of plates :   ISBN 5-7775-0209-1 :
ND699.H57 Z37 1990

Darst, Diane W., 1948- Massey, Sue J., 1947- Learning to look . Englewood Cliffs, N.J. , c1991. p. cm. ISBN 0-13-528795-2 DDC 701/.1/071273 20
N353 .M37 1991

Darstellungen alter Frauen in der griechischen Kunst /. Pfisterer-Haas, Susanne. Frankfurt am Main , 1989. xii, 237 p. :   ISBN 3-631-41559-1
NYPL [3-MAMZ 91-4214]

Darstellungen Berliner Künstler. (Bd. 2) Timner, Carl, 1933- Carl Timner . Berlin , 1988. 109 p. :   DDC 760/.092 20
N6888.T55 A4 1988
NYPL [3-MCK T578 91-6122]

Darstellungen des Achilleus in griechischer und römischer Kunst /. Kemp-Lindemann, Dagmar. Bern , Frankfurt/M. , 1975. v, 287 p., [1] leaf of plates :   ISBN 3-261-01770-8 :
N7760 .K45   *NYPL [3-MAMZ 90-12607]*

Dart, Richard Pousette- see Pousette-Dart, Richard, 1916-

Das alte Mühlhausen . Badstübner, Ernst. Leipzig , c1989. 205 p. :   ISBN 3-7338-0055-9
N6886.M78 B34 1989

Das antike Rathaus . Gneisz, Doris. Wien , 1990. viii, 369 p. :   ISBN 3-85369-786-0 DDC 725/.13/0938 20
NA278.P6 G58 1990

Das bildnerische Denken /. Klee, Paul, 1879-1940. Basel , c1990. 555 p. :   ISBN 3-7965-0889-8
N7454 .K58 Bd. 1, 1990 N6888.K55

Das Engadin Ferdinand Hodlers und anderer Künstler des 19. und 20. Jahrhunderts : Bündner Kunstmuseum Chur, 31. März bis 10. Juni 1990 : Segantini Museum, St. Moritz, 19. Juni bis 15. September 1990 / [Konzept, Gestaltung und Redaktion, Beat Stutzer]. [Chur] : Bündner Kunstmuseum Chur ; St. Moritz : Segantini Museum, c1990. 122 p. : ill. (some col.) ; 28 cm. Spine title: Das Engadin Ferdinand Hodlers. Includes bibliographical references.   ISBN 3-905240-15-7 DDC 759.9494 20
1. Hodler, Ferdinand, 1853-1918 - Exhibitions. 2. Art, Swiss - Exhibitions. 3. Art, Modern - 19th century - Switzerland - Exhibitions. 4. Art, Modern - 20th century - Switzerland - Exhibitions. 5. Graubünden (Switzerland) in art - Exhibitions. I. Hodler, Ferdinand, 1853-1918. II. Stutzer, Beat. III. Bündner Kunstmuseum Chur. IV. Segantini-Museum St. Moritz. V. Title:

Engadin Ferdinand Hodlers.
ND853.H6 A4 1990

Das Hauptportal des Regensburger Domes . Fuchs, Friedrich. München , c1990. 175 p. :   ISBN 3-7954-0652-8
NA5586.R385 F8 1990

Das Leben Walter Leistikows . Corinth, Lovis, 1858-1925. Berlin , 1910. 129 p., [2] leaves of plates :   DDC 709/.2 B 20
N6888.L362 C67 1910

Das Menschenbild der neuen Sachlichkeit /. Matt, Georgia. Konstanz , 1989. 168 p., xv leaves of plates :   ISBN 3-89191-308-7
ND568.5.E9 M37 1989

Das, R. K., 1906- Temples of Vrindaban / by R.K. Das. Delhi : Sandeep Prakashan, 1990. xii, 292 p., [8] p. of plates : ill., 1 folded map ; 25 cm. Includes bibliographical references (p. [286]-287)   ISBN 81-85067-47-3 :   DDC 294.5/35/09542 20
1. Temples, Hindu - India - Vrindávan. 2. Vrindávan (India) - Religion. I. Title.
BL1243.76.V75 D37 1990
NYPL [3-MQWS 90-11587]

Das Selbstportrait im Zeitalter der Photographie : Maler und Photographen im Dialog mit sich selbst / herausgegeben von Erika Billeter ; mit einem Vorwort von Michel Tournier ; Textbeiträge von Erika Billeter ... [et al.] = L'autoportrait à l'âge de la photographie : peintres et photographes en dialogue avec leur propre image / publié par Erika Billeter ; avec une préface de Michel Tournier ; contributions de Erika Billeter ... [et al.]. Bern : Benteli, c1985. 523 p. : chiefly ill. (some col.) ; 29 cm. French and German. Catalog of an exhibition held at the Musée cantonal des beaux-arts, Lausanne, Jan. 18-Mar. 24, 1985, the Württembergischer Kunstverein, Stuttgart, Apr. 19-June 9, 1985, and the Akademie der Künste, Berlin, Sept. 1-Oct. 6, 1985. Includes bibliographies.
1. Self-portraits - Exhibitions. 2. Photographers - Portraits - Exhibitions. 3. Artists - Portraits - Exhibitions. 4. Photography - Portraits - Exhibitions. I. Billeter, Erika, 1927-. II. Musée cantonal des beaux-arts Lausanne. III. Württembergischer Kunstverein. IV. Akademie der Künste (Berlin, Germany). V. Title: Autoportrait à l'âge de la photographie.
NYPL [MFW 91-2389]

Das Stiftergrabmal in Maria Laach /. Dölling, Regine. Worms , c1990. 73 p. :   ISBN 3-88462-069-X
NB1870 .D6 1990

Das, Surendra Kumar, 1907- Mahābidyā =. [Cuttack , 1978] [23] leaves of plates :
ND2048.O75 M34 1978

Das Unverständnis gegenüber moderner Malerei /. Untner, Alois. Wien , 1990. 312 p. ;   ISBN 3-85369-793-3
ND195 .U58 1990

Dash, Evette. Leake, Jerry. Far fetched /. [Boston, MA , c1986] 1 v. (unpaged) :   DDC 741.5/973 20
NC1429.L373 A4 1986

Dass, Christiane. Kriester, Rainer. Rainer Kriester, Steinplastiken 1984-1989 =. Berlin [1989] 216 p. :   ISBN 3-87584-278-2
NYPL [3-MGO+ (Kriester) 91-6677]

DATACAD (COMPUTER PROGRAM) Buehrens, Carol. DataCAD for the architect /. Blue Ridge Summit, PA , c1991. xxi, 450 p. :   ISBN 0-8306-3746-X (pbk.) :   DDC 720/.28/402855369 20
NA2728 .B84 1991

DataCAD for the architect /. Buehrens, Carol. Blue Ridge Summit, PA , c1991. xxi, 450 p. :   ISBN 0-8306-3746-X (pbk.) :   DDC 720/.28/402855369 20
NA2728 .B84 1991

Datos históricos sobre la plástica hondureña /. Fiallos S., Raúl (Fiallos Salgado), 1917- [Tegucigalpa, Honduras?] c1989 (Tegucigalpa, Honduras, C.A. : Litografía López) 129 p. :   DDC 709/.7283 20
N6579 .F5 1989

Datta, Birendranātha. Folk toys of Assam / Birendranath Datta. Guwahati, Assam : Directorate of Cultural Affairs, Govt. of Assam, 1986. 40 p., [1] p. of plates : ill. (some col.) ; 22 x 29 cm. Bibliography: p. [16] at end. DDC 745.592 20

1. Toys - India - Assam. 2. Folk art - India - Assam. I.
Title.
NK9509.65.I52 A84 1986
                    NYPL [3-MNE 91-6912]

Daugelis, Oswaldas. Bialopetravičienė, Laima.
Ciurlionis und die litauische Malerei,
1900-1940 . Duisburg , c1989. 105 p. :   ISBN
3-923576-57-9   **NYPL [3-MCY 90-10676]**

Daum dans les musées de Nancy /. Pétry-Parisot,
Claude. [Nancy , 1989] 183 p. :   ISBN
2-901408-03-6   **NYPL [3-MPW 91-6650]**

Daumier, Honoré, 1808-1879.
Honoré Daumier : Gemälde, Graphik / Text
von Benno Fleischmann. Wien : Otto Lorenz,
[1938] xxxxviii p., 196 p. of plates : ill. (some
col.) ; 26 cm. "Tofelverzeichnis": [4] p.; 25 x 11
inserted.
1. Daumier, Honoré, 1808-1879 - Catalogs. I.
Fleischmann, Benno. II. Title.
                    NYPL [3-MCO D24 89-27412]

Honoré Daumier : peintures, dessins,
lithographies, sculptures : [exposition]. 2e éd.
Ingelheim am Rhein : [s.n], 1971. 1 v.
(unpaged) : ill. ; 21 cm. Exhibition held at the Villa
Schneider, Ingelheim from April 24 to May 31, 1971.
French; catalog in German. Includes bibliographies.
1. Daumier, Honoré, 1808-1897 - Exhibitions. I. Villa
Schneider. II. Title.
                    NYPL [3-MCO D24 90-6296]

DAUMIER, HONORÉ, 1808-1879 -
        CATALOGS.
Daumier, Honoré, 1808-1879. Honoré
Daumier. Wien [1938] xxxxviii p., 196 p. of
plates :   **NYPL [3-MCO D24 89-27412]**

DAUMIER, HONORÉ, 1808-1879 -
        EXHIBITIONS.
Femmes d'esprit . Middlebury, Vt. , Hanover ,
c1990. 146 p. :   ISBN 0-9625262-0-7   DDC
741.5/.944 20
NC1499.D3 A4 1990
                    NYPL [MDG (Daumier) 90-11002]

Picture this! . [New York] , c1990. 36 p. :
                    NYPL [MDG (Daumier) 91-4770]

DAUMIER, HONORÉ, 1808-1897 -
        EXHIBITIONS.
Daumier, Honoré, 1808-1879. Honoré
Daumier. Ingelheim am Rhein , 1971. 1 v.
(unpaged) :   **NYPL [3-MCO D24 90-6296]**

Dautel, Jean-Marie. Les Vanités dans la peinture
au XVIIe siècle . [Paris] , Caen , c1990. 351
p. :   ISBN 2-226-04877-4   DDC 759.04/6/0744422
20
ND1452.E8515 V3 1990
                    NYPL [MBT+ 91-6843]

DAUZATS, ADRIEN, 1804-1868 -
        CATALOGUES RAISONNÉS.
Plessier, Ghislaine. Adrien Dauzats, ou, La
tentation de l'Orient . Bordeaux , c1990. 227
p. :   ISBN 2-902067-15-1 :   DDC 759.4 20
ND553.D245 A4 1990

Daval, Jean Luc.
Bazaine, Jean, 1904- Bazaine /. Genève ,
Paris , c1990. 178 p. :   ISBN 2-605-00162-8
DDC 759.4 20
ND553.B42 A4 1990

Raynaud, Jean Pierre, 1939- Jean-Pierre
Raynaud . Houston, Tex. , c1991. 135 p. :
ISBN 0-939594-23-4 :   DDC 709/.2 20
N6853.R33 A4 1991
                    NYPL [3-MGO (Raynaud) 91-7980]

Davanzo Poli, Doretta. Tessuti : inventario / a
cura di Doretta Davanzo Poli. Venezia :
Fondazione Scientifica Querini Stampalia, 1987.
[30] p. : ill. (some col.) ; 30 cm. (Collana
Queriniana . 2)
1. Fondazione scientifica Querini Stampalia - Catalogs.
2. Textile fabrics - Italy - Venice - Catalogs. I.
Fondazione Scientifica Querini Stampalia. II. Title. III.
Series.   **NYPL [3-MON+ 90-10944]**

Davenport . Lockett, Terence A. London , 1989.
302 p. :   ISBN 0-7126-2002-8 :   DDC 738.0942463
20   **NYPL [3-MPGO+ 90-11562]**

DAVENPORT PORCELAIN.
Lockett, Terence A. Davenport . London ,
1989. 302 p. :   ISBN 0-7126-2002-8 :   DDC
738.0942463 20
                    NYPL [3-MPGO+ 90-11562]

DAVENPORT POTTERY.
Lockett, Terence A. Davenport . London ,

1989. 302 p. :   ISBN 0-7126-2002-8 :   DDC
738.0942463 20
                    NYPL [3-MPGO+ 90-11562]

Davezac, Bertrand, 1930- Four Byzantine and
Russian icons in the Menil Collection /.
Houston, Tex. , c1991. p. cm.   ISBN
0-939594-21-8   DDC 704.9/.482 20
N8186.U6 M474 1991

David. Lévêque, Jean Jacques. La vie et l'œuvre
de Jacques-Louis David /. Courbevoie (Paris) ,
c1989. 239 p. :   ISBN 2-86770-036-1
                    NYPL [3-MCO D25 90-13274]

The David and Alfred Smart Museum of Art .
David and Alfred Smart Museum of Art. New
York , c1990. 216 p. :   ISBN 1-555-95061-2
DDC 708.173/11 20
N531.D38 D38 1990
                    NYPL [3-MAVZ (Chicago) 91-4808]

David and Alfred Smart Museum of Art.
The David and Alfred Smart Museum of Art :
a guide to the collection / edited by Sue Taylor
and Richard A. Born.1st ed. New York :
Hudson Hills Press in association with the
Museum, c1990. 216 p. : ill. (some col.) ; 28
cm. Includes index. Includes bibliographical references
(p. 178-190). ISBN 1-555-95061-2   DDC 708.173/11
20
1. David and Alfred Smart Museum of Art - Catalogs.
2. Art - Illinois - Chicago - Catalogs. I. Taylor, Sue,
1949-. II. Born, Richard A. III. Title.
N531.D38 D38 1990
                    NYPL [3-MAVZ (Chicago) 91-4808]

DAVID AND ALFRED SMART MUSEUM OF
        ART - CATALOGS.
David and Alfred Smart Museum of Art. The
David and Alfred Smart Museum of Art . New
York , c1990. 216 p. :   ISBN 1-555-95061-2
DDC 708.173/11 20
N531.D38 D38 1990
                    NYPL [3-MAVZ (Chicago) 91-4808]

David B. Holmes . Holmes, David B. (David
Bryan), 1936- New York [1987?] 20 p. :
                    NYPL [3-MCZ H75 90-11603]

David Bates . Bates, David, 1952- New York,
NY , c1990. [42] p. :
                    NYPL [3-MCX B329 91-4403]

David Burluik. Burliūk, David, 1882-1967. Long
Beach, N.Y [c1962] 12, [20] p.
                    NYPL [3-MCZ B95 90-7138]

David, Catherine. Lam, Wifredo. Wifredo Lam /.
Paris , c1991. 31 p. :   ISBN 2-85587-191-3
                    NYPL [3-MCZ+ L213 91-7544]

David d'Angers . De Caso, Jacques, 1928- [David
d'Angers. English.] Princeton, N.J. , c1992. p.
cm.   ISBN 0-691-04078-8 :   DDC 730/.92 20
NB553.D3 D413 1992

DAVID D'ANGERS, PIERRE-JEAN, 1788-
        1856 - CRITICISM AND
        INTERPRETATION.
De Caso, Jacques, 1928- [David d'Angers.
English.] David d'Angers . Princeton, N.J. ,
c1992. p. cm.   ISBN 0-691-04078-8 :   DDC
730/.92 20
NB553.D3 D413 1992

DAVID D'ANGERS, PIERRE-JEAN, 1788-
        1856 - ART COLLECTIONS -
        EXHIBITIONS.
Miniatures indiennes de la collection
David-d'Angers . Angers [France] [1986] 58
p. :   ISBN 2-901297-08-5
MLCS 90/02237 (N)
                    NYPL [3-MAF 90-12754]

David Gentleman's Paris. Gentleman, David.
London , 1991. 192 p. :   ISBN 0-340-51869-3 :
DDC 914.43604838 20
DC707   **NYPL [3-MCV+ G337 91-7455]**

David Hockney . Hockney, David. New York ,
c1990. 1 v. (unpaged) :
                    NYPL [3-MCV H678 91-4234]

David Hockney, things recent, and a catalogue
with new kinds of reproduction. Hockney,
David. David Hockney . New York , c1990. 1
v. (unpaged) :
                    NYPL [3-MCV H678 91-4234]

David, Jacques-Louis, 1748-1825.
Jacques-Louis David, 1748-1825 : Musée du
Louvre, Département des peintures, Paris [et]
Musée national du château, Versailles, 26
octobre 1989-12 février 1990. Paris :Ministère

de la culture, de la communication, des grands
travaux et du Bicentenaire, Editions de la
Réunion des musées nationaux, c1989. 655 p. :
ill. (some col.) ; 32 cm. Cette exposition a été
organisée par la Réunion des musées nationaux, le
Musée du Louvre et le Musée du château de Versailles.
Includes bibliographical references (p. 639-647). ISBN
2-7118-2258-3   DDC 759.4 20
1. David, Jacques-Louis, 1748-1825 - Exhibitions. I.
Musée du Louvre. Département des peintures. II.
Musée national de Versailles. III. Réunion des musées
nationaux (France). IV. Title.
N6853.D315 A4 1989

DAVID, JACQUES LOUIS, 1748-1825 -
        CRITICISM AND INTERPRETATION.
Thévoz, Michel. Le théâtre du crime . Paris ,
c1989. 61 p. :   ISBN 2-7073-1312-2   DDC 759.4
20
ND553.D25 T44 1989

DAVID, JACQUES-LOUIS, 1748-1825 -
        EXHIBITIONS.
David, Jacques-Louis, 1748-1825. Jacques-Louis
David, 1748-1825 . Paris :Ministère de la
culture, de la communication, des grands
travaux et du Bicentenaire, Editions de la
Réunion des musées nationaux, c1989. 655 p. :
ISBN 2-7118-2258-3   DDC 759.4 20
N6853.D315 A4 1989

David Jones . Jones, David Michael, 1895-1974.
London , c1989. 48 p. :   ISBN 1-85332-040-4
(pbk.)   **NYPL [3-MCV+ J765 89-19109]**

David, Louis. see **David, Jacques-Louis, 1748-**
        1825.

David McKee Gallery. Guston, Philip, 1913-
Philip Guston, drawings, 1947-1977. New
York , c1978. [48] p. :
                    NYPL [3-MCX G982 91-1369]

David Milne (1882-1953) . Milne, David,
1882-1953. Toronto, Ont. [1982] [28] p. :
                    NYPL [3-MCZ M642 91-5654]

David Nash, sculpture 1971-90 . Nash, David,
1945- [London , 1990?] 62 p. :   ISBN
1-87081-475-4   **NYPL [3-MGO 91-6747]**

David, Zdeněk V. Ehrenberg, Ralph E., 1937-
Scholars' guide to Washington, D.C., for
cartography and remote sensing imagery .
Washington, D.C. , 1987. xx, 385 p. :   ISBN
0-87474-406-7   DDC 026/.912/025753 19
GA193.U5 E37 1987
                    NYPL [Map Div. 87-819]

Davidov, Corinne. Dawes, Ginny Redington.
Victorian jewelry . New York , 1991. p. cm.
ISBN 1-558-59135-4   DDC 739.27/09/034 20
NK7309.85 V53.D38 1991

Davidson, Bernice F. Frick Collection. Paintings
from the Frick Collection /. New York , 1990.
[146] p. :   ISBN 0-8109-3710-7   DDC 750/.74/7471
20
N620.F6 A87 1990
                    NYPL [3-MAVZ+ (New York) 91-4472]

Davidson, Clifford. On tradition : essays on the
use and valuation of the past / Clifford
Davidson. New York : AMS Press, 1991. p.
cm. (AMS studies in the Middle Ages . no. 20)
Includes bibliographical references and index. ISBN
0-404-64160-1   DDC 700/.9 20
1. Arts - History. I. Title. II. Series.
NX440 .D38 1991

Davidson, Gail S., 1941- Public art program,
1985-1988 /. [Brookville, N.Y.] [1989] 64 p. :
ISBN 0-933699-13-1   DDC
709/.04/80740147245 19
NB235.B73 P83 1989
                    NYPL [3-MGI 90-11532]

Davidson, Harold G., 1912- Edward Borein, the
update : the watercolors, etchings, and drawings
/ Harold G. Davidson.1st ed. Santa Barbara,
Calif. : H.G. Davidson, 1991. 219 p. : ill. (some
col.) ; 29 cm. Includes bibliographical references (p.
211-212) and index. ISBN 0-9627674-0-9 :   DDC
760/.092 20
1. Borein, Edward, 1872-1945 - Criticism and
interpretation. I. Borein, Edward, 1872-1945. II. Title.
N6537.B63 D39 1991

Davidson, Richard. Furniture /. New York,
N.Y. , 1991. p. cm.   ISBN 0-670-83957-4   DDC
749/.1/075 20
NK2240 .F87 1991

Davidson, Steef, 1943- Beeldenstorm : de
ontwikkeling van de politieke strip (1965-1975)

/ samengesteld door Steef Davidson.
Amsterdam : Van Gennep, 1978. 176 p. : ill. ;
31 cm. Bibliography: p. [5] ISBN 90-6012-315-8 :
1. Comic books, strips, etc. - Political aspects. 2.
Political satire - History and criticism. I. Title.
PN6714 .D3   NYPL [3-MDY+ 90-4753]

Davies, Alan, 1946- At work & play : our past in
pictures / Alan Davies. [Sydney] : State Library
of New South Wales, 1989. 128 p. : chiefly ill. ;
22 x 30 cm. ISBN 0-7305-6293-X
1. Recreation - Australia - History - Pictorial works. 2.
Working class - Australia - History - Pictorial works. 3.
Australia - Social life and customs - Pictorial works. I.
Title.   NYPL [MFW+ 90-1035]

Davies, Arthur B. (Arthur Bowen), 1862-1928.
M. Knoedler & Co. Arthur B. Davies . New
York , c1975. 55 p. :
NYPL [3-MCX D25 91-905]

**DAVIES, ARTHUR B. (ARTHUR BOWEN),
1862-1928 - CATALOGUES RAISONNES.**
Czestochowski, Joseph S. Arthur B. Davies .
Newark , London , c1987. 258 p., [12] p. of
plates : ISBN 0-87413-242-8 DDC 769.92/4 19
NE539.D3 A4 1987
NYPL [MDG+ (Davies) 87-4836]

**DAVIES, ARTHUR B. (ARTHUR BOWEN),
1862-1928 - EXHIBITIONS.**
M. Knoedler & Co. Arthur B. Davies . New
York , c1975. 55 p. :
NYPL [3-MCX D25 91-905]

Davies, David. El Greco, mystery and
illumination . [Edinburgh] [1989] 96 p. : ISBN
0-903148-90-0
NYPL [3-MCQ T39 90-10831]

Davies, Marie Thérèse Jones- see Jones-Davies,
Marie Thérèse.

Davies, Peter. Josef Herman : drawings and
studies / Peter Davies. Bristol [England] :
Redcliffe, 1990. 136 p. : ill. ; 24 cm. Includes
bibliographical references (p. 131-134). ISBN
1-87297-150-4
1. Herman, Josef, 1911-. I. Herman, Josef, 1911-. II.
Title.   NYPL [3-MCZ H545 91-5532]

Davis Allen . Slavin, Maeve. New York , c1990.
136 p. : ISBN 0-8478-1255-3 DDC 729/.092 20
NK2004.3.A45 S5 1990
NYPL [3-MLO 91-3724]

Davis & Langdale Company. Gore, Spencer
Frederick, 1878-1914. Spencer Frederick Gore,
1878-1914 . New York [1990] [23] p. :
NYPL [3-MCV G666 90-13021]

Davis & Long Company. Charles Conder, Robert
Henri, James Morrice, Maurice Prendergast .
New York [1975] [54] p. :
NYPL [3-MC 90-5453]

Davis, Bruce, 1951- Robert Gore Rifkind Center
for German Expressionist Studies. German
expressionist prints and drawings . Los Angeles,
Calif. : Munich, Federal Republic of Germany :
2 v. : ISBN 3-7913-0959-5 (Prestel Verlag : set)
DDC 760/.0943 19
N6868.5.E9 R6 1989
NYPL [MDE+ 91-5830]

Davis, Courtney, 1946- Celtic designs and motifs
/ Courtney Davis. New York : Dover, 1991. 44
p. : chiefly ill. ; 28 cm. (Dover pictorial archive
series) Dover design library ISBN 0-486-26718-0
(pbk.) : DDC 745.4/41/09364 20
1. Decoration and ornament, Celtic - Themes, motives.
I. Title.
NK1264 .D38 1991

Davis, Jacqueline E. American artists of the
bookplate, 1970-1990 /. Cambridge, Mass. ,
c1990. xi, 155 p. : ISBN 0-9627290-0-0
NYPL [MDVK 91-6220]

Davis, Keith F., 1952-
Clarence John Laughlin : visionary
photographer / by Keith F. Davis ; with
contributions by Nancy C. Barrett and John H.
Lawrence. Kansas City, Mo. : Hallmark Cards,
Inc., c1990. 166 p. : ill. ; 30 cm. "With the
exception of figures 1-9, 14, 16, 17, 19, 22, 24, 25, 27,
and 28, all reproductions in this volume are from
original prints in the Hallmark Photographic Collection.
The reproductions noted above are from works in the
holdings of the Historic New Orleans Collection"--T.p.
verso. Includes bibliographical references. ISBN
0-87529-629-7
1. Laughlin, Clarence John. I. Laughlin, Clarence John.
II. Barrett, Nancy. III. Lawrence, John H. IV. Hallmark

Photographic Collection. V. Historic New Orleans
Collection. VI. Title.
NYPL [MFX+ (Laughlin) 91-7437]

George N. Barnard, photographer of Sherman's
campaign / Keith F. Davis. Kansas City, Mo. :
Hallmark Cards ; Albuquerque, N.M. :
Distributed by the University of New Mexico
Press, c1990. 232 p. : ill. ; 25 x 32 cm. Includes
bibliographical references (p. 217-231). ISBN
0-87529-627-0
1. Barnard, George N., 1819-1902. 2. Photographers -
United States - Biography. I. Barnard, George N.,
1819-1902. II. Title.
IN PROCESS (ONLINE)
NYPL [MFX+ (Barnard) 91-6015]

Davis, Lynn, 1944-
Lynn Davis : Frankfurter Kunstverein,
Steinernes Haus am Römerberg, 11. April-13.
Mai 1990, Frankfurt am Main. Frankfurt am
Main : Der Kunstverein, 1990. [10] p., 56
leaves of plates : ill. ; 24 cm.
1. Davis, Lynn, 1944-- Exhibitions. 2. Photography of
the nude - Exhibitions. I. Frankfurter Kunstverein. II.
Title.   NYPL [MFX (Davis) 91-4676]

DAVIS, LYNN, 1944- - EXHIBITIONS.
Davis, Lynn, 1944- Lynn Davis . Frankfurt am
Main , 1990. [10] p., 56 leaves of plates :
NYPL [MFX (Davis) 91-4676]

Davis, Miles. The art of Miles Davis / Miles
Davis and Scott Gutterman. 1st ed. New York :
Prentice Hall Editions, c1991. 89 p. : col. ill. ;
38 cm. "A Bryon Preiss book." "ARTS." ISBN
0-13-608704-3 : DDC 759.13 B 20
1. Davis, Miles. 2. Painters - United States - Biography.
I. Gutterman, Scott. II. Title.
ND237.D3326 A2 1991
NYPL [3-MCX+ D259 91-6131]

DAVIS, MILES.
Davis, Miles. The art of Miles Davis /. New
York , c1991. 89 p. : ISBN 0-13-608704-3 :
DDC 759.13 B 20
ND237.D3326 A2 1991
NYPL [3-MCX+ D259 91-6131]

Davis, Nancy, 1959- Handling with care :
preserving your heirlooms / text by Nancy
Davis ; illustrated by Patricia L. Miller.
Rochester, NY : Rochester Museum & Science
Center, c1991. 31 p. : ill. ; 28 cm. ISBN
0-938551-02-7 DDC 702/.8/8 20
1. Art - Handling - Handbooks, manuals, etc. 2. Art -
Conservation and restoration - Handbooks, manuals,
etc. I. Rochester Museum and Science Center.
N8585 .D38 1991

Davis, Robert P. Stobart, John, 1929- American
maritime paintings of John Stobart /. New
York, N.Y. , 1991. p. cm. ISBN 0-525-93355-7
DDC 759.2 20
ND497.S797 A4 1991

Davis, Sally Prince, 1942- The graphic artist's
guide to marketing and self-promotion / Sally
Prince Davis. Rev. ed. Cincinnati, Ohio : North
Light Books, 1991. p. cm. (Artist's market business
series) Includes bibliographical references and index.
ISBN 0-89134-416-0 : DDC 741.6/068/8 20
1. Graphic arts - United State - Marketing. 2.
Commercial art - United States - Marketing. I. Title. II.
Series.
NC1001.6 .D38 1991

Davis, Stuart, 1892-1964.
Sims, Lowery Stokes. Stuart Davis . New
York , 1991. p. cm. ISBN 0-87099-627-4 DDC
759.13 20
ND237.D333 A4 1991

Stuart Davis : graphic work and related
paintings with a catalogue raisonné of the prints
/ edited by Jane Myers ; essay by Diane
Kelder ; catalogue raisonné by Sylvan Cole and
Jane Myers. Fort Worth, Tex. : Amon Carter
Museum, 1986. viii, 96 p. : ill. (some col.) ; 26
cm. Exhibition catalog published on the occasion of the
exhibition at the Amon Carter Museum, Aug. 29-Oct.
26, 1986. Includes index. Bibliography: p. 90-92.
ISBN 0-88360-054-4 DDC 760/.092/4 19
1. Davis, Stuart, 1892-1964 - Exhibitions. I. Myers,
Jane, 1955-. II. Kelder, Diane. III. Cole, Sylvan. IV.
Amon Carter Museum of Western Art. V. Title.
N6537.D345 A4 1986
NYPL [MDG (Davis) 90-12799]

**DAVIS, STUART, 1892-1964 - CRITICISM
AND INTERPRETATION.**
Sims, Lowery Stokes. Stuart Davis . New

York , 1991. p. cm. ISBN 0-87099-627-4 DDC
759.13 20
ND237.D333 A4 1991

DAVIS, STUART, 1892-1964 - EXHIBITIONS.
Davis, Stuart, 1892-1964. Stuart Davis . Fort
Worth, Tex. , 1986. viii, 96 p. : ISBN
0-88360-054-4 DDC 760/.092/4 19
N6537.D345 A4 1986
NYPL [MDG (Davis) 90-12799]

Sims, Lowery Stokes. Stuart Davis . New
York , 1991. p. cm. ISBN 0-87099-627-4 DDC
759.13 20
ND237.D333 A4 1991

Davis, Whitney. Masking the blow : scenes of
representation in late prehistoric Egyptian art /
Whitney Davis. Berkeley : University of
California Press, 1992. p. cm. (California studies in
the history of art. 30) Includes bibliographical
references and index. ISBN 0-520-07488-2 DDC
709/.32 20
1. Art, Prehistoric - Egypt - Themes, motives. 2. Art,
Egyptian - Themes, motives. I. Title.
N5310.5.E3 D38 1992

Davison Art Center.
Alvin Lucier /. Middletown, Conn. , c1988. 23
p. ; ISBN 0-929687-01-9 (pbk.).
NYPL [3-MGO+ (Lucier) 89-21332]

D'Oench, Ellen. Jim Dine prints, 1977-1985 /.
New York , c1986. 182 p. : ISBN
0-06-431501-0 : DDC 769/.92/4 19
NE539.D5 A4 1986
NYPL [MDG (Dine) 86-1962]

Friends of the Davison Art Center acquisitions,
1962-1988 / by Ellen G. D'Oench and Richard
H. Wood. Middletown, Conn. : The Center,
c1988. 72 p. : ill. ; 28 cm. Published in conjunction
with an exhibition held March 28-June 4, 1989.
1. Davison Art Center, Friends. 2. Prints - Exhibitions.
I. D'Oench, Ellen. II. Wood, Richard H., 1935-1988.
III. Title.   NYPL [MDE 89-17470]

DAVISON ART CENTER, FRIENDS.
Davison Art Center. Friends of the Davison
Art Center acquisitions, 1962-1988 /.
Middletown, Conn. , c1988. 72 p. :
NYPL [MDE 89-17470]

Dawes, Ginny Redington. Victorian jewelry :
unexplored treasures / Ginny Redington
Dawes, Corinne Davidov ; photographsy by
Tom Dawes. New York : Abbeville Press
Publishers, 1991. p. cm. Includes bibliographical
references and index. ISBN 1-558-59135-4 DDC
739.27/09/034 20
1. Jewelry, Victorian. I. Davidov, Corinne. II. Title.
NK7309.85 V53.D38 1991

Dawson, Doug, 1944- Capturing light and color
with pastel / Doug Dawson. 1st ed. Cincinnati,
Ohio : North Light Books, c1991. p. cm.
Includes index. ISBN 0-89134-376-8 (hrdcvr) :
DDC 741.2/35 20
1. Pastel drawing - Technique. 2. Light in art. 3. Color
in light. I. Title.
NC880 .D35 1991

Dawson, Joan, 1932- The mapmaker's eye : Nova
Scotia through early maps / Joan Dawson.
Halifax, N.S. : Nimbus ; Nova Scotia Museum,
1988. x, 156 p. : ill., maps, facsims. ; 23 x 31
cm. Includes index. Includes bibliographical references
(p. 151-154). ISBN 0-921054-12-2
1. Cartography - Nova Scotia - History. 2. Nova
Scotia - Maps - To 1800. I. Nova Scotia Museum. II.
Title.   NYPL [Map Div. 90-11404]

Day, Holliday T. Power : its myths and mores in
American art, 1961-1991 / Holliday T. Day ;
with essays by Brian Wallis, Anna C. Chave,
and George E. Marcus ...1st ed. Indianapolis,
Ind. : Indianapolis Museum of Art in
cooperation with Indiana University Press,
1991. p. cm. "This book is a debate in the form an
exhibition catalogue"--Foreword. Exhibition organized
by the Indiana Museum of Art. Includes bibliographical
references and index. ISBN 0-253-31658-8 DDC
709/.73/07477252 20
1. Art, American - Exhibitions. 2. Art - Political
aspects - United States - Exhibitions. 3. Art and
society - United States - Exhibitions. 4. Mass media
and art - United States - Exhibitions. 5. Art, Modern -
20th century - United States - Exhibitions. I.
Indianapolis Museum of Art.
N72.P6 D38 1991

A Day in the life of China / photographed by 90
of the world's leading photojournalists on one

day, April 15, 1989 ; [project director, David Cohen]. San Francisco : Collins, 1989. 220 p. : col. ill. ; 37 cm. ISBN 0-00-215321-1 (returnable ed.) : DDC 951.05/8/0222 20
1. China - Description and travel - 1976- - Views. 2. China - Social life and customs - 1976- - Pictorial works. I. Cohen, David, 1955-.
DS712 .D39 1989
NYPL [MFW+ 90-11175]

A Day in the life of Italy / photographed by 100 of the world's leading photojournalists on one day, April 27, 1990. San Francisco, Calif. : Collins Publishers San Francisco, 1990. 220 p. : col. ill. ; 37 cm. ISBN 0-00-215729-2 : DDC 945/.0022/2 20
1. Italy - Description and travel - 1975- - Views. 2. Italy - Social life and customs - Pictorial works. I. Collins Publishers San Francisco.
DG420 .D35 1990 **NYPL [MFW+ 91-3408]**

Day, Michael, 1938- Discipline-based art education . Santa Monica, Calif. , 1991. p. cm. ISBN 0-89236-171-9 : DDC 700 20
N362 .C6 1991

A day spent with Josephine and her friends /. Prince, Pamela. New York, NY , 1992. p. cm. ISBN 0-517-58303-8 : DDC 741.6/42 20
NC978.5.A67 P75 1992

DAYLIGHTING.
Yáñez Parareda, Guillermo. Arquitectura solar . Madrid , 1988. 192 p. : ISBN 84-7433-542-6 DDC 720/.472 20
NA2542.S6 Y35 1988

Dayton, Linnea, 1944-
Gosney, Michael, 1954- The Verbum book of digital painting /. Redwood City, Calif. , 1990. ix, 211 p. : ISBN 1-558-51090-7 DDC 760 20
N7433.8 .G68 1990

Gosney, Michael, 1954- The Verbum book of scanned imagery /. Redwood City, CA , 1990. p. cm. ISBN 1-558-51091-5 : DDC 760 20
N7433 .G68 1990

The DBAE handbook . Dobbs, Stephen M. Santa Monica, CA , 1991. p. cm. ISBN 0-89236-214-6 : DDC 707/.073 20
N105 .D63 1991

DCP .
(89, 50-61) New York (N.Y.). Dept. of City Planning. Block & lot maps-- Manhattan Community District ... atlas /. New York, N.Y. , c1989. 12 v. :
NYPL [Map Div. 91-7469]

(90, no. 30, etc) New York (N.Y.). Dept. of City Planning. Block & lot maps-- Brooklyn Community District ... atlas /. New York, N.Y. , c1990. 18 v. :
NYPL [Map Div. 91-6366]

(90, 01-12) New York (N.Y.). Dept. of City Planning. Block & lot maps-- Bronx Community District ... atlas /. New York, N.Y. , c1990. 12 v. :
NYPL [Map Div. 91-7471]

(90, 17-34) New York (N.Y.). Dept. of City Planning. Block & lot maps-- Brooklyn Community District ... atlas /. New York, N.Y. , c1990. 18 v. :
NYPL [Map Div. 91-6366]

(90, 45 etc) New York (N.Y.). Dept. of City Planning. Block & lot maps-- Queens Community District ... atlas /. New York, N.Y. , c1991- v. :
NYPL [Map Div. 91-7475]

(90, 45-51) New York (N.Y.). Dept. of City Planning. Block & lot maps-- Queens Community District ... atlas /. New York, N.Y. , c1991- v. :
NYPL [Map Div. 91-7475]

De Albentiis, Emidio, 1958- La casa dei Romani / di Emidio De Albentiis. 1. ed. Milano : Longanesi, c1990. 348 p., [8] p. of plates : ill. ; 21 cm. (Biblioteca di archeologia . v. 13) Includes bibliographical references (p. [323]-330) and index. ISBN 88-304-0930-8 : DDC 728/.0937 20
1. Architecture, Domestic - Rome. 2. Architecture, Ancient. I. Series: Biblioteca di archeologia (Milan, Italy) , v. 13. II. Title.
NA324 .D44 1990 **NYPL [JFD 91-5342]**

De år i Rom . Andersen, Jørgen, 1922- København , 1989. 301 p. : ISBN 87-7241-576-2 :
ND723.A2 A86 1989

De architectvra. Vitruvius Pollio. [De architectvra. Spanish.] M. Vitrvvio Pollion De architectvra /. Valencia , 1978. 21, 178, [15] p. : ISBN 84-7274-032-3
NA2515 .V618 1978
NYPL [3-MQD+ 87-3849]

De blauwe gitaar /. Tilroe, Anna. Amsterdam , 1990. 192 p. : ISBN 90-214-8367-X
N6490 .T556 1990

De Bona . De Bona, Theodoro, 1904- [Curitiba, Brazil] [1989?] 69 p. : ISBN 85-85132-36-1 DDC 759.981 20
ND359.D4 A4 1989
NYPL [3-MCZ D287 91-5630]

De Bona, Theodoro, 1904-
De Bona : um exercício de criação. [Curitiba, Brazil] : Scientia et Labor, Editora da UFPR, [1989?] 69 p. : ill. (some col.) ; 29 cm. ISBN 85-85132-36-1 DDC 759.981 20
1. De Bona, Theodoro, 1904- - Catalogs. I. Universidade Federal do Paraná. II. Title.
ND359.D4 A4 1989
NYPL [3-MCZ D287 91-5630]

DE BONA, THEODORO, 1904- - CATALOGS.
De Bona, Theodoro, 1904- De Bona . [Curitiba, Brazil] [1989?] 69 p. : ISBN 85-85132-36-1 DDC 759.981 20
ND359.D4 A4 1989
NYPL [3-MCZ D287 91-5630]

De Bray, Lys. The art of botanical illustration : the classic illustrators and their achievements from 1550 to 1900 / Lys de Bray. Bromley, Kent : C. Helm, c1989. 191 p. : ill. (chiefly col.) ; 34 cm. Includes index. "A Quarto book." Bibliography: p. 187. ISBN 0-7470-0232-0
1. Botanical illustration - History. I. Title.
NYPL [MDT+ 91-3771]

De Carlo, Giancarlo, 1919-
Zucchi, Benedict. The architecture of Giancarlo De Carlo /. Oxford , Boston , 1991. p. cm. ISBN 0-7506-1275-4 : DDC 720/.92 20
NA1123.D29 Z8 1991

DE CARLO, GIANCARLO, 1919- - CRITICISM AND INTERPRETATION.
Zucchi, Benedict. The architecture of Giancarlo De Carlo /. Oxford , Boston , 1991. p. cm. ISBN 0-7506-1275-4 : DDC 720/.92 20
NA1123.D29 Z8 1991

De Caro, F. A. Folklife in Louisiana photography : images of tradition / Frank de Caro. Baton Rouge : Louisiana State University Press, c1990. viii, 213 p. : ill. ; 29 cm. Includes bibliographical references (p. 201-206) and index. ISBN 0-8071-1633-5 (cloth : alk. paper) : DDC 398/.09763 20
1. Folklore - Louisiana - Pictorial works - Exhibitions. 2. Louisiana - Social life and customs - Pictorial works - Exhibitions. I. Title.
GR110.L5 D4 1990 **NYPL [MFW 91-6803]**

De Carolis, Ernesto. Lucerne greche e romane / Ernesto De Carolis. 3a ed. Roma : Gruppo archeologico romano, 1982. 84 p. : ill. ; 21 cm. (Pubblicazioni del G.A.R. Monografie . 3) Quaderni del G.A.R. ; n. 3. Bibliography: p. 84. DDC 738.8 19
1. Lamps, Classical. 2. Classical antiquities. I. Series. II. Series: Quaderni del G.A.R. , n. 3. III. Title.
DE61.L34 D43 1982
NYPL [3-MNHL 90-6882]

De Caso, Jacques, 1928-
[David d'Angers. English]
David d'Angers : sculptural communication in the age of romanticism / Jacques de Caso ; translated by Dorothy Johnson and Jacques de Caso. Princeton, N.J. : Princeton University Press, c1992. p. cm. Translation of: David d'Angers. Includes bibliographical references and index. ISBN 0-691-04078-8 : DDC 730/.92 20
1. David d'Angers, Pierre-Jean, 1788-1856 - Criticism and interpretation. 2. Portrait sculpture, French. 3. Romanticism in art - France. 4. Public sculpture - France. I. Title.
NB553.D3 D413 1992

De Chiara, Joseph, 1929- Time-saver standards for interior design and space planning / Joseph De Chiara, Julius Panero, Martin Zelnik. New York : McGraw-Hill, c1991. p. cm. Includes index. ISBN 0-07-016299-9 DDC 729 20
1. Interior decoration - Standards - Handbooks, manuals, etc. 2. Interior architecture - Standards - Handbooks, manuals, etc. I. Panero, Julius. II. Zelnik,

Martin, 1939-. III. Title.
NK2110 .D35 1991

De Chirico, Giorgio, 1888-
Dalla Chiesa, Giovanna. De Chirico scultore /. Milano , c1988. 111 p. : ISBN 88-374-1036-0
NYPL [3-MGO+ (De Chirico) 91-6552]

Giorgio de Chirico, 1920-1950 / a cura di Massimo Di Carlo ... [et al.] ; contributi critici di Francesco Gallo, Paolo Levi, Francesco Poli. Milano : Electa, c1990. 166 p. : ill. (chiefly col.) ; 25 cm. Italian and English. Catalog published in conjunction with an exhibition held in New York, Nov. 29, 1990-Jan. 15, 1991. "This exhibition is an extended edition of the exhibition shown in September 1989 in Montecarlo, Monaco"--P. [37] Includes bibliographical references (p. 165-166). ISBN 88-435-3403-3 (jacket)
1. De Chirico, Giorgio, 1888- - Exhibitions. I. Di Carlo, Massimo. II. Gallo, Francesco. III. Levi, Paolo, 1919-. IV. Poli, Francesco, 1949-. V. Title.
NYPL [3-MCF C535 91-6458]

DE CHIRICO, GIORGIO, 1888-
Chirico, Giorgio, 1888- Mémoires /. Paris , 1965. 307 p. ; **NYPL [3-MCF C535 91-6673]**

Dalla Chiesa, Giovanna. De Chirico scultore /. Milano , c1988. 111 p. : ISBN 88-374-1036-0
NYPL [3-MGO+ (De Chirico) 91-6552]

DE CHIRICO, GIORGIO, 1888- - EXHIBITIONS.
De Chirico, Giorgio, 1888- Giorgio de Chirico, 1920-1950 /. Milano , c1990. 166 p. : ISBN 88-435-3403-3 (jacket)
NYPL [3-MCF C535 91-6458]

De Chirico scultore /. Dalla Chiesa, Giovanna. Milano , c1988. 111 p. : ISBN 88-374-1036-0
NYPL [3-MGO+ (De Chirico) 91-6552]

De Clouet à Matisse : dessins français des collections américaines : Musée de l'Orangerie, Paris, 1958-1959. Paris : Le Musée, [1958] 1 v. (unpaged) : ill. ; 21 cm. Includes bibliographical references.
1. Drawing, French - Exhibitions. I. Musée de l'Orangerie.
MLCS 90/03647 (P)
NYPL [3-MBH 91-6247]

De Europa : John Weber Gallery, April 29-May 24, 1972 : Anselmo ... New York : The Gallery, [1972] [52] p. : ill. ; 20 cm.
1. Conceptual art - Europe - Exhibitions. I. John Weber Gallery. **NYPL [3-MAL 91-639]**

De Felicis Orlandi, Simonetta. Dipinti dei musei e gallerie di Roma. Roma , 1978- v. ;
N4035.G33 D56 1981
NYPL [MAVZ+ (Rome) 91-6377]

De Fusco, Renato, 1929- Le nuove idee di architettuta : storia della critica da Rogers a Jencks / Renato De Fusco, Cettina Lenza.1. ed. Milano : ETASLIBRI, 1991. ix, 326 p. ; 24 cm. (Scienze del territorio) Includes bibliographical references and index. ISBN 88-453-0435-3
1. Architecture, Modern - 20th century Themes, motives. I. Lenza, Cettina, 1954-. II. Title. III. Series.
NA680 .D38 1991

De Glehn, Wilfrid-Gabriel, 1870-1951.
Wilfrid-Gabriel de Glehn (1870-1951) : paintings and watercolors : March 4 to April 15, 1989 / introduction by Laura Wortley. New York, N.Y. : Hirschl & Adler Galleries, c1989. 48 p. : ill. (some col.) ; 27 cm. ISBN 0-915057-27-1
1. De Glehn, Wilfrid-Gabriel, 1870-1951 - Exhibitions. I. Wortley, Laura. II. Title.
NYPL [3-MCV D318 90-10955]

DE GLEHN, WILFRID-GABRIEL, 1870-1951 - EXHIBITIONS.
De Glehn, Wilfrid-Gabriel, 1870-1951. Wilfrid-Gabriel de Glehn (1870-1951) . New York, N.Y. , c1989. 48 p. : ISBN 0-915057-27-1
NYPL [3-MCV D318 90-10955]

De Grada, Raffaele, 1885-1957. Pittura '800 /. Novara , c1989. 487 p. : ISBN 88-402-0088-6 : DDC 759.05 20
ND457 .P58 1989 **NYPL [3-MC 90-12798]**

De Grauwe, Paul. see Grauwe, Paul de.

De Gruchy, Graham. Architecture in Brisbane / Graham de Gruchy. Bowen Hills, Brisbane, Qld. : Boolarong Publications with Kookaburra Books, 1988. 132 p. : ill. (some col.), maps, plans ; 31 cm. Includes bibliographical references. ISBN 0-86439-078-5

1. Architecture - Australia - Brisbane (Qld.). 2. Brisbane (Qld.) - Buildings, structures, etc. I. Title.
NYPL [3-MQWZ+ 89-21433]

De humani corporis fabrica. Montréal, Québec, Canada : Artextes, 1988, c1985-c1986. 3 v. in 1 case : ill. (some col.) ; 26 cm. Title from case. Vol. 2 has text in English with French translation; vol. 3 has captions in English and a poem in French, German, and Italian. Includes bibliographical references (v. [1], p. [91]). CONTENTS. - Contents: [1] Charcot, deux concepts de nature / Nicole Jolicoeur -- [2] Oceania = Océanie / Anne Ramsden -- [3] Vitality / John Di Stefano. DDC 700/.92/271428 20
1. Artists' books - Québec (Province) - Montréal. I. Jolicoeur, Nicole. Charcot, deux concepts de nature. 1988. II. Ramsden, Anne, 1952- Oceania. 1988. III. Di Stefano, John. Vitality. 1988. IV. Title: Charcot, deux concepts de nature. V. Title: Oceania. VI. Title: Vitality.
N7433.35.C2 D4 1988
NYPL [MEMZ 90-11163]

De Kay, Charles. Tiffany, Louis Comfort, 1848-1933. The art work of Louis C. Tiffany. Poughkeepsie, NY , 1987. xxxi, 90 p., [60] p. of plates : ISBN 0-938290-06-1 DDC 709.2 20
N6537.T5 A4 1987
NYPL [3-MPW+ 90-11567]

De Kooning, Willem, 1904- Willem de Kooning, Jean Dubuffet . New York, NY , c1990. 29, [84] p. : **NYPL [3-MAMZ 91-5530]**

DE KOONING, WILLEM, 1984- - EXHIBITIONS.
Willem de Kooning, Jean Dubuffet . New York, NY , c1990. 29, [84] p. :
NYPL [3-MAMZ 91-5530]

De La Croix, Horst. Gardner, Helen. [Art through the ages.] Gardner's art through the ages. San Diego , c1991. xvi, 1135 p. : ISBN 0-15-503769-2 **NYPL [MAD 91-4710]**

De L'Empire romain aux villes impériales = 6000 ans d'art au Maroc = Min al-Imbarāṭūriyah al-Rūmāniyah ilá-al-'awāṣim al-'atiqah : sittat ālāf sanah min al-funūn bi-al-Maghrib. Paris : Musée du Petit Palais, c1990. xxiii, 474 p. : ill. (some col.), maps ; 32 cm. Catalog of an exhibition to have been held at the Musée du Petit Palais, Paris, in early 1991. The exhibition was cancelled. French and Arabic. Includes bibliographical references (p. 469-473).
1. Art, Moroccan - Exhibitions. 2. Art, Islamic - Morocco - Exhibitions. I. Musée du Petit-Palais (Paris, France). II. Title: Min al-Imbarāṭūriyah al-Rūmāniyah ilá-al-'awāṣim al-'atiqah.
NYPL [3-MAM+ 91-6786]

De Long, David Gilson, 1939- Brownlee, David Bruce. Louis I. Kahn, architect of the American century /. New York , 1991. p. cm. ISBN 0-8478-1330-4 DDC 720/.92 20
NA737.K32 B76 1991

De l'origine des lanternes des morts /. Bougoux, Christian. Bordeaux , c1989. 151 p. : ISBN 2-9503805-0-6
NA6165 .B68 1989

De Lory, Peter. The wild and the innocent / a story and photographs by Peter de Lory ; song by Terry Allen. Riverside, Calif. : California Museum of Photography, University of California, 1987. [46] p. : col. ill. ; 25 cm. "Also published as: CMP bulletin, volume 6, number 3"--P. [46]. ISBN 0-9619038-2-1
1. Artists' books - United States. I. Allen, Terry, 1943-. II. California Museum of Photography. III. CMP bulletin. IV. Title.
NYPL [MFX (De Lory) 90-11264]

De Lue, Donald, 1897-1988. Howlett, D. Roger. The sculpture of Donald De Lue . Boston , 1990. xxi, 234 p. : ISBN 0-87923-820-8
NYPL [3-MGO+ (De Lue) 91-3674]

DE LUE, DONALD, 1897-1988.
Howlett, D. Roger. The sculpture of Donald De Lue . Boston , 1990. xxi, 234 p. : ISBN 0-87923-820-8
NYPL [3-MGO+ (De Lue) 91-3674]

De Marchi, Andrea. Le fontanelle di Roma / Andrea De Marchi. 1a ed. Roma : Anthropos, 1988. 61 p. : col. ill. ; 21 cm. (I Gioielli di Roma . 3)
1. Fountains - Italy - Rome. I. Title. II. Series.
NYPL [3-MRN 90-10437]

De Marco, Vittorio. La vela di Gio Ponti / Vittorio De Marco ; grafica, Michelangelo De Franchis ; fotografie, Carmine La Fratta.

Taranto : Scorpione, [1990] 94 p. : ill. ; 31 cm. (Il Meridione nell'arte . 3)
1. Ponti, Gio, 1891-. I. Title. II. Series.
IN PROCESS (ONLINE)
NYPL [3-MQZ+ (Ponti) 91-3777]

De Maria, Nicola, 1954-
Nicola De Maria, fiori ed usignoli miei. Saarbrücken : Saarland Museum, [1990]. 87 p. : col. ill. ; 29 cm. "Herausgegeben von Ernst-Gerhard Güse"--Colophon. Catalog of an exhibition held at the Saarland Museum, Saarbrücken, April 8-May 20, 1990. ISBN 3-925303-46-4
1. De Maria, Nicola, 1954- - Exhibitions. I. Güse, Ernst-Gerhard. II. Saarland-Museum Saarbrücken. III. Title. IV. Title: Fiori ed usignoli miei.
NYPL [3-MCF D372 91-5202]

DE MARIA, NICOLA, 1954- - EXHIBITIONS.
De Maria, Nicola, 1954- Nicola De Maria, fiori ed usignoli miei. Saarbrücken [1990]. 87 p. : ISBN 3-925303-46-4
NYPL [3-MCF D372 91-5202]

De Marly, Diana. Dress in North America / Diana de Marly. New York : Holmes & Meier, 1990- v. : ill. (some col.) ; 26 cm. Includes bibliographical references and index. CONTENTS. - v. 1. The New World, 1492-1800. ISBN 0-8419-1199-1 DDC 391/.0097 20
1. Costume - United States - History. 2. Costume - Canada - History. 3. United States - Social conditions - To 1865. 4. Canada - Social conditions - To 1763. I. Title.
GT603 .D4 1990   **NYPL [3-MMP 91-3984]**

De' Medici Stucchi, Lorenza, 1926- The Renaissance of Italian gardens / Lorenza de' Medici ; text in association with Giuppi Pietromarchi ; photographs by John Ferro Sims. London : Pavilion, 1990. 192 p. : col. ill. ; 26 cm. Includes index. Bibliography: p. 190. ISBN 1-85145-392-X : DDC 712.60945 20
1. Gardens, Italian. 2. Gardens, Renaissance - Italy. 3. Gardens - Italy. 4. Gardens, Italian - Pictorial works. 5. Gardens, Renaissance - Italy - Pictorial works. 6. Gardens - Italy - Pictorial works. I. Pietromarchi, Giuppi. II. Sims, John Ferro. III. Title.
SB466.I8   **NYPL [3-MSK 91-3348]**

De Mesa, José. Gisbert, Teresa, 1926- La tradición bíblica en el arte virreinal /. La Paz, Bolivia , 1987. viii, 33 p. :
NYPL [3-MAM 90-12522]

De Micheli, Mario.
Guastalla, Giorgio. Marino Marini . Livorno , c1990. 268 p. :
NYPL [MDG+ (Marini) 91-5689]

Mascherini, Marcello, 1906- Mascherini, scultore europeo /. [Italy] , Pordenone , c1988. 126 p., [101] p. of plates : DDC 730/.92 20
NB623.M454 A4 1988
NYPL [3-MGO (Mascherini) 91-3748]

La Scuola di Mons . Brescia , Milano , c1989. 103 p. : DDC 709/.493/42 20
N6968 .S37 1989
NYPL [3-MAME 90-10713]

De Nachtwacht in het donker . Grauwe, Paul de. Tielt [1990] 180 p. : ISBN 90-209-1766-8 :
N8600 .G73 1990

De Nittis, Giuseppe, 1846-1884.
Giuseppe De Nittis, dipinti 1864-1884 / testi di Raffaele Monti ... [et al.] ; [mostra a cura di Rossana Bossaglia ... [et al.]. Firenze : Artificio, 1990. 205 p. : ill. (some col.), ports. ; 28 cm. Catalog of an exhibition held at the Palazzo della permanente, Milan, Apr. 11-May 27, 1990 and the Pinacoteca provinciale, Bari, June 2-Sept. 29, 1990. Includes bibliographical references (p. 203-205).
1. De Nittis, Giuseppe, 1846-1884 - Exhibitions. I. Monti, Raffaele. II. Bossaglia, Rossana. III. Palazzo della permanente (Milan, Italy). IV. Bari (Italy : Province). Pinacoteca provinciale. V. Title.
NYPL [3-MCF N73 91-6553]

DE NITTIS, GIUSEPPE, 1846-1884.
Lamacchia, Giovanni. Giuseppe De Nittis . Firenze [1990] 257 p., [9] leaves, [23] p. of plates : **NYPL [3-MCF N73 90-12002]**

Lamacchia, Giovanni. Giuseppe De Nittis, capolista degli impressionisti /. Firenze [1990] 257 p., [39] p. of plates : DDC 759.5 B 20
ND623.D417 L5 1990

DE NITTIS, GIUSEPPE, 1846-1884 - EXHIBITIONS.
De Nittis, Giuseppe, 1846-1884. Giuseppe De

Nittis, dipinti 1864-1884 /. [Firenze , 1990. 205 p. : **NYPL [3-MCF N73 91-6553]**

De Paoli, Geri. Gelburd, Gail. The trans parent thread . [Hempstead, N.Y.] , Philadelphia, Pa. , c1990. 124 p. : ISBN 0-8122-1376-9 (pbk.)
NYPL [3-MAMT 91-4984]

De Paz, Alfredo. Goya : arte e condizione umana / Alfredo De Paz.1. ed italiana. Napoli : Liguori, 1990. 490 p., [16] p. of plates : ill. (some col.) ; 21 cm. (Storia dell'arte e della critica d'arte . 1) Includes bibliographical references (p. [463]-490). ISBN 88-20-71734-4 : DDC 760/.092 20
1. Goya, Francisco, 1746-1828 - Criticism and interpretation. I. Goya, Francisco, 1746-1828. II. Title. III. Series.
N7113.G68 A4 1990
NYPL [3-MCQ G72 91-4505]

De Piro, Nicholas, 1941- The international dictionary of artists who painted Malta / Nicholas de Piro. Valletta, Malta : Said International, 1988. 207 p. : chiefly col. ill. ; 30 cm. ISBN 1-87168-400-5 DDC 758/.994585 20
1. Malta in art. 2. Artists - Biography - Dictionaries. I. Title.
N8213 .D4 1988

De Pisis, Filippo, 1896-1956. Malabotta, Manlio, 1907- L'opera grafica di Filippo De Pisis. [Milano, c1969] 171 p., incl. 71 plates.
NE2352.5.P5 M3
NYPL [MDG (DePisis) 90-6243]

DE PISIS, FILIPPO, 1896-1956.
Malabotta, Manlio, 1907- L'opera grafica di Filippo De Pisis. [Milano, c1969] 171 p., incl. 71 plates.
NE2352.5.P5 M3
NYPL [MDG (DePisis) 90-6243]

De Pury, Simon. Novak, Barbara. Nineteenth-century American painting /. New York , 1991. p. cm. ISBN 0-89660-026-2 : DDC 759.13/074/49478 20
ND210 .N686 1991

De Ranitz, Louise Barnouw- see Barnouw-De Ranitz, Louise.

De Rocco . De Rocco, Federico. [Pordenone] , c1984. 59 p., [36] p. of plates :
NYPL [3-MCF D439 91-5210]

De Rocco, Federico.
De Rocco : opera grafica : con tre testi e due lettere di Pier Paolo Pasolini / [a cura di] Giancarlo Pauletto. [Pordenone] : Edizioni Concordia 7, c1984. 59 p., [36] p. of plates : ill. ; 27 cm. (Edizioni d'arte. nuova serie 13) Exhibition held at the Palazzo Altan, San Vito al Tagliamento, Nov. 1983-Jan. 1984. Includes bibliographical references (p. 56-59).
1. De Rocco, Federico - Exhibitions. 2. Pasolini, Pier Paolo, 1922-1975 - Correspondence. I. Pauletto, Giancarlo. II. Pasolini, Pier Paolo, 1922-1975. III. Palazzo Altan (San Vito al Tagliamento, Italy). IV. Series: Edizioni d'arte (Pordenone, Italy) , nuova serie 13. V. Title. **NYPL [3-MCF D439 91-5210]**

DE ROCCO, FEDERICO - EXHIBITIONS.
De Rocco, Federico. De Rocco . [Pordenone] , c1984. 59 p., [36] p. of plates :
NYPL [3-MCF D439 91-5210]

De Rosa, Pier Andrea. Alisio, Giancarlo, 1930- Napoli com'era nelle gouaches del Sette e Ottocento . Roma , 1990. 262 p. : DDC 758/.994573 20
ND2243.I8 A44 1990

De Saye Hutton, Anthony. A guide to New Hall porcelain patterns / A. de Saye Hutton. London : Barrie & Jenkins, c1990. 240 p., [8] p. of plates : ill. (some col.) ; 25 cm. Includes indexes. Includes bibliographical references (p.85) ISBN 0-7126-3579-3 : DDC 738.2/7 19
1. New Hall porcelain - Patterns. 2. New Hall porcelain - Collectors and collecting. 3. New Hall porcelain - Guide-books. 4. Porcelain, English. I. Title.
NK4399.N4   **NYPL [3-MPGO 90-12008]**

De Stefano, Nino. immagini da una rivoluzione, Napoli 1799 / Nino D'Antonio ... [et al.]. [Napoli] : A. Guida, [1989] 1 v. (unpaged) : ill. (some col., some folded) ; 33 cm. Includes bibliographical references.
1. De Stefano, Armando, 1926- - Criticism and interpretation. 2. Parthenopean Republic in art. 3. Naples (Italy) in art. I. De Stefano, Armando, 1926-. II.

D'Antonio, Nino.
N6923.D395 D4 1989
        NYPL [3-MCF+ D476 90-11563]

De Stefano, Armando, 1926-
De Stefano . [Napoli] [1989] 1 v. (unpaged) :
N6923.D395 D4 1989
        NYPL [3-MCF+ D476 90-11563]

**DE STEFANO, ARMANDO, 1926- -
    CRITICISM AND INTERPRETATION.**
De Stefano . [Napoli] [1989] 1 v. (unpaged) :
N6923.D395 D4 1989
        NYPL [3-MCF+ D476 90-11563]

**DE STIJL (ART MOVEMENT) - EUROPE -
    EXHIBITIONS.**
Mondrian e De Stijl . Milano , c1990. 273 p. :
    ISBN 88-435-3172-7
        NYPL [3-MCH M741 91-6318]

De Strobel, Anna Maria. Le arazzerie romane dal
XVII al XIX secolo / Anna Maria de Strobel.
[Roma] : Istituto Nazionale di Studi Romani,
c1989. 99 p., [91] p. of plates : ill. ; 24 cm.
(Quaderni di storia dell'arte. 22) Includes
bibliographical references (p. [75]-78) and index.
    1. Tapestry, Baroque - Italy - Rome. 2. Tapestry -
    Italy - Rome. 3. Church decoration and ornament -
    Italy - Rome. I. Title.   **NYPL [3-MOR 91-3766]**

De Tolnay, Charles, 1899- Michelangelo
Buonarroti, 1475-1564. Michelangelo Buonarroti
/. Würzburg , c1964. 236 p. :
        NYPL [3-MCE B9 90-6774]

**DE UNGER, EDMUND - ART
    COLLECTIONS - CATALOGS.**
King, Monique. European textiles in the Keir
collection . London , Boston , 1990. 311 p. :
    ISBN 0-571-13371-1 :   DDC 746/.094/07442132
    20
NK8942 .K56 1990

De Versailles à Paris : le destin des collections
royales / ouvrage collectif sous la direction de
Jacques Charles. Paris : Centre Culturel du
Panthéon, 1989. 288 p., [38] p. of plates : ill.
(some col.) ; 29 cm. Exhibition held at the Mairie
du Ve arrondissement, Paris. Bibliography: p. 283-284.
    ISBN 2-9504070-0-5
    1. Royal houses - France - Art collections - Exhibitions.
    2. Furniture - France - History - 18th century -
    Exhibitions. 3. France - Royal household - Exhibitions.
    4. France - Kings and rulers - Dwellings - Exhibitions.
    I. Charles, Jacques. II. Paris (France). Mairie du 5e
    Arrondissement. III. Title: Destin des collections
    royales.   NYPL [3-MAWC (Paris) 90-12345]

De Vries, Jan, 1943 Nov. 14- Art in
history/history in art . Santa Monica, CA
[Chicago, Ill.] , 1991. p. cm.
    0-89236-201-4 :   DDC 701/.03/0949209032 20
N72.S6 A746 1991

De Wain Valentine, new work . Los Angeles
County, Calif. Museum of Art, Los Angeles.
Los Angeles, Calif. , c1979. [12] p. :
NB237.V28 A4 1979
        NYPL [3-MGO (Valentine) 81-769]

De Wevers en Vincent van Gogh / samenstelling
en redactie, G.J.M. van den Brink, W.Th.M.
Frijhoff. Zwolle : Waanders, c1990. 127 p. : ill.
(some col.) ; 28 cm. "Uitgave naar aanleiding van de
tentoonstelling 'De wevers en Vincent van Gogh', van 2
juni tot en met 7 oktober 1990 in het Nederlands
Textielmuseum te Tilburg"--Colophon. Summary in
English. Includes bibliographical references (p.
123-127).   ISBN 90-6630-222-4 :
    1. Gogh, Vincent van, 1853-1890 - Criticism and
    interpretation. 2. Weavers in art. I. Gogh, Vincent van,
    1853-1890. II. Brink, G. J. M. van den (Gabriël J. M.).
    III. Frijhoff, Willem. IV. Nederlands Textielmuseum
    Tilburg.
N6953.G63 D4 1990

Deacon, Richard, 1949-
Richard Deacon : sculptures, 1989-90. New
York : Marian Goodman Gallery, 1991. p. cm.
Catalog of the exhibition.   ISBN 0-944219-09-8
    DDC 730/.92 20
    1. Deacon, Richard, 1949- - Exhibitions. I. Marian
    Goodman Gallery. II. Title.
NB497.D44 A4 1991

DEACON, RICHARD, 1949- - EXHIBITIONS.
Deacon , Richard, 1949- Richard Deacon . New
York , 1991. p. cm.   ISBN 0-944219-09-8   DDC
    730/.92 20
NB497.D44 A4 1991

DEAD, LANTERNS OF THE. see **LANTERNS
    OF THE DEAD.**

**DEAD - PORTRAITS - HISTORY - 19TH
    CENTURY.**
Burns, Stanley B. Sleeping beauty . Altadena,
Calif. , 1990. 1 v. (unpaged) :   ISBN
    0-942642-32-5   **NYPL [MFW+ 91-6778]**

deAk, Edit. Spero, Nancy, 1926- Nancy Spero .
Kyoto, Japan , c1989. 1 v. (unpaged) :   ISBN
    4-7636-8548-1 :   DDC 760 20
N6537.S648 A4 1989

El Deán López-Cepero y su colección pictórica /.
Merchán Cantisán, Regla. Sevilla , 1979. 102
p., [9] leaves of plates :   ISBN 84-85268-53-9
ND804 .M47   **NYPL [3-MCP 81-534]**

Dean, Peter, 1934-
Peter Dean / introduction by Laurel Reuter;
essay by Carter Ratcliff. Grand Forks, N.D. :
North Dakota Museum of Art, 1989. 16, [52]
p. : ill., (some col.) ; 23 cm. Exhibition organized
by the North Dakota Museum of Art.   ISBN
    0-943107-02-4
    1. Dean, Peter 1934- - Exhibitions. I. Ratcliff, Carter.
    II. North Dakota Museum of Art. III. Title.
        NYPL [3-MCX D2785 90-12360]

Peter Dean : a retrospective : Alternative
Museum, September 28-October 27, 1990. 1st
ed. [New York] : The Museum, [1990?] 16 p. :
ill. ; 28 cm.   ISBN 0-932075-31-2
    1. Dean, Peter 1934- - Exhibitions. I. Alternative
    Museum (New York, N.Y.) II. Title.
        NYPL [3-MCX D2785 90-13373]

DEAN, PETER 1934- - EXHIBITIONS.
Dean, Peter, 1934- Peter Dean /. Grand Forks,
N.D. , 1989. 16, [52] p. :   ISBN 0-943107-02-4
        NYPL [3-MCX D2785 90-12360]

Dean, Peter, 1934- Peter Dean . [New York]
[1990?] 16 p. :   ISBN 0-932075-31-2
        NYPL [3-MCX D2785 90-13373]

Dean, Tom, 1947-
Tom Dean drawings, 1985-1990 : June 10-July
29, 1990. Kingston, Ont. : Agnes Etherington
Art Centre, Queen's University, [c1990] 1 v.
(unpaged) : ill. ; 23 cm. Includes bibliographical
references.   ISBN 0-88911-502-2   DDC 741.971 20
    1. Dean, Tom, 1947- - Exhibitions. I. Agnes
    Etherington Art Centre. II. Title.
NC143.D43 A4 1990

DEAN, TOM, 1947- - EXHIBITIONS.
Dean, Tom, 1947- Tom Dean drawings,
1985-1990 . Kingston, Ont. [c1990] 1 v.
(unpaged) :   ISBN 0-88911-502-2   DDC 741.971 20
NC143.D43 A4 1990

DeAngelus, Michele D. Okulick, John, 1947-
Transformation in perspective . Wilmington,
DE , 1991. 92 p. :   DDC 709/.2 20
NB237.O4 A4 1991
        NYPL [3-MGO+ (Okulick) 91-7465]

Dear happy ghosts . Hunter, William. Edinburgh ,
1990. 191 p. :   ISBN 1-85158-371-8 :   DDC
    941.443082 20   **NYPL [MFW 91-3480]**

Dear M . Pollock, Jack. Toronto, Ont. , c1989.
308 p. ;   ISBN 0-7710-7027-6 :
MLCM 90/06755 (N)
        NYPL [3-MAVC 91-5609]

Dear Nan . Carr, Emily, 1871-1945.
[Correspondence.] Vancouver , 1990. xlvi, 436
p., [24] p. of plates :   ISBN 0-7748-0348-7 (cloth)
        NYPL [3-MCZ c28 91-7320]

Deas, Malcolm D., 1941- Tipos y costumbres de
la Nueva Granada : la colección de pinturas
formada por Joseph Brown entre
1825 y 1841 y el diario de su excursión a
Girón, 1834 = Types and customs of New
Granada : the collection of paintings made in
Colombia by Joseph Brown between 1825 and
1841, and the journal of his excursion to Girón,
1834 / Malcolm Deas, Efraín Sánchez, Aída
Martínez.1a ed. Bogotá : Fondo Cultural
Cafetero, 1989. 229 p. : ill. (some col.) ; 31 cm.
Spanish and English. Includes bibliographical references
(p. 227-229).   ISBN 958-9144-25-X
    1. Brown, Joseph, 1802-1874. I. Brown, Joseph,
    1802-1874. II. Sánchez, Efraín. III. Martínez, Aída. IV.
    Title. V. Title: Types and customs of New Granada.
IN PROCESS (ONLINE)
        NYPL [3-MCV+ B8785 90-13354]

Death, Dance of. see **Dance of death.**

DEATH IN ART.
Der Totentanz auf der Spreuerbrücke in Luzern
=. Luzern [195-?] [64] p. :
        NYPL [3-MBO 89-20195]

DEATH IN ART - CATALOGS.
Universität Düsseldorf. Graphiksammlung.
Mensch und Tod . Düsseldorf , c1989. xxi, 525
p. :   ISBN 3-7998-0053-0
NE55.G4 D878 1989

DEATH IN ART - EXHIBITIONS.
Ashes to ashes . New York, N.Y. , c1982. 16
p. :   **NYPL [3-MAMZ 90-12622]**

Images of death in contemporary art .
Milwaukee, Wis. , c1990. 56 p. :   ISBN
    0-87462-902-X   **NYPL [3-MAMZ 91-7063]**

Totentanzfolgen . Braunschweig , 1989. 98 p. ;
    ISBN 3-927288-04-7
IN PROCESS (ONLINE)
        NYPL [3-MAMZ 90-12755]

Il "Trionfo della morte" di Palermo . Palermo ,
c1989. 88 p., [62] p. of plates :   ISBN
    88-7681-040-4   **NYPL [3-MLP 90-11764]**

DEATH-MASKS. see **MASKS (SCULPTURE)**

A Debate on abstraction : the Bertha and Karl
Leubsdorf Art Gallery, Hunter College. [New
York] : The Gallery, [1988?] 79 p. : ill. ; 22
cm. Catalog published in conjunction with the
following exhibitions at Hunter College: Systems and
abstraction, curated by Susan Edwards, Nov. 15-Dec.
22, 1988, The Persistence of painting, curated by
Vincent Longo, Feb. 1-Mar. 10, 1989, Anti-simulation:
materialism and abstraction, curated by Maurice Berger,
Mar. 16-Apr. 21, 1989, Photography and abstraction,
curated by Rosalind Krauss, May 1-June 2, 1989.
Includes bibliographical references.
    1. Art, Abstract - Exhibitions. 2. Photography,
    Abstract - Exhibitions. 3. Arts, Modern - 20th century -
    Exhibitions. I. Edwards, Susan. II. Longo, Vincent. III.
    Berger, Maurice. IV. Krauss, Rosalind E. V. Hunter
    College. Art Gallery.   NYPL [3-MAL 90-12609]

Debenham, Frank, 1883-1965.
Reader's Digest Association (Great Britain) The
Reader's Digest great world atlas. London,
Sydney [etc.] 1968. 179 p.   DDC 912
G1019 .R555 1968
        NYPL [Map Div. 90-12412]

Reader's Digest Association (Great Britain)
[Reader's digest great world atlas. Swedish.]
Det Bästas stora världsatlas. Stockholm , c1978.
1 atlas (215 p.) :   ISBN 91-7030-070-4
        NYPL [Map Div. 91-7523]

**Déblaiement d'art ; suivi de, La triple offense à
la beauté ; Le nouveau ; Max Elskamp ; La
voie sacrée ; La colonne** /. Velde, Henry van
de, 1863-1957. [Essays. Selections. 1979.]
Bruxelles , 1979. 198 p. ;   DDC 700 19
N70 .V38 1979   **NYPL [3-MAB 91-456]**

Debo, Sarat Chandra, 1911-1973.
Sarat Chandra Debo / editor, Dinanath Pathy.
1st ed. Bhubaneswar : Working Artists'
Association of Orissa, 1987. [22] p., [21] p. of
plates : ill. (some col.) ; 19 x 26 cm.
(Contemporary artists of Orissa series . 2) Cover title:
Saratchandra Debo. Reproduction of paintings; includes
biography of the painter.   DDC 759.954 20
    1. Debo, Sarat Chandra, 1911-1973 - Catalogs. I. Pathy,
    Dinanath. II. Working Artists' Association of Orissa.
    III. Title. IV. Title: Saratchandra Debo. V. Series.
ND2049.D36 A4 1987
        NYPL [3-MAF 91-4520]

**DEBO, SARAT CHANDRA, 1911-1973 -
    CATALOGS.**
Debo, Sarat Chandra, 1911-1973. Sarat
Chandra Debo /. Bhubaneswar , 1987. [22] p.,
[21] p. of plates :   DDC 759.954 20
ND2049.D36 A4 1987
        NYPL [3-MAF 91-4520]

Debrie, Christine. Richesses de la peinture
flamande et hollandaise des XVIe et XVIIe
siècles au Musée Jeanne d'Aboville de La Fère
/ par Christine Debrie. [La Fère] : Le Musée,
1988. 59 leaves, 33 leaves of plates : ill. ; 30
cm.
    1. Musée Jeanne d'Aboville - Catalogs. I. Title.
IN PROCESS (ONLINE)
        NYPL [MAVZ+ (La Fère) 91-5902]

Debroise, Olivier. Sussman, Elisabeth, 1939- El
corazón sangrante =. Boston, Mass. , Seattle,
Wash. , c1991. p.   ISBN 0-910663-50-5 (paperback)

DDC 704.9/46 20
N8217.H53 S87 1991

A decade in the contemporary galleries, 1949-1959. Pasadena Art Museum. [Pasadena, 1959] 76 p.   *NYPL [3-MAMT 91-287]*

The Decade show : frameworks of identity in the 1980s. [New York] : Museum of Contemporary Hispanic Art, c1990. 364 p. : ill. (some col.) ; 28 cm. Catalog of an exhibition held at the Museum of Contemporary Hispanic Art, May 16-Aug. 19, 1990, the New Museum of Contemporary Art, May 12-Aug. 19, 1990, and at the Studio Museum in Harlem, May 18 to Aug. 19, 1990. Includes bibliographical references.
ISBN 0-915557-68-1
1. Art, American - Exhibitions. 2. Art, Modern - 20th century - United States - Exhibitions. 3. Minorities as artists - United States - Exhibitions. I. Museum of Contemporary Hispanic Art (New York, N.Y.). II. New Museum of Contemporary Art (New York, N.Y.). III. Studio Museum in Harlem.
NYPL [3-MAMT 90-12484]

Deccan College Post-graduate and Research Institute, Poona India. American Institute of Indian Studies. see **American Institute of Indian Studies.**

Dech, Jula. Hannah Höch, Schnitt mit dem Küchenmesser Dada durch die letzte weimarer Bierbauchkulturepoche Deutschlands / von Jula Dech. Originalausg. Frankfurt am Main : Fischer Taschenbuch, 1989. 89 p., [1] folded leaf of plates : ill. (1 col.) ; 19 cm. (Kunststück) Bibliography: p. 88-89. ISBN 3-596-23970-2 :
1. Höch, Hannah, 1889- - Criticism and interpretation. 2. Höch, Hannah, 1889- Cut with the kitchen knife. 3. Dadaism - Germany. I. Title. II. Series.
NYPL [3-MCK H691 91-4661]

Decimo cuarto Salon de Grabado. XIV Salón de Grabado, diciembre de 1964 . [Madrid] [1964] [64] p. :
MLCS 83/618 (N)   NYPL [MDBF 90-5976]

Decker, Emile. Céramique lorraine . Nancy , Metz , c1990. 367 p. : ISBN 2-86480-458-1 :
DDC 738/.0944/38074758231 20
NK4098.L67 C47 1990

Deconstruction : omnibus volume / edited by Andreas Papadakis, Catherine Cooke & Andrew Benjamin. London : Academy Editions, 1989. 264 p. : ill. (some col.) ; 32 cm. Includes bibliographical references. ISBN 0-85670-996-4
1. Deconstructivism (Architecture). 2. Architecture, Modern - 20th century. I. Papadakēs, A. II. Cooke, Catherine. III. Benjamin, Andrew E.
NYPL [MQV+ 89-27959]

DECONSTRUCTION.
Miller, J. Hillis (Joseph Hillis), 1928- Illustration /. Cambridge, Mass. , 1992. p. cm. ISBN 0-674-44357-8 DDC 700/.1 20
NX640 .M55 1992

The New modernism . [[London] , New York , 1988. 80 p. : ISBN 0-85670-940-9
NYPL [3-MAL 90-4522]

DECONSTRUCTIVISM (ARCHITECTURE)
Deconstruction . London , 1989. 264 p. : ISBN 0-85670-996-4 *NYPL [MQV+ 89-27959]*

Decorating style. Garey, Carol Cooper. House beautiful decorating style /. New York , 1991. p. cm. ISBN 0-688-09734-0 : DDC 747.213 20
NK2115 .G25 1991

Decorating with fabric Liberty style /. Watkins, Charmian. London , 1987. 144 p. : ISBN 0-85223-595-X : DDC 747/.9 19
NK2115.5.F3   NYPL [3-MON 90-11077]

Decorating with pictures /. Hoppen, Stephanie. New York , 1991. p. cm. ISBN 0-517-58168-X : DDC 747/.9 20
NK2115.5.P48 H66 1991

Décoration . Dorn, Roland. Hildesheim , New York , 1990. xxxii, 622 p. : ISBN 3-487-09098-8
ND653.G7 D64 1990

DECORATION AND ORNAMENT.
Soulillou, Jacques. Le décoratif /. Paris , 1990. 91 p., 12 p. of plates : ISBN 2-252-02703-7
NK1510 .S68 1990

DECORATION AND ORNAMENT - 1900 STYLE. see **DECORATION AND ORNAMENT - ART NOUVEAU.**

DECORATION AND ORNAMENT - ANIMAL FORMS - INDIA.
The Decorative art of India /. New York ,

1990. 214 p., 102 p. of plates : ISBN 0-517-01489-0 DDC 745.4/4954 20
NK1476.A1 D43 1990

DECORATION AND ORNAMENT, ARCHITECTURAL.
Audsley, W. (William), b. 1833. [Polychromatic decoration as applied to buildings in the mediaeval styles.] Victorian sourcebook of medieval decoration /. New York , 1991. p. cm. ISBN 0-486-26834-9 (pbk.) DDC 729/.4 20
NK1548 .A84 1991

Soulillou, Jacques. Le décoratif /. Paris , 1990. 91 p., 12 p. of plates : ISBN 2-252-02703-7
NK1510 .S68 1990

DECORATION AND ORNAMENT, ARCHITECTURAL - ARAB COUNTRIES.
Hessemer, Friedrich Maximilian, 1800-1860. [Arabische und Alt-Italienische Bau-Verzierungen. English.] Historic designs and patterns in color from Arabic and Italian sources /. New York , c1990. 120 p. : ISBN 0-486-26425-4 DDC 745.4 20
NA3573 .H4713 1990
NYPL [3-MRX+ 91-6246]

DECORATION AND ORNAMENT, ARCHITECTURAL - BRAZIL - MINAS GERAIS.
Negro, Carlos del. Escultura ornamental barrôca do Brasil. [Belo Horizonte, 1967] 2 v.,
NB1285 .N4   NYPL [3-MRX 91-6337]

DECORATION AND ORNAMENT, ARCHITECTURAL - BRAZIL - MINAS GERAIS - DICTIONARIES.
Avila, Affonso, 1928- Barroco mineiro, glossário de arquitetura e ornamentação /. [Rio de Janeiro?] . 220 p. :
NA3533.A3 M563 1980

DECORATION AND ORNAMENT, ARCHITECTURAL - CALIFORNIA - LOS ANGELES.
Breeze, Carla. L.A. deco /. New York , 1991. p. cm. ISBN 0-8478-1434-3 DDC 720/.9794/9409042 20
NA735.L55 B74 1991

DECORATION AND ORNAMENT, ARCHITECTURAL - CATALOGS.
Fuhring, Peter. Design into art . London , New York , 1989. 2 v. (792 p.) : ISBN 0-85667-354-4
(London)   *NYPL [MLD+ 89-23146]*

DECORATION AND ORNAMENT, ARCHITECTURAL - CZECHOSLOVAKIA.
Hrady a zámky v Československu . Praha , Martin , 1990. 383 p. : ISBN 80-7038-100-0 :
NA7720 .H73 1990

DECORATION AND ORNAMENT, ARCHITECTURAL - EUROPE.
Tafelmaier, Walter, 1935- Architekturmalerei an Fassaden . Stuttgart , 1988. 159 p. : ISBN 3-421-02937-7   *NYPL [3-MRX 90-12633]*

Tahara, Keiichi, 1951- [Seikimatsu no kenchiku. English.] Images of fin-de-siècle architecture and interior decoration /. London , New York , 1988. 263 p. : ISBN 0-00-215354-8 : DDC 724.9/1 19
NA3485   *NYPL [3-MRX+ 91-3382]*

DECORATION AND ORNAMENT, ARCHITECTURAL - FRANCE - CONSERVATION AND RESTORATION - CONGRESSES.
L'Ornementation architecturale en pierre dans les monuments historiques . [Paris] [1989] 280 p. : ISBN 2-11-085558-4
NA3549.A1 O76 1989

DECORATION AND ORNAMENT, ARCHITECTURAL - FRANCE - MARSEILLE - THEMES, MOTIVES.
Architectures historiques à Marseille . Aix-en-Provence , c1987. 141 p. : ISBN 2-85744-290-4 : DDC 720/.944/912 19
NA1051.M37 U73 1987
NYPL [3-MQWF+ 90-12768]

DECORATION AND ORNAMENT, ARCHITECTURAL - FRANCE - PARIS.
Goy-Truffaut, Françoise. Paris façade /. Paris , c1989. 245 p. : ISBN 2-85025-208-5
NYPL [3-MRX 90-5327]

DECORATION AND ORNAMENT, ARCHITECTURAL - GERMANY - REGENSBURG.
Fuchs, Friedrich. Das Hauptportal des

Regensburger Domes . München , c1990. 175 p. : ISBN 3-7954-0652-8
NA5586.R385 F8 1990

DECORATION AND ORNAMENT, ARCHITECTURAL - GERMANY (WEST) - MÜNDEN.
Konovaloff, Arpád. Ornament am Fachwerk . Münster [1985?] 86 p., [83] p. of plates : ISBN 3-88660-169-2 DDC 728/.0943/59 19
NA7351.M83 K66 1985
NYPL [3-MRN 90-10411]

DECORATION AND ORNAMENT, ARCHITECTURAL - GREECE.
Oppermann, Manfred. Vom Medusabild zur Athenageburt . Leipzig , 1990. 195 p. : ISBN 3-363-00471-0 DDC 733/.3 20
NB133 .O6 1990

DECORATION AND ORNAMENT, ARCHITECTURAL - ITALY.
Hessemer, Friedrich Maximilian, 1800-1860. [Arabische und Alt-Italienische Bau-Verzierungen. English.] Historic designs and patterns in color from Arabic and Italian sources /. New York , c1990. 120 p. : ISBN 0-486-26425-4 DDC 745.4 20
NA3573 .H4713 1990
NYPL [3-MRX+ 91-6246]

DECORATION AND ORNAMENT, ARCHITECTURAL - ITALY - FLORENCE.
Firenze, frammenti di memoria /. Firenze , c1990. 200 p. :
NA3552.F57 F56 1990

DECORATION AND ORNAMENT, ARCHITECTURAL - ITALY - MANTUA.
Suitner Nicolini, Gianna. Palazzo Te, Mantova /. Milano , c1990. 114 p. : ISBN 88-435-3099-2
NA7756.M3 S8 1990

Zuccoli, Noris. Mantova . Firenze , 1986. 60 p. :   *NYPL [3-MQWB 90-12550]*

DECORATION AND ORNAMENT, ARCHITECTURAL - ITALY - SANTA MARIA CAPUA VETERE - CONSERVATION AND RESTORATION.
Vargas, Davide. Colore e arredo urbano . Napoli [Santa Maria Capua Vetere] [1990] 154 p. :
NA3552.S27 V3 1990

DECORATION AND ORNAMENT, ARCHITECTURAL - ITALY - TREVISO.
Botter, Mario. Affreschi decorativi di antiche case trivigiane, dal XIII al XV secolo /. Treviso , 1979 (1987 printing) 162 p. :
NYPL [3-MLP+ 91-4495]

DECORATION AND ORNAMENT, ARCHITECTURAL - LAOS - THEMES, MOTIVES.
D [Vientiane] [1959?] [100] p. :
NA3578.6.L3 D64 1959

DECORATION AND ORNAMENT, ARCHITECTURAL - MEXICO - MEXICO (CITY)
Rangel, Magdalena E. de. La Casa de los Azulejos . [Mexico] , 1986. 131 p., [10] p. of plates :
NA3511.M65 R35 1986

DECORATION AND ORNAMENT, ARCHITECTURAL - MOROCCO.
Terrasse, Henri, 1895-1971. Les arts décoratifs au Maroc /. Casablanca , c1988. 198 p. :
NK1487.75.A1 T47 1988

DECORATION AND ORNAMENT, ARCHITECTURAL - NEW YORK (N.Y.)
Tunick, Susan. Ceramic ornament in the New York subway system /. New York, N.Y. , Italy [1989?] [14] p. :
NYPL [3-MRXZ+ 90-10715]

DECORATION AND ORNAMENT, ARCHITECTURAL - PORTUGAL.
Meco, José, 1952- O azulejo em Portugal /. Lisboa , c1989. 256 p. : DDC 738.6/09469 20
NK4670.7.P6 M43 1989

Simões, J. M. dos Santos (João Miguel dos Santos), 1907-1972. Azulejaria em Portugal nos séculos XV e XVI. Lisboa , 1990. 197 p. : DDC 738.6/09469/09024 20
NK4670.7.P6 S57 1990

DECORATION AND ORNAMENT, ARCHITECTURAL - PORTUGAL - COIMBRA.
Anacleto, Regina. O artista conimbricense

Miguel Costa, 1859-1914 /. Coimbra , 1989.
113 p. : ISBN 972-90380-6-6   DDC 738/.092 20
NK4670.7.P63 C673 1989

**DECORATION AND ORNAMENT,
  ARCHITECTURAL - RÉUNION -
  THEMES, MOTIVES.**
Egon, J. Paul (Jean-Paul) Lambroquins à la
Réunion /. Saint-Denis [1985] 95 p. : DDC
728.3/7/096981 19
NK9789.84.R48 E36 1985
                    NYPL [3-MRX+ 90-11044]

**DECORATION AND ORNAMENT,
  ARCHITECTURAL - SAUDI ARABIA -
  MEDINA.**
Ṭāhā, Ḥātim ʻUmar, 1957- Ṭaybah wa-fannuhā
al-rafiʻ /. [Medina] [198-] 140 p. :
NA7419.S2 T27 1980z

**DECORATION AND ORNAMENT,
  ARCHITECTURAL - TERMINOLOGY.**
White, Antony, 1941- Architecture &
ornament . New York , 1991. p. cm. ISBN
0-8306-3352-9 : DDC 720/.14 20
NA31 .W44 1991

**DECORATION AND ORNAMENT,
  ARCHITECTURAL - THEMES,
  MOTIVES.**
Sullivan, Louis H., 1856-1924. [System of
architectural ornament according with a
philosophy of man's powers.] Louis H.
Sullivan . New York , 1990. 159 p. : ISBN
0-8478-1109-3 DDC 720/.22/22 20
NA2707.S94 A4 1990
                    NYPL [3-MRX++ 91-4221]

**DECORATION AND ORNAMENT,
  ARCHITECTURAL - TURKEY.**
Schneider, Gerd. Pflanzliche Bauornamente der
Seldschuken in Kleinasien /. Wiesbaden ,
c1989. 278 p. : ISBN 3-88226-472-1
NA3565.A1 S36X1989

**DECORATION AND ORNAMENT,
  ARCHITECTURAL - TURKEY - KONYA -
  THEMES, MOTIVES.**
Sarre, Friedrich Paul Theodor, 1865-1945.
Konia . Berlin [1921] 30 p., 12 leaves of plates
(some folded) : DDC 720/.9564 20
NA5871.k86 S27 1921

**DECORATION AND ORNAMENT,
  ARCHITECTURAL - UKRAINE -
  THEMES, MOTIVES.**
Skliarenko, G. IA. (Galina IAkovlevna)
Khudozhnik i gorod . Kiev , 1990. 102 p., [32]
p. of plates : ISBN 5-12-001093-8 :
ND2768.U37 S54 1990

**DECORATION AND ORNAMENT,
  ARCHITECTURAL - YEMEN - ṢANʻĀʼ.**
Bonnenfant, Guillemette. L'art du bois à
Sanaa . Aix-en-Provence , c1987. 208 p. :
    ISBN 2-85744-315-3
NA3573.6.Y42 S254 1987
                    NYPL [3-MRX+ 91-4933]

**DECORATION AND ORNAMENT - ART
  DECO.**
Pelichet, Edgar. La céramique art déco /.
Lausanne , Paris , c1988. 199 p. : ISBN
2-88148-007-1 DDC 738/.09/041 20
NK3930.3.A77 P4 1988
                    NYPL [3-MPC+ 90-11744]

Starr, Steve. Picture perfect . New York , 1991.
p. cm. ISBN 0-8478-1332-0 DDC 749/.7/09041 20
N8550 .S73 1991

**DECORATION AND ORNAMENT - ART
  DECO - COLLECTORS AND
  COLLECTING - CATALOGS.**
Art deco /. New York, NY , 1991. p. cm.
    ISBN 0-670-83956-6 DDC 709/.04/012075 20
NK1396.A76 A78 1991

**DECORATION AND ORNAMENT - ART
  NOUVEAU - CATALOGS.**
The Complete "Masters of the poster" . New
York , 1990. xv, 240, [16] p. : ISBN
0-486-26309-6 DDC 741.6/74/09034 20
NC1845.A7 C6 1990
                    NYPL [3-MDW+ 90-12311]

Landesmuseum Mainz. Jugendstil . Mainz ,
c1990. 396 p. : ISBN 3-8053-1141-9
NK5109.85.A7 L35 1990

**DECORATION AND ORNAMENT - ART
  NOUVEAU - EXHIBITIONS.**
Le Bijou 1900 . Bruxelles , 1965. 102 p., [26] p.
of plates : **NYPL [3-MNR 90-6082]**

**DECORATION AND ORNAMENT - BALTIC
  STATES - THEMES, MOTIVES.**
Innes, Jocasta. Scandinavian painted decor /.
New York , 1990. 256 p. : ISBN 0-8478-1235-9
    DDC 729/.4/0948 20
ND2770 .I55 1990   **NYPL [3-MLP 91-3275]**

**DECORATION AND ORNAMENT -
  BELGIUM - ART NOUVEAU.**
Watelet, Jacques Grégoire, 1917-
Serrurier-Bovy . Paris [1989, c1987] 134 p. :
                    NYPL [MOF 91-6858]

**DECORATION AND ORNAMENT -
  BULGARIA - EXHIBITIONS.**
Bulgaria . [Liverpool] , 1989. 79 p. : ISBN
    0-906367-38-7 (pbk.) : DDC 949.770074 20
                    NYPL [3-MNE+ 90-11535]

**DECORATION AND ORNAMENT -
  CATALOGS.**
Fuhring, Peter. Design into art . London , New
York , 1989. 2 v. (792 p.) : ISBN 0-85667-354-4
(London)   **NYPL [MLD+ 89-23146]**

**DECORATION AND ORNAMENT, CELTIC -
  THEMES, MOTIVES.**
Davis, Courtney, 1946- Celtic designs and
motifs /. New York , 1991. 44 p. : ISBN
0-486-26718-0 (pbk.) : DDC 745.4/41/09364 20
NK1264 .D38 1991

**DECORATION AND ORNAMENT - CHILE -
  HISTORY - 20TH CENTURY.**
Lago, Tomás. Arte popular chileno /. Santiago
de Chile [1985] 136 p. :
NK901 .L33 1985

**DECORATION AND ORNAMENT - CHINA -
  EXHIBITIONS.**
Magic, art and order . Palm Springs, Calif. ,
c1990. 155 p. : **NYPL [3-MNW+ 90-13208]**

**DECORATION AND ORNAMENT - CHINA -
  THEMES, MOTIVES.**
Jones, Owen, 1809-1874. The complete
"Chinese ornament" . New York , 1990. 100 p.
of plates : ISBN 0-486-26259-6 : DDC 745.4/4951
20
NK1483.A1 J64 1990
                    NYPL [3-MLF+ 91-3685]

**DECORATION AND ORNAMENT - EMPIRE
  STYLE.**
Il Palazzo del Quirinale . Roma, 1989. 2 v. :
                    NYPL [3-MQWB+ 90-12794]

**DECORATION AND ORNAMENT -
  ENGLAND - CONGRESSES.**
The Fashioning and functioning of the British
country house /. Washington, D.C. , Hanover
[N.H.] , 1989. 417 p. : ISBN 0-89468-128-1
                    NYPL [3-MRG 90-12992]

**DECORATION AND ORNAMENT -
  EUROPE - ART NOUVEAU.**
Tahara, Keiichi, 1951- [Seikimatsu no kenchiku.
English.] Images of fin-de-siècle architecture
and interior decoration /. London , New York ,
1988. 263 p. : ISBN 0-00-215354-8 : DDC
724.9/1 19
NA3485   **NYPL [3-MRX+ 91-3382]**

**DECORATION AND ORNAMENT -
  EUROPE - CHINESE INFLUENCES -
  EXHIBITIONS.**
Drömmen om Kina. [Göteborg] , 1984. 55 p. :
                    NYPL [3-MAM 90-12530]

**DECORATION AND ORNAMENT -
  EUROPE - HISTORY - 16TH CENTURY -
  CATALOGS.**
Museum für Kunsthandwerk Frankfurt am
Main. Ornament und Entwurf . Frankfurt am
Main , c1983. 199 p., [8] p. of plates : ISBN
3-88270-021-1 DDC 745.4/494//0740341 19
NK1530 .M87 1983   **NYPL [MDE 85-3207]**

**DECORATION AND ORNAMENT -
  EUROPE - HISTORY - 17TH CENTURY -
  CATALOGS.**
Museum für Kunsthandwerk Frankfurt am
Main. Ornament und Entwurf . Frankfurt am
Main , c1983. 199 p., [8] p. of plates : ISBN
3-88270-021-1 DDC 745.4/494//0740341 19
NK1530 .M87 1983   **NYPL [MDE 85-3207]**

**DECORATION AND ORNAMENT -
  EUROPE - HISTORY - 18TH CENTURY -
  CATALOGS.**
Museum für Kunsthandwerk Frankfurt am
Main. Ornament und Entwurf . Frankfurt am
Main , c1983. 199 p., [8] p. of plates : ISBN

3-88270-021-1 DDC 745.4/494/0740341 19
NK1530 .M87 1983   **NYPL [MDE 85-3207]**

**DECORATION AND ORNAMENT -
  EUROPE - HISTORY - 19TH CENTURY -
  CATALOGS.**
Museum für Kunsthandwerk Frankfurt am
Main. Ornament und Entwurf . Frankfurt am
Main , c1983. 199 p., [8] p. of plates : ISBN
3-88270-021-1 DDC 745.4/494/0740341 19
NK1530 .M87 1983   **NYPL [MDE 85-3207]**

**DECORATION AND ORNAMENT -
  EUROPE - PRIVATE COLLECTIONS -
  NEW YORK (N.Y.) - EXHIBITIONS.**
Metropolitan Museum of Art (New York, N.Y.)
The Lesley and Emma Sheafer collection . New
York , 1975. [26] p. :
                    NYPL [3-MAX (Sheafer) 90-5897]

DECORATION AND ORNAMENT - FRANCE.
Feray, Jean. Architecture intérieure et
décoration en France, des origines à 1875 /.
Paris , c1988. 399 p. : ISBN 2-7013-0752-X
    DDC 729/.0944 20
NA2850 .F4 1988
                    NYPL [3-MLF+ 90-12087]

**DECORATION AND ORNAMENT -
  FRANCE - ART DECO.**
Kjellberg, Pierre. Art déco . [Paris] [1986] 247
p. : ISBN 2-85917-054-5 : DDC 749.24 19
NK2549 .K59 1986
                    NYPL [3-MOF+ 91-5321]

**DECORATION AND ORNAMENT -
  FRANCE - ART DECO - CATALOGS.**
Montry, Annie de. Voyages, avec Roger
Broders . Paris , c1991. 117 p. : ISBN
2-86738-595-4
NC1850.B76 A4 1991

**DECORATION AND ORNAMENT -
  FRANCE - ART NOUVEAU.**
Duncan, Alastair. Louis Majorelle . New York ,
1991. p. cm. ISBN 0-8109-3617-8 DDC
    745.4/492 20
NK1535.M24 D8 1991

Mortimer, Tony L. Lalique. . London , 1989.
128 p. : ISBN 1-87130-764-3
                    NYPL [3-MNR 90-5089]

**DECORATION AND ORNAMENT -
  FRANCE - ART NOUVEAU -
  EXHIBITIONS.**
Guimard, Hector, 1867-1942. Hector Guimard .
Paris , 1971. 45 p. :
                    NYPL [3-MRX 90-7184]

**DECORATION AND ORNAMENT -
  FRANCE - EMPIRE STYLE.**
Percier,Charles, 1764-1838. [Recueil de
décorations intérieures. English.] Empire
stylebook of interior design . New York , 1991.
p. cm. ISBN 0-486-26754-7 DDC 747.24/09/034
20
NK1449.A1 P4713 1991

**DECORATION AND ORNAMENT -
  FRANCE - HISTORY - 18TH CENTURY -
  EXHIBITIONS.**
Myers, Mary L., 1940- Architectural and
ornament drawings . New York , 1991. p. cm.
    ISBN 0-87099-625-8 DDC
    741.944/09/0330747471 20
NC246 .M94 1991

**DECORATION AND ORNAMENT -
  FRANCE - HISTORY - 19TH CENTURY.**
Duncan, Alastair. Louis Majorelle . New York ,
1991. p. cm. ISBN 0-8109-3617-8 DDC
    745.4/492 20
NK1535.M24 D8 1991

**DECORATION AND ORNAMENT -
  FRANCE - VERSAILLES -
  EXHIBITIONS.**
Charles Le Brun, 1619-1690, célébration du
tricentenaire de la mort de l'artiste . Paris ,
c1990. 102 p. : ISBN 2-7118-2393-8
                    NYPL [3-MCO L454 91-5557]

**DECORATION AND ORNAMENT -
  GERMANY - DARMSTADT.**
Darmstadt Künstler-Kolonie. Museum
Künstlerkolonie Darmstadt /. Darmstadt
[1989?] lv, 253 p. :   **NYPL [3-MLF 91-5455]**

**DECORATION AND ORNAMENT, GOTHIC -
  THEMES, MOTIVES.**
Pugin, Augustus, 1762-1832. [Gothic ornament.]
Pugin's gothic ornament . New York , 1987.
100 p. : ISBN 0-486-25500-X (pbk.) DDC

745.4/42 19
NK1295 .P84 1987
NYPL [3-MLEC+ 91-3947]

**DECORATION AND ORNAMENT -
HISTORY.**
Riegl, Alois, 1858-1905. [Stilfragen. English.]
Problems of style . Princeton, NJ , 1993. p. cm.
ISBN 0-8071-1706-4 :   DDC 745.4/4 20
NK1175 .R513 1993

**DECORATION AND ORNAMENT -
HISTORY - 20TH CENTURY.**
Woodham, Jonathan M. Twentieth-century
ornament /. New York , 1990. 335 p. : ISBN
0-8478-1221-9 DDC 745.4/442 20
NK1390 .W6 1990
NYPL [3-MLD 90-13196]

**DECORATION AND ORNAMENT -
INTERNATIONAL STYLE -
EXHIBITIONS.**
Design 1935-1965 . [Montréal] , 1991. 424 p. :
ISBN 0-8109-3205-9 DDC 745/.09/0407471428
20
NK1394 .D47 1991
NYPL [3-MNH+ 91-7472]

**DECORATION AND ORNAMENT, ISLAMIC -
ARAB COUNTRIES.**
Hessemer, Friedrich Maximilian, 1800-1860.
[Arabische und Alt-Italienische
Bau-Verzierungen. English.] Historic designs
and patterns in color from Arabic and Italian
sources /. New York , c1990. 120 p. : ISBN
0-486-26425-4 DDC 745.4 20
NA3573 .H4713 1990
NYPL [3-MRX+ 91-6246]

**DECORATION AND ORNAMENT, ISLAMIC -
MOROCCO.**
Terrasse, Henri, 1895-1971. Les arts décoratifs
au Maroc /. Casablanca , c1988. 198 p. :
NK1487.75.A1 T47 1988

**DECORATION AND ORNAMENT, ISLAMIC -
TURKEY.**
Schneider, Gerd. Pflanzliche Bauornamente der
Seldschuken in Kleinasien /. Wiesbaden ,
c1989. 278 p. : ISBN 3-88226-472-1
NA3565.A1 S36X1989

**DECORATION AND ORNAMENT, ISLAMIC -
YEMEN - ṢANʻAʼ.**
Bonnenfant, Guillemette. L'art du bois à
Sanaa . Aix-en-Provence , c1987. 208 p. :
ISBN 2-85744-315-3
NA3573.6.Y42 S254 1987
NYPL [3-MRX+ 91-4933]

DECORATION AND ORNAMENT - ITALY.
Hessemer, Friedrich Maximilian, 1800-1860.
[Arabische und Alt-Italienische
Bau-Verzierungen. English.] Historic designs
and patterns in color from Arabic and Italian
sources /. New York , c1990. 120 p. : ISBN
0-486-26425-4 DDC 745.4 20
NA3573 .H4713 1990
NYPL [3-MRX+ 91-6246]

**DECORATION AND ORNAMENT - ITALY -
TREVISO.**
Botter, Mario. Affreschi decorativi di antiche
case trivigiane, dal XIII al XV secolo /.
Treviso , 1979 (1987 printing) 162 p. :
NYPL [3-MLP+ 91-4495]

DECORATION AND ORNAMENT - JAPAN.
Yanagi, Muneyoshi, 1889-1961. The unknown
craftsman. [Tokyo, Palo Alto, Calif., 1972] 230
p. ISBN 0-87011-184-1 DDC 745.4/49/52
NK1071 .Y34 1972
NYPL [3-MNE 90-5442]

**DECORATION AND ORNAMENT - JAPAN -
EXHIBITIONS.**
Artes decorativas modernas del Japón .
México , 1964. [14] p. :
NYPL [3-MNE 91-833]

**DECORATION AND ORNAMENT,
MEDIEVAL.**
Audsley, W. (William), b. 1833. [Polychromatic
decoration as applied to buildings in the
mediaeval styles.] Victorian sourcebook of
medieval decoration /. New York , 1991. p.
cm. ISBN 0-486-26834-9 (pbk.) DDC 729/.4 20
NK1548 .A84 1991

**DECORATION AND ORNAMENT,
MEDIEVAL - ITALY.**
Hessemer, Friedrich Maximilian, 1800-1860.
[Arabische und Alt-Italienische

Bau-Verzierungen. English.] Historic designs
and patterns in color from Arabic and Italian
sources /. New York , c1990. 120 p. : ISBN
0-486-26425-4 DDC 745.4 20
NA3573 .H4713 1990
NYPL [3-MRX+ 91-6246]

**DECORATION AND ORNAMENT -
MOROCCO.**
Terrasse, Henri, 1895-1971. Les arts décoratifs
au Maroc /. Casablanca , c1988. 198 p. :
NK1487.75.A1 T47 1988

**DECORATION AND ORNAMENT, MUSLIM.
see DECORATION AND ORNAMENT,
ISLAMIC.**

**DECORATION AND ORNAMENT -
NEBRASKA - LINCOLN.**
A Harmony of the arts . Lincoln , c1990. x,
119 p. : ISBN 0-8032-2887-2 (alk. paper) DDC
725/.11/09782293 19
NA4413.L56 H37 1990
NYPL [3-MQWO 90-11994]

**DECORATION AND ORNAMENT - PLANT
FORMS.**
Hofmann, Richard, of Plauen im Vogtland.
Decorative flower and leaf designs /. New
York , 1991. p. cm. ISBN 0-486-26869-1 DDC
745.4 20
NK1560 .H57 1991

**DECORATION AND ORNAMENT - PLANT
FORMS - INDIA.**
The Decorative art of India /. New York ,
1990. 214 p., 102 p. of plates : ISBN
0-517-01489-0 DDC 745.4/4954 20
NK1476.A1 D43 1990

**DECORATION AND ORNAMENT - PLANT
FORMS - JAPAN - THEMES, MOTIVES.**
Japanese floral stencil designs /. New York ,
1991. 94 p. : ISBN 0-486-26655-9 : DDC 746.6
20
NK1484.A1 J37 1991

**DECORATION AND ORNAMENT -
PORTUGAL.**
Lino, António. O homem e a casa, a casa e o
tempo /. [Lisboa] , 1990. 131 p. :
NK1103 .L56 1990

**DECORATION AND ORNAMENT,
PRIMITIVE.**
Bossert, Helmuth Theodor, 1889-1961.
[Ornamente der Völker. English.] Folk art of
primitive peoples . New York [1955] 15 p., 40
leaves of plates : DDC 745
NK1177 .B612   *NYPL [3-MNE+ 91-5923]*

**DECORATION AND ORNAMENT - QUEEN
ANNE STYLE.**
Vandal, Norman L., 1948- Queen Anne
furniture . Newtown, Conn. , c1990. 247 p. :
ISBN 0-942391-07-1 : DDC 749.214 20
TT197 .V36 1990   *NYPL [3-MOF 91-3711]*

**DECORATION AND ORNAMENT,
RENAISSANCE - EXHIBITIONS.**
Auch kleine Dinge . [Cambridge] [1971] [174]
p. :   *NYPL [3-MNC 90-5886]*

Byrne, Janet S. Renaissance ornament prints
and drawings /. New York , c1981. 143 p. :
ISBN 0-87099-288-0 DDC 760/.094/07401471
19
NE441 .B97   *NYPL [MDB 83-1989]*

**DECORATION AND ORNAMENT,
RENAISSANCE - ITALY.**
Rosa, Gilda. La decorazione rinascimentale /.
Milano , c1966. 156 p. :
NYPL [3-MNC 90-6051]

**DECORATION AND ORNAMENT, ROCOCO -
UNITED STATES - EXHIBITIONS.**
Heckscher, Morrison H. American rococo,
1750-1775 . New York : [Los Angeles] : p. cm.
ISBN 0-87099-630-4 DDC
745.4/4974/090330747471 20
NK1403.5 .H4 1992

**DECORATION AND ORNAMENT, RUSTIC -
SCANDINAVIA.**
Barwick, JoAnn. Scandinavian country /. New
York , c1991. p. cm. ISBN 0-517-57661-9 :
DDC 745.4/4948 20
NK1457 .B37 1991

**DECORATION AND ORNAMENT -
SCANDINAVIA - THEMES, MOTIVES.**
Innes, Jocasta. Scandinavian painted decor /.
New York , 1990. 256 p. : ISBN 0-8478-1235-9

DDC 729/.4/0948 20
ND2770 .I55 1990   *NYPL [3-MLP 91-3275]*

**DECORATION AND ORNAMENT, SELJUK -
TURKEY.**
Schneider, Gerd. Pflanzliche Bauornamente der
Seldschuken in Kleinasien /. Wiesbaden ,
c1989. 278 p. : ISBN 3-88226-472-1
NA3565.A1 S36X1989

**DECORATION AND ORNAMENT -
SWEDEN - NEOCLASSICISM.**
Groth, Håkan. Neo-classicism in the North .
New York , 1990. 224 p. : ISBN 0-8478-1273-1
DDC 728/.37/09485 20
NK1461.A1 G76 1990
NYPL [3-MLO 91-3368]

**DECORATION AND ORNAMENT - THEMES,
MOTIVES.**
Flat ornament. Treasury of historic pattern and
design /. New York , 1990. 150 p. : ISBN
0-486-26274-X DDC 745.4 20
NK1175 .F5 1990
NYPL [3-MLD+ 90-11804]

**DECORATION AND ORNAMENT - UNITED
STATES - ART DECO - THEMES,
MOTIVES.**
Baker, Eric, 1949- Trademarks of the 40's and
50's /. San Francisco , c1988. 156 p. : ISBN
0-87701-485-X : DDC 741.6 19
NC998.5.A1 B36 1988
NYPL [MNF 88-3842]

**DECORATION AND ORNAMENT - UNITED
STATES - HISTORY - 18TH CENTURY -
EXHIBITIONA.**
Heckscher, Morrison H. American rococo,
1750-1775 . New York : [Los Angeles] : p. cm.
ISBN 0-87099-630-4 DDC
745.4/4974/090330747471 20
NK1403.5 .H4 1992

**DECORATION AND ORNAMENT,
VICTORIAN - UNITED STATES.**
Creating a dignified past . Savage, Md. , c1991.
ix, 129 p. : ISBN 0-8476-7690-0
NYPL [3-MLF 91-6907]

**DECORATION AND ORNAMENT -
WINDSOR STYLE.**
Santore, Charles. The Windsor style in
America . Philadelphia, Pa. , c1991. p. ISBN
1-561-38057-1 DDC 749.214 20
NK2406 .S37 1991

**DECORATION, INTERIOR. see INTERIOR
DECORATION.**

Decoration U. S.A. Wilson, José. New York
[c1965] 278 p. DDC 747.213
NK2002 .W53   *NYPL [3-MLO+ 91-6753]*

**DECORATIVE ART IN ARCHITECTURE. see
DECORATION AND ORNAMENT,
ARCHITECTURAL.**

The Decorative art of India / introduction by
Susan Stronge. New York : Portland House,
1990. 214 p., 102 p. of plates : chiefly ill. (some
col.) ; 34 cm. "Compilation of material from the
following publications: the Journal of Indian art ...
India, photographs and drawings of historical
buildings ... and Jaipur enamels, by S.S. Jacobs and
T.H. Hendley"--T.p. verso. ISBN 0-517-01489-0
DDC 745.4/4954 20
*1. Decoration and ornament - Plant forms - India. 2.
Decoration and ornament - Animal forms - India. I.
Portland House (Firm).*
NK1476.A1 D43 1990

DECORATIVE ARTS.
Jockel, Nils. Alles Plastik . [Hamburg] , 1985.
36 p. :   *NYPL [3-MGF 86-364]*

**DECORATIVE ARTS, AMERICAN -
MICHIGAN - DEARBORN.**
Popular antiques at the Henry Ford Museum.
[Westfield, N.Y.? , 1959?] 36 p. :
*NYPL [3-MAVZ+ (Dearborn, Mi.)
90-5439]*

**DECORATIVE ARTS, ANCIENT - THRACE -
EXHIBITIONS.**
Traci . Milano , c1989. 347 p. :
NK1000.T48 T73 1989
NYPL [3-MAE+ 91-6582]

**DECORATIVE ARTS - ARKANSAS -
HISTORY - 19TH CENTURY.**
Bennett, Swannee, 1949- Arkansas made .
Fayetteville , c1990-1991. 2 v. : ISBN
1-557-28138-6 (v. 1 : alk. paper) DDC

709/.767/09034 20
NK835.A8 B4 1990

DECORATIVE ARTS, BUDDHIST - SOUTH ASIA - EXHIBITIONS.
Arts from the rooftop of Asia . New York
[1971] 4, [46] p. : *NYPL [3-MAE 91-302]*

DECORATIVE ARTS - BULGARIA - HISTORY - 20TH CENTURY.
Sŭvremenni dekorativno-prilozhni izkustva v Bŭlgariĭa /. Sofiĭa , 1989. 262 p. :
NK1019 .S95 1989

DECORATIVE ARTS - CATALOGS.
Mace, O. Henry. Collector's guide to Victoriana /. Radnor, Pa. , c1991. p. cm. ISBN
0-87069-600-9 (hc) : DDC 745.1/09/034075 20
NK1378 .M3 1991

DECORATIVE ARTS - COMPETITIONS - JAPAN - EXHIBITIONS.
Santori Bijutsukan taishō ten '88 =. Tōkyō , 1988. 84 p. : *NYPL [3-MLF 90-13007]*

DECORATIVE ARTS - CZECHOSLOVAKIA - HISTORY.
Medková, Jiřina. Řeč věcí . Praha , 1990. 153, [4] p. : ISBN 80-7012-026-6 :
NK600 .M4 1990

DECORATIVE ARTS - DOMINICAN REPUBLIC.
Castillo, José del, 1947- Artesanía dominicana /. Santo Domingo, República Dominicana , 1989. 125 p. : DDC 745/.097293 20
NK886.D65 C38 1989

DECORATIVE ARTS, EARLY AMERICAN - SOUTHERN STATES - CATALOGS.
Museum of Early Southern Decorative Arts. The regional arts of the early South . Winston-Salem, N.C. , 1991. p. ISBN
0-945578-02-4 : DDC 745/.0975/07475667 20
NK811 .M87 1991

DECORATIVE ARTS - EUROPE - CATALOGS.
Art Institute of Chicago. European decorative arts in the Art Institute of Chicago /. Chicago, Ill. , New York , c1991. p. ISBN 0-8109-3253-9
(Abrams : hardcover) DDC 745/.094/07477311 20
NK925 .A78 1991

DECORATIVE ARTS - EUROPE - CONGRESSES.
Internationaler Kongress Europäisches Kunsthandwerk (1988 : Stuttgart, Germany) Internationaler Kongress Europäisches Kunsthandwerk 1988, Stuttgart . Frankfurt , 1988. 56 p. ; ISBN 3-87864-176-1
NYPL [3-MNC+ 90-12554]

DECORATIVE ARTS - EUROPE - HISTORY.
Calloway, Stephen. Royal style . Boston , 1991. p. ISBN 0-316-12509-1 : DDC 745/.094 20
NK925 .C35 1991

DECORATIVE ARTS - EXHIBITIONS.
Heirlooms [microform] . Manchester, N.H. [1985] [5] leaves : *NYPL [*ZM-218 no.2]*

DECORATIVE ARTS - FINLAND - HISTORY.
Kruskopf, Erik. Finlands konstindustri . Borgå , c1989. 268 p. : ISBN 951-0-15964-6
NK1035.F5 K78 1989

DECORATIVE ARTS - FRANCE - EXHIBITIONS.
Les Années UAM, 1929-1958 . Paris , c1988. 268 p. : ISBN 2-901422-11-X
NYPL [3-MLF 90-10798]

DECORATIVE ARTS - FRANCE - HISTORY - 19TH CENTURY.
Troy, Nancy J. Modernism and the decorative arts in France . New Haven , c1991. xx, 300 p., [16] p. of plates : ISBN 0-300-04554-9 (alk. paper)
DDC 745/.0944/09041 20
NK947 .T76 1991   *NYPL [3-MLF 91-5453]*

DECORATIVE ARTS - FRANCE - HISTORY - 20TH CENTURY.
Brunhammer, Yvonne. [Artistes décorateurs. English.] The decorative arts in France,
·1900-1942 . New York , 1990. 288 p. : ISBN
0-8478-1251-0 DDC 745/.0944/09041 20
NK1396.S63 A7813 1990
NYPL [3-MNE+ 91-3934]

Troy, Nancy J. Modernism and the decorative arts in France . New Haven , c1991. xx, 300 p., [16] p. of plates : ISBN 0-300-04554-9 (alk. paper)

DDC 745/.0944/09041 20
NK947 .T76 1991   *NYPL [3-MLF 91-5453]*

DECORATIVE ARTS - FRANCE - PARIS - CATALOGS.
Musée du Louvre . Paris , 1985. 300 p. : ISBN 2-7118-2365-2
NYPL [3-MAVZ (Paris) 91-5074]

DECORATIVE ARTS, FRISIAN.
Fries Museum (Leeuwarden, Netherlands) Fries Museum /. Haarlem , c1978. 110 p. : ISBN
90-70024-07-1   *NYPL [3-MAVZ (Leeuwarden, Netherlands) 90-5650]*

DECORATIVE ARTS - GEORGIA - EXHIBITIONS.
Hidden heritage . Atlanta , 1990. 127 p. : ISBN 0-939802-62-7
NYPL [3-MNE 91-48]

DECORATIVE ARTS - GERMANY - BERLIN - CATALOGS.
Kunsthandwerk der Gegenwart . [Berlin] , 1989. 152 p. :
NK954.6.A1 K86 1989

DECORATIVE ARTS - GERMANY (EAST) - HISTORY - 20TH CENTURY - CATALOGS.
Kunsthandwerk der Gegenwart . [Berlin] , 1989. 152 p. :
NK954.6.A1 K86 1989

DECORATIVE ARTS - GERMANY - HISTORY - 20TH CENTURY.
Design in Deutschland, 1933-45 . Giessen , 1990. 141 p. : ISBN 3-87038-146-9
N14 .W454 vol. 20 NK951

DECORATIVE ARTS - GERMANY - HISTORY - 20TH CENTURY - EXHIBITIONS.
Zeitgenössisches deutsches Kunsthandwerk . München , c1990. 443 p. : ISBN 3-7913-1090-9
DDC 745/.0943/07443 20
NK951 .Z364 1990

DECORATIVE ARTS - GERMANY (WEST) - HAMBURG - CATALOGS.
Museum für Kunst und Gewerbe Hamburg. Kunst für Hamburg . Hamburg , c1990. 251 p. :
NYPL [3-MLF 91-6790]

DECORATIVE ARTS - GERMANY (WEST) - MITTELFRANKEN - HISTORY - 20TH CENTURY - EXHIBITIONS.
Kunsthandwerk im Stadtmuseum . [Nürnberg] [1987] 55 p. : DDC 730/.0943/320740332 19
NK952.M58 K86 1987
NYPL [3-MLF 90-12631]

DECORATIVE ARTS - GERMANY (WEST) - NUREMBERG - HISTORY - 20TH CENTURY - EXHIBITIONS.
Kunsthandwerk im Stadtmuseum . [Nürnberg] [1987] 55 p. : DDC 730/.0943/320740332 19
NK952.M58 K86 1987
NYPL [3-MLF 90-12631]

DECORATIVE ARTS - GREAT BRITAIN - HISTORY - 19TH CENTURY.
Haslam, Malcolm. Arts & crafts /. London , 1988. 168 p. : ISBN 0-356-15633-8 : DDC 745/.0941/075 20
NK1142 .H38 1988

DECORATIVE ARTS - GREAT BRITAIN - HISTORY - 20TH CENTURY.
Haslam, Malcolm. Arts & crafts /. London , 1988. 168 p. : ISBN 0-356-15633-8 : DDC 745/.0941/075 20
NK1142 .H38 1988

DECORATIVE ARTS - HEW HAMPSHIRE - EXHIBITIONS.
Heirlooms [microform] . Manchester, N.H. [1985] [5] leaves : *NYPL [*ZM-218 no.2]*

DECORATIVE ARTS - HISTORY.
Medková, Jiřina. Řeč věcí . Praha , 1990. 153, [4] p. : ISBN 80-7012-026-6 :
NK600 .M4 1990

DECORATIVE ARTS - HISTORY - 19TH CENTURY.
Mielke, Heinz-Peter. Kriegsgefangenen Arbeiten aus zwei Jahrunderten /. Viersen [1987] 232 p. : ISBN 3-924568-00-6
NYPL [3-MLE 91-6772]

DECORATIVE ARTS - HISTORY - 20TH CENTURY.
Capella, Juli. [Diseño de arquitectos en los 80. English.] Designed by architects in the 1980s /.

New York , 1988. 191 p. : ISBN 0-8478-0941-2 :
DDC 749.2/0498 19
NK2702 .C3713 1988
NYPL [3-MOI 91-6559]

Levin, Marianne, 1942- Plagiat, stöld, förebild, inspiration /. [Solna] , c1990. 138 p. : ISBN
91-7332-505-8 :
NK789 .L48 1990

Mielke, Heinz-Peter. Kriegsgefangenen Arbeiten aus zwei Jahrunderten /. Viersen [1987] 232 p. : ISBN 3-924568-00-6
NYPL [3-MLE 91-6772]

DECORATIVE ARTS - HISTORY - 20TH CENTURY - COLLECTORS AND COLLECTING - CATALOGS.
Art deco /. New York, NY , 1991. p. cm. ISBN 0-670-83956-6 DDC 709/.04/012075 20
NK1396.A76 A78 1991

DECORATIVE ARTS - HISTORY - 20TH CENTURY - EXHIBITIONS.
Design 1935-1965 . [Montréal] , 1991. 424 p. : ISBN 0-8109-3205-9 DDC 745/.09/0407471428 20
NK1394 .D47 1991
NYPL [3-MNH+ 91-7472]

DECORATIVE ARTS - ILLINOIS - CHICAGO - CATALOGS.
Art Institute of Chicago. European decorative arts in the Art Institute of Chicago /. Chicago, Ill. , New York , c1991. p. ISBN 0-8109-3253-9
(Abrams : hardcover) DDC 745/.094/07477311 20
NK925 .A78 1991

The decorative arts in France, 1900-1942 .
Brunhammer, Yvonne. [Artistes décorateurs. English.] New York , 1990. 288 p. : ISBN
0-8478-1251-0 DDC 745/.0944/09041 20
NK1396.S63 A7813 1990
NYPL [3-MNE+ 91-3934]

DECORATIVE ARTS - IRELAND - EXHIBITIONS.
National Museum of Ireland. Irish decorative arts, 1550-1928 /. [Dublin] 1990. 94 p. : ISBN 0-901777-21-8
NYPL [3-MNE 90-13211]

DECORATIVE ARTS, ISLAMIC - CATALOGS.
Islamic art in the Keir collection /. London , Boston , 1988. xviii, 316 p., [60] p. of plates :
ISBN 0-571-13753-9 DDC 745/.0917/67107442176 20
NK720 .I84 1988   *NYPL [3-MAF 91-3908]*

DECORATIVE ARTS, ISLAMIC - PAKISTAN - SWAT RIVER VALLEY.
Kalter, Johannes. The arts and crafts of the Swat Valley . New York, NY , 1991. 180 p. :
ISBN 0-500-97384-9
NYPL [3-MNE 91-7551]

DECORATIVE ARTS - ITALY.
Thornton, Peter, 1926- The Italian Renaissance interior, 1400-1600 /. New York , 1991. p. cm.
ISBN 0-8109-3459-0 DDC 747.25/09/024 20
NK959 .T47 1991

DECORATIVE ARTS - ITALY - ALPS, ITALIAN - HISTORY - 20TH CENTURY.
Artigianato di tradizione nelle Alpi occidentali italiane . Ivrea, Italy , c1990. 305 p. : DDC 745/.0945/1 20
NK960.A536 A78 1990

DECORATIVE ARTS - JAPAN - COLLECTORS AND COLLECTING - CATALOGS.
Florence, Gene, 1944- The collector's encyclopedia of Occupied Japan collectibles . Paducah, KY , c1990. 127 p. : ISBN
0-89145-401-2 : DDC 738/.0952/075 20
NK1071 .F583 1990

DECORATIVE ARTS - JAPAN - EXHIBITIONS.
Japanska konstskatter från Tokyo Fuji Art Museum /. Stockholm , 1990. 78 p.:
NK1071 .J37 1990

DECORATIVE ARTS - JAPAN - HISTORY - 20TH CENTURY - EXHIBITIONS.
Santori Bijutsukan taishō ten '88 =. Tōkyō , 1988. 84 p. : *NYPL [3-MLF 90-13007]*

DECORATIVE ARTS - LATVIA.
Latviešu lietišķā māksla /. Riga , 1987. 153 p., [32] p. of plates :
NK976.L3 L254 1987

DECORATIVE ARTS - LIBRARY RESOURCES - DELAWARE - WILMINGTON.
Winterthur Library. American cornucopia . Winterthur, Del. , 1990. 115 p. : ISBN 0-912724-20-X DDC 026.973 20
Z733.W785 W55 1990
NYPL [3-MAVZ (Wilmington) 91-3457]

DECORATIVE ARTS - MADAGASCAR - EXHIBITIONS.
Salon de l'artisanat de Madagascar (1989) Salon de l'artisanat de Madagascar, 25 août au 03 septembre 1989. [Madagascar] [1989] 3 v. in 2 ;
NK1086.6.M3 S25 1989

DECORATIVE ARTS - MADAGASCAR - HISTORY.
Salon de l'artisanat de Madagascar (1989) Salon de l'artisanat de Madagascar, 25 août au 03 septembre 1989. [Madagascar] [1989] 3 v. in 2 ;
NK1086.6.M3 S25 1989

DECORATIVE ARTS, MAORI - EXHIBITIONS.
Mau mahara . Auckland, N.Z. , 1990. 130 p. : ISBN 1-86941-093-9
NYPL [3-MNE 91-5081]

DECORATIVE ARTS, MEDIEVAL - GERMANY - CHIEMSEE.
Dannheimer, Hermann. Torhalle auf Frauenchiemsee . München , 1983, c1980. 118 p. : ISBN 3-7954-0818-0
NYPL [3-MRBB 91-6996]

DECORATIVE ARTS - MEXICO.
Sayer, Chloë. Arts and crafts of Mexico /. London , 1990. 160 p. : ISBN 0-87701-781-6 :
NYPL [3-MNE 91-4573]

DECORATIVE ARTS - MEXICO - MICHOACÁN DE OCAMPO.
El Quehacer de un pueblo . Morelia, Michoacán , 1986. 183, [9] p. : ISBN 968-667-045-9 DDC 745/.0972/37 20
NK845.M53 Q44 1986

DECORATIVE ARTS - NEW ZEALAND - EXHIBITIONS.
Mau mahara . Auckland, N.Z. , 1990. 130 p. : ISBN 1-86941-093-9
NYPL [3-MNE 91-5081]

DECORATIVE ARTS - NORTH CAROLINA - WINSTON-SALEM - CATALOGS.
Museum of Early Southern Decorative Arts. The regional arts of the early South . Winston-Salem, N.C. , 1991. p. ISBN 0-945578-02-4 : DDC 745/.0975/07475667 20
NK811 .M87 1991

DECORATIVE ARTS - NORTHWESTERN STATES - HISTORY - 20TH CENTURY - EXHIBITIONS.
Yard art . Boise, Idaho , c1991. 1 v. (unpaged) : DDC 745/.0979/07479628 20
NK824 .Y37 1991

DECORATIVE ARTS - PAKISTAN - SWAT RIVER VALLEY.
Kalter, Johannes. The arts and crafts of the Swat Valley . New York, NY , 1991. 180 p. : ISBN 0-500-97384-9
NYPL [3-MNE 91-7551]

DECORATIVE ARTS - PORTUGAL.
Artesanato da região norte . Porto , 1989. 406 p. : ISBN 972-90030-0-9 DDC 745/.09469 20
NK1003 .A83 1989

DECORATIVE ARTS - PRIVATE COLLECTIONS - CALIFORNIA - LOS ANGELES - EXHIBITIONS.
Bowman, Leslie Greene. American arts & crafts . Los Angeles, Calif. , Boston , c1990. 255 p. : ISBN 0-8212-1824-7 (hardback) : DDC 745/.0973/07479494 20
NK1141 .B64 1990
NYPL [3-MNE+ 91-4630]

DECORATIVE ARTS - PRIVATE COLLECTIONS - QUÉBEC (PROVINCE) - MONTRÉAL - EXHIBITIONS.
Design 1935-1965 . [Montréal] , 1991. 424 p. : ISBN 0-8109-3205-9 DDC 745/.09/0407471428 20
NK1394 .D47 1991
NYPL [3-MNH+ 91-7472]

DECORATIVE ARTS, RENAISSANCE - ITALY.

Thornton, Peter, 1926- The Italian Renaissance interior, 1400-1600 /. New York , 1991. p. cm. ISBN 0-8109-3459-0 DDC 747.25/09/024 20
NK959 .T47 1991

DECORATIVE ARTS - RUSSIAN S.F.S.R.
Cerwinske, Laura. Russian imperial style /. New York , 1990. 223 p. : ISBN 0-13-784810-2 : DDC 745/.0947 20
NK975 .C45 1990
NYPL [3-MLF+ 91-3951]

DECORATIVE ARTS - RUSSIAN S.F.S.R. - DAGESTANSKAIA A.S.S.R. - HISTORY.
Mammaev, M. M. Dekoratino-prikladnoe iskusstvo Dagestana . Makhachkala , 1989. 345 p. :
NK1045.D3 M36 1989

DECORATIVE ARTS, SHAKER - NEW YORK (STATE) - EXHIBITIONS.
Kramer, Fran. Simply Shaker . Rochester, NY , c1991. 86 p. : ISBN 0-938551-01-9 DDC 745/.08/8288 20
NK838.G76 K73 1991

DECORATIVE ARTS, SHAKER - NEW YORK (STATE) - GROVELAND - EXHIBITIONS.
Kramer, Fran. Simply Shaker . Rochester, NY , c1991. 86 p. : ISBN 0-938551-01-9 DDC 745/.08/8288 20
NK838.G76 K73 1991

DECORATIVE ARTS - SOVIET UNION.
Sbornik khudozhestvenno-promyshlennykh risunkov. S.-Peterburg , 1889. [2] p., [60] plates in portfolio : ***NYPL [Slav. Reserve 90-4456 no. 73 (Bates).]***

DECORATIVE ARTS - SOVIET UNION - HISTORY - 20TH CENTURY.
Art décoratif soviétique 1917-1937 /. Paris , c1989. 436 p. : ISBN 2-903370-46-X DDC 745/.0947/09041 20
NK975 .A79 1989
NYPL [3-MLF+ 90-2331]
Tolstoĭ, Vladimir Pavlovich. Russian decorative arts, 1917-1937 /. New York , 1990. 439 p. : ISBN 0-8478-1242-1 DDC 745/.0947/09041 20
NK975 .T6 1990 ***NYPL [3-MLF+ 91-2690]***

DECORATIVE ARTS - STUDY AND TEACHING - GERMANY - HISTORY.
Heller, Dieter. Die Entwicklung des Werkens und seiner Didaktik von 1880 bis 1914 . Bad Heilbrunn/Obb. , 1990. 322 p. : ISBN 3-7815-0652-5 :
NK249 .H44 1990

DECORATIVE ARTS - THRACE - EXHIBITIONS.
Traci . Milano , c1989. 347 p. :
NK1000.T48 T73 1989
NYPL [3-MAE+ 91-6582]

DECORATIVE ARTS - TURKEY - EXHIBITIONS.
Diplomaten und Wesire . München , 1988. 187 p., [24] p. of plates :
NYPL [3-MAF 90-12662]

DECORATIVE ARTS - TURKEY - THEMES, MOTIVES.
Żygulski, Zdzisław. Ottoman art in the service of the empire /. New York , c1991. p. cm. ISBN 0-8147-9671-0 : DDC 745/.09561 20
NK1011 .Z94 1991

DECORATIVE ARTS - UKRAINE - EXHIBITIONS.
Ukrainian Museum (New York, N.Y.) Ukrainian folk art /. New York , c1984. [28] p. ; ***NYPL [*QGA 89-3075 (1984)]***

DECORATIVE ARTS - UNITED STATES - CATALOGS.
Layton Art Collection. American furniture with related decorative arts, 1660-1830 /. New York , c1991. p. ISBN 1-555-95068-X : DDC 749.213/074/77595 20
NK2406 .L38 1991

United States. Dept. of State. Treasures of State . New York , 1991. p. cm. ISBN 0-8109-3911-8 (cloth) DDC 709/.73/074753 20
N6505 .U48 1991

DECORATIVE ARTS - UNITED STATES - HISTORY - 19TH CENTURY - EXHIBITIONS.
Bowman, Leslie Greene. American arts & crafts . Los Angeles, Calif. , Boston , c1990. 255 p. : ISBN 0-8212-1824-7 (hardback) : DDC

745/.0973/07479494 20
NK1141 .B64 1990
NYPL [3-MNE+ 91-4630]

DECORATIVE ARTS - UNITED STATES - HISTORY - 20TH CENTURY.
Conway, Patricia. Art for everyday . New York, N.Y. , 1990. 264 p. : ISBN 0-517-57381-4 DDC 745/.0973/0904 20
NK808 .C64 1990 ***NYPL [3-MLO 90-12856]***

DECORATIVE ARTS - UNITED STATES - HISTORY - 20TH CENTURY - CATALOGS.
Fine woodworking design book five . Newtown, Conn. , c1990. 185 p. : ISBN 0-942391-28-4 : DDC 674/.8 20
NK2408 .F57 1990

DECORATIVE ARTS - UNITED STATES - HISTORY - 20TH CENTURY - COLLECTIBLES.
Kerr, Ann, 1921- The collector's encyclopedia of Russel Wright designs /. Paducah, KY , c1990. 189 p. : ISBN 0-89145-423-3 : DDC 745.4/492 20
NK839.W75 K47 1990

DECORATIVE ARTS - UNITED STATES - HISTORY - 20TH CENTURY - EXHIBITIONS.
Bowman, Leslie Greene. American arts & crafts . Los Angeles, Calif. , Boston , c1990. 255 p. : ISBN 0-8212-1824-7 (hardback) : DDC 745/.0973/07479494 20
NK1141 .B64 1990
NYPL [3-MNE+ 91-4630]

DECORATIVE ARTS, VICTORIAN.
Wissinger, Joanna. Victorian details . New York , c1990. 160 p . : ISBN 0-525-24844-7 (cloth) ***NYPL [3-MLE 90-12318]***

DECORATIVE ARTS, VICTORIAN - GREAT BRITAIN.
Victoria, the intimate home. New York , 1991. p. cm. ISBN 0-688-13489-0 DDC 747.2/048 20
NK2115.5.V53 V49 1991

DECORATIVE ARTS - WASHINGTON (D.C.) - CATALOGS.
United States. Dept. of State. Treasures of State . New York , 1991. p. cm. ISBN 0-8109-3911-8 (cloth) DDC 709/.73/074753 20
N6505 .U48 1991

DECORATIVE ARTS - WISCONSIN - MILWAUJEE - CATALOGS.
Layton Art Collection. American furniture with related decorative arts, 1660-1830 /. New York , c1991. p. ISBN 1-555-95068-X : DDC 749.213/074/77595 20
NK2406 .L38 1991

Decorative flower and leaf designs /. Hofmann, Richard, of Plauen im Vogtland. New York , 1991. p. cm. ISBN 0-486-26869-1 DDC 745.4 20
NK1560 .H57 1991

Decorative frames and borders . Gillon, Edmund Vincent. New York [1973] 173 p. : ISBN 0-486-22928-9 DDC 741.6
NK1530 .G54 1973
NYPL [3-MLD 90-12472]

Decorative ironwork /. Zimelli, Umberto. [Ferro battuto. English.] [London , 1987. 154 p. : ISBN 0-304-32158-3 (pbk.) : DDC 739/.474 19
NK8242 ***NYPL [3-MNK 91-5042]***

Decorative maps /. Barron, Roderick. London , 1990,c1989. 8 p., 40 leaves of plates : ISBN 1-85170-298-9 ***NYPL [Map Div. 91-4236]***

DECORATIVE METAL-WORK. see ART METAL-WORK.

The decorator /. Dampierre, Florence de. New York , 1989. 255 p. : ISBN 0-08-478118-2 DDC 729/.092/2 B 20
NK2115.8 .D36 1989
NYPL [3-MLO+ 91-3369]

La decorazione rinascimentale /. Rosa, Gilda. Milano , c1966. 156 p. : ***NYPL [3-MNC 90-6051]***

DECOYS (HUNTING)
Levinson, John M., 1927- Shorebirds . Centreville, Md. , 1991. p. ISBN 0-87033-424-7 : DDC 745.593/6 20
NK9704 .L56 1991

Dedert, Hartmut. Pariser Opern- und Konzerthäuser . Tübingen , c1989. 71 p. :

ISBN 3-8030-0149-8
NA6840.F72 P3736 1989

Dedicatòries /. Dali, Salvador, 1904- Barcelona
[1990] 223 p. : ISBN 84-85984-55-2
NC287.D3 A4 1990
           NYPL   [3-MCQ D14 91-4506]

Dedora, B. (Brian) With WK in the workshop : a
memoir of William Kurelek / Brian Dedora ;
introduction by Ramsay Cook ; with paintings,
drawings, and photographs by William Kurelek.
Stratford, Ont. : Aya Press/Mercury Press,
1989. 64 p. : ill. (some col.) ; 23 cm. Spine title:
A memoir of William Kurelek. ISBN 0-920544-68-1 :
DDC 759.11 20
*1. Kurelek, William, 1927-. 2. Painters - Canada -
Biography. I. Kurelek, William, 1927-. II. Title. III.
Title: Memoir of William Kurelek.*
           NYPL   [3-MCZ K971 91-6555]

Dee, Elaine Evans. Fuhring, Peter. Design into
art . London , New York , 1989. 2 v. (792 p.) :
ISBN 0-85667-354-4 (London)
           NYPL   [MLD+ 89-23146]

**DEFACEMENT OF ART. see ART -
MUTILATION, DEFACEMENT, ETC.**

DeFeo, Jay, 1929-
Stich, Sidra. Jay DeFeo . Berkeley, Calif. ,
1989. 89 p. :
IN PROCESS (ONLINE)
           NYPL   [3-MCX+ D313 90-11686]

DEFEO, JAY, 1929- - EXHIBITIONS.
Stich, Sidra. Jay DeFeo . Berkeley, Calif. ,
1989. 89 p. :
IN PROCESS (ONLINE)
           NYPL   [3-MCX+ D313 90-11686]

Definición y clasificación del arte popular /.
Ortiz Angulo, Ana. México, D.F. , 1990. 150
p. : ISBN 968-606-893-7 DDC 709/.72 20
NK844 .O78 1990

The Definitively unfinished Marcel Duchamp /
edited by Thierry de Duve. Halifax, N.S. :
Nova Scotia College of Art and Design ;
Cambridge, Mass. : MIT Press, 1991. p. cm.
Includes bibliographical references and index. ISBN
0-262-04117-0 DDC 709/.2 20
*1. Duchamp, Marcel, 1887-1968 - Criticism and
interpretation. I. Duve, Thierry de.*
N6853.D8 D44 1991

Defossez, Freddy, 1952-
Dervin, Sylvie, 1953- Defossez, peintures,
lithographies /. [Paris] , c1990. 190 p. : ISBN
2-87736-098-9 : DDC 760/.092 20
N6853.D327 A4 1990

DEFOSSEZ, FREDDY, 1952- - CATALOGS.
Dervin, Sylvie, 1953- Defossez, peintures,
lithographies /. [Paris] , c1990. 190 p. : ISBN
2-87736-098-9 : DDC 760/.092 20
N6853.D327 A4 1990

Defossez, peintures, lithographies /. Dervin,
Sylvie, 1953- [Paris] , c1990. 190 p. : ISBN
2-87736-098-9 : DDC 760/.092 20
N6853.D327 A4 1990

DEFRAOUI, CHERIF - EXHIBITIONS.
Defraoui, Silvie. Orient/occident /. Genève ,
c1989. 53 p. :
           NYPL   [3-MCZ + D316 89-27977]

Defraoui, Silvie.
Orient/occident / Silvie Defraoui, Cherif
Defraoui ; [rédaction : Sylvie Matthey,
Lysiane Lechot, Babina Chaillot]. Genève :
Centre d'art contemporain, c1989. 53 p. : ill.
(some col.) ; 25 x 31 cm. Catalog of an exhibition
held at Musee Rath, Genève, January, February 1989;
Museum van Hedendaagse Kunst, Antwerp,
March-April 1989; Centre de création contemporaine,
Tours, May-June 1989, and other cities. Includes
bibliographical references.
*1. Defraoui, Silvie - Exhibitions. 2. Defraoui, Cherif -
Exhibitions. 3. Art, Swiss - Exhibitions. 4. Art,
Modern - 20th century - Switzerland - Exhibitions. I. Matthey,
Sylvie. II. Lechot, Lysiane. III. Chaillot, Babina. IV.
Museum van Hedendaagse Kunst. V. Centre de création
contemporaihe (Tours, France). VI. Title. VII. Title:
Silvie and Cherif Defraoui. VIII. Title: Orient occident.*
           NYPL   [3-MCZ + D316 89-27977]

DEFRAOUI, SILVIE - EXHIBITIONS.
Defraoui, Silvie. Orient/occident /. Genève ,
c1989. 53 p. :
           NYPL   [3-MCZ + D316 89-27977]

Degand, Léon. Abstraction, figuration : langage et
signification de la peinture / Léon Degand ;
introduction de Daniel Abadie. Paris : Editions
Cerle d'art, c1988. 273 p. : ill. ; 23 cm.
(Diagonales, 0985-0619) Includes index. ISBN
2-7022-0226-8
*1. Figure painting. 2. Painting, Abstract. 3. Painting -
Language. I. Title.*
ND1290 .D44 1988

Degano, E. (Enrico) Architettura in pietra a
secco . Fasano, Br , c1990. 578 p. : ISBN
88-7514-413-3 : DDC 721/.0441 20
NA4130 .A73 1990

Degas /. Bouret, Jean. Paris , c1987. 223 p. :
ISBN 2-85056-186-X :
           NYPL   [3-MCO D31 90-13587]

Degas . Degas, Edgar, 1834-1917. New York ,
Ottawa , 1988. 640 p. : ISBN 0-87099-519-7
DDC 709.2 19
N6853.D33 A4 1988
           NYPL   [3-MCO+ D31 90-12588]

Degas /. Loyrette, Henri. [Paris] , c1991. vii, 851
p., [16] p. of plates : ISBN 2-213-02086-8
           NYPL   [3-MCO D31 91-4275]

Degas. Terrasse, Antoine. Edgar Degas /.
London , 1988. 94 p. : ISBN 0-304-32165-6
           NYPL   [3-MCO+ D31 90-5412]

Degas, Edgar, 1834-1917.
Bouret, Jean. Degas /. Paris , c1987. 223 p. :
ISBN 2-85056-186-X :
           NYPL   [3-MCO D31 90-13587]

Degas : [an exhibition held at the] Galeries
nationales du Grand Palais, Paris, 9
February-16 May 1988, National Gallery of
Canada, Ottawa, 16 June-28 August 1988, the
Metropolitan Museum of Art, New York, 27
September 1988-8 January 1989 / Jean
Sutherland Boggs ... [et al.]. New York :
Metropolitan Museum of Art ; Ottawa :
National Gallery of Canada, 1988. 640 p. : ill.
(some col.) ; 31 cm. Includes index. Bibliography: p.
614-620. ISBN 0-87099-519-7 DDC 709.2 19
*1. Degas, Edgar, 1834-1917 - Exhibitions. I. Boggs,
Jean Sutherland. II. Galeries nationales du Grand Palais
(France). III. Metropolitan Museum of Art (New York,
N.Y.). IV. Title.*
N6853.D33 A4 1988
           NYPL   [3-MCO+ D31 90-12588]

Degas, images of women. [Liverpool] [1989]
72 p. : ISBN 1-85437-025-1 (pbk.) : DDC 709.24
20
N6853.D33
           NYPL   [3-MCO+ D31 90-11609]

Edgar Degas : esculturas, Biblioteca Luis-Angel
Arango, Bogotá, colección Museo de Arte
Moderno de Sao Paulo Assis Chateaubriand,
mayo-junio 1990. Bogotá, D.E., Colombia :
Banco de la República, [1990] 1 v. (unpaged) :
ill. (some col.) ; 28 cm. DDC 730/.92 20
*1. Degas, Edgar, 1834-1917 - Exhibitions. I. Biblioteca
Luis-Angel Arango. II. Museu de Arte de São Paulo
Assis Chateaubriand. III. Title.*
NB553.D4 A4 1990

Terrasse, Antoine. Edgar Degas /. London ,
1988. 94 p. : ISBN 0-304-32165-6
           NYPL   [3-MCO+ D31 90-5412]

DEGAS, EDGAR, 1834-1917.
Loyrette, Henri. Degas /. [Paris] , c1991. vii,
851 p., [16] p. of plates : ISBN 2-213-02086-8
           NYPL   [3-MCO D31 91-4275]

Terrasse, Antoine. Edgar Degas /. London ,
1988. 94 p. : ISBN 0-304-32165-6
           NYPL   [3-MCO+ D31 90-5412]

DEGAS, EDGAR, 1834-1917 - EXHIBITIONS.
Degas, Edgar, 1834-1917. Degas . New York ,
Ottawa , 1988. 640 p. : ISBN 0-87099-519-7
DDC 709.2 19
N6853.D33 A4 1988
           NYPL   [3-MCO+ D31 90-12588]

Degas, Edgar, 1834-1917. Edgar Degas .
Bogotá, D.E., Colombia [1990] 1 v.
(unpaged) : DDC 730/.92 20
NB553.D4 A4 1990

Degas, images of women. [Liverpool] [1989]
72 p. : ISBN 1-85437-025-1 (pbk.) : DDC 709.24
20
N6853.D33
           NYPL   [3-MCO+ D31 90-11609]

**DEGAS, EDGAR, 1834-1917 - CRITICISM
AND INTERPRETATION.**
Bouret, Jean. Degas /. Paris , c1987. 223 p. :
ISBN 2-85056-186-X :
           NYPL   [3-MCO D31 90-13587]

Degas, images of women. [Liverpool] : Tate
Gallery Liverpool, [1989] 72 p. : ill. (some
col.), ports. ; 32 cm. Bibliography: p. 71. ISBN
1-85437-025-1 (pbk.) : DDC 709.24 20
*1. Degas, Edgar, 1834-1917 - Exhibitions. I. Degas,
Edgar, 1834-1917. II. Tate Gallery Liverpool.*
N6853.D33
           NYPL   [3-MCO+ D31 90-11609]

Degenerate art : the fate of the avant-garde in
Nazi Germany / [edited by] Stephanie Barron ;
with contributions by Peter Guenther ... [et al.].
Los Angeles, Calif. : Los Angeles County
Museum of Art ; New York : H.N. Abrams,
c1991. 423 p. : ill. (some col.) ; 31 cm. Published
in conjunction with the exhibition to be held at the Los
Angeles County Museum of Art, Feb. 17-May 12,
1991, and at the Art Institute of Chicago, June 22-Sept.
8, 1991. Includes bibliographical references and index.
ISBN 0-8109-3653-4 DDC 709/.43/07477311 20
*1. Art, German - Exhibitions. 2. Art, Modern - 20th
century - Germany - Exhibitions. 3. National socialism
and art - Exhibitions. 4. Germany - Cultural policy -
Exhibitions. I. Barron, Stephanie. II. Guenther, Peter
W. III. Los Angeles County Museum of Art. IV. Art
Institute of Chicago.*
N6868 .D3388 1991

Degenerate art : the fate of the avant-garde in
Nazi Germany / [edited by] Stephanie Barron ;
with contributions by Peter Guenther ... [et al.].
Los Angeles, Calif. : Los Angeles County
Museum of Art ; New York : H.N. Abrams,
c1991. p. cm. Published in conjunction with the
exhibition to be held at the Los Angeles County
Museum of Art, Feb. 17-May 12, 1991, and at the Art
Institute of Chicago, June 22-Sept. 8, 1991. Includes
bibliographical references and index. ISBN
0-87587-158-5 DDC 709/.43/07477311 20
*1. Art, German - Exhibitions. 2. Art, Modern - 20th
century - Germany - Exhibitions. 3. National socialism
and art - Exhibitions. 4. Germany - Cultural policy -
Exhibitions. I. Barron, Stephanie. II. Guenther, Peter
W. III. Los Angeles County Museum of Art. IV. Art
Institute of Chicago.*
N6868 .D3388 1991b

Degn, Ole. Scandinavian atlas of historic towns.
Odense , 1977- portfolios : ISBN 87-7492-216-5
(no. 1)   **NYPL   [Map Div. 82-813]**

Degrees of discovery . Historic New Orleans
Collection. [New Orleans, La.] [1977] 31 p. :
DDC 912/.763 19
GA427 .H57 1977 Rosenwald Coll
           NYPL   [Map Div. 91-140]

Dehejia, Vidya. Art of the imperial Cholas /
Vidya Dehejia. New York : Columbia
University Press, c1990. xviii, 148 p. : ill. ; 27
cm. (The Polsky lectures in Indian and Southeast
Asian art and archaeology) Includes bibliographical
references (p. 135-137) and index. ISBN
0-231-07188-4 DDC 726/.145/09548 20
*1. Architecture, Chola. 2. Sculpture, Chola. 3.
Temples - India, South. 4. Temples, Hindu - India,
South. 5. Sculpture, Hindu - India, South. 6. Sculpture
- India, South. I. Title. II. Series.*
NA6007.S6 D44 1990
           NYPL   [3-MAF 90-12973]

Dehio-Handbuch.
Niederösterreich . Wien , c1990. xxxviii, 1414
p., [13] leaves of plates : ISBN 3-7031-0652-2
           NYPL   [3-MQWD 91-3702]

Niederösterreich nördlich der Donau /. Wien ,
c1990. xxxviii, 1414 p., 6 p. of plates : ISBN
3-7031-0652-2 DDC 720/.946/12 20
NA1009.L68 N54 1990

Deichman-Sørensen, Trine. Kulturanalyse /.
[Oslo] , c1990. 236 p. ; ISBN 82-05-18967-6
NX456 .K77 1990

Deichtorhallen Hamburg. Einleuchten . Hamburg
[1989] 289 p. : ISBN 3-7672-1102-5 DDC
709/.04/507443515 20
N6488.G3 H2832 1989

Dekoratino-prikladnoe iskusstvo Dagestana .
Mammaev, M. M. Makhachkala , 1989. 345
p. :
NK1045.D3 M36 1989

Del arte religioso a lo religioso del arte /.
Taverna Irigoyen, J. M. Rosario [Argentina] ,

1990. 111 p. :
N7790 .T3 1990

Del barro al metal. Castro, Raquel. Fruto Vivas .
[Caracas] , 1989. 176 p., [16] p. of plates :
ISBN 980-300-866-8   DDC 720/.92 20
NA939.V57 C37 1989

Del Buono, Oreste, 1923- Giorgio Armani .
Milano , c1989. 229 p. :   ISBN 88-435-2946-3
IN PROCESS (ONLINE)
NYPL [3-MME+ 91-4011]

Del Guercio, Antonio. Grosz, George, 1893-1959.
George Grosz, Deutschland über Alles . Roma ,
1963. 19 p., [84] leaves of plates :
NYPL [3-MCK G879 91-1374]

Del-Prete, Sandro, 1937-
Illusoria : ein Reisebericht und unglaubliche
Bilder aus dem neuentdeckten Illusorialand /
Sandro Del-Prete. Bern : Benteli, c1987. 115
p. : ill. ; 30 cm.
1. Del-Prete, Sandro, 1937- - Catalogs. I. Title.
NYPL [3-MCZ + D363 88-3591]

DEL-PRETE, SANDRO, 1937- - CATALOGS.
Del-Prete, Sandro, 1937- Illusoria . Bern ,
c1987. 115 p. :
NYPL [3-MCZ + D363 88-3591]

Del Re, Marc'Antonio, 1697-1766. Castello di
Belgioioso . Milano , 1987. 15 p. :   ISBN
88-7111-010-2
NYPL [MDG+ (Dal Re) 90-10839]

Del Vitto, Francesca. Abruzzes Molise romans /.
La Pierre-qui-Vire (Yonne) , 1990. 304 p. :
ISBN 2-7369-0182-7
NYPL [3-MQWB 91-4524]

Delaborde, Yves. Bloch-Dermant, Janine. G.
Argy-Rousseau . Paris , c1990. 229 p. :   ISBN
2-85917-105-3   DDC 748.294 20
NK5198.A74 A4 1990

Delacroix et la gravure romantique. Bibliothèque
nationale (France). Cabinet des estampes.
Paris , 1963. 9, [36] p. :
NYPL [MDBF 90-7193]

Delacroix, Eugène, 1798-1863.
Journal. Selections. 1990. Guillerm,
Jean-Pierre. Couleurs du noir : le Journal de
Delacroix / Jean-Pierre Guillerm. [Lille] ,
c1990. 197 p. :   ISBN 2-85939-379-X :   DDC
759.4 20
ND553.D33 A2 1990

[Letters. Selections]
Eugène Delacroix, further correspondence,
1817-1863 / edited with a preface and notes
by Lee Johnson. Oxford : Clarendon Press ;
New York : Oxford University Press, 1991.
p. cm.   ISBN 0-19-817395-4   DDC 759.4 B 20
*1. Delacroix, Eugène, 1798-1863 - Correspondence. 2.
Painters - France - Correspondence. I. Johnson, Lee, art
historian. II. Title.*
ND553.D33 A3 1991

**DELACROIX, EUGÈNE, 1798-1863 -
CORRESPONDENCE.**
Delacroix, Eugène, 1798-1863. [Letters.
Selections.] Eugène Delacroix, further
correspondence, 1817-1863 /. Oxford , New
York , 1991. p. cm.   ISBN 0-19-817395-4   DDC
759.4 B 20
ND553.D33 A3 1991

**DELACROIX, EUGÈNE, 1798-1863 -
CRITICISM AND INTERPRETATION.**
Guillerm, Jean-Pierre. Couleurs du noir .
[Lille] , c1990. 197 p. :   ISBN 2-85939-379-X :
DDC 759.4 20
ND553.D33 A2 1990

**DELACROIX, EUGÈNE, 1798-1863 -
DIARIES.**
Guillerm, Jean-Pierre. Couleurs du noir .
[Lille] , c1990. 197 p. :   ISBN 2-85939-379-X :
DDC 759.4 20
ND553.D33 A2 1990

**DELACROIX, EUGÈNE, 1798-1863 -
EXHIBITIONS.**
Bibliothèque nationale (France). Cabinet des
estampes. Delacroix et la gravure romantique.
Paris , 1963. 9, [36] p. :
NYPL [MDBF 90-7193]

Loan exhibition of masterpieces by Delacroix
and Renoir . New York , c1948. 84 p. :
NYPL [3-MCN 90-6958]

**DELACROIX, EUGÈNE, 1798-1863 -
POLITICAL AND SOCIAL VIEWS.**

Athanassoglou-Kallmyer, Nina M., 1945-
Eugène Delacroix . New Haven, CT , 1991. p.
cm.   ISBN 0-300-04931-5   DDC 741.5/092 20
NC1499.D36 A9 1991

**DELACROIX, EUGÈNE, 1798-1863 -
LITERARY ART.**
Sieber-Meier, Christine. Untersuchungen zum
"oeuvre litteraire" von Eugène Delacroix /.
Bern , c1963. 112 p., [7] p. of plates :
NYPL [MCO D33 90-7051]

Delacroix, Ferdinand Victor Eugène. see
Delacroix, Eugène, 1798-1863.

Delafond, Marianne. Le Sidaner, Henri,
1862-1939. Henri Le Sidaner, 1862-1939 . Paris
[1989] 119 p. :   DDC 759.4 20
ND553.L837 A4 1989

Delaney, J. G. Paul. Charles Ricketts : a
biography / J.G.P. Delaney. Oxford, England :
Clarendon Press ; New York, NY : Oxford
University Press, 1990. xxiii, 429 p. : ill., port. ;
24 cm. Includes index. Bibliography: p. [402]-413.
ISBN 0-19-817212-5 :   DDC 709/.2/4 B 19
*1. Ricketts, Charles S., 1866-1931. 2. Artists -
England - Biography. I. Ricketts, Charles S., 1866-1931.
II. Title.*
N6797.R5 D45 1989
NYPL [3-MCV R55 90-11599]

Delano, Jack. Doty, C. Stewart (Charles Stewart)
Acadian hard times . Orono, Me. , 1991. xiv,
184 p. :   ISBN 0-89101-070-X   DDC 338.1/09741/1
20
HD1775.M2 D67 1991
NYPL [MFW 91-7984]

Delarbre, Léon, 1889-1974.
Billot, Renée. Léon Delarbre, le peintre
déporté . Jarville-La Malgrange [1989] 125 p. :
ISBN 2-86955-088-X :
N6853.D3385 B55 1989

**DELARBRE, LÉON, 1889-1974 -
APPRECIATION.**
Billot, Renée. Léon Delarbre, le peintre
déporté . Jarville-La Malgrange [1989] 125 p. :
ISBN 2-86955-088-X :
N6853.D3385 B55 1989

Delarbre, Léon, 1889- Billot, Renée. Léon
Delarbre, le peintre déporté . Jarville-La
Malgrange [1989] 125 p. :   ISBN 2-86955-088-X
NYPL [3-MCO+ D339 91-6125]

DELARBRE, LÉON, 1889-
Billot, Renée. Léon Delarbre, le peintre
déporté . Jarville-La Malgrange [1989] 125 p. :
ISBN 2-86955-088-X
NYPL [3-MCO+ D339 91-6125]

Delau, Reinhard. Kunstguss . Lauchhammer,
DDR [1984?] 119 p. :
NYPL [3-MGI 91-4446]

Delaunay, Sonia.
Sonia Delaunay, dessins / [teks en
samenstelling], Yvonne Brentjens. Tilburg :
Nederlands Textielmuseum, 1988. 96 p. : ill.
(some col.), ports. ; 30 cm. Published on the
occasion of an exhibition held at the Nederlands
Textielmuseum Tilburg, March 18-May 29, 1988.
Bibliography: p. 94-95.   ISBN 90-70962-03-9 (pbk.)
*1. Delaunay, Sonia. 2. Delaunay, Sonia - Exhibitions. I.
Brentjens, Yvonne. II. Nederlands Textielmuseum
Tilburg. III. Title.*
NYPL [3-MCO+ D344 90-10425]

Tapisseries : [exposition] / Sonia Delaunay.
Paris : Musée d'art moderne de la ville de
Paris, [1972] 35 p. : ill. ; 29 cm.
*1. Delaunay, Sonia - Exhibitions. I. Musée d'art
moderne de la ville de Paris. II. Title.*
NYPL [3-MOR 90-6281]

DELAUNAY, SONIA.
Delaunay, Sonia. Sonia Delaunay, dessins /.
Tilburg , 1988. 96 p. :   ISBN 90-70962-03-9 (pbk.)
NYPL [3-MCO+ D344 90-10425]

DELAUNAY, SONIA - EXHIBITIONS.
Delaunay, Sonia. Sonia Delaunay, dessins /.
Tilburg , 1988. 96 p. :   ISBN 90-70962-03-9 (pbk.)
NYPL [3-MCO+ D344 90-10425]

Delaunay, Sonia. Tapisseries . Paris [1972] 35
p. :   NYPL [3-MOR 90-6281]

Delaunay-Terk, Sonia. see Delaunay, Sonia.

Delaware Art Museum. Stackhouse, Robert.
Robert Stackhouse . Wilmington, DE , 1991. p.
cm.   DDC 709/.2 20
NB237.S5785 A4 1991

Delbourg-Delphis, Marylène. Le chic et le look :
histoire de la mode féminine et des mœurs, de
1850 à nos jours / Marylène Delbourg-Delphis.
[Paris] : Hachette, c1981. 279 p., [8] p. of
plates : ill. ; 23 cm. Includes index. Bibliography: p.
[257]-265.   ISBN 2-01-008276-1 :   DDC 391/.2/0944
19
*1. Fashion - France - History. 2. Fashion - History. I.
Title.*
GT853 .D37 1981   NYPL [3-MME 90-6057]

**Délégation à l'action artistique de la ville de
Paris.** Auburtin, Jean-Francis, 1866-1930.
Jean-Francis Auburtin, 1866-1930 . Paris
[1990?] 158 p. :   ISBN 2-905118-27-X
NYPL [3-MCO A897 91-7473]

**Délégation régionale à l'architecture et à
l'environnement Nord-Pas-de-Calais.** Etude
du site de l'Abbaye de Liessies /. [Fourmies,
France] [1984] [82] leaves :   DDC
726/.7/094428 19
NA5551.L4693 E88 1984
NYPL [3-MRBB+ 90-12771]

Delehanty, Randolph. In the Victorian style /
Randolph Delehanty ; photography by Richard
Sexton. San Francisco : Chronicle Books,
c1991. p. cm. Includes bibliographical references.
ISBN 0-87701-750-6 (hc) :   DDC
720/.9794/6109034 20
*1. Architecture, Victorian - California - San Francisco.
2. Architecture, Domestic - California - San Francisco.
3. Architecture - California - San Francisco - Details. 4.
San Francisco (Calif.) - Buildings, structures, etc. I.
Sexton, Richard. II. Title.*
NA7238.S35 D4 1991

DELESSERT, ETIENNE - APPRECIATION.
Etienne Delessert /. New York , 1992. p. cm.
ISBN 1-556-70224-8   DDC 741.6/092 20
NC988.5.D45 E8 1992

Delevoy, Robert L.
[Bosch. English]
Bosch / Robert L. Delevoy. 1st pbk. ed.
Geneva : Skira ; New York : Rizzoli, 1990.
139 p. : col. ill. ; 28 cm. Translation of: Bosch.
Originally published: 1960. Includes bibliographical
references (p. 129-136).   ISBN 0-8478-1348-7
DDC 759.9492 20
*1. Bosch, Hieronymus, d. 1516. 2. Painters -
Netherlands - Biography. I. Bosch, Hieronymus, d.
1516. II. Title.*
ND653.B65 D353 1991

[Brueghel. English]
Bruegel / Robert L. Delevoy ; [translated
from the French by Stuart Gilbert]. 1st pbk.
ed. New York : Rizzoli, 1990. 138 p. : ill.
(some col.) ; 28 cm. Translation of: Brueghel.
"First published 1959"--T.p. verso.   ISBN
0-8478-1349-5 (pbk.)   DDC 760/.092 20
*1. Bruegel, Pieter, ca. 1525-1569 - Criticism and
interpretation. I. Title.*
ND673.B73 D6613 1991

Delgado Mercado, Osiris. Ramón Frade León,
pintor puertorriqueño (1875-1954) : un virtuoso
del intelecto / Osiris Delgado Frade. 1a ed. San
Juan : Centro de Estudios Avanzados de Puerto
Rico y el Caribe, con la colaboración Instituto
de Cultura Puertorriqueñ, Academia
Puertorriqueña de la Historia, 1989. 277 p. : ill.
(some col.) ; 28 cm. Includes index. Includes
bibliographical references (209-215).
*1. Frade León , Ramón. 2. Painters - Puerto Rico -
Biography. I. Title.*
NYPL [3-MCZ F799 90-10392]

Delgado, Osiris. see Delgado Mercado, Osiris.

A delight to all who know it . Reed, Roger G.
Augusta, Me. , 1990. 144 p. :   ISBN
0-935447-07-5   DDC 720/.92 20
NA7575 .R4 1990

Dell, Elizabeth. Images of wood .
[Johannesburg] , 1989. 188 p. :   ISBN
0-620-13867-X   DDC 730/.968/07468221 20
NB1255.S6 I46 1989

Della Bella, Stefano, 1610-1664.
Gabinetto delle stampe di Milano. Disegni di
Stefano della Bella. Milano [1976?] 70 p. :
NYPL [3-MCF B367 91-1368]

**DELLA BELLA, STEFANO, 1610-1664 -
EXHIBITIONS.**
Gabinetto delle stampe di Milano. Disegni di
Stefano della Bella. Milano [1976?] 70 p. :
NYPL [3-MCF B367 91-1368]

Della Grazia, Paolo.
Archivio Della Grazia di nuova scrittura /.
Milano , 1989. 96 p., [39] p. of plates :
N7433.35.I8 A73 1989

DELLA GRAZIA, PAOLO - ART COLLECTIONS - CATALOGS.
Archivio Della Grazia di nuova scrittura /.
Milano , 1989. 96 p., [39] p. of plates :
N7433.35.I8 A73 1989

Della Peruta, Franco, 1924- Chiappori, Alfredo,
1943- Storie d'Italia . Milano , 1978. 174 p. :
DDC 945.081/02/07
DG552 .C47
NYPL [3-MEM (Chiappori) 90-4348]

Della Torre, Enrico, 1931-
Enrico della Torre : Arbeiten aus den Jahren
1958 bis 1986 : Bayerische
Staatsgemäldesammlungen München 7. Juli
1987 bis 23. August 1987, Kunstverein
Ludwigshafen am Rhein e.V., Ludwigshafen 3.
September 1987 bis 4. Oktober 1987,
Fritz-Winter-Haus, Ahlen/Westfalen, 24,
Oktober 1987 bis 31. Dezember 1987 /
[Redaktion, Annegret Hoberg]. München : Die
Sammlungen, c1987. 64 p. : ill. (chiefly col.) ;
31 cm. Includes bibliographical references (p. 60).
1. Della Torre, Enrico, 1931- - Exhibitions. I. Hoberg,
Annegret. II. Bayerische Staatsgemäldesammlung. III.
Kunstverein Ludwigshafen am Rhein. IV.
Fritz-Winter-Haus. V. Title.
NYPL [3-MCF+ D343 90-5284]

DELLA TORRE, ENRICO, 1931- - EXHIBITIONS.
Della Torre, Enrico, 1931- Enrico della Torre .
München , c1987. 64 p. :
NYPL [3-MCF+ D343 90-5284]

Della Torre, Renato. Vita di Michelangelo :
l'uomo, l'artista / Renato Della Torre.1a ed.
Firenze : Arnaud, 1990. v, 341 p., 16 p. of
plates : col. ill. ; 21 cm. Includes bibliographical
references (p. 313-318) and index. DDC 700/.92 B 20
1. Michelangelo Buonarroti, 1475-1564. 2. Artists -
Italy - Biography. I. Title.
N6923.B9 D36 1990
NYPL [3-MCF B9 91-4624]

Dell'Arco, Maurizio Fagiolo. see Fagiolo
dell'Arco, Maurizio, 1939-

Delluc, Brigitte. Cadouin, une aventure
cistercienne en Périgord /. Le Bugue [France] ,
1990. 167 p. : ISBN 2-86952-017-4 DDC
726/.7/094472 20
NA5551.C28 C3 1990

Delluc, Gilles.
Cadouin, une aventure cistercienne en Périgord.
Cadouin, une aventure cistercienne en
Périgord / Brigitte Delluc ... [et al.], avec la
collaboration du père Albert C. de Veer, de
Guy Ponceau et de Marcel Berthier ; préfaces
du président Pierre Merlhiot et de Jean
Briquet. Nouv. éd. rev. et augm. Le Bugue
[France] , 1990. 167 p. : ISBN 2-86952-017-4
DDC 726/.7/094472 20
NA5551.C28 C3 1990

Deloche, Jean. Military technology in Hoysala
sculpture : twelfth and thirteenth century /
Jean Deloche. New Delhi : Sitaram Bhartia
Institute of Scientific Research, 1989. 50 p., 36
p. of plates : ill., map ; 29 cm. Includes
bibliographical references (p. 49-50) DDC
730/.954/8709022 20
1. Sculpture, Hoysala. 2. Sculpture, Indic - India -
Karnataka. 3. Military art and science in art. I. Sitaram
Bhartia Institute of Scientific Research. II. Title.
NB1007.K37 D45 1988
NYPL [3-MAF 90-3730]

Delons, André, 1909-1940. Au carrefour du
Grand jeu et du surréalisme / André Delons ;
textes polémiques et artistiques réunis et
présentés par Odette et Alain Virmaux.
[Mortemart, Mézière-sur-Issoire] : Rougerie,
[1988] 201 p. ; 23 cm. Includes bibliographical
references.
1. Surrealism - France. 2. Arts, Modern - 20th
century - France. I. Virmaux, Odette. II. Virmaux,
Alain. III. Title.
NX549.A1 D45 1988
NYPL [3-MAMI 90-11123]

DeLorme Mapping Company.
Oregon atlas & gazetteer. lst ed. Freeport, Me. :
DeLorme Mapping Company, c1991. 1 atlas
(88 p.) : col. maps ; 40 cm. Relief shown by

contours. Includes index. ISBN 0-89933-235-8
1. Outdoor recreation - Oregon - Maps. 2. Oregon -
Maps. 3. Oregon - Description and travel -
Guide-books. I. Title. II. Title: Oregon atlas and
gazetteer. *NYPL [Map Div. 91-7316]*
Pennsylvania atlas & gazetteer. 3rd ed.
Freeport, Me. : DeLorme Mapping Company,
c1990. 1 atlas (96 p.) : col. maps ; 40 cm. Relief
shown by contours. Includes index. Subtitle on cover:
Topographic maps of the entire state; back roads and
outdoor recreation. ISBN 0-89933-236-6 :
1. Outdoor recreation - Pennsylvania - Maps. 2.
Pennsylvania - Maps. 3. Pennsylvania - Description and
travel - Guide-books. I. Title. II. Title: Pennsylvania
atlas and gazetteer. *NYPL [Map Div. 90-11808]*
Upstate New York city street maps. Freeport,
Me. : The Company, 1990. 1 atlas (40 p.) : col.
maps ; 40 cm. ISBN 0-89933-300-1 :
1. New York (State) - Maps. I. Title.
NYPL [Map Div. 90-11948]

Delouche, Denise.
Artistes étrangers à Pont-Aven, Concarneau et
autres lieux de Bretagne /. [Rennes] [1989]
233 p. : ISBN 2-86847-026-2
NYPL [3-MAM 91-3261]
Les peintres et le paysan breton / Denise
Delouche. Baillé : Ursa-Le Chasse-Marée, 1988.
xii, 216 p. : ill. (some col.), 1 map ; 23 cm. (Les
peintres de la Bretagne) Includes bibliographical
references and indexes. ISBN 2-86934-011-7
1. Brittany (France) in art. 2. Painting, French -
France - Brittany. I. Series: Peintres de la Bretagne. II.
Title. *NYPL [3-MAMY 91-7021]*
Puget, Catherine. Gauguin et ses amis à
Pont-Aven /. Douarnenez , 1989. 113 p. :
ISBN 2-903708-22-3
IN PROCESS (ONLINE)
NYPL [3-MAMI 91-6154]

**Delphindarstellungen von der minoischen bis zur
geometrischen Zeit /.** Czernohaus, Karola.
Göteborg , 1988. 235, 111 p., 121 p. of plates :
ISBN 91-86098-76-4
NYPL [3-MAH 90-10819]

**DELPY, HIPPOLYTE-CAMILLE, 1842-1910 -
CRITICISM AND INTERPRETATION.**
Lannoy-Duputel, Michèle. Hippolyte-Camille
Delpy, 1842-1910. [Paris] [1989] 141 p., [28]
p. of plates : ISBN 2-86377-076-4 : DDC 759.4
20
ND553.D3596 L36 1989

Delval, Ralph. Pelichet, Edgar. La céramique art
déco /. Lausanne , Paris , c1988. 199 p. :
ISBN 2-88148-007-1 DDC 738/.09/041 20
NK3930.3.A77 P4 1988
NYPL [3-MPC+ 90-11744]

Delvaux, Paul.
Hommage à Paul Delvaux . Bruxelles, [r. du
Musée 9] [1977] [68] p. :
N6973.D44 A4 1977
NYPL [3-MCH D32 81-766]
Paul Delvaux : [exhibition], Staempfli Gallery,
47 East 77 Street, New York, October
20-November 7, 1959. New York : The
Gallery, [1959] [42] p. : chiefly ill. (some col.) ;
1. Delvaux, Paul - Exhibitions. I. Staempfli Gallery
(New York, N.Y.). II. Title.
NYPL [3-MCH D32 90-4983]
Rombaut, Marc. Paul Delvaux /. New York ,
1990. 128 p. : ISBN 0-8478-1201-4
IN PROCESS(ONLINE)
NYPL [3-MCH+ D32 91-5799]

DELVAUX, PAUL.
Rombaut, Marc. Paul Delvaux /. New York ,
1990. 128 p. : ISBN 0-8478-1201-4
IN PROCESS(ONLINE)
NYPL [3-MCH+ D32 91-5799]

DELVAUX, PAUL - EXHIBITIONS.
Delvaux, Paul. Paul Delvaux . New York
[1959] [42] p. :
NYPL [3-MCH D32 90-4983]
Hommage à Paul Delvaux . Bruxelles, [r. du
Musée 9] [1977] [68] p. :
N6973.D44 A4 1977
NYPL [3-MCH D32 81-766]

Demange, F. Cogniet, Léon, 1794-1880. Léon
Cogniet, 1794-1880 . Orléans [1990] 197 p. :
NYPL [3-MCO C676 91-6494]

Demchinsky, Bryan. Grassroots, greystones, and
glass towers . Montréal , Buffalo, N.Y. , c1989.

211 p. : ISBN 1-550-65001-7 : DDC 720/.9714/28
20
NA747.M66 G7 1989

Dēmētrēs Mytaras--zōgraphikē, 1948-1983.
Mytaras, Dēmētrēs. Athēna [1984?] 195 p. :
NYPL [3-MCZ M999 88-3865]

Demeure (Art gallery) Muze'on Tel Aviv.
Tapisseries françaises contemporaines de la
Galerie "La Demeure"-Paris. Tel-Aviv [1971]
[24] p. *NYPL [3-MOR 90-6931]*

D'Emilio, Sandra, 1939- Visions and visionaries :
the art and artists of the Santa Fe Railway /
Sandra D'Emilio and Suzan Campbell. Salt
Lake City : Peregrine Smith Books, 1991. p.
cm. Includes bibliographical references and index.
ISBN 0-87905-383-6 : DDC 758/.9978 20
1. Southwest, New, in art. 2. Railroads in art. 3.
Painting, American. 4. Painting, Modern - 20th
century - United States. 5. Atchinson, Topeka, and
Santa Fe Railway Company. 6. Fred Harvey (Firm). I.
Campbell, Suzan. II. Title.
N8214.5.U6 D46 1991

Demma, Maria Pia. Pietro Novelli e il suo
ambiente /. Palermo , c1990. 550 p. : ISBN
88-7804-048-7
NYPL [3-MCF N9385 91-3641]

Demornex, Jacqueline. Madeleine Vionnet /
Jacqueline Demornex ; préface, Madeleine
Chapsal ; photographies, Patricia Canino ;
coordination et iconographie, Anne Bony, avec
la collaboration de Jacques Griffe et d'Azzedine
Alaïa. Paris : Editions du Regard, c1990. 305
p. : ill. ; 33 cm. ISBN 2-903370-58-3
1. Vionnet, Madeleine. I. Title.
IN PROCESS (ONLINE)
NYPL [3-MME+ 91-5778]

Demotte Inc. Blochet, Edgar, 1870- Catalogue of
an exhibition of Persian paintings from the
XIIth to the XVIIIth cent. . [s.l. , 1930?]. 79
p. : *NYPL [3-MAF 83-2314]*

Dempsey, Charles. Gli Scritti dei Carracci .
Bologna , 1990. 202 p. ; ISBN 88-7779-139-X
NYPL [3-MCF C32 91-5526]

Den Åbne dør, polsk nutidskunst, 1989 :
Udstillingsbygningen ved Charlottenborg,
København, 28.-4. til 18.-6. 1989 / [kataloget et
redigeret af Henning Damgård-Sørensen og
Bent Karl Jacobsen ; oversættelse, Lone
Ramskov Larsen]. [Copenhagen :
Udstillingsbygningen, 1989] 56 p. : col. ill. ; 28
cm. "Arrangeret i samarbejde med Centralne Biuro
Wystaw Artystycznych"--P. 2 cover. ISBN
87-88944-07-7
1. Art, Polish - Exhibitions. 2. Art, Modern - 20th
century - Poland - Exhibitions. I. Damgård-Sørensen,
Henning. II. Jacobsen, Bent Karl. III.
Udstillingsbygningen ved Charlottenborg. IV. Poland.
Centralne Biuro Wystaw Artystycznych.
N7255.P6 A36 1989

DeNeve, Rose. Promo 1 . Cincinnati, Ohio ,
c1990. 163 p. : ISBN 0-89134-344-X : DDC
741.6/068/8 20
NC1001.6 .P7 1990
NYPL [3-MDW+ 91-4332]

Denk, Wolfgang, 1947-
Wolfgang Denk : Malerei 1982 bis 1986 /
[Katalogredaktion, Joachim Rössl]. Wien : NÖ
Landesmuseum, Blau-Gelbe Galerie der NÖ
Kulturabt. ; Rastenfeld : Galerie Schloss
Ottenstein, 1986. 1 v. (unpaged) : chiefly ill.
(chiefly col.) ; 27 cm. (Katalog des
Niederösterreichischen Landesmuseums . n.F., Nr. 175)
Katalog / Blau-Gelbe Galerie der NÖ Kulturabteilung ;
5 "Blau-Gelbe Galerie der NÖ Kulturabteilung ... 7.
Mai 1986-30. Mai 1986, Galerie Schloss Ottenstein ...
Juni, Juli, August 1986"--Colophon.
1. Denk, Wolfgang, 1947- - Exhibitions. I. Rössl,
Joachim. II. Blau-Gelbe Galerie der NÖ
Kulturabteilung. III. Galerie Schloss Ottenstein. IV.
Title. V. Title: Malerei 1982 bis 1986. VI. Series. VII.
Series: Katalog (Blau-Gelbe Galerie der NÖ
Kulturabteilung) , 5.
AM101 .V5344 n.F., Nr. 175 ND511.5.D45
NYPL [3-MCK D396 91-5501]

DENK, WOLFGANG, 1947- - EXHIBITIONS.
Denk, Wolfgang, 1947- Wolfgang Denk .
Wien , Rastenfeld , 1986. 1 v. (unpaged) :
AM101 .V5344 n.F., Nr. 175 ND511.5.D45
NYPL [3-MCK D396 91-5501]

Denker, Winnie. La sentinelle de Paris / Winnie
Denker, Françoise Sagan. Paris : R. Laffont,

Denkmalkunde in Bamberg :

c1988. 111 p. : chiefly col. ill. ; 36 cm.
"Centenaire de la Tour Eiffel, 1989." Bibliography: p.
111. ISBN 2-221-05516-0
1. Tour Eiffel (Paris, France) - Pictorial works. 2. Paris
(France) - Buildings, structures, etc. - Pictorial works. I.
Sagan, Françoise, 1935-. II. Title.
NYPL [MFX+ (Denker) 91-3483]

Denkmalkunde in Bamberg : eine Ausstellung des
Bayerischen Landesamtes für Denkmalpflege in
München/Seehof und des Historischen
Museums Bamberg, 4.4-16.4.1990 /
[Herausgeber, Tilmann Breuer und Lothar
Hennig]. Bamberg : Das Museum, [1990] 77
p. : ill. ; 21 cm. (Schriften des Historischen Museums
Bamberg, 0936-4277 . Nr. 15) Includes bibliographical
references. DDC 720/.28/80943318 20
1. Architecture - Germany - Bamberg - Conservation
and restoration - Congresses. 2. Bamberg (Germany) -
Buildings, structures, etc. - Congresses. I. Breuer,
Tilmann. II. Hennig, Lothar. III. Bayerisches Landesamt
für Denkmalpflege. IV. Historisches Museum (Bamberg,
Germany). V. Series.
NA109.G3 D44 1990

Denkmalpflege Hamburg. Speckter-Fresken .
Hamburg , 1990. 20 p. : DDC 759.3 20
ND588.S58 S6 1990

Denkmalpflege in Rheinland-Pfalz.
Forschungsberichte .
(Bd. 1) Dölling, Regine. Das Stiftergrabmal in
Maria Laach /. Worms , c1990. 73 p. : ISBN
3-88462-069-X
NB1870 .D6 1990

Denkmalpflege und Forschung in Westfalen .
(Bd. 18) Böker, Hans Josef. Die
Marktpfarrkirche St. Lamberti zu Münster .
Bonn , 1989. 229 p. : ISBN 3-7749-2382-5
NA5586.M853 B65 1989

Denkmaltopographie Bundesrepublik Deutschland.
Kulturdenkmäler in Hessen.
Kreis Kassel /. Braunschweig/Wiesbaden ,
1990- v. <1 > : ISBN 3-528-06239-8 DDC
720/.943/412 20
NA1076.K37 K7 1990

Denkmaltopographie Bundesrepublik Deutschland.
Kulturdenkmäler in Rheinland-Pfalz .
(Bd. 2) Stadt Mainz /. Düsseldorf , 1986-1988.
2 v. : ISBN 3-590-31032-4 (Bd. 1) DDC
720/.943/43 19
NA1086.M26 S38 1986
NYPL [3-MQWD+ 90-1818]

(Bd. 8) Oexner, Mara. Stadt Ludwigshafen am
Rhein /. Düsseldorf , 1990. 194 p. :
NYPL [3-MQWD+ 91-4455]

Denmark. Planstyrelsen. Boderne i Næstved /.
[Næstved] [Copenhagen] , 1988. 111 p. :
ISBN 87-05-03735-60
NA9053.C6 B63 1988

Dennis Adams . Adams, Dennis. New York, NY ,
c1990. 94 p. : ISBN 1-87860-707-3
NYPL [3-MGO (Adams, D.) 91-4565]

Dennis Adams--street vanities. Adams, Dennis.
Dennis Adams . New York, NY , c1990. 94
p. : ISBN 1-87860-707-3
NYPL [3-MGO (Adams, D.) 91-4565]

Dennis the Menace--his first 40 years /.
Ketcham, Hank, 1920- New York , 1991. p.
cm. ISBN 1-558-59157-5 DDC 741.5/973 20
NC1429.K52 A4 1991

Dennison, Lisa. Da van Gogh a Picasso, Da
Kandinsky a Pollock . Milano , c1990. 391 p. :
DDC 709/.04/10744531 20
N6488.5.T55 D3 1990

Denscher, Bernhard. Slama, Victor Th.,
1890-1973. Von der Sinnlichkeit der roten
Farbe . [Wien] [1990?] 112 p. :
NC1850.S56 A4 1990

Dentan, Yves. Giono, Jean, 1895-1970. Yves
Brayer /. Paris , c1990. 171 p. : ISBN
2-85047-154-2 DDC 759.4 20
ND553.B875 G48 1990

Dentro la natura . Ventrone, Luciano, 1942-
[Roma] , 1990. 60 p. : DDC 759.5 20
ND623.V3826 A4 1990

Denver. Art Museum.
Colorado, 1990 . Denver, Colo. , c1990. 143
p. : ISBN 0-914738-39-9 (pbk.)
IN PROCESS (ONLIN)
NYPL [3-MAMT 90-13383]

Fibre structures; an exhibition of contemporary

textiles. The Denver Art Museum, May 9-June
18, 1972. Denver, 1972. 56 p. illus. 21 cm.
Caption title.
1. Textile fabrics - Exhibitions. 2. Fiberwork -
Exhibitions. I. Title. **NYPL [3-MON 91-240]**

German expressionist paintings . [S.l. , 196-]
[60] p. : **NYPL [3-MCI 90-5896]**

The West as America . Washington , c1991.
xiv, 389 p. : ISBN 1-560-98023-0 (h-cover : alk.
paper) DDC 978/.02/074753 20
F596 .W493 1991
NYPL [3-MAMY 91-5810]

Denvir, Bernard, 1917-
The Thames and Hudson encyclopaedia of
Impressionism / Bernard Denvir. London ;
New York, N.Y. : Thames and Hudson, 1990.
240 p. : ill. (some col.), maps ; 22 cm. (World of
art) Includes indexes. Includes bibliographical references
(p. 232-233). ISBN 0-500-20239-7 :
1. Impressionism (Art) - Dictionaries and encyclopedias.
I. Title. II. Title: Encyclopaedia of Impressionism.
NYPL [MBK 90-12515]

Toulouse-Lautrec / Bernard Denvir. London :
Thames and Hudson, c1991. 216 p. : ill. ; 21
cm. (World of art) ISBN 0-500-20250-8
1. Toulouse-Lautrec, Henri de, 1864-1901. I. Title.
NYPL [3-MCO T72 91-7558]

DEPARTMENT STORES - AUSTRIA -
VIENNA - HISTORY.
Lehne, Andreas. Wiener Warenhäuser,
1865-1914 /. Wien , 1990. 195 p. : ISBN
3-7005-4488-X
NA6227.D45 L44 1990

Dépenses de l'administration publique provinciale
au titre de la culture, 1984-1988. Québec,
Québec : Bureau de la statistique du Québec,
[1989] 29 p. : ill. ; 28 cm. (Statistiques culturelles)
ISBN 2-550-19744-5
1. Arts - Québec (Province) - Finance - Statistics. 2.
Art and state - Québec (Province). I. Bureau de la
statistique du Québec. II. Series.
NX750.C2 D47 1989

Depression glass & American dinnerware price
list. Kovel, Ralph M. [Depression glass &
American dinnerware price list.] Kovels'
depression glass & American dinnerware price
list /. New York , c1991. 250 p. : ISBN
0-517-58444-1 : DDC 738/.0973/075 20
NK5439.D44 K67 1991

Depression glass and American dinnerware price
list. Kovel, Ralph M. [Depression glass &
American dinnerware price list.] Kovels'
depression glass & American dinnerware price
list /. New York , c1991. 250 p. : ISBN
0-517-58444-1 : DDC 738/.0973/075 20
NK5439.D44 K67 1991

DEPRESSION GLASS - CATALOGS.
Kovel, Ralph M. [Depression glass & American
dinnerware price list.] Kovels' depression
glass & American dinnerware price list /. New
York , c1991. 250 p. : ISBN 0-517-58444-1 :
DDC 738/.0973/075 20
NK5439.D44 K67 1991

DEPRESSION GLASS - COLLECTORS AND
COLLECTING - CATALOGS.
Florence, Gene, 1944- Elegant glassware of the
depression era /. Paducah, KY , c1991. 191 p. :
ISBN 0-89145-436-5 : DDC 748.2913/075 20
NK5439.D44 F563 1991

DePuma, Richard D. Etruscan and Villanovan
Pottery : a catalogue of Italian ceramics from
midwestern collections / by Richard D.
DePuma. [Iowa City] : University of Iowa
Museum of Art, 1971. 35 p. : ill. ; 27 cm.
March 17 to April 30, 1971.
1. Pottery, Etruscan - Exhibitions. 2. Pottery - Italy -
Exhibitions. I. University of Iowa. Museum of Art. II.
Title. **NYPL [3-MPEK 90-5449]**

Der Alltag. 1/1990. Grazda, Ed. Afghanistan,
1980-1989 /. Zürich, Switzerland : Zürich,
Switzerland ; 139 p. : **NYPL [MFX (Grazda) 91-3488]**
(Parkett)

Der barocke Franziskuszyklus von Frater Lukas
Plazer in Innichen /. Plazer, Lukas, 1663-1723.
Innichen , 1990. 259 p. : ISBN 88-85226-00-0
ND623.P696 A4 1990

Der Expressionismus und Westfalen /
herausgegeben von Reinhold Happel im Auftrag
des Landschaftsverbandes Westfalen-Lippe.
Münster : Westfälisches Landesmuseum für

Kunst und Kulturgeschichte, [1990] 239 p. : ill.
(chiefly col.) ; 28 cm. "Eine Ausstellung des
Westfälischen Landesmuseums für Kunst und
Kulturgeschichte Münster. Haus Nordrhein-Westfalen,
Bonn, 11. Juni-15. Juli 1990; Verbindungsbüro
Nordrhein-Westfalen, Brüssel, 20. September-12.
Oktober 1990; Städtische Galerie Lüdenscheid, 9.
Dezember 1990-27. Januar 1991"--P. opposite t.p.
Includes bibliographical references. ISBN
3-88789-096-5
1. Art, German - Germany - North Rhine-Westphalia -
Exhibitions. 2. Art, Modern - 20th century - Germany -
North Rhine-Westphalia - Exhibitions. 3. Expressionism
(Art) - Germany - North Rhine-Westphalia -
Exhibitions. I. Happel, Reinhold. II. Landschaftsverband
Westfalen-Lippe. III. Westfälisches Landesmuseum für
Kunst und Kulturgeschichte Münster.
N6879 .E97 1990

Der Geist der Gotik und die expressionistische
Kunst . Bushart, Magdalena. München , c1990.
255 p. : ISBN 3-88960-018-2 :
N6848.5.E9 B8 1990

Der heilige Berg [sound recording] . Sinding,
Christian, 1856-1941. [Norway] , p1988. 2
sound discs :
Norwegian Music Productions CDN 31002

Der Kunsthund knurrt : die Geschichte von
Langheim : der neue Spiritismus in der Kunst /
[Textbeiträge von Rudolf Gütlein]. Düsseldorf :
Allgemeiner Freundes- und Förderkreis für
Junge Kunst, c1983. 1 v. (unpaged) : chiefly
ill. ; 21 cm. (Reihe Enthüllungen und Forschen in der
klaffenden Moderne . 3. Bd.)
1. Art, German - Germany. 2. Art, Modern - 20th
century - Germany. I. Gütlein, Rudolf. II. Series.
N6868 .K7876 1983

Der Künstler als Märtyrer . Heusinger von
Waldegg, Joachim. Worms , c1989. 112 p., [48]
p. of plates : ISBN 3-88462-073-8
N6490 .H468 1989

Der Magdeburger Dom : ottonische Gründung
und staufischer Neubau : Bericht über ein
wissenschaftliches Symposion in Magdeburg
vom 7.10. bis 11.10.1986 / herausgegeben von
Ernst Ullmann ; unter Mitwirkung der
Braunschweigischen Wissenschaftlichen
Gesellschaft, Kommission für Niedersächsische
Bau- und Kunstgeschichte. Leipzig : E.A.
Seemann, 1989. 229 p., [120] p. of plates : ill. ;
28 cm. (Schriftenreihe der Kommission für
Niedersächsische Bau- und Kunstgeschichte bei der
Braunschweigischen Wissenschaftlichen Gesellschaft .
Bd. 5) German, English and Italian. Includes
bibliographical references (p. [226]-[230]). ISBN
3-363-00425-7 DDC 726/.6/09431822 20
1. Magdeburger Dom - Congresses. 2. Cathedrals -
Germany - Magdeburg - Congresses. 3. Magdeburg
(Germany) - Buildings, structures, etc. - Congresses. I.
Ullmann, Ernst. II. Braunschweigische Wissenschaftliche
Gesellschaft. Kommission für Niedersächsische Bau-
und Kunstgeschichte. III. Series.
NA5586.M15 M34 1989

Der Zeichner Wilhelm Schnabl /. Schaffer,
Nikolaus. Salzburg , c1988. 60 p. :
NC245.S36 A4 1988

DERBY PORCELAIN.
Bradley, Gilbert, 1917- Derby porcelain
1750-1798 /. London , 1990. 180 p. : ISBN
0-946708-25-8 : DDC 738.207 20
NK4399.D4 **NYPL [3-MPGO 91-5746]**

Bradshaw, Peter, 1922- Derby porcelain figures
1750-1848 /. London , Boston , 1990. xxvii,
484 p., [16] p. of plates : ISBN 0-571-15332-1 :
DDC 738.8/2/0942517 20
NK4399.D4 B74 1990
NYPL [3-MPGO 91-2617]

Derby porcelain figures 1750-1848 /. Bradshaw,
Peter, 1922- London , Boston , 1990. xxvii, 484
p., [16] p. of plates : ISBN 0-571-15332-1 :
DDC 738.8/2/0942517 20
NK4399.D4 B74 1990
NYPL [3-MPGO 91-2617]

Derby porcelain 1750-1798 /. Bradley, Gilbert,
1917- London , 1990. 180 p. : ISBN
0-946708-25-8 : DDC 738.207 20
NK4399.D4 **NYPL [3-MPGO 91-5746]**

Dercon, Chris. Theatergarden Bestiarium .
Cambridge, Mass. , Long Island City, N.Y. ,
c1990. 176 p. : ISBN 0-262-04105-7 DDC

701/.03 20
N6494.E6 T4 1990
                    NYPL [3-MAL+ 90-12503]

Dercsényi, Dezső. Nekcsei-Lipócz Bible. A
Nekcsei-Biblia legszebb lapjai. Budapest ,
Washington , 1988. 231 [5] p. : ISBN
963-207-955-8
IN PROCESS (ONLINE) Rare Bk Coll
                    NYPL [JFH 91-4]

Deri, Max, b. 1878. Sarre, Friedrich Paul
Theodor, 1865-1945. Konia . Berlin [1921] 30
p., 12 leaves of plates (some folded) : DDC
720/.9564 20
NA5871.k86 S27 1921

Dermant, Janine Bloch- see **Bloch-Dermant,
Janine.**

Dernières parutions.
Conquet, Jean. Bénévent L'Abbaye /. Guéret,
Creuse , c1988. 126 p. : ISBN 2-903870-28-4
NA5551.B514 C6 1988

Derniers domiciles connus . Léger, Jean-Michel.
Paris , c1990. 168 p. : ISBN 2-907150-18-9 :
     DDC 728/.314/094409047 20
NA7346 .L44 1990

Les derniers jours de Saint-Exupéry . Phillips,
John, 1914- Zurich , New York , c1989. 1 v.
(unpaged) : ISBN 3-907509-05-6 (Parkett)
MLCL 90/00740 (T)
                    NYPL [MFX+ (Phillips) 90-13603]

Derouet, Christian.
Gris, Juan, 1887-1927. Juan Gris . [Valencia,
Spain] [Paris, France] [1990] 150 p. : ISBN
2-85850-595-0
NC287.G76 A4 1990

Musée national d'art moderne (France). Cabinet
d'art graphique. Le Musée national d'art
moderne . Paris , c1990. 125, [3] p. : ISBN
2-85850-557-8   *NYPL [3-MBH 91-3585]*

Derrida, Jacques. The New modernism .
[[London] , New York , 1988. 80 p. : ISBN
0-85670-940-9   *NYPL [3-MAL 90-4522]*

Dervin, Sylvie, 1953- Defossez, peintures,
lithographies / texte de Sylvie Dervin. [Paris] :
Séguier, c1990. 190 p. : ill. (some col.) ; 31 cm.
     ISBN 2-87736-098-9 : DDC 760/.092 20
1. Defossez, Freddy, 1952- - Catalogs. I. Defossez,
Freddy, 1952-. II. Title.
N6853.D327 A4 1990

The Dervish lodge : architecture, art, and Sufism
in Ottoman Turkey / edited by Raymond
Lifchez ; contributors, Ayla Algar ... [et al.].
Berkeley : University of California Press, c1992.
p. cm. (Comparative studies on Muslim societies)
Includes index. ISBN 0-520-07060-7 (alk. paper)
     DDC 700/.9561 20
1. Arts, Turkish. 2. Arts, Islamic - Turkey. 3.
Architecture, Ottoman. 4. Sufism - Turkey. 5.
Dervishes - Turkey - Civilization. I. Lifchez, Raymond,
1932-. II. Algar, Ayla Esen. III. Series.
NX688.T9 D47 1992

DERVISHES - TURKEY - CIVILIZATION.
The Dervish lodge . Berkeley , c1992. p. cm.
     ISBN 0-520-07060-7 (alk. paper) DDC
700/.9561 20
NX688.T9 D47 1992

**Des graffiti de 1947 aux monuments du 3e
millénaire.** Lambert, Jean Clarence. Bernard
Quentin . Paris , c1991. 215 p. : DDC 709/.2 20
N6853.Q46 A4 1991

Des Moines Art Center.
Between spring and summer . Tacoma, Wash. ,
Boston, Mass. , c1990. x, 206 p. : ISBN
0-910663-49-1
N6988.5.C62 B48 1990
                    NYPL [3-MAM 90-12998]
Dunlap, David, 1940- This is always finished
(David Dunlap) . Des Moines, Iowa , c1989. 42
p. : ISBN 0-9614615-9-4
                    NYPL [3-MCX D919 91-6455]
Shapiro, Joel. Joel Shapiro . Des Moines, Ia. ,
1990. 80 p. : ISBN 1-87900-300-7
                    NYPL [3-MGO (Shapiro) 91-7050]
Twombly, Cy, 1928- Cy Twombly. Houston,
TX , 1990. 129 p. : ISBN 0-939594-22-6 DDC
709/.2 20
N6537.T96 A4 1990
                    NYPL [3-MCX T965 90-11580]

Desarrollo Orinoco-Apure. Eje de desarrollo

Orinoco-Apure atlas /. Caracas , 1987. 1 Atlas
([16] leaves) :   *NYPL [Map Div. 91-50]*

Descargues, Pierre. Rembrandt / Pierre
Descargues. [Paris] : J.-C. Lattès, c1990. 304 p.,
[8] p. of plates : ill. ; 25 cm. Includes
bibliographical references (p. [295]-296) and index.
     DDC 759.9492 B 20
1. Rembrandt Harmenszoon van Rijn, 1606-1669. 2.
Artists - Netherlands - Biography. I. Title.
ND653.R4 D39 1990

Deschênes-Damian, Luce. Atlas transcanadien /
Luce Deschênes Damian, Raymond Damian.
Montréal : Guérin, c1988. 1 atlas (145 p.) : ill.,
maps, plans ; 32 cm. Includes index. Includes
bibliographical references (p. 139). ISBN
2-7601-1923-8 : DDC 912/.71 19
1. Atlases, Canadian. 2. Canada - Maps. I. Damian,
Raymond. II. Title.   *NYPL [Map Div. 91-7753]*

Descobrimentos portugueses do século XV /.
Vidigal, Ana. Lisboa , 1987. 1 v. (unpaged) :
     DDC 741.9469 20
NC288.V54 A4 1987

**Description de l'arc de triomphe de l'Étoile, et
des bas-reliefs dont ce monument est décoré.**
Lafitte, Louis, 1770-1828. Paris, 1810. 12 p. 10
pl.   *NYPL [MRI 90-12815]*

Description de San Marco /. Butor, Michel.
[Paris] [1989], c1963. 111 p., [1] folded leaf of
plates : ISBN 2-07-021099-5
                    NYPL [3-MRBN 91-4656]

**Descrizione delle pitture, scolture, e architetture,
ecc., che trovansi in alcune città, borghi, e
castelli delle due riviere dello stato Ligure :**
qui disposti per ordine alfabetico : coll'aggiunta
de' saggi cronologici riguardanti il dominio tutto
della serenissima repubblica di Genova.
Genova : Presso Ivone Gravier ..., 1780. 256,
[i.e. 258], VII, [1] p., [4] leaves of plates (1
folded) : 3 ill., 1 map (engravings) ; 19 cm.
(8vo) Signatures: a-k⁸ l⁸(l1+1) m-q⁸ [cross]⁴. LC copy
has binder's title: Instruz. di Genova. Tom. II. DLC
     DDC 709/.45/18 20
1. Art, Italian - Italy - Liguria. 2. Art - Italy - Liguria.
N6919.L54 D47 1780

Desde la vigilia . Martínez, Cesáreo. [Peru?]
1989. 212 p. ;
N6718 .M37 1989

Desenho brasileiro . Margutti, Mário. Rio de
Janeiro , 1988. 136 p. : DDC 741.981 20
NC198 .M37 1988

Deshoulières, Dominique. Vitou, Elisabeth.
Gabriel Guévrékian, 1900-1970 . Paris , c1987.
150 p. : ISBN 2-86649-003-7 : DDC 720/.92/4 19
NA1053.G77 V5 1987
                    NYPL [3-MQZ (Guévrékian) 91-4588]

Design . Myerson, Jeremy. London , c1990. 255
p. : ISBN 0-904866-77-7
                    NYPL [3-MNF 91-6321]

DESIGN.
Bang, Molly. Picture this . Boston , 1991. p.
cm. ISBN 0-8212-1855-7 DDC 741.6 20
NK1510 .B258 1991

Bothwell, Dorr. Notan . New York , 1991. p.
cm. ISBN 0-486-26856-X (pbk.) DDC 745.4 20
NK1510 .B67 1991

Hiebert, Kenneth J. Graphic design processes .
New York , c1992. 208 p. : ISBN 0-442-00839-2
     DDC 741.6 20
NC1000 .H54 1991

Lawson, Bryan. How designers think /.
London , Boston , 1990. vii, 243 p. : ISBN
0-408-50072-7 DDC 745.4 20
NK1510 .L4 1990 *NYPL [3-MNF 90-10740]*

The Plastics age . [London] , 1990. 159 p. :
     ISBN 1-85177-066-6 (pbk.) : DDC 668.4 20
TP1120   *NYPL [3-MNF 90-11058]*

Potter, Norman. Models & constructs .
London , 1990. 310 p. ISBN 0-907259-04-9 :
     DDC 745.4 20
NK1510   *NYPL [3-MNF 90-13184]*

Potter, Norman. What is a designer . London ,
1989. 19 p. ; ISBN 0-907259-03-0 (pbk.) : DDC
745.4 20
NK1510   *NYPL [3-MNC 91-6671]*

Design & marketing /. Swann, Alan, 1946-
London , 1990. 144 p. : ISBN 0-7148-2647-2
                    NYPL [3-MNC 90-12596]

Design and marketing. Swann, Alan, 1946-

Design & marketing /. London , 1990. 144 p. :
     ISBN 0-7148-2647-2
                    NYPL [3-MNC 90-12596]

DESIGN, ARCHITECTURAL. see
ARCHITECTURAL DESIGN.

DESIGN, BOOK. see **BOOK DESIGN.**

Design book five. Fine woodworking design book
five . Newtown, Conn. , c1990. 185 p. : ISBN
0-942391-28-4 : DDC 674/.8 20
NK2408 .F57 1990

**A design catalogue of Chinese export porcelain
for the American market /.** Crossman, Carl L.
Salem, Mass. , 1969. 48 p. : ISBN 0-87577-019-3
                    NYPL [3-MPFF 90-6436]

Design Center, Stockholm. Levin, Marianne,
1942- Plagiat, stöld, förebild, inspiration /.
[Solna] , c1990. 138 p. : ISBN 91-7332-505-8 :
NK789 .L48 1990

Design Center Stuttgart. Frauen im Design .
Stuttgart [1989] 2 v. : DDC 745.4/442/082 20
NK1174 .F7 1989   *NYPL [3-MNF 90-725]*

DESIGN COORDINATION, INDUSTRIAL.
see **INDUSTRIAL DESIGN
COORDINATION.**

**DESIGN, DECORATIVE - DENMARK -
EXHIBITIONS.**
Dansk 50-tal . Stockholm , 1981. 36, [1] p. :
     ISBN 91-7100-198-0
                    NYPL [3-MNE 90-5648]

DESIGN, DECORATIVE - UNITED STATES.
Hanks, David A. The decorative designs of
Frank Lloyd Wright /. New York , c1979. xx,
[1], 232 p., [8] leaves of plates : ISBN
0-525-08958-6 :
                    NYPL [3-MQZ (Wright) 90-10664]

Design drawing techniques . Porter, Tom. New
York : Toronto : p. cm. ISBN 0-684-19045-1
     DDC 720/.28/4 20
NA2714 .P67 1991

DESIGN, ENGINEERING. see
ENGINEERING DESIGN.

Design for the environment /. Mackenzie,
Dorothy. New York , 1991. 176 p. : ISBN
0-8478-1390-8 DDC 720/.47 20
NA2542.35 .M34 1991

**DESIGN - FRANCE - HISTORY - 20TH
CENTURY.**
Colin, Christine. Starck /. Liège [1988?] 348
p. : ISBN 2-87009-332-2
                    NYPL [3-MLO + 90-2824]

Entre deux guerres . Paris , c1990. 631 p. ;
     ISBN 2-87686-057-0 : DDC 700/.944/09041 20
NX549.A1 E5 1990

**DESIGN - GERMANY (EAST) - HISTORY -
20TH CENTURY.**
Deutsches Design 1950-1990 . München ,
c1990. 280 p. : ISBN 3-7913-1079-8
                    NYPL [3-MNF+ 91-3891]

**DESIGN - GERMANY (WEST) - HISTORY -
20TH CENTURY.**
Deutsches Design 1950-1990 . München ,
c1990. 280 p. : ISBN 3-7913-1079-8
                    NYPL [3-MNF+ 91-3891]

DESIGN - GREAT BRITAIN.
Plans and elevations /. London , 1990. [84] p. :
     ISBN 1-85454-052-1 (pbk.) : DDC 745.44941 20
NK1443   *NYPL [3-MNE 90-11636]*

DESIGN - HISTORY - 20TH CENTURY.
Aldersey-Williams, Hugh. World design . New
York , 1992. p. cm. ISBN 0-8478-1461-0 DDC
745.4/442 20
NK1390 .A43 1992

Capella, Juli. [Diseño de arquitectos en los 80.
English.] Designed by architects in the 1980s /.
New York , 1988. 191 p. : ISBN 0-8478-0941-2 :
     DDC 749.2/0498 19
NK2702 .C3713 1988
                    NYPL [3-MOI 91-6559]

Levin, Marianne, 1942- Plagiat, stöld, förebild,
inspiration /. [Solna] , c1990. 138 p. : ISBN
91-7332-505-8 :
NK789 .L48 1990

Lloyd-Jones, Peter, 1940- Taste today .
Oxford , New York , 1991. p. cm. ISBN
0-08-040251-8 : DDC 745.4/442 20
NK1520 .L46 1991

Sudjic, Deyan. Cult objects . London , 1985.

159 p. :   ISBN 0-586-08483-5 (pbk.) :   DDC
745.2/09/04 19
NK1390 .S83 1985   NYPL [3-MNF 91-5813]

**DESIGN - HISTORY - 20TH CENTURY -
CATALOGS.**
Metropolitan Museum of Art (New York, N.Y.)
Modern design in the Metropolitan Museum of
Art, 1890-1990 /. New York , c1990. xiii, 312
p. :   ISBN 0-87099-598-7 DDC 745/.09/040747471
20
NK1390 .M54 1990
NYPL [3-MNH+ 91-3314]

**DESIGN - HISTORY - 20TH CENTURY -
DICTIONARIES.**
Contemporary designers /. Chicago , 1990. x,
[6], 641 p. :   ISBN 0-912289-69-4
NYPL [MNF+ 91-4858]

Pile, John F. Dictionary of 20th-century design
/. New York , 1990. viii, 312 p. :   ISBN
0-8160-1811-1 DDC 745.4/442/03 20
NK1390 .P53 1990   NYPL [MNF 91-3301]

**DESIGN - HISTORY - 20TH CENTURY -
EXHIBITIONS.**
Classic plastic . London [1989] 36 p. :
NYPL [3-MNF 91-7530]

La Coppia =. Milano , c1989. 205 p. :   DDC
745.4/442 20
NK1390 .C66 1989
NYPL [3-MNF 90-11125]

Frauen im Design . Stuttgart [1989] 2 v. :
DDC 745.4/442/082 20
NK1174 .F7 1989   NYPL [3-MNF 90-725]

**DESIGN - HISTORY - 20TH CENTURY -
THEMES, MOTIVES.**
Bangert, Albrecht, 1944- 80s style, designs of
the decade /. New York , 1990. 240 p. :   ISBN
1-558-59117-6 DDC 745.4/442 20
NK1390 .B26 1990
NYPL [3-MNF+ 90-13410]

Design in exile. Pawley, Martin. Eva Jiricna,
design in exile /. London , 1990. 112 p. :
ISBN 1-87218-016-7
NYPL [3-MQZ (Jiriena) 91-5084]

**DESIGN, INDUSTRIAL - DENMARK -
EXHIBITIONS.**
Dansk 50-tal . Stockholm , 1981. 36, [1] p. :
ISBN 91-7100-198-0
NYPL [3-MNE 90-5648]

DESIGN, INDUSTRIAL - EXHIBITIONS.
Kramer, Friso. Friso Kramer . [Amsterdam]
1978 (Amsterdam : Stadsdrukkerij) [36] p. :
NYPL [3-MNF 90-6852]

DESIGN, INDUSTRIAL - GERMANY.
Hochschule für Gestaltung Ulm. English. Ulm
design . Cambridge, Mass. , 1991, c1990. 287
p. :   ISBN 0-262-12147-6 DDC 745.2/0943/473 20
NK430.G4 H57813 1990
NYPL [3-MNE 91-5537]

**DESIGN, INDUSTRIAL - GERMANY -
ESSEN - EXHIBITIONS.**
Design--Schnittpunkt--Essen 1949-1989 . Berlin
[1990] 368 p. :   ISBN 3-433-02539-8
NYPL [3-MNF 91-7403]

**DESIGN, INDUSTRIAL - HISTORY - 20TH
CENTURY.**
Sudjic, Deyan. Cult objects . London , 1985.
159 p. :   ISBN 0-586-08483-5 (pbk.) :   DDC
745.2/09/04 19
NK1390 .S83 1985   NYPL [3-MNF 91-5813]

DESIGN, INDUSTRIAL - ITALY.
Casciani, Stefano, 1955- Arte industriale .
Milano , c1988. 194 p. :   ISBN 88-85684-21-1
NYPL [3-MNE+ 90-12329]

**DESIGN, INDUSTRIAL - ITALY -
EXHIBITIONS.**
Contenir, regarder, jouer . [Paris , 1970] [58]
p. :   *NYPL [3-MNF 90-6809]*

**DESIGN, INDUSTRIAL - ITALY - HISTORY -
20TH CENTURY.**
Vercelloni, Virgilio. [Avventura del design,
Gavina. English.] The adventure of design .
New York , 1989. 220 p. :   ISBN 0-8478-1039-9
DDC 749/.245 20
TS79 .V4713 1989
NYPL [3-MNE+ 90-12985]

DESIGN, INDUSTRIAL - SOCIAL ASPECTS.
Sudjic, Deyan. Cult objects . London , 1985.
159 p. :   ISBN 0-586-08483-5 (pbk.) :   DDC

745.2/09/04 19
NK1390 .S83 1985   NYPL [3-MNF 91-5813]

**DESIGN, INDUSTRIAL - SPAIN - HISTORY -
20TH CENTURY.**
Julier, Guy. New Spanish design /. London ,
c1991. 191 p. :   ISBN 0-500-23599-6
NYPL [3-MNF 91-5804]

**DESIGN, INDUSTRIAL - UNITED STATES -
EXHIBITIONS.**
Found industrial objects . Rochester, Mich.
[1973?] [24] p. :   *NYPL [3-MNF 91-4231]*

**DESIGN, INDUSTRIAL - UNITED STATES -
HISTORY - EXHIBITIONS.**
Aesthetics of progress . Cambridge, Mass. ,
c1984. 28 p. :
TS23 .A47 1984   NYPL [3-MNE 90-10675]

**DESIGN, INDUSTRIAL - UNITED STATES -
PICTORIAL WORKS.**
Sideli, John. Classic plastic radios of the 1930s
and 1940s . New York , c1990. 127 p. :   ISBN
0-525-24608-8 (cloth)
NYPL [3-MNF 91-6800]

Design into art . Fuhring, Peter. London , New
York , 1989. 2 v. (792 p.) :   ISBN 0-85667-354-4
(London)   *NYPL [MLD+ 89-23146]*

**DESIGN - ITALY - HISTORY - 20TH
CENTURY.**
Bellati, Nally. New Italian design /. New
York , c1990. 203 p. :   ISBN 0-8478-1258-8
DDC 745.4/4945/09048 20
NK1452.A1 B4 1990
NYPL [3-MNE 91-4847]

**DESIGN - ITALY - HISTORY - 20TH
CENTURY - EXHIBITIONS.**
Design, Kunst, Spiele . Geisenheim , 1989. 96
p. :   ISBN 3-9802208-0-X
NYPL [MNE 91-3753]

**DESIGN - ITALY - MILAN - HISTORY -
20TH CENTURY.**
Aldersey-Williams, Hugh. King and Miranda .
New York , 1991. p. cm.   ISBN 0-8478-1358-4 (pbk.)
DDC 745.4/4922 20
NK1535.K52 A84 1991

DESIGN - JAPAN.
Goshi-tada, Fuji Hara. Gwa-hon shu kan
[microform] . [S.l. , 19--?] 6 v. :
*NYPL [*ZM-229]*

Yanagi, Muneyoshi, 1889-1961. The unknown
craftsman. [Tokyo, Palo Alto, Calif., 1972] 230
p. ISBN 0-87011-184-1 DDC 745.4/49/52
NK1071 .Y34 1972
NYPL [3-MNE 90-5442]

DESIGN - JAPAN - HISTORY.
Thornton, Richard S. The graphic spirit of
Japan /. New York , 1991. p. cm.   ISBN
0-442-30376-9 DDC 741.6/0952 20
NK1484.A1 T47 1991

**DESIGN - JAPAN - HISTORY - 20TH
CENTURY - CATALOGS.**
Bottle & label design /. Tokyo , 1990. 219 p. :
ISBN 4-568-50104-0
NK5440.B6 B578 1990

Design, Kunst, Spiele : Danese Milano 1957 bis
heute / [Redaktion, Wolfgang Schepers].
Geisenheim : Teunen & Teunen, 1989. 96 p. :
ill. ; 17 x 18 cm. Issued at back cover : letter opener
designed by Enzo Mari. Catalog of an exhibition held
at the Kunstmuseum Düsseldorf, Oct. 21-Dec. 3, 1989
and the Wilhelm-Hack-Museum, Ludwigshafen, Feb.
11-Mar. 25, 1990. Includes bibliographical references.
ISBN 3-9802208-0-X
*I. Danese (Firm) - Exhibitions. 2. Design - Italy -
History - 20th century - Exhibitions. I. Schepers,
Wolfgang. II. Kunstmuseum Düsseldorf. III.
Wilhelm-Hack-Museum. IV. Title: Danese Milano 1957
bis heute.*   *NYPL [MNE 91-3753]*

Design lines meet in Essen.
Design--Schnittpunkt--Essen 1949-1989 . Berlin
[1990] 368 p. :   ISBN 3-433-02539-8
NYPL [3-MNF 91-7403]

Design management : papers from the London
Business School / Peter Gorb, editor. London :
Architecture Design and Technology, 1990. viii,
184 p. ; 21 cm. ISBN 1-85453-156-6 :   DDC
745.4068 20
I. Gorb, Peter. II. London Business School.
NYPL [3-MNF 90-12036]

Design Museum (London, England) Devětsil .
[Oxford] , London , c1990. 115 p. :   ISBN

0-905836-70-7
NYPL [3-MAM+ 90-12482]

Design of warning labels and instructions /.
Ryan, Joseph P. New York , c1991. xiv, 201
p. :   ISBN 0-442-31953-3 DDC 741.6/92 20
NC1002.L3 R94 1990

Design--Schnittpunkt--Essen 1949-1989 : von der
Folkwangschule für Gestaltung zur Universität
Essen : 40 Jahre Industriedesign in Essen /
herausgegeben von Stefan Lengyel und
Hermann Sturm = Design lines meet in Essen,
1949-1989 : from the Folkwangschule für
Gestaltung to the University of Essen : 40 years
industrial design in Essen / edited by Stefan
Lengyel [and] Hermann Sturm. Berlin : Ernst &
Sohn, [1990] 368 p. : ill. (some col.) ; 27 cm.
German and English. Exhibition held May 17-June 10,
1990 at the Museum Folkwang Essen. Includes
bibliographical references. ISBN 3-433-02539-8
*1. Design, Industrial - Germany - Essen - Exhibitions.
I. Lengyel, Stefan, 1937-. II. Sturm, Hermann, 1936-.
III. Folkwangschule für Gestaltung. IV. Universität
Essen. V. Museum Folkwang Essen. VI. Title: Design
lines meet in Essen.*   *NYPL [3-MNF 91-7403]*

DESIGN - SCOTLAND.
Scottish art and design . New York , 1991,
c1990. 200 p. :   ISBN 0-8109-3818-9 DDC
709/.411/07441443 20
N6772 .S37 1991
NYPL [3-MAMR 91-6763]

**DESIGN SERVICES - ESTIMATES - UNITED
STATES.**
Sampson, Carol A. Estimating for interior
designers . New York , 1991. p. cm.   ISBN
0-8230-1600-5 DDC 729/.029/9 20
NK2116.2 .S26 1991

DESIGN SERVICES - MANAGEMENT.
Mott, Richard. Managing a design practice /.
London , 1989. 129 p. :   ISBN 1-85454-145-5
(pbk.) :   DDC 745.4/068 19
NYPL [3-MQD 90-12491]

**DESIGN SERVICES - UNITED STATES -
MANAGEMENT - HANDBOOKS,
MANUALS, ETC.**
Stewart, Joyce M., 1962- How to make your
design business profitable /. Cincinnati, Ohio ,
c1992. p. cm.   ISBN 0-89134-391-1 (paper) :   DDC
745.4/068 20
NK1403 .S74 1992

**DESIGN SERVICES - UNITED STATES -
MARKETING.**
Stasiowski, Frank, 1948- Staying small
successfully . New York , c1991. xv, 297 p. :
ISBN 0-471-50652-4 DDC 720/.68 20
NA1996 .S75 1991

**DESIGN SERVICES - UNITED STATES -
MARKETING - HANDBOOKS,
MANUALS, ETC.**
Stewart, Joyce M., 1962- How to make your
design business profitable /. Cincinnati, Ohio ,
c1992. p. cm.   ISBN 0-89134-391-1 (paper) :   DDC
745.4/068 20
NK1403 .S74 1992

DESIGN - SOCIAL ASPECTS.
Sudjic, Deyan. Cult objects . London , 1985.
159 p. :   ISBN 0-586-08483-5 (pbk.) :   DDC
745.2/09/04 19
NK1390 .S83 1985   NYPL [3-MNF 91-5813]

**DESIGN - SPAIN - HISTORY - 20TH
CENTURY.**
Julier, Guy. New Spanish design /. London ,
c1991. 191 p. :   ISBN 0-500-23599-6
NYPL [3-MNF 91-5804]

**DESIGN - STUDY AND TEACHING -
GERMANY - ULM.**
Hochschule für Gestaltung Ulm. English. Ulm
design . Cambridge, Mass. , 1991, c1990. 287
p. :   ISBN 0-262-12147-6 DDC 745.2/0943/473 20
NK430.G4 H57813 1990
NYPL [3-MNE 91-5537]

Seckendorff, Eva von. Die Hochschule für
Gestaltung in Ulm . Marburg , c1989. 184 p. :
ISBN 3-922561-81-0 :
N332.G33 U467 1989

**DESIGN - STUDY AND TEACHING - GREAT
BRITAIN.**
Critical studies in art and design education /.
Portsmouth, NH , 1991. p. cm.   ISBN
0-435-08592-1 DDC 707/.041 20
N185 .C68 1991

**DESIGN - STUDY AND TEACHING -
MICHIGAN - BLOOMFIELD HILLS.**
Cranbrook design . New York , 1990. 207 p. :
    ISBN 0-8478-1252-9 DDC 745.4/071/177439 20
NK1170 .C7 1990   NYPL [3-MNF 91-4482]

DESIGN - TECHNIQUE.
Visuelle Kommunikation . Berlin , c1989. 344
p. : ISBN 3-496-01061-4
NC1000 .V58 1989

DESIGN - THEMES, MOTIVES.
Elements =. [Tokyo] , 1989. 12 v. : ISBN
4-87210-018-2 (v. 1) : DDC 745.4 20
NK1530 .E44 1989

**DESIGN - UNITED STATES - HISTORY -
20TH CENTURY.**
Conway, Patricia. Art for everyday . New
York, N.Y. , 1990. 264 p. : ISBN 0-517-57381-4
DDC 745/.0973/0904 20
NK808 .C64 1990 NYPL [3-MLO 90-12856]

**DESIGN - UNITED STATES - HISTORY -
20TH CENTURY - THEMES, MOTIVES.**
Cabarga, Leslie, 1954- Trademark designs of the
twenties /. New York , 1991. p. cm. ISBN
0-486-26858-6 (pbk.) DDC 741.6 20
NC998.5.A1 C33 1991

Design 1. Colani, Luigi. Luigi Colani . Zofingen ,
c1986. 1 v. (unpaged) : ISBN 3-906460-01-2
    NYPL [3-MNF 91-6398]

Design 1935-1965 : what modern was : selections
from the Liliane and David M. Stewart
Collection / edited by Martin Eidelberg ; essay
by Paul Johnson ; contributors, Kate Carmel ...
[et al.]. [Montréal] : Musée des arts décoratifs
de Montréal in association with H.N. Abrams,
New York, 1991. 424 p. : ill. (some col) ; 31
cm. Exhibition catalog. Includes bibliographical
references and index. ISBN 0-8109-3205-9 DDC
745/.09/0407471428 20
*1. Stewart, David M. - Art collections - Exhibitions. 2.
Stewart, Liliane - Art collections - Exhibitions. 3.
Musée des arts décoratifs de Montréal - Exhibitions. 4.
Decorative arts - History - 20th century - Exhibitions.
5. Decoration and ornament - International style -
Exhibitions. 6. Postmodernism - Exhibitions. 7.
Decorative arts - Private collections - Québec
(Province) - Montréal - Exhibitions. I. Eidelberg,
Martin P. II. Musée des arts décoratifs de Montréal.
NK1394 .D47 1991*
    NYPL [3-MNH+ 91-7472]

Designed by architects in the 1980s /. Capella,
Juli. [Diseño de arquitectos en los 80. English.]
New York , 1988. 191 p. : ISBN 0-8478-0941-2 :
DDC 749.2/0498 19
NK2702 .C3713 1988
    NYPL [3-MOI 91-6559]

Designer catalogs. London College of Fashion.
The London College of Fashion designer files.
Bath , c1991. 309 microfiches :
    *NYPL [*XMC-772]*

Designer china . Harle, Lesley. New York , 1991.
p. cm. ISBN 0-688-10923-3 DDC 738.1/5 20
NK4605 .H36 1991

**DESIGNERS - BIOGRAPHY -
DICTIONARIES.**
Contemporary designers /. Chicago , 1990. x,
[6], 641 p. : ISBN 0-912289-69-4
    NYPL [MNF+ 91-4858]

The designer's commonsense business book /.
Ganim, Barbara. Cincinnati, Ohio , c1991. p.
cm. ISBN 0-89134-373-3 (pbk.) : DDC 741.6/068
20
NC1001 .G36 1991

DESIGNERS - IRELAND - BIOGRAPHY.
Johnson, J. Stewart. Eileen Gray, designer /.
London , c1979. 67 p. : ISBN 0-87070-307-2 :
NK1535.G68 J63   NYPL [MOI 80-2273]

Designers' self image . Marcus, Joshua. New
York , c1991. 224 p. : DDC
741.6/09/048074569442 20
NC997.A4 J46 1991

Designi del Figino /. Gallerie dell'Accademia di
Venezia. Milano , c1987. 227 p. : ISBN
88-435-2240-X
    NYPL [3-MCF F472 88-4259]

Designing for industry. Hildebrand, Grant, 1934-
Cambridge, Mass. [1974] xvii, 232 p. ISBN
0-262-08054-0 DDC 720/.92/4
NA737.K28 H54
    NYPL [MQZ (Kahn) 74-1827]

Designing interiors /. Kilmer, Rosemary. Fort
Worth, TX , 1992. p. cm. ISBN 0-03-032233-2
DDC 729 20
NK2110 .K45 1992

Designing with two colors /. Binns, Betty, 1929-
New York , 1991. 127 p. : ISBN 0-8230-1334-0 :
DDC 741.6 20
NK1548 .B56 1991

Designing with 2 colors. Binns, Betty, 1929-
Designing with two colors /. New York , 1991.
127 p. : ISBN 0-8230-1334-0 : DDC 741.6 20
NK1548 .B56 1991

Designing your practice . Kaderlan, Norman S.
New York , c1991. xii, 191 p. : ISBN
0-07-033254-1 DDC 720/.68 20
NA1996 .K3 1991   NYPL [JBE 91-659]

**DESIGNS, ARCHITECTURE. see
ARCHITECTURE - DESIGNS AND
PLANS.**

**DESIGNS (INDUSTRIAL PUBLICITY) see
INDUSTRIAL DESIGN
COORDINATION.**

Desjardijn, Dave. 301 lithoos, 1802-1981.
Amsterdam , c1983. 331 p. : ISBN
90-70604-02-7   *NYPL [MDP+ 90-11340]*

Desjardijn, Harry. 301 lithoos, 1802-1981.
Amsterdam , c1983. 331 p. : ISBN
90-70604-02-7   *NYPL [MDP+ 90-11340]*

Desmarais, Charles, 1949- Ilene Segalove : why I
got into TV and other stories / Charles
Desmarais. Laguna Beach, Calif. : Laguna Art
Museum, c1990. 79 p. : ill. (some col.) ; 24 cm.
Catalog of an exhibition held at the Laguna Art
Museum, Laguna Beach, Apr. 27-July 8, 1990, and at 4
other locations through Oct. 13, 1991. Includes
bibliographical references (p. 76-78) ISBN
0-940872-15-3 DDC 700/.92 20
*1. Segalove, Ilene, 1950- - Exhibitions. 2. Video art -
United States - Exhibitions. I. Laguna Art Museum
(Laguna Beach, Calif.) II. Title.
N6537.S38 D47 1990*
    NYPL [3-MAL 91-3691]

**Desmarest, Jean, sieur de Saint Sorlin. see
Desmarets de Saint Sorlin, Jean, 1595-1676.**

**Desmarests, Jean. see Desmarets de Saint Sorlin,
Jean, 1595-1676.**

**DESMARETS DE SAINT SORLIN, JEAN,
1595-1676.**
Hall, H. Gaston. Richelieu's Desmarets and the
century of Louis XIV /. Oxford , New York ,
1990. 399 p. : ISBN 0-19-815157-8 : DDC 841/.4
B 20
PQ1794.D6 H35 1990
    NYPL [3-MAVZ (Hamburg) 91-3450]

**Desmaretz, Jean. see Desmarets de Saint Sorlin,
Jean, 1595-1676.**

Desroches-Noblecourt, Christiane, 1913- Grand
temple d'Abou Simbel : la bataille de Qadech :
description et inscriptions, dessins et
photographies / Ch. Desroches Noblecourt, S.
Donadoni, E. Edel, avec la collaboration de Ch.
Nims ... [et al.]. Le Caire : Centre de
documentation et d'études sur l'ancienne
Egypte, 1971. vi, 65 leaves, xlii leaves of
plates : ill. ; 29 cm. (Collection scientifique) Issued
in case. Includes transcriptions of the inscriptions (in
Egyptian hieroglyphs).
*1. Mural painting and decoration, Egyptian - Egypt -
Abū Sunbul. 2. Kadesh, Battle of, 1300 B. C. (?), in art.
3. Great Temple (Abū Sunbul, Egypt). I. Donadoni,
Sergio. II. Edel, Elmar, 1914-. III. Markaz Tasjīl
al-Āthār al-Miṣriyah. IV. Series: Collection scientifique
(Markaz Tasjīl al-Āthār al-Miṣriyah). V. Title.
ND2865.A2 D4 1971*

Dessins . Malevich, Kazimir Severinovich,
1878-1935. Paris [1970] [40] p. :
    NYPL [3-MCZ M248 90-6042]

Les dessins de Caillebotte /. Caillebotte, Gustave,
1848-1894. Paris , c1989. 127 p. : ISBN
2-86665-084-0 DDC 759.4 20
NC248.C27 A4 1989
    NYPL [3-MCO+ C134 91-3741]

Dessins de Taddeo et Federico Zuccaro. Musée
du Louvre. Cabinet des dessins. Paris, 1969. 79
p.   *NYPL [3-MBH 91-1497]*

Dessins italiens du Musée de Rennes. Disegno .
[Rennes], France [1990] 253 p. : ISBN
2-901430-22-8 DDC 741.945/074/4415 20
NC255 .D54 1990

Dessins-pastels, peintures, lithographies /.
Bourrié, André, 1936- Paris , c1990. 163 p. :
    ISBN 2-87736-085-7 DDC 760/.092 20
N6853.B625 A4 1990
    NYPL [3-MCO+ B774 90-13050]

Dessins politiques. Siné. [Paris, 1972 printing,
c1965] 186 p.
DC412 .S527 1972
    NYPL [3-MEM (Siné) 90-7137]

**Les Dessins vénitiens des collections de l'École
des beaux-arts :** 3 mai-15 juillet 1990, École
nationale supérieure des beaux-arts /
[commissaire, Emmanuelle Brugerolles]. Paris :
L'École, c1990. xlii, 257 p. : ill. ; 31 cm. ISBN
2-903639-68-X
*1. Drawing, Italian - Italy - Venice - Exhibitions. I.
Brugerolles, Emmanuelle. II. Ecole nationale supérieure
des beaux-arts (France).*
    NYPL [3-MBH+ 90-12996]

Destin des collections royales. De Versailles à
Paris . Paris , 1989. 288 p., [38] p. of plates :
    ISBN 2-9504070-0-5
    NYPL [3-MAWC (Paris) 90-12345]

Destins d'objets / sous la direction de Jean
Cuisenier. Paris : Documentation française,
1988. 474 p. : ill., ports. ; 24 cm. (Collection
études et travaux . no 1) At head of title: Ecole du
Louvre, Ecole du patrimoine. Includes bibliographical
references. ISBN 2-11-002009-1 (pbk.)
*1. Art - Collectors and collecting - France. 2. Art -
Private collections - France. 3. Cultural property,
Protection of - France. I. Cuisenier, Jean, 1927-. II.
Ecole du patrimoine. III. Series.*
    NYPL [3-MAVC 90-9455]

Det brændende nu, Axel Salto . Salto, Axel,
1889-1961. [Copenhagen] [1989] 78 p. : ISBN
87-87075-60-1
N7023.S25 A4 1989

**DETAILS, ARCHITECTURAL. see
ARCHITECTURE - DETAILS.**

The details of modern architecture /. Ford,
Edward R. Cambridge, Mass. , c1990. ix, 371
p. : ISBN 0-262-06121-X DDC 724/.5 20
NA2840 .F67 1989
    NYPL [3-MRN 90-12073]

The Detective's eye : investigating the Old
Masters. [Milwaukee] : Milwaukee Art
Museum, c1989. 124 p. : ill. (some col.) ; 28
cm. Catalog of an exhibition held at the Milwaukee
Art Museum, Jan. 20-March 19, 1989. Guest curators,
Isabel and Alfred Bader. Pages 123-124 are blank.
Bibliography: p. 122.
*1. Painting, Dutch - Expertising - Exhibitions. 2.
Painting, Modern - 17th-18th centuries - Netherlands -
Expertising - Exhibitions. 3. Painting - Forgeries -
Exhibitions. I. Bader, Alfred, 1924-. II. Bader, Alfred,
Mrs. III. Milwaukee Art Museum.*
    NYPL [MCG 89-19048]

Dethier, Hubert. Cultural hermeneutics of
modern art . Amsterdam , Atlanta, GA , 1989.
307 p., [1] p. of plates : ISBN 90-6203-645-7
    NYPL [3-MAS 90-10857]

Detroit and vicinity. Rand McNally and
Company. Rand McNally StreetFinder. Detroit
and vicinity. Chicago , c1988. 1 atlas (165, 108
p.) : ISBN 0-528-91787-0 : DDC 912.774/3 19
G1414.D4 R33 1988
    NYPL [Map Div. 90-12401]

Detroit [convention] 1970. United Federation of
Doll Clubs. [Detroit, 1970] 152 p. DDC
745.59/22
NK4893 .U5

**Detroit. Donald Morris Gallery. see Donald
Morris Gallery.**

Detroit Focus Gallery. Kamrowski, Gerome.
Gerome Kamrowski . Detroit, Mich. [1990] 15
p. :   *NYPL [3-MCX K155 91-6272]*

Detroit. Founders Society. see Founders Society.

The Detroit Institute of Arts . Detroit. Institute
of Arts. Detroit, Mich. , c1991. p. cm. ISBN
0-89558-135-3 : DDC 708.174/34 20
N560 .A83 1991

Detroit. Institute of Arts.
American paintings in the Detroit Institute of
Arts / introduction by Nancy Rivard Shaw ;
essays by Mary Black ... [et al.]. 1st ed. New
York : Hudson Hills Press : Rizzoli
[distributor], c1991- p. cm. (The collections of the
Detroit Institute of Arts) "In association with the

Founders Society, Detroit Institute of Arts." Includes bibliographical references and index. CONTENTS. - v. 1. Works by artists born before 1816. ISBN 1-555-95044-2 (alk. paper) : DDC 759.13/074/77434 20
1. Painting, American - Catalogs. 2. Painting - Michigan - Detroit - Catalogs. 3. Detroit. Institute of Arts - Catalogs. I. Shaw, Nancy Rivard, 1945-. II. Black, Mary (Mary C.). III. Founders Society. IV. Series: Detroit Institute of Arts. Collections of the Detroit Institute of Arts. V. Title.
ND205 .D298 1991

Collections of the Detroit Institute of Arts.
Detroit. Institute of Arts. American paintings in the Detroit Institute of Arts /. New York , c1991- p. ISBN 1-555-95044-2 (alk. paper) : DDC 759.13/074/77434 20
ND205 .D298 1991

The Detroit Institute of Arts : a brief history / William H. Peck. Detroit, Mich. : The Institute : Distributed by Wayne State University Press, c1991. p. cm. Includes bibliographical references and index. ISBN 0-89558-135-3 : DDC 708.174/34 20
1. Detroit Institute of Arts - History. I. Peck, William H. II. Title.
N560 .A83 1991

Greene, Alison de Lima. Arman 1955-1991 . Houston, Tex. , c1991. p. cm. ISBN 0-89090-050-7 : DDC 709/.2 20
N6853.A69 A4 1991

DETROIT. INSTITUTE OF ARTS - CATALOGS.
Detroit. Institute of Arts. American paintings in the Detroit Institute of Arts /. New York , c1991- p. ISBN 1-555-95044-2 (alk. paper) : DDC 759.13/074/77434 20
ND205 .D298 1991

DETROIT INSTITUTE OF ARTS - HISTORY.
Detroit. Institute of Arts. The Detroit Institute of Arts . Detroit, Mich. , c1991. p. cm. ISBN 0-89558-135-3 : DDC 708.174/34 20
N560 .A83 1991

DETROIT METROPOLITAN AREA (MICH.) - MAPS.
Rand McNally and Company. Rand McNally StreetFinder. Detroit and vicinity. Chicago , c1988. 1 atlas (165, 168 p.) : ISBN 0-528-91787-0 : DDC 912.774/3 19
G1414.D4 R33 1988
NYPL [Map Div. 90-12401]

DETROIT PUBLISHING COMPANY.
Lowe, James L. Detroit Publishing Company collectors' guide /. Newton Square, Pa. , c1975. 288 p. : ISBN 0-913782-07-6
NC1872 .L59 **NYPL [JFF 76-522]**

Detroit Publishing Company collectors' guide /. Lowe, James L. Newton Square, Pa. , c1975. 288 p. : ISBN 0-913782-07-6
NC1872 .L59 **NYPL [JFF 76-522]**

Deuchler, Florens, 1931-
Ars Helvetica . Disentis , 1987- v. : ISBN 3-85637-130-3 (set)
NYPL [3-MAM 91-6348]
Stiftung Langmatt Sidney und Jenny Brown. Sammlungskataloge. Baden , c1990- v. : ISBN 3-85545-044-7 (Bd. 1)
NYPL [3-MAX+ (Brown) 91-1053]

DEUTCHES TEXTILMUSEUM KREFELD - EXHIBITIONS.
Deutsches Textilmuseum Krefeld. "Und Blumen sing' ich ungestört, von ihrem Shawl herunter" . Krefeld , 1988. 159 p., [8] leaves of plates :
NK2809.P4 D4 1988

Deutsch-Amerikanisches Institut. Art-- made in USA . [Regensburg] [1988?] 90 p. :
NYPL [3-MAMT 89-28438]

Deutsche Akademie der Künste zu Berlin.
Mexikanische Graphik. Berlin , 1956. 70 p. :
NYPL [MDBF 90-6611]

Deutsche Expressionisten aus der Sammlung Morton D. May, St. Louis, USA /. Syamken, Georg. [Bielefeld] [1968] 106 p. : DDC 759.3
ND568 .R5 **NYPL [3-MCI 90-5742]**

Deutsche Fayencen im Museum des Kunsthandwerks Leipzig, Grassimuseum . Museum des Kunsthandwerks Leipzig. Leipzig [1986] 84 p. : DDC 738.3/0943/074432122 20
NK4305.5.G3 M87 1986
NYPL [3-MPGK 90-12397]

Deutsche Gesellschaft für Holografie. Holografie in der Bundesrepublik Deutschland . [Osnabrück] , c1989. 114 p. : ISBN 3-88984-102-3 DDC 621.36/75/0943 20
QC449 .H57 1989 **NYPL [MFW 90-11263]**

Deutsche Gruppe Textilkunst. Textil im Freien . Nürnberg , c1989. [53] p. :
MLCM 89/00525 (N)
NYPL [3-MGI 91-6975]

Deutsche Kirchenbaukunst des zwanzigsten Jahrhunderts. Kahle, Barbara. Deutsche Kirchenbaukunst des 20. Jahrhunderts /. Darmstadt , c1990. viii, 271 p. : ISBN 3-534-03614-X : DDC 726/.5/09430904 20
NA5568 .K35 1990

Deutsche Kirchenbaukunst des 20. Jahrhunderts /. Kahle, Barbara. Darmstadt , c1990. viii, 271 p. : ISBN 3-534-03614-X : DDC 726/.5/09430904 20
NA5568 .K35 1990

Deutsche Kunstausstellung (1962 : Dresden, Germany) Germany (West). Bundesministerium für Gesamtdeutsche Fragen. Polit-kunst in der Sowjetischen Besatzungszone Deutschlands. Bonn [1963?] 64 p. :
NYPL [3-MAMG 90-6808]

Deutsche Maler in Brasilien im XIX Jahrhundert. Peixoto, Maria Elizabete Santos. Pintores alemães no Brasil durante o século XIX =. Rio de Janeiro , 1989. 244 p. : ISBN 85-7191-001-4 **NYPL [3-MCI+ 90-8914]**

Deutsche Maler in Brasilien in XIX Jahrhundert. Peixoto, Maria Elizabete Santos. Pintores alemães no Brasil durante o século XIX =. Rio de Janeiro , 1989. 244 p. : ISBN 85-7191-001-4 DDC 750/.89/31081 20
ND354 .P45 1989

Deutsche Malerei des neunzehnten Jahrhunderts. Neidhardt, Hans Joachim. Deutsche Malerei des 19. Jahrhunderts /. Leipzig , c1990. 264 p. : ISBN 3-363-00468-0 DDC 759.3/09/034 20
ND567 .N44 1990

Deutsche Malerei des 19. Jahrhunderts /. Neidhardt, Hans Joachim. Leipzig , c1990. 264 p. : ISBN 3-363-00468-0
NYPL [3-MCI+ 91-4273]

Deutsche Malerei des 19. Jahrhunderts /. Neidhardt, Hans Joachim. Leipzig , c1990. 264 p. : ISBN 3-363-00468-0 DDC 759.3/09/034 20
ND567 .N44 1990

Deutsche Malerei und Graphik im 20. Jahrhundert. Hütt, Wolfgang. Berlin, 1969. 602 p. DDC 760/.0943
N6868 .H78 **NYPL [3-MAMG 90-6799]**

Deutsche Messe AG. Industriearchitektur in Europa =. Hannover , c1990. 128 p. : ISBN 3-87870-350-3 DDC 725/.4/09409048 20
NA6403.E85 I53 1990

Die deutsche Stadt des Absolutismus im Spiegel barocker Veduten und zeitgenössischer Pläne . Gerlach, Siegfried. Stuttgart , c1990. 80 p. : ISBN 3-515-05600-9
IN PROCESS (ONLINE)
NYPL [3-MQWD 91-3447]

Deutscher Akademischer Austauschdienst. Berliner Künstlerprogramm. Torres, Francesc, 1948- Francesc Torres, Plus ultra /. Berlin , c1988. 60, [4] p. : ISBN 3-89357-010-1
NYPL [3-MGO (Torres) 90-13375]

DEUTSCHER ALPENVEREIN (1950-) Zebhauser, Helmuth. Alpine Exlibris =. München , c1985. 192 p. : ISBN 3-7654-2043-3 DDC 769.5 19
Z994.5.A38 Z43 1985
NYPL [MDVC 91-5221]

Deutscher Kartographentag (38th : 1989 : Vienna, Austria) Kartographenkongress (1989 : Vienna, Austria) Kartographenkongress Wien 1989 . [Wien] , c1990. 288 p. : ISBN 3-900830-04-5 **NYPL [Map Div. 91-5664]**

Deutscher Kunstrat. Frühe irische Kunst . [Germany , 1959] (Mainz : Eggebrecht-Presse) 1 v. (unpaged) :
N6240 .F7 **NYPL [3-MAMR 91-303]**

DEUTSCHER WERKBUND.
Design in Deutschland, 1933-45 . Giessen , 1990. 141 p. : ISBN 3-87038-146-9
N14 .W454 vol. 20 NK951

Deutsches Archäologisches Institut. Römisch-Germanische Kommission. Conspectus formarum terrae sigillatae Italico modo confectae /. Bonn , 1990. ix, 213 p. : ISBN 3-7749-2456-2 **NYPL [3-MPA+ (Materialien zur römisch-germanischen Keramik. Heft 10)]**

Deutsches Architekturmuseum.
Hannes Meyer, 1889-1954 . Berlin , c1989. 368 p. : ISBN 3-433-02053-1 : DDC 720/.92 20
NA1353.M4 H35 1989
Klotz, Heinrich. Architektur des 20. Jahrhunderts . Frankfurt am Main , c1989. 351 p. : **NYPL [3-MQV 90-11330]**
New York Architektur, 1970-1990 /. München , c1989. 335 p., [1] leaf of plates : ISBN 3-7913-0923-4
NYPL [3-MQWO+ 89-22879]

Deutsches Design 1950-1990 : designed in Germany / herausgegeben von Michael Erlhoff für den Rat für Formgebung ; Redaktion, Bernd Busch ; mit Beiträgen von Helge Aszmoneit ... [et al.]. München : Prestel, c1990. 280 p. : ill. ; 31 cm. ISBN 3-7913-1079-8
1. Design - Germany (West) - History - 20th century. 2. Design - Germany (East) - History - 20th century. I. Erlhoff, Michael. **NYPL [3-MNF+ 91-3891]**

Deutsches Elfenbeinmuseum Erbach. Schnitzkunst aus der Südsee . Erbach/Odenwald [1974] 47 p. : **NYPL [3-MADF 91-5898]**

Deutsches Goldschmiedehaus. Treskow, Elisabeth, 1898- Elisabeth Treskow, Goldschmiedekunst des 20. Jahrhunderts . Köln [1990] 168 p. : DDC 739.2/272 20
NK7198.T734 A4 1990

DEUTSCHES HISTORISCHES MUSEUM (PROJECTED) - DESIGNS AND PLANS - EXHIBITIONS.
Ferlenga, Alberto. Aldo Rossi . Milano , 1990. 118 p. : ISBN 88-435-3088-7
NYPL [3-MQZ (Rossi) 91-6524]

Deutsches Informel : Malerei nach 1945 / Peter Brüning ...[et al.]. Düsseldorf : Galerie Zimmer, [1987] 39 p. : ill. (chiefly col.) ; 30 cm.
1. Painting, Modern - 20th century - Germany (West) - Exhibitions. I. Brüning, Peter. II. Galerie Zimmer.
NYPL [3-MCI+ 91-4284]

Deutsches Klingenmuseum, Solingen, Ger. see Solingen, Ger. Deutsches Klingenmuseum.

Deutsches Plakat Museum Essen. Baumberger, Otto, 1889-1961. Otto Baumberger, 1889-1961 . Zürich , c1988. 127 p. : ISBN 3-907065-27-1 DDC 741.6/74/092 20
NC1850.B38 A4 1988
NYPL [3-MDW 90-13136]

Deutsches Textilmuseum Krefeld. "Und Blumen sing' ich ungestört, von ihrem Shawl herunter" : persische Seiden des 16.-18. Jahrhunderts aus dem Besitz des Deutschen Textilmuseums Krefeld : Ausstellung vom 19. Juni bis zum 28. August 1988 / [Katalogbearbeitung, Brigitte Tietzel]. Krefeld : Stadt Krefeld, der Oberstadtdirektor, 1988. 159 p., [8] leaves of plates : ill. (some col.) ; 24 cm. Cover title: Persische Seiden. Includes bibliographical references (p. 158).
1. Rugs, Persian - Exhibitions. 2. Deutches Textilmuseum Krefeld - Exhibitions. I. Tietzel, Brigitte. II. Title. III. Title: Persische Seiden.
NK2809.P4 D4 1988

Deutschland, Deutschland /. Haitzinger, Horst, 1939- München , c1990. 125 p. : ISBN 3-7654-2311-4
NYPL [3-MEM (Haitzinger) 91-3584]

Deutschland im Frühjahr 1990, Ost sieht West, West sieht Ost, eine Fotodokumentation. Ost sieht West, West sieht Ost . Stuttgart , c1990. 179 p. : ISBN 3-89322-215-4
NYPL [MFW+ 91-6972]

Deutschland über Alles. Grosz, George, 1893-1959. George Grosz, Deutschland über Alles . Roma , 1963. 19 p., [84] leaves of plates : **NYPL [3-MCK G879 91-1374]**

DEUTSCHMANN, JOSEPH, 1717-1787 - CRITICISM AND INTERPRETATION.
Vogl, Hubert. Joseph Deutschmann 1717-1787 . Weissenhorn in Bayern , c1989. 223 p., 3 leaves of plates ISBN 3-87437-223-5 DDC 730/.92 20
NB588.D434 V63 1989
NYPL [3-MGO (Deutschmann) 90-6255]

Deutschsprachige Gemeinschaft (Eupen, Belgium) Prokop, Eva. Bauen im Grenzland . Aachen [1989] 227 p. : ISBN 3-89399-092-5 *NA7350.A23 P76 1989*

Deux, Fred, 1924- Fred Deux : l'œuvre graphique : Musées de Marseille. Marseille [France] : Les Musées ; [Arles] : Actes sud, c1989. 103 p. : ill. (some col.) ; 22 cm. "A l'occasion de l'exposition Fred Deux: l'œuvre graphique, au Musée Cantini, Marseille, du 27 février au 30 avril 1989"--Prelim. p. "Catalogue par Olivier Cousinou"--T.p. verso. ISBN 2-86869-298-2 : *1. Deux, Fred, 1924- - Exhibitions. I. Cousinou, Olivier. II. Title.* *MLCS 90/03392 (N)* ***NYPL [MDG (Deux) 90-11000]***

DEUX, FRED, 1924- - EXHIBITIONS. Deux, Fred, 1924- Fred Deux . Marseille [France] [Arles], c1989. 103 p. : ISBN 2-86869-298-2 : *MLCS 90/03392 (N)* ***NYPL [MDG (Deux) 90-11000]***

Devade, Marc, 1943-1983. Marc Devade : écrits théoriques / textes réunis et présentés par Camille Saint-Jacques. Paris : Lettres modernes, 1989-1990. 3 v. (479 p.) ; 19 cm. (Archives des arts modernes . 5-7) Archives d'art contemporain ; 3 Includes bibliographical references. ISBN 2-256-90867-4 DDC 701 20 *1. Art - Philosophy. I. Saint-Jacques, Camille. II. Title. III. Title: Écrits théoriques. IV. Series.* *N70 .D458 1989*

The development of roof revetment in the Peloponnese /. Cooper, Nancy Kelly. Jonsered [Sweden] , 1989. v, 135 p., 57 p. of plates (1 folded) : ISBN 91-85058-44-0 ***NYPL [3-MLEC 90-11039]***

Devětsil : Czech avant-garde art, architecture and design of the 1920s and 30s : Museum of Modern Art Oxford, Design Museum London. [Oxford] : Museum of Modern Art Oxford ; London : Design Museum, c1990. 115 p. : ill., ports. ; 30 cm. Cover title. Half-title: The Czech avant-garde of the 1920s and 30s. Bibliography: p. 112-113. ISBN 0-905836-70-7 *1. Devětsil (Society). 2. Art, Czech - Exhibitions. 3. Art, Modern - 20th century - Exhibitions. 4. Avant-garde (Aesthetics) - Czechoslovakia - History - 20th century - Exhibitions. I. Museum of Modern Art (Oxford, England). II. Design Museum (London, England). III. Title: Czech avant-garde of the 1920s and 30s.* ***NYPL [3-MAM+ 90-12482]***

Devětsil . Devětsil (Society) Łódź [1989]. 105 p. : *N6831.5.D48 D4 1989*

Devětsil (Society) Devětsil : czeska awangarda artystyczna lat dwudziestych / [wystawa przygotowana we współpracy z Galerie hlavního města Prahy ; redakcja katalogu Urszula Czartoryska]. Łódź : Muzeum Sztuki w Łodzi, [1989]. 105 p. : ill. ; 24 cm. Mostly translated from the Czech. Includes bibliographical references (p. 94-95). *1. Devětsil (Society) - Exhibitions. 2. Avant-garde (Aesthetics) - Czechoslovakia - History - 20th century - Exhibitions. 3. Art, Czech - Exhibitions. 4. Art, Modern - 20th century - Czechoslovakia - Exhibitions. I. Czartoryska, Urszula. II. Muzeum Sztuki w Łodzi. III. Galerie hlavního města Prahy. IV. Title.* *N6831.5.D48 D4 1989*

DEVĚTSIL (SOCIETY) Devětsil . [Oxford] , London , c1990. 115 p. : ISBN 0-905836-70-7 ***NYPL [3-MAM+ 90-12482]***

DEVĚTSIL (SOCIETY) - EXHIBITIONS. Devětsil (Society) Devětsil . Łódź [1989]. 105 p. : *N6831.5.D48 D4 1989*

DEVEY, GEORGE, 1820-1886. Allibone, Jill. George Devey, architect, 1820-1886 /. Cambridge, England , c1991. 189 p. : ISBN 0-7188-2785-6 : DDC 720.92 20 ***NYPL [3-MQZ (Devey) 91-6770]***

The devil at Isenheim . Mellinkoff, Ruth. Berkeley , c1988. xv, 109 p. : ISBN 0-520-06204-3 (alk. paper) DDC 759.3 19 *ND588.G7 A645 1988* ***NYPL [3-MCK+ G88 90-10399]***

Devlin, Harry. Mitnick, Barbara J. Harry Devlin . Morristown, N.J. , c1991. 68 p. : ISBN 0-9613046-4-2 ***NYPL [3-MCX D497 91-3433]***

Portraits of American architecture : monuments to a romantic mood, 1830-1900 / by Harry Devlin.1st ed. Boston : D. Godine, 1989. 191 p. : ill. (some col.) ; 29 x 30 cm. Includes index. ISBN 0-87923-793-7 : DDC 759.13 19 *1. Devlin, Harry. 2. Dwellings in art. 3. Architecture, Victorian, in art. 4. Dwellings - United States - History - 19th century. 5. Architecture, Victorian - United States. I. Title.* *ND237.D43 A4 1989* ***NYPL [3-MRG+ 90-2829]***

Portraits of American architecture, November 4th to December 2nd, 1979, Morris Museum of Arts and Sciences, Morristown, N.J. / by Harry Devlin. Morristown, N.J. : The Museum, c1979. [38] p. : ill. (some col.) ; 20 x 23 cm. DDC 759.13 *1. Devlin, Harry - Exhibitions. 2. Architecture in art - Exhibitions. 3. Architecture - United States - Pictorial works - Exhibitions. I. Morris Museum of Arts and Sciences. II. Title.* *ND237.D43 A4 1979* ***NYPL [3-MCX D497 90-12735]***

DEVLIN, HARRY. Devlin, Harry. Portraits of American architecture . Boston , 1989. 191 p. : ISBN 0-87923-793-7 : DDC 759.13 19 *ND237.D43 A4 1989* ***NYPL [3-MRG+ 90-2829]***

DEVLIN, HARRY - EXHIBITIONS. Devlin, Harry. Portraits of American architecture, November 4th to December 2nd, 1979, Morris Museum of Arts and Sciences, Morristown, N.J. /. Morristown, N.J. , c1979. [38] p. : DDC 759.13 *ND237.D43 A4 1979* ***NYPL [3-MCX D497 90-12735]***

Mitnick, Barbara J. Harry Devlin . Morristown, N.J. , c1991. 68 p. : ISBN 0-9613046-4-2 ***NYPL [3-MCX D497 91-3433]***

Devon /. Cherry, Bridget. Harmondsworth , 1989. 976 p., [96] p. of plates : ISBN 0-14-071050-7 : ***NYPL [3-MQWK 90-12006]***

Devon Editions : [first collection catalog]. Corte Madera, Calif. (770 Tomalipas Dr. 94925) : Devon Editions, c1989. 328 p. : ill. (chiefly col.) ; 32 cm. 'Supplements,' [52] p. including "Pricing" index, inserted. *1. Devon Editions - Catalogs. 2. Prints - Collectors and collecting - United States - Catalogs.* ***NYPL [MDS+ 90-198]***

DEVON EDITIONS - CATALOGS. Devon Editions . Corte Madera, Calif. (770 Tomalipas Dr. 94925) , c1989. 328 p. : ***NYPL [MDS+ 90-198]***

Devon, Karbon, Perm . Schobinger, Bernhard. [Zürich?] c1988. [64] p. : ***NYPL [3-MNR+ 89-28258]***

Devoto, Guido, 1935- Archeogemmologia : pietre antiche, glittica, magia e litoterapia / Guido Devoto, Albert Molayem. Roma : La Meridiana, [1990] 247 p. : col. ill. ; 31 cm. Includes bibliographical references (p. 241-242) and index. ISBN 88-7222-008-4 DDC 736/.2/093 20 *1. Glyptics. I. Molayem, Albert. II. Title.* *NK5500 .D48 1990*

Dewitz, Bodo von. An den süssen Ufern Asiens . Köln , 1988. 171 p. : *TR790 .A5 1988* ***NYPL [MFW 91-6019]***

So wird bei uns der Krieg geführt! : Amateurfotografie im Ersten Weltkrieg / Bodo von Dewitz. München : Tuduv-Verlagsgesellschaft, c1989. 435, 29 p., 90 p. of plates : ill. ; 21 cm. (Tuduv-Studien. Reihe Kunstgeschichte . Bd. 32) Originally presented as the author's thesis (doctoral)--Universität Hamburg, 1985. Includes bibliographical references (p. 412-435). ISBN 3-88073-303-1 *1. World War, 1914-1918 - Photography. I. Title. II. Series.* *TR820.6 .D49 1989* ***NYPL [MFW 91-7998]***

Dexel, Thomas, 1890- Frühe Keramik in China; die Entwicklung der Hauptformen vom Neolithikum bis in die T'ang-Zeit. Braunschweig, Klinkhardt & Biermann [c1973]

84, [48] p. 80 p. of illus. 28 cm. *1. Pottery, Chinese - History. 2. Pottery, Prehistoric - China. 3. China - Civilization. I. Title.* *GN799.P6 D49* ***NYPL [3-MPFF 90-6053]***

Dexeus, Victoria Combalía. see Combalía Dexeus, Victoria, 1952-

Dézélus, Robert. L'art de Transcaucasie / Robert Dézélus. Vienne, Autriche : Edition Méchithariste, c1989. 368 p. : ill. (some col.) ; 28 cm. Includes bibliographical references (p. 353-356). *1. Art, Armenian. 2. Art, Georgian (Georgian S.S.R.). I. Title.* *N7292.6 .D49 1989*

DGE-LUGS-PA (SECT) - EXHIBITIONS. Kreijger, Hugo. Godenbeelden uit Tibet . ['s-Gravenhage] [Amsterdam] , c1989. 129, [1] p. : ISBN 90-12-06219-5 ***NYPL [3-MAF 91-5465]***

Dhaky, Madhusudan A. Encyclopaedia of Indian temple architecture /. New Delhi , Philadelphia , 1983- v. : ISBN 0-8122-7840-2 (U. S. : v. 1, pt. 1) DDC 726/.14/0954 19 *NA6001 .E53 1983* ***NYPL [3-MQWS 87-1248]***

Dharmasiri, Albert. Modern art in Sri Lanka : the Anton Wickremasinghe collection / Albert Dharmasiri. Colombo, Sri Lanka : Associated Newspapers of Ceylon, 1988. 80 p. : ill. (some col.) ; 29 cm. Includes a brief biography of the painters represented. Includes bibliographical references. ISBN 955-9034-01-4 : DDC 709/.5493/0745493 20 *1. Wickremasinghe, Anton - Art collections - Catalogs. 2. Art, Sri Lankan - Catalogs. 3. Art, Modern - 20th century - Sri Lanka - Catalogs. 4. Artists - Sri Lanka - Biography. 5. Art - Private collections - Sri Lanka - Catalogs. I. Wickremasinghe, Anton. II. Title. III. Title: Anton Wickremasinghe collection.* *N7310.6 .D47 1988* ***NYPL [3-MAF 91-6910]***

Di Bonaventura, Adriano. Atti del convegno di Pescara, 27-29 gennaio 1989, su il sacro, l'architettura sacra oggi /. Rimini , c1990. 319 p., [36] p. of plates : *NA4795 .A8 1990*

Di Carlo, Massimo. De Chirico, Giorgio, 1888-Giorgio de Chirico, 1920-1950 /. Milano , c1990. 166 p. : ISBN 88-435-3403-3 (jacket) ***NYPL [3-MCF C535 91-6458]***

Di castello in castello . Bosi, Enrico. Milano , c1990. 279 p. : ISBN 88-85271-02-2 *IN PROCESS (ONLINE)* ***NYPL [3-MQWB 91-7180]***

Di Castro, Federica. La Linea astratta dell'incisione italiana . Milano , c1989. 209 p. : ISBN 88-435-3024-0 : *IN PROCESS (ONLINE)* ***NYPL [MDBF 90-13122]***

Di Genova, Alauzen. Antoine Ferrari / Alauzen di Genova. La Calade, Aix-en-Provence : Edisud, c1990. 136 p. : ill. (some col.) ; 29 cm. Includes bibliographical references (p. 129). ISBN 2-85744-497-4 DDC 759.4 20 *1. Ferrari, Antoine - Criticism and interpretation. 2. Expressionism (Art) - France. I. Ferrari, Antoine. II. Title.* *ND553.F44 D5 1990*

Di Piero, W. S. Out of Eden : essays on modern art / W.S. Di Piero. Berkeley : University of California Press, c1991. 257 p. : ill. (some col.) ; 24 cm. Includes bibliographical references (p. 249-251) and index. ISBN 0-520-07065-8 (cloth) DDC 709/.04 20 *1. Art, Modern - 20th century - Themes, motives. I. Title.* *N6490 .D44 1991*

Di San Luca, Guido Clemente. Three papers / Guido Clemente di San Luca. Napoli : Editoriale scientifica, c1990. 84 p. : ill. ; 24 cm. (Ricerche giuridiche . 28) Includes bibliographical references. CONTENTS. - Government and the arts in Italy -- Brief remarks upon a comparative analysis between Italian and U. S.A. systems of supporting the arts -- Legal perspectives for the institutional government of the metropolitan area of Naples in Italy. DDC 700/.1/03 20 *1. Art and state - Italy. I. Title. II. Series.* *N8846.I8 D5 1990*

Di Stefano, Guido. Pietro Novelli, : monrealese / Guido Di Stefano ; prefazione di Giulio Carlo

Di Stefano, John.
Argan ; catalogo delle opere e repertori a cura di Angela Mazzè. Palermo : Flaccovio, 1989. ix, 347 p. : ill. (some col.) ; 29 cm. Includes indexes. Bibliography: p. 325-335. ISBN 88-7804-038-X
1. Novelli, Pietro, 1603-1647 - Catalogs. I. Mazzè, Angela. ***NYPL [3-MCF N9385 90-12325]***

Di Stefano, John.
Vitality. 1988. De humani corporis fabrica. Montréal, Québec, Canada , 1988, c1985-c1986. 3 v. in 1 case : DDC 700/.92/271428 20
N7433.35.C2 D4 1988
NYPL [MEMZ 90-11163]

Di villa in villa : guida alla visita delle ville Venete = a visitor's guide to the Veneto villas / a cura di Antonio Canova. Treviso : Canova, c1990. 235 p. : ill. (chiefly col.), maps ; 25 cm. Italian and English. Includes bibliographical references (p. 235) and indexes. ISBN 88-85066-98-4
1. Country homes - Italy - Veneto. 2. Historic buildings - Italy - Veneto. 3. Veneto, Italy - Description and travel. I. Canova, Antonio.
NYPL [3-MQWB 91-4915]

Di villa in villa : guida alla visita delle ville venete = A visitors' guide to the Veneto villas / a cura di Antonio Canova. Treviso : Edizioni Canova, c1990. 235 p. : ill. (some col.), col. maps ; 25 cm. Text in Italian and English. Includes bibliographical references (p. 235) and index. ISBN 88-85066-98-4 : DDC 728.8/0945/3 20
1. Architecture, Domestic - Italy - Veneto - Guide-books. I. Canova, Antonio. II. Title: Visitors' guide to the Veneto villas.
NA7594 .D54 1990

Dia Art Foundation. Discussions in contemporary culture /. Seattle , 1987- v. : ISBN 0-941920-07-0 (no. 1 : pbk.) : DDC 700/.1/03 19
N72.S6 D57 1987 ***NYPL [3-MAS 88-1789]***

Diakrona (Firm) Milan . Bologna, Italy [1990?] 157 p. : ISBN 88-7193-601-9 : DDC 709/.45/21 20
N6921.M6 M48 1990

Dialogues with nature . Kaelin, Charles Salis, 1858-1929. New York , c1990. 41 p., [30] p. of plates : ISBN 0-945936-09-5
NYPL [3-MCX K118 90-13101]

Diamond, David, 1915-
Rounds, string orchestra. 1980. American music for strings [sound recording]. Los Angeles, Calif. , p1980. 1 sound disc :
Nonesuch D-79002

Diamonds in the rust . Kytola, Pat, 1951- Osceola, WI , 1989. 128 p. : ISBN 0-87938-368-2 DDC 779/.9629222 20
TD795.4 .K98 1989
NYPL [MFX (Kytola, L.) 91-2394]

Diane Brown Gallery. Levine, Erik, 1960- Erik Levine . Genève , c1989. 1 v. (unpaged) :
NYPL [3-MGO (Levine) 91-7405]

Diary of a Victorian cat . Herbert, Susan, 1945- Boston , c1991. p. cm. ISBN 0-8212-1865-4 DDC 759.2 20
ND497.H49 A4 1991

Diary of an art dealer. Gimpel, René. [Journal d'un collectionneur. English.] New York, 1966. xii, 465 p. : DDC 706.50924
N8660.G5 A313 ***NYPL [3-MAVC 91-3867]***

Dias, Antonio, 1944-
Antonio Dias : Malerei : 12. März-16. April 1989, Städtisches Museum Mülheim in der alten Post / [Herausgeber, Städtisches Museum Mülheim an der Ruhr]. Mülheim an der Ruhr : Das Museum, 1989. 70 p. : ill. ; 21 x 30 cm. ISBN 3-9802023-2-1
1. Dias, Antonio, 1944- Exhibitions. I. Mülheim an der Ruhr (Germany). Städtisches Museum. II. Title.
NYPL [3-MCX+ D525 91-4585]

DIAS, ANTONIO, 1944- EXHIBITIONS.
Dias, Antonio, 1944- Antonio Dias . Mülheim an der Ruhr , 1989. 70 p. : ISBN 3-9802023-2-1
NYPL [3-MCX+ D525 91-4585]

El dibujo /. López-Nussa, Leonel, 1916- La Habana , 1964. 138 p., [49] p. of plates :
NYPL [3-MBB 90-12526]

Dibujos /. García Lorca, Federico, 1898-1936. [Madrid] . 155 p. : ISBN 84-86691-00-1 DDC 741.946 20
NC287.G383 A4 1987a

Dibujos de José María Velasco /. Velasco, José Maria, 1840-1912. México , 1989. 1 v. (unpaged) : DDC 741.792 20
NC146.V45 A4 1989

Dibujos de la guerra /. Souto, Arturo, 1902- Madrid [1937?]. [7] leaves. :
NC1185 .S7A42
NYPL [3-MCQ S728 90-10971]

Diccionario geográfico de Honduras. Instituto Geográfico Nacional (Honduras). Sección Diccionario Geográfico. Nombres geográficos de Honduras /. [Tegucigalpa] [1976?- v. :
F1502 .I57 1976a ***NYPL [Map Div. 91-81]***

Diccionarios antiquaria .
(6) García Gutiérrez, Pedro Francisco. La escultura /. Madrid [1990?]- v. <1 > : ISBN 84-86508-00-2 DDC 730 20
NB60 .G3 1990

Dice thrown /. Gianni, Benjamin, 1958- New York, N.Y. , c1989. 56 p. : ISBN 0-910413-62-2 : DDC 728/.92/09730747468 20
NA8201 .G47 1989
NYPL [3-MQV 90-12464]

Dicionário da arte barroca em Portugal / direcção de José Fernandes Pereira ; coordenação de Paulo Pereira. 1a. ed. Lisboa : Editorial Presença, 1989. 542 p. : ill. (some col.) ; 31 cm. Includes bibliographical references. ISBN 972-231-088-7
1. Art - Portugal - Dictionaries. 2. Art, Baroque - Portugal - Dictionaries. 3. Artists - Portugal - Biography - Dictionaries. I. Pereira, José Fernandes, 1953-. II. Pereira, Paulo.
NYPL [3-MAML+ 91-4315]

The Dick Tracy casebook . Dick Tracy (Comic strip). Selections. 1990. New York , 1990. x, 273 p. : ISBN 0-312-04461-5 (deluxe) : DDC 741.5/0973 20
PN6728.D53 D534 1990
NYPL [3-MEM (Gould) 90-10998]

Dick Tracy (Comic strip). Selections. 1990. The Dick Tracy casebook : favorite adventures, 1931-1990 / selected by Max Allan Collins and Dick Locher.1st ed. New York : St. Martin's Press, 1990. x, 273 p. : ill. ; 28 cm. Reproduces strips by Chester Gould and subsequent artists. ISBN 0-312-04461-5 (deluxe) : DDC 741.5/0973 20
I. Gould, Chester. II. Collins, Max Allan. III. Locher, Dick, 1929-. IV. Title.
PN6728.D53 D534 1990
NYPL [3-MEM (Gould) 90-10998]

DICKENS, CHARLES, 1812-1870 - CRITICISM AND INTERPRETATION - JUVENILE LITERATURE.
Giants of the arts . New York , 1991. p. cm. ISBN 1-85435-414-0 : DDC 700/.92/24 20
NX633 .G53 1991

Dickinson, Duo. Nolon, John R. Common walls/private homes . New York , c1990. x, 196 p. : ISBN 0-07-016819-9 DDC 728/.312/0973 20
NA7520 .N6 1990
NYPL [3-MQWO 90-10404]

DICKINSON, EDWIN WALTER, 1891- - EXHIBITIONS.
Burchfield Center. Edwin Dickinson . [Buffalo] [c1977] 35 p. :
ND237.D46 A4 1977
NYPL [3-MCX D563 80-2252]

Dickinson, Gary. Imperial wardrobe / Gary Dickinson & Linda Wrigglesworth. London : Bamboo, 1990. 203 p. : ill. (some col.) ; 31 cm. Bibliography: p. 201-202. ISBN 1-87007-607-9 : DDC 391.0220951 20
1. Costume - China - History - Ming-Ch'ing dynasties, 1368-1912. 2. China - Court and courtiers - Pictorial works. 3. China - Kings and rulers - Pictorial works. I. Wrigglesworth, Linda. II. Title.
NYPL [3-MMR+ 91-4972]

Dicksion, Rhonda, 1959- Lesbian survival manual : cartoons / by Rhonda Dicksion. Tallahassee, FL : Naiad Press, 1990. 94 p. : ill. ; 22 cm. ISBN 0-941483-71-1 DDC 741.5/973 20
1. Lesbians - Caricatures and cartoons. 2. American wit and humor, Pictorial. I. Title.
NC1429.D45 A4 1990
NYPL [3-MEM (Dicksion) 90-13132]

Dickson, Harold E., 1900- Poor, Henry Varnum, 1887-1970. Henry Varnum Poor, 1887-1970 .

[University Park, Pa.] , c1983. 168 p. : ISBN 0-911209-29-8
NYPL [3-MCX+ P82 90-13379]

Dickson, Harold Edward, 1900- Pennsylvania State University. Museum of Art. Portraits USA 1776-1976 . University Park, Pa. [1976] 133 p. : ***NYPL [3-MCW 90-5890]***

Dickson, Jane.
Jane Dickson life under neon : paintings and drawings of Times Square, 1981-1988 : Goldie Paley Gallery, Moore College of Art and Design, May 24-July 7, 1989 / catalog essay by Gary Indiana. Philadelphia, PA : The Gallery, c1989. 12 p. : ill. (some col.) ; 28 cm. Includes bibliographical references.
1. Dickson, Jane - Exhibitions. 2. Time Square (New York, N.Y.) in art. I. Indiana, Gary. II. Goldie Paley Gallery. III. Title. IV. Title: Life under neon.
NYPL [3-MCX D568 91-4639]

DICKSON, JANE - EXHIBITIONS.
Dickson, Jane. Jane Dickson life under neon . Philadelphia, PA , c1989. 12 p. :
NYPL [3-MCX D568 91-4639]

Dictionary of artists and their work in the summer exhibitions of the Royal Academy of Arts. Royal Academy exhibitors 1971-1989 . Calne, Wiltshire, England , 1989. 546 p. ; ISBN 0-904722-19-8
NYPL [MAO 90-9340]

Dictionary of British eighteenth century painters in oils and crayons. Waterhouse, Ellis Kirkham, 1905- The dictionary of British 18th century painters in oils and crayons /. Woodbridge , 1981. 443 p. : ISBN 0-902028-93-6 : DDC 759.2 B 19
N6766 .W29 ***NYPL [MAO 91-6317]***

The dictionary of British 18th century painters in oils and crayons /. Waterhouse, Ellis Kirkham, 1905- Woodbridge , 1981. 443 p. : ISBN 0-902028-93-6 : DDC 759.2 B 19
N6766 .W29 ***NYPL [MAO 91-6317]***

Dictionary of floristry and flower arranging /. Gatrell, Anthony. London , 1988. 184 p., [2] p. of plates : ISBN 0-7134-5904-2 :
NYPL [MLT 90-12341]

The dictionary of Minton /. Atterbury, Paul. Woodbridge, Suffolk, England , 1990. 370 p. : ISBN 1-85149-073-6 : DDC 738/.0942 19
NYPL [3-MPGO 90-10594]

Dictionary of North Carolina biography / edited by William S. Powell. Chapel Hill : University of North Carolina Press, c1979- v. ; 29 cm. Includes bibliographies. ISBN 0-8078-1329-X (v. 1)
1. North Carolina - Biography - Dictionaries. I. Powell, William Stevens, 1919-.
CT252 .D5 ***NYPL [JFM 80-102]***

Dictionary of painters and engravers. Bryan, Michael, 1757-1821. Bryan's dictionary of painters and engravers. New York , London , 1903-1905. 5 v. : ***NYPL [MCA 91-4552]***

The dictionary of Scottish painters, 1600-1960 /. Halsby, Julian. Edinburgh , Oxford , 1990. xii, 236 p. : ISBN 0-86241-328-1 : DDC 759.2911 20
ND475 ***NYPL [3-MCT+ 91-3993]***

Dictionary of signatures & monograms of American artists . Falk, Peter H. Madison, Conn. , Land O'Lakes, FL , 1988. 556 p., [1] leaf of plates : ISBN 0-932087-04-3 (alk. paper) : DDC 702/.78 20
N45 .F35 1988 ***NYPL [MAO 90-11577]***

Dictionary of signatures and monograms of American artists. Falk, Peter H. Dictionary of signatures & monograms of American artists . Madison, Conn. , Land O'Lakes, FL , 1988. 556 p., [1] leaf of plates : ISBN 0-932087-04-3 (alk. paper) : DDC 702/.78 20
N45 .F35 1988 ***NYPL [MAO 90-11577]***

Dictionary of twentieth-century design. Pile, John F. Dictionary of 20th-century design /. New York , 1990. viii, 312 p. : ISBN 0-8160-1811-1 DDC 745.4/442/03 20
NK1390 .P53 1990 ***NYPL [MNF 91-3301]***

Dictionary of 20th-century design /. Pile, John F. New York , 1990. viii, 312 p. : ISBN 0-8160-1811-1 DDC 745.4/442/03 20
NK1390 .P53 1990 ***NYPL [MNF 91-3301]***

Dictionnaire biographique illustré des artistes en Belgique depuis 1830. [Bruxelles] : Arto, 1987. 416 p., [31] p. of plates : ill. (some col.) ; 26

cm.
1. Artists - Belgium - Biography - Dictionaries. 2. Art,
Modern - 19th century - Belgium. 3. Art, Modern -
20th century - Belgium. 4. Belgium - Biography -
Dictionaries.   **NYPL [3-MAO 91-4886]**

Dictionnaire de la peinture allemande et
d'Europe centrale / [direction éditoriale,
conception, réalisation et sélection
iconographique, Jean-Philippe Breuille]. Paris :
Larousse, c1990. 415 p. : col. ill. ; 23 cm.
(Essentiels) ISBN 2-03-740017-9 DDC 759.3/03 20
1. Painting, German - Dictionaries. 2. Painting,
European - Central Europe - Dictionaries. I. Breuille,
Jean-Philippe. II. Series.
ND561 .D53 1990   **NYPL [3-MAO 91-7701]**

Dictionnaire de la peinture espagnole et
portugaise du Moyen Âge à nos jours / préface
d'Alfonso E. Pérez Sánchez ; [conception
éditoriale, réalisation et sélection
iconographique, Jean-Philippe Breuille]. Paris :
Larousse, c1989. 319 p. ; 23 cm. (Essentiels)
    ISBN 2-03-740016-0
1. Painters - Spain - Biography - Dictionaries. 2.
Painters - Portugal - Biography - Dictionaries. I. Series.
                  NYPL [MAO 90-9370]

Dictionnaire de la peinture flamande et
hollandaise du Moyen Âge à nos jours /
[conception éditoriale, réalisation et sélection
iconographique, Jean-Philippe Breuille]. Paris :
Larousse, c1989. 493 p. ; 23 cm. (Essentiels)
    ISBN 2-03-740015-2
1. Painters - Flanders - Biography - Dictionaries. 2.
Painters - Netherlands - Biography - Dictionaries. 3.
Painters - Belgium - Biography - Dictionaries. I. Series.
                  NYPL [MAO 90-9371]

Dictionnaire des ébénistes et des menuisiers.
Ledoux-Lebard, Denise. Le mobilier français du
XIXe siècle . Paris , c1989. 700 p., xxxii p. of
plates :   **NYPL [3-MOF 90-11782]**

Dictz moraulx pour faire tapisserie /. Baude,
Henri, 15th century. Paris , 1988. 89 p. : ISBN
2-903920-04-4
      NYPL [3-MCO B328 89-89984]

Diderot, Denis, 1713-1784.
  [Salons. Russian]
  Salony : v dvukh tomakh / Deni Didro ;
  [vstupitelʹnaia statʹia, sostavlenie, obshchaia
  redaktsiia L.IA. Reĭngardt ; perevody s
  frantsuzskogo I.IA. Volevich ... et al. ;
  primechaniia E.IU. Saprykinoĭ ; podbor
  illiustratsiĭ N.IU. Zolotovoĭ]. Moskva :
  "Iskusstvo", 1989. 2 v. : ill. (some col.) ; 25
  cm. On leaf preceding t.p.: Ordena Lenina
  Akademiia khudozhestv SSSR,
  Nauchno-issledovatelʹskiĭ institut teorii i istorii
  izobrazitelʹnykh iskusstv. "Opyt o zhivopisi": v. 1, p.
  [203]-[242]. "Razroznennye mysli o zhivopisi,
  skulʹpture, arkhitekture i poėzii, sluzhashchie
  prodolzheniem Salonov": v. 2, p. [325]-[357].
  Includes bibliographical references and index.
  1. Art, Modern - 17th-18th centuries - France -
  Exhibitions. 2. Art, French - Exhibitions. 3. Salon
  (Exhibition : Paris, France). I. Reĭngardt, L. IA. (Lidiia
  IAkovlevna). II. Saprykina, E. IU. (Elena IUrʹevna). III.
  Title.
  N6846 .D4617 1989

DIDEROT, DENIS, 1713-1784 - AESTHETICS.
Kohle, Hubertus. Ut pictura poesis non erit .
Hildesheim , New York , 1989. 191 p. : ISBN
3-487-09096-1 :   DDC 111/.85/092 20
B2018.A4 K64 1989

          NYPL [3-MAB 91-4602]

Didi-Huberman, Georges. Fra Angelico :
dissemblance et figuration / Georges
Didi-Huberman. Paris : Flammarion, c1990. 263
p. : ill. (some col.) ; 29 cm. (Idées et recherches)
Includes bibliographical references (p. 242-259) and
index. ISBN 2-08-012614-8 DDC 759.5 20
1. Angelico, fra, ca. 1400-1455 - Criticism and
interpretation. I. Angelico, fra, ca. 1400-1455. II. Title.
ND623.A5393 D53 1990

          NYPL [3-MCF A58 91-6120]

Die archaische Plastik der Griechen /. Martini,
Wolfram. Darmstadt , c1990. vi, 300 p. : ISBN
3-534-03175-X DDC 733/.3 20
NB94 .M38 1990

Die Bauernhäuser der Schweiz .
  (Bd. 7) Anderegg, Jean Pierre. Die
  Bauernhäuser des Kantons Freiburg =. Basel ,
  1979-1987. 2 v. : DDC 728/.67/09494 s

728/.67/094945
NA8206.S9 B38 Bd. 7, etc. NA8210
          NYPL [3-MRGF 84-1334]

Die Bauwerke und Kunstdenkmäler von Berlin.
Beiheft .
  (15) Klinkott, Manfred. Die Backsteinbaukunst
  der Berliner Schule . Berlin , c1988. 479 p., 9
  leaves of plates : ISBN 3-7861-1438-2 DDC
  721/.04421/094315509034 20
  NA1085 .K57 1988

          NYPL [3-MQWD 90-11025]

Die Botschaft der Graphik . Oberösterreichische
Landesausstellung (1989 : Benediktinerstift
Lambach) Linz , 1989. 211 p. :
NE45.A8 L366 1989

Die Denkmalpflege als Plage und Frage :
Festgabe für August Gebessler / herausgegeben
von Georg Mörsch und Richard Strobel.
München : Deutscher Kunstverlag, 1989. xii,
196 p. : ill. ; 26 cm. Includes bibliographical
references. ISBN 3-422-06037-5
1. Architecture - Germany - Conservation and
restoration. I. Gebessler, August, 1929-. II. Mörsch,
Georg. III. Strobel, Richard.
NA109.G3 D446 1989

Die deutschen Hugenottenstädte /. Stubenvoll,
Willi. Frankfurt am Main , c1990. 208 p. :
    ISBN 3-524-69093-9
NA9199 .S78 1990

Die Eisenbahn in der deutschen Kunst . Meurer,
Thomas. Witterschlick/Bonn , 1989. 172, [76]
p. : ISBN 3-925267-28-X
N6867 .M48 1989

Die Entwicklung des Werkens und seiner
Didaktik von 1880 bis 1914 . Heller, Dieter.
Bad Heilbrunn/Obb. , 1990. 322 p. : ISBN
3-7815-0652-5 :
NK249 .H44 1990

Die Faszination des Fremden . Günther, Erika.
Münster [1990] i, 193 p., [56] p. of plates :
    ISBN 3-88660-542-6
ND567 .G86 1990

Die Geburt Christi in der russischen
Ikonenmalerei . Stichel, Rainer. Stuttgart ,
1990. 176 p., 92 p. of plates : ISBN
    3-515-04273-3 DDC 755/.53/0947 20
N8189.S62 R9773 1990

Die Geistesgeschichte und ihre Methoden :
Quellen und Forschung .
  (Bd. 7) Steiner, Reinhard A. Theorie und
  Wirklichkeit der Kunst bei Leonardo da Vinci
  /. München , 1979. 93 p. : ISBN 3-7705-1845-4
  N6923.L33 S73   **NYPL [3-MCF V7 81-452]**

Die Gestalt des Menschen in der Kunst und im
Spiegel der Wissenschaft /. Herzog, Karl.
Darmstadt , c1990. xii, 234 p. : ISBN
    3-534-11010-2 DDC 704.9/421 20
N7572 .H47 1990

Die Herrlichkeit des Herrn . Scheele,
Paul-Werner. Würzburg , c1990. 136 p. : ISBN
    3-429-01316-X
ND2750.L36 S34 1990

Die Hochschule für Gestaltung in Ulm .
Seckendorff, Eva von. Marburg , c1989. 184
p. : ISBN 3-922561-81-0 :
N332.G33 U467 1989

Die Kultur der Abtei Sankt Gallen /
herausgegeben von Werner Vogler. Zürich :
Belser, c1990. 223 p. : ill. (some col.) ; 30 cm.
Includes bibliographical references and index. ISBN
    3-7630-1220-6
1. Arts, Medieval - Switzerland - St. Gall. 2. Christian
art and symbolism - Medieval, 500-1500 - Switzerland -
St. Gall. 3. Kloster St. Gallen. 4. St. Gall
(Switzerland) - Buildings, structures, etc. I. Vogler,
Werner.
NX663.S9 K84 1990

Die Kunst Dalmatiens . Höfler, Janez.
Graz/Austria , 1989. 338 p. : ISBN
    3-201-01466-4 DDC 709/.497/2 20
N7249.D34 H64 1989

Die Kunstdenkmale des Regierungsbezirkes
Oberbayern /. Bezold, Gustav von. München ,
1982. 10 v. : ISBN 3-486-50421-5 (v. 1)
N6873 .K86 1980 vol. 1 N6873

Die Kunstdenkmäler von Bayern .
  (1) Bezold, Gustav von. Die Kunstdenkmale des
  Regierungsbezirkes Oberbayern /. München ,

1982. 10 v. : ISBN 3-486-50421-5 (v. 1)
N6873 .K86 1980 vol. 1 N6873

  (2) Die Kunstdenkmäler von Oberpfalz &
  Regensburg /. München , 1981-<1983. v.
  <1-2, 4-11, 14-21 > : ISBN 3-486-50431-2 (v. 1)
  N6873 .K86 1980 vol. 2 N6876.O23

  (3) Die Kunstdenkmäler von Unterfranken &
  Aschaffenburg /. München , 1981-<1983. v.
  <1-2, 4-5, 7-8, 10, 12-18, 21-24 > : ISBN
    3-486-50455-X (v. 1)
  N6873 .K86 1980 vol. 3 N6882.U54

  (4) Die Kunstdenkmäler von Niederbayern /.
  München , 1980-<1983. v. <1-5, 7-8, 10-18,
  20-22 > : ISBN 3-486-50479-7 (v. 1)
  N6873 .K86 1980 vol. 4 N6876.N54

  (5) Die Kunstdenkmäler von Mittelfranken /.
  München , <1982-. v. <2 > : ISBN
    3-486-50505-X (v. 2)
  N6873 .K86 1980 vol. 5 N6876.M58

  (7) Die Kunstdenkmäler von Schwaben /.
  München , 1981-<1982. <v. 1-2 > : ISBN
    3-486-50514-9 (v. 1)
  N6873 .K86 1980 vol. 7 N6876.N58

Die Kunstdenkmäler von Mittelfranken /
[herausgegeben im Auftrag des Landesamtes für
Denkmalpflege von Felix Mader]. München : R.
Oldenbourg, <1982- > v. <2 > : ill. ; 26 cm.
(Die Kunstdenkmäler von Bayern . 5) Title on added
t.p.: Regierungsbezirk Mittelfranken. Reprint. Originally
published: München : R. Oldenbourg, <1928- >. (Die
Kunstdenkmäler von Bayern ; 5). Includes
bibliographical references and indexes. ISBN
    3-486-50505-X (v. 2)
1. Art, German - Germany - Mittelfranken. 2.
Mittelfranken (Germany) - Description and travel. I.
Mader, Felix, b. 1867. II. Bayerisches Landesamt für
Denkmalpflege. III. Title: Regierungsbezirk
Mittelfranken. IV. Series.
N6873 .K86 1980 vol. 5 N6876.M58

Die Kunstdenkmäler von Niederbayern /
[herausgegeben vom Kgl.
Generalkonservatorium der Kunstdenkmale und
Altertümer Bayerns]. München : R.
Oldenbourg, 1980-<1983 > v. <1-5, 7-8,
10-18, 20-22 > : ill. ; 26 cm. (Die
Kunstdenkmäler von Bayern . 4) Title on added t.p.:
Regierungsbezirk Niederbayern. Vols. 3-<5, 7-8, 10-18,
20-22 > edited by Felix Mader. Reprint. Originally
published: München : R. Oldenbourg, 1912-<1930 >.
(v. 1-2:Die Kunstdenkmäler des Königreichs Bayern ;
3. Bd.)(v. 3-<5, 7-8, 10-18, 20-22 > : Die
Kunstdenkmäler von Bayern ; 3). Includes
bibliographical references and indexes. ISBN
    3-486-50479-7 (v. 1)
1. Art, German - Germany - Niederbayern. 2.
Niederbayern (Germany) - Description and travel. I.
Mader, Felix, b. 1867. II. Kgl. Generalkonservatorium
der Kunstdenkmale und Altertümer Bayerns. III. Title:
Regierungsbezirk Niederbayern. IV. Series.
N6873 .K86 1980 vol. 4 N6876.N54

Die Kunstdenkmäler von Oberpfalz &
Regensburg / [herausgegeben von Georg
Hager]. München : R. Oldenbourg,
1981-<1983 > v. <1-2, 4-11, 14-21 > : ill. ;
26 cm. (Die Kunstdenkmäler von Bayern . 2) Title on
added t.p.: Regierungsbezirk Oberpfalz und Regensburg.
Reprint. Originally published: München : R.
Oldenbourg, 1905-<1914 >. (Die Kunstdenkmäler des
Königreichs Bayern ; 2. Bd.). Includes bibliographical
references and indexes. ISBN 3-486-50431-2 (v. 1)
1. Art, German - Germany - Oberpfalz. 2. Oberpfalz
(Germany) - Description and travel. I. Hager, Georg, b.
1863. II. Title: Kunstdenkmäler von Oberpfalz und
Regensburg. III. Title: Regierungsbezirk Oberpfalz und
Regensburg. IV. Series.
N6873 .K86 1980 vol. 2 N6876.O23

Die Kunstdenkmäler von Schwaben /
[herausgegeben von Georg Lill]. München : R.
Oldenbourg, 1981-<1982 > <v. 1-2 > : ill. ;
26 cm. (Die Kunstdenkmäler von Bayern . 7) Vol. <2
> has title: Die Kunstdenkmäler von Schwaben u.
Neuburg. Title on added t.p. of v. 1: Regierungsbezirk
Schwaben; v. <2 > : Regierungsbezirk Schwaben und
Neuburg. Reprint. Originally published: München : R.
Oldenbourg, 1938-<1940 >. (Die Kunstdenkmäler von
Bayern ; 7). Includes bibliographical references and
indexes. ISBN 3-486-50514-9 (v. 1)
1. Art, German - Germany - Nördlingen Region. 2.
Nördlingen Region (Germany) - Description and travel.
I. Lill, Georg, 1883-1951. II. Title: Kunstdenkmäler von
Schwaben u. Neuburg. III. Title: Regierungsbezirk
Schwaben. IV. Title: Regierungsbezirk Schwaben und

Neuburg. V. Series.
N6873 .K86 1980 vol. 7 N6876.N58

**Die Kunstdenkmäler von Unterfranken &
Aschaffenburg /** [herausgegeben vom Kgl.
Generalkonservatorium der Kunstdenkmale und
Altertümer Bayerns]. München : R.
Oldenbourg, 1981-<1983 > < 1-2, 4-5, 7-8,
10, 12-18, 21-24 > : ill. ; 26 cm. (Die
Kunstdenkmäler von Bayern . 3) Title on added t.p.:
Regierungsbezirk Unterfranken & Aschaffenburg. Vols.
8, <10, 12-18, 21-24 > edited by Felix Mader.
Reprint. Originally published: München :
Oldenbourg, 1911-1927. (v. 1-<2, 4-5, 7-8, 10, 12-18
>: Die Kunstdenkmäler des Königreichs Bayern ; 3.
Bd.)(v. <21 >-24: Die Kunstdenkmäler von Bayern ;
3). Includes bibliographical references and indexes.
ISBN 3-486-50455-X (v. 1)
*1. Art, German - Germany - Unterfranken. 2.
Unterfranken (Germany) - Description and travel. I.
Mader, Felix, b. 1867. II. Kgl. Generalkonservatorium
der Kunstdenkmale und Altertümer Bayerns. III. Title:
Kunstdenkmäler von Unterfranken und Aschaffenburg.
IV. Title: Regierungsbezirk Unterfranken &
Aschaffenburg. V. Series.*
N6873 .K86 1980 vol. 3 N6882.U54

**Die kurkölnische Bruderschafts-, Ritterordens-
und Hofkirche St. Michael in Berg im Laim .**
Stalla, Robert. Weissenhorn , c1989. 279 p. :
ISBN 3-87437-271-5
NA5586.M8 S73 1989

Die Marktpfarrkirche St. Lamberti zu Münster .
Böker, Hans Josef. Bonn , 1989. 229 p. : ISBN
3-7749-2382-5
NA5586.M853 B65 1989

Die Popoloca von Tepexi (Puebla) Jäcklein,
Klaus. Los popolocas de Tepexi (Puebla) .
Wiesbaden , 1978. xv, 316 p. : ISBN
3-515-02888-9
F1203 .D46 vol. 15 F1221.P6
NYPL [HTC 74-1117 [Bd.] 15]

Die Re-Dekade . Brock, Bazon, 1936- München ,
c1990. 298 p. : ISBN 3-7814-0288-6 :
NX550.A1 B76 1990

Die Schreinmadonna "Vierge ouvrante". Radler,
Gudrun. Frankfurt am Main , 1990. 366 p.,
[184] p. of plates : ISBN 3-923813-05-8 :
NB1912.M37 R33 1990

Die Schwierigen . Seibert, Ingrit. Wien , c1986.
199 p. : ISBN 3-7046-0053-9
NX548.Z8 S45 1986

**Die Vor- und frühgeschichtlichen Altertümer im
Germanischen Nationalmuseum .**
(Heft 4) Pülhorn, Wolfgang. Antike
Kleinkunst . Nürnberg , 1987. 163 p. : ISBN
3-9801529-0-1 DDC 738.3/82/093807443324 20
NK3835 .P85 1987
NYPL [3-MPE 90-11122]

**Die Wahrheit der Kunst : wider die Banalität :
für Günter Rombold zum 65. Geburtstag /**
Monika Leisch-Kiesl, Enrico Savio (Hrsg.).
Stuttgart : Katholisches Bibelwerk, c1989. 198
p. : ill. ; 24 cm. "Bibliographie Günter Rombold": p.
191-194. Includes bibliographical references. ISBN
3-460-32881-9 DDC 701 20
*1. Art - Philosophy. 2. Art - Themes, motives. 3.
Symbolism in art. I. Rombold, Günter, 1925-. II.
Leisch-Kiesl, Monika, 1960-. III. Savio, Enrico, 1954-.*
N68 .W24 1989

Die Wallfahrtskirche Birnau . Knapp, Ulrich,
1956- Friedrichshafen , c1989. 219 p. : ISBN
3-922137-58-X
NA5586.W266 K58 1989

Die Zwanziger Jahre in Dresden .
(T. 1) Barth, Peter. Conrad Felixmüller, die
Dresdner Jahre 1913-1933 /. Düsseldorf , 1987.
128 p. : **NYPL [3-MCK F316 89-18042]**

**Die 100 Radierungen zu den Fabeln von La
Fontaine /.** Chagall, Marc, 1887- Salzburg
[1989] 223 p. : DDC 769.92 20
NE2056.5.C45 A4 1989

Die 100 schönsten Speisekarten Österreichs :
ausgewählt beim 1. Speisekartenwettbewerb des
Fachverbandes Gastronomie und des
Fachverbandes der Hotel- und
Beherbergungsbetriebe. Graz : Mangold, [1982?]
160 p. : chiefly ill. (some col.) ; 29 cm. ISBN
3-900301-16-6
*1. Menu design - Austria - Awards. I. Fachverband
Gastronomie (Austria). II. Fachverband der Hotel- und
Beherbergungsbetriebe (Austria). III. Title: Hundert*

schönsten Speisekarten Österreichs.
NC1002.M4 A14 1982

Diebenkorn, Richard, 1922-
Richard Diebenkorn monotypes : Frederick S.
Wight Art Gallery, University of California, Los
Angeles, February 1 to February 29, 1976 / by
Gerald Nordland. Los Angeles : Frederick S.
Wight Art Gallery, University of California,
1976. 50 p. : ill. ; 28 cm. Bibliography: p. 50.
*1. Diebenkorn, Richard, 1922- - Exhibitions. I.
Nordland, Gerald. II. Title.*
NYPL [MDG (Diebenkorn) 90-7014]

**DIEBENKORN, RICHARD, 1922- -
EXHIBITIONS.**
Diebenkorn, Richard, 1922- Richard
Diebenkorn monotypes . Los Angeles , 1976.
50 p. : **NYPL [MDG (Diebenkorn) 90-7014]**

Dieckmann, Christoph, 1956- Olle DDR . Berlin ,
c1990. 168 p. : ISBN 3-362-00521-7
NYPL [MFW 91-8049]

Diederichs, Joachim, 1949- Wyczółkowski, Leon,
1852-1936. Leon Wyczółkowski, 1852-1936 .
[Wilhelmshaven] c1989. 77 p. :
N7255.P63 W892 1989
NYPL [3-MCZ+ W97 91-7562]

Diego /. Winter, Jeanette. New York , 1991. p.
cm. ISBN 0-679-81987-8 (trade) DDC 759.972 92
20
ND259.R5 W48 1991

Diego, Estrella de. Madrid (Spain). Museo
Municipal. Gabinete de Estampas. Catálogo del
Gabinete de Estampas del Museo Municipal de
Madrid /. [Madrid] , 1985- v. in : ISBN
84-398-4272-4 (set) DDC 769.946/074/0641 19
NE699 .M33 1985 **NYPL [MDE 91-282]**

Diego Rivera /. Cockcroft, James D. New York ,
c1991. 119 p., [8] p. of col. plates : ISBN
0-7910-1252-2 : DDC 759.972 B 92 20
ND259.R5 C57 1991

Diego Rivera . Rivera, Diego, 1886-1957.
[M´exico, D.F.] , 1988. 339 p. : ISBN
968-290-640-7 (pbk.)
NYPL [3-MCZ R62 90-12543]

Diego Rivera . Rivera, Diego, 1886-1957.
[Mexico City, Mexico] , 1988. 387 p. : ISBN
968-292-277-1 DDC 759.972 20
ND259.R5 A4 1988

Diego Rivera . Rivera, Diego, 1887-1957.
[Mexico City, Mexico] , 1989. 339 p. : ISBN
968-290-640-7 DDC 760/.092 20
N6559.R55 A4 1989

Diego Rivera, artist of the people /. Neimark,
Anne E. New York, NY , 1992. p. cm. ISBN
0-06-021783-9 DDC 759.972 B 20
ND259.R5 N37 1992

Diehl, Gaston.
[Max Ernst. English]
Max Ernst / by Gaston Diehl ; [translated
from the French by Eileen B. Hennessy].
New York : Crown Publishers, 1991. p. cm.
Translation of: Max Ernst. Includes bibliographical
references. ISBN 0-517-50004-3 : DDC 759.4 20
*1. Ernst, Max, 1891-1976 - Criticism and interpretation.
I. Title.*
N6888.E7 D513 1991

Poleo / Gastón Diehl ; traducción del francés
al español por Bélgica Rodríguez. [Caracas] :
Ernesto Armitano, [1989] 131 p. : col. ill. ; 27
cm. Includes index. ISBN 980-216-054-7 DDC
759.987 20
*1. Poleo, Héctor - Criticism and interpretation. I. Poleo,
Héctor. II. Title.*
ND439.P6 D54 1989

[Vasarely. English]
Vasarely / by Gaston Diehl ; [translated from
the French by Eileen B. Hennessy]. New
York : Crown, 1991. p. cm. ISBN
0-517-50800-1 : DDC 759.4 20
*1. Vasarely, Victor, 1908- - Criticism and interpretation.
2. Kinetic art - France. I. Title.*
ND553.V35 D513 1991

Diehl, Ursula. Werkstattbesuche bei Künstlern in
Berlin-Wedding /. Berlin , c1989. 2 v. : ISBN
3-9801875-9-4 :
N6885 .W46 1989

Diehl, Wolfgang. Hermann Croissant : Maler
zwischen Tradition und Moderne : eine
Monographie / von Wolfgang Diehl.
Landau/Pfalz : Pfälzische Verlagsanstalt, c1987.

200 p. : ill. (some col.) ; 28 cm. Includes
bibliographical references (p. 200). ISBN
3-87629-120-8 DDC 759.3 B 20
*1. Croissant, Hermann, 1897-1963. 2. Painters -
Germany, West - Biography. I. Croissant, Hermann,
1897-1963. II. Title.*
ND588.C85 D53 1987
NYPL [3-MCK C942 90-10583]

Dieter Crumbiegel . Crumbiegel, Dieter, 1938-
Montabaur , c1988. 107 p. : ISBN
3-921548-39-X
MLCM 89/07955 (N)
NYPL [3-MPGK 90-8715]

Dieter Hacker . Hacker, Dieter, 1942- Köln ,
c1988. 48 p. : **NYPL [3-MCK H118 91-5907]**

Diether Kressel . Kressel, Diether, 1925-
Hamburg , c1988. 64, [7] p. : ISBN
3-920365-10-0
NC251.K7 A4 1988

Dietrich, Sarolta. Gott erhalte Österreich .
Eisenstadt [1990] 239 p. :
N6807 .G67 1990

Điêu kh T Hà N 1988. 232 p., [1] leaf of plates :
NB1910 .T36 1988

Diez y seis dibujos de guerra /. Rodríguez Luna,
Antonio. Valencia , 1937. [20] p. :
NYPL [3-MCQ R696 88-10683]

Digesting the child within /. Callahan, John. New
York, N.Y. , 1991. p. cm. ISBN 0-688-09488-0
DDC 741.5/973 20
NC1429.C23 A4 1991

Dillen, Rainer, 1938-
Rainer Dillen : Retrospektive : Bilder,
Gouachen, Grafik 1959-1989 : Städtische
Galerie Rosenheim, 3.11-10.12.89.
[Rosenheim] : Die Galerie, [1989?] 100 p. : ill. ;
28 cm.
*1. Dillen, Rainer, 1938- - Exhibitions. I. Städtische
Galerie Rosenheim. II. Title.*
NYPL [3-MCK D5786 90-13533]

DILLEN, RAINER, 1938- - EXHIBITIONS.
Dillen, Rainer, 1938- Rainer Dillen .
[Rosenheim] [1989?] 100 p. :
NYPL [3-MCK D5786 90-13533]

Dillenberger, Jane. Image and spirit in sacred and
secular art / by Jane Dillenberger ; edited by
Diane Apostolos-Cappadona. New York :
Crossroad, 1990. xiii, 217 p., [8] p. of plates :
ill. (some col.) ; 24 cm. Spine title: Image & spirit
in sacred & secular art. "Bibliography of the writings of
Jane Dillenberger": p. 205-206. Includes bibliographical
references (p. 191-204) and index. ISBN
0-8245-1036-4 : DDC 701 20
*1. Women in art. I. Apostolos-Cappadona, Diane. II.
Title. III. Title: Image & spirit in sacred & secular art.*
N72.R4 D45 1990
NYPL [3-MAMZ 91-3989]

Diller, Burgoyne, 1906-1965.
Haskell, Barbara. Burgoyne Diller /. New
York , c1990. 180 p. : ISBN 0-87427-071-5
DDC 759.13 20
ND237.D47 A4 1990
NYPL [3-MCX D578 91-4631]

**DILLER, BURGOYNE, 1906-1965 -
EXHIBITIONS.**
Haskell, Barbara. Burgoyne Diller /. New
York , c1990. 180 p. : ISBN 0-87427-071-5
DDC 759.13 20
ND237.D47 A4 1990
NYPL [3-MCX D578 91-4631]

Dillon, Gianvittorio. Il Genio di Giovanni
Benedetto Castiglione, il Grechetto /. Genova ,
c1990. 267 p. : ISBN 88-7058-351-1
NYPL [3-MCF C35 90-11510]

Dimension--petit. Grösse--klein . Bern , c1989.
292 p. : **NYPL [3-MGI 91-5536]**

Dimensione futuro . Biennale di Venezia (44th :
1990) [Venezia] [Milano] , c1990. 348 p. :
ISBN 88-20-80356-9 DDC 709/.04/80744531 20
N6488.I8 V43 1990

Dimensions and directions : Black artists of the
South : a survey exhibition of works by
contemporary Black artists from 11
southeastern states / organized by the
Mississippi Museum of Art and funded in part
by the National Endowment for the Arts.
Jackson, MS : The Museum, c1980. ii, 46 p. :
ill. ; 22 cm. Catalog editor: Ruth C. Poulsen.

Exhibition held Feb. 8-Mar. 30, 1980, at the Mississippi Museum of Art in Jackson, Miss. DDC 704/.0396073075/07476251 20
1. Afro-American art - Southern States - Exhibitions. 2. Art, Modern - 20th century - Southern States - Exhibitions. I. Mississippi Museum of Art. II. Title: Black artists of the South.
N6538.N5 D47 1980

Dimitri Hadzi /. Hadzi, Dimitri, 1921- New York, N.Y. , 1989. 23 p. :
NYPL [3-MGO (Hadzi) 91-5082]

Dimitrov, Dimitŭr G. Liŭben Zidarov / Dimitŭr G. Dimitrov. 1. izd. Sofiĭa : Izd-vo Bŭlgarski khudozhnik, 1990. 159 p. : ill. (some col.) ; 31 cm. (Poreditsa Maĭstori na izobrazitelnoto izkustvo) Summary in German. Includes bibliographical references (p. 159).
1. Zidarov, Liŭben - Criticism and interpretation. I. Title.
ND893.Z53 D56 1990

Dine, Jim, 1935-
D'Oench, Ellen. Jim Dine prints, 1977-1985 /. New York , c1986. 182 p. : ISBN 0-06-431501-0 : DDC 769/.92/4 19
NE539.D5 A4 1986
NYPL [MDG (Dine) 86-1962]

Jim Dine : [Ausstellung], Kunsthalle Nürnberg am Marientor, 12. Dez. 1969 bis 14. Jan. 1970. [Munich] : Kunstverein München, c1969. 28 p. : ill. ; 24 cm. Catalog of an exhibition organized by The Museum of Modern Art, New York, under the auspices of the International Council of the Museum. Bibliography: p. 23.
1. Dine, Jim, 1935- - Exhibitions. I. Kunsthalle Nürnberg. II. Museum of Modern Art (New York, N.Y.). III. Title. *NYPL [3-MCX D58 90-6937]*

Jim Dine : Youth and the Maiden / [essay by Dr. Konrad Oberhuber]. London : Waddington Graphics, 1988. 67 p. (some folded) : ill. (some col.) ; 30 cm. Exhibition at Albertina Museum, Vienna, Jan.-Feb. 1989 and Waddington Graphics, London, 30 Mar.-22 Apr. 1989. Bibliography: p. 66.
1. Dine, Jim, 1935- - Exhibitions. I. Oberhuber, Konrad. II. Graphische Sammlung Albertina. III. Waddington Graphics (Firm). IV. Title. V. Title: Youth and the Maiden.
NYPL [MDG+ (Dine) 90-10861]

Jim Dine, drawings : February 16-March 17, 1990. New York : Pace Gallery, 1990. 1 v. (unpaged) : chiefly col. ill. ; 30 cm. ISBN 1-89828-304-9
1. Dine, Jim, 1935- - Exhibitions. I. Title.
MLCM 90/00383 (N)
NYPL [3-MCX+ D58 90-12022]

Rogers-Lafferty, Sarah. Jim Dine . Cincinnati , c1988. 119 p. : ISBN 0-917562-50-X DDC 741.973 20
NC139.D56 A4 1988

DINE, JIM, 1935- - EXHIBITIONS.
Dine, Jim, 1935- Jim Dine . [Munich] , c1969. 28 p. : *NYPL [3-MCX D58 90-6937]*
Dine, Jim, 1935- Jim Dine . London , 1988. 67 p. (some folded) :
NYPL [MDG+ (Dine) 90-10861]
Dine, Jim, 1935- Jim Dine, drawings . New York , 1990. 1 v. (unpaged) : ISBN 1-89828-304-9
MLCM 90/00383 (N)
NYPL [3-MCX+ D58 90-12022]
D'Oench, Ellen. Jim Dine prints, 1977-1985 /. New York , c1986. 182 p. : ISBN 0-06-431501-0 : DDC 769/.92/4 19
NE539.D5 A4 1986
NYPL [MDG (Dine) 86-1962]
Rogers-Lafferty, Sarah. Jim Dine . Cincinnati , c1988. 119 p. : ISBN 0-917562-50-X DDC 741.973 20
NC139.D56 A4 1988

Diners . Kittel, Gerd. London , 1990. 80 p. :
NYPL [MFX (Kittel) 90-11265]

DINERS (RESTAURANTS) - NORTHEASTERN STATES - PICTORIAL WORKS.
Kittel, Gerd. Diners . London , 1990. 80 p. :
NYPL [MFX (Kittel) 90-11265]

Dini, Francesca. Dini, Piero. I macchiaioli e la scuola di Castiglioncello /. [Rosignano Marittimo] [1990] 217 p. :
ND617.5.M3 D57 1990

Dini, Massimo, 1946- Renzo Piano, progetti e architetture, 1964-1983 / Massimo Dini. Milano : Electa, c1983. 246 p. : ill. (some col.) ; 24 cm. (Architettura. I Contemporanei) Bibliography: p. 244-245. ISBN 88-435-0921-7 : DDC 720/.92/4 19
1. Piano, Renzo. 2. Architecture, Modern - 20th century - Italy. I. Piano, Renzo. II. Series: Architettura. Contemporanei. III. Title.
NA1123.P47 D5 1983
NYPL [3-MQS (Piano) 90-129970]

Dini, Piero. I macchiaioli e la scuola di Castiglioncello / Piero Dini, Francesca Dini ; prefazione di Giovanni Spadolini. [Rosignano Marittimo] : Comune di Rosignano Marittimo, Assessorato alla cultura, [1990] 217 p. : ill. (some col.) ; 30 cm. Exhibition catalog. Includes bibliographical references (p. 205-214) and index.
1. Macchiaioli - Exhibitions. 2. Painting, Italian - Exhibitions. 3. Painting, Modern - 19th century - Italy - Exhibitions. 4. Artist colonies - Italy - Castiglioncello. I. Dini, Francesca. II. Title.
ND617.5.M3 D57 1990

DINING. see DINNERS AND DINING.

Dining design : informal restaurant interiors / by the editors of PBC International. New York : PBC International, 1991. p. cm. Includes indexes. DDC 725/.71/097309048 20
1. Restaurants, lunch rooms, etc. - United States - Decoration. I. PBC International.
NK2195.R4 D56 1991

Dining on rails . Luckin, Richard W. Golden, CO (621 Cascade Ct., Golden 80403-1581) , 1990- v. <1- > : DDC 738/.0973/075 20
NK4005 .L83 1990

DINNERS AND DINING - CARICATURES AND CARTOONS.
Robinson, W. Heath (William Heath), 1872-1944. Meals on wheels . London , c1989. 64 p. : ISBN 0-285-62932-8
NYPL [3-MEM+ (Robinson) 90-2152]

DINNERS AND DINING IN ART - EXHIBITIONS.
Art what thou eat . Mount Kisco, N.Y. , c1991. 191 p. : ISBN 1-559-21051-6 : DDC 704.9/49641/0973 20
N6512 .A763 1991
NYPL [3-MAMZ+ 91-5410]

Dinnerstein, Simon, 1943-
The art of Simon Dinnerstein / introduction by Albert Boime ; foreword by Thomas M. Messer. Fayetteville : University of Arkansas Press, 1990. xii, 254 p. : ill. (some col.) ; 24 x 31 cm. Includes bibliographical references (p. 239-246) and index. ISBN 1-557-28142-4 (alk. paper) : DDC 760/.092 20
1. Dinnerstein, Simon, 1943- - Catalogs. I. Title.
N6537.D53 A4 1990
NYPL [3-MCX+ D587 91-3991]

DINNERSTEIN, SIMON, 1943- - CATALOGS.
Dinnerstein, Simon, 1943- The art of Simon Dinnerstein /. Fayetteville , 1990. xii, 254 p. : ISBN 1-557-28142-4 (alk. paper) : DDC 760/.092 20
N6537.D53 A4 1990
NYPL [3-MCX+ D587 91-3991]

DINZ RIALTO, DELFINO - ART COLLECTIONS.
Museo delle arti primitive. Museo delle arti primitive. Cinisello Balsamo [1972?] [124] p., incl. plates.
N5310.8.I8 R55 *NYPL [3-MADF 90-6283]*

Dinzelbacher, Peter. Nitschke, August, 1926- Körper in Bewegung . Stuttgart , c1989. 399 p. : ISBN 3-7831-0955-8 DDC 704.9/42 20
N7625.5 .N58 1989

Diözesanmuseum St. Pölten, 1888-1988.
Diözesanmuseum St. Pölten (Austria) 100 Jahre Diözesanmuseum St. Pölten, 1888-1988 . St. Pölten, [Austria] , 1988. 96 p., [76] p. of plates : *NYPL [3-MAIH 91-6668]*

Das dionysische Schmuckrelief /. Hundsalz, Brigitte. München , c1987. xvii, 311 p., [32] p. of plates : ISBN 3-88073-236-1 (Deut. Bibl.) DDC 733 19
NB133 .H86 1987 *NYPL [3-MGH 91-4608]*

Dionysos 1987. Arte orafa e iconografia dionisiaca . [Italy , 1987] 88 p. :
NYPL [3-MNO+ 89-27461]

DIONYSUS (GREEK DEITY) - ART.
Hundsalz, Brigitte. Das dionysische Schmuckrelief /. München , c1987. xvii, 311 p., [32] p. of plates : ISBN 3-88073-236-1 (Deut. Bibl.) DDC 733 19
NB133 .H86 1987 *NYPL [3-MGH 91-4608]*

DIONYSUS (GREEK DEITY) - ART - EXHIBITIONS.
Arte orafa e iconografia dionisiaca . [Italy , 1987] 88 p. : *NYPL [3-MNO+ 89-27461]*

DIONYSUS (GREEK DEITY) - CULT.
Hundsalz, Brigitte. Das dionysische Schmuckrelief /. München , c1987. xvii, 311 p., [32] p. of plates : ISBN 3-88073-236-1 (Deut. Bibl.) DDC 733 19
NB133 .H86 1987 *NYPL [3-MGH 91-4608]*

DIOR, CHRISTIAN.
De Marly, Diana. Christian Dior /. New York , 1990. 96 p., [8] p. of plates : ISBN 0-8419-1260-2 : DDC 746.9/2/092 20
TT507 .D47 1990 *NYPL [3-MME 90-12028]*

Diözesan-Museum Hildesheim.
Kirchenkunst des Mittelalters . Hildesheim , c1989. 275 p. : ISBN 3-87065-528-3
NYPL [3-MAIH 90-12031]
Kirchenkunst des Mittelalters, erhalten und erforschen . Hildesheim , 1989. 275 p. : ISBN 3-87065-528-3 DDC 704.9/482/0907435958 20
N7850 .K57 1989

DIÖZESAN-MUSEUM HILDESHEIM - CATALOGS.
Kirchenkunst des Mittelalters . Hildesheim , c1989. 275 p. : ISBN 3-87065-528-3
NYPL [3-MAIH 90-12031]

Diözesanmuseum Friesing (Germany) Molzahn, Johannes, 1892-1965. Johannes Molzahn . München , 1985. 72 p. : ISBN 3-7954-0635-8
NYPL [3-MCK M731 91-6581]

Diözesanmuseum St. Pölten (Austria)
100 Jahre Diözesanmuseum St. Pölten, 1888-1988 : Sonderausstellung 1988 / bearbeiter von Johann Kronbichler unter Mitarbeit von Susanne Kronbichler-Skacha. St. Pölten, [Austria] : Bischöfliches Ordinariat St. Pölten, 1988. 96 p., [76] p. of plates : ill. (some col.) ; 21 cm. On cover and spine: Diözesanmuseum St. Pölten, 1888-1988. At head of title: Diözesanmuseum St. Pölten. Includes bibliographical references.
1. Diözesanmuseum St. Pölten (Austria) - Exhibitions. 2. Christian art and symbolism - Austria - Exhibitions. 3. Christian art and symbolism - Germany - Exhibitions. 4. Christian art and symbolism - Austria - St. Pölten - Exhibitions. 5. Art - Austria - St. Pölten - Exhibitions. 6. St, Pölten (Austria) - Church history - Exhibitions. I. Kronbichler, Johann. II. Kronbichler-Skacha, Susanne. III. Title. IV. Title: Hundert Jahre Diözesanmuseum St. Pölten, 1888-1988. V. Title: Diözesanmuseum St. Pölten, 1888-1988.
NYPL [3-MAIH 91-6668]

DIÖZESANMUSEUM ST. PÖLTEN (AUSTRIA) - EXHIBITIONS.
Diözesanmuseum St. Pölten (Austria) 100 Jahre Diözesanmuseum St. Pölten, 1888-1988 . St. Pölten, [Austria] , 1988. 96 p., [76] p. of plates : *NYPL [3-MAIH 91-6668]*

DiPerna, Frank, 1947- Terra sancta . Washington, D.C. , c1990. [32] p. : ISBN 0-88675-034-2
NYPL [MFW 91-4044]

I dipinti dal X secolo fino a Giotto /. Vatican. Pinacoteca. [Città del Vaticano] , 1979. 66 p., [71] p. of plates : ISBN 88-20-90009-2
NYPL [MAVZ (Vatican) 82-938]

I Dipinti dei Guarino e le arti decorative nella Collegiata di Solofra / Renato Ruotolo ... [et al.] ; fotografie di Francesco Tanasi. Napoli : Edizioni scientifiche italiane, c1987. 205 p. : ill. (some col.) ; 32 cm. (Collana Arte, cultura, artigianato dell'Irpinia . 1) "A cura di Vincenzo Pacelli"--Jacket. Includes bibliographies.
1. Guarino, Giovan Tommaso, 1573-1637 - Catalogs. 2. Guarino, Francesco, 1611-1654 - Catalogs. 3. Collegiata di San Michele (Solofra, Italy). 4. Painting, Italian - Catalogs. 5. Painting, Modern - 17th-18th centuries - Italy - Catalogs. I. Ruotolo, Renato. II. Pacelli, Vincenzo, 1939-. III. Series.
ND616 .D5 1987
NYPL [3-MCF+ G924 90-12954]

Dipinti dei musei e gallerie di Roma. Roma : Ministero per i beni culturali e ambientali,

Istituto centrale per il catalogo e la documentazione, 1978- v. ; 30 cm. (Repertorio delle fotografie del Gabinetto fotografico nazionale) Includes indexes. CONTENTS. - pt. 1. Galleria dell'Accademia di San Luca, Galleria nazionale d'arte antica, Galleria Borghese, Galleria Colonna, Galleria Doria Pamphilj, Galleria Pallavicini, Galleria Spada / a cura di Aldo Cicinelli, Sandra Vasco Rocca -- pt. 2. Museo di Palazzo Venezia, Museo di Roma, Pinacoteca capitolina, Quadreria della Cassa depositi e prestiti / a cura di Sandra Vasco Rocca, Simonetta De Felicis Orlandi -- pt. 4. Galleria Borghese, Galleria Colonna, Galleria dell'Accademia di S. Luca, Galleria Doria Pamphili, Galleria nazionale d'arte antica, Galleria Pallavicini, Galleria Spada : aggiornamento e revisione / a cura di Paola Callegari.
1. Gabinetto fotografico nazionale - Catalogs. 2. Painting - Italy - Rome - Catalogs. 3. Pictures - Italy - Rome - Catalogs. 4. Photography - Italy - Rome - Catalogs. 5. Photographs - Catalogs. I. Cicinelli, Aldo. II. Vasco Rocca, Sandra. III. De Felicis Orlandi, Simonetta. IV. Callegari, Paola. V. Series.
N4035.G33 D56 1981
NYPL [MAVZ+ (Rome) 91-6377]

Dipinti della Civica galleria "Anna e Luigi Parmeggiani." Civica galleria "Anna e Luigi Parmeggiani." Reggio Emilia [Italy] , 1988- v. :
NYPL [3-MCE 91-6861]

Dipinti e sculture in casa Martelli . Civai, Alessandra. Firenze , c1990. 219 p. :
NYPL [3-MAVC+ 91-6773]

Dipinti fiamminghi in Italia 1420-1570 . Ragghianti Collobi, Licia. Bologna , c1990. x, 318 p. : ISBN 88-7019-478-7
NYPL [3-MCG 91-7394]

Dipinti murali di Piero della Francesca . Centauro, Giuseppe. Milano , c1990. 317 p. : ISBN 88-435-3147-6
NYPL [3-MCF F81 91-7303]

Dipinti murali di Piero della Francesca . Centauro, Giuseppe. Milano , c1990. 317 p. : ISBN 88-435-3147-6 DDC 759.5 20
ND623.P548 C45 1990

Dipinti, sculture e oggetti d'arte di età romanica e gotica. Galleria nazionale dell'Umbria. Galleria nazionale dell'Umbria /. Roma , 1969- v. : **NYPL [MAVY (Perugia) 91-5431]**

Dipinti, sculture e oggetti dei secoli XV-XVI. Galleria nazionale dell'Umbria. Galleria nazionale dell'Umbria /. Roma , 1969- v. :
NYPL [MAVY (Perugia) 91-5431]

Diplomaten und Wesire : Krieg und Frieden im Spiegel türkischen Kunsthandwerks / herausgegeben von Peter W. Schienerl ; unter Mitarbeit von Christine Stelzig.1. Aufl. München : Staatliches Museum für Völkerkunde, 1988. 187 p., [24] p. of plates : ill. (some col.), maps ; 22 cm. First exhibition held at the newly opened branch of the Staatliches Museum für Völkerkunde München, Zweigmuseum Oettingen, Neues Schloss in 1988. Includes bibliographical references.
1. Art, Turkish - Exhibitions. 2. Decorative arts - Turkey - Exhibitions. 3. Turkey - Foreign relations - Europe - Exhibitions. I. Schienerl, Peter W. II. Stelzig, Christine. III. Staatliches Museum für Völkerkunde München. **NYPL [3-MAF 90-12662]**

Dippie, Brian W. Catlin and his contemporaries : the politics of patronage / Brian W. Dippie. Lincoln : University of Nebraska Press, c1990. xix, 553 p., [16] p. of plates : ill. (some col.), ports. ; 27 cm. Includes index. Bibliography: p. [527]-533. ISBN 0-8032-1683-1 (alk. paper) DDC 759.13 20
1. Catlin, George, 1796-1872 - Finance, Personal. 2. Art patronage - History - 19th century. I. Title.
N8835 .D57 1990
NYPL [3-MCX C36 90-10763]

DIPTYCHS - EXHIBITIONS.
Polyptyques . Paris , c1990. 293 p. : ISBN 2-7118-2331-8 **NYPL [3-MAK 90-11625]**

Dirāsāt fī al-ʻimārah wa-al-funūn al-Qibṭiyah /. Shīḥah, Muṣṭafá ʻAbd Allāh. [Cairo] [1988] 412 p., [1] folded leaf plates : ISBN 977-15-8516-9
NA6082 .S55 1988

Directors Guild Publishers.
Directory of artist associations and exhibition spaces, art commissions, museum curators & art critics /. Renaissance, CA , c1990. 208 p. ;

ISBN 0-940899-14-0
NYPL [MAV 91-6690]
Directory of galleries for the fine artist /. Renaissance, CA , c1990. 359 p. ; ISBN 0-940899-08-6 **NYPL [MA 90-11525]**
Erotic art by living artists . Renaissance, CA , c1988. 111 p. : ISBN 0-940899-02-7 (pbk.) : DDC 704.9/428/0973074 20
N8217.E6 E665 1988
NYPL [3-MAMZ 90-10946]

Directory of artist associations and exhibition spaces, art commissions, museum curators & art critics / edited by Constance Franklin. Renaissance, CA : Directors Guild Publishers, c1990. 208 p. ; 22 cm. Includes index. ISBN 0-940899-14-0
1. Art critics - United States - Directories. 2. Art commissions - United States - Directories. 3. Arts facilities - United States - Directories. I. Franklin, Constance. II. Directors Guild Publishers. III. Title: Artist associations and exhibition spaces, art commissions, museum curators & art critics.
NYPL [MAV 91-6690]

Directory of Boston architects, 1846-1970 : compiled from Boston city directories and related works / Massachusetts Committee for the Preservation of Architectural Records. Cambridge, Mass. (P.O. Box 129, Cambridge 02142) : Massachusetts Committee for the Preservation of Architectural Records, [1984]. 72 p. ; 29 cm. Cover title. "Cambridge, 1984." DDC 720/.25/74461 20
1. Architects - Massachusetts - Boston - Directories. I. Massachusetts Committee for the Preservation of Architectural Records.
NA55.B67 D57 1984

Directory of galleries for the fine artist / edited by Constance Franklin. 1st ed. Renaissance, CA : Directors Guild Publishers, c1990. 359 p. ; 22 cm. Includes index. ISBN 0-940899-08-6
1. Art galleries, Commercial - Directories. I. Franklin, Constance. II. Directors Guild Publishers. III. Title: Galleries for the fine artist.
NYPL [MA 90-11525]

Directory of master glass-painters. Thomas, Brian. Newcastle upon Tyne, 1972. [6], 122 p. ISBN 0-85362-147-0 DDC 748.5/92
NK5300.7 .T48 **NYPL [3-MRY 90-5473]**

Diruf, Hermann. Paläste Venedigs vor 1500 : baugeschichtliche Untersuchungen zur venezianischen Palastarchitektur im 15. Jahrhundert / Hermann Diruf. München : Scaneg, c1990. 224 p. : ill. ; 21 cm. (Beiträge zur Kunstwissenschaft, 0175-7202 . Bd. 33) Originally presented as the author's thesis (doctoral)--Universität München, 1978. Includes bibliographical references (p. 211-224). ISBN 3-89235-033-7
1. Palaces - Italy - Venice. 2. Architecture, Gothic - Italy - Venice. 3. Architecture, Renaissance - Italy - Venice.I. 4. Venice (Italy) - Buildings, structures, etc. I. Title. II. Series.
NA7756.V4 D57 1990

Discerning tastes . Brooke, Janet M. Montréal, Québec, Canada , c1989. 254 p. : ISBN 2-89192-123-2 **NYPL [3-MAVC 90-12883]**

Discher, Fritz, 1880-1983.
Fritz Discher (1880-1983) : Rügen-Impressionen : Gemälde, Aquarelle, Zeichnungen, Radierungen : 31. Mai-19. August 1990, Kiel, Gemäldegalerie / [Katalog und Ausstellung, Thorsten Rodiek]. Kiel : Stiftung Pommern, c1990. 64 p. : ill. (some col.) ; 24 cm. Includes bibliographical references (p. 63-64). DDC 760/.092 20
1. Discher, Fritz, 1880-1983 - Exhibitions. 2. Rügen Island (Germany) in art - Exhibitions. I. Rodiek, Thorsten. II. Stiftung Pommern. Gemäldegalerie. III. Title. IV. Title: Rügen-Impressionen.
N6888.D466 A4 1990

DISCHER, FRITZ, 1880-1983 - EXHIBITIONS.
Discher, Fritz, 1880-1983. Fritz Discher (1880-1983) . Kiel , c1990. 64 p. : DDC 760/.092 20
N6888.D466 A4 1990

Disciples of light . Smith, Graham, 1942- Malibu [Calif.] , 1990. 170 p. : ISBN 0-89236-158-1 DDC 779/.074 20
TR654 .S555 1990 **NYPL [MFW 91-3475]**

Discipline-based art education : a curriculum sampler / edited by Michael Day, Kay

Alexander. Santa Monica, Calif. : J. Paul Getty Museum, 1991. p. cm. "The Getty Center for Education in the Arts." Includes bibliographical references. ISBN 0-89236-171-9 : DDC 700 20
1. Art - Study and teaching (Elementary) - United States. 2. Art - Study and teaching (Secondary) - United States. I. Day, Michael, 1938-. II. Alexander, Kay. III. Getty Center for Education in the Arts.
N362 .C6 1991

Disciplines in art education.
Levi, Albert William, 1911- Art education . Urbana , c1991. p. cm. ISBN 0-252-01813-3 (cl) DDC 707/.073 20
N105 .L48 1991

Discourses : conversations in postmodern art and culture / edited by Russell Ferguson ... [et al.] ; foreword by Marcia Tucker ; a photographic sketchbook by John Baldessari. Cambridge, Mass. : MIT Press ; New York, N.Y. : New Museum of Contemporary Art, 1990. 471 p. : ill. ; 25 cm. (Documentary sources in contemporary art . v. 3) Includes bibliographical references (p. 454-464) and index. ISBN 0-262-06125-2 DDC 700/.9/048 20
1. Postmodernism. I. Ferguson, Russell. II. Baldessari, John, 1931-. III. Series.
NX456.5.P66 D57 1990
NYPL [3-MAL 91-3360]

DISCOVERERS. see DISCOVERIES (IN GEOGRAPHY)

DISCOVERIES (IN GEOGRAPHY) - MAPS.
Nebenzahl, Kenneth, 1927- Atlas of Columbus and the great discoveries /. Chicago , c1990. viii, 168 p. : **NYPL [Map Div. 91-7246]**

DISCOVERIES (IN SCIENCE) see INVENTIONS; SCIENCE.

DISCOVERIES, MARITIME. see DISCOVERIES (IN GEOGRAPHY)

Discovering American folk art /. Schaffner, Cynthia V. A. New York, N.Y. , 1991. p. cm. ISBN 0-8109-3206-7 DDC 745/.0973 20
NK805 .S28 1991

Discovering Turner /. Cumming, Robert, 1943- London , 1990. 72 p. : ISBN 1-85437-039-1
NYPL [3-MCV T94 91-6306]

Discrimination by design . Weisman, Leslie. Urbana , c1992. p. cm. ISBN 0-252-01849-4 (cl) DDC 720/.1/03 20
NA2543.W65 W45 1992

Discursos (Córdoba, Spain) .
(1) Vicent Zaragoza, Ana María. Retratos romanos femeninos del Museo Arqueológico de Córdoba /. Córdoba, España , 1989. 54 p. : ISBN 84-600-3110-1 DDC 733/.5/0744684 20
NB1296.3 .V53 1989

Discussions in contemporary culture / Dia Art Foundation. Seattle : Bay Press, 1987- v. : ill. ; 21 cm. Editors vary. Includes bibliographies. CONTENTS. - no. 1. [without special title] / edited by Hal Foster -- no. 6. If you lived here: the city in art, theory, and social activism: a project / by Martha Rosler; edited by Brian Wallis. ISBN 0-941920-07-0 (no. 1 : pbk.) : DDC 700/.1/03 19
1. Aesthetics, Modern - 20th century. I. Dia Art Foundation.
N72.S6 D57 1987 **NYPL [3-MAS 88-1789]**

I disegni di figura nell'Archivio storico dell'Accademia di San Luca / Accademia nazionale di San Luca. Archivio Storico. Roma , 1988- v. : ISBN 88-7140-011-9 (v. 2)
NYPL [3-MBH 90-2410]

Disegni di Giandomenico Tiepolo /. Pedrocco, Filippo. Milano , c1990. 94 p. : ISBN 88-85215-02-5
NYPL [3-MCF+ T56 91-4612]

Disegni di Salvadori /. Salvadori, Aldo. Milano , c1962. 44 leaves of plates :
NYPL [3-MCF+++ S174 90-12039]

Disegni di Stefano della Bella. Gabinetto delle stampe di Milano. Milano [1976?] 70 p. :
NYPL [3-MCF B367 91-1368]

Disegni emiliani del Sei-Settecento : i grandi cicli di affreschi / a cura di Jadranka Bentini, Angelo Mazza ; introduzione di Renato Roli ; schede di Prisco Bagni ... [et al.] ; fotografie di Marco Ravenna ; coordinamento editoriale, Graziano Manni. [Cinisello Balsamo, Milano] : Silvana, [1990] 318 p. : ill. ; 31 cm. ISBN 88-366-0306-8

1. Artists' preparatory studies - Italy - Emilia-Romagna. 2. Mural painting and decoration, Italian - Italy - Emilia-Romagna. 3. Mural painting and decoration - 17th century - Italy - Emilia-Romagna. 4. Mural painting and decoration - 18th century - Italy - Emilia-Romagna. I. Bentini, Jadranka.
NYPL [3-MLP+ 91-7177]

Disegni toscani e umbri del primo Rinascimento . Gabinetto nazionale delle stampe. Roma [1979] 183 p. :
NC256.T8 G32 1979
NYPL [3-MBH 81-532]

Disegni umbri . Venice. Gallerie dell'Accademia. Milano , c1984. 211 p. : ISBN 88-435-0801-6
NYPL [3-MBH 86-3573]

Disegni veneti e lombardi dal XVI al XVIII secolo. Ruggieri, Ugo. Disegni veneti e lombardi dal XVI al XVIII secolo dalle collezioni del Gabinetto dei disegni e delle stampe /. Roma , 1989. 226 p. : ISBN 88-7597-101-3
NYPL [3-MBH 90-12366]

Disegni veneti e lombardi dal XVI al XVIII secolo dalle collezioni del Gabinetto dei disegni e delle stampe /. Ruggieri, Ugo. Roma , 1989. 226 p. : ISBN 88-7597-101-3
NYPL [3-MBH 90-12366]

Disegno : les dessins italiens du Musée de Rennes : Galleria estense, Modène, 27 mai-29 juillet 1990, Musée des beaux-arts, Rennes, novembre-décembre 1990 : catalogue de l'exposition, suivi d'un inventaire de la collection. [Rennes], France : Le Musée, [1990] 253 p. : ill. (some col.) ; 30 cm. Errata slip inserted. Includes bibliographical references (p. 241-247) and index. ISBN 2-901430-22-8 DDC 741.945/074/4415 20
1. Drawing, Italian - Exhibitions. 2. Musée des beaux-arts de Rennes - Exhibitions. I. Musée des beaux-arts de Rennes. II. Galleria, museo e medagliere estense (Modena, Italy). III. Title: Dessins italiens du Musée de Rennes.
NC255 .D54 1990

DISHES. see POTTERY.

Disler, Martin. Geneva (Switzerland). Musée d'art et d'histoire. Cabinet des estampes. Martin Disler . Genève , 1989- v. : ISBN 2-8306-0060-6 DDC 769.92 20
NE710.D57 A4 1989
NYPL [MDG (Disler) 91-5106]

DISLER, MARTIN - CATALOGUES RAISONNÉS. Geneva (Switzerland). Musée d'art et d'histoire. Cabinet des estampes. Martin Disler . Genève , 1989- v. : ISBN 2-8306-0060-6 DDC 769.92 20
NE710.D57 A4 1989
NYPL [MDG (Disler) 91-5106]

Disney's Art of animation . Thomas, Bob, 1922- New York , c1991. p. cm. ISBN 1-562-82997-1 : DDC 741.5/8/0979493 20
NC1766.U52 D568 1991

Dispenza, Joseph, 1942- Will Shuster : a Santa Fe legend / by Joseph Dispenza and Louise Turner ; introduction by Richard Bradford. Santa Fe, N.M. : Museum of New Mexico Press, c1989. xvi, 135 p., [32] p. of plates : ill. (some col.) ; 27 cm. Includes index. ISBN 0-89013-198-8 DDC 759.13 B 19
1. Shuster, Will. 2. Artists - New Mexico - Santa Fe - Biography. 3. Santa Fe, N. M. - Biography. I. Turner, Louise. II. Title.
N6537.S537 D57 1989
NYPL [3-MCX S566 90-12340]

Displaying the Orient . Çelik, Zeynep. Berkeley , c1992. p. cm. ISBN 0-520-07494-7 (alk. paper) DDC 725/.91 20
NA957 .C44 1992

DISPOSAL OF REFUSE. see REFUSE AND REFUSE DISPOSAL.

Dissertationen der Universität Salzburg, 0259-0700 . (28) Untner, Alois. Das Unverständnis gegenüber moderner Malerei /. Wien , 1990. 312 p. : ISBN 3-85369-793-3
ND195 .U58 1990

Dissertationen der Universität Wien, 0379-1424 . (205) Gneisz, Doris. Das antike Rathaus . Wien , 1990. viii, 369 p. : ISBN 3-85369-786-0 DDC 725/.13/0938 20
NA278.P6 G58 1990

A distanced land . Pfahl, John, 1939- [Albuquerque] , 1990. xvi, 204 p. : ISBN 0-8263-1214-4 DDC 779/.36/092 20
TR647 .P494 1990
NYPL [MFX (Pfahl) 91-7438]

A distant city . Frugoni, Chiara, 1940- [Lontana città. English.] Princeton, N.J. , 1991. xv, 206 p., [80] p. of plates : ISBN 0-691-04083-4 (cloth : alk. paper) : DDC 709/.02 20
N5975 .F7813 1991
NYPL [3-MAK 91-6315]

Distel, Anne. Les collectionneurs des impressionnistes : amateurs et marchands / Anne Distel. [Paris] : Bibliothèque des Arts, c1989. 283 p. : ill. (some col.), facsims., ports. ; 31 cm. Includes index. Bibliography: p. 264-269. ISBN 2-85047-042-2
1. Art - Collectors and collecting - France. 2. Art dealers - France. 3. Impressionism (Art) - France. I. Title.
NYPL [MAVC+ 91-6788]

Seurat / Anne Distel. [Paris] : Chêne, c1991. 159, [1] p. : ill. (some col.) ; 33 cm. (Profils de l'art) "Documentation, commentaires, légendes et chronologie de Emmanuel Lévy"--T.p. verso. Includes bibliographical references (p. [160]). DDC 759.4 20
1. Seurat, Georges, 1859-1891 - Criticism and interpretation. 2. Neo-impressionism (Art) - France. I. Seurat, Georges, 1859-1891. II. Lévy, Emmanuel. III. Title. IV. Series.
N6853.S48 D5 1991

Distel, Herbert. Spoon River anthology / [Texte von] Edgar Lee Masters ; [Photographien von] Herbert Distel ; [Übersetzungen, Eileen Walliser]. Bern : Benteli, 1990. 87 p. : col. ill. ; 28 x 32 cm. Issued in conjunction with the exhibit "Herbert Distel : Diesseits, Jenseits : Menschen aus Edgar Lee Masters' Spoon River anthology" im Kunstmuseum Bern (23. Januar bis 4. März 1990) und in der "Stücki" (Galerie Klaus Littmann) in Basel (April/Mai 1990). German and English. ISBN 3-7165-0702-4
1. Distel, Herbert - Exhibitions. 2. Photography, Artistic - Exhibitions. I. Masters, Edgar Lee, 1868-1950. Spoon River anthology. Selections. II. Kunstmuseum Bern. III. Galerie Klaus Littmann. IV. Title.
NYPL [MFX (Distel) 90-2736]

DISTEL, HERBERT - EXHIBITIONS. Distel, Herbert. Spoon River anthology /. Bern , 1990. 87 p. : ISBN 3-7165-0702-4
NYPL [MFX (Distel) 90-2736]

Distelberger, Rudolf. National Gallery of Art (U. S.) Sculpture and decorative arts . Washington, D.C. [New York] , 1992. p. cm. ISBN 0-89468-162-1 DDC 708.153 20
N5963.W18 N382 1992

DISTRIBUTION (ECONOMICS) see MARKETING.

DISTRICTING (IN CITY PLANNING) see ZONING.

Dittler, Ingeborg. Seligenstädter Perlenstickerei : Ausstellung vom 15. Aug.-30. Spet. [i.e. Sept.] 1981 / Zusammengetragen und vorgestellt von Ingeborg Dittler. Seligenstadt : Verein für Forderung des Landschaftsmuseums Seligenstadt, 1981. 87 p. : ill. ; 21 cm. At head of title: Landschaftsmuseum Seligenstadt. Bibliography: p. 85.
1. Beadwork - Germany (West) - Exhibitions. I. Landschaftsmuseum Seligenstadt.
NYPL [3-MOT 89-27386]

Dittmer, Kathrin. Baudenkmale in Niedersachsen /. Hannover , c1990. 356 p. : ISBN 3-87706-322-5 DDC 720/.943/59 20
NA1081 .B38 1990

Divenuto, Francesco. Napoli sacra del XVI secolo : repertorio delle fabbriche religiose napoletane nella Cronaca del gesuita Giovan Francesco Araldo / Francesco Divenuto. Napoli : Edizioni scientifiche italiane, c1990. 317 p., [32] p. of plates : ill. (some col.) ; 25 cm. Includes bibliographical references (p. 289-294) and indexes. ISBN 88-7104-562-9 : DDC 726/.5/094573 20
1. Church architecture - Italy - Naples. 2. Architecture, Jesuit - Italy - Naples. 3. Naples (Italy) - Buildings, structures, etc. I. Araldi, Giovan Francesco, 1528-1599. Chronico della Compagnia di Giesù di Napoli. Selections. 1990. II. Title.
NA5621.N2 D58 1990

The Divided heritage : themes and problems in German modernism / edited by Irit Rogoff.

Cambridge [England] ; New York : Cambridge University Press, 1991. xvi, 390 p. : ill. ; 26 cm. At head of title on preliminary t.p.: Royal Academy Symposia volume. Includes bibliographical references and index. ISBN 0-521-34553-7 DDC 709.43/09/04 20
1. Modernism (Art) - Germany. 2. Modernism (Art) - Germany (West). 3. Art, Modern - 20th century - Germany. 4. Art, Modern - 20th century - Germany, West. I. Rogoff, Irit. II. Royal Academy of Arts (Great Britain).
N6868.5.M63 D58 1990
NYPL [3-MAMG 91-6532]

A divina arte negra e o livro português . Pacheco, José, 1954- Lisboa [1988?] 282 p. :
NE1163 .P33 1988
NYPL [MDOH 90-12803]

Divine comedy . Cameron, Eric, 1935- Ottawa , 1990. 75 p., 27 p. of plates : ISBN 0-88884-594-4 DDC 709/.2 20
N6549.C35 A4 1990
NYPL [3-MGO (Cameron)]

La divine et l'impure . Haddad, Michèle. Paris , c1990. 191 p. : ISBN 2-86950-174-9
IN PROCESS (ONLINE)
NYPL [3-MAMZ 91-5801]

Divisible by two. Whiteman, John E. M. Divisible by 2 /. [Chicago] , Cambridge, Mass. , 1990. 61 p. : ISBN 0-262-73093-6 (pbk.) DDC 728/.092 20
NA7125 .W48 1990
NYPL [3-MRG 91-6702]

Divisible by 2 /. Whiteman, John E. M. [Chicago] , Cambridge, Mass. , 1990. 61 p. : ISBN 0-262-73093-6 (pbk.) DDC 728/.092 20
NA7125 .W48 1990
NYPL [3-MRG 91-6702]

Divisionismo italiano / [direzione della mostra, Gabriella Belli. Milano : Electa, 1990. 480 p. : ill. (some col.) ; 24 cm. Catalog of an exhibition held at the Palazzo delle Albere, Trento, Italy, Apr. 21-July 15, 1990. Includes bibliographical references (p. 469-480). ISBN 88-435-3178-6
1. Neo-impressionism (Art) - Italy - Exhibitions. 2. Painting, Italian - Exhibitions. 3. Painting, Modern - 19th century - Italy - Exhibitions. I. Belli, Gabriella. II. Palazzo delle Albere (Trento, Italy).
NYPL [3-MCE 90-12999]

Divulgación (Alicante, Spain). (9) Hernández Guardiola, Lorenzo, 1953- Pintura decorativa barroca en la provincia de Alicante /. Alicante [1990- v. <1 > : ISBN 84-7784-037-7
ND2786.A43 H4 1990

Diwa--buhay, ritwal at sining. Museo ng Kalinangang Pilipino . Maynila, Pilipinas , 1989. 190, [1] p. :
NX581.A1 M88 1989

Dix, Jan, 1928- Nuremberg. Germanisches Nationalmuseum. Archiv für Bildende Kunst. Dokumente zu Leben und Werk des Malers Otto Dix . Nürnberg , 1977. 80 p. :
N6888.D5 A4 1977
NYPL [3-MCK D619 81-446]

Dix, Otto, 1891-1969. Kunsthalle zu Kiel. Otto Dix, Zeichnungen aus dem Nachlass, 1911-1942 . Kiel [1980?] [71] p. : *NYPL [3-MCK+ D619 90-5743]*

DIX, OTTO, 1891-1969 - EXHIBITIONS. Kunsthalle zu Kiel. Otto Dix, Zeichnungen aus dem Nachlass, 1911-1942 . Kiel [1980?] [71] p. : *NYPL [3-MCK+ D619 90-5743]*

Nuremberg. Germanisches Nationalmuseum. Archiv für Bildende Kunst. Dokumente zu Leben und Werk des Malers Otto Dix . Nürnberg , 1977. 80 p. :
N6888.D5 A4 1977
NYPL [3-MCK D619 81-446]

Dixon Gallery and Gardens. Misfeldt, Willard E. J. J. Tissot . Alexandria, Va. , 1991. p. cm. ISBN 0-88397-097-X DDC 769.92 20
NE650.T56 M57 1991

Dixon, Maurice, 1947- Coulter, Lane, 1944- New Mexican tinwork, 1840-1940 /. Albuquerque , c1990. xxii, 189 p. : ISBN 0-8263-1180-6 DDC 739.5/32/09789 20
TS600 .C68 1990 *NYPL [3-MNK 90-11509]*

Dixon, Roger, 1935- Victorian architecture /Roger Dixon, Stefan Muthesius. New York : Oxford University Press, 1978. 288 p. : ill. ; 22 cm. (The World of art) Bibliography: p. 250-251.

Includes index.　ISBN 0-19-520048-9　DDC 720/.941
1. Architecture, Victorian - Great Britain. 2.
Architecture - Great Britain. I. Muthesius, Stefan, joint
author. II. Title.
NA967 .D59

Dizionario degli scultori italiani dell'Ottocento /.
Panzetta, Alfonso. Torino , Milano, c1989. 228
p. :　ISBN 88-422-0224-X
　　　NYPL　[3-MGI+ 90-11558]

Dizionario degli scultori italiani dell'Ottocento /.
Panzetta, Alfonso. Torino , 19. 228 p. :　ISBN
88-422-0224-X :　DDC 730/.92/245 B 20
NB622 .P36 1989

Dizionario della pittura e dei pittori /. Petit
Larousse de la peinture. Italian. Torino , c1989-
v. :　ISBN 88-06-11573-1 (v. 1)
　　　NYPL　[MAO 90-2147]

Dmitrievskiĭ, Vitaliĭ Nikolaevich. Iskusstvo v
khudozhestvennoĭ zhizni sotsialisticheskogo
obshchestva /. Moskva , 1990. 173 p. ;　ISBN
5-02-012744-2 :
NX556.A1 185 1990

**DMOCHOWSKI, Z. R. (ZBIGNIEW R.) , 1906-
1982 - EXHIBITIONS.**
Dmochowski, Z. R. (Zbigniew R.), 1906-1982.
The work of Z.R. Dmochowski . London ,
1988. 80 p. :　ISBN 0-905788-90-7
　　NYPL　[3-MQZ+ (Dmochowski) 90-95]

Dmochowski, Z. R. (Zbigniew R.), 1906-1982.
The work of Z.R. Dmochowski : Nigerian
traditional architecture / edited and introduced
by J.C. Moughtin. London : Ethnographica,
1988. 80 p. : ill., maps, plans ; 31 cm. "First
published in 1988 as a catalogue to the exhibition of
photographs and drawings by Z.R. Dmochowski,
Nigeria's architectural achievement ... [which] ... tours
several venues in USA and United Kingdom from April
1988-December 1989"--T.p. verso. Includes
bibliographical references (p. 78). CONTENTS. -
Foreword / J.C. Moughtin -- Nigeria's architectural
achievement / Z.R. Dmochowski -- The work of Z.R.
Dmochowski / J.C. Moughtin.　ISBN 0-905788-90-7
1. Dmochowski, Z. R. (Zbigniew R.) , 1906-1982 -
Exhibitions. 2. Architecture - Nigeria - Exhibitions. I.
Moughtin, J. C. II. Dmochowski, Zbigniew, 1906-1982.
Nigeria's architectural achievement. III. Title. IV. Title:
Nigeria's architectural achievement. V. Title: Nigerian
traditional architecture.
　　NYPL　[3-MQZ+ (Dmochowski) 90-95]

Dmochowski, Zbigniew, 1906-1982.
Nigeria's architectural achievement.
Dmochowski, Z. R. (Zbigniew R.),
1906-1982. The work of Z.R. Dmochowski :
Nigerian traditional architecture / edited and
introduced by J.C. Moughtin. London , 1988.
80 p. :　ISBN 0-905788-90-7
　　NYPL　[3-MQZ+ (Dmochowski) 90-95]

Do Mosteiro dos Jerónimos . Carvalho, Artur
Marques de. [Lisbon] [1990] 281 p. :
NA5830.M67 C37 1990

**DOANE TURK, SANDRA - ART
COLLECTIONS - EXHIBITIONS.**
The Sandra Doane Turk collection of Western
art . St. Petersburg, Florida , 1985. 42 p. :
　　　NYPL　[3-MAMZ 90-11526]

Dobbels, Daniel. Bazaine, Jean, 1904- Bazaine.
Paris , c1990. 178 p. :　ISBN 2-605-00162-8
　　　NYPL　[3-MCO B35 90-12858]

Dobbie, Ian. Sudjic, Deyan. Cult objects .
London , 1985. 159 p. :　ISBN 0-586-08483-5
(pbk.) :　DDC 745.2/09/04 19
NK1390 .S83 1985　NYPL　[3-MNF 91-5813]

Dobbs, Stephen M. The DBAE handbook : an
overview of discipline-based art education / by
Stephen Mark Dobbs. Santa Monica, CA :
Getty Center for Education in the Arts, 1991.
p. cm. Includes bibliographical references.　ISBN
0-89236-214-6 :　DDC 707/.073 20
1. Art - Study and teaching - United States -
Handbools, manuals, etc. I. Title.
N105 .D63 1991

Döbele, Hedwig. Ackermann, Max. Max
Ackermann, Klang der Farbe . Stuttgart ,
c1989. 61 p. :
ND588.A313 A4 1989

Döbele, Johannes. Ackermann, Max. Max
Ackermann, Klang der Farbe . Stuttgart ,
c1989. 61 p. :
ND588.A313 A4 1989

Dobrez, Patricia. The art of the Boyds :
generations of artistic achievement / Patricia
Dobrez and Peter Herbst. Sydney : Bay Books,
1990. 232 p. : ill. ; 33 cm.　ISBN 1-86256-426-4
1. Boyd family. I. Title.
　　　NYPL　[3-MAM+ 90-13433]

Dobson, S. Gaston. (ill) Historic Blacks in the arts
/. Chicago, IL , c1990. p. cm.　ISBN
0-922162-58-1 :　DDC 700/.92/2 B 20
NX164.B55 H57 1990

Dr. Atl . Atl, Dr., 1875-1964. México , 1974. 137
p. :　DDC 759.972 20
N6559.A85 A4 1974

Doctor Atl. Atl, Dr., 1875-1964. Dr. Atl .
México , 1974. 137 p. :　DDC 759.972 20
N6559.A85 A4 1974

Doctorow, E. L., 1931- Fischl, Eric, 1948- Scenes
and sequences . Hanover, NH , New York ,
1990. 118 p. :　ISBN 0-944722-04-0　DDC 769.92
20
NE2246.F5 A4 1990
　　　NYPL　[MDG (Fischl) 90-12797]

DOCTORS. see PHYSICIANS.

**DOCUMENTARY PHOTOGRAPHY. see
PHOTOGRAPHY, DOCUMENTARY.**

Documentary sources in contemporary art .
(v. 3) Discourses . Cambridge, Mass. , New
York, N.Y. , 1990. 471 p. :　ISBN 0-262-06125-2
　　DDC 700/.9/048 20
NX456.5.P66 D57 1990
　　　NYPL　[3-MAL 91-3360]

(v. 4) Out there . New York, N.Y. , Cambridge,
Mass. , c1990. 446 p. :　ISBN 0-262-06132-5
　　DDC 700/.1/0308693 20
NX180.S6 O97 1990　NYPL　[3-MA 91-3296]

Documenti di architettura.
Olanda 1870-1940 . Milano , 1990, c1980. 208
p. :　ISBN 88-435-3094-1
　　　NYPL　[3-MQW 91-6563]

Documenti di architettura armena .
(16) Gandolfo, Francesco. Ptghni/Arudch /.
Milano, Italia , 1986. 74 p. :　ISBN
88-85822-03-7　DDC 720/.9566/2 s
726/.5/094792 19
NA1474 .D6 no. 16 NA5998.P84
　　　NYPL　[3-MQW 90-11667]

(19) Gharabagh /. Milano, Italia , 1988. 107
p. :　ISBN 88-85822-09-6
　　　NYPL　[3-MQW 91-4235]

**Documenti geocartografici nelle bibiloteche e
negli archivi privati e pubblici della Liguria.**
Firenze : L.S. Olschki, 1990- v. : ill. (some
col.), maps ; 30 cm. (Catalogazione di cimeli
geocartografici . 5) Includes bibliographical references.
CONTENTS. - 1. Museo navale di Genova / a cura di
Alberto Capacci.　ISBN 88-22-23788-9 (v. 1)
1. Maps - Bibliography - Catalogs. 2. Libraries - Italy -
Liguria - Catalogs. 3. Archives - Italy - Liguria -
Catalogs. I. Capacci, Alberto.
　　　NYPL　[Map Div. 91-69]

**Documenti geocartografici nelle bibiloteche e
negli archivi privati e pubblici della Toscana.**
Firenze : L.S. Olschki, 1987- v. : ill. (some
col.) ; 30 cm. (Catalogazione di cimeli
geocartografici . 2-4) Includes bibliographical references
and indexes. CONTENTS. - 1. Le piante dell'ufficio
fiumi e fossi di Pisa / a cura di Danilo Barsanti -- 2. I
fondi cartografici dell'Archivio di Stato di Firenze. 1.
Miscellanea di piante / a cura di Leonardo Rombai,
Diana Toccafondi e Carlo Vivoli -- 3. Introduzione allo
studio delle geocarte nautiche di tipo medievale e la
racconta della Biblioteca comunale di Siena / a cura di
Osvaldo Baldacci.　ISBN 88-22-23511-8 (v. 1)　DDC
016.91245/5 20
1. Tuscany (Italy) - Maps - Bibliography - Catalogs. 2.
Tuscany (Italy) - Archival resources - Italy - Tuscany -
Catalogs. 3. Tuscany (Italy) - Library resources - Italy -
Tuscany - Catalogs. I. Series: Catalogazione di cimeli
geocartografici , 2, etc.
Z6027.I82 T873 1987 GA895.T8
　　　NYPL　[Map Div. 90-16]

Documenti (Turin, Italy)
Poli, Francesco, 1949- Giulio Paolini /. Torino ,
c1990. 171 p. :　ISBN 88-7180-006-0 :　DDC
709/.2 20
N6923.P27 A4 1990

Documentos de escultura contemporánea.
Arte conceptual revisado =. [Valencia] [1990?]
286 p. :　ISBN 84-7721-108-6　DDC 709/.04/075

20
N6494.C63 A76 1990

Documentos de Querétaro .
(7) Ramírez Montes, Guillermina. Pedro de
Rojas y su taller de escultura en Querétaro /.
Querétaro, Qro., México , 1988. 113 p. :　ISBN
968-614-020-4　DDC 730/.92 20
NB259.R58 R35 1988

**Documentos internacionales sobre patrimonio
arquitectónico.** [Bogotá, Colombia] : Facultad
de Arquitectura, Universidad de los Andes :
Ediciones PROA, [1989 or 1990] 35 p. ; 28
cm. (Colección Patrimonio arquitectónico colombiano .
1)
1. Architecture - Colombia. I. Universidad de los Andes
(Bogotá, Colombia). Facultad de Arquitectura. II.
Series.
NA870 .D6 1989

Documents d'architecture. OMA-Rem Koolhaas .
Paris , c1990. 167 p. :　ISBN 2-86653-080-2
　　DDC 720/.92 20
NA1153.K64 O45 1990

Dodd, Jeremy. Lisney, Adrian. Landscape design
guide /. Aldershot, Hants, England ; Brookfield,
Vt., USA : 2 v. :　ISBN 0-566-09017-1 (v. 1) :
　　DDC 712 19
SB472　　　*NYPL　[3-MSD 90-13255]*

Dodd, Philip. Buck, Louisa. Relative values, or
What's art worth? /. London , 1991. 176 p. :
　　ISBN 0-563-36118-2 (cased) :　DDC 700.1 20
N7425　　　*NYPL　[MA 91-5744]*

Dodds, Jerrilynn D. Architecture and ideology in
early medieval Spain / Jerrilynn D. Dodds.
University Park : Pennsylvania State University
Press, c1990. xiv, 174 p., [72] p. of plates : ill.,
map ; 29 cm. Includes bibliographical references (p.
[117]-170) and index.　ISBN 0-271-00671-4　DDC
720/.946/09021 20
1. Architecture - Spain. 2. Architecture, Medieval -
Spain. 3. Architecture and society - Spain. I. Title.
NA1303 .D63 1989
　　　NYPL　[3-MQWH 91-4942]

Dodgson, Campbell, 1867-1948. The etchings of
Charles Meryon / by Campbell Dodgson ;
edited by Geoffrey Holme. London : "The
Studio," 1921. vii, 28 p., 47 leaves of plates :
ill. ; 30 cm.
1. Meryon, Charles, 1821-1868. I. Meryon, Charles,
1821-1868. II. Holme, C. Geoffrey (Charles Geoffrey),
1887-1954. III. Title.
NF2115.M6 D6
　　　NYPL　[MDG+ (Méryon) 91-6349]

Dölling, Regine.
Das Stiftergrabmal in Maria Laach / Regine
Dölling, Reinhold Elenz. Worms : Werner,
c1990. 73 p. : ill. (some col.) ; 26 cm.
(Denkmalpflege in Rheinland-Pfalz.
Forschungsberichte . Bd. 1) Includes bibliographical
references (p. 69-73).　ISBN 3-88462-069-X
1. Sepulchral monuments - Germany -
Rhineland-Palatinate. 2. Sculpture, German -
Germany - Rhineland-Palatinate. 3. Sculpture, Gothic -
Germany - Rhineland-Palatinate. 4. Abtei Maria Laach.
I. Elenz, Reinhold. II. Title. III. Series.
NB1870 .D6 1990

Hindorf, Heinz. Heinz Hindorf, Glasfenster /.
Freiburg , c1989. 176 p. :　ISBN 3-451-21540-3 :
　　DDC 748.593 20
NK5398.H56 A4 1989

D'Oench, Ellen.
Davison Art Center. Friends of the Davison
Art Center acquisitions, 1962-1988 .
Middletown, Conn. , c1988. 72 p. :
　　　NYPL　[MDE 89-17470]

Jim Dine prints, 1977-1985 / Ellen G.
D'Oench and Jean E. Feinberg. 1st ed. New
York : Harper & Row, c1986. 182 p. : ill. ; 29
cm. (Icon editions) "Published in association with an
exhibition organized for the Davison Art Center and
the Ezra and Cecile Zilkha Gallery, Wesleyan
University, Middletown, Connecticut." Includes index.
Bibliography: p. 178-180.　ISBN 0-06-431501-0 :
　　DDC 769/.92/4 19
1. Dine, Jim, 1935- - Exhibitions. I. Feinberg, Jean E.
II. Dine, Jim, 1935-. III. Davison Art Center. IV. Ezra
and Cecile Zilkha Gallery. V. Title.
NE539.D5 A4 1986
　　　NYPL　[MDG (Dine) 86-1962]

Doerr, Carl, 1777-1842.
Biedermeierliches Württemberg : Carl Doerr als
Landschaftsmaler : [Austellung], Städtische

Museen Heilbronn, Deutschhof, 21. September bis 28. Oktober 1979 / [Katalog, Andreas Pfeiffer]. Heilbronn : Städtische Museen, c1979. 94 p. : chiefly ill. (some col.) ; 21 x 30 cm. (Heilbronner Museumskatalog. Nr. 10) Bibliography: p. 32.
1. Doerr, Carl, 1777-1842 - Exhibitions. 2. Württemberg in art - Exhibitions. 3. Biedermeier (Art) - Germany, West - Württemberg - Exhibitions. I. Pfeiffer, Andreas. II. Title.
N6888.D63 A4 1979
NYPL [3-MCK D672 81-1042]

DOERR, CARL, 1777-1842 - EXHIBITIONS.
Doerr, Carl, 1777-1842. Biedermeierliches Württemberg . Heilbronn , c1979. 94 p. :
N6888.D63 A4 1979
NYPL [3-MCK D672 81-1042]

Doerr, Josef, 1914-
Meuser, Bernhard. Josef Doerr /. Speyer am Rhein , 1989. 96 p. : ISBN 3-87637-040-X DDC 709/. 20
N6888.D634 M4 1989

DOERR, JOSEF, 1914- - CRITICISM AND INTERPRETATION.
Meuser, Bernhard. Josef Doerr /. Speyer am Rhein , 1989. 96 p. : ISBN 3-87637-040-X DDC 709/. 20
N6888.D634 M4 1989

Doesburg, Theo van, 1883-1931.
Théo Van Doesburg /. Paris , c1990. 240 p. : ISBN 2-904057-45-5
NYPL [3-MCH D645 91-3770]

DOESBURG, THEO VAN, 1883-1931 - CONGRESSES.
Théo Van Doesburg /. Paris , c1990. 240 p. : ISBN 2-904057-45-5
NYPL [3-MCH D645 91-3770]

Doezema, Marianne, 1950-
George Bellows and urban America / Marianne Doezema. New Haven, CT : Yale University Press, c1991. p. cm. Includes bibliographical references and index. ISBN 0-300-05043-7 DDC 759.13 20
1. Bellows, George, 1882-1925 - Criticism and interpretation. 2. United States in art. 3. Cities and towns in art. I. Title.
ND237.B45 D6 1991

Marlais, Michael Andrew. Americans and Paris . Waterville, Me. , c1990. 62 p. : DDC 759.13/074/7416 20
N6510 .M27 1990
NYPL [3-MAMT 90-13006]

Doherty, Willie, 1959-
Willie Doherty, unknown depths. Cardiff : Ffotogallery, in association with Orchard Gallery and Third Eye Centre, c1990. [39] p. : ill. (some col.) ; 29 cm. Exhibition held at Ffotogallery, Cardiff, April 3-May 12, 1990; Third Eye Centre, Glasgow, June 30-July 29, 1990; Orchard Gallery, Derry, Sept. 12-Oct. 25, 1990; and at other galleries. Includes bibliographical references. ISBN 1-87277-101-7
1. Doherty, Willie, 1959- - Exhibitions. 2. Great Britain - Description and travel - 1971- - Views - Exhibitions. 3. Ireland - Description and travel - 1981- - Views - Exhibitions. I. Ffotogallery (Cardiff, Wales). II. Title. III. Title: Unknown depths.
NYPL [MFX (Doherty) 90-13467]

DOHERTY, WILLIE, 1959- - EXHIBITIONS.
Doherty, Willie, 1959- Willie Doherty, unknown depths. Cardiff , c1990. [39] p. : ISBN 1-87277-101-7
NYPL [MFX (Doherty) 90-13467]

Doisneau, Robert. Bonnet, Serge, 1924- Automne, hiver de l'homme du fer /. [Nancy] [Metz] , c1986. 102 p. : ISBN 2-86480-255-4
HD8039.I52 F823 1986
NYPL [MFW+ 89-20431]

Dokumentation der Museumsgesellschaft Kronberg e.V. Schriften .
(Bd. 4) Wilhelm Busch und seine Freunde in Frankfurt und Kronberg /. Frankfurt am Main , c1984. 104 p. : ISBN 3-7829-0289-0 : DDC 831/.8 19
PT2603.U8 Z895 1984
NYPL [3-MCK B97 86-1055]

Dokumente unserer Zeit (Mainz, Rhineland-Palatinate, Germany) .
(Bd. 4) Uecker, Günther, 1930- Günther Uecker . Mainz , c1988. 84 p. : ISBN

3-926663-04-9
N6888.U37 A4 1988
NYPL [3-MCK+ U125 91-7298]

Dokumente zu Leben und Werk des Malers Otto Dix . Nuremberg. Germanisches Nationalmuseum. Archiv für Bildende Kunst. Nürnberg , 1977. 80 p. :
N6888.D5 A4 1977
NYPL [3-MCK D619 81-446]

Dokumente zur modernen Schweizer Architektur. Mehlau-Wiebking, Friederike. Schweizer Typenmöbel, 1925-1935 . Zürich , c1989. 231 p. : ISBN 3-85676-029-6
NYPL [3-MOF+ 89-26582]

Dolfin, Marceline J. Utrecht : de huizen binnen de singels / door Marceline J. Dolfin, E.M. Kylstra en Jean Penders ; met bijdragen van T.J. Hoekstra ... [et al.]. 's-Gravenhage : SDU Uitgeverij, 1989. 2 v. : ill., plans ; 30 cm. (De Nederlandse monumenten van geschiedenis en kunst. De provincie Utrecht. De gemeente Utrecht . deel 3A-3B) "Samengesteld vanwege de gemeente Utrecht." Includes bibliographical references and index.
CONTENTS. - [v. 1] Beschrijving -- [v. 2] Overzicht. ISBN 90-12-05876-7 (set)
1. Architecture, Domestic - Netherlands - Utrecht. 2. Dwellings - Netherlands - Utrecht. 3. Utrecht (Netherlands) - Buildings, structures, etc. I. Kylstra, E. M. II. Penders, Jean. III. Series: Nederlandse monumenten van geschiedenis en kunst. IV. Title.
NYPL [3-MRG+ 90-12086]

DOLL CLOTHES - CATALOGS.
Pilkenton, Linda. Skipper fashion value guide, 1964-1976 /. [Albuquerque, N.M.] , c1990. 59 p. : DDC 688.7/221/0979493 20
NK4894.2.M37 A4 1990

Doll, Nancy. Plous, Phyllis. PULSE 2 . Santa Barbara , Seattle , c1990. 76 p. : ISBN 0-942006-19-4 DDC 709/.73/07479491 20
N72.T4 P85 1990 **NYPL [3-MGI 91-5051]**

Doll, Nancy, 1947-
Inner natures : four contemporary painters : Gregory Amenoff, Brenda Goodman, Mary Hambleton, Michael Kessler / Nancy Doll. Santa Barbara, Calif. : Santa Barbara Museum of Art, 1990. 40 p. : ill. (some col.) ; 28 cm. Catalog of an exhibition held at the Santa Barbara Museum of Art Nov. 23, 1990 to Feb. 10, 1991. Includes bibliographical references. ISBN 0-89951-080-9 DDC 759.14/074/79491 20
1. Painting, American - Exhibitions. 2. Painting, Modern - 20th century - United States - Exhibitions. 3. Painters - United States - Biography. I. Santa Barbara Museum of Art. II. Title.
ND212 .D65 1990

Santa Barbara Museum of Art. Santa Barbara Museum of Art . Santa Barbara, Calif. [1991] 109 p. : ISBN 0-89951-078-7 : DDC 708.194/91 20
N742.S15 A195 1991

DOLLHOUSES - SPECIMENS.
Lellie, Herman. A Victorian dollhouse /. New York , 1991. p. cm. ISBN 0-312-06228-1 : DDC 688.7/23 20
NK4893 .L39 1991

DOLLMAKING - UNITED STATES - HISTORY - 19TH CENTURY - EXHIBITIONS.
Dolls and duty--Martha Chase and the progressive agenda, 1889-1925 /. Providence, R.I. (110 Benevolent St., Providence 02906) , 1989. 48 p. : DDC 688.7/221/097451 20
NK4894.2.C43 A4 1989

DOLLMAKING - UNITED STATES - HISTORY - 20TH CENTURY - EXHIBITIONS.
Dolls and duty--Martha Chase and the progressive agenda, 1889-1925 /. Providence, R.I. (110 Benevolent St., Providence 02906) , 1989. 48 p. : DDC 688.7/221/097451 20
NK4894.2.C43 A4 1989

Dolls . Werner, Vivian L. New York, NY , c1991. 120 p. : ISBN 0-380-76044-4 : DDC 688.7/221/09 20
NK4894.A2 W43 1991

Dolls and duty--Martha Chase and the progressive agenda, 1889-1925 / Paul G. Bourcier, curator ; Miriam Formanek-Brunell, academic consultant. Providence, R.I. (110 Benevolent St., Providence 02906) : Rhode Island Historical Society, 1989. 48 p. : ill. ; 23

cm. Catalog of an exhibition held at the Rhode Island Historical Society, Sept. 20, 1989-Aug. 12, 1990. Includes bibliographical references. DDC 688.7/221/097451 20
1. Chase, Martha Jenks, 1851-1925 - Exhibitions. 2. Dollmaking - United States - History - 19th century - Exhibitions. 3. Dollmaking - United States - History - 20th century - Exhibitions. I. Chase, Martha Jenks, 1851-1925. II. Bourcier, Paul G. III. Formanek-Brunell, Miriam. IV. Rhode Island Historical Society.
NK4894.2.C43 A4 1989

DOLLS - COLLECTORS AND COLLECTING.
Seeley, Mildred. Judging dolls . Livonia, Mich. (30595 8 Mile Rd., Livonia 46152-1798) [c1991] 166 p. : DDC 688.7/221/075 20
NK4893 .S384 1991

United Federation of Doll Clubs. Detroit [convention] 1970. [Detroit, 1970] 152 p. DDC 745.59/22
NK4893 .U5

DOLLS - HISTORY - JUVENILE LITERATURE.
Werner, Vivian L. Dolls . New York, NY , c1991. 120 p. : ISBN 0-380-76044-4 : DDC 688.7/221/09 20
NK4894.A2 W43 1991

Dolph and Stewart. Dolph's Atlas of Westchester county, N. Y., showing streets, roads, parkways, golf and country clubs, parks, schools, land owners. New York, N. Y., Dolph & Stewart [1942] 72 p. incl. maps (part col.) illus. 38 cm. Cover title. "Historic landmarks in Westchester county": p. 12. Includes advertising matter.
1. Westchester County, N. Y. - Maps. 2. Real property - Westchester county, N. Y. - Maps.
NYPL [Map Div. 90-12850]

Dolph Map Company. Dolph's street atlas of Dade County, Florida. Fort Lauderdale, Florida , 1991. 141 p. :
NYPL [Map Div. 91-7313]

DOLPHINS.
Czernohaus, Karola. Delphindarstellungen von der minoischen bis zur geometrischen Zeit /. Göteborg , 1988. 235, 111 p., 121 p. of plates : ISBN 91-86098-76-4
NYPL [3-MAH 90-10819]

DOLPHINS - FOLKLORE.
Czernohaus, Karola. Delphindarstellungen von der minoischen bis zur geometrischen Zeit /. Göteborg , 1988. 235, 111 p., 121 p. of plates : ISBN 91-86098-76-4
NYPL [3-MAH 90-10819]

Dolph's street atlas of Dade County, Florida. Fort Lauderdale, Florida : Dolph Map Co., 1991. 141 p. : chiefly maps (some col.) ; 31 cm. Includes index.
1. Real property - Florida - Dade County. 2. Dade County, Fla. - Maps. I. Dolph Map Company. II. Title: Street atlas of Dade County, Florida.
NYPL [Map Div. 91-7313]

DOM ZU ERFURT (GERMANY)
Drachenberg, Erhard. Die mittelalterliche Glasmalerei in Erfurt. Berlin, Wien, 1976- v in. ISBN 3-205-00581-3 (v. 2, pt. 1)
NYPL [MRY+ 77-1943 Bd.1, T.1-2]

DOM ZU XANTEN - EXHIBITIONS.
Brandt, C. F. (Christian Friedrich), 1823-1891. C.F. Brandt . Kleve , c1991. 122 p. : ISBN 3-89413-192-6
NYPL [MFX+ (Brandt) 91-7695]

Domenico Beccafumi e il suo tempo. Milano : Electa, c1990. 732 p. : ill. (some col.) ; 28 cm. Catalog of an exhibition held in various locations in Siena in 1990. Bibliography: p. 716-731. ISBN 88-435-3173-5
1. Beccafumi, Domenico, 1486-1551 - Exhibitions.
NYPL [3-MCF B365 91-2303]

Domenico Beccafumi e il suo tempo. Beccafumi, Domenico, 1486-1551. Milano , c1990. 732 p. : ISBN 88-435-3173-5 DDC 759.5 20
ND623.B34 A4 1990

Domenico Bianchi . Bianchi, Domenico, 1955- [Turin] [1989] 1 v. (unpaged) :
N6923.B557 A4 1989

DOMENICO, DI BARTOLO, CA. 1400-CA. 1445.
Torriti, Piero. Il Pellegrinaio nello Spedale di Santa Maria della Scala a Siena /. Siena , 1987. 93 p. : **NYPL [3-MCF+ D668 90-11012]**

Domenico Fiasella /. Fiasella, Domenico,
1589-1669. Genova , c1990. 287 p. :
NYPL [3-MCF F464 90-13082]

Domenico Gnoli . Gnoli, Domenico, 1933-1970.
[Madrid] , c1990. 151 p. : ISBN 84-7664-248-2
NYPL [3-MCF+ G572 90-12300]

Domenico Mazzone, sculptor. Mazzone,
Domenico, 1927- [New York City?] c1971. 48
p. : *NYPL [3-MGO (Mazzone) 91-874]*

Domenig, Gerald, 1953-
BCLIK / Gerald Domenig. [S.l.] : G. Domenig,
c1988. 1 v. (unpaged) : all ill. ; 30 cm. Catalog
of an exhibition held at Portikus, Frankfurt am Main,
June 17-July 24, 1988, and at the Kunstverein
München, July 8-17, 1988.
*1. Domenig, Gerald, 1953- - Exhibitions. I. Portikus
(Museum). II. Kunstverein München. III. Title. IV.
Title: B.C.L.I.K.*
NYPL [MFX+ (Domenig) 91-2386]

Gerald Domenig, Merciette : Portikus,
Frankfurt am Main, 17. Juni-24. Juli 1988,
Kunstverein München, 8. Juli-17. Juli 1988.
[S.l.] : G. Domenig, c1988. 1 v. (unpaged) : all
ill. ; 20 x 30 cm.
*1. Domenig, Gerald, 1953- - Exhibitions. I. Portikus
(Museum). II. Kunstverein München. III. Title. IV.
Title: Merciette.*
NYPL [MFX+ (Domenig) 90-13478]

DOMENIG, GERALD, 1953- - EXHIBITIONS.
Domenig, Gerald, 1953- BCLIK /. [S.l.] ,
c1988. 1 v. (unpaged) :
NYPL [MFX+ (Domenig) 91-2386]

Domenig, Gerald, 1953- Gerald Domenig,
Merciette . [S.l.] , c1988. 1 v. (unpaged) :
NYPL [MFX+ (Domenig) 90-13478]

Domènikos Theotokópoulos. El Greco .
Rethymno , 1990. 416 p. : ISBN 960-7309-00-6
DDC 759.6 20
ND813.T4 E524 1990

DOMESTIC ARCHITECTURE. see
ARCHITECTURE, DOMESTIC.

Domestic architecture in the Lebanon /.
El-Khoury, Fouad. London [1975] 25 p. :
NYPL [3-MRG 90-12551]

The domestic architecture of Sir Edwin Lutyens
/. Butler, A. S. G. (Arthur Stanley George),
1888-1965. [Architecture of Sir Edwin Lutyens.
Vol. 1.] Woodbridge, Suffolk , 1989. 61 p., 110,
[120] p. of plates : ISBN 1-85149-100-7
NYPL [3-MQZ++ (Lutyens) 90-12076]

Dominguez, Antonio. see Dominguez Ortiz,
Antonio.

Dominguez Ortiz, Antonio. Resplendence of the
Spanish monarchy . New York , 1991. p. cm.
ISBN 0-87099-621-5 DDC 739.7/0946/0747471
20
NK3062.A1 R47 1991

Dominik, Janet B. American scene painting .
Irvine, Calif. , 1991. p. : ISBN 0-9610520-3-1 :
DDC 758/.99794052 20
ND230.C3 A44 1991

Dominikanerkirche (Osnabrück, Germany) Teepe,
Friedrich, 1929- Friedrich Teepe .
[Osnabrück] , 1988. 73 p. :
NYPL [3-MGO+ (Teepe) 89-27029]

DOMON, KEN, 1909- - EXHIBITIONS.
The Beauty of Japan. Tokyo, Japan , c1987.
[12], 118 p. : *NYPL [MFW 91-3529]*

Domröse, Ulrich. Bilderlust . Heidelberg , 1991.
200 p. : ISBN 3-925835-74-1
NYPL [MFW+ 91-6341]

DON QUIXOTE (FICTITIOUS CHARACTER)
IN ART - CATALOGS.
Museo Iconográfico del Quijote. Museo
Iconográfico del Quijote /. México, D.F. ,
1987. 103 p. : ISBN 968-7037-31-8
N910.G78 A6 1987

Donadoni, Sergio. Desroches-Noblecourt,
Christiane, 1913- Grand temple d'Abou
Simbel . Le Caire , 1971. vi, 65 leaves, xlii
leaves of plates :
ND2865.A2 D4 1971

Donald Friend, 1915-1989 . Friend, Donald.
Sydney , 1990. 160 p. : ISBN 0-7305-6929-2
(pbk.) *NYPL [3-MCZ+ F87 90-11801]*

Donald Friend, 1915-1989 . Pearce, Barry.
[Sydney, N.S.W.] , 1990. 160 p. : ISBN

0-7305-6929-2 (pbk.) DDC 709/.2 20
N7405.F7 A4 1990

Donald Friend's Bali : an exhibition arranged in
conjunction with the Donald Friend
retrospective, 9 February-25 March 1990, Art
Gallery of New South Wales / sponsored by
the Australia-Indonesia Institute. Sydney :
Trustees of the Art Gallery of New South
Wales, 1990. 65 p. : ill. (some col.) ; 21 x 22
cm. ISBN 0-7305-6574-2
*1. Friend, Donald - Art collections - Exhibitions. 2.
Art, Balinese - Exhibitions. I. Art Gallery of New
South Wales.*
MLCS 90/15244 (N)
NYPL [3-MAF 91-6722]

Donald Judd . Judd, Donald, 1928-
Baden-Baden , 1989. 215 p. : ISBN
3-89322-168-9
NYPL [3-MGO (Judd) 90-12983]

Donald Judd . Judd, Donald, 1928- Stuttgart-Bad
Cannstatt [1989] 215 p. : ISBN 3-89322-168-9 :
DDC 709/.2 20
NB237.J76 A4 1989

Donald Morris Gallery. Brockmann, Gottfried,
1903- Gottfried Brockmann, drawings
1921-1931 . Birmingham, Mich. , c1975. [32]
p. : *NYPL [3-MCK B862 91-1178]*

Donald Sultan . Sultan, Donald. London , c1989.
31 p. : ISBN 1-87071-502-0
NYPL [3-MCX S954 91-5893]

Donatello . Donatello, 1386?-1466. Padova ,
c1989. 185 p. (some folded) : ISBN
88-7026-883-7
NYPL [3-MGO+ (Donatello) 91-3657]

Donatello, 1386?-1466. Donatello : le sculture al
Santo di Padova / foto di Elio Ciol ; testo di
Giuseppe Mazzariol, Attilia Dorigato. Padova :
Messaggero, c1989. 185 p. (some folded) : col.
ill. ; 34 cm. Includes bibliographical references.
ISBN 88-7026-883-7
*1. Donatello, 1386?-1466. 2. Basilica di Sant'Antonio
(Padua, Italy). 3. Sculpture - Italy - Padua. I. Ciol, Elio.
II. Mazzariol, Giuseppe. III. Dorigato, Attilia. IV.
Basilica di Sant'Antonio (Padua, Italy). V. Title. VI.
Title: Sculture al Santo Padova.*
NYPL [3-MGO+ (Donatello) 91-3657]

DONATELLO, 1386?-1466.
Donatello, 1386?-1466. Donatello . Padova ,
c1989. 185 p. (some folded) : ISBN
88-7026-883-7
NYPL [3-MGO+ (Donatello) 91-3657]

Donath, Joachim. Olle DDR . Berlin , c1990. 168
p. : ISBN 3-362-00521-7
NYPL [MFW 91-8049]

Donati, Piero. Fiasella, Domenico, 1589-1669.
Domenico Fiasella /. Genova , c1990. 287 p. :
NYPL [3-MCF F464 90-13082]

Donati, Valentino. Pietre dure e medaglie del
Rinascimento : Giovanni da Castel Bolognese /
Valentino Donati ; introduzione di Massimo
Griffo. Ferrara : Belriguardo, [1989]. 291 p. :
ill. (some col.) ; 31 cm. English and Italian.
Includes bibliographgical references (p. 289-291).
*1. Bernardi, Giovanni, 1494-1553. 2. Glyptics - Italy. 3.
Intaglios - Italy. I. Title.*
NYPL [3-MGW+ 91-7173]

Donatio et memoria . Schleif, Corine.
[München] , 1990. 288 p., [4] leaves of plates :
ISBN 3-422-06031-6
NYPL [3-MRBB 91-7159]

Donation Gerard Bonnier / redaktör, Nina
Öhman ; författare, Werner Aspenström ... [et
al.]. Stockholm : Rabén & Sjögren, [1989] 106
p. : ill. (some col.) ; 23 cm. (Årsbok för statens
konstmuseer . 35) Includes bibliographical references.
ISBN 91-29-59355-7
*1. Art, Modern - 20th century. 2. Bonnier, Gerard,
1917- - Art collections. 3. Art - Private collections -
Sweden. 4. Nationalmuseet (Stockholm, Sweden). I.
Bonnier, Gerard, 1917-. II. Öhman, Nina. III.
Aspenström, Werner, 1918-. IV. Moderna museet
(Stockholm, Sweden). V. Series.*
N6488.S8 S74 1989

Donation Maurice et Pauline Feuillet de Borsat
/. Musée Borély. Marseille, 1969. 1 v.
(unpaged)
NC27.F7 M355
NYPL [3-MAVZ (Marseilles) 91-291]

Donauer, Georg. Tafelmaier, Walter, 1935-
Architekturmalerei an Fassaden . Stuttgart ,
1988. 159 p. : ISBN 3-421-02937-7
NYPL [3-MRX 90-12633]

Dong son drums in Viet Nam / [Betonamu Kōko
Kenkyūjo, Betonamu Shakai Kagaku Iinkai
Kokusai Kyōryokubu]. [Shohan]. Tōkyō : Rocco
Shuppan, 1990. 282 p. : ill. (some col.) ; 38 cm.
+ 1 suppl. (35 p.) Text in English, Japanese, and
Vietnamese. Colophon title: Betonamu dōko zuroku.
Colophon inserted. ISBN 4-8453-3038-5 :
*1. Bronzes, Vietnamese - Catalogs. 2. Drums
(Containers) - Vietnam - Catalogs. I. Betonamu Kōko
Kenkyūjo. II. Betonamu Shakai Kagaku Iinkai. Kokusai
Kyōryokubu. III. Title: Betonamu dōko zuroku.*
NK7978.6.V5 D66 1990

Donihue, David. Luminosity . New York, NY ,
c1986. 20 p. : ISBN 0-932075-11-8
NYPL [3-MAL 90-10424]

Donizetti, Gaetano, 1797-1848.
[Alina, regina di Golconda]
Alina [sound recording] / Donizetti.
Pontelambro, Italy : Nuova era, p1988. 2
sound discs (134 min.) : digital ; 4 3/4 in.
Opera semiseria in 2 acts. Libretto by Felice Romani,
based on: La reine de Golconde / le chevalier de
Boufflers. Daniela Dessì, Adelisa Tabiadon, Rockwell
Blake, Paolo Coni, Andrea Martin, Sergio Bertocchi,
singers ; Gruppo giovanile "Artisti del coro" del
Teatro regio di Parma ; Orchestra "Arturo
Toscanini" ; Antonello Allemandi, conductor.
Recorded in Teatro Alighieri, Ravenna, July 15-17,
1987. "World premiere recording"--Container.
Compact discs. Program notes and synopsis in Italian
with English translation and Italian libretto (56 p. :
ill.) in container.
1. Operas. I. Title.
Nuova era 033.6701

Anna Bolena [sound recording] / Gaetano
Donizetti ; [libretto di Felice Romani].
Pontelambro (Como) Italy : Nuova Era, p1988.
2 sound discs (2 hr., 12 min.) : digital ; 4 3/4
in. Tragic opera in 2 acts. Leyla Gencer, Giulietta
Simionato, Plinio Clabassi, Aldo Bertocci, singers ;
Orchestra Sinfonica e Coro di Milano della
Radiotelevisione Italiana ; Gianandrea Gavazzeni,
conductor. "1958 original recording." Compact disc.
Analog recording. Text in Italian (38 p.) in container.
*1. Operas. 2. Anne Boleyn, Queen, consort of Henry
VIII, King of England, 1507-1536 - Drama. I. Title.*
Nuova Era 6713-DM

Donnadieu, Jean-Claude. Trülzsch, Holger. Le
garage de Hegel /. [Paris] , c1989. 108 p. :
ISBN 2-86234-050-2 DDC 709/.2 20
N6888.T697 A4 1989

Donnelly, Marian C. (Marian Card) Architecture
in the Scandinavian countries / Marian C.
Donnelly. Cambridge, Mass. : MIT Press,
c1991. p. cm. Includes bibliographical references and
index. ISBN 0-262-04118-9 DDC 720/.948 20
1. Architecture - Scandinavia - History. I. Title.
NA1201 .D66 1991

D'Onofrio, Cesare, 1921- Visitiamo Roma nel
Quattrocento : la città degli umanisti / Cesare
D'Onofrio. Roma : Romano società editrice,
1989. 307 p. : ill. ; 25 cm. (Studi e testi per la
storia della città di Roma. 9) Texts in Italian and Latin
in parallel columns. Includes bibliographical references
(p. 294-296) and index.
*1. Historic buildings - Italy - Rome. 2. Architecture -
Italy - Rome. 3. Architecture - Italy - Rome. 4. Rome
(Italy) - History. 5. Rome (Italy) - Buildings, structures,
etc. 6. Rome (Italy) - Buildings, Structures etc. -
History. 7. Rome (Italy) - Antiquities. I. Series: Studi e
testi per la storia della città di Roma, 9. II. Title.*
NYPL [3-MQWB 91-4311]

Donovan, Fiona. Nordfeldt, Bror Julius Olsson,
1878-1955. The woodblock prints of B.J.O.
Nordfeldt . Minneapolis , c1991. 72 p. : ISBN
0-938713-08-6 DDC 769.92 20
NE1300.6.N6 A4 1991

DÖNSELMANN, KARL - EXHIBITIONS.
Dunkel, Trimborn, Dönselmann . [Emden,
Germany , 1988] 87 p. : ISBN 3-925564-02-0
NYPL [3-MAMG + 89-11596]

Donzel, Catherine.
Palaces et grands hôtels d'Amérique du Nord /
par Catherine Donzel, Alexis Gregory et Marc
Walter ; préface par Yves Berger. Paris :
Flammarion, c1989. 255 p. : ill. (some col.) ; 32
cm. Includes bibliographical references (p. 253).
ISBN 2-08-201846-6 DDC 728/.5/0973 20

1. Hotels, taverns, etc. - United States. 2. Hotels, taverns, etc. - Canada. I. Gregory, Alexis. II. Walter, Marc. III. Title.
NA7840 .D67 1989

Saint-Laurent, Cécil, 1919- Histoire imprévue des dessous féminins /. Paris , 1988. 280 p. :
  ISBN 2-7335-0126-7 :
GT2703 .S25 1988
  NYPL [3-MMV+ 91-5460]

DOOR COUNTY (WIS.) - MAPS.
Rockford Map Publishers. Door County, Wisconsin, land atlas & plat book. Rockford, Ill. , c1990. 1 atlas (63 p.) :
  NYPL [Map Div. 90-12838]

Door County, Wisconsin, land atlas & plat book.
Rockford Map Publishers. Rockford, Ill. , c1990. 1 atlas (63 p.) :
  NYPL [Map Div. 90-12838]

DOORS.
Meyer-Bohe, Walter. Türen und Tore /. Stuttgart , 1977. 142 p. : ISBN 3-87422-581-X :
TH2278 .M43   **NYPL [3-MRR 80-2183]**

DOORS - GERMANY - FRIESLAND.
Jessel, Hans, 1956- Friesenhaustüren /. Hamburg , c1990. 56 p. : ISBN 3-89234-159-1
NA7350.F84 J4 1990

DOORWAYS - BRAZIL - MINAS GERAIS.
Negro, Carlos del. Escultura ornamental barrôca do Brasil. [Belo Horizonte, 1967] 2 v.,
NB1285 .N4   **NYPL [3-MRX 91-6337]**

Döpping, Marga. Laabs, Hans, 1915- Hans Laabs . Berlin , c1990. 189 p. : ISBN 3-87584-294-4 DDC 759.3 20
ND588.L25 A4 1990

D'Orazio, Maria Pia. Dorazio, Piero, 1927- Piero Dorazio . Todi , 1975. [178] p. : DDC 759.5
ND623.D64 A53
  NYPL [3-MCF+ D693 91-1152]

Dorazio, Piero, 1927-
Piero Dorazio : mostra retrospettiva 1946-1975, marzo-maggio 1975 : Sala delle pietre, Palazzo del popolo, Todi. Todi : Associazione Piazza Maggiore, 1975. [178] p. : ill. (some col.) ; 30 cm. Catalog edited by Maria Pia D'Orazio. Bibliography: p. [166] DDC 759.5
1. Dorazio, Piero, 1927- - Exhibitions. 2. Dorazio, Piero, 1927- - Criticism and interpretation. I. D'Orazio, Maria Pia. II. Palazzo del popolo (Todi, Italy). III. Title.
ND623.D64 A53
  NYPL [3-MCF+ D693 91-1152]

DORAZIO, PIERO, 1927- - EXHIBITIONS.
Dorazio, Piero, 1927- Piero Dorazio . Todi , 1975. [178] p. : DDC 759.5
ND623.D64 A53
  NYPL [3-MCF+ D693 91-1152]

DORAZIO, PIERO, 1927- - CRITICISM AND INTERPRETATION.
Dorazio, Piero, 1927- Piero Dorazio . Todi , 1975. [178] p. : DDC 759.5
ND623.D64 A53
  NYPL [3-MCF+ D693 91-1152]

Đorđević, Kosta.
Kosta Đorđević : izložba keramike, mart-april 1976 / Muzej primenjene umetnosti = Kosta Đorđeviv : exhibition of ceramics, March-April 1976. Beograd : Muzej, 1976. 1 v. (unpaged) : ill. ; 24 cm. Serbo-Croatian (Roman) and English.
1. Đorđević, Kosta - Exhibitions. I. Muzej primenjene umetnosti (Belgrade, Serbia). II. Title.
  NYPL [3-MPG 91-884]

ĐORĐEVIĆ, KOSTA - EXHIBITIONS.
Đorđević, Kosta. Kosta Đorđević . Beograd , 1976. 1 v. (unpaged) :
  NYPL [3-MPG 91-884]

Dörflinger, Johannes, 1941-
Johannes Dörflinger : Pastelle und Zeichnungen : Katalog zur Ausstellung vom 9. März bis 28. April 1989, Galerie Döbele, Stuttgart / [Autorin, Jill Lloyd ; Übersetzung, Heide-Marie Reindl-Scheuering]. Stuttgart : Die Galerie, c1989. [37] p. : col. ill. ; 30 cm. German and English. Double-folded leaves.
1. Dörflinger, Johannes, 1941- - Exhibitions. I. Lloyd, Jill. II. Galerie Döbele. III. Title.
  NYPL [3-MCK+ D663 89-25787]

DÖRFLINGER, JOHANNES, 1941- - EXHIBITIONS.
Dörflinger, Johannes, 1941- Johannes Dörflinger . Stuttgart , c1989. [37] p. :
  NYPL [3-MCK+ D663 89-25787]

Dorfman, Ariel. Chile from within, 1973-1988 /. New York , 1990. 143 p. : ISBN 0-393-02817-8 (cl.) DDC 983.06/5 20
F3100 .F4722 1990   **NYPL [MFW 91-4452]**

Dorfstecher, Dietrich. América Latina . [Berlin , 1988?] 144 p. :
N6884.5 .A44 1988
  NYPL [3-MAMG 91-5083]

Dorigato, Attilia. Donatello, 1386?-1466. Donatello . Padova , c1989. 185 p. (some folded) : ISBN 88-7026-883-7
  NYPL [3-MGO+ (Donatello) 91-3657]

Döring, Volker, 1952- Olle DDR . Berlin , c1990. 168 p. : ISBN 3-362-00521-7
  NYPL [MFW 91-8049]

Doris Chase, artist in motion . Failing, Patricia. Seattle , c1991. p. cm. ISBN 0-295-97112-6 DDC 700/.92 B 20
N6537.C4638 F35 1991

Dorman, John Frederick. Virginia Revolutionary pension applications, abstracted. Washington, 1958- v. 28 cm. Vol. 38-44: "Abstracted and compiled by John Frederick Dorman." Vols. 42-44 published in Falmouth, Virginia.
1. Pensions, Military - United States - Revolution, 1775-1783. 2. United States - History - Revolution, 1775-1783 - Biography. 3. Virginia - Biography. 4. Virginia - Genealogy. I. Title.   **NYPL [APR (Virginia) (Dorman, J. F. Virginia Revolutionary pensions applications)]**

Dormant lines. Andō, Tadao, 1941- Tadao Ando . New York, N.Y. , c1991. 32 p. : ISBN 0-8478-1339-8 DDC 720/.22/22 20
NA2707.A53 A4 1991

Dorn, Günter. Junge Berliner Künstler . Ludwigshafen , c1987. 103 p. :
IN PROCESS (ONLINE)
  NYPL [3-MAMG 90-12473]

Dorn, Roland.
Décoration : Vincent van Goghs Werkreihe für das Gelbe Haus in Arles / Roland Dorn. Hildesheim ; New York : G. Olms, 1990. xxxii, 622 p. : ill. ; 21 cm. (Studien zur Kunstgeschichte, 0175-9558 . Bd. 45) "Kunstliteratur-Preis 1987 der Confédération internationale des négociants en œuvres d'art (CINOA)." Originally presented as the author's thesis (doctoral)--Johannes-Gutenberg Universität, Mainz, 1986. Includes catalog of the "Décoration" (p. 331-475). Includes bibliographical references (p. 531-599). ISBN 3-487-09098-8
1. Gogh, Vincent van, 1853-1890 - Homes and haunts - France - Arles. 2. Artists - Netherlands - Biography. 3. Arles (France) in art. 4. Gogh, Vincent van, 1853-1890 - Catalogs. I. Title. II. Series.
ND653.G7 D64 1990

Festschrift für Hartmut Biermann /. Weinheim , c1990. 400 p. : ISBN 3-527-17712-4
  NYPL [3-MAS 91-5197]

Vincent van Gogh and the modern movement, 1890-1914 /. Freren [Germany] , 1990. 436 p. : ISBN 3-923641-33-8 (Hard cover)
  NYPL [3-MCH G61 91-4493]

Dornauf, Moritz, 1953- Quintessenz . [Darmstadt] [1989] 76 p. :
N668 .Q55 1989

Dornier, Christoph M., 1938-
Kluckert, Ehrenfried. Von der Kunst die Phantasie zu leben . Stuttgart , c1989. 93 p. : ISBN 3-89322-172-7 DDC 709/.2 20
N6888.D665 K58 1989

DORNIER, CHRISTOPH M., 1938- - CRITICISM AND INTERPRETATION.
Kluckert, Ehrenfried. Von der Kunst die Phantasie zu leben . Stuttgart , c1989. 93 p. : ISBN 3-89322-172-7 DDC 709/.2 20
N6888.D665 K58 1989

Dorny, Bertrand, 1931- Cortot, Jean. Morand--memorandum /. 1989. [13] p. : DDC 700/.92 20
N7433.4.C66 A4 1989

Dorothea Rockburne . Rockburne, Dorothea. Waltham, Mass. , c1989. 63 p. :
  NYPL [3-MCX R6825 91-6138]

Dorothea Tanning . Tanning, Dorothea, 1910- London , 1989. 59 p. : ISBN 1-87071-506-3 (pbk.)

DDC 760.092 20
  NYPL [3-MCX T167 91-5915]

DOROTHEA VON STETTEN-KUNSTPREIS - EXHIBITIONS.
Dorothea von Stetten-Kunstpreis 1988 . Bonn , 1988. 126 p. : DDC 730/.943/074435518 20
NB568 .D74 1988   **NYPL [3-MGI 91-7194]**

Dorothea von Stetten-Kunstpreis 1988 :
Städtisches Kunstmuseum Bonn, 4. Mai bis 5. Juni 1988 / Stephan Balkenhol ... [et al. ; Direktorin, Katharina Schmidt ; Katalogredaktion, Klaus Schrenk, Elke Bratke]. Bonn : Das Kunstmuseum, 1988. 126 p. : chiefly ill. (some col.) ; 28 cm. DDC 730/.943/074435518 20
1. Sculpture, German - Germany (West) - Exhibitions. 2. Sculpture, Modern - 20th century - Germany (West) - Exhibitions. 3. Dorothea von Stetten-Kunstpreis - Exhibitions. I. Balkenhol, Stephan, 1957-. II. Schrenk, Klaus. III. Bratke, Elke. IV. Städtisches Kunstmuseum Bonn.
NB568 .D74 1988   **NYPL [3-MGI 91-7194]**

Dorset. Estate Publications (Firm) Estate Publications Dorset . Tenterden, Kent [1980?] 1 atlas (34, [6] p.) : ISBN 0-86084-108-1
  NYPL [Map Div. 91-1161]

DORSET (ENGLAND) - MAPS.
Estate Publications (Firm) Estate Publications Dorset . Tenterden, Kent [1980?] 1 atlas (34, [6] p.) : ISBN 0-86084-108-1
  NYPL [Map Div. 91-1161]

Dortmunder Museumsgesellschaft zur Pflege der Bildenden Kunst. Französische Illustrationen des 18. und 19. Jahrhunderts . Dortmund , 1985. 267 p. : ISBN 3-924302-16-2 DDC 741.64/074/0356 s 741.64/0944/0740356 19
NC980 .B54 1985 vol. 1
  NYPL [MDT 91-2511]

Dos broncos conmemorativos y una gesta heroica . Pujol, Annie Lemistre. Alajuela, Costa Rica , 1988. 171 p. : ISBN 997-7953-10-4
  NYPL [3-MGI 89-24636]

Dos Santos, Deoscoredes Maximiliano. see Santos, Deoscoredes Maximiliano dos.

DOSHI, BALKRISHNA V. - CRITICISM AND INTERPRETATION.
Curtis, William J. R. Balkrishna Doshi . New York , 1988. 191 p. : ISBN 0-8478-0937-4 DDC 720/.92 20
NA1510.D67 C87 1988
  NYPL [3-MQZ (Doshi) 89-22893]

Doss, Erika Lee. Benton, Pollock, and the politics of modernism : from regionalism to abstract expressionism / Erika Doss. Chicago : University of Chicago Press, 1991. p. cm. Includes bibliographical references and index. ISBN 0-226-15942-6 (alk. paper) DDC 759.13 20
1. Benton, Thomas Hart, 1889-1975 - Criticism and interpretation. 2. Regionalism in art - United States. 3. Pollock, Jackson. 1912-1956 - Criticism and interpretation. 4. Abstract expressionism - United States. 5. Modernism (Art) - Political aspects - United States - History - 20th century. I. Title.
ND237.B47 D67 1991

Dossier Québec series.
Grassroots, greystones, and glass towers . Montréal , Buffalo, N.Y. , c1989. 211 p. : ISBN 1-550-65001-7 : DDC 720/.9714/28 20
NA747.M66 G7 1989

Dossier Rembrandt . Dudok van Heel, Sebastien A. C. Amsterdam , 1987. 88 p. :
  NYPL [3-MCH R3 91-6725]

Dossiers du Musée d'Orsay .
(19) Paris. Musée d'Orsay. Un Sculpteur-écrivain Ernst Barlach . Paris , 1988. 64 p. : ISBN 2-7118-2181-1 :
  NYPL [3-MGO (Barlach) 90-4429]

Dotterer, Ronald L., 1948- Sexuality, the female gaze, and the arts . Selinsgrove [N.J.] , London , 1992. p. cm. ISBN 0-945636-32-6 (alk. paper) DDC 700/.1/03 20
NX180.F4 S49 1992

Dottori, Gerardo, 1884-
Gerardo Dottori, 1884-1977 : Palazzo Ancaiani, Spoleto, 27 giugno-15 luglio 1979 / Ministero per i beni culturali e ambientali, Soprintendenza speciale alla Galeria nazionale d'arte moderna e contemporanea. Roma : De Luca, c1979. 71 p. : ill., 1 port. ; 24 cm. Includes bibliographical references.

1. Dottori, Gerardo, 1884- - Exhibitions. I. Italy.
Soprintendanza speciale alla Galeria nazionale d'arte
moderna e contemporanea. II. Title.
MLCM 80/99 NYPL [3-MCF D725 91-878]

DOTTORI, GERARDO, 1884- -
EXHIBITIONS.
Dottori, Gerardo, 1884- Gerardo Dottori,
1884-1977 . Roma , c1979. 71 p. :
MLCM 80/99 NYPL [3-MCF D725 91-878]

Doty, C. Stewart (Charles Stewart) Acadian hard
times : the Farm Security Administration in
Maine's St. John Valley, 1940-1943 / C.
Stewart Doty ; photographs by John Collier, Jr.,
Jack Delano, and Jack Walas.1st ed. Orono,
Me. : University of Maine Press, 1991. xiv, 184
p. : ill. ; 29 cm. Includes bibliographical references.
ISBN 0-89101-070-X DDC 338.1/09741/1 20
1. United States. Farm Security Administration -
History. 2. Agriculture and state - Maine - History. 3.
Agriculture and state - Saint John River Valley (Me.
and N.B.) - History. 4. Agriculture - Economic
aspects - Maine - History. 5. Agriculture - Economic
aspects - Saint John River Valley (Me.and N.B.) -
History. 6. Saint John River Valley (Me. and N.B.) -
Description and travel - Views. I. Collier, John, 1913-.
II. Delano, Jack. III. Walas, Jack. IV. Title.
HD1775.M2 D67 1991
NYPL [MFW 91-7984]

Douard, Christel. Châteaux de Haut-Léon .
Saint-Brice-en Coglès , c1987. 32 p. : ISBN
2-86934-006-0
NYPL [3-MQWF+ 90-5362]

Double negative. Heizer, Michael, 1944- Michael
Heizer . New York , 1991. p. cm. ISBN
0-8478-1426-2 DDC 709/.2 20
N6537.H384 A635 1991

D'Oudry à Le Sidaner . Salmon, Marie José.
Beauvais , 1990. 171 p. : ISBN 2-901290-06-X
N8214.5.F8 S25 1990

DOUGLAS COUNTY (ILL.) - DIRECTORIES.
Rockford Map Publishers. Douglas County,
Illinois, land atlas & plat book . Rockford, Ill. ,
1976, c1969. 1 atlas (32 p.) :
NYPL [Map Div. 90-5519]

DOUGLAS COUNTY (ILL.) - MAPS.
Rockford Map Publishers. Douglas County,
Illinois, land atlas & plat book . Rockford, Ill. ,
1976, c1969. 1 atlas (32 p.) :
NYPL [Map Div. 90-5519]

Douglas County, Illinois, land atlas & plat book .
Rockford Map Publishers. Rockford, Ill. , 1976,
c1969. 1 atlas (32 p.) :
NYPL [Map Div. 90-5519]

**Douglas County, Illinois, land atlas and plat
book.** Rockford Map Publishers. Douglas
County, Illinois, land atlas & plat book .
Rockford, Ill. , 1976, c1969. 1 atlas (32 p.) :
NYPL [Map Div. 90-5519]

DOUGLAS COUNTY, MINN. - MAPS.
(1990) Rockford Map Publishers. Douglas
County, Minnesota, land atlas & plat book .
Rockford, Ill. [c1990] 1 atlas (47 p.) :
NYPL [Map Div. 90-11382]

**Douglas County, Minnesota, land atlas & plat
book .** Rockford Map Publishers. Rockford, Ill.
[c1990] 1 atlas (47 p.) :
NYPL [Map Div. 90-11382]

Douglas Hyde Gallery.
Kiefer, Anselm, 1945- Jason /. Dublin , c1990.
1 v. (unpaged) : ISBN 0-907660-36-3
MLCM 90/06234 (N)
NYPL [3-MGO (Kiefer) 91-5151]

A new tradition . Dublin , 1990. 139 p. : ISBN
0-907660-37-1 : DDC 709.415 20
NYPL [3-MAMR 91-5078]

**DOUGLAS, WILLIAM O. (WILLIAM
ORVILLE), 1898-**
Bowdoin College. Museum of Art. As Maine
goes. Brunswick, Maine, 1966. 1 v. (unpaged)
NYPL [MFX (McKee) 90-5881]

**DOUGLASS, FREDERICK, 1817?-1895 -
PORTRAITS.**
Wheat, Ellen Harkins. Jacob Lawrence .
Hampton, Va. , 1991. p. cm. ISBN
0-9616982-4-1 : DDC 759.13 20
ND237.L29 W48 1991

Douglass, John M. (John Michael) The lost
language / John M. Douglass, Sue N. Peters.
Bell Canyon, Calif. : WNL Communications,

1990. 2 v. : ill. (some col.) ; 32 cm. Includes
bibliographical references. CONTENTS. - v. 1. Value &
symbolism in oriental rugs -- v. 2. The lost language
collection. ISBN 0-9627930-0-0 (set) DDC
746.7/5/095 20
1. Rugs, Oriental - Themes, motives. 2. Signs and
symbols. I. Peters, Sue N. II. Title.
NK2808 .D65 1990

Doumato, Lamia.
American drawing : a guide to information
sources / Lamia Doumato. Detroit : Gale
Research Co., c1979. x, 246 p. ; 23 cm. (Art and
architecture information guide series. v. 11) Gale
information guide library Includes index. ISBN
0-8103-1441-X : DDC 016.741/0973
1. Drawing, American - Bibliography. I. Title.
Z5956.D7 D68 NC105
NYPL [3-MAC 91-7864]

Augustus Northmore Welby Pugin, 1812-1852
[microform] / Lamia Doumato. Monticello,
Ill. : Vance Bibliographies, 1983. 9 p. ; 28 cm.
(Architecture series--bibliography, 0194-1356 . A-1082)
Cover title. Microfiche. New York : New York Public
Library, 1986. 1 microfiche : negative ; 11 x 15 cm.
(FSN 41,215) ISBN 0-88066-732-X (pbk.) : DDC
016.72/092/4 19
1. Pugin, Augustus Welby Northmore, 1812-1852 -
Bibliography. 2. Architecture, Modern - 19th century -
Great Britain - Bibliography. I. Title.
Z8716.2 .D68 1983 NA997.P9
*NYPL [*XMC-615]*

Dovaz, Claude. Guide Christie's du collectionneur
/. Paris , c1986. 223 p. : ISBN 2-7000-2140-1
NYPL [3-MAVC 89-25308]

Dove, Rita. The other side of the house / Rita
Dove, Tamarra Kaida. Tempe : VARI
Studios/Pyracantha Press, School of Art,
Arizona State University, 1988. [11] leaves :
ill. ; 34 x 47 cm. Poems. Limited ed. of 50 signed
and numbered copies. Library's copy is no. 40.
I. Kaida, Tamarra. II. Title.
NYPL [MFX++ (Kaida) 91-2637]

Dover art library.
Canaletto, 1697-1768. Canaletto drawings .
New York , 1991. 44 p. : ISBN 0-486-26647-8
(pbk.) : DDC 741.945 20
NC257.C27 A4 1991

Matisse, Henri, 1869-1954. Matisse portrait
drawings /. New York , 1990. 44 p. : ISBN
0-486-26438-6 : DDC 714.944 20
NC248.M4 A4 1990
NYPL [3-MCO M43 91-5312]

Old master portrait drawings . New York ,
c1990. 44 p. : ISBN 0-486-26364-9 : DDC 743.94
20
NC773 .O4 1990 NYPL [3-MBH 91-3424]

Dover design library.
Hofmann, Richard, of Plauen im Vogtland.
Decorative flower and leaf designs /. New
York , 1991. p. cm. ISBN 0-486-26869-1 DDC
745.4 20
NK1560 .H57 1991

Down river. Pennington, Estill Curtis.
Downriver . Gretna, La. , 1991. 208 p. : ISBN
0-88289-800-0 DDC 759.163 20
ND230.L8 P46 1991
NYPL [3-MCW+ 91-7305]

Downing, Joseph. Brockmann, Gottfried, 1903-
Gottfried Brockmann, drawings 1921-1931 .
Birmingham, Mich. , c1975. [32] p. :
NYPL [3-MCK B862 91-1178]

Downriver . Pennington, Estill Curtis. Gretna,
La. , 1991. 208 p. : ISBN 0-88289-800-0 DDC
759.163 20
ND230.L8 P46 1990
NYPL [3-MCW+ 91-7305]

Doyle, Richard, 1824-1883.
Richard Doyle's journal, 1840 / introd. and
notes by Christopher Wheeler. Edinburgh : J.
Bartholomew in association with British
Museum Publications, 1980. xvii, 156 p. : ill. ;
27 cm. Includes bibliographical references. ISBN
0-7028-8280-1 : DDC 741.6/092/4 B 19
1. Doyle, Richard, 1824-1883 - Diaries. 2. Illustrators -
England - Diaries. 3. England - Social life and
customs - 19th century. I. Title.
NC978.5.D68 A2 1980
NYPL [MDG (Doyle) 81-1248]

DOYLE, RICHARD, 1824-1883 - DIARIES.
Doyle, Richard, 1824-1883. Richard Doyle's

journal, 1840 /. Edinburgh , 1980. xvii, 156 p. :
ISBN 0-7028-8280-1 : DDC 741.6/092/4 B 19
NC978.5.D68 A2 1980
NYPL [MDG (Doyle) 81-1248]

Doyon, Roy. Historical atlas of Massachusetts /.
Amherst , c1991. 152 p. : ISBN 0-87023-697-0
(alk. paper) : DDC 912.744 20
G1230 .H5 1990
NYPL [Map Div.+ 91-7396]

Drache und Phoenix . Lee, King Tsi. [Köln] ,
c1990. 229 p. : DDC 745.7/26/0951074435514 20
NK9900.7.C6 L44 1990
NYPL [3-MNX 91-4182]

Drache und Schmetterling. Schack, Gerhard,
1929- Horst Janssen . München , c1989. 1 v.
(unpaged) : ISBN 3-7913-1042-9 DDC 760/.092
20
N6888.J37 A4 1989

Drachenberg, Erhard.
Die mittelalterliche Glasmalerei in Erfurt [von]
Erhard Drachenberg, Karl-Joachim Maercker,
Christa Schmidt. Hrsg. vom Institut für
Denkmalpflege in der DDR. Berlin, Akademie
Verlag; Wien, Verlag Hermann Böhlaus Nachf.;
1976- v in. illus. (part col.) 32 cm. (Corpus
vitrearum Medii Aevi: Deutsche Demokratische
Republik. Bd. 1, T. 1-2) Includes bibliographies.
CONTENTS. - T. 1. Die mittelalterliche Glasmalerei in
den Ordenskirchen und im Angermuseum zu Erfurt.--T.
2. Die mittelalterliche Glasmalerei im Erfurter Dom. 2
v. ISBN 3-205-00581-3 (v. 2, pt. 1)
1. Dom zu Erfurt (Germany). 2. Glass painting and
staining, Medieval - Germany, East - Erfurt. I.
Maercker, Karl-Joachim. II. Schmidt, Christa. III.
Institut für Denkmalpflege in der DDR. IV. Title. V.
Series. *NYPL [MRY+ 77-1943 Bd.1, T.1-2]*

Mittelalterliche Glasmalerei in Erfurt / Erhard
Drachenberg ; Aufnahmen von Fritz Strauss.
Dresden : Verlag der Kunst, c1990. 296 p. : ill
(some col.) ; 31 cm. Includes bibliographical
references (p. 282-287) and indexes. ISBN
3-364-00044-1
1. Glass painting and staining, Medieval - Germany,
East - Erfurt. 2. Glass painting and staining - Germany
(East) - Erfurt. I. Title.
NYPL [3-MRY+ 91-4383]

**DRAFT HORSES - GREAT BRITAIN -
HISTORY.**
Heiney, Paul. George Soper's horses /.
London , 1990. 143 p. : ISBN 0-85493-200-3 :
DDC 636.15 20
SF311.3.G7 NYPL [3-MCV S712 91-3373]

Drafz, Helge. Ettl, Georg, 1940- Georg Ettl,
Arbeiten 1968-1989 =. Düsseldorf , 1990. 102
p. : ISBN 3-925974-14-8
NYPL [3-MGO (ETTL) 91-4445]

**DRAGHI, UMBERTO - ART COLLECTIONS -
EXHIBITIONS.**
Art chinois . [Morlanwelz, Belgium] , 1990. 216
p. : DDC 730/.0951/07449342 20
NK4165 .A714 1990

Dragomirov, Ivan. Bulgaria. Upravlenie po
geodeziia i kartografiia. Geografski atlas .
Sofiia , 1969. 1 atlas (65 p. :
NYPL [Map Div. 91-1090]

Dragon and phoenix. Lee, King Tsi. Drache und
Phoenix . [Köln] , c1990. 229 p. : DDC
745.7/26/0951074435514 20
NK9900.7.C6 L44 1990
NYPL [3-MNX 91-4182]

Drain, Francita L. The quilt primer : a guide to
quilt identification / by Francita L. Drain,
Charlene Hoschouer. Benkelman, NE : Broken
Star Pub., c1991. 138 p. : ill. ; 22 cm. Includes
bibliographical references (p. 137-138) and index.
ISBN 0-9629407-0-4 DDC 746.9/7041/0973 20
1. Quilts - United States - Identification. I. Hoschouer,
Charlene Ketler. II. Title.
NK9112 .D73 1991

Drake, W. Avon. Alfredo Jaar . Richmond, VA ,
c1991. p. cm. ISBN 0-917046-32-3 DDC 709/.2
20
N6537.J26 A4 1991

Dramatik des Alltags /. Hinniger, Volker,
1947-1988. Kassel , c1990. 160 p. : ISBN
3-925272-22-4 DDC 759.3 20
N6888.H556 A4 1990

Drammens museum. By og bygd i Buskerud.
[Drammen] : Drammens museum, [1990] 36
p. : ill. (some col.) ; 30 cm.

1. Folk art - Norway - Buskerud fylke. 2. Drammens museum. I. Title.
NK992.B8 D73 1990

DRAMMENS MUSEUM.
Drammens museum. By og bygd i Buskerud. [Drammen] [1990] 36 p. :
NK992.B8 D73 1990

Dramp'yan, R. G. (Ruben Grigorovich)
Hovnat'anyan, Hakob, 1806-1881. Hakob Hovnat'anyan /. Erevan [197-?] 64p. :
NYPL [3-MCZ H833 90-8404]

DRAPERY IN INTERIOR DECORATION.
Expressions of style . Middleton, WI (7549 Graber Road, Middleton 53562-1096) , c1990. 95 p. : DDC 747/.3 20
NK2115.5.D73 E95 1990

Draw! . Hanks, Kurt, 1947- Los Altos, Calif. , 1990. p. cm. ISBN 1-560-52054-X : DDC 741.2 20
NC730 .H27 1990

Draw! /. Solga, Kim. Cincinnati, Ohio , c1991. p. cm. ISBN 0-89134-385-7 (paper) : DDC 741.2 20
NC730 .S66 1991

Draw fifty creepy crawlies. Ames, Lee J. Draw 50 creepy crawlies /. New York , c1991. p. cm. ISBN 0-385-41189-8 DDC 743/.6 20
NC783 .A44 1991

Draw from your head . Jamieson, Doug. New York , 1991. p. cm. ISBN 0-8230-1374-X DDC 743/.49 20
NC760 .J34 1991

Draw horses with Sam Savitt. Savitt, Sam. Middletown, Md. , 1991. p. cm. ISBN 0-939481-23-5: DDC 743/.69725 20
NC783.8.H65 S38 1991

Draw 50 creepy crawlies /. Ames, Lee J. New York , c1991. p. cm. ISBN 0-385-41189-8 DDC 743/.6 20
NC783 .A44 1991

DRAWIGN - 17TH CENTURY - ITALY - CATALOGS.
Forlani Tempesti, Anna. Italian fifteenth- to seventeenth-century drawings /. New York , Princeton , 1991. p. cm. ISBN 0-87099-606-1 DDC 741.945/074/7471 20
NC255 .F6 1991

Drawing . Betti, Claudia. Fort Worth, TX , 1991. p. cm. ISBN 0-03-053147-0 DDC 741.2 20
NC730 .B43 1991

DRAWING.
Studien zur Künstlerzeichnung . Stuttgart , c1990. 334 p. : ISBN 3-7757-0306-3
NC40 .S78 1990

DRAWING - 15TH CENTURY - ITALY - CATALOGS.
Forlani Tempesti, Anna. Italian fifteenth- to seventeenth-century drawings /. New York , Princeton , 1991. p. cm. ISBN 0-87099-606-1 DDC 741.945/074/7471 20
NC255 .F6 1991

DRAWING - 16TH CENTURY - EUROPE - EXHIBITIONS.
Kunstmuseum Düsseldorf. Akademiesammlung. Facetten des Barock . Düsseldorf , 1990. 295 p. : DDC 741.94/09/032074435534 20
NC225 .K87 1990

DRAWING - 16TH CENTURY - ITALY - CATALOGS.
Forlani Tempesti, Anna. Italian fifteenth- to seventeenth-century drawings /. New York , Princeton , 1991. p. cm. ISBN 0-87099-606-1 DDC 741.945/074/7471 20
NC255 .F6 1991

DRAWING - 16TH CENTURY - ITALY - EXHIBITIONS.
Ruggieri, Ugo. Disegni veneti e lombardi dal XVI al XVIII secolo dalle collezioni del Gabinetto dei disegni e delle stampe /. Roma , 1989. 226 p. : ISBN 88-7597-101-3
NYPL [3-MBH 90-12366]

DRAWING - 16TH CENTURY - ITALY - FLORENCE - EXHIBITIONS.
Feinberg, Larry J. From studio to studiolo . Oberlin , Seattle , 1991. p. cm. ISBN 0-295-97145-2 : DDC 741.945/51/0903107474 20
NC256.F5 F4 1991

DRAWING - 16TH CENTURY - ITALY - VENICE (PROVINCE) - EXHIBITIONS.
Stockholm. Nationalmuseum. Venetianska teckningar, 1400-1600-talen. [Stockholm] , 1979. 15 p. : ISBN 91-7100-154-9
N3540 .A27 nr. 421 NC256.V4
NYPL [3-MBH 81-953]

DRAWING - 16TH CENTURY - ITALY - VERONA - EXHIBITIONS.
Stockholm. Nationalmuseum. Venetianska teckningar, 1400-1600-talen. [Stockholm] , 1979. 15 p. : ISBN 91-7100-154-9
N3540 .A27 nr. 421 NC256.V4
NYPL [3-MBH 81-953]

DRAWING - 16TH CENTURY - NETHERLANDS - EXHIBITIONS.
Niederländische Zeichnungen des 16. Jahrhunderts in der Staatlichen Graphischen Sammlung München . München , 1989. 219 p. : ISBN 3-927803-00-6
NYPL [3-MBH 91-4571]

DRAWING - 17TH CENTURY - EUROPE - EXHIBITIONS.
Kunstmuseum Düsseldorf. Akademiesammlung. Facetten des Barock . Düsseldorf , 1990. 295 p. : DDC 741.94/09/032074435534 20
NC225 .K87 1990

I Premiati dell'Accademia, 1682-1754 /. Roma , c1989. 189 p. : ISBN 88-7140-010-0
NYPL [3-MBH 91-4486]

DRAWING - 17TH CENTURY - EXHIBITIONS.
Prize winning drawings from the Roman Academy 1682-1754 =. Roma , c1990. 189 p. : ISBN 88-7140-013-5
NYPL [3-MBH 91-5071]

DRAWING - 17TH CENTURY - ITALY - EXHIBITIONS.
Ruggieri, Ugo. Disegni veneti e lombardi dal XVI al XVIII secolo dalle collezioni del Gabinetto dei disegni e delle stampe /. Roma , 1989. 226 p. : ISBN 88-7597-101-3
NYPL [3-MBH 90-12366]

DRAWING - 17TH CENTURY - ITALY - ROME - CATALOGS.
Blunt, Anthony, 1907-1983. The Roman drawings of the XVII & XVIII centuries in the collection of Her Majesty the Queen at Windsor Castle /. London , c1960. 197 p. : DDC 741.945/632/093207442296 20
NC256.R6 B4 1960

DRAWING - 17TH CENTURY - ITALY - SAN LUCA.
Accademia nazionale di San Luca. Archivio Storico. I disegni di figura nell'Archivio storico dell'Accademia di San Luca /. Roma , 1988- v. : ISBN 88-7140-011-9 (v. 2)
NYPL [3-MBH 90-2410]

DRAWING - 17TH CENTURY - ITALY - VENICE (PROVINCE) - EXHIBITIONS.
Stockholm. Nationalmuseum. Venetianska teckningar, 1400-1600-talen. [Stockholm] , 1979. 15 p. : ISBN 91-7100-154-9
N3540 .A27 nr. 421 NC256.V4
NYPL [3-MBH 81-953]

DRAWING - 17TH CENTURY - ITALY - VERONA - EXHIBITIONS.
Stockholm. Nationalmuseum. Venetianska teckningar, 1400-1600-talen. [Stockholm] , 1979. 15 p. : ISBN 91-7100-154-9
N3540 .A27 nr. 421 NC256.V4
NYPL [3-MBH 81-953]

DRAWING - 18TH CENTURY - DENMARK - COPENHAGEN - EXHIBITIONS.
Kongelige Kobberstiksamling (Statens museum for kunst) Von Abildgaard bis Marstrand . [München] , 1985. 87 p., 114 p. of plates : DDC 741.9489/1 19
NC274.C67 K66 1985
NYPL [3-MBH 90-12465]

DRAWING - 18TH CENTURY - EUROPE - EXHIBITIONS.
I Premiati dell'Accademia, 1682-1754 /. Roma , c1989. 189 p. : ISBN 88-7140-010-0
NYPL [3-MBH 91-4486]

DRAWING - 18TH CENTURY - EXHIBITIONS.
Prize winning drawings from the Roman Academy 1682-1754 =. Roma , c1990. 189 p. : ISBN 88-7140-013-5
NYPL [3-MBH 91-5071]

DRAWING - 18TH CENTURY - FRANCE - EXHIBITIONS.
Metropolitan Museum of Art (New York, N.Y.) French drawings & prints of the eighteenth century . [New York , 1972] [19] p., [4] p. of plates :
NYPL [3-MBH 91-409]

Myers, Mary L., 1940- Architectural and ornament drawings . New York , 1991. p. cm. ISBN 0-87099-625-8 DDC 741.944/09/0330747471 20
NC246 .M94 1991

DRAWING - 18TH CENTURY - ITALY - CATALOGS.
Metropolitan Museum of Art (New York, N.Y.) 18th century Italian drawings in the Metropolitan Museum of Art /. New York , 1990. 288 p. : ISBN 0-87099-585-5 DDC 741.945/074/7471 20
NC255 .M4 1990
NYPL [3-MAVZ (New York) 91-3640]

DRAWING - 18TH CENTURY - ITALY - EXHIBITIONS.
Ruggieri, Ugo. Disegni veneti e lombardi dal XVI al XVIII secolo dalle collezioni del Gabinetto dei disegni e delle stampe /. Roma , 1989. 226 p. : ISBN 88-7597-101-3
NYPL [3-MBH 90-12366]

DRAWING - 18TH CENTURY - ITALY - ROME - CATALOGS.
Blunt, Anthony, 1907-1983. The Roman drawings of the XVII & XVIII centuries in the collection of Her Majesty the Queen at Windsor Castle /. London , c1960. 197 p. :
NC256.R6 B4 1960

DRAWING - 19TH CENTURY - DENMARK - COPENHAGEN - EXHIBITIONS.
Kongelige Kobberstiksamling (Statens museum for kunst) Von Abildgaard bis Marstrand . [München] , 1985. 87 p., 114 p. of plates : DDC 741.9489/1 19
NC274.C67 K66 1985
NYPL [3-MBH 90-12465]

DRAWING - 19TH CENTURY - FRANCE - CATALOGS.
Mráz, Bohumír. Aquarelles et dessins impressionnistes . [Gennevilliers?] , 1987. 206 p. : ISBN 2-86901-027-3
NYPL [3-MBH+ 89-28607]

DRAWING - 19TH CENTURY - FRANCE - EXHIBITIONS.
Hyldest til Fransk Kunst . København, 1967. 115 p. : *NYPL [3-MBH 90-5670]*

DRAWING - 20TH CENTURY - BRAZIL - CATALOGS.
Margutti, Mário. Desenho brasileiro . Rio de Janeiro , 1988. 136 p. : DDC 741.981 20
NC198 .M37 1988

DRAWING - 20TH CENTURY - CALIFORNIA - SANTA BARBARA - EXHIBITIONS.
Santa Barbara Museum of Art. Santa Barbara drawings, 1976. [Santa Barbara] [1976] [20] p. : DDC 741.9/794/91074019491
NC138.S26 S26 1976
NYPL [3-MBH 91-6988]

DRAWING - 20TH CENTURY - CANADA - EXHIBITIONS.
Boyanoski, Christine, 1955- The 1950s . Toronto, Canada , 1988. iii, 48 p. : ISBN 0-919777-65-1 DDC 741.971/074/0113541 19
NYPL [3-MCY 90-12731]

DRAWING - 20TH CENTURY - EUROPE - EXHIBITIONS.
Kubin, Alfred, 1877-1959. Alfred Kubin. [Stockholm] , 1990. 31, 29 p. : ISBN 91-7100-386-X
NYPL [3-MCK K95 90-11683]

DRAWING - 20TH CENTURY - EXHIBITIONS.
Kunsten å tegne . Oslo [1990] 64 p. :
N8640 .O8 nr. 532 NC95

DRAWING - 20TH CENTURY - FRANCE - EXHIBITIONS.
Hyldest til Fransk Kunst . København, 1967. 115 p. : *NYPL [3-MBH 90-5670]*

DRAWING - 20TH CENTURY - QUÉBEC (PROVINCE) - EXHIBITIONS.

BIBLIOGRAPHIC GUIDE
Drawing - 20th century - Québec (Province) - Exhibitions. (cont.)

288

Cent-onze dessins du Québec . [Québec, Québec] , c1976. 54 p. :
NYPL [3-MBH+ 90-6892]

DRAWING - 20TH CENTURY - UNITED STATES - EXHIBITIONS.
Amerikanische Zeichnungen in den achtziger Jahren . München , c1990. 190 p. : DDC 741.973/09/04807443551 20
NC108 .A55 1990

Minimalism and post-minimalism . Hanover, N.H. , 1990. 104 p. : ISBN 0-944722-05-9 DDC 741.973/074/7423 20
NC108 .M528 1990
NYPL [3-MBH 91-3948]

Wolfe, Townsend. National drawing invitational, March 1-April 8, 1990 /. Little Rock, Ark. (P.O. Box 2137, Little Rock 72203) , c1990. 48 p. : DDC 741.973/09/04807476773 20
NC108 .W65 1990

DRAWING, AMERICAN - BIBLIOGRAPHY.
Doumato, Lamia. American drawing . Detroit , c1979. x, 246 p. ; ISBN 0-8103-1441-X : DDC 016.741/0973
Z5956.D7 D68 NC105
NYPL [3-MAC 91-7864]

DRAWING, AMERICAN - EXHIBITIONS.
Amerikanische Zeichnungen in den achtziger Jahren . München , c1990. 190 p. : DDC 741.973/09/04807443551 20
NC108 .A55 1990

Minimalism and post-minimalism . Hanover, N.H. , 1990. 104 p. : ISBN 0-944722-05-9 DDC 741.973/074/7423 20
NC108 .M528 1990
NYPL [3-MBH 91-3948]

Santa Barbara Museum of Art. Santa Barbara drawings, 1976 . [Santa Barbara] [1976] [20] p. : DDC 741.9/794/91074019491
NC138.S26 S26 1976
NYPL [3-MBH 91-6988]

Wolfe, Townsend. National drawing invitational, March 1-April 8, 1990 /. Little Rock, Ark. (P.O. Box 2137, Little Rock 72203) , c1990. 48 p. : DDC 741.973/09/04807476773 20
NC108 .W65 1990

100 American drawings and watercolors from 200 years . New York [1976] [26] p. :
NYPL [3-MAMT 90-6431]

DRAWING, AMERICAN - PRIVATE COLLCTIONS - EXHIBITIONS.
American drawings . New York, 1980. [40] p. :
NYPL [3-MBH 90-6350]

DRAWING, AMERICAN - WASHINGTON (STATE) - 20TH CENTURY - EXHIBITIONS.
Northwest impressions [microform] . Seattle [1986] [12] p. ; *NYPL [*ZM-218 no.1]*

Drawing and cartooning 1,001 faces, places, and things /. Hamm, Jack. New York, NY , c1991. p. cm. ISBN 0-399-51687-5 (alk. paper) DDC 741.2 20
NC730 .H25 1991

DRAWING, ARCHITECTURAL. see ARCHITECTURAL DRAWING.

DRAWING - AUSTRALIA - CANBERRA (A.C. T.) - CATALOGS.
Australian National Gallery. Australian drawings and watercolours . Canberra , c1988. 64 p. : ISBN 0-642-13032-9
NYPL [3-MBH+ 90-10417]

DRAWING, AUSTRALIAN - CATALOGS.
Australian National Gallery. Australian drawings and watercolours . Canberra , c1988. 64 p. : ISBN 0-642-13032-9
NYPL [3-MBH+ 90-10417]

DRAWING, BAROQUE - CZECHOSLOVAKIA - BOHEMIA - EXHIBITIONS.
Barockmaler in Böhmen. München [1961] 36 p.
N6832.B3 H8 *NYPL [3-MCY 90-5883]*

DRAWING, BAROQUE - EUROPE - EXHIBITIONS.
Kunstmuseum Düsseldorf. Akademiesammlung. Facetten des Barock . Düsseldorf , 1990. 295 p. : DDC 741.94/09/032074435534 20
NC225 .K87 1990

DRAWING, BAROQUE - FRANCE - LILLE - EXHIBITIONS.

Renaissance et baroque . Milano , c1989. 159 p. : ISBN 2-902092-10-5
NYPL [3-MBH+ 91-6534]

DRAWING, BAROQUE - ITALY - EXHIBITIONS.
Loisel-Legrand, Catherine. La Rome baroque de Maratti à Piranèse . Paris , c1990. 144 p. : ISBN 2-7118-2392-X
NYPL [3-MBH 91-6654]

DRAWING, BAROQUE - PRIVATE COLLECTIONS - ITALY.
Drawings from Tuscany and Umbria, 1350-1700 . [Oakland?] , 1961. [24] p., [14] p. of plates : *NYPL [3-MCE 90-7042]*

DRAWING - BERLIN (GERMANY) - EXHIBITIONS.
Nationalgalerie (Germany : East) Von Caspar David Friedrich bis Adolph Menzel . München , 1990. 283 p. : ISBN 3-7913-1047-X
NYPL [3-MCI+ 91-3367]

DRAWING, BRAZILIAN - CATALOGS.
Margutti, Mário. Desenho brasileiro . Rio de Janeiro , 1988. 136 p. : DDC 741.981 20
NC198 .M37 1988

Drawing/building/text : essays in architectural theory / Andrea Kahn, editor. New York, N.Y. : Princeton Architectural Press, c1991. 175 p. : ill. ; 24 cm. Includes bibliographical references. ISBN 0-910413-71-1 : DDC 720/.1 20
1. Architecture - Philosophy. I. Kahn, Andrea, 1958-.
NA2500 .D7 1990 *NYPL [3-MQ 91-7053]*

Drawing/building/text : essays in architectural theory / Andrea Kahn, editor. New York : Princeton Architectural Press, c1991. 175 p. : ill. ; 24 cm. Includes bibliographical references. ISBN 0-910413-71-1 : DDC 720/.1 20
1. Architecture - Philosophy. I. Kahn, Andrea, 1958-.
NA2500 .D7 1990

DRAWING, CANADIAN - EXHIBITIONS.
Boyanoski, Christine, 1955- The 1950s . Toronto, Canada , 1988. iii, 48 p. : ISBN 0-919777-65-1 DDC 741.971/074/0113541 19
NYPL [3-MCY 90-12731]

DRAWING, CANADIAN - QUÉBEC (PROVINCE) - EXHIBITIONS.
Cent-onze dessins du Québec . [Québec, Québec] , c1976. 54 p. :
NYPL [3-MBH+ 90-6892]

DRAWING - CATALOGS.
Fuhring, Peter. Design into art . London , New York , 1989. 2 v. (792 p.) : ISBN 0-85667-354-4 (London) *NYPL [MLD+ 89-23146]*

Drawing Center (New York, N.Y.) Wagner, Otto, 1841-1918. Masterdrawings of Otto Wagner . New York , c1987. 135 p. :
NYPL [3-MQZ+ (Wagner) 91-4283]

DRAWING - COMPETITIONS - ITALY - EXHIBITIONS.
I Premiati dell'Accademia, 1682-1754 /. Roma , c1989. 189 p. : ISBN 88-7140-010-0
NYPL [3-MBH 91-4486]

DRAWING, DANISH - DENMARK - COPENHAGEN - EXHIBITIONS.
Kongelige Kobberstiksamling (Statens museum for kunst) Von Abildgaard bis Marstrand . [München] , 1985. 87 p., 114 p. of plates : DDC 741.9489/1 19
NC274.C67 K66 1985
NYPL [3-MBH 90-12465]

DRAWING, DUTCH - EXHIBITIONS.
Niederländische Zeichnungen des 16. Jahrhunderts in der Staatlichen Graphischen Sammlung München . München , 1989. 219 p. : ISBN 3-927803-00-6
NYPL [3-MBH 91-4571]

DRAWING, EUROPEAN - CATALOGS.
Gallerie dell'Accademia di Venezia. Catalogo dei disegni antichi . Milano , c1982- v. : ISBN 88-435-0801-6 (v. 1) DDC 741.94/074/0531 19
NC255 .G35 1982 *NYPL [3-MBH 85-260]*

Meisterzeichnungen . [Leipzig] , c1990. 352 p. : ISBN 3-361-00241-0
IN PROCESS (ONLINE)
NYPL [3-MBH+ 91-6466]

Metropolitan Museum of Art (New York, N.Y.) European drawings recently acquired, 1972-1975. [New York] [1975] [52] p. :
NYPL [3-MBH 90-5754]

DRAWING, EUROPEAN - EXHIBITIONS.
Da Leonardo a Rembrandt. English. From Leonardo to Rembrandt . Torino , c1990. 409 p. : ISBN 88-422-0260-6
NYPL [3-MBH+ 91-5774]

Kunstmuseum Düsseldorf. Meisterzeichnungen der Sammlung Lambert Krahe. [Düsseldorf] , c1969. 199 p. : *NYPL [3-MBH 90-6620]*

Kunstmuseum Düsseldorf. Akademiesammlung. Facetten des Barock . Düsseldorf , 1990. 295 p. : DDC 741.94/09/032074435534 20
NC225 .K87 1990

Museum Boymans-Van Beuningen. From Pisanello to Cézanne . Rotterdam , New York , c1990. 276 p. : ISBN 0-521-40105-4
NYPL [3-MBH+ 90-13057]

National Gallery of Scotland. Old master drawings from the National Gallery of Scotland /. Washington , c1990. 191 p. : ISBN 0-89468-151-6 DDC 741.94/074/4134 20
NC15 .N3755 1990
NYPL [3-MBH 91-6402]

Rijksmuseum Kröller-Müller. Cent dessins du Musée Kröller-Müller. Bruxelles, c1971. [viii], 100, [xvi] p. DDC 741.9/074/04582
NC17.N4 O8773 *NYPL [3-MBH 90-6298]*

Thos. Agnew and Sons Ltd. Master drawings and prints . London , 1975. 60 p., [12] p. of plates : *NYPL [3-MAL 90-6894]*

DRAWING, EUROPEAN - HISTORY - EXHIBITIONS.
Winner, Matthias, 1931- Zeichner sehen die Antike. Berlin-Dahlem [1967] 134 p. DDC 741/.094
NC225 .W5 *NYPL [3-MBH 91-1293]*

DRAWING, EUROPEAN - PRIVATE COLLECTIONS - EXHIBITIONS.
Zeichnungen des 16. bis 18. Jahrhunderts . [Stuttgart , 1989?] 207 p. :
IN PROCESS (ONLINE)
NYPL [3-MBH 90-12017]

DRAWING - EXHIBITIONS.
Die Albertina und das Dresdner Kupferstich-Kabinett . Dresden , 1978. 181 p. :
NC17.A8 V52 *NYPL [MBH 80-591]*

Universität Göttingen. Kunstsammlung. Handzeichnungen alter Meister aus dem Besitz der Kunstsammlung der Georg-August-Universität Göttingen. [Kiel? 1966] 1 v. (unpaged)
NC15 .K5 *NYPL [3-MBH 91-232]*

DRAWING, FIGURE. see ANATOMY, ARTISTIC; FIGURE DRAWING.

DRAWING, FLEMISH - EXHIBITIONS.
Niederländische Zeichnungen des 16. Jahrhunderts in der Staatlichen Graphischen Sammlung München . München , 1989. 219 p. : ISBN 3-927803-00-6
NYPL [3-MBH 91-4571]

Drawing for older children, teens, and adult beginners /. Brookes, Mona, 1937- Los Angeles , New York , c1991. p. cm. ISBN 0-87477-660-0 : DDC 741.2 20
NC730 .B657 1991

DRAWING - FRANCE - PARIS - CATALOGS.
Musée national d'art moderne (France). Cabinet d'art graphique. Le Musée national d'art moderne . Paris , c1990. 125, [3] p. : ISBN 2-85850-557-8 *NYPL [3-MBH 91-3585]*

DRAWING, FRENCH - CATALOGS.
Mráz, Bohumír. Aquarelles et dessins impressionnistes . [Gennevilliers?] , 1987. 206 p. : ISBN 2-86901-027-3
NYPL [3-MBH+ 89-28607]

Musée Borély. Donation Maurice et Pauline Feuillet de Borsat /. Marseille, 1969. 1 v. (unpaged)
NC27.F7 M355
NYPL [3-MAVZ (Marseilles) 91-291]

DRAWING, FRENCH - EXHIBITIONS.
De Clouet à Matisse . Paris [1958] 1 v. (unpaged)
MLCS 90/03647 (P)
NYPL [3-MBH 91-6247]

Hyldest til Fransk Kunst . København, 1967. 115 p. : *NYPL [3-MBH 90-5670]*

Maîtres français, 1550-1800 . Paris , c1989. 313

p. :   ISBN 2-903639-64-7
NYPL [3-MBH+ 89-26750]

Myers, Mary L., 1940- Architectural and ornament drawings . New York , 1991. p. cm.
ISBN 0-87099-625-8 DDC 741.944/09/0330747471 20
NC246 .M94 1991

Rosenberg, Pierre. Masterful studies . New York , c1990. 277 p. :
IN PROCESS (ONLINE)
NYPL [3-MBH+ 91-4237]

Drawing from life /. Brown, Clint. Fort Worth , c1992. p. cm. ISBN 0-03-028934-3 DDC 743/.4 20
NC760 .B86 1992

DRAWING, GERMAN - CATALOGS.
Robert Gore Rifkind Center for German Expressionist Studies. German expressionist prints and drawings . Los Angeles, Calif. : Munich, Federal Republic of Germany : 2 v. :
ISBN 3-7913-0959-5 (Prestel Verlag : set) DDC 760/.0943 19
N6868.5.E9 R6 1989
NYPL [MDE+ 91-5830]

DRAWING - GERMANY (WEST) - MÜNICH - EXHIBITIONS.
Niederländische Zeichnungen des 16. Jahrhunderts in der Staatlichen Graphischen Sammlung München . München , 1989. 219 p. :
ISBN 3-927803-00-6
NYPL [3-MBH 91-4571]

Drawing in color . Lorenz, Albert, 1941- New York , 1991. p. cm. ISBN 0-8230-1384-7 DDC 741.2 20
NC758 .L67 1991

DRAWING, ITALIAN - CATALOGS.
Forlani Tempesti, Anna. Italian fifteenth- to seventeenth-century drawings /. New York , Princeton , 1991. p. cm. ISBN 0-87099-606-1 DDC 741.945/074/7471 20
NC255 .F6 1991

Metropolitan Museum of Art (New York, N.Y.) 18th century Italian drawings in the Metropolitan Museum of Art /. New York , 1990. 288 p. : ISBN 0-87099-585-5 DDC 741.945/074/7471 20
NC255 .M4 1990
NYPL [3-MAVZ (New York) 91-3640]

DRAWING, ITALIAN - EXHIBITIONS.
Disegno . [Rennes], France [1990] 253 p. :
ISBN 2-901430-22-8 DDC 741.945/074/4415 20
NC255 .D54 1990

Wolk-Simon, Linda, 1958- Italian old master drawings from the collection of Jeffrey E. Horvitz /. Gainesville, Fla. , 1991. v, 175 p. :
ISBN 0-9629384-0-8 (alk. paper) DDC 741.945/074/73 20
NC255 .W6 1991

DRAWING, ITALIAN - FRANCE - EXHIBITIONS.
Loisel-Legrand, Catherine. La Rome baroque de Maratti à Piranèse . Paris , c1990. 144 p. :
ISBN 2-7118-2392-X
NYPL [3-MBH 91-6654]

DRAWING, ITALIAN - FRANCE - LILLE - EXHIBITIONS.
Renaissance et baroque . Milano , c1989. 159 p. : ISBN 2-902092-10-5
NYPL [3-MBH+ 91-6534]

DRAWING, ITALIAN - ITALY - EXHIBITIONS.
Ruggieri, Ugo. Disegni veneti e lombardi dal XVI al XVIII secolo dalle collezioni del Gabinetto dei disegni e delle stampe /. Roma , 1989. 226 p. : ISBN 88-7597-101-3
NYPL [3-MBH 90-12366]

DRAWING, ITALIAN - ITALY - FLORENCE - EXHIBITIONS.
Feinberg, Larry J. From studio to studiolo . Oberlin , Seattle , 1991. p. cm. ISBN 0-295-97145-2 : DDC 741.945/51/0903107474 20
NC256.F5 F4 1991

DRAWING, ITALIAN - ITALY - ROME - CATALOGS.
Blunt, Anthony, 1907-1983. The Roman drawings of the XVII & XVIII centuries in the collection of Her Majesty the Queen at Windsor Castle /. London , c1960. 197 p. :

DDC 741.945/632/093207442296 20
NC256.R6 B4 1960

DRAWING, ITALIAN - ITALY - TUSCANY - EXHIBITIONS.
Gabinetto nazionale delle stampe. Disegni toscani e umbri del primo Rinascimento . Roma [1979] 183 p. :
NC256.T8 G32 1979
NYPL [3-MBH 81-532]

DRAWING, ITALIAN - ITALY - TUSCANY - PRIVATE COLLECTIONS - EXHIBITIONS.
Drawings from Tuscany and Umbria, 1350-1700 . [Oakland?] , 1961. [24] p., [14] p. of plates :
NYPL [3-MCE 90-7042]

DRAWING, ITALIAN - ITALY - UMBRIA - CATALOGS.
Venice. Gallerie dell'Accademia. Disegni umbri . Milano , c1984. 211 p. : ISBN 88-435-0801-6
NYPL [3-MBH 86-3573]

DRAWING, ITALIAN - ITALY - UMBRIA - EXHIBITIONS.
Gabinetto nazionale delle stampe. Disegni toscani e umbri del primo Rinascimento . Roma [1979] 183 p. :
NC256.T8 G32 1979
NYPL [3-MBH 81-532]

DRAWING, ITALIAN - ITALY - UMBRIA - PRIVATE COLLECTIONS - EXHIBITIONS.
Drawings from Tuscany and Umbria, 1350-1700 . [Oakland?] , 1961. [24] p., [14] p. of plates :
NYPL [3-MCE 90-7042]

DRAWING, ITALIAN - ITALY - VENICE - EXHIBITIONS.
Les Dessins vénitiens des collections de l'École des beaux-arts . Paris , c1990. xlii, 257 p. :
ISBN 2-903639-68-X
NYPL [3-MBH+ 90-12996]

Venetianska teckningar från École des beaux-arts, Paris . Stockholm [1990] 165 p. :
ISBN 90-71003-80-0
NC256.V4 V4 1990

DRAWING, ITALIAN - ITALY - VENICE (PROVINCE) - EXHIBITIONS.
Stockholm. Nationalmuseum. Venetianska teckningar, 1400-1600-talen. [Stockholm] , 1979. 15 p. : ISBN 91-7100-154-9
N3540 .A27 nr. 421 NC256.V4
NYPL [3-MBH 81-953]

DRAWING, ITALIAN - ITALY - VERONA - EXHIBITIONS.
Stockholm. Nationalmuseum. Venetianska teckningar, 1400-1600-talen. [Stockholm] , 1979. 15 p. : ISBN 91-7100-154-9
N3540 .A27 nr. 421 NC256.V4
NYPL [3-MBH 81-953]

DRAWING - ITALY - SAN LUCA - EXHIBITIONS.
Prize winning drawings from the Roman Academy 1682-1754 =. Roma , c1990. 189 p. :
ISBN 88-7140-013-5
NYPL [3-MBH 91-5071]

DRAWING - ITALY - TURIN - EXHIBITIONS.
Da Leonardo a Rembrandt. English. From Leonardo to Rembrandt . Torino , c1990. 409 p. : ISBN 88-422-0260-6
NYPL [3-MBH+ 91-5774]

DRAWING - ITALY - VENICE - CATALOGS.
Gallerie dell'Accademia di Venezia. Catalogo dei disegni antichi /. Milano , c1982- v. :
ISBN 88-435-0801-6 (v. 1) DDC 741.94/074/0531 19
NC255 .G35 1982 *NYPL [3-MBH 85-260]*

Venice. Gallerie dell'Accademia. Disegni umbri . Milano , c1984. 211 p. : ISBN 88-435-0801-6
NYPL [3-MBH 86-3573]

DRAWING, MODERN - 17TH-18TH CENTURIES - EXHIBITIONS.
Kunstmuseum Düsseldorf. Meisterzeichnungen der Sammlung Lambert Krahe. [Düsseldorf] , c1969. 199 p. : *NYPL [3-MBH 90-6620]*

DRAWING - NETHERLANDS - AMSTERDAM - CATALOGS.
Rijksmuseum (Netherlands). Rijksprentenkabinet. Selected drawings from the Printroom. Amsterdam, 1965. 71 p.
NC27.N4 A47 *NYPL [3-MBH 90-7038]*

DRAWING - NETHERLANDS - ROTTERDAM - EXHIBITION.
Museum Boymans-Van Beuningen. From Pisanello to Cézanne . Rotterdam , New York , c1990. 276 p. : ISBN 0-521-40105-4
NYPL [3-MBH+ 90-13057]

DRAWING - NEW YORK (N.Y.) - CATALOGS.
Forlani Tempesti, Anna. Italian fifteenth- to seventeenth-century drawings /. New York , Princeton , 1991. p. cm. ISBN 0-87099-606-1 DDC 741.945/074/7471 20
NC255 .F6 1991

Metropolitan Museum of Art (New York, N.Y.) 18th century Italian drawings in the Metropolitan Museum of Art /. New York , 1990. 288 p. : ISBN 0-87099-585-5 DDC 741.945/074/7471 20
NC255 .M4 1990
NYPL [3-MAVZ (New York) 91-3640]

Drawing portraits in all mediums /. Parramón, José María. [Dibujando retratos. English.] New York , 1991. p. cm. ISBN 0-8230-1457-6 : DDC 743/.42 20
NC773 .P3813 1991

DRAWING - PRIVATE COLLECTIONS - CALIFORNIA - SAN MARINO - EXHIBITIONS.
Bloch, E. Maurice. Focusing on nature . San Marino, Calif. , c1991. p. cm. ISBN 0-87328-133-0 : DDC 741.973/074/79493 20
NC790 .B58 1991

DRAWING - PRIVATE COLLECTIONS - ENGLAND - WINDSOR (BERKSHIRE) - CATALOGS.
Blunt, Anthony, 1907-1983. The Roman drawings of the XVII & XVIII centuries in the collection of Her Majesty the Queen at Windsor Castle /. London , c1960. 197 p. :
DDC 741.945/632/093207442296 20
NC256.R6 B4 1960

DRAWING - PRIVATE COLLECTIONS - UNITED STATES - EXHIBITIONS.
Wolk-Simon, Linda, 1958- Italian old master drawings from the collection of Jeffrey E. Horvitz /. Gainesville, Fla. , 1991. v, 175 p. :
ISBN 0-9629384-0-8 (alk. paper) DDC 741.945/074/73 20
NC255 .W6 1991

DRAWING, PSYCHOLOGY OF.
Hanks, Kurt, 1947- Rapid viz . Los Altos, CA , c1990. 149 p. : ISBN 1-560-52055-8 (pbk.) :
DDC 741.6 20
NC877.8 .H36 1990

DRAWING, RENAISSANCE - EXHIBITIONS.
Byrne, Janet S. Renaissance ornament prints and drawings /. New York , c1981. 143 p. :
ISBN 0-87099-288-0 DDC 760/.094/07401471 19
NE441 .B97 *NYPL [MDB 83-1989]*

Kunstmuseum Düsseldorf. Meisterzeichnungen der Sammlung Lambert Krahe. [Düsseldorf] , c1969. 199 p. : *NYPL [3-MBH 90-6620]*

DRAWING, RENAISSANCE - FRANCE - LILLE - EXHIBITIONS.
Renaissance et baroque . Milano , c1989. 159 p. : ISBN 2-902092-10-5
NYPL [3-MBH+ 91-6534]

DRAWING, RENAISSANCE - ITALY.
Wethey, Harold E. (Harold Edwin), 1902-1984. Titian and his drawings . Princeton, N.J. , c1987. xxiii, 267 p., [159] p. of plates : ISBN 0-691-04040-0 (alk. paper) : DDC 741/.092/4 19
NC257.T58 W47 1987
NYPL [3-MCF+ T63 90-10773]

DRAWING, RENAISSANCE - ITALY - TUSCANY - EXHIBITIONS.
Gabinetto nazionale delle stampe. Disegni toscani e umbri del primo Rinascimento . Roma [1979] 183 p. :
NC256.T8 G32 1979
NYPL [3-MBH 81-532]

DRAWING, RENAISSANCE - ITALY - UMBRIA - CATALOGS.
Venice. Gallerie dell'Accademia. Disegni umbri . Milano , c1984. 211 p. : ISBN 88-435-0801-6 *NYPL [3-MBH 86-3573]*

DRAWING, RENAISSANCE - ITALY - UMBRIA - EXHIBITIONS.
Gabinetto nazionale delle stampe. Disegni

toscani e umbri del primo Rinascimento . Roma
[1979] 183 p. :
NC256.T8 G32 1979
NYPL [3-MBH 81-532]

**DRAWING, RENAISSANCE - ITALY -
VENICE - CATALOGS.**
Gallerie dell'Accademia di Venezia. Designi del
Figino /. Milano , c1987. 227 p. : ISBN
88-435-2240-X
NYPL [3-MCF F472 88-4259]

**DRAWING, RENAISSANCE - PRIVATE
COLLECTIONS - ITALY.**
Drawings from Tuscany and Umbria,
1350-1700 . [Oakland?] , 1961. [24] p., [14] p.
of plates :   **NYPL [3-MCE 90-7042]**

DRAWING - STUDY AND TEACHING.
López-Nussa, Leonel, 1916- El dibujo /. La
Habana , 1964. 138 p., [49] p. of plates :
NYPL [3-MBB 90-12526]

**DRAWING - STUDY AND TEACHING
(ELEMENTARY) - JUVENILE
LITERATURE.**
DuBosque, D. C. Learn to draw now! /.
Molalla, OR , 1991. p. cm. ISBN 0-939217-16-3 :
DDC 741.2/4 20
NC630 .D8 1991

DRAWING - TECHNIQUE.
Albert, Greg, 1953- Basic drawing techniques /.
Cincinnati, Ohio , c1991. p. cm. ISBN
0-89134-388-1 (pbk.) : DDC 741.2 20
NC730 .A52 1991

Betti, Claudia. Drawing . Fort Worth, TX ,
1991. p. cm. ISBN 0-03-053147-0 DDC 741.2 20
NC730 .B43 1991

Blake, Wendon. Getting started in drawing /.
Cincinnati, Ohio , c1991. vi, 137 p. : ISBN
0-89134-361-X (hrdcvr.) : DDC 741.2 20
NC730 .B535 1991

Brookes, Mona, 1937- Drawing for older
children, teens, and adult beginners /. Los
Angeles , New York , c1991. p. cm. ISBN
0-87477-660-0 : DDC 741.2 20
NC730 .B657 1991

Brown, Clint. Drawing from life /. Fort Worth ,
c1992. p. cm. ISBN 0-03-028934-3 DDC 743/.4
20
NC760 .B86 1992

Hamm, Jack. Drawing and cartooning 1,001
faces, places, and things /. New York, NY ,
c1991. p. cm. ISBN 0-399-51687-5 (alk. paper)
DDC 741.2 20
NC730 .H25 1991

Hanks, Kurt, 1947- Draw! . Los Altos, Calif. ,
1990. p. cm. ISBN 1-560-52054-X : DDC 741.2
20
NC730 .H27 1990

Jamieson, Doug. Draw from your head . New
York , 1991. p. cm. ISBN 0-8230-1374-X DDC
743/.49 20
NC760 .J34 1991

Martin, Judy (Frances Judy) Sketching school
/. Pleasantville, N.Y. , c1992. p. cm. ISBN
0-89577-405-4 DDC 741.2 20
NC730 .M294 1992

Nelms, Henning, 1900- Thinking with a pencil
/. Berkeley, Calif. , 1991. p. cm. ISBN
0-89815-052-3 DDC 741.5/994 20
NC730 .N4 1991

Parramón, José María. [Así se dibuja. English.]
How to draw . New York , 1991. 112 p. :
ISBN 0-8230-2352-4 : DDC 741.2 20
NC730 .P2713 1991

Parramón, José María. [Cómo dibujar la
anatomía del cuerpo humano. English.] Human
anatomy /. New York , 1991. p. cm. ISBN
0-8230-2499-7 : DDC 743/.49 20
NC760 .P3413 1991

Parramón, José María. [Dibujando pintando
apuntes. English.] Sketching people and places
in all mediums /. New York , 1991. p. cm.
ISBN 0-8230-4852-7 : DDC 741.2 20
NC730 .P28313 1991

Powell, Dick. Presentation techniques .
London , 1990. 160 p. : ISBN 0-356-17584-7 :
DDC 745.2 19
TS171   **NYPL [3-MDW 90-11572]**

Sheppard, Joseph, 1930- Drawing the living
figure /. New York , 1991. 144 p. : ISBN

0-486-26723-7 (pbk.) :   DDC 743/.4 20
NC765 .S436 1991

**DRAWING - TECHNIQUE - JUVENILE
LITERATURE.**
Ames, Lee J. Draw 50 creepy crawlies /. New
York , 1991. p. cm. ISBN 0-385-41189-8 DDC
743/.6 20
NC783 .A44 1991

Savitt, Sam. Draw horses with Sam Savitt.
Middletown, Md. , 1991. p. cm. ISBN
0-939481-23-5: DDC 743/.69725 20
NC783.8.H65 S38 1991

Simpson, Anne. How to draw wild animals /.
Mahwah, N.J. [1991] p. cm. ISBN
0-8167-2481-4 (lib. bdg.) : DDC 743/.6 20
NC780 .S54 1991

Solga, Kim. Draw! /. Cincinnati, Ohio , c1991.
p. cm. ISBN 0-89134-385-7 (paper) DDC 741.2
20
NC730 .S66 1991

Soloff-Levy, Barbara. How to draw clowns /.
Mahwah, N.J. , c1992. p. cm. ISBN
0-8167-2477-6 (lib. bdg.) : DDC 743/.8979133
20
NC765 .S65 1992

Soloff-Levy, Barbara. How to draw fairy-tale
characters /. Mahwah, N.J. , c1992. p. cm.
ISBN 0-8167-2378-8 (library) : DDC 743/.89398
20
NC655 .S65 1992

Drawing the living figure /. Sheppard, Joseph,
1930- New York , 1991. 144 p. : ISBN
0-486-26723-7 (pbk.) : DDC 743/.4 20
NC765 .S436 1991

Drawings. Keyt, George. George Keyt drawings /.
Colombo , 1990. xxviii, 90 p. : ISBN
955-9065-01-7 : DDC 741.95493 20
NC330.Z9 K492 1990

DRAWINGS. see DRAWING.

Drawings and graphics.
Coe, Sue, 1951- Paintings and drawings /.
Metuchen, N.J. , 1985. x, 150 p. : ISBN
0-8108-1782-9 DDC 759.2 19
N6797.C55 A4 1985
NYPL [3-MCV C672 91-6814]

Drawings by Saul Steinberg . Steinberg, Saul.
New York , 1969. [24] p. :
NYPL [3-MCX S813 91-1179]

Drawings from the estate. Smithson, Robert.
Robert Smithson . [Münster] [1989?] 140 p. :
ISBN 3-88789-087-6
NC139.S57 A4 1989
NYPL [3-MCX S664 91-6132]

Drawings from the Le Corbusier archive /.
Fondation Le Corbusier. London , New York ,
c1986. 88 p. : DDC 720/.22/22 20
NA2707.L4 A4 1986

Drawings from Tuscany and Umbria, 1350-1700 /.
[exhibition] Mills College Art Gallery, Oakland;
University of California, Berkeley, 1961.
[Oakland?] : The Gallery, 1961. [24] p., [14] p.
of plates : ill. ; 25 cm. From the collection of Janos
Scholz. Includes bibliographical references.
*1. Scholz, Janos - Art collections - Exhibitions. 2.
Drawing, Italian - Italy - Tuscany - Private collections -
Exhibitions. 3. Drawing, Italian - Italy - Umbria -
Private collections - Exhibitions. 4. Drawing,
Renaissance - Private collections - Italy. 5. Drawing,
Baroque - Private collections - Italy. I. Mills College.
Art Gallery. II. University of California, Berkeley.
University Art Gallery.*   **NYPL [3-MCE 90-7042]**

The drawings of Anthony van Dyck /. Brown,
Christopher, 1948- New York , 1991. 294 p. :
ISBN 0-87598-091-0
NYPL [3-MCH+ D99 91-5935]

**The drawings of Antonio Canaletto in the
collection of Her Majesty the Queen at
Windsor Castle /.** Parker, K. T. (Karl
Theodore), 1895- Bologna, Italy , 1990. 174 p. :
ISBN 88-7779-105-5
NYPL [3-MCF+ C21 91-5238]

The drawings of Bruno Schulz /. Schulz, Bruno,
1892-1942. Evanston, Ill. , 1990. 271 p. : ISBN
0-8101-0964-6 (lib. bdg.) DDC 741.9438 20
NC312.P63 S382 1990
NYPL [3-MCZ S388 91-3910]

The drawings of Thomas Gainsborough /. Hayes,
John T. New Haven , 1971, c1970. 2 v. (x, 368

p., [143] leaves of plates) : ISBN 0-300-01425-2
DDC 741/.092/4
NC242.G3 A4 1970
NYPL [MCV+ G14.H4d]

Drawings recently acquired, 1972-1975.
Metropolitan Museum of Art (New York, N.Y.)
European drawings recently acquired,
1972-1975. [New York] [1975] [52] p. :
NYPL [3-MBH 90-5754]

Dream rooms, decorating with flair /. Sherrow,
Victoria. Mahwah, N.J. , c1991. 114 p. : ISBN
0-8167-2293-5 (lib. bdg.) : DDC 747.7/7 20
NK2115 .S48 1991

Dreams and responsibilities . Kennedy, Brian P.
[Dublin, Ireland] [1990?] xiii, 292 p. : ISBN
0-906627-32-X DDC 700/.1/03 20
NX750.I7 K4 1990   **NYPL [JFE 91-2989]**

Dreams in dry places /. Bruhn, Roger, 1941-
Lincoln , c1990. xix, 143 p. : ISBN
0-8032-1214-3 : DDC 779/.4782/092 20
TR660 .B784 1990
NYPL [MFX (Bruhn) 91-3589]

Drechsler, Marika, 1942-
Egger, Gerhart, 1916- Graphiken von Marika
Drechsler /. Wien , 1978. 15 p., 32 p. of
plates :   **NYPL [MDG (Drechsler) 90-6047]**

**DRECHSLER, MARIKA, 1942- -
EXHIBITIONS.**
Egger, Gerhart, 1916- Graphiken von Marika
Drechsler /. Wien , 1978. 15 p., 32 p. of
plates :   **NYPL [MDG (Drechsler) 90-6047]**

Dreher, Anselm.
Grass, Günter, 1927- [Selections. English.
1985.] Etchings and words, 1972-1982 /. San
Diego , c1985. 148 p. : ISBN 0-15-129150-0
DDC 769.92/4 19
NX550.Z9 G725 1983 vol. 2
NYPL [MDG+ (Grass) 91-2286]

Grass, Günter, 1927- [Selections. 1982.]
Zeichnen und Schreiben . Darmstadt ,
c1982-1984. 2 v. : ISBN 3-472-90002-4 (Bd. II)
DDC 700/.92/4 19
NX550.Z9 G725 1982
NYPL [MCK++ G76 85-327]

Grass, Günter, 1927- [Selections. 1982.]
Zeichnungen und Texte 1954-1977 /.
Darmstadt , c1982. 133 p. : ISBN 3-472-90001-6
DDC 700/.92/4 s 741.943 19
NX550.Z9 G725 1982 Bd. 1
NYPL [MCK++ G76 85-327]

Grass, Günter, 1927- [Selections. 1982.]
Radierungen und Texte 1972-1982 /.
Darmstadt , c1984. 146 p. : ISBN 3-472-90002-4
DDC 700/.92/4 s 769.92/4 19
NX550.Z9 G725 1982 Bd. 2
NYPL [MDG+ (Grass) 91-2285]

Dreher, Peter, 1932-
Tag um Tag ist guter Tag : Peter Dreher :
Städtische Museen Freiburg, 27.1.-4.3.1990 :
Kunst, 27.1.-4.3.1990 : Städtische Kunsthalle
Mannheim, 5.8.-23.9.1990 / [Redaktion, Jochen
Ludwig und Detlef Zinke]. Freiburg im
Breisgau : Museum für Neue Kunst ;
[Mannheim] : Städtische Kunsthalle Mannheim,
c1990. 707 p. : chiefly ill. ; 20 cm. Includes
bibliographical references. DDC 759.3 20
*1. Dreher, Peter, 1932- - Exhibitions. I. Ludwig,
Jochen. II. Zinke, Detlef. III. Museum für Neue Kunst
(Freiburg im Breisgau, Germany). IV. Städtische
Kunsthalle Mannheim. V. Title.*
ND588.D69 A4 1990

DREHER, PETER, 1932- - EXHIBITIONS.
Dreher, Peter, 1932- Tag um Tag ist guter
Tag : Peter Dreher . Freiburg im Breisgau
[Mannheim] , c1990. 707 p. : DDC 759.3 20
ND588.D69 A4 1990

Drei Generationen Prachensky . Hauser, Krista.
[Austria] , 1986. 50 p. :
NYPL [3-MQWD+ 89-27463]

Dreishpoon, Douglas. Benton, Thomas Hart,
1889-1975. Benton's America . New York,
N.Y. , c1991. 63 p. : ISBN 0-915057-39-5
NYPL [3-MCX B47 91-6240]

Dreissinger, Sepp. Hausmeisterportraits : Wien,
Paris, Berlin / photographiert und
herausgegeben von Sepp Dreissinger ; Texte
von Erol Akdag ... [et al.]. Salzburg : O.
Müller, c1989. 107 p. : ill. ; 30 cm. ISBN

3-7013-0764-4
1. Photography - Portraits. I. Title.
NYPL [MFX+ (Dreissinger) 90-11180]

Dreissinger, Sepp, 1946- Seibert, Ingrit. Die
Schwierigen . Wien , c1986. 199 p. : ISBN
3-7046-0053-9
NX548.Z8 S45 1986

Drepper, Uwe. Robert Vorhoelzer, ein
Architektenleben . München , c1990. 296 p. :
ISBN 3-7667-0960-7
NA1088.V67 R6 1990

Dresch, Jutta. Kunst in der Residenz .
[Karlsruhe] [1990] 399 p. : ISBN 3-925835-58-X
DDC 709/.43/4643074434643 20
N6886.K33 K85 1990

Drescher, Tim. San Francisco murals : community
creates its muse, 1914-1990 / Timothy W.
Drescher. [St. Paul, Minn.] : Pogo Press,cc1991.
104 p., [32] p. of plates : ill. (some col.), maps ;
28 cm. Includes lists of San Francisco and East Bay
murals with maps. Includes bibliographical references
(p. 104) and index. ISBN 0-9617767-7-3
1. Mural painting and decoration, American -
California - San Francisco - Catalogs. 2. Mural painting
and decoration - 20th century - California - San
Francisco - Catalogs. I. Title.
NYPL [3-MLP 91-6587]

Dresden : von der Königlichen Kunstakademie
zur Hochschule für Bildende Künste,
1764-1989 : die Geschichte einer Institution /
[Autoren, Manfred Altner ... et al. ;
herausgegeben von der Hochschule für Bildende
Künste Dresden]. Dresden : Verlag der Kunst,
1990. 684 p. : ill. (some col.) ; 31 cm. Cover
title: 1764-1989. Includes bibliographical references (p.
665-672) and index. ISBN 3-364-00145-6
1. Hochschule für Bildende Künste Dresden. 2. Art -
Study and teaching (Higher) - Germany - Dresden. 3.
Dresden (Germany) - Buildings, structures, etc. 4.
Artists - Germany - Dresden - Biography. I. Altner,
Manfred. II. Hochschule für Bildende Künste Dresden.
III. Title: 1764-1989.
N333.G33 D744 1990

**DRESDEN (GERMANY) - BUILDINGS,
STRUCTURES, ETC.**
Dresden . Dresden , 1990. 684 p. : ISBN
3-364-00145-6
N333.G33 D744 1990

Dresden. Kupferstichkabinett. Die Albertina und
das Dresdner Kupferstich-Kabinett . Dresden ,
1978. 181 p. :
NC17.A8 V52 **NYPL [MBH 80-591]**

**Dresden. Staatliche Kunstsammlungen.
Kupferstichkabinett. see Dresden.
Kupferstichkabinett.**

**Dresden. Staatliches Kupferstich-Kabinett. see
Dresden. Kupferstichkabinett.**

DRESS DESIGN. see COSTUME DESIGN.

Dress in North America /. de Marly, Diana.
New York , 1990- v. : ISBN 0-8419-1199-1
DDC 391/.0097 20
GT603 .D4 1990 **NYPL [3-MMP 91-3984]**

**DRESSAGE - BIBLIOGRAPHY -
EXHIBITIONS.**
Reitkunst in Bild und Schrift des 16.-19.
Jahrhunderts /. Hamburg [1982] 44 p. :
Z6240 .R44 1982 SF309
NYPL [MDZ 87-5069]

**DRESSAGE - PICTORIAL WORKS -
EXHIBITIONS.**
Reitkunst in Bild und Schrift des 16.-19.
Jahrhunderts /. Hamburg [1982] 44 p. :
Z6240 .R44 1982 SF309
NYPL [MDZ 87-5069]

Dresser, Christopher. Halén, Widar. Christopher
Dresser /. Oxford , 1990. 208 p. : ISBN
0-07-148008-5 DDC 745.20924 20
NYPL [3-MNE 91-3313]

DRESSER, CHRISTOPHER.
Halén, Widar. Christopher Dresser /. Oxford ,
1990. 208 p. : ISBN 0-07-148008-5 DDC
745.20924 20 **NYPL [3-MNE 91-3313]**

**Drevniaia i srednevekovaia arkhitektura
Dagestana :** sbornik statei [sostavitel' M.S.
Gadzhiev ; otvetstvennyi redaktor A.I.
Islammagomedov]. Makhachkala : Dagestanskii
filial AN SSSR, In-t istorii, iazyka i lit-ry im.
G. TSadasy, 1989. 184, [4] p. : ill. ; 23 cm.
Includes bibliographical references (p. 183-[185]).

1. Architecture, Ancient - Russian S.F.S.R. -
Dagestanskaia A.S.S.R. 2. Architecture, Islamic -
Russian S.F.S.R. - Dagestanskaia A.S.S.R. 3.
Architecture - Russian S.F.S.R. - Dagestanskaia
A.S.S.R. I. Gadzhiev, M. S. II. Islammagomedov, A. I.
III. Institut istorii, iazyka i literatury im. G. TSadasy.
NA1492.8 .D7 1989

Drexel University. Museum. Eirich, E. C.
(Edward Conrad), 1877-1929. E.C. Eirich
(1877-1929) . [Philadelphia, Pa.] , c1991. 48
p. : **NYPL [3-MCX E35 91-7603]**

Dreyfus, Dominique, 1954- Emaux de Longwy /
Dominique Dreyfus. Paris : Massin, [1990?] 95
p. : col. ill. ; 29 cm. ISBN 2-7072-0162-6
1. Pottery - France. 2. Enamel and enameling -
France - Longwy. I. Title.
NYPL [3-MPGG 91-5541]

Dreyfus, John. Rogerson, Ian. Agnes Miller
Parker, wood-engraver and book illustrator,
1895-1990 /. Wakefield, West Yorkshire , 1990.
88 p., [6] leaves of plates : ISBN 0-948375-23-X
(quarter cloth) DDC 769.92 20
NE1147.6.P37 R64 1990

Dri, Giorgio. Ermes Midena, architetto moderno
in Friuli /. Udine , 1988. 94 p. : ISBN
88-7772-012-3 (pbk.)
NYPL [3-MQZ + (Midena) 90-2526]

Drie lagen diep. Lucebert, 1924- Amsterdam
[1969] [10] p.,
NC263.S95 A48
NYPL [3-MCH S961 90-6370]

DRIED FLOWER ARRANGEMENT.
Scott, Margaret Kennedy. Pressed flowers and
flower pictures /. London , 1988. 118 p. :
ISBN 0-7134-5245-5 DDC 745.92/8 19
SB449.3.P7 S362 1988
NYPL [3-MLT 90-10805]

Driehonderdteneen lithoos, 1802-1981. 301
lithoos, 1802-1981. Amsterdam , c1983. 331
p. : ISBN 90-70604-02-7
NYPL [MDP+ 90-11340]

**DRINKING VESSELS - ASIA,
SOUTHEASTERN - CATALOGS.**
Khoo, Joo Ee, 1940- Kendi . Singapore , New
York , 1991. p. cm. ISBN 0-19-588939-8 : DDC
738/.095/0745951 20
NK4163 .K48 1991

**DRINKING VESSELS - EAST ASIA -
CATALOGS.**
Khoo, Joo Ee, 1940- Kendi . Singapore , New
York , 1991. p. cm. ISBN 0-19-588939-8 : DDC
738/.095/0745951 20
NK4163 .K48 1991

**DRINKING VESSELS - SINGAPORE -
CATALOGS.**
Khoo, Joo Ee, 1940- Kendi . Singapore , New
York , 1991. p. cm. ISBN 0-19-588939-8 : DDC
738/.095/0745951 20
NK4163 .K48 1991

Dripps, Matthew. Map of the city of Brooklyn :
being the former cities of Brooklyn &
Williamsburgh and the town of Bushwick, as
consolidated January 1st, 1855 by an act of the
legislature of the State of New York ... showing
also a part of the City of New York. New
York : M. Dripps, 1869. 1 atlas (8 leaves) : 8
col. maps ; 56 cm.
1. Brooklyn (New York, N.Y.) - Maps. I. Title.
NYPL [Map Div. 87-470]

Driskel, Michael Paul. Representing belief :
religion, art, and society in ninteenth-century
France / Michael Paul Driskel. University
Park : Pennsylvania State University Press,
c1991. p. cm. Includes bibliographical references and
index. ISBN 0-271-00747-8 DDC 709/.44/09034 20
1. Art, French. 2. Art and religion - France. 3. Art and
society - France. 4. Art, Modern - 19th century -
France. I. Title.
N6847 .D75 1991

Drocourt, Daniel. Architectures historiques à
Marseille . Aix-en-Provence , c1987. 141 p. :
ISBN 2-85744-290-4 : DDC 720/.944/912 19
NA1051.M37 U73 1987
NYPL [3-MQWF+ 90-12768]

Drohojowska, Hunter, 1952- Shire, Peter.
Tempest in a teapot . New York , 1991. 144
p. : ISBN 0-8478-1322-3 DDC 738/.092 20
NK4210.S534 D76 1991

Drömmen om Kina. [Göteborg] : Röhsska
Konstslöjdmuseet, 1984. 55 p. : ill. ; 21 cm.

Accompanies an exhibition held at the museum from
June 15 to November 18, 1984. Includes bibliographical
references (p. 54-55).
1. Art, European - Chinese influences - Exhibitions. 2.
Decoration and ornament - Europe - Chinese
influences - Exhibitions. I. Röhsska konstslöjdmuseet
(Göteborg, Sweden). **NYPL [3-MAM 90-12530]**

Drost, Dietrich. Ornament und Plastik fremder
Völker. English. Ornament and sculpture in
primitive society. New York [1966] [138] p. :
DDC 709.011
N7380 .O713 1966b
NYPL [3-MADF 90-6405]

Droysen Keramikgalerie, Kattrin Kühn. Penck A.
R., 1939- A.R. Penck, Keramik. Berlin , c1989.
1 v. (unpaged) :
NK4210.P446 A4 1989

**Dru, Line, 1957-
[Cafés. English]**
Cafes / Line Dru, Carlo Aslan. New York,
NY : Princeton Architectural Press, 1990.
118 p. : ill. (some col.) ; 28 cm. (Thematic
architecture) Translation of: Les Cafés. Includes
bibliographical references (p. 118). ISBN
0-910413-66-5
1. Restaurants, lunch rooms, etc. - Design. 2.
Restaurant, lunch rooms, etc. - Decoration. 3. Hotels,
taverns, etc. - Design. 4. Interior architecture -
History - 20th century. I. Aslan, Carlo, 1953-. II. Title.
III. Series. **NYPL [3-MLO 90-10718]**

Drucker, Malka. Frida Kahlo : torment and
triumph in her life and art / Malka Drucker ;
with an introduction by Laurie Anderson. New
York : Bantam, 1991. p. cm. (A Bantam-Barnard
biography) Includes index. A detailed account of the
often turbulent life and career of Mexico's most famous
woman artist. ISBN 0-553-07165-3 DDC 759.972 B
92 20
1. Kahlo, Frida. 2. Artists - Mexico - Biography. I.
Title. II. Series.
N6559.K34 D7 1991

Die Druckgrafik und Monotypisches /.
Thomkins, André. Zürich , c1977. [17] p., [83]
leaves of plates :
NE710.T47 A4 1977
NYPL [MDG+ (Thomkins) 91-6204]

**Druckgrafische Ortsansichten des Wallis
1548-1850 /.** Gattlen, Anton. [Switzerland] ,
1987. 264 p., 18 leaves of plates :
NYPL [MDZ 91-5819]

Druckgraphik. Grieshaber, Helmut A. P., 1909-
Grieshaber . Stuttgart , 1984-c1986. 2 v. :
ISBN 3-7757-0221-0 (Bd. 1) DDC 769.92/4 19
NE1150.5.G7 A4 1984a
NYPL [MDG+ (Grieshaber) 91-1093]

Druckgraphikl, Handzeichnungen, Plastik.
Kollwitz, Käthe, 1867-1945. Käthe Kollwitz,
Druckgraphik, Handzeichnungen, Plastik /.
Stuttgart , 1990. 255 p. : ISBN 3-7757-0300-4
DDC 709/.2 20
N6868.K62 A4 1990

Das druckgraphische Werk Max Pechsteins /.
Krüger, Günter. Tökendorf , c1988. 368 p. :
ISBN 3-926483-00-8
NYPL [MDG (Pechstein) 90-10978]

Druckgraphische Werke und illustrierte Bücher.
Ernst, Max, 1891-1976. Max Ernst,
druckgraphische Werke und illustrierte Bücher .
Köln , 1990. 312 p. : DDC 769.92 20
NE654.E7 A4 1990

Drugstore tins & their prices /. Bergevin, Al.
Radnor, Pa. , c1990. 282 p., [10] p. of plates :
ISBN 0-87069-568-1 : DDC 741.6/7/0973075
20
NK8425 .B45 1990
NYPL [3-MNH 91-3998]

Drugstore tins and their prices. Bergevin, Al.
Drugstore tins & their prices /. Radnor, Pa. ,
c1990. 282 p., [10] p. of plates : ISBN
0-87069-568-1 : DDC 741.6/7/0973075 20
NK8425 .B45 1990
NYPL [3-MNH 91-3998]

Druks, Michael, 1940-
Kent, Sarah. Catalogue /. London , 1978. [36]
p. :
N7279.D78 A4 1978
NYPL [3-MCV D758 81-443]

DRUKS, MICHAEL, 1940- - EXHIBITIONS.
Kent, Sarah. Catalogue /. London , 1978. [36]

p. :
N7279.D78 A4 1978
NYPL [3-MCV D758 81-443]

DRUMS (CONTAINERS) - VIETNAM - CATALOGS.
Dong son drums in Viet Nam /. Tōkyō , 1990.
282 p. : ISBN 4-8453-3038-5 :
NK7978.6.V5 D66 1990

Drutt, Matthew. Norton, Deborah. Albert Paley .
Washington, D.C. , 1991. p. cm. ISBN
0-295-97152-5 DDC 739.27/092 20
NK7398.P35 A4 1991

Druzhestvo na khudozhnitsite--Kiustendil.
30 godini Druzhestvo na
khudozhnitsite--Kiustendil, 1959-1989 /. [S.l. ,
1989] (Sofiā : Ofsetgrafik) 47 p. :
N7191.K58 A15 1989

DRUZHESTVO NA KHUDOZHNITSITE--KIUSTENDIL - ANNIVERSARIES, ETC.
30 godini Druzhestvo na
khudozhnitsite--Kiustendil, 1959-1989 /. [S.l. ,
1989] (Sofiā : Ofsetgrafik) 47 p. :
N7191.K58 A15 1989

DRY MARKER DRAWING - TECHNIQUE.
Gleason, John A. Illustration with markers .
New York , 1991. p. cm. ISBN 0-8230-2536-5 :
DDC 741.6 20
NC878 .G57 1991

Du Bourguet, Pierre. Die Kopten, von P. du
Bourguet. [Aus dem Französischen übers. von
Eva Rapsilber] Baden-Baden, Holle Verlag
[1967] 237 p. illus., map, plates (part col.) 24
cm. (Kunst der Welt; ihre geschichtlichen,
soziologischen und religiösen Grundlagen. Die
aussereuropäischen Kulturen) Bibliography: p. 221-224.
DDC 709/.32
1. Art, Coptic. I. Title.
N7988 .D815   *NYPL [3-MAE 91-329]*

'DU KHAN (TEMPLE : ALCHI GŌMPA, INDIA) - EXHIBITIONS.
Goepper, Roger. Alchi . Köln, c1982. 110 p. :
ISBN 3-7701-1479-5 DDC 755/.943/09546 19
ND2829.A415 G64 1982
NYPL [3-MAF 90-12370]

Du Pont, Diana C., 1953- Florence Henri,
artist-photographer the avant-garde / Diana
C. du Pont. San Francisco : San Francisco
Museum of Modern Art, c1990. 158 p. : ill. ;
31 cm. "Published on the occasion of the exhibition ...
organized by the San Francisco Museum of Modern
Art, San Francisco Museum of Modern Art, December
13, 1990-February 10, 1991 ... [and other
museums]"--T.p. verso. Includes bibliographical
references (p. 145-152). ISBN 0-918471-17-6
(softcover) : DDC 779/.092 20
*1. Henri, Florence, 1893-- Exhibitions. 2. Photography,
Artistic - Exhibitions. I. Henri, Florence, 1893-. II. San
Francisco. Museum of Modern Art. III. Title.*
TR647 .H46 1990
NYPL [MFX+ (Henri) 91-4579]

**Du Pont Museum, Winterthur, Del. see Henry
Francis du Pont Winterthur Museum.**

Duane Hanson, Skulpturen /. Bush, Martin H.
[Stuttgart] , c1990. 111 p. : ISBN 3-89322-205-7
NYPL [3-MGO (Hanson) 91-7453]

Duarte, António.
Gastão, Marques, 1914- Encontros com
António Duarte /. [Lisbon, Portugal] [1989]
128 p. : DDC 730/.92 20
NB833.D8 G37 1989

DUARTE, ANTÓNIO - CRITICISM AND INTERPRETATION.
Gastão, Marques, 1914- Encontros com
António Duarte /. [Lisbon, Portugal] [1989]
128 p. : DDC 730/.92 20
NB833.D8 G37 1989

Duarte, Carlos F. El arte de la platería en
Venezuela : período hispánico / Carlos F.
Duarte. Caracas, Venezuela : Fundación
Pampero, 1988. 438 p. : ill. (some col.) ; 33 cm.
Includes bibliographical references (p. 396-397) and
index. ISBN 980-300-084-5 DDC 739.2/3787 20
*1. Silverwork, Colonial - Venezuela. 2. Silverwork -
Venezuela. 3. Church plate - Venezuela. I. Title.*
NK7141.A1 D8 1988

Duarte, Carlota. Odella : a hidden survivor : a
photographic essay / by Carlota Duarte.
Albuquerque, N.M. : Distributed by the
University of New Mexico Press ; c1990. [56]
p. : ill. ; 23 cm. "An exhibition of the photographs

will take place at the CityPlace Gallery, Artists
Foundation, Boston, April 1990 in collaboration with
Tufts University"--P. [56] ISBN 0-9624109-0-X
*1. Photography of women - Exhibitions. 2. Women -
Portraits - Exhibitions. I. CityPlace Gallery (Boston,
Mass.). II. Tufts University. III. Title.*
NYPL [MFX (Duarte) 90-13481]

DUBLIN (DUBLIN) - DESCRIPTION - VIEWS.
Brooking, Charles. [Map of the city and suburbs
of Dublin.] The city of Dublin, 1728 /. Dublin ,
1983. 1 portfolio : ISBN 0-904720-14-4 : DDC
941.8/35 19
DA995.D8 B76 1983
NYPL [Map Div. 87-655]

DUBLIN (DUBLIN) - MAPS.
Brooking, Charles. [Map of the city and suburbs
of Dublin.] The city of Dublin, 1728 /. Dublin ,
1983. 1 portfolio : ISBN 0-904720-14-4 : DDC
941.8/35 19
DA995.D8 B76 1983
NYPL [Map Div. 87-655]

**DUBLIN (IRELAND) - SOCIAL LIFE AND
CUSTOMS - PICTORIAL WORKS.**
O'Shea, Tony, 1947- Dubliners /. London ,
1990. 160 p. : ISBN 0-356-17641-X : DDC
941.8350824 20
DA995.D75
NYPL [MFX (O'Shea) 91-3472]

Dubliners /. O'Shea, Tony, 1947- London , 1990.
160 p. : ISBN 0-356-17641-X : DDC 941.8350824
20
DA995.D75
NYPL [MFX (O'Shea) 91-3472]

DuBosque, D. C. Learn to draw now! / by D.C.
DuBosque. Molalla, OR : Peel Productions,
1991. p. cm. (Learn to draw) Includes index.
Introduces techniques and exercises for rendering the
basic three-dimensional forms essential for realistic
drawing: the cylinder, cone, sphere, and box. ISBN
0-939217-16-3 : DDC 741.2/4 20
*1. Drawing - Study and teaching (Elementary) -
Juvenile literature. I. Title. II. Series.*
NC630 .D8 1991

DUBROVNIK, YUGOSLAVIA - HISTORY.
Beritićev zbornik . Dubrovnik , 1960. 335 p.,
[1] folded leaf of plates :
*NYPL [*QKK 83-2704]*

Dubuffet /. Franzke, Andreas. Köln , c1990. 207
p. : ISBN 3-7701-2523-1 DDC 709/.2 20
N6853.D78 F72 1990

Dubuffet, Jean, 1901-
Jean Dubuffet : [exposición] 9 febrero-31 marzo
1976, / textos, Jean Dubuffet ; traducidos por
José Luis Alonso. Madrid : Fundación Juan
March, 1976. 64 p. : ill. (some col.) ; 29 cm.
ISBN 84-7075-026-7 :
*1. Dubuffet, Jean, 1901-- Exhibitions. I. Fundación
Juan March.*
N6853.D78 A4 1976
NYPL [3-MCO D82 81-175]

Jean Dubuffet: paintings. A retrospective
exhibition organized by the Arts Council of
Great Britain at the Tate Gallery, London 23
April-30 May. London, Arts Council, 1966. 63
p. illus. (part col.) port. 23 cm. Bibliography: p.
11-14.
*1. Dubuffet, Jean, 1901-- Exhibitions. I. Tate Gallery.
II. Title.*
ND553.D772 A9
NYPL [3-MCO D82 90-5661]

Willem de Kooning, Jean Dubuffet . New York,
NY , c1990. 29, [84] p. :
NYPL [3-MAMZ 91-5530]

DUBUFFET, JEAN, 1901-
Franzke, Andreas. Dubuffet /. Köln , c1990.
207 p. : ISBN 3-7701-2523-1 DDC 709/.2 20
N6853.D78 F72 1990

DUBUFFET, JEAN, 1901-- EXHIBITIONS.
Dubuffet, Jean, 1901- Jean Dubuffet . Madrid ,
1976. 64 p. : ISBN 84-7075-026-7 :
N6853.D78 A4 1976
NYPL [3-MCO D82 81-175]

Dubuffet, Jean, 1901- Jean Dubuffet: paintings.
London, 1966. 63 p.
ND553.D772 A9
NYPL [3-MCO D82 90-5661]

Willem de Kooning, Jean Dubuffet . New York,
NY , c1990. 29, [84] p. :
NYPL [3-MAMZ 91-5530]

Duby, Georges.
[Sculpture. English]
Sculpture : the great art of the Middle Ages
from the fifth to the fifteenth century / by
Georges Duby, Xavier Barral i Altet, Sophie
Guillot de Suduiraut. New York :
Skira/Rizzoli, 1990. 318 p. : ill. (some col.) ;
35 cm. "Translated from the French by Michael
Hero"--T.p. verso. ISBN 0-8478-1285-5 DDC 734
20
*1. Sculpture, Medieval. I. Barral i Altet. Xavier. II.
Guillot de Suduiraut, Sophie. III. Title.*
NB170 .D813 1990
NYPL [3-MGF+ 91-3656]

Duccio . Ragionieri, Giovanna. Firenze , c1989.
159 p. : ISBN 88-7737-058-0
NYPL [MCF D82 91-4998]

Duccio di Buoninsegna, d. 1319.
La Maestà di Duccio restaurata. Firenze
[1990] 89 p. : ISBN 88-7038-187-0
NYPL [MCF D82 90-10935]

Ragionieri, Giovanna. Duccio . Firenze , c1989.
159 p. : ISBN 88-7737-058-0
NYPL [MCF D82 91-4998]

MAESTÀ.
La Maestà di Duccio restaurata. Firenze
[1990] 89 p. : ISBN 88-7038-187-0
NYPL [MCF D82 90-10935]

**DUCCIO, DI BUONINSEGNA, D. 1319 -
CATALOGUES RAISONNÉS.**
Ragionieri, Giovanna. Duccio . Firenze , c1989.
159 p. : ISBN 88-7737-058-0
NYPL [MCF D82 91-4998]

**DUCHAMP, MARCEL, 1887-1968 -
CRITICISM AND INTERPRETATION.**
The Definitively unfinished Marcel Duchamp /.
Halifax, N.S. , Cambridge, Mass. , 1991. p. cm.
ISBN 0-262-04117-0 DDC 709/.2 20
N6853.D8 D44 1991

Paz, Octavio, 1914- Marcel Duchamp,
appearance stripped bare /. New York , 1990.
vii, 211 p. : ISBN 1-559-70138-2 : DDC 759.4 20
ND553.D774 P352 1990

Duchamp, Suzanne, 1889-1963.
Tabu Dada . Bern , c1983. 139 p. : DDC
709/.04/062074094945 19
N6853.C86 A4 1983
NYPL [3-MCZ C946 83-2831]

**DUCHAMP, SUZANNE, 1889-1963 -
EXHIBITIONS.**
Tabu Dada . Bern , c1983. 139 p. : DDC
709/.04/062074094945 19
N6853.C86 A4 1983
NYPL [3-MCZ C946 83-2831]

**Duchamp-Villon, Marcel. see Duchamp, Marcel,
1887-1968.**

Duchamp's trans/formers /. Lyotard,
Jean-François. [Transformateurs Duchamp.
English.] Venice, Calif. , c1990. 199 p. , [1] leaf
(folded) : ISBN 0-932499-63-5
NYPL [3-MCO D827 90-12009]

Duchamp's transformers. Lyotard, Jean-François.
[Transformateurs Duchamp. English.]
Duchamp's trans/formers /. Venice, Calif. ,
c1990. 199 p. , [1] leaf (folded) : ISBN
0-932499-63-5
NYPL [3-MCO D827 90-12009]

Duchet-Suchaux, Gaston.
La Bible et les saints : guide iconographique /
Gaston Duchet-Suchaux, Michel Pastoureau.
Paris : Flammarion, c1990. 319 p., xxxii p. of
plates : ill. (some col.) ; 22 cm. Includes
bibliographical references. ISBN 2-08-011725-4
*1. Bible - Illustrations. 2. Bible - Dictionaries. 3.
Christian art and symbolism - Dictionaries. I.
Pastoureau, Michel, 1947-. II. Title.*
NYPL [3-MAIH 91-6578]

Iconographie médiévale . Paris , 1990. 207 p. :
ISBN 2-222-04344-1 : DDC 709/.02 20
N5970 .I26 1990

DUCKS IN ART - CATALOGS.
Worthen, Amy N. The prints of J.N. Darling /.
Ames, Iowa , 1991. 126 p. : ISBN 0-8138-1996-2
IN PROCESS (ONLINE)
NYPL [MDG (Darling) 91-6947]

Ducrey, Marina. Félix Vallotton : la vie, la
technique, l'œuvre peint / Marina Ducrey.
Lausanne : Edita, c1989. 163 p. : ill. (some
col.) ; 31 cm. (Collection "Biographie") Includes

bibliographical references (p. 157-160). ISBN
2-88001-248-1 DDC 759.9494 20
*1. Vallotton, Félix, 1865-1925. 2. Painters -
Switzerland - Biography. I. Vallotton, Félix, 1865-1925.
II. Series: Collection "Biographie" (Edita (Firm)). III.
Title.*
ND853.V3 D8 1989
        NYPL [3-MCZ+ V19 90-11783]

**DUDERSTADT (GERMANY) - BUILDINGS,
STRUCTURES, ETC.**
Das Rathaus in Duderstadt /. Hameln , c1989.
304 p. :   ISBN 3-87585-096-3
        NYPL [3-MQWD+ 91-5449]

Dudok van Heel, Sebastien A. C. Dossier
Rembrandt : documenten, tekeningen en
prenten = The Rembrandt papers : documents,
drawings and prints / S.A.C. Dudok van Heel ;
with contributions by P. Schatborn, drawings,
E. Ornstein-van Slooten, prints. Amsterdam :
Museum het Rembrandthuis in collaboration
with Gemeentearchief, Amsterdam, 1987. 88
p. : ill. ; 21 x 24 cm. Exhibition held Oct. 17,
1987-Jan. 4, 1988. Dutch and English.
*1. Rembrandt, Harmenszoon van Rijn, 1606-1669 -
Exhibitions. 2. Rembrandt Harmenszoon van Rijn,
1606-1669 - Archives. I. Schatborn, Peter. II.
Ornstein-van Slooten, E. (Eva). III. Museum het
Rembrandthuis (Amsterdam, Netherlands). IV.
Amsterdam (Netherlands). Gemeentearchief. V. Title.
VI. Title: Rembrandt papers.*
        NYPL [3-MCH R3 91-6725]

Dückers, Alexander, 1939- Bilder aus der grossen
Stadt . Berlin-Dahlem , 1977. [96] p. :
N6885 .B55   *NYPL [3-MAMG 81-424]*

**Düren, Ger. (City). Leopold-Hoesch-Museum. see
Leopold-Hoesch-Museum.**

**DÜRER, ALBRECHT, 1471-1528 -
CONGRESSES.**
Schutt-Kehm, Elke M., 1954- Albrecht Dürer
und die Frühzeit der Exlibriskunst .
Wiesbaden , c1990. 39 p. :   ISBN 3-922835-18-X
        NYPL [MDVF 91-7231]

**DÜRER, ALBRECHT, 1471-1528 -
EXHIBITIONS.**
Albert Dürer aux Pays-Bas . Bruxelles , 1977.
xxiii, 211, 144 p., [14] leaves of plates :
N6888.D8 A4 1977
        NYPL [3-MCK D85 81-320]

Düreriana . Nürnberg , c1990. 296 p. :   ISBN
3-418-00349-4
N6888.D8 A4 1990
        NYPL [3-MCK+ D85 91-7549]

Schutt-Kehm, Elke M., 1954- Albrecht Dürer
und die Frühzeit der Exlibriskunst .
Wiesbaden , c1990. 39 p. :   ISBN 3-922835-18-X
        NYPL [MDVF 91-7231]

**DÜRER, ALBRECHT, 1471-1528 -
INFLUENCE - EXHIBITIONS.**
Albert Dürer aux Pays-Bas . Bruxelles , 1977.
xxiii, 211, 144 p., [14] leaves of plates :
N6888.D8 A4 1977
        NYPL [3-MCK D85 81-320]

Auch kleine Dinge . [Cambridge] [1971] [174]
p. :   *NYPL [3-MNC 90-5886]*

Düreriana . Nürnberg , c1990. 296 p.   ISBN
3-418-00349-4
N6888.D8 A4 1990
        NYPL [3-MCK+ D85 91-7549]

**Dürer-Verein, Nuremberg. see Albrecht-Dürer-
Gesellschaft.**

Düreriana : Neuerwerbungen der
Albrecht-Dürer-Haus-Stiftung e.V., Nürnberg /
[herausgegeben von der Albrecht-Dürer-Haus
Stiftung e.V. Nürnberg ... ; bearbeitet von
Matthias Mende]. Nürnberg : H. Carl, c1990.
296 p. : ill. (some col.) ; 32 cm. Catalog published
on the occasion of an exhibition held at the
Albrecht-Dürer-Haus, Nürnberg, May 21-Sept. 30,
1990. Includes index. ISBN 3-418-00349-4
*1. Dürer, Albrecht, 1471-1528 - Exhibitions. 2. Dürer,
Albrecht, 1471-1528 - Influence - Exhibitions. 3.
Albrecht Dürerhaus Stiftung - Exhibitions. 4. Art,
Modern - Exhibitions. I. Mende, Matthias. II. Albrecht
Dürerhaus Stiftung. III. Albrecht-Dürer-Haus.*
N6888.D8 A4 1990
        NYPL [3-MCK+ D85 91-7549]

**Düsseldorf. Grabbeplate Kunsthalle. see
Städtische Kunsthalle Düsseldorf.**

**Düsseldorf. Hetjens-Museum. see Hetjens-
Museum.**

**Düsseldorf. Kunsthalle. see Städtische Kunsthalle
Düsseldorf.**

**Düsseldorf. Städtische Kunsthalle. see Städtische
Kunsthalle Düsseldorf.**

Dufek, Antonín. Linie, barva, tvar v českém
výtvarném umění třicátých let . [Prague ,
1990?] 152 p. :
N6831 .L54 1990

Duff, Roger. (ed) Art Galleries and Museums
Association of New Zealand. No sort of iron.
[Christchurch, 1969] 91 p.   DDC 709.01/1
N7410 .A73

Duffek, Karen, 1956- Bob Boyer : a blanket
statement / by Karen Duffek. [Vancouver] :
UBC Museum of Anthropology, c1988. 1 folded
sheet (8) p. ; ill. (some col.), port. ; 26 cm.
(UBC Museum of Anthropology museum note . no. 23)
Catalog of traveling exhibition produced by the
University of British Columbia Museum of
Anthropology. ISBN 0-88865-111-2 (pbk.)
*1. Boyer, Bob, 1948- - Exhibitions. I. Boyer, Bob,
1948-. II. University of British Columbia. Museum of
Anthropology. III. Title. IV. Title: Blanket statement. V.
Series: Museum note (Vancouver, B.C.) no. 23.*
        NYPL [3-MON 89-19266]

Dufour, Gary, 1954- Jeff Wall, 1990 / Gary
Dufour ; with an essay by Jerry Zaslove.
[Vancouver : Vancouver Art Gallery, 1990] 119
p. : ill. (some col., some folded) ; 27 cm.
Catalogue of an exhibition held at the Vancouver Art
Gallery. Bibliography: p. 112-118. ISBN
0-920095-83-6 DDC 779/.092/4 19
*1. Wall, Jeff, 1946- - Exhibitions. I. Wall, Jeff, 1946-.
II. Zaslove, Jerry, 1934-. III. Vancouver Art Gallery.
IV. Title.*   *NYPL [MFX (Wall) 90-11194]*

Dufresne, Charles, 1876-1936.
Charles Dufresne (1876-1936) a retrospective
exhibition. Introduction by Jean Bouret. New
York, Hirschl and Adler Galleries, 1971. [18] p
illus. (part col.) 26 cm. Exhibition held at Hirschl
and Adler Galleries, New York, Apr. 27-May 21, 1971.
*1. Dufresne, Charles, 1876-1936 - Exhibitions. I.
Bouret, Jean. II. Title.*
        NYPL [3-MCO D846 91-890]

**DUFRESNE, CHARLES, 1876-1936 -
EXHIBITIONS.**
Dufresne, Charles, 1876-1936. Charles Dufresne
(1876-1936) New York, 1971. [18] p
        NYPL [3-MCO D846 91-890]

**Duisburg. Lehmbruck Museum. see Wilhelm-
Lehmbruck-Museum der Stadt Duisburg.**

**Duisburg. Wilhelm-Lehmbruck-Museum. see
Wilhelm-Lehmbruck-Museum der Stadt
Duisburg.**

Duits, Thimo te. Baldwin, Gordon. Gordon
Baldwin . Rotterdam [1989] 39 p. :   ISBN
90-6918-044-8
NK4210.B33 A4 1989

**DUKE UNIVERSITY - ART COLLECTIONS -
EXHIBITIONS.**
Moeller, Robert C. Sculpture and decorative
art. Raleigh [1967] 97 p.
        NYPL [3-MAK 90-6857]

Duke University, Durham, N. C. Art Museum.
Selected works from the Benenson Collection :
an exhibition of works from the private art
collection of Mr. and Mrs. Edward H.
Benenson. Durham, N.C. : Duke University
Museum of Art, 1976. [24] p. : col. ill. ; 22 cm.
DDC 750/.74/0156563 19
*1. Benenson, Edward H. - Art collections - Exhibitions.
2. Benenson, Gladys - Art collections - Exhibitions. 3.
Painting, Modern - 19th century - Exhibitions. 4.
Painting, Modern - 20th century - Exhibitions. I. Title.*
ND189 .D84 1976   *NYPL [3-MAL 81-352]*

Duke University. Museum of Art.
The Brummer collection of medieval art, the
Duke University Museum of Art / by Caroline
Bruzelius with Jill Meredith ; essays by Ilene H.
Forsyth ... [et al.]. Durham : Duke University
Press, in association with the Museum, 1991.
xix, 297 p., 16 p. of plates : ill. (some col.) ; 29
cm. Includes bibliographical references (p. 287-291)
and indexes. ISBN 0-8223-1055-4 DDC
709/.02/074756563 20
*1. Brummer, Ernest - Art collections - Catalogs. 2.
Duke University. Museum of Art - Catalogs. 3. Art,
Medieval - Catalogs. 4. Art - North Carolina -
Durham - Catalogs. I. Bruzelius, Caroline Astrid. II.*

Meredith, Jill. III. Forsyth, Ilene H. IV. Title.
N5963.D87 D854 1991
        NYPL [3-MAK 91-5627]

García Lorca, Federico, 1898-1936. [Dibujos.
English.] Line of light and shadow . Durham ,
1991. 273 p. :   ISBN 0-8223-1122-4 DDC 741.946
20
NC287.G389 A4 1991

**DUKE UNIVERSITY. MUSEUM OF ART -
CATALOGS.**
Duke University. Museum of Art. The
Brummer collection of medieval art, the Duke
University Museum of Art /. Durham , 1991.
xix, 297 p., 16 p. of plates :   ISBN 0-8223-1055-4
DDC 709/.02/074756563 20
N5963.D87 D854 1991
        NYPL [3-MAK 91-5627]

Duluc, Anne. Bazzana, Andrés. La céramique
islamique du Musée archéologique provincial de
Jaén (Espagne) /. Madrid , Paris , 1985. 78 p. :
DDC 738.3/0946/83 20
DP302.J1 B38 1985
        NYPL [3-MPG+ 91-5911]

DULWICH PICTURE GALLERY - HISTORY.
Waterfield, Giles. Rich summer of art .
[London] , 1988. 47 p. :   DDC 708/.21/64 19
        NYPL [MAVZ (London) 91-6984]

Dům umění města Brna. Knížák, Milan. Milan
Knížák . [Brno , 1990?] 1 v. (unpaged) :
N6834.5.K56 A4 1990

Dumarçay, Jacques.
Borobudur / Jacques Dumarçay ; translated and
edited by Michael Smithies. 2nd ed. Singapore ;
New York : Oxford University Press, 1992. p.
cm. (Images of Asia) Includes bibliographical
references and index. ISBN 0-19-588550-3 : DDC
726/.143/095982 20
*1. Borobudur (Temple : Magelang, Indonesia). 2.
Temples - Indonesia - Magelang - Conservation and
restoration. I. Smithies, Michael, 1932-. II. Title. III.
Series.*
NA6026.6.B6 D8513 1992

Le savoir des maîtres d'œuvre javanais aux
XIIIe et XIVe siècles / par Jacques Dumarçay.
Paris : Editions d'Amérique et d'Orient, 1986.
122 p. : ill., maps, plans ; 35 cm. (Publications de
l'Ecole française d'Extrême-Orient. Mémoires
archéologiques . 17) Five folded leaves in pocket.
Includes bibliographical references and indexes. ISBN
2-85539-417-1 (pbk.)
1. Architecture - Indonesia - Java. I. Title. II. Series.
        NYPL [3-MQWS+ 90-11045]

Dumas, Ann. Vuillard, Édouard, 1868-1940.
Vuillard . Paris , c1990. 237 p. :   ISBN
2-08-011730-0 DDC 760/.092 20
N6853.V85 A4 1990

Dumas, Charles. Mast, Michiel van der. Van
Gogh en Den Haag /. Zwolle , c1990. 191 p. :
ISBN 90-6630-240-2
        NYPL [3-MCH G61 91-6680]

Dümmler, Elfriede, d. 1937.
Kirchner, Ernst Ludwig, 1880-1938. Ernst
Ludwig Kirchner . Bern , 1989. 147 p. :   ISBN
3-85773-022-6
N6888.K45 A3 1989
        NYPL [3-MCK K58 90-11101]

**DÜMMLER, ELFRIEDE, D. 1937 -
CORRESPONDENCE.**
Kirchner, Ernst Ludwig, 1880-1938. Ernst
Ludwig Kirchner . Bern , 1989. 147 p. :   ISBN
3-85773-022-6
N6888.K45 A3 1989
        NYPL [3-MCK K58 90-11101]

Dumond, D. E. (joint author) Spranz, Bodo. Die
Pyramiden vom Cerro Xochitecatl, Tlaxcala
(Mexico) /. Wiesbaden , 1977. 109 p. :   ISBN
3-515-02697-5
F1203 .D46 vol. 12 F1219.1.T623
        NYPL [HTC 74-1117 Bd. 12]

Dumont, Pierre, 1884-1936. Knyff, Gilbert de.
Pierre Dumont (1884-1936) /. Paris , 1976. 61,
[vii] p., 55 leaves of col. plates :   ISBN
84-399-4832-8
        NYPL [3-MCO D912 91-3677]

DUMONT, PIERRE, 1884-1936.
Knyff, Gilbert de. Pierre Dumont (1884-1936)
/. Paris , 1976. 61, [vii] p., 55 leaves of col.
plates :   ISBN 84-399-4832-8
        NYPL [3-MCO D912 91-3677]

Dunbar, Prescott N. The New Orleans Museum of Art : the first seventy-five years / Prescott N. Dunbar. Baton Rouge : Louisiana State University Press, c1990. xviii, 386 p., [18] p. of plates : ill. ; 24 cm. Includes bibliographical references. ISBN 0-8071-1604-1 (alk. paper) DDC 708.163/35/09 20
1. New Orleans Museum of Art - History. I. Title.
N598 .D86 1990
    NYPL [3-MAVZ (New Orleans) 91-3668]

Duncan, Alastair. Louis Majorelle : master of art nouveau design / Alastair Duncan ; foreword by Iloyd Macklowe. New York : Abrams, 1991. p. cm. Includes bibliographical references and index. ISBN 0-8109-3617-8 DDC 745.4/492 20
1. Majorelle, Louis, 1859-1900 - Criticism and interpretation. 2. Decoration and ornament - France - Art nouveau. 3. Decoration and ornament - France - History - 19th century. I. Title.
NK1535.M24 D8 1991

Duncan, David Douglas. This is war! : a photo-narrative of the Korean War / by David Douglas Duncan ; with a foreword by Harrison E. Salisbury. Boston : Little, Brown, c1990. [152] p. : ill. ; 31 cm. Reprint. Originally published: New York : Harper, 1951. ISBN 0-316-19565-0 : DDC 951.904/2 20
1. Korean War, 1950-1953 - Pictorial works. I. Title.
DS918.15 .D86 1990
    NYPL [MFX+ (Duncan) 91-3478]

Duncan, John. (artist) Phallus : a book of dreams / John Duncan. [S.l. : s.n.], 1979. 1 v. (unpaged) : ill. ; 26 cm. Cover title.
I. Title.   *NYPL [MEMZ 90-13233]*

Duncan Phillips collects . Phillips Collection. Washington, D.C. , c1991. p. cm. ISBN 0-943044-16-2 : DDC 759.4/361/09041074753 20
N6850 .P45 1991

DUNIKOWSKI, XAWERY, 1875-1964 - EXHIBITIONS.
Nie wieder! . [Düsseldorf] , 1989. 251 p. :
    NYPL [3-MAM+ 91-6409]

DUNKEL, HERBERT - EXHIBITIONS.
Dunkel, Trimborn, Dönselmann . [Emden, Germany , 1988] 87 p. : ISBN 3-925564-02-0
    NYPL [3-MAMG + 89-11596]

Dunkel, Trimborn, Dönselmann : Ostfriesland und die Kunst des 20. Jahrhunderts : eine Ausstellung der Ludolf Backhuysen Gesellschaft in der Kunsthalle in Emden, Stiftung Henri Nannen / [Katalog und Redaktion] Gerhard Finckh, Jost Galle. [Emden, Germany : Die Kunsthalle, 1988] 87 p. : ill. (some col.) ; 30 cm. ISBN 3-925564-02-0
1. Dunkel, Herbert - Exhibitions. 2. Trimborn, Hans - Exhibitions. 3. Dönselmann, Karl - Exhibitions. 4. Art, Modern - 20th century - Germany, West - Exhibitions. 5. Art, German - Germany, West - Exhibitions. I. Finckh, Gerhard. II. Galle, Jost. III. Kunsthalle in Emden--Stiftung Henri Nannen. IV. Ludolf Backhuysen Gesellschaft. *NYPL [3-MAMG + 89-11596]*

Dunlap, David, 1940-
This is always finished (David Dunlap) : Des Moines Art Center, December 9, 1989-January 28, 1990. Des Moines, Iowa : The Center, c1989. 42 p. : ill. ; 18 cm. ISBN 0-9614615-9-4
1. Dunlap, David, 1940- - Exhibitions. I. Des Moines Art Center. II. Title.
    NYPL [3-MCX D919 91-6455]

DUNLAP, DAVID, 1940- - EXHIBITIONS.
Dunlap, David, 1940- This is always finished (David Dunlap) . Des Moines, Iowa , c1989. 42 p. : ISBN 0-9614615-9-4
    NYPL [3-MCX D919 91-6455]

Dunlop, Beth, 1947- Arquitectonica / foreword by Rem Koolhaas ; introduction and text by Beth Dunlop ; design by Massimo Vignelli. Washington, D.C. : American Institute of Architects Press, c1991. p. cm. ISBN 1-558-35043-8 : DDC 720/.92/2 20
1. Arquitectonica (Firm : Coral Gables, Fla.). 2. Architecture, Modern - 20th century - United States. I. Title.
NA737.A77 D8 1991

Dunlop, Ian, 1925- Mondrian, Piet, 1872-1944. Piet Mondrian /. Paulton [England] , c1967. 8 p., xvi p. of plates :
    NYPL [3-MCH+ M741 89-6448]

Dunnan, Nancy.
Collectibles / Nancy Dunnan. Englewood

Cliffs, NJ : Silver Burdett Press, c1990. 128 p. : ill. ; 25 cm. (The Inside track library) Includes index. ISBN 0-382-09918-4 DDC 745.1 20
1. Antiques - Handbooks, manuals, etc. 2. Collectors and collecting - Handbooks, manuals, etc. I. Series: Dunnan, Nancy. Inside track library. II. Title.
NK1125 .D786 1990
    NYPL [MAVC 91-5516]

Inside track library.
Dunnan, Nancy. Collectibles /. Englewood Cliffs, NJ , c1990. 128 p. : ISBN 0-382-09918-4 DDC 745.1 20
NK1125 .D786 1990
    NYPL [MAVC 91-5516]

Dunning, William, 1933- Changing images of pictorial space : a history of spatial illusion in painting / William V. Dunning.1st ed. Syracuse : Syracuse University Press, 1991. xi, 254 p. : ill. ; 24 cm. Includes bibliographical references (p. 237-243) and index. ISBN 0-8156-2505-7 (cloth : alk. paper) DDC 750/.1/8 20
1. Painting - Technique. 2. Visual perception. I. Title.
ND1475 .D86 1991   *NYPL [3-MC 91-5767]*

Dunoyer, Pierre, 1949-
Pierre Dunoyer, new paintings : [exhibition], April 3-May 4, 1985. New York, N.Y. (1000 Madison Ave., New York 10021) : Nohra Haime Gallery, [1985] [8] p. : ill. (some col.) ; 28 cm. Bibliography: p. [3] of cover.
1. Dunoyer, Pierre, 1949- - Exhibitions. I. Nohra Haime Gallery (New York, N.Y.). II. Title.
    NYPL [3-MCO D924 90-12769]

DUNOYER, PIERRE, 1949- - EXHIBITIONS.
Dunoyer, Pierre, 1949- Pierre Dunoyer, new paintings . New York, N.Y. (1000 Madison Ave., New York 10021) [1985] [8] p. :
    NYPL [3-MCO D924 90-12769]

Dunster, David. Key buildings of the twentieth century / David Dunster. New York : Rizzoli, c1985- v. : chiefly ill., plans ; 21 x 30 cm. Vol. 2 has imprint: London ; Boston : Butterworth Architecture. Includes bibliographical references. CONTENTS. - v. 1. Houses, 1900-1944 -- v. 2. Houses 1945-1989. ISBN 0-8478-0642-1 (pbk. : v. 1) : DDC 724.9/1 19
1. Architecture, Modern - 20th century. 2. Buildings - Designs and plans. I. Title. II. Title: Key buildings of the 20th century.
NA680 .D86 1985
    NYPL [3-MQV+ 86-3952]

Duomo. Il Duomo di Pisa . Firenze , c1989. 236 p. : ISBN 88-404-1204-2 DDC 726/.6/094555 20
NA5621.P713 D86 1989
    NYPL [3-MRBN+ 90-10929]

DUOMO DI MESSINA.
Barbera, Gioacchino. I bozzetti di Sartorio per il Duomo di Messina /. Palermo , c1989. 158 p. : ISBN 88-7681-048-X :
NC257.S2685 B37 1989

DUOMO DI MONZA.
Il Duomo di Monza /. Milano , 1990. 2 v. : DDC 726/.6/09451 20
NA5621.M954 D8 1990

DUOMO DI ORVIETO.
Testa, Giusi. La Cattedrale di Orvieto . [Roma] , c1990. 249, [2] p. : ISBN 88-24-00040-1 DDC 726/.6/0945652 20
NA5621.O426 T4 1990

DUOMO DI PAVIA.
Gianani, Faustino. Il Duomo di Pavia 1488-1932 /. Pavia , c1989. 108 p. : ISBN 88-7129-191-3
    NYPL [3-MRBN+ 91-3663]

Il Duomo di Pavia 1488-1932 /. Gianani, Faustino. Pavia , c1989. 108 p. : ISBN 88-7129-191-3
    NYPL [3-MRBN+ 91-3663]

Il Duomo di Pisa : il Battistero, il Campanile / a cura di Enzo Carli ; presentazione di Giuseppe Toniolo ; [testi di Enzo Carli ... et al.]. Firenze : Nardini, c1989. 236 p. : col. ill. ; 32 cm. (Chiese monumentali d'Italia) Spine title: Il Duomo. Includes bibliographical references (p. 233-236). ISBN 88-404-1204-2 DDC 726/.6/094555 20
1. Duomo (Pisa, Italy). Battistero. 2. Christian art and symbolism - Medieval, 500-1500 - Italy - Pisa. 3. Duomo (Pisa, Italy). 4. Leaning Tower (Pisa, Italy). 5. Pisa (Italy) - Buildings, structures, etc. I. Carli, Enzo,

1910-. II. Title: Duomo. III. Series.
NA5621.P713 D86 1989
    NYPL [3-MRBN+ 90-10929]

Duomo di Siena. Carli, Enzo, 1910- Il Museo dell'opera del duomo /. Siena , 1989. 63 p., [16] p. of plates :
    NYPL [3-MAVZ (Siena) 90-12388]

Il duomo di Tolmezzo . Marcolini, Silvia. Udine , c1990. 137, [4] p. :
IN PROCESS (ONLINE)
    NYPL [3-MRBD+ 91-6937]

DUOMO DI TOLMEZZO.
Marcolini, Silvia. Il duomo di Tolmezzo . Udine , c1990. 137, [4] p. :
IN PROCESS (ONLINE)
    NYPL [3-MRBD+ 91-6937]

DUOMO (PISA, ITALY)
Il Duomo di Pisa . Firenze , c1989. 236 p. : ISBN 88-404-1204-2 DDC 726/.6/094555 20
NA5621.P713 D86 1989
    NYPL [3-MRBN+ 90-10929]

DUOMO (PISA, ITALY). BATTISTERO.
Il Duomo di Pisa . Firenze , c1989. 236 p. : ISBN 88-404-1204-2 DDC 726/.6/094555 20
NA5621.P713 D86 1989
    NYPL [3-MRBN+ 90-10929]

Duperrex, Michèle. Pelichet, Edgar. La céramique art déco /. Lausanne , Paris , c1988. 199 p. : ISBN 2-88148-007-1 DDC 738/.09/041 20
NK3930.3.A77 P4 1988
    NYPL [3-MPC+ 90-11744]

Dupin, Jacques. Michaux, Henri, 1899- Henri Michaux /. Paris , c1990. 31 p. : ISBN 2-85587-182-4
    NYPL [3-MCO+ M61 90-13365]

Duplani Tucci, Giuliana. Venini . Milano [1989] 222 p. : ISBN 88-21-60127-7
    NYPL [3-MPW+ 91-4803]

Dupont, Jacques. The seventeenth century; the new developments in art from Caravaggio to Vermeer. Text by Jacques Dupont and François Mathey. Translated by S. J. C. Harrison. Geneva, New York, Skira [1951] 136 p. : mounted col. illus. ; 29 cm. (The Great centuries of painting) Includes index. Bibliography: p. 132. DDC 750.903
1. Painting - History. 2. Paintings. 3. Painters. I. Mathey, François. II. Title. III. Series.
ND180 .D8   *NYPL [MC 90-11578]*

Duppen, L. M. J. Klement, Fon, 1930- Fon Klement /. Venlo, Nederland , c1990. 136 p. : ISBN 90-6216-195-2 :
N6953.K48 A4 1990

Dupré-Lafon. Couvrat Desvergnes, Thierry, 1945- Paul Dupré-Lafon, décorateur des millionnaires /. Paris, France , c1990. 206, [2] p. : ISBN 2-901151-45-0 (Editions de l'Amateur) DDC 747.24 20
NK2049.Z9 D8633 1990

Dupré Lafon, décorateur des millionnaires. Couvrat Desvergnes, Thierry, 1945- Paul Dupré-Lafon, décorateur des millionnaires /. Paris, France , c1990. 206, [2] p. : ISBN 2-901151-45-0 (Editions de l'Amateur) DDC 747.24 20
NK2049.Z9 D8633 1990

Dupré-Lafon, Paul, 1900-1971.
Couvrat Desvergnes, Thierry, 1945- Paul Dupré-Lafon, décorateur des millionnaires /. Paris, France , c1990. 206, [2] p. : ISBN 2-901151-45-0 (Editions de l'Amateur) DDC 747.24 20
NK2049.Z9 D8633 1990

DUPRÉ-LAFON, PAUL, 1900-1971 - CRITICISM AND INTERPRETATION.
Couvrat Desvergnes, Thierry, 1945- Paul Dupré-Lafon, décorateur des millionnaires /. Paris, France , c1990. 206, [2] p. : ISBN 2-901151-45-0 (Editions de l'Amateur) DDC 747.24 20
NK2049.Z9 D8633 1990

DURACAMPS, RAFAEL, 1891-1979 - EXHIBITIONS.
Durancamps, Rafael, 1891-1979. Rafael Durancamps entre 1915-1945 . Barcelona , c1990. 166 p. : ISBN 84-7664-268-7
ND813.D87 A4 1990

Durancamps, Rafael, 1891-1979. Rafael Durancamps entre 1915-1945 : exposició

organitzada per la Caixa de Pensions. 1. ed.
Barcelona : Sala d'Exposicions de la Caixa de
Pensions, c1990. 166 p. : ill. (some col.) ; 22
cm. Catalan and Spanish.   ISBN 84-7664-268-7
*1. Duracamps, Rafael, 1891-1979 - Exhibitions. I.
Fundació Caixa de Pensions (Barcelona, Spain). II.
Title.*
ND813.D87 A4 1990

Durand, Régis. Pascal Kern : icônes & sculptures
/ Régis Durand. [Paris] : Marval, c1989. [16]
p., 15 plates : ill. (chiefly col., some folded),
port. ; 22 x 24 cm. Includes bibliographical
references (p. [16]).   ISBN 2-86234-035-9
*1. Kern, Pascal, 1952-. I. Kern, Pascal, 1952-. II. Title.
III. Title: Icônes & sculptures. IV. Title: Icônes et
sculptures.*   **NYPL [3-MGO (Kern) 91-3283]**

**DURANGO (MEXICO) - BUILDINGS,
    STRUCTURES, ETC.**
Guerrero Romero, Javier. El Palacio Escárzaga,
Durango /. Durango, Dgo., México , 1988. xii,
82 p. :   ISBN 968-609-400-8
NA757.D87 G84 1986

Duras, Marguerite. Gibson, Ralph. L'histoire de
France /. New York, N.Y., c1991. 119 p. :
ISBN 0-89381-471-7
                NYPL [MFX+ (Gibson) 91-7448]

Durch den Tag laufen : Gedichte, Geschichten,
Bilder / [die Auswahl besorgten Helmut
Preissler (Lyrik), Wolfgang Speer (Bild), Martin
Viertel (Prosa) ; das Nachwort schrieb Hannes
Würtz].1. Aufl. Berlin : Verlag Tribüne, 1989.
287 p. : ill. (some col.) ; 23 cm.   ISBN
3-7303-0434-8
*1. German literature - Germany, East. 2. German
literature - 20th century. 3. Art, German - Germany,
East. 4. Art, Modern - 20th century - Germany, East.
I. Preissler, Helmut. II. Speer, Wolfgang. III. Viertel,
Martin.*
PT3732 .D87 1989
                NYPL [3-MAMG 90-10453]

Durer, Albert. see Dürer, Albrecht, 1471-1528.

**DÜRER, ALBRECHT, 1471-1528 - CRITICISM
    AND INTERPRETATION.**
Eisler, Colin. Dürer's animals /. Washington ,
1991. p. cm.   ISBN 0-87474-408-3 DDC 760/.092
20
N6888.D8 E57 1991

Rebel, Ernst. Die Modellierung der Person .
Stuttgart , 1990. 151 p. :   ISBN 3-515-05690-4
                        NYPL [3-MCK D85 91-7043]

Dürer aux Pays-Bas. Albert Dürer aux Pays-Bas .
Bruxelles , 1977. xxiii, 211, 144 p., [14] leaves
of plates :
N6888.D8 A4 1977
                        NYPL [3-MCK D85 81-320]

Dürer's animals /. Eisler, Colin. Washington ,
1991. p. cm.   ISBN 0-87474-408-3 DDC 760/.092
20
N6888.D8 E57 1991

Duret-Robert, François, 1932- Le Grand livre des
ventes aux enchères /. Paris [1988] 288 p. :
ISBN 2-7144-2265-9 (Belfond)   DDC 707/.5 20
N8675 .G68 1988

**DUREZ, LISE - CRITICISM AND
    INTERPRETATION.**
Cruysmans, Philippe, 1925- Lise Durez peint
Victor Hugo /. Bruxelles [1986] 183 p. :   ISBN
2-87103-023-5
N6973.D85 C7 1986

DURHAM (ENGLAND) - MAPS.
Geographers' A-Z Map Company.
Newcastle-Upon-Tyne, Sunderland, City of
Durham . Sevenoaks, Kent , c1988. 1 atlas
(144, [86] p.) :   **NYPL [Map Div. 90-13146]**

Durham indological series, 0951-7863 .
(no. 2) Symbols in art and religion . London ,
Glenn Dale, MD , 1990. xiii, 221 p. :   ISBN
0-913215-69-4 DDC 704.94894 20
N7301   **NYPL [3-MAF 91-6383]**

Durham, Jimmie.
Jimmie Durham : the bishop's moose and the
pinkerton men : November 1-December 2, 1989
/ curator Jeanette Ingberman ; texts, Papo
Colo ... [et al.]. New York : Exit Art, c1990. 37
p. : ill. ; 28 cm. Includes bibliographical references.
*1. Durham, Jimmie - Exhibitions. I. Colo, 1946-. II.
Ingberman, Jeanette, 1952-. III. Exit Art (Gallery :
New York, N.Y.). IV. Title. V. Title: Bishop's moose
and the pinkerton men.*
                        NYPL [3-MGO (Durham) 90-10679]

DURHAM, JIMMIE - EXHIBITIONS.
Durham, Jimmie. Jimmie Durham . New York ,
c1990. 37 p. :
                        NYPL [3-MGO (Durham) 90-10679]

Durliat, Marcel. La sculpture romane de la route
de Saint-Jacques : de Conques à Compostelle /
Marcel Durliat. Mont-de-Marsan : Comité
d'études sur l'histoire et l'art de la Gascogne,
c1990. 508 p. : ill. ; 32 cm. Includes bibliographical
references (p. [471]-491) and index.   ISBN
2-9501584-1-2 :
*1. Sculpture, Romanesque - France, Southwest. 2.
Sculpture, French - France, Southwest. 3. Sculpture,
Romanesque - Spain, Northern. 4. Sculpture, Spanish -
Spain, Northern. 5. Christian pilgrims and pilgrimages -
Spain - Santiago de Compostela. I. Title.*
NB549.S7 D87 1990

Duró, Gábor. Erdély és a Részek térképe és
helységnévtára . Szeged , 1987 ([Budapest] :
Franklin Nyomda) 1 atlas (41, 214 p., [9] p. of
plates) :   ISBN 963-481-771-8 :   DDC 912/.4984 19
G2037.T7 E7 1987
                        NYPL [Map Div. 91-145]

Durozoi, Gérard. Matisse / par Gérard Durozoi.
Paris : Hazan, c1989. 138, [5] p. : ill. (some
col.) ; 31 cm. Bibliography: p. [140]   ISBN
2-85025-194-1
*1. Matisse, Henri, 1869-1954. I. Matisse, Henri,
1869-1954. II. Title.*
                        NYPL [3-MCO+ M43 91-2641]

Durrell, Julie. (ill) Werner, Vivian L. Dolls . New
York, NY , c1991. 120 p. :   ISBN
0-380-76044-4 :   DDC 688.7/221/09 20
NK4894.A2 W43 1991

Duschek, Karl.
Visuelle Kommunikation . Berlin , c1989. 344
p. :   ISBN 3-496-01061-4
                        NYPL [3-MDW 90-12434]
Visuelle Kommunikation . Berlin , c1989. 344
p. :   ISBN 3-496-01061-4
NC1000 .V58 1989

Dušek, Bohuslav, 1886-1957.
Národní galerie V Praze. Sbírka Bohuslava
Duška . [Prague] [1990?] 131 p. :
N5280.C952 D876 1990

**DUŠEK, BOHUSLAV, 1886-1957 - ART
    COLLECTIONS - EXHIBITIONS.**
Národní galerie V Praze. Sbírka Bohuslava
Duška . [Prague] [1990?] 131 p. :
N5280.C952 D876 1990

Dusserudorufu Shiritsukindai Bijutsukan. see
Städtische Kunsthalle Düsseldorf.

DUTCH ART. see ART, DUTCH.

Dutch arts.
Visual arts in the Netherlands /. The Hague
[1989] 46 p. :   DDC 709/.492 20
N6947 .V57 1989
                        NYPL [3-MAME 91-5917]

Dutch church painters : Saenredam's Great
Church at Haarlem in context : National
Gallery of Scotland, 6 July-9 September 1984.
Edinburgh : National Galleries of Scotland,
c1984. 64 p. : ill. (some col.) ; 30 cm. Catalog of
a loan exhibition. "Festival of Architecture." Includes
index. Bibliography: p. 62.   ISBN 0-903148-54-4 (pbk.)
DDC 758/.7/09492074029134 19
*1. Saenredam, Pieter Jansz, 1597-1665. Sint Bavo-kerk
te Haarlem (1648) - Exhibitions. 2. Churches in art -
Exhibitions. 3. Painting, Dutch - Exhibitions. 4.
Painting, Modern - 17th-18th centuries - Netherlands -
Exhibitions. 5. Perspective - Exhibitions. I. National
Gallery of Scotland.*
ND1412.N43 D88 1984
                        NYPL [3-MCG+ 91-5468]

Dutch houses and castles /. Guillermo, Jorge.
London , New York, N.Y. , c1990. 208 p. :
ISBN 1-85043-237-6 DDC 720.9492 20
                        NYPL [3-MQW+ 91-3636]

DUTCH PAINTING. see PAINTING, DUTCH.

Dutch silver. Nederlands zilver =.
's-Gravenhage , 1979. L, 390 p. :   ISBN
90-12-02571-0 (pbk.) :   DDC 739.2/37492/074
NK7154.A1 N42   **NYPL [MNO 80-2184]**

DUTCH WIT AND HUMOR, PICTORIAL.
Straaten, Peter van. This literary life /.
Minneapolis , 1991. p. cm.   ISBN 0-918273-92-7
(pbk.) :   DDC 741.5/9492 20
NC1549.S8 A4 1991

Dutta, Monoranjan, 1961- Sculpture of Assam /
Monoranjan Dutta. Delhi : Agam Kala
Prakashan, 1990. 173 p., [53] p. of plates : ill. ;
25 cm. From the earliest time to 1826. Includes index.
Includes bibliographical references (p. [142]-145)
ISBN 81-7186-001-X :   DDC 730/.954/162 20
1. Sculpture, Indic - India - Assam. I. Title.
NB1007.A5 D88 1990
                        NYPL [3-MGI 91-4454]

Düttmann, W. Werner Düttmann . Basel ,
Boston , c1990. 322 p. :   ISBN 3-7643-2413-9
                        NYPL [3-MQZ (Düttmann) 91-5517]

DÜTTMANN, W.
Werner Düttmann . Basel , Boston , c1990. 322
p. :   ISBN 3-7643-2413-9
                        NYPL [3-MQZ (Düttmann) 91-5517]

Dutton, Thomas A. Voices in architectural
education . New York , 1991. p. cm.   ISBN
0-89789-253-4 (alk. paper) DDC 720/.7/073 20
NA2105 .V65 1991

Duval-Carrié, Edouard, 1954-
Revolution française sous les tropiques . [Paris ,
1989] 74 p. :   **NYPL [3-MCY 91-5057]**

**DUVAL-CARRIÉ, EDOUARD, 1954- -
    EXHIBITIONS.**
Revolution française sous les tropiques . [Paris ,
1989] 74 p. :   **NYPL [3-MCY 91-5057]**

Duve, Thierry de. The Definitively unfinished
Marcel Duchamp /. Halifax, N.S. , Cambridge,
Mass. , 1991. p. cm.   ISBN 0-262-04117-0 DDC
709/.2 20
N6853.D8 D44 1991

**Dvadeset i chetiri tvorbi ot Bachkovskiĭa
manastir.** Santova, Mila. 24 zlatarski tvorbi ot
Bachkovskiĭa manastir /. Sofiĭa , 1990. 47 p. :
NK7215 .S34 1990

Dwellings : Institute of Contemporary Art,
University of Pennsylvania, Philadelphia,
Pennsylvania, 20 October to 25 November
1978. Philadelphia : The Institute, c1978. 16
p. : ill. ; 30 cm. "[Lenders to the exhibition]: Alice
Adams ... [et al.]" ISBN 0-88454-050-2
*1. Art, American - Exhibitions. 2. Art, Modern - 20th
century - United States - Exhibitions. 3. Architecture
in art - Exhibitions. I. Pennsylvania. University. Institute
of Contemporary Art.*
N6512 .D85   **NYPL [3-MAMT+ 79-2026]**

DWELLINGS - ALGERIA - ALGIERS.
Golvin, Lucien. Palais et demeures d'Alger à la
période ottomane /. Aix-en-Provence [1988]
141 p., [16] p. of plates :   ISBN 2-85744-307-2
                        NYPL [3-MQT+ 90-4959]

DWELLINGS - FRANCE.
Loyer, François. Henri Sauvage . Bruxelles ,
1987. 159 p. :   ISBN 2-87009-304-7 (pbk.)
                        NYPL [3-MQZ (Savage) 90-12030]

DWELLINGS - FRANCE - MOSELLE.
Massel, Christiane, 1953- Couleurs &
architecture . [Sarreguemines] , c1989. 157 p. :
ISBN 2-7085-0075-9 DDC 728/.0944/3825 20
NA3549.A3 M676 1989

**DWELLINGS - GERMANY (WEST) -
    COLOGNE.**
Heinen, Werner. Köln . Köln , 1988. 327 p. :
ISBN 3-7616-0929-9
                        NYPL [3-MQWD 91-5588]

DWELLINGS - GREECE.
Schattner, Thomas G. Griechische
Hausmodelle . Berlin , c1990. 229 p., [29] p. of
plates :   ISBN 3-7861-1585-0
                        NYPL [3-MQM 91-6516]

DWELLINGS IN ART.
Devlin, Harry. Portraits of American
architecture . Boston , 1989. 191 p. :   ISBN
0-87923-793-7 :   DDC 759.13 19
ND237.D43 A4 1989
                        NYPL [3-MRG+ 90-2829]

DWELLINGS - ITALY - VENICE.
Zorzi, Alvise. I palazzi veneziani /. Udine ,
c1989. 537 p. :   ISBN 88-7057-083-5
                        NYPL [3- MQWB+ 90-10932]

DWELLINGS - LAYOUT. see ROOM LAYOUT
(DWELLINGS)

DWELLINGS - LEBANON.
El-Khoury, Fouad. Domestic architecture in the
Lebanon /. London [1975] 25 p. :
                        NYPL [3-MRG 90-12551]

DWELLINGS - NETHERLANDS - UTRECHT.
Dolfin, Marceline J. Utrecht . 's-Gravenhage ,
1989. 2 v. : ISBN 90-12-05876-7 (set)
NYPL [3-MRG+ 90-12086]

**DWELLINGS - PLANNING - HANDBOOKS,
MANUALS, ETC.**
Myrvang, June Cotner. The home design
handbook . New York , c1992. p. cm. ISBN
0-8050-1833-6 DDC 728 20
NA7115 .M97 1992

**DWELLINGS - PURCHASING -
HANDBOOKS, MANUALS, ETC.**
Myrvang, June Cotner. The home design
handbook . New York , c1992. p. cm. ISBN
0-8050-1833-6 DDC 728 20
NA7115 .M97 1992

**DWELLINGS - REMODELING -
HANDBOOKS, MANUALS, ETC.**
Myrvang, June Cotner. The home design
handbook . New York , c1992. p. cm. ISBN
0-8050-1833-6 DDC 728 20
NA7115 .M97 1992

DWELLINGS - ROME.
Roman art in the private sphere . Ann Arbor ,
c1991. 156 p. : ISBN 0-472-10196-X (alk. paper)
DDC 747.2937 20
N5760 .R66 1991

**DWELLINGS - UNITED STATES - ACCESS
FOR THE PHYSICALLY
HANDICAPPED.**
The Accessible housing design file /. New
York, N.Y. , c1991. p. cm. ISBN 0-442-00775-2
DDC 728/.042 20
NA2545.P5 A34 1991

**DWELLINGS - UNITED STATES -
HISTORY - 19TH CENTURY.**
Devlin, Harry. Portraits of American
architecture . Boston , 1989. 191 p. : ISBN
0-87923-793-7 : DDC 759.13 19
ND237.D43 A4 1989
NYPL [3-MRG+ 90-2829]

**DWELLINGS - UNITED STATES -
JUVENILE LITERATURE.**
Seltzer, Isadore. The house I live in /. New
York : Toronto : p. cm. ISBN 0-02-781801-2
DDC 728/.0973 20
NA7205 .S375 1992

Dwyer, Nancy. In other words . [Stuttgart]
[1989] 107 p. : ISBN 3-89322-159-X
NYPL [3-MAL 90-8164]

Dybdahl, Lars. Salto, Axel, 1889-1961. Det
brændende nu, Axel Salto . [Copenhagen]
[1989] 78 p. : ISBN 87-87075-60-1
N7023.S25 A4 1989

Dyer, Rod. Coast to coast : the best of travel
decal art / Rod Dyer, Brad Benedict, and
David Lees. New York : Abbeville Press, 1991.
p. cm. ISBN 1-558-59156-7 DDC 741.6/92/0973
20
*1. Travel labels - United States - Themes, motives. I.
Benedict, Brad. II. Lees, David, 1950-. III. Title.*
NC1002.L3 D94 1991

E. A. Seemann Verlag. Allgemeines
Künstlerlexikon . Leipzig , 1983- v. : ISBN
3-363-00114-2 (v. 1) DDC 709/.2/2 B 19
N40 .A63 1983   *NYPL [MAO 85-1702]*

E.C. Eirich (1877-1929) . Eirich, E. C. (Edward
Conrad), 1877-1929. [Philadelphia, Pa.] , c1991.
48 p. : *NYPL [3-MCX E35 91-7603]*

E.G. Bührle collection, master paintings. The
passionate eye . [Zurich?] , Zurich , c1990. 244
p. : ISBN 0-8478-1215-4
NYPL [3-MAX (Bührle) 90-12982]

E.L. Kirchner. Moeller, Magdalena M. Ernst
Ludwig Kirchner . Stuttgart , c1990. 344 p. :
ISBN 3-7757-0301-2 DDC 769.92 20
NE654.K4 A4 1990

E. M. Donahue Gallery.
Cyphers, Peggy, 1954- Peggy Cyphers . New
York [1990] [12] p. :
NYPL [3-MCX C996 91-6446]
Schmit, Randall. Randall Schmit . New York,
N.Y. [1990] [12] p. :
NYPL [3-MCX S357 91-6439]

E.W. Nay, a retrospective. Nay, E. W. (Ernst
Wilhelm), 1902-1968. E.W. Nay, Retrospektive
/. Köln , c1990. 210 p. : ISBN 3-7701-2726-9
NYPL [3-MCK+ N331 91-5930]

E.W. Nay, Retrospektive /. Nay, E. W. (Ernst
Wilhelm), 1902-1968. Köln, c1990. 210 p. :
ISBN 3-7701-2726-9
NYPL [3-MCK+ N331 91-5930]

Eadie, William, 1948- Movements of modernity :
the case of Glasgow and art nouveau / William
Eadie. London : New York, NY : Routledge,
1990. viii, 292 p. ; 23 cm. Includes bibliographical
references (p. 274-285) and index. ISBN
0-415-03243-1 DDC 709/.414/4309034 20
*1. Mackintosh, Charles Rennie, 1868-1928 - Influence.
2. Glasgow School of Art. 3. Art nouveau - Scotland -
Glasgow. 4. Art, Modern - 19th century - Scotland -
Glasgow. 5. Art, Modern - 20th century - Scotland -
Glasgow. I. Title.*
N6781.G55 E26 1991
NYPL [3-MAMR 90-13191]

Eagle, Mary, 1944-
Australian modern painting : between the wars :
1914-1939 / Mary Eagle ; general editor,
Jennifer Phipps. Sydney : Bay Books, 1990. 216
p. : ill. ; 33 cm. ISBN 1-86256-427-2
1. Painting, Modern - 20th century - Australia. I. Title.
NYPL [3-MCY+ 90-13348]
1990 Adelaide Biennial of Australian art / by
Mary Eagle ; with essays by Merlin Brown ...
[et al.]. Adelaide : Art Gallery Board of South
Australia, 1990. 113 p. : ill. (some col.) ; 30
cm. Exhibition held at the Art Gallery of South
Australia, Mar. 2 - Apr. 22, 1990. ISBN
0-7308-0773-8
*1. Art, Australian - Exhibitions. 2. Art, Modern - 20th
century - Australia - Exhibitions. I. Art Gallery of
South Australia. II. Adelaide Biennial of Australian Art
(1990). III. Title.* *NYPL [3-MAM+ 91-5044]*

Eagles . Goggin, Bill. New Market, MD (Box
277, New Market 21774) [1990] xv, 319 p. :
DDC 749.214/09/033075 20
NK2406 .G6 1990

Eagles, Americana at auction. Goggin, Bill.
Eagles . New Market, MD (Box 277, New
Market 21774) [1990] xv, 319 p. : DDC
749.214/09/033075 20
NK2406 .G6 1990

Eagles (New Market, Frederick County, Md.)
Goggin, Bill. Eagles . New Market, MD (Box
277, New Market 21774) [1990] xv, 319 p. :
DDC 749.214/09/033075 20
NK2406 .G6 1990

Eakins, Susan Macdowell. Foster, Kathleen A.
Writing about Eakins . Philadelphia , c1989.
xiv, 411 p. : ISBN 0-8122-8107-1 DDC 016.7/092
20
Z6616.E23 F67 1989 ND237.E15
NYPL [3-MCX E12 90-10747]

EAKINS, SUSAN MACDOWELL.
Foster, Kathleen A. Writing about Eakins .
Philadelphia , c1989. xiv, 411 p. : ISBN
0-8122-8107-1 DDC 016.7/092 20
Z6616.E23 F67 1989 ND237.E15
NYPL [3-MCX E12 90-10747]

Eakins, Thomas, 1844-1916. Foster, Kathleen A.
Writing about Eakins . Philadelphia , c1989.
xiv, 411 p. : ISBN 0-8122-8107-1 DDC 016.7/092
20
Z6616.E23 F67 1989 ND237.E15
NYPL [3-MCX E12 90-10747]

EAKINS, THOMAS, 1844-1916.
Foster, Kathleen A. Writing about Eakins .
Philadelphia , c1989. xiv, 411 p. : ISBN
0-8122-8107-1 DDC 016.7/092 20
Z6616.E23 F67 1989 ND237.E15
NYPL [3-MCX E12 90-10747]

Eames, Sarah Sink. Barbie fashion / Sarah Sink
Eames. Paducah, Ky. : Collector Books, c1990-
v. <1- > : col. ill. ; 29 cm. CONTENTS. - v. 1.
1959-1967 ISBN 0-89145-418-7 (v. 1) : DDC
688.7/221/0979493075 20
1. Barbie dolls - Clothing - Catalogs. I. Title.
NK4894.3.B37 E17 1990

Earl, Ralph, 1751-1801.
Kornhauser, Elizabeth Mankin, 1950- Ralph
Earl . New Haven : Yale University Press ; p.
cm. ISBN 0-300-05041-0 (cloth) DDC 759.13 20
ND1329.E23 A4 1991

EARL, RALPH, 1751-1801 - EXHIBITIONS.
Kornhauser, Elizabeth Mankin, 1950- Ralph
Earl . New Haven : Yale University Press ; p.
cm. ISBN 0-300-05041-0 (cloth) DDC 759.13 20
ND1329.E23 A4 1991

Earle, Ralph [i. e., Earl Ralph, 1751-1801] see
Earl, Ralph, 1751-1801.

Earll, Ralph [i. e., Earl Ralph, 1751-1801] see
Earl, Ralph, 1751-1801.

Early American homes for today . Congdon,
Herbert Wheaton, 1876-1965. Dublin, N.H. ,
c1985. xv, 236 p. : ISBN 0-87233-065-6 (pbk.)
DDC 728.3/7/0974 19
NA7210 .C6 1985

Early American pattern glass, 1850-1910 . Jenks,
Bill. Radnor, Pa. , c1990. xv, 602 p. : ISBN
0-87069-545-2 : DDC 748.2913/075 20
NK5439.P36 E18 1990
NYPL [3-MPW 90-11097]

The early art of the West Riding of Yorkshire .
Palmer, Barbara D. Kalamazoo, Mich. , 1990.
xxii, 363 p., [44] p. of plates : ISBN
0-918720-32-X (case) DDC
704.9/482/0942810902 20
N7944.W47 P35 1990

Early Caucasian rugs /. Ellis, Charles Grant,
1908- Washington, D.C. [1975?] 112 p. :
NYPL [3-MOP 90-12476]

EARLY CHRISTIAN ARCHITECTURE. see
ARCHITECTURE, EARLY CHRISTIAN.

EARLY CHRISTIAN ART. see **ART, EARLY
CHRISTIAN.**

**Early colonial homes of the Sydney region,
1788-1838 /.** Kingston, Daphne. Kenthurst,
N.S.W. , 1990. 96 p. : ISBN 0-86417-352-0
NYPL [3-MRG+ 91-3712]

The early criticism of André Salmon .
Gersh-Nešić, Beth S. New York , 1991. p. cm.
ISBN 0-8153-0115-4 (alk. paper) DDC
759.4/09/041 20
N6848.5.C82 G46 1991

Early drama, art, and music reference series .
(5) Sheingorn, Pamela. The Easter sepulchre in
England /. Kalamazoo, MI , 1987. 426 p., [36]
p. of plates : ISBN 0-918720-79-6 (hardbound)
DDC 730/.942/0902 20
NB1912.J47 S48 1987
(6) Palmer, Barbara D. The early art of the
West Riding of Yorkshire . Kalamazoo, Mich. ,
1990. xxii, 363 p., [44] p. of plates : ISBN
0-918720-32-X (case) DDC
704.9/482/0942810902 20
N7944.W47 P35 1990

Early Gothic Saint-Denis . Blum, Pamela Z.
Berkeley , 1992. p. cm. ISBN 0-520-07371-1
(cloth) DDC 730/.944/362 20
NB1910 .B58 1992

Early Italian painting, 1290-1470. Boskovits,
Miklós. The Thyssen-Bornemisza Collection .
London , New York, N.Y., U. S.A. , 1990. 226
p. : ISBN 0-85667-381-1
NYPL [3-MCE+ 91-7306]

**Early medieval wall painting and painted
sculpture in England :** based on the
proceedings of a symposium at the Courtauld
Institute of Art, February 1985 / edited by
Sharon Cather, David Park and Paul
Williamson. Oxford, England : B.A.R., 1990.
xxii, 262 p. ; ill. ; 30 cm. (BAR British series. 216)
ISBN 0-86054-719-1
*1. Mural painting and decoration, Medieval - England -
Congresses. 2. Sculpture, Medieval - England -
Congresses. I. Cather, Sharon.*
NYPL [3-MAMR+ 91-3440]

Early Meissen porcelain in Dresden /.
Menzhausen, Ingelore. [Alt-Meissner Porzellan
in Dresden. English.] New York , 1990. 212
p. : ISBN 0-500-01482-5
NYPL [3-MPGK 90-11978]

Early Mexican houses . Garrison, G. Richard
(George Richard), 1898- [Mexican houses.]
Stamford, Conn. , 1990. xvii, 173 p. : ISBN
0-942655-03-0 : DDC 728/.0972 20
NA7244 .G3 1990
NYPL [3-MQWN+ 91-4465]

**Early photographs of architecture and views in
two Copenhagen libraries.** Bramsen, Henrik
Boe, 1908- Copenhagen , 1957. 92 p. : DDC
779.4
N4015 .B67   *NYPL [MFW 91-4572]*

**Early portrait of San Diego from an artist's
portfolio.** Messenger, Ivan. Not for tourists

only . [San Diego?] c1969 (Los Angeles : Anderson, Ritchie & Simon) 94 p. :
NYPL [3-MAMY 90-7015]

EARLY PRINTED BOOKS. see INCUNABULA.

Early Soviet photography, 1917-1940. 20 Sowjetische Photographen . Amsterdam , 1990. 287 p. : ISBN 90-900327-6-2
NYPL [MFW 91-6715]

Early temples of central Tibet /. Vitali, Roberto. London , 1990. 150 p. : ISBN 0-906026-25-3 :
DDC 951.5 20 **NYPL [3-MAF+ 91-4702]**

Early works by Charles-Edouard Jeanneret-Gris. Le Corbusier, early works by Charles-Edouard Jeanneret-Gris / . London , New York , 1987. 136 p. : ISBN 0-312-47583-7 (paper)
NYPL [3-MQZ+ (Le Corbusier) 87-3750]

The early works of Piet Mondrian. Noah Goldowsky Gallery. New York [1971] [31] p.
NYPL [3-MCH M741 91-876]

Earnshaw, Anthony. An eighth secret alphabet / conceived and drawn by Tony Earnshaw. Church Hanborough, Oxford : Hanborough Parrot Pieces, 1988 ([Didcot? England] : Didcot Press) [23] p. : ill. (chiefly col.) ; 23 cm. "An edition of 95 copies, of which 25 have been hand-coloured by the artist and are numbered with roman numerals"--P. [23]. Sequel to: Seven secret alphabets. "First published by Surrealist Transformations of Sidmouth in 1974"--P. [23]. Printed on double leaves. Ill. on lining papers. LC has copy no. XXI, signed by the artist. DLC Source: Purchase, July 27, 1990. DLC DDC 741.5/942 20
1. Alphabets - Caricatures and cartoons. 2. English wit and humor, Pictorial. 3. Surrealism - England. I. Title. II. Title: 8th secret alphabet.
NC1479.E37 A4 1988

Earp, Thomas. Mitchell, Anthony. Thomas Earp, master of stone . Buckingham (England) , 1990. 112 p. : ISBN 0-86023-463-0
NYPL [3-MGO (Earp) 91-4519]

EARP, THOMAS.
Mitchell, Anthony. Thomas Earp, master of stone . Buckingham (England) , 1990. 112 p. : ISBN 0-86023-463-0
NYPL [3-MGO (Earp) 91-4519]

EARTH, EFFECT OF MAN ON. see MAN - INFLUENCE ON NATURE.

The earth mother /. Jayakar, Pupul. New Delhi, India , New York, N.Y., U. S. A. , 1989. 229 p., [32] p. of plates : ISBN 0-14-012352-0 : DDC 704.9/4894/0954 20
NX576.A1 J38 1989
NYPL [3-MAF 91-3706]

The earth mother . Jayakar, Pupul. San Francisco, Calif. , c1990. xxx, 248 p., [32] p. of plates : ISBN 0-06-250405-3 : DDC 700/.954 20
N8191.I4 J39 1990 **NYPL [3-MAF 91-5051]**

EARTH SHELTERED HOUSES - CHINA.
Golany, Gideon. Chinese earth-sheltered dwellings . Honolulu , c1992. p. cm. ISBN 0-8248-1369-3 DDC 728/.0473/0951 20
NA7448 .G6 1992

EARTHENWARE. see POTTERY.

The earthly paradise . Hofmann, Werner, 1928- New York , 1961. 436 p. :
ND457 .H613 **NYPL [3-MAL+ 90-10772]**

EARTHWORKS (ART)
Adcock, Craig E. James Turrell . Berkeley , c1990. xxiv, 272 p., [32] p. of plates : ISBN 0-520-06728-2 (alk. paper) DDC 709/.2 20
N6537.T78 A84 1990
NYPL [3-MCX+ T941 91-5229]

Goldsworthy, Andy. Andy Goldsworthy. London , 1990. [120] p. : ISBN 0-670-83213-8 : DDC 709.2 20 **NYPL [3-MGO+ (Goldsworthy) 90-11987]**

EARTHWORKS (ART) - UNITED STATES - CATALOGS.
Sonfist, Alan. Alan Sonfist, 1969-1989 . Brookville, N.Y. [1990] 80 p. : ISBN 0-933699-16-6 DDC 709/.2 20
N6537.S64 A4 1990
NYPL [3-MGO (Sonfist) 91-4000]

East Asian lacquer . Metropolitan Museum of Art (New York, N.Y.) New York , 1991. p. cm. ISBN 0-87099-622-3 DDC

745.7/26/09510747471 20
NK9900.7.E15 M47 1991

EAST FLANDERS (BELGIUM) - ROAD MAPS.
Alle straten en straatjes van Oost-Vlaanderen. De Pinte , 1985. 1 atlas (267 p.) :
NYPL [Map Div. 90-11660]

East Hampton avant-garde : a salute to the Signa Gallery, 1957-1960 : Guild Hall Museum, East Hampton Center for Contemporary Art, East Hampton, New York, 12 August-23 September 1990 / Helen A. Harrison, guest curator. [East Hampton] : Guild Hall of East Hampton, c1990. 68 p. : ill. ; 21 x 23 cm. ISBN 0-933793-14-6
1. Signa Gallery - Exhibitions. I. Harrison, Helen A. II. Guild Hall of East Hampton. III. East Hampton Center for Contemporary Art. **NYPL [3-MAW (East Hampton) 90-13535]**

East Hampton Center for Contemporary Art. East Hampton avant-garde . [East Hampton] , c1990. 68 p. : ISBN 0-933793-14-6
NYPL [3-MAW (East Hampton) 90-13535]

East Hampton, N. Y. Guild Hall. see Guild Hall of East Hampton.

EAST INDIANS IN NORTH AMERICA - POLITICS AND GOVERNMENT.
Josh, Sohan Singh, 1898- Hindustan Gadar Party . New Delhi , 1977. 1 v. ;
DS480.45 .J66 **NYPL [JLK 80-148]**

EAST INDIANS - NORTH AMERICA - POLITICS AND GOVERNMENT.
Josh, Sohan Singh, 1898- Hindustan Gadar Party . New Delhi , 1977-1978. 2 v. ;
DS480.45 .J66 **NYPL [JLL 79-458]**

East Kent street atlas : 3 1/2 inches to 1 mile. Maybush, Southampton : Ordnance Survey ; London : George Philip, 1989. 1 atlas (viii, 238 p.) : maps ; 28 cm. "East of the Medway, including all of Rochester and Maidstone."--Cover. Includes indexes. ISBN 0-540-05559-X : DDC 912.4223 20
1. Streets - England - Kent - Maps. 2. Kent (England) - Maps. I. Great Britain. Ordnance Survey.
NYPL [Map Div. 91-174]

East Meets West Cultural International. East meets west in design . New York, NY , c[1987] 85 p. : ISBN 0-9621872-0-8
NYPL [3-MNF + 89-25263]

East meets west in design : archaeology of the present / [editor, Allan Klusacek]. New York, NY : East Meets West Cultural International, c[1987] 85 p. : col. ill. ; 34 cm. Cover title. "The exhibition is the culmination of an international design competition among Japanese and Western architects, artists and designers, submitting works reflecting cross-cultural influences, accelerated by today's increasing economic interdependence between countries"--Foreword. One article in Japanese. ISBN 0-9621872-0-8
I. Klusacek, Allan. II. East Meets West Cultural International. **NYPL [3-MNF + 89-25263]**

EASTER EGGS - RUSSIAN S.F.S.R. - THEMES, MOTIVES.
Fabergé, Peter Carl, 1846-1920. Fabergé and the Russian master goldsmiths /. New York , 1991. p. cm. ISBN 0-517-02733-X DDC 739.2/092 20
NK7398.F32 A4 1991

EASTER EGGS - UKRAINE - THEMES, MOTIVES.
Shcherbakivs´kyĭ, V. Osnovni elementy ornamentatsiï ukraïns´kykh pysanok ta ïkhniē pokhodzhennia /. Ottava , Philadelphia , 1990. 32 p. :
NK4900 .S47 1990

The Easter sepulchre in England /. Sheingorn, Pamela. Kalamazoo, MI , 1987. 426 p., [36] p. of plates : ISBN 0-918720-79-6 (hardbound) DDC 730/.942/0902 20
NB1912.J47 S48 1987

Easterling, Keller, 1959- Seaside /. New York, N.Y. , c1991. p. cm. ISBN 0-910413-26-6 (paper) : DDC 720/.9759/41 20
NA735.S44 S43 1991

Eastern Orthodox Church. see Orthodox Eastern Church.

Eastman Kodak Company.
Young America . New York , 1990. 144 p. : ISBN 0-8264-0479-0 : DDC 779/.2/097307473

20
TR681.F28 Y68 1990
NYPL [MFW 91-3590]

EASTMAN KODAK COMPANY - HISTORY.
Collins, Douglas, 1945- The story of Kodak /. New York , 1990. 392 p. : ISBN 0-8109-1222-8 DDC 338.7/681418/0973 20
HD9708.U64 E273 1990
NYPL [MFW+ 91-5847]

EATING. see DINNERS AND DINING.

Eatwell, John. New Palgrave. Selections. The New Palgrave . London , 1991. xi, 756 p. : ISBN 0-333-55177-X (pbk.) : DDC 330 20
HB171 **NYPL [*R-Econ. HB171 .N48]**

EAU CLAIRE COUNTY (WIS.) - MAPS.
Rockford Map Publishers. Eau Claire County, Wisconsin, land atlas & plat book . Rockford, Ill. , Altoona, Wis. [c1990] 1 atlas (69 p.) :
NYPL [Map Div. 91-4028]

Eau Claire County, Wisconsin, land atlas & plat book . Rockford Map Publishers. Rockford, Ill. , Altoona, Wis. [c1990] 1 atlas (69 p.) :
NYPL [Map Div. 91-4028]

Euclaire, Sally. The cat in photography / Sally Euclaire. 1st ed. Boston : Little, Brown, c1990. 198 p. : ill. ; 25 cm. "A Bulfinch Press book." ISBN 0-8212-1782-8 DDC 779/.092 20
1. Photography of cats. I. Title.
TR729.C3 E28 1990 **NYPL [MFW 91-2489]**

E.B. Crocker Art Gallery. West Coast watercolor [transparent watercolor paintings, by members of the West Coast Watercolor Society. Sacramento, 1970] [28] p. illus. 23cm. Cover title. Exhibition held Dec. 13, 1970-Jan. 9, 1971.
1. Watercolor painting, American - Pacific Coast (U. S.) - Exhibitions. 2. Painting, Modern - 20th century - Pacific Coast (U. S.) - Exhibitions. 3. Painting - Pacific Coast (U. S.) - Exhibitions. I. West Coast Watercolor Society. II. Title. **NYPL [3-MCW 91-794]**

Ebenezer Society. see Amana Society.

Eberhard Viegener . Kerber, Bernhard. Soest , c1990. 198 p. : ISBN 3-87902-503-7
IN PROCESS (ONLINE)
NYPL [MDG (Viegener) 91-7277]

Eberhard Viegener, 1890-1967 /. Viegener, Eberhard, 1890-1967. Soest , c1990. 207 p. : ISBN 3-87902-551-7
NYPL [3-MCK V65 91-5324]

Eberhard Viegener, 1890-1967 /. Viegener, Eberhard, 1890-1967. Soest , c1990. 207 p. : ISBN 3-87902-551-7 DDC 760/.092 20
N6888.V485 A4 1990

Eberhard Wenzel . Herrmann, Ursula. Berlin , c1989. 210 p. ; ISBN 3-374-00804-6 DDC 780/.92 B 20
NK410.W464 H5 1989

Eberlein, K. Die Bonnerinnen . [Bonn , 1988. 333 p. : **NYPL [3-MAMG+ 89-25284]**

The Eccentric painters of Yangzhou /. Giacalone, Vito. New York City , 1990. 92 p. : ISBN 0-295-97087-1 **NYPL [3-MAG 91-6594]**

ECCLESIASTICAL ARCHITECTURE. see CHURCH ARCHITECTURE.

ECCLESIASTICAL ART. see CHRISTIAN ART AND SYMBOLISM.

ECCLESIASTICAL EMBROIDERY - CONSERVATION AND RESTORATION - ITALY - ASCOLI PICENO.
Il Piviale duecentesco di Ascoli Piceno . Firenze , 1991. 180 p. : ISBN 88-7737-143-9 :
NK9310 .P58 1991

ECCLESIASTICAL EMBROIDERY, MEDIEVAL - CONSERVATION AND RESTORATION - ITALY - ASCOLI PICENO.
Il Piviale duecentesco di Ascoli Piceno . Firenze , 1991. 180 p. : ISBN 88-7737-143-9 :
NK9310 .P58 1991

ECCLESIASTICAL EMBROIDERY - RUSSIAN S.F.S.R. - EXHIBITIONS.
Gosudarstvennye muzei Moskovskogo Kremlia. Russkoe khudozhestvennoe shit´e XIV-nachala XVIII veka . Moskva , 1989. 135 p. :
NK9310 .G67 1989

ECCLESIASTICAL FURNITURE. see CHURCH FURNITURE.

ECCLESIASTICAL RITES AND CEREMONIES. see RITES AND CEREMONIES.

Echo Press : a decade of printmaking. Bloomington : Indiana University Art Museum, c1990. 95 p. : ill. ; 31 cm. "Published in conjunction with the exhibition held at the Indiana University Art Museum, October 23, 1990-January 6, 1991"--T.p. verso.
1. Echo Press - Exhibitions. 2. Prints - 20th century - Exhibitions. I. Indiana. University. Museum of Art.
NYPL [MDF+ 91-3853]

ECHO PRESS - EXHIBITIONS.
Echo Press . Bloomington , c1990. 95 p. :
NYPL [MDF+ 91-3853]

Echoes of New York . Bernstein, Theresa. New York, NY [1990?] [16] p. :
NYPL [3-MCX B531 91-3442]

Ecker, Ferdinand van den. In unnachahmlicher Treue . Köln , 1979. 370 p. :
TR6.G3 C644 **NYPL [MFW 81-577]**

Eckersley, Sarah. Art at the edge . Oxford , 1988. 43 p. : ISBN 0-905836-66-9 (pbk.) DDC 709/.438/074 19
N7255.P6 **NYPL [3-MAM+ 90-4738]**

ECLECTICISM IN ARCHITECTURE - CALIFORNIA.
Harris, Bill, 1933- Great homes of California /. New York , 1990. 160 p. : ISBN 0-517-62377-3 DDC 728.8/09794 20
NA7511.3.C2 H3 1990

ECLECTICISM IN ARCHITECTURE - FLORIDA.
Mizner, Addison, 1872-1933. Florida architecture of Addison Mizner /. Boulder, Colo. , 1991. p. cm. ISBN 1-87865-002-5 : DDC 720/.92 20
NA737.M59 A4 1991

ECLECTICISM IN ARCHITECTURE - FLORIDA - PALM BEACH.
Schezen, Roberto. Palm Beach houses /. New York , 1991. 324 p. : ISBN 0-8478-1313-4 DDC 728.8/09759/32 20
NA7238.P235 S34 1991

ECLECTICISM IN ARCHITECTURE - GERMANY.
Schinkel, Karl Friedrich, 1781-1841. [Sammlung Architecktonischer Entwürfe. English.] Collection of architectural designs . New York , 1989. 54, 11 p., 174 p. of plates : ISBN 0-910413-56-8 DDC 720/.92/4 19
NA1088.S3 A4 1989
NYPL [3-MQZ (Schinkel) 91-6053]

ECLECTICISM IN ARCHITECTURE - GREAT BRITAIN.
Lutyens, Edwin Landseer, Sir, 1869-1944. Edwin Lutyens. London , New York , 1986. 112 p., [7] folded leaves of plates : ISBN 0-85670-422-9 (paper) DDC 728.8/092/4 19
NA997.L8 I57 1986
NYPL [3-MQZ+ (Lutyens) 87-2200]

ECLECTICISM IN ARCHITECTURE - HUNGARY.
Bakonyi, Tibor. Magyar Ede /. Budapest , 1989. 28 p., [48] p. of plates : ISBN 963-05-4981-6 :
NA1022.5.M337 B3 1989

ECLECTICISM IN ARCHITECTURE - PORTUGAL.
Mestre José Luiz Monteiro . [Lisbon] [1990] 93 p. : DDC 720/.92 20
NA1333.M65 M48 1990

ECLECTICISM IN ARCHITECTURE - RUSSIAN S.F.S.R.
Brumfield, William Craft, 1944- The origins of modernism in Russian architecture /. Berkeley , c1991. xxv, 343 p., [24] p. of plates : ISBN 0-520-06929-3 (alk. paper) DDC 720/.947/09041 20
NA1187 .B78 1991
NYPL [3-MQW 91-6488]

ECLECTICISM IN ARCHITECTURE - SPAIN.
Arrechea, Julio I. Arquitectura y romanticismo . Valladolid, España [Salamanca] , c1989. 330 p. : ISBN 84-7762-086-5 DDC 720/.946/09034 20
NA1307 .A7 1989

ECLECTICISM IN ARCHITECTURE - UNITED STATES.
Foreman, John, 1945- The Vanderbilts and the

gilded age . New York , 1991. viii, 340 p. : ISBN 0-312-05984-1 : DDC 728.8/0973 20
NA7207 .F67 1991 **NYPL [ILD 91-6528]**

Smith, Daisy M. (Daisy Mullett) A.B. Mullett . Washington, D.C. , c1990. xii, 128 p. : ISBN 0-9611410-2-6 (hardcover) DDC 720/.92 20
NA737.M78 S65 1990

ECLECTICISM IN ART - YUGOSLAVIA - SLOVENIA.
Žitko, Sonja. Historizem v kiparstvu 19. stoletja na Slovenskem /. Ljubljana , 1989. 188 p. :
NB949.S5 Z58 1989

Ecole d'architecture de Clermont-Ferrand.
L'Architecture entre nos sens et le sens /. Clermont-FD , 1986. 167 p. : ISBN 2-09-510800-2
NA2542.35 .A69 1986

ÉCOLE DE PARIS - EXHIBITIONS.
Phillips Collection. Duncan Phillips collects . Washington, D.C. , c1991. p. cm. ISBN 0-943044-16-2 : DDC 759.4/361/09041074753 20
N6850 .P45 1991

Ecole du patrimoine. Destins d'objets /. Paris , 1988. 474 p. : ISBN 2-11-002009-1 (pbk.)
NYPL [3-MAVC 90-9455]

Bulletin de Correspondance hellénique. Supplément. see Bulletin de correspondance hellénique. Supplément.

Ecole nationale supérieure des beaux-arts (France)
Les Architectes de la liberté, 1789-1799 . Paris , c1989. 396 p. : ISBN 2-903639-65-5
NYPL [3-MQWF 90-11622]

Les Dessins vénitiens des collections de l'École des beaux-arts . Paris , c1990. xlii, 257 p. : ISBN 2-903639-68-X
NYPL [3-MBH+ 90-12996]

Les Architectes de la liberté, 1789-1799 . Paris , c1989. 396 p. : ISBN 2-903639-65-5 DDC 720/.944/07444361 20
NA1046.5.N4 A7 1989

Maîtres français, 1550-1800 . Paris , c1989. 313 p. : ISBN 2-903639-64-7
NYPL [3-MBH+ 89-26750]

Venetianska teckningar från École des beaux-arts, Paris . Stockholm [1990] 165 p. : ISBN 90-71003-80-0
NC256.V4 V4 1990

ECOLE NATIONALE SUPÉRIEURE DES BEAUX-ARTS (FRANCE) - EXHIBITIONS.
Venetianska teckningar från École des beaux-arts, Paris . Stockholm [1990] 165 p. : ISBN 90-71003-80-0
NC256.V4 V4 1990

ECOLOGY, HUMAN. see HUMAN ECOLOGY.

ECOLOGY, SOCIAL. see HUMAN ECOLOGY.

Economic Community Information Service. The European community in maps. Bruxelles : European Community Information Service, [1962] 1 atlas (1 portfolio ([4] p., 12 leaves of plates)) : col. maps ; 28 cm. Title from portfolio cover. "Maps ... prepared by Dr. I.B.F. Kormoss ... with the advice of M. Gabriel Quencez"--P. 2 of cover. Bibliography: p. 3. of portfolio cover. CONTENTS. - Administrative regions and units -- Density of population -- Land utilization and main crops -- Livestock and fishing -- Energy and steel -- The nuclear industry -- Selected industries -- Main industrial regions and distribution of manpower by activities -- Railways and navigation -- Roads and aviation -- External trade -- Associated overseas countries. DDC 330.94055/0223 20
1. European Economic Community countries - Economic Conditions - Maps. 2. Europe - Economic conditions - 1945- - Maps. I. Kormoss, I. B. F. II. Title.
G1802.E9G1 E3 1962
NYPL [Map Div. 91-5515]

ECONOMIC GEOGRAPHY - MAPS.
Soviet Union. Glavnoe upravlenie geodezii i kartografii. Atlas zarubezhnykh stran dlia srednei shkoly . [Moskva , 1964]. 1 atlas (40 p. : **NYPL [Map Div. 91-1092]**

ECONOMIC GEOLOGY. see GEOLOGY, ECONOMIC.

Economic Research, National Bureau of. see National Bureau of Economic Research.

ECONOMIC THEORY. see ECONOMICS.

ECONOMICS - DICTIONARIES.
New Palgrave. Selections. The New Palgrave . London , 1991. xi, 756 p. : ISBN 0-333-55177-X (pbk.) : DDC 330 20
HB171 **NYPL [*R-Econ. HB171 .N48]**

The Economics of art museums / edited and with an introduction by Martin Feldstein. Chicago : University of Chicago Press, 1991. p. cm. (A National Bureau of Economic Research conference report) Includes bibliographical references and index. ISBN 0-226-24073-8 (alk. paper) DDC 338.4/770813 20
1. Art museums - Economic aspects - United States. I. Feldstein, Martin S. II. National Bureau of Economic Research. III. Series: Conference report (National Bureau of Economic Research).
N510 .E27 1991

Economist (London, England) The Economist world atlas and almanac. New York , 1989. 384 p. : ISBN 0-13-234964-7
NYPL [Map Div. 90-11363]

The Economist world atlas and almanac. 1st Prentice Hall Press ed. New York : Prentice Hall, 1989. 384 p. : col. ill., col. maps ; 26 cm. "The Economist Books." CONTENTS. - World maps -- World comparisons -- World encyclopedia. ISBN 0-13-234964-7
1. Geography, Economic - Maps. 2. World politics - Maps. I. Economist (London, England). II. Title: World atlas and almanac. **NYPL [Map Div. 90-11363]**

Ecostoria .
(4) Pierotti, Piero. Una torre da non salvare . Ospedaletto (Pisa) , 1990. 191 p. :
NYPL [3-MRI 90-10810]

Ecrits /. Borduas, Paul Emile. [Selections. 1987.] Montréal, Qué., Canada , 1987- v. : ISBN 2-7606-0761-5 (v. 1)
NYPL [3-MAS 88-2798]

Ecrits sur l'art /. Severini, Gino, 1883-1966. Paris , c1987. 414 p. : ISBN 2-7022-0213-6
N6923.S495 A2 1987

Ecrits théoriques. Devade, Marc, 1943-1983. Marc Devade . Paris , 1989-1990. 3 v. (479 p.) ; ISBN 2-256-90867-4 DDC 701 20
N70 .D458 1989

Ecritures et les images de la musique. L'Œil musicien . Charleroi , 1985. 106 p. :
NYPL [3-MAMZ 86-4322]

Ecsedy, Csaba. Boglár, Lajos. Tribal art in Africa and Oceania . [Budapest] , 1971. 8, 8 p., 8, 8 p. of plates :
enghun **NYPL [3-MADF 90-5887]**

ECUADOR - SURVEYS.
Smith, James R. (James Raymond), 1935- From plane to spheroid . Rancho Cordova, CA, U.S.A. , c1986. xii, 219 p. : ISBN 0-910845-29-8 DDC 526/.1/09 19
QB283 .S64 1986
NYPL [Map Div. 91-4222]

Ed Epping, echoed events. Epping, Ed, 1948- Ed Epping, events echoed . New York , c1984. 16 p. : DDC 709/.2/4 19
N6537.E66 A4 1984
NYPL [3-MGO (Epping) 90-12638]

Ed Epping, events echoed . Epping, Ed, 1948- New York , c1984. 16 p. : DDC 709/.2/4 19
N6537.E66 A4 1984
NYPL [3-MGO (Epping) 90-12638]

Ed Rossbach . Rossbach, Ed. Asheville, N.C. , Washington, D.C. , 1990. 164 p. : ISBN 0-937274-52-6 : DDC 746/.092 20
NK8998.R68 A4 1990
NYPL [3-MON 90-11617]

Eddie Figge /. Figge, Eddie, 1904- Stockholm, Sweden [1989?] 1 v. (unpaged) : ISBN 91-86164-10-4 DDC 709/.2 20
N7093.F54 A4 1989

Edel, Elmar, 1914- Desroches-Noblecourt, Christiane, 1913- Grand temple d'Abou Simbel . Le Caire , 1971. vi, 65 leaves, xlii leaves of plates :
ND2865.A2 D4 1971

Edelenbos, P. (Peter) Velden, R. K. W. van der. Letteren in arbeidsmarkt /. Groningen , 's-Gravenhage [1989] 129 p. ;
NX554.A1 V4 1989

Edelstein, T. J. Perspectives on Morisot . New
York , c1990. 120 p. : ISBN 1-555-95049-3 (alk.
paper) : DDC 759.4 20
ND553.M88 P47 1990
        NYPL [3-MCO M86 91-4616]

Edgar Degas . Degas, Edgar, 1834-1917. Bogotá,
D.E., Colombia [1990] 1 v. (unpaged) : DDC
730/.92 20
NB553.D4 A4 1990

Edgar Degas /. Terrasse, Antoine. London , 1988.
94 p. : ISBN 0-304-32165-6
        NYPL [3-MCO+ D31 90-5412]

Edge of a city /. Holl, Steven. New York , 1991.
p. cm. ISBN 1-87827-156-3 : DDC 711/.4/09048
20
NA9095 .H65 1991

Edgerton, Samuel Y. The heritage of Giotto's
geometry : art and science on the eve of the
scientific revolution / Samuel Y. Edgerton, Jr.
Ithaca : Cornell University Press, 1991. p. cm.
Includes bibliographical references (p.) and index.
        ISBN 0-8014-2573-5 (cloth : alk. paper) DDC
701/.8 20
        *1. Perspective. 2. Visual perception. 3. Space (Art). 4.
Art, Medieval. 5. Art, Renaissance. 6. Giotto,
1266?-1337 - Themes, motives. I. Title.*
N7430.5 .E34 1991

Edice Výstavy .
    (78) Alšova jihočeská galerie. Gotické umění v
jižních Cechách . Praha [1990] 101 p. : ISBN
80-7035-013-X :
N6832.J53 A48 1990

    (81) Národní galerie V Praze. Sbírka Bohuslava
Duška . [Prague] [1990?] 131 p. :
N5280.C952 D876 1990

    (83) Maďarské výtvarné umění XX. století
(1945-1988) . V Praze , 1989. 40 p. : ISBN
80-7035-009-1 :
N6820 .M25 1989

Edícia Orientácia.
    Kamenistý, Ján. Ako kopú múzy . Bratislava ,
1990. 263 p. : ISBN 80-221-0036-6 :
NX571.C92 S54 1990

Edilizia in Toscana dal XV al XVII secolo /.
Giusti, Maria Adriana. Firenze [1990] 254 p. :
IN PROCESS (ONLINE)
        NYPL [3-MQWB+ 91-6836]

Edilizia medievale in Toscana /. Redi, Fabio.
Firenze , 1989. 237 p. :
IN PROCESS (ONLINE)
        NYPL [3-MQWB+ 90-11747]

Edinburgh Festival Society. The Blue Rider
group; an exhibition, sponsored by the
Edinburgh Festival Society and arranged jointly
with the Royal Scottish Academy and the Arts
Council of Great Britain. Edinburgh, Royal
Scottish Academy, 1960. 32 p. 44 plates (part
col.) 25 cm. On cover: Edinburgh International
Festival, 1960. Includes bibliographical references.
        *1. Painting, Modern - 20th century - Germany -
Munich - Exhibitions. 2. Blaue Reiter (Group of
artists) - Exhibitions. I. Title.*
ND586.M9 E3   ***NYPL [3-MC 91-285]***

Edinburgh. Fruit Market Gallery. see **Fruit
Market Gallery.**

Edinburgh International Festival. El Greco,
mystery and illumination . [Edinburgh] [1989]
96 p. : ISBN 0-903148-90-0
        NYPL [3-MCQ T39 90-10831]

Edinburgh. Stills (Gallery) see **Stills (Gallery)**

**Edinburgh. The Scottish Photography Group
Gallery.** see **Stills (Gallery)**

Edith C. Blum Art Institute.
    Art what thou eat . Mount Kisco, N.Y. , c1991.
191 p. : ISBN 1-559-21051-6 : DDC
704.9/49641/0973 20
N6512 .A763 1991
        NYPL [3-MAMZ+ 91-5410]

    Gelburd, Gail. The trans parent thread .
[Hempstead, N.Y.] , Philadelphia, Pa. , c1990.
124 p. : ISBN 0-8122-1376-9 (pbk.)
        NYPL [3-MAMT 91-4984]

Edition Fotohof .
    (Bd. 1) Kaindl, Kurt. Harald P. Lechenperg .
Salzburg , 1990. 127 p. : ISBN 3-7013-0801-2
        NYPL [MFX (Lechenperg) 91-3519]

    (Bd. 2) Fotoseite . Salzburg , 1990. 159 p. :
        ISBN 3-7013-0802-0   ***NYPL [MFW+]***

Edition Galerie Buchmann .
    (Vol. 1) Mang, Rainer, 1943- Mang /. Basel ,
c1989. 61 p. :
        NYPL [3-MGO (Mang) 90-10231]

    (Vol. 4) Kopf, Willi, 1949- Kopf /. Basel ,
c1989. 35 p. :
        NYPL [3-MGO (Kopf) 90-13399]

Edition Privatvergnügen .
    (Bd. 3) Nechwatal, Norbert. Richard Wagner
im Exlibris . Wiesbaden , c1988. 124 p. : ISBN
3-922835-11-2   ***NYPL [MDVF 90-10990]***

EDITION ROTHE - CATALOGS.
    Rothe, Gesamtverzeichnis der
Originaldruckgraphik 1958-1989 . Frankfurt ,
c1989. 199 p. :   ***NYPL [MDF+ 90-13674]***

Edition Schellmann.
    Edition Schellmann, 1969-1989. Munich ; New
York : Edition Schellmann, c1989. 309 p. : all
ill. (chiefly col.) ; 27 cm. "Published ... on the
occasion of the exhibition, For 20 years: Editions
Schellmann, in the Tatyana Grosman Gallery, the
Museum of Modern Art, New York, November 16,
1989-March 13, 1990"--T.p. verso. Cover title: Edition
Schellmann, 1969-1989. Includes index. ISBN
        3-921629-40-3 DDC 709/.04/50747471 20
        *1. Edition Schellmann - Catalogs. 2. Prints - 20th
century - Catalogs. I. Museum of Modern Art (New
York, N.Y.) II. Title. III. Title: Edition Schellmann,
1969-1989.*
N6487.N4 M845 1989
        NYPL [MDF 90-8257]

EDITION SCHELLMANN - CATALOGS.
    Edition Schellmann. Edition Schellmann,
1969-1989. Munich , New York , c1989. 309
p. : ISBN 3-921629-40-3 DDC 709/.04/50747471
20
N6487.N4 M845 1989
        NYPL [MDF 90-8257]

Edition Schellmann, 1969-1989. Edition
Schellmann. Munich , New York , c1989. 309
p. : ISBN 3-921629-40-3 DDC 709/.04/50747471
20
N6487.N4 M845 1989
        NYPL [MDF 90-8257]

Edition Schellmann, 1969-1989. Edition
Schellmann. Edition Schellmann, 1969-1989.
Munich , New York , c1989. 309 p. : ISBN
        3-921629-40-3 DDC 709/.04/50747471 20
N6487.N4 M845 1989
        NYPL [MDF 90-8257]

EDITIONS DARGAUD - HISTORY.
    Filippini, Henri. Histoire du journal Pilote et
des publications des Editions Dargaud /.
Grenoble , c1977. 141 p. : ISBN 2-7234-0038-7
        NYPL [3-MDY 90-3530]

Editorial La Pulga. Chile 1973: ni reforma, ni
revolución! Medellín [1973] 1 v.
        NYPL [HIO 75-1240]

**Editorials and resolutions in memory of Samuel
Putnam Avery;** born March 17th, 1823, died
August 11th, 1904. New York, Privately
printed [The Gilliss press] 1905. 3 p.l., 3-81, [1]
p., 1 l. front. (port.) 23 cm. Limited ed. of 100
copies.
        1. Avery, Samuel Putnam, 1822-1904.
N8384 .A8   ***NYPL [3-MAS 91-331]***

Edizioni d'arte (Pordenone, Italy) .
    (nuova ser., 17) Giannelli, Angelo, 1922-
Giannelli /. Pordenone , c1986. 61 p., [30] p.
of plates :
ND623.G484 A4 1986
        NYPL [3-MCF G4453 91-4199]

    (nuova ser., 21) Mascherini, Marcello, 1906-
Mascherini, scultore europeo /. [Italy] ,
Pordenone , c1988. 126 p., [101] p. of plates :
        DDC 730/.92 20
NB623.M454 A4 1988
        NYPL [3-MGO (Mascherini) 91-3748]

    (nuova ser., 22) Pauletto, Giancarlo. Kosta
Angeli Radovani /. Pordenone , c1988. 84 p.,
[66] p. of plates :
        NYPL [3-MGO (Radovani) 91-6969]

    (nuova serie 13) De Rocco, Federico. De
Rocco . [Pordenone] , c1984. 59 p., [36] p. of
plates :   ***NYPL [3-MCF D439 91-5210]***

Edmondo Pizzi /. Pizzi, Edmondo. Poggibonsi ,
1989. 118 p. :
        NYPL [3-MCF P6933 90-12591]

Edmonds, Mary Jaene. Samplers &
samplermakers : an American schoolgirl art,
1700-1850 / Mary Jaene Edmonds. [Los
Angeles] : Los Angeles County Museum of
Art ; New York : Rizzoli, 1991. p. cm. Published
in conjunction with the exhibition held at Los Angeles
County Museum of Art Nov. 7, 1991-Feb. 2, 1992.
Includes bibliographical references. ISBN
        0-8478-1396-7 DDC 746.39/73 20
        *1. Samplers - United States - History - 18th century. 2.
Samplers - United States - History - 19th century. I.
Los Angeles County Museum of Art. II. Title. III. Title:
Samplers and samplermakers.*
NK9112 .E3 1991

Edna Manley, sculptor /. Boxer, David, 1946-
[Kingston] , c1990. 204 p. : ISBN 9623836-2-7
        NYPL [3-MGO+ (Manley) 91-7698]

Edouard Pingret . Ortiz Macedo, Luis. México ,
1989. xiii, 160 p. : ISBN 968-7009-20-9 DDC
759.4 20
ND553.P5375 O78 1989

Eduard Angeli. Angeli, Eduard, 1942- Wien
[1983?] [21] leaves : DDC 759.36 19
ND511.5.A53 A4 1982
        NYPL [3-MCK+ A597 85-3252]

Eduard Bischoff, 1890-1974 . Lankau,
Hans-Helmut. Husum , c1990. 96 p. : ISBN
        3-88042-460-8 DDC 759.3 20
ND588.B5 A4 1990

Eduardo Arroyo /. Calvo Serraller, F. (Francisco),
1948- Madrid , 1991. 283 p. : ISBN
        84-87798-00-4
        NYPL [3-MCQ+ A778 91-5775]

Eduardo Chillida . Chillida, Eduardo, 1924-
[Venezia] [1990] 199 p. : ISBN 88-20-80358-5
        DDC 709/.2 20
N7113.C555 A4 1990

**Eduardo Chillida, Zeichnung als Skulptur
1948-1989** . Chillida, Eduardo, 1924- Bonn ,
Münster , c1989. 161 p. : DDC 709/.2 20
N6913 .C48 1989
        NYPL [3-MGO+ (Chillida) 90-12885]

Eduardo Kingman /. Kingman, Eduardo. [Quito? ,
1985. 253 p. :
        NYPL [3-MCZ+ K524 88-4055]

Eduardo Sanguinetti . Espartaco, Carlos. Buenos
Aires, Argentina , 1989. 110 p. : ISBN
        950-9004-98-7 DDC 700/.92 20
NX531.Z9 S254 1989

EDUCATION AND STATE - EGYPT.
    Khiṭṭat al-nashāṭ li-'ām 1974 /. al-Qāhirah ,
1974. 9, 108 p. ;
NX750.E3 K45 1974

EDUCATION, ART. see **ART - STUDY AND
TEACHING.**

**EDUCATION - CARICATURES AND
CARTOONS.**
    Harris, Sidney. Can't you guys read? cartoons
on academia /. New Brunswick , c1991. p. cm.
        ISBN 0-8135-1733-8 (pbk.) : DDC 741.5/973 20
NC1429.H33315 A4 1991a

EDUCATION, HUMANISTIC.
    Kulturens dekningsbidrag . [Oslo] , c1991. 179
p. : ISBN 82-02-12832-3
NX456 .K78 1991

**EDUCATION, HUMANISTIC -
NETHERLANDS.**
    Velden, R. K. W. van der. Letteren en
arbeidsmarkt /. Groningen , 's-Gravenhage
[1989] 129 p. ;
NX554.A1 V4 1989

EDUCATION, LIBERAL. see **EDUCATION,
HUMANISTIC.**

**EDUCATIONAL EVALUATION - UNITED
STATES.**
    Clarke, David, 1942- Frank Lloyd Wright and
the Laffer curve . Wakefield, N.H. , 1991. p.
cm. ISBN 0-89341-655-X DDC 720/.71/173 20
NA2105 .C58 1991

EDUCATIONAL POLICY. see **EDUCATION
AND STATE.**

Educational series (Buckner, Mo.) .
    (1) Britt, John. Heart of American Carnival
Glass Association. [Buckner, MO] [c1990] 150
p. : DDC 748.2913/09/041 20
NK5439.C35 B75 1990

Edvard Munch . Eggum, Arne. [Oslo] , c1990.

303 p. : ISBN 82-7201-164-6
N7073.M8 E34 1990

Edvard Munch . Munch, Edvard, 1863-1944.
Washington , c1990. 144 p. : ISBN
0-89468-150-8 DDC 769.92 20
NE694.M8 A4 1990
    NYPL [MDG+ (Munch) 90-11909]

Edvard Munch Holzschnitte . Munch, Edvard,
1863-1944. [Reutlingen] [1991] 125 p. : ISBN
3-927228-31-1 DDC 769.92 20
NE1160.5.M86 A4 1991

Edward Borein, the update . Davidson, Harold
G., 1912- Santa Barbara, Calif. , 1991. 219 p. :
ISBN 0-9627674-0-9 : DDC 760/.092 20
N6537.B63 D39 1991

**The Edward Burr Van Vleck collection of
Japanese prints.** Elvehjem Museum of Art.
Madison , 1990. vi, 352 p. : ISBN
0-932990-24-0 : DDC 769.952/074/77583 20
NE1321.8 .E48 1990

**Edward Hopper, selections from the permanent
collection .** Hopper, Edward, 1882-1967. New
York, NY , c1989. 32 p. :
    NYPL [3-MCX H79 91-5552]

Edward James, poet, patron, eccentric . Lowe,
John, 1928- London , 1991. xix, 262 p. : ISBN
0-00-217941-5 : DDC 700.92 20
N5247.J3
    NYPL [3-MAX (James, E.) 91-4883]

Edward Ruscha . Ruscha, Edward. Rotterdam
[1989] 152 p : ISBN 90-6918-048-0
    NYPL [3-MCX R95 90-11542]

Edward Ruscha Los Angeles apartments, 1965 /.
Marshall, Richard, 1947- [New York, N.Y.] ,
c1990. 63 p. : ISBN 0-87427-074-X
    NYPL [3-MCX R95 90-13010]

Edward W. Root Art Center. Bloch, Albert,
1882-1961. Albert Bloch, 1882-1961 . [Utica,
N.Y.] , c1974. 36 p. :
    NYPL [3-MCX B643 91-6562]

Edward Wadsworth, 1889-1949. Wadsworth,
Edward, 1889-1949. A genius of industrial
England . [Bradford] , c1990. 128 p. : ISBN
0-9505532-7-1
    NYPL [3-MCV W12 91-6333]

Edward Wadsworth, 1889-1949. Wadsworth,
Edward, 1889-1949. A genius of industrial
England . [London] : [Bradford] : 128 p. :
ISBN 0-9505532-7-1 DDC 760/.092 20
N6797.W26 A4 1990

Edward Weston, his life /. Maddow, Ben, 1909-
New York, N.Y. , c1989. 281 p. : ISBN
0-89381-369-9 :
    NYPL [MFX (Weston) 90-11262]

Edwards C., Hernán (Edwards Cruchaga)
Monumentos nacionales y arquitectura
tradicional : V Región Valparaíso, Chile /
Hernán Edwards C., Rómolo Trebbi del T.,
Alvaro Mora D. [Santiago, Chile] : E. Novoa
Castro, [1990?] 80 p. : ill. (some col.) ; 21 x 26
cm. Spine title: Monumentos nacionales. Includes
bibliographical references (flap of back cover). DDC
720/.983/255 20
*1. Architecture - Chile - Valparaíso Bay Region -
Catalogs. 2. Architecture, Modern - 19th century -
Chile - Valparaíso Bay Region - Catalogs. 3.
Architecture, Modern - 20th century - Chile -
Valparaíso Bay Region - Catalogs. I. Trebbi del
Trevigiano, Rómolo. II. Mora Donoso, Alvaro. III.
Title. IV. Title: Monumentos nacionales.*
NA866.V3 E3 1990

Edwards, Clive, 1947- Gloag, John, 1896- A
complete dictionary of furniture /. Woodstock,
N.Y. , 1991. 828 p. : ISBN 0-87951-414-0 DDC
749 20
NK2205 .G54 1991   *NYPL [MOF 91-6208]*

Edwards, Deborah. Stampede of the lower gods :
classical mythology in Australian art,
1890s-1930s : Art Gallery of New South Wales,
19th October-26th November 1989 / Deborah
Edwards. Sydney : Trustees of the Art Gallery
of New South Wales, [1989] vi, 66 p. : ill.
(some col.) ; 26 cm. Catalogue of an exhibition.
"September 1989"--Verso t.p. Includes bibliographical
references. ISBN 0-7305-6555-6 DDC
709/.94/0749441 20
*1. Art, Australian - Exhibitions. 2. Mythology,
Classical, in art - Exhibitions. 3. Art, Modern - 19th
century - Australia - Exhibitions. 4. Art, Modern - 20th
centuiry - Australia - Exhibitions. I. Art Gallery of*

New South Wales. II. Title.
N7760 .E38 1989

Edwards, Geoffrey. Clifford Last sculpture, a
retrospective exhibition : 23 November 1989-29
January 1990 / by Geoffrey Edwards ; with an
essay by Noel Hutchison. Melbourne : National
Gallery of Victoria, 1989. 71 p. : ill. ; 30 cm.
*1. Last, Clifford, 1918- - Exhibitions. I. Last, Clifford,
1918-. II. National Gallery of Victoria. III. Title.*
    NYPL [3-MGO+ (Last) 91-4348]

Edwards, Richard, 1916- The world around the
Chinese artist : aspects of realism in Chinese
painting / Richard Edwards. Ann Arbor :
University of Michigan, 1987. 158 p. : ill. ; 26
cm. (The Distinguished senior faculty lecture series)
Includes bibliographical references. CONTENTS. - Hsia
Kuei and the Late Sung -- Shen Chou and the Ming --
Shih-t'ao and the Early Ch'ing. ISBN 0-472-10130-7
*1. Hsia, Kuei, fl. 1190-1224. 2. Shen, Chou, 1427-1509.
3. Shih-t'ao, 17th/18th cent. 4. Realism in art - China.
I. Title.*   *NYPL [3-MAF 90-4955]*

Edwards, Susan. A Debate on abstraction . [New
York] [1988?] 79 p. :
    NYPL [3-MAL 90-12609]

Edwin Lutyens. Lutyens, Edwin Landseer, Sir,
1869-1944. London , New York , 1986. 112 p.,
[7] folded leaves of plates : ISBN 0-85670-422-9
(paper) DDC 728.8/092/4 19
NA997.L8 I57 1986
    NYPL [3-MQZ+ (Lutyens) 87-2200]

Eekhoud, Georges, 1854-1927. Les peintres
animaliers belges. Bruxelles, Librairie nationale
d'art et d'histoire, 1911. 125 p. plates. 26cm.
(Collection de l'art belge au XIXe siècle)
*1. Animal painters - Belgium. 2. Animals in art. 3.
Painting, Modern - 19th century - Belgium. I. Title.*
    NYPL [3-MCG 90-6348]

Eero Saarinen. Saarinen, Eero, 1910-1961. New
York [1971] 130 p. ISBN 0-671-20879-9 ; DDC
720/.924
NA737.S28 S6

Eesti kunsti sidemeid XX sajandi algupoolelt :
artiklite kogumik. Tallinn : Kunst, 1978. 271
p. : ill. ; 22 cm. At head of title: ENSV TA Ajaloo
Instituut. Summaries in German and Russian. Includes
bibliographical references and index.
*1. Art, Estonian - Addresses, essays, lectures. 2. Art,
Modern - 20th century - Estonia - Addresses, essays,
lectures. I. Eesti NSV Teaduste Akadeemia. Ajaloo
Instituut.*
N6995.E8 E365   *NYPL [3-MAM 81-512]*

Eesti NSV Ajakirjanike Liit. Pliiatsi ja blokiga
mööda Nõukogude Eestit. [Tallinn] , 1960. [74]
leaves :   *NYPL [3-MAMY 84-1245]*

Eesti NSV Teaduste Akadeemia. Ajaloo Instituut.
Eesti kunsti sidemeid XX sajandi algupoolelt .
Tallinn , 1978. 271 p. :
N6995.E8 E365   *NYPL [3-MAM 81-512]*

**Eesti NSV Teaduste Akadeemia. Institut für
Geschichtsforschung. see Eesti NSV Teaduste
Akadeemia. Ajaloo Instituut.**

**Eesti NSV Teaduste Akadeemia. Institut istorii.
see Eesti NSV Teaduste Akadeemia. Ajaloo
Instituut.**

**Eesti NSV Teaduste Akadeemia. Institute of
History. see Eesti NSV Teaduste Akadeemia.
Ajaloo Instituut.**

**Eesti Teaduste Akadeemia. Kodu-uurimise
Komisjon.** Tartu ja kultuur /. Tallinn , 1990.
215 p. :
NX556.T37 T37 1990

**EFFIGIES, SEPULCHRAL. see SEPULCHRAL
MONUMENTS.**

Effigy tumuli . Heizer, Michael, 1944- New
York , 1990. 131 p. : ISBN 0-8109-1166-3 DDC
709/.2/4 19
N6537.H384 A64 1988
    NYPL [3-MGO (Heizer) 90-11298]

Effleurage /. Bartolini, Anna Maria. [Leeds,
Mass.] , 1989. [13] p., [26] leaves of plates :
DDC 769.92 20
NE2052.5.B364 A4 1989

Egeland, Erik. Kai Fjell / Erik Egeland ;
[fotografier, Per Petterson, Helene Fjell].
[Oslo] : Stenersen, c1990. 136 p. : ill. (some
col.) ; 30 cm. ISBN 82-7201-169-7 :
*1. Fjell, Kai, 1907-. 2. Painters - Norway - Biography.
I. Fjell, Kai, 1907-. II. Title.*
ND773.F53 E35 1990

Eger und das Egerland : Volkskunst und
Brauchtum / Lorenz Schreiner, Hrsg.
München : Langen Müller, c1988. 671 p. : ill.
(some col.), maps, music, ports. ; 31 cm. Col.
maps on lining papers. Includes bibliographical
references. ISBN 3-7844-2178-4
*1. Folk art - Czechoslovakia - Cheb. 2. Folk art -
Czechoslovakia - Cheb Region. 3. Cheb
(Czechoslovakia) - Social life and customs. 4. Cheb
Region (Czechoslovakia) - Social life and customs. I.
Schreiner, Lorenz.*   *NYPL [3-MNE+ 90-597]*

Egerländer Trachtenfibel / herausgegeben von
der Egerland-Jugend im Bund der Eghalanda
Gmoin e.V. (BdEG) ; mit Unterstützung der
Bundesbeauffragten für Trachten, Leni Fritsch ;
Zusammenstellung und Gestaltung, Sabine
Müller. Frankfurt / M. : Münker & Schmidt,
1986. 136 p. : ill. (some col.) ; 30 cm. Includes
bibliographical references.
*1. Costume - Czechoslovakia - Cheb Region. I. Fritsch,
Leni. II. Müller, Sabina. III. Egerland-Jugend im Bund
der Eghalanda Gmoin (Marktredwitz, Germany).*
    NYPL [3-MMM+ 89-25288]

**Egerland-Jugend im Bund der Eghalanda Gmoin
(Marktredwitz, Germany)** Egerländer
Trachtenfibel /. Frankfurt / M. , 1986. 136 p. :
    NYPL [3-MMM+ 89-25288]

Egerton, Judy. Wright of Derby / Judy Egerton.
London : Tate Gallery, 1990. 294 p. : ill. (some
col.) ; 31 cm. Includes bibliographical references and
index. "Published by order of the Trustees 1990 on the
occasion of the exhibition at the Tate Gallery: 7
February-22 April 1990, Grand Palais, Paris: 17
May-23 July 1990 [and] Metropolitan Museum of Art,
New York: 6 September-2 December 1990"--T.p. verso.
ISBN 1-85437-037-5 (paper)
*1. Wright, Joseph, 1734-1797 - Exhibitions. I. Wright,
Joseph, 2734-1797. II. Tate Gallery. III. Grand Palais
(Paris, France). IV. Metropolitan Museum of Art (New
York, N.Y.). V. Title.*
    NYPL [3-MCV+ W95 90-11565]

Egger, Gerhart, 1916- Graphiken von Marika
Drechsler / Gerhart Egger. Wien :
Österreichisches Museum für angewandte
Kunst, 1978. 15 p., 32 p. of plates : ill. ; 23 cm.
(Schriften der Bibliothek des Österreichischen Museums
für Angewandte Kunst . 4) Exhibition catalog.
*1. Drechsler, Marika, 1942- - Exhibitions. I. Drechsler,
Marika, 1942-. II. Title. III. Series.*
    NYPL [MDG (Drechsler) 90-6047]

Eggum, Arne. Edvard Munch : livsfrisen fra
maleri til grafikk / Arne Eggum. [Oslo] : J.M.
Stenersens forlag, c1990. 303 p. : ill. (some
col.) ; 29 cm. Includes bibliographical references (p.
292-297) and index. ISBN 82-7201-164-6
*1. Munch, Edvard, 1863-1944. 2. Artists - Norway -
Biography. I. Munch, Edvard, 1863-1944. II. Title.*
N7073.M8 E34 1990

Egle, Arvīds, 1905-1977. Lāce, Rasma. Arvīds
Egle /. Rīga , 1985. 108 p. :
    NYPL [3-MCZ E299 90-11091]

EGLE, ARVĪDS, 1905-1977.
Lāce, Rasma. Arvīds Egle /. Rīga , 1985. 108
p. :   *NYPL [3-MCZ E299 90-11091]*

EGLISE ABBATIALE DE SAINT-DENIS.
Crosby, Sumner McK. (Sumner McKnight),
1909- The Royal Abbey of Saint-Denis . New
Haven , c1987. xxiii, 525 p., 3 folded leaves of
plates : ISBN 0-300-03143-2 (alk. paper) DDC
726/.5/0944362 19
NA5551.S214 C76 1987
    NYPL [3-MRBB 91-6920]

EGLISE DE NEVILLY-EN-DONJON.
Rodriguez, Jean. Nevilly-en-Donjon /. [France ,
1973] [20] p. :   *NYPL [3-MRBB 86-3728]*

Eglise Saint-Germain : Argentan-Orne /
[rédaction, Marie-Hélène Since ; photographies,
Pascal Corbierre ; réalisée par la Direction
régionale des affaires culturelles de
Basse-Normandie]. [Caen, France] : Association
de développement culturel en Basse-Normandie,
[1990] 16 p. : ill. ; 30 cm. (Images du patrimoine ;
no 71) Cover title. Includes bibliographical references
(p. 5). ISBN 2-908621-00-2 : DDC 726/.5/094423
20
*1. Eglise Saint-Germain (Argentan, France). 2.
Argentan (France) - Buildings, structures, etc. I. Since,
Marie-Hélène. II. Corbierre, Pascal. III. France.
Direction régionale des affaires culturelles de
Basse-Normandie. IV. Series.*
NA5551.A674 E36 1990

EGLISE SAINT-GERMAIN (ARGENTAN, FRANCE)
Eglise Saint-Germain . [Caen, France] [1990]
16 p. :   ISBN 2-908621-00-2 :   DDC 726/.5/094423
20
NA5551.A674 E36 1990

EGLISE ST-JEAN-BAPTISTE DE KEMBS (KEMBS, FRANCE)
Abel, Louis. Kembs en Sundgau rhénan .
[Kembs, France] , c1986. 285 p. :
NA1053.Z45 A83 1986

Egloff, Anton.
Galerie Raeber zeigt Plastiken, Objekte und
Collagen von Anton Egloff. [Luzern, Die
Galerie, 1970] 1 v. (unpaged) illus. 21 cm.
Exhibition held Aug. 7-Sept. 1970.
1. Egloff, Anton - Exhibitions. I. Galerie Raeber. II.
Title.   ***NYPL [3-MGO (Egloff) 90-6858]***

EGLOFF, ANTON - EXHIBITIONS.
Egloff, Anton. Galerie Raeber zeigt Plastiken,
Objekte und Collagen von Anton Egloff.
[Luzern, 1970] 1 v. (unpaged)
NYPL [3-MGO (Egloff) 90-6858]

Egon, J. Paul (Jean-Paul) Lambroquins à la
Réunion / J. Paul Egon. Saint-Denis : Ministère
de l'éducation nationale, CNDP, C.D.D.P. de la
Réunion, [1985] 95 p. : ill. ; 30 cm. Cover title.
Includes bibliographical references. DDC
728.3/7/096981 19
1. Wood-carving - Réunion - Themes, motives. 2.
Decoration and ornament, Architectural - Réunion -
Themes, motives. I. Title.
NK9789.84.R48 E36 1985
NYPL [3-MRX+ 90-11044]

Egon Schiele . Schiele, Egon, 1890-1918. [Wien]
[1990?] 104 p. :   DDC 709/.2 20
N6811.5.S34 A4 1990
NYPL [3-MCK S332 91-5564]

Egon Schiele, a centennial retrospective.
Sabarsky, Serge. Egon Schiele, 1890-1918 .
[Roslyn Harbor, N.Y.] , c1990. 183 p. :
NYPL [3-MCK S332 91-3690]

Egon Schiele, the complete works . Kallir, Jane.
New York , 1990. 687 p. :   ISBN 0-8109-3802-2
DDC 709/.2 B 20
N6811.5.S34 K35 1990
NYPL [MCK+ S332 91-5491]

Egon Schiele, 1890-1918 . Sabarsky, Serge.
[Roslyn Harbor, N.Y.] , c1990. 183 p. :
NYPL [3-MCK S332 91-3690]

Egoumenidou, Frosso.
London, Gloria. Töpferei auf Zypern damals -
heute =. Mainz am Rhein , c1990. 84 p. :
ISBN 3-8053-1028-5
NYPL [3-MPC 90-12781]

London, Gloria. [Traditional pottery in Cyprus.
German.] Töpferei auf Zypern, damals--heute
=. Mainz am Rhein , c1990. 84 p. :   ISBN
3-8053-1028-5   DDC 738.3/095645 20
NK4146.C9 L6615 1990

Egyesült Allamok. see United States.

Egypt : the source and the legacy : ancient
Egyptian and Egyptian Revival objects, Sarah
Lawrence College Art Gallery, February
13-April 22, 1990. [Bronxville, N.Y.] : Sarah
Lawrence College, Art Gallery, c1989. 22 p. :
ill. ; 31 cm. Includes bibliographical references: P. 22.
1. Art objects, Egyptian - Exhibitions. 2. Egyptian
Revial (Art) - Exhibitions. 3. Egypt in art - Exhibitions.
I. Sarah Lawrence College. Art Gallery.
IN PROCESS (ONLINE)
NYPL [3-MAMY+ 90-10613]

Egypt . Pare, Richard. New York , 1990. [96] p. :
ISBN 0-943221-08-0 :
DT70 .P37 1990
NYPL [MFX (Pare) 91-3479]

EGYPT - ANTIQUITIES - EXHIBITIONS.
Beyond the pyramids . Atlanta, Ga. , c1990. 95
p. :   ***NYPL [3-MAE 91-4240]***

Egypt - Archaeology. see Egypt - Antiquities.

EGYPT - CIVILIZATION - PICTORIAL WORKS.
Pare, Richard. Egypt . New York , 1990. [96]
p. :   ISBN 0-943221-08-0 :
DT70 .P37 1990
NYPL [MFX (Pare) 91-3479]

EGYPT - CULTURAL POLICY.
Khiṭṭat al-nashāṭ li-'ām 1974 /. al-Qāhirah ,

1974. 9, 108 p. ;
NX750.E3 K45 1974

EGYPT - DESCRIPTION AND TRAVEL - 1981- - VIEWS.
Pare, Richard. Egypt . New York , 1990. [96]
p. :   ISBN 0-943221-08-0 :
DT70 .P37 1990
NYPL [MFX (Pare) 91-3479]

EGYPT IN ART - EXHIBITIONS.
Egypt . [Bronxville, N.Y.] , c1989. 22 p. :
IN PROCESS (ONLINE)
NYPL [3-MAMY+ 90-10613]

Egypt. Wizārat al-Thaqāfah. Thaqāfah al-Jamāhīriyah. Khiṭṭat al-nashāṭ li-'ām 1974 /.
al-Qāhirah , 1974. 9, 108 p. ;
NX750.E3 K45 1974

EGYPTIAN ART. see ART, EGYPTIAN.

EGYPTIAN ART OBJECTS. see ART OBJECTS, EGYPTIAN.

EGYPTIAN CHRONOLOGY. see CHRONOLOGY, EGYPTIAN.

EGYPTIAN REVIAL (ART) - EXHIBITIONS.
Egypt . [Bronxville, N.Y.] , c1989. 22 p. :
IN PROCESS (ONLINE)
NYPL [3-MAMY+ 90-10613]

EGYPTIAN REVIVAL (ART)
Humbert, Jean, conservateur. L'Egyptomanie
dans l'art occidental /. Courbevoie, Paris ,
c1989. 336 p. :   ISBN 2-86770-037-X
N6351.2.E39 H86 1989
NYPL [3-MAL 91-2337]

Egyptian rural house. Abū al-'Ulá, Muḥammad
Farīd. al-Maskan al-rīfī al-Miṣrī . al-Qāhirah ,
1990. 231, 3, 11 p. :   ISBN 977-373-128-6 :
NA7463.A1 A28 1990

L'Egyptomanie dans l'art occidental /. Humbert,
Jean, conservateur. Courbevoie, Paris , c1989.
336 p. :   ISBN 2-86770-037-X
N6351.2.E39 H86 1989
NYPL [3-MAL 91-2337]

Ehlers, Chad. Sweden / photography by Chad
Ehlers ; text by Lars Nordström. Portland, Or. :
Graphic Arts Center Pub. Co., c1990. 159 p. :
chiefly col. ill. ; 35 cm. ISBN 1-558-68023-3
1. Sweden - Description and travel - 1981- - Views. I.
Nordström, Lars. II. Title.
IN PROCESS (ONLINE)
NYPL [MFX+ (Ehlers) 91-3403]

Ehrenberg, Ralph E., 1937- Scholars' guide to
Washington, D.C., for cartography and remote
sensing imagery : maps, charts, aerial
photographs, satellite images, cartographic
literature, and geographic information systems /
Ralph E. Ehrenberg ; preface by Alan K.
Henrikson ; consultants, Joseph W. Wiedel,
John A. Wolter ; editor, Zdeněk V. David.
Washington, D.C. : Smithsonian Institution
Press, 1987. xx, 385 p. ; 24 cm. (Scholar's guide
to Washington, D. C. no. 12) "Woodrow Wilson
International Center for Scholars." Includes indexes.
Bibliography: p. [327]-328. ISBN 0-87474-406-7
DDC 026/.912/025753 19
1. Map collections - Washington (D.C.) - Directories. I.
David, Zdeněk V. II. Title. III. Title: Cartography and
remote sensing imagery.
GA193.U5 E37 1987
NYPL [Map Div. 87-819]

Ehrens, Susan. Alma Lavenson photographs /
Susan Ehrens. 1st ed. Berkeley, Calif. :
Wildwood Arts, c1990. 106 p. : ill.; 30 cm.
Includes bibliographical references (p. 104-106).   ISBN
0-8263-1237-3
1. Lavenson, Alma, 1897-. I. Lavenson, Alma, 1897-. II.
Title.   ***NYPL [MFX+ (Lavenson) 91-5848]***

Ehrentraut, R. P. Restauriertes Kulturgut aus den
Werkstätten des Bezirkes Karl-Marx-Stadt .
Glauchau , 1986. 68 p. ;
NYPL [3-MAW (Glauchau) 90-10827]

Ehrlich, George, 1925- Technology and the artist
[microform] : a study of the interaction of
technological growth and nineteenth century
American pictorial art / by George Ehrlich.
1960. iv, 243 leaves : ill. Thesis (Ph.D.)--University
of Illinois, 1960. Bibliography: (leaves 238-242)
Microfilm. Ann Arbor, Mich. : University Microfilms
International, 1961. 1 microfilm reel ; 35 mm.
1. Art, Modern - 19th century - United States. 2. Art
and technology - United States. I. Title.
NYPL [*ZM-231]

Eidelberg, Martin P. Design 1935-1965 .
[Montréal] , 1991. 424 p. :   ISBN 0-8109-3205-9
DDC 745/.09/0407471428 20
NK1394 .D47 1991
NYPL [3-MNH+ 91-7472]

**Eidgenössische Technische Hochschule Zürich.
Institut für Geschichte und Theorie der
Architektur.** Hannes Meyer, 1889-1954 .
Berlin , c1989. 368 p. :   ISBN 3-433-02053-1 :
DDC 720/.92 20
NA1353.M4 H35 1989

The Eiffel Tower /. Ryan, Christopher, 1952-
Mankato, MN, U. S.A. , c1991. p. cm.   ISBN
1-560-65026-5 :   DDC 725/.97/0944361 20
NA2930 .R93 1991

**EIGHT ECCENTRICS OF YANG-CHOU
(GROUP OF PAINTERS) -
EXHIBITIONS.**
Giacalone, Vito. The Eccentric painters of
Yangzhou /. New York City , 1990. 92 p. :
ISBN 0-295-97087-1
NYPL [3-MAG 91-6594]

**EIGHT (GROUP OF AMERICAN ARTISTS) -
EXHIBITIONS.**
Men of the rebellion . Washington, D.C. ,
c1990. 32 p. :   ***NYPL [3-MCW 91-4249]***

Milroy, Elizabeth, 1954- Painters of a new
century . Milwaukee, WI , 1991. p. cm.   ISBN
0-944110-08-8   DDC 759.03/09/04107477595 20
ND212.5.E4 M5 1991

Eight hundred years of Japanese printmaking :
from the collection of Dr. and Mrs. James B.
Austin. Pittsburgh : Museum of Art, Carnegie
Institute, c1976. 126 p. : ill. (some col.) ; 29
cm. Catalog of an exhibition held October 22,
1976-January 2, 1977, at the Museum of Art, Carnegie
Institute, Pittsburgh. Introduction by Roger S. Keyes.
1. Austin, James Bliss, 1904- - Art Collections -
Exhibitions. 2. Prints, Japanese - Private collections -
United States - Exhibitions. I. Keyes, Roger S. II.
Carnegie Institute. Museum of Art.
NYPL [MDBV 90-6041]

Eight Irish paintings. [S.l. : s.n., 1985?] [11], 8 p.,
[8] leaves of plates : col. ill. ; 32 cm. Three
artcles signed by Brendan Kennelly, Brian Quinn and
Max Wykes-Joyce respectively. Paintings by Arthur
Armstrong ... [et. al]
1. Armstrong, Arthur, Irish painter. 2. Painting, Irish -
Catalogs. 3. Painting, Modern - 20th century - Ireland -
Catalogs. I. Kennelly, Brendan.
NYPL [3-MCY+ 89-3282]

Eighteen contemporary masters : United States
Embassy, Ottawa. [Ottawa : The Embassy,
1977] 23 p. : col. ill. ; 23 cm. Cover title.
1. Art, Modern - 20th century - United States. 2. Art,
Modern - 20th century - Canada. I. United States.
Embassy (Canada).   ***NYPL [3-MAL 90-5655]***

**Eighteenth century Italian drawings in the
Metropolitan Museum of Art.** Metropolitan
Museum of Art (New York, N.Y.). 18th century
Italian drawings in the Metropolitan Museum of
Art /. New York , 1990. 288 p. :   ISBN
0-87099-585-5   DDC 741.945/074/7471 20
NC255 .M4 1990
NYPL [3-MAVZ (New York) 91-3640]

**Eighteenth century Venetian art in Canadian
collections.** Knox, George. 18th century
Venetian art in Canadian collections =.
Vancouver, B.C., Canada , c1989. 108 p. :
ISBN 0-920095-81-X
IN PROCESS (ONLINE)
NYPL [3-MAMC+ 91-6265]

An eighth secret alphabet /. Earnshaw, Anthony.
Church Hanborough, Oxford , 1988 ([Didcot?
England] : Didcot Press) [23] p. :   DDC
741.5/942 20
NC1479.E37 A4 1988

Eighties style, designs of the decade. Bangert,
Albrecht, 1944- 80s style, designs of the decade
/. New York , 1990. 240 p. :   ISBN
1-558-59117-6   DDC 745.4/442 20
NK1390 .B26 1990
NYPL [3-MNF+ 90-13410]

Eighty years of Australian painting. The D.R.
Sheumack collection . Paddington, NSW , 1988.
[153] p. :   ***NYPL [3-MCY 89-11925]***

Eikaas, Ludvig, 1920- Portrett av jeg /. Oslo ,
c1990. 131 p. :   ISBN 82-504-1793-3
N7073.E36 P67 1990

EIKAAS, LUDVIG, 1920-
Portrett av jeg /. Oslo , c1990. 131 p. : ISBN
82-504-1793-3
N7073.E36 P67 1990

EIKONS. see ICONS.

Eileen Gray, designer /. Johnson, J. Stewart.
London , c1979. 67 p. : ISBN 0-87070-307-2 :
NK1535.G68 J63 　　**NYPL [MOI 80-2273]**

Eilenberg, Natasha. Boisselier, Jean. [Tendances
de l'art khmèr. English.] Trends in Khmer art /.
Ithaca, N.Y. , 1989. 118 p. : ISBN
0-87727-705-2 DDC 730/.9596/074596 20
NB1015 .B6213 1989
　　　　　　　　　NYPL [3-MAF 91-3339]

**EILENBERG, SAMUEL - ART
COLLECTIONS - EXHIBITIONS.**
Metropolitan Museum of Art (New York, N.Y.)
The lotus transcendent . New York , 1991. p.
cm. ISBN 0-87099-613-4 DDC 730/.0954/0747471
20
N7300 .M47 1991

Ein Frisör aus Lingen, Harry Kramer : Stuttgart,
9. August bis 16. September 1990,
Württembergischer Kunstverein Stuttgart :
Lingen, 29. September bis 28. Oktober 1990,
Kunstverein Lingen in der Galerie im Theater :
Kassel, 13. Januar bis 1. April 1991, Museum
Fridericianum Kassel und Gesamthochschule
Kassel / Ausstellungsorganisation, Kunstverein
Lingen ; [Herausgeber, Michael Willhardt ;
Redaktion, Michael Willhardt, unter Mitarbeit
von Anne Fingerling, Wolfgang Hahn, Felicitas
Noeske]. Freren : Luca, c1990. ix, 198 p., [1] p.
of plates : ill. ; 28 cm. Exhibition catalog issued on
the occasion of the 65th birthday of Harry Kramer.
Cover title: Ein Frisör aus Lingen. Includes texts by
Harry Kramer. Filmography: p. 180. Includes
bibliographical references (p. 180-181). ISBN
3-923641-30-3 DDC 700/.92 20
*1. Kramer, Harry, 1925- - Exhibitions. I. Kramer,
Harry, 1925-. II. Willhardt, Michael, 1956-. III.
Württembergischer Kunstverein. IV. Kunstverein
Lingen. V. Title: Frisör aus Lingen.*
NX550.Z9 K7352 1990

Eingartner, Johannes. Isis und ihre Dienerinnen
in der Kunst der römischen Kaiserzeit / von
Johannes Eingartner. Leiden ; New York : E.J.
Brill, 1991. 197 p., [97] p. of plates : ill. ; 24
cm. (Mnemosyne, bibliotheca classica Batava.
Supplementum, 0169-8958 . 115) Revision of the
author's thesis
(doctoral)--Ludwig-Maximilians-Universität München,
1982. Includes bibliographical references and indexes.
ISBN 90-04-09312-5 DDC 733/.5 20
*1. Sculpture, Roman - Themes, motives. 2. Isis
(Egyptian deity) - Art. 3. Goddesses, Egyptian, in art. I.
Title. II. Series.*
NB115 .E37 1990

Eingreifendes Fotografieren : Geschichte, Theorie,
Projekte / hrsg. von Wolfgang Kunde u.
Lienhard Wawrzyn. Berlin : Verlag Ästhetik u.
Kommunikation, 1979. 240 p. : numerous ill. ;
21 cm. (Schriften des Instituts für Kultur und Ästhetik
(IKAe) ; Bd. 2) Includes bibliographical references.
*I. Kunde, Wolfgang. II. Wawrzyn, Lienhard, 1941-. III.
Series: Institut für kultur und Ästhetik. Schriften, Bd.2.*
TR820.5 .E38 　　**NYPL [MFW 81-506]**

Einholz, Sibylle. Ethos und Pathos . Berlin ,
c1990. 419 p. : ISBN 3-7861-1597-4
　　　　　　　NYPL [3-MGI 90-12677]

Einleuchten : Will, Vorstel & Simul in HH : 11.
November 1989 bis 18. Februar 1990 /
[Kataloggestaltung, Harald Szeemann, Carsten
Best ; redaktionelle Mitarbeit, Renate Cornu,
Uta Grosenick]. Hamburg : Christians, [1989]
289 p. : ill. (chiefly col.) ; 32 cm. Catalog of an
exhibition held at the Deichtorhallen Hamburg. ISBN
3-7672-1102-5 DDC 709/.04/507443515 20
*1. Art, Modern - 20th century - Exhibitions. I.
Szeemann, Harald. II. Best, Carsten. III. Cornu, Renate.
IV. Grosenick, Uta. V. Deichtorhallen Hamburg.*
N6488.G3 H2832 1989

Einsichten. Thomann, Ernst, 1910- Ernst
Thomann--Einsichten . Emmendingen , c1990.
69 p. : ISBN 3-925928-13-8
NB588.T39 A4 1990

Einsmann, Elke. Die Malerin Elke Einsmann /
Dino Larese. Amriswil : Amriswiler Bücherei,
[1988] [72] p. : col. ill. ; 27 cm. Introductory text
in German and English.

1. Einsmann, Elke. I. Larese, Dino. II. Title.
MLCM 89/00586 (N)
　　　　　　　NYPL [3-MCZ E352 90-12593]

EINSMANN, ELKE.
Einsmann, Elke. Die Malerin Elke Einsmann /.
Amriswil [1988] [72] p. :
MLCM 89/00586 (N)
　　　　　　　NYPL [3-MCZ E352 90-12593]

Einzelbilder vom Niederrhein. Quedenfeldt,
Erwin, 1869-1948. Erwin Quedenfeldt . Kleve ,
c1989. 119 p. : ISBN 3-89413-180-2
　　　　NYPL [MFX+ (Quedenfeldt) 90-13431]

Einzelkarten des Matthias Quad (1557-1613) /.
Quad, Matthias, 1557-1613. Mönchengladbach ,
1984. 1 atlas (1 portfolio ([10] folded leaves of
plates)) : DDC 911/.43 19
G1912.2 .Q8 1984 **NYPL [Map Div. 87-177]**

Eirich, E. C. (Edward Conrad), 1877-1929.
E.C. Eirich (1877-1929) : a Drexel technical
illustrator / essays by Jack Becker ; co-curators,
Jack Becker and Jean Henry. [Philadelphia,
Pa.] : Museum at Drexel University, c1991. 48
p. : ill. ; 28 cm. Catalog of an exhibition held at the
Museum at Drexel University. Jan. 1991-Jan. 1992.
Includes bibliographical references.
*1. Eirich, E. C. (Edward Conrad), 1877-1929 -
Exhibitions. I. Becker, Jack. II. Henry, Jean. III. Drexel
University. Museum. IV. Title.*
　　　　　　NYPL [3-MCX E35 91-7603]

**EIRICH, E. C. (EDWARD CONRAD), 1877-
1929 - EXHIBITIONS.**
Eirich, E. C. (Edward Conrad), 1877-1929. E.C.
Eirich (1877-1929) . [Philadelphia, Pa.] , c1991.
48 p. : 　　**NYPL [3-MCX E35 91-7603]**

Eisenman, Peter, 1932-
Peter Eisenman : Guardiola House =
Guardiola Haus : Ausstellung vom 16. Januar
bis. 14. Februar 1989, Aedes Galerie für
Architektur und Raum. Berlin : Die Galerie,
1989. [46] p. : ill. ; 19 cm. English and German.
*1. Eisenman, Peter, 1932- - Exhibitions. 2. Guardiola
House (Puerto de Santa Maria, Spain). 3. Architectural
drawing - 20th century - United States. I. Aedes
Galerie für Architektur und Raum. II. Title.*
　　　　NYPL [3-MQZ (Eisenman) 90-12528]

EISENMAN, PETER, 1932- - EXHIBITIONS.
Eisenman, Peter, 1932- Peter Eisenman .
Berlin , 1989. [46] p. :
　　　　NYPL [3-MQZ (Eisenman) 90-12528]

Eisenplastik. Kunsthalle Bern, Eisenplastik .
[Bern , 1955] 1 v. (unpaged) :
　　　　　　NYPL [3-MGF 91-395]

**Eisenwerth, J. Adolf Schmoll gen. see Schmoll
gen. Eisenwerth, J. Adolf, 1915-**

Eisler, Colin. Dürer's animals / Colin Eisler.
Washington : Smithsonian Institution Press,
1991. p. cm. Includes bibliographical references and
index. ISBN 0-87474-408-3 DDC 760/.092 20
*1. Dürer, Albrecht, 1471-1528 - Criticism and
interpretation. 2. Animals in art. I. Title.*
N6888.D8 E57 1991

Eisler, Colin T. American drawings . New York,
1980. [40] p. : 　　**NYPL [3-MBH 90-6350]**

Eitle, Hans-Dieter. Eitle, Ruth. Ruth Eitle .
Tübingen , 1989. 222 p. : ISBN 3-924123-13-6
　　　　　NYPL [3-MCK+ E39 89-27955]

Eitle, Peter. Eitle, Ruth. Ruth Eitle . Tübingen ,
1989. 222 p. : ISBN 3-924123-13-6
　　　　　NYPL [3-MCK+ E39 89-27955]

Eitle, Ruth.
Ruth Eitle : Malerei und Graphik : [Kunsthalle
Tübingen, 23. April-28. Mai 1989 /
Kataloggestaltung, Hans-Dieter Eitle, Peter
Eitle]. Tübingen : Gulde-Verlag, 1989. 222 p. :
ill. (some col., some folded), music, ports. ; 31
cm. ISBN 3-924123-13-6
*1. Eitle, Ruth - Exhibitions. I. Eitle, Hans-Dieter. II.
Eitle, Peter. III. Title.*
　　　　　NYPL [3-MCK+ E39 89-27955]

EITLE, RUTH - EXHIBITIONS.
Eitle, Ruth. Ruth Eitle . Tübingen , 1989. 222
p. : ISBN 3-924123-13-6
　　　　　NYPL [3-MCK+ E39 89-27955]

Eje de desarrollo Orinoco-Apure atlas /
Ministerio del Ambiente y de los Recursos
Naturales Renovables, Dirección General
Sectorial de Planificación y Ordenación del
Ambiente, Proyecto Orinoco-Apure. Caracas :
El Ministerio, 1987. 1 Atlas ([16] leaves) : 13

col. maps ; 46 x 92 cm. Cover title: Atlas eje de
desarrollo Orinoco-Apure. At head of title:
PROA/Projecto Orinoco-Apure. "Agosto 1987."
"Publicación especial DGSPOA/PE/17."
*1. Regional planning - Venezuela - Maps. 2.
Venezuela - Maps. 3. Apure (Venezuela) - Maps. I.
Venezuela. Ministerio del Ambiente y de los Recursos
Naturales Renovables. Proyecto Orinoco-Apure. II.
Title: Proyecto Orinoco-Apure. III. Title: Atlas eje de
desarrollo Orinoco-Apure. IV. Title: Desarrollo
Orinoco-Apure.* 　　**NYPL [Map Div. 91-50]**

Ekklēsies tou Nomou Pellēs. Moutsopoulos,
Nikolaos K., 1927- Churches in the prefecture
of Pella /. Thessaloniki , 1973. xi, 504 p., [1]
folded leaf of plates :
NA5599.M34 M6 1973

EKKT 1956-1990 art album /. Society of
Estonian Artists in Toronto. [Toronto] [1990]
180 p. : DDC 709/.2/2713541 B 20
N6547.T67 S65 1990

El aporte friulano a la arquitectura argentina /.
Brandariz, Gustavo A. Buenos Aires , 1987. 52
leaves :
NA830 .B7 1987

El arte colombiano en el siglo XX /. Mejía de
Millán, Beatriz Amelia. Pereira, Colombia ,
1988. 155 p. : DDC 709/.861/0904 20
N6675 .M45 1988

El arte de la platería en Venezuela . Duarte,
Carlos F. Caracas, Venezuela , 1988. 438 p. :
ISBN 980-300-084-5 DDC 739.2/3787 20
NK7141.A1 D8 1988

El Arte de la platería mexicana, 500 años :
noviembre 1989-febrero 1990. [Mexico] :
Centro Cultural Arte Contemporáneo, [c1989]
595 p. : ill. (some col.) ; 31 cm. Includes
bibliographical references (p. 588-592). ISBN
968-619-120-8 DDC 739.2/3772 20
*1. Silverwork - Mexico. 2. Silversmiths - Mexico. 3.
Hallmarks - Mexico. I. Centro Cultural/Arte
Contemporáneo (Mexico).*
NK7114.A1 A73 1989

El arte genial de Víctor Mideros . Almeida,
Enrique. Quito , 1988 (Quito, Ecuador : Tall.
Gráf. del Instituto Andino de Artes Populares
del Convenio Andrés Bello) 156 p. : DDC
759.9866 20
ND389.M5 A84 1988

El barroco en Hidalgo. Vergara Vergara, José.
[Pachuca, Mexico?] , 1988. 177, [5] p. :
N7914.A3 H538 1988

El cartel taurino . Zaldívar, Rafael. Madrid ,
1990. 370 p. : ISBN 84-239-5426-9 DDC
741.6/74/0946 20
NC1849.B84 Z35 1990

El color humano . Abinade, José, 1922- Caracas ,
1990. 170 p. ; ISBN 980-222-520-7 DDC 759.987
B 20
ND435 .A24 1990

El corazón sangrante =. Sussman, Elisabeth,
1939- Boston, Mass. , Seattle, Wash. , c1991. p.
ISBN 0-910663-50-5 (paperback) DDC 704.9/46
20
N8217.H53 S87 1991

El descubrimiento de Miró . Combalía Dexeus,
Victoria, 1952- Barcelona , 1990. 302 p., [24] p.
of plates : ISBN 84-233-1921-0 DDC 759.6 20
N7113.M54 C66 1990

El escultor Ortells . Gasco Sidro, Antonio J.
(Antonio José) [Castelló] , 1989. 191 p. : ISBN
84-86895-11-1 DDC 730/.92 B 20
NB813.O697 G37 1989

El Espíritu erótico / Fernando Guinard,
Jotamario, Alvaro Chaves M. [editores]. 1. ed.
Bogotá : Taller De-Mente Colombiano, 1990.
207 p. : ill. (some col.) ; 29 cm. Includes
bibliographical references (p. 206) and index. DDC
704.9/428/098610904 20
*1. Erotic art - Colombia. 2. Art, Colombian. 3. Art,
Modern - 20th century - Colombia. I. Guinard,
Fernando. II. Jotamario. III. Chaves, Alvaro.*
N8217.E6 E87 1990

El Goulli, Sophie. Ammar Farhat et son œuvre /
Sophie El Goulli. Tunis : Union internationale
de banques, c1979. 140 p. : chiefly ill. (some
col.), ports. ; 30 cm. French and Arabic. ISBN
2-85119-021-0
1. Farhat, Ammar. I. Farhat, Ammar. II. Title.
　　　　　NYPL [3-MCZ+ F215 90-11030]

El Grabado : historia y trascendencia / Cristina Rodríguez García ... [et al.].1. ed. México, D.F. : Universidad Autónoma Metropolitana-Xochimilco, 1989. 141 p. : ill. ; 31 cm. Includes bibliographical references (p. 136-141). ISBN 968-8405-20-5 DDC 769.972 20
1. Prints, Mexican. 2. Prints - History. I. Rodríguez García, Cristina.
NE544 .G66 1989

El grabado en la ciudad de Puebla de los Angeles /. Pérez Salazar, Francisco, 1888-1941. Puebla , 1990. 68 p. :
NE545.P8 P4 1990

El Greco : documents on his life and work / edited by Nicos Hadjinicolaou = Domēnikos Theotokopoulos : tekmēria gia tē zōē kai to ergo tou / epimeleia Nikou Chadzēnikolaou. Rethymno : Crete University Press, 1990. 416 p. : ill. ; 25 x 35 cm. (Literary sources of art history = Pēges tēs historias tēs technēs) English, French, Greek, Italian, and Spanish. Includes bibliographical references. ISBN 960-7309-00-6 DDC 759.6 20
1. Greco, 1541?-1614 - Criticism and interpretation. I. Hadjinicolaou, Nicos, 1938-. II. Title: Domēnikos Theotokopoulos. III. Series: Literary sources of art history.
ND813.T4 E524 1990

El Greco . Greco, 1541?-1614. New York , c1941. [41] p. :
                              NYPL [3-MCQ+ T39 88-3794]

El Greco, mystery and illumination : [exhibition National Gallery of Scotland, Edinburgh, July 29-Oct. 15, 1989] / National Gallery of Scotland in collaboration with the Edinburgh International Festival. [Edinburgh] : Trustees of the National Galleries of Scotland, [1989] 96 p. : ill. (some col.) ; 23 cm. Exhibition "selected and catalogued by David Davies"--p. 7. Includes bibliographical references. ISBN 0-903148-90-0
1. Greco, 1541?-1614 - Exhibitions. 2. Monkeys in art - Exhibitions. 3. Light in art - Exhibitions. I. Greco, 1541?-1614. II. Davies, David. III. National Gallery of Scotland. IV. Edinburgh International Festival. V. Title: Mystery and illumination.
          NYPL [3-MCQ T39 90-10831]

El Greco to Murillo . Mallory, Nina A. New York , c1990. xx, 316 p. : ISBN 0-06-435531-4 : DDC 759.6/09/032 20
ND805 .M35 1990
                              NYPL [3-MCP 90-13189]

El-Khoury, Fouad. Domestic architecture in the Lebanon / Fouad El-Khoury. London : Art and Archaeology Research Papers, [1975] 25 p. : ill., map, plans ; 29 cm. (AARP, Art and archaeology research papers) Cover title. "June 1975."
1. Architecture, Domestic - Lebanon. 2. Dwellings - Lebanon. I. Title. II. Series.
                              NYPL [3-MRG 90-12551]

El Lissitzky . Hemken, Kai-Uwe. Köln , c1990. 211 p. : ISBN 3-7701-2613-0
          NYPL [3-MCZ L772 91-6410]

El mundo desconocido de José Luis Cuevas /. Cajigas R., María de los Angeles. México , c1990. 154 p. : ISBN 968-409-526-0 DDC 760/.092 B 20
N6559.C8 C34 1990

El negro /. Alberti, Rafael, 1902- [Negro Motherwell. English.] Bedford, N.Y. , 1983. [24] leaves (some folded) : DDC 769.92 20
NE2312.M68 A4 1983

El Palacio de Minería. 4. ed. México, D.F. : Universidad Nacional Autónoma de México, Sociedad de Ex-alumnos de la Facultad de Ingeniería de la UNAM, 1988. 231 p. : ill. (some col., some folded) ; 31 cm. Includes bibliographical references.
1. Palacio de Minería (Mexico City). 2. Neoclassicism (Architecture) - Mexico - Mexico City - Conservation and restoration. 3. Mexico City (Mexico) - Buildings, structures, etc. 4. Tolsá, Manuel, 1757-1816. I. Universidad Nacional Autónoma de México. Facultad de Ingeniería. Sociedad de Ex-alumnos.
NA4425.M62 M494 1988

El Palacio Escárzaga, Durango /. Guerrero Romero, Javier. Durango, Dgo., México , 1988. xii, 82 p. : ISBN 968-609-400-8
NA757.D87 G84 1986

El Paso Museum of Art. Schriever, George. American masters in the West . [S.l.] , c1976. 67 p. :   NYPL [3-MCW 90-5762]

El Quehacer de un pueblo : artesanías Michoacán / [texto documental, Octavio Vázquez, alfarería ... et al. ; texto narrativo, Miguel Angel Pardo ; fotografía, Luis Arias ... et al. ; canciones y adivinanzas, Unidad Regional de Culturas Populares ; poesía, Alejandro Aura ; coordinación, Porfirio Aguilera ; diseño, Marcela Meurehg, Raúl Mercado]. Morelia, Michoacán : Casa de las Artesanías del Estado de Michoacán, 1986. 183, [9] p. : ill. (some col.) ; 27 cm. Includes bibliographical references (p. [187]-[190]). ISBN 968-667-045-9   DDC 745/.0972/37 20
1. Decorative arts - Mexico - Michoacán de Ocampo. 2. Folk art - Mexico - Michoacán de Ocampo. 3. Handicraft - Mexico - Michoacán de Ocampo. I. Vázquez, Octavio. II. Aguilera, Porfirio. III. Casa de las Artesanías del Estado de Michoacán.
NK845.M53 Q44 1986

El retablo neoclásico en Cádiz /. Alonso de la Sierra Fernández, Lorenzo. [Cádiz] [1989?] 177 p., [24] p. of plates : ISBN 84-87144-02-0
NB1910 .A48 1989

El Románico en Silos : IX centenario de la consagración de la iglesia y claustro, 1088-1988. Burgos : Abadía de Silos, 1990. 606 p. : ill. (some col.); 30 cm. (Studia Silensia. Series maior . 1) Includes bibliographical references. ISBN 0-8470-0317-7   DDC 726/.7/0946353 20
1. Santo Domingo de Silos (Benedictine Abbey). 2. Architecture, Romanesque - Spain - Burgos (Province) - Congresses. 3. Christian art and symbolism - Medieval, 500-1500 - Spain - Burgos (Province) - Congresses. I. Series.
NA5811.S48 R66 1990

El Salvador /. Kufeld, Adam. New York , c1990. 183 p. : ISBN 0-393-02811-9 (cloth) : DDC 972.8405/3 20
F1488.3 .K84 1990
                              NYPL [MFX (Kufeld) 91-5007]

EL SALVADOR - DESCRIPTION AND TRAVEL - 1981- - VIEWS.
Kufeld, Adam. El Salvador /. New York , c1990. 183 p. : ISBN 0-393-02811-9 (cloth) : DDC 972.8405/3 20
F1488.3 .K84 1990
                              NYPL [MFX (Kufeld) 91-5007]

EL SALVADOR - GEOGRAPHY.
Geografía de El Salvador. San Salvador , 1986- v. : DDC 917.284/02 19
F1484.3 .G46 1986 NYPL [Map Div. 90-69]

El Salvador. Ministerio de Cultura y Comunicaciones. Dirección de Publicaciones e Impresos. Geografía de El Salvador. San Salvador , 1986- v. : DDC 917.284/02 19
F1484.3 .G46 1986 NYPL [Map Div. 90-69]

EL SALVADOR - POETRY.
Kufeld, Adam. El Salvador /. New York , c1990. 183 p. : ISBN 0-393-02811-9 (cloth) : DDC 972.8405/3 20
F1488.3 .K84 1990
                              NYPL [MFX (Kufeld) 91-5007]

EL SALVADOR - POLITICS AND GOVERNMENT - 1979- - PICTORIAL WORKS.
Kufeld, Adam. El Salvador /. New York , c1990. 183 p. : ISBN 0-393-02811-9 (cloth) : DDC 972.8405/3 20
F1488.3 .K84 1990
                              NYPL [MFX (Kufeld) 91-5007]

El Surrealismo entre Viejo y Nuevo Mundo : 6 marzo-22 abril 1990 : Sala de Exposiciones de la Fundación Cultural Mapfre Vida. [Madrid] : Quinto Centenario, [1990] 346 p. : ill. (some col.) ; 28 cm. (Colección Encuentros. Serie Catálogos) Spanish and English. Includes bibliographical references. ISBN 84-86022-51-2
1. Surrealism - United States - Exhibitions. 2. Art, Modern - 20th century - United States - Exhibitions. 3. Avant-garde (Aesthetics) - United States - History - 20th century - Exhibitions. 4. Surrealism - Mexico - Exhibitions. 5. Art, Modern - 20th century - Mexico - Exhibitions. 6. Avant-garde (Aesthetics) - Mexico - History - 20th century - Exhibitions. I. Comisión Nacional del Quinto Centenario del Descubrimiento de América (Spain). II. Fundación Mapfre. III. Series: Colección Encuentros (Turner (Firm)). Serie Catálogos.
N6512.5.S87 S8 1990

El Taller Torres-García : the School of the South and its legacy / edited by Mari Carmen Ramírez.1st ed. Austin : Published for the Archer M. Huntington Art Gallery, College of Fine Arts, the University of Texas at Austin by University of Texas Press, 1991. p. cm. Catalogue of the exhibition held June 1991-Jan. 1993 at the Archer M. Huntington Art Gallery and other locations. Includes bibliographical references (p.) and index. ISBN 0-292-78121-0 DDC 709/.8/074 20
1. Art, Latin American - Exhibitions. 2. Asociación de Arte Constructivo - Exhibitions. 3. Taller Torres-García - Exhibitions. 4. Art, Modern - 20th century - Latin America - Exhibitions. I. Ramírez, Mari Carmen, 1955-. II. Archer M. Huntington Art Gallery.
N6502.5 .T35 1991

El Templo de la Purísima en Monterrey /. Ravizé Rodríguez, Armando. Monterrey, N.L. [Mexico] , 1986. 1 v. (unpaged) :
NA5257.M66 R38 1986

Elaborati urbanistici : piani e progetti per piccoli e medi comuni / progetto dell'edizione Luigi Galletti ; coordinamento editoriale Luigi Galletti e Antonia Izzo. Milano : Over, [1987?] 10 pamphlets in portfolio : ill. ; 29 cm. (Architettura, edilizia, urbanistica . v. 5)
1. City planning - Italy. 2. Architecture - Italy - Designs and plans. I. Galletti, Luigi. II. Izzo, Antonia. III. Title: Piani e progetti per piccoli e medi comuni. IV. Series. NYPL [3-MQWB 90-11014]

ELDERLY PERSONS. see AGED.

Eldredge, Charles C. Georgia O'Keeffe / Charles C. Eldredge. New York : H.N. Abrams in association with the National Museum of American Art, Smithsonian Institution, 1991. 160 p. : ill. (some col.) ; 32 cm. (The Library of American art) Includes bibliographical references (p. 157) and index. Errata slip inserted. ISBN 0-8109-3657-7 DDC 759.13 20
1. O'Keeffe, Georgia, 1887-1986 - Criticism and interpretation. I. O'Keeffe, Georgia, 1887-1986. II. Series: Library of American art (Harry N. Abrams, Inc.). III. Title.
ND237.O5 E43 1991
                              NYPL [3-MCX+ 041 91-7249]

ELECTIONS - JAMAICA.
Stone, Carl. Electoral behaviour and public opinion in Jamaica /. Mona , 1974. 107 p. :
HN230.Z9 P817   NYPL [JLE 77-1420]

Electoral behaviour and public opinion in Jamaica /. Stone, Carl. Mona , 1974. 107 p. :
HN230.Z9 P817   NYPL [JLE 77-1420]

ELECTORAL COLLEGE. see PRESIDENTS - UNITED STATES - ELECTION.

ELECTRIC LAMPS, INCANDESCENT - HISTORY.
Myerson, Jeremy. Lamps and lighting /. New York , 1990. 80 p. : ISBN 0-442-30302-5 DDC 749/.63 20
TK4351 .C66 1990
                              NYPL [3-MNHL 91-3445]

ELECTRIC LIGHT IN PHOTOGRAPHY. see PHOTOGRAPHY - PORTRAITS - LIGHTING AND POSING.

ELECTRONIC ART. see VIDEO ART.

Elegant glassware of the depression era /. Florence, Gene, 1944- Paducah, KY , c1991. 191 p. : ISBN 0-89145-436-5 : DDC 748.2913/075 20
NK5439.D44 F563 1991

Elektrifizierung in Westfalen : Fotodokumente aus dem Archiv der VEW / im Auftrag der Vereinigte Elektrizitätswerke Westfalen AG ; herausgegeben von Theo Horstmann. Hagen : v.d. Linnepe, c1990. 168 p. : ill. ; 29 cm. ISBN 3-89431-005-7
1. Vereinigte Elektrizitätswerke Westfalen - Photograph collections - Exhibitions. I. Horstmann, Theo. II. Museum für Kunst und Kulturgeschichte der Stadt Dortmund.
IN PROCESS (ONLINE)
                              NYPL [MFW 91-2652]

Elemente der Bilder und Bücher. Watts, Harriett. Hans Arp und Sophie Taeuber-Arp . Wolfenbüttel [1989] 54 p. : ISBN 3-88373-054-8 DDC 700/.92 20
N6853.A7 A4 1989

Elements = [Patān seisatsushū erementsu]. [Shohan]. [Tokyo] : AIM, 1989. 12 v. : all ill. ; 28 cm. Cover title. Parallel title on v. 2-12: Irasuto patān-shū "erementsu." CONTENTS. - 1-3. Trends: African. Japanesque. Fancy & goods -- 4-6. Neo natural: Botanical. Animal. Organic -- 7-9. Basic: Basic. 2 dimensions. 3 dimensions -- 10-12. Communication:

Signal. Event. Wave.   ISBN 4-87210-018-2 (v. 1) :
DDC 745.4 20
1. Design - Themes, motives. I. Ēmu Kurieitibu
Purodakutsu, Kabushiki Kaisha. II. Title: Patän
seisatsushü erementsu. III. Title: Irasuto patän-shū
"erements.".
NK1530 .E44 1989

The elements of architecture . Meiss, Pierre von,
1938- [De la forme au lieu. English.] London ,
New York, NY , 1990. xiv, 211 p. :   ISBN
0-442-31151-6 (U. S.)   DDC 720 20
NA2760 .M4413 1989
                              NYPL [3-MQD 90-10808]

The Elements of style : a practical encyclopedia
of interior architectural details, from 1485 to
the present / Stephen Calloway, general editor,
Elizabeth Cromley, American editor. New
York : Simon and Schuster, c1991. p. cm.
Includes bibliographical references and index.   ISBN
0-671-73981-6   DDC 721 20
1. Interior architecture. 2. Architecture - Details. 3.
Interior architecture - United States. 4. Architecture -
United States - Details. I. Calloway, Stephen. II.
Cromley, Elizabeth C.
NA2850 .E44 1991

Elenz, Reinhold. Dölling, Regine. Das
Stiftergrabmal in Maria Laach /. Worms ,
c1990. 73 p. :   ISBN 3-88462-069-X
NB1870 .D6 1990

Elf steden, elf landen. 11 steden, 11 landen .
Leeuwarden, The Netherlands , 1990. xxvii, 263
p. :   ISBN 90-900348-9-7 :
N6758 .A113 1990

Elffers, Joost. Meller, Susan. Textile designs .
New York , 1991. p. cm.   ISBN 0-8109-3853-7
DDC 746.6/2041 20
NK9500 .M45 1991

Elg, Margareta, 1944- Svenska kartor /
Margareta Elg ; teckning, Karin Feltzin, Ina
Lehman ; foto, Pål-Nils Nilsson. Stockholm :
Svenska turistföreningen, 1979. 63, [1] p. : ill.
(some col.), maps (some col.) ; 25 cm. (Känn ditt
land . nr. 1) Caption title. Includes index. Includes
bibliographical references.   ISBN 91-7156-008-4 (pbk.)
1. Sweden - Maps. I. Title. II. Series.
GA991 .E43   NYPL [Map Div. 90-11679]

Elger, Dietmar.
Neonstücke / Dietmar Elger. Buchhandelsausg.
[Stuttgart] : Edition Cantz, [1990?] 103 p. : ill. ;
29 cm. Published on the occasion of an exhibition
held at the Sprengel Museum Hannover. German and
English. ISBN 3-89322-206-5
1. Neon sculpture - Exhibitions. I. Sprengel Museum
Hannover. II. Title.   NYPL [3-MAL 91-6468]

Steinitz, Kate Traumann, 1880-1975. Kate
Steinitz, eine Dokumentation . Hannover ,
c1989. 106 p. :   ISBN 3-89169-051-7
                       NYPL [3-MCK S8225 91-4564]

Eliash, Humberto. Fernando Castillo : de lo
moderno a lo real / Humberto Eliash.
[Santiago, Chile] : Colegio de Arquitectos de
Chile : Facultad de Arquitectura, Universidad
Católica de Chile ; 237 p. : ill. (some col.) ; 23
x 24 cm. (Colección SomoSur . t. 7) Spanish and
English. Includes bibliographical references (p. 235).
ISBN 958-9082-44-0 (colección)   DDC 720/.92
20
1. Castillo Velasco, Fernando, 1918- - Catalogs. 2.
Architecture, Modern - 20th century - Chile - Catalogs.
I. Title.
NA869.C37 A4 1990

Eliot Clark (1883-1980) : artist, scholar, world
traveler / Mildred Thaler Cohen. New York,
N.Y. : Marbella Gallery, [1990] 53 p. : ill.
(some col.) ; 23 cm. Exhibition catalog.
1. Clark, Eliot Candee, 1883- - Exhibitions. I. Clark,
Eliot Candee, 1883-. II. Cohen, Mildred Thaler. III.
Marbella Gallery.
MLCM 90/01921 (N)
                       NYPL [3-MCX C592 91-7404]

Eliot, T. S. (Thomas Stearns), 1888-1965.
Four quartets. Finn, David, 1921- Evocations
of Four quartets : paintings / by David Finn.
Redding Ridge, CT, U. S.A. , c1990. 96 p. :
ISBN 0-933806-61-2 (cloth) :   DDC 759.13 20
ND237.F433 A4 1990

FOUR QUARTETS - INFLUENCE.
Finn, David, 1921- Evocations of Four
quartets . Redding Ridge, CT, U. S.A. ,
c1990. 96 p. :   ISBN 0-933806-61-2 (cloth) :

DDC 759.13 20
ND237.F433 A4 1990

Eliovson, Sima. The gardens of Roberto Burle
Marx / Sima Eliovson ; foreword by Roberto
Burle Marx. New York : H.N.
Abrams/Sagapress, c1991. 237 p. : ill. (chiefly
col.) ; 29 cm. "A Ngaere Macray book." Includes
index.   ISBN 0-8109-3357-8   DDC 712/.092 B 20
1. Burle Marx, Roberto, 1909-. 2. Gardens - Brazil. 3.
Landscape architects - Brazil - Biography. I. Title.
SB470.B87 E45 1991
                       NYPL [3-MSCC 91-6489]

Elisabeth Kmölniger, Zeichnungen /. Kmölniger,
Elisabeth, 1947- Frankfurt am Main , 1987. 146
p. :
          NYPL [3-MEM+ (Kmölniger) 90-10838]

Elisabeth Treskow, Goldschmiedekunst des 20.
Jahrhunderts . Treskow, Elisabeth, 1898- Köln
[1990] 168 p. :   DDC 739.2/272 20
NK7198.T734 A4 1990

ELISABETHKIRCHE (MARBURG, GRMANY)
Schneider Berrenberg, Rüdiger. Sie bauten ein
Abbild der Seele . München , Solingen , 1988.
xii, 149 p. :
NA5586.M23 S36 1988

Elizabeth II, Queen of Great Britain, 1926-
Millar, Oliver, Sir, 1923- The Victorian pictures
in the collection of Her Majesty the Queen .
Cambridge [England] , New York , 1992. p.
cm.   ISBN 0-521-26522-3 (hardcover)   DDC
759.2/074/41 20
ND192.V5 M55 1992

ELIZABETH, II, QUEEN OF GREAT
BRITAIN, 1926- - ART COLLECTIONS -
CATALOGS.
Blunt, Anthony, 1907-1983. The Roman
drawings of the XVII & XVIII centuries in the
collection of Her Majesty the Queen at
Windsor Castle /. London , c1960. 197 p. :
DDC 741.945/632/093207442296 20
NC256.R6 B4 1960

Millar, Oliver, Sir, 1923- The Victorian pictures
in the collection of Her Majesty the Queen .
Cambridge [England] , New York , 1992. p.
cm.   ISBN 0-521-26522-3 (hardcover)   DDC
759.2/074/41 20
ND192.V5 M55 1992

Parker, K. T. (Karl Theodore), 1895- The
drawings of Antonio Canaletto in the collection
of Her Majesty the Queen at Windsor Castle /.
Bologna, Italy , 1990. 174 p. :   ISBN
88-7779-105-5
                       NYPL [3-MCF+ C21 91-5238]

Elizabeth, Queen of Great Britain, 1926- see
Elizabeth II, Queen of Great Britain, 1926-

ELK COUNTY (PA.) - MAPS.
Rockford Map Publishers. Elk County,
Pennsylvania, land atlas & plat book .
Rockford, Ill. , Bradford, Pa. [c1990] 1 atlas
(79 p.) :   *NYPL [Map Div. 90-11385]*

Elk County, Pennsylvania, land atlas & plat
book . Rockford Map Publishers. Rockford,
Ill. , Bradford, Pa. [c1990] 1 atlas (79 p.) :
                       NYPL [Map Div. 90-11385]

Elling, Wilhelm. Der Antwerpener Altar in St.
Georg Vreden /. Vreden , 1989. 247 p. :   ISBN
3-926627-03-4
                       NYPL [3-MAIH+ 91-6544]

Elliot, Robert S. Reflections of an eras : portraits
of 19th century New Brunswick ships =
Reflets d'une époque : portraits de navires du
Nouveau-Brunswick au XIXe siècle / Robert S.
Elliot, Alan D. McNairn. Saint John, [N.B.]
Canada : New Brunswick Museum, 1987. [108]
p. : chiefly ill. (some col.) ; 22 x 28 cm. English
and French on parallel columns. Catalog of paintings at
the New Brunswick Museum. ISBN 0-919326-25-0
(pbk.)
1. New Brunswick Museum - Catalogs. 2. Sailing ships
in art - Catalogs. 3. Sailing ships - New Brunswick -
History - Catalogs. I. McNairn, Alan D. II. New
Brunswick Museum. III. Title.
                       NYPL [3-MAMZ 90-244]

Elliott, James. The perfect thought : works by
James Lee Byars / James Elliott. Berkeley,
Calif. : University Art Museum, University of
California at Berkeley, 1990. 154 p. : ill. (some
col.) ; 28 cm. Catalog of an exhibition held at the
University Art Museum, University of California at
Berkeley, Apr. 18-June 24, 1990 and at the

Contemporary Arts Museum, Houston, Tex., Sept.
8-Oct. 28, 1990. Includes bibliographical references (p.
147-154).
1. Byars, James Lee - Exhibitions. I. Byars, James Lee.
II. University of California, Berkeley. University Art
Museum. III. Title.
          NYPL [3-MGO (Byars) 91-6418]

Elliott, Julia. Art at the edge . Oxford , 1988. 43
p. :   ISBN 0-905836-66-9 (pbk.)   DDC 709/.438/074
19
N7255.P6   NYPL [3-MAM+ 90-4738]

Ellis, Anita J. The Fine art of folk art /.
[Cincinnati] , c1990. 43 p. :   ISBN 0-931537-12-6
DDC 709/.73/07477178 20
NK806 .F56 1990

Ellis, Charles Grant, 1908- Early Caucasian rugs
/ Charles Grant Ellis. Washington, D.C. : the
Textile Museum, [1975?] 112 p. : ill. (some
col.) ; 28 cm. Catalogue of an exhibition held at the
Textile Museum, Nov. 11, 1975 - Mar. 6, 1976, in
honor of its fiftieth anniversary. Exhibition consists
principally of items from the collections of the Textile
Museum. Bibliography: p. 107-109.
1. Textile Museum (Washington, D.C.) - Exhibitions. 2.
Rugs, Caucasian - Exhibitions. I. Textile Museum
(Washington, D.C.). II. Title.
                       NYPL [3-MOP 90-12476]

Ellis, Elizabeth Garrity. Novak, Barbara.
Nineteenth-century American painting /. New
York , 1991. p. cm.   ISBN 0-89660-026-2 :   DDC
759.13/074/49478 20
ND210 .N686 1991

Ellis, Harvey, b. 1852.
A rediscovery--Harvey Ellis, artist, architect : a
joint exhibition of Memorial Art Gallery of the
University of Rochester and Margaret
Woodbury Strong Museum, Rochester, New
York : exhibited at Memorial Art Gallery,
December 8, 1972-January 14, 1973. Rochester,
N.Y. : The Gallery, c1991. p. cm. Includes
bibliographical references.   ISBN 0-918098-04-1 :
DDC 709/.2 20
1. Ellis, Harvey, b. 1852 - Exhibitions. I. University of
Rochester. Memorial Art Gallery. II. Margaret
Woodbury Strong Museum. III. Title.
N6537.E5416 A4 1991

ELLIS, HARVEY, B. 1852 - EXHIBITIONS.
Ellis, Harvey, b. 1852. A rediscovery--Harvey
Ellis, artist, architect . Rochester, N.Y. , c1991.
p. cm.   ISBN 0-918098-04-1 :   DDC 709/.2 20
N6537.E5416 A4 1991

Ellis, Ray G. Westwind / Ray Ellis, Walter
Cronkite. 1st ed. Birmingham, Ala. : Oxmoor
House, c1990. 125 p. : col. ill. ; 32 x 40 cm.
ISBN 0-8487-0763-X
1. Pacific Coast (United States) in art. 2. Pacific Coast
(United States) - Description and travel - Views. I.
Cronkite, Walter. II. Title.
                       NYPL [3-MCX+ E473 91-3383]

Ellsworth Kelly, Gemälde und Skulpturen
1966-1979 . Kelly, Ellsworth, 1923-
[Baden-Baden] [1980] 125 p. :
                       NYPL [3-MCX K297 91-872]

Elmira, N. Y. Arnot Art Museum. see Arnot Art
Museum.

Eloge de la navigation hollandaise au XVIIe
siécle : tableaux, dessins et gravures de la mer
et de ses rivages dans la collection Frits Lugt.
Paris : Fondation Custodia, 1989. xix, 181 p.,
[150] p. of plates : ill. (some col.) ; 26 cm.
Catalog of an exhibition held at Institut néerlandais,
Nov. 3-Dec. 17, 1989. The exhibited works were
selected from the collection of Fondation Custodia.
Includes index. Bibliography: p. 165-179.
1. Lugt, Frits, 1884-1970 - Art collections - Exhibitions.
2. Marine art, Dutch - Exhibitions. 3. Marine art - 17th
century - Netherlands - Exhibitions. 4. Marine art -
Private collections - France - Paris - Exhibitions. I.
Fondation Custodia. II. Institut néerlandais (Paris,
France).   NYPL [3-MAME 91-7020]

The eloquence of color . Lichtenstein, Jacqueline.
[Couleur éloquente. English.] Berkeley , 1992.
p. cm.   ISBN 0-520-06907-2   DDC 759.4/09/032 20
ND546 .L6613 1992

The eloquent brush /. Laxman, R. K. [Bombay] ,
c1988. 303 p. :
                       NYPL [3-MEM+ (Laxman) 89-25506]

Els Llibres de l'Institut d'Humanitats. Estudis .
(2) Gaudí i el seu temps /. Barcelona , 1990.

255 p. ; ISBN 84-7533-567-5
NA1313.G3 G39 1990

Elsa Gullberg, textil pionjär. Stockholm :
Nationalmuseum, 1989. 105 p. : ill. ; 22 cm.
(Nationalmusei utställningskatalog . nr 523) ISBN
91-7100-378-9
1. Gullberg, Elsa - Exhibitions. I. GUllberg, Elsa. II.
Nationalmuseum (Sweden).
IN PROCESS (ONLINE)
NYPL [3-MON 91-4317]

Elsam, Richard, Esq. An essay on rural
architecture, illustrated with original and
œconomical designs ..., designed by Richard
Elsam. Farnborough, Gregg, 1972. [5], v, 54 p.,
[31] leaves. illus., plans. 29 cm. Reprint of the
1803 ed., London. ISBN 0-576-15164-5 DDC 728.6
1. Cottages - England. 2. Country homes - England. I.
Title.
NA7562 .E73 1803a
NYPL [3-MQZ (Elsam) 90-6797]

Else Alfelt . Stabell, Annette. København , c1990.
93 p. : ISBN 87-418-5910-3
ND723.A4 S73 1990

Eluère, Christiane. Secrets of ancient gold /
Christiane Eluère ; translated by Ann
Greening-Sautier and Peter Northover and with
the collaboration of Elisabeth Saunier for
Chapter IX. Düdingen, Switzerland : Trio,
c1989. 239 p. : ill. (some col.) ; 32 cm. Includes
bibliographical references (p. 228-231) and index.
ISBN 3-908573-08-4
1. Goldwork, Ancient. I. Title.
NYPL [3-MNO+ 90-9347]

Elvehjem Museum of Art.
The Edward Burr Van Vleck collection of
Japanese prints. Madison : Elvehjem Museum
of Art, University of Wisconsin--Madison, 1990.
vi, 352 p. : ill. ; 31 cm. ISBN 0-932900-24-0 :
DDC 769.952/074/77583 20
1. Colot prints, Japanese - Edo period, 1600-1868 -
Catalogs. 2. Color prints, Japanese - Meiji period,
1868-1912 - Catalogs. 3. Ukiyoe - Catalogs. 4. Van
Vleck, Edward Burr, 1863-1943 - Art collections -
Catalogs. 5. Color prints - Private collections -
Wisconsin - Madison - Catalogs. 6. Color prints -
Wisconsin - Madison - Catalogs. 7. Elvehjem Museum
of Art - Catalogs. I. Title.
NE1321.8 .E48 1990

Handbook of the collection / Elvehjem
Museum of Art, University of
Wisconsin--Madison. Madison, Wis. : The
Museum, c1990. xvi p., 154 p. of plates :
chiefly ill. (some col.) ; 26 cm. Includes index.
ISBN 0-932900-23-2 DDC 708.175/83 20
1. Elvehjem Museum of Art - Catalogs. 2. Art -
Wisconsin - Madison - Catalogs. I. Title.
N582.M22 A6 1990
NYPL [3-MAVZ (Madison) 91-4867]

Wright, Frank Lloyd, 1867-1959. Frank Lloyd
Wright and Madison . Madison, Wis. , 1990.
vii, 218 p. : ISBN 0-932900-22-4 DDC 720/.92
20
NA737.W7 A4 1990
NYPL [3-MQZ+ (Wright) 90-12072]

**ELVEHJEM MUSEUM OF ART -
CATALOGS.**
Elvehjem Museum of Art. The Edward Burr
Van Vleck collection of Japanese prints.
Madison , 1990. vi, 352 p. : ISBN
0-932900-24-0 : DDC 769.952/074/77583 20
NE1321.8 .E48 1990

Elvehjem Museum of Art. Handbook of the
collection / . Madison, Wis. , c1990. xvi p., 154
p. of plates : ISBN 0-932900-23-2 DDC
708.175/83 20
N582.M22 A6 1990
NYPL [3-MAVZ (Madison) 91-4867]

Elvira Bach /. Bach, Elvira, 1951- München ,
c1990. 103 p. : ISBN 3-7913-1093-3
NYPL [3-MCK+ B118 91-3385]

Ely, Timothy. Totem / T. Ely. 1989. [24] p. : all
col. ill. ; 35 cm. An original art work. "The paintings
and drawings in Totem were executed on archival
paper, in various media, including: watercolor, gouache,
airbrush, pen, pencil, and foil stamping. These have
been bound in full-leather decorated in many colors by
means of dyeing, tooling, painting and affixing. The
doublures have been painted with acrylic medium mixed
with ground marble, further painted, and then waxed;
acrylic medium and ground marble was also used to
model the topographic reliefs on the covers, which were

then painted"--Dealer's description accompanying the
work. Art work on most pages includes artist's invented
script. Source: Purchase, Aug. 21, 1990. DLC DDC
700/.92 20
1. Ely, Timothy. 2. Artists' books - United States. I.
Title.
N7433.4.E35 A4 1989

ELY, TIMOTHY.
Ely, Timothy. Totem /. 1989. [24] p. : DDC
700/.92 20
N7433.4.E35 A4 1989

Em torno da escultura no Brasil /. Bardi, P. M.
(Pietro Maria), 1900- [São Paulo, Brazil] , 1989.
119 p. :
NB350 .B37 1989

Email im frühen Mittelalter . Haseloff, Günther.
Marburg , c1990. 244 p. : ISBN 3-89398-020-2
NYPL [3-MNV 91-5235]

Emailkunst aus Wien, 1900-1989 /. Vogelsberger,
Vera. [Wien] , c1990. 27 p., [60] p. of plates :
ISBN 3-85063-193-1 DDC 738.4/09436/130904
20
NK5004.A9 V64 1990

Emanuelli, Oreste.
Oreste Emanuelli : mostra antologica / a cura
di Marzio Dall'Acqua. Parma : Libreria, c1985.
124 p. : ill. ; 23 cm.
1. Emanuelli, Oreste - Exhibitions. I. Biblioteca
comunale di Fidenza (Italy). II. Title.
NYPL [3-MCF E53 91-6419]

EMANUELLI, ORESTE - EXHIBITIONS.
Emanuelli, Oreste. Oreste Emanuelli . Parma ,
c1985. 124 p. : NYPL [3-MCF E53 91-6419]

Emaux de Longwy /. Dreyfus, Dominique, 1954-
Paris [1990?] 95 p. : ISBN 2-7072-0162-6
NYPL [3-MPGG 91-5541]

**EMBARRASS (MINN.) - BUILDINGS,
STRUCTURES, ETC.**
Gudmundson, Wayne. Testaments in wood . St.
Paul , 1991. p. cm. ISBN 0-87351-268-5 (paper) :
DDC 720/.9776/77 20
NA7235.M62 E454 1991

EMBLEM BOOKS, GERMAN.
Rollos, Peter, 17th cent. Vita Corneliana, sive
Cytherea studiosorum . [S.l.] 1639. [4] p., 58
[i.e. 59] leaves of plates :
NE654.R57 A4 1639

**EMBLEMS - GERMANY (WEST) -
WRISBERGHOLZEN.**
Köhler, Johannes. Angewandte Emblematik im
Fliesensaal von Wrisbergholzen bei Hildesheim
/. Hildesheim , 1988. 165 p. : ISBN
3-7848-3757-3 NYPL [3-MRXZ 90-13016]

Emboden, William A. Jean Cocteau and the
illustrated book / by William A. Emboden. 1st
ed. [Northridge, Calif.] : Santa Susana Press,
California State University Northridge Libraries,
1990. 29 p. : ill. (some col.) ; 37 cm. (California
masters series . no. 10) Spine title: Jean Cocteau & the
illustrated book. "This first edition ... was ... printed ...
in an edition of 226 copies of which 125 contain an
illustrated leaf from the 1923 first edition of
Dessins"--Colophon. NYPL has no. 148, signed by the
author and by the editor of the Press, Norman Tanis.
1. Cocteau, Jean, 1889-1963. 2. Illustrated books -
France - 20th century. 3. Illustration of books - 20th
century - France. I. Title. II. Title: Jean Cocteau & the
illustrated book. III. Series.
NYPL [MDG+ (Cocteau) 90-11895]

Embroidered textiles /. Paine, Sheila. New York ,
1990. 192 p. : ISBN 0-8478-1231-6 : DDC 746.44
20
NK8806 .P35 1990
NYPL [3-MON 90-13400]

EMBROIDERY.
The Golden hands book of embroidery.
Sydney , New York , 1972. 125 p. :
NYPL [3-MOT 79-376]

**EMBROIDERY - CANADA - HISTORY -
20TH CENTURY - THEMES, MOTIVES.**
Smith, Barbara Lee. Celebrating the stitch .
Newtown, CT , c1991. p. cm. ISBN
0-942391-39-X : DDC 746.44/0973/09045 20
NK9212 .S64 1991

EMBROIDERY - EXHIBITIONS.
Embroidery in women's lives, 1300-1900.
Women and textiles today /. [Manchester,
England]s , 1988. 64 p. : ISBN 0-903261-24-3
(pbk.) NYPL [3-MOT+ 89-23508]

**EMBROIDERY, HMONG (ASIAN PEOPLE) -
THAILAND - THEMES, MOTIVES.**
MacDowell, Marsha. Stories in thread . [East
Lansing, Mich.] , 1989. v, 50 p. : ISBN
0-944311-02-4 DDC 746.44/089/95 20
NK9278.7.A1 M33 1989

**Embroidery in women's lives, 1300-1900. Women
and textiles today /** selected by Pennina
Barnett. [Manchester, England]s : Cornerhouse
and The Whitworth Art Gallery, 1988. 64 p. :
ill., (some col.) ; 30 cm. Catalog of an exhibition-
"Embroidery in women's lives..." held at Whitworth Art
Gallery 27 May-29 August 1988 and "Women and
Textiles..." held at Cornerhouse 27 May-17 July 1988.
Cover title: The subversive stitch. "List of exhibits"
inserted. Includes bibliographical references. ISBN
0-903261-24-3 (pbk.)
1. Embroidery - Exhibitions. 2. Women artists. 3.
Women artisans. 4. Textile crafts - History. I. Barnett,
Pennina. II. Whitworth Art Gallery. III. Cornerhouse
(Gallery : Manchester, England). IV. Title: Women and
textiles today. V. Title: Subversive Stitch.
NYPL [3-MOT+ 89-23508]

EMBROIDERY - MALAYSIA.
Selvanayagam, Grace Inpam, 1933- Songket .
Singapore ; New York , 1990. xxii, 204 p. :
ISBN 0-19-588928-2 DDC 746.1/4/09595 20
NK8979.A1 S45 1990
NYPL [3-MON 91-6537]

**EMBROIDERY - RUSSIAN S.F.S.R. -
MOSCOW - EXHIBITIONS.**
Gosudarstvennyĭ istoricheskiĭ muzeĭ (Moscow,
R.S.F.S.R.) Meraviglie sconosciute dal Museo
storico di Mosca . Milano , c1989. 198 p. :
NYPL [3-MNR+ 91-4646]

**EMBROIDERY - SWITZERLAND - SAINT
GALL - HISTORY - 19TH CENTURY -
EXHIBITIONS.**
Stickerei-Zeit . St. Gallen , c1989. 270 p. :
ISBN 3-7291-1052-7
NYPL [3-MOT+ 91-4274]

**EMBROIDERY - SWITZERLAND - SAINT
GALL - HISTORY - 20TH CENTURY -
EXHIBITIONS.**
Stickerei-Zeit . St. Gallen , c1989. 270 p. :
ISBN 3-7291-1052-7
NYPL [3-MOT+ 91-4274]

EMBROIDERY - THEMES, MOTIVES.
Paine, Sheila. Embroidered textiles . New
York , 1990. 192 p. : ISBN 0-8478-1231-6 :
DDC 746.44 20
NK8806 .P35 1990
NYPL [3-MON 90-13400]

**EMBROIDERY - UNITED STATES -
HISTORY - 20TH CENTURY - THEMES,
MOTIVES.**
Smith, Barbara Lee. Celebrating the stitch .
Newtown, CT , c1991. p. cm. ISBN
0-942391-39-X : DDC 746.44/0973/09045 20
NK9212 .S64 1991

Emerenciano, ou, O teor das actas /. Cláudio,
Mário. Lisboa , 1989. 115 p. :
ND833.R63 A4 1989

Emerging Japanese architects of the 1990s /
edited by Jackie Kestenbaum. New York :
Columbia University Press, 1991. 121 p. : ill. ;
31 cm. (Columbia studies on art . no. 3) Catalog of an
exhibition held at the Wallach Art Gallery, Columbia
University, Sept. 14-Nov. 3, 1990 and at the Canadian
Center for Architecture, Montreal, Apr. 15-June 30,
1991. Includes bibliographical references (p. 118-120).
DDC 720/.952/09045 20
1. Architecture, Modern - 20th century - Japan -
Exhibitions. 2. Architecture - Japan - Exhibitions. 3.
Architects - Japan - Psychology - Exhibitions. I.
Kestenbaum, Jackie, 1959-. II. Wallach Art Gallery. III.
Centre canadien d'architecture. IV. Series.
NA1555 .E44 1991
NYPL [3-MQWS+ 91-6807]

Emerging patterns in the Southern Highlands .
Lovingood, Paul E. [Boone, N.C.] [1986?]- v. :
ISBN 0-913239-36-4 (pbk.)
NYPL [Map Div. 88-2045]

Emerich, A. D. Community industries of the
Shakers . [Colonie, N.Y.] , c1983. 48 p. : DDC
338/.008288 19
BX9784 .C66 1983
NYPL [3-MNE 90-12552]

**EMERSON, WILLIAM RALPH, 1833-1917 -
CRITICISM AND INTERPRETATION.**
Reed, Roger G. A delight to all who know it .

Augusta, Me. , 1990. 144 p. : ISBN
0-935447-07-5 DDC 720/.92 20
NA7575 .R4 1990

Emery, Sergio, 1928-
Bilder von Sergio Emery in der Galerie Medici,
27. August bis 14. Oktober 1989 / [Texte,
Umberto Galimberti, John Matheson].
Solothurn : Die Galerie, [1989] 1 v. (unpaged) :
chiefly ill. (chiefly col.) ; 30 cm.
1. Emery, Sergio, 1928- - Exhibitions. I. Galerie
Medici. II. Title.
MLCM 90/03081 (N)
NYPL [3-MCZ+ E515 91-5903]

EMERY, SERGIO, 1928- - EXHIBITIONS.
Emery, Sergio, 1928- Bilder von Sergio Emery
in der Galerie Medici, 27. August bis 14.
Oktober 1989 /. Solothurn [1989] 1 v.
(unpaged) :
MLCM 90/03081 (N)
NYPL [3-MCZ+ E515 91-5903]

Émil´ Nol´de . Nolde, Emil, 1867-1956.
[Neukirchen] , 1990. 177 p. :
N6888.N6 A4 1990

Emil Torday and the art of the Congo, 1900-1909
/. Mack, John. London , 1990. 96 : ISBN
0-7141-1594-0 (pbk) : DDC 709.6724 20
NYPL [Sc E 91-236]

Emile Bernard, 1868-1941 . Bernard, Émile,
1868-1941. Mannheim : Amsterdam : 384 p. :
ill. (some col.) ; ISBN 90-6630-151-1 (glued)
DDC 760/.092 20
N6853.B386 A4 1990

Emile Stahl, 1847-1938 /. Metz, René,
professeur. Saint-Dié [France] , 1987. 182 p. :
ISBN 2-906849-02-2
ND553.S835 M4 1987
NYPL [3-MCO S781 91-4473]

Emiliani, Andrea.
Crespi, Giuseppe Maria, 1665-1747. Giuseppe
Maria Crespi, 1665-1747 . Bologna , c1990.
xxcvi, 278 p. : ISBN 88-7779-148-9 DDC 759.5
20
ND623.C8 A4 1990

Crespi, Giuseppe Maria, 1665-1747. Giuseppe
Maria Crespi, 1665-1747 . [Bologna] , c1990.
ccxvi, 278 p. : ISBN 88-7779-148-9
NYPL [3-MCF C922 91-5467]

Emiliozzi, Adriana. Le Ciste prenestine /.
[Roma] , 1979- v. :
DG70.P33 C57 1979
NYPL [3-MGR+ 83-2202]

Emily Carr /. Shadbolt, Doris. Vancouver ,
Seattle , c1990. 240 p. : ISBN 0-295-97003-0
(University of Washington Press) : DDC 759.11
B 20
ND249.C3 S54 1990
NYPL [3-MCZ C28 90-13014]

Emily Lowe Gallery. Landscape & discovery : an
exhibition of photography, January 29-March 7,
1973 / the Emily Lowe Gallery, Hofstra
University, Hempstead, Long Island, N.Y.
Hempstead, N. Y. : Gallery, 1973. [24] p. : ill. ;
24 x 21 cm.
1. Photography, Artistic - Exhibitions. 2. Photography -
Landscapes - Exhibitions. 3. Photographers - Biography.
I. Title. II. Title: Landscape and discovery.
NYPL [MFW 90-5755]

Emisora H.J.C.K. (Bogotá, Colombia) Cronología
de la cultura, 1950-1990 /. [Bogotá, Colombia] ,
1990. 524 p. : ISBN 958-9138-62-4 DDC
700/.9/045 20
NX535.B64 C76 1990

EMISORA H.J.C.K. (BOGOTÁ, COLOMBIA)
Cronología de la cultura, 1950-1990 /. [Bogotá,
Colombia] , 1990. 524 p. : ISBN 958-9138-62-4
DDC 700/.9/045 20
NX535.B64 C76 1990

Emmanuel Gondouin, 1883-1934. La Frégonnière,
Jacques de. [Paris, c1969] 190 p.
ND553.G665 L3
NYPL [3-MCO G637 90-6359]

Emmanuel-Rebuffat, Denise. Corpus speculorum
Etruscorum. France. Roma , c1988- v. : ISBN
88-7062-645-8
NYPL [3-MAE+ 89-23865]

Emmerling, Mary Ellisor.
Mary Emmerling's American country flags /.
New York , 1991. p. cm. ISBN 0-517-58366-6 :

DDC 929.9/2/0973 20
NK839.E46 A4 1991

EMMERLING, MARY ELLISOR - THEMES,
MOTIVES.
Mary Emmerling's American country flags /.
New York , 1991. p. cm. ISBN 0-517-58366-6 :
DDC 929.9/2/0973 20
NK839.E46 A4 1991

Emmet Gowin, photographs. Gowin, Emmet,
1941- Philadelphia, Pa. , Boston , c1990. 127
p. : ISBN 0-8212-1835-2 (Bulfinch : cloth) : DDC
779/.092 20
NYPL [MFX+ (Gowin) 91-4964]
TR647 .G69 1990

Emory University. Museum of Art and
Archaeology. Beyond the pyramids . Atlanta,
Ga. , c1990. 95 p. : **NYPL [3-MAE 91-4240]**

Emotope : Ausstellung 21.-27. September 1987 /
Geneviève Cadieux ... [et al.] ; Büro Berlin in
Zusammenarbeit mit Künstlerhaus Bethanien.
[Berlin] : Das Künstlerhaus, c1988. 43 p. : ill.
(some col.) ; 33 cm. German and English : ISBN
3-923479-27-1
1. Art, Modern - 20th century - Berlin (Germany) -
Exhibitions. I. Cadieux, Geneviève. II. Künstlerhaus
Bethanien. **NYPL [3-MAL+ 90-10665]**

Empfindung und Reflexion : ein Problem des 18.
Jahrhunderts / herausgegeben von Hans
Körner ... [et al.] ; Schriftleitung Ludwig
Tavernier. Hildesheim ; New York : Olms,
1986. vi, 374 p. : 60 ill. ; 21 cm. (Münchner
Beiträge zur Geschichte und Theorie der Künste,
0931-5160 . Bd. 1) Errata slip laid in. Includes
bibliographies and index. CONTENTS. - Cognitio
sensitiva / Constanze Peres -- L'imitation de la belle
nature / Ludwig Tavernier -- Gefühlsschauspieler und
Verstandesschauspieler / Ulrike Stephan -- Empfindung,
Reflexion und "ästhetischer Sinn" / Kai Puntel -- Die
Wirksamkeit des Raumes / Reinhard Steiner --
Architektur und Natur / Eckart Bergmann -- Watteaus
Bild / Hermann Bauer -- "Das Mädchen mit dem
zerbrochenen Krug" und sein Betrachter / Hans
Körner -- "La richesse est la mort du sublime" /
Gabriele Oberreuter-Kronabel -- Nachahmung zwischen
Authentizität und Wahrheit / Ernst Rebel. ISBN
3-487-07845-7
1. Arts, European. 2. Arts, Modern - 18th century -
Europe. 3. Aesthetics, Modern - 18th century. 4.
Sentimentalism in art. 5. Self-knowledge in art. I.
Körner, Hans. II. Tavernier, Ludwig. III. Series.
NX542 .E46 1986 **NYPL [3-MC 90-12618]**

EMPIRE STYLE (DECORATION AND
ORNAMENT) see DECORATION AND
ORNAMENT - EMPIRE STYLE.

Empire stylebook of interior design .
Percier,Charles, 1764-1838. [Recueil de
décorations intérieures. English] New York ,
1991. p. cm. ISBN 0-486-26754-7 DDC
747.24/09/034 20
NK1449.A1 P4713 1991

Empires restored, Elysium revisited . Lovett,
Jennifer Gordon. Williamstown, Mass. , 1991.
p. cm. ISBN 0-931102-30-8 (pbk.) DDC 759.2 20
ND497.A4 A4 1991

EMPOLI (ITALY) - CHURCH HISTORY.
Pagni, Lucia. La chiesa e il convento di S.
Maria a Ripa . Tirrenia (Pisa) , 1988. 238 p. :
NYPL [MRBD 91-3395]

Empordà . Pujolboira, 1949- Figueres, Alt
Empordà [1990] [161] p. : ISBN 84-85874-33-1
N7113.P84 A4 1990

Empty places . Anderson, Laurie, 1947- New
York, NY , 1991. p. ISBN 0-06-096586-X
(paper) : DDC 700/.92 20
NX512.A54 A4 1991

Emslandmuseum. Crumbiegel, Dieter, 1938-
Dieter Crumbiegel . Montabaur , c1988. 107
p. : ISBN 3-921548-39-X
MLCM 89/07955 (N)
NYPL [3-MPGK 90-8715]

Ēmu Kurieitibu Purodakutsu, Kabushiki Kaisha.
Elements =. [Tokyo] , 1989. 12 v. : ISBN
4-87210-018-2 (v. 1) : DDC 745.4 20
NK1530 .E44 1989

En plein air : the art colonies at East Hampton
and Old Lyme, 1880-1930. East Hampton,
N.Y. : Guild Hall of East Hampton, c1989. 72
p. : ill. (some col.), maps ; 22 x 27 cm. Catalog
of an exhibition held at the Florence Griswold
Museum, Old Lyme, Conn. 10 June-30 July 1989 and

Guild Hall Museum, East Hampton, N.Y., 18 June-30
July 1989. Includes bibliographical references. ISBN
0-933793-12-X (pbk.)
1. Painting, American - Exhibitions. 2. Painting -
Connecticut - Old Lyme. 3. Painting - New York
(State) - East Hampton. I. Florence Griswold Museum.
II. Guild Hall of East Hampton.
NYPL [3-MCW 90-399]

En tiempos de la posmodernidad. [Mexico City] :
Dirección de Estudios Históricos, INAH :
Universidad Iberoamericana : 116 p. : ill. (some
col.) ; 22 x 23 cm. Catalog of an exhibition held at
the Museo de Arte Moderno, Mexico City, June 1988.
Includes bibliographical references. ISBN
968-8405-58-2
1. Art, Mexican - Exhibitions. 2. Art, Modern - 20th
century - Mexico - Exhibitions. I. Museo de Arte
Moderno (Mexico). II. Instituto Nacional de
Antropología e Historia (Mexico). Dirección de
Estudios Históricos.
N6555 .E5 1989

ENAMEL AND ENAMELING - AUSTRIA -
VIENNA - HISTORY - 20TH CENTURY.
Vogelsberger, Vera. Emailkunst aus Wien,
1900-1989 /. [Wien] , c1990. 27 p., [60] p. of
plates : ISBN 3-85063-193-1 DDC
738.4/09436/130904 20
NK5004.A9 V64 1990

ENAMEL AND ENAMELING - EUROPE.
Belli Barsali, Isa. [Smalto in Europa. English.]
European enamels /. London , 1988. 157 p. :
ISBN 0-304-32179-6 (pbk) DDC 738.4/094 19
NYPL [3-MNV 90-9465]

ENAMEL AND ENAMELING - FRANCE -
LONGWY.
Dreyfus, Dominique, 1954- Emaux de Longwy
/. Paris [1990?] 95 p. : ISBN 2-7072-0162-6
NYPL [3-MPGG 91-5541]

ENAMEL AND ENAMELING, MEDIEVAL -
EUROPE.
Haseloff, Günther. Email im frühen Mittelalter .
Marburg , c1990. 244 p. : ISBN 3-89398-020-2
NYPL [3-MNV 91-5235]

Enciclopedia dei pittori e scultori italiani del
Novecento : quotazione degli artisti nati dal
1900 ai nostri giorni / a cura di Giorgio
Falossi. Milano : Il Quadrato, [1991] 2 v. (1261
p.) : ill. (some col.) ; 27 cm. Previous ed. published
under the title: Pittori e scultori italiani del 900. 1981.
DDC 709/.2/.2450904 B 20
1. Art, Italian - Prices. 2. Art, Modern - 20th century -
Italy - Prices. 3. Artists - Italy - Biography -
Dictionaries. I. Falossi, Giorgio. II. Pittori e scultori
italiani del 900.
N6918 .E58 1991

Encontros com António Duarte /. Gastão,
Marques, 1914- [Lisbon, Portugal] [1989] 128
p. : DDC 730/.92 20
NB833.D8 G37 1989

Encounters & reflections . Danto, Arthur
Coleman, 1924- New York , 1990. 355 p. ;
ISBN 0-374-14819-8 DDC 709/.04 20
N6490 .D237 1990
NYPL [3-MAL 90-11092]

Encounters and reflections. Danto, Arthur
Coleman, 1924- Encounters & reflections . New
York , 1990. 355 p. ; ISBN 0-374-14819-8 DDC
709/.04 20
N6490 .D237 1990
NYPL [3-MAL 90-11092]

Encouraging the artist in yourself . Warner, Sally.
New York , 1991. p. cm. ISBN 0-312-04667-7 :
DDC 702/.8 20
N7430 .W37 1991

Encyclopaedia of Impressionism. Denvir, Bernard,
1917- The Thames and Hudson encyclopaedia
of Impressionism /. London , New York, N.Y. ,
1990. 240 p. : ISBN 0-500-20239-7 :
NYPL [MBK 90-12515]

Encyclopaedia of Indian temple architecture /
edited by Michael W. Meister ; coordinated by
M.A. Dhaky. New Delhi : American Institute
of Indian Studies ; Philadelphia : University of
Pennsylvania Press, 1983- v. : ill. ; 29 cm. Spine
title: Indian temple architecture. CONTENTS. - v. 1.
South India, pt. 1. Lower Drāvidadésa, 200 B.C.--A.D.
1324 (2 v.). -- v. 1. Lower Drāvidadésa, 200 B.C.--A.D.
1324 (2 v.). ISBN 0-8122-7840-2 (U. S. : v. 1, pt. 1)
DDC 726/.14/0954 19
1. Temples - India. I. Meister, Michael W. II. Dhaky,
Madhusudan A. III. American Institute of Indian

Studies. IV. Title: Indian temple architecture.
NA6001 .E53 1983
NYPL [3-MQWS 87-1248]

The encyclopedia of animated cartoons /.
Lenburg, Jeff. New York , c1990. p. cm. ISBN
0-8160-2252-6 (acid-free paper) DDC
791.43/75/0973 20
NC1766.U5 L46 1990

Encyclopedia of sculpture techniques /. Mills,
John W. London , 1990. 239 p. : ISBN
0-7134-5133-5   **NYPL [MGD 90-9552]**

**Encyclopedia of twentieth-century American folk
art and artists.** Rosenak, Chuck. Museum of
American Folk Art encyclopedia of
twentieth-century American folk art and artists
/. New York , c1990. 416 p. : ISBN
1-558-59041-2 DDC 709/.2/2730904 B 20
NK808 .R6 1990   **NYPL [MAMT 91-5742]**

The encyclopedia of watercolor techniques /.
Harrison, Hazel. Philadelphia, Pa. , 1990. 192
p. : ISBN 0-89471-893-2 DDC 751.4/2 20
ND2420 .H37 1990

Encyklopedia wiedzy o Śląsku.
Kowal-Moik, Katarzyna. "Maluję dla ludzi
czujących--" . Opole , 1990. 75 p., [28] p. of
plates :
ND955.P63 B385 1990

The end and the myth /. Time-Life Books.
Alexandria, Va. , c1979. 240 p. : ISBN
0-8094-2314-6
F591 .T57 1979   **NYPL [IW 79-2698]**

End, Eevi. Jõesaar, Ernst, 1905- Ernst Jõesaar .
Stockholm , 1975. 25 p. [132] p. of plates :
NB955.F53 J642 1975

The end of expressionism . Weinstein, Joan.
Chicago , 1990. xiv, 332 p. : ISBN
0-226-89059-7 DDC 701/.03 19
N6868.5.E9 W45 1989
NYPL [3-MAMG 90-11096]

Endangered species . Luzwick, Dierdre. San
Francisco, Calif. , 1992. p. ISBN 0-06-250419-3
DDC 741.973 20
NC139.L89 A4 1992

**ENDANGERED SPECIES - PICTORIAL
WORKS.**
Balog, James. Survivors . New York , 1990. 144
p. : ISBN 0-8109-3908-8 DDC 779/.32/092 20
TR727 .B25 1990
NYPL [MFX+ (Balog) 91-5850]

Endara Crow, Gonzalo, 1936-
Gonzalo Endara Crow. [2. ed.]. [Quito,
Ecuador : Pintores Ecuatorianos, 1990] 225 p. :
ill. (some col.) ; 20 cm. Texts by Hernán Rodríguez
Castelo et al. DDC 759.9866 20
1. Endara Crow, Gonzalo, 1936- Catalogs. 2. Fantasy
in art - Catalogs. I. Rodríguez Castelo, Hernán, 1933-.
II. Title.
ND389.E53 A4 1990

**ENDARA CROW, GONZALO, 1936- -
CATALOGS.**
Endara Crow, Gonzalo, 1936- Gonzalo Endara
Crow. [Quito, Ecuador , 1990] 225 p. : DDC
759.9866 20
ND389.E53 A4 1990

Enderlein, Volkmar. Islamische Kunst / Volkmar
Enderlein. Dresden : Verlag der Kunst, 1990.
324 p. : chiefly ill. (some col.) ; 24 cm. Includes
bibliographical references (p. [280]-319) and index.
ISBN 3-364-00195-2 DDC 709/.17/671 20
1. Art, Islamic - History. I. Title.
N6260 .E64 1990

Endre Nemes . Nemes, Endre, 1909-
[Stockholm] , 1990. 112 p. : ISBN 91-7100-400-9
N5078.S8 S8 Nr. 237 N7093.N45

Energétique de l'insolence. Conil-Lacoste, Michel.
Tinguely, l' énergétique de l'insolence /. Paris
[1989?] 2 v. : ISBN 2-7291-0389-9 (set)
NYPL [3-MGO (Tinguely) 90-266]

Enfance de l'art. Sur les murs. L'Art fun, ou,
L'enfance de l'art. Ateliers en liberté.
Jouy-en-Josas [France] [1986] 77 p. : ISBN
2-86925-004-5
N6488.F8 J687 1986
NYPL [3-MAL+ 90-10669]

Engadin Ferdinand Hodlers. Das Engadin
Ferdinand Hodlers und anderer Künstler des
19. und 20. Jahrhunderts . [Chur] , St. Moritz ,
c1990. 122 p. : ISBN 3-905240-15-7 DDC

759.9494 20
ND853.H6 A4 1990

Engel, Carl Ludvig, 1778-1840.
Pöykkö, Kalevi, 1933- Carl Ludvig Engel
1778-1840 . [Helsinki] [1990] 159 p. : ISBN
951-772-066-1
NA1088.E6 P69 1990

**ENGEL, CARL LUDVIG, 1778-1840 -
CRITICISM AND INTERPRETATION.**
Pöykkö, Kalevi, 1933- Carl Ludvig Engel
1778-1840 . [Helsinki] [1990] 159 p. : ISBN
951-772-066-1
NA1088.E6 P69 1990

**Die Engel in der altchristlichen Kunst
[microform]** ... /. Stuhlfauth, Georg, b. 1870.
Freiburg i. B. , 1896. 40 p. ;
NYPL [*ZM-219]

Engelhorn, J. Flat ornament. Treasury of historic
pattern and design /. New York , 1990. 150
p. : ISBN 0-486-26274-X DDC 745.4 20
NK1175 .F5 1990
NYPL [3-MLD+ 90-11804]

Engelmann, Manfred, 1956- Banater Künstler in
der Bundesrepublik Deutschland . Berlin , 1988.
60 p. : ISBN 3-922131-57-8
N6868 .B33 1988
NYPL [3-MAMG 91-6298]

Engels, Pieter, 1938-
Engels: The selfportrait of this century.
[Stedelijk Museum, Amsterdam, Prentenkabinet,
29 September-19 november 1972. Amsterdam,
Stedelijk Museum, 1972] 18 p. illus. 28 cm.
Cover title. English and Dutch. "Stedelijk Museum
Amsterdam: Cat. nr. 528." DDC
704.94/28/074094923 s 709/.2/4
1. Engels, Pieter, 1938- - Exhibitions. I. Amsterdam
(Netherlands). Stedelijk Museum. II. Title.
N5072.A55 A3 nr. 528 N6953.E53
NYPL [3-MCH E571 90-6259]

ENGELS, PIETER, 1938- - EXHIBITIONS.
Engels, Pieter, 1938- Engels: The selfportrait of
this century. [Amsterdam, 1972] 18 p. DDC
704.94/28/074094923 s 709/.2/4
N5072.A55 A3 nr. 528 N6953.E53
NYPL [3-MCH E571 90-6259]

Engels: The selfportrait of this century. Engels,
Pieter, 1938- [Amsterdam, 1972] 18 p. DDC
704.94/28/074094923 s 709/.2/4
N5072.A55 A3 nr. 528 N6953.E53
NYPL [3-MCH E571 90-6259]

Engen, Rodney K. Sir John Tenniel : Alice's
white knight / Rodney Engen. Aldershot,
Hants, England : Scolar Press ; Brookfield, Vt.,
USA : Gower Pub. Co., c1991. ix, 232 p. : ill. ;
26 cm. Includes bibliographical references (p. 179-182)
and index. ISBN 0-85967-872-5 : DDC 741.6/092
20
1. Tenniel, John, Sir, 1820-1914 - Criticism and
interpretation. I. Tenniel, John, Sir, 1820-1914. II. Title.
N6797.T44 E54 1991
NYPL [MDG (Tenniel) 91-8040]

**ENGINEERING, ARCHITECTURAL. see
BUILDING; BUILDING, IRON AND
STEEL.**

ENGINEERING DESIGN - SWEDEN.
When people matter /. Sweden , Solna, Sweden
[1989] 223 p. : ISBN 91-540-5059-6 DDC
725/.4/09485 20
NA6403.S8 W47 1989

ENGINEERING - MANAGEMENT.
Stasiowski, Frank, 1948- Project management
for the design professional /. New York , 1991.
p. cm. ISBN 0-8230-4413-0 DDC 720/.68 20
NA1996 .S74 1991

**ENGINEERING, MUNICIPAL. see
MUNICIPAL ENGINEERING.**

ENGINEERING - PHILOSOPHY.
Picon, Antoine. [Architectes et ingénieurs au
siècle des Lumières. English.] French architects
and engineers in the Age of Enlightenment /.
Cambridge , New York , 1991. p. cm. ISBN
0-521-38253-X DDC 720/.944/09033 20
NA1046.5.N4 P513 1991

**ENGINEERING SERVICES MARKETING -
UNITED STATES.**
Stasiowski, Frank, 1948- Staying small
successfully . New York , c1991. xv, 297 p. :
ISBN 0-471-50652-4 DDC 720/.68 20
NA1996 .S75 1991

**ENGLAND - DESCRIPTION AND TRAVEL -
1701-1800.**
Forrest, Ebenezer, fl. 1774. [Hogarth's
peregrination.] An account of what seem'd most
remarkable in the five days peregrination of the
five following persons, vizt. Messieurs Tothall,
Scott, Hogarth, Thornhill & Forrest, begun on
Saturday, May 27th, 1723 and finished on the
31st of the same month /. Church Hanborough,
Oxford , 1989 ([Didcot? England] : Didcot
Press) [35] p. : DDC 760/.092 20
ND497.H7 F6 1989

England - History. see Great Britain - History.

**ENGLAND - SOCIAL LIFE AND CUSTOMS -
18TH CENTURY - EXHIBITIONS.**
Fairman, Elisabeth R. Pleasures and pastimes .
New Haven, Conn. , c1990. 39 p. : ISBN
0-930606-62-0
NYPL [3-MAMZ 90-11038]

**ENGLAND - SOCIAL LIFE AND CUSTOMS -
19TH CENTURY.**
Doyle, Richard, 1824-1883. Richard Doyle's
journal, 1840 /. Edinburgh , 1980. xvii, 156 p. :
ISBN 0-7028-8280-1 : DDC 741.6/092/4 B 19
NC978.5.D68 A2 1980
NYPL [MDG (Doyle) 81-1248]

**ENGLAND - SOCIAL LIFE AND CUSTOMS -
19TH CENTURY - EXHIBITIONS.**
Fairman, Elisabeth R. Pleasures and pastimes .
New Haven, Conn. , c1990. 39 p. : ISBN
0-930606-62-0
NYPL [3-MAMZ 90-11038]

**ENGLAND - SOCIAL LIFE AND CUSTOMS -
CONGRESSES.**
The Fashioning and functioning of the British
country house /. Washington, D.C. , Hanover
[N.H.] , 1989. 417 p. : ISBN 0-89468-128-1
NYPL [3-MRG 90-12992]

Engler, Herbert. Kermer, Wolfgang, 1935- Willi
Baumeister . Stuttgart [1989] 350 p. : ISBN
3-89322-145-X
NYPL [3-MCK+ B35 90-12548]

ENGLISH ARTS. see ARTS, ENGLISH.

**ENGLISH BOOK-PLATES. see BOOK-
PLATES, ENGLISH.**

English country houses /. Hussey, Christopher,
1899- London , 1988. 3 v. : ISBN 1-85149-029-9
(set : pbk.)   **NYPL [3-MRG 90-12887]**

English extremists . Sudjic, Deyan. London ,
c1988. 112 p. : ISBN 0-947795-68-5 (pbk.)
NYPL [3-MQWK 89-4432]

**ENGLISH FOLK-SONGS. see FOLK-SONGS,
ENGLISH.**

English Gothic choir-stalls, 1400-1540 /. Tracy,
Charles, 1938- Woodbridge, Suffolk [England] ,
Rochester, NY, USA , 1990. xx, 75 p., [112] p.
of plates : ISBN 0-85115-272-4 (hardback : acid-free
paper) : DDC 726/.5293 20
NA5463 .T74 1990
NYPL [3-MRBV+ 91-4462]

English Heritage book of abbeys and priories /.
Coppack, Glyn. London , 1990. 159 p., [8] p.
of plates : ISBN 0-7134-6308-2 (cased) : DDC 942
20   **NYPL [3-MRBR 91-6767]**

**ENGLISH LANDSCAPE PAINTING. see
LANDSCAPE PAINTING, ENGLISH.**

**ENGLISH LITERATURE - 19TH CENTURY -
BIBLIOGRAPHY.**
Vries, Leonard de. A treasury of illustrated
children's books . New York , 1989. 285 p. :
ISBN 0-89659-939-6 DDC 011/.62 19
Z1037 .V75 1989 PN1009.A1
NYPL [MDTO+ 90-9497]

ENGLISH LITERATURE - 20TH CENTURY.
Hockney, David. Hockney's alphabet /. New
York, NY, c1991. p. cm. ISBN 0-679-41066-X :
DDC 741.942 20
NC242.H6 A4 1991a

**ENGLISH PAINTING. see PAINTING,
ENGLISH.**

**ENGLISH PORCELAIN. see PORCELAIN,
ENGLISH.**

ENGLISH WIT AND HUMOR, PICTORIAL.
Bentley, Nicolas, 1907- Nicolas Bentley drew
the pictures /. Aldershot, Hants, England ,
Brookfield, Vt., USA , 1990. xxvi, 133 p. :
ISBN 0-85967-843-1 DDC 741.5/942 20
NC1479.B485 A4 1990

Earnshaw, Anthony. An eighth secret alphabet
/. Church Hanborough, Oxford , 1988
([Didcot? England] : Didcot Press) [23] p. :
DDC 741.5/942 20
NC1479.E37 A4 1988

Giles, Carl Ronald, 1916- Nurse! /. London ,
1975. [96] p. :   ISBN 0-85079-066-2 :   DDC
741.5/942
NC1479.G48 A53
              NYPL   [3-MEM (Giles) 90-4867]

Jackson, Cath. Visibly Vera . London , 1986.
[62] p. :   ISBN 0-7043-4029-1 (pbk.) :   DDC
741.5/942 19
NC1479 NC1479
              NYPL   [3-MEM (Jackson) 90-10991]

Robinson, W. Heath (William Heath),
1872-1944. Meals on wheels . London , c1989.
64 p. :   ISBN 0-285-62932-8
              NYPL   [3-MEM+ (Robinson) 90-2152]

Engraved bookplates. Severin, Mark. Pinner,
1972. 176 p. (chiefly facsims.)   ISBN
0-900002-91-3   **NYPL   [MDVC 90-7007]**

Engraven desire . Stewart, Philip. Durham , 1992.
p. cm.   ISBN 0-8223-1177-1   DDC 769.944/09/033
20
NE647.2 .S73 1992

Engravers and etchers. Carrington, Fitz Roy,
1869-1954. [Chicago] 1917. 9 p. L., 13-278 p.
incl. front., plates, ports.
NE400 .C3   **NYPL   [MDB 91-7805]**

ENGRAVERS - DICTIONARIES.
Bryan, Michael, 1757-1821. Bryan's dictionary
of painters and engravers. New York , London ,
1903-1905. 5 v. :   **NYPL   [MCA 91-4552]**

ENGRAVING - 15TH CENTURY - INDEXES.
Vanderwielen, Betty. An index of woodcuts and
engravings in incunabula and early printed
books (to 1600) in the Library of the Institute
of Cistercian Studies /. Kalamazoo, Mich. ,
1988. viii, 284 leaves ;   ISBN 0-918720-92-3
DDC 769.94/09/03107477417 20
NE1052 .V36 1988

ENGRAVING - 16TH CENTURY - INDEXES.
Vanderwielen, Betty. An index of woodcuts and
engravings in incunabula and early printed
books (to 1600) in the Library of the Institute
of Cistercian Studies /. Kalamazoo, Mich. ,
1988. viii, 284 leaves ;   ISBN 0-918720-92-3
DDC 769.94/09/03107477417 20
NE1052 .V36 1988

**ENGRAVING - 17TH CENTURY - EUROPE -
EXHIBITIONS.**
Graphische Sammlung Albertina. Claude
Lorrain und die Meister der römischen
Landschaft im XVII Jahrhundert . [Wien, 1965]
xv, 187 p. :   **NYPL   [3-MBH 91-1175]**

**ENGRAVING - 18TH CENTURY - FRANCE -
THEMES, MOTIVES.**
Stewart, Philip. Engraven desire . Durham ,
1992. p. cm.   ISBN 0-8223-1177-1   DDC
769.944/09/033 20
NE647.2 .S73 1992

ENGRAVING, BAROQUE - GERMANY.
Appuhn-Radtke, Sibylle. Das Thesenblatt im
Hochbarock . Weissenhorn , 1988. 307 p. :
ISBN 3-87437-251-0
              NYPL   [MDG+ (Kilian) 90-13673]

ENGRAVING - CATALOGS.
Bartsch, Adam von, 1757-1821. [Peintre
graveur. English.] The illustrated Bartsch /.
New York , 1978- v. :   ISBN 0-89835-000-X
DDC 769/.074
NE90 .B213   **NYPL   [MDD+ 80-258]**

ENGRAVING, ENGLISH.
Le Keux, John, 1783-1846. [Engravings of
Victorian Cambridge.] Le Keux's Engravings of
Victorian Cambridge. Cambridge , New York ,
1985. 135 p. :   ISBN 0-521-30350-8   DDC
914.26/59/00222 19
DA690.C2 L45 1985
              NYPL   [MDG (Le Keux) 87-4848]

ENGRAVING - FRANCE - HISTORY.
Lehrs, Max, 1855-1938. Geschichte und
kritischer Katalog des deutschen,
niederländischen und französischen Kupferstichs
im xv. Jahrhundert. [New York, 1970?] 9 v.
NE1450 .L513

**ENGRAVING, FRENCH - THEMES,
MOTIVES.**

Stewart, Philip. Engraven desire . Durham ,
1992. p. cm.   ISBN 0-8223-1177-1   DDC
769.944/09/033 20
NE647.2 .S73 1992

ENGRAVING, GERMAN.
Appuhn-Radtke, Sibylle. Das Thesenblatt im
Hochbarock . Weissenhorn , 1988. 307 p. :
ISBN 3-87437-251-0
              NYPL   [MDG+ (Kilian) 90-13673]

ENGRAVING - GERMANY - HISTORY.
Lehrs, Max, 1855-1938. Geschichte und
kritischer Katalog des deutschen,
niederländischen und französischen Kupferstichs
im xv. Jahrhundert. [New York, 1970?] 9 v.
NE1450 .L513

ENGRAVING - HISTORY.
Carrington, Fitz Roy, 1869-1954. Engravers and
etchers. [Chicago] 1917. 9 p. L., 13-278 p. incl.
front., plates, ports.
NE400 .C3   **NYPL   [MDB 91-7805]**

ENGRAVING, MEXICAN.
Pérez Salazar, Francisco, 1888-1941. El grabado
en la ciudad de Puebla de los Angeles /.
Puebla , 1990. 68 p. :
NE545.P8 P4 1990

**ENGRAVING - MEXICO - PUEBLA - 17TH
CENTURY.**
Pérez Salazar, Francisco, 1888-1941. El grabado
en la ciudad de Puebla de los Angeles /.
Puebla , 1990. 68 p. :
NE545.P8 P4 1990

ENGRAVING - NETHERLANDS - HISTORY.
Lehrs, Max, 1855-1938. Geschichte und
kritischer Katalog des deutschen,
niederländischen und französischen Kupferstichs
im xv. Jahrhundert. [New York, 1970?] 9 v.
NE1450 .L513

**ENGRAVING - PRIVATE COLLECTIONS -
FRANCE - PARIS - EXHIBITIONS.**
Fondation Custodia. Le héraut du dix-septième
siècle . Paris , 1985. xi, 153 p., 80 p. of plates :
NE670.G74 A4 1985

ENGRAVINGS - CATALOGS.
Lehrs, Max, 1855-1938. Geschichte und
kritischer Katalog des deutschen,
niederländischen und französischen Kupferstichs
im xv. Jahrhundert. [New York, 1970?] 9 v.
NE1450 .L513

The engravings of John Buckland Wright /.
Buckland Wright, John, 1897-1954. Aldershot,
Hants , 1990. 160 p. :   ISBN 0-85967-850-4 :
DDC 769.92 20
NE642.B8 A4 1990   **NYPL   [MDG (Buckland
                                Wright) 91-7278]**

Engravings of Victorian Cambridge. Le Keux,
John, 1783-1846. [Engravings of Victorian
Cambridge.] Le Keux's Engravings of Victorian
Cambridge. Cambridge , New York , 1985. 135
p. :   ISBN 0-521-30350-8   DDC 914.26/59/00222 19
DA690.C2 L45 1985
              NYPL   [MDG (Le Keux) 87-4848]

ENLIGHTENMENT - EUROPE.
Herding, Klaus. Im Zeichen der Aufklärung .
Frankfurt am Main , 1989. 242, [1] p. :   ISBN
3-596-23615-0   **NYPL   [3-MAL 90-13019]**

**ENLIGHTENMENT - INFLUENCE -
EXHIBITIONS.**
Gianni, Benjamin, 1958- Dice thrown /. New
York, N.Y. , c1989. 56 p. :   ISBN
0-910413-62-2 :   DDC 728/.92/09730747468 20
NA8201 .G47 1989
              NYPL   [3-MQV 90-12464]

Enrici, Michel. Rose, Barbara. Jean-Pierre
Pincemin /. [Aubusson] [Paris] [1986] 79 p. :
ISBN 2-7291-0207-4 :
MLCM 89/01361 (N)
              NYPL   [3-MCO P643 90-12613]

Enrico Baj . Baudrillard, Jean. Paris , c1990. 55
p. :   ISBN 2-7291-0617-0 :   DDC 759.5 20
ND623.B17 B38 1990

Enrico della Torre . Della Torre, Enrico, 1931-
München , c1987. 64 p. :
              NYPL   [3-MCF+ D343 90-5284]

Enrique Chagoya . Chagoya, Enrique. New York,
N.Y. , c1989. 24 p. ;   ISBN 0-932075-25-8 (pbk.)
              NYPL   [3-MCX C433 91-4634]

Enrique Nieto Ulibarri, 1860-1963 . Zugaza
Miranda, Miguel. Bilbao , 1989. 143 p. ;   ISBN

84-87184-01-4
IN PROCESS (ONLINE)
              NYPL   [3-MCQ N677 91-6904]

Enrique Zañartu. Jurado, María Cristina. Zañartu
/. Santiago de Chile , 1989. 64 p. :   DDC
759.983 20
ND369.D38 A4 1989

ENRIQUILLO, D. 1535.
Peña Batlle, Manuel Arturo. La rebelión del
bahoruco. Santo Domingo, 1970. 257,[5] p.
              NYPL   [HBC 76-2412]

L'Enrôlement des volontaires de 1792 : Thomas
Couture, 1815-1879 : les artistes au service de
la patrie en danger : [exposition] Musée
départemental de l'Oise, Ancien Palais
Épiscopal, Beauvais, 5 octobre - 31 décembre
1989. Beauvais : Le Musée, [1989] 258 p. : ill.
(some col.) ; 21 cm. Bibliography: p. 252-255.
ISBN 2-901290-05-1
*1. France - History - Revolution, 1789-1799 - Art and
the Revolution - Exhibitions. 2. Artists' preparatory
studies - France - Exhibitions. I. Title: Artistes au
service de la patrie en danger.*
              NYPL   [3-MCO C87 91-5550]

Ensayo biográfico de Octavio Pinto /. Pinto,
Adelina. [Córdoba, Argentina] [1974] 150 p.,
[6] leaves of plates :   DDC 759.982 B 20
ND339.P54 P56 1974

**Ensayo sobre el rigen y significación del arte
prehistórico /.** Beltrán Martínez, Antonio,
1916- Zaragoza, España , 1989. 199 p. ;   ISBN
84-7733-136-7
IN PROCESS (ONLINE)
              NYPL   [3-MADF 91-4516]

Ensayos sobre fotografía /. Beceyro, Raúl.
México , 1978. 91 p., [7] leaves of plates :
TR185 .B35   **NYPL   [MFW 81-439]**

L'enseigne de Gersaint. Maurel, André, 1863-
Paris, 1913. 2 p. ., 116, [1] p.   DDC 759.4
ND553.W3 M35
              NYPL   [3-MCO W34 90-6342]

Enseigner la conception / Ph. Boudon ... [et al.].
Paris : LAREA, 1986-<1989 > v. <1, 4 > :
ill. ; 30 cm. Cover title. Includes bibliographical
references.
*1. Architectural design - Study and teaching. I. Boudon,
Philippe.*
NA2750 .E58 1986

Ensko, Stephen Guernsey Cook, 1896- American
silversmiths and their marks IV / by Stephen
Guernsey Cook Ensko ; a revised and enlarged
edition compiled by Dorothea Ensko Wyle. 1st
ed. Boston : Godine, 1989, c1988. xiii, 477 p. :
ill., facsims. ; 24 cm. Bibliography: p. 393-399.
ISBN 0-87923-778-3
*1. Silversmithing - United States. 2. Hallmarks - United
States. I. Wyle, Dorothea Ensko. II. Title.*
              NYPL   [MNP 90-11585]

Ensor /. Janssens, Jacques. [James Ensor.
English.] New York , c1990. p. cm.   ISBN
0-517-53284-0 :   DDC 760/.092 20
N6973.E5 J3613 1990

ENSOR, JAMES, 1860-1949 - CATALOGS.
Hoozee, Robert. [James Ensor, tekeningen en
prenten. French.] James Ensor, dessins et
estampes /. Antwerpen , Paris , c1987. 271 p. :
ISBN 90-6153-177-2 (Fonds Mercator)   DDC
760/.092 20
N6973.E5 A4 1987

**ENSOR, JAMES, 1860-1949 - CRITICISM
AND INTERPRETATION.**
Janssens, Jacques. [James Ensor. English.]
Ensor /. New York , c1990. p. cm.   ISBN
0-517-53284-0 :   DDC 760/.092 20
N6973.E5 J3613 1990

Entenza, John, 1903- Arts & architecture .
Cambridge, Mass. , c1990. 248 p. :   ISBN
0-262-07131-2 :   DDC 700/.9/04 20
NX456.5.M64 A7 1990
              NYPL   [3-MAL+ 91-3679]

An enterprising life . Leonoff, Cyril Edel.
Vancouver , 1990. 176 p. :   ISBN 0-88922-283-5 :
DDC 779/.9871103 20
              NYPL   [MFX+ (Frank) 91-7431]

**ENTERTAINERS - UNITED STATES -
PORTRAITS.**
Avery, Sid. Hollywood at home . New York ,
c1990. 144 p. :   ISBN 0-517-57696-1 :
PN1998.2 .A85 1990
              NYPL   [MFX (Avery) 91-5134]

ENTOURAGE (ARCHITECTURAL RENDERING)
McGarry, Richard M., 1948- Scale elements for design elevations /. New York , c1991. 160 p. : ISBN 0-442-00694-2   DDC 720/.28/4 20
NA2780 .M37 1991

Porter, Tom. Design drawing techniques . New York : Toronto : p. cm.   ISBN 0-684-19045-1
DDC 720/.28/4 20
NA2714 .P67 1991

ENTRANCE HALLS.
Espacios de comunicación =. Barcelona , 1976. 265 p. :   ISBN 84-7031-447-5
NA2853 .E86   *NYPL [3-MRN 81-422]*

Entre deux guerres : la création française entre 1919 et 1939 / sous la direction de Olivier Barrot et Pascal Ory. Paris : F. Bourin, c1990. 631 p. ; 23 cm. Includes bibliographical references and index.   ISBN 2-87686-057-0 :   DDC 700/.944/09041 20
1. Arts, French. 2. Arts, Modern - 20th century - France. 3. Design - France - History - 20th century. 4. France - Civilization - 20th century. I. Barrot, Olivier. II. Ory, Pascal. III. Title: Entre 2 guerres.
NX549.A1 E5 1990

Entre 2 guerres. Entre deux guerres . Paris , c1990. 631 p. ;   ISBN 2-87686-057-0 :   DDC 700/.944/09041 20
NX549.A1 E5 1990

Entwicklungen . Narbutt-Lieven, Wladimir, 1918- Vienna , 1978. [30] p. :
NYPL [MFX (Narbutt-Lieven) 91-1496]

Entwistle Gallery.
Lowenthal, Anne W. Netherlandish mannerism in British collections . London , c1990. 87 p. :
NYPL [3-MAME 91-3425]

Spilliaert, Léon, 1881-1946. Léon Spilliaert, 1881-1946 . London , 1989. 61 p. :
NYPL [3-MCH S756 90-10667]

ENVIRONMENT. see HUMAN ECOLOGY; MAN - INFLUENCE ON NATURE.

ENVIRONMENT (ART) - EXHIBITIONS.
Theatergarden Bestiarium . Cambridge, Mass. , Long Island City, N.Y. , c1990. 176 p. :   ISBN 0-262-04105-7   DDC 701/.03 20
N6494.E6 T4 1990
NYPL [3-MAL+ 90-12503]

ENVIRONMENT (ART) - OHIO - EXHIBITIONS.
Quintessence--the alternative spaces residency program, the City Beautiful Council of Dayton, Ohio, the Wright State University, Department of Art. Dayton , c1978- v. :   ISBN 0-9602550-0-1 (v. 2)   DDC 709/.73/074017173
N6530.O3 Q56   *NYPL [3-MAMT 79-2025]*

ENVIRONMENT (ART) - UNITED STATES - CATALOGS.
Sonfist, Alan. Alan Sonfist, 1969-1989 . Brookville, N.Y. [1990] 80 p. :   ISBN 0-933699-16-6   DDC 709/.2 20
N6537.S64 A4 1990
NYPL [3-MGO (Sonfist) 91-4000]

Environmental figuration : contemporary views of the figure in an exterior : Bill Cass ... [et al.] / Cheryl Hahn, exhibition curator. Springfield, Ill. : Illinois State Museum, c1990. 31 p. : ill. ; 23 cm. "Illinois State Museum Lockport, December 9, 1990-February 24, 1991; Illinois State Museum, Springfield, April 7-June 30, 1991." Includes bibliographical references (p. 28-29).   ISBN 0-89792-130-5   DDC 757/.09773/1107477325 20
1. Human figure in art - Exhibitions. 2. Painting, American - Exhibitions. 3. Painting, Modern - 20th century - United States - Exhibitions. I. Cass, Bill. II. Hahn, Cheryl. III. Illinois State Museum Lockport Gallery (Lockport, Ill.). IV. Illinois State Museum.
ND1292 .E59 1990

ENVIRONMENTAL POLLUTION. see POLLUTION.

ENVIRONMENTAL PROTECTION IN ART - EXHIBITIONS.
Wadden, Mary Ann. The political landscape . Brookville, N.Y. , 1990. 32 p. :   ISBN 0-933699-17-4   DDC 709/.73/074747245 20
N8835 .W34 1990
NYPL [3-MAMT 91-4586]

ENVIRONMENTAL PROTECTION - OREGON - MAPS.
Oregon environmental atlas /. [Portland] , Portland, Or. , 1988. 1 atlas (64 p.) :   DDC 363.73/2/09795022 20
G1491.N85 O7 1988
NYPL [Map Div. 91-2711]

ENVIRONMENTAL PSYCHOLOGY - CARICATURES AND CARTOONS.
Phillips, Steve, 1953- Farmer Johnson's psycho dairy farm for environmentally aware barnyard animals /. New York, N.Y. , 1992. p. cm.   ISBN 0-385-30495-1 :   DDC 741.5/973 20
NC1429.P57 A4 1992

Enzo Cucchi, etchings and lithographs, 1979-1985. Cucchi, Enzo. Munich , c1985. 1 v. (unpaged) :   ISBN 3-921629-12-8
NYPL [MDG (Cucchi) 90-11907]

Enzo Cucchi testa /. Cucchi, Enzo. München , c1987. 2 v. :   ISBN 3-88645-076-7 (v. 1)
NYPL [3-MCF C952 88-3505]

Epiphanies /. Arnold, Steven. Pasadena, CA. , 1987. [88] p. :   ISBN 0-942642-33-3
NYPL [MFX (Arnold) 90-9103]

Epítészet az osztrák-magyar monarchiában, 1867-1918 /. Moravánszky, Ákos. [Budapest] , c1988. 226 p. :   ISBN 963-13-2096-0
NYPL [3-MQW 91-6539]

Epping, Ed, 1948-
Ed Epping, events echoed : [exhibition] October 17-November 3, 1984. New York : Alternative Museum, c1984. 16 p. : ill. ; 28 cm. Title on cover and t.p. verso: Ed Epping, echoed events. "Curator, Geno Rodriguez ... ; essays, David J. Langston & George Aitken"--T.p. verso.   DDC 709/.2/4 19
1. Epping, Ed, 1948- - Exhibitions. I. Rodriguez, Geno. II. Langston, David J. III. Aitken, George. IV. Alternative Museum (New York, N.Y.). V. Title. VI. Title: Ed Epping, echoed events.
N6537.E66 A4 1984
NYPL [3-MGO (Epping) 90-12638]

EPPING, ED, 1948- - EXHIBITIONS.
Epping, Ed, 1948- Ed Epping, events echoed . New York , c1984. 16 p. :   DDC 709/.2/4 19
N6537.E66 A4 1984
NYPL [3-MGO (Epping) 90-12638]

Epstein, Cheryl. Halley, Peter [Essays. Selections.] Collected essays, 1981-1987 /. New York , Venice, CA , 1989, c1988. 302 p. :   ISBN 3-905173-24-2
NYPL [3-MC 89-19486]

Epstein, Diana.
Buttons / Diana Epstein, Millicent Safro ; photography by John Parnell. New York : H.N. Abrams, 1991. p. cm. Includes bibliographical references (p.) and index.   ISBN 0-8109-3113-3 :   DDC 646/.19 20
1. Buttons - Catalogs. 2. Epstein, Diana - Art collections - Catalogs. 3. Safro, Millicent, 1934- - Art collections - Catalogs. 4. Buttons - Private collections - New York (N.Y.) - Catalogs. I. Safro, Millicent, 1934-. II. Title.
NK3668.5 .E665 1991

The collector's guide to buttons / Diana Epstein. New York : Walker, 1990. 84 p. : ill. ; 21 cm. Cover title: A collector's guide to buttons. Includes bibliographical references.   ISBN 0-8027-7342-7 :   DDC 646/.19 20
1. Buttons - Collectors and collecting. I. Title. II. Title: Buttons.
NK3668.5 .E67 1990
NYPL [3-MNH 91-6705]

EPSTEIN, DIANA - ART COLLECTIONS - CATALOGS.
Epstein, Diana. Buttons /. New York , 1991. p. cm.   ISBN 0-8109-3113-3 :   DDC 646/.19 20
NK3668.5 .E665 1991

EPSTEIN FAMILY - ART COLLECTIONS - EXHIBITIONS.
Munch, Edvard, 1863-1944. Edvard Munch . Washington , c1990. 144 p. :   ISBN 0-89468-150-8   DDC 769.92 20
NE694.M8 A4 1990
NYPL [MDG+ (Munch) 90-11909]

EQUESTRIAN STATUES.
Calcani, Giuliana. Cavalieri di bronzo . Roma , c1989. 182 p. :   ISBN 88-7062-671-7
NYPL [3-MGO (Lysippus) 91-5330]

EQUESTRIAN STATUES - EUROPE.
Otto, Rudolf, 1910- Europäische Reiterdenkmäler . [S.l.] 1986 (Raunheim : Druckhaus Sahm) [19] p. :
NYPL [3-MGF 90-4503 Suppl.]

EQUESTRIAN STATUES - EUROPE - HISTORY.
Marco Aurelio . [Italy] , c1989. 277 p. :   ISBN 88-366-0280-0   *NYPL [3-MGR+ 91-5599]*

EQUESTRIAN STATUES - ITALY - ROME.
Marco Aurelio . [Italy] , c1989. 277 p. :   ISBN 88-366-0280-0   *NYPL [3-MGR+ 91-5599]*

EQUESTRIAN STATUES - ROME.
Bergemann, Johannes. Römische Reiterstatuen . Mainz am Rhein , c1990. xii, 196 p., 96 p. of plates :   ISBN 3-8053-1149-4
NYPL [3-MGH+ 91-5688]

Erasmus Grasser und der Meister des Blutenburger Apostelzyklus . Otto, Kornelius. München , 1988. 268 p., [20] p. of plates :   ISBN 3-87821-270-4
NB586.M77 O8 1988

Eraud, Dominique. Laval, Mayenne / recherches et texte, Dominique Eraud ; photographies, François Lasa. [Nantes] : Association pour le développement de l'Inventaire général des Pays de la Loire, [1990] 138 p. : col. ill. ; 30 cm. (Images du patrimoine . no 68) "Ministère de la culture, de la communication, des grands travaux et du bicentenaire, Inventaire général des monuments et des richesses artistiques de la France, Région des Pays de la Loire, Ville de Laval."   ISBN 2-906344-24-9   DDC 709/.44/16 20
1. Art, French - France - Laval (Mayenne). I. Lasa, François. II. Inventaire général des monuments et des richesses artistiques de la France. Région des Pays de la Loire. III. Laval (Mayenne, France). IV. Title. V. Series.
N6851.L36 E7 1990

Erber, Wolfram. 10X . [Berlin] [1984] 1 portfolio (10 pieces) :   *NYPL [3-MAMG+ 88-4811]*

Erdély és a Részek térképe és helységnévtára : készült Lipszky János 1806-ban megjelent műve alapján / szerkesztette, Herner János ; [készítette a József Attila Tudományegyetem I. sz. Magyar Irodalomtörténeti Tanszékének diák-munkaközössége, Duró Gábor ... et al.]. Szeged : [s.n.], 1987 ([Budapest] : Franklin Nyomda) 1 atlas (41, 214 p., [9] p. of plates) : ill., coats of arms, maps ; 29 cm. Title on added t.p.: Mappa Transilvaniae et Partium Regni Hungariae repertoriumque locorum objectorum. Summary in German. Includes bibliographical references and index.   ISBN 963-481-771-8 :   DDC 912/.4984 19
1. Names, Geographical - Romania - Transylvania. 2. Cartography - Romania - Transylvania - History. 3. Crests - Romania - Transylvania. 4. Transylvania (Romania) - Maps. I. Herner, János. II. Duró, Gábor. III. Lipszky, János, báró, 1766-1826. Mappa generalis Regni Hungariae Partiumque adnexarum Croatiae, Slavoniae, et Confiniorum Militarium, magni item Principatus Transylvaniae... IV. József Attila Tudományegyetem. I. sz.--Magyar Irodalomtörténeti Tanszék. V. Title: Mappa Transilvaniae et Partium Regni Hungariae repertoriumque locorum objectorum.
G2037.T7 E7 1987
NYPL [Map Div. 91-145]

Ereignis Karikaturen : Geschichte in Spottbildern 1600-1930 : Landschaftsverband Westfalen-Lippe, Westfälisches Landesmuseum für Kunst und Kulturgeschichte Münster, 11. September bis 13. November 1983 / [herausgegeben von Siegfried Kessemeier im Auftrage des Landschaftsverbandes Westfalen-Lippe ; Ausstellung und Katalog, Siegfried Kessemeier, Heiko K.L. Schulze in Zusammenarbeit mit Alfred Pohlmann und Carin Gentner]. Münster : Der Landschaftsverband, c1983. 384 p. : ill. (some col.) ; 23 cm. Bibliography: p. 381-384.   ISBN 3-88789-061-2   DDC 940/.0207 19
1. Political satire - Exhibitions. 2. Wit and humor, Pictorial - Exhibitions. 3. Europe - Politics and government - Caricatures and cartoons - Exhibitions. I. Kessemeier, Siegfried. II. Schulze, Heiko K. L.
D217 .E74 1983   *NYPL [MDY 84-1349]*

Erftemeijer, A. (Antoon) Bellec, François. Sillages néerlandais . Zutphen , c1989. 172 p. :   ISBN 90-6011-657-7   *NYPL [3-MAME 91-6109]*

Erfurter Kunstverein. Leverkühne, Silke, 1953- Silke Leverkühne aus anderer Perspektive . Münster [1990] 46 p. :   ISBN 3-925047-09-3
NYPL [3-MCK+ L661 91-6474]

Ergänzungsband der Mitteilungen der Berliner Gesellschaft für Anthropologie, Ethnologie und Urgeschichte .

(2) Frühe Bergvölker in Armenien und im Kaukasus . Berlin , 1984. 84 p. :
NYPL [3-MAE 90-10823]

Eric Fischl . Fischl, Eric, 1948- New York, N.Y. , 1990. 1 v. (unpaged) : ISBN 0-941863-17-4 DDC 759.13 20
ND237.F434 A4 1990

Eric Hosking's birds . Hosking, Eric John. London , 1979. 224 p. : ISBN 0-7207-1163-0 :
TR729.B5 H67 1979b
NYPL [MFX (Hosking) 81-890]

Eric Owen Moss, buildings and projects /. Moss, Eric Owen, 1943- New York , 1991. p. ISBN 0-8478-1431-9 DDC 720/.92 20
NA737.M73 A4 1991

Erich Mendelsohn . Mendelsohn, Erich, 1887-1953. [Works. English. 1991.] New York, N.Y. , 1991. p. cm. ISBN 0-910413-91-6 : DDC 720/.92 20
NA1088.M57 A4 1991

Erich Mendelsohn [sound recording] . Mendelsohn, Erich, 1887-1953. Oklahoma City [1976] 2 sound cassettes :
NA1088

Erich Müller-Santis . Huggler, Max, 1903- Bern , c1990. 107 p. : ISBN 3-7165-0684-2 DDC 759.9494 20
ND853.M778 H84 1990

ERICSON, A. W. (AUGUSTUS WILLIAM), 1848-1927.
Palmquist, Peter E. The photographers of the Humboldt Bay Region /. Arcata, CA , c1985- v. ;
NYPL [MFW 87-4565]

Erie Canal; history of the canal that made New York the Empire State from 1817 to the present. [Introductory statement by Louise Broeckar. New York, New York State Council on the Arts, c1971] [4] p., 50 plates. 37 cm. Issued in a case. "An exhibit portfolio produced by the New York State Council on the Arts for the New York Museums Collaborative." DDC 917.47/04
1. Erie Canal (N.Y.) - History - Pictorial works. I. New York State Council on the Arts. II. Museums Collaborative.
F127.E5 E74 *NYPL [MFW+ 91-6808]*

ERIE CANAL (N.Y.) - HISTORY - PICTORIAL WORKS.
Erie Canal; history of the canal that made New York the Empire State from 1817 to the present. [New York, c1971] [4] p., 50 plates. DDC 917.47/04
F127.E5 E74 *NYPL [MFW+ 91-6808]*

Erik Johan Löfgren . Löfgren, Erik Johan, 1825-1884. Helsinki , 1989. 1 v. (unpaged) : ISBN 951-9075-31-3
ND955.F53 L642 1989

Erik Levine . Levine, Erik, 1960- Genève , c1989. 1 v. (unpaged) :
NYPL [3-MGO (Levine) 91-7405]

ERIKSSON, FRITZ H. - ART COLLECTIONS - EXHIBITIONS.
Fritz H. Erikssons samling . Stockholm , 1943. 26 p., [64] p. of plates :
NYPL [3-MAX (Eriksson) 90-6849]

Eriksson, Leif. Beck & Jung. Chromo cube /. Bjärred, Sweden (Box 123, S-237 00 Bjärred) , c1982. 49 p., [24] leaves of plates : ISBN 91-85752-30-4 *NYPL [3-MAL 88-3799]*

Erlach, Johann Bernhard Fischer von. see Fischer von Erlach, Johann Bernhard, 1656-1723.

Erlangen. Städtische Galerie. see Städtische Galerie, Erlangen.

Das Erlernen der Malerei . Corinth, Lovis, 1858-1925. Berlin , c1920. 205 p. :
NYPL [MEM C798 91-5924]

Erlhoff, Michael. Deutsches Design 1950-1990 . München , c1990. 280 p. : ISBN 3-7913-1079-8
NYPL [3-MNF+ 91-3891]

Erm, Voldemar. Köler, Johann, 1826-1899. Johann Köler . Tallinn , 1976. 1 portfolio ([2] leaves, [14] leaves of plates :
ND699.K54 E75
NYPL [3-MCZ K797 79-583]

Ermes Midena, architetto moderno in Friuli / a cura di Luisa Mangilli ; contributi di Giorgio Dri, Sergio Polano. Udine : Cooperativa Alea, 1988. 94 p. : ill. ; 30 cm. (Alea contemporanea. 1)

Italian and English. Includes bibliographical references. ISBN 88-7772-012-3 (pbk.)
1. Midena, Ermes, 1895-1972. I. Mangilli, Luisa. II. Dri, Giorgio. III. Polano, Sergio. IV. Midena, Ermes, 1895-1972. V. Series.
NYPL [3-MQZ + (Midena) 90-2526]

Ermilov, Vasilii Dmitrievich, 1894-1968.
Vasily Dmitrievich Ermilov, 1894-1968 : gouaches, sculpture, reliefs : [exhibition] April 27-June 8, 1990, Leonard Hutton Galleries. New York : The Galleries, 1990. [64] p. : ill. (chiefly col.) ; 31 cm.
1. Ermilov, Vasilii Dmitrievich, 1894-1968 - Exhibitions. I. Leonard Hutton Galleries. II. Title.
NYPL [3-MCZ+ E685 90-8443]

ERMILOV, VASILII DMITRIEVICH, 1894-1968 - EXHIBITIONS.
Ermilov, Vasilii Dmitrievich, 1894-1968. Vasily Dmitrievich Ermilov, 1894-1968 . New York , 1990. [64] p. :
NYPL [3-MCZ+ E685 90-8443]

Ėrmitazh : istoriiạ stroitel´stva i arkhitektura zdaniĭ = Hermitage : history of buildings erection and architecture / pod obshcheĭ redaktsieĭ B.B. Piotrovskogo ; [V.M. Glinka ... et al.]. Leningrad : Stroĭizdat, 1989. 560 p. : ill. (some col.) ; 35 cm. Captions also in English. Includes bibliographical references (p. 554-557) and index. ISBN 5-274-00375-3 :
1. Gosudarstvennyĭ Ėrmitazh (Soviet Union) - History. 2. Architecture, Baroque - Russian S.F.S.R. - Leningrad. 3. Neoclassicism (Architecture) - Russian S.F.S.R. - Leningrad. 4. Leningrad (R.S.F.S.R.) - Buildings, structures, etc. I. Piotrovskiĭ, B. B. (Boris Borisovich), 1908-. II. Glinka, V. M. (Vladislav Mikhaĭlovich), 1903-. III. Title: Hermitage.
N3350 .E76 1989

Ernest Cormier and the Université de Montréal /. Ernest Cormier et l'Université de Montréal. English. Montréal , 1990. 179 p. : ISBN 0-920785-30-1
NA749.C67 E7613 1990
NYPL [3-MQZ (Cormier) 91-6585]

Ernest Cormier et l'Université de Montréal. English. Ernest Cormier and the Université de Montréal / edited by Isabelle Gournay. Montréal : Centre canadien d'architecture, 1990. 179 p. : ill. ; 27 cm. Translation of: Ernest Cormier et l'Université de Montréal. Includes bibliographical references (p. 177-179). ISBN 0-920785-30-1
1. Cormier, Ernest - Criticism and interpretation. 2. Université de Montréal - Buildings. 3. Architecture, Modern - 20th century - Québec (Province) - Montréal. 4. Montréal (Québec) - Buildings, structures, etc. I. Gournay, Isabelle. II. Title.
NA749.C67 E7613 1990
NYPL [3-MQZ (Cormier) 91-6585]

Ernest Pignon Ernest /. Pignon Ernest, Ernest. [Paris] , c1990. 157, [3] p. : ISBN 2-7335-0160-7
NYPL [3-MCO+ P633 91-5885]

Ernest Pignon Ernest /. Pignon Ernest, Ernest. [Paris] , c1990. 157, [3] p. : ISBN 2-7335-0160-7 DDC 709/.2 20
N6853.P53 A4 1990

Ernestine Ruben . Ruben, Ernestine, 1931- Schaffhausen , c1989. 95 p. : ISBN 3-7231-0392-8
NYPL [MFX (Ruben) 91-7939]

Ernestine Ruben : photographies. Ruben, Ernestine, 1931- Ernestine Ruben . Schaffhausen , c1989. 95 p. : ISBN 3-7231-0392-8
NYPL [MFX (Ruben) 91-7939]

Ernestine Ruben : photographs. Ruben, Ernestine, 1931- Ernestine Ruben . Schaffhausen , c1989. 95 p. : ISBN 3-7231-0392-8
NYPL [MFX (Ruben) 91-7939]

Ernesto Maldarelli (1850-1930). Maldarelli, Ernesto, 1850-1930. Un artista ferrarese del legno, Ernesto Maldarelli (1850-1930) /. Ferrara , c1989. 107 p. :
NYPL [3-MOC 90-12376]

Ernesto Saemisch . Saemisch, Ernesto, 1902-1984. [Mexico] [1989] 63 p. : ISBN 968-8405-96-5 DDC 759.3 20
N6888.S22 A4 1989

Erni, Hans, 1909-
Erni, vie et mythologie : [exposition] Fondation Pierre Giahadda, Martigny, 7 avril au 15 mai

1989. Martigny : Fondation Pierre Gianadda, [1989] 159 p. : ill. (some col.) ; 24 cm. Includes Bibliographical references.
1. Erni, Hans, 1909- - Exhibitions. I. Fondation Pierre-Gianadda. II. Title.
NYPL [3-MCZ E71 89-27325]

ERNI, HANS, 1909- - EXHIBITIONS.
Erni, Hans, 1909- Erni, vie et mythologie . Martigny [1989] 159 p. :
NYPL [3-MCZ E71 89-27325]

Erni, vie et mythologie . Erni, Hans, 1909- Martigny [1989] 159 p. :
NYPL [3-MCZ E71 89-27325]

Ernst Barlach: 1870-1938. Reiser, Katharyn D. [n.p., 1970] 1 v. (unpaged)
N6888.B35 R4

Ernst Geitlinger . Geitlinger, Ernst, 1895-1972. Ludwigshafen a. Rh. , c1989. 119 p. :
NYPL [3-MCK+ G316 90-5281]

Ernst Jõesaar . Jõesaar, Ernst, 1905- Stockholm , 1975. 25 p. [132] p. of plates :
NB955.F53 J642 1975

Ernst Ludwig Kirchner . Kirchner, Ernst Ludwig, 1880-1938. Bern , 1989. 147 p. : ISBN 3-85773-022-6
N6888.K45 A3 1989
NYPL [3-MCK K58 90-11101]

Ernst Ludwig Kirchner . Moeller, Magdalena M. Stuttgart , c1990. 344 p. : ISBN 3-7757-0301-2
NYPL [MDG+ (Kirchner) 91-3597]

Ernst Ludwig Kirchner . Moeller, Magdalena M. Stuttgart , c1990. 344 p. : ISBN 3-7757-0301-2 DDC 769.92 20
NE654.K4 A4 1990

Ernst, Max, 1891-1976.
Histoires de forêt . [Nantes] [1987] 100 p. : ISBN 2-906211-01-X DDC 760/.092 20
N6888.E7 A4 1987a

Histoires de forêt : Max Ernst : Musée des beaux arts de Nantes, juin-septembre 1987. [Nantes] : Le Musée, c1987. 100 p. : ill. (some col.) ; 23 cm. (Lectura . 1) Bibliography: p. 99. ISBN 2-906211-01-X
1. Ernst, Max, 1891-1976 - Exhibitions. I. Nantes (France). Musée des beaux-arts. II. Title.
NYPL [3-MCK E71 91-7033]

Max Ernst, druckgraphische Werke und illustrierte Bücher : Museum Ludwig Köln, 18. Juli-16. September 1990, Pfalzgalerie Kaiserslautern, 30. September-11. November 1990, Nassauischer Kunstverein Wiesbaden, 25. November 1990-6. Januar 1991, Neue Galerie der Stadt Linz, 24. Januar-31. März 1991 / [Ausstellung und Katalog, A.M. Fischer, Gabriele Lohberg]. Köln : Museum Ludwig, 1990. 312 p. : ill. (some col.) ; 31 cm. Exhibition catalog. Includes bibliographical references (p. 311-312). DDC 769.92 20
1. Ernst, Max, 1891-1976 - Exhibitions. I. Fischer, Alfred M. II. Lohberg, Gabriele, 1954-. III. Museum Ludwig. IV. Title. V. Title: Druckgraphische Werke und illustrierte Bücher.
NE654.E7 A4 1990

Spies, Werner, 1937- Max Ernst collages . New York , 1991. 540 p. : ISBN 0-8109-3251-2 DDC 709/.2 20
N6888.E7 M43 1991
NYPL [3-MCK+ E71 91-5153]

ERNST, MAX, 1891-1976.
Spies, Werner, 1937- Max Ernst collages . New York , 1991. 540 p. : ISBN 0-8109-3251-2 DDC 709/.2 20
N6888.E7 M43 1991
NYPL [3-MCK+ E71 91-5153]

ERNST, MAX, 1891-1976 - CRITICISM AND INTERPRETATION.
Diehl, Gaston. [Max Ernst. English.] Max Ernst /. New York , 1991. p. cm. ISBN 0-517-50004-3 : DDC 759.4 20
N6888.E7 D513 1991

ERNST, MAX, 1891-1976 - EXHIBITIONS.
Ernst, Max, 1891-1976. Histoires de forêt . [Nantes] , c1987. 100 p. : ISBN 2-906211-01-X
NYPL [3-MCK E71 91-7033]

Ernst, Max, 1891-1976. Max Ernst, druckgraphische Werke und illustrierte Bücher . Köln , 1990. 312 p. : DDC 769.92 20
NE654.E7 A4 1990

Histoires de forêt . [Nantes] [1987] 100 p. :

ISBN 2-906211-01-X   DDC 760/.092 20
N6888.E7 A4 1987a

Ernst Thomann. Thomann, Ernst, 1910- Ernst
Thomann--Einsichten . Emmendingen , c1990.
69 p. :   ISBN 3-925928-13-8
NB588.T39 A4 1990

Ernst Thomann--Einsichten . Thomann, Ernst,
1910- Emmendingen , c1990. 69 p. :   ISBN
3-925928-13-8
NB588.T39 A4 1990

Erotic art by living artists : a veritable gallery of
art of the erotic genre. Renaissance, CA :
Directors Guild Publishers, c1988. 111 p. : col.
ill. ; 22 cm.   ISBN 0-940899-02-7 (pbk.) :   DDC
704.9/428/0973074 20
1. Erotic art - Catalogs. I. Directors Guild Publishers.
N8217.E6 E665 1988
       NYPL [3-MAMZ 90-10946]

EROTIC ART - CATALOGS.
Erotic art by living artists . Renaissance, CA ,
c1988. 111 p. :   ISBN 0-940899-02-7 (pbk.) :
DDC 704.9/428/0973074 20
N8217.E6 E665 1988
       NYPL [3-MAMZ 90-10946]

EROTIC ART - COLOMBIA.
El Espíritu erótico /. Bogotá , 1990. 207 p. :
DDC 704.9/428/098610904 20
N8217.E6 E87 1990

EROTIC ART - EXHIBITIONS.
Kinsey Institute for Research in Sex, Gender,
and Reproduction. Selections from the
collections of the Kinsey Institute .
[Bloomington, Ind.]   [1990?] [40] p. :
       NYPL [3-MAMZ 91-7035]
Liebe, Dokumente unserer Zeit /. [Darmstadt]
Gütersloh , 1980. 191 p. :
       NYPL [3-MAMZ 90-6445]

EROTIC ART - PRIVATE COLLECTIONS -
GERMANY - CATALOGS.
Die Erotica und Priapea aus den Sammlungen
Goethes /. Frankfurt am Main , 1990. 298 p. :
       NYPL [3-MAMZ 91-4510]

EROTIC DRAWING.
Henric, Jacques. Pierre Klossowski /. Paris ,
c1989. 167 p. :   ISBN 2-87660-039-0   DDC
741/.092 20
NC248.K55 H46 1989

EROTIC DRAWING - POLAND - CATALOGS.
Schulz, Bruno, 1892-1942. The drawings of
Bruno Schulz /. Evanston, Ill. , 1990. 271 p. :
ISBN 0-8101-0964-6 (lib. bdg.)   DDC 741.9438
20
NC312.P63 S382 1990
       NYPL [3-MCZ S388 91-3910]

The erotic sculpture of Khajuraho /. Pacaurī,
Lakshmīnarāyaṇa. Calcutta, India , 1989. xvi,
218 p., [8] p. of plates :   ISBN 81-85109-79-6 :
DDC 730/.954/2 20
NB1952.E76 P3 1989
       NYPL [3-MAF 90-12490]

Die Erotica und Priapea aus den Sammlungen
Goethes / herausgegeben und erläutert von
Gerhard Femmel und Christoph Michel.
Frankfurt am Main : Insel, 1990. 298 p. : ill.
(some col.) ; 25 cm. Includes bibliographical
references (p. 82-122).
1. Goethe, Johann Wolfgang von, 1749-1832 - Art
collections - Catalogs. 2. Erotic art - Private
collections - Germany - Catalogs. I. Femmel, Gerhard.
II. Michel, Christoph. III. Title.
       NYPL [3-MAMZ 91-4510]

Die Erotische postkarte : das beste aus der
Foto-Sammlung Robert Lebeck / [redaktion
und texte, Robert Züblin]. Schaffhausen :
Edition Stemmle, c1988. [39] p. : ill. (some
col.) ; 24 cm.   ISBN 3-7231-0378-2
1. Lebeck, Robert - Photograph collections. I. Züblin,
Robert.   *NYPL [MFW 91-5010]*

Errázuriz, Paz. Chile from within, 1973-1988 /.
New York , 1990. 143 p. :   ISBN 0-393-02817-8
(cl.)   DDC 983.06/5 20
F3100 .F4722 1990   *NYPL [MFW 91-4452]*

Ersichtliches. Chaimowicz, Georg, 1929- Georg
Chaimowicz . Lüdenscheid , c1988. 100 p. :
MLCS 88/02633 (N)
       NYPL [3-MCK+ C434 91-5888]

Értekezések, emlékezések, 0236-6258.
Finta, József. A funkció társkeresései,
szerződéseim Budapesttel . Budapest , c1990.

---

34 p., [24] p. of plates :   ISBN 963-05-5571-9 :
NA682.F8 F5 1990

ERUDITION. see LEARNING AND
SCHOLARSHIP.

Ervand K'och'ar. K'och'ar, Ervand, 1899-
Erevan , 1972. 89 p. :
       NYPL [3-MCZ K762 89-27399]

Ervin Bossanyi. Hayes, Dagmar. [Canterbury]
1965. 37 p.   *NYPL [3-MRY 90-7119]*

Erwin Holl . Holl, Erwin, 1957- Stuttgart , 1989.
64 p. :   ISBN 3-89322-107-7
       NYPL [3-MCK+ H733 91-7978]

Erwin Lang . Lang, Erwin, 1886- Wien [1990?]
150 p. :   ISBN 3-85211-007-6
       NYPL [MDG+ (Lang) 91-4287]

Erwin Quedenfeldt . Quedenfeldt, Erwin,
1869-1948. Kleve , c1989. 119 p. :   ISBN
3-89413-180-2
       NYPL [MFX+ (Quedenfeldt) 90-13431]

Erythropel, Ilse, 1911-1967. Ilse Erythropel.
[Text von] Sahl Swarz [und] F. G. Winter.
Krefeld, Scherpe, 1968. 59 p. illus (part col.) 20
cm. In English and German.
1. Erythropel, Ilse, 1911-1967. I. Swarz, Sahl. II.
Winter, F. G. III. Title.
NB237.E7 S9
       NYPL [3-MGO (Erythropel) 90-6760]

ERYTHROPEL, ILSE, 1911-1967.
Erythropel, Ilse, 1911-1967. Ilse Erythropel.
Krefeld, 1968. 59 p. :
NB237.E7 S9
       NYPL [3-MGO (Erythropel) 90-6760]

Erzbischöfliches Diözesan-Museum (Cologne,
Germany) Religiöse Graphik aus der Zeit des
Kölner Dombaus 1842-1880 . Köln [1980] 63
p. , [52] p. of plates :
       NYPL [MDET 91-1492]

Erzen, Jale N. Berkel, Sabri, 1907- Sabri Berkel
/. [Turkey] [1988] 167 p. :   DDC 760/.092 20
ND873.B47 A4 1988

Es war einmal-- . Schleusing, Thomas. Berlin ,
c1979. 70 p. :
MLCM 84/5378 (P)
       NYPL [3-MDY 90-6651]

Escales du Baroque. Barocco mediterraneo .
[Naples] , c1989. 245 p. :   ISBN 88-435-2807-6
       NYPL [3-MCE 91-3396]

Esch-sur-Alzette (Luxembourg). Galerie d'art
municipale. Klötzer, Bernd, 1941- Bernd
Klötzer, Zeichnungen /. Nürnberg , c1988. 152
p. :   ISBN 3-922531-60-1
       NYPL [3-MGO+ (Klötzer) 90-8494]

Escher, Rolf, 1936- Polgar, Alfred, 1875-1955.
Auf dem Balkon . Reinbek bei Hamburg , 1989
(Neu-Isenburg : Druck der Edition Tiessen) 33
p. :   ISBN 3-920947-89-4
       NYPL [MEM+ E735 90-2434]

Escobar, Mario. see Escobar Ortiz, Mario.

Escobar, Marisol. see Marisol, 1930-

Escobar Ortiz, Mario. Museo Rayo Dibujo y
Grabado Latinoamericano, Roldanillo, Valle,
Colombia /. [Colombia? , 198-?] 95 p., [12]
leaves of plates :
N910.R58 A6 1980z

ESCOLA GUIGNARD (BELO HORIZONTE,
BRAZIL) - HISTORY.
Vieira, Ivone Luzia. A Escola Guignard na
cultura modernista de Minas, 1944-1962 /.
[Pedro Leopoldo, Minas Gerais] [1988] 164
p. :   DDC 709/.81/51 20
N6656.M5 V54 1988

A Escola Guignard na cultura modernista de
Minas, 1944-1962 /. Vieira, Ivone Luzia.
[Pedro Leopoldo, Minas Gerais] [1988] 164
p. :   DDC 709/.81/51 20
N6656.M5 V54 1988

Escott, Florence. University of Texas. Bureau of
Business Research. 1965 industrial atlas of
Texas. Austin, 1965. 20, 20 p. :
G1371.G1 A32 1965
       NYPL [Map Div. 90-6571]

Escritos sobre arte y artistas valencianos /.
Azcárraga, Adolfo de. Valencia , 1989. 330 p. :
ISBN 84-505-8230-X
       NYPL [3-MAML 90-11103]

Escuela de Buenos Aires . Glusberg, Jorge.
Buenos Aires, Argentina [between 1984 and

1990] 31 p. :
NA2706.A7 G58 1984

Escuela de Madrid : exposición antológica, Sala
de Exposiciones Casa del Monte, Madrid,
Mayo-Julio 1990. [Madrid] : Fundación
Humanismo y Democracia : Caja de Madrid,
[1990?] 293 p. : col. ill. ; 30 cm. Spine title:
Exposición antológica de la Escuela de Madrid.
"Comisarios de la exposición y editores del catálogo,
Javier Tusell Gómez, Alvaro Martínez-Novillo
González"--P. 293. Includes bibliographical references
(p. 287)   ISBN 84-505-9356-5   DDC
759.6/41/090450744641 20
1. Madrid school of painting - Exhibitions. 2. Painting,
Modern - 20th century - Spain - Exhibitions. I. Tusell,
Javier, 1945-. II. Martínez-Novillo González, Alvaro.
III. Fundación Humanismo y Democracia (Madrid,
Spain). IV. Caja de Ahorros y Monte de Piedad de
Madrid. V. Title: Exposición antológica de la Escuela
de Madrid.
ND808.5.M28 E83 1990

Escuela Nacional de Artes Plásticas (Mexico).
División de Estudios de Posgrado. Luis
Gutiérrez, Javier Cruz, Luis René Alva .
[Mexico City, Mexico] , 1988. 61 p. :
NE544 .L85 1988

Escultores españoles.
Ortega Coca, María Teresa. Francisco Barón /.
[Valladolid] [1989?] 60 p., [64] p. of plates :
ISBN 84-7852-010-4   DDC 730/.92 20
NB813.B29 A4 1989
       NYPL [3-MGO (Barón) 91-6088]
Ortega Coca, María Teresa. Venancio Blanco /.
[Valladolid] [1989?] 57 p., [46] p. of plates :
ISBN 84-7852-008-2   DDC 730/.92 20
NB813.B52 A4 1989
       NYPL [3-MGO (Blanco) 91-6429]

Escultura catalana del segle XIX. Escultura
catalana del segle XIX . Barcelona [1989?] 246
p. :   DDC 730/.946/70744672 20
NB809.C3 E83 1989

Escultura catalana del segle XIX : del
neoclassicisme al realisme : [exposició] del 2 al
23 de novembre de 1989, Casa Llotja de Mar
de Barcelona / [catàleg edició i direcció,
Fundació Caixa de Catalunya ; textos, Santiago
Alcolea i Gil ... et al.]. [Barcelona] : Fundació
Caixa de Catalunya, [1989] 246 p. : ill. (some
col.) ; 31 cm. Text also in Spanish and English.
Bibliography: p. 201.
1. Sculpture, Spanish - Spain - Catalonia. 2. Sculpture,
Modern - 19th century - Spain - Catalonia. I. Alcolea,
Santiago. II. Fundació Caixa de Catalunya. III. Casa
Llotja de Mar (Barcelona, Spain).
       NYPL [3-MGI+ 91-6802]

Escultura catalana del segle XIX : del
neoclassicisme al realisme / [textos, Santiago
Alcolea i Gil ... et al. ; traductors, Santiago
Alcolea i Gil, Antonia Kerrigan, José Enrique
Martínez]. Barcelona : Fundació Caixa de
Catalunya, [1989?] 246 p. : ill. (some col.) ; 30
cm. Catalan, English, and Spanish. "Del 2 al 23 de
novembre de 1989, Casa Llotja de Mar de Barcelona,
carrer Consolat del Mar 2." Includes bibliographical
references (p. 201).   DDC 730/.946/70744672 20
1. Sculpture, Spanish - Spain - Catalonia - Exhibitions.
2. Sculpture, Modern - 19th century - Spain -
Catalonia - Exhibitions. 3. Sculptors - Spain -
Catalonia - Biography. I. Alcolea, Santiago. II. Fundació
Caixa de Catalunya. III. Title: Escultura catalana del
segle 19. IV. Title: Escultura catalana del segle dinou.
NB809.C3 E83 1989

Escultura catalana del segle 19. Escultura
catalana del segle XIX . Barcelona [1989?] 246
p. :   DDC 730/.946/70744672 20
NB809.C3 E83 1989

Escultura gótica funeraria en Burgos /. Gómez
Barcena, María Jesús. [Burgos] , 1988. 261 p.,
[2] folded leaves of plates :   ISBN 84-86841-01-1
       NYPL [3-MRIF+ 91-6774]

A escultura mágico-erótica de Chico Tabibuia /.
Pardal, Paulo. Rio de Janeiro , 1989. 143 p. :
ISBN 85-7107-002-4   DDC 730/.92 20
NB359.T33 P3 1990

La escultura monumental en Madrid . Salvador
Prieto, Ma. del Socorro (María del Socorro)
Madrid , c1990. 523 p. :   ISBN 84-381-0147-X
    DDC 730/.946/4109034 20
NB810 .S25 1990   *NYPL [3-MGI 91-3250]*

Escultura ornamental barrôca do Brasil. Negro,

Carlos del. [Belo Horizonte, 1967] 2 v.,
NB1285 .N4   *NYPL [3-MRX 91-6337]*

Església de Santa Càndia d'Orpí / [direcció,
Antoni González ; autors, Antoni González ...
et al.]. [Barcelona] : Diputació de Barcelona,
Servei del Patrimoni Arquitectònic, c1989. 64
p. : ill. (some col.) ; 30 cm. (Monografies . 1)
Includes bibliographical references.   ISBN
   84-7794-049-5
*1. Església de Santa Càndia d'Orpí (Santa Càndia,
Spain). 2. Christian art and symbolism - Spain - Santa
Càndia. 3. Santa Càndia (Spain) - Buildings, structures,
etc. I. González, Antoni. II. Series: Monografies
(Barcelona (Spain : Province). Servei del Patrimoni
Arquitectònic) , 1.*
NA5821.S26 E8 1989

**ESGLÉSIA DE SANTA CÀNDIA D'ORPÍ
(SANTA CÀNDIA, SPAIN)**
Església de Santa Càndia d'Orpí /. [Barcelona] ,
c1989. 64 p. :   ISBN 84-7794-049-5
NA5821.S26 E8 1989

Eshaurren, Roberto, Sebastián Matta. see **Matta
Echaurren, Roberto Sebastián, 1911-**

Esher, Lionel, 1913- The glory of the English
house : one hundred architectural masterpieces
/ Lionel Esher ; photographs by Clay Perry.1st
U. S. ed. Boston, Mass. : Little, Brown, 1991.
p. cm. "A Bulfinch Press book."   ISBN
   0-8212-1851-4 :   DDC 728/.0942 20
1. Architecture, Domestic - England. I. Title.
NA7328 .E74 1991

Espace niçois d'art et de culture. "Peindre et
photographier?" . [Nice] , c1983. [44] p., [4]
leaves of plates :   *NYPL [MFW+ 91-7018]*

Espaces des autres : lectures anthropologiques
d'architectures. [Paris] : Editions de La Villette,
c1987. 270 p. : ill. ; 21 cm. (Penser l'espace)
Papers presented at a conference which was held Nov.
8-10, 1983 at the Musée de l'homme and was organized
by the Ecole d'architecture de Paris-La Villette (Unité
pédagogique d'architecture no 6). Includes
bibliographical references.   ISBN 2-903539-13-8
*1. Architecture, Domestic. 2. Personal space. 3. Space
(Architecture). 4. Ethnic architecture. I. Unité
pédagogique d'architecture no 6. II. Series.*
NA7125 .E83 1987

Espacios de comunicación = Areas of
communication = Surfaces de communication /
Director Marta Ribalta.1. ed. Barcelona :
Blume, 1976. 265 p. : ill. (some col.) ; 26 cm.
(Nuevo ambiente ; 3) "Distributed by ... Universe
Books ... New York." In English, French, and Spanish.
   ISBN 84-7031-447-5
*1. Entrance halls. 2. Halls. 3. Staircases. I. Ribalta,
Marta. II. Title: Areas of communication. III. Title:
Surfaces de communication.*
NA2853 .E86   *NYPL [3-MRN 81-422]*

España. see **Spain.**

Espartaco, Carlos. Eduardo Sanguinetti : la
experiencia de los límites / Carlos
Espartaco.Ed. bilingüe español-inglés. Buenos
Aires, Argentina : Ediciones de Arte
Gaglianone, 1989. 110 p. : ill. ; 23 cm.
(Colección Ensayo)   ISBN 950-9004-98-7   DDC
700/.92 20
*1. Sanguinetti, Eduardo, 1951- - Criticism and
interpretation. 2. Performance art - Argentina. I. Title.*
NX531.Z9 S254 1989

Espejo, Beatriz. Historia de la pintura mexicana /
texto, Beatriz Espejo ; prólogos, Rufino
Tamayo ... [et al.]. [S.l.] : Comermex, c1989. 3
v. : ill. (some col.) ; 28 cm. Bibliography: v. 3, p.
[251]-[254]
I. Title.   *NYPL [3-MCY 91-2619]*

Espinola, Vera B. Russian copper icons and
crosses from the Kunz Collection . Washington,
D.C. , 1990. p. cm.   DDC 730/.947 20
NK1653.S65 R8 1990

Esposizioni e "stile nazionale" (1861-1925) .
Buscioni, Maria Cristina. Firenze , c1990. xv,
303 p. :   DDC 725/.91 20
NA6750.A1 B8 1990

Espressione fotografica .
(1) Nicaragua, una realtà delle Americhe /.
Palermo (Italia) , c1987. 206 p. :   ISBN
   88-7704-010-6 :   *NYPL [MFW+ 91-3429]*

L'esprit de Genève . Jaxa, Piotr. Lausanne ,
c1988. 150 p. :   ISBN 2-8265-1051-7
      NYPL [MFX+ (Jaxa) 89-17890]

ESPRIT NOUVEAU.
Gabetti, Roberto. Le Corbusier e L'Esprit
nouveau /. [Torino] [c1975] x, 273 p., [12] p.
of plates :
NA1053.J4 G22
      NYPL [3-MCO J42 90-6619]

An essay on rural architecture. Elsam, Richard,
Esq. Farnborough, 1972. [5], v, 54 p., [31]
leaves.   ISBN 0-576-15164-5   DDC 728.6
NA7562 .E73 1803a
      NYPL [3-MQZ (Elsam) 90-6797]

Essays in aesthetic education. Swanger, David.
San Francisco , 1991. p. cm.   ISBN
   0-7734-9900-8   DDC 700/.7/073 20
NX303 .S94 1991

Esselte Map Service. The Botswana Society
social studies atlas /. Stockholm , 1988. 1 atlas
(48 [i.e. 50] p.) :   ISBN 999-12-6003-X   DDC
912.6883 20
G2579.7 B6 1988
      NYPL [Map Div. 91-7948]

Essen. Universität. see **Universität Essen.**

Essentielle Malerei in Deutschland . Bleyl,
Matthias. Nürnberg , c1988. 252 p. :   ISBN
   3-922531-56-3   *NYPL [3-MCI 90-12463]*

Essentielle Malerei in Deutschland . Bleyl,
Matthias. Nürnberg , c1988. 252 p. :   ISBN
   3-922531-56-3
ND568.5.A14 B57 1988

Essentiels.
Dictionnaire de la peinture allemande et
d'Europe centrale /. Paris , c1990. 415 p. :
   ISBN 2-03-740017-9   DDC 759.3/03 20
ND561 .D53 1990   NYPL [3-MAO 91-7701]
Dictionnaire de la peinture espagnole et
portugaise du Moyen Âge à nos jours /. Paris ,
c1989. 319 p. ;   ISBN 2-03-740016-0
      NYPL [MAO 90-9370]
Dictionnaire de la peinture flamande et
hollandaise du Moyen Âge à nos jours /. Paris ,
c1989. 493 p. ;   ISBN 2-03-740015-2
      NYPL [MAO 90-9371]

Essex Co., N.J. Outline & index map of Newark,
New Jersey. Newark, N.J. , 1926-1928. 4 v. :
      NYPL [Map Div. 91-4095]

Essex County atlas. Hagstrom Map Company.
Hagstrom's atlas of Essex County, New Jersey.
New York , c1961. 1 atlas (36 p.) :
      NYPL [Map Div. 90-67]

ESSEX COUNTY, N. J. - MAPS.
(1904) Robinson, E. (Elisha) Atlas of the
Oranges Essex County, N.J. . Philadelphia, Pa. ,
1904. 1 atlas ([4] leaves of plates, 26 double
leaves of plates) :   *NYPL [Map Div. 91-4093]*
(1926) Outline & index map of Newark, New
Jersey. Newark, N.J. , 1926-1928. 4 v. :
      NYPL [Map Div. 91-4095]
(1961) Hagstrom Map Company. Hagstrom's
atlas of Essex County, New Jersey. New York ,
c1961. 1 atlas (36 p.) :
      NYPL [Map Div. 90-67]

**Essex County, New Jersey outline and index
map.** Outline & index map of Newark, New
Jersey. Newark, N.J. , 1926-1928. 4 v. :
      NYPL [Map Div. 91-4095]

Essick, Robert N. William Blake's commercial
book illustrations : a catalogue and study of the
plates engraved by Blake after designs by other
artists / Robert N. Essick. Oxford [England] :
Clarendon Press ; New York : Oxford
University Press, 1991. p. cm. Includes index.
   ISBN 0-19-817390-3 :   DDC 769.92 20
*1. Blake, William, 1757-1827 - Catalogs. 2. Blake,
William, 1757-1827 - Criticism and interpretation. 3.
Artists' preparatory studies - England - Catalogs. 4.
Illustration of books - 18th century - England -
Catalogs. 5. Illustration of books - 19th century -
England - Catalogs. I. Blake, William, 1757-1827. II.
Title.*
NE2047.6.B55 A4 1991

Esslingen. Künstlergilde. see **Künstlergilde.**

Estados Unidos de Colombia. see **Colombia.**

Estampas, 1984-1985 : elenco de estampas
realizadas en España durante los años 1984 y
1985, mediante las técnicas de xilografía,
grabado calcográfico, litografía y serigrafía.
Madrid : Real Academia de Bellas Artes de San
Fernando, Calcografía Nacional, 1988. 331 p. :

ill. ; 23 cm. "Autores, Clemente Barrena, María
Martín, Elvira Villena"--T.p. verso. Includes index.
   ISBN 84-600-5307-5
*1. Prints, Spanish. 2. Prints - 20th century - Spain. I.
Barrena, Clemente. II. Martin, Maria. III. Villena,
Elvira. IV. Calcografía Nacional (Spain).*
      NYPL [MDBF 91-5842]

Estate Publications Dorset . Estate Publications
(Firm) Tenterden, Kent [1980?] 1 atlas (34, [6]
p.) :   ISBN 0-86084-108-1
      NYPL [Map Div. 91-1161]

Estate Publications (Firm) Estate Publications
Dorset : street maps of 22 towns with index,
road map with index, population gazetteer,
administrative districts / Street plans prepared
and published by Estate Publications.
Tenterden, Kent : Estate Publications, [1980?] 1
atlas (34, [6] p.) : col. maps ; 21 cm. Indexed.
Scale of Dorset road map [1:316,800]. 5 miles to 1 in.
Cover title: Estate Publications red book Dorset.
"136A."   ISBN 0-86084-108-1
*1. Cities and towns - England - Dorset - Maps. 2.
Dorset (England) - Maps. I. Title. II. Title: Estate
Publications red book Dorset. III. Title: Dorset.*
      NYPL [Map Div. 91-1161]

Estate Publications red book Dorset. Estate
Publications (Firm) Estate Publications Dorset .
Tenterden, Kent [1980?] 1 atlas (34, [6] p.) :
   ISBN 0-86084-108-1
      NYPL [Map Div. 91-1161]

Esteban Chartrand . Ruiz, Raúl R. La Habana,
Cuba , 1987. 85 p. :
      NYPL [3-MCZ C486 89-26612]

Esteban Leal, Paloma. Tesoros de las colecciones
particulares madrileñas . [Madrid] [1989?] 282
p. :   ISBN 84-451-0090-4   DDC 759.06/074/41 20
N6488.S7 M38 1989   NYPL [3-MC 90-8478]

Esterle, Max von, 1870-1947. Karikaturen und
Kritiken / Max von Esterle ; herausgegeben
von Wilfried Kirschl und Walter Methlagl.
Salzburg : O. Müller, c1971. 237 p. : 92 ill. ; 24
cm. (Brenner-Studien. Sonderreihe . Bd. 1) Reviews
and caricatures were originally published in the
periodicals Der Föhn and Der Brenner. Includes index.
Bibliography: p. 235-236.   ISBN 3-7013-0455-6
*1. Austrian wit and humor, Pictorial. 2. Austria -
Biography - Caricatures and cartoons. I. Kirschl,
Wilfried, 1930-. II. Methlagl, Walter. III. Title. IV.
Series.*
NC1489.E85 A4 1971
      NYPL [MEM (Esterle) 90-6541]

Estética y semiótica /. Ravera, Rosa María.
[Rosario, Santa Fe, Argentina] [1988] 250 p. ;
NX180.S46 R38 1988

Estetická výchova ve společenské práci /. Klivar,
Miroslav. Praha , 1989. 122 p. :
N69.C95 K58 1989

Esteveny, François. Catalogue de base des cartes
postales belges = Basis katalogus van de
Belgische postkaarten / ouvrage de François
Esteveny. [Bruxelles] : F. Esteveny, [1987] 269,
[2] p. : ill. ; 30 cm. Includes bibliographical
references (p. [271]).
*1. Postcards - Belgium - Catalogs. I. Title. II. Title:
Basis katalogus van de Belgische postkaarten.*
NC1878.7.B4 E88 1987

Esther Altorfer, 1936-1988. Altorfer, Esther,
1936-1988. [Bern] , c1989. 82 p. :   ISBN
   3-907991-13-3
      NYPL [3-MCZ A469 91-6665]

ESTHETICS. see **AESTHETICS.**

Esthétiques du dix-huitième siècle. Saint Girons,
Baldine. Esthétiques du XVIIIe siècle . Paris ,
c1990. 724 p. :   ISBN 2-904057-31-5
      NYPL [3-MAB 91-2669]

Esthétiques du XVIIIe siècle . Saint Girons,
Baldine. Paris , c1990. 724 p. :   ISBN
   2-904057-31-5   *NYPL [3-MAB 91-2669]*

Esthétiques du 18e siècle. Saint Girons, Baldine.
Esthétiques du XVIIIe siècle . Paris , c1990.
724 p. :   ISBN 2-904057-31-5
      NYPL [3-MAB 91-2669]

Estienne, Charles. Gauguin / Charles Estienne.
[Paris] : Nathan, [1989?] 157 p. : ill. (some
col.), ports. ; 34 cm. (Grands peintres)   ISBN
   2-09-284699-X
*1. Gauguin, Paul, 1848-1903 - Criticism and
interpretation. I. Title.*
      NYPL [3-MCO+ G26 89-28011]

Estilo y naturaleza . Arnaldo, Javier. Madrid ,
c1990. 284 p. : ISBN 84-7774-536-6
N6867.5.R6 A76 1990

Estimating for interior designers . Sampson,
Carol A. New York , 1991. p. cm. ISBN
0-8230-1600-5 DDC 729/.029/9 20
NK2116.2 .S26 1991

ESTONIA IN ART.
Pliiatsi ja blokiga mööda Nõukogude Eestit.
[Tallinn] , 1960. [74] leaves :
                    NYPL [3-MAMY 84-1245]

ESTONIAN ARTS. see ARTS, ESTONIAN.

Estructura y ciudad /. Munizaga, Gustavo.
Santiago de Chile , 1985. 147 p. :
NA9168.S3 M8 1985

Estructuralismo plástico mexicano . Martorrev.
Guadalajara, Jalisco, México , 1987. 120, [3]
p. :   *NYPL [3-MCY 89-11595]*

Estuardo Maldonado . Montana, Guido.
[Ecuador] , 1989. 251 p. : DDC 709/.2 20
N6689.M35 A4 1989

Estudios y fuentes del arte en México .
(51) Rivera, Diego, 1886-1957. Textos de arte
/. México , 1986. 430 p., [22] p. of plates :
  ISBN 968-8379-10-7
N6559.R58 A35 1986

Estudos de história da arte da Renascença /.
Gonçalves, António Nogueira, 1901- Aveiro
[Portugal] [between 1975 and 1987] 311 p. :
N7963.C65 G66 1975

Estudos de pintura maneirista e barroca /.
Serrão, Vítor, 1952- Lisboa , c1989. 416 p., [32]
p. of plates : ISBN 972-210-454-3 : DDC
759.69/09/031 20
ND825 .S47 1989

Et la lumière fut! . Bonnard, Olivier. Lausanne,
Suisse , c1989. 1 v. (unpaged) : ISBN
2-88074-166-1
                    NYPL [MFX+ (Bonnard) 91-5994]

L'Età del divisionismo / a cura di Gabriella Belli
e Franco Rella. Milano : Electa, c1990. 295 p.,
[2] p. of plates : ill. ; 24 cm. "Pubblicato in
occasione della mostra Divisionismo italiano, Trento,
Museo d'arte moderna e contemporanea, aprile-luglio
1990"--Verso t.p. Includes bibliographical references.
  ISBN 88-435-3179-4 DDC 700 20
1. Neo-impressionism (Art) - Italy - Exhibitions. 2.
Arts, Italian - Exhibitions. 3. Arts, Modern - 19th
century - Italy - Exhibitions. 4. Arts, Modern - 20th
century - Italy - Exhibitions. I. Belli, Gabriella. II.
Rella, Franco, 1944-. III. Museo d'arte moderna e
contemporanea di Trento e Rovereto.
NX552.A1 E78 1990
                    NYPL [3-MAMC 91-4384]

L'Età di Masaccio : il primo Quattrocento a
Firenze / a cura di Luciano Berti e Antonio
Paolucci. Milano : Electa, c1990. 265 p. : ill.
(some col.) ; 28 cm. Catalog of an exhibition held at
the Palazzo vecchio, Florence, June 7-Sept. 16, 1990.
Includes bibliographical references. ISBN
88-435-3211-1
1. Masaccio, 1401-1428? - Exhibitions. 2. Art, Italian -
Italy - Florence - Exhibitions. 3. Art, Renaissance -
Italy - Florence - Exhibitions. I. Berti, Luciano. II.
Paolucci, Antonio. III. Palazzo vecchio.
                    NYPL [3-MAMC 90-12878]

Etched in memory . Lang, Gladys Engel. Chapel
Hill , 1990. xviii, 437 p., [46] p. of plates :
  ISBN 0-8078-1908-5 (alk. paper) DDC
767/.2/094209034 20
NE2043.25 .L36 1990
                    NYPL [MDN 90-13667]

**ETCHERS - UNITED STATES -
BIOGRAPHY.**
Saunders, Boyd. Alfred Hutty and the
Charleston renaissance /. Orangeburg, S.C. ,
c1990. 127 p. : ISBN 0-87844-089-5 DDC 769.92
B 20
NE2012.H88 S28 1990
                    NYPL [MDG+ (Hutty) 91-5803]

**ETCHING - 19TH CENTURY - GREAT
BRITAIN.**
Lang, Gladys Engel. Etched in memory .
Chapel Hill , 1990. xviii, 437 p., [46] p. of
plates : ISBN 0-8078-1908-5 (alk. paper) DDC
767/.2/094209034 20
NE2043.25 .L36 1990
                    NYPL [MDN 90-13667]

**ETCHING - 19TH CENTURY - UNITED
STATES.**
Lang, Gladys Engel. Etched in memory .
Chapel Hill , 1990. xviii, 437 p., [46] p. of
plates : ISBN 0-8078-1908-5 (alk. paper) DDC
767/.2/094209034 20
NE2043.25 .L36 1990
                    NYPL [MDN 90-13667]

**ETCHING - 19TH CENTURY - UNITED
STATES - EXHIBITIONS.**
Schneider, Rona. American painter etchings,
1853-1908 . New York City [1989] 48 p. :
  ISBN 0-910672-06-7 (pbk.)
                    NYPL [MDBF 89-19631]

ETCHING - 20TH CENTURY - CATALOGS.
Kunstverlag Möller. Original-Radierungen mit
Motiven europäischer Städte /. Lübeck [198-?]
80 p. :   *NYPL [MDZ + 90-1093]*

**ETCHING - 20TH CENTURY - ENGLAND -
BRISTOL.**
Stoddard, Sheena. City impressions . Bristol ,
1990. 120 p. : ISBN 1-87297-120-2 (pbk.) : DDC
758.9942393 20
ND1354.4   *NYPL [MDNH 91-4822]*

**ETCHING - 20TH CENTURY - GREAT
BRITAIN.**
Lang, Gladys Engel. Etched in memory .
Chapel Hill , 1990. xviii, 437 p., [46] p. of
plates : ISBN 0-8078-1908-5 (alk. paper) DDC
767/.2/094209034 20
NE2043.25 .L36 1990
                    NYPL [MDN 90-13667]

**ETCHING - 20TH CENTURY - UNITED
STATES.**
Lang, Gladys Engel. Etched in memory .
Chapel Hill , 1990. xviii, 437 p., [46] p. of
plates : ISBN 0-8078-1908-5 (alk. paper) DDC
767/.2/094209034 20
NE2043.25 .L36 1990
                    NYPL [MDN 90-13667]

ETCHING, AMERICAN.
Lang, Gladys Engel. Etched in memory .
Chapel Hill , 1990. xviii, 437 p., [46] p. of
plates : ISBN 0-8078-1908-5 (alk. paper) DDC
767/.2/094209034 20
NE2043.25 .L36 1990
                    NYPL [MDN 90-13667]

ETCHING, AMERICAN - EXHIBITIONS.
Schneider, Rona. American painter etchings,
1853-1908 . New York City [1989] 48 p. :
  ISBN 0-910672-06-7 (pbk.)
                    NYPL [MDBF 89-19631]

ETCHING, BRITISH.
Jackson, Christine E. (Christine Elisabeth),
1936- Bird etchings . Ithaca , 1985. 292 p., [4]
leaves of plates : ISBN 0-8014-1695-7 (alk paper)
  DDC 598/.022/2 19
NE2043 .J33 1985   *NYPL [MDZ 85-4087]*

Lang, Gladys Engel. Etched in memory .
Chapel Hill , 1990. xviii, 437 p., [46] p. of
plates : ISBN 0-8078-1908-5 (alk. paper) DDC
767/.2/094209034 20
NE2043.25 .L36 1990
                    NYPL [MDN 90-13667]

ETCHING - HISTORY.
Carrington, Fitz Roy, 1869-1954. Engravers and
etchers. [Chicago] 1917. 9 p. L., 13-278 p. incl.
front., plates, ports.
NE400 .C3   *NYPL [MDB 91-7805]*

Etchings and words, 1972-1982 /. Grass, Günter,
1927- [Selections. English. 1985.] San Diego ,
c1985. 148 p. : ISBN 0-15-129150-0 DDC
769.92/4 19
NX550.Z9 G725 1983 vol. 2
                    NYPL [MDG+ (Grass) 91-2286]

Etchings by Clara Mairs. Mairs, Clara,
1878-1963. Clara . St. Paul, Minn. , c1976. 47
p. :   *NYPL [MDG (Mairs) 90-5656]*

The etchings of Charles Meryon /. Dodgson,
Campbell, 1867-1948. London , 1921. vii, 28 p.,
47 leaves of plates :
NF2115.M6 D6
                    NYPL [MDG+ (Méryon) 91-6349]

The etchings of Claude Lorrain /. Lorrain,
Claude, 1600-1682. New Haven , 1988. ix, 310
p. : ISBN 0-300-04222-1 DDC 769.92/4 19
NE2049.5.L67 A4 1988
                    NYPL [MDG (Gelée) 89-6552]

The etchings of Wilfred Fairclough /. Lowe, Ian.
Aldershot [England] , 1990. 112 p. : ISBN

0-85967-846-6
                    NYPL [MDG (Fairclough) 91-4725]

The etchings of Wilfred Fairclough /. Lowe, Ian.
Aldershot, Hants , 1990. 112 p. : ISBN
0-85967-846-6 DDC 769.92 20
NE2047.6.F35 L68 1990

Eternal metaphors . Sollins, Susan. New York,
N.Y. , c1989. 72 p. : ISBN 0-916365-28-X
                    NYPL [3-MAMC 90-11056]

ETHNIC ARCHITECTURE.
Espaces des autres . [Paris] , c1987. 270 p. :
  ISBN 2-903539-13-8
NA7125 .E83 1987

**ETHNIC ARCHITECTURE - MINNESOTA -
EMBARRASS.**
Gudmundson, Wayne. Testaments in wood . St.
Paul , 1991. p. cm. ISBN 0-87351-268-5 (paper) :
  DDC 720/.9776/77 20
NA7235.M62 E454 1991

ETHNIC ART.
Barnard, Nicholas. Living with folk art .
Boston , 1991. p. ISBN 0-8212-1840-9 DDC
745/.089 20
N5313 .B37 1991

ETHNIC ART - INDIA.
Koppar, D. H. Forgotten art of India /.
Baroda , 1989. xxiii, 266, [4] p. : DDC 709/.54
20
N7301 .K58 1989   *NYPL [3-MAF 91-6940]*

**ETHNIC ART - INDONESIA -
EXHIBITIONS.**
Taylor, Paul Michael. Beyond the Java Sea .
Washington, D.C. , New York , 1991. p. cm.
  ISBN 0-8109-3112-5 (hardcover : Abrams) :
  DDC 709/.598 20
N7326 .T39 1991

ETHNIC ART - UNITED STATES.
Lippard, Lucy R. Mixed blessings . New York ,
c1990. viii, 278 p., [40] p. of plates : ISBN
0-394-57759-0; 0-06-797296-6 DDC
704/.0693/0973 20
N6537.5 .L5 1990
                    NYPL [3-MAMT 91-2488]

Ethnic Arts Council of Los Angeles. Kalb, Laurie
Beth. Santos statues & sculpture . Los Angeles ,
c1988. [24] p., [2] leaves of plates (some
folded) : DDC 704.9/482 19
NK9712 .K35 1988
                    NYPL [3-MNE 90-12649]

ETHNIC ARTS - CYPRUS.
Gökçeoğlu, M. (Mustafa), 1942- Tezler ve
sözler /. [Cyprus] [1985?]- v. < 1 > :
NX573.6.C9 G64 1985

ETHNIC ARTS - PHILIPPINES.
Museo ng Kalinangang Pilipino . Maynila,
Pilipinas , 1989. 190, [1] p. :
NX581.A1 M88 1989

**ETHNIC JEWELRY - ITALY - HISTORY -
18TH CENTURY - EXHIBITIONS.**
Museo nazionale delle arti e tradizioni popolari
(Italy) Oreficeria popolare italiana e costumi
regionali del '700 . Lugano , 1978. 57 p., 36
leaves of plates :   *NYPL [3-MNR 90-5751]*

**Ethnikē Pinakothēkē, Mouseion Alexandrou
Soutsou.** Chartographēsē tou Hellēnikou
paraliou kai nēsiōtikou chōrou . [Athēna] ,
c1989. 84 p. :
GA881 .C43 1989
                    NYPL [Map Div. 91-3879]

**ETHNOLOGY - LITHUANIA -
CONGRESSES.**
Liaudies kūrybos palikimas dabarties kultūroje .
Kaunas , 1989. 220 p. : ISBN 5-430-00541-X :
NX180.S6 L5 1989

Ethos und Pathos : die Berliner Bildhauerschule,
1786-1914 Ausstellungskatalog / herausgegeben
von Peter Bloch, Sibylle Einholz, Jutta von
Simson. Berlin : Gebr. Mann, c1990. 419 p. :
ill. ; 27 cm. Published on the occasion of the
exhibition of the same name organized by the
Skulpturengalerie der Staatlichen Museen Preussischer
Kulturbesitz and held May 19-July 29, 1990, at the
Hamburger Bahnhof. Includes index. Includes
bibliographical references (p. 407-409). ISBN
3-7861-1597-4
1. Sculpture, German - Berlin (Germany) - Exhibitions.
2. Neoclassicism (Art) - Berlin (Germany) -
Exhibitions. 3. Sculptors - Berlin (Germany) -
Exhibitions. I. Bloch, Peter, 1925-. II. Einholz, Sibylle.
III. Simson, Jutta von. IV. Staatliche Museen

Preussischer Kulturbesitz. Skulpturengalerie. V. Hamburger Bahnhof (Exhibition hall : Berlin, Germany).   **NYPL   [3-MGI 90-12677]**

Etienne Delessert / designed by Rita Marshall. New York : Stewart, Tabori & Chang, 1992. p. cm. Includes bibliographical references.   ISBN 1-556-70224-8   DDC 741.6/092 20
1. Delessert, Etienne - Appreciation. I. Marshall, Rita.
NC988.5.D45 E8 1992

ETRURIANS. see ETRUSCANS.

Etruscan and Villanovan Pottery . DePuma, Richard D. [Iowa City] , 1971. 35 p. :
NYPL   [3-MPEK 90-5449]

ETRUSCAN MIRRORS. see MIRRORS, ETRUSCAN.

ETRUSCAN VASES. see VASES, ETRUSCAN.

The Etruscans . Newall, Christopher. Stoke-on-Trent , 1989. 78 p. :   ISBN 0-905080-83-1   **NYPL   [3-MCT 90-10817]**

ETRUSCANS - ITALY - CERVETERI - EXHIBITIONS.
Civiche raccolte numismatiche di Milano. Gli Etruschi e Cerveteri . Milano , c1980. 267 p. :   DDC 937/.5 19
DG70.C12 E88 1980
NYPL   [3-MPEK 89-13643]

ETRUSCANS - ITALY - PALESTRINA - CATALOGS.
Le Ciste prenestine /. [Roma] , 1979- v. :
DG70.P33 C57 1979
NYPL   [3-MGR+ 83-2202]

Gli Etruschi e Cerveteri . Civiche raccolte numismatiche di Milano. Milano , c1980. 267 p. :   DDC 937/.5 19
DG70.C12 E88 1980
NYPL   [3-MPEK 89-13643]

Etrusker, vad menade ni egentligen? . Säflund, Gösta, 1903- Partille [Sweden] , 1989. 154 p. :   ISBN 91-86098-88-8
NYPL   [3-MAH 91-6667]

Die Etrusker--Volterra . Cateni, Gabriele. Solingen , 1986. 90 p. :
NYPL   [3-MAE 90-12646]

Ettinghausen, Richard. Prayer rugs /. Washington, D.C. , c1974. 139 p. :
NYPL   [3-MOP 90-12309]

Ettl, Georg, 1940-
Georg Ettl, Arbeiten 1968-1989 = Georg Ettl, works, 1968-1989 / mit Texten von Johannes Cladders, Helge Drafz, Jiri Svestka. Düsseldorf : Kunstverein für die Rheinlande und Westfalen, 1990. 102 p. : ill. (some col.) ; 28 cm. German and English. Catalog of an exhibition held at the Kunstverein für die Rheinlande und Westfalen, Düsseldorf, Jan. 27-Mar. 4, 1990. Includes bibliographical references (p. 98-99).   ISBN 3-925974-14-8
1. Ettl, Georg, 1940- - Exhibitions. I. Cladders, Johannes. II. Drafz, Helge. III. Švestka, Jiří. IV. Kunstverein für die Rheinlande und Westfalen. V. Title. VI. Title: Georg Ettl, works, 1968-1989.
NYPL   [3-MGO (ETTL) 91-4445]

ETTL, GEORG, 1940- - EXHIBITIONS.
Ettl, Georg, 1940- Georg Ettl, Arbeiten 1968-1989 =. Düsseldorf , 1990. 102 p. :   ISBN 3-925974-14-8
NYPL   [3-MGO (ETTL) 91-4445]

Ettlinger, Elisabeth. Conspectus formarum terrae sigillatae Italico modo confectae /. Bonn , 1990. ix, 213 p. :   ISBN 3-7749-2456-2
NYPL   [3-MPA+ (Materialien zur römisch-germanischen Keramik. Heft 10)]

Ettlinger, John R. T. A Checklist of Canadian copyright deposits in the British Museum, 1895-1923 /. Halifax, N.S., Canada , 1984- v. :   ISBN 0-7703-0179-7 (pbk. : v. 1) :   DDC 015.71 19
Z1365 .C48 1984   **NYPL   [Map Div. 85-549]**

Etude de topographie du palais sacré de Byzance . Miranda, Salvador. [Paris?] 1976. 184 p., [43] p. of plates :
NYPL   [3-MQP 90-4929]

Etude du site de l'Abbaye de Liessies / étude réalisée pour la D.R.A.E. par Michel Schuermans ... [et al.]. [Fourmies, France] : Ecomusée de la région de Fourmies-Trélon, [1984] [82] leaves : ill. ; 30 cm. Bibliography: leaves [2]-[3] DDC 726/.7/094428 19

1. Abbaye de Liessies. 2. Church architecture - France - Liessies - Expertising. 3. Liessies (France) - Buildings, structures, etc. I. Schuermans, Michel. II. Délégation régionale à l'architecture et à l'environnement Nord-Pas-de-Calais.
NA5551.L4693 E88 1984
NYPL   [3-MRBB+ 90-12771]

Etudes québécoises.
(12) Lacroix, Jean-Guy, 1945- La condition d'artiste . Outremont, Québec , Ville Saint-Laurent, Québec , c1990. 249 p. ;   ISBN 2-89005-389-X   DDC 338.4/77/00971409048 20
NX513.A3 Q35 1990

Études sur l'orfèvrerie antique = Studies in ancient jewelry / éditées par Tony Hackens. Louvain-la-Neuve : Institut supérieur d'archéologie et d'histoire de l'art, 1980. viii, 154 p. : ill. (some col.) ; 27 cm. (Publications d'histoire de l'art et d'archéologie de l'Université catholique de Louvain ; 14. Aurifex . 1) Includes bibliographical references.
1. Jewelry, Ancient. I. Hackens, Tony, 1939-. II. Series: Publications d'histoire de l'art et d'archéologie de l'Universit catholique de Louvain. Aurifex , 1.
NYPL   [3-MNR 83-1678]

Eudora Welty . MacNeil, Robert, 1931- Jackson , c1990. 15 p. ;   ISBN 0-87805-471-5   DDC 770/.92 20
TR140.W43 M33 1990
NYPL   [MFW 91-4663]

Eugen Batz . Batz, Eugen, 1905- Ravensburg , c1989. 65 p. :
NYPL   [3-MCK B3365 90-262]

Eugene and Agnes E. Meyer Memorial exhibition. Freer Gallery of Art. Washington, 1971. 77 p.   **NYPL   [3-MAG 90-7182]**

Eugène Carrière . Bantens, Robert James. New York , c1990. 131 p. :   ISBN 1-87860-708-1
NYPL   [3-MCO C31 90-11584]

Eugène Delacroix . Athanassoglou-Kallmyer, Nina M., 1945- New Haven, CT , 1991. p. cm. ISBN 0-300-04931-5   DDC 741.5/092 20
NC1499.D36 A9 1991

Eugène Delacroix, further correspondence, 1817-1863 /. Delacroix, Eugène, 1798-1863. [Letters. Selections.] Oxford , New York , 1991. p. cm.   ISBN 0-19-817395-4   DDC 759.4 B 20
ND553.D33 A3 1991

Euler-Schmidt, Michael. Oellers, Adam C. Barthel Gilles, 1891-1977 . Recklinghausen , c1987. 326 p. :   ISBN 3-7647-0387-3
ND588.G46 O45 1987
NYPL   [3-MCK G475 91-4613]

Eun Nim Ro . Ro, Eun Nim, 1946- Berlin , Stuttgart , c1990. 79 p. :   ISBN 3-89322-301-0
N7369.R6 A4 1990

Euphronios.
Euphronios, peintre à Athènes au VIe siècle avant J.-C. [Paris] , 1990. 270 p. :   ISBN 2-7118-2348-2   **NYPL   [3-MPEK 91-3338]**

EUPHRONIOS - EXHIBITIONS.
Euphronios, peintre à Athènes au VIe siècle avant J.-C. [Paris] , 1990. 270 p. :   ISBN 2-7118-2348-2   **NYPL   [3-MPEK 91-3338]**

Euphronios, peintre à Athènes au VIe siècle avant J.-C. [Paris] : Editions de la Réunion des musées nationaux, 1990. 270 p. : ill. (some col.) ; 28 cm. Exhibition at Musée du Louvre, 18 septembre-31 décembre 1990. Includes index. Includes bibliographical references (p. 252-258) ISBN 2-7118-2348-2
1. Euphronios - Exhibitions. 2. Vases, Greek - Exhibitions. 3. Vase-painting, Greek - Exhibitions. I. Euphronios II. Musée du Louvre. III. Réunion des musées nationaux (France).
NYPL   [3-MPEK 91-3338]

Europa. Touring club italiano. Servizio cartografico. Atlante enciclopedico Touring. Volume 2, Europa /. Milano , c1987. 1 atlas (xi, 180 p.) :   ISBN 88-365-0299-7   DDC 912/.4 19
G1797.2 .T64 1987
NYPL   [Map Div. 90-10885]

L'Europa dei razionalisti : pittura, scultura, architettura negli anni trenta / a cura di Luciano Caramel. Milano : Electa, c1989. 383 p. : ill. (some col.) ; 24 cm. "Como, Palazzo Volpi, San Francesco, 27 maggio-3 settembre 1989"--P. [5] Includes bibliographical references (p. 336-374).   ISBN

88-435-2847-5
1. Art, European - Exhibitions. 2. Art, Modern - 20th century - Europe - Exhibitions. I. Caramel, Luciano.
NYPL   [3-MAL 91-4900]

Europa oggi : arte contemporanea nell'Europa occidentale / a cura di Amnon Barzel ; con la collaborazione di Giorgio Maragliano = Europe now : contemporary art in Western Europe / edited by Amnon Barzel ; with the collaboration of Giorgio Maragliano. Firenze : Centro Di ; Milano : Electa, c1988. 253 p. : ill. (some col.) ; 27 cm. (Cataloghi / Prato Museo d'arte contemporanea . 1) Cat. / Centro di ; 226 Catalog of an exhibition held at Museo d'arte contemporanea, Prato, June 25-Oct. 20, 1988. English and Italian.   ISBN 88-435-2560-3
1. Art, European - Exhibitions. 2. Art, Modern - 20th century - Europe - Exhibitions. I. Barzel, Amnon. II. Maragliano, Giorgio. III. Museo d'arte contemporanea (Prato, Italy). IV. Title: Europe now. V. Series: Cat. (Centro Di) , 226.   **NYPL   [3-MAL 89-1689]**

Europäische Reiterdenkmäler . Otto, Rudolf, 1910- [S.l.] 1986 (Raunheim : Druckhaus Sahm) [19] p. :
NYPL   [3-MGF 90-4503 Suppl.]

Eurōpaikē zōgraphikē tou dekatou hevdomou aiōna. Chrēstou, Chrysanthos, 1922- Hē Eurōpaikē zōgraphikē tou 17ou aiōna . Thessalonikē , 1989. 516 p. :
ND456 .C47 1989

Europäische Hochschulschriften. Reihe 38, Archäologie .
(Bd. 15) Roik, Elke. Das altägyptische Wohnhaus und seine Darstellung im Flachbild /. Frankfurt am Main , New York , c1988. 2 v. :   ISBN 3-8204-0163-6
NA215 .R65 1988
NYPL   [3-MQL+ 90-8068]

(Bd. 21) Pfisterer-Haas, Susanne. Darstellungen alter Frauen in der griechischen Kunst /. Frankfurt am Main , 1989. xii, 237 p. :   ISBN 3-631-41559-1   **NYPL   [3-MAMZ 91-4214]**

Europäische Kulturtage (1988 : Karlsruhe, Germany) Odenbach, Marcel, 1953- Marcel Odenbach . Karlsruhe , c1988. 100 p. :   ISBN 3-922531-57-1
N6888.O237 A4 1988
NYPL   [3-MCK 0245 90-11059]

Europalia (1987 : Brussels, Belgium) Rainer, Arnulf, 1929- Arnulf Rainer, masqué-démasqué . Vienne [1987] 143 p. :   ISBN 3-85127-000-2
NYPL   [3-MCK R155 90-12023]

Europalia (1989 : Brussels, Belgium)
Tokyo project . Bruxelles [1989] 189 p. :
NYPL   [3-MQWS+ 90-11043]

Vos, Ken. Assignment Japan . The Hague , 1989. 107 p. :   ISBN 90-12-06415-5
NYPL   [3-MAG+ 90-12025]

Europalia 87 Österreich. Tresors de la toison d'or . Bruxelles , 1987. 209 p. :   ISBN 2-87193-044-9
NYPL   [3-MAMZ+ 90-11054]

Europarådet. see Council of Europe.

Europarat. see Council of Europe.

EUROPE, EASTERN - GAZETTEERS.
Mokotoff, Gary. Where once we walked . Teaneck, N.J. , c1991. xxviii, 514 p. :   ISBN 0-9626373-1-9 (acid-free paper) :   DDC 914.7/0003 20
DS135.E83 M65 1991
NYPL   [*PWA 91-4243]

EUROPE, EASTERN - MAPS.
Sozialistische Staaten Mittel- und Südosteuropas /. Gotha , 1986. 1 atlas (190 p.) :   ISBN 3-7301-0032-7   **NYPL   [Map Div. 91-3783]**

EUROPE - ECONOMIC CONDITIONS - 1945- - MAPS.
Economic Community Information Service. The European community in maps. Bruxelles [1962] 1 atlas (1 portfolio ([4] p., 12 leaves of plates)) :   DDC 330.94055/0223 20
G1802.E9G1 E3 1962
NYPL   [Map Div. 91-5515]

EUROPE (GREEK MYTHOLOGY) IN ART - CATALOGS.
Die Verführung der Europa . Frankfurt am Main , 1988. 303 p. [16] p. of plates :   ISBN 3-549-05872-1   **NYPL   [3-MAMZ 89-1483]**

EUROPE IN ART.
Hodgkinson, Frank. Frank Hodgkinson's European sketchbooks. Kenthurst, N.S.W., Australia , c1990- v. : ISBN 0-646-01520-6 (set)
NYPL [3-MCZ H6895 91-3616]

EUROPE IN ART - EXHIBITIONS.
Bellotto, Bernardo, 1721-1780. Bernardo Bellotto . Milano , c1990. 172 p. : ISBN 88-435-3242-1
ND623.B43 A4 1990

EUROPE - KINGS AND RULERS - ART PATRONAGE.
Calloway, Stephen. Royal style . Boston , 1991. p. ISBN 0-316-12509-1 : DDC 745/.094 20
NK925 .C35 1991

EUROPE - MAPS.
(1987) Touring club italiano. Servizio cartografico. Atlante enciclopedico Touring. Volume 2, Europa /. Milano , c1987. 1 atlas (xi, 180 p.) : ISBN 88-365-0299-7 DDC 912/.4 19
G1797.2 .T64 1987
NYPL [Map Div. 90-10885]

Europe now. Europa oggi . Firenze , Milano , c1988. 253 p. : ISBN 88-435-2560-3
NYPL [3-MAL 89-1689]

EUROPE - POLITICS AND GOVERNMENT - CARICATURES AND CARTOONS - EXHIBITIONS.
Ereignis Karikaturen . Münster , c1983. 384 p. : ISBN 3-88789-061-2 DDC 940/.0207 19
D217 .E74 1983   NYPL [MDY 84-1349]

EUROPE - ROAD MAPS.
(1965) Mairs Geographischer Verlag. Der Grosse Shell Atlas. Stuttgart , c1965-1966. viii, 283, [166], x-xxii p. :
NYPL [Map Div. 90-5904]

Europe - Rulers. see **Europe - Kings and rulers.**

European and American carpets and rugs /. Faraday, Cornelia Bateman. Woodbridge, Suffolk, England , c1990. 484 p. : ISBN 1-85149-092-2 : DDC 746.7 19
NK2795   NYPL [3-MOP 90-11733]

EUROPEAN ART. see **ART, EUROPEAN.**

EUROPEAN ARTS. see **ARTS, EUROPEAN.**

EUROPEAN BOOK-PLATES. see **BOOK-PLATES, EUROPEAN.**

European common market countries. see **European Economic Community countries.**

The European community in maps. Economic Community Information Service. Bruxelles [1962] 1 atlas (1 portfolio ([4] p., 12 leaves of plates)) : DDC 330.94055/0223 20
G1802.E9G1 E3 1962
NYPL [Map Div. 91-5515]

European decorative arts in the Art Institute of Chicago /. Art Institute of Chicago. Chicago, Ill. , New York , c1991. p. ISBN 0-8109-3253-9 (Abrams : hardcover) DDC 745/.094/07477311 20
NK925 .A78 1991

European drawings recently acquired, 1972-1975. Metropolitan Museum of Art (New York, N.Y.) [New York] [1975] [52] p. :
NYPL [3-MBH 90-5754]

EUROPEAN ECONOMIC COMMUNITY COUNTRIES - ECONOMIC CONDITIONS - MAPS.
Economic Community Information Service. The European community in maps. Bruxelles [1962] 1 atlas (1 portfolio ([4] p., 12 leaves of plates)) : DDC 330.94055/0223 20
G1802.E9G1 E3 1962
NYPL [Map Div. 91-5515]

European enamels /. Belli Barsali, Isa. [Smalto in Europa. English.] London , 1988. 157 p. : ISBN 0-304-32179-6 (pbk) DDC 738.4/094 19
NYPL [3-MNV 90-9465]

European ex libris 1950-70. Severin, Mark. Engraved bookplates. Pinner, 1972. 176 p. (chiefly facsims.) ISBN 0-900002-91-3
NYPL [MDVC 90-7007]

European Graphic Arts, Biennial of. see **Biennial of European Graphic Arts, 1st, Heidelberg, 1979.**

EUROPEAN PAINTING. see **PAINTING, EUROPEAN.**

European paintings before 1900 in the Fogg Art Museum . Fogg Art Museum. Cambridge , c1991. p. cm. ISBN 0-916724-76-X (hardcover : acid-free paper) : DDC 759.94/074/7444 20
ND450 .F64 1991

European pigeon pennies . Pollack, Steven. [New York] , c1989. [24] p. :
NYPL [3-MGO+ (Pollack) 89-5996]

EUROPEAN POTTERY. see **POTTERY, EUROPEAN.**

EUROPEAN PRINTS. see **PRINTS, EUROPEAN.**

European sketchbooks. Hodgkinson, Frank. Frank Hodgkinson's European sketchbooks. Kenthurst, N.S.W., Australia , c1990- v. : ISBN 0-646-01520-6 (set)
NYPL [3-MCZ H6895 91-3616]

European textiles in the Keir collection . King, Monique. London , Boston , 1990. 311 p. : ISBN 0-571-13371-1 : DDC 746/.094/07442132 20
NK8942 .K56 1990

EUROPEAN WAR, 1914-1918 - ART AND THE WAR.
Nejedlý, Otakar, 1883-1957. Francouzská bojiště československých legií . Praze [1920?] [4] p., [8] leaves of plates :
NYPL [3-MAMY+++ 83-2786]

EUROPEAN WAR, 1914-1918 - CAMPAIGNS - FRANCE - PICTORIAL WORKS.
Nejedlý, Otakar, 1883-1957. Francouzská bojiště československých legií . Praze [1920?] [4] p., [8] leaves of plates :
NYPL [3-MAMY+++ 83-2786]

EUROPEAN WAR, 1914-1918 - CZECHOSLOVAKIA - PICTORIAL WORKS.
Nejedlý, Otakar, 1883-1957. Francouzská bojiště československých legií . Praze [1920?] [4] p., [8] leaves of plates :
NYPL [3-MAMY+++ 83-2786]

EUROPEAN WAR, 1914-1918 - INVENTIONS. see **INVENTIONS.**

EUROPEAN WAR, 1939-1945. see **WORLD WAR, 1939-1945.**

Eva/Ave . Russell, H. Diane (Helen Diane) Washington : New York, N.Y. : 238 p. : ISBN 0-89468-157-5 (pbk.) : DDC 769/.424/094074753 20
NE962.W65 R87 1990
NYPL [MDZ 91-4755]

Eva Gonzalès, 1849-1883 . Sainsaulieu, Marie-Caroline. Paris , c1990. 297 p. : ISBN 2-85047-115-0 DDC 759.4 20
N6853.G597 A4 1990

Eva Jiricna, design in exile /. Pawley, Martin. London , 1990. 112 p. : ISBN 1-87218-016-7
NYPL [3-MQZ (Jiriena) 91-5084]

Evaluating and predicting design performance / edited by Yehuda E. Kalay. New York, N.Y. : Wiley, c1991. p. cm. (Principles of computer-aided design) A selection of the papers were originally presented at a symposium. Includes bibliographical references and index. ISBN 0-471-85385-2 DDC 721/.0285 20
1. Architectural design - Data processing - Evaluation. 2. Computer-aided design - Evaluation. I. Kalay, Yehuda E. II. Series: Kalay, Yehuda E. Principles of computer-aided design.
NA2728 .E94 1991

EVANGELIARIES - ILLUSTRATIONS.
Anderson, Jeffrey C. The New York Cruciform Lectionary /. University Park , 1991. p. cm. ISBN 0-271-00743-5 DDC 745.6/7487 20
ND3359.N48 A44 1991

Evangelisti, Silvia. Crespi, Giuseppe Maria, 1665-1747. Giuseppe Maria Crespi, 1665-1747 . [Bologna] , c1990. ccxvi, 278 p. : ISBN 88-7779-148-9
NYPL [3-MCF C922 91-5467]

Evans, Dorinda. Benjamin West and his American students / by Dorinda Evans. Washington, D.C. : Published for the National Portrait Gallery by the Smithsonian Institution Press : for sale by the Supt. of Docs., U. S. Govt. Print. Off., 1980. 203 p. : ill. (some col.) ; 28 cm. "[Published for] an exhibition at the National Portrait Gallery, October 16, 1980 to January 4, 1981; and at the Pennsylvania Academy of the Fine Arts,

January 30 to April 19, 1981." Includes index. Bibliography: p. 191-197. ISBN 0-87474-418-0 DDC 759.13/074/0153
1. West, Benjamin, 1738-1820 - Influence - Exhibitions. 2. Painting, American - Exhibitions. 3. Painting, Modern - 17th-18th centuries - United States - Exhibitions. 4. Painting, Modern - 19th century - United States - Exhibitions. I. National Portrait Gallery (Smithsonian Institution). II. Pennsylvania Academy of the Fine Arts. III. Title.
ND207 .E94   NYPL [3-MCW 91-6652]

EVANS, JODIE - ART COLLECTIONS - EXHIBITIONS.
Bowman, Leslie Greene. American arts & crafts . Los Angeles, Calif. , Boston , c1990. 255 p. : ISBN 0-8212-1824-7 (hardback) : DDC 745/.0973/07479494 20
NK1141 .B64 1990
NYPL [3-MNE+ 91-4630]

Evans, Mark L. The Royal collection . Cardiff , 1990. 136 p. : ISBN 0-85331-589-2 (cased) : DDC 750.74 20   *NYPL [3-MC 91-4388]*

Evans, Walker, 1903-1975.
Mora, Gilles, 1945- [Walker Evans, Havana 1933. English.] Walker Evans, Havana 1933 /. New York , c1989. 111 p. : ISBN 0-394-57493-1 : DDC 972.91/23062/0222 19
F1799.H34 M6713 1989
NYPL [MFX (Evans) 90-1064]

Walker Evans / introduction par Gilles Mora. [Paris] : Centre national de la photographie, c1990. 1 v. (unpaged) : ill. ; 19 cm. (Photo poche . 45) ISBN 2-86754-065-8
1. Evans, Walker, 1903-1975. I. Title. II. Series.
NYPL [MFX (Evans) 91-2707]

EVANS, WALKER, 1903-1975.
Evans, Walker, 1903-1975. Walker Evans /. [Paris] , c1990. 1 v. (unpaged) : ISBN 2-86754-065-8
NYPL [MFX (Evans) 91-2707]

Mora, Gilles, 1945- [Walker Evans, Havana 1933. English.] Walker Evans, Havana 1933 /. New York , c1989. 111 p. : ISBN 0-394-57493-1 : DDC 972.91/23062/0222 19
F1799.H34 M6713 1989
NYPL [MFX (Evans) 90-1064]

Southall, Thomas, 1951- Of time & place . San Francisco , Fort Worth , c1990. 88 p. : ISBN 0-933286-57-0 (cloth)
NYPL [MFW 91-3397]

EVANS, WALKER, 1903-1975 - EXHIBITIONS.
Rosenheim, Jeff. Walker Evans and Jane Ninas in New Orleans, 1935-1936 /. New Orleans, La. , 1991. 24 p. : ISBN 0-917860-31-4
NYPL [MFX+ (Evans) 91-4936]

Evasions sur les traces du passe, les Poyas dans le canton de Fribourg. Spuren, die ins Freie führen . [Kiesen, Switzerland] , 1986. 40 p. :
NYPL [3-MAMZ 90-10960]

Everett, Gwen. Li'l Sis and Uncle Willie : a story based on the life and paintings of William H. Johnson / by Gwen Everett. Washington, DC : National Museum of American Art, Smithsonian Institution ; New York : Rizzoli International, c1991. p. cm. Surveys the life of African-American artist William H. Johnson as his young niece might have told it. The artist's paintings provide the illustrations. ISBN 0-8478-1462-9 DDC 759.13 B 20
1. Johnson, William H., 1901-1970 - Juvenile literature. 2. Afro-American artists - Biography - Juvenile literature. I. National Museum of American Art (U. S.). II. Title.
ND237.J73 E94 1991

Everett, Sally, 1941- Art theory and criticism . Jefferson, N.C. , c1991. xiii, 282 p. : ISBN 0-89950-595-3 (lib. bdg. : alk. paper) DDC 701 20
N71 .A7475 1991

Everson Museum of Art. Levine, Les, 1935- Public mind, Les Levine's media sculpture and mass ad campaigns 1969-1990, Everson Museum of Art /. Syracuse, NY , c1990. 127 p. : ISBN 0-914407-14-7
NYPL [3-MCX L659 91-6648]

Everything you do is a portrait of yourself . Reynolds, Marjorie, 1914- Rosebank, S.A. , 1989. xiii, 490 p. : ISBN 0-620-12883-6 DDC

760/.092 B 20
N7396.K38 R48 1989

Evocations of Four quartets . Finn, David, 1921-
Redding Ridge, CT, U. S.A. , c1990. 96 p. :
ISBN 0-933806-61-2 (cloth) : DDC 759.13 20
ND237.F433 A4 1990

Evolución de la arquitectura en México . Anda,
Enrique X. de. México, D.F. , 1987 [i.e. 1988]
235 p. : ISBN 968-380-186-2 DDC 720/.972 20
NA750 .A49 1988

Evolution de la professionnalité des architectes .
Benjamin, Isabelle. Paris [1990] 109 p. ; ISBN
2-11-085420-0 :
NA1996 .B46 1990

Evrard, Jacques. Watelet, Jacques Grégoire, 1917-
Serrurier-Bovy . Paris [1989, c1987] 134 p. :
NYPL [MOF 91-6858]

Ewald Mataré . Mataré, Sonja. Kleve , 1990. 503
p. : ISBN 3-89413-330-9
NYPL [MDG+ (Mataré) 91-3717]

Ewel, Markus. Thoma, Hans, 1839-1924. Hans
Thoma, Lebensbilder . Königstein im Taunus ,
c1989. 336 p. : ISBN 3-7845-7870-X DDC 759.3
20
ND588.T4 A4 1989

Ewenfält, Helena. Japanska konstskatter från
Tokyo Fuji Art Museum /. Stockholm , 1990.
78 p. :
NK1071 .J37 1990

Ewing, Elizabeth. Fashion in underwear, with
illustrations by Jean Webber. London, Batsford
[1971] 160 p. illus. 25 cm. Bibliography: p.
[155]-156. ISBN 0-7134-0857-X DDC 391/.42
1. Underwear - History. I. Title.
GT2073 .E9 1971 *NYPL [MMV 90-7022]*

EX-CONVICTS - SERVICES FOR.
al-Ri'āyah al-lāḥiqah lil-mufraj 'anhum bayna
al-naẓariyah wa-al-taṭbīq. al-Riyāḍ , 1988. 175
p. :
NV9275 .R52 1988

EX-OFFENDERS. see EX-CONVICTS.

EX-PRISONERS. see EX-CONVICTS.

**EXCAVATIONS (ARCHAEOLOGY) -
EUROPE.**
Le Verre préromain en Europe occidentale /.
Montagnac , 1989. 191 p. : ISBN 2-907303-00-7
NYPL [3-MPW+ 91-7509]

**EXCAVATIONS (ARCHAEOLOGY) - ITALY -
TERRACINA - EXHIBITIONS.**
Coppola, Maria Rosaria. Terracina . Roma ,
1986. 42 p. : ISBN 88-85020-74-7
NYPL [3-MQM 90-13012]

**EXCAVATIONS (ARCHAEOLOGY) - SPAIN -
ALBACETE (PROVINCE)**
Mosaicos romanos de Lérida y Albacete /.
Madrid , 1989. 124 p. : ISBN 84-00-06983-8
NYPL [3-MRXZ 90-12594]

**EXCAVATIONS (ARCHAEOLOGY) - SPAIN -
LÉRIDA (PROVINCE)**
Mosaicos romanos de Lérida y Albacete /.
Madrid , 1989. 124 p. : ISBN 84-00-06983-8
NYPL [3-MRXZ 90-12594]

**EXCAVATIONS (ARCHAEOLOGY) -
THAILAND.**
Thailand. Krom Sinlapākōn. Kānphatthanā
phiphitthaphanthasathān læ ngān bōrānnakhadī
kh [Bangkok] , 2508 [1965] 70, [30] p., [3]
leaves of plates :
N7321 .T46 1965

**EXCHANGES, STOCK. see STOCK-
EXCHANGE.**

**EXECUTIONS AND EXECUTIONERS IN
ART.**
Puppi, Lionello. [Splendore dei supplizi.
English.] Torment in art . New York , 1991. p.
ISBN 0-8478-1406-8 DDC 758/.936466/094 20
ND1452.E8515 P8713 1991

EXHIBITION BUILDINGS.
Buscioni, Maria Cristina. Esposizioni e "stile
nazionale" (1861-1925) . Firenze , c1990. xv,
303 p. : DDC 725/.91 20
NA6750.A1 B8 1990

**EXHIBITION BUILDINGS - EUROPE -
HISTORY - 19TH CENTURY.**
Çelik, Zeynep. Displaying the Orient .
Berkeley , c1992. p. cm. ISBN 0-520-07494-7

(alk. paper) DDC 725/.91 20
NA957 .C44 1992

**EXHIBITION BUILDINGS - UNITED
STATES - HISTORY - 19TH CENTURY.**
Çelik, Zeynep. Displaying the Orient .
Berkeley , c1992. p. cm. ISBN 0-520-07494-7
(alk. paper) DDC 725/.91 20
NA957 .C44 1992

Exhibition of British Paintings, 1750-1950 : June
13-July 11, 1990 ... Henry Wyndham Fine Art
of St. James's Art Group. London : St. James's
Art Group, 1990. 1 v. (unpaged) : ill. ; 26 cm.
*1. Painting, British - Exhibitions. I. St. James Art
Group. II. Henry Wyndham Fine Art.*
NYPL [3-MCT 90-13366]

**An Exhibition of five recent works by Larry Bell,
John McCracken, DeWain Valentine, Ron
Cooper [and] Peter Alexander;** an exhibition
organized for the Edmonton Art Gallery,
Edmonton, Canada by the Ace Gallery,
Vancouver and Los Angeles. July 2-31, 1971.
Edmonton, 1971. 44 p. illus. 26 cm.
*1. Black in art. 2. Art, American - Exhibitions. 3. Art,
Modern - 20th century - Los Angeles. I. Ace Gallery.*
N6535.L6 E89 *NYPL [3-MAMT 81-415]*

Exhibition of paintings by Walt Kuhn . Kuhn,
Walt, 1877-1949. New York , 1930. [31] p. :
NYPL [3-MCX K96 90-6805]

**An exhibition of prints, paintings and lacquer by
Shibata Zeshin, 25 June-9 July 1976, Milne
Henderson, London.** Zeshin, 1807-1891.
London [1976] [74] p. :
NYPL [MDG (Zeshin) 90-5668]

**An exhibition of works acquired from the G.
David Thompson Collection.** Alcoa Collection
of Contemporary Art. [Pittsburgh , 1967?] [32]
p. : *NYPL [3-MC 90-6343]*

An exhibition of works by Pierre Bonnard .
Bonnard, Pierre, 1867-1947. London [1978] 30
p. : *NYPL [3-MCO B716 90-6128]*

Exit Art (Gallery : New York, N.Y.)
Durham, Jimmie. Jimmie Durham . New York ,
c1990. 37 p. :
NYPL [3-MGO (Durham) 90-10679]

Wodiczko, Krzysztof. Krzysztof Wodiczko .
New York [1990?] 46 p. : ISBN 0-913263-29-X :
DDC 709/.2 20
N7255.P63 W642 1990
NYPL [MFX (Wodiczko) 91-4633]

Exlibris. Rother, Richard. Richard Rother und
sein Werk . Würzburg , c1987. 88 p. : ISBN
3-429-01100-0 DDC 769.5 19
Z996 .R65 1987
NYPL [MDVK (Rother) 89-26556]

Das Exlibris von heute 1988-1990 . Thoms,
Klaus. Wiesbaden , c1990. 286 p. : ISBN
3-922835-20-1 *NYPL [MDVF 91-7229]*

Exlibris-Werkverzeichnisse .
(1) Witte, Klaus. Martin E. Philipp, 1881-1978 .
Frederikshavn , 1984. [73] p. :
NYPL [MDVK (Philipp) 90-13583]

(3) Witte, Klaus. Georg Broel, 1884-1940 .
Frederikshavn , 1984. 86 p. : ISBN
87-7317-116-6
NYPL [MDVK (bBroel) 90-13584]

**EXOTICISM IN ARCHITECTURE -
EUROPE.**
Çelik, Zeynep. Displaying the Orient .
Berkeley , c1992. p. cm. ISBN 0-520-07494-7
(alk. paper) DDC 725/.91 20
NA957 .C44 1992

Mărgineanu-Cârstoiu, Monica. Romantismul în
arhitectură /. Bucureşti , 1990. 261, [3] p., [48]
p. of plates : ISBN 973-330-080-2 :
NA957 .M37 1990

**EXOTICISM IN ARCHITECTURE - UNITED
STATES.**
Çelik, Zeynep. Displaying the Orient .
Berkeley , c1992. p. cm. ISBN 0-520-07494-7
(alk. paper) DDC 725/.91 20
NA957 .C44 1992

EXOTICISM IN ART.
Günther, Erika. Die Faszination des Fremden .
Münster [1990] i, 193 p., [56] p. of plates :
ISBN 3-88660-542-6
ND567 .G86 1990

EXOTICISM IN ART - EUROPE.
Daftari, Fereshteh. The influence of Persian art

on Gauguin, Matisse, and Kandinsky /. New
York , 1991. p. cm. ISBN 0-8153-0715-2 (alk.
paper) DDC 709/.2/24 20
N7280 .D34 1991

Ionescu, Adrian-Silvan. Artă şi document .
Bucureşti , 1990. 318 p., [48] p. of plates :
ISBN 973-330-072-1 :
N8214.5.R6 I55 1990

**EXOTICISM IN ART - FRANCE -
CATALOGS.**
Plessier, Ghislaine. Adrien Dauzats, ou, La
tentation de l'Orient . Bordeaux , c1990. 227
p. : ISBN 2-902067-15-1 : DDC 759.4 20
ND553.D245 A4 1990

EXOTICISM IN ART - ROMANIA.
Ionescu, Adrian-Silvan. Artă şi document .
Bucureşti , 1990. 318 p., [48] p. of plates :
ISBN 973-330-072-1 :
N8214.5.R6 I55 1990

**EXPANSION (U. S. POLITICS) see UNITED
STATES - TERRITORIAL EXPANSION.**

**EXPATRIATE PAINTERS - BRAZIL -
CATALOGS.**
Peixoto, Maria Elizabete Santos. Pintores
alemães no Brasil durante o século XIX =. Rio
de Janeiro , 1989. 244 p. : ISBN 85-7191-001-4
DDC 750/.89/31081 20
ND354 .P45 1989

EXPERIENCE.
Csikszentmihalyi, Mihaly. The art of seeing .
Malibu, Calif. , 1990. xvii, 203 p. : ISBN
0-89236-156-5 : DDC 111/.85 20
BH301.E8 C75 1990
NYPL [3-MAB 91-6221]

Expérience esthétique et ontologie de l'œuvre .
Lories, D. (Danielle) Bruxelles [1989] 286 p. ;
ISBN 2-8031-0074-6 DDC 701 20
N67 .L76 1989

Experimental architecture in Los Angeles /
introduction by Frank Gehry ; essays by Aaron
Betsky, John Chase, and Leon Whiteson. New
York : Rizzoli International, 1991. p. cm.
ISBN 0-8478-1424-6 (HC) DDC
720/.9794/9409045 20
*1. Architecture, Modern - 20th century - California -
Los Angeles. 2. Avant-garde (Aesthetica) - California -
Los Angeles - History - 20th century. 3. Architecture -
California - Los Angeles. 4. Los Angeles (Calif.) -
Buildings, structures, etc. I. Betsky, Aaron. II. Chase,
John, 1953-. III. Whiteson, Leon.*
NA735.L55 E97 1991

**EXPERIMENTAL TELEVISION. see VIDEO
ART.**

Exploring abstraction. Wege zur Abstraktion /.
Basel , c1989. [74] p. :
NYPL [3-MAL+ 90-13078]

Exploring the past.
Giants of the arts . New York , 1991. p. cm.
ISBN 1-85435-414-0 : DDC 700/.92/24 20
NX653 .G53 1991

Exposição vida e obra de Stuart, 1982.
Carvalhais, Stuart, b. 1887. Vida e obra de
Stuart Carvalhais /. Lisboa , 1982. 244 p., [54]
p. of plates :
N7133.C34 A4 1982

Exposición antológica de la Escuela de Madrid.
Escuela de Madrid . [Madrid] [1990?] 293 p. :
ISBN 84-505-9356-5 DDC
759.6/41/09450744641 20
ND808.5.M28 E83 1990

Exposición barroco latinoamericano. [Buenos
Aires, Argentina] : Facultad de Arquitectura y
Urbanismo, Instituto de Arte Americano e
Investigaciones Estéticas "Mario J.
Buschiazzo" : Museo Nacional de Bellas Artes,
[between 1983 and 1989] 116 p. : ill. ; 23 cm.
The essays in this book were originally presented at
Simposio internacional sul Barocco latino americano,
Rome, Apr. 21-24, 1982. DDC 724/.16 20
*1. Architecture - Latin America - Congresses. 2.
Architecture, Baroque - Latin America - Congresses. I.
Museo Nacional de Bellas Artes (Argentina). II.
Instituto de Arte Americano-Mario J. Buschiazzo. III.
Simposio internacional sul Barocco latino americano
(1980 : Rome, Italy).*
NA702.2 .E97 1983

Exposition Claude Monet, 1840-1926 . Monet,
Claude, 1840-1926. Paris , 1959. 31 p. :
NYPL [3-MCO M74 90-6413]

Exposition de l'oeuvre lithographique d'Albert de Belleroche . Belleroche, Albert de. Bruxelles , 1933 (Renaix : J. Leherte-Courtin) [37] p., [8] leaves of plates :
NYPL [MDG (Belleroche) 90-5547]

Exposition des oeuvres récemment acquises par le Musée Fabre. [Montpellier , 1965] 40 p., [5] leaves of plates :
NYPL [3-MAVZ (Montpellier) 90-4843]

Exposition Mille ans d'art du vitrail. Beyer, Victor. Les vitraux des musées de Strasbourg /. Strasbourg , 1965. 2 v. in 1 :
NYPL [3-MRY 85-4411]

EXPRESSIONISM (ART) - EUROPE - EXHIBITIONS.
Wilhelm-Hack-Museum. Graphik des Expressionismus aus den Beständen des Museums /. Ludwigshafen am Rhein , c1989. 130 p. : DDC 769.94/09/07443435 20
NE625 .W54 1989

EXPRESSIONISM (ART) - FRANCE.
Di Genova, Alauzen. Antoine Ferrari /. La Calade, Aix-en-Provence , c1990. 136 p. : ISBN 2-85744-497-4 DDC 759.4 20
ND553.F44 D5 1990

EXPRESSIONISM (ART) - GERMANY.
Bushart, Magdalena. Der Geist der Gotik und die expressionistische Kunst . München , c1990. 255 p. : ISBN 3-88960-018-2 :
N6848.5.E9 B8 1990

The Ideological crisis of expressionism . Columbia, S.C. , c1990. 299 p. : ISBN 0-938100-77-7 (alk. paper) DDC 700 20
NX550.A1 I33 1990
NYPL [3-MAMG 90-11742]

Taylor, Seth, 1955- Left-wing Nietzscheans . Berlin , New York , 1990. x, 254 p. : ISBN 0-89925-695-3 (U. S.) : DDC 700/.944/09041 20
NX550.A1 T39 1990
NYPL [3-MAMG 91-3362]

Weinstein, Joan. The end of expressionism . Chicago , 1990. xiv, 332 p. : ISBN 0-226-89059-7 DDC 701/.03 19
N6868.5.E9 W45 1989
NYPL [3-MAMG 90-11096]

EXPRESSIONISM (ART) - GERMANY - CATALOGS.
Robert Gore Rifkind Center for German Expressionist Studies. German expressionist prints and drawings . Los Angeles, Calif. : Munich, Federal Republic of Germany : 2 v. : ISBN 3-7913-0959-5 (Prestel Verlag : set) DDC 760/.0943 19
N6868.5.E9 R6 1989
NYPL [MDE+ 91-5830]

EXPRESSIONISM (ART) - GERMANY - EXHIBITIONS.
Beckmann, Max, 1884-1950. Max Beckmann . [Italy] [1985] 141 p. : DDC 769.92/4 19
NE654.B37 A4 1985
NYPL [MDG (Beckmann) 86-4332]

German expressionist paintings . [S.l. , 196-] [60] p. : *NYPL [3-MCI 90-5896]*

German expressionist prints . Stuttgart , 1984. 1 portfolio (47, 151 p.) :
NYPL [MDBF 85-1960]

Meisterwerke des Expressionismus . Stuttgart , c1990. 251 p. : ISBN 3-7757-0302-0
IN PROCESS (ONLINE)
NYPL [3-MAMG+ 91-7962]

Pasadena Art Museum. The Blue Four. Pasadena [1954?] [32] p.
N6868.5.E9 P37 1954 *NYPL [3-MC 91-406]*

Vincent van Gogh and the modern movement, 1890-1914 /. Freren [Germany] , 1990. 436 p. : ISBN 3-923641-33-8 (Hard cover)
NYPL [3-MCH G61 91-4493]

EXPRESSIONISM (ART) - GERMANY - NORTH RHINE-WESTPHALIA - EXHIBITIONS.
Der Expressionismus und Westfalen /. Münster [1990] 239 p. : ISBN 3-88789-096-5
N6879 .E97 1990

EXPRESSIONISM (ART) - GERMANY - PRIVATE COLLECTIONS - MISSOURI - ST. LOUIS - EXHIBITIONS.
Syamken, Georg. Deutsche Expressionisten aus der Sammlung Morton D. May, St. Louis, USA

/. [Bielefeld] [1968] 106 p. : DDC 759.3
ND568 .R5 *NYPL [3-MCI 90-5742]*

EXPRESSIONISM (ART) - GERMANY - SOCIETIES, ETC. - EXHIBITIONS.
Kunsthalle Bern. Chronik KGBrücke, 1913 [microform] . Bern , 1948. 32 p., [16] leaves of plates : *NYPL [*ZM-202]*

EXPRESSIONISM (ART) - GERMANY (WEST) - MUNICH.
Zweite, Armin. The Blue Rider in the Lenbachhaus, Munich . Munich , 1989. 288 p. : ISBN 3-7913-0850-0
NYPL [3-MAMG+ 90-11017]

EXPRESSIONISM - GERMANY.
Lepovitz, Helena Waddy, 1945- Images of faith . Athens , c1991. xviii, 228 p. : ISBN 0-8203-1256-8 (alk. paper) DDC 760/.04482/094336 20
NK5435.G3 L4 1991
NYPL [3-MRY 91-4876]

The Expressionist landscape : North American modernist painting, 1920-1947 / organized by Ruth Stevens Appelhof, with the assistance of Cumbee Wilson ; with essays by Ruth Stevens Appelhof, Barbara Haskell, Jeffrey R. Hayes. Birmingham, Ala. : Birmingham Museum of Art, ; Seattle : distributed by the University of Washington Press, 1988, c1987. 216 p. : ill. (some col.) ; 28 cm. Bibliography: p. 200-215. DDC 759.1 19
1. Steiglitz, Alfred, 1864-1946 - Art patronage - Exhibitions. 2. Steiglitz, Alfred, 1864-1946 - Friends and associates - Exhibitions. 3. Landscape painting, American - Exhibitions. 4. Landscape painting - 20th century - United States - Exhibitions. 5. Landscape painting, Canadian - Exhibitions. 6. Landscape painting - 20th century - Canada - Exhibitions. I. Appelhof, Ruth Ann. II. Haskell, Barbara. III. Hayes, Jeffrey Russell, 1946-. IV. Birmingham Museum of Art.
ND1351.6 .E97 1987
NYPL [3-MCW 88-3335]

The expressionist surface . Matilsky, Barbara C. New York , c1990. 48 p. : ISBN 0-9604514-2-0
IN PROCESS (ONLINE)
NYPL [3-MAMT+ 91-4360]

Expressions of a new spirit . Warren, Elizabeth V. New York , c1989. 168 p. : ISBN 0-912161-01-9 DDC 745/.0973/0747471 20
NK805 .W33 1989
NYPL [3-MNE 90-12958]

Expressions of life . Zerbe, Karl, 1903-1972. Tallahassee, Fla. (125 N. Gadsden St., Tallahassee 32301) , c1989. 95 p. : DDC 760/.092 20
N6537.Z46 A4 1989
NYPL [3-MCX Z58 90-10828]

Expressions of style : window fashions / by Graber. Middleton, WI (7549 Graber Road, Middleton 53562-1096) : Graber Industries, c1990. 95 p. : ill. (some col.) ; 26 cm. Includes index. DDC 747/.3 20
1. Drapery in interior decoration. 2. Windows in interior decoration. I. Graber (Firm).
NK2115.5.D73 E95 1990

Exquisite corpse . Sorkin, Michael, 1948- London , New York , 1991. p. cm ISBN 0-86091-323-6 DDC 724/.6 20
NA682.P67 S67 1991

Extended photo media series .
(#2) Reilly, James M., 1946- The albumen & salted paper book /. Rochester, N.Y. , 1980. 133 p. : ISBN 0-87992-014-9 (pbk.) :
TR400 .R44 *NYPL [MFW 81-800]*

Exteriors, interiors, objects, people. Hamilton, Richard, 1922- Richard Hamilton . Hannover [1990] 153 p. : DDC 708.3/5954 s 709/.2 20
N5070.H3 K4 1990/5 N6797.H3

Exuberance now. Minder kan het niet . Groningen , c1989. 103 p. :
NYPL [3-MAL 90-12610]

EYCK, JAN VAN, 1390-1440.
Baldass, Ludwig, 1887-1963. Jan van Eyck /. New York , 1952. 297 p. : DDC 927.5
ND673.E9 B33 1952a
NYPL [3-MCH+ E97 91-4308]

Eye Level Gallery (Halifax, N.S.) Forster, Andrew, 1942- Andrew Forster (1942-) . Halifax, N.S. , 1983. 46 p. :
NYPL [3-MCZ F717 88-2150]

Eye on Washington . Tames, George, 1919- New

York , c1990. 159 p. : ISBN 0-06-016031-4 : DDC 973.9/092/2 20
E176.5 .T36 1990
NYPL [MFX+ (Tames) 90-13437]

Eyewitness . Lacayo, Richard. New York , c1990. 192 p. : ISBN 0-8487-1022-3 DDC 778.9/907049 20
TR820 .L34 1990 *NYPL [MFW+ 91-5849]*

Eyice, Semavi. Fotoğraflarla Fatih anıtları / metin, Semavi Eyice, Mehmet İ. Tunay, M. Baha Tanman ; fotoğraflar, Sabit Kalfagil. Fatih [Istanbul, Turkey] : Fatih Belediyesi, [1989?] 126 p. : col. ill. ; 28 cm.
1. Architecture, Islamic - Turkey - Fatih (Istanbul). 2. Architecture - Turkey - Fatih (Istanbul). 3. Istanbul (Turkey) - Buildings, structures, etc. 4. Fatih (Istanbul, Turkey) - Buildings, structures, etc. I. Tunay, Mehmet İ. II. Tanman, M. Baha. III. Kalfagil, Sabit. IV. Title. V. Title: Fatih anıtları.
NA1370 .E88 1989

Ezequiel Linares : comentarios críticos, 1959-1990. San Miguel de Tucumán, Argentina : Centro Cultural Dr. Albert Rouges, Fundación Miguel Lillo, [1990] 1 v. (unpaged) : ill. ; 21 cm. Cover title. Includes bibliographical references.
1. Linares, Ezequiel, 1927- - Criticism and interpretation. I. Linares, Ezequiel, 1927-. II. Centro Cultural Dr. Alberto Rouges.
ND339.L5 A4 1990

Ezra and Cecile Zilkha Gallery.
Alvin Lucier /. Middletown, Conn. , c1988. 23 p. ; ISBN 0-929687-01-9 (pbk.)
NYPL [3-MGO+ (Lucier) 89-21332]

D'Oench, Ellen. Jim Dine prints, 1977-1985 /. New York , c1986. 182 p. : ISBN 0-06-431501-0 : DDC 769/.92/4 19
NE539.D5 A4 1986
NYPL [MDG (Dine) 86-1962]

F. Busoni International Piano Competition.
Concorso pianistico internazionale "Busoni" [sound recording] =. Pontelambro (Co), Italy , p1988. 6 sound discs :
Nuova era 6716-DM--6721 DM

F. SCHUMACHER & CO.
Slavin, Richard E. Opulent textiles . New York , 1992. p. cm. ISBN 0-517-58255-4 : DDC 677/.02864/097471 20
NK8998.F2 S5 1992

Fabbri, Pier Giovanni. L'abbigliamento popolare italiano /. Brescia [1986] 160 p. :
NYPL [3-MMO 90-8664]

Faber, Monika, 1954- Furuya, Seiichi, 1950- Mémoires 1978-1988 /. Graz , c1989. 1 v. (unpaged) : ISBN 3-900508-06-2
NYPL [MFX (Furuya) 90-9132]

Fabergé and the Russian master goldsmiths / edited by Gerard Hill ; with introductions by Gerard Hill, G.G. Smorodinova and B.L. Ulyanova. [New York] : H.L. Levin Associates : Distributed by Macmillan Pub. Co., c1989. 320 p. : ill. (chiefly col.) ; 34 cm. Col. ill. on lining papers. ISBN 0-88363-889-4
1. Fabergé, Peter Carl, 1846-1920. 2. Goldwork - Soviet Union. I. Hill, Gerard.
NYPL [3-MNO+ 89-26729]

Fabergé and the Russian master goldsmiths /.
Fabergé, Peter Carl, 1846-1920. New York , 1991. p. cm. ISBN 0-517-02733-X DDC 739.2/092 20
NK7398.F32 A4 1991

FABERGÉ FAMILY.
Moore, Andrew, 1951- Theo Fabergé and the St. Petersburg Collection /. London , 1989. 161 p. : ISBN 1-87235-700-8 : DDC 929/.2/094 19
NYPL [3-MNE+ 90-11785]

Fabergé (Firm) see Faberzhe (Firm)

Fabergé, Peter Carl, 1846-1920.
Fabergé and the Russian master goldsmiths / edited by Gerard Hill. New York : Wings Books : Distributed by Outlet Book Co., 1991. p. cm. Includes bibliographical references and index. ISBN 0-517-02733-X DDC 739.2/092 20
1. Fabergé, Peter Carl, 1846-1920 - Themes, motives. 2. Faberzhe (Firm). 3. Art objects, Russian - Themes, motives. 4. Easter eggs - Russian S.F.S.R. - Themes, motives. 5. Goldwork - Russian S.F.S.R. - Themes, motives. I. Hill, Gerard. II. Title.
NK7398.F32 A4 1991

FABERGÉ, PETER CARL, 1846-1920.
Fabergé and the Russian master goldsmiths /.
[New York] , c1989. 320 p. :   ISBN
0-88363-889-4
NYPL [3-MNO+ 89-26729]

**FABERGÉ, PETER CARL, 1846-1920 -
THEMES, MOTIVES.**
Fabergé, Peter Carl, 1846-1920. Fabergé and
the Russian master goldsmiths /. New York ,
1991. p. cm.   ISBN 0-517-02733-X   DDC
739.2/092 20
NK7398.F32 A4 1991

**FABERGÉ, PETER CARL, 1846-1920 -
CATALOGS.**
Moore, Andrew, 1951- Theo Fabergé and the
St. Petersburg Collection /. London , 1989. 161
p. :   ISBN 1-87235-700-8 :   DDC 929/.2/094 19
NYPL [3-MNE+ 90-11785]

FABERGÉ, THEO, 1922- - CATALOGS.
Moore, Andrew, 1951- Theo Fabergé and the
St. Petersburg Collection /. London , 1989. 161
p. :   ISBN 1-87235-700-8 :   DDC 929/.2/094 19
NYPL [3-MNE+ 90-11785]

FABERZHE (FIRM)
Fabergé, Peter Carl, 1846-1920. Fabergé and
the Russian master goldsmiths /. New York ,
1991. p. cm.   ISBN 0-517-02733-X   DDC
739.2/092 20
NK7398.F32 A4 1991

Fabio Sargentini. Milano : Giancarlo Politi,
c1990. 125 p. : ill. ; 24 cm. (Lo Specchio)
Interview by Giancarlo Politi.   ISBN 88-7816-032-6
1. Sargentini, Fabio - Interviews. 2. Conceptual art -
Italy. 3. Performance art - Italy. I. Sargentini, Fabio. II.
Politi, Giancarlo.
IN PROCESS (ONLINE)
NYPL [MWES (Sargentini, F.) 91-4430]

A fable of modern art /. Ashton, Dore. Berkeley ,
c1991. p. cm.   ISBN 0-520-07301-0   DDC
700/.9/04 20
NX454 .A8 1991

Fabled cloths of Minangkabau /. Summerfield,
Anne, 1917- Santa Barbara, CA , 1991. p. cm.
ISBN 0-89951-082-5   DDC 746/.089/992 20
NK8980.A3 S87376 1991

Fables : five hundred years of illustration and text
/ edited by Anne Stevenson Hobbs. Savannah,
Ga. : F.C. Beil, 1991. p. cm. Originally published:
South Kensington : Victoria and Albert Museum, 1986.
"Attempts to show a cross-section of fable illustration in
printed books from the collections of the National Art
Library"--Apologia. Includes bibliographical references
and index. Presents selected fables from around the
world illustrated with artwork from the National Art
Library of London.   ISBN 0-913720-75-5 (hardcover) :
DDC 741.6/4 398.2 20
1. Fables - Illustrations. 2. Illustration of books. 3.
Fables. 4. National Art Library (Great Britain). I.
Hobbs, Anne Stevenson. II. National Art Library
(Great Britain).
NC961.7.F34 F3 1991

FABLES.
Fables . Savannah, Ga. , 1991. p. cm.   ISBN
0-913720-75-5 (hardcover) :   DDC 741.6/4 398.2
20
NC961.7.F34 F3 1991

Fables, formes, figures /. Chastel, André, 1912-
Paris , c1978. 2 v. :   DDC 701
N7560 .C46   *NYPL [3-MA 81-444]*

FABLES - ILLUSTRATIONS.
Fables . Savannah, Ga. , 1991. p. cm.   ISBN
0-913720-75-5 (hardcover) :   DDC 741.6/4 398.2
20
NC961.7.F34 F3 1991

Fabre, Gladys C. Arte abstracto, arte concreto .
[Valencia?] , c1990. 439 p. :   ISBN 84-7890-151-5
N6494.A2 A78 1990

FABRIC CRAFTS. see TEXTILE CRAFTS.

**FABRIC PICTURES - AUSTRIA -
EXHIBITIONS.**
Riedl, Fritz, 1923- Fritz Riedl . Vienna , 1978.
1 v. (unpaged) :   *NYPL [3-MOR 91-1456]*

**FABRIC PICTURES - SPAIN -
EXHIBITIONS.**
Royo, Josep. Josep Royo . Barcelona , 1972. 1
v. (unpaged) :   *NYPL [3-MON 90-6888]*

Fabric vibrations. . American Crafts Council.
Museum of Contemporary Crafts. New York ,
1972. [16] p. :   *NYPL [3-MON 90-5448]*

**FÁBRICA DE PORCELANA DA VISTA
ALEGRE - CATALOGS.**
Vista Alegre . [Lisbon] , c1989. 267 p. :   ISBN
972-90191-9-3   DDC 738.2/09469/35 20
NK4210.F3175 V5 1989

FABRICS. see TEXTILE FABRICS.

Fabrics and wallpapers . Phillips, Barty. Boston ,
c1991. p.   ISBN 0-8212-1871-9 :   DDC 747/.3 20
NK8806 .P48 1991

Fabris, Annateresa. Portinari, pintor social /
Annateresa Fabris. São Paulo, SP, Brasil :
Editora Perspectiva : Secretaria de Estado da
Cultura : xvi, 147 p. : ill. ; 23 cm. (Coleção
Estudos. 112.) Includes bibliographical references (p.
[141]-147).   ISBN 85-27-30027-3   DDC 759.981 20
1. Portinari, Cândido, 1903-1962 - Criticism and
interpretation. I. Series: Coleção Estudos (São Paulo,
Brazil) , 112. II. Title.
ND359.P6 F3 1990

Fabrizio Clerici /. Clerici, Fabrizio, 1913- Roma ,
1990. 260 p. :   ISBN 88-7813-268-3
NYPL [3-MCF C625 91-5535]

Fabro, Luciano, 1936-
Luciano Fabro : Castello di Rivoli, 28
giugno-17 settembre 1989 / a cura di Johannes
Gachnang, Rudi Fuchs, Cristina Mundici.
Bompiani : Fabbri ; [Turin] : Il Castello, c1989.
254 p. :: ill. ; 23 cm. In Italian; essays also in
English. Includes bibliographical references (p. 215-231)
1. Fabro, Luciano, 1936- - Exhibitions. I. Fuchs, Rudolf
Herman, 1942-. II. Gachnang, Johannes, 1939-. III.
Mundici, Maria Cristina. IV. Castello di Rivoli
(Museum : Turin, Italy). V. Title.
NYPL [3-MGO (Fabro) 90-11538]

FABRO, LUCIANO, 1936- - EXHIBITIONS.
Fabro, Luciano, 1936- Luciano Fabro .
Bompiani [Turin] , c1989. 254 p. ::
NYPL [3-MGO (Fabro) 90-11538]

Fabula üksi. Fabula 1 /. Helsinki [1989] 61 p. :
ISBN 951-861-843-7
N7255.F5 F28 1989

Fabula 1 / Lauri Astala ... [et al. ; taiteilijoitten
esittelytekstit, Juha Siltanen ; toimittanut Eero
Markuksela]. Helsinki : Valtion painatuskeskus :
Kuvataideakatemia, [1989] 61 p. : ill. (some
col.) ; 27 cm.   ISBN 951-861-843-7
1. Art, Finnish - Exhibitions. 2. Art, Modern - 20th
century - Finland - Exhibitions. I. Astala, Lauri. II.
Siltanen, Juha. III. Markuksela, Eero. IV.
Kuvataideakatemia (Helsinki, Finland). V. Title: Fabula
üksi.
N7255.F5 F28 1989

The fabulous life of Diego Rivera /. Wolfe,
Bertram David, 1896-1977. Chelsea, MI , 1990,
c1963. xxi, 457 p., [96] p. of plates :   ISBN
0-8128-1259-X :   DDC 759.972 B 20
ND259.R5 W56 1990
NYPL [3-MCZ R62 91-4860]

FACADES - EUROPE.
Tafelmaier, Walter, 1935- Architekturmalerei an
Fassaden . Stuttgart , 1988. 159 p. :   ISBN
3-421-02937-7   *NYPL [3-MRX 90-12633]*

FAÇADES - FRANCE - MOSELLE.
Massel, Christiane, 1953- Couleurs &
architecture . [Sarreguemines] , c1989. 157 p. :
ISBN 2-7085-0075-9   DDC 728/.0944/3825 20
NA3549.A3 M676 1989

FAÇADES - FRANCE - PARIS.
Goy-Truffaut, Françoise. Paris façade /. Paris ,
c1989. 245 p. :   ISBN 2-85025-208-5
NYPL [3-MRX 90-5327]

FAÇADES - ITALY - MANTUA.
Zuccoli, Noris. Mantova . Firenze , 1986. 60
p. :   *NYPL [3-MQWB 90-12550]*

**FAÇADES - ITALY - SANTA MARIA CAPUA
VETERE - CONSERVATION AND
RESTORATION.**
Vargas, Davide. Colore e arredo urbano .
Napoli [Santa Maria Capua Vetere] [1990]
154 p. :
NA3552.S27 V3 1990

FAÇADES - PORTUGAL - PORTO.
Brochado, Alexandrino. O Porto e suas igrejas
azulejadas /. Porto , 1990. 102 p. :
NK4670.7.P62 P673 1990

**FAÇADES - SPAIN - BARCELONA -
CATALOGS.**
Barcelona fi de segle . Barcelona [198-] 1

portfolio ([10] leaves of plates) :
NA2706.S7 B37 1980z

Face au silence. Begegnung mit der Stile =.
Bern , 1988. [35] leaves :
NYPL [3-MAL 89-11598]

Face farces. Rainer, Arnulf, 1929- München,
1970. 1 v.   DDC 709/.24
N6811.5.R3 A45

The face of Australia . Hansen, David. Frenchs
Forest, NSW, Australia , 1988. 127 p. :   ISBN
0-86777-181-X   DDC 760/.0449994 19
N7400 .H3 1988   NYPL [3-MAM+ 91-2242]

Facetten des Barock . Kunstmuseum Düsseldorf.
Akademiesammlung. Düsseldorf , 1990. 295 p. :
DDC 741.94/09/032074435534 20
NC225 .K87 1990

Fachterminologie für den historischen Holzbau :
Fachwerk, Dachwerk / herausgegeben von
Günter Binding, in Zusammenarbeit mit
Annette Roggatz. Köln : Vertrieb, Abt.
Architekturgeschichte des Kunsthistorischen
Instituts, 1990. 49 p. : 51 ill. ; 21 cm.
(Veröffentlichung der Abteilung Architekturgeschichte
des Kunsthistorischen Instituts der Universität zu Köln ,
38.) "Im Rahmen des am 8. Sept. 1987 unterzeichneten
'Abkommens zwischen der Regierung der
Bundesrepublik Deutschland und der Regierung der
Deutschen Demokratischen Republik über die
Zusammenarbeit auf den Gebieten der Wissenschaft und
Technik' (WTZ) wurde ... in einem Expertengespräch
am 27./28. März 1990 in Köln eine Fachterminologie
erarbeitet"--P. 1. Includes bibliographical references (p.
47-48).
1. Half-timbered buildings - Terminology. 2. German
language - Terminology. I. Binding, Günter. II. Roggatz,
Annette. III. Series.
NA4115 .F34 1990

**Fachverband der Hotel- und
Beherbergungsbetriebe (Austria)** Die 100
schönsten Speisekarten Österreichs . Graz
[1982?] 160 p. :   ISBN 3-900301-16-6
NC1002.M4 A14 1982

Fachverband Gastronomie (Austria) Die 100
schönsten Speisekarten Österreichs . Graz
[1982?] 160 p. :   ISBN 3-900301-16-6
NC1002.M4 A14 1982

Facial expression. Faigin, Gary, 1950- The artist's
complete guide to facial expression /. New
York , 1990. 287, [1] p. :   ISBN 0-8230-1628-5 :
DDC 704.9/42 20
N7573.3 .F35 1990

FACIAL EXPRESSION IN ART.
Faigin, Gary, 1950- The artist's complete guide
to facial expression /. New York , 1990. 287,
[1] p. :   ISBN 0-8230-1628-5 :   DDC 704.9/42 20
N7573.3 .F35 1990

Facility management (Stuttgart, Germany) .
(2) Kahlen, Hans. CAD-Einsatz in der
Architektur /. Stuttgart , c1989. 200 p. :   ISBN
3-17-010297-4
NA2728 .K38 1989

Facius, Antonio Ríus. see Ríus Facius, Antonio.

**Faculté des lettres de Fès. Département de
géographie.** Atlas de la médina de Fès .
Toulouse , 1990. 1 atlas (46 p.) :   ISBN
2-85816-137-2   *NYPL [Map Div. 91-161]*

Faden, William, 1750?-1836. Faden's map of
Norfolk / introduction by J.C. Barringer ; small
maps drawn by David Yaxley. 1st ed. Dereham,
Norfolk : Larks Press, 1989. 11 p., [37] p. of
plates : maps ; 22 x 31 cm. "First printed in
1797"--Cover.   ISBN 0-948400-09-9 (pbk.) :   DDC
911/.426/1 19
1. Norfolk (England) - Maps. I. Barringer, J. C. II.
Title.   *NYPL [Map Div. 91-8124]*

Faden's map of Norfolk /. Faden, William,
1750?-1836. Dereham, Norfolk , 1989. 11 p.,
[37] p. of plates :   ISBN 0-948400-09-9 (pbk.) :
DDC 911/.426/1 19
NYPL [Map Div. 91-8124]

Fagiolo dell'Arco, Maurizio, 1939-
Fonti, Daniela. Gino Severini . Milano , 1988.
655 p. :   *NYPL [MCF+ S49 90-485]*
Savinio, Alberto, 1891-1952. Alberto Savinio .
Ferrara , 1980. ca. 250 p. :
NYPL [3-MCF S265 90-6458]

**Fagiolo, Maurizio. see Fagiolo dell'Arco,
Maurizio, 1939-**

Fagone, Vittorio. L'immagine video : arti visuali e nuovi media elettronici / Vittorio Fagone.1. ed. in "Campi del sapere". Milano : Feltrinelli, 1990. 239 p., 32 p. of plates : ill. (some col.) ; 23 cm. (Campi del sapere. I Segni e la critica) Includes bibliographical references and index.   ISBN 88-07-10132-7 :   DDC 700/.9/04 20
1. Video art. 2. Art, Modern - 20th century. I. Title.
N6494.V53 F34 1990

Fahr, Friedrich. Molzahn, Johannes, 1892-1965. Johannes Molzahn . München , 1985. 72 p. :   ISBN 3-7954-0635-8
　　　　　　NYPL [3-MCK M731 91-6581]

FAIENCE - CATALOGS.
Musée de l'hôtel Sandelin. Chefs-d'œuvre de la faïence du Musée de Saint-Omer. Saint-Omer , c1988. 245 p. :   DDC 738.3/7/0940744427 20
NK4305 .M78 1988
　　　　　　NYPL [3-MPGG+ 90-12652]

Faïence de Marseille au dix-huitième siècle. La Faïence de Marseille au XVIIIe siècle . [Marseille] , 1990. 311 p. :   DDC 738.3/0944/912 20
NK4210.L28 F35 1990

La Faïence de Marseille au XVIIIe siècle : la manufacture de la Veuve Perrin / [commissariat général Danielle Maternati-Baldouy]. Marseille : Musées de Marseille : Agep, 1990. 311 p. : ill. (some col.), maps, plans ; 32 cm. Exhibition held at the Centre de la Vieille Charité, Marseille, Oct. 20-Jan. 20, 1991. Includes index. Includes bibliographical references (p. 304-305).
1. Perrin, Pierette, d. 1793 - Exhibitions. 2. La Veuve Perrin (Firm) - Exhibitions. 3. Faience - France - History - 18th century - Exhibitions. I. Maternati-Baldouy, Danielle. II. Galerie de la Vieille Charité.　　*NYPL [3-MPGG+ 91-7172]*

Faïence de Marseille au 18e siècle. La Faïence de Marseille au XVIIIe siècle . [Marseille] , 1990. 311 p. :   DDC 738.3/0944/912 20
NK4210.L28 F35 1990

FAIENCE - FRANCE - CATALOGS.
Musée de l'hôtel Sandelin. Chefs-d'œuvre de la faïence du Musée de Saint-Omer. Saint-Omer , c1988. 245 p. :   DDC 738.3/7/0940744427 20
NK4305 .M78 1988
　　　　　　NYPL [3-MPGG+ 90-12652]

FAIENCE - FRANCE - HISTORY - 18TH CENTURY - EXHIBITIONS.
La Faïence de Marseille au XVIIIe siècle . Marseille , 1990. 311 p. :
　　　　　　NYPL [3-MPGG+ 91-7172]
Faïences et objets révolutionnaires . Gagny , 1989. 150 p. :   *NYPL [3-MPGG+ 90-252]*
Faïences révolutionnaires . Paris , Rouen , 1989. 76 p. :   *NYPL [3-MPGG+ 90-71]*

FAIENCE - FRANCE - MARSEILLE - HISTORY - 18TH CENTURY.
La Faïence de Marseille au XVIIIe siècle . [Marseille] , 1990. 311 p. :   DDC 738.3/0944/912 20
NK4210.L28 F35 1990

FAIENCE - FRANCE - SAINT-OMER - CATALOGS.
Musée de l'hôtel Sandelin. Chefs-d'œuvre de la faïence du Musée de Saint-Omer. Saint-Omer , c1988. 245 p. :   DDC 738.3/7/0940744427 20
NK4305 .M78 1988
　　　　　　NYPL [3-MPGG+ 90-12652]

FAIENCE - GERMANY (EAST) - LEIPZIG - CATALOGS.
Museum des Kunsthandwerks Leipzig. Deutsche Fayencen im Museum des Kunsthandwerks Leipzig, Grassimuseum . Leipzig [1986] 84 p. :   DDC 738.3/0943/074432122 20
NK4305.5.G3 M87 1986
　　　　　　NYPL [3-MPGK 90-12397]

FAIENCE - GERMANY - HISTORY - 18TH CENTURY - CATALOGS.
Museum des Kunsthandwerks Leipzig. Deutsche Fayencen im Museum des Kunsthandwerks Leipzig, Grassimuseum . Leipzig [1986] 84 p. :   DDC 738.3/0943/074432122 20
NK4305.5.G3 M87 1986
　　　　　　NYPL [3-MPGK 90-12397]

FAIENCE - GERMANY (WEST) - DURLACH.
Das Pfinzgaumuseum in Karlsruhe-Durlach . Karlsruhe , 1976. 80 p. :   ISBN 3-7880-9565-2 :
N2307.K65 P34　*NYPL [3-MAMG 90-9226]*

FAIENCE - GERMANY (WEST) - WRISBERGHOLZEN.
Köhler, Johannes. Angewandte Emblematik im Fliesensaal von Wrisbergholzen bei Hildesheim /. Hildesheim , 1988. 165 p. :   ISBN 3-7848-3757-3   *NYPL [3-MRXZ 90-13016]*

FAÏENCERIES DE QUIMPER - CATALOGS.
Cahn, Laurent. Vierges et saints . [Quimper] [1990] 159 p. :
NK4210.F345 C35 1990

Faïences et objets révolutionnaires : collection P.M. Sestié : Conservatoire François Joseph Gossec, 4 Février-27 mars 1989. Gagny : La ville de Gagny, 1989. 150 p. : ill. (some col.) ; 30 cm.
1. Sestié, P. M. - Art collections - Exhibitions. 2. Faience - France - History - 18th century - Exhibitions. 3. France - History - Revolution, 1789-1799 - Art and the Revolution - Exhibitions. I. Conservatoire François Joseph Gossec.　　*NYPL [3-MPGG+ 90-252]*

Faïences révolutionnaires : collections du Musée de la céramique de Rouen : expositions, Rouen, Musée de la céramique, du 25 février au 31 août 1989, Auxerre, Musée Leblanc-Duvernoy, du 15 septembre 1989 au 8 janvier 1990 / [par Jacques Garnier et Catherine Vaudour]. Paris : Varia ; Rouen : Amis de la céramique, 1989. 76 p. : col. ill. ; 30 cm. Supplement ([4] p.) inserted. Includes bibliographical references.
1. Faience - France - History - 18th century - Exhibitions. 2. France - History - Revolution, 1789-1799 - Art and the Revolution - Exhibitions. I. Garnier, Jacques. II. Vaudour, Catherine. III. Rouen (France). Musée de la céramique. IV. Musée Leblanc-Duvernoy.　*NYPL [3-MPGG+ 90-71]*

Faigin, Gary, 1950- The artist's complete guide to facial expression / Gary Faigin. New York : Watson-Guptill Publications, 1990. 287, [1] p. : ill. (some col.) ; 29 cm. Includes bibliographical references (p. [288]) and index.   ISBN 0-8230-1628-5 :   DDC 704.9/42 20
1. Facial expression in art. 2. Art - Technique. I. Title. II. Title: Facial expression.
N7573.3 .F35 1990

Failing, Patricia. Doris Chase, artist in motion : from painting and sculpture to video art / by Patricia Failing ; introduction by Ann-Sargent Wooster. Seattle : University of Washington Press, c1991. p. cm. "A Samuel and Althea Stroum book." Includes bibliographical references and index.   ISBN 0-295-97112-6   DDC 700/.92 B 20
1. Chase, Doris, 1923-. 2. Artists - United States - Biography. 3. Video art - United States. I. Title.
N6537.C4638 F35 1991

Fain, Stephen M., 1940. Scheinbaum, David, 1951- Miami Beach . Miami , Gainsville, FL , c1990. 1 v. (unpaged) :   ISBN 0-8130-0933-2 (cloth)   DDC 975.9/381 20
F319.M6 S34 1990
　　　　　　NYPL [MFX (Scheinbaum) 91-3587]

Fair wilderness . Mandel, Patricia C. F. Blue Mountain Lake, N.Y. , 1990. 175 p. :   ISBN 0-910020-40-X   *NYPL [3-MCW 90-11114]*

Fairbrother, Nan. The nature of landscape design: as an art form, a craft, a social necessity. With a foreword by F. Fraser Darling.[1st American ed.] New York, Knopf, 1974. xii, 252 p. illus. 25 cm.   ISBN 0-394-47046-X   DDC 712
I. Title.
SB472 .F3 1974　　*NYPL [3-MSD 90-11372]*

Fairclough, Wilfred.
Lowe, Ian. The etchings of Wilfred Fairclough /. Aldershot [England] , 1990. 112 p. :   ISBN 0-85967-846-6
　　　　　　NYPL [MDG (Fairclough) 91-4725]

Fairclough, Wilfred, 1907-
Lowe, Ian. The etchings of Wilfred Fairclough /. Aldershot, Hants , 1990. 112 p. :   ISBN 0-85967-846-6   DDC 769.92 20
NE2047.6.F35 L68 1990

FAIRCLOUGH, WILFRED, 1907- - CATALOGS.
Lowe, Ian. The etchings of Wilfred Fairclough /. Aldershot, Hants , 1990. 112 p. :   ISBN 0-85967-846-6   DDC 769.92 20
NE2047.6.F35 L68 1990

FAIRCLOUGH, WILFRED - CATALOGUES RAISONNÉS.
Lowe, Ian. The etchings of Wilfred Fairclough /. Aldershot [England] , 1990. 112 p. :   ISBN

0-85967-846-6
　　　　　　NYPL [MDG (Fairclough) 91-4725]

FAIRFIELD COUNTY, CONN. - MAPS.
(1966) Hagstrom Company, inc., New York. Hagstrom's atlas of Fairfield County, Conneticut. New York, 1966. 70 p. :
G1243.F3 H3 1966   *NYPL [Map Div. 90-61]*

Fairley, John, 1940- Racing in art / John Fairley. London : John Murray, 1990. 224 p. : ill. (mostly col.) ; 28 cm. Includes index.   ISBN 0-7195-4723-7
1. Race horses in art. I. Title.
　　　　　　NYPL [3-MAMZ 90-13348]

Fairley, Robert. Blackburn, Jemima, 1823-1909. Jemima . Edinburgh , 1988. 207 p. :   ISBN 0-86241-186-6
　　　　　　NYPL [3-MCV B628 90-12435]

Fairman, Elisabeth R. Pleasures and pastimes : an exhibition / organized by Elisabeth R. Fairman. New Haven, Conn. : Yale Center for British Art, c1990. 39 p. : ill. ; 21 cm. "This catalogue was published on the occasion of an exhibition at the Yale Center for British Art, New Haven, Connecticut, February 21-April 29, 1990"--P. [4].   ISBN 0-930606-62-0
1. Leisure in art. 2. Games in art. 3. England - Social life and customs - 18th century - Exhibitions. 4. England - Social life and customs - 19th century - Exhibitions. I. Title.
　　　　　　NYPL [3-MAMZ 90-11038]

FAIRY TALES - CARICATURES AND CARTOONS.
Schleusing, Thomas. Es war einmal-- . Berlin , c1979. 70 p. :
MLCM 84/5378 (P)
　　　　　　NYPL [3-MDY 90-6651]

Fake? : the art of deception / edited by Mark Jones with Paul Craddock and Nicolas Barker. London : Published for the Trustees of the British Museum by British Museum Publications, 1990. 312 p. : ill. (some col.) ; 29 cm. Catalog of an exhibition at the British Museum. Includes bibliographical references (p. 308-309) and index.   ISBN 0-7141-1703-X
1. Art - Forgeries - Exhibitions. I. Jones, Mark, 1951-. II. Craddock, Paul. III. Barker, Nicolas. IV. British Museum.
N8790 .F3 1990b

Fakonstrukciók, fotogramok, rajzok. Megyik, János, 1938- János Megyik . Wien [1988] 39 p. :   ISBN 3-900776-02-8   DDC 709.2 20
N6822.5.M48 A4 1988
　　　　　　NYPL [3-MGO+ (Megyik) 90-11666]

Falaise, Calvados / [réalisé par le Service régional de l'Inventaire général ; rédaction, Jean-Louis Libourel ; photographies, Pascal Corbierre]. [Caen, France] : Association de développement culturel en Basse-Normandie, [1990] 64 p. : ill. (some col.) ; 30 cm. (Images du patrimoine . no 76) Cover title.   ISBN 2-908621-01-0 :   DDC 709/.44/22 20
1. Art, French - France - Falaise. I. Libourel, Jean-Louis. II. Corbierre, Pascal. III. Inventaire général des monuments et des richesses artistiques de la France. Service régional (Basse-Normandie, France). IV. Series.
N6851.F35 F35 1990

Falcón, Jorge, 1908- Centenario del nacimiento de José Sabogal, 1888-19 marzo-1988 /. Lima, Perú , 1989 (Miraflores : Librería Editorial "Minerva") 68 p. :
N6719.S23 C46 1989

Falconer, John, 1951- A vision of the past : a history of early photography in Singapore and Malaya : the photographs of G.R. Lambert & Co., 1880-1910 / by John Falconer. Singapore : Times Eds., 1987. 192 p. : ill., facsims., ports. ; 27 x 29 cm. Bibliography: p. 188.   ISBN 997-14-0105-3   DDC 770/.95957 20
1. G.R. Lambert & Co. 2. Photography - Singapore - History. 3. Photography - Malaya - History. I. G.R. Lambert & Co. II. Title.
TR113.S53 F35 1987
　　　　　　NYPL [MFW 91-3302]

Falk, Gathie, 1928- Lind, Jane. Gathie Falk /. Vancouver , c1989. 40 p. :   ISBN 0-88894-815-8 :   DDC 709.2 20   *NYPL [3-MAL 90-12811]*

Falk, Peter H. Dictionary of signatures & monograms of American artists : from the colonial period to the mid 20th century / by Peter Hastings Falk. Madison, Conn. : Sound View Press ; Land O'Lakes, FL : Distributed by

Dealer's Choice Books, 1988. 556 p., [1] leaf of
plates : ill. ; 29 cm. ISBN 0-932087-04-3 (alk.
paper) : DDC 702/.78 20
  1. Artists' marks - United States - Dictionaries. 2.
  Autographs - United States - Dictionaries. 3.
  Monograms - United States - Dictionaries. I. Title. II.
  Title: Dictionary of signatures and monograms of
  American artists.
  N45 .F35 1988   **NYPL** *[MAO 90-11577]*

Fallai, Aldo. Martin, Richard. Giorgio Armani .
New York , 1990. 224 p. : ISBN 0-8478-1298-7
  DDC 746.9/2/092 20
  TT580 .M37 1990
                    NYPL *[3-MME+ 91-3312]*

The Falmer Press library on aesthetic education.
Taylor, Rod. The visual arts in education /.
London , New York , 1992. p. cm. ISBN
1-85000-769-1 DDC 707/.041 20
  N88 .T38 1992

Falossi, Giorgio. Enciclopedia dei pittori e scultori
italiani del Novecento . Milano [1991] 2 v.
(1261 p.) : DDC 709/.2/.2450904 B 20
  N6918 .E58 1991

Falvey, William D. The official collector's guide
to Kentucky Derby mint julep glasses / by
William D. Falvey and Aaron Chase. Louisville,
Ky. (301 S. 30th St., Louisville 40212) :
Louisville Manufacturing Co., c1991. 81 p. :
col. ill. ; 22 cm. DDC 748.8/3/097713 20
  1. Advertising drinking glasses - Collectors and
  collecting - United States - Catalogs. 2. Kentucky
  Derby, Louisville, Ky. - Collectibles - Catalogs. I.
  Chase, Aaron. II. Title.
  NK5440.D75 F3 1991

Una Famiglia di architetti e costruttori a Roma,
1887-1987 / a cura di Stefano Mariani e
Corrado Cocconi. Roma : De Luca, 1987. xxiv,
75 p. : chiefly ill. (some col.), facsims., plans ;
30 cm. ISBN 88-7813-027-3
  1. Mariani, Giuseppe, 1863-1932. 2. Mariani family. 3.
  Impresa Mariani. 4. Architecture - Italy - Rome. 5.
  Rome (Italy) - Buildings, structures, etc. I. Mariani,
  Stefano. II. Cocconi, Corrado.
                    NYPL *[3-MQWB+ 90-9457]*

Family circus. Keane, Bil, 1922- [Family circus.
Selections.] I had a frightmare! /. New York ,
1990. 1 v. (unpaged) : ISBN 0-449-14615-4 :
  DDC 741.5/973 20
  NC1429.K29 A4 1990

FAMILY FARMS - UNITED STATES -
JUVENILE LITERATURE.
Ancona, George. The American family farm .
San Diego , c1989. 1 v. (unpaged) : ISBN
0-15-203025-5 : DDC 630/.973 19
  S519 .A53 1989
                    NYPL *[MFX (Ancona) 90-11254]*

FAMILY-OWNED BUSINESS
ENTERPRISES - CARICATURES AND
CARTOONS.
Danco, Léon A., 1923- Someday, it'll all be--
whos's? /. Cleveland , c1990. vi, 196 p. : ISBN
0-915601-09-3 (Jamieson) : DDC 741.5/973 20
  NC1429.D2344 A4 1990

Family snaps : the meaning of domestic
photography / edited by Jo Spence and Patricia
Holland. London : Virago, 1991. 252 p. : ill.,
ports. ; 24 cm. Includes bibliographical references (p.
249-252). ISBN 1-85381-270-6 (pbk) : DDC
778.92619 20
  1. Photography of families - History. I. Spence, Jo. II.
  Holland, Patricia.
  TR681.F28   **NYPL** *[MFW 91-6707]*

FAMILY - UNITED STATES - PICTORIAL
WORKS.
Young America . New York , 1990. 144 p. :
  ISBN 0-8264-0479-0 : DDC 779/.2/097307473
  20
  TR681.F28 Y68 1990
                    NYPL *[MFW 91-3590]*

Famouz . Corbijn, Anton. München , c1989. [146]
p. : ISBN 3-88814-313-6
                    NYPL *[MFX+ (Corbijn) 89-28153]*

Fan aur muṭāla'ah-yi fan /. Rafiq, Sa'id Aḥmad.
Karāci , 1988. 271 p. ;
  N7425.8.U73 R34 1988

FAN PAINTING - 18TH CENTURY -
CATALOGS.
Müller-Krumbach, Renate. Alte Fächer /.
Weimar , c1988. 87 p. : ISBN 3-7443-0066-8
                    NYPL *[3-MMW 90-10782]*

FANCY DRESS. see **COSTUME.**

FANEFJORD KIRKE.
Hammer, Karen Elisabeth, 1959- Sakrale
Wandmalerei in Dänemark und
Norddeutschland im ausgehenden Mittelalter .
Ammersbek bei Hamburg , c1990. 324 p. :
  ISBN 3-926987-18-9
  ND2773 .H36 1990

Fanelli, Giovanni.
Carl Otto Czeschka : dalla Secession viennese
all'art déco / Giovanni Fanelli. Firenze :
Cantini, [1990?] 127 p. : ill. (some col.) ; 22
cm. (Album Cantini) Bibliography: p. 28-29. ISBN
88-7737-079-3
  1. Czeschka, Carl Otto, 1878-1960 - Catalogs. I.
  Czeschka, Carl Otto, 1878-1960. II. Title.
      NYPL *[MDG (Czeschka) 91-3839]*

Il Palazzo Medici Riccardi di Firenze /.
Firenze , c1990. 379 p. : ISBN 88-09-20180-9
  DDC 725/.17/094551 20
  NA7756.F65 P35 1990

L'illustrazione Art nouveau / Giovanni Fanelli,
Ezio Godoli. Roma : Laterza, 1989. 332 p. : ill.
(some col.) ; 24 cm. (Grandi opere) Includes index.
Bibliography): p. [307]-322. ISBN 88-420-3476-2
  1. Illustration of books - 20th century. 2. Art nouveau.
  I. Godoli, Ezio. II. Title.
                    NYPL *[MDTT 90-10984]*

Il Palazzo Medici Riccardi di Firenze /.
Florence , c1990. x, 379 p. : ISBN
88-09-20180-9
                    NYPL *[3-MQWB+ 91-3377]*

Perret e Le Corbusier : confronti / Giovanni
Fanelli, Roberto Gargiani.1. ed. Roma : Laterza,
1990. 255 p. : ill. ; 22 cm. (Biblioteca di cultura
moderna. 985) Includes bibliographical references and
index. ISBN 88-420-3596-3 :
  1. Functionalism (Architecture) - France. 2.
  Architecture, Modern - 20th century - France. 3.
  Perret, Auguste, 1874-1954 - Criticism and
  interpretation. 4. Le Corbusier, 1887-1965 - Criticism
  and interpretation. I. Gargiani, Roberto, 1956-. II.
  Series: Biblioteca di cultura moderna (Editori Laterza) ,
  985. III. Title.
  NA1048.5.F85 F36 1990

Polano, Sergio. [Hendrik Petrus Berlage, opera
completa. English.] Hendrik Petrus Berlage,
complete works /. New York , 1988. 266 p. :
  ISBN 0-8478-0901-3 DDC 720/.92 20
  NA1153.B4 A4 1988
                    NYPL *[3-MQZ (Berlage) 90-11983]*

Fanelli, Rosalia Bonito. see **Bonito Fanelli,**
Rosalia.

FANFANI, AMINTORE.
Ragghianti, Carlo Ludovico. Dalla pittura al
pittore . Milano , c1987. 166 p. :
                    NYPL *[3-MCF+ F211 90-12787]*

Fang Chün-pi kuo hua chi /. Fang, Chün-pi,
1898- [S.l. , 1938] 2 v., [32] p. of plates :
                    NYPL *[3-MAG 90-6901]*

Fang, Chün-pi, 1898- Fang Chün-pi kuo hua chi /
Fang Chün-pi. [S.l. : s.n.] [1938] 2 v., [32] p. of
plates : chiefly ill. ; 27 cm. Added t.p. in English :
Chinese paintings, by Fan Tchun Pi.
  1. Painting, Chinese - 20th century. I. Title. II. Title:
  Chinese paintings. **NYPL** *[3-MAG 90-6901]*

Fanlights /. Gray, Alexander Stuart. London ,
1990. 148 p. : ISBN 0-7136-3077-9 : DDC
  721.823 20   **NYPL** *[3-MRR 91-3295]*

FANLIGHTS - GREAT BRITAIN.
Gray, Alexander Stuart. Fanlights /. London ,
1990. 148 p. : ISBN 0-7136-3077-9 : DDC
  721.823 20   **NYPL** *[3-MRR 91-3295]*

FANLIGHTS - UNITED STATES.
Gray, Alexander Stuart. Fanlights /. London ,
1990. 148 p. : ISBN 0-7136-3077-9 : DDC
  721.823 20   **NYPL** *[3-MRR 91-3295]*

FANS - HISTORY - 18TH CENTURY -
CATALOGS.
Müller-Krumbach, Renate. Alte Fächer /.
Weimar , c1988. 87 p. : ISBN 3-7443-0066-8
                    NYPL *[3-MMW 90-10782]*

FANS IN ART.
Sefrioui, Anne. Impressionist fans /. New
York , 1991. p. cm. ISBN 0-86565-129-9 DDC
  759.4/09/034 20
  N6847.5.I4 S44 1991

FANS - ITALY - HISTORY - EXHIBITIONS.
Ventagli italiani . Venezia , 1990. 167 p. :

  ISBN 88-317-5398-3
IN PROCESS (ONLINE)
                    NYPL *[3-MMW 91-5409]*

La Fantastique contemporain : 60 peintres,
graveurs, sculpteurs : [exposition] / présentés
par Jean-Claude Gaubert ; préface, Alain
Bosquet. Paris : Galerie de l'université, 1972.
[126] p. : ill. ; 28 cm.
  1. Surrealism - Exhibitions. 2. Fantasy in art -
  Exhibitions. I. Bosquet, Alain, 1919-. II. Gaubert, Jean
  Claude. III. Galerie de l'université (Paris, France).
                    NYPL *[3-MAL 91-288]*

FANTASY IN ART.
Breton, André, 1896-1966. L'art magique /.
[Paris] [c1991] 358 p. : ISBN 2-85940-215-2
  N8222.M3 B7 1991

Kluckert, Ehrenfried. Von der Kunst die
Phantasie zu leben . Stuttgart , c1989. 93 p. :
  ISBN 3-89322-172-7 DDC 709/.2 20
  N6888.D665 K58 1989

Rof Carballo, Juan. Los duendes del Prado /.
Madrid [1990?] 376 p. : ISBN 84-239-5300-9
  DDC 709/.4/0744641 20
  N8217.F28 R64 1990

Tronche, Anne. Ljuba /. [Paris] [c1988] 250
p. : ISBN 2-226-03498-6 DDC 759.9497 20
  ND953.L55 T76 1988

FANTASY IN ART - CATALOGS.
Endara Crow, Gonzalo, 1936- Gonzalo Endara
Crow. [Quito, Ecuador , 1990] 225 p. : DDC
  759.9866 20
  ND389.E53 A4 1990

FANTASY IN ART - EXHIBITIONS.
La Fantastique contemporain . Paris , 1972.
[126] p. :   **NYPL** *[3-MAL 91-288]*

Faoro, Victoria. Award-winning quilts & their
makers / edited by Victoria Faoro. Paducah,
KY : American Quilter's Society, c1991- v. <1
> : col. ill. ; 28 cm. Includes indexes.
  CONTENTS. - v. 1. The best of American Quilter's
  Society shows, 1985-1987. ISBN 0-89145-972-3 (v.
  1) : DDC 746.9/7/097309048 20
  1. Quilts - United States - Awards. 2. Quiltmakers -
  United States - Biography. 3. Quilts - Awards. I.
  American Quilter's Society. II. Title: Award-winning
  quilts and their makers. III. Title: Quilts & their
  makers.
  NK9112 .F36 1991

Far Eastern Association. see **Association for**
Asian Studies.

Far fetched /. Leake, Jerry. [Boston, MA , c1986]
1 v. (unpaged) : DDC 741.5/973 20
  NC1429.L373 A4 1986

Faraday, Cornelia Bateman. European and
American carpets and rugs / Cornelia Bateman
Faraday. New ed. Woodbridge, Suffolk,
England : Antique Collector's Club, c1990. 484
p. : ill. (some col.) ; 28 cm. Reprint of the 1929
edition, published by the Dean-Hicks Co., Decorative
Arts Press, Grand Rapids, Mich., with 80 additional
color plates, new introduction and bibliography.
Includes bibliographical references (p. 475-479) and
index. ISBN 1-85149-092-2 : DDC 746.7 19
  1. Carpets - Europe. 2. Carpets - United States. 3.
  Rugs - Europe. 4. Rugs - United States. I. Title.
  NK2795   **NYPL** *[3-MOP 90-11733]*

Farago, Claire J. Leonardo da Vinci's Paragone :
a critical interpretation with a new edition of
the text in the Codex Urbinas / by Claire J.
Farago. Leiden, The Netherlands ; New York :
E.J. Brill, 1991. p. cm. (Brill's studies in intellectual
history, 0920-8607 . v. 25) Revision of author's thesis.
Includes bibliographical references (p.) and index.
  ISBN 90-04-09415-6 (cloth) DDC 750 20
  1. Painting - Philosophy. 2. Codex Vaticanus Urbinas
  1270. 3. Leonardo, da Vinci, 1452-1519 - Aesthetics. 4.
  Ut pictura poesis (Aesthetics). I. Leonardo, da Vinci,
  1452-1519. Trattato della pittura. 1991. II. Title. III.
  Series.
  ND1140 .F35 1991

Die Farbe Purpur im frühen Griechentum . Stulz,
Heinke. Stuttgart , 1990. 205 p. ; ISBN
3-519-07455-9 **NYPL** *[3-MBM 91-4521]*

Farbe schwarz--das Licht. Walter, Hans-Albert,
1925- Hans-Albert Walter . Hannover , 1990.
54 p. : ISBN 3-89169-056-8
                    NYPL *[3-MCK+ W226 91-6801]*

Farbe Schwarz, das Licht. Walter, Hans-Albert,
1925- Hans-Albert Walter, die Farbe Schwarz,
das Licht . Hannover [1990] 54 p. : ISBN

3-89169-056-8
N6888.W32 A4 1990

Farbholzschnitte. Grieshaber, Helmut A. P.,
1909- HAP Grieshaber, Farbholzschnitte .
Stuttgart , c1983. 43 p., 73 leaves of plates :
NYPL [MDG (Grieshaber) 90-13133]

Farhat, Ammar. El Goulli, Sophie. Ammar Farhat
et son œuvre /. Tunis , c1979. 140 p. : ISBN
2-85119-021-0
NYPL [3-MCZ+ F215 90-11030]

FARHAT, AMMAR.
El Goulli, Sophie. Ammar Farhat et son œuvre
/. Tunis , c1979. 140 p. : ISBN 2-85119-021-0
NYPL [3-MCZ+ F215 90-11030]

Farías, Ixca. Pintores jaliscienses / Ixca Farías. 1a
ed. Guadalajara, Jalisco, México : Gobierno del
Estado de Jalisco, 1969. 93 p. ; 18 cm. (Temas
jaliscienses . 2) On half t.p.: Biografías de pintores
jaliscienses. On series t.p.: Biografía de pintores
jaliscienses.
*1. Artists - Mexico - Jalisco - Biography. I. Title. II.
Title: Biografías de pintores jaliscienses. III. Title:
Biografía de pintores jaliscienses. IV. Series.*
N6556.J3 F37 1969

Fariba Hajamadi . Hajamadi, Fariba, 1957-
[Philadelphia] , c1988. 1 folded sheet (7 p.) :
ISBN 0-88454-045-6
NYPL [3-MCX H152 90-12728]

Farina, Federico. L'architettura cistercense e
l'Abbazia di Casamari / Federico Farina,
Benedetto Fornari ; prefazione di Angiola
Maria Romanini. 2a ed. Casamari : Edizioni
Casamari, 1981, c1978. xii, 187 p. : ill. (some
col.) ; 31 cm. Includes indexes. Bibliography: p.
171-177. DDC 726/.7/0945622 19
*1. Abbazia di Casamari. 2. Architecture, Cistercian -
Italy - Lazio. I. Fornari, Benedetto. II. Title.*
NA5621.A22 F37 1981
NYPL [3-MRBD+ 90-12587]

Farish Gallery. Le Corbusier, 1887-1965. Le
Corbusier . New York, NY , c1990. 37 p. :
ISBN 1-87827-122-9
NYPL [3-MCO J42 91-4349]

Fārisī, Zakī Muḥammad 'Alī. National guide &
atlas of the kingdom of Saudi Arabia. [Jeddah,
Saudi Arabia , 1989] 1 v. (various pagings) :
NYPL [Map Div. 91-5950]

FARM BUILDING - SWITZERLAND.
Gschwend, Max. Bauernhäuser der Schweiz =.
Blauen , c1988. 306 p. : ISBN 3-907080-07-6
NYPL [3-MRGF+ 89-25516]

**FARM BUILDINGS - FRANCE -
NORMANDY.**
Fréal, Jacques. La Normandie /. [Paris] ,
c1980. 110 p. : ISBN 2-7050-0260-X : DDC
392/.36/009442 19
NA8203 .F693   *NYPL [3-MQWF 81-936]*

**FARM BUILDINGS - FRANCE - PÉRIGORD -
CONSERVATION AND RESTORATION.**
Simon, Jean-Paul, 1947- L'architecture
paysanne en Périgord et sa restauration /.
[Périgueux] , c1991. 207 p. : ISBN
2-86577-148-2 : DDC 728/.6/0288094472 20
NA8203 .S55 1991

**FARM BUILDINGS - FRANCE - SAINT-
VÉRAN - CONSERVATION AND
RESTORATION.**
Perron, Claude. Saint-Véran . La Calade,
Aix-en-Provence , c1990. 159 p. : ISBN
2-85744-465-6
NA8203 .P47 1990

FARM BUILDINGS - NETHERLANDS.
Molen, S. J. van der. Boerderijen van het
Noordererf /. Zutphen , c1979. 159 p. : ISBN
90-6011-065-X
NA8206.N4 M597   *NYPL [3-MRGF 81-908]*

**FARM BUILDINGS - UNITED STATES -
THEMES, MOTIVES - EXHIBITIONS.**
Gianni, Benjamin, 1958- Dice thrown /. New
York, N.Y. , c1989. 56 p. : ISBN
0-910413-62-2 : DDC 728/.92/09730747468 20
NA8201 .G47 1989
NYPL [3-MQV 90-12464]

FARM LIFE - PICTORIAL WORKS.
Ancona, George. The American family farm .
San Diego , c1989. 1 v. (unpaged) : ISBN
0-15-203025-5 : DDC 630/.973 19
S519 .A53 1989
NYPL [MFX (Ancona) 90-11254]

**FARM LIFE - UNITED STATES - JUVENILE
LITERATURE.**
Ancona, George. The American family farm .
San Diego , c1989. 1 v. (unpaged) : ISBN
0-15-203025-5 : DDC 630/.973 19
S519 .A53 1989
NYPL [MFX (Ancona) 90-11254]

Farmer, Gene (Eugene Davis) Architectural
detailing for commercial construction / Gene
Davis. New York : McGraw-Hill, c1991. p. cm.
ISBN 0-07-019983-3 DDC 725/.21/028 20
*1. Architectural drawing - Detailing. 2. Commercial
buildings - Designs and plans. I. Title.*
NA2718 .F37 1991

**Farmer Johnson's psycho dairy farm for
environmentally aware barnyard animals /.**
Phillips, Steve, 1953- New York, N.Y. , 1992.
p. cm. ISBN 0-385-30495-1 : DDC 741.5/973 20
NC1429.P57 A4 1992

Farmer, W. D. (William Davis)
[Homes for pleasant living]
W.D. Farmer presents homes for pleasant
living. NAHB show special ed. Atlanta, Ga.
(P.O. Box 450025, Atlanta 30345) : W.D.
Farmer, c1989. 16 p. : all ill. ; 28 cm. Cover
title. "16 new plans from 1400 to 3700 sq. ft."
DDC 728/.37/0223 20
*1. Architecture, Domestic - United States - Designs and
plans. I. Title. II. Title: Homes for pleasant living.*
NA7205 .F37 1989

FARMHOUSES - CYPRUS.
Ionas, Ioannis. La maison rurale de Chypre
(XVIIIe-XXe siècle) . Nicosie , 1988. 238 p. :
ISBN 996-308-012-X DDC 728/.095645 20
NA8210.C93 I57 1988

**FARMHOUSES - ENGLAND -
CUMBERLAND.**
Ramm, Herman Gabriel. Shielings and bastles.
London, 1970. xv, 104 p., 41 plates (2 fold.).
ISBN 0-11-700468-5 DDC 914.28
GT287.C8 R3   *NYPL [3-MRGF 90-6851]*

**FARMHOUSES - ENGLAND -
NORTHUMBERLAND.**
Ramm, Herman Gabriel. Shielings and bastles.
London, 1970. xv, 104 p., 41 plates (2 fold.).
ISBN 0-11-700468-5 DDC 914.28
GT287.C8 R3   *NYPL [3-MRGF 90-6851]*

FARMHOUSES - FRANCE.
Laws, Bill. Traditional houses of rural France /.
New York , 1991. p. cm. ISBN 1-558-59222-9
DDC 728/.0944/091734 20
NA8210.F8 L38 1991

**FARMHOUSES - FRANCE - FRANCHE-
COMTÉ.**
Garneret, Jean. La maison du montagnon /.
Besançon , 1981. 557 p., [2] p. of plates :
DDC 728/.67/094445 s 728/.67/094445 19
NA8208.52.F8 M34 1981, t. 1
NYPL [3-MQWF 90-5444]

FARMHOUSES - FRANCE - LORRAINE.
Gérard, Claude, professeur. La maison rurale en
Lorraine /. Nonette [France] [1990] 151 p. :
ISBN 2-902894-66-X : DDC 728/.0944/38 20
NA8210.F8 G47 1990

FARMHOUSES - GREAT BRITAIN.
Rice, Matthew. Traditional houses of rural
Britain /. New York , 1992. p. cm. ISBN
1-558-59338-1 DDC 728/.0941 20
NA8210.G67 R5 1992

FARMHOUSES - HUNGARY.
Balassa, M. Iván. A parasztház évszázadai .
Békéscsaba , 1985. 188 p. : ISBN 963-01-6472-8
NA8210.H9 B35 1985
NYPL [3-MRGF 90-12492]

**FARMHOUSES - JURA MOUNTAIN
REGION (FRANCE AND
SWITZERLAND)**
Garneret, Jean. La maison du montagnon /.
Besançon , 1981. 557 p., [2] p. of plates :
DDC 728/.67/094445 s 728/.67/094445 19
NA8208.52.F8 M34 1981, t. 1
NYPL [3-MQWF 90-5444]

FARMHOUSES - NETHERLANDS.
Post, Kees. Het boerenhuis in Nederland /.
S'Gravenhage , c1975. 119 p. : ISBN
90-239-2895-4   *NYPL [3-MRGF 90-5859]*

FARMHOUSES - SWITZERLAND.
Gschwend, Max. Bauernhäuser der Schweiz =.
Blauen , c1988. 306 p. : ISBN 3-907080-07-6
NYPL [3-MRGF+ 89-25516]

**FARMHOUSES - SWITZERLAND -
FRIBOURG (CANTON)**
Anderegg, Jean Pierre. Die Bauernhäuser des
Kantons Freiburg =. Basel , 1979-1987. 2 v. :
DDC 728/.67/09494 s 728/.67/094945
NA8206.S9 B38 Bd. 7, etc. NA8210
NYPL [3-MRGF 84-1334]

FARMING. see AGRICULTURE.

**FARNESE, ALESSANDRO, 1520-1589 - ART
PATRONAGE.**
Robertson, Clare. Il gran cardinale . New
Haven , 1992. p. cm. ISBN 0-300-05045-3 DDC
709/.2 20
N6915 .R66 1992

**FARNESE FAMILY - ART COLLECTIONS -
CATALOGS.**
Ajello, Raffaele. Classicismo d'età Romana .
Napoli , c1988. 203 p. : ISBN 88-7042-955-5
NYPL [3-MGH+ 90-10570]

Fárová, Anna. Sudek, Josef, 1896-1976. Josef
Sudek . New York, N.Y. , c1990. 159 p. :
ISBN 0-89381-386-9
NYPL [MFX+ (Sudek) 90-9102]

Farr, Dennis, 1929-
Courtauld Institute Galleries. The Courtauld
Institute Galleries, University of London /.
London , 1990. 128 p. : ISBN 1-87024-839-2
NYPL [3-MAVZ (London) 90-12082]

Lynn Chadwick sculptor : with a complete
illustrated catalogue, 1947-1988 / Dennis Farr
and Eva Chadwick. Oxford [England] :
Clarendon Press ; New York : Oxford
University Press, 1990. 347 p., [12] p. of
plates : ill. (some col.) ; 29 cm. Includes
bibliographical references (p. [39]-43). ISBN
0-19-817213-3 : DDC 730/.92 20
*1. Chadwick, Lynn, 1914- - Catalogues raisonnés. I.
Chadwick, Eva. II. Title.*
NB497.C45 A4 1990
NYPL [3-MGO (Chadwick) 91-4618]

Farrer, Anne. 'The brush dances & the ink sings' :
Chinese paintings and calligraphy from the
British Museum : 6 September to 4 November
1990, Hayward Gallery, London / Anne Farrer.
London : South Bank Centre, c1990. 143 p. :
ill. ; 20 cm. ISBN 1-85332-058-7
*1. Painting, Chinese - Exhibitions. I. Hayward Gallery.
II. Title. III. Title: Brush dances and the ink sings.*
NYPL [3-MAG 91-6891]

FARRIERY. see HORSES.

FARUFFINI, FEDERICO, 1831-1869.
Finocchi, Anna. Federico Faruffini . [Italy] ,
1989. 238 p. : ISBN 88-366-0268-1
NYPL [3-MCF+ F247 91-5543]

FASCISM AND ARCHITECTURE - ITALY.
Adalberto Libera. English. Adalberto Libera /.
New York, N.Y. , c1991. p. cm. ISBN
1-87827-114-8 : DDC 720/.92 20
NA1123.L46 A4 1991

**FASCISM AND ARCHITECTURE - ITALY -
LATINA.**
Latina /. Roma , 1990. 94 p. : ISBN
88-7597-124-2 : DDC 711/.4/0945623 20
NA9204.L37 L37 1990

**FASCISM AND ARCHITECTURE - ITALY -
ROME.**
Schumacher, Thomas L. [Danteum di Terragni.
English.] The Danteum . Princeton, NJ , c1985.
169 p. : ISBN 0-910413-09-6
NA2707.T466 S3713 1985
NYPL [3-MQZ (Terragni) 86-3775]

FASCISM AND ART - ITALY.
Golomshtok, Igor. Totalitarian art in the Soviet
Union, the Third Reich, Fascist Italy and the
People's Republic of China /. New York,
N.Y. , c1990. xv, 416 p., [15] p. of plates :
ISBN 0-06-433266-7
NYPL [3-MAL 91-7447]

FASHION - ARGENTINA.
Saulquin, Susana. La moda en la Argentina /.
Buenos Aires, Argentina , c1990. 284 p., [26] p.
of plates : ISBN 950-0-41007-9
TT504.6.A7 S38 1990
NYPL [3-MMP 91-6766]

FASHION - AUSTRALIA.
Australian fashion . Sydney , 1989. 64 p. :
ISBN 1-86317-002-2
NYPL [3-MME+ 91-6591]

FASHION - AUSTRIA - VIENNA - EXHIBITIONS.
Historiches Museum der Stadt Wien. 200 Jahre Mode in Wien . Wien , 1976. 120 p., [34] leaves of plates : *NYPL [3-MMM 90-6048]*

FASHION - CATALOGS.
London College of Fashion. The London College of Fashion designer files. Bath , c1991. 309 microfiches : *NYPL [*XMC-772]*

The fashion cycle . Daria, Irene. New York , c1990. 240 p., [16] p. of plates : ISBN 0-671-66729-7 DDC 746.9/2/092273 20 *TT507 .D345 1990 NYPL [3-MMP 91-3812]*

FASHION DESIGN. see COSTUME DESIGN.

FASHION DESIGNERS - AUSTRIA - VIENNA - BIOGRAPHY.
Fischer, Wolfgang Georg, 1933- [Gustav Klimt und Emilie Flöge. English.] Klimt and Emilie . Woodstock, N.Y. , 1992. p. cm. ISBN 0-87951-451-5 : DDC 709/.2 B 20 *N6811.5.K55 F513 1992*

FASHION DESIGNERS - FRANCE - PARIS - HISTORY - 20TH CENTURY.
Le Théâtre de la Mode . Paris , c1990. 166 p. : ISBN 2-906450-41-3
NYPL [3-MME+ 90-13056]

FASHION DRAWING - HISTORY - 20TH CENTURY.
Gruau, René, 1909- Gruau /. Paris , c1989. 191 p. : ISBN 2-7335-0172-0 DDC 741.6/092 20 *TT509 .G77 1989*
NYPL [3-MME+ 91-5612]

FASHION - FRANCE - HISTORY.
Delbourg-Delphis, Marylène. Le chic et le look . [Paris] , c1981. 279 p., [8] p. of plates : ISBN 2-01-008276-1 : DDC 391/.2/0944 19 *GT853 .D37 1981 NYPL [3-MME 90-6057]*

FASHION - FRANCE - HISTORY - 20TH CENTURY - EXHIBITIONS.
Musée des arts de la mode (France) Histoires de mode d'hier et d'aujourd'hui . Paris , c1988. 55 p. : ISBN 2-901422-13-6 :
NYPL [3-MME+ 91-5058]

FASHION - FRANCE - PARIS - HISTORY - 20TH CENTURY.
Le Théâtre de la Mode /. Paris , c1990. 166 p. : ISBN 2-906450-41-3
NYPL [3-MME+ 90-13056]

FASHION - HISTORY.
Delbourg-Delphis, Marylène. Le chic et le look . [Paris] , c1981. 279 p., [8] p. of plates : ISBN 2-01-008276-1 : DDC 391/.2/0944 19 *GT853 .D37 1981 NYPL [3-MME 90-6057]*

Peacock, John. The chronicle of western costume . London , c1991. 224 p. : ISBN 0-500-01490-6 *NYPL [3-MMC 91-5165]*

FASHION - HISTORY - 20TH CENTURY.
Beurden, Leontien van. Mode in de 20ste eeuw /. Nijmegen , c1988. 143 p. (some col.) ; ISBN 90-6168-291-6 :
GT596 .B48 1988 NYPL [3-MME 90-10712]

FASHION - HISTORY - COLLECTED WORKS.
Parisian fashion, from the "Journal des dames et des modes," vol. 1, 1912-1913 /. New York , c1979. [12] p., [93] p. of plates : ISBN 0-8478-0253-1 : DDC 391/.2/0944361 *GT887 .P3 NYPL [MML 81-188]*

FASHION ILLUSTRATORS - FRANCE.
Gruau, René, 1909- Gruau /. Paris , c1989. 191 p. : ISBN 2-7335-0172-0 DDC 741.6/092 20 *TT509 .G77 1989*
NYPL [3-MME+ 91-5612]

Fashion in underwear. Ewing, Elizabeth. London [1971] 160 p. ISBN 0-7134-0857-X DDC 391/.42 *GT2073 .E9 1971 NYPL [MMV 90-7022]*

Fashion Institute of Technology (New York, N.Y.) Martin, Richard. Giorgio Armani . New York , 1990. 224 p. : ISBN 0-8478-1298-7 DDC 746.9/2/092 20 *TT580 .M37 1990*
NYPL [3-MME+ 91-3312]

FASHION - ITALY - EXHIBITIONS.
Moda Italia . Milano , 1988. 200 p. :
NYPL [3-MME+ 89-6593]

FASHION PHOTOGRAPHY - EXHIBITIONS.
Ray, Man, 1890-1976. Man Ray in fashion /. New York City , 1990. 95 p. : ISBN

0-933642-14-8
NYPL [MFX (Ray) 91-3335]

FASHION PHOTOGRAPHY - GERMANY (EAST) - EXHIBITIONS.
Ausgeblendete Realität . Wien , 1989. 95 p. :
NYPL [MFW+ 90-11185]

FASHION PHOTOGRAPHY - HISTORY - 20TH CENTURY - EXHIBITIONS.
Modefotografie . Wien , c1990. 240 p. :
NYPL [MFW 91-4480]

The Fashioning and functioning of the British country house / edited by Gervase Jackson-Stops ... [et al.]. Washington, D.C. : National Gallery of Art ; Hanover [N.H.] : Distributed by the University Press of New England, 1989. 417 p. : ill. (some col.) ; 27 cm. (Studies in the history of art, 00917338 . 25. 10) "Proceedings of the symposium "The Fashioning and Functioning of the British Country House" jointly sponsored by the Center for Advanced Studyin the Visual Arts, National Gallery of Art, Washington, The Folger Institute, The Folger Shakespeare Library, and Program of Studies in Landscape Architecture, Dumbarton Oaks, 5-8 February 1986"--T.p. verso. Includes bibliographical references. ISBN 0-89468-128-1
1. Country homes - England - Congresses. 2. Manors - England - Congresses. 3. Interior architecture - England - Congresses. 4. Decoration and ornament - England - Congresses. 5. Country life - England - Congresses. 6. England - Social life and customs - Congresses. I. Jackson-Stops, Gervase. II. Series: Studies in the history of art (Washington, D.C.) , 25.
NYPL [3-MRG 90-12992]

Fassbar-anfassbar-unfassbar / Sabine Adam ... [et al.] [München?] : Arbeitskreis für Gemeinsame Kultwarbeit Bayerische Städte, [1981?] 1 portfolio ([13] pieces) : ill. ; 30 cm. Exhibition held at Künstlerwerkstätte Lothringer Strasse 13, München-Haidhausen, September 1981, [and at other places]. "Redaktion: Karl Manfred Fischer, Lisa Puyplat."
1. Adam, Sabine, 1957-. 2. Textile design - Exhibitions. 3. Art, Modern - 20th century - Germany, West - Exhibitions. I. Künstlerwerkstätte Lothringer Strasse 13 (Munich, Ger.). **NYPL [3-MAL+ 82-1845]**

Fassbender, Joseph, 1903-1974.
Joseph Fassbender, Malerei zurischen Figuration und Abstraktion / herausgegeben von Wulf Merzegegrath ; mit einem Werkverzeichnis der farbigen Arbciten von Uwe Haupenthal ; mit Beitragen von Bernh. joh. Blume --- [et al.]. Köln : Wienand, 1988. 171 p. : ill. (some col.), ports. ; 32 cm. "Dieses Buch erscheint anlässlich der Ausstellung --- im Kölnischen Kunstverein vom 11.12.1988 bis 15.1.1989. Includes index of names (Personenregister). Bibliography: p. 167-169. ISBN 3-87909-203-6
1. Fassbender, Joseph, 1903-1974 - Exhibitions. I. Herzogenrath, Wulf. II. Haupenthal, Uwe. III. Kölnischer Kunstverein. IV. Title.
NYPL [3-MCK+ F249 89-11746]

FASSBENDER, JOSEPH, 1903-1974 - EXHIBITIONS.
Fassbender, Joseph, 1903-1974. Joseph Fassbender, Malerei zurischen Figuration und Abstraktion /. Köln , 1988. 171 p. : ISBN 3-87909-203-6
NYPL [3-MCK+ F249 89-11746]

Fassbind, Franz. Balz Camenzind : Versuch einer Annäherung / von Franz Fassbind. [Schwyz] : Kulturkommission des Kantons Schwyz, 1982. 32 p. : ill. (some col.) ; 21 cm. (Schwyzer Hefte. 26)
1. Camenzind, Balz, 1907-. I. Series.
NYPL [3-MCZ C178 88-4435]

Fassianos. Phasianos. Athens , c1990. 221 p. :
ND603.P34 A4 1990

Fast so alt wie das Jahrhundert /. Posener, Julius. Berlin , c1990. 312 p. : ISBN 3-88680-381-3 : DDC 720/.92 B 20 *NA2599.8.P67 A2 1990*

FASTS AND FEASTS - PORTUGAL.
Ferreira, Jaime M. M. Bilhetes postais e cartões de boas festas /. Lisboa , 1989- v. <1 > : DDC 741.6/83/09469075 20 *NC1878.7.P8 F4 1989*

Fatal consequences : Callot, Goya, and the horrors of war. Hanover, N.H. : Hood Museum of Art, Dartmouth College, 1990. 92 p. : ill. ;

31 cm. Catalog of an exhibition at the Hood Museum of Art, Sept. 8-Dec. 9, 1990, written by Hilliard T. Goldfarb and Reva Wolf. Includes bibliographical references. ISBN 0-944722-04-0 DDC 769.92 20 *1. Callot, Jacques, 1592-1635. Miseries of war - Exhibitions. 2. Goya, Francisco, 1746-1828. Disasters of war - Exhibitions. 3. War in art - Exhibitions. 4. Etching - 17th century - Exhibitions. 5. Etching - 19th century - Exhibitions. I. Callot, Jacques, 1592-1635. II. Goya, Francisco, 1746-1828. III. Goldfarb, Hilliard T. IV. Wolf, Reva, 1956-. V. Hood Museum of Art. NE2149.W37 F38 1990*
NYPL [MDG+ (Callot) 91-4763]

Fathpur-sikri and its architecture. Husain, A. B. M., 1934- Dacca [1970] x, 169 p. DDC 722/.4 *NA1508.F3 H8*

FATHY, HASSAN - CRITICISM AND INTERPRETATION.
Steele, James. Hassan Fathy /. London , New York , 1988. 149 p. : ISBN 0-312-01140-7 (U. S. : pbk.) : DDC 720/.92/4 19 *NA1585.F37 S74 1988*
NYPL [3-MQZ+ (Fathy) 88-4615]

Fatih anıtları. Eyice, Semavi. Fotoğraflarla Fatih anıtları /. Fatih [Istanbul, Turkey] [1989?] 126 p. : *NA1370 .E88 1989*

FATIH (ISTANBUL, TURKEY) - BUILDINGS, STRUCTURES, ETC.
Eyice, Semavi. Fotoğraflarla Fatih anıtları /. Fatih [Istanbul, Turkey] [1989?] 126 p. : *NA1370 .E88 1989*

Fattorini, Tommaso. I meravigliosi bronzi del Giappone : antichi e moderni = The marvellous bronzes of Japan : antique and modern / Tommaso Fattorini. Milano : Electa, c1990. 147 p. : ill. ; 29 cm.
1. Bronzes, Japanese. I. Title. II. Title: Marvellous bronzes of Japan. *NYPL [3-MAG 91-7721]*

Faucheux, Pierre. Totems et tabous . Paris , 1968. 1 v. (unpaged) : *NYPL [3-MC 90-6212]*

Faucon, Bernard, 1950- "Peindre et photographier?" . [Nice] , c1983. [44] p., [4] leaves of plates : *NYPL [MFW+ 91-7018]*

FAUNA. see ZOOLOGY.

Faure, Philippe. Fer d'art roman / Philippe Faure ; préface, Alain Gislot ; traductions, Ursula Wagner-Kuon (allemand), Dominique Parizot (espagnol), Danièle Enselme (anglais), Jean-Marie Roussel (italien). [Dijon] : Centre régional de documentation pédagogique de l'Académie de Dijon, 1988- v. <1 > : ill. ; 31 cm. English, French, German, and Spanish. Includes bibliographical references (v. 1, p. 196-209). CONTENTS. - [1] De 1000 à 1250 -- ISBN 2-86621-112-X (v. 1)
1. Art metal-work, Romanesque - France. 2. Art metal-work - France. I. Title. NK6449.A1 F38 1988

Faust, Wolfgang Max, 1944-
Art today in the Federal Republic of Germany /. Bonn , c1988. 114 p. :
NYPL [3-MAMG+ 90-12546]

Blanchette, Manon, 1952- Blickpunkte . Montréal, Québec , c1989. 2 v. : ISBN 2-551-12161-2 *N6868.5.C63 B55 1989*

Fausto Pirandello /. Gian Ferrari, Claudia. Roma , c1991. 162 p. : ISBN 88-7813-321-3
NYPL [3-MCF+ P6667 91-7465]

Fautrier. Peyré, Yves. Fautrier, ou, Les outrages de l'impossible /. Paris , c1990. 437 p. : ISBN 2-903370-54-0 DDC 709/.2 20 *N6853.F3 P48 1990*

Fautrier, Jean, 1898-1964.
Cabanne, Pierre. Jean Fautrier /. Paris , c1988. 167 p. : ISBN 2-7291-0346-5 DDC 759.4 20 *ND553.F36 A4 1988*

Peyré, Yves. Fautrier, ou, Les outrages de l'impossible /. Paris , c1990. 437 p. : ISBN 2-903370-54-0 DDC 709/.2 20 *N6853.F3 P48 1990*

FAUTRIER, JEAN, 1898-1964 - CATALOGS.
Cabanne, Pierre. Jean Fautrier /. Paris , c1988. 167 p. : ISBN 2-7291-0346-5 DDC 759.4 20 *ND553.F36 A4 1988*

FAUTRIER, JEAN, 1898-1964 - CRITICISM AND INTERPRETATION.
Cabanne, Pierre. Jean Fautrier /. Paris , c1988.

167 p. : ISBN 2-7291-0346-5 DDC 759.4 20
ND553.F36 A4 1988

Peyré, Yves. Fautrier, ou, Les outrages de
l'impossible /. Paris, c1990. 437 p. : ISBN
2-903370-54-0 DDC 709/.2 20
N6853.F3 P48 1990

Fautrier, ou, Les outrages de l'impossible /.
Peyré, Yves. Paris, c1990. 437 p. : ISBN
2-903370-54-0 DDC 709/.2 20
N6853.F3 P48 1990

The fauve landscape /. Freeman, Judi. Los
Angeles, Calif. , New York , 1990. 350 p. :
ISBN 1-558-59025-0 DDC
758/.1/094407479494 20
ND1356.6 .F74 1990
              NYPL [3-MCN 90-13060]

FAUVISM - FRANCE - EXHIBITIONS.
Freeman, Judi. The fauve landscape /. Los
Angeles, Calif. , New York , 1990. 350 p. :
ISBN 1-558-59025-0 DDC
758/.1/094407479494 20
ND1356.6 .F74 1990
              NYPL [3-MCN 90-13060]

Vincent van Gogh and the modern movement,
1890-1914 /. Freren [Germany] , 1990. 436 p. :
ISBN 3-923641-33-8 (Hard cover)
              NYPL [3-MCH G61 91-4493]

Favier, Philippe, 1957-
Philippe Favier, gravures 1981-1990 : du 18
mars au 03 juin 1990, Musée du dessin et de
l'estampe originale de Gravelines [et] du 15 juin
au 15 septembre 1990, Musée de la cohue,
Vannes [et] du 28 septembre au 31 octobre
1990, Nouveau Théâtre d'Angers. [Gravelines] :
Musée de Gravelines, c1990. 168 p. : chiefly
ill. ; 30 cm. Envelope containing 19 prints and 1
portrait of Favier inserted. Includes bibliographical
references (p. 166). DDC 769.92 20
*1. Favier, Philippe, 1957- - Exhibitions. I. Musée du
dessin et de l'estampe originale en l'Arsenal de
Gravelines. II. Musée de la cohue (Vannes, France). III.
Nouveau Théâtre d'Angers. IV. Title.*
NE2049.5.F39 A4 1990

FAVIER, PHILIPPE, 1957- - EXHIBITIONS.
Favier, Philippe, 1957- Philippe Favier, gravures
1981-1990. [Gravelines] , c1990. 168 p. :
DDC 769.92 20
NE2049.5.F39 A4 1990

Favole, Paolo. Abruzzes Molise romans /. La
Pierre-qui-Vire (Yonne) , 1990. 304 p. : ISBN
2-7369-0182-7   ***NYPL [3-MQWB 91-4524]***

Faxon, Susan C. Homer, Winslow, 1836-1910.
Winslow Homer at the Addison . Andover,
Mass. , 1990. 95 p. :
              NYPL [3-MCX H76 90-13073]

FAYETTE COUNTY (ILL.) - MAPS.
Rockford Map Publishers. Fayette County,
Illinois, land atlas & plat book . Rockford, Ill. ,
c1990. 1 atlas (45 p.) :
              NYPL [Map Div. 90-12841]

Fayette County, Illinois, land atlas & plat book .
Rockford Map Publishers. Rockford, Ill. ,
c1990. 1 atlas (45 p.) :
              NYPL [Map Div. 90-12841]

A feast of colour . Sillevis, John. [Feest van kleur.
English.] Zwolle , c1990. 260 p. : ISBN
90-6630-232-1   ***NYPL [3-MC 91-3415]***

The Feast of the gods . Bull, David, 1934-
Washington , Hanover, N.H. , 1990. 106 p. :
ISBN 0-89468-144-3 DDC 709 s 759.5 20
N386.U5 S78 vol. 40 ND623.B39
              NYPL [3-MCF B39 90-8050]

**FEDERAL AID TO ART - UNITED STATES -
EXHIBITIONS.**
Fowler, Harriet W. New Deal art .
[Lexington] , c1985. 119 p. : DDC
760/.0973/074016947 19
N8838 .F69 1985   ***NYPL [MDBF 87-1170]***

**FEDERAL AID TO THE ARTS - UNITED
STATES.**
Arts in Education Special Projects Handbook
update, 1986-1990 /. Washington, DC , 1991.
p. cm. DDC 700/.7/073 20
NX398 .A82 1991

Public money and the muse . New York ,
c1991. p. cm. ISBN 0-393-03015-6 DDC
353/.0085/4 20
NX735 .P83 1991

FEDERAL ART PROJECT - EXHIBITIONS.
Fowler, Harriet W. New Deal art .
[Lexington] , c1985. 119 p. : DDC
760/.0973/074016947 19
N8838 .F69 1985   ***NYPL [MDBF 87-1170]***

Federal Republic of Nigeria. see Nigeria.

**Fédération des architectes hongrois. see Magyar
Építőművészek Szövetsége.**

**Fédération internationale des sociétés d'amateurs
d'ex-libris.**
Schutt-Kehm, Elke M., 1954- Albrecht Dürer
und die Frühzeit der Exlibriskunst .
Wiesbaden , c1990. 39 p. : ISBN 3-922835-18-X
              NYPL [MDVF 91-7231]

Thoms, Klaus. Das Exlibris von heute
1988-1990 . Wiesbaden , c1990. 286 p. : ISBN
3-922835-20-1   ***NYPL [MDVF 91-7229]***

Federation of Nigeria. see Nigeria.

**Federativna Narodna Republika Jugoslavije. see
Yugoslavia.**

Federici, Renzo. Grafica russa 1917/1930 .
Firenze , c1990. 192 p. :
IN PROCESS (ONLINE)
              NYPL [MDBF+ 90-11003]

Federico, Jean Taylor, 1940. Clues to American
furniture / Jean Taylor Federico ; illustrated by
Judith Curcio. Rev. ed. Washington DC :
Starhill Press, 1991. p. cm. Includes bibliographical
references. ISBN 0-913515-75-2 : DDC
749.213/075 20
*1. Furniture - United States - Styles. I. Curcio, Judith.
II. Title.*
NK2405 .F43 1991

Feeney, Kelly, 1961- Josef Albers : works on
paper / Kelly Feeney. Alexandria, Va. : Art
Services International, 1991. p. cm. Catalog of an
exhibition organized and circulated by Art Services
International. Includes bibliographical references.
ISBN 0-88397-100-3 DDC 760/.092 20
*1. Albers, Josef - Notebooks, sketchbooks, etc. -
Exhibitions. I. Albers, Josef. II. Art Services
International. III. Title.*
NC251.A36 A4 1991

Fehérvári, Géza. 1400 years of Islamic art : a
descriptive catalogue / Géza Fehérvári & Yasin
H. Safadi. London : Khalili Gallery, 1984. 247
p. : col. ill., 1 map ; 32 cm. Bibliography: p.
245-247.
*1. Art, Islamic - Catalogs. I. Safadi, Yasin Hamid. II.
Khalili Gallery (London, England). III. Title. IV. Title:
Fourteen hundred years of Islamic art.*
              NYPL [3-MAF+ 90-12505]

Fehl, Philipp P. Birds of a feather / Philipp P.
Fehl ; essay by Maurice E. Cope ; Krannert Art
Museum, University of Illinois at
Urbana-Champaign. Urbana : University of
Illinois Press, c1991. p. cm. ISBN 0-252-06241-8
(alk. paper) DDC 741.973 20
*1. American wit and humor, Pictorial. I. Krannert Art
Museum. II. Title.*
NC1429.F2955 A4 1991

FEHLING, HEINZ.
Küster, Bernd, 1952- Heinz Fehling . [S.l.] ,
c1990. 127 p. : ISBN 3-89299-152-9
              NYPL [3-MDWS (Fehling) 91-4830]

Fehling, Heinz, 1912-1989.
Küster, Bernd, 1952- Heinz Fehling,
Plakatkunst und Werbung /. [Worpswede] ,
c1990. 127 p. : ISBN 3-89299-152-9
NC1850.F37 K8 1990

**FEHLING, HEINZ, 1912-1989 - CRITICISM
AND INTERPRETATION.**
Küster, Bernd, 1952- Heinz Fehling,
Plakatkunst und Werbung /. [Worpswede] ,
c1990. 127 p. : ISBN 3-89299-152-9
NC1850.F37 K8 1990

Fehling, Irene. 10X . [Berlin] [1984] 1 portfolio
(10 pieces) :   ***NYPL [3-MAMG+ 88-4811]***

Fehr, Michael. Meyer-Rogge, Jan, 1935-
Stillwasser . Bochum [1980] 117 p. : ISBN
3-8093-0056-X
              NYPL [3-MGO (Meyer-Rogge) 90-6349]

Feick, Susanne. Speckter-Fresken . Hamburg ,
1990. 20 p. : DDC 759.3 20
ND588.S58 S6 1990

Feinberg, Jean E. D'Oench, Ellen. Jim Dine
prints, 1977-1985 /. New York , c1986. 182

p. : ISBN 0-06-431501-0 : DDC 769/.92/4 19
NE539.D5 A4 1986
              NYPL [MDG (Dine) 86-1962]

Feinberg, Larry J.
From studio to studiolo : Florentine
draftsmanship under the first Medici grand
dukes / Larry J. Feinberg ; with and essay by
Karen-edis Barzman. Oberlin : Allen Memorial
Art Museum, Oberlin College ; Seattle :
Distributed by University of Washington Press,
1991. p. cm. Exhibition schedule: Allen Memorial Art
Museum, Oberlin College, Oct. 14-Dec. 1, 1991;
Bowdoin College Museum of Art, Jan. 27-March 15,
1992; Hood Museum of Art, Dartmouth College, April
6-May 24, 1992. Includes bibliographical references.
ISBN 0-295-97145-2 : DDC
741.945/51/0903107474 20
*1. Drawing, Italian - Italy - Florence - Exhibitions. 2.
Mannerism (Art) - Italy - Florence - Exhibitions. 3.
Drawing - 16th century - Italy - Florence - Exhibitions.
I. Allen Memorial Art Museum. II. Title.*
NC256.F5 F4 1991

The Metamorphic medium . [Oberlin, Ohio]
c1989. ix, 46 p. :   ***NYPL [MFW 90-11187]***

Feinblatt, Ebria. Seventeenth-century Bolognese
ceiling decorators / Ebria Feinblatt. Santa
Barbara, Calif. : Fithian Press, 1991. p. cm.
Includes bibliographical references and index. ISBN
0-931832-89-6 : DDC 729/.4/09454109032 20
*1. Ceilings - Italy - Bologna. 2. Mural painting and
decoration, Italian - Italy - Bologna. 3. Mural painting
and decoration, Baroque - Italy - Bologna. 4. Interior
decoration - Italy - Bologna - History - 17th century. I.
Title.*
ND2757.B54 F45 1991

Feininger. Feininger, Lyonel, 1871-1956. Lyonel
Feininger, 1871-1956 . Köln , c1989. 70 p. :
              NYPL [3-MCX F29 91-5551]

Feininger, Lyonel, 1871-1956.
Lyonel Feininger, 1871-1956 : 27. Februar bis
23. März 1989. Köln : Galerie Gmurzynska,
c1989. 70 p. : ill. (some col.) ; 24 cm. Cover
title: Feininger. "Texte und Zitatauswahl: Rochus von
Stolzmann."--p. 70. Includes bibliographies.
*1. Feininger, Lyonel, 1871-1956 - Exhibitions. I.
Stolzmann, Rochus von. II. Galerie
Gmurzynska-Bargera. III. Title. IV. Title: Feininger.*
              NYPL [3-MCX F29 91-5551]

Thüringen und die See : Druckgrafik--Aquarelle
/ Lyonel Feininger Galerie Quedlinburg; [Texte,
Roland März, Johannes Wend]. Quedlinburg :
Die Galerie, 1987. 95 p. : ill. (some col.) ; 20
cm.
*1. Feininger, Lyonel, 1871-1956 - Catalogs. 2. Lyonel
Feininger Galerie Quedlinburg - Catalogs. 3. Thüringen
(Germany) in art - Catalogs. I. März, Roland. II. Wend,
Johannes. III. Lyonel Feininger Galerie Quedlinburg.
IV. Title.*
              NYPL [3-MDG (Feininger) 89-6002]

**FEININGER, LYONEL, 1871-1956 -
CATALOGS.**
Feininger, Lyonel, 1871-1956. Thüringen und
die See . Quedlinburg , 1987. 95 p. :
              NYPL [3-MDG (Feininger) 89-6002]

**FEININGER, LYONEL, 1871-1956 -
EXHIBITIONS.**
Feininger, Lyonel, 1871-1956. Lyonel Feininger,
1871-1956 . Köln , c1989. 70 p. :
              NYPL [3-MCX F29 91-5551]

Feireiss, Kristin. 14x Amerika-Gedenkbibliothek .
Berlin , c1989. 132 p. : ISBN 3-433-02288-7
(pbk.)   ***NYPL [3-MQWO+ 90-11060]***

Feischen, Claudia. Gorenflo, Roger M.
Verzeichnis der bildenden Künstler von 1880
bis heute . Rüsselsheim , 1988. 3 v. (989 p.) ;
ISBN 3-926759-00-3 (set)
              NYPL [3-MAO 90-10802]

Fekner, John. Artist as apolitical sensor : Andrew
Castrucci ... [et al.] : October 10-November 18,
1990, Hillwood Art Museum, Long Island
University, C.W. Post Campus / curator, John
Kekner. Brookville, N.Y. : The Museum, 1990.
28 p. : ill. (some col.) ; 23 cm.
*1. Castrucci, Andrew - Exhibitions. 2. Art, American -
Exhibitions. 3. Art, Modern - 20th century - United
States - Exhibitions. I. Hillwood Art Gallery. II. Title.*
              NYPL [3-MAMT 91-5026]

Feld, Stuart P. Neo-classicism in America . New
York, N.Y. , c1991. 136 p. : ISBN
0-915057-41-7   ***NYPL [3-MAMT 91-7337]***

Feldstein, Martin S. The Economics of art museums /. Chicago , 1991. p. cm. ISBN 0-226-24073-8 (alk. paper) DDC 338.4/770813 20
N510 .E27 1991

Felice Levini . Levini, Felice, 1956- Milano , 1988. 77 p. :
N6923.L345 A4 1988
NYPL [3-MCF L665 90-12541]

Félicien Rops, 1833-1898 : Aquarelle, Zeichnungen, Druckgraphik : Städtische Kunsthalle Düsseldorf, 16. Februar-25. März 1979 / [Katalogredaktion Catherine De Croës, Katharina Schmidt]. Brüssel : Ministère de la culture française, 1979. 88 p. : ill. (some col.) ; 20 x 21 cm. Catalog of the exhibition sponsored jointly by the Ministère de la culture française, Service de la diffusion des arts, and the Städtische Kunsthalle Düsseldorf. Includes some text in French. Bibliography: p. 76-81.
1. Rops, Félicien Victor Joseph, 1833-1898 - Exhibitions. I. Rops, Félicien Victor Joseph, 1833-1898. II. Croës, Catherine de, 1941-. III. Schmidt, Katharina. IV. Belgium. Ministère de la culture française. V. Belgium. Service de la diffusion des arts.
N6973.R67 A4 1979
NYPL [3-MCH R78 81-420]

Felix Nussbaum . Nussbaum, Felix, 1904-1944. Bramsche , c1990. 440 p. : ISBN 3-922469-46-9 DDC 759.3 20
ND588.N8 A4 1990

Félix Vallotton . Ducrey, Marina. Lausanne , c1989. 163 p. : ISBN 2-88001-248-1 DDC 759.9494 20
ND853.V3 D8 1989
NYPL [3-MCZ+ V19 90-11783]

Felix, Zdenik. Gober, Halley, Kessler, Wool . [Munich] , c1989. 89 p. : ISBN 3-923357-24-9
NYPL [3-MAMT 90-12879]

Felixmüller, Conrad, 1897-1977.
Barth, Peter. Conrad Felixmüller, die Dresdner Jahre 1913-1933 /. Düsseldorf , 1987. 128 p. :
NYPL [3-MCK F316 89-18042]

Conrad Felixmüller, 1897-1977 : Aquarelle, Zeichnungen, Skulpturen, Graphik : Ausstellung zum 85. Geburtstag, Mai-Juli 1982, Graphik-Salon Gerhart Sohn, Dusseldorf. Dusseldorf : Das Graphik-Salon, [1982?] [38] p. : ill. (some col.) ; 24 cm.
1. Felixmüller, Conrad, 1897-1977 - Exhibitions. I. Graphik-Salon Gerhart Sohn, III. Title.
NYPL [3-MCK F316 91-868]

Rathke, Christian. Conrad Felixmüller . [Schleswig] [1990] 282 p. :
NYPL [3-MCK F316 91-7198]

FELIXMÜLLER, CONRAD, 1897-1977 - EXHIBITIONS.
Barth, Peter. Conrad Felixmüller, die Dresdner Jahre 1913-1933 /. Düsseldorf , 1987. 128 p. :
NYPL [3-MCK F316 89-18042]

Felixmüller, Conrad, 1897-1977. Conrad Felixmüller, 1897-1977 . Dusseldorf [1982?] [38] p. : *NYPL [3-MCK F316 91-868]*

Rathke, Christian. Conrad Felixmüller . [Schleswig] [1990] 282 p. : *NYPL [3-MCK F316 91-7198]*

Fell, Derek. Renoir's garden / Derek Fell ; foreword by Jacques Renoir. New York : Simon and Schuster, c1991. p. cm. Includes bibliographical references and index. ISBN 0-671-74444-5 DDC 759.4 20
1. Renoir, Auguste, 1841-1919 - Homes and haunts - France - Cagnes-sur-Mer. 2. Gardens - France - Cagnes-sur-Mer. 3. Maison de Renoir (Cagnes-sur-Mer, France). I. Title.
ND553.R45 F415 1991

Felsch, J. Eugene. Milwaukee. Art Center. Photography 68. Milwaukee , 1968. [36] p. :
NYPL [MFW 90-6743]

FELT MARKER DRAWING.
Hanks, Kurt, 1947- Rapid viz . Los Altos, CA , c1990. 149 p. : ISBN 1-560-52055-8 (pbk.) : DDC 741.6 20
NC877.8 .H36 1990

FELT MARKER DRAWING - TECHNIQUE.
Gleason, John A. Illustration with markers . New York , 1991. p. cm. ISBN 0-8230-2536-5 : DDC 741.6 20
NC878 .G57 1991

FEMALE. see WOMEN.

Female trouble /. Rheims, Bettina. München , c1989. 151 p. : ISBN 3-88814-305-5
NYPL [MFX+ (Rheims) 89-26830]

Female trouble /. Rheims, Bettina, 1952- Munich , c1989. 151 p. : ISBN 3-88814-537-6
NYPL [MFX+ (Rheims) 90-2146]

FEMININE BEAUTY (AESTHETICS) - ENGLAND.
Renaissance bodies . London , 1990. x, 294 p. : ISBN 0-948462-09-4 DDC 700 20
NX650.F45 R46 1990

FEMININE BEAUTY (AESTHETICS) - ROME - EXHIBITIONS.
Bellezza e seduzione nella Roma imperiale . [Roma] [c1990] 122 p. : ISBN 88-7813-283-7 :
N7629.2.I8 R663 1990

FEMINISM AND ART - EAST (U. S.) - HISTORY.
McCarthy, Kathleen D. Women's culture . Chicago , 1991. p. cm. ISBN 0-226-55583-6 (alk. paper) DDC 701/.03 20
N72.F45 M34 1991

FEMINISM AND ART - EXHIBITIONS.
Garrard, Rose. Rose Garrard . Birmingham [England] [1983?] 32 p. :
N6797.G37 I5 1983
NYPL [3-MGO (Garrard) 90-10680]

FEMINISM AND ART - FRANCE.
Broude, Norma. Impressionism . New York , 1991. p. cm. ISBN 0-8478-1397-5 DDC 759.05/4 20
ND547.5.I4 B76 1991

FEMINISM AND ART - MIDDLE WEST - HISTORY.
McCarthy, Kathleen D. Women's culture . Chicago , 1991. p. cm. ISBN 0-226-55583-6 (alk. paper) DDC 701/.03 20
N72.F45 M34 1991

FEMINISM AND ART - UNITED STATES.
Feminist art criticism . New York, NY , c1991. p. ISBN 0-06-430216-4 (paperback) : DDC 701/.03 20
N72.F45 F445 1991

FEMINISM AND THE ARTS.
Bornay, Erika. Las hijas de Lilith /. Madrid , c1990. 404 p. : ISBN 84-376-0868-6
NX652.F45 B6 1990

Göttner-Abendroth, Heide, 1941- [Tanzende Göttin. English.] The dancing goddess . Boston , c1991. p. cm. ISBN 0-8070-6753-9 (alk.) DDC 700/.1/03 20
NX180.F4 G613 1991

The Helicon nine reader . Kansas City , c1990. 512 p. : ISBN 0-9627460-0-2 DDC 700/.82 20
NX180.F4 H44 1990

Surrealism and women /. Cambridge, Mass. , 1991. 240 p. : ISBN 0-262-53098-8 : DDC 700 20
NX456.5.S8 S87 1991

FEMINISM AND THE ARTS - CONGRESSES.
Sexuality, the female gaze, and the arts . Selinsgrove [N.J.] , London , 1992. p. cm. ISBN 0-945636-32-6 (alk. paper) DDC 700/.1/03 20
NX180.F4 S49 1992

Feminist art criticism : an anthology / edited by Arlene Raven, Cassandra L. Langer, and Joanna Frueh.1st Icon ed. New York, NY : Icon Editions, c1991. p. cm. Originally published: Ann Arbor, Mich. : UMI Research Press, c1988. (Studies in the fine arts. Criticism ; no. 27). ISBN 0-06-430216-4 (paperback) : DDC 701/.03 20
1. Feminism and art - United States. 2. Feminist art criticism - United States. I. Raven, Arlene. II. Langer, Cassandra L. III. Frueh, Joanna.
N72.F45 F445 1991

FEMINIST ART CRITICISM - UNITED STATES.
Feminist art criticism . New York, NY , c1991. p. ISBN 0-06-430216-4 (paperback) : DDC 701/.03 20
N72.F45 F445 1991

Femmel, Gerhard. Die Erotica und Priapea aus den Sammlungen Goethes /. Frankfurt am Main , 1990. 298 p. :
NYPL [3-MAMZ 91-4510]

Femmes d'artistes /. Clébert, Jean Paul. Paris , c1989. 415 p. ; ISBN 2-85616-499-4 :
NX165 .C6 1989

Les Femmes de Vogue hommes / [préface, Gérald Asaria]. Paris : A. Michel, c1988. 110 p. : chiefly ill. ; 30 cm. ISBN 2-226-03004-2
1. Photography of women. I. Vogue hommes.
NYPL [MFW+ 89-26844]

Femmes d'esprit : women in Daumier's caricature / [edited by] Kirsten H. Powell and Elizabeth C. Childs ; with contributions by Janis Bergman-Carton, Lucette Czyba, and Judith Wechsler. Middlebury, Vt. : C.A. Johnson Memorial Gallery, Middlebury College ; Hanover : Distributed by University Presses of New England, c1990. 146 p. : ill. ; 28 cm. Catalog of an exhibition held at the Christian A. Johnson Memorial Gallery, Middlebury College, Middlebury, Vt., June 16-July 15, 1990, and at the Neuberger Museum, State University of New York at Purchase, Purchase, N.Y., Sept. 9-Dec. 10, 1990. Includes bibliographical references. ISBN 0-9625262-0-7 DDC 741.5/944 20
1. Daumier, Honoré, 1808-1879 - Exhibitions. 2. Women - Caricatures and cartoons - Exhibitions. 3. French wit and humor, Pictorial - Exhibitions. I. Powell, Kirsten H., 1951-. II. Childs, Elizabeth C. III. Christian A. Johnson Memorial Gallery. IV. Neuberger Museum.
NC1499.D3 A4 1990
NYPL [MDG (Daumier) 90-11002]

FEMMES FATALES IN ART.
Bornay, Erika. Las hijas de Lilith /. Madrid , c1990. 404 p. : ISBN 84-376-0868-6
NX652.F45 B6 1990

Fendel, Ute. Landschaft im Licht . Köln , Zürich , c1990. 519 p. : DDC 759.05/4/074435514 20
ND192.I4 L27 1990
NYPL [3-MC+ 91-5272]

Fensch, Angela, 1953- Kind Frau : ein fotografisches Essay aus der DDR / von Angela Fensch. Bern : Benteli, c1989. ca. 103 p. : ill. 31 cm. Sw90-01 ISBN 3-7165-0685-0 :
1. Fensch, Angela, 1953-. 2. Mother and child - Germany (East) - Pictorial works. I. Title.
IN PROCESS (ONLINE)
NYPL [MFX+ (Fensch) 91-2503]

FENSCH, ANGELA, 1953-
Fensch, Angela, 1953- Kind Frau . Bern , c1989. ca. 103 p. : ISBN 3-7165-0685-0 :
IN PROCESS (ONLINE)
NYPL [MFX+ (Fensch) 91-2503]

Fensch, Helmut. Olle DDR . Berlin , c1990. 168 p. : ISBN 3-362-00521-7
NYPL [MFW 91-8049]

FENZONI, FERRAÙ, 1562-1645.
Pittura del Seicento in Umbria . Todi , 1990. 351 p., [20] p. of plates :
NYPL [3-MCE+ 91-4970]

Le fer à Paris . Marrey, Bernard. [Paris] , 1989. 209 p., [1] leaf of plates : ISBN 2-7084-0379-6
NYPL [3-MQWF+ 90-243]

Fer d'art roman /. Faure, Philippe. [Dijon] , 1988- v. <1 > : ISBN 2-86621-112-X (v. 1)
NK6449.A1 F38 1988

Feray, Jean. Architecture intérieure et décoration en France, des origines à 1875 / Jean Feray ; [iconographie, Dominique Paul-Boncour]. Paris : Berger-Levrault : Caisse nationale des monuments historiques et des sites, c1988. 399 p. : ill. (some col.) ; 31 cm. Includes bibliographical references (p. 365-367) and index. ISBN 2-7013-0752-X DDC 729/.0944 20
1. Interior architecture - France. 2. Decoration and ornament - France. 3. Interior decoration - France. I. Paul-Boncour, Dominique. II. Caisse nationale des monuments historiques et des sites (France). III. Title.
NA2850 .F4 1988
NYPL [3-MLF+ 90-12087]

Ferazzini, Pierre-Alain. Musée Barbier-Müller. Ancient art from the Barbier-Mueller Museum /. New York , c1991. 183 p. : 0-8109-1904-4 *NYPL [3-MAE+ 91-6535]*

Ferber, Linda S. Anderson, Nancy K. Albert Bierstadt . New York , c1990. 327 p. : ISBN 1-555-95059-0 : DDC 759.13 20
ND237.B585 A4 1991
NYPL [3-MCX+ B585 91-5808]

Ferdinand Georg Waldmüller /. Schröder, Klaus

Albrecht. München , c1990. 260 p. : ISBN 3-7913-1078-X
NYPL [3-MCK+ W16 90-13356]

Ferdinand Parpan. Lévêque, Jean Jacques. Ferdinand Parpan, sculpteur /. Paris , c1989. 179 p. : ISBN 2-85917-092-8 DDC 730/.92 20
NB553.P35 L48 1989

Ferdinand Parpan, sculpteur /. Lévêque, Jean Jacques. Paris , c1989. 179 p. : ISBN 2-85917-092-8 DDC 730/.92 20
NB553.P35 L48 1989

Ferdinand Tietz und seine Bildhauerschule . Utz, Hildegard. Trier , 1976. 96 p. : ISBN 3-87760-411-0
NB588.T53 U89
NYPL [3-MGO (Tietz) 91-6414]

Ferdinand von Quast. Buch, Felicitas. Studien zur Preussischen Denkmalpflege am Beispiel konservatorischer Arbeiten Ferdinand von Quasts /. Worms , c1990. 250 p. : ISBN 3-88462-929-8
NA109.G3 B83 1990

Ferenc Martyn. see Martyn, Ferenc, 1899-

Ferguson, Bruce. Sherrie Levine--Fountain : 4 May to 25 May 1991 / text by Bruce Ferguson. New York : Mary Boone Gallery, 1991. p. cm. Includes bibliographical references.
ISBN 0-941863-20-4 DDC 709/.2 20
1. Levine, Sherrie - Exhibitions. 2. Conceptual art - United States - Exhibitions. I. Levine, Sherrie. II. Mary Boone Gallery (New York, N.Y.). III. Title.
N6537.L453 A4 1991

Ferguson, Russell.
Discourses . Cambridge, Mass. , New York, N.Y. , 1990. 471 p. : ISBN 0-262-06125-2 DDC 700/.9/048 20
NX456.5.P66 D57 1990
NYPL [3-MAL 91-3360]

Out there . New York, N.Y. , Cambridge, Mass. , c1990. 446 p. : ISBN 0-262-06132-5 DDC 700/.1/0308693 20
NX180.S6 O97 1990 *NYPL [3-MA 91-3296]*

Ferino Pagden, Sylvia. Venice. Gallerie dell'Accademia. Disegni umbri . Milano , c1984. 211 p. : ISBN 88-435-0801-6
NYPL [3-MBH 86-3573]

Ferkai, András. Konsztantyin Melnyikov / írta, Ferkai András. Budapest : Akadémiai Kiadó, 1988. 43 p., [59] p. of plates : 81 ill. ; 23 cm. (Architektúra, 0066-6270) Includes bibliographical references (p. 42-43). ISBN 963-05-4517-9
1. Mel'nikov, Konstantin Stepanovich, 1890- - Criticism and interpretation. 2. Constructivism (Architecture) - Russian S.F.S.R. I. Title. II. Series.
NA1199.M37 F4 1988

Ferlenga, Alberto. Aldo Rossi : Deutsches Historisches Museum, Berlino / Alberto Ferlenga. Milano : Electa, 1990. 118 p. : ill. (some col.), plans ; 25 cm. (Opere e progetti ; 2) ISBN 88-435-3088-7
1. Rossi, Aldo, 1931- - Exhibition. 2. Deutsches Historisches Museum (Projected) - Designs and plans - Exhibitions. 3. Historical museums - Berlin (Germany) - Designs and plans - Exhibitions. I. Rossi, Aldo, 1931-. II. Title. III. Series.
NYPL [3-MQZ (Rossi) 91-6524]

Fermo . Pupilli, Laura. Bologna , c1990. v, 272 p. : ISBN 88-7019-449-3
NYPL [MAVZ (Femo, Italy) 91-5714]

Fern, Dan, 1945- Dan Fern : works with paper / edited by Rick Poynor. London : Architecture Design and Technology Press, 1990. 108 p. : ill. (some col.) ; 21 cm. "An ADT designfile"--P. [2] Includes bibliographical references (p. 108). ISBN 1-85454-149-8 (pbk.) DDC 760.092 20
1. Fern, Dan, 1945-. I. Poynor, Rick. II. Title.
NYPL [3-MDWS (Fern) 91-6335]

FERN, DAN, 1945-
Fern, Dan. Dan Fern : works with paper /. London , 1990. 108 p. : ISBN 1-85454-149-8 (pbk.) DDC 760.092 20 *NYPL [3-MDWS (Fern) 91-6335]*

Fernan Lez'eh. Léger, Fernand, 1881-1955. Fernand Léger . Jérusalem , c1989. 212 p. : ISBN 965-278-059-6 DDC 759.4 20
NC248.L43 A4 1989

Fernand Léger . Léger, Fernand, 1881-1955. Jérusalem , c1989. 212 p. : ISBN 965-278-059-6 DDC 759.4 20
NC248.L43 A4 1989

Fernand Léger . Léger, Fernand, 1881-1955. [Paris] , c1990- v. : ISBN 2-86941-098-0 (v. 1) DDC 759.4 20
ND553.L58 A4 1990a
NYPL [MCO L512 91-826]

Fernand Léger . Léger, Fernand, 1881-1955. Köln , c1990. 102 p. :
ND553.L58 A4 1990

Fernand Léger, study for three portraits, 1910-11 /. Danoff, I. Michael. [Milwaukee] , c1977. 17 p. : *NYPL [3-MCO L512 90-7194]*

Fernand Toussaint . Berko, P. [Knokke-Heist, Belgium , 1986] 112 p. : ISBN 90-70481-94-4 DDC 759.9493 20
ND673.T68 A4 1986
NYPL [3-MCH T725 90-10766]

Fernández, Antonio. Historia visual del arte /. Barcelona , <1989-. v. <3-4 > : ISBN 84-316-2704-3 (v. 3)
N5300 .H58 1989

FERNÁNDEZ LEDESMA, GABRIEL, 1900- - CRITICISM AND INTERPRETATION.
Alanís, Judith. Gabriel Fernández Ledesma /. México , 1985. 219 p. : ISBN 968-8373-78-8
N6559.F46 A83 1985

Fernández, Martha (Fernández García) La arquitectura de la Ciudad de México en el siglo XVII / Martha Fernández. [Mexico] : Departamento del Distrito Federal, Secretaría General de Desarrollo Social, Comité Interno de Ediciones Gubernamentales, 1987. 43 p. : ill. ; 21 cm. (Ciudad y cultura . 2) Includes bibliographical references. ISBN 968-8160-77-6 DDC 720/.972/5309032 20
1. Architecture - Mexico - Mexico City. 2. Architecture, Baroque - Mexico - Mexico City. 3. Mexico City (Mexico) - Buildings, structures, etc. I. Title. II. Series.
NA757.M4 F46 1987

Fernández Martínez, Carlos María. Trinidad Cuartara Cassinello, arquitecto : Almería, 1871-1912 / Carlos María Fernández Martínez.1a ed. Almería : Cajal, 1989. 392 p. : ill., facsim., plans, port. ; 24 cm. (Biblioteca de autores y temas almerienses. Serie mayor . 16) Accompanied by one folded plan and "Addenda y corrigenda". Includes bibliographical references (p. 301-312). ISBN 84-85219-75-9
1. Cuartara Cassinello, Trinidad, 1847-1912. I. Title. II. Series. *NYPL [MQZ (Cuartara Cassinello) 91-5988]*

Fernández, Miguel Angel. García Sáiz, Maria Concepción. Las castas mexicanas . [S.l.] , 1989 (Milano) 253 p. : *NYPL [3-MCY+ 91-4969]*

Fernando Botero . Cau, Jean, 1925- Paris , c1990. 161 p. : ISBN 2-85047-159-3 DDC 759.9861 20
N6679.B6 A4 1990b

Fernando Botero /. Soavi, Giorgio, 1923- Milano , c1988. 275 p. :
ND379.B6 S63 1988
NYPL [3-MCZ+ B74 90-12665]

Fernando Castillo . Eliash, Humberto. [Santiago, Chile] . 237 p. : ISBN 958-9082-44-0 (colección) DDC 720/.92 20
NA869.C37 A4 1990

Fernando Ureña Rib /. Tolentino, Marianne. Santo Domingo, República Dominicana , 1989. 1 v. (unpaged) :
NYPL [3-MCZ+ U795 90-8607]

Fernando Ureña Rib /. Tolentino, Marianne. Santo Domingo, República Dominicana , 1989. 134 p. : DDC 759.97293 20
ND315.U74 A4 1989

Fernie, E. C. Medieval architecture and its intellectual context . London , Ronceverte, WV , 1990. xxvii, 304 p. : ISBN 1-85285-034-5 : DDC 723 20
NA350 *NYPL [3-MQO 90-11593]*

Fernier, Jean-Jacques. Courbet et Ornans / Jean-Jacques Fernier, Jean-Luc Mayaud, Patrick Le Nouëne et le Musée Gustave Courbet à Ornans. Paris : Herscher, 1989. 126 p. : ill. (some col.), ports. ; 29 cm. Bibliography: p. 126. ISBN 2-7335-0170-4
1. Ornans (France) in art. I. Mayaud, Jean Luc. II. Le Nouëne, Patrick. III. Musée Gustave Courbet. IV. Title.
NYPL [3-MCO C858 91-5529]

Ferran García Sevilla . Cameron, Dan. New

York , c1990. [24] p. :
NYPL [3-MCQ+ G236 91-4299]

Ferran, Pierre, fl. 1966- L'Amour à la carte /. Paris , [c1980] ca 150 p. : ISBN 2-7058-0095-6 :
NC1878.L68 A45 *NYPL [3-MAMZ 81-962]*

Ferrara. Centro attività visive. see Centro attività visive.

Ferrara. Civica raccolta d'arte moderna. see Galleria civica d'arte moderna, Ferrara.

Ferrara. Galleria civica d'arte moderna. see Galleria civica d'arte moderna, Ferrara.

Ferrara (Italy). Assessorato alle istituzioni culturali.
Aspetti dell'arte contemporanea spagnola. Barcelona , c1990. 47, [1] p. : ISBN 84-87433-11-1 DDC 709/.46/0744545 20
N7108 .A87 1990

Rubio, Miguel. Rafael Canogar /. Barcelona , c1990. 47, [1] p. : ISBN 84-87433-10-3
N6913.C36 A4 1990

Ferrara (Italy). Galleria civica d'arte moderna.
Aspetti dell'arte contemporanea spagnola. Barcelona , c1990. 47, [1] p. : ISBN 84-87433-11-1 DDC 709/.46/0744545 20
N7108 .A87 1990

Campigli, Massimo, 1895-1971. Massimo Campigli . Ferrara , 1979. 1 v. (unpaged) :
NYPL [3-MCF C19 90-5911]

Rubio, Miguel. Rafael Canogar /. Barcelona , c1990. 47, [1] p. : ISBN 84-87433-10-3
N6913.C36 A4 1990

Savinio, Alberto, 1891-1952. Alberto Savinio . Ferrara , 1980. ca. 250 p. :
NYPL [3-MCF S265 90-6458]

FERRARI, AGOSTINO, 1938-
Caramel, Luciano. Agostino Ferrari /. Milano , c1991. 151 p. : ISBN 88-435-3445-9
IN PROCESS (ONLINE)
NYPL [3-MCF F366 91-7167]

Ferrari, Antoine.
Di Genova, Alauzen. Antoine Ferrari /. La Calade, Aix-en-Provence , c1990. 136 p. : ISBN 2-85744-497-4 DDC 759.4 20
ND553.F44 D5 1990

FERRARI, ANTOINE - CRITICISM AND INTERPRETATION.
Di Genova, Alauzen. Antoine Ferrari /. La Calade, Aix-en-Provence , c1990. 136 p. : ISBN 2-85744-497-4 DDC 759.4 20
ND553.F44 D5 1990

Ferrari, Enrique Lafuente. see Lafuente Ferrari, Enrique.

Ferrari, Germana. Matta Echaurren, Roberto Sebastián, 1911- Matta . Roma , c1980. [10], 111 p. : *NYPL [MDG+ (Matta) 90-7102]*

Ferrari, Giovanni Battista, 1829-1906.
Ferrari, Roberto. Gio Batta Ferrari, 1829-1906 /. Brescia , 1990. 110 p. : ISBN 88-7385-059-6
NYPL [3-MCF F372 91-5212]

FERRARI, GIOVANNI BATTISTA, 1829-1906 - EXHIBITIONS.
Ferrari, Roberto. Gio Batta Ferrari, 1829-1906 /. Brescia , 1990. 110 p. : ISBN 88-7385-059-6
NYPL [3-MCF F372 91-5212]

Ferrari, Oreste. Bozzetti italiani dal manierismo al barocco / Oreste Ferrari. Napoli : Electa, c1990. 285 p. : ill. (some col.) ; 29 cm. Includes bibliographical references and indexes.
1. Painting - 16th century - Italy - Catalogs. 2. Painting, Italian - Catalogs. 3. Painting, Modern - 17th-18th centuries - Italy - Catalogs. 4. Artists' preparatory studies - Italy - Catalogs. I. Title.
ND615 .F47 1990 *NYPL [3-MCE 91-4960]*

Ferrari, Roberto. Gio Batta Ferrari, 1829-1906 / Roberto Ferrari ; contributi di Eleonora Bairati, Francesco Rovetta, Monica Rovetta ; prefazione di Gaetano Panazza. Brescia : Grafo, 1990. 110 p. : ill. (some col.) ; 26 cm. Catalog of an exhibition held Sale ex Monte di pietà, Brescia, May 1990. Includes bibliographical references (p. 91-93). ISBN 88-7385-059-6
1. Ferrari, Giovanni Battista, 1829-1906 - Exhibitions. I. Ferrari, Giovanni Battista, 1829-1906. II. Bairati, Eleonora. III. Rovetta, Monica. IV. Rovetta, Francesco. V. Sale ex Monte di pietà (Brescia, Italy). VI. Title.
NYPL [3-MCF F372 91-5212]

Ferrazzi, Ferruccio, 1891-
VORTICE DELLO SPIRITO SANTO.
Fornaro, Cosimo, 1928- Il mosaico di
Ferruccio Ferrazzi nella Chiesa di S. Antonio
in Taranto /. Fasano, Brindisi , c1987. 95 p. :
   ISBN 88-7514-199-1 :   DDC 726/.527/092 20
NA3860.F47 A4 1987
         NYPL [3-MRXZ+ 90-12439]

Ferre, Mathilde. Groupes, mouvements,
tendances de l'art contemporain depuis 1945 /.
Paris , 1990. 183 p. ;   ISBN 2-903639-61-2 :
   DDC 709/.04/5 20
N6490 .G724 1990

Ferreira, Fátima Cordeiro G. Mestre José Luiz
Monteiro . [Lisbon] [1990] 93 p. :   DDC
   720/.92 20
NA1333.M65 M48 1990

Ferreira, Jaime M. M. Bilhetes postais e cartões
de boas festas / Jaime M.M. Ferreira, L.M.
Barata das Neves ; colaboração de Miguel
Pessanha. Lisboa : Filatelia Barata das Neves,
1989- v. <1 > : ill. ; 21 cm. Vol. 1 cover title:
Bilhetes postais de boas festas, cartões de boas festas.
Includes bibliographical references (v. 1, p. 223-224).
   DDC 741.6/83/09469075 20
  *1. Postcards - Portugal - Catalogs. 2. Fasts and feasts -
Portugal. I. Neves, L. M. Barata das. II. Pessanha,
Miguel. III. Title. IV. Title: Bilhetes postais de boas
festas, cartões de boas festas.*
NC1878.7.P8 F4 1989

Ferrer, Eulalio. see **Ferrer Rodríguez, Eulalio.**

Ferrer Rodríguez, Eulalio. La Mona Lisa : una
fascinante historia / Eulalio Ferrer Rodríguez.1.
ed. española. Madrid : Maeva Ediciones, c1990.
82 p. : ill. ; 23 cm. Originally published under the
title: Mona Lisa. Includes bibliographical references (p.
79-82).   ISBN 84-86478-32-4   DDC 759.5 20
  *1. Leonardo da Vinci, 1452-1519. Mona Lisa. 2.
Leonardo da Vinci, 1452-1519 - Influence. I. Title.*
ND623.L5 A7 1990

Ferrez, Gilberto.
[Fotografia no Brasil, 1840-1900. English]
Photography in Brazil, 1840-1900 / Gilberto
Ferrez ; translated by Stella de Sá Rego. 1st
U. S. ed. Albuquerque : University of New
Mexico Press, [1990] c1984. xvii, 243 p. :
ill. ; 30 cm. Translation of: A fotografia no Brasil.
Includes bibliographical references (p. [235]-237) and
index.   ISBN 0-8263-1211-X   DDC
   770/.981/09034 20
  *1. Photography - Brazil - History - 19th century. I.
Title.*
TR41 .F4313 1990   *NYPL [MFW+ 91-4968]*

Ferrone (Firm : Milan, Italy) Appunti per piazze
d'Italia /. [Milano] , c1988. 79 p. :
        NYPL [3-MQWB+ 90-12352]

FERRONE (FIRM : MILAN, ITALY)
Appunti per piazze d'Italia /. [Milano] , c1988.
79 p. :   *NYPL [3-MQWB+ 90-12352]*

FÈS (MOROCCO) - INDUSTRIES - MAPS.
Atlas de la médina de Fès . Toulouse , 1990. 1
atlas (46 p.) :   ISBN 2-85816-137-2
        NYPL [Map Div. 91-161]

FÈS (MOROCCO) - MAPS.
Atlas de la médina de Fès . Toulouse , 1990. 1
atlas (46 p.) :   ISBN 2-85816-137-2
        NYPL [Map Div. 91-161]

FÈS (MOROCCO) - POPULATION - MAPS.
Atlas de la médina de Fès . Toulouse , 1990. 1
atlas (46 p.) :   ISBN 2-85816-137-2
        NYPL [Map Div. 91-161]

FESTIVALS IN ART.
Bowles, Edmund A. (Edmund Addison), 1925-
Musical ensembles in festival books,
1500-1800 . Ann Arbor, Mich. , c1989. xxii,
583 p. :   ISBN 0-8357-1872-7 (alk. paper)   DDC
   704.9/49785 19
ML85 .B66 1989   *NYPL [JMD 89-232]*

Festschrift für Georg Hoeltje / herausgegeben
vom Institut für Bau- und Kunstgeschichte der
Universität Hannover ; bearbeitet von Sid
Auffarth ; unter Mitarbeit von Olaf Thielecke.
Hannover : Das Institut, 1988. 160 p. : ill. ; 30
cm. (Schriften des Instituts für Bau- und
Kunstgeschichte der Universität Hannover . Bd. 5)
Includes bibliographical references.
  *1. Hoeltje, Georg, 1906-. 2. Architecture - Germany -
History. I. Hoeltje, Georg, 1906-. II. Auffarth, Sid,*

*1938-. III. Thielecke, Olaf. IV. Universität Hannover.
Institut für Bau- und Kunstgeschichte. V. Series.*
        NYPL [3-MQWD+ 90-12015]

Festschrift für Hartmut Biermann /
herausgegeben von Christoph Andreas, Maraike
Bückling und Roland Dorn. Weinheim : VCH,
Acta Humaniora, c1990. 400 p. : ill, plans ; 25
cm. Includes bibliographical references.   ISBN
   3-527-17712-4
  *1. Biermann, Hartmut, 1925-. 2. Art - Europe. 3.
Architecture - Europe. I. Andreas, Christoph. II.
Bückling, Maraike. III. Dorn, Roland. IV. Biermann,
Hartmut, 1925-.*   *NYPL [3-MAS 91-5197]*

Festschrift für Peter Bloch zum 11. Juli 1990 /
herausgegeben von Hartmut Krohm und
Christian Theuerkauff. Mainz am Rhein : P.
von Zabern, c1990. xviii, 420 p. : ill. ; 30 cm.
Chiefly German; some contributions in English or
French. Includes bibliographical references.   ISBN
   3-8053-1120-6
  *1. Bloch, Peter, 1925-. I. Bloch, Peter, 1925-. II.
Krohm, Hartmut, Dr. III. Theuerkauff, Christian, 1936-.*
        NYPL [3-MAS+ 91-4807]

Feuchtmayr, Andrea. Kulissenheiliggräber im
Barock : Entstehungsgeschichte und Typologie
/ Andrea Feuchtmayr. München : Tuduv
Verlag, c1989. 139, [26] p. of plates : ill. ; 21
cm. (Schriften aus dem Institut für Kunstgeschichte der
Universität München . Bd. 38) Includes bibliographical
references (p. 116-123).   ISBN 3-88073-309-0
  *1. Mural painting and decoration, European. 2. Mural
painting and decoration, Baroque - Europe. 3. Holy
sepulcher in art. 4. Church decoration and ornament -
Europe. 5. Trompel'oeil painting - Europe. I. Title. II.
Series.*
ND2725 .F48 1989

FEUDAL CASTLES. see CASTLES.

FEUDAL TENURE. see LAND TENURE.

Feuer, Gábor. Madarské výtvarné umění XX.
století (1945-1988) . V Praze , 1989. 40 p. :
   ISBN 80-7035-009-1 :
N6820 .M25 1989

Feugère, Michel. Le Verre préromain en Europe
occidentale /. Montagnac , 1989. 191 p. :
   ISBN 2-907303-00-7
        NYPL [3-MPW+ 91-7509]

**FEUILLET, MAURICE, 1873- - ART
COLLECTIONS - CATALOGS.**
Musée Borély. Donation Maurice et Pauline
Feuillet de Borsat /. Marseille, 1969. 1 v.
(unpaged)
NC27.F7 M355
        NYPL [3-MAVZ (Marseilles) 91-291]

**FEUILLET, PAULINE - ART COLLECTIONS -
CATALOGS.**
Musée Borély. Donation Maurice et Pauline
Feuillet de Borsat /. Marseille, 1969. 1 v.
(unpaged)
NC27.F7 M355
        NYPL [3-MAVZ (Marseilles) 91-291]

Feyt, Henri.
Marcel Arnaud : peintre de Provence :
1877-1956 / Henri Feyt, Jean-Marc Pontier ;
préface de André Alauzen di Genova. La
Calade, Aix-en-Provence : Edisud, c1990. 111
p. : ill. (some col.) ; 29 cm. Includes bibliographical
references (p. 110).   ISBN 2-85744-463-X   DDC
   759.4 20
  *1. Arnaud, Marcel, 1877-1956 - Criticism and
interpretation. 2. Provence (France) in art. I. Arnaud,
Marcel, 1877-1956. II. Pontier, Jean-Marc. III. Title.*
ND553.A589 F49 1990

Marcel Arnaud : peintre de Provence,
1877-1956 / Henri Feyt, Jean-Marc Pontier ;
préface de André Alauzen di Genova.
Aix-en-Provence : Edisud, c1990. 111 p. : ill.
(some col.) ; 29 cm. Includes bibliographical
references (p. 110).   ISBN 2-85744-463-X
  *1. Arnaud, Marcel, 1877-1956. I. Arnaud, Marcel,
1877-1956. II. Pontier, Jean-Marc.*
        NYPL [3-MCO A744 91-6751]

Ffolliott, Sheila. Hancock, Jane H., 1949-
Homecoming . St. Paul , c1991. x, 116 p. :
   ISBN 0-87351-259-6   DDC
   759.05/074/74776581 20
N6450 .H298 1991

Ffotogallery (Cardiff, Wales) Doherty, Willie,
1959- Willie Doherty, unknown depths.
Cardiff , c1990. [39] p. :   ISBN 1-87277-101-7
        NYPL [MFX (Doherty) 90-13467]

Fiallos S., Raúl (Fiallos Salgado), 1917- Datos
históricos sobre la plástica hondureña / Raúl
Fiallos S. [Tegucigalpa, Honduras? : s.n.], c1989
(Tegucigalpa, Honduras, C.A. : Litografía
López) 129 p. : ill. (some col.) ; 22 cm. Errata
slip mounted on p. [3] of cover. Includes bibliographical
references (p. 106-107).   DDC 709/.7283 20
  *1. Art, Honduran. 2. Art, Modern - 20th century -
Honduras. 3. Artists - Honduras - Biography. I. Title.
II. Title: Plástica hondureña.*
N6579 .F5 1989

Fiasella, Domenico, 1589-1669.
Domenico Fiasella / a cura di Piero Donati ;
saggi di Carlo Bitossi ... [et al.]. Genova :
Sagep, c1990. 287 p. : ill. (some col.) ; 27 cm.
Catalog of an exhibition held at the Palazzo Reale,
Genoa, June 9-Aug. 5, 1990. At head of title:
Ministerio per i beni culturali e ambientali - Comune di
Genova. Includes bibliographical references (p.
279-287).
  *1. Fiasella, Domenico, 1589-1669 - Exhibitions. I.
Donati, Piero. II. Bitossi, Carlo. III. Palazzo reale
(Genoa, Italy). IV. Title.*
        NYPL [3-MCF F464 90-13082]

**FIASELLA, DOMENICO, 1589-1669 -
EXHIBITIONS.**
Fiasella, Domenico, 1589-1669. Domenico
Fiasella /. Genova , c1990. 287 p. :
        NYPL [3-MCF F464 90-13082]

**FIBERWORK - CALIFORNIA -
EXHIBITIONS.**
Transformation . [Los Angeles , 1979] [37] p. :
        NYPL [3-MON 91-290]

FIBERWORK - EXHIBITIONS.
Denver. Art Museum. Fibre structures. Denver,
1972. 56 p.   *NYPL [3-MON 91-240]*

**FIBERWORK - SOUTHERN STATES -
HISTORY - 20TH CENTURY.**
Ramsey, Bets, 1923- Southern quilts . Mclean,
Va. , c1991. p. cm.   ISBN 0-939009-52-8   DDC
   746.3975/09/049 20
NK9112 .R37 1991

**FIBERWORK - UNITED STATES -
HISTORY - 20TH CENTURY.**
Rossbach, Ed. Ed Rossbach . Asheville, N.C. ,
Washington, D.C. , 1990. 164 p. :   ISBN
0-937274-52-6 :   DDC 746/.092 20
NK8998.R68 A4 1990
        NYPL [3-MON 90-11617]

Fibre . M'Closkey, Kathy, 1943- Windsor, Ont. ,
c1988. [56] p. :   ISBN 0-919837-16-6   DDC
   746.9/7 19   *NYPL [3-MOT 90-8017]*

Fibre structures. Denver. Art Museum. Denver,
1972. 56 p.   *NYPL [3-MON 91-240]*

Ficarolo, Niccolò da. see **Niccolò da Ficarolo,
12th cent.**

Fichner-Rathus, Lois, 1953- Understanding art /
Lois Fichner-Rathus. 3rd ed. Englewood Cliffs,
N.J. : Prentice Hall, 1992. p. cm. Includes index.
   ISBN 0-13-932235-5 (pbk.)   DDC 701/.1 20
  *1. Visual perception. 2. Composition (Art). 3. Art -
History. I. Title.*
N7430.5 .F5 1992

Fickle, Dorothy H. Images of the Buddha in
Thailand / Dorothy H. Fickle. Singapore ; New
York : Oxford University Press, 1989. ix, 86
p. : ill. (some col.) ; 20 cm. (Images of Asia)
Includes bibliographical references (p. 84) and index.
   ISBN 0-19-588920-7 (U. S.)   DDC
   704.9/4894363/09593 20
  *1. Gautama Buddha - Art. 2. Sculpture, Buddhist -
Thailand. 3. Sculpture, Thai. I. Title. II. Series.*
NB1912.G38 F53 1989

Ficowski, Jerzy. Schulz, Bruno, 1892-1942. The
drawings of Bruno Schulz /. Evanston, Ill. ,
1990. 271 p. :   ISBN 0-8101-0964-6 (lib. bdg.)
   DDC 741.9438 20
NC312.P63 S382 1990
        NYPL [3-MCZ S388 91-3910]

Fictions of culture : essays in honor of Walter H.
Sokel / edited by Steven Taubeneck. New
York : P. Lang, 1991. p. cm. Includes papers
presented at a conference held in April, 1988 at the
University of Virginia. Includes bibliographical
references.   ISBN 0-8204-1714-9   DDC 700 20
  *1. Arts, Modern - Congresses. 2. Aesthetics, Modern -
Congresses. I. Taubeneck, Steven A. II. Sokel, Walter
Herbert, 1917-.*
NX449.5 .F53 1991

FIDENZA (ITALY) - BUILDINGS, STRUCTURES, ETC.
Appunti per piazze d'Italia /. [Milano] , c1988.
79 p. : *NYPL [3-MQWB+ 90-12352]*

Fiedermutz-Laun, Annemarie. Aus Erde geformt .
Mainz [1990] 171 p. : ISBN 3-8053-1107-9 :
NA1588 .A97 1990 *NYPL [Sc F 91-122]*

Fiedler, Jeannine.
Fotografie am Bauhaus /. [Berlin] , c1990. 362
p. : ISBN 3-88940-045-0
NYPL [MFW+ 91-3409]

Fotografie am Bauhaus. English. Photography at
the Bauhaus /. Cambridge, Mass. , 1990. 362
p. : ISBN 0-262-06126-0 DDC 779/.09431/84 20
TR653 .F66513 1990
NYPL [MFW+ 91-189]

FIEFS. see LAND TENURE.

FIELD CROPS - MAPS.
Atlas des cultures vivrières. Paris [1971] 41 p.
NYPL [Map Div. 73-116]

Field of vision . Burke, Janine. Ringwood, Vic.,
Australia , 1990. xi, 148 p., [16] p. of plates :
ISBN 0-670-83586-2
NYPL [3-MAM 90-13438]

Field, Richard S. Metropolitan Museum of Art
(New York, N.Y.) Fifteenth-century woodcuts
and other relief prints in the collection of the
Metropolitan Museum of Art . [New York] ,
c1977. [28] p. ; *NYPL [MDE 91-3607]*

FIELD SPORTS. see SPORTS.

Fieldhouse, Ken. Lisney, Adrian. Landscape
design guide /. Aldershot, Hants, England ;
Brookfield, Vt., USA : 2 v. : ISBN 0-566-09017-1
(v. 1) : DDC 712 19
SB472 *NYPL [3-MSD 90-13255]*

Fields, Darell Wayne. Andō, Tadao, 1941- Tadao
Ando . New York, N.Y. , c1991. 32 p. : ISBN
0-8478-1339-8 DDC 720/.22/22 20
NA2707.A53 A4 1991

Fiesta, poder y arquitectura . Bonet Correa,
Antonio. Madrid, España , c1990. 182 p. :
ISBN 84-7600-446-6 DDC 720/.946/09033 20
NA1306 .B57 1990

Fiets en mode : [tentoonstelling]. [Netherlands :
s.n.], 1966 (Ijsselstein : Drukkerij De Kroon) 1
v. (unpaged) : ill. ; 24 cm. Exhibition opened Nov.
29, 1966 at het Nederlands Textielmuseum te Tilburg.
*1. Cyclists - Costume - History - Exhibitions. I.
Nederlands Textielmuseum Tilburg.*
NYPL [3-MMED 91-294]

**Fifteenth century Italian woodcuts from the
Biblioteca Classense in Ravenna.** Ravenna :
Longo, c1989. 13 p., [46] p. of plates : ill.
(chiefly col.) ; 29 cm. (Interventi classensi . 11)
Text by Luigi Malkowski, translated by Manuela
Farneti.
*1. Biblioteca comunale classense (Ravenna, Italy) -
Catalogs. 2. Wood-engraving - 15th century - Italy -
Catalogs. 3. Wood-engraving, Italian - Catalogs. 4.
Wood-engraving - Italy - Ravenna - Catalogs. I.
Malkowski, Luigi. II. Biblioteca comunale classense
(Ravenna, Italy). III. Series.*
NYPL [MDOH 90-11354]

Fifteenth-century Persian painting . Robinson, B.
W. (Basil William) New York , 1991. p. cm.
ISBN 0-8147-7417-2 DDC 745.6/7/095509024
20
ND3241 .R597 1991

**Fifteenth-century woodcuts and other relief
prints in the collection of the Metropolitan
Museum of Art .** Metropolitan Museum of Art
(New York, N.Y.) [New York] , c1977. [28]
p. ; *NYPL [MDE 91-3607]*

Fifty etchings /. Lebrun, Christopher. London ,
1991. 123 p. : ISBN 0-904866-88-2
NYPL [MDG+ (Lebrun) 91-8018]

Fifty four master photographers of 1960-1979. 54
master photographers of 1960-1979. Tokyo ,
c1989. 560 p. : *NYPL [MFW 91-7942]*

**Fifty masterpieces of ancient Near Eastern art in
the Department of Western Asiatic Antiquities,
the British Museum.** British Museum. Dept. of
Western Asiatic Antiquities. London, 1969. 96
p. ISBN 0-7141-1069-8 DDC 732/.5
N5345 .B7 1969 *NYPL [3-MAF 90-6059]*

Fifty years of British art, 1914-64. London
Group. [London, 1964] 1 v. (unpaged)
N6768 .L65

Fifty years of Perceval drawings /. Perceval,
John, 1923- Sydney [1989] 256 p. : ISBN
1-86256-411-6 DDC 741.994 20
NC371.P47 A4 1989

Figari . Anastasía, Luis V. Montevideo , 1976. 92
p., [15] leaves of plates :
NYPL [3-MAM 90-5569]

Figari, Pedro, 1861-1938. Anastasía, Luis V.
Figari . Montevideo , 1976. 92 p., [15] leaves of
plates : *NYPL [3-MAM 90-5569]*

FIGARI, PEDRO, 1861-1938.
Anastasía, Luis V. Figari . Montevideo , 1976.
92 p., [15] leaves of plates :
NYPL [3-MAM 90-5569]

Figge, Eddie, 1904-
Eddie Figge / [XX Bienal de São Paulo, 1989].
Stockholm, Sweden : NUNSKU, [1989?] 1 v.
(unpaged) : col. ill. ; 22 cm. Portuguese with
English translation. Exhibition catalog. ISBN
91-86164-10-4 DDC 709/.2 20
*1. Figge, Eddie, 1904- - Exhibitions. I. Bienal
Internacional de São Paulo (20th : 1989). II. NUNSKU
(Organization : Sweden). III. Title.*
N7093.F54 A4 1989

FIGGE, EDDIE, 1904- - EXHIBITIONS.
Figge, Eddie, 1904- Eddie Figge /. Stockholm,
Sweden [1989?] 1 v. (unpaged) : ISBN
91-86164-10-4 DDC 709/.2 20
N7093.F54 A4 1989

FIGHTING. see WAR.

Fighting fish, fighting birds . Hiro. New York ,
1990. 66 p. : ISBN 0-8109-3403-5 DDC 779/.32
20
TR729.F5 H57 1990
NYPL [MFX+ (Hiro) 91-3304]

Figino, Giovan Ambrogio, 1548?-1608. Gallerie
dell'Accademia di Venezia. Disegni del Figino
/. Milano , c1987. 227 p. :
NYPL [3-MCF F472 88-4259]

FIGINO, GIOVAN AMBROGIO, 1548?-1608.
Gallerie dell'Accademia di Venezia. Disegni del
Figino /. Milano , c1987. 227 p. : ISBN
88-435-2240-X
NYPL [3-MCF F472 88-4259]

Figueiredo, Guilherme. Patrimônio histórico do
Rio de Janeiro / Guilherme Figueiredo, Riva
Bernstein. [Rio de Janeiro] : Europa, c1988. 1
portfolio : col. ill. ; 46 cm. Includes bibliographical
references.
*1. Historic buildings - Brazil - Rio de Janeiro. 2. Rio de
Janeiro (Brazil) - Buildings, structures, etc. I. Bernstein,
Riva. II. Title.*
NYPL [3-MQWN++ 89-26567]

Figueroa, Enrique, d. 1930.
Loredano, Cássio. Guevara e Figueroa . Rio de
Janeiro, RJ , 1988. 131 p. :
NC1460.G84 A4 1988

**FIGUEROA, ENRIQUE, D. 1930 -
CATALOGS.**
Loredano, Cássio. Guevara e Figueroa . Rio de
Janeiro, RJ , 1988. 131 p. :
NC1460.G84 A4 1988

La Figura e l'opera di Giovanni Morelli.
Bergamo : Biblioteca civica Angelo Mai, 1987.
2 v. : ill., facsims. ; 24 cm. Papers from the
Convegno su Giovanni Morelli e la cultura dei
conoscitori held in Bergamo at the Ex Chiesa di S.
Agostino, June 4-7, 1987. Text also published in
Bergomum, n. 2-3, 1987. "Repertorio bibliografico di
studi e pubblicazioni sulla figura e l'opera di Giovanni
Morelli": v. 1, p. [349]-372. Includes bibliographical
references and indexes. CONTENTS. - 1. Materiali di
ricerca / a cura di Matteo Panzeri e Giulio Orazio
Bravi -- 2. Studi e ricerche / Hans Ebert, Donata Levi,
Giacomo Agosti.
*1. Morelli, Giovani, 1816-1891 - Congresses. 2. Morelli,
Giovanni, 1816-1891 - Library - Catalogs. 3. Art
critics - Italy - Biography - Congresses. I. Panzeri,
Matteo. II. Convegno su Giovanni Morelli e la cultura
dei conoscitori (1987 : Bergamo, Italy).*
NYPL [3-MAVC 90-10867]

FIGURATION. see FIGURATIVE ART.

Figuration critique (Association : France)
Figuration critique 1990 . [Vélizy-Villacoublay]
[Séoul, Corée] [1990] 332 p. : DDC
709/.04/807444361 20
N6494.F5 F5188 1990

**FIGURATION CRITIQUE (ASSOCIATION :
FRANCE) - EXHIBITIONS.**

Figuration critique 1990 . [Vélizy-Villacoublay]
[Séoul, Corée] [1990] 332 p. : DDC
709/.04/807444361 20
N6494.F5 F5188 1990

Figuration critique 1990 : Paris, Leningrad,
Moscou. [Vélizy-Villacoublay] : Editions
Figuration critique ; [Séoul, Corée] : Editions
API, [1990] 332 p. : chiefly col. ill. ; 31 cm.
"Au Grand Palais du 5 au 25 septembre 1990." Includes
index. DDC 709/.04/807444361 20
*1. Figuration critique (Association : France) -
Exhibitions. 2. Figurative art - Exhibitions. 3. Art,
Modern - 20th century - Exhibitions. I. Figuration
critique (Association : France). II. Galeries nationales
du Grand Palais (France).*
N6494.F5 F5188 1990

Figuration und Bildformat . Bott, Gudrun, 1957-
Frankfurt am Main , New York , c1990. 208
p. ; ISBN 3-631-42715-8 DDC 759.3 20
ND588.B35 B6 1990

FIGURATIVE ART - EXHIBITIONS.
Figuration critique 1990 . [Vélizy-Villacoublay]
[Séoul, Corée] [1990] 332 p. : DDC
709/.04/807444361 20
N6494.F5 F5188 1990

**FIGURATIVE ART - SPAIN - HISTORY AND
CRITICISM.**
García-Viñó, Manuel. Pintura española
neofigurativa. Madrid [c1968] 203 p.
ND808 .G34 *NYPL [3-MCP 91-787]*

FIGURATIVE ART - UNITED STATES.
Adams, Doug. Transcendence with the human
body in art . New York , 1991. p. cm. ISBN
0-8245-1104-2 (cloth) DDC 701/.04 20
N6512.5.F5 A34 1991

**FIGURATIVE PAINTING, BRITISH -
EXHIBITIONS.**
The pursuit of the real . London , c1990. 127
p. : ISBN 0-85331-571-X (pbk.)
NYPL [3-MCT 90-11527]

Figure . Panizza, Mario. Roma , 1989. 238 p. :
ISBN 88-26-70066-4 :
IN PROCESS (ONLINE)
NYPL [3-MQV 90-11026]

Figure and abstraction. Paulson, Ronald. Figure
and abstraction in contemporary painting /.
New Brunswick [N.J.] , c1990. xi, 283 p. :
ISBN 0-8135-1604-8 DDC 759.06/09/045 20
ND196.F5 P38 1990
NYPL [3-MAL 91-3353]

Figure and abstraction in contemporary painting
/. Paulson, Ronald. New Brunswick [N.J.] ,
c1990. xi, 283 p. : ISBN 0-8135-1604-8 DDC
759.06/09/045 20
ND196.F5 P38 1990
NYPL [3-MAL 91-3353]

**FIGURE DRAWING - PRIVATE
COLLECTIONS - EXHIBITIONS.**
American drawings . New York [1979?] [40]
p. : *NYPL [3-MAX (Magriel) 90-6859]*

FIGURE DRAWING - TECHNIQUE.
Sheppard, Joseph, 1930- Realistic figure
drawing /. Cincinnati, Ohio , c1991. 136 p. :
ISBN 0-89134-374-1 : DDC 743/.4 20
NC765 .S445 1991

The figure in action . Gordon, Louise. London ,
1989. 128 p. : ISBN 0-7134-5946-8 DDC 743/.49
20
NC760 .G72 1989

FIGURE PAINTING.
Degand, Léon. Abstraction, figuration . Paris ,
c1988. 273 p. : ISBN 2-7022-0226-8
ND1290 .D44 1988

**FIGURE SCULPTURE - 20TH CENTURY -
UNITED STATES - EXHIBITIONS.**
Segal, George, 1924- George Segal, sculptures
/. Minneapolis , c1978. 99 p. : DDC 730/.92/4
NB237.S44 A4 1978
NYPL [3-MGO (Segal) 91-5273]

**FIGURE SCULPTURE, AMERICAN -
EXHIBITIONS.**
Segal, George, 1924- George Segal, sculptures
/. Minneapolis , c1978. 99 p. : DDC 730/.92/4
NB237.S44 A4 1978
NYPL [3-MGO (Segal) 91-5273]

Figuren 1947-1989. Luginbühl, Bernhard, 1929-
Bernhard Luginbühl, Figuren 1947-1989 /.
Bern , c1989. 511 p. : ISBN 3-7165-0692-3

DDC 730/.92 20
NB853.L8 A4 1989
NYPL [3-MGO+ (Luginbühl) 91-5929]

Figures of architecture and thought . Dal Co,
Francesco, 1945- New York , 1990. 344 p. :
ISBN 0-8478-0654-5 (pbk.) : DDC 720/.943 19
NA1067 .D35 1990
NYPL [3-MQWD 90-10690]

FIGURINES.
Bartman, Elizabeth. Ancient sculpture copies in
miniature /. Leiden , New York , 1992. p. cm.
ISBN 90-04-09532-2 DDC 733/.3 20
NB94 .B37 1992

Filed maps of Hudson County, N.J. Spielmann &
Brush. Hoboken, N.J. , 1881. 1 atlas (76
leaves) :   **NYPL [Map Div. 90-4088]**

FILIGRAINS. see WATER-MARKS.

Filipowicz, Diane. Wright, Frank Lloyd,
1867-1959. Frank Lloyd Wright and Madison .
Madison, Wis. , 1990. vii, 218 p. : ISBN
0-932900-22-4 DDC 720/.92 20
NA737.W7 A4 1990
NYPL [3-MQZ+ (Wright) 90-12072]

Filippi, Elena. Maarten van Heemskerck :
inventio urbis / Elena Filippi. Milano :
Berenice, c1990. 121 p. : ill. ; 34 cm. (Le Grandi
raccolte dei disegni di architettura) ISBN
88-85215-03-3
*1. Heemskerck, Martin van, 1498-1574. I. Title. II.
Series.* **NYPL [3-MCH+ H45 91-4260]**

Filippini, Henri. Histoire du journal Pilote et des
publications des Editions Dargaud / Henri
Filippini. Grenoble : J. Glénat, c1977. 141 p. :
ill. ; 29 cm. ISBN 2-7234-0038-7
*1. Editions Dargaud - History. 2. Pilote - History. 3.
Comic books, strips, etc. - France - Publishing. I. Title.*
NYPL [3-MDY 90-3530]

Filippo Avalle /. Monteforte, Franco. Milano :
1990. 124 p. : ISBN 88-444-1147-4 : DDC 709/.2
20
N6923.A89 M66 1990

Filippo Brunelleschi . Klotz, Heinrich. London ,
1990. 175 p. : ISBN 0-85670-986-7
NYPL [3-MQZ (Brunelleschi) 90-11571]

Fillin-Yeh, Susan. The Technological muse .
Katonah, N.Y. , c1990. 96 p. : ISBN
0-915171-19-8
NYPL [3-MAMT+ 91-7609]

Filliozat, Pierre Sylvain. Hampi-Vijayanagar :
Temple of Vithala / Pierre-Sylvain Filliozat and
Vasundhara Filliozat. New Delhi : Sitaram
Bhartia Institute of Scientific Research, 1988. 1
portfolio : ill. ; 30 cm. + 1 book (viii, 91, [4]
p. : ill. ; 29 cm.) Title from portfolio cover.
Architectural drawings by Pierre-Sylvain Filliozat and
text by Pierre-Sylvain Filliozat and Vasundhara
Filliozat. Includes index. Includes bibliographical
references (book, p. [93]-[95]) DDC 726/.145/095487
20
*1. Filliozat, Pierre Sylvain. 2. Temple of Vithala
(Hampi, India). 3. Architecture, Hindu - India - Hampi.
4. Hampi (India) - Buildings, structures, etc. I. Filliozat,
Vasundhara. II. Sitaram Bhartia Institute of Scientific
Research. III. Title.*
NA6008.H35 F53 1988
NYPL [3-MQWS+ 91-6052]

FILLIOZAT, PIERRE SYLVAIN.
Filliozat, Pierre Sylvain. Hampi-Vijayanagar .
New Delhi , 1988. 1 portfolio : DDC
726/.145/095487 20
NA6008.H35 F53 1988
NYPL [3-MQWS+ 91-6052]

Filliozat, Vasundhara. Filliozat, Pierre Sylvain.
Hampi-Vijayanagar . New Delhi , 1988. 1
portfolio : DDC 726/.145/095487 20
NA6008.H35 F53 1988
NYPL [3-MQWS+ 91-6052]

FILM POSTERS, ITALIAN - EXHIBITIONS.
Il Cinema nei manifesti di Silvano Campeggi
Nano, 1945-1969 . Firenze [1988] 158 p. :
DDC 741.6/74/092 20
NC1850.C36 A4 1988

**Filomarino, Anna Maria Cito. see Cito
Filomarino, Anna Maria.**

Filonov /. Filonov, Pavel Nikolaevich, 1883-1941.
[Paris] , 1990]. 248, [12] p. : ISBN
2-85850-531-4 : DDC 759.7 20
N6999.F55 A4 1990

Filonov, Pavel Nikolaevich, 1883-1941.
Filonov / [organisé en collaboration avec le
Musée russe de Léningrad]. [Paris] : Centre
Georges Pompidou, 1990]. 248, [12] p. : ill.
(some col.) ; 30 cm. "Conception et réalisation,
Evgueni Kovtoune, Stanislas Zadora, Nicole
Ouvrard"--P. [6]. Includes bibliographical references (p.
[254]) and index. ISBN 2-85850-531-4 : DDC 759.7
20
*1. Filonov, Pavel Nikolaevich, 1883-1941 - Exhibitions.
I. Kovtun, E. F. (Evgeniĭ Fedorovich). II. Zadora,
Stanislas. III. Ouvrard, Nicole. IV. Gosudarstvennyĭ
russkiĭ muzeĭ (Leningrad, R.S.F.S.R.). V. Title.*
N6999.F55 A4 1990

**FILONOV, PAVEL NIKOLAEVICH, 1883-
1941 - EXHIBITIONS.**
Filonov, Pavel Nikolaevich, 1883-1941. Filonov
/. [Paris] , 1990]. 248, [12] p. : ISBN
2-85850-531-4 : DDC 759.7 20
N6999.F55 A4 1990

Finamore, Daniel. Boudin, Eugène, 1824-1898.
Boudin . Salem, Mass. , 1991. p. DDC 759.4 20
ND553.B73 A4 1991

**FINANCIAL TIMES PRINT WORKS
(LONDON, ENGLAND)**
Jenkins, David. Financial Times Print Works,
London, 1988 . London , New York , 1991. ca.
60 p. : ISBN 1-85454-255-9 (pbk.) : DDC 725.4 20
NA6400
NYPL [3-MQZ+ (Grimshaw) 91-6989]

Financial Times Print Works, London, 1988 .
Jenkins, David. London , New York , 1991. ca.
60 p. : ISBN 1-85454-255-9 (pbk.) : DDC 725.4 20
NA6400
NYPL [3-MQZ+ (Grimshaw) 91-6989]

Fincardi, Marco. L'abbigliamento popolare
italiano /. Brescia [1986] 160 p. :
NYPL [3-MMO 90-8664]

Finch, Christopher. Nineteenth-century
watercolors / by Christopher Finch. New
York : Abbeville Press, 1991. p. cm. Includes
bibliographical references and index. ISBN
1-558-59019-6 DDC 759.05 20
*1. Watercolor painting - 19th century - History. I. Title.
II. Title: 19th-century watercolors.*
ND1797 .F56 1991

**Finck (Robert) Gallery, Brussels. see Galerie
Robert Finck.**

Finckh, Gerhard. Dunkel, Trimborn,
Dönselmann . [Emden, Germany , 1988] 87 p. :
ISBN 3-925564-02-0
NYPL [3-MAMG + 89-11596]

The Fine art of folk art / by Anita J. Ellis ... [et
al.]. [Cincinnati] : Cincinnati Art Museum,
c1990. 43 p. : col. ill. ; 26 cm. "Exhibition dates:
May 11-September 2, 1990"--T.p. verso. ISBN
0-931537-12-6 DDC 709/.73/07477178 20
*1. Folk art - United States - History - 19th century -
Exhibitions. 2. Folk art - United States - History - 20th
century - Exhibitions. I. Ellis, Anita J. II. Cincinnati.
Art Museum.*
NK806 .F56 1990

Fine art value guide. Huxford's fine art value
guide. Paducah, KY , <c1991-. v. <2 > :
ISBN 0-89145-427-6 (v. 2) : DDC 707/.5 20
N8675 .H88 1991

FINE ARTS. see ART; ARTS.

**Fine Arts Gallery, University of British
Columbia. see University of British Columbia.
Fine Arts Gallery.**

Fine Arts Museums of San Francisco.
Anderson, Nancy K. Albert Bierstadt . New
York , c1990. 327 p. : ISBN 1-555-95059-0 :
DDC 759.13 20
ND237.B585 A4 1991
NYPL [3-MCX+ B585 91-5808]

Broos, B. P. J. Great Dutch paintings from
America . The Hague, Zwolle , c1990. 561 p. :
ISBN 90-6630-253-4 (paperback)
NYPL [3-MCG 91-5531]

Fine arts series (Newton Abbot, England)
Cortel, Tine. Basic principles & language of fine
art /. Newton Abbot , New York, N.Y. , 1989.
116 p. : ISBN 0-7153-9475-4 DDC 750/.18 20
ND1500 .C67 1989

Fine arts series (Newton Abbot, London)
How to use oil paints . Newton Abbot , New
York, N.Y. , 1989. 116 p. : ISBN 0-7153-9474-6

DDC 751.45 20
ND1500 .H67 1989

**Fine Arts Society, Seattle. see Seattle. Art
Museum.**

Fine European paintings. Frank S. Schwarz &
Son. Philadelphia , c1988. 1 v. (unpaged)
NYPL [3-MC 90-13536]

Fine homebuilding. Craftsman-style houses.
Newton, Conn. , c1991. p. cm. ISBN
1-561-58014-7 : DDC 728/.373/09730904 20
NA7208 .C68 1991

Fine, Irving, 1914-1962.
Serious song. 1980. American music for strings
[sound recording]. Los Angeles, Calif. ,
p1980. 1 sound disc :
Nonesuch D-79002

Fine, Ruth, 1941- National Gallery of Art (U. S.)
Graphicstudio . Washington , 1991. p. cm.
ISBN 0-89468-164-8 DDC 769.9759/65/074753
20
NE538.T35 N37 1991

Fine woodworking. Fine woodworking design
book five . Newtown, Conn. , c1990. 185 p. :
ISBN 0-942391-28-4 : DDC 674/.8 20
NK2408 .F57 1990

Fine woodworking design book five : 259
photographs of the best work in wood : with an
essay by Scott Landis on Northwest
woodworkers. Newtown, Conn. : Taunton Press,
c1990. 185 p. : chiefly col. ill. ; 31 cm. "A Fine
woodworking book"--T.p. verso. "Design in
context--woodworkers of the Northwest, by Scott
Landis" (p. [146]-183). Includes index. ISBN
0-942391-28-4 : DDC 674/.8 20
*1. Furniture - United States - History - 20th century -
Catalogs. 2. Decorative arts - United States - History -
20th century - Catalogs. 3. Wood-carving - United
States - History - 20th century - Catalogs. I. Landis,
Scott. II. Fine woodworking. III. Title: Design book
five. IV. Title: Fine woodworking design book 5.*
NK2408 .F57 1990

Fine woodworking design book 5. Fine
woodworking design book five . Newtown,
Conn. , c1990. 185 p. : ISBN 0-942391-28-4 :
DDC 674/.8 20
NK2408 .F57 1990

Fineberg, Jonathan David. Aycock, Alice.
Complex visions . Mountainville, N.Y. , c1990.
47, [1] p. :
NYPL [3-MGO (Aycock) 91-7401]

FINISHES AND FINISHING - TECHNIQUE.
Marx, Ina Brosseau, 1929- Professional painted
finishes . New York , 1991. p. cm. ISBN
0-8230-4418-1 : DDC 667/.9 20
NK2175 .M37 1991

Finizio, Luigi Paolo. L'astrattismo costruttivo :
suprematismo e costruttivismo / Luigi Paolo
Finizio. Roma : Laterza, 1990. vii, 237 p., [16]
p. of plates : ill. (some col.) ; 24 cm. (Grandi
opere) L'Arte contemporanea Includes bibliographical
references (p. [215]-229) and index. ISBN
88-420-3642-0 : DDC 709/.47/09041 20
*1. Constructivism - Soviet Union. 2. Suprematism in
art. 3. Art, Russian. 4. Art, Modern - 20th century -
Soviet Union. I. Series: Arte contemporanea (Editori
Laterza). II. Title.*
N6988.5.C64 F56 1990

Fink, Lois Marie. American art at the
nineteenth-century Paris Salons / Lois Marie
Fink. Washington, D.C. : National Museum of
American Art, Smithsonian Institution ;
Cambridge ; xxiv, 430 p. : ill. (some col.) ; 26
cm. Includes bibliographical references (p. 410-420)
and index. ISBN 0-521-38499-0 DDC
709/.73/0903407444361 20
*1. Salon (Exhibition : Paris, France). 2. Art, American -
Exhibitions. 3. Art, Modern - 19th century - United
States - Exhibitions. I. Title.*
N6510 .F57 1990 **NYPL [3-MCW 90-11536]**

Finkel, Kenneth. Legacy in light . [Philadelphia,
Pa.] , c1990. 72 p. :
IN PROCESS (ONLINE)
NYPL [MFW+ 91-8029]

**Finland. Central Statistical Office. see Finland.
Tilastokeskus.**

**Finland. Statistikcentralen. see Finland.
Tilastokeskus.**

Finland. Tilastokeskus. Koordinointitoimisto.
Veikkola, Eeva-Sisko. Kulttuurin julkinen

rahoitus . Helsinki , 1989. 51 p. : ISBN
951-47-2866-1 :
NX750.F5 V45 1989

Finland. Ympäristöministeriö. Kautto, Jussi, 1942-
Suomalaista kaupunkiarkkitehtuuria =.
Helsinki , 1990. 233 p. : ISBN 951-9229-63-9
NA9241.F5 K38 1990

Finlands konstindustri . Kruskopf, Erik. Borgå ,
c1989. 268 p. : ISBN 951-0-15964-6
NK1035.F5 K78 1989

Finlands stadsförbund. see **Suomen
kaupunkiliitto.**

Finlay, Ian Hamilton.
Homage to Ian Hamilton Finlay : an exhibition
of works, 14 July-29 Agust 1987 : an essay /
by Yves Abrioux. London : Victoria Miro
Gallery : Coracle Distribution, [1987] 22 p., 22
p. of plates : ill. (chiefly col.) ; 17 cm. Includes
bibliographical references.
*1. Finlay, Ian Hamilton - Exhibitions. I. Abrioux, Yves.
II. Victoria Miro Gallery. III. Coracle Press. IV. Title.*
NYPL [MEMZ 91-2445]

Ian Hamilton Finlay / [Herausgeber, Thomas
Kellein]. [Basel] : Kunsthalle Basel, 1990. [79]
p. : ill. (some col.) ; 31 cm. Catalog of an
exhibition held at the Kunsthalle Basel, Feb. 4-Apr. 16,
1990. Includes bibliographical references.
*1. Finlay, Ian Hamilton - Exhibitions. I. Kellein,
Thomas. II. Kunsthalle Basel. III. Title.*
MLCL 90/00821 (N)
NYPL [MDG+ (Finlay) 91-4829]

FINLAY, IAN HAMILTON - EXHIBITIONS.
Finlay, Ian Hamilton. Homage to Ian Hamilton
Finlay . London [1987] 22 p., 22 p. of plates :
NYPL [MEMZ 91-2445]

Finlay, Ian Hamilton. Ian Hamilton Finlay /.
[Basel] , 1990. [79] p. :
MLCL 90/00821 (N)
NYPL [MDG+ (Finlay) 91-4829]

Finley, Robert J. Atlas of major Texas gas
reservoirs /. Chicago, Ill. , Austin, Tex. , 1989.
1 atlas (ix, 161 p.) :
NYPL [Map Div. 90-11657]

Finn, David, 1921-
Evocations of Four quartets : paintings / by
David Finn. Redding Ridge, CT, U.S.A. :
Black Swan Books, c1990. 96 p. : chiefly col.
ill. ; 29 cm. Thirty-eight paintings accompanied by
quotes from T.S. Eliot's Four quartets. "Published on
the occasion of an exhibition at the Yale Center for
British Art, New Haven, Connecticut, September
22-November 18, 1990"--T.p. verso. ISBN
0-933806-61-2 (cloth) : DDC 759.13 20
*1. Finn, David, 1921-. 2. Eliot, T. S. (Thomas Stearns),
1888-1965. Four quartets - Influence. I. Eliot, T. S.
(Thomas Stearns), 1888-1965. Four quartets. II. Yale
Center for British Art. III. Title.*
ND237.F433 A4 1990

Hunter, Sam, 1923- In the mountains of Japan .
New York, NY [1988?] 288 p. : ISBN
0-89659-949-3 DDC 735/.23/00740952136 19
NB198 .H86 1988
NYPL [3-MGI+ 90-11775]

Morand, Kathleen. Claus Sluter, artist at the
Court of Burgundy /. Austin , 1991. 399 p., 8
p. of plates : ISBN 0-292-71117-4
NYPL [3-MGO (Sluter) 91-6518]

FINN, DAVID, 1921-
Finn, David, 1921- Evocations of Four
quartets . Redding Ridge, CT, U.S.A. , c1990.
96 p. : ISBN 0-933806-61-2 (cloth) : DDC 759.13
20
ND237.F433 A4 1990

Finne, Ferdinand, 1910- Vandrer mot en annen
strand : en reise mellom øyer : en bok om tro
og kunst / Ferdinand Finne. Oslo : Dreyer,
c1990. 187 p. : ill. (some col.) ; 30 cm. ISBN
82-09-10612-0
*1. Finne, Ferdinand, 1910-. 2. Artists - Norway -
Biography. I. Title.*
N7073.F56 A2 1990

FINNE, FERDINAND, 1910-
Finne, Ferdinand, 1910- Vandrer mot en annen
strand . Oslo , c1990. 187 p. : ISBN
82-09-10612-0
N7073.F56 A2 1990

FINNISH ART. see **ART, FINNISH.**

Finnish glass lives 2. Suomen lasi elää 2 =.

[Riihimäki] [1990] 89 p. : ISBN 951-895-209-4
NK5171.F5 S94 1990

Finnish town planning and architecture. Kautto,
Jussi, 1942- Suomalaista kaupunkiarkkitehtuuria
=. Helsinki , 1990. 233 p. : ISBN 951-9229-63-9
NA9241.F5 K38 1990

Finnish wooden church. Pettersson, Lars.
Suomalainen puukirkko =. Helsinki , c1989.
160 p. : ISBN 951-9229-59-0
NA5955.F5 P48 1989

Fino, Lucio. Il vedutismo a Napoli : nella grafica
dal XVII al XIX secolo : con cenni sulla
pittura, l'architettura e le trasformazioni urbane
/ Lucio Fino. Napoli : Grimaldi, 1990. 218 p. :
ill. (some col.) ; 35 cm. Includes bibliographical
references (p. 205-209) and index. DDC
769/.444573//094 20
1. Naples (Italy) in art. I. Title.
NE954.3.I8 F55 1990
NYPL [MDZ+ 91-3596]

Finocchi, Anna. Federico Faruffini : un pittore tra
Romanticismo e Realismo / Anna Finocchi.
[Italy] : Silvana, 1989. 238 p. : ill. (some col.) ;
31 cm. "Errata corrige" slip inserted. Includes
bibliographical references (p. 235-238). Library's copy
lacks errata slip. ISBN 88-366-0268-1
1. Faruffini, Federico, 1831-1869.
NYPL [3-MCF+ F247 91-5543]

Finsen, Hanne.
Hyldest til Fransk Kunst . København, 1967.
115 p. :
NYPL [3-MBH 90-5670]

Wivel, Mikael. Manet . København , 1989. 173
p. : ISBN 87-88692-04-3
ND553.M3 A4 1989

Finsterlin, Hermann, 1887-1973.
FINSTERLIN, HERMANN, 1887-1973.
Finsterlin, Hermann, 1887-1973. [Selections.
Italian & German. 1969.] Hermann Finsterlin .
Firenze , 1969, c1968. 382 p. :
NYPL [3-MQZ (Finsterlin) 90-5737]

[Selections. Italian & German. 1969]
Hermann Finsterlin : idea dell'architettura =
Architektur in seiner Idee / a cura di Franco
Borsi. Firenze : Libreria Editrice Fiorentina,
1969, c1968. 382 p. : ill. (some col.) ; 20 cm.
(L'occhio e le seste . 2) German and Italian.
Bibliography: p. 369-374.
*1. Finsterlin, Hermann, 1887-1973. I. Borsi, Franco. II.
Title.* **NYPL [3-MQZ (Finsterlin) 90-5737]**

Finta, József. A funkció társkeresései,
szerződéseim Budapesttel : akadémiai
székfoglaló, 1986, február 6. / Finta József.
Budapest : Akadémiai Kiadó, c1990. 34 p., [24]
p. of plates : ill. ; 20 cm. (Értekezések,
emlékezések, 0236-6258) Includes bibliographical
references (p. 32-34). ISBN 963-05-5571-9 :
1. Functionalism (Architecture). I. Title. II. Series.
NA682.F8 F5 1990

Fiori ed usignoli miei. De Maria, Nicola, 1954-
Nicola De Maria, fiori ed usignoli miei.
Saarbrücken [1990]. 87 p. : ISBN 3-925303-46-4
NYPL [3-MCF D372 91-5202]

Firenze, frammenti di memoria / a cura di Egidio
Mucci ; introduzione di Franco Cardini.
Firenze : Ponte alle Grazie, c1990. 200 p. : ill. ;
24 cm. Includes bibliographical references.
*1. Decoration and ornament, Architectural - Italy -
Florence. I. Mucci, Egidio.*
NA3552.F57 F56 1990

Firenze restaura : il laboratorio nel suo
quarantennio : guida alla mostra / a cura di
Umberto Baldini e Paolo Dal Poggetto.2. ed.
Firenze : G.C. Sansoni, 1973, c1972. 154 p.,
[168] p. of plates : ill., plans ; 26 cm. "Mostra di
Opere restaurate dalla Soprintendenza alle Gallerie
sotto l'alto patronato del Presidente della Repubblica
Giovanni Leone." Exhibition held March 18-June 4,
1972 at Fortezza da Basso. Bibliography: p. 141-144.
*1. Painting - Italy - Florence - Conservation and
restoration - Exhibition. 2. Art objects - Italy -
Florence - Conservation and restoration - Exhibition. 3.
Art - Conservation and restoration - Exhibitions. I.
Baldini, Umberto, 1893-. II. Dal Poggetto, Paolo. III.
Fortezza da Basso. IV. Soprintendenza alle Gallerie di
Firenze.* **NYPL [3-MBK 90-5749]**

Fireogtyve exlibris med vin-motiver. Rhebergen,
Jan. 24 exlibris med vin-motiver.
Frederikshavn , 1979. 56 p. : ISBN
87-7317-034-8 :
Z994.5.W5 R48 **NYPL [MDVF 81-622]**

Firmo, Walter, 1937- Walter Firmo. Rio de
Janeiro : Dazibao, c1989. [15] p., [46] leaves of
plates : ill. ; 19 cm. (Antologia fotográfica . 1)
Portuguese and English.
1. Firmo, Walter, 1937-. I. Title. II. Series.
NYPL [MFX (Firmo) 91-3319]

FIRMO, WALTER, 1937-
Firmo, Walter, 1937- Walter Firmo. Rio de
Janeiro , c1989. [15] p., [46] leaves of plates :
NYPL [MFX (Firmo) 91-3319]

**First exhibition of oil and water colors by
English painters /** Jordan Art Gallery. Boston :
Jordan, Marsh & Co., 1897. 49 p., [5] leaves of
plates : ill. ; 18 cm.
*1. Painting, English - Massachusetts - Boston -
Exhibitions. 2. Painting, Modern - 19th century -
England - Exhibitions. I. Jordan Art Gallery (Boston,
Mass.).* **NYPL [3-MCT 90-5919]**

The First five years : an exhibition of the
Kaldeweey Press at Harvard University.
Poestenkill, N.Y. : Kaldeweey Press, [1990] 53
p. : col. ill. ; 29 cm. Catalog of an exhibition held at
the Widener Memorial Room Rotunda, Widener
Library, Nov. 28-Dec. 24, 1990. Includes bibliographical
references.
*1. Kaldeweey Press - Exhibitions. I. Harvard University.
Library.* **NYPL [MDTT 91-3883]**

First hundred years. Whitworth Art Gallery. The
Whitworth Art Gallery . Manchester
[England] , 1989. v, 152 p. : ISBN
0-09-032612-6
NYPL [3-MAVZ (Manchester) 90-11602]

First impressions (New York, N.Y.)
Beardsley, John. Pablo Picasso /. New York ,
1991. p. cm. ISBN 0-8109-3713-1 DDC 709/.2 B
20
N6853.P5 B43 1991

Schwartz, Gary, 1940- Rembrandt /. New
York, N.Y. , 1992. p. cm. ISBN 0-8109-3760-3
DDC 759.9492 B 20
N6953.R4 S437 1992

First International Exhibition of Architecture.
Biennale di Venezia (1980). Settore architettura.
The presence of the past . Venice , Milan ,
c1980. 350 p. : ISBN 88-20-80266-X
NYPL [3-MQV 91-420]

First National Bank of Arizona. Metro Phoenix
street atlas / First National Bank of Arizona.
[Phoenix] : The Bank, 1976. 25, [9] p. : chiefly
col. maps ; 27 cm. Cover title.
1. Phoenix Metropolitan Area (Ariz.) - Maps. I. Title.
NYPL [Map Div. 90-5614]

First steps in paint . Robb, Tom. New York ,
1991. p. cm. ISBN 0-87663-619-9 DDC 751.4/2
20
ND1500 .R538 1991

First steps in painting /. Parramón, José María.
[Primeros pasos en pintura. English.] New
York , 1991. p. cm. ISBN 0-8230-1826-1 : DDC
751.4 20
ND1500 .P2913 1991

Fischer, Alfred M. Ernst, Max, 1891-1976. Max
Ernst, druckgraphische Werke und illustrierte
Bücher . Köln , 1990. 312 p. : DDC 769.92 20
NE654.E7 A4 1990

Fischer, Bernard, 1965- Foto . Hannover , c1989.
147, 139 p. : ISBN 3-7716-1504-6
NYPL [MFW 91-7548]

Fischer, Chris. Fra Bartollommeo : master
draughtsman of the high renaissance : a
selection from the Rotterdam albums and
landscape drawings from various collections /
by Chris Fischer. Rotterdam : Museum
Boymans-van Beuningen Rotterdam ; Seattle :
Distribution in U.S.A., University of
Washington Press, c1990. 415 p. : ill. (some
col.) ; 30 cm. Includes bibliographical references (p.
401-410) and index. ISBN 90-6918-070-7 DDC
741.945 20
*1. Bartolomeo, fra, 1472-1517 - Catalogs. I. Museum
Boymans-Van Beuningen. II. Title.*
NC257.B3418 A4 1990

Fischer, Eberhard, 1941- Das Gold in der Kunst
Westafrikas. Zurich , 1981. 58 p. :
NYPL [3-MNO 90-12398]

Fischer, Erik, 1920- Kongelige Kobberstiksamling
(Statens museum for kunst) Von Abildgaard bis
Marstrand . [München] , 1985. 87 p., 114 p. of

plates : DDC 741.9489/1 19
NC274.C67 K66 1985
NYPL [3-MBH 90-12465]

Fischer Fine Art Limited. Classic plastic .
London [1989] 36 p. :
NYPL [3-MNF 91-7530]

**FISCHER, FRANK - ART COLLECTIONS -
EXHIBITIONS.**
Aus einem Guss . Berlin , c1988. 248 p. :
ISBN 3-87584-203-0 DDC
730/.0943/074431554 20
NK8250.A3 P784 1988
NYPL [3-MNK 91-3716]

Fischer, Knut. Beuys, Joseph. Joseph Beuys im
Gespräch mit Knut Fischer und Walter
Smerling. Köln , c1989. 75 p. : ISBN
3-462-01970-8
NYPL [3-MGO (Beuys) 90-2524]

Fischer, Lili, 1947-
Hausgeister : Installationen, Objekte,
Zeichnungen : Lili Fischer [Ausstellung],
Heidelberger Kunstverein, 18.9.-16.10. 1988,
Koblenzer Kunstverein, 22.10.-20.11. 1988.
Heidelberg : Der Kunstverein, 1988. 67 p. :
chiefly ill. ; 30 cm. Edition of 500 copies. Includes
bibliographical references. ISBN 3-926905-02-6 (pbk.)
*1. Fischer, Lili, 1947- - Exhibitions. I. Koblenzer
Kunstverein. II. Title.*
NYPL [3-MGO+ (Fisher) 89-21325]

FISCHER, LILI, 1947- - EXHIBITIONS.
Fischer, Lili, 1947- Hausgeister . Heidelberg ,
1988. 67 p. : ISBN 3-926905-02-6 (pbk.)
NYPL [3-MGO+ (Fisher) 89-21325]

Fischer, R. M., 1947-
R.M. Fischer : new sculpture : February
28-March 23, 1991. New York, N.Y. : Sidney
Janis Gallery, 1991. [20] p. : ill. ; 28 cm.
*1. Fischer, R. M., 1947- - Exhibitions. I. Sidney Janis
Gallery. II. Title.*
NYPL [3-MGO (Fischer) 91-4295]

FISCHER, R. M., 1947- - EXHIBITIONS.
Fischer, R. M., 1947- R.M. Fischer . New
York, N.Y. , 1991. [20] p. :
NYPL [3-MGO (Fischer) 91-4295]

Fischer von Erlach, Johann Bernhard, 1656-1723.
Aurenhammer, Hans. J. B. Fischer von Erlach.
Cambridge, Mass., 1973. 193 p. ISBN
0-674-46988-7 DDC 720/.92/4
NA1011.5.F57 A94 1973b **NYPL [3-MQZ
(Fischer von Erlach) 90-5573]**

**FISCHER VON ERLACH, JOHANN
BERNHARD, 1656-1723.**
Aurenhammer, Hans. J. B. Fischer von Erlach.
Cambridge, Mass., 1973. 193 p. ISBN
0-674-46988-7 DDC 720/.92/4
NA1011.5.F57 A94 1973b **NYPL [3-MQZ
(Fischer von Erlach) 90-5573]**

Fischer, Wolfgang Georg, 1933-
[Gustav Klimt und Emilie Flöge. English]
Klimt and Emilie : a painter and his muse /
Wolfgang Fischer. Woodstock, N.Y. : The
Overlook Press, 1992. p. cm. Translation of:
Gustav Klimt und Emilie Flöge. Includes
bibliographical references and index. ISBN
0-87951-451-5 : DDC 709/.2 B 20
*1. Klimt, Gustav, 1862-1918. 2. Flöge, Emilie,
1874-1952. 3. Wiener Secession. 4. Artists - Austria -
Vienna - Biography. 5. Fashion designers - Austria -
Vienna - Biography. 6. Art, Austrian - Austria - Vienna.
7. Art, Modern - 19th century - Austria - Vienna. 8.
Art, Modern - 20th century - Austria - Vienna. 9.
Vienna (Austria) - Intellectual life. I. Title.*
N6811.5.K55 F513 1992

Fischer, Yona. Léger, Fernand, 1881-1955.
Fernand Léger . Jérusalem , c1989. 212 p. :
ISBN 965-278-059-6 DDC 759.4 20
NC248.L43 A4 1989

Fischl, Eric, 1948-
Eric Fischl : 17 November to 22 December,
1990. New York, N.Y. : Mary Boone Gallery,
1990. 1 v. (unpaged) : chiefly col. ill. ; 34 cm.
Includes bibliographical references and index. ISBN
0-941863-17-4 DDC 759.13 20
*1. Fischl, Eric, 1948- - Exhibitions. I. Mary Boon
Gallary (New York, N.Y.). II. Title.*
ND237.F434 A4 1990

Kincaid, Jamaica. Annie, Gwen, Lilly, Pam, and
Tulip /. New York , 1989. [20] p. : ISBN

0-394-58035-4   DDC 813 20
PR9275.A585 K5633 1989
NYPL [MEMZ+ 91-3772]

Scenes and sequences : recent monotypes by
Eric Fischl. Hanover, NH : Hood Museum of
Art, Dartmouth College ; New York :
Distributed by Harry N. Abrams, 1990. 118 p. :
ill. (some col.) ; 25 x 29 cm. Text by E.L.
Doctorow and others. Exhibition organized by Hood
Museum of Art. Includes bibliographical references.
ISBN 0-944722-04-0 DDC 769.92 20
*1. Fischl, Eric, 1948- - Catalogs. I. Doctorow, E. L.,
1931-. II. Hood Museum of Art. III. Title.*
NE2246.F5 A4 1990
NYPL [MDG (Fischl) 90-12797]

FISCHL, ERIC, 1948- - EXHIBITIONS.
Fischl, Eric, 1948- Eric Fischl . New York,
N.Y. , 1990. 1 v. (unpaged) : ISBN
0-941863-17-4 DDC 759.13 20
ND237.F434 A4 1990

FISCHL, ERIC, 1948- - CATALOGS.
Fischl, Eric, 1948- Scenes and sequences .
Hanover, NH , New York , 1990. 118 p. :
ISBN 0-944722-04-0 DDC 769.92 20
NE2246.F5 A4 1990
NYPL [MDG (Fischl) 90-12797]

Fisette, Jean. Borduas, Paul Emile. [Selections.
1987.] Ecrits /. Montréal, Qué., Canada , 1987-
v. : ISBN 2-7606-0761-5 (v. 1)
NYPL [3-MAS 88-2798]

Fisher, Joel. Ein unwiderruflicher Schritt = It is
an irrevocable action : [Ausstellung, Städtisches
Museum Mönchengladbach, 23. September bis
26. Oktober 1975 : Katalog / Text, Fotos, Joel
Fisher ; Übersetzung der Texte vom Englischen
ins Deutsche, Clara Weyergraf]. [s.l. : s.n.,
1975?] (Mönchengladbach : H. Schlechtriem)
48 p. : ill. ; 19 cm. English and German. "Zur
Eröffnung der Ausstellung Joel Fisher" by J. Cladders
([3] leaves inserted)
*1. Fisher, Joel. 2. Paper work - Exhibitions. I. Cladders,
Johannes. II. Mönchen-Gladbach, Ger. Städtisches
Museum. III. Title. IV. Title: It is an irrevocable action.
V. Title: Ausstellung Joel Fisher.*
N6537.F48 A58
NYPL [3-MCX F532 81-643]

FISHER, JOEL.
Fisher, Joel. Ein unwiderruflicher Schritt =.
[s.l. , 1975?] (Mönchengladbach : H.
Schlechtriem) 48 p. :
N6537.F48 A58
NYPL [3-MCX F532 81-643]

Fisher, Kurt A. (collector) Kurt Fisher collection of
letters and papers related to the history of
Haiti, 1728-1958 [microform] New York, 1976.
14 reels (ca. 2300 items)
NYPL [Sc Micro R-2228]

Fisher, Philip. Making and effacing art : modern
American art in a culture of museums / Philip
Fisher. New York : Oxford University Press,
1991. p. cm. Includes bibliographical references and
index. ISBN 0-19-506046-6 DDC 709/.73/0904 20
*1. Art, American. 2. Art, American. 3. Art, Modern -
20th century - United States. 4. Art museum
architecture - United States - Psychological aspects. 5.
Space (Architecture) - United States - Psychological
aspects. I. Title.*
N6512. .F57 1991

FISHES.
(1991) Troll, Ray, 1954- [Shocking fish tales.]
Ray Troll's shocking fish tales . Anchorage ,
1991. p. cm. ISBN 0-88240-416-4 : DDC
760/.092 20
N6537.T69 A4 1991

FISHES IN ART.
Troll, Ray, 1954- [Shocking fish tales.] Ray
Troll's shocking fish tales . Anchorage , 1991.
p. cm. ISBN 0-88240-416-4 : DDC 760/.092 20
N6537.T69 A4 1991

FISHING.
Troll, Ray, 1954- [Shocking fish tales.] Ray
Troll's shocking fish tales . Anchorage , 1991.
p. cm. ISBN 0-88240-416-4 : DDC 760/.092 20
N6537.T69 A4 1991

**FISHING - CARICATURES AND
CARTOONS.**
Cochran, Bruce. Bass fever . Minocqua, WI ,
c1991. p. cm. ISBN 1-559-71126-4 (hardcover) :
DDC 741.5/973 20
NC1429.C619 A4 1991

FISHING - LITERARY COLLECTIONS.
Traub, Charles, 1945- An angler's album . New
York , 1990. 215 p. : ISBN 0-8478-1256-1 DDC
779/.979912 20
PN6071.F47 T7 1990
NYPL [MFW 91-4963]

FISHING - PICTORIAL WORKS.
Traub, Charles, 1945- An angler's album . New
York , 1990. 215 p. : ISBN 0-8478-1256-1 DDC
779/.979912 20
PN6071.F47 T7 1990
NYPL [MFW 91-4963]

**FISHMAN, JANET - ART COLLECTIONS -
EXHIBITIONS.**
Art in Germany 1909-1936 . Munich , c1990.
271 p. : ISBN 0-944110-02-9 (pbk.) :
N6868 .F74 1990
NYPL [3-MAMG+ 91-4806]

**FISHMAN, MARVIN - ART COLLECTIONS -
EXHIBITIONS.**
Art in Germany 1909-1936 . Munich , c1990.
271 p. : ISBN 0-944110-02-9 (pbk.) :
N6868 .F74 1990
NYPL [3-MAMG+ 91-4806]

Fita, Domènec, 1927-
Fita pintura, 1942-1989. 1. ed. [Girona] :
Diputació de Girona, 1990. 207 p. : ill. (some
col.) ; 31 cm. Catalan and Spanish. ISBN
84-86812-18-6
*1. Fita, Domènec, 1927- - Catalogs. I. Gerona (Spain :
Province). Diputación Provincial. II. Title.*
ND813.F58 A4 1990

FITA, DOMÈNEC, 1927- - CATALOGS.
Fita, Domènec, 1927- Fita pintura, 1942-1989.
[Girona] , 1990. 207 p. : ISBN 84-86812-18-6
ND813.F58 A4 1990

Fita pintura, 1942-1989. Fita, Domènec, 1927-
[Girona] , 1990. 207 p. : ISBN 84-86812-18-6
ND813.F58 A4 1990

Fitoussi, Brigitte, 1956-
[Boutiques. English]
Showrooms / Brigitte Fitoussi ; [English
translation, Lois Nesbitt] New York, NY :
Princeton Architectural Press, 1989. 118 p. :
ill. (some col.) ; 28 cm. (Thematic architecture)
Translation of: Boutiques. Includes bibliographical
references (p. 118). ISBN 0-910413-67-3
*1. Stores, Retail - Design. 2. Store decoration. 3.
Showrooms - Decoration. 4. Showrooms - Design. 5.
Interior architecture - History - 20th century. I. Title.
II. Series.* **NYPL [3-MLO 90-10719]**

Fitzbauer, Erich. Das Südlicht / Erich Fitzbauer ;
Farbholzschnitte, Alfred Pohl. Wien : Edition
Graphischer Zirkel, 1990. [15] p. : col. ill. ; 20
x 25 cm. Limited ed. of 250 copies. Library has copy
no. 202.
I. Pohl, Alfred. II. Title.
NYPL [MEM P748 91-4749]

FitzGerald, Desmond. Vanishing country houses
of Ireland / The Knight of Glin, David J.
Griffin, Nicholas K. Robinson. [Dublin] : Irish
Architectural Archive ; [Leixlip] : Irish
Georgian Society, 1988. vi, 161 p. : ill. ; 29 cm.
Includes bibliographical references and index. ISBN
0-948018-04-6
*1. Country homes - Ireland. I. Griffin, David J. II.
Robinson, Nicholas K. III. Irish Architectural Archive.
IV. Irish Georgian Society. V. Title.*
NYPL [3-MRGF 89-17124]

Fitzpatrick, Kelly (John Kelly)
A symphony of color : the world of Kelly
Fitzpatrick. Montgomery, Ala. : Montgomery
Museum of Fine Arts, 1991. p. cm. Exhibition
held at the Montgomery Museum of Fine Arts,
Montgomery, Alabama, March 10-May 19, 1991 and
the Greenville County Museum of Art, Greenville,
South Carolina, August 27-October 6, 1991. Includes
bibliographical references. ISBN 0-89280-028-3
DDC 759.13 20
*1. Fitzpatrick, Kelly (John Kelly) - Exhibitions. I.
Montgomery Museum of Fine Arts. II. Greenville
County Museum of Art. III. Title.*
ND237.F455 A4 1991

**FITZPATRICK, KELLY (JOHN KELLY) -
EXHIBITIONS.**
Fitzpatrick, Kelly (John Kelly) A symphony of
color . Montgomery, Ala. , 1991. p. cm. ISBN
0-89280-028-3 DDC 759.13 20
ND237.F455 A4 1991

Fitzwilliam Museum.
Gainsborough, English music, and the

Fitzwilliam : a collection of essays and a catalogue of an exhibition of the work of Thomas Gainsborough and of English music in the Fitzwilliam Museum in May 1977. Cambridge : The Museum, 1977. 39 p., [4] p. of plates : ill. ; 25 cm. Includes bibliographical references.
1. Gainsborough, Thomas, 1727-1788 - Exhibitions. 2. Fitzwilliam, Richard Fitzwilliam, 7th Viscount, 1745-1816 - Exhibitions. 3. Music - England - Exhibitions. I. Title.
NYPL [3-MCV G14 90-6810]

Webb, Joseph, 1908-1962. Joseph Webb, 1908-1962 . [Cambridge , 1989] 26 p. : ISBN 0-09-045425-8
NYPL [MDG+ (Webb) 90-11352]

FITZWILLIAM, RICHARD FITZWILLIAM, 7TH VISCOUNT, 1745-1816 - EXHIBITIONS.
Fitzwilliam Museum. Gainsborough, English music, and the Fitzwilliam . Cambridge , 1977. 39 p., [4] p. of plates :
NYPL [3-MCV G14 90-6810]

Fiume, Laura, 1953-
Barletta, Riccardo. Laura Fiume . Bologna [1989] 1 v. (unpaged) : ISBN 88-85638-89-9 DDC 759.5 20
ND623.F558 B37 1989

FIUME, LAURA, 1953- - CRITICISM AND INTERPRETATION.
Barletta, Riccardo. Laura Fiume . Bologna [1989] 1 v. (unpaged) : ISBN 88-85638-89-9 DDC 759.5 20
ND623.F558 B37 1989

Five centuries of artists in Sutton . Beasley, Maureen. Sutton, Surrey , 1989. 144 p. : ISBN 0-907335-19-5 DDC 709/.2/242192 B 20
N6770 .B43 1989

Five contemporary aboriginal artists. On the edge . [Perth, W.A.] , c1989. 64 p. : ISBN 0-7309-0703-1
NYPL [3-MADF+ 90-12876]

Five hundred small houses of the twenties. Smith, Henry Atterbury, b. 1872. [Books of a thousand homes. Volume 1.] 500 small houses of the twenties /. New York , 1990. 312 p. : ISBN 0-486-26300-2 : DDC 728/.37/0222 20
NA7205 .S6525 1990
NYPL [3-MRG 91-6727]

Five years of interior architecture awards. 5 years of interior architecture awards /. Chicago, Ill. , c1985. 104 p. : DDC 729/.09773/1109048 20
NA2850 .A14 1985

Fjell, Kai, 1907- Egeland, Erik. Kai Fjell /. [Oslo] , c1990. 136 p. : ISBN 82-7201-169-7 :
ND773.F53 E35 1990

FJELL, KAI, 1907-
Egeland, Erik. Kai Fjell /. [Oslo] , c1990. 136 p. : ISBN 82-7201-169-7 :
ND773.F53 E35 1990

Flämische Malerei von 1550 bis 1650 /. Mai, Ekkehard. Köln , 1987. 68 p. :
NYPL [3-MCG 90-9224]

FLAGS IN ART.
Mary Emmerling's American country flags /. New York , 1991. p. cm. ISBN 0-517-58366-6 : DDC 929.9/2/0973 20
NK839.E46 A4 1991

Flagstaff House Museum of Tea Ware (Hong Kong) Chinese export porcelain . Hong Kong , 1989. 303 p. : ISBN 962-215-094-2
NYPL [3-MPFF 91-5164]

Flanagan, Barry, 1941-
Barry Flanagan : September 14-October 13, 1990. New York, (N.Y.) : Pace Gallery, c1990. 1 v. (unpaged) : chiefly col. ill. ; 30 cm. ISBN 1-87828-308-1
1. Flanagan, Barry, 1941- - Exhibitions.
NYPL [3-MGO+ (Flanagan) 91-5568]

FLANAGAN, BARRY, 1941- - EXHIBITIONS.
Flanagan, Barry, 1941- Barry Flanagan . New York, (N.Y.) , c1990. 1 v. (unpaged) : ISBN 1-87828-308-1
NYPL [3-MGO+ (Flanagan) 91-5568]

Flandria extra muros.
La Peinture flamande au Prado /. Anvers , Paris , c1989. 318 p. : ISBN 90-6153-199-3 (Fonds Mercator) DDC 759.9493/1/0744641 20
ND669.F5 P43 1989

Flash [sound recording]. Stockholm : Nostalgia, p1984. 1 sound disc : analog, 33 1/3 rpm, stereo. ; 12 in. Brief record. CONTENTS. - Signature/Flash -- Jumpin' at the Woodside -- Miss Annabelle Lee -- St. Louis blues -- Swingminded -- Sweet Georgia Brown -- All of me -- South Rampart Street parade -- Sonny boy -- On the sunny side of the street -- Don't be that way -- Night and day -- Just a dixie -- Swanee River -- Rockin' the rag -- He's the last word.
1. Big band music.
Nostalgia NOST 7655

Flat ornament. Treasury of historic pattern and design / edited by J. Engelhorn. Dover ed. New York : Dover, 1990. 150 p. : all ill. (some col.) ; 31 cm. (Dover pictorial archive series) Reprint. Originally published: Flat ornament. Stuttgart, Germany : Printed for J. Engelhorn ; London : Sold by B.T. Batsford. ISBN 0-486-26274-X DDC 745.4 20
1. Decoration and ornament - Themes, motives. I. Engelhorn, J. II. Title.
NK1175 .F5 1990
NYPL [3-MLD+ 90-11804]

Flatiron : a photographic history of the world's first steel frame skyscraper, 1901-1990 / photographs and commentary collected by Peter Gwillim Kreitler ; foreword by Weston J. Naef. Washington, D.C. : American Institute of Architects Press, [c1990] xiii, 216 p. : ill. (some col.) ; 32 cm. Includes bibliographical references (p. 214-215). ISBN 1-558-35060-8 DDC 779/.47471/074 20
1. Kreitler, Peter Gwillim - Photograph collections. 2. Flatiron Building (New York, N.Y.) - Pictorial works. 3. Photography, Architectural - New York (N.Y.). I. Kreitler, Peter Gwillim.
TR659 .F57 1990 **NYPL [MFW+ 91-5158]**

FLATIRON BUILDING (NEW YORK, N.Y.) - PICTORIAL WORKS.
Flatiron . Washington, D.C. [c1990] xiii, 216 p. : ISBN 1-558-35060-8 DDC 779/.47471/074 20
TR659 .F57 1990 **NYPL [MFW+ 91-5158]**

Flavin, Dan, 1933-
Neue Anwendungen fluoreszierenden Lichts mit Diagrammen, Zeichnungen und Drucken von Dan Flavin : 26.2-16.4.1989, Staatliche Kunsthalle Baden-Baden / [herausgegeben von Jochen Poetter ; Katalog-Redaktion, Jochen Poetter] = New uses for fluorescent light with diagrams, drawings and prints from Dan Flavin : 2/26-4/16/1989, Staatliche Kunsthalle Baden-Baden. [Baden-Baden] : Die Kunsthalle, [1989] 168 p. : ill. (some col.) ; 30 cm. English and German. ISBN 3-89322-156-5
1. Flavin, Dan, 1933- - Exhibitions. I. Poetter, Jochen. II. Staatliche Kunsthalle Baden-Baden. III. Title.
NYPL [3-MCX+ F589 90-12621]

FLAVIN, DAN, 1933- - EXHIBITIONS.
Flavin, Dan, 1933- Neue Anwendungen fluoreszierenden Lichts mit Diagrammen, Zeichnungen und Drucken von Dan Flavin . [Baden-Baden] [1989] 168 p. : ISBN 3-89322-156-5
NYPL [3-MCX+ F589 90-12621]

Flavio Paolucci / Ivo Monighetti, Werner Jehle, Peter F. Althaus. Lugano : G. Casagrande, c1989. 2 v. : ill. (some col.) ; 27 cm. Cover title. Texts in English, German and Italian. Vol. [2]: chiefly col. ill. by Alberto Flammer. Includes bibliographical references (v. [1], p. [77]-[79]). ISBN 88-7795-032-3 DDC 709/.2 20
1. Paolucci, Flavio, 1934- - Criticism and interpretation. 2. Paolucci, Flavio, 1934- - Catalogs. I. Paolucci, Flavio, 1934-. II. Monighetti, Ivo, 1938-.
N7153.P28 F57 1989

Fleischer, Roland E. Ludolf de Jongh (1616-1679) : painter of Rotterdam / Roland E. Fleischer. Doornspijk, The Netherlands : Davaco, c1989. 100 p., [93] p. of plates : ill. (some col.) ; 24 cm. (Ars picturae . no. 1) Includes bibliographical references (p. [87]-96) and index. ISBN 90-70288-53-2 DDC 759.9492 20
1. Jongh, Ludolf de, 1616-1679 - Criticism and interpretation. 2. Painting, Modern - 17th-18th centuries - Netherlands - Rotterdam . I. Jongh, Ludolf de, 1616-1679. II. Title. III. Series.
ND653.J4 F54 1989
NYPL [3-MCH J763 91-6586]

Fleischmann, Benno. Daumier, Honoré, 1808-1879. Honoré Daumier . Wien [1938] xxxxviii p., 196 p. of plates :
NYPL [3-MCO D24 89-27412]

Fleischmann, Kaspar Manuel. Strand, Paul, 1890-1976. Paul Strand /. Zürich, Switzerland , c1987-c1990. 2 v. :
NYPL [MFX (Strand) 91-3461]

FLEISCHMANN, OTTO - ART COLLECTIONS - EXHIBITIONS.
University of Kansas. Museum of Art. Paintings, drawings, and prints of the 19th and 20th centuries. Lawrence [1960] 24 p. DDC 707.4
N5220.F56 **NYPL [3-MAL 90-6052]**

Fleissner, Herbert. (ed) Brauer, Erich, 1929- Brauer. München [1968] c1963. 59 p. DDC 759.36
ND588.B72 F55
NYPL [3-MCK B823 91-396]

Fleming, Gordon H., 1920- Whistler : the man and his work / Gordon Fleming. New York : St. Martin's Press, 1991. p. cm. "A Thomas Dunne book." ISBN 0-312-05995-7 : DDC 760/.092 B 20
1. Whistler, James McNeill, 1834-1903. 2. Artists - United States - Biography. I. Title.
N6537.W4 F57 1991

Fleming, John, 1919-
Honour, Hugh. The Venetian hours of Henry James, Whistler, Sargent /. Boston , c1991. p. ISBN 0-8212-1861-1 DDC 700 20
NX653.V46 H66 1991

Honour, Hugh. The visual arts . New York , 1991. ISBN 0-8109-3913-4 (cloth) DDC 709 20
N5300 .H68 1991

Fleming-Williams, Ian. Constable and his drawings / Ian Fleming-Williams. London : Philip Wilson, 1990. 328 p. : ill. (some col.) ; 30 cm. Includes bibliographical references and index. ISBN 0-85667-380-3 (cased) : DDC 741.942 20
1. Constable, John, 1776-1837. I. Constable, John, 1776-1837. II. Title.
NC242.C5 **NYPL [3-MCV+ C75 91-3316]**

FLEMISH ART. see ART, FLEMISH.

FLEMISH PAINTING. see PAINTING, FLEMISH.

FLEMISH TAPESTRY. see TAPESTRY, FLEMISH.

Flemming, Klaus.
Baukhage, Gerd, 1911- Gerd Baukhage . [Köln] [1989] 114 p. :
MLCM 90/03723 (N)
NYPL [3-MCK B339 91-2508]

Schober, Helmut, 1947- Helmut Schober . München , c1989. 153 p. : ISBN 3-7913-1013-5
NYPL [3-MCK+ S3627 89-26518]

Fletcher, Colin. Sexton, John, 1953- Quiet light /. Boston , c1990. 121 p. : ISBN 0-8212-1775-5 : DDC 779/.092 20
TR654 .S4719 1990
NYPL [MFX+ (Sexton) 90-11257]

Fletcher, Valerie J. Museum of Contemporary Art (Los Angeles, Calif.) The Rita and Taft Schreiber collection /. Los Angeles, Calif. , c1991. 1 v. (unpaged) : ISBN 0-914357-24-7 DDC 709/.04/007479494 20
N6487.L67 L677 1991

Fletcher-Watson, James. The magic of watercolour / James Fletcher-Watson. New York : Dover Publications, 1991. 128 p. : ill. (some col.) ; 29 cm. Reprint. Originally published: London : Batsford, 1987. ISBN 0-486-26776-8 (pbk.) DDC 751.42/2436 20
1. Watercolor painting - Technique. I. Title.
ND2420 .F58 1991

Fleurent, Maurice. Villandry : le jardin du bonheur / Maurice Fleurent ; photographies de l'auteur. Paris : Sous le vent : Stendhal diffusion, c1990. 105 p. : ill. (some col.) ; 23 cm. (Collection L'esprit des lieux) Includes bibliographical references. ISBN 2-85889-052-1
1. Château de Villandry (Villandry, France). 2. Gardens, Renaissance - France - Villandry - Pictorial works. 3. Gardens, French - France - Villandry - Pictorial works. I. Title. II. Series. **NYPL [3-MSK 91-3221]**

Fligny, Laurence. Le mobilier en Picardie : 1200-1700 / par Laurence Fligny. [Paris] : Picard, c1990. 358 p. : ill. (some col.) ; 31 cm. Includes bibliographical references (355-357). ISBN 2-7084-0390-7 : DDC 749.24/26 20
1. Furniture - France - Picardy - History. 2. Furniture, Medieval - France - Picardy. 3. Furniture,

Renaissance - France - Picardy. 4. Furniture, Baroque - France - Picardy. I. Title.
NK2548 .F57 1990
NYPL [3-MOF+ 91-6459]

Flint Institute of Arts. Four painters . Flint, Mich. , c1989. 40 p. : ISBN 0-939896-09-5 (pbk.)
NYPL [MCW 89-24559]

Flint, Mich. Institute of Arts. see Flint Institute of Arts.

FLÖGE, EMILIE, 1874-1952.
Fischer, Wolfgang Georg, 1933- [Gustav Klimt und Emilie Flöge. English.] Klimt and Emilie . Woodstock, N.Y. , 1992. p. cm. ISBN 0-87951-451-5 : DDC 709/.2 B 20
N6811.5.K55 F513 1992

FLOOR PLANS. see ARCHITECTURE, DOMESTIC - DESIGNS AND PLANS.

Flora y vegetación en los tapices de La Seo /.
Bosqued Lacambra, Pilar. Zaragoza , 1989. 123 p. ; ISBN 84-505-8690-9
IN PROCESS (ONLINE)
NYPL [3-MOR+ 90-12501]

FLORAL DECORATION. see FLOWER ARRANGEMENT.

Florea, Vasile. Gheorghe Petrașcu / Vasile Florea ; [translated into English by Andrei Bantaș]. Bucharest : Meridiane Pub. House, 1990. 109 p. : ill. (some col.) ; 33 cm. Includes bibliographical references (p. 99-104). ISBN 973-330-041-1 DDC 759.9498 20
1. Petrașcu, Gheorghe, 1872-1949 - Criticism and interpretation. I. Petrașcu, Gheorghe, 1872-1949. II. Title.
ND933.P4 F55 1990

Florence. Galleria Menghelli. see Galleria Menghelli.

Florence, Gene, 1944-
The collector's encyclopedia of Occupied Japan collectibles : fourth series / by Gene Florence. Paducah, KY : Collector Books, c1990. 127 p. : col. ill. ; 28 cm. ISBN 0-89145-401-2 : DDC 738/.0952/075 20
1. Decorative arts - Japan - Collectors and collecting - Catalogs. 2. Japan - History - Allied occupation, 1945-1952 - Collectibles - Catalogs. I. Title. II. Title: Occupied Japan collectibles.
NK1071 .F583 1990

Elegant glassware of the depression era / by Gene Florence. Rev. 4th ed. Paducah, KY : Collector Books, c1991. 191 p. : col. ill. ; 29 cm. Includes index. ISBN 0-89145-436-5 : DDC 748.2913/075 20
1. Depression glass - Collectors and collecting - Catalogs. I. Title.
NK5439.D44 F563 1991

Florence Griswold Museum. En plein air . East Hampton, N.Y. , c1989. 72 p. : ISBN 0-933793-12-X (pbk.)
NYPL [3-MCW 90-399]

Florence Henri, artist-photographer of the avant-garde /. Du Pont, Diana C., 1953- San Francisco , c1990. 158 p. : ISBN 0-918471-17-6 (softcover) : DDC 779/.092 20
TR647 .H46 1990
NYPL [MFX+ (Henri) 91-4579]

Florence (Italy)
Gruppo Donatello, XXVII edizione . Firenze , 1989. 111, [34] p. :
N6921.F7 G78 1989
NYPL [3-MAMC 90-11322]

FLORENCE (ITALY) - ANTIQUITIES - CATALOGS.
Centro di Firenze restituito . Firenze , c1989. 614 p., 8 p. of plates :
NYPL [3-MAVZ+ (Florence) 90-12442]

FLORENCE (ITALY) - BUILDINGS, STRUCTURES, ETC.
La Chiesa e il Convento di San Marco a Firenze. [Firenze?] , c1989- v. :
NYPL [3-MRBD+ 90-2804]

Il Palazzo Medici Riccardi di Firenze /. Firenze , c1990. 379 p. : ISBN 88-09-20180-9 DDC 725/.17/094551 20
NA7756.F65 P35 1990

Maffei, Gian Luigi. La casa fiorentina nella storia della città dalle origini all'Ottocento /. Venezia , 1990. 383 p. : ISBN 88-317-5346-0
NA9053.B58 M3 1990

Il Palazzo Medici Riccardi di Firenze /. Florence , c1990. x, 379 p. : ISBN 88-09-20180-9
NYPL [3-MQWB+ 91-3377]

FLORENCE (ITALY) - BUILDINGS, STRUCTURES, ETC. - HISTORY.
Centro di Firenze restituito . Firenze , c1989. 614 p., 8 p. of plates :
NYPL [3-MAVZ+ (Florence) 90-12442]

FLORENCE (ITALY) - HISTORY.
Breidecker, Volker. Florenz, oder, "die Rede, die zum Auge spricht" . München , c1990. 446 p., lvi p. of plates : ISBN 3-7705-2600-7
NYPL [3-MAMC 91-6316]

FLORENCE (ITALY) - HISTORY - 1421-1737.
Il Palazzo Medici Riccardi di Firenze /. Firenze , c1990. 379 p. : ISBN 88-09-20180-9 DDC 725/.17/094551 20
NA7756.F65 P35 1990

FLORENCE (ITALY) - INTELLECTUAL LIFE.
Breidecker, Volker. Florenz, oder, "die Rede, die zum Auge spricht" . München , c1990. 446 p., lvi p. of plates : ISBN 3-7705-2600-7
NYPL [3-MAMC 91-6316]

FLORENCE (ITALY) - SOCIAL LIFE AND CUSTOMS.
Breidecker, Volker. Florenz, oder, "die Rede, die zum Auge spricht" . München , c1990. 446 p., lvi p. of plates : ISBN 3-7705-2600-7
NYPL [3-MAMC 91-6316]

Florence. Museo mediceo. see Museo mediceo.

Florenz, oder, "die Rede, die zum Auge spricht" . Breidecker, Volker. München , c1990. 446 p., lvi p. of plates : ISBN 3-7705-2600-7
NYPL [3-MAMC 91-6316]

Flores, Angel, 1900- (tr) Sabartés, Jaime, 1881-1968. Picasso, an intimate portrait. New York [1948] x, 230 p. DDC 927.5
ND553.P5 S315
NYPL [3-MCQ P58 91-6769]

Flores-Antúnez, Ignacio. Arte y artistas : veinte años de periodismo y crítica / Flores-Antúnez. México, D.F. : I. Flores-Antúnez, 1989. 385 p. : ill. (some col.) ; 24 cm. Includes index.
1. Art, Mexican. 2. Art, Modern - 20th century - Mexico. I. Title.
N6555 .F57 1989

Flores d'Arcais, Francesca. Magagnato, Licisco. La pittura a Verona tra Sei e Settecento . [Vicenza] , 1978. 301 p., [68] leaves of plates :
ND621.V6 M32   *NYPL [3-MCE 80-3084]*

Flores, Inés María. 100 artistas del Ecuador /. Quito , 1990. 285 p. : DDC 709/.2/2866 B 20
N6985 .A15 1990

Flores Kaperotxipi, M. Pintores vascos y no vascos / M. Flores Kaperotxipi ; [traducción al Euskera, José Luis Alvarez Emparanza]. San Sebastián : Caja de Ahorros Municipal, c1989. 242 p. ; 28 cm. ISBN 84-7173-139-6
1. Flores Kaperotxipi, M. I. Title.
IN PROCESS (ONLINE)
NYPL [3-MCQ F634 91-4475]

FLORES KAPEROTXIPI, M.
Flores Kaperotxipi, M. Pintores vascos y no vascos /. San Sebastián , c1989. 242 p. ; ISBN 84-7173-139-6
IN PROCESS (ONLINE)
NYPL [3-MCQ F634 91-4475]

Florian, Paul. Betsky, Aaron. Violated perfection . New York , 1990. 208 p. : ISBN 0-8478-1269-3 DDC 724/.6 20
NA680 .B497 1990 *NYPL [3-MQV 91-3682]*

Florida architecture of Addison Mizner /. Mizner, Addison, 1872-1933. Boulder, Colo. , 1991. p. cm. ISBN 1-87865-002-5 : DDC 720/.92 20
NA737.M59 A4 1991

FLORIDA IN ART.
Florida visionaries, 1870-1930 . Gainesville, Fla. , c1989. 80 p. : ISBN 0-8130-0929-4 (pbk.)
NYPL [3-MAMY 90-12386]

FLORIDA RECREATION - GUIDE-BOOKS.
Rand McNally and Company. Rand McNally Florida road atlas and travel guide. St. Petersburg, Fla. , c1991. 1 atlas (102 p.) : ISBN 0-528-90285-7
NYPL [Map Div. 91-72]

Florida road atlas and travel guide. Rand

McNally and Company. Rand McNally Florida road atlas and travel guide. St. Petersburg, Fla. , c1991. 1 atlas (102 p.) : ISBN 0-528-90285-7   *NYPL [Map Div. 91-72]*

FLORIDA - ROAD MAPS.
Rand McNally and Company. Rand McNally Florida road atlas and travel guide. St. Petersburg, Fla. , c1991. 1 atlas (102 p.) : ISBN 0-528-90285-7
NYPL [Map Div. 91-72]

Trakker Maps, Inc. Trakker's state atlas Florida. Miami, Florida , 1990. 1 atlas (56 p.) :
NYPL [Map Div. 90-13045]

A Florida sand dollar book.
Manucy, Albert C. The houses of St. Augustine, 1565-1821 /. Jacksonville , c1992. p. cm. ISBN 0-8130-1103-5 DDC 728/.09759/18 20
NA7238.S27 M3 1992

Florida visionaries, 1870-1930 : February 19-March 26, 1989 / introduction by Ruth K. Beesch ; graduate research assistants Carol Jentsch, E. Michael Whittington ; research intern Blair S. Sands. Gainesville, Fla. : University Presses of Florida, c1989. 80 p. : ill. (some col.) ; 23 cm. At head of title: Florida Arts Celebration, the Gallery Guild, and the University of Florida present ... Catalog of an exhibition held at the University Gallery, College of Fine Arts, University of Florida, Feb. 19-Mar. 26, 1989. Includes bibliographies. ISBN 0-8130-0929-4 (pbk.)
1. University of Florida. University Gallery - Exhibitions. 2. Florida in art. 3. Landscape painting, American - Florida - Exhibitions. 4. Landscape painting - 19th century - Florida - Exhibitions. 5. Landscape painting - 20th century - Florida - Exhibitions. 6. Landscape painters - Florida - Exhibitions. 7. Painting, American - Exhibitions. I. Beesch, Ruth K. (Ruth Konnan), 1958-. II. University of Florida. University Gallery.
NYPL [3-MAMY 90-12386]

Flow blue. Blake, Sylvia Dugger. [Des Moines, c1971] v, [48] p. DDC 738.2
NYPL [3-MPGO 90-6862]

FLOWER ARRANGEMENT - DICTIONARIES.
Gatrell, Anthony. Dictionary of floristry and flower arranging /. London , 1988. 184 p., [2] p. of plates : ISBN 0-7134-5904-2 :
NYPL [MLT 90-12341]

FLOWER ARRANGEMENT, JAPANESE.
Allen, Ellen G. (Ellen Gordon), 1897- Japanese flower arrangement . Rutland, Vt. , 1963, cc1962. 86 p. : *NYPL [3-MLT 90-5857]*

FLOWER DRAWING. see FLOWER PAINTING AND ILLUSTRATION.

FLOWER PAINTING AND ILLUSTRATION.
Tableaux de fleurs du XVIIe siècle . [Brussels] , 1989. 104 p. :   *NYPL [3-MBT 91-5569]*

FLOWER PAINTING AND ILLUSTRATION - EUROPE - EXHIBITIONS.
Symbolique & botanique . Caen [1987] 30, [68] p. :   *NYPL [3-MBT 90-12364]*

FLOWER PAINTING AND ILLUSTRATION - NETHERLANDS - EXHIBITIONS.
Segal, Sam. Flowers and nature . Amstelveen , 1990. 302 p. : ISBN 90-12-06632-8
NYPL [3-MCG+ 91-4196]

FLOWER PAINTING AND ILLUSTRATIONS.
Anderson, Frank J., 1912- A treasury of flowers . Boston , c1990. 175 p. : ISBN 0-8212-1758-5 : DDC 582.13/022/2 20
QK98.3 .A53 1990 *NYPL [MDZ+ 91-6182]*

FLOWER PRINTS. see FLOWERS IN ART.

Flowering in the shadows : women in the history of Chinese and Japanese painting / edited by Marsha Weidner. Honolulu : University of Hawaii Press, c1990. xvi, 315 p. : ill. ; 27 cm. Includes bibliographical references and index. ISBN 0-8248-1149-6 (alk. paper) DDC 759.951/082 20
1. Women painters - China. 2. Women painters - Japan. I. Weidner, Marsha Smith.
ND1040 .F58 1990   *NYPL [MAG 91-5098]*

The flowering of art nouveau graphics /. King, Julia, 1943- London , 1990. 144 p. : ISBN 0-86294-170-9 :   *NYPL [3-MDW 91-3586]*

Flowers. Anderson, Frank J., 1912- A treasury of flowers . Boston , c1990. 175 p. : ISBN 0-8212-1758-5 : DDC 582.13/022/2 20
QK98.3 .A53 1990 *NYPL [MDZ+ 91-6182]*

Flowers . Bukovnik, Gary, 1947- New York , 1990. 119 p. :   ISBN 0-8109-3105-2   DDC 760/.092 20
N6537.B835 A4 1990
NYPL [3-MCX B924 90-11081]

Flowers /. Mapplethorpe, Robert. Boston , c1990. 1 v. (unpaged) :   ISBN 0-8212-1781-X   DDC 779/.34 20
TR724 .M36 1990
NYPL [MFX+ (Mapplethorpe) 91-200]

Flowers . Penn, Irving. New York , c1980. 94 p. :   ISBN 0-517-54074-6 :
SB407 .P44 1980
NYPL [MFX (Penn) 81-867]

Flowers and nature . Segal, Sam. Amstelveen , 1990. 302 p. :   ISBN 90-12-06632-8
NYPL [3-MCG+ 91-4196]

FLOWERS - ARRANGEMENT. see FLOWER ARRANGEMENT.

FLOWERS IN ART.
Hofmann, Richard, of Plauen im Vogtland. Decorative flower and leaf designs /. New York , 1991. p. cm.   ISBN 0-486-26869-1   DDC 745.4 20
NK1560 .H57 1991

La Flor imaginaria . Caracas , 1989. 160 p. :   ISBN 980-255-018-3   DDC 700 20
NX650.F57 F58 1989

Moran, Patricia, 1944- Painting the beauty of flowers with oils /. Cincinnati, Ohio , c1991. p. cm.   ISBN 0-89134-382-2 :   DDC 751.45/434 20
ND1400 .M67 1991

Nonomura, Akira, 1934- Active design . Kyoto, Japan , c1990. 5 v. :   ISBN 4-7636-8071-4 (v. 1) :   DDC 746.6/2 20
NK9502.2.N65 A4 1990

Pike, Joyce, 1929- Painting flowers with Joyce Pike. Cincinnati, Ohio , 1992. p. cm.   ISBN 0-89134-419-5 :   DDC 751.45/434 20
ND1400 .P55 1992

Shapiro, David, 1947- Mondrian flowers . New York , 1991. 79, [1] p. :   ISBN 0-8109-3615-1   DDC 759.9492 20
ND653.M76 S53 1991

FLOWERS IN ART - EXHIBITIONS.
Peters, Anna, 1843-1926. Anna Peters, 1843-1926 . Biberach an der Riss , c1990. 55 p. :   ISBN 3-924392-13-7   DDC 759.3 20
ND588.P467 A4 1990

Flowers of fire. Kakiemon porcelain from the English country house . London , 1989. 64 p. :   ISBN 0-903432-35-8
NYPL [3-MPFK 91-4566]

Flowers of the Yayla . Landreau, Anthony N., 1930- Washington, D.C. , c1983. 108 p. :   DDC 746.1/4/089943 19
TT848 .L372 1983
NYPL [3-MOP+ 90-12467]

FLOWERS, PAINTING OF. see FLOWER PAINTING AND ILLUSTRATION.

FLOWERS - PICTORIAL WORKS.
(1980) Penn, Irving. Flowers . New York , c1980. 94 p. :   ISBN 0-517-54074-6 :
SB407 .P44 1980
NYPL [MFX (Penn) 81-867]

(1990) Mapplethorpe, Robert. Flowers /. Boston , c1990. 1 v. (unpaged) :   ISBN 0-8212-1781-X   DDC 779/.34 20
TR724 .M36 1990
NYPL [MFX+ (Mapplethorpe) 91-200]

Flushing, N. Y. Queens County Art and Cultural Center. see Queens Museum.

Flushing, N. Y. Queens Museum. see Queens Museum.

Flynn (Gallery) Stout, Myron, 1908- Myron Stout /. [New York, N.Y.] , 1990. 64 p. :   ISBN 0-9624258-2-6
NYPL [3-MCX S889 91-6242]

Focarino, Joseph. Holmes, Mary Tavener. Nicolas Lancret, 1690-1743 . New York , 1992. p. cm.   ISBN 0-8109-3559-7   DDC 759.4 20
ND553.L2293 A4 1991

Focillon, Henri, 1881-1943. Giovanni-Battista Piranesi : essai de catalogue raisonné de son œuvre / par Henri Focillon. Paris : Libr. Renouard, H. Laurens, 1918. 74 p. ; 27 cm. Includes index.

1. Piranesi, Giambattista, 1720-1778 - Catalogs. I. Title.
NE2052.5.P5 A4 1918

Focusing on nature . Bloch, E. Maurice. San Marino, Calif. , c1991. p. cm.   ISBN 0-87328-133-0 :   DDC 741.973/074/79493 20
NC790 .B58 1991

Fogg Art Museum.
Cohn, Marjorie B. Wash and gouache . [Cambridge, Mass.] , c1977. 116 p. :   ISBN 0-916724-06-9   DDC 751.4/22
ND2430 .C63   *NYPL [MBO 79-96]*

European paintings before 1900 in the Fogg Art Museum : a summary catalogue including paintings in the Busch-Reisinger Museum / Edgar Peters Bowron. Cambridge : Harvard University Art Museums, c1991. p. cm. Includes bibliographical references and index.   ISBN 0-916724-76-X (hardcover : acid-free paper) :   DDC 759.94/074/7444 20
1. Painting, European - Catalogs. 2. Fogg Art Museum - Catalogs. 3. Busch-Reisinger Museum - Catalogs. 4. Art - Massachusetts - Cambridge - Catalogs. I. Bowron, Edgar Peters. II. Busch-Reisinger Museum. III. Title.
ND450 .F64 1991

FOGG ART MUSEUM - CATALOGS.
Fogg Art Museum. European paintings before 1900 in the Fogg Art Museum . Cambridge , c1991. p. cm.   ISBN 0-916724-76-X (hardcover : acid-free paper) :   DDC 759.94/074/7444 20
ND450 .F64 1991

Foggi, Rossella. Berti, Luciano. Masaccio . Firenze , c1989. 159 p. :   ISBN 88-7737-059-9
NYPL [MCF M39 90-13563]

Fogh, Dorte. Billedkunst : ismer i dansk maleri efter 1870 / Dorte Fogh, Hans Struve, Irene Søndergaard.1. udg. Copenhagen : Gyldendal, 1990. 231 p. : ill. (some col.) ; 26 cm. Includes bibliographical references (p. 225-[227]) and index.   ISBN 87-00-48782-1 :
1. Painting, Danish. 2. Painting, Modern - 19th century - Denmark. 3. Painting, Modern - 20th century - Denmark. I. Struve, Hans. II. Søndergaard, Irene. III. Title.
ND717 .F69 1990

Foire international d'art de Zürich. Forum Internationale Kunstmesse Zürich (1984) Forum Internationale Kunstmesse Zürich =. Zürich [1984] [124] leaves :
NYPL [3-MAL+ 90-11547]

Földes, Mihály. The folk art and customs of a people / Mihály Földes. [Budapest] : Pannonia Press, 1964. 134 p., [12] leaves of plates : ill. ; 17 cm. (New Hungary)   DDC 943.9
1. Folk art - Hungary. 2. Hungary - Social life and customs. I. Title. II. Series.
DB868 .F613   *NYPL [MNE 90-6194]*

Folgen. Lüpertz, Markus. Markus Lüpertz . Berlin , c1989. 1 v. (unpaged) :
N6888.L8 A4 1989

FOLK ARCHITECTURE. see VERNACULAR ARCHITECTURE.

FOLK ART.
Barnard, Nicholas. Living with folk art . Boston , 1991. p.   ISBN 0-8212-1840-9   DDC 745/.089 20
N5313 .B37 1991

The folk art and customs of a people /. Földes, Mihály. [Budapest] , 1964. 134 p., [12] leaves of plates :   DDC 943.9
DB868 .F613   *NYPL [MNE 90-6194]*

FOLK ART - ARKANSAS - HISTORY - 19TH CENTURY.
Bennett, Swannee, 1949- Arkansas made . Fayetteville , c1990-1991. 2 v. :   ISBN 1-557-28138-6 (v. 1 : alk. paper)   DDC 709/.767/09034 20
NK835.A8 B4 1990

FOLK ART - BULGARIA - EXHIBITIONS.
Bulgaria . [Liverpool] , 1989. 79 p. :   ISBN 0-906367-38-7 (pbk.)   DDC 949.770074 20
NYPL [3-MNE+ 90-11535]

FOLK ART - CHILE.
Lago, Tomás. Arte popular chileno /. Santiago de Chile [1985] 136 p. :
NK901 .L33 1985

FOLK ART - COLOMBIA - EXHIBITIONS.
Colombian art in Canada =. Bogotá, Colombia , 1990. 24 p. :   DDC

709/.861/07486148 20
N6675 .C65 1990

FOLK ART - CZECHOSLOVAK - MORAVIA.
Vondrušková, Alena. Tradice lidové tvorby . V Praze , 1988. 191 p. :
NK1035.C92 B649 1988

FOLK ART - CZECHOSLOVAKIA - BOHEMIA.
Vondrušková, Alena. Tradice lidové tvorby . V Praze , 1988. 191 p. :
NK1035.C92 B649 1988

FOLK ART - CZECHOSLOVAKIA - CHEB.
Eger und das Egerland . München , c1988. 671 p. :   ISBN 3-7844-2178-4
NYPL [3-MNE+ 90-597]

FOLK ART - CZECHOSLOVAKIA - CHEB REGION.
Eger und das Egerland . München , c1988. 671 p. :   ISBN 3-7844-2178-4
NYPL [3-MNE+ 90-597]

FOLK ART - DOMINICAN REPUBLIC.
Castillo, José del, 1947- Artesanía dominicana /. Santo Domingo, República Dominicana , 1989. 125 p. :   DDC 745/.097293 20
NK886.D65 C38 1989

FOLK ART - GERMANY (EAST) - MECKLENBURG.
Peesch, Reinhard. Mecklenburgische Volkskunst /. Leipzig , 1988- 280 p. :   ISBN 3-363-00358-7
NYPL [3-MNE+ 89-22898]

FOLK ART - GERMANY - EXHIBITIONS.
Leinweber, Ulf. Karl Rumpf (1885-1968) . [Kassel] , 1989. 621 p. :   ISBN 3-87280-057-4
NK951.R86 A4 1989
NYPL [3-MNE 91-5812]

FOLK ART - GERMANY - INFLUENCE.
Lepovitz, Helena Waddy, 1945- Images of faith . Athens , c1991. xviii, 228 p. :   ISBN 0-8203-1256-8 (alk. paper)   DDC 760/.04482/094336 20
NK5435.G3 L4 1991
NYPL [3-MRY 91-4876]

FOLK ART - GERMANY, WEST - BAVARIA.
Paukner, Josef. Bartholomäus-Schmucker-Heimatmuseum Ruhpolding /. München , c1987. 64 p. :   ISBN 3-7954-0755-9
NK480.R84 P38 1987
NYPL [3-MNE 91-3452]

FOLK ART - HUNGARY.
Földes, Mihály. The folk art and customs of a people /. [Budapest] , 1964. 134 p., [12] leaves of plates :   DDC 943.9
DB868 .F613   *NYPL [MNE 90-6194]*

Folk art in the Soviet Union /. Razina, T. M. (Tat´iana Mikhaĭlovna) New York , Leningrad , 1990. 459 p. :   ISBN 0-8109-0944-8   DDC 745/.0947 19
NK975 .R35 1987   NYPL [3-MNE 90-11088]

FOLK ART - INDIA.
Jayakar, Pupul. The earth mother /. New Delhi, India , New York, N.Y., U. S. A. , 1989. 229 p., [32] p. of plates :   ISBN 0-14-012352-0 :   DDC 704.9/4894/0954 20
NX576.A1 J38 1989
NYPL [3-MAF 91-3706]

FOLK ART - INDIA - ASSAM.
Datta, Birendranātha. Folk toys of Assam /. Guwahati, Assam , 1986. 40 p., [15] p. of plates :   DDC 745.592 20
NK9509.65.I52 A84 1986
NYPL [3-MNE 91-6912]

FOLK ART - INDIA - MADHUBANI - THEMES, MOTIVES.
Thakur, Upendra. Madhubani painting /. New Delhi [1981 or 1982] xii, 158 p., [36] p. of plates :   ISBN 0-391-02411-6 :
NK1476.M34 T47 1981
NYPL [3-MAF 90-5433]

FOLK ART - LITHUANIA.
Galaunė, Paulius, 1890- Lietuvių liaudies menas . Vilnius , 1988. 301 p., [42] leaves of plates :   ISBN 5-420-00625-1 :
NK976.L5 G3 1988

FOLK ART - MEXICO.
Kaplan, Flora S. Urban potters of La Luz . Carbondale , c1992. p. cm.   ISBN 0-8093-1730-3   DDC 738.3/0972/48 20
NK4031 .K3 1992

Oettinger, Marion. Folk treasures of Mexico .
New York , 1990. 223 p. : ISBN 0-8109-1182-5 :
DDC 745/.0972/07473 20
NK844 .O35 1990
                    NYPL [3-MNE 90-11777]

Ortiz Angulo, Ana. Definición y clasificación
del arte popular /. México, D.F. , 1990. 150
p. : ISBN 968-606-893-7 DDC 709/.72 20
NK844 .O78 1990

Sayer, Chloë. Arts and crafts of Mexico /.
London , 1990. 160 p. : ISBN 0-87701-781-6 :
                    NYPL [3-MNE 91-4573]

FOLK ART - MEXICO - EXHIBITIONS.
San Antonio Museum Association. Con cariño,
Mexican folk art . [San Antonio] [1986] 69 p. :
DDC 745/.0972/0740164351 19
NK844 .S26 1986   NYPL [3-MNE 88-2957]

**FOLK ART - MEXICO - MICHOACÁN DE
OCAMPO.**
El Quehacer de un pueblo . Morelia,
Michoacán , 1986. 183, [9] p. : ISBN
968-667-045-9 DDC 745/.0972/37 20
NK845.M53 Q44 1986

FOLK ART - NEW MEXICO - EXHIBITIONS.
Kalb, Laurie Beth. Santos statues & sculpture .
Los Angeles , c1988. [24] p., [2] leaves of
plates (some folded) : DDC 704.9/482 19
NK9712 .K35 1988
                    NYPL [3-MNE 90-12649]

**FOLK ART - NEW YORK (N.Y.) -
CATALOGS.**
Warren, Elizabeth V. Expressions of a new
spirit . New York , c1989. 168 p. : ISBN
0-912161-01-9 DDC 745/.0973/0747471 20
NK805 .W33 1989
                    NYPL [3-MNE 90-12958]

**FOLK ART - NEW YORK (N.Y.) -
EXHIBITIONS.**
Folklore! . New York, N.Y. [1988?] 31 p. :
                    NYPL [3-MNE 90-11620]

FOLK ART - NORWAY - BUSKERUD FYLKE.
Drammens museum. By og bygd i Buskerud.
[Drammen] [1990] 36 p. :
NK992.B8 D73 1990

Folk art of primitive peoples . Bossert, Helmuth
Theodor, 1889-1961. [Ornamente der Völker.
English.] New York [1955] 15 p., 40 leaves of
plates : DDC 745
NK1177 .B612   NYPL [3-MNE+ 91-5923]

Folk art of the Soviet Union : reflections of a
rich cultural diversity of the fifteen republics /
designed and edited by Martha Longenecker ;
photography by Lynton Gardiner. San Diego,
Calif. : Mingei International Museum of World
Folk Art, c1989. 167 p. : ill. ; 28 cm. ISBN
0-914155-06-7
*1. Folk art - Soviet Union - Exhibitions. I.
Longenecker, Martha. II. Mingei International Museum
of World Folk Art.*   *NYPL [3-MNE 90-13387]*

**FOLK ART - PERU - HISTORY - 20TH
CENTURY.**
Salas, María Angélica. Mates de Cochas . Lima,
Perú , 1987. 166 p. :
NK6075 .S25 1987

FOLK ART - PORTUGAL - ESTREMOZ.
Vermelho, Joaquim. Barros de Estremoz .
[Portugal] , 1990. 145 p. : DDC 738.8/2/0946952
20
NK4660 .V47 1990

FOLK ART - SOVIET UNION.
Bobrinskoĭ, Aleksei Alekseevich, graf.
Narodnyĭa russkiĭa derevi͡annyĭa izdi͡eliĭa
predmety domashni͡ago, khozi͡aĭstvennago i
otchasti tserkovnago obikhoda. Moskva , 1910.
7, 18, [7, 5, 6, 5, 5, 7, 163 leaves of plates :
                    *NYPL [Slav. Reserve 90-4456 no. 37
                              (Bates)]*

Chekalov, A. K. (Aleksandr Kalimovich),
1928-1970. Bäuerliche russische Holzskulptur.
Dresden [c1967] 110 p.
NK9756.A1 C4515 NYPL [3-MOC 90-5991]

Razina, T. M. (Tat´i͡ana Mikhaĭlovna) Folk art
in the Soviet Union /. New York , Leningrad ,
1990. 459 p. : ISBN 0-8109-0944-8 DDC
745/.0947 19
NK975 .R35 1987 NYPL [3-MNE 90-11088]

**FOLK ART - SOVIET UNION -
EXHIBITIONS.**

Folk art of the Soviet Union . San Diego,
Calif. , c1989. 167 p. : ISBN 0-914155-06-7
                    NYPL [3-MNE 90-13387]

**FOLK ART - SWITZERLAND - FRIBOURG
(CANTON)**
Spuren, die ins Freie führen . [Kiesen,
Switzerland] , 1986. 40 p. :
                    NYPL [3-MAMZ 90-10960]

FOLK ART - UKRAINE - EXHIBITIONS.
Ukrainian Museum (New York, N.Y.)
Ukrainian folk art /. New York , c1984. [28]
p. ;   *NYPL [*QGA 89-3075 (1984)]*

FOLK ART - UNITED STATES.
Lavitt, Wendy. Animals in American folk art /.
New York , 1990. x, 244 p. : ISBN
0-394-57156-8 : DDC 745/.0973 20
NK805 .L38 1990
                    NYPL [3-MAMT 90-13276]

Linsley, Leslie. The hooked rug . New York ,
1991. p. cm. ISBN 0-517-58102-7 : DDC
746.7/4/0973 20
NK9112 .L56 1991

Mary Emmerling's American country flags /.
New York , 1991. p. cm. ISBN 0-517-58366-6 :
DDC 929.9/2/0973 20
NK839.E46 A4 1991

Schaffner, Cynthia V. A. Discovering American
folk art /. New York, N.Y. , 1991. p. cm.
ISBN 0-8109-3206-7 DDC 745/.0973 20
NK805 .S28 1991

FOLK ART - UNITED STATES - CATALOGS.
Warren, Elizabeth V. Expressions of a new
spirit . New York , c1989. 168 p. : ISBN
0-912161-01-9 DDC 745/.0973/0747471 20
NK805 .W33 1989
                    NYPL [3-MNE 90-12958]

**FOLK ART - UNITED STATES - HISTORY -
19TH CENTURY - EXHIBITIONS.**
The Fine art of folk art /. [Cincinnati] , c1990.
43 p. : ISBN 0-931537-12-6 DDC
709/.73/07477178 20
NK806 .F56 1990

**FOLK ART - UNITED STATES - HISTORY -
20TH CENTURY - DICTIONARIES.**
Rosenak, Chuck. Museum of American Folk
Art encyclopedia of twentieth-century American
folk art and artists /. New York , c1990. 416
p. : ISBN 1-558-59041-2 DDC 709/.2/2730904 B
20
NK808 .R6 1990   NYPL [MAMT 91-5742]

**FOLK ART - UNITED STATES - HISTORY -
20TH CENTURY - EXHIBITIONS.**
The Fine art of folk art /. [Cincinnati] , c1990.
43 p. : ISBN 0-931537-12-6 DDC
709/.73/07477178 20
NK806 .F56 1990

**FOLK ART - VENEZUELA - HISTORY -
20TH CENTURY - CATALOGS.**
Raúl Santana y su museo criollo. [Caracas]
[198-?] 1 v. (unpaged) :
NK922 .R38 1980z

Folk art weather vanes . Nelson, John A., 1935-
Harrisburg, PA , c1990. 160 p. : ISBN
0-8117-2406-9 : DDC 736/.4 20
TT200 .N36 1990 NYPL [3-MNE 91-3290]

**FOLK ARTISTS - UNITED STATES -
BIOGRAPHY - DICTIONARIES.**
Rosenak, Chuck. Museum of American Folk
Art encyclopedia of twentieth-century American
folk art and artists /. New York , c1990. 416
p. : ISBN 1-558-59041-2 DDC 709/.2/2730904 B
20
NK808 .R6 1990   NYPL [MAMT 91-5742]

FOLK COSTUME. see COSTUME.

FOLK DANCING - WEST INDIES.
Gilbert, Will G. Rumbamuziek [microform].
s-Gravenhage [1947?] 119 p.
                    NYPL [Sc Micro R-5903 no.2]

FOLK MUSIC - JAMAICA.
Jekyll, Walter. (ed) Jamaican song and story.
New York [1966] xv, 288 p.
                    NYPL [JMD 74-129]

**FOLK MUSIC - WEST INDIES - HISTORY
AND CRITICISM.**
Gilbert, Will G. Rumbamuziek [microform].
s-Gravenhage [1947?] 119 p.
                    NYPL [Sc Micro R-5903 no.2]

FOLK-SONGS, ENGLISH - JAMAICA.
Jekyll, Walter. (ed) Jamaican song and story.
New York [1966] xv, 288 p.
                    NYPL [JMD 74-129]

Folk toys of Assam /. Datta, Birendranātha.
Guwahati, Assam , 1986. 40 p., [15] p. of
plates : DDC 745.592 20
NK9509.65.I52 A84 1986
                    NYPL [3-MNE 91-6912]

Folk treasures of Mexico . Oettinger, Marion.
New York , 1990. 223 p. : ISBN 0-8109-1182-5 :
DDC 745/.0972/07473 20
NK844 .O35 1990
                    NYPL [3-MNE 90-11777]

Folklife in Louisiana photography . De Caro, F.
A. Baton Rouge , c1990. viii, 213 p. : ISBN
0-8071-1633-5 (cloth : alk. paper) : DDC
398/.09763 20
GR110.L5 D4 1990   NYPL [MFW 91-6803]

Folklore! : traditional crafts from Cuba, the
Dominican Republic & Puerto Rico made in
New York : December 16, 1988-February 19,
1989, a presentation of the Association of
Hispanic Arts, Inc. in collaboration with El
Museo del Barrio / [text, Ana Negrón ;
translation, Alma Rodríguez]. New York, N.Y. :
The Association, [1988?] 31 p. : ill. ; 25 cm.
English and Spanish.
*1. Folk art - New York (N.Y.) - Exhibitions. I. Negrón,
Ana. II. Association of Hispanic Arts (New York,
N.Y.).*   *NYPL [3-MNE 90-11620]*

FOLKLORE - JAMAICA.
Jekyll, Walter. (ed) Jamaican song and story.
New York [1966] xv, 288 p.
                    NYPL [JMD 74-129]

**FOLKLORE - LOUISIANA - PICTORIAL
WORKS - EXHIBITIONS.**
De Caro, F. A. Folklife in Louisiana
photography . Baton Rouge , c1990. viii, 213
p. : ISBN 0-8071-1633-5 (cloth : alk. paper) : DDC
398/.09763 20
GR110.L5 D4 1990   NYPL [MFW 91-6803]

**FOLKLORE - YUGOSLAVIA - KUPINEC
(CROATIA)**
Bakrač, Ivanka. Narodna nošnja Kupinca .
Zagreb , 1986. 69 p., [28] p. of plates : ISBN
86-80825-06-9
NK4771.Y82 K863 1986

Folkwang series.
Biermann, Aenne, 1898-1933. Aenne
Biermann . London , c1988. 141 p. : ISBN
1-85378-004-9
TR654 .B54 1988
                    NYPL [MFX (Biermann) 91-8099]

Folkwangschule für Gestaltung.
Design--Schnittpunkt--Essen 1949-1989 . Berlin
[1990] 368 p. : ISBN 3-433-02539-8
                    NYPL [3-MNF 91-7403]

**FOLLES (ARCHITECTURE) - GREAT
BRITAIN.**
Stamp, Gavin. Telephone boxes /. London ,
1989. 106 p. : ISBN 0-7011-3366-X (pbk.) DDC
363.6/9 19   *NYPL [3-MQWK 90-12389]*

**FOLLIES (ARCHITECTURE) - FRANCE -
PARIS.**
Portzamparc, Christian de, 1944- La Cité de la
musique . Seyssel, France [1986] 47 p. : ISBN
2-903528-76-4 : DDC 725/.81/0924 19
*NA1053.P655 A4 1986   NYPL [3-MQZ+
                              (Portzamparc) 90-12557]*

Folly & vice : the art of satire and social
criticism : exhibition tour, Bolton Museum and
Art Gallery, 16 December 1989-3 February
1990; York City Art Gallery, 10 February-18
March; Exeter, Royal Albert Memorial
Museum, 31 March-6 May; Birmingham
Museum and Art Gallery, 12 May-24 June.
London : South Bank Center, c1989. 63 p. :
ill. ; 28 cm. Addendum and erratum slip inserted.
ISBN 1-85332-053-6 DDC 741.5/94/07442 20
*1. Wit and humor, Pictorial - Exhibitions. I. Bolton
Museum and Art Gallery. II. Title: Folly and vice.*
NC1312.G7 B664 1989

Folly and vice. Folly & vice . London , c1989. 63
p. : ISBN 1-85332-053-6 DDC 741.5/94/07442 20
NC1312.G7 B664 1989

Folon and Topor. Folon, Jean Michel. [Chicago?,
1972] [16] p.   *NYPL [3-MCN 90-6752]*

Folon, Jean Michel.
Folon and Topor. [Chicago?, 1972] [16] p.

chiefly illus. 21 cm. Cover title. Exhibition held at The Arts Club of Chicago, April 4-May 11, 1972; Museum of Art, University of Iowa, July 3-August 15, 1972; and University Gallery, University of Minnesota, Sept. 1-Sept. 30, 1972.
1. Folon, Jean Michel - Exhibitions. 2. Topor, Roland, 1938- - Exhibitions. I. Topor, Roland, 1938-. II. Arts Club of Chicago. III. University of Iowa. Museum of Art. IV. University of Minnesota. University Gallery. V. Title. **NYPL [3-MCN 90-6752]**

FOLON, JEAN MICHEL - EXHIBITIONS.
Folon, Jean Michel. Folon and Topor. [Chicago?, 1972] [16] p.
NYPL [3-MCN 90-6752]

Fomento Cultural Banamex. Mogilner, Mark. Edificaciones del Banco Nacional de México. México , 1988. 191 p. : ISBN 968-7009-18-7 DDC 725/.24/0972 20
NA6245.M6 M64 1988

Fon Klement /. Klement, Fon, 1930- Venlo, Nederland , c1990. 136 p. : ISBN 90-6216-195-2 :
N6953.K48 A4 1990

Fonatti, Franco, 1942-
Architektur als Erkenntnis = Architettura come cognizione / Franco Fonatti & Helmut Hempel. Wien : Edition Tusch, c1989. 189 p. : ill. (some col.) ; 23 cm.
1. Fonatti, Franco, 1942- - Catalogs. 2. Architecture, Modern - 20th century - Italy - Catalogs. I. Hempel, Helmut, 1949-. II. Title. III. Title: Architettura come cognizione.
NA1123.F59 A4 1989

FONATTI, FRANCO, 1942- - CATALOGS.
Fonatti, Franco, 1942- Architektur als Erkenntnis =. Wien , c1989. 189 p. :
NA1123.F59 A4 1989

Fondation Alfred et Eugénie Baur-Duret. see Collections Baur.

FONDATION CARTIER (JOUY-EN-JOSAS, FRANCE)
Sur les murs. L'Art fun, ou, L'enfance de l'art. Ateliers en liberté. Jouy-en-Josas [France] [1986] 77 p. : ISBN 2-86925-004-5
N6488.F8 J687 1986
NYPL [3-MAL+ 90-10669]

Fondation Custodia.
Eloge de la navigation hollandaise au XVIIe siècle . Paris , 1989. xix, 181 p., [150] p. of plates : **NYPL [3-MAME 91-7020]**

Le héraut du dix-septième siècle : dessins et gravures de Jacques de Gheyn II et III de la Fondation Custodia, Collection Frits Lugt. Paris : Institut néerlandais, 1985. xi, 153 p., 80 p. of plates : ill. ; 26 cm. "Le catalogue a été établi par Carlos van Hasselt ... et par Mària van Berge-Gerbaud." Catalog of an exhibition held May 9 to June 16, 1985 at the Institut néerlandais. Includes bibliographical references (p. 139-153) and index.
1. Gheyn, Jacob de, 1565-1629 - Exhibitions. 2. Gheyn, Jacquesde, 1595-1641 - Exhibitions. 3. Lugt, Frits, 1884-1970 - Art collections - Exhibitions. 4. Engraving - Private collections - France - Paris - Exhibitions. 5. Fondation Custodia - Exhibitions. I. Gheyn, Jacob de, 1565-1629. II. Gheyn, Jacques de, 1595-1641. III. Berge-Gerbaud, Mària van. V. Institut néerlandais (Paris, France). VI. Title. VII. Title: Héraut du 17. siècle.
NE670.G74 A4 1985

Quimper, France. Musée des beaux-arts. Tableaux flamands et hollandais du Musée des beaux-arts de Quimper. Paris , Quimper , 1987. xxxiv, 101 p. : ISBN 2-906739-10-3 DDC 759.9492/074/44361 20
ND636 .Q5 1987

FONDATION CUSTODIA - EXHIBITIONS.
Fondation Custodia. Le héraut du dix-septième siècle . Paris , 1985. xi, 153 p., 80 p. of plates :
NE670.G74 A4 1985

Fondation de Coubertin. Rinuy, Paul-Louis. Pierres et marbres de Joseph Bernard /. Saint-Rémy-lès-Chevreuse , 1989. 95 p. : ISBN 2-908115-04-2
NYPL [3-MGO (Bernard) 91-5897]

Fondation de l'Hermitage. Brianchon, Maurice, 1899-1979. Maurice Brianchon, 1899-1979 . Lausanne , c1989. 201 p. :
IN PROCESS (ONLINE)
NYPL [3-MCO B85 91-4217]

Fondation Gottfried Keller. Landolt, Hanspeter.

Gottfried Keller-Stiftung . Bern , c1990. 627 p. : ISBN 3-7165-0696-6
N5279.2.G68 L3 1990
NYPL [3-MAK 91-4989]

Fondation Jean-Louis Prevost.
Mille objets pour Genève, un patrimoine enrichi . Genève , c1989. 213 p. : ISBN 2-8306-0055-X
NYPL [3-MAVZ+ (Geneva) 90-12623]

FONDATION JEAN-LOUIS PREVOST - CATALOGS.
Mille objets pour Genève, un patrimoine enrichi . Genève , c1989. 213 p. : ISBN 2-8306-0055-X
NYPL [3-MAVZ+ (Geneva) 90-12623]

Fondation Jos Albert. Roberts-Jones, Philippe. Jos Albert /. Bruxelles [1986] 154 p. : DDC 759.9493 20
ND673.A35 R6 1986

Fondation Le Corbusier.
Drawings from the Le Corbusier archive / Fondation Le Corbusier in Paris ; guest-edited by Alexander Tzonis. London : Garland Architectural Archives ; New York : Distributed in the U. S.A. by St Martin's Press, c1986. 88 p. : ill. ; 28 cm. (Architectural design profile, 0003-8504 . 60) Includes bibliographical references. DDC 720/.22/22 20
1. Le Corbusier, 1887-1965 - Catalogs. 2. Architectural drawing - 20th century - France - Catalogs. 3. Fondation Le Corbusier - Catalogs. I. Le Corbusier, 1887-1965. II. Tzonis, Alexander. III. Title. IV. Series.
NA2707.L4 A4 1986

FONDATION LE CORBUSIER - CATALOGS.
Fondation Le Corbusier. Drawings from the Le Corbusier archive /. London , New York , c1986. 88 p. : DDC 720/.22/22 20
NA2707.L4 A4 1986

Fondation Maeght.
Hartung, Hans, 1904- Hartung . Saint-Paul [1971] [12] p. : DDC 759.3
ND588.H34 F65
NYPL [3-MCK H336 90-6261]

L'œuvre ultime de Cézanne à Dubuffet . Saint-Paul , c1989. 269 p. : ISBN 2-900923-01-60 DDC 709/.04/007444941 20
N6757 .O43 1989

Miró, Joan, 1893- Joan Miró . Saint-Paul , c19. 205 p. : ISBN 2-900923-01-87 DDC 759.6 20
N7113.M54 A4 1990

Miró, Joan, 1893- Joan Miro, Skulpturen /. München , c1990. 246, [1] p. : ISBN 3-7774-5300-5 DDC 730/.92 20
NB813.M5 A4 1990

L'œuvre ultime de Cézanne à Dubuffet . Saint-Paul , 1989. 269 p. :
NYPL [3-MC 91-3351]

Fondation nationale de la photographie (France)
Weiss, Sabine, 1924- Sabine Weiss, intimes convictions /. Paris , c1989. 163 p. : ISBN 2-85949-091-4
TR654 .W416 1989
NYPL [MFX+ (Weiss) 91-5841]

Fondation Pierre-Gianadda.
Botero, Fernando, 1932- Botero . Martigny , c1990. 139 p. :
NYPL [3-MCZ B74 91-4899]

Claudel, Camille, 1864-1943. C. Claudel . Martigny, Suisse , c1990. 167 p. : DDC 730/.92 20
NB553.C44 A4 1990b

Claudel, Camille, 1864-1943. C. Claudel . Martigny, Suisse , c1990. 167 p. :
NYPL [3-MGO (Claudel) 91-7335]

Erni, Hans, 1909- Erni, vie et mythologie . Martigny [1989] 159 p. :
NYPL [3-MCZ E71 89-27325]

Modigliani, Amedeo, 1884-1920. Modigliani . Martigny , c1990. 263 p. :
NYPL [3-MCF M69 90-11614]

Modigliani, Amedeo, 1884-1920. Modigliani . Martigny , 1990. 263 p. : DDC 709/.2 20
N6923.M55 A4 1990a

Moore, Henry, 1898-1986. Henry Moore . Martigny , Milano , c1990. 319 p. :
NYPL [3-MGO (Moore) 90-12634]

Soutter, Louis, 1871-1942. Louis Soutter .

Martigny [1990] 199 p. :
NYPL [3-MCZ S728 91-4290]

Fondation pour l'architecture (Brussels, Belgium)
Louis Herman de Koninck, architecte des années modernes =. Bruxelles , 1989. 284 p. : ISBN 2-87143-066-7
IN PROCESS (ONLINE)
NYPL [3-MQZ+ (Koninck) 91-4894]

Maisons sur l'île d'Ibiza. Bruxelles , 1990. 127 p. : ISBN 2-87143-072-6
NA7386.I25 M35 1990

Fondation Singer-Polignac. Barrière, C. L'art pariétal de Rouffignac . Paris , 1982. 205 p., [4] folded leaves of plates : ISBN 2-900927-10-2 DDC 709/.01/12094472 19
GN772.22.F7 B343 1982
NYPL [3-MADF+ 91-6417]

Fondazione Antonio Mazzotta. Warhol, Andy, 1928- Le cento immagini di Andy Warhol . Milano , c1989. 116 p. : ISBN 88-20-20906-3
NYPL [3-MCX W27 90-11112]

Fondazione Cagli.
Cagli, Corrado, 1910- La Fondazione Cagli per Firenze . [Florence] , c1979. 77 p., [183] p. of plates : **NYPL [3-MCF C125 90-5873]**

Cagli, Corrado, 1910- La Fondazione Cagli per Firenze . [Florence] , c1979. 77 p., [183] p. of plates : **NYPL [3-MCF C125 90-5873]**

FONDAZIONE CAGLI - EXHIBITIONS.
Cagli, Corrado, 1910- La Fondazione Cagli per Firenze . [Florence] , c1979. 77 p., [183] p. of plates : **NYPL [3-MCF C125 90-5873]**

La Fondazione Cagli per Firenze . Cagli, Corrado, 1910- [Florence] , c1979. 77 p., [183] p. of plates : **NYPL [3-MCF C125 90-5873]**

Fondazione "Giorgio Cini."
Mondrian e De Stijl . Milano , c1990. 273 p. : ISBN 88-435-3172-7
NYPL [3-MCH M741 91-6318]

Tiziano e la silografia veneziana del Cinquecento /. Vicenza , 1976. xviii, 166 p., [71] leaves of plates :
NE1152.5.T59 T58
NYPL [MDG+ (Titian) 81-1039]

Fondazione Lerici. Civiche raccolte numismatiche di Milano. Gli Etruschi e Cerveteri . Milano , c1980. 267 p. : DDC 937/.5 19
DG70.C12 E88 1980
NYPL [3-MPEK 89-13643]

FONDAZIONE LERICI.
Civiche raccolte numismatiche di Milano. Gli Etruschi e Cerveteri . Milano , c1980. 267 p. : DDC 937/.5 19
DG70.C12 E88 1980
NYPL [3-MPEK 89-13643]

Fondazione Magnani Rocca.
Capolavori dalle collezioni della Fondazione Magnani Rocca / a cura di Simona Tosini Pizzetti. Bologna : Nuova Alfa, 1990. xxxi, 131 p. : col. ill. ; 23 cm. Includes bibliographical references (p. 125) and index. ISBN 88-7779-116-0
1. Fondazione Magnani Rocca - Catalogs. 2. Art - Private collections - Italy - Parma - Catalogs. 3. Art - Italy - Parma - Catalogs. I. Tosini Pizzetti, Simona. II. Title. **NYPL [MAVZ (Parma, Italy) 91-6194]**

FONDAZIONE MAGNANI ROCCA - CATALOGS.
Fondazione Magnani Rocca. Capolavori dalle collezioni della Fondazione Magnani Rocca /. Bologna , 1990. xxxi, 131 p. : ISBN 88-7779-116-0
NYPL [MAVZ (Parma, Italy) 91-6194]

Fondazione Scientifica Querini Stampalia.
Davanzo Poli, Doretta. Tessuti . Venezia , 1987. [30] p. : **NYPL [3-MON+ 90-10944]**

Fotografie di Ikona Gallery . Venezia , 1989. 54 p. : **NYPL [3-MFW+ 91-7282]**

I Querini Stampalia . Venezia , 1987. 255 p. : **NYPL [3-MAX+ (Querini Stampalia) 90-12441]**

FONDAZIONE SCIENTIFICA QUERINI STAMPALIA - CATALOGS.
Davanzo Poli, Doretta. Tessuti . Venezia , 1987. [30] p. : **NYPL [3-MON+ 90-10944]**

Fontaine, Isabelle Monod - see Monod-Fontaine, Isabelle.

Fontaine, Pierre François Léonard, 1762-1853.
Percier,Charles, 1764-1838. [Recueil de décorations intérieures. English.] Empire stylebook of interior design . New York , 1991. p. cm.   ISBN 0-486-26754-7 DDC 747.24/09/034 20
NK1449.A1 P4713 1991

Fontana, Franco, 1933- Franco Fontana : kaleidoscope / con un saggio di Franco Lefèvre ; presentazione di Christian Caujolle. Udine : Art&, c1990. 251 p. : ill. ; 31 cm.   ISBN 88-85893-21-X
1. Fontana, Franco, 1933-. I. Title. II. Title: Kaleidoscope.
NYPL   [MFX+ (Fontana) 91-3996]

FONTANA, FRANCO, 1933-
Fontana, Franco, 1933- Franco Fontana . Udine , c1990. 251 p. :   ISBN 88-85893-21-X
NYPL   [MFX+ (Fontana) 91-3996]

Le fontanelle di Roma /. De Marchi, Andrea. Roma , 1988. 61 p. :
NYPL   [3-MRN 90-10437]

FONTCUBERTA, JOAN, 1955- - EXHIBITIONS.
Pitts, Terence. 4 Spanish photographers . [Tucson, Ariz.] , c1988. 23 p. :
NYPL   [MFW+ 89-1448]

Fontein, Jan, 1927- The sculpture of Indonesia / Jan Fontein ; with essays by R. Soekmono, Edi Sedyawati. Washington, [D.C.] : National Gallery of Art ; New York, N.Y. : H.N. Abrams, c1990. 312 p. : ill. (some col.), facsims., maps ; 30cm. Catalog of an exhibition held at the National Gallery of Art, Washington, D.C., July 1-Nov. 4, 1990; Houston Museum of Fine Arts, Dec. 9, 1990-Mar. 17., 1991; Metropolitan Museum of Art, Apr. 21-Aug. 18, 1991; and at 1 other institution. Includes bibliographical references (p. 303-311).   ISBN 0-89468-141-9 DDC 730/.9598/07473 20
1. Sculpture, Indonesian - Exhibitions. I. Soekmono, R. II. Sedyawati, Edi, 1938-. III. National Gallery of Art (U. S.). IV. Metropolitan Museum of Art (New York, N.Y.). V. Museum of Fine Arts, Houston. VI. Title.
NB1026 .F6 1990
NYPL   [3-MAF+ 90-11766]

Fontenaille, Guy Felix. Réplique aux ténèbres. Paris, Editions Cujas, [1965] 190 p. 19 cm. (Ouvertures)
1. Man. I. Title.
N70 .F65
NYPL   [3-MAB 90-5820]

Fontes historiae artis Neerlandicae .
(2) Schouteet, Albert. De vlaamse primitieven te Brugge . Brussel , 1989- v. ;   ISBN 90-6569-381-5
NYPL   [3-MCG 90-12723]

Fonti, Daniela. Gino Severini : catalogo ragionato / Daniela Fonti ; consulenza di Maurizio Fagiolo dell'Arco, Gina Severini Franchina ; biografia di Maurizio Fagiolo dell'Arco ; testi critici di Maurizio Fagiolo dell'Arco ... [et al.]. Milano : A. Mondadori : P. Daverio, 1988. 655 p. : ill. (some col.) ; 30 cm. Includes index. Bibliography: p. 642-647. "Scritti di Gino Severini": p. 648-651.
1. Severini, Gino, 1883-1966 - Catalogues raisonnés. I. Severini, Gino, 1883-1966. II. Fagiolo dell'Arco, Maurizio, 1939-. III. Severini, Gina. IV. Title.
NYPL   [MCF+ S49 90-485]

FOOD - CARICATURES AND CARTOONS.
Robinson, W. Heath (William Heath), 1872-1944. Meals on wheels . London , c1989. 64 p. :   ISBN 0-285-62932-8
NYPL   [3-MEM+ (Robinson) 90-2152]

FOOD IN ART - EXHIBITIONS.
Art what thou eat . Mount Kisco, N.Y. , c1991. 191 p. :   ISBN 1-559-21051-6 :   DDC 704.9/49641/0973 20
N6512 .A763 1991
NYPL   [3-MAMZ+ 91-5410]

A fool in paradise . McCarthy, Doris, 1910- Toronto , 1990. 257 p., [14] p. of plates :   ISBN 0-921912-03-X :   DDC 759.11 20
NYPL   [3-MCZ M117 91-6026]

Foot, M. R. D. (Michael Richard Daniel), 1919-
Art and war : twentieth century warfare as depicted by war artists / M.R.D. Foot. London : Headline, 1990. 240 p. : ill. (some col.) ; 27 cm. Spine title: Art & war. "Published in association with the Imperial War Museum." Includes bibliographical references and index.   ISBN 0-7472-0286-9 DDC 758/.994053 20
1. Art, British. 2. Art, Modern - 20th century - Great

Britain. 3. World War, 1914-1918 - Art and the war. 4. World War, 1939-1945 - Art and the war. 5. Imperial War Museum (Great Britain). I. Imperial War Museum (Great Britain). II. Title. III. Title: Art & war.
N8260 .F58 1990

Foote, Lisa H. Haines, Carol L. "Forms to sett on" . Concord, Mass. [1984?] 36 p. :
NK2715 .H35 1984
NYPL   [3-MOF 90-12018]

For God, country, and the thrill of it . Noggle, Anne, 1922- College Station , c1990. xi, 160 p. :   ISBN 0-89096-401-7 (alk. paper) DDC 940.54/4973/092 B 20
D790 .N64 1990
NYPL   [MFX+ (Noggle) 91-3591]

Forbidden city. De Verboden Stad . Rotterdam , New York, NY , c1990. 245 p. :   ISBN 90-6918-065-0
NYPL   [3-MAG 91-6651]

FORBIDDEN CITY (PEKING, CHINA) - EXHIBITIONS.
De Verboden Stad . Rotterdam , New York, NY , c1990. 245 p. :   ISBN 90-6918-065-0
NYPL   [3-MAG 91-6651]

FORCE (POLITICAL AND SOCIAL SCIENCE, ETC.) see VIOLENCE.

Ford, Barbara Brennan.
Metropolitan Museum of Art (New York, N.Y.) East Asian lacquer . New York , 1991. p. cm.   ISBN 0-87099-622-3 DDC 745.7/26/09510747471 20
NK9900.7.E15 M47 1991

Metropolitan Museum of Art (New York, N.Y.) Japanese art from the Gerry collection in the Metropolitan Museum of Art /. New York , c1989. 141 p. :   ISBN 0-87099-556-1 DDC 738/.0952/0747471 20
N7352 .F67 1989   **NYPL   [3-MAG 89-28868]**

Ford, Charles Henri. View . New York , Emeryville, CA , c1991. p. cm.   ISBN 1-560-25013-5 :   DDC 700/.9/04 20
NX456 .V49 1991

FORD COUNTY, ILL. - MAPS.
(1990) Rockford Map Publishers. Ford County, Illinois, land atlas & plat book . Rockford, Ill. [c1990] 1 atlas (37 p.) :
NYPL   [Map Div. 90-11386]

Ford County, Illinois, land atlas & plat book . Rockford Map Publishers. Rockford, Ill. [c1990] 1 atlas (37 p.) :
NYPL   [Map Div. 90-11386]

Ford, Edward R. The details of modern architecture / Edward R. Ford. Cambridge, Mass. : MIT Press, c1990. ix, 371 p. : ill. ; 29 cm. Includes index. Includes bibliographical references (p. 361-363)   ISBN 0-262-06121-X DDC 724/.5 20
1. Architecture, Modern - 19th century. 2. Architecture, Modern - 20th century. I. Title.
NA2840 .F67 1989
NYPL   [3-MRN 90-12073]

FORD, O'NEIL, 1905- - CRITICISM AND CRITICISM.
George, Mary Carolyn Hollers. O'Neil Ford, architect /. College Station , c1992. p. cm.   ISBN 0-89096-433-5 DDC 720/.92 20
NA737.O5 G46 1992

Foreman, John, 1945- The Vanderbilts and the gilded age : architectural aspirations, 1879-1901 / John Foreman and Robbe Pierce Stimson ; introduction by Louis Auchincloss.1st ed. New York : St. Martin's Press, 1991. viii, 340 p. : ill., ports., plans, geneal. tables ; 29 cm. Includes index. Includes bibliographical references (p. 324-329).   ISBN 0-312-05984-1 :   DDC 728.8/0973 20
1. Vanderbilt family. 2. Mansions - United States. 3. Eclecticism in architecture - United States. 4. Architecture, Modern - 19th century - United States. 5. United States - Social life and customs - 1865-1918. I. Stimson, Robbe Pierce. II. Title.
NA7207 .F67 1991   **NYPL   [ILD 91-6528]**

Forente stater. see United States.

A foreshadowing of 21st century art . Alexander, Christopher. New York , 1990. p. cm.   ISBN 0-19-520866-8 DDC 746.7/561 20
NK2865.A1 A44 1990

FOREST PLANTING. see FORESTS AND FORESTRY.

FORESTATION. see FORESTS AND FORESTRY.

Forestier, Sylvie. Chagall e la ceramica / Sylvie Forestier, Meret Meyer ; campagna fotografica 1989, Giorgio Dettori ; [traduzione dal francese, Chiara Formis]. 1a ed. italiana. Milano : Jaca Book, 1990. 187 p. : ill. ; 38 cm. (I Contemporanei)   ISBN 88-16-60103-5
I. Meyer, Meret. II. Title.
NYPL   [3-MCZ+ C43]

FORESTS AND FORESTRY - COLOMBIA - MAPS.
Instituto Geográfico "Agustín Codazzi." Subdirección Agrológica. Suelos y bosques de Colombia. Bogotá , 1988. 1 atlas (133 p.) :
NYPL   [Map Div. 91-13234]

FORESTS AND FORESTRY IN ART - EXHIBITIONS.
Histoires de forêt . [Nantes] [1987] 100 p. :   ISBN 2-906211-01-X DDC 760/.092 20
N6888.E7 A4 1987a

Förg, Günther, 1952-
Günther Förg / [Ausstellung, Günther Förg, Veit Loers ; Herausgeber des Katalogs, Veit Loers]. Ausg. für den Buchhandel. Stuttgart : Edition Cantz, c1990. 202 p. : ill. ; 31 cm. German and English. "Museum Fridericianum Kassel, Museum van Hedendaagse Kunst Gent, Museum der Bildenden Künste Leipzig, Kunsthalle Tübingen, Kunstraum München."   ISBN 3-89322-214-6
1. Förg, Günther, 1952- Exhibitions. I. Loers, Veit. II. Museum Fridericianum. III. Title.
NYPL   [3-MCK+ F635 91-6911]

Günther Förg : Castello di Rivoli, 6 ottobre-3 dicembre 1989 / a cura di Rudi Fuchs, Johannes Gachnang, Cristina Mundici. [Turin] : Castello di Rivoli, museo d'arte contemporanea [1989] 1 v. (unpaged) : col. ill. ; 23 cm. Text also in English. Includes bibliographical references. DDC 709/.2 20
1. Förg, Günther, 1952- - Exhibitions. I. Castello di Rivoli (Museum : Turin, Italy).
N6888.F62 A4 1989a

FÖRG, GÜNTHER, 1952- - EXHIBITIONS.
Förg, Günther, 1952- Günther Förg /. Stuttgart , c1990. 202 p. :   ISBN 3-89322-214-6
NYPL   [3-MCK+ F635 91-6911]

Förg, Günther, 1952- Günther Förg . [Turin] [1989] 1 v. (unpaged) :   DDC 709/.2 20
N6888.F62 A4 1989a

FORGERY OF WORKS OF ART. see ART - FORGERIES.

Forgotten art of India /. Koppar, D. H. Baroda , 1989. xxiii, 266, [4] p. :   DDC 709/.54 20
N7301 .K58 1989   **NYPL   [3-MAF 91-6940]**

The Forgotten arts.
Bacon, Richard M. Wall stenciling /. Camden, Me. , 1991. p. cm.   ISBN 0-89909-326-4 :   DDC 745.7/3 20
NK8662 .B3 1991

The forgotten hermitage of Skellig Michael /. Horn, Walter William, 1908- Berkeley , c1990. xi, 111 p. :   ISBN 0-520-06410-0 (alk. paper) DDC 941.9/6 19
BX2602.S54 H67 1989
NYPL   [3-MRBB+ 91-3376]

Forlani Tempesti, Anna. Italian fifteenth- to seventeenth-century drawings / Anna Forlani Tempesti. New York : Metropolitan Museum of Art ; Princeton : Princeton University Press, 1991. p. cm. (The Robert Lehman collection . 5) Includes bibliographical references (p.) and indexes.   ISBN 0-87099-606-1 DDC 741.945/074/7471 20
1. Drawing, Italian - Catalogs. 2. Drawing - 15th century - Italy - Catalogs. 3. Drawing - 16th century - Italy - Catalogs. 4. Drawing - 17th century - Italy - Catalogs. 5. Drawing - New York (N.Y.) - Catalogs. 6. Lehman, Robert, 1892-1969 - Art collections - Catalogs. 7. Metropolitan Museum of Art (New York, N.Y.) - Catalogs. I. Metropolitan Museum of Art (New York, N.Y.). II. Title. III. Series.
NC255 .F6 1991

Form- und Gestaltungslehre, von Paul Klee. see Klee, Paul, 1879-1940. Form- und Gestaltungslehre.

FORM (AESTHETICS)
Kell, Klaus. Formuntersuchungen zu spät- und nachhellenistischen Gruppen /. [Saarbrücken] [1988] 136 p. :   ISBN 3-925036-26-1
NB94 .K35 1988   **NYPL   [3-MGH 90-12808]**

Martorrev. Estructuralismo plástico mexicano .

337

Guadalajara, Jalisco, México , 1987. 120, [3]
p. : *NYPL [3-MCY 89-11595]*

FORMAL GARDENS. see GARDENS.

Formalhaut Architektur Skulptur . Formalhaut
(Group) Darmstadt , c1989. 54 p. : ISBN
3-925376-40-2 *NYPL [3-MGI 91-7331]*

Formalhaut (Group) Formalhaut Architektur
Skulptur : double knight game / Ottmar Hörl,
Gabriela Seifert, Götz G. Stöckmann.1. Aufl.
Darmstadt : Verlag der G. Büchner Buchh.,
c1989. 54 p. : ill. (some col.) ; 24 cm. German
and English. Includes bibliographical references. ISBN
3-925376-40-2
1. Formalhaut (Group). 2. Sculpture, Modern - 20th
century - Germany. 3. Architecture - Germany. 4.
Architecture, Modern - 20th century - Germany. I.
Hörl, Ottmar, 1950-. II. Seifert, Gabriela, 1954-. III.
Stöckmann, Götz, 1953-. IV. Title.
NYPL [3-MGI 91-7331]

FORMALHAUT (GROUP)
Formalhaut (Group) Formalhaut Architektur
Skulptur . Darmstadt , c1989. 54 p. : ISBN
3-925376-40-2 *NYPL [3-MGI 91-7331]*

FORMALISM (ART) - AUSTRIA.
Olin, Margaret Rose, 1948- Forms of
representation in Alois Riegl's theory of art /.
University Park, Pa. , 1992. p. cm. ISBN
0-271-00777-X DDC 709/.2 20
N7483.R54 O35 1992

Forman, Henry Chandlee, 1904- The architecture
of the Old South : the medieval style,
1585-1850 / by Henry Chandlee Forman.
Cambridge : Harvard University Press, 1948.
203 p., [7] p. of plates : ill. ; 26 cm. Includes
index. Bibliography: p. [185]-191. DDC 720.975
1. Architecture, Colonial - Southern States. 2.
Architecture - Southern States. I. Title.
NA720 .F6 *NYPL [3-MQWO 91-6780]*

Formanek-Brunell, Miriam. Dolls and
duty--Martha Chase and the progressive agenda,
1889-1925 /. Providence, R.I. (110 Benevolent
St., Providence 02906) , 1989. 48 p. : DDC
688.7/221/097451 20
NK4894.2.C43 A4 1989

The formation of Nabatean art . Patrich, J.
(Joseph) Jerusalem : Leiden ; 231 p. : ISBN
90-04-09285-4 (Brill) DDC 709/.39/48 20
DS154.22 .P38 1990
NYPL [3-MAE 91-3363]

Forme e tecniche dell'architettura moderna /.
Morabito, Giovanni. Roma , c1990. 206 p. :
IN PROCESS (ONLINE)
NYPL [3-MQV 91-6531]

Formica & design : from the counter top to high
art / editor, Susan Grant Lewin ; introduction
by R. Craig Miller ; essays by Sarah Bayliss ...
[et al.] ; afterword by Vincent P. Langone. New
York : Rizzoli, 1991. 191 p. : ill. (some col.) ;
26 cm. Includes bibliographical references (p.
[184]-185) and index. ISBN 0-8478-1334-7 DDC
729 20
1. Formica Corporation. 2. Laminated plastics. 3.
Plastics in interior decoration. 4. United States -
Popular culture - History - 20th century. I. Lewin,
Susan Grant. II. Title: Formica and design.
NK2004.3.F67 F67 1991

Formica and design . Formica & design . New
York , 1991. 191 p. : ISBN 0-8478-1334-7 DDC
729 20
NK2004.3.F67 F67 1991

FORMICA CORPORATION.
Formica & design . New York , 1991. 191 p. :
ISBN 0-8478-1334-7 DDC 729 20
NK2004.3.F67 F67 1991

The forms of color . Gerstner, Karl. Cambridge,
Mass. , c1986. 179 p. : ISBN 0-262-07100-2
DDC 701/.8 19
ND1489 .G4713 1986
NYPL [3-MAMZ 91-6985]

Forms of representation in Alois Riegl's theory
of art /. Olin, Margaret Rose, 1948- University
Park, Pa. , 1992. p. cm. ISBN 0-271-00777-X
DDC 709/.2 20
N7483.R54 O35 1992

Forms of the Goddess Lajjā Gauri in Indian art
/. Bolon, Carol R. University Park, PA , 1991.
p. cm. ISBN 0-271-00761-3 DDC 730/.954 20
NB1912.L34 .B65 1991

"Forms to sett on" . Haines, Carol L. Concord,

Mass. [1984?] 36 p. :
NK2715 .H35 1984
NYPL [3-MOF 90-12018]

**Formuntersuchungen zu spät- und
nachhellenistischen Gruppen** /. Kell, Klaus.
[Saarbrücken] [1988] 136 p. : ISBN
3-925036-26-1
NB94 .K35 1988 *NYPL [3-MGH 90-12808]*

Fornari, Benedetto. Farina, Federico.
L'architettura cistercense e l'Abbazia di
Casamari /. Casamari , 1981, c1978. xii, 187
p. : DDC 726/.7/0945622 19
NA5621.A22 F37 1981
NYPL [3-MRBD+ 90-12587]

Fornari Schianchi, Lucia. Parma : history, art,
and monuments / by Lucia Fornari Schianchi ;
Maria Cristina Alfieri, Rossella Cattani, Milena
Fornari. Bologna, Italy : Italcards, [1991?] 158
p. : col. ill. ; 24 cm. ISBN 88-7193-650-7 DDC
709/.45/44 20
1. Art, Italian - Italy - Parma. 2. Parma (Italy) -
Description - Guide-books. I. Title.
N6951.P35 F67 1991

Fornaro, Cosimo, 1928- Il mosaico di Ferruccio
Ferrazzi nella Chiesa di S. Antonio in Taranto
/ Cosimo Fornaro. Fasano, Brindisi : Schena,
c1987. 95 p. : col. ill., port. ; 32 cm. ISBN
88-7514-199-1 : DDC 726/.527/092 20
1. Ferrazzi, Ferruccio, 1891- Vortice dello Spirito
Santo. 2. Chiesa di S. Antonio (Taranto, Italy). 3.
Church decoration and ornament - Italy - Taranto -
History - 20th century. 4. Holy Spirit - Art. I. Title.
NA3860.F47 A4 1987
NYPL [3-MRXZ+ 90-12439]

Fornasetti, designer of dreams /. Mauriès,
Patrick. Boston, Mass. , 1991. p. ISBN
0-8212-1872-7 DDC 745.4/492 20
N6923.F637 M38 1991

**FORNASETTI, PIERO, D. 1988 - CRITICISM
AND INTERPRETATION.**
Mauriès, Patrick. Fornasetti, designer of dreams
/. Boston, Mass. , 1991. p. ISBN 0-8212-1872-7
DDC 745.4/492 20
N6923.F637 M38 1991

Forneck, Gerd Martin. Bischöfliches Dom- und
Diözesanmuseum Trier. Das neue Bischöfliche
Dom- und Diözesanmuseum . Trier , 1988. 123
p. : *NYPL [3-MAIH 90-10260]*

Fornells Angelats, Montserrat, 1953- Los lienzos
de José María Sert en la Iglesia de San Telmo,
de San Sebastián / por Montserrat Fornells
Angelats. San Sebastián : Edición patrocinada
por la Excma. Diputación Foral de Guipúzcoa,
1985. 206, [12] p. : ill. (some col.) ; 25 cm.
Originally presented as the author's thesis (tesis de
licenciatura--Universidad Complutense de Madrid)
Bibliography: p. [215]-[218]
1. Sert, José María, 1874-1945 - Criticism and
interpretation. 2. Iglesia de San Telmo (San Sebastián,
Spain). 3. Museo de San Telmo. 4. Basques in art. I.
Title.
ND813.S47 F67 1985
NYPL [3-MCQ S49 90-13288]

Forni, Pierre. Les Bronzes antiques de Paris /.
Paris , 1989. 512 p. : ISBN 2-901414-34-6 DDC
730/.09364 20
NK7949.P2 B7 1989

**FORO EMILIANO (TERRACINA, ITALY) -
EXHIBITIONS.**
Coppola, Maria Rosaria. Terracina . Roma ,
1986. 42 p. : ISBN 88-85020-74-7
NYPL [3-MQM 90-13012]

Foro 2000.
Tibol, Raquel. Gráficas y neográficas en México
/. México, D.F. , 1987. 302 p. : ISBN
968-291-357-8
NE544.4 .T5 1987

Forrest, Ebenezer, fl. 1774.
[Hogarth's peregrination]
An account of what seem'd most remarkable
in the five days peregrination of the five
following persons, vizt. Messieurs Tothall,
Scott, Hogarth, Thornhill & Forrest, begun on
Saturday, May 27th, 1723 and finished on
the 31st of the same month / with an
introduction by Nick Savage and vinyl
engravings by Michaela Kidney. Church
Hanborough, Oxford : Hanborough Parrot
Press, 1989 ([Didcot? England] : Didcot
Press) [35] p. : ill. (chiefly col.) ; 23 cm. Half
title: Hogarth's peregrination. Text signed at end: E.

Fforrest [sic]. "Written by Ebenezer Forrest"--Introd.
"First published in 1759 ... An edition of 125 copies,
of which 25 are specially hand-coloured"--P. [35].
Printed on double leaves. Ill. on lining papers. LC
has copy no. V/XXV, signed by N. Savage and M.
Kidney. DLC Source: Purchase, July 27, 1990. DLC
DDC 760/.092 20
1. Hogarth, William, 1697-1764 - Journeys - England.
2. England - Description and travel - 1701-1800. I.
Hogarth, William 1697-1764. II. Savage, Nick. III.
Kidney, Michaela. IV. Title. V. Title: Account of what
seemed most remarkable in the five days
peregrination ... VI. Title: Hogarth's peregrination.
ND497.H7 F6 1989

**Forschungen der Denkmalpflege in
Niedersachsen** .
(6) Das Rathaus in Duderstadt /. Hameln ,
c1989. 304 p. : ISBN 3-87585-096-3
NYPL [3-MQWD+ 91-5449]

**Forschungen und Beiträge zur Wiener
Stadtgeschichte.**
(Bd. 20) Lehne, Andreas. Wiener Warenhäuser,
1865-1914 /. Wien , 1990. 195 p. : ISBN
3-7005-4488-X
NA6227.D45 L44 1990

**Forschungen und Berichte des Institutes für
Kunstgeschichte der Karl-Franzens-
Universität Graz.**
(VIII) Höfler, Janez. Die Kunst Dalmatiens .
Graz , 1989. 338 p. : ISBN 3-201-01466-4
NYPL [3-MAM+ 90-8024]
(8) Höfler, Janez. Die Kunst Dalmatiens .
Graz/Austria , 1989. 338 p. : ISBN
3-201-01466-4 DDC 709/.497/2 20
N7249.D34 H64 1989

Forschungen zur deutschen Landeskunde.
(Bd. 206) Plapper, Wolfgang. Die
kartographische Darstellung von
Bevölkerungsentwicklungen . Bonn-Bad
Godesberg , 1975. 49 p. : ISBN 3-87994-206-4
G58 .F73 Bd. 206 HB3596.S33
NYPL [Map Div. 80-63]

Forseth, Kevin. Rendering the visual field :
illusion becomes reality / Kevin Forseth. New
York, N.Y. : Van Nostrand Reinhold, c1991. p.
cm. Includes bibliographical references and index.
ISBN 0-442-20042-0 DDC 720/.28/4 20
1. Architectural rendering. I. Title.
NA2780 .F67 1991

Forster, Andrew, 1942-
Andrew Forster (1942-) : retrospective.
Halifax, N.S. : Eye Level Gallery, 1983. 46 p. :
ill. ; 24 cm. "Published 1983 for the exhibition June
7-June 25, 1983, Eye Level Gallery, Halifax, Nova
Scotia."--T.p. verso.
1. Forster, Andrew, 1942- - Exhibitions. I. Eye Level
Gallery (Halifax, N.S.). II. Title.
NYPL [3-MCZ F717 88-2150]

FORSTER, ANDREW, 1942- - EXHIBITIONS.
Forster, Andrew, 1942- Andrew Forster
(1942-) . Halifax, N.S. , 1983. 46 p. :
NYPL [3-MCZ F717 88-2150]

Forster, Michael. Talos, Kurt, 1942-1976. Kurt
Talos, 1942-1976 . Wien [1978?] [24], 60 p. :
N6811.5.T34 A4 1978
NYPL [3-MCK+ T152 81-334]

Forsyth, Elliot William. Baudin in Australian
waters . Melbourne , 1988. 347 p. : ISBN
0-19-554787-X
NYPL [3-MAMY+ 90-10770]

Forsyth, Ilene H. Duke University. Museum of
Art. The Brummer collection of medieval art,
the Duke University Museum of Art /.
Durham , 1991. xix, 297 p., 16 p. of plates :
ISBN 0-8223-1055-4 DDC 709/.02/074756563
20
N5963.D87 D854 1991
NYPL [3-MAK 91-5627]

**FORT APACHE INDIAN RESERVATION
(ARIZ.) - EXHIBITIONS.**
McAuley, Skeet. Sign language . New York,
N.Y. , c1989. 78 p. : ISBN 0-89381-333-8 :
DDC 979.1/35 20
E99.N3 M515 1989
NYPL [MFX (McAuley) 89-26792]

Fort, Ilene Susan. Los Angeles County Museum
of Art. American art . Los Angeles, Calif. ,
Seattle , 1991. p. cm. ISBN 0-87587-155-0 DDC
759.13/074/79494 20
N6505 .L6 1991

Fort Worth Art Center-Museum. Stella, Frank.
Frank Stella . [Fort Worth] , 1984. vi, 45 p. :
   DDC 769.92/4 19
NE539.S72 A4 1984
         NYPL [MDG (Stella) 85-2527]

**Fort Worth, Tex. Art Center-Museum. see Fort
Worth Art Center-Museum.**

**Fort Worth, Tex. Kimbell Art Museum. see
Kimbell Art Museum.**

Fortezza da Basso. Firenze restaura . Firenze ,
1973, c1972. 154 p., [168] p. of plates :
         NYPL [3-MBK 90-5749]

Fortier, Bruno. Paris, la ville et ses projets .
Paris , c1989. 253 p. :   ISBN 2-907742-04-3
         NYPL [3-MQWF+ 90-10864]

Fortier, Ivanhoë, 1931-
Ivanhoë Fortier : inter-modulaires : [exposition]
Musée d'art contemporain, 18 janvier au 4 mars
1979. Montréal : Le Musée, 1980. 22 p. : ill. (4
col.) ; 21 x 27 cm. Bibliography: p. 16, 19. ISBN
2-551-03707-7
  *1. Fortier, Ivanhoë, 1931- - Exhibitions. I. Québec
(Province). Musée d'art contemporain. II. Title.*
         NYPL [3-MGO (Fortier) 90-6907]

FORTIER, IVANHOË, 1931- - EXHIBITIONS.
Fortier, Ivanhoë, 1931- Ivanhoë Fortier .
Montréal , 1980. 22 p. :   ISBN 2-551-03707-7
         NYPL [3-MGO (Fortier) 90-6907]

**Fortieth anniversary of Gene Heier Orchestra,
1947-1987.** 1947-1987, 40th anniversary of
Gene Heier Orchestra [sound recording]. Green
Bay, Wisc. [198-]. 1 sound disc :
North Star Appli NSA 140

Forty-five. Baselitz, Georg, 1938- [Dresdner
Frauen. English.] The women of Dresden . New
York , c1990. 43 p., 1 folded sheet of plates
(20 leaves) :   ISBN 1-87828-311-1   DDC 730/.92
20
NB588.B358 A4 1990

Forty Texas printmakers. [Fort Worth] : Modern
Art Museum of Fort Worth, 1990. vi, 146 p. :
ill. (some col.) ; 28 cm.   ISBN 0-929865-06-5
   DDC 769.92/2764 20
  *1. Prints, American - Texas. 2. Prints - 20th century -
Texas. 3. Printmakers - Texas - Biography. I. Modern
Art Museum of Fort Worth. II. Title: 40 Texas
printmakers.*
NE535.T4 F67 1990
         NYPL [MDBF 91-5248]

Forum Gallery. Gillespie, Gregory, 1936- Gregory
Gillespie, paintings (Italy 1962-1970). New
York , 1970. 55 p. :
         NYPL [3-MCX+ G477 91-1181]

Forum Internationale Kunstmesse Zürich (1984)
Forum Internationale Kunstmesse Zürich =
Foire internationale d'art de Zurich :
International Art Fair Zurich : 22.-27.
November 1984. Zürich : Forum Internationale
Kunstmesse Zürich, [1984] [124] leaves : ill. ;
42 cm. Title also in Italian. Cover title.
  *1. Art, Modern - 20th century - Exhibitions. I. Title:
Foire international d'art de Zürich. II. Title:
International Art Fair Zürich. III. Title: Internationale
Kunstmesse Zürich.*
         NYPL [3-MAL+ 90-11547]

**FORUMS, ROMAN - ITALY - TERRACINA -
EXHIBITIONS.**
Coppola, Maria Rosaria. Terracina . Roma ,
1986. 42 p. :   ISBN 88-85020-74-7
         NYPL [3-MQM 90-13012]

Foshay, Ella M., 1948-
Art in bloom / Ella M. Foshay. New York :
Phaidon Universe ; Oxford : Phaidon, 1990. 80
p. : ill. (chiefly col.) ; 32 cm. "With paintings from
the Museum of Fine Arts, Boston." Includes
bibliographical references (p. 80).   ISBN 0-87663-603-2
(Phaidon Universe)   DDC 758/.42/09 20
  I. Museum of Fine Arts, Boston. II. Title.
ND1400 .F67 1990
         NYPL [3-MAMZ+ 91-4872]

Mr. Luman Reed's picture gallery : a pioneer
collection of American art / by Ella M.
Foshay ; introduction by Wayne Craven ;
catalogue by Timothy Anglin Burgard. New
York : Abrams in association with the
New-York Historical Society, 1990. 228 p. : ill.,
ports. ; 25 cm. Includes bibliographical references
and index.   ISBN 0-8109-3751-4   DDC
759.14/074/7471 20
  1. Reed, Luman, 1785-1836 - Art collections - Catalogs.

*2. Painting, American - Catalogs. 3. Painting, Modern -
19th century - United States - Catalogs. 4. Painting,
European - Catalogs. 5. Painting - Private collections -
New York (N.Y.) - Catalogs. I. Reed, Luman,
1785-1836. II. Craven, Wayne. III. Burgard, Timothy
Anglin, 1963-. IV. New York Historical Society. V.
Title.*
ND210 .F65 1990
         NYPL [3-MCW 90-12446]

Foss, Gloria. How to paint : a course in the art of
oil painting / Gloria Foss. New York :
Watson-Guptill, 1991. p. cm. includes
bibliographical references and index.   ISBN
0-8230-2456-3 :   DDC 751.45/435 20
  1. Painting - Technique. I. Title.
ND1500 .F67 1991

Fossati, Paolo 1938-
Giorgio Griffa / Paolo Fossati, Mario Bertoni.
Ravenna : Essegi, c1990. 161 p. : ill. ; 24 cm.
(Artisti contemporanei)
  1. Griffa, Giorgio. I. Title.
IN PROCESS (ONLINE)
         NYPL [3-MCF G847 91-2466]

Rama, Carol. Carol Rama /. Torino , c1989.
117 p. :   ISBN 88-422-0173-1
         NYPL [3-MCF+ R165 89-26726]

Vago, Valentino, 1931- Valentino Vago /.
Milano [1975] [48] p. :
         NYPL [3-MCF+ V126 91-6299]

Fossier, François. Il fiore dell'impressionismo =
La fleur de l'impressionnisme / testo e schede a
cura di François Fossier ; con un testo
introduttivo di Renato Barilli. Milano : Fabbri,
c1990. 388 p. : ill. (some col.) ; 30 cm.
Exhibition held in Aosta July 13-Oct. 31, 1990. Text
also in French. Includes bibliographical references (p.
385).
  *1. Impressionism (Art) - France - Exhibitions. 2. Prints,
French - Exhibitions. 3. Prints - 19th century - France -
Exhibitions. 4. Bibliothèque nationale (France). Cabinet
des estampes - Exhibitions. I. Title.*
NE647.6.14 F67 1990

Foster. Foster, Norman, 1935- Barcelona , c1989.
128 p. :   ISBN 84-252-1385-1
         NYPL [3-MQZ (Foster) 90-12468]

**FOSTER ASSOCIATES (LONDON,
ENGLAND)**
Williams, Stephanie. Hongkong Bank . Boston ,
c1989. 302 p. :   ISBN 0-316-94238-3 :   DDC
725/.24/095125 20
NA6245.C62 H668 1989
         NYPL [3-MQZ (Foster) 91-4484]

Foster, Kathleen A. Writing about Eakins : the
manuscripts in Charles Bregler's Thomas Eakins
Collection / Kathleen A. Foster, Cheryl
Leibold. Philadelphia : Published for the
Pennsylvania Academy of the Fine Arts by the
University of Pennsylvania Press, c1989. xiv,
411 p. : ill., facsims., geneal. table, ports. ; 24
cm. Companion volume to: Charles Bregler's Thomas
Eakins collection [microform]. Includes bibliographical
references (p. [373]-374) and indexes. CONTENTS. -
The manuscripts of Thomas Eakins -- The manuscripts
of Susan Macdowell Eakins -- The manuscripts of
Charles Bregler.   ISBN 0-8122-8107-1   DDC
016.7/092 20
  *1. Eakins, Thomas, 1844-1916. 2. Eakins, Susan
Macdowell. 3. Bregler, Charles. 4. Bregler, Charles -
Library - Catalogs. 5. Pennsylvania Academy of the
Fine Arts - Catalogs. 6. Manuscripts - Pennsylvania -
Philadelphia - Catalogs. I. Eakins, Thomas, 1844-1916.
II. Eakins, Susan Macdowell. III. Bregler, Charles. IV.
Leibold, Cheryl. V. Pennsylvania Academy of the Fine
Arts. VI. Pennsylvania Academy of the Fine Arts.
Charles Bregler's Thomas Eakins collection. VII. Title.*
Z6616.E23 F67 1989 ND237.E15
         NYPL [3-MCX E12 90-10747]

Foster, Norman, 1935-
Foster. Barcelona : G.Gili : Col·legi
d'Arquitectes de Catalunya c1989. 128 p. : ill.
(some col.) ; 27 cm. (Quaderns monografías)
English and Spanish. "Edición con motivo de la
exposición N. Foster, presentada en el Colegio de
Arquitectos del 17 de enero de 1989 hasta el 28 de
febrero de 1989"--P. preceding t.p. "Norman Foster,
obras y proyectos, 1981-1988"--P. [1].   ISBN
84-252-1385-1
  *1. Foster, Norman, 1935- - Exhibitions. 2. Architecture,
Modern - 20th century - Exhibitions. I. Title. II. Title:
Norman Foster, obras y proyectos, 1981-1988. III.
Series.*   *NYPL [3-MQZ (Foster) 90-12468]*

[Norman Foster. German & English]
Norman Foster : sketches = Zeichnungen /
edited by Werner Blaser ; [translation into
German by Claudia Neuenschwander]. Basel ;
Boston : Birkhäuser Verlag, c1992. p. cm.
  ISBN 3-7643-2546-1 :   DDC 720/.22/22 20
  *1. Foster, Norman, 1935- - Themes, motives. I. Blaser,
Werner, 1924-. II. Title.*
NA2707.F67 A4 1992

**FOSTER, NORMAN, 1935- - THEMES,
MOTIVES.**
Foster, Norman, 1935- [Norman Foster.
German & English.] Norman Foster . Basel ,
Boston , c1992. p. cm.   ISBN 3-7643-2546-1 :
  DDC 720/.22/22 20
NA2707.F67 A4 1992

**FOSTER, NORMAN, 1935- - CRITICISM
AND INTERPRETATION.**
Abel, Chris. Renault centre . London , New
York , 1991. [60] p. :   ISBN 1-85454-776-3 (pbk.) :
  DDC 720.92 20
NA997.F6
         NYPL [3-MQZ+ (Foster) 91-6980]

Williams, Stephanie. Hongkong Bank . Boston ,
c1989. 302 p. :   ISBN 0-316-94238-3 :   DDC
725/.24/095125 20
NA6245.C62 H668 1989
         NYPL [3-MQZ (Foster) 91-4484]

FOSTER, NORMAN, 1935- - EXHIBITIONS.
Foster, Norman, 1935- Foster. Barcelona ,
c1989. 128 p. :   ISBN 84-252-1385-1
         NYPL [3-MQZ (Foster) 90-12468]

Foster, Stephen C. The Avant-garde and the
text . Providence, RI , c1988. p. 306-507 :
         NYPL [MDT 91-5721]

Fostoria American . Seligson, Sidney P. [U.
S.A.] , c1990. 63 p. :   DDC 748.29154/16 20
NK5198.F6 A4 1990

FOSTORIA GLASS COMPANY - CATALOGS.
Seligson, Sidney P. Fostoria American . [U.
S.A.] , c1990. 63 p. :   DDC 748.29154/16 20
NK5198.F6 A4 1990

Foto : Annäherung an die Sowjetunion : ein
fotografischer Dialog / HerausgeberInnen,
Bernard Fischer ... [et al.]. Hannover :
Fackelträger, c1989. 147, 139 p. : ill. ; 29 cm.
German and Russian.   ISBN 3-7716-1504-6
  *1. Photographers - Germany - Biography. 2.
Photographers - Soviet Union - Biography. 3. Soviet
Union - Description and travel - 1970- - Views. 4.
Soviet Union - Social life and customs - 1970- -
Pictorial works. I. Fischer, Bernard, 1965-.*
         NYPL [MFW 91-7548]

Foto-Historama Agfa-Gevaert Leverkusen. In
unnachahmlicher Treue . Köln , 1979. 370 p. :
TR6.G3 C644   *NYPL [MFW 81-577]*

Foto in omslag : het Nederlandse documentaire
fotoboek na 1945 / [redactie: Mattie Boom,
Frans van Burko, Jenny Smets; tekst: Mattie
Boom, Rik Suermondt] = Photography between
covers : the Dutch documentary photobook
after 1945 / [editing: Mattie Boom, Frans van
Burkom, Jenny Smets; text: Mattie Boom, Rik
Suermondt]. Amsterdam : Fragment in
samenwerking met de Rijksdienst Beeldende
Kunst, 1989. 143 p. : ill. ; 30 cm. Text in Dutch
and English. Exhibition catalog. Includes index.
Includes bibliographical references.   ISBN
90-6579-033-0 (pbk.)
  *1. Photography, Documentary - Netherlands -
Exhibitions. 2. Illustrated books - Netherlands -
Exhibitions. I. Boom, Mattie. II. Burkom, Frans van.
III. Smets, Jenny. IV. Suermondt, Rik. V. Netherlands.
Rijksdienst Beeldende Kunst. VI. Title: Photography
between covers.*   *NYPL [MFW+ 91-3603]*

FotoFest 90 . FotoFest 90 (1990 : Houston, Tex.)
Houston, Tex. , c1990. 276 p. :   ISBN
0-9619766-1-6   DDC 779/.074/7641411 20
TR645.H8 F67 1990   *NYPL [MFW 91-3434]*

FOTOFEST 90 (HOUSTON, TEX.)
FotoFest 90 (1990 : Houston, Tex.) FotoFest
90 . Houston, Tex. , c1990. 276 p. :   ISBN
0-9619766-1-6   DDC 779/.074/7641411 20
TR645.H8 F67 1990   *NYPL [MFW 91-3434]*

FotoFest 90 (1990 : Houston, Tex.) FotoFest 90 :
the international month of photography :
[exhibition] February 10-March 10. Houston,
Tex. : Houston FotoFest : Distributed by Texas
Monthly Press, c1990. 276 p. : ill. (some col.) ;
25 cm. Includes index.   ISBN 0-9619766-1-6   DDC

779/.074/7641411 20
1. *FotoFest 90 (Houston, Tex.). 2. Photography,*
Artistic - Exhibitions. I. Title.
TR645.H8 F67 1990   **NYPL [MFW 91-3434]**

La fotografia antagonista /. Beltrame, Aldo,
1932- Piombino , 1989. 67 p., [6] leaves of
plates :   DDC 770 20
TR185 .B42 1989   **NYPL [MFW 91-3721]**

Fotografie am Bauhaus / herausgegeben für das
Bauhaus-Archiv von Jeannine Fiedler. [Berlin] :
Das Archiv, c1990. 362 p. : ill. ; 31 cm.   ISBN
3-88940-045-0
1. *Photography, Artistic - Exhibitions. I. Fiedler,*
Jeannine.   **NYPL [MFW+ 91-3409]**

Fotografie am Bauhaus. English. Photography at
the Bauhaus / edited for the Bauhaus-Archiv by
Jeannine Fiedler. 1st MIT Press ed. Cambridge,
Mass. : MIT Press, 1990. 362 p. : ill. (some
col.) ; 30 cm. Translation of: Fotografie am Bauhaus.
Includes index. Bibliography: p. 358-359.   ISBN
0-262-06126-0   DDC 779/.09431/84 20
1. *Bauhaus - Exhibitions. 2. Photography, Artistic -*
Exhibitions. I. Fiedler, Jeannine.
TR653 .F66513 1990
                      NYPL [MFW+ 91-189]

Fotografie di Ikona Gallery : fotografie di Felice
Beato, Carlo Naya, Gisèle Freund, Robert
Doisneau, Helen Levitt, Rosalind Solomon,
William Klein, Franco Fontana, John Batho,
Chuck Freedman, Herbert Midgoll / a cura di
Živa Kraus. Venezia : Fondazione scientifica
Querini Stampalia, 1989. 54 p. : ill. (some
col.) ; 30 cm. (Collana Queriniana . 10) Italian and
English. Exhibition catalog.
1. *Photography, Artistic - Exhibitions. I. Kraus, Živa. II.*
Ikona Gallery. III. Fondazione Scientifica Querini
Stampalia. IV. Series.
                      NYPL [3-MFW+ 91-7282]

Fotografie, Wissenschaft, Neue Technologien :
Facetten der Interaktion : Kunstmuseum
Düsseldorf, 8.12.1989-14.1.1990 /
[Katalogredaktion, Johannes auf der Lake].
[Düsseldorf : Landeshauptstadt Düsseldorf, der
Oberstadtdirektor, 1990]. 128 p. : ill. ; 27 cm.
1. *Photography, Artistic - Exhibitions. I. Lake, Johannes*
auf der. II. Kunstmuseum Düsseldorf.
                      NYPL [MFW 91-3438]

Het Fotografisch Museum van Auguste Grégoire .
Rijksuniversiteit te Leiden. Prentenkabinet.
s'Gravenhage , 1989. 208 p.:   ISBN
90-12-06303-5   **NYPL [MFW 91-3485]**

Fotoğraflarla Fatih anıtları /. Eyice, Semavi.
Fatih [Istanbul, Turkey] [1989?] 126 p. :
NA1370 .E88 1989

De foto's van Breitner /. Hefting, Paul.
's-Gravenhage , 1989. 142 p. :   ISBN
90-12-06046-X (pbk.)
                NYPL [MFX (Hefting) 91-2475]

Fotoschule. Le Louarn, Yvan Francis, 1915-1968.
Chaval's Fotoschule . Zürich , 1975. 45 p. :
ISBN 3-257-00788-4
                NYPL [3-MEM (Le Louarn) 84-2309]

Fotosecuencia /. Segall, Thea. Caracas,
Venezuela , 1988. 3 v. :   ISBN 980-615-106-2 (v.
1)   **NYPL [MFX+ (Segall) 90-13452]**

Fotoseite : kommentierte Beiträge zur Fotografie
aus der Wiener Zeitung Extra / von Carl
Aigner ... [et al.]. Salzburg : O. Müller, 1990.
159 p. : ill. ; 31 cm. (Edition Fotohof . Bd. 2)
ISBN 3-7013-0802-0
1. *Photojournalism - Austria - Vienna. I. Aigner, Carl.*
II. Wiener Zeitung. Extra. III. Series.
                      NYPL [MFW+]

Foucart, Bruno. Landowski / Bruno Foucart,
Michèle Lefrançois, Gérard Caillet. Paris :
Editions Van Wilder, c1989. 111 p. : ill. (some
col.) ; 30 cm. Includes bibliographical references.
ISBN 2-85299-009-1   DDC 730/.92 20
1. *Landowski, Paul Maximilien, 1875-1961 - Criticism*
and interpretation. I. Landowski, Paul Maximilien,
1875-1961. II. Lefrançois, Michèle. III. Caillet, Gérard,
1920-. IV. Title.
NB553.L25 F6 1989
                NYPL [3-MGO+ (Landowski) 91-3328]

Foucart-Walter, Elisabeth. La Collection A.P. de
Mirimonde . Paris , 1987. 137 p. :   ISBN
2-7118-2151-X
                NYPL [3-MAX (Mirimonde) 90-10806]

Found industrial objects : unintended art : an
exhibition presented by Meadow Brook Art

Gallery, Oakland University, Rochester,
Michigan, October 14-November 25, 1973.
Rochester, Mich. : The Gallery, [1973?] [24]
p. : ill. ; 22 cm.
1. *Design, Industrial - United States - Exhibitions. I.*
Meadow Brook Art Gallery.
                      NYPL [3-MNF 91-4231]

FOUND OBJECTS (ART) IN INTERIOR
DECORATION.
Wissinger, Joanna. Lost & found /. New York ,
c1991. p. cm.   ISBN 0-02-630590-9   DDC 747/.9
20
NK2115.5.F68 W5 1991

FOUND OBJECTS (ART) - JUVENILE
LITERATURE.
Lancaster, John, 1930- Art with found materials
/. New York , 1992. p. cm.   ISBN 0-531-14204-3
DDC 745.5 20
N7433.7 .L36 1992

Founders Society. Detroit. Institute of Arts.
American paintings in the Detroit Institute of
Arts /. New York , c1991- p.   ISBN
1-555-95044-2 (alk. paper) :   DDC
759.13/074/77434 20
ND205 .D298 1991

FOUNTAINS - GERMANY - MAINZ.
Hanfgarn, Werner, 1925- Mainzer Brunnen .
Mainz , 1990. 180 p. :   ISBN 3-87439-210-4 :
NA9415.M35 H36 1990

FOUNTAINS - GERMANY - WAGHÄUSEL.
Ringwald, Klaus. Der Marienbrunnen in
Waghäusel /. Stuttgart , c1990. 84 p. :   ISBN
3-7630-1977-4
MLCL 90/00744 (N)
                      NYPL [3-MRK+ 91-7607]

FOUNTAINS - GERMANY - WEIMAR.
Hemmann, Paul, 1895-1977. Die Brunnen in
Weimar . Weimar , 1990. 96 p. :   ISBN
3-910053-43-0   **NYPL [3-MRK 91-7023]**

FOUNTAINS - ITALY - ROME.
De Marchi, Andrea. Le fontanelle di Roma /.
Roma , 1988. 61 p. :
                      NYPL [3-MRN 90-10437]

FOUQUET, NICOLAS, 1615-1680.
France, Anatole, 1844-1924. Le château de
Vaux-le-Vicomte /. Etrépilly , c1987. v, 212 p.,
[8] p. of plates :   ISBN 2-905563-19-2
                      NYPL [3-MQWF 90-12695]

Four abstract artists . Fruit Market Gallery.
Edinburgh , 1977. [14] p. :   ISBN 0-902989-44-8
ND479 .F78 1977   **NYPL [3-MCT 79-734]**

Four Byzantine and Russian icons in the Menil
Collection / edited by Bertrand Davezac.
Houston, Tex. : Menil Collection, c1991. p. cm.
(The Menil Collection monographs . v. 1)   ISBN
0-939594-21-8   DDC 704.9/482 20
1. *Icons, Byzantine - Themes, motives. 2. Christian*
saints in art. 3. Uspenie (Icon). 4. Mary, Blessed Virgin,
Saint - Art. 5. Icons, Russian - Themes, motives. 6.
Orthodox Eastern Church and art. 7. Menil Collection
(Houston, Tex.). I. Davezac, Bertrand, 1930-. II. Series.
N8186.U6 M474 1991

Four painters : Michael Kessler, Archie Rand,
Mark Schlesinger, Lynton Wells / curated with
an essay by John Yau. Flint, Mich. ; Flint
Institute of Arts, c1989. 40 p. : ill. (some col.) ;
28 cm. Catalog of exhibition held Jan. 22-Feb. 26,
1989, at Flint Institute of Arts. Includes bibliographies.
ISBN 0-939896-09-5 (pbk.)
1. *Kessler, Michael, 1954-- Exhibitions. 2. Rand,*
Archie, 1949-- Exhibitions. 3. Schlesinger, Mark,
1949-- Exhibitions. 4. Wells, Lynton, 1940-–
Exhibitions. 5. Painting, American - Exhibitions. I. Yau,
John, 1950-. II. Flint Institute of Arts.
                      NYPL [MCW 89-24559]

Four Spanish photographers. Pitts, Terence. 4
Spanish photographers . [Tucson, Ariz.] , c1988.
23 p. :   **NYPL [MFW+ 89-1448]**

Fourcade, Dominique. Olitski, Jules, 1922- Jules
Olitski /. [New York] , c1990. 5 v. :
                      NYPL [3-MCX O47 91-6724]

Fourteen American monuments /. Friedlander,
Lee. [New York] , c1977. 13 p. :
                NYPL [MFX (Friedlander) 91-7115]

Fourteen hundred years of Islamic art. Fehérvári,
Géza. 1400 years of Islamic art . London ,
1984. 247 p. :   **NYPL [3-MAF+ 90-12505]**

Fourteen paintings : De Kooning, Dubuffet,
Ossorio, Pollock, Still. London : Thomas

Gibson Fine Art Ltd., [1976] [44] p. : ill. (14
col.), ports. ; 31 cm. "The catalogue notes have been
written by Alfonso Ossorio."--T.p. verso. Sales catalog.
Includes bibliographical references.
1. *Painting, Modern - 20th century - Catalogs. I.*
Ossorio, Alfonso. II. Thomas Gibson Fine Art Ltd.
                      NYPL [3-MC 90-7100]

Fowble, E. McSherry, 1933- To please every
taste : eighteenth-century prints from the
Winterthur Museum / E. McSherry Fowble.
Alexandria, Va. : Art Services International,
1991. p. cm. Exhibition catalog. Includes
bibliographical references.   ISBN 0-88397-098-8
DDC 769/.974/07474 20
1. *Prints, American - Exhibitions. 2. Prints - 18th*
century - United States - Exhibitions. 3. United States
in art - Exhibitions. 4. Henry Francis du Pont
Winterthur Museum - Exhibitions. I. Henry Francis du
Pont Winterthur Museum. II. Title.
NE506 .F6 1991

FOWLER, FRANCIS E., 1892-1975 - ART
COLLECTIONS - CATALOGS.
University of California, Los Angeles. Fowler
Museum of Cultural History. The Francis E.
Fowler, Jr., collection of silver /. Los Angeles,
Calif., USA , c1991. p.   ISBN 0-930741-19-6
(hard) :   DDC 739.2/3/07479494 20
NK7103.F68 U5 1991

Fowler, Harriet W. New Deal art : WPA works
at the University of Kentucky : University of
Kentucky Art Museum, August 25--October 27,
1985 / by Harriet W. Fowler ; with research
assistance by Sophia Wallace. [Lexington] : The
Museum, c1985. 119 p. : ill. ; 24 x 26 cm.
Bibliography: p. 119.   DDC 760/.0973/074016947 19
1. *Federal Art Project - Exhibitions. 2. Art, American -*
Exhibitions. 3. Social realism - Exhibitions. 4. Art,
Modern - 20th century - United States - Exhibitions. 5.
Federal aid to art - United States - Exhibitions. I.
Wallace, Sophia. II. University of Kentucky. Art
Museum. III. Title.
N8838 .F69 1985   **NYPL [MDBF 87-1170]**

Fowler, P. J. Images of prehistory / text by Peter
Fowler ; photographs by Mick Sharp.
Cambridge ; New York : Cambridge University
Press, 1990. 223 p. : ill. ; 27 cm. Includes
bibliographical references and index.
0-521-35646-6   DDC 936.1/0022/2 20
1. *Man, Prehistoric - Great Britain - Pictorial works. 2.*
Great Britain - Antiquities - Pictorial works. I. Sharp,
Mick. II. Title.
GN805 .F69 1990
                NYPL [MFX (Sharp) 91-4460]

Fox, Sandi. Wrapped in glory : figurative quilts &
bedcovers, 1700-1900 / Sandi Fox. New York :
Thames and Hudson ; Los Angeles : Los
Angeles County Museum of Art, c1990. 167
p. : ill. (some col.) ; 28 cm. Catalogue of the
exhibition held at the Los Angeles County Museum of
Art. Includes bibliographical references.   ISBN
0-500-01499-X   DDC 746.9/7/097307479494 20
1. *Quilts - United States - Exhibitions. 2. Quilts -*
England - Exhibitions. 3. Coverlets - United States -
Exhibitions. 4. Human figure in art - Exhibitions. I. Los
Angeles County Museum of Art. II. Title.
NK9112 .F698 1990
                      NYPL [3-MOT 91-3344]

Foye, Raymond, 1957- Percy, Ann. Francesco
Clemente . Philadelphia, Pa. , New York ,
1990. 184, [1] p. :   ISBN 0-87633-084-7
(Philadelphia Museum)   DDC 709/.2 20
NC257.C575 A4 1990
                NYPL [3-MCF+ C621 91-3673]

FOYERS. see ENTRANCE HALLS.

Fra Angelico . Didi-Huberman, Georges. Paris ,
c1990. 263 p. :   ISBN 2-08-012614-8   DDC 759.5
20
ND623.A5393 D53 1990
                NYPL [3-MCF A58 91-6120]

Fra Bartolommeo . Fischer, Chris. Rotterdam ,
Seattle , c1990. 415 p. :   ISBN 90-6918-070-7
DDC 741.945 20
NC257.B3418 A4 1990

Fra Galgario, Carlo Ceresa, Giacomo Ceruti.
Milesi, Silvana. Fra Galgario tra Seicento e
Settecento . Bergamo , c1990. 206 p. :
ND1318.3 .M5 1990

Fra Galgario tra Seicento e Settecento . Milesi,
Silvana. Bergamo , c1990. 206 p. :
ND1318.3 .M5 1990

Fra Galgario tra Seicento e Settecento . Milesi,
Silvana. Bergamo , c1990. 206 p. :
NYPL [3-MCF+ G43 91-5343]

Fra jord til fjell med Reidar Fritzvold /. Telnes,
Sigurd, 1925- Bø i Telemark , 1990. 111 p. :
ISBN 82-992118-0-8
ND773.F68 T4 1990

Frach, Petra. P40 . [Berlin] [1989?] 160 p. :
NYPL [3-MDW+ 90-11546]

Frackmann, Bilder 1980-1988. Frackmann,
Harald, 1944- Harald Frackmann, Bilder
1980-1988 . [Hamburg] [1988] [52] p. :
NYPL [3-MCK+ F797 91-4628]

Frackmann, Harald, 1944-
Harald Frackmann, Bilder 1980-1988 :
[Austellung] Hamburger Kunsthalle.
[Hamburg] : Die Kunsthalle, [1988] [52] p. :
chiefly ill. (some col.) ; 29 cm. Catalog of an
exhibition held at the Hamburger Kunsthalle, Sept.
14-Oct. 9, 1988. Cover title: Frackmann, Bilder
1980-1988.
1. Frackmann, Harald, 1944- - Exhibitions. I.
Hamburger Kunsthalle. II. Title. III. Title: Frackmann,
Bilder 1980-1988.
NYPL [3-MCK+ F797 91-4628]

FRACKMANN, HARALD, 1944- -
EXHIBITIONS.
Frackmann, Harald, 1944- Harald Frackmann,
Bilder 1980-1988 . [Hamburg] [1988] [52] p. :
NYPL [3-MCK+ F797 91-4628]

FRADE LEÓN , RAMÓN.
Delgado Mercado, Osiris. Ramón Frade León,
pintor puertorriqueño (1875-1954) . San Juan ,
1989. 277 p. :
NYPL [3-MCZ F799 90-10392]

Fraenkel Gallery. The Kiss of Apollo . San
Francisco , c1991. 105 p. : ISBN 0-938491-66-0 :
DDC 779/.973 20
TR658.3 .K57 1991   NYPL [MFW 91-6782]

Fragments of Chicago's past . Art Institute of
Chicago. Chicago, IL , 1990. 180 p. : ISBN
0-86559-088-5 DDC 720/.9773/1107477311 20
NA735.C4 A77 1990
NYPL [3-MQWO 91-3419]

Fragonard. Rosenberg, Pierre. Tout l'œuvre peint
de Fragonard /. Paris , c1989. 140 p. : ISBN
2-08-011227-9 DDC 759.4 20
ND553.F7 A4 1989

Fragonard, Honoré. see Fragonard, Jean Honoré,
1732-1806.

Fragonard, Jean Honoré, 1732-1806.
Rosenberg, Pierre. Tout l'œuvre peint de
Fragonard /. Paris , c1989. 140 p. : ISBN
2-08-011227-9 DDC 759.4 20
ND553.F7 A4 1989

FRAGONARD, JEAN-HONORÉ, 1732-1806 -
CATALOGUES RAISONNÉS.
Rosenberg, Pierre. Tout l'œuvre peint de
Fragonard /. Paris , c1989. 140 p. : ISBN
2-08-011227-9 DDC 759.4 20
ND553.F7 A4 1989

Fralin, Frances. Livingston, Jane. Odyssey .
Charlottesville, Va. , c1988. 363 p. : ISBN
0-934738-45-9 : DDC 779/.074/0153 19
TR790 .L58 1988   NYPL [MFW+ 90-556]

The frame in America, 1700-1900 . Adair,
William. Washington, D.C. , c1983. ix, 50 p. :
DDC 749/.7/0973074753 20
N8551.U6 A3 1983

Frameworks for international co-operation /
edited by A.J.R. Groom and Paul Taylor.
London : Pinter, 1990. x, 293 p. ; 24 cm.
Includes bibliographical references and index. ISBN
0-86187-537-0 : DDC 327.17 20
I. Groom, A. J. R. II. Taylor, Paul Graham.
JX1954   NYPL [JLE 90-2359]

Framing art . Carter, Michael, 1944- Sydney,
NSW , c1990. 211 p. : ISBN 0-86806-354-1
NYPL [3-MAD 91-2237]

FRAMING OF PICTURES. see PICTURE
FRAMES AND FRAMING.

Framke, Gisela. Französische Illustrationen des
18. und 19. Jahrhunderts . Dortmund , 1985.
267 p. : ISBN 3-924302-16-2 DDC
741.64/074/0356 s 741.64/0944/0740356 19
NC980 .B54 1985 vol. 1
NYPL [MDT 91-2511]

Frampton, Kenneth.
Frank Lloyd Wright . New York, N.Y. , c1991.
308 p. : ISBN 1-87827-126-1 (cloth) DDC 720/.92
20
NA737.W7 F678 1990
NYPL [3-MQZ (Wright) 91-6794]

Mas Serra, Elías, 1945- 50 Años de
arquitectura en Euskadi /. [Vitoria] , 1990.
xviii, 347 p. : ISBN 84-7542-854-1 DDC
720/.946/609045 20
NA1309.P33 M37 1990

Santiago Calatrava . Basel , Boston , 1991. p.
cm. ISBN 0-8176-2460-0 DDC 720/.92 20
NA1313.C35 S26 1991

Från svenska sagor till amerikansk fantasi .
Tenggren, Gustaf, 1896- Stockholm [1990] 77
p. : ISBN 91-7100-389-4
NC986.5.T46 A4 1990

FRANCE - REVOLUTION, 1789-1799 -
INFLUENCE - EXHIBITIONS.
Les Architectes de la liberté, 1789-1799 .
Paris , c1989. 396 p. : ISBN 2-903639-65-5
DDC 720/.944/07444361 20
NA1046.5.N4 A7 1989

France, Anatole, 1844-1924. Le château de
Vaux-le-Vicomte / Anatole France. Suivi d'une
étude historique par Jean Cordey. Etrépilly :
Presses du village, c1987. v, 212 p., [8] p. of
plates : ill. ; 22 cm. Includes bibliographical
references. Reprint, with new plates. Originally
published : Paris : Calmann-Lévy, 1933. ISBN
2-905563-19-2
1. Fouquet, Nicolas, 1615-1680. 2. Château de
Vaux-le-Vicomte (Maincy, France). 3. Castles - France -
Maincy. I. Cordey, Jean. II. Title.
NYPL [3-MQWF 90-12695]

France. Centre Georges Pompidou. see Centre
Georges Pompidou.

France. Centre national d'art et de culture
Georges Pompidou. see Centre Georges
Pompidou.

France, Christine, 1939-
Justin O'Brien, image and icon / Christine
France. Seaforth, NSW, Australia : Craftsman
House, 1987. 125 p. : ill. (some col.) ; 30 cm.
Bibliography: p. [121]-123. ISBN 0-947131-04-3
DDC 759.994 19
1. O'Brien, Justin, 1917- - Catalogs. I. Title.
ND1105.O27 A4 1987
NYPL [3-MCZ+ O129 89-1698]

Margaret Olley / Christine France. Roseville,
NSW, Australia : Craftsman House, c1990. 180
p. : ill. ; 30 cm. ISBN 0-947131-36-1
1. Olley, Margaret, 1923-. I. Title.
NYPL [3-MCZ+ O495 90-13349]

FRANCE - CIVILIZATION - 20TH
CENTURY.
Entre deux guerres . Paris , c1990. 631 p. ;
ISBN 2-87686-057-0 : DDC 700/.944/09041 20
NX549.A1 E5 1990

FRANCE - COLONIES - NORTH AMERICA.
Boucher, Philip P., 1944- Les nouvelles
Frances . Providence, RI , 1989. xxi, 122 p. :
ISBN 0-916617-32-7
NYPL [Map Div. 90-11548]

FRANCE - COURT AND COURTIERS -
BIOGRAPHY.
Hall, H. Gaston. Richelieu's Desmarets and the
century of Louis XIV /. Oxford , New York ,
1990. 399 p. : ISBN 0-19-815157-8 : DDC 841/.4
B 20
PQ1794.D6 H35 1990
NYPL [3-MAVZ (Hamburg) 91-3450]

FRANCE - DESCRIPTION AND TRAVEL -
1975- - VIEWS.
Le Château en France /. Paris , 1988. 448 p.,
[16] p. of plates : ISBN 2-7013-0741-4
NYPL [3-MQWF+ 90-11996]

FRANCE - DESCRIPTION AND TRAVEL -
GUIDE-BOOKS.
Lurie, Patty, 1944- A guide to the impressionist
landscape . Boston , c1990. 135 p. : ISBN
0-8212-1796-8 DDC 758/.144/094409034 20
ND1355.5 .L8 1990
NYPL [3-MCN 91-2248]

France. Direction du patrimoine. Les Enjeux du
patrimoine architectural du XXe siècle . [Paris]
[1988?] 186 p. : ISBN 2-11-085013-2
NA109.F8 E55 1988

France. Direction générale des relations
culturelles, scientifiques et techniques.
Histoire de la photographie française : des
origines à 1920 : [exposition itinérante, 1978-]
/ catalogue ... réalisé par la Direction générale
des relations culturelles, scientifiques et
techniques du Ministère des affaires étrangères ;
avec le concours du Musée français de la
photographie ... Paris (19, rue du Départ,
75014) : Créatis, 1978. 1 v. (unpaged) : ill.
(some col.) ; 30 cm.
1. Photography - France - History - Exhibitions. I.
Musée français de la photographie. II. Title.
TR71 .F69 1978   NYPL [MFX+ 81-584]

France. Direction régionale des affaires
culturelles de Basse-Normandie. Eglise
Saint-Germain . [Caen, France] [1990] 16 p. :
ISBN 2-908621-00-2 : DDC 726/.5/094423 20
NA5551.A674 E36 1990

France - Government. see France - Politics and
government.

France - Guidebooks. see France - Description
and travel - Guide-books.

FRANCE - HISTORY - LOUIS XIV, 1643-
1715.
Hall, H. Gaston. Richelieu's Desmarets and the
century of Louis XIV /. Oxford , New York ,
1990. 399 p. : ISBN 0-19-815157-8 : DDC 841/.4
B 20
PQ1794.D6 H35 1990
NYPL [3-MAVZ (Hamburg) 91-3450]

FRANCE - HISTORY - REVOLUTION, 1789-
1799 - ART AND THE REVOLUTION.
Herding, Klaus. Im Zeichen der Aufklärung .
Frankfurt am Main , 1989. 242, [1] p. : ISBN
3-596-23615-0   *NYPL [3-MAL 90-13019]*

FRANCE - HISTORY - REVOLUTION, 1789-
1799 - ART AND THE REVOLUTION -
EXHIBITIONS.
L'Enrôlement des volontaires de 1792 .
Beauvais [1989] 258 p. : ISBN 2-901290-05-1
NYPL [3-MCO C87 91-5550]

Faïences et objets révolutionnaires . Gagny ,
1989. 150 p. :   *NYPL [3-MPGG+ 90-252]*

Faïences révolutionnaires . Paris , Rouen ,
1989. 76 p. :   *NYPL [3-MPGG+ 90-71]*

Hould, Claudette. Images of the French
Revolution /. Québec , c1989. 446 p. : ISBN
2-551-08407-5   *NYPL [MDZ+ 90-12786]*

Robert, Hubert, 1733-1808. Hubert Robert et la
Révolution /. Valence , 1989. 179 p. :
NYPL [3-MCO R641 90-11133]

FRANCE - HISTORY - REVOLUTION, 1789-
1799 - EXHIBITIONS.
Le Panthéon, symbole des révolutions .
[Montréal] : [Paris] : 339 p. : ISBN
2-7084-0386-9 (Picard)
IN PROCESS (ONLINE)
NYPL [3-MQWF 90-10797]

FRANCE - HISTORY - REVOLUTION, 1789-
1799 - PICTORIAL WORKS -
EXHIBITIONS.
Les Architectes de la liberté, 1789-1799 . Paris ,
c1989. 396 p. : ISBN 2-903639-65-5
NYPL [3-MQWF 90-11622]

FRANCE - HISTORY - REVOLUTION, 1789-
1799 - PORTRAITS.
Kessemeier, Siegfried. Köpfe der französischen
Revolution . Münster , 1989. 121 p. : ISBN
3-88789-088-4   *NYPL [MDZ 91-5816]*

FRANCE - HISTORY - RESTORATION, 1814-
1830 - CARICATURES AND CARTOONS.
Athanassoglou-Kallmyer, Nina M., 1945-
Eugène Delacroix . New Haven, CT , 1991. p.
cm. ISBN 0-300-04931-5 DDC 741.5/092 20
NC1499.D36 A9 1991

FRANCE - HISTORY - GERMAN
OCCUPATION, 1940-1945.
Cone, Michèle S., 1932- Art, prejudice, and
persecution . Princeton, N.J. , c1992. p. cm.
ISBN 0-691-04088-5 : DDC 701/.03 20
N6848 .C66 1992

FRANCE - HISTORY - PICTORIAL WORKS.
Gaehtgens, Thomas W., 1940- Versailles .
Paris , c1981. 407 p. : ISBN 2-226-02168-X
N2180.2.G34 G3 1981

FRANCE - INTELLECTUAL LIFE - 18TH
CENTURY.
Picon, Antoine. [Architectes et ingénieurs au

siècle des Lumières. English.] French architects
and engineers in the Age of Enlightenment /.
Cambridge , New York , 1991. p. cm.   ISBN
0-521-38253-X   DDC 720/.944/09033 20
NA1046.5.N4 P513 1991

**France. Inventaire général des monuments et des
richesses artistiques de la France.** see
**Inventaire général des monuments et des
richesses artistiques de la France.**

**FRANCE - KINGS AND RULERS -
DWELLINGS - EXHIBITIONS.**
De Versailles à Paris . Paris , 1989. 288 p., [38]
p. of plates :   ISBN 2-9504070-0-5
        NYPL [3-MAWC (Paris) 90-12345]

FRANCE. MARINE. SOUS-MARINS.
Rusbridger, James. Who sank Surcouf? .
London , 1991. xiii, 209 p., [8] of plates :
        ISBN 0-7126-3975-6 :   DDC 940.5451 20
D780   *NYPL [JFE 91-5695]*

**France. Ministère de la culture, de la
communication, des grands travaux et du
Bicentenaire.**
Arabesques et jardins de paradis . Paris , c1989.
334 p. :   ISBN 2-7118-2294-X :   DDC
        709/.17/67107444361 20
N6264.F8 P317 1990

Les Architectes de la liberté, 1789-1799 .
Paris , c1989. 396 p. :   ISBN 2-903639-65-5
        DDC 720/.944/07444361 20
NA1046.5.N4 A7 1989

Le Meuble régional en France : Musée national
des arts et traditions populaires 19 octobre
1990/25 février 1991. Paris : Editions de la
Réunion des musées nationaux, 1990. 189 p. :
ill. (some col.) ; 24 cm. "Ministère de la culture, de
la communication, des grands travaux et du
Bicentenaire." Includes bibliographical references.
        ISBN 2-7118-2374-1
*1. Furniture - France - Exhibitions. 2. Furniture, -
France - History. I. Musée national des arts et
traditions populaires (France). II. Réunion des musées
nationaux (France).*   *NYPL [3-MOF 91-3999]*

Picasso, Pablo, 1881-1973. Picasso, une
nouvelle dation. Paris , c1990. 298 p. :   ISBN
        2-7118-2369-5 :   DDC 709/.2 20
N6853.P5 A4 1990a

**France. Ministère de la France d'outre-mer.
Office de la recherche scientifique et
technique outre-mer.** see **France. Office de la
recherche scientifique et technique outre-mer.**

**France. Ministère des affaires étrangères.
Direction générale des relations culturelles,
scientifiques et techniques.** see **France.
Direction générale des relations culturelles,
scientifiques et techniques.**

**France. Ministère d'État chargé des affaires
culturelles. Inventaire général des
monuments et des richesses artistiques de la
France.** see **Inventaire général des
monuments et des richesses artistiques de la
France.**

**France. Office de la recherche scientifique et
technique outre-mer.** Atlas del inventario de
tierras del territorio federal Amazonas /.
Caracas, Venezuela [1985]. 1 v. (various
pagings) :   ISBN 980-04-0053-2
        NYPL [Map Div. 91-7664]

**France. Office de la recherche scientifique outre-
mer.** see **France. Office de la recherche
scientifique et technique outre-mer.**

**FRANCE - POLITICS AND GOVERNMENT -
1852-1870.**
Friedrich, Otto, 1929- Olympia . New York ,
NY , c1992. p.   ISBN 0-06-016318-6 (cloth) :
        DDC 701/.03 20
N6847 .F75 1992

**FRANCE - POLITICS AND GOVERNMENT -
1958- - CARICATURES AND CARTOONS.**
Siné. Dessins politiques. [Paris, 1972 printing,
c1965] 186 p.
DC412 .S527 1972
        NYPL [3-MEM (Siné) 90-7137]

**FRANCE - POLITICS AND GOVERNMENT -
1981- - CARICATURES AND CARTOONS.**
Cabu. Le gros blond avec sa chemise noire /.
Paris , c1987. 1 v. (unpaged) :   ISBN
2-226-03167-7
        NYPL [3-MEM+ (Cabu) 89-27328]

FRANCE - POPULAR CULTURE.
Rigby, Brian. Popular culture in modern
France . London , New York , 1992. p. cm.
        ISBN 0-415-01246-5   DDC 700/.1/0309440904
        20
NX180.S6 R54 1992

**France. Recherche scientifique et technique outre-
mer, Office de la.** see **France. Office de la
recherche scientifique et technique outre-mer.**

**France. Relations culturelles, scientifiques et
techniques, Direction générale des.** see
**France. Direction générale des relations
culturelles, scientifiques et techniques.**

**FRANCE - RELIGIOUS LIFE AND
CUSTOMS.**
Bougoux, Christian. De l'origine des lanternes
des morts /. Bordeaux , c1989. 151 p. :   ISBN
2-9503805-0-6
NA6165 .B68 1989

FRANCE - ROYAL HOUSEHOLD.
Verlet, Pierre. Le mobilier royal français /.
[Paris] , 1990- v. <4 > :   ISBN 2-7084-0389-3
        (v. 4)   DDC 749.24 20
NK2548 .V44 1990

**FRANCE - ROYAL HOUSEHOLD -
EXHIBITIONS.**
De Versailles à Paris . Paris , 1989. 288 p., [38]
p. of plates :   ISBN 2-9504070-0-5
        NYPL [3-MAWC (Paris) 90-12345]

Frances Anne Hopkins, 1838-1919 . Clark, Janet
E. Thunder Bay, Ont. , 1989. 112 p. :   ISBN
0-920539-30-0 :   DDC 759.11 20
        NYPL [3-MCV H762 90-10799]

Frances Benjamin Johnston . Johnston, Frances
Benjamin, 1864-1952. York [1984] [20] p. :
        ISBN 0-906361-45-1 (pbk.)
TR820.5 M544 1984
        NYPL [MFX (Johnston) 91-3499]

Frances Brundage post cards . Budd, Ellen H.
[Cincinnati, OH] (6910 Tenderfoot La.,
Cincinnati 45249) [1990] 140 p. :   DDC
741.6/83/092 20
NC1879.B76 A4 1990

Frances Wolfson Art Gallery. Presser, Elena,
1940- Elena Presser, Bach's Goldberg
variations . Miami , c1985. [28] p. :   ISBN
0-916203-09-3
        NYPL [3-MDG (Presser) 88-4568]

Franceschini, Marcantonio, 1648-1729.
Miller, Dwight C. (Dwight Cameron), 1923-
Marcantonio Franceschini and the
Liechtensteins . Cambridge , New York , 1991.
xx, 296 p., [16] p. of plates :   ISBN
0-521-36503-1   DDC 759.5 B 20
ND623.F78125 A3 1990
        NYPL [3-MCF F813 91-7475]

**FRANCESCHINI, MARCANTONIO, 1648-
1729 - CORRESPONDENCE.**
Miller, Dwight C. (Dwight Cameron), 1923-
Marcantonio Franceschini and the
Liechtensteins . Cambridge , New York , 1991.
xx, 296 p., [16] p. of plates :   ISBN
0-521-36503-1   DDC 759.5 B 20
ND623.F78125 A3 1990
        NYPL [3-MCF F813 91-7475]

Francesco Clemente . Clemente, Francesco, 1952-
New York , 1991. p. cm.   ISBN 0-8478-1469-6
        DDC 759.5 20
ND1962.C58 A4 1991

Francesco Clemente . Percy, Ann. Philadelphia,
Pa. , New York , 1990. 184, [1] p. :   ISBN
0-87633-084-7 (Philadelphia Museum)   DDC
709/.2 20
NC257.C575 A4 1990
        NYPL [3-MCF+ C621 91-3673]

FRANCHISE. see ELECTIONS.

Francia, François-Thomas-Louis, 1772-1839.
Louis Francia, 1772-1839 : Calais, Musée des
beaux-arts, 15 octobre 1988-9 janvier 1989.
Calais : Le Musée, 1988. 156 p. : ill. (some
col.) ; 27 cm. Cover title: Louis Francia.
Bibliography: p. 148-155.
*1. Francia, François-Thomas-Louis, 1772-1839 -
Exhibitions. I. Musée des beaux-arts de Calais. II. Title.
III. Title: Louis Francia.*
N6797.F736 A4 1988
        NYPL [3-MCO F832 90-11618]

Louis Francia, 1772-1839 : Calais, Musée des
beaux-arts, 15 octobre 1988-9 janvier 1989.

Calais : Le Musée, 1988. 156 p. : ill. (some
col.) ; 28 cm. Produced under the direction of
Patrick Le Nouëne. Includes bibliographical references
(p. 148-15).   ISBN 2-7118-... DDC 760/.092 20
*1. Francia, François-Thomas-Louis, 1772-1839 -
Exhibitions. 2. Sea in art - Exhibitions. 3. Ships in art -
Exhibitions. I. Le Nouëne, Patrick. II. Musée des
beaux-arts de Calais. III. Title.*
N6853.F695 A4 1988

**FRANCIA, FRANÇOIS-THOMAS-LOUIS,
1772-1839 - EXHIBITIONS.**
Francia, François-Thomas-Louis, 1772-1839.
Louis Francia, 1772-1839 . Calais , 1988. 156
p. :   DDC 760/.092 20
N6853.F695 A4 1988

Francia, François-Thomas-Louis, 1772-1839.
Louis Francia, 1772-1839 . Calais , 1988. 156
p. :
N6797.F736 A4 1988
        NYPL [3-MCO F832 90-11618]

Francis Bott, das Gesamtwerk /. Henze,
Wolfgang, 1944- Stuttgart , Zürich , c1988. 395
p. :   ISBN 3-7630-2062-4
        NYPL [3-MCK+ B7895 90-11079]

Francis, Carolyn A., 1956- People places . New
York, N.Y. , 1990. xvii, 295 p. :   ISBN
0-442-31929-0 :   DDC 711/.4 20
NA9070 .P45 1990
        NYPL [3-MQWO 90-11592]

**Francis, Dennis Steadman.
Architects in practice, New York City, 1840-
1900.** Ward, James. Architects in practice,
New York City, 1900-1940 / James Ward for
the Committee for the Preservation of
Architectural Records. Union, N.J. [1989]
xviii, 87 p. ;   DDC 720/.25/7471 20
NA55.N5 W3 1989

The Francis E. Fowler, Jr., collection of silver /.
University of California, Los Angeles. Fowler
Museum of Cultural History. Los Angeles,
Calif., USA , c1991. p.   ISBN 0-930741-19-6
        (hard)   DDC 739.2/3/07479494 20
NK7103.F68 U5 1991

Francis Graham-Dixon Gallery. Olitski, Jules,
1922- Jules Olitski /. [New York] , c1990. 5
v. :   *NYPL [3-MCX O47 91-6724]*

Francis, Mark, 1950- The Meaning of gardens .
Cambridge, Mass. , c1990. ix, 283 p. :   ISBN
0-262-06127-9   DDC 712 20
SB470.7 .M43 1990
        NYPL [3-MSC 90-11705]

**FRANCIS, OF ASSISI, SAINT, 1182-1226 -
ART.**
Plazer, Lukas, 1663-1723. Der barocke
Franziskuszyklus von Frater Lukas Plazer in
Innichen /. Innichen , 1990. 259 p. :   ISBN
        88-85226-00-0
ND623.P696 A4 1990

Francis, Sam, 1923-
Sam Francis, Los Angeles County Museum of
Art, March 13 - May 11, 1980. Los Angeles,
Calif. : Los Angeles County Museum of Art,
c1980. 44 p. : ill. (some col.) ; 31 cm. Includes
bibliographical references.   ISBN 0-87587-094-5
*1. Francis, Sam, 1923- - Exhibitions. I. Los Angeles
County, Calif. Museum of Art, Los Angeles. II. Title.*
NE2246.F72 A4 1980
        NYPL [3-MCX+ F819 81-339]

FRANCIS, SAM, 1923- - EXHIBITIONS.
Francis, Sam, 1923- Sam Francis, Los Angeles
County Museum of Art, March 13 - May 11,
1980. Los Angeles, Calif. , c1980. 44 p. :   ISBN
0-87587-094-5
NE2246.F72 A4 1980
        NYPL [3-MCX+ F819 81-339]

Francisco Amighetti /. Amighetti, Francisco. San
José, Costa Rica , c1989. 167 p. :   ISBN
997-7671-12-5   DDC 760/.092 20
N6575.A45 A4 1989

Francisco Barón /. Ortega Coca, María Teresa.
[Valladolid] , [1989?] 60 p., [64] p. of plates :
        ISBN 84-7852-010-4   DDC 730/.92 20
NB813.B29 A4 1989
        NYPL [3-MGO (Barón) 91-6088]

Francisco Corzas. Corzas, Francisco, 1936-
México, D.F. [1985] 137 p. :   ISBN
968-8400-43-2
N6559.C65 A4 1985

Francisco de Zurbarán /. Brown, Jonathan, 1939-
New York [1991] p. cm.   ISBN 0-8109-3962-2

DDC 759.6 20
ND813.Z85 B76 1991

Francisco Goya /. Venezia, Mike. Chicago , 1991.
p. cm. ISBN 0-516-02292-X DDC 759.6 B 92 20
ND813.G7 V4 1991

Francisco Montoya de la Cruz. Montoya de la
Cruz, Francisco, 1909- [Durango] [1984] 70
p. : DDC 759.972 20
ND259.M63 A4 1984

Francisco Toledo . Toledo, Francisco, 1940- New
York, N.Y. [1974] [30] p. :
NYPL [3-MCZ T649 91-6243]

Francisco Toledo . Toledo, Francisco, 1940- New
York, N.Y. [1990?] [48] p. :
NYPL [3-MCZ T649 90-13384]

Franciscono, Marcel. Paul Klee : his work and
thought / Marcel Franciscono. Chicago :
University of Chicago Press, 1991. x, 395 p. :
ill. ; 24 cm. Includes bibliographical references (p.
375-383) and index. ISBN 0-226-25990-0 (alk. paper)
DDC 760/.092 20
1. Klee, Paul, 1879-1940 - Criticism and interpretation.
N6888.K55 F7 1991
NYPL [3-MCZ K63 91-6530]

Franck, Irene M. Brownstone, David M. 20th
century culture . [New York?] , 1991. p. cm.
ISBN 0-13-210519-5 : DDC 700/.9/04 20
NX456 .B76 1991

Franco Albini, architecture and design,
1934-1977 : Marco Albini, Franca Helg,
Antonio Piva / [edited by] Stephen Leet ;
foreword, Ignazio Gardella ; preface, Julio M.
San Jose ; with essays by Franca Helg, Stephen
Leet, Alberto Sartoris. New York, NY :
Princeton Architectural Press, c1990. 138 p. :
ill., plans ; 26 cm. Catalog of an exhibition held at
the New York Institute of Technology and other
institutions, Oct. 2, 1989-Mar. 7, 1991. Includes
bibliographical references. ISBN 0-910413-79-7 (pbk. :
alk. paper) : DDC 720/.92 20
1. Albini, Franco - Exhibitions. 2. Functionalism
(Architecture) - Italy - Exhibitions. I. Leet, Stephen. II.
New York Institute of Technology. III. Title:
Architecture and design, 1934-1977.
NA1123.A525 A4 1990
NYPL [3-MQZ (Albini) 91-6735]

Franco Fontana . Fontana, Franco, 1933- Udine ,
c1990. 251 p. : ISBN 88-85893-21-X
NYPL [MFX+ (Fontana) 91-3996]

Franco Torrijos, Enrique. Herrán, Saturnino,
1887-1918. Saturnino Herrán /. México , 1988
143 p. : ISBN 968-665-809-2
NYPL [3-MCZ++ H564 89-26935]

François, André. André François / [traduit de
l'anglais par Vicky Hayward et Jean-Marie
Clarke]. Paris : Herscher, c1986. 240 p. : ill.
(some col.) ; 29 cm. ISBN 2-7335-0116-X
1. François, André. I. Title.
NYPL [3-MDWS (François) 91-5326]

FRANÇOIS, ANDRÉ.
François, André. André François /. Paris ,
c1986. 240 p. : ISBN 2-7335-0116-X
NYPL [3-MDWS (François) 91-5326]

François Bouillon . Bouillon, François, 1944-
[Labège, France , 1990] 160 p. : ISBN
2-905992-32-8 : DDC 709/.2 20
N6853.B588 A4 1990

François Maréchal, 1861-1945 . Maréchal,
François, 1861- Köln , 1979. [74] p. :
NE2055.5.M37 A4 1979
NYPL [MDG (Maréchal) 81-1028]

Françoise Bujold . Bujold, Françoise, 1933-1981.
[Québec] , c1982. 55 p. : ISBN 2-550-02474-5
MLCS 82/8466
NYPL [MDG (Bujold) 91-891]

FRANCONIA (GERMANY) - DESCRIPTION
AND TRAVEL - GUIDE-BOOKS.
Stolz, Georg. Franken. [München] [1989] 371
p. : ISBN 3-422-03012-3 DDC 709/.43/32 20
N6874.F7 S76 1989

Francouzská bojiště československých legií .
Nejedlý, Otakar, 1883-1957. Praze [1920?] [4]
p., [8] leaves of plates :
NYPL [3-MAMY+++ 83-2786]

Frandsen, Jan Würtz. Mertz, Albert. Giv agt .
København , c1987. [16] p. : ISBN
87-87273-62-4
NYPL [3-MCH M565 90-12521]

Franger, Gaby.
Akkent, Meral. Das Kopftuch . Frankfurt a.M. ,
1987. 286 p. : ISBN 3-924320-61-6 :
GT2113 .A35 1987
NYPL [3-MMV+ 91-4637]

[Arpilleras : Bilder die sprechen Organisation
und Alltag der Frauen in den Slums von
Lima. Spanish]
Arpilleras : cuadros que hablan vida cotidiana
y organización de mujeres / Gaby Franger.
Lima, Peru : Betaprint, 1988. 110 p. : ill.
(some col.), ports. ; 21 cm. Translation of:
Arpilleras : Bilder die sprechen Organisation und
Alltag der Frauen in den Slums von Lima. Organized
by Mujeres Creativas.
1. Canvas embroidery - Peru - Lima. 2. Women artists -
Peru - Lima. 3. Women - Peru - Lima - Societies and
clubs. I. Mujeres Creativas. II. Title. III. Title: Cuadros
que hablan vida cotidiana y organización de mujeres.
NYPL [3-MOT 90-12715]

Frangi, Giuseppe. Moroni in Val Seriana /.
Brescia , 1978. 69 p. :
ND623.M76 M67
NYPL [3-MCF M86 81-635]

Frangos, Seva. Miriam Stannage, perception
1969-1989 : 20 April to 25 May, 1989 / Seva
Frangos, Margaret Moore. Perth, W.A. : Art
Gallery of Western Australia, [1989] 64 p. : ill.
(some col.) ; 30 cm. Catalog of an exhibition held at
the Art Gallery of Western Australia, 20 April to 25
May 1989. Includes bibliographical references (p. 53).
ISBN 0-7309-0719-8 DDC 760/.092 20
1. Stannage, Miriam, 1939- - Exhibitions. I. Moore,
Margaret, 1958-. II. Title.
N7405.S73 A4 1989
NYPL [3-MCZ+ S787 91-4200]

Frank and Ernest. Thaves, Bob. [Frank and
Ernest. Selections.] Assemble the hyenas-- I feel
a pun coming on! . New York , 1991. ca. 130
p. : ISBN 0-88687-529-3 : DDC 741.5/973 20
NC1429.T44 A4 1991

Frank Buchser 1828-1890 . Buchser, Frank,
1828-1890. Einsiedeln , c1990. 284 p. :
NYPL [3-MCZ+ B92 91-8120]

Frank, Folker. Bauen im Dritten Reich /.
Stuttgart [1989] 73 p. ; ISBN 3-8167-0278-3
NYPL [3-MQWD 90-10818]

Frank Furness . Thomas, George E. New York,
N.Y. , c1991. p. cm. ISBN 1-87827-104-0 :
DDC 720/.92 20
NA737.F84 A4 1991

Frank, Hartmut, 1942- Nordlicht . Hamburg ,
1989. 415 p. : ISBN 3-88506-174-0 DDC
709/.43/51507443515 20
N332.G33 H355 1989

Frank, Hilmar. Asmus Jakob Carstens und Joseph
Anton Koch, zwei Zeitgenossen der
Französischen Revolution . Berlin [1989] 160
p. :
NC249 .A835 1989

Frank Hodgkinson's European sketchbooks.
Hodgkinson, Frank. Kenthurst, N.S.W.,
Australia , c1990- v. : ISBN 0-646-01520-6 (set)
NYPL [3-MCZ H6895 91-3616]

Frank, Leonard. Leonoff, Cyril Edel. An
enterprising life . Vancouver , 1990. 176 p. :
ISBN 0-88922-283-5 : DDC 779/.9871103 20
NYPL [MFX+ (Frank) 91-7431]

FRANK, LEONARD.
Leonoff, Cyril Edel. An enterprising life .
Vancouver , 1990. 176 p. : ISBN 0-88922-283-5 :
DDC 779/.9871103 20
NYPL [MFX+ (Frank) 91-7431]

Frank Lloyd Wright : a primer on architectural
principles / Robert McCarter, editor ; Kenneth
Frampton ... [et al.]. New York, N.Y. :
Princeton Architectural Press, c1991. 308 p. :
ill. ; 26 cm. Includes bibliographical references.
ISBN 1-87827-126-1 (cloth) DDC 720/.92 20
1. Wright, Frank Lloyd, 1867-1959 - Criticism and
interpretation. 2. Prairie school (Architecture). I.
McCarter, Robert, 1955-. II. Frampton, Kenneth.
NA737.W7 F678 1990
NYPL [3-MQZ (Wright) 91-6794]

Frank Lloyd Wright . Laseau, Paul, 1937- New
York, N.Y. , c1991. p. cm. ISBN 0-442-23478-3
DDC 720/.92 20
NA737.W7 L37 1991

Frank Lloyd Wright /. McDonough, Yona Zeldis.
New York , 1991. p. cm. ISBN 0-7910-1626-9

DDC 720/.92 B 20
NA737.W7 M37 1991

Frank Lloyd Wright and Madison . Wright,
Frank Lloyd, 1867-1959. Madison, Wis. , 1990.
vii, 218 p. : ISBN 0-932900-22-4 DDC 720/.92
20
NA737.W7 A4 1990
NYPL [3-MQZ+ (Wright) 90-12072]

Frank Lloyd Wright and the Laffer curve .
Clarke, David, 1942- Wakefield, N.H. , 1991. p.
cm. ISBN 0-89341-655-X DDC 720/.71/173 20
NA2105 .C58 1991

Frank Lloyd Wright in lecture delivered, May 2,
1952, at the University of Oklahoma [sound
recording]. Wright, Frank Lloyd, 1867-1959.
Oklahoma City [1976] 1 sound cassette :
NA737

Frank Lloyd Wright in Michigan /. Northup, A.
Dale, 1941- Algonac, Mich. , 1991. 100 p. :
ISBN 0-917256-51-4 DDC 728/.373/092 20
NA737.W7 N6 1991

Frank Lloyd Wright remembered /. Meehan,
Patrick Joseph. Washington, DC , 1991. p. cm.
ISBN 0-89133-187-5 DDC 720/.92 20
NA737.W7 M44 1991

Frank Lloyd Wright versus America . Johnson,
Donald Leslie. Cambridge, Mass. , c1990. xi,
436 p. : ISBN 0-262-10044-4 DDC 720/.92 B 20
NA737.W7 J6 1990
NYPL [3-MQZ (Wright) 91-4307]

Frank O'Meara and his contemporaries.
Campbell, Julian. Frank O'Meara, 1853-1888 /.
Dublin , c1989. xii, 90 p., [6] p. of plates :
ISBN 0-9514246-0-2 (pbk.) DDC 709/.415/074
19
N6789
NYPL [3-MCZ O54 91-4562]

Frank O'Meara, 1853-1888 /. Campbell, Julian.
Dublin , c1989. xii, 90 p., [6] p. of plates :
ISBN 0-9514246-0-2 (pbk.) DDC 709/.415/074
19
N6789
NYPL [3-MCZ O54 91-4562]

Frank S. Schwarz & Son.
A Century of Philadelphia artists. Philadelphia ,
1988. 64 p. : *NYPL [3-MCW 90-13578]*

Fine European paintings. Philadelphia : F.S.
Schwarz & Son, c1988. 1 v. (unpaged) : ill. ; 25
cm. (Philadelphia collection . 38)
1. Painting, European - Exhibitions. I. Title.
NYPL [3-MC 90-13536]

Hall, Audrey. American miniatures.
Philadelphia, Pa. (1806 Chestnut St.,
Philadelphia 19103) , 1990. 1 v. (unpaged) :
DDC 757/.7/09740903307474811 20
ND1337.U5 H34 1990

Hall, Audrey. American paintings. Philadelphia,
PA (1806 Chestnut St., Philadelphia 19103)
[c1990] 1 v. : DDC 759.13/09/03407474811 20
ND210 .H34 1990

Frank Stella . Stella, Frank. [Fort Worth] , 1984.
vi, 45 p. : DDC 769.92/4 19
NE539.S72 A4 1984
NYPL [MDG (Stella) 85-2527]

Franke, Michael. Wehling, Hans-Werner, 1949-
Werks- und Genossenschaftssiedlungen im
Ruhrgebiet 1844-1939. Essen , 1990- v. <1
> : ISBN 3-88474-344-9 DDC 728/.0943/5509034
20
NA7553 .W44 1990

Franken. Stolz, Georg. [München] [1989] 371
p. : ISBN 3-422-03012-3 DDC 709/.43/32 20
N6874.F7 S76 1989

Franken, Franz Hermann. Hans Meid : Leben
und Werk / F.H. Franken ; herausgegeben von
Ralph Jentsch. Stuttgart-Bad Cannstatt : Cantz,
c1987. 462 p. : ill. (some col.) ; 31 cm. Includes
bibliographical references (p. 438-442) and index.
ISBN 3-922608-58-2
1. Meid, Hans, 1883-1957. 2. Artists - Germany, West -
Biography. I. Meid, Hans, 1883-1957. II. Jentsch,
Ralph. III. Title.
NYPL [3-MCK+ M4978 90-11755]

Frankenthaler, Helen, 1928-
Helen Frankenthaler, works on paper :
gouaches and prints. Vancouver :
Buschlen-Mowatt Gallery, c1989. 43 p. : chiefly
col. ill. ; 28 cm. Catalogue of an exhibition held Dec.
1989 at the Buschlen-Mowatt Gallery, Vancouver.
Introduction in English and French. Includes
bibliographical references. ISBN 0-9693328-7-4 :

DDC 759.13 20
1. Frankenthaler, Helen, 1928- - Exhibitions. I.
Buschlen-Mowatt Gallery. II. Title.
NYPL [3-MCX F825 91-3252]

**FRANKENTHALER, HELEN, 1928- -
EXHIBITIONS.**
Frankenthaler, Helen, 1928- Helen
Frankenthaler, works on paper . Vancouver ,
c1989. 43 p. : ISBN 0-9693328-7-4 : DDC 759.13
20 **NYPL [3-MCX F825 91-3252]**

Frankfurt am Main. Frankfurter Kunstverein. see
Frankfurter Kunstverein, Frankfurt am Main.

**FRANKFURT AM MAIN (GERMANY) -
BIOGRAPHY.**
Wilhelm Busch und seine Freunde in Frankfurt
und Kronberg /. Frankfurt am Main , c1984.
104 p. : ISBN 3-7829-0289-0 : DDC 831/.8 19
PT2603.U8 Z895 1984
NYPL [3-MCK B97 86-1055]

**Frankfurt am Main (Germany). Dezernat Kultur
und Freizeit.** Avitabile, Gunhild. Chao
Shao-an . Frankfurt am Main , c1988. 58 p. :
ISBN 3-88270-046-7 DDC 759.951 20
ND1049.C4527 A4 1988
NYPL [3-MAG+ 91-6442]

Frankfurt am Main. Liebieghaus. see **Liebieghaus.**

**Frankfurt am Main. Städelsches Kunstinstitut
und Städtische Galerie.** see **Städelsches
Kunstinstitut und Städtische Galerie
Frankfurt am Main.**

**Frankfurter Fundamente der Kunstgeschichte,
0175-3517 .**
(Bd. 6) Radler, Gudrun. Die Schreinmadonna
"Vierge ouvrante" . Frankfurt am Main , 1990.
366 p., [184] p. of plates : ISBN 3-923813-05-8 :
NB1912.M37 R33 1990
(Bd. 7) Schwarz, Jürgen. Bildannoncen aus der
Jahrhundertwende . Frankfurt [am Main] ,
1990. 224 p. : ISBN 3-923813-06-6 :
NC998.6.G4 S38 1990

Frankfurter Kunstverein.
Bourgeois, Louise, 1911- Louise Bourgeois .
Frankfurt , Schaffhausen , c1989. 194 p. :
ISBN 3-7231-0401-0 DDC 730/.92 20
NB237.B65 A4 1989
Coplans, John. John Coplans . Frankfurt am
Main [1990] 60 p. :
NYPL [MFX (Coplans) 91-7947]
Croissant, Michael, 1928- Michael Croissant .
Frankfurt am Main [1990] 121 p. :
NYPL [3-MGO (Croissant) 91-4350]
Davis, Lynn, 1944- Lynn Davis . Frankfurt am
Main , 1990. [10] p., 56 leaves of plates :
NYPL [MFX (Davis) 91-4676]
Kunst in Frankfurt 1987 . [Frankfurt am Main]
[1987?] 122 p. : **NYPL [MCI 89-28315]**
Vom Impressionismus zum Bauhaus .
Frankfurt/Main , c1966. [48] p., 82 leaves of
plates : **NYPL [3-MC 90-6950]**

Frankfurter Kunstverein, Frankfurt am Main.
Gerz, Jochen. Jochen Gerz, 5 Installationen
1975-1979 . Frankfurt , 1980. 1 portfolio ([24]
pieces) : **NYPL [3-MCK++ G288 82-855]**

Franklin, Constance.
Directory of artist associations and exhibition
spaces, art commissions, museum curators & art
critics /. Renaissance, CA , c1990. 208 p. ;
ISBN 0-940899-14-0
NYPL [MAV 91-6690]
Directory of galleries for the fine artist /.
Renaissance, CA , c1990. 359 p. ; ISBN
0-940899-08-6 **NYPL [MA 90-11525]**

Franklin Furnace Archive. Stein, Donna.
Contemporary illustrated books . New York,
N.Y. , c1989. 72 p. : ISBN 0-916365-00-X
NYPL [MDTT+ 91-6216]

Franklin Survey Company. Property atlas of
Bergen County, N. J. . Philadelphia, Pa. , 1936-
4 v. : **NYPL [Map Div. 91-4090]**

Frans Hals /. Hals, Frans, 1584-1666. Munich ,
New York, NY, USA , c1989. 437 p. : ISBN
3-7913-1032-1 DDC 759.9492 20
ND1329.H33 A4 1989

**Frans Hals and the groupportraits at Harlem,
1528-1737 /.** Baard, H. P. (Henricus Petrus),
1906- [Frans Hals en het Haarlemse

groepportret in het Gemeentemuseum
1528-1737. English.] Harlem , 1952. 72 p. :
NYPL [3-MCH H2 90-5924]

Frans Hals--the complete work /. Grimm, Claus.
[Frans Hals--das Gesamtwerk. English.] New
York , 1990. 296 p. : ISBN 0-8109-3404-3 DDC
759.9492 20
ND653.H2 G7313 1990
NYPL [MCH+ H2 91-3380]

Frans Halsmuseum. Hals, Frans, 1584-1666.
Frans Hals /. Munich , New York, NY, USA ,
c1989. 437 p. : ISBN 3-7913-1032-1 DDC
759.9492 20
ND1329.H33 A4 1989

FRANS HALSMUSEUM.
Baard, H. P. (Henricus Petrus), 1906- [Frans
Hals en het Haarlemse groepportret in het
Gemeentemuseum 1528-1737. English.] Frans
Hals and the groupportraits at Harlem,
1528-1737 /. Harlem , 1952. 72 p. :
NYPL [3-MCH H2 90-5924]

Frans Masereel. Masereel, Frans, 1889-1972.
[Belgium] [1990?] 175 p. : ISBN 90-506-6064-9
NYPL [MDG+ (Masereel) 90-11001]

Frans-Masereel-Stiftung.
Frans Masereel, 1889-1972 . Saarbrücken ,
1989. 279 p. : ISBN 3-922807-40-2
NYPL [3-MCZ M396 91-4464]
Masereel, Frans, 1889-1972. Frans Masereel
(1889-1972) . Saarbrücken , 1989. 280 p. :
ISBN 3-922807-40-2 DDC 760/.092 20
N6973.M32 A4 1989

Frans Masereel, 1889-1972 : zur Verwirklichung
des Traums von einer freien Gesellschaft /
Karl-Ludwig Hofmann, Peter Riede (Hrsg.)
Saarbrücken : Saarbrücker Zeitung, 1989. 279
p. : ill. (some col.) ; 28 cm. "Herausgegeben von
der Frans-Masereel-Stiftung, Saarbrücken, anlässlich der
Ausstellungen im Saarland-Museum in Saarbrücken und
in der Städtischen Galerie Homburg/Saar." Includes
bibliographical references (p. 274) and index. ISBN
3-922807-40-2
1. Masereel, Frans, 1889-1972 - Notebooks,
sketchbooks, etc. - Exhibitions. 2. Social problems in
art - Exhibitions. I. Hofmann, Karl Ludwig. II.
Masereel, Frans, 1889-1972. III. Reide, Peter. IV.
Frans-Masereel-Stiftung. V. Saarland-Museum. VI.
Städtischen Galerie Homburg/Saar. VII. Title: Zur
Verwirklichung des Traums von einer freien
Gesellschaft. **NYPL [3-MCZ M396 91-4464]**

Frans Masereel (1889-1972) . Masereel, Frans,
1889-1972. Saarbrücken , 1989. 280 p. : ISBN
3-922807-40-2 DDC 760/.092 20
N6973.M32 A4 1989

Frans Molenaar . Meij, Letse. De Bilt , c1986.
176 p. : ISBN 90-213-0378-7 (speciale luxe ed.)
NYPL [3-MMO 89-19034]

Frans Post, 1612-1680 /. Post, Frans, 1612
(ca.)-1680. [Basel] [Tübingen] , 1990. 99 p. :
DDC 759.9492 20
ND653.P6 A4 1990

**Frans Snyders, Stilleben- und Tiermaler,
1579-1657 /.** Robels, Hella. München [1989]
592 p., 8 leaves of plates : ISBN 3-422-06052-9
NYPL [3-MCH S693 90-12494]

Frans Widerberg . Widerberg, Frans, 1934- Oslo,
Norway , c1990. 248 p. : ISBN 82-7393-008-4
DDC 769.92 20
NE694.W55 A4 1990

Franta. Franta, 1930- Bronx, N.Y. , 1989. [32]
p. : **NYPL [3-MCZ+ F836 91-5469]**

Franta, 1930-
Franta. Bronx, N.Y. : Bronx Museum of the
Arts, 1989. [32] p. : ill. (some col.) ; 29 cm.
Cover title: Franta, paintings and works on paper,
1986-1989. "This catalogue is published on the occasion
of two solo exhibitions of the work of Franta: The
Bronx Museum of the Arts ... June 8 to August 31,
1989; Terry Dintenfass Gallery, Inc. ... June 5 to June
30, 1989"--P. [2] of cover. Includes bibliographical
references.
1. Franta, 1930- - Exhibitions. I. Bronx Museum of the
Arts. II. Terry Dintenfass, inc. III. Title. IV. Title:
Franta, paintings and works on paper, 1986-1989. V.
Title: Paintings and works on paper, 1986-1989.
NYPL [3-MCZ+ F836 91-5469]

Franta, paintings and works on paper, 1986-1989.
Franta, 1930- Franta. Bronx, N.Y. , 1989. [32]
p. : **NYPL [3-MCZ+ F836 91-5469]**

FRANTA, 1930- - EXHIBITIONS.
Franta, 1930- Franta. Bronx, N.Y. , 1989. [32]
p. : **NYPL [3-MCZ+ F836 91-5469]**

Frantz, Susanne K. Charleston, R. J. (Robert
Jesse), 1916- Masterpieces of glass . New
York , 1990. 256 p. : ISBN 0-8109-3607-0
NYPL [3-MPW+ 91-5598]

**Frantzuzkīa polīa strazheuii cheshskoslovatzkikh
lehīï.** Nejedlý, Otakar, 1883-1957. Francouzská
bojiště československých legií . Praze [1920?]
[4] p., [8] leaves of plates :
NYPL [3-MAMY+++ 83-2786]

Franz, Erich. Klee, Paul, 1879-1940. Paul Klee .
Essen , 1989. 163 p. :
NYPL [3-MCZ+ K63 90-12860]

Franz Karl Palko (1724-1767) . Palko, Franz
Anton, 1724-1767. Salzburg , 1989. 131 p. :
NYPL [3-MCK P1567 91-5023]

Franz Krautgasser . Reichart, Helga. Innsbruck ,
1989. 112 p. : ISBN 3-7022-1729-0 DDC 759.36
20
N6811.5.K68 A4 1989
NYPL [3-MCK K9127 91-7554]

Franz Marc . Pese, Claus. Stuttgart , c1989. 224
p. : ISBN 3-7630-1968-5
NYPL [3-MCK+ M31 91-6787]

Franz Rosei . Rosei, Franz, 1947- [Salzburg] ,
c1990. [48] p. :
NYPL [3-MGO (Rosei) 91-6970]

Franz Schuster, 1892-1972 / [Gestaltung des
Katalogs, Herbert Sommer] Wien : Hochschule
für Angewandte Kunst, 1976. 136 p. : ill. ; 30
cm. "11"--Cover. DDC 720/.92/4 19
1. Schuster, Franz, 1892-1972. 2. Architecture,
Modern - 20th century - Austria. I. Schuster, Franz,
1892-1972. II. Sommer, Herbert, Oberassistent Mag.
arch. III. Hochschule für Angewandte Kunst (Vienna,
Austria).
NA1011.5.S38 A4 1976
NYPL [3-MQZ+ (Schuster) 90-12651]

Franz Secky, 1895-1950 /. Secky, Franz. Wien
[1987?] 96 p. :
NYPL [3-MCK+ S444 90-205]

Franz Weiss, eine Künstlermonographie /. Weiss,
Franz, 1921- Graz , c1988. 119 p. : ISBN
3-222-11820-5 DDC 709/.2 B 20
N6811.5.W45 A4 1988
NYPL [3-MCK W43195 90-11992]

Franz Wiegele, 1887-1944 . Rohsmann, Arnulf.
Klagenfurt , 1989. 23, viii, 102 p. : ISBN
3-85366-583-7 DDC 741.9436 20
NC245.W48 A4 1989

Franzen, Georg, 1958- Kunstbetrachtung aus der
Sicht der humanistischen Psychologie : eine
Fresko des Malers Wilhelm von Schadow /
Georg Franzen. Regensburg : S. Roderer, 1989.
42 p. : ill. ; 21 cm. (Theorie und Forschung . Bd.
83) Psychologie ; Bd. 30 Includes bibliographical
references (p. 40-42). ISBN 3-89073-435-9
1. Schadow, Wilhelm von 1788-1862 - Criticism and
interpretation. I. Title.
NYPL [MCK S275 90-12393]

Franziskanerkloster Innichen. Plazer, Lukas,
1663-1723. Der barocke Franziskuszyklus von
Frater Lukas Plazer in Innichen /. Innichen ,
1990. 259 p. : ISBN 88-85226-00-0
ND623.P696 A4 1990

FRANZISKANERKLOSTER INNICHEN.
Plazer, Lukas, 1663-1723. Der barocke
Franziskuszyklus von Frater Lukas Plazer in
Innichen /. Innichen , 1990. 259 p. : ISBN
88-85226-00-0
ND623.P696 A4 1990

Franzke, Andreas. Dubuffet / Andreas Franzke.
Köln : DuMont Buchverlag, c1990. 207 p. : ill.
(some col.) ; 18 cm (Dumont Taschenbücher . 249)
Includes bibliographical references (p. 198-199). ISBN
3-7701-2523-1 DDC 709/.2 20
1. Dubuffet, Jean, 1901-. 2. Artists - France -
Biography. I. Title.
N6853.D78 F72 1990

**Französische Graphik, neunzehntes und
zwanzigstes Jahrhundert, Ecole de Paris.**
Pfalzgalerie Kaiserslautern. Graphische
Sammlung. Französische Graphik, 19. und 20.
Jahrhundert, Ecole de Paris /. Kaiserslautern ,
1989. 212 p. : ISBN 3-89422-002-3 DDC

769/.074/43435 s 769.944/361/07443435 20
NE55.G4 K346 1985 vol. 3 NE647.3
NYPL [MDE 91-4020]

Französische Graphik, 19. und 20. Jahrhundert,
Ecole de Paris /. Pfalzgalerie Kaiserslautern.
Graphische Sammlung , Kaiserslautern , 1989.
212 p. : ISBN 3-89422-002-3 DDC
769/.074/43435 s 769.944/361/07443435 20
NE55.G4 K346 1985 vol. 3 NE647.3
NYPL [MDE 91-4020]

Französische Illustrationen des 18. und 19.
Jahrhunderts : aus der Sammlung von Kritter :
15.12. 1985 bis 16.2. 1986 / [herausgegeben im
Auftrag der Dortmunder Museumsgesellschaft
zur Pflege der Bildenden Kunst e.V. für das
Museum für Kunst und Kulturgeschichte der
Stadt Dortmund von Gerhard Langemeyer ; mit
Beiträgen von Gisela Framke ... et al. ; Katalog,
Jutta von Simson ... et al. ; Redaktion, Sepp
Hiekisch-Picard, Gisela Marenk]. Dortmund :
Das Museum, 1985. 267 p. : ill. (some col.) ;
28 cm. (Bilderwelten.) 1) Includes indexes.
Bibliography: p. 262-265. ISBN 3-924302-16-2 DDC
741.64/074/0356 s 741.64/0944/0740356 19
1. Kritter, Ulrich von - Art collections - Exhibitions. 2.
Illustration of books - France - Exhibitions. 3.
Illustration of books - 18th century - France -
Exhibitions. 4. Illustration of books - 19th century -
France - Exhibitions. 5. Illustrated books - France -
18th century - Exhibitions. 6. Illustrated books -
France - 19th century - Exhibitions. 7. Illustrated
books - Private collections - Germany (West) -
Dortmund - Exhibitions. I. Kritter, Ulrich von. II.
Langemeyer, Gerhard. III. Framke, Gisela. IV. Simson,
Jutta von. V. Dortmunder Museumsgesellschaft zur
Pflege der Bildenden Kunst. VI. Museum für Kunst und
Kulturgeschichte der Stadt Dortmund. VII. Series.
NC980 .B54 1985 vol. 1
NYPL [MDT 91-2511]

Französische Landschaften. Schweizer, Helmut.
Helmut Schweizer . Düsseldorf , 1989. 39 p. :
ISBN 3-925974-09-1
NYPL [MFX+ (Schweizer) 91-7486]

Französische Lithographien des 19.
Jahrhunderts . Städtische Galerie im
Städelschen Kunstinstitut Frankfurt am Main.
Frankfurt am Main , c1990. 87 p. :
NYPL [MDE 91-6189]

Französische Photographie, 1840-1871 :
Schweizerische Stiftung für die Photographie,
Kunsthaus Zürich, 5. Juni-23. August 1987 /
[Konzept und Realisation von Ausstellung und
Katalog, Walter Binder]. [Zürich] : Die
Stiftung : Das Kunsthaus, [1987] 104 p. :
chiefly ill., ports. ; 27 cm. Bibliography: p. 103.
1. Photography - France - History - 19th century -
Exhibitions. 2. Photography - Portraits - Exhibitions. I.
Binder, Walter, 1931-. II. Stiftung für die Photographie
(Switzerland). III. Kunsthaus Zürich.
TR71 .F675 1987 *NYPL [MFW 91-2388]*

Franzoi, Umberto.
L'armeria del Palazzo ducale a Venezia /
Umberto Franzoi. Dosson (Treviso) : Canova,
[1990] 273 p. : ill. (some col.) ; 28 cm. Includes
bibliographical references (p. 271-273). ISBN
88-85066-74-7
1. Arms and armor - Italy - Venice - Catalogs. 2.
Palazzo ducale (Venice, Italy) - Catalogs. I. Title.
NK6702.5.I8 F7 1990

Il Palazzo ducale di Venezia / U. Franzoi e F.
Valcanover. 5a ed. Roma : Istituto poligrafico e
zecca dello stato, Libreria dello stato, 1987. 170
p., [24] p. of plates (2 folded) : ill. (some col.),
plans ; 19 cm. (Itinerari dei musei, gallerie e
monumenti d'Italia . n. 23) Bibliography: p. 169-170.
1. Palazzo ducale (Venice, Italy) - Guide-books. 2. Art -
Italy - Venice - Guide-books. 3. Venice (Italy) -
Buildings, structures, etc. - Guide-books. I. Valcanover,
Francesco. II. Series.
NYPL [3-MQWB 90-10853]

Il Palazzo ducale di Venezia / Umberto
Franzoi, Terisio Pignatti, Wolfgang Wolters.
Treviso : Canova, c1990. 382 p. : ill. ; 28 cm.
ISBN 88-85066-97-6
1. Palazzo ducale (Venice, Italy). I. Title.
IN PROCESS (ONLINE)
NYPL [3-MQWB 91-5236]

Fraser, Ted, 1946- Caven Atkins, the Winnipeg
years / Ted Fraser. Windsor, Canada : Art
Gallery of Windsor, c1987. [40] p. : ill. (some
col.) ; 23 x 29 cm. Catalog of an exhibition held at
the Winnipeg Art Gallery, Winnipeg, Man., Nove. 15,

1987-Jan. 10, 1988 and 3 other Canadian locations
through Oct. 30, 1968. ISBN 0-919837-10-7
1. Atkins, Caven - Exhibitions. I. Atkins, Caven. II.
Winnipeg Art Gallery. III. Art Gallery of Windsor. IV.
Title.
MLCM 90/03385 (N)
NYPL [3-MCZ A865 90-8692]

Frases espontáneas /. Badii, Líbero, 1916- Buenos
Aires, Argentina , 1982. 47 p. : DDC 700 20
N6639.B32 A35 1982

Fratadocchi, Tommaso Breccia. see Breccia
Fratadocchi, Tommaso.

Frati, Tiziana. Greco, 1541?-1614. L'opera
completa del Greco /. Milano : Rizzoli Editore,
1978. 128 p. :
NYPL [3-MCQ + T39 88-3246]

Frau in der Gesellschaft.
Breitling, Gisela. Der verborgene Eros .
Frankfurt am Main , 1990. 242 p. : ISBN
3-596-24740-3
NYPL [3-MAMZ 90-11131]

Frau Republik geht pleite . Haese, Klaus. Berlin ,
c1990. 144 p. : ISBN 3-361-00251-6 :
IN PROCESS (ONLINE)
NYPL [MDY 91-3467]

Frauen im Design : Berufsbilder und Lebenswege
seit 1900 / [Redaktion, Angela
Oedekoven-Gerischer ... et al. ; Übersetzungen,
Martin Crellin] = Women in design : careers
and life histories since 1900 / [editors, Angela
Oedekoven-Gerischer ... et al. ; translation,
Martin Crellin]. Stuttgart : Design Center
Stuttgart, [1989] 2 v. : ill. ; 21 cm. Catalog of a
traveling exhibit first presented by Design Center
Stuttgart, Haus der Wirtschaft, June 28-Oct. 1, 1989.
German and English. Includes bibliographical
references. DDC 745.4/442/082 20
1. Women designers - Exhibitions. 2. Design - History -
20th century - Exhibitions. 3. Women designers -
Biography. I. Oedekoven-Gerischer, Angela. II. Design
Center Stuttgart. III. Title: Women in design.
NK1174 .F7 1989 *NYPL [3-MNF 90-725]*

Frauen Museum (Bonn, Germany) Die
Rheinkonferenz . Bonn , 1990. 1 v. (unpaged) :
NYPL [3-MAMY+ 91-7965]

Das Frauenbild /. Hrdlička, Alfred, 1928- Wien
[198-?] 131 p. : ISBN 3-900318-48-4
NYPL [3-MCK+ H857 90-5270]

Frauenbildnisse, 1947-1988 /. Janssen, Horst,
1929- Hamburg , c1988. 1 v. (unpaged) : ISBN
3-923848-22-6 DDC 760/.092 20
N6888.J37 A4 1988 <fol.>

Frauenmuseum Bonn (Germany) Die
Bonnerinnen . [Bonn , 1988. 333 p. :
NYPL [3-MAMG+ 89-25284]

Fraunhofer-Gesellschaft. Informationszentrum
Raum und Bau.
Architekten, Atelier 5, Bern. Stuttgart [1988]
49 p. ; ISBN 3-8167-1816-7 (pbk.)
NYPL [3-MQWD 90-12512]

Architekten, Rem Koolhaas und OMA.
Stuttgart [1988] 66 p. ; ISBN 3-8167-1844-2
(pbk.)
NYPL [3-MQZ (Koolhaas) 90-12511]

Architekten, Rolf Gutbrod. Stuttgart [1988]. 51
p. ; ISBN 3-8167-1847-7 (pbk.)
NYPL [3-MQZ (Gutbrad) 90-12742]

Architektur und Städtebau des Islam /.
Stuttgart , 1985- v. ; ISBN 3-8167-0105-1 DDC
016.72/0917/671 19
Z5943.I84 A73 1984 NA380
NYPL [3-MQT 91-826]

Bauen im Dritten Reich /. Stuttgart [1989] 73
p. ; ISBN 3-8167-0278-3
NYPL [3-MQWD 90-10818]

Fraústo, Isabel. Vidigal, Ana. Descobrimentos
portugueses do século XV /. Lisboa , 1987. 1 v.
(unpaged) DDC 741.9469 20
NC288.V54 A4 1987

Fréal, Jacques. La Normandie / texte de Jacques
Fréal ; ill. de l'auteur. [Paris] : Garnier, c1980.
110 p. : ill. ; 24 cm. (Témoins de la vie paysanne)
Bibliography: p. 110. ISBN 2-7050-0260-X : DDC
392/.36/009442 19
1. Vernacular architecture - France - Normandy. 2.
Farm buildings - France - Normandy. 3. Furniture -
France - Normandy. 4. Implements, utensils, etc. -
France - Normandy. 5. Peasantry - France - Normandy.

I. Title.
NA8203 .F693 *NYPL [3-MQWF 81-936]*

Frèches-Thory, Claire. Les nabis / Claire
Frèches-Thory, Antoine Terrasse. Paris :
Flammarion, c1990. 319 p. : ill. (some col.) ; 32
cm. Includes bibliographical references (p. 309-310)
and index. ISBN 2-08-010941-3 DDC
709/.44/36109034 20
1. Nabi (Group of artists). 2. Art, French. 3. Art,
Modern - 19th century - France. I. Terrasse, Antoine.
II. Title.
N6847.5.N3 F735 1990

Frechko, Irina. Gauguin, Paul, 1848-1903. Paul
Gauguin . Paris , c1988. 186 p. : ISBN
2-7022-0218-7 DDC 759.4 20
ND553.G27 A4 1988

Freckmann, Karl-Heinz. Wehling, Hans-Werner,
1949- Werks- und Genossenschaftssiedlungen
im Ruhrgebiet 1844-1939. Essen , 1990- v. <1
> : ISBN 3-88474-344-9 DDC 728/.0943/5509034
20
NA7553 .W44 1990

Frecot, Janos, 1937- Missmann, Max, ca.
1870-1948. Max Missmann . Berlin , 1989. 75
p. : *NYPL [MFX (Missmann) 91-2390]*

Fred Baier . Houston, John. London , 1990. 64
p. : ISBN 0-947792-46-5 (pbk.) : DDC 749.22 20
NYPL [3-MOF 90-11124]

Fred Deux . Deux, Fred, 1924- Marseille [France]
[Arles] , c1989. 103 p. : ISBN 2-86869-298-2 :
MLCS 90/03392 (N)
NYPL [MDG (Deux) 90-11000]

FRED HARVEY (FIRM)
D'Emilio, Sandra, 1939- Visions and
visionaries . Salt Lake City , 1991. p. cm.
ISBN 0-87905-383-6 : DDC 758/.9978 20
N8214.5.U6 D46 1991

Fred Hoffman Gallery. Penck A. R., 1939- A.R.
Penck, Venice paintings. Santa Monica , c1989.
[33] p. : ISBN 0-927442-00-0
NYPL [3-MCK+ P41 91-7059]

Frederic Edwin Church /. Kelly, Franklin.
Washington , c1989. 211 p. : ISBN
0-89468-136-2 DDC 759.13 20
ND237.C52 A4 1989
NYPL [3-MCX C56 90-10398]

Frederic Remington . Shapiro, Michael Edward.
New York [1991] p. cm. ISBN 0-8109-8104-1
DDC 709/.2 20
N6537.R4 S5 1991

Frederick C. Frieseke . Frieseke, Frederick C.
(Frederick Carl), 1874-1939. New York, N.Y.
(11 E. 70th St., New York 10021) , c1990. 47
p. :
IN PROCESS (ONLINE)
NYPL [3-MCX F916 91-6495]

Frederick Gore on Piero della Francesca's 'The
baptism'. Gore, Frederick. London , 1990. 32 p.,
fold plate. ISBN 0-304-93279-5 DDC 759.5
ND623.F78 G6
NYPL [3-MCF F81 90-6257]

Frederick S. Wight Art Gallery.
Almaraz, Carlos. Moonlight theater . Los
Angeles , c1991. p. cm. ISBN 0-9628162-0-5
(pbk.) DDC 769.92 20
NE539.A44 M66 1991

Chicano art . Los Angeles , 1991. p. cm. ISBN
0-943739-16-0 : DDC
704/.0368/7207307479494 20
N6538.M4 C45 1991

Fredericksburg and Spotsylvania National
Military Park. Wilshin, Francis F. Tour of
the battlefields of Fredericksburg,
Chancellorsville, Wilderness, Spotsylvania
C.H. . [Fredericksburg, Va.] [1955?] [17]
leaves : *NYPL [Map Div. 90-949]*

FREDERICKSBURG, BATTLE OF, 1862 -
MAPS.
Wilshin, Francis F. Tour of the battlefields of
Fredericksburg, Chancellorsville, Wilderness,
Spotsylvania C.H. . [Fredericksburg, Va.]
[1955?] [17] leaves :
NYPL [Map Div. 90-949]

The Fredric Wertham collection . Harvard
University. Art Museums. [Cambridge] , 1990.
101 p. : ISBN 0-916724-75-1
IN PROCESS (ONLINE)
NYPL [3-MAX (Wertham) 91-5499]

FREDRICKS, CHARLES DEFOREST.
Levine, Robert M. Cuba in the 1850s . Tampa ,
c1990. xv, 86 p. : ISBN 0-8130-1010-1 (alk. paper)
DDC 779/.99729105 20
F1763 .L65 1990
NYPL *[MFX (Fredricks) 91-3474]*

Fredrickson, Thomas. Julia Wachtel /. Chicago ,
c1991. p. cm. ISBN 0-933856-33-4 DDC 759.13
20
ND237.W24 A4 1991

**FREE HAND TECHNICAL DRAWING -
TECHNIQUE.**
Sutherland, Martha, 1927- Graphic
fundamentals . New York, N.Y. , 1991. p. cm.
ISBN 0-8306-3480-0 : DDC 720/.28/4 20
NA2708 .S88 1991

Free money for people in the arts /. Blum,
Laurie. New York , Toronto , 1991. p. cm.
ISBN 0-02-028175-7 DDC 700/.79/73 20
NX398 .B58 1991

Free, Renée.
Lloyd Rees : the last twenty years / Renée
Free in collaboration with Lloyd Rees.
Roseville, N.S.W., Australia : Craftsman House,
1990. 176 p. : ill. (some col.) ; 30 cm. Includes
bibliographical references (p. 172). ISBN
0-947131-34-5 DDC 759.994 20
*1. Rees, Lloyd Frederic, 1895- - Catalogs. I. Rees,
Lloyd Frederic, 1895-. II. Title.*
N7405.R4 A4 1990

Thomas, Daniel, fl. 1962- Tony Tuckson /.
Roseville, NSW, Australia , 1989. 188 p. :
ISBN 0-947131-22-1
NYPL *[3-MCZ+ T893 91-3381]*

Freedberg, David.
Art in history/history in art . Santa Monica,
CA [Chicago, Ill.] , 1991. p. cm. ISBN
0-89236-201-4 : DDC 701/.03/0949209032 20
N72.S6 A746 1991

Iconoclasts and their motives / David
Freedberg. Maarssen : G. Schwartz ; Montclair,
N.J. : Distributed in North America by A.
Schram, c1985. 60 p. : ill. ; 21 cm. (Gerson
lecture . 2nd) Bibliography: p. 55-60. ISBN
90-6179-056-5 (pbk.) DDC 709 19
1. Art - Mutilation, defacement, etc. I. Title. II. Series.
N8557 .F74 1985 **NYPL** *[3-MAS 91-5030]*

Freedman Gallery (Reading, Pa.)
Contemporary Hispanic shrines . Reading, Pa. ,
c1989. 24 p. : ISBN 0-941972-09-7
IN PROCESS (ONLINE)
NYPL *[3-MAMT 91-7297]*

Lipski, Donald, 1947- Donald Lipski, poetic
sculpture . Reading, Penn. , c1990. 51 p. :
ISBN 0-941972-10-0
NYPL *[3-MGO (Lipski) 90-12553]*

Selections from the Edward Albee collection .
Reading, Penn. , 1988. 28 p. : ISBN
0-941972-07-0
NYPL *[3-MAX (Albee) 90-12382]*

Freedman, Luba, 1953- Titian's independent
self-portraits / Luba Freedman. [Firenze] : L.S.
Olschki, 1990. 126 p. : ill. ; 21 cm. (Pocket
library of studies in art. 26) Includes bibliographical
references (p. 109-119) and index. ISBN
88-22-23745-5
*1. Titian, ca. 1488-1576 - Self-portraits. 2. Self-portraits,
Italian. I. Titian, ca. 1488-1576. II. Title.*
NYPL *[3-MCF T63 91-3793]*

Freedman, Richard, 1964- Hersey, George L.
Possible Palladian villas . Cambridge, Mass. ,
c1992. p. cm. ISBN 0-262-08210-1 DDC
728.8/092 20
NA7125 .H47 1992

**FREEHOLD. see LAND TENURE; REAL
PROPERTY.**

Freeland, J. M. (John Maxwell), 1920-
Architecture in Australia : a history / J.M.
Freeland. Ringwood, Victoria, Australia :
Penguin Books Australia ; New York, N.Y., U.
S.A. : Viking Penguin, 1972 328 p. : ill. ; 21
cm. (Pelican books) Includes bibliographical references
(p. [315]) and index. ISBN 0-14-021152-7
1. Architecture - Australia - History. I. Title.
NA1600 .F7 1972

Freeman, Jennifer. W.D. Caröe, RStO, FSA : his
architectural achievement / Jennifer M.
Freeman. Manchester, UK ; New York, NY,
USA : Manchester University Press ; xiii, 258

p., [4] p. of plates : ill. (some col.) ; 25 cm.
Includes bibliographical references (p. [253]-254) and
index. ISBN 0-7190-2449-8 DDC 720/.92 20
*1. Caröe, William Douglas, 1857-1938 - Criticism and
interpretation. I. Title.*
NA997.C325 F7 1990
NYPL *[3-MQZ (Caröe) 91-4076]*

Freeman, Judi.
Conisbee, Philip. Monet to Matisse . Los
Angeles, Calif. , c1991. 144 p. : ISBN
0-87587-159-3 DDC 709/.44/09034 20
N6847 .C6 1991

The fauve landscape / Judi Freeman ; with
contributions by Roger Benjamin ... [et al.] ;
Los Angeles County Museum of Art. 1st ed.
Los Angeles, Calif. : Los Angeles County
Museum of Art ; New York : Abbeville Press,
1990. 350 p. : ill. (some col.) ; 29 cm. Published
in conjunction with an exibition held at the Los
Angeles County Museum of Art, Oct. 4-Dec. 30, 1990,
The Metropolitan Museum of Art, New York, Feb.
19-May 5, 1991, and Royal Academy of Arts, London,
June 10-Sept. 1, 1991. Includes index. Includes
bibliographical references (p. 324-330). ISBN
1-558-59025-0 DDC 758/.1/094407479494 20
*1. Fauvism - France - Exhibitions. 2. Landscape
painting, French - Exhibitions. 3. Landscape painting -
20th century - France - Exhibitions. I. Los Angeles
County Museum of Art. II. Royal Academy of Arts
(Great Britain). III. Metropolitan Museum of Art (New
York, N.Y.). IV. Title.*
ND1356.6 .F74 1990
NYPL *[3-MCN 90-13060]*

Freeman, Phyllis.
New art /. New York , 1990. 205 p. : ISBN
0-8109-2443-9 DDC 709/.04 20
N6493 1980 .N48 1990
NYPL *[3-MAL+ 90-11610]*

Sarab´iānov, Dmitriĭ Vladimirovich. [Lioubov
Popova. English.] Popova /. New York , 1990.
396 p. : ISBN 0-8109-3701-8 (soft) DDC 709/.2/4
B 19
N6999.P67 S27 1989
NYPL *[3-MCZ+ P828 91-3662]*

FREEMASONS, AFRO-AMERICAN.
Williamson, Harry Albro, 1875- Chips from the
quarries /. New York, 1971. 407 ft. of
microfilm. **NYPL** *[Sc Micro R-1295-1299]*

Freer Gallery of Art.
Eugene and Agnes E. Meyer Memorial
exhibition. Freer Gallery of Art. Washington,
Smithsonian Institution, 1971. 77 p. 32 plates.
25 cm.
*1. Art, Chinese - Exhibitions. I. Meyer, Eugene. II.
Meyer, Agnes Elizabeth Ernst, 1887-. III. Title.*
NYPL *[3-MAG 90-7182]*

Merrill, Linda, 1959- An ideal country .
Washington, D.C. , Hanover [N.H.] , c1990.
200 p. : ISBN 0-87451-538-6 (alk. paper) DDC
759.13 20
ND237.T83 A4 1990
NYPL *[3-MCX T87 91-4949]*

FREER GALLERY OF ART - CATALOGS.
Cort, Louise Allison, 1944- Seto and Mino
ceramics /. Washington, D.C. , Honolulu,
Hawaii , 1992. p. cm. ISBN 0-08-248143-1 :
DDC 738/.0952/16 20
NK4168.S4 C67 1992

Merrill, Linda, 1959- An ideal country .
Washington, D.C. , Hanover [N.H.] , c1990.
200 p. : ISBN 0-87451-538-6 (alk. paper) DDC
759.13 20
ND237.T83 A4 1990
NYPL *[3-MCX T87 91-4949]*

Frei, Hans, 1937- Historischer Atlas von
Bayerisch-Schwaben /. Augsburg ,
Weissenhorn , 1982- 1 atlas (1 v. (loose-leaf)) :
ISBN 3-922518-96-6 DDC 911/.433 19
G1923.B3 H35 1982
NYPL *[Map Div. 84-179]*

Frei, Urs-Beat. Post, Frans, 1612 (ca.)-1680.
Frans Post, 1612-1680 /. [Basel] [Tübingen] ,
1990. 99 p. : DDC 759.9492 20
ND653.P6 A4 1990

**Freiburg i. B. Kunstverein. see Kunstverein
Freiburg.**

Freie und Hansestadt Hamburg . Hipp, Hermann.
Köln , 1990. 608 p. : ISBN 3-7701-1590-2 DDC
720/.943/515 20
NA1086.H3 H57 1990

Freilichtmuseum des Bezirks Oberbayern.
Groth-Schmachtenberger, Erika. Volks-trachten
aus Oberbayern, Österreich, Ungarn,
Jugoslawien, mit den Donauschwaben,
Rumänien, mit den Siebenbürger Sachsen /.
[München?] , 1980. 181 p., 6 leaves of plates :
NYPL *[3-MMM 90-10816]*

Freire, J. Moreira (José Moreira) Un problème
d'art : l'école portugaise, créatrice des grandes
écoles / par J. Moreira Freire.2. éd. Lisboa :
José A. Rodrigues, 1898. 190 p., [12] leaves of
plates : ill., ports. ; 21 cm. Source: Purchase from
Israel Perlstein, Mar. 24, 1931 (DLC #409629, 1931).
DLC DDC 709/.469 20
*1. Art Portuguese. 2. Art, Portuguese - Influence. I.
Title.*
N7121 .F74 1898

Fremdbild Heimat . Zaunschirm, Thomas, 1943-
Wien , c1989. 101 p. : ISBN 3-900606-12-9
N6809.C3 Z36 1989

Frémion, Yves. Images interdites / Yves Fremion,
Bernard Joubert. Paris : Syros/Alternatives,
c1989. 125 p. : ill. ; 28 cm. ISBN
2-86738-423-0 :
1. Sex in art. I. Title.
MLCM 90/04283 (H)
NYPL *[3-MAMZ 90-12310]*

Frémon, Jean, 1946- Brown, James, 1951- James
Brown . Paris , c1990. 42 p. : ISBN
2-85587-184-0
NYPL *[3-MCX+ B8765 90-13074]*

The French Academy : classicism and its
antagonists / edited by June Hargrove.
Newark : University of Delaware Press ;
London ; 231 p. : ill. ; 25 cm. Includes
bibliographical references and index. ISBN
0-87413-343-2 (alk. paper) DDC 706/.044 19
*1. Académie des beaux-arts (France). 2. Classicism in
art - France. I. Hargrove, June Ellen.*
N332.F83 P345 1990
NYPL *[3-MAMI 90-11304]*

**French architects and engineers in the Age of
Enlightenment** /. Picon, Antoine. [Architectes
et ingénieurs au siècle des Lumières. English.]
Cambridge , New York , 1991. p. cm. ISBN
0-521-38253-X DDC 720/.944/09033 20
NA1046.5.N4 P513 1991

FRENCH ART. see ART, FRENCH.

FRENCH ARTS. see ARTS, FRENCH.

**FRENCH AUTHORS. see AUTHORS,
FRENCH.**

French battlefields of the Czechoslovak legies.
Nejedlý, Otakar, 1883-1957. Francouzská
bojiště československých legií . Praze [1920?]
[4] p., [8] leaves of plates :
NYPL *[3-MAMY+++ 83-2786]*

French ceramics. Céramique lorraine . Nancy ,
Metz , c1990. 367 p. : ISBN 2-86480-458-1 :
DDC 738/.0944/38074758231 20
NK4098.L67 C47 1990

**French ceramics : 18th and 19th century
masterpieces from Lorraine.** Céramique
lorraine . Nancy , Metz , c1990. 367 p. : ISBN
2-86480-458-1 **NYPL** *[3-MPGG 91-7166]*

French, Chris. Anastos, Phillip. Illegal . New
York , 1991. 128 p. : ISBN 0-8478-1367-3 DDC
305.9/0693 20
F392.R5 A53 1991
NYPL *[MFW+ 91-6710]*

French, Christopher C.
Sultan, Terrie, 1952- Inability to endure or
deny the world . Washington, D.C. , c1990. 65
p. : ISBN 0-88675-036-9 : DDC 760/.092 20
ND237.M74 A4 1990
NYPL *[3-MCX+ M877 91-4930]*

Wiley, William T., 1937- William T. Wiley:
struck! sure? sound/unsound /. Washington,
D.C. , c1991. p. cm. ISBN 0-88675-037-7 DDC
709/.2 20
N6537.W47 A4 1991

The French crown jewels . Morel, Bernard.
Antwerp [1988] 417 p. ; ISBN 90-6153-188-8
DDC 739.27/0944 20
NK7415.F8 M67 1988

**French drawings & prints of the eighteenth
century .** Metropolitan Museum of Art (New
York, N.Y.) [New York , 1972] [19] p., [4] p.
of plates : **NYPL** *[3-MBH 91-409]*

FRENCH ENGRAVING. see ENGRAVING, FRENCH.

FRENCH ILLUMINATION OF BOOKS AND MANUSCRIPTS. see ILLUMINATION OF BOOKS AND MANUSCRIPTS, FRENCH.

FRENCH LANDSCAPE PAINTING. see LANDSCAPE PAINTING, FRENCH.

FRENCH LITERATURE - ILLUSTRATIONS.
Stewart, Philip. Engraven desire . Durham ,
1992. p. cm. ISBN 0-8223-1177-1 DDC
769.944/09/033 20
NE647.2 .S73 1992

FRENCH LITHOGRAPHY. see LITHOGRAPHY, FRENCH.

French masters, Rococo to Romanticism : an
exhibition of paintings, drawings & prints /
sponsored by the UCLA Art Council. [Los
Angeles] : UCLA Art Galleries, 1961. 72 p. :
ill. ; 30 cm. Exhibition held Mar. 5-Apr. 18, 1961,
the UCLA Art Galleries.
*1. Art, French - Exhibitions. 2. Art, Modern - 18th
century - France - Exhibitions. 3. Art, Modern - 19th
century - France - Exhibitions. I. UCLA Art Council.
II. UCLA Art Galleries.*
      NYPL [3-MAMI+ 90-6906]

FRENCH PAINTING. see PAINTING, FRENCH.

FRENCH POSTERS. see POSTERS, FRENCH.

FRENCH REVOLUTION. see FRANCE - HISTORY - REVOLUTION, 1789-1799.

FRENCH WIT AND HUMOR, PICTORIAL.
Cham, 1819-1879. Croquis Parisiens /. Paris ,
c[18--] [15] leaves :
      NYPL [3-MEM (Cham) 88-3113]

Le Louarn, Yvan Francis, 1915-1968. Chaval's
Fotoschule . Zürich , 1975. 45 p. : ISBN
3-257-00788-4
      NYPL [3-MEM (Le Louarn) 84-2309]

Samivel, 1907- Bonhommes de neige /. [Paris] ,
1987. 95 p. : ISBN 2-905292-13-X
      NYPL [3-MEM+ (Samivel) 90-2327]

Sempé, Jean Jacques, 1932- Luxe, calme &
volupté /. Paris , c1987. 102 p. : ISBN
2-207-23419-3
      NYPL [3-MEM+ (Sempé) 90-2504]

FRENCH WIT AND HUMOR, PICTORIAL - EXHIBITIONS.
Charpin, Catherine. Les arts incohérents
(1882-1893) /. Paris , c1990. 128 p. : ISBN
2-86738-465-6 : DDC 741.5/0944/09034 20
NC1495 .C58 1990

Femmes d'esprit . Middlebury, Vt. , Hanover ,
c1990. 146 p. : ISBN 0-9625262-0-7 DDC
741.5/944 20
NC1499.D3 A4 1990
      NYPL [MDG (Daumier) 90-11002]

Die Politische Lithographie im Kampf um die
Pariser Kommune /. [Stuttgart , 1976. 110 p.,
[33] fold. leaves of plates :
      NYPL [MDY 90-7009]

FRENCH WIT AND HUMOR, PICTORIAL - HISTORY - 19TH CENTURY.
Athanassoglou-Kallmyer, Nina M., 1945-
Eugène Delacroix . New Haven, CT , 1991. p.
cm. ISBN 0-300-04931-5 DDC 741.5/092 20
NC1499.D36 A9 1991

French 19th century paintings : 23rd March-6th
April 1977 / presented by Shepherd Gallery
Associates and Jan G. Milner. London : Alpine
Club Gallery, 1977. 101 p. : all ill. ; 25 cm.
Catalog of an exhibition.
*1. Painting, Modern - 19th century - France -
Exhibitions. 2. Painting, French - Exhibitions. I. Milner,
Jan G. II. Shepherd Gallery. III. Alpine Club Gallery
(London, England).*   *NYPL [3-MCN 90-7134]*

The Frenchwoman's bedroom /. Ladd,
Mary-Sargent. New York , c1991. p. cm. ISBN
0-385-26558-1 : DDC 747.7/7 20
NK2117.B4 L33 1991

Frenzel, Ursula. Marcks, Gerhard. Gerhard
Marcks 1889-1981 . München , c1988. 220 p. :
ISBN 3-7913-0777-0 DDC 730/.92 B 20
NB588.M35 A3 1988
      NYPL [3-MGO (Marcks) 90-12499]

Frere, Sheppard Sunderland. Cichorius, Conrad,
1863- Trajan's Column . Gloucester, UK ,

Wolfboro, N.H., USA , 1988. xviii, 339 p. [94]
p. of plates : ISBN 0-86299-467-5 : DDC 937/.07
19
DG59.D3 C63 1988
      NYPL [3-MGH 91-6949]

Fresella-Lee, Nancy. The American paintings in
the Pennsylvania Academy of the Fine Arts :
an illustrated checklist / compiled by Nancy
Fresella-Lee ; edited by Jacolyn A. Mott.
Philadelphia : Pennsylvania Academy of the
Fine Arts ; Seattle : In association with the
University of Washington Press, c1989. xviii,
204 p. : ill. (some col.) ; 29 cm. Includes index.
ISBN 0-943836-11-5 : DDC 759.13/074/74811
20
*1. Pennsylvania Academy of the Fine Arts - Catalogs.
2. Painting, American - Catalogs. 3. Painting -
Pennsylvania - Philadelphia - Catalogs. I. Mott, Jacolyn
A., 1935- II. Pennsylvania Academy of the Fine Arts.
III. Title.*
ND205 .F728 1989   *NYPL [3-MAVZ
(Philadelphia) 90-13075]*

Fresh start (London, England)
Lancaster, John, 1930- Art with found materials
/. New York , 1992. p. cm. ISBN 0-531-14204-3
DDC 745.5 20
N7433.7 .L36 1992

FREUD, SIGMUND, 1856-1939 - INFLUENCE.
Taboo and totem . New York , 1991. p. cm.
ISBN 0-8419-1249-1 (cloth) DDC 701/.05 20
N72.P74 T33 1991

FREUD, SIGMUND, 1856-1939 - INFLUENCE - EXHIBITIONS.
Wiener Diwan . Klagenfurt , c1989. 219 p. :
ISBN 3-85415-069-5 :
N6488.A9 V6 1989
      NYPL [3-MAL+ 91-5876]

Freudenthal, Dan. 10X . [Berlin] [1984] 1
portfolio (10 pieces) :
      NYPL [3-MAMG+ 88-4811]

Freund, Gisela.
Neyer, Hans Joachim, 1947- Gisèle Freund /.
Berlin , c1988. 80 p. : ISBN 3-87024-143-8 (pbk.)
      NYPL [MFX+ (Freund) 89-24612]

FREUND, GISELA - EXHIBITIONS.
Neyer, Hans Joachim, 1947- Gisèle Freund /.
Berlin , c1988. 80 p. : ISBN 3-87024-143-8 (pbk.)
      NYPL [MFX+ (Freund) 89-24612]

Mainfränkische Studien. see Mainfränkische Studien.

Frey, Jean-Pierre. Recherches sur la typologie et
les types architecturaux. [Paris] , c1991. 367
p. : ISBN 2-7384-0903-2
NA2000 .R38 1991

Frey, Stefan. Klee, Paul, 1879-1940. Paul Klee,
das Schaffen im Todesjahr /. Stuttgart , 1990.
303 p. : ISBN 3-7757-0297-0 : DDC 759.9494 20
N6888.K55 A4 1990a

Frey, Susan R. (Susan Rademacher), 1954-
Oehme, Wolfgang, 1930- Bold romantic
gardens . Reston, Va. , 1990. 310 p. : ISBN
0-87491-950-9 : DDC 712/.0973 20
SB473 .O44 1990   *NYPL [3-MSK+ 91-4459]*

Freyer-Schauenburg, Brigitte. Corpus vasorum
antiquorum. Deutschland. Kiel. Kunsthalle,
Antikensammlung. München , c1988- v. :
ISBN 3-406-32830-X
      NYPL [MPEK+ C8.K54]

Fribourg dans l'œuvre gravé de Henri Robert.
Robert, Henri, 1881-1961. Fribourg , 1989. 1 v.
(unpaged) :
      NYPL [MDG+ (Robert) 90-11166]

FRIBOURG (SWITZERLAND) IN ART.
Robert, Henri, 1881-1961. Fribourg dans
l'œuvre gravé de Henri Robert. Fribourg , 1989.
1 v. (unpaged) :
      NYPL [MDG+ (Robert) 90-11166]

Frick Collection.
Holmes, Mary Tavener. Nicolas Lancret,
1690-1743 . New York , 1992. p. cm. ISBN
0-8109-3559-7 DDC 759.4 20
ND553.L2293 A4 1991

Paintings from the Frick Collection /
introduction by Charles Ryskamp ; text by
Bernice Davidson, Edgar Munhall, and Nadia
Tscherny. New York : H.N. Abrams in
association with the Frick Collection, 1990.
[146] p. : col. ill. (some folded), ports. ; 34 cm.

Includes index. Erratum slip inserted. ISBN
0-8109-3710-7 DDC 750/.74/7471 20
*1. Frick Collection - Catalogs. 2. Painting - New York
(N.Y.) - Catalogs. I. Davidson, Bernice F. II. Munhall,
Edgar. III. Tscherny, Nadia. IV. Title.*
N620.F6 A87 1990
      NYPL [3-MAVZ+ (New York) 91-4472]

FRICK COLLECTION - CATALOGS.
Frick Collection. Paintings from the Frick
Collection /. New York , 1990. [146] p. :
ISBN 0-8109-3710-7 DDC 750/.74/7471 20
N620.F6 A87 1990
      NYPL [3-MAVZ+ (New York) 91-4472]

Fricker, H. R.
I am a Networker (sometimes) : Mail-Art und
Tourism im Network der 80er Jahre / H.R.
Fricker ; [Redaktion, Roland Wäspe, H.R.
Fricker]. St. Gallen : Vexer, c1989. 125 p. : ill.
(some col.) ; 30 cm. "Dieses Buch erscheint
anlässlich der Ausstellung, H.R. Fricker, I am a
Networker (Sometimes), Kunstverein St. Gallen, 2. Juli
bis 28. August 1989."--Verso of t.p. Includes
bibliographical references. ISBN 3-909090-07-9 :
*1. Fricker, H. R. - Exhibitions. 2. Mail art -
Exhibitions. I. Wäspe, Roland. II. Kunstverein St.
Gallen. III. Title.*
IN PROCESS (ONLINE)
      NYPL [3-MAL+ 90-12013]

FRICKER, H. R. - EXHIBITIONS.
Fricker, H. R. I am a Networker (sometimes) .
St. Gallen , c1989. 125 p. : ISBN
3-909090-07-9 :
IN PROCESS (ONLINE)
      NYPL [3-MAL+ 90-12013]

Frida Kahlo . Drucker, Malka. New York , 1991.
p. cm. ISBN 0-553-07165-3 DDC 759.972 B 92 20
N6559.K34 D7 1991

Frida Kahlo . Herrera, Hayden. New York, NY ,
c1991. p. ISBN 0-06-016699-1 : DDC 759.972 20
ND1329.K33 H4 1991

Frida Kahlo /. Lowe, Sarah M. New York, NY ,
1991. p. cm. ISBN 0-87663-607-5 (pbk.) : DDC
759.972 20
ND259.K33 L69 1991

Frida Kahlo . Museum of Contemporary Art
(Chicago, Ill.) Chicago , c1978. 28 p. :
      NYPL [3-MCZ K122 90-7091]

Frida Kahlo /. Turner, Robyn. Boston , 1992. p.
cm. ISBN 0-316-85651-7 : DDC 759.972 B 20
ND259.K33 T87 1992

Frie udstilling (Copenhagen, Denmark) Kitsch &
konkret . København , 1990. 95 p. : ISBN
87-89556-00-3 :
NX558.A1 K58 1990

Fried, Pankraz. Historischer Atlas von
Bayerisch-Schwaben /. Augsburg ,
Weissenhorn , 1982- 1 atlas (1 v. (loose-leaf)) :
ISBN 3-922518-96-6 DDC 911/.433 19
G1923.B3 H35 1982
      NYPL [Map Div. 84-179]

Friedel, Helmut.
Cucchi, Enzo. Enzo Cucchi testa /. München ,
c1987. 2 v. : ISBN 3-88645-076-7 (v. 1)
      NYPL [3-MCF C952 88-3505]

McKeever, Ian, 1946- Ian McKeever, a history
of rocks, 1986-1988 /. München [1990] 49 p. :
DDC 759.2 20
ND497.M5 A4 1990

Städtische Galerie im Lenbachhaus München /.
Braunschweig , 1978. 130 p. :
N2339.S7 S7
      NYPL [MAVZ (Munich) 81-634]

Friedemann Hahn . Schilling, Jürgen, 1949-
Stuttgart , c1990. 183 p. : ISBN 3-89322-210-3
      NYPL [MDG+ (Hahn) 91-6100]

Friedemann Hahn, Zeichnungen und Aquarelle /.
Hahn, Friedemann, 1949- Stuttgart , 1990. 196
p. : ISBN 3-89322-181-6 : DDC 759.3 20
N6888.H256 A4 1990

Friedemann Hahn, Zeichnungen und Aquarelle /.
Hahn, Friedemann, 1949- Stuttgart , 1990. 196
p. : ISBN 3-89322-181-6 (Normalausg.)
      NYPL [3-MCK+ H137 90-12445]

Die Friedenspfeife . Leskoschek, Axl. Wien ,
1990. 1 v. (unpaged) :
      NYPL [MDG (Leskoschek) 91-6211]

Friedlaender . Friedlaender Johnny, 1912-
Krefeld , 1988. 120 p. : ISBN 3-922195-11-3
   NYPL [MDG+ (Friedlaender) 91-3995]

**Friedlaender : catalogue de l'oeuvre gravé, tome
IV 1982-1988.** Friedlaender Johnny, 1912-
Friedlaender . Krefeld , 1988. 120 p. : ISBN
3-922195-11-3
   NYPL [MDG+ (Friedlaender) 91-3995]

**Friedlaender : catalogue of the printed graphic
work, volume IV 1982-1988.** Friedlaender
Johnny, 1912- Friedlaender . Krefeld , 1988.
120 p. : ISBN 3-922195-11-3
   NYPL [MDG+ (Friedlaender) 91-3995]

Friedlaender Johnny, 1912-
Friedlaender : Werkverzeichnis der
Radierungen, Band IV 1982-1988 = Catalogue
de l'oeuvre gravé, Tome IV 1982-1988 =
Catalogue of the printed graphic work, Volume
IV 1982-1988. Krefeld : Verlag Galerie
Peerlings, 1988. 120 p. : chiefly ill (chiefly
col.) ; 37 cm. German; artist's statement also in
English and French. Bibliography: p. 115-117. ISBN
3-922195-11-3
   *1. Friedlaender, Johnny, 1912- - Catalogs. I. Title. II.
Title: catalogue de l'oeuvre gravé, tome
IV 1982-1988. III. Title: Friedlaender : catalogue of the
printed graphic work, volume IV 1982-1988.*
   NYPL [MDG+ (Friedlaender) 91-3995]

**FRIEDLAENDER, JOHNNY, 1912- -
   CATALOGS.**
Friedlaender Johnny, 1912- Friedlaender .
Krefeld , 1988. 120 p. : ISBN 3-922195-11-3
   NYPL [MDG+ (Friedlaender) 91-3995]

Friedlander, Lee.
Fourteen American monuments / Lee
Friedlander. [New York] : Eakins Press
Foundation, c1977. 13 p. : chiefly ill. ; 15 x 23
cm. Cover title.
   *1. Friedlander, Lee. 2. Historic sites - United States -
Pictorial works. 3. Monuments - United States -
Pictorial works. I. Title.*
   NYPL [MFX (Friedlander) 91-7115]

Lee Friedlander / introduction par Loïc Malle.
Paris : Centre national de la photographie,
c1987. 1 v. (unpaged), [60] leaves of plates :
ill. ; 20 cm. (Photo poche. 29) Includes
bibliographical references. ISBN 2-86754-039-9
   1. Friedlander, Lee. I. Title. II. Series.
   NYPL [MFX (Friedlander) 91-3487]

FRIEDLANDER, LEE.
Friedlander, Lee. Fourteen American
monuments /. [New York] , c1977. 13 p. :
   NYPL [MFX (Friedlander) 91-7115]

Friedlander, Lee. Lee Friedlander /. Paris ,
c1987. 1 v. (unpaged), [60] leaves of plates :
ISBN 2-86754-039-9
   NYPL [MFX (Friedlander) 91-3487]

Friedli, Bendicht, 1930-
Killer, Peter, 1945- Bendicht Friedli, oder, Der
Weg entsteht im Gehen /. Bern , c1989. 112
p. : ISBN 3-258-04138-5 DDC 759.9494 20
ND853.F69 A4 1989
   NYPL [3-MCZ F869 91-4185]

FRIEDLI, BENDICHT, 1930- - CATALOGS.
Killer, Peter, 1945- Bendicht Friedli, oder, Der
Weg entsteht im Gehen /. Bern , c1989. 112
p. : ISBN 3-258-04138-5 DDC 759.9494 20
ND853.F69 A4 1989
   NYPL [3-MCZ F869 91-4185]

Friedman, Drew. Warts and all / Drew Friedman
and Josh Alan Friedman ; edited and designed
by Art Spiegelman, R. Sikoryak and Francoise
Mouly. New York, N.Y. : Penguin Books,
1990. [80] p. : chiefly ill. ; 19 cm. ISBN
0-14-013086-1 (pbk.)
   *1. American wit and humor, Pictorial. I. Friedman, Josh
Alan. II. Title.*
   NYPL [3-MEM (Friedman) 90-13588]

Friedman, Josh Alan. Friedman, Drew. Warts and
all /. New York, N.Y. , 1990. [80] p. : ISBN
0-14-013086-1 (pbk.)
   NYPL [3-MEM (Friedman) 90-13588]

Friedman, Martin L.
Segal, George, 1924- George Segal, sculptures
/. Minneapolis , c1978. 99 p. : DDC 730/.92/4
NB237.S44 A4 1978
   NYPL [3-MGO (Segal) 91-5273]

Walker Art Center. Walker Art center .
Minneapolis , New York , 1990. 568 p. : ISBN

0-8478-1267-7   DDC 708.176/579 20
N583 .A884 1990
   NYPL [MAVZ+ (Minneapolis) 91-4981]

Friedman, Mildred S. Ades, Dawn. The
20th-century poster . Minneapolis , New York
[1990] 227 p. : ISBN 1-558-59130-3 DDC
741.6/74/0904 20
NC1815 .A33 1990

Friedrich, Caspar David, 1774-1840.
Caspar David Friedrich : seine Zeichnungen in
der Hamburger Kunsthalle / [Text und
Redaktion, Jenns E. Howoldt ;
Katalogbearbeitung, Eckhard Schaar, Jenns E.
Howoldt, Ulrich Rüter]. [Hamburg] : Die
Kunsthalle, [1990] 35 p. : ill. ; 22 cm.
(Bilderhefte der Hamburger Kunsthalle . 11) "Mai
1990."
   *1. Friedrich, Caspar David, 1774-1840 - Exhibitions. 2.
Hamburger Kunsthalle - Exhibitions. I. Howoldt, Jenns
E. II. Title. III. Series.*
NC251.F66 A4 1990

**FRIEDRICH, CASPAR DAVID, 1774-1840 -
   EXHIBITIONS.**
Friedrich, Caspar David, 1774-1840. Caspar
David Friedrich . [Hamburg] [1990] 35 p. :
NC251.F66 A4 1990

Leighton, John. Caspar David Friedrich .
London , 1990. 72 p. : ISBN 0-947645-75-6 (pbk)
   NYPL [3-MCK F91 90-12688]

**FRIEDRICH, CASPAR DAVID, 1774-1840 -
   CRITICISM AND INTERPRETATION.**
Koerner, Joseph Leo. Caspar David Friedrich
and the subject of landscape /. New Haven ,
1990. 256 p. : ISBN 0-300-04926-9 DDC 759.3
20
ND588.F75 K64 1990
   NYPL [3-MCK F91 91-7554]

**Friedrich, Kaspar David. see Friedrich, Caspar
David, 1774-1840.**

Friedrich Knupper . Knupper, Friedrich,
1947-1987. Nürnberg , c1990. 103 p. : ISBN
3-926982-20-9   *NYPL [3-MNR 91-6999]*

Friedrich, Otto, 1929- Olympia : Paris in the age
of Manet / by Otto Friedrich.1st ed. New
York, NY : HarperCollins, c1992. p. cm.
Includes bibliographical references and index. ISBN
0-06-016318-6 (cloth) : DDC 701/.03 20
   *1. Art - Political aspects - France - Paris. 2. Art,
French - France - Paris. 3. Art, Modern - 19th
century - France - Paris. 4. Art and state - France -
Paris. 5. Manet, Edouard, 1832-1883 - Criticism and
interpretation. 6. France - Politics and government -
1852-1870. I. Title.*
N6847 .F75 1992

Friedrich Preller . Preller, Friedrich, 1804-1878.
Weimar [1978?] [96] p. : DDC 760/.092/4 19
N6888.P735 A4 1978
   NYPL [3-MCK P925 90-6361]

Friedrich Teepe . Teepe, Friedrich, 1929-
[Osnabrück] , 1988. 73 p. :
   NYPL [3-MGO+ (Teepe) 89-27029]

Friedrich von Gärtner und das Bad Kissingen /.
Wegner, Ewald. Würzburg , 1981. v, 78 p., [12]
p. of plates : DDC 720/.92/4 19
NA1088.G3 W43 1981
   NYPL [3-MQWD 90-5440]

Friedrich Vordemberge-Gildewart .
Vordemberge-Gildewart, Friedrich, 1899-1962.
[Bottrop] , 1980. [43] p. :
MLCS 87/4613 (N)
   NYPL [3-MCK V953 90-5864]

Friend, Donald.
Donald Friend, 1915-1989 : retrospective /
Barry Pearce ; with contributions by Lou
Klepac ... [et al.]. Sydney : Art Gallery of New
South Wales, 1990. 160 p. : ill. (some col.) ; 32
cm. Catalog of an exhibition at the Art Gallery of New
South Wales, Feb. 9-Mar. 25, 1990; National Gallery of
Victoria, Apr. 14-June 6, 1990; and Tasmanian Museum
and Art Gallery, June 26- Aug. 19, 1990. Includes
bibliographical references (p. 155-159). ISBN
0-7305-6929-2 (pbk.)
   *1. Friend, Donald - Exhibitions. I. Pearce, Barry. II.
Art Gallery of New South Wales. III. National Gallery
of Victoria. IV. Title.*
   NYPL [3-MCZ+ F87 90-11801]

Pearce, Barry. Donald Friend, 1915-1989 .
[Sydney, N.S.W.] , 1990. 160 p. : ISBN
0-7305-6929-2 (pbk.) DDC 709/.2 20
N7405.F7 A4 1990

**FRIEND, DONALD - ART COLLECTIONS -
   EXHIBITIONS.**
Donald Friend's Bali . Sydney , 1990. 65 p. :
ISBN 0-7305-6574-2
MLCS 90/15244 (N)
   NYPL [3-MAF 91-6722]

FRIEND, DONALD - EXHIBITIONS.
Friend, Donald. Donald Friend, 1915-1989 .
Sydney , 1990. 160 p. : ISBN 0-7305-6929-2
(pbk.)   *NYPL [3-MCZ+ F87 90-11801]*

Pearce, Barry. Donald Friend, 1915-1989 .
[Sydney, N.S.W.] , 1990. 160 p. : ISBN
0-7305-6929-2 (pbk.) DDC 709/.2 20
N7405.F7 A4 1990

**Friends of the Davison Art Center acquisitions,
1962-1988 /.** Davison Art Center. Middletown,
Conn. , c1988. 72 p. :
   NYPL [MDE 89-17470]

Fries Museum (Leeuwarden, Netherlands) Fries
Museum / written by the staff of the museum.
Haarlem : Joh. Enschedé, c1978. 110 p. : ill.
(some col.), map, plans ; 23 cm. (Dutch museums
= Niederländische Museen . 2) English and German.
ISBN 90-70024-07-1
   *1. Fries Museum (Leeuwarden, Netherlands). 2. Art,
Frisian. 3. Decorative arts, Frisian. 4. Friesland,
Netherlands. I. Series: Nederlandse musea, 2.*
   *NYPL [3-MAVZ (Leeuwarden,
                        Netherlands) 90-5650]*

**FRIES MUSEUM (LEEUWARDEN,
   NETHERLANDS)**
Fries Museum (Leeuwarden, Netherlands) Fries
Museum /. Haarlem , c1978. 110 p. : ISBN
90-70024-07-1   *NYPL [3-MAVZ
   (Leeuwarden, Netherlands) 90-5650]*

**Frieseke, Frederick C. (Frederick Carl), 1874-
1939.**
Frederick C. Frieseke : women in repose : May
2-June 23, 1990. New York, N.Y. (11 E. 70th
St., New York 10021) : Berry-Hill Galleries,
c1990. 47 p. : col. ill. ; 23 cm. Includes
bibliographical references (p. 13).
   *1. Frieseke, Frederick C. (Frederick Carl), 1874-1939 -
Exhibitions. I. Berry-Hill Galleries. II. Title.*
IN PROCESS (ONLINE)
   NYPL [3-MCX F916 91-6495]

**FRIESEKE, FREDERICK C. (FREDERICK
   CARL), 1874-1939 - EXHIBITIONS.**
Frieseke, Frederick C. (Frederick Carl),
1874-1939. Frederick C. Frieseke . New York,
N.Y. (11 E. 70th St., New York 10021) ,
c1990. 47 p. :
IN PROCESS (ONLINE)
   NYPL [3-MCX F916 91-6495]

Friesenhaustüren /. Jessel, Hans, 1956-
Hamburg , c1990. 56 p. : ISBN 3-89234-159-1
NA7350.F84 J4 1990

FRIESLAND, NETHERLANDS.
Fries Museum (Leeuwarden, Netherlands) Fries
Museum /. Haarlem , c1978. 110 p. : ISBN
90-70024-07-1   *NYPL [3-MAVZ
   (Leeuwarden, Netherlands) 90-5650]*

Frieslandhal. 11 steden, 11 landen . Leeuwarden,
The Netherlands , 1990. xxvii, 263 p. : ISBN
90-900348-9-7 :
N6758 .A113 1990

Friis-Hansen, Dana, 1961- Not so simple
pleasures . Cambridge, Mass. , 1990. 32 p. :
ISBN 0-938437-34-8 (pbk.) : DDC
709/.73/0747444 20
N6512 .N635 1990

Frijhoff, Willem. De Wevers en Vincent van
Gogh / Zwolle , c1990. 127 p. : ISBN
90-6630-222-4 :
N6953.G63 D4 1990

Frisby, David. Sociological impressionism : a
reassessment of Georg Simmel's social theory /
David Frisby.2nd ed., rev. and enl. London ;
New York, NY : Routledge, 1991. p. cm.
Includes bibliographical references (p.) and index.
ISBN 0-415-05795-7 (pb) DDC 301/.01 20
   *1. Simmel, Georg, 1858-1918. 2. Sociology - Germany -
History. 3. Sociology - Methodology. I. Title.*
NM22.G3 S483 1991

Frisia, Netherlands. see Friesland, Netherlands.

Friso Kramer . Kramer, Friso. [Amsterdam] 1978
(Amsterdam : Stadsdrukkerij) [36] p. :
   NYPL [3-MNF 90-6852]

Frisör aus Lingen. Ein Frisör aus Lingen, Harry

Kramer . Freren , c1990. ix, 198 p., [1] p. of
plates : ISBN 3-923641-30-3 DDC 700/.92 20
NX550.Z9 K7352 1990

Fritsch, Leni. Egerländer Trachtenfibel /.
Frankfurt / M. , 1986. 136 p. :
NYPL [3-MMM+ 89-25288]

**Fritz Brunner, geboren am 24. April 1908 in
Glarus.** Brunner, Fritz, 1908- Glarus , c1989.
131 p. : ISBN 3-85546-040-X
IN PROCESS (ONLINE)
NYPL [3-MCZ B8975 91-2454]

Fritz Discher (1880-1983) . Discher, Fritz,
1880-1983. Kiel , c1990. 64 p. : DDC 760/.092
20
N6888.D466 A4 1990

Fritz H. Erikssons samling : nutida Svensk
konst : Kungl. Akademien för de fria konsterna,
april-maj 1943. Stockholm : Caslon Press, 1943.
26 p., [64] p. of plates : ill. ; 23 cm. (Katalog /
Föreningen för nutida konst . no. 6)
*1. Eriksson, Fritz H. - Art collections - Exhibitions. 2.
Art, Swedish - Private collections - Exhibitions. 3. Art,
Modern - 20th century - Sweden - Private collections -
Exhibitions. I. Kungl. Akademien för de fria konsterna
(Stockholm, Sweden).*
NYPL [3-MAX (Eriksson) 90-6849]

Fritz Heeg-Erasmus, 1901-1986. Heeg-Erasmus,
Fritz, 1901-1986. [Stuttgart] , c1989. 67 p. :
NYPL [3-MCK+ H451 90-12477]

Fritz Riedl. Riedl, Fritz, 1923- Vienna , 1978. 1
v. (unpaged) :   *NYPL [3-MOR 91-1456]*

Fritz Steisslinger, 1891-1957 . Imiela,
Hans-Jürgen, 1927- Stuttgart , c1990. 342 p. :
ISBN 3-8062-0840-9
NYPL [3-MCK+ S8232 90-13357]

Fritz Steisslinger, 1891-1957, Leben und Werk /.
Imiela, Hans-Jürgen, 1927- Stuttgart , c1990.
342 p. : ISBN 3-8062-0840-9 : DDC 759.3 B 20
ND588.S7127 145 1990

Fritz Winter /. Winter, Fritz, 1905- Stuttgart ,
c1990. 309 p. : ISBN 3-7757-0310-1 DDC 759.3
20
ND588.W65 A4 1990

Fritz Winter /. Winter, Fritz, 1905- [Stuttgart] ,
c1990. 309 p. : ISBN 3-7757-0310-1
NYPL [3-MCK+ W78 91-4957]

Fritz-Winter-Haus. Della Torre, Enrico, 1931-
Enrico della Torre . München , c1987. 64 p. :
NYPL [3-MCF+ D343 90-5284]

Fritzvold, Reidar.
Telnes, Sigurd, 1925- Fra jord til fjell med
Reidar Fritzvold /. Bø i Telemark , 1990. 111
p. : ISBN 82-992118-0-8
ND773.F68 T4 1990

**FRITZVOLD, REIDAR - CRITICISM AND
INTERPRETATION.**
Telnes, Sigurd, 1925- Fra jord til fjell med
Reidar Fritzvold /. Bø i Telemark , 1990. 111
p. : ISBN 82-992118-0-8
ND773.F68 T4 1990

Friuli-Venezia Giulia (Italy)
I Longobardi /. Milano , c1990. 492 p. : ISBN
88-435-3210-3
N6919.L8 L67 1990

Trionfo barocco . [Monfalcone] [1990] 265 p. :
ISBN 88-85296-00-9 DDC 759.04/6/07445392
20
ND182.B3 T75 1990

Friz, Richard. The official identification and price
guide to collectible toys / Richard Friz. 5th ed.
New York : House of Collectibles, 1990. 533
p., [8] p. of plates : ill. (some col.) ; 21 cm.
Includes bibliographical references (p. 516-525) and
index. ISBN 0-87637-803-3 : DDC 688.7/2/075 20
*1. Toys - Collectors and collecting - Catalogs. I. Title.
II. Title: Toys.*
NK9509 .F75 1990

Frodel, Gerbert. Geschichtsbilder aus dem alten
Österreich . Wien , 1989. [100] p. :
*NYPL [3-MAW (Vienna) (Vienna.
Österreichische Galerie.
Wechselausstellung. Nr.133)]*

Frogs . Ribuoli, Patrizia. [Rana. English.] Boston ,
c1991. p. ISBN 0-8212-1876-X : DDC 704.9/432
20
N7668.F76 R3613 1991

FROGS - COLLECTIBLES.
Ribuoli, Patrizia. [Rana. English.] Frogs .

Boston , c1991. p. ISBN 0-8212-1876-X : DDC
704.9/432 20
N7668.F76 R3613 1991

FROGS - HISTORY.
Ribuoli, Patrizia. [Rana. English.] Frogs .
Boston , c1991. p. ISBN 0-8212-1876-X : DDC
704.9/432 20
N7668.F76 R3613 1991

FROGS IN ART.
Ribuoli, Patrizia. [Rana. English.] Frogs .
Boston , c1991. p. ISBN 0-8212-1876-X : DDC
704.9/432 20
N7668.F76 R3613 1991

FROGS - LEGENDS.
Ribuoli, Patrizia. [Rana. English.] Frogs .
Boston , c1991. p. ISBN 0-8212-1876-X : DDC
704.9/432 20
N7668.F76 R3613 1991

Fröhlich, Max. Das Gold in der Kunst
Westafrikas. Zürich , 1981. 58 p. :
NYPL [3-MNO 90-12398]

From abacus to Zeus . Pierce, James Smith.
Englewood Cliffs, N.J. , c1991. p. cm. ISBN
0-13-338021-1 : DDC 703 20
N33 .P5 1991

From Adams to Stieglitz . Newhall, Nancy
(Wynne) New York, NY , c1989. [xvi], 172 p. :
ISBN 0-89381-372-9
NYPL [MFW 91-3294]

**From Alexander to Cleopatra, Greek art of the
Hellenistic Age.** Part one, The age of
Alexander [videorecording] / Astoria, NY :
Go-Telecom, c1989. 1 videocassette (28 min.,
30 sec.) : sd., col. ; 1/2 in. (Illuminations . 22)
Cataloged from contributor's data. Photographer, James
Nicholas ; editor, Stuart Neal ; narrator, Yanni
Simonides. VHS. Presents a tour of the permanent
collection of statues, vases, art objects, and jewelry form
the Hellenistic Age at the Walters Art Gallery in
Baltimore, Md. The conservator of the museum explains
the techniques for preserving and restoring these
priceless artifacts and explains their significance from an
art historian's point of view. DDC 709.38 11
*1. Art, Hellenistic. 2. Art, Hellenistic - Conservation
and restoration. 3. Walters Art Gallery (Baltimore,
Md.). I. Go-Telecom (Firm). II. Title: Age of
Alexander. III. Series: Illuminations (Astoria, N.Y.) ,
22.*
N5633

From expressionism to resistance. Art in
Germany 1909-1936 . Munich , c1990. 271 p. :
ISBN 0-944110-02-9 (pbk.) :
NYPL [3-MAMG+ 91-4806]

From idea to building . Brawne, Michael.
Oxford , Boston , 1991. p. cm. ISBN
0-7506-1271-1 : DDC 720 20
NA2750 .B66 1991

From Pisanello to Cézanne . Museum
Boymans-Van Beuningen. Rotterdam , New
York , c1990. 276 p. : ISBN 0-521-40105-4
NYPL [3-MBH+ 90-13057]

From plane to spheroid . Smith, James R. (James
Raymond), 1935- Rancho Cordova, CA, U.
S.A. , c1986. xii, 219 p. : ISBN 0-910845-29-8
DDC 526/.1/09 19
QB283 .S64 1986
NYPL [Map Div. 91-4222]

From sea charts to satellite images : interpreting
North American history through maps / edited
by David Buisseret. Chicago : University of
Chicago Press, 1990. xvi, 324 p., [8] p. of
plates : ill., maps (some col.) ; 25 cm. Includes
bibliographical references and index.
0-226-07991-0 (alk. paper) DDC 973/.022/3 20
*1. Cartography - History. 2. United States - History -
Maps. 3. North America - History - Maps. I. Buisseret,
David.*
E179 .F84 1990   NYPL [Map Div. 90-12430]

From signs to design . Burroughs, Charles.
Cambridge, Mass. , c1990. xii, 344 p., [54] p. of
plates : ISBN 0-262-02298-2 DDC
307.76/0945/63209024 20
NA1120 .B87 1990
NYPL [MQWB 91-4224]

From studio to studiolo . Feinberg, Larry J.
Oberlin , Seattle , 1991. p. cm. ISBN
0-295-97145-2 : DDC 741.945/51/0903107474
20
NC256.F5 F4 1991

From the karkhana to the studio . Chatterjee,
Ratnabali, 1941- New Delhi , 1990. xi, 144 p.,
[12] p. of plates : ISBN 81-85016-28-3 : DDC
701/.03/095414 20
N72.S6 C35 1990   NYPL [3-MAF 91-6048]

From the wild. French. D'après nature : les
meilleurs peintres animaliers d'Amérique du
Nord / sous la direction de Christopher Hume ;
avec une introduction de David M. Lank ;
traduit de l'anglais par Jean Chapdelaine
Gagnon. Saint-Laurent, Québec : Editions du
Trécarré, c1986. 192 p. : ill. (some col.) ; 29 x
32 cm. Translation of: From the wild. Errata slip
inserted. Includes index. ISBN 2-89249-128-2 :
DDC 704.9/432/0971 19
*1. Wildlife art - Canada. 2. Wildlife art - United States.
3. Animal painters - Canada. 4. Animal painters -
United States. I. Hume, Christopher.*
NYPL [3-MAMZ+ 91-4177]

From Titian to Tiepolo. Van Titiaan tot Tiepolo .
Rotterdam [1990] 143 p. : ISBN 90-6918-047-2
NYPL [3-MCE 90-11770]

Frønes, Ivar. Kulturanalyse /. [Oslo] , c1990. 236
p. ; ISBN 82-05-18967-6
NX456 .K77 1990

Froning, Hubertus. Gotsch, Friedrich Karl, 1900-
Friedrich Karl Gotsch, 1900-1984 . [Essen] ,
1990. 95 p. :   *NYPL [3-MCK G684 91-4563]*

**FRONT NATIONAL (FRANCE: 1972-) -
CARICATURES AND CARTOONS.**
Cabu. Le gros blond avec sa chemise noire /.
Paris , c1987. 1 v. (unpaged) : ISBN
2-226-03167-7
NYPL [3-MEM+ (Cabu) 89-27328]

**FRONTIER AND PIONEER LIFE - THE
WEST - MISCELLANEA.**
Time-Life Books. The end and the myth /.
Alexandria, Va. , c1979. 240 p. : ISBN
0-8094-2314-6
F591 .T57 1979   NYPL [IW 79-2698]

**FRONTIER AND PIONEER LIFE - WEST (U.
S.) - EXHIBITIONS.**
The West as America . Washington , c1991.
xiv, 389 p. : ISBN 1-560-98023-0 (h-cover : alk.
paper) DDC 978/.02/074753 20
F596 .W493 1991
NYPL [3-MAMY 91-5810]

Frost & Reed.
Catalogue. Bristol [England] : Frost & Reed,
1913. 92 p. : chiefly ill. ; 29 cm.
*1. Frost & Reed - Catalogs. 2. Prints - 20th century -
England - Catalogs. 3. Prints, English - Catalogs. I.
Title. II. Title: Catalogue of etchings, engravings and
color prints. NYPL [MDF 89-12517]*

FROST & REED - CATALOGS.
Frost & Reed. Catalogue. Bristol [England] ,
1913. 92 p. :   *NYPL [MDF 89-12517]*

Frottier, Elisabeth, 1959- Michael Powolny :
Keramik und Glas aus Wien 1900 bis 1950 :
Monografie und Werkverzeichnis / Elisabeth
Frottier. Wien : Böhlau, c1990. 289 p. : ill.
(some col.) ; 29 cm. (Stichwort Kunstgeschichte)
Originally presented as the author's thesis
(doctoral--Hochschule für Angewandte Kunst in Wien)
under the title: Michael Powolny (1871-1954). Includes
bibliographical references (p. 275-283). Includes index.
ISBN 3-205-05268-4 :
*1. Powolny, Michael, 1871-1954 - Criticism and
interpretation. 2. Powolny, Michael, 1871-1954 -
Catalogs. 3. Pottery - 20th century - Austria - Catalogs.
4. Glassware - Austria - History - 20th century -
Catalogs. I. Powolny, Michael, 1871-1954. II. Title. III.
Title: Keramik und Glas aus Wien 1900 bis 1950. IV.
Series.*
NK4210.P68 F76 1990

Frueh, Joanna. Feminist art criticism . New York,
NY , c1991. p. ISBN 0-06-430216-4 (paperback) :
DDC 701/.03 20
N72.F45 F445 1991

Frühe Bergvölker in Armenien und im Kaukasus :
Berliner Forschungen des 19. Jahrhunderts :
Ausstellung des Museums für Vor- und
Frühgeschichte Berlin, Staatliche Museen
Preussischer Kulturbesitz und der Berliner
Gesellschaft für Anthropologie, Ethnologie und
Urgeschichte / [Texte und Abbildungen
zusammengestellt und kommentiert, Kay
Kohlmeyer und Geraldine Saherwala].2. erg.
Aufl. Berlin : Die Gesellschaft, 1984. 84 p. : ill.
(some col.), maps ; 23 cm. (2. Ergänzungsband der
Mitteilungen der Berliner Gesellschaft für

Anthropologie, Ethnologie und Urgeschichte)
Bibliography: p. 4.
1. Art, Ancient - Armenia. 2. Art, Ancient - Caucasus.
3. Bronze age - Armenia. 4. Bronze age - Caucasus. 5.
Iron age - Armenia. 6. Iron age - Caucasus. 7.
Armenia - Antiquities. 8. Caucasus - Antiquities. I.
Kohlmeyer, Kay. II. Saherwala, Geraldine. III. Museum
für Vor- und Frühgeschichte (Berlin, Germany : West).
IV. Berliner Gesellschaft für Anthropologie, Ethnologie
und Urgeschichte. V. Series: Ergänzungsband der
Mitteilungen der Berliner Gesellschaft für
Anthropologie, Ethnologie und Urgeschichte , 2.
                    NYPL [3-MAE 90-10823]

Frühe irische Kunst : eine Ausstellung des
Deutschen Kunstrates in Zusammenarbeit mit
dem Irischen National-Museum. [Germany :
s.n., 1959] (Mainz : Eggebrecht-Presse) 1 v.
(unpaged) : ill. ; 21 cm. Chiefly a catalog of the
exhibition held in 1959 at the Schloss Charlottenburg,
Berlin; the Bayerisches Nationalmuseum, Munich, and
the Museum für Kunst und Gewerbe, Hamburg.
1. Art, Celtic - Ireland - Exhibitions. 2. Art, Irish -
Exhibitions. I. Deutscher Kunstrat. II. National
Museum of Ireland. III. Schloss Charlottenburg. IV.
Bayerisches Nationalmuseum. V. Museum für Kunst
und Gewerbe Hamburg.
N6240 .F7   *NYPL [3-MAMR 91-303]*

Frühe Keramik in China. Dexel, Thomas, 1890-
Braunschweig [c1973] 84, [48] p.
GN799.P6 D49   *NYPL [3-MPFF 90-6053]*

Frühe Reife, ewige Kindheit. Schiele, Egon,
1890-1918. Egon Schiele . [Wien] [1990?] 104
p. :   DDC 709/.2 20
N6811.5.S34 A4 1990
                    NYPL [3-MCK S332 91-5564]

Frugoni, Chiara, 1940-
[Lontana città. English]
    A distant city : images of urban experience in
the medieval world / Chiara Frugoni ;
translated by William McCuaig. Princeton,
N.J. : Princeton University Press, 1991. xv,
206 p., [80] p. of plates : ill. ; 24 cm.
Translation of: Una lontana città. Includes
bibliographical references and index.   ISBN
0-691-04083-4 (cloth : alk. paper) :   DDC
709/.02 20
1. Art, Medieval - Themes, motives. I. Title.
N5975 .F7813 1991
                    NYPL [3-MAK 91-6315]

Frühe und späte Bilder. Laabs, Hans, 1915- Hans
Laabs . Berlin , c1990. 189 p. :   ISBN
3-87584-294-4   DDC 759.3 20
ND588.L25 A4 1990

Frühgeschichte und frühe Hochkulturen /.
Wetzel, Christoph. Darmstadt , c1990. 448 p. :
    ISBN 3-7630-1971-5
N5330 .W54 1990

Fruit Market Gallery.
    Four abstract artists : Abercrombie, Gouk,
McLean, Pollock : [catalogue of an exhibition
held at] the Fruit Market Gallery, 29 Market
Street, Edinburgh, Scotland, 19 November - 17
December 1977. Edinburgh : Scottish Arts
Council, 1977. [14] p. : col. ill. ; 21 x 23 cm.
    ISBN 0-902989-44-8
1. Abercrombie, Douglas, 1934- - Exhibitions. 2. Gouk,
Alan, 1934- - Exhibitions. 3. McLean, John, 1939- -
Exhibitions. 4. Pollock, Fred, 1937- - Exhibitions. 5.
Painting, Abstract - Exhibitions. 6. Painting, Scottish -
Exhibitions. I. Abercrombie, Douglas, 1934-. II. Title.
ND479 .F78 1977   *NYPL [3-MCT 79-734]*

Lafontaine, Marie-Jo. Marie-Jo Lafontaine /.
Edinburgh , London , c1989. 86 p. :   ISBN
0-947912-36-3 (Fruitmarket Gallery)
                    NYPL [3-MCH+ L166 90-8490]

Fruitmarket Gallery. Cucchi, Enzo. Enzo Cucchi
testa /. München , c1987. 2 v. :   ISBN
3-88645-076-7 (v. 1)
                    NYPL [3-MCF C952 88-3505]

Fruto Vivas. Castro, Raquel. [Caracas] , 1989.
176 p., [16] p. of plates :   ISBN 980-300-866-8
    DDC 720/.92 20
NA939.V57 C37 1989

Fry, Gladys-Marie. Stitched from the soul : slave
quilts from the ante-bellum South /
Gladys-Marie Fry. New York : Dutton Studio
Books : in association with the Museum of
American Folk Art, c1990. ix, 101 p. : ill.
(some col.) ; 29 cm. Research for this book initially
resulted in an exhibition of the same title held at the
Museum of American Folk Art, New York, in the

summer of 1989. Includes bibliographical references (p.
96-101).   ISBN 0-525-24842-0 (cloth)
1. Afro-American quilts - Southern States - History -
19th century. 2. Quilts - Southern States - history -
19th century. 3. Slaves - Southern States - Social life
and customs. I. Title.   *NYPL [3-MOT 91-4318]*

Fry, Philip, 1938- Parsons, Bruce. Bruce Parsons,
United Technologies and gardens . Montréal
[1986] 55 p. :   DDC 709/.2/4 19
                    NYPL [3-MCZ P267 90-10791]

ftograf a dielo .
    (7) Kollar, François, 1904- František Kollár /.
Martin , 1989. 171 p. :   ISBN 80-217-0032-7
                    NYPL [MFX+ (Kollár) 90-9109]

Fu, Shen, 1937- Challenging the past : the
paintings of Chang Dai-chien / by Shen C.Y.
Fu ; with major contributions and translated by
Jan Stuart ; selected poems and inscriptions
translated by Stephen D. Allee. Washington,
D.C. : Arthur M. Sackler Gallery, Smithsonian
Institution ; Seattle : University of Washington
Press, c1991. p. cm. Catalog of an exhibition held at
the Arthur M. Sackler Gallery, Nov. 24, 1991-Apr. 5,
1992, and at the Asia Society and the St. Louis Art
Museum. Includes bibliographical references (p.) and
index.   ISBN 0-295-97124-X (cloth : alk. paper)
    DDC 759.951 20
1. Chang, Ta-ch'ien, 1899- - Exhibitions. 2. Chang,
Ta-ch'ien, 1899- - Criticism and interpretation. I.
Chang, Ta-ch'ien, 1899-. II. Stuart, Jan, 1955-. III.
Arthur M. Sackler Gallery (Smithsonian Institution).
IV. Asia Society. V. St. Louis Art Museum. VI. Title.
ND1049.C4523 A4 1991

Fuchs, Friedrich. Das Hauptportal des
Regensburger Domes : Portal, Vorhalle,
Skulptur / Friedrich Fuchs. München :
Schnell & Steiner, c1990. 175 p. : 176 ill. ; 31
cm. (Kataloge und Schriften / Kunstsammlungen des
Bistums Regensburg, Diözesanmuseum Regensburg .
Bd. 9) Includes bibliographical references (p. 109-117).
    ISBN 3-7954-0652-8
1. Regensburger Dom. 2. Church doorways -
Germany - Regensburg. 3. Decoration and ornament,
Architectural - Germany - Regensburg. 4. Regensburg
(Germany) - Buildings, structures, etc. I. Series:
Kataloge und Schriften , Bd. 9. II. Title.
NA5586.R385 F8 1990

Fuchs, Martin. Türk, K. H., 1928- Werkbericht .
[Stuttgart , c1988. 209 p. :   ISBN 3-930-2067-5
                    NYPL [3-MGO+ (Türk) 89-26927]

Fuchs, Rainer, Dr. Gironcoli, Bruno, 1936- Bruno
Gironcoli, Arbeiten auf Papier . Graz [1990]
120 p. :   DDC 709/.2 20
N6811.5.G57 A4 1990

Fuchs, Rudolf Herman, 1942-
Fabro, Luciano, 1936- Luciano Fabro .
Bompiani [Turin] , c1989. 254 p. :
                    NYPL [3-MGO (Fabro) 90-11538]

Yeats, Jack Butler, 1871-1957. Jack B. Yeats .
Bristol : London : 111 p. :   ISBN 0-907738-29-X
(Arnolfini Gallery)
                    NYPL [3-MCV Y41 91-6477]

Fuchsberg, E. K., 1957- Zeichnungen 1987 :
Halten und Vergehen / E.K. Fuchsberg. Wien :
Museum moderner Kunst : Edition Tusch,
c1988. 85 p. : chiefly col. ill., port. ; 28 cm.
Cover title: Zeichnungen. Prelim. matter in German and
Italian.   ISBN 3-85063-184-2
1. Fuchsberg, E. K., 1957-. I. Title. II. Title:
Zeichnungen. III. Title: Halten und Vergehen.
                    NYPL [3-MCK F946 90-8110]

FUCHSBERG, E. K., 1957-
Fuchsberg, E. K., 1957- Zeichnungen 1987 .
Wien , c1988. 85 p. :   ISBN 3-85063-184-2
                    NYPL [3-MCK F946 90-8110]

Fünftausend Jahre Aegyptische Kunst. 5000 Jahre
Aegyptische Kunst . Zürich [1961] 141 p., [73]
p. of plates (1 folded) :
                    NYPL [3-MAE 90-7095]

Fünfundsiebzig Jahre Maerz. 75 Jahre Maerz .
Linz , 1988. 142 p. :   ISBN 3-900762-08-2
                    NYPL [3-MAMG+ 90-9954]

Fünfzig Jahre Bauhaus. 50 Jahre Bauhaus .
Stuttgart , 1968. 369 p. :
                    NYPL [3-MAL 90-6848]

Fuente, Alvaro de la. Retrato de un pintor /
Alvaro de la Fuente. Santiago de Chile :
Publicaciones "Dial", 1980. 305 p. ; 21 cm.
1. Guevara, Alvaro, 1894-1951. 2. Painters - Chile -

Biography. I. Title.
ND369.G77 F8 1980

Fuente, Beatriz de la. Coloquio Internacional de
Historia del Arte (1980 : Mexico City, Mexico)
Arte funerario /. México , 1987- v. :   ISBN
968-360-243-6 (set)
NB1800 .C65 1980
                    NYPL [3-MRIF 90-2698]

Fuentes, Carlos. Calderwood, Michael. Mexico, a
higher vision . La Jolla, Calif. , c1990. 192 p. :
    ISBN 0-9625399-5-3
                    NYPL [MFX+ (Calderwood) 91-3343]

Fuentes-Pérez, Ileana. Outside Cuba. [New
Brunswick, N.J.] , Miami, Fla. , 1989. 366 p. :
    ISBN 0-935501-13-4
                    NYPL [3-MAM 90-12497]

Fuera de Cuba. Outside Cuba. [New Brunswick,
N.J.] , Miami, Fla. , 1989. 366 p. :   ISBN
0-935501-13-4   *NYPL [3-MAM 90-12497]*

Füssli, Hans Heinrich. see Fuseli, Henry, 1741-
1825.

Füssli, Heinrich. see Fuseli, Henry, 1741-1825.

Füssli, Johann Heinrich. see Fuseli, Henry, 1741-
1825.

Führer des Niederrheinischen Museums für
Volkskunde und Kulturgeschichte Kevelaer .
(22) Gold- und Silberschmiede am Niederrhein,
1854-1987 . [Kevelaer] [1987] 42 p. :   DDC
739.2/0943/550740355 19
NK7150.A3 R544 1987
                    NYPL [3-MNO 91-5028]

Fuhring, Peter. Design into art : drawings for
architecture and ornament : the Lodewijk
Houthakker collection / Peter Fuhring [with
essays contributed by Elaine Evans Dee ... et
al.]. London : P. Wilson ; New York :
Distributed in the USA by Harper & Row,
1989. 2 v. (792 p.) : ill. (some col.) ; 31 cm.
Includes bibliographical references.   ISBN
0-85667-354-4 (London)
1. Houthakker, Lodewijk - Art collections - Catalogs. 2.
Decoration and ornament - Catalogs. 3. Decoration and
ornament, Architectural - Catalogs. 4. Interior
decoration rendering - Catalogs. 5. Drawing - Catalogs.
I. Houthakker, Lodewijk. II. Dee, Elaine Evans. III.
Title.   *NYPL [MLD+ 89-23146]*

Fuhrmann, Franz. Die Chorkrypta des
romanischen Domes in Salzburg : ein Führer
mit Hinweisen auf die neue Gruft der
Erzbischöfe / Franz Fuhrmann. Salzburg :
Salzburger Museum Carolino Augusteum, 1962.
32 p. : ill. ; 17 cm. (Schriftenreihe des Salzburger
Museums Carolino Augusteum . Bd. 3) Cover title: Die
Chorkrypta des romanischen Domes zu Salzburg.
Bibliography: p. 32.
1. Salzburger Dom. 2. Crypts - Austria - Salzburg. I.
Salzburger Museum Carolino Augusteum. II. Title. III.
Title: Chorkrypta des romanischen Domes zu Salzburg.
                    NYPL [3-MRIF 90-4729]

Fuksas, Massimiliano, 1944- La Biblioteca
ritrovata . Roma , 1990. 50 p. :
                    NYPL [3-MQWB 91-5054]

Fukuoka. Art Museum. see Fukuoka-shi
Bijutsukan.

Fukuoka-shi Bijutsukan. Furansu kaiga no seika .
[Tokyo] , c1989. 314 p. :
ND546 .F873 1989   NYPL [3-MCN 90-9786]

Full circle . Snelson, Kenneth, 1927- New York,
N.Y. , 1990. 95 p. :   ISBN 0-89381-438-5
                    NYPL [MFX (Snelson) 91-3355]

A função social do arquiteto /. Artigas, João
Batista Vilanova. São Paulo, SP , 1989. 93 p. :
    ISBN 85-21-30621-0   DDC 720/.1/0309810904
20
NA2543.S6 A76 1989

FUNCTIONALISM (ARCHITECTURE)
Finta, József. A funkció társkeresései,
szerződéseim Budapesttel . Budapest , c1990.
34 p., [24] p. of plates :   ISBN 963-05-5571-9 :
NA682.F8 F5 1990

FUNCTIONALISM (ARCHITECTURE) -
BRAZIL.
Harris, Elizabeth Davis, 1950- Le Corbusier .
São Paulo, SP , 1987. 218 p. :   ISBN
85-21-30469-2 :
                    NYPL [3-MQZ (Le Corbusier) 90-10663]

FUNCTIONALISM (ARCHITECTURE) -
FRANCE.

Fanelli, Giovanni. Perret e Le Corbusier .
Roma , 1990. 255 p. : ISBN 88-420-3596-3 :
NA1048.5.F85 F36 1990

**FUNCTIONALISM (ARCHITECTURE) -
INFLUENCE - EXHIBITIONS.**
Gianni, Benjamin, 1958- Dice thrown /. New
York, N.Y. , c1989. 56 p. : ISBN
0-910413-62-2 : DDC 728/.92/09730747468 20
NA8201 .G47 1989
                NYPL [3-MQV 90-12464]

**FUNCTIONALISM (ARCHITECTURE) -
ITALY.**
Adalberto Libera. English. Adalberto Libera /.
New York, N.Y. , c1991. p. cm.   ISBN
1-87827-114-8 : DDC 720/.92 20
NA1123.L46 A4 1991

**FUNCTIONALISM (ARCHITECTURE) -
ITALY - EXHIBITIONS.**
Franco Albini, architecture and design,
1934-1977 . New York, NY , c1990. 138 p. :
ISBN 0-910413-79-7 (pbk. : alk. paper) : DDC
720/.92 20
NA1123.A525 A4 1990
                NYPL [3-MQZ (Albini) 91-6735]

**FUNCTIONALISM (ARCHITECTURE) -
ITALY - ROME.**
Schumacher, Thomas L. [Danteum di Terragni.
English.] The Danteum . Princeton, NJ , c1985.
169 p. : ISBN 0-910413-09-6
NA2707.T466 S3713 1985
                NYPL [3-MQZ (Terragni) 86-3775]

**FUNCTIONALISM (ARCHITECTURE) -
RUSSIAN S.F.S.R. - MOSCOW.**
Cohen, Jean-Louis. [Le Corbusier et la mystique
de l'URSS. English.] Le Corbusier and the
mystique of the USSR . Princeton, N.J. [1991]
p. cm.   ISBN 0-691-04076-1 : DDC 720/.92 20
NA1053.J4 C55 1991

**Fundação Casa de Rui Barbosa. Centro de
Estudos Históricos.**
O Clero no Parlamento brasileiro /. Brasília ,
Rio de Janeiro , 1978-79. 2 v. : ISBN
85-7004-002-4
JL2454 .C53   *NYPL [HFE 80-1465]*

O Clero no Parlamento brasileiro /. Brasília ,
Rio de Janeiro , 1978- v. : ISBN 85-7004-002-4
JL2454 .C53   *NYPL [HFE 80-1378]*

**Fundação Centro de Preservação dos Sítios
Históricos de Olinda.** Bajado, 1912- Bajado,
um artista de Olinda /. Olinda [Brasil] , 1985.
48 p. : DDC 759.981 19
ND359.B34 A35 1985
                NYPL [3-MCZ B1583 90-9450]

Fundação Joaquim Nabuco.
Arquitetura nos trópicos . Recife , 1985. 161
p. : ISBN 85-7019-095-6
NA2542.T7 A77 1985
                NYPL [3-MQD 90-11121]

Atlas histórico cartográfico do Recife /. Recife ,
1988. 1 atlas (114, [10] p.) : ISBN 85-7019-172-3
                NYPL [Map Div. 91-7611]

Fundação Memorial da América Latina.
Integração das artes . São Paulo , 1990. 113 p. :
N6655 .I58 1990

Memorial da América Latina. São Paulo-S.P.
[1990] 127 p. : DDC 725/.8042/098161 20
NA6813.B62 S265 1990

Fundació Caixa de Catalunya.
Escultura catalana del segle XIX . [Barcelona]
[1989] 246 p. :   *NYPL [3-MGI+ 91-6802]*

Escultura catalana del segle XIX . Barcelona
[1989?] 246 p. : DDC 730/.946/70744672 20
NB809.C3 E83 1989

Fundació Caixa de Pensions (Barcelona, Spain)
Durancamps, Rafael, 1891-1979. Rafael
Durancamps entre 1915-1945 . Barcelona ,
c1990. 166 p. : ISBN 84-7664-268-7
ND813.D87 A4 1990

Puig i Cadafalch, Josep, 1869-1957. Josep Puig
i Cadafalch . Barcelona , 1989. 193 p. : ISBN
84-7664-239-3
*IN PROCESS (ONLINE)   NYPL [3-MQZ+
              (Puig i Cadafalch) 91-4264]*

Vuillard, Édouard, 1868-1940. Vuillard . Paris ,
c1990. 237 p. : ISBN 2-08-011730-0 DDC
760/.092 20
N6853.V85 A4 1990

**Fundació Caixa de Pensions (Barcelona, Spain).
Centre Cultural.** Puig i Cadafalch, Josep,
1869-1957. Josep Puig i Cadafalch . Barcelona ,
1989. 193 p. : ISBN 84-7664-239-3
*IN PROCESS (ONLINE)   NYPL [3-MQZ+
              (Puig i Cadafalch) 91-4264]*

**Fundació Joan Miró-Centre d'Estudis d'Art
Contemporani.** Levine, Erik, 1960- Erik
Levine . Genève , c1989. 1 v. (unpaged) :
                NYPL [3-MGO (Levine) 91-7405]

Fundación Caja de Pensiones (Madrid, Spain)
Gnoli, Domenico, 1933-1970. Domenico
Gnoli . [Madrid] , c1990. 151 p. : ISBN
84-7664-248-2
                NYPL [3-MCF+ G572 90-12300]

Fundación Caja de Pensiones (Madrid, Spin) La
Razón revisada = Reason revised . Madrid ,
c1988. 135 p. : ISBN 84-7664-183-4
                NYPL [3-MAMG 91-7022]

Fundación Caja de Pensiones (Valencia, Spain)
Ribera, José de, 1588?-1652. Jusepe de Ribera,
grabador, 1591-1652 . [Valencia] , c1989. 113
p. : ISBN 84-7664-196-6 DDC 769.92 20
NE2062.5.R52 A4 1989
                NYPL [MDG (Ribera) 91-3604]

**Fundación Humanismo y Democracia (Madrid,
Spain)** Escuela de Madrid . [Madrid]
[1990?] 293 p. : ISBN 84-505-9356-5 DDC
759.6/41/090450744641 20
ND808.5.M28 E83 1990

Fundación Juan March. Dubuffet, Jean, 1901-
Jean Dubuffet . Madrid , 1976. 64 p. : ISBN
84-7075-026-7 :
N6853.D78 A4 1976
                NYPL [3-MCO D82 81-175]

Fundación Mapfre.
El Surrealismo entre Viejo y Nuevo Mundo .
[Madrid] [1990] 346 p. : ISBN 84-86022-51-2
N6512.5.S87 S8 1990

Penagos (1889-1954). [Madrid , 1989] 270 p. :
ISBN 84-404-4727-2 DDC 741.6/092 20
NC1850.P44 A4 1989

Fundamentals of Chinese floral painting. Chou,
Shih-hsin. Chung-kuo hua hui hua chi ch'u =.
[Taipei?] [1976?] 263 p. :
                NYPL [3-MAF+ 90-6353]

Funde aus Asciburgium .
(Heft 9) Bechert, Tilmann. Töpferstempel aus
Südgallien /. Duisburg , 1988. 102 p. :
IN PROCESS (ONLINE)
                NYPL [3-MPK+ 91-4448]

**FUNERAL RIGHTS AND CEREMONIES -
FRANCE.**
Plault, Michel. Les lanternes des morts .
Poitiers , 1988. 198 p. : ISBN 2-902170-58-0
                NYPL [3-MRIF+ 89-26506]

**FUNERAL RITES AND CEREMONIES -
CHINA - HISTORY - CONGRESSES.**
Ancient mortuary traditions of China . Los
Angeles, Calif. [Honolulu?] , c1991. p. cm.
ISBN 0-87587-157-7 (pbk.)   DDC
732/.71/07479494 20
NK4165 .A53 1991

Fünfzig Werke aus fünfzig Jahren (1890-1940)
Klee, Paul, 1879-1940. Paul Klee . [Hamburg]
[1990] 130 p. :
N6888.K55 A4 1990

**A funkció társkeresései, szerződéseim
Budapesttel .** Finta, József. Budapest , c1990.
34 p., [24] p. of plates : ISBN 963-05-5571-9 :
NA682.F8 F5 1990

**FUNNIES. see COMIC BOOKS, STRIPS,
ETC.**

Furansu kaiga no seika : ru saron no
kyoshōtachi : 1989-nen 6-gatsu 6-nichi--7-gatsu
16-nichi, Kyōto Kokuritsu Kindai Bijutsukan /
[Kanshū Ikegami Chūji ; henshū Fukuoka-shi
Bijutsukan, Yasunaga Kōichi, Ushiroshōji
Masahiro] = La tradition et l'innovation dans
l'art français par les peintres des Salons : 6
juin-16 juillet 1989, Musée national d'art
moderne de Kyoto / [sous la direction de Chūji
Ikegami ; édition, Musée d'art de Fukuoka,
Kōichi Yasunaga, Masahiro Ushiroshōji].
[Tokyo] : Nihon Keizai Shinbunsha, c1989. 314
p. : ill. (some col.) ; 29 cm. French and Japanese.
Includes bibliographical references.
*1. Société des artistes français. Salon - Exhibitions. 2.
Salon (Exhibition : Paris, France) - Exhibitions. 3.*

*Painting, French - Exhibitions. 4. Painting, Modern -
17th-18th centuries - France - Exhibitions. 5. Painting,
Modern - 19th century - France - Exhibitions. I.
Fukuoka-shi Bijutsukan. II. Title: Tradition et
l'innovation dans l'art français par les peintres des
Salons.*
ND546 .F873 1989   NYPL [3-MCN 90-9786]

La fureur poétique, du 15 mars au 23 avril 1967.
Paris. Musée d'art moderne de la ville de Paris.
Paris , 1967. 1 v. (unpaged)
N6494.S8 P3   *NYPL [3-MAL 83-2155]*

**Furnace (Franklin) Archive. see Franklin Furnace
Archive.**

FURNESS, FRANK, 1839-1912 - CATALOGS.
Thomas, George E. Frank Furness . New York,
N.Y. , c1991. p. cm.   ISBN 1-87827-104-0 :
DDC 720/.92 20
NA737.F84 A4 1991

Furnishing Williamsburg's historic buildings.
Gilliam, Jan (Jan Kirsten) Williamsburg, Va. ,
1991. p. cm.   ISBN 0-87935-083-0 DDC
747.2155/4252/09033 20
NK2438.W54 G5 1991

Furniture / consultant, Richard Davidson ;
general editors, Judith and Martin Miller. New
York, N.Y. : Viking Studio Books, 1991. p. cm.
(Miller's antiques checklists) Includes index. ISBN
0-670-83957-4 DDC 749/.1/075 20
*1. Furniture - Collectors and collecting - Catalogs. I.
Davidson, Richard. II. Miller, Judith. III. Miller,
Martin. IV. Series.*
NK2240 .F87 1991

FURNITURE.
White, Antony, 1941- Furniture & furnishings .
New York , 1991. p. cm.   ISBN 0-8306-1832-5 :
DDC 749 20
NK2230 .W48 1991

Furniture & furnishings . White, Antony, 1941-
New York , 1991. p. cm.   ISBN 0-8306-1832-5 :
DDC 749 20
NK2230 .W48 1991

FURNITURE, AMANA.
Albers, Marjorie K. The Amana people and
their furniture /. Ames , 1990. xii, 221 p. :
ISBN 0-8138-1238-0 (pbk. : alk. paper)   DDC
749.2177/653 20
NK2435.I8 A4 1990
                NYPL [3-MOF 91-4695]

Furniture and furnishings. White, Antony, 1941-
Furniture & furnishings . New York , 1991. p.
cm. ISBN 0-8306-1832-5 : DDC 749 20
NK2230 .W48 1991

**FURNITURE - AUSTRALIA - HISTORY -
20TH CENTURY.**
Bogle, Michael. Modern Australian furniture .
Roseville, NSW, Australia , 1989. 144 p. :
ISBN 0-947131-26-4 DDC 749.2994/09048 20
NK2689 .B64 1989
                NYPL [3-MOF+ 90-8166]

**FURNITURE, BAROQUE - FRANCE -
PICARDY.**
Fligny, Laurence. Le mobilier en Picardie .
[Paris] , c1990. 358 p. : ISBN 2-7084-0390-7 :
DDC 749.24/26 20
NK2548 .F57 1990
                NYPL [3-MOF+ 91-6459]

**FURNITURE, BAROQUE - NEW JERSEY -
EXHIBITIONS.**
Kenny, Peter (Peter M.) American kasten .
New York , c1991. viii, 80 p. : ISBN
0-87099-605-3 (pbk.) DDC 749/.3 20
NK2727 .K46 1991 NYPL [3-MOF 91-6596]

**FURNITURE, BAROQUE - NEW YORK
(STATE) - EXHIBITIONS.**
Kenny, Peter (Peter M.) American kasten .
New York , c1991. viii, 80 p. : ISBN
0-87099-605-3 (pbk.) DDC 749/.3 20
NK2727 .K46 1991 NYPL [3-MOF 91-6596]

**FURNITURE - BELGIUM - HISTORY - 19TH
CENTURY.**
Watelet, Jacques Grégoire, 1917-
Serrurier-Bovy . Paris [1989, c1987] 134 p. :
                NYPL [MOF 91-6858]

**FURNITURE - BELGIUM - HISTORY - 20TH
CENTURY.**
Watelet, Jacques Grégoire, 1917-
Serrurier-Bovy . Paris [1989, c1987] 134 p. :
                NYPL [MOF 91-6858]

FURNITURE - BELGIUM - LIEGE - HISTORY - 18TH CENTURY.
Philippe, Joseph, 1919- Le meuble liégeois à son âge d'or . Liège , 1990. 173 p. : ISBN 2-87114-044-8 *NYPL [3-MOF+ 91-4973]*

FURNITURE - BUILDING. see FURNITURE MAKING.

FURNITURE - CHINA - EXHIBITIONS.
Museu Nacional de Arte Antiga (Portugal) Catalogue of furniture in the exhibition of embroidered quilts from the Museu de Arte Antiga, Lisboa . London , 1978. 1 v. (unpaged) : *NYPL [3-MOF 91-296]*

FURNITURE - CHINA - EXPERTISING.
Wang, Shih-hsiang, 1914- [Ming shih chia chü yen chiu. English.] Connoisseurship of Chinese furniture . Chicago, Ill. , 1990. 2 v. : ISBN 1-87852-901-3 *NYPL [3-MOF+ 91-4916]*

FURNITURE - CHINA - HISTORY - MING-CH'ING DYNASTIES, 1368-1912.
Wang, Shih-hsiang, 1914- [Ming shih chia chü yen chiu. English.] Connoisseurship of Chinese furniture . Chicago, Ill. , 1990. 2 v. : ISBN 1-87852-901-3 *NYPL [3-MOF+ 91-4916]*

FURNITURE, CHURCH. see CHURCH FURNITURE.

FURNITURE - COLLECTORS AND COLLECTING - CATALOGS.
Furniture /. New York, N.Y. , 1991. p. cm. ISBN 0-670-83957-4 DDC 749/.1/075 20
NK2240 .F87 1991

FURNITURE, COLONIAL - NEW ZEALAND.
Northcote-Bade, Stanley. Colonial furniture in New Zealand. Wellington [1971] 164 p. ISBN 0-589-00683-5 DDC 749.2/9931
NK2692.A1 N67 NYPL [3-MOF 90-5434]

FURNITURE - DENMARK - HISTORY - 20TH CENTURY.
Karlsen, Arne. Dansk møbelkunst i det 20. århundrede /. København , 1990- v. <1 > : ISBN 87-7241-677-7 (set)
NK2585 .K37 1990

Sieck, Frederik, 1916- [Nutidig dansk møbeldesign. English.] Contemporary Danish furniture design . [Copenhagen] , c1990. 231 p. : ISBN 87-17-06121-0 (pbk.) : DDC 749.289/09/045 20
NK2585 .S513 1990

FURNITURE DESIGN.
White, Antony, 1941- Furniture & furnishings . New York , 1991. p. cm. ISBN 0-8306-1832-5 : DDC 749 20
NK2230 .W48 1991

FURNITURE DESIGN - BELGIUM - LIEGE.
Philippe, Joseph, 1919- Le meuble liégeois à son âge d'or . Liège , 1990. 173 p. : ISBN 2-87114-044-8 *NYPL [3-MOF+ 91-4973]*

Watelet, Jacques-Grégoire, 1917- [Serrurier-Bovy. English.] Serrurier-Bovy . London , 1987. 133 p. : ISBN 0-85331-508-6 *NYPL [3-MOI+ 88-3631]*

FURNITURE DESIGN - BRITAIN.
Morrison, Jasper, 1959- Jasper Morrison . London , 1990. 82 p. : ISBN 1-85454-435-7 (pbk) : DDC 749.22 20
NYPL [3-MOF 90-11539]

FURNITURE DESIGN - EUROPE - EXHIBITIONS.
'90 Möbeldesign aus Europa . Köln , 1990. 1 v. (unpaged) : *NYPL [3-MOF 91-6579]*

FURNITURE DESIGN - FRANCE - HISTORY - 20TH CENTURY.
Goguel, Solange. René Herbst /. Paris , c1990. 363 p. : ISBN 2-903370-56-7 DDC 720/.92 20
NK2049.Z9 H4734 1990

FURNITURE DESIGN - HISTORY - 20TH CENTURY.
Benje, Peter. Die Produktionsleitlinie /. Bremen , 1989. 63 leaves ; *NYPL [3-MOF+ 91-4271]*

International furniture design for the '90s /. New York, N.Y. , 1991. p. cm. ISBN 0-86636-136-7 : DDC 749.2/0499 20
NK2395 .I57 1991

Sembach, Klaus-Jürgen. Möbeldesign des 20. Jahrhunderts /. Köln [1988] 255 p. : ISBN 3-8228-0097-X *NYPL [3-MOI+ 91-3916]*

FURNITURE DESIGN - ITALY - HISTORY - 20TH CENTURY.
Pasca, Vanni. [Vico Magistretti, disegno. English.] Vico Magistretti, designer /. N.Y. , 1991. p. ISBN 0-8478-1342-8 (pbk.) : DDC 749.25 20
NK2562.M34 V513 1991

Vercelloni, Virgilio. [Avventura del design, Gavina. English.] The adventure of design . New York , 1989. 220 p. : ISBN 0-8478-1039-9 DDC 749/.245 20
TS79 .V4713 1989
NYPL [3-MNE+ 90-12985]

FURNITURE DESIGNERS - AUSTRALIA - BIOGRAPHY.
Bogle, Michael. Modern Australian furniture . Roseville, NSW, Australia , 1989. 144 p. : ISBN 0-947131-26-4 DDC 749.2994/09048 20
NK2689 .B64 1989
NYPL [3-MOF+ 90-8166]

FURNITURE DESIGNERS - ENGLAND.
Houston, John. Fred Baier . London , 1990. 64 p. : ISBN 0-947792-46-5 (pbk.) : DDC 749.22 20
NYPL [3-MOF 90-11124]

FURNITURE DESIGNERS - ITALY - BIOGRAPHY.
The Italian furniture /. Tokyo, Japan , c1991. 273 p. : ISBN 4-7661-0609-1
NYPL [3-MOF+ 91-5637]

FURNITURE - DICTIONARIES.
Gloag, John, 1896- A complete dictionary of furniture /. Woodstock, N.Y. , 1991. 828 p. : ISBN 0-87951-414-0 DDC 749 20
NK2205 .G54 1991 NYPL [MOF 91-6208]

FURNITURE, DUTCH COLONIAL - NEW JERSEY - EXHIBITIONS.
Kenny, Peter (Peter M.) American kasten . New York , c1991. viii, 80 p. : ISBN 0-87099-605-3 (pbk.) DDC 749/.3 20
NK2727 .K46 1991 NYPL [3-MOF 91-6596]

FURNITURE, DUTCH COLONIAL - NEW YORK (STATE) - EXHIBITIONS.
Kenny, Peter (Peter M.) American kasten . New York , c1991. viii, 80 p. : ISBN 0-87099-605-3 (pbk.) DDC 749/.3 20
NK2727 .K46 1991 NYPL [3-MOF 91-6596]

FURNITURE, EARLY AMERICAN - PRICES.
Goggin, Bill. Eagles . New Market, MD (Box 277, New Market 21774) [1990] xv, 319 p. : DDC 749.214/09/033075 20
NK2406 .G6 1990

FURNITURE, ECCLESIASTICAL. see CHURCH FURNITURE.

FURNITURE - ENGLAND - HISTORY.
Macquoid, Percy, d. 1925. A history of English furniture . London , 1988. 416 p., lx p. of plates : ISBN 1-85170-080-3 : DDC 749.22 19
NK2529 NYPL [3-MOF+ 91-4219]

FURNITURE - EUROPE - EXHIBITIONS.
'90 Möbeldesign aus Europa . Köln , 1990. 1 v. (unpaged) : *NYPL [3-MOF 91-6579]*

FURNITURE - EUROPE - HISTORY - 19TH CENTURY.
İrez, Feryal. XIX. yüzyıl Osmanlı saray mobilyası /. Ankara , 1988. 110 p., [83] p. of plates : ISBN 975-16-0039-1
NK2525 .I7 1988

FURNITURE - EXHIBITIONS.
Sotheby Parke Bernet Inc. The Benjamin Sonnenberg collection . New York , 1979. 2 v. :
NYPL [3-MAX (Sonnenberg) 90-5888]

FURNITURE - FRANCE.
Janneau, Guillaume, 1887- Le meuble d'ébénisterie /. Paris , c1989. 236 p. : ISBN 2-85917-083-9 *NYPL [3-MOI 91-6666]*

Verlet, Pierre. Le mobilier royal français /. [Paris] , 1990- v. <4 > : ISBN 2-7084-0389-3 (v. 4) : DDC 749.24 20
NK2548 .V44 1990

FURNITURE - FRANCE - EXHIBITIONS.
France. Ministère de la culture, de la communication, des grands travaux et du Bicentenaire. Le Meuble régional en France . Paris , 1990. 189 p. : ISBN 2-7118-2374-1
NYPL [3-MOF 91-3999]

FURNITURE - FRANCE - HISTORY.
France. Ministère de la culture, de la communication, des grands travaux et du

Bicentenaire. Le Meuble régional en France . Paris , 1990. 189 p. : ISBN 2-7118-2374-1
NYPL [3-MOF 91-3999]

FURNITURE - FRANCE - HISTORY - 18TH CENTURY.
Kjellberg, Pierre. Le mobilier français du XVIIIe siècle . Paris , c1989. 887 p. : ISBN 2-85917-087-1 *NYPL [3-MOF 90-11781]*

FURNITURE - FRANCE - HISTORY - 18TH CENTURY - EXHIBITIONS.
De Versailles à Paris . Paris , 1989. 288 p., [38] p. of plates : ISBN 2-9504070-0-5
NYPL [3-MAWC (Paris) 90-12345]

FURNITURE - FRANCE - HISTORY - 20TH CENTURY.
Kjellberg, Pierre. Art déco . [Paris] [1986] 247 p. : ISBN 2-85917-054-5 : DDC 749.24 19
NK2549 .K59 1986
NYPL [3-MOF+ 91-5321]

FURNITURE - FRANCE - NORMANDY.
Fréal, Jacques. La Normandie /. [Paris] , c1980. 110 p. : ISBN 2-7050-0260-X : DDC 392/.36/009442 19
NA8203 .F693 NYPL [3-MQWF 81-936]

FURNITURE - FRANCE - PARIS - HISTORY - 19TH CENTURY.
Ledoux-Lebard, Denise. Le mobilier français du XIXe siècle . Paris , c1989. 700 p., xxxii p. of plates : *NYPL [3-MOF 90-11782]*

FURNITURE - FRANCE - PICARDY - HISTORY.
Fligny, Laurence. Le mobilier en Picardie . [Paris] , c1990. 358 p. : ISBN 2-7084-0390-7 : DDC 749.24/26 20
NK2548 .F57 1990
NYPL [3-MOF+ 91-6459]

FURNITURE, GEORGIAN - IRELAND - DUBLIN - CATALOGS.
Hinckley, F. Lewis. The more significant Georgian furniture /. New York , c1990. 125 p. : ISBN 0-8147-3461-8 : DDC 749.22/91835/074 20
NK2538.D8 H554 1989
NYPL [3-MOF 90-12955]

FURNITURE - GERMANY - HISTORY - 18TH CENTURY - CATALOGS.
Möbel von Abraham und David Roentgen . [Neuwied] , 1990. 56 p. :
NK2554.R6 A4 1990

FURNITURE - GERMANY - HISTORY - 19TH CENTURY.
Hampel, Frithjof Detlev Paul. Schinkels Möbelwerk und seine Voraussetzungen /. Witterschlick/Bonn , 1989. 255 p., [8] p. of plates : ISBN 3-925267-29-8
NK2554.S35 H35 1989

Rammert-Götz, Michaela. Richard Riemerschmid, Möbel und Innenräume von 1895-1900 /. München , c1987. 185 p. ; ISBN 3-88073-253-1
NK2554.R54 R36 1987
NYPL [3-MOF 90-11037]

FURNITURE - GERMANY - NEUWIED - CATALOGS.
Möbel von Abraham und David Roentgen . [Neuwied] , 1990. 56 p. :
NK2554.R6 A4 1990

FURNITURE - GERMANY (WEST) - MAINZ - HISTORY - 18TH CENTURY.
Zinnkann, Heidrun. Meisterstücke, Mainzer Möbel des 18. Jahrhunderts . Frankfurt am Main , 1988. 154 p. : ISBN 3-88270-039-4
NYPL [3-MOF 89-25235]

FURNITURE - HISTORY - 20TH CENTURY.
Capella, Juli. [Diseño de arquitectos en los 80. English.] Designed by architects in the 1980s /. New York , 1988. 191 p. : ISBN 0-8478-0941-2 : DDC 749.2/0498 19
NK2702 .C3713 1988
NYPL [3-MOI 91-6559]

Sembach, Klaus-Jürgen. Möbeldesign des 20. Jahrhunderts /. Köln [1988] 255 p. : ISBN 3-8228-0097-X
NK2395 .S44 1988

Furniture in studio. Houston, John. Fred Baier . London , 1990. 64 p. : ISBN 0-947792-46-5 (pbk.) : DDC 749.22 20
NYPL [3-MOF 90-11124]

FURNITURE - INDIA - EXHIBITIONS.
Museu Nacional de Arte Antiga (Portugal)
Catalogue of furniture in the exhibition of
embroidered quilts from the Museu de Arte
Antiga, Lisboa . London , 1978. 1 v.
(unpaged) :   *NYPL [3-MOF 91-296]*

**FURNITURE INDUSTRY AND TRADE -
BELGIUM - LIÈGE.**
Watelet, Jacques-Grégoire, 1917-
[Serrurier-Bovy. English.] Serrurier-Bovy .
London , 1987. 133 p. : ISBN 0-85331-508-6
        NYPL [3-MOI+ 88-3631]

FURNITURE - IOWA - HISTORY.
Albers, Marjorie K. The Amana people and
their furniture /. Ames , 1990. xii, 221 p. :
    ISBN 0-8138-1238-0 (pbk. : alk. paper)   DDC
    749.2177/653 20
NK2435.I8 A4 1990
        NYPL [3-MOF 91-4695]

**FURNITURE - IRELAND - DUBLIN -
STYLES - CATALOGS.**
Hinckley, F. Lewis. The more significant
Georgian furniture /. New York , c1990. 125
p. : ISBN 0-8147-3461-8 : DDC 749.22/91835/074
    20
NK2538.D8 H554 1989
        NYPL [3-MOF 90-12955]

**FURNITURE - ITALY - HISTORY - 19TH
CENTURY.**
Cito Filomarino, Anna Maria. L'ottocento.
[Milano, c1969]. 255 p.
NK2561 .C58   *NYPL [3-MOF 90-6347]*

**FURNITURE - ITALY - HISTORY - 20TH
CENTURY.**
The Italian furniture /. Tokyo, Japan , c1991.
273 p. : ISBN 4-7661-0609-1
        NYPL [3-MOF+ 91-5637]

FURNITURE MAKING - HISTORY.
Vandal, Norman L., 1948- Queen Anne
furniture . Newtown, Conn. , c1990. 247 p. :
    ISBN 0-942391-07-1 : DDC 749.214 20
TT197 .V36 1990   *NYPL [3-MOF 91-3711]*

FURNITURE - MARKS - FRANCE - PARIS.
Ledoux-Lebard, Denise. Le mobilier français du
XIXe siècle . Paris , c1989. 700 p., xxxii p. of
plates :   *NYPL [3-MOF 90-11782]*

**FURNITURE, MEDIEVAL - FRANCE -
PICARDY.**
Fligny, Laurence. Le mobilier en Picardie .
[Paris] , c1990. 358 p. : ISBN 2-7084-0390-7 :
    DDC 749.24/26 20
NK2548 .F57 1990
        NYPL [3-MOF+ 91-6459]

**FURNITURE - NEW YORK (STATE) -
HISTORY - 18TH CENTURY -
CATALOGS.**
Scherer, John L. New York furniture . Albany,
N.Y. , c1988. 29 p. : ISBN 1-555-57180-8
        NYPL [3-MOF 90-10811]

**FURNITURE - NEW YORK (STATE) -
HISTORY - 19TH CENTURY -
CATALOGS.**
Scherer, John L. New York furniture . Albany,
N.Y. , c1988. 29 p. : ISBN 1-555-57180-8
        NYPL [3-MOF 90-10811]

FURNITURE - NEW ZEALAND.
Northcote-Bade, Stanley. Colonial furniture in
New Zealand. Wellington [1971] 164 p. ISBN
0-589-00683-5 DDC 749.2/9931
NK2692.A1 N67   *NYPL [3-MOF 90-5434]*

**FURNITURE - NORTH AMERICA -
HISTORY.**
Bomchil, Sara. El mueble colonial de las
Américas y su circunstancia histórica /. Buenos
Aires , c1987. 919 p., [24] p. of plates : ISBN
950-0-70386-6 DDC 749.297 19
NK2401.A1 B66 1987
        NYPL [3-MOF 91-2686]

**FURNITURE, OAK - UNITED STATES -
CATALOGS.**
Swedberg, Robert W. American oak furniture .
Radnor, Pa. , 1991. p. ISBN 0-87069-588-6 (pbk.)
    DDC 749.213/075 20
NK2405 .S89 1991a

Swedberg, Robert W. American oak furniture .
Radnor, Pa. , 1991. p. cm. ISBN 0-87069-621-1
    (hc) DDC 749.213/075 20
NK2405 .S89 1991b

Swedberg, Robert W. American oak furniture .
Radnor, Pa. , c1991. ix, 195 p. : ISBN

0-87069-587-8 (pbk.) : DDC 749.213/075 20
NK2405 .S89 1991

Furniture of today. Rhode Island School of
Design. Museum of Art. Providence [c1948] 30
p.   *NYPL [3-MOF 90-7196]*

FURNITURE - PORTUGAL.
Guimarães, Alfredo, b. 1882. [Mobiliário
artístico português. 2. Guimarães.] Mobiliário
artístico português . Porto , 1989. xvi, 181, [6]
p., [170] p. of plates : DDC 749.269 20
NK2604 .G825 1989

FURNITURE - PORTUGAL - EXHIBITIONS.
Museu Nacional de Arte Antiga (Portugal)
Catalogue of furniture in the exhibition of
embroidered quilts from the Museu de Arte
Antiga, Lisboa . London , 1978. 1 v.
(unpaged) :   *NYPL [3-MOF 91-296]*

**FURNITURE, RENAISSANCE - FRANCE -
PICARDY.**
Fligny, Laurence. Le mobilier en Picardie .
[Paris] , c1990. 358 p. : ISBN 2-7084-0390-7 :
    DDC 749.24/26 20
NK2548 .F57 1990
        NYPL [3-MOF+ 91-6459]

FURNITURE, SHAKER - EXHIBITIONS.
Community industries of the Shakers . [Colonie,
N.Y.] , c1983. 48 p. : DDC 338/.008288 19
BX9784 .C66 1983
        NYPL [3-MNE 90-12552]

**FURNITURE - SOUTH AMERICA -
HISTORY.**
Bomchil, Sara. El mueble colonial de las
Américas y su circunstancia histórica /. Buenos
Aires , c1987. 919 p., [24] p. of plates : ISBN
950-0-70386-6 DDC 749.297 19
NK2401.A1 B66 1987
        NYPL [3-MOF 91-2686]

**FURNITURE - SOVIET UNION - HISTORY -
18TH CENTURY.**
Chenevière, Antoine. [Russian furniture.
French.] Splendeurs du mobilier russe,
1780-1840 /. Paris , 1989. 312 p. : ISBN
2-08-010916-2   *NYPL [3-MOF+ 91-6353]*

**FURNITURE - SOVIET UNION - HISTORY -
19TH CENTURY.**
Chenevière, Antoine. [Russian furniture.
French.] Splendeurs du mobilier russe,
1780-1840 /. Paris , 1989. 312 p. : ISBN
2-08-010916-2   *NYPL [3-MOF+ 91-6353]*

FURNITURE - SPAIN.
Paz Aguilo, María. El mueble clásico español /.
Madrid , 1987. 237 p. : ISBN 84-376-0679-9
    DDC 749.26 19
NK2599 .P38 1987   *NYPL [3-MOF 91-6670]*

FURNITURE - STYLES.
Miller, Judith. Period style /. London , c1989.
240 p. : ISBN 0-85533-731-1 : DDC 747 19
NK2115   *NYPL [MLO 90-12678]*

White, Antony, 1941- Furniture & furnishings .
New York , 1991. p. cm. ISBN 0-8306-1832-5 :
    DDC 749 20
NK2230 .W48 1991

FURNITURE - SWEDEN - STYLES.
Groth, Håkan. Neo-classicism in the North .
New York , 1990. 224 p. : ISBN 0-8478-1273-1
    DDC 728/.37/09485 20
NK1461.A1 G76 1990
        NYPL [3-MLO 91-3368]

**FURNITURE - SWITZERLAND - HISTORY -
20TH CENTURY.**
Mehlau-Wiebking, Friederike. Schweizer
Typenmöbel, 1925-1935 . Zürich , c1989. 231
p. : ISBN 3-85676-029-6
        NYPL [3-MOF+ 89-26582]

FURNITURE - UNITED STATES.
Wilson, José. Decoration U. S.A. New York
[c1965] 278 p. DDC 747.213
NK2002 .W53   *NYPL [3-MLO+ 91-6753]*

**FURNITURE - UNITED STATES -
CATALOGS.**
Layton Art Collection. American furniture with
related decorative arts, 1660-1830 /. New
York , c1991. p. ISBN 1-555-95068-X: DDC
    749.213/074/77595 20
NK2406 .L38 1991

Swedberg, Robert W. Collector's encyclopedia
of American furniture /. Paducah, KY , c1991-
v. <1 > : ISBN 0-89145-441-1 (v. 1) : DDC

749.213/075 20
NK2405 .S894 1991

**FURNITURE - UNITED STATES -
EXHIBITIONS.**
Rhode Island School of Design. Museum of
Art. Furniture of today. Providence [c1948] 30
p.   *NYPL [3-MOF 90-7196]*

**FURNITURE - UNITED STATES - HISTORY -
18TH CENTURY.**
Perspectives on American furniture /. New
York , c1988. vi, 360 p. : ISBN 0-393-02654-X
    DDC 749.213 19
NK2406 .P44 1988
        NYPL [3-MOF 89-21203]

Santore, Charles. The Windsor style in
America . Philadelphia, Pa. , c1991. p. ISBN
1-561-38057-1 DDC 749.214 20
NK2406 .S37 1991

**FURNITURE - UNITED STATES - HISTORY -
19TH CENTURY.**
Perspectives on American furniture /. New
York , c1988. vi, 360 p. : ISBN 0-393-02654-X
    DDC 749.213 19
NK2406 .P44 1988
        NYPL [3-MOF 89-21203]

**FURNITURE - UNITED STATES - HISTORY -
19TH CENTURY - PRICES.**
Goggin, Bill. Eagles . New Market, MD (Box
277, New Market 21774) [1990] xv, 319 p. :
    DDC 749.214/09/033075 20
NK2406 .G6 1990

**FURNITURE - UNITED STATES - HISTORY -
20TH CENTURY.**
Perspectives on American furniture /. New
York , c1988. vi, 360 p. : ISBN 0-393-02654-X
    DDC 749.213 19
NK2406 .P44 1988
        NYPL [3-MOF 89-21203]

**FURNITURE - UNITED STATES - HISTORY -
20TH CENTURY - CATALOGS.**
Fine woodworking design book five . Newtown,
Conn. , c1990. 185 p. : ISBN 0-942391-28-4 :
    DDC 674/.8 20
NK2408 .F57 1990

Stickley, Gustav, 1858-1942. [Catalogue of
craftsman furniture.] The 1912 and 1915
Gustav Stickley craftsman furniture catalogs /.
Philadelphia , New York , 1991. p. cm. ISBN
0-486-26676-1 (pbk.) DDC 749.213 20
NK2439.S8 A4 1991

**FURNITURE - UNITED STATES - HISTORY -
20TH CENTURY - EXHIBITIONS.**
Castle, Wendell, 1932- Angel chairs . New
York , 1991. 111 p. : ISBN 0-9628849-0-1 DDC
    749.213 20
NK2439.C3 A4 1991

FURNITURE - UNITED STATES - STYLES.
Federico, Jean Taylor, 1940. Clues to American
furniture /. Washington DC , 1991. p. cm.
    ISBN 0-913515-75-2 : DDC 749.213/075 20
NK2405 .F43 1991

**FURNITURE - VIRGINIA -
WILLIAMSBURG - HISTORY - 18TH
CENTURY.**
Gilliam, Jan (Jan Kirsten) Furnishing
Williamsburg's historic buildings. Williamsburg,
Va. , 1991. p. cm. ISBN 0-87935-083-0 DDC
    747.2155/4252/09033 20
NK2438.W54 G5 1991

**FURNITURE - WISCONSIN - MILWAUKEE -
CATALOGS.**
Layton Art Collection. American furniture with
related decorative arts, 1660-1830 /. New
York , c1991. ISBN 1-555-95068-X : DDC
    749.213/074/77595 20
NK2406 .L38 1991

Furrer, Bruno, 1929- Carybé, 1911- Carybé /.
[Salvador] , 1989. 452 p. : DDC 709/.2 20
N6659.C39 A4 1989

Fürst, Margot.
Grieshaber, Helmut A. P., 1909- Grieshaber .
Stuttgart , 1984-c1986. 2 v. : ISBN
3-7757-0221-0 (Bd. 1) DDC 769.92/4 19
NE1150.5.G7 A4 1984a
        NYPL [MDG+ (Grieshaber) 91-1093]

Grieshaber, Helmut A. P., 1909- Grieshaber,
das Werk . Stuttgart , c1989. 309, [1] p. :
    ISBN 3-7757-0280-6 DDC 760/.092 20
NE1150.5.G7 A4 1989
        NYPL [MDG+ (Grieshaber) 90-5070]

Fŭrtunov, Stefan. Ralin, Radoĭ, 1923- Svetŭt e otseliăl, zashtoto se e smiăl =. Sofiiă , 1989. 239 p. :
NC1355 .R34 1989

Furtwängler, Andreas E. Studien zur klassischen Archäologie . Saarbrücken , Amsterdam , 1986. 219 p. : ISBN 3-925384-00-6
NYPL [3-MAH 90-12469]

Furtwängler, Felix Martin, 1954-
Aus-Druck : Bücher und Graphik von Felix Martin Furtwängler : Museum für Kunsthandwerk Frankfurt am Main, 31. August bis 5. November 1989 / [Katalog und Ausstellungskonzept, Stefan Soltek ; Textbeitrag, Joachim Kruse ; Autorenbiographien, Margret Soltek]. Frankfurt am Main : Museum für Kunsthandwerk Frankfurt am Main, [1989] 112 p. : ill. (some col.) ; 24 cm. Exhibition catalog. Includes bibliographical references (p. 110). ISBN 3-88270-048-3 DDC 769.92 20
1. Furtwängler, Felix Martin, 1954- - Exhibitions. I. Soltek, Stefan. II. Museum für Kunsthandwerk Frankfurt am Main. III. Title. IV. Title: Ausdruck.
NE654.F84 A4 1989
NYPL [MDG (Furtwängler) 90-13668]

FURTWÄNGLER, FELIX MARTIN, 1954- - EXHIBITIONS.
Furtwängler, Felix Martin, 1954- Aus-Druck . Frankfurt am Main [1989] 112 p. : ISBN 3-88270-048-3 DDC 769.92 20
NE654.F84 A4 1989
NYPL [MDG (Furtwängler) 90-13668]

Furuya, Seiichi, 1950-
Mémoires 1978-1988 / Seiichi Furuya ; mit Texten von Monika Faber ... [et al.]. Graz : Camera Austria, c1989. 1 v. (unpaged) : ill. (some col.) ; 29 cm. Catalog of an exhibition held at the Neue Galerie am Landesmuseum Joanneum. Includes bibliographical references. ISBN 3-900508-06-2
1. Furuya, Seiichi, 1950- - Exhibitions. 2. Photography, Artistic - Exhibitions. I. Faber, Monika, 1954-. II. Neue Galerie am Landesmuseum Joanneum. III. Title.
NYPL [MFX (Furuya) 90-9132]

FURUYA, SEIICHI, 1950- - EXHIBITIONS.
Furuya, Seiichi, 1950- Mémoires 1978-1988 /. Graz , c1989. 1 v. (unpaged) : ISBN 3-900508-06-2
NYPL [MFX (Furuya) 90-9132]

Fusco, Peter, 1945- The Romantics to Rodin . Los Angeles, Calif. , New York , c1980. 368 p. : ISBN 0-8076-0953-4 (Braziller) DDC 730/.944
NB547 .R65   NYPL [MGI 80-2189]

Fusco, Tony. The official identification and price guide to posters / by Tony Fusco ; with special guest contributors, Robert K. Brown ... [et al.] ; photographs by Robert Four. 1st ed. New York : House of Collectibles, 1990. xiv, 562 p., [8] p. of plates : ill. ; 21 cm. ISBN 0-87637-797-5
1. Posters - Collectors and collecting. I. Title.
IN PROCESS (ONLINE)
NYPL [3-MDW 91-6106]

Fuseli, Henry, 1741-1825.
Andersen, Jørgen, 1922- De år i Rom . København , 1989. 301 p. : ISBN 87-7241-576-2 :
ND723.A2 A86 1989

FUSELI, HENRY, 1741-1825 - FRIENDS AND ASSOCIATES.
Andersen, Jørgen, 1922- De år i Rom . København , 1989. 301 p. : ISBN 87-7241-576-2 :
ND723.A2 A86 1989

Fuseli, John Henry. see Fuseli, Henry, 1741-1825.

Fusi Aizpurúa, Juan Pablo, 1945- Mas Serra, Elías, 1945- 50 Años de arquitectura en Euskadi /. [Vitoria] , 1990. xviii, 347 p. : ISBN 84-7542-854-1 DDC 720/.946/609045 20
NA1309.P33 M37 1990

Fusi, Juan Pablo. see Fusi Aizpurúa, Juan Pablo, 1945-

Fusscas, Helen K., 1943- Cummings, Hildegard. J. Alden Weir . Storrs , c1991. p. cm. ISBN 0-918386-43-8 DDC 759.13 20
ND237.W4 A4 1991

Fussell, G. E. (George Edwin), 1889- Landscape painting and the agricultural revolution / G.E.

Fussell. London : Pindar Press, 1984. 83 p., [16] p. of plates : ill. ; 25 cm. Includes index. Bibliography: p. [73]-78. ISBN 0-907132-17-0 DDC 758/.1/0942 19
1. Landscape painting, English. 2. Landscape painting - 18th century - England. 3. Landscape painting - 19th century - England. 4. Agriculture in art. 5. Agricultural innovations in art. 6. Agriculture - England - History. 7. Agricultural innovations - England - History. I. Title.
ND1354.4 .F87 1984
NYPL [3-MCT 91-5610]

Futagawa, Yukio, 1932-
(illus) Shingū, Susumu, 1937- Shingu. New York [1973] 15 p., 152 plates (part col.) ISBN 0-8109-0481-0 DDC 730/.92/4
NB1059.S5 O3713
NYPL [3-MGO (Shingu) 90-5446]
Takamatsu, Shin, 1948- Shin Takamatsu /. Tokyo , c1990. 193 p. : ISBN 4-87140-415-3
NYPL [3-MQZ+ (Takamatsu) 90-11765]

Future tense . Hewison, Robert, 1943- London , 1990. 190 p. : ISBN 0-413-63430-2 : DDC 700 20
N7425   NYPL [3-MAL 90-11326]

FUTURISM (ART) - ITALY.
Agnese, Gino. Marinetti . Milano , c1990. 373 p., [16] p. of plates : ISBN 88-7767-094-0 :
N6923.M269 A85 1990

FUTURISM (ART) - ITALY - CATALOGS.
Scudiero, Maurizio. R.M. Baldessari, opere futuriste /. [Roma] , 1989. 231 p. : ISBN 88-7165-004-2 : DDC 709/.2 20
N6923.B257 A4 1989

FUTURISM (ART) - ITALY - EXHIBITIONS.
Archivi futuristi /. Modena , Milano , c1990. 189 p. : DDC 709/.45/0744542 20
N6918.5.F8 A74 1990

FUTURISM (ART) - ITALY - SOURCES.
Testimonianze e polemiche figurative in Italia . Messina [1974] 507 p. ;
N6917.5.N44 B37
NYPL [3-MAMC 90-5898]

FUTURISM (ART) - RUSSIA.
Canevari, D. Russian futurism, 1910-1916 . Cambridge, [Cambridgeshire] Eng. [1977?] 18 leaves :   *NYPL [Desk-Slav. Div. 85-672]*

FUTURISM (LITERARY MOVEMENT) - RUSSIA.
Canevari, D. Russian futurism, 1910-1916 . Cambridge, [Cambridgeshire] Eng. [1977?] 18 leaves :   *NYPL [Desk-Slav. Div. 85-672]*

Fyman, Vladimír. Mezi klasickým řádem a selankou . [Prague] , <1990?-. v. <2 > :
N6831.5.N46 M4 1990

G. Argy-Rousseau . Bloch-Dermant, Janine. Paris , c1990. 229 p. : ISBN 2-85917-105-3 DDC 748.294 20
NK5198.A74 A4 1990

GA architect .
(9) Takamatsu, Shin, 1948- Shin Takamatsu /. Tokyo , c1990. 193 p. : ISBN 4-87140-415-3
NYPL [3-MQZ+ (Takamatsu) 90-11765]

Gabetti, Roberto. Le Corbusier e L'Esprit nouveau / Roberto Gabetti e Carlo Olmo. [Torino] : G. Einaudi, [c1975] x, 273 p., [12] p. of plates : ill. ; 22 cm. (Saggi. 555) Includes bibliographical references and index.
1. Le Corbusier, 1887-1965. 2. Esprit nouveau. I. Olmo, Carlo Maria, 1944- joint author. II. Title.
NA1053.J4 G22
NYPL [3-MCO J42 90-6619]

Gabinetto dei disegni e delle stampe (Italy)
Ruggieri, Ugo. Disegni veneti e lombardi dal XVI al XVIII secolo dalle collezioni del Gabinetto dei disegni e delle stampe /. Roma , 1989. 226 p. : ISBN 88-7597-101-3
NYPL [3-MBH 90-12366]

Gabinetto delle stampe di Milano. Disegni di Stefano della Bella. Milano : Gabinetto delle stampe, [1976?] 70 p. : chiefly ill. ; 28 cm. Catalog of an exhibition held Nov. 12-Dec. 4, 1976 at the Gabinetto delle stampe, Milan; Dec. 6, 1976-Jan. 8, 1977 at Arte Antica, Torino; and Jan. 12-Feb. 5, 1977 at Antiquaria Romana, Rome.
1. Della Bella, Stefano, 1610-1664 - Exhibitions. I. Della Bella, Stefano, 1610-1664. II. Arte antica di Torino. III. Antiquaria Romana (Art gallery). IV. Title.
NYPL [3-MCF B367 91-1368]

Gabinetto disegni e stampe degli Uffizi.
Cappugi, Luana. Bruno Innocenti . Firenze , 1991. 79 p., [51] p. of plates : ISBN 88-22-23837-0
NYPL [3-MCF I57 91-5735]

GABINETTO DISEGNI E STAMPE DEGLI UFFIZI - CATALOGS.
Cappugi, Luana. Bruno Innocenti . Firenze , 1991. 79 p., [51] p. of plates : ISBN 88-22-23837-0
NYPL [3-MCF I57 91-5735]

GABINETTO FOTOGRAFICO NAZIONALE - CATALOGS.
Dipinti dei musei e gallerie di Roma. Roma , 1978- v. ;
N4035.G33 D56 1981
NYPL [MAVZ+ (Rome) 91-6377]

Gabinetto nazionale delle stampe.
Disegni toscani e umbri del primo Rinascimento : dalle collezioni del Gabinetto nazionale delle stampe : [Istituto nazionale per la grafica, Gabinetto nazionale delle stampe, Roma, villa alla Farnesina alla Lungara, 22 marzo-31 maggio 1979] : catalogo / Enrichetta Beltrame Quattrocchi. Roma : De Luca, [1979] 183 p. : ill. ; 21 cm. Bibliography: p. 172-181. Includes index.
1. Gabinetto nazionale delle stampe - Exhibitions. 2. Drawing, Italian - Italy - Tuscany - Exhibitions. 3. Drawing, Renaissance - Italy - Tuscany - Exhibitions. 4. Drawing, Italian - Italy - Umbria - Exhibitions. 5. Drawing, Renaissance - Italy - Umbria - Exhibitions. I. Beltrame Quattrocchi, Enrichetta. II. Title.
NC256.T8 G32 1979
NYPL [3-MBH 81-532]

Immagini dal Veronese : incisioni dal sec. XVI al XIX dalle collezioni del Gabinetto nazionale delle stampe : Roma, Villa alla Farnesina alla Lungara, 21 novembre 1978-31 gennaio 1979 / catalogo di Paolo Ticozzi. Roma : De Luca, [1978] 127 p. : ill. ; 21 cm. At head of title: Istituto nazionale per la grafica, Gabinetto nazionale delle stampe. Includes indexes. Bibliography: p. 115-120.
1. Veronese, 1528-1588 - Exhibitions. 2. Prints - Exhibitions. I. Veronese, 1528-1588. II. Ticozzi, Paolo. III. Villa della Farnesina. IV. Title.
ND623.V5 A4 1978
NYPL [MDG (Veronese) 80-1248]

GABINETTO NAZIONALE DELLE STAMPE - EXHIBITIONS.
Gabinetto nazionale delle stampe. Disegni toscani e umbri del primo Rinascimento . Roma [1979] 183 p. :
NC256.T8 G32 1979
NYPL [3-MBH 81-532]

Gabo, Naum, 1890-
Naum Gabo, 1890-1977 : centenary exhibition. London : Annely Juda Fine Art, c1990. 127 p. : ill. (some col.) ; 26 cm. Catalog of an exhibition held at Annely Juda Fine Art, June 28-Sept. 29, 1990. Cover title. ISBN 1-87028-022-9
1. Gabo, Naum, 1890- - Exhibitions. I. Annely Juda Fine Art. II. Title.
NYPL [3-MGO (Gabo) 91-3725]

GABO, NAUM, 1890- - EXHIBITIONS.
Gabo, Naum, 1890- Naum Gabo, 1890-1977 . London , c1990. 127 p. : ISBN 1-87028-022-9
NYPL [3-MGO (Gabo) 91-3725]

Gabriel Fernández Ledesma /. Alanís, Judith. México , 1985. 219 p. : ISBN 968-8373-78-8
N6559.F46 A83 1985

Gabriel Guévrékian, 1900-1970 . Vitou, Elisabeth. Paris , c1987. 150 p. : ISBN 2-86649-003-7 : DDC 720/.92/4 19
NA1053.G77 V5 1987
NYPL [3-MQZ (Guévrékian) 91-4588]

Gabriele Münter und ihre Zeit . Münter, Gabriele, 1877-1962. Essen , 1990. 184 p. : ISBN 3-923806-14-0
NYPL [3-MCK M93 91-6711]

Gabriele Münter und Wassily Kandinsky . Kleine, Gisela, 1926- Frankfurt am Main , 1990. 813 p., 16 p. of plates : ISBN 3-458-16090-6
ND588.M83 K5 1990

Gachet, Paul, 1873-1962. Van Gogh et les peintres d'Auvers-sur-Oise. [Paris] , 1954. xl, 100 p., xxxii p. of plates :
N6847.5.I4 V36 1954

GACHET, PAUL FERDINAND, 1828-1909 -
ART COLLECTIONS - EXHIBITIONS.
Van Gogh et les peintres d'Auvers-sur-Oise .
[Paris] , 1954. xl, 100 p., xxxii p. of plates :
N6847.5.I4 V36 1954

Gachnang, Johannes, 1939- Fabro, Luciano, 1936-
Luciano Fabro . Bompiani [Turin] , c1989. 254
p. ::   *NYPL [3-MGO (Fabro) 90-11538]*

Gädeke, Thomas. Wolfgang Klähn / von Thomas
Gädeke und Bernd Seydel. Recklinghausen : A.
Bongers, c1990. 144 p. : 75 ill. (chiefly col.) ;
25 cm. Includes bibliographical references (p.
139-140). ISBN 3-7647-0410-1 DDC 759.3 20
*1. Klähn, Wolfgang, 1929- - Criticism and
interpretation. I. Klähn, Wolfgang, 1929-. II. Seydel,
Bernd. III. Title.*
ND1954.K493 G3 1990

Gadliger, Werner, 1950- Nachtbubenwerk /
Werner Gadliger. Zürich : Edition WerGa,
c1988. 132 p. : ill. ; 31 cm. Cover title. ISBN
3-909146-05-8 : DDC 709/.2 20
1. Gadliger, Werner, 1950-. I. Title.
N7153.G27 A4 1988
     NYPL [3-MCZ+ G126 90-10623]

GADLIGER, WERNER, 1950-
Gadliger, Werner, 1950- Nachtbubenwerk /.
Zürich , c1988. 132 p. : ISBN 3-909146-05-8 :
DDC 709/.2 20
N7153.G27 A4 1988
     NYPL [3-MCZ+ G126 90-10623]

Gadzhiev, M. S. Drevni͡ai͡a i srednevekova͡ia
arkhitektura Dagestana . Makhachkala , 1989.
184, [4] p. :
NA1492.8 .D7 1989

Gaebler, Volkhard. Sozialistische Staaten Mittel-
und Südosteuropas /. Gotha , 1986. 1 atlas
(190 p.) : ISBN 3-7301-0032-7
     NYPL [Map Div. 91-3783]

Gaedicke, Claus-Lutz, 1943- Skulptur, Grafik,
Zeichnung aus der Deutschen Demokratischen
Republik . Berlin [1984] [44] p. :
MLCM 87/97 (N)
     NYPL [3-MAMG 90-10659]

Gaehtgens, Thomas W., 1940- Versailles : de la
résidence royale au Musée historique : la
Galerie des batailles dans le Musée historique
de Louis-Philippe / Thomas W. Gaehtgens ;
préface par Pierre Lemoine ; [traduit de
l'allemand par Patrick Poirot]. Paris : A.
Michel, c1981. 407 p. : ill. (some col.) ; 34 cm.
Includes bibliographical references (p. 399-402) and
index. ISBN 2-226-02168-X
*1. Musée national de Versailles. Galerie des batailles -
History. 2. France - History - Pictorial works. I. Title.*
N2180.2.G34 G3 1981

GÄRTNER, FRIEDRICH VON, 1792-1847.
Wegner, Ewald. Friedrich von Gärtner und das
Bad Kissingen /. Würzburg , 1981. v, 78 p.,
[12] p. of plates : DDC 720/.92/4 19
NA1088.G3 W43 1981
     NYPL [3-MQWD 90-5440]

Gaeta Bertelà, Giovanna.
Luca, Andrea, Giovanni Della Robbia / G.
Gaeta Bertelà. Firenze : Becocci Editore, c1977.
64 p. : ill. (some col.) ; 28 cm. Bibliography: p. 24.
*1. Robbia family. 2. Robbia, Luca della, 1400?-1482. 3.
Robbia, Andrea della, 1435?-1525?. 4. Robbia, Giovanni
della, 1469-1529?. 5. Sculpture, Renaissance - Italy -
Florence. I. Title.*   *NYPL [3-MGI 90-6050]*

Museo nazionale di Firenze. Acquisti e
donazioni del Museo nazionale del Bargello,
1970-1987 /. Firenze , c1988. xv, 158 p. :
DDC 708.5/51 19
N2555 .A515 1988
     NYPL [3-MAVZ (Florence) 90-11120]

Gagnon, Carolle. Marcel Barbeau : fugato / by
Carolle Gagnon and Ninon Gauthier ;
translation by Liliane Busby. [Canada] :
Editions du Centre d'étude et de
communication sur l'art, c1990. 243 p. : ill. ; 32
cm. ISBN 2-9802034-5-9 (prestige ed.)
1. Barbeau, Marcel, 1925-. I. Gauthier, Ninon. II. Title.
     NYPL [3-MCZ+ B233 91-7596]

Gagosian Gallery.
Clemente, Francesco, 1952- Francesco
Clemente . New York , 1991. p. cm. ISBN
0-8478-1469-6 DDC 759.5 20
ND1962.C58 A4 1991

Klein, Yves, 1928-1962. Yves Klein, sponge
reliefs . New York , c[1989] 30 p. : ISBN

0-9624347-0-1
     NYPL [3-MCOX K64 91-4627]

Marden, Brice, 1938- Brice Marden . New
York , c1991. 63 p. : ISBN 0-9624347-6-0
     NYPL [3-MCX+ M315 91-6583]

Salle, David, 1952- David Salle . New York ,
1991. 1 v. (unpaged) : ISBN 0-9624347-7-9
     NYPL [3-MCX+ S167 91-6681]

Gainsborough, English music, and the
Fitzwilliam . Fitzwilliam Museum. Cambridge ,
1977. 39 p., [4] p. of plates :
     NYPL [3-MCV G14 90-6810]

Gainsborough in Bath : a bicentenary exhibition 1
July-14 August 1988, Holborne Museum and
Crafts Study Centre. Bath [England] : Holborne
Museum, [1988] 40 p. : ill. (some col.) ; 30 cm.
Essays by Ann Sumner and Philippa Bishop. Includes
bibliographical references. ISBN 0-86197-081-0 (pbk.)
*1. Gainsborough, Thomas, 1727-1788 - Exhibitions. I.
Sumner, Ann. II. Bishop, Philippa. III. Holburne of
Menstrie Museum.*
     NYPL [3-MCV+ G14 89-28866]

Gainsborough, Thomas, 1727-1788.
Hayes, John T. The drawings of Thomas
Gainsborough /. New Haven , 1971, c1970. 2
v. (x, 368 p., [143] leaves of plates) : ISBN
0-300-01425-2 DDC 741/.092/4
NC242.G3 A4 1970
     NYPL [MCV+ G14.H4d]

GAINSBOROUGH, THOMAS, 1727-1788.
Leonard, Jonathan Norton, 1903-1975. The
world of Gainsborough, 1727-1788. New York
[1969] 192 p. DDC 759.2
ND497.G L4

GAINSBOROUGH, THOMAS, 1727-1788 -
CATALOGS.
Cormack, Malcolm. The paintings of Thomas
Gainsborough /. Cambridge , New York , 1991.
p. cm. ISBN 0-521-38241-6 DDC 759.2 20
ND497.G2 A4 1991

Hayes, John T. The drawings of Thomas
Gainsborough /. New Haven , 1971, c1970. 2
v. (x, 368 p., [143] leaves of plates) : ISBN
0-300-01425-2 DDC 741/.092/4
NC242.G3 A4 1970
     NYPL [MCV+ G14.H4d]

GAINSBOROUGH, THOMAS, 1727-1788 -
EXHIBITIONS.
Fitzwilliam Museum. Gainsborough, English
music, and the Fitzwilliam . Cambridge , 1977.
39 p., [4] p. of plates :
     NYPL [3-MCV G14 90-6810]

Gainsborough in Bath . Bath [England] [1988]
40 p. : ISBN 0-86197-081-0 (pbk.)
     NYPL [3-MCV+ G14 89-28866]

Galanti, María Luisa. Catálogo nacional de arte
contemporáneo. Barcelona , c1989. 4 v. : ISBN
84-87433-00-6 (obra completa)
N7108 .C29 1989

Galassi, Peter. Corot in Italy : open-air painting
and the classical landscape tradition / Peter
Galassi. New Haven, Conn. : Yale University
Press, c1991. viii, 258 p. : ill. (some col.), map ;
30 cm. Includes bibliographical references and index.
ISBN 0-300-04957-9 DDC 759.4 20
*1. Corot, Jean-Baptiste Camille, 1796-1875 - Criticism
and interpretation. 2. Corot, Jean-Baptiste-Camille,
1796-1875 - Journeys - Italy. 3. Italy in art. 4. Italy -
Description and travel - 1801-1860. I. Title. II. Title:
Open-air painting and the classical-landscape tradition.*
ND553.C8 G245 1991
     NYPL [3-MCO+ C82 91-7307]

Galaunė, Paulius, 1890- Lietuvių liaudies menas :
jo meninių formų plėtojimosi pagrindai /
Paulius Galaunė. Vilnius : Mokslas, 1988. 301
p., [42] leaves of plates : ill. ; 23 cm. Title from
colophon: Litovskoe narodnoe iskusstvo. Reprint.
Originally published: Kaunas : L.U. Humanitarinių
mokslų fakulteto leidinys, 1930. One folded leaf
inserted. Includes bibliographical references (p.
275-287). ISBN 5-420-00625-1 :
*1. Folk art - Lithuania. I. Title. II. Title: Litovskoe
narodnoe iskusstvo.*
NK976.L5 G3 1988

Gale, Adrian. Mies van der Rohe . London , New
York , 1986. 112 p. : ISBN 0-85670-685-X
DDC 720/.92/4 19
NA1088.M65 M54 1986   *NYPL [3-MQZ+*
     (Mies van der Rohe) 86-3545]

Galeano, Eduardo H., 1940- Salgado, Sebastião,
1944- An uncertain grace /. New York , c1990.
155, [1] p. : ISBN 0-89381-421-0 (Hardcover)
     NYPL [MFX+ (Salgado) 91-3484]

Galeria Afinsa. Olitski, Jules, 1922- Jules Olitski
/. [New York] , c1990. 5 v. :
     NYPL [3-MCX O47 91-6724]

Galeria Almirante. Olitski, Jules, 1922- Jules
Olitski /. [New York] , c1990. 5 v. :
     NYPL [3-MCX O47 91-6724]

Galería Barbié. 1er aniversario, 1975. Barcelona,
Spain : La Galería, 1975. 31 p. : ill. ; 22 cm.
*1. Art, Spanish - Exhibitions. 2. Art, Modern - 20th
century - Spain - Exhibitions. I. Galería Barbié.*
     NYPL [3-MAML 90-7109]

Galería Barbié. Galería Barbié . Barcelona,
Spain , 1975. 31 p. :
     NYPL [3-MAML 90-7109]

Galeria Bonino (New York, N.Y.) Italy, new
tendencies. New York, N.Y. [1966] [16] p. :
     NYPL [3-MAMC 90-6953]

**Galeria d'arte morerna Fratelli Falsetti (Cortina
d'Ampezzo, Italy)** Severini, Gino, 1883-1966.
Omaggio a Gino Severini . Cortina
d'Ampezzo , 1970. 27 p., 23 leaves of plates :
     NYPL [3-MCF S49 90-6460]

Galería de Arte Nacional (Venezuela) Proyecto
nueva sede, Galería de Arte Nacional, Caracas
=. [Caracas, Venezuela] [1986] 77 p. : ISBN
980-603-006-0
N910.C22 P76 1986
     NYPL [3-MQWN+ 90-11046]

GALERÍA DE ARTE NACIONAL
(VENEZUELA)
Proyecto nueva sede, Galería de Arte Nacional,
Caracas =. [Caracas, Venezuela] [1986] 77 p. :
ISBN 980-603-006-0
N910.C22 P76 1986
     NYPL [3-MQWN+ 90-11046]

Galería de artistas .
([10]) Manzano, Rafael, 1917- Coll Bardolet /.
Barcelona [1977?] 119 p. : ISBN 84-85321-52-1
DDC 759.6 20
ND813.C59 A4 1977

Galería de pintores . Ríus Facius, Antonio.
México, D.F. , 1981. 120 p., [24] p. of plates :
ISBN 968-400-207-6
ND255 .R5 1981

Galería Durbán. Arte para los ochenta =.
Caracas, Venezuela , c1980. [24] p. :
     NYPL [3-MAL 90-4430]

Galería "Los Espacios Cálidos." La Flor
imaginaria . Caracas , 1989. 160 p. : ISBN
980-255-018-3 DDC 700 20
NX650.F57 F58 1989

Galería Praxis (Santiago, Chile) Jurado, María
Cristina. Zañartu /. Santiago , 1989. 64 p. :
     NYPL [3-MCZ+ Z449 90-12332]

Galería Vandrés. Smith, Robert, 1944- Robert
Smith . Madrid [1971] 1 v. (unpaged) :
     NYPL [3-MCX S6575 91-4232]

Galerie Alexandre Iolas (Paris, France) Ghika,
1906- Ghika. [Paris, 1973?] 1 v. (chiefly illus.)
DDC 741.9/495
NC254.C45 G34
     NYPL [3-MCZ C495 90-6263]

Galerie am Finkenbusch. Werner, Josef, 1945-
Josef Werner, Bilder und Radierungen /.
Böchölt [between 1980 and 1989] [34] leaves :
     NYPL [3-MCK W493 88-3632]

Galerie Ars Polona. Nie wieder! . [Düsseldorf] ,
1989. 251 p. :   *NYPL [3-MAM+ 91-6409]*

Galerie Aubes 3935. Living in NY . Montréal,
Qc. [1988] [16] p. :
     NYPL [3-MAMT 89-27022]

Galerie Barlach. Carr, Tom, 1956- Tom Carr.
Hamburg , 1987. 33 p. : ISBN 3-89018-029-9
     NYPL [3-MGO (Carr) 91-4300]

Galerie Benedikta Rejta. Knížák, Milan. Milan
Knížák . [Brno , 1990?] 1 v. (unpaged) :
N6834.5.K56 A4 1990

Galerie Beyeler.
Giacometti, Alberto, 1901-1966. Alberto
Giacometti. Basel , c1989. 139 p. :
     NYPL [3-MGO+ (Giacometti) 90-13215]

Giacometti, Alberto, 1901-1966. Alberto
Giacometti . Basel , c1989. 139 p. : DDC

709/.2 20
N6853.G5 A4 1989
Wege zur Abstraktion /. Basel , c1989. [74] p. :
     NYPL [3-MAL+ 90-13078]

Galerie Brockstedt. Kressel, Diether, 1925-
Diether Kressel . Hamburg , c1988. 64, [7] p. :
ISBN 3-920365-10-0
NC251.K7 A4 1988

Galerie Bruno Bischofberger. Bidlo, Mike. Mike
Bidlo, masterpieces. Zurich/Switzerland , c1989.
1 v. (unpaged) : ISBN 3-905173-26-3
     NYPL [3-MCX+ B582 90-11086]

Galerie Brusberg. Botero, Fernando, 1932-
Botero, der Maler . Berlin , 1991. 72 p. : ISBN
3-87972-071-1
     NYPL [3-MCZ+ B74 91-7449]

Galerie Buchmann (Basel, Switzerland)
Kopf, Willi, 1949- Kopf /. Basel , c1989. 35 p. :
     NYPL [3-MGO (Kopf) 90-13399]

Mang, Rainer, 1943- Mang /. Basel , c1989. 61
p. :   *NYPL [3-MGO (Mang) 90-10231]*

Galerie Carinthia. Zaunschirm, Thomas, 1943-
Fremdbild Heimat . Wien , c1989. 101 p. :
ISBN 3-900606-12-9
N6809.C3 Z36 1989

Galerie CGER. Tokyo project . Bruxelles [1989]
189 p. :   *NYPL [3-MQWS+ 90-11043]*

Galerie Charpentier. Catalogue des objets d'art et
d'ameublement du XVIIIe siècle : tableaux
anciens, gravures du XVIIIe et du XIXe
siècle ... objets d'art d'extrême-orient,
composant la collection de Madame André
Saint, et dont la vente aux enchères publiques
aura lieu à Paris, Galerie Jean Charpentier, 20
et 21 mai 1935. Paris : La Galerie, 1935. 88 p.,
44 leaves of plates : ill. ; 32 cm.
1. Saint, André, Mme. - Art collections - Exhibitions. 2.
Art - Private collections - France - Exhibitions. I. Title.
     NYPL [3-MAX+ (Saint) 91-404]

Galerie Claude Lafitte. Maîtres canadiens .
Montréal, Québec, Canada , c1988. 34 p. :
ISBN 2-9800685-6-X
MLCM 89/00906 (N)
     NYPL [3-MCY 91-7978]

Galerie de France (Paris, France) Bergman,
Anna-Eva, 1909- Anna Eva Bergman. Paris
[1962] [33] p. :
     NYPL [3-MCZ+ B495 91-4580]

Galerie de la Vieille Charité. La Faïence de
Marseille au XVIIIe siècle . Marseille , 1990.
311 p. :   *NYPL [3-MPGG+ 91-7172]*

Galerie de l'université (Paris, France) La
Fantastique contemporain . Paris , 1972. [126]
p. :   *NYPL [3-MAL 91-288]*

Galerie de poche. Schlatter, Christian. Art
conceptuel, formes conceptuelles =. Paris ,
1990. 598 p. :   *NYPL [3-MAL 91-3664]*

Galerie de Seine.
Bozzolini, Silvano, 1911- Bozzolini . Paris
[1971?] 64 p. :
     NYPL [3-MCF B785 90-6085]

Tyszblat, Michel, 1936- Tyszblat. Paris [1973?]
35 p. DDC 759.4
ND553.T9 G34
     NYPL [3-MCO T994 91-5024]

Galerie Defet. Lang, Nikolaus, 1941- Nikolaus
Lang . Münster , Nürnberg , 1978. 68 p. :
N6923.L25 A4 1978
     NYPL [3-MCK+ L271 81-770]

Galerie Denise René.
Kupka, František, 1871-1957. Kupka . New
York , c1975. [20] p. :
     NYPL [3-MCZ K965 91-869]

Vasarely, Victor, 1908- Vasarely, duo-exhibition
recent works. [New York? 1972] [28] p. DDC
759.4
ND553.V35 G283
     NYPL [3-MCO V328 90-6940]

Galerie der Stadt Esslingen. Graubner, Gotthard,
1930- Gotthard Graubner . Bremen , c1989.
145 p. (5 folded) :
     NYPL [3-MCK+ G773 91-6686]

Galerie der Stadt Kornwestheim. Beuys, Joseph.
Joseph Beuys . Stuttgart , c1990. 135 p. : ISBN
3-7757-0313-6
     NYPL [3-MCK+ B569 91-3920]

Galerie der Stadt Stuttgart. Winter, Fritz, 1905-
Fritz Winter /. Stuttgart , c1990. 309 p. :
ISBN 3-7757-0310-1 DDC 759.3 20
ND588.W65 A4 1990

Galerie Döbele.
Ackermann, Max. Max Ackermann . Stuttgart
[1989]. 61 p. :
     NYPL [3-MCK+ A178 90-13009]

Ackermann, Max. Max Ackermann, Klang der
Farbe . Stuttgart , c1989. 61 p. :
ND588.A313 A4 1989

Batz, Eugen, 1905- Eugen Batz . Ravensburg ,
c1989. 65 p. :
     NYPL [3-MCK B3365 90-262]

Dörflinger, Johannes, 1941- Johannes
Dörflinger . Stuttgart , c1989. [37] p. :
     NYPL [3-MCK+ D663 89-25787]

Galerie Dorothea van der Koelen. Uecker,
Günther, 1930- Günther Uecker . Mainz ,
c1988. 84 p. : ISBN 3-926663-04-9
N6888.U37 A4 1988
     NYPL [3-MCK+ U125 91-7298]

Galerie du Luxembourg (Paris, France) Guimard,
Hector, 1867-1942. Hector Guimard . Paris ,
1971. 45 p. :   *NYPL [3-MRX 90-7184]*

Galerie Durand-Ruel. Monet, Claude, 1840-1926.
Exposition Claude Monet, 1840-1926 . Paris ,
1959. 31 p. :   *NYPL [3-MCO M74 90-6413]*

**Galerie française de femmes célèbres par leurs
talens, leur rang ou leur beauté.** La Mésangère,
Pierre de, 1761-1831. Costumes des femmes
françaises du XIIe au XVIIIe siècle /. Paris ,
1900. [5] leaves, [70] col. leaves of plates :
     NYPL [3-MML+ 84-1125]

Galerie Georg Nothelfer. Adochi, 1954- Adochi .
Berlin , c1989. 73, [2] p. : ISBN 3-87329-934-8
DDC 759.9498 20
N7233.A36 A4 1989

Galerie Gilles Gheerbrant. Mohr, Manfred, 1938-
Manfred Mohr . [S.l.] c1974. [24] p. :
     NYPL [3-MCK M6893 91-5180]

Galerie Gmurzynska.
Léger, Fernand, 1881-1955. Fernand Léger .
Köln , c1990. 102 p. :
ND553.L58 A4 1990

Röhl, Karl Peter, 1890-1975. Karl Peter Röhl,
Bauhausjahre . Köln , c1990. 109 p. :
NC251.R62 A4 1990

Galerie Gmurzynska-Bargera. Feininger, Lyonel,
1871-1956. Lyonel Feininger, 1871-1956 .
Köln , c1989. 70 p. :
     NYPL [3-MCX F29 91-5551]

Galerie Gottschick. Gröne, Ulla. Helmuth Seible .
Tübingen , c1991. 48 p. : DDC 803/.1 s 759.3 20
N390.G32 T8 Nr. 34 ND588.S447

Galerie Hartl & Klier. Spicher, Stephan, 1950-
Stephan Spicher. Tübingen , c1989. [40] p. :
     NYPL [3-MCZ+ S754 91-4060]

Galerie Heike Curtze. Rainer, Arnulf, 1929-
Strassenräuber . Wien , 1981. [8], 41 p. :
N6811.5.R3 A4 1981
     NYPL [3-MCK R155 90-6258]

Galerie Heimeshoff. Lakner, László. László
Lakner . Essen , c1982. 22 p. :
     NYPL [3-MCZ L185 88-3717]

Galerie Hennemann. Götz, K. O. (Karl Otto),
1914- K.O. Götz /. Bonn , c1978. 360 p., [1]
folded leaf of plates :
     NYPL [3-MCK G612 91-996]

Galerie hlavního města Prahy.
Český neoklasicismus dvacátých let . [Prague]
[1986?] 1 v. (unpaged):
N6831.5.N46 C47 1986

Devětsil (Society) Devětsil . Łódź [1989]. 105
p. :
N6831.5.D48 D4 1989

Linie, barva, tvar v českém výtvarném umění
třicátých let . [Prague , 1990?] 152 p. :
N6831 .L54 1990

Mezi klasickým řádem a selankou . [Prague] ,
<1990?-. v. <2 > :
N6831.5.N46 M4 1990

Galerie Holtmann (Cologne, Germany) Hacker,
Dieter, 1942- Dieter Hacker . Köln , c1988. 48
p. :   *NYPL [3-MCK H118 91-5907]*

Galerie im Ganserhaus. Jawlensky, Alexej von,
1864-1941. Alexej Jawlensky, vom Abbild zum
Urbild . Wasserburg am Inn , 1979. 107 p. :
N6999.J38 A4 1979
     NYPL [3-MCZ J41 81-398]

Galerie im Körnerpark (Berlin, Germany) 10X.
[Berlin] [1984] 1 portfolio (10 pieces) :
     NYPL [3-MAMG+ 88-4811]

**Galerie im Stadthaus (Bad Homburg vor der
Höhe, Germany)** Sassu, Aligi, 1912- Aligi
Sassu, Malerei, Skulpturen, Grafik. Bad
Homburg [1984] [84] p. :
MLCS 86/5629 (N)
     NYPL [3-MCF S263 90-10657]

Galerie Jean Chauvelin. Malevich, Kazimir
Severinovich, 1878-1935. Dessins . Paris
[1970] [40] p. :
     NYPL [3-MCZ M248 90-6042]

Galerie Johanna Ricard. Cotosman, Roman.
Cotosman, Valenta /. Nürnberg , c1981. [25]
p. :   *NYPL [3-MGO (Cotosman) 90-2044]*

Galerie Klaus Littmann. Distel, Herbert. Spoon
River anthology /. Bern , 1990. 87 p. : ISBN
3-7165-0702-4
     NYPL [MFX (Distel) 90-2736]

Galerie Klewan.
Baumer, Dorothea. Attersee . München
[1987?] 26 leaves :
MLCM 88/01498 (N)
     NYPL [3-MCK+ A88 90-9373]

Giacometti, Alberto, 1901-1966. Alberto
Giacometti, 10.10.1901-11.1.1966 . München ,
c1989. [40] p. :
     NYPL [3-MGO (Giacometti) 91-7078]

Wiener, Oswald. Maria Lassnig . München
[1989?] 1 v. (unpaged) :
     NYPL [3-MCK+ L348 91-5906]

Galerie Krinzinger.
Rainer, Arnulf, 1929- Arnulf Rainer, "Alte
Meister." Innsbruck , 1989. 124 p. :
     NYPL [3-MCK+ R155 90-340]

Wakolbinger, Manfred, 1952- Skulpturen .
Innsbruck , 1988. 39 p. :
     NYPL [3-MGO (Wakolbinger) 91-5905]

Galerie Lavignes-Bastille. Brach, Paul, 1924-
Kacere /. [Paris] , c1989. 169 p. : ISBN
2-85018-313-X
     NYPL [3-MCX+ K115 90-2574]

Galerie Lelong (New York, N.Y.) Cameron, Dan.
Ferran García Sevilla . New York , c1990. [24]
p. :   *NYPL [3-MCQ+ G236 91-4299]*

Galerie Lelong (Paris, France)
Brown, James. James Brown . Paris , 1989. 32
p. : ISBN 2-85587-173-5
     NYPL [3-MGO+ (Brown) 90-10558]

Brown, James, 1951- James Brown . Paris ,
c1990. 42 p. : ISBN 2-85587-184-0
     NYPL [3-MCX+ B8765 90-13074]

Kounellis, Jannis, 1946- Jannis Kounellis /.
Paris , 1989. 31 p. : ISBN 2-85587-177-8
     NYPL [3-MCZ+ K865 90-11632]

Lam, Wifredo. Wifredo Lam /. Paris , c1991.
31 p. : ISBN 2-85587-191-3
     NYPL [3-MCZ+ L213 91-7544]

Michaux, Henri, 1899- Henri Michaux /. Paris ,
c1990. 31 p. : ISBN 2-85587-182-4
     NYPL [3-MCO+ M61 90-13365]

Miró, Joan, 1893- Joan Miró . Paris , c1990. 63
p. : ISBN 2-85587-185-9
     NYPL [MDG+ (Miró) 91-4765]

Galerie Linssen. Calder, Alexander, 1898-1976.
[Calder. English.] Calder . Köln , c1987. 120
p. : ISBN 3-926835-03-6 DDC 709/.2 20
N6537.C33 A4 1987

Galerie Littmann Basel. Le Musée sentimental de
Bâle / erausgegeben von Barbara Huber-Greub
und Stephen Andreae ; [Idee und künstlerische
Leitung: Daniel Spoerri]. Basel , c1989. 332 p. :
ISBN 3-85700-006-X
     NYPL [3-MAVZ (Basel) 90-13397]

Galerie Louis Carré.
Calder, Alexander, 1898-1976. Alexander
Calder, mobiles, Fernand Léger, peintures.
Paris , c1988. 69 p. : ISBN 2-86574-012-9
MLCM 90/03707 (N)
     NYPL [3-MGO+ (Calder) 91-3331]

Galerie Louis Carré. (cont.)

Lapicque, Charles, 1898- Charles Lapicque .
Paris , c1989. 85 p. : ISBN 2-86574-014-5
NYPL [3-MCO+ L305 91-3426]

Galerie Maeght Lelong (New York, N.Y.)
Coplans, John. Hand . New York , c1988. 1 v.
(unpaged) : **NYPL [MFX (Coplans) 91-4595]**

Galerie Marcel Guiot. Albert André, 1869-1954;
œuvres exécutées de 1892 à 1900. [Exposition]
du 19 octobre au 10 novembre, 1960. Paris
[1960] 17 p. illus. 21 cm. Text by George Besson.
*1. André, Albert, 1869-1954 - Exhibitions. I. André,
Albert, 1869-1954. II. Besson, George. III. Title.*
ND553.A5 G33 1960
NYPL [3-MCO A55 90-7046]

Galerie Mathias Fels.
Galerie Mathias Fels. Nouveau réalisme,
1960-1970. Paris, 1970. [34] p.
N6494.R4 G3   **NYPL [3-MAL 90-5761]**

Nouveau réalisme, 1960-1970; Arman, César,
Christo, Deschamps ...[et al.] Galerie Mathias
Fels, Paris. [27 octobre-27 novembre 1970].
Paris, Galerie Mathias Fels, 1970. [34] p. illus.
26 cm. Essay by Pierre Restany.
*1. Realism in art - Exhibitions. 2. Art, Modern - 20th
century - Exhibitions. I. Restany, Pierre. II. Galerie
Mathias Fels. III. Title.*
N6494.R4 G3   **NYPL [3-MAL 90-5761]**

Galerie Medici. Emery, Sergio, 1928- Bilder von
Sergio Emery in der Galerie Medici, 27. August
bis 14. Oktober 1989 /. Solothurn [1989] 1 v.
(unpaged) :
MLCM 90/03081 (N)
NYPL [3-MCZ+ E515 91-5903]

Galerie Metropol. Secessionismus und
Abstraktion = Secessionism and abstraction .
Wien , New York , 1989. 81 p. :
NYPL [3-MAMG+ 90-12363]

Galerie Michael. Robbe, Manuel, 1872-1936.
Manuel Robbe . Beverly Hills, Calif. (430 N.
Rodeo Dr., Beverly Hills) , c1987. 83 p. :
DDC 769.92/4 19
NE2049.5.R64 A4 1987
NYPL [MDG (Robbe) 90-10996]

Galerie Michael Neumann. Antes, Horst, 1936-
Horst Antes . Kiel , c1990. 84 p. : ISBN
3-923701-41-1
NYPL [3-MCK+ A62 91-6789]

Galerie Montaigne. Olitski, Jules, 1922- Jules
Olitski /. [New York] , c1990. 5 v. :
NYPL [3-MCX O47 91-6724]

**Galerie nationale du Canada, Ottawa. see
National Gallery of Canada.**

**Galerie nationale Hongroise, Budapest. see
Budapest. Magyar Nemzeti Galéria.**

Galerie Neher Essen. Münter, Gabriele,
1877-1962. Gabriele Münter und ihre Zeit .
Essen , 1990. 184 p. : ISBN 3-923806-14-0
NYPL [3-MCK M93 91-6711]

Galerie Neiriz. Kelims der Nomaden und Bauern
Persiens /. Berlin , 1990. [29] p., 70 leaves of
plates :   **NYPL [3-MOP+ 91-6927]**

Galerie Nierendorf.
Jaenisch, Hans, 1907- Hans Jaenisch. [Berlin ,
1987] [20] p. :
NYPL [3-MCK J225 90-5359]

Marcks, Gerhard. Gerhard Marcks zum
einhundertsten Geburtstag . Berlin , 1989. iii,
[1] p., [2] p. of plates :
NYPL [3-MGO+ (Marcks) 89-25923]

Rohlfs, Christian, 1849-1938. Christian Rohlfs
zum einhundertvierzigsten Geburtstag . Berlin ,
1989. 72 p. :
NYPL [3-MCK+ R738 91-4220]

Galerie Norbert Blaeser (Düsseldorf, Germany)
Pillhofer, Josef, 1921- Josef Pillhofer .
Düsseldorf [1989?] [76] p. :
NB511.P5 A4 1989

Galerie Nothelfer. see Galerie Georg Nothelfer.

Galerie Palazzo. Matter, Carlos, 1951- Layout .
Liestal , c1987. [68] p. :
MLCM 88/00507 (N)
NYPL [3-MCZ M4368 90-12748]

Galerie Patrick Cramer. Miró, Joan, 1893- Joan
Miró . Genève , 1979. [120] p. : DDC
741.64/092/4 19
NC987.5.M57 A4 1979
NYPL [MDG (Miró) 81-676]

Galerie Paul Maenz (Cologne, Germany) Scholte,
Rob, 1958- Rob Scholte, Amsterdam .
Cologne , 1988. [48] p. :
NYPL [3-MCH S349 89-11,526]

Galerie Pels-Leusden. Heiliger, Bernhard, 1915-
Bernhard Heiliger . Berlin , 1987. 48 p. :
NYPL [3-MGO+ (Heiliger) 90-254]

Galerie Raeber. Egloff, Anton. Galerie Raeber
zeigt Plastiken, Objekte und Collagen von
Anton Egloff. [Luzern, 1970] 1 v. (unpaged)
NYPL [3-MGO (Egloff) 90-6858]

**Galerie Raeber zeigt Plastiken, Objekte und
Collagen von Anton Egloff.** Egloff, Anton.
[Luzern, 1970] 1 v. (unpaged)
NYPL [3-MGO (Egloff) 90-6858]

Galerie Remmert und Barth. Barth, Peter. Conrad
Felixmüller, die Dresdner Jahre 1913-1933 /.
Düsseldorf , 1987. 128 p. :
NYPL [3-MCK F316 89-18042]

Galerie Renée Ziegler. Bury, Pol, 1922- Pol
Bury . Zürich [1989] 54 p. :
NYPL [3-MGO (Bury) 90-12639]

Galerie Robert Finck. Bruegel, Pieter, 1564-1638.
Galerie Robert Finck présente l'exposition de
trente-trois tableaux de Pierre Breughel le jeune
dans les collections privées belges. Bruxelles ,
1969. 1 v. (unpaged) :
NYPL [3-MCH B891 91-305]

**Galerie Robert Finck présente l'exposition de
trente-trois tableaux de Pierre Breughel le
jeune dans les collections privées belges.**
Bruegel, Pieter, 1564-1638. Bruxelles , 1969. 1
v. (unpaged) **NYPL [3-MCH B891 91-305]**

Galerie Scheffel. Sassu, Aligi, 1912- Aligi Sassu,
Malerei, Skulpturen, Grafik. Bad Homburg
[1984] [84] p. :
MLCS 86/5629 (N)
NYPL [3-MCF S263 90-10657]

Galerie Schlégl. Suter, Paul, 1926- Paul Suter,
Eisenplastiken. Zürich , 1988. 135 p. :
NYPL [3-MGO (Sutter) 89-24566]

Galerie Schlichtenmaier.
Graf, Gottfried, 1881-1938. Gottfried Graf,
1881-1938 . Schloss Dätzingen, 7031 Grafenau
2 (bei Sindelfingen) [1985] [44] p. :
MLCM 86/1201 (N)
NYPL [3-MCK G7352 87-826]

Graf, Gottfried, 1881-1938. Gottfried Graf,
1881-1938, Arbeiten auf Papier, 1915-1925 .
Grafenau , 1987. 64 p. : ISBN 3-89298-017-9
NYPL [3-MCK G7352 88-4413]

Ziegler, Richard, 1891- Richard Ziegler .
Grafenau , c1988. 104 p. : ISBN 3-89298-033-0
NC251.Z54 A4 1988

Galerie Schloss Ottenstein. Denk, Wolfgang,
1947- Wolfgang Denk . Wien , Rastenfeld ,
1986. 1 v. (unpaged) :
AM101 .V5344 n.F., Nr. 175 ND511.5.D45
NYPL [3-MDH D396 91-5501]

Galerie Schrade. Ungarische Avantgarde in der
Malerei der achtziger Jahre . [Mannheim]
[Budapest] , c1989. 55 p. : ISBN 3-927224-01-4
ND520 .U54 1989

Galerie Springer, Berlin. Penck A. R., 1939-
A.R. Penck, Keramik. Berlin , c1989. 1 v.
(unpaged)
NK4210.P446 A4 1989

Galerie St. Etienne. Moses, Grandma, 1860-1961.
Grandma Moses (1860-1961) . New York,
N.Y. , c1962. 32 p. : DDC 759.13 19
ND237.M78 A4 1962
NYPL [3-MCX M89 91-6296]

Galerie Stübler. Rolf Münzner, Peter Schnürpel,
Reiner Schwarz . Hannover , c1988. 1 v.
(unpaged)
NYPL [MDG+ (Münzner) 89-23658]

Galerie Taménaga. La peinture figurative
contemporaine du Japon : [exposition]. Paris :
Galerie Taménaga France, 1971. 1 v.
(unpaged) : ill. ; 25 x 26 cm.
*1. Painting, Modern - 20th century - Japan -
Exhibitions.* **NYPL [3-MCY 91-457]**

Galerie van De Loo. Rainer, Arnulf, 1929- Face
farces. München, 1970. 1 v. DDC 709/.24
N6811.5.R3 A45

Galerie Vita. Begegnung mit der Stile =. Bern ,
1988. [35] leaves : **NYPL [3-MAL 89-11598]**

Galerie Vömel.
Bargheer, Eduard, 1901-1979. Eduard Bargheer,
1901-1979, Ölbilder, Aquarelle, Graphik .
Düsseldorf , 1982. [16] p. :
NYPL [3-MCK B245 90-10707]

Kolle, Helmut, 1899-1931. Kolle . Düsseldorf ,
c1988. 59 p. :
MLCM 89/07398 (N)
NYPL [3-MCZ K799 90-10673]

Galerie Weiller. Mohr, Manfred, 1938- Manfred
Mohr . [S.l.] c1974. [24] p. :
NYPL [3-MCK M6893 91-5180]

Galerie Welz Salzburg. Alfred Hrdlicka.
Druckgraphik und zeichnungen. Salzburg, 1969.
86 p. illus. (some col.) 21 cm. Catalog of an
exhibition July 24-Sept. 7, 1969. Includes
bibliographical refernces.
*1. Hrdlička, Alfred, 1928- - Exhibitions. I. Hrdlička,
Alfred, 1928-. II. Title.*
NYPL [MDG (Hrdlicka) 91-394]

Galerie Wolfgang Ketterer. Rauh, Caspar Walter,
1912-1983. Caspar Walter Rauh, 1912-1983 .
München [1987] 16 p. :
NYPL [MDG (Rauh) 90-11352]

Galerie Würthle.
Angeli, Eduard, 1942- Eduard Angeli. Wien
[1983?] [21] leaves : DDC 759.36 19
ND511.5.A53 A4 1982
NYPL [3-MCK+ A597 85-3252]

Kokoschka, Oskar, 1886- Das Konzert .
Salzburg , c1988. 67 p. :
NYPL [3-MCZ K79 89-4191]

Lehmden, Anton, 1929- Lehmden . Wien
[1989] 1 v. (unpaged) : ISBN 3-900567-07-7
NYPL [3-MCK L516 91-6421]

Galerie Yoshii. Rouault, Isabelle. Isabelle
Rouault . Paris [1984] [39] p. :
MLCS 86/4499 (N)
NYPL [3-MCO R853 90-721]

Galerie "Zem Specht" Basel. His, Andreas, 1928-
Andreas His . [Basel] , c1984. [65] p. :
NYPL [3-MCZ H673 90-2126]

Galerie Zimmer. Deutsches Informel . Düsseldorf
[1987] 1 v. : **NYPL [3-MCI+ 91-4284]**

Galerie Zur Stockeregg. Strand, Paul, 1890-1976.
Paul Strand /. Zürich, Switzerland ,
c1987-c1990. 2 v. :
NYPL [MFX (Strand) 91-3461]

Galerie 1900-2000 (Paris, France)
Breer, Robert. Robert Breer . Paris , c1990. 28
p. :   **NYPL [3-MCX+ B832 91-7234]**

Schlatter, Christian. Art conceptuel, formes
conceptuelles =. Paris , 1990. 598 p. :
NYPL [3-MAL 91-3664]

Galerie 6. Holenstein, Werner. Werner
Holenstein . Aarau , 1987. 92 p. : ISBN
3-7941-2937-7
NYPL [3-MCZ+ H729 89-28257]

**Galeries nationales d'exposition du Grand Palais
(France)** Québec (Province). Musée d'art
contemporain. Borduas et les automatistes,
Montréal, 1942-1955. [Montréal] [1971] 154 p.
ND246.Q4 M88   **NYPL [3-MCY 90-5662]**

Galeries nationales du Grand Palais (France)
Bazaine, Jean, 1904- Bazaine /. Genève ,
Paris , c1990. 178 p. : ISBN 2-605-00162-8
DDC 759.4 20
ND553.B42 A4 1990

Bazaine, Jean, 1904- Bazaine. Paris , c1990.
178 p. : ISBN 2-605-00162-8
NYPL [3-MCO B35 90-12858]

Degas, Edgar, 1834-1917. Degas . New York ,
Ottawa , 1988. 640 p. : ISBN 0-87099-519-7
DDC 709.2 19
N6853.D33 A4 1988
NYPL [3-MCO+ D31 90-12588]

Figuration critique 1990 . [Vélizy-Villacoublay]
[Séoul, Corée] [1990] 332 p. : DDC
709/.04/807444361 20
N6494.F5 F5188 1990

Picasso, Pablo, 1881-1973. Picasso, une
nouvelle dation. Paris , c1990. 298 p. : ISBN
2-7118-2369-5 : DDC 709/.2 20
N6853.P5 A4 1990a

31 artistes suisses contemporains. Paris , 1972.
[72] p. :   **NYPL [3-MAM 90-6430]**

GALGARIO, FRA, 1655-1743.
Milesi, Silvana. Fra Galgario tra Seicento e
Settecento . Bergamo , c1990. 206 p. :
NYPL [3-MCF+ G43 91-5343]

GALGARIO, FRA, 1655-1743 - CATALOGS.
Milesi, Silvana. Fra Galgario tra Seicento e
Settecento . Bergamo , c1990. 206 p. :
ND1318.3 .M5 1990

Galicia (Series) (Santiago de Compostela, Spain)
Bozal Fernández, Valeriano. Arte y ciudad en
Galicia, siglo XIX /. Santiago de Compostela
[1990] 133 p. :   ISBN 84-505-9217-8   DDC
709/.46/109034 20
N72.S6 B6 1990

Galinou, Mireille. London's pride . London ,
1990. 224 p. :   ISBN 1-85470-032-4 (cased) :
DDC 712.609421 20
NYPL [3-MSK+ 90-11162]

Galizia, Fede, 1578-1630.
Caroli, Flavio. Fede Galizia /. Torino , c1989.
102 p. :   ISBN 88-422-0217-7
NYPL [3-MCF+ G155 90-12321]

GALIZIA, FEDE, 1578-1630 - CATALOGS.
Caroli, Flavio. Fede Galizia /. Torino , c1989.
102 p. :   ISBN 88-422-0217-7
NYPL [3-MCF+ G155 90-12321]

Gallardo, Jesús, 1931-
Cuaderno de dibujos / Jesús Gallardo. 1. ed. en
la Colección Artistas de Guanajuato.
Guanajuato, Gto. [i.e. Guanajuato, Mexico] :
Gobierno del Estado de Guanajuato, 1989. 112
p. : chiefly ill. (some col.) ; 28 cm. (Artistas de
Guanajuato) ISBN 968-617-017-0   DDC 741.972 20
1. Gallardo, Jesús, 1931- - Catalogs. I. Title. II. Title:
Jesús Gallardo. III. Series.
NC146.G35 A4 1989

GALLARDO, JESÚS, 1931- - CATALOGS.
Gallardo, Jesús, 1931- Cuaderno de dibujos /.
Guanajuato, Gto. [i.e. Guanajuato, Mexico] ,
1989. 112 p. :   ISBN 968-617-017-0   DDC 741.972
20
NC146.G35 A4 1989

Gallati, Barbara Dayer. Brooklyn Museum.
Curator's choice . [Brooklyn, N.Y. , 1990] 1
folded sheet ([8] p.) :
NYPL [3-MCX H76 91-7969]

Gallaudet University. Redmond, Granville,
1871-1935. Granville Redmond. Oakland, Calif.
[1989?] xv, 111 p., [6] leaves of plates :
NYPL [3-MCX R318 89-7639]

Gallavotti Cavallero, Daniela. Palazzi di Roma
dal XIV al XX secolo / Daniela Gallavotti
Cavallero ; presentazione di Carlo Pietrangeli.
Roma : NER, c1989. 268 p. : ill. ; 32 cm.
Includes bibliographical references (p. 249-258) and
index. ISBN 88-85085-03-2
1. Architecture - Italy - Rome. 2. Rome (Italy) -
Buildings, structures, etc. 3. Palaces - Italy - Rome. I.
Pietrangeli, Carlo. II. Title.
IN PROCESS (ONLINE)
NYPL [3-MQWB+ 90-12319]

Galle, Jost. Dunkel, Trimborn, Dönselmann .
[Emden, Germany , 1988] 87 p. :   ISBN
3-925564-02-0
NYPL [3-MAMG + 89-11596]

Galleria A. Jannone. Bellini, Mario, 1935- Mario
Bellini, architetture /. Milano , 1988. 115 p. :
ISBN 88-435-2665-0
NYPL [3-MQZ (Bellini) 90-12540]

Galleria Bellini (Florence, Italy) Collezione del
Palazzo dei Dogi Mocenigo di S. Samuele a
Venezia di proprietà del conde Andrea di
Robilant . Firenze , 1933. 38 p., 54 leaves of
plates :
NYPL [3-MAX+ (Robilant) 87-3088]

Galleria civica d'arte moderna, Ferrara.
Boni, Paolo, 1926- Boni . Roma [1977] [70]
p. :
ND623.B5688 A4 1977
NYPL [3-MCF B704 81-336]

Morandi, Giorgio, 1890-1964. Giorgio
Morandi . Cento [1978] [213] p. :
N6923.M6 A4 1978
NYPL [3-MCF M82 81-718]

GALLERIA CIVICA DI PALAZZO TE.
Suitner Nicolini, Gianna. Palazzo Te, Mantova
/. Milano , c1990. 114 p. :   ISBN 88-435-3099-2
NA7756.M3 S8 1990

Galleria d'arte moderna (Paternò, Italy) Scianna,
Ferdinando. Città del mondo /. Milano , c1988.
95 p. :   *NYPL [MFX (Scianna) 91-5705]*

Galleria d'arte sagittaria.
Murtić, Edo. Murtić /. Pordenone , 1978. x, 81
p., [61] leaves of plates :   DDC 759.9497 19
ND953.M8 A4 1978
NYPL [3-MCZ M978 91-3581]

Pauletto, Giancarlo. Kosta Angeli Radovani /.
Pordenone , c1988. 84 p., [66] p. of plates :
NYPL [3-MGO (Radovani) 91-6969]

Galleria degli Uffizi. Botticelli, Sandro, 1444 or
5-1510. L'incoronazione della Vergine del
Botticelli . Firenze , 1990. 141 p. :
IN PROCESS (ONLINE)
NYPL [3-MCF B75 90-11619]

La Galleria del Costume. Firenze : Centro Di,
c1983- v. : ill. (some col.) ; 29 cm. (Centro Di
cat. . 169, 219, 245) Edited by Kirsten Aschengreen
Piacenti. At head of title: Ministero per i beni culturali
e ambienti ... "Palazzo Pitti, Firenze. Galleria del
costume"--P. [1] of each vol. Includes bibliographical
references.   ISBN 88-7038-077-7 (v. 1)
1. Galleria del costume - Catalogs. 2. Costume - Italy -
Catalogs. 3. Costume - Europe - Catalogs. I. Piacenti
Aschengreen, Cristina. II. Series: Cat. (Centro Di)
169, etc.   *NYPL [3-MME 84-2509]*

La Galleria del costume / [redazione del catalogo,
Kirsten Aschengreen Piacenti]. Firenze : Centro
di, 1988. 93 p. : ill. (some col.) ; 29 cm.
(Galleria del costume . 3) Centro di cat. ; 219 At head
of title: Ministero per i beni culturali e ambientali ... [et
al.]. Bibliography: p. 93.   ISBN 88-7038-145-5
1. Galleria del costume - Catalogs. 2. Costume - Italy -
Florence - Catalogs. I. Piacenti Aschengreen, Cristina.
II. Series: Galleria del costume (Series) ; 3.
NYPL [3-MMO 88-4827]

GALLERIA DEL COSTUME - CATALOGS.
La Galleria del Costume. Firenze , c1983- v. :
ISBN 88-7038-077-7 (v. 1)
NYPL [3-MME 84-2509]

La Galleria del costume /. Firenze , 1988. 93
p. :   ISBN 88-7038-145-5
NYPL [3-MMO 88-4827]

Galleria del costume (Series) .
(3) La Galleria del costume /. Firenze , 1988.
93 p. :   ISBN 88-7038-145-5
NYPL [3-MMO 88-4827]

La Galleria estense . Galleria, museo e
medagliere estense (Modena, Italy) Modena
[1990] 197 p. :   ISBN 88-7686-154-8 :
NYPL [3-MAVZ+ (Modena) 91-4947]

Galleria Fonte d'Abisso (Modena, Italy) Archivi
futuristi /. Modena , Milano , c1990. 189 p. :
DDC 709/.45/0744542 20
N6918.5.F8 A74 1990

Galleria Menghelli. Raphaël Mafai, Antonietta,
1900-1975. Antonietta Raphael Mafai, Mario
Mafai . Firenze , 1971. [51] p. :
NYPL [3-MCE 91-1300]

Galleria Morone sei. Vago, Valentino, 1931-
Valentino Vago. Milano [1973] [24] p. :
NYPL [3-MCF+ V126 91-6601]

Galleria Morone 6. Vago, Valentino, 1931-
Valentino Vago /. Milano [1975] [48] p. :
NYPL [3-MCF+ V126 91-6299]

**Galleria, museo e medagliere estense (Modena,
Italy)**
Disegno . [Rennes], France [1990] 253 p. :
ISBN 2-901430-22-8   DDC 741.945/074/4415 20
NC255 .D54 1990

La Galleria estense : doni, lasciti, acquisti
1884-1990 / a cura di Gaetano Ghiraldi ;
presentazione di Jadranka Bentini. Modena :
F.C. Panini, [1990] 197 p. : ill. ; 30 cm. At head
of title: Ministero per i beni culturali ambientali,
Soprintendenza per i beni artistici e storici di Modena e
Reggio Emilia. Includes bibliographical references (p.
195-197) and index.   ISBN 88-7686-154-8 :
1. Galleria, museo e medagliere estense (Modena,
Italy) - Catalogs. 2. Painting - Italy - Modena -
Catalogs. I. Ghiraldi, Gaetano. II. Italy. Soprintendenza
per i beni artistici e storici di Modena e Reggio. III.
Title.   *NYPL [3-MAVZ+ (Modena) 91-4947]*

**GALLERIA, MUSEO E MEDAGLIERE
ESTENSE (MODENA, ITALY) -
CATALOGS.**
Galleria, museo e medagliere estense (Modena,
Italy) La Galleria estense . Modena [1990] 197

p. :   ISBN 88-7686-154-8 :
NYPL [3-MAVZ+ (Modena) 91-4947]

Galleria nazionale d'arte moderna (Italy)
Galleria nazionale d'arte moderna (Italy) Clerici,
Fabrizio, 1913- Fabrizio Clerici /. Roma , 1990.
260 p. :   ISBN 88-7813-268-3
NYPL [3-MCF C625 91-5535]

Individualités . Milano , c1984. 107 p. :
NYPL [3-MAMI 90-12643]

Galleria nazionale delle Marche. Il restauro della
Città ideale di Urbino . [Urbino , 1978] 39 p. :
NYPL [3-MBK 90-5658]

Galleria nazionale dell'Umbria /. Galleria
nazionale dell'Umbria. Roma , 1969- v. :
NYPL [MAVY (Perugia) 91-5431]

Galleria nazionale dell'Umbria.
Galleria nazionale dell'Umbria / Francesco
Santi. Roma : Istituto poligrafico dello Stato,
Libreria dello Stato, 1969- v. : ill. ; 27 cm.
(Cataloghi dei musei e gallerie d'Italia) Includes
bibliographical references and indexes. CONTENTS. -
[1] Dipinti, sculture e oggetti d'arte di età romanica e
gotica -- [2] Dipinti, sculture e oggetti dei secoli
XV-XVI.
1. Galleria nazionale dell'Umbria - Catalogs. 2. Art -
Italy - Perugia - Catalogs. I. Santi, Francesco. II. Title.
III. Title: Dipinti, sculture e oggetti d'arte di età
romanica e gotica. IV. Title: Dipinti, sculture e oggetti
dei secoli XV-XVI.
NYPL [MAVY (Perugia) 91-5431]

**GALLERIA NAZIONALE DELL'UMBRIA -
CATALOGS.**
Galleria nazionale dell'Umbria. Galleria
nazionale dell'Umbria /. Roma , 1969- v. :
NYPL [MAVY (Perugia) 91-5431]

Galleria regionale della Sicilia.
Pietro Novelli e il suo ambiente /. Palermo ,
c1990. 550 p. :   ISBN 88-7804-048-7
NYPL [3-MCF N9385 91-3641]

Pittori del Seicento a Palazzo Abatellis /.
Milano , c1990. 192 p. :   ISBN 88-435-3177-8
NYPL [3-MC 91-7058]

Il "Trionfo della morte" di Palermo . Palermo ,
c1989. 88 p., [62] p. of plates :   ISBN
88-7681-040-4   *NYPL [3-MLP 90-11764]*

Gallerie dell'Accademia di Venezia.
Catalogo dei disegni antichi / Gallerie
dell'Accademia di Venezia ; coordinatori,
Giovanna Nepi Sciré e Francesco Valcanover.
Milano : Electa, c1982- v. : ill. (some col.) ; 25
cm. Includes bibliographies and indexes.
CONTENTS. - [1] Storia della collezione dei disegni /
Giovanna Nepi Sciré -- [2] Disegni lombardi / Ugo
Ruggeri -- [4] Disegni del Figino / Annalisa Perissa
Torrini -- [7] Disegni umbri / Sylvia Ferino Pagden --
[8] Disegni romani, toscani e napoletani / Simonetta
Prosperi Valenti Rodinò   ISBN 88-435-0801-6 (v. 1)
DDC 741.94/074/0531 19
1. Gallerie dell'Accademia di Venezia - Catalogs. 2.
Drawing, European - Catalogs. 3. Drawing - Italy -
Venice - Catalogs. I. Nepi Sciré, Giovanna. II.
Valcanover, Francesco. III. Title.
NC255 .G35 1982   *NYPL [3-MBH 85-260]*

Catalogo dei disegni antichi .
(3) Venice. Gallerie dell'Accademia. Disegni
umbri . Milano , c1984. 211 p. :   ISBN
88-435-0801-6   *NYPL [3-MBH 86-3573]*

(4) Gallerie dell'Accademia di Venezia.
Designi del Figino /. Milano , c1987. 227 p. :
ISBN 88-435-2240-X
NYPL [3-MCF F472 88-4259]

Designi del Figino / Annalisa Perissa Torrini.
Milano : Electa, c1987. 227 p. : ill. (some
col.) ; 25 cm. (Catalogo dei disegni antichi . [4]) At
head of title: Gallerie dell'Accademia di Venezia.
Includes indexes. Bibliography: p. 221-224.   ISBN
88-435-2240-X
1. Figino, Giovan Ambrogio, 1548?-1608. 2. Gallerie
dell'Accademia di Venezia - Catalogs. 3. Drawing,
Renaissance - Italy - Venice - Catalogs. I. Perissa
Torrini, Annalisa. II. Figino, Giovan Ambrogio,
1548?-1608. III. Series: Gallerie dell'Accademia di
Venezia. Catalogo dei disegni antichi , 4. IV. Title.
NYPL [3-MCF F472 88-4259]

**GALLERIE DELL'ACCADEMIA DI
VENEZIA - CATALOGS.**
Gallerie dell'Accademia di Venezia. Catalogo
dei disegni antichi /. Milano , c1982- v. :
ISBN 88-435-0801-6 (v. 1)   DDC

741.94/074/0531 19
NC255 .G35 1982 **NYPL [3-MBH 85-260]**
Gallerie dell'Accademia di Venezia. Designi del
Figino /. Milano , c1987. 227 p. : ISBN
88-435-2240-X
NYPL [3-MCF F472 88-4259]

**GALLERIE DELL'ACCADEMIA (VENICE,
ITALY) - CATALOGS.**
Nepi Sciré, Giovanna. [Gallerie dell'Accademia.
English.] Treasures of Venetian painting . New
York , 1991. p. cm. ISBN 0-86565-127-2 DDC
759.5/31/0744531 20
ND621.V5 N4613 1991

GALLERIES (ART) see ART MUSEUMS.

Galleries for the fine artist. Directory of galleries
for the fine artist /. Renaissance, CA , c1990.
359 p. ; ISBN 0-940899-08-6
NYPL [MA 90-11525]

Gallery 5610. Iwaki, Nobuyoshi. Nobuyoshi
Iwaki, private exhibition. [s.l. , 1978] (Tokyo :
Mainichi Printing Company) 31 p. :
NB1059.I95 A4 1978
NYPL [3-MGO (Iwaki) 81-791]

Gallery going . Perl, Jed. San Diego , c1991. xxiv,
431 p., [16] p. of plates : ISBN 0-15-134260-1 :
DDC 709/.04/0074 20
N6447 .P38 1991 **NYPL [3-MAV 91-7445]**

**Gallery of Modern Art Including the Huntington
Hartford Collection, New York. see New
York (City). Gallery of Modern Art
Including the Huntington Hartford
Collection.**

**Gallery of Modern Art, New York. see New
York (City). Gallery of Modern Art
Including the Huntington Hartford
Collection.**

Galletti, Luigi. Elaborati urbanistici . Milano
[1987?] 10 pamphlets in portfolio :
NYPL [3-MQWB 90-11014]

Galli, Giovanna. Il mosaico : nella tradizione di
Ravenna : storia, materiali, tecniche / Giovanna
Galli.1. ed. Torino : Ulisse, 1989. 115 p. : ill. ;
27 cm. (Atelier, che cosa, con che cosa . 12) ISBN
88-414-2039-2
1. Mosaics - Italy - Ravenna. 2. Mosaics - Technique. I.
Title. II. Series. **NYPL [3-MRXZ 91-7273]**

Gallo, Francesco. De Chirico, Giorgio, 1888-
Giorgio de Chirico, 1920-1950 /. Milano ,
c1990. 166 p. : ISBN 88-435-3403-3 (jacket)
NYPL [3-MCF C535 91-6458]

Gallo, Vincent, 1961-
Vincent Gallo : paintings and drawings,
1982-1988. Kyoto, Japan : Kyoto Shoin, c1989.
25 leaves : chiefly col. ill. ; 31 cm. (Art random .
5) ISBN 4-7636-8523-6 : DDC 709/.2 20
1. Gallo, Vincent, 1961- - Catalogs. I. Title. II. Series.
N6537.G35 A4 1989

GALLO, VINCENT, 1961- - CATALOGS.
Gallo, Vincent, 1961- Vincent Gallo . Kyoto,
Japan , c1989. 25 leaves : ISBN 4-7636-8523-6 :
DDC 709/.2 20
N6537.G35 A4 1989

Gallwitz, Klaus.
Beckmann, Max, 1884-1950. Max Beckmann .
Stuttgart , c1990. 258 p. : ISBN 3-7757-0314-4
NYPL [3-MCK B39 91-7591]
Kiefer, Anselm, 1945- Über Räume und Völker
/. Frankfurt am Main , 1990. 174 p. :
3-518-38305-1
NC251.K44 A4 1990
Luginbühl, Bernhard, 1929- Bernhard Luginbühl
im Städel . Frankfurt am Main [1979] [68] p. :
N7153.T56 A4 1979 **NYPL [3-MGO
(Luginbühl) 80-865 [pt. 1]]**

Gambardella, Carmine. Bacoli : il disegno, il
progetto / Carmine Gambardella ; introduzione
di Marcello Angrisani. Napoli : Società editrice
napoletana, [1982] 70 p. : ill. (some col.) ; 22 x
24 cm. (Architettura, storia e progetto . 1)
Bibliography: p. 67-68.
1. Solar buildings - Italy - Bacoli - Design and
construction. 2. Solar energy - Passive systems - Design
and construction. I. Title. II. Series.
TH7413 .G36 1982 **NYPL [MQWB 91-840]**

Gambee, Robert. Wall Street Christmas / Robert
Gambee. New York : Norton, c1990. 272 p. :
col. ill. ; 28 cm. Includes index. ISBN
0-393-02835-6 DDC 394.2/68282/097471 20

1. Christmas - New York (N.Y.) - Pictorial works. 2.
Stock-exchange - New York (N.Y.). 3. Wall Street
(New York, N.Y.) - Social life and customs. 4. New
York (N.Y.) - Social life and customs. I. Title.
GT4986.A2 N484 1990
NYPL [MFX (Gambee) 91-3471]

Gambier, Madile. I Querini Stampalia . Venezia ,
1987. 255 p. : **NYPL [3-MAX+ (Querini
Stampalia) 90-12441]**

Gambuti, Alessandro. La Tribuna di Galileo /
Alessandro Gambuti. Firenze : Alinea, c1990.
99 p. : ill. ; 23 cm. (Saggi e documenti. 95)
1. Tribuna di Galileo. I. Series: Saggi e documenti
(Alinea editrice) , 95. II. Title.
IN PROCESS (ONLINE)
NYPL [3-MQWB 91-7100]

GAME FOWL - PICTORIAL WORKS.
Hiro. Fighting fish, fighting birds . New York ,
1990. 66 p. : ISBN 0-8109-3403-5 DDC 779/.32
20
TR729.F5 H57 1990
NYPL [MFX+ (Hiro) 91-3304]

GAMES IN ART.
Fairman, Elisabeth R. Pleasures and pastimes .
New Haven, Conn. , c1990. 39 p. : ISBN
0-930606-62-0
NYPL [3-MAMZ 90-11038]

Gamet, Pierre. Henri Rivière : peintre et imagier
de la Bretagne / Pierre Gamet. Douarnenez :
Editions Le Chasse-Marée, 1989. 40 p., 48
leaves of plates : ill. (some col.) ; 26 x 33 cm.
Includes bibliographical references (p. 33). ISBN
2-903708-20-7 DDC 769.92 20
1. Rivière, Henri, 1864-1951 - Catalogs. 2. Brittany in
art - Catalogs. I. Title.
N6853.R5 A4 1989

Gammon, Mitzi. The south / text by Mitzi
Gammon ; photographs by Jon Jensen ;
introduction by Virginia and Lee McAlester.
New York : Bantam Books, 1991. p. cm.
(American design) Includes bibliographical references.
ISBN 0-553-07550-0 DDC 728/.37/0975 20
1. Architecture, Domestic - Southern States. 2.
Vernacular architecture - Southern States. 3. Interior
decoration - Southern States. I. Jensen, Jon. II. Title.
III. Series.
NA7211 .G35 1991

Gandelsonas, Mario, 1938-
Pelli, Cesar. Cesar Pelli . New York , 1990. 288
p. : ISBN 0-8478-1262-6 DDC 720/.92 20
NA737.P39 A4 1990
NYPL [3-MQZ (Pelli) 91-5464]
The urban text / Mario Gandelsonas. London,
England ; Boston, Mass. : Chicago Institute for
Architecture and Urbanism ; p. cm. ISBN
0-262-57084-X (pbk.) DDC 711/.4/0977311 20
1. City planning - Illinois - Chicago. 2. Architecture -
Illinois - Chicago - Human factors. I. Title.
NA9127.C4 G36 1990

Gandini, Manuela. Taking the picture . New
York, N.Y. [1990?] 1 v. (unpaged)
NYPL [MFW 91-4296]

Gandolfo, Francesco.
Matthiae, Guglielmo. Pittura romana del
Medioevo /. Roma , c1987-c1988. 2 v. : ISBN
88-7621-234-5 (v. 1) DDC
751.7/3/09456320902 20
ND2757.R6 M34 1987
NYPL [3-MLP+ 90-12085]
Ptghni/Arudch / [testi, Francesco Gandolfo,
Armen Zarian]. 1a ed. Milano, Italia : OEMME
edizioni, 1986. 74 p. : ill. (some col.), plans ; 27
x 28 cm. (Documenti di architettura armena =
Documents of Armenian architecture . 16) Armenian,
English, and Italian. Bibliography: p. 34-35. ISBN
88-85822-03-7 DDC 720/.9566/2 s
726./5/094792 19
1. Ptghavank' (Ptykhni, Armenian S.S.R.). 2. Surb
Grigor Ekeghets'i (Talish, Armenian S.S.R.). 3.
Architecture, Medieval - Armenian S.S.R. - Ptykhni. 4.
Architecture, Medieval - Armenian S.S.R. - Talish. 5.
Ptykhni (Armenian S.S.R.) - Buildings, structures, etc.
6. Talish (Armenian S.S.R.) - Buildings, structures, etc.
I. Zaryan, Armen, 1914-. II. Title. III. Title:
Arudch/Ptghni. IV. Title: Ptghni, Arudch. V. Series:
Documenti di architettura armena , 16.
NA1474 .D6 no. 16 NA5998.P84
NYPL [3-MQW 90-11667]

Ganim, Barbara. The designer's commonsense
business book / by Barbara Ganim. Cincinnati,
Ohio : North Light Books, c1991. p. cm.

Includes index. ISBN 0-89134-373-3 (pbk.) : DDC
741.6/068 20
1. Commercial art - United States - Practice -
Handbooks, manuals, etc. I. Title.
NC1001 .G36 1991

GANYMEDE (GREEK MYTHOLOGY) - ART.
Barkan, Leonard. Transuming passion .
Stanford, Calif. , 1991. 147 p. : ISBN
0-8047-1851-2 (cloth : acid-free paper) : DDC
700 20
NX652.G35 B37 1991
NYPL [3-MAMZ 91-6123]

Ganz tief unten : ein Gesamtkunstwerk in der
Tiefgarage der Kreissparkasse Recklinghausen,
7. bis 12. April 1989 / Veranstalter, Vestischer
Künstlerbund ; Durchführung, K.I.R., Kultur im
Ruhrgebiet e.V. ; Organisationskomitee, Jochem
Ahmann ... [et al.] ; Organisation,
Kreissparkasse Recklinghausen, Vestischer
Künstlerbund, Kunsthalle Recklinghausen ;
Kataloggestaltung und -bearbeitung, Gerhard
Reinert, Ferdinand Ullrich ; Fotografien, Martin
Grothusmann, Ferdinand Ullrich]. [Germany :
s.n., 1989?] 1 v. (unpaged) : chiefly ill. (some
col.) ; 27 cm.
1. Art, German - Exhibitions. 2. Art, Modern - 20th
century - Germany - Exhibitions. 3. Installations (Art) -
Germany - Exhibitions. I. Ahmann, Jochem. II. Reinert,
Gerhard. III. Ullrich, Ferdinand. IV. Kreissparkasse
Recklinghausen. V. Vestischer Künstlerbund
Recklinghausen. VI. Städtische Kunsthalle
Recklinghausen.
N6868 .G34 1989

--Die ganze Welt im kleinen-- : Kunst und
Kunstgeschichte in Leipzig / herausgegeben von
Ernst Ullmann.1. Aufl. Leipzig : E.A. Seemann,
1989. 300 p. : ill. (some col.) ; 20 cm.
(Seemann-Beiträge zur Kunstwissenschaft) Includes
bibliographical references. ISBN 3-363-00419-2
1. Art - Germany - Leipzig. 2. Arts - Germany -
Leipzig. 3. Architecture - Germany - Leipzig. 4. Art -
Historiography. I. Ullmann, Ernst. II. Title: Kunst und
Kunstgeschichte in Leipzig. III. Series.
NYPL [MAMG 91-6223]

Garas, Klára. Szépművészeti Múzeum. English.
The Budapest Museum of Fine Arts /.
[Budapest] , c1985. 171 p. : ISBN 963-13-2297-1
NYPL [MAVZ+ (Budapest) 91-4223]

Garavaglia, Niny. Mantegna, Andrea, 1431-1506.
L'opera completa del Mantegna. Milano, 1967.
128 p. :
ND623.M3 B42
NYPL [3-MCF+ M29 91-5642]

**GARBAGE. see REFUSE AND REFUSE
DISPOSAL.**

Garbisch, Edgar William. American naive
painting of the 18th and 19th centuries: lll
masterpieces from the collection of Edgar
William and Bernice Chrysler Garbisch.
Foreword by John Walker. Preface by Lloyd
Goodrich. Introd. by Albert Ten Eyck Gardner.
[New York] American Federation of Arts
[1969] 159 p. illus. (part col.), ports. 25 cm.
Exhibition shown in the United States and in Europe
under the auspices of the American Federation of Arts,
1968-1970.
1. Paintings, American - Exhibitions. 2. Paintings -
Private collections. 3. Primitivism in art. I. Title.
NYPL [3-MCW 91-7028]

**García, Antonio [i. e. Antonio García Cubas] see
García Cubas, Antonio, 1832-1912.**

García Arévalo, Manuel Antonio. Castillo, José
del, 1947- Artesanía dominicana /. Santo
Domingo, República Dominicana , 1989. 125
p. : DDC 745/.097293 20
NK886.D65 C38 1989

García Cubas, Antonio, 1832-1912. Atlas
geográfico, estadístico e histórico de la
República Mexicana / formado por Antonio
García y Cubas. 2a facsimilar. Mexico : Miguel
Angel Porrúa, 1989, c1988. 1 atlas (various
pagings) : ill. (some col.), maps ; 56 cm. Issued
in portfolio. Title on cover: Atlas de la República
Mexicana. Includes bibliographical references. Facsimile
reprint. Originally published : Mexico: Imprenta de José
Mariano Fernandez de Lara, 1858. ISBN
968-8421-57-X
1. Mexico - Maps. I. Title. II. Title: Atlas de la
República Mexicana. **NYPL [Map Div. 91-131]**

García, Elena. Daroczi, Isabel. Atlas de la
República Oriental del Uruguay /. Montevideo ,

1990. 1 atlas (109 p.) :
NYPL [Map Div. 90-13118]

García, Federico. see **García Lorca, Federico, 1898-1936.**

García Grinda, José Luis. Arquitectura popular de Burgos : crítica y teoría de la arquitectura popular, tipos y caracterización de la arquitectura rural autóctona castellano-leonesa, el caso burgalés / José Luis García Grinda. [Burgos] : Colegio Oficial de Arquitectos de Burgos, [1988] 322 p. : ill. (some col.), maps, plans ; 31 cm. Includes bibliographical references. ISBN 84-505-7747-0
1. Vernacular architecture - Spain - Burgos (Province). I. Title. *NYPL [3-MQWH+ 90-791]*

García Gutiérrez, Pedro Francisco. La escultura / Pedro F. García Gutiérrez y José Landa Bravo. Madrid : Antiquaria, [1990?]- v. <1 > : ill. (some col.) ; 25 cm. (Diccionarios antiquaria . 6) Includes index. CONTENTS. - 1. De la prehistoria al gótico ISBN 84-86508-00-2 DDC 730 20
1. Sculpture. I. Landa Bravo, José. II. Title. III. Series.
NB60 .G3 1990

García Iglesias, José Manuel, 1950- A Catedral de Santiago e o barroco / por Xosé Manuel García Iglesias. Santiago de Compostela : Colexio Oficial de Arquitectos de Galicia, 1990. 228 p. : ill. (some col.) ; 31 cm. Text in Gallegan; summaries in English and Spanish. Includes bibliographical references (p. 142-146). ISBN 84-85665-20-1
1. Catedral de Santiago de Compostela. 2. Architecture, Baroque - Spain - Santiago de Compostela. 3. Church decoration and ornament - Spain - Santiago de Compostela. 4. Santiago de Compostela (Spain) - Buildings, structures, etc. I. Title.
NA5811.S46 G37 1990
NYPL [3-MRBN+ 91-3888]

García, Juan. see **García Ponce, Juan.**

García Lorca, Federico, 1898-1936.
Dibujos / Federico García Lorca ; proyecto y catalogación, Mario Hernández. [Madrid] : Ministerio de Asuntos Exteriores de España, Dirección General de Relaciones Culturales : Instituto de Cooperación Iberoamericana : 155 p. : ill. (some col.) ; 29 cm. Catalog of an exhibition held in Caracas, Buenos Aires, Montevideo, Mexico City, and New York in 1987. Includes bibliographical references. ISBN 84-86691-00-1 DDC 741.946 20
1. García Lorca, Federico, 1898-1936 - Exhibitions. I. Hernández, Mario. II. Title.
NC287.G383 A4 1987a

[Dibujos. English]
Line of light and shadow : the drawings of Federico García Lorca / [edited, with an introduction by] Mario Hernández ; translated by Christopher Maurer. Durham : Published by the Duke University Press in association with the Duke University Museum of Art, 1991. 273 p. : ill. (some col.) ; 31 cm. Rev. translation of: Dibujos. 1987. Includes bibliographical references (p. 33-34) and indexes. ISBN 0-8223-1122-4 DDC 741.946 20
1. García Lorca, Federico, 1898-1936 - Exhibitions. I. Hernández, Mario. II. Duke University. Museum of Art. III. Title.
NC287.G389 A4 1991

GARCÍA LORCA, FEDERICO, 1898-1936 - EXHIBITIONS.
García Lorca, Federico, 1898-1936. Dibujos /. [Madrid] . 155 p. : ISBN 84-86691-00-1 DDC 741.946 20
NC287.G383 A4 1987a

García Lorca, Federico, 1898-1936. [Dibujos. English.] Line of light and shadow . Durham , 1991. 273 p. : ISBN 0-8223-1122-4 DDC 741.946 20
NC287.G389 A4 1991

García, Luis Reyes. see **Reyes García, Luis.**

García, Manuel. see **García-Viñó, Manuel.**

García, Miguel A. Núñez Borda, Luis, 1872-1970. L. Núñez Borda, el pintor de Bogotá /. [Bogotá, Colombia?] 1988 (Bogotá, Colombia : Litográficos de Escala) 116 p. : ISBN 958-9082-41-6 DDC 759.9861 20
ND379.N85 A4 1988

Garcia, Nicolas B. Learning architectural drafting & design / Nicolas B. Garci and Diana Pratt Howe. Albany, N.Y. : Delmar Publishers, c1992. p. cm. Includes index. ISBN 0-8273-4633-6 (textbook) DDC 720/.28/4 20
1. Architectural drawing - Technique. 2. Architectural design - Technique. I. Howe, Diana Pratt. II. Title. III. Title: Learning architectural drafting and design.
NA2708 .G3 1992

García Orozco, Aurora. Catálogo del patrimonio artístico cultural de Michoacán / recopilación, ordenamiento, registro, catalogación y notas, Aurora García Orozco ; revisión y corrección, Rosalía Santín. Morelia, Michoacán, México : Comité Editorial del Gobierno del Estado de Michoacán, 1986. 180 p. : ill. ; 22 cm. ISBN 968-667-047-5
1. Art - Mexico - Michoacán de Ocampo - Catalogs. I. Santín, Rosalía. II. Title.
N6556M5 G3 1986

García Ponce, Juan. Una lectura pseudognóstica de la pintura de Balthus / Juan García Ponce. México : Ediciones del Equilibrista, 1987. 39 p. : col. ill. ; 28 cm.
1. Balthus, 1908- - Criticism and interpretation. I. Title.
ND553.B23 G37 1987

GARCIA RODERO, CRISTINA, 1949- - EXHIBITIONS.
Pitts, Terence. 4 Spanish photographers . [Tucson, Ariz.] , c1988. 23 p. :
NYPL [MFW+ 89-1448]

García Sáiz, Maria Concepción. Las castas mexicanas : un género pictórico americano = The castes : a genre of Mexican painting / María Concepción García Sáiz ; prólogos de Diego Angulo Iñiguez, Roberto Moreno de los Arcos, Miguel Angel Fernández. [S.l.] : Olivetti, 1989 (Milano) 253 p. : col. ill. ; 31 cm. Spanish and English. Exhibition held at the Museo de Monterrey, Monterrey, Nuevo León, México, 21 Septiembre-24 Diciembre, 1989; at the San Antonio Art Museum, San Antonio, Texas, January 26-April 1, 1990; and at the Museo Franz Mayer, Ciudad de México, México, 3 Mayo-5 Agosto, 1990. Includes bibliographical references (p. 253).
1. Painting, Mexican - Catalogs. 2. Painting, Modern - 17th-18th centuries. 3. Miscegenation - Mexico - Exhibitions - Catalogs. 4. Art and race - Exhibitions - Catalogs. 5. Mexico - Race relations - Exhibitions - Catalogs. I. Angulo Iñiguez, Diego. II. Moreno, Roberto. III. Fernández, Miguel Angel. IV. Museo de Monterrey. V. San Antonio Museum of Art. VI. Museo Franz Mayer (Mexico City, Mexico). VII. Title. VIII. Title: Castes, a genre of Mexican painting.
NYPL [3-MCY+ 91-4969]

GARCÍA SEVILLA, FERRAN, 1949- - EXHIBITIONS.
Cameron, Dan. Ferran García Sevilla . New York , c1990. [24] p. :
NYPL [3-MCQ+ G236 91-4299]

García-Viñó, Manuel. Pintura española neofigurativa [por] M. García-Viñó. Prefacio de José Camón Aznar. Madrid, Ediciones Guadarrama [c1968] 203 p. plates 19 cm. (Colección Punto omega. 17) Includes bibliographical references.
1. Figurative art - Spain - History and criticism. 2. Painting, Modern - 20th century - Spain - History and criticism. I. Title.
ND808 .G34
NYPL [3-MCP 91-787]

Gardelles, Jacques. Bordeaux, cité médiévale / Jacques Gardelles ; photographies de Alain Béguerie. Bordeaux : Horizon chimérique, c1989. 221 p. : ill. ; 25 cm. Includes bibliographical references (p. 214-218). ISBN 2-907202-13-8
1. Christian art and symbolism - Medieval, 500-1500 - France - Bordeaux. I. Title.
N7949.B67 G37 1989

GARDEN ARCHITECTURE. see **ARCHITECTURE, DOMESTIC; LANDSCAPE GARDENING.**

GARDEN FIXTURES. see **GARDEN ORNAMENTS AND FURNITURE.**

GARDEN FURNITURE. see **GARDEN ORNAMENTS AND FURNITURE.**

Garden ornament . Plumptre, George. [London] , c1989. 256 p. : ISBN 0-500-01477-9
NYPL [3-MSF+ 89-26932]

GARDEN ORNAMENTS AND FURNITURE - NORTHWESTERN STATES - EXHIBITIONS.
Yard art . Boise, Idaho , c1991. 1 v. (unpaged) . DDC 745/.0979/07479628 20
NK824 .Y37 1991

GARDEN STRUCTURES - SCOTLAND.
Buxbaum, Tim. Scottish garden buildings . Edinburgh , 1988. 192 p. : ISBN 1-85158-113-8 : DDC 717 19 *NYPL [3-MSK 90-11993]*

Garden styles : an illustrated history of design and tradition / general editor, David Joyce. London : Pyramid Books, c1989. 192 p. : ill. (chiefly col.) ; 29 cm. "Based on The Oxford companion to gardens." ISBN 1-87130-778-3
1. Gardens - History. 2. Landscape gardening - History. I. Joyce, David. II. Oxford companion to gardens.
NYPL [3-MSC 90-8787]

GARDENERS - GREAT BRITAIN - BIOGRAPHY.
Allan, Mea. William Robinson, 1838-1935 . London , 1982. 255 p. : ISBN 0-571-11865-8 :
NYPL [3-MSCC 83-2793]

GARDENING, LANDSCAPE. see **LANDSCAPE GARDENING.**

GARDENS, AMERICAN.
Oehme, Wolfgang, 1930- Bold romantic gardens . Reston, Va. , 1990. 310 p. : ISBN 0-87491-950-9 : DDC 712/.0973 20
SB473 .O44 1990 *NYPL [3-MSK+ 91-4459]*

GARDENS - BRAZIL.
Eliovson, Sima. The gardens of Roberto Burle Marx /. New York , c1991. 237 p. : ISBN 0-8109-3357-8 DDC 712/.092 B 20
SB470.B87 E45 1991
NYPL [3-MSCC 91-6489]

GARDENS - DESIGN.
The Meaning of gardens . Cambridge, Mass. , c1990. ix, 283 p. : ISBN 0-262-06127-9 DDC 712 20
SB470.7 .M43 1990
NYPL [3-MSC 90-11705]

GARDENS - ENGLAND - HISTORY.
Robinson, John Martin. Temples of delight . London , 1990. 176 p. : ISBN 0-540-01217-3 : DDC 712.60942 20
SB477.G7 *NYPL [3-MSK 91-2633]*

GARDENS - ENGLAND - KENT.
Brown, Jane. Sissinghurst . London , 1990. 136 p. : ISBN 0-297-83043-0
NYPL [3-MSK 90-11984]

GARDENS - ENGLAND - LONDON - HISTORY.
London's pride . London , 1990. 224 p. : ISBN 1-85470-032-4 (cased) : DDC 712.609421 20
NYPL [3-MSK+ 90-11162]

GARDENS - FRANCE - CAGNES-SUR-MER.
Fell, Derek. Renoir's garden /. New York , c1991. p. cm. ISBN 0-671-74444-5 DDC 759.4 20
ND553.R45 F415 1991

GARDENS - FRANCE - DESIGN - HISTORY - 17TH CENTURY - EXHIBITONS.
Bibliothèque nationale (France) Le Notre et l'art des jardins. Paris , 1964. 62 p. :
NYPL [3-MSCC 91-517]

GARDENS - FRANCE - VERSAILLES.
Pérouse de Montclos, Jean-Marie. [Versailles. English.] Versailles /. New York , 1991. p. cm. ISBN 1-558-59228-8 DDC 725/.17/0944366 20
NA7736.V5 P4713 1991

GARDENS - FRANCE - YERRES.
Wittmer, Pierre. Caillebotte au jardin . Saint-Rémy-en-l'Eau , c1990. 344 p. : ISBN 2-903824-15-0 DDC 759.4 20
ND553.C243 W58 1990

Wittmer, Pierre. [Caillebotte au jardin. English.] Caillebotte and the garden at Yerres /. New York , 1991. p. cm. ISBN 0-8109-3167-2 (cloth) DDC 759.4 20
ND553.C243 W5813 1991

GARDENS, FRENCH - FRANCE - VILLANDRY - PICTORIAL WORKS.
Fleurent, Maurice. Villandry . Paris , c1989. 105 p. : ISBN 2-85889-052-1
NYPL [3-MSK 91-3221]

GARDENS - HISTORY.
Garden styles . London , c1989. 192 p. : ISBN 1-87130-778-3 *NYPL [3-MSC 90-8787]*

GARDENS IN ART.
Bumpus, Judith. Impressionist gardens /. Oxford , 1990. 80 p. : ISBN 0-7148-2660-X : DDC 759.054 20
ND192.I4 *NYPL [3-MCN+ 90-13280]*

GARDENS, ITALIAN.
De' Medici Stucchi, Lorenza, 1926- The
Renaissance of Italian gardens /. London ,
1990. 192 p. : ISBN 1-85145-392-X : DDC
712.60945 20
SB466.I8   *NYPL [3-MSK 91-3348]*

GARDENS, ITALIAN - PICTORIAL WORKS.
De' Medici Stucchi, Lorenza, 1926- The
Renaissance of Italian gardens /. London ,
1990. 192 p. : ISBN 1-85145-392-X : DDC
712.60945 20
SB466.I8   *NYPL [3-MSK 91-3348]*

GARDENS - ITALY.
De' Medici Stucchi, Lorenza, 1926- The
Renaissance of Italian gardens /. London ,
1990. 192 p. : ISBN 1-85145-392-X : DDC
712.60945 20
SB466.I8   *NYPL [3-MSK 91-3348]*

GARDENS - ITALY - PICTORIAL WORKS.
De' Medici Stucchi, Lorenza, 1926- The
Renaissance of Italian gardens /. London ,
1990. 192 p. : ISBN 1-85145-392-X : DDC
712.60945 20
SB466.I8   *NYPL [3-MSK 91-3348]*

GARDENS - JAPAN - HISTORY.
Hennig, Karl. Der Karesansui-Garten als
Ausdruck der Kultur der Muromachi-Zeit /.
Hamburg , 1982. vi, 412 p. :
          NYPL [3-MSK 90-6887]

GARDENS - NEW YORK (N.Y.)
Harrison, Marina, 1939- Artwalks in New
York . New York , 1991. p. cm. ISBN
0-935576-40-1 DDC 709/.747/1 20
N8845.N7 H3 1991

The gardens of Roberto Burle Marx /. Eliovson,
Sima. New York , c1991. 237 p. : ISBN
0-8109-3357-8 DDC 712/.092 B 20
SB470.B87 E45 1991
          NYPL [3-MSCC 91-6489]

The gardens of Tuscany /. Clarke, Ethne.
London , 1990. 160 p. : ISBN 0-297-83044-9 :
          NYPL [3-MSK 91-3390]

GARDENS - RELIGIOUS ASPECTS.
The Meaning of gardens . Cambridge, Mass. ,
c1990. ix, 283 p. : ISBN 0-262-06127-9 DDC
712 20
SB470.7 .M43 1990
          NYPL [3-MSC 90-11705]

**GARDENS, RENAISSANCE - FRANCE -
VILLANDRY - PICTORIAL WORKS.**
Fleurent, Maurice. Villandry . Paris , c1989.
105 p. : ISBN 2-85889-052-1
          NYPL [3-MSK 91-3221]

GARDENS, RENAISSANCE - ITALY.
De' Medici Stucchi, Lorenza, 1926- The
Renaissance of Italian gardens /. London ,
1990. 192 p. : ISBN 1-85145-392-X : DDC
712.60945 20
SB466.I8   *NYPL [3-MSK 91-3348]*

**GARDENS, RENAISSANCE - ITALY -
PICTORIAL WORKS.**
De' Medici Stucchi, Lorenza, 1926- The
Renaissance of Italian gardens /. London ,
1990. 192 p. : ISBN 1-85145-392-X : DDC
712.60945 20
SB466.I8   *NYPL [3-MSK 91-3348]*

GARDENS - SCOTLAND.
Buxbaum, Tim. Scottish garden buildings .
Edinburgh , 1988. 192 p. : ISBN 1-85158-113-8 :
DDC 717 19   *NYPL [3-MSK 90-11993]*

GARDENS - SOCIAL ASPECTS.
The Meaning of gardens . Cambridge, Mass. ,
c1990. ix, 283 p. : ISBN 0-262-06127-9 DDC
712 20
SB470.7 .M43 1990
          NYPL [3-MSC 90-11705]

GARDENS - SYMBOLIC ASPECTS.
The Meaning of gardens . Cambridge, Mass. ,
c1990. ix, 283 p. : ISBN 0-262-06127-9 DDC
712 20
SB470.7 .M43 1990
          NYPL [3-MSC 90-11705]

GARDENS - TUSCANY REGION.
Clarke, Ethne. The gardens of Tuscany /.
London , 1990. 160 p. : ISBN 0-297-83044-9 :
          NYPL [3-MSK 91-3390]

GARDENS - TUSCANY REGION - HISTORY.
Clarke, Ethne. The gardens of Tuscany /.
London , 1990. 160 p. : ISBN 0-297-83044-9 :
          NYPL [3-MSK 91-3390]

GARDENS - UNITED STATES.
Oehme, Wolfgang, 1930- Bold romantic
gardens . Reston, Va. , 1990. 310 p. : ISBN
0-87491-950-9 : DDC 712/.0973 20
SB473 .O44 1990   NYPL [3-MSK+ 91-4459]

Gardner, Donald. De Verboden Stad .
Rotterdam , New York, NY , c1990. 245 p. :
ISBN 90-6918-065-0
          NYPL [3-MAG 91-6651]

Gardner, Helen.
[Art through the ages]
Gardner's art through the ages. 9th ed. /
Horst de la Croix, Richard G. Tansey, Diane
Kirkpatrick. San Diego : Harcourt Brace
Jovanovich, c1991. xvi, 1135 p. : ill. (some
col.) ; 29 cm. Includes bibliographical references
(p. 1107-1117) and index. ISBN 0-15-503769-2
*1. Art - History. I. De La Croix, Horst. II. Tansey,
Richard G. III. Kirkpatrick, Diane. IV. Title.*
          NYPL [MAD 91-4710]

Gardner's art through the ages. Gardner, Helen.
[Art through the ages.] San Diego , c1991. xvi,
1135 p. : ISBN 0-15-503769-2
          NYPL [MAD 91-4710]

Garduño, Blanca. Los Zapatas de Diego Rivera /.
Ciudad de México , Cuernavaca, Morelos ,
1989. 117 p., [2] folded leaves of plates : ISBN
968-292-333-6 DDC 760/.092 20
N6559.R58 Z37 1989
          NYPL [3-MCZ R62 91-4245]

Garet, Jedd, 1955-
Jedd Garet : [exhibition]. New York : Robert
Miller Gallery, [1981] [43] p. : ill. (1 col.) ; 23
cm. "Published to accompany and exhibition at the
Robert Miller Gallery from March 24 to April 11,
1981"--T.p. verso.
*1. Garet, Jedd, 1955- - Exhibitions. I. Robert Miller
Gallery. II. Title.   NYPL [3-MCX G229 91-849]*

GARET, JEDD, 1955- - EXHIBITIONS.
Garet, Jedd, 1955- Jedd Garet . New York
[1981] [43] p. :
          NYPL [3-MCX G229 91-849]

Garey, Carol Cooper. House beautiful decorating
style / by the editors of House beautiful. New
York : Hearst Books, 1991. p. cm. Author: Carol
Cooper Garey. ISBN 0-688-09734-0 : DDC 747.213
20
*1. Interior decoration - Handbooks, manuals, etc. I.
House beautiful. II. Title. III. Title: Decorating style.*
NK2115 .G25 1991

Garff, Jan. Rubens Cantoor : the drawings of
Willem Panneels : a critical catalogue / by Jan
Garff and Eva de la Fuente Pedersen ; with an
introduction by Jan Garff ; [translation by
Ernest Dupont]. Copenhagen : Royal Museum
of Fine Arts, 1988. 2 v. : ill. ; 20 cm. At head of
title: Department of Prints and Drawings. Published in
connection with an exhibition titled "Christian IV and
Europe", held March 30-Sept. 25, 1988. Includes
bibliographical references (v. 1, p. 193-197) and index.
ISBN 87-87273-88-8 (set)
*1. Panneels, Willem, b.1600? - Catalogues raisonnés. I.
Pedersen, Eva de la Fuente. II. Panneels, Willem, b.
1600?. III. Kongelige Kobberstiksamling (Statens
museum for kunst). IV. Title.*
NC266.P36 A4 1988

Garfias, Hernán.
Antúnez, Nemesio. Carta aérea /. Santiago de
Chile , 1988. 65 p. : DDC 759.983 20
ND369.A58 A4 1988

Jurado, María Cristina. Zañartu /. Santiago ,
1989. 64 p. :
          NYPL [3-MCZ+ Z449 90-12332]

Garfinkel, Martin. Sturgis, South Dakota :
motorcycle mecca / photographs & text by
Martin Garfinkel.1st ed. Carbondale, Colo. :
ZG Pub. Co., c1990. [160] p. : chiefly ill. ; 28
cm. Spine title: Sturgis motorcylce mecca. ISBN
1-87862-701-5 (softcover)
*1. Motorcyclists - United States - Pictorial works. 2.
Sturgis (S.D.) - Description - Views. I. Title. II. Title:
Sturgis motorcycle mecca.*
          NYPL [MFX (Garfinkel) 91-3583]

Gargerle, Christian. Nitsch, Hermann, 1938-
[Works. 1986.] Gesamtverzeichnis der Malerei
und Grafik /. Wien , c1986. v. : ISBN

3-85449-011-9 (Bd. 1) DDC 760/.092/4 19
N6811.5.N58 A4 1986
          NYPL [3-MCK N772 90-11453]

Gargiani, Roberto, 1956- Fanelli, Giovanni. Perret
e Le Corbusier . Roma , 1990. 255 p. : ISBN
88-420-3596-3 :
NA1048.5.F85 F36 1990

Gari Melchers . Melchers, Gari, 1860-1932. St.
Petersburg, Fla. , c1990. 239 p. : ISBN
1-87839-000-7
          NYPL [3-MCX+ M51 90-12354]

Garín Ortiz de Taranco, Felipe María. La visión
de España de Sorolla, por Felipe M.a Garín.
[Valencia] Diputación Provincial de Valencia
[1965] 44 p. illus. (part col.), port. 32 cm.
*1. Sorolla, Joaquín, 1863-1923 - Criticism and
interpretation. 2. Spain in art. I. Sorolla, Joaquín,
1863-1923. II. Title.*
ND813.S7 G3
          NYPL [3-MCQ+ S71 88-5170]

Garland publications in the fine arts.
Daftari, Fereshteh. The influence of Persian art
on Gauguin, Matisse, and Kandinsky /. New
York , 1991. p. cm. ISBN 0-8153-0715-2 (alk.
paper) DDC 709/.2/24 20
N7280 .D34 1991

Garms, Jörg. Skulptur und Grabmal des
Spätmittelalters in Rom und Italien . Wien ,
1990. 464 p[.], [212] p. of plates : ISBN
3-7001-1717-5
          NYPL [3-MRIF+ 90-13377]

Garner, John S., 1945- The Midwest in American
architecture /. Urbana , c1991. xv, 259 p., [1]
p. of plates : ISBN 0-252-01743-9 (alk. paper)
DDC 720/.977 20
NA722 .M53 1991
          NYPL [3-MQWO 91-6382]

Garner, Lawrence. The buildings of Shropshire /
Lawrence Garner. Shrewsbury, England : Swan
Hill Press, <1989- > v. <2 > : ill. ; 22 cm.
Includes bibliographical references (v. 2, p. 94).
CONTENTS. - -- v. 2. The Tudor and Stuart legacy,
1530-1730. ISBN 1-85310-091-9 (v. 2) : DDC
720/.9424/5 20
1. Architecture - England - Shropshire. I. Title.
NA969.S3 G37 1989

Garneret, Jean. La maison du montagnon / Jean
Garneret, Pierre Bourgin, Bernard Guillaume.
2e éd. Besançon : Folklore comtois, 1981. 557
p., [2] p. of plates : ill. ; 30 cm. (Maisons
paysannes en Franche-Comté . t. 1) Includes index.
Bibliography: p. 551-552. DDC 728/.67/094445 s
728/.67/094445 19
*1. Farmhouses - Jura Mountain Region (France and
Switzerland). 2. Farmhouses - France - Franche-Comté.
3. Vernacular architecture - Jura Mountain Region
(France and Switzerland). 4. Vernacular architecture -
France - Franche-Comté. I. Bourgin, Pierre. II.
Guillaume, Bernard. III. Title. IV. Series.*
NA8208.52.F8 M34 1981, t. 1
          NYPL [3-MQWF 90-5444]

Garnier, Charles, 1825-1898.
Le théâtre / Charles Garnier ; précédé de
Garnier et la mise en place des corps par
Georges Banu ; Garnier, esquisse d'une
biographie par Martine Kahane. 1re éd. Arles :
Actes sud, c1990. 254 p. ; 22 cm. (Le Temps du
théâtre) A reprint of the 1871 ed. published by
Hachette from which the chapters having to do with
the technology of the time have been omitted. ISBN
2-86869-530-2 DDC 725/.822 20
*1. Theater architecture. I. Banu, Georges. II. Kahane,
Martine. III. Title. IV. Series.*
NA6821 .G3 1990

**GARNIER, CHARLES, 1825-1898 -
CRITICISM AND INTERPRETATION.**
Mead, Christopher Curtis. Charles Garnier's
Paris Opéra . New York, N.Y. , Cambridge,
Mass. , c1991. p. cm. ISBN 0-262-13275-3 DDC
725/.822/092 20
NA6840.F72 P379 1991

**GARNIER, CHARLES, 1825-1898 -
EXHIBITIONS.**
L'Opéra de Monte-Carlo au temps du Prince
Albert Ier de Monaco /. Paris , c1990. 72 p. :
ISBN 2-7118-2321-0
          NYPL [3-MQW 91-7009]

Garnier, Jacques. Faïences révolutionnaires .
Paris , Rouen , 1989. 76 p. :
          NYPL [3-MPGG+ 90-71]

Garnier, Tony, 1869-1948.
Tony Garnier, l'œuvre complète /. Paris ,
c1989. 254 p. : ISBN 2-85850-527-6 DDC
720/.92 20
NA1053.G37 A4 1989

**GARNIER, TONY, 1869-1948 -
EXHIBITIONS.**
Tony Garnier, l'œuvre complète /. Paris ,
c1989. 254 p. : ISBN 2-85850-527-6 DDC
720/.92 20
NA1053.G37 A4 1989

Garnock, Jamie. Plumptre, George. Garden
ornament . [London] , c1989. 256 p. : ISBN
0-500-01477-9 **NYPL [3-MSF+ 89-26932]**

Garofalo, Francesco. Adalberto Libera. English.
Adalberto Libera /. New York, N.Y. , c1991. p.
cm. ISBN 1-87827-114-8 : DDC 720/.92 20
NA1123.L46 A4 1991

Garrard, Rose.
Rose Garrard : between ourselves. Birmingham
[England] : Ikon Gallery, [1983?] 32 p. : ill.
(some col.) ; 27 cm. Catalog of an exhibition held at
the Ikon Gallery, Birmingham, Jan. 18-Feb. 18, 1984,
and at other locations.
*1. Garrard, Rose - Exhibitions. 2. Feminism and art -
Exhibitions. I. Ikon Gallery. II. Title. III. Title: Between
ourselves.*
N6797.G37 I5 1983
NYPL [3-MGO (Garrard) 90-10680]

GARRARD, ROSE - EXHIBITIONS.
Garrard, Rose. Rose Garrard . Birmingham
[England] [1983?] 32 p. :
N6797.G37 I5 1983
NYPL [3-MGO (Garrard) 90-10680]

Garrett, Wendell. Neo-classicism in America .
New York, N.Y. , c1991. 136 p. : ISBN
0-915057-41-7 **NYPL [3-MAMT 91-7337]**

Garrido, Felipe. Herrán, Saturnino, 1887-1918.
Saturnino Herrán /. México , 1988. 143 p. :
ISBN 968-665-809-2 DDC 759.972 20
N6559.H47 A4 1988

Garrido, Luis, 1898- Herrán, Saturnino,
1887-1918. Saturnino Herrán /. México , 1988
143 p. : ISBN 968-665-809-2
NYPL [3-MCZ++ H564 89-26935]

Garriga, Joseph Grau- see **Grau-Garriga, Josep,
1929-**

Garrigou, Marcel. La culture, richesse de
l'entreprise : ces murs qu'on abat ... / Marcel
Garrigou ; préface de Jean Matteoli ;
témoignages de Francis Ballagna ... [et al.].
[Paris] : Aubier, c1990. 272 p. ; 22 cm. Includes
bibliographical references (p. [260]-263). ISBN
2-7007-2836-X :
*1. Arts - Economic aspects - France. 2. Art patronage -
France. 3. Arts - Economic aspects. 4. Art patronage. I.
Ballagna, Francis. II. Title.*
NX634 .G37 1990

Garrison, G. Richard (George Richard), 1898-
[Mexican houses]
Early Mexican houses : a book of
photographs & measured drawings / by G.
Richard Garrison and George W. Rustay ;
with a new preface by David Gebhard.
Stamford, Conn. : Architectural Book Pub.
Co., 1990. xvii, 173 p. : ill. ; 31 cm. Previously
published as: Mexican houses. c1930. Includes
bibliographical references. ISBN 0-942655-03-0 :
DDC 728/.0972 20
*1. Architecture, Domestic - Mexico. 2. Architecture,
Spanish colonial - Mexico. I. Rustay, George W.
(George Warren), 1902-. II. Title.*
NA7244 .G3 1990
NYPL [3-MQWN+ 91-4465]

Garruba, Caio. Russian revolutionary posters,
1917-1929 /. New York , c1967. [14] p. :
NYPL [3-MDW 90-4813]

Gärtner, Martin. Sergius Ruegenberg : eine
Monographie : Bauten und Entwürfe zur
Berliner Architektur seit 1925 / Martin
Gärtner. Berlin : Mann, c1990. 115 p. : 55 ill. ;
26 cm. Cover subtitle: Bauten und Pläne seit 1925.
Originally presented as the author's
thesis--Philipps-Universität, Marburg, 1988. Includes
bibliographical references (p. 109-111). Includes index.
ISBN 3-7861-1581-8 DDC 720/.92 20
*1. Ruegenberg, Sergius, 1903- - Criticism and
interpretation. 2. Architecture, Modern - 20th century -
Germany. I. Ruegenberg, Sergius, 1903-. II. Title.*
NA1088.R83 G37 1990

G'arts. Guid'arts . Nice [1989] 174 p. : ISBN
2-87720-040-X :
N6485.3 .G85 1989

Garver, Thomas H. Joseph Raffael . [San
Francisco] , c1978. 64 p. :
N6537.R23 A4 1978
NYPL [3-MCX+ R136 79-2011]

Garwer, Cornelia. Sammlung Köhler-Osbahr /.
Duisburg , c1990- v. <1 > : ISBN
3-923576-75-7
N5267.K64 S26 1990

Gary Bukovnik watercolors & monotypes.
Bukovnik, Gary, 1947- Flowers . New York ,
1990. 119 p. : ISBN 0-8109-3105-2 DDC
760/.092 20
N6537.B835 A4 1990
NYPL [3-MCX B924 90-11081]

GAS FIELDS - TEXAS - MAPS.
Atlas of major Texas gas reservoirs /. Chicago,
Ill. , Austin, Tex. , 1989. 1 atlas (ix, 161 p.) :
NYPL [Map Div. 90-11657]

Gas Research Institute. Atlas of major Texas gas
reservoirs /. Chicago, Ill. , Austin, Tex. , 1989.
1 atlas (ix, 161 p.) :
NYPL [Map Div. 90-11657]

GAS RESERVOIRS - TEXAS - MAPS.
Atlas of major Texas gas reservoirs /. Chicago,
Ill. , Austin, Tex. , 1989. 1 atlas (ix, 161 p.) :
NYPL [Map Div. 90-11657]

Gasaitéar na hÉireann : ainmneacha ionad daonra
agus gnéithe aiceanta / arna ullmhú ag Brainse
Logainmneacha na Suirhéireachta Ordanáis =
Gazetteer of Ireland : names of centres of
population and physical features / prepared by
the Placenames Branch of the Ordnance
Survey. Baile Atha Cliath : Oifig an tSoláthair,
1989. xxxiv, 283 p. : ill., 2 maps ; 21 cm.
English and Irish. ISBN 0-7076-0076-6
*1. Names, Geographical - Ireland. 2. Ireland -
Gazetteers. I. Ireland. Placenames Branch. II. Title:
Gazetteer of Ireland.*
NYPL [Map Div. 91-3800]

Gasca, Luis. Tebeo y cultura de masas. Prólogo
del Dr. Juan J. López Ibor. Madrid, Editorial
Prensa Española, 1966. 249 p. illus. 19 cm.
(Colección "Vislumbres". 2) Includes bibliographical
references.
*1. Comic books, strips, etc. - History and criticism. I.
Title.*
NC1355 .G36 **NYPL [MDY 91-418]**

Gasco Sidro, Antonio J. (Antonio José) El
escultor Ortells : apuntes para una biografía /
Antonio J. Gasco Sidro, Ma. Teresa Vives
Agost. [Castelló] : Diputació de Castelló, 1989.
191 p. : ill. ; 21 cm. (Col·lecció universitària.
Geografia e historia . 16) Includes bibliographical
references. ISBN 84-86895-11-1 DDC 730/.92 B 20
*1. Ortells i López, Josep, 1887-1961. 2. Sculptors -
Spain - Biography. I. Vives Agost, Ma. Teresa (María
Teresa). II. Title. III. Series.*
NB813.O697 G37 1989

Gaspar Gallery, Barcelona. see **Sala Gaspar.**

Gasparri, Carlo. Ajello, Raffaele. Classicismo
d'età Romana . Napoli , c1988. 203 p. : ISBN
88-7042-955-5
NYPL [3-MGH+ 90-10570]

Gassen, Richard W. Wilhelm-Hack-Museum.
Graphik des Expressionismus aus den
Beständen des Museums /. Ludwigshafen am
Rhein , c1989. 130 p. : DDC
769.94/09/07443435 20
NE625 .W54 1989

GASSER, MARTIN, 1955- - EXHIBITIONS.
Installation, Klangraum, Musik . [St. Gallen]
[1983] [29] p. : **NYPL [3-MAL 90-12516]**

GASSER, ULRICH, 1950- - EXHIBITIONS.
Installation, Klangraum, Musik . [St. Gallen]
[1983] [29] p. : **NYPL [3-MAL 90-12516]**

Gassier, Pierre.
[Goya. English]
Goya / Pierre Gassier. New York :
Skira/Rizzoli, 1989. 129 p. : ill. (chiefly
col.) ; 28 cm. Translation of: Goya. Originally
published: 1955. ISBN 0-8478-1108-5 DDC
760/.092 B 20
*1. Goya, Francisco, 1746-1828. 2. Artists - Spain -
Biography. I. Title.*
N7113.G68 G3713 1989
NYPL [3-MCQ 91-2506]

Gassner, Hubertus, 1950- Klutsis, Gustav
Gustavovich, 1895-1944. Gustav Klucis .
Stuttgart , c1991. 395 p. : ISBN 3-7757-0327-6
NYPL [3-MCZ K6585 91-7281]

Gastaldi, Andrea, 1826-1889.
Maggio Serra, Rosanna. Andrea Gastaldi,
1826-1889 . Torino , c1988. 232 p. : ISBN
88-422-0169-3 : DDC 759.5 20
N6923.G365 A4 1988
NYPL [3-MCF+ G253 90-10922]

**GASTALDI, ANDREA, 1826-1889 -
CATALOGS.**
Maggio Serra, Rosanna. Andrea Gastaldi,
1826-1889 . Torino , c1988. 232 p. : ISBN
88-422-0169-3 : DDC 759.5 20
N6923.G365 A4 1988
NYPL [3-MCF+ G253 90-10922]

Gastão, Marques, 1914- Encontros com António
Duarte / Marques Gastão. [Lisbon, Portugal] :
Impr. Nacional-Casa da Moeda, [1989] 128 p. :
ill. ; 24 cm. (Colecção Arte e artistas) DDC
730/.92 20
*1. Duarte, António - Criticism and interpretation. I.
Duarte, António. II. Title. III. Series.*
NB833.D8 G37 1989

Gasteig Betriebsgesellschaft. Pariser Opern- und
Konzerthäuser . Tübingen , c1989. 71 p. :
ISBN 3-8030-0149-8
NA6840.F72 P3736 1989

Gaston, Mary Frank. Blue willow / Mary Frank
Gaston. Rev. 2nd ed. Paducah, Ky. : Collector
Books, c1990. 191 p. : ill. (some col.) ; 28 cm.
"Price guide": p. 189-191. Includes indexes. Includes
bibliographical references (p. 182-183). ISBN
0-89145-396-2 : DDC 738 20
*1. Willowware - Collectors and collecting - Catalogs. I.
Title.*
NK4277 .G37 1990
NYPL [3-MPK 90-12474]

Gatbonton, Esperanza Bunag. A heritage of saints
/ Esperanza Bunag Gatbonton. Manila :
Editorial Associates, 1979. xii, 195 p. : ill.
(some col.) ; 29 cm. Bibliography: p. [186]-190.
1. Santos (Art) - Philippines. I. Title.
MLCM 81/1350 **NYPL [3-MOC 89-5146]**

Gately, George.
[Heathcliff. Selections]
Heathcliff thinks big / by Geo. Gately. Jove
trade pbk. ed. New York : Jove Books, 1990.
1 v. (unpaged) : chiefly ill. ; 14 x 21 cm.
Selections from the comic strip Heathcliff. ISBN
0-515-10431-0 : DDC 741.5/973 20
1. American wit and humor, Pictorial. I. Title.
NC1429.G3 A4 1990

GATES - ITALY - MILAN - HISTORY.
Pifferi, Enzo, 1940- Milano, le porte : la storia
di Milano attraverso le porte /. Como , c1989.
137 p. : DDC 945/.21 20
DG664 .P54 1989
NYPL [3-MQWB+ 91-4912]

Gathered visions . Hall, Robert L., 1950-
Washington, D.C. , c1991. 86 p. ISBN 1-560-98106-7
(pbk.) : DDC 704/.042/09753074753 20
N6538.N5 H26 1991

Gathie Falk /. Lind, Jane. Vancouver , c1989. 40
p. : ISBN 0-88894-815-8 : DDC 704/.042 20
NYPL [3-MAL 90-12811]

Gatine, Georges Jacques, b. 1773. La Mésangère,
Pierre de, 1761-1831. Costumes des femmes
françaises du XIIe au XVIIIe siècle /. Paris ,
1900. [5] leaves, [70] col. leaves of plates :
NYPL [3-MML+ 84-1125]

Gatodo Gallery. Kawara, On. On Kawara .
Tokyo , c1986. [36] p. :
NYPL [3-MCZ K221 89-25604]

Gatodo Gallery (Tokyo, Japan) Seven boxes by
Joseph Cornell. [Tokyo] , c1978. 41 p. :
NYPL [3-MGO (Cornell) 88-4763]

Gatrell, Anthony. Dictionary of floristry and
flower arranging / Anthony Gatrell ;
illustrations by the author. London : Batsford,
1988. 184 p., [2] p. of plates : ill. ; 22 cm.
(Batsford vocational handbooks) ISBN
0-7134-5904-2 :
1. Flower arrangement - Dictionaries. I. Title. II. Series.
NYPL [MLT 90-12341]

Gatti Perer, Maria Luisa. Dal monastero di S.
Ambrogio all'Università Cattolica /. Milano ,

1990. 301 p. : ISBN 88-343-3007-2
IN PROCESS (ONLINE)
NYPL [3-MRBD+ 91-5237]

Gattiker, Nell, 1906- Nell Gattiker :
Werkverzeichnis, Auswahl 1950-1980 : Bilder,
Antiklas-Kompositionen, Plastiken /
[Mitarbeiter, Antiklas, H.R. Suess-Naegeli,
Bronze, Ernst Matt, Metall, K. Diem und H.
Haug]. [Zürich : N. Gattiker, 1982?] 54 p. :
chiefly ill. (some col.) ; 23 cm. DDC 709/.2/4
19
*1. Gattiker, Nell, 1906-. I. Title. II. Title:
Werkverzeichnis, Auswahl 1950-1980.*
N7153.G336 A4 1982
NYPL [3-MCZ G263 90-10825]

GATTIKER, NELL, 1906-
Gattiker, Nell, 1906- Nell Gattiker . [Zürich ,
1982?] 54 p. : DDC 709/.2/4 19
N7153.G336 A4 1982
NYPL [3-MCZ G263 90-10825]

Gattlen, Anton. Druckgrafische Ortsansichten des
Wallis 1548-1850 / Anton Gattlen.
[Switzerland] : Editions Gravures, 1987. 264 p.,
18 leaves of plates : ill. ; 25 x 29 cm.
*1. Valais (Switzerland) - Description and travel - Views.
I. Title.* **NYPL [MDZ 91-5819]**

Gaube du Gers, Olivier. Pinçon, Jean-Marie.
Odiot, l'orfèvre /. Paris , c1990. 217 p. : ISBN
2-85889-054-4 **NYPL [3-MNO+ 91-5777]**

Gaube du Gers, Olivier, 1948- Pinçon,
Jean-Marie. Odiot l'orfèvre /. Paris , c1990.
217 p. : ISBN 2-85889-054-4 : DDC
739.2/0944/361 20
NK7198.O35 P56 1990

Gaubert, Jean Claude. La Fantastique
contemporain . Paris , 1972. [126] p. :
NYPL [3-MAL 91-288]

Gaudens, Augustus Saint- see **Saint-Gaudens,
Augustus, 1848-1907.**

GAUDÍ, ANTONI, 1852-1926.
Jimeno, Oswaldo, 1928- La magia del muro .
Lima, Peru , 1973. 151 p. :
NYPL [3-MQV 91-819]

Masini, Lara Vinca. [Antonia Gaudí. English.]
Gaudí [translated from the Italian]. London,
New York, 1970. 96 p. ISBN 0-600-33811-5
DDC 720/.92
NA1313.G3 M3213

El Palau Güell /. [Barcelona] , 1990. 230 p. :
ISBN 84-7794-130-0
NYPL [3-MQZ+ (Gaudí) 91-5154]

**GAUDÍ, ANTONI, 1852-1926 - CRITICISM
AND INTERPRETATION.**
Gaudí i el seu temps /. Barcelona , 1990. 255
p. ; ISBN 84-7533-567-5
NA1313.G3 G39 1990

Gaudí i el seu temps / Juan José Lahuerta (ed.).
1. ed. Barcelona : Barcanova, 1990. 255 p. ; 21
cm. (Els Llibres de l'Institut d'Humanitats. Estudis . 2)
Includes bibliographical references. ISBN
84-7533-567-5
*1. Gaudí, Antoni, 1852-1926 - Criticism and
interpretation. 2. Architecture, Modern - 19th century -
Spain - Catalonia. 3. Architecture, Modern - 20th
century - Spain - Catalonia. 4. Catalonia (Spain) -
Intellectual life - 19th century. 5. Catalonia (Spain) -
Intellectual life - 20th century. I. Lahuerta, Juan José,
1945-. II. Series.*
NA1313.G3 G39 1990

Gaudí [translated from the Italian]. Masini, Lara
Vinca. [Antonia Gaudí. English.] London, New
York, 1970. 96 p. ISBN 0-600-33811-5 DDC
720/.92
NA1313.G3 M3213

Gaudibert, Pierre. Ipoustéguy / texte de Pierre
Gaudibert ; conversation avec Évelyne Artaud ;
les portraits de Michel Chassat. Paris : Editions
Cercle d'art, c1989. 204 p. : ill. (some col.) ; 33
cm. (Grands peintres et sculpteurs, 0750-5922)
Bibliography: p. 198-199. ISBN 2-7022-0246-2
*1. Ipoustéguy, Jean, 1920-. I. Artaud, Evelyne. II.
Ipoustéguy, Jean, 1920-. III. Chassat, Michel. III.
Chassat, Michel. III. Ipoustéguy, Jean, 1920-. IV. Title.*
NYPL [3-MGO+ (Ipoustéguy) 91-3898]

Gauditz, Peter. Bilder aus der Bundesrepublik .
Hannover , c1982. [92] p. :
NYPL [MFW 84-1657]

Gaudy Dutch and Welsh. Shuman, John A. The
collector's encyclopedia of Gaudy Dutch and
Welsh /. [Paducah, KY] (P.O. Box 300,

Paducah 42002-3009) [c1991] 175 p. : DDC
738.3/0942/0973 20
NK4340.G38 S5 1991

**GAUDY WARE - COLLECTORS AND
COLLECTING.**
Shuman, John A. The collector's encyclopedia
of Gaudy Dutch and Welsh /. [Paducah, KY]
(P.O. Box 300, Paducah 42002-3009) [c1991]
175 p. : DDC 738.3/0942/0973 20
NK4340.G38 S5 1991

GAUDY WARE - UNITED STATES.
Shuman, John A. The collector's encyclopedia
of Gaudy Dutch and Welsh /. [Paducah, KY]
(P.O. Box 300, Paducah 42002-3009) [c1991]
175 p. : DDC 738.3/0942/0973 20
NK4340.G38 S5 1991

Gaugh, Harry F. Henning, Anton, 1964- Anton
Henning, new work . Norman, Okla. [1990] 1
v. (unpaged) :
NYPL [3-MCK H5166 91-4640]

Gauguin /. Estienne, Charles. [Paris] [1989?] 157
p. : ISBN 2-09-284699-X
NYPL [3-MCO+ G26 89-28011]

Gauguin et ses amis à Pont-Aven /. Puget,
Catherine. Douarnenez , 1989. 113 p. : ISBN
2-903708-22-3
IN PROCESS (ONLINE)
NYPL [3-MAMI 91-6154]

Gauguin, Eugène Henry Paul. see **Gauguin, Paul,
1848-1903.**

Gauguin, Paul, 1848-1903.
Paul Gauguin : Musée de l'Ermitage, Musée
des beaux-arts Pouchkine / [rédacteur, Irina
Frechko]. Paris : Editions Cercle d'art, c1988.
186 p. : ill. (some col.) ; 35 cm. Title from
colophon: Pol´ Gogen v muzeiākh sovetskogo soiūza.
Includes bibliographical references (p. 186). ISBN
2-7022-0218-7 DDC 759.4 20
*1. Gauguin, Paul, 1848-1903 - Catalogs. 2.
Gosudarstvennyĭ Ėrmitazh (Soviet Union) - Catalogs. 3.
Gosudarstvennyĭ muzeĭ izobrazitel´nykh iskusstv imeni
A.S. Pushkina - Catalogs. I. Frechko, Irina. II.
Gosudarstvennyĭ Ėrmitazh (Soviet Union). III.
Gosudarstvennyĭ muzeĭ izobrazitel´nykh iskusstv imeni
A.S. Pushkina. IV. Title. V. Title: Pol´ Gogen v
muzeiākh sovetskogo soiūza.*
ND553.G27 A4 1988

GAUGUIN, PAUL, 1848-1903 - CATALOGS.
Gauguin, Paul, 1848-1903. Paul Gauguin .
Paris , c1988. 186 p. : ISBN 2-7022-0218-7
DDC 759.4 20
ND553.G27 A4 1988

**GAUGUIN, PAUL, 1848-1903 -
CORRESPONDENCE.**
Merlhès, Victor. Paul Gauguin et Vincent van
Gogh 1887-1888 . Taravao, Tahiti , 1989. 277
p., [3] folded leaves of plates : ISBN
2-907716-02-6 (pbk.)
NYPL [3-MCO G26 91-7602]

**GAUGUIN, PAUL, 1848-1903 - CRITICISM
AND INTERPRETATION.**
Daftari, Fereshteh. The influence of Persian art
on Gauguin, Matisse, and Kandinsky /. New
York , 1991. p. cm. ISBN 0-8153-0715-2 (alk.
paper) DDC 709/.2/24 20
N7280 .D34 1991

Estienne, Charles. Gauguin /. [Paris] [1989?]
157 p. : ISBN 2-09-284699-X
NYPL [3-MCO+ G26 89-28011]

Gauss, Ulrike. Baumeister, Willi, 1889-1955. Willi
Baumeister . Stuttgart [1989?] 275 p. : ISBN
3-89322-130-1
NYPL [3-MCK+ B35 89-21287]

Gaustad, Randi, 1942- Samtidskeramikk : norsk
keramikk fra 1940 til i dag / Randi Gaustad,
Gunnar Danbolt. Oslo : Dreyer, c1990. 127 p. :
ill. (some col.) ; 29 cm. ISBN 82-09-10613-9
*1. Pottery, Norwegian. 2. Pottery - 20th century -
Norway. 3. Ceramic sculpture - 20th century - Norway.
I. Danbolt, Gunnar. II. Title. III. Title: Norsk keramikk
fra 1940 til i dag.*
NK4119 .G38 1990

GAUTAMA BUDDHA - ART.
Fickle, Dorothy H. Images of the Buddha in
Thailand /. Singapore , New York , 1989. ix,
86 p. : ISBN 0-19-588920-7 (U. S.) DDC
704.9/4894363/09593 20
NB1912.G38 F53 1989

Kānsāng Phraphutthawachiramongkut .

[Bangkok] [2511 i.e. 1968] 44 p. :
NK7978.7.A1 K36 1968

Nehru, Lolita. Origins of the Gandhāran style .
Delhi , New York , 1989. xxii, 230 p. : ISBN
0-19-562472-6 (U. S.) DDC 732/.44 20
NB1912.G38 N44 1989

Pramūan phāp pratimā =. [Bangkok , 2508 i.e.
1965] 4, 43, 3, 42 p., 100 leaves of plates :
NB1912.G38 P7 1965

GAUTAMA BUDDHA - ICONOGRAPHY.
Bhattacharyya, Benoytosh, 1897-1964. The
Indian Buddhist iconography. Calcutta [1968]
xxxiii, 478 p. **NYPL [3-MAF 75-368]**

Gauthier, Ninon. Gagnon, Carolle. Marcel
Barbeau . [Canada] , c1990. 243 p. : ISBN
2-9802034-5-9 (prestige ed.)
NYPL [3-MCZ+ B233 91-7596]

Gauthron, Bernard. Boucheix, F. (François) Le
rêve et la lumière . Craponne-sur-Arzon, France
[1991?] 207 p. : ISBN 2-907858-00-9 DDC 759.4
20
ND553.B698 A4 1991

Gavazza, Ezia. Lo spazio dipinto : il grande
affresco genovese nel '600 / Ezia Gavazza.
Genova : Sagep, c1989. 406 p. : ill. (some
col.) ; 28 cm. "Collana di strada nuova"--Jacket.
Includes bibliographical references (p. 389-396) and
indexes. ISBN 88-7058-334-1 : DDC
751.7/3/094518209032 20
*1. Mural painting and decoration, Italian - Italy -
Genoa. 2. Mural painting - 17th century - Italy -
Genoa. I. Title.*
ND2757.G46 G39 1989
NYPL [3-MBO 91-4982]

Gaveman, Aleksandr Vasil´evich, 1903- Soviet
Union. Glavnoe upravlenie geodezii i
kartografii. Atlas Kalininskoĭ oblasti /. Moskva ,
1964. 1 atlas ([8] p., 34 p. :
NYPL [Map Div. 91-1093]

**GAVINA, DINO - RELATIONS WITH
INDUSTRIAL DESIGNERS.**
Vercelloni, Virgilio. [Avventura del design,
Gavina. English.] The adventure of design .
New York , 1989. 220 p. : ISBN 0-8478-1039-9
DDC 749/.245 20
TS79 .V4713 1989
NYPL [3-MNE+ 90-12985]

Gaya, Ramón.
[Works. 1990]
Obra completa / Ramón Gaya. Valencia :
Pre-Textos, c1990- v. <1 > ; 20 cm.
(Pre-textos. 124-) Subseries from jacket. ISBN
84-87101-33-X (obra completa)
*1. Arts, Spanish. I. Series: Pre-textos. Letras hispánicas.
II. Title.*
NX440 .G3 1990

Gaynor, Elizabeth, 1946- Russian houses / by
Elizabeth Gaynor and Kari Haavisto ; with
essays by Darra Goldstein. New York :
Stewart, Tabori & Chang : Distributed in the U.
S. by Workman Pub., 1991. p. cm. Includes index.
ISBN 1-556-70163-2 (cloth) : DDC 728/.0947
20
*1. Architecture, Domestic - Russian S.F.S.R. - Themes,
motives. I. Haavisto, Kari. II. Goldstein, Darra. III.
Title.*
NA7367 .G3 1991

Gazda, Elaine K., 1943- Roman art in the private
sphere . Ann Arbor , c1991. 156 p. : ISBN
0-472-10196-X (alk. paper) DDC 747.2937 20
N5760 .R66 1991

Gazetteer of Ireland. Gasaitéar na hÉireann .
Baile Atha Cliath , 1989. xxxiv, 283 p. : ISBN
0-7076-0076-6 **NYPL [Map Div. 91-3800]**

Gazzera, Romano, 1906-1985. La rosa di Clarissa
/ Romano Gazzera. Milano : Mediolanum
editori associati, c1990. 279 p., [16] p. of
plates : ill. (some col.) ; 24 cm. ISBN
88-7712-078-9 :
*1. Gazzera, Romano, 1906-1985. 2. Artists - Italy -
Biography. I. Title.*
N6923.G394 A2 1990
NYPL [3-MCF G284 91-5003]

GAZZERA, ROMANO, 1906-1985.
Gazzera, Romano, 1906-1985. La rosa di
Clarissa . Milano , c1990. 279 p., [16] p. of
plates : ISBN 88-7712-078-9 :
N6923.G394 A2 1990
NYPL [3-MCF G284 91-5003]

Gebessler, August, 1929- Die Denkmalpflege als Plage und Frage . München , 1989. xii, 196 p. : ISBN 3-422-06037-5
NA109.G3 D446 1989

Gebouwd in Arnhem . Lavooij, Wim. Zutphen , c1990. 166 p. : ISBN 90-6011-684-4 :
NA1151.A76 L38 1990

GEBRÜDER THONET - EXHIBITIONS.
Sitz-Gelegenheiten . Nürnberg , c1989. 263 p. : ISBN 3-926982-13-6
IN PROCESS (ONLINE)
NYPL [3-MOF 91-6263]

Die Geburt Christi in der russischen Ikonenmalerei . Stichel, Rainer. Stuttgart , 1990. 176 p., 92 p. of plates : ISBN 3-515-04273-3
NYPL [3-MAIH+ 91-4218]

Das Gedächtnis der Ehren Albrecht Dürers /. Arend, Henrich Conrad. Unterschneidheim , 1978. [159] p. : ISBN 3-921503-53-1
NYPL [3-MCK D85 90-6660]

Gedeon, Lucinda H. Collaborations and connections . Tempe, Ariz. , c1990. viii, 36 p. :
NYPL [MDTT 91-4768]

Geer van Velde /. Viatte, Germain. [Paris] , c1989. 221 p. : ISBN 2-85117-104-6
NYPL [3-MCH+ V424 89-26499]

Gegenwart Ewigkeit. Schmied, Wieland, 1929- GegenwartEwigkeit . Stuttgart , c1990. 341 p. : ISBN 3-89322-179-4 : DDC 709/.04/5074431554 20
N6488.G3 S8565 1990

Gegenwart Museum .
([13]) Berlinische Galerie. Berliner Kunststücke /. Stuttgart [1990] 459 p. : ISBN 3-89322-176-X
N6868 .B44 1990

Höch, Hannah, 1889- Hannah Höch 1889-1978 . [Berlin] , 1989. 223, [24] p. : ISBN 3-87024-156-X (Argon)
NYPL [3-MCK H691 90-12356]

Missmann, Max, ca. 1870-1948. Max Missmann . Berlin , 1989. 75 p. :
NYPL [MFX (Missmann) 91-2390]

GegenwartEwigkeit . Schmied, Wieland, 1929- Stuttgart , c1990. 341 p. : ISBN 3-89322-179-4 : DDC 709/.04/5074431554 20
N6488.G3 S8565 1990

Geheime Staatspolizei. see Germany. Geheime Staatspolizei.

Gehring, Wes D. Laurel & Hardy : a bio-bibliography / Wes D. Gehring. New York : Greenwood Press, 1990. xvi, 307 p. : ill. ; 24 cm. (Popular culture bio-bibliographies, 0193-6891) Includes bibliographical references, discography, filmography, and index. ISBN 0-313-25172-X (lib. bdg. : alk. paper) DDC 791.43/028/0922 B 20
1. Laurel, Stan. 2. Hardy, Oliver, 1892-1957. 3. Laurel, Stan - Bibliography. 4. Hardy, Oliver, 1892-1957 - Bibliography. 5. Comedians - United States - Biography. 6. Motion picture actors and actresses - United States - Biography. I. Title. II. Title: Laurel and Hardy. III. Series.
PN2287.L285 G4 1990
NYPL [MMES (Laurel, DS.) 90-10877]

GEIGER, CONRAD, 1751-1808 - CATALOGS.
Schneider, Erich, Dr. Conrad Geiger . Nürnberg , 1990. 213 p. : ISBN 3-924461-09-0 : DDC 759.3 20
ND588.G33 A4 1990

Geiger, Rupprecht, 1908-
RupprechtGeiger : "Rot Form" Bilder : 20. Oktober bis 10. Dezember 1989, Kunstverein Braunschweig. Braunschweig : Der Kunstverein, [1989?] 118 p. ; 21 cm.
1. Geiger, Rupprecht, 1908- - Exhibitions. I. Title.
NYPL [3-MCK G311 90-12399]

GEIGER, RUPPRECHT, 1908- - EXHIBITIONS.
Geiger, Rupprecht, 1908- Rupprecht Geiger . Braunschweig [1989?] 118 p. ;
NYPL [3-MCK G311 90-12399]

Geisert, Helmut, 1951- Wände aus farbigem Glas . Berlin , 1989. 218 p. : ISBN 3-927873-01-2
NYPL [3-MPW 91-4800]

Geissberger, Hans. Übergänge : Aquarelle / von Hans Geissberger ; mit Texten von Hans Bischof. Stuttgart : Urachhaus, c1990. 135 p. :

ill. ; 25 x 28 cm. ISBN 3-87838-641-9
1. Geissberger, Hans. I. Bischof, Hans. II. Title.
NYPL [3-MCZ G314 91-4261]

GEISSBERGER, HANS.
Geissberger, Hans. Übergänge . Stuttgart , c1990. 135 p. : ISBN 3-87838-641-9
NYPL [3-MCZ G314 91-4261]

Geissler, Heinrich. Zeichnungen des 16. bis 18. Jahrhunderts . [Stuttgart , 1989?] 207 p. :
IN PROCESS (ONLINE)
NYPL [3-MBH 90-12017]

Geissler, Paul.
Kunstverlag Möller. Original-Radierungen mit Motiven europäischer Städte /. Lübeck [198-?] 80 p. :   *NYPL [MDZ + 90-1093]*

GEISSLER, PAUL - CATALOGS.
Kunstverlag Möller. Original-Radierungen mit Motiven europäischer Städte /. Lübeck [198-?] 80 p. :   *NYPL [MDZ + 90-1093]*

Geitlinger, Ernst, 1895-1972.
Ernst Geitlinger : 1895-1972 Retrospektive : von der Natur zur Abstraktion : 28. Mai bis 2. Juli 1989, Wilhelm-Hack-Museum, Ludwigshafen am Rhein / [Katalogredaktion, Lida von Mengden, Beatrix Altmann]. Ludwigshafen a. Rh. : Das Museum, c1989. 119 p. : ill. (some col.) ; 30 cm. (Künstler und Autoren) Includes bibliographical references (p. 115).
1. Geitlinger, Ernst, 1895-1972 - Exhibitions. I. Mengden, Lida von. II. Altmann, Beatrix. III. Wilhelm-Hack-Museum. IV. Title.
NYPL [3-MCK+ G316 90-5281]

GEITLINGER, ERNST, 1895-1972 - EXHIBITIONS.
Geitlinger, Ernst, 1895-1972. Ernst Geitlinger . Ludwigshafen a. Rh. , c1989. 119 p. :
NYPL [3-MCK+ G316 90-5281]

Gelburd, Gail. The trans parent thread : Asian philosophy in recent American art / by Gail Gelburd and Geri De Paoli ; organized by the Hofstra Museum, Hofstra University and the Edith C. Blum Art Institute, Bard College. [Hempstead, N.Y.] : Published by Hofstra University and Bard College ; Philadelphia, Pa. : Distributed by University of Pennsylvania Press, c1990. 124 p. : ill. (some col.) ; 29 cm. Tour itinerary: Hofstra Museum, Hofstra University, Hempstead, New York, September 16 - November 11, 1990; Edith C. Blum Art Institute, Bard College, Annandale-on-Hudson, New York, December 2, 1990 - February 14, 1991 ... [and 4 other museums and galleries]. Includes bibliographical references (p. 120-123). ISBN 0-8122-1376-9 (pbk.)
1. Art, American - Exhibitions. 2. Art, Modern - 20th century - United States - Exhibitions. 3. Taoism - Influence - Exhibitions. 4. Zen Buddhism - Influence - Exhibitions. I. De Paoli, Geri. II. Hofstra Museum. III. Edith C. Blum Art Institute. IV. Title. V. Title: Transparent thread. *NYPL [3-MAMT 91-4984]*

Geld spielt keine Rolle /. Herold, Georg, 1947- Köln , c1990. 78 p. :
NYPL [3-MCK H556 91-6202]

Geldzahler, Henry.
Charles Bell : the complete works, 1970-1990 / by Henry Geldzahler ; with an essay by Louis K. Meisel. New York : Abrams, 1991. p. cm. Includes bibliographical references and index. ISBN 0-8109-3114-1 (cloth) DDC 759.13 20
1. Bell, Charles, 1935- - Catalogs. 2. Photo-realism - United States - Catalogs. I. Bell, Charles, 1935-. II. Meisel, Louis K. III. Title.
N6537.B447 A4 1991

Olitski, Jules, 1922- Jules Olitski /. [New York] , c1990. 5 v. :
NYPL [3-MCX O47 91-6724]

Stout, Myron, 1908- Myron Stout /. [New York, N.Y.] , 1990. 64 p. : ISBN 0-9624258-2-6
NYPL [3-MCX S889 91-6242]

Gelius, William. Kongelige Kobberstiksamling (Statens museum for kunst) Von Abildgaard bis Marstrand. [München] , 1985. 87 p., 114 p. of plates : DDC 741.9489/1 19
NC274.C67 K66 1985
NYPL [3-MBH 90-12465]

GELUGPA (SECT) see DGE-LUGS-PA (SECT)

GELUKPA (SECT) see DGE-LUGS-PA (SECT)

Gemälde, Zeichnungen, Aquarelle, Druckgrafik.
Stein, Hans, 1935- Hans Stein, Gemälde, Zeichnungen, Aquarelle, Druckgrafik /. Berlin ,

1988. 1 v. (unpaged) : DDC 760/.092 20
N6888.S68527 A4 1988
NYPL [3-MCK+ S815 90-12765]

Gemälde, Zeichnungen, Radierungen. Jaeger, Heino, 1938- Heino Jaeger . Hamburg , 1988. 99 p. : ISBN 3-7672-1072-X DDC 760/.092 20
NC251.J265 A4 1988
NYPL [3-MCK+ J221 91-4186]

Gemälde 1945-1989. Schall, Lothar, 1924- Lothar Schall, Gemälde 1945-1989 =. Stuttgart , c1989. 186 p. : ISBN 3-89322-186-7 DDC 759.3 20
N6888.S326 A4 1989

Gemäldegalerie Neue Meister. Richter, Rainer. Carl Christian Vogel von Vogelstein, 1788-1868 . Dresden , c1988. 93, [1] p. :
N6888.V57 A4 1988

GEMÄLDEGALERIE NEUE MEISTER (DRESDEN, GERMANY) - EXHIBITIONS.
Schätze aus Dresden. [Gera] [1987?] 108 p. : ISBN 3-910051-30-8
NYPL [MAVZ (Dresden) 91-5904]

Gemeentekrediet van België. see Crédit communal de Belgique.

Gemin, Massimo.
Ca' Vendramin Calergi / Massimo Gemin, Filippo Pedrocco. Milano : Berenice, c1990. 147 p. : ill. (some col.) ; 29 cm. (Palazzi e monumenti) Includes index. Includes bibliographical references (p. 141-143). ISBN 88-85215-01-7
1. Ca' Vendramin Calergi (Venice, Italy) - History. 2. Venice (Italy) - Buildings, structures, etc. I. Pedrocco, Filippo. II. Title. III. Series.
NYPL [3-MQWB 90-13059]

Nuovi studi su Paolo Veronese /. Venezia , c1990. xi, 422 p. : ISBN 88-7743-056-7
NYPL [3-MCF V54 91-3715]

GEMS - CATALOGS.
Casal García, Raquel. Colección de glíptica del Museo Arqueológico Nacional (serie de entalles romanos) /. [Spain] [1990?] 2 v. : ISBN 84-7483-657-3 (set)
NK5511.S67 M344 1990

Gems of costume jewelry /. Greindl, Gabriele. [Strass. English.] New York , 1991. p. cm. ISBN 1-558-59207-5 DDC 391/.7 20
NK4890.C67 G7413 1991

GENERAL MOTORS CORPORATION - HISTORY.
Butman, John. Car wars . London , 1991. 236 p., [16] p. of plates : ISBN 0-246-13541-7 : DDC 338.76292222094
TL240   *NYPL [JBE 91-1425]*

Geneva as seen in prints and watercolours /. Loës, Barbara de. [Genève par la gravure et l'aquarelle. English.] Geneva , c1990. 401 p. : ISBN 2-88338-001-5
NYPL [MDZ+ 91-2361]

Geneva. Collection Baur. see Collections Baur.

Geneva. Galeria Patrick Cramer. see Galerie Patrick Cramer.

GENEVA (SWITZERLAND) - DESCRIPTION - VIEWS.
Interfoto (Agency) Contes de la ville quotidienne /. Genève , c1987. 123 p. :
NYPL [MFW 90-13469]

Jaxa, Piotr. L'esprit de Genève . Lausanne , c1988. 150 p. : ISBN 2-8265-1051-7
NYPL [MFX+ (Jaxa) 89-17890]

GENEVA (SWITZERLAND) IN ART.
Loës, Barbara de. [Genève par la gravure et l'aquarelle. English.] Geneva as seen in prints and watercolours /. Geneva , c1990. 401 p. : ISBN 2-88338-001-5
NYPL [MDZ+ 91-2361]

Geneva (Switzerland). Musée d'art et d'histoire.
Peintures et pastels de l'ancienne école genevoise : XVIIe-début XIXe siècle : Musée d'art et d'histoire, catalogue des peintures et pastels / Danielle Buyssens. Genève : Le Musée, 1988. 270 p., [83] p. of plates : ill. (some col.) ; 26 cm. "Catalogues, bibliographie et expositions": p. [213]-229. Includes indexes. ISBN 2-8306-0056-8
1. Painting, Swiss - Switzerland - Geneva - Catalogs. 2. Painting, Modern - Switzerland - Geneva - Catalogs. 3. Painting - Switzerland - Geneva - Catalogs. 4. Geneva (Switzerland). Musée d'art et d'histoire - Catalogs. I.

Geneva (Switzerland). Musée d'art et d'histoire. (cont.)

BIBLIOGRAPHIC GUIDE

364

Buyssens, Danièlle. II. Title.
ND851.G4 G45 1988

Russell, Margarita. Images of reality, images of Arcadia . Winterthur [Switzerland] , Washington, D.C. , c1989. 131 p. : ISBN 3-907798-01-5 *NYPL [3-MCG 90-11767]*

Sculptures en pierre du Musée de Genève /. Mainz am Rhein , c1989- v. : ISBN 3-8053-1130-3 (t. 1)
NYPL [MGH+ 89-24649]

Geneva (Switzerland). Musée d'art et d'histoire. Cabinet des estampes. Martin Disler : l'œuvre gravé = Martin Disler : die Druckgraphik = Martin Disler : the prints / Juliane Willi-Cosandier, Rainer Michael Mason. Genève : Cabinet des estampes, Musée d'art et d'histoire, 1989- v. : ill. (some col.) ; 28 cm. French, English and German. Includes bibliographical references (v. 1, p. 169-172) and index. CONTENTS. - 1. 1978-1988. ISBN 2-8306-0060-6 DDC 769.92 20
1. Disler, Martin - Catalogues raisonnés. I. Disler, Martin. II. Willi-Cosandier, Juliane. III. Mason, Rainer Michael. IV. Title. V. Title: Martin Disler : die Druckgraphik. VI. Title: Martin Disler : the prints.
NE710.D57 A4 1989
NYPL [MDG (Disler) 91-5106]

GENEVA (SWITZERLAND). MUSÉE D'ART ET D'HISTOIRE - CATALOGS. Geneva (Switzerland). Musée d'art et d'histoire. Peintures et pastels de l'ancienne école genevoise . Genève , 1988. 270 p., [83] p. of plates : ISBN 2-8306-0056-8
ND851.G4 G45 1988

Sculptures en pierre du Musée de Genève /. Mainz am Rhein , c1989- v. : ISBN 3-8053-1130-3 (t. 1)
NYPL [MGH+ 89-24649]

Geneviève Claisse . Claisse, Geneviève, 1935- Le Cateau-Cambrésis [1989] 95 p. : ISBN 2-907545-08-6
MLCM 90/03414 (N)
NYPL [3-MCO C585 91-7060]

Il Genio di Giovanni Benedetto Castiglione, il Grechetto / saggi di Gianvittorio Dillon ... [et al.]. Genova : Sagep, c1990. 267 p. : ill. (some col.), facsims., port. ; 27 cm. Catalogue of an exhibition held at the Accademia ligustica di belle arti, Jan. 27-Apr. 1, 1990. At head of title: Ministero per i beni culturali e ambientali, Comune di Genova, Università degli studi di Genova, Accademia ligustica di belle arti. Bibliography: p. 257-265. ISBN 88-7058-351-1
1. Castiglione, Giovanni Benedetto, 1610?-1670? - Exhibitions. I. Dillon, Gianvittorio. II. Castiglione, Giovanni Benedetto, 1610?-1670?. III. Accademia ligustica di belle arti. IV. Title: Grechetto.
NYPL [3-MCF C35 90-11510]

A genius of industrial England . Wadsworth, Edward, 1889-1949. [Bradford] , c1990. 128 p. : ISBN 0-9505532-7-1
NYPL [3-MCV W12 91-6333]

A genius of industrial England . Wadsworth, Edward, 1889-1949. [London] : [Bradford] : 128 p. : ISBN 0-9505532-7-1 DDC 760/.092 20
N6797.W26 A4 1990

Gennaro, Paola. Burelli, Augusto Romano, 1938- La moschea di Sinan . Venezia , 1988. 127 p. : ISBN 88-85067-56-5 (pbk.)
NYPL [3-MQT+ 90-10684]

GENOA (ITALY) - DESCRIPTION - TOURS. Testimonianze Liberty a Genova /. Genova , c1986. 46 p. : ISBN 88-7058-218-3
NYPL [3-MAMC 90-11119]

GENRE PAINTING - 17TH CENTURY - EUROPE - EXHIBITIONS. Les Vanités dans la peinture au XVIIe siècle . [Paris] , Caen , c1990. 351 p. : ISBN 2-226-04877-4 DDC 759.04/6/0744422 20
ND1452.E8515 V3 1990
NYPL [MBT+ 91-6843]

GENRE PAINTING - 19TH CENTURY - UNITED STATES. Johns, Elizabeth, 1937- American genre painting . New Haven , c1991. p. cm. ISBN 0-300-05019-4 DDC 754/.0973/09034 20
ND1451.5 .J64 1991

GENRE PAINTING, AMERICAN. Johns, Elizabeth, 1937- American genre painting . New Haven , c1991. p. cm. ISBN

0-300-05019-4 DDC 754/.0973/09034 20
ND1451.5 .J64 1991

GENRE PAINTING - AUSTRIA - 19TH CENTURY - EXHIBITIONS. Geschichtsbilder aus dem alten Österreich . Wien , 1989. [100] p. : *NYPL [3-MAW (Vienna) (Vienna. Österreichische Galerie. Wechselausstellung. Nr.133)]*

GENRE PAINTING, EUROPEAN. Puppi, Lionello. [Splendore dei supplizi. English.] Torment in art . New York , 1991. p. ISBN 0-8478-1406-8 DDC 758/.936466/094 20
ND1452.E8515 P8713 1991

GENRE PAINTING, EUROPEAN - EXHIBITIONS. Les Vanités dans la peinture au XVIIe siècle . [Paris] , Caen , c1990. 351 p. : ISBN 2-226-04877-4 DDC 759.04/6/0744422 20
ND1452.E8515 V3 1990
NYPL [MBT+ 91-6843]

Gent (Belgium) Open mind . Milano , c1989. 318 p. : *NYPL [3-MAMZ 90-11011]*

Gent, Lucy.
Renaissance bodies . London , 1990. x, 294 p. : ISBN 0-948462-09-4 DDC 700 20
NX650.F45 R46 1990

Renaissance bodies . London , 1990. x, 294 p. : ISBN 0-948462-09-4 (cased) : DDC 700 20
NYPL [3-MAMZ 90-11501]

Gente de Olinda .
(1) Bajado, 1912- Bajado, um artista de Olinda /. Olinda [Brasil] , 1985. 48 p. : DDC 759.981 19
ND359.B34 A35 1985
NYPL [3-MCZ B1583 90-9450]

Gente do aço / apresentação e poemas, Affonso Romano de Sant'Anna ; crônica de ferro e aço, Antônio Houaiss ; pequena história da siderurgia, Herculano Gomes Mathias ; fotos de Jamie Stewart-Granger. [Rio de Janeiro, RJ] : Editora Index, c1989. 147 p. : ill. ; 30 cm. ISBN 85-7083-026-2
1. Iron and steel workers - Brazil - Pictorial works. I. Houaiss, Antônio. II. Mathias, Herculano Gomes. III. Stewart-Granger, Jamie. *NYPL [MFX+ (Stewart-Granger) 91-7436]*

Genth, Lillian Mathilde, 1876-1953. Lillian Mathilde Genth : a retrospective. Hickory, N.C. : Hickory Museum of Art, [1990?] 36 p. : ill. ; 26 cm.
1. Genth, Lillian Mathilde, 1876-1953 - Exhibitions. I. Hickory Museum of Art (Hickory, N.C.). II. Title.
NYPL [3-MCX G337 91-5913]

GENTH, LILLIAN MATHILDE, 1876-1953 - EXHIBITIONS. Genth, Lillian Mathilde, 1876-1953. Lillian Mathilde Genth . Hickory, N.C. [1990?] 36 p. : *NYPL [3-MCX G337 91-5913]*

Gentili, Augusto. Sebastiano del Piombo : pala di San Giovanni Crisostomo / Augusto Gentili e Chiara Bertini. Venezia : Arsenale editrice, 1985. 32 p., [16] p. of plates : ill. ; 15 cm. (Hermia . 4) Bibliography: p. 31-32.
1. Sebastiano del Piombo, 1485-1547. Pala di San Giovanni Crisostomo. I. Bertini, Chiara.
NYPL [3-MCF P66 90-12518]

Gentleman, David. David Gentleman's Paris. London : Hodder & Stoughton, 1991. 192 p. : col. ill. ; 30 cm. "A John Curtis book." Includes index. ISBN 0-340-51869-3 : DDC 914.43604838 20
1. Paris (France) in art. 2. Paris (France) - Description - 1975-. I. Title. II. Title: Paris.
DC707 *NYPL [3-MCV+ G337 91-7455]*

Geo. Herriman's Krazy + Ignatz /. Herriman, George, 1880-1944. Forestville, CA , 1988- v. : ISBN 0-913035-48-3 (pbk. : v. 1)
NYPL [3-MEM+ (Herriman) 91-610]

Geoff Winningham, photographs . Winningham, Geoff. Houston , c1974. 23 p. :
NYPL [MFX+ (Winningham) 91-1458]

Geografía de El Salvador. 1a ed. San Salvador : Dirección de Publicaciones, Ministerio de Cultura y Comunicaciones, 1986- v. : ill. (some col.) ; 35 cm. Bibliography: v. 1, p. 248-249. DDC 917.284/02 19
1. Physical geography - El Salvador. 2. El Salvador - Geography. I. El Salvador. Ministerio de Cultura y Comunicaciones. Dirección de Publicaciones e

Impresos.
F1484.3 .G46 1986 *NYPL [Map Div. 90-69]*

Geografía humana .
(1) La Cerámica tradicional del Perú /. Lima , 1989. 228 p. : ISBN 84-89291-21-7
Nk4077 .C47 1989

Geografski atlas . Bulgaria. Upravlenie Geodeziĭa i kartografiĭa. Sofiĭa , 1961. 1 atlas (14 p. :
NYPL [Map Div. 91-1091]

Geografski atlas . Bulgaria. Upravlenie po geodeziĭa i kartografiĭa. Sofiĭa , 1969. 1 atlas (65 p.) : *NYPL [Map Div. 91-1090]*

Geographers' A to Z street atlas of Liverpool. Geographers' A-Z Map Company. Liverpool . Sevenoaks , c1990. 1 atlas (239 p.) :
NYPL [Map Div. 90-13145]

Geographers' A-Z Map Company.
Liverpool : Birkenhead, Wallasey, Warrington, Bootle, Crosby, Heswall, Hoylake, Huyton, Runcorn, St. Helens, Kirby, Maghull, Prescot ... : AZ street atlas. Ed. 5. Sevenoaks : Geographers' A-Z Map Co., c1990. 1 atlas (239 p.) : maps ; 20 cm. Cover title. Scale 1:15,840. 4 in. to 1 mile. Earlier eds. published under title: Geographers' A to Z street atlas of Liverpool, by the company under its earlier name Geographers' Map Company, ltd. Includes index. On cover: New ed. P. 236-239 blank for notes.
1. Liverpool (England) - Maps. 2. Liverpool Suburban Area (Merseyside) - Maps. I. Title. II. Title: Geographers' A to Z street atlas of Liverpool.
NYPL [Map Div. 90-13145]

Newcastle-Upon-Tyne, Sunderland, City of Durham : Gateshead, North & South Shields, Tynemouth, Chester-le-Street, Peterlee, Seaham, Stanley, Wallsend, Washington, Whitley Bay : AZ street atlas. Ed. 3. Sevenoaks, Kent : Geographers' A-Z Map Co., c1988. 1 atlas (144, [86] p.) : maps ; 20 cm. Cover title. Spine title: AZ Newcastle-upon-Tyne. Includes index.
1. Newcastle upon Tyne (England) - Maps. 2. Sunderland (Tyne and Wear, England) - Maps. 3. Durham (England) - Maps. I. Title. II. Title: AZ Newcastle-upon-Tyne. III. Title: AZ street atlas, Newcastle-Upon-Tyne.
NYPL [Map Div. 90-13146]

Sheffield : Barnsley, Doncaster, Rotherham, Chesterfield, Mexborough, Conisbrough, Dronfield, Stocksbridge, Wombwell, Dearne, Maltby, Rawmarsh, Wath upon Dearne, Adwick le Street : AZ street atlas. Ed. 1. Sevenoaks, Kent : Geographers' A-Z Map Co., c1988. 1 atlas (200 p.) : maps ; 20 cm. Cover title. Spine title: AZ Sheffield. Scales: 1:18,103, 1:9,051. Includes index. ISBN 0-85039-212-8 :
1. Sheffield (England) - Maps. I. Title. II. Title: AZ Sheffield. *NYPL [Map Div. 90-13147]*

Geographers' Map Company, ltd. AZ Geographers' London atlas /. Sevenoaks , 1991. 259 p. : ISBN 0-85039-000-1
NYPL [Map Div. 91-7553]

Geographic names & the federal government . Orth, Donald J. Washington, D.C. : Geography and Map Division, The Library of Congress, 1990. ii, 59 p. ; *NYPL [Map Div. 91-5514]*

Geographic names and the federal government. Orth, Donald J. Geographic names & the federal government . Washington, D.C. : Geography and Map Division, The Library of Congress, 1990. ii, 59 p. ;
NYPL [Map Div. 91-5514]

GEOGRAPHICAL ATLASES. see ATLASES.

GEOGRAPHICAL DISTRIBUTION OF MAN. see ETHNOLOGY.

GEOGRAPHICAL MYTHS IN ART. Leason, Percy, 1889- Wiregrass . Melbourne , 1986. 80 p. : ISBN 0-85091-249-0 DDC 741.5/994 20
NC371.L42 A4 1986

GEOGRAPHICAL NAMES. see NAMES, GEOGRAPHICAL.

GEOGRAPHICAL PATHOLOGY. see MEDICAL GEOGRAPHY.

Geographisch-Kartographisches Institut Meyer. Meyers neuer weltatlas /. Mannheim , 1989. 321 p. : ISBN 3-411-02354-6
NYPL [Map Div. 90-11958]

Geographisch-landeskundlicher Atlas von Westfalen /. Landschaftsverband

Westfalen-Lippe. Geographische Kommission für Westfalen. Münster , 1985- 1 atlas : DDC 912/.4355 19
G1923.N6E1 L3 1985
NYPL [Map Div. 89-18]

Geographisches-Kartographisches Institut Meyer.
Meyers Universal Atlas . Mannheim , c1990. 1 atlas (224 p.) : ISBN 3-411-07285-7
NYPL [Map Div. 91-7165]

GEOGRAPHY - 400-1400. see GEOGRAPHY, MEDIEVAL.

GEOGRAPHY - ATLASES. see ATLASES.

GEOGRAPHY, BIBLICAL. see BIBLE - GEOGRAPHY.

GEOGRAPHY - DISCOVERIES. see DISCOVERIES (IN GEOGRAPHY)

GEOGRAPHY - EARLY WORKS. see GEOGRAPHY, MEDIEVAL.

GEOGRAPHY, ECONOMIC - MAPS.
The Economist world atlas and almanac. New York , 1989. 384 p. : ISBN 0-13-234964-7
NYPL [Map Div. 90-11363]

Larousse, firm, publishers, Paris. Atlas international Larousse. Paris [1950] xix, [144], 42, 41 p. **NYPL [Map Div. 90-64]**

Prévot, Victor. Géopolitique transparente . [Paris] , 1987. 1 atlas (255 p.) : ISBN 2-210-98004-6 **NYPL [Map Div. 91-6046]**

GEOGRAPHY, HISTORICAL - MAPS.
Atlas of classical history /. London , New York , c1985, 1988. 1 atlas (217 p.) : ISBN 0-415-03463-9 (pbk.)
NYPL [Map Div. 91-5122]

Vallés Perdrix, Edmundo. Atlas de historia universal /. Barcelona , c1973. [86] p. :
NYPL [Map Div. 81-234]

GEOGRAPHY, HISTORICAL - MAPS - CATALOGS.
R. V. Tooley Ltd. An introduction to the history of maps and mapmaking. London , 1980. 68 p. : **NYPL [Map Div. 91-4077]**

GEOGRAPHY, MEDICAL. see MEDICAL GEOGRAPHY.

GEOGRAPHY, MEDIEVAL - MAPS.
The Atlas of the Crusades /. New York , 1991, c1990. 192 p. : ISBN 0-8160-2186-4 DDC 911 20
G1034 .R5 1990 **NYPL [Map Div. 91-4709]**

Touring club italiano. Servizio cartografico. Atlante enciclopedico Touring. Volume 4, Storia antica e medievale /. Milano , c1987. 1 atlas (143 p.) : ISBN 88-365-0301-2
NYPL [Map Div. 91-7773]

GEOGRAPHY - NAMES. see NAMES, GEOGRAPHICAL.

GEOGRAPHY - NETWORK ANALYSIS.
Prévot, Victor. Géopolitique transparente . [Paris] , 1987. 1 atlas (255 p.) : ISBN 2-210-98004-6 **NYPL [Map Div. 91-6046]**

GEOGRAPHY, POLITICAL - MAPS.
Prévot, Victor. Géopolitique transparente . [Paris] , 1987. 1 atlas (255 p.) : ISBN 2-210-98004-6 **NYPL [Map Div. 91-6046]**

GEOGRAPHY - TERMINOLOGY - BIBLIOGRAPHY.
Orth, Donald J. Geographic names & the federal government . Washington, D.C. : Geography and Map Division, The Library of Congress, 1990. ii, 59 p. :
NYPL [Map Div. 91-5514]

Geological Survey bulletin .
(1532) Snyder, John Parr, 1926- Map projections used by the U. S. Geological Survey /. Washington , 1982 [i.e. 1983] xiii, 313 p. : DDC 557.3 s 526.8 19
QE75 .B9 no. 1532 GA110
NYPL [Map Div. 90-11151]

Geological Survey (U. S.)
The National gazetteer of the United States of America. Washington , Denver, C0 , 1990. xxxii, 526 p. : DDC 917.3/003 20
E154 .N38 1990 **NYPL [Map Div. 91-7315]**

Stark, Peter L. (Peter LeRoy), 1953- A cartobibliography of separately published U. S. Geological Survey special maps and river surveys /. Santa Cruz, Calif. , 1989. xxii, 336

p. : ISBN 0-939112-14-0 DDC 016.91273 20
Z6027.U5 S7 1989 GA405
NYPL [Map Div. 90-11842]

GEOLOGICAL SURVEY (U. S.)
Snyder, John Parr, 1926- Map projections used by the U. S. Geological Survey /. Washington , 1982 [i.e. 1983] xiii, 313 p. : DDC 557.3 s 526.8 19
QE75 .B9 no. 1532 GA110
NYPL [Map Div. 90-11151]

GEOLOGICAL SURVEY (U. S.) - CATALOGS.
Stark, Peter L. (Peter LeRoy), 1953- A cartobibliography of separately published U. S. Geological Survey special maps and river surveys /. Santa Cruz, Calif. , 1989. xxii, 336 p. : ISBN 0-939112-14-0 DDC 016.91273 20
Z6027.U5 S7 1989 GA405
NYPL [Map Div. 90-11842]

GEOLOGY, ECONOMIC - QATAR - MAPS.
Yaḥyá, Muḥammad 'Ādil Aḥmad. Aṭlas al-ṣuwar al-faḍā'iyah li-Dawlat Qaṭar min al-qamar al-ṣinā'ī "Landsāt" /. al-Dawḥah , 1983. 1 atlas (vii, 166 p.) : DDC 912/.5363 19
G2249.81.C2 Y2 1983
NYPL [Map Div. 91-2599]

GEOLOGY, STRUCTURAL - MAPS.
Atlas of major Texas gas reservoirs /. Chicago, Ill. , Austin, Tex. , 1989. 1 atlas (ix, 161 p.) :
NYPL [Map Div. 90-11657]

La Geometria in funzione nell'architettura e nella costruzione della città / a cura di Pierluigi Grandinetti ; scritti di, Armando dal Fabbro ... [et al.]. Venezia : C.L.U.V.A. università, c1985. 157 p. : ill. ; 30 cm. (Quaderni del Dipartimento di architettura e progettazione urbana, Istituto universitario di architettura di Venezia . 10) Includes bibliographical references. ISBN 88-85067-29-8
I. Grandinetti, Pierluigi. II. Dal Fabbro, Armando. III. Series.
NA2760 .G38 1985
NYPL [3-MQD+ 90-12625]

Geometrie del disordine. Levini, Felice, 1956- Felice Levini . Milano , 1988. 77 p. :
N6923.L345 A4 1988
NYPL [3-MCF L665 90-12541]

Géométries du désordre. Levini, Felice, 1956- Felice Levini . Milano , 1988. 77 p. :
N6923.L345 A4 1988
NYPL [3-MCF L665 90-12541]

Geometrix . Hornung, Clarence Pearson. New York , c1991. vii, 115 p. : ISBN 0-486-26674-5 : DDC 745.4 20
NK1570 .H595 1991

GEOMETRY.
(1986) Gerstner, Karl. The forms of color . Cambridge, Mass. , c1986. 179 p. : ISBN 0-262-07100-2 DDC 701/.8 19
ND1489 .G4713 1986
NYPL [3-MAMZ 91-6985]

GEOPOLITICS - MAPS.
Prévot, Victor. Géopolitique transparente . [Paris] , 1987. 1 atlas (255 p.) : ISBN 2-210-98004-6 **NYPL [Map Div. 91-6046]**

Géopolitique transparente . Prévot, Victor. [Paris] , 1987. 1 atlas (255 p.) : ISBN 2-210-98004-6 **NYPL [Map Div. 91-6046]**

Georg Baselitz . Baselitz, Georg, 1938- New York [1990?] 9 p., [11] leaves of plates :
NYPL [3-MCK B299 91-3832]

Georg Baselitz . Baselitz, Georg, 1938- München , c1991. 111 p. :
NYPL [MDG+ (Baselitz) 91-8026]

Georg Baselitz, Bilder aus Berliner Privatbesitz . Baselitz, Georg, 1938- Berlin (West) , c1990. 94 p. : ISBN 3-87584-312-6
NYPL [3-MCK+ B299 90-11612]

Georg Broel, 1884-1940 . Witte, Klaus. Frederikshavn , 1984. 86 p. : ISBN 87-7317-116-6
NYPL [MDVK (bBroel) 90-13584]

Georg Chaimowicz . Chaimowicz, Georg, 1929- Lüdenscheid , c1988. 100 p. :
MLCS 88/02633 (N)
NYPL [3-MCK+ C434 91-5888]

Georg Ettl, Arbeiten 1968-1989 =. Ettl, Georg, 1940- Düsseldorf , 1990. 102 p. : ISBN 3-925974-14-8
NYPL [3-MGO (ETTL) 91-4445]

Georg Ettl, works, 1968-1989. Ettl, Georg, 1940- Georg Ettl, Arbeiten 1968-1989 =. Düsseldorf , 1990. 102 p. : ISBN 3-925974-14-8
NYPL [3-MGO (ETTL) 91-4445]

Georg Herold. Herold, Georg, 1947- Geld spielt keine Rolle /. Köln , c1990. 78 p. :
NYPL [3-MCK H556 91-6202]

Georg Karl Pfahler . Pfahler, Georg Karl, 1926- Stuttgart , c1990. 126 p. : ISBN 3-89322-180-8
ND588.P523 A4 1990

Georg Klusemann, La meccanica della illusione. Klusemann, Georg, 1942- Milano , c1988. 77 p. : ISBN 88-85684-22-X
NYPL [3-MCK+ K658 89-25779]

Georg Kolbe, Leben und Werk . Berger, Ursel. Berlin , 1990. 429 p. : ISBN 3-7861-1589-3 DDC 730/.92 20
NB588.K6 B38 1990
NYPL [MGO (Kolbe) 91-5528]

Georg-Kolbe-Museum Berlin.
Berger, Ursel. Georg Kolbe, Leben und Werk . Berlin , 1990. 429 p. : ISBN 3-7861-1589-3 DDC 730/.92 20
NB588.K6 B38 1990
NYPL [MGO (Kolbe) 91-5528]

GEORG-KOLBE-MUSEUM BERLIN - CATALOGS.
Berger, Ursel. Georg Kolbe, Leben und Werk . Berlin , 1990. 429 p. : ISBN 3-7861-1589-3 DDC 730/.92 20
NB588.K6 B38 1990
NYPL [MGO (Kolbe) 91-5528]

Georg Muche--Leise sagen . Muche, Georg, 1895- Kassel , 19. 143 p. :
NYPL [3-MCK MGO 88-2455]

George Bellows : paintings / by Michael Quick ... [et al.], with an introduction by John Wilmerding. Fort Worth, Tex. : Amon Carter Museum ; Los Angeles, Calif. : Los Angeles County Museum of Art ; p. cm. Published in conjunction with the exhibition, The paintings of George Bellows; Los Angeles County Museum of Art, Whitney Museum of Art, Columbus Museum of Art, Amon Carter Museum. Includes index. ISBN 0-8109-3119-2 DDC 759.13 20
1. Bellows, George, 1882-1925 - Exhibitions. I. Quick, Michael.
ND237.B45 A4 1992

George Bellows and urban America /. Doezema, Marianne, 1950- New Haven, CT , c1991. p. cm. ISBN 0-300-05043-7 DDC 759.13 20
ND237.B45 D6 1991

George Bellows (1882-1925) . Bellows, George, 1882-1925. New York, N.Y. [1984] 30 p. :
NYPL [3-MCX B44 91-6268]

George Catlin . Sufrin, Mark. New York : Toronto : p. cm. ISBN 0-689-31608-9 DDC 759.13 B 92 20
ND237.C35 S8 1991

George Cooke, 1793-1849 /. Keyes, Donald D. [Athens, Ga.] , 1991. 104 p. : ISBN 0-915977-07-9 DDC 759.13 20
ND237.C6785 A4 1991

George Cress . Cress, George. Chattanooga, Tenn. , c1990. 56 p. :
NYPL [3-MCX C922 91-7066]

George Devey, architect, 1820-1886 /. Allibone, Jill. Cambridge, England , c1991. 189 p. : ISBN 0-7188-2785-6 : DDC 720.92 20
NYPL [3-MQZ (Devey) 91-6770]

George Grosz . Lewis, Beth Irwin. Princeton, N.J. , c1991. p. cm. ISBN 0-691-00291-6 (pb.) : DDC 741/.092 B 20
NC251.G66 L48 1991

George Grosz, Deutschland über Alles . Grosz, George, 1893-1959. Roma , 1963. 19 p., [84] leaves of plates :
NYPL [3-MCK G879 91-1374]

George Keyt drawings /. Keyt, George. Colombo , 1990. xxviii, 90 p. : ISBN 955-9065-01-7 : DDC 741.95493 20
NC330.Z9 K492 1990

George, Mary Carolyn Hollers. O'Neil Ford, architect / Mary Carolyn Hollers George ; foreword by Hugh A. Stubbins ; color photographs by W. Eugene George. College Station : Texas A&M University Press, c1992. p. cm. (The John and Sara Lindsey series in

architectural studies . no. 1) Includes bibliographical references and index. ISBN 0-89096-433-5 DDC 720/.92 20
1. Ford, O'Neil, 1905- - Criticism and criticism. I. Title. II. Series.
NA737.O5 G46 1992

George N. Barnard, photographer of Sherman's campaign /. Davis, Keith F., 1952- Kansas City, Mo. , Albuquerque, N.M. , c1990. 232 p. : ISBN 0-87529-627-0
IN PROCESS (ONLINE)
NYPL [MFX+ (Barnard) 91-6015]

George Outram & Co.
Hunter, William. Dear happy ghosts .
Edinburgh , 1990. 191 p. : ISBN 1-85158-371-8 : DDC 941.443082 20
NYPL [MFW 91-3480]

GEORGE OUTRAM & CO. - PHOTOGRAPH COLLECTIONS.
Hunter, William. Dear happy ghosts .
Edinburgh , 1990. 191 p. : ISBN 1-85158-371-8 : DDC 941.443082 20
NYPL [MFW 91-3480]

George Philip & Son. Philip's Road atlas of Great Britain : with special London section / George Philip. [London] : G. Philip, c1980. 1 atlas (vii, 80, [61] p.) : col. ill., col. maps ; 29 cm. Includes indexes. ISBN 0-540-05364-3 DDC 912/.41 19
1. Great Britain - Road maps. 2. London (England) - Maps. I. Title. II. Title: Road atlas of Great Britain.
G1812.21.P2 G6 1980
NYPL [Map Div. 90-5738]

George S. & Nancy B. Parker Collection. The mapping of the Great Lakes in the seventeenth century. . Providence, R. I, 1989. xix, [3], 85 p. incl. maps : *NYPL [Map Div. 90-65]*

George Segal . Price, Marla. [Fort Worth] , 1990. vi, 58 p. : ISBN 0-929865-04-9
IN PROCESS
NYPL [3-MGO (Segal) 90-11611]

George Soper's horses /. Heiney, Paul. London , 1990. 143 p. : ISBN 0-85493-200-3 : DDC 636.15 20
SF311.3.G7 *NYPL [3-MCV S712 91-3373]*

George Soper's horses /. Heiney, Paul. Boston , 1991. 143 p. : ISBN 0-395-58040-4 : DDC 759.2 20
N6797.S64 A4 1990

George Tsutakawa /. Kingsbury, Martha, 1941- Seattle , Bellevue, Wash. , c1990. 156 p. : ISBN 0-295-97020-0 (alk. paper) DDC 709/.2 20
N6537.T74 A4 1990
NYPL [3-MGO (Tsutakawa) 91-6230]

George Washington Wilson . Wilson, George Washington, 1823-1893. [Edinburgh] [1979?] 32 p. : ISBN 0-902989-57-X
NYPL [MFX (Wilson) 90-7092]

Georges Braque /. Wilkin, Karen. New York , 1991. p. cm. ISBN 0-89659-944-2 (cloth) DDC 759.4 20
N6853.B7 W53 1991

Georges Rouault, 1871-1958 . Rouault, Georges, 1871-1958. Berlin , 1988. 263 p. : DDC 760/.092 20
NE2049.5.R6 A4 1988
NYPL [3-MCO+ R852 90-10814]

Georges Sabbagh . Sabbagh, Georges, 1887-1951. Thonon-les-Bains, c1990. 141 p. : ISBN 2-908528-09-6 : DDC 759.4 20
ND553.S23 A4 1990

Georges Seurat, 1859-1891 /. Seurat, Georges, 1859-1891. New York , 1991. p. cm. ISBN 0-87099-618-5 DDC 759.4 20
ND553.S5 A4 1991

Georges von Swetlik /. Swetlik, Georges von, 1912- Helsingfors , c1989. 128 p. : ISBN 952-9014-15-5
ND955.F53 A4 1989

Georgetown University.
Catalogue of the art collection, Georgetown University, Washington,D.C. Washington, D.C. : The University, 1963. 119 p., 33 p. of plates : ill. (some col.) ; 22 cm. Preface signed: Erik Larsen. Includes bibliographical references and index.
1. Georgetown University - Art collections - Catalogs.

2. Art - Washington, D.C. - Catalogs. I. Larsen, Erik, 1911-. II. Title. *NYPL [3-MAVZ (Washington, D.C.) 91-821]*

Leonardo, Michelangelo, and Raphael in Renaissance Florence, 1500-1508 /. Washington, D.C. , 1991. p. cm. ISBN 0-87840-219-5 DDC 709/.2/2455109031 20
N6923.L33 L456 1991

GEORGETOWN UNIVERSITY - ART COLLECTIONS - CATALOGS.
Georgetown University. Catalogue of the art collection, Georgetown University, Washington,D.C. Washington, D.C. , 1963. 119 p., 33 p. of plates : *NYPL [3-MAVZ (Washington, D.C.) 91-821]*

Georgia Museum of Art.
Art of the Cameroon . Athens, Ga. , c1990. 40 p. : ISBN 0-915977-05-2 DDC 730/.096711/0747582311 20
NB1099.C3 A7 1990

Keyes, Donald D. George Cooke, 1793-1849 /. [Athens, Ga.] , 1991. 104 p. : ISBN 0-915977-07-9 DDC 759.13 20
ND237.C6785 A4 1991

Georgia O'Keeffe /. Eldredge, Charles C. New York , 1991. 160 p. : ISBN 0-8109-3657-7 DDC 759.13 20
ND237.O5 E43 1991
NYPL [3-MCX+ 041 91-7249]

Georgia O'Keeffe /. Turner, Robyn. Boston , c1991. p. cm. DDC 759.13 B 92 20
ND237.O5 T87 1991

Georgia O'Keeffe, paintings of Hawai'i /. Saville, Jennifer, 1955- Honolulu , 1990. 79 p. : ISBN 0-937426-11-3 DDC 759.13 20
ND237 .O5A4 1990
NYPL [3-MCX O41 90-12481]

Georgia. University. Georgia Museum of Art. see **Georgia Museum of Art.**

GEORGIAN CHURCH AT IŞHAN.
Kadiroğlu, Mine, 1944- The architecture of the Georgian Church at Işhan /. Frankfurt am Main , New York , 1991. p. cm. ISBN 3-631-42828-6 DDC 726/.5/095662 20
NA5871.I84 K33 1991

The Georgians . Shawe - Taylor, Desmond. London , 1990. 239 p. : ISBN 0-7126-3827-X : DDC 757.0941 20
ND1314.5 *NYPL [3-MCT 91-5013]*

GEORGIANS (TRANSCAUCASIANS) - TURKEY - IŞHAN - MONUMENTS.
Kadiroğlu, Mine, 1944- The architecture of the Georgian Church at Işhan /. Frankfurt am Main , New York , 1991. p. cm. ISBN 3-631-42828-6 DDC 726/.5/095662 20
NA5871.I84 K33 1991

GEOTECTONICS. see GEOLOGY, STRUCTURAL.

Gerald Domenig, Merciette . Domenig, Gerald, 1953- [S.l.] , c1988. 1 v. (unpaged) :
NYPL [MFX+ (Domenig) 90-13478]

Gérald Minkoff, Muriel Olesen . Minkoff, Gérald. [Solothurn] , 1988. 48 p. : ISBN 3-906663-14-0
NYPL [3-MCZ + M6435 90-132]

Gerald Peters Gallery.
Gorky, Arshile, 1904-1948. Arshile Gorky . [Santa Fe, N.M.] , c1990. 11 p., [30] leaves of plates : ISBN 0-935037-38-1
NYPL [3-MCZ G669 91-4351]

Modernist themes in New Mexico . Santa Fe , 1989. 56 p. : ISBN 0-03-503729-2
NYPL [3-MCW 90-12647]

Prythero, Tim, 1962- Tim Prythero. Santa Fe , c1990. 1 v. (unpaged) : ISBN 0-935037-34-9 DDC 709/.2 20
N6537.P79 A4 1990

Gérard, Claude, professeur. La maison rurale en Lorraine / Claude Gérard. Nonette [France] : CREER, [1990] 151 p. : ill. ; 24 cm. (Les Cahiers de construction traditionnelle, 0182-2853 . v. no 14) Includes bibliographical references (p. 150). ISBN 2-902894-66-X : DDC 728/.0944/38 20
1. Farmhouses - France - Lorraine. 2. Vernacular architecture - France - Lorraine. I. Title. II. Series.
NA8210.F8 G47 1990

Gérard Trignac . Trignac, Gérard, 1955- [Clermont-Ferrand, France] , c1990. 1 v.

(unpaged) : ISBN 2-903792-15-1 : DDC 769.92 20
NE650.T75 A4 1990
NYPL [MDG+ (Trignac) 90-13672]

Gérard, Yves. L'Opéra de Monte-Carlo au temps du Prince Albert Ier de Monaco /. Paris , c1990. 72 p. : ISBN 2-7118-2321-0
NYPL [3-MQW 91-7009]

Gerardo Dottori, 1884-1977 . Dottori, Gerardo, 1884- Roma , c1979. 71 p. :
MLCM 80/99 *NYPL [3-MCF D725 91-878]*

Gerber, Bärbel. Kultur und Kunst in Berlin : ein Wegweiser / [Autor, Bärbel Gerber ; Redakteur, Erika Grünberg]. Berlin : Berlin-Information, 1988. 248 p. : ill. (chiefly col.) ; 20 cm. One folded map entitled Kulturstätten im Stadtzentrum Berlins laid in. Includes index. ISBN 3-7442-0022-1
1. Arts - Germany - Berlin - Guide-books. 2. Berlin (Germany) - Intellectual life - Guide-books. I. Berlin-Information. II. Title.
NX550.B4 G4 1988

Gerchman, Rubens, 1942- [Rio de Janeiro-RJ] [c1989] 208 p. : DDC 759.981 20
ND359.G47 A4 1989

Gerchman, Rubens, 1942-
Gerchman. [Rio de Janeiro-RJ] : Salamandra, [c1989] 208 p. : ill. (chiefly col.) ; 28 cm. Portuguese and English. "Texto, Wilson Coutinho"--P. [7]. DDC 759.981 20
1. Gerchman, Rubens, 1942- - Catalogs. I. Coutinho, Wilson. II. Title.
ND359.G47 A4 1989

GERCHMAN, RUBENS, 1942- - CATALOGS.
Gerchman, Rubens, 1942- Gerchman. [Rio de Janeiro-RJ] [c1989] 208 p. : DDC 759.981 20
ND359.G47 A4 1989

Gercke, Hans, 1941-
Blau, Farbe der Ferne /. Heidelberg , c1990. 615 p. : ISBN 3-88423-062-X DDC 709/.04/0074434645 20
N6488.G3 H442 1990

Uematsu, Keiji, 1947- Keiji Uematsu . Heidelberg , 1979. 59, [1] p. :
NB1059.U3 A4 1979
NYPL [3-MGO (Uematsu) 81-772]

Gerd Baukhage . Baukhage, Gerd, 1911- [Köln] [1989] 114 p. :
MLCM 90/03723 (N)
NYPL [3-MCK B339 91-2508]

Gerd-Möller-Stiftung. Wyczołkowski, Leon, 1852-1936. Leon Wyczółkowski, 1852-1936 . [Wilhelmshaven] , c1989. 77 p. :
N7255.P63 W892 1989
NYPL [3-MCZ+ W97 91-7562]

Gerd Utescher, 1912-1983 /. Utescher, Gerd, 1912-1983. Alassio, Italy , c1987. 1 v. (unpaged) :
NYPL [3-MGO+ (Utescher) 90-12478]

Gerdts, William H.
American Impressionism : masterworks from public and private collections in the United States : exhibition catalogue / by William H. Gerdts. [Lugano-Castagnola] : Thyssen-Bornemisza Foundation ; [Einsiedeln, Switzerland] : Eidolon, c1990. 161 p. : col. ill. ; 29 cm. Exhibition held at the Villa Favorita, Thyssen-Bornemisza Foundation, Lugano-Castagnola, July 22-October 28, 1990. Includes bibliographical references. DDC 759.13/09/03407449478 20
1. Impressionism (Art) - United States - Exhibitions. 2. Painting, American - Exhibitions. 3. Painting, Modern - 19th century - United States - Exhibitions. 4. Painting, Modern - 20th century - United States - Exhibitions. I. Title.
ND210.5.I4 G474 1990a

Art across America : two centuries of regional painting in America, 1710-1920 / William H. Gerdts. New York : Abbeville Press, 1990. 3 v. : ill. (some col.), maps ; 34 cm. Includes bibliographical references and indexes. CONTENTS. - v. 1. New England, New York, the Mid-Atlantic -- v. 2. The South, the Near Midwest -- v. 3. The Far Midwest, the Rocky Mountain West, the Southwest, the Pacific. DDC 759.13 20
1. Painting, Colonial - United States. 2. Painting, Modern - 19th century - United States. 3. Regionalism in art. I. Title.
ND212 .G47 1990
NYPL [MCW+ 90-11405]

Masterworks of American impressionism / by William H. Gerdts. Lugano-Castagnola,

Switzerland : Thyssen-Bornemisza Foundation ;
Einsiedeln, Switzerland : Eidolon ; 163 p. : ill.
(some col.) ; 30 cm. "A publication of the
Thyssen-Bornemisza Foundation in cooperation with
Eidolon AG in Einsiedeln (Switzerland) and in
conjunction with the exhibition, held in 1990 at the
Villa Favorita, Thyssen-Bornemisza Foundation,
Lugano-Castagnola (Switzerland)"--T.p. verso. Includes
bibliographical references and index. ISBN
    0-8109-3614-3   DDC 759.13/074/49478 20
*1. Impressionism (Art) - United States - Exhibitions. 2.
Painting, American - Exhibitions. 3. Painting, Modern -
19th century - United States - Exhibitions. 4. Painting,
Modern - 20th century - United States - Exhibitions. I.
Title.*
ND210.5.I4 G476 1991
              NYPL [3-MCW+ 91-7414]
Ten American painters /. New York , c1990.
187 p. : ISBN 0-945936-07-9
              NYPL [3-MCW 90-11805]

Gere, Charlotte. Artists' jewellery : Pre-Raphaelite
to Arts and Crafts / Charlotte Gere and
Geoffrey C. Munn. Woodbridge [England] :
Antique Collectors' Club, c1989. 244 p. : ill.
(some col.) ; 29 cm. Includes index. Bibliography: p.
240. ISBN 1-85149-024-8
*1. Jewelry - History - 19th century. 2. Jewelry -
History - 20th century. 3. Preraphaelites. I. Munn,
Geoffrey C. II. Antique Collectors' Club. III. Title.*
              NYPL [MNR 89-11557]

Gere, John A. Musée du Louvre. Cabinet des
dessins. Dessins de Taddeo et Federico
Zuccaro. Paris, 1969. 79 p. :
              NYPL [3-MBH 91-1497]

Gerhard Hoehme, Bilder . Hoehme, Gerhard,
1920- Düsseldorf , 1979. 200 p. :
N6888.H63 A4 1979
              NYPL [3-MCK H6931 81-779]

Gerhard Hofmann . Hofmann, Gerhard, 1960-
Stuttgart , 1990. 63 p. :
              NYPL [MDG+ (Hofmann) 91-7588]

Gerhard-Marcks-Haus.
Keramik und Bauhaus /. Berlin [1989] 286 p. :
    ISBN 3-89181-404-6
              NYPL [3-MPGK 90-11031]
Keramik und Bauhaus . Berlin [1989] 286 p. :
    ISBN 3-89181-404-6
NK4099 .K446 1989

Gerhard Marcks zum einhundertsten Geburtstag .
Marcks, Gerhard. Berlin , 1989. iii, [1] p., [2] p.
of plates :
              NYPL [3-MGO+ (Marcks) 89-25923]

Gerhard Marcks zum 100. Geburtstag. Marcks,
Gerhard. Gerhard Marcks zum einhundertsten
Geburtstag . Berlin , 1989. iii, [1] p., [2] p. of
plates :
              NYPL [3-MGO+ (Marcks) 89-25923]

Gerhard Marcks zum 90. Geburtstag . Marcks,
Gerhard. Bremen , 1979. [4], 82 p. :
N6888.M344 A4 1979
              NYPL [3-MGO (Marcks) 81-691]

Gerhard Marcks 1889-1981 . Marcks, Gerhard.
München , c1988. 220 p. : ISBN 3-7913-0777-0
    DDC 730/.92 B 20
NB588.M35 A3 1988
              NYPL [3-MGO (Marcks) 90-12499]

Gerhard Richter, Atlas /. Richter, Gerhard, 1932-
München , c1989. 232 p. :
              NYPL [3-MCK+ R528 91-3384]

Gerhard Richter, 1988/89 . Richter, Gerhard,
1932- Rotterdam [1990] 166 p. : ISBN
    90-6918-046-4
ND588.R48 A4 1990

Gerhardus, Dietfried. Bild, Schema,
Konstruktion : zum Begriff des Konstruierens in
der Konkreten Kunst am Beispiel der
Bodenplastik "Halbzylinder III" von Diethelm
Koch : mit der Erstveröffentlichung der
Werkgruppe, "Halbzylinder" I-XIII / Dietfried
Gerhardus. St. Ingbert : W.J. Röhrig, 1989. 72
p. : ill. ; 20 cm. (Kunst im Röhrig Verlag . Bd. 1)
    ISBN 3-924555-33-8
1. Koch, Diethelm. I. Title. II. Series.
IN PROCESS (ONLINE)
              NYPL [3-MGO (Koch) 91-7233]

Gericault . Carril, Bonifacio del. [Buenos Aires?] ,
1989. 27, [3] p. : ISBN 950-0-40910-0 DDC
769.92 20
NE2349.5.G44 C37 1989
              NYPL [MDG+ (Géricault) 90-11344]

Géricault, Théodore, 1791-1824.
Bazin, Germain. Théodore Géricault . Paris ,
c1987-c1990. 4 v. : ISBN 2-85047-016-3 (t. 1)
    DDC 759.4 20
N6853.G355 B39 1987
              NYPL [MCO+ G36 89-6652]

**GÉRICAULT, THÉODORE, 1791-1824 -
CATALOGUES RAISONNÉS.**
Bazin, Germain. Théodore Géricault . Paris ,
c1987-c1990. 4 v. : ISBN 2-85047-016-3 (t. 1)
    DDC 759.4 20
N6853.G355 B39 1987
              NYPL [MCO+ G36 89-6652]

**GÉRICAULT, THÉODORE, 1791-1824 -
CRITICISM AND INTERPRETATION.**
Bazin, Germain. Théodore Géricault . Paris ,
c1987-c1990. 4 v. : ISBN 2-85047-016-3 (t. 1)
    DDC 759.4 20
N6853.G355 B39 1987
              NYPL [MCO+ G36 89-6652]

Carril, Bonifacio del. Gericault . [Buenos
Aires?] , 1989. 27, [3] p. : ISBN 950-0-40910-0
    DDC 769.92 20
NE2349.5.G44 C37 1989
              NYPL [MDG+ (Géricault) 90-11344]

Geringer, Laura. Yours 'til the ice cracks : a book
of valentines / by Laura Geringer ; illustrated
by Andrea Baruffi. New York : HarperCollins
Publishers, 1992. p. cm. A book of whimsical
Valentine's Day sayings and pictures. ISBN
    0-06-020399-4   DDC 741.6/84 20
*1. Valentines - Juvenile literature. I. Baruffi, Andrea, ill.
II. Title.*
NC1860 .G47 1992

Gerken, J. Ellen. Click 1 . Cincinnati, Ohio ,
c1990. 149 p. : ISBN 0-89134-348-2 : DDC 700
20
N7433.8 .C55 1990
              NYPL [3-MAL+ 91-4501]

Gerkens, Gerhard. Greune, Karl Heinrich, 1933-
Karl Heinrich Greune . Bremen [1979] [80]
p. :
N6888.G733 A4 1979
              NYPL [3-MCK G837 81-784]

Gerlach, Siegfried. Die deutsche Stadt des
Absolutismus im Spiegel barocker Veduten und
zeitgenössischer Pläne : erweiterte Fassung
eines Vortrags am 11. November 1986 im
Reutlinger Spitalhof / Siegfried Gerlach.
Stuttgart : F. Steiner, c1990. 80 p. : ill. (some
col.) ; 24 cm. (Erdkundliches Wissen. Heft 101)
Includes bibliographical references. ISBN
3-515-05600-9
*1. Architecture, Baroque - Germany - History. 2. Cities
and towns - Germany - History. I. Reutlinger Spitalhof.
II. Title.*
IN PROCESS (ONLINE)
              NYPL [3-MQWD 91-3447]

Gerlinde Beck . Beck, Gerlinde, 1930- Stuttgart ,
c1990. 120 p. : ISBN 3-87346-093-9
              NYPL [3-MGO+ (Beck) 91-5636]

Gerlovin, Valeriy.
Gerlovina, Rimma. Still performances /.
Cambridge, Mass. , 1989. 39 p. : ISBN
    0-938437-27-5   DDC 779/.092/2 20
NX556.Z9 G472 1989
              NYPL [MFW 90-4189]

GERLOVIN, VALERIY - EXHIBITIONS.
Gerlovina, Rimma. Still performances /.
Cambridge, Mass. , 1989. 39 p. : ISBN
    0-938437-27-5   DDC 779/.092/2 20
NX556.Z9 G472 1989
              NYPL [MFW 90-4189]

Gerlovina, Rimma.
Still performances / Rimma Gerlovina and
Valeriy Gerlovin. Cambridge, Mass. : MIT List
Visual Arts Center, 1989. 39 p. : ill. ; 22 x 23
cm. Catalog of an exhibition held at the MIT List
Visual Arts Center, Sept. 5-Oct. 8, 1989 and Anderson
Gallery, Virginia Commonwealth University, Nov. 21,
1989-Jan. 14, 1990. Includes bibliographical references.
    ISBN 0-938437-27-5   DDC 779/.092/2 20
*1. Gerlovina, Rimma - Exhibitions. 2. Gerlovin,
Valeriy - Exhibitions. 3. Performance art - Russian
S.F.S.R. - Exhibitions. 4. Conceptual art - Russian
S.F.S.R. - Exhibitions. I. Gerlovin, Valeriy. II. Albert
and Vera List Visual Arts Center. III. Anderson
Gallery. IV. Title.*
NX556.Z9 G472 1989
              NYPL [MFW 90-4189]

GERLOVINA, RIMMA - EXHIBITIONS.
Gerlovina, Rimma. Still performances /.
Cambridge, Mass. , 1989. 39 p. : ISBN
    0-938437-27-5   DDC 779/.092/2 20
NX556.Z9 G472 1989
              NYPL [MFW 90-4189]

Germaine, Ina M. (Ina May) Bowman, Irving. A
portfolio of interiors . [New York] [1941?] 17,
17 leaves :   ***NYPL [3-MLO+ 90-2451]***

Germaine, Max, 1914- Artists & galleries of
Australia / Max Germaine. Rev. and enl. 3rd
ed. Roseville, NSW, Australia : Craftsman
House, c1990. 2 v. (xii, 832 p.) : ill. ; 31 cm.
    ISBN 976-8097-02-7
*1. Artists - Australia - Biography. 2. Art museums -
Australia - Directories. 3. Art galleries, Commercial -
Australia - Directories. I. Title. II. Title: Artists and
galleries of Australia.* ***NYPL [MAO+ 91-2667]***

GERMAN ART. see ART, GERMAN.

GERMAN ARTS. see ARTS, GERMAN.

**GERMAN BOOK-PLATES. see BOOK-PLATES,
GERMAN.**

**GERMAN EMBLEM BOOKS. see EMBLEM
BOOKS, GERMAN.**

**GERMAN ENGRAVING. see ENGRAVING,
GERMAN.**

German expressionist paintings : from the
collection of Mr. and Mrs. Morton D. May /
[foreword, Vincent Price]. [S.l. : s.n.], [196-]
[60] p. : ill. ; 28 cm. Includes essay, "German
expressionism," by Otto Karl Bach. Cover title. Catalog
of an exhibition held at the Denver Art Museum and 9
other locations, 1960-62.
*1. May, Morton D., 1914- Art collections -
Exhibitions. 2. May, Marge Wolcott - Art collections -
Exhibitions. 3. Expressionism (Art) - Germany -
Exhibitions. 4. Painting, Modern - 20th century -
Germany - Private collections - Missouri - St. Louis -
Exhibitions. 5. Painting, German - Exhibitions. I. Bach,
Otto Karl. II. Denver. Art Museum. III. Chicago. Art
Institute.*   ***NYPL [3-MCI 90-5896]***

German expressionist prints : Grafik des
deutschen Expressionismus / [responsible,
Hermann Pollig, Viola Suhle ; editor of the
catalogue and preface, Bernd Rau ; translation,
John Anthony Thwaites, Merle Roczen].
Stuttgart : Institute for Foreign Cultural
Relations, 1984. 1 portfolio (47, 151 p.) :
chiefly ill. (some col.) ; 24 cm. "An exhibition of
the Institute for Foreign Cultural Relations,
Stuttgart"--P. [3] (1st set) English and German. Includes
bibliographies.
*1. Prints, German - Exhibitions. 2. Prints - 20th
century - Germany - Exhibitions. 3. Expressionism
(Art) - Germany - Exhibitions. I. Pollig, Hermann. II.
Suhle, Viola. III. Rau, Bernd. IV. Title: Grafik des
deutschen Expressionismus.*
              NYPL [MDBF 85-1960]

German expressionist prints and drawings .
Robert Gore Rifkind Center for German
Expressionist Studies. Los Angeles, Calif. :
Munich, Federal Republic of Germany : 2 v. :
    ISBN 3-7913-0959-5 (Prestel Verlag : set) DDC
    760/.0943 19
N6868.5.E9 R6 1989
              NYPL [MDE+ 91-5830]

GERMAN LANGUAGE - TERMINOLOGY.
Fachterminologie für den historischen Holzbau .
Köln , 1990. 49 p. :
NA4115 .F34 1990

GERMAN LITERATURE - 20TH CENTURY.
Durch den Tag laufen . Berlin , 1989. 287 p. :
    ISBN 3-7303-0434-8
PT3732 .D87 1989
              NYPL [3-MAMG 90-10453]

GERMAN LITERATURE - GERMANY, EAST.
Durch den Tag laufen . Berlin , 1989. 287 p. :
    ISBN 3-7303-0434-8
PT3732 .D87 1989
              NYPL [3-MAMG 90-10453]

**GERMAN MURAL PAINTING AND
DECORATION. see MURAL PAINTING
AND DECORATION, GERMAN.**

**GERMAN NEWSPAPERS - BERLIN -
HISTORY - EXHIBITIONS.**
Berliner Pressezeichner der Zwanziger Jahre .
Berlin , 1977. [68] p. :
NC970 .B47   ***NYPL [3-MAMG 81-294]***

German painters in Brazil during the XIX century. Peixoto, Maria Elizabete Santos. Pintores alemães no Brasil durante o século XIX =. Rio de Janeiro , 1989. 244 p. : ISBN 85-7191-001-4 *NYPL [3-MCI+ 90-8914]*

German painters in Brazil during the XIX century. Peixoto, Maria Elizabete Santos. Pintores alemães no Brasil durante o século XIX =. Rio de Janeiro , 1989. 244 p. : ISBN 85-7191-001-4 DDC 750/.89/31081 20 *ND354 .P45 1989*

GERMAN PAINTING. see PAINTING, GERMAN.

GERMAN PRINTS. see PRINTS, GERMAN.

GERMAN SATIRE. see SATIRE, GERMAN.

GERMAN SCULPTURE. see SCULPTURE, GERMAN.

GERMAN WIT AND HUMOR, PICTORIAL.
Busch, Wilhelm, 1832-1908. Gesammelte Werke /. München , c1959. 996 p. : *NYPL [3-MEM (Busch) 91-6173]*

Haitzinger, Horst, 1939- Deutschland, Deutschland /. München , c1990. 125 p. : ISBN 3-7654-2311-4 *NYPL [3-MEM (Haitzinger) 91-3584]*

Kmölniger, Elisabeth, 1947- Elisabeth Kmölniger, Zeichnungen /. Frankfurt am Main , 1987. 146 p. : *NYPL [3-MEM+ (Kmölniger) 90-10838]*

Rauch, Hans-Georg, 1939- Neue Zeitzeichen /. Hamburg , c1990. [144] p. : ISBN 3-89315-028-5 DDC 741.5/943 20 *NC1509.R34 A4 1990*

Schade, Rainer. Rainer Schade . Berlin , c1989. 158 p. : ISBN 3-359-00341-1 *NC1509.S275 A4 1989*

Verstappen, Andreas, 1960- Waechters Erzählungen . Köln , c1990. 209 p., 11 p. of plates : ISBN 3-7701-2420-0 : *NC1509.W3 V47 1990*

GERMAN WIT AND HUMOR, PICTORIAL - EXHIBITIONS.
Humorist Walter Trier . [Toronto] [c1980] 48 p. : ISBN 0-919876-56-0 (pbk.) *NC1509.T74 A4 1980* *NYPL [3-MEM (Trier) 81-644]*

Papan. Karikaturen . [Mannheim] , 1988. [50] p. : ISBN 3-926857-01-3 *NYPL [3-MEM+ (Papan) 89-11634]*

Germanisches National-Museum zur Deutschen Kunst- und Kulturgeschichte, Nuremberg. see Nuremberg. Germanisches Nationalmuseum.

Germanisches Nationalmuseum. Werner, Martina, 1929- Der graue Fetisch . Nürnberg , c1987. 44 p. : *MLCS 88/03971 (N)* *NYPL [3-MGO (Werner) 90-13400]*

Germanisches Nationalmuseum, Nuremberg. see Nuremberg. Germanisches Nationalmuseum.

Germanisches Nationalmuseum Nürnberg. Barockmaler in Böhmen. München [1961] 36 p. *N6832.B3 H8* *NYPL [3-MCY 90-5883]*

Knupper, Friedrich, 1947-1987. Friedrich Knupper . Nürnberg , c1990. 103 p. : ISBN 3-926982-20-9 *NYPL [3-MNR 91-6999]*

Pülhorn, Wolfgang. Antike Kleinkunst . Nürnberg , 1987. 163 p. : ISBN 3-9801529-0-1 DDC 738.3/82/093807443324 20 *NK3835 .P85 1987* *NYPL [3-MPE 90-11122]*

Sitz-Gelegenheiten . Nürnberg , c1989. 263 p. : ISBN 3-926982-13-6 *IN PROCESS (ONLINE)* *NYPL [3-MOF 91-6263]*

Textil im Freien . Nürnberg , c1989. [53] p. : *MLCM 89/00525 (N)* *NYPL [3-MGI 91-6975]*

Germanisches Nationalmuseum Nürnberg. Archiv für Bildende Kunst. Marcks, Gerhard. Gerhard Marcks 1889-1981 . München , c1988. 220 p. : ISBN 3-7913-0777-0 DDC 730/.92 B 20 *NB588.M35 A3 1988* *NYPL [3-MGO (Marcks) 90-12499]*

GERMANISCHES NATIONALMUSEUM NÜRNBERG - CATALOGS.
Pülhorn, Wolfgang. Antike Kleinkunst .

Nürnberg , 1987. 163 p. : ISBN 3-9801529-0-1 DDC 738.3/82/093807443324 20 *NK3835 .P85 1987* *NYPL [3-MPE 90-11122]*

GERMANS - BELGIUM - BIOGRAPHY.
The Ideological crisis of expressionism . Columbia, S.C. , c1990. 299 p. : 0-938100-77-7 (alk. paper) DDC 700 20 *NX550.A1 I33 1990* *NYPL [3-MAMG 90-11742]*

GERMANY - CULTURAL POLICY - EXHIBITIONS.
Degenerate art . Los Angeles, Calif. , New York , c1991. 423 p. : ISBN 0-8109-3653-4 DDC 709/.43/07477311 20 *N6868 .D3388 1991*

Degenerate art . Los Angeles, Calif. , New York , c1991. p. cm. ISBN 0-87587-158-5 DDC 709/.43/07477311 20 *N6868 .D3388 1991b*

GERMANY - CULTURAL POLICY - HISTORY - 20TH CENTURY.
Brock, Bazon, 1936- Die Re-Dekade . München , c1990. 298 p. : ISBN 3-7814-0288-6 : *NX550.A1 B76 1990*

Kunst auf Befehl? . München , c1990. 275 p. : ISBN 3-7814-0285-1 DDC 701/.03 20 *N6868.5.N37 K85 1990*

Kunst und Kunstkritik der dreissiger Jahre . Dresden , c1990. 353 p. : ISBN 3-364-00190-1 *N6868 .K7865 1990*

GERMANY - DESCRIPTION AND TRAVEL - VIEWS.
Ost sieht West, West sieht Ost . Stuttgart , c1990. 179 p. : ISBN 3-89322-215-4 *NYPL [MFW+ 91-6972]*

GERMANY, EAST - DESCRIPTION AND TRAVEL - VIEWS.
Olle DDR . Berlin , c1990. 168 p. : ISBN 3-362-00521-7 *NYPL [MFW 91-8049]*

Germany, East - Government. see Germany, East - Politics and government.

GERMANY (EAST) - POLITICS AND GOVERNMENT - 1989-1990.
Olle DDR . Berlin , c1990. 168 p. : ISBN 3-362-00521-7 *NYPL [MFW 91-8049]*

GERMANY (EAST) - SOCIAL CONDITIONS - PICTORIAL WORKS.
Olle DDR . Berlin , c1990. 168 p. : ISBN 3-362-00521-7 *NYPL [MFW 91-8049]*

GERMANY. GEHEIME STAATSPOLIZEI - BUILDINGS.
Zum Umgang mit dem Gestapo-Gelände . [Berlin , 1988] 105, 25, 73 p. : *NA1068.5.N37 Z85 1988*

Germany. Gestapo. see Germany. Geheime Staatspolizei.

GERMANY - HISTORICAL GEOGRAPHY - MAPS.
Historische Karten aus der Sammlung der Ernst-Moritz-Arndt-Universität Greifswald in der Sektion Geographie /. Greifswald , 1981. 1 portfolio (20 maps (some col.)) ; *NYPL [Map Div. 86-337]*

Jähnig, Bernhart. Kleiner Atlas zur deutschen Territorialgeschichte /. Bonn , 19. 192 p. : ISBN 3-88557-057-2 *NYPL [Map Div. 91-67]*

Quad, Matthias, 1557-1613. Einzelkarten des Matthias Quad (1557-1613) /. Mönchengladbach , 1984. 1 atlas (1 portfolio ([10] folded leaves of plates)) : DDC 911/.43 19 *G1912.2 .Q8 1984 NYPL [Map Div. 87-177]*

GERMANY - HISTORY - 20TH CENTURY - EXHIBITIONS.
Berliner Pressezeichner der Zwanziger Jahre . Berlin , 1977. [68] p. : *NC970 .B47* *NYPL [3-MAMG 81-294]*

GERMANY - HISTORY - 1918-1933 - ANECDOTES, FACETIAE, SATIRE, ETC.
Haese, Klaus. Frau Republik geht pleite . Berlin , c1990. 144 p. : ISBN 3-361-00251-6 : *IN PROCESS (ONLINE)* *NYPL [MDY 91-3467]*

GERMANY - HISTORY - 1918-1933 - CARCATURES AND CARTOONS.
Lewis, Beth Irwin. George Grosz . Princeton, N.J. , c1991. p. cm. ISBN 0-691-00291-6 (pbk.) :

DDC 741/.092 B 20 *NC251.G66 L48 1991*

GERMANY - HISTORY - 1918-1933 - EXHIBITIONS.
Die Zwanziger Jahre in München . München , 1979. xxiii, 768 p. : *NX550.M86 Z9 NYPL [3-MAMG 81-913]*

GERMANY - HISTORY - REVOLUTION, 1918 - ART AND THE REVOLUTION.
Weinstein, Joan. The end of expressionism . Chicago , 1990. xiv, 332 p. : 0-226-89059-7 DDC 701/.03 19 *N6868.5.E9 W45 1989* *NYPL [3-MAMG 90-11096]*

Germany - History - Atlases. see Germany - Historical geography - Maps.

Germany - History - Maps. see Germany - Historical geography - Maps.

GERMANY IN ART - EXHIBITIONS.
Berliner Pressezeichner der Zwanziger Jahre . Berlin , 1977. [68] p. : *NC970 .B47* *NYPL [3-MAMG 81-294]*

GERMANY - MAPS, EARLY - TO 1800.
Quad, Matthias, 1557-1613. Einzelkarten des Matthias Quad (1557-1613) /. Mönchengladbach , 1984. 1 atlas (1 portfolio ([10] folded leaves of plates)) : DDC 911/.43 19 *G1912.2 .Q8 1984 NYPL [Map Div. 87-177]*

GERMANY - ROAD MAPS.
(1924) Continental Gummi-Werke AG. Continental Atlas für Mittel-Europa. Hannover [1924] viii, 65 (i.e. 66) fold. col. maps. *G1881.P2 C6 1924* *NYPL [Map Div. 83-672]*

(1965) Mairs Geographischer Verlag. Der Grosse Shell Atlas. Stuttgart , c1965-1966. viii, 283, [166], x-xxii p. : *NYPL [Map Div. 90-5904]*

Germany (West). Bundesministerium für Gesamtdeutsche Fragen. Polit-kunst in der Sowjetischen Besatzungszone Deutschlands. Die "Deutsche Kunstausstellung 1962" in Dresden und ihre vorgänger. Bonn [1963?] 64 p., ill., plates, 21 cm. Dritte überarbeitete und ergänzte auflage.
1. Art, Modern - 20th century - Germany, East. I. Deutsche Kunstausstellung (1962 : Dresden, Germany). II. Title. *NYPL [3-MAMG 90-6808]*

GERMANY, WEST - DESCRIPTION AND TRAVEL - VIEWS.
Reinartz, Dirk, 1947- Kein schöner Land . Göttingen , 1989. ca. 180 p. : ISBN 3-88243-127-X *NYPL [MFX+ (Reinartz) 90-13430]*

GERMANY (WEST) - DESCRIPTION AND TRAVEL - VIEWS - EXHIBITIONS.
Bilder aus der Bundesrepublik . Hannover , c1982. [92] p. : *NYPL [MFW 84-1657]*

GERMANY, WEST - POLITICS AND GOVERNMENT - CARICATURES AND CARTOONS.
Haitzinger, Horst, 1939- Deutschland, Deutschland /. München , c1990. 125 p. : ISBN 3-7654-2311-4 *NYPL [3-MEM (Haitzinger) 91-3584]*

Germany, Western. see Germany, West.

Gerome Kamrowski . Kamrowski, Gerome. Detroit, Mich. [1990] 15 p. : *NYPL [3-MCX K155 91-6272]*

Gerón, Cándido, 1950-
Antología de la pintura dominicana = Anthology of Dominican painting / Cándido Gerón ; [traducción al inglés y al francés, Doña Guillermina Nadal]. [Santo Domingo, Dominican Republic? : s.n., 1990] [Santo Domingo, República Dominicana : Editora Tele 3) 148 p. : ill. (some col.) ; 29 cm. Text in Spanish, English, and French. DDC 759.97293 20
1. Painting, Dominican - Themes, motives. 2. Painting, Modern - 19th century - Dominican Republic - Themes, motives. 3. Painting, Modern - 20th century - Dominican Republic - Themes, motives. I. Title. II. Title: Anthology of Dominican painting. *ND315.D6 G45 1990*

Antología de la pintura dominicana = Anthology of Dominican painting = Anthologie de la peinture dominicaine / Cándido Gerón. [S.l. : s.n.], 1990. 148 p. : ill. ; 30 cm. Spanish, English and French.

1. Painting, Dominican. I. Title. II. Title: Anthology of Dominican painting. III. Title: Anthologie de la peinture dominicaine.
NYPL [3-MCY+ 90-13378]

Gerona (Spain : Province). Diputación Provincial. Fita, Domènec, 1927- Fita pintura, 1942-1989. [Girona] , 1990. 207 p. : ISBN 84-86812-18-6
ND813.F58 A4 1990

Gerrit Rietveld Academie. The Other side of photography . Amsterdam , c1989. 220 p. : ISBN 90-6617-055-7 (pbk.)
NYPL [MFW 91-2504]

GERRY, PEGGY - ART COLLECTIONS - EXHIBITIONS. Metropolitan Museum of Art (New York, N.Y.) Japanese art from the Gerry collection in the Metropolitan Museum of Art / . New York , c1989. 141 p. : ISBN 0-87099-556-1 DDC 738/.0952/0747471 20
N7352 .F67 1989 **NYPL [3-MAG 89-28868]**

GERRY, ROGER, 1916- - ART COLLECTIONS - EXHIBITIONS. Metropolitan Museum of Art (New York, N.Y.) Japanese art from the Gerry collection in the Metropolitan Museum of Art / . New York , c1989. 141 p. : ISBN 0-87099-556-1 DDC 738/.0952/0747471 20
N7352 .F67 1989 **NYPL [3-MAG 89-28868]**

Gersh-Nešić, Beth S. The early criticism of André Salmon : a study of his thoughts on Cubism / Beth S. Gersh-Nešić. New York : Garland, 1991. p. cm. (Studies in the fine arts) Originally presented as the author's thesis (Ph. D.)--City University of New York, 1989. Includes bibliographical references and index. ISBN 0-8153-0115-4 (alk. paper) DDC 759.4/09/041 20
1. Cubism - France. 2. Art, Modern - 20th century - France. 3. Salmon, André, 1881- . 4. Art criticism - France - History - 20th century. I. Title. II. Series.
N6848.5.C82 G46 1991

Gerson Gallery, New York. see Marlborough-Gerson Gallery.

Gerson lecture. (2nd) Freedberg, David. Iconoclasts and their motives / . Maarssen , Montclair, N.J. , c1985. 60 p. : ill. ISBN 90-6179-056-5 (pbk.) DDC 709 19
N8557 .F74 1985 **NYPL [3-MAS 91-5030]**

Gerson (Otto) Gallery, New York. see Marlborough-Gerson Gallery.

Gerstler, Amy. Past lives / Amy Gerstler and Alexis Smith. 1st ed. Santa Monica, Calif. : Santa Monica Museum of Art, c1989. 40 p. : ill. (some col.) ; 23 cm. Accompanies an exhibition held at the Santa Monica Museum of Art. ISBN 0-929335-01-5 DDC 700/.92 20
1. Gerstler, Amy - Exhibitions. 2. Smith, Alexis, 1949- - Exhibitions. 3. Artists' books - United States - Exhibitions. I. Smith, Alexis, 1949-. II. Santa Monica Museum of Art. III. Title.
N7433.4.G45 A4 1989

Smith, Alexis, 1949- Alexis Smith / . New York , 1991. p. cm. ISBN 0-87427-076-6 DDC 700/.92 20
N6537.S58 A4 1991

GERSTLER, AMY - EXHIBITIONS. Gerstler, Amy. Past lives / . Santa Monica, Calif. , c1989. 40 p. : ISBN 0-929335-01-5 DDC 700/.92 20
N7433.4.G45 A4 1989

Gerstner, Karl. The forms of color : the interaction of visual elements / Karl Gerstner. Cambridge, Mass. : MIT Press, c1986. 179 p. : ill. (some col.) ; 25 cm. Translation of: Die Formen der Farben. ISBN 0-262-07100-2 DDC 701/.8 19
1. Color in art. 2. Geometry. I. Title.
ND1489 .G4713 1986
NYPL [3-MAMZ 91-6985]

Gertraud Möhwald . Möhwald, Gertraud, 1929- Halle , 1989. 182 p. : ISBN 3-86105-026-9 DDC 730/.092 20
NK4210.M585 A4 1989
NYPL [3-MPGK 91-5045]

Gertrude Abercrombie : an exhibition / organized for the Illinois State Museum by Kent J. Smith with Susan Weininger ; with an essay by Susan Weininger. Springfield, IL : Illinois State Museum, 1991. p. cm. Includes bibliographical references. ISBN 0-89792-132-1 DDC 759.13 20

1. Abercrombie, Gertrude, 1909-1977 - Exhibitions. I. Smith, Kent, 1949-. II. Weininger, Susan. III. Illinois State Museum.
ND237.A235 A4 1991

Gertrude Stein . Stavitsky, Gail, 1954- New York, N.Y. , c1990. 52 p. :
NYPL [3-MAMT 91-7537]

Gertrude Stein on Picasso. Stein, Gertrude, 1874-1946. New York [1970] 122, [16] p. : ISBN 0-87140-513-X DDC 759.6
ND553.P5 S76
NYPL [3-MCQ P58 90-11647]

Gervasoni, Marie-George. Biennale di Venezia (44th : 1990) Dimensione futuro . [Venezia] [Milano] , c1990. 348 p. : ISBN 88-20-80356-9 DDC 709/.04/80744531 20
N6488.I8 V43 1990

Gerz, Jochen. Jochen Gerz, 5 Installationen 1975-1979 : [Ausstellung] 18. Januar bis 2. März Frankfurter Kunstverein Steineres Haus am Römberg. Frankfurt : Der Kunstverein, 1980. 1 portfolio ([24] pieces) : ill. ; 42 cm. This work includes the catalog of the exhibition at the Frankfurter Kunstverein (1 part) and a facsimile of the "Venedig-Manuskript" Biennale Venedig 1976 (23 parts)
1. Gerz, Jochen. I. Gerz, Jochen Venedig-Manuskript. II. Frankfurter Kunstverein, Frankfurt am Main.
NYPL [3-MCK++ G288 82-855]

Venedig-Manuskript. Gerz, Jochen. Jochen Gerz, 5 Installationen 1975-1979 : [Ausstellung] 18. Januar bis 2. März Frankfurter Kunstverein Steineres Haus am Römberg. Frankfurt , 1980. 1 portfolio ([24] pieces) : **NYPL [3-MCK++ G288 82-855]**

GERZ, JOCHEN. Gerz, Jochen. Jochen Gerz, 5 Installationen 1975-1979 . Frankfurt , 1980. 1 portfolio ([24] pieces) : **NYPL [3-MCK++ G288 82-855]**

Gesammelte Werke /. Busch, Wilhelm, 1832-1908. München , c1959. 996 p. :
NYPL [3-MEM (Busch) 91-6173]

Gesamtverzeichnis der Malerei und Grafik /. Nitsch, Hermann, 1938- [Works. 1986.] Wien , c1986. v. : ISBN 3-85449-011-9 (Bd. 1) DDC 760/.092/4 19
N6811.5.N58 A4 1986
NYPL [3-MCK N772 90-11453]

Geschichte und kritischer Katalog des deutschen, niederländischen und französischen Kupferstichs im xv. Jahrhundert. Lehrs, Max, 1855-1938. [New York, 1970?] 9 v.
NE1450 .L513

Geschichtete Momente /. Kaufhold, Enno, 1944- Berlin , c1989. 112 p. : ISBN 3-88940-035-3
NYPL [MFX (Kaufhold) 91-3330]

Geschichtsbilder aus dem alten Österreich : unbekannte Historienmalerei des 19. Jahrhunderts : eine Ausstellung der Österreichischen Galerie Wien in Schloss Halbturn, 3. Mai bis 26. Oktober 1989 / [Redaktion und Gestaltung, Gerbert Frodel]. Wien : Die Galerie, 1989. [100] p. : col. ill. ; 21 x 24 cm. (Wechselausstellung der Österreichischen Galerie. 133) Includes bibliographical references.
1. History in art - Exhibitions. 2. Genre painting - Austria - 19th century - Exhibitions. I. Frodel, Gerbert. II. Österreichische Galerie. III. Schloss Halbturn (Halbturn, Austria). IV. Title: Unbekannte Historienmalerei des 19. Jahrhunderts.
NYPL [3-MAW (Vienna) (Vienna. Österreichische Galerie. Wechselausstellung. Nr.133)]

Gesellschaft der Berliner Sezession. see Berliner Secession.

Gesellschaft für Deutsch-Sowjetische Freundschaft. Skulptur, Grafik, Zeichnung aus der Deutschen Demokratischen Republik . Berlin [1984] [44] p. :
MLCM 87/97 (N)
NYPL [3-MAMG 90-10659]

Gesellschaft für Ausbildungsforschung und Berufsentwicklung (Munich, Germany) Künstlerisch handeln . Stuttgart , c1989. 170 p. : ISBN 3-7725-0914-2
N199 .K857 1989

Gesetze des Sehens /. Metzger, Wolfgang, 1899-1979. Frankfurt am Main , 1975, c1953. 676 p. : ISBN 3-7829-1047-8 : DDC 152.1/4
BF241 .M4 1975 **NYPL [3-MA 91-1148]**

Geslotten circuits. Open mind . Milano , c1989. 318 p. : **NYPL [3-MAMZ 90-11011]**

Gespräch . Böhmer, Gunter, 1911- [Memmingen] , 1989. 1 v. (unpaged) : ISBN 3-922406-43-2
NYPL [3-MCK+ B671 91-5538]

Gestapo. see Germany. Geheime Staatspolizei.

GESTURE IN ART. Nitschke, August, 1926- Körper in Bewegung . Stuttgart , c1989. 399 p. : ISBN 3-7831-0955-8 DDC 704.9/42 20
N7625.5 .N58 1989

Getscher, Robert H. Whistler, James McNeill, 1834-1903. James Abbott McNeill Whistler--pastels / . New York , 1991. p. cm. ISBN 0-8076-1266-9 : DDC 741.973 20
NC139.W45 A4 1991

Getting started in drawing /. Blake, Wendon. Cincinnati, Ohio , c1991. vi, 137 p. : ISBN 0-89134-361-X (hrdcvr.) : DDC 741.2 20
NC730 .B535 1991

Getting to know the world's greatest artists. Venezia, Mike. Francisco Goya / . Chicago , 1991. p. cm. ISBN 0-516-02292-X DDC 759.6 B 92 20
ND813.G7 V4 1991

Venezia, Mike. Michelangelo / . Chicago , 1991. p. cm. ISBN 0-516-02293-8 DDC 700/.92 B 20
N6923.B9 V44 1991

Venezia, Mike. Paul Klee / . Chicago , 1991. p. cm. ISBN 0-516-02294-6 DDC 759.9494 B 20
ND588.K5 V46 1991

Venezia, Mike. Sandro Botticelli / . Chicago , 1991. p. cm. ISBN 0-516-02291-1 DDC 759.5 B 92 20
ND623.B7 V37 1991

The Getty Center : design process / Harold Williams ... [et al.]. Los Angeles : J. Paul Getty Trust, 1991. p. cm. ISBN 0-89236-210-3 (paper) : DDC 727 20
1. Getty Center (Los Angeles, Calif.). 2. Art centers - California - Los Angeles - Designs and plans. 3. Richard Meier & Partners. 4. The Getty Center (Calif.) - Buildings, structures, etc. I. Williams, Harold Marvin, 1928-.
NA6813.U6 L674 1991

Getty Center for Education in the Arts. Discipline-based art education . Santa Monica, Calif. , 1991. p. cm. ISBN 0-89236-171-9 : DDC 700 20
N362 .C6 1991

GETTY CENTER (LOS ANGELES, CALIF.) The Getty Center . Los Angeles , 1991. p. cm. ISBN 0-89236-210-3 (paper) : DDC 727 20
NA6813.U6 L674 1991

Getty Conservation Institute. The Conservation of the Orpheus Mosaic at Paphos, Cyprus. Marinadel Rey, CA , 1991. p. cm. ISBN 0-89236-188-3 (paperback) : DDC 738.5/2 20
NA3770 .C65 1991

The Conservation of wall paintings . Marina del Rey, CA , 1991. p. cm. ISBN 0-89236-162-X (pbk.) DDC 751.6/2 20
ND2552 .C64 1991

Getty Museum studies on art. Lippincott, Louise, 1953- Lawrence Alma Tadema . Malibu, Calif. , 1991. p. cm. ISBN 0-89236-186-7 : DDC 759.2 20
ND497.A4 A755 1991

Gewerbemuseum Basel. Baumberger, Otto, 1889-1961. Otto Baumberger, 1889-1961 . Zürich , c1988. 127 p. : ISBN 3-907065-27-1 DDC 741.6/74/092 20
NC1850.B38 A4 1988
NYPL [3-MDW 90-13136]

Le Musée sentimental de Bâle / erausgegeben von Barbara Huber-Greub und Stephen Andreae ; [Idee und künstlerische Leitung: Daniel Spoerri]. Basel , c1989. 332 p. : ISBN 3-85700-006-X
NYPL [3-MAVZ (Basel) 90-13397]

Gharabagh / [texts, Maria Adelaide ... et al.]. 1st ed. Milano, Italia : OEMME, 1988. 107 p. : chiefly col. ill., maps, plans ; 27 x 28 cm. (Documenti di architettura armena = Documents of Armenian architecture . 19) English and Italian. Bibliography: p. 24-31. ISBN 88-85822-09-6

1. Architecture, Armenian - Azerbaijan S.S.R. - Nagorno-Karabakhskaiā avtonomnaiā oblast'. 2. Church architecture - Azerbaijan S.S.R. - Nagorno-Karabakhskaiā avtonomnaiā oblast'. 3. Nagorno-Karabakhskaiā avtonomnaiā oblast' (Azerbaijan S.S.R.) - Antiquities. I. Adelaide, Maria. II. Series: Documenti di architettura armena , 19.
NYPL [3-MQW 91-4235]

Gheorghe M. Tattarescu, un pictor Romîn şi veacul său. Wertheimer-Ghika, Jacques. [Bucureşti] 1958. 288 p.
NYPL [3-MCZ T22 91-1177]

Gheorghe Petraşcu /. Florea, Vasile. Bucharest , 1990. 109 p. : ISBN 973-330-041-1 DDC 759.9498 20
ND933.P4 F55 1990

Gheyn, Jacob de, 1565-1629. Fondation Custodia. Le héraut du dix-septième siècle . Paris , 1985. xi, 153 p., 80 p. of plates :
NE670.G74 A4 1985

GHEYN, JACOB DE, 1565-1629 - EXHIBITIONS. Fondation Custodia. Le héraut du dix-septième siècle . Paris , 1985. xi, 153 p., 80 p. of plates :
NE670.G74 A4 1985

Gheyn, Jacques de, 1595-1641. Fondation Custodia. Le héraut du dix-septième siècle . Paris , 1985. xi, 153 p., 80 p. of plates :
NE670.G74 A4 1985

GHEYN, JACQUESDE, 1595-1641 - EXHIBITIONS. Fondation Custodia. Le héraut du dix-septième siècle . Paris , 1985. xi, 153 p., 80 p. of plates :
NE670.G74 A4 1985

Ghika. Ghika, 1906- [Paris, 1973?] 1 v. (chiefly illus.) DDC 741.9/495
NC254.C45 G34
NYPL [3-MCZ C495 90-6263]

Ghika, Jacques Wertheimer- see **Wertheimer-Ghika, Jacques.**

Ghika, 1906- Ghika. [Paris] Alexander Iolas Gallery [1973?] 1 v. (chiefly illus.) 20 x 31 cm. DDC 741.9/495
1. Ghika, 1906-. I. Galerie Alexandre Iolas (Paris, France). II. Title.
NC254.C45 G34
NYPL [3-MCZ C495 90-6263]

GHIKA, 1906- Ghika, 1906- Ghika. [Paris, 1973?] 1 v. (chiefly illus.) DDC 741.9/495
NC254.C45 G34
NYPL [3-MCZ C495 90-6263]

Ghiraldi, Gaetano. Galleria, museo e medagliere estense (Modena, Italy) La Galleria estense . Modena [1990] 197 p. : ISBN 88-7686-154-8 :
NYPL [3-MAVZ+ (Modena) 91-4947]

Ghirardo, Diane Yvonne. Out of site . Seattle , 1991. 251 p. : ISBN 0-941920-20-8 : DDC 720/.1/03 20
NA2543.S6 O9 1991   NYPL [JFD 91-5955]

Ghozland, F. Mémoire de l'affiche : une année de créations françaises / Freddy Ghozland. Toulouse : Milan, c1990. 101 p. : col. ill. ; 23 x 28 cm. ISBN 2-86726-619-X
1. Posters, French - Catalogs. 2. Posters - 20th century - France - Catalogs. I. Title.
NC1807.F7 G47 1990

Già e non ancora. Arte . (90) Beigbeder, Olivier. [Lexique des symboles. Italian.] Lessico dei simboli medievali /. Milano , 1989. 304 p., [114] p. of plates : ISBN 88-16-60090-X
NYPL [3-MAMZ 91-5818]

Giacalone, Vito. The Eccentric painters of Yangzhou / Vito Giacalone ; with an essay by Ginger Cheng-chi Hsü. New York City : China House Gallery, China Institute in America, 1990. 92 p. : ill. (some col., 1 folded), 1 map ; 29 cm. Catalog of the exhibition held at China House Gallery, New York City, Oct. 20-Dec. 15, 1990. Bibliography: p. 86-88. ISBN 0-295-97087-1
1. Eight Eccentrics of Yang-chou (Group of painters) - Exhibitions. 2. Painting, Chinese - Ming-Ch'ing dynasties, 1368-1912 - Exhibitions. I. Hsü, Ginger Cheng-chi. II. China House Gallery. III. China Institute in America. IV. Title. *NYPL [3-MAG 91-6594]*

Giacomelli, Mario. Costabile, Franco, 1924-1965. Il canto dei nuovi emigranti /. Vibo Valentia, CZ , Milano , 1989. 64 p., [62] p. of plates :

ISBN 88-16-64013-8   DDC 851/.914 20
PQ4863.O767 C36 1989
NYPL [MFX+ (Giacomelli) 91-3400]

Giacometti, Alberto, 1901-1966. Alberto Giacometti. Basel : Galerie Beyeler, c1989. 139 p. : ill. ; 31 cm. Catalog of an exhibition held June-Sept. 1990.
1. Giacometti, Alberto, 1901-1966 - Exhibitions. I. Galerie Beyeler. II. Title.
NYPL [3-MGO+ (Giacometti) 90-13215]

Alberto Giacometti : Galerie Beyeler. Basel : La Galerie, c1989. 139 p. : ill. (some col.) ; 31 cm. French and German. Catalog of an exhibition held June-Sept. 1990. DDC 709/.2 20
1. Giacometti, Alberto, 1901-1966 - Exhibitions. I. Galerie Beyeler. II. Title.
N6853.G5 A4 1989

Alberto Giacometti, 10.10.1901-11.1.1966 : Sammlung Klewan : Salzburger Landessammlungen Rupertinum, Salzburg, Wiener-Philharmoniker-Gasse 9, 23. Februar-2. April 1989 / [Text, Otto Breicha ; Katalog, Helmut Klewan]. München : Galerie Klewan, c1989. [40] p. : ill. (some col.) ; 21 x 30 cm.
1. Giacometti, Alberto, 1901-1966 - Exhibitions. I. Breicha, Otto. II. Klewan, Helmut. III. Galerie Klewan. IV. Salzburger Landessammlungen Rupertinum. V. Title.
NYPL [3-MGO (Giacometti) 91-7078]

GIACOMETTI, ALBERTO, 1901-1966. Lord, James. A Giacometti portrait /. New York [c1965] 68 p., [4] p. of plates :
ND853.G44 L6
NYPL [3-MCZ G427 90-7105]

GIACOMETTI, ALBERTO, 1901-1966 - EXHIBITIONS. Giacometti, Alberto, 1901-1966. Alberto Giacometti. Basel , c1989. 139 p. :
NYPL [3-MGO+ (Giacometti) 90-13215]

Giacometti, Alberto, 1901-1966. Alberto Giacometti . Basel , c1989. 139 p. : DDC 709/.2 20
N6853.G5 A4 1989

Giacometti, Alberto, 1901-1966. Alberto Giacometti, 10.10.1901-11.1.1966 . München , c1989. [40] p. :
NYPL [3-MGO (Giacometti) 91-7078]

A Giacometti portrait /. Lord, James. New York [c1965] 68 p., [4] p. of plates :
ND853.G44 L6
NYPL [3-MCZ G427 90-7105]

Giacomo Caneva e la scuola fotografica romana (1847/1855) /. Becchetti, Piero. Firenze , c1989. 197 p. : ISBN 88-7292-106-8
NYPL [MFX+ (Caneva) 91-6016]

Giagiannos, Apostolos. Stephanidēs, Manos S., 1954- Apostolos Giagiannos . Athēna , 1986. 62 p. : *NYPL [3-MCZ G43 90-8058]*

GIAGIANNOS, APOSTOLOS. Stephanidēs, Manos S., 1954- Apostolos Giagiannos . Athēna , 1986. 62 p. :
NYPL [3-MCZ G43 90-8058]

Giambattista and Lorenzo Bregno . Schulz, Anne Markham, 1938- Cambridge [England] , New York , 1991. xi, 564 p. : ISBN 0-521-38406-0 DDC 730/.92 20
NB623.B746 S38 1991

Giambologna : il Mercurio volante e altre opere giovanili / [a cura di H. Keutner]. Firenze : Museo nazionale del Bargello, c1984. 35 p. : ill. ; 21 cm. (Lo Specchio del Bargello . 17) Bibliography: p. 35.
1. Giambologna, 1529-1608. 2. Mercury (Roman deity) - Art. I. Keutner, H. (Herbert). II. Museo nazionale di Firenze. III. Series.
NYPL [3-MGO (Giambologna) 86-955]

GIAMBOLOGNA, 1529-1608. Giambologna . Firenze , c1984. 35 p. :
NYPL [3-MGO (Giambologna) 86-955]

Gian Ferrari, Claudia. Casorati, Felice, 1883-1963. Casorati . Milano , 1989. 171 p. : ISBN 88-435-3139-5
NYPL [3-MCF C338 90-13079]

Fausto Pirandello / Claudia Gian Ferrari. Roma : Leonardo-De Luca, c1991. 162 p. : ill. ; 34 cm. ISBN 88-7813-321-3
1. Pirandello, Fausto, 1899-1975. I. Title.
NYPL [3-MCF+ P6667 91-7465]

Gianani, Faustino. Il Duomo di Pavia 1488-1932 / Faustino Gianani, Ottorino Modesti. Pavia :

EMI, c1989. 108 p. : ill. ; 30 cm. Reprint of the 1932 ed. ISBN 88-7129-191-3
1. Duomo di Pavia. I. Modesti, Ottorino. II. Title.
NYPL [3-MRBN+ 91-3663]

Gianella, Victor, 1918- Victor Gianella : abstractions / [edited by Helmut Gernsheim ; translated by Esther Lüthy]. [Ennetbaden] : Edition Schmid, c1988. 1 v. (unpaged) : ill. ; 28 cm. Introduction also in German. ISBN 3-908028-07-3
1. Gianella, Victor, 1918-. 2. Photography, Abstract. I. Title. II. Title: Abstractions.
NYPL [MFX (Gianella) 91-2650]

GIANELLA, VICTOR, 1918- Gianella, Victor, 1918- Victor Gianella . [Ennetbaden] , c1988. 1 v. (unpaged) : ISBN 3-908028-07-3
NYPL [MFX (Gianella) 91-2650]

Gianlorenzo Bernini /. Scribner, Charles. New York , 1991. 128 p. : ISBN 0-8109-3111-7 DDC 709/.2 20
N6923.B5 S37 1991
NYPL [3-MGO+ (Bernini) 91-7243]

Giannelli /. Giannelli, Angelo, 1922- Pordenone , c1986. 61 p., [30] p. of plates :
ND623.G484 A4 1986
NYPL [3-MCF G4453 91-4199]

Giannelli, Angelo, 1922- Giannelli / [a cura di] Franco Solmi. Pordenone : Concordia 7, c1986. 61 p., [30] p. of plates : ill. (some col.) ; 27 cm. (Edizioni d'arte. nuova ser., 17) Exhibition held Nov. 1986-Jan. 1987 in Maniago. Bibliography: p. 61.
1. Giannelli, Angelo, 1922- - Exhibitions. I. Solmi, Franco. II. Series: Edizioni d'arte (Pordenone, Italy) , nuova ser., 17. III. Title.
ND623.G484 A4 1986
NYPL [3-MCF G4453 91-4199]

GIANNELLI, ANGELO, 1922- - EXHIBITIONS. Giannelli, Angelo, 1922- Giannelli /. Pordenone , c1986. 61 p., [30] p. of plates :
ND623.G484 A4 1986
NYPL [3-MCF G4453 91-4199]

Gianni, Benjamin, 1958- Dice thrown / Benjamin Gianni, Bryan Shiles, Kevin Kemner ; with an introduction by Elysabeth Yates-Burns. New York, N.Y. : Princeton Architectural Press, c1989. 56 p. : ill. ; 22 cm. Catalogue of an exhibition held at the following galleries: the University Gallery, Ohio State University, Columbus, Ohio, February 29-March 11, 1988; the Arts and Architecture Gallery, Yale University, New Haven, Connecticut, October 24-November 4, 1988. ISBN 0-910413-62-2 : DDC 728/.92/09730747468 20
1. Farm buildings - United States - Themes, motives - Exhibitions. 2. Vernacular architecture - United States - Themes, motives - Exhibitions. 3. Architecture, Modern - 20th century - Europe - Themes, motives - Exhibitions. 4. Architecture - Europe - Themes, motives - Exhibitions. 5. Functionalism (Architecture) - Influence - Exhibitions. 6. Enlightenment - Influence - Exhibitions. I. Shiles, Bryan, 1959-. II. Kemner, Kevin, 1959-. III. Ohio State University. Gallery of Fine Art. IV. Yale University. Art and Architecture Gallery. V. Title.
NA8201 .G47 1989
NYPL [3-MQV 90-12464]

Giannoulēs Chalepas . Kairophylas, Giannēs, 1927- Athēna , 1986. 79 p. :
NYPL [3-MGO (Chalepas) 90-4715]

Giants of the arts : Ludwig van Beethoven, Charles Dickens, Vincent van Gogh. Reference ed. New York : M. Cavendish Corp., 1991. p. cm. (Exploring the past) Includes bibliographical references and index. Traces the lives of three prominent figures in the world of the arts: Ludwig van Beethoven, Charles Dickens, and Vincent van Gogh.
ISBN 1-85435-414-0 : DDC 700/.92/24 20
1. Artists - Europe - Juvenile literature. 2. Beethoven, Ludwig von, 1770-1827 - Criticism and interpretation - Juvenile literature. 3. Dickens, Charles, 1812-1870 - Criticism and interpretation - Juvenile literature. 4. Gogh, Vincent van, 1853-1890 - Criticism and interpretation - Juvenile literature. I. Marshall Cavendish Corporation. II. Series.
NX633 .G53 1991

Giatti, Natalia. Iconografia mariana nei masi dell'Alto Adige / Natalia Giatti. 2a ed. Calliano [Trento] : Manfrini, c1990. 256 p. : col. ill. ; 33 cm. ISBN 88-7024-408-3
1. Mary, Blessed Virgin, Saint - Art. 2. Christian art

and symbolism - Italy - Trentino-Alto Adige. 3. Mural painting and decoration, Italian - Italy - Trentino-Alto Adige. I. Title.   **NYPL [3-MAIH+ 91-4956]**

Gibbes Museum of Art (Charleston, S.C.) Henrietta Johnston . Winston-Salem, N.C. , c1991. p.   DDC 741.973 20
NC139.J6 H4 1991

Hollander, John. Landscape painting, 1960-1990 . Charleston, S.C. , 1990. 70 p. :
     NYPL [3-MCW 91-4635]

Giboire, Clive. O'Keeffe, Georgia, 1887-1986. Lovingly, Georgia . New York , c1990. xxvii, 365 p. :   ISBN 0-671-69236-4 (hardcover) :   DDC 759.13 B 20
N6537.O39 A3 1990
     NYPL [3-MCX O41 90-11778]

Gibson, Ann Eden, 1944- Issues in abstract expressionism : the artist-run periodicals / by Ann Eden Gibson. Ann Arbor, Mich. : UMI Research Press, c1990. xvi, 430 p. : ill. ; 24 cm. (Studies in the fine arts. Avant-garde . no. 66) Includes bibliographical references.   ISBN 0-8357-1944-8 (alk. paper)   DDC 709.747/1/09044 20
1. Abstract expressionism - New York (N.Y.). 2. New York school of art. 3. Art criticism - New York (N.Y.) - History - 20th century. 4. Art - Periodicals. I. Title. II. Series.
N6535.N5 G53 1989
     NYPL [3-MAMT 90-11594]

Gibson, Ralph. L'histoire de France / [Ralph Gibson] ; introduction by Marguerite Duras. New York, N.Y. : Aperture, c1991. 119 p. : col. ill. ; 37 cm. Text in English. "Accompanies an exhibition by the same name, which opens at Leo Castelli Gallery in New York in May 1991 and will be travelling internationally"--T.p. verso.   ISBN 0-89381-471-7
1. Gibson, Ralph - Exhibitions. 2. Photography, Artistic - Exhibitions. I. Duras, Marguerite. II. Leo Castelli Gallery. III. Title.
     NYPL [MFX+ (Gibson) 91-7448]

GIBSON, RALPH - EXHIBITIONS. Gibson, Ralph. L'histoire de France /. New York, N.Y. , c1991. 119 p. :   ISBN 0-89381-471-7
     NYPL [MFX+ (Gibson) 91-7448]

Gibson, Robin. Madame Yevonde : colour, fantasy and myth / Robin Gibson and Pam Roberts. London : National Portrait Gallery, 1990. 119 p. : ill. (some col.) ; 31 cm. Published to accompany an exhibition held at the Royal Photographic Society, Bath, 1990, and the National Portrait Gallery, London, 1990. Includes index. Bibliography: p. 106.   ISBN 1-85514-024-1 (pbk) :   DDC 779.092 20
1. Yevonde, Madame - Exhibitions. 2. Photography - Portraits - Exhibitions. I. Roberts, Pam. II. Yevonde, Madame. III. National Portrait Gallery (Great Britain). IV. Title.   **NYPL [MFX+ (Yevonde) 91-3496]**

Gibson, Sarah Scott. Sterling and Francine Clark Art Institute. Library. Book illustrations from six centuries in the Library of the Sterling & Francine Clark Art Institute /. Williamstown, Mass. , 1990. 116 p. :   ISBN 0-931102-29-4 (paper)   DDC 741.6/4/0747441 20
NC961.W55 S747 1990
     NYPL [MDT 91-2365]

Gidal, Peter. Andy Warhol : films and paintings, the Factory years / Peter Gidal. New York, N.Y. : Da Capo Press, [1991] c1971. xiii, 158 p. : ill. ; 22 cm. (A Da Capo paperback) Originally published: London : Studio Vista, 1971. With new preface. Includes index.   ISBN 0-306-80456-5 :   DDC 700/.92 20
1. Warhol, Andy, 1928- - Criticism and interpretation. I. Title.
NX512.W37 G5 1991

Giebelbilder der Kapellbrücke in Luzern = Les peintures du Pont de la Chapelle à Lucerne = The paintings in the Chapel-Bridge à Lucerne. Luzern : Räber, 1966. [12] p., 74 p. of plates : ill. ; 15x21 cm. In German, French, and English. Reduced offset re-edition of the first illustrated album of the paintings (started in 1614 by Hans Heinrich Wägmann and his school) decorating the "Kapellbrücke" in Lucerne, Switzerland. The original ed. was issued in 1828, by the lithographic press Eglin Bros. of Lucerne, after drawings by Jakob Schwegler."--Cf. English introd., p. [11]. Introduction signed by Adolf Reinle.
1. Mural painting and decoration - Switzerland - Lucerne. 2. Mural painting and decoration - 17th century - Switzerland - Lucerne. 3. Kapellbrücke

(Lucerne, Switzerland). I. Reinle, Adolf. II. Schwegler, Jakob, 1793-1866. III. Wägmann, Hans Heinrich. IV. Title: Peintures du Pont de la Chapelle à Lucerne. V. Title: Paintings in the Chapel-Bridge at Lucerne.
     NYPL [3-MLP 89-6482]

Giedion, S. (Sigfried), 1888-1968. Wege in die Öffentlichkeit : Aufsätze und unveröffentlichte Schriften aus den Jahren 1926-1956 / Sigfried Giedion ; herausgegeben und kommentiert von Dorothee Huber. Zürich : GTA/Ammann, c1987. 231 p. : ill. ; 26 cm. Includes texts in English. Includes bibliographical references and index.   ISBN 3-250-50104-2   DDC 700 19
I. Huber, Dorothee. II. Title.
N7445.4 .G54 1987   **NYPL [3-MAS 91-3933]**

GIEDION, S. (SIGFRIED), 1888-1968. Mehlau-Wiebking, Friederike. Schweizer Typenmöbel, 1925-1935 . Zürich , c1989. 231 p. :   ISBN 3-85676-029-6
     NYPL [3-MOF+ 89-26582]

Giehler, H. G. (Hans-Georg) Braun, Dietrich. Nikolauskirche Beuren . Villingen , c1988. 96 p. :   ISBN 3-7883-1904-6
NA5586.B4395 B73 1988

GIERDZIEJEWSKI, IGNACY, 1826-1860 - CATALOGS. Kozakiewicz, Stefan. Ignacy Gierdziejewski /. Wrocław , 1958. 175 p. :
ND955.P63 G4835 1958

GIERDZIEJEWSKI, IGNACY, 1826-1860 - CRITICISM AND INTERPRETATION. Kozakiewicz, Stefan. Ignacy Gierdziejewski /. Wrocław , 1958. 175 p. :
ND955.P63 G4835 1958

Giesen, Hans 1942- Hans Giesen, junge Malerei aus Amsterdam : Landesmuseum Oldenburg : 23.10.-21.11.1988 / [Katalog Bearbeitung und Redaktion, Peter Reindl] Oldenburg : Das Museum, c1988. 75 p. : ill. (chiefly col.). port. ; 20 x 22 cm. Text in Dutch and German.
1. Giesen, Hans, 1942- - Exhibitions. I. Reindl, Peter. II. Landesmuseum für Kunst- und Kulturgeschichte Oldenburg. III. Title.
     NYPL [3-MCH G456 90-12615]

GIESEN, HANS, 1942- - EXHIBITIONS. Giesen, Hans 1942- Hans Giesen, junge Malerei aus Amsterdam . Oldenburg , c1988. 75 p. :
     NYPL [3-MCH G456 90-12615]

Gifkins, Michael, 1945- McCahon, Colin. Colin McCahon . Auckland, New Zealand , c1988. 157 p. :   ISBN 0-86463-165-0
     NYPL [3-MCZ+ M116 91-6649]

Gift of the Morgan Guaranty Trust Endowment for the Economics and Public Affairs Division. Brown, Jane. Sissinghurst . London , 1990. 136 p. :   ISBN 0-297-83043-0
     NYPL [3-MSK 90-11984]

Mansfield, Howard. Cosmopolis . New Brunswick, N.J. , c1990. vii, 165 p. :   ISBN 0-88285-131-4   DDC 307.76/4 20
HT330 .M34 1990
     NYPL [3-MQV 90-13391]

People places . New York, N.Y. , 1990. xvii, 295 p. :   ISBN 0-442-31929-0 :   DDC 711/.4 20
NA9070 .P45 1990
     NYPL [3-MQWO 90-11592]

Public policy under Thatcher /. Houndmills, Basingstoke, Hampshire , 1990. xviii, 291 p. ;   ISBN 0-333-53659-2 (cased) :   DDC 336.390941 20
HJ2096   **NYPL [JLD 90-2067]**

GIFTED CHILDREN - EDUCATION - ART. Gray, Donna B., 1944- A parent's guide to teaching art . White Hall, Va. , c1991. p. cm.   ISBN 1-558-70202-4 (pbk.) :   DDC 700 20
N351 .G73 1991

Giger, H. R. (Hansruedi), 1940- **[Biomechanics. English]**
H.R. Giger's Biomechanics / color illustrations, Roland Gretler ; black and white illustrations, Louis Stalder ; English translation by Clara Höricht Frame ; Harlan Ellison, introduction. 1st American ed. Beverly Hills, CA : Morpheus International, 1990. 95 p. : chiefly ill. (some col.) ; 43 cm. Translation of: H.R. Giger's biomechanics. Includes bibliographical references (p. [96-97]).   ISBN 0-9623447-1-0   DDC 709/.2 20

1. Giger, H. R (Hansruedi), 1940- - Themes, motives. I. Title. II. Title: Biomechanics.
N7153.G48 A4 1990

H.R. Giger's Biomechanics. 1. Aufl. Zug, Switzerland : Edition C, 1988. 95 p. : chiefly ill. (some col.) ; 42 cm. "Juni, 1988." Includes bibliographical references.   ISBN 3-89082-527-3
1. Giger, H. R. (Hansruedi), 1940-. I. Title. II. Title: Biomechanics.
     NYPL [3-MCZ++ G455 89-25898]

GIGER, H. R. (HANSRUEDI), 1940- Giger, H. R. (Hansruedi), 1940- H.R. Giger's Biomechanics. Zug, Switzerland , 1988. 95 p. :   ISBN 3-89082-527-3
     NYPL [3-MCZ++ G455 89-25898]

GIGER, H. R (HANSRUEDI), 1940- - THEMES, MOTIVES. Giger, H. R. (Hansruedi), 1940- [Biomechanics. English.] H.R. Giger's Biomechanics /. Beverly Hills, CA , 1990. 95 p. :   ISBN 0-9623447-1-0   DDC 709/.2 20
N7153.G48 A4 1990

Gil Imaná . Imaná, Gil, 1933- [La Paz, Bolivia , 1989?] 1 v. (unpaged) :   DDC 759.984 20
ND349.I43 A4 1989

Gila, Miguel. El libro de quejas / de Gila. 1. ed. Madrid : Sedmay, 1975. 187 p. : chiefly ill. ; 25 cm. Cartoons.   ISBN 84-7380-065-6 :
1. Spanish wit and humor, Pictorial. I. Title.
NC1639.G5 A49
     NYPL [3-MEM (Gila) 90-4764]

Gilardoni, Arturo. X-rays in art : physics, technique, applications / Arturo Gilardoni, Riccardo Ascani Orsini, Silvia Taccani. Mandello Lario, Italy : Gilardoni, 1977. 231 p. : ill. (1 col.) ; 31 cm. Includes index. Bibliography: p. 213-224.
1. Art - Expertising. I. Ascani Orsini, Riccardo, 1940-. II. Taccani, Silvia, 1956-. III. Title.
     NYPL [3-MAS+ 90-7036]

GILBERT, ADELE - ART COLLECTIONS - EXHIBITIONS. Miller, Debra. Art and life in Northern Europe, 1500-1800 . St. Petersburg, Fla. , c1990. 46 p. :
     NYPL [3-MAX (Gilbert) 91-5565]

Gilbert Collection. Miller, Debra. Art and life in Northern Europe, 1500-1800 . St. Petersburg, Fla. , c1990. 46 p. :
     NYPL [3-MAX (Gilbert) 91-5565]

GILBERT COLLECTION - CATALOGS. Miller, Debra. Art and life in Northern Europe, 1500-1800 . St. Petersburg, Fla. , c1990. 46 p. :
     NYPL [3-MAX (Gilbert) 91-5565]

GILBERT, GORDON - ART COLLECTIONS - EXHIBITIONS. Miller, Debra. Art and life in Northern Europe, 1500-1800 . St. Petersburg, Fla. , c1990. 46 p. :
     NYPL [3-MAX (Gilbert) 91-5565]

Gilbert, Rita, 1942- Living with art / Rita Gilbert. 3rd ed. New York : McGraw-Hill, c1992. p. cm. Includes bibliographical references and index.   ISBN 0-07-023454-X :   DDC 701/.1 20
1. Art appreciation. I. Title.
N7477 .G55 1992

Gilbert, Will G. Rumbamuziek [microform], volksmuziek van de Midden-Amerikaansche Negers. s-Gravenhage, J. P. Kruseman [1947?] 119 p. illus., music. 16 cm. (De Muziek. 19) Bibliography: p. 115-118. Microfilm. New York : New York Public Library. 1 microfilm reel ;35 mm. (MN *ZZ-30393)
1. Folk music - West Indies - History and criticism. 2. Folk dancing - West Indies. 3. Blacks - West Indies - Songs and music - History and criticism. 4. Jazz music - West Indies. I. Title.
     NYPL [Sc Micro R-5903 no.2]

Gildewart, Friedrich Vordemberge- see **Vordemberge-Gildewart, Friedrich, 1899-1962.**

Giles, Carl Ronald, 1916- Nurse! / by Giles. London : Daily Express, 1975. [96] p. : of ill. ; 22 x 27 cm.   ISBN 0-85079-066-2 :   DDC 741.5/942
1. Nursing - Caricatures and cartoons. 2. English wit and humor, Pictorial. I. Title.
NC1479.G48 A53
     NYPL [3-MEM (Giles) 90-4867]

Gilhooly, Sheila, 1951- Blackbridge, Persimmon, 1951- Still sane /. Vancouver, B.C., Canada , 1985. 101 p. :   ISBN 0-88974-028-3 :   DDC

730/.971 19
NYPL [3-MGO (Blackbridge) 90-12979]

GILHOOLY, SHEILA, 1951-
Blackbridge, Persimmon, 1951- Still sane /.
Vancouver, B.C., Canada , 1985. 101 p. : ISBN
0-88974-028-3 : DDC 730/.971 19
NYPL [3-MGO (Blackbridge) 90-12979]

GILKEY, GORDON W. - ART COLLECTIONS - EXHIBITIONS.
Portland Art Museum (Or.) Master prints from
the Gilkey collection . [Portland, Or.] , c1980.
[35] p. : *NYPL [MDE 91-5247]*

GILKEY, VIVIAN - ART COLLECTIONS - EXHIBITIONS.
Portland Art Museum (Or.) Master prints from
the Gilkey collection . [Portland, Or.] , c1980.
[35] p. : *NYPL [MDE 91-5247]*

Gille, Marianne. Levin, Marianne, 1942- Plagiat,
stöld, förebild, inspiration /. [Solna] , c1990.
138 p. : ISBN 91-7332-505-8 :
NK789 .L48 1990

Gille, Sighard, 1941-
Sighard Gille 1962-1989 : Gemälde, Objekte,
Zeichnungen, Grafik : Städtische Galerie
Schloss Oberhausen, 27. Oktober bis 10.
Dezember 1989, Kunststation Kleinsassen, 6417
Kleinsassen/Rhön, 17. Februar bis 16. April
1990, Haus Ludwig für Kunst der DDR,
Saarlouis, 12. August bis 24. September 1990 /
herausgegeben vom Ludwig-Institut für Kunst
der DDR, Oberhausen ; [Katalogredaktion,
Bernhard Mensch, Inge Ludescher].1. Aufl.
Oberhausen : Plitt-Verlag, [1989?] 186 p. : ill. ;
28 cm.
*1. Gille, Sighard, 1941- - Exhibitions. I. Städtische
Galerie Schloss Oberhausen. II. Title.*
NYPL [3-MCK G473 91-5896]

GILLE, SIGHARD, 1941- - EXHIBITIONS.
Gille, Sighard, 1941- Sighard Gille 1962-1989 .
Oberhausen [1989?] 186 p. :
NYPL [3-MCK G473 91-5896]

Gillen, Eckhart, 1947- Kunst in der DDR /.
Köln , c1990. 470 p. : ISBN 3-462-02068-4
DDC 709/.431/09045 20
N6889 .K862 1990

Gilles, Barthel, 1891-1977. Oellers, Adam C.
Barthel Gilles, 1891-1977 . Recklinghausen ,
c1987. 326 p. : ISBN 3-7647-0387-3
ND588.G46 O45 1987
NYPL [3-MCK G475 91-4613]

GILLES, BARTHEL, 1891-1977.
Oellers, Adam C. Barthel Gilles, 1891-1977 .
Recklinghausen , c1987. 326 p. : ISBN
3-7647-0387-3
ND588.G46 O45 1987
NYPL [3-MCK G475 91-4613]

Gillespie, Gregory, 1936- Gregory Gillespie,
paintings (Italy 1962-1970). New York : Forum
Gallery, 1970. 55 p. : all ill. (some col.) ; 30
cm. Includes "List of reproductions".
1. Gillespie, Gregory, 1936-. I. Forum Gallery. II. Title.
NYPL [3-MCX+ G477 91-1181]

GILLESPIE, GREGORY, 1936-
Gillespie, Gregory, 1936- Gregory Gillespie,
paintings (Italy 1962-1970). New York , 1970.
55 p. : *NYPL [3-MCX+ G477 91-1181]*

Gilliam, Jan (Jan Kirsten) Furnishing
Williamsburg's historic buildings. Williamsburg,
Va. : Colonial Williamsburg Foundation, 1991.
p. cm. (Williamsburg decorative arts series) Prepared
by Jan Gilliam and Betty Leviner. Includes
bibliographical references and index. ISBN
0-87935-083-0 DDC 747.2155/4252/09033 20
*1. Furniture - Virginia - Williamsburg - History - 18th
century. 2. House furnishings - Virginia - Williamsburg -
History - 18th century. I. Leviner, Betty (Betty Crowe).
II. Title. III. Series.*
NK2438.W54 G5 1991

Gillies, Linda Boyer. Metropolitan Museum of
Art (New York, N.Y.) French drawings &
prints of the eighteenth century . [New York ,
1972] [19] p., [4] p. of plates :
NYPL [3-MBH 91-409]

Gillon, Edmund Vincent.
Decorative frames and borders : 396 examples
from the Renaissance to the present day.
Selected by Edmund V. Gillon, Jr. New York,
Dover Publications [1973] 173 p. : ill. ; 29 cm.
(Dover pictorial archives series) ISBN 0-486-22928-9
DDC 741.6

I. Title.
NK1530 .G54 1973
NYPL [3-MLD 90-12472]

Victorian houses : a treasury of lesser-known
examples / Edmund V. Gillon, Jr. and Clay
Lancaster. New York : Dover Publications,
c1973. 1 v. (unpaged) : ill. ; 25 x 29 cm.
Includes index. ISBN 0-486-22966-1
*1. Architecture, Domestic - United States. 2.
Architecture, Victorian - United States. 3. United
States - Description and travel - Views. I. Lancaster,
Clay. II. Title.* *NYPL [3-MQWO 90-7005]*

Gillow, John. Traditional Indian textiles / John
Gillow and Nicholas Barnard. London : Thames
and Hudson, c1991. 160 p. : ill. ; 31 cm. ISBN
0-500-01491-4
1. Textile fabrics - India. I. Barnard, Nicholas. II. Title.
NYPL [3-MON+ 91-5640]

Gilman, John, 1941- Heide, Robert, 1939-
Popular art deco . New York , 1991. 228 p. :
ISBN 1-558-59030-7 DDC 709/.73/09041 20
N6512.5.A7 H45 1991
NYPL [3-MAMT 91-8075]

Gilman, Sander L. Taboo and totem . New
York , 1991. p. cm. ISBN 0-8419-1249-1 (cloth)
DDC 701/.05 20
N72.P74 T33 1991

Gilot, Françoise, 1921- Matisse and Picasso : a
friendship in art / Françoise Gilot.1st ed. New
York : Doubleday, c1990. xii, 339 p., [8] p. of
plates : ill. (some col.) ; 27 cm. Includes index.
ISBN 0-385-26044-X : DDC 709/.2/244 B 20
*1. Matisse, Henri, 1869-1954 - Friends and associates.
2. Picasso, Pablo, 1881-1973 - Friends and associates. I.
Title.*
N6853.M33 G45 1990
NYPL [3-MCO M43 90-12867]

Giltay, J. Museum Boymans-Van Beuningen.
Rubens en zijn tijd . Rotterdam , 1990. 176 p. :
ISBN 90-6918-063-4
ND673.R9 A4 1990

Giménez, Carmen. Modern masterpieces from the
collection of Jacques Hachuel . [New York,
N.Y.] [1990?] 123 p. : ISBN 84-86022-41-X
NYPL [3-MAX (Hachuel) 91-3852]

Gimpel, René.
[Journal d'un collectionneur. English]
Diary of an art dealer. Translated from the
French by John Rosenberg. Introd. by Sir
Herbert Read. New York, Farrar, Straus and
Giroux, 1966. xii, 465 p. : ill., ports. ; 23 cm.
Translation of: Journal d'un collectionneur. DDC
706.50924
*1. Gimpel, René - Diaries. 2. Art dealers - France -
Diaries. I. Title. II. Title: René Gimpel, diary of an art
dealer.*
N8660.G5 A313 *NYPL [3-MAVC 91-3867]*

GIMPEL, RENÉ - DIARIES.
Gimpel, René. [Journal d'un collectionneur.
English.] Diary of an art dealer. New York,
1966. xii, 465 p. : DDC 706.50924
N8660.G5 A313 *NYPL [3-MAVC 91-3867]*

Gingold, Diane J. A sense of place .
Montgomery, Ala. , 1990. p. cm. ISBN
0-89280-027-5 DDC 759.15/074/76147 20
N6520 .S46 1990

Gino Severini . Fonti, Daniela. Milano , 1988.
655 p. : *NYPL [MCF+ S49 90-485]*

Gintz, Claude.
L'Art conceptuel, une perspective . Paris ,
c1989. 260 p. : *NYPL [3-MAL 90-11049]*

L'Art conceptuel, une perspective . Paris ,
c1989. 260 p. : ISBN 2-85534-607-1 DDC
709/.04/07507444361 20
N6494.C63 A75 1989

Gio Batta Ferrari, 1829-1906 /. Ferrari, Roberto.
Brescia , 1990. 110 p. : ISBN 88-7385-059-6
NYPL [3-MCF F372 91-5212]

Gio Ponti . Licitra Ponti, Lisa. Milano , 1990.
287 p. : ISBN 88-355-0083-4: DDC 709/.2 20
N6923.P6226 A4 1990a

Gio Ponti . Ponti, Lisa Licitra. [Gio Ponti.
English.] Cambridge, Mass. , 1990. 288 p. :
ISBN 0-262-16118-4 DDC 720/.92 20
N6923.P6226 A4 1990
NYPL [3-MQZ (Ponti) 90-12861]

Il Gioco dell'amore : le cortigiane di Venezia dal
Trecento al Settecento : catalogo della mostra :
Venezia, Casinò municipale Ca'Vendramin

Calergi, 2 febbraio-16 aprile 1990. Milano :
Berenice, 1990. 216 p. : ill. (some col.) ; 28 cm.
Texts by Giovanni Scarabello ... [et al.] Includes
bibliographical references (p. 214-216) ISBN
88-85215-00-9
*1. Courtesans - Italy - Venice - Exhibitions. 2.
Courtesans in art - Exhibitions. 3. Art, Italian - Italy -
Venice - Exhibitions. I. Scarabello, Giovanni. II. Ca'
Vendramin Calergi (Venice, Italy). III. Title. IV. Title:
Cortigiane di Venezia dal Trecento al Settecento.*
IN PROCESS (ONLINE)
NYPL [3-MAMC 91-4481]

Giono, Jean, 1895-1970. Yves Brayer / par Jean
Giono et Yves Dentan. Paris : La Bibliothèque
des arts, c1990. 171 p. : ill. (some col.) ; 35 cm.
(Collection Art moderne) ISBN 2-85047-154-2
DDC 759.4 20
*1. Brayer, Yves, 1907-. 2. Painters - France -
Biography. I. Brayer, Yves, 1907-. II. Dentan, Yves. III.
Title.*
ND553.B875 G48 1990

Giordani Aragno, Bonizza. Moda Italia . Milano ,
1988. 200 p. : *NYPL [3-MME+ 89-6593]*

Giorgieri, Pietro. Itinerari apuani di architettura
moderna / Pietro Giorgieri ; presentazione di
Grazia Gobbi Sica. Firenze : Alinea, 1989. 263
p. : ill. (some col.), maps, plans ; 22 cm. + 1
folded map. (Saggi e documenti. 87. Sezione Guide di
architettura moderna ; 2) On cover: A guide to modern
architecture in Apuania. Text also in English. Includes
indexes. Folded map inserted in pocket. Bibliography: p.
253-257.
*1. Architecture, Modern - 20th century - Italy -
Massa-Carrara (Province) - Guide-books. 2.
Architecture - Italy - Massa-Carrara - Guide-books. 3.
City planning - Italy - Massa-Carrara - History. I. Title.
II. Title: Guide to modern architecture in Apuania. III.
Series: Saggi e documenti (Alinea editrice) ; 87.*
NYPL [3-MQWB 90-11118]

Giorgio Armani : collezione autunno inverno
1989-90 / testo di Oreste del Buono. Milano :
Electa, c1989. 229 p. : ill. ; 32 cm. ISBN
88-435-2946-3
*1. Armani, Giorgio. I. Armani, Giorgio. II. Del Buono,
Oreste, 1923-.*
IN PROCESS (ONLINE)
NYPL [3-MME+ 91-4011]

Giorgio Armani . Martin, Richard. New York ,
1990. 224 p. : ISBN 0-8478-1298-7 DDC
746.9/2/092 20
TT580 .M37 1990
NYPL [3-MME+ 91-3312]

Giorgio de Chirico, 1920-1950 /. De Chirico,
Giorgio, 1888- Milano , c1990. 166 p. : ISBN
88-435-3403-3 (jacket)
NYPL [3-MCF C535 91-6458]

Giorgio Griffa /. Fossati, Paolo 1938- Ravenna ,
c1990. 161 p. :
IN PROCESS (ONLINE)
NYPL [3-MCF G847 91-2466]

Giorgio Morandi, 1890-1990. Morandi, Giorgio,
1890-1964. Milano , c1990. 419 p. : DDC
760/.092 20
N6923.M6 A4 1990

Giorgio Morandi, 1890-1990 /. Morandi, Giorgio,
1890-1964. Milano , c1990. 419 p. : ISBN
88-435-3185-9
NYPL [3-MCF M82 90-12991]

**Giorgio Morandi, 1890-1990, mostra del
centenario.** Morandi, Giorgio, 1890-1964.
Giorgio Morandi, 1890-1990 /. Milano , c1990.
419 p. : ISBN 88-435-3185-9
NYPL [3-MCF M82 90-12991]

Giorgione, la pittura /. Giorgione, 1477-1511.
Firenze , c1987. 156 p. :
NYPL [3-MCF G49 90-8925]

Giorgione, 1477-1511.
Giorgione, la pittura / a cura di Francesco
Valcanover. Firenze : Giunti : Nardini, c1987.
156 p. : chiefly col. ill. ; 11 cm. (Le Giade . 52)
Includes bibliographical references.
*1. Giorgione, 1477-1511. I. Valcanover, Francesco. II.
Title. III. Series. NYPL [3-MCF G49 90-8925]*

TEMPESTA.
Settis, Salvatore. [Tempesta interpretata.
English.] Giorgione's Tempest . Chicago ,
1990. xi, 189 p. : ISBN 0-226-74893-6 (alk.
paper) DDC 759.5 20
ND623.G5 A763813 1990
NYPL [3-MCF G49 90-10874]

GIORGIONE, 1477-1511.
Giorgione, 1477-1511. Giorgione, la pittura /.
Firenze , c1987. 156 p. :
NYPL [3-MCF G49 90-8925]

GIORGIONE, 1477-1511 - CATALOGS.
Wethey, Harold E. (Harold Edwin), 1902-1984.
Titian and his drawings . Princeton, N.J. ,
c1987. xxiii, 267 p., [159] p. of plates : ISBN
0-691-04040-0 (alk. paper) : DDC 741/.092/4
19
NC257.T58 W47 1987
NYPL [3-MCF+ T63 90-10773]

**GIORGIONE, 1477-1511 - CRITICISM AND
INTERPRETATION.**
Wethey, Harold E. (Harold Edwin), 1902-1984.
Titian and his drawings . Princeton, N.J. ,
c1987. xxiii, 267 p., [159] p. of plates : ISBN
0-691-04040-0 (alk. paper) : DDC 741/.092/4
19
NC257.T58 W47 1987
NYPL [3-MCF+ T63 90-10773]

Giorgione's Tempest . Settis, Salvatore. [Tempesta
interpretata. English.] Chicago , 1990. xi, 189
p. : ISBN 0-226-74893-6 (alk. paper) DDC 759.5
20
ND623.G5 A763813 1990
NYPL [3-MCF G49 90-10874]

Giotto, 1266?-1337.
Giotto di Bondone /. Konstanz , 1970. 292 p. :
ND623.G6 G5 NYPL [3-MCF G52 90-5664]

GIOTTO, 1266?-1337.
Giotto di Bondone /. Konstanz , 1970. 292 p. :
ND623.G6 G5 NYPL [3-MCF G52 90-5664]
Gosebruch, Martin. Giotto und die Entwicklung
des neuzeitlichen Kunstbewusstseins. Köln
[1962] 235 p. : *NYPL [3-MCF G52 91-520]*

GIOTTO, 1266?-1337 - THEMES, MOTIVES.
Edgerton, Samuel Y. The heritage of Giotto's
geometry . Ithaca , 1991. p. cm. ISBN
0-8014-2573-5 (cloth : alk. paper) DDC 701/.8
20
N7430.5 .E34 1991

Giotto di Bondone / mit Beiträgen von Martin
Gosebruch ... [et al.] Konstanz : L. Leonhardt,
1970. 292 p. : ill. ; 24 cm. (Persönlichkeit und
Werk . Bd. 3) Each essay is followed by a summary in
English. Includes bibliographical references and index.
*1. Giotto, 1266?-1337. I. Gosebruch, Martin. II. Giotto,
1266?-1337. III. Series.*
ND623.G6 G5 NYPL [3-MCF G52 90-5664]

Giotto's father and the family of Vasari's lives /.
Barolsky, Paul, 1941- University Park, PA ,
c1991. p. cm. ISBN 0-271-00762-1 (alk. paper)
DDC 709/.2/245 B 20
N6915 .B28 1991

Il Giovane Arturo Martini : opere dal 1905 al
1921 / [catalogo, Eugenio Manzato, Nico
Stringa]. Roma : De Luca Edizioni d'Arte,
c1989. 183 p. : ill. (some col.), ports. ; 27 cm.
Catalogue of an exhibition held in Treviso at the Museo
Civico "Luigi Bailo", Oct. 15, 1989-Jan. 10, 1990.
Includes bibliographical references (p. 181-183). ISBN
88-7813-250-0
*1. Martini, Arturo, 1889-1947 - Exhibitions. I.
Manzato, Eugenio. II. Stringa, Nico. III. Martini,
Arturo, 1889-1947. IV. Museo civico "L. Bailo"
(Treviso, Italy).*
NYPL [3-MGO (Martini) 90-11108]

Giovane pittura d'Europa. Milano : Electa, c1991.
132 p. : ill. (some col.) ; 28 cm. Italian, English,
French, and German. Catalog of an exhibition held in
Trento's Palazzo delle Albere, 1-19/3-3/1991. Includes
bibliographical references (p. 116-124). ISBN
88-435-3436-X DDC 759.06/09/04807445385
20
*1. Painting, European - Exhibitions. 2. Painting,
Modern - 20th century - Europe - Exhibitions. I.
Palazzo delle Albere (Trento, Italy).*
ND458 .G56 1991

Giovanni-Battista Piranesi . Focillon, Henri,
1881-1943. Paris , 1918. 74 p. ;
NE2052.5.P5 A4 1918

**Giovanni Gerolamo Savoldo tra Foppa, Giorgione
e Caravaggio.** Milano : Electa, c1990. 356 p. :
ill. (some col.) ; 28 cm. Spine title: Savoldo.
"Brescia, Monastero di Santa Giulia, 3 marzo-31 maggio
1990, Francoforte, Schirn Kunsthalle, 8 giugno-3
settembre 1990"--P. [5]. Includes bibliographical
references (p. 325-356). ISBN 88-435-3093-3
1. Savoldo, Gian Girolamo, b. ca. 1480 - Exhibitions. I.

*Savoldo, Gian Girolamo, b. ca. 1480. II. Monastero di
San Salvatore-Santa Giulia (Brescia, Italy). III. Schirn
Kunsthalle Frankfurt. IV. Title: Savoldo.*
N6923.S3584 A4 1991 *NYPL [3-MCF S268 90-12994]*

Giovanni Morelli da collezionista a conoscitore :
catalogo della mostra, Bergamo, 4 giugno-31
luglio 1987. [Bergamo] : Accademia Carrara,
c1987. 79 p. : ill., facsims., ports. ; 22 cm.
(Quaderni / Accademia Carrara . 9) Catalog of an
exhibition held in conjunction with the Convegno su
Giovanni Morelli e la cultura dei conoscitori held in
Bergamo at the Ex Chiesa di S. Agostino, June 4-7,
1987.
*1. Morelli, Giovanni, 1816-1891 - Art collections -
Exhibitions. I. Accademia Carrara. II. Convegno su
Giovanni Morelli e la cultura dei conoscitori (1987 :
Bergamo, Italy). III. Series: Quaderni / Accademia
Carrara , 9.*
NYPL [3-MAX (Morelli) 90-10868]

Giovannoni, Giannino. Mantova e i tarocchi del
Mantegna / Giannino Giovannoni. Mantova :
Provincia di Mantova, Casa del Mantegna ;
Faenza : Associazione culturale le tarot, [1987]
78 p. : ill. (some col.) ; 24 cm. "3"--Spine.
Bibliography: p. 31-32.
*1. Mantegna, Andrea, 1431-1506 - Exhibitions. 2. Art,
Italian - Italy - Mantua - Themes, motives -
Exhibitions. 3. Art, Renaissance - Italy - Mantua -
Themes, motives - Exhibitions. 4. Tarot - Exhibitions. I.
Casa del Mantegna. II. Associazione culturale Le tarot
(Faenza, Italy). III. Title.*
N6923.M249 A4 1987
NYPL [3-MCF M29 91-7036]

Gippenreiter, Vadim Evgen´evich. The golden
ring : cities of old Russia / photographs by
Vadim Gippenreiter ; text by Alexei Komech.
New York : Abbeville Press, 1991. p. cm.
Translated from the Russian. ISBN 1-558-59216-4
DDC 720/.947 20
*1. Architecture - Russian S.F.S.R. 2. Church
architecture - Russian S.F.S.R. 3. City planning -
Russian S.F.S.R. - History. 4. Russian S.F.S.R. -
History. I. Komech, A. I. (Aleksei I.). II. Title.*
NA1181 .G56 1991

Girard, Xavier. Musée Matisse. Henri Matisse .
Nice , 1988. 366 p. : ISBN 2-86941-071-9
NYPL [3-MCO+ M43 91-5314]

Gironcoli. Gironcoli, Bruno, 1936- Bruno
Gironcoli, Arbeiten auf Papier . Graz [1990]
120 p. : DDC 709/.2 20
N6811.5.G57 A4 1990

Gironcoli, Bruno, 1936-
Bruno Gironcoli, Arbeiten auf Papier : Neue
Galerie, Graz, 20. 4.-20. 5. 1990, Kärntner
Landesgalerie, Klagenfurt, 30. 5.-30. 6. 1990,
Galerija grada Zagreba, Zagreb, 1991, Mestna
Galerija, Ljubljana, 1991 / [Ausstellung und
Katalog, Neue Galerie am Landesmuseum
Joanneum, Wilfried Skreiner ; Katalogredaktion,
Rainer Fuchs, Christa Steinle]. Graz : Die
Galerie, [1990] 120 p. : chiefly ill. (all col.) ; 30
cm. Cover title: Gironcoli. "Herausgegeben von der
Gesellschaft der Freunde der Neuen Galerie, Graz, und
der Kärtner Landesgalerie Klagenfurt"--T.p. verso.
Includes bibliographical references (p. 118). DDC
709/.2 20
*1. Gironcoli, Bruno, 1936- - Exhibitions. I. Skreiner,
Wilfried. II. Fuchs, Rainer, Dr. III. Steinle, Christa. IV.
Neue Galerie am Landesmuseum Joanneum. V. Title.
VI. Title: Arbeiten auf Papier. VII. Title: Gironcoli.*
N6811.5.G57 A4 1990

**GIRONCOLI, BRUNO, 1936- -
EXHIBITIONS.**
Gironcoli, Bruno, 1936- Bruno Gironcoli,
Arbeiten auf Papier . Graz [1990] 120 p. :
DDC 709/.2 20
N6811.5.G57 A4 1990

Gisbert de Mesa, Teresa. (joint author) Mesa, José
de. El pintor Mateo Pérez de Alesio. La Paz,
1972. 130 p.
ND623.P3843 M47
NYPL [3-MCZ P437 81-673]

Gisbert, Teresa. see Gisbert de Mesa, Teresa.

Gisbert, Teresa, 1926- La tradición bíblica en el
arte virreinal / Teresa Gisbert, José de Mesa.
1a ed. La Paz, Bolivia : Los Amigos del Libro,
1987. viii, 33 p. : ill. ; 14 x 22 cm. (Colección
Texto y documento) Bibliography: p. 33.
*1. Bible - Bolivia - Influence. 2. Art, Bolivian -
Influence. I. De Mesa, José. II. Title.*
NYPL [3-MAM 90-12522]

Gisela Breitling /. Breitling, Gisela. Stuttgart ,
c1987. 95 p. : ISBN 3-88059-280-2 DDC 759.3
20
ND588.B757 A4 1987
NYPL [3-MCK B835 90-12642]

Gisèle Freund /. Neyer, Hans Joachim, 1947-
Berlin , c1988. 80 p. : ISBN 3-87024-143-8 (pbk.)
NYPL [MFX+ (Freund) 89-24612]

Gisske, Ehrhardt. Behr, Adalbert. Bauen in
Berlin, 1973 bis 1987 /. Leipzig , 1987. 199 p. :
ISBN 3-7338-0040-0 DDC 720/.9431/55 20
NA1085 .B437 1987

Gittinger, Mattiebelle. To speak with cloth . Los
Angeles , c1989. 256 p. : ISBN 0-930741-17-X
(pbk.) *NYPL [3-MON 90-11591]*

Gittings, Kirk. Chaco body / photographs by Kirk
Gittings ; poems by V.B. Price ; with a
foreword by Michael P. Marshall. Albuquerque,
N.M. : Artspace Press : Distributed by the
University of New Mexico Press, 1991. 85 p. :
ill. ; 24 x 26 cm. ISBN 0-8263-1277-2
*1. Chaco Canyon (N.M.) - Description and travel -
Views. I. Price, V. B. (Vincent Barrett). II. Title.*
NYPL [MFX (Gittings) 91-6549]

Giulio Paolini /. Poli, Francesco, 1949- Torino ,
c1990. 171 p. : ISBN 88-7180-006-0 : DDC
709/.2 20
N6923.P27 A4 1990

Giulio Paolini /. Poli, Francesco, 1949- Torino ,
c1990. 171 p. : ISBN 88-7180-006-0
NYPL [3-MCF P198 90-11802]

Giuseppe De Nittis . Lamacchia, Giovanni.
Firenze [1990] 257 p., [9] leaves, [23] p. of
plates : *NYPL [3-MCF N73 90-12002]*

Giuseppe De Nittis, capolista degli impressionisti
/. Lamacchia, Giovanni. Firenze [1990] 257 p.,
[39] p. of plates : DDC 759.5 B 20
ND623.D417 L5 1990

Giuseppe De Nittis, dipinti 1864-1884 /. De
Nittis, Giuseppe, 1846-1884. [Firenze , 1990.
205 p. : *NYPL [3-MCF N73 91-6553]*

Giuseppe Maria Crespi, 1665-1747 . Crespi,
Giuseppe Maria, 1665-1747. [Bologna] , c1990.
ccxvi, 278 p. : ISBN 88-7779-148-9
NYPL [3-MCF C922 91-5467]

Giuseppe Santomaso . Santomaso, Giuseppe.
Torino , c1988. 101 p. : ISBN 88-381-0057-8
NYPL [3-MCF S235 90-234]

Giuseppe Zocchi : Veduten der Villen und
anderer Orte der Toscana 1744 : Staatliche
Graphische Sammlung München, 7. Dezember
1988-12. Februar 1989 / [Katalogbearbeitung,
Richard Harprath]. München : Die Sammlung,
c1988. 132 p. : ill. ; 20 x 27 cm. Includes
bibliographical references (p. 131-132).
*1. Zocchi, Giuseppe, 1711-1767 - Exhibitions. 2.
Tuscany (Italy) in art - Exhibitions. 3. Tuscany (Italy) -
Description and travel - Views - Exhibitions. I. Zocchi,
Giuseppe, 1711-1767. II. Harprath, Richard. III.
Staatliche Graphische Sammlung München.*
IN PROCESS (ONLINE)
NYPL [MDG (Zocchi) 91-4741]

Giusti, Maria Adriana. Edilizia in Toscana dal
XV al XVII secolo / Maria Adriana Giusti.
Firenze : EDIFIR, [1990] 254 p. : ill. ; 30 cm.
(Strutture edilizie e organizzazione dello spazio in
Toscana . 2)
1. Architecture - Italy - Tuscany. I. Title. II. Series.
IN PROCESS (ONLINE)
NYPL [3-MQWB+ 91-6836]

Giverny. Götz, K. O. (Karl Otto), 1914- K.O.
Götz . Düsseldorf , 1989. 101 p. :
NYPL [3-MCK+ G612 89-26570]

Gizzi, Corrado.
Alberto Martini e Dante /. Milano , c1989. 431
p. : ISBN 88-435-2984-6
IN PROCESS (ONLINE)
NYPL [3-MCF+ M383 90-11582]

Botticelli e Dante /. Milano , c1990. 361 p. :
ISBN 88-435-3329-0
N6923.B67 A4 1990
NYPL [3-MCF+ B75 91-5452]

GLADNESS. see HAPPINESS.

GLADWIN COUNTY (MICH.) - MAPS.
Rockford Map Publishers. Gladwin County,
Michigan, land atlas & plat book . Rockford,
Ill. [c1990] 1 atlas (49 p.) :
NYPL [Map Div. 90-11381]

Gladwin County, Michigan, land atlas & plat book . Rockford Map Publishers. Rockford, Ill. [c1990] 1 atlas (49 p.) :
NYPL [Map Div. 90-11381]

Glancey, Jonathan. The new moderns / by Jonathan Glancey ; photographs by Richard Bryant ; foreword by Charles Gwarthmey. 1st American ed. New York : Crown, c1990. 191 p. : col. ill. ; 30 cm. Title on spine: The new moderns, architects and interior designers of the 1990's. ISBN 0-517-57662-7 : DDC 728/.09/045 20
1. Architecture, Modern - 20th century. 2. Interior decoration - History - 20th century. I. Bryant, Richard. II. Title.
NA680 .G57 1990
NYPL [3-MLO+ 91-4945]

Glanville, Philippa. Women silversmiths, 1685-1845 : works from the collection of the National Museum of Women in the Arts / Philippa Glanville, Jennifer Faulds Goldsborough. New York, N.Y. : Thames and Hudson, 1990. 176 p. : ill. ; 30 cm. ISBN 0-500-23578-3
1. Silverwork - Great Britain - Exhibitions. I. National Museum of Women in the Arts (U. S.). II. Title.
NYPL [3-MNO+ 90-11566]

Glas aus der Sammlung des Kunstgewerbemuseums Zürich. Kunstgewerbemuseum Zürich. Zürich, c1969. 239 p. : *NYPL [3-MPW 90-6938]*

Glas aus fünf Jahrhunderten. Glas aus 5 Jahrhunderten /. Wien, 1990. 423 p. : ISBN 3-900605-05-X : DDC 748.2994/074/43613 20
NK5142 .G59 1990

Glas aus 5 Jahrhunderten / [Beschreibung der Gläser, Walter Spiegl, Regine und Michael Kovacek ; japanische Übersetzung, Megumi Maderdonner]. Wien : Glasgalerie Michael Kovacek, 1990. 423 p. : ill. (chiefly col.), 1 map ; 31 cm. Catalog of the exhibition held at the Glasgalerie Michael Kovacek, Vienna, 1990. Supplementary leaf inserted between p. 54 and p. 55. Includes bibliographical references. ISBN 3-900605-05-X : DDC 748.2994/074/43613 20
1. Glassware - Europe - Exhibitions. 2. Glasgalerie Michael Kovacek (Vienna, Austria) - Exhibitions. I. Spiegl, Walter. II. Kovacek, Regine. III. Kovacek, Michael. IV. Glasgalerie Michael Kovacek (Vienna, Austria). V. Title: Glas aus fünf Jahrhunderten.
NK5142 .G59 1990

Glas in lood in Nederland, 1817-1968 / hoofdredactie, Carine Hoogveld, eindredactie, Ellinoor Bergvelt en Frans van Burkom ; tekstbijdragen van Ellinoor Bergvelt ...[et al.]. 's-Gravenhage : SDU, [1990?] 414 p. : ill. (some col.) ; 31 cm. Includes bibliographical references (p. 375-384) and index. ISBN 90-12-06146-6
1. Glass painting and staining - Netherlands - History - 19th century. 2. Glass painting and staining - Netherlands - History - 20th century. I. Hoogveld, Carine. II. Bergvelt, Ellinoor. III. Burkom, Frans van.
NK5354.A1 G57 1990

Glaser, Rainer. Thomann, Ernst, 1910- Ernst Thomann--Einsichten . Emmendingen, c1990. 69 p. : ISBN 3-925928-13-8
NB588.T39 A4 1990

GLASFABRIK JOH. LOETZ WITWE IN KLOSTERMÜHLE - EXHIBITIONS. Lötz . München, c1989. 2 v. : ISBN 3-7913-0984-6 (Bd.1)
NYPL [3-MPW+ 90-13666]

Glasfenster. Hindorf, Heinz. Heinz Hindorf, Glasfenster /. Freiburg, c1989. 176 p. : ISBN 3-451-21540-3 : DDC 748.593 20
NK5398.H56 A4 1989

Glasgalerie Michael Kovacek (Vienna, Austria) Glas aus 5 Jahrhunderten /. Wien, 1990. 423 p. : ISBN 3-900605-05-X : DDC 748.2994/074/43613 20
NK5142 .G59 1990

GLASGALERIE MICHAEL KOVACEK (VIENNA, AUSTRIA) - EXHIBITIONS. Glas aus 5 Jahrhunderten /. Wien, 1990. 423 p. : ISBN 3-900605-05-X : DDC 748.2994/074/43613 20
NK5142 .G59 1990

Glasgow : 24 hours in the life of a city. London : Chapmans, 1990. 186 p. : ill. (some col.) ; 32 cm. ISBN 1-85592-505-2 : DDC 941.4430859 20

1. Glasgow (Scotland) - Description - Views.
DA890.G5 NYPL [MFW 91-6199]

Glasgow . Armstrong, Anthony, 1935- Glasgow, 1990. 132 p. : ISBN 0-9516481-0-1 : DDC 759.2911 20
NYPL [3-MCV+ A689 91-4953]

Glasgow Art Gallery and Museum. The pursuit of the real . London, c1990. 127 p. : ISBN 0-85331-571-X (pbk.)
NYPL [3-MCT 90-11527]

Rowlandson, Thomas, 1756-1827. The rumbustious world of Thomas Rowlandson . London, 1989. 16 p. ;
NYPL [MDG+ (Rowlandson) 90-13687]

Smith, Sheenah. Horatio McCulloch, 1805-1867 /. [Glasgow], c1988. 112 p. : ISBN 0-902752-35-9 (pbk.)
ND497.M493 S65 1988
NYPL [3-MCV M129 90-11544]

Glasgow Museums and Art Galleries. Hamilton, Vivien. Joseph Crawhall, 1861-1913 . London, 1990. xiii, 177 p. : ISBN 0-7195-4827-6 : DDC 759.2/911 20
ND1942.C89 A4 1990

GLASGOW SCHOOL OF ART. Eadie, William, 1948- Movements of modernity . London, 1990. viii, 292 p. ; ISBN 0-415-03243-1 DDC 709/.414/4309034 20
N6781.G55 E26 1991
NYPL [3-MAMR 90-13191]

GLASGOW SCHOOL OF PAINTING - EXHIBITIONS. Hamilton, Vivien. Joseph Crawhall, 1861-1913 . London, 1990. xiii, 177 p. : ISBN 0-7195-4827-6 : DDC 759.2/911 20
ND1942.C89 A4 1990

GLASGOW (SCOTLAND) - DESCRIPTION - VIEWS. Glasgow . London, 1990. 186 p. : ISBN 1-85592-505-2 : DDC 941.4430859 20
DA890.G5 NYPL [MFW 91-6199]

GLASGOW (SCOTLAND) - SOCIAL LIFE AND CUSTOMS - PICTORIAL WORKS. Hunter, William. Dear happy ghosts . Edinburgh, 1990. 191 p. : ISBN 1-85158-371-8 : DDC 941.443082 20
NYPL [MFW 91-3480]

Glaskunst vom Empire bis zum Historismus . Bremer Landesmuseum für Kunst- und Kulturgeschichte. Bremen, 1988. 214 p. :
NYPL [3-MPW 91-4604]

Glasmalereien für Jerusalem /. Chagall, Marc, 1887- [Vitraux pour Jerusalem. German.] Monte Carlo, c1962. 211 p. :
NYPL [3-MCZ+ C43 91-7160]

Glasmeier, Michael, 1951- Buchstäblich Nürnberger wörtliche Tage . [Nürnberg], c1990. 80 p. : ISBN 3-922531-77-6
NX458 .B83 1990

GLASNOST. Artaud, Evelyne. Perestroïk'art . [Paris], c1990. 118 p. : ISBN 2-7022-0269-1 DDC 709/.47/09048 20
N6988 .A7635 1990
NYPL [3-MAM 90-13376]

Glass . Morris, William. Seattle, c1989. 88 p. : ISBN 0-295-96917-2 DDC 730/.92 20
NK5198.M585 A4 1989
NYPL [3-MPW+ 90-12438]

GLASS ART - EUROPE - HISTORY - 20TH CENTURY - EXHIBITIONS. Ricke, Helmut. Neues Glas in Europa . Düsseldorf, c1990. 352 p. : ISBN 3-87864-205-9
NYPL [3-MPW 91-5638]

GLASS ART - FRANCE - NANCY - CATALOGS. Pétry-Parisot, Claude. Daum dans les musées de Nancy /. [Nancy, 1989] 183 p. : ISBN 2-901408-03-6 *NYPL [3-MPW 91-6650]*

GLASS ART - NORTHWESTERN STATES - HISTORY - 20TH CENTURY. Miller, Bonnie J. Out of the fire . San Francisco, CA, c1991. p. cm. ISBN 0-87701-893-6 (hb) DDC 730/.0979 20
NK5109 .M5 1991

GLASS ART - SOVIET UNION - EXHIBITIONS. Asharina, N. A. (Nina Aleksandrovna) Russian

glass of the 17th-20th centuries /. Corning, N.Y., c1990. 191 p. : ISBN 0-87290-123-8
NYPL [3-MPW 90-11677]

GLASS ART - UNITED STATES - HISTORY - 20TH CENTURY - CATALOGS. Morris, William. Glass . Seattle, c1989. 88 p. : ISBN 0-295-96917-2 DDC 730/.92 20
NK5198.M585 A4 1989
NYPL [3-MPW+ 90-12438]

GLASS ART - UNITED STATES - HISTORY - 20TH CENTURY - THEMES, MOTIVES. Chihuly, Dale, 1941- Venetians /. Altadena, Calif., 1989. 1 v. : ISBN 0-944092-08-X DDC 730/.92 20
NK5198.C43 A4 1989

GLASS BEADS - EUROPE. Le Verre préromain en Europe occidentale /. Montagnac, 1989. 191 p. : ISBN 2-907303-00-7
NYPL [3-MPW+ 91-7509]

GLASS CONTAINERS - CZECHOSLOVAKIA - HISTORY - 20TH CENTURY - CATALOGS. North, Jacquelyn Y. Jones. Czechoslovakian perfume bottles and boudoir accessories /. Marietta, Ohio, c1990. 128 p. : ISBN 0-915410-65-6 (hardbound) DDC 748.8/2/094370904075 20
NK5440.B65 N67 1990

GLASS CRAFT - GERMANY - HISTORY - EXHIBITIONS. Wände aus farbigem Glas . Berlin, 1989. 218 p. : ISBN 3-927873-01-2
NYPL [3-MPW 91-4800]

Glass, five thousand years. Glass, 5,000 years /. New York, 1991. p. cm. ISBN 0-8109-3361-6 DDC 748.29 20
NK5106 .G54 1991

Glass glossary. Jones, Olive R. The Parks Canada glass glossary for the description of containers, tableware, flat glass, and closures /. Ottawa, Ont., 1989. 184 p. : ISBN 0-660-13245-1 DDC 748.2/014 20
NK5104 .J66 1989

Glass in jewelry . Jargstorf, Sibylle. West Chester, Pa., c1991. 174 p. : ISBN 0-88740-295-X DDC 748.8 20
NK5440.J48 J37 1991

GLASS INDUSTRY. see GLASS MANUFACTURE.

Glass, Ingo, 1941- Banater Künstler in der Bundesrepublik Deutschland . Berlin, 1988. 60 p. : ISBN 3-922131-57-8
N6868 .B33 1988
NYPL [3-MAMG 91-6298]

GLASS JEWELRY. Jargstorf, Sibylle. Glass in jewelry . West Chester, Pa., c1991. 174 p. : ISBN 0-88740-295-X DDC 748.8 20
NK5440.J48 J37 1991

GLASS MANUFACTURE - GERMANY - HISTORY - EXHIBITIONS. Wände aus farbigem Glas . Berlin, 1989. 218 p. : ISBN 3-927873-01-2
NYPL [3-MPW 91-4800]

GLASS MANUFACTURE - UNITED STATES. John Frederick Amelung, early American glassmaker /. Corning : London ; 243 p., [4] p. of plates : ISBN 0-87290-075-4 (alk. paper) DDC 748.2913 19
NK5198.A44 A4 1988
NYPL [3-MPW 91-6798]

GLASS PAINTERS AND STAINERS. see GLASS PAINTING AND STAINING.

GLASS PAINTERS - DIRECTORIES. Thomas, Brian. Directory of master glass-painters. Newcastle upon Tyne, 1972. [6], 122 p. : ISBN 0-85362-147-0 DDC 748.5/92
NK5300.7 .T48 NYPL [3-MRY 90-5473]

GLASS PAINTERS - ENGLAND - SUFFOLK - DIRECTORIES. Haward, Birkin, 1912- Nineteenth century Suffolk stained glass . Woodbridge, 1989. xxv, 334 p. : ISBN 0-85115-529-4 : DDC 748.592 19
NYPL [3-MRY 91-2235]

GLASS PAINTING AND STAINING - ENGLAND - DIRECTORIES. Haward, Birkin, 1912- Nineteenth century

Suffolk stained glass . Woodbridge , 1989. xxv,
334 p. : ISBN 0-85115-529-4 : DDC 748.592 19
NYPL [3-MRY 91-2235]

**GLASS PAINTING AND STAINING -
ENGLAND - SUFFOLK - HISTORY -
19TH CENTURY.**
Haward, Birkin, 1912- Nineteenth century
Suffolk stained glass . Woodbridge , 1989. xxv,
334 p. : ISBN 0-85115-529-4 : DDC 748.592 19
NYPL [3-MRY 91-2235]

**GLASS PAINTING AND STAINING -
FRANCE - ANGERS - HISTORY - 19TH
CENTURY.**
Boisléve, Jacques, 1943- Les vitraux vendéens
et les maîtres verriers angevins /. [Maulevrier,
France] , c1987. 110 p. : DDC 748.594/18 19
NK5349.A54 B65 1987
NYPL [3-MRY 90-12359]

**GLASS PAINTING AND STAINING -
FRANCE - ANGERS - HISTORY - 20TH
CENTURY.**
Boisléve, Jacques, 1943- Les vitraux vendéens
et les maîtres verriers angevins /. [Maulevrier,
France] , c1987. 110 p. : DDC 748.594/18 19
NK5349.A54 B65 1987
NYPL [3-MRY 90-12359]

**GLASS PAINTING AND STAINING -
FRANCE - BRAINE.**
Caviness, Madeline Harrison, 1938- Sumptuous
arts at the royal abbeys in Reims and Braine .
Princeton, N.J. , 1990. xxv, 401 p. : ISBN
0-691-04058-3 : DDC 748.594/32 20
NK5349.R3 C38 1990
NYPL [3-MRY+ 91-4463]

**GLASS PAINTING AND STAINING -
FRANCE - LORRAINE.**
Lillich, Meredith P., 1932- Rainbow like an
emerald . University Park , c1991. xix, 161 p.,
[102] p. of plates : ISBN 0-271-00702-8 : DDC
748.594/38/09022 20
NK5349.A3 L675 1991
NYPL [3-MRY 91-5798]

**GLASS PAINTING AND STAINING -
FRANCE - REIMS.**
Caviness, Madeline Harrison, 1938- Sumptuous
arts at the royal abbeys in Reims and Braine .
Princeton, N.J. , 1990. xxv, 401 p. : ISBN
0-691-04058-3 : DDC 748.594/32 20
NK5349.R3 C38 1990
NYPL [3-MRY+ 91-4463]

**GLASS PAINTING AND STAINING -
FRANCE - STRASBOURG -
EXHIBITIONS.**
Beyer, Victor. Les vitraux des musées de
Strasbourg /. Strasbourg , 1965. 2 v. in 1 :
NYPL [3-MRY 85-4411]

**GLASS PAINTING AND STAINING -
GERMANY (EAST) - ERFURT.**
Drachenberg, Erhard. Mittelalterliche
Glasmalerei in Erfurt /. Dresden , c1990. 296
p. : ISBN 3-364-00044-1
NYPL [3-MRY+ 91-4383]

**GLASS PAINTING AND STAINING -
GERMANY - HISTORY - 20TH
CENTURY - CATALOGS.**
Hindorf, Heinz. Heinz Hindorf, Glasfenster /.
Freiburg , c1989. 176 p. : ISBN 3-451-21540-3 :
DDC 748.593 20
NK5398.H56 A4 1989

**GLASS PAINTING AND STAINING,
GOTHIC - FRANCE - LORRAINE.**
Lillich, Meredith P., 1932- Rainbow like an
emerald . University Park , c1991. xix, 161 p.,
[102] p. of plates : ISBN 0-271-00702-8 : DDC
748.594/38/09022 20
NK5349.A3 L675 1991
NYPL [3-MRY 91-5798]

**GLASS PAINTING AND STAINING -
HISTORY.**
Reyntiens, Patrick. The beauty of stained glass
/. London , 1990. 224 p. : ISBN 1-87156-925-7 :
DDC 748.59 20
NK5306   *NYPL [3-MRY 91-3631]*

**GLASS PAINTING AND STAINING -
JERUSALEM - HISTORY - 20TH
CENTURY.**
Chagall, Marc, 1887- [Vitraux pour Jerusalem.
German.] Glasmalereien für Jerusalem /. Monte
Carlo , c1962. 211 p. :
NYPL [3-MCZ+ C43 91-7160]

**GLASS PAINTING AND STAINING,
MEDIEVAL - AUSTRIA - VIENNA -
EXHIBITIONS.**
Mittelalterliche Glasmalereien aus St. Stephan .
Wien , 1990. 16 p. :
NYPL [3-MRY 91-4404]

**GLASS PAINTING AND STAINING,
MEDIEVAL - GERMANY, EAST -
ERFURT.**
Drachenberg, Erhard. Die mittelalterliche
Glasmalerei in Erfurt. Berlin, Wien, 1976- v in.
ISBN 3-205-00581-3 (v. 2, pt. 1)
NYPL [MRY+ 77-1943 Bd.1, T.1-2]

Drachenberg, Erhard. Mittelalterliche
Glasmalerei in Erfurt /. Dresden , c1990. 296
p. : ISBN 3-364-00044-1
NYPL [3-MRY+ 91-4383]

**GLASS PAINTING AND STAINING -
NETHERLANDS - HISTORY - 19TH
CENTURY.**
Glas in lood in Nederland, 1817-1968 /.
's-Gravenhage [1990?] 414 p. : ISBN
90-12-06146-6
NK5354.A1 G57 1990

**GLASS PAINTING AND STAINING -
NETHERLANDS - HISTORY - 20TH
CENTURY.**
Glas in lood in Nederland, 1817-1968 /.
's-Gravenhage [1990?] 414 p. : ISBN
90-12-06146-6
NK5354.A1 G57 1990

**GLASS PAINTING AND STAINING,
RENAISSANCE - SPAIN.**
Nieto Alcaide, Víctor Manuel. La vidriera del
Renacimiento en España /. Madrid , 1970. 63
p., 48 p. of plates : DDC 748.596 19
NK5362.A1 N53 1970
NYPL [3-MRY 90-5629]

**GLASS PAINTING AND STAINING,
ROMANESQUE - FRANCE - BRAINE.**
Caviness, Madeline Harrison, 1938- Sumptuous
arts at the royal abbeys in Reims and Braine .
Princeton, N.J. , 1990. xxv, 401 p. : ISBN
0-691-04058-3 : DDC 748.594/32 20
NK5349.R3 C38 1990
NYPL [3-MRY+ 91-4463]

**GLASS PAINTING AND STAINING,
ROMANESQUE - FRANCE - REIMS.**
Caviness, Madeline Harrison, 1938- Sumptuous
arts at the royal abbeys in Reims and Braine .
Princeton, N.J. , 1990. xxv, 401 p. : ISBN
0-691-04058-3 : DDC 748.594/32 20
NK5349.R3 C38 1990
NYPL [3-MRY+ 91-4463]

GLASS PAINTING AND STAINING - SPAIN.
Nieto Alcaide, Víctor Manuel. La vidriera del
Renacimiento en España /. Madrid , 1970. 63
p., 48 p. of plates : DDC 748.596 19
NK5362.A1 N53 1970
NYPL [3-MRY 90-5629]

**GLASS PAINTING AND STAINING -
SWITZERLAND - CATALOGS.**
Schneider, Jenny, 1924- Kabinettscheiben des
16. und 17. Jahrhunderts /. Bern , c1956. 12 p.,
[16] p. of plates :   *NYPL [3-MRY 91-521]*

**GLASS PAINTING AND STAINING -
UNITED STATES - HISTORY - 19TH
CENTURY.**
Clark, Willene B. The stained glass art of
William Jay Bolton /. Syracuse, N.Y. , 1992. p.
cm. ISBN 0-8156-2553-7 DDC 748.5913 20
NK5398.B65 C53 1992

Glass paperweights. Bergstrom-Mahler Museum.
Glass paperweights of the Bergstrom-Mahler
Museum /. Richmond, Va. , New York , c1989.
xxxv, 112, [16] p. : ISBN 0-927997-00-2 DDC
748.8/4/07477564 20
NK5440.P3 B44 1989
NYPL [3-MPW 91-6422]

**GLASS SCULPTURE - 20TH CENTURY -
EXHIBITIONS.**
Opalescence . Bruxelles , 1986. 1 v. (unpaged) :
NYPL [3-MPW+ 90-4506]

GLASS SCULPTURE - EXHIBITIONS.
Aldridge, Peter. New sculpture by Peter
Aldridge /. New York , 1981. [24] p. :
NYPL [3-MGO (Aldridge) 90-6401]

GLASS, STAINED. see **GLASS PAINTING
AND STAINING.**

GLASS, STAINED AND PAINTED. see
GLASS PAINTING AND STAINING.

**GLASS UNDERPAINTING - GERMANY -
HISTORY.**
Lepovitz, Helena Waddy, 1945- Images of
faith . Athens , c1991. xviii, 228 p. : ISBN
0-8203-1256-8 (alk. paper) DDC
760/.04482/094336 20
NK5435.G3 L4 1991
NYPL [3-MRY 91-4876]

**GLASS UNDERPAINTING - GERMANY -
HISTORY - 20TH CENTURY.**
Lepovitz, Helena Waddy, 1945- Images of
faith . Athens , c1991. xviii, 228 p. : ISBN
0-8203-1256-8 (alk. paper) DDC
760/.04482/094336 20
NK5435.G3 L4 1991
NYPL [3-MRY 91-4876]

**GLASS UNDERPAINTING -
MASSACHUSETTS - NEW BEDFORD -
HISTORY - 20TH CENTURY -
CATALOGS.**
Malakoff, Edward. Pairpoint lamps /. West
Chester, Pa. , c1990. 155 p. : ISBN
0-88740-281-X DDC 749/.63 20
NK5436.P35 A4 1990

Glass, 5,000 years / edited by Hugh Tait. New
York : H.N. Abrams, 1991. p. cm. Includes
bibliographical references and index. ISBN
0-8109-3361-6 DDC 748.29 20
1. Glassware - History. I. Tait, Hugh. II. Title: Glass,
five thousand years.
NK5106 .G54 1991

Glassammlung des Kunstmuseums Düsseldorf.
Kunstmuseum Düsseldorf. Reflex der
Jahrhunderte . Düsseldorf , 1989. 352 p. :
NYPL [3-MPW 91-7179]

GLASSWARE, ANCIENT - EUROPE.
Le Verre préromain en Europe occidentale /.
Montagnac , 1989. 191 p. : ISBN 2-907303-00-7
NYPL [3-MPW+ 91-7509]

**GLASSWARE - AUSTRIA - HISTORY - 20TH
CENTURY - CATALOGS.**
Frottier, Elisabeth, 1959- Michael Powolny .
Wien , c1990. 289 p. : ISBN 3-205-05268-4 :
NK4210.P68 F76 1990

GLASSWARE - CATALOGS.
Bremer Landesmuseum für Kunst- und
Kulturgeschichte. Glaskunst vom Empire bis
zum Historismus . Bremen , 1988. 214 p. :
NYPL [3-MPW 91-4604]

Kunstgewerbemuseum Zürich. Glas aus der
Sammlung des Kunstgewerbemuseums Zürich.
Zürich , c1969. 239 p. :
NYPL [3-MPW 90-6938]

Kunstmuseum Düsseldorf. Reflex der
Jahrhunderte . Düsseldorf , 1989. 352 p. :
NYPL [3-MPW 91-7179]

**GLASSWARE - COLLECTORS AND
COLLECTING.**
Lee, Ruth Webb, 1894-1958. Victorian glass
handbook. Wellesley Hills, Mass. [1946] 1 v.
(chiefly illus., 260 plates) DDC 748.8
NK5112 .L48   *NYPL [3-MPW 90-5568]*

Sotheby's concise encyclopedia of glass /.
Boston , c1991. p. ISBN 0-316-08374-7 : DDC
748.29 20
NK5104 .S66 1991

**GLASSWARE - CZECHOSLOVAKIA -
BOHEMIA - HISTORY - 19TH
CENTURY - EXHIBITIONS.**
Lötz . München , c1989. 2 v. : ISBN
3-7913-0984-6 (Bd.1)
NYPL [3-MPW+ 90-13666]

**GLASSWARE - CZECHOSLOVAKIA -
BOHEMIA - HISTORY - 20TH
CENTURY - EXHIBITIONS.**
Lötz . München , c1989. 2 v. : ISBN
3-7913-0984-6 (Bd.1)
NYPL [3-MPW+ 90-13666]

GLASSWARE - EUROPE - EXHIBITIONS.
Glas aus 5 Jahrhunderten /. Wien , 1990. 423
p. : ISBN 3-900605-05-X : DDC
748.2994/074/43613 20
NK5142 .G59 1990

GLASSWARE - EXHIBITIONS.
Kunstmuseum Düsseldorf. Reflex der
Jahrhunderte . [Düsseldorf] , c1989. 352 p. :

DDC 748.2/074/432122 20
NK5102.5.G3 D885 1989

GLASSWARE - FINLAND - HISTORY - 20TH CENTURY - EXHIBITIONS.
Suomen lasi elää 2 =. [Riihimäki] [1990] 89 p. : ISBN 951-895-209-4
NK5171.F5 S94 1990

GLASSWARE - FRANCE - HISTORY - 20TH CENTURY.
Mortimer, Tony L. Lalique. . London , 1989. 128 p. : ISBN 1-87130-764-3
NYPL [3-MNR 90-5089]

GLASSWARE - FRANCE - NANCY - CATALOGS.
Pétry-Parisot, Claude. Daum dans les musées de Nancy /. [Nancy , 1989] 183 p. : ISBN 2-901408-03-6 *NYPL [3-MPW 91-6650]*

GLASSWARE - GERMANY - DÜSSELDORF - CATALOGS.
Kunstmuseum Düsseldorf. Reflex der Jahrhunderte . Düsseldorf , 1989. 352 p. :
NYPL [3-MPW 91-7179]

GLASSWARE - GERMANY - MAINZ - CATALOGS.
Landesmuseum Mainz. Jugendstil . Mainz , c1990. 396 p. : ISBN 3-8053-1141-9
NK5109.85.A7 L35 1990

GLASSWARE - GERMANY (WEST) - BAVARIA - HISTORY - 19TH CENTURY.
Gropplero di Troppenburg, Elianna. Das bayerische Glas des Historismus dargestellt an der Hütte Theresienthal . München , c1988. 285 p., [32] p. of plates : ISBN 3-88073-275-2 DDC 338.7/6661/094336 19
NK5198.H78 G76 1988
NYPL [3-MPW 91-5027]

GLASSWARE - GERMANY (WEST) - BREMEN - CATALOGS.
Bremer Landesmuseum für Kunst- und Kulturgeschichte. Glaskunst vom Empire bis zum Historismus . Bremen , 1988. 214 p. :
NYPL [3-MPW 91-4604]

GLASSWARE - HISTORY.
Charleston, R. J. (Robert Jesse), 1916- Masterpieces of glass . New York , 1990. 256 p. : ISBN 0-8109-3607-0
NYPL [3-MPW+ 91-5598]

Glass, 5,000 years /. New York , 1991. p. cm. ISBN 0-8109-3361-6 DDC 748.29 20
NK5106 .G54 1991

GLASSWARE - HISTORY - 19TH CENTURY - CATALOGS.
Landesmuseum Mainz. Jugendstil . Mainz , c1990. 396 p. : ISBN 3-8053-1141-9
NK5109.85.A7 L35 1990

GLASSWARE - HISTORY - 20TH CENTURY - CATALOGS.
Landesmuseum Mainz. Jugendstil . Mainz , c1990. 396 p. : ISBN 3-8053-1141-9
NK5109.85.A7 L35 1990

GLASSWARE - HISTORY - 20TH CENTURY - EXHIBITIONS.
Opalescence . Bruxelles , 1986. 1 v. (unpaged) :
NYPL [3-MPW+ 90-4506]

GLASSWARE - ITALY - VENICE - HISTORY.
Barovier Mentasti, Rosa. Il vetro veneziano . Milano , 1988, c1982. 346 p. :
NYPL [3-MPW 90-11729]

GLASSWARE - MASSACHUSETTS - SANDWICH - CATALOGS.
Barlow, Raymond E. A guide to Sandwich glass . West Chester, PA , Windham, NH , c1989. 1 v. (unpaged) : ISBN 0-88740-171-6 DDC 749/.63 20
NK5112 .B335 1989
NYPL [3-MPW+ 90-10804]

GLASSWARE - NEW HAMPSHIRE - HISTORY.
Yankee glass . Keene, NH (P.O. Box 702, Keene 03431) , c1990. xvi, 76 p. : DDC 748.29142/09/034 20
NK5112 .Y36 1990

GLASSWARE - NEW YORK (STATE) - CORNING.
Charleston, R. J. (Robert Jesse), 1916- Masterpieces of glass . New York , 1990. 256 p. : ISBN 0-8109-3607-0
NYPL [3-MPW+ 91-5598]

GLASSWARE - PENNSYLVANIA - INDIANA - HISTORY.
Heacock, William. Harry Northwood--the early years, 1881-1900 /. Marietta, Ohio [1990] viii, 151 p. : ISBN 0-915410-39-7 (softbound) DDC 748.2913 20
NK5198.N59 H4 1990

GLASSWARE - PORTUGAL - EXHIBITIONS.
O Vidro em Portugal . [Lisbon] [1989] 75 p. : DDC 748.2969/074469425 20
NK5143.A1 V5 1989

GLASSWARE, RUSSIAN - EXHIBITIONS.
Asharina, N. A. (Nina Aleksandrovna) Russian glass of the 17th-20th centuries /. Corning, N.Y. , c1990. 191 p. :
NYPL [3-MPW 90-11677]

GLASSWARE - SWEDEN - HISTORY - 20TH CENTURY - EXHIBITIONS.
Svenskt glas 86 . [Göteborg] [1986] 82 p. : ISBN 91-970533-4-1
MLCS 88/02246 (N)
NYPL [3-MPW 91-6219]

GLASSWARE - TERMINOLOGY.
Jones, Olive R. The Parks Canada glass glossary for the description of containers, tableware, flat glass, and closures /. Ottawa, Ont. , 1989. 184 p. : ISBN 0-660-13245-1 DDC 748.2/014 20
NK5104 .J66 1989

GLASSWARE - UNITED STATES.
Lee, Ruth Webb, 1894-1958. Victorian glass handbook. Wellesley Hills, Mass. [1946] 1 v. (chiefly illus., 260 plates) DDC 748.8
NK5112 .L48 *NYPL [3-MPW 90-5568]*

GLASSWARE - UNITED STATES - HISTORY - 18TH CENTURY.
John Frederick Amelung, early American glassmaker /. Corning : London ; 243 p., [4] p. of plates : ISBN 0-87290-075-4 (alk. paper) DDC 748.2913 19
NK5198.A44 A4 1988
NYPL [3-MPW 91-6798]

GLASSWARE - UNITED STATES - HISTORY - 19TH CENTURY.
Couldrey, Vivienne. The art of Louis Comfort Tiffany /. Secaucus, N.J. , c1989. 191 p. : ISBN 1-555-21447-9 DDC 748/.092 20
NK5198.T5 C68 1989

GLASSWARE - UNITED STATES - HISTORY - 20TH CENTURY.
Couldrey, Vivienne. The art of Louis Comfort Tiffany /. Secaucus, N.J. , c1989. 191 p. : ISBN 1-555-21447-9 DDC 748/.092 20
NK5198.T5 C68 1989

GLASSWARE - WEST VIRGINIA - MOUNDSVILLE - HISTOTY - 20TH CENTURY - CATALOGS.
Seligson, Sidney P. Fostoria American . [U.S.A.] , c1990. 63 p. : DDC 748.29154/16 20
NK5198.F6 A4 1990

GLASTONBURY ABBEY - HISTORY.
Willis, Robert, 1800-1875. The architectural history of Glastonbury Abbey /. Lampeter , 1990. x, 91 p., [6] leaves of plates : ISBN 0-947992-44-8 *NYPL [3-MRBH 91-7084]*

GLAZES.
Mansfield, Janet. Salt-glaze ceramics . Tortola, BVI , c1991. vii, 134 p. : ISBN 976-8097-11-6
NYPL [3-MPO+ 91-8072]

Tailor, Heather. Lustre for china painters and potters /. Kenthurst , 1990. 47 p. : ISBN 0-86417-294-X DDC 738.1/5 20
NK4605 .T25 1990

GLAZING.
Rankin, Don. Answers to 50 of the most often asked questions about watercolor glazing techniques /. New York , 1991. 144 p. : ISBN 0-8230-4489-0 : DDC 751.42/2 20
ND2430 .R36 1991

GLAZING (CERAMICS)
Mansfield, Janet. Salt-glaze ceramics . Tortola, BVI , c1991. vii, 134 p. : ISBN 976-8097-11-6
NYPL [3-MPO+ 91-8072]

Gleason, David K. Over Miami / aerial photographs and text by David King Gleason. Baton Rouge : Louisiana State University Press, c1990. vii, 136 p. : (chiefly col.) ill. ; 27 x 37 cm. Includes index. DDC 917.59/381/00222 20 (alk. paper)
1. Miami (Fla.) - Aerial photographs. 2. Miami Region

(Fla.) - Aerial photographs. 3. Miami (Fla.) - Description - Views. 4. Miami Region (Fla.) - Description and travel - Views. I. Title.
F319.M6 G57 1990
NYPL [MFX+ (Gleason) 91-4499]

Gleason, John A. Illustration with markers : time-saving techniques for design professionals / John A. Gleason. New York : Whitney Library of Design, 1991. p. cm. Includes index. ISBN 0-8230-2536-5 : DDC 741.6 20
1. Dry marker drawing - Technique. 2. Felt marker drawing - Technique. I. Title.
NC878 .G57 1991

Gleick, James. Porter, Eliot, 1901- Nature's chaos /. New York, N.Y., U. S.A. , 1990. 125, [1] p. : ISBN 0-670-83532-3 : DDC 779/.3 20
TR721 .G58 1990
NYPL [MFX+ (Porter) 91-6781]

Gleisberg, Dieter.
Kunstschätze aus Sachsen : Meisterwerke aus Leipziger Museen vom Mittelalter bis zur Gegenwart / Dieter Gleisberg. Karlsruhe : G. Braun, [1991] 399 p. : ill. ; 29 cm. "Dieses Buch erschien anlässlich der Ausstellung ... in der Städtischen Galerie im Prinz-Max-Palais Karlsruhe vom 6. April bis 30. Juni 1991"--P. [6] ISBN 3-7650-8091-8
1. Art, German - Germany - Saxony - Exhibitions. I. Städtische Galerie im PrinzMaxPalais Karlsruhe. II. Title. *NYPL [3-MAMG 91-8019]*

Meisterzeichnungen . [Leipzig] , c1990. 352 p. : ISBN 3-361-00241-0
IN PROCESS (ONLINE)
NYPL [3-MBH+ 91-6466]

Merkur & die Musen . [Wien] [1989] 627 p. : ISBN 3-900926-02-6
NYPL [3-MAMG+ 90-13617]

Merkur & die Musen . Wien , 1989. 627 p. : ISBN 3-900926-02-6 DDC 707/.4/43613 20
N6886.L4 M47 1989

Glendening, Elaine. Oregon environmental atlas /. [Portland] , Portland, Or. , 1988. 1 atlas (64 p.) : DDC 363.73/2/09795022 20
G1491.N85 O7 1988
NYPL [Map Div. 91-2711]

Glenn, Constance. Barnes, Lucinda. Imágenes líricas =. Long Beach , c1990. 119 p. : ISBN 0-936270-30-6
NYPL [3-MAML+ 91-5035]

Gli Archivi del progetto.
Nizzoli, Marcello, 1887-1969. Marcello Nizzoli /. Milano , 1990. 391 p. : ISBN 88-435-3064-X *NYPL [3-MCF+ N737 91-6520]*

Quintavalle, Arturo Carlo. Arnaldo Pomodoro . Milano , 1990. 163 p. : ISBN 88-435-3379-7
IN PROCESS (ONLINE)
NYPL [3-MGO+ (Pomodoro) 91-7181]

Gli Uffizi. Studi e ricerche .
(6) La Maestà di Duccio restaurata. Firenze [1990] 89 p. : ISBN 88-7038-187-0
NYPL [MCF D82 90-10935]

Glibota, Ante. Olympiade des arts =. [Seoul] [1988] 839 p. : DDC 709/.04/80745195 20
N6488.K6 S467 1988

Glimcher, Marc. The Art of Mark Rothko . New York , c1991. p. cm. ISBN 0-517-58148-5 : DDC 759.13 20
ND237.R725 A9 1991

Glimcher, Mildred, 1939- Willem de Kooning, Jean Dubuffet . New York, NY , c1990. 29, [84] p. : *NYPL [3-MAMZ 91-5530]*

Glinka, V. M. (Vladislav Mikhaĭlovich), 1903- Ermitazh . Leningrad , 1989. 560 p. : ISBN 5-274-00375-3 :
N3350 .E76 1989

Gloag, John, 1896- A complete dictionary of furniture / John Gloag ; revised and expanded by Clive Edwards. Rev. ed. Woodstock, N.Y. : Overlook Press, 1991. 828 p. : ill. ; 24 cm. Includes bibliographical references (p. 779-784). ISBN 0-87951-414-0 DDC 749 20
1. Furniture - Dictionaries. I. Edwards, Clive, 1947-. II. Title.
NK2205 .G54 1991 *NYPL [MOF 91-6208]*

GLOBES - CONSERVATION AND RESTORATION.
Baynes-Cope, A.D. The study and conservation of globes /. Wien , 1985. 80 p., [15] p. of plates : *NYPL [Map Div. 86-526]*

GLOBES - JUVENILE LITERATURE.
Broekel, Ray. Maps and globes /. Chicago ,
c1983. 45 p. : ISBN 0-516-01695-4   DDC 912 19
GA105.6 .B76 1983
                              NYPL [Map Div. 91-2532]

GLOBES, TERRESTRIAL. see GLOBES.

Glöckner, Hermann, 1889-
Hermann Glöckner : Raum, Zeit, Figur : ein
Dresdner Beitrag zur Moderne : Ulmer
Museum, 3. Februar-17. März 1991. Stuttgart :
B. Wilhelm, [1991] 130 p. : ill. ; 31 cm. ISBN
3-923717-65-2
  *1. Glöckner, Hermann, 1889- - Exhibitions. I. Ulmer
  Museum. II. Title.*
                        NYPL [3-MCK+ G562 91-8028]

GLÖCKNER, HERMANN, 1889- -
  EXHIBITIONS.
Glöckner, Hermann, 1889- Hermann Glöckner .
Stuttgart [1991] 130 p. : ISBN 3-923717-65-2
                        NYPL [3-MCK+ G562 91-8028]

Glöckner, Wolfgang. Grieshaber, Helmut A. P.,
1909- Grieshaber . Bonn , c1989. 190 p. :
ISBN 3-416-02188-6 (Katalog)
                          NYPL [3-MCK G84 91-5878]

Glories of the past : ancient art from the Shelby
White and Leon Levy collection / edited by
Dietrich von Bothmer. New York :
Metropolitan Museum of Art : Distributed by
H.N. Abrams, c1990. x, 280 p. : ill. (some
col.) ; 29 cm. Includes bibliographical references and
index. ISBN 0-87099-593-6   DDC 709/.01 20
  *1. White, Shelby - Art collections - Exhibitions. 2.
  Levy, Leon - Art collections - Exhibitions. 3. Art,
  Ancient - Exhibitions. 4. Art - Private collections -
  United States - Exhibitions. I. Von Bothmer, Dietrich,
  1918-. II. Metropolitan Museum of Art (New York,
  N.Y.).*
N5337.W47 G57 1990
                          NYPL [3-MAE+ 91-5037]

Glorious cats . Ivory, Lesley Anne. New York ,
1992. p. cm. ISBN 0-517-58692-4 : DDC 759.13
20
ND237.I94 A4 1992

The glory of the English house . Esher, Lionel,
1913- Boston, Mass. , 1991. p. ISBN
0-8212-1851-4 : DDC 728/.0942 20
NA7328 .E74 1991

GLOUCESTER (MASS.) IN ART -
  EXHIBITIONS.
Homer, Winslow, 1836-1910. Winslow Homer
in Gloucester /. Chicago, Ill. , c1990. 112 p. :
ISBN 0-8478-1315-0
                          NYPL [3-MCX+ H76 91-5348]

**Gloutchenko, Nicolas. see Hlushchenko, Mykola
Petrovych, 1901-**

Glózer, László, 1936- Wols Photograph / Laszlo
Glozer. 2. Aufl. München : Schirmer/Mosel,
c1978. 117 p., 102 p. of plates : ill. ; 21 cm.
Includes bibliographical references. ISBN
3-921375-30-4
  *1. Wols, 1913-1951. 2. Photography, Artistic -
  Exhibitions. I. Wols, 1913-1951. II. Title.*
                        NYPL [3-MFX (Wols) 90-6352]

Glusberg, Jorge.
The architecture of Mario Botta : between
history and memory : the past as friend / by
Jorge Glusberg. Buenos Aires : Center of Art
and Communication, [1980] 37 p. : ill. ; 24 cm.
Cover title: Mario Botta. DDC 720/.92 20
  *1. Botta, Mario, 1943- - Criticism and interpretation. 2.
  Architecture, Modern - 20th century - Switzerland. I.
  Title: Mario Botta.*
NA1353.B67 G58 1980

Escuela de Buenos Aires : dibujos de
arquitectos / Jorge Glusberg. Buenos Aires,
Argentina : Ediciones Union Carbide, [between
1984 and 1990] 31 p. : ill. ; 30 cm. (Cuadernos
de arquitectura de la Unión Internacional de
Arquitectos)
  *1. Architectural drawing - 20th century - Argentina -
  Buenos Aires - Exhibitions. I. Title. II. Series.*
NA2706.A7 G58 1984

Miguel Angel Roca, arquitecto / Jorge
Glusberg. Buenos Aires, Argentina : Ediciones
Union Carbide, [between 1985 and 1990] 39
p. : ill. ; 30 cm. (Cuadernos de arquitectura de la
Unión Internacional de Arquitectos) DDC 720/.92 20
  *1. Roca, Miguel Angel - Catalogs. 2. Architecture,
  Postmodern - Argentina. I. Title. II. Series.*
NA839.R62 A4 1990

**Glushchenko, Nikolaï. see Hlushchenko, Mykola
Petrovych, 1901-**

GLYPTICS.
Devoto, Guido, 1935- Archeogemmologia .
Roma [1990] 247 p. : ISBN 88-7222-008-4
DDC 736/.2/093 20
NK5500 .D48 1990

GLYPTICS - ITALY.
Donati, Valentino. Pietre dure e medaglie del
Rinascimento . Ferrara [1989]. 291 p. :
                          NYPL [3-MGW+ 91-7173]

GLYPTOGRAPHY. see GLYPTICS.

Glyptothek München, 1830-1980 :
Jubiläumsausstellung zur Entstehungs- und
Baugeschichte, 17. September bis 23. November
1980, Glyptothek München, Königsplatz /
[herausgegeben von Klaus Vierneisel und
Gottlieb Leinz ; Gestaltung des Kataloges,
Klaus-Jürgen Sembach]. München : Glyptothek,
c1980. 640 p. : ill. (some col.) ; 23 cm. Includes
bibliographies.
  *1. Glyptothek München - Exhibitions. 2. Art
  museums - Germany (West) - Munich - Exhibitions. 3.
  Architecture, Modern - 19th century - Germany
  (West) - Munich - Exhibitions. 4. Sculpture, Classical -
  Collectors and collecting - Germany (West) -
  Exhibitions. 5. Munich (Germany) - Buildings,
  structures, etc. - Exhibitions. I. Vierneisel, Klaus, 1929-.
  II. Leinz, Gottlieb. III. Sembach, Klaus-Jürgen. IV.
  Glyptothek München.*
NB87.M8 G55 1980
                          NYPL [3-MQWD 90-5627]

Glyptothek München.
Glyptothek München, 1830-1980 . München ,
c1980. 640 p. :
NB87.M8 G55 1980
                          NYPL [3-MQWD 90-5627]

GLYPTOTHEK MÜNCHEN - CATALOGS.
Vierneisel-Schlörb, Barbara. Klassische
Grabdenkmäler und Votivreliefs /. München ,
c1988. viii, 239 p. : ISBN 3-406-32911-X   DDC
730/.74/43364 s 733/.3/07443364 20
NB27.G4 M864 1979 Bd. 3 NB133.5.S46
                          NYPL [MGH 91-3807]

GLYPTOTHEK MÜNCHEN - EXHIBITIONS.
Glyptothek München, 1830-1980 . München ,
c1980. 640 p. :
NB87.M8 G55 1980
                          NYPL [3-MQWD 90-5627]

G.M. Hopkins Company. Atlas of Hudson
County, New Jersey. Philadelphia, Pa. ,
1908-1909. 2 atlases :
                          NYPL [Map Div. 91-4092]

Gmurzynska-Bscher, Krystyna. Röhl, Karl Peter,
1890-1975. Karl Peter Röhl, Bauhausjahre .
Köln , c1990. 109 p. :
NC251.R62 A4 1990

Gneisz, Doris. Das antike Rathaus : das
griechische Bouleuterion und die frührömische
Curia / Doris Gneisz. Wien : VWGÖ, 1990.
viii, 369 p. : ill. ; 21 cm. (Dissertationen der
Universität Wien, 0379-1424 . 205) Originally
presented as the author's thesis (doctoral)--Universität
Wien, 1987. Includes bibliographical references. ISBN
3-85369-786-0   DDC 725/.13/0938 20
  *1. City halls - Greece. 2. City halls - Rome. I. Title. II.
  Series.*
NA278.P6 G58 1990

Gnoli, Domenico, 1933-1970.
Domenico Gnoli : últimas obras 1963-1969 : 16
de enero-4 de marzo de 1990, Sala de
Exposiciones de la Fundación Caja de
Pensiones, Madrid : exposición / organizada
por la Fundación Caja de Pensiones ;
[traducciones, Laurel Berger ... et al.].1a ed.
[Madrid] : La Fundación, c1990. 151 p. : ill.
(some col.) ; 30 cm. "Bajo los auspicios del
Ministerio de Asuntos Exteriores de Italia dentro del
marco del Festival de la Cooperación Cultural
Ítalo-Española 1990-91." Spanish and English.
Bibliography: p. 145-147. ISBN 84-7664-248-2
  *1. Gnoli, Domenico, 1933-1970 - Exhibitions. I.
  Fundación Caja de Pensiones (Madrid, Spain). II. Title.*
                          NYPL [3-MCF+ G572 90-12300]

GNOLI, DOMENICO, 1933-1970 -
  EXHIBITIONS.
Gnoli, Domenico, 1933-1970. Domenico
Gnoli . [Madrid] , c1990. 151 p. : ISBN
84-7664-248-2
                          NYPL [3-MCF+ G572 90-12300]

Gnos, Hans Peter. Schweizer Kunst, 1900-1990 .
[Zug] , c1990. 144 p. : ISBN 3-908215-01-5
DDC 709/.494/074494756 20
N7148 .S253 1990

Go-Telecom (Firm)
From Alexander to Cleopatra, Greek art of the
Hellenistic Age. Astoria, NY , c1989. 1
videocassette (28 min., 30 sec.) : DDC 709.38
11
N5633

Holy image, holy space--icons & frescoes from
Greece. Astoria, NY , c1988. 1 videocassette
(28 min., 30 sec.) : DDC 704.9 11
N7852.5

Goa . Hutt, Antony. Buckhurst Hill, Essex,
England , 1988. 192 p. : ISBN 0-905906-66-7
                          NYPL [3-MQWS 89-17186]

GOA - DESCRIPTION AND TRAVEL.
Hutt, Antony. Goa . Buckhurst Hill, Essex,
England , 1988. 192 p. : ISBN 0-905906-66-7
                          NYPL [3-MQWS 89-17186]

Goa, folk art rediscovered. Panaji-Goa : Dept. of
Information & Publicity, Govt. of Goa, 1988.
[32] p. of plates : chiefly col. ill. ; 22 cm.
Pictorial work. DDC 751.7/3/0954799 20
  *1. Mural painting and decoration - India - Goa (State).
  2. Primitivism in art - India - Goa (State). I. Goa
  (India : State). Dept. of Information and Publicity.*
ND2828.G6 G6 1988
                          NYPL [3-MAF 91-6905]

GOA - HISTORY.
Hutt, Antony. Goa . Buckhurst Hill, Essex,
England , 1988. 192 p. : ISBN 0-905906-66-7
                          NYPL [3-MQWS 89-17186]

**Goa (India : State). Dept. of Information and
Publicity.** Goa, folk art rediscovered.
Panaji-Goa , 1988. [32] p. of plates : DDC
751.7/3/0954799 20
ND2828.G6 G6 1988
                          NYPL [3-MAF 91-6905]

Gobbi, Elmar, 1962- Plazer, Lukas, 1663-1723.
Der barocke Franziskuszyklus von Frater Lukas
Plazer in Innichen /. Innichen , 1990. 259 p. :
ISBN 88-85226-00-0
ND623.P696 A4 1990

Göbel, Johannes. Grieshaber, Helmut A. P., 1909-
Grieshaber . Bonn , c1989. 190 p. : ISBN
3-416-02188-6 (Katalog)
                          NYPL [3-MCK G84 91-5878]

Gober, Halley, Kessler, Wool : four artists from
New York / [Idee und Organisation, Zdenik
Felix]. [Munich] : Kunstverein München,
c1989. 89 p. : col. ill. ; 25 cm. Catalog of an
exhibition held Sept. 15-Oct. 22, 1989 at the
Kunstverein München. English and German. Includes
bibliographical references. ISBN 3-923357-24-9
  *1. Gober, Robert, 1954- - Exhibitions. 2. Halley, Peter -
  Exhibitions. 3. Kessler, Jon, 1957- - Exhibitions. 4.
  Wool, Christoher, 1955- - Exhibitions. 5. Art,
  American - New York (N.Y.) - Exhibitions. 6. Art,
  Modern - 20th century - New York (N.Y.) -
  Exhibitions. I. Felix, Zdenik. II. Kunstverein München.*
                          NYPL [3-MAMT 90-12879]

Gober, Halley, Kessler, Wool : four artists fron
New York. München : Kunstverein, c1989. 89
p. : ill. (some col.) ; 25 cm. English and German.
ISBN 3-923357-24-9
  *1. Art, American - New York (N.Y.) - Exhibitions. 2.
  Art, Modern - 20th century - New York (N.Y.) -
  Exhibitions. I. Gober, Robert, 1954-.*
N6535.N5 G63 1989

Gober, Robert, 1954-
Gober, Halley, Kessler, Wool . München ,
c1989. 89 p. : ISBN 3-923357-24-9
N6535.N5 G63 1989

New sculpture. [Chicago] , c1986. [12] p. :
ISBN 0-941548-11-2
                          NYPL [3-MGI+ 90-12556]

Robert Gober : Museum Boymans-Van
Beuningen, Rotterdam, 13/5-1/7/90, Kunsthalle
Bern, 1/9-14/10/90 / [organisatie
tentoonstelling en redactie catalogus, Robert
Gober, Ulrich Loock, Karel Schampers].
Rotterdam : Museum Boymans-Van Beuningen ;
Bern : Kunsthalle, [1990] 85 p. : ill. (some
col.) ; 28 cm. Dutch and English. Includes
bibliographical references (p. 84). ISBN 90-6918-054-5
  *1. Gober, Robert, 1954- - Exhibitions. I. Loock, Ulrich.
  II. Schampers, Karel. III. Museum Boymans-Van*

Beuningen. IV. *Kunsthalle Bern. V. Title.*
N6537.G56 A4 1990

GOBER, ROBERT, 1954- - EXHIBITIONS.
Gober, Halley, Kessler, Wool . [Munich] ,
c1989. 89 p. :   ISBN 3-923357-24-9
          NYPL [3-MAMT 90-12879]

Gober, Robert, 1954- Robert Gober .
Rotterdam , Bern [1990] 85 p. :   ISBN
90-6918-054-5
N6537.G56 A4 1990

New sculpture . [Chicago] , c1986. [12] p. :
ISBN 0-941548-11-2
          NYPL [3-MGI+ 90-12556]

Goddard, Donald Letcher. American painting /
Donald Goddard ; introduction by Robert
Rosenblum. New York : Hugh Lauter Levin
Associates : Distributed by Macmillan Pub. Co.,
c1990. 319 p. : col. ill. ; 37 cm. Includes index.
ISBN 0-88363-590-9
*1. Painting, Modern - 17th-18th centuries - United
States. 2. Painting, Modern - 19th century - United
States. 3. Painting, Modern - 20th century - United
States. I. Title.* **NYPL** *[MCW+ 91-2640]*

Godden, Geoffrey A.
The concise guide to British pottery and
porcelain / Geoffrey A. Godden. London :
Barrie & Jenkins, 1990. 224 p. : ill. (some
col.) ; 18 cm. An enlarged, up-dated, and reillustrated
version of Mary and Geoffrey Payton's The observer's
book of pottery and porcelain. Includes bibliographical
references (p. 206-213) and index.   ISBN
0-7126-3600-5   DDC 738/.0941/075 20
*1. Pottery, British - Dictionaries. 2. Porcelain, British -
Dictionaries. I. Payton, Mary. The observer's book of
pottery and porcelain. II. Title.*
NK4085 .G62 1990

Lockett, Terence A. Davenport . London ,
1989. 302 p. :   ISBN 0-7126-2002-8 :   DDC
738.0942463 20
          NYPL [3-MPGO+ 90-11562]

GODDESSES, EGYPTIAN, IN ART.
Eingartner, Johannes. Isis und ihre Dienerinnen
in der Kunst der römischen Kaiserzeit /.
Leiden , New York , 1991. 197 p., [97] p. of
plates :   ISBN 90-04-09312-5   DDC 733/.5 20
NB115 .E37 1990

GODDESSES IN ART. see GODS IN ART.

Godenbeelden uit Tibet . Kreijger, Hugo.
['s-Gravenhage] [Amsterdam] , c1989. 129, [1]
p. :   ISBN 90-12-06219-5
          NYPL [3-MAF 91-5465]

Godey's Lady's book. Kunciov, Robert. Mr.
Godey's ladies. Princeton [N.J.] 1971. viii, 183
p.   ISBN 0-87861-009-X   DDC 391/.07/20973
GT610 .K8   **NYPL** *[3-MMP 90-5497]*

Godfrey, Honor. Colman Foods. The Colman
Collection of silver mustard pots /. Norwich ,
1979. 143 p. :   ISBN 0-9506456-0-5 (pbk.) :
NK7236.M88 C64 1979
          NYPL [MNO 81-450]

Godoli, Ezio. Fanelli, Giovanni. L'illustrazione
Art nouveau /. Roma , 1989. 332 p. :   ISBN
88-420-3476-2   **NYPL** *[MDTT 90-10984]*

Godoy, José-A. Resplendence of the Spanish
monarchy . New York , 1991. p. cm.   ISBN
0-87099-621-5   DDC 739.7/0946/0747471 20
NK3062.A1 R47 1991

Godrej, Pheroza. India, a pageant of prints /.
Bombay , c1990. xii, 240 p. :   ISBN
81-85026-08-4 :   DDC 769/.49954 20
NE954.3.G7 I5 1989
          NYPL [MDZ+ 91-6181]

Gods and heroes in late archaic Greek art /.
Schefold, Karl. [Götter- und Heldensagen der
Griechen in der spätarchaischen Kunst.
English.] Cambridge , New York , 1992. p. cm.
ISBN 0-521-32718-0   DDC 704.94/7/0938 20
N7760 .S27313 1992

**GODS, BUDDHIST, IN ART -
EXHIBITIONS.**
Kreijger, Hugo. Godenbeelden uit Tibet .
['s-Gravenhage] [Amsterdam] , c1989. 129, [1]
p. :   ISBN 90-12-06219-5
          NYPL [3-MAF 91-5465]

GODS - DICTIONARIES.
Shaw, Marvin S. A viewer's guide to art . Santa
Fe, N.M. , 1991. p. cm.   ISBN 0-945465-66-1
DDC 704.9/48 20
N7760 .S4 1991

GODS, HINDU, IN ART.
Yadu, Hemūlāla, 1953- Dakshiṇa Kosala kī
kalā . Naī Dillī , 1990. xiv, 200 p., [29] p. of
plates :
NB1912.H55 Y33 1990

GODS IN ART.
Schefold, Karl. [Götter- und Heldensagen der
Griechen in der spätarchaischen Kunst.
English.] Gods and heroes in late archaic Greek
art /. Cambridge , New York , 1992. p. cm.
ISBN 0-521-32718-0   DDC 704.94/7/0938 20
N7760 .S27313 1992

Shaw, Marvin S. A viewer's guide to art . Santa
Fe, N.M. , 1991. p. cm.   ISBN 0-945465-66-1
DDC 704.9/48 20
N7760 .S4 1991

GODS IN ART - EXHIBITIONS.
Herrscher, Krieger und Geliebte . Innsbruck ,
c1989. 95 p., [6] p. of plates :
          NYPL [3-MGR 91-3460]

Godwin-Ternbach Museum. Herschman, Joel,
1936- Un voyage héliographique à faire . [S.l. ,
1981] 37 p. :   DDC 779/.4/0740147243 19
DC20 .H47   *NYPL [MFW 91-8054]*

Göknil, Ulya Vogt- see Vogt-Göknil, Ulya.

Goepper, Roger.
Alchi : Buddhas, Göttinnen, Mandalas :
Wandmalerei in einem Himalaya-Kloster / Text
von Roger Goepper ; Fotos von Barbara
Lutterbeck und Jaroslav Poncar. Köln :
DuMont, c1982. 110 p. : 32 col. ill. ; 27 cm. Ill.
of art works in the temples of Sumtsek and Dukhang.
Legends in English and German. "Dieses Buch erscheint
aus Anlass der Ausstellung selben Titels vom 9.
Oktober 1982 bis zum 30. Januar 1983 im Museum für
Ostasiatische Kunst der Stadt Köln"--T.p. verso.
Bibliography: p. 46-47.   ISBN 3-7701-1479-5   DDC
755/.943/09546 19
*1. Gsum-rtsegs (Temple : Alchi Gömpa, India) -
Exhibitions. 2. 'Du Khaṅ (Temple : Alchi Gömpa,
India) - Exhibitions. 3. Mural painting and decoration,
Buddhist - India - Alchi Gömpa - Exhibitions. 4. Mural
painting and decoration - India - Alchi Gömpa -
Exhibitions. 5. Temples, Buddhist - India - Alchi
Gömpa - Exhibitions. 6. Alchi Gömpa (India) -
Buildings, structures, etc. - Exhibitions. I. Lutterbeck,
Barbara. II. Poncar, Jaroslav. III. Museum für
Ostasiatische Kunst der Stadt Köln. IV. Title.*
ND2829.A415 G64 1982
          NYPL [3-MAF 90-12370]

Lee, King Tsi. Drache und Phoenix . [Köln] ,
c1990. 229 p. :   DDC 745.7/26/0951074435514 20
NK9900.7.C6 L44 1990
          NYPL [3-MNX 91-4182]

Goerigk, Wolfgang. Reitkunst in Bild und Schrift
des 16.-19. Jahrhunderts /. Hamburg [1982] 44
p. :
Z6240 .R44 1982 SF309
          NYPL [MDZ 87-5069]

Goethe-Institut Montréal. Blanchette, Manon,
1952- Blickpunkte . Montréal, Québec , c1989.
2 v. :   ISBN 2-551-12161-2
N6868.5.C63 B55 1989

Goethe-Institut (Munich, Germany)
Chargesheimer, 1924-1972. Chargesheimer
1924-1972 . [München] [1983] 24 p. :
          NYPL [MFX (Chargesheimer) 90-13458]

**GOETHE, JOHANN WOLFGANG VON, 1749-
1832 - INFLUENCE.**
Lichtenstern, Christa. Metamorphose in der
Kunst des 19. und 20. Jahrhunderts /.
Weinheim , 1990- v. :   ISBN 3-527-17707-8
          NYPL [3-MAMZ 91-236]

**GOETHE, JOHANN WOLFGANG VON, 1749-
1832 - ART COLLECTIONS - CATALOGS.**
Die Erotica und Priapea aus den Sammlungen
Goethes /. Frankfurt am Main , 1990. 298 p. :
          NYPL [3-MAMZ 91-4510]

Goethel, Paul, 1952- Gosney, Michael, 1954- The
Verbum book of digital painting /. Redwood
City, Calif. , 1990. ix, 211 p. :   ISBN
1-558-51090-7   DDC 760 20
N7433.8 .G68 1990

Goettl, Helmut. Kunstsituation und Künstler sein
heute . Karlsruhe , 1988. 342 p. :
N6886.K33 K88 1988
          NYPL [3-MAMG 90-10706]

Göttlicher, Arvid. Materialien für ein Corpus der
Schiffsmodelle im Altertum / Arvid Göttlicher.
Mainz am Rhein : P. von Zabern, c1978. 128

p., [56] p. of plates : ill. ; 32 cm. Includes index.
Bibliography: p. 114-128.   ISBN 3-8053-0249-5   DDC
730
*1. Art objects, Ancient. 2. Ships, Ancient - Models. 3.
Ship models. I. Title.*
VM6.A1 G63   *NYPL [3-MAE 90-6881]*

Goetz, Mary Anna, 1946- Painting landscapes in
oils / Mary Anna Goetz. Cincinnati, Ohio :
North Light Books, 1991. p. cm. Includes index.
ISBN 0-89134-377-6 :   DDC 751.45/436 20
1. Landscape painting - Technique. I. Title.
ND1342 .G64 1991

Goggin, Bill. Eagles : market & price guide, pre
1840 American furniture, sold in public estate
auctions, 1988 through 1990 / Bill & Karen
Goggin. New Market, MD (Box 277, New
Market 21774) : Copies from Eagles, [1990] xv,
319 p. : ill. ; 23 cm. Cover title: Eagles, Americana
at auction. "Compilation of photos and descriptions
appearing from 1988 through 1990 in Eagles Americana
review"--p. vi.   DDC 749.214/09/033075 20
*1. Furniture, Early American - Prices. 2. Furniture -
United States - History - 19th century - Prices. I.
Goggin, Karen. II. Eagles (New Market, Frederick
County, Md.). III. Title. IV. Title: Eagles, Americana at
auction.*
NK2406 .G6 1990

Goggin, Karen. Goggin, Bill. Eagles . New
Market, MD (Box 277, New Market 21774)
[1990] xv, 319 p. :   DDC 749.214/09/033075 20
NK2406 .G6 1990

**GOGH, THEO VAN, 1857-1891 -
CORRESPONDENCE.**
Gogh, Vincent van, 1853-1890 -
Correspondence. The complete letters of
Vincent van Gogh . Greenwich, Conn. , 1958. 3
v. :   *NYPL [3-MCH G61 90-11512]*

**GOGH, VINCENT VAN, 1853 - INFLUENCE -
EXHIBITIONS.**
Vincent van Gogh und die Moderne. English.
Vincent van Gogh and the modern movement,
1890-1914 . Freren , 1990. 436 p. :   ISBN
3-923641-33-8 (hard cover):   DDC 759.9492 20
ND653.G7 A4 1990a

Gogh, Vincent van, 1853-1890.
Bronkhorst, Hans. Vincent van Gogh . Weert ,
c1990. 200 p. :   ISBN 90-6590-394-1 :   DDC
759.9492 B 20
ND653.G7 B724 1990

De Wevers en Vincent van Gogh /. Zwolle ,
c1990. 127 p. :   ISBN 90-6630-222-4 :
N6953.G63 D4 1990

[Provence]
Van Gogh's Provence. New York, NY :
Universe Pub., 1992. p. cm.   ISBN
0-87663-621-0   DDC 759.9492 20
*1. Gogh, Vincent van, 1853-1890 - Themes, motives. 2.
Provence (France) in art. I. Title.*
ND653.G7 A4 1992

Van Gogh, vertigo of light / by Jacqueline and
Maurice Guillaud ; text of Vincent van Gogh's
letters selected by Jacqueline Guillaud. Paris ;
New York : Guillaud Éditions ; p. cm. Includes
index.   ISBN 0-517-58306-2   DDC 759.9492 20
*1. Gogh, Vincent van, 1853-1890. 2. Gogh, Vincent
van, 1853-1890 - Homes and haunts - France -
Provence. 3. Provence (France) in art. I. Guillaud,
Jacqueline. II. Guillaud, Maurice. III. Title.*
ND653.G7 A4 1991

Vincent van Gogh und die Moderne. English.
Vincent van Gogh and the modern movement,
1890-1914 . Freren , 1990. 436 p. :   ISBN
3-923641-33-8 (hard cover):   DDC 759.9492 20
ND653.G7 A4 1990a

GOGH, VINCENT VAN, 1853-1890.
Bronkhorst, Hans. Vincent van Gogh . Weert ,
c1990. 200 p. :   ISBN 90-6590-394-1 :   DDC
759.9492 B 20
ND653.G7 B724 1990

Gogh, Vincent van, 1853-1890. Van Gogh,
vertigo of light /. Paris ; New York : p. cm.
ISBN 0-517-58306-2   DDC 759.9492 20
ND653.G7 A4 1991

Sweetman, David. Van Gogh . New York ,
1991. p. cm.   ISBN 0-671-74338-4   DDC 759.9492
B 20
ND653.G7 S94 1991

Wilkie, Kenneth, 1942- [Van Gogh assignment.]
In search of van Gogh /. Rocklin, CA , 1991.

p. cm. ISBN 1-559-58101-8 : DDC 759.9492 B 20
ND653.G7 W54 1991

**GOGH, VINCENT VAN, 1853-1890 -
CATALOGS.**
Dorn, Roland. Décoration . Hildesheim , New
York , 1990. xxxii, 622 p. : ISBN 3-487-09098-8
ND653.G7 D64 1990

Gogh, Vincent van, 1853-1890 - Correspondence.
The complete letters of Vincent van Gogh :
with reproductions of all the drawings in the
correspondence. Greenwich, Conn. : New York
Graphic Society, 1958. 3 v. : ill. (some col.) ;
25 cm. Includes index (v. 3) Includes bibliographical
references.
*1. Gogh, Theo van, 1857-1891 - Correspondence. 2.
Painters - Netherlands - Correspondence. I. Title.*
    NYPL **[3-MCH G61 90-11512]**

**GOGH, VINCENT VAN, 1853-1890 -
CORRESPONDENCE.**
Gogh, Vincent van, 1853-1890.
[Correspondence. English. Selections.] Van
Gogh, letters from Provence /. New York ,
c1990. 160 p. : ISBN 0-517-58144-2 : DDC
759.9492 B 20
ND653.G7 A3 1990
    NYPL **[3-MCH G61 91-2645]**

Merlhès, Victor. Paul Gauguin et Vincent van
Gogh 1887-1888 . Taravao, Tahiti , 1989. 277
p., [3] folded leaves of plates : ISBN
2-907716-02-6 (pbk.)
    NYPL **[3-MCO G26 91-7602]**

**GOGH, VINCENT VAN, 1853-1890 -
CRITICISM AND INTERPRETATION.**
De Wevers en Vincent van Gogh /. Zwolle ,
c1990. 127 p. : ISBN 90-6630-222-4 :
N6953.G63 D4 1990

**GOGH, VINCENT VAN, 1853-1890 -
CRITICISM AND INTERPRETATION -
JUVENILE LITERATURE.**
Giants of the arts . New York , 1991. p. cm.
ISBN 1-85435-414-0 : DDC 700/.92/24 20
NX633 .G53 1991

**GOGH, VINCENT VAN, 1853-1890 -
EXHIBITIONS.**
Mast, Michiel van der. Van Gogh en Den Haag
/. Zwolle , c1990. 191 p. : ISBN 90-6630-240-2
    NYPL **[3-MCH G61 91-6680]**

Van Gogh et les peintres d'Auvers-sur-Oise .
[Paris] , 1954. xl, 100 p., xxxii p. of plates :
N6847.5.I4 V36 1954

Vincent van Gogh and the modern movement,
1890-1914 /. Freren [Germany] , 1990. 436 p. :
ISBN 3-923641-33-8 (Hard cover)
    NYPL **[3-MCH G61 91-4493]**

Vincent van Gogh und die Moderne. English.
Vincent van Gogh and the modern movement,
1890-1914 . Freren , 1990. 436 p. : ISBN
3-923641-33-8 (hard cover): DDC 759.9492 20
ND653.G7 A4 1990a

**GOGH, VINCENT VAN, 1853-1890 - HOMES
AND HAUNTS - FRANCE - ARLES.**
Dorn, Roland. Décoration . Hildesheim , New
York , 1990. xxxii, 622 p. : ISBN 3-487-09098-8
ND653.G7 D64 1990

**GOGH, VINCENT VAN, 1853-1890 - HOMES
AND HAUNTS - FRANCE - PROVENCE.**
Gogh, Vincent van, 1853-1890. Van Gogh,
vertigo of light /. Paris ; New York : p. cm.
ISBN 0-517-58306-2 DDC 759.9492 20
ND653.G7 A4 1991

Gogh, Vincent van, 1853-1890.
[Correspondence. English. Selections.] Van
Gogh, letters from Provence /. New York ,
c1990. 160 p. : ISBN 0-517-58144-2 : DDC
759.9492 B 20
ND653.G7 A3 1990
    NYPL **[3-MCH G61 91-2645]**

**GOGH, VINCENT VAN, 1853-1890 - HOMES
AND HAUNTS - NETHERLANDS -
AMSTERDAM.**
Groot, Reindert. Vincent van Gogh in
Amsterdam /. Amsterdam , c1990. 128 p. :
ISBN 90-6274-045-6 :
ND653.G7 G74 1990

**GOGH, VINCENT VAN, 1853-1890 - THEMES,
MOTIVES.**
Gogh, Vincent van, 1853-1890. [Provence.] Van
Gogh's Provence. New York, NY , 1992. p.
cm. ISBN 0-87663-621-0 DDC 759.9492 20
ND653.G7 A4 1992

[Correspondence. English. Selections]
Van Gogh, letters from Provence / selected
and introduced by Martin Bailey. 1st
American ed. New York : Clarkson Potter,
c1990. 160 p. : ill. (chiefly col.) ; 20 x 26 cm.
Translation of letters written in French; with two
letters originally written in English. Includes
bibliographical references (p. 158). ISBN
0-517-58144-2 : DDC 759.9492 B 20
*1. Gogh, Vincent van, 1853-1890 - Correspondence. 2.
Gogh, Vincent van, 1853-1890 - Homes and haunts -
France - Provence. 3. Painters - Netherlands -
Correspondence. I. Bailey, Martin, 1947-. II. Title. III.
Title: Letters from Provence.*
ND653.G7 A3 1990
    NYPL **[3-MCH G61 91-2645]**

Goglia, Luigi, 1943- Colonialismo e fotografia .
Messina [1989?] 354 p. :
IN PROCESS (ONLINE)
    NYPL **[MFW 91-8015]**

Goguel, Solange.
René Herbst / Solange Goguel ; iconographie
réunie et établie par Anne Bony et l'auteur.
Paris : Editions du Regard, c1990. 363 p. : ill.
(some col.) ; 31 cm. Includes bibliographical
references (p. 360-361). ISBN 2-903370-56-7
    NYPL **[3-MLH+ 91-5789]**

René Herbst / Solange Goguel ; iconographie
réunie et établie par Anne Bony et l'auteur.
Paris : Editions du Regard, c1990. 363 p. : ill.
(some col.) ; 31 cm. Includes bibliographical
references (p. 360-361). ISBN 2-903370-56-7 DDC
720/.92 20
*1. Herbst, René - Criticism and interpretation. 2.
Interior decoration - France - History - 20th century. 3.
Interior architecture - France - History - 20th century.
4. Furniture design - France - History - 20th century. I.
Title.*
NK2049.Z9 H4734 1990

Gohr, Siegfried. Nay, E. W. (Ernst Wilhelm),
1902-1968. E.W. Nay, Retrospektive /. Köln ,
c1990. 210 p. : ISBN 3-7701-2726-9
    NYPL **[3-MCK+ N331 91-5930]**

Gojowy, Detlef. Schleswig-Holstein, Ingeborg zu.
Weg ins Licht . Hamburg , c1988. 78 p. :
ISBN 3-7672-1062-2
ND588.S2819 A4 1988
    NYPL **[3-MCK+ S343 90-10580]**

Gökçeoğlu, M. (Mustafa), 1942- Tezler ve sözler
/ M. Gökçeoğlu. [Cyprus] : Gençlik Merkezi,
[1985?]- v. <1 > : ill. ; 21 cm. Includes
bibliographical references (v. 1, p. 233).
*1. Ethnic arts - Cyprus. 2. Arts, Turkish - Cyprus. 3.
Turks - Cyprus - Social life and customs. I. Title.*
NX573.6.C9 G64 1985

Gokhale, D. V. (Dinkar Vinayak), 1923- Laxman,
R. K. The eloquent brush /. [Bombay] , c1988.
303 p. :
    NYPL **[3-MEM+ (Laxman) 89-25506]**

Golany, Gideon. Chinese earth-sheltered
dwellings : indigenous lessons for modern urban
design / Gideon S. Golany. Honolulu :
University of Hawaii Press, c1992. p. cm.
Includes bibliographical references and index. ISBN
0-8248-1369-3 DDC 728/.0473/0951 20
1. Earth sheltered houses - China. I. Title.
NA7448 .G6 1992

Das Gold in der Kunst Westafrikas. 2., stark
ver-anderte Aufl. Z-urich : Museum Rietbert
Z-urich, 1981. 58 p. : ill. (some col.) ; 22cm.
Bibliography: p. 27. CONTENTS. - Kunstwerke der
Akan-V-olker im Museum Rietberg Z-urich / von
Eberhard Fischer und Hans Himmelheber -- Zur
Technik des Goldgusses bei den Ashanti (Ghana) / von
Max Fr-ohlich.
*1. Goldwork - Africa, West. I. Fischer, Eberhard,
1941-. II. Himmelheber, Hans, 1908-. III. Fröhlich,
Max. IV. Museum Rietberg.*
    NYPL **[3-MNO 90-12398]**

GOLD JEWELRY, ANCIENT - CATALOGS.
Museum für Kunst und Gewerbe Hamburg.
Antiker Gold- und Silberschmuck . Mainz am
Rhein , c1968. x, 246 p. :
NK7307 .H6   *NYPL* **[3-MNR 90-7024]**

**Gold- und Silberschmiede am Niederrhein,
1854-1987 :** Sonderausstellung vom 8.
November bis 27. Dezember 1987 :
Niederrheinisches Museum für Volkskunde und
Kulturgeschichte Kevelaer / [Redaktion und
Texte, Robert Plötz]. [Kevelaer] : Kreis Kleve,

[1987] 42 p. : ill. (some col.) ; 20 x 22 cm.
(Führer des Niederrheinischen Museums für
Volkskunde und Kulturgeschichte Kevelaer . 22)
DDC 739.2/0943/550740355 19
*1. Goldwork - Germany (West) - Rhineland - History -
19th century - Exhibitions. 2. Goldwork - Germany
(West) - Rhineland - History - 20th century -
Exhibitions. 3. Silverwork - Germany (West) -
Rhineland - History - 19th century - Exhibitions. 4.
Silverwork - Germany (West) - Rhineland - History -
20th century - Exhibitions. I. Plötz, Robert. II.
Niederrheinisches Museum für Volkskunde und
Kulturgeschichte Kevelaer. III. Series.*
NK7150.A3 R544 1987
    NYPL **[3-MNO 91-5028]**

Goldberg, Beth. Photographs updated : similar
images/dissimilar motives / Beth Goldberg,
curator ; Amy Paldi, curatorial assistant.
Rohnert Park, Calif. : University Art Gallery,
Sonoma State University, c1990. 30 p. : ill. ; 30
cm. Catalog of an exhibition held at University Art
Gallery, Sonoma St. Univ., 3/15-4/12/90 and Santa
Barbara Museum of Art, 4/28-6/17/90. Includes
bibliographical references (p. 29). DDC
779/.074/79418 20
*1. Photography, Artistic - Exhibitions. I. Sonoma State
University. University Art Gallery. II. Santa Barbara
Museum of Art. III. Title.*
TR645.R652 U654 1990
    NYPL **[MFW+ 91-3329]**

Goldberg, Rube, 1883-1970. The best of Rube
Goldberg / compiled by Charles Keller.
Englewood Cliffs, N.J. : Prentice-Hall, [1979]
xiii, 130 p. : ill. ; 22 x 27 cm. A collection of
more than 90 humorous inventions which have
appeared in the author's cartoons during his career.
ISBN 0-13-074807-2 : DDC 741.5/973
*1. Inventions - Caricatures and cartoons - Juvenile
literature. 2. American wit and humor, Pictorial -
Juvenile literature. I. Keller, Charles. II. Title.*
NC1429.G46 A4 1979
    NYPL **[3-MEM (Goldberg) 81-1046]**

Goldberg, Vicki. Photography in print .
Albuquerque , 1988, c1981. 570 p. ; ISBN
0-8263-1091-5 DDC 770 19
TR185 .P49 1988   *NYPL* **[MFW 91-5039]**

The Golden Age of painting in Spain /. Brown,
Jonathan, 1939- New Haven , 1991. ix, 330 p. :
ISBN 0-300-04760-6 DDC 759.6/09/03 20
ND804 .B74 1991
    NYPL **[3-MCP+ 91-4955]**

Golden hands. The Golden hands book of
embroidery. Sydney , New York , 1972. 125
p. :   *NYPL* **[3-MOT 79-376]**

The Golden hands book of embroidery. Sydney ;
New York : P. Hamlyn, 1972. 125 p. : ill. ; 29
cm. "The greater part of the material published in this
book was first published in 'Golden hands'."
1. Embroidery. I. Golden hands.
    NYPL **[3-MOT 79-376]**

The golden relationship . Boles, Martha.
Bradford, Mass. , c1990- v. <1 > : ISBN
0-9614504-3-6 (bk. 1) DDC 701 20
N72.M3 B65 1990

The golden ring . Gippenreïter, Vadim
Evgen'evich. New York , 1991. p. cm. ISBN
1-558-59216-4 DDC 720/.947 20
NA1181 .G56 1991

Goldenberg, Yvonne. Joly, Raymond, 1911-
Raymond Joly, un médailleur d'aujourd'hui.
Paris, 1967. 133 p. : DDC 709/.2/4
N6853.J64 G64
    NYPL **[3-MGP (Joly) 90-7101]**

Goldfarb, Hilliard T. Fatal consequences .
Hanover, N.H. , 1990. 92 p. : ISBN
0-944722-04-0 DDC 769.92 20
NE2149.W37 F38 1990
    NYPL **[MDG+ (Callot) 91-4763]**

Goldfinger, Eliot. A guide to human anatomy for
artists : a complete reference / by Eliot
Goldfinger. New York : Oxford University
Press, 1991. p. cm. Includes bibliographical
references and indexes. ISBN 0-19-505206-4 DDC
702/.8 20
1. Anatomy, Artistic. 2. Human figure in art. I. Title.
NC760 .G67 1991

Goldie Paley Gallery. Dickson, Jane. Jane
Dickson life under neon . Philadelphia, PA ,
c1989. 12 p. :
    NYPL **[3-MCX D568 91-4639]**

Golding, John.
John Golding : Yale Center for British Art.
New Haven, Conn. : The Center, 1989. 39 p. :
ill. (some col.) ; 20 cm. "Catalog published on the
occasion of an exhibition at the Yale Center for British
Art, New Haven, Connecticut, September 16-November
12, 1989"--Label mounted on p. [2] of cover.   ISBN
0-930606-60-4
   1. Golding, John - Exhibitions. I. Title.
                    NYPL [3-MCV G618 90-12734]

GOLDING, JOHN - EXHIBITIONS.
Golding, John. John Golding . New Haven,
Conn. , 1989. 39 p. :   ISBN 0-930606-60-4
                    NYPL [3-MCV G618 90-12734]

Goldman, Judith. Rosenquist, James, 1933- James
Rosenquist . [Mount Kisco, N.Y.] , 1989. 48
p. :   ISBN 0-9625185-0-6
                    NYPL [3-MCX+ R797 90-12772]

Goldovskiĭ, G. N. (Grigoriĭ Naumovich) La
Pittura russa nell'età romantica /. Bologna ,
c1990. lx, 190 p. :   ISBN 88-7779-129-2
IN PROCESS (ONLINE)
                    NYPL [3-MCY 90-11768]

Goldscheider, Cécile. Auguste Rodin : catalogue
raisonné de l'œuvre sculpté / Cécile
Goldscheider. Paris : Wildenstein Institute ;
Lausanne : Bibliothèque des arts, c1989- v. :
ill. ; 39 cm. Title on spine: Rodin. Includes
bibliographical references and indexes. CONTENTS. -
t. 1. 1840-1886.   ISBN 2-908063-03-4 (set)   DDC
730/.92 20
   1. Rodin, Auguste, 1840-1917 - Catalogues raisonnés. I.
   Title. II. Title: Rodin.
NB553.R7 A4 1989
                    NYPL [3-MGO+ (Rodin) 91-391]

**GOLDSCHMIDT, ALLA, D. 1989 - ART
COLLECTIONS - EXHIBITIONS.**
Musée d'art moderne (Musées royaux des
beaux-arts de Belgique) Collection Alla et
Bénédict Goldschmidt . Bruxelles [1990] 426
p. :   *NYPL [3-MAL 91-5716]*

**GOLDSCHMIDT, BÉNÉDICT LÉOPOLD,
1905-1972 - ART COLLECTIONS -
EXHIBITIONS.**
Musée d'art moderne (Musées royaux des
beaux-arts de Belgique) Collection Alla et
Bénédict Goldschmidt . Bruxelles [1990] 426
p. :   *NYPL [3-MAL 91-5716]*

Goldschmiedekunst des 20. Jahrhunderts.
Treskow, Elisabeth, 1898- Elisabeth Treskow,
Goldschmiedekunst des 20. Jahrhunderts . Köln
[1990] 168 p. :   DDC 739.2/272 20
NK7198.T734 A4 1990

Goldsmith, Lloyd, 1945-
Lloyd Goldsmith, cityviews : 13 February-6
March, 1982. New York, N.Y. : Hirschl &
Adler Modern, [1982] [16] p. : ill. ; 27 cm.
   *1. Goldsmith, Lloyd, 1945- - Exhibitions. 2. New York
   (N.Y.) in art. I. Hirschl & Adler Modern. II. Title. III.*
   Title: Cityviews.   NYPL [3-MAMY 91-1159]

**GOLDSMITH, LLOYD, 1945- -
EXHIBITIONS.**
Goldsmith, Lloyd, 1945- Lloyd Goldsmith,
cityviews . New York, N.Y. [1982] [16] p. :
                    NYPL [3-MAMY 91-1159]

**GOLDSMITHS - ENGLAND - LONDON -
BIOGRAPHY.**
Grimwade, Arthur. London goldsmiths,
1697-1837 . London , 1990. ix, 773 p., [5] p. of
plates :   ISBN 0-571-15238-4   DDC 739.2/092/2 19
NK7144.L66   *NYPL [MNO 90-13187]*

GOLDSMITHS - FRANCE - BIOGRAPHY.
Pinçon, Jean-Marie. Odiot l'orfèvre /. Paris ,
c1990. 217 p. :   ISBN 2-85889-054-4 :   DDC
739.2/0944/361 20
NK7198.O35 P56 1990

Goldsmiths' Hall (London, England) Paul de
Lamerie . [London] , 1990. 181 p. :   ISBN
0-907814-19-0   *NYPL [3-MNO+ 91-5049]*

Goldstein, Barbara. Arts & architecture .
Cambridge, Mass. , c1990. 248 p. :   ISBN
0-262-07131-2 :   DDC 700/.9/04 20
NX456.5.M64 A7 1990
                    NYPL [3-MAL+ 91-3679]

Goldstein, Darra. Gaynor, Elizabeth, 1946-
Russian houses /. New York , 1991. p. cm.
   ISBN 1-556-70163-2 (cloth) :   DDC 728/.0947
20
NA7367 .G3 1991

Goldstein, Richard, 1944- Zeitlin, Marilyn. South
Bronx Hall of Fame . Houston, Tex. , c1991. p.
cm.   ISBN 0-936080-21-3 (pbk.) :   DDC 730/.92 20
NB237.A35 A4 1991

Goldsworthy, Andy.
Andy Goldsworthy. London : Viking, 1990.
[120] p. : chiefly col. ill. ; 32 cm.   ISBN
0-670-83213-8 :   DDC 709.2 20
   1. Goldsworthy, Andy - Catalogs. 2. Earthworks (Art).
   3. Avant-garde (Aesthetics) - 20th century - Great
   Britain. I. Title.   *NYPL [3-MGO+
                    (Goldsworthy) 90-11987]*

GOLDSWORTHY, ANDY - CATALOGS.
Goldsworthy, Andy. Andy Goldsworthy.
London , 1990. [120] p. :   ISBN 0-670-83213-8 :
   DDC 709.2 20   *NYPL [3-MGO+
                    (Goldsworthy) 90-11987]*

GOLDWORK - AFRICA, WEST.
Das Gold in der Kunst Westafrikas. Zürich ,
1981. 58 p. :   *NYPL [3-MNO 90-12398]*

GOLDWORK, ANCIENT.
Eluère, Christiane. Secrets of ancient gold /.
Düdingen, Switzerland , c1989. 239 p. :   ISBN
3-908573-08-4   *NYPL [3-MNO+ 90-9347]*

**GOLDWORK, ANCIENT - ROMANIA -
SÎNNICOLAU MARE.**
László, Gyula. [Nagyszentmiklósi kincs.
English.] The treasure of Nagyszentmiklós /.
[Budapest] [1984] 182, [2] p. ;   DDC
739.2/274984 20
NK7169.S26 L3713 1984

GOLDWORK, ANCIENT - SPAIN.
Nicolini, Gérard. Techniques des ors antiques .
[Paris] , 1990. 2 v. :   ISBN 2-7084-0405-9 (set)
   DDC 739.27/09366/09014 20
NK7162.A1 N53 1990

**GOLDWORK - GERMANY - HISTORY -
20TH CENTURY - CATALOGS.**
Rudolph, Monika, 1956- Naum Slutzky .
Stuttgart [1990] 273 p. :   ISBN 3-925369-06-6
NK7198.S58 A4 1990

**GOLDWORK - GERMANY - HISTORY -
20TH CENTURY - EXHIBITIONS.**
Treskow, Elisabeth, 1898- Elisabeth Treskow,
Goldschmiedekunst des 20. Jahrhunderts . Köln
[1990] 168 p. :   DDC 739.2/272 20
NK7198.T734 A4 1990

**GOLDWORK - GERMANY (WEST) -
RHINELAND - HISTORY - 19TH
CENTURY - EXHIBITIONS.**
Gold- und Silberschmiede am Niederrhein,
1854-1987 . [Kevelaer] [1987] 42 p. :   DDC
739.2/0943/550740355 19
NK7150.A3 R544 1987
                    NYPL [3-MNO 91-5028]

**GOLDWORK - GERMANY (WEST) - 20TH
RHINELAND - HISTORY - 20TH
CENTURY - EXHIBITIONS.**
Gold- und Silberschmiede am Niederrhein,
1854-1987 . [Kevelaer] [1987] 42 p. :   DDC
739.2/0943/550740355 19
NK7150.A3 R544 1987
                    NYPL [3-MNO 91-5028]

**GOLDWORK - ITALY - FLORENCE -
EXHIBITIONS.**
Ori e argenti nelle collezioni del Museo
archeologico di Firenze. Firenze [1990] xiv, 75
p. :   ISBN 88-7038-195-1
                    NYPL [3-MNO+ 91-3414]

GOLDWORK - LATIN AMERICA - HISTORY.
Orfebreria hispanoamericana, siglos XVI-XIX .
Madrid , 1986. 123 p. :
                    NYPL [3-MNO+ 90-8754]

GOLDWORK, MEDIEVAL - GERMANY.
Medding-Alp, Emma. Rheinische
Goldschmiedekunst in ottonischer Zeit. Koblenz
am Rhein [1952] 84 p.
                    NYPL [3-MNO+ 91-321]

**GOLDWORK - NORWAY - HISTORY - 20TH
CENTURY.**
Opstad, Jan-Lauritz. Ny norsk gullsmedkunst /.
Oslo , c1983. 88 p., [4] p. of plates :   ISBN
82-7003-039-2 :
NK7160.A1 O67 1983
                    NYPL [3-MNO 91-4207]

GOLDWORK - POLAND - EXHIBITIONS.
Polonia, gioielli, ornamenti e arredi . [Arezzo ,
1989] xxxi, 197 p. :
                    NYPL [3-MNO+ 90-13368]

**GOLDWORK - ROMANIA - SÎNNICOLAU
MARE.**
László, Gyula. [Nagyszentmiklósi kincs.
English.] The treasure of Nagyszentmiklós /.
[Budapest] [1984] 182, [2] p. ;   DDC
739.2/274984 20
NK7169.S26 L3713 1984

**GOLDWORK - RUSSIAN S.F.S.R. - THEMES,
MOTIVES.**
Fabergé, Peter Carl, 1846-1920. Fabergé and
the Russian master goldsmiths /. New York ,
1991. p. cm.   ISBN 0-517-02733-X   DDC
739.2/092 20
NK7398.F32 A4 1991

GOLDWORK - SOVIET UNION.
Fabergé and the Russian master goldsmiths /.
[New York] , c1989. 320 p. :   ISBN
0-88363-889-4
                    NYPL [3-MNO+ 89-26729]

**GOLDWORK - THEMES, MOTIVES -
EXHIBITIONS.**
Arte orafa e iconografia dionisiaca . [Italy ,
1987] 88 p. :   *NYPL [3-MNO+ 89-27461]*

Golling, Günter. Hemmann, Paul, 1895-1977. Die
Brunnen in Weimar . Weimar , 1990. 96 p. :
   ISBN 3-910053-43-0
                    NYPL [3-MRK 91-7023]

Golomshtok, Igor. Totalitarian art in the Soviet
Union, the Third Reich, Fascist Italy and the
People's Republic of China / Igor Golomstock ;
translated from the Russian by Robert
Chandler. 1st U. S. ed. New York, N.Y. :
IconEditions, c1990. xv, 416 p., [15] p. of
plates : ill. (some col.) ; 26 cm. Includes
bibliographical references (p. 387-394) and index.
   ISBN 0-06-433266-7
   *1. Socialist realism in art - Soviet Union. 2. Fascism
   and art - Italy. 3. Socialist realism in art - China. I.*
   Title.   *NYPL [3-MAL 91-7447]*

**GOLUB, LEON, 1922- - CRITICISM AND
INTERPRETATION.**
Marzorati, Gerald. A painter of darkness . New
York , 1990. 271 p. :   ISBN 0-670-81979-4   DDC
759.13 20
ND237.G6113 M37 1990
                    NYPL [3-MCX G629 90-10755]

Golvin, Lucien. Palais et demeures d'Alger à la
période ottomane / Lucien Golvin.
Aix-en-Provence : Edisud, [1988] 141 p., [16]
p. of plates : ill. (some col.), plans ; 31 cm.
Bibliography: p. 137.   ISBN 2-85744-307-2
   *1. Dwellings - Algeria - Algiers. 2. Palaces - Algeria -
   Algiers. 3. Architecture, Ottoman - Algeria - Algiers. 4.*
   Algiers (Algeria) - Buildings, structures, etc. I. Title.
                    NYPL [3-MQT+ 90-4959]

Gombrich, E. H. (Ernst Hans), 1909-
Art, perception and reality [by] E. H.
Gombrich, Julian Hochberg [and] Max Black.
Baltimore, Johns Hopkins University Press
[1972] x, 132 p. illus. 24 cm. (The Alvin and
Fanny Blaustein Thalheimer lectures. 1970) Includes
bibliographies.   ISBN 0-8018-1354-9   DDC 701/.17
   *1. Art - Psychology. 2. Visual perception. I. Hochberg,
   Julian E. II. Black, Max, 1909-. III. Title.*
N71 .G64   *NYPL [3-MAB 90-5472]*

Topics of our time : comments on
twentieth-century issues in learning and in the
art / E.H. Gombrich. Berkeley : University of
California Press, 1991. p. cm. Includes index.
   ISBN 0-520-07516-1   DDC 001.3 20
   *1. Art, Modern - 20th century. 2. Learning and
   scholarship - History - 20th century. 3. Cultural
   relativism. I. Title.*
N6490 .G595 1991

Gombrich, Ernst Hans Josef, Sir, 1909- Aby
Warburg: an intellectual biography, by E. H.
Gombrich; with a memoir on the history of the
library by F. Saxl. London, The Warburg
Institute, 1970. vi, 376 p., 65 plates. illus.,
facsims., ports. 27 cm. Bibliography: p. [339]-352.
   ISBN 0-85481-001-3
   1. Warburg, Aby, 1866-1929. I. Saxl, Fritz, 1890-1948.
   II. London. University. Warburg Institute.
N7483.W36 G6   *NYPL [JFF 81-532]*

Gomes, Maria Calado Albuquerque. Santinho, M.
Manuela (Maria Manuela) A arte em Portugal e
os Descobrimentos . Porto , 1989. 164 p. :
   DDC 709/.469 20
N7121 .S27 1989

Gómez Arriola, Ignacio. Comala : estudio de
fisonomía urbana / Ignacio Gómez Arriola.

Colima, Col. [Mexico] : Coordinación General de Comunicación Social, Universidad de Colima, [1985] 75 p. : ill. ; 21 cm. (Colección Rajuela)
1. Vernacular architecture - Mexico - Comala. 2. Comala (Mexico) - Buildings, structures, etc. I. Title. II. Series.
NA757.C66 G66 1985

Gómez Barcena, María Jesús. Escultura gótica funeraria en Burgos / Ma. Jesús Gómez Barcena. 1a ed. [Burgos] : Excma. Diputacíon Provincial de Burgos, 1988. 261 p., [2] folded leaves of plates : ill., plans ; 30 cm. (Publicaciones de la Excma. Diputación Provincial de Burgos. Serie Monografías burgalesas) Includes indexes. Bibliography: p. 235-245. ISBN 84-86841-01-1
1. Sculpture, Gothic - Spain - Burgos. 2. Sepulchral monuments - Spain - Burgos. I. Title. II. Series.
                    NYPL [3-MRIF+ 91-6774]

Gómez, Carmen. see **Gómez-Moreno, Carmen.**

Gómez Jaramillo, Ignacio, 1910-1970. Anotaciones de un pintor / Ignacio Gómez Jaramillo ; cronología, Santiago Londoño V. 1a ed. completa. Medellín : Ediciones Autores Antioqueños, 1987. 313 p. : ill. ; 21 cm. (Colección Autores antioqueños . v. 39) Includes bibliographical references.
1. Gómez Jaramillo, Ignacio, 1910-1970 - Aesthetics. 2. Art criticsim - Colombia - History - 20th century. I. Title. II. Series.
N7483.G64 A2 1987
                    NYPL [3-MCZ G632 90-12606]

GÓMEZ JARAMILLO, IGNACIO, 1910-1970 - AESTHETICS.
Gómez Jaramillo, Ignacio, 1910-1970. Anotaciones de un pintor /. Medellín , 1987. 313 p. :
N7483.G64 A2 1987
                    NYPL [3-MCZ G632 90-12606]

Gómez-Moreno Calera, José Manuel. La arquitectura religiosa granadina en la crisis del Renacimiento (1560-1650) : diócesis de Granada y Guadix-Baza / José Manuel Gómez-Moreno Calera. Granada : Universidad de Granada : Diputación Provincial de Granada, 1989. 486 p. : ill. ; 25 cm. (Monográfica Arte y arqueología . 4) ISBN 84-338-0944-X
1. Church architecture - Spain - Granada (Province). I. Title. II. Series.
IN PROCESS (ONLINE)
                    NYPL [3-MRBB 91-6097]

Gómez-Moreno, Carmen. Sculpture from Notre-Dame, Paris : a dramatic discovery : exhibited September 6-November 25, 1979, the Metropolitan Museum of Art, New York December 15, 1979-January 27, 1980, the Cleveland Museum of Art / by Carmen Gómez-Moreno. New York : Metropolitan Museum of Art, c1979. 32 p. : ill. ; 27 cm. Catalog of an exhibition. Includes bibliographical references. ISBN 0-87099-211-2
1. Paris. Notre-Dame (Cathedral) - Exhibitions. 2. Sculpture, Gothic - France - Paris - Exhibitions. 3. Sculpture, French - France - Paris - Exhibitions. 4. Head in art - Exhibitions. I. New York (City). Metropolitan Museum of Art. II. Title.
NB550 .G65   NYPL [MGI 80-2163]

Gomide /. Vernaschi, Elvira. São Paulo-Brazil . 247 p. :
ND359.G6 V47 1989

GOMIDE, ANTONIO GONÇALVES, 1895-1967 - CRITICISM AND INTERPRETATION.
Vernaschi, Elvira. Gomide /. São Paulo-Brazil . 247 p. :
ND359.G6 V47 1989

Gomringer, Eugen, 1925- Hajek, Otto Herbert, 1927- O.H. Hajek . Stuttgart , c1989. x, 98, xix p. : ISBN 3-7630-1607-4
IN PROCESS (ONLINE)
                    NYPL [3-MGO+ (Hajek) 91-3854]

Gonçalves, António Nogueira, 1901- Estudos de história da arte da Renascença / [A. Nogueira Gonçalves]. Aveiro [Portugal] : Livraria Estante Editora, [between 1975 and 1987] 311 p. : ill. ; 24 cm. (Paisagem-arte . no. 4) Includes bibliographical references.
1. Art, Portuguese - Portugal - Coimbra. 2. Art, Renaissance - Portugal - Coimbra. 3. Christian art and symbolism - Renaissance, 1450-1600 - Portugal -

Coimbra. I. Series: Colecção Paisagem-arte , 4. II. Title.
N7963.C65 G66 1975

Gonçalves, Flávio. História da arte : iconografia e crítica / Flávio Gonçalves. [Lisbon] : Impr. Nacional-Casa da Moeda, [1990] 353 p. : ill. ; 24 cm. (Colecção Arte e artistas) Includes bibliographical references. DDC 709/.469 20
1. Art Portuguese. I. Title. II. Series.
N7121 .G6 1990

Gonçalves, Nuno, fl. 1450-1471. Scarlatti, Lita. Os painéis de Nuno Gonçalves /. Lisboa , 1990. 127 p. :
ND833.3.P35 S27 1990

GONÇALVES, NUNO, FL. 1450-1471 - CRITICISM AND INTERPRETATION.
Scarlatti, Lita. Os painéis de Nuno Gonçalves /. Lisboa , 1990. 127 p. :
ND833.3.P35 S27 1990

Gonçalves, Rui Mário. 100 pintores portugueses do século XX / Rui Mário Gonçalves. Lisboa : Publicações Alfa, c1986. 268 p. : col. ill. ; 30 cm.
1. Painting, Portuguese - Catalogs. 2. Painting, Modern - 20th century - Portugal - Catalogs. 3. Painters - Portugal - Biography. I. Title. II. Title: Cem pintores portugueses do século XX.
ND828 .G66 1986

GONCHAROVA, NATALIIA SERGEEVNA, 1881-1962 - EXHIBITIONS.
Pari no joryū gaka 6-nin ten . [Tokyo] 1983. 190 p. :   NYPL [3-MC 90-9733]

Gondouin, Emmanuel, 1883-1934. La Frégonnière, Jacques de. Emmanuel Gondouin, 1883-1934. [Paris, c1969] 190 p.
ND553.G665 L3
                    NYPL [3-MCO G637 90-6359]

GONDOUIN, EMMANUEL, 1883-1934.
La Frégonnière, Jacques de. Emmanuel Gondouin, 1883-1934. [Paris, c1969] 190 p.
ND553.G665 L3
                    NYPL [3-MCO G637 90-6359]

Gonschior, Kuno, 1935-
Kuno Gonschior : Städtische Galerie Lüdenscheid, 20. Januar-19. Februar 1989. Lüdenscheid : Die Galerie, 1989. 76 leaves : col. ill. ; 30 cm. Bibliography: p. 74.
1. Gonschior, Kuno, 1935- - Exhibitions. I. Städtische Galerie Lüdenscheid. II. Title.
                    NYPL [3-MCK+ G645 89-11778]

GONSCHIOR, KUNO, 1935- - EXHIBITIONS.
Gonschior, Kuno, 1935- Kuno Gonschior . Lüdenscheid , 1989. 76 leaves :
                    NYPL [3-MCK+ G645 89-11778]

Gontijo, João Marcos Machado. Avila, Affonso, 1928- Barroco mineiro, glossário de arquitetura e ornamentação /. [Rio de Janeiro?] . 220 p. :
NA3533.A3 M563 1980

Gönül Öney. see **Öney, Gönül.**

GONZAGA, LUDOVICO, MARCHESE, 1414-1478 - ART PATRONAGE.
Woods-Marsden, Joanna, 1936- The Gonzaga of Mantua and Pisanello's Arthurian frescoes /. Princeton, N.J. , 1988. xxv, 274 p., [129] p. of plates : ISBN 0-691-04048-6 (alk. paper) : DDC 758/.980880351/094528 19
N6923.P497 W66 1988
                    NYPL [3-MCF P67 91-4621]

The Gonzaga of Mantua and Pisanello's Arthurian frescoes /. Woods-Marsden, Joanna, 1936- Princeton, N.J. , 1988. xxv, 274 p., [129] p. of plates : ISBN 0-691-04048-6 (alk. paper) : DDC 758/.980880351/094528 19
N6923.P497 W66 1988
                    NYPL [3-MCF P67 91-4621]

Gonzalès, Eva, 1849-1883.
Sainsaulieu, Marie-Caroline. Eva Gonzalès, 1849-1883 . Paris , c1990. 297 p. : ISBN 2-85047-115-0 DDC 759.4 20
N6853.G597 A4 1990

GONZALÈS, EVA, 1849-1883 - CATALOGUES RAISONNÉS.
Sainsaulieu, Marie-Caroline. Eva Gonzalès, 1849-1883 . Paris , c1990. 297 p. : ISBN 2-85047-115-0 DDC 759.4 20
N6853.G597 A4 1990

GONZALÈS, EVA, 1849-1883 - EXHIBITIONS.
Pari no joryū gaka 6-nin ten . [Tokyo] 1983. 190 p. :   NYPL [3-MC 90-9733]

Gonzàlez, Antoni. Església de Santa Càndia d'Orpí /. [Barcelona] , c1989. 64 p. : ISBN 84-7794-049-5
NA5821.S26 E8 1989

Història i arquitectura . Barcelona [1986?] 260 p. : ISBN 84-505-2551-9
NA1309.B29 H57 1986
                    NYPL [3-MQWH+ 90-12046]

Lacuesta, Raquel. Arquitectura modernista en Cataluña /. Barcelona , c1990. 213 p. : ISBN 84-252-1430-0 DDC 720/.946/70904 20
NA1309.C2 L33 1990

González de Durana, Javier, 1951- Mas Serra, Elías, 1945- 50 Años de arquitectura en Euskadi /. [Vitoria] , 1990. xviii, 347 p. : ISBN 84-7542-854-1 DDC 720/.946/609045 20
NA1309.P33 M37 1990

González, Eduardo. see **González Lanuza, Eduardo,**

González Franco, Glorinela. Catálogo de artistas y artesanos de México /. México, D.F. , 1986 [i.e. 1987] 292 p. : ISBN 968-603-853-1
N6547.M56 C37 1986

González Goyri, Roberto. Homenaje a Carlos Mérida : pionero y renovador del arte latinoamericano : Guatemala-México, septiembre 1985. [Guatemala] : Editorial Universitaria, Universidad de San Carlos de Guatemala, [1985?] 17, [2] p. : ill. (some col.) ; 27 cm. Includes bibliographical references (p. [18]).
1. Mérida, Carlos, 1891- - Catalogs. I. Mérida, Carlos, 1891-. II. Title.
N6578.M47 A4 1985

González, Juan José Martín. see **Martín González, Juan José.**

González, Julio, 1876-1942.
Sculpture, drawings, collages, by Julio Gonzalez. [Chicago, Arts Club of Chicago, 1969] 1 v.(unpaged) illus. 26 cm. Exhibition held Sept. 22-Oct. 18, 1969, the Arts Club of Chicago. Caption title. Cover title: Julio González.
1. González, Julio, 1876-1942 - Exhibitions. I. Arts Club of Chicago. II. Title. III. Title: Julio González.
                    NYPL [3-MGO (González) 90-6908]

GONZÁLEZ, JULIO, 1876-1942 - EXHIBITIONS.
González, Julio, 1876-1942. Sculpture, drawings, collages. [Chicago, 1969] 1 v.(unpaged)
                    NYPL [3-MGO (González) 90-6908]

González Lanuza, Eduardo, 1900- Alva Negri, Tomás. Julio E. Payró /. Buenos Aires , c1976. 68 p. :
N6639.P38 A94 1976

González Pérez, Clodio. Castelao, 1886-1950. Castelao . Sada, A Coruña , 1982. 183 p. : ISBN 84-7492-114-7
                    NYPL [3-MEM (Castelao) 90-5990]

Gonzalo Endara Crow. Endara Crow, Gonzalo, 1936- [Quito, Ecuador , 1990] 225 p. : DDC 759.9866 20
ND389.E53 A4 1990

A good planet is hard to find /. Heine, John, 1950- Birmingham, Ala. , 1991. p. cm. ISBN 0-89732-108-1 DDC 741.5/973 20
NC1429.H377 A4 1991

GOODHUE, BERTRAM GROSVENOR, 1869-1924 - THEMES, MOTIVES.
A Harmony of the arts . Lincoln , c1990. x, 119 p. : ISBN 0-8032-2887-2 (alk. paper) DDC 725/.11/09782293 19
NA4413.L56 H37 1990
                    NYPL [3-MQWO 90-11994]

Gooding, Mel. John Hoyland / Mel Gooding. Hatfield, Herts : J. Taylor in association with Lund Humphries, London, 1990. 39 p., 80 leaves of plates : ill. (some col.) ; 30 cm. Bibliography: p. 34-37. ISBN 0-85331-564-7
1. Hoyland, John, 1934-. I. Title.
                    NYPL [3-MCV+ H867 91-6325]

Goodman, Cynthia. Hans Hofmann / Cynthia Goodman ; with essays by Cynthia Goodman, Irving Sandler, Clement Greenberg. New York : Whitney Museum of American Art in association with Prestel-Verlag, Munich, 1990. 200 p. : ill. ; 30 cm. Includes bibliographical references (p. 182-185) and index. ISBN 0-87427-070-7 DDC 759.13 20
1. Hofmann, Hans, 1880-1966 - Exhibitions. I.

Hofmann, Hans, 1880-1966. II. Greenberg, Clement, 1909-. III. Sandberg, Irving, 1925-. IV. Whitney Museum of American Art. V. Title.
ND237.H667 A4 1990
NYPL [3-MCK+ H71 90-12024]

Goodman, Sue. Porter, Tom. Design drawing techniques . New York : Toronto : p. cm.
ISBN 0-684-19045-1 DDC 720/.28/4 20
NA2714 .P67 1991

Goodrich, Lloyd, 1897- Corcoran Gallery of Art. Albert Pinkham Ryder . Washington, D.C.
[1961] 53 p. : **NYPL [3-MCX R99 91-850]**

Goodwin, Betty, 1923-
Betty Goodwin, steel notes : Canada 20th São Paulo International Biennial, 14-10-89 - 10-12-89 / commissioner, France Morin. [Ottawa] : National Gallery of Canada, c1989. 151 p. : ill. (some col.) ; 25 cm. English, French and Portuguese. "Published in conjunction with an exhibition of the same title shown as part of Canada's participation in the XX São Paulo International Biennial ...."--verso of t.p. Includes an interview with the artist. ISBN 0-88884-602-9
1. Goodwin, Betty, 1923- - Exhibitions. I. Morin, France. II. Bienal Internacional de São Paulo (20th : 1989). III. Title: Steel notes.
NYPL [3-MCZ G658 91-6759]

GOODWIN, BETTY, 1923- - EXHIBITIONS.
Goodwin, Betty, 1923- Betty Goodwin, steel notes . [Ottawa] , c1989. 151 p. : ISBN 0-88884-602-9
NYPL [3-MCZ G658 91-6759]

Goodwin, Emily, 1948- Krasner, Melvin I. New York City community health atlas 1988 /. New York, N.Y. , 1988. 1 atlas (230 p.) : ISBN 0-934459-51-7 : DDC 912/.13621/097471 19
G1254.N4E55 K7 1988
NYPL [Map Div. 91-5382]

Goonetileke, H. A. I. Keyt, George. George Keyt drawings /. Colombo , 1990. xxviii, 90 p. : ISBN 955-9065-01-7 : DDC 741.95493 20
NC330.Z9 K492 1990

Gopal Bajpai, Shiva. see Bajpai, Shiva Gopal.

Gopnik, Adam.
Modern art and popular culture . New York , 1990. 255 p., [81] p. of plates : ISBN 0-8109-2466-8 (pbk.) DDC 700/.9/04 20
N6447 .M63 1991 **NYPL [3-MAL 91-3688]**

Varnedoe, Kirk, 1946- High & low . New York , c1990. 460 p. : ISBN 0-87070-353-6 (MoMA : hard)
NYPL [3-MAL+ 91-3655]

Gorb, Peter. Design management . London , 1990. viii, 184 p. ; ISBN 1-85454-153-6 : DDC 745.4068 20 **NYPL [3-MNF 90-12036]**

Gorbals children . McKenzie, Joseph, 1929- Glasgow , 1990. [128] p. : ISBN 0-86267-269-4 (pbk) : DDC 779/.092/4 19
NYPL [MFX (McKensie) 90-11268]

GORBALS (GLASGOW, SCOTLAND) - DESCRIPTION - VIEWS.
McKenzie, Joseph, 1929- Gorbals children . Glasgow , 1990. [128] p. : ISBN 0-86267-269-4 (pbk) : DDC 779/.092/4 19
NYPL [MFX (McKensie) 90-11268]

Gordon, Alastair. Beaux Arch '89 . Sag Harbor, N.Y. , 1989. 119 p. : ISBN 0-9623542-0-1
IN PROCESS **NYPL [3-MQWO 91-3337]**

Gordon Baldwin . Baldwin, Gordon. Rotterdam [1989] 39 p. : ISBN 90-6918-044-8
NK4210.B33 A4 1989

Gordon, Douglas E.
How architecture works / Douglas E. Gordon, Stephanie Stubbs ; illustrated by Timothy B. McDonald. New York : Van Nostrand Reinhold, c1991. xii, 190 p. : ill. ; 24 cm. Includes bibliographical references (p. 185-186) and index. ISBN 0-442-23951-3 DDC 720 20
1. Architecture. I. Stubbs, M. Stephanie. II. Title.
NA2520 .G58 1991

Rowan, Bob, 1944- A capital perspective . Chatsworth, Calif. , 1991. p. cm. ISBN 0-89781-427-4 DDC 720/.9753 20
NA735.W3 R69 1991

Gordon, Judith. Bukovnik, Gary, 1947- Flowers . New York , 1990. 119 p. : ISBN 0-8109-3105-2 DDC 760/.092 20
N6537.B835 A4 1990
NYPL [3-MCX B924 90-11081]

Gordon, Louise. The figure in action : anatomy for artist / Louise Gordon. London : B.T. Batsford, 1989. 128 p. : ill. ; 28 cm. Includes index. ISBN 0-7134-5946-8 DDC 743/.49 20
1. Anatomy, Artistic. 2. Human anatomy. I. Title.
NC760 .G72 1989

Gore, Frederick. Frederick Gore on Piero della Francesca's 'The baptism'. London, Cassell, 1969. 32 p., fold plate. illus. (incl. 1 col.) 26 cm. (Painters on painting) Includes bibliographical references. ISBN 0-304-93279-5 DDC 759.5
1. Piero, della Francesca, 1416?-1492. Baptism. I. Title. II. Series.
ND623.F78 G6
NYPL [3-MCF F81 90-6257]

Gore, Spencer Frederick, 1878-1914.
Spencer Frederick Gore, 1878-1914 : drawings and watercolors. New York : Davis & Langdale, [1990] [23] p. : ill. ; 23 cm. Catalogue of an exhibition held at Davis & Langdale Co., Inc., October 9-November 10, 1990, in association with Anthony D'Offay Gallery, London.
1. Gore, Spencer Frederick, 1878-1914 - Exhibitions. I. Davis & Langdale Company. II. Anthony d'Offay (Firm). **NYPL [3-MCV G666 90-13021]**

GORE, SPENCER FREDERICK, 1878-1914 - EXHIBITIONS.
Gore, Spencer Frederick, 1878-1914. Spencer Frederick Gore, 1878-1914 . New York [1990] [23] p. : **NYPL [3-MCV G666 90-13021]**

Gorenflo, Roger M. Verzeichnis der bildenden Künstler von 1880 bis heute : ein biographisch-bibliographisches Nachschlagewerk zur Kunst der Gegenwart / Roger M. Gorenflo ; [unter zeitweiser Mitarbeit von Claudia Feischen]. Rüsselsheim : Brün, 1988. 3 v. (989 p.) ; 21 cm. Contents and abbreviations in German and English. Key to bibliographic sources in vol. 3: p. 961-989. Vols. 2-3: 2. unveränderte Aufl., have 1988 imprint. ISBN 3-926759-00-3 (set)
1. Artists - Biography - Indexes. I. Feischen, Claudia. II. Title. **NYPL [3-MAO 90-10802]**

Gorey, Edward, 1925- La balade troublante / Edward Gorey. [New York] : Fantod Press, 1991. [32] leaves : chiefly ill. ; 15 cm. Small stick-figure drawings, with one-word or two-word French captions. DDC 741.5/973 20
1. Gorey, Edward, 1925-. I. Title.
NC139.G63 A4 1991

GOREY, EDWARD, 1925-
Gorey, Edward, 1925- La balade troublante /. [New York] , 1991. [32] leaves : DDC 741.5/973 20
NC139.G63 A4 1991

Gorizia (Italy)
Marieschi tra Canaletto e Guardi . Torino , c1989. 329 p. : ISBN 88-422-0194-4
N6923.M268 A4 1989

Gorizia (Italy). Assessorato alle attività culturali.
Marieschi tra Canaletto e Guardi . Torino , c1989. 329 p. : ISBN 88-422-0194-4
N6923.M268 A4 1989

Trionfo barocco . [Monfalcone] [1990] 265 p. : ISBN 88-85296-00-9 DDC 759.04/6/07445392 20
ND182.B3 T75 1990

Gorky, Arshile, 1904-1948.
Arshile Gorky : three decades of drawings / essay by Melvin P. Lader. [Santa Fe, N.M.] : Gerald Peters Gallery, in association with John Van Doren, New York, c1990. 11 p., [30] leaves of plates : col. ill. ; 27 cm. Catalog of an exhibition held in Santa Fe, Sept. 22-Oct. 4, 1990, Dallas, Oct. 11-31, 1990 and New York, Nov. 5-21, 1990. Includes bibliographical references. ISBN 0-935037-38-1
1. Gorky, Arshile, 1904-1948 - Exhibitions. I. Lader, Melvin P. II. Gerald Peters Gallery. III. Title.
NYPL [3-MCZ G669 91-4351]

GORKY, ARSHILE, 1904-1948 - EXHIBITIONS.
Gorky, Arshile, 1904-1948. Arshile Gorky . [Santa Fe, N.M.] , c1990. 11 p., [30] leaves of plates : ISBN 0-935037-38-1
NYPL [3-MCZ G669 91-4351]

Görlitz (Germany). Rat.
Johannes-Wüsten-Symposium (1976 : Görlitz, Dresden, Germany) Protokollband Johannes-Wüsten-Symposium, Görlitz, 1976, 2.

Oktober /. Görlitz , 1978. 109 p. : *NX550.Z9 W875 1976*
NYPL [3-MCK W953 90-13398]

Gorman, R. C. (Rudolph Carl), 1932-
Monthan, Doris Born, 1924- R.C. Gorman--a retrospective /. Flagstaff, AZ , c1990. ix, 193 p. : ISBN 0-87358-505-4 (hardcover) : DDC 709/.2 20
N6537.G66 M66 1990
NYPL [3-MCX+ G670 91-2497]

GORMAN, R. C. (RUDOLPH CARL), 1932- - CRITICISM AND INTERPRETATION.
Monthan, Doris Born, 1924- R.C. Gorman--a retrospective /. Flagstaff, AZ , c1990. ix, 193 p. : ISBN 0-87358-505-4 (hardcover) : DDC 709/.2 20
N6537.G66 M66 1990
NYPL [3-MCX+ G670 91-2497]

Gosebruch, Martin.
Giotto di Bondone /. Konstanz , 1970. 292 p. : *ND623.G6 G5* **NYPL [3-MCF G52 90-5664]**

Giotto und die Entwicklung des neuzeitlichen Kunstbewusstseins. Köln, M. DuMont Schauberg [1962] 235 p. plates 21 cm. (DuMont Dokumente) Includes bibliography.
1. Giotto, 1266?-1337.
NYPL [3-MCF G52 91-520]

Goshi-tada, Fuji Hara. Gwa-hon shu kan [microform] : japanese-chinese sketches and designs / collected by Fuji Hara Goshi-tada. [S.l. : s.n., 19--?] 6 v. : chiefly ill. Title page handwritten. Microfilm. New York : New York Public Library, 1990. 1 microfilm reel ; 35 mm. (MN *ZZ-30,971)
1. Design - Japan. I. Title. **NYPL [*ZM-229]**

Gosney, Michael, 1954-
The Verbum book of digital painting / Michael Gosney, Linnea Dayton, Paul Goethel. 1st ed. Redwood City, Calif. : M&T Pub., 1990. ix, 211 p. : ill. (some col.) ; 28 cm. (The Verbum electronic art & design series) Includes index. ISBN 1-558-51090-7 DDC 760 20
1. Computer art - Technique. I. Dayton, Linnea, 1944-. II. Goethel, Paul, 1952-. III. Title. IV. Series.
N7433.8 .G68 1990

The Verbum book of scanned imagery / Michael Gosney, Linnea Dayton, Phil Inje Chang. 1st ed. Redwood City, CA : M&T Books, 1990. p. cm. (The Verbum electronic art and design series) Includes index. ISBN 1-558-51091-5 : DDC 760 20
1. Computer art - Study and teaching. I. Dayton, Linnea, 1944-. II. Chang, Phil Inje. III. Verbum (San Diego, Calif.). IV. Title. V. Series.
N7433 .G68 1990

GOSS & CRESTED CHINA LTD. - CATALOGS.
Pine, Nicholas. The 1989 price guide to Crested China . Horndean, Portsmouth, Hants , c1988. 377 p. : ISBN 1-85265-101-6 DDC 738/.029/442274 20
NK4210.G58 A4 1988

Gössel, Peter, 1956-
Sembach, Klaus-Jürgen. Möbeldesign des 20. Jahrhunderts /. Köln [1988] 255 p. : ISBN 3-8228-0097-X
NK2395 .S44 1988

Sembach, Klaus-Jürgen. Möbeldesign des 20. Jahrhunderts /. Köln [1988] 255 p. : ISBN 3-8228-0097-X **NYPL [3-MOI+ 91-3916]**

Gosudarstvennaia akademiia khudozhestv Latviiskoi SSR. see Latvijas PSR Valsts mākslas akadēmija.

Gosudarstvennaia akademiia khudozhestv Latviiskoi SSR. Latvijas PSR Valsts Mākslas akadēmija /. Riga , c1989. 279 p. :
N332.L33 R57 1989

Gosudarstvennaia biblioteka SSSR imeni V.I. Lenina.
Russian revolutionary posters, 1917-1929 /. New York , c1967. [14] p. :
NYPL [3-MDW 90-4813]

Sovetskii zrelishchnyi plakat. English. The Soviet arts poster . London, England , New York, N.Y., USA , 1990. 207 p. : ISBN 0-14-012018-1: DDC 741.6/74/09470904 20
NC1807.S65 S6613 1990

Gosudarstvennaia Tret´iakovskaia galereia.
Art into life . Seattle, Wash. , New York, NY , c1990. 276 p. : ISBN 0-935558-27-6 (pbk.) DDC

709/.47/074 20
N6988.5.C64 A68 1990
NYPL [3-MAM 90-11568]

Russische Malerei im 19. Jahrhundert .
[Zürich , 1989] 321 p. : DDC 759.7/074/49457
20
ND687 .R744 1989
NYPL [3-MCY 90-12884]

Gosudarstvennye muzei Moskovskogo Kremlīā.
Russkoe khudozhestvennoe shit´e XIV-nachala
XVIII veka : katalog vystavki / [avtory
vstupitel´nykh stateī i sostaviteli kataloga N.A.
Maīāsova, I.I. Vishnevskaīā]. Moskva : Gos.
muzei Moskovskogo Kremlīā, 1989. 135 p. : ill.
(some col.) ; 29 cm.
1. Ecclesiastical embroidery - Russian S.F.S.R. -
Exhibitions. 2. Gosudarstvennye muzei Moskovskogo
Kremlīā - Exhibitions. I. Maīāsova, Natalīiā Andreevna.
II. Vishnevskaīā, I. I. III. Title. IV. Title: Russkoe
khudozhestvennoe shit´e 14.-nachala 18. veka. V. Title:
Russkoe khudozhestvennoe shit´e
chetyrnadtsatogo-nachala vosemnadtsatogo veka.
NK9310 .G67 1989

**GOSUDARSTVENNYE MUZEI
MOSKOVSKOGO KREMLĪĀ -
EXHIBITIONS.**
Gosudarstvennye muzei Moskovskogo Kremlīā.
Russkoe khudozhestvennoe shit´e XIV-nachala
XVIII veka . Moskva , 1989. 135 p. :
NK9310 .G67 1989

Gosudarstvennyī Ėrmitazh (Soviet Union)
Les Costumes historiques russes du Musée de
l'Ermitage de Léningrad. [Paris?] [1989] 78
p. : **NYPL [3-MMO 89-8777]**

Gauguin, Paul, 1848-1903. Paul Gauguin .
Paris , c1988. 186 p. : ISBN 2-7022-0218-7
DDC 759.4 20
ND553.G27 A4 1988

Grigorovich, D. V. (Dmitriī Vasil´evich),
1822-1899. [Novye priobretenia Ėrmitazha.]
Novyīā priobrīeteniīā Ėrmitazha . S. Peterburg ,
1865. 61 p. ;
ND615 .G75 1985

The Hermitage . [London] , c1990. 164 p. :
ISBN 0-904866-85-8
NYPL [3-MAVZ (Leningrad) 91-4483]

The Hermitage . New York , c1991. 164 p. :
ISBN 0-385-41966-X : DDC 708.7/453 20
N3350 .H48 1991

Muril´o i khudozhniki Andalusii XVII veka v
sobranii Ėrmitazha : katalog vystavki / [avtor
vstupitel´noī stat´i i sostavitel´ kataloga L.L.
Kaganė]. Leningrad : Izd-vo "Iskusstvo,"
Leningradskoe otd-nie, 1984. 73 p. : ill. ; 22
cm. At head of title: Gosudarstvennyī ordena Lenina
Ėrmitazh. Includes bibliographical references.
1. Murillo, Bartolomé Esteban, 1617-1682 - Exhibitions.
2. Murillo, Bartolomé Esteban, 1617-1682 - Influence -
Exhibitions. 3. Painting, Spanish - Spain - Andalusia -
Exhibitions. 4. Painting, Modern - 17th-18th centuries -
Spain - Andalusia - Exhibitions. 5. Gosudarstvennyī
Ėrmitazh (Soviet Union) - Exhibitions. I. Kaganė,
Līūdmila L. (Līūdmila L´ovna). II. Title. III. Title:
Muril´o i khudozhniki Andalusii 17. veka v sobranii
Ėrmitazha. IV. Title: Muril´o i khudozhniki Andalusii
semnadtsatogo veka v sobranii Ėrmitazha.
ND806 .G67 1984

Nauchnaīā konferentsīiā Rol´ pamīātnikov
antichnogo iskusstva v reshenii problem
ėsteticheskogo vospitanīiā naselenīiā (1988 :
Leningrad, R.S.F.S.R.) Kratkie tezisy dokladov
Nauchnoī konferentsii Rol´ pamīātnikov
antichnogo iskusstva v reshenii problem
ėsteticheskogo vospitanīiā naselenīiā .
Leningrad , 1988. 148 p. ;
N5327 .N38 1988

St. Petersburg um 1800 . Recklinghausen ,
c1990. 568 p. : ISBN 3-7647-0401-2
N6996 .S7 1990

St. Petersburg um 1800 . Recklinghausen ,
c1990. 568 p. : ISBN 3-7647-0401-2
NYPL [3-MAVZ (Leningrad) 90-13200]

Sobranie zapadnoevropeīskoī zhivopisi .
(15) Asvarishch, B. (Boris) Nemetskaīā i
avstriīskaīā zhivopis´ XIX-XX veka .
Leningrad , 1988. 370 p. :
ND450 .G67 1983 vol. 15 ND567

(5) Nikulin, Nikolaī Nikolaevich.
Niderlandskaīā zhivopis´ XV-XVI veka .

Leningrad , 1989. 220 p. :
ND450 .G67 1983 vol. 5 ND669.F5

**[Sobranie zapadnoevropeīskoī zhivopisi.
English. (Florence, Italy)]**
The Hermitage catalogue of Western
European painting / The Hermitage. 1st ed.
Florence : Giunti, <c1988- > v. <15 > :
ill. ; 34 cm. Translation of: Sobranie
zapadnoevropeīskoī zhivopisi. Includes bibliographical
references and indexes. CONTENTS. - -- v. 15.
German and Austrian painting / by Boris I.
Asvarishch. ISBN 88-09-20028-4 DDC
759.94/074/47435 20
1. Painting, European - Catalogs. 2. Painting - Russian
S.F.S.R. - Leningrad - Catalogs. 3. Gosudarstvennyī
Ėrmitazh (Soviet Union) - Catalogs. I. Title.
ND450 .G6713 1988

**GOSUDARSTVENNYĪ ĖRMITAZH (SOVIET
UNION)**
Grigorovich, D. V. (Dmitriī Vasil´evich),
1822-1899. [Novye priobretenie Ėrmitazha.]
Novyīā priobrīeteniīā Ėrmitazha . S. Peterburg ,
1865. 61 p. ;
ND615 .G75 1985

**GOSUDARSTVENNYĪ ĖRMITAZH (SOVIET
UNION) - CATALOGS.**
Asvarishch, B. (Boris) Nemetskaīā i avstriīskaīā
zhivopis´ XIX-XX veka . Leningrad, 1988. 370
p. :
ND450 .G67 1983 vol. 15 ND567

Gauguin, Paul, 1848-1903. Paul Gauguin .
Paris , c1988. 186 p. : ISBN 2-7022-0218-7
DDC 759.4 20
ND553.G27 A4 1988

Gosudarstvennyī Ėrmitazh (Soviet Union)
[Sobranie zapadnoevropeīskoī zhivopisi. English.
(Florence, Italy)] The Hermitage catalogue of
Western European painting /. Florence ,
<c1988-. v. <15 > : ISBN 88-09-20028-4
DDC 759.94/074/47435 20
ND450 .G6713 1988

The Hermitage . [London] , c1990. 164 p. :
ISBN 0-904866-85-8
NYPL [3-MAVZ (Leningrad) 91-4483]

The Hermitage . New York , c1991. 164 p. :
ISBN 0-385-41966-X : DDC 708.7/453 20
N3350 .H48 1991

**GOSUDARSTVENNYĪ ĖRMITAZH (SOVIET
UNION) - EXHIBITIONS.**
Gosudarstvennyī Ėrmitazh (Soviet Union)
Muril´o i khudozhniki Andalusii XVII veka v
sobranii Ėrmitazha . Leningrad , 1984. 73 p. :
ND806 .G67 1984

St. Petersburg um 1800 . Recklinghausen ,
c1990. 568 p. : ISBN 3-7647-0401-2
N6996 .S7 1990

**GOSUDARSTVENNYĪ ĖRMITAZH (SOVIET
UNION) - HISTORY.**
Ėrmitazh . Leningrad , 1989. 560 p. : ISBN
5-274-00375-3 :
N3350 .E76 1989

**Gosudarstvennyī istoricheskiī muzeī (Moscow, R.
S.F.S.R.)**
Meraviglie sconosciute dal Museo storico di
Mosca : gioielli, costumi, tessuti : XVI - XIX
secolo / [Nina Ašarina ... et al.]. Milano :
Fabbri, c1989. 198 p. : col. ill. ; 30 cm. "Mostra
promossa da Museo storico statale ... Comune di
Milano, Settore Cultura e Spettacolo, Gruppo
Rinascente, Milano." Includes bibliographical references
(p. 198).
1. Gosudarstvennyī istoricheskiī muzeī (Moscow,
R.S.F.S.R.) - Exhibitions. 2. Art, Russian - Exhibitions.
3. Embroidery - Russian S.F.S.R. - Moscow -
Exhibitions. 4. Jewelry - Russian S.F.S.R. - Moscow -
Exhibitions. I. Ašarina, Nina. II. Milan (Italy).
Ripartizione cultura turismo spettacolo. III. Title.
NYPL [3-MNR+ 91-4646]

**GOSUDARSTVENNYĪ ISTORICHESKIĪ
MUZEĪ (MOSCOW, R.S.F.S.R.) -
EXHIBITIONS.**
Gosudarstvennyī istoricheskiī muzeī (Moscow,
R.S.F.S.R.) Meraviglie sconosciute dal Museo
storico di Mosca . Milano , c1989. 198 p. :
NYPL [3-MNR+ 91-4646]

**Gosudarstvennyī muzeī izobrazitel´nykh iskusstv
imeni A.S. Pushkina.**
Crespi, Giuseppe Maria, 1665-1747. Giuseppe

Maria Crespi, 1665-1747 . [Bologna] , c1990.
ccxvi, 278 p. : ISBN 88-7779-148-9
NYPL [3-MCF C922 91-5467]

Gauguin, Paul, 1848-1903. Paul Gauguin .
Paris , c1988. 186 p. : ISBN 2-7022-0218-7
DDC 759.4 20
ND553.G27 A4 1988

**GOSUDARSTVENNYĪ MUZEĪ
IZOBRAZITEL´NYKH ISKUSSTV IMENI
A.S. PUSHKINA - CATALOGS.**
Gauguin, Paul, 1848-1903. Paul Gauguin .
Paris , c1988. 186 p. : ISBN 2-7022-0218-7
DDC 759.4 20
ND553.G27 A4 1988

**GOSUDARSTVENNYĪ MUZEĪ
IZOBRAZITELNYKH ISKUSSTV IMENI
A.S. PUSHKINA - EXHIBITIONS.**
Ryska skillingtryck . [Stockholm] , 1989. 79 p. :
ISBN 91-7100-377-0
NYPL [MDON 91-5473]

**Gosudarstvennyī muzeī izobrazitel'nykh iskussty
imeni A.S. Pushkina.** Crespi, Giuseppe
Maria, 1665-1747. Giuseppe Maria Crespi,
1665-1747 . Bologna , c1990. xxcvi, 278 p. :
ISBN 88-7779-148-9 DDC 759.5 20
ND623.C8 A4 1990

**Gosudarstvennyī nauchno-issledovatel´skiī muzeī
arkhitektury imeni A.V. Shchuseva.**
Neuvostomaan arkkitehtuuria . [Helsinki , 1988]
81 p. : ISBN 951-9229-56-6
NA1188 .N48 1988

**Gosudarstvennyī russkiī muzeī (Leningrad, R.S.F.
S.R.)**
Filonov, Pavel Nikolaevich, 1883-1941. Filonov
/. [Paris] , 1990]. 248, [12] p. : ISBN
2-85850-531-4 : DDC 759.7 20
N6999.F55 A4 1990

Russische Malerei im 19. Jahrhundert .
[Zürich , 1989] 321 p. : DDC 759.7/074/49457
20
ND687 .R744 1989
NYPL [3-MCY 90-12884]

**GOSUDARTSVENNYĪ ĖRMITAZH (SOVIET
UNION) - CATALOGS.**
Nikulin, Nikolaī Nikolaevich. Niderlandskaīā
zhivopis´ XV-XVI veka . Leningrad , 1989. 220
p. :
ND450 .G67 1983 vol. 5 ND669.F5

Göteborgs historiska museums skrifter :
(1) Hasselgréen, Ingmar, 1938- Ostindiska
huset, Göteborgs museum /. [Gothenburg] ,
1984 (Göteborg : Rundqvist, 1983) 95 p. :
ISBN 91-7236-025-9
AM101.G63 H37 1984
NYPL [MAVZ (Göteborg) 85-3424]

GÖTEBORGS MUSEUM.
Hasselgréen, Ingmar, 1938- Ostindiska huset,
Göteborgs museum /. [Gothenburg] , 1984
(Göteborg : Rundqvist, 1983) 95 p. : ISBN
91-7236-025-9
AM101.G63 H37 1984
NYPL [MAVZ (Göteborg) 85-3424]

**GOTHIC ARCHITECTURE. see
ARCHITECTURE, GOTHIC.**

Gothic art. Bracons i Clapés, Josep. [Claves del
arte gótico. English.] The key to gothic art /.
Minneapolis , 1990. 80 p. : ISBN 0-8225-2051-6
(lib. bdg.) DDC 709.02/2 20
N6310 .B7313 1990
NYPL [3-MAK 90-11597]

The Gothic cathedral . Wilson, Christopher.
London , c1990. 304 p. : ISBN 0-500-34105-2
NYPL [3-MQS 90-8030]

**GOTHIC ILLUMINATION OF BOOKS AND
MANUSCRIPTS. see ILLUMINATION
OF BOOKS AND MANUSCRIPTS,
GOTHIC.**

**GOTHIC REVIVAL (ARCHITECTURE) -
CONGRESSES.**
Il Neogotico nel XIX e XX secolo /. Milano
[1990] 2 v. : ISBN 88-20-20863-6 (set) DDC
724/.3 20
NA645.5.G68 N46 1990

Gotické umění v jižních Čechách . Alšova
jihočeská galerie. Praha [1990] 101 p. : ISBN
80-7035-013-X :
N6832.J53 A48 1990

**Gotik : Prag um 1400 : der Schöne Stil,
Böhmische Malerei und Plastik in der Gotik :**

Sonderausstellung des Historischen Museums der Stadt Wien in Zusammenarbeit mit der Nationalgalerie Prag, 19. April 1990 bis 1. Juli 1990. Wien : Eigenverlag der Museen der Stadt Wien, [1990] 141 p. : ill. ; 27 cm.
(Sonderausstellung des Historischen Museums der Stadt Wien . 131)
1. Art, Gothic - High Gothic - Czechoslovakia - Bohemia - Exhibitions. 2. Bohemian School of Art - Exhibitions. I. Historisches Museum der Stadt Wien. II. Title: Prag um 1400. III. Series.
NYPL [3-MAM 90-11533]

Gotik : Prag um 1400 : der schöne Stil, böhmische Malerei und Plastik in der Gothik : 131. Sonderausstellung des Historischen Museums der Stadt Wien in Zusammenarbeit mit der Nationalgalerie Prag, 19. April 1990 bis 1. Juli 1990. [Wien : Wien Kultur, 1990] 141 p., [62] p. of plates : col. ill. ; 27 cm.
(Sonderausstellung des Historischen Museums der Stadt Wien . 131) Includes bibliographical references (p. 137-141).
1. Art, Gothic - Czechoslovakia - Bohemia - Exhibitions. 2. Art - Czechoslovakia - Bohemia - Exhibitions. I. Národní galerie V Praze. II. Series.
N6832.B63 G68 1990

GOTLIEB, ALLAN - ART COLLECTIONS - EXHIBITIONS.
Misfeldt, Willard E. J. J. Tissot . Alexandria, Va. , 1991. p. cm. ISBN 0-88397-097-X DDC 769.92 20
NE650.T56 M57 1991

Gotsch, Friedrich Karl, 1900-
Friedrich Karl Gotsch, 1900-1984 : Aquarelle, Zeichnungen, Druckgraphik : 17. Dezember 1989 bis 4. Februar 1990, Museum Folkwang / [Hubertus Froning]. [Essen] : Die Museum, 1990. 95 p. : chiefly ill. (some col.) ; 21 cm.
Includes bibliographical references.
1. Gotsch, Friedrich Karl, 1900- - Exhibitions. I. Froning, Hubertus.
NYPL [3-MCK G684 91-4563]

GOTSCH, FRIEDRICH KARL, 1900- - EXHIBITIONS.
Gotsch, Friedrich Karl, 1900- Friedrich Karl Gotsch, 1900-1984 . [Essen] , 1990. 95 p. :
NYPL [3-MCK G684 91-4563]

Gott erhalte Österreich : Religion und Staat in der Kunst des 19. Jahrhunderts : Ausstellung in Schloss Halbturn, 6. April bis 28. Oktober 1990 / [Verfasser des Katalogteiles, Sarolta Dietrich, Elisabeth Hülmbauer]. Eisenstadt : Amt der Burgenländischen Landesregierung, [1990] 239 p. : ill. (some col.) ; 21 x 24 cm. Includes bibliographical references (p. 235).
1. Art, Austrian - Exhibitions. 2. Art, Modern - 19th century - Austria - Exhibitions. 3. Art and religion - Austria - Exhibitions. 4. Art and state - Austria - Exhibitions. I. Dietrich, Sarolta. II. Hülmbauer, Elisabeth. III. Schloss Halbturn (Halbturn, Austria).
N6807 .G67 1990

Götte, Gisela. Neuhaus, Josef, 1923- Josef Neuhaus, Plastiken und Reliefs . Neuss , 1988. 77 p. : *NYPL [3-MGO (Neuhaus) 89-25259]*

Götterdämmerung. Wagner, Richard, 1813-1883. [Operas. Selections.] Die Meistersinger von Nürnberg ; Tristan und Isolde ; Die Götterdämmerung ; Parsifal [sound recording] /. Pontelambro, Italy , N.Y. [i.e. New York] , p1988. 1 sound disc :
Nuova Era 013.6337

Gottfried Brockmann, drawings 1921-1931 .
Brockmann, Gottfried, 1903- Birmingham, Mich. , c1975. [32] p. :
NYPL [3-MCK B862 91-1178]

Gottfried Graf, 1881-1938. Graf, Gottfried, 1881-1938. Schloss Dätzingen, 7031 Grafenau 2 (bei Sindelfingen) [1985] [44] p. :
MLCM 86/1201 (N)
NYPL [3-MCK G7352 87-826]

Gottfried Helnwein . Helnwein. Heidelberg [1988] 1 v. (unpaged) : ISBN 3-925835-07-5
N6811.5.H45 A4 1988

Gottfried Keller, Landschaftsmaler /. Weber, Bruno. Zürich , c1990. 194 p. : ISBN 3-85823-265-3
NYPL [3-MCZ K29 90-12339]

GOTTFRIED-KELLER-STIFTING - ART COLLECTIONS - CATALOGS.
Landolt, Hanspeter. Gottfried Keller-Stiftung .

Bern , c1990. 627 p. : ISBN 3-7165-0696-6
N5279.2.G68 L3 1990
NYPL [3-MAK 91-4989]

Gottfried Keller-Stiftung . Landolt, Hanspeter.
Bern , c1990. 627 p. : ISBN 3-7165-0696-6
N5279.2.G68 L3 1990
NYPL [3-MAK 91-4989]

Gottfried-Keller-Stiftung.
Landolt, Hanspeter. Gottfried Keller-Stiftung .
Bern , c1990. 627 p. : ISBN 3-7165-0696-6
N5279.2.G68 L3 1990
NYPL [3-MAK 91-4989]

GOTTFRIED-KELLER-STIFTUNG - HISTORY.
Landolt, Hanspeter. Gottfried Keller-Stiftung .
Bern , c1990. 627 p. : ISBN 3-7165-0696-6
N5279.2.G68 L3 1990
NYPL [3-MAK 91-4989]

Gottfried Pilz . Pilz, Gottfried. [Heidelberg] , 1990. 135 p. : ISBN 3-925835-59-8
NYPL [3-MGO+ (Pilz) 91-5633]

Gottfried Stein. Stein, Gottfried, 1915- Gottfried Stein zum 75. Geburtstag . [Göttingen] , c1990. 31 p. : DDC 759.3 20
ND588.S67 A4 1990

Gottfried Stein zum 75. Geburtstag . Stein, Gottfried, 1915- [Göttingen] , c1990. 31 p. : DDC 759.3 20
ND588.S67 A4 1990

Gotthard Graubner /. Graubner, Gotthard, 1930- Hannover [c1969] 102 p. :
NYPL [3-MCK G773 91-906]

Gotthard Graubner . Graubner, Gotthard, 1930- Bremen , c1989. 145 p. (5 folded) :
NYPL [3-MCK+ G773 91-6686]

Gotthard Schuh . Schuh, Gotthard, 1897-1969.
Bern , c1982. 218, [5] p. : ISBN 3-7165-0405-X : DDC 779/.092/4 19
TR820 .S34 1982
NYPL [MFX+ (Schuh) 90-11176]

Gottlieb, Adolph, 1903-1974.
Adolph Gottlieb : major paintings, October 6 to November 3, 1990. New York : Knoedler & Co., c1990. [20] p. : col. ill. (1 folded) ; 28 cm.
1. Gottlieb, Adolph, 1903-1974 - Exhibitions. I. M. Knoedler & Co. II. Title.
NYPL [3-MCX G686 91-3416]

GOTTLIEB, ADOLPH, 1903-1974 - EXHIBITIONS.
Gottlieb, Adolph, 1903-1974. Adolph Gottlieb .
New York , c1990. [20] p. :
NYPL [3-MCX G686 91-3416]

Gottlieb Christian Bernhard Heller und seine Musterbücher in der Universitätsbibliothek Jena /. Heller, Gottlieb Christian Bernhard.
Jena , 1988. 141 p. : ISBN 3-910014-02-X
IN PROCESS (ONLINE)
NYPL [MDG (Heller) 90-13678]

Gottlieb, Robert. Solid waste management .
[Chicago, IL (1313 E. 60th St., Chicago, 60637) , c1990. 71 p. : DDC 361.6/0973 s 363.72/85 20
NA9108 .A545 no. 424/425 TD788

Göttner-Abendroth, Heide, 1941-
[Tanzende Göttin. English]
The dancing goddess : principles of a matriarchal aesthetic / Heide Göttner-Abendroth ; translated by Maureen T. Krause.1st English ed. Boston : Beacon Press, c1991. p. cm. Translation of: Die Tanzende Göttin. Includes bibliographical references. ISBN 0-8070-6753-9 (alk.) DDC 700/.1/03 20
1. Feminism and the arts. 2. Women and spiritualism. I. Title.
NX180.F4 G613 1991

Götz, K. O. (Karl Otto), 1914-
K.O. Götz / herausgegeben von Manfred de la Motte. Bonn : Galerie Hennemann, c1978. 360 p., [1] folded leaf of plates : ill. (some col.), ports. ; 22 cm. (Taschenbuchreihe . 18) "Diese Dokumentation erscheint aus Anlass der Ausstellung im Oktober 1978." Bibliography: p. 346-357.
1. Götz, K. O. (Karl Otto), 1914- - Exhibitions. I. La Motte, Manfred de. II. Galerie Hennemann. III. Series: Taschenbuchreihe (Galerie Hennemann) , 18.
NYPL [3-MCK G612 91-996]

K.O. Götz : Giverny : Gemälde, Gouachen, Steindrucke, 1985-1989. Düsseldorf : Concept Verlag, 1989. 101 p. : chiefly ill. (some col.) ;

43 cm.
1. Götz, K. O. (Karl Otto), 1914- - Catalogs. I. Title. II. Title: Giverny.
NYPL [3-MCK++ G612 89-26570]

GÖTZ, K. O. (KARL OTTO), 1914- - CATALOGS.
Götz, K. O. (Karl Otto), 1914- K.O. Götz .
Düsseldorf , 1989. 101 p. :
NYPL [3-MCK++ G612 89-26570]

GÖTZ, K. O. (KARL OTTO), 1914- - EXHIBITIONS.
Götz, K. O. (Karl Otto), 1914- K.O. Götz /.
Bonn , c1978. 360 p., [1] folded leaf of plates :
NYPL [3-MCK G612 91-996]

Goüin, Henry. Royaumont : Mons Regalis / Henry Goüin, descriptif et historique ; Claude Jacques-Dammé, photographies et textes ; préface de Jean-Philippe Lachenaud. [Paris] : Editions du Valhermeil, c1990. 94 p. : col. ill. ; 25 cm. Includes bibliographical references. ISBN 2-905674-28-3 DDC 726/.7/0944367 20
1. Abbaye de Royaumont. 2. Royaumont (France) - Buildings, structures, etc. I. Dammé, Claude Jacques. II. Title.
NA5551.R65 G64 1990

GOUK, ALAN, 1934- - EXHIBITIONS.
Fruit Market Gallery. Four abstract artists .
Edinburgh , 1977. [14] p. : ISBN 0-902989-44-8
ND479 .F78 1977 *NYPL [3-MCT 79-734]*

GOULANDRIS, N. P. - ART COLLECTIONS.
Renfrew, Colin, 1937- The Cycladic spirit .
New York , 1991. p. cm. ISBN 0-8109-3169-9 DDC 732/.3/093915 20
NB130.C78 R4 1991

Gould, Chester. Dick Tracy (Comic strip). Selections. 1990. The Dick Tracy casebook .
New York , 1990. x, 273 p. : ISBN 0-312-04461-5 (deluxe) : DDC 741.5/0973 20
PN6728.D53 D534 1990
NYPL [3-MEM (Gould) 90-10998]

Gould, Stephen Jay. Kelly, Franklin. Frederic Edwin Church /. Washington , c1989. 211 p. : ISBN 0-89468-136-2 DDC 759.13 20
ND237.C52 A4 1989
NYPL [3-MCX C56 90-10398]

Goulet, Patrice.
Six projets /. Paris , c1990. 509 p. :
NA2707.O34 A4 1990

Speidel, Manfred. Team Zoo . New York , 1991. p. cm. ISBN 0-8478-1402-5 DDC 720/.952/09045 20
NA1559.T4 S64 1991

40 architectes de moins de quarante ans, Paris /. [Paris] , c1990. 311 p. : ISBN 2-281-15116-6
NA1048 .A13 1990

GOURD CRAFT - PERU.
Salas, María Angélica. Mates de Cochas . Lima, Perú , 1987. 166 p. :
NK6075 .S25 1987

Gournay, Isabelle. Ernest Cormier et l'Université de Montréal. English. Ernest Cormier and the Université de Montréal /. Montréal , 1990. 179 p. : ISBN 0-920785-30-1
NA749.C67 E7613 1990
NYPL [3-MQZ (Cormier) 91-6585]

Gousha California road atlas. Gousha California road atlas and visitor's guide. San Jose, Calif. , c1991. 56 p. : ISBN 0-13-110891-3 :
NYPL [Map Div. 90-13143]

Gousha California road atlas and visitor's guide.
San Jose, Calif. : H.M. Gousha, c1991. 56 p. : col. maps ; 28 cm. Cover title: Gousha California road atlas. Includes index. ISBN 0-13-110891-3 :
1. California - Description and travel - 1981- - Guide-books. 2. California - Road maps. I. H.M. Gousha (Firm). II. Title: California road atlas and visitor's guide. III. Title: Gousha California road atlas.
NYPL [Map Div. 90-13143]

Gousha Colorado road atlas. H.M. Gousha Company. Gousha Colorado road atlas and visitor's guide /. New York, NY , c1991. 1 atlas (56 p.) : ISBN 0-13-151275-7
NYPL [Map Div. 90-11950]

Gousha Colorado road atlas and visitor's guide /.
H.M. Gousha Company. New York, NY , c1991. 1 atlas (56 p.) : ISBN 0-13-151275-7
NYPL [Map Div. 90-11950]

Gousha Kansas City street atlas. H.M. Gousha Company. [New York] [1989] 1 atlas (xii, 86

p.) : ISBN 0-13-362187-1
NYPL [Map Div. 90-11941]

Gousha pocket road atlas, United States, Canada, Mexico. H.M. Gousha Company. Pocket road atlas, United States, Canada, Mexico. San Jose, CA , 1990. 1 atlas (64 p.) : ISBN 0-13-622465-2
NYPL [Map Div. 90-12566]

Gousha Texas road atlas. H.M. Gousha Company. Gousha Texas road atlas and visitor's guide /. New York, NY , c1991. 1 atlas (56 p.) : ISBN 0-13-932112-8
NYPL [Map Div. 90-11949]

Gousha Texas road atlas and visitor's guide /. H.M. Gousha Company. New York, NY , c1991. 1 atlas (56 p.) : ISBN 0-13-932112-8
NYPL [Map Div. 90-11949]

Govan, Michael. Mondrian e De Stijl . Milano , c1990. 273 p. : ISBN 88-435-3172-7
NYPL [3-MCH M741 91-6318]

GOVERNMENT BUILDINGS. see PUBLIC BUILDINGS.

Government Central Museum (Jaipur, India) Jaipur brassware in Government Central Museum, Jaipur. Jaipur : Dept. of Archaeology & Museums, Govt. of Rajasthan, 1955. 61 p. : ill. ; 12 x 19 cm. Cover title.
1. Government Central Museum (Jaipur, India). 2. Brassware - India - Jaipur. I. Title.
NYPL [3-MNK 90-7182]

GOVERNMENT CENTRAL MUSEUM (JAIPUR, INDIA) Government Central Museum (Jaipur, India) Jaipur brassware in Government Central Museum, Jaipur , 1955. 61 p. :
NYPL [3-MNK 90-7182]

GOVERNMENT CONTRACTS. see PUBLIC CONTRACTS.

GOVERNMENT, MUNICIPAL. see MUNICIPAL GOVERNMENT.

Government Museum, Udaipur. Vatsyayan, Kapila. Mewari Gita-Govinda /. New Delhi , c1987. xi, 276 p. :
ND1337.I5 V38 1987
NYPL [3-MAF+ 91-4471]

GOVERNMENT PUBLICATIONS - BIBLIOGRAPHY. Orth, Donald J. Geographic names & the federal government . Washington, D.C. : Geography and Map Division, The Library of Congress, 1990. ii, 59 p. ;
NYPL [Map Div. 91-5514]

Gowan, James. Mies van der Rohe . New York , 1986. 112 p. : ISBN 0-85670-685-X DDC 720/.92/4 19
NA1088.M65 M54 1986 *NYPL [3-MQZ+ (Mies van der Rohe) 86-3545]*

Gowin, Emmet, 1941- Emmet Gowin, photographs. 1st U. S. trade ed. Philadelphia, Pa. : Philadelphia Museum of Art ; Boston : Bulfinch Press, c1990. 127 p. : chiefly ill ; 29 x 32 cm. "Published on the occasion of an exhibition shown at the Philadelphia Museum of Art, December 8, 1990-February 24, 1991..." Includes bibliographical references. ISBN 0-8212-1835-2 (Bulfinch : cloth) : DDC 779/.092 20
1. Gowin, Emmet, 1941- - Exhibitions. 2. Photography, Artistic - Exhibitions. I. Title.
TR647 .G69 1990
NYPL [MFX+ (Gowin) 91-4964]

GOWIN, EMMET, 1941- - EXHIBITIONS. Gowin, Emmet, 1941- Emmet Gowin, photographs. Philadelphia, Pa. , Boston , c1990. 127 p. : ISBN 0-8212-1835-2 (Bulfinch : cloth) : DDC 779/.092 20
TR647 .G69 1990
NYPL [MFX+ (Gowin) 91-4964]

Goy-Truffaut, Françoise. Paris façade / Françoise Goy-Truffaut. Paris : Hazan, c1989. 245 p. : ill. ; 29 cm. Includes bibliographical references (p. [241]-243). ISBN 2-85025-208-5
1. Decoration and ornament, Architectural - France - Paris. 2. Façades - France - Paris. 3. Paris (France) - Buildings, structures, etc. I. Title.
NYPL [3-MRX 90-5327]

Goya . De Paz, Alfredo. Napoli , 1990. 490 p., [16] p. of plates : ISBN 88-20-71734-4 : DDC

760/.092 20
N7113.G68 A4 1990
NYPL [3-MCQ G72 91-4505]

Goya /. Gassier, Pierre. [Goya. English.] New York , 1989. 129 p. : ISBN 0-8478-1108-5 DDC 760/.092 B 20
N7113.G68 G3713 1989
NYPL [3-MCQ 91-2506]

Goya . Goya, Francisco, 1746-1828. [Madrid] , 1951. 1 v. (unpaged) :
NYPL [3-MCQ G72 91-669]

Goya . Goya, Francisco, 1746-1828. [Madrid] , c1990. 161 p. : ISBN 84-7483-633-6
NYPL [3-MCQ G72 91-3635]

Goya /. Perez Sanchez, Alfonso E. [Goya. English.] London , 1990. 160 p. : ISBN 0-7126-3926-8 : DDC 759.6 20
ND813.G7 *NYPL [3-MCQ+ G72 90-11752]*

Goya and the satirical print in England and on the Continent, 1730 to 1850 /. Wolf, Reva, 1956- Boston , c1991. viii, 109 p. : ISBN 0-87923-897-6 (hardcover : acid-free) DDC 769.92 20
NC1639.G6 A4 1991

Goya, Francisco, 1746-1828. CAPRICHOS - EXHIBITIONS. Wolf, Reva, 1956- Goya and the satirical print in England and on the Continent, 1730 to 1850 /. Boston , c1991. viii, 109 p. : ISBN 0-87923-897-6 (hardcover : acid-free) DDC 769.92 20
NC1639.G6 A4 1991

De Paz, Alfredo. Goya . Napoli , 1990. 490 p., [16] p. of plates : ISBN 88-20-71734-4 : DDC 760/.092 20
N7113.G68 A4 1990
NYPL [3-MCQ G72 91-4505]

Fatal consequences . Hanover, N.H. , 1990. 92 p. : ISBN 0-944722-04-0 DDC 769.92 20
NE2149.W37 F38 1990
NYPL [MDG+ (Callot) 91-4763]

Goya : [exposición] / Museo del Prado. [Madrid] : El Museo, 1951. 1 v. (unpaged) : ill. ; 22 cm.
1. Goya, Francisco, 1746-1828 - Exhibitions. I. Museo del Prado. II. Title.
NYPL [3-MCQ G72 91-669]

Goya : toros y toreros : Real Academia de Bellas Artes de San Fernando, del 15 de junio al 29 de julio de 1990. [Madrid] : Ministerio de Cultura : Comunidad de Madrid, c1990. 161 p. : ill. ; 28 cm. ISBN 84-7483-633-6
1. Goya, Francisco, 1746-1828 - Exhibitions. 2. Bullfights in art - Exhibitions. I. Real Academia de Bellas Artes de San Fernando. II. Title.
NYPL [3-MCQ G72 91-3635]

Perez Sanchez, Alfonso E. [Goya. English.] Goya /. London , 1990. 160 p. : ISBN 0-7126-3926-8 : DDC 759.6 20
ND813.G7 *NYPL [3-MCQ+ G72 90-11752]*

Wolf, Reva, 1956- Goya and the satirical print in England and on the Continent, 1730 to 1850 /. Boston , c1991. viii, 109 p. : ISBN 0-87923-897-6 (hardcover : acid-free) DDC 769.92 20
NC1639.G6 A4 1991

GOYA, FRANCISCO, 1746-1828. Gassier, Pierre. [Goya. English.] Goya /. New York , 1989. 129 p. : ISBN 0-8478-1108-5 DDC 760/.092 B 20
N7113.G68 G3713 1989
NYPL [3-MCQ 91-2506]

Perez Sanchez, Alfonso E. [Goya. English.] Goya /. London , 1990. 160 p. : ISBN 0-7126-3926-8 : DDC 759.6 20
ND813.G7 *NYPL [3-MCQ+ G72 90-11752]*

Pita Andrade, José Manuel. Goya y sus primeras visiones de la historia . Madrid , 1989. 63 p. ; ISBN 84-7392-315-4
IN PROCESS (ONLINE)
NYPL [3-MCQ G72 91-4507]

GOYA, FRANCISCO, 1746-1828 - APPRECIATION - JUVENILE LITERATURE. Venezia, Mike. Francisco Goya /. Chicago , 1991. p. cm. ISBN 0-516-02292-X DDC 759.6 B 92 20
ND813.G7 V4 1991

GOYA, FRANCISCO, 1746-1828 - CATALOGUES RAISONNÉS. Morales y Marín, José Luis, 1946- Goya, pintor religioso /. [Zaragoza] [1990] 354 p. : ISBN 84-7753-132-3 DDC 759.6 20
ND813.G7 A4 1990

GOYA, FRANCISCO, 1746-1828 - CRITICISM AND INTERPRETATION. De Paz, Alfredo. Goya . Napoli , 1990. 490 p., [16] p. of plates : ISBN 88-20-71734-4 : DDC 760/.092 20
N7113.G68 A4 1990
NYPL [3-MCQ G72 91-4505]

Mestre Sancho, Juan Antonio. Juego y deporte en la pintura de Goya /. [Valencia] [1990?] 294 p. : ISBN 84-7890-087-X DDC 760/.092 20
N7113.G68 A4 1990a

CAPRICHOS. Cela, Camilo José, 1916- Los Caprichos de Francisco de Goya y Lucientes /. [Madrid] , c1989. 172 p. : ISBN 84-7737-018-4
NYPL [MDG (Goya) 90-10979]

Caprichos. 1989. Cela, Camilo José, 1916- Los Caprichos de Francisco de Goya y Lucientes / Camilo José Cela. [Madrid] , c1989. 172 p. : ISBN 84-7737-018-4
NYPL [MDG (Goya) 90-10979]

GOYA, FRANCISCO, 1746-1828 - EXHIBITIONS. Goya, Francisco, 1746-1828. Goya . [Madrid] , 1951. 1 v. (unpaged) :
NYPL [3-MCQ G72 91-669]

Goya, Francisco, 1746-1828. Goya . [Madrid] , c1990. 161 p. : ISBN 84-7483-633-6
NYPL [3-MCQ G72 91-3635]

Goya, pintor religioso /. Morales y Marín, José Luis, 1946- [Zaragoza] [1990] 354 p. : ISBN 84-7753-132-3 DDC 759.6 20
ND813.G7 A4 1990

Goya y sus primeras visiones de la historia . Pita Andrade, José Manuel. Madrid , 1989. 63 p. ; ISBN 84-7392-315-4
IN PROCESS (ONLINE)
NYPL [3-MCQ G72 91-4507]

G.R. Lambert & Co. Falconer, John, 1951- A vision of the past . Singapore , 1987. 192 p. : ISBN 997-14-0105-3 DDC 770/.95957 20
TR113.S53 F35 1987
NYPL [MFW 91-3302]

G.R. LAMBERT & CO. Falconer, John, 1951- A vision of the past . Singapore , 1987. 192 p. : ISBN 997-14-0105-3 DDC 770/.95957 20
TR113.S53 F35 1987
NYPL [MFW 91-3302]

Graber (Firm) Expressions of style . Middleton, WI (7549 Graber Road, Middleton 53562-1096) , c1990. 95 p. : DDC 747/.3 20
NK2115.5.D73 E95 1990

Grabski, Józef. Opus sacrum . Vienna , c1990. 399 p. : ISBN 3-900731-29-2
NYPL [3-MAIH 91-4343]

Grace, Arthur. Choose me : portraits of a presidential race / photographs by Arthur Grace ; foreword by Sam Donaldson ; text by Jim Wooten ; afterword by Jane Livingston. [Waltham, Mass. : Brandeis University Press] ; Hanover, NH : Distributed for Brandeis University Press by University Press of New England, c1989. 127 p. : chiefly ill. ; 29 cm. "A Newsweek book." ISBN 0-87451-491-6
1. Presidential candidates - United States - Portraits. 2. Presidents - United States - Elections - 1988. 3. Presidents - United States - Election - 1988 - Pictorial works. 4. Photography, Journalistic - United States. 5. United States - Politics and government - 1981-1989. 6. United States - Politics and government - 1981-1989 - Pictorial works. I. Wooten, Jim. II. Title.
NYPL [MFX (Grace) 89-28159]

Grace Cossington Smith /. James, Bruce. Roseville, NSW, Australia , 1990. 189 p. : ISBN 0-947131-35-3
NYPL [3-MCZ+ S6485 90-13355]

Grace Hartigan, four decades of painting . Hartigan, Grace. New York, N.Y. (23 East 73 Street, New York, 10021) , 1989. 32 p. :
NYPL [3-MCX+ H329 91-4638]

Gradl, Hermann, 1883-1964. Hermann Gradl : der Malerromantiker und Landschaftsmaler /

ausgewählt und herausgegeben von Horst
Bröstler. Marktheidenfeld am Main : H.
Bröstler, 1989. 190 p. : ill. ; 32 cm. ISBN
3-927439-06-1
1. Gradl, Hermann, 1883-1964. I. Bröstler, Horst. II.
Title.   *NYPL [3-MCK+ G73 91-5156]*

GRADL, HERMANN, 1883-1964.
Gradl, Hermann, 1883-1964. Hermann Gradl .
Marktheidenfeld am Main , 1989. 190 p. :
ISBN 3-927439-06-1
          NYPL [3-MCK+ G73 91-5156]

Graeber, Laurel. Kaufman, Donald. Color
atmospheres . New York , 1991. p. cm. ISBN
0-517-57660-0 :   DDC 728 20
NK2115.5.C6 K38 1991

Graeder, Hans, 1919-
Hans Graeder, Re-Visionen : Städtische
Kunsthalle Mannheim, 14. Juli bis 9. September
1990 / [Katalogredaktion, Jochen Kronjäger,
Antje Terrahe]. Mannheim : Die Kunsthalle,
c1990. 57 p. : ill. (some col.) ; 26 cm. Exhibition
catalog. Includes bibliographical references (p. 56).
ISBN 3-89165-071-X
1. Graeder, Hans, 1919- - Exhibitions. I. Städtische
Kunsthalle Mannheim. II. Title. III. Title: Re-Visionen.
N6888.G658 A4 1990

GRAEDER, HANS, 1919- - EXHIBITIONS.
Graeder, Hans, 1919- Hans Graeder,
Re-Visionen . Mannheim , c1990. 57 p. : ISBN
3-89165-071-X
N6888.G658 A4 1990

Graefe, Julius Meier- see **Meier-Graefe, Julius,**
1867-1935.

Graetz, René, 1908-1974.
René Graetz, 1908-1974 : Grafik & Plastik :
Gedenkausstellung zum 70. Geburtstag,
Staatliche Museen zu Berlin, National-Galerie,
Kupferstichkabinett & Sammlung der
Zeichnungen, August-Oktober, 1978 /
[Bearbeitung, Gottfried Riemann, Ilse Oschütz].
Berlin : Staatliche Museen zu Berlin, 1978. 149
p. : ill. (some col.), ports. ; 20 cm. Bibliography:
p. 149.
1. Graetz, René, 1908-1974 - Exhibitions. I. Riemann,
Gottfried. II. Oschütz, Ilse. III. Staatliche Museen zu
Berlin (Germany : East). Kupferstichkabinett.
          NYPL [MDG (Graetz) 90-5669]

GRAETZ, RENÉ, 1908-1974. - EXHIBITIONS.
Graetz, René, 1908-1974. René Graetz,
1908-1974 . Berlin , 1978. 149 p. :
          NYPL [MDG (Graetz) 90-5669]

Graf, Gottfried, 1881-1938.
Gottfried Graf, 1881-1938 : Ausstellung 17.
März bis 13. April 1985 : Galerie
Schlichtenmaier, Schloss Dätzingen, 7031
Grafenau 2 (bei Sindelfingen) : Die Galerie,
[1985] [44] p. : ill. (some col.) ; 23 cm. (Katalog
(Galerie Schlichtenmaier) ; 29) Bibliography: p. [42-44].
1. Graf, Gottfried, 1881-1938 - Exhibitions. I. Galerie
Schlichtenmaier. II. Series. III. Series: Katalog (Galerie
Schlichtenmaier) ; 29. IV. Title.
MLCM 86/1201 (N)
          NYPL [3-MCK G7352 87-826]

Gottfried Graf, 1881-1938, Arbeiten auf Papier,
1915-1925 : [Ausstellung] Galerie
Schlichtenmaier, Grafenau, 30. August bis 26.
September, 1987. Grafenau : Die Galerie, 1987.
64 p. : ill. (some col.) ; 23 cm. (Katalog (Galerie
Schlichtenmaier) . 58) "Redaktion und Gestaltung: Bert,
Harry und Kuno Schlichtenmaier." Bibliography: p. 29.
ISBN 3-89298-017-9
1. Graf, Gottfried, 1881-1938 - Exhibitions. I. Galerie
Schlichtenmaier. II. Series. III. Series: Katalog (Galerie
Schlichtenmaier) ; 58.
          NYPL [3-MCK G7352 88-4413]

GRAF, GOTTFRIED, 1881-1938 -
EXHIBITIONS.
Graf, Gottfried, 1881-1938. Gottfried Graf,
1881-1938 . Schloss Dätzingen, 7031 Grafenau
2 (bei Sindelfingen) [1985] [44] p. :
MLCM 86/1201 (N)
          NYPL [3-MCK G7352 87-826]
Graf, Gottfried, 1881-1938. Gottfried Graf,
1881-1938, Arbeiten auf Papier, 1915-1925 .
Grafenau , 1987. 64 p. : ISBN 3-89298-017-9
          NYPL [3-MCK G7352 88-4413]

Graf, Otto Antonia. Wagner, Otto, 1841-1918.
Masterdrawings of Otto Wagner . New York ,
c1987. 135 p. :
          NYPL [3-MQZ+ (Wagner) 91-4283]

Graffenried, Michael von, 1957- Swiss image /
Michael von Graffenried. Bern : Benteli, c1989.
183 p. : ill. (some col., some folded) ; 31 cm.
Text in English, French and German. Includes
bibliographical references. ISBN 3-7165-0679-6
1. Graffenried, Michael von, 1957-. 2. Photography,
Documentary - Switzerland. 3. Switzerland -
Description and travel - Views. I. Title.
          NYPL [MFX+ (Graffenried) 91-3592]

GRAFFENRIED, MICHAEL VON, 1957-
Graffenried, Michael von, 1957- Swiss image /.
Bern , c1989. 183 p. : ISBN 3-7165-0679-6
          NYPL [MFX+ (Graffenried) 91-3592]

GRAFFITI - BERLIN (GERMANY)
Tillman, Terry. The writings on the wall . Santa
Monica, Calif. , Emeryville, Calif. , c1990. 152
p. : ISBN 0-9626551-0-4
          NYPL [MFX (Tillman) 91-2668]
Waldenburg, Hermann, 1940- The Berlin Wall
book /. London , 1990. 119 p. : ISBN
0-500-97385-7   *NYPL [3-MLP 90-12020]*

GRAFFITI - NEW YORK (N.Y.)
Robinson, David, 1936 Dec. 9- Soho walls .
New York , 1990. 96 p. : ISBN 0-500-27602-1
          NYPL [MFX (Robinson) 90-13454]

Grafica russa 1917/1930 : manifesti, stampe, libri
da collezioni private russe / [catalogo a cura di
Renzo Federici ; con testi di Giovanni
Spadolini ... et al.]. Firenze : Vallecchi : Centro
culturale Il Bisonte, c1990. 192 p. : ill. ; 30 cm.
1. Graphic arts - Soviet Union - History - 20th
century - Exhibitions. I. Federici, Renzo. II. Palazzo
Strozzi.
IN PROCESS (ONLINE)
          NYPL [MDBF+ 90-11003]

Gráficas y neográficas en México /. Tibol,
Raquel. México, D.F. , 1987. 302 p. : ISBN
968-291-357-8
NE544.4 .T5 1987

Grafik des deutschen Expressionismus. German
expressionist prints . Stuttgart , 1984. 1
portfolio (47, 151 p.) :
          NYPL [MDBF 85-1960]

Grafik des Kapitalistischen Realismus. Block,
René. KP Brehmer, KH Hödicke, Sigmar Polke,
Gerhard Richter, Wolf Vostell . Berlin , 1976.
p. 200-266 :
          NYPL [MDBF (Block, R. Grafik)]

Grafiken /. Hauffe, Hans, 1916- Berlin - West
[1979?] [12] p. :
          NYPL [MDG+ (Hauffe) 90-2831]

Grafiken, Plastik. Kollwitz, Käthe, 1867-1945.
Käthe Kollwitz . Stuttgart , 1990. 113 p. :
DDC 709/.2 20
N6888.K62 A4 1990a

Grafische Werk. Rohsmann, Arnulf. Franz
Wiegele, 1887-1944 . Klagenfurt , 1989. 23, viii,
102 p. : ISBN 3-85366-583-7 DDC 741.9436 20
NC245.W48 A4 1989

Grafton, Carol Belanger. Trades and
occupations . New York , 1990. 202 p. : ISBN
0-486-26362-2 : DDC 760/.04493059 20
NE962.O25 T73 1990
          NYPL [3-MDZ+ 91-5602]

GRAHAM, ANDERSON, PROBST, WHITE.
Chappell, Sally Anderson. Architecture and
planning of Graham, Anderson, Probst, and
White, 1912-1936 . Chicago , 1991. p. cm.
ISBN 0-226-10134-7 DDC 720/.92/2 20
NA737.G7 C48 1991

Graham-Campbell, James. Philpott, Fiona A.,
1961- A silver saga . [Liverpool] , 1990. 87 p. :
ISBN 0-906367-41-7 (pbk.) : DDC 948.02 20
DL31   *NYPL [3-MNO 91-6595]*

Graham, Rigby, 1931- Sketchbook drawings /
Rigby Graham ; with an introduction by Alan
Tucker. Church Hanborough, Oxford : :
Hanborough Parrot Press, 1989 ([Didcot?
England] : Didcot Press) [56] p. : ill. (some
col.) ; 24 cm. "An edition of 170 copies, of which 85
are uncoloured and 85 are pochoir coloured by Sylvia
Stokeld and numbered with roman
numerals"--Colophon. Printed on double leaves. Ill. on
lining papers. LC has copy no. XXXVIII, signed by
Graham and Tucker. DLC Source: Purchase, July 23,
1990. DLC DDC 741.942 20
1. Graham, Rigby, 1931-. I. Tucker, Alan. II. Title.
NC242.G67 A4 1989

GRAHAM, RIGBY, 1931-
Graham, Rigby, 1931- Sketchbook drawings /.
Church Hanborough, Oxford , 1989 ([Didcot?
England] : Didcot Press) [56] p. : DDC 741.942
20
NC242.G67 A4 1989

Graham, Robert, 1938-
Twenty-one figures by Robert Graham :
[exhibition] October 1990, Robert Miller, New
York. New York : Robert Miller, 1990. [58]
p. : col. ill. ; 29 cm. Includes bibliographical
references (p. [50-54]). ISBN 0-944680-09-7
1. Graham, Robert, 1938- - Exhibitions. I. Robert
Miller Gallery (New York, N.Y.). II. Title.
          NYPL [3-MGO+ (Graham) 91-4645]

GRAHAM, ROBERT, 1938- - EXHIBITIONS.
Graham, Robert, 1938- Twenty-one figures by
Robert Graham . New York , 1990. [58] p. :
ISBN 0-944680-09-7
          NYPL [3-MGO+ (Graham) 91-4645]

GRAHIC ARTS - TECHNIQUE.
Hiebert, Kenneth J. Graphic design processes .
New York , c1992. 208 p. : ISBN 0-442-00839-2
DDC 741.6 20
NC1000 .H54 1991

Grainger's Worcester porcelain /. Sandon, Henry.
London , 1989. 288 p., [8] p. of plates : ISBN
0-7126-2052-4 : DDC 738.2/7 19
          NYPL [3-MPGO 90-11586]

GRAMERCY PARK FOUNDATION - ART
COLLECTIONS - EXHIBITIONS.
Sotheby Parke Bernet Inc. The Benjamin
Sonnenberg collection . New York , 1979. 2 v. :
          NYPL [3-MAX (Sonnenberg) 90-5888]

Gran Colombia. see **Colombia.**

Granadine Confederation. see **Colombia.**

Grand Central Art Galleries. Henri & Ryerson .
New York, NY , c1990. [32] p. :
          NYPL [3-MCX H51 90-11633]

Le grand livre de Carl Larsson /. Lindwall, Bo,
1915- Paris [1989] 193 p. : ISBN 2-7335-0042-2
          NYPL [3-MCZ L329 91-7556]

Grand Palais (Paris, France) Egerton, Judy.
Wright of Derby /. London , 1990. 294 p. :
ISBN 1-85437-037-5 (paper)
          NYPL [3-MCV+ W95 90-11565]

Grand Rapids Art Museum. Cameron, John B.
Photography's beginnings . Rochester, Mich. ,
Albuquerque , c1989. 176 p. : ISBN
0-925859-00-1 (softbound) DDC 770/.9 20
TR15 .C36 1989   *NYPL [MFW 91-6729]*

Grand temple d'Abou Simbel .
Desroches-Noblecourt, Christiane, 1913- Le
Caire , 1971. vi, 65 leaves, xlii leaves of plates :
ND2865.A2 D4 1971

La Grande Arche Tête Défense,
Paris-la-Défense . Andreu, Paul. Paris , c1989.
80 p. : ISBN 2-907757-08-3
IN PROCESS (ONLINE) *NYPL [3-MQZ+*
          (Spreckelsen) 90-13216]

GRANDES CHRONIQUES DE FRANCE -
ILLUSTRATIONS.
Hedeman, Anne Dawson. The royal image .
Berkeley , c1991. p. cm. ISBN 0-520-07069-0
DDC 745.6/7/09440902 20
ND3399.G67 H44 1991

GRANDI, GIAN GEROLAMO.
Cessi, Francesco. Vincenzo e Gian Gerolamo
Grandi, scultori (secolo XVI) /. Trento , 1967.
116 p. :   *NYPL [3-MGO (Grandi) 90-6345]*

Grandi monografie. Scultori d'oggi.
Argan, Giulio Carlo. Henry Moore /. Milano ,
c1987. 247 p. :
          NYPL [3-MGO+ (Moore) 91-6102]

GRANDI, VINCENZO.
Cessi, Francesco. Vincenzo e Gian Gerolamo
Grandi, scultori (secolo XVI) /. Trento , 1967.
116 p. :   *NYPL [3-MGO (Grandi) 90-6345]*

Grandinetti, Pierluigi. La Geometria in funzione
nell'architettura e nella costruzione della città /.
Venezia , c1985. 157 p. : ISBN 88-85067-29-8
NA2760 .G38 1985
          NYPL [3-MQD+ 90-12625]

GRANDJEAN DE MONTIGNY, AUGUSTE
HENRI VICTOR, 1776-1850.
Levy, Carlos Roberto Maciel, 1951- Rio
imperial /. [São Paulo, Brazil?] [1988] 176 p.,

[2] p. of plates :
NA857.R5 L4 1988

GRANDJEAN DE MONTIGNY, AUGUSTE HENRI VICTOR, 1776-1850 - INFLUENCE.
Levy, Carlos Roberto Maciel, 1951- Rio imperial /. [São Paulo, Brazil?] [1988] 176 p., [2] p. of plates :
NA857.R5 L4 1988

Grandma Moses (1860-1961) . Moses, Grandma, 1860-1961. New York, N.Y. , c1962. 32 p. : DDC 759.13 19
ND237.M78 A4 1962
NYPL [3-MCX M89 91-6296]

Grandma Moses (1860-1961) . Moses, Grandma, 1860-1961. New York, N.Y. (33 W. 57th St., New York 10019) , c1990. 24 p. : DDC 759.13 20
ND237.M78 A4 1990

Grands naïfs. De Grote naïeven =. Amsterdam , 1974. [41] p. : **NYPL [3-MCN 90-6044]**

Grant Wood . Czestochowski, Joseph S. Cedar Rapids, Iowa , c1991. p. cm. ISBN 0-942982-10-X DDC 760/.092 20
NE2312.W66 A4 1991

Granville Redmond. Redmond, Granville, 1871-1935. Oakland, Calif. [1989?] xv, 111 p., [6] leaves of plates :
NYPL [3-MCX R318 89-7639]

Granzotto, Giovanni. Nono, Luigi, 1850-1918. Luigi Nono . [Italy] [1990] 206 p. :
ND623.N59 A4 1990

The graphic artist's guide to marketing and self-promotion /. Davis, Sally Prince, 1942- Cincinnati, Ohio , 1991. p. cm. ISBN 0-89134-416-0 : DDC 741.6/068/8 20
NC1001.6 .D38 1991

Graphic Artists Guild handbook . Graphic Artists Guild (U. S.) New York, NY , c1991. 235 p. ; ISBN 0-932102-07-7
NYPL [3-MDW+ 91-5861]

Graphic Artists Guild (U. S.) Graphic Artists Guild handbook : pricing & ethical guidelines. 7th ed. New York, NY : The Guild ; Cincinnatti, OH : Distributors to the trade in the U. S. and Canada: North Light Books, c1991. 235 p. ; 31 cm. Includes bibliographical references and index. ISBN 0-932102-07-7
1. Graphic arts - United States - Marketing. 2. Artists - Professional ethics - United States. 3. Artists - Legal status, laws, etc. - United States. I. Title. II. Title: Pricing & ethical guidelines. III. Title: Pricing and ethical guidelines. **NYPL [3-MDW+ 91-5861]**

GRAPHIC ARTS.
Berryman, Gregg, 1942- Notes on graphic design and visual communication /. Los Altos, Calif. , 1990. p. cm. ISBN 1-560-52044-2 DDC 741.6 20
NC997 .B43 1990

Radice, Judi. Shopping bag design 2 /. New York [1991] p. cm. ISBN 0-86636-143-X DDC 741.6 20
NK8643.3 .R34 1991

GRAPHIC ARTS - COLOMBIA - 20TH CENTURY - EXHIBITIONS.
Archer M. Huntington Gallery. Colombian figurative graphics /. Austin [1976] 47 p. :
NYPL [MDBF 90-5877]

GRAPHIC ARTS - EXHIBITIONS.
Collaborations and connections . Tempe, Ariz. , c1990. viii, 36 p. : **NYPL [MDTT 91-4768]**

GRAPHIC ARTS - GERMANY (WEST) - HISTORY - 20TH CENTURY - EXHIBITIONS.
Idee . [Braunschweig] , 1988. 169 p. : ISBN 3-88895-025-2
IN PROCESS (ONLINE)
NYPL [3-MDW 91-6406]

GRAPHIC ARTS - HISTORY - 19TH CENTURY.
King, Julia, 1943- The flowering of art nouveau graphics /. London , 1990. 144 p. : ISBN 0-86294-170-9 : **NYPL [3-MDW 91-3586]**

GRAPHIC ARTS - HISTORY - 20TH CENTURY.
King, Julia, 1943- The flowering of art nouveau graphics /. London , 1990. 144 p. : ISBN 0-86294-170-9 : **NYPL [3-MDW 91-3586]**

Labuz, Ronald, 1953- Contemporary graphic design /. New York , c1991. xi, 156 p. : ISBN 0-442-31887-1 DDC 741.6/09/048 20
NK1505 .L24 1991
NYPL [3-MDW 91-4184]

Visuelle Kommunikation . Berlin , c1989. 344 p. : ISBN 3-496-01061-4
NYPL [3-MDW 90-12434]

GRAPHIC ARTS - HISTORY - 20TH CENTURY - EXHIBITIONS.
Marcus, Joshua. Designers' self image . New York , c1991. 224 p. : DDC 741.6/09/048074569442 20
NC997.A4 J46 1991

GRAPHIC ARTS - ITALY - HISTORY - 20TH CENTURY.
Altea, Giuliana. Le matite di un popolo barbaro . Cinisello Balsamo (Milano), c1990. 190 p. : ISBN 88-366-0285-1
NC998.6.I8 A48 1990

GRAPHIC ARTS - JAPAN - HISTORY.
Thornton, Richard S. The graphic spirit of Japan /. New York , 1991. p. cm. ISBN 0-442-30376-9 DDC 741.6/0952 20
NK1484.A1 T47 1991

GRAPHIC ARTS - NETHERLANDS.
Brattinga, Pieter, 1931- The activities of Pieter Brattinga, a portrait of an era /. Tokyo , The Hague , 1989. 287 p. : ISBN 90-12-06213-6
(SDU) **NYPL [3-MDWS+ (Brattinga) 90-9941 Suppl.]**

GRAPHIC ARTS - RUSSIAN S.F.S.R. - HISTORY - 19TH CENTURY.
Chernevich, Elena, 1939- Russian graphic design /. New York, NY , 1990. 160 p. : ISBN 1-558-59016-1 DDC 741.6/0947 20
NC998.6.R9 C47 1990
NYPL [3-MDW+ 90-11977]

GRAPHIC ARTS - SOVIET UNION - HISTORY - 20TH CENTURY - EXHIBITIONS.
Grafica russa 1917/1930 . Firenze , c1990. 192 p. :
IN PROCESS (ONLINE)
NYPL [MDBF+ 90-11003]

GRAPHIC ARTS - STUDY AND TEACHING.
Wilde, Judith. Visual literacy . New York , 1991. 191 p. : ISBN 0-8230-5619-8 : DDC 741.6 20
NC845 .W55 1991

GRAPHIC ARTS - TECHNIQUE.
Hanks, Kurt, 1947- Rapid viz . Los Altos, CA , c1990. 149 p. : ISBN 1-560-52055-8 (pbk.) : DDC 741.6 20
NC877.8 .H36 1990

Wood, John Rowland, 1937- Handbook of illustration /. New York, N.Y. , 1991. p. cm. ISBN 0-8306-3560-2 : DDC 741.6 20
NC1000 .W66 1991

GRAPHIC ARTS - UNITED STATE - MARKETING.
Davis, Sally Prince, 1942- The graphic artist's guide to marketing and self-promotion /. Cincinnati, Ohio , 1991. p. cm. ISBN 0-89134-416-0 : DDC 741.6/068/8 20
NC1001.6 .D38 1991

GRAPHIC ARTS - UNITED STATES - EXHIBITIONS.
Princeton University. Library. Dept. of Rare Books and Special Collections. American graphic arts . Princeton, N.J. , 1990. xi, 213 p. : ISBN 0-87811-033-X
NYPL [MDBF 90-10992]

Roylance, Dale. American graphic arts . Princeton, N.J. , 1990. xi, 213 p. : DDC 760/.0973/07474965 20
NE954.3.U6 R68 1990

GRAPHIC ARTS - UNITED STATES - HUMOR.
Heller, Steven. Graphic wit . New York , 1991. p. cm. ISBN 0-8230-2161-0 : DDC 741.6 20
NC998.5.A1 H44 1991

GRAPHIC ARTS - UNITED STATES - MARKETING.
Graphic Artists Guild (U. S.) Graphic Artists Guild handbook . New York, NY , Cincinnatti, OH , c1991. 235 p. ; ISBN 0-932102-07-7
NYPL [3-MDW+ 91-5861]

GRAPHIC ARTS - UNITED STATES - THEMES, MOTIVES.
Greiman, April. Hybrid imagery . New York , 1990. 158 p. : ISBN 0-8230-2518-7 : DDC 741.6 20
NC998.5.A1 G75 1990
NYPL [3-MDW 90-10910]

GRAPHIC DATA PROCESSING. see COMPUTER GRAPHICS.

Graphic design . Rosentswieg, Gerry. New York, N.Y. , c1988. 299 p. : ISBN 0-8230-4891-8 : DDC 741.6/0794/94 19
NC998.5.C22 L677 1988
NYPL [3-MDW+ 90-11018]

Graphic design processes . Hiebert, Kenneth J. New York , c1992. 208 p. : ISBN 0-442-00839-2 DDC 741.6 20
NC1000 .H54 1991

Graphic excursions. Graphic excursions--American prints in black and white, 1900-1950 . Boston, Mass. , 1991. 155 p. : ISBN 0-87923-902-6 DDC 769.973/074/73 20
NE508 .G74 1991 **NYPL [MDE 91-5862]**

Graphic excursions--American prints in black and white, 1900-1950 : selections from the collection of Reba & Dave Williams / essays by Karen F. Beall and David W. Kiehl. Boston, Mass. : D.R. Godine in association with The American Federation of Arts, 1991. 155 p. : ill. ; 23 X 25 cm. Published in conjunction with an exhibition organized and circulated by the American Federation of Arts at the Weatherspoon Art Gallery, University of North Carolina, Greensboro, North Carolina, Apr. 6-June 1, 1991, and 7 other locations through Apr. 4, 1993. Spine title: Graphic excursions. Includes bibliographical references and index. ISBN 0-87923-902-6 DDC 769.973/074/73 20
1. Williams, Dave, 1932- - Art collections - Exhibitions. 2. Williams, Reba - Art collections - Exhibitions. 3. Prints, American - Exhibitions. 4. Prints - 20th century - United States - Exhibitions. 5. Prints - Private collections - United States - Exhibitions. I. Williams, Reba. II. Williams, Dave, 1932-. III. Beall, Karen F. IV. Kiehl, David W. V. Weatherspoon Art Gallery. VI. Title: Graphic excursions.
NE508 .G74 1991 **NYPL [MDE 91-5862]**

Graphic fundamentals . Sutherland, Martha, 1927- New York, N.Y. , 1991. p. cm. ISBN 0-8306-3480-0 : DDC 720/.28/4 20
NA2708 .S88 1991

The graphic spirit of Japan /. Thornton, Richard S. New York , 1991. p. cm. ISBN 0-442-30376-9 DDC 741.6/0952 20
NK1484.A1 T47 1991

Graphic wit . Heller, Steven. New York , 1991. p. cm. ISBN 0-8230-2161-0 : DDC 741.6 20
NC998.5.A1 H44 1991

Graphic work. Kipniss, Robert. Robert Kipniss . Saint Louis, Mo. , c1981. 64 p. :
NYPL [MDG (Kipniss) 91-3728]

The graphic work of René Magritte /. Kaplan, Gilbert E. New York, N.Y. , c1982. [50] p. : DDC 769.92/4 19
NE2049.5.M29 A4 1982
NYPL [MDG (Magritte) 83-207]

Graphic works. Paulson, Ronald. Hogarth's graphic works /. London , 1989. xviii, 479 p. : ISBN 0-9514808-0-4 : DDC 769.92 20
NE642.H6 A4 1989

Graphic works 1965-1990. Brandstätter, Karl, 1946- Graphisches Werk 1965-1990 =. Klagenfurt , c1989. 1 v. (unpaged) : ISBN 3-85391-088-2 DDC 769.92 20
NE646.B7 A4 1989

GRAPHICS, COMPUTER. see COMPUTER GRAPHICS.

Graphicstudio . National Gallery of Art (U. S.) Washington , 1991. p. cm. ISBN 0-89468-164-8 DDC 769.9759/65/074753 20
NE538.T35 N37 1991

Graphicstudio.
National Gallery of Art (U. S.) Graphicstudio . Washington , 1991. p. cm. ISBN 0-89468-164-8 DDC 769.9759/65/074753 20
NE538.T35 N37 1991

GRAPHICSTUDIO - EXHIBITIONS.
National Gallery of Art (U. S.) Graphicstudio . Washington , 1991. p. cm. ISBN 0-89468-164-8

DDC 769.9759/65/074753 20
NE538.T35 N37 1991

Graphik des deutschen Impressionismus .
Pfalzgalerie Kaiserslautern. Graphische
Sammlung. Kaiserslautern , 1985. 91 p. :   DDC
769/.074/0343 s 769.943/074/0343 19
NE55.G4 K346 1985 vol. 1 NE651.6.14
                    NYPL [MDE 91-4007]

**Graphik des Expressionismus aus den Beständen
des Museums /.** Wilhelm-Hack-Museum.
Ludwigshafen am Rhein , c1989. 130 p. :   DDC
769.94/09/07443435 20
NE625 .W54 1989

Graphik-Salon Gerhart Sohn. Felixmüller,
Conrad, 1897-1977. Conrad Felixmüller,
1897-1977 . Dusseldorf [1982?] [38] p. :
                    NYPL [3-MCK F316 91-868]

Graphiken von Marika Drechsler /. Egger,
Gerhart, 1916- Wien , 1978. 15 p., 32 p. of
plates :   ***NYPL [MDG (Drechsler) 90-6047]***

**Die Graphiksammlung des Humanisten
Hartmann Schedel /** [Katalog, Béatrice
Hernad]. München : Prestel, c1990. 336 p. : ill.
(some col.) ; 29 cm. (Ausstellungskataloge /
Bayerische Staatsbibliothek . 52) Catalog of an
exhibition held at the Bayerische Staatsbibliothek in
München, June 20-Sept. 15, 1990. Includes
bibliographical references (p. 320-330) and index.
  ISBN 3-7913-1083-6   DDC
  769.94/09/02407443364 20
  *1. Schedel, Hartmann, 1440-1514 - Art collections -
  Exhibitions. 2. Prints, European - Exhibitions. 3.
  Prints - 15th century - Europe - Exhibitions. 4. Prints -
  16th century - Europe - Exhibitions. 5. Prints - Private
  collections - Germany - Nuremberg - Exhibitions. I.
  Schedel, Hartmann, 1440-1514. II. Hernad, Béatrice.
  III. Bayerische Staatsbibliothek. IV. Series:
  Ausstellungskataloge / Bayerische Staatsbibliothek , 52.*
NE59.G4 S324 1990   ***NYPL [MDE 91-7276]***

Graphische Sammlung. Universität Osnabrück .
Osnabrück , 1988. [99] p. :
                    NYPL [MDE+90-269]

Graphische Sammlung Albertina.
Amerikanische Zeichnungen in den achtziger
Jahren . München , c1990. 190 p. :   DDC
741.973/09/04807443551 20
NC108 .A55 1990

Claude Lorrain und die Meister der römischen
Landschaft im XVII Jahrhundert : Ausstellung
16. November 1964 bis 15. Februar 1965.
[Wien, 1965] xv, 187 p. : 51 plates ; 21 cm.
Bibliography: p.12-22.
  *1. Lorrain, Claude, 1600-1682 - Exhibitions. 2.
  Landscape drawing - 17th century - Europe -
  Exhibitions. 3. Engraving - 17th century - Europe -
  Exhibitions. 4. Campagna di Roma (Italy) - Description
  and travel - Views - Exhibitions. I. Title.*
                    NYPL [3-MBH 91-1175]

Dine, Jim, 1935- Jim Dine . London , 1988. 67
p. (some folded) :
                    NYPL [MDG+ (Dine) 90-10861]

Ingres, Jean-Auguste-Dominique, 1780-1867.
J.A.D. Ingres 1780-1867 . Wien [1991] 297
p. :   ISBN 3-900656-14-2
                    NYPL [3-MCO+ I55 91-6971]

Oberhuber, Konrad. Herbert Brandl, Josef
Danner, Otto Zitko /. Wien , 1988. 4 v. in 1 :
                    NYPL [3-MCK B818 90-8683]

Oberösterreichische Landesausstellung (1989 :
Benediktinerstift Lambach) Die Botschaft der
Graphik . Linz , 1989. 211 p. :
NE45.A8 L366 1989

Der Zertrümmerte Spiegel . Klagenfurt , 1989.
392 p. :   ISBN 3-85415-062-8
                    NYPL [3-MAL 91-7188]

Das graphische Werk. Jones, Allen, 1937- [Köln,
1969?] [74] p.
NE642.J6 A46
                    NYPL [MDG (Jones, A.) 90-6297]

Graphische Werk. Magnus, Günter Hugo.
Magnus . Heidelberg , c1989. 131 p. :   ISBN
3-925835-50-4
NC999.6.G4 M342 1989

Graphische Werk. Weidensdorfer, Claus, 1931-
Claus Weidensdorfer . [Leipzig] [1989?] 95 p. :
  ISBN 3-86060-007-9   DDC 769.92 20
NE654.W39 A4 1989

**Graphisches Kabinett Kunsthandel Wolfgang
Werner.** Skulpturen 1925-1950 . Bremen
[1989] 1 v. (unpaged) :
                    NYPL [3-MGF+ 91-6497]

Graphisches Kabinett Wolfgang Werner. see
**Graphisches Kabinett Kunsthandel Wolfgang
Werner.**

Graphisches Werk 1965-1990 =. Brandstätter,
Karl, 1946- Klagenfurt , c1989. 1 v. (unpaged) :
  ISBN 3-85391-088-2   DDC 769.92 20
NE646.B7 A4 1989

Grass, Günter, 1927-
Nicaragua, una realtà delle Americhe /.
Palermo (Italia) , c1987. 206 p. :   ISBN
88-7704-010-6 :   ***NYPL [MFW+ 91-3429]***

Totes Holz : ein Nachruf / Günter Grass.1.
Aufl. Göttingen : Steidl, 1990. 110 p. : chiefly
ill. ; 28 cm.   ISBN 3-88243-155-5
  *1. Grass, Günter, 1927-. 2. Acid rain - Environmental
  aspects - Germany - Pictorial works. I. Title.*
NX550.Z9 G72 1990

GRASS, GÜNTER, 1927-
Grass, Günter, 1927- Totes Holz . Göttingen ,
1990. 110 p. :   ISBN 3-88243-155-5
NX550.Z9 G72 1990

Grass, Günter, 1927- [Selections. English.
1985.] Etchings and words, 1972-1982 /. San
Diego , c1985. 148 p. :   ISBN 0-15-129150-0
  DDC 769.92/4 19
NX550.Z9 G725 1983 vol. 2
                    NYPL [MDG+ (Grass) 91-2286]

Grass, Günter, 1927- [Selections. 1982.]
Zeichnungen und Texte 1954-1977 /.
Darmstadt , c1982. 133 p. :   ISBN 3-472-90001-6
  DDC 700/.92/4 s 741.943 19
NX550.Z9 G725 1982 Bd. 1
                    NYPL [MCK++ G76 85-327]

Grass, Günter, 1927- [Selections. 1982.]
Zeichnen und Schreiben . Darmstadt ,
c1982-1984. 2 v. :   ISBN 3-472-90002-4 (Bd. II)
  DDC 700/.92/4 19
NX550.Z9 G725 1982
                    NYPL [MCK++ G76 85-327]

Grass, Günter, 1927- [Selections. 1982.]
Radierungen und Texte 1972-1982 /.
Darmstadt , c1984. 146 p. :   ISBN 3-472-90002-4
  DDC 700/.92/4 s 769.92/4 19
NX550.Z9 G725 1982 Bd. 2
                    NYPL [MDG+ (Grass) 91-2285]

Selections. English. 1983. .
(2) Grass, Günter, 1927- [Selections. English.
1985.] Etchings and words, 1972-1982 /. San
Diego , c1985. 148 p. :   ISBN 0-15-129150-0
  DDC 769.92/4 19
NX550.Z9 G725 1983 vol. 2
                    NYPL [MDG+ (Grass) 91-2286]

[Selections. English. 1985]
Etchings and words, 1972-1982 / Günter
Grass ; edited by Anselm Dreher ; text
selection and afterword by Sigrid Mayer. 1st
American ed. San Diego : Harcourt Brace
Jovanovich, c1985. 148 p. : ill. ; 41 cm.
(Graphics and writing . 2) Translation of:
Radierungen und Texte 1972-1982. "A Helen and
Kurt Wolff book." Bibliography: p. 142-143.   ISBN
0-15-129150-0   DDC 769.92/4 19
  *1. Grass, Günter, 1927-. I. Dreher, Anselm. II. Mayer,
  Sigrid. III. Series: Grass, Günter, 1927- Selections.
  English. 1983. , 2. IV. Title.*
NX550.Z9 G725 1983 vol. 2
                    NYPL [MDG+ (Grass) 91-2286]

[Selections. 1982]
Zeichnungen und Texte 1954-1977 / Günter
Grass ; herausgegeben von Anselm Dreher ;
Textauswahl und Nachwort von Sigrid
Mayer. Darmstadt : Luchterhand, c1982. 133
p. : ill. ; 41 cm. (Zeichnen und Schreiben : das
bildnerische Werk des Schriftstellers Günter Grass .
Bd. 1)   ISBN 3-472-90001-6   DDC 700/.92/4 s
741.943 19
  *1. Grass, Günter, 1927-. I. Dreher, Anselm. II. Mayer,
  Sigrid. III. Title.*
NX550.Z9 G725 1982 Bd. 1
                    NYPL [MCK++ G76 85-327]

Zeichnen und Schreiben : das bildnerische
Werk des Schriftstellers Günter Grass /
herausgegeben von Anselm Dreher.
Darmstadt : Luchterhand, c1982-1984. 2 v. :
ill. ; 41 cm. No more published. CONTENTS. -
Bd. 1. Zeichnungen und Texte 1954-1977 -- Bd. 2.

Radierungen und Texte 1972-1982.   ISBN
3-472-90002-4 (Bd. II)   DDC 700/.92/4 19
  1. Grass, Günter, 1927-. I. Dreher, Anselm. II. Title.
NX550.Z9 G725 1982
                    NYPL [MCK++ G76 85-327]

Radierungen und Texte 1972-1982 / Günter
Grass ; herausgegeben von Anselm Dreher ;
Textauswahl und Nachwort von Sigrid
Mayer. Darmstadt : Luchterhand, c1984. 146
p. : ill. ; 41 cm. (Zeichnen und Schreiben : das
bildnerische Werk des Schriftstellers Günter Grass .
Bd. 2)   ISBN 3-472-90002-4   DDC 700/.92/4 s
769.92/4 19
  *1. Grass, Günter, 1927-. I. Dreher, Anselm. II. Mayer,
  Sigrid. III. Title.*
NX550.Z9 G725 1982 Bd. 2
                    NYPL [MDG+ (Grass) 91-2285]

GRÄSSEL, HANS, 1860-1939.
Krieg, Nina A. Schon Ordnung ist Schönheit .
München , 1990. xix, 304 p. :   ISBN
3-87821-286-0
NA6166 .K75 1990

**GRASSER, ERASMUS, CA. 1450-1518 -
CRITICISM AND INTERPRETATION.**
Otto, Kornelius. Erasmus Grasser und der
Meister des Blutenburger Apostelzyklus .
München , 1988. 268 p., [20] p. of plates :
  ISBN 3-87821-270-4
NB586.M77 O8 1988

Grassroots, greystones, and glass towers :
Montreal urban issues and architecture /
[edited by Bryan Demchinsky]. Montréal :
Véhicule Press ; Buffalo, N.Y. : U.S.
distribution, University of Toronto Press, c1989.
211 p. : ill. ; 23 cm. (Dossier Québec series)
Includes index.   ISBN 1-550-65001-7 :   DDC
720/.9714/28 20
  *1. Architecture - Quebec (Province) - Montreal. 2.
  Urban renewal - Québec (Province) - Montréal. 3.
  Montréal (Québec) - Buildings, structures, etc. I.
  Demchinsky, Bryan. II. Series.*
NA747.M66 G7 1989

GRATIOT COUNTY, MICH. - MAPS.
(1990) Rockford Map Publishers. Gratiot
County, Michigan, land atlas & plat book .
Rockford, Ill. , Ithaca, Mich. , c1990. 1 atlas
(53 p.) :   ***NYPL [Map Div. 90-12843]***

**Gratiot County, Michigan, land atlas & plat
book .** Rockford Map Publishers. Rockford,
Ill. , Ithaca, Mich. , c1990. 1 atlas (53 p.) :
                    NYPL [Map Div. 90-12843]

Grau-Garriga à Angers . Grau-Garriga, Josep,
1929- Angers [1989] 175 p. :   ISBN
2-901287-20-4
NK3062.A3 G722 1989

Grau-Garriga, Josep, 1929-
Grau-Garriga à Angers : Musée Jean Lurçat et
de la tapisserie contemporaine, 19 mai-29
octobre [et] Musée des beaux-arts, 23 juin-29
octobre [et] Abbaye du Ronceray, 23 juin-24
septembre [et] Château, 23 juin-29 octobre /
[organisation, Musées, Service des affaires
culturelles, ville d'Angers]. Angers : Mairie
d'Angers [1989] 175 p. : ill. (some col.) ; 30
cm. Exhibition catalog. Includes bibliographical
references (p. 172-175).   ISBN 2-901287-20-4
  *1. Grau-Garriga, Josep, 1929- - Exhibitions. 2.
  Tapestry - Spain - History - 20th century - Exhibitions.
  I. Musée Jean Lurçat et de la tapisserie contemporaine
  (Angers, France). II. Musées d'Angers. Service des
  affaires culturelles. III. Title.*
NK3062.A3 G722 1989

**GRAU-GARRIGA, JOSEP, 1929- -
EXHIBITIONS.**
Grau-Garriga, Josep, 1929- Grau-Garriga à
Angers . Angers [1989] 175 p. :   ISBN
2-901287-20-4
NK3062.A3 G722 1989

Graubner, Gotthard, 1930-
Gotthard Graubner / [Katalogredaktion:
Wieland Schmied] Hannover :
Kestner-Gesellschaft, [c1969] 102 p. : ill. ; 21
cm. (Katalog . 6, Ausstellungsjahr 1969) Catalog of an
exhibition held at the Kestner-Gesellschaft, Hanover,
Oct. 9-Nov. 2, 1969. Bibliography: p. 25.
  *1. Graubner, Gotthard, 1930-. I. Scmied, Wieland,
  1929-. II. Series: Katalog (Kestner-Gesellschaft) ,
  1969/6. III. Title.*
                    NYPL [3-MCK G773 91-906]

Gotthard Graubner : Malerei auf Papier ;
Kunsthalle Bremen 3.12.1989-18.2.1990 ;

Kunstverein Braunschweig 16.3.1990-29.4.1990 ; Galerie der Stadt Esslingen, Villa Merkel 8.6.1990-8.7.1990 / [herausgeber, Siegfried Salzmann ; ausstellung und katalog, Ulrike Lehmann, Gotthard Graubner]. Bremen : Kunsthalle Bremen, c1989. 145 p. (5 folded) : chiefly ill. (chiefly col.), 1 port. ; 29 cm. Bibliography: p. 139-144.
1. Graubner, Gotthard, 1930- - Exhibitions. I. Salzmann, Siegfried. II. Lehmann, Ulrike. III. Kunsthalle Bremen. IV. Galerie der Stadt Esslingen. V. Title. NYPL [3-MCK+ G773 91-6686]

GRAUBNER, GOTTHARD, 1930-
Graubner, Gotthard, 1930- Gotthard Graubner /. Hannover [c1969] 102 p. :
NYPL [3-MCK G773 91-906]

GRAUBNER, GOTTHARD, 1930- - EXHIBITIONS.
Graubner, Gotthard, 1930- Gotthard Graubner . Bremen , c1989. 145 p. (5 folded) :
NYPL [3-MCK+ G773 91-6686]

GRAUBÜNDEN (SWITZERLAND) IN ART - EXHIBITIONS.
Das Engadin Ferdinand Hodlers und anderer Künstler des 19. und 20. Jahrhunderts . [Chur] , St. Moritz , c1990. 122 p. : ISBN 3-905240-15-7 DDC 759.9494 20
ND853.H6 A4 1990

Der graue Fetisch . Werner, Martina, 1929- Nürnberg , c1987. 44 p. :
MLCS 88/03971 (N)
NYPL [3-MGO (Werner) 90-13400]

Graulich, Gerhard. Die Sammlung Woty und Theodor Werner /. München , c1990. 131 p. : ISBN 3-7774-5460-5
NYPL [3-MAX (Werner, W.) 91-6703]

Graupner, Stefan. Köchl, Alois, 1951- Alois Köchl, Stadtzeichner von Nürnberg 1984 . [Nürnberg] [1985] 37 p. :
MLCM 86/3093 (N)
NYPL [3-MCK K768 90-10681]

Grauwe, Paul de. De Nachtwacht in het donker : over kunst en economie / Paul de Grauwe. Tielt : Lannoo, [1990] 180 p. : ill. ; 21 cm. Includes bibliographical references. ISBN 90-209-1766-8 :
1. Art - Economic aspects. I. Title.
N8600 .G73 1990

Gravalos, Mary Evans O'Keefe. Bertha Lum / Mary Evans O'Keefe Gravalos and Carol Pulin. Washington, D.C. : Smithsonian Institution Press, c1991. 112 p. : ill. (some col.), port. ; 26 cm. (Smithsonian series) American printmakers Includes bibliographical references (105-108) and index. ISBN 1-560-98008-7 (pbk.) DDC 769.92 20
1. Lum, Bertha Boynton, 1869-1954 - Criticism and interpretation. 2. Prints - 20th century - United States - Japanese influences. I. Pulin, Carol. II. Series. III. Series: American printmakers (Washington, D.C.). IV. Title.
NE1112.L86 G73 1990
NYPL [MDG (Lum) 91-5860]

GRAVELINES (FRANCE) IN ART.
Lee, Ellen Wardwell. Seurat at Gravelines, the last landscapes /. Indianapolis, Ind. , c1990. 80 p. : ISBN 0-936260-55-6
NYPL [3-MCO+ S49 91-4490]

The graven image . Ben Yosef, Ute. Cape Town , c1989. 128 p. : ISBN 0-628-03407-5 DDC 730/.92 B 20
NB1096.K67 B46 1989

GRAVES. see SEPULCHRAL MONUMENTS.

GRAVESTONES. see SEPULCHRAL MONUMENTS.

A gravura de Lasar Segall. Segall, Lasar, 1891-1957. São Paulo, Brasil [1988] xxii, 183 p. : ISBN 85-85163-01-1 DDC 769.92 20
NE600.S44 A4 1988
NYPL [MDG (Segall) 90-10985]

Gravures d'Edwin Holgate. Thom, Ian M. (Ian MacEwan), 1952- The prints of Edwin Holgate =. Kleinburg, Ont. , c1989. [69] p. : ISBN 0-7729-6098-4 DDC 769.92 20
NYPL [MDG (Holgate) 91-5843]

Gray, Alexander Stuart. Fanlights / Alexander Stuart Gray, John Sambrook, Tony Birks-Hay ; drawings by Charlotte Halliday ; photographs by Jane Whitton. London : Alphabooks : A & C Black, 1990. 148 p. : ill. ; 26 cm. Includes index. Bibliography: p. 144-145. ISBN

0-7136-3077-9 : DDC 721.823 20
1. Fanlights - Great Britain. 2. Architecture, Georgian - Great Britain. 3. Architecture, Domestic - Great Britain. 4. Fanlights - United States. 5. Architecture, Georgian - United States. 6. Architecture, Domestic - United States. I. Sambrook, John. II. Birks-Hay, Tony. III. Halliday, Charlotte. IV. Title.
NYPL [3-MRR 91-3295]

Gray, Bill. Tips on making greeting cards / Bill Gray and Jan Van Milligen. 1st ed. New York, NY : Design Press, c1991. 136 p. : ill. (some col.) ; 24 cm. Includes bibliographical references (p. 134) and index. ISBN 0-8306-0595-9 : DDC 741.6/84 20
1. Greeting cards - Design. I. Van Milligen, Jane. II. Title.
NC1860 .G64 1991

Gray, Donna B., 1944- A parent's guide to teaching art : how to encourage your child's artistic talent and ability / Donna B. Gray. White Hall, Va. : Betterway Publications, c1991. p. cm. Includes bibliographical references and index. ISBN 1-558-70202-4 (pbk.) : DDC 700 20
1. Children as artists. 2. Youth as artists. 3. Gifted children - Education - Art. I. Title.
N351 .G73 1991

Gray, Eileen, 1879-1976. Johnson, J. Stewart. Eileen Gray, designer /. London , c1979. 67 p. : ISBN 0-87070-307-2 :
NK1535.G68 J63 NYPL [MOI 80-2273]

GRAY, EILEEN, 1879-1976.
Johnson, J. Stewart. Eileen Gray, designer /. London , c1979. 67 p. : ISBN 0-87070-307-2 :
NK1535.G68 J63 NYPL [MOI 80-2273]

GRAY, EILEEN, 1878-1976.
On rigor /. Cambridge, Mass. , c1989. 188 p. : ISBN 0-262-52138-5
NYPL [3-MQV+ 91-6328]

Gray, Milton, 1942- Cartoon animation : introduction to a career / Milton Gray. Northridge, CA : Lion's Den Publications, c1991. iv, 124 p. : ill. ; 28 cm. Includes bibliographical references (p. 109-114) and index. ISBN 0-9628444-5-4 : DDC 741.5/8/02373 20
1. Animation (Cinematography) - Vocational guidance - United States. I. Title.
NC1765 .G7 1991

Graz. Universität. Kunsthistorisches Institut. Forschungen und Berichte.
(8) Höfler, Janez. Die Kunst Dalmatiens . Graz , 1989. 338 p. : ISBN 3-201-01466-4
NYPL [3-MAM+ 90-8024]

Grazda, Ed. Afghanistan, 1980-1989 / Ed Grazda. Zürich, Switzerland : Der Alltag ; Zürich, Switzerland ; 139 p. : ill. ; 28 cm. "Published as a special issue of Der Alltag magazine, 1/1990"--Colophon. English and German. ISBN 3-907509-12-9 (Parkett)
1. Grazda, Ed. 2. Photojournalism - Afghanistan. 3. Afghanistan - History - Soviet occupation, 1979-1989 - Pictorial works. I. Der Alltag. 1/1990. II. Title.
NYPL [MFX (Grazda) 91-3488]

GRAZDA, ED.
Grazda, Ed. Afghanistan, 1980-1989 /. Zürich, Switzerland : Zürich, Switzerland ; 139 p. : ISBN 3-907509-12-9 (Parkett)
NYPL [MFX (Grazda) 91-3488]

The great art hoax . Huer, Jon. Bowling Green, Ohio , c1990. 173 p. ; ISBN 0-87972-491-9
NYPL [3-MAAZ 90-12001]

Great Australian paintings / selected by Laura Murray. 1st ed. Frenchs Forest, NSW, Australia : Child & Associates, 1989. 64 p. : ill. ; 32 cm. ISBN 0-86777-247-6
I. Murray, Laura. NYPL [3-MCY+ 91-4467]

GREAT BRITAIN - ANTIQUITIES - PICTORIAL WORKS.
Fowler, P. J. Images of prehistory /. Cambridge , New York , 1990. 223 p. : ISBN 0-521-35646-6 DDC 936.1/0022/2 20
GN805 .F69 1990
NYPL [MFX (Sharp) 91-4460]

GREAT BRITAIN - ANTIQUITIES, ROMAN - MAPS.
Jones, Barri. An atlas of Roman Britain /. Oxford , Cambridge, Mass., USA , 1990. vii, 341 p. : ISBN 0-631-13791-2 : DDC 911.41 20
NYPL [Map Div. 90-10987]

Great Britain - Archaeology. see Great Britain - Antiquities.

Great Britain - Archaeology - Roman remains. see Great Britain - Antiquities, Roman.

Great Britain. Arts Council. see Arts Council of Great Britain.

GREAT BRITAIN - CIVILIZATION - 19TH CENTURY - PICTORIAL WORKS.
Barr, John, 1934- Britain portrayed . London , 1989. 126 p. : ISBN 0-7123-0174-7 :
NYPL [3-MAMY+ 91-4983]

Great Britain. Department of the Environment. Property Services Agency. see Great Britain. Property Services Agency.

GREAT BRITAIN - DESCRIPTION AND TRAVEL - 1901-1945 XEXHIBITIONS.
Mellor, David. Recording Britain . Newton Abbot , 1990. 160 p. : ISBN 0-7153-9798-2 : DDC 941.084 20
NYPL [3-MAMY 91-6793]

GREAT BRITAIN - DESCRIPTION AND TRAVEL - 1971- - VIEWS - EXHIBITIONS.
Doherty, Willie, 1959- Willie Doherty, unknown depths. Cardiff , c1990. [39] p. : ISBN 1-87277-101-7
NYPL [MFX (Doherty) 90-13467]

GREAT BRITAIN - DESCRIPTION AND TRAVEL - VIEWS - EXHIBITIONS.
Mellor, David. Recording Britain . Newton Abbot , 1990. 160 p. : ISBN 0-7153-9798-2 : DDC 941.084 20
NYPL [3-MAMY 91-6793]

GREAT BRITAIN - ECONOMIC POLICY - 1945-
Public policy under Thatcher /. Houndmills, Basingstoke, Hampshire , 1990. xviii, 291 p. ; ISBN 0-333-53659-2 (cased) : DDC 336.390941 20
HJ2096 NYPL [JLD 90-2067]

Great Britain - Government. see Great Britain - Politics and government.

GREAT BRITAIN - HISTORY - ROMAN PERIOD, 55 A.D.-449 A.D. - MAPS.
Jones, Barri. An atlas of Roman Britain /. Oxford , Cambridge, Mass., USA , 1990. vii, 341 p. : ISBN 0-631-13791-2 : DDC 911.41 20
NYPL [Map Div. 90-10987]

Great Britain - History, Political. see Great Britain - Politics and government.

GREAT BRITAIN IN ART.
Barr, John, 1934- Britain portrayed . London , 1989. 126 p. : ISBN 0-7123-0174-7 :
NYPL [3-MAMY+ 91-4983]

Mellor, David. Recording Britain . Newton Abbot , 1990. 160 p. : ISBN 0-7153-9798-2 : DDC 941.084 20
NYPL [3-MAMY 91-6793]

Wood, Christopher, 1941- Victorian panorama . London , 1990. 260 p. : ISBN 0-571-14375-X DDC 758/.9941081 20
ND1452.G75 W66 1990

GREAT BRITAIN - MAPS, MANUSCRIPT - BIBLIOGRAPHY - CATALOGS.
Hodson, Yolande. Ordnance surveyors' drawings, 1789-c.1840 . Reading, England , 1989. 154 p. : ISBN 0-86257-101-4 DDC 016.91242 20
Z6027.G7 H66 1989 GA791
NYPL [Map Div. 91-169]

Great Britain. Museums and Galleries Commission. The National museums . London , 1988. 64 p. : ISBN 0-11-290457-2 (pbk.) : DDC 069/.0941 708.2 19
AM41 N1020 NYPL [MAV 90-11367]

Great Britain. Ordnance Survey.
East Kent street atlas . Maybush, Southampton , London , 1989. 1 atlas (viii, 238 p.) : ISBN 0-540-05559-X : DDC 912.4223 20
NYPL [Map Div. 91-174]

West Kent street atlas . London , 1989. 1 atlas (viii, 226 p.) : ISBN 0-540-05560-3 : DDC 912.4223 20 *NYPL [Map Div. 91-158]*

GREAT BRITAIN - POLITICS AND GOVERNMENT - 1979-
Public policy under Thatcher /. Houndmills, Basingstoke, Hampshire , 1990. xviii, 291 p. ; ISBN 0-333-53659-2 (cased) : DDC 336.390941 20
HJ2096 NYPL [JLD 90-2067]

Great Britain. Property Services Agency. Lisney, Adrian. Landscape design guide /. Aldershot, Hants, England ; Brookfield, Vt., USA : 2 v. :
    ISBN 0-566-09017-1 (v. 1) :   DDC 712 19
SB472   *NYPL [3-MSD 90-13255]*

GREAT BRITAIN - ROAD MAPS.
(1980) George Philip & Son. Philip's Road atlas of Great Britain . [London] , c1980. 1 atlas (vii, 80, [61] p.) :   ISBN 0-540-05364-3 DDC 912/.41 19
G1812.21.P2 G6 1980
        NYPL [Map Div. 90-5738]

(1986) William Collins Sons and Co. Road atlas, Britain. Glasgow , c1986. 1 atlas (129 p.) :   *NYPL [Map Div. 91-5505]*

GREAT BRITAIN - SOCIAL LIFE AND CUSTOMS - PICTORIAL WORKS.
Wood, Christopher, 1941- Victorian panorama . London , 1990. 260 p. :   ISBN 0-571-14375-X
    DDC 758/.9941081 20
ND1452.G75 W66 1990

GREAT BRITAIN - SOCIAL POLICY - 1979-
Public policy under Thatcher /. Houndmills, Basingstoke, Hampshire , 1990. xviii, 291 p. ;
    ISBN 0-333-53659-2 (cased) :   DDC 336.390941 20
HJ2096   *NYPL [JLD 90-2067]*

The Great centuries of painting.
Dupont, Jacques. The seventeenth century. Geneva, New York [1951] 136 p. :   DDC 750.903
ND180 .D8   *NYPL [MC 90-11578]*

Great Dutch paintings from America. Broos, B. P. J. The Hague , Zwolle , c1990. 561 p. :
    ISBN 90-6630-253-4 (paperback)
        NYPL [3-MCG 91-5531]

Great homes of California /. Harris, Bill, 1933- New York , 1990. 160 p. :   ISBN 0-517-62377-3
    DDC 728.8/09794 20
NA7511.3.C2 H3 1990

Great housewives of art revisited /. Swain, Sally. New York , 1992. p. cm.   ISBN 0-14-015837-5 :
    DDC 741.5/994 20
NC1759.S93 A4 1992

GREAT LAKES - MAPS.
The mapping of the Great Lakes in the seventeenth century. . Providence, R. I, 1989. xix, [3], 85 p. incl. maps :
        NYPL [Map Div. 90-65]

GREAT PALACE OF THE BYZANTINE EMPERORS (ISTANBUL, TURKEY)
Miranda, Salvador. Etude de topographie du palais sacré de Byzance . [Paris?] 1976. 184 p., [43] p. of plates :   *NYPL [3-MQP 90-4929]*

The Great plains photography series.
Bruhn, Roger, 1941- Dreams in dry places /. Lincoln , c1990. xix, 143 p. :   ISBN 0-8032-1214-3 :   DDC 779/.4782/092 20
TR660 .B784 1990
        NYPL [MFX (Bruhn) 91-3589]

A Harmony of the arts . Lincoln , c1990. x, 119 p. :   ISBN 0-8032-2887-2 (alk. paper) DDC 725/.11/09782293 19
NA4413.L56 H37 1990
        NYPL [3-MQWO 90-11994]

GREAT POWERS - MAPS.
Prévot, Victor. Géopolitique transparente . [Paris] , 1987. 1 atlas (255 p.) :   ISBN 2-210-98004-6   *NYPL [Map Div. 91-6046]*

Great prints of the world. Peterdi, Gabor. [New York, 1969] xii, 265, [2] p.   DDC 769
NE430 .P47

Great restaurant design / by the editors of PBC International. New York : PBC International, 1991. p. cm. Includes index. DDC 725/.71/0973 20
1. Restaurants, lunch rooms, etc. - United States - Designs and plans. 2. Restaurants, lunch rooms, etc. - United States - Decoration. I. PBC International.
NA7840 .G7 1991

GREAT SKELLIG ISLAND (IRELAND) - ANTIQUITIES.
Horn, Walter William, 1908- The forgotten hermitage of Skellig Michael /. Berkeley , c1990. xi, 111 p. :   ISBN 0-520-06410-0 (alk. paper) DDC 941.9/6 19
BX2602.S54 H67 1989
        NYPL [3-MRBB+ 91-3376]

GREAT TEMPLE (ABÙ SUNBUL, EGYPT)
Desroches-Noblecourt, Christiane, 1913- Grand

temple d'Abou Simbel . Le Caire , 1971. vi, 65 leaves, xlii leaves of plates :
ND2865.A2 D4 1971

Great world atlas. Reader's Digest Association (Great Britain) The Reader's Digest great world atlas. London, Sydney [etc.] 1968. 179 p.   DDC 912
G1019 .R555 1968
        NYPL [Map Div. 90-12412]

Grechetto. Il Genio di Giovanni Benedetto Castiglione, il Grechetto /. Genova , c1990. 267 p. :   ISBN 88-7058-351-1
        NYPL [3-MCF C35 90-11510]

Grecian Heritage Foundation "Orpheus." New voices in Greek-American art . Brooklyn, N.Y. [1990] [40] p. :   *NYPL [MAMT 91-6992]*

Greco, 1541?-1614.
El Greco : loan exhibition for the benefit of the Greek War Relief Association, January 17 to February 15, 1941 : commemorating the 400th anniversary of the birth of El Greco : at the galleries of M. Knoedler and Company, Inc. New York : Art Aid Corporation, c1941. [41] p. : ill. ; 31 cm.
1. Greco, 1541?-1614 - Exhibitions. I. Greek War Relief Association. II. M. Knoedler & Co. III. Title.
        NYPL [3-MCQ+ T39 88-3794]

El Greco, mystery and illumination . [Edinburgh] [1989] 96 p. :   ISBN 0-903148-90-0
        NYPL [3-MCQ T39 90-10831]

L'opera completa del Greco / presentazione di Ganna Manzini ; apparati critici e filologici di Tiziana Frati. Nuova serie. Milano : Rizzoli Editore, 1978. 128 p. : ill. (some col.) ; 31 cm. (Classici dell' arte. 35) Bibliography: p. 82.
1. Greco, 1541?-1614 - Catalogues raisonnés. I. Manzini, Gianna. II. Frati, Tiziana. III. Title.
        NYPL [3-MCQ + T39 88-3246]

GRECO, 1541?-1614 - CRITICISM AND INTERPRETATION.
El Greco . Rethymno , 1990. 416 p. :   ISBN 960-7309-00-6 DDC 759.6 20
ND813.T4 E524 1990

GRECO, 1541?-1614 - CATALOGUES RAISONNÉS.
Greco, 1541?-1614. L'opera completa del Greco /. Milano : Rizzoli Editore, 1978. 128 p. :
        NYPL [3-MCQ + T39 88-3246]

GRECO, 1541?-1614 - EXHIBITIONS.
El Greco, mystery and illumination . [Edinburgh] [1989] 96 p. :   ISBN 0-903148-90-0
        NYPL [3-MCQ T39 90-10831]

Greco, 1541?-1614. El Greco . New York , c1941. [41] p. :
        NYPL [3-MCQ+ T39 88-3794]

GREECE - ANTIQUITIES.
Pfisterer-Haas, Susanne. Darstellungen alter Frauen in der griechischen Kunst /. Frankfurt am Main , 1989. xii, 237 p. :   ISBN 3-631-41559-1   *NYPL [3-MAMZ 91-4214]*

Schattner, Thomas G. Griechische Hausmodelle . Berlin , c1990. 229 p., [29] p. of plates :   ISBN 3-7861-1585-0
        NYPL [3-MQM 91-6516]

GREECE - ANTIQUITIES - PRIVATE COLLECTIONS - GERMANY - MÜNSTER IN WESTFALEN - CATALOGS.
Stupperich, Reinhard, 1951- Die Antiken der Sammlung Werner Peek /. Münster , 1990. 77 p., [16] leaves of plates :
        NYPL [3-MPEK 91-4659]

Greece - Archaeology. see Greece - Antiquities.

GREECE - BIOGRAPHY - PORTRAITS.
Ritratti greci /. Firenze [1990] 148 p., 48 p. of plates :   *NYPL [3-MGH 91-7395]*

GREECE - HISTORICAL GEOGRAPHY - MAPS.
Kontorlès, Kōnstantinos P. Historikos atlas . Athēnai , 1962. 39 p. :
        NYPL [Map Div. 86-229]

Greece. Hypourgeio Politismou. Athènes affaire européenne . Athènes , c1985. 2 v. :
NA1100 .A84 1985

GREECE IN ART - EXHIBITIONS.
Tsigakou, Fani-Maria. Through romantic eyes . Alexandria, Va. , 1991. p. cm.   ISBN

    0-88397-099-6 DDC 758/.9949506 20
N8214.5.G8 T784 1991

GREEK AMERICAN ARTISTS - BIOGRAPHY.
New voices in Greek-American art . Brooklyn, N.Y. [1990] [40] p. :
        NYPL [MAMT 91-6992]

GREEK ARCHITECTURE. see ARCHITECTURE, GREEK.

GREEK ART. see ART, GREEK.

Greek art of the Aegean Islands . New York (City). Metropolitan Museum of Art. New York , c1979. 238 p. :   ISBN 0-87099-216-3
N5640 .N48 1979   *NYPL [MAH 80-2168]*

GREEK BRONZES. see BRONZES, GREEK.

Greek church. see Orthodox Eastern Church.

GREEK MYTHOLOGY. see MYTHOLOGY, GREEK.

Greek pottery . Sparkes, Brian A. Manchester ; New York : p. cm.   ISBN 0-7190-2236-3 (cloth)   DDC 666/.3938 20
NK3840 .S65 1991

GREEK POTTERY. see POTTERY, GREEK.

GREEK SCULPTURE. see SCULPTURE, GREEK.

GREEK VASES. see VASES, GREEK.

Greek vases in the J. Paul Getty Museum.
Malibu, Calif. : The Museum, 1983- v. : ill. ; 28 cm. (Occasional papers on antiquities . v. 1-3, 5) English, French, and German. Includes bibliographical references.   ISBN 0-89236-058-5 (v. 1 : pbk.) DDC 738.3/0938/074019493 19
1. Vases, Greek. 2. Vase-painting, Greek. 3. Vases, Etruscan. 4. Vase-painting, Etruscan. 5. Vases - California - Malibu. I. J. Paul Getty Museum. II. Series: Occasional papers on antiquities , v. 1, etc.
NK4623.M37 G7 1983
        NYPL [3-MPEK 86-4692]

Greek War Relief Association. Greco, 1541?-1614. El Greco . New York , c1941. [41] p. :   *NYPL [3-MCQ+ T39 88-3794]*

Green architecture . Vale, Brenda. Boston , c1991. p. cm.   ISBN 0-8212-1866-2 DDC 720/.472 20
NA2542.3 .V35 1991

Green, Candida Lycett. see Lycett Green, Candida.

GREEN COUNTY (WIS.) - MAPS.
Rockford Map Publishers. Green County, Wisconsin, land atlas & plat book . Rockford, Ill. [c1990] 1 atlas (51 p.) :
        NYPL [Map Div. 91-4030]

Green County, Wisconsin, land atlas & plat book . Rockford Map Publishers. Rockford, Ill. [c1990] 1 atlas (51 p.) :
        NYPL [Map Div. 91-4030]

Green County, Wisconsin, land atlas and plat book. Rockford Map Publishers. Green County, Wisconsin, land atlas & plat book . Rockford, Ill. [c1990] 1 atlas (51 p.) :
        NYPL [Map Div. 91-4030]

Green, Marilyn V. The button lover's book / Marilyn V. Green. Radnor, Pa. : Chilton Book Co., c1991. p. cm. (Creative machine arts series) Includes bibliographical references and index.   ISBN 0-8019-8184-0 (hc) :   DDC 646/.19 20
1. Buttons - History. 2. Buttons - Collectors and collecting. I. Title. II. Series.
NK3668.5 .G7 1991

Green, Oliver. Underground art : London Transport posters, 1908 to the present / Oliver Green. London : Studio Vista, 1990. 144 p. : ill. (chiefly col.) ; 30 cm. Bibliography: p. 144.   ISBN 0-289-80037-4 :   DDC 769.4938842809421 20
1. London Regional Transport (Agency) - Posters. 2. Posters, British. 3. Posters - 20th century - Great Britain. I. Title.
HE311.G72L   *NYPL [3-MDW+ 90-11793]*

Green, Richard L. Historic Blacks in the arts /. Chicago, IL , c1990. p. cm.   ISBN 0-922162-58-1 :   DDC 700/.92/2 B 20
NX164.B55 H57 1990

Green, Richard, M. A. Murray, Hugh, M. A. York through the eyes of the artist /. York , c1990. 174 p. :   ISBN 0-903281-10-4 (pbk.) DDC 760.044442843 20
        NYPL [3-MAMY 91-5206]

Greenaway, Kate, 1846-1901.
Taylor, Ina. The art of Kate Greenaway .
Gretna, La. , 1991. 128 p. :   ISBN 0-88289-867-1
DDC 741.6/42/092 B 20
NC978.5.G7 T37 1991

Taylor, Ina. The art of Kate Greenaway .
Exeter, Devon , 1991. 128 p. :   ISBN
0-86350-397-7
NYPL [MDG (Greenaway) 91-8041]

GREENAWAY, KATE, 1846-1901.
Taylor, Ina. The art of Kate Greenaway .
Gretna, La. , 1991. 128 p. :   ISBN 0-88289-867-1
DDC 741.6/42/092 B 20
NC978.5.G7 T37 1991

Taylor, Ina. The art of Kate Greenaway .
Exeter, Devon , 1991. 128 p. :   ISBN
0-86350-397-7
NYPL [MDG (Greenaway) 91-8041]

Greenberg, Clement, 1909- Goodman, Cynthia.
Hans Hofmann /. New York , 1990. 200 p. :
ISBN 0-87427-070-7   DDC 759.13 20
ND237.H667 A4 1990
NYPL [3-MCK+ H71 90-12024]

Greene, Alison de Lima. Arman 1955-1991 : a
retrospective, the Museum of Fine Arts,
Houston / essays by Alison de Lima Greene
and Pierre Restany ; foreword by Peter C.
Marzio. Houston, Tex. : Museum of Fine Arts,
Houston, c1991. p. cm. Catalog of an exhibition
held at the Museum of Fine Arts, Houston, the
Brooklyn Museum, and the Detroit Institute of Arts.
Includes bibliographical references.   ISBN
0-89090-050-7 :   DDC 709/.2 20
*1. Arman, 1928- - Exhibitions. I. Restany, Pierre. II.
Museum of Fine Arts, Houston. III. Brooklyn Museum.
IV. Detroit. Institute of Arts. V. Title.*
N6853.A69 A4 1991

Greene, Joshua. Mary Emmerling's American
country flags /. New York , 1991. p. cm.   ISBN
0-517-58366-6 :   DDC 929.9/2/0973 20
NK839.E46 A4 1991

Greenfield-Sanders, Timothy. Salle, David, 1952-
David Salle . New York , 1991. 1 v.
(unpaged) :   ISBN 0-9624347-7-9
NYPL [3-MCX+ S167 91-6681]

Greenhouse, Wendy, 1955- The art of Archibald
J. Motley, Jr. / by Wendy Greenhouse and
Jontyle T. Robinson ; with an introduction by
Floyd Coleman. Chicago, IL : Chicago
Historical Society, 1991. p. cm. Accompanies an
exhibition by the Chicago Historical Society. Includes
index.   ISBN 0-913820-15-6 :   DDC 759.13 20
*1. Motley, Archibald John, 1891- - Exhibitions. I.
Robinson, Jontyle Theresa. II. Motley, Archibald John,
1891-. III. Chicago Historical Society. IV. Title.*
ND237.M8524 A4 1991

GREENOUGH, HORATIO, 1805-1852.
Crane, Sylvia E. White silence . Coral Gables
[Fla., 1972] xviii, 499 p. :   ISBN 0-87024-199-0
DDC 730/.973
NB236 .C72   ***NYPL [3-MGI 90-11552]***

Greenough, Sarah, 1951- Paul Strand : an
American vision / Sarah Greenough. New
York, NY : Aperture Foundation, in association
with the National Gallery of Art, Washington.
171 p. : ill., ports. ; 34 cm. Catalog of an
exhibition held at the National Gallery of Art, Dec. 2,
1990-Feb. 3, 1991 ; Art Institute of Chicago, May
26-July 21, 1991 ; St. Louis Art Museum, Aug. 11-Oct.
6, 1991, and at 4 other locations through Nov. 1992.
Includes bibliographical references (p. 169-171).   ISBN
0-89381-442-3
*1. Strand, Paul, 1890-1976 - Exhibitions. 2.
Photography, Artistic - Exhibitions. I. Strand, Paul,
1890-1976. II. National Gallery of Art (U. S.). III.
Aperture Foundation. IV. Title.*
NYPL [MFX+ (Strand) 91-4965]

Greenstein, Jack Matthew. Mantegna and
painting as historical narrative / Jack M.
Greenstein. Chicago : University of Chicago
Press, 1992. p. cm. Includes bibliographical
references (p.) and index.   ISBN 0-226-30707-7
DDC 759.5 20
*1. Mantegna, Andrea, 1431-1506 - Criticism and
interpretation. 2. History in art. 3. Jesus Christ - Art. I.
Title.*
ND623.M3 G7 1992

Greenville Co., S. C. Museum of Art. see
Greenville County Museum of Art.

Greenville County Museum of Art. Fitzpatrick,
Kelly (John Kelly) A symphony of color .
Montgomery, Ala. , 1991. p. cm.   ISBN
0-89280-028-3   DDC 759.13 20
ND237.F455 A4 1991

Greenville, S. C. County Museum of Art. see
Greenville County Museum of Art.

Greer, Nora Richter. Rowan, Bob, 1944- A
capital perspective . Chatsworth, Calif. , 1991.
p. cm.   ISBN 0-89781-427-4   DDC 720/.9753 20
NA735.W3 R69 1991

GREETING CARDS - DESIGN.
Gray, Bill. Tips on making greeting cards /.
New York, NY , c1991. 136 p. :   ISBN
0-8306-0595-9 :   DDC 741.6/84 20
NC1860 .G64 1991

Gref, Franz Heinrich, 1872-1957.
Franz Heinrich Gref : Aspekte zu seinem
Leben und seinem Werk : Werkverzeichnis. 1.
Aufl. Bierlingen : Donzelli-Kluckert, 1987. 167
p. : ill. (some col.) ; 22 cm.   ISBN 3-9801521-2-X
1. Gref, Franz Heinrich, 1872-1957 - Catalogs.
NYPL [3-MCK G792 90-12342]

GREF, FRANZ HEINRICH, 1872-1957 -
CATALOGS.
Gref, Franz Heinrich, 1872-1957. Franz
Heinrich Gref . Bierlingen , 1987. 167 p. :
ISBN 3-9801521-2-X
NYPL [3-MCK G792 90-12342]

Greff, Jean-Pierre. Bazaine, Jean, 1904- Bazaine.
Paris , c1990. 178 p. :   ISBN 2-605-00162-8
NYPL [3-MCO B35 90-12858]

GRÉGOIRE, AUGUSTE, 1888-1971 -
PHOTOGRAPH COLLECTIONS.
Rijksuniversiteit te Leiden. Prentenkabinet. Het
Fotografisch Museum van Auguste Grégoire .
s'Gravenhage , 1989. 208 p.:   ISBN
90-12-06303-5   ***NYPL [MFW 91-3485]***

Gregori, Mina. La Pittura in Italia . [Milano ,
1989, c1988. 2 v. (967 p.) :
NYPL [3-MCE 90-11795]

Gregory, Alexis. Donzel, Catherine. Palaces et
grands hôtels d'Amérique du Nord /. Paris ,
c1989. 255 p. :   ISBN 2-08-201846-6   DDC
728/.5/0973 20
NA7840 .D67 1989

Gregory Gillespie, paintings (Italy 1962-1970).
Gillespie, Gregory, 1936- New York , 1970. 55
p. :   ***NYPL [3-MCX+ G477 91-1181]***

Greifswald. Universität. Sektion Geographie.
Historische Karten aus der Sammlung der
Ernst-Moritz-Arndt-Universitat Greifswald in
der Sektion Geographie /. Greifswald , 1981. 1
portfolio (20 maps (some col.)) ;
NYPL [Map Div. 86-337]

Greiman, April.
April Greiman, large scale posters. [Cullowhee,
N.C.] , c1987. v, 27 p. :
NYPL [3-MDWS (Greiman) 90-12807]

Hybrid imagery : the fusion of technology and
graphic design / April Greiman ; with
overviews by Eric Martin. New York :
Watson-Guptill, 1990. 158 p. : ill. (some col.) ;
27 cm.   ISBN 0-8230-2518-7 :   DDC 741.6 20
*1. Commercial art - United States - Themes, motives. 2.
Computer art - United States - Themes, motives. 3.
Graphic arts - United States - Themes, motives. I. Title.*
NC998.5.A1 G75 1990
NYPL [3-MDW 90-10910]

GREIMAN, APRIL - EXHIBITIONS.
April Greiman, large scale posters. [Cullowhee,
N.C.] , c1987. v, 27 p. :
NYPL [3-MDWS (Greiman) 90-12807]

Greindl, Gabriele.
[Strass. English]
Gems of costume jewelry / Gabriele
Greindl ; with an introduction by Dominica
Volkert ; translated from the German by
Laura Lindgren. New York : Abbeville Press,
1991. p. cm. Translation of: Strass. Includes
bibliographical references and index.   ISBN
1-558-59207-5   DDC 391/.7 20
1. Costume jewelry. I. Title.
NK4890.C67 G7413 1991

Greiner, P. Sozialistische Staaten Mittel- und
Südosteuropas /. Gotha , 1986. 1 atlas (190
p.) :   ISBN 3-7301-0032-7
NYPL [Map Div. 91-3783]

Les Grès contemporains en France : [exposition]

Sèvres, Musée national de céramique,
mai-juillet, 1963. [Paris] : Ministère d'Etat
affaires culteurelles, [1963] 29 p., [4] leaves of
plates : ill. ; 21 cm. "Avant-propos" signed: H.P.
Fourest.
*1. Pottery - France - Exhibitions. 2. Pottery - 20th
century - France - Marks. I. Musée national de
céramique (France).*   ***NYPL [3-MPGG 90-6052]***

Greune, Karl Heinrich, 1933-
Karl Heinrich Greune : Gemälde, Handzeichn.,
Druckgraphik : Ausstellung, Kunsthalle Bremen,
19. August-16. September 1979 /
[Katalogbearb., Gerhard Gerkens]. Bremen :
Kunsthalle, [1979] [80] p. : chiefly ill. (some
col.) ; 22 cm.
*1. Greune, Karl Heinrich, 1933- - Exhibitions. I.
Gerkens, Gerhard. II. Bremen. Kunsthalle.*
N6888.G733 A4 1979
NYPL [3-MCK G837 81-784]

GREUNE, KARL HEINRICH, 1933- -
EXHIBITIONS.
Greune, Karl Heinrich, 1933- Karl Heinrich
Greune . Bremen [1979] [80] p. :
N6888.G733 A4 1979
NYPL [3-MCK G837 81-784]

Grewe, Cordula. Thomann, Ernst, 1910- Ernst
Thomann--Einsichten . Emmendingen , c1990.
69 p. :   ISBN 3-925928-13-8
NB588.T39 A4 1990

Grewenig, Meinrad Maria, 1954- Der Akt in der
deutschen Renaissance : die Einheit von
Nacktheit und Leib in der bildenden Kunst /
Meinrad Maria Grewenig. Freren : Luca, 1987.
143 p., [100] p. of plates : 150 ill. ; 22 cm.
(Wissenschaft und Forschung ; Bd. 1) Originally
presented as the author's thesis (doctoral)--Paris Lodron
Universität in Salzburg, 1983. Includes index.
Bibliography: p. 129-137.   ISBN 3-923641-07-9   DDC
704.9/421/0943 19
*1. Art, Renaissance - Germany. I. Series: Wissenschaft
und Forschung (Freren, Germany) , Bd. 1. II. Title.*
N6865 .G74 1987
NYPL [3-MAMG 91-4610]

Grey, Alex.
Sacred mirrors : the visionary art of Alex Grey
/ with essays by Ken Wilber, Carlo
McCormick, Alex Grey. Rochester, Vt. : Inner
Traditions International, c1990. 96 p. : ill.
(some col.) ; 35 cm. Includes bibliographical
references (p. 96).   ISBN 0-89281-257-5   DDC
759.13 20
*1. Grey, Alex - Philosophy. 2. Grey, Alex - Criticism
and interpretation. I. Wilber, Ken. II. McCormick,
Carlo. III. Title.*
N6537.G718 S23 1990
NYPL [3-MCX+ G842 90-13202]

GREY, ALEX - CRITICISM AND
INTERPRETATION.
Grey, Alex. Sacred mirrors . Rochester, Vt. ,
c1990. 96 p. :   ISBN 0-89281-257-5   DDC 759.13
20
N6537.G718 S23 1990
NYPL [3-MCX+ G842 90-13202]

GREY, ALEX - PHILOSOPHY.
Grey, Alex. Sacred mirrors . Rochester, Vt. ,
c1990. 96 p. :   ISBN 0-89281-257-5   DDC 759.13
20
N6537.G718 S23 1990
NYPL [3-MCX+ G842 90-13202]

Grey Art Gallery & Study Center. Hujar, Peter,
1934- Peter Hujar /. New York, N.Y. , 1990.
95 p. :   ISBN 0-934349-07-X (pbk.)
IN PROCESS (ONLINE)
NYPL [MFX (Hujar) 91-830]

Griechische Hausmodelle . Schattner, Thomas G.
Berlin , c1990. 229 p., [29] p. of plates :   ISBN
3-7861-1585-0   ***NYPL [3-MQM 91-6516]***

Griechische Skulpturen und Fragmente .
Staatliche Kunstsammlungen Dresden.
Skulpturensammlung. [Dresden] , c1989. 96 p. :
DDC 733/.3/074432142 20
NB87.D73 S737 1989

Griechisches Bauwesen in der Antike /.
Müller-Wiener, Wolfgang. München , c1988.
221 p. :   ISBN 3-406-32993-4
NYPL [3-MQM 90-12379]

Grieco, Romy. Lucca : town of art / Romy
Grieco. Bologna, Italy : Italcards ; Lucca :
Distribution Renzo Santori, [1990?] 99 p. : col.
ill. ; 29 cm. Includes index.   DDC 709/.45/53 20
1. Art, Italian - Italy - Lucca - Guide-books. 2.

Architecture - Italy - Lucca - Guide-books. 3. Lucca (Italy) - Description - Guide-books. 4. Lucca (Italy) - Buildings, structures, etc. - Guide-books. I. Title.
N6921.L82 G74 1990

Griesebach, Lucius. Buchstäblich Nürnberger wörtliche Tage . [Nürnberg] , c1990. 80 p. :   ISBN 3-922531-77-6
NX458 .B83 1990

Grieshaber . Grieshaber, Helmut A. P., 1909- Stuttgart , 1984-c1986. 2 v. :   ISBN 3-7757-0221-0 (Bd. 1)   DDC 769.92/4 19
NE1150.5.G7 A4 1984a
        NYPL [MDG+ (Grieshaber) 91-1093]

Grieshaber . Grieshaber, Helmut A. P., 1909- Bonn , c1989. 190 p. :   ISBN 3-416-02188-6 (Katalog)   ***NYPL [3-MCK G84 91-5878]***

Grieshaber, das Werk . Grieshaber, Helmut A. P., 1909- Stuttgart , c1989. 309, [1] p. :   ISBN 3-7757-0280-6   DDC 760/.092 20
NE1150.5.G7 A4 1989
        NYPL [MDG+ (Grieshaber) 90-5070]

Grieshaber, Helmut A. P., 1909-
Grieshaber : die Druckgraphik : Werkverzeichnis / [herausgegeben von] Margot Fürst ; Einleitung, Heinz Spielmann. Stuttgart : G. Hatje, 1984-c1986. 2 v. : ill. (some col.) ; 33 cm. Includes indexes. Vol. 1 issued 1986. CONTENTS. - Bd. 1. 1932-1965 -- Bd. 2. 1966-1981. ISBN 3-7757-0221-0 (Bd. 1)   DDC 769.92/4 19
1. Grieshaber, Helmut A. P., 1909- - Catalogs. I. Fürst, Margot. II. Spielmann, Heinz. III. Title. IV. Title: Druckgraphik.
NE1150.5.G7 A4 1984a
        NYPL [MDG+ (Grieshaber) 91-1093]

Grieshaber : der Holzschneider als Maler : Gouachen, Malbriefe, Aquarelle, Holzschnitte, Zeichnungen / herausgegeben von Johannes Göbel und Wolfgang Glöckner. Bonn : Bouvier, c1989. 190 p. : chiefly ill. (chiefly col.) ; 24 x 27 cm. ISBN 3-416-02188-6 (Katalog)
1. Grieshaber, Helmut A. P., 1909-. I. Göbel, Johannes. II. Glöckner, Wolfgang. III. Title.
        NYPL [3-MCK G84 91-5878]

Grieshaber, das Werk : Hommage zum 80. Geburtstag / herausgegeben von Margot Fürst. Stuttgart : Hatje, c1989. 309, [1] p. : chiefly ill. (some col.) ; 32 cm. Includes bibliographical references (p. 308-[310]). ISBN 3-7757-0280-6   DDC 760/.092 20
1. Grieshaber, Helmut A. P., 1909- - Catalogs. I. Fürst, Margot. II. Title.
NE1150.5.G7 A4 1989
        NYPL [MDG+ (Grieshaber) 90-5070]

HAP Grieshaber, Farbholzschnitte : [eine Ausstellung des Instituts für Auslandsbeziehungen, Stuttgart / verantwortlich, Hermann Pollig, Viola Suhle ; mit Beiträgen von Wilhelm Boeck, Margarete Hannsmann].Veränderte Aufl. Stuttgart : Das Institut, c1983. 43 p., 73 leaves of plates : chiefly ill. (chiefly col.) ; 25 cm. In portfolio.
1. Grieshaber, Helmut A. P., 1909- - Exhibitions. I. Institut für Auslandbeziehungen. II. Title. III. Title: H.A.P. Grieshaber, Farbholzschnitte. IV. Title: Farbholzschnitte.
        NYPL [MDG (Grieshaber) 90-13133]

GRIESHABER, HELMUT A. P., 1909-
Grieshaber, Helmut A. P., 1909- Grieshaber . Bonn , c1989. 190 p. :   ISBN 3-416-02188-6 (Katalog)   ***NYPL [3-MCK G84 91-5878]***

GRIESHABER, HELMUT A. P., 1909- - CATALOGS.
Grieshaber, Helmut A. P., 1909- Grieshaber . Stuttgart , 1984-c1986. 2 v. :   ISBN 3-7757-0221-0 (Bd. 1)   DDC 769.92/4 19
NE1150.5.G7 A4 1984a
        NYPL [MDG+ (Grieshaber) 91-1093]

Grieshaber, Helmut A. P., 1909- Grieshaber, das Werk . Stuttgart , c1989. 309, [1] p. :   ISBN 3-7757-0280-6   DDC 760/.092 20
NE1150.5.G7 A4 1989
        NYPL [MDG+ (Grieshaber) 90-5070]

GRIESHABER, HELMUT A. P., 1909- - EXHIBITIONS.
Grieshaber, Helmut A. P., 1909- HAP Grieshaber, Farbholzschnitte . Stuttgart , c1983. 43 p., 73 leaves of plates :
        NYPL [MDG (Grieshaber) 90-13133]

GRIFFA, GIORGIO.
Fossati, Paolo 1938- Giorgio Griffa /.

Ravenna , c1990. 161 p. :
IN PROCESS (ONLINE)
        NYPL [3-MCF G847 91-2466]

Griffin, David J. FitzGerald, Desmond. Vanishing country houses of Ireland /. [Dublin] [Leixlip] , 1988. vi, 161 p. :   ISBN 0-948018-04-6
        NYPL [3-MRGF 89-17124]

Griffin, Lillian Baynes. One thousand and twenty, Fifth Avenue, New York. [New York, c1912] [56] leaves :
NA7238.N6 S2
        NYPL [3-MQWO+ 84-2021]

Griffin, Marion Mahony, 1871-1962.
Walter Burley Griffin . Clayton, Vic. , 1988. 75 p. :   ISBN 0-86746-860-2
        NYPL [3-MQZ+ (Griffin) 90-2584]

GRIFFIN, MARION MAHONY, 1871-1962 - EXHIBITIONS.
Walter Burley Griffin . Clayton, Vic. , 1988. 75 p. :   ISBN 0-86746-860-2
        NYPL [3-MQZ+ (Griffin) 90-2584]

Griffin, Walter Burley, 1876-1937.
Walter Burley Griffin . Clayton, Vic. , 1988. 75 p. :   ISBN 0-86746-860-2
        NYPL [3-MQZ+ (Griffin) 90-2584]

GRIFFIN, WALTER BURLEY, 1876-1937 - EXHIBITIONS.
Walter Burley Griffin . Clayton, Vic. , 1988. 75 p. :   ISBN 0-86746-860-2
        NYPL [3-MQZ+ (Griffin) 90-2584]

Grigor Tatevats'i ev Ananun Syunets'i = Grigor Tatevatsi i Anonim iz Siūnika = Grigor Tatevatsi and Anonymous painter of Syunig / kazmets', arajabanˇev tsanot'ag. grets' Alvida Mirzoyanē]. Erevan : "Sovetakan grogh", 1987. 165 p. : ill. (some col.) ; 33 cm. In Armenian, Russian and English. "Matenadaran, Hayk. SSH Ministrneri Khoshrdin a rēnt'er Mashtots'i anvan Hin Dze ragreri Institut." "Explanations of the miniatures": p. 162-165. Bibliography:p. [167].
1. Illuminations of books and manuscripts - Armenian S.S.R. 2. Miniature painting - Armenian S.S.R. I. Mirzoyan, Alvida.   ***NYPL [3-MCY+ 90-4058]***

GRIGORESCU, LUCIAN, 1894- - CRITICISM AND INTERPRETATION.
Cârneci, Magda. Lucian Grigorescu /. [Bucharest] , 1989. 77 p., [64] p. of plates :
        NYPL [3-MCZ+ G849 89-24509]

Grigorovich, D. V. (Dmitriĭ Vasil′evich), 1822-1899.
[Novye priobretenie Ėrmitazha]
Novyĭa priobrietenīīa Ėrmitazha : "Madonna" Līonardo da Vinchi. "Sud Apollona nad Marsiem" Korredzhio / D.V. Grigorovicha. S. Peterburg : V tip. V.N. Maĭkova, 1865. 61 p. ; 16 cm. Source: Purchase from Gennadiĭ Vasil′evich Yudin. 1906. DLC Includes bibliographical references.
1. Painting, Renaissance - Italy. 2. Painting, Italian. 3. Painting - Russian S.F.S.R. - Leningrad. 4. Gosudarstvennyĭ Ėrmitazh (Soviet Union). I. Gosudarstvennyĭ Ėrmitazh (Soviet Union). II. Title.
ND615 .G75 1985

Grimm, Claus.
[Frans Hals--das Gesamtwerk. English]
Frans Hals--the complete work / Claus Grimm ; translated from the German by Jürgen Riehle. New York : H.N. Abrams, 1990. 296 p. : ill. (some col.) ; 35 cm. Includes index. Translation of: Frans Hals--das Gesamtwerk. Includes bibliographical references.   ISBN 0-8109-3404-3   DDC 759.9492 20
1. Hals, Frans, 1584-1666 - Criticism and interpretation. 2. Hals, Frans, 1584-1666 - Catalogs. I. Hals, Frans, 1584-1666. II. Title.
ND653.H2 G7313 1990
        NYPL [MCH+ H2 91-3380]

Grimm, Günter. Kunst der Ptolemäer- und Römerzeit im Ägyptischen Museum Kairo / Günter Grimm ; unter Mitarbeit von Mohiy Ibrahim und Mohammed Mohsen ; Aufnahmen von Dieter Johannes. Mainz : Philip von Zabern, [1975] 34 p, 118 p., [6] leaves of plates : ill. (some col.), map ; 32 cm. Bibliography: p. 15.
1. Mathaf al-Misri. 2. Art, Hellenistic - Egypt - Catalogs. 3. Art, Roman - Egypt - Catalogs. 4. Art - Egypt - Catalogs. I. Johannes, Dieter. II. Mathaf al-Misri. III. Title.
N5888.A1 G74   ***NYPL [3-MAH 90-5474]***

Grimm, Reinhold. Laughter unlimited . Madison, Wis. , 1991. vii, 135 p. :   ISBN 0-299-97073-6 :   DDC 837.009 20
NX550.A1 L38 1991   ***NYPL [JFE 91-3649]***

Grimme, Ernst Günther. Sammlung Teo Matthéy, Aachen . [Aachen] , c1989. 109 p.
        NYPL [3-MAX (Matthéy) 91-3454]

Grimmer, Anne E. The Secretary of the Interior's standards for rehabilitation and Illustrated guidelines for rehabilitating historic buildings /. Washington, D.C. , 1991. p. cm.   DDC 720/.28/8021873 20
NA106 .S4 1991

GRIMSHAW, NICHOLAS.
Jenkins, David. Financial Times Print Works, London, 1988 . London , New York , 1991. ca. 60 p. :   ISBN 1-85454-255-9 (pbk.) :   DDC 725.4 20
NA6400
        NYPL [3-MQZ+ (Grimshaw) 91-6989]

Grimwade, Arthur. London goldsmiths, 1697-1837 : their marks and lives : from the original registers at Goldsmiths' Hall and other sources / by Arthur G. Grimwade.3rd rev. and enl. ed. London : Faber and Faber, 1990. ix, 773 p., [5] p. of plates : ill. ; 26 cm.   ISBN 0-571-15238-4   DDC 739.2/092/2 19
1. Goldsmiths - England - London - Biography. 2. Silversmiths - England - London - Biography. 3. Hallmarks - England - London. 4. London (England) - Biography. I. Title.
NK7144.L66   ***NYPL [MNO 90-13187]***

GRINTEN, JOSEPH VAN DER - ART COLLECTIONS - EXHIBITIONS.
Beuys, Joseph. Joseph Beuys . Hannover [1990] 267 p. :   DDC 759.3 20
N6888.B463 A4 1990

Gris, Juan, 1887-1927.
Juan Gris : correspondance, dessins 1915-1921 : IVAM Centre Julio González du 23 octobre 1990 au 13 janvier 1991, Centre Georges Pompidou, Musée national d'art moderne du 29 janvier 1991 au 1er avril 1991 / texte établi et annoté par Christian Derouet. [Valencia, Spain] : IVAM Centre Julio González ; [Paris, France] : Centre Georges Pompidou, [1990] 150 p. : ill. (some col.) ; 24 cm. "Correspondance Juan Gris - Léonce Rosenberg": p. [23]-73. Includes bibliographical references (p. 101-102) and index. ISBN 2-85850-595-0
1. Gris, Juan, 1887-1927 - Exhibitions. 2. Gris, Juan, 1887-1927 - Correspondence. 3. Artists - Spain - Correspondence. I. Derouet, Christian. II. Rosenberg, Léonce, 1879-1947. III. IVAM Centre Julio González. IV. Musée national d'art moderne (France). V. Title.
NC287.G76 A4 1990

GRIS, JUAN, 1887-1927 - CORRESPONDENCE.
Gris, Juan, 1887-1927. Juan Gris . [Valencia, Spain] [Paris, France] [1990] 150 p. :   ISBN 2-85850-595-0
NC287.G76 A4 1990

GRIS, JUAN, 1887-1927 - EXHIBITIONS.
Gris, Juan, 1887-1927. Juan Gris . [Valencia, Spain] [Paris, France] [1990] 150 p. :   ISBN 2-85850-595-0
NC287.G76 A4 1990

Grisebach, Renate. Neuer Berliner Kunstverein. 20 Jahre NBK . Berlin [1989] 233 p. :
        NYPL [3-MAVZ (Berlin) 91-6480]

Grisi, Laura.
Laura Grisi : a selection of works and notes by the artist / essay-interview by Germano Celant. New York : Rizzoli International Publications, 1990. 276 p. : ill. (some col.) ; 31 cm. Includes bibliographical references (p. [265]-273).   ISBN 0-8478-1222-7   DDC 709/.2 20
1. Grisi, Laura - Interviews. 2. Artists - Italy - Interviews. I. Celant, Germano. II. Title.
N6923.G73 A35 1990
        NYPL [3-MGO+ (Grisi) 91-3273]

GRISI, LAURA - INTERVIEWS.
Grisi, Laura. Laura Grisi . New York , 1990. 276 p. :   ISBN 0-8478-1222-7   DDC 709/.2 20
N6923.G73 A35 1990
        NYPL [3-MGO+ (Grisi) 91-3273]

Grisoli-Struve, Marie-Catherine, 1917-1987.
Marie-Catherine Grisoli-Struve : oeuvres : poémes, dessins, peintures 1917-1987. Paris : L. Laget, 1988. 1 v. (unpaged) : ill. (chiefly col.) ;

31 cm. ISBN 2-85204-114-6
1. Grisoli-Struve, Marie-Catherine, 1917-1987. I. Title.
NYPL [3-MCO+ G85 90-8022]

GRISOLI-STRUVE, MARIE-CATHERINE, 1917-1987.
Grisoli-Struve, Marie-Catherine, 1917-1987. Marie-Catherine Grisoli-Struve . Paris , 1988. 1 v. (unpaged) : ISBN 2-85204-114-6
NYPL [3-MCO+ G85 90-8022]

Griswold del Castillo, Richard. Chicano art . Los Angeles , 1991. p. cm. ISBN 0-943739-16-0 : DDC 704/.0368/7207307479494 20
N6538.M4 C45 1991

Griswold, William. Metropolitan Museum of Art (New York, N.Y.) 18th century Italian drawings in the Metropolitan Museum of Art /. New York , 1990. 288 p. : ISBN 0-87099-585-5 DDC 741.945/074/7471 20
NC255 .M4 1990
NYPL [3-MAVZ (New York) 91-3640]

Gritchenko, Alexis, 1883- Alexis Gritchenko . Paris , c1964. 83 p. :
NYPL [3-MCZ G874 91-903]

GRITCHENKO, ALEXIS, 1883-
Alexis Gritchenko . Paris , c1964. 83 p. :
NYPL [3-MCZ G874 91-903]

Gritton, Joy L. Archuleta, Margaret, 1950- Shared visions . Phoenix, Ariz. , 1991. 110 p. : ISBN 0-934351-21-X : DDC 704/.0397/0904 20
N6538.A4 A7 1991

Grobman. Grobman, Mikhail. Michail Grobman, Künstler und Sammler . Bochum [1988] 1 v. (unpaged) : ISBN 3-8093-0123-X
N6999.G76 A4 1988

Grobman, Mikhail.
Michail Grobman, Künstler und Sammler : [Ausstellung], Museum Bochum, 11.6-7.8.1988, Museum Tel Aviv / [Redaktion und graphische Gestaltung, Peter Spielmann ; Textbeiträge, Michail Grobman, Peter Spielmann, Marc Scheps ; Übersetzung aus dem Russischen, Peter Spielmann]. Bochum : Oberstadtdirektor : Das Museum, [1988] 1 v. (unpaged) : chiefly ill. (some col.) ; 25 cm. (Veröffentlichungen zur osteuropäischen Kultur. Reihe Dokumente und Beiträge zur russischen bildenden Kunst und Literatur . Bd. 2) Half title: Grobman. Includes bibliographical references. ISBN 3-8093-0123-X
1. Grobman, Mikhail - Exhibitions. 2. Grobman, Mikhail - Art collections - Exhibitions. 3. Art, Russian - Exhibitions. 4. Art - Private collections - Israel - Exhibitions. I. Spielmann, Peter, Dr. II. Scheps, Marc. III. Museum Bochum. IV. Muze'on Tel Aviv. V. Title. VI. Title: Künstler und Sammler. VII. Title: Grobman. VIII. Series.
N6999.G76 A4 1988

GROBMAN, MIKHAIL - ART COLLECTIONS - EXHIBITIONS.
Grobman, Mikhail. Michail Grobman, Künstler und Sammler . Bochum [1988] 1 v. (unpaged) : ISBN 3-8093-0123-X
N6999.G76 A4 1988

GROBMAN, MIKHAIL - EXHIBITIONS.
Grobman, Mikhail. Michail Grobman, Künstler und Sammler . Bochum [1988] 1 v. (unpaged) : ISBN 3-8093-0123-X
N6999.G76 A4 1988

Grodecki, Louis, 1910- Le Moyen Age retrouvé / Louis Grodecki. Paris : Flammarion, c1986- v. : ill. ; 24 cm. (Idées et recherches) "Bibliographie de Louis Grodecki", v. 1, p. 15-[29] Includes bibliographical references and indexes. CONTENTS. - 1. De l'an mil à l'an 1200 -- 2. De Saint Louis à Viollet-le-Duc ISBN 2-08-012607-5 (v. 1) DDC 709/.02/1 19
I. Title.
N6280 .G76 1986   **NYPL [3-MAK 87-1158]**

Groenhart, Barbara. Henderikse, Jan, 1937- Modern times . Kiel , c1990. 65 p. :
NYPL [MFX (Henderikse) 91-4590]

Grösse--klein : Schweizer Kunst zwischen Kleinplastik und Objekt von Alberto Giacometti bis heute = Dimension--petit : l'art suisse entre petite sculpture et objet d'Alberto Giacometti à nos jours / herausgegeben von Erika Billeter ; Beiträge von Erika Billeter, Reinhold Hohl, Dieter Honisch. Bern : Benteli Verlag, c1989. 292 p. : ill. (some col.) ; 28 cm. German and French. Catalog of an exhibition held Oct. 7-Dec. 24, 1989, at the Musée cantonal des Beaux-arts, Lausanne.

Includes bibliographical references.
1. Small sculpture - 20th century - Switzerland - Exhibitions. 2. Sculpture, Modern - 20th century - Exhibitions. I. Billeter, Erika, 1927-. II. Hohl, Reinhold. III. Honisch, Dieter. IV. Musée cantonal des beaux-arts Lausanne. V. Title: Dimension--petit.
NYPL [3-MGI 91-5536]

Die Grötzinger Malerkolonie : die erste Generation, 1890-1920, Karl Biese, Jenny Fikentscher, Otto Fikentscher, Franz Hein, Margarethe Hormuth-Kallmorgen, Friedrich Kallmorgen, Gustav Kampmann : Ausstellung in der Staatlichen Kunsthalle Karlsruhe vom 28. November 1975 bis zum 1. Februar 1976. Karlsruhe : Staatliche Kunsthalle Karlsruhe, c1975. 239 p. : ill. (some col.) ; 21 cm. Includes bibliographies.
1. Grötzinger Malerkolonie. 2. Painting, Modern - 19th century - Germany - Exhibitions. 3. Painting, Modern - 20th century - Germany - Exhibitions. 4. Painting, German - Exhibitions. I. Biese, Karl, 1863-1926. II. Staatliche Kunsthalle Karlsruhe.
N6867.5.G7 G76   **NYPL [3-MCI 90-7040]**

Groh, Klaus, 1936- Der neue Dadaismus in Nordamerika / Klaus Groh. Augsburg : Maro Verlag, 1979. 221 p. : ill. ; 21 cm. (Reihe wissenschaftlicher Texte . Bd. 13) Originally presented as the author's thesis (doctoral--Oldenburg, 1979) under the title: Untersuchungen über Erscheinungsformen und Kommunikationsformen des "Neuen Dadaismus" in Nordamerika und seine pädagogische Bedeutung. Bibliography: p. 205-214. ISBN 3-87512-113-9
1. Dadaism - United States. 2. Dadaism - Canada. 3. Art, Modern - 20th century - United States. 4. Art, Modern - 20th century - Canada. I. Title.
NYPL [3-MAL 90-7185]

Grohs, Fritz.
   Josef Danner. 1988. Oberhuber, Konrad. Herbert Brandl, Josef Danner, Otto Zitko / Konrad Oberhuber. Wien , 1988. 4 v. in 1 :
NYPL [3-MCK B818 90-8683]

Grolier Club. Schneider, Rona. American painter etchings, 1853-1908 . New York City [1989] 48 p. : ISBN 0-910672-06-7 (pbk.)
NYPL [MDBF 89-19631]

Gromer, Alfred. Kunst des Abendlandes /. Karlsruhe , c1960-<c1963. v. <1-3 > : DDC 709 20
N5300 .K96 1960

Gromme, Owen J. The world of Owen Gromme / introduction by Roger Tory Peterson ; biography by Michael Mentzer ; commentaries by Judith Redline Coopey. 2nd ed. Minocqua, WI : NorthWord, 1991. p. cm. Includes index. ISBN 1-559-71130-2 : DDC 759.13 B 20
1. Gromme, Owen J. 2. Painters - United States - Biography. 3. Birds in art. 4. Animals in art. I. Mentzer, Michael. II. Coopey, Judith Redline. III. Title.
ND237.G665 A2 1991

GROMME, OWEN J.
Gromme, Owen J. The world of Owen Gromme /. Minocqua, WI , 1991. p. cm. ISBN 1-559-71130-2 : DDC 759.13 B 20
ND237.G665 A2 1991

Gröne, Ulla. Helmuth Seible : ein schwäbischer Maler im Aufbruch vom Impressionismus zur Moderne : eine Ausstellung in der Galerie Gottschick im Frühjahr 1991 in Verbindung mit der Universitätsstadt Tübingen / bearbeitet von Ulla Gröne. Tübingen : Universitätsstadt Tübingen, c1991. 48 p. : col. ill. ; 20 x 21 cm. (Tübinger Kataloge . Nr. 34) DDC 803/.1 s 759.3 20
1. Seible, Helmuth, 1889-1955 - Exhibitions. I. Seible, Helmuth, 1889-1955. II. Galerie Gottschick. III. Title. IV. Series.
N390.G32 T8 Nr. 34 ND588.S447

GRÖNINGER, GERHARD, 1582-1652.
Jászai, Géza, 1931- Das Werk des Bildhauers Gerhard Gröninger, 1582-1652 /. Münster , 1989. 207 p. : ISBN 3-88789-090-6
NYPL [3-MGO (Gröninger) 91-6968]

Groninger Museum. Minder kan het niet . Groningen , c1989. 103 p. :
NYPL [3-MAL 90-12610]

Groom, A. J. R. Frameworks for international co-operation /. London , 1990. x, 293 p. ; ISBN 0-86187-537-0 : DDC 327.17 20
JX1954
NYPL [JLE 90-2359]

Groot, Elbrig. Ruscha, Edward. Edward Ruscha . Rotterdam [1989] 152 p : ISBN 90-6918-048-0
NYPL [3-MCX R95 90-11542]

Groot, Irene de. Maritime prints by the Dutch Masters / selected, introduced and annotated by Irene de Groot and Robert Vorstman ; translated from the Dutch by Michael Hoyle. London : Gordon Fraser, 1980. 284 p. : ill. (some folded) ; 31 cm. Most prints illustrated in this work are from the printroom of the Rijksmuseum, Amsterdam. This is a companion volume to Landscape etchings by the Dutch masters of the seventeenth century. "Glossary:" p. 279-281. "Biographies:" p. 272-276. Includes index. Bibliography: p. 277-278. ISBN 0-86092-052-6
1. Marine art - Netherlands - Catalogs. 2. Prints, Dutch - Catalogs. 3. Naval prints - Catalogs. 4. Ships in art. 5. Artists - Netherlands - Biography. I. Vorstman, Robert. II. Rijksmuseum (Netherlands). Rijksprentenkabinet. III. Title.
NYPL [MDBF+ 90-12796]

Groot, Reindert. Vincent van Gogh in Amsterdam / Reindert Groot, fotografie & Sjoerd de Vries, tekst. Amsterdam : Stadsuitgeverij Amsterdam, c1990. 128 p. : ill. ; 24 cm. Includes bibliographical references (p. 125) and index. ISBN 90-6274-045-6 :
1. Gogh, Vincent van, 1853-1890 - Homes and haunts - Netherlands - Amsterdam. 2. Artists - Netherlands - Biography. 3. Amsterdam (Netherlands) - History. I. Vries, Sjoerd de. II. Title.
ND653.G7 G74 1990

Groover, Jan, 1943- Pure invention--the table top still life : photographs / by Jan Groover.1st ed. Washington : Smithsonian Institution Press, c1990. 63 p. : ill. ; 26 cm. (Photographers at work) "Published in association with Constance Sullivan Editions." ISBN 1-560-98005-2 DDC 770/.92 20
1. Groover, Jan, 1943-. 2. Still-life photography. 3. Photography, Table-top. I. Title. II. Series.
TR656.5 .G76 1990
NYPL [MFX (Groover) 91-3321]

GROOVER, JAN, 1943-
Groover, Jan, 1943- Pure invention--the table top still life . Washington , c1990. 63 p. : ISBN 1-560-98005-2 DDC 770/.92 20
TR656.5 .G76 1990
NYPL [MFX (Groover) 91-3321]

Gropius . Isaacs, Reginald R., 1911- Boston , c1991. xix, 344 p. : ISBN 0-8212-1753-4 : DDC 720/.92 B 20
NA1088.G85 I79 1991
NYPL [3-MQZ (Gropius) 91-5539]

Gropius, Ise, comp. Gropius, Walter, 1883-1969. Walter Gropius. [Zürich, 1971] 73 p. ISBN 0-262-57023-8 DDC 720/.924
NA1088.G85 G7
NYPL [3-MQZ (Gropius) 90-5748]

Gropius, Walter, 1883-1969.
Walter Gropius: Bauten und Projekte 1906-1969. [Zürich, Kunstgewerbemuseum, 1971] 73 p. illus. 20 x 23 cm. (Wegleitung des Kunstgewerbemuseums der Stadt Zürich. Nr. 283) Catalog of the exhibition held at the Kunstgewerbemuseum Zürich, June 26-Aug. 22, 1971. "Die Texte über das Werk von Gropius sind von Ise Gropius speziell für diesen Katalog neu zusammengestellt worden." Bibliography: p. 28. ISBN 0-262-57023-8 DDC 720/.924
1. Gropius, Walter, 1883-1969 - Exhibitions. I. Gropius, Ise, comp. II. Kunstgewerbemuseum Zürich. III. Series: Wegleitung, v. 283.
NA1088.G85 G7

GROPIUS, WALTER, 1883-1969.
Isaacs, Reginald R., 1911- Gropius . Boston , c1991. xix, 344 p. : ISBN 0-8212-1753-4 : DDC 720/.92 B 20
NA1088.G85 I79 1991
NYPL [3-MQZ (Gropius) 91-5539]

GROPIUS, WALTER, 1883-1969 - ARCHIVES - CATALOGS.
Busch-Reisinger Museum. The Walter Gropius Archive . New York , Cambridge, Mass. , 1990. 3 v. : ISBN 0-8240-3340-X (v. 1) : DDC 720/.22/2 20
NA1088.G85 A4 1990
NYPL [3-MQZ+ (Gropius) 90-12990]

GROPIUS, WALTER, 1883-1969 - EXHIBITIONS.
Gropius, Walter, 1883-1969. Walter Gropius. [Zürich, 1971] 73 p. ISBN 0-262-57023-8 DDC 720/.924
NA1088.G85 G7
NYPL [3-MQZ (Gropius) 90-5748]

Gropper Art Gallery. Hoffbauer, Charles, 1875-1957. Charles Hoffbauer (1875-1957) . W. Sommerville, Mass. [1977] [29] p. : DDC 759.4
N6853.H63 G76
NYPL [3-MCO H698 81-412]

Gropper, Joseph. Hoffbauer, Charles, 1875-1957. Charles Hoffbauer (1875-1957) . W. Sommerville, Mass. [1977] [29] p. : DDC 759.4
N6853.H63 G76
NYPL [3-MCO H698 81-412]

Gropplero di Troppenburg, Elianna. Das bayerische Glas des Historismus dargestellt an der Hütte Theresienthal : Kunstgewerbe und Kunsttheorie im 19. Jahrhundert / Elianna Gropplero di Troppenburg. München : Tuduv-Verlagsgesellschaft, c1988. 285 p., [32] p. of plates : ill. ; 21 cm. (Tuduv-Studien. Reihe Kunstgeschichte . Bd. 28) Originally presented as the author's thesis (doctoral)--Münchner Ludwig-Maximilians-Universität, 1977. Bibliography: p. 183-202. ISBN 3-88073-275-2 DDC 338.7/6661/094336 19
1. Hütte Theresienthal. 2. Glassware - Germany (West) - Bavaria - History - 19th century. I. Title. II. Series.
NK5198.H78 G76 1988
NYPL [3-MPW 91-5027]

Le gros blond avec sa chemise noire /. Cabu. Paris , c1987. 1 v. (unpaged) : ISBN 2-226-03167-7
NYPL [3-MEM+ (Cabu) 89-27328]

Grosenick, Uta. Einleuchten . Hamburg [1989] 289 p. : ISBN 3-7672-1102-5 DDC 709/.04/507443515 20
N6488.G3 H2832 1989

Gross, Friedrich. Jesus, Luther und der Papst im Bilderkampf 1871 bis 1918 : zur Malereigeschichte der Kaiserzeit / Friedrich Gross. Marburg : Jonas, c1989. 588 p. : ill. ; 31 cm. Originally presented as the author's thesis (doctoral)--Universität Hamburg, 1982. Includes bibliographical references (p. 531-566) and indexes. ISBN 3-922561-37-3
1. Painting, German. 2. Painting, Modern - 17th-18th centuries - Germany. 3. Painting, Modern - 19th century - Germany. 4. Christian art and symbolism - Modern period, 1500- - Germany. 5. Jesus Christ - Art. I. Title.
ND566 .G75 1989

GROSS, FRITZ, 1895-1969 - ART COLLECTIONS - EXHIBITIONS.
Whistler, Catherine. Impressionist and modern . Oxford , 1990. 128 p. : ISBN 0-907849-97-0 (pbk) *NYPL [3-MAX (Gross) 90-11583]*

Gross, Marianne. Schilder, Bilder, Moritaten . [Berlin] [1987] 96 p. :
ND2880 .S35 1987 NYPL [3-MBO 91-7047]

Gross, Steve. Old houses / photographs by Steve Gross and Susan Daley ; text by Henry Wiencek. New York : Stewart, Tabori & Chang, 1991. p. cm. Includes bibliographical references. ISBN 1-556-70184-5 : DDC 728/.0973 20
1. Architecture, Domestic - United States. 2. Architecture, Domestic - United States - Conservation and restoration. 3. Interior decoration - United States. I. Daley, Susan, 1953-. II. Wiencek, Henry. III. Title.
NA7205 .G764 1991

Grosse Ausstellungsführer (Prähistorische Staatssamlung (Bavaria, Germany)) .
(Bd. 2) Dannheimer, Hermann. Torhalle auf Frauenchiemsee . München , 1983, c1980. 118 p. : ISBN 3-7954-0818-0
NYPL [3-MRBB 91-6996]

Grosse Hovest, Benedikt. Die Wiedenbrücker Schule : Kunst und Kunsthandwerk des Historismus / Benedikt Grosse Hovest, Marita Heinrich. Paderborn : Bonifatius, c1991. 124 p. : ill. ; 28 cm. ISBN 3-87088-662-5
1. Christian art and symbolism - Modern period, 1500- - Germany - Wiedenbrück. I. Heinrich, Marita. II. Title. *NYPL [3-MAIH 91-7956]*

Der Grosse Shell Atlas. Mairs Geographischer Verlag. Stuttgart , c1965-1966. viii, 283, [166], x-xxii p. : *NYPL [Map Div. 90-5904]*

Grosser Bibelstudien Atlas. Karṭa (Firm) Stuttgart , 1987. 1 atlas (17 p.) : ISBN 3-7675-7760-7 *NYPL [Map Div. 90-9723]*

Grossman, Nancy.
Raven, Arlene. Nancy Grossman /. Brookville, N.Y. , 1991. p. cm. ISBN 0-933699-22-0 DDC 709.2 20
N6537.G75 A4 1991

GROSSMAN, NANCY - CATALOGS.
Raven, Arlene. Nancy Grossman /. Brookville, N.Y. , 1991. p. cm. ISBN 0-933699-22-0 DDC 709.2 20
N6537.G75 A4 1991

Grossmann, G. Ulrich (Georg Ulrich) Renaissance im Weserraum . München , 1989. 2 v. : ISBN 3-422-06039-1 (Bd. 1)
N6882.W38 R4 1989
NYPL [3-MAMG 89-28831]

Grosz, George, 1893-1959. George Grosz, Deutschland über Alles : 85 opere tra il 1913 e il 1936 / scelte da Antonio Del Guercio ; presentazione di Ulrich Becher. Roma : Editori Riuniti, 1963. 19 p., [84] leaves of plates : ill. (some col.) ; 28 cm.
1. Grosz, George, 1893-1959. I. Del Guercio, Antonio. II. Becher, Ulrich, 1910-. III. Title. IV. Title: Deutschland über Alles.
NYPL [3-MCK G879 91-1374]

GROSZ, GEORGE, 1893-1959.
Grosz, George, 1893-1959. George Grosz, Deutschland über Alles . Roma , 1963. 19 p., [84] leaves of plates :
NYPL [3-MCK G879 91-1374]

GROSZ, GEORGE, 1893-1959 - CRITICISM AND INTERPRETATION.
Lewis, Beth Irwin. George Grosz . Princeton, N.J. , c1991. p. cm. ISBN 0-691-00291-6 (pb.) : DDC 741/.092 B 20
NC251.G66 L48 1991

De Grote naïeven = [Les grands naïfs : Stedelijk Museum Amsterdam, 24.8 - 20.10.1974 / voorbereiding katalogus en tentoonstelling, Marja Bloem, Ad Petersen]. Amsterdam : Stedelijk Museum, 1974. [41] p. : ill. (some col.), ports. ; 28 cm. Cover title. In Dutch or French. "Katalogusnummer 564." Includes bibliographies.
1. Primitivism in art - Exhibitions. 2. Primitivism in art - France - Exhibitions. 3. Painting, Modern - 20th century - France - Exhibitions. I. Bloem, Marja. II. Petersen, Ad. III. Amsterdam (Netherlands). Stedelijk Museum. IV. Title: Grands naïfs.
NYPL [3-MCN 90-6044]

GROTESQUE IN ART.
Breton, André, 1896-1966. L'art magique /. [Paris] [c1991] 358 p. : ISBN 2-85940-215-2
N8222.M3 B7 1991

Rof Carballo, Juan. Los duendes del Prado /. Madrid [1990?] 376 p. : ISBN 84-239-5300-9 DDC 709/.4/0744641 20
N8217.F28 R64 1990

Groth, Håkan. Neo-classicism in the North : Swedish furniture and interiors, 1770-1850 / Håkan Groth ; photographs by Fritz Von der Schulenburg ; with a catalog of furniture types and styles and notes on the architects, artists, and craftsmen. New York : Rizzoli, 1990. 224 p. : ill. (some col.), plans ; 29 cm. Includes bibliographical references: (p.221) and index. ISBN 0-8478-1273-1 DDC 728/.37/09485 20
1. Decoration and ornament - Sweden - Neoclassicism. 2. Furniture - Sweden - Styles. 3. Interior decoration - Sweden - History - 18th century. 4. Interior architecture - Sweden - History - 18th century. I. Von der Schulenburg, Fritz. II. Title.
NK1461.A1 G76 1990
NYPL [3-MLO 91-3368]

Groth, Jan, 1938- Jan Groth, tegn . Oslo , 1988. 84 p. : ISBN 82-7418-154-9
NK3060.A3 G7635 1988

GROTH, JAN, 1938-
Jan Groth, tegn . Oslo , 1988. 84 p. : ISBN 82-7418-154-9
NK3060.A3 G7635 1988

Groth-Schmachtenberger, Erika. Volks-trachten aus Oberbayern, Österreich, Ungarn, Jugoslawien, mit den Donauschwaben, Rumänien, mit den Siebenbürger Sachsen / Fotos von Erika Groth-Schmachtenberger ; Texte von Heide Nixdorff ; mit Beiträgen von Erika Groth-Schmachtenberger, Ottmar Schuberth. [München?] : Bezirk Oberbayern, 1980. 181 p., 6 leaves of plates : ill. (some col.), maps ; 21 cm. (Schriften des Freilichtmuseums des

Bezirks Oberbayern an der Glentleiten . Nr. 6) "Ausstellung im Freilichtmuseum des Bezirks Oberbayern an der Glentleiten, 15. Mai-14. September 1980." Bibliography: p. 181.
1. Costume - Germany, (West) - Oberbayern - Exhibitions. 2. Costume - Austria - Exhibitions. 3. Costume - Hungary - Exhibitions. 4. Costume - Yugoslavia - Exhibitions. 5. Costume - Romania - Exhibitions. I. Schuberth, Ottmar. II. Nixdorff, Heide. III. Freilichtmuseum des Bezirks Oberbayern. IV. Title. V. Series.
NYPL [3-MMM 90-10816]

GRÖTZINGER MALERKOLONIE.
Die Grötzinger Malerkolonie . Karlsruhe , c1975. 239 p. :
N6867.5.G7 G76
NYPL [3-MCI 90-7040]

GROUP WORK IN ARCHITECTURE - CONGRESSES.
Building Arts Forum/New York. Symposium (1989 : Guggenheim Museum) Bridging the gap . New York , c1991. xv, 183 p. : ISBN 0-442-00135-5 DDC 720 20
NA2543.T43 B8 1991
NYPL [3-MQV 91-3950]

GROUP WORK IN ART - EXHIBITIONS.
Team spirit /. New York, N.Y. , c1990. 84 p. : ISBN 0-916365-30-1
NYPL [3-MAL 91-6734]

GROUP WORK IN ART - FLORIDA - TAMPA - EXHIBITIONS.
National Gallery of Art (U. S.) Graphicstudio . Washington , 1991. p. cm. ISBN 0-89468-164-8 DDC 769.9759/65/074753 20
NE538.T35 N37 1991

GROUP WORK IN ART - NEW YORK (N.Y.) - EXHIBITIONS.
Zeitlin, Marilyn. South Bronx Hall of Fame . Houston, Tex. , c1991. p. cm. ISBN 0-936080-21-3 (pbk.) : DDC 730/.92 20
NB237.A35 A4 1991

Groupes, mouvements, tendances de l'art contemporain depuis 1945 / [sous la direction de Mathilde Ferrer, avec Marie-Hélène Colas-Adler]. 2. éd. rev. et augm. Paris : Ecole nationale supérieure des beaux-arts, 1990. 183 p. ; 21 cm. Includes bibliographical references and index. ISBN 2-903639-61-2 : DDC 704/.5 20
1. Art, Modern - 20th century - Themes, motives. I. Ferre, Mathilde. II. Colas-Adler, Marie-Hélène.
N6490 .G724 1990

Grove, Nancy. Magical mixtures--Marisol portrait sculpture / Nancy Grove. Washington, D.C. : Published by the Smithsonian Institution Press for the National Portrait Gallery, c1991. 96 p. : ill. (some col.) ; 28 cm. "An exhibition at the National Portrait Gallery, April 5 to August 11, 1991"--T.p. verso. Includes bibliographical references (p. 89-94) and index. ISBN 1-560-98042-7 DDC 709/.2 20
1. Marisol, 1930- - Exhibitions. I. Marisol, 1930-. II. National Portrait Gallery (Smithsonian Institution). III. Title.
NB439.M3 A4 1991

Groves, E. B. (Edward Bebb), 1928- Postcode marketing gazetteer of Great Britain / E. B. Groves. Shrewsbury : Management Update, 1989. vi, 122 p. ; 30 cm. Errata slip inserted. Includes index. Bibliography: p. 103-104. ISBN 0-946679-37-1 (pbk.) : DDC 914.1/003/21 19
1. Zip code - Great Britain. 2. Marketing - Great Britain. I. Title.
DA640
NYPL [Map Div. 91-149]

Growth of Manchester, Lancashire and North Cheshire. The Village atlas . [London] , 1989. 1 atlas (203 p.) : ISBN 0-946619-34-4 : DDC 911/.4273 19 *NYPL [Map Div. 90-12411]*

Groys, Boris. Herold, Georg, 1947- Geld spielt keine Rolle /. Köln , c1990. 78 p. :
NYPL [3-MCK H556 91-6202]

Gruau /. Gruau, René, 1909- Paris , c1989. 191 p. : ISBN 2-7335-0172-0 DDC 741.6/092 20
TT509 .G77 1989
NYPL [3-MME+ 91-5612]

Gruau, René, 1909- Gruau / préface de Gilles de Bure. Paris : Herscher, c1989. 191 p. : ill. (some col.) ; 33 cm. "Cet ouvrage est publié à l'occasion de l'exposition présentée de juin à septembre 1989 à Paris, au Palais Galliéra, Musée de la mode et du costume." Includes bibliographical references (p. 20). ISBN 2-7335-0172-0 DDC 741.6/092 20
1. Gruau, René, 1909-. 2. Fashion drawing - History - 20th century. 3. Fashion illustrators - France. I. Bure,

Gilles de. II. Musée de la mode et du costume (Paris, France). III. Title.
TT509 .G77 1989
NYPL [3-MME+ 91-5612]

GRUAU, RENÉ, 1909-
Gruau, René, 1909- Gruau /. Paris , c1989. 191 p. : ISBN 2-7335-0172-0 DDC 741.6/092 20
TT509 .G77 1989
NYPL [3-MME+ 91-5612]

Grubair, Hélène. Musée du Panthéon national haïtien. [Port-au-Prince] : République d'Haïti, Institut national haïtien de la culture et des arts, [1984] 3 v. : ill. ; 21 x 25 cm. Title from portfolio. "Ce catalogue a été conçu et réalisé par Hélène Grubair."--V. 1, p. 18. Issued in portfolio. CONTENTS. - [1] Aux pères de la patrie -- [2] Autour du vodou -- [3] Un âge d'or. DDC 069/.097294 19
1. Musée du Panthéon national haïtien - Catalogs. I. Musée du Panthéon national haïtien. II. Institut national haïtien de la culture et des arts. III. Title.
AM101.H1466 G78 1984
NYPL [3-MAV 86-3034]

Grubert, Beate. Munch, Edvard, 1863-1944. Edvard Munch Holzschnitte . [Reutlingen] [1991] 125 p. : ISBN 3-927228-31-1 DDC 769.92 20
NE1160.5.M86 A4 1991

Gruen, John. The artist observed : 28 interviews with contemporary artists, 1972-1978 / John Gruen. Chicago, IL : A Cappella Books, c1991. p. cm. Includes bibliographical references and index. ISBN 1-556-52103-0 : DDC 709/.2/2 B 20
1. Artists - Interviews. 2. Art, Modern - 20th century. I. Title.
N6490 .G725 1991

Gruenebaum Gallery (New York, N.Y.) James Brooks, Giorgio Cavallon . New York , 1979. 24 p. : **NYPL [3-MCW 91-284]**

Grüger, Johannes, 1906- Johannes Grüger--Grafiken / [herausgegeben von Paul Böhringer]. 1. aufl. Düsseldorf : Pädagogischer Verlag Schwann, 1981. 55 p. : ill. ; 24 cm. "Bibliographic Johannes Grüger: eine Auswahl aus 120 Büchern."
1. Grüger, Johannes, 1906-.
NYPL [MDG (Grüger) 88-533]

GRÜGER, JOHANNES, 1906-
Grüger, Johannes, 1906- Johannes Grüger--Grafiken /. Düsseldorf , 1981. 55 p. :
NYPL [MDG (Grüger) 88-533]

Grundberg, Andy. Mike and Doug Starn / Andy Grundberg ; introduction, Robert Rosenblum. New York : H.N. Abrams, 1990. 144 p. : ill. (some col.) ; 26 x 27 cm. Includes bibliographical references (p. 138-139). ISBN 0-8109-3815-4 DDC 779/.092/2 20
1. Starn, Mike. 2. Starn, Doug. I. Starn, Mike. II. Starn, Doug. III. Title.
TR647 .S73 1990
NYPL [MFX (Starn) 91-3582]

Grundkredit Bank (Berlin, Germany).
Kunstforum. Torres, Francesc, 1948- Francesc Torres, Plus ultra /. Berlin , c1988. 60, [4] p. : ISBN 3-89357-010-1
NYPL [3-MGO (Torres) 90-13375]

Grundy, Milton. Atroshenko, V. I. Mediterranean vernacular . New York , 1991. p. cm. ISBN 0-8478-1386-X DDC 720/.9182/2 20
NA1458 .A87 1991

Grünewald, Matthias, 16th cent.
ISENHEIM ALTAR.
Mellinkoff, Ruth. The devil at Isenheim . Berkeley , c1988. xv, 109 p. : ISBN 0-520-06204-3 (alk. paper) DDC 759.3 19
ND588.G7 A645 1988
NYPL [3-MCK+ G88 90-10399]

Grunow, Heinz. Schmeck, Ingrid M. Wundersames Wolfenbüttel /. Wolfenbüttel , 1982. [46] p. :
NYPL [3-MCK S348 88-4592]

Grunwald Center for the Graphic Arts. Almaraz, Carlos. Moonlight theater . Los Angeles , c1991. p. cm. ISBN 0-9628162-0-5 (pbk.) DDC 769.92 20
NE539.A44 M66 1991

GRUPA "A.R." (GROUP OF ARTISTS) - CATALOGS.
Płauszewski, Andrzej. "a.r.", mit urzeczywistniony . Łódź , 1989. 156 p. : ISBN 83-218-0237-0 **NYPL [3-MAM 90-11923]**

Grupo X Promoções e Empreendimentos Artísticos. Catálogo pernambucano de arte . Recife-PE-Brasil , c1987. 1 v. (unpaged) : DDC 709/.2/28134 B 20
N6656.P47 C38 1987

Gruppe Odious.
Odious . [München , 1988] 245 p. : ISBN 3-923244-05-3 **NYPL [3-MGI 89-28056]**

GRUPPE ODIOUS - EXHIBITIONS.
Odious . [München , 1988] 245 p. : ISBN 3-923244-05-3 **NYPL [3-MGI 89-28056]**

Gruppo Donatello.
Gruppo Donatello, XXVII edizione . Firenze , 1989. 111, [34] p. :
N6921.F7 G78 1989
NYPL [3-MAMC 90-11322]

GRUPPO DONATELLO - EXHIBITIONS.
Gruppo Donatello, XXVII edizione . Firenze , 1989. 111, [34] p. :
N6921.F7 G78 1989
NYPL [3-MAMC 90-11322]

Gruppo Donatello, XXVII edizione : mostra all'aperto, 7-17 settembre 1989 / Comune di Firenze ... [et al.]. Firenze : ALINEA, 1989. 111, [34] p. : ill. ; 22 cm. (Il Donatello . 7-8) Title on cover: Mostra d'arte del Piazzale Donatello. Issued (back-to-back, head-to-toe) with: Gruppo Donatello, 7 monumenti per Firenze.
1. Gruppo Donatello - Exhibitions. 2. Art, Italian - Italy - Florence - Exhibitions. 3. Art, Modern - 20th century - Italy - Florence - Exhibitions. I. Gruppo Donatello. II. Florence (Italy). III. Title: Gruppo Donatello, 7 monumenti per Firenze. 1989. IV. Title: 7 monumenti per Firenze. V. Title: Sette monumenti per Firenze. VI. Title: Mostra d'arte del Piazzale Donatello. VII. Series.
N6921.F7 G78 1989
NYPL [3-MAMC 90-11322]

Gruppo Donatello, 7 monumenti per Firenze. 1989. Gruppo Donatello, XXVII edizione . Firenze , 1989. 111, [34] p. :
N6921.F7 G78 1989
NYPL [3-MAMC 90-11322]

Gruyaert, Harry, 1941- Morocco : Photographien / Harry Gruyaert. München : Schirmer/Mosel, c1990. 45 leaves of plates : ill. ; 31 x 33 cm. ISBN 3-88814-323-3
1. Morocco - Description and travel - Views. 2. Morocco - Description and travel - 1981- - Views. I. Title. **NYPL [MFX+ (Gruyaert) 91-7938]**

Grzechca-Mohr, Ursula. Schlemmer, Oskar, 1888-1943. Oskar Schlemmer . Frankfurt am Main , c1989. 79 p. :
IN PROCESS (ONLINE)
NYPL [3-MCK S341 91-7616]

Grzesiák, Angela. Mehnert-Pfabe, Elisabeth, 1905- Klöppelspitzen . [Leipzig] [1988] 82 p. : DDC 746.2/22/092 20
NK9498.M44 A4 1988
NYPL [3-MOX 91-6977]

Grzimek, Waldemar, 1918-
Waldemar Grzimek 1918-1984 : Plastik, Zeichnungen, Grafik : Museen, Gedenkstätten und Sammlungen der Stadt Magdeburg, Kloster Unser Lieben Frauen, 12. Februar bis 14. Mai 1989, Zentrum für Kunstausstellungen der DDR, Neue Berliner Galerie im Alten Museum, Juni-Juli 1989 / [Katalogregie und Redaktion, Renate Schmidt, Uta Tietze]. Berlin : Das Zentrum : Neue Berliner Galerie, c1988. 115 p. : ill. (some col.) ; 26 cm.
1. Grzimek, Waldemar, 1918- - Exhibitions. I. Kloster Unser Lieben Frauen Magdeburg. II. Title.
MLCM 90/06352 (N)
NYPL [3-MGO (Grzimek) 91-5353]

GRZIMEK, WALDEMAR, 1918- - EXHIBITIONS.
Grzimek, Waldemar, 1918- Waldemar Grzimek 1918-1984 . Berlin , c1988. 115 p. :
MLCM 90/06352 (N)
NYPL [3-MGO (Grzimek) 91-5353]

Gschwend, Max. Bauernhäuser der Schweiz = Maisons rurales en Suisse Case rurali in Svizzera / Max Gschwend.1. Aufl. Blauen : Schweizer Baudokumentation, c1988. 306 p. : ill., maps, plans ; 31 cm. French, German, and Italian. ISBN 3-907080-07-6
1. Farmhouses - Switzerland. 2. Farm building - Switzerland. I. Schweizer Baudokumentation (Firm). II. Title. III. Title: Maisons rurales en Suisse. IV. Title:

Case rurali in Svizzera.
NYPL [3-MRGF+ 89-25516]

GSUM-RTSEGS (TEMPLE : ALCHI GÖMPA, INDIA) - EXHIBITIONS.
Goepper, Roger. Alchi . Köln , c1982. 110 p. : ISBN 3-7701-1479-5 DDC 755/.943/09546 19
ND2829.A415 G64 1982
NYPL [3-MAF 90-12370]

Guadalupe Posada, José. see Posada, José Guadalupe, 1852-1913.

Guanajuato, Mexico (State) Chávez Morado, José, 1909- José Chávez Morado . Guanajuato, Gto. , 1988. 215 p. : ISBN 968-617-012-X
NYPL [3-MCZ C51 90-11331]

Guarda, Gabriel. Colchagua, arquitectura tradicional / Gabriel Guarda. Santiago de Chile : Ediciones Universidad Católica de Chile, 1988. 177 p. : ill. (some col.) ; 27 x 37 cm. At head of title: Arte. Includes bibliographical references (p. 66-69). ISBN 956-1-40220-7 DDC 720/.983/33 20
1. Architecture - Chile - Colchagua. 2. Architecture, Colonial - Chile - Colchagua. I. Title.
NA866.C64 G83 1988

Guardi /. Pleşu, Andrei. [Guardi. English.] Bucharest , 1981. 27 p., [56] p. of plates : DDC 759.5 20
N6923.G8165 A4 1981

Guardi, Francesco, 1712-1793.
Pleşu, Andrei. [Guardi. English.] Guardi /. Bucharest , 1981. 27 p., [56] p. of plates : DDC 759.5 20
N6923.G8165 A4 1981

GUARDI, FRANCESCO, 1712-1793 - CATALOGS.
Pleşu, Andrei. [Guardi. English.] Guardi /. Bucharest , 1981. 27 p., [56] p. of plates : DDC 759.5 20
N6923.G8165 A4 1981

GUARDIOLA HOUSE (PUERTO DE SANTA MARIA, SPAIN)
Eisenman, Peter, 1932- Peter Eisenman . Berlin , 1989. [46] p. :
NYPL [3-MQZ (Eisenman) 90-12528]

GUARINO, FRANCESCO, 1611-1654 - CATALOGS.
I Dipinti dei Guarino e le arti decorative nella Collegiata di Solofra /. Napoli , c1987. 205 p. :
ND616 .D5 1987
NYPL [3-MCF+ G924 90-12954]

GUARINO, GIOVAN TOMMASO, 1573-1637 - CATALOGS.
I Dipinti dei Guarino e le arti decorative nella Collegiata di Solofra /. Napoli , c1987. 205 p. :
ND616 .D5 1987
NYPL [3-MCF+ G924 90-12954]

Guastalla, Giorgio.
Marino Marini : catalogo ragionato dell'opera grafica (incisioni e litografie) 1919-1980 / Giorgio e Guido Guastalla ; saggio critico, Mario De Micheli. Livorno : Graphis arte, c1990. 268 p. : ill. ; 31 cm.
1. Marini, Marino, 1901- - Catalogues raisonnés. I. Marini, Marino, 1901-. II. Guastalla, Guido. III. De Micheli, Mario. IV. Title.
NYPL [MDG+ (Marini) 91-5689]
Parisot, Christian. Modigliani . Livorno , c1990- v. : **NYPL [MCF+ M69 91-7510]**

Guastalla, Guido.
Guastalla, Giorgio. Marino Marini . Livorno , c1990. 268 p. :
NYPL [MDG+ (Marini) 91-5689]
Parisot, Christian. Modigliani . Livorno , c1990- v. : **NYPL [MCF+ M69 91-7510]**

GUATEMALAN ART. see ART, GUATEMALAN.

Gubler, Jacques. Le Corbusier, early works by Charles-Edouard Jeanneret-Gris /. London , New York , 1987. 136 p. : ISBN 0-312-47583-7 (paper) **NYPL [3-MQZ+ (Le Corbusier) 87-3750]**

Guckel, Peter, Dr. Hahn, Siegbert, 1937- Siegbert Hahn . Solingen , Koblenz , 1978. 93 p. :
ND588.H253 A4 1978
NYPL [3-MCK H147 81-775]

GUDEWERDT, HANS, CA. 1600-1671.
Behling, Holger. Hans Gudewerdt der jüngere (um 1600-1671) . Neumünster , 1990. 375 p. :

ISBN 3-529-02515-1
NYPL [3-MGO+ (Gudewerdt) 91-6536]

Gudmundson, Wayne. Testaments in wood :
Finnish log structures at Embarrass, Minnesota
/ photographs by Wayne Gudmundson ; text by
Suzanne Winckler. St. Paul : Minnesota
Historical Society Press, 1991. p. cm. Includes
bibliographical references. ISBN 0-87351-268-5
(paper) :   DDC 720/.9776/77 20
*1. Log cabins - Minnesota - Embarrass. 2. Ethnic
architecture - Minnesota - Embarrass. 3. Embarrass
(Minn.) - Buildings, structures, etc. I. Winckler,
Suzanne. II. Title.*
NA7235.M62 E454 1991

Gudrun von Leitner . Leitner, Gudrun von, 1940-
München , c1988. 216 p. : ISBN 3-7913-0897-1
DDC 709.2 20
N6888.L365 A4 1988
NYPL [3-MCK+ L543 90-11791]

Güell, Xavier.
Arquitectura española contemporánea .
Barcelona , c1990. 192 p. : ISBN 84-252-1429-7
DDC 720/.946/09048 20
NA1308 .A84 1990
NYPL [3-MQWH 91-3890]

Linazasoro, José Ignacio. J. I. Linazasoro /.
Barcelona , c1989. 96 p. : ISBN 84-252-1388-6
NYPL [3-MQZ (Linazasoro) 90-11075]

Guéné, Hélène. Loyer, François. Henri Sauvage .
Bruxelles , 1987. 159 p. : ISBN 2-87009-304-7
(pbk.)
NYPL [3-MQZ (Savage) 90-12030]

Günter Brus . Brus, Günter. [Bern] , c1976. [36]
p. :   *NYPL [3-MCK B895 91-1317]*

Günther Förg /. Förg, Günther, 1952- Stuttgart ,
c1990. 202 p. : ISBN 3-89322-214-6
NYPL [3-MCK+ F635 91-6911]

Guenther, Peter W.
Degenerate art . Los Angeles, Calif. , New
York , c1991. p. cm. ISBN 0-87587-158-5 DDC
709/.43/07477311 20
N6868 .D3388 1991b

Degenerate art . Los Angeles, Calif. , New
York , c1991. 423 p. : ISBN 0-8109-3653-4
DDC 709/.43/07477311 20
N6868 .D3388 1991

Günther Uecker . Uecker, Günther, 1930-
Mainz , c1988. 84 p. : ISBN 3-926663-04-9
N6888.U37 A4 1988
NYPL [3-MCK+ U125 91-7298]

Günther Wizemann. Wizemann, Günther, 1953-
Kartause Ittingen , Reutlingen , c1989. 64 p. :
IN PROCESS (ONLINE)
NYPL [3-MCZ+ W835 91-7402]

Guernica : Kunst und Politik am Beispiel
Guernica : Picasso und der Spanische
Bürgerkrieg : eine Ausstellung der Neuen
Gesellschaft für Bildende Kunst Berlin :
Juni/Juli 1975, Stadt Schwäbisch Hall,
September/Oktober 1975, Kunstverein
Ingolstadt, Oktober/November 1975, Städtische
Galerie Erlangen / [herausgegeben von der
Arbeitsgruppe Guernica ; Redaktion des
Katalogs und Tafeltexte, Wolfgang Virmond].3.
Aufl. Berlin : Neue Gesellschaft für Bildende
Kunst e.V., c1975. 160 p. : ill. ; 24 cm.
Bibliography: p. 129-130.
*1. Picasso, Pablo, 1881-1973. Guernica - Exhibitions. 2.
Politics in art - Exhibitions. 3. Spain - History - Civil
War, 1936-1939 - Art and the war - Exhibitions. I.
Virmond, Wolfgang. II. Neue Gesellschaft für Bildende
Kunst. Arbeitsgruppe Guernica.*
NYPL [3-MCQ P58 79-2649]

Guerrero Romero, Javier. El Palacio Escárzaga,
Durango / por Javier Guerrero Romero ;
fotografías de Jaime Andrade Ramírez. 1. ed.
Durango, Dgo., México : H. Ayuntamiento,
1986-1989, 1988. xii, 82 p. : ill. ; 28 cm. ISBN
968-609-400-8
*1. Palacio Escárzaga (Durango, Mexico). 2.
Architecture, Modern - 19th century - Mexico -
Durango. 3. Durango (Mexico) - Buildings, structures,
etc. I. Andrade Ramírez, Jaime. II. Title.*
NA757.D87 G84 1986

**Guerry, Liliane Brion- see Brion-Guerry, Liliane,
1916-**

GUEVARA, ALVARO, 1894-1951.
Fuente, Alvaro de la. Retrato de un pintor /.
Santiago de Chile , 1980. 305 p. ;
ND369.G77 F8 1980

Guevara, Andrés, d. 1964.
Loredano, Cássio. Guevara e Figueroa . Rio de
Janeiro, RJ , 1988. 131 p. :
NC1460.G84 A4 1988

GUEVARA, ANDRÉS, D. 1964 - CATALOGS.
Loredano, Cássio. Guevara e Figueroa . Rio de
Janeiro, RJ , 1988. 131 p. :
NC1460.G84 A4 1988

Guevara e Figueroa . Loredano, Cássio. Rio de
Janeiro, RJ , 1988. 131 p. :
NC1460.G84 A4 1988

Guévrékian, Gabriel, 1900-1970.
Vitou, Elisabeth. Gabriel Guévrékian,
1900-1970 . Paris , c1987. 150 p. : ISBN
2-86649-003-7 : DDC 720/.92/4 19
NA1053.G77 V5 1987
NYPL [3-MQZ (Guévrékian) 91-4588]

**GUÉVRÉKIAN, GABRIEL, 1900-1970 -
CRITICISM AND INTERPRETATION.**
Vitou, Elisabeth. Gabriel Guévrékian,
1900-1970 . Paris , c1987. 150 p. : ISBN
2-86649-003-7 : DDC 720/.92/4 19
NA1053.G77 V5 1987
NYPL [3-MQZ (Guévrékian) 91-4588]

Guglielmo Borremans tra Napoli e Sicilia /.
Siracusano, Citti, 1948- Palermo , c1990. 186
p. : ISBN 88-7177-009-9 : DDC 759.5 20
ND623.B684 A4 1990

Guha-Thakurta, Tapati. The making of a new
"Indian" art : artists, aesthetics, and nationalism
in Bengal, c1850-1920 / Tapati Guha-Thakurta.
Cambridge [England] ; New York : Cambridge
University Press, 1992. p. cm. (Cambridge South
Asian studies) Includes bibliographical references (p.)
and index. ISBN 0-521-39247-0 DDC
709/.54/1409034 20
*1. Art, Bengali. 2. Art, Modern - 19th century - India -
Bengal. 3. Art, Modern - 20th century - India - Bengal.
4. Nationalism and art - India - Bengal. I. Title.*
N7307.B4 G84 1992

Guía de la cerámica romana /. Beltrán Lloris,
Miguel. Zaragoza , 1990. 373 p. : ISBN
84-85264-80-5
IN PROCESS (ONLINE)
NYPL [3-MPEK+ 91-2666]

Guia dos bens tombados Brasil / coordenação de
Maria Elisa Carrazzoni ; [ilustrações, Jimmy
Scott ... et al.]. 2. ed. Rio de Janeiro, RJ :
Expressão e Cultura, c1987. 512, [24] p. : ill. ;
28 cm. Includes bibliographical references (p.
[517]-[521]) and index. DDC 720/.981 20
*1. Architecture - Brazil - Guide-books. 2. Architecture,
Colonial - Brazil - Guide-books. 3. Historic buildings -
Brazil - Guide-books. I. Carrazzoni, Maria Elisa.*
NA853 .G85 1987

Guías de arquitectura.
Lacuesta, Raquel. Arquitectura modernista en
Cataluña /. Barcelona , c1990. 213 p. : ISBN
84-252-1430-0 DDC 720/.946/70904 20
NA1309.C2 L33 1990

Guida alla città di Venezia /. Pizzarello, Ugo,
1940- Venezia , 1986- v. :
NYPL [3-MQWB 91-653]

Guid'arts : musées et galeries, art moderne et
contemporain, de Marseille à Menton / [textes,
Alain Amiel ... et al. ; photos, Béatrice
Heyligers ... et al.]. Nice : Z'éditions, [1989]
174 p. : ill. (some col.) ; 21 cm. (Collection
Découverte) Cover title. Half title: G'arts. ISBN
2-87720-040-X :
*1. Art, Modern - 20th century - Directories. 2. Art
museums - France - Provence - Directories. 3. Art
galleries, Commercial - France - Provence - Directories.
I. Amiel, Alain. II. Title: Musées et galeries, art
moderne et contemporaine, de Marseille à Menton. III.
Title: G'arts. IV. Series: Collection Découverte (Nice,
France).*
N6485.3 .G85 1989

Guide all'architettura moderna.
Trevisiol, Robert. Otto Wagner /. Bari , 1990.
202 p. : ISBN 88-420-3527-0
NYPL [3-MQZ (Wagner) 91-4449]

Guide and plan of Lisbon. Portugália Editora.
[Lisbon?, 1971?] 1 v. (unpaged)
G1979.L5 P6 1971
NYPL [Map Div. 90-13144]

Guide artistiche Electa.
Battilotti, Donata. Le ville di Palladio /.
Milano , c1990. 139 p. : ISBN 88-435-3085-2

DDC 728.8/092 20
NA7594 .B34 1990
NYPL [3-MQZ (Palladio, A.) 91-5518]
Suitner Nicolini, Gianna. Palazzo Te, Mantova
/. Milano , c1990. 114 p. : ISBN 88-435-3099-2
NA7756.M3 S8 1990

Guide Christie's du collectionneur / sous la
direction de Robert Cumming ; adaptation
française de Claude Dovaz. Paris : Gründ,
c1986. 223 p. : ill. ; 25 cm. French adaptation of:
Christie's guide to collecting. Includes bibliographical
references. ISBN 2-7000-2140-1
I. Cumming, Robert, 1943-. II. Dovaz, Claude.
NYPL [3-MAVC 89-25308]

Guide de l'architecture moderne à Paris =.
Martin, Hervé. Paris , c1990. 318 p. : ISBN
2-86738-483-4 : DDC 720/.944/3610904 20
NA1050 .M35 1990

Guide de production. Benje, Peter. Die
Produktionsleitlinie /. Bremen , 1989. 63
leaves ;   *NYPL [3-MOF+ 91-4271]*

Guide of production. Benje, Peter. Die
Produktionsleitlinie /. Bremen , 1989. 63
leaves ;   *NYPL [3-MOF+ 91-4271]*

A guide to human anatomy for artists /.
Goldfinger, Eliot. New York , 1991. p. cm.
ISBN 0-19-505206-4 DDC 702/.8 20
NC760 .G67 1991

Guide to modern architecture in Apuania.
Giorgieri, Pietro. Itinerari apuani di architettura
moderna /. Firenze , 1989. 263 p. :
NYPL [3-MQWB 90-11118]

Guide to modern architecture in Paris. Martin,
Hervé. Guide de l'architecture moderne à Paris
=. Paris , c1990. 318 p. : ISBN 2-86738-483-4 :
DDC 720/.944/3610904 20
NA1050 .M35 1990

A guide to modern Australian painting. Luck,
Ross K. Melbourne [1969] 119 p. DDC 759.994
ND1100 .L8

A guide to New Hall porcelain patterns /. De
Saye Hutton, Anthony. London , c1990. 240 p.,
[8] p. of plates : ISBN 0-7126-3579-3 : DDC
738.2/7 19
NK4399.N4   *NYPL [3-MPGO 90-12008]*

**Guide to research in classical art and mythology
/.** Van Keuren, Frances Dodds, 1946- Chicago ,
1991. p. cm. ISBN 0-8389-0564-1 DDC 709/.38
20
N7760 .V3 1991

A guide to Sandwich glass . Barlow, Raymond E.
West Chester, PA , Windham, NH , c1989. 1 v.
(unpaged) : ISBN 0-88740-171-6 DDC 749/.63 20
NK5112 .B335 1989
NYPL [3-MPW+ 90-10804]

A guide to the impressionist landscape . Lurie,
Patty, 1944- Boston , c1990. 135 p. : ISBN
0-8212-1796-8 DDC 758/.144/094409034 20
ND1355.5 .L8 1990
NYPL [3-MCN 91-2248]

Guide to the Musée d'Orsay . Musée d'Orsay.
Paris , 1987. 280 p. : ISBN 2-7118-2123-4
NYPL [3-MAVZ (Paris) 90-13020]

**Guide to the photographic collections at the
Historic New Orleans Collection.** Historic New
Orleans Collection. New Orleans, La. , 1989. 1
v. (unpaged) : ISBN 0-917860-29-2
NYPL [MFW 90-11189]

**Guide to the Ram Khamhaeng National Museum,
Sukhothai.** Subhadradis Diskul, M.C.
[Namchom Phiphịtthaphanthasathān hǣng Chāt
Rāmkhamhǣng, Changwat Sukhōthai.
English & Thai.] Namchom
Phiphịtthaphanthạsathān hǣng Chāt
Rāmkhamhǣng, Changwat Sukhōthai /.
[Bangkok] [1964] 60 p., [25] p. of plates (some
folded) :
N7322.S84 S83 1964

Guide to the records of the Bahamas /. Saunders,
D. Gail. [Nassau , 1973] xvi, 109, 28 p. ;
CD3882 .S27   *NYPL [HRG 76-607]*

**Guides of the Institute for Balkan Studies (I.M.
X.A.).**
(10) Tsigaridas, Euth. N. Latomou monastery .
Thessaloniki , 1988. 89 p., 32 p. of plates :
NYPL [3-MRBN 89-25752]

Guides to information sources (London, England)
Information sources in cartography /. London

[England] , New York , c1990. xiii, 540 p. ;
ISBN 0-408-02458-5 (U. S.) DDC 016.526 20
Z6021 .I53 1990 GA105.3
NYPL [Map Div. 91-2555]

**GUIGNARD, ALBERTO DA VEIGA, 1896-
1962 - INFLUENCE.**
Vieira, Ivone Luzia. A Escola Guignard na
cultura modernista de Minas, 1944-1962 /.
[Pedro Leopoldo, Minas Gerais] [1988] 164
p. : DDC 709/.81/51 20
N6656.M5 V54 1988

Guigou, Paul, 1834-1871.
Bonnici, Claude-Jeanne. Paul Guigou . La
Calade, Aix-en-Provence , c1989. 235 p. :
ISBN 2-85744-436-2 DDC 759.4 B 20
ND553.G893 B66 1989

Bonnici, Claude-Jeanne. Paul Guigou,
1834-1871 /. Aix-en-Provence [France] , c1989.
235 p. : ISBN 2-85744-436-2
NYPL [3-MCO+ G945 91-3279]

GUIGOU, PAUL, 1834-1871.
Bonnici, Claude-Jeanne. Paul Guigou . La
Calade, Aix-en-Provence , c1989. 235 p. :
ISBN 2-85744-436-2 DDC 759.4 B 20
ND553.G893 B66 1989

**GUIGOU, PAUL, 1834-1871 - CATALOGUES
RAISONNÉS.**
Bonnici, Claude-Jeanne. Paul Guigou . La
Calade, Aix-en-Provence , c1989. 235 p. :
ISBN 2-85744-436-2 DDC 759.4 B 20
ND553.G893 B66 1989

Bonnici, Claude-Jeanne. Paul Guigou,
1834-1871 /. Aix-en-Provence [France] , c1989.
235 p. : ISBN 2-85744-436-2
NYPL [3-MCO+ G945 91-3279]

Guiheux, A. Tony Garnier, l'œuvre complète /.
Paris , c1989. 254 p. : ISBN 2-85850-527-6
DDC 720/.92 20
NA1053.G37 A4 1989

Guilbaut, Serge. Reconstructing modernism .
Cambridge, Mass. , 1990. xvii, 418 p. : ISBN
0-262-07120-7 DDC 759.06/09/045 20
N6535.N5 R4 1990
NYPL [3-MAL 90-11100]

Guild Hall of East Hampton.
East Hampton avant-garde . [East Hampton] ,
c1990. 68 p. : ISBN 0-933793-14-6
**NYPL [3-MAW (East Hampton)
90-13535]**

En plein air . East Hampton, N.Y. , c1989. 72
p. : ISBN 0-933793-12-X (pbk.)
NYPL [3-MCW 90-399]

Tucker, Toba. Toba Tucker . East Hampton,
N.Y. , c1987. 23 p. : ISBN 0-933793-07-3 DDC
779/.2/092 20
E99.S38 T83 1987 **NYPL [MFW 91-6717]**

**Guildford, Eng. Borough Council. Leisure &
Recreation Section.** A Picturesque ride
through Surrey . Guildford [1978] 42 p., [6] p.
of plates :
MLCS 82/10141 **NYPL [3-MCT 90-6056]**

Guildford House Gallery. A Picturesque ride
through Surrey . Guildford [1978] 42 p., [6] p.
of plates :
MLCS 82/10141 **NYPL [3-MCT 90-6056]**

Guiliani, Luca. Schefold, Karl. [Götter- und
Heldensagen der Griechen in der
spätarchaischen Kunst. English.] Gods and
heroes in late archaic Greek art /. Cambridge ,
New York , 1992. p. cm. ISBN 0-521-32718-0
DDC 704.94/7/0938 20
N7760 .S27313 1992

Guillaud, Jacqueline.
Gogh, Vincent van, 1853-1890. Van Gogh,
vertigo of light /. Paris ; New York : p. cm.
ISBN 0-517-58306-2 DDC 759.9492 20
ND653.G7 A4 1991

La peinture à fresque au temps de Pompéi / par
Jacqueline et Maurice Guillaud ; avec la
collaboration de Alix Barbet, et la coopération
de Baldassare Conticello et de Mimmo Jodice.
Paris ; New York : Guillaud, 1990. 255 p. : col.
ill. ; 30 cm. Includes bibliographical references (p.
52-53). ISBN 2-907895-12-5 DDC 751.7/3/09377
20
1. *Mural painting and decoration, Greco-Roman -
Italy - Pompeii (Ancient city). 2. Mural painting and
decoration - Italy - Pompeii (Ancient city). I. Guillaud,*

Maurice. II. Title.
ND2575 .G832 1990

Guillaud, Maurice.
Gogh, Vincent van, 1853-1890. Van Gogh,
vertigo of light /. Paris ; New York : p. cm.
ISBN 0-517-58306-2 DDC 759.9492 20
ND653.G7 A4 1991

Guillaud, Jacqueline. La peinture à fresque au
temps de Pompéi /. Paris , 1990. 255 p. :
ISBN 2-907895-12-5 DDC 751.7/3/09377 20
ND2575 .G832 1990

Guillaume, Bernard. Garneret, Jean. La maison
du montagnon /. Besançon , 1981. 557 p., [2]
p. of plates : DDC 728/.67/094445 s
728/.67/094445 19
NA8208.52.F8 M34 1981, t. 1
NYPL [3-MQWF 90-5444]

Guillerm, Jean-Pierre. Couleurs du noir : le
Journal de Delacroix / Jean-Pierre Guillerm.
[Lille] : Presses universitaires de Lille, c1990.
197 p. : ill. ; 24 cm. (Objet) Includes bibliographical
references, and texts and reproductions of sketches
extracted from the Journal of Eugène Delacroix.
ISBN 2-85939-379-X : DDC 759.4 20
1. *Delacroix, Eugène, 1798-1863 - Diaries. 2. Painters -
France - Diaries. 3. Delacroix, Eugène, 1798-1863 -
Criticism and interpretation. I. Delacroix, Eugène,
1798-1863. Journal. Selections. 1990. II. Title.*
ND553.D33 A2 1990

Guillermo, Jorge. Dutch houses and castles / text
by Jorge Guillermo ; photographs by Nicolas
Sapieha ; introduction by Heimerick Tromp,
Adriaan W. Vliegenthart. London : Tauris Parke
Books ; New York, N.Y. : Distributed in the U.
S. and Canada by Rizzoli International
Publications, c1990. 208 p. : ill. ; 32 cm.
Bibliography: p. 206-207. ISBN 1-85043-237-6 DDC
720.9492 20
1. *Country homes - Netherlands. 2. Castles -
Netherlands. I. Title.*
NYPL [3-MQW+ 91-3636]

Guillot de Suduiraut, Sophie. Duby, Georges.
[Sculpture. English.] Sculpture . New York ,
1990. 318 p. : ISBN 0-8478-1285-5 DDC 734 20
NB170 .D813 1990
NYPL [3-MGF+ 91-3656]

Guimarães, Alfredo, b. 1882.
[Mobiliário artístico português. 2. Guimarães]
Mobiliário artístico português : em fac-simile
/ [Alfredo Guimarães]. Porto : Sòlivros de
Portugal, 1989. xvi, 181, [6] p., [170] p. of
plates : ill. ; 26 cm. Reprint of v. 2: Guimarães.
Originally published: [S.l.] : Edições Pátria, 1935.
Includes bibliographical references (p. [185]). DDC
749.269 20
1. *Furniture - Portugal. I. Title.*
NK2604 .G825 1989

Guimard, Hector, 1867-1942. Hector Guimard :
fontes artistiques : Galérie du Luxembourg,
Paris, avril-mai, 1971. Paris : La Galerie, 1971.
45 p. : ill. ; 25 cm. Text written by Alain Blondel
and Yves Plantin. Bibliography: p. 20.
1. *Guimard, Hector, 1867-1942. 2. Architectural
ironwork - France - Exhibitions. 3. Decoration and
ornament - France - Art nouveau - Exhibitions. 4. Art
metal-work - France - Exhibitions. I. Blondel, Alain. II.
Plantin, Yves. III. Galerie du Luxembourg (Paris,
France). IV. Title.* **NYPL [3-MRX 90-7184]**

GUIMARD, HECTOR, 1867-1942.
Guimard, Hector, 1867-1942. Hector Guimard .
Paris , 1971. 45 p. :
NYPL [3-MRX 90-7184]

Guinan, Robert, 1934- Krehbiel, Albert,
1873-1945. Krehbiel, life and works of an
American artist /. Washington, D.C. , Lanham,
MD , c1991. p. cm. ISBN 0-89526-533-8
(acid-free paper) DDC 759.13 20
N6537.K726 A4 1991

Guinard, Fernando. El Espíritu erótico /. Bogotá ,
1990. 207 p. : DDC 704.9/428/098610904 20
N8217.E6 E87 1990

Guiton, Jacques. A life in three lands : memoirs
of an architect / by Jacques E. Guiton.
Boston : Branden Pub. Co., c1991. 175 p. : ill. ;
23 cm. Includes bibliographical references (p.
[173]-175). ISBN 0-8283-1937-5 : DDC 720/.92 B
20
1. *Guiton, Jacques. 2. Architects - United States -
Biography. I. Title.*
NA737.G8 A2 1991
NYPL [3-MQZ (Guiton) 91-5761]

GUITON, JACQUES.
Guiton, Jacques. A life in three lands . Boston ,
c1991. 175 p. : ISBN 0-8283-1937-5 : DDC
720/.92 B 20
NA737.G8 A2 1991
NYPL [3-MQZ (Guiton) 91-5761]

Gujarat (India). Dept. of Museums. Koppar, D.
H. Forgotten art of India /. Baroda , 1989.
xxiii, 266, [4] p. : DDC 709/.54 20
N7301 .K58 1989 **NYPL [3-MAF 91-6940]**

Gulbransson, Olaf, 1873-1958.
Olaf Gulbransson : Graphik, Gemälde aus der
Privatsammlung Dagny Björnson-Gulbransson
und den Bayerischen
Staatsgemäldesammlungen :
Wilhelm-Busch-Museum Hannover, Ausstellung
vom 13. März bis 4. Juni 1979 / [Katalog,
Herwig Guratzsch]. Hannover :
Wilhelm-Busch-Gesellschaft, c1979. 72 p. : ill. ;
24 cm. Bibliography of works by and about the author:
p. 37. ISBN 3-921752-08-6
1. *Gulbransson, Olaf, 1873-1958 - Exhibitions. 2.
Björnson-Gulbransson, Dagny - Art collections -
Exhibitions. I. Guratzsch, Herwig. II. Bavaria.
Bayerische Staatsgemäldesammlungen.*
NC1619.G85 A4 1979
NYPL [3-MCZ G971 81-538]

**GULBRANSSON, OLAF, 1873-1958 -
EXHIBITIONS.**
Gulbransson, Olaf, 1873-1958. Olaf
Gulbransson . Hannover , c1979. 72 p. : ISBN
3-921752-08-6
NC1619.G85 A4 1979
NYPL [3-MCZ G971 81-538]

Guldan, Bożena. Muzeum Narodowe we
Wrocławiu. Sztuka Śląska XV-XVIII w. ze
zbiorów Muzeum Narodowego we Wrocławiu .
Opole , 1990. 30 p., [20] p. of plates :
N7255.P62 S545 1990

Guliānitskiĭ, N. F. (Nikolaĭ Feodos´evich)
Arkhitekturnoe nasledie Moskvy . Moskva ,
1988. 100 p. :
NA1197.M6 A78 1988

Gullalderens Mestere . Moen, Arve. Olso , 1964.
139, 165 p. **NYPL [3-MAM+ 90-2909]**

GUllberg, Elsa.
Elsa Gullberg, textil pionjär. Stockholm , 1989.
105 p. : ISBN 91-7100-378-9
IN PROCESS (ONLINE)
NYPL [3-MON 91-4317]

GULLBERG, ELSA - EXHIBITIONS.
Elsa Gullberg, textil pionjär. Stockholm , 1989.
105 p. : ISBN 91-7100-378-9
IN PROCESS (ONLINE)
NYPL [3-MON 91-4317]

Gunn, Thom. Mandrakes / Thom Gunn ;
illustrated by Leonard Baskin. [London] :
Rainbow Press, c1973. 33, [3] p. : ill. ; 30 cm.
Hagstrom & Bixby. Gunn, A21a Carter, S. Rampant
Lions Press, 56 Poems. The ill. are printed from line
blocks after drawings by Baskin. Binding, publisher's, by
Sangorski and Sutcliffe, of quarter white goat vellum
and reddish brown textured paper boards; issued in a
slipcase. DDC 821/.9/14
1. *Baskin, Leonard, 1922-. II. Title.*
PR6013.U65 M3
NYPL [*KP+ (Rampant) 76-52]

Gunn, Virginia. Lasansky, Jeannette. Bits and
pieces . Lewisburg, Pa. , c1991. 120 p. : ISBN
0-917127-06-4 : DDC 746.9/7/0973 20
NK9112 .L33 1991

Gunter, Ann Clyburn, 1951- Investigating artistic
environments in the ancient Near East /.
Washington, D.C. , c1990. xii, 153 p. : ISBN
0-299-97070-1 (alk. paper) : DDC 709/.35 20
N7265 .I58 1990 **NYPL [3-MAE 90-12590]**

Günter, Karin. Städtische Galerie Würzburg.
Würzburg--Künstler sehen eine Stadt .
[Würzburg] [1989?] 102 p. : ISBN
3-926916-04-4
N6886.W87 S73 1989

Günther, Erika. Die Faszination des Fremden :
der malerische Orientalismus in Deutschland /
Erika Günther. Münster : Lit, [1990] i, 193 p.,
[56] p. of plates : ill. ; 24 cm. (Kunstgeschichte ;
Bd. 29) Originally presented as the author's thesis
(doctoral)--Universität Münster, 1988. Includes
bibliographical references (p. 175-193). ISBN
3-88660-542-6
1. *Painting, German. 2. Painting, Modern - 19th*

century - Germany. 3. Exoticism in art. 4. Orient in art. 5. Africa, North, in art. I. Series: Kunstgeschichte (Münster in Westfalen, Germany) , Bd. 29. II. Title.
ND567 .G86 1990

GÜNTHER, MATTHÄUS, 1705-1788 - CRITICISM AND INTERPRETATION.
Hamacher, Bärbel, 1957- Arbeitssituation und Werkprozess in der Freskomalerei von Matthäus Günther (1705-1788) /. München , c1987. ii, 198 p., [30] p. of plates : ISBN 3-88073-277-9 (Deut. Bibl.) DDC 759.3 19
ND588.G9 H36 1987
NYPL [3-MCK G928 91-7030]

Guratzsch, Herwig.
Gulbransson, Olaf, 1873-1958. Olaf Gulbransson. Hannover , c1979. 72 p. : ISBN 3-921752-08-6
NC1619.G85 A4 1979
NYPL [3-MCZ G971 81-538]

Kollwitz, Käthe, 1867-1945. Käthe Kollwitz . Stuttgart , 1990. 255 p. : ISBN 3-7757-0300-4
NYPL [3-MCK+ K81 91-3893]

Kollwitz, Käthe, 1867-1945. Käthe Kollwitz, Druckgraphik, Handzeichnungen, Plastik /. Stuttgart , 1990. 255 p. : ISBN 3-7757-0300-4 DDC 709/.2 20
N6888.K62 A4 1990

Gürtner, Werner.
Scheffczyk, Marie-Theres. Werner Gürtner, Bildhauer /. Konstanz , 1987. 75 p. :
NYPL [3-MGO (Gürtner) 90-8485]

GÜRTNER, WERNER - CATALOGS.
Scheffczyk, Marie-Theres. Werner Gürtner, Bildhauer /. Konstanz , 1987. 75 p. :
NYPL [3-MGO (Gürtner) 90-8485]

Güse, Ernst-Gerhard.
Böckstiegel, Peter August, 1889-1951. P.A. Böckstiegel /. [Münster] , 1989. 237 p. : ISBN 3-7757-0236-9 DDC 760/.092 20
N6888.B58 A4 1989
NYPL [3-MCK B663 90-10619]

De Maria, Nicola, 1954- Nicola De Maria, fiori ed usignoli miei. Saarbrücken [1990]. 87 p. : ISBN 3-925303-46-4
NYPL [3-MCF D372 91-5202]

Gushchina, A. G. Soviet Union. Glavnoe upravlenie geodezii i kartografii. Irkutsk . Moskva , 1977. [14] p. :
NYPL [Map Div. 91-1089]

Gustafson, Donna. Art what thou eat . Mount Kisco, N.Y. , c1991. 191 p. : ISBN 1-559-21051-6 : DDC 704.9/49641/0973 20
N6512 .A763 1991
NYPL [3-MAMZ+ 91-5410]

Gustav Kiepenheuer Bücherei, 0433-0153 .
(65) Meier-Graefe, Julius, 1867-1935. Kunst-Schreiberei . Leipzig , 1987. 331 p. ; ISBN 3-378-00163-1
N7445.4 M45 1987

Gustav Klucis. Klutsis, Gustav Gustavovich, 1895-1944. Stuttgart , c1991. 395 p. : ISBN 3-7757-0327-6
NYPL [3-MCZ K6585 91-7281]

Gustav-Lübcke-Museum Hamm. Kätelhön, Hermann, 1884-1940. Radierungen . [Hamm] [1978] [42] p. :
MLCS 84/15697 (N)
NYPL [MDG (Kätelhön) 90-5865]

Gustave Caillebotte, 1848-1894 . Wildenstein & Co. (London, England) [London, 1966] 35 p. :
NYPL [3-MCO C134 91-1182]

Gustave Serrurier-Bovy à l'aube de l'esthetique industrielle. Watelet, Jacques Grégoire, 1917- Serrurier-Bovy . Paris [1989, c1987] 134 p. :
NYPL [MOF 91-6858]

Gustavison, Susan J. Robert J. Wickenden (1861-1931) and the late nineteenth-century print revival / Susan J. Gustavison. [S.l.] : S.J. Gustavison, c1989. ix, 297 leaves, [39] leaves of plates : ill. ; 28 cm. "A thesis in the Department of Art History." "Presented in partial fulfillment of the requirements for the degree of master of arts at Concordia University, Montréal, Québec, Canada, July 1989."
1. Wickenden, Robert J. I. Title.
NYPL [MDG (Wickenden) 90-13688]

Gustinus Ambrosi-Museum. Gustinus Ambrosi, Pläne und Entwürfe : Gustinus

Ambrosi-Museum, Wien, 13. Juni bis 2. September 1990 /. Wien [1990] 31 p. :
NYPL [3-MGO (Ambrosi) 91-4660]

Gustinus Ambrosi, Pläne und Entwürfe : Gustinus Ambrosi-Museum, Wien, 13. Juni bis 2. September 1990 / Regine Schmidt. Wien : Österreichische Galerie Wien, [1990] 31 p. : ill. (some col.) ; 14 x 21 cm. (145. Wechselausstellung der Österreichischen Galerie)
1. Ambrosi, Gustinus, 1893-1975 - Exhibitions. I. Ambrosi, Gustinus, 1893-1975. II. Schmidt, Regine. III. Gustinus Ambrosi-Museum. IV. Österreichische Galerie. V. Title: Pläne und Entwürfe. VI. Series: Wechselausstellung der Österreichischen Galerie, 145.
NYPL [3-MGO (Ambrosi) 91-4660]

Gustinus Ambrosi, Pläne und Entwürfe . Schmidt, Regine. Wien [1990] 31 p. :
N1708 .A54 nr.145 N6811.5.A48A4

Guston, Philip, 1913-
Philip Guston, drawings, 1947-1977. New York : David McKee Gallery, c1978. [48] p. : ill. ; 26 cm. Catalog of an exhibition held at the David McKee Gallery, New York.
1. Guston, Philip, 1913- - Exhibitions. I. David McKee Gallery. *NYPL [3-MCX G982 91-1369]*

GUSTON, PHILIP, 1913- - EXHIBITIONS.
Guston, Philip, 1913- Philip Guston, drawings, 1947-1977. New York , c1978. [48] p. :
NYPL [3-MCX G982 91-1369]

GUSTON, PHILIP, 1913- - CRITICISM AND INTERPRETATION.
Ashton, Dore. A critical study of Philip Guston /. Berkeley [1990], c1976. xvii, 216 p., 15 p. of plates : ISBN 0-520-06931-5 (alk. paper) DDC 759.13 20
ND237.G8 A82 1990
NYPL [3-MCX G982 91-5624]

GUTBROD, ROLF - BIBLIOGRAPHY.
Architekten, Rolf Gutbrod. Stuttgart [1988]. 51 p. ; ISBN 3-8167-1847-7 (pbk.)
NYPL [3-MQZ (Gutbrad) 90-12742]

Gutenberg-Museum Mainz. Bert, Lore, 1936- Lore Bert . [Mainz] , c1989. 40 p. :
MLCM 89/00848 (N)
NYPL [3-MCK B536 91-5899]

Gutfreund, Oto, 1889-1927.
Oto Gutfreund : 7.XXI.1969-25.I.1970, Städtische Kunstgalerie Bochum. Bochum : Die Kunstgalerie, 1970. 1 v. (unpaged) : ill. ; 26 cm.
1. Gutfreund, Oto, 1889-1927 - Exhibitions. I. Städtische Kunstgalerie Bochum. II. Title.
NYPL [3-MGO (Gutfreund) 90-6935]

GUTFREUND, OTO, 1889-1927 - EXHIBITIONS.
Gutfreund, Oto, 1889-1927. Oto Gutfreund . Bochum , 1970. 1 v. (unpaged) :
NYPL [3-MGO (Gutfreund) 90-6935]

Kotalík, Jiří. Kupka, Gutfreund & C. . Venezia , c1980. 114 p. : ISBN 88-20-80273-2 DDC 709/.437/0740531 19
N6831 .K67 1980   *NYPL [3-MAM 90-5445]*

Gutiérrez, Fernando G. Japón y Occidente : influencias recíprocas en el arte / Fernando Ga. Gutiérrez. Sevilla : Guadalquivir, 1990. 245 p. : col. ill. ; 29 cm. Includes bibliographical references (p. 235) and index. ISBN 84-86080-27-4 DDC 709/.52 20
1. Art, Japanese. 2. Art, Japanese - European influences. I. Title.
N7350 .G88 1990

Gutiérrez, Luis, 1944-
Luis Gutiérrez, Javier Cruz, Luis René Alva . [Mexico City, Mexico] , 1988. 61 p. :
NE544 .L85 1988

GUTIÉRREZ, LUIS, 1944- - CATALOGS.
Luis Gutiérrez, Javier Cruz, Luis René Alva . [Mexico City, Mexico] , 1988. 61 p. :
NE544 .L85 1988

Gutiérrez, Ramón. Cabildos y ayuntamientos en América /. [Mar del Plata, Argentina?] : [Azcapotzalco, Mexico] : 134 p. : ISBN 968-636-305-X
NA4202.A1 C33 1990

Gutiérrez Zaldívar, Ignacio, 1951- Squirru, Rafael F. 40 maestros del arte de los argentinos /. Buenos Aires , 1990. 297 p. : ISBN 950-99493-1-0 DDC 759.982 B 20
ND335 .S63 1990   *NYPL [3-MCY 91-5611]*

Gütlein, Rudolf. Der Kunsthund knurrt . Düsseldorf , c1983. 1 v. (unpaged) :
N6868 .K7876 1983

Gütmane, Margita. Veronika Strēlerte . [Stockholm] , c1982. 128 p. :
NX556.Z9 S778 1982

GUTMANN, BESSIE PEASE.
Christie, Victor J. W. Bessie Pease Gutmann . Radnor, Pa. , c1990. xv, 199 p. : ISBN 0-87069-561-4 : DDC 741.6/092 B 20
N6537.G88 C4 1990
NYPL [3-MCX G983 91-3649]

Gutsell, Barbara J. The Purpose and use of national and regional atlases . Toronto, Canada , 1979. vii, 100 p. : ISBN 0-919870-23-6 (pbk.)
GA101.2 .P87   *NYPL [Map Div. 81-199]*

GUTTA-PERCHA.
Moyer, Susan Louise. Silk painting . New York , 1991. p. cm. ISBN 0-8230-4828-4 DDC 746.6 20
ND1572 .M68 1991

Gutterman, Scott. Davis, Miles. The art of Miles Davis /. New York , c1991. 89 p. : ISBN 0-13-608704-3 : DDC 759.13 B 20
ND237.D3326 A2 1991
NYPL [3-MCX+ D259 91-6131]

GUTTMANN, MARTIN, 1957- - EXHIBITIONS.
Clegg & Guttmann . [Bremerhaven] , Velbert-Neviges , 1989. 73 p. : ISBN 3-926133-17-1   *NYPL [MFW+ 91-2570]*

Guttuso e la Sicilia . Guttuso, Renato, 1912- Palermo , c1985. iii, 159 p. :
NYPL [3-MCF+ G985 88-4362]

Guttuso, il testamento /. Crispolti, Enrico. [Roma] [1987] 97 p. :
ND623.G97 C65 1987
NYPL [3-MCF G985 90-12762]

Guttuso, Renato, 1912-
Crispolti, Enrico. Guttuso, il testamento /. [Roma] [1987] 97 p. :
ND623.G97 C65 1987
NYPL [3-MCF G985 90-12762]

Guttuso e la Sicilia : opere dal 1970 ad oggi : [mostra] Palermo, Palazzo Comitini. 2a ed. Palermo : Provincia di Palermo : Banca popolare siciliana, c1985. iii, 159 p. : ill. (some col.), ports. ; 31 cm. "Organizzata dall'Amministrazione provinciale di Palermo ed allestita a Palazzo Comitini, in Palermo, dal 20 aprile al 31 maggio 1985"--P. 2. Addendum (8 p.) inserted at end. Bibliography: p. 19.
1. Guttuso, Renato, 1912- - Exhibitions. 2. Sicily in art. I. Palermo (Sicily : Province). Amministrazione provinciale. II. Palazzo Comitini (Palermo, Sicily). III. Title.   *NYPL [3-MCF+ G985 88-4362]*

GUTTUSO, RENATO, 1912-
Crispolti, Enrico. Guttuso, il testamento /. [Roma] [1987] 97 p. :
ND623.G97 C65 1987
NYPL [3-MCF G985 90-12762]

GUTTUSO, RENATO, 1912- - EXHIBITIONS.
Guttuso, Renato, 1912- Guttuso e la Sicilia . Palermo , c1985. iii, 159 p. :
NYPL [3-MCF+ G985 88-4362]

Guy, John, 1949- Arts of India, 1550-1900 /. London , c1990. 240 p. : ISBN 1-85177-022-4 DDC 709.54 20
N7301   *NYPL [3-MAF 91-6685]*

Gwa-hon shu kan [microform] . Goshi-tada, Fuji Hara. [S.l. , 19--?] 6 v. :   *NYPL [*ZM-229]*

Gwinner, Schnuppe von.
[Die Geschichte des patchworkquilts. English]
The history of the patchwork quilt : origins, traditions and symbols of a textile art / Shnuppe von Gwinner. West Chester, Pa. : Schiffer Pub. Co., 1988. 196 p. : ill. (some col.) ; 27 cm. Translation of: Die Geschichte des Patchworkquilts. Includes index. Bibliography: p. 191-194. ISBN 0-88740-136-8
1. Patchwork quilts - United States - History. 2. Patchwork quilts - History. 3. Quilting - History. I. Title.   *NYPL [3-MOT 90-4539]*

Gyuon, Madeline H.
Folk art projects. Schaffner, Cynthia V. A. Discovering American folk art / by Cynthia V.A. Schaffner. Folk art projects / Madeline H. Gyuon. New York, N.Y. , 1991. p. cm.

ISBN 0-8109-3206-7   DDC 745/.0973 20
NK805 .S28 1991

GYZĒS, NIKOLAOS, 1842-1901.
Kairophylas, Giannēs, 1927- Nikolaos Gyzēs, ho ethnikos zōgraphos /. Athēna , 1990. 79 p. ;
ND603.G9 K35 1990
     NYPL [3-MCZ G99 91-7003]

H.A.P. Grieshaber, Farbholzschnitte. Grieshaber, Helmut A. P., 1909- HAP Grieshaber, Farbholzschnitte . Stuttgart , c1983. 43 p., 73 leaves of plates :
     NYPL [MDG (Grieshaber) 90-13133]

H. F. AHMANSON & COMPANY - ART COLLECTIONS - CATALOGS.
Los Angeles County Museum of Art. The Ahmanson gifts . Los Angeles, Calif. , c1991. p. cm.   ISBN 0-87587-160-7 (pbk.)   DDC 759.94/074/79494 20
ND454 .L6 1991

[H] GDWLY HAMNWT HMWDRNYT. [R]
Masters of modern art . [Tel Aviv] , 1982.
[112] p. :   *NYPL [3-MC 89-18785]*

H.H. Steffens /. Marteau, Robert. Gifkendorf , 1988. 87 p. :   ISBN 3-926112-09-3
     NYPL [3-MCK+ S8045 90-12584]

H.P. Harr . Harr, H. P. Velbert-Neviges , c1989. 131 p. :   ISBN 3-926133-14-7
     NYPL [3-MGO (Harr) 89-27491]

H.R. Giger's Biomechanics. Giger, H. R. (Hansruedi), 1940- Zug, Switzerland , 1988. 95 p. :   ISBN 3-89082-527-3
     NYPL [3-MCZ++ G455 89-25898]

H.R. Giger's Biomechanics /. Giger, H. R. (Hansruedi), 1940- [Biomechanics. English.] Beverly Hills, CA , 1990. 95 p. :   ISBN 0-9623447-1-0   DDC 709/.2 20
N7153.G48 A4 1990

H.Th. Baumann . Kapp, Volker. Marburg , c1989. 228 p. :   ISBN 3-89398-004-0
IN PROCESS (ONLINE)
     NYPL [3-MNF+ 90-11083]

[H] 12 CYYRY Y'SRAL [R] Twelve Israeli painters. Tel-Aviv : Lion the Printer, 1965. 1 portfolio ([12] leaves of plates) : all col. ill. ; 35 cm. English and Hebrew.
1. Painting, Israeli. 2. Painting, Modern - 20th century - Israel. I. Title: Twelve Israeli painters. II. Title: 12 Israeli painters.   *NYPL [3-MCY+ 84-2732]*

Haack Atlas.
Sozialistische Staaten Mittel- und Südosteuropas /. Gotha , 1986. 1 atlas (190 p.) :   ISBN 3-7301-0032-7   *NYPL [Map Div. 91-3783]*

Haack Atlas Weltmeer /. Hermann Haack Geographisch-Kartographische Anstalt Gotha. Gotha [1989] 1 atlas (viii, 136 p.) :   ISBN 3-7301-0010-6   *NYPL [Map Div. 91-7352]*

Haags Gemeente museum. Meij, Letse. Frans Molenaar . De Bilt , c1986. 176 p. :   ISBN 90-213-0378-7 (speciale luxe ed.)
     NYPL [3-MMO 89-19034]

Haags Gemeentemuseum.
Yeats, Jack Butler, 1871-1957. Jack B. Yeats . Bristol : London : 111 p. :   ISBN 0-85488-091-7 (Arnolfini)   DDC 759.2/915 20
ND497.Y42 A4 1991

Yeats, Jack Butler, 1871-1957. Jack B. Yeats . Bristol : London : 111 p. :   ISBN 0-907738-29-X (Arnolfini Gallery)
     NYPL [3-MCV Y41 91-6477]

Haags Historisch Museum. Mast, Michiel van der. Van Gogh en Den Haag /. Zwolle , c1990. 191 p. :   ISBN 90-6630-240-2
     NYPL [3-MCH G61 91-6680]

Haarmann, Rainer. Kunst in der DDR /. Köln , c1990. 470 p. :   ISBN 3-462-02068-4   DDC 709/.431/09045 20
N6889 .K862 1990

Haase, Otto. Steinböck, Wilhelm. Luigi Coppa /. Graz, Austria , c1990. 149 p. :   ISBN 3-201-01502-4   DDC 759.5 20
ND623.C694 A4 1990

Haavisto, Kari. Gaynor, Elizabeth, 1946- Russian houses /. New York , 1991. p. cm.   ISBN 1-556-70163-2 (cloth) :   DDC 728/.0947 20
NA7367 .G3 1991

L'Habitat égéen préhistorique : actes de la table ronde internationale organisée par le Centre national de la recherche scientifique, l'Université de Paris I et l'École française d'Athènes (Athènes, 23-25 juin 1987) / édités par Pascal Darcque et René Treuil. Athènes : Ecole française d'Athènes ; Paris : Dépositaire, Diffusion de Boccard, 1990. 495 p. : ill., maps ; 25 cm. (Bulletin de correspondance hellénique. Supplément. 19) Papers in French, English, German or Italian; summaries primarily in modern Greek. Includes bibliographical references.   ISBN 2-86958-031-2
1. Architecture, Prehistoric - Aegean Sea Region - Congresses. 2. Architecture, Domestic - Aegean Sea Region - Congresses. I. Darcque, Pascal. II. Treuil, René. III. Series.   *NYPL [3-MQL 91-5181]*

Hachet, Jean-Charles. César, ou, Les métamorphoses d'un grand art / Jean-Charles Hachet. Paris : Editions Varia, 1989. 92 p. : ill. ; 31 cm. (Collection "Les Grands sculpteurs contemporains")
I. Title. II. Title: Métamorphoses d'un grand art. III. Series.
IN PROCESS (ONLINE)
     NYPL [3-MGO+ (Baldaccini) 90-11990]

HACHUEL, JACQUES - ART COLLECTIONS - EXHIBITIONS.
Modern masterpieces from the collection of Jacques Hachuel . [New York, N.Y.] [1990?] 123 p. :   ISBN 84-86022-41-X
     NYPL [3-MAX (Hachuel) 91-3852]

HACIENDAS - BRAZIL - ESPÍRITO SANTO (STATE)
Muniz, Maria Izabel Perini. Arquitetura rural do século XIX no Espírito Santo /. Vitória-ES , 1989 ([Vitória?] : Gráfica e Editora São José) 239 p. :
NA8210.B69 M86 1989

HACIENDAS - MEXICO - ATOYAC VALLEY - HISTORY.
Prem, Hanns J., 1941- Milpa y hacienda . Wiesbaden , 1978. x, 325 p. ;   ISBN 3-515-02698-3
F1203 .D46 vol. 13 HD329.A84
     NYPL [HTC 74-1117 Bd. 13]

HACIENDAS - MEXICO - HISTORY.
Nickel, Herbert J. Soziale Morphologie der mexikanischen Hacienda =. Wiesbaden , [1978. xvii, 432 p.   ISBN 3-515-02699-1
F1203 .D46 vol. 14 HD1471.M6
     NYPL [HTC 74-1117 Bd. 14]

HACIENDAS - MEXICO - PUEBLA (STATE) - HISTORY.
Nickel, Herbert J. Soziale Morphologie der mexikanischen Hacienda =. Wiesbaden , 1978. xvii, 432 p.   ISBN 3-515-02699-1
F1203 .D46 vol. 14 HD1471.M6
     NYPL [HTC 74-1117 Bd. 14]

HACIENDAS - MEXICO - TLAXCALA.
Torre Villalpando, Guadalupe de la. Las calpanerías de las haciendas tlaxcaltecas . [Mexico] , 1988. 124 p. :
NA7555.M6 T67 1988

HACIENDAS - MEXICO - TLAXCALA (STATE) - HISTORY.
Nickel, Herbert J. Soziale Morphologie der mexikanischen Hacienda =. Wiesbaden , 1978. xvii, 432 p.   ISBN 3-515-02699-1
F1203 .D46 vol. 14 HD1471.M6
     NYPL [HTC 74-1117 Bd. 14]

Hackenbroch, Yvonne. Metropolitan Museum of Art (New York, N.Y.) The Lesley and Emma Sheafer collection . New York , 1975. [26] p. :
     NYPL [3-MAX (Sheafer) 90-5897]

Hackens, Tony, 1939- Études sur l'orfèvrerie antique =. Louvain-la-Neuve , 1980. viii, 154 p. :   *NYPL [3-MNR 83-1678]*

Hacker, Dieter, 1942-
Dieter Hacker : Bilder und Skulpturen : November-Dezember 1988 / [Text, Stephan Schmidt-Wulffen]. Köln : H. Holtmann, c1988. 48 p. : ill. (some col.) ; 28 cm.
1. Hacker, Dieter, 1942- - Exhibitions. I. Galerie Holtmann (Cologne, Germany). II. Title.
     NYPL [3-MCK H118 91-5907]

HACKER, DIETER, 1942- - EXHIBITIONS.
Hacker, Dieter, 1942- Dieter Hacker . Köln , c1988. 48 p. :
     NYPL [3-MCK H118 91-5907]

Haddad, Alejandro. México y su paisaje / [visto por la acuarela de Alejandro Haddad]. 1a ed. México : Taller de Alejandro Haddad, 1981. 95 p. : col. ill. ; 31 cm. (Ediciones de arte mexicano = Mexican art editions . l) Text in English and Spanish.   ISBN 968-499-067-7 (jkt.)
1. Mexico in art. I. Title.
     NYPL [3-MCZ+ H125 90-12506]

Haddad, Michèle. La divine et l'impure : le nu au XIXe / Michèle Haddad. Paris : Jaguar, c1990. 191 p. : ill. ; 29 cm.   ISBN 2-86950-174-9
I. Title.
IN PROCESS (ONLINE)
     NYPL [3-MAMZ 91-5801]

Haddock, a painter's life /. Mayans, Ernesto. Seattle , c1989. xvi, 193 p. :   ISBN 0-295-96921-0
     NYPL [3-MCX H127 90-5086]

Haddock, Arthur. Mayans, Ernesto. Haddock, a painter's life /. Seattle , c1989. xvi, 193 p. :   ISBN 0-295-96921-0
     NYPL [3-MCX H127 90-5086]

HADDOCK, ARTHUR, 1895-1980.
Mayans, Ernesto. Haddock, a painter's life /. Seattle , c1989. xvi, 193 p. : 0-295-96921-0
     NYPL [3-MCX H127 90-5086]

HADEN, FRANCIS SEYMOUR, SIR, 1818-1910 - EXHIBITIONS.
Corcoran Gallery of Art. Haden, Whistler, and Pennell . Washington, D.C. , c1990. [18] p., [18] leaves of plates :   ISBN 0-88675-035-0   DDC 769.92/2/074753 20
NE2043.25 .C67 1990
     NYPL [MDE+ 91-4773]

Haden, Francis Seymour, Sir 1818-1910.
Corcoran Gallery of Art. Haden, Whistler, and Pennell . Washington, D.C. , c1990. [18] p., [18] leaves of plates :   ISBN 0-88675-035-0   DDC 769.92/2/074753 20
NE2043.25 .C67 1990
     NYPL [MDE+ 91-4773]

Haden, Whistler, and Pennell . Corcoran Gallery of Art. Washington, D.C. , c1990. [18] p., [18] leaves of plates :   ISBN 0-88675-035-0   DDC 769.92/2/074753 20
NE2043.25 .C67 1990
     NYPL [MDE+ 91-4773]

Hadfield, Charles, 1909- D'Agapeyeff, A. (Alexander) Maps /. London , 1950 (1953 printing) 199 p., [8] leaves of plates :
     NYPL [Map Div. 91-1013]

Hadjinicolaou, Nicos, 1938- El Greco . Rethymno , 1990. 416 p. :   ISBN 960-7309-00-6   DDC 759.6 20
ND813.T4 E524 1990

Hadjipaschalis, A. J. Cyprus . Nicosia , 1986. 12 p., [1] folded leaf of plates :
     NYPL [Map Div. 90-11332]

Hadzi, Dimitri, 1921-
Dimitri Hadzi / [text, Dore Ashton]. New York, N.Y. : Kouros, 1989. 23 p. : ill. (some col.), port. ; 22 cm. Catalog of an exhibition held at the Kouros Gallery, May 1989. Bibliography: p. 23.
1. Hadzi, Dimitri, 1921- - Exhibitions. I. Ashton, Dore. II. Kouros Gallery. III. Title.
     NYPL [3-MGO (Hadzi) 91-5082]

HADZI, DIMITRI, 1921- - EXHIBITIONS.
Hadzi, Dimitri, 1921- Dimitri Hadzi /. New York, N.Y. , 1989. 23 p. :
     NYPL [3-MGO (Hadzi) 91-5082]

Haeckl, Anne E. Roman art in the private sphere . Ann Arbor , c1991. 156 p. :   ISBN 0-472-10196-X (alk. paper)   DDC 747.2937 20
N5760 .R66 1991

Haedeke, Hanns Ulrich. Kunstgewerbemuseum der Stadt Köln. Cimelien /. Köln , 1960. 96 p., 32 p. of plates :   *NYPL [3-MNE 90-6793]*

Haenlein, Carl Albrecht.
Basquiat, Jean Michel. Jean-Michel Basquiat . Hannover , 1989. [122] p. :   *NYPL [3-MAW (Hanover) 73-2900 1989/4]*

Beuys, Joseph. Joseph Beuys . Hannover [1990] 267 p. :   DDC 759.3 20
N6888.B463 A4 1990

Das Buch des Künstlers . [Hannover] [1989] 179 p. :   DDC 708.3/5954 s 769.9/04/074435954 20
N5070.H3 K4 1989/3 NE890
     NYPL [3-MAW (Hanover) 73-2900 1989/3]

Haese, Klaus. Frau Republik geht pleite : deutsche Karikaturen der zwanziger Jahre / Klaus Haese, Wolfgang U. Schütte. Berlin :

Neuer Malik Verlag, c1990. 144 p. : ill. (some
col.) ; 28 cm. Includes index. Includes bibliographical
references (p. 140-141).
*1. Caricatures and cartoons - Germany. 2. Germany -
History - 1918-1933 - Anecdotes, facetiae, satire, etc. I.
Schütte, Wolfgang U. II. Title.*
IN PROCESS (ONLINE)
NYPL [MDY 91-3467]

Haese, Roël d', 1921-
Popelier, Bert, 1945- Roel D'Haese . Gent
[1987] 63 p. :
NB673.H3 P67 1987

**HAESE, ROEL D', 1921- - CRITICISM AND
INTERPRETATION.**
Popelier, Bert, 1945- Roel D'Haese . Gent
[1987] 63 p. :
NB673.H3 P67 1987

Häuser, Bäume, Boote, Meer. Sammer, Luis,
1936- Luis Sammer--Häuser, Bäume, Boote,
Meer . Graz , 1982. [8]p., [24]p. of plates :
NYPL [3-MCK S182 88-3625]

Haezrahi, Yehudah. Katz, Shemuel, 1926-
Jerusalem, holy business as usual. Tel Aviv
[1970] 1 v. (unpaged)
NYPL [*PXLL (Jerusalem) 90-1882]

Hafertepe, Kenneth, 1955- Abner Cook : master
builder on the Texas frontier / by Kenneth
Hafertepe. Austin : Texas State Historical
Association, c1991. p. cm. Includes bibliographical
references and index.   ISBN 0-87611-102-9 (cloth)
DDC 720/.92 B 20
*1. Cook, Abner, 1814-1884. 2. Architects - Texas -
Biography. I. Title.*
NA737.C66 H3 1991

Hafner, German. Corpus vasorum antiquorum.
Deutschland. Karlsruhe--Badisches
Landesmuseum. München, 1951-1952. v.
NK4640.C6 G4 Bd. 7-8
NYPL [MPEK+ C8.K2]

Haftmann, Werner.
Der Bildhauer Martin Mayer / Werner
Haftmann. München : Callwey, c1988. 269 p. :
chiefly ill. ; 31 cm. Bibliography: p. 268.   ISBN
3-7667-0900-3   DDC 730/.92 20
*1. Mayer, Martin, 1931- - Catalogs. I. Mayer, Martin,
1931-. II. Title.*
NB588.M384 A4 1988
NYPL [3-MGO+ (Mayer) 90-10579]

Nay, E. W. (Ernst Wilhelm), 1902-1968. E.W.
Nay, Retrospektive /. Köln , c1990. 210 p. :
ISBN 3-7701-2726-9
NYPL [3-MCK+ N331 91-5930]

Sax, Ursula, 1935- Ursula Sax . Berlin [1989]
xxii, 155, [4] p. :
NB588.S3 A4 1989

Hagan, Tere. Silverplated flatware, an
identification & value guide / by Tere Hagan ;
drawings by Alfred J. Hagan. Rev. 4th ed.
Paducah, Ky. : Collector Books, c1990. 372 p. :
chiefly ill. ; 28 cm. Includes indexes.   ISBN
0-89145-428-4 :   DDC 739.2/3773/075 20
*1. Silver-plated flatware - United States - Patterns -
Catalogs. 2. Silver-plated flatware - United States -
History - 19th century - Catalogs. 3. Silver-plated
flatware - United States - History - 20th century -
Catalogs. I. Title. II. Title: Silverplated flatware, an
identification and value guide. III. Title: Silverplated
flatware.*
NK7242.F55 H3 1990

Hageney, Wolfgang. Textile patternbook . Rome,
Italy , 1989. xxi, 79, 79, 79 p. :   ISBN
88-7070-076-3   **NYPL [3-MON+ 91-4270]**

Hagenlocher, Alfred. Böhmer, Gunter, 1911-
Gunter Böhmer . Albstadt , 1980. 220 p. :
NYPL [3-MCK B671 91-1151]

Hager, Georg, b. 1863.
Bezold, Gustav von. Die Kunstdenkmale des
Regierungsbezirkes Oberbayern /. München ,
1982. 10 v. :   ISBN 3-486-50421-5 (v. 1)
N6873 .K86 1980 vol. 1 N6873

Die Kunstdenkmäler von Oberpfalz &
Regensburg /. München , 1981-<1983. v.
<1-2, 4-11, 14-21 >   ISBN 3-486-50431-2 (v. 1)
N6873 .K86 1980 vol. 2 N6876.O23

Hager, Serafina. Leonardo, Michelangelo, and
Raphael in Renaissance Florence, 1500-1508 /.
Washington, D.C. , 1991. p. cm.   ISBN
0-87840-219-5   DDC 709/.2/2455109031 20
N6923.L33 L456 1991

Hagstrom Company, inc., New York. Hagstrom's
atlas of Fairfield County, Conneticut. 2d. ed.
New York, 1966. 70 p. : col. maps ; 34 cm.
"Atlas No. 3035A. Scale of sectionalmaps ca. 1:30,000
or ca. 1:39,000.
*1. Fairfield County, Conn. - Maps. I. Title. II. Title:
Atlas of Fairfield County, Connecticut.*
G1243.F3 H3 1966   **NYPL [Map Div. 90-61]**

Hagstrom Map Company. Hagstrom's atlas of
Essex County, New Jersey. New York :
Hagstrom Map Co., c1961. 1 atlas (36 p.) : col.
maps ; 33 cm. "Atlas no. 2800A." Includes index.
*1. Essex County, N. J. - Maps. I. Title. II. Title: Essex
County atlas.*   **NYPL [Map Div. 90-67]**

Hagstrom's atlas of Essex County, New Jersey.
Hagstrom Map Company. New York , c1961. 1
atlas (36 p.) :   **NYPL [Map Div. 90-67]**

Hagstrom's atlas of Fairfield County, Conneticut.
Hagstrom Company, inc., New York. New
York, 1966. 70 p. :
G1243.F3 H3 1966   **NYPL [Map Div. 90-61]**

Hague. Museum Bredius. see Museum Bredius.

Hahn, Cheryl. Environmental figuration .
Springfield, Ill. , c1990. 31 p. :   ISBN
0-89792-130-5   DDC 757/.09773/1107477325 20
ND1292 .E59 1990

Hahn, Friedemann, 1949-
Friedemann Hahn, Zeichnungen und Aquarelle
/ herausgegeben von Werner Meyer. Stuttgart :
Ed. Cantz, 1990. 196 p. : chiefly ill. (some
col.) ; 31 cm. "Dieses Buch erscheint anlässlich der
Ausstellung Friedemann Hahn, Zeichnungen und
Aquarelle: Kunstkreis Südliche Bergstrasse Kraichgau,
Wiesloch; Städtische Galerie Bietigheim-Bissingen;
Städtische Galerie Villingen-Schwenningen;
Stadtmuseum Ratingen; Kunstmuseum Heidenheim,
Galerie der Stadt"--Colophon. Includes bibliographical
references (p. 193-194).   ISBN 3-89322-181-6 :   DDC
759.3 20
*1. Hahn, Friedemann, 1949- - Exhibitions. I. Meyer,
Werner. II. Kunstkreis Südliche Bergkreis-Kraichgau.
III. Title. IV. Title: Zeichnungen und Aquarelle.*
N6888.H256 A4 1990

Friedemann Hahn, Zeichnungen und Aquarelle
/ herausgegeben von Werner Meyer. Stuttgart :
Edition Cantz, 1990. 196 p. : ill. (chiefly col.) ;
31 cm. Published in conjunction with an exhibition
held at Kunstkreis Südliche Bergstrasse Kraichgau,
Wiesloch and at four other locations. Includes
bibliographical references (p. 193-194).   ISBN
3-89322-181-6 (Normalausg.)
*1. Hahn, Friedemann, 1949- - Exhibitions. I. Meyer,
Werner. II. Kunstkreis Südliche Bergstrasse-Kraichgau.
III. Title. IV. Title: Zeichnungen und Aquarelle.*
NYPL [3-MCK+ H137 90-12445]

**HAHN, FRIEDEMANN, 1949- -
EXHIBITIONS.**
Hahn, Friedemann, 1949- Friedemann Hahn,
Zeichnungen und Aquarelle /. Stuttgart , 1990.
196 p. :   ISBN 3-89322-181-6 :   DDC 759.3 20
N6888.H256 A4 1990

Hahn, Friedemann, 1949- Friedemann Hahn,
Zeichnungen und Aquarelle /. Stuttgart , 1990.
196 p. :   ISBN 3-89322-181-6 (Normalausg.)
NYPL [3-MCK+ H137 90-12445]

HAHN, FRIEDEMANN, 1949- - CATALOGS.
Schilling, Jürgen, 1949- Friedemann Hahn .
Stuttgart , c1990. 183 p. :   ISBN 3-89322-210-3
NYPL [MDG+ (Hahn) 91-6100]

Hahn, Otto.
Daniel Spoerri / Otto Hahn. Paris :
Flammarion, c1990. 190 p. : ill. (some col.) ; 26
cm. (La Création contemporaine) Filmography: p. 187.
Includes bibliographical references (p. 189-190).   ISBN
2-08-012140-5 :   DDC 709/.2 20
*1. Spoerri, Daniel, 1930-. 2. Artists - France -
Biography. I. Spoerri, Daniel, 1930-. II. Title. III.
Series.*
N6853.S6 H34 1990

Daniel Spoerri / Otto Hahn. Paris :
Flammarion, c1990. 190 p. : ill. (some col.) ; 26
cm. (Création contemporaine) Includes bibliographical
references (p. 189-190).   ISBN 2-08-012140-5
*1. Spoerri, Daniel, 1930-. 2. Spoerri, Daniel, 1930-
Criticism and interpretation. 3. Conceptual art - France.
I. Spoerri, Daniel, 1930-. II. Title. III. Series.*
NYPL [3-MGO (Spoerri) 90-13083]

Hahn, Siegbert, 1937-
Siegbert Hahn : Ölbilder = Oil paintings : [Dt.
Klingenmuseum Solingen, 20. Aug.-15. Okt.

1978 : Mittelrhein-Museum Koblenz, 5.
Nov.-30. Dez. 1978 / Autoren, Peter Guckel ...
et al.]. Solingen : Dt. Klingenmuseum ;
Koblenz : Mittelrhein-Museum, 1978. 93 p. :
chiefly ill. (all col.) ; 24 x 25 cm. Text in English
and German. Exhibition catalog.
*1. Hahn, Siegbert, 1937- - Exhibitions. I. Guckel, Peter,
Dr. II. Solingen, Ger. Deutsches Klingenmuseum. III.
Mittelrhein-Museum Koblenz.*
ND588.H253 A4 1978
NYPL [3-MCK H147 81-775]

HAHN, SIEGBERT, 1937- - EXHIBITIONS.
Hahn, Siegbert, 1937- Siegbert Hahn .
Solingen , Koblenz , 1978. 93 p. :
ND588.H253 A4 1978
NYPL [3-MCK H147 81-775]

Hahnloser, Margrit. The passionate eye .
[Zurich?] , Zurich , c1990. 244 p. :   ISBN
0-8478-1215-4
NYPL [3-MAX (Bührle) 90-12982]

Haig, Catherine. Hoppen, Stephanie. Decorating
with pictures /. New York , 1991. p. cm.   ISBN
0-517-58168-X :   DDC 747/.9 20
NK2115.5.P48 H66 1991

Hainard, Robert. Quand le Rhône coulait libre /
Robert Hainard. 2e éd. rev. et augm. [Genève] :
Tribune éditions, c1989. 141 p. : chiefly ill.
(some col.) ; 30 cm. Col. map on lining papers.
Includes bibliographical references (p. 139).   ISBN
2-8297-0043-0
1. Hainard, Robert. 2. Rhone River in art. I. Title.
NYPL [3-MCZ+ H1523 90-12988]

HAINARD, ROBERT.
Hainard, Robert. Quand le Rhône coulait libre
/. [Genève] , c1989. 141 p. :   ISBN
2-8297-0043-0
NYPL [3-MCZ+ H1523 90-12988]

Hainaut, Jean. Terrasse, Henri, 1895-1971. Les
arts décoratifs au Maroc /. Casablanca , c1988.
198 p. :
NK1487.75.A1 T47 1988

Haines, Carol L. "Forms to sett on" : a social
history of Concord seating furniture / Carol L.
Haines, Lisa H. Foote. Concord, Mass. :
Concord Antiquarian Museum, [1984?] 36 p. :
ill. ; 28 cm. Includes bibliographical references.
*1. Chairs - Massachusetts - Concord - Exhibitions. I.
Foote, Lisa H. II. Concord Antiquarian Society.
Museum. III. Title. IV. Title: Concord seating furniture.*
NK2715 .H35 1984
NYPL [3-MOF 90-12018]

Haining, Peter. Robinson, W. Heath (William
Heath), 1872-1944. Meals on wheels . London ,
c1989. 64 p. :   ISBN 0-285-62932-8
NYPL [3-MEM+ (Robinson) 90-2152]

**HAINS, RAYMOND, 1926- - CRITICISM
AND INTERPRETATION.**
Sur les murs. L'Art fun, ou, L'enfance de l'art.
Ateliers en liberté. Jouy-en-Josas [France]
[1986] 77 p. :   ISBN 2-86925-004-5
N6488.F8 J687 1986
NYPL [3-MAL+ 90-10669]

HAIR-DRESSING. see HAIRDRESSING.

HAIRDRESSING.
(1967) Maurice, Don. The new look for men.
[San Diego?] , c1967. 32 p. :
NYPL [3-MMX 90-7028]

**HAITI - DESCRIPTION AND TRAVEL - 1981-
- VIEWS.**
Webb, Alex. Under a grudging sun . New
York , London , 1989. 85 p. :   ISBN
0-500-27544-0 (pbk.)
NYPL [MFX+ (Webb) 89-21399]

Haïti et ses peintres . Lerebours, Michel Philippe.
Port-au-Prince, Haïti [1989] 2 v. :   DDC
759.97294/09/034 20
ND306 .L47 1989   **NYPL [Sc E 91-316]**

HAITI - HISTORY - 1986-
Webb, Alex. Under a grudging sun . New
York , London , 1989. 85 p. :   ISBN
0-500-27544-0 (pbk.)
NYPL [MFX+ (Webb) 89-21399]

HAITI - HISTORY - SOURCES.
Kurt Fisher collection of letters and papers
related to the history of Haiti, 1728-1958
[microform] New York, 1976. 14 reels (ca.
2300 items)   **NYPL [Sc Micro R-2228]**

Haitzinger, Horst, 1939- Deutschland,
Deutschland / Horst Haitzinger ; mit einem

Vorwort von Werner Schneyder. München :
Bruckmann, c1990. 125 p. : chiefly col. ill. ; 29
cm. ISBN 3-7654-2311-4
1. German wit and humor, Pictorial. 2. Germany,
West - Politics and government - Caricatures and
cartoons. I. Title.
NYPL [3-MEM (Haitzinger) 91-3584]

HAJAMADI, FARIBA, 1957- - EXHIBITIONS.
Hajamadi, Fariba, 1957- Fariba Hajamadi .
[Philadelphia] , c1988. 1 folded sheet (7 p.) :
ISBN 0-88454-045-6
NYPL [3-MCX H152 90-12728]

Hajdu, István. Les ateliers de Budapest = The
studios of Budapest = Die Ateliers in Budapest
= Budapesti műtermek / István Hajdu,
introduction and essais biographiques. Paris :
Editions E. Navarra, c1990. 240 p. : ill. ; 30
cm. French, English, German and Hungarian. ISBN
978-290-807-2006
1. Art, Hungarian - Hungary - Budapest - Exhibitions.
2. Art, Modern - 20th century - Hungary - Budapest -
Exhibitions. I. Magyar Nemzeti Galéria. II. Title. III.
Title: Studios of Budapest. IV. Title: Ateliers in
Budapest. V. Title: Budapesti műtermek.
NYPL [3-MAM+ 91-3623]

Hajek, Otto Herbert, 1927- O.H. Hajek :
Farbwege in Moskau : Begegnung mit einer
Ausstellung / [Herausgeber, Eugen Gomringer].
Stuttgart : Belser, c1989. x, 98, xix p. : ill. ; 33
cm. ISBN 3-7630-1607-4
1. Hajek, Otto Herbert, 1927-. I. Gomringer, Eugen,
1925-. II. Title.
IN PROCESS (ONLINE)
NYPL [3-MGO+ (Hajek) 91-3854]

HAJEK, OTTO HERBERT, 1927-
Hajek, Otto Herbert, 1927- O.H. Hajek .
Stuttgart , c1989. x, 98, xix p. : ISBN
3-7630-1607-4
IN PROCESS (ONLINE)
NYPL [3-MGO+ (Hajek) 91-3854]

Hajós, Géza.
Niederösterreich . Wien , c1990. xxxviii, 1414
p., [13] leaves of plates : ISBN 3-7031-0652-2
NYPL [3-MQWD 91-3702]
Niederösterreich nördlich der Donau /. Wien ,
c1990. xxxviii, 1414 p., 6 p. of plates : ISBN
3-7031-0652-2 DDC 720/.946/12 20
NA1009.L68 N54 1990

Hakob Hovnat'anyan /. Hovnat'anyan, Hakob,
1806-1881. Erevan [197-?] 64p. :
NYPL [3-MCZ H833 90-8404]

Hakob Kojoyan. Kojoyan, Hakob, 1883-1959.
Erevan , 1983. 215 p. :
NYPL [3-MCZ K784 89-27414]

**Hakone Open-air Museum. see Chōkoku no Mori
Bijutsukan.**

Halahmy, Oded, 1938-
Oded Halahmy : bronze sculptures, 1986-1990 :
exhibition March 1991. New York (141 Prince
St., New York 10012) : Louis K. Meisel
Gallery, 1991. 30 p. : ill. ; 28 cm. Introduction by
Peter Frank. Includes bibliographical references (p. 28).
1. Halahmy, Oded, 1938- - Exhibitions. I. Louis K.
Meisel Gallery. II. Title.
NYPL [3-MGO (Halahmy) 91-6647]

HALAHMY, ODED, 1938- - EXHIBITIONS.
Halahmy, Oded, 1938- Oded Halahmy . New
York (141 Prince St., New York 10012) , 1991.
30 p. : **NYPL [3-MGO (Halahmy) 91-6647]**

Haldemann, Matthias. Schweizer Kunst,
1900-1990 . [Zug] , c1990. 144 p. : ISBN
3-908215-01-5 DDC 709/.494/074494756 20
N7148 .S253 1990

**HALE COUNTY (ALA.) - DESCRIPTION
AND TRAVEL - VIEWS.**
Southall, Thomas, 1951- Of time & place . San
Francisco , Fort Worth , c1990. 88 p. : ISBN
0-933286-57-0 (cloth)
NYPL [MFW 91-3397]

Hale, J. R. (John Rigby), 1923- Artists and
warfare in the Renaissance / J.R. Hale. New
Haven : Yale University Press, 1990. ix, 278
p. : ill., (some col.) ; 29 cm. Includes indexes.
Bibliography: p. 271-275. ISBN 0-300-04840-8 DDC
760/.09/024 20
1. Art and war. I. Title.
N6370 .H25 1990 **NYPL [3-MAL 91-6322]**

Halén, Widar. Christopher Dresser / Widar
Halén. Oxford : Phaidon-Christie's, 1990. 208
p. : ill. (some col.) ; 28 cm. Includes bibliographical

references (p. [204]-206) and index. ISBN
0-07-148008-5 DDC 745.20924 20
1. Dresser, Christopher. I. Dresser, Christopher. II.
Title.
NYPL [3-MNE 91-3313]

Hales, Peter B. (Peter Bacon) Muybridge,
Eadweard, 1830-1904. One city/two visions .
San Francisco, CA , c1990. [1] p. of plates
(folded into 28 p.), 11, [1], p. : ISBN
0-938491-42-3
F869.S343 M89 1990
NYPL [MFX+ (Muybridge) 91-4539]

Haley, Christine. National Gallery of Art (U. S.)
Joie de vivre . New York, NY , 1991. p. cm.
ISBN 0-87663-608-3 DDC 759.4/074/753 20
ND547 .N38 1991

Haley, Mary Jean, 1945- Oakland Museum. A
time and place . Oakland, Calif. , c1990. iv, 175
p. : **NYPL [3-MCW+ 91-7175]**

Haley, Russell, 1934- Hanly, a New Zealand
artist / Russell Haley. Auckland : Hodder &
Stoughton, 1989. xi, 240 p., 56 p. of plates :
ill. ; 27 cm. ISBN 0-340-43129-6
1. Hanly, Patrick, 1932-. I. Title.
IN PROCESS (Online)
NYPL [3-MCZ H227 91-5639]

**HALF-TIMBERED BUILDINGS - GERMANY
(WEST) - MÜNDEN.**
Konovaloff, Arpád. Ornament am Fachwerk .
Münster [1985?] 86 p., [83] p. of plates :
ISBN 3-88660-169-2 DDC 728/.0943/59 19
NA7351.M83 K66 1985
NYPL [3-MRN 90-10411]

**HALF-TIMBERED BUILDINGS -
TERMINOLOGY.**
Fachterminologie für den historischen Holzbau .
Köln , 1990. 49 p. :
NA4115 .F34 1990

**HALF-TIMBERED HOUSES - GERMANY
(WEST) - MÜNDEN.**
Konovaloff, Arpád. Ornament am Fachwerk .
Münster [1985?] 86 p., [83] p. of plates :
ISBN 3-88660-169-2 DDC 728/.0943/59 19
NA7351.M83 K66 1985
NYPL [3-MRN 90-10411]

Hall, Audrey.
American miniatures. Philadelphia, Pa. (1806
Chestnut St., Philadelphia 19103) : Schwarz,
1990. 1 v. (unpaged) : col. ill. ; 16 cm.
(Philadelphia collection . 44) Catalogue organized,
researched, and written by Audrey Hall. DDC
757/.7/09740903307474811 20
1. Portrait miniatures, American - Catalogs. 2. Portrait
miniatures - 18th century - United States - Catalogs. 3.
Portrait miniatures - 19th century - United States -
Catalogs. 4. United States - Biography - Portraits -
Catalogs. I. Frank S. Schwarz & Son. II. Series:
Philadelphia collection , no. 44. III. Title.
ND1337.U5 H34 1990
American paintings. Philadelphia, PA (1806
Chestnut St., Philadelphia 19103) : Schwarz,
[c1990] 1 v. : col. ill. ; 22 x 24 cm. (Philadelphia
collection . 43) Catalog organized, researched, and
written by Audrey Hall. DDC
759.13/09/03407474811 20
1. Painting, American - Catalogs. 2. Painting, Modern -
19th century - United States - Catalogs. I. Frank S.
Schwarz & Son. II. Series: Philadelphia collection , no.
43. III. Title.
ND210 .H34 1990
A Century of Philadelphia artists. Philadelphia ,
1988. 64 p. : **NYPL [3-MCW 90-13578]**

Hall, Christopher. Tookey, John. The Cotswolds .
London , 1990. 60 p. : ISBN 0-233-98554-9 :
DDC 759.2 20
ND1942.T66 A4 1990

Hall, Dickson. Chinese paintings in the Palace
Museum, Beijing, 4th-14th century / Dickson
Hall. Hong Kong : Joint Pub. (H.K.) Co., 1989.
viii, 175 p., [12] p. of plates : ill. (some col.) ;
27 cm. Includes bibliographical references (p. 171).
ISBN 962-04-0691-5 : DDC 759.951/074/51156
20
1. Ku kung po wu yüan (China) - Catalogs. 2. Ink
painting, Chinese - Catalogs. 3. Scrolls, Chinese -
Catalogs. 4. Ink painting - China - Beijing - Catalogs. 5.
Scrolls - China - Beijing - Catalogs. I. Ku kung po wu
yüan (China). II. Title.
ND2068 .H35 1989
NYPL [3-MAG 91-5448]

Hall, Donald, 1928- Anecdotes of modern art :
from Rousseau to Warhol / Donald Hall, Pat
Corrington Wykes. New York : Oxford
University Press, 1990. xix, 377 p. ; 24 cm.
Includes index. ISBN 0-19-503813-4 (alk. paper) :
DDC 709.04 20
1. Art, Modern - 19th century - Anecdotes. 2. Art,
Modern - 20th century - Anecdotes. 3. Artists -
Anecdotes. I. Wykes, Pat Corrington. II. Title.
N6447 .H34 1990 **NYPL [3-MAL 90-11303]**

Hall, Douglas, 1926- 20th century Scottish
painting . [London?] , 1963. [21] p. :
NYPL [3-MCT 91-410]

Hall, H. Gaston. Richelieu's Desmarets and the
century of Louis XIV / Hugh Gaston Hall.
Oxford : Clarendon Press ; New York : Oxford
University Press, 1990. 399 p. : ill. ; 23 cm.
Includes bibliographical references (p. [357]-378) and
index. ISBN 0-19-815157-8 : DDC 841/.4 B 20
1. Desmarets de Saint Sorlin, Jean, 1595-1676. 2.
Richelieu, Armand Jean Du Plessis, duc de,
1585-1642 - Friends and associates. 3. Académie
Française - History. 4. Authors, French - 17th century -
Biography. 5. Performing art - France - History - 17th
century. 6. Ancients and moderns, Quarrel of. 7.
France - Court and courtiers - Biography. 8. France -
History - Louis XIV, 1643-1715. I. Title.
PQ1794.D6 H35 1990
NYPL [3-MAVZ (Hamburg) 91-3450]

Hall, Lee. Betty Parsons : artist, dealer collector
/ Lee Hall. New York : H.N. Abrams, 1991.
192 p. : ill. (some col.) ; 29 cm. Includes index.
Include bibliographical references. ISBN
0-8109-3712-3 DDC 709/.2 B 20
1. Parsons, Betty. 2. Art dealers - United States -
Biography. 3. Sculptors - United States - Biography. I.
Title.
N8660.P37 H35 1990
NYPL [3-MAVC 91-7302]

Hall, Marcia B. Color and meaning : practice and
theory in Renaissance painting / Marcia B.
Hall. Cambridge ; New York : Cambridge
University Press, 1991. p. cm. Includes
bibliographical references and index.
0-521-39222-5 DDC 759.03 20
1. Painting, Renaissance. I. Title.
ND170 .H3 1991

HALL-MARKS.
Colman Foods. The Colman Collection of silver
mustard pots /. Norwich , 1979. 143 p. : ISBN
0-9506456-0-5 (pbk.) :
NK7236.M88 C64 1979
NYPL [MNO 81-450]

Hall, Michael D.
Michael Hall, sculpture, 1964-1970 : the J.B.
Speed Art Museum, May 12-June 7, 1970.
[Louisville, Ky. : J.B. Speed Art Museum,
1970] [16] p. : chiefly ill. ; 28 cm.
1. Hall, Michael D. - Exhibitions. I. J.B. Speed Art
Museum. II. Title.
NYPL [3-MGO (Hall) 91-7024]

HALL, MICHAEL D. - EXHIBITIONS.
Hall, Michael D. Michael Hall, sculpture,
1964-1970 . [Louisville, Ky. , 1970] [16] p. :
NYPL [3-MGO (Hall) 91-7024]

Hall, Murray G. Die Muskete . Wien , c1983.
235 p. : ISBN 3-85063-137-0
DB30 .M87x 1983 **NYPL [MDY 87-1108]**

Hall of Fame for Great Americans. Zeitlin,
Marilyn. South Bronx Hall of Fame . Houston,
Tex. , c1991. p. cm. ISBN 0-936080-21-3 (pbk.) :
DDC 730/.92 20
NB237.A35 A4 1991

Hall, Robert L., 1950- Gathered visions : selected
works by African American women artists /
Robert L. Hall. Washington, D.C. : Anacostia
Museum, Smithsonian Institution, 1991. p. cm.
"Published on the occasion of ... an exhibition at the
Anacostia Museum from November 18, 1990, to April
28, 1991"--T.p. verso. ISBN 1-560-98106-7 (pbk.) :
DDC 704/.042/09753074753 20
1. Afro-American art - Washington Metropolitan Area -
Exhibitions. 2. Afro-American women artists -
Washington Metropolitan Area - Exhibitions. I.
Anacostia Neighborhood Museum. II. Title.
N6538.N5 H26 1991

Hall, Thomas. Scandinavian atlas of historic
towns. Odense , 1977- portfolios : ISBN
87-7492-216-5 (no. 1)
NYPL [Map Div. 82-813]

Hall, Tom. Williams, Valerie J. The nudes of Jon
Reich /. Chicago , 1991. 126 p. :   ISBN
0-9627203-0-5   DDC 741.973 20
NC139.R395 A4 1991

Halle Sud Genève. Levine, Erik, 1960- Erik
Levine . Genève , c1989. 1 v. (unpaged) :
NYPL [3-MGO (Levine) 91-7405]

Haller, Rudolf, 1929- Schwarz, Hannes, 1926-
Landschaften /. Graz , 1984. 87 p. :   ISBN
3-85420-046-3 (Normalausg.)   DDC 741.9436 20
NC245.S38 A4 1984
NYPL [3-MCK+ S407 91-5457]

Halley, Peter.
[Essays. Selections]
Collected essays, 1981-1987 / Peter Halley ;
[editor, Cheryl Epstein]. New York :
Sonnabend Gallery ; Venice, CA : Distributed
by Lapis Press, 1989, c1988. 302 p. : ill. ; 18
cm. "First published in 1988 by Edition Gallery
Bruno Bischofberger"--Colophon. Includes
bibliographical references. CONTENTS. - Beat,
minimalism, new wave, and Robert Smithson --
Notes on the paintings -- Statement (1983) -- Against
postmodernism: reconsidering Ortega -- Ross
Bleckner: painting at the end of history -- Nature
and culture -- The crisis in geometry -- After art --
The deployment of the geometric -- Notes on
nostalgia -- Frank Stella ... and the Simulacrum -- On
line -- Essence and model (1986) -- Response to
Barnett Newman's "The sublime is now" -- Notes on
abstraction. ISBN 3-905173-24-2
I. Epstein, Cheryl. II. Title.
NYPL [3-MC 89-19486]

Images of death in contemporary art .
Milwaukee, Wis. , c1990. 56 p. :   ISBN
0-87462-902-X *NYPL [3-MAMZ 91-7063]*

HALLEY, PETER - EXHIBITIONS.
Gober, Halley, Kessler, Wool . [Munich] ,
c1989. 89 p. :   ISBN 3-923357-24-9
NYPL [3-MAMT 90-12879]

Halliday, Charlotte. Gray, Alexander Stuart.
Fanlights /. London , 1990. 148 p. :   ISBN
0-7136-3077-9 :   DDC 721.823 20
NYPL [3-MRR 91-3295]

Hallmark Photographic Collection. Davis, Keith
F., 1952- Clarence John Laughlin . Kansas City,
Mo. , c1990. 166 p. :   ISBN 0-87529-629-7
NYPL [MFX+ (Laughlin) 91-7437]

HALLMARKS - ENGLAND - LONDON.
Grimwade, Arthur. London goldsmiths,
1697-1837 . London , 1990. ix, 773 p., [5] p. of
plates :   ISBN 0-571-15238-4   DDC 739.2/092/2 19
NK7144.L66   *NYPL [MNO 90-13187]*

**HALLMARKS - FRANCE - NANTES -
DICTIONARIES.**
Orfèvrerie nantaise . Paris , 1989. xlviii, 395
p. :   ISBN 2-11-081040-8   DDC 739.2/0944/14 20
NK7210 .O74 1989
NYPL [3-MNP 91-3349]

HALLMARKS - MEXICO.
El Arte de la platería mexicana, 500 años .
[Mexico] [c1989] 595 p. :   ISBN 968-619-120-8
DDC 739.2/3772 20
NK7114.A1 A73 1989

HALLMARKS ON PLATE. see HALL-MARKS.

HALLMARKS - UNITED STATES.
Ensko, Stephen Guernsey Cook, 1896-
American silversmiths and their marks IV /.
Boston , 1989, c1988. xiii, 477 p. :   ISBN
0-87923-778-3   *NYPL [MNP 90-11585]*

HALLS.
Espacios de comunicación =. Barcelona , 1976.
265 p. :   ISBN 84-7031-447-5
NA2853 .E86   *NYPL [3-MRN 81-422]*

HALLS - ITALY.
Starn, Randolph. Arts of power . Berkeley ,
c1992. p. cm.   ISBN 0-520-07383-5 (cloth)   DDC
725/.17/0945 20
NA6815 .S787 1992

Halper, Vicki. McQueen, John, 1943- John
McQueen . Washington, D.C. , 1991. p.   ISBN
0-295-97153-3   DDC 746.41/2/092 20
NK3649.55.U64 M372 1991

Hals, Frans, 1584-1666.
Frans Hals / [introduced and] edited by
Seymour Slive ; with contributions by Pieter
Biesboer ... [et al.]. Munich : Prestel ; New
York, NY, USA : Distributed in the USA and
Canada by Neues Pub. Co., c1989. 437 p. : ill.

(some col.) ; 31 cm. Catalog of an exhibition which
opened at the National Gallery of Art, Washington,
D.C., Oct. 1 - Dec. 31, 1989; traveled to the Royal
Academy of Arts, London, Jan 13, 1990; and closed at
the Frans Halsmuseum, Haarlem, July 1990. Includes
bibliographical references and index. ISBN
3-7913-1032-1   DDC 759.9492 20
*1. Hals, Frans, 1584-1666 - Exhibitions. 2. Hals, Frans,
1584-1666 - Criticism and interpretation. I. Slive,
Seymour, 1920-. II. Biesboer, P. III. National Gallery of
Art (U. S.). IV. Royal Academy of Arts (Great Britain).
V. Frans Halsmuseum. VI. Title.*
ND1329.H33 A4 1989

Grimm, Claus. [Frans Hals--das Gesamtwerk.
English.] Frans Hals--the complete work /.
New York , 1990. 296 p. :   ISBN 0-8109-3404-3
DDC 759.9492 20
ND653.H2 G7313 1990
NYPL [MCH+ H2 91-3380]

HALS, FRANS, 1584-1666.
Baard, H. P. (Henricus Petrus), 1906- [Frans
Hals en het Haarlemse groepportret in het
Gemeentemuseum 1528-1737. English.] Frans
Hals and the groupportraits at Harlem,
1528-1737 /. Harlem , 1952. 72 p. :
NYPL [3-MCH H2 90-5924]

**HALS, FRANS, 1584-1666 - CRITICISM AND
INTERPRETATION.**
Grimm, Claus. [Frans Hals--das Gesamtwerk.
English.] Frans Hals--the complete work /.
New York , 1990. 296 p. :   ISBN 0-8109-3404-3
DDC 759.9492 20
ND653.H2 G7313 1990
NYPL [MCH+ H2 91-3380]

Hals, Frans, 1584-1666. Frans Hals /. Munich ,
New York, NY, USA , c1989. 437 p. :   ISBN
3-7913-1032-1   DDC 759.9492 20
ND1329.H33 A4 1989

HALS, FRANS, 1584-1666 - EXHIBITIONS.
Hals, Frans, 1584-1666. Frans Hals /. Munich ,
New York, NY, USA , c1989. 437 p. :   ISBN
3-7913-1032-1   DDC 759.9492 20
ND1329.H33 A4 1989

HALS, FRANS, 1584-1666 - CATALOGS.
Grimm, Claus. [Frans Hals--das Gesamtwerk.
English.] Frans Hals--the complete work /.
New York , 1990. 296 p. :   ISBN 0-8109-3404-3
DDC 759.9492 20
ND653.H2 G7313 1990
NYPL [MCH+ H2 91-3380]

Halsby, Julian.
The dictionary of Scottish painters, 1600-1960 /
Julian Halsby and Paul Harris. Edinburgh :
Canongate ; Oxford : Phaidon Press, 1990. xii,
236 p. : ill. (some col.) ; 31 cm. "In association
with Bourne Fine Art." Includes bibliographical
references (p. x-xi). ISBN 0-86241-328-1 :   DDC
759.2911 20
*1. Painters - Scotland - Biography - Dictionaries. I.
Harris, Paul, M.A. II. Title.*
ND475   *NYPL [3-MCT+ 91-3993]*

Venice : the artist's vision : a guide to British
and American painters / Julian Halsby.
London : B.T. Batsford, 1990. 223 p., [32] p. of
plates : ill. (some col.), map ; 26 cm. Includes
index. Bibliography: p. 180-182. ISBN 0-7134-6606-5
DDC 758.745310922 20
1. Venice (Italy) in art. 2. Art, British. I. Title.
NYPL [3-MAMY 91-4188]

Halten und Vergehen. Fuchsberg, E. K., 1957-
Zeichnungen 1987 . Wien , c1988. 85 p. :
ISBN 3-85063-184-2
NYPL [3-MCK F946 90-8110]

Hamacher, Bärbel, 1957- Arbeitssituation und
Werkprozess in der Freskomalerei von
Matthäus Günther (1705-1788) / Bärbel
Hamacher. München : Tuduv, c1987. ii, 198 p.,
[30] p. of plates : ill., map ; 21 cm. (Schriften aus
dem Institut für Kunstgeschichte der Universität
München . Bd. 29) A revision of the author's thesis
(M.A.)--Ludwig-Maximilians-Universität München,
1983. Bibliography: p. 176-192. ISBN 3-88073-277-9
(Deut. Bibl.)   DDC 759.3 19
*1. Günther, Matthäus, 1705-1788 - Criticism and
interpretation. 2. Mural painting and decoration -
Technique. I. Title. II. Series.*
ND588.G9 H36 1987
NYPL [3-MCK G928 91-7030]

HAMAYA, HIROSHI, 1915- - EXHIBITIONS.
The Beauty of Japan. Tokyo, Japan , c1987.
[12], 118 p. :   *NYPL [MFW 91-3529]*

Hamburg. Ernst Barlach Haus. Paris. Musée
d'Orsay. Un Sculpteur-écrivain Ernst Barlach .
Paris , 1988. 64 p. :   ISBN 2-7118-2181-1 :
NYPL [3-MGO (Barlach) 90-4429]

**Hamburg. Galerie Brockstedt. see Galerie
Brockstedt.**

**HAMBURG (GERMANY) - BUILDINGS,
STRUCTURES, ETC. - GUIDE-BOOKS.**
Hipp, Hermann. Freie und Hansestadt
Hamburg . Köln , 1990. 608 p. :   ISBN
3-7701-1590-2   DDC 720/.943/515 20
NA1086.H3 H57 1990

**HAMBURG (GERMANY) - DESCRIPTION -
GUIDE-BOOKS.**
Hipp, Hermann. Freie und Hansestadt
Hamburg . Köln , 1990. 608 p. :   ISBN
3-7701-1590-2   DDC 720/.943/515 20
NA1086.H3 H57 1990

**HAMBURG (GERMANY) - DESCRIPTION -
VIEWS.**
Kaufhold, Enno, 1944- Geschichtete Momente
/. Berlin , c1989. 112 p. :   ISBN 3-88940-035-3
NYPL [MFX (Kaufhold) 91-3330]

HAMBURG (GERMANY) - HISTORY.
Hipp, Hermann. Freie und Hansestadt
Hamburg . Köln , 1990. 608 p. :   ISBN
3-7701-1590-2   DDC 720/.943/515 20
NA1086.H3 H57 1990

Hamburg (Germany). Landesplanungsamt.
Stadtbild Hamburg. Hamburg [1990] 64 p. :
NA9053.C6 S72 1990

**HAMBURG-HARBURG (HAMBURG,
GERMANY) - BUILDINGS,
STRUCTURES, ETC.**
Stadtbild Hamburg. Hamburg [1990] 64 p. :
NA9053.C6 S72 1990

**Hamburg. Kunstverein. see Kunstverein in
Hamburg.**

Hamburg Messe und Congress GmbH. Art
Maritim '88 (1988 : Hamburg, Germany)
Ostseeschiffahrt in der Kunst /. Hamburg ,
c1988. 140 p. :   ISBN 3-87700-058-4   DDC
758/.2/094307443515 20
ND1373.5.G3 A78 1988
NYPL [3-MAMZ 91-6580]

**Hamburger Bahnhof (Exhibition hall : Berlin,
Germany)** Ethos und Pathos . Berlin , c1990.
419 p. :   ISBN 3-7861-1597-4
NYPL [3-MGI 90-12677]

Hamburger Kunsthalle.
Frackmann, Harald, 1944- Harald Frackmann,
Bilder 1980-1988 . [Hamburg] [1988] [52] p. :
NYPL [3-MCK+ F797 91-4628]

Hofmann, Werner, 1928- Jürgen Partenheimer .
Hamburg , c1990. 1 v. (unpaged) :
N6888.P24 A4 1990

Huene, Stephan von, 1932- Stephan von
Huene . [Hamburg] , c1990. 1 v. (unpaged) :
N6537.H77 A4 1990

Klee, Paul, 1879-1940. Paul Klee . [Hamburg]
[1990] 130 p. :
N6888.K55 A4 1990

Kubin, Alfred, 1877-1959. Alfred Kubin
1877-1959 /. München [1990] 400 p. :   ISBN
3-88645-092-9 (Ausstellungskatalog)
IN PROCESS (ONLINE)
NYPL [3-MCK K95 91-8111]

Reden zur Jahrhundertfeier der Hamburger
Kunsthalle am 28. und 29. August 1969.
(Hamburg, 1969.) 42 p. 3 l. of illus. 25 cm.
I. Title.
N2305.H3 A86
NYPL [MAVZ (Hamburg) 83-2308]

Russische Ikonen 1400-1700 . [Hamburg]
[1990] 74, [2] p. :   DDC 704.9/482 20
N8189.S62 R9757 1990

**HAMBURGER KUNSTHALLE -
EXHIBITIONS.**
Friedrich, Caspar David, 1774-1840. Caspar
David Friedrich . [Hamburg] [1990] 35 p. :
NC251.F66 A4 1990

HAMILTON COUNTY (ILL.) - MAPS.
Rockford Map Publishers. Hamilton County,
Illinois, land atlas & plat book . Rockford, Ill.
[c1990] 1 atlas (37 p.) :
NYPL [Map Div. 91-4032]

Hamilton County, Illinois, land atlas & plat book . Rockford Map Publishers. Rockford, Ill. [c1990] 1 atlas (37 p.) :
NYPL [Map Div. 91-4032]

Hamilton County, Illinois, land atlas and plat book. Rockford Map Publishers. Hamilton County, Illinois, land atlas & plat book . Rockford, Ill. [c1990] 1 atlas (37 p.) :
NYPL [Map Div. 91-4032]

Hamilton, Helen, 1889-1970. Love, Richard H. Helen Hamilton (1889-1970) . Chicago , c1986. 72 p. : ISBN 0-940114-24-0 (pbk.) : DDC 759.13 B 19 *ND237.H259 A4 1986*
NYPL [3-MCX H2184 90-12509]

HAMILTON, HELEN, 1889-1970 - CRITICISM AND INTERPRETATION. Love, Richard H. Helen Hamilton (1889-1970) . Chicago , c1986. 72 p. : ISBN 0-940114-24-0 (pbk.) : DDC 759.13 B 19 *ND237.H259 A4 1986*
NYPL [3-MCX H2184 90-12509]

HAMILTON, HELEN, 1889-1970 - EXHIBITIONS. Love, Richard H. Helen Hamilton (1889-1970) . Chicago , c1986. 72 p. : ISBN 0-940114-24-0 (pbk.) : DDC 759.13 B 19 *ND237.H259 A4 1986*
NYPL [3-MCX H2184 90-12509]

Hamilton, Mary Jane. Wright, Frank Lloyd, 1867-1959. Frank Lloyd Wright and Madison . Madison, Wis. , 1990. vii, 218 p. : ISBN 0-932900-22-4 DDC 720/.92 20 *NA737.W7 A4 1990*
NYPL [3-MQZ+ (Wright) 90-12072]

Hamilton, Richard, 1922- Richard Hamilton : exteriors, interiors, objects, people / [Ausstellung und Katalog, Richard Hamilton und Dieter Schwarz]. Hannover : Kestner-Gesellschaft, [1990] 153 p. : ill. (chiefly col.) ; 24 cm. (Katalog . 5/1990) Catalog of an exhibition held at the Kunstmuseum Winterthur, Sept. 15-Nov. 11, 1990, at the Kestner-Gesellschaft, Hannover, Dec. 7, 1990-Feb. 3, 1991, and at the IVAM, Centre Julio González, Valencia, Feb. 25-Apr. 4, 1991. German and English. Includes bibliographical references (p. 127-130). DDC 708.3/5954 s 709/.2 20 *1. Hamilton, Richard, 1922- - Exhibitions. I. Schwarz, Dieter. II. Kunstmuseum Winterthur. III. Kestner-Gesellschaft. IV. IVAM Centre Julio González. V. Title. VI. Title: Exteriors, interiors, objects, people. VII. Series: Katalog (Kestner-Gesellschaft) , 1990/5.* *N5070.H3 K4 1990/5 N6797.H3*

HAMILTON, RICHARD, 1922- - EXHIBITIONS. Hamilton, Richard, 1922- Richard Hamilton . Hannover [1990] 153 p. : DDC 708.3/5954 s 709/.2 20 *N5070.H3 K4 1990/5 N6797.H3*

Hamilton, Vivien. Joseph Crawhall, 1861-1913 : one of the Glasgow boys / by Vivien Hamilton. London : J. Murray in association with Glasgow Museums and Art Galleries, 1990. xiii, 177 p. : ill. (some col.) ; 29 cm. Joseph Crawhall exhibition held 5 July-26 August 1990, the Burrell Collection, Glasgow and 4-29 September 1990, the Fine Art Society, London. Includes bibliographical references (p. [159]-160) and index. ISBN 0-7195-4827-6 : DDC 759.2/911 20 *1. Crawhall, Joseph, 1861-1913 - Exhibitions. 2. Glasgow school of painting - Exhibitions. 3. Crawhall, Joseph, 1861-1913 - Criticism and interpretation. I. Crawhall, Joseph, 1861-1913. II. Glasgow Museums and Art Galleries. III. Title.* *ND1942.C89 A4 1990*

Hamm, Ger. Gustav-Lübcke Museum. see Gustav-Lübcke-Museum Hamm.

Hamm, Jack. Drawing and cartooning 1,001 faces, places, and things / Jack Hamm. New York, NY : Perigee books, c1991. p. cm. Includes index. Provides instructions for making serious cartoons or drawings of hundreds of subjects from people to animals. ISBN 0-399-51687-5 (alk. paper) DDC 741.2 20 *1. Drawing - Technique. 2. Cartooning - Technique. I. Title.* *NC730 .H25 1991*

HAMMAN, JOHANN FRIEDRICH, 1655?-1718? Reuter, Fritz. Peter und Johann Friedrich Hamman . [Worms] [1989] 117 p. : ISBN

3-925518-05-3
IN PROCESS (ONLINE)
NYPL [3-MAMY 91-6283]

HAMMAN, PETER, 1624-1692. Reuter, Fritz. Peter und Johann Friedrich Hamman . [Worms] [1989] 117 p. : ISBN 3-925518-05-3
IN PROCESS (ONLINE)
NYPL [3-MAMY 91-6283]

Hammer Galleries. Moses, Grandma, 1860-1961. Grandma Moses (1860-1961) . New York, N.Y. (33 W. 57th St., New York 10019) , c1990. 24 p. : DDC 759.13 20 *ND237.M78 A4 1990*

Hammer, Karen Elisabeth, 1959- Sakrale Wandmalerei in Dänemark und Norddeutschland im ausgehenden Mittelalter : eine Studie zu den Malereien der Elmelundegruppe in Sakralräumen Süddänemarks unter besonderer Berücksichtigung der Kirche zu Fanefjord sowie der norddeutschen Wandmalerei / Karen Elisabeth Hammer. Ammersbek bei Hamburg : Verlag an der Lottbek, c1990. 324 p. : ill. ; 21 cm. Includes bibliographical references (p. 303-322). ISBN 3-926987-18-9 *1. Mural painting and decoration, Danish. 2. Mural painting and decoration, Medieval - Denmark. 3. Mural painting and decoration, German - Germany, Northern. 4. Mural painting and decoration, Medieval - Germany, Northern. 5. Fanefjord kirke. I. Title.* *ND2773 .H36 1990*

Hammerstiel, Robert F., 1957- Stand-Orte / Robert F. Hammerstiel. [Wien] : Amt der NÖ Landesregierung, Abt. III/2, Kulturabt., c1988. 1 v. (unpaged) : ill. ; 29 cm. (Katalog des Niederösterreichischen Landesmuseums . n.F., Nr. 223) *1. Hammerstiel, Robert F., 1957- - Exhibitions. I. Blau-Gelbe Galerie der NÖ Kulturabteilung. II. Series. III. Series: Medium (Vienna, Austria) , 8. IV. Title.* *NYPL [MFX (Hammerstiel) 90-13462]*

HAMMERSTIEL, ROBERT F., 1957- - EXHIBITIONS. Hammerstiel, Robert F., 1957- Stand-Orte /. [Wien] , c1988. 1 v. (unpaged) : ISBN 3-900464-91-1
NYPL [MFX (Hammerstiel) 90-13462]

Hammond past worlds. Past worlds . Maplewood, N.J. , 1988. 319 p.: ISBN 0-7230-0306-8 : DDC 912 19 *G1046.E15 P3 1988*
NYPL [Map Div. 90-11840]

Hammond-Tooke, David. African art in Southern Africa . Johannesburg , 1989. 252 p. : ISBN 0-86852-158-2 DDC 704/.03968 20 *N7392 .A57 1989*

Hampel, Frithjof Detlev Paul. Schinkels Möbelwerk und seine Voraussetzungen / Frithjof Detlev Paul Hampel. 1. Aufl. Witterschlick/Bonn : Wehle, 1989. 255 p., [8] p. of plates : ill. ; 21 cm. (Beiträge zur Kunstgeschichte. Bd. 4) Originally presented as the author's thesis (doctoral)--Universität Bonn, 1989. Includes bibliographical references (p. 232-242). ISBN 3-925267-29-8 *1. Schinkel, Karl Friedrich, 1781-1841 - Criticism and interpretation. 2. Furniture - Germany - History - 19th century. 3. Classicism in art - Germany. I. Series: Beiträge zur Kunstgeschichte (Witterschlick, Germany) , Bd. 4. II. Title.* *NK2554.S35 H35 1989*

Hampel, Lucie. Historiches Museum der Stadt Wien. 200 Jahre Mode in Wien . Wien , 1976. 120 p., [34] leaves of plates :
NYPL [3-MMM 90-6048]

HAMPI (INDIA) - BUILDINGS, STRUCTURES, ETC. Filliozat, Pierre Sylvain. Hampi-Vijayanagar . New Delhi , 1988. 1 portfolio : DDC 726/.145/095487 20 *NA6008.H35 F53 1988*
NYPL [3-MQWS+ 91-6052]

Hampi-Vijayanagar . Filliozat, Pierre Sylvain. New Delhi , 1988. 1 portfolio : DDC 726/.145/095487 20 *NA6008.H35 F53 1988*
NYPL [3-MQWS+ 91-6052]

Hampton, Mark. Legendary decorators of the twentieth century / Mark Hampton. 1st ed. New York : Doubleday, 1992. p. cm. ISBN

0-385-26361-9 : DDC 747.213/09/04 20 *1. Interior decoration - United States - History - 20th century. 2. Interior decorators - United States - Biography. I. Title.* *NK2004 .H36 1992*

Hancock, Jane H., 1949- Homecoming : the art collection of James J. Hill / Jane H. Hancock, Sheila Ffolliott, Thomas O'Sullivan. St. Paul : Minnesota Historical Society Press, c1991. x, 116 p. : ill. (some col.) ; 28 cm. "Published in conjunction with an exhibition of the same name ... at the James J. Hill House, St. Paul, Minnesota, May 18-September 21, 1991." "Catalogue of the exhibition": p.67-100. Includes bibliographical references (p. 65-66) and index. ISBN 0-87351-259-6 DDC 759.05/074/74776581 20 *1. Art, Modern - 19th century - Exhibitions. 2. Hill, James Jerome, 1838-1916 - Art collections - Exhibitions. 3. Art - Private collections - Minnesota - Saint Paul - Exhibitions. 4. Hill, James Jerome, 1838-1916 - Homes and haunts - Minnesota - Saint Paul - Exhibitions. I. Ffolliott, Sheila. II. O'Sullivan, Thomas, 1951-. III. Minnesota Historical Society. IV. Title.* *N6450 .H298 1991*

Hand . Coplans, John. New York , c1988. 1 v. (unpaged) : *NYPL [MFX (Coplans) 91-4595]*

HAND WEAVING - INDONESIA. Marah, Soerisman. Berbagai pola kain tenun dan kehidupan pengrajinnya /. [Jakarta] [1989?] v, 68 p. : *NK8980.A1 M37 1989*

HAND WEAVING - TURKEY - TAURUS MOUNTAINS REGION - EXHIBITIONS. Landreau, Anthony N., 1930- Flowers of the Yayla . Washington, D.C. , c1983. 108 p. : DDC 746.1/4/089943 19 *TT848 .L372 1983*
NYPL [3-MOP+ 90-12467]

Handbook of American paintings in the Nelson-Atkins Museum of Art, Kansas City, Missouri /. Nelson-Atkins Museum of Art. Kansas City, Mo. , 1991. p. cm. ISBN 0-942614-17-8 DDC 759.13/074/778411 20 *ND205 .N34 1991*

Handbook of architectural contract administration /. Pachner, Edmond, 1916- New York , 1992. p. cm. ISBN 0-471-55004-3 DDC 720/.68/7 20 *NA1996 .P3 1992*

A handbook of Chinese ceramics /. Valenstein, Suzanne G. New York , c1989. xiii, 331 p., [32] p. of plates : ISBN 0-87099-514-6 DDC 738/.0951 19 *NK4165 .V34 1989*
NYPL [3-MPFF 91-3954]

Handbook of painting. Kugler, Franz, 1808-1858. London, 1898. St. Clair Shores, Mich., 1972. 2 v. (xi, 586 p.) ISBN 0-403-01059-4 DDC 759.3 *ND625 .K8 1972*

Handbook of the Cleveland Museum of Art. Cleveland Museum of Art. Cleveland, Ohio , 1991. x, 161 p. : ISBN 0-940717-00-X : DDC 708.171/32 20 *N552 .A6 1991*

Handbook of the collection /. Elvehjem Museum of Art. Madison, Wis. , c1990. xvi p., 154 p. of plates : ISBN 0-932900-23-2 DDC 708.175/83 20 *N582.M22 A6 1990*
NYPL [3-MAVZ (Madison) 91-4867]

Handbook of the collections in the Blanden Memorial Art Museum, Fort Dodge, Iowa /. Blanden Memorial Art Museum. Fort Dodge, Iowa (920 3rd Ave., South, Fort Dodge 50501) , 1989. 132 p. : DDC 708.177/51 20 *N570.29 .A6 1989*

Handelshögskolan i Stockholm. Centrum för immaterialrätt och medierätt. Levin, Marianne, 1942- Plagiat, stöld, förebild, inspiration /. [Solna] , c1990. 138 p. : ISBN 91-7332-505-8 : *NK789 .L48 1990*

HANDICAPPED AND ARCHITECTURE. see ARCHITECTURE AND THE HANDICAPPED.

HANDICRAFT (BEADWORK) see BEADWORK.

HANDICRAFT - DOMINICAN REPUBLIC. Castillo, José del, 1947- Artesanía dominicana /. Santo Domingo, República Dominicana ,

1989. 125 p. :   DDC 745/.097293 20
NK886.D65 C38 1989

HANDICRAFT - ITALY - ALPS, ITALIAN - HISTORY - 20TH CENTURY.
Artigianato di tradizione nelle Alpi occidentali italiane . Ivrea, Italy , c1990. 305 p. :   DDC 745/.0945/1 20
NK960.A536 A78 1990

HANDICRAFT - JAPAN - OKINAWA.
Okamura, Kichiemon, 1916- Okinawa no kōgei. Tōkyō, 1946. 143, 30 p. :
NYPL   [3-MNH 91-800]

HANDICRAFT - MEXICO.
Sayer, Chloë. Arts and crafts of Mexico /. London , 1990. 160 p. :   ISBN 0-87701-781-6 :
NYPL   [3-MNE 91-4573]

HANDICRAFT - MEXICO - MICHOACÁN DE OCAMPO.
El Quehacer de un pueblo . Morelia, Michoacán , 1986. 183, [9] p. :   ISBN 968-667-045-9   DDC 745/.0972/37 20
NK845.M53 Q44 1986

HANDICRAFT - NEW ZEALAND - EXHIBITIONS.
Kahurangi . Los Angeles [1984] 63 p. :   ISBN 0-477-01518-2 (pbk.)
NK1092.A1 K35 1984
NYPL   [3-MNE 90-10614]

HANDICRAFT - PORTUGAL.
Artesanato da região norte . Porto , 1989. 406 p. :   ISBN 972-90030-0-9   DDC 745/.09469 20
NK1003 .A83 1989

HANDICRAFT - VIETNAM.
Vietnamese handicrafts. Hanoi , 1959. 48 p., [21] p. of plates :   DDC 745/.09597
TT113.V5 V53   *NYPL   [3-MNE 90-7047]*

HANDICRAFTS - INDIA - ORISSA.
Arts and artisans of Orissa /. Bhubaneswar [1981?] 106 p. ;   DDC 338.4/77/095413 19
N7307.O74 A77 1981
NYPL   [3-MNE 90-5470]

Handicrafts of Okinawa. Okamura, Kichiemon, 1916- Okinawa no kōgei. Tōkyō, 1946. 143, 30 p. :   *NYPL   [3-MNH 91-800]*

Handloik, Volker. Leichtmetall . [Berlin?] [1990?] 190 p. :   ISBN 3-86163-003-6
NYPL   [3-MDY+ 91-5809]

Hands-on, hands-off . Stone, Harris, 1934- New York , c1991. 191 p. :   ISBN 0-85345-824-3 (pbk.) :   DDC 720/.1/04 20
NA2543.H55 S7 1991

Handtekeningen van belgische kunstenaars uit de XIX en XXe eeuwen. Piron, Paul-L. Belgian artists' signatures /. [Brussels] [1989] 544 p. :
NYPL   [3-MAME 91-5520]

Handzeichnungen alter Meister aus dem Besitz der Kunstsammlung der Georg-August-Universität Göttingen. Universität Göttingen. Kunstsammlung. [Kiel?] 1966] 1 v. (unpaged)
NC15 .K5   *NYPL   [3-MBH 91-232]*

Hanebutt-Benz, Eva-Maria. Museum für Kunsthandwerk Frankfurt am Main. Ornament und Entwurf . Frankfurt am Main , c1983. 199 p., [8] p. of plates :   ISBN 3-88270-021-1   DDC 745.4/494/0740341 19
NK1530 .M87 1983   *NYPL   [MDE 85-3207]*

Hanefi Yeter /. Yeter, Hanefi, 1947- Berlin , 1989. 159 p. :   ISBN 3-88520-323-5
N7173.Y4 A4 1989

Hanfgarn, Werner, 1925- Mainzer Brunnen : was sie uns erzählen / Werner Hanfgarn. Mainz : H. Schmidt, 1990. 180 p. : ill. (some col.) ; 20 cm. Includes bibliographical references (p. 180).
ISBN 3-87439-210-4 :
1. Fountains - Germany - Mainz. 2. Mainz (Germany) - Buildings, structures, etc. 3. Mainz (Germany) - History. I. Title.
NA9415.M35 H36 1990

Hangartner, Urs, 1958- "Mit Pikasso macht man Kasso" . Zürich , c1990. 155 p., [5] p. of plates :   ISBN 3-907010-50-7
IN PROCESS (ONLINE)
NYPL   [MDY+ 90-12785]

Han'guk misul Chŏnjip. The Arts of Korea. Seoul , c1979. 6 v. :   DDC 709/.519
N7363 .A79   *NYPL   [3-MAF+ 83-1615]*

Han'guk ŭi ko kŏnch'uk. Korean architecture.

Seoul , 1982- v. :   DDC 722/.13 19
NA1563 .K67 1982
NYPL   [3-MQWS+ 87-1952]

Hanhardt, John G. Haskell, Barbara. Yoko Ono, arias, and objects /. Salt Lake City , 1991. p. cm.   ISBN 0-87905-386-0 (pbk.) :   DDC 700/.92 20
NX512.O56 H37 1991

Hanhart, Rudolf. Installation, Klangraum, Musik . [St. Gallen] [1983] [29] p. :
NYPL   [3-MAL 90-12516]

Hanke, Stefan, 1961- Menschen einer deutschen Stadt : 99 Photographien aus Regensburg / Stefan Hanke. Nördlingen : DELPHI Verlegt bei Greno, 1988. 109 p. : ill- ; 30 cm.   ISBN 3-89130-621-8
1. Hanke, Stefan, 1961-. I. Title.
NYPL   [MFX+ (Hanke) 89-20458]

HANKE, STEFAN, 1961-
Hanke, Stefan, 1961- Menschen einer deutschen Stadt . Nördlingen , 1988. 109 p. :   ISBN 3-89130-621-8
NYPL   [MFX+ (Hanke) 89-20458]

Hanks, David A. The decorative designs of Frank Lloyd Wright / David A. Hanks. 1st ed. New York : Dutton, c1979. xx, [1], 232 p., [8] leaves of plates : ill. (some col.) ; 24 cm. "Published in association with an exhibition originated by Renwick Gallery of the National Collection of Fine Arts, Smithsonian Institution, Washington, D.C." Includes index. Bibliography: p. [xxi]   ISBN 0-525-08958-6 :
1. Wright, Frank Lloyd, 1867-1959. 2. Design, Decorative - United States.
NYPL   [3-MQZ (Wright) 90-10664]

Hanks, Kurt, 1947-
Draw! : a visual approach to thinking, learning and communicating / Kurt Hanks and Larry Belliston. Los Altos, Calif. : Crisp Publications, 1990. p. cm. Previously published: Los Altos, Calif. : William Kaufmann, 1977. Includes bibliographical references and index.   ISBN 1-560-52054-X :   DDC 741.2 20
1. Drawing - Technique. 2. Visualperception. I. Belliston, Larry, 1949-. II. Title.
NC730 .H27 1990

Rapid viz : a new method for the rapid visualization of ideas / Hanks and Belliston. Los Altos, CA : Crisp Publications, c1990. 149 p. : ill. ; 22 x 28 cm. Reprint. Originally published: Experimental ed. Los Altos, Calif. : W. Kaufmann, c1980. Includes bibliographical references (p. [151]).
ISBN 1-560-52055-8 (pbk.) :   DDC 741.6 20
1. Graphic arts - Technique. 2. Felt marker drawing. 3. Visual communication. 4. Drawing, Psychology of. I. Belliston, Larry, 1949-. II. Title.
NC877.8 .H36 1990

Hanle, Adolf.
Meyers neuer weltatlas /. Mannheim , 1989. 321 p. :   ISBN 3-411-02354-6
NYPL   [Map Div. 90-11958]

Meyers Universal Atlas . Mannheim , c1990. 1 atlas (224 p.) :   ISBN 3-411-07285-7
NYPL   [Map Div. 91-7165]

Hanly, a New Zealand artist /. Haley, Russell, 1934- Auckland , 1989. xi, 240 p., 56 p. of plates :   ISBN 0-340-43129-6
IN PROCESS (Online)
NYPL   [3-MCZ H227 91-5639]

HANLY, PATRICK, 1932-
Haley, Russell, 1934- Hanly, a New Zealand artist /. Auckland , 1989. xi, 240 p., 56 p. of plates :   ISBN 0-340-43129-6
IN PROCESS (Online)
NYPL   [3-MCZ H227 91-5639]

Hann, Edith. Lehne, Andreas. Wiener Warenhäuser, 1865-1914 /. Wien , 1990. 195 p. :   ISBN 3-7005-4488-X
NA6227.D45 L44 1990

Hann Trier . Trier, Hann, 1915- Köln , c1990. 183 p. :   DDC 759.3 20
ND588.T833 A4 1990

Hannah, Duncan.
Duncan Hannah, mythic times : April 24-May 27, 1990, University Galleries of Illinois State University. Normal, Ill. : The Galleries, 1990. 55 p. : ill. (some col.) ; 28 cm. Exhibition also travels to Moody Gallery of University of Alabama, Tuscaloosa, Aug. 24-Sept. 30, 1990. Includes bibliographical references.   ISBN 0-945558-08-2
1. Hannah, Duncan - Exhibitions. I. Illinois State University. University Galleries. II. Moody Gallery. III.

Title: Mythic times.
NYPL   [3-MCX H244 91-39]

HANNAH, DUNCAN - EXHIBITIONS.
Hannah, Duncan. Duncan Hannah, mythic times . Normal, Ill. , 1990. 55 p. :   ISBN 0-945558-08-2
NYPL   [3-MCX H244 91-39]

Hannah Höch, Schnitt mit dem Küchenmesser Dada durch die letzte weimarer Bierbauchkulturepoche Deutschlands /. Dech, Jula. Frankfurt am Main , 1989. 89 p., [1] folded leaf of plates :   ISBN 3-596-23970-2 :
NYPL   [3-MCK H691 91-4661]

Hannah Höch 1889-1978 . Höch, Hannah, 1889- [Berlin] , 1989. 223, [24] p. :   ISBN 3-87024-156-X (Argon)
NYPL   [3-MCK H691 90-12356]

Hannah Villiger . Villiger, Hannah. Basel , c1989. 72 p. :   ISBN 3-909158-34-X
IN PROCESS (ONLINE)
NYPL   [MFX (Villiger) 90-13438]

Hannes Meyer . Kieren, Martin. Heiden , c1990. 195 p. :   ISBN 3-7212-0224-4   DDC 720/.92 20
NA1353.M4 K54 1990

Hannes Meyer, 1889-1954 : Architekt, Urbanist, Lehrer / [Herausgeber, Bauhaus-Archiv, Berlin, und Deutsches Architekturmuseum, Frankfurt am Main, in Verbindung mit dem Institut fur Geschichte und Theorie der Architektur an der ETH Zürich; Bearbeiter, Werner Kleinerüschkamp]. Berlin : Ernst, c1989. 368 p. : ill. (some col.) ; 29 cm. Includes bibliographical references and index.   ISBN 3-433-02053-1 :   DDC 720/.92 20
1. Meyer, Hannes, 1889-1954. 2. Architecture, Modern - 20th century - Switzerland. 3. Architects - Switzerland - Biography. I. Meyer, Hannes, 1889-1954. II. Kleinerüschkamp, Werner. III. Bauhaus Archiv, Museum für Gestaltung. IV. Deutsches Architekturmuseum. V. Eidgenössische Technische Hochschule Zürich. Institut für Geschichte und Theorie der Architektur.
NA1353.M4 H35 1989

Hannoosh, Michele, 1954- Baudelaire and caricature : from the comic to an art of modernity / Michele Hannoosh. University Park, Pa. : Pennsylvania State University Press, c1992. p. cm. Includes bibliographical references (p.) and index.   ISBN 0-271-00804-0 (acid-free paper) :   DDC 741.5/09 20
1. Caricature - History. 2. Modernism (Art). 3. Baudelaire, Charles, 1821-1867 - Philosophy. I. Title.
NC1325 .H36 1992

Hanns Schimansky, Zeichnungen /. Schimansky, Hanns, 1949- Berlin , c1990. 24 p. :   ISBN 3-88609-248-8
NC251.S3277 A4 1990

Hanover. Kestner-Gesellschaft. see Kestner-Gesellschaft.

Hanover. Kunstmuseum Hannover mit Sammlung Sprengel. see Kunstmuseum Hannover mit Sammlung Sprengel.

Hanover. Wilhelm-Busch-Museum. see Wilhelm-Busch-Museum.

Hans-Albert Walter . Walter, Hans-Albert, 1925- Hannover , 1990. 54 p. :   ISBN 3-89169-056-8
NYPL   [3-MCK+ W226 91-6801]

Hans-Albert Walter, die Farbe Schwarz, das Licht . Walter, Hans-Albert, 1925- Hannover [1990] 54 p. :   ISBN 3-89169-056-8
N6888.W32 A4 1990

Hans-Albert Walter zum 65. Geburtstag. Walter, Hans-Albert, 1925- Hans-Albert Walter, die Farbe Schwarz, das Licht . Hannover [1990] 54 p. :   ISBN 3-89169-056-8
N6888.W32 A4 1990

Hans Arp und Sophie Taeuber-Arp . Watts, Harriett. Wolfenbüttel [1989] 54 p. :   ISBN 3-88373-054-8   DDC 700/.92 20
N6853.A7 A4 1989

Hans Böhler, Gemälde und Graphik /. Breicha, Otto. Salzburg , c1981. 119 p. of plates :   ISBN 3-85349-084-0 :   DDC 741.9436 19
N6811.5.B64 A4 1981
NYPL   [3-MCK B68 91-5395]

Hans Burkhardt . Burkhardt, Hans Gustav, 1904- Long Beach, Calif. [1972] [20] p. :   DDC

759.13
ND237.B896 L66
NYPL [3-MCX B953.L849]

Hans Giesen, junge Malerei aus Amsterdam .
Giesen, Hans 1942- Oldenburg , c1988. 75 p. :
NYPL [3-MCH G456 90-12615]

Hans Graeder, Re-Visionen . Graeder, Hans,
1919- Mannheim , c1990. 57 p. : ISBN
3-89165-071-X
N6888.G658 A4 1990

Hans Gudewerdt der jüngere (um 1600-1671) .
Behling, Holger. Neumünster , 1990. 375 p. :
ISBN 3-529-02515-1
NYPL [3-MGO+ (Gudewerdt) 91-6536]

Hans Hartung, premières peintures 1922-1949.
Hartung, Hans, 1904- Antibes , 1987. 74 p. :
ISBN 2-905315-10-5
NYPL [3-MCK H336 91-4238]

Hans Hofmann /. Goodman, Cynthia. New
York , 1990. 200 p. : ISBN 0-87427-070-7 DDC
759.13 20
ND237.H667 A4 1990
NYPL [3-MCK+ H71 90-12024]

**Hans Hofmann, paintings on paper from the
1940s** . Hofmann, Hans, 1880-1966. New
York , c1990. [21] p., 8 leaves of plates :
NYPL [3-MCK+ H71 91-6604]

**Hans Jürgen Kallmann, oder, Das Prinzip des
Unbeirrbaren** /. Keller, Horst. München ,
c1972. 114 p. : ISBN 3-7654-1496-4
ND1329.K34 K44
NYPL [3-MCK K139 91-1299]

Hans Körnig, Aquatintaradierungen . Körnig,
Hans, 1905- Reutlingen , 1980. 66 p. :
MLCM 87/1650 (N)
NYPL [MDG (Körnig) 91-1316]

Hans Kuhn. Kuhn, Hans, 1905- Köln [1968] 105,
[6] p. DDC 759.3
ND588.K88 B3
NYPL [3-MCK K956 91-880]

Hans Laabs . Laabs, Hans, 1915- Berlin , c1990.
189 p. : ISBN 3-87584-294-4 DDC 759.3 20
ND588.L25 A4 1990
NYPL [3-MCK+ B126 89-28417]

Hans Matthäus Bachmayer. Bachmayer, Hans
Matthäus. München , 1988. 51 p. :
NYPL [3-MCK+ B126 89-28417]

Hans Meid . Franken, Franz Hermann.
Stuttgart-Bad Cannstatt , c1987. 462 p. : ISBN
3-922608-58-2
NYPL [3-MCK+ M4978 90-11755]

Hans Purrmann, Hans, 1880-1966.
Heidelberg , c1990. 178 p. : ISBN 3-925835-29-6
DDC 759.3 20
ND588.P86 A4 1990

**Hans Stein, Gemälde, Zeichnungen, Aquarelle,
Druckgrafik** /. Stein, Hans, 1935- Berlin ,
1988. 1 v. (unpaged) : DDC 760/.092 20
N6888.S68527 A4 1988
NYPL [3-MCK+ S815 90-12765]

Hans Thoma-Gesellschaft. Körnig, Hans, 1905-
Hans Körnig, Aquatintaradierungen .
Reutlingen , 1980. 66 p. :
MLCM 87/1650 (N)
NYPL [MDG (Körnig) 91-1316]

Hans Thoma, Lebensbilder . Thoma, Hans,
1839-1924. Königstein im Taunus , c1989. 336
p. : ISBN 3-7845-7870-X DDC 759.3 20
ND588.T4 A4 1989

Hans Thoma, 1839-1924, zum 150. Geburtstag .
Thoma, Hans, 1839-1924. Karlsruhe , c1989.
169 p. : ISBN 3-925212-08-6
NYPL [3-MCK T45 90-12555]

Hanscomb, Brian.
Sun, sea & earth / copper-engravings by Brian
Hanscomb ; with texts by Richard Jefferies,
John Clare, Edward Thomas & the artist.
Andoversford, Gloucestershire : Whittington
Press, 1989. [21] p. : ill. ; 26 cm. "Edition of 125
copies ... 100 copies are printed on hand-made paper,
and 25 copies are printed on Hammer and Anvil
hand-made paper, with an extra set of proofs of the
engravings"--P. [21]. Printed on double leaves. LC has
copy no. 6 of the regular issue. DLC Source: Purchase,
July 27, 1990. DLC CONTENTS. - The pageant of
summer / Richard Jefferies -- On Long Knoll, Wiltshire
/ Brian Hanscomb -- A dream / Edward Thomas --
The hedgehog / John Clare -- The story of my heart /

Richard Jefferies -- A Mendip spring / Brian
Hanscomb -- I am / John Clare. ISBN 1-85428-004-X
DDC 769.92 20
1. Hanscomb, Brian - Themes, motives. I. Jefferies,
Richard, 1848-1887. II. Thomas, Edward, 1878-1917.
III. Clare, John, 1793-1864. IV. Title. V. Title: Sun, sea,
and earth.
NE642.H34 A4 1989

HANSCOMB, BRIAN - THEMES, MOTIVES.
Hanscomb, Brian. Sun, sea & earth /.
Andoversford, Gloucestershire , 1989. [21] p. :
ISBN 1-85428-004-X DDC 769.92 20
NE642.H34 A4 1989

Hansen, David. The face of Australia : the land &
the people, the past & the present / text by
David Hansen in association with the
Australian Bicentennial Authority.1st ed.
Frenchs Forest, NSW, Australia : Child &
Associates, 1988. 127 p. : ill. (some col.) ; 31
cm. Catalog of a traveling exhibition presented by the
Australian Bicentennial Authority in 1988. Includes
bibliographical references and index. ISBN
0-86777-181-X DDC 760/.0449994 19
1. Art, Australian - Exhibitions. 2. Australia in art -
Exhibitions. I. Australian Bicentennial Authority. II.
Title.
N7400 .H3 1988 **NYPL [3-MAM+ 91-2242]**

Hansen, Emil. see Nolde, Emil, 1867-1956.

Hansen, Judith W., 1953- Pennsylvania prints
from the Collection of John C. O'Connor and
Ralph M. Yeager : lithographs, engravings,
aquatints and watercolors from the Tavern
Restaurant : catalog / compiled by Judith W.
Hansen ; entry information from notes by John
C. O'Connor and Ralph M. Yeager. University
Park : Museum of Art, Pennsylvania State
University ; distributed by Pennsylvania State
University Press, c1980. [176] p. : ill. (some
col.) ; 24 x 31 cm. Includes bibliography. DDC
769.9748/074/014853
1. O'Connor, John C. - Art collections - Exhibitions. 2.
Yeager, Ralph M. - Art collections - Exhibitions. 3.
Tavern Restaurant (State College, Pa.) - Art
collections - Exhibitions. 4. Prints, American -
Exhibitions. 5. Prints - 19th century - United States -
Exhibitions. 6. Pennsylvania in art - Exhibitions. I.
Pennsylvania State University. Museum of Art. II. Title.
NE507 .H36 **NYPL [MDBF+ 82-159]**

Hansen, Trudy V. Intaglio printing in the 1980s :
prints, plates and proofs from the Rutgers
Archives for Printmaking Studios : the Jane
Voorhees Zimmerli Art Museum, December 9,
1990-February 24, 1991 / Trudy V. Hansen.
[New Brunswick, N.J.] : The Museum, c1990.
v, 45 p. : ill. ; 28 cm. Bibliography: p. 44.
1. Rutgers Archives for Printmaking Studios -
Exhibitions. 2. Intaglio printing - Exhibitions. I. Jane
Voorhees Zimmerli Art Museum. II. Title.
IN PROCESS (ONLINE)
NYPL [MDE 91-3493]

Hanson, Duane.
Bush, Martin H. Duane Hanson, Skulpturen /.
[Stuttgart] , c1990. 111 p. : ISBN 3-89322-205-7
NYPL [3-MGO (Hanson) 91-7453]

HANSON, DUANE - EXHIBITIONS.
Bush, Martin H. Duane Hanson, Skulpturen /.
[Stuttgart] , c1990. 111 p. : ISBN 3-89322-205-7
NYPL [3-MGO (Hanson) 91-7453]

Hanson, F. Allan, 1939- Art and identity in
Oceania /. Honolulu , c1990. viii, 315 p., [8] p.
of plates : ISBN 0-8248-1304-9 : DDC 700/.995
20
N7399.7 .A78 1990
NYPL [3-MADF 91-5014]

Hanson, John M. Minnesota atlas : a complete
guide to public lands and water accesses / by
John M. Hanson. Cambridge, MN : Adventure
Publications, Inc., 1990. 1 atlas (216 p.) :
maps ; 43 cm. ISBN 0-934860-61-0
1. Recreation areas - Minnesota - Maps - 1990. 2.
Minnesota - Public lands - Maps - 1990. 3. Minnesota -
Maps - 1990. I. Adventure Publications (Firm :
Cambridge, Minn.). II. Title. III. Title: A complete
guide to public lands and water accesses.
NYPL [Map Div. 91-7525]

Hanson, Louise, 1940- Art and identity in
Oceania /. Honolulu , c1990. viii, 315 p., [8] p.
of plates : ISBN 0-8248-1304-9 : DDC 700/.995
20
N7399.7 .A78 1990
NYPL [3-MADF 91-5014]

HAP Grieshaber, Farbholzschnitte . Grieshaber,
Helmut A. P., 1909- Stuttgart , c1983. 43 p., 73
leaves of plates :
NYPL [MDG (Grieshaber) 90-13133]

Happel, Ralph. Wilshin, Francis F. Tour of the
battlefields of Fredericksburg, Chancellorsville,
Wilderness, Spotsylvania C.H. . [Fredericksburg,
Va.] [1955?] [17] leaves :
NYPL [Map Div. 90-949]

Happel, Reinhold. Der Expressionismus und
Westfalen /. Münster [1990] 239 p. : ISBN
3-88789-096-5
N6879 .E97 1990

**HAPPENING (ART) - ARGENTINA -
HISTORY AND CRITICISM.**
Happenings. [Buenos Aires, c1967] 206 p.
DDC 709.04
PN3203 .H33   **NYPL [3-MAL 91-230]**

**HAPPENING (ART) - HISTORY AND
CRITICISM.**
Happenings. [Buenos Aires, c1967] 206 p.
DDC 709.04
PN3203 .H33   **NYPL [3-MAL 91-230]**

Happenings [por] Oscar Masotta y otros. Con
hechos y textos de Marta Minujin [et al.
Buenos Aires] Editorial J. Alvares [c1967] 206
p. plates 20cm. Includes bibliographical references.
DDC 709.04
1. Happening (Art) - History and criticism. 2.
Happening (Art) - Argentina - History and criticism. I.
Masotta, Oscar, 1930-.
PN3203 .H33   **NYPL [3-MAL 91-230]**

HAPPINESS.
Stürmer, Michael. Scherben des Glücks .
Berlin , c1987. 99 p. : ISBN 3-88680-180-2
N6425.N4 S78 1987

Happy families. Applebroog, Ida. Ida
Applebroog . Houston , Seattle, Wash. , c1990.
96 p. : ISBN 0-936080-20-5 DDC 700/.92 20
ND237.A646 A4 1990
NYPL [3-MCX A649 90-12475]

Harald Frackmann, Bilder 1980-1988 .
Frackmann, Harald, 1944- [Hamburg] [1988]
[52] p. : **NYPL [3-MCK+ F797 91-4628]**

Harald Jegodzienski . Jegodzienski, Harald, 1952-
Rotterdam [1989] 48 p. : ISBN 90-6918-051-0
NYPL [3-MGO (Jegodzienski) 90-11665]

Harald P. Lechenperg . Kaindl, Kurt. Salzburg ,
1990. 127 p. : ISBN 3-7013-0801-2
NYPL [MFX (Lechenperg) 91-3519]

Harald Vike, 1906-1987 . Vike, Harald,
1906-1987. Perth, W.A. , 1990. 100 p. : ISBN
0-7316-9673-5
NYPL [3-MCZ+ V695 91-5560]

Haraszti-Takács, Marianne. Rubens and his age.
[Translated by Elisabeth Hoch] [Budapest]
Corvina [c1972] 32 p. 48 col. plates. 24 cm.
Half t.p.: Museum of Fine Arts.
1. Rubens, Peter Paul, Sir, 1577-1640. 2. Painting,
Flemish - History and criticism. I. Title.
NYPL [3-MCG 90-6280]

HARBIN (CHINA) - MAPS.
Al'bom planov i diagramm, otnosīāshchikhsīā k
dīelu sooruzhenīīā élevatorov na Kitaĭskoĭ
Vostochnoĭ zh.[eleznoĭ] d.[oroge]. [S.l. , 192-?].
6 leaves (some folded) :
NYPL [Map Div. 91-1086]

Harbison, Craig S. Symbols in transformation;
iconographic themes at the time of the
Reformation. [Princeton, N.J., 1969] 110 p.
illus. 26 cm. "An exhibition of prints in memory of
Erwin Panofsky, The Art Museum, Princeton
University, March 15-April 13, 1969." Introduction and
catalogue entries by Craig Harbison. Bibliography: p.
35-[37] DDC 769/.4/6094
1. Prints - Exhibitions. I. Panofsky, Erwin, 1892-1968.
II. Princeton University. Art Museum. III. Title.
NE42.P7 P75   **NYPL [MDET 91-980]**

Harbison, Robert. The built, the unbuilt, and the
unbuildable : in pursuit of architectural meaning
/ Robert Harbison.1st MIT Press ed.
Cambridge, Mass. : MIT Press, 1991. 192 p. :
ill. ; 24 cm. Includes bibliographical references (p.
179-188) and index. ISBN 0-262-08204-7 : DDC
720/.1 20
1. Architecture - Philosophy. 2. Signs and symbols in
architecture. 3. Architecture and history. I. Title.
NA2500 .H37 1991

HARBORS - NEW JERSEY - MAPS.
United States. Army. Corps of Engineers. New
York District. Project maps . New York, N.Y.
[1967?] 1 v. (various pagings) :
NYPL [Map Div. 86-562]

HARBORS - NEW YORK (N.Y.) - MAPS.
National Ocean Survey. New York Harbor tidal
current charts. Rockville, Md. [1979] 1 atlas
(34 p.) :   DDC 912/.15514708/097471 19
G1254.N4C75 N3 1979
NYPL [Map Div. 91-5021]

HARBORS - NEW YORK (STATE) - MAPS.
United States. Army. Corps of Engineers. New
York District. Project maps . New York, N.Y.
[1967?] 1 v. (various pagings) :
NYPL [Map Div. 86-562]

Harburger Binnenhafen. Stadtbild Hamburg.
Hamburg [1990] 64 p. :
NA9053.C6 S72 1990

Harcus Gallery. Points along the Côte d'Azur
triangle /. New York, c1985. 36 p. :   ISBN
0-935581-00-6   *NYPL [3-MAMT 90-4521]*

Hard traveling . McGraw, DeLoss. San Diego ,
c1989. [25] sheets :   DDC 769.92 20
NE539.M34 A4 1989

Harden, Renate. Boulboullé, Guido. Worpswede .
Köln , c1989. 223 p. :   ISBN 3-7701-1847-2
NYPL [3-MAMG 90-12605]

Hardie, William R. Scottish painting, 1837 to the
present / William Hardie. London : Studio
Vista, 1990. 223 p. : ill. (some col.) ; 30 cm.
"Parts of the text first appeared in the author's Scottish
painting, 1837-1939"--T.p. verso. Includes
bibliographical references (p. 217-219) and index.
  ISBN 0-289-80022-6 :   DDC 759.2911 20
*1. Painting, Scottish. 2. Painting, Modern - 19th
century - Scotland. 3. Painting, Modern - 20th
century - Scotland. I. Title.*
ND475   *NYPL [3-MCT+ 91-5407]*

Hardy Holzman Pfeiffer Associates : buildings
and projects, 1967-1992 / preface by Michael
Sorkin ; introduction by Mildred F. Schmertz.
New York : Rizzoli International, [1992] p. cm.
Includes bibliographical references.   ISBN
0-8478-1480-7   DDC 720/.92/2 20
*1. Hardy Holzman Pfeiffer Associates. 2. Architecture,
Modern - 20th century - United States. I. Schmertz,
Mildred F.*
NA737.H29 A4 1992

**HARDY HOLZMAN PFEIFFER
ASSOCIATES.**
Hardy Holzman Pfeiffer Associates . New York
[1992] p. cm.   ISBN 0-8478-1480-7   DDC
720/.92/2 20
NA737.H29 A4 1992

HARDY, OLIVER, 1892-1957.
Gehring, Wes D. Laurel & Hardy . New York ,
1990. xvi, 307 p. :   ISBN 0-313-25172-X (lib. bdg. :
alk. paper)   DDC 791.43/028/0922 B 20
PN2287.L285 G4 1990
NYPL [MMES (Laurel, DS.) 90-10877]

**HARDY, OLIVER, 1892-1957 -
BIBLIOGRAPHY.**
Gehring, Wes D. Laurel & Hardy . New York ,
1990. xvi, 307 p. :   ISBN 0-313-25172-X (lib. bdg. :
alk. paper)   DDC 791.43/028/0922 B 20
PN2287.L285 G4 1990
NYPL [MMES (Laurel, DS.) 90-10877]

**Hardy Strid's work and Swedish modernism in
art from 1935 to 1980 /.** Sellem, Jean.
Munich , c1981. 224 p. :   ISBN 3-923091-00-1
NYPL [3-MCZ S917 85-1125]

Hare, Susan. Paul de Lamerie . [London] , 1990.
181 p. :   ISBN 0-907814-19-0
NYPL [3-MNO+ 91-5049]

Hargrove, June Ellen. The French Academy .
Newark : London ; 231 p. :   ISBN 0-87413-343-2
(alk. paper)   DDC 706/.044 19
N332.F83 P345 1990
NYPL [3-MAMI 90-11304]

Haring, Keith.
Keith Haring : a memorial exhibition, early
works on paper, May 4-June 2, 1990. New
York (163 Mercer St., New York 10012) :
Shafrazi Gallery, c1990. 44 p. : ill. (some col.) ;
32 cm.   DDC 741.973 20
*1. Haring, Keith - Exhibitions. I. Tony Shafrazi Gallery.
II. Title.*
NC139.H3 A4 1990

Keith Haring, a memorial exhibition : early
works on paper : May 4-June 2, 1990. New
York : Shafrazi Gallery, c1990. 44 p. : ill. ; 32
cm.
*1. Haring, Keith - Exhibitions. I. Tony Shafrazi Gallery.
II. Title.*   *NYPL [3-MCX+ H281 90-13385]*

HARING, KEITH - EXHIBITIONS.
Haring, Keith. Keith Haring . New York (163
Mercer St., New York 10012) , c1990. 44 p. :
  DDC 741.973 20
NC139.H3 A4 1990

Haring, Keith. Keith Haring, a memorial
exhibition . New York , c1990. 44 p. :
NYPL [3-MCX+ H281 90-13385]

Harlan Hubbard . Berry, Wendell, 1934- New
York , 1992. p.   ISBN 0-679-73858-4 (pbk.) :
  DDC 759.13 B 20
NX512.H82 B47 1992

Harle, Lesley. Designer china : hand-painting
ceramics to decorate your home / Lesley Harle.
New York : Morrow, 1991. p. cm. Includes
bibliographical references and index.   ISBN
0-688-10923-3   DDC 738.1/5 20
*1. China painting - Themes, motives. 2. Interior
decoration - Themes, motives. I. Title.*
NK4605 .H36 1991

Harling, Robert. The House & garden book of
living rooms / by Robert Harling, Leonie
Highton, and John Bridges. New York :
Vendome Press : Distributed in the USA and
Canada by Rizzoli International Publications,
1991. p. cm.   ISBN 0-86565-125-6   DDC 747.7/5
20
*1. Living rooms. 2. Interior decoration. I. Highton,
Leonie. II. Bridges, John. III. House & garden. IV.
Title. V. Title: House and garden book of living rooms.
VI. Title: Book of living rooms.*
NK2117.L5 H37 1991

Harmon, Byron, 1876-1934. The Canadian Pacific
Rockies : a series of twenty-four Vandyck
photogravures / published by Byron
Harmon.4th ed. Banff [Alta.] : B. Harmon,
[1928?] 24 leaves of plates : chiefly ill. ; 22 x
32 cm. "Printed in England." Cover title: Rocky
Mountains of Canada: a series of twenty-four sepia
Vandyck photogravures.
*1. Canadian Rockies (B.C. and Alta.) - Description and
travel - Views. I. Title. II. Title: Rocky Mountains of
Canada.*   *NYPL [MFX+ (Harmon) 87-132]*

Harmony & discord : American landscape
painting today : August 7-September 30, 1990,
Virginia Museum of Fine Arts, Richmond.
Richmond : The Museum, c1990. 32 p. : ill.
(some col.) ; 21 cm. Includes bibliographical
references (p. 29).
*1. Landscape painting, American - Exhibitions. 2.
Landscape painting - 20th century - United States -
Exhibitions. I. Virginia Museum of Fine Arts. II. Title:
Harmony and discord. III. Title: American landscape
painting today.*
MLCS 91/06468 (N)
NYPL [3-MCW 91-4406]

Harmony and discord. Harmony & discord .
Richmond , c1990. 32 p. :
MLCS 91/06468 (N)
NYPL [3-MCW 91-4406]

A Harmony of the arts : the Nebraska state
capitol / edited by Frederick C. Luebke.
Lincoln : University of Nebraska Press, c1990.
x, 119 p. : ill. (some col.) ; 27 (The Great plains
photography series) Includes index. Includes
bibliographical references (p. 115-118). CONTENTS. -
The capitals and capitols of Nebraska / Frederick C.
Luebke -- The architectural vision of Bertram
Grosvenor Goodhue / H. Keith Sawyers -- Symbolism
and inscriptions / David Murphy -- Art, architecture,
and humanism / Dale L. Gibbs -- The decorative art of
Hildreth Meiere / Joan Woodside and Betsy Gabb --
The capitol murals / Norman Geske and Jon Nelson --
Landscape architecture / Robert C. Ripley.   ISBN
0-8032-2887-2 (alk. paper)   DDC
725/.11/09782293 19
*1. Goodhue, Bertram Grosvenor, 1869-1924 - Themes,
motives. 2. Nebraska State Capitol (Lincoln, Neb.). 3.
Interior architecture - Nebraska - Lincoln. 4.
Decoration and ornament - Nebraska - Lincoln. 5.
Lincoln (Neb.) - Buildings, structures, etc. I. Luebke,
Frederick C., 1927-. II. Title: Nebraska state capitol.
III. Series.*
NA4413.L56 H37 1990
NYPL [3-MQWO 90-11994]

Harms, Klaus B. Stuttgart, Kunst & Kultur .
Stuttgart , 1988. 480 p. :   ISBN 3-925860-08-8
  DDC 700/.943/47109048 20
NX550.S77 S77 1988

**HARNETT, WILLIAM MICHAEL, 1848-1892 -
CRITICISM AND INTERPRETATION.**
William M. Harnett /. Fort Worth : New
York : p. cm.   ISBN 0-8109-3410-8   DDC 759.13
20
ND237.H315 A4 1992

**HARNETT, WILLIAM MICHAEL, 1848-1892 -
EXHIBITIONS.**
William M. Harnett /. Fort Worth : New
York : p. cm.   ISBN 0-8109-3410-8   DDC 759.13
20
ND237.H315 A4 1992

Harper, Jenny. Kruger, Barbara, 1945- Barbara
Kruger . Wellington, N.Z. , c1988. 73 p. :
  ISBN 0-9597785-5-1
NYPL [3-MCX+ K935 90-10674]

Harprath, Richard. Giuseppe Zocchi . München ,
c1988. 132 p. :
IN PROCESS (ONLINE)
NYPL [MDG (Zocchi) 91-4741]

Harpur, Jerry. Robinson, John Martin. Temples
of delight . London , 1990. 176 p. :   ISBN
0-540-01217-3 :   DDC 712.60942 20
SB477.G7   *NYPL [3-MSK 91-2633]*

Harr, H. P.
H.P. Harr : Bild-Gebilde : 13. November-31.
Dezember 1988, Kunstverein Bochum, 26.
Februar-23. April 1989, Museum Schloss
Hardenberg, Velbert-Neviges. Velbert-Neviges :
Das Museum, c1989. 131 p. : chiefly ill. (some
col.), port. ; 22 x 30 cm. Includes bibliographical
references.   ISBN 3-926133-14-7
*1. Harr, H. P. - Exhibitions. I. Kunstverein Bochum. II.
Städtische Museen Schloss Hardenberg. III. Title.*
NYPL [3-MGO (Harr) 89-27491]

HARR, H. P. - EXHIBITIONS.
Harr, H. P. H.P. Harr . Velbert-Neviges ,
c1989. 131 p. :   ISBN 3-926133-14-7
NYPL [3-MGO (Harr) 89-27491]

Harrap's illustrated dictionary of art & artists.
Bromley, Kent : Harrap Books, 1990. 589 p. :
ill. ; 25 cm. "Harrap's reference."   ISBN
0-245-54692-8
*1. Art - Dictionaries. 2. Artists - Biography -
Dictionaries. I. Title: Harrap's illustrated dictionary of
art and artists. II. Title: Illustrated dictionary of art &
artists. III. Title: Illustrated dictionary of art and artists.*
NYPL [MAO 91-4216]

Harrap's illustrated dictionary of art and artists.
Harrap's illustrated dictionary of art & artists.
Bromley, Kent , 1990. 589 p. :   ISBN
0-245-54692-8   *NYPL [MAO 91-4216]*

Harriet Hosmer, American sculptor, 1830-1908 /.
Sherwood, Dolly. Columbia , c1991. p. cm.
  ISBN 0-8262-0766-9 (alk. paper)   DDC 730/.92
B 20
NB237.H6 S53 1991

Harris, Bill, 1933- Great homes of California /
text by Bill Harris ; [photography, Ric
Pattison]. New York : Crescent Books :
Distributed by Outlet Book Co., 1990. 160 p. :
chiefly col. ill. ; 37 cm. Includes index.   ISBN
0-517-62377-3   DDC 728.8/09794 20
*1. Eclecticism in architecture - California. 2. Mansions -
California. 3. Interior decoration - California. I.
Pattison, Ric. II. Title.*
NA7511.3.C2 H3 1990

Harris, Eileen. British architectural books and
writers, 1556-1785 / Eileen Harris ; assisted by
Nicholas Savage. Cambridge [England] ; New
York : Cambridge University Press, 1990. 571
p. : ill. ; 27 cm. Includes index. Includes
bibliographical references.   ISBN 0-521-38551-2
  DDC 016.72 20
*1. Architecture, Renaissance - Great Britain -
Bibliography. 2. Architecture, Modern - 17th-18th
centuries - Great Britain - Bibliography. 3.
Architecture - Great Britain - Bibliography. I. Savage,
Nicholas. II. Title.*
NA965 .H37 1990
NYPL [MQWK 90-13195]

Harris, Elizabeth Davis, 1950- Le Corbusier :
riscos brasileiros / Elizabeth D. Harris ;
[tradução, Antonio de Pádua Danesi e Gilson
César Cardoso de Sousa]. São Paulo, SP :
Nobel 1987. 218 p. : ill. ; 21 cm. Includes

bibliographical references. ISBN 85-21-30469-2 :
*1. Le Corbusier, 1887-1965 - Influence - Brazil. 2.
Functionalism (Architecture) - Brazil. 3. Architecture,
Modern - 20th century - Brazil. I. Le Corbusier,
1887-1965. II. Title. III. Title: Corbusier.*
NYPL [3-MQZ (Le Corbusier) 90-10663]

Harris, Nathaniel. The paintings of Manet /
Nathaniel Harris. London : Hamlyn, 1989. 128
p. : ill. (some col.), ports. (some col.) ; 29 cm.
ISBN 0-600-56457-6 : DDC 759.4 19
*1. Manet, Édouard, 1832-1883. I. Manet, Édouard,
1832-1883. II. Title. III. Title: Manet.*
ND553.M3 **NYPL [3-MCO M27 90-12443]**

Harris, Paul, M.A. Halsby, Julian. The dictionary
of Scottish painters, 1600-1960 /. Edinburgh ,
Oxford , 1990. xii, 236 p. : ISBN 0-86241-328-1 :
DDC 759.2911 20
ND475 **NYPL [3-MCT+ 91-3993]**

Harris, R. Cole. Historical atlas of Canada.
Toronto , Buffalo [1987]- v. : ISBN
0-8020-2495-5 (v. 1)
NYPL [Map Div. 87-990]

Harris, Sidney.
Can't you guys read? cartoons on academia /
Sidney Harris. New Brunswick : Rutgers
University Press, c1991. p. cm. ISBN
0-8135-1733-8 (pbk.) : DDC 741.5/973 20
*1. Education - Caricatures and cartoons. 2. American
wit and humor, Pictorial. I. Title.*
NC1429.H33315 A4 1991a

You want proof? I'll give you proof! : more
cartoons / from Sidney Harris. New York :
W.H. Freeman, c1991. [150] p. : ill. ; 24 cm.
ISBN 0-7167-2159-7 : DDC 741.5/973 20
*1. Science - Caricatures and cartoons. 2. American wit
and humor, Pictorial. I. Title.*
NC1429.H33315 A4 1991
NYPL [3-MEM (Harris) 90-13677]

Harris, Victor, 1942- Smith, Lawrence. Japanese
art . Bloomsbury , c1990. 256 p. : ISBN
0-7141-1446-4 : DDC 709/.52/074 19
N7350 **NYPL [3-MAG 90-11503]**

Harrison, Hazel. The encyclopedia of watercolor
techniques / Hazel Harrison. Philadelphia, Pa. :
Running Press, 1990. 192 p. : col. ill. ; 23 x 24
cm. "A Quarto book"--T.p. verso. Includes index.
ISBN 0-89471-893-2 DDC 751.4/2 20
*1. Watercolor painting - Technique - Dictionaries. 2.
Watercolor painting - Themes, motives. I. Title.*
ND2420 .H37 1990

Harrison, Helen A. East Hampton avant-garde .
[East Hampton] , c1990. 68 p. : ISBN
0-933793-14-6 **NYPL [3-MAW (East
Hampton) 90-13535]**

Harrison, Henry S. Houses : the illustrated guide
to construction, design, and systems / Henry S.
Harrison.2nd ed. Chicago, IL : Residential Sales
Council : Real Estate Education Co., 1991. p.
cm. Includes bibliographical references and index.
ISBN 0-7931-0332-0 (pbk.) DDC 728 20
*1. Architecture, Domestic - Handbooks, manuals, etc. 2.
Building materials - Handbooks, manuals, etc. I. Title.*
NA7110 .H33 1991

Harrison, Marina, 1939- Artwalks in New York :
delightful discoveries of public art and gardens
in Manhattan, Brooklyn, the Bronx, Queens,
and Staten Island / Marina Harrison and Lucy
D. Rosenfeld ; illustrations by Lucy D.
Rosenfeld. New York : M. Kesend Pub., 1991.
p. cm. Includes index. ISBN 0-935576-40-1 DDC
709/.747/1 20
*1. Public art - New York (N.Y.). 2. Gardens - New
York (N.Y.). I. Rosenfeld, Lucy D., 1939-. II. Title.*
N8845.N7 H3 1991

Harrison, Martin, 1945- Appearances : fashion
photography since 1945 / Martin Harrison.
London : Cape, 1991. 312 p. : ill. (some col.),
ports. ; 33 cm. Includes bibliographical references (p.
308-310). ISBN 0-224-03067-1 (cased) : DDC
779.93912 20
1. Photography of women. I. Title.
TR679 **NYPL [MFW+ 91-4961]**

Harry Benson's people. Benson, Harry.
Edinburgh , 1990. 167 p. : ISBN 1-85158-322-X
(cased) : DDC 779.2 20
NYPL [MFX+ (Benson) 91-8014]

Harry Devlin . Mitnick, Barbara J. Morristown,
N.J. , c1991. 68 p. : ISBN 0-9613046-4-2
NYPL [3-MCX D497 91-3433]

Harry Northwood--the early years, 1881-1900 /.

Heacock, William. Marietta, Ohio [1990] viii,
151 p. : ISBN 0-915410-39-7 (softbound) DDC
748.2913 20
NK5198.N59 H4 1990

Harry Rosenthal, scultore /. Cajani, Franco,
1943- [Italy] , c1988. 223 p. : DDC 730/.92 20
NB979.R67 A4 1988

Hart, Pro, 1928-
HART, PRO, 1928-
Hart, Pro, 1928- [Legendary Tasmania.] Pro
Hart's Legendary Tasmania /. Adelaide , New
York , 1982. 71 p. : ISBN 0-7270-1539-7 : DDC
994.6/01 19
ND1105.H37 A4 1982
NYPL [3-MAMY 90-6913]

[Legendary Tasmania]
Pro Hart's Legendary Tasmania / text by
Paul White. Adelaide ; New York : Rigby,
1982. 71 p. : col. ill. ; 22 x 26 cm. Includes
bibliographical references. ISBN 0-7270-1539-7 :
DDC 994.6/01 19
*1. Hart, Pro, 1928-. 2. Tasmania in art. 3. Tasmania -
History. I. White, Paul, 1944-. II. Title.*
ND1105.H37 A4 1982
NYPL [3-MAMY 90-6913]

Hartdegen, Paddy. Our building heritage . [South
Africa] , 1988. iv, 312, [5] p. : ISBN
0-620-12738-4 DDC 720/.968 20
NA1592 .O94 1988

Harten, Jürgen. Sowjetische Kunst um 1990 :
Binationale, Yiśra'el-SSSR / Jürgen Harten.
Köln : DuMont, c1991. 299 p. : ill. ; 29 cm.
German and Russian. Catalog of an exhibition held at
the Städtische Kunsthalle, Düsseldorf, Apr. 12-June 2,
1991; Israel Museum, Weisbord Pavilion, Jerusalem,
Aug.-Nov. 1991; TSentral´nyĭ dom khudozhnika,
Moscow, 1992. ISBN 3-7701-2733-1
*1. Art, Soviet - Exhibitions. 2. Art, Modern - 20th
century - Soviet Union - Exhibitions. I. Muze'on
Yiśra'el (Jerusalem). II. TSentral´nyĭ dom khudozhnika
(Soviet Union). III. Title. IV. Title: Binationale,
Yiśra'el-SSSR. V. Title: Binationale, Israel-UdSSR.*
NYPL [3-MAM 91-8020]

**Hartford, Huntington, Collection, New York. see
New York (City). Gallery of Modern Art
Including the Huntington Hartford
Collection.**

Harthorn, Sandy, 1945-
One hundred years of Idaho art, 1850-1950 :
Boise Art Museum, June 23-August 19, 1990 /
Sandy Harthorn and Kathleen Bettis. Boise,
ID : Boise Art Museum, c1990. 134 p. : ill.
(some col.) ; 28 cm. Includes bibliographical
references (p. 128-130) and index. DDC
709/.796/07479628 20
*1. Art, American - Idaho - Exhibitions. 2. Art,
Modern - 19th century - Idaho - Exhibitions. 3. Art,
Modern - 20th century - Idaho - Exhibitions. 4. Idaho
in art - Exhibitions. I. Bettis, Kathleen, 1947-. II. Boise
Art Museum. III. Title.*
N6530.I2 H37 1990
NYPL [3-MAMT 90-11110]

Yard art . Boise, Idaho , c1991. 1 v.
(unpaged) : DDC 745/.0979/07479628 20
NK824 .Y37 1991

Hartigan, Grace.
Grace Hartigan, four decades of painting :
[exhibition], April 7-May 6, 1989, Kouros. New
York, N.Y. (23 East 73 Street, New York,
10021) : Kouros Gallery, 1989. 32 p. : ill.
(some col.) ; 23 x 31 cm. Edited by Robert
Saltonstall Mattison. Bibliography: p. 31.
*1. Hartigan, Grace - Exhibitions. I. Mattison, Robert
Saltonstall. II. Kouros Gallery. III. Title.*
NYPL [3-MCX+ H329 91-4638]

HARTIGAN, GRACE - EXHIBITIONS.
Hartigan, Grace. Grace Hartigan, four decades
of painting . New York, N.Y. (23 East 73
Street, New York, 10021) , 1989. 32 p. :
NYPL [3-MCX+ H329 91-4638]

Hartmann, Krieg, Kristiansen, Vogt : 4 Beiträge
zur neuen Malerei : [Ausstellung] Von der
Heydt-Museum Wuppertal, 18. Januar-22.
Februar 1981. Wuppertal : Das Museum, [1981]
[49] p. : ill. (4 col.) ; 26 cm. Essays by Günter
Aust and Karl Hans Müller.
*1. Hartmann, Robert, 1949- - Exhibitions. 2. Krieg,
Dieter, 1937- - Exhibitions. 3. Vogt, Peter, 1944- -
Exhibitions. 4. Kristiansen, Nils, 1943- - Exhibitions. 5.
Painting, German - Germany (West) - Exhibitions. 6.*

*Painting, Modern - 20th century - Germany (West) -
Exhibitions.* **NYPL [3-MCI 90-5657]**
**HARTMANN, ROBERT, 1949- -
EXHIBITIONS.**
Hartmann, Krieg, Kristiansen, Vogt . Wuppertal
[1981] [49] p. : **NYPL [3-MCI 90-5657]**

Hartmann, Thomas, 1950-
Nord, Sued / Thomas Hartmann. [Freiburg im
Breisgau] : Kunstverein Freiburg : Kunsthalle
Wilhelmshaven, c1988. 55 p. : ill. (some col.,
some folded) ; 32 cm. "Die Ausstellung im
Kunstverein Freiburg findet vom 17. 12. 1988 bis 15. 1.
1989, die in der Kunsthalle Wilhelmshaven vom 26. 1.
bis 5. 3. 1989 statt"--Colophon.
*1. Hartmann, Thomas, 1950- - Exhibitions. I.
Kunstverein Freiburg. II. Title.*
NYPL [3-MCK+ H331 90-5135]

**HARTMANN, THOMAS, 1950- -
EXHIBITIONS.**
Hartmann, Thomas, 1950- Nord, Sued /.
[Freiburg im Breisgau] , c1988. 55 p. :
NYPL [3-MCK+ H331 90-5135]

Hartmann, William K. In the stream of stars .
New York , 1990. 183 p. : ISBN 0-89480-705-6
(paper) : DDC 758/.96294 20
N8234.O8 I5 1990
NYPL [3-MAMZ 91-5459]

Hartmann, Wolfgang, 1938- Das
Bildhauersymposion . Stuttgart , c1988. 163 p. :
ISBN 3-7757-0263-6
NYPL [3-MGI 90-11129]

Hartt, Frederick. New light on Michelangelo in
the Sistine Chapel. German. Der neue
Michelangelo . Luzern, Schweiz , c1989-c1991.
3 v. : ISBN 3-85672-033-2 (set)
NYPL [MCF++ B9 91-6340]

Hartung . Hartung, Hans, 1904- Saint-Paul
[1971] [12] p. : DDC 759.3
ND588.H34 F65
NYPL [3-MCK H336 90-6261]

Hartung, Hans, 1904-
Hans Hartung, premières peintures 1922-1949.
Antibes : Musée Picasso, 1987. 74 p. : ill. ; 24
cm. ISBN 2-905315-10-5
*1. Hartung, Hans, 1904- - Exhibitions. I. Musée Picasso
(Antibes, France). II. Title.* **NYPL [3-MCK H336 91-4238]**

Hartung : grands formats, 1961-1971.
Saint-Paul : Fondation Maeght, [1971] [12] p. :
col. ill. ; 21 cm. Cover title. Exhibition catalog.
Filmography: p. [10] DDC 759.3
*1. Hartung, Hans, 1904- - Exhibitions. I. Fondation
Maeght. II. Title.*
ND588.H34 F65
NYPL [3-MCK H336 90-6261]

HARTUNG, HANS, 1904- - EXHIBITIONS.
Hartung, Hans, 1904- Hans Hartung, premières
peintures 1922-1949. Antibes , 1987. 74 p. :
ISBN 2-905315-10-5
NYPL [3-MCK H336 91-4238]

Hartung, Hans, 1904- Hartung . Saint-Paul
[1971] [12] p. : DDC 759.3
ND588.H34 F65
NYPL [3-MCK H336 90-6261]

HARTWELL HOUSE (ENGLAND)
Smyth, W. H. (William Henry), 1788-1865.
Ædes Hartwellianæ. London, 1851. vii, 414 p.,
1 l.
N5245 .H4

Hartwig, Werner. Ornament und Plastic fremder
Völker. English. Ornament and sculpture in
primitive society. New York [1966] [138] p.
DDC 709.011
N7380 .O713 1966b
NYPL [3-MADF 90-6405]

Harvard College. see Harvard University.

Harvard dissertations in philosophy.
Batkin, Norton. Photography and philosophy /.
New York , 1990, c1981. xiii, 219 p. : ISBN
0-8240-3389-2 (alk. paper) DDC 770/.1 20
TR183 .B27 1990 **NYPL [MFW 91-3465]**

**HARVARD UNIVERSITY. ART MUSEUM -
CATALOGS.**
Harvard University. Art Museums. Stone
sculptures . Cambridge [Mass.] , 1990. 184 p. :
ISBN 0-916724-70-0 DDC 733/.074/7444 20
NB87 .H37 1990 **NYPL [3-MGH 91-3444]**

Harvard University. Art Museums.
The Fredric Wertham collection : gift of his

wife Hesketh. [Cambridge] : Busch-Reisinger Museum, Harvard University, 1990. 101 p. : ill. (some col.) ; 28 cm. Catalog of an exhibition held at the Arthur M. Sackler Museum, May 26-July 22, 1990. Errata slip inserted. Includes bibliographical references. ISBN 0-916724-75-1
1. Wertham, Fredric, 1895-1981 - Art collections - Exhibitions. 2. Art - Private collections - United States - Exhibitions. I. Arthur M. Sackler Museum. II. Busch-Reisinger Museum. III. Title.
IN PROCESS (ONLINE)
NYPL [3-MAX (Wertham) 91-5499]

Stone sculptures : the Greek, Roman, and Etruscan collections of the Harvard University Art Museums / Cornelius C. Vermeule and Amy Brauer. Cambridge [Mass.] : The Museums, 1990. 184 p. : ill. ; 28 cm. Includes bibliographical references (p. 171-183). ISBN 0-916724-70-0 DDC 733/.074/7444 20
1. Harvard University. Art Museum - Catalogs. 2. Sculpture, Classical - Catalogs. 3. Sculpture - Massachusetts - Cambridge - Catalogs. I. Vermeule, Cornelius Clarkson, 1925-. II. Brauer, Amy. III. Title.
NB87 .H37 1990   NYPL [3-MGH 91-3444]

Harvard University. Design, Faculty of. see **Harvard University. Graduate School of Design.**

Harvard University. Faculty of Design. see **Harvard University. Graduate School of Design.**

Harvard University. Graduate School of Design. Andō, Tadao, 1941- Tadao Ando . New York, N.Y. , c1991. 32 p. : ISBN 0-8478-1339-8 DDC 720/.22/22 20
NA2707.A53 A4 1991

Harvard University. Graduate Schools of Design. Thinking the present . New York, NY , c1990. 136 p. : ISBN 0-910413-93-2
NYPL [3-MQWO 90-13419]

Harvard University. Harvard College Library. see **Harvard University. Library.**

Harvard University. Library. The First five years . Poestenkill, N.Y. [1990] 53 p. :
NYPL [MDTT 91-3883]

Harvey, Bunny, 1946-
Bunny Harvey : October 25-November 17, 1990. New York, N.Y. : Berry-Hill Galleries, c1990. 32 p. : ill. ; 23 cm.
1. Harvey, Bunny, 1946- - Exhibitions. I. Berry-Hill Galleries. II. Title.
NYPL [3-MCX H341 90-13537]

HARVEY, BUNNY, 1946- - EXHIBITIONS. Harvey, Bunny, 1946- Bunny Harvey . New York, N.Y. , c1990. 32 p. :
NYPL [3-MCX H341 90-13537]

Harvey Wang's New York /. Wang, Harvey. New York , c1990. 112 p. : ISBN 0-393-02914-X DDC 974.7/1 20
F128.37 .W36 1990
NYPL [MFX (Wang) 91-4993]

Hasegawa, Sadao. Sadao Hasegawa : paintings and drawings / introduced by Frits Staal. London : GMP ; Boston, MA : Distributed in North America by Alyson Publications, 1990. 76 p. : ill. ; 32 cm. ISBN 0-85449-142-2 : DDC 305.31 20
1. Hasegawa, Sadao. I. Title.
HQ1090   NYPL [3-MAG+ 91-5629]

HASEGAWA, SADAO. Hasegawa, Sadao. Sadao Hasegawa . London , Boston, MA , 1990. 76 p. : 0-85449-142-2 : DDC 305.31 20
HQ1090   NYPL [3-MAG+ 91-5629]

Haseloff, Günther. Email im frühen Mittelalter : frühchristiliche Kunst von der Spätantike bis zu den Karolingern / Günther Haseloff. Marburg : Hitzeroth, c1990. 244 p. : ill. (some col.), maps ; 27 x 28 cm. (Marburger Studien zur Vor- und Frühgeschichte. Sonderband . 1) Includes indexes. Includes bibliographical references (p. 228-236). ISBN 3-89398-020-2
1. Enamel and enameling, Medieval - Europe. 2. Champlevé, Medieval - Europe. 3. Cloisonné, Medieval - Europe. 4. Art metal-work, Medieval - Europe. 5. Christian art and symbolism - Medieval, 500-1500 - Europe. I. Title. II. Series.
NYPL [3-MNV 91-5235]

Hasior, Władysław, 1928-
Władysław Hasior, Camiel Van Breedam : 22/12/1989-25/2/1990. Bruxelles : Atelier 340,

c1989. 287 p. : ill. (some col.) ; 30 cm. Polish, French, Dutch, English and German. Catalog of an exhibition held at the Kunsthalle Darmstadt, March 3 - Apr. 29, 1990 and at 4 other locations through 1991. ISBN 90-71386-13-9
1. Breedam, Camiel van, 1936- - Exhibitions. 2. Hasior, Władysław, 1936- - Exhibitions. I. Breedam, Camiel van, 1936-. II. Title.
NYPL [3-MGO+ (Hasior) 91-6879]

HASIOR, WŁADYSŁAW, 1928- - EXHIBITIONS. Hasior, Władysław, 1928- Władysław Hasior, Camiel Van Breedam . Bruxelles , c1989. 287 p. : ISBN 90-71386-13-9
NYPL [3-MGO+ (Hasior) 91-6879]

Haskell, Barbara.
Burgoyne Diller / Barbara Haskell. New York : Whitney Museum of American Art, c1990. 180 p. : ill. (some col.) ; 28 cm. Catalog of an exhibition held at the Whitney Museum of American Art, Sept. 13-Nov. 25, 1990. Includes bibliographical references (p. 176-177). ISBN 0-87427-071-5 DDC 759.13 20
1. Diller, Burgoyne, 1906-1965 - Exhibitions. I. Diller, Burgoyne, 1906-1965. II. Whitney Museum of American Art.
ND237.D47 A4 1990
NYPL [3-MCX D578 91-4631]

The Expressionist landscape . Birmingham, Ala. , Seattle , 1988, c1987. 216 p. : DDC 759.1 19
ND1351.6 .E97 1987
NYPL [3-MCW 88-3335]

Yoko Ono, arias, and objects / Barbara Haskell and John Hanhardt. Salt Lake City : Gibbs-Smith Pub., 1991. p. cm. ISBN 0-87905-386-0 (pbk.) : DDC 700/.92 20
1. Ono, Yōko - Criticism and interpretation. I. Hanhardt, John G. II. Title.
NX512.O56 H37 1991

Haskell, Francis, 1928- Ajello, Raffaele. Classicismo d'età Romana . Napoli , c1988. 203 p. : ISBN 88-7042-955-5
NYPL [3-MGH+ 90-10570]

Haslam, Malcolm.
Arts & crafts / Malcolm Haslam. London : Macdonald Orbis, 1988. 168 p. : ill. (some col.) ; 21 cm. Includes bibliographical references (p. 163) and index. ISBN 0-356-15633-8 : DDC 745/.0941/075 20
1. Arts and crafts movement - Great Britain. 2. Decorative arts - Great Britain - History - 19th century. 3. Decorative arts - Great Britain - History - 20th century. I. Title. II. Title: Arts and crafts.
NK1142 .H38 1988

Arts & crafts carpets / Malcolm Haslam. New York : Rizzoli, 1991. p. cm. Includes bibliographical references and index. ISBN 0-8478-1388-6 DDC 746.7/2 20
1. Carpets - England - History - 19th century. 2. Carpets - England - History - 20th century. 3. Arts and crafts movement - England. I. Title. II. Title: Arts and crafts carpets.
NK2843 .H37 1991

Hassam, Childe, 1859-1935.
Catalogue of the etchings and dry-points of Childe Hassam, N.A., of the American Academy of Arts and Letters / Royal Cortissoz and the Leonard Clayton Gallery. Rev. ed. San Francisco : Alan Wofsy Fine Arts, 1989. 224 p. : ill. ; 32 cm. "This work combines and revises the catalogues first published in 1925 and 1933 with the addition of several new descriptions and many new illustrations."--P. [4] Spine title: Childe Hassam: etchings & dry-points. ISBN 1-556-60029-1
1. Hassam, Childe, 1859-1935 - Catalogs. I. Cortissoz, Royal, 1869-1948. II. Leonard Clayton Gallery. III. Title. IV. Title: Childe Hassam: etchings & dry-points.
NYPL [MDG+ (Hassam) 89-27271]

HASSAM, CHILDE, 1859-1935 - CATALOGS. Hassam, Childe, 1859-1935. Catalogue of the etchings and dry-points of Childe Hassam, N.A., of the American Academy of Arts and Letters /. San Francisco , 1989. 224 p. : ISBN 1-556-60029-1
NYPL [MDG+ (Hassam) 89-27271]

Hassam, Frederick Childe. see **Hassam, Childe, 1859-1935.**

Hassan Fathy /. Steele, James. London , New York , 1988. 149 p. : ISBN 0-312-01140-7 (U. S. :

pbk.) : DDC 720/.92/4 19
NA1585.F37 S74 1988
NYPL [3-MQZ+ (Fathy) 88-4615]

Hassan Fathy. see **Fathy, Hassan.**

Hassebrauk, Ernst, 1905-
Die Wiederbegegnung : Ernst Hassebrauk zeichnet zurückgekehrte Kunstwerke : Ausstellung zum 30. Jahrestag ihrer Rückgabe durch die UdSSR vom 2. Juli 1988 bis 12. Oktober 1988 im Albertinum, Staatliche Kunstsammlungen Dresden ; [Gesamtleitung, Manfred Bachmann ; Konzeption und wissenschaftliche Leitung, Joachim Menzhausen ; Redaktion des Katalogs, Ulli Arnold, Joachim Menzhausen, Gerd Spitzer]. [Dresden] : Staatliche Kunstsammlungen Dresden, c1988. 80 p. : ill. (some col.) ; 26 cm. Exhibition catalog. Bibliography: p. [3] of cover. DDC 741.943 20
1. Hassebrauk, Ernst, 1905- - Exhibitions. 2. Staatliche Kunstsammlungen Dresden - Exhibitions. 3. Art - Germany - Dresden - Influence - Exhibitions. I. Bachmann, Manfred, 1928-. II. Albertinum (Dresden, Germany). III. Staatliche Kunstsammlungen Dresden. IV. Title.
NC251.6.Z9 H372 1988
NYPL [3-MCK H354 91-4570]

HASSEBRAUK, ERNST, 1905- - EXHIBITIONS. Hassebrauk, Ernst, 1905- Die Wiederbegegnung . [Dresden] , c1988. 80 p. : DDC 741.943 20
NC251.6.Z9 H372 1988
NYPL [3-MCK H354 91-4570]

Hasselgréen, Ingmar, 1938- Ostindiska huset, Göteborgs museum / Ingmar Hasselgréen. [Gothenburg] : Göteborgs historiska museum, 1984 (Göteborg : Rundqvist, 1983) 95 p. : ill. ; 21 x 23 cm. (Göteborgs historiska museums skrifter . 1) Bibliography: p. 94. ISBN 91-7236-025-9
1. Göteborgs museum. 2. Ostindiska huset (Göteborg, Sweden). I. Title. II. Series.
AM101.G63 H37 1984
NYPL [MAVZ (Göteborg) 85-3424]

HASSELL, EDWARD - EXHIBITIONS. A Picturesque ride through Surrey . Guildford [1978] 42 p., [6] p. of plates :
MLCS 82/10141   NYPL [3-MCT 90-6056]

HASSELL, J. (JOHN), D. 1825 - EXHIBITIONS. A Picturesque ride through Surrey . Guildford [1978] 42 p., [6] p. of plates :
MLCS 82/10141   NYPL [3-MCT 90-6056]

Hasselt, Carlos van. Fondation Custodia. Le héraut du dix-septième siècle . Paris , 1985. xi, 153 p., 80 p. of plates :
NE670.G74 A4 1985

Hassi Romi /. Voth, Hannsjörg, 1940- Nürnberg , c1989. 259 p. : ISBN 3-922531-68-7
NYPL [3-MGO+ (Voth) 91-7441]

Hassis . Hassis, 1926- Fpolis [i.e. Florianópolis], Sta. Catarina [1968?] [11] p. :
N6659.H37 A4 1968

Hassis, 1926-
Hassis : em intercâmbio com o Departamento de Educação e Cultura da Universidade Federal de S.C. [i.e. Santa Catarina] : de 19 a 30 de abril de 1968. Fpolis [i.e. Florianópolis], Sta. Catarina : Museu de Arte Moderna de Florianópolis, [1968?] [11] p. : ill. ; 16 cm. Catalog of exhibition.
1. Hassis, 1926- - Exhibitions. I. Museu de Arte Moderna de Florianópolis. II. Title.
N6659.H37 A4 1968

HASSIS, 1926- - EXHIBITIONS. Hassis, 1926- Hassis . Fpolis [i.e. Florianópolis], Sta. Catarina [1968?] [11] p. :
N6659.H37 A4 1968

Hassrick, Peter H. Shapiro, Michael Edward. Frederic Remington . New York [1991] p. cm. ISBN 0-8109-8104-1 DDC 709/.2 20
N6537.R4 S5 1991

Hathaway, Nancy, 1946- Native American portraits, 1862-1918 : photographs from the collection of Kurt Koegler / Nancy Hathaway. San Francisco : Chronicle Books, c1990. 115, [1] p. : ill. ; 25 x 26 cm. Bibliography: p. [116]. ISBN 0-87701-766-2
1. Koegler, Kurt - Photograph collections. 2. Indians of

North America - Portraits. I. Title.
E89 .H38 1990   *NYPL [MFW 91-3605]*

HATS.
Campione, Adele. Il cappello da donna =.
Milano , 1989. 143 p. : ISBN 88-7143-086-7
                       NYPL [3-MMV 91-7599]

Hattat Aziz Efendi /. Aziz Efendi, 1871 or
2-1934. İstanbul , 1988. 119 p. :
NK3636.5.A95 A2 1988

Hatton Gallery. Whistler, Catherine. Impressionist
and modern . Oxford , 1990. 128 p. : ISBN
0-907849-97-0 (pbk.)
                   NYPL [3-MAX (Gross) 90-11583]

Hatzack, Irmgard, 1907- Aichelburg, Wolf.
Irmgard Hatzack, Leben und Werk . München ,
1988. 19 p., [26] p. of plates : ISBN
3-88356-057-X   DDC 730/.92 20
NB933.H38 A87 1988
          NYPL [3-MGO (Hatzack) 90-10824]

HATZACK, IRMGARD, 1907-
Aichelburg, Wolf. Irmgard Hatzack, Leben und
Werk . München , 1988. 19 p., [26] p. of
plates : ISBN 3-88356-057-X   DDC 730/.92 20
NB933.H38 A87 1988
          NYPL [3-MGO (Hatzack) 90-10824]

Haubenreisser, Wolfgang. Wörterbuch der Kunst
/ begründet von Johannes Jahn ; fortgeführt
von Wolfgang Haubenreisser. 11. durchgesehene
und erw. Aufl. Stuttgart : A. Kröner, c1989. ix,
932 p. : ill. ; 18 cm. (Kröners Taschenausgabe. Bd.
165) ISBN 3-520-16511-2 :   DDC 703 20
1. Art - Dictionaries - German. I. Jahn, Johannes,
1892-. II. Title.
N33 .H35 1989

HAUBENSACK, PIERRE, 1935- -
EXHIBITIONS.
Haubensack, Pierre, 1935- Pierre Haubensak .
[Winterthur] , 1990. 64 p. :
MLCM 90/03436 (N)
                   NYPL [3-MCZ H375 91-5179]

Haubensak, Pierre, 1935- Pierre Haubensak :
Bilder 1985-1989 : [Ausstellung], 28. Januar-18.
März 1990 / [Ausstellung und Katalog, Rudolf
Koella]. [Winterthur] : Kunstmuseum
Winterthur, 1990. 64 p. : ill. (some col.) ; 27
cm.
1. Haubensack, Pierre, 1935- - Exhibitions. I.
Kunstmuseum Winterthur. II. Title.
MLCM 90/03436 (N)
                   NYPL [3-MCZ H375 91-5179]

Hauck, Eldon, 1914- American capitols : an
encyclopedia of the state, national, and
territorial capital edifices of the United States /
by Eldon Hauck. Jefferson, N.C. : McFarland,
c1991. ix, 310 p. : ill. ; 24 cm. Includes
bibliographical references (p. 289-296) and index.
    ISBN 0-89950-551-1 (lib bdg. : alk. paper)   DDC
    725/.11/0973 20
1. United States - Capital and capitol - History. 2.
Public buildings - United States. I. Title.
NA4411 .H38 1991

Hauffe, Hans, 1916- Grafiken / von Hans Hauffe.
Berlin - West : H. Hauffe, [1979?] [12] p. : all
ill. ; 40 cm. Cover title.
1. Hauffe, Hans, 1916-. I. Title.
                   NYPL [MDG+ (Hauffe) 90-2831]

HAUFFE, HANS, 1916-
Hauffe, Hans, 1916- Grafiken /. Berlin - West
[1979?] [12] p. :
                   NYPL [MDG+ (Hauffe) 90-2831]

Haun, Declan. Livingston, Jane. Odyssey .
Charlottesville, Va. , c1988. 363 p. : ISBN
0-934738-45-9 :   DDC 779/.074/0153 19
TR790 .L58 1988   *NYPL [MFW+ 90-556]*

Haunfelder, bernd. Münster und das Münsterland
in Frühen photographien, 1841 bis 1900 /
Bernd Haunfelder. Münster : Aschendorff,
1988. 107 p. : ill., ports. ; 25 x 30 cm. ISBN
3-402-05208-3
1. Münster in Westfalen (Germany) - Description -
Views. 2. Münsterland (Germany) - Description and
travel - Views. I. Title.
                   NYPL [MFW+ 90-9117]

Haupenthal, Uwe. Fassbender, Joseph, 1903-1974.
Joseph Fassbender, Malerei zurischen
Figuration und Abstraktion /. Köln , 1988. 171
p. : ISBN 3-87909-203-6
                   NYPL [3-MCK+ F249 89-11746]

**HAUPTKIRCHE ST. KATHARINEN
(HAMBURG, GERMANY)**

Schleswig-Holstein, Ingeborg zu. Weg ins
Licht . Hamburg , c1988. 78 p. : ISBN
3-7672-1062-2
ND588.S2819 A4 1988
                   NYPL [3-MCK+ S343 90-10580]

Haus am Checkpoint Charlie (Berlin, Germany)
Hildebrandt, Rainer, 1914- Die Mauer . Berlin ,
1989. 52 p. : ISBN 3-922484-22-0
IN PROCESS (ONLINE)
                   NYPL [MFW+ 91-7248]

Lusici, 1942- Lusici . Berlin , 1988. 88 p. :
    ISBN 3-922484-19-0
                   NYPL [3-MCK L971 91-6721]

Haus am Waldsee (Zehlendorf, Berlin, Germany)
Lüpertz, Markus. Markus Lüpertz . Berlin ,
c1989. 1 v. (unpaged) :
N6888.L8 A4 1989

**Haus der Bayerischen Geschichte (Munich,
Germany)**
Henker, Michael. Von Senefelder zu Daumier .
München , New York , 1988. 260 p. : ISBN
3-598-10804-4 (pbk.)
                   NYPL [MDP+ 91-3593]

Schneider, Erich. Balthasar Neumann,
1687-1753 . München , c1987. 48 p. :
                   NYPL [3-MQZ+ (Neumann) 91-6584]

Haus der Kulturen der Welt. Ro, Eun Nim,
1946- Eun Nim Ro . Berlin , Stuttgart , c1990.
79 p. : ISBN 3-89322-301-0
N7369.R6 A4 1990

Hausberg, Margaret Dunwoody. The prints of
Theodore Roussel : a catalogue raisonné /
Margaret Dunwoody Hausberg. Bronxville,
N.Y. : M. Hausberg, 1991. vii, 242 p., [8] p. of
plates : ill. (some col.) ; 32 cm. Includes index.
Bibliography: p. 235-236.   ISBN 0-9628234-0-6
1. Roussel, Theodore, 1847-1926 - Catalogues raisonnés.
I. Roussel, Theodore, 1847-1926. II. Title.
                   NYPL [MDG+ (Roussel) 91-4756]

Hauser, Krista. Drei Generationen Prachensky :
[Prachensky Theodor, Prachensky Wilhelm
Nikolas, Baumann Franz, Prachensky Manfred,
Prachensky Hubert, Prachensky Markus,
Prachensky Michael / Krista Hauser ; I
Herausgegeben und für den Inhalt
verantwortlich, Michael Prachensky]. [Austria] :
M. Prachensky, 1986. 50 p. : ill. ; 34 cm. cover
title.
1. Prachensky family. 2. Architecture, Modern - 20th
century - Austria. 3. Painting, Modern - 20th century -
Austria. I. Prachensky, Michael. II. Title.
                   NYPL [3-MQWD+ 89-27463]

Hausgeister . Fischer, Lili, 1947- Heidelberg ,
1988. 67 p. : ISBN 3-926905-02-6 (pbk.)
                   NYPL [3-MGO+ (Fisher) 89-21325]

Hausmann, Till, 1953-
Till Hausmann, Skulpturen und Zeichnungen
1986-1989 : [Ausstellung] Mannheimer
Kunstverein, 12. Februar bis 12. März 1989.
Mannheim : Der Kunstverein, [1989] [39] p. :
chiefly ill. (some col.) ; 28 cm. Includes
bibliographical references (p. [39]).
1. Hausmann, Till, 1953- - Exhibitions. I. Mannheimer
Kunstverein. II. Title.
                   NYPL [3-MGO (Hausmann) 90-8109]

HAUSMANN, TILL, 1953- - EXHIBITIONS.
Hausmann, Till, 1953- Till Hausmann,
Skulpturen und Zeichnungen 1986-1989 .
Mannheim [1989] [39] p. :
                   NYPL [3-MGO (Hausmann) 90-8109]

Hausmarken in Friedrichstadt . Stolz, Gerd.
Husum , 1987. 54 p. : ISBN 3-88042-362-8
                   NYPL [3-MRX 90-12732]

Hausmeisterportraits . Dreissinger, Sepp.
Salzburg , c1989. 107 p. : ISBN 3-7013-0764-4
                   NYPL [MFX+ (Dreissinger) 90-11180]

Hauswald, Harald, 1954- Rathenow, Lutz, 1952-
Berlin-Ost . Berlin , c1990. 133 p. : ISBN
3-86163-006-0
                   NYPL [MFX (Rathenow) 91-6720]

"Haut und Hülle" : 3 Fotoprojekte aus der
Hochschule für Angewandte Kunst in Wien,
Meisterklasse für Graphik, Gast-Prof. Ernst
Caramelle / [Ausstellungskonzept und für den
Inhalt verantwortlich, Eva Choung-Fux]. Wien :
Rektorat der Hochschule für Angewandte Kunst
in Wien, [1989?] 82 p. : ill. ; 30 cm.
CONTENTS. - Moda povera -- Experimentum imago
specularis -- Modus vivendi.
1. Photography, Artistic - Exhibitions. I. Choung-Fux,

Eva. II. Hochschule für Angewandte Kunst (Vienna,
Austria).   *NYPL [MFW+ 91-2502]*

Hautecoeur, Louis, 1884- Bibliothèque nationale
(France) Le Notre et l'art des jardins. Paris ,
1964. 62 p. :   *NYPL [3-MSCC 91-517]*

Hauteville, Isabelle d'. Art décoratif soviétique
1917-1937 /. Paris , c1989. 436 p. : ISBN
2-903370-46-X   DDC 745/.0947/09041 20
NK975 .A79 1989
                   NYPL [3-MLF+ 90-2331]

Hava Mehutan. Mehutan, Hava. [Tel Aviv] , 738
[1977 or 1978] 10, 100, 10 p. : DDC 730/.92 20
NB979.M44 A4 1977

Hayah Mehutan. Mehutan, Hava. Hava Mehutan.
[Tel Aviv] , 738 [1977 or 1978] 10, 100, 10 p. :
DDC 730/.92 20
NB979.M44 A4 1977

HAVANA (CUBA) - DESCRIPTION - VIEWS.
Mora, Gilles, 1945- [Walker Evans, Havana
1933. English.] Walker Evans, Havana 1933 /.
New York , c1989. 111 p. : ISBN
0-394-57493-1 :   DDC 972.91/23062/0222 19
F1799.H34 M6713 1989
                   NYPL [MFX (Evans) 90-1064]

**HAVANA (CUBA) - SOCIAL CONDITIONS -
PICTORIAL WORKS.**
Mora, Gilles, 1945- [Walker Evans, Havana
1933. English.] Walker Evans, Havana 1933 /.
New York , c1989. 111 p. : ISBN
0-394-57493-1 :   DDC 972.91/23062/0222 19
F1799.H34 M6713 1989
                   NYPL [MFX (Evans) 90-1064]

Havana 1933. Mora, Gilles, 1945- [Walker Evans,
Havana 1933. English.] Walker Evans, Havana
1933 /. New York , c1989. 111 p. : ISBN
0-394-57493-1 :   DDC 972.91/23062/0222 19
F1799.H34 M6713 1989
                   NYPL [MFX (Evans) 90-1064]

Havanna : das Nationalmuseum der Schönen
Künste / [Einleitung von Miguel Luis Núñez
Gutiérrez ; Übertragung aus dem Spanischen
von Renate Petrahn ; bearbeitet von Christine
Baitinger].1. Aufl. Leipzig : E.A. Seemann,
1990. 187 p. : ill. ; 31 cm. ISBN 3-363-00469-9
1. Museo Nacional de Bellas Artes (Cuba). I. Núñez
Gutiérrez, Miguel Luis.
                   NYPL [3-MAVZ+ (Havana) 91-2658]

Haveli . Pramar, V. S. Middletown, NJ , 1989.
238 p. : ISBN 0-944142-15-X
                   NYPL [3-MQWS+ 90-2291]

Havinga, Anne. Ackley, Clifford S. The unique
print . Boston , c1990. 34 p. : ISBN
0-87846-325-9
IN PROCESS (ONLINE)
                   NYPL [MDET 91-4771]

HAWAII IN ART - EXHIBITIONS.
Saville, Jennifer, 1955- Georgia O'Keeffe,
paintings of Hawai'i . Honolulu , 1990. 79 p. :
    ISBN 0-937426-11-3   DDC 759.13 20
ND237 .O5A4 1990
                   NYPL [3-MCX O41 90-12481]

Haward, Birkin, 1912- Nineteenth century
Suffolk stained glass : gazetteer, directory, an
account of Suffolk stained glass painters /
Birkin Haward. Woodbridge : Boydell, 1989.
xxv, 334 p. : ill., 1 map ; 25 cm. - + 4
microfiches (all col. ill. ; 11 x 15 cm.) Map on
lining paper. Includes bibliographical references (p.
xxiii-xxv) and indexes. ISBN 0-85115-529-4 :   DDC
748.592 19
1. Glass painting and staining - England - Suffolk -
History - 19th century. 2. Glass painters - England -
Suffolk - Directories. 3. Glass painting and staining -
England - Directories. I. Title.
                   NYPL [3-MRY 91-2235]

Hawkins, J. B. 19th century Australian silver / J.
B. Hawkins. Woodbridge, [England] : Antique
Collectors' Club, 1990. 2 v. : ill.(some col.) ; 28
cm. Includes indexes. Includes bibliographical
references (v. 2, p. 332-335). ISBN 1-85149-002-7 :
DDC 739.23794 20
1. Silverwork - 19th century - Australia. 2. Silverware -
Australia. I. Antique Collectors' Club. II. Title. III.
Title: Nineteenth century Australian silver. IV. Title:
Nineteenth-century Australian silver.
                   NYPL [3-MNO 90-12680]

Hawkins, William, 1895-1990.
Popular images, personal visions : the art of
William Hawkins, 1895-1990 : May 6-July 1,
1990, Columbus Museum of Art. [Columbus] :

The Museum, c1990. 32 p. : ill. ; 23 cm. ISBN 0-918881-23-4
1. Hawkins, William, 1895-1990 - Exhibitions. I. Columbus Museum of Art. II. Title.
NYPL [3-MCX H424 90-13390]

HAWKINS, WILLIAM, 1895-1990 - EXHIBITIONS.
Hawkins, William, 1895-1990. Popular images, personal visions . [Columbus] , c1990. 32 p. :
ISBN 0-918881-23-4
NYPL [3-MCX H424 90-13390]

Haworth-Booth, Mark. Yeats, Jack Butler, 1871-1957. Jack B. Yeats . Bristol : London : 111 p. : ISBN 0-907738-29-X (Arnolfini Gallery)
NYPL [3-MCV Y41 91-6477]

Hayastani eritasard nkarich'nerĕ / kazmogh P'. M. Mirzoyan ; tek'sti heghinak, A.V. Aghasyan = Molodye khudozhniki Armenii / sostavitel', F.M. Mirzoĭan ; avtor teksta, A.V. Agasīan. Erevan : "Sovetakan Grogh", 1987. 166 p. : ill. (some col.) ; 27 cm. Armenian and Russian. "Albom"--Colophon. Col. ill. on lining papers.
1. Art, Armenian - Catalogs. 2. Art, Modern - 20th century - Armenian S.S.R. - Catalogs. 3. Artists - Armenian S.S.R. - Catalogs. I. Mirzoyan, P'. M. (P'aravon M.), 1949-. II. Aghasyan, A. V. (Ara V.). III. Title: Molodye khudozhniki Armenii.
N7292.6 .H37 1987

Hayden Gallery. Aesthetics of progress . Cambridge, Mass. , c1984. 28 p. :
TS23 .A47 1984   **NYPL [3-MNE 90-10675]**

Haydon, Benjamin Robert, 1786-1846. Neglected genius : the diaries of Benjamin Robert Haydon, 1808-1846 / edited by John Jolliffe. London : Hutchinson, 1990. xii, 260 p. : ill., ports. ; 24 cm. Includes index. ISBN 0-09-173546-7 : DDC 759.2 20
1. Haydon, Benjamin Robert, 1786-1846 - Diaries. 2. Painters - Great Britain - Diaries. I. Jolliffe, John. II. Title.   **NYPL [3-MCV H41 90-11598]**

HAYDON, BENJAMIN ROBERT, 1786-1846 - DIARIES.
Haydon, Benjamin Robert, 1786-1846. Neglected genius . London , 1990. xii, 260 p. : ISBN 0-09-173546-7 : DDC 759.2 20
NYPL [3-MCV H41 90-11598]

Hayes, Dagmar. Ervin Bossanyi; the splendour of stained glass. [Canterbury] Friends of Canterbury Cathedral, 1965. 37 p. plates, illus. (part col.) 23 cm.
1. Bossanyi, Ervin, 1891-1975 - Criticism and interpretation. I. Title. **NYPL [3-MRY 90-7119]**

Hayes, Jeffrey Russell, 1946- The Expressionist landscape . Birmingham, Ala. , Seattle , 1988, c1987. 216 p. : DDC 759.1 19
ND1351.6 .E97 1987
NYPL [3-MCW 88-3335]

Hayes, John T. The art of Thomas Rowlandson / John Hayes. Alexandria, Va. : Art Services International, c1990. 196 p. : ill. (some col.) ; 25 x 30 cm. "February 6-April 8, 1990, the Frick Collection, New York, NY; April 21-June, 1990, the Frick Art Museum, Pittsburgh, PA; June 23-August 5, 1990, Baltimore, MD. This exhibition was organized and is circulated by Art Services International, Alexandria, Virginia"--T.p. verso. Includes bibliographical references and index. DDC 741.942 20
1. Rowlandson, Thomas, 1756-1827 - Exhibitions. I. Rowlandson, Thomas, 1756-1827. II. Art Services International. III. Title.
NC242.R66 A4 1990
NYPL [MDG+ (Rowlandson) 91-6401]

The drawings of Thomas Gainsborough / John Hayes. New Haven : Published for the Paul Mellon Centre for Studies in British Art (London) by Yale University Press, 1971, c1970. 2 v. (x, 368 p., [143] leaves of plates) : ill. ; 30 cm. Includes index. Bibliography: v. 1, p. 327-333. CONTENTS. - 1. Text.--2. Plates. ISBN 0-300-01425-2 DDC 741/.092/4
1. Gainsborough, Thomas, 1727-1788 - Catalogs. I. Gainsborough, Thomas, 1727-1788. II. Title.
NC242.G3 A4 1970
NYPL [MCV+ G14.H4d]

National Gallery of Art (U. S.) British paintings of the sixteenth through nineteenth centuries /. Washington, D.C. [New York] , 1991. p. cm.
ISBN 0-89468-156-7 DDC 759.2/074/753 20
ND464 .N38 1991

Hayes, William Christopher, 1903-1963. The scepter of Egypt : a background for the study of the Egyptian antiquities in the Metropolitan Museum of Art / by William C. Hayes.5th printing, rev. New York : The Museum : distributed by Harry N. Abrams, Inc., 1990. 2 v. : ill., fold. maps ; 26 cm. Includes bibliographical references and indexes. CONTENTS. - Pt. 1. From the earliest times to the end of the Middle Kingdom -- Pt. 2. The Hyksos period and the New Kingdom (1675-1080 B.C.) (4th printing, rev.) ISBN 0-87099-572-2 (v. 1)
1. Metropolitan Museum of Art (New York, N.Y.). 2. Art, Egyptian - New York (N.Y.). I. Title.
NYPL [MAE 90-12062]

Haykakan SSH Gitut'yunneri Akademia. Atlas Armīanskoĭ Sovetskoĭ Sotsialisticheskoĭ Respubliki / [redaktsionnaīa kollegiīa Arutīunīan (Arents) A.B. ... et al.]. Erevan : Glav. upravlenie geodezii i kartografii MGiON SSSR, 1961. 1 atlas (viii, 111 p. : col. maps) ; 34 x 35 cm. At head of title: Akademiīa nauk Armīanskoĭ SSR.
1. Armenian S.S.R. - Maps. 2. Armenian S.S.R. - Economic conditions - Maps. I. Arutīunīan, Aramais Bagrotovich. II. Soviet Union. Glavnoe upravlenie geodezii i kartografii. III. Title.
G2157.A7 A5 1961
NYPL [Map Div. 91-1095]

Hayman, John, 1935- John Ruskin and Switzerland / John Hayman. Waterloo, Ont., Canada : Wilfrid Laurier University Press, c1990. ix, 141 p. : ill., map ; 29 cm. Includes bibliographical references (p. 139) and index. ISBN 0-88920-966-9 DDC 759.2 20
1. Ruskin, John, 1819-1900 - Catalogs. 2. Switzerland in art - Catalogs. I. Ruskin, John, 1819-1900. II. Title.
NC242.R8 A4 1990

Hayman, Patrick, 1915-
Patrick Hayman, a voyage of discovery : a South Bank Centre touring exhibition. London : The Centre, c1990. 60 p. : ill. (some col.) ; 21 x 22 cm. Catalog of a exhibition held at the Camden Arts Centre, London, 9 May to 17 June 1990, and at four other galleries to the first of December. ISBN 1-85332-056-0
1. Hayman, Patrick, 1915- - Exhibitions. I. Camden Arts Centre. II. South Bank Centre. III. Title. IV. Title: Voyage of discovery.
NYPL [3-MCV H4155 91-5046]

HAYMAN, PATRICK, 1915- - EXHIBITIONS.
Hayman, Patrick, 1915- Patrick Hayman, a voyage of discovery . London , c1990. 60 p. : ISBN 1-85332-056-0
NYPL [3-MCV H4155 91-5046]

Hayots' Aybybenĕ /. Khanjian, Grigor, 1926- Erevan , 1981. 1 portfolio ([4 p.], [12] leaves of plates) :   **NYPL [3-MOR 86-4591]**

Hays, K. Michael. Thinking the present . New York, NY , c1990. 136 p. : ISBN 0-910413-93-2
NYPL [3-MQWO 90-13419]

HAYTER, STANLEY WILLIAM, 1901- - EXHIBITIONS.
Anderson, Susan M. (Susan Mary) Pursuit of the marvelous . Laguna Beach, Calif. , c1990. 64 p. : ISBN 0-940872-16-1 DDC 760/.09794/607479496 20
N6530.C2 A58 1990
NYPL [3-MCW+ 91-6334]

Hayward Gallery. Farrer, Anne. 'The brush dances & the ink sings' . London , c1990. 143 p. : ISBN 1-85332-058-7
NYPL [3-MAG 91-6891]

Hayward, J. F. (John Forrest), 1916- University of California, Los Angeles. Fowler Museum of Cultural History. The Francis E. Fowler, Jr., collection of silver /. Los Angeles, Calif., USA , c1991. p. ISBN 0-930741-19-6 (hard) : DDC 739.2/3/07479494 20
NK7103.F68 U5 1991

Hazel, Kennedy, Betty. Hurricane Hazel /. Toronto , 1979. viii, 176 p., [16] leaves of plates : ISBN 0-7705-1821-4 :
QC959.C2 K46   **NYPL [JSE 91-664]**

Hazlitt Gallery (London, England) Seventeenth and eighteenth century oil sketches. [Exhibition] May 1961. [London] 1961. [19 p.] illus. 26 cm.
1. Painting Baroque - Exhibitions. I. Title. II. Title: Oil sketches.   **NYPL [3-MC 90-6627]**

Hazlitt, Gooden & Fox. Indian painting for British patrons, 1770-1860 . London , c1991. 1 v. (unpaged) : ISBN 1-87327-701-6
NYPL [3-MAF 91-5920]

Hē Eurōpaikē zōgraphikē tou 17ou aiōna . Chrēstou, Chrysanthos 1922- Thessalonikē , 1989. 516 p. :
ND456 .C47 1989

Heacock, William. Harry Northwood--the early years, 1881-1900 / William Heacock, James Measell, Berry Wiggins. Marietta, Ohio : Antique Publications, [1990] viii, 151 p. : ill. (some col.) ; 28 cm. Includes bibliographical references (p. 147-149) and index. ISBN 0-915410-39-7 (softbound) DDC 748.2913 20
1. Northwood, Harry, 1860-1919 - Criticism and interpretation. 2. Northwood Glass Company. 3. Glassware - Pennsylvania - Indiana - History. I. Measell, James S. II. Wiggins, Berry A. III. Title.
NK5198.N59 H4 1990

HEAD-GEAR - FRANCE - POITOU-CHARENTES.
Piot, Michel. Coiffes & bonnets en Charentes, Poitou, Vendée . Poitiers , c1989. 350 p. :
ISBN 2-902170-61-0
GT885.P64 P56 1989
NYPL [3-MMV+ 91-5346]

HEAD IN ART - EXHIBITIONS.
Gómez-Moreno, Carmen. Sculpture from Notre-Dame, Paris . New York , c1979. 32 p. :
ISBN 0-87099-211-2
NB550 .G65   **NYPL [MGI 80-2163]**

HEADDRESS. see HAIRDRESSING.

HEADINGS, SUBJECT. see SUBJECT HEADINGS.

Headley, Somers G., 1911- Levinson, John M., 1927- Shorebirds . Centreville, Md. , 1991. p.
ISBN 0-87033-424-7 : DDC 745.593/6 20
NK9704 .L56 1991

HEALTH CARE. see MEDICAL CARE.

HEALTH RESORTS, WATERING PLACES, ETC. - FRANCE - ARCACHON.
Arcachon, la ville d'hiver /. Liège , 1988. 238 p. : ISBN 2-87009-372-1
NA1051.A73 A73 1988

Heard Museum.
Archuleta, Margaret, 1950- Shared visions . Phoenix, Ariz. , 1991. 110 p. : ISBN 0-934351-21-X : DDC 704/.0397/0904 20
N6538.A4 A7 1991

Cotter, Holland, 1947- Kay WalkingStick . Brookville, NY , 1991. p. cm. ISBN 0-933699-20-4 : DDC 759.13 20
ND237.W316 A4 1991

HEART IN ART - EXHIBITIONS.
Sussman, Elisabeth, 1939- El corazón sangrante =. Boston, Mass. , Seattle, Wash. , c1991. p.
ISBN 0-910663-50-5 (paperback) DDC 704.9/46 20
N8217.H53 S87 1991

Heart of American Carnival Glass Association.
Britt, John. [Buckner, MO] [c1990] 150 p. :
DDC 748.2913/09/041 20
NK5439.C35 B75 1990

Heath, Charles, 1785-1848. Neue Shakspeare-Galerie. Leipzig, 1848. [192] p. 45 pl.
PR2991 .N4   **NYPL [MEB 83-2445]**

Heathcliff thinks big /. Gately, George. [Heathcliff. Selections.] New York , 1990. 1 v. (unpaged) : ISBN 0-515-10431-0 : DDC 741.5/973 20
NC1429.G3 A4 1990

Heavenly pottery. Hull, Joan Gray. Hull, the heavenly pottery /. Huron, SD (1376 Nevada SW, Huron 57350) , c1990. 128 p. : DDC 738.3/09771/59 20
NK4210.H84 A4 1990

Hebecker, Inge. Kunsthandwerk im Stadtmuseum . [Nürnberg] [1987] 55 p. :
DDC 730/.0943/320740332 19
NK952.M58 K86 1987
NYPL [3-MLF 90-12631]

Hebel, Johann Peter, 1760-1826. Kannitverstan : acht Kalendergeschichten / Johann Peter Hebel ; mit sieben Originalholzstichen von Karl-Georg Hirsch. Neu-Isenburg : Edition Tiessen, [1989?] 25 p. : ill. ; 25 cm. Limited

edition of 175 copies Library has copy no. 81. ISBN 3-920947-88-6
I. Hirsch, Karl-Georg. II. Title.
NYPL [MEM H668 90-10306]

HEBREW ART. see ART, JEWISH.

HEBREWS. see JEWS.

HÉBUTERNE, JEANNE.
Chaplin, Patrice. Into the darkness laughing .
London , 1990. 151 p., [8] p. of plates : ISBN
1-85381-235-8
NYPL [3-MCF M69 91-4515]

H.E.C. Robinson Pty. Ltd. Robinson's official
Blue Mountains (N.S.W.) street directory and
tourist guide : with street maps from Emu
Plains ... / compiled and published by H.E.C.
Robinson.7th ed. Sydney, Australia : H.E.C.
Robinson, [196-?] 64 p. : ill., maps ; 22 cm.
1. Blue Mountains (N.S.W.) - Maps. I. Title.
NYPL [Map Div. 90-6266]

Heckmann, Hermann. Matthäus Daniel
Pöppelmann : Leben und Werk / Hermann
Heckmann. München : Deutscher Kunstverlag,
1972. 387 p. : ill. ; 28 cm. Includes indexes.
Bibliography: p. 376-380. ISBN 3-422-00651-6
1. Pöppelmann, Matthäus Daniel, 1662-1736. I. Title.
NA1088.P6 H35
NYPL [3-MQZ (Pöppelmann) 74-573]

**Heckscher Art Museum, Huntington, N. Y. see
Heckscher Museum.**

Heckscher, Morrison H. American rococo,
1750-1775 : elegance in ornament / Morrison
H. Heckscher, Leslie Greene Bowman. New
York : Metropolitan Museum of Art ; [Los
Angeles] : Los Angeles County Museum of
Art ; p. cm. Includes bibliographical references and
index. ISBN 0-87099-630-4 DDC
745.4/4974/090330747471 20
*1. Decoration and ornament, Rococo - United States -
Exhibitions. 2. Decoration and ornament - United
States - History - 18th century - Exhibitiona. I.
Bowman, Leslie Greene. II. Title.*
NK1403.5 .H4 1992

Heckscher Museum. Hirschland, Ellen B. Henri
Matisse, Jazz and other illustrated books,
Heckscher Museum, Huntington, New York,
January 12--February 18, 1979 / H. Huntington,
N.Y. [1979] 20 p. : DDC 741.9/44
NC980.5.M35 A4 1979
NYPL [MDG (Matisse) 80-305]

Héctor Basaldúa /. Whitelow, Guillermo. [Buenos
Aires, Argentina ? [1980] 65 p. : DDC 759.982
20
ND339.B3 A4 1980

Hector Guimard . Guimard, Hector, 1867-1942.
Paris , 1971. 45 p. :
NYPL [3-MRX 90-7184]

Héctor Poleo, a retrospective exhibition . Poleo,
Héctor. New York [1974?] [44] p. :
NYPL [3-MCZ P756 91-871]

Hedeman, Anne Dawson. The royal image :
illustrations of the Grandes chroniques de
France, 1274-1422 / Anne Dawson Hedeman.
Berkeley : University of California Press, c1991.
p. cm. (California studies in the history of art. 28)
Based on the author's thesis (Ph. D., Johns Hopkins
University) under title: The illustrations of the Grandes
chroniques de France from 1274 to 1422. Includes
bibliographical references. ISBN 0-520-07069-0
DDC 745.6/7/09440902 20
*1. Grandes chroniques de France - Illustrations. 2.
Illumination of books and manuscripts, French. 3.
Illumination of books and manuscripts, Gothic - France.
4. Kings and rulers in art. 5. Allegories. I. Title.*
ND3399.G67 H44 1991

Heeg-Erasmus, Fritz, 1901-1986.
Fritz Heeg-Erasmus, 1901-1986. [Stuttgart] :
Staatsgalerie Suttgart, c1989. 67 p. : col. ill. ;
30 cm. Catalog of an exhibition held at Staatsgalerie
Stuttgart, July 11-Aug. 6, 1989. Includes bibliographical
references (p. 65).
*1. Heeg-Erasmus, Fritz, 1901-1986 - Exhibitions. I.
Staatsgalerie Stuttgart. II. Title.*
NYPL [3-MCK+ H451 90-12477]

**HEEG-ERASMUS, FRITZ, 1901-1986 -
EXHIBITIONS.**
Heeg-Erasmus, Fritz, 1901-1986. Fritz
Heeg-Erasmus, 1901-1986. [Stuttgart] , c1989.
67 p. : **NYPL [3-MCK+ H451 90-12477]**

**Heemskerck, Martin van. see Heemskerk,
Martin van, 1498-1574.**

HEEMSKERK, MARTIN VAN, 1498-1574.
Filippi, Elena. Maarten van Heemskerck .
Milano , c1990. 121 p. : ISBN 88-85215-03-3
NYPL [3-MCH+ H45 91-4260]

Heer, Jan de. Polano, Sergio. [Hendrik Petrus
Berlage, opera completa. English.] Hendrik
Petrus Berlage, complete works /. New York ,
1988. 266 p. : ISBN 0-8478-0901-3 DDC 720/.92
20
NA1153.B4 A4 1988
NYPL [3-MQZ (Berlage) 90-11983]

Hefte des Focke-Museums .
(Nr. 77) Bremer Landesmuseum für Kunst- und
Kulturgeschichte. Glaskunst vom Empire bis
zum Historismus . Bremen , 1988. 214 p. :
NYPL [3-MPW 91-4604]

Hefte zur bayerischen Geschichte und Kultur .
(Bd. 4) Schneider, Erich. Balthasar Neumann,
1687-1753 . München , c1987. 48 p. :
NYPL [3-MQZ+ (Neumann) 91-6584]

Hefting, Paul. De foto's van Breitner / Paul
Hefting. 's-Gravenhage : SDU uitgeverij, 1989.
142 p. : chiefly ill. ; 29 cm. The photographs
reproduced in this book have been exhibited at the
Teylers Museum in Haarlem, Apr. 8-June 11, 1989.
Includes bibliographical references. ISBN
90-12-06046-X (pbk.)
*1. Breitner, George Hendrik, 1857-1923 - Exhibitions.
2. Photography - Netherlands - Exhibitions. I. Teylers
Museum. II. Title.*
NYPL [MFX (Hefting) 91-2475]

Hegyi, Lóránd. Ungarische Avantgarde in der
Malerei der achtziger Jahre . [Mannheim]
[Budapest] , c1989. 55 p. : ISBN 3-927224-01-4
ND520 .U54 1989

Heide Park and Art Gallery. Tuckson, Tony,
1921-1973. Tony Tuckson . Bulleen, Australia ,
1989. 28 cm. : ISBN 0-947104-08-9
NYPL [3-MCZ T893 90-12756]

Heide, Robert, 1939- Popular art deco :
depression era style and design / Robert Heide
and John Gilman. New York : Abbeville Press,
1991. 228 p. : ill. (some col.) ; 26 cm. Includes
bibliographical references (p. 221-222) and index.
ISBN 1-558-59030-7 DDC 709/.73/09041 20
*1. Art deco - United States. 2. Art, Modern - 20th
century - United States. I. Gilman, John, 1941-. II.
Title.*
N6512.5.A7 H45 1991
NYPL [3-MAMT 91-8075]

**Heidelberg. Kunstverein. see Heidelberger
Kunstverein.**

Heidelberger Kunstverein. Blau, Farbe der Ferne
/. Heidelberg , c1990. 615 p. : ISBN
3-88423-062-X DDC 709/.04/0074434645 20
N6488.G3 H442 1990

Hejdt, Renate. Bialopetraviĉiené, Laima.
Ciurlionis und die litauische Malerei,
1900-1940 . Duisburg , c1989. 105 p. : ISBN
3-923576-57-9 **NYPL [3-MCY 90-10676]**

Heijbroek, Jan Frederik. Hoozee, Robert. [James
Ensor, tekeningen en prenten. French.] James
Ensor, dessins et estampes /. Antwerpen ,
Paris , c1987. 271 p. : ISBN 90-6153-177-2
(Fonds Mercator) DDC 760/.092 20
N6973.E5 A4 1987

Heilbrun, Françoise.
Meisterwerke der Photographie im Musée
d'Orsay /. Stuttgart , 1987. ca. 200 p. : ISBN
3-608-76240-X **NYPL [MFW+ 89-24590]**

Musée d'Orsay : masterpieces of the
photographic collection / by Françoise
Heilbrun, Philippe Néagu ; [translated from the
French by Carol Pratl]. Amsterdam :
Meulenhoff/Landshoff, c1987. [186] p. : chiefly
ill. (some col.) ; 31 cm. ISBN 90-290-8344-1
*1. Musée d'Orsay - Photograph collections - Catalogs. I.
Néagu, Philippe. II. Musée d'Orsay. III. Title.*
NYPL [MFW+ 89-28266]

Les paysages des impressionnistes / par
Françoise Heilbrun. Paris : Hazan : Réunion
des Musées nationaux, c1986. 95 p. : ill. ; 24
cm. (Collection "XIXe siècle / Photographie" . 1) Most
of the photographs are in the collection of the Musée
d'Orsay. Bibliography: p. 95. ISBN 2-85025-116-X
*1. Photography - France - Landscapes. I. Musée
d'Orsay. II. Title. III. Series.*
NYPL [MFW 90-11191]

Pierre Bonnard photographe / par Françoise
Heilbrun et Philippe Néagu ; préface d'Antoine

Terrasse. Paris : P. Sers : Réunion des musées
nationaux, 1987. 148 p. : ill. (some col.) ; 31
cm. "Réalisé à l'occasion de l'exposition 'Bonnard
photographe' au Musée d'Orsay--T.p. verso.
Bibliography: p. 147. ISBN 2-904057-24-2 DDC
779/.092 20
*1. Bonnard, Pierre, 1867-1947 - Exhibitions. 2.
Photography, Artistic - Exhibitions. I. Bonnard, Pierre,
1867-1947. II. Néagu, Philippe. III. Musée d'Orsay. IV.
Title.*
TR647 .B647 1987
NYPL [MFX+ (Bonnard) 91-2568]

[Pierre Bonnard photographe. English]
Pierre Bonnard : photographs and paintings /
by Françoise Heilbrun and Philippe Néagu.
New York : Aperture Foundation :
Distributed to the general book trade by
Farrar, Straus and Giroux, c1988. 148 p. : ill.
(some col.) ; 31 cm. Translation of: Pierre
Bonnard photographe. "Originally published in France
in conjunction with the exhibition 'Bonnard
photographe' at the Musée d'Orsay"--T.p. verso. "An
Aperture book." Bibliography: p. 147. ISBN
0-89381-322-2 : DDC 779/.092/4 19
*1. Bonnard, Pierre, 1867-1947 - Exhibitions. 2.
Photography, Artistic - Exhibitions. I. Bonnard, Pierre,
1867-1947. II. Néagu, Philippe. III. Musée d'Orsay. IV.
Title.*
TR647 .B64713 1988
NYPL [MFX+ (Bonnard) 89-17895]

Heilfurth, Gerhard, 1909- Heuchler, Eduard,
1801-1879. Album für Freunde des Bergbaues .
Frankfurt am Main [1977] 1 portfolio (6 p.,
[14] leaves of plates) :
NYPL [MEM+ H595 89-6071]

Heilig Kreuz in Donauwörth / Werner
Schiedermair (Hrsg.) ; Beiträge von Franz
Xaver Aninger ... [et al.] ; Photographien von
Wolf-Christian von der Mülbe. 1, Aufl.
Donauwörth : L. Auer, 1987. 203 p. : col. ill. ;
31 cm. On lining papers. "Herausgegeben im
Auftrag der Pädagogischen Stiftung Cassianeum in
Donauwörth"--T.p. verso. Includes bibliographical
references (p. 186-198). ISBN 3-403-01848-2
*1. Benediktinerkloster Heilig Kreuz zu Donauwörth. I.
Schiedermair, Werner. II. Aninger, Franz Xaver. III.
Pädagogische Stiftung Cassianeum.*
NYPL [3-MRBB+ 90-2728]

Heiliger, Bernhard, 1915-
Bernhard Heiliger : Skulpturen, Reliefobjekte,
Collagen : 6. April bis 30. Mai 1987,
Ausstellung in der Galerie Pels-Leusden, Berlin
/ [Redaktion, Verena Tafel]. Berlin : Die
Galerie, 1987. 48 p. : chiefly ill. (some col.),
port. ; 30 cm. Includes bibliographical references.
*1. Heiliger, Bernhard, 1915- - Exhibitions. I. Tafel,
Verena. II. Galerie Pels-Leusden. III. Title.*
NYPL [3-MGO+ (Heiliger) 90-254]

Salzmann, Siegfried. Bernhard Heiliger /.
Berlin , c1989. 356 p. : ISBN 3-549-05308-8
NYPL [3-MGO+ (Heiliger) 91-5239]

HEILIGER, BERNHARD, 1915-
Salzmann, Siegfried. Bernhard Heiliger /.
Berlin , c1989. 356 p. : ISBN 3-549-05308-8
NYPL [3-MGO+ (Heiliger) 91-5239]

**HEILIGER, BERNHARD, 1915- -
EXHIBITIONS.**
Heiliger, Bernhard, 1915- Bernhard Heiliger .
Berlin , 1987. 48 p. :
NYPL [3-MGO+ (Heiliger) 90-254]

Heilmann, Angela. Archipenko, Alexander,
1887-1964. Alexander Archipenko.
Saarbrücken , 1986- 2 v. : ISBN 3-925303-31-6
(Bd. 1)
NYPL [3-MGO (Archipenko) 87-1303]

Hein Semke . Semke, Hein, 1899- Lisboa [1989]
153 p. :
NB833.S46 S46 1989

Heine, John, 1950- A good planet is hard to find
/ drawings by John Heine. Birmingham, Ala. :
Menashe Ridge Press, 1991. p. cm. ISBN
0-89732-108-1 DDC 741.5/973 20
*1. Human ecology - Caricatures and cartoons. 2.
American wit and humor, Pictorial. I. Title.*
NC1429.H377 A4 1991

Heinemann, Sue, 1948- Binns, Betty, 1929-
Designing with two colors /. New York , 1991.
127 p. : ISBN 0-8230-1334-0 : DDC 741.6 20
NK1548 .B56 1991

Heinemeyer, Elfriede. Wand- und Bodenfliesen im Landesmuseum Oldenburg . [Oldenburg] , c1988. 84 p. : *NYPL [3-MRXZ 89-26971]*

Heinen, Werner. Köln : Siedlungen 1888-1938 / Werner Heinen, Anne-Marie Pfeffer.1. Aufl. Köln : J.P. Bachem, 1988. 327 p. : ill., map, plans ; 25 cm. (Stadtspuren, Denkmäler in Köln . Bd. 10, 1) Map on lining papers. Includes bibliographical references (p. 305-327) ISBN 3-7616-0929-9
1. Dwellings - Germany (West) - Cologne. 2. Planned communities - Germany (West) - Cologne. 3. Cologne (Germany) - Buildings, structures, etc. I. Pfeffer, Anne-Marie. II. Title. III. Series.
NYPL [3-MQWD 91-5588]

Heiney, Paul.
George Soper's horses / Paul Heiney ; illustrations by George Soper. London : Witherby, 1990. 143 p. : ill. (some col.) ; 25 x 27 cm. Includes bibliographical references (p. 143).
ISBN 0-85493-200-3 : DDC 636.15 20
1. Soper, George, 1870-1942. 2. Draft horses - Great Britain - History. 3. Horses - Great Britain - History. 4. Horses in art. I. Soper, George, 1870-1942. II. Title.
SF311.3.G7 NYPL [3-MCV S712 91-3373]

George Soper's horses / Paul Heiney ; illustrations by George Soper. Boston : Houghton Mifflin, 1991. 143 p. : ill. (some col.) ; 25 x 27 cm. "First published in Great Britain in 1990 by H.F. & G. Witherby Ltd. ... London"--T.p. verso. Includes bibliographical references (p. 143).
ISBN 0-395-58040-4 : DDC 759.2 20
1. Soper, George, 1870-1942 - Themes, motives. 2. Horses in art. I. Soper, George, 1870-1942. II. Title.
N6797.S64 A4 1990

Heinle, Erwin.
[Türme aller Zeiten, aller Kulturen. English]
Towers : a historical survey / Erwin Heinle, Fritz Leonhardt ; [translation by Martha Humphreys]. New York : Rizzoli, 1989. 343 p. : ill. (some col.) ; 30 cm. Translation of: Türme aller Zeiten, aller Kulturen. Ill. on lining papers. Includes indexes. Bibliography: p. 332-334. ISBN 0-8478-1076-3 : DDC 720 19
I. Leonhardt, Fritz, 1909-. II. Title.
NA2930 .H4513 1989
NYPL [MRA+ 91-4474]

Heino Jaeger . Jaeger, Heino, 1938- Hamburg , 1988. 99 p. : ISBN 3-7672-1072-X DDC 760/.092 20
NC251.J265 A4 1988
NYPL [3-MCK+ J221 91-4186]

Heinrich Bürkel . Bühler, Hans-Peter. München , c1989. 343 p. : ISBN 3-7654-2232-0
NYPL [3-MCK B928 90-13435]

Heinrich Campendonk . Campendonk, Heinrich, 1889-1957. Krefeld , c1989. 159 p. : ISBN 3-926530-38-3
N6888.C35 A4 1989

Heinrich, Marita. Grosse Hovest, Benedikt. Die Wiedenbrücker Schule . Paderborn , c1991. 124 p. : ISBN 3-87088-662-5
NYPL [3-MAIH 91-7956]

Heinz, Erich. Johann Heinrich Tischbein d.Ä. (1722-1789) . Kassel [1989] 204 p. : ISBN 3-925272-20-8
NYPL [3-MCK T598 90-10764]

Heinz Fehling . Küster, Bernd, 1952- [S.l.] , c1990. 127 p. : ISBN 3-89299-152-9
NYPL [3-MDWS (Fehling) 91-4830]

Heinz Fehling, Plakatkunst und Werbung /. Küster, Bernd, 1952- [Worpswede] , c1990. 127 p. : ISBN 3-89299-152-9
NC1850.F37 K8 1990

Heinz Hindorf, Glasfenster /. Hindorf, Heinz. Freiburg , c1989. 176 p. : ISBN 3-451-21540-3 : DDC 748.593 20
NK5398.H56 A4 1989

Heinz, Marianne.
Johann Heinrich Tischbein d.Ä. (1722-1789) . Kassel [1989] 204 p. : ISBN 3-925272-20-8
NYPL [3-MCK T598 90-10764]

Muche, Georg, 1895- Georg Muche--Leise sagen . Kassel , 19. 143 p. :
NYPL [3-MCK MGO 88-2455]

Heinz Wieck . Wieck, Heinz, 1935- [Recklinghausen] , c1989. [63] p. :
MLCS 89/16960 (N)
NYPL [3-MGO (Wieck) 90-12381]

Heirlooms [microform] : historical art and decorative arts from New Hampshire collectors : The Currier Gallery of Art, Manchester, New Hampshire, September 7-October 13, 1985. Manchester, N.H. : The Gallery, [1985] [5] leaves : ill. ; 28 cm. Cover title. Microfilm. New York : New York Public Library, 1989. 1 microfilm reel ; 35 mm. (MN *ZZ-30,250)
1. Decorative arts - Exhibitions. 2. Decorative arts - Hew Hampshire - Exhibitions. I. Currier Gallery of Art. II. Title: Historical art and decorative arts from New Hampshire collectors. *NYPL [*ZM-218 no.2]*

Heizer, Michael, 1944-
DOUBLE NEGATIVE.
Heizer, Michael, 1944- Michael Heizer . New York , 1991. p. cm. ISBN 0-8478-1426-2 DDC 709/.2 20
N6537.H384 A635 1991

Effigy tumuli : the reemergence of ancient mound building / Michael Heizer ; essay by Douglas C. McGill ; photographs and explanatory captions by Michael Heizer. New York : Abrams, 1990. 131 p. : ill. (some col.) ; 26 cm. ISBN 0-8109-1166-3 DDC 709/.2/4 19
1. Heizer, Michael, 1944- Effigy tumuli. 2. Earthworks (Art) - United States. 3. Conceptual art - United States. 4. Buffalo Rocks State Park (Ill.). I. McGill, Douglas C. II. Title.
N6537.H384 A64 1988
NYPL [3-MGO (Heizer) 90-11298]

Michael Heizer : double negative / foreword by Richard Koshalek and Kerry Brougher ; essay by Mark C. Taylor. New York : Rizzoli, 1991. p. cm. Includes bibliographical references. ISBN 0-8478-1426-2 DDC 709/.2 20
1. Heizer, Michael, 1944- Double negative. 2. Heizer, Michael, 1944- - Criticism and interpretation. I. Taylor, Mark C., 1945-. II. Title. III. Title: Double negative.
N6537.H384 A635 1991

EFFIGY TUMULI.
Heizer, Michael, 1944- Effigy tumuli . New York , 1990. 131 p. : ISBN 0-8109-1166-3 DDC 709/.2/4 19
N6537.H384 A64 1988
NYPL [3-MGO (Heizer) 90-11298]

Hejduk, John, 1929-
John Hejduk : Riga : Ausstellung, vom 16. Juni bis 9. Juli 1988. Berlin : Aedes Galerie für Architektur und Raum, c1988. [43] p. : ill. (some col.) ; 19 cm. German and English.
1. Hejduk, John, 1929- - Exhibitions. 2. Riga (Latvia) in art - Exhibitions. I. Aedes Galerie für Architektur und Raum. II. Title. *NYPL [3-MCX H458 91-7235]*

Riga, Vladivostok, Lake Baikal : a work / by John Hejduk ; edited by Kim Shkapich. New York : Rizzoli, 1989. 272 p. : ill. (some col.) ; 31 cm. English and Russian. Includes index. ISBN 0-8478-1129-8 (hardbound) DDC 700/.92 20
1. Hejduk, John, 1929- - Themes, motives. 2. Architecture - Philosophy. I. Shkapich, Kim. II. Title. III. Title: Vladivostok.
NA737.H36 A4 1989
NYPL [3-MQZ+ (Hejduk) 91-4487]

Whiteman, John E. M. Divisible by 2 /. [Chicago] , Cambridge, Mass. , 1990. 61 p. : ISBN 0-262-73093-6 (pbk.) DDC 728/.092 20
NA7125 .W48 1990
NYPL [3-MRG 91-6702]

HEJDUK, JOHN, 1929- - EXHIBITIONS.
Hejduk, John, 1929- John Hejduk . Berlin , c1988. [43] p. :
NYPL [3-MCX H458 91-7235]

HEJDUK, JOHN, 1929- - THEMES, MOTIVES.
Hejduk, John, 1929- Riga, Vladivostok, Lake Baikal . New York , 1989. 272 p. : ISBN 0-8478-1129-8 (hardbound) DDC 700/.92 20
NA737.H36 A4 1989
NYPL [3-MQZ+ (Hejduk) 91-4487]

Heland Wetterling Gallery.
Ken Tyler, 25 glorious years . Stockholm, Sweden , c1989. 31 p. :
NYPL [MDBF 90-11072]

Rosenquist, James, 1933- James Rosenquist . [Mount Kisco, N.Y.] , 1989. 48 p. : ISBN 0-9625185-0-6
NYPL [3-MCX+ R797 90-12772]

Held, Al, 1928-
Al Held, new paintings : [exhibition] March 2-25, 1989 / introduction by Donald Kuspit. New York, N.Y. (41 E. 57th St., New York, N.Y. 10022) : André Emmerich Gallery, c1989.
[7] p., 11 leaves of plates (1 folded) : chiefly col. ill. ; 28 cm.
1. Held, Al, 1928- - Exhibitions. I. Kuspit, Donald B. (Donald Burton), 1935-. II. André Emmerich Gallery. III. Title. *NYPL [3-MCX H465 91-4593]*

HELD, AL, 1928- - EXHIBITIONS.
Held, Al, 1928- Al Held, new paintings . New York, N.Y. (41 E. 57th St., New York, N.Y. 10022) , c1989. [7] p., 11 leaves of plates (1 folded) : *NYPL [3-MCX H465 91-4593]*

Held, Julius Samuel, 1905-
The oil sketches of Peter Paul Rubens : a critical catalogue / by Julius S. Held. Princeton, N.J. : Princeton University Press, c1980. 2 v. : ill. (some col.) ; 29 cm. (Kress Foundation studies in the history of European art. no. 7) Includes index. Bibliography: v. 1, p. 649-672. ISBN 0-691-03929-4 : DDC 759.9493
1. Rubens, Peter Paul, Sir, 1577-1640 - Catalogs. I. Rubens, Peter Paul, Sir, 1577-1640. II. Title. III. Series.
ND673.R9 A4 1979
NYPL [MCH R8 81-1504]

Rubens and the book . [Williamstown, Mass.] [c1977] ix, 307 p. : DDC 741.64/092/4
NC984.5.R8 A4 1977a
NYPL [MDG (Rubens) 86-4489]

Helen Foresman Spencer Museum of Art.
Baekeland, Frederick. Images of America . Birmingham, Ala. , 1991. p. cm. ISBN 0-931394-31-7 : DDC 759.13/09/03407473 20
ND1460.U54 B34 1991

Helen Frankenthaler, works on paper . Frankenthaler, Helen, 1928- Vancouver , c1989. 43 p. : ISBN 0-9693328-7-4 : DDC 759.13 20
NYPL [3-MCX F825 91-3252]

Helen Hamilton (1889-1970) . Love, Richard H. Chicago , c1986. 72 p. : ISBN 0-940114-24-0 (pbk.) : DDC 759.13 B 19
ND237.H259 A4 1986
NYPL [3-MCX H2184 90-12509]

Helen Hyde /. Mason, Tim, 1934- Washington , c1991. 120 p. : ISBN 1-560-98009-5 (pbk.) DDC 769.92 20
NE539.H9 M37 1991
NYPL [MDG (Hyde) 91-7232]

Helene Schjerfbeck, Hugo Simberg, Tyko Sallinen / [artikkelit, Marianne Koskimies-Envall, Jorma Mikola, Leena Karttunen]. Vaasa : Pohjanmaan museo, 1989. 69 p. : ill. (some col.) ; 21 cm. (Pohjanmaan museon julkaisuja . no 2 = nr. 2) Finnish and Swedish. Includes bibliographical references (p. 69). ISBN 951-99914-3-3
1. Painting, Finnish - Exhibitions. 2. Painting, Modern - 19th century - Finland - Exhibitions. 3. Schjerfbeck, Helene, 1862-1946 - Exhibitions. 4. Simberg, Hugo, 1873-1917 - Exhibitions. 5. Sallinen, Tyko Konstantin, 1879-1955 - Exhibitions. I. Schjerfbeck, Helene, 1862-1946. II. Simberg, Hugo, 1873-1917. III. Sallinen, Tyko Konstantin, 1879-1955. IV. Koskimies-Envall, Marianne. V. Mikola, Jorma. VI. Karttunen, Leena. VII. Pohjanmaan museo (Vaasa, Finland). VIII. Series: Skrifter utgivna av Österbottens museum , nr. 2.
ND955.F5 H4 1989

Helfand, William H.
The picture of health : images of medicine and pharmacy from the William H. Helfand Collection / commentaries by William H. Helfand ; essays by Patricia Eckert Boyer ; Judith Wechsler, and Maurice Rickards. Philadelphia : Philadelphia Museum of Art ; Distributed by the University of Pennsylvania Press, c1991. p. cm. Includes bibliographical references and index. ISBN 0-8122-7962-X (University of Pennsylvania Press) DDC 769/.4961 20
1. Medicine in art - Exhibitions. 2. Pharmacy in art - Exhibitions. 3. Art - Exhibitions. 4. Helfand, William H. - Art collections - Exhibitions. 5. Art - Private collections - Pennsylvania - Philadelphia - Exhibitions. 6. Philadelphia Museum of Art - Exhibitions. I. Boyer, Patricia Eckert. II. Wechsler, Judith, 1940-. III. Rickards, Maurice, 1919-. IV. Philadelphia Museum of Art. V. Title.
N8223 .H44 1991

HELFAND, WILLIAM H. - ART COLLECTIONS - EXHIBITIONS.
Helfand, William H. The picture of health . Philadelphia , c1991. p. cm. ISBN 0-8122-7962-X (University of Pennsylvania Press) : DDC 769/.4961 20
N8223 .H44 1991

Helfenstein, Josef. Klee, Paul, 1879-1940. Paul Klee, das Schaffen im Todesjahr /. Stuttgart , 1990. 303 p. : ISBN 3-7757-0297-0 : DDC 759.9494 20
N6888.K55 A4 1990a

Helicon nine. The Helicon nine reader . Kansas City , c1990. 512 p. : ISBN 0-9627460-0-2 DDC 700/.82 20
NX180.F4 H44 1990

The Helicon nine reader : a celebration of women in the arts : the best selections from 10 years of Helicon nine, the journal of women's arts & letters / edited by Gloria Vando Hickok ; designed by Tim Barnhart. Kansas City : Helicon Nine Editions, c1990. 512 p. : ill. ; 26 cm. Includes bibliographical references and index. ISBN 0-9627460-0-2 DDC 700/.82 20
1. Feminism and the arts. 2. Arts, Modern - 20th century. I. Hickok, Gloria Vando. II. Barnhart, Tim. III. Helicon nine.
NX180.F4 H44 1990

HELIOCHROMY. see COLOR PHOTOGRAPHY.

HELIOGRAVURE. see PHOTOGRAVURE.

Hellebranth, Robert. Alcide Le Beau, 1873-1943 / Robert Hellebranth, Anne Burdin. [S.l.] : Editions Matute, c1988. 73 p. : ill. ; 32 cm.
1. Le Beau, Alcide. I. Title.
       NYPL [3-MCO+ L442 91-5884]

Hoi Hellēnes naiph zōgraphoi =. Lydakēs, Stelios, 1933- [Athēna] , 1987. 143 p. : ISBN 960-7588-01-0   *NYPL [3-MCY 89-27265]*

Hellēnikē Hetaireia Chartographias. Chartographēsē tou Hellēnikou paraliou kai nēsiōtikou chōrou . [Athēna] , c1989. 84 p. :
GA881 .C43 1989
            NYPL [Map Div. 91-3879]

HELLENISTIC ART. see ART, HELLENISTIC.

HELLENISTIC SCULPTURE. see SCULPTURE, HELLENISTIC.

Hellenistic sculpture I . Ridgway, Brunilde Sismondo, 1929- Madison, Wis. , c1990. xxvi, 405 p., [169] p. of plates : ISBN 0-299-11820-7 : DDC 733.3 20
NB94 .R535 1989 *NYPL [3-MGH 90-11504]*

Hellenistic sculpture one. Ridgway, Brunilde Sismondo, 1929- Hellenistic sculpture I . Madison, Wis. , c1990. xxvi, 405 p., [169] p. of plates : ISBN 0-299-11820-7 : DDC 733.3 20
NB94 .R535 1989 *NYPL [3-MGH 90-11504]*

Hellenistic sculpture 1. Ridgway, Brunilde Sismondo, 1929- Hellenistic sculpture I . Madison, Wis. , c1990. xxvi, 405 p., [169] p. of plates : ISBN 0-299-11820-7 : DDC 733.3 20
NB94 .R535 1989 *NYPL [3-MGH 90-11504]*

Heller, Amy, 1951- Newark Museum. Catalogue of the Newark Museum Tibetan collection /. Newark, N.J. , 1983- v. : ISBN 0-932828-12-4 (pbk.) : DDC 709/.51/5074014932 19
N7346.T5 N48 1983   *NYPL [MAF 91-997]*

Heller, Dieter. Die Entwicklung des Werkens und seiner Didaktik von 1880 bis 1914 : zur Verflechtung von Kunsterziehung und Arbeitsschule / von Dieter Heller. Bad Heilbrunn/Obb. : Klinkhardt, 1990. 322 p. : ill. ; 21 cm. Includes bibliographical references (p. 277-312). Includes index. ISBN 3-7815-0652-5 :
1. Decorative arts - Study and teaching - Germany - History. 2. Art - Study and teaching - Germany - History. 3. Vocational education - Germany - History. I. Title.
NK249 .H44 1990

Heller, Gottlieb Christian Bernhard. Gottlieb Christian Bernhard Heller und seine Musterbücher in der Universitätsbibliothek Jena / [Auswahl, Artur Liebig ; Kommentar, Irmgard Kratzsch]. Jena : Die Universitätsbibliothek, 1988. 141 p. : ill. ; 20 x 22 cm. ISBN 3-910014-02-X
1. Heller, Gottlieb Christian Bernhard. I. Title.
IN PROCESS (ONLINE)
          NYPL [MDG (Heller) 90-13678]

HELLER, GOTTLIEB CHRISTIAN BERNHARD.
Heller, Gottlieb Christian Bernhard. Gottlieb Christian Bernhard Heller und seine Musterbücher in der Universitätsbibliothek Jena

/. Jena , 1988. 141 p. : ISBN 3-910014-02-X
IN PROCESS (ONLINE)
          NYPL [MDG (Heller) 90-13678]

Heller, Martin. Baumberger, Otto, 1889-1961. Otto Baumberger, 1889-1961 . Zürich , c1988. 127 p. : ISBN 3-907065-27-1 DDC 741.6/74/092 20
NC1850.B38 A4 1988
             NYPL [3-MDW 90-13136]

"Mit Pikasso macht man Kasso" . Zürich , c1990. 155 p., [5] p. of plates : ISBN 3-907010-50-7
IN PROCESS (ONLINE)
          NYPL [MDY+ 90-12785]

Heller, Reinhold. Art in Germany 1909-1936 . Munich , c1990. 271 p. : ISBN 0-944110-02-9 (pbk.) :
N6868 .F74 1990
            NYPL [3-MAMG+ 91-4806]

Heller, Steven. Graphic wit : the art of humor in design / Steven Heller and Gail Anderson. New York : Watson-Guptill, 1991. p. cm. Includes index. ISBN 0-8230-2161-0 : DDC 741.6 20
1. Graphic arts - United States - Humor. 2. American wit and humor, Pictorial. I. Anderson, Gail, 1962-. II. Title.
NC998.5.A1 H44 1991

Helman, Włodzimierz. Wkład Polaków i Polonii do światowej sztuki / Włodzimierz Helman. Warszawa : Tow. Wiedzy Powszechnej, Zarząd Główny, 1988. 70 p. ; 21 cm. (Polacy w kulturze i cywilizacji)
1. Arts, Polish. I. Title. II. Series.
NX571.P6 H45 1988

Helmhaus Zürich. Das Leben zur Kunst machen . Zürich , c1989. 151 p. : ISBN 3-906396-02-9
                  NYPL [3-MAM+ 91-6598]

Helms, Dietrich. Vordemberge-Gildewart, Friedrich, 1899-1962. Vordemberge-Gildewart, the complete works /. Munich, Federal Republic of Germany , New York, NY, USA , 1990. 427 p. : ISBN 3-7913-0978-1
                  NYPL [3-MCK V953 90-12857]

Helmut Bönitz /. Bönitz, Helmut, 1914- [Göttingen] , c1990. 119 p. :
N6888.B6165 A4 1990

Helmut Newton . Newton, Helmut, 1920- 's-Gravenhage , 1986. 54 p. : ISBN 90-12-05217-3
                  NYPL [MFX (Newton) 89-17853]

Helmut Newton portraits. Newton, Helmut, 1920- Helmut Newton . 's-Gravenhage , 1986. 54 p. : ISBN 90-12-05217-3
                  NYPL [MFX (Newton) 89-17853]

Helmut Schober . Schober, Helmut, 1947- München , c1989. 153 p. : ISBN 3-7913-1013-5
                  NYPL [3-MCK+ S3627 89-26518]

Helmut Schweizer . Schweizer, Helmut, Düsseldorf , 1989. 39 p. : ISBN 3-925974-09-1
                  NYPL [MFX+ (Schweizer) 91-7486]

Helmuth Seible . Gröne, Ulla. Tübingen , c1991. 48 p. : DDC 803/.1 s 759.3 20
N390.G32 T8 Nr. 34 ND588.S447

Helnwein.
Gottfried Helnwein : Selbstbildnisse = Self-portraits : 1970-1987. Heidelberg : Braus, [1988] 1 v. (unpaged) : chiefly ill. (some col.) ; 33 cm. German, English, and French. Cover title: Der Untermensch. Includes bibliographical references. ISBN 3-925835-07-5
1. Helnwein - Self-portraits. I. Title. II. Title: Selbstbildnisse. III. Title: Untermensch.
N6811.5.H45 A4 1988

HELNWEIN - SELF-PORTRAITS.
Helnwein. Gottfried Helnwein . Heidelberg [1988] 1 v. (unpaged) : ISBN 3-925835-07-5
N6811.5.H45 A4 1988

Helsingin kaupungin tietokeskuksen tutkimuksia.
(1991:4) Sakari, Marja. Helsinki kuvataidekaupunkina. Helsinki , 1991. 104 p. : ISBN 951-772-148-X
N7255.F52 H47 1991

Helsinki. Helsinki, Espoo, Kauniainen, Vantaa . Helsingissä , c1990. 195 p. : ISBN 951-1-10582-5
NA1455.F52 H4575 1990

Helsinki, Espoo, Kauniainen, Vantaa :

arkkitehtuuriopas / [toimittanut] Arvi Ilonen.[Uud. painos]. Helsingissä : Otava, c1990. 195 p. : ill. (some col.), maps ; 29 x 13 cm. Published in conjunction with Suomen Rakennustaiteen Museo. Includes 10 maps on folded pages. Includes indexes. ISBN 951-1-10582-5
1. Architecture - Finland - Helsinki - Guide-books. 2. Helsinki (Finland) - Buildings, structures, etc. - Guide-books. I. Ilonen, Arvi. II. Suomen Rakennustaiteen Museo. III. Title: Helsinki.
NA1455.F52 H4575 1990

HELSINKI (FINLAND) - BUILDINGS, STRUCTURES, ETC.
Pöykkö, Kalevi, 1933- Carl Ludvig Engel 1778-1840 . [Helsinki] [1990] 159 p. : ISBN 951-772-066-1
NA1088.E6 P69 1990

HELSINKI (FINLAND) - BUILDINGS, STRUCTURES, ETC. - GUIDE-BOOKS.
Helsinki, Espoo, Kauniainen, Vantaa . Helsingissä , c1990. 195 p. : ISBN 951-1-10582-5
NA1455.F52 H4575 1990

Helsinki kuvataidekaupunkina . Sakari, Marja. Helsinki , 1991. 104 p. : ISBN 951-772-148-X
N7255.F52 H47 1991

Helvetic Confederation. see Switzerland.

Hemelrijk, Jaap M. Corpus vasorum antiquorum. The Netherlands. Amsterdam, Allard Pierson Museum, University of Amsterdam /. Amsterdam , 1988- v. : ISBN 90-71211-13-4 (v. 1)   *NYPL [MPEK+ C8.A5]*

Hemin, Yves. Pascin, Jules, 1885-1930. Pascin . Paris [1984-1990] 3 v. : ISBN 2-906565-01-6 (t. 2) DDC 759.13 19
N7193.P37 A4 1984
            NYPL [MCZ P27 84-2664]

Hemingway, Andrew. Naturalism and modernity : landscape imagery and urban culture in Britain, 1800-1830 / Andrew Hemingway. Cambridge [England] ; New York : Cambridge University Press, 1992. p. cm. Based on the author's thesis. ISBN 0-521-39118-0 (hardback) DDC 758/.1/41094109034 20
1. Landscape painting, British. 2. Landscape painting - 19th century - Great Britain. 3. Naturalism in art - Great Britain. 4. City and town life in art. I. Title.
ND1354.5 .H46 1992

Hemken, Kai-Uwe. El Lissitzky : Revolution und Avantgarde / Kai-Uwe Hemken. Köln : DuMont, c1990. 211 p. : ill. ; 18 cm. ISBN 3-7701-2613-0
1. Lissitzky, El, 1890-1941. I. Title.
                  NYPL [3-MCZ L772 91-6410]

Hemmann, Gisela. Hemmann, Paul, 1895-1977. Die Brunnen in Weimar . Weimar , 1990. 96 p. : ISBN 3-910053-43-0
                  NYPL [3-MRK 91-7023]

Hemmann, Paul, 1895-1977. Die Brunnen in Weimar : Geschichte und Geschichten zum Entstehen dem teilweisen Verfall und dem Wiederingangsetzen der Laufbrunnen in Weimar/ Paul Hemmann, Günter Golling, Gisela Hemmann. Weimar : Stadtmuseum Weimar, 1990. 96 p. : ill. ; 23 cm. (Tradition und Gegenwart = Weimarer Schriften . Heft 38) Includes bibliographical references (p. 92). ISBN 3-910053-43-0
1. Fountains - Germany - Weimar. 2. Weimar (Germany) - Buildings, structures, etc. I. Golling, Günter. II. Hemmann, Gisela. III. Title. IV. Series.
                  NYPL [3-MRK 91-7023]

Hempel, Eberhard. Jockel, Nils. Alles Plastik . [Hamburg] , 1985. 36 p. :
                  NYPL [3-MGF 86-364]

Hempel, Helmut, 1949- Fonatti, Franco, 1942- Architektur als Erkenntnis =. Wien , c1989. 189 p. :
NA1123.F59 A4 1989

Henderikse, Jan, 1937-
Modern times : Jan Henderikse : Stadtgalerie im Sophienhof Kiel, 28. Januar-25 Februar 1990 : Stedelijk Museum Het Prinsenhof Delft, 10. März- 16. April 1990. Kiel : Die Stadtgalerie, c1990. 65 p. : ill. (chiefly col.) ; 27 cm. Text in English and German. Includes essays by Renate Damsch-Wiehager, Knut Nievers and Barbara Groenhart. Includes bibliographical references.
1. Henderikse, Jan, 1937- - Exhibitions. I. Damsch-Wiehager, Renate. II. Groenhart, Barbara. III. Nievers, Knut. IV. Stadtgalerie im Sophienhof (Kiel,

Germany). V. Stedelijk Museum "Het Prinsenhof". VI.
Title. **NYPL [MFX (Henderikse) 91-4590]**

HENDERIKSE, JAN, 1937- - EXHIBITIONS.
Henderikse, Jan, 1937- Modern times . Kiel ,
c1990. 65 p. :
NYPL [MFX (Henderikse) 91-4590]

Henderson, R. Henderson's sign painter,
originally published in 1906 ; and, The Signist,
originally published in 1905 /. Cincinnati, OH ,
1991. p. cm.   ISBN 0-911380-94-9 :   DDC 741.6/7
20
NK3630.3.S54 H46 1991

Henderson's sign painter, originally published in
1906 ; and, The Signist, originally published in
1905 / [compiled] by R. Henderson. Cincinnati,
OH : Reprinted by ST Publications, 1991. p.
cm.   ISBN 0-911380-94-9 :   DDC 741.6/7 20
1. Signs and signboards - UnitedStates - Lettering. I.
Henderson, R. II. Signist. 1991. III. Title: Sign painter.
NK3630.3.S54 H46 1991

Hendra, Tony. Saget, Bob. [Tales from the crib.]
Bob Saget's Tales from the crib /. New York,
NY , c1991. 95 p. :   ISBN 0-399-51676-X :   DDC
741.5/973 20
NC1429.S315 A4 1991

Hendrick, Jacques. La peinture au pays de
Liège : XVIe, XVIIe et XVIIIe siècles /
Jacques Hendrick. Liège : Perron-Wahle, [1987]
287 p. : ill. (some col.) ; 32 cm. Includes
bibliographical references (p. 277-283)   ISBN
2-87114-026-X
1. Painting, Walloon - Belgium - Liège (Province). 2.
Painting, Modern - Belgium - Liège (Province). I. Title.
ND669.L7 H47 1987
NYPL [3-MCG+ 90-12089]

Hendrik Chabot . Chabot, Hendrik, 1894-1949.
Rotterdam [1990] 24 p. :   ISBN 90-6918-057-X
NYPL [3-MCH C42 91-7291]

Hendrik Petrus Berlage, complete works /.
Polano, Sergio. [Hendrik Petrus Berlage, opera
completa. English.] New York , 1988. 266 p. :
ISBN 0-8478-0901-3   DDC 720/.92 20
NA1153.B4 A4 1988
NYPL [3-MQZ (Berlage) 90-11983]

Henkel, Gabriele.
Tafelbilder / Gabriele Henkel. Köln : DuMont,
c1990. 1 v. (unpaged) : col. ill. ; 30 cm.   ISBN
3-7701-2418-9   DDC 709/.2 20
1. Henkel, Gabriele - Catalogs. I. Title.
N6888.H457 A4 1990

Tafelbilder / Gabriele Henkel. Köln : DuMont,
c1990. 236 p. : ill. ; 30 cm.   ISBN 3-7701-2418-9
1. Henkel, Gabriele. I. Title.
NYPL [3-MGO+ (Henkel) 91-5880]

HENKEL, GABRIELE.
Henkel, Gabriele. Tafelbilder /. Köln , c1990.
236 p. :   ISBN 3-7701-2418-9
NYPL [3-MGO+ (Henkel) 91-5880]

HENKEL, GABRIELE - CATALOGS.
Henkel, Gabriele. Tafelbilder /. Köln , c1990. 1
v. (unpaged) :   ISBN 3-7701-2418-9   DDC 709/.2
20
N6888.H457 A4 1990

Henker, Michael. Von Senefelder zu Daumier :
die Anfänge der lithographischen Kunst /
Michael Henker, Karlheinz Scherr, Elmar
Stolpe. München ; New York : K. G. Saur,
1988. 260 p. : ill. ; 31 cm. (Veröffentlichungen zur
bayerischen Geschichte und Kultur . Nr. 16) Catalog of
an exhibit held at the Haus der Bayerischen Geschichte,
June 21-July 9, 1988. Includes bibliographical
references.   ISBN 3-598-10804-4 (pbk.)
1. Lithography - 19th century - Exhibitions. I. Scherr,
Karlheinz. II. Stolpe, Elmar. III. Haus der Bayerischen
Geschichte (Munich, Germany). IV. Title. V. Series.
NYPL [MDP+ 91-3593]

Henkes, Robert. American women painters of the
1930s and 1940s : the lives and work of ten
artists / by Robert Henkes. Jefferson, N.C. :
McFarland, c1991. xv, 236 p. : ill. ; 27 cm.
Includes bibliographical references and index.   ISBN
0-89950-474-4 (lib. bdg. : alk. paper)   DDC
759.13/082 20
1. Women painters - United States - Biography. 2.
Painting, American. 3. Painting, Modern - 20th
century - UnitedStates. I. Title.
ND212 .H46 1991

Henle, Fritz, 1909- Paris vor 50 Jahren / Fritz
Henle ; [Ausstellung und Katalog, Kurt
Wettengl]. Heidelberg : Edition Braus, c1989.

132 p. : ill. ; 31 cm. Published in conjunction with
the exhibition "Fritz Henle, Paris 1938," held at the
Museum für Kunst und Kulturgeschichte der Stadt
Dortmund from June 23-Aug. 27, 1989.   ISBN
3-925835-75-X
1. Paris (France) - Description - Views. I. Wettengl,
Kurt. II. Museum für Kunst und Kulturgeschichte der
Stadt Dortmund. III. Title. IV. Title: Paris vor fünfzig
Jahren.   **NYPL [MFX+ (Henle) 90-8408]**

Henner, Jean-Jacques, 1829-1905.
J.J. Henner. Mulhouse : Musée des beaux-arts
de Mulhouse ; [Steinbrunn-le-Haut] : Editions
du Rhin, [1989-] v. <1 > : ill. ; 26 cm.
Exhibition catalog. Title on spine: Jean-Jacques Henner.
Includes bibliographical references. CONTENTS. - 1.
La jeunesse d'un peintre, de 1847 à 1864, du Sundgau à
la Villa Medicis.   ISBN 2-86339-059-7 (v. 1) :   DDC
759.4 20
1. Henner, Jean-Jacques, 1829-1905 - Exhibitions. I.
Mulhouse (France). Musée des beaux-arts. II. Title. III.
Title: Jean-Jacques Henner.
ND553.H4 A3 1989

HENNER, JEAN-JACQUES, 1829-1905 -
EXHIBITIONS.
Henner, Jean-Jacques, 1829-1905. J.J. Henner.
Mulhouse [Steinbrunn-le-Haut] [1989-] v. <1
> : ill.   ISBN 2-86339-059-7 (v. 1) :   DDC 759.4 20
ND553.H4 A3 1989

Hennessy, John Wyndham Pope- see Pope-
Hennessy, John Wyndham, Sir, 1913-

Hennig, Karl. Der Karesansui-Garten als
Ausdruck der Kultur der Muromachi-Zeit / von
Karl Hennig. Hamburg : Gesellschaft für Natur-
und Völkerkunde Ostasiens, 1982. vi, 412 p. :
ill. ; 22 cm. (Mitteilungen / Gesellschaft für Natur-
und Völkerkunde Ostasiens . Bd. 92) Includes index.
Bibliography: p. 385-396.
1. Gardens - Japan - History. 2. Japan - Civilization -
1185-1600. I. Series: Mitteilungen der Deutschen
Gesellschaft für Natur- und Völkerkunde Ostasiens ;
Bd. 92. II. Title.   **NYPL [3-MSK 90-6887]**

Hennig, Lothar. Denkmalkunde in Bamberg .
Bamberg [1990] 77 p. :   DDC 720/.28/80943318
20
NA109.G3 D44 1990

Hennig, Wolfgang W. Lötz . München , c1989. 2
v. :   ISBN 3-7913-0984-6 (Bd.1)
NYPL [3-MPW+ 90-13666]

Henning, Anton, 1964-
Anton Henning, new work : [exhibition]
August 30-September 30, 1990, the University
of Oklahoma, Museum of Art, November
24-December 22, 1990, Vrej Baghoomian
Gallery. Norman, Okla. : The Museum, [1990]
1 v. (unpaged) : col. ill. ; 28 cm. Text by Harry F.
Gaugh. Includes bibliographical references.
1. Henning, Anton, 1964- - Exhibitions. I. Gaugh,
Harry F. II. University of Oklahoma. Museum of Art.
III. Vrej Baghoomian Gallery. IV. Title.
NYPL [3-MCK H5166 91-4640]

HENNING, ANTON, 1964- - EXHIBITIONS.
Henning, Anton, 1964- Anton Henning, new
work . Norman, Okla. [1990] 1 v. (unpaged) :
NYPL [3-MCK H5166 91-4640]

Henning, Randolph C. Wright, Frank Lloyd,
1867-1959. "At Taliesin" . Carbondale , c1992.
p. cm.   ISBN 0-8093-1709-5   DDC 720/.7/077576
20
NA2127.G74 W75 1992

Henning, Robert. Santa Barbara Museum of Art.
Santa Barbara Museum of Art . Santa Barbara,
Calif. [1991] 109 p. :   ISBN 0-89951-078-7 :
DDC 708.194/91 20
N742.S15 A195 1991

Henri & Ryerson : the art spirit : an exhibition
organized by Grand Central Art Galleries, April
24-May 26, 1990. New York, NY : The
Galleries, c1990. [32] p. : ill. ; 28 cm.
1. Henri, Robert, 1865-1929 - Exhibitions. 2. Ryerson,
Margery - Exhibitions. I. Grand Central Art Galleries.
II. Title: Henri and Ryerson.
NYPL [3-MCX H51 90-11633]

Henri and Ryerson. Henri & Ryerson . New
York, NY , c1990. [32] p. :
NYPL [3-MCX H51 90-11633]

Henri, Florence, 1893-
Du Pont, Diana C., 1953- Florence Henri,
artist-photographer of the avant-garde /. San
Francisco , c1990. 158 p. :   ISBN 0-918471-17-6

(softcover) :   DDC 779/.092 20
TR647 .H46 1990
NYPL [MFX+ (Henri) 91-4579]

HENRI, FLORENCE, 1893- - EXHIBITIONS.
Du Pont, Diana C., 1953- Florence Henri,
artist-photographer of the avant-garde /. San
Francisco , c1990. 158 p. :   ISBN 0-918471-17-6
(softcover) :   DDC 779/.092 20
TR647 .H46 1990
NYPL [MFX+ (Henri) 91-4579]

Henri Le Sidaner, 1862-1939 . Le Sidaner, Henri,
1862-1939. Paris [1989] 119 p. :   DDC 759.4 20
ND553.L837 A4 1989

Henri Matisse . Musée Matisse. Nice , 1988. 366
p. :   ISBN 2-86941-071-9
NYPL [3-MCO+ M43 91-5314]

Henri Matisse, Jazz and other illustrated books,
Heckscher Museum, Huntington, New York,
January 12--February 18, 1979 /. Hirschland,
Ellen B. Huntington, N.Y. [1979] 20 p. :
DDC 741.9/44
NC980.5.M35 A4 1979
NYPL [MDG (Matisse) 80-305]

Henri Matisse, l'art du livre. Matisse, Henri,
1869-1954. Nice , 1989. 143 p. :   ISBN
2-901412-05-X
NYPL [MDG (Matisse) 91-6192]

Henri Michaux /. Michaux, Henri, 1899- Paris ,
c1990. 31 p. :   ISBN 2-85587-182-4
NYPL [3-MCO+ M61 90-13365]

Henri Rivière . Gamet, Pierre. Douarnenez ,
1989. 40 p., 48 leaves of plates :   ISBN
2-903708-20-7   DDC 769.92 20
N6853.R5 A4 1989

HENRI, ROBERT, 1865-1929.
Perlman, Bennard B. Robert Henri . New
York , 1991. xv, 176 p. :   ISBN 0-486-26722-9 :
DDC 759.13 B 20
ND237.H5 P4 1991

HENRI, ROBERT, 1865-1929 -
EXHIBITIONS.
Charles Conder, Robert Henri, James Morrice,
Maurice Prendergast . New York [1975] [54]
p. :   **NYPL [3-MC 90-5453]**

Henri & Ryerson . New York, NY , c1990.
[32] p. :   **NYPL [3-MCX H51 90-11633]**

Henri Rousseau /. Vallier, Dora. [Henri
Rousseau. English.] New York , c1990. 95 p. :
ISBN 0-517-53697-8 :   DDC 759.4 20
ND553.R67 V33 1991

Henri Sauvage . Loyer, François. Bruxelles ,
1987. 159 p. :   ISBN 2-87009-304-7 (pbk.)
NYPL [3-MQZ (Savage) 90-12030]

Henric, Jacques. Pierre Klossowski / par Jacques
Henric. Paris : A. Biro, c1989. 167 p. : ill.
(some col.) ; 30 cm. Includes bibliographical
references (p. 166).   ISBN 2-87660-039-0   DDC
741/.092 20
1. Klossowski, Pierre - Criticism and interpretation. 2.
Erotic drawing. I. Klossowski, Pierre. II. Title.
NC248.K55 H46 1989

Henrietta Johnston : who greatly helped ... by
drawing pictures. Winston-Salem, N.C. :
Museum of Early Southern Decorative Arts,
c1991. p. cm. "The Museum of Early Southern
Decorative Arts, Winston-Salem North Carolina,
October 12-December 8, 1991, the Gibbes Museum of
Art, Charleston, South Carolina, December 12,
1991-February 2, 1992." Edited by Forsyth Alexander;
photography by Bradford L. Rauschenberg and Wesley
Stewart.   DDC 741.973 20
1. Johnston, Henrietta - Exhibitions. I. Alexander,
Forsyth, 1960-. II. Museum of Early Southern
Decorative Arts. III. Gibbes Museum of Art
(Charleston, S.C.).
NC139.J6 H4 1991

Henry Art Gallery. The Revolution and the
avant-garde . Seattle , 1991. p.   ISBN
0-935558-30-6   DDC 700/.947/09041 20
NX556.A1 R48 1991

Henry, Daniel, pseud. see Kahnweiler, Daniel
Henry, 1884-

Henry E. Huntington Library and Art Gallery.
Bloch, E. Maurice. Focusing on nature . San
Marino, Calif. , c1991. p. cm.   ISBN
0-87328-133-0 :   DDC 741.973/074/79493 20
NC790 .B58 1991

**HENRY E. HUNTINGTON LIBRARY AND
ART GALLERY - EXHIBITIONS.**
Bloch, E. Maurice. Focusing on nature . San
Marino, Calif. , c1991. p. cm.   ISBN
0-87328-133-0 :   DDC 741.973/074/79493 20
NC790 .B58 1991

**HENRY FORD MUSEUM AND
GREENFIELD VILLAGE.**
Popular antiques at the Henry Ford Museum.
[Westfield, N.Y.? , 1959?] 36 p. :
*NYPL [3-MAVZ+ (Dearborn, Mi.)
90-5439]*

Henry Francis du Pont Winterthur Museum.
Fowble, E. McSherry, 1933- To please every
taste . Alexandria, Va. , 1991. p. cm.   ISBN
0-88397-098-8   DDC 769/.974/07474 20
NE506 .F6 1991

**HENRY FRANCIS DU PONT WINTERTHUR
MUSEUM - EXHIBITIONS.**
Fowble, E. McSherry, 1933- To please every
taste . Alexandria, Va. , 1991. p. cm.   ISBN
0-88397-098-8   DDC 769/.974/07474 20
NE506 .F6 1991

Henry Gallery. see Henry Art Gallery.

Henry Hamilton Bennett 1843-1908. Bennett, H.
H. (Henry Hamilton), 1843-1908. New York ,
c1978. [12] p. :
NYPL [MFX (Bennett) 90-5652]

Henry, Hélène. Max Jacob et les artistes de son
temps . Orléans [1989] 240 p. :
NYPL [3-MCO J15 91-6271]

Henry, Jean. Eirich, E. C. (Edward Conrad),
1877-1929. E.C. Eirich (1877-1929) .
[Philadelphia, Pa.] , c1991. 48 p. :
NYPL [3-MCX E35 91-7603]

Henry Miller--the painting : a centennial
retrospective / preface by Gary Koeppel ; with
commentary by collectors and writings by
Henry Miller. Carmel, CA : Coast Pub., 1991.
p. cm.   ISBN 0-9600554-3-6 (limited ed., numbered,
handsigned, clothbound) :   DDC 759.13 20
1. Miller, Henry, 1891- - Exhibitions. I. Miller, Henry,
1891-.
ND1839.M57 A4 1991

Henry Moore /. Argan, Giulio Carlo. Milano ,
c1987. 247 p. :
NYPL [3-MGO+ (Moore) 91-6102]

Henry Moore . Moore, Henry, 1898- London ,
1990. 32 p. :   ISBN 1-85332-055-2
NYPL [3-MGO+ (Moore) 91-6697]

Henry Moore . Moore, Henry, 1898-1986.
Martigny , Milano , c1989. 319 p. :
NYPL [3-MGO (Moore) 90-12634]

Henry Moore at the Serpentine . Moore, Henry
Spencer, 1898- [London] , 1978. [60] p. :   ISBN
0-7287-0177-4 :
NB497.M6 A4 1978b
NYPL [3-MGO (Moore) 79-2019]

Henry Ossawa Tanner . Mosby, Dewey F., 1942-
Philadelphia, PA , New York, NY , 1991. 307
p. :   ISBN 0-8478-1346-0 :   DDC 759.13 20
N6537.T35 A4 1991   *NYPL [Sc G 91-19]*

Henry-Thiébaut, Pierre. Blues / Pierre
Henry-Thiebaut ; André Blondel [dessin].
Paris : Nidot, 1949. [14] p. : ill. ; 19 cm.
1. Blondel, André. I. Title.
NYPL [MEM B658 89-4051]

Henry Varnum Poor, 1887-1970 . Poor, Henry
Varnum, 1887-1970. [University Park, Pa.] ,
c1983. 168 p. :   ISBN 0-911209-29-8
NYPL [3-MCX+ P82 90-13379]

Henry Wyndham Fine Art. Exhibition of British
Paintings, 1750-1950 . London , 1990. 1 v.
(unpaged) :   *NYPL [3-MCT 90-13366]*

**HENTRICH, HELMUT, 1905- - ART
COLLECTIONS.**
Kunstmuseum Düsseldorf. Reflex der
Jahrhunderte . Düsseldorf , 1989. 352 p. :
NYPL [3-MPW 91-7179]

Henze, Wolfgang, 1944- Francis Bott, das
Gesamtwerk / Wolfgang Henze. Stuttgart ;
Zürich : Belser, c1988. 395 p. : ill. (some col.),
ports. ; 36 cm. Includes index. Bibliography: p. 388.
ISBN 3-7630-2062-4
1. Bott, Francis, 1904- - Catalogue raisonné. I. Title.
NYPL [3-MCK+ B7895 90-11079]

Héraut du 17. siècle. Fondation Custodia. Le
héraut du dix-septième siècle . Paris , 1985. xi,

153 p., 80 p. of plates :
NE670.G74 A4 1985

[Herb Ritts: Men/women] Ritts, Herb. Altadena,
Cailf. , c1989. 2 v. :   ISBN 0-944092-11-X
NYPL [MFX (Ritts) 90-11182]

Herbert Beck . Beck, Herbert, 1920- New York,
NY (33 East 74th Street, New York 10021) ,
c1989. 32 p. :
MLCL 89/00926 (N)
NYPL [3-MCK+ B3862 91-4293]

Herbert Brandl, Josef Danner, Otto Zitko /.
Oberhuber, Konrad. Wien , 1988. 4 v. in 1 :
NYPL [3-MCK B818 90-8683]

Herbert, John, 1924- Inside Christie's / John
Herbert. London : Hodder & Stoughton, 1990.
407 p., [16] p. of plates : ill. (some col.) ; 25
cm. Includes index.   ISBN 0-340-43043-5 :   DDC
381/.1 19
1. Christie's International Group. I. Title.
NYPL [3-MAZ 90-10748]

Herbert, Robert L., 1929- Seurat, Georges,
1859-1891. Georges Seurat, 1859-1891 /. New
York , 1991. p. cm.   ISBN 0-87099-618-5   DDC
759.4 20
ND553.S5 A4 1991

Herbert, Susan, 1945- Diary of a Victorian cat :
30 paintings / by Susan Herbert ; text by
Stanley Baron.1st U. S. ed. Boston : Little,
Brown, c1991. p. cm. "A Bulfinch Press book."
ISBN 0-8212-1865-4   DDC 759.2 20
1. Herbert, Susan, 1945-. 2. Cats in art. I. Baron,
Stanley. II. Title.
ND497.H49 A4 1991

HERBERT, SUSAN, 1945-
Herbert, Susan, 1945- Diary of a Victorian cat .
Boston , c1991. p. cm.   ISBN 0-8212-1865-4
DDC 759.2 20
ND497.H49 A4 1991

Herbert, Zbigniew.
[Stomme van Kampen. English]
Still life with a bridle : essays and apocryphas
/ by Zbigniew Herbert ; translated [from the
Polish] by John and Bogdana Carpenter.1st
ed. New York : Ecco Press, c1991. p. cm.
Translation of: De Stomme van Kampen.   ISBN
0-88001-306-0 :   DDC 709/.492/09032 20
1. Art, Dutch. 2. Art, Modern - 17th-18th centuries -
Netherlands. I. Title.
N6946 .H4713 1991

Herbie Knott, black and white. Knott, Herbie.
Black and white /. London , 1990. 128 p. :
ISBN 1-85283-283-5 :   DDC 779.0942 20
NYPL [MFX (Knott) 91-3406]

Herbst, Helmut, 1945- Zwischen den Ruinen .
Stuttgart , c1989. 143 p. :   ISBN 3-87516-511-X
NYPL [3-MAMG+ 91-3257]

HERBST, RENÉ.
Goguel, Solange. René Herbst /. Paris , c1990.
363 p. :   ISBN 2-903370-56-7
NYPL [3-MLH+ 91-5789]

**HERBST, RENÉ - CRITICISM AND
INTERPRETATION.**
Goguel, Solange. René Herbst /. Paris , c1990.
363 p. :   ISBN 2-903370-56-7   DDC 720/.92 20
NK2049.Z9 H4734 1990

Herdies, Paul.
Adolfo-Mario Marizza : le sens caché de la
beauté / Paul Herdies. Bruxelles : Editeurs d'art
associés, [1985] 94 p. : ill. (some col.) ; 28 cm.
(Collection "La Mémoire de l'art") French, Dutch,
German, and Italian.   ISBN 2-87103-011-1   DDC
759.36 20
1. Marizza, Adolfo-Mario, d. 1982 - Catalogs. I. Title.
II. Series.
N6811.5.M34 A4 1985

Lodew Bosscke : "ce lyrique contrôlé" / Paul
Herdies, Georges-Marie Matthijs.Ed. originale.
Bruxelles : Editeurs d'art associés, [1985] 120
p. : ill. (some col.) ; 28 cm. (Collection "La
Mémoire de l'art") Summary in English, Dutch, and
German.   ISBN 2-87103-016-2   DDC 759.9493 20
1. Bosscke, Lodew, 1900-1980 - Catalogs. 2. Bosscke,
Lodew, 1900-1980 - Appreciation. I. Matthijs,
Georges-Marie. II. Title. III. Series.
N6673.B5393 A4 1985

Herding, Klaus.
Courbet : to venture independence / Klaus
Herding ; translated by John William Gabriel.
New Haven : Yale University Press, 1991. p.
cm. Includes bibliographical references and index.

ISBN 0-300-03744-9   DDC 759.4 20
1. Courbet, Gustave, 1819-1877 - Psychology. 2.
Autonomy (Psychology). I. Title.
ND553.C9 H47 1991

Im Zeichen der Aufklärung : Studien zur
Moderne / Klaus Herding.Originalausg.
Frankfurt am Main : Fischer Taschenbuch
Verlag, 1989. 242, [1] p. : ill. ; 19 cm.
"Bibliograpie Klaus Herding": p. 233-[243]. Includes
bibliographical references (p. 183-231). CONTENTS. -
Kondrete Utopie im Weltmassstab : Davids "Narat als
dernier appel à l'unité révolutionnaire -- Visuelle
Zeichensysteme in der Graphik der Französischen
Revolution -- "Die Schönheit wandelt auf den
Strassen" : Lichtenberg zur Bildsatire seiner Zeit --
Diogenes als Bürgerheld.   ISBN 3-596-23615-0
1. Art, Modern - 17th-18th centuries. 2.
Enlightenment - Europe. 3. France - History -
Revolution, 1789-1799 - Art and the revolution. I.
Title.   *NYPL [3-MAL H-13019]*

Hering, Karl Heinz. Küchenmeister, Rainer,
1926- Rainer Küchenmeister . Düsseldorf ,
1980. [108] p. :   DDC 759.3 19
N6888.K8 A4 1980
NYPL [3-MCK K9533 90-5916]

Héritage de France; French painting 1610-1760.
An exhibition ... The Montreal Museum of Fine
Arts, October 6th-November 6th, 1961; Le
Musée de la province de Québec, November
16th-December 16th, 1961; The National
Gallery of Canada, January 4th-February 4th,
1962; The Art Gallery of Toronto, February
16th-March 18th, 1962. [Catalogue. Montreal,
Museum of Fine Arts, 1961] 156 p. 87 illus. (1
col.) 25 cm. "France--the country and its art during
the seventeenth and eighteenth centuries, by Linda
Murray": p. 13-24. Bibliography: p. 68-69.
1. Painting, French - Exhibitions. 2. Painting, Modern -
17th-18th centuries - France - Exhibitions.
ND546 .H4   *NYPL [3-MCN 90-6060]*

The heritage of Giotto's geometry . Edgerton,
Samuel Y. Ithaca , 1991. p. cm.   ISBN
0-8014-2573-5 (cloth : alk. paper)   DDC 701/.8
20
N7430.5 .E34 1991

A heritage of saints /. Gatbonton, Esperanza
Bunag. Manila , 1979. xii, 195 p. :
MLCM 81/1350   *NYPL [3-MOC 89-5146]*

Herman, Jerry. Time and space concepts in art /.
New York , 1980. viii, 157 p., 4 leaves of
plates :
NX650.S8 T55   *NYPL [3-MAMZ 80-2228]*

Herman, Josef, 1911- Davies, Peter. Josef
Herman . Bristol [England] , 1990. 136 p. :
ISBN 1-87297-150-4
NYPL [3-MCZ H545 91-5532]

HERMAN, JOSEF, 1911-
Davies, Peter. Josef Herman . Bristol
[England] , 1990. 136 p. :   ISBN 1-87297-150-4
NYPL [3-MCZ H545 91-5532]

Hermand, Jost. Laughter unlimited . Madison,
Wis. , 1991. vii, 135 p. :   ISBN 0-299-97073-6 :
DDC 837.009 20
NX550.A1 L38 1991   *NYPL [JFE 91-3649]*

Hermann Croissant . Diehl, Wolfgang.
Landau/Pfalz , c1987. 200 p. :   ISBN
3-87629-120-8   DDC 759.3 B 20
ND588.C85 D53 1987
NYPL [3-MCK C942 90-10583]

Hermann Finsterlin . Finsterlin, Hermann,
1887-1973. [Selections. Italian & German.
1969.] Firenze , 1969, c1968. 382 p. :
NYPL [3-MQZ (Finsterlin) 90-5737]

Hermann Glöckner . Glöckner, Hermann, 1889-
Stuttgart [1991] 130 p. :   ISBN 3-923717-65-2
NYPL [3-MCK+ G562 91-8028]

Hermann Gradl . Gradl, Hermann, 1883-1964.
Marktheidenfeld am Main , 1989. 190 p. :
ISBN 3-927439-06-1
NYPL [3-MCK+ G73 91-5156]

**Hermann Haack Geographisch-Kartographische
Anstalt Gotha.**
Haack Atlas Weltmeer / Herausgeber, VEB
Hermann Haack Geographisch-Kartographische
Anstalt Gotha. 1. Aufl. Gotha : H. Haack,
[1989] 1 atlas (viii, 136 p.) : col. ill., 162 col.
maps ; 36 cm. "Redaktionsschluss, Januar 1989"--T.p.
verso. Flags on lining papers. Includes bibliographical
references (p. 134-135) and indexes.   ISBN
3-7301-0010-6

1. Oceanography - Maps. 2. Oceanography - Charts, diagrams, etc. 3. Shipping - Maps. 4. Marine resources - Maps. I. Title. II. Title: Atlas Weltmeer.
NYPL [Map Div. 91-7352]

Sozialistische Staaten Mittel- und Südosteuropas /. Gotha , 1986. 1 atlas (190 p.) : ISBN 3-7301-0032-7 **NYPL [Map Div. 91-3783]**

Hermary, Antoine. Musée du Louvre. Département des antiquités orientales. Catalogue des antiquités de Chypre . Paris , 1989. 496 p. : ISBN 2-7118-2279-6 DDC 732/.973/07444361 20
NB130.C8 M87 1989

Hermeneutics of art, 0899-9856 . (vol. 2) Weyl, Martin. Passion for reason and reason of passion . New York , c1989. 314 p. ; ISBN 0-8204-0981-2 : DDC 709.44/09/032 20
N6846 .W49 1989
NYPL [3-MAMI 91-6906]

The Hermitage : selected treasures from a great museum / text written by the curatorial staff of the State Hermitage Museum ; commissioned by the Hermitage Joint Venture. [London] : Booth-Clibborn Editions, c1990. 164 p. : ill. ; 26 cm. ISBN 0-904866-85-8
1. Gosudarstvennyĭ Ėrmitazh (Soviet Union) - Catalogs. I. Gosudarstvennyĭ Ėrmitazh (Soviet Union).
NYPL [3-MAVZ (Leningrad) 91-4483]

The Hermitage : selected treasures from one of the world's great museums / text written by the curatorial staff of the State Hermitage Museum ; commissioned by the Hermitage Joint Venture.1st ed. in the U. S. New York : Doubleday, c1991. 164 p. : col. ill. ; 26 cm. Includes index. ISBN 0-385-41966-X : DDC 708.7/453 20
1. Art - Russian S.F.S.R. - Leningrad - Catalogs. 2. Gosudarstvennyĭ Ėrmitazh (Soviet Union) - Catalogs. I. Gosudarstvennyĭ Ėrmitazh (Soviet Union).
N3350 .H48 1991

Hermitage . Ėrmitazh . Leningrad , 1989. 560 p. : ISBN 5-274-00375-3 :
N3350 .E76 1989

The Hermitage catalogue of Western European painting /. Gosudarstvennyĭ Ėrmitazh (Soviet Union) [Sobranie zapadnoevropeĭskoĭ zhivopisi. English. (Florence, Italy)] Florence , <c1988-. v. <15 > : ISBN 88-09-20028-4 DDC 759.94/074/47435 20
ND450 .G6713 1988

Hernad, Béatrice. Die Graphiksammlung des Humanisten Hartmann Schedel . München , c1990. 336 p. : ISBN 3-7913-1083-6 DDC 769.94/09/02407443364 20
NE59.G4 S324 1990 **NYPL [MDE 91-7276]**

Hernán Merino . Merino, Hernán, 1922-1973. Bogotá [1986?] 107 p. :
NC1460.M47 A4 1986

Hernández Guardiola, Lorenzo, 1953- Pintura decorativa barroca en la provincia de Alicante / Lorenzo Hernández Guardiola. Alicante : Instituto de Cultura "Juan Gil-Albert", Diputación de Alicante, [1990- v. ill ; 20 cm. (Colección Divulgación. 9) Includes indexes. Includes bibliographical references. CONTENTS. - t. 1. El último tercio del siglo XVII y primeros años del XVIII. ISBN 84-7784-037-7
1. Painting, Spanish - Spain - Alicante (Province). 2. Painting, Baroque - Spain - Alicante (Province). 3. Painting, Modern - 17th-18th centuries - Spain - Alicante (Province). I. Title. II. Series.
NYPL [3-MCP 91-858]

Pintura decorativa barroca en la provincia de Alicante / Lorenzo Hernández Guardiola. Alicante : Instituto de Cultura "Juan Gil-Albert," Diputación de Alicante, [1990- v. <1 > : ill. ; 19 cm. (Divulgación . 9) Includes bibliographical references (v. 1, p. 251-258) and index. CONTENTS. - v. 1. El último tercio del siglo XVII y primeros años del XVIII ISBN 84-7784-037-7
1. Mural painting and decoration, Spanish - Spain - Alicante (Province). 2. Mural painting and decoration, Baroque - Spain - Alicante (Province). I. Series: Divulgación (Alicante, Spain) , 9. II. Title.
ND2786.A43 H4 1990

Hernández, Mario. García Lorca, Federico, 1898-1936. Dibujos /. [Madrid] . 155 p : ISBN 84-86691-00-1 DDC 741.946 20
NC287.G383 A4 1987a

García Lorca, Federico, 1898-1936. [Dibujos. English.] Line of light and shadow . Durham , 1991. 273 p. : ISBN 0-8223-1122-4 DDC 741.946 20
NC287.G389 A4 1991

Hernández-Porto, Ana. Outside Cuba . [New Brunswick, N.J.] , Miami, Fla. , 1989. 366 p. : ISBN 0-935501-13-4
NYPL [3-MAM 90-12497]

Herner, János. Erdély és a Részek térképe és helységnévtára . Szeged , 1987 ([Budapest] : Franklin Nyomda) 1 atlas (41, 214 p., [9] p. of plates) : ISBN 963-481-771-8 : DDC 912/.4984 19
G2037.T7 E7 1987
NYPL [Map Div. 91-145]

HEROINES. see WOMEN.

Herold, Georg, 1947- Geld spielt keine Rolle / Georg Herold. Köln : Kölnischer Kunstverein, c1990. 78 p. : ill. (chiefly col., some folded) ; 24 cm. "Katalog zur Ausstellung, Georg Herold, 'Geld spielt keine Rolle,' Kölnischer Kunstverein, 2. Juni bis 29. Juli 1990."--Colophon. Essays by Marianne Stockebrand and Boris Groys in English and German. Includes bibliographical references (p. 77-78).
1. Herold, Georg, 1947- - Exhibitions. I. Stockebrand, Marianne. II. Groys, Boris. III. Kölnischer Kunstverein. IV. Title. V. Title: Georg Herold.
NYPL [3-MCK H556 91-6202]

HEROLD, GEORG, 1947- - EXHIBITIONS. Herold, Georg, 1947- Geld spielt keine Rolle /. Köln , c1990. 78 p. :
NYPL [3-MCK H556 91-6202]

Heron, Patrick, 1920- Patrick Heron : gouaches, 1961-1989. London : Waddington Galleries, 1989. 40 p. : col. ill. ; 23 x 29 cm. Catalog of an exhibition held Apr. 26-May 20, 1989. Includes bibliographical references (p. 38-39).
1. Heron, Patrick, 1920- - Exhibitions. I. Waddington Galleries. **NYPL [3-MCV H562 90-10958]**

HERON, PATRICK, 1920- - EXHIBITIONS. Heron, Patrick, 1920- Patrick Heron . London , 1989. 40 p. :
NYPL [3-MCV H562 90-10958]

Heron, Roy. The sporting art of Cecil Aldin / Roy Heron. London : Sportsman's Press, 1990. 126 p., [20] p. of plates : ill. (some col.) ; 28 cm. Includes bibliography and index. ISBN 0-948253-50-9 : DDC 760.092 20
1. Aldin, Cecil Charles Windsor, 1870-1935. 2. Artists - England - Biography. 3. Sports in art. I. Aldin, Cecil Charles Windsor, 1870-1935. II. Title.
NC242.A4 **NYPL [3-MCV A36 91-5523]**

Herr, Harald, 1951- Kunstsituation und Künstler sein heute . Karlsruhe , 1988. 342 p. :
N6886.K33 K88 1988
NYPL [3-MAMG 90-10706]

Herrán, Saturnino, 1887-1918. Saturnino Herrán / acompañado pr textos de Ramón López Velarde ; presentación y selección de textos, Felipe Garrido ; fotografía, Enrique Franco Torrijos. 1a ed. México : Fondo Editorial de la Plástica Mexicana, 1988 143 p. : ill. (chiefly col.) ; 46 cm. Includes bibliographical references. ISBN 968-665-809-2
1. Herrán, Saturnino, 1887-1918 - Catalogs. I. Garrido, Luis, 1898-. II. Franco Torrijos, Enrique. III. Title.
NYPL [3-MCZ++ H564 89-26935]

Saturnino Herrán / acompañado por textos de Ramón López Velarde ; presentación y selección de textos, Felipe Garrido. 1. ed. México : Fondo Editorial de la Plástica Mexicana, 1988. 143 p. : ill. (some col.) ; 46 cm. Includes bibliographical references. ISBN 968-665-809-2 DDC 759.972 20
1. Herrán, Saturnino, 1887-1918 - Catalogs. I. López Velarde, Ramón, 1888-1921. II. Garrido, Felipe. III. Title.
N6559.H47 A4 1988

HERRÁN, SATURNINO, 1887-1918 - CATALOGS. Herrán, Saturnino, 1887-1918. Saturnino Herrán /. México , 1988 143 p. : ISBN 968-665-809-2
NYPL [3-MCZ++ H564 89-26935]

Herrán, Saturnino, 1887-1918. Saturnino Herrán /. México , 1988. 143 p. : ISBN 968-665-809-2 DDC 759.972 20
N6559.H47 A4 1988

Herrera, Hayden. Frida Kahlo : the paintings / by Hayden

Herrera.1st ed. New York, NY : HarperCollins Publishers, c1991. p. cm. Includes index. ISBN 0-06-016699-1 : DDC 759.972 20
1. Kahlo, Frida - Self-portraits. 2. Kahlo, Frida - Criticism and interpretation. I. Title.
ND1329.K33 H4 1991

Museum of Contemporary Art (Chicago, Ill.) Frida Kahlo . Chicago , c1978. 28 p. :
NYPL [3-MCZ K122 90-7091]

Herrero Carretero, Concha. Resplendence of the Spanish monarchy . New York , 1991. p. cm. ISBN 0-87099-621-5 DDC 739.7/0946/0747471 20
NK3062.A1 R47 1991

Herriman, George, 1880-1944. Geo. Herriman's Krazy + Ignatz / introduction by Bill Blackbeard. Forestville, CA : Eclipse Books/Turtle Island Foundation, 1988- v. : chiefly ill. ; 32 cm. Spine title: Krazy & Ignatz. "The Komplete Kat Komics"--Cover. CONTENTS. - v. 1. 1916 -- v. 4. 1919: Howling among the halls of night -- v. 5. 1920: Pilgrims on the road to nowhere -- v. 6 1921: Sure as moons in cheeses. ISBN 0-913035-48-3 (pbk. : v. 1)
1. Krazy Kat (Comic strip). I. Title. II. Title: Krazy + Ignatz. III. Title: Krazy & Ignatz. IV. Title: Krazy and Ignatz. V. Title: Komplete Kat Komics.
NYPL [3-MEM+ (Herriman) 91-610]

Herrmann, Ursula. Eberhard Wenzel : Komponist, Pädagoge, Interpret / Ursula Herrmann.1. Aufl. Berlin : Evangelische Verlagsanstalt, c1989. 210 p. ; 20 cm. "Verzeichnis der Kompositionen Eberhard Wenzels"--p. 146-205. Includes bibliographical references (p. 206-207). Includes index. ISBN 3-374-00804-6 DDC 780/.92 B 20
1. Wenzel, Eberhard, 1896-1982. 2. Composers - Germany - Biography. 3. Church musicians - Germany - Biography. I. Title.
NK410.W464 H5 1989

Herrmann, Wolfgang, 1899- In what style should we build? . Santa Monica, Calif. , 1991. p. cm. ISBN 0-89236-199-9 : DDC 720/.1 20
NA2500 .I5 1991

Herron Museum of Art. see Indianapolis Museum of Art.

Herrscher, Krieger und Geliebte : antike Götter und ihr Himmel : Sonderausstellung Tiroler Landesmuseum Ferdinandeum, Innsbruck, 30. Mai bis 27. August 1989 / [Katalog, Liselotte Zemmer-Plank]. Innsbruck : Tiroler Landesmuseum Ferdinandeum, c1989. 95 p., [6] p. of plates : ill. (some col.) ; 23 cm. Includes bibliographical references.
1. Mythology, Greek, in art - Exhibitions. 2. Mythology, Roman, in art - Exhibitions. 3. Mythology, Classical, in art - Exhibitions. 4. Idols and images - Exhibitions. 5. Bronzes, Classical - Exhibitions. 6. Gods in art - Exhibitions. 7. Sculpture, Classical - Exhibitions. I. Tiroler Landesmuseum Ferdinandeum.
NYPL [3-MGR 91-3460]

Herschman, Joel, 1936- Un voyage héliographique à faire : the mission of 1851 : the first photographic survey of historical monuments in France : inaugural exhibition, sponsored by the National Endowment for the Arts, Godwin-Ternbach Museum at Queens College, Mattis Room, Paul Klapper Library, Queens College, Flushing, NY 11367, 4 March-3 April 1981 : catalogue / by Joel A. Herschman and William W. Clark. [S.l. : s.n., 1981] 37 p. : ill. ; 17 x 22 cm. Bibliography: p. 23. DDC 779/.4/0740147243 19
1. Photography, Architectural - France - Exhibitions. I. Clark, William W., 1940-. II. Godwin-Ternbach Museum. III. Paul Klapper Library. IV. Title.
DC20 .H47 **NYPL [MFW 91-8054]**

Hersey, George L. Possible Palladian villas : (plus a few instructively impossible ones) / George Hersey and Richard Freedman. Cambridge, Mass. : MIT Press, c1992. p. cm. Includes bibliographical references (p.) and index. ISBN 0-262-08210-1 DDC 728.8/092 20
1. Architecture, Domestic - Data processing. 2. Architectural design - Data processing. 3. Palladio, Andrea, 1508-1580. I. Freedman, Richard, 1964-. II. Title.
NA7125 .H47 1992

Hersey, Irwin. Indonesian primitive art / Irwin Hersey. Singapore ; New York : Oxford University Press, 1991. p. cm. (The Asia collection) Includes bibliographical references. ISBN

0-19-588553-8 : DDC 730/.089/9922 20
1. Art, Primitive - Indonesia. 2. Art, Indonesian. I.
Title. II. Series.
N7326 .H47 1991

Hershkowitz, Robert. The British photographer
abroad . London , 1980. 95 p. : ISBN
0-9507057-0-5 :
TR790 .B74 **NYPL [MFW 81-889]**

Hertle, Gisela.
Nahua-Dialekte in Puebla-Tlaxcala. Marschall,
Wolfgang. Beiträge zur Ethnographie der
Sierra-Totonaken. Wiesbaden, 1972. 112 p.:
NYPL [HTC 74-1117 Bd. 4]

HERVE REGION (BELGIUM) -
DESCRIPTION AND TRAVEL - VIEWS.
Lambiet, Thomas. Le pays de Herve .
[Belgium] , 1978. 343 p., [2] leaves of plates :
NYPL [3-MQW+ 89-10507]

Hervey, John. Collector's guide to cartoon &
promotional drinking glasses / by John Hervey.
Gas City, IN : L-W Book Sales, c1990. x, 180
p. : ill. (some col.) ; 28 cm. Spine title: Cartoon &
promotional drinking glasses. "Pepsi, McDonalds, sports,
Disney, Coco-Cola, much more. Over 3000
glasses"--Cover. ISBN 0-89145-443-8 : DDC
760/.0951/07479493 20
1. Advertising glasses - United States - Catalogs. 2.
Advertising specialities - United States - Catalogs. I.
Title. II. Title: Collector's guide to cartoon and
promotional drinking glasses. III. Title: Cartoon &
promotional drinking glasses. IV. Title: Cartoon and
promotional drinking glasses.
NK5440.D75 H4 1990

HERZMANOVSKY-ORLANDO, FRITZ,
RITTER VON, 1877-1954 - CRITICISM
AND INTERPRETATION.
Van Zon, Gabriele, 1937- Word and picture .
New York , 1991. p. cm. ISBN 0-8204-1475-1
DDC 700/.92 20
NX548.Z9 K838 1991

Herzog & de Meuron : projects and buildings
1982-1990 / editor, Wilfried Wang. Cambridge,
Mass. : Harvard University Graduate School of
Design ; New York : Rizzoli, 1990. 96 p. : ill ;
29 cm. "Published in connection with the joint
appointment of Jacques Herzog and Pierre de Meuron
as the Kenzo Tange Visiting Professors of Architecture,
Spring 1989." Includes bibliographical references (p.
87-89). ISBN 0-8478-1187-5
1. Herzog, Jacques. 2. Meuron, Pierre de. 3.
Architecture, Modern - 20th century - Switzerland. I.
Herzog, Jacques. II. Meuron, Pierre de. III. Wang,
Wilfried. IV. Title: Herzog and de Meuron.
NYPL [3-MQZ (Herzog) 90-12645]

Herzog and de Meuron . Herzog & de Meuron .
Cambridge, Mass. , New York , 1990. 96 p. :
ISBN 0-8478-1187-5
NYPL [3-MQZ (Herzog) 90-12645]

Herzog August Bibliothek.
Das Buch des Künstlers . [Hannover] [1989]
179 p. : DDC 708.3/5954 s 769.9/04/074435954 20
N5070.H3 K4 1989/3 NE890
NYPL [3-MAW (Hanover) 73-2900
1989/3]

Die Porträtsammlung der Herzog August
Bibliothek Wolfenbüttel /. München , New
York , 1986- v. : ISBN 3-598-31480-9 (Reihe A)
NYPL [MDE+ 88-1441]

Watts, Harriett. Hans Arp und Sophie
Taeuber-Arp . Wolfenbüttel [1989] 54 p. :
ISBN 3-88373-054-8 DDC 700/.92 20
N6853.A7 A4 1989

HERZOG AUGUST BIBLIOTHEK -
CATALOGS.
Die Porträtsammlung der Herzog August
Bibliothek Wolfenbüttel /. München , New
York , 1986- v. : ISBN 3-598-31480-9 (Reihe A)
NYPL [MDE+ 88-1441]

HERZOG AUGUST BIBLIOTHEK -
EXHIBITIONS.
Das Buch des Künstlers . [Hannover] [1989]
179 p. : DDC 708.3/5954 s 769.9/04/074435954 20
N5070.H3 K4 1989/3 NE890
NYPL [3-MAW (Hanover) 73-2900
1989/3]

Herzog, Erich. Unbekannte Schätze der Kasseler
Gemälde-Galerie. [Ausstellung.
Katalogbearbeitung: Erich Herzog und Jürgen
Lehmann.] [Kassel] Staatliche
Kunstsammlungen Kassel [1968] 92 p. illus. 22

cm.
1. Staatliche Kunstsammlungen Kassel. Gemäldegalerie
Alte Meister - Catalogs. 2. Painting, European -
Catalogs. 3. Painting, Modern - 17th-18th centuries -
Europe - Catalogs. I. Lehmann, Jürgen M. II. Staatliche
Kunstsammlungen Kassel. Gemäldegalerie Alte Meister.
III. Title.
N2308.4 .H4 **NYPL [3-MAVZ (Kassel,**
Germany) 90-6612]

Herzog, Jacques. Herzog & de Meuron .
Cambridge, Mass. , New York , 1990. 96 p. :
ISBN 0-8478-1187-5
NYPL [3-MQZ (Herzog) 90-12645]

HERZOG, JACQUES.
Herzog & de Meuron . Cambridge, Mass. ,
New York , 1990. 96 p. : ISBN 0-8478-1187-5
NYPL [3-MQZ (Herzog) 90-12645]

Herzog, Jesús Silva. see Silva Herzog, Jesús,
1893-

Herzog, Karl. Die Gestalt des Menschen in der
Kunst und im Spiegel der Wissenschaft / Karl
Herzog. Darmstadt : Wissenschaftliche
Buchgesellschaft, c1990. xii, 234 p. : ill. ; 29
cm. Includes bibliographical references and index.
ISBN 3-534-11010-2 DDC 704.9/421 20
1. Nude in art. 2. Human figure in art. 3. Art -
Themes, motives. 4. Body, Human. I. Title.
N7572 .H47 1990

Herzogenrath, Wulf.
Berlin, März 1990 . Berlin , Braunschweig
[1990] 88 p. :
MLCM 91/00973 (N)
NYPL [3-MAL 91-6662]

Fassbender, Joseph, 1903-1974. Joseph
Fassbender, Malerei zurischen Figuration und
Abstraktion /. Köln , 1988. 171 p. : ISBN
3-87909-203-6
NYPL [3-MCK+ F249 89-11746]

50 Jahre Bauhaus . Stuttgart , 1968. 369 p. :
NYPL [3-MAL 90-6848]

Heslip, Colleen Cowles. Between the rivers :
itinerant painters from the Connecticut to the
Hudson / by Colleen Cowles Heslip ; with an
introduction by Mary Black. Williamstown,
Mass. : Sterling and Francine Clark Art
Institute, c1990. 95 p. : ill. (some col.) ; 28 cm.
Catalog of an exhibition held at the Sterling and
Francine Clark Art Institute Apr. 7-July 22, 1990, the
Museum of Fine Arts, Springfield, Mass. Sept. 9-Nov.
4, 1990, and the Hudson River Museum Jan. 20-Mar.
10, 1991. Includes bibliographical references. ISBN
0-931102-28-6 : DDC 759.14/074/744 20
1. Primitivism in art - New England - Exhibitions. 2.
Painting, American - New England - Exhibitions. 3.
Painting, Colonial - New England - Exhibitions. 4.
Painting, Modern - 19th century - New England -
Exhibitions. 5. Primitivism in art - New York (State) -
Exhibitions. 6. Painting, Colonial - New York (State) -
Exhibitions. 7. Painting, Modern - 19th century - New
York (State) - Exhibitions. I. Sterling and Francine
Clark Art Institute. II. Museum of Fine Arts
(Springfield, Mass.). III. Hudson River Museum. IV.
Title.
ND215 .H47 1990 **NYPL [3-MCW 91-4583]**

Hess, G. Historische Karten aus der Sammlung
der Ernst-Moritz-Arndt-Universitat Greifswald
in der Sektion Geographie /. Greifswald , 1981.
1 portfolio (20 maps (some col.)) ;
NYPL [Map Div. 86-337]

Hessemer, Friedrich Maximilian, 1800-1860.
[Arabische und Alt-Italienische Bau-
Verzierungen. English]
Historic designs and patterns in color from
Arabic and Italian sources / F.M. Hessemer.
New York : Dover Publications, c1990. 120
p. : chiefly col. ill. ; 31 cm. Translation of:
Arabische und Alt-Italienische Bau-Verzierungen.
ISBN 0-486-26425-4 DDC 745.4 20
1. Decoration and ornament, Architectural - Arab
countries. 2. Decoration and ornament, Architectural -
Italy. 3. Decoration and ornament, Islamic - Arab
countries. 4. Decoration and ornament, Medieval -
Italy. 5. Decoration and ornament - Italy. I. Title.
NA3573 .H4713 1990
NYPL [3-MRX+ 91-6246]

Hessischer Rundfunk.
Programm im Plakat . Frankfurt/Main , c1988.
103 p. : ISBN 3-8218-1718-6
NC1807.G3 P76 1988
NYPL [3-MDW+ 90-12547]

HESSISCHER RUNDFUNK - POSTERS -
EXHIBITIONS.
Programm im Plakat . Frankfurt/Main , c1988.
103 p. : ISBN 3-8218-1718-6
NC1807.G3 P76 1988
NYPL [3-MDW+ 90-12547]

Hessisches Landesmuseum (Darmstadt, Germany)
Joseph Beuys . Darmstadt , c1989. 179 p. :
ISBN 3-925376-30-5 (trade ed.)
NYPL [3-MGO (Beuys) 91-6704]

Rainer, Arnulf, 1929- Strassenräuber . Wien ,
1981. [8], 41 p. :
N6811.5.R3 A4 1981
NYPL [3-MCK R155 90-6258]

HESSISCHES LANDESMUSEUM
(DARMSTADT, GERMANY) -
CATALOGS.
Joseph Beuys . Darmstadt , c1989. 179 p. :
ISBN 3-925376-30-5 (trade ed.)
NYPL [3-MGO (Beuys) 91-6704]

Hessisches Landesmusuem (Kassel, Germany)
Klee, Paul, 1879-1940. Paul Klee . Essen ,
1989. 163 p. :
NYPL [3-MCZ+ K63 90-12860]

Hester, Randolph T. The Meaning of gardens .
Cambridge, Mass. , c1990. ix, 283 p. : ISBN
0-262-06127-9 DDC 712 20
SB470.7 .M43 1990
NYPL [3-MSC 90-11705]

Hestvold, Thomas, 1957-
Thomas Hestvold, Jakob Schmidt, Sverre
Wyller : Kunstnernes hus, 20. jan-18. febr.
1990. Oslo : Kunstnernes hus, [1990] 31 p. : ill.
(some col.) ; 28 cm. (KH kat. . nr. 530) Cover title.
Norwegian and English. Includes bibliographical
references (p. 29-30).
1. Hestvold, Thomas, 1957- - Exhibitions. I. Schmidt,
Jakob, 1947-. II. Wyller, Sverre, 1953-. III. Kunstnernes
hus (Oslo, Norway). IV. Series: Katalog (Kunstnernes
hus (Oslo, Norway)) . nr. 530. V. Title.
N8640 .O8 nr. 530 ND773.H43A4

HESTVOLD, THOMAS, 1957- -
EXHIBITIONS.
Hestvold, Thomas, 1957- Thomas Hestvold,
Jakob Schmidt, Sverre Wyller . Oslo [1990] 31
p. :
N8640 .O8 nr. 530 ND773.H43A4

Hetjens-Museum. Keramik und Bauhaus . Berlin
[1989] 286 p. : ISBN 3-89181-404-6
NK4099 .K446 1989

Hetjensmuseum. see Hetjens-Museum.

Hetzer, Theodor, 1890-1946.
Italienische Architektur / Theodor Hetzer.
Stuttgart : Urachhaus, c1990. 472 p. : ill. ; 24
cm. (Schriften Theodor Hetzers . Bd. 6) Includes
bibliographical references (p. 445-459). Includes
indexes. ISBN 3-87838-905-1 DDC 720/.945/09024
20
1. Architecture, Renaissance - Italy. 2. Architecture -
Italy. I. Series: Hetzer, Theodor, 1890-1946. Works.
1981 . Bd. 6. II. Title.
NA1115 .H48 1990

Works. 1981 .
(Bd. 6) Hetzer, Theodor, 1890-1946.
Italienische Architektur /. Stuttgart , c1990.
472 p. : ISBN 3-87838-905-1 DDC
720/.945/09024 20
NA1115 .H48 1990

Hetzler, Florence M. Art and philosophy . New
York , 1991. p. cm. ISBN 0-8204-1599-5 DDC
730/.92 20
NB933.B7 A78 1991

Heuchler, Eduard, 1801-1879. Album für Freunde
des Bergbaues : vierzehn Bilder aus dem Leben
des Freiberger Berg- und Hüttenmannes /
Eduard Heuchler ; herausgegeben von Gerhard
Heilfurth. Frankfurt am Main : W. Weidlich,
[1977] 1 portfolio (6 p., [14] leaves of plates) :
ill. ; 29 x 40 cm. (Mohnkopf-Steinolrucke) Reprint.
Originally published: Freiberg J. G. Engelhardt, 1855.
1. Heuchler, Eduard, 1801-1879. 2. Miners in art. I.
Heilfurth, Gerhard, 1909-. II. Title.
NYPL [MEM+ H595 89-6071]

HEUCHLER, EDUARD, 1801-1879.
Heuchler, Eduard, 1801-1879. Album für
Freunde des Bergbaues . Frankfurt am Main
[1977] 1 portfolio (6 p., [14] leaves of plates) :
NYPL [MEM+ H595 89-6071]

Heuser, August, 1949- Christus in der bildenden
Kunst . München , c1989. 150 p. : ISBN

3-466-36334-9
N8050 .C44 1989

Heusinger von Waldegg, Joachim. Der Künstler als Märtyrer : Sankt Sebastian in der Kunst des 20. Jahrhunderts / Joachim Heusinger von Waldegg. Worms : Wernersche Verlagsgesellschaft, c1989. 112 p., [48] p. of plates : ill. ; 24 cm. Includes bibliographical references (p. 89-107) and index. ISBN 3-88462-073-8
1. Art, Modern - 20th century. 2. Sebastian, Saint - Art. I. Title.
N6490 .H468 1989

Heuzé, Jean Jacques. Image latente présente Jean-Jacques Heuzé : [exposition], Musée des beaux-arts de Lyon, Palais Saint-Pierre, du 26 avril au 26 mai 1979. Lyon : Image latente, 1979. 32 p. : ill. ; 29 cm.
1. Heuzé, Jean Jacques. 2. Photography, Artistic - Exhibitions. I. Lyons. Musée des beaux-arts. II. Title.
TR647 .H49 1979
NYPL [MFX (Heuzé) 81-585]

HEUZÉ, JEAN JACQUES.
Heuzé, Jean Jacques. Image latente présente Jean-Jacques Heuzé . Lyon , 1979. 32 p. :
TR647 .H49 1979
NYPL [MFX (Heuzé) 81-585]

Hewison, Robert, 1943- Future tense : a new art for the nineties / Robert Hewison. London : Methuen, 1990. 190 p. : ill. ; 25 cm. Includes bibliographical references and index. ISBN 0-413-63430-2 : DDC 700 20
I. Title. II. Title: New art for the nineties.
N7425 **NYPL [3-MAL 90-11326]**

Hewitt, Mark A. The architecture of Mott B. Schmidt / Mark Alan Hewitt ; introduction by Robert A.M. Stern. New York : Rizzoli International Publications, 1991. p. cm. Includes bibliographical references. ISBN 0-8478-1399-1 DDC 720/.92 20
1. Schmidt, Mott B., 1889-1977 - Criticism and interpretation. 2. Architecture, Domestic - United States. 3. Architecture, Georgian - United States. I. Title.
NA737.S355 H4 1991

Heydt-Museum, Wuppertal. see **Von der Heydt-Museum.**

Heyer, Hans Rudolf. Bauen vor der Stadt. English & German. Bauen vor der Stadt . Basel , Boston , c1991. p. cm. ISBN 3-7643-2629-8 : DDC 720/.9494/33 20
NA1349.B38 B3813 1991

HEYSEN, NORA.
Klepac, Lou. Nora Heysen /. Sydney , 1989. 80 p. : ISBN 0-947349-01-4
IN PROCESS (ONLINE)
NYPL [3-MCZ+ H621 90-11028]

Hickok, Gloria Vando. The Helicon nine reader . Kansas City , c1990. 512 p. : ISBN 0-9627460-0-2 DDC 700/.82 20
NX180.F4 H44 1990

Hickory Museum of Art (Hickory, N.C.) Genth, Lillian Mathilde, 1876-1953. Lillian Mathilde Genth . Hickory, N.C. [1990?] 36 p. :
NYPL [3-MCX G337 91-5913]

Hidden heritage : recent discoveries in Georgia decorative art, 1733-1915 / Pamela Wagner, guest curator ; Mary Carolyn Pindar, photographer. Atlanta : High Museum of Art, 1990. 127 p. : ill. ; 28 cm. ISBN 0-939802-62-7
1. Decorative arts - Georgia - Exhibitions. I. Wagner, Pamela. II. High Museum of Art.
NYPL [3-MNE 91-48]

Hidden impressions. Verborgene Impressionen =. [Wien] , c1990. 445 p. : ISBN 3-900688-13-3 (Katalogausgabe) **NYPL [3-MAM 91-3678]**

Hidryma Meletōn Chersonēsou tou Haimou (Series) .
(231) Moutsopoulos, Nikolaos K., 1927- Churches in the prefecture of Pella /. Thessaloniki , 1973. xi, 504 p., [1] folded leaf of plates :
NA5599.M34 M6 1973

Hidryma Nikolaou P. Goulandrē. Renfrew, Colin, 1937- The Cycladic spirit . New York , 1991. p. cm. ISBN 0-8109-3169-9 DDC 732/.3/093915 20
NB130.C78 R4 1991

Hiebert, Kenneth J. Graphic design processes : universal to unique / Kenneth J. Hiebert. New York : Van Nostrand Reinhold, c1992. 208 p. :

ill. (some col.) ; 28 cm. Includes index. ISBN 0-442-00839-2 DDC 741.6 20
1. Grahic arts - Technique. 2. Design. 3. Computer graphics - Technique. I. Title.
NC1000 .H54 1991

Hieronyus Bosch /. Linfert, Carl, 1900- [Hieronymus Bosch. English.] New York , 1989. 126 p. : ISBN 0-8109-0719-4 DDC 759.9492 19
ND653.B65 L513 1989
NYPL [MCH+ B74 89-26502]

Hiesinger, Ulrich W., 1943- Impressionism in America : the Ten American Painters / Ulrich W. Hiesinger. Munich : Prestel ; New York, NY : Distributed in the USA and Canada by te Neues, c1991. 255 p. : ill. (some col.) ; 32 cm. Published in conjuction with an exhibition held at the Jordan-Volpe Gallery, New York, May 18-June 28, 1991. Includes bibliographical references (p. 251-253) and index. ISBN 3-7913-1142-5
1. Ten American Painters (New York, N.Y.) - Exhibitions. 2. Impressionism (Art) - United States - Exhibitions. 3. Painting, American - Exhibitions. 4. Painting, Modern - 19th century - United States - Exhibitions. 5. Painting, Modern - 20th century - United States - Exhibitions. I. Jordan-Volpe Gallery. II. Title. **NYPL [3-MCW+ 91-7730]**

Higashiyama, Kaii, 1908- Kaii Higashiyama / [editor-in-chief, Yukimori Akanoma]. 1st ed. Sandy Hook, Conn. : Shorewood Fine Art Books, 1989. 260 p. : ill. (some col.) ; 29 cm. Includes bibliographical references (p. 14). ISBN 0-88185-029-2
1. Higashiyama, Kaii, 1908-. I. Akanoma, Yukimori. II. Title. **NYPL [3-MAG 91-3347]**

HIGASHIYAMA, KAII, 1908-
Higashiyama, Kaii, 1908- Kaii Higashiyama /. Sandy Hook, Conn. , 1989. 260 p. : ISBN 0-88185-029-2 **NYPL [3-MAG 91-3347]**

Higgins, Nancy M. South Carolina State Museum. South Carolina art . Columbia, S.C. [1991] 90 p. : DDC 709/.757/07475771 20
N6530.S6 S68 1991

HIGGINS, VICTOR, 1884-1949 - EXHIBITIONS.
Porter, Dean A. Victor Higgins . Salt Lake City , 1991. 304 p. : ISBN 0-87905-362-3 : DDC 759.13 B 20
ND237.H584 P67 1991
NYPL [3-MCX H636 91-5525]

High & low. Modern art and popular culture . New York , 1990. 255 p., [81] p. of plates : ISBN 0-8109-2466-8 (pbk). DDC 700/.9/04 20
N6447 .M63 1991 **NYPL [3-MAL 91-3688]**

High and low. Modern art and popular culture . New York , 1990. 255 p., [81] p. of plates : ISBN 0-8109-2466-8 (pbk). DDC 700/.9/04 20
N6447 .M63 1991 **NYPL [3-MAL 91-3688]**

High & low . Varnedoe, Kirk, 1946- New York , c1990. 460 p. : ISBN 0-87070-353-6 (MoMA : hard) **NYPL [3-MAL+ 91-3655]**

High and low. Varnedoe, Kirk, 1946- High & low . New York , c1990. 460 p. : ISBN 0-87070-353-6 (MoMA : hard)
NYPL [3-MAL+ 91-3655]

High Museum of Art.
Céramique lorraine . Nancy , Metz , c1990. 367 p. : ISBN 2-86480-458-1
NYPL [3-MPGG 91-7166]

Hidden heritage . Atlanta , 1990. 127 p. : ISBN 0-939802-62-7
NYPL [3-MNE 91-48]

Pfahl, John, 1939- A distanced land . [Albuquerque] , 1990. xvi, 204 p. : ISBN 0-8263-1214-4 DDC 779/.36/092 20
TR647 .P494 1990
NYPL [MFX (Pfahl) 91-7438]

The high priestess /. Kiefer, Anselm, 1945- New York , 1989. 226 p. : ISBN 0-8109-1216-3 DDC 709/.2/4 19
NB588.K43 A65 1989
NYPL [3-MGO+ (Kiefer) 89-23144]

HIGH SCHOOL STUDENTS - CARICATURES AND CARTOONS.
McPherson, John, 1959- Life at McPherson High . Grand Rapids, Mich. , 1991. p. cm. ISBN 0-310-71161-4 (paper) DDC 741.5/973 20
NC1429.M275 A4 1991

HIGHLANDS COUNTY (FLA.) - DIRECTORIES.
Rockford Map Publishers. Highlands County, Florida, land atlas and plat book . Rockford, Ill. , 1980, c1975. 1 atlas (40 p.) : DDC 912/.75955 19
G1318.H6 R58 1980
NYPL [Map Div. 90-5880]

HIGHLANDS COUNTY, FLA. - MAPS.
(1980) Rockford Map Publishers. Highlands County, Florida, land atlas and plat book . Rockford, Ill. , 1980, c1975. 1 atlas (40 p.) : DDC 912/.75955 19
G1318.H6 R58 1980
NYPL [Map Div. 90-5880]

Highlands County, Florida, land atlas and plat book . Rockford Map Publishers. Rockford, Ill. , 1980, c1975. 1 atlas (40 p.) : DDC 912/.75955 19
G1318.H6 R58 1980
NYPL [Map Div. 90-5880]

Highton, Leonie. Harling, Robert. The House & garden book of living rooms . New York , 1991. p. cm. ISBN 0-86565-125-6 DDC 747.7/5 20
NK2117.L5 H37 1991

Higonnet, Anne, 1959-
Berthe Morisot, une biographie / par Anne Higonnet ; traduit de l'américan par Isabelle Chapman]. Paris : Adam Biro, c1989. 236 p., [16] p. of plates : ill., ports. ; 25 cm. Includes bibliographical references (p. [229]) and index. ISBN 2-87660-048-7 (cover):
1. Artists - France - Biography. I. Title.
NYPL [3-MCO M86 90-13217]

Berthe Morisot's images of women / Anne Higonnet. Cambridge, Mass. : Harvard University Press, 1992. p. cm. Includes bibliographical references and index. ISBN 0-674-06798-3 (acid-free) DDC 759.4 20
1. Morisot, Berthe, 1841-1895 - Criticism and interpretation. 2. Women in art. I. Title.
ND553.M88 H53 1992

Hikade, Karl, 1942-
Karl Hikade : Kärntner Landesgalerie Klagenfurt, Landesmuseum Joanneum, Graz / [Fotos, Gerold Zugmann]. Klagenfurt : Die Landesgalerie ; Graz : Neue Galerie, Landesmuseum Joanneum, 1990. 1 v. : col. ill. ; 21 x 29 cm. Issued in two booklets, one of text (14 p., 21 x 11 cm.) and the other of illustrations (17 p., 21 x 17 cm.), mounted side by side on a board. DDC 759.36 20
1. Hikade, Karl, 1942- - Exhibitions. I. Kärntner Landesgalerie. II. Neue Galerie am Landesmuseum Joanneum. III. Title.
ND511.5.H55 A4 1990

HIKADE, KARL, 1942- - EXHIBITIONS.
Hikade, Karl, 1942- Karl Hikade . Klagenfurt , Graz , 1990. 1 v. : DDC 759.36 20
ND511.5.H55 A4 1990

HIKING - HIMALAYA MOUNTAINS - MAPS.
Bawa, Manmohan Singh. Himalayan trekking maps /. [Bombay?] [New Delhi, India , 1985]. 1 atlas (unpaged) :
NYPL [Map Div. 90-11639]

Hilbert, Peter Paul. (joint author) Spranz, Bodo. Die Pyramiden vom Cerro Xochitecatl, Tlaxcala (Mexico) /. Wiesbaden , 1977. 109 p. : ISBN 3-515-02697-5
F1203 .D46 vol. 12 F1219.1.T623
NYPL [HTC 74-1117 Bd. 12]

Hilda Uccusic . Uccusic, Hilda, 1938- Oberpullendorf, c1988. 129 p. :
N6811.5.U23 A4 1988

Hildebrand, Grant, 1934- Designing for industry: the architecture of Albert Kahn. Cambridge, Mass., The MIT Press [1974] xvii, 232 p. illus. 21 x 27 cm. Includes bibliographical references. ISBN 0-262-08054-0 DDC 720/.92/4
1. Kahn, Albert, 1869-1942. I. Title.
NA737.K28 H54
NYPL [MQZ (Kahn) 74-1827]

Hildebrandt, Rainer, 1914- Die Mauer : Faszination der Fotokunst : Katalog des gleichnamigen Fotowettbewerbes, veranstaltet vom Museum Haus am Checkpoint Charlie : Ausstellung, Oktober 1988 bis August 1989 / Text und Bildzusammenstellung, Rainer Hildebrandt.1. Aufl. Berlin : Verlag Haus am

Checkpoint Charlie, 1989. 52 p. : ill. ; 21 x 30 cm. ISBN 3-922484-22-0
1. Berlin Wall, Berlin, Germany, 1961-1989 - Pictorial works - Exhibitions. I. Haus am Checkpoint Charlie (Berlin, Germany). II. Title.
IN PROCESS (ONLINE)
         NYPL [MFW+ 91-7248]

Hilger, Ernst.
Bäumer, Angelica. Josef Bramer /. [Wien] [1990] 89 p. : ISBN 3-203-51094-4 DDC 759.36 20
ND511.5.B69 A4 1990

Hrdlička, Alfred, 1928- Das Frauenbild /. Wien [198-?] 131 p. : ISBN 3-900318-48-4
    NYPL [3-MCK+ H857 90-5270]

Hill, Charles Christopher. The smells of summer / Charles Christopher Hill, Kristine McKenna. Santa Monica : Jacob Samuel, 1989. [15] leaves : col. ill. ; 29 cm. "Edition is limited to ten bound copies"--Colophon. LC has copy no. 10, signed by Charles Christopher Hill. DLC Source: Purchase, July 31, 1990. DLC DDC 769.92 20
1. Hill, Charles Christopher. I. McKenna, Kristine. II. Title.
NE2012.H55 A4 1989

HILL, CHARLES CHRISTOPHER.
Hill, Charles Christopher. The smells of summer /. Santa Monica , 1989. [15] leaves : DDC 769.92 20
NE2012.H55 A4 1989

Hill, Gerard.
Fabergé and the Russian master goldsmiths /. [New York] , c1989. 320 p. : ISBN 0-88363-889-4
    NYPL [3-MNO+ 89-26729]

Fabergé, Peter Carl, 1846-1920. Fabergé and the Russian master goldsmiths /. New York , 1991. p. cm. ISBN 0-517-02733-X DDC 739.2/092 20
NK7398.F32 A4 1991

HILL, JAMES JEROME, 1838-1916 - ART COLLECTIONS - EXHIBITIONS.
Hancock, Jane H., 1949- Homecoming . St. Paul , c1991. x, 116 p. : ISBN 0-87351-259-6 DDC 759.05/074/74776581 20
N6450 .H298 1991

HILL, JAMES JEROME, 1838-1916 - HOMES AND HAUNTS - MINNESOTA - SAINT PAUL - EXHIBITIONS.
Hancock, Jane H., 1949- Homecoming . St. Paul , c1991. x, 116 p. : ISBN 0-87351-259-6 DDC 759.05/074/74776581 20
N6450 .H298 1991

Hill, John T. Mora, Gilles, 1945- [Walker Evans, Havana 1933. English.] Walker Evans, Havana 1933 /. New York , c1989. 111 p. : ISBN 0-394-57493-1 : DDC 972.91/23062/0222 19
F1799.H34 M6713 1989
    NYPL [MFX (Evans) 90-1064]

Hill, Rick (Richard) Brach, Paul, 1924- Our land/ourselves . Albany, N.Y. , 1991. p. ISBN 0-910763-05-4 : DDC 760/.089/97073 20
N6538.A4 B67 1991

Hiller, Friedrich. Studien zur klassischen Archäologie . Saarbrücken , Amsterdam , 1986. 219 p. : ISBN 3-925384-00-6
    NYPL [3-MAH 90-12469]

HILLER, FRIEDRICH.
Studien zur klassischen Archäologie . Saarbrücken , Amsterdam , 1986. 219 p. : ISBN 3-925384-00-6
    NYPL [3-MAH 90-12469]

Hillman, James. Team spirit /. New York, N.Y. , c1990. 84 p. : ISBN 0-916365-30-1
    NYPL [3-MAL 91-6734]

HILLSBOROUGH COUNTY, FLA. - MAPS
(1989) Trakker Maps, Inc. Trakker's street atlas of West Pasco, Pinellas, and Hillsborough counties, Florida. Miami, Florida , 1989. 1 atlas (57 p.) : *NYPL [Map Div. 90-13047]*

Hillwood Art Gallery.
Fekner, John. Artist as apolitical sensor . Brookville, N.Y. , 1990. 28 p. :
    NYPL [3-MAMT 91-5026]

Public art program, 1985-1988 /. [Brookville, N.Y.] [1989] 64 p. : ISBN 0-933699-13-1 DDC 709/.04/80740147245 19
NB235.B73 P83 1989
    NYPL [3-MGI 90-11532]

Hillwood Art Museum.
Cotter, Holland, 1947- Kay WalkingStick . Brookville, NY , 1991. p. cm. ISBN 0-933699-20-4 : DDC 759.13 20
ND237.W316 A4 1991

Raven, Arlene. Nancy Grossman /. Brookville, N.Y. , 1991. p. cm. ISBN 0-933699-22-0 DDC 709.2 20
N6537.G75 A4 1991

Wadden, Mary Ann. The political landscape . Brookville, N.Y. , 1990. 32 p. : ISBN 0-933699-17-4 DDC 709/.73/074747245 20
N8835 .W34 1990
    NYPL [3-MAMT 91-4586]

Weyhe, Arthur. Arthur Weyhe--sculpture, 1972-1989 /. Brookville, N.Y. , c1990. 48 p. : ISBN 0-933699-19-0 DDC 709/.2 20
NB237.W443 A4 1990

Hilschenz-Mlynek, Helga. Zeitgenössisches deutsches Kunsthandwerk . München , c1990. 443 p. : ISBN 3-7913-1090-9 DDC 745/.0943/07443 20
NK951 .Z364 1990

HILSDORF, JACOB, 1872-1916 - EXHIBITIONS.
Nicola Perscheid, Theodor und Jacob Hilsdorf, August Sander . Mainz [1989] 80 p. : ISBN 3-87439-204-X
IN PROCESS (ONLINE)
    NYPL [MFW+ 91-5892]

HILSDORF, THEODOR, 1868-1944 - EXHIBITIONS.
Nicola Perscheid, Theodor und Jacob Hilsdorf, August Sander . Mainz [1989] 80 p. : ISBN 3-87439-204-X
IN PROCESS (ONLINE)
    NYPL [MFW+ 91-5892]

Hilton McConnico /. McConnico, Hilton, 1943- Marseille , c1990. 160 p. : ISBN 2-907010-07-7
    NYPL [3-MLH+ 90-11601]

Hilton, Tim. Olitski, Jules, 1922- Jules Olitski /. [New York] , c1990. 5 v. :
    NYPL [3-MCX O47 91-6724]

HIMALAYA MOUNTAINS - MAPS.
Bawa, Manmohan Singh. Himalayan trekking maps /. [Bombay?] [New Delhi, India , 1985]. 1 atlas (unpaged) :
    NYPL [Map Div. 90-11639]

Himalayan trekking maps /. Bawa, Manmohan Singh. [Bombay?] [New Delhi, India , 1985]. 1 atlas (unpaged) :
    NYPL [Map Div. 90-11639]

Himmelheber, Hans, 1908- Das Gold in der Kunst Westafrikas. Zürich , 1981. 58 p. :
    NYPL [3-MNO 90-12398]

Himstedt, Anton, 1952-
Anton Himstedt, Skulpturen : Kunsthalle Winterthur 22.1-4.3.1990 : Westfälisches Landesmuseum für Kunst und Kulturgeschichte Münster, Landschaftsverband Westfalen-Lippe, 24.3-20.5.1990. Münster : Das Landesmuseum, c1990. 60 p. : ill. (some col.) ; 28 cm. Includes bibliographical references (p. 60). ISBN 3-88789-092-2
1. Himstedt, Anton, 1952- - Exhibitions. I. Kunsthalle Waaghaus (Winterthur, Switzerland). II. Title.
    NYPL [3-MGO (Himstedt) 91-6714]

HIMSTEDT, ANTON, 1952- - EXHIBITIONS.
Himstedt, Anton, 1952- Anton Himstedt, Skulpturen . Münster , c1990. 60 p. : ISBN 3-88789-092-2
    NYPL [3-MGO (Himstedt) 91-6714]

Hinckley, F. Lewis. The more significant Georgian furniture / F. Lewis Hinckley. New York : Washington Mews Books, c1990. 125 p. : ill. ; 29 cm. Includes index. ISBN 0-8147-3461-8 : DDC 749.22/91835/074 20
1. Furniture, Georgian - Ireland - Dublin - Catalogs. 2. Furniture - Ireland - Dublin - Styles - Catalogs. I. Title.
NK2538.D8 H554 1989
    NYPL [3-MOF 90-12955]

Hind, Arthur Mayger, 1880-1957.
EARLY ITALIAN ENGRAVING - INDEXES.
Straten, Roelof van. Iconclass indexes. Italian prints /. Doornspijk, The Netherlands , c1987- v. ; ISBN 90-70288-35-4
    NYPL [MDBF 89-1708]

Hindorf, Heinz.
Heinz Hindorf, Glasfenster / mit Beiträgen von Suzanne Beeh-Lustenberger, Regine Dölling und

Dieter Stoodt und Farbbildern von Wolfgang Müller. Freiburg : Herder, c1989. 176 p. : ill. (chiefly col.) ; 27 cm. "Werkverzeichnis Heinz Hindorf": p. 162-176. Includes bibliographical references. ISBN 3-451-21540-3 : DDC 748.593 20
1. Hindorf, Heinz - Catalogs. 2. Glass painting and staining - Germany - History - 20th century - Catalogs. I. Beeh-Lustenberger, Suzanne. II. Dölling, Regine. III. Stoodt, Dieter. IV. Title. V. Title: Glasfenster.
NK5398.H56 A4 1989

HINDORF, HEINZ - CATALOGS.
Hindorf, Heinz. Heinz Hindorf, Glasfenster /. Freiburg, c1989. 176 p. : ISBN 3-451-21540-3 : DDC 748.593 20
NK5398.H56 A4 1989

HINDU SYMBOLISM.
Symbols in art and religion . London , Glenn Dale, MD , 1990. xiii, 221 p. : ISBN 0-913215-69-4 DDC 704.94894 20
N7301   *NYPL [3-MAF 91-6383]*

Hindustan Gadar Party . Josh, Sohan Singh, 1898- New Delhi , 1977-1978. 2 v. :
DS480.45 .J66   *NYPL [JLL 79-458]*

HINDUSTAN GADAR PARTY - HISTORY.
Josh, Sohan Singh, 1898- Hindustan Gadar Party . New Delhi , 1977-1978. 2 v. :
DS480.45 .J66   *NYPL [JLL 79-458]*

Josh, Sohan Singh, 1898- Hindustan Gadar Party . New Delhi , 1977. 1 v. ;
DS480.45 .J66   *NYPL [JLK 80-148]*

Hine, Alvaro Cardona- see Cardona-Hine, Alvaro.

Hinniger, Volker, 1947-1988. Dramatik des Alltags / Volker Hinniger ; [Herausgeber, Gretel Hinniger] Kassel : Weber & Weidemeyer, c1990. 160 p. : ill. (some col.) ; 27 cm. ISBN 3-925272-22-4 DDC 759.3 20
1. Hinniger, Volker, 1947-1988. I. Title.
N6888.H556 A4 1990

HINNIGER, VOLKER, 1947-1988.
Hinniger, Volker, 1947-1988. Dramatik des Alltags /. Kassel , c1990. 160 p. : ISBN 3-925272-22-4 DDC 759.3 20
N6888.H556 A4 1990

Hinson, Tom E. The invitational--artists of northeast Ohio : an invitational exhibition of the works of fifteen artists : the Cleveland Museum of Art, February 27-April 21, 1991 / selected by Tom E. Hinson. [Cleveland] : The Museum, c1991. vii, 64 p. : ill. (some col.) ; 22 x 28 cm. ISBN 0-940717-07-7 : DDC 709/.771/307477132 20
1. Art, American - Ohio - Exhibitions. 2. Art, Modern - 20th century - Ohio - Exhibitions. I. Cleveland Museum of Art. II. Title.
N6530.O3 H56 1991

Hinton, Mark. Kakiemon porcelain from the English country house . London , 1989. 64 p. : ISBN 0-903432-35-8
    NYPL [3-MPFK 91-4566]

Hintzenstern, Herbert von. Die Marienaltäre in Lippersdorf und Münchenbernsdorf / Herbert von Hintzenstern ; Fotos von Klaus G. Beyer und Günther Ziegler ; [herausgegeben von der Pressestelle der Ev.-Luth. Kirche in Thüringen]. [Berlin] : Evangelische Verlagsanstalt Berlin, 1963. 21, [3] p., [48] p. of plates : ill. ; 21 cm. Includes bibliographical references (p. 21-[22]).
1. Mary, Blessed Virgin, Saint - Art. 2. Altarpieces, Gothic - Germany (East) - Thuringia. I. Title.
MLCS 87/955 (N)   *NYPL [MRBV 91-277]*

Hiort, Esbjørn. Arkitekten Finn Juhl : møbelkunst, arkitektur, brugskunst : en biografi / af Esbjørn Hiort. København : Arkitektens forlag, 1990. 143, [1] p. : ill. (some col.) ; 31 cm. Includes bibliographical references (p. 143-[144]). ISBN 87-7407-093-2 :
1. Juhl, Finn, 1912-. 2. Artists - Denmark - Biography. I. Juhl, Finn, 1912-. II. Title.
N7023.J84 H5 1990

Hipp, Hermann. Freie und Hansestadt Hamburg : Geschichte, Kultur und Stadtbaukunst an Elbe und Alster / Hermann Hipp. 2. Aufl. Köln : DuMont Buchverlag, 1990. 608 p. : ill. (some col.), maps (some col.) ; 21 cm. (Kunst-Reiseführer in der Reihe DuMont Dokumente) Includes bibliographical references (p. 547-550) and indexes. ISBN 3-7701-1590-2 DDC 720/.943/515 20
1. Architecture - Germany (West) - Hamburg - Guide-books. 2. Art - Germany (West) - Hamburg -

Guide-books. 3. Hamburg (Germany) - History. 4. Hamburg (Germany) - Description - Guide-books. 5. Hamburg (Germany) - Buildings, structures, etc. - Guide-books. I. Title.
NA1086.H3 H57 1990

HIPPOLOGY. see HORSES.

Hippolyte-Camille Delpy, 1842-1910 . Lannoy-Duputel, Michèle. [Paris] [1989] 141 p., [28] p. of plates :   ISBN 2-86377-076-4 :   DDC 759.4 20
ND553.D3596 L36 1989

Hirner-Schüssele, René. Von der Anschauung zur Formerfindung : Studien zu Willi Baumeisters Theorie moderner Kunst / René Hirner-Schüssele. Worms : Wernersche Verlagsgesellschaft, c1990. 283 p. ; 24 cm. (Manuskripte zur Kunstwissenschaft in der Wernerschen Verlagsgesellschaft . Bd. 32) Originally presented as the author's thesis (doctoral)--Universität Tübingen. Includes bibliographical references (p. 261-283).   ISBN 3-88462-931-X
1. Baumeister, Willi, 1889-1955. Unbekannte in der Kunst. 2. Art - Philosophy. 3. Modernism (Art). 4. Aesthetics, Modern - 20th century. I. Title. II. Series.
N68.B323 H57 1990

Hiro. Fighting fish, fighting birds : photographs / by Hiro ; essay by Susanna Moore. New York : H.N. Abrams, 1990. 66 p. : ill. (some col.) ; 28 x 30 cm.   ISBN 0-8109-3403-5   DDC 779/.32 20
1. Hiro. 2. Photography of fishes. 3. Siamese fighting fish - Pictorial works. 4. Game fowl - Pictorial works. I. Moore, Susanna. II. Title.
TR729.F5 H57 1990
NYPL [MFX+ (Hiro) 91-3304]

HIRO.
Hiro. Fighting fish, fighting birds . New York , 1990. 66 p. :   ISBN 0-8109-3403-5   DDC 779/.32 20
TR729.F5 H57 1990
NYPL [MFX+ (Hiro) 91-3304]

Hirsch, Karl-Georg. Hebel, Johann Peter, 1760-1826. Kannitverstan . Neu-Isenburg [1989?] 25 p. :   ISBN 3-920947-88-6
NYPL [MEM H668 90-10306]

Hirsch, Richard. West, Benjamin, 1738-1820. The world of Benjamin West . Allentown, Pa. , 1962. 96 p. :
ND237.W45 A65
NYPL [3-MCX W51 90-7090]

Hirschfeld . Hirschfeld, Al. New York : Toronto : p. cm.   ISBN 0-684-19365-5   DDC 741.5/092 B 20
NC1429.H527 A2 1991

Hirschfeld, Al. Hirschfeld : art and recollections from eight decades / Al Hirschfeld. New York : Scribner ; Toronto : Maxwell Macmillan Canada ; p. cm. Includes index.   ISBN 0-684-19365-5   DDC 741.5/092 B 20
1. Hirschfeld, Al. 2. Cartoonists - United States - Biography. I. Title. II. Title: Art and recollections from eight decades.
NC1429.H527 A2 1991

HIRSCHFELD, AL.
Hirschfeld, Al. Hirschfeld . New York : Toronto : p. cm.   ISBN 0-684-19365-5   DDC 741.5/092 B 20
NC1429.H527 A2 1991

Hirschl & Adler Modern.
Goldsmith, Lloyd, 1945- Lloyd Goldsmith, cityviews . New York, N.Y. [1982] [16] p. :
NYPL [3-MAMY 91-1159]

Manzoni, Piero, 1933-1963. Piero Manzoni . New York , 1990. 102 p. :   ISBN 0-942051-29-7
NYPL [3-MCF M294 91-6741]

Wilmarth, Christopher. Christopher Wilmarth, drawings 1963-1987 . New York [1989] 48 p. :   ISBN 0-942051-17-3
NYPL [3-MCX W735 90-12637]

Hirschland, Ellen B. Henri Matisse, Jazz and other illustrated books, Heckscher Museum, Huntington, New York, January 12--February 18, 1979 / [Ellen B. Hirschland, author]. Huntington, N.Y. : The Museum, [1979] 20 p. : ill. ; 21 cm. "Catalogue of the exhibition": p. 13-15. Bibliography: p. 19-20.   DDC 741.9/44
1. Matisse, Henri, 1869-1954 - Jazz - Exhibitions. 2. Matisse, Henri, 1869-1954 - Exhibitions. I. Matisse, Henri, 1869-1954. II. Heckscher Museum. III. Title.
NC980.5.M35 A4 1979
NYPL [MDG (Matisse) 80-305]

HIRSHHORN, JOSEPH H. - ART COLLECTIONS.
Arnason, H. Harvard. Paintings from the Joseph H. Hirshhorn Foundation Collection . New York , c1962. 47 p. :   DDC 759.06/074/0153
ND195 .A72
NYPL [3-MAX (Hirshhorn) 85-1211]

Hirt, Aloys, 1759-1836. Osservazioni istorico-architettoniche sopra il Panteon. In Roma : Nella stamperia Pagliarini, 1791. V, [3], 40 p., [3] leaves of plates : 5 plans (engravings) ; 25 cm. (4to) Dedicatory letter bears the author's name, Luigi Hirt. Signatures: pi⁴ a-e⁴. Illustration of the Pantheon (metal cut) on t.p. Includes bibliographical references.   DDC 726/.1207/09376 20
1. Pantheon (Rome, Italy). 2. Rome (Italy) - Buildings, structures, etc. I. Title.
NA323 .H57 1791

His, Andreas, 1928-
Andreas His : Pariser Bilder, 1979-1984 : Ausstellung vom 8. November bis l. Dezember 1984, Galerie "zem Specht" Basel / [Text, Aurel Schmidt]. [Basel] : Editions Galerie "zem Specht" Basel, c1984. [65] p. : ill. (some col.), port. ; 22 cm. Includes bibliographical references.
1. His, Andreas, 1928- - Exhibitions. 2. Paris (France) in art - Exhibitions. I. Schmidt, Aurel, 1935-. II. Galerie "Zem Specht" Basel. III. Title. IV. Title: Pariser Bilder, 1979-1984.
NYPL [3-MCZ H673 90-2126]

HIS, ANDREAS, 1928- - EXHIBITIONS.
His, Andreas, 1928- Andreas His . [Basel] , c1984. [65] p. :
NYPL [3-MCZ H673 90-2126]

HISPANIC AMERICAN ART - CALIFORNIA - LOS ANGELES - EXHIBITIONS.
Le Démon des anges . [Barcelona] , Nantes [1989] 245 p. :   DDC 704/.036872079494/0744672 20
N6538.M4 D46 1989

HISPANIC AMERICAN ART - EXHIBITIONS.
Ceremony of memory . Santa Fe, N.M. , c1988. 48 p. :   ISBN 0-929762-00-2
NYPL [3-MAMT+ 91-7407]

Contemporary Hispanic shrines . Reading, Pa. , c1989. 24 p. :   ISBN 0-941972-09-7
IN PROCESS (ONLINE)
NYPL [3-MAMT 91-7297]

HISPANIC AMERICAN WOOD-CARVERS - NEW MEXICO - EXHIBITIONS.
Kalb, Laurie Beth. Santos statues & sculpture . Los Angeles , c1988. [24] p., [2] leaves of plates (some folded) :   DDC 704.9/482 19
NK9712 .K35 1988
NYPL [3-MNE 90-12649]

HISPANIC AMERICAN WOOD-CARVING - NEW MEXICO - EXHIBITIONS.
Kalb, Laurie Beth. Santos statues & sculpture . Los Angeles , c1988. [24] p., [2] leaves of plates (some folded) :   DDC 704.9/482 19
NK9712 .K35 1988
NYPL [3-MNE 90-12649]

Hispanics of achievement.
Cockcroft, James D. Diego Rivera / . New York , c1991. 119 p., [8] p. of col. plates :   ISBN 0-7910-1252-2 :   DDC 759.972 B 92 20
ND259.R5 C57 1991

HISPANO-AMERICAN WAR, 1898. see UNITED STATES - HISTORY - WAR OF 1898.

HISPANOS. see MEXICAN AMERICANS.

Histoire de la photographie française . France. Direction générale des relations culturelles, scientifiques et techniques. Paris (19, rue du Départ, 75014) , 1978. 1 v. (unpaged) :
TR71 .F69 1978   ***NYPL [MFX+ 81-584]***

Histoire du journal Pilote et des publications des Editions Dargaud /. Filippini, Henri. Grenoble , c1977. 141 p. :   ISBN 2-7234-0038-7
NYPL [3-MDY 90-3530]

Histoire imprévue des dessous féminins /. Saint-Laurent, Cécil, 1919- Paris , 1988. 280 p. :   ISBN 2-7335-0126-7 :
GT2703 .S25 1988
NYPL [3-MMV+ 91-5460]

Histoires de forêt . Max Ernst : Musée des beaux arts de Nantes, juin-septembre 1987. [Nantes] : Le Musée, [1987] 100 p. : ill. (some col.) ; 23 cm. (Lectura . 1) Exhibition catalog with texts by and about Max Ernst, and with reproductions of Max Ernst's works. Includes bibliographical references (p. 99).   ISBN 2-906211-01-X   DDC 760/.092 20
1. Ernst, Max, 1891-1976 - Exhibitions. 2. Forests and forestry in art - Exhibitions. I. Ernst, Max, 1891-1976. II. Nantes. Musée des beaux-arts. III. Series: Lectura (Nantes, France) , 1.
N6888.E7 A4 1987a

Histoires de forêt . Ernst, Max, 1891-1976. [Nantes] , c1987. 100 p. :   ISBN 2-906211-01-X
NYPL [3-MCK E71 91-7033]

Histoires de mode d'hier et d'aujourd'hui . Musée des arts de la mode (France) Paris , c1988. 55 p. :   ISBN 2-901422-13-6 :
NYPL [3-MME+ 91-5058]

Histoires (Flammarion (Firm))
Matthews Grieco, Sara F. Ange ou diablesse . [Paris] , c1991. 495 p. :   ISBN 2-08-211187-3   DDC 769/.424/0940931 20
NE962.W65 M38 1991

Historia argentina de la vivienda de interés social. Capital Federal [Argentina] : Escuela Arte, Ciencia, Técnica y Comunidad Nacional, [between 1986 and 1990- v. <1- > : ill. ; 30 cm. (Arquitectura y comunidad nacional) Map of Ciudad Evita inserted. Includes bibliographical references. CONTENTS. - pt. 1. 1943/1955
1. Architecture, Domestic - Argentina. 2. Architecture, Modern - 20th century - Argentina. 3. Architecture and society - Argentina. I. Series.
NA7292 .H57 1990

História da arte . Gonçalves, Flávio. [Lisbon] [1990] 353 p. :   DDC 709/.469 20
N7121 .G6 1990

Historia de la arquitectura colombiana /. Arango, Silvia, 1948- Bogota , 1989. 291 p. :   ISBN 958-1-70061-7
NYPL [3-MQWN+ 90-12805]

Historia de la arquitectura en Colombia /. Arango, Silvia, 1948- Bogotá , 1989 [i.e. 1990] 291 p. :   ISBN 958-1-70061-7   DDC 720/.9861 20
NA870 .A73 1990

Historia de la caricatura en Colombia .
(3) Merino, Hernán, 1922-1973. Hernán Merino . Bogotá [1986?] 107 p. :
NC1460.M47 A4 1986

(5) Bogotá en caricatura . [Bogotá] [1988] 235 p. :   DDC 986.1/48 20
F2291.B62 B64 1988
NYPL [3-MDY+ 91-6190]

Historia de la Casa del Cordón de Burgos /. Ibáñez Pérez, Alberto C. [Burgos] , 1987. 359 p. :   ISBN 84-505-5944-8
NYPL [3-MQWH 91-7280]

Historia de la pintura mexicana /. Espejo, Beatriz. [S.l.] , c1989. 3 v. :   ***NYPL [3-MCY 91-2619]***

Historia de la pintura nicaragüense /. Arellano, Jorge Eduardo. [Managua, Nicaragua] 1990. 200 p. :
ND282 .A74 1990

Historia de la teoría de la arquitectura, el porfirismo /. Vargas, Ramón. [Mexico City] , 1989. 221 p. :   ISBN 968-8406-73-2
NA200 .V37 1989

Historia de Valladolid .
(8, pt. 1) Virgili Blanquet, María Antonia. Arquitectura y urbanismo de Valladolid en el siglo XX /. Valladolid , 1988. 190 p. :   ISBN 84-404-2435-3   ***NYPL [3-MQWH 90-9439]***

Historia del arte en Andalucía / [dirigida por Enrique Pareja López]. Sevilla : Gever, [1988]- v. : ill. (some col.) ; 30 cm. Includes bibliographical references and indexes. CONTENTS. - v. 1. La antigüedad / por Ramón Corzo Sánchez -- v. 2. El arte en el sur de Al-Andalus / por Enrique Pareja López -- v. 3. El arte de la Reconquista cristiana / por Enrique Pareja López, Matilde Megía Navarro -- v. 4. El arte del Renacimiento : Urbanismo y arquitectura / por Jorge Bernales Ballesteros ... [et al.] -- v. 5. El arte del Renacimiento : Escultura-pintura y artes decorativas / por Jorge Bernales Ballesteros, José Hernández Díaz, Matilde Megia Navarro -- v. 6. El arte del Barroco : Urbanismo y arquitectura / Jorge Bernales Ballesteros ... [et al.].   ISBN 84-7566-015-0 (obra completa)   DDC 709/.46/8 20
1. Art - Spain - Andalusia. 2. Art, Spanish - Spain - Andalusia. I. Pareja López, Enrique.
N7109.A6 H57 1988
NYPL [3-MAML+ 91-417]

Historia del arte iberoamericano /. Castedo, Leopoldo. Madrid , c1988. 2 v. : ISBN 84-206-9597-1 (obra completa)
NYPL [3-MAM 89-11457]

Història i arquitectura : la recerca històrica en el procés d'intervenció en els monuments : memòria 1984 / A. González ... [et al.] ; [traduccions al català i al castellá, Raquel Lacuesta ; traduccions a l'anglès, James Charles Townsend]. Barcelona : Diputació de Barcelona, Servei de Catalogació i Conservació de Monuments, [1986?] 260 p. : ill., plans ; 24 x 31 cm. Catalan, English, and Spanish. Proceedings from the Simposi sobre Historia i Arquitectura, held Dec. 12-14, 1984, Vic, organized by the Comissió de Defensa del Patrimoni Arquitectònic del Col·legi d'Arquitectes in collaboration with the Servei de Catalogació i Conservació de Monuments de la Diputació de Barcelona. Errata slip inserted.   ISBN 84-505-2551-9
1. Architecture - Spain - Barcelona (Province) - Congresses. I. González, Antoni. II. Colegio Oficial de Arquitectos de Cataluña y Baleares. Delegación de Barcelona. Comisión de Defensa del Patrimonio Arquitectónico. III. Barcelona (Spain : Province). Servei de Catalogació i Conservació de Monuments. IV. Simposi sobre Història i Arquitectura (1984 : Vich, Spain).
NA1309.B29 H57 1986
NYPL [3-MQWH+ 90-12046]

Historia visual del arte / dirección, A. Fernández, F. Olaguer-Feliú. 1. ed. Barcelona : Vicens-Vives, <1989- > v. <3-4 > : col. ill. ; 21 cm. Includes bibliographical references.
CONTENTS. - - 3. La pintura y el mosaico romanos / F. de Olaguer-Feliú -- 4. La pintura románica / F. de Olaguer-Feliú   ISBN 84-316-2704-3 (v. 3)
1. Art. I. Fernández, Antonio. II. Olaguer-Feliú Alonso, Fernando de.
N5300 .H58 1989

Historia visual del arte .
(12) Portela Sandoval, Francisco. La pintura del siglo XVIII /. Barcelona , 1990. vi, 202 p. : ISBN 84-316-2727-1
N5300 .H58 1989 vol. 12 ND456

(3) Olaguer-Feliú Alonso, Fernando de. La pintura y el mosaico romanos /. Barcelona , 1989. ix, 182 p. : ISBN 84-316-2703-5
N5300 .H58 1989 vol. 3 ND2575

(4) Olaguer-Feliú Alonso, Fernando de. La pintura románica /. Barcelona , 1989. xi, 182 p. : ISBN 84-316-2704-3
N5300 .H58 1989 vol. 4 ND2580

Historias del viajero /. Cuevas, José Luis, 1934- México, D.F. , 1987. 78 p. : ISBN 968-434-446-5 DDC 760/.092/4 B 19
N6559.C8 A2 1987
NYPL [3-MCZ C955 90-12616]

Historias para una exposición /. Cuevas, José Luis, 1934- Tlahuapan, Puebla [Mexico] , 1988. 95 p. : DDC 760/.092 B 20
N6559.C8 A2 1988
NYPL [3-MCZ C955 91-5025]

Historic and prehistoric perceptions . Layton, Robert, 1944- [London] , 1990. 18 p. ; ISBN 1-85507-020-0 DDC 709/.01/130994 20
N5310.5.A83 L39 1990

Historic Blacks in the arts / publisher & editor, Richard L. Green ; senior editor, Judith Conaway ; illustrators, Steve Clay & S. Gaston Dobson ; preface, Empak Publishing Co. Chicago, IL : Empak Pub. Co., c1990. p. cm. (Black history publications series . v. 8) Includes bibliographical references and index. Provides biographies of famous black writers, singers, musicians, etc.   ISBN 0-922162-58-1 : DDC 700/.92/2 B 20
1. Artists, Black - Biography - Juvenile literature. 2. Arts - Juvenile literature. 3. Blacks - Biography. I. Green, Richard L. II. Conaway, Judith, 1948-. III. Clay, Steve, ill. IV. Dobson, S. Gaston, ill. V. Series.
NX164.B55 H57 1990

HISTORIC BUILDINGS.
Lorange, Erik, 1919- Historiske byer . [Oslo] , c1990. 310 p. : ISBN 82-00-21048-0 DDC 720/.9 20
NA200 .L65 1990

HISTORIC BUILDINGS - BELGIUM - BRUSSELS - GUIDE-BOOKS.
Le Patrimoine monumental de la Belgique. Liège [1989- <v. 1, pt. 1 > : ISBN

2-8021-0092-0 (v. 1)   DDC 720/.9493/32 20
NA1170 .P37 1989

HISTORIC BUILDINGS - BRAZIL - GUIDE-BOOKS.
Guia dos bens tombados Brasil /. Rio de Janeiro, RJ , c1987. 512, [24] p. : DDC 720/.981 20
NA853 .G85 1987

HISTORIC BUILDINGS - BRAZIL - RIO DE JANEIRO.
Figueiredo, Guilherme. Patrimônio histórico do Rio de Janeiro /. [Rio de Janeiro] , c1988. 1 portfolio :   *NYPL [3-MQWN++ 89-26567]*

HISTORIC BUILDINGS - CARIBBEAN AREA - CONSERVATION AND RESTORATION.
Pérez Montas, Eugenio. Carimos . Santo Domingo, República Dominicana , 1989. 358 p. :
NA791 .P47 1989

HISTORIC BUILDINGS - FRANCE.
Profils de corniches de plafonds /. [Paris] , 1990- v. <1 > : ISBN 2-11-086067-7
NA2960 .P76 1990

HISTORIC BUILDINGS - FRANCE - TOURAINE - ADDRESSES, ESSAYS, LECTURES.
Montoux, André. Vieux logis de Touraine /. [Chambray-les-Tours] (42 av. des Platanes) , 1974- v. : DDC 944/.54
DC611.T728 M6   *NYPL [JFL 76-344]*

HISTORIC BUILDINGS - GERMANY - KASSEL (LANDKREIS)
Kreis Kassel /. Braunschweig/Wiesbaden , 1990- v. <1 > : ISBN 3-528-06239-8 DDC 720/.943/412 20
NA1076.K37 K7 1990

HISTORIC BUILDINGS - ITALY - ROME.
D'Onofrio, Cesare, 1921- Visitiamo Roma nel Quattrocento . Roma , 1989. 307 p. :
NYPL [3-MQWB 91-4311]

HISTORIC BUILDINGS - ITALY - VENETO.
Di villa in villa . Treviso , c1990. 235 p. : ISBN 88-85066-98-4
NYPL [3-MQWB 91-4915]

HISTORIC BUILDINGS - LOUISIANA - GARYVILLE - CONSERVATION AND RESTORATION.
Return to elegance . Reserve, La. [1979?] [32] p. :
MLCM 83/7334 (N)
NYPL [3-MQWO 91-297]

HISTORIC BUILDINGS - NETHERLANDS - AMSTERDAM - CONSERVATION AND RESTORATION.
Amsterdam (Netherlands). Gemeentelijk bureau Monumentenzorg. Bewaard in het hart . Amsterdam , 1965. 174 p. :
NYPL [3-MQW 90-6245]

HISTORIC BUILDINGS - NEW BRUNSWICK - WOODSTOCK - PICTORIAL WORKS.
Connell, Allison. A view of Woodstock . Fredericton, N.B. , c1988. 74 p. : ISBN 0-920483-19-4 : DDC 971.5/52/0208 19
NYPL [3-MQWM 90-12592]

HISTORIC BUILDINGS - NEW YORK (N.Y.) - CONSERVATION AND RESTORATION.
The Restoration directory . New York, NY , 1990. 110 p. :   *NYPL [3-MQWO 91-6663]*

HISTORIC BUILDINGS - TENNESSEE - JONESBORO - CONSERVATION AND RESTORATION.
Tennessee State Planning Commission. Upper East Tennessee Office. Historic district plan, Jonesborough, Tennessee /. Johnson City, Tenn. , Springfield, Va. , 1972. 115 p. :
NYPL [3-MQWO 90-6607]

HISTORIC BUILDINGS - UNITED STATES - CONSERVATION AND RESTORATION - BIBLIOGRAPHY.
Landmark yellow pages . Washington, D.C. , 1990. 319 p. : ISBN 0-89133-154-9 DDC 363.6/9/0973 20
E159 .L28 1990
NYPL [Desk-USLHG 90-10086]

HISTORIC BUILDINGS - UNITED STATES - CONSERVATION AND RESTORATION - HANDBOOKS, MANUALS, ETC.
Landmark yellow pages . Washington, D.C. ,

1990. 319 p. : ISBN 0-89133-154-9 DDC 363.6/9/0973 20
E159 .L28 1990
NYPL [Desk-USLHG 90-10086]

HISTORIC BUILDINGS - UNITED STATES - CONSERVATION AND RESTORATION - SOCIETIES, ETC. - DIRECTORIES.
Landmark yellow pages . Washington, D.C. , 1990. 319 p. : ISBN 0-89133-154-9 DDC 363.6/9/0973 20
E159 .L28 1990
NYPL [Desk-USLHG 90-10086]

HISTORIC BUILDINGS - UNITED STATES - CONSERVATION AND RESTORATION - STANDARDS.
The Secretary of the Interior's standards for rehabilitation and Illustrated guidelines for rehabilitating historic buildings /. Washington, D.C. , 1991. p. cm. DDC 720/.28/8021873 20
NA106 .S4 1991

Historic Cherry Hill (Corporation) Creating a dignified past . Savage, Md. , c1991. ix, 129 p. : ISBN 0-8476-7690-0
NYPL [3-MLF 91-6907]

Historic designs and patterns in color from Arabic and Italian sources /. Hessemer, Friedrich Maximilian, 1800-1860. [Arabische und Alt-Italienische Bau-Verzierungen. English.] New York , c1990. 120 p. : ISBN 0-486-26425-4 DDC 745.4 20
NA3573 .H4713 1990
NYPL [3-MRX+ 91-6246]

Historic district plan, Jonesborough, Tennessee /. Tennessee State Planning Commission. Upper East Tennessee Office. Johnson City, Tenn. , Springfield, Va. , 1972. 115 p. :
NYPL [3-MQWO 90-6607]

HISTORIC HOUSES, ETC. see **HISTORIC BUILDINGS.**

Historic New Orleans Collection.
Davis, Keith F., 1952- Clarence John Laughlin . Kansas City, Mo. , c1990. 166 p. : ISBN 0-87529-629-7
NYPL [MFX+ (Laughlin) 91-7437]

Degrees of discovery : from New World to New Orleans. [New Orleans, La.] : Historic New Orleans Collection, [1977] 31 p. : maps (some col.) ; 22 x 28 cm. Published in association with an exhibition of the same name, held Sept. 14-Dec. 10, 1977. DDC 912/.763 19
1. Louisiana - Maps - Exhibitions. 2. Louisiana - Discovery and exploration - Exhibitions. I. Title.
GA427 .H57 1977 Rosenwald Coll
NYPL [Map Div. 91-140]

Guide to the photographic collections at the Historic New Orleans Collection. New Orleans, La. : The Collection, 1989. 1 v. (unpaged) : ill. ; 22 cm. ISBN 0-917860-29-2
1. Historic New Orleans Collection - Catalogs. 2. Photograph collections - Louisiana - New Orleans - Catalogs. I. Title.   *NYPL [MFW 90-11189]*

Rosenheim, Jeff. Walker Evans and Jane Ninas in New Orleans, 1935-1936 /. New Orleans, La. , 1991. 24 p. : ISBN 0-917860-31-4
NYPL [MFX+ (Evans) 91-4936]

HISTORIC NEW ORLEANS COLLECTION - CATALOGS.
Historic New Orleans Collection. Guide to the photographic collections at the Historic New Orleans Collection. New Orleans, La. , 1989. 1 v. (unpaged) : ISBN 0-917860-29-2
NYPL [MFW 90-11189]

Historic preservation tomorrow . National Trust for Historic Preservation in the United States. [Williamsburg, Va.] 1967. xi, 57 p.
NYPL [3-MQWO 90-5564]

HISTORIC SITES - CONSERVATION AND RESTORATION.
Hlobil, Ivo. Teorie městských památkových rezervací, 1900-1975 /. Praha , 1985. 123 p. ;
NA9050 .H58 1985

HISTORIC SITES - TENNESSEE - JONESBORO - CONSERVATION AND RESTORATION.
Tennessee State Planning Commission. Upper East Tennessee Office. Historic district plan, Jonesborough, Tennessee /. Johnson City, Tenn. , Springfield, Va. , 1972. 115 p. :
NYPL [3-MQWO 90-6607]

HISTORIC SITES - UNITED STATES - PICTORIAL WORKS.
Friedlander, Lee. Fourteen American monuments /. [New York] , c1977. 13 p. :
NYPL [MFX (Friedlander) 91-7115]

HISTORICAL ART. see HISTORY IN ART.

Historical art and decorative arts from New Hampshire collectors. Heirlooms [microform] . Manchester, N.H. [1985] [5] leaves :
*NYPL [*ZM-218 no.2]*

Historical art index, A.D. 400-1650 . Rochelle, Mercedes, 1955- Jefferson, N.C. , c1989. v, 217 p. ; ISBN 0-89950-449-3 (lib. bdg. : alk. paper) : DDC 704.9/499 20
N8210 .R6 1989 **NYPL [*R-MAC 90-419]**

Historical atlas of Canada. Toronto ; Buffalo : University of Toronto Press, [1987]- v. : ill. (some col.), col. maps ; 38 cm. Includes bibliographies. CONTENTS. - v. 1. From the beginning to 1800 / R. Cole Harris, editor ; Geoffrey J. Matthews, cartographer/designer -- v. 3. Addressing thetwentieth century, 1891-1961. ISBN 0-8020-2495-5 (v. 1)
1. Canada - Historical geography - Maps. I. Harris, R. Cole. II. Matthews, Geoffrey J.
NYPL [Map Div. 87-990]

Historical atlas of Massachusetts / edited by Richard W. Wilkie and Jack Tager ; cartographic production directed by Roy Doyon. Amherst : University of Massachusetts Press, c1991. 152 p. : ill. (some col.), maps. ; 32 x 41 cm. Two transparencies inserted in pocket. Includes bibliographical references and index. ISBN 0-87023-697-0 (alk. paper) : DDC 912.744 20
1. Massachusetts - Maps. 2. Massachusetts - History - Maps. 3. Massachusetts - Social conditions - Maps. I. Wilkie, Richard W., 1938-. II. Tager, Jack. III. Doyon, Roy.
G1230 .H5 1990
NYPL [Map Div.+ 91-7396]

A historical atlas of South Asia; / edited by Joseph E. Schwartzberg, with the collaboration of Shiva G. Bajpai ... [et al]. Chicago : University of Chicago Press, 1978. xxxix, 352 p. illus., maps (part col.) 42 cm. (Association for Asian Studies. Reference series) Two overlay maps and three chronological charts inserted in pocket. Bibliography: p. 267-304. Includes index. ISBN 0-226-74221-0
1. South Asia - History. 2. South Asia - Historical geography - Maps. I. Schwartzberg, Joseph E. II. Bajpai, Shiva Gopal. III. Series.
G2661.S1 H5 1978 **NYPL [Map Div. 79-12]**

HISTORICAL ATLASES. see GEOGRAPHY, HISTORICAL - MAPS.

Historical center of Salvador. Verger, Pierre. Centro histórico de Salvador . São Paulo , 1989. 1 v. (unpaged) :
NYPL [MFX+ (Verger) 90-13439]

Historical costumes of Turkish women. 1st ed. Istanbul, Turkey : Middle East Video Corp., 1986. 175 p. : chiefly col. ill., maps ; 32 cm. Bibliography: p. 15.
1. Costume - Turkey. I. Orta Doğu Video İşletmeleri A.Ş. **NYPL [3-MMR + 89-19091]**

HISTORICAL MUSEUMS - BERLIN (GERMANY) - DESIGNS AND PLANS - EXHIBITIONS.
Ferlenga, Alberto. Aldo Rossi . Milano , 1990. 118 p. : ISBN 88-435-3088-7
NYPL [3-MQZ (Rossi) 91-6524]

HISTORICAL MUSEUMS - UNITED STATES.
Creating a dignified past . Savage, Md. , c1991. ix, 129 p. : ISBN 0-8476-7690-0
NYPL [3-MLF 91-6907]

HISTORICAL RECORDS - PRESERVATION. see ARCHIVES.

HISTORICAL SITES. see HISTORIC SITES.

Historical society architectural publications, Georgia, Hawaii, Idaho, Illinois, and Indiana /. Vance, Mary A. Monticello, Ill. , 1980. 54 p. ;
Z5944.U5 V353 NA705
NYPL [3-MQWO 81-771]

Historical Society of Berks County. Machmer, Richard S. Just for nice . [Reading, PA] (940 Centre Ave., Reading 19601) , c1991. 88 p. : DDC 730/.09748/107474816 20
NK9710.P4 M33 1991

Historiches Museum der Stadt Wien. 200 Jahre Mode in Wien : aus des Modesammlungen des Historischen Museums der Stadt Wien : 42. Sonderausstellung des Historischen Museums der Stadt Wien, 10. April bis 31. Oktober 1976 / gemeinsame Veranstaltung des Kulturamts und der Museen der Stadt Wien ; durchgeführt vom Verein der Freunde der Hermesvilla, Lainzer Tiergarten, Hermesvilla. Wien : Verein der Freunde der Hermesvilla, 1976. 120 p., [34] leaves of plates : ill. (some col.) ; 22 cm. Includes essays by Susanne Walther, Lucie Hampel, and Otto Koening. Includes bibliographical references.
1. Fashion - Austria - Vienna - Exhibitions. 2. Costume - Austria - Vienna - History - Exhibitions. I. Walther, Susanne. II. Hampel, Lucie. III. Koenning, Otto. IV. Vienna (Austria) Kulturamt. V. Title. VI. Title: Zwei hundert Jahre Mode in Wien.
NYPL [3-MMM 90-6048]

HISTORICISM.
Lavin, Irving, 1927- Past-present . Berkeley , c1992. p. cm. ISBN 0-520-06816-5 (cloth) DDC 709 20
N72.H58 L38 1992

Historienmalerei in Europa : Paradigmen in Form, Funktion und Ideologie / herausgegeben von Ekkehard Mai ; unter Mitarbeit von Anke Repp-Eckert. Mainz am Rhein : P.v. Zabern, c1990. 439 p. : ill. ; 29 cm. Papers presented at a conference held in Cologne in December 1987 on the occasion of an exhibition at the Wallraf-Richartz-Museum. Includes articles in English. Includes bibliographical references and index. ISBN 3-8053-1113-3
1. Painting, European - Congresses. 2. Painting, Modern - Europe - Congresses. 3. History in art - Congresses. I. Mai, Ekkehard. II. Repp-Eckert, Anke.
ND454 .H55 1990

Historikos atlas . Kontorlēs, Kōnstantinos P. Athēnai , 1962. 39 p. :
NYPL [Map Div. 86-229]

Historisch-geographischer Atlas des Preussenlandes. Mortensen, Hans, 1894-1964. Wiesbaden, 1968. 15 v. DDC 911/.438/3
G1918.E2 M6 1968
NYPL [Map Div. 72-266]

Historische Karten aus der Sammlung der Ernst-Moritz-Arndt-Universitat Greifswald in der Sektion Geographie / Einführung und Erlauterung. Greifswald : Die Sektion, 1981. 1 portfolio (20 maps (some col.)) ; 40 cm. + 1 booklet (25 p. ; 30 cm.) Introductory text in German, Russian, and English.
1. Germany - Historical geography - Maps. I. Hess, G. II. Greifswald. Universität. Sektion Geographie. III. Title. **NYPL [Map Div. 86-337]**

Historische Photographie in Chemnitz /. Voigt, May. [Karl-Marx-Stadt] , 1988. 96 p. :
NYPL [MFW 91-6682]

Historischer Atlas von Bayerisch-Schwaben / im Auftrag der Schwäbischen Forschungsgemeinschaft, unter Mitwirkung der Kommission für Bayerische Landesgeschichte, in Verbindung mit Wolfgang Zorn, herausgegeben von Hans Frei, Pankraz Fried, Franz Schaffer. 2., neu bearbeitet und erg. Aufl. Augsburg : Verlag der Schwäbischen Forschungsgemeinschaft ; Weissenhorn : Auslieferung, A.H. Konrad, 1982- 1 atlas (1 v. (loose-leaf)) : maps (some col.) ; 36 cm. (Veröffentlichungen der Schwäbischen Forschungsgemeinschaft bei der Kommission für Bayerische Landesgeschichte) Issued in parts. Issued in portfolio. "1. Auflage, in Verbindung mit zahlreichen Mitarbeitern herausgegeben vom Wolfgang Zorn." ISBN 3-922518-96-6 DDC 911/.433 19
1. Bavaria (Germany) - Historical geography - Maps. 2. Bavaria (Germany) - History. 3. Swabia (Germany) - Historical geography - Maps. 4. Swabia (Germany) - History. I. Zorn, Wolfgang. II. Frei, Hans, 1937-. III. Fried, Pankraz. IV. Schaffer, Franz. V. Schwäbische Forschungsgemeinschaft. VI. Bayerische Akademie der Wissenschaften. Kommission für Bayerische Landesgeschichte. VII. Series.
G1923.B3 H35 1982
NYPL [Map Div. 84-179]

Historischer Atlas von Wien / Herausgeber, Wiener Stadt- und Landesarchiv, Ludwig Boltzmann Institut für Stadtgeschichtsforschung ; wissenschaftliche Gesamtleitung, Felix Czeike, Renate Banik-Schweitzer ; ständige wissenschaftliche Mitarbeit, Gerhard Meissl ; redaktionelle Leitung, Renate Banik-Schweitzer ; kartographische und technische Leitung, Erich Kopecky ; Kartographie, Wiener Stadt- und Landesarchiv, Wien, Ludwig Boltzmann Institut für Stadtgeschichtsforschung, Linz-Wien. Wien : Jugend und Volk Verlagsgesellschaft, 1981- 1 atlas (v. (loose-leaf)) : col. ill., col. maps (some folded) ; 50 cm. Issued in parts. "Inhaltsverzeichnis der 1. bis 3. Lieferung", inserted in Lfg. 3. ISBN 3-7141-6044-2 (1. Lfg.) DDC 911/.43613 19
1. Vienna (Austria) - Historical geography - Maps. 2. Vienna (Austria) - Maps. I. Czeike, Felix. II. Banik-Schweitzer, Renate, 1939-. III. Kopecky, Erich. IV. Wiener Stadt- und Landesarchiv. V. Ludwig Boltzmann-Institut für Stadtgeschichtsforschung.
G1939.V4S1 H5 1981
NYPL [Map Div. 90-56]

Historischer Teil, 900 Jahre Klosterkirche Lambach. Oberösterreichische Landesausstellung (1989 : Benediktinerstift Lambach) 900 Jahre Klosterkirche Lambach . Linz , 1989. 231 p. :
NA5510.L355 O23 1989
NYPL [3-MRBB 91-7295]

Mainfränkische Studien. see Mainfränkische Studien.

Historisches Museum (Bamberg, Germany) Denkmalkunde in Bamberg . Bamberg [1990] 77 p. : DDC 720/.28/80943318 20
NA109.G3 D44 1990

Historisches Museum der Pfalz (Speyer, Germany) Von Constantin zu Karl dem Grossen . Mainz , 1990. 71 p., [5] leaves of plates : ISBN 3-88467-025-5
N5760 .V57 1990

Historisches Museum der Stadt Wien. Biedermeier in Wien 1815-1848 . Mainz , c1990. 251 p. : ISBN 3-8053-1128-1
NX548.V53 B54 1990

Gotik . Wien [1990] 141 p. :
NYPL [3-MAM 90-11533]

Modes romantiques viennoises, 1800-1860 : collections de modes du Musée de l'histoire de la ville de Vienne présentées sous le patronage de l'Institut autrichien de Paris : [exposition] décembre 1969-avril 1970. Paris : Musée du costume de la ville de Paris, 1970. [28] p., 16 p. of plates : ill. ; 21 cm.
1. Historisches Museum der Stadt Wien - Exhibitions. 2. Costume - Austria - Vienna - History - 19th century - Exhibitions. I. Musée du costume de la ville de Paris. II. Title.
GT821.V5 P3 **NYPL [3-MMM 91-516]**

Schiele, Egon, 1890-1918. Egon Schiele . [Wien] [1990?] 104 p. : DDC 709/.2 20
N6811.5.S34 A4 1990
NYPL [3-MCK S332 91-5564]

HISTORISCHES MUSEUM DER STADT WIEN - EXHIBITIONS.
Historisches Museum der Stadt Wien. Modes romantiques viennoises, 1800-1860 . Paris , 1970. [28] p., 16 p. of plates :
GT821.V5 P3 **NYPL [3-MMM 91-516]**

Historiske byer . Lorange, Erik, 1919- [Oslo] , c1990. 310 p. : ISBN 82-00-21048-0 DDC 720/.9 20
NA200 .L65 1990

Historizem v kiparstvu devetnajstega stoletja na Slovenskem. Žitko, Sonja. Historizem v kiparstvu 19. stoletja na Slovenskem /. Ljubljana , 1989. 188 p. :
NB949.S5 Z58 1989

Historizem v kiparstvu 19. stoletja na Slovenskem /. Žitko, Sonja. Ljubljana , 1989. 188 p. :
NB949.S5 Z58 1989

HISTORY, ANCIENT.
Atlas of classical history /. London , New York , c1985, 1988. 1 atlas (217 p.) : ISBN 0-415-03463-9 (pbk.)
NYPL [Map Div. 91-5122]

HISTORY AND ART. see ART AND HISTORY.

History and critical catalog of German, Netherlandish, and French copper engravings in the 15th century. Lehrs, Max, 1855-1938. Geschichte und kritischer Katalog des deutschen, niederländischen und französischen Kupferstichs im xv. Jahrhundert. [New York,

1970?] 9 v.
NE1450 .L513

History and design of interior decoration.
Ottolini, Gianni, 1943- Storia e progetto di
arredamento =. Milano , c1989. 63 p. : ISBN
88-7080-255-8 :
IN PROCESS (ONLINE)
NYPL [3-MLO+ 90-11115]

**HISTORY - ATLASES. see GEOGRAPHY,
HISTORICAL - MAPS.**

History in art. Art in history/history in art .
Santa Monica, CA [Chicago, Ill.] , 1991. p.
cm. ISBN 0-89236-201-4 : DDC
701/.03/0949209032 20
N72.S6 A746 1991

HISTORY IN ART.
Greenstein, Jack Matthew. Mantegna and
painting as historical narrative /. Chicago ,
1992. p. cm. ISBN 0-226-30707-7 DDC 759.5 20
ND623.M3 G7 1992

HISTORY IN ART - CONGRESSES.
Historienmalerei in Europa . Mainz am Rhein ,
c1990. 439 p. : ISBN 3-8053-1113-3
ND454 .H55 1990

HISTORY IN ART - EXHIBITIONS.
Geschichtsbilder aus dem alten Österreich .
Wien , 1989. [100] p. : **NYPL [3-MAW
(Vienna) (Vienna. Österreichische Galerie.
Wechselausstellung. Nr.133)]**

HISTORY IN ART - INDEXES.
Rochelle, Mercedes, 1955- Historical art index,
A.D. 400-1650 . Jefferson, N.C. , c1989. v, 217
p. ; ISBN 0-89950-449-3 (lib. bdg. : alk. paper) :
DDC 704.9/499 20
N8210 .R6 1989 **NYPL [*R-MAC 90-419]**

The history of architecture in India . Tadgell,
Christopher, 1939- London , 1990. ix, 336 p. :
ISBN 1-85454-350-4 : DDC 720.95 20
NA1501 **NYPL [3-MAF 90-12863]**

History of art for young people /. Janson, H. W.
(Horst Woldemar), 1913- New York , 1992. p.
cm. ISBN 0-8109-3405-1 DDC 709 20
N5300 .J33 1992

A history of English furniture . Macquoid, Percy,
d. 1925. London , 1988. 416 p., lx p. of plates :
ISBN 1-85170-080-3 : DDC 749.22 19
NK2529 **NYPL [3-MOF+ 91-4219]**

A history of Maltese architecture . Mahoney,
Leonard. [Zabbar , 1988] 360 p., 120 p. of
plates : DDC 720/.9458/5 20
NA1455.M3 M3 1988

History of rocks, 1986-1988. McKeever, Ian,
1946- Ian McKeever, a history of rocks,
1986-1988 /. München [1990] 49 p. : DDC
759.2 20
ND497.M5 A4 1990

History of the British landscape.
Howard, Peter, 1944- Landscapes . London ,
New York , 1991. xiv, 260 p. : ISBN
0-415-00775-5 DDC 758/.141/0941 20
ND1354 .H79 1990 **NYPL [3-MCT 91-4509]**

History of the comic strip. Kunzle, David.
Berkeley [c1973- v. ; ISBN 0-520-01865-6 (v. 1)
DDC 741.5/909 s 741.5/909
PN6710 .K85 **NYPL [MDY+ 75-691]**

The history of the patchwork quilt . Gwinner,
Schnuppe von. [Die Geschichte des
patchworkquilts. English.] West Chester, Pa. ,
1988. 196 p. : ISBN 0-88740-136-8
NYPL [3-MOT 90-4539]

The history of travel . Wegman, William.
Cincinnati, Ohio , Youngstown, Ohio [1990]
36 p. : ISBN 0-915577-19-4
NYPL [3-MCX W411 91-3443]

History through art and architecture.
American art and architecture [videorecording]
/. Boulder, CO , 1990. 5 videocassettes (140
min.) : DDC 709.73 11
N6505

HISTRIONICS. see THEATER.

Hitchens, Ivon, 1893- Khoroche, Peter. Ivon
Hitchens /. London , 1990. viii, 277 p. : ISBN
0-233-98607-3 : DDC 759.2 20
NYPL [3-MCV H674 91-5928]

HITCHENS, IVON, 1893-
Khoroche, Peter. Ivon Hitchens /. London ,

1990. viii, 277 p. : ISBN 0-233-98607-3 : DDC
759.2 20 **NYPL [3-MCV H674 91-5928]**

Hittorff, Jacques Ignace, 1792-1867.
Architectural drawings and watercolors by
Jakob Ignaz Hittorff, 1792-1867 /. Cologne ,
Washington, D.C. , 1990. 64 p. : ISBN
0-86528-040-1 DDC 720/.22/22 20
NA2707.H58 A4 1990
NYPL [3-MQZ (Hittorff) 91-5615]

**HITTORFF, JACQUES IGNACE, 1792-1867 -
EXHIBITIONS.**
Architectural drawings and watercolors by
Jakob Ignaz Hittorff, 1792-1867 /. Cologne ,
Washington, D.C. , 1990. 64 p. : ISBN
0-86528-040-1 DDC 720/.22/22 20
NA2707.H58 A4 1990
NYPL [3-MQZ (Hittorff) 91-5615]

**Hiwsisayin Amerikayi Miats'eal Tērut'iwnk'. see
United States.**

Hlaváček, Luboš. Ota Janeček / Luboš Hlaváček.
Vyd. 1. Praha : Odeon, 1989. 213 p. : ill. (some
col.) ; 27 cm. (Umělecké profily. sv. 35) Summary in
English, French, German, and Russian. Includes
bibliographical references (p. 200-201). ISBN
80-207-0082-X :
*1. Janeček, Ota - Criticism and interpretation. I.
Janeček, Ota. II. Title.*
ND534.5.J27 H58 1989

Hlobil, Ivo. Teorie městských památkových
rezervací, 1900-1975 / Ivo Hlobil. Praha :
Ústav teorie a dějin umění ČSAV v Praze,
1985. 123 p. ; 24 cm. (Uměnovědné studie . 6)
Includes bibliographical references (p. 97-120).
*1. Cities and towns - Conservation and restoration. 2.
Historic sites - Conservation and restoration. I. Title. II.
Series.*
NA9050 .H58 1985

**HLUSHCHENKO, MYKOLA PETROVYCH,
1901-**
Zaremba, Volodymyr. Podarovana krasa .
Dnipropetrovs'k , 1990. 284 p., [16] p. of
plates : ISBN 5-7775-0209-1 :
ND699.H57 Z37 1990

**Hlustschenko, Mykola. see Hlushchenko, Mykola
Petrovych, 1901-**

H.M. Gousha Company.
Gousha Colorado road atlas and visitor's guide
/ text, Naomi V. Cutner ; design, Edward P.
O'Dell. New York, NY : H.M. Gousha, c1991.
1 atlas (56 p.) : col. maps ; 28 cm. ISBN
0-13-151275-7
*1. Colorado - Road maps. I. Title. II. Title: Colorado
road atlas. III. Title: Gousha Colorado road atlas.*
NYPL [Map Div. 90-11950]

Gousha Kansas City street atlas. [New York] :
H.M. Gousha, [1989] 1 atlas (xii, 86 p.) :
maps ; 28 cm. ISBN 0-13-362187-1
*1. Zip code - Missouri - Kansas City. 2. Kansas City,
Mo. - Maps. I. Title.*
NYPL [Map Div. 90-11941]

Gousha Texas road atlas and visitor's guide /
text, Mary T. Mulkerin ; design, Edward P.
O'Dell. New York, NY : H.M. Gousha, c1991.
1 atlas (56 p.) : col. maps ; 28 cm. ISBN
0-13-932112-8
*1. Texas - Road maps. I. Title. II. Title: Texas road
atlas. III. Title: Gousha Texas road atlas.*
NYPL [Map Div. 90-11949]

Pocket road atlas, United States, Canada,
Mexico. San Jose, CA : H.M. Gousha, 1990,
c1989. 1 atlas (64 p.) : col. maps ; 16 cm. Cover
title: Gousha pocket road atlas, United States, Canada,
Mexico. ISBN 0-13-622465-2
*1. United States - Road maps. 2. Canada - Road maps.
3. Mexico - Road maps. I. Title. II. Title: Gousha
pocket road atlas, United States, Canada, Mexico.*
NYPL [Map Div. 90-12566]

H.M. Gousha (Firm) Gousha California road atlas
and visitor's guide. San Jose, Calif. , c1991. 56
p. : ISBN 0-13-110891-3 :
NYPL [Map Div. 90-13143]

Ho, Wai-kam. The Century of Tung Ch'i-ch'ang
/. Kansas City, Mo. , 1992. p. cm. ISBN
0-295-97157-6 DDC 759.951 20
N7349.T86 A4 1992

Hoare, William, 1707-1792.
Newby, Evelyn. William Hoare of Bath R. A.,
1707-1792 . Bath [England] , c1990. 62 p., [8]
p. of plates : ISBN 0-86299-897-2
NYPL [3-MCV H677 91-6664]

**HOARE, WILLIAM, 1707-1792 -
EXHIBITIONS.**
Newby, Evelyn. William Hoare of Bath R. A.,
1707-1792 . Bath [England] , c1990. 62 p., [8]
p. of plates : ISBN 0-86299-897-2
NYPL [3-MCV H677 91-6664]

Hobart atlas. Tasmania. Lands and Surveys Dept.
[Hobart, 1969] 64 p. (p. 13-41 col. maps) DDC
912.94/6
G2754.H6 T3 1969
NYPL [Map Div. 90-5986]

HOBART (TAS.) - MAPS.
Tasmania. Lands and Surveys Dept. Hobart
atlas. [Hobart, 1969] 64 p. (p. 13-41 col. maps)
DDC 912.94/6
G2754.H6 T3 1969
NYPL [Map Div. 90-5986]

**Hobart. Tasmanian Museum and Art Gallery. see
Tasmanian Museum and Art Gallery.**

Hobbs, Anne Stevenson. Fables . Savannah, Ga. ,
1991. p. cm. ISBN 0-913720-75-5 (hardcover) :
DDC 741.6/4 398.2 20
NC961.7.F34 F3 1991

Hobbs, Robert Carleton, 1946- Pousette-Dart,
Richard, 1916- Richard Pousette-Dart /.
Indianapolis, Ind. , c1990. 195 p. : ISBN
0-936260-51-3
NYPL [3-MCX+ P878 91-3358]

Hoberg, Annegret.
Della Torre, Enrico, 1931- Enrico della Torre .
München , c1987. 64 p. :
NYPL [3-MCF+ D343 90-5284]

Kubin, Alfred, 1877-1959. Alfred Kubin
1877-1959 /. München [1990] 400 p. : ISBN
3-88645-092-9 (Ausstellungskatalog)
IN PROCESS (ONLINE)
NYPL [3-MCK K95 91-8111]

Zweite, Armin. The Blue Rider in the
Lenbachhaus, Munich . Munich , 1989. 288 p. :
ISBN 3-7913-0850-0
NYPL [3-MAMG+ 90-11017]

Hobson, Charles, 1943- Leonardo da Vinci,
1452-1519. Leonardo knows baseball /. San
Francisco , c1991. p. cm. ISBN 0-8118-0013-X
DDC 700/.92 20
NC257.L4 A4 1991

Hobzek, Josef. Mapa hradů a zámků
Československé republiky /. [Praha] , 1959. 80
p., [16] p. of plates :
NYPL [Map Div. 88-934]

HÖCH, HANNA, 1889- - EXHIBITIONS.
Höch, Hannah, 1889- Colagens, Hannah Höch,
1889-1978 /. Lisboa , 1989. 134 p. :
N6888.H6 A4 1989a

CUT WITH THE KITCHEN KNIFE.
Dech, Jula. Hannah Höch, Schnitt mit dem
Küchenmesser Dada durch die letzte
weimarer Bierbauchkulturepoche
Deutschlands /. Frankfurt am Main , 1989.
89 p., [1] folded leaf of plates : ISBN
3-596-23970-2 :
NYPL [3-MCK H691 91-4661]

**HÖCH, HANNAH, 1889- - CRITICISM AND
INTERPRETATION.**
Dech, Jula. Hannah Höch, Schnitt mit dem
Küchenmesser Dada durch die letzte weimarer
Bierbauchkulturepoche Deutschlands /.
Frankfurt am Main , 1989. 89 p., [1] folded leaf
of plates : ISBN 3-596-23970-2 :
NYPL [3-MCK H691 91-4661]

Hochberg, Julian E. Gombrich, E. H. (Ernst
Hans), 1909- Art, perception and reality.
Baltimore [1972] x, 132 p. ISBN 0-8018-1354-9
DDC 701/.17
N71 .G64 **NYPL [3-MAB 90-5472]**

Hochöfen /. Becher, Bernd, 1931- München ,
c1990. 15 p., 223 p. of plates : ISBN
3-88814-352-7
NYPL [MFX+ (Becher) 91-7985]

Hochschule für Grafik und Buchkunst Leipzig :
Abteilung Buchgestaltung / Redaktion, Peter
Pachnicke, Walter Schiller, Gert Wunderlich.
Leipzig : [Hochschule für Grafik und Buchkunst,
1985?]. 136 p. : ill. ; 25 cm.
*1. Hochschule für Grafik und Buchkunst Leipzig. 2.
Illustration of books - Germany, East. I. Pachnicke,
Peter. II. Schiller, Walter, 1920-. III. Wunderlich, Gert.
IV. Hochschule für Grafik und Buchkunst Leipzig.*
NYPL [MDTT 91-6738]

Hochschule für Angewandte Kunst (Vienna, Austria)
Franz Schuster, 1892-1972 /. Wien , 1976. 136 p. : DDC 720/.92/4 19
NA1011.5.S38 A4 1976
NYPL [3-MQZ+ (Schuster) 90-12651]

"Haut und Hülle" . Wien [1989?] 82 p. :
NYPL [MFW+ 91-2502]

Lang, Erwin, 1886- Erwin Lang . Wien [1990?] 150 p. : ISBN 3-85211-007-6
NYPL [MDG+ (Lang) 91-4287]

Vogelsberger, Vera. Emailkunst aus Wien, 1900-1989 /. [Wien] , c1990. 27 p., [60] p. of plates : ISBN 3-85063-193-1 DDC 738.4/09436/130904 20
NK5004.A9 V64 1990

Hochschule für Angewandte Kunst (Vienna, Austria). Institut für Kostümkunde.
Ausgeblendete Realität . Wien , 1989. 95 p. :
NYPL [MFW+ 90-11185]

Hochschule für Bildende Künste Braunschweig.
Idee . [Braunschweig] , 1988. 169 p. : ISBN 3-88895-025-2
IN PROCESS (ONLINE)
NYPL [3-MDW 91-6406]

Hochschule für Bildende Künste Dresden.
Dresden . Dresden , 1990. 684 p. : ISBN 3-364-00145-6
N333.G33 D744 1990

HOCHSCHULE FÜR BILDENDE KÜNSTE DRESDEN.
Dresden . Dresden , 1990. 684 p. : ISBN 3-364-00145-6
N333.G33 D744 1990

Hochschule für Bildende Künste Hamburg.
Nordlicht . Hamburg , 1989. 415 p. : ISBN 3-88506-174-0 DDC 709/.43/51507443515 20
N332.G33 H355 1989

HOCHSCHULE FÜR BILDENDE KÜNSTE HAMBURG - HISTORY - EXHIBITIONS.
Nordlicht . Hamburg , 1989. 415 p. : ISBN 3-88506-174-0 DDC 709/.43/51507443515 20
N332.G33 H355 1989

Hochschule für Gestaltung Ulm. English. Ulm design : the morality of objects : Hochschule für Gestaltung Ulm 1953-1968 / edited by Herbert Lindinger ; translated by David Britt.1st MIT Press ed. Cambridge, Mass. : MIT Press, 1991, c1990. 287 p. : ill. (some col.), ports. ; 27 cm. Translation of: Hochschule für Gestaltung Ulm. Includes bibliographical references.
ISBN 0-262-12147-6 DDC 745.2/0943/473 20
1. Design - Study and teaching - Germany - Ulm. 2. Design, Industrial - Germany. I. Lindinger, Herbert, 1933-. II. Hochschule für Gestaltung (Ulm, Germany). III. Title.
NK430.G4 H57813 1990
NYPL [3-MNE 91-5537]

Hochschule für Gestaltung (Ulm, Germany)
Hochschule für Gestaltung Ulm. English. Ulm design . Cambridge, Mass. , 1991, c1990. 287 p. : ISBN 0-262-12147-6 DDC 745.2/0943/473 20
NK430.G4 H57813 1990
NYPL [3-MNE 91-5537]

HOCHSCHULE FÜR GESTALTUNG (ULM, GERMANY)
Seckendorff, Eva von. Die Hochschule für Gestaltung in Ulm . Marburg , c1989. 184 p. : ISBN 3-922561-81-0 :
N332.G33 U467 1989

Hochschule für Grafik und Buchkunst Leipzig.
Hochschule für Grafik und Buchkunst Leipzig . Leipzig [1985?]. 136 p. :
NYPL [MDTT 91-6738]

HOCHSCHULE FÜR GRAFIK UND BUCHKUNST LEIPZIG.
Hochschule für Grafik und Buchkunst Leipzig . Leipzig [1985?]. 136 p. :
NYPL [MDTT 91-6738]

Höchst (Frankfurt am Main, Germany) Jahrhunderthalle. Aus der Werkstatt des Künstlers . [S.l. , 1969?] (München : R. Koehler) ca. 100 p. :
NYPL [MDBF 90-5879]

HÖCHSTER PORZELLANMANUFAKTUR GMBH - EXHIBITIONS.
Höchster Porzellan des 18. Jahrhunderts aus Privatbesitz . Hoechst (Frankfurt am Main) , c1984. 183 p. : *NYPL [3-MPGK 90-10661]*

Hockney, David.
David Hockney : December 5, 1990 to January 5, 1991. New York : André Emmerich Gallery, c1990. 1 v. (unpaged) : all col. ill. ; 22 x 28 cm. Title on cover: David Hockney, things recent, and a catalogue with new kinds of reproduction.
1. Hockney, David - Exhibitions. I. André Emmerich Gallery. II. Title. III. Title: David Hockney, things recent, and a catalogue with new kinds of reproduction.
NYPL [3-MCV H678 91-4234]

Hockney's alphabet / drawings by David Hockney ; edited by Stephen Spender. New York, NY : Random House for the AIDS Crisis Trust, c1991. p. cm. "First published in 1991 by Faber and Faber Limited ... London"--T.p. verso.
ISBN 0-679-41066-X : DDC 741.942 20
1. Hockney, David. 2. Alphabets in art. 3. English literature - 20th century. 4. American literature - 20th century. I. Spender, Stephen, 1909-. II. Title.
NC242.H6 A4 1991a

HOCKNEY, DAVID.
Hockney, David. Hockney's alphabet /. New York, NY , c1991. p. cm. ISBN 0-679-41066-X : DDC 741.942 20
NC242.H6 A4 1991a

HOCKNEY, DAVID - EXHIBITIONS.
Hockney, David. David Hockney . New York , c1990. 1 v. (unpaged) :
NYPL [3-MCV H678 91-4234]

Hockney's alphabet /. Hockney, David. New York, NY , c1991. p. cm. ISBN 0-679-41066-X : DDC 741.942 20
NC242.H6 A4 1991a

Hocquél, Wolfgang. Leipzig : Baumeister und Bauten : von der Romanik bis zur Gegenwart / von Wolfgang Hocquél.1. Aufl. Leipzig : Tourist Verlag, c1990. 284 p. : ill. (some col.), maps ; 22 cm. Includes bibliographical references (p. 268-270) and indexes. ISBN 3-350-00333-8 DDC 720/.9432/122 20
1. Architecture - Germany - Leipzig - Guide-books. 2. Leipzig (Germany) - Buildings, structures, etc. - Guide-books. 3. Architects - Germany - Leipzig - Biography. I. Title.
NA1086.L4 H63 1990

Hodgkinson, Frank. Frank Hodgkinson's European sketchbooks. Kenthurst, N.S.W., Australia : Geebung Studios, c1990- v. : ill. ; 28 cm. CONTENTS. - v. 1. Paris, 1947-1950 ISBN 0-646-01520-6 (set)
1. Hodgkinson, Frank. 2. Europe in art. I. Title. II. Title: European sketchbooks.
NYPL [3-MCZ H6895 91-3616]

HODGKINSON, FRANK.
Hodgkinson, Frank. Frank Hodgkinson's European sketchbooks. Kenthurst, N.S.W., Australia , c1990- v. : ISBN 0-646-01520-6 (set)
NYPL [3-MCZ H6895 91-3616]

Hodler, Ferdinand, 1853-1918.
Das Engadin Ferdinand Hodlers und anderer Künstler des 19. und 20. Jahrhunderts . [Chur] , St. Moritz , 1990. 122 p. : ISBN 3-905240-15-7 DDC 759.9494 20
ND853.H6 A4 1990

HODLER, FERDINAND, 1853-1918 - EXHIBITIONS.
Das Engadin Ferdinand Hodlers und anderer Künstler des 19. und 20. Jahrhunderts . [Chur] , St. Moritz , c1990. 122 p. : ISBN 3-905240-15-7 DDC 759.9494 20
ND853.H6 A4 1990

Hódmezővásárhely, Hungary. Tornyai János Múzeum. see **Tornyai János Múzeum.**

Hodson, Yolande. Ordnance surveyors' drawings, 1789-c.1840 : the original manuscript maps of the first ordnance survey of England and Wales from the British Library Map Library / by Yolande Hodson ; with an introduction, summary listing, and indexes by Tony Campbell. Reading, England : Research Publications, 1989. 154 p. : map ; 30 cm. Col. map on folded leaf in pocket. Includes bibliographical references. ISBN 0-86257-101-4 DDC 016.91242 20
1. Map Library (British Library) - Catalogs. 2. Great Britain - Maps, Manuscript - Bibliography - Catalogs. I. Campbell, Tony. II. Map Library (British Library). III. Title.
Z6027.G7 H66 1989 GA791
NYPL [Map Div. 91-169]

Höch, Hannah, 1889-
Colagens, Hannah Höch, 1889-1978 /

[concepção e elaboração, Götz Adriani ; textos, Götz Adriani ... et al. ; tradução, Virgínia Blanc de Sousa]. Lisboa : Fundação Calouste Gulbenkian, Centro de Arte Moderna, 1989. 134 p. : ill. (some col.) ; 24 cm. Based on: Hannah Höch : Fotomontagen, Gemälde, Aquarelle. "Uma exposição do Instituto de Relações Culturais com o Exterior, Estugarda"--Verso t.p. Includes bibliographical references (p. 96-97).
1. Höch, Hanna, 1889- - Exhibitions. I. Adriani, Götz, 1940-. II. Institut für Auslandsbeziehungen. III. Title.
N6888.H6 A4 1989a

Hannah Höch 1889-1978 : ihr Werk, ihr Leben, ihre Freunde / Berlinische Galerie, Museum für Moderne Kunst, Photographie und Architektur im Martin-Gropius-Bau, Museumspädigogischer Dienst Berlin ; [Redaktion, Elisabeth Moortgat, Cornelia Thater-Schulz ; Mitarbeit, Armin Schulz]. [Berlin] : Berlinische Galerie : Argon, 1989. 223, [24] p. : ill. (some col.) ; 24 cm. (Gegenwart Museum) Exhibition held at the Berlinische Galerie, 25 Nov. 1989-14 Jan. 1990, on the 100th anniversary of Hannah Höch's birth. ISBN 3-87024-156-X (Argon)
1. Höch, Hannah, 1889- - Exhibitions. 2. Dadaism - Germany - Exhibitions. I. Moortgat, Elisabeth. II. Thater-Schulz, Cornelia. III. Schulz, Armin. IV. Museumspädagogischer Dienst Berlin (Germany). V. Title. VI. Series.
NYPL [3-MCK H691 90-12356]

HÖCH, HANNAH, 1889- - EXHIBITIONS.
Höch, Hannah, 1889- Hannah Höch 1889-1978 . [Berlin] , 1989. 223, [24] p. : ISBN 3-87024-156-X (Argon)
NYPL [3-MCK H691 90-12356]

Höchster Porzellan des 18. Jahrhunderts aus Privatbesitz : [Ausstellung] Jahrhunderthalle Hoechst, 9. Dezember 1984 bis 9. Januar 1985 / [Wiss. Bearbeitung und Katalog, Horst Reber]. Hoechst (Frankfurt am Main) : Jahrhunderthalle, c1984. 183 p. : ill. ; 24 cm. Bibliography: p. 182-183.
1. Höchster Porzellanmanufaktur GmbH - Exhibitions. 2. Porcelain, German - Germany (West) - Höchst (Frankfurt am Main) - Exhibitions. 3. Porcelain - 18th century - Germany (West) - Höchst (Frankfurt am Main) - Exhibitions. 4. Porcelain - Private collections - Germany (West) - Exhibitions. I. Reber, Horst. II. Jahrhunderthalle Hoechst (Frankfurt am Main, Germany).
NYPL [3-MPGK 90-10661]

Höck, Alfred. Leinweber, Ulf. Karl Rumpf (1885-1968) . [Kassel] , 1989. 621 p. : ISBN 3-87280-057-4
NK951.R86 A4 1989
NYPL [3-MNE 91-5812]

Höfler, Janez.
Die Kunst Dalmatiens : vom Mittelalter bis zur Renaissance (800-1520) / Janez Höfler. Graz/Austria : Akademische Druck- u. Verlagsanstalt, 1989. 338 p. : 312 ill. (some col.) ; 29 cm. (Forschungen und Berichte des Institutes für Kunstgeschichte der Karl-Franzens-Universität Graz . 8) Includes bibliographical references (p. 324-326) and index. ISBN 3-201-01466-4 DDC 709/.497/2 20
1. Art - Yugoslavia - Dalmatia (Croatia). I. Title. II. Series.
N7249.D34 H64 1989

Die Kunst Dalmatiens : vom Mittelalter bis zur Renaissance (800-1520) / Janez Höfler. Graz : Akademische Druck, 1989. 338 p. : ill. (some col.) ; 30 cm. (Forschungen und Berichte des Institutes für Kunstgeschichte der Karl-Franzens-Universität Graz . VIII) Bibliography: p. 318-326. ISBN 3-201-01466-4
1. Art, Medieval - Yugoslavia - Dalmatia (Croatia). 2. Art, Renaissance - Yugoslavia - Dalmatia (Croatia). 3. Architecture, Medieval - Yugoslavia - Dalmatia (Croatia). 4. Architecture, Renaissance - Yugoslavia - Dalmatia (Croatia). 5. Dalmatia (Croatia) - Art. I. Series. II. Series: Graz. Universität. Kunsthistorisches Institut. Forschungen und Berichte, 8. III. Title.
NYPL [3-MAM+ 90-8024]

Hoehme, Gerhard, 1920-
Gerhard Hoehme, Bilder : [Ausstellung] Städtische Kunsthalle Düsseldorf 30. März bis 2. Mai 1979, Heidlelberger Kunstverein e. V., Heidelberger Schloss, Ottheinrichsbau 13. Mai bis 17. Juni 1979 / [hrsg. von der Städtischen Kunsthalle Düsseldorf, in Zusammenarbeit mit dem Institut für Moderne Kunst Nürnberg ; Katalog, Jürgen Partenheimer]. Düsseldorf : Städtische Kunsthalle, 1979. 200 p. : chiefly ill.

(some col.) ; 28 cm. Bibliography: p. 192.
1. Hoehme, Gerhard, 1920- - Exhibitions. I.
Partenheimer, Jürgen. II. Institut für Moderne Kunst
Nürnberg. III. Title.
N6888.H63 A4 1979
        NYPL [3-MCK H6931 81-779]

**HOEHME, GERHARD, 1920- -
    EXHIBITIONS.**
Hoehme, Gerhard, 1920- Gerhard Hoehme,
Bilder . Düsseldorf , 1979. 200 p. :
N6888.H63 A4 1979
        NYPL [3-MCK H6931 81-779]

Hoeltje, Georg, 1906- Festschrift für Georg
Hoeltje /. Hannover , 1988. 160 p. :
        NYPL [3-MQWD+ 90-12015]

HOELTJE, GEORG, 1906-
Festschrift für Georg Hoeltje /. Hannover ,
1988. 160 p. :
        NYPL [3-MQWD+ 90-12015]

Hölzel, Adolf, 1853-1934.
Adolf Hölzel von seinen Schülern . Stuttgart ,
1978. 61 p. :
N6868 .A38   NYPL [3-MCK H693 81-755]

**HÖLZEL, ADOLF, 1853-1934 - INFLUENCE -
    EXHIBITIONS.**
Adolf Hölzel von seinen Schülern . Stuttgart ,
1978. 61 p. :
N6868 .A38   NYPL [3-MCK H693 81-755]

Hoeneveld, Herman. Newton, Helmut, 1920-
Helmut Newton . 's-Gravenhage , 1986. 54 p. :
    ISBN 90-12-05217-3
        NYPL [MFX (Newton) 89-17853]

**Hoesch (Leopold) Museum. see Leopold-Hoesch-
    Museum.**

Hoetink, Hans. Broos, B. P. J. Great Dutch
paintings from America . The Hague , Zwolle ,
c1990. 561 p. :   ISBN 90-6630-253-4 (paperback)
        NYPL [3-MCG 91-5531]

Hoey, Carole Clew. Modersohn-Becker, Paula,
1876-1907. [Paula Modersohn-Becker in Briefen
und Tagebüchern. English.] Paula
Modersohn-Becker, the letters and journals /.
Evanston, Ill. , 1990. ix, 576 p., [22] p. of
plates :   ISBN 0-8101-0902-6   DDC 739.3 B 20
ND588.M58 A3 1990
        NYPL [3-MCK M68 90-12461]

Höfchen, Heinz.
Pfalzgalerie Kaiserslautern. Graphische
Sammlung. Französische Graphik, 19. und 20.
Jahrhundert, Ecole de Paris /. Kaiserslautern ,
1989. 212 p. :   ISBN 3-89422-002-3   DDC
769/.074/43435 s 769.944/361/07443435 20
NE55.G4 K346 1985 vol. 3 NE647.3
        NYPL [MDE 91-4020]

Pfalzgalerie Kaiserslautern. Graphische
Sammlung. Graphik des deutschen
Impressionismus . Kaiserslautern , 1985. 91 p. :
    DDC 769/.074/0343 s 769.943/074/0343 19
NE55.G4 K346 1985 vol. 1 NE651.6.I4
        NYPL [MDE 91-4007]

Hofer, Diethelm, 1945- Muscheln und Schnecken
aus der Sicht des Malers :
Niederösterreichisches Landesmuseum,
Sonderausstellung, 24. September bis 17-
Oktober 1982 / Diethelm Hofer ; [Herausgeber
und Verleger, Amt der Niederösterreichischen
Landesregierung, Abt. III/2 -- Kulturabteilung].
Wien : Das Amt, 1982. [18] p. : ill. (some
col.) ; 20 cm. (Katalog des Niederösterreichischen
Landesmuseums Neue Folge. 128)
1. Hofer, Diethelm, 1945- - Exhibitions. 2. Mussels in
art - Exhibitions. 3. Snails in art - Exhibitions. I. Series:
Vienna. Niederösterreichisches Landesmuseum. Katalog,
n.F., 128. II. Title.
        NYPL [MAVZ (Vienna) 75-791 Nr.128]

HOFER, DIETHOLM, 1945- - EXHIBITIONS.
Hofer, Diethelm, 1945- Muscheln und
Schnecken aus der Sicht des Malers . Wien ,
1982. [18] p. :
        NYPL [MAVZ (Vienna) 75-791 Nr.128]

Hoffbauer, Charles, 1875-1957. Charles Hoffbauer
(1875-1957) : drawings, temperas & oil
paintings. W. Sommerville, Mass. : Gropper Art
Gallery, [1977] [29] p. : ill. ; 21 x 27 cm.
"Research, text, and catalog design [by] Joseph
Gropper." Bibliography: p. [28]-[29]   DDC 759.4
1. Hoffbauer, Charles, 1875-1957. I. Gropper, Joseph.
II. Gropper Art Gallery.
N6853.H63 G76
        NYPL [3-MCO H698 81-412]

HOFFBAUER, CHARLES, 1875-1957.
Hoffbauer, Charles, 1875-1957. Charles
Hoffbauer (1875-1957) . W. Sommerville, Mass.
[1977] [29] p. :   DDC 759.4
N6853.H63 G76
        NYPL [3-MCO H698 81-412]

Hoffenberg, H. L.
Levine, Robert M. Cuba in the 1850s . Tampa ,
c1990. xv, 86 p. :   ISBN 0-8130-1010-1 (alk. paper)
    DDC 779/.99729105 20
F1763 .L65 1990
        NYPL [MFX (Fredricks) 91-3474]

**HOFFENBERG, H. L. - PHOTOGRAPH
    COLLECTIONS.**
Levine, Robert M. Cuba in the 1850s . Tampa ,
c1990. xv, 86 p. :   ISBN 0-8130-1010-1 (alk. paper)
    DDC 779/.99729105 20
F1763 .L65 1990
        NYPL [MFX (Fredricks) 91-3474]

Hoffman, Donald H. Arts for older adults : an
enhancement of life / Donald H. Hoffman.
Englewood Cliffs, N.J. : Prentice Hall, 1992. p.
cm. Includes bibliographical references and index.
    ISBN 0-13-048182-3   DDC 700/.1/03 20
1. Art and the aged - United States. I. Title.
NX180.A35 H64 1992

Hoffman, Moshe, 1938-1983.
Moshe Hoffman, woodcuts, 1966-1980 /
[editor, Uri Katz ; translation, Peretz Kidron].
Jerusalem : Jerusalem Print Workshop, c1989.
223 p. : ill. ; 32 cm.   ISBN 965-222-160-0
1. Hoffman, Moshe, 1938-1983 - Catalogues raisonnés.
I. Title.   NYPL [MDG+ (Hoffman) 90-10981]

**HOFFMAN, MOSHE, 1938-1983 -
    CATALOGUES RAISONNÉS.**
Hoffman, Moshe, 1938-1983. Moshe Hoffman,
woodcuts, 1966-1980 /. Jerusalem , c1989. 223
p. :   ISBN 965-222-160-0
        NYPL [MDG+ (Hoffman) 90-10981]

Hoffmann, Carla Schulz- see Schulz-Hoffmann,
Carla.

Hoffmann, Herbert, 1930- Museum für Kunst
und Gewerbe Hamburg. Antiker Gold- und
Silberschmuck . Mainz am Rhein , c1968. x,
246 p. :
NK7307 .H6   *NYPL [3-MNR 90-7024]*

**HOFFMANN, JOSEF FRANZ MARIA, 1870-
    1956.**
Muntoni, Alessandra. Il Palazzo Stoclet di Josef
Hoffmann, 1905-1911 /. Roma , 1989. 175 p. :
    ISBN 88-7597-102-1
        NYPL [MQW 91-4190]

Rochowanski, L. W. (Leopold Wolfgang), 1885-
Josef Hoffmann. Wien [c1950] 67 p.
NA1038.H6 R6
        NYPL [3-MQZ (Hoffmann) 90-6083]

Hoflehner, Rudolf, 1916-
Schmied, Wieland, 1929- Hoflehner, Wandel
und Kontinuität . [Stuttgart] , c1988. 316 p. :
    ISBN 3-608-76250-7
        NYPL [3-MGO+ (Hoflehner) 90-11980]

HOFLEHNER, RUDOLF, 1916- - CATALOGS.
Schmied, Wieland, 1929- Hoflehner, Wandel
und Kontinuität . [Stuttgart] , c1988. 316 p. :
    ISBN 3-608-76250-7
        NYPL [3-MGO+ (Hoflehner) 90-11980]

**HOFLEHNER, RUDOLF, 1916- - CRITICISM
    AND INTERPRETATION.**
Schmied, Wieland, 1929- Hoflehner, Wandel
und Kontinuität . [Stuttgart] , c1988. 316 p. :
    ISBN 3-608-76250-7
        NYPL [3-MGO+ (Hoflehner) 90-11980]

Hoflehner, Wandel und Kontinuität . Schmied,
Wieland, 1929- [Stuttgart] , c1988. 316 p. :
    ISBN 3-608-76250-7
        NYPL [3-MGO+ (Hoflehner) 90-11980]

Höfliger-Griesser, Yvonne. Spescha, Matias, 1925-
Matias Spescha /. Chur , 1987. 46 p. :
MLCS 89/21018 (N)
        NYPL [3-MCZ S751 90-2847]

Hofmaier, James. Max Beckmann : catalogue
raisonné of his prints / James Hofmaier. Bern :
Gallery Kornfeld, c1990. 2 v. (894 p.) : ill. ; 32
cm. Includes indexes. Bibliography: p. 878.
CONTENTS. - v 1. No. 1-179 -- v. 2. No. 180-373.
    ISBN 3-85773-024-2
1. Beckmann, Max, 1884-1950 - Catalogues raisonnés.
I. Beckmann, Max, 1884-1950. II. Title.
        NYPL [MDG+ (Beckmann) 90-11722]

Hofmann, Andrea, 1956- Bilder vom Bodensee .
Konstanz , 1987. 192 p. :   ISBN 3-7621-8000-8
    DDC 943/.462 20
DD801.C74 B5 1987
        NYPL [3-MAMY 90-11013]

Hofmann, Erich, 1924- Bilder vom Bodensee .
Konstanz , 1987. 192 p. :   ISBN 3-7621-8000-8
    DDC 943/.462 20
DD801.C74 B5 1987
        NYPL [3-MAMY 90-11013]

Hofmann, Gerhard, 1960-
Gerhard Hofmann : Werkverzeichnis der
Druckgraphik 1982-1990. Stuttgart : Manus
Presse, 1990. 63 p. : ill. ; 33 cm. "Preisliste der
Graphiken" (2 p.) inserted.
1. Hofmann, Gerhard, 1960- - Catalogs. I. Manus
Presse. II. Title.
        NYPL [MDG+ (Hofmann) 91-7588]

HOFMANN, GERHARD, 1960- - CATALOGS.
Hofmann, Gerhard, 1960- Gerhard Hofmann .
Stuttgart , 1990. 63 p. :
        NYPL [MDG+ (Hofmann) 91-7588]

Hofmann, Hans, 1880-1966.
Goodman, Cynthia. Hans Hofmann /. New
York , 1990. 200 p. :   ISBN 0-87427-070-7   DDC
    759.13 20
ND237.H667 A4 1990
        NYPL [3-MCK+ H71 90-12024]

Hans Hofmann, paintings on paper from the
1940s : January 6 to 27, 1990. New York :
André Emmerich Gallery, c1990. [21] p., 8
leaves of plates : ill. (chiefly col.) ; 30 cm.
1. Hofmann, Hans, 1880-1966 - Exhibitions. I. André
Emmerich Gallery. II. Title. III. Title: Paintings on
paper from the 1940s.
        NYPL [3-MCK+ H71 91-6604]

**HOFMANN, HANS, 1880-1966 -
    EXHIBITIONS.**
Goodman, Cynthia. Hans Hofmann /. New
York , 1990. 200 p. :   ISBN 0-87427-070-7   DDC
    759.13 20
ND237.H667 A4 1990
        NYPL [3-MCK+ H71 90-12024]

Hofmann, Hans, 1880-1966. Hans Hofmann,
paintings on paper from the 1940s . New
York , c1990. [21] p., 8 leaves of plates :
        NYPL [3-MCK+ H71 91-6604]

Hofmann, Karl Ludwig.
Frans Masereel, 1889-1972 . Saarbrücken ,
1989. 279 p. :   ISBN 3-922807-40-2
        NYPL [3-MCZ M396 91-4464]

Kunstsituation und Künstler sein heute .
Karlsruhe , 1988. 342 p. :
N6886.K33 K88 1988
        NYPL [3-MAMG 90-10706]

Masereel, Frans, 1889-1972. Frans Masereel
(1889-1972) . Saarbrücken , 1989. 280 p. :
    ISBN 3-922807-40-2   DDC 760/.092 20
N6973.M32 A4 1989

Hofmann, Richard, of Plauen im Vogtland.
Blätter und Blumen für Flächen-Decoration.
Selections. Hofmann, Richard, of Plauen
im Vogtland. Decorative flower and leaf
designs / Richard Hofmann. New York ,
1991. p. cm.   ISBN 0-486-26869-1   DDC 745.4
    20
NK1560 .H57 1991

Decorative flower and leaf designs / Richard
Hofmann. New York : Dover Publications,
1991. p. cm. (Dover design library) "A New selection
of motifs from the portfolio Blätter und Blumen für
Flächen-Decoration ... originally published ...
1885"--T.p. verso.   ISBN 0-486-26869-1   DDC 745.4
    20
1. Decoration and ornament - Plant forms. 2. Flowers
in art. 3. Leaves in art. I. Hofmann, Richard, of Plauen
im Vogtland. Blätter und Blumen für
Flächen-Decoration. Selections. II. Title. III. Series.
NK1560 .H57 1991

Hofmann, Werner, 1928-
The earthly paradise : art in the nineteenth
century / Werner Hofmann ; [translated from
the German by Brian Battershaw]. New York :
G. Braziller, 1961. 436 p. : ill. (some col.) ; 30
cm. Includes bibliographical references and indexes.
1. Art, Modern - 19th century. I. Title.
ND457 .H613   NYPL [3-MAL 90-10772]

Jürgen Partenheimer : Vasts apart : ein Zyklus
von 34 Zeichnungen und 11 Aquarellen /
Werner Hofmann. Hamburg : Hamburger

Kunsthalle, c1990. 1 v. (unpaged) : chiefly ill. (col.) ; 32 cm. Catalog of an exhibition held at the Hamburger Kunsthalle from Mar. 23 to Apr. 29, 1990. *1. Partenheimer, Jürgen - Exhibitions. I. Partenheimer, Jürgen. II. Hamburger Kunsthalle. III. Title. IV. Title: Vasts apart.*
N6888.P24 A4 1990

Klee, Paul, 1879-1940. Paul Klee . [Hamburg] [1990] 130 p. :
N6888.K55 A4 1990

Hofstätter, Hans Hellmut, 1928- Van Look : Lichthorizonte : Malerei 1982-86 / Hans H. Hofstätter. Waldkirch : Waldkircher Verlagsgesellschaft, 1987. 84 p. : ill. ; 32 cm. ISBN 3-87885-155-3
1. Look, Hans-Günther van, 1939-. I. Title.
IN PROCESS (ONLINE)
　　　　NYPL [3-MCK+ L863 91-4263]

Hofstra Museum.
Gelburd, Gail. The trans parent thread . [Hempstead, N.Y.] , Philadelphia, Pa. , c1990. 124 p. : ISBN 0-8122-1376-9 (pbk.)
　　　　NYPL [3-MAMT 91-4984]

New art van Amsterdam /. Hempstead, N.Y. , c1990. 16 p. : *NYPL [3-MAME 91-7061]*

Hofstra University, Hempstead, N. Y. Emily Lowe Gallery. see Emily Lowe Gallery.

Hogan, Janet, 1941- Balance 1990 . South Brisbane, Qld., Australia , c1990. 95 p. : ISBN 0-7242-3855-7　*NYPL [3-MADF 91-7104]*

Hogarth. Paulson, Ronald. New Haven, 1971. 2 v. ISBN 0-300-01388-4 DDC 760/.092 B 20
ND497.H7 P38　*NYPL [MCV H72.P33]*

Hogarth /. Paulson, Ronald. New Brunswick , c1991- v. <1- > : ISBN 0-8135-1694-3 (v. 1) DDC 760/.092 B 20
N6797.H6 P38 1991

HOGARTH PRESS.
Kennedy, Richard, 1910- A boy at the Hogarth Press /. London , 1972. x, 85 p., [1] folded leaf of plates : ISBN 0-435-18510-1
　　　　NYPL [3-MEM (Kennedy) 90-11892]

Hogarth, William 1697-1764.
Forrest, Ebenezer, fl. 1774. [Hogarth's peregrination.] An account of what seem'd most remarkable in the five days peregrination of the five following persons, vizt. Messieurs Tothall, Scott, Hogarth, Thornhill & Forrest, begun on Saturday, May 27th, 1723 and finished on the 31st of the same month /. Church Hanborough, Oxford , 1989 ([Didcot? England] : Didcot Press) [35] p. : DDC 760/.092 20
ND497.H7 F6 1989

Paulson, Ronald. Hogarth. New Haven, 1971. 2 v. ISBN 0-300-01388-4 DDC 760/.092 B 20
ND497.H7 P38　*NYPL [MCV H72.P33]*

Paulson, Ronald. Hogarth's graphic works /. London , 1989. xviii, 479 p. : ISBN 0-9514808-0-4 : DDC 769.92 20
NE642.H6 A4 1989

HOGARTH, WILLIAM 1697-1764.
Paulson, Ronald. Hogarth. New Haven, 1971. 2 v. ISBN 0-300-01388-4 DDC 760/.092 B 20
ND497.H7 P38　*NYPL [MCV H72.P33]*

Paulson, Ronald. Hogarth /. New Brunswick , c1991- v. <1- > : ISBN 0-8135-1694-3 (v. 1) DDC 760/.092 B 20
N6797.H6 P38 1991

HOGARTH, WILLIAM, 1697-1764 - CATALOGUES RAISONNÉS.
Paulson, Ronald. Hogarth's graphic works /. London , 1989. xviii, 479 p. : ISBN 0-9514808-0-4 : DDC 769.92 20
NE642.H6 A4 1989

HOGARTH, WILLIAM, 1697-1764 - JOURNEYS - ENGLAND.
Forrest, Ebenezer, fl. 1774. [Hogarth's peregrination.] An account of what seem'd most remarkable in the five days peregrination of the five following persons, vizt. Messieurs Tothall, Scott, Hogarth, Thornhill & Forrest, begun on Saturday, May 27th, 1723 and finished on the 31st of the same month /. Church Hanborough, Oxford , 1989 ([Didcot? England] : Didcot Press) [35] p. : DDC 760/.092 20
ND497.H7 F6 1989

Hogarth's graphic works /. Paulson, Ronald. London , 1989. xviii, 479 p. : ISBN

0-9514808-0-4 : DDC 769.92 20
NE642.H6 A4 1989

Hogarth's peregrination. Forrest, Ebenezer, fl. 1774. [Hogarth's peregrination.] An account of what seem'd most remarkable in the five days peregrination of the five following persons, vizt. Messieurs Tothall, Scott, Hogarth, Thornhill & Forrest, begun on Saturday, May 27th, 1723 and finished on the 31st of the same month /. Church Hanborough, Oxford , 1989 ([Didcot? England] : Didcot Press) [35] p. : DDC 760/.092 20
ND497.H7 F6 1989

Hogg, Ingeborg.
Zubillaga, Francisco. La Cartuja de Jerez de la Frontera =. Salzburg, Austria , 1978. [97] p. :
　　　　NYPL [3-MRBB 90-4725]

Zubillaga, Francisco. Las cartujas de las Cuevas, Cazalla de la Sierra y Granada =. Salzburg , 1979. [109] p. : DDC 726/.7/094682
NA5811.S4876 Z8
　　　　NYPL [3-MRBB+ 81-645]

Hogg, James.
Zubillaga, Francisco. La Cartuja de Jerez de la Frontera =. Salzburg, Austria , 1978. [97] p. :
　　　　NYPL [3-MRBB 90-4725]

Zubillaga, Francisco. Las cartujas de las Cuevas, Cazalla de la Sierra y Granada =. Salzburg , 1979. [109] p. : DDC 726/.7/094682
NA5811.S4876 Z8
　　　　NYPL [3-MRBB+ 81-645]

Hohl, Reinhold. Grösse–klein . Bern , c1989. 292 p. :　　　　*NYPL [3-MGI 91-5536]*

Hokusai. see Katsushika, Hokusai, 1760-1849.

Holabird & Roche (Chicago, Ill.)
Bruegmann, Robert. Holabird & Roche, Holabird & Root . New York , 1991. 3 v. : ISBN 0-8240-3974-2 : DDC 720/.92/2 20
NA737.H558 A4 1991
　　　　NYPL [MQWO+ 91-6811]

HOLABIRD & ROCHE (CHICAGO, ILL.) - CATALOGS.
Bruegmann, Robert. Holabird & Roche, Holabird & Root . New York , 1991. 3 v. : ISBN 0-8240-3974-2 : DDC 720/.92/2 20
NA737.H558 A4 1991
　　　　NYPL [MQWO+ 91-6811]

Holabird & Roche, Holabird & Root .
Bruegmann, Robert. New York , 1991. 3 v. : ISBN 0-8240-3974-2 : DDC 720/.92/2 20
NA737.H558 A4 1991
　　　　NYPL [MQWO+ 91-6811]

Holabird and Roche, Holabird and Root.
Bruegmann, Robert. Holabird & Roche, Holabird & Root . New York , 1991. 3 v. : ISBN 0-8240-3974-2 : DDC 720/.92/2 20
NA737.H558 A4 1991
　　　　NYPL [MQWO+ 91-6811]

Holabird & Root (Chicago, Ill.)
Bruegmann, Robert. Holabird & Roche, Holabird & Root . New York , 1991. 3 v. : ISBN 0-8240-3974-2 : DDC 720/.92/2 20
NA737.H558 A4 1991
　　　　NYPL [MQWO+ 91-6811]

HOLABIRD & ROOT (CHICAGO, ILL.) - CATALOGS.
Bruegmann, Robert. Holabird & Roche, Holabird & Root . New York , 1991. 3 v. : ISBN 0-8240-3974-2 : DDC 720/.92/2 20
NA737.H558 A4 1991
　　　　NYPL [MQWO+ 91-6811]

Holan, Jerri. Norwegian wood : a tradition of building / Jerri Holan ; foreword by Christian Norberg-Schulz. New York : Rizzoli, 1990. 208 p., [16] p. of plates : ill. (some col.), map, plans ; 26 cm. Includes index. Includes bibliographical references (p. 204-205). ISBN 0-8478-0954-4 : DDC 721/.0448/09485 19
1. Building, Wooden - Norway. 2. Architecture - Norway. I. Title.
NA1261 .H65 1989
　　　　NYPL [3-MQWE 91-4988]

Holanda, Francisco de. see Hollanda, Francisco de, 1517-1584.

Holberton, Paul. Palladio's villas : life in the Renaissance countryside / Paul Holberton. London : Murray, 1990. xiii, 256 p. : ill. ; 24 cm. Includes bibliography and index. ISBN 0-7195-4782-2 : DDC 720/.92/4 19

---

1. Palladio, Andrea, 1508-1580. 2. Architecture, Renaissance - Italy. 3. Architecture, Domestic - Italy. I. Title.
NA1123.P2
　　　　NYPL [3-MQZ (Palladio) 90-11020]

Holburne of Menstrie Museum. Gainsborough in Bath . Bath [England] [1988] 40 p. : ISBN 0-86197-081-0 (pbk.)
　　　　NYPL [3-MCV+ G14 89-28866]

Holeczek, Bernhard, 1941- Schumacher, Emil, 1912- Emil Schumacher . Braunschweig [1978] 204 p. :
N6888.S412 A4 1978
　　　　NYPL [3-MCK S389 81-546]

Holenstein, Werner. Werner Holenstein : [Venedig] / Herausgeber, Edition Galerie 6, Aarau. Aarau : Sauerländer, 1987. 92 p. : ill. (chiefly col.), port. ; 30 cm. Includes bibliographical references. ISBN 3-7941-2937-7
1. Holenstein, Werner. 2. Venice (Italy) in art. I. Galerie 6. II. Title. III. Title: Venedig.
　　　　NYPL [3-MCZ+ H729 89-28257]

HOLENSTEIN, WERNER.
Holenstein, Werner. Werner Holenstein . Aarau , 1987. 92 p. : ISBN 3-7941-2937-7
　　　　NYPL [3-MCZ+ H729 89-28257]

Holešovský, František. Čeští ilustrátoři v současné knize pro děti a mládež / František Holešovský. 1. vyd. Praha : Albatros, 1989. 455 p. : ill. ; 21 cm. Includes bibliographical references.
1. Illustrators - Czechoslovakia - Biography. 2. Children's literature, Czech - Illustrations. 3. Illustration of books - Czechoslovakia. I. Title.
NC989.C9 H62 1989

Holfeld, Anke, 1934-
Anke Holfeld : Aquarelle, 1977-1980 : Kunsthaus Hamburg, Galerie Elke Dröscher Hamburg, Overbeck-Gesellschaft Lübeck. [Hamburg] : Das Kunsthaus, [1980] 37 p. : ill. (some col.) ; 19 x 21 cm.
1. Holfeld, Anke, 1934- - Exhibitions. I. Kunsthaus Hamburg. II. Title.
MLCS 87/3478 (N)
　　　　NYPL [3-MCK H729 90-6357]

HOLFELD, ANKE, 1934- - EXHIBITIONS.
Holfeld, Anke, 1934- Anke Holfeld . [Hamburg] [1980] 37 p. :
MLCS 87/3478 (N)
　　　　NYPL [3-MCK H729 90-6357]

Holgate, Edwin, 1892-1977.
Thom, Ian M. (Ian MacEwan), 1952- The prints of Edwin Holgate =. Kleinburg, Ont. , c1989. [69] p. : ISBN 0-7729-6098-4 DDC 769.92 20
　　　　NYPL [MDG (Holgate) 91-5843]

HOLGATE, EDWIN, 1892-1977 - EXHIBITIONS.
Thom, Ian M. (Ian MacEwan), 1952- The prints of Edwin Holgate =. Kleinburg, Ont. , c1989. [69] p. : ISBN 0-7729-6098-4 DDC 769.92 20
　　　　NYPL [MDG (Holgate) 91-5843]

Holger, Lena.
Tenggren, Gustaf, 1896- Från svenska sagor till amerikansk fantasi . Stockholm [1990] 77 p. : ISBN 91-7100-389-4
NC986.5.T46 A4 1990

Venetianska teckningar från École des beaux-arts, Paris . Stockholm [1990] 165 p. : ISBN 90-71003-80-0
NC256.V4 V4 1990

Holl, Erwin, 1957-
Erwin Holl : Landschaften. Stuttgart : Edition Cantz, 1989. 64 p. : ill. (some col.) ; 30 cm. "Eine Debütantenausstellung der Staatlichen Akademie der Bildenden Künste Stuttgart im September 1989 im Künstlerhaus Stuttgart e.V."--Colophon. ISBN 3-89322-107-7
1. Holl, Erwin, 1957- - Exhibitions. I. Staatliche Akademie der Bildenden Künste Stuttgart. II. Künstlerhaus Stuttgart. III. Title.
　　　　NYPL [3-MCK+ H733 91-7978]

HOLL, ERWIN, 1957- - EXHIBITIONS.
Holl, Erwin, 1957- Erwin Holl . Stuttgart , 1989. 64 p. : ISBN 3-89322-107-7
　　　　NYPL [3-MCK+ H733 91-7978]

Holl, Steven.
Edge of a city / Steven Holl. New York : Princeton Architectural Press, 1991. p. cm. (Pamphlet architecture . #13) ISBN 1-87827-156-3 :

DDC 711/.4/09048 20
1. City planning - History - 20th century. 2. Architecture and society. I. Series: Pamphlet architecture , no. 13. II. Title.
NA9095 .H65 1991

14x Amerika-Gedenkbibliothek . Berlin , c1989. 132 p. :   ISBN 3-433-02288-7 (pbk.)
NYPL [3-MQWO+ 90-11060]

Hollamby, Edward. Red House : Bexleyheath 1859 : architect, Philip Webb / text, Edward Hollamby ; photographs, Charlotte Wood ; foreword, Sir Hugh Casson. London : Architecture and Design Technology Press : New York : Van Nostrand Reinhold, 1991. [60] p. : ill. (some col.), plans ; 30 cm. (Architecture in detail . 03) Includes bibliographical references.
ISBN 1-85454-704-6 (pbk.) :   DDC 724.6 20
1. Webb, Philip, 1831-1915. 2. Architecture, Modern - 19th century. 3. Architecture, Modern - 20th century. I. Title. II. Series.
NA645.5.A
NYPL [3-MQZ+ (Webb) 91-6981]

Holland. see Netherlands.

Holland, Patricia. Family snaps . London , 1991. 252 p. :   ISBN 1-85381-270-6 (pbk)   DDC 778.92619 20
TR681.F28   *NYPL [MFW 91-6707]*

Holland, Stephanie K. All about creative textiles / Stephanie K. Holland. Oxford : Oxford University Press, 1988, c1987. 80 p. : ill. (some col.) ; 25 cm. Includes index.   ISBN 0-19-832737-4 (pbk)   DDC 746 19
I. Title.
TT699   *NYPL [3-MON 90-12316]*

Hollanda, Francisco de, 1517-1584. Album dos desenhos das antigualhas de Francisco de Holanda / introdução e notas, José da Felicidade Alves. Lisboa : Livros Horizonte, c1989. 54, 54, 73 p., [5] folded leaves of plates : ill. (some col.) ; 29 cm. Includes bibliographical references (p. 15, 3rd group).
ISBN 972-240-733-3   DDC 741.9469 20
1. Hollanda, Francisco de, 1517-1584 - Catalogs. 2. Classicism in art - Catalogs. I. Alves, José da Felicidade. II. Title.
NC290.H65 A4 1989

HOLLANDA, FRANCISCO DE, 1517-1584 - CATALOGS.
Hollanda, Francisco de, 1517-1584. Album dos desenhos das antigualhas de Francisco de Holanda / . Lisboa , c1989. 54, 54, 73 p., [5] folded leaves of plates :   ISBN 972-240-733-3   DDC 741.9469 20
NC290.H65 A4 1989

Hollander, John.
Briganti, Giuliano. William Bailey / . New York , 1991. 195 p. :   ISBN 0-8478-1345-2 :   DDC 759.13 20
N6537.B16 A4 1991

Landscape painting, 1960-1990 : the Italian tradition in American art / catalog essay by John Hollander. Charleston, S.C. : Gibbes Museum of Art, 1990. 70 p. : col. ill. ; 28 cm. Catalog of an exhibition held in conjunction with the Spoleto Festival USA 1990. Exhibition held at Gibbes Museum of Art, Charleston, South Carolina, May 25-July 4, 1990 and Bayly Museum of Art, University of Virginia, Charlottesville, Virginia, August 7-September 30, 1990. Bruno Civitico, Guest curator. Bibliography: p. 64-69.
1. Landscape painting - 20th century - United States - Exhibitions. 2. Landscape painting, American - Exhibitions. I. Gibbes Museum of Art (Charleston, S.C.). II. University of Virginia. Art Museum. III. Spoleto Festival U. S.A. (1990). IV. Title. V. Title: Italian tradition in American art.
NYPL [3-MCW 91-4635]

Hollander, Stacy C. Warren, Elizabeth V. Expressions of a new spirit . New York , c1989. 168 p. :   ISBN 0-912161-01-9   DDC 745/.0973/0747471 20
NK805 .W33 1989
NYPL [3-MNE 90-12958]

Holländische Malerei des siebzehnten Jahrhunderts. Olbrich, Harald. Holländische Malerei des 17. Jahrhunderts / . Leipzig , c1990. 300 p. :   ISBN 3-7338-0059-1   DDC 759.9492/09/032 20
ND646 .O4 1990

Holländische Malerei des 17. Jahrhunderts / . Olbrich, Harald. Leipzig , c1990. 300 p. :

ISBN 3-7338-0059-1   DDC 759.9492/09/032 20
ND646 .O4 1990

Hollandse en vlaamse kunst uit de 17e eeuw : hoogtepunten van minder bekende meesters / schilderijen en tekeningen uit de verzameling F. C. Butôt ; Museum Boymans-van Beuningen, 16 Februari--1 April 1973. [Rotterdam, The Museum, 1973?] 183 p. : chiefly ill. ; 25 cm. Bibliography : p. [7]
1. Butôt, F. C. - Art collections - Exhibitions. 2. Art, Flemish - Private collections - Exhibitions. 3. Art, Dutch - Private collections - Exhibitions. 4. Art, Modern - 17th-18th centuries - Netherlands - Private collections - Exhibitions. I. Museum Boymans-van Beuningen.   *NYPL [3-MAME 90-5901]*

Hollar, Wenceslaus, 1607-1677.
Berge, Mària van. Wenzel Hollar, 1607-1677 . Paris , 1979. 77 p., [15] leaves of plates :
NE642.H7 A4 1979
NYPL [3-MCZ H737 81-151]

HOLLAR, WENCESLAUS, 1607-1677 - EXHIBITIONS.
Berge, Mària van. Wenzel Hollar, 1607-1677 . Paris , 1979. 77 p., [15] leaves of plates :
NE642.H7 A4 1979
NYPL [3-MCZ H737 81-151]

Hollenstein, Roman. Buchser, Frank, 1828-1890. Frank Buchser 1828-1890 . Einsiedeln , c1990. 284 p. :   *NYPL [3-MCZ+ B92 91-8120]*

Hollweck, Ludwig. Joseph Kaspar Sattler : ein Wegbereiter des Judgendstils / Ludwig Hollweck, Hannes Schultes ; mit Beiträgen von Dieter Distl, Klaus Englert und Reinhard Horn. Pfaffenhofen : W. Ludwig, c1988. 156 p. : ill. (some col.) ; 21 cm. (Schrobenhausener Kunstreihe . vol.2) Includes bibliographical references.   ISBN 3-7787-2090-2
1. Sattler, Joseph, 1867-1931. 2. Art nouveau - Germany. I. Schultes, Hannes. II. Title. III. Series.
IN PROCESS (ONLINE)
NYPL [MDG (Sattler) 90-5109]

Hollywood at home . Avery, Sid. New York , c1990. 144 p. :   ISBN 0-517-57696-1 :
PN1998.2 .A85 1990
NYPL [MFX (Avery) 91-5134]

Holm, Lars. Kitsch & konkret . København , 1990. 95 p. :   ISBN 87-89556-00-3 :
NX558.A1 K58 1990

Holme, C. Geoffrey (Charles Geoffrey), 1887-1954. Dodgson, Campbell, 1867-1948. The etchings of Charles Meryon / . London , 1921. vii, 28 p., 47 leaves of plates :
NF2115.M6 D6
NYPL [MDG+ (Méryon) 91-6349]

HOLMES À COURT, ROBERT - ART COLLECTIONS - EXHIBITIONS.
Contemporary aboriginal art from the Robert Holmes à Court Collection . Perth , 1990. 125 p. :   ISBN 0-7316-8569-5
NYPL [3-MADF+ 91-4291]

Holmes, David B. (David Bryan), 1936- David B. Holmes : an American journey : recent paintings commemorating the bicentennial of the United States Constitution : November 12 through December 12, 1987. New York : Wally Findlay Galleries, [1987?] 20 p. : ill. ; 21 cm.
1. Holmes, David B. (David Bryan), 1936- - Exhibitions. I. Wally Findlay Galleries. II. Title. III. Title: American journey.
NYPL [3-MCZ H75 90-11603]

HOLMES, DAVID B. (DAVID BRYAN), 1936- - EXHIBITIONS.
Holmes, David B. (David Bryan), 1936- David B. Holmes . New York [1987?] 20 p. :
NYPL [3-MCZ H75 90-11603]

Holmes, Kristin, 1955- The Victorian express / text and photography by Kristin Holmes & David Watersun. Wilsonville, Or. : Beautiful America Pub. Co., c1991. p. cm. Includes bibliographical references and index.   ISBN 0-89802-568-0 :   DDC 728/.37/097309034 20
1. Architecture, Victorian - United States. 2. Architecture, Modern - 19th century - United States. 3. Architecture - United States. 4. Architecture - United States. I. Watersun, David, 1952-. II. Title.
NA710.5.V5 H64 1991

Holmes, Mary Tavener. Nicolas Lancret, 1690-1743 : by Mary Tavener Holmes ; edited by Joseph Focarino. New York : H.N. Abrams

in association with the Frick Collection, 1992. p. cm. Includes bibliographical references and index.
ISBN 0-8109-3559-7   DDC 759.4 20
1. Lancret, Nicolas, 1690-1743 - Exhibitions. I. Focarino, Joseph. II. Frick Collection. III. Title.
ND553.L2293 A4 1991

Holmila, Ilkka. Kautto, Jussi, 1942- Suomalaista kaupunkiarkkitehtuuria =. Helsinki , 1990. 233 p. :   ISBN 951-9229-63-9
NA9241.F5 K38 1990

Holografie in der Bundesrepublik Deutschland : Ausstellung im Konzertsaal des Kurhauses Bad Rothenfelde / Schirmherr, Johann-Tönnjes Cassens ; [Herausgeber, Deutsche Gesellschaft für Holografie e.V. und HolografieGalerie Bad Rothenfelde ; Katalogredaktion, Peter Zec ; Assistenz, Claudia Oražem]. [Osnabrück] : Deutsche Gesellschaft für Holografie, c1989. 114 p. : ill. (some col.) ; 21 cm. Catalog of an exhibition held Sept. 1-30, 1989. One hologram pasted on added t.p. Includes bibliographical references (p. 71-75).   ISBN 3-88984-102-3   DDC 621.36/75/0943 20
1. Holography - Germany (West) - History - Exhibitions. I. Zec, Peter. II. Oražem, Claudia. III. Kurhaus Bad Rothenfelde. Konzertsaal. IV. Deutsche Gesellschaft für Holografie. V. HolografieGalerie Bad Rothenfelde.
QC449 .H57 1989   *NYPL [MFW 90-11263]*

HolografieGalerie Bad Rothenfelde. Holografie in der Bundesrepublik Deutschland . [Osnabrück] , c1989. 114 p. :   ISBN 3-88984-102-3   DDC 621.36/75/0943 20
QC449 .H57 1989   *NYPL [MFW 90-11263]*

HOLOGRAPHY - GERMANY (WEST) - HISTORY - EXHIBITIONS.
Holografie in der Bundesrepublik Deutschland . [Osnabrück] , c1989. 114 p. :   ISBN 3-88984-102-3   DDC 621.36/75/0943 20
QC449 .H57 1989   *NYPL [MFW 90-11263]*

Holsten, Siegmar. Kunst in der Residenz . [Karlsruhe] [1990] 399 p. :   ISBN 3-925835-58-X   DDC 709/.43/4643074434643 20
N6886.K33 K85 1990

Holten, Ragnar von, 1934- Nemes, Endre, 1909- Endre Nemes . [Stockholm] , 1990. 112 p. :   ISBN 91-7100-400-9
N5078.S8 S8 Nr. 237 N7093.N45

Holtje, Adrienne Kriebel. Szeglin, Charles B. Creativities! . West Nyack, N.Y. , c1991. p. cm.   ISBN 0-13-189804-3   DDC 372.5/044 20
N362 .S95 1991

Hołubiec, Jerzy. Polskie lampy i świeczniki / Jerzy W. Hołubiec. Wrocław : Zakład Narodowy im. Ossolińskich, Wydawn., 1990. 176 p., [190] p. of plates : ill. (some col.) ; 19 x 21 cm. "Polskie rzemiosło i polski przemysł"--Jacket. Includes bibliographical references (p. 155-[158]).
ISBN 83-04-02227-3
1. Lamps - Poland - History. 2. Candlesticks - Poland - History. 3. Lighting - Poland - History. I. Title.
NK6196 .H65 1990

HOLY CARDS - GERMANY - HISTORY.
Lepovitz, Helena Waddy, 1945- Images of faith . Athens , c1991. xviii, 228 p. :   ISBN 0-8203-1256-8 (alk. paper)   DDC 760/.04482/094336 20
NK5435.G3 L4 1991
NYPL [3-MRY 91-4876]

HOLY CARDS - TRANSYLVANIA - EXHIBITIONS.
Xilogravura populară din Transilvania în sec. XVIII-XIX /. [Bucureşti] 1970. [143] p. :
NE958.3.R6 X54   *NYPL [MDON 90-5753]*

Holy image, holy space--icons & frescoes from Greece. Part II, A theology in colors [videorecording] / Astoria, NY : Go-Telecom, c1988. 1 videocassette (28 min., 30 sec.) : sd., col. ; 1/2 in. (Illuminations . 11) Cataloged from contributor's data. Photographer, John Krol ; editor, Stuart Neal. VHS. This is the second part of a documentary taped at the Walters Art Gallery in Baltimore, Md., and hosted by medieval and Byzantine art curator Dr. Gary Vikan, which focuses on icons as objects of religious worship and artistic achievement.   DDC 704.9 11
1. Art, Byzantine. 2. Christian art and symbolism - Medieval, 500-1500. 3. Orthodox Eastern Church and art. I. Vikan, Gary. II. Go-Telecom (Firm). III. Title: Theology in colors. IV. Series: Illuminations (Astoria,

N.Y.) , 11.
N7852.5

Holy Orthodox Eastern Catholic and Apostolic Church. see Orthodox Eastern Church.

Holy Scriptures. see Bible.

HOLY SEPULCHER IN ART.
Feuchtmayr, Andrea. Kulissenheiliggräber im Barock . München , c1989. 139, [26] p. of plates :   ISBN 3-88073-309-0
ND2725 .F48 1989

Holz, Irmgard.
Josef Wopfner, 1843-1927 / Irmgard Holz ; Text, Alexander Rauch. Rosenheim : Rosenheimer Verlagshaus, c1989. 255 p. : ill. (some col.) ; 26 x 30 cm. (Rosenheimer Raritäten) Includes bibliographical references (p. 46-47).   ISBN 3-475-52594-1 :   DDC 759.3 20
1. Wopfner, Josef, 1843-1927 - Catalogs. I. Wopfner, Josef, 1843-1927. II. Rauch, Alexander. III. Title.
ND588.W76 A4 1989

Josef Wopfner 1843-1927 / Irmgard Holz ; Text, Alexander Rauch. Rosenheim : Rosenheimer, c1989. 255 p. : ill. (some col.) ; 26 x 30 cm. (Rosenheimer Raritäten) Includes bibliographical references.   ISBN 3-475-52594-1
1. Wopfner, Josef, 1843-1927 - Catalogues raisonnés. 2. Wopfner, Josef, 1843-1927. II. Rauch, Alexander. III. Title.
NYPL [3-MCK+ W915 90-12081]

HOLZER, JENNY, 1950- - EXHIBITIONS.
Auping, Michael. Jenny Holzer . Buffalo, N.Y. , 1991. p. cm. ISBN 0-914782-80-0 DDC 709/.2 20
N6537.H577 A4 1991

Holzkonstruktionen, Fotogramme, Zeichnungen.
Megyik, János, 1938- János Megyik . Wien [1988] 39 p. :   ISBN 3-900776-02-8 DDC 709.2 20
N6822.5.M48 A4 1988
NYPL [3-MGO+ (Megyik) 90-11666]

Die Holzskulpturen des Mittelalters (1000-1400) /. Schnütgen-Museum. Köln , 1989. 381 p. :
NYPL [3-MGI 91-4187]

Homage to Béla Czóbel, 1883-1976 . Czóbel, Béla, 1883- Chicago, Ill. , 1990. 64 p. :
NYPL [3-MCZ C998 91-6706]

Homage to Ian Hamilton Finlay. Finlay, Ian Hamilton. London [1987] 22 p., 22 p. of plates :   **NYPL [MEMZ 91-2445]**

Homburger Gespräche (9th : 1987 : Kiel, Germany) Austausch und Verbindungen in der Kunstgeschichte des Ostseeraums . Kiel , 1988. 207 p., [8] p. of plates :
IN PROCESS (ONLINE)
NYPL [3-MAM+ 91-4693]

HOME.
Rockness, Miriam Huffman, 1944- Home, God's design . Grand Rapids, Mich. , c1990. 245 p. ; ISBN 0-310-59081-7 DDC 728/.01 20
NA7125 .R55 1990 **NYPL [3-MRG 91-5022]**

HOME DECORATION. see INTERIOR DECORATION.

HOME DESIGN. see ARCHITECTURE, DOMESTIC.

The home design handbook . Myrvang, June Cotner. New York , c1992. p. cm. ISBN 0-8050-1833-6 DDC 728 20
NA7115 .M97 1992

HOME FURNISHINGS. see HOUSE FURNISHINGS.

Home, God's design . Rockness, Miriam Huffman, 1944- Grand Rapids, Mich. , c1990. 245 p. ;   ISBN 0-310-59081-7 DDC 728/.01 20
NA7125 .R55 1990 **NYPL [3-MRG 91-5022]**

HOME REMODELING. see DWELLINGS - REMODELING.

Homecoming . Hancock, Jane H., 1949- St. Paul , c1991. x, 116 p. : ISBN 0-87351-259-6 DDC 759.05/074/74776581 20
N6450 .H298 1991

Homecoming . Powell, Richard J., 1953- Washington, D.C. [1991] p. ISBN 0-8478-1421-1 : DDC 759.13 20
ND237.J73 P69 1991

Homenaje a Carlos Mérida . González Goyri, Roberto. [Guatemala] [1985?] 17, [2] p. :
N6578.M47 A4 1985

Homenaje a Federico Sescosse : un hombre, un

destino y un lugar / Clara Bargellini ... [et al.].1. ed. [Zacatecas, Mexico] : Gobierno del Estado de Zacatecas, 1990. xi, 140 p., [46] p. of plates : ill. (some col.) ; 24 cm. Includes bibliographical references. DDC 709/.72 20
1. Art, Mexican - Themes, motives. I. Sescosse, Federico. II. Bargellini, Clara.
N6550 .H65 1990

Homenaje a Jorge Luis Borges. Toledo, Francisco, 1940- Zoología fantástica . México , 1989. 58 p. :   **NYPL [3-MCZ T649 91-6144]**

Homenaje a Santos Balmori en su nonagésimo aniversario. Balmori, Santos. Homenaje a Santos 90 Balmori en su nonagésimo aniversario . [Mexico] [1989] 1 v. (unpaged) : DDC 709/.2 20
N6559.B35 A4 1989
NYPL [3-MCZ B193 91-5072]

Homenaje a Santos 90 Balmori en su nonagésimo aniversario . Balmori, Santos. [Mexico] [1989] 1 v. (unpaged) : DDC 709/.2 20
N6559.B35 A4 1989
NYPL [3-MCZ B193 91-5072]

Homer Watson, R.C.A., 1855-1936 . Watson, Homer, 1855-1936. Ottawa , 1963. 1 v. (unpaged) : DDC 759.11 20
N6549.W37 A4 1963

Homer, Winslow, 1836-1910.
Robertson, Bruce, 1955- Reckoning with Winslow Homer . Cleveland, Ohio , 1990. xvi, 196 p. : ISBN 0-940717-02-6 DDC 759.13 20
ND237.H7 A4 1990
NYPL [3-MCX H76 91-3391]

Winslow Homer at the Addison : [exhibition] April 12 through June 10, 1990. Andover, Mass. : Addison Gallery of American Art, 1990. 95 p. : ill. (some col.) ; 23 x 28 cm. Essay by Jock Reynolds and Susan C. Faxon. Includes bibliographical references (p. 70).
1. Homer, Winslow, 1836-1910 - Exhibitions. I. Reynolds, Jock. II. Faxon, Susan C. III. Addison Gallery of American Art. IV. Title.
NYPL [3-MCX H76 90-13073]

Winslow Homer in Gloucester / essays by D. Scott Atkinson and Jochen Wierich ; edited by Sue Taylor. Chicago, Ill. : Terra Museum of American Art, c1990. 112 p. : ill. (some col.) ; 24 x 31 cm. Catalog of an exhibition held at the Terra Museum of American Art, Oct. 20-Dec. 30, 1990. Includes bibliographical references (p. 110-111).   ISBN 0-8478-1315-0
1. Homer, Winslow, 1836-1910 - Exhibitions. 2. Gloucester (Mass.) in art - Exhibitions. I. Atkinson, D. Scott, 1953-. II. Wierich, Jochen. III. Taylor, Sue, 1949-. IV. Terra Museum of American Art. V. Title.
NYPL [3-MCX+ H76 91-5348]

HOMER, WINSLOW, 1836-1910.
Cikovsky, Nicolai. Winslow Homer /. New York , 1990. 156 p. : ISBN 0-8109-1193-0 DDC 759.13 B 20
ND237.H7 C54 1990
NYPL [3-MCX+ H76 91-6394]

HOMER, WINSLOW, 1836-1910 - CRITICISM AND INTERPRETATION.
Tatham, David. Winslow Homer and the illustrated book /. Syracuse, N.Y. , 1992. p. cm.   ISBN 0-8156-2550-2 DDC 741.6/4/092 20
NC975.5.H65 T38 1992

HOMER, WINSLOW, 1836-1910 - CRITICISM AND INTERPRETATION - CONGRESSES.
Winslow Homer . Washington , Hanover, N.H. , 1990. 156 p. : ISBN 0-89468-132-X DDC 759.13 20
ND237.H7 W56 1990

HOMER, WINSLOW, 1836-1910 - EXHIBITIONS.
Brooklyn Museum. Curator's choice . [Brooklyn, N.Y. , 1990] 1 folded sheet ([8] p.) :
NYPL [3-MCX H76 91-7969]

Homer, Winslow, 1836-1910. Winslow Homer at the Addison . Andover, Mass. , 1990. 95 p. :
NYPL [3-MCX H76 90-13073]

Homer, Winslow, 1836-1910. Winslow Homer in Gloucester /. Chicago, Ill. , c1990. 112 p. :   ISBN 0-8478-1315-0
NYPL [3-MCX+ H76 91-5348]

Robertson, Bruce, 1955- Reckoning with Winslow Homer . Cleveland, Ohio , 1990. xvi,

196 p. : ISBN 0-940717-02-6 DDC 759.13 20
ND237.H7 A4 1990
NYPL [3-MCX H76 91-3391]

Winslow Homer in the 1890s . New York , c1990. 154 p. : ISBN 1-555-95042-6 (alk. paper) : DDC 759.13 20
ND237.H7 A4 1990b
NYPL [3-MCX H76 90-13349]

HOMER, WINSLOW, 1836-1910 - HOMES AND HAUNTS - MAINE - PROUTS NECK.
Winslow Homer in the 1890s . New York , c1990. 154 p. : ISBN 1-555-95042-6 (alk. paper) : DDC 759.13 20
ND237.H7 A4 1990b
NYPL [3-MCX H76 90-13349]

HOMER, WINSLOW, 1836-1910 - INFLUENCE - EXHIBITIONS.
Robertson, Bruce, 1955- Reckoning with Winslow Homer . Cleveland, Ohio , 1990. xvi, 196 p. : ISBN 0-940717-02-6 DDC 759.13 20
ND237.H7 A4 1990
NYPL [3-MCX H76 91-3391]

HOMES. see DWELLINGS.

Homes for pleasant living. Farmer, W. D. (William Davis) [Homes for pleasant living.] W.D. Farmer presents homes for pleasant living. Atlanta, Ga. (P.O. Box 450025, Atlanta 30345) , c1989. 16 p. : DDC 728/.37/0223 20
NA7205 .F37 1989

HOMESITES - ISRAEL.
Israel builds. [Jerusalem , 1964] 1 v. (unpaged) :
NA9051 .I77 1964

Hommage a l'art français. Hyldest til Fransk Kunst . København, 1967. 115 p. :
NYPL [3-MBH 90-5670]

Hommage à Paul Delvaux : [exposition], 8 juillet - 25 septembre 1977. Bruxelles, [r. du Musée 9] : Musées royaux des beaux-arts de Belgique, [1977] [68] p. : Ill. (some col.) ; 19 x 21 cm. Catalog by S. Houbart-Wilkin. Bibliography: p. [66]
1. Delvaux, Paul - Exhibitions. I. Delvaux, Paul. II. Houbart-Wilkin, Suzanne. III. Brussels. Musées royaux des beaux-arts de Belgique.
N6973.D44 A4 1977
NYPL [3-MCH D32 81-766]

Hommage au Millénaire du baptême de la Russie. Icônes et merveilles . Paris , c[1988] [116] p. : ISBN 2-905197-10-2
NYPL [3-MAIH 91-5048]

HOMOSEXUALITY IN ART.
Barkan, Leonard. Transuming passion . Stanford, Calif. , 1991. 147 p. : ISBN 0-8047-1851-2 (cloth : acid-free paper) : DDC 700 20
NX652.G35 B37 1991
NYPL [3-MAMZ 91-6123]

HONDURAS - CARICATURES AND CARTOONS.
Banegas, Angel Darío. Y reír es de sabios /. Tegucigalpa, Honduras , 1989. 1 v. (unpaged) :
NYPL [3-MDY 90-11033]

HONDURAS - GAZETTEERS.
Instituto Geográfico Nacional (Honduras). Sección Diccionario Geográfico. Nombres geográficos de Honduras /. [Tegucigalpa] [1976?- v. :
F1502 .I57 1976a **NYPL [Map Div. 91-81]**

Honegger, Gottfried, 1917- Lemoine, Serge. Aurélie Nemours /. Zürich , Reutlingen , c1989. 254 p. : ISBN 3-908080-28-2
NYPL [3-MCO N436 90-8474]

Honegger, Karl Lukas, 1902- Mein Leben und Werk : Maler und Bildhauer wider den Zeitgeist / Karl Lukas Honegger.1. Aufl. Stein am Rhein : Christiana-Verlag, 1990. 528 p. : ill. (some col.) ; 22 cm. ISBN 3-7171-0934-0 DDC 709/.2 B 20
1. Honegger, Karl Lukas, 1902-. 2. Artists - Switzerland - Biography. I. Title.
N7153.H654 A2 1990

HONEGGER, KARL LUKAS, 1902-
Honegger, Karl Lukas, 1902- Mein Leben und Werk . Stein am Rhein , 1990. 528 p. : ISBN 3-7171-0934-0 DDC 709/.2 B 20
N7153.H654 A2 1990

Honey, Sandra. Mies van der Rohe . London ,
New York , 1986. 112 p. : ISBN 0-85670-685-X
DDC 720/.92/4 19
NA1088.M65 M54 1986 ***NYPL [3-MQZ+***
(Mies van der Rohe) 86-3545]

Hong Kong Bank. Williams, Stephanie. Hongkong
Bank . Boston, c1989. 302 p. : ISBN
0-316-94238-3 : DDC 725/.24/095125 20
NA6245.C62 H668 1989
NYPL [3-MQZ (Foster) 91-4484]

HONGKONG AND SHANGHAI BANKING
CORPORATION - BUILDINGS.
Williams, Stephanie. Hongkong Bank . Boston ,
c1989. 302 p. : ISBN 0-316-94238-3 : DDC
725/.24/095125 20
NA6245.C62 H668 1989
NYPL [3-MQZ (Foster) 91-4484]

Hongkong Bank . Williams, Stephanie. Boston ,
c1989. 302 p. : ISBN 0-316-94238-3 : DDC
725/.24/095125 20
NA6245.C62 H668 1989
NYPL [3-MQZ (Foster) 91-4484]

Honisch, Dieter.
Grösse--klein . Bern , c1989. 292 p. :
NYPL [3-MGI 91-5536]

[Uecker. English]
Uecker / Dieter Honisch ; translated from
the German by Robert Erich Wolf. New
York : Abrams, [1986] 268 p. : ill. (some
col.) ; 34 cm. Translation of: Uecker. Includes
index. Bibliography: p. 265-267. ISBN
0-8109-1707-6 DDC 709/.2/4 19
1. Uecker, Günther, 1930- - Criticism and
interpretation. 2. Uecker, Günther, 1930- - Catalogs. I.
Title.
N6888.U37 H6613 1986
NYPL [3-MCK+ U125 86-4379]

Honnef, Klaus.
Andy Warhol 1928-1987 : Kunst als Kommerz
/ Klaus Honnef. Köln : B. Taschen, c1989. 95
p. : ill. ; 31 cm. ISBN 3-8228-0255-7
1. Warhol, Andy, 1928-. I. Title.
NYPL [3-MCX+ W27 91-4180]

Tony Munzlinger : ich bin ein Dinosaurier /
Klaus Honnef. Bad Honnef : K.H. Bock,
[1990?]. 240 p. : ill. ; 22 x 24 cm. ISBN
3-87066-217-4
1. Munzlinger, Tony - Exhibitions. I. Munzlinger, Tony.
II. Rheinisches Landesmuseum in Bonn. III. Title.
NYPL [3-MCK M975 90-13085]

Honolulu Academy of Arts.
Brandon, Reiko Mochinaga. Textile art of
Okinawa /. Honolulu , 1990. viii, 46 p. : ISBN
0-937426-12-1 DDC 746.9/2/09522907496931
20
NK8984.A3 O383 1990
NYPL [3-MON 91-3749]

Saville, Jennifer, 1955- Georgia O'Keeffe,
paintings of Hawai'i /. Honolulu , 1990. 79 p. :
ISBN 0-937426-11-3 DDC 759.13 20
ND237 .O5A4 1990
NYPL [3-MCX O41 90-12481]

Visions of the Dharma : Japanese Buddhist
paintings and prints in the Honolulu Academy
of Arts / [compiled by] Stephen Little.
Honolulu : The Academy, 1991. p. cm. Includes
bibliographical references and index. ISBN
0-937426-14-8 (alk. paper) : DDC
760/.048943/09520749693 1 20
1. Art, Japanese - Catalogs. 2. Art, Buddhist - Japan -
Catalogs. 3. Art - Hawaii - Honolulu - Catalogs. 4.
Honolulu Academy of Arts - Catalogs. I. Little,
Stephen, 1954-. II. Title.
N7352 .H66 1991

HONOLULU ACADEMY OF ARTS -
CATALOGS.
Honolulu Academy of Arts. Visions of the
Dharma . Honolulu , 1991. p. cm. ISBN
0-937426-14-8 (alk. paper) : DDC
760/.048943/09520749693 1 20
N7352 .H66 1991

Shibata, Zeshin, 1807-1891. The art of Shibata
Zeshin . [London] [Honolulu] , c1979. 195 p. :
ISBN 0-903697-05-X DDC 709/.2/4
N7359.S46 A4 1979
NYPL [3-MAG+ 91-6922]

Honoré Daumier . Daumier, Honoré, 1808-1879.
Wien [1938] xxxxviii p., 196 p. of plates :
NYPL [3-MCO D24 89-27412]

Honoré Daumier . Daumier, Honoré, 1808-1879.
Ingelheim am Rhein , 1971. 1 v. (unpaged) :
NYPL [3-MCO D24 90-6296]

Honour, Hugh.
The Venetian hours of Henry James, Whistler,
Sargent / Hugh Honour & John Fleming. 1st
U. S. ed. Boston : Little, Brown, c1991. p. cm.
"A Bulfinch Press book." Includes index. ISBN
0-8212-1861-1 DDC 700 20
1. Arts, American. 2. James, Henry, 1843-1916 -
Criticism and interpretation. 3. Sargent, John Singer,
1856-1925 - Criticism and interpretation. 4. Whistler,
James McNeill, 1834-1903 - Criticism and interpretion.
5. Venice in art. 6. Venice in literature. I. Fleming,
John, 1919-. II. Title.
NX653.V46 H66 1991

The visual arts : a history / Hugh Honour and
John Fleming. 3rd ed. New York : Abrams,
1991. p. cm. Includes bibliographical references and
index. ISBN 0-8109-3913-4 (cloth) DDC 709 20
1. Art - History. I. Fleming, John, 1919-. II. Title.
N5300 .H68 1991

HONZÍK, KAREL, 1900-
Prušáková-Honzíková, Marie. Když hoří
obrazy . Praha , 1989. 247 p. ; ISBN
80-7023-021-5 :
NA1034.5.H6 A2 1989

Hood Museum of Art.
Fatal consequences . Hanover, N.H. , 1990. 92
p. : ISBN 0-944722-04-0 DDC 769.92 20
NE2149.W37 F38 1990
NYPL [MDG+ (Callot) 91-4763]

Fischl, Eric, 1948- Scenes and sequences .
Hanover, NH , New York , 1990. 118 p. :
ISBN 0-944722-04-0 DDC 769.92 20
NE2246.F5 A4 1990
NYPL [MDG (Fischl) 90-12797]

Images of paradise in Islamic art /. Hanover,
N.H. , 1991. p. cm. ISBN 0-944722-07-5
(hardcover) DDC 704.9/489723 20
N6263.D37 H664 1991

The Independent Group . Cambridge, Mass. ,
c1990. 256 p. : ISBN 0-262-18139-8 DDC
709/.41/074 20
N6768.5.I53 I53 1990
NYPL [3-MAMR+ 90-11745]

Minimalism and post-minimalism . Hanover,
N.H. , 1990. 104 p. : ISBN 0-944722-05-9 DDC
741.973/074/7423 20
NC108 .M528 1990
NYPL [3-MBH 91-3948]

Hoogveld, Carine. Glas in lood in Nederland,
1817-1968 /. 's-Gravenhage [1990?] 414 p. :
ISBN 90-12-06146-6
NK5354.A1 G57 1990

The hooked rug . Linsley, Leslie. New York ,
1991. p. cm. ISBN 0-517-58102-7 : DDC
746.7/4/0973 20
NK9112 .L56 1991

HOOKED RUGS. see RUGS, HOOKED.

Hooper, Juliana. Hooper, Toby. Australian
country furniture /. South Yarra, Vic.,
Australia , 1988. 138 p., [24] p. of plates :
ISBN 0-670-90074-5
NYPL [3-MOF+ 91-7961]

Hooper, Toby. Australian country furniture /
Toby and Juliana Hooper. South Yarra, Vic.,
Australia : Viking O'Neil, 1988. 138 p., [24] p.
of plates : ill. ; 30 cm. ISBN 0-670-90074-5
1. Country furniture - Australia. I. Hooper, Juliana. II.
Title. ***NYPL [3-MOF+ 91-7961]***

Hoozee, Robert.
[James Ensor, tekeningen en prenten. French]
James Ensor, dessins et estampes / Robert
Hoozee, Sabine Bown-Taevernier, J.F.
Heijbroek ; [traduit du néerlandais par
Catherine Warnant, John Rossbach, Marnix
Vincent]. Antwerpen : Fonds Mercator ;
Paris : A. Michel, c1987. 271 p. : ill. (some
col.) ; 30 cm. Translation of: James Ensor,
tekeningen en prenten. Includes bibliographical
references (p. 268). ISBN 90-6153-177-2 (Fonds
Mercator) DDC 760/.092 20
1. Ensor, James, 1860-1949 - Catalogs. I.
Bown-Taevernier, Sabine. II. Heijbroek, Jan Frederik.
III. Title. IV. Title: James Ensor.
N6973.E5 A4 1987

Hope, Shoshana Lev.
Shoshana Lev Hope. [Israel] : Printed by
Grafika Omanim, [1982?] [8] p. : ill. (some
col.) ; 21 cm. Cover title. Added cover title in
Hebrew: Shoshanah Lev Hop. Catalog of an exhibition
held May 1982, Yad-Labanim Museum, Petach Tikva.
English and Hebrew.
1. Hope, Shoshana Lev - Exhibitions. I. Yad-Labanium
Museum. II. Title. III. Title: Shoshanah Lev Hop.
NYPL [3-MCZ H791 88-3770]

HOPE, SHOSHANA LEV - EXHIBITIONS.
Hope, Shoshana Lev. Shoshana Lev Hope.
[Israel] [1982?] [8] p. :
NYPL [3-MCZ H791 88-3770]

Hopfengart, Christine. Loewig, Roger, 1930-
Roger Loewig, Zeichnungen und Lithographien
/. Berlin [1988] 134 p. :
NYPL [MDG (Loewig) 90-10854]

Hopkins, Frances Anne, 1838-1919.
Clark, Janet E. Frances Anne Hopkins,
1838-1919 . Thunder Bay, Ont. , 1989. 112 p. :
ISBN 0-920539-30-0 : DDC 759.11 20
NYPL [3-MCV H762 90-10799]

HOPKINS, FRANCES ANNE, 1838-1919 -
EXHIBITIONS.
Clark, Janet E. Frances Anne Hopkins,
1838-1919 . Thunder Bay, Ont. , 1989. 112 p. :
ISBN 0-920539-30-0 : DDC 759.11 20
NYPL [3-MCV H762 90-10799]

Hopkins, Rupert, 1949- Peace snapped / by
Rupert Hopkins. Clifton, Bristol : Podivin
Books, c1986. 112 p. : ill. ; 30 cm. "A series of
black and white photographs of peace camps and the
peace movement in Britain. Taken between December
1982 and September 1986." ISBN 0-9511816-0-2
1. Peace movements - Great Britain - Pictorial works. I.
Title. ***NYPL [MFX+ (Hopkins) 90-13477]***

Hopkinson, Martin J. James McNeill Whistler at
the Hunterian Art Gallery . [Glasgow] [1990].
56 p. : ISBN 0-904254-11-9
NYPL [3-MCX W57 91-6660]

Hoppen, Stephanie. Decorating with pictures / by
Stephanie Hoppen ; text by Catherine Haig.
New York : Clarkson Potter, 1991. p. cm.
ISBN 0-517-58168-X : DDC 747/.9 20
1. Pictures in interior decoration. I. Haig, Catherine. II.
Title.
NK2115.5.P48 H66 1991

Hopper, Edward, 1882-1967.
Edward Hopper, selections from the permanent
collection : Whitney Museum of American Art,
July 21-November 5, 1989. New York, NY :
The Museum, c1989. 32 p. : ill. ; 23 cm. Essays
by Susan C. Larsen and Deborah Lyons.
1. Hopper, Edward, 1882-1967 - Exhibitions. 2.
Whitney Museum of American Art - Exhibitions. I.
Larsen, Susan C. II. Lyons, Deborah. III. Whitney
Museum of American Art. IV. Title.
NYPL [3-MCX H79 91-5552]

HOPPER, EDWARD, 1882-1967 -
EXHIBITIONS.
Hopper, Edward, 1882-1967. Edward Hopper,
selections from the permanent collection . New
York, NY , c1989. 32 p. :
NYPL [3-MCX H79 91-5552]

Hopps, Walter.
Raynaud, Jean Pierre, 1939- Jean-Pierre
Raynaud . Houston, Tex. , c1991. 135 p. :
ISBN 0-939594-23-4 : DDC 709/.2 20
N6853.R33 A4 1991
NYPL [3-MGO (Raynaud) 91-7980]

Robert Rauschenberg : the early 1950s / text
by Walter Hopps. Houston : The Menil
Collection ; Houston Fine Art Press, 1991. p.
cm. Includes bibliographical references and index.
ISBN 0-939594-25-0 DDC 709/.2 20
1. Rauschenberg, Robert, 1925- - Exhibitions. I. Title.
N6537.R27 A4 1991a

Horatio McCulloch, 1805-1867 /. Smith,
Sheenah. [Glasgow] , c1988. 112 p. : ISBN
0-902752-35-9 (pbk.)
ND497.M493 S65 1988
NYPL [3-MCV M129 90-11544]

Horbachova, I. O. ĪAblonsʹka, Tetīāna Nylivna,
1917- Tatʹīāna Nilovna ĪAblonskaīā . Moskva ,
1989. 1 v. (unpaged) : ISBN 5-269-00340-6 :
N7193.I13 A4 1989

Hore, Somnath, 1921- Tebhaga : an artist's diary
and sketchbook / Somnath Hore ; translated
from the Bengali by Somnath Zutshi. Calcutta :
Seagull Books, 1990. xiii, 61 p. : ill. ; 26 cm.
ISBN 81-7046-078-6

1. Hore, Somnath, 1921-. 2. Artists - India - Biography.
I. Title.   **NYPL [3-MCZ H792 91-4053]**

HORE, SOMNATH, 1921-
Hore, Somnath, 1921- Tebhaga . Calcutta ,
1990. xiii, 61 p. :   ISBN 81-7046-078-6
NYPL [3-MCZ H792 91-4053]

Hörl, Ottmar, 1950- Formalhaut (Group)
Formalhaut Architektur Skulptur . Darmstadt ,
c1989. 54 p. :   ISBN 3-925376-40-2
NYPL [3-MGI 91-7331]

HORN CARVING.
Krzyszkowska, O. (Olga) Ivory and related
materials . London , 1990. xv, 109 p., [70] p. of
plates :   ISBN 0-900587-62-8
NYPL [3-MNW 91-7005]

Horn, Rebecca, 1944-
Rebecca Horn : diving through Buster's
bedroom. Los Angeles : Museum of
Contemporary Art ; Milan : Fabbri Editori,
c1990. 111 p. : ill. (some col.) ; 29 cm.
"Published on the occasion of the exhibition 'Diving
through Buster's bedroom' by Rebecca Horn, organized
by Elizabeth A.T. Smith and presented at the Museum
of Contemporary Art, Los Angeles, September 30,
1990-January 5, 1991"--T.p. verso. Includes
bibliographical references (p. 111). ISBN
0-914357-22-0   DDC 700/.92 20
1. Horn, Rebecca, 1944- - Exhibitions. 2. Keaton,
Buster, 1895-1966 - Influence - Exhibitions. I. Smith,
Elizabeth A. T., 1958-. II. Museum of Contemporary
Art (Los Angeles, Calif.). III. Title.
NX550.Z9 H67 1990
NYPL [3-MGO+ (Horn) 91-6589]

HORN, REBECCA, 1944- - EXHIBITIONS.
Horn, Rebecca, 1944- Rebecca Horn . Los
Angeles , Milan , c1990. 111 p. :   ISBN
0-914357-22-0   DDC 700/.92 20
NX550.Z9 H67 1990
NYPL [3-MGO+ (Horn) 91-6589]

Horn, Roni, 1955-
Roni Horn. Los Angeles : Museum of
Contemporary Art, c1990. 1 v. (unpaged) : ill.
(some col.) ; 27 cm.   ISBN 0-914357-20-4
1. Horn, Roni, 1955- - Exhibitions. I. Museum of
Contemporary Art (Los Angeles, Calif.). II. Title.
MLCM 90/00740 (N)
NYPL [3-MGO (Horn) 90-11634]

To place : folds / Roni Horn. New York :
Mary Boone Gallery, 1991- p. cm.   ISBN
0-941863-21-2   DDC 709.2 20
1. Horn, Roni, 1955-. 2. Conceptual art - United States.
I. Mary Boone Gallery (New York, N.Y.). II. Title.
N6537.H644 A4 1991

HORN, RONI, 1955-
Horn, Roni, 1955- To place . New York , 1991-
p. cm.   ISBN 0-941863-21-2   DDC 709.2 20
N6537.H644 A4 1991

HORN, RONI, 1955- - EXHIBITIONS.
Horn, Roni, 1955- Roni Horn. Los Angeles ,
c1990. 1 v. (unpaged) :   ISBN 0-914357-20-4
MLCM 90/00740 (N)
NYPL [3-MGO (Horn) 90-11634]

Horn, Walter William, 1908- The forgotten
hermitage of Skellig Michael / Walter Horn,
Jenny White Marshall, Grellan D. Rourke with
Paddy O'Leary and Lee Snodgrass. Berkeley :
University of California Press, c1990. xi, 111
p. : ill. (chiefly col.) ; 31 cm. (California studies in
the history of art. Discovery series . 2) "A Centennial
book." Includes index. Includes bibliographical
references (p. 100-107). ISBN 0-520-06410-0 (alk.
paper) DDC 941.9/6 19
1. Skellig Michael (Monastery : Ireland). 2. Christian
antiquities - Ireland - Great Skellig Island. 3. Great
Skellig Island (Ireland) - Antiquities. 4. Ireland -
Antiquities. I. Marshall, Jenny White. II. Rourke,
Grellan D. III. Title. IV. Series.
BX2602.S54 H67 1989
NYPL [3-MRBB+ 91-3376]

Horn, Wolfgang. Köchl, Alois, 1951- Alois Köchl,
Stadtzeichner von Nürnberg 1984 . [Nürnberg]
[1985] 37 p. :
MLCM 86/3093 (N)
NYPL [3-MCK K768 90-10681]

Hornbostel, Wilhelm. Museum für Kunst und
Gewerbe Hamburg. Kunst für Hamburg .
Hamburg , c1990. 251 p. :
NYPL [3-MLF 91-6790]

Horne, Catherine Wilson, 1957- Crossroads of
clay . Columbia, S.C. , 1990. xi, 129 p. :   ISBN

0-938983-08-3 :   DDC 738.3/0975/07475771 20
NK3634 .C76 1990
NYPL [3-MPH 90-11055]

Horníček, Miroslav, 1918- Miloslav Stibor /
Miroslav Horníček, Ludvík Baran. Vyd. 1.
Ostrava : Profil, 1990. 1 v. (unpaged) : ill. ; 30
cm. ISBN 80-7034-045-2
1. Stibor, Miloslav. I. Title.
IN PROCESS (ONLINE)
NYPL [MFX+ (Stibor) 91-4479]

Hornstein, Sari R., 1955- Beverley R. Robinson
Collection. Naval prints from the Beverley R.
Robinson Collection /. Annapolis, Md. , 1991-
p. ISBN 0-9628260-0-6 (hardcover) DDC
769/.493594/07475256 20
NE957 .B48 1991

Hornung, Clarence Pearson. Geometrix : 161
patterns and motifs for artists and designers /
by Clarence P. Hornung. New York : Dover
Publications, c1991. vii, 115 p. : chiefly ill. ; 31
cm. (Dover pictorial archive series)   ISBN
0-486-26674-5 :   DDC 745.4 20
1. Borders, Ornamental (Decorative arts). 2.
Repetitive patterns (Decorative arts). 3. Stars in art. 4.
Polyhedra in art. I. Title.
NK1570 .H595 1991

**HOROSCOPES - CARICATURES AND
CARTOONS.**
Olson, Eric, 1958- Horrorscope . Stamford,
Conn. , 1991. p. cm.   ISBN 0-681-41165-1 :
DDC 741.5/973 20
NC1429.O45 A4 1991

Horrorscope . Olson, Eric, 1958- Stamford,
Conn. , 1991. p. cm.   ISBN 0-681-41165-1 :
DDC 741.5/973 20
NC1429.O45 A4 1991

HORSE. see HORSES.

**HORSE RAILROADS - GREAT BRITAIN -
MAPS.**
Crowther, G. L. National atlas showing canals,
navigable rivers, mineral tramroads, railways,
and street tramways /. Preston, Lancs. , 1985-
1 atlas (v.) :   ISBN 0-948850-50-7 (lib. ed. : v. 1)
DDC 912/.41 19
G1812.21.P1 C7 1985
NYPL [Map Div. 90-2]

HORSE RIDING. see HORSEMANSHIP.

**HORSEBACK RIDING. see
HORSEMANSHIP.**

**HORSEMANSHIP - BIBLIOGRAPHY -
EXHIBITIONS.**
Reitkunst in Bild und Schrift des 16.-19.
Jahrhunderts /. Hamburg [1982] 44 p. :
Z6240 .R44 1982 SF309
NYPL [MDZ 87-5069]

**HORSEMANSHIP - PICTORIAL WORKS -
EXHIBITIONS.**
Reitkunst in Bild und Schrift des 16.-19.
Jahrhunderts /. Hamburg [1982] 44 p. :
Z6240 .R44 1982 SF309
NYPL [MDZ 87-5069]

HORSEMEN AND HORSEWOMEN IN ART.
Calcani, Giuliana. Cavalieri di bronzo . Roma ,
c1989. 182 p. :   ISBN 88-7062-671-7
NYPL [3-MGO (Lysippus) 91-5330]

Horses . Butterfield, Deborah, 1949- Coral
Gables, Fla. , San Francisco , 1992. p. cm.
ISBN 0-8118-0137-3 (hard) :   DDC 730/.92 20
NB237.B87 A4 1992

HORSES - GREAT BRITAIN - HISTORY.
Heiney, Paul. George Soper's horses /.
London , 1990. 143 p. :   ISBN 0-85493-200-3 :
DDC 636.15 20
SF311.3.G7   **NYPL [3-MCV S712 91-3373]**

HORSES IN ART.
Heiney, Paul. George Soper's horses /.
London , 1990. 143 p. :   ISBN 0-85493-200-3 :
DDC 636.15 20
SF311.3.G7   **NYPL [3-MCV S712 91-3373]**

Heiney, Paul. George Soper's horses /. Boston ,
1991. 143 p. :   ISBN 0-395-58040-4 :   DDC 759.2
20
N6797.S64 A4 1990

HORSES IN ART - EXHIBITIONS.
Butterfield, Deborah, 1949- Horses . Coral
Gables, Fla. , San Francisco , 1992. p. cm.
ISBN 0-8118-0137-3 (hard) :   DDC 730/.92 20
NB237.B87 A4 1992

**HORSES IN ART - JUVENILE
LITERATURE.**
Savitt, Sam. Draw horses with Sam Savitt.
Middletown, Md. , 1991. p. cm.   ISBN
0-939481-23-5:   DDC 743/.69725 20
NC783.8.H65 S38 1991

**HORSEWOMANSHIP. see
HORSEMANSHIP.**

Horst Antes . Antes, Horst, 1936- Kiel , c1990.
84 p. :   ISBN 3-923701-41-1
NYPL [3-MCK+ A62 91-6789]

Horst Janssen . Schack, Gerhard, 1929-
München , c1989. 1 v. (unpaged) :   ISBN
3-7913-1042-9   DDC 760/.092 20
N6888.J37 A4 1989

Horstmann, Theo. Elektrifizierung in Westfalen .
Hagen , c1990. 168 p. :   ISBN 3-89431-005-7
IN PROCESS (ONLINE)
NYPL [MFW 91-2652]

Horta, Joaquim. Napols i el Barroc Mediterrani .
[Barcelona] [1990?] 168 p. :   ISBN
84-7609-344-6   **NYPL [3-MCE 90-12335]**

Horton, David. Luminous perceptions / by David
Horton. [New Milford, N.Y.] : Flying Pyramid
Press, [1988] 1 strip ; 18 x 194 cm. "A 16 page
accordion fold visual book ... From its 7"7"2" slipcase,
this book ... unfolds into a 6'4" long sequence of
photographs and three dimensional panoramas. Each of
the pages was printed by the artist on photographic
paper, mounted on 4 ply museum board ... The edition
is limited to twenty signed and numbered copies and
four artist's proofs"--Explanatory sheet. Accompanied by
a folded explanatory sheet attached to a paper cover
(sheet unfolds to 18 x 35 cm.). LC has copy no. 20.
DLC Source: Purchase, Aug. 2, 1990. DLC   DDC
709/.2 20
1. Horton, David. 2. Artists' books - United States. I.
Title.
N7433.4.H658 A4 1988

HORTON, DAVID.
Horton, David. Luminous perceptions /. [New
Milford, N.Y.] [1988] 1 strip ;   DDC 709/.2 20
N7433.4.H658 A4 1988

**HORVITZ, JEFFREY E. - ART
COLLECTIONS - EXHIBITIONS.**
Wolk-Simon, Linda, 1958- Italian old master
drawings from the collection of Jeffrey E.
Horvitz /. Gainesville, Fla. , 1991. v, 175 p. :
ISBN 0-9629384-0-8 (alk. paper)   DDC
741.945/074/73 20
NC255 .W6 1991

Hoschouer, Charlene Ketler. Drain, Francita L.
The quilt primer . Benkelman, NE , c1991. 138
p. :   ISBN 0-9629407-0-4   DDC 746.9/7041/0973 20
NK9112 .D73 1991

Hosking, Eric John. Eric Hosking's birds : fifty
years of photographing wildlife / [by] Eric
Hosking with Kevin MacDonnell ; foreword by
Roger Tory Peterson. London : Pelham, 1979.
224 p. : chiefly ill. (some col.) ; 29 cm.
American ed. published under title: A passion for birds.
Includes index.   ISBN 0-7207-1163-0 :
1. Birds. I. MacDonnell, Kevin, joint author. II. Title.
III. Title: Birds.
TR729.B5 H67 1979b
NYPL [MFX (Hosking) 81-890]

Hosley, William. The Japan idea : art and life in
Victorian America / by William Hosley.
Hartford, Conn. : Wadsworth Atheneum, 1990.
211 p. : ill. (some col.) ; 30 cm. Catalog of an
exhibition held at the Wadsworth Atheneum, Oct.
21-Dec. 30, 1990. Includes bibliographical references (p.
201-207) and index.   ISBN 0-918333-07-5
1. Art, Victorian - United States - Japanese influences -
Exhibitions. 2. Art, American - Japanese influences -
Exhibitions. 3. Art, Modern - 19th century - United
States - Japanese influences - Exhibitions. 4. Art,
Japanese - Exhibitions. I. Wadsworth Atheneum. II.
Title.   **NYPL [3-MAMT+ 91-3289]**

HOSMER, HARRIET.
Sherwood, Dolly. Harriet Hosmer, American
sculptor, 1830-1908 /. Columbia , c1991. p. cm.
ISBN 0-8262-0766-9 (alk. paper)   DDC 730/.92
B 20
NB237.H6 S53 1991

Hosoda, Eishi, 1756-1829. The thirty-six immortal
women poets : introduction, commentaries, and
translations of the poems / by Andrew J.
Pekarik. New York : G. Braziller, 1991. p. cm.
Includes bibliographical references and index.   ISBN

0-8076-1256-1   DDC 769.92 20
1. Hosoda, Eishi, 1756-1829. 2. Women poets, Japanese - Portraits. 3. Japanese poetry. I. Pekarik, Andrew J. II. Title.
NE1325.H69 A4 1991

HOSODA, EISHI, 1756-1829.
Hosoda, Eishi, 1756-1829. The thirty-six immortal women poets . New York , 1991. p. cm.   ISBN 0-8076-1256-1   DDC 769.92 20
NE1325.H69 A4 1991

HOSTILITIES. see WAR.

Hot shots . Seeff, Norman. New York [1974] 90 p. :   ISBN 0-8256-3903-4 :   DDC 779/.2/0924
TR680 .S38   *NYPL [JFD 79-382]*

Hôtel de Sully (Paris, France)
Le Panthéon, symbole des révolutions . [Montréal] : [Paris] : 339 p. :   ISBN 2-7084-0386-9 (Picard)
IN PROCESS (ONLINE)
        NYPL [3-MQWF 90-10797]
Saint-Sernin de Toulouse, trésors et métamorphoses . [Toulouse] , 1989. 259 p. :   ISBN 2-9500977-7-4
        NYPL [3-MRBB 91-5050]

Hôtel Solvay. Le Bijou 1900 . Bruxelles , 1965. 102 p., [26] p. of plates :
        NYPL [3-MNR 90-6082]

HOTELS, TAVERNS, ETC. - CANADA.
Donzel, Catherine. Palaces et grands hôtels d'Amérique du Nord /. Paris , c1989. 255 p. :   ISBN 2-08-201846-6   DDC 728/.5/0973 20
NA7840 .D67 1989

HOTELS, TAVERNS, ETC. - DESIGN.
Dru, Line, 1957- [Cafés. English.] Cafes /. New York, NY , c1989. 118 p. :   ISBN 0-910413-66-5
        NYPL [3-MLO 90-10718]

HOTELS, TAVERNS, ETC., IN ART.
Zaid, Barry. Wish you were here . New York , c1990. 95 p. :   ISBN 0-517-58009-8 :   DDC 741.6/83/0973074 20
NC1878.7.U6 Z35 1990
        NYPL [3-MDW 91-4875]

HOTELS, TAVERNS, ETC. - UNITED STATES.
Donzel, Catherine. Palaces et grands hôtels d'Amérique du Nord /. Paris , c1989. 255 p. :   ISBN 2-08-201846-6   DDC 728/.5/0973 20
NA7840 .D67 1989

HOTELS, TAVERNS, ETC. - UNITED STATES - PICTORIAL WORKS.
Zaid, Barry. Wish you were here . New York , c1990. 95 p. :   ISBN 0-517-58009-8 :   DDC 741.6/83/0973074 20
NC1878.7.U6 Z35 1990
        NYPL [3-MDW 91-4875]

Houaiss, Antônio. Gente do aço /. [Rio de Janeiro, RJ] , c1989. 147 p. :   ISBN 85-7083-026-2   *NYPL [MFX+ (Stewart-Granger) 91-7436]*

Houbart-Wilkin, Suzanne. Hommage à Paul Delvaux . Bruxelles, [r. du Musée 9] [1977] [68] p. :
N6973.D44 A4 1977
        NYPL [3-MCH D32 81-766]

Hough, Katherine Plake. Northwest by southwest . Palm Springs, Calif. (P.O. Box 2288, 101 Museum Dr.) , c1990. 116 p. :   DDC 758/.9978/007479497 20
ND1451.6 .N67 1990
        NYPL [3-MCW+ 90-11042]

HOUGHTON COUNTY (MICH.) - MAPS.
Rockford Map Publishers. Houghton County, Michigan, land atlas, plat book, sportsman's guide . Rockford, Ill. , Hancock, Mich. , c1991. 1 atlas (63 p.) :   *NYPL [Map Div. 91-7460]*

Houghton County, Michigan, land atlas, plat book, sportsman's guide . Rockford Map Publishers. Rockford, Ill. , Hancock, Mich. , c1991. 1 atlas (63 p.) :
        NYPL [Map Div. 91-7460]

Hould, Claudette. Images of the French Revolution / Claudette Hould. Québec : Musée du Québec : Publications du Québec, c1989. 446 p. : ill. (some col.) ; 31 cm. Published in conjunction with an exhibition of the same title held at the Musée du Québec, February 9-March 26, 1989 and three other museums in Canada through December 10, 1989. Bibliography: p. [441]-446.   ISBN 2-551-08407-5
1. Politics in art - France - Exhibitions. 2. Prints - 18th

century - France - Themes, motives - Exhibitions. 3. Prints, French - Themes, motives - Exhibitions. 4. France - History - Revolution, 1789-1799 - Art and the Revolution - Exhibitions. I. Musée du Québec. II. Title.
        NYPL [MDZ+ 90-12786]

The House & garden book of living rooms /. Harling, Robert. New York , 1991. p. cm.   ISBN 0-86565-125-6   DDC 747.7/5 20
NK2117.L5 H37 1991

House & garden. Harling, Robert. The House & garden book of living rooms /. New York , 1991. p. cm.   ISBN 0-86565-125-6   DDC 747.7/5 20
NK2117.L5 H37 1991

House and garden book of living rooms. Harling, Robert. The House & garden book of living rooms /. New York , 1991. p. cm.   ISBN 0-86565-125-6   DDC 747.7/5 20
NK2117.L5 H37 1991

House beautiful.
Barwick, JoAnn. Scandinavian country /. New York , c1991. p. cm.   ISBN 0-517-57661-9 :   DDC 745.4/4948 20
NK1457 .B37 1991
Garey, Carol Cooper. House beautiful decorating style /. New York , 1991. p. cm.   ISBN 0-688-09734-0 :   DDC 747.213 20
NK2115 .G25 1991

House beautiful decorating style /. Garey, Carol Cooper. New York , 1991. p. cm.   ISBN 0-688-09734-0 :   DDC 747.213 20
NK2115 .G25 1991

HOUSE DECORATION. see INTERIOR DECORATION.

HOUSE FURNISHINGS - ITALY - HISTORY - 20TH CENTURY.
Vercelloni, Virgilio. [Avventura del design, Gavina. English.] The adventure of design . New York , 1989. 220 p. :   ISBN 0-8478-1039-9   DDC 749/.245 20
TS79 .V4713 1989
        NYPL [3-MNE+ 90-12985]

HOUSE FURNISHINGS - TURKEY - ISTANBUL - HISTORY - 19TH CENTURY.
İrez, Feryal. XIX. yüzyıl Osmanlı saray mobilyası /. Ankara , 1988. 110 p., [83] p. of plates :   ISBN 975-16-0039-1
NK2525 .I7 1988

HOUSE FURNISHINGS - VIRGINIA - WILLIAMSBURG - HISTORY - 18TH CENTURY.
Gilliam, Jan (Jan Kirsten) Furnishing Williamsburg's historic buildings. Williamsburg, Va. , 1991. p. cm.   ISBN 0-87935-083-0   DDC 747.2155/4252/09033 20
NK2438.W54 G5 1991

The house I live in /. Seltzer, Isadore. New York : Toronto : p. cm.   ISBN 0-02-781801-2   DDC 728/.0973 20
NA7205 .S375 1992

HOUSE MARKS - GERMANY (WEST) - FRIEDRICHSTADT.
Stolz, Gerd. Hausmarken in Friedrichstadt . Husum , 1987. 54 p. :   ISBN 3-88042-362-8
        NYPL [3-MRX 90-12732]

A house not made with hands /. Stedman, Myrtle. Santa Fe, N.M. , c1990. 110 p. ;   ISBN 0-86534-145-1 :   DDC 720/.92 B 20
NA737.S637 A2 1990
        NYPL [3-MQZ (Stedman) 91-6674]

The house of God . Norman, Edward R. New York, N.Y. , 1990. 312 p. :   ISBN 0-500-25108-8 :   DDC 726/.5/09 20
NA4800 .N587 1990
        NYPL [3-MRB+ 91-3658]

A house of one's own . Stageberg, James. New York , c1991. vii, 200 p. :   ISBN 0-517-58214-7 :   DDC 728/.37 20
NA7115 .S7 1991

House of Representatives of the United States [microform]. Brady, Mathew B., 1823 (ca.)-1896. [New York , 1864] 1 album (193 carte-de-visite photoprints) :
        *NYPL [*ZM-233]*

House of Representatives (U. S.) see United States. Congress. House.

The house of the singing winds . Steele, Selma N.

(Selma Neubacher), ca. 1870-1945. Indianapolis [1990] 209 p., [45] p. of plates :   ISBN 0-87195-053-7 (cloth) :   DDC 759.13 B 20
ND237.S68 S7 1990
        NYPL [3-MCX S79 91-3988]

HOUSE STYLE. see INDUSTRIAL DESIGN COORDINATION.

HOUSEHOLD GOODS. see HOUSE FURNISHINGS.

HOUSEHOLD LINENS - COLLECTORS AND COLLECTING.
Johnson, Frances. Collecting antique linens, lace, and needlework /. Radnor, Pa. , c1991. p. cm.   ISBN 0-87069-634-3 (hc) :   DDC 746/.075 20
NK8904 .J64 1991

Houses . Harrison, Henry S. Chicago, IL , 1991. p. cm.   ISBN 0-7931-0332-0 (pbk.)   DDC 728 20
NA7110 .H33 1991

HOUSES. see ARCHITECTURE, DOMESTIC; DWELLINGS.

Houses by Bart Prince . Mead, Christopher Curtis. Albuquerque , c1991. xiii, 100 p., [8] p. of col. plates :   ISBN 0-8263-1254-3   DDC 728.8/092 20
NA737.P69 M4 1991
        NYPL [3-MQZ (Prince) 91-6791]

The houses of Roman Italy, 100 B.C.-A.D. 250 . Clarke, John R., 1945- Berkeley , c1991. p. cm.   ISBN 0-520-07267-7 (alk. paper)   DDC 728/.0937 20
NA324 .C57 1991

Houses of Saint Augustine, 1565-1821. Manucy, Albert C. The houses of St. Augustine, 1565-1821 /. Jacksonville , c1992. p. cm.   ISBN 0-8130-1103-5   DDC 728/.09759/18 20
NA7238.S27 M3 1992

Houses of Southold . Langhart, Nicholas. Southold, N.Y. , c1990. vi, 66 p. :   ISBN 0-8488-0870-3 :   DDC 728/.37/0974725 20
NA7238.S62 L36 1990

The houses of St. Augustine, 1565-1821 /. Manucy, Albert C. Jacksonville , c1992. p. cm.   ISBN 0-8130-1103-5   DDC 728/.09759/18 20
NA7238.S27 M3 1992

HOUSING, RURAL - CYPRUS.
Ionas, Ioannis. La maison rurale de Chypre (XVIIIe-XXe siècle) . Nicosie , 1988. 238 p. :   ISBN 996-308-012-X   DDC 728/.095645 20
NA8210.C93 I57 1988

Housing the arts in Great Britain. Arts Council of Great Britain. London, 1959-61. 2 v.
NA6813.G7 A77

Houston, John.
Fred Baier : furniture in studio / John Houston. London : Bellew, 1990. 64 p. : ill. (some col.) ; 22 cm. (Craft in studio) Includes bibliographical references.   ISBN 0-947792-46-5 (pbk.) :   DDC 749.22 20
1. Baier, Fred. 2. Furniture designers - England. I. Title. II. Title: Furniture in studio. III. Series.
        NYPL [3-MOF 90-11124]
Richard Slee : Ceramics in studio / John Houston. London : Bellew, 1990. 64 p. : ill. (some col.) ; 22 cm. Includes bibliographical references.   ISBN 0-947792-47-3 (pbk.) :   DDC 738.092 20
1. Slee, Richard. 2. Ceramic sculpture - England - 20th century. I. Title. II. Title: Ceramics in studio.
        NYPL [3-MPGO 90-12737]

Houston, John, 1935- Caroline Broadhead : jewellery in studio / John Houston. London : Bellew, 1990. 64 p. : ill. (some col.) ; 22 cm. (Craft in studio) Includes bibliographical references (p. 63-64).   ISBN 0-947792-48-1 (pbk.) :   DDC 739.27092 20
1. Broadhead, Caroline. 2. Jewelry - Design. I. Broadhead, Caroline. II. Title. III. Title: Jewellery in studio. IV. Series.   *NYPL [3-MNR 90-12744]*

HOUSTON (TEX.) - BUILDINGS, STRUCTURES, ETC.
Nicholson, Patrick James, 1921- William Ward Watkin and the Rice Institute /. Houston, Tex. , c1991. p. cm.   ISBN 0-88415-012-7   DDC 727/.3/092 20
NA737.W39 N5 1991

Houston, Tex. Contemporary Arts Museum. see Contemporary Arts Museum.

Houthakker, Lodewijk.
Fuhring, Peter. Design into art . London , New York , 1989. 2 v. (792 p.) : ISBN 0-85667-354-4
(London) *NYPL [MLD+ 89-23146]*

HOUTHAKKER, LODEWIJK - ART COLLECTIONS - CATALOGS.
Fuhring, Peter. Design into art . London , New York , 1989. 2 v. (792 p.) : ISBN 0-85667-354-4
(London) *NYPL [MLD+ 89-23146]*

HOVE, FRANCINE VAN, 1942- - CATALOGS.
Hove, Francine van, 1942- Van Hove . Paris , c1991. 95 p. : ISBN 2-85956-931-6 : DDC 759.4
20
ND553.H68 A4 1991

Hovhannes Minasian . Minasian, Hovhannes, 1928-1972. Erevan , 1974. 109p. :
NYPL [3-MCZ M643 86-4492]

Hovnat'anyan, Hakob, 1806-1881. Hakob Hovnat'anyan / [Kazmets'ev dzevavorets' Ashot Tonikyan~; neratsakan khosk Ruben Drambyani]. Erevan : Hayastani nkarch'i tan hratarakut'yun ; [197-?] 64p. : ill. (some col.) ; 24cm. Armenian, Russian, English and French. Added t.p. in Russian and English: Akop Ovnatanian, Hakop Hovnatanian.
1. Hovnat'anyan, Hakob, 1806-1881. 2. Portrait painting, Armenian. I. Tonikyan, Ashot. II. Dramp'yan, R. G. (Ruben Grigorovich). III. Title.
NYPL [3-MCZ H833 90-8404]

HOVNAT'ANYAN, HAKOB, 1806-1881.
Hovnat'anyan, Hakob, 1806-1881. Hakob Hovnat'anyan /. Erevan [197-?] 64p. :
NYPL [3-MCZ H833 90-8404]

Hovstadius, Barbro, 1937- Svenskt silver : från renässans till rokoko : en konstbok från Nationalmuseum / av Barbro Hovstadius. Stockholm : Rabén & Sjögren, c1990. 149 p., [4] leaves of plates : ill. (some col.) ; 23 cm. (Årsbok för statens konstmuseer . 36) Includes bibliographical references (p. 146-147) and index.
ISBN 91-29-59391-3
1. Silverwork - Sweden - History - 16th century. 2. Silverwork - Sweden - History - 17th century. 3. Silverwork - Sweden - History - 18th century. 4. Nationalmuseum (Sweden). I. Nationalmuseum (Sweden). II. Series.
NK7161.A1 H68 1990

How architecture works /. Gordon, Douglas E. New York , c1991. xii, 190 p. : ISBN 0-442-23951-3 DDC 720 20
NA2520 .G58 1991

How art becomes history . Berger, Maurice. New York, N.Y. , c1992. p. ISBN 0-06-430385-3 : DDC 700/.1/03 20
NX180.S6 B47 1992

How designers think /. Lawson, Bryan. London ; Boston , 1990. vii, 243 p. : ISBN 0-408-50072-7 DDC 745.4 20 *NYPL [3-MNF 90-10740]*
NK1510 .L4 1990

How the Metropolitan Museum misteaches art /. Shaw, Theodore L. [Hypocrisy about art. Selections.] [Boston, Mass. , 195-?] 15 p.
NYPL [3-MAB 90-5666]

How things were built. Brown, David J. The Random House book of how things were built /. New York , 1992. p. cm. ISBN 0-679-82044-2
(trade) DDC 720 20
NA2555 .B68 1992

How to draw . Parramón, José María. [Así se dibuja. English.] New York , 1991. 112 p. : ISBN 0-8230-2352-4 : DDC 741.2 20
NC730 .P2713 1991

How to draw clowns /. Soloff-Levy, Barbara. Mahwah, N.J. , c1992. p. cm. ISBN 0-8167-2477-6 (lib. bdg.) : DDC 743/.8979133
20
NC765 .S65 1992

How to draw fairy-tale characters /. Soloff-Levy, Barbara. Mahwah, N.J. , c1992. p. cm. ISBN 0-8167-2378-8 (library) : DDC 743/.89398 20
NC655 .S65 1992

How to draw (Mahwah, N.J.)
Simpson, Anne. How to draw wild animals /. Mahwah, N.J. [1991] p. cm. ISBN 0-8167-2481-4 (lib. bdg.) : DDC 743/.6 20
NC780 .S54 1991

Soloff-Levy, Barbara. How to draw fairy-tale characters /. Mahwah, N.J. , c1992. p. cm. ISBN 0-8167-2378-8 (library) : DDC 743/.89398

20
NC655 .S65 1992

How to draw wild animals /. Simpson, Anne. Mahwah, N.J. [1991] p. cm. ISBN 0-8167-2481-4 (lib. bdg.) : DDC 743/.6 20
NC780 .S54 1991

How to look at modern art /. Yenawine, Philip. New York , 1991. p. cm. ISBN 0-8109-2485-4
DDC 701/.1 20
N6490 .Y46 1991

How to make watercolor work for you /. Nofer, Frank, 1929- Cincinnati, Ohio , c1991. p. cm. ISBN 0-89134-379-2 : DDC 751.42/2 20
ND2420 .N64 1991

How to make your design business profitable /. Stewart, Joyce M., 1962- Cincinnati, Ohio , c1992. p. cm. ISBN 0-89134-391-1 (paper) : DDC 745.4/068 20
NK1403 .S74 1992

How to paint . Foss, Gloria. New York , 1991. p. cm. ISBN 0-8230-2456-3 : DDC 751.45/435 20
ND1500 .F67 1991

How to paint buildings /. Sicilia, Manel Plana. [Cómo pintar el paisaje urbano a la acuarela. English.] New York , 1991. p. cm. ISBN 0-8230-2474-1 : DDC 751.42/244 20
ND2310 .S513 1991

How to paint seascapes /. Crespo, Francesc. [Cómo pintar marinas. English.] New York , 1991. 96 p. : ISBN 0-8230-2472-5 : DDC 751.42/2437 20
ND1370 .C7413 1991

How to recognize and refinish antiques for pleasure and profit /. Peake, Jacquelyn. Chester, Conn. , c1992. p. cm. ISBN 1-564-40020-4 DDC 745.1/028/8 20
NK1125 .P39 1992

How to use oil paints : basic techniques / [translation by Carla van Splunteren and Tony Burrett]. Newton Abbot : David & Charles ; New York, N.Y. : Distributed by Sterling Pub. Co., 1989. 116 p. : ill. (some col.) ; 27 cm. (The Fine arts series : theory and practice) Translation from the Dutch. Distributor info. from label on t.p. ISBN 0-7153-9474-6 DDC 751.45 20
1. Painting - Technique. I. Splunteren, Carla van. II. Burrett, Tony. III. Series: Fine arts series (Newton Abbot, London)
ND1500 .H67 1989

Howard Ben Tré . Johnson, Linda L., 1961- Washington, D.C. , 1989. 48 p. : ISBN 0-943044-14-6 : DDC 730/.92 20
NB237.B434 J64 1989
NYPL [3-MGO (Ben Tré) 91-6438]

HOWARD, CHARLES, 1899-1978 - EXHIBITIONS.
Anderson, Susan M. (Susan Mary) Pursuit of the marvelous . Laguna Beach, Calif. , c1990. 64 p. : ISBN 0-940872-16-1 DDC 760/.09794/607479496 20
N6530.C2 A58 1990
NYPL [3-MCW+ 91-6334]

Howard, Hugh, 1952- The preservationist's progress : architectural adventures in conserving yesterday's houses / Hugh Howard.1st ed. New York : Farrar, Straus and Giroux, c1991. x, 272 p. : ill. ; 25 cm. Includes bibliographical references and index. ISBN 0-374-17303-6 : DDC 728/.028/8 20
1. Architecture, Domestic - United States - Conservation and restoration. I. Title.
NA7205 .H735 1991
NYPL [3-MRG 91-7075]

Howard, Ken, 1932- The Complete artist . New York, NY , 1991. p. cm. ISBN 0-8230-0771-5
(cloth) : DDC 751.4 20
N7430 .C58 1991

Howard, Peter, 1944- Landscapes : the artists' vision / Peter Howard. London ; New York : Routledge, 1991. xiv, 260 p. : ill. ; 24 cm. (History of the British landscape) Includes bibliographical references (p. [238]-245) and index. ISBN 0-415-00775-5 DDC 758/.141/0941 20
1. Landscape - Great Britain - History. I. Title. II. Series.
ND1354 .H79 1990 NYPL [3-MCT 91-4509]

Howard, Seymour, 1928- Antiquity restored : essays on the afterlife of the antique / Seymour Howard ; with a preface by Ernst H. Gombrich. Vienna : IRSA, 1990. 344 p. : ill. ; 29 cm.

(Bibliotheca artibus et historiae) Includes bibliographical references (p. 297-314) and index. ISBN 3-900731-11-X
1. Classicism in art. I. Title. II. Series.
NYPL [3-MAH 91-4921]

Howard University. Libraries. Lois Mailou Jones . Washington, DC [1988?] 29 p. : DDC 759.13 20
N6537.J68 A4 1988

Howat, John K. The Hudson River and its painters / by John K. Howat ; pref. by James Biddel, foreword by Carl Carmer. Harmondsworth, Eng. ; New York : Penguin Books, 1978, c1972. 208 p. : ill. (some col.) ; 31 cm. Includes index. Bibliography: p. 193-201. ISBN 0-14-005080-9 DDC 758/.1/097473
1. Hudson River school of landscape painting. 2. Landscape painting - 19th century - United States. 3. Hudson River Valley (N.Y. and N.J.) - Description and travel - Views. I. Title.
ND1351.5 .H6 1978
NYPL [3-MAMT+ 90-11628]

Howe, Diana Pratt. Garcia, Nicolas B. Learning architectural drafting & design /. Albany, N.Y. , c1992. p. cm. ISBN 0-8273-4633-6
(textbook) DDC 720/.28/4 20
NA2708 .G3 1992

Howett, John. Southern exposure . New York, NY , c1985. 55 p. : ISBN 0-932075-02-9 (pbk.) DDC 709/.75/07401471 19
N6520 .S67 1985
NYPL [3-MAMT 90-12368]

Howlett, D. Roger. The sculpture of Donald De Lue : gods, prophets, and heroes / by D. Roger Howlett ; with contributions by Joseph Veach Noble ... [et al.].1st ed. Boston : Godine, 1990. xxi, 234 p. : ill. (some col.) ; 32 cm. Includes bibliographical references (p. 223-226) and index. ISBN 0-87923-820-8
1. De Lue, Donald, 1897-1988. I. De Lue, Donald, 1897-1988. II. Noble, Joseph Veach, 1920-. III. Title.
NYPL [3-MGO+ (De Lue) 91-3674]

Howoldt, Jenns E. Friedrich, Caspar David, 1774-1840. Caspar David Friedrich . [Hamburg] [1990] 35 p. :
NC251.F66 A4 1990

Høyer, Kurt Rosenkrans. Boderne i Næstved /. [Næstved] [Copenhagen] , 1988. 111 p. : ISBN 87-05-03735-60
NA9053.C6 B63 1988

HOYLAND, JOHN, 1934-
Gooding, Mel. John Hoyland /. Hatfield, Herts , 1990. 39 p., 80 leaves of plates : ISBN 0-85331-564-7
NYPL [3-MCV+ H867 91-6325]

Hoyos, Ana Mercedes, 1942-
Ana Mercedes Hoyos, de la luz al palenque / [texto] Eduardo Serrano. 1. ed. Bogotá : Ediciones Alfredo Wild, 1990. 123 p. : ill. (some col.) ; 34 cm. Cover title: Ana Mercedes Hoyos. Includes bibliographical references (p. 116-119). ISBN 958-95327-0-5 DDC 759.9861 20
1. Hoyos, Ana Mercedes, 1942- - Catalogs. I. Serrano, Eduardo. II. Title.
N6679.H6 A4 1990

HOYOS, ANA MERCEDES, 1942- - CATALOGS.
Hoyos, Ana Mercedes, 1942- Ana Mercedes Hoyos, de la luz al palenque /. Bogotá , 1990. 123 p. : ISBN 958-95327-0-5 DDC 759.9861 20
N6679.H6 A4 1990

HOYSALA SCULPTURE. see SCULPTURE, HOYSALA.

Hrady a zámky v Československu : proměny slohu a životního stylu / Dalibor Kusák ... [et al.].1. vyd. Praha : Panorama ; Martin : Osveta, 1990. 383 p. : chiefly ill. (some col.) ; 31 cm. (Edice Naše vlast) Summary in English, French, German, Russian, and Spanish. ISBN 80-7038-100-0 :
1. Castles - Czechoslovakia. 2. Decoration and ornament, Architectural - Czechoslovakia. I. Kusák, Dalibor.
NA7720 .H73 1990

Hrdlička, Alfred, 1928-
Das Frauenbild / Alfred Hrdlicka ; mit Beiträgen von Eva Blimlinger ... [et al.] ; herausgegeben von Ernst Hilger. Wien : Galerie Hilger, [198-?] 131 p. : ill. (some col.) ; 31 cm. ISBN 3-900318-48-4

*1. Women in art. I. Blimlinger, Eva. II. Hilger, Ernst.
III. Title.*   **NYPL [3-MCK+ H857 90-5270]**
Galerie Welz Salzburg. Alfred Hrdlicka.
Salzburg, 1969. 86 p.
                 NYPL [MDG (Hrdlicka) 91-394]
HRDLIČKA, ALFRED, 1928- - EXHIBITIONS.
Galerie Welz Salzburg. Alfred Hrdlicka.
Salzburg, 1969. 86 p.
                 NYPL [MDG (Hrdlicka) 91-394]
HRH the Prince of Wales watercolours. Charles,
Prince of Wales, 1948- Boston , 1991. p.   ISBN
0-8212-1881-6 :   DDC 759.2 20
ND1942.C46 A4 1991

Hrůza, Jiří. Město Praha / Jiří Hrůza. Vyd. 1.
Praha : Odeon, 1989. 421 p. : ill. (some col.) ;
29 cm. Summary in English, French, German, and
Russian. Includes bibliographical references (p. 411).
     ISBN 80-207-0065-X :
*1. Architecture - Czechoslovakia - Prague. 2. City
planning - Czechoslovakia - Prague - History. 3. Prague
(Czechoslovakia) - Buildings, structures, etc. I. Title.*
NA1033.P7 H78 1989

HSIA, KUEI, FL. 1190-1224.
Edwards, Richard, 1916- The world around the
Chinese artist . Ann Arbor , 1987. 158 p. :
     ISBN 0-472-10130-7
                              NYPL [3-MAF 90-4955]
Hsieh, Li-fa, 1938- The Twentieth century
Taiwanese paintings =. Long Beach, CA, U.
S.A. , T'ai-pei shih , 1983- v. :   ISBN
0-941942-14-7 (v. 1) :   DDC
759.951/249/074019493 19
ND1049.8 .T85 1983
                              NYPL [3-MAG+ 85-2718]
Hsü, Ginger Cheng-chi. Giacalone, Vito. The
Eccentric painters of Yangzhou /. New York
City , 1990. 92 p. :   ISBN 0-295-97087-1
                              NYPL [3-MAG 91-6594]
**HSÜ, HUNG-YÜAN - ART COLLECTIONS -
     CATALOGS.**
The Twentieth century Taiwanese paintings =.
Long Beach, CA, U. S.A. , T'ai-pei shih , 1983-
v. :   ISBN 0-941942-14-7 (v. 1) :   DDC
759.951/249/074019493 19
ND1049.8 .T85 1983
                              NYPL [3-MAG+ 85-2718]
Hu, Shih Chang. Lee, King Tsi. Drache und
Phoenix . [Köln] , c1990. 229 p. :   DDC
745.7/26/0951074435514 20
NK9900.7.C6 L44 1990
                              NYPL [3-MNX 91-4182]
Hubala, Erich, 1920- Barockmaler in Böhmen.
München [1961] 36 p.
N6832.B3 H8   **NYPL [3-MCY 90-5883]**
**HUBBARD, HARLAN - CRITICISM AND
     INTERPRETATION.**
Berry, Wendell, 1934- Harlan Hubbard . New
York , 1992. p.   ISBN 0-679-73858-4 (pbk.) :
     DDC 759.13 B 20
NX512.H82 B47 1992

Huber, Dorothee.
Giedion, S. (Sigfried), 1888-1968. Wege in die
Öffentlichkeit . Zürich , c1987. 231 p. :   ISBN
3-250-50104-2   DDC 700 19
N7445.4 .G54 1987   **NYPL [3-MAS 91-3933]**
Senn, Otto H. (Otto Heinrich), 1902- Otto
Senn . Basel , c1990. 137 p. :   ISBN
3-905065-12-4
NA1353.S46 A4 1990

Huber-Greub, Barbara. Le Musée sentimental de
Bâle / erausgegeben von Barbara Huber-Greub
und Stephen Andreae ; [Idee und künstlerische
Leitung: Daniel Spoerri]. Basel , c1989. 332 p. :
     ISBN 3-85700-006-X
                              NYPL [3-MAVZ (Basel) 90-13397]
Huber, Hans Dieter, 1953- System und
Wirkung : Rauschenberg, Twombly, Baruchello :
Fragen der Interpretation und Bedeutung
zeitgenössischer Kunst : ein systemtheoretischer
Ansatz / Hans Dieter Huber. München : W.
Fink, c1989. 191 p., 29 p. of plates : ill. (some
col.) ; 25 cm. Includes bibliographical references (p.
182-191).   ISBN 3-7705-2504-3
*1. Rauschenberg, Robert, 1925- - Criticism and
interpretation. 2. Twombly, Cy, 1928- - Criticism and
interpretation. 3. Baruchello, Gianfranco - Criticism and
interpretation. I. Title.*
N6490 .H796 1989   **NYPL [3-MAL 91-4622]**

Huber, Thomas.
Rede zur Schöpfung / Thomas Huber. [Bern] :
Kunsthalle Bern, [1983] 41 p. : ill. (1 col.) ; 21
cm. Folded col. ill. (11 x 41 cm.) in pocket.
"Anlässlich der Ausstellung 'Konstruierte Orte' in der
Kunsthalle Bern vom 29. Oktober bis zum 27.
November 1983 erscheint diese Rede ..."
*1. Huber, Thomas - Exhibitions. I. Kunsthalle Bern. II.
Title.*   **NYPL [3-MCK H869 90-12739]**
HUBER, THOMAS - EXHIBITIONS.
Huber, Thomas. Rede zur Schöpfung /. [Bern]
[1983] 41 p. :
                              NYPL [3-MCK H869 90-12739]
Hubert Robert et la Révolution /. Robert,
Hubert, 1733-1808. Valence , 1989. 179 p. :
                              NYPL [3-MCO R641 90-11133]
Hübner, Birgitta. Ikonographische Untersuchung
zum Motivschatz der stadtrömischen
mythologischen Sarkophage des 2. Jhs. n. Chr.
/ Brigitta Hübner. Münster : Archäologisches
Seminar der Universität, 1990. 217 p. : ill. ; 21
cm. (Boreas, 0344-810X. Beiheft . 5) Spine title:
Motivschatz stadtröm. mythol. Sarkophage. Originally
presented as the author's thesis (doctoral)--Westfälische
Wilhelms-Universität in Münster, 1988. Includes
bibliographical references.
*1. Sarcophagi, Roman - Themes, motives. 2. Mythology,
Classical, in art. 3. Relief (Sculpture), Classical -
Themes, motives. 4. Rome - Antiquities. I. Title. II.
Title: Motivschatz stadtrömischer mythologischer
Sarkophage. III. Series: Boreas (Münster, Germany).
Beiheft , 5.*   **NYPL [3-MGH 91-5059]**
Hübner, Eberhard, 1922- Wirth, Günther.
Botschaft der Taube . Stuttgart , c1989. 327 p. :
     ISBN 3-7831-1004-1
                              NYPL [3-MCK+ O279 89-28163]
Hübsch, Heinrich, 1795-1863. In what style
should we build? . Santa Monica, Calif. , 1991.
p. cm.   ISBN 0-89236-199-9 :   DDC 720/.1 20
NA2500 .I5 1991

**Huc, Reinhold Bethusy- see Bethusy-Huc,
     Reinhold, Graf.**

**Hudson Bay Company. see Hudson's Bay
     Company.**

HUDSON COUNTY, N. J. - MAPS.
(1908) Atlas of Hudson County, New Jersey.
Philadelphia, Pa. , 1908-1909. 2 atlases :
                              NYPL [Map Div. 91-4092]
**HUDSON COUNTY (N.J.) - HISTORICAL
     GEOGRAPHY - MAPS.**
Spielmann & Brush. Filed maps of Hudson
County, N.J. Hoboken, N.J. , 1881. 1 atlas (76
leaves) :   **NYPL [Map Div. 90-4088]**
Hudson, Jennifer. Bullivant, Lucy. International
interior design /. New York , 1991. p. cm.
     ISBN 1-558-59235-0   DDC 725/.09/048 20
NK1980 .B84 1991
The Hudson River and its painters /. Howat,
John K. Harmondsworth, Eng. , New York ,
1978, c1972. 208 p. :   ISBN 0-14-005080-9   DDC
758/.1/097473
ND1351.5 .H6 1978
                              NYPL [3-MAMT+ 90-11628]
Hudson River Museum.
Heslip, Colleen Cowles. Between the rivers .
Williamstown, Mass. , c1990. 95 p. :   ISBN
0-931102-28-6 :   DDC 759.14/074/744 20
ND215 .H47 1990   **NYPL [3-MCW 90-4583]**
A New consciousness . Yonkers, N.Y. , c1971.
[12] p. :
                              NYPL [3-MAX (CIBA-GEIGY) 90-7135]
Yarnall, James L. John La Farge, watercolors
and drawings /. Yonkers, N.Y. , c1990. 143 p. :
     ISBN 0-943651-24-7 :   DDC 759.13 20
N6537.L28 A4 1990
**HUDSON RIVER SCHOOL OF LANDSCAPE
     PAINTING.**
Howat, John K. The Hudson River and its
painters /. Harmondsworth, Eng. , New York ,
1978, c1972. 208 p. :   ISBN 0-14-005080-9   DDC
758/.1/097473
ND1351.5 .H6 1978
                              NYPL [3-MAMT+ 90-11628]
Powell, Earl A. Thomas Cole /. New York ,
1990. 144 p. (some col.) ;   ISBN 0-8109-3158-3
     DDC 759.13 20
ND237.C6 A4 1990
                              NYPL [3-MCX C68 90-12862]

**HUDSON RIVER SCHOOL OF LANDSCAPE
     PAINTING - EXHIBITIONS.**
American light . [Laurenceville, NJ] ,
Washington, [D.C.] , c1989. 330 p. :   ISBN
0-691-04074-5 (alk. paper) :   DDC
758/.1/09730740153 19
N8214.5.U6 A47 1989
                              NYPL [3-MAMT 90-12012]
**HUDSON RIVER VALLEY (N.Y. AND N.J.) -
     DESCRIPTION AND TRAVEL - VIEWS.**
Howat, John K. The Hudson River and its
painters /. Harmondsworth, Eng. , New York ,
1978, c1972. 208 p. :   ISBN 0-14-005080-9   DDC
758/.1/097473
ND1351.5 .H6 1978
                              NYPL [3-MAMT+ 90-11628]
**HUDSON'S BAY COMPANY - MAP
     COLLECTIONS.**
Ruggles, Richard I., 1923- A country so
interesting . Montreal , Buffalo , c1991. xix,
300 p. :   ISBN 0-7735-0679-9 :   DDC 912.71 20
                              NYPL [Map Div. 91-6178]
HUDSON'S BAY COMPANY - MAPS.
Ruggles, Richard I., 1923- A country so
interesting . Montreal , Buffalo , c1991. xix,
300 p. :   ISBN 0-7735-0679-9 :   DDC 912.71 20
                              NYPL [Map Div. 91-6178]
Huelsenbeck, Richard, 1892-1974.
Als Dada begann . [Zürich] , c1957. 92 p. :
                              NYPL [3-MAM 90-7093]

Memoirs of a Dada drummer / by Richard
Huelsenbeck ; edited, with an introduction,
notes, and bibliography by Hans J.
Kleinschmidt ; foreword by Richard Kuenzli ;
translated by Joachim Neugroschel. Berkeley :
University of California Press, 1991. liv, 202 p.,
[12] p. of plates : ill. ; 21 cm. Reprint, with new
introd. Originally published: New York : Viking Press,
1974. Includes bibliographical references (p. 191-194)
and index.   ISBN 0-520-07370-3 (pbk.)   DDC 700 20
*1. Dadaism. 2. Arts, Modern - 20th century. I.
Kleinschmidt, Hans J. II. Title.*
NX600.D3 H79 1991   **NYPL [MAL 91-7694]**

Huene, Stephan von, 1932-
Stephan von Huene : Lexichaos : vom
Verstehen des Missverstehens zum
Missverstehen des Verständlichen : eine
Klanginstallation im Kuppelsaal der Hamburger
Kunsthalle vom 8. Juni bis 8. Juli 1990.
[Hamburg] : Hamburger Kunsthalle, c1990. 1 v.
(unpaged) : ill. ; 30 cm.
*1. Huene, Stephan von, 1932- - Exhibitions. I.
Hamburger Kunsthalle. II. Title. III. Title: Lexichaos.*
N6537.H77 A4 1990

**HUENE, STEPHAN VON, 1932- -
     EXHIBITIONS.**
Huene, Stephan von, 1932- Stephan von
Huene . [Hamburg] , c1990. 1 v. (unpaged) :
N6537.H77 A4 1990

Huer, Jon. The great art hoax : essays in the
comedy and insanity of collectible art / Jon
Huer. Bowling Green, Ohio : Bowling Green
State University Popular Press, c1990. 173 p. ;
24 cm. Includes bibliographical references.   ISBN
0-87972-491-9
1. Art, Modern - Collectors and collecting. I. Title.
                              NYPL [3-MAAZ 90-12001]
Hürlimann, Martin, 1897- Italy; 225 pictures in
photogravure, introductory essay, historical
notes. London, Thames and Hudson [1953] xiii,
248 p. illus. 32 cm. Includes index.
1. Italy - Description and travel - Views. I. Title.
                              NYPL [3-MQWB+ 90-11464]
Hütt, Wolfgang. Deutsche Malerei und Graphik
im 20. Jahrhundert. [Mit 396 Abbildungen im
Text und 36 Farbtafeln]. Berlin, Henschelverlag,
1969. 602 p. illus. 28 cm. Bibliography: p. 567-589.
     DDC 760/.0943
1. Art, Modern - 20th century - Germany. I. Title.
N6868 .H78   **NYPL [3-MAMG 90-6799]**
Huggler, Max, 1903- Erich Müller-Santis : das
malerische Werk = L'oeuvre peint / Max
Huggler ; traduction française de Daniel
Hartmann. Bern : Benteli, c1990. 107 p. : ill.
(some col.) ; 27 cm. German and French.   ISBN
3-7165-0684-2   DDC 759.9494 20
*1. Müller-Santis, Erich, 1927- - Criticism and
interpretation. I. Müller-Santis, Erich, 1927-. II. Title.*
ND853.M778 H84 1990

Hugh Lane Municipal Gallery of Modern Art.
Campbell, Julian. Frank O'Meara, 1853-1888 /.

Dublin , c1989. xii, 90 p., [6] p. of plates :
ISBN 0-9514246-0-2 (pbk.)   DDC 709/.415/074
19
N6789   *NYPL [3-MCZ O54 91-4562]*

Hughes, Robert, 1936-
Amish, the art of the quilt / text, Robert
Hughes ; plate commentary, Julie Silber. 1st ed.
New York : Knopf in association with
Callaway, 1990. 207 p. : 82 col. ill. ; 36 cm.
ISBN 0-394-58781-2 : DDC 746.9/708/8287 20
1. Quilts, Amish. I. Silber, Julie, 1944-. II. Title.
NK9112 .H8 1990
          NYPL [3-MOT+ 90-12042]

Nothing if not critical : selected essays on art
and artists / Robert Hughes. 1st ed. New York :
Knopf, 1990. xii, 429 p. ; 24 cm. Includes index.
ISBN 0-394-58026-5 : DDC 709 20
1. Artists - Biography - History and criticism. I. Title.
N7445.2 .H83 1990
          NYPL [3-MAN 90-13402]

Stella, Frank. Frank Stella . [Fort Worth] ,
1984. vi, 45 p. : DDC 769.92/4 19
NE539.S72 A4 1984
          NYPL [MDG (Stella) 85-2527]

HUGO, VICTOR, 1802-1885 - INFLUENCE.
Cruysmans, Philippe, 1925- Lise Durez peint
Victor Hugo /. Bruxelles [1986] 183 p. : ISBN
2-87103-023-5
N6973.D85 C7 1986

Hugué, Manuel, 1872-1945.
Manolo Hugué : 16 febrer/15 abril, 1990,
Museu d'Art Modern, Parc de la Ciutadella,
Barcelona / [comissària de l'exposició, Mercè
Doñate ; traducció al francès, Rosa Bonvehí].
[Catalunya] : Fundació Caixa de Catalunya ;
[Barcelona] : Ajuntament de Barcelona, [1990?]
269 p. : ill. ; 28 cm. (Col·lecció Catàlegs
d'exposicions . 84) Catalan and French. ISBN
84-7609-342-X
1. Hugué, Manuel, 1872-1945 - Exhibitions. I.
Barcelona (Spain). Museo de Arte Moderno. II. Title.
IN PROCESS (ONLINE)
          NYPL [3-MGO (Hugué) 91-6103]

**HUGUÉ, MANUEL, 1872-1945 -
EXHIBITIONS.**
Hugué, Manuel, 1872-1945. Manolo Hugué .
[Catalunya] [Barcelona] [1990?] 269 p. :
ISBN 84-7609-342-X
IN PROCESS (ONLINE)
          NYPL [3-MGO (Hugué) 91-6103]

**HUGUENOTS - GERMANY - HISTORY -
16TH CENTURY.**
Stubenvoll, Willi. Die deutschen
Hugenottenstädte /. Frankfurt am Main ,
c1990. 208 p. : ISBN 3-524-69093-9
NA9199 .S78 1990

**HUGUENOTS - GERMANY - HISTORY -
17TH CENTURY.**
Stubenvoll, Willi. Die deutschen
Hugenottenstädte /. Frankfurt am Main ,
c1990. 208 p. : ISBN 3-524-69093-9
NA9199 .S78 1990

Huguet, Jean, 1925- Paul-Emile Pajot
(1873-1929) : marin-pêcheur et peintre / Jean
Huguet. Douarnenez : Le
Chasse-Marée/ArMen, 1989. 62 p., 41 leaves of
plates : ill. (some col.) ; 25 x 32 cm. Includes
bibliographical references (p. [52]). ISBN
2-903708-24-X
1. Pajot, Paul Émile, 1873-1929. I. Title.
IN PROCESS (ONLINE)
          NYPL [3-MCO+ P15 91-4805]

Huguette Berès (Art Gallery) Art graphique de la
Chine : exposition du 18 février au 12 mars
1960. Paris : Huguette Berès, 1960. [26] p. : 8
mounted ill. ; 27 cm.
1. Prints - China - Exhibitions. 2. Painting, Chinese -
Ming-Ch'ing dynasties, 1368-1912 - Exhibitions. I.
Title.   *NYPL [MDBF 90-6890]*

Hugunin, James. Spectrum . Honolulu, Hawaii ,
c1979. [32] p. :   *NYPL [MFW 91-1278]*

Huish, Marcus Bourne, 1845-1921. Samplers &
tapestry embroideries / by Marcus B. Huish.
London : B.T. Batsford, 1990. xiv, 176 p. : ill.
(some col.) ; 25 cm. Originally published: 2nd ed.
London ; New York : Longmans, Green, 1913. Includes
index. ISBN 0-7134-6463-1 DDC 746.3942 20
1. Samplers - England. 2. Tapestry - England. I. Title.
II. Title: Samplers and tapestry embroideries.
NK9143 .H8 1990

Hujar, Peter, 1934-
Peter Hujar / essays by Stephen Koch and
Thomas Sokolowski ; interviews with Fran
Lebowitz and Vince Aletti. New York, N.Y. :
Grey Art Gallery & Study Center, New York
University, 1990. 95 p. : ill. ; 28 cm. Catalog of
an exhibition held at the Grey Art Gallery & Study
Center, New York University, Jan. 17-Feb. 24, 1990
and the Fine Arts Gallery, University of British
Columbia, Vancouver, Aug. 1-Sept. 15, 1990. ISBN
0-934349-07-X (pbk.)
1. Hujar, Peter, 1934- - Exhibitions. 2. Photography,
Artistic - Exhibitions. I. Koch, Stephen. II. Sokolowski,
Thomas W. III. Lebowitz, Fran. IV. Aletti, Vince. V.
Grey Art Gallery & Study Center. VI. University of
British Columbia. Fine Arts Gallery. VII. Title.
IN PROCESS (ONLINE)
          NYPL [MFX (Hujar) 91-830]

HUJAR, PETER, 1934- - EXHIBITIONS.
Hujar, Peter, 1934- Peter Hujar /. New York,
N.Y. , 1990. 95 p. : ISBN 0-934349-07-X (pbk.)
IN PROCESS (ONLINE)
          NYPL [MFX (Hujar) 91-830]

Huldt, Åke. Svenskt glas 86 . [Göteborg] [1986]
82 p. : ISBN 91-970533-4-1
MLCS 88/02246 (N)
          NYPL [3-MPW 91-6219]

Hull, David Stewart. Cafferty, James H.,
1819-1869. James Henry Cafferty, N.A.
(1819-1869) /. New York , c1986. 55 p. :
          NYPL [3-MCX C129 91-6656]

Hull, Joan Gray. Hull, the heavenly pottery / by
Joan Gray Hull with John Burks and Dee
Konyha ; Darlene Kutzler, photographer. 1st
ed. Huron, SD (1376 Nevada SW, Huron
57350) : May be ordered from J.G. Hull,
c1990. 128 p. : ill. (some col.) ; 21 cm. "An
alphabetical, numerical, pictorial, pocket size price guide
for Hull pottery lovers." Includes bibliographical
references (p. 124) and index. DDC 738.3/09771/59
20
1. Hull Pottery Company - Catalogs. 2. Pottery - 20th
century - Ohio - Crookville - Catalogs. I. Burks, John
(John H.). II. Konyha, Dee. III. Title. IV. Title:
Heavenly pottery.
NK4210.H84 A4 1990

HULL POTTERY COMPANY - CATALOGS.
Hull, Joan Gray. Hull, the heavenly pottery /.
Huron, SD (1376 Nevada SW, Huron 57350) ,
c1990. 128 p. : DDC 738.3/09771/59 20
NK4210.H84 A4 1990

**HULL (QUÉBEC) - BUILDINGS,
STRUCTURES, ETC.**
The Architecture of Douglas Cardinal /.
Edmonton , 1989. 150 p. : ISBN 0-920897-46-0
(bound)   DDC 720/.92/4 19
          NYPL [3-MQZ+ (Cardinal) 90-10573]

Hull, the heavenly pottery /. Hull, Joan Gray.
Huron, SD (1376 Nevada SW, Huron 57350) ,
c1990. 128 p. : DDC 738.3/09771/59 20
NK4210.H84 A4 1990

Hulls and hulks in the tide of time . Urban, Erin,
1948- Staten Island, N.Y. , 1991. p. cm. ISBN
0-9623017-0-1 DDC 769.92 B 20
N6537.N64 U7 1991

Hülmbauer, Elisabeth. Gott erhalte Österreich .
Eisenstadt [1990] 239 p. :
N6807 .G67 1990

Hülsmann, Boda. Paula Modersohn-Becker : in
Freiheit zu sich selbst / Boda Hülsmann.
Stuttgart : Verlag Urachhaus, c1988. 75 p. : ill.
(chiefly col.) ; 22 cm. ISBN 3-87838-586-2
1. Modersohn-Becker, Paula, 1876-1907 - Criticism and
interpretation. I. Title. II. Title: In Freiheit zu sich
selbst.   *NYPL [3-MCK M68 90-4525]*

Hulst, Roger Adolf d'. Rubenshuis (Antwerp,
Belgium) Tekeningen van Jacob Jordaens,
1593-1678. [Antwerp, 1966] 133 p.
          NYPL [3-MCH J82 91-564]

Hultén, Björn.
Björn Hultén : möbelformgivare : en utställning
på Röhsska konstslöjdmuseet 1988 /
sammanställd av Lennart Larsson &
Marie-Louise Sundén. [S.l. : s.n., 1988?] [24]
p. : ill. ; 26 cm. Title from cover. Addenda (2 leaves
inserted. ISBN 91-7360-161-6
1. Hultén, Björn - Exhibitions. I. Röhsska
konstslöjdmuseet (Göteborg, Sweden). II. Title.
IN PROCESS (ONLINE)
          NYPL [3-MOF 91-7025]

HULTÉN, BJÖRN - EXHIBITIONS.
Hultén, Björn. Björn Hultén . [S.l. , 1988?] [24]
p. : ISBN 91-7360-161-6
IN PROCESS (ONLINE)
          NYPL [3-MOF 91-7025]

Hultén, Karl Gunnar Pontus, 1924- The
surrealists look at art : Eluard, Aragon,
Soupault, Breton, Tzara / Pontus Hulten.
Venice, CA : Lapis Press, 1990. 220 p. : ill. ;
26 cm. ISBN 0-932499-08-2
I. Title.   *NYPL [3-MAL 90-13246]*

Human anatomy /. Parramón, José María. [Cómo
dibujar la anatomía del cuerpo humano.
English.] New York , 1991. p. cm. ISBN
0-8230-2499-7 : DDC 743/.49 20
NC760 .P3413 1991

HUMAN ANATOMY.
Gordon, Louise. The figure in action . London ,
1989. 128 p. : ISBN 0-7134-5946-8 DDC 743/.49
20
NC760 .G72 1989

HUMAN BODY. see **BODY, HUMAN.**

**HUMAN ECOLOGY - CARICATURES AND
CARTOONS.**
Heine, John, 1950- A good planet is hard to
find /. Birmingham, Ala. , 1991. p. cm. ISBN
0-89732-108-1 DDC 741.5/973 20
NC1429.H377 A4 1991

HUMAN FACTORS IN ARCHITECTURE. see
ARCHITECTURE - HUMAN FACTORS.

HUMAN FIGURE IN ART.
Goldfinger, Eliot. A guide to human anatomy
for artists . New York , 1991. p. cm. ISBN
0-19-505206-4 DDC 702/.8 20
NC760 .G67 1991

Herzog, Karl. Die Gestalt des Menschen in der
Kunst und im Spiegel der Wissenschaft /.
Darmstadt , c1990. xii, 234 p. : ISBN
3-534-11010-2 DDC 704.9/421 20
N7572 .H47 1990

Jamieson, Doug. Draw from your head . New
York , 1991. p. cm. ISBN 0-8230-1374-X DDC
743/.49 20
NC760 .J34 1991

Leonardo da Vinci, 1452-1519. Leonardo knows
baseball /. San Francisco , c1991. p. cm. ISBN
0-8118-0013-X DDC 700/.92 20
NC257.L4 A4 1991

Nitschke, August, 1926- Körper in Bewegung .
Stuttgart , c1989. 399 p. : ISBN 3-7831-0955-8
DDC 704.9/42 20
N7625.5 .N58 1989

Parramón, José María. [Pintando figura al óleo.
English.] Painting figures in oil and acrylic /.
New York , 1991. p. cm. ISBN 0-8230-3632-4 :
DDC 751.45/42 20
ND1290 .P3713 1991

Renaissance bodies . London , 1990. x, 294 p. :
ISBN 0-948462-09-4 DDC 700 20
NX650.F45 R46 1990

Sheppard, Joseph, 1930- Drawing the living
figure /. New York , 1991. 144 p. : ISBN
0-486-26723-7 (pbk.) : DDC 743/.4 20
NC765 .S436 1991

HUMAN FIGURE IN ART - ENGLAND.
Renaissance bodies . London , 1990. x, 294 p. :
ISBN 0-948462-09-4 (cased) : DDC 700 20
          NYPL [3-MAMZ 90-11501]

HUMAN FIGURE IN ART - EXHIBITIONS.
Environmental figuration . Springfield, Ill. ,
c1990. 31 p. : ISBN 0-89792-130-5 DDC
757/.09773/1107477325 20
ND1292 .E59 1990

Fox, Sandi. Wrapped in glory . New York , Los
Angeles , c1990. 167 p. : ISBN 0-500-01499-X
DDC 746.9/7/097307479494 20
NK9112 .F698 1990
          NYPL [3-MOT 91-3344]

**HUMAN FIGURE IN ART - JUVENILE
LITERATURE.**
Soloff-Levy, Barbara. How to draw clowns /.
Mahwah, N.J. , c1992. p. cm. ISBN
0-8167-2477-6 (lib. bdg.) : DDC 743/.8979133
20
NC765 .S65 1992

**HUMAN FIGURE IN LITERATURE -
ENGLAND.**

Renaissance bodies . London , 1990. x, 294 p. :
ISBN 0-948462-09-4 (cased) : DDC 700 20
NYPL [3-MAMZ 90-11501]

Humanes Bustamante, Alberto. Intervenciones en
el patrimonio arquitectónico (1980-1985) /.
[Madrid] [1990] 465 p. : ISBN 84-7483-661-1
DDC 720/.28/8094609048 20
NA1301 .I57 1990

HUMANISM.
Smith, Christine (Christine Hunnikin)
Architecture in the culture of early humanism .
New York , 1991. p. cm. ISBN 0-19-506128-4
(alk. paper) DDC 724/.12 20
NA510 .S65 1991

HUMANISM IN ART.
Maiorino, Giancarlo, 1943- The cornucopian
mind and the baroque unity of the arts /.
University Park , c1990. x, 210 p. : ISBN
0-271-00679-X : DDC 700/.1 20
NX451.5.B3 M35 1990
NYPL [3-MAK 90-10647]

HUMANISTIC EDUCATION. see
EDUCATION, HUMANISTIC.

HUMANS IN ART.
Luzwick, Dierdre. Endangered species . San
Francisco, Calif. , 1992. p. ISBN 0-06-250419-3
DDC 741.973 20
NC139.L89 A4 1992

Matt, Georgia. Das Menschenbild der neuen
Sachlichkeit /. Konstanz , 1989. 168 p., xv
leaves of plates : ISBN 3-89191-308-7
ND568.5.E9 M37 1989

Parramón, José María. [Dibujando pintando
apuntes. English.] Sketching people and places
in all mediums /. New York , 1991. p. cm.
ISBN 0-8230-4852-7 : DDC 741.2 20
NC730 .P28313 1991

Pavón, Herminia. Personajes de nuestra ciudad .
Ciudad de México , 1983. 80 p. : ISBN
968-499-137-1 DDC 759.972 20
N6559.P38 A4 1983

Schwalm, Hans-Jürgen, 1955- Individuum und
Gruppe . Essen , c1990. 230 p., [36] p. of
plates : ISBN 3-89206-329-X
N6490 .S3335 1990

Shaw, Marvin S. A viewer's guide to art . Santa
Fe, N.M. , 1991. p. cm. ISBN 0-945465-66-1
DDC 704.9/48 20
N7760 .S4 1991

HUMANS IN ART - EXHIBITIONS.
M. H. De Young Memorial Museum. Man:
glory, jest, and riddle. San Francisco, 1964. 1 v.
(unpaged) *NYPL [3-MAMZ 90-7043]*

Recent painting USA. Garden City, N.Y, 19.
[43] p. *NYPL [3-MCW 90-6761]*

HUMANS IN ART - PRIVATE
COLLECTIONS - EXHIBITIONS.
American drawings . New York, 1980. [40] p. :
NYPL [3-MBH 90-6350]

Humbert, Jean, conservateur. L'Egyptomanie
dans l'art occidental / Jean-Marcel Humbert ;
préface de Jean Tulard ; avant-propos de Jean
Leclant. Courbevoie, Paris : ACR, c1989. 336
p. : ill. (some col.) ; 29 cm. An abridgement of the
author's thesis (doctoral)--Université de Paris-Sorbonne.
Includes bibliographical references (p. 321-329). ISBN
2-86770-037-X
1. Egyptian revival (Art). I. Title.
N6351.2.E39 H86 1989
NYPL [3-MAL 91-2337]

Humboldt Bay photographers. Palmquist, Peter
E. The photographers of the Humboldt Bay
Region /. Arcata, CA , c1985- v. :
NYPL [MFW 87-4565]

HUMBOLDT COUNTY (CALIF.) -
DESCRIPTION AND TRAVEL - VIEWS.
Palmquist, Peter E. The photographers of the
Humboldt Bay Region /. Arcata, CA , c1985-
v. ; *NYPL [MFW 87-4565]*

HUMBOLDT COUNTY (CALIF.) - HISTORY.
Palmquist, Peter E. The photographers of the
Humboldt Bay Region /. Arcata, CA , c1985-
v. ; *NYPL [MFW 87-4565]*

Hume, Christopher. From the wild. French.
D'après nature . Saint-Laurent, Québec , c1986.
192 p. : ISBN 2-89249-128-2 : DDC
704.9/432/0971 19
NYPL [3-MAMZ+ 91-4177]

Humfrey, Peter, 1947- The Altarpiece in the
Renaissance /. Cambridge [England] , New
York , 1990. xiv, 273 p. : ISBN 0-521-36061-7
DDC 726/.5296 20
N7862 .A48 1990 NYPL [3-MAIH 91-4497]

Humorist Walter Trier : selections from the
Trier-Fodor Foundation gift / circulated by the
Art Gallery of Ontario Extension Services,
1980-81. [Toronto] : Art Gallery of Ontario,
[c1980] 48 p. : ill. (some col.) ; 21 x 23 cm.
Bibliography: p. 44-45. "Books illustrated by Walter
Trier": p. 46-47. ISBN 0-919876-56-0 (pbk.)
1. Trier, Walter, 1890-1951 - Exhibitions. 2. German
wit and humor, Pictorial - Exhibitions. 3. Toys -
Germany - Exhibitions. I. Trier, Walter, 1890-1951. II.
Trier-Fodor Foundation. III. Art Gallery of Ontario.
Extension Dept.
NC1509.T74 A4 1980
NYPL [3-MEM (Trier) 81-644]

HUMOROUS ILLUSTRATIONS. see
CARICATURES AND CARTOONS; WIT
AND HUMOR, PICTORIAL.

HUMOROUS SONGS.
The J. Russell Young School of Expression
Class song ; The J. Russell Young School of
Expression Hymn [sound recording]. [New
York] [194-] 1 sound disc :
NCP 4246

Hundert Jahre Diözesanmuseum St. Pölten,
1888-1988. Diözesanmuseum St. Pölten
(Austria) 100 Jahre Diözesanmuseum St.
Pölten, 1888-1988 . St. Pölten, [Austria] , 1988.
96 p., [76] p. of plates :
NYPL [3-MAIH 91-6668]

Hundert Jahre Österreichisches Museum für
angewandte Kunst. Österreichisches Museum
für Angewandte Kunst. 100 Jahre
Österreichisches Museum für angewandte
Kunst. [Wien, 1964] xxxxv, 109 p.
NK520.V5 V5 NYPL [3-MNC 90-6955]

Hundert Radierungen zu den Fabeln von La
Fontaine. Chagall, Marc, 1887- Die 100
Radierungen zu den Fabeln von La Fontaine /.
Salzburg [1989] 223 p. : DDC 769.92 20
NE2056.5.C45 A4 1989

Hundert schönsten Speisekarten Österreichs. Die
100 schönsten Speisekarten Österreichs . Graz
[1982?] 160 p. : ISBN 3-900301-16-6
NC1002.M4 A14 1982

Hundertfünfzig Jahre Antikensammlungen in
Karlsruhe. 150 Jahre Antikensammlungen in
Karlsruhe . Karlsruhe , 1988. 170 p. : ISBN
3-923132-15-8
N5336.G3 K3715 1988
NYPL [3-MAE 90-12538]

Hundertwasser. Hundertwasser, 1928- Glarus,
Switzerland, c1973. 97 p.
NYPL [3-MCK H933 90-5895]

Hundertwasser, 1928-
Hundertwasser. 1973, New Zealand. 1st ed.
Glarus, Switzerland, Gruener Janura, c1973. 97
p. col. illus. 16 cm. "Hundertwasser is in the South
Pacific as the guest of honour of the City of Auckland
and the City of Auckland Art Gallery. This catalogue
was published on the event of the Hundertwasser
Exhibition in New Zealand and Australia 1973."
Accompanied by: Catalogue, exhibited originals and
water colour. 1 folded leaf.
1. Hundertwasser, 1928- - Exhibitions. I. Auckland City
Art Gallery. II. Title.
NYPL [3-MCK H933 90-5895]

HUNDERTWASSER, 1928- - EXHIBITIONS.
Hundertwasser, 1928- Hundertwasser. Glarus,
Switzerland, c1973. 97 p.
NYPL [3-MCK H933 90-5895]

Hundsalz, Brigitte. Das dionysische
Schmuckrelief / Brigitte Hundsalz. München :
Tuduv, c1987. xvii, 311 p., [32] p. of plates :
ill. ; 21 cm. (Tuduv-Studien. Reihe Archäologie . Bd.
1) Originally presented as the author's thesis
(doctoral)--Universität zu Köln, Wintersemester
1985/86. Bibliography: p. xiii-xvii. ISBN
3-88073-236-1 (Deut. Bibl.) DDC 733 19
1. Relief (Sculpture), Classical. 2. Dionysus (Greek
deity) - Art. 3. Dionysus (Greek deity) - Cult. I. Title.
II. Series.
NB133 .H86 1987 NYPL [3-MGH 91-4608]

Hüneke, Andreas. Schlemmer, Oskar, 1888-1943.
Idealist der Form . Leipzig , 1990. 429 p., xxxii
p. of plates : ISBN 3-379-00473-1 DDC 709/.2 B

20
ND588.S2818 A3 1990

HUNGARIAN ART. see ART, HUNGARIAN.

Hungarian folk jewelry /. Baloghné Horváth,
Terézia. [Népi ékszerek. English.] Budapest ,
1983. 66 p., [56] p. of plates : ISBN
963-13-1762-5 DDC 739.27/09439 19
GT2252.H9 B3513 1983
NYPL [3-MNR 90-11105]

HUNGARIAN PAINTING. see PAINTING,
HUNGARIAN.

HUNGARY - SOCIAL LIFE AND CUSTOMS.
Földes, Mihály. The folk art and customs of a
people /. [Budapest] , 1964. 134 p., [12] leaves
of plates : DDC 943.9
DB868 .F613 NYPL [MNE 90-6194]

Hünnekens, Ludger. 150 Jahre
Antikensammlungen in Karlsruhe . Karlsruhe ,
1988. 170 p. : ISBN 3-923132-15-8
N5336.G3 K3715 1988
NYPL [3-MAE 90-12538]

Hunt, Richard, 1935-
Richard Hunt : sculpture--past, present, future :
an exhibition organized by the Kalamazoo
Institute of Arts in cooperation with Kalamazoo
College : March 30-May 6, 1990, Kalamazoo
Institute of Arts, Kalamazoo, Michigan.
Kalamazoo, Mich. : The Institute, c1990. 16
p. : ill. ; 28 cm. (Bulletin / Kalamazoo Institute of
Arts . no. 77) ISBN 0-933742-17-7 DDC
708.174/17 s 730/.92 20
1. Hunt, Richard, 1935- - Exhibitions. I. Kalamazoo
Institute of Arts. II. Kalamazoo College. III. Series:
Bulletin / Kalamazoo Institute of Arts , no. 77. IV.
Title.
N582.K24 A25a no. 77 NB237.H79

HUNT, RICHARD, 1935- - EXHIBITIONS.
Hunt, Richard, 1935- Richard Hunt .
Kalamazoo, Mich. , c1990. 16 p. : ISBN
0-933742-17-7 DDC 708.174/17 s 730/.92 20
N582.K24 A25a no. 77 NB237.H79

HUNT, WILLIAM MORRIS, 1824-1879.
Webster, Sally. William Morris Hunt,
1824-1879 /. Cambridge , New York , 1991. p.
cm. ISBN 0-521-34583-9 DDC 759.13 B 20
ND237.H9 W4 1991

Hunter College. Art Gallery.
A Debate on abstraction . [New York] [1988?]
79 p. : *NYPL [3-MAL 90-12609]*

Picture this! . [New York] , c1990. 36 p. :
NYPL [MDG (Daumier) 91-4770]

Hunter Museum of Art. Cress, George. George
Cress . Chattanooga, Tenn. , c1990. 56 p. :
NYPL [3-MCX C922 91-7066]

Hunter, Sam, 1923-
American masters of the 60's . New York, NY
(130 Prince St., New York 10012) , c1990. 76
p. : DDC 709/.73/0747471 20
N6512 .A6156 1990

In the mountains of Japan : the open air
museums of Hakone and Utsukushi-ga-hara /
text by Sam Hunter ; photographs by David
Finn. New York, NY : Abbeville Press, [1988?]
288 p. : col. ill. ; 34 cm. Includes bibliographical
references and index. ISBN 0-89659-949-3 DDC
735/.23/00740952136 19
1. Chōkoku no Mori Bijutsukan - Catalogs. 2. Sculpture,
Modern - 20th century - Catalogs. 3. Sculpture -
Japan - Hakone-machi - Catalogs. 4. Open-air
museums - Japan - Hakone-machi - Catalogs. 5.
Sculpture gardens - Japan - Hakone-machi - Catalogs. I.
Finn, David, 1921-. II. Chōkoku no Mori Bijutsukan.
III. Utsukushigahara Kōgen Bijutsukan. IV. Title.
NB198 .H86 1988
NYPL [3-MGI+ 90-11775]

Modern art : painting, sculpture, architecture /
Sam Hunter and John Jacobus.3rd ed. New
York : H.N. Abrams, 1992. p. cm. "Produced by
the Vendome Press/an Alexis Gregory book." Includes
bibliographical references (p.) and index. ISBN
0-8109-3609-7 DDC 709/.04 20
1. Art, Modern - 19th century. 2. Art, Modern - 20th
century. I. Jacobus, John M. II. Title.
N6447 .H86 1992

Modern art : painting, sculpture, architecture /
Sam Hunter and John Jacobus.3rd ed.
Englewood Cliffs, N.J. : Prentice Hall ; New
York : H.N. Abrams, 1992. p. cm. Includes
bibliographical references and index. ISBN
0-13-596073-8 (pbk.) DDC 709/.04 20

1. Art, Modern - 19th century. 2. Art, Modern - 20th century. I. Jacobus, John M. II. Title.
N6447 .H86 1992b

Hunter, William. Dear happy ghosts : scenes from the Outram Picture Archive 1898-1990 / commentary by William Hunter ; introduction by Arnold Kemp. Edinburgh : Mainstream, 1990. 191 p. : ill. ; 29 cm. ISBN 1-85158-371-8 : DDC 941.443082 20
1. George Outram & Co. - Photograph collections. 2. Photojournalism - Scotland. 3. Glasgow (Scotland) - Social life and customs - Pictorial works. I. George Outram & Co. II. Title. **NYPL [MFW 91-3480]**

Hunterian Art Gallery (University of Glasgow) James McNeill Whistler at the Hunterian Art Gallery. [Glasgow] [1990]. 56 p. : ISBN 0-904254-11-9
NYPL [3-MCX W57 91-6660]

Prints & printmaking / Hunterian Art Gallery, University of Glasgow. [Glasgow] : The Gallery, c1990. 52 p. : ill. ; 24 cm. "Sponsored by Mitchells Roberton, solicitors." Includes bibliographical references (p. 52). ISBN 0-904254-08-9 DDC 760/.7441443 20
1. Prints - Scotland - Glasgow - Catalogs. 2. Hunterian Art Gallery (University of Glasgow) - Catalogs. 3. Prints - Technique. I. Title. II. Title: Prints and printmaking.
NE55.G68 G534 1990

HUNTERIAN ART GALLERY (UNIVERSITY OF GLASGOW) - CATALOGS.
Hunterian Art Gallery (University of Glasgow) Prints & printmaking /. [Glasgow] , c1990. 52 p. : ISBN 0-904254-08-9 DDC 760/.7441443 20
NE55.G68 G534 1990

Huntington Hartford Collection, New York. see New York (City). Gallery of Modern Art Including the Huntington Hartford Collection.

Huntington, N. Y. Heckscher Museum. see Heckscher Museum.

Hurlimann, Martin. see Hürlimann, Martin, 1897-

HURON COUNTY, MICH. - MAPS.
(1990) Rockford Map Publishers. Huron County, Michigan, land atlas & plat book . Rockford, Ill. [c1990] 1 atlas (65 p.) :
NYPL [Map Div. 90-11384]

Huron County, Michigan, land atlas & plat book . Rockford Map Publishers. Rockford, Ill. [c1990] 1 atlas (65 p.) :
NYPL [Map Div. 90-11384]

Hurricane Hazel /. Kennedy, Betty. Toronto , 1979. viii, 176 p., [16] leaves of plates : ISBN 0-7705-1821-4 :
QC959.C2 K46   **NYPL [JSE 91-664]**

Husain, A. B. M., 1934- Fathpur-sikri and its architecture [by] A.B.M. Husain. Dacca, Bureau of national Reconstruction [1970] x, 169 p. illus. 28 cm. Bibliography: p. [155]-163. DDC 722/.4
1. Architecture, Mogul - Fatehpur-Sikri. 2. Architecture - Fatehpur-Sikri. I. Title.
NA1508.F3 H8

Husar, Irene. Johann Joachim Winckelmann in den ostslawischen Ländern / Irene Husar. Winckelmann und Böhmen / Hugo Rokyta. Stendal : [s.n.], 1979. 98 p. ; 21 cm. (Beiträge zu der internationalen Wirkung Johann Joachim Winckelmanns . T. 2/3) Band 9 der "Beiträge der Winckelmann-Gesellschaft" Includes bibliographical references. DDC 709/.2/4 19
1. Winckelmann, Johann Joachim, 1717-1768 - Influence. 2. Art criticism - Slavic countries - Historiography. I. Rokyta, Hugo. Winckelmann und Böhmen. 1979. II. Title. III. Title: Winckelmann und Böhmen. IV. Series. V. Series: Beiträge der Winckelmann-Gesellschaft , Bd. 9.
N7483.W5 H8 1979
NYPL [3-MAB 90-12523]

HUSBANDRY. see AGRICULTURE.

Huse, Norbert.
[Venedig, die Kunst der Renaissance. English] The art of Renaissance Venice : architecture, sculpture, and painting, 1460-1590 / Norbert Huse, Wolfgang Wolters ; translated by Edmund Jephcott. Chicago : University of Chicago Press, 1990. 382 p., [32] p. of plates : ill. (some col.) ; 28 cm. Translation of: Venedig, die Kunst der Renaissance. Includes index.

Includes bibliographical references (p. 353-369) ISBN 0-226-36107-1 (alk. paper) DDC 709/.45/3109024 20
1. Art, Italian - Italy - Venice. 2. Art, Renaissance - Italy - Venice. 3. Venice (Italy) - Buildings, structures, etc. I. Wolters, Wolfgang. II. Title.
N6921.V5 H8713 1990
NYPL [3-MAMC 91-3259]

Huseboe, Arthur R., 1931- An illustrated history of the arts in South Dakota / by Arthur R. Huseboe. Sioux Falls, S.D. : Center for Western Studies, Augustana College, 1989. xiii, 396 p. : ill. (some col.) ; 29 cm. "Commissioned by the South Dakota Committee on the Humanities and the South Dakota Arts Council, with a section on Sioux Indian arts by Arthur Amiotte." Includes bibliographical references (p. 385-386) and index. ISBN 0-931170-44-3 : DDC 700/.9783 20
1. Arts, American - South Dakota. 2. Dakota Indians - Arts. 3. Indians of North America - South Dakota - Arts. 4. South Dakota Committee on the Humanities. 5. South Dakota Arts Council. I. Title.
NX510.S8 H87 1989

Hussey, Christopher, 1899- English country houses / Christopher Hussey. Softback ed. London : Antique Collector's Club, 1988. 3 v. : ill., plans ; 28 cm. Includes indexes. Includes bibliographical references. Reprint. Originally published: London : Country Life, 1955-1958. CONTENTS. - [1] Early Georgian, 1715-1760 -- [2] Mid Georgian, 1760-1800 -- [3] Late Georgian, 1800-1840. ISBN 1-85149-009-9 (set : pbk.)
1. Country homes - England. 2. Architecture, Georgian - England. 3. Interior decoration - England. I. Antique Collectors' Club. II. Title.
NYPL [3-MRG 90-12887]

Hussey, Christopher, 1899-1970. Butler, A. S. G. (Arthur Stanley George), 1888-1965. [Architecture of Sir Edwin Luytens. Vol. 1.] The domestic architecture of Sir Edwin Lutyens /. Woodbridge, Suffolk , 1989. 61 p., 110, [120] p. of plates : ISBN 1-85149-100-7
NYPL [3-MQZ++ (Lutyens) 90-12076]

Hutchinson, Garrie. Leason, Percy, 1889- Wiregrass . Melbourne , 1986. 80 p. : ISBN 0-85091-249-0 DDC 741.5/994 20
NC371.L42 A4 1986

Hutt, Antony. Goa ; a traveller's historical and architectural guide / Antony Hutt. Buckhurst Hill, Essex, England : Scorpion Publishing Ltd., 1988. 192 p. : ill. (some col.), maps, plans ; 25 cm. Includes index. Bibliography: p. [187]-188. ISBN 0-905906-66-7
1. Architecture - India - Goa. 2. Goa - History. 3. Goa - Description and travel. I. Title.
NYPL [3-MQWS 89-17186]

HÜTTE THERESIENTHAL.
Gropplero di Troppenburg, Elianna. Das bayerische Glas des Historismus dargestellt an der Hütte Theresienthal . München , c1988. 285 p., [32] p. of plates : ISBN 3-88073-275-2 DDC 338.7/6661/094336 19
NK5198.H78 G76 1988
NYPL [3-MPW 91-5027]

Hutton, Leonard, Galleries. see Leonard Hutton Galleries.

HUTTY, ALFRED, 1877-1954.
Saunders, Boyd. Alfred Hutty and the Charleston renaissance /. Orangeburg, S.C. , c1990. 127 p. : ISBN 0-87844-089-5 DDC 769.92 B 20
NE2012.H88 S28 1990
NYPL [MDG+ (Hutty) 91-5803]

Huvenne, Paul. Nieuwdorp, Hans M. J. Peter Paul Rubens, Graphiken . Andernach , 1988. 60 p. : DDC 769.92 20
NE674.R9 A4 1988
NYPL [MDG (Rubens) 90-13679]

Huxford's fine art value guide. Paducah, KY : Collector Books, <c1991- > v. <2 > : ill. ; 29 cm. ISBN 0-89145-427-6 (v. 2) : DDC 707/.5 20
1. Art - Prices. I. Collector Books. II. Title: Fine art value guide.
N8675 .H88 1991

Huyghe, René. Psychologie de l'art : résumé des cours du collège de France, 1951-1976 / René Huyghe. Monaco : Editions du Rocher, c1991. 366 p. ; 23 cm. ISBN 2-268-01023-6 : DDC 701/.15 20

1. Art - Psychology. I. Collège de France. II. Title.
N71 .H79 1991

Huyn, Marie Christine. Das Plakat in der Münchener Prinzregentenzeit / Marie Christine Huyn. München : Tuduv Verlag, c1988. 65 p., [9] p. of plates : ill. ; 21 cm. (Schriften aus dem Institut für Kunstgeschichte der Universität München . Bd. 28) Bibliography: p. 54-61. ISBN 3-88073-274-4
1. Posters - 19th century - Germany (West) - Munich. 2. Posters - 20th century - Germany (West) - Munich. 3. Posters, German - Germany (West) - Munich. I. Title. II. Series. **NYPL [3-MDW 91-6997]**

H.V. Allison Galleries.
American art : a selection of paintings, watercolors and sculpture, February 2-March 9, 1985. New York, N.Y. : H.V. Allison Galleries, 1985. 22 p. : ill. (some col.) ; 23 cm.
1. H.V. Allison Galleries - Catalogs. 2. Art, American - Catalogs. I. Title. **NYPL [3-MAMT 91-6712]**

Bellows, George, 1882-1925. George Bellows (1882-1925) . New York, N.Y. [1984] 30 p. :
NYPL [3-MCX B44 91-6268]

H.V. ALLISON GALLERIES - CATALOGS.
H.V. Allison Galleries. American art . New York, N.Y. , 1985. 22 p. :
NYPL [3-MAMT 91-6712]

Hyams, Jay, 1949- Moore, Gene. My time at Tiffany's /. New York , c1990. 232 p. : ISBN 0-312-03473-3 DDC 659.1/57 B 20
HF5849.J6 M66 1990
NYPL [3-MLT+ 91-3269]

Hybrid imagery . Greiman, April. New York , 1990. 158 p. : ISBN 0-8230-2518-7 : DDC 741.6 20
NC998.5.A1 G75 1990
NYPL [3-MDW 90-10910]

HYBRIDITY OF RACES. see MISCEGENATION.

HYDE, HELEN, 1868-1919 - CRITICISM AND INTERPRETATION.
Mason, Tim, 1934- Helen Hyde /. Washington , c1991. 120 p. : ISBN 1-560-98009-5 (pbk.) DDC 769.92 20
NE539.H9 M37 1991
NYPL [MDG (Hyde) 91-7232]

The hydrogen jukebox . Schjeldahl, Peter. Berkeley , c1991. p. cm. ISBN 0-520-06731-2 (alk. paper) DDC 709/.04 20
N6447 .S345 1991

HYDROGRAPHIC CHARTS. see NAUTICAL CHARTS.

HYDROGRAPHY - CHILE - MAPS.
Instituto Hidrográfico de la Armada. Atlas hidrográfico de Chile /. [Valparaíso] , 1974. 37, [14], [212] p. : DDC 623.89/2
G1751.C3 I5 1974
NYPL [Map Div. 91-6470]

Hyldest til Fransk Kunst : fra Courbet til Soulages. Franske tegninger fra Musée du Louvre og Musée National d'Art Moderne, Paris, samt Den kongelige Kobberstikamsling, København. Katalog ved Hanne Finsen. København, Statens Museum for Kunst, 1967. 115 p. : ill. ; 21 cm. Danish and French. "Den Kongelige Kobberstiksammling. Udstilling no. 121-sommeren 1967." Added t.p. title: Hommage à l'art français: de Courbet à Soulages. Includes bibliographical references.
1. Drawing, French - Exhibitions. 2. Drawing - 19th century - France - Exhibitions. 3. Drawing - 20th century - France - Exhibitions. I. Finsen, Hanne. II. Kongelige Kobberstiksamling (Statens museum for kunst). III. Musée du Louvre. IV. Musée national d'art moderne (France). V. Title: Hommage a l'art français.
NYPL [3-MBH 90-5670]

Hylton, Jane. Adelaide angries : South Australian painting of the 1940s / Jane Hylton. Adelaide : Art Gallery Board of South Australia, 1989. 80 p. : ill. (some col.) ; 30 cm. Catalog of an exhibition held at the Art Gallery of South Australia, Nov. 10, 1989-Jan. 29, 1990 and at 2 other locations through June 3, 1990. Bibliography: p. 80. ISBN 0-7308-0772-X
1. Painting, Australian - Australia - Adelaide (S. Aust.) - Exhibitions. 2. Painting, Modern - 20th century - Australia - Adelaide (S. Aust.) - Exhibitions. I. Art Gallery of South Australia. II. Title.
NYPL [3-MCY+ 90-13322]

Hynais, Vojtěch, 1854-1925. Mžyková, Marie. Vojtěch Hynais /. Praha , 1990. 108 p. : ISBN

80-207-0007-2 :
ND534.5.H96 M99 1990

HYNAIS, VOJTĚCH, 1854-1925.
Mžyková, Marie. Vojtěch Hynais /. Praha ,
1990. 108 p. : ISBN 80-207-0007-2 :
ND534.5.H96 M99 1990

Hypo-Kulturstiftung (Munich, Germany).
Kunsthalle.
Königliches Dresden . München , c1990. 216
p. : ISBN 3-7913-1113-1
NYPL [3-MAMG+ 91-4691]

Miró, Joan, 1893- Joan Miro, Skulpturen /.
München , c1990. 246, [1] p. : ISBN
3-7774-5300-5 DDC 730/.92 20
NB813.M5 A4 1990

Zorn, Anders, 1860-1920. Anders Zorn,
1860-1920 . [München] , 1989. 237 p. : ISBN
3-923701-36-5
NYPL [3-MCZ Z89 90-11754]

I am a Networker (sometimes) . Fricker, H. R.
St. Gallen , c1989. 125 p. : ISBN
3-909090-07-9 :
IN PROCESS (ONLINE)
NYPL [3-MAL+ 90-12013]

I bozzetti di Sartorio per il Duomo di Messina /.
Barbera, Gioacchino. Palermo , c1989. 158 p. :
ISBN 88-7681-048-X :
NC257.S2685 B37 1989

ICOM. see **International Council of Museums.**

I chiostri di Brescia . Terraroli, Valerio. [Brescia]
[1989] 171 p. : ISBN 88-7385-052-9 DDC
726/.7/094526 20
NA5621.B8 T47 1989

I dipinti dell'Ottocento e Novecento . Torresi,
Antonio P., 1951- Ferrara [1990] 168 p. :
DDC 751.6/2/0945 20
ND617 .T66 1990

I dipinti olandesi del Seicento e del Settecento /.
Chiarini, Marco. Roma , 1989. xxiii, 671 p. :
ISBN 88-24-00001-0 DDC 759.9492/074/4551
20
ND646 .C48 1989

I don't want to play cards with Cézanne, and
other works : selections from the Chinese New
Wave and Avant-Garde art of the eighties /
edited by Richard E. Strassberg. Pasadena,
Calif. : Pacific Asia Museum, 1991. xii, 104 p. :
ill. (some col.) ; 28 cm. Includes bibliographical
references. ISBN 1-87792-105-X DDC
760/.0951/07479493 20
1. Painting, Chinese - Exhibitions. 2. Painting,
Modern - 20th century - China - Exhibitions. 3. Prints -
20th century - China - Exhibitions. 4. Avant-garde
(Aesthetics) - China - History - 20th century -
Exhibitions. I. Strassberg, Richard E. II. Pacific Asia
Museum.
ND1045 .I16 1991

I draw, I paint.
Rouira, Albert. [Yo dibujo, yo pinto ceras.
English.] Wax crayons . New York , c1991. p.
cm. ISBN 0-8120-4718-4 DDC 741.2/3 20
NC870 .R6813 1991

Sánchez Sánchez, Isidro. [Yo dibujo, yo pinto
acuarela. English.] Water color . New York ,
c1991. p. cm. ISBN 0-8120-4717-6 DDC
751.42/2 20
ND2420 .S2613 1991

Sánchez Sánchez, Isidro. [Yo dibujo, yo pinto
lápices de colores. English.] Colored pencils .
New York , c1991. p. cm. ISBN 0-8120-4719-2
DDC 741.2/4 20
NC892 .S2613 1991

I Gigli dell'arte .
([5]) Leone de Castris, Pierluigi. Simone
Martini . Firenze , c1989. 159 p. : ISBN
88-7737-051-3
NYPL [MCF M38 90-12598]

(12) Paolucci, Antonio. Piero della Francesca .
Firenze , c1990. 159 p. : ISBN 88-7737-071-8 :
DDC 759.5 20
ND623.P548 A4 1990

(4) Ragionieri, Giovanna. Duccio . Firenze ,
c1989. 159 p. : ISBN 88-7737-058-0
NYPL [MCF D82 91-4998]

(6) Natali, Antonio. Andrea del Sarto .
Firenze , c1989. 159 p. : ISBN 88-7737-068-8
NYPL [3-MCF S24 90-12007]

(7) Berti, Luciano. Masaccio . Firenze , c1989.

---

159 p. : ISBN 88-7737-059-9
NYPL [MCF M39 90-13563]

(8) Verzotti, Giorgio. Boccioni . Firenze ,
c1989. 159 p. : ISBN 88-7737-055-6
NYPL [3-MCF B665 90-12871]

I Gioielli di Roma .
(3) De Marchi, Andrea. Le fontanelle di Roma
/. Roma , 1988. 61 p. :
NYPL [3-MRN 90-10437]

I Grandi.
Brandi, Cesare. Morandi /. Roma , 1990. 249
p., [37] p. of plates : ISBN 88-359-3363-3 :
N6923.M6 B7 1990

I had a frightmare! /. Keane, Bil, 1922- [Family
circus. Selections.] New York , 1990. 1 v.
(unpaged) : ISBN 0-449-14615-4 : DDC
741.5/973 20
NC1429.K29 A4 1990

I. K. Ae. Reihe. see **Institut für kultur und**
Ästhetik. Schriften.

I. K. Ae. Schriften. see **Institut für kultur und**
Ästhetik. Schriften.

I Libri blu.
Sinisgalli, Leonardo, 1908- Promenades
architecturales /. Bergamo , c1987. 125 p. ;
ISBN 88-7766-013-9 :
NA1111 .S48 1987
NYPL [3-MQWB 91-6903]

I Longobardi / a cura di Gian Carlo Menis ;
scritti di E.A. Arslan ... [et al.]. Milano :
Electa, c1990. 492 p. : ill. (some col.), maps ;
28 cm. "Mostra promossa dalla Regione Friuli-Venezia
Giulia"--P. [13]. Exhibition held at various sites in
Cividale, Italy, and Passariano, Italy. Includes
bibliographical references (p. 478-492). ISBN
88-435-3210-3
1. Lombard - Italy - Exhibitions. I. Menis, Gian
Carlo. II. Arslan, Ermanno A. III. Friuli-Venezia Giulia
(Italy).
N6919.L8 L67 1990

I.M. Pei . Wiseman, Carter. New York , 1990.
320 p. : ISBN 0-8109-3709-3 DDC 720/.92 B 20
NA737.P365 W57 1990
NYPL [3-MQZ (Pei) 90-12859]

I macchiaioli e la scuola di Castiglioncello /.
Dini, Piero. [Rosignano Marittimo] [1990] 217
p. :
ND617.5.M3 D57 1990

I miei ricordi, 1851-1924 . Broggi, Luigi,
1851-1926. Milano, Italy , c1989. 301 p. :
ISBN 88-20-43560-8 : DDC 720/.92 B 20
NA1123.B76 A2 1989

I Palazzi del Senato.
Borsi, Franco. Palazzo Cenci /. Roma , c1989.
119 p. : ISBN 88-7060-222-2
IN PROCESS (ONLINE)
NYPL [3-MQWB+ 91-4178]

I Supporti nelle arti pittoriche : storia, tecnica,
restauro / E.I. Basile ... [et al.] ; a cura di
Corrado Maltese. Milano : Mursia, c1990. 2 v. ;
22 cm. (Strumenti per una nuova cultura. Guide e
manuali) Includes bibliographical references and index.
CONTENTS. - pt. 1. Supporti parietali per graffiti e
dipinti, mosaici e tarsie, supporti lapidei e vitrei,
supporti metallici, gli smalti, supporti lignei -- pt. 2.
Introduzione ai supporti tessili, le tele per la pittura, gli
arazzi, i tappeti, il cuoio, la pergamena, la carta. DDC
702/.8/8 20
1. Painting - Conservation and restoration. I. Basile, E.
I. (Elisabetta Ingrid). II. Maltese, Corrado, 1921-.
ND1640 .S89 1990

I tawt I taw a puddy tat . Beck, Jerry. New
York , c1991. p. cm. ISBN 0-8050-1644-9 DDC
741.5/09794/03 20
NC1766.U52 W37334 1991

I Tiepolo e il Settecento vicentino / a cura di
Fernando Rigon ... [et al.]. Milano : Electa,
c1990. 404 p. : ill. (some col.) ; 28 cm. Catalog
of exhibitions held in Vicenza, Montecchio Maggiore
and Bassano del Grappa, Italy, May 26-Sept. 20, 1990.
Includes bibliographical references. ISBN
88-435-3180-8
1. Tiepolo, Giovanni Battista, 1696-1770 - Exhibitions.
2. Tiepolo, Giovanni Domenico, 1726?-1804 -
Exhibitions. 3. Art, Italian - Italy - Vicenza (Province) -
Exhibitions. 4. Art, Modern - 17th-18th centuries -
Italy - Vicenza (Province) - Exhibitions. I. Tiepolo,
Giovanni Battista, 1696-1770. II. Tiepolo, Giovanni
Domenico, 1726?-1804. III. Rigon, Fernando.
N6923.T5 A4 1990

Īablons'ka, Tetīāna Nylivna, 1917-
Tat′iāna Nilovna Iablonskaīa : zhivopis′,
risunok / [avtor vstupitel′noī stat′i A.I.
Solov′ev ; sostaviteli kataloga I.E. Gorbacheva,
L.S. Koval′skaīa]. Moskva : Sov. khudozhnik,
1989. 1 v. (unpaged) : chiefly col. ill. ; 29 cm.
ISBN 5-269-00340-6 :
1. Īablons′ka, Tetīāna Nylivna, 1917- - Catalogs. I.
Horbachova, I. O. II. Koval′skaīa, Līudmila. III. Title.
N7193.I13 A4 1989

Īablons'ka, Tetīāna Nylivna, 1917- -
CATALOGS.
Īablons′ka, Tetīāna Nylivna, 1917- Tat′iāna
Nilovna Iablonskaīa . Moskva , 1989. 1 v.
(unpaged) : ISBN 5-269-00340-6 :
N7193.I13 A4 1989

Īablonskaīa, M. (Mīuda) Women artists of
Russia's new age, 1900-1935 / M.N.
Yablonskaya ; edited by Anthony Parton.
London : Thames and Hudson, c1990. 248 p. :
ill. (some col.) 29 cm. Includes index. Bibliography:
p. 237-238. ISBN 0-500-23559-7
1. Avant-garde (Aesthetics) - Russian S.F.S.R. -
History - 20th century. 2. Constructivism (Art) -
Russian S.F.S.R. 3. Women artists - Russian S.F.S.R. I.
Parton, Anthony. II. Title.
NYPL [3-MAM 90-12322]

Ian Hamilton Finlay /. Finlay, Ian Hamilton.
[Basel] , 1990. [79] p. :
MLCL 90/00821 (N)
NYPL [MDG+ (Finlay) 91-4829]

Ian McKeever, a history of rocks, 1986-1988 /.
McKeever, Ian, 1946- München [1990] 49 p. :
DDC 759.2 20
ND497.M5 A4 1990

Ianelli, Arcangelo, 1922-
Arcangelo Ianelli : Staatliche Kunsthalle Berlin,
Ausstellung vom 5. Mai bis 5. Juni 1988 /
[Redaktion und Kataloggestaltung, Dieter
Ruckhaberle ... et al. ; Übersetzung, Sarita
Brandt]. 1. Aufl. Berlin : Die Kunsthalle, c1988.
79 p. : chiefly ill. (chiefly col.) ; 32 cm. German
and Portuguese. Includes bibliographical references (p.
13).
1. Ianelli, Arcangelo, 1922- - Exhibitions. I.
Ruckhaberle, Dieter. II. Staatliche Kunsthalle Berlin.
III. Title.
ND359.I15 A4 1988

Beuttenmüller, Alberto, 1935- Volpi, Ianelli,
Aldir . [São Paulo , 1989] 1 v. (unpaged) :
ND355 .B48 1989

IANELLI, ARCANGELO, 1922- -
EXHIBITIONS.
Ianelli, Arcangelo, 1922- Arcangelo Ianelli .
Berlin , c1988. 79 p. :
ND359.I15 A4 1988

IANELLI, ARCANGELO, 1922- - THEMES,
MOTIVES.
Beuttenmüller, Alberto, 1935- Volpi, Ianelli,
Aldir . [São Paulo , 1989] 1 v. (unpaged) :
ND355 .B48 1989

Ibáñez Pérez, Alberto C. Historia de la Casa del
Cordón de Burgos / Alberto C. Ibáñez Pérez.
[Burgos] : Caja de Ahorros Municipal de
Burgos, 1987. 359 p. : ill. (some col.) ; 28 cm.
Includes bibliographical references (p. 348-349). ISBN
84-505-5944-8
1. Casa del Cordón (Burgos, Spain). 2. Palaces - Spain -
Burgos. 3. Burgos, Spain - History. I. Title.
NYPL [3-MQWH 91-7280]

Die iberischen Bronzevotive. Nicolini, Gérard.
Kallmünz/Opf., 1967. 49 p. with illus.
NYPL [L-11 3436 Nr. 10]

IBM Gallery of Science and Art. The Rise of a
great tradition . New York [1990?] 112 p. :
ISBN 0-913304-30-1
NYPL [3-MPFK+ 91-5067]

Icaza. Icaza, Ernesto. Un charro pintor .
[Monterrey, Mexico] [1986] 1 v. (unpaged) :
DDC 759.972 20
ND259.I28 A4 1986

Icaza, Ernesto.
Un charro pintor : Ernesto Icaza : Museo de
Monterrey, septiembre-noviembre 1986.
[Monterrey, Mexico] : El Museo, [1986] 1 v.
(unpaged) : col. ill. ; 20 x 27 cm. Cover title:
Icaza. Spanish and English. Text by Xavier Moyssén.
DDC 759.972 20
1. Icaza, Ernesto - Exhibitions. 2. Charros in art -
Exhibtions. 3. Mexico - Social life and customs -

Pictorial works - Exhibitions. I. Moyssén Echeverría,
Xavier. II. Museo de Monterrey. III. Title. IV. Title:
Icaza.
ND259.I28 A4 1986

ICAZA, ERNESTO - EXHIBITIONS.
Icaza, Ernesto. Un charro pintor. [Monterrey,
Mexico] [1986] 1 v. (unpaged) : DDC 759.972
20
ND259.I28 A4 1986

ICE CARVING.
Matsuo, Yukio. [Hyōchōbi. English.] Ice
sculpture /. New York , 19. p. cm. ISBN
0-471-55409-X DDC 736/.94 20
NK6030 .M3813 1992

Ice sculpture /. Matsuo, Yukio. [Hyōchōbi.
English.] New York , 19. p. cm. ISBN
0-471-55409-X DDC 736/.94 20
NK6030 .M3813 1992

Ich bin mit dir . Mayer, Klaus. Würzburg , 1989.
115 p. : ISBN 3-429-01137-3
NYPL [MDG+ (Chagall) 89-18773]

ICON VENERATION. see ICONS - CULT.

Iconclass indexes. Italian prints /. Straten,
Roelof van. Doornspijk, The Netherlands ,
c1987- v. ; ISBN 90-70288-35-4
NYPL [MDBF 89-1708]

Icônes & sculptures. Durand, Régis. Pascal Kern .
[Paris] , c1989. [16] p., 15 plates : ISBN
2-86234-035-9
NYPL [3-MGO (Kern) 91-3283]

Icônes et merveilles : mille ans de tradition
chrétienne : collections françaises et
européennes : Musée Cernuschi, 26 nov.
1988-19 fév. 1989. Paris : Le Musée, c[1988]
[116] p. : ill. (some col.), 1 map ; 28 cm. At
head of title: Hommage au Millénaire du baptême de la
Russie. Includes bibliographical references (p. [116]).
ISBN 2-905197-10-2
*1. Icons, Russian - Exhibitions. 2. Christian art and
symbolism - Russian S.F.S.R. - Exhibitions. I. Musée
Cernuschi. II. Title: Hommage au Millénaire du
baptême de la Russie.*
NYPL [3-MAIH 91-5048]

Icônes et sculptures. Durand, Régis. Pascal
Kern . [Paris] , c1989. [16] p., 15 plates :
ISBN 2-86234-035-9
NYPL [3-MGO (Kern) 91-3283]

Iconoclasts and their motives /. Freedberg,
David. Maarssen , Montclair, N.J. , c1985. 60
p. : ISBN 90-6179-056-5 (pbk.) DDC 709 19
N8557 .F74 1985   *NYPL [3-MAS 91-5030]*

Iconografía de Sevilla, 1650-1790 /. Serrera
Contreras, Juan Miguel. Madrid , c1989. 292
p. : ISBN 84-86022-35-2
NYPL [3-MAML+ 91-2661]

Iconografía mariana nei masi dell'Alto Adige /.
Giatti, Natalia. Calliano [Trento] , c1990. 256
p. : ISBN 88-7024-408-3
NYPL [3-MAIH+ 91-4956]

**Iconografía y fiesta durante el lustro real,
1729-1733** /. León, Aurora. Sevilla , 1990. 189
p. : ISBN 84-7798-045-4
N7111.S5 L46 1990

Iconographie médiévale : image, texte, contexte /
sous la direction de Gaston Duchet-Suchaux.
Paris : Editions du Centre national de la
recherche scientifique : Diffusion, Presses du
CNRS, 1990. 207 p. : ill. ; 24 cm. At head of
title: Centre régional de publication de Paris, Institut de
recherche et d'histoire des textes. Includes
bibliographical references. ISBN 2-222-04344-1 :
DDC 709/.02 20
*1. Art, Medieval - Themes, motives. I. Duchet-Suchaux,
Gaston. II. Institut de recherche et d'histoire des textes
(France).*
N5970 .I26 1990

**ICONOGRAPHY. see ART; CHRISTIAN ART
AND SYMBOLISM; IDOLS AND
IMAGES; PORTRAITS.**

**The iconography of the Maltese Islands,
1400-1900** . Buhagiar, Mario, 1945- Valletta,
Malta , 1988. 202 p. : DDC 759.58/5 20
ND955.M3 B84 1988

**The iconography of the sarcophagus of Junius
Bassus** /. Malbon, Elizabeth Struthers.
Princeton, N.J. , c1990. xix, 256 p., [22] p. of
plates : ISBN 0-691-07355-4 (alk. paper) : DDC

733/.5/09376 20
NB1810 .M26 1990
NYPL [3-MGH 91-4522]

Icons and their history /. Rice, David Talbot,
1903-1972. Woodstock, N.Y. , 1974. 192 p., [4]
leaves of plates : ISBN 0-87951-021-8 : DDC
755/.2
N8187 .R52 1974   *NYPL [MAIH 76-974]*

**ICONS, BULGARIAN - BULGARIA -
MELNIK.**
Bakalova, Elka. Rozhenskiĭat manastir /.
Sofiia , 1990. 107 p. :
ND2802.M45 B3 1990

ICONS, BYZANTINE - THEMES, MOTIVES.
Four Byzantine and Russian icons in the Menil
Collection /. Houston, Tex. , c1991. p. cm.
ISBN 0-939594-21-8 DDC 704.9/482 20
N8186.U6 M474 1991

ICONS - CULT.
Belting, Hans, 1935- Bild und Kult . München ,
c1990. 700 p. : ISBN 3-406-34367-8
NYPL [3-MAIH 90-12870]

ICONS - EXHIBITIONS.
Ikonen und ostkirchliches Kultgerät aus
rheinischem Privatbesitz . Köln , 1990. 205 p. :
DDC 704.9/482 20
N8186.G3 C655 1990

ICONS - HISTORY.
Rice, David Talbot, 1903-1972. Icons and their
history /. Woodstock, N.Y. , 1974. 192 p., [4]
leaves of plates : ISBN 0-87951-021-8 : DDC
755/.2
N8187 .R52 1974   *NYPL [MAIH 76-974]*

**ICONS - PRIVATE COLLECTIONS -
GERMANY - RHINELAND -
EXHIBITIONS.**
Ikonen und ostkirchliches Kultgerät aus
rheinischem Privatbesitz . Köln , 1990. 205 p. :
DDC 704.9/482 20
N8186.G3 C655 1990

**ICONS - PRIVATE COLLECTIONS -
SWITZERLAND - GENEVA -
EXHIBITIONS.**
Russische Ikonen 1400-1700 . [Hamburg]
[1990] 74, [2] p. : DDC 704.9/482 20
N8189.S62 R9757 1990

ICONS, RUSSIAN.
Russian copper icons and crosses from the
Kunz Collection . Washington, D.C. , 1990. p.
cm. DDC 730/.947 20
NK1653.S65 R8 1990

Stichel, Rainer. Die Geburt Christi in der
russischen Ikonenmalerei . Stuttgart , 1990. 176
p., 92 p. of plates : ISBN 3-515-04273-3 DDC
755/.53/0947 20
N8189.S62 R9773 1990

ICONS, RUSSIAN - EXHIBITIONS.
Icônes et merveilles . Paris , c[1988] [116] p. :
ISBN 2-905197-10-2
NYPL [3-MAIH 91-5048]

Russische Ikonen 1400-1700 . [Hamburg]
[1990] 74, [2] p. : DDC 704.9/482 20
N8189.S62 R9757 1990

ICONS, RUSSIAN - THEMES, MOTIVES.
Four Byzantine and Russian icons in the Menil
Collection /. Houston, Tex. , c1991. p. cm.
ISBN 0-939594-21-8 DDC 704.9/482 20
N8186.U6 M474 1991

ICONS - WASHINGTON (D.C.)
Russian copper icons and crosses from the
Kunz Collection . Washington, D.C. , 1990. p.
cm. DDC 730/.947 20
NK1653.S65 R8 1990

IDAHO IN ART - EXHIBITIONS.
Harthorn, Sandy, 1945- One hundred years of
Idaho art, 1850-1950 . Boise, ID , c1990. 134
p. : DDC 709/.796/07479628 20
N6530.I2 H37 1990
NYPL [3-MAMT 90-11110]

The idea of Rococo /. Park, William, 1930-
Newark , 1992. p. cm. ISBN 0-87413-434-X
DDC 700/.9/033 20
NX452.5.R6 P37 1992

An ideal country . Merrill, Linda, 1959-
Washington, D.C. , Hanover [N.H.] , c1990.
200 p. : ISBN 0-87451-538-6 (alk. paper) DDC
759.13 20
ND237.T83 A4 1990
NYPL [3-MCX T87 91-4949]

IDEALISM IN ART.
Marlais, Michael Andrew. Conservative echoes
in Fin de siècle Parisian art criticism /.
University Park, Pa. , c1992. p. cm. ISBN
0-271-00773-7 (acid-free paper) DDC
701/.18/094436109034 20
N7476 .M37 1992

IDEALISM IN ART - CONGRESSES.
Proudy české umělecké tvorby 19. století .
Praha , 1990. 262 p. :
NX650.I34 P76 1990

IDEALISM IN ART - EXHIBITIONS.
Michel, Régis. Le beau idéal . Paris , 1989. 176
p. : ISBN 2-7118-2317-2
NYPL [3-MA 90-12383]

Idealist der Form . Schlemmer, Oskar,
1888-1943. Leipzig , 1990. 429 p., xxxii p. of
plates : ISBN 3-379-00473-1 DDC 709/.2 B 20
ND588.S2818 A3 1990

Ideas e imágenes en la Argentina de hoy.
[Buenos Aires, Argentina] : Ministerio de
Relaciones Exteriores y Culto, República
Argentina, [between 1984 and 1987] 1 v.
(unpaged) : ill. ; 24 cm. Exhibition catalog.   DDC
759.982/09/048074 20
*1. Painting, Argentine - Exhibitions. 2. Painting,
Modern - 20th century - Argentina - Exhibitions. I.
Argentina. Ministerio de Relaciones Exteriores y Culto.*
ND335 .I34 1987

Idee : HBK Grafikdesign : Braunschweigisches
Landesmuseum, Mai-Juli 88, Niedersächsischer
Landtag Hannover, März-April 89, Deutsches
Plakat Museum Essen, Juni-Sept. 89 /
[Herausgeber, Rektor der Hochschule für
Bildende Künste Braunschweig, Referat für
Öffentlichkeitsarbeit und Weiterbildung ;
Redaktionelle Betreuung, Gerhard Baller ;
Textverarbeitung, Inge Cramm ... et al.].
[Braunschweig] : Die Hochschule, 1988. 169
p. : ill. ; 20 x 21 cm. ISBN 3-88895-025-2
*1. Graphic arts - Germany (West) - History - 20th
century - Exhibitions. I. Hochschule für Bildende
Künste Braunschweig. II. Braunschweigisches
Landesmuseum für Geschichte und Volkskum.*
IN PROCESS (ONLINE)
NYPL [3-MDW 91-6406]

Identidade e convulsión . Seoane, Xavier, 1954-
Sada, A Coruña [1990] 322 p. : ISBN
84-7492-461-8 DDC 709/.46/109048 20
N7109.G3 S46 1990

Identidade. Série Cultura portuguesa, 0871-4428.
Lino, António. O homem e a casa, a casa e o
tempo /. [Lisboa] , 1990. 131 p. :
NK1103 .L56 1990

**Identification d'oeuvres ayant fait partie de la
succession de Madame Veuve Edouard Manet.**
Mathey, Jacques. Paris [1964] [30] p.
NYPL [3-MCO M27 90-5874]

Identifying American brillant cut glass /.
Boggess, Bill. West Chester, Pa. , c1991. x, 283
p. : ISBN 0-88740-296-8 DDC 748.2913/075 20
NK5203 .B64 1991

The Ideological crisis of expressionism : the
literary and artistic German war colony in
Belgium 1914-1918 / edited by Rainer Rumold
and O.K. Werckmeister.1st ed. Columbia, S.C. :
Camden House, c1990. 299 p. : ill. ; 24 cm.
(Studies in German literature, linguistics, and culture ;
v. 51) Includes bibliographical references. ISBN
0-938100-77-7 (alk. paper) DDC 700 20
*1. Expressionism (Art) - Germany. 2. Arts, Modern -
20th century - Germany. 3. Germans - Belgium -
Biography. 4. Belgium - History - German occupation,
1914-1918. I. Rumold, Rainer. II. Werckmeister, O. K.
(Otto Karl), 1934-.*
NX550.A1 I33 1990
NYPL [3-MAMG 90-11742]

Idiens, Dale. Cook Islands art / Dale Idiens.
Princes Risborough, Buckinghamshire, UK :
Shire, 1990. 64 p. : ill. ; 21 cm. (Shire
ethnography . 18) Includes bibliography and index.
ISBN 0-7478-0061-8 (pbk.) : DDC 709.0110996
20
1. Art, Polynesian. I. Title. II. Series.
NYPL [3-MADF 91-6597]

IDOLS AND IMAGES - EXHIBITIONS.
Herrscher, Krieger und Geliebte . Innsbruck ,
c1989. 95 p., [6] p. of plates :
NYPL [3-MGR 91-3460]

ÏErmilov, Vasyl', 1894-1968.
Vasily Dmitrievich Ermilov, 1894-1968 :
gouaches, sculpture, reliefs. New York :
Leonard Hutton Galleries, 1990. 64 p. : ill.
(some col.), ports. ; 31 cm. Catalog of an
exhibition held at Leonard Hutton Galleries, New York,
April 27-June 8, 1990.
*1. ÏErmilov, Vasyl', 1894-1968 - Exhibitions. I. Leonard
Hutton Galleries. II. Title.*
        NYPL [3-MCZ+ I215 91-6688]

**ÏERMILOV, VASYL', 1894-1968 -
    EXHIBITIONS.**
IErmilov, Vasyl', 1894-1968. Vasily Dmitrievich
Ermilov, 1894-1968 . New York , 1990. 64 p. :
        NYPL [3-MCZ+ I215 91-6688]

If cats could talk! /. Vey, P. C. (Peter C.) New
York, N.Y., U. S.A., c1991. 1 v. (unpaged) :
        ISBN 0-452-26642-4 :   DDC 741.5/973 20
NC1429.V57 A4 1991

If pictures could talk . Coran, James L. Oakland,
Calif., c1989. 382 p. :   ISBN 0-938842-07-2
        NYPL [3-MCW+ 90-12851]

Igirisu bijutsu wa ima : uchinaru shigaku /
[henshū Setagaya Bijutsukan ... [et al.] =
British art now : a subjective view / [edited by
Setagaya Art Museum ... et al.]. Tōkyō : Asahi
Shinbunsha, c1990. 151 p. : ill. (some col.) ; 28
cm. Japanese and English. Catalog of an exhibition
held at Setagaya Bijutsukan, Aug. 25-Oct. 7, 1990 and
at other 5 locations through June 1991. Includes
bibliographical references.
*1. Art, British - Exhibitions. 2. Art, Modern - 20th
century - Great Britain - Exhibitions. I. Setagaya
Bijutsukan. II. Title: British art now.*
        NYPL [3-MAMR 91-7545]

Igit'yan, Henrik. K'och'ar, Ervand, 1899- Ervand
K'och'ar. Erevan , 1972. 89 p. :
        NYPL [3-MCZ K762 89-27399]

**IGLESIA DE SAN TELMO (SAN SEBASTIÁN,
    SPAIN)**
Fornells Angelats, Montserrat, 1953- Los
lienzos de José María Sert en la Iglesia de San
Telmo, de San Sebastián /. San Sebastián ,
1985. 206, [12] p. :
ND813.S47 F67 1985
        NYPL [3-MCQ S49 90-13288]

Ignacy Gierdziejewski /. Kozakiewicz, Stefan.
Wrocław , 1958. 175 p. :
ND955.P63 G4835 1958

**II centenario de la Plaza Ochavada de Archidona
/.** Coloquio de Urbanismo Barroco (1986 :
Archidona, Spain) [Málaga] [1989] 350 p. :
        ISBN 84-7496-177-7
NA1306 .C6 1986

**IKE, TAIGA, 1723-1776 - CRITICISM AND
    INTERPRETATION.**
Takeuchi, Melinda. Taiga's true views .
Stanford, Calif. , 1991. p. cm. ISBN
0-8047-1915-2 DDC 759.952 20
ND1059.I4 T35 1991

**IKEBANA. see FLOWER ARRANGEMENT,
    JAPANESE.**

Ikon Gallery.
Brett, Guy. Transcontinental . London ; New
York : 112 p. :   ISBN 0-86091-511-5
        NYPL [3-MAM 91-7008]

Garrard, Rose. Rose Garrard . Birmingham
[England] [1983?] 32 p. :
N6797.G37 I5 1983
        NYPL [3-MGO (Garrard) 90-10680]

Ikona Gallery. Fotografie di Ikona Gallery .
Venezia , 1989. 54 p. :
        NYPL [3-MFW+ 91-7282]

**Ikonen und ostkirchliches Kultgerät aus
rheinischem Privatbesitz :** Katalog zur
Ausstellung im Schnütgen-Museum /
[Redaktion: Ulrich Bock ... et al.]. Köln : Das
Museum, 1990. 205 p. : chiefly col. ill. ; 28 cm.
Includes bibliographical references (p. 203-205). DDC
704.9/482 20
*1. Icons - Exhibitions. 2. Orthodox Eastern Church and
art - Exhibitions. 3. Icons - Private collections -
Germany - Rhineland - Exhibitions. I. Bock, Ulrich. II.
Schnütgen-Museum.*
N8186.G3 C655 1990

Eine Ikonographie des tibetischen Buddhismus /.
Lauf, Detlef Ingo. Graz, Austria , 1979. 204
p. :   ISBN 3-201-01092-8 :   DDC 704.9/48943923
    19
N8193.T52 L38   ***NYPL [3-MAF 91-4701]***

**Ikonographische Untersuchung zum Motivschatz
der stadtrömischen mythologischen Sarkophage
des 2. Jhs. n. Chr. /.** Hübner, Birgitta.
Münster , 1990. 217 p. :
        NYPL [3-MGH 91-5059]

IKONS. see ICONS.

Il Campidoglio nel Cinquecento . Pecchiai, Pio, b.
1882. Roma , 1950. xxvii, 310 p. :
N2830 .P4 1950

**Il Cinema nei manifesti di Silvano Campeggi
Nano, 1945-1969 :** Firenze, Museo mediceo,
Palazzo medici Riccardi, 18 marzo-16 aprile
1988. Firenze : Giunti : Opus libri, [1988] 158
p. : ill. (some col.) ; 24 cm. At head of title:
Comune di Firenze, Provincia di Firenze, Mediateca
regionale toscana. Bibliography: p. 29. Includes indexes.
        DDC 741.6/74/092 20
*1. Campeggi, Silvano - Exhibitions. 2. Film posters,
Italian - Exhibitions. I. Campeggi, Silvano. II. Museo
mediceo.*
NC1850.C36 A4 1988

Il Donatello .
(7-8) Gruppo Donatello, XXVII edizione .
Firenze , 1989. 111, [34] p. :
N6921.F7 G78 1989
        NYPL [3-MAMC 90-11322]

Il Duomo di Monza / [contributi di Ermanno A.
Arslan ... et al. ; a cura di Roberto Conti].
Nuova ed. Milano : Electa, 1990. 2 v. : ill.
(some col.) ; 29 cm. Includes bibliographical
references and index. CONTENTS. - t. 1. La storia e
l'arte -- t. 2. I tesori.   DDC 726/.6/09451 20
*1. Duomo di Monza. 2. Christian art and symbolism -
Italy - Monza. 3. Church decoration and ornament -
Italy - Monza. 4. Monza (Italy) - Buildings, structures,
etc. I. Arslan, Ermanno A. II. Conti, Roberto.*
NA5621.M954 D8 1990

Il fiore dell'impressionismo =. Fossier, François.
Milano , c1990. 388 p. :
NE647.6.I4 F67 1990

Il gran cardinale . Robertson, Clare. New
Haven , 1992. p. cm. ISBN 0-300-05045-3 DDC
709/.2 20
N6915 .R66 1992

Il Lauro e il bronzo : la scultura celebrativa in
Italia, 1800-1900 : Torino, Circolo ufficiali, 30
aprile-8 luglio 1990 / a cura di Maurizio
Corgnati, di Gianlorenzo Mellini e di Francesco
Poli. [Italy : s.n., 1990] 182 p. ; 28 cm. Includes
bibliographical references (p. 177-180).   DDC
730/.945/0744512 20
*1. Sculpture, Italian - Exhibitions. 2. Sculpture,
Modern - 19th century - Italy - Exhibitions. 3.
Sculpture, Modern - 20th century - Italy - Exhibitions.
I. Corgnati, Maurizio, 1917-. II. Mellini, Gian Lorenzo.
III. Poli, Francesco, 1949-.*
NB617 .L3 1990

Il Meridione nell'arte .
(2) La Cripta della Cattedrale di Taranto /.
Taranto [1986] 94 p. :
        NYPL [3-MRBN+ 90-10741]
(3) De Marco, Vittorio. La vela di Gio Ponti /.
Taranto [1990] 94 p. :
IN PROCESS (ONLINE)
        NYPL [3-MQZ+ (Ponti) 91-3777]

Il Neogotico nel XIX e XX secolo / a cura di
Rossana Bossaglia e Valerio Terraroli. Milano :
Mazzotta, [1990] 2 v. : ill. ; 24 cm. Italian,
English, and French. Proceedings of the Convegno
internazionale su "Il neogotico nel XIX e XX secolo",
held at the Università di Pavia in Sept., 1985. Includes
bibliographical references. ISBN 88-20-20863-6 (set)
DDC 724/.3 20
*1. Gothic revival (Architecture) - Congresses. 2.
Architecture, Modern - 19th century - Congresses. 3.
Architecture, Modern - 20th century - Congresses. I.
Bossaglia, Rossana. II. Terraroli, Valerio. III. Università
di Pavia. Dipartimento di scienza della letteratura e
dell'arte medievale e moderna. IV. Convegno
internazionale su "Il neogotico nel XIX e XX secolo
(1985 : Pavia, Italy). V. Title: Neogotico nel 19. e 20.
secolo.*
NA645.5.G68 N46 1990

Il Palazzo Medici Riccardi di Firenze / a cura di
Giovanni Cherubini e Giovanni Fanelli ; testi di
Cristina Acidini Luchinat ... [et al.]. Firenze :
Giunti, c1990. 379 p. : ill. (some col.) ; 32 cm.
Includes bibliographical references (p. 360-363) and
index. ISBN 88-09-20180-9 DDC 725/.17/094551
20
1. Palazzo Medici Riccardi. 2. Architecture,

*Renaissance - Italy - Florence. 3. Medici, House of. 4.
Florence (Italy) - History - 1421-1737. 5. Florence
(Italy) - Buildings, structures, etc. I. Cherubini,
Giovanni. II. Fanelli, Giovanni. III. Acidini, Cristina.*
NA7756.F65 P35 1990

Il Piviale duecentesco di Ascoli Piceno : storia e
restauro / a cura di Rosalia Bonito Fanelli ;
testi di Dante Cecchi ... [et al.]. Firenze :
Cantini, 1991. 180 p. : ill. (some col.) ; 31 cm.
Includes bibliographical references (p. 177-180). ISBN
88-7737-143-9 :
*1. Ecclesiastical embroidery - Conservation and
restoration - Italy - Ascoli Piceno. 2. Ecclesiastical
embroidery, Medieval - Conservation and restoration -
Italy - Ascoli Piceno. 3. Pinacoteca civica di Ascoli
Piceno. I. Bonito Fanelli, Rosalia. II. Cecchi, Dante.*
NK9310 .P58 1991

IL sixty. IL 60 . New York , c1990. xviii, 284
p. :   ISBN 0-934977-18-6 :   DDC 709/.45 20
N6911 .I34 1990
        NYPL [3-MAMC 90-11305]

Il Tesoro dell'architettura : gioielli, argenti, vetri,
orologi : 1980/1990 Cleto Munari / [a cura di]
Alessandro Vezzosi ; introduzione di Gillo
Dorfles. Firenze : EDIFIR, [1990] 149 p. : ill.
(some col.) ; 30 cm. Cover title. An exhibition held
in Florence May 12-June 14, 1990. Errata slip inserted.
        DDC 739.27/09/0480744551 20
*1. Architect-designed jewelry - History - 20th century -
Exhibitions. 2. Architect-designed decorative arts -
History - 20th century - Exhibitions. 3. Jewelry -
Private collections - Italy - Exhibitions. 4. Munari,
Cleto - Art collections - Exhibitions. I. Vezzosi,
Alessandro.*
NK7310 .T47 1990

IL 60 : essays honoring Irving Lavin on his
sixtieth birthday / edited by Marilyn Aronberg
Lavin. New York : Italica Press, c1990. xviii,
284 p. : ill. ; 24 cm. "Bibliography of the works of
Irving Lavin": p. xiii-xviii. Includes bibliographical
references and index. CONTENTS. - The coordination
of wall, floor, and ceiling decoration in the houses of
Roman Italy, 100 BCE-235 CE / John R. Clarke --
Pegasos and the seasons in a pavement from Caesarea
Maritima / Marie Spiro -- The Madonna del Coazzone
and the Cult of the Virgin Immaculate in Milan and
Pavia / Edith W. Kirsch -- Donatello and the high altar
in the Santo, Padua / Sarah Blake McHam -- Medici
patronage and the festival of 1589 / Arthur
Blumenthal -- The Vatican tower of the winds and the
architectural legacy of the Counter Reformation /
Nicola Courtright -- Drawing and collaboration in the
Carracci Academy / Gail Feigenbaum -- Clement VIII,
the Lateran and Christian concord / Jack Freiberg --
Lelio Pasqualini, a late sixteenth-century antiquarian /
Alexandra Herz -- The Bentvueghels / David Levine --
The king, the poet, and the nation / Michael
Mezzatesta -- Marble revetment in the late
sixteenth-century Roman chapels / Steven Ostrow.
        ISBN 0-934977-18-6 :   DDC 709/.45 20
*1. Lavin, Irving, 1927-. 2. Art, Medieval - Italy. 3. Art,
Modern - Italy. 4. Relief (Sculpture), French. I. Lavin,
Irving, 1927-. II. Lavin, Marilyn Aronberg. III. Title: IL
sixty.*
N6911 .I34 1990
        NYPL [3-MAMC 90-11305]

Ilene Segalove . Desmarais, Charles, 1949-
Laguna Beach, Calif. , c1990. 79 p. :   ISBN
0-940872-15-3 DDC 700/.92 20
N6537.S38 D47 1990
        NYPL [3-MAL 91-3691]

Iles, Chrissie. Art at the edge . Oxford , 1988. 43
p. :   ISBN 0-905836-66-9 (pbk.) DDC 709/.438/074
19
N7255.P6   ***NYPL [3-MAM+ 90-4738]***

Iliazd, 1894-1975. Rogelio Lacourière pêcheur de
cuivres / Iliazd. Aux quatre coins de la pièce /
Pablo Picasso. [Paris] : Degré quarante et un,
c1968. [46] leaves : 13 ill. (3 col.) ; 26 x 32
cm. Cover title: Hommage à Roger Lacourière.
Contains full-page prints by various artists in addition
to the texts by Iliazd and Picasso. Issued in 23 loose
bifolia in a parchment cover, in a slipcase. The bifolia
(except 1, 3, and 23) are numbered. "10 exemplaires sur
parchemin rustique ... 50 sur vieux Japon chiffrés de 1
à 50, XV sur le même de compagnons, 10 suites signées
sur Chine ..."--Colophon. DDC 769.9/04 20
*1. Artists' illustrated books. 2. Prints - 20th century. 3.
Lacourière, Roger, 1892-1966. I. Picasso, Pablo,
1881-1973. Aux quatre coins de la pièce. 1968. II.
Title. III. Title: Aux quatre coins de la pièce.*
NE890 .I45 1968

Ilkjær, Marianne Olsson. Postmodernismen i dansk arkitektur : international baggrund, dansk debat og praksis / Marianne Olsson Ilkjær. [København : Byggeriets studiearkiv, 1987] 104 leaves : ill. ; 30 cm. (BSA/arkitektur, 0109-6885 . 6) Includes bibliographical references (leaves 99-104). ISBN 87-87448-52-1
1. Architecture - Denmark. 2. Architecture, Postmodern - Denmark. I. Title. II. Series.
NA1218 .I43 1987

Illegal . Anastos, Phillip. New York , 1991. 128 p. : ISBN 0-8478-1367-3 DDC 305.9/0693 20
F392.R5 A53 1991
NYPL [MFW+ 91-6710]

ILLINOIS - ROAD MAPS.
Rockford Map Publishers, Rockford, Ill. Illinois State atlas. Rockford, Ill. , 1980, c1965. 232 p. : **NYPL [Map Div. 81-239]**

Illinois State atlas. Rockford Map Publishers, Rockford, Ill. Rockford, Ill. , 1980, c1965. 232 p. : **NYPL [Map Div. 81-239]**

Illinois State Museum.
Environmental figuration . Springfield, Ill. , c1990. 31 p. : ISBN 0-89792-130-5 DDC 757/.09773/1107477325 20
ND1292 .E59 1990

Gertrude Abercrombie . Springfield, IL , 1991. p. cm. ISBN 0-89792-132-1 DDC 759.13 20
ND237.A235 A4 1991

Illinois State Museum Lockport Gallery (Lockport, Ill.) Environmental figuration . Springfield, Ill. , c1990. 31 p. : ISBN 0-89792-130-5 DDC 757/.09773/1107477325 20
ND1292 .E59 1990

Illinois State University. University Galleries.
Hannah, Duncan. Duncan Hannah, mythic times . Normal, Ill. , 1990. 55 p. : ISBN 0-945558-08-2
NYPL [3-MCX H244 91-39]

Illinois. University. Krannert Art Museum. see **Krannert Art Museum.**

ILLUMINATION. see **LIGHTING.**

ILLUMINATION OF BOOKS AND MANUSCRIPTS - AUSTRIA - CATALOGS.
Buluță, Gheorghe. Manuscrise miniate și ornate românești în colecții din Austria /. București , 1990. 142 p. : ISBN 973-330-070-5 :
ND3227 .B84 1990

ILLUMINATION OF BOOKS AND MANUSCRIPTS, BYZANTINE.
Anderson, Jeffrey C. The New York Cruciform Lectionary /. University Park , 1991. p. cm. ISBN 0-271-00743-5 DDC 745.6/7487 20
ND3359.N48 A44 1991

Lowden, John. The Octateuches . University Park, Pa. , c1992. p. cm. ISBN 0-271-00771-0 DDC 745.6/7487 20
ND3358.O27 L68 1992

ILLUMINATION OF BOOKS AND MANUSCRIPTS, CISTERCIAN - FRANCE.
Załuska, Yolanta. L'enluminure et le scriptorium de Cîteaux au XIIe siècle /. Nuits-Saint-Georges [France] , 1989. 453 p. : DDC 745.6/7/094409021 20
ND3149.C5 Z35 1989

ILLUMINATION OF BOOKS AND MANUSCRIPTS, CZECH.
Krása, Josef. České iluminované rukopisy 13./16. století /. Praha , 1990. 455 p. : ISBN 80-207-0114-1 : DDC 745.6/7/094370902 20
ND3235.C9 K69 1990

ILLUMINATION OF BOOKS AND MANUSCRIPTS - EXHIBITIONS.
Morello, Giovanni. Libri d'ore della Biblioteca apostolica vaticana /. Zürich , c1988. 143 p. : DDC 745.6/7/09407445634 20
ND2899.V36 M6 1988

ILLUMINATION OF BOOKS AND MANUSCRIPTS - FRANCE.
Załuska, Yolanta. L'enluminure et le scriptorium de Cîteaux au XIIe siècle /. Nuits-Saint-Georges [France] , 1989. 453 p. : DDC 745.6/7/094409021 20
ND3149.C5 Z35 1989

ILLUMINATION OF BOOKS AND MANUSCRIPTS, FRENCH.
Hedeman, Anne Dawson. The royal image .

Berkeley , c1991. p. cm. ISBN 0-520-07069-0 DDC 745.6/7/09440902 20
ND3399.G67 H44 1991

ILLUMINATION OF BOOKS AND MANUSCRIPTS, GOTHIC - FRANCE.
Hedeman, Anne Dawson. The royal image . Berkeley , c1991. p. cm. ISBN 0-520-07069-0 DDC 745.6/7/09440902 20
ND3399.G67 H44 1991

ILLUMINATION OF BOOKS AND MANUSCRIPTS, INDIC - CATALOGS.
Indian miniature painting series 2. New Delhi , 1986. 1 portfolio ([4] p., 8 leaves of col. ; 11.);
NYPL [3-MAF+ 87-3545]

ILLUMINATION OF BOOKS AND MANUSCRIPTS, IRANIAN.
Robinson, B. W. (Basil William) Fifteenth-century Persian painting . New York , 1991. p. cm. ISBN 0-8147-7417-2 DDC 745.6/7/095509024 20
ND3241 .R597 1991

ILLUMINATION OF BOOKS AND MANUSCRIPTS, IRANIAN - CATALOGS.
Beldescu, Alexandra. Manuscrise persane în colecții din România /. București , 1987. 77 p., 40 leaves of plates :
ND3241 .B353 1987

ILLUMINATION OF BOOKS AND MANUSCRIPTS, ISLAMIC - CATALOGS.
Islamic art in the Keir collection /. London , Boston , 1988. xviii, 316 p., [60] p. of plates : ISBN 0-571-13753-9 DDC 745/.0917/67107442176 20
NK720 .I84 1988 **NYPL [3-MAF 91-3908]**

Topkapı Sarayı. Manuscrits et miniatures /. Paris , 1986. 294 p. : ISBN 2-86950-015-0
NYPL [3-MAF+ 90-12903]

ILLUMINATION OF BOOKS AND MANUSCRIPTS, ISLAMIC - IRAN.
Robinson, B. W. (Basil William) Fifteenth-century Persian painting . New York , 1991. p. cm. ISBN 0-8147-7417-2 DDC 745.6/7/095509024 20
ND3241 .R597 1991

ILLUMINATION OF BOOKS AND MANUSCRIPTS, MEDIEVAL - CZECHOSLOVAKIA.
Krása, Josef. České iluminované rukopisy 13./16. století /. Praha , 1990. 455 p. : ISBN 80-207-0114-1 : DDC 745.6/7/094370902 20
ND3235.C9 K69 1990

ILLUMINATION OF BOOKS AND MANUSCRIPTS, MEDIEVAL - HUNGARY.
Nekcsei-Lipócz Bible. A Nekcsei-Biblia legszebb lapjai. Budapest , Washington , 1988. 231 [5] p. : ISBN 963-207-955-8
IN PROCESS (ONLINE) Rare Bk Coll
NYPL [JFH 91-4]

ILLUMINATION OF BOOKS AND MANUSCRIPTS, ROMANESQUE - FRANCE.
Załuska, Yolanta. L'enluminure et le scriptorium de Cîteaux au XIIe siècle /. Nuits-Saint-Georges [France] , 1989. 453 p. : DDC 745.6/7/094409021 20
ND3149.C5 Z35 1989

ILLUMINATION OF BOOKS AND MANUSCRIPTS - ROMANIA - CATALOGS.
Beldescu, Alexandra. Manuscrise persane în colecții din România /. București , 1987. 77 p., 40 leaves of plates :
ND3241 .B353 1987

ILLUMINATION OF BOOKS ANDMANUSCRPTS, ROMANIAN - CATALOGS.
Buluță, Gheorghe. Manuscrise miniate și ornate românești în colecții din Austria /. București , 1990. 142 p. : ISBN 973-330-070-5 :
ND3227 .B84 1990

Illuminations (Astoria, N.Y.) .
(11) Holy image, holy space--icons & frescoes from Greece. Astoria, NY , c1988. 1 videocassette (28 min., 30 sec.) : DDC 704.9 11
N7852.5

(22) From Alexander to Cleopatra, Greek art of the Hellenistic Age. Astoria, NY , c1989. 1 videocassette (28 min., 30 sec.) : DDC 709.38

11
N5633

ILLUMINATIONS OF BOOKS AND MANUSCRIPTS - ARMENIAN S.S.R.
Grigor Tatevats'i ev Ananun Syunets'i =] Erevan , 1987. 165 p. :
NYPL [3-MCY+ 90-4058]

ILLUSION IN ART.
Chambers, Karen S. Trompe l'oeil at home . New York , c1991. p. ISBN 0-8478-1420-3 DDC 751.7/3 20
N7430.5 .C48 1991

ILLUSIONS, OPTICAL. see **OPTICAL ILLUSIONS.**

Illusoria . Del-Prete, Sandro, 1937- Bern , c1987. 115 p. : **NYPL [3-MCZ + D363 88-3591]**

The illustrated Bartsch /. Bartsch, Adam von, 1757-1821. [Peintre graveur. English.] New York , 1978- v. : ISBN 0-89835-000-X DDC 769/.074
NE90 .B213 **NYPL [MDD+ 80-258]**

ILLUSTRATED BOOKS - 20TH CENTURY - EXHIBITIONS.
Das Buch des Künstlers . [Hannover] [1989] 179 p. : DDC 708.3/5954 s 769.9/04/074435954 20
N5070.H3 K4 1989/3 NE890
NYPL [3-MAW (Hanover) 73-2900 1989/3]

ILLUSTRATED BOOKS - CATALOGS.
Pomeroy, Jane R. Alexander Anderson's life and engravings . Worcester [Mass.] , 1990. p, 137-230 : ISBN 0-944026-25-7
NYPL [MDG (Anderson) 91-4737]

ILLUSTRATED BOOKS, CHILDREN'S.
Children's book illustration and design /. New York , 1991. p. cm. ISBN 0-86636-147-2 DDC 741.6/42/09048 20
NC965 .C43 1991

ILLUSTRATED BOOKS, CHILDREN'S - ARAB COUNTRIES - BIBLIOGRAPHY.
Malaș, Muḥammad. Kutub al-atfāl al-muṣawwarah . 'Ammān, al-Mamlakah al-Urduniyah al-Hāshimiyah , 1989. 90 p. ;
NC965 .M33 1989

ILLUSTRATED BOOKS, CHILDREN'S - BRAZIL - EXHIBITIONS.
Mostra de Ilustrações para Crianças (1987 : Rio de Janeiro, Brazil) Mostra de Ilustrações para Crianças, Rio 87 /. Rio de Janeiro [1987] 87 p. : DDC 741.6/42/09810748153 20
NC976.B6 M6 1987

ILLUSTRATED BOOKS, CHILDREN'S - CZECHOSLOVAKIA - CATALOGS.
Ševčíková, Hana. Ilustrátoři dětské knihy /. Olomouc , 1989. 1 portfolio (3, [1] p., [12] leaves) ;
NC989.C9 S48 1989

ILLUSTRATED BOOKS, CHILDREN'S - ENGLAND.
Taylor, Ina. The art of Kate Greenaway . Gretna, La. , 1991. 128 p. : ISBN 0-88289-867-1 DDC 741.6/42/092 B 20
NC978.5.G7 T37 1991

Taylor, Ina. The art of Kate Greenaway . Exeter, Devon , 1991. 128 p. : ISBN 0-86350-397-7
NYPL [MDG (Greenaway) 91-8041]

ILLUSTRATED BOOKS, CHILDREN'S - EXHIBITIONS.
Artists of books for children . Milwaukee, Wis. , c1987. 56 p. :
NYPL [MDTT 91-2512]

ILLUSTRATED BOOKS, CHILDREN'S - GREAT BRITAIN - BIBLIOGRAPHY.
Vries, Leonard de. A treasury of illustrated children's books . New York , 1989. 285 p. : ISBN 0-89659-939-6 DDC 011/.62 19
Z1037 .V75 1989 PN1009.A1
NYPL [MDTO+ 90-9497]

ILLUSTRATED BOOKS, CHILDREN'S - LIBRARY RESOURCES - ONTARIO - TORONTO.
Vries, Leonard de. A treasury of illustrated children's books . New York , 1989. 285 p. : ISBN 0-89659-939-6 DDC 011/.62 19
Z1037 .V75 1989 PN1009.A1
NYPL [MDTO+ 90-9497]

ILLUSTRATED BOOKS, CHILDREN'S - SOVIET UNION - EXHIBITIONS.

Kinderbuchillustrationen aus der Sowjetunion .
Berlin [1989] 71 p. : ISBN 3-86050-003-1 DDC
741.6/42/0947074431552 20
NC985 .K49 1989   NYPL [MDTT 91-4009]

ILLUSTRATED BOOKS - EXHIBITIONS.
Artists of the book 1988 . Boston, Mass. ,
c1988. 40 p. : ISBN 0-934552-53-3
                NYPL [MDTT 91-4772]

Stein, Donna. Contemporary illustrated books .
New York, N.Y. , c1989. 72 p. : ISBN
0-916365-00-X   *NYPL [MDTT+ 91-6216]*

**ILLUSTRATED BOOKS - FRANCE - 18TH
CENTURY - EXHIBITIONS.**
Französische Illustrationen des 18. und 19.
Jahrhunderts . Dortmund , 1985. 267 p. :
    ISBN 3-924302-16-2 DDC 741.64/074/0356 s
    741.64/0944/0740356 19
NC980 .B54 1985 vol. 1
                NYPL [MDT 91-2511]

**ILLUSTRATED BOOKS - FRANCE - 19TH
CENTURY - EXHIBITIONS.**
Französische Illustrationen des 18. und 19.
Jahrhunderts . Dortmund , 1985. 267 p. :
    ISBN 3-924302-16-2 DDC 741.64/074/0356 s
    741.64/0944/0740356 19
NC980 .B54 1985 vol. 1
                NYPL [MDT 91-2511]

**ILLUSTRATED BOOKS - FRANCE - 20TH
CENTURY.**
Emboden, William A. Jean Cocteau and the
illustrated book /. [Northridge, Calif.] , 1990.
29 p. :   *NYPL [MDG+ (Cocteau) 90-11895]*

**ILLUSTRATED BOOKS - GERMANY (WEST)
- DÜSSELDORF - HISTORY - 20TH
CENTURY - EXHIBITIONS.**
Illustrierte Bücher und Mappenwerke des
Jungen Rheinlands . Düsseldorf , 1985. ii, 56
p., xvii leaves of plates :
                NYPL [MDTT 88-673]

**ILLUSTRATED BOOKS - GREAT BRITAIN -
19TH CENTURY - BIBLIOGRAPHY.**
Vries, Leonard de. A treasury of illustrated
children's books . New York , 1989. 285 p. :
    ISBN 0-89659-939-6 DDC 011/.62 19
Z1037 .V75 1989 PN1009.A1
                NYPL [MDTO+ 90-9497]

**ILLUSTRATED BOOKS - NETHERLANDS -
EXHIBITIONS.**
Foto in omslag . Amsterdam , 1989. 143 p. :
    ISBN 90-6579-033-0 (pbk.)
                NYPL [MFW+ 91-3603]

**ILLUSTRATED BOOKS - PRIVATE
COLLECTIONS - GERMANY (WEST) -
DORTMUND - EXHIBITIONS.**
Französische Illustrationen des 18. und 19.
Jahrhunderts . Dortmund , 1985. 267 p. :
    ISBN 3-924302-16-2 DDC 741.64/074/0356 s
    741.64/0944/0740356 19
NC980 .B54 1985 vol. 1
                NYPL [MDT 91-2511]

Illustrated catalogue, Alte Pinakothek Munich.
Alte Pinakothek (Munich, Germany) Alte
Pinakothek Munich. Munich , 1938. xv, 320 p.,
196 p. of plates :
        NYPL [3-MAVZ (Munich) 90-7035]

Illustrated children's books. Malas, Muḥammad.
Kutub al-aṭfāl al-muṣawwarah . 'Ammān,
al-Mamlakah al-Urdunīyah al-Hāshimīyah ,
1989. 90 p. ;
NC965 .M33 1989

**ILLUSTRATED CHILDREN'S BOOKS. see
ILLUSTRATED BOOKS, CHILDREN'S.**

Illustrated dictionary of art & artists. Harrap's
illustrated dictionary of art & artists. Bromley,
Kent , 1990. 589 p. : ISBN 0-245-54692-8
                NYPL [MAO 91-4216]

Illustrated dictionary of art and artists. Harrap's
illustrated dictionary of art & artists. Bromley,
Kent , 1990. 589 p. : ISBN 0-245-54692-8
                NYPL [MAO 91-4216]

**The Illustrated encyclopedia of architects and
architecture** / edited by Dennis Sharp. New
York, NY :Whitney Library of Design, 1991. p.
cm. Includes bibliographical references and index.
    ISBN 0-8230-2539-X : DDC 720/.3 20
1. Architects - Biography - Dictionaries. 2.
Architecture - History. I. Sharp, Dennis.
NA40 .I45 1991

The illustrated encyclopedia of cartoon animals /.

Rovin, Jeff. New York , 1991. p. cm. ISBN
0-13-275561-0 DDC 741.5/0973 20
NC1766.U5 R6 1991

**Illustrated guidelines for rehabilitating historic
buildings.** The Secretary of the Interior's
standards for rehabilitation and Illustrated
guidelines for rehabilitating historic buildings /.
Washington, D.C. , 1991. p. cm. DDC
720/.28/8021873 20
NA106 .S4 1991

The Illustrated history of antiques : the essential
reference for all antique lovers and collectors /
general editor, Huon Mallalieu. Philadelphia,
Pa. : Running Press, 1991. p. cm. Includes index.
    ISBN 0-89471-888-6 : DDC 745.1 20
1. Antiques - History. I. Mallalieu, Huon.
NK1125 .I45 1991

**An illustrated history of the arts in South
Dakota** /. Huseboe, Arthur R., 1931- Sioux
Falls, S.D. , 1989. xiii, 396 p. : ISBN
0-931170-44-3 : DDC 700/.9783 20
NX510.S8 H87 1989

Illustration /. Miller, J. Hillis (Joseph Hillis),
1928- Cambridge, Mass. , 1992. p. cm. ISBN
0-674-44357-8 DDC 700/.1 20
NX640 .M55 1992

**ILLUSTRATION, BOTANICAL. see
BOTANICAL ILLUSTRATION.**

Illustration du vieux Bordeaux /. Avisseau, Jean
Paul. Avignon , c1990. 1 v. (unpaged) : ISBN
2-7006-0141-6
N8214.5.F8 A95 1990

ILLUSTRATION OF BOOKS.
Fables . Savannah, Ga. , 1991. p. cm. ISBN
0-913720-75-5 (hardcover) : DDC 741.6/4 398.2
20
NC961.7.F34 F3 1991

**ILLUSTRATION OF BOOKS - 15TH
CENTURY - PORTUGAL - CATALOGS.**
Pacheco, José, 1954- A divina arte negra e o
livro português . Lisboa [1988?] 282 p. :
NE1163 .P33 1988
                NYPL [MDOH 90-12803]

**ILLUSTRATION OF BOOKS - 16TH
CENTURY - PORTUGAL - CATALOGS.**
Pacheco, José, 1954- A divina arte negra e o
livro português . Lisboa [1988?] 282 p. :
NE1163 .P33 1988
                NYPL [MDOH 90-12803]

**ILLUSTRATION OF BOOKS - 18TH
CENTURY - ENGLAND - CATALOGS.**
Essick, Robert N. William Blake's commercial
book illustrations . Oxford [England] , New
York , 1991. p. cm. ISBN 0-19-817390-3 : DDC
769.92 20
NE2047.6.B55 A4 1991

**ILLUSTRATION OF BOOKS - 18TH
CENTURY - FRANCE - EXHIBITIONS.**
Französische Illustrationen des 18. und 19.
Jahrhunderts . Dortmund , 1985. 267 p. :
    ISBN 3-924302-16-2 DDC 741.64/074/0356 s
    741.64/0944/0740356 19
NC980 .B54 1985 vol. 1
                NYPL [MDT 91-2511]

**ILLUSTRATION OF BOOKS - 19TH
CENTURY - ENGLAND - CATALOGS.**
Essick, Robert N. William Blake's commercial
book illustrations . Oxford [England] , New
York , 1991. p. cm. ISBN 0-19-817390-3 : DDC
769.92 20
NE2047.6.B55 A4 1991

**ILLUSTRATION OF BOOKS - 19TH
CENTURY - FRANCE - EXHIBITIONS.**
Französische Illustrationen des 18. und 19.
Jahrhunderts . Dortmund , 1985. 267 p. :
    ISBN 3-924302-16-2 DDC 741.64/074/0356 s
    741.64/0944/0740356 19
NC980 .B54 1985 vol. 1
                NYPL [MDT 91-2511]

**ILLUSTRATION OF BOOKS - 19TH
CENTURY - GREAT BRITAIN.**
Vries, Leonard de. A treasury of illustrated
children's books . New York , 1989. 285 p. :
    ISBN 0-89659-939-6 DDC 011/.62 19
Z1037 .V75 1989 PN1009.A1
                NYPL [MDTO+ 90-9497]

**ILLUSTRATION OF BOOKS - 19TH
CENTURY - GREAT BRITAIN -
EXHIBITIONS.**
Lilly Library (Indiana University, Bloomington)

Changing images . Bloomington, Ind. , 1991. 62
p. : ISBN 1-87959-800-0 DDC
741.6/4/09034074772255 20
NC978 .L55 1991

**ILLUSTRATION OF BOOKS - 19TH
CENTURY - UNITED STATES.**
Tatham, David. Winslow Homer and the
illustrated book /. Syracuse, N.Y. , 1992. p. cm.
    ISBN 0-8156-2550-2 DDC 741.6/4/092 20
NC975.5.H65 T38 1992

**ILLUSTRATION OF BOOKS - 20TH
CENTURY.**
Children's book illustration and design /. New
York , 1991. p. cm. ISBN 0-86636-147-2 DDC
741.6/42/09048 20
NC965 .C43 1991

Fanelli, Giovanni. L'illustrazione Art nouveau /.
Roma , 1989. 332 p. : ISBN 88-420-3476-2
                NYPL [MDTT 90-10984]

**ILLUSTRATION OF BOOKS - 20TH
CENTURY - BRAZIL - EXHIBITIONS.**
Mostra de Ilustrações para Crianças (1987 : Rio
de Janeiro, Brazil) Mostra de Ilustrações para
Crianças, Rio 87 /. Rio de Janeiro [1987] 87
p. : DDC 741.6/42/09810748153 20
NC976.B6 M6 1987

**ILLUSTRATION OF BOOKS - 20TH
CENTURY - EXHIBITIONS.**
Artists of books for children . Milwaukee,
Wis. , c1987. 56 p. :
                NYPL [MDTT 91-2512]

**ILLUSTRATION OF BOOKS - 20TH
CENTURY - FRANCE.**
Emboden, William A. Jean Cocteau and the
illustrated book /. [Northridge, Calif.] , 1990.
29 p. :   *NYPL [MDG+ (Cocteau) 90-11895]*

**ILLUSTRATION OF BOOKS - 20TH
CENTURY - SOVIET UNION -
EXHIBITIONS.**
Kinderbuchillustrationen aus der Sowjetunion .
Berlin [1989] 71 p. : ISBN 3-86050-003-1 DDC
741.6/42/0947074431552 20
NC985 .K49 1989   NYPL [MDTT 91-4009]

**ILLUSTRATION OF BOOKS - ARAB
COUNTRIES - PSYCHOLOGICAL
ASPECTS.**
Malas, Muḥammad. Kutub al-aṭfāl
al-muṣawwarah . 'Ammān, al-Mamlakah
al-Urdunīyah al-Hāshimīyah , 1989. 90 p. ;
NC965 .M33 1989

**ILLUSTRATION OF BOOKS -
CZECHOSLOVAKIA.**
Holešovský, František. Čeští ilustrátoři v
současné knize pro děti a mládež /. Praha ,
1989. 455 p. :
NC989.C9 H62 1989

**ILLUSTRATION OF BOOKS - ENGLAND -
CATALOGS.**
Ray, Gordon Norton, 1915- The illustrator and
the book in England from 1790 to 1914 /. New
York , 1991. p. cm. ISBN 0-486-26955-8 (pbk.)
    DDC 741.6/4/09420747471 20
NC978 .R37 1991

**ILLUSTRATION OF BOOKS -
EXHIBITIONS.**
Sterling and Francine Clark Art Institute.
Library. Book illustrations from six centuries in
the Library of the Sterling & Francine Clark
Art Institute /. Williamstown, Mass. , 1990.
116 p. : ISBN 0-931102-29-4 (paper) DDC
741.6/4/0747441 20
NC961.W55 S747 1990
                NYPL [MDT 91-2365]

**ILLUSTRATION OF BOOKS - FRANCE -
EXHIBITIONS.**
Französische Illustrationen des 18. und 19.
Jahrhunderts . Dortmund , 1985. 267 p. :
    ISBN 3-924302-16-2 DDC 741.64/074/0356 s
    741.64/0944/0740356 19
NC980 .B54 1985 vol. 1
                NYPL [MDT 91-2511]

**ILLUSTRATION OF BOOKS - GERMANY,
EAST.**
Hochschule für Grafik und Buchkunst Leipzig .
Leipzig [1985?]. 136 p. :
                NYPL [MDTT 91-6738]

**ILLUSTRATION OF BOOKS - GREAT
BRITAIN - EXHIBITIONS.**
Berg Collection. Pen & brush . [New York] ,
c1969 (Lunenburg, Vt. : Stinehour Press) 59 p. :

ISBN 0-87104-142-1   DDC 741.942
NC15.N43 N47   **NYPL [MAMZ 75-566]**

ILLUSTRATION OF BOOKS - SOVIET UNION - CATALOGS.
Schmidt, Werner, art critic. Russische Graphik des XIX. und XX. Jahrhunderts. Leipzig, 1967. xxx, 476 p.
NC985 .S4   **NYPL [MDBF 90-6661]**

ILLUSTRATION OF BOOKS - UNITED STATES - EXHIBITIONS.
Berg Collection. Pen & brush . [New York] , c1969 (Lunenburg, Vt. : Stinehour Press) 59 p. :   ISBN 0-87104-142-1   DDC 741.942
NC15.N43 N47   **NYPL [MAMZ 75-566]**

Illustration with markers . Gleason, John A. New York , 1991. p. cm.   ISBN 0-8230-2536-5 :   DDC 741.6 20
NC878 .G57 1991

ILLUSTRATION, ZOOLOGICAL. see ZOOLOGICAL ILLUSTRATION.

ILLUSTRATIONS, HUMOROUS. see CARICATURES AND CARTOONS; WIT AND HUMOR, PICTORIAL.

The illustrator and the book in England from 1790 to 1914 /. Ray, Gordon Norton, 1915- New York , 1991. p. cm.   ISBN 0-486-26955-8 (pbk.)   DDC 741.6/4/09420747471 20
NC978 .R37 1991

ILLUSTRATORS - ARGENTINA - BIOGRAPHY.
Criollos for export . Buenos Aires, Argentina [1990] 149 p., [5] p. of plates :
NC976.A7 C75 1990

ILLUSTRATORS - BIOGRAPHY.
Children's book illustration and design /. New York , 1991. p. cm.   ISBN 0-86636-147-2   DDC 741.6/42/09048 20
NC965 .C43 1991

ILLUSTRATORS - CZECHOSLOVAKIA - BIOGRAPHY.
Holešovský, František. Čeští ilustrátoři v současné knize pro děti a mládež /. Praha , 1989. 455 p. :
NC989.C9 H62 1989

Ševčíková, Hana. Ilustrátoři dětské knihy /. Olomouc , 1989. 1 portfolio (3, [1] p., [12] leaves) ;
NC989.C9 S48 1989

ILLUSTRATORS - ENGLAND - BIOGRAPHY.
Kennedy, Richard, 1910- A boy at the Hogarth Press /. London , 1972. x, 85 p., [1] folded leaf of plates :   ISBN 0-435-18510-1
           NYPL [3-MEM (Kennedy) 90-11892]

Rogerson, Ian. Agnes Miller Parker, wood-engraver and book illustrator, 1895-1980 /. Wakefield, West Yorkshire , 1990. 88 p., [6] leaves of plates :   ISBN 0-948375-23-X (quarter cloth)   DDC 769.92 20
NE1147.6.P37 R64 1990

Taylor, Ina. The art of Kate Greenaway . Gretna, La. , 1991. 128 p. :   ISBN 0-88289-867-1   DDC 741.6/42/092 B 20
NC978.5.G7 T37 1991

Taylor, Ina. The art of Kate Greenaway . Exeter, Devon , 1991. 128 p. :   ISBN 0-86350-397-7
           NYPL [MDG (Greenaway) 91-8041]

ILLUSTRATORS - ENGLAND - CATALOGS.
Ray, Gordon Norton, 1915- The illustrator and the book in England from 1790 to 1914 /. New York , 1991. p. cm.   ISBN 0-486-26955-8 (pbk.)   DDC 741.6/4/09420747471 20
NC978 .R37 1991

ILLUSTRATORS - ENGLAND - DIARIES.
Doyle, Richard, 1824-1883. Richard Doyle's journal, 1840 /. Edinburgh , 1980. xvii, 156 p. :   ISBN 0-7028-8280-1 :   DDC 741.6/092/4 B 19
NC978.5.D68 A2 1980
           NYPL [MDG (Doyle) 81-1248]

ILLUSTRATORS - FINLAND - BIOGRAPHY.
Salonen, Marja. Rudolf Koivu, 1890-1946 /. [Espoo] , c1990. 83 p. :   ISBN 951-35-5022-2
NC989.F5 K37 1990

ILLUSTRATORS - FRANCE - BIOGRAPHY.
Kochert, Françis. Morette l'enchanteur /. Metz , c1985. 175 p. :   ISBN 2-901647-69-3
           NYPL [MDG+ (Morette) 90-8256]

ILLUSTRATORS - GREAT BRITAIN - BIOGRAPHY.
Lilly Library (Indiana University, Bloomington) Changing images . Bloomington, Ind. , 1991. 62 p. :   ISBN 1-87959-800-0   DDC 741.6/4/09304074772255 20
NC978 .L55 1991

ILLUSTRATORS - SPAIN - BIOGRAPHY.
Alfageme Ruano, Pedro. El romanticismo Sevillano . Sevilla , 1989. 176 p., [21] p. of plates :   ISBN 84-87039-13-8
           NYPL [3-MCQ B39 91-4517]

ILLUSTRATORS - UNITED STATES - BIOGRAPHY - JUVENILE LITERATURE.
Carle, Eric. The art of Eric Carle . Saxonville, MA , c1991. p. cm.   ISBN 0-88708-176-2 :   DDC 741.6/42/092 20
NC975.5.C36 A2 1991

Talking with artists . New York : Toronto : p. cm.   ISBN 0-02-724245-5   DDC 741.6/42/092273 B 20
NC975 .T34 1991

L'illustrazione Art nouveau /. Fanelli, Giovanni. Roma , 1989. 332 p. :   ISBN 88-420-3476-2
           NYPL [MDTT 90-10984]

Illustrierte Bücher und Mappenwerke des Jungen Rheinlands : eine Ausstellung der Universitätsbibliothek Düsseldorf, 15. Februar bis 30. April 1985. Düsseldorf : Universitätsbibliothek, 1985. ii, 56 p., xvii leaves of plates : ill. ; 25 cm. Errata slip inserted. Includes bibliographical references and index.
1. Junge Rheinland (Association) - Exhibitions. 2. Illustrated books - Germany (West) - Düsseldorf - History - 20th century - Exhibitions. 3. Prints, German - Germany (West) - Düsseldorf - Exhibitions. 4. Prints - 20th century - Germany (West) - Düsseldorf - Exhibitions. I. Universitätsbibliothek Düsseldorf.   **NYPL [MDTT 88-673]**

Ilonen, Arvi. Helsinki, Espoo, Kauniainen, Vantaa . Helsingissä , c1990. 195 p. :   ISBN 951-1-10582-5
NA1455.F52 H4575 1990

Ilse Erythropel. Erythropel, Ilse, 1911-1967. Krefeld, 1968. 59 p.
NB237.E7 S9
           NYPL [3-MGO (Erythropel) 90-6760]

Ilustrátoři dětské knihy /. Ševčíková, Hana. Olomouc , 1989. 1 portfolio (3, [1] p., [12] leaves) ;
NC989.C9 S48 1989

Ilya Kabakov . Kabakov, Il'i͡a Iosifovich, 1933- London [1989] 72 p. :   ISBN 0-905263-47-2 (pbk.)
           NYPL [3-MGO (Kabakov) 90-12888]

Im Zeichen der Aufklärung . Herding, Klaus. Frankfurt am Main , 1989. 242, [1] p. :   ISBN 3-596-23615-0   **NYPL [3-MAL 90-13019]**

Image and presence /. Shapiro, Estela. Mexico , 1985. 155 p. :   ISBN 968-610-601-4
           NYPL [3-MAM 91-4913]

Image and spirit in sacred and secular art /. Dillenberger, Jane. New York , 1990. xiii, 217 p., [8] p. of plates :   ISBN 0-8245-1036-4 :   DDC 701 20
N72.R4 D45 1990
           NYPL [3-MAMZ 91-3989]

Image & spirit in sacred & secular art. Dillenberger, Jane. Image and spirit in sacred and secular art /. New York , 1990. xiii, 217 p., [8] p. of plates :   ISBN 0-8245-1036-4 :   DDC 701 20
N72.R4 D45 1990
           NYPL [3-MAMZ 91-3989]

Image latente présente Jean-Jacques Heuzé . Heuzé, Jean Jacques. Lyon , 1979. 32 p. :
TR647 .H49 1979
           NYPL [MFX (Heuzé) 81-585]

The Image of man in modern Japanese art from the Museum collection : July 22-Sept. 11, 1988, The National Museum of Modern Art, Tokyo. [Tokyo] : The Museum, 1988. [36] p. : ill. (some col.) ; 24 cm. Title page and text in English and Japanese. Japanese title reads: Kindai bijutsu miru ningenzō: shozō sakuhin ni yoru zenkan chinretsu.
1. Art, Japanese - 1868- - Exhibitions. 2. Art, Modern - 20th century - Japan - Exhibitions. I. Tōkyō Kokuritsu Kindai Bijutsukan. II. Title: Kindai bijutsu miru ningenzō: shozō sakuhin ni yoru zenkan chinretsu.
           NYPL [3-MAG 89-6015]

The image of the Jew in Byzantine art /. Revel-Neher, Elisabeth. Oxford, England , New York , 1991. p. cm.   ISBN 0-08-040655-6 (HC)   DDC 704.9/499495004924 20
N6250 .R44 1991

Imagen femenina : en las artes visuales en Chile. 1a ed. Santiago, Chile : Editorial Lord Cochrane, 1989. 159 p. : ill. (some col.) ; 31 cm. Includes index. Includes bibliographical references.
1. Women - Chile - Portraits - Exhibitions. 2. Women in art - Exhibitions. 3. Portrait painting, Chilean - Exhibitions.   **NYPL [3-MAMZ+ 91-7168]**

Imágenes líricas =. Barnes, Lucinda. Long Beach , c1990. 119 p. :   ISBN 0-936270-30-6
           NYPL [3-MAML+ 91-5035]

Imagens do Sagrado. Lisboa : Fundação Calouste Gulbenkian, Centro de Arte Moderna, 1989. 47 p. : ill. (chiefly col.) ; 24 cm. "Exposição organizada pelo Centro de Arte Moderna com a colaboração de Emília Nadal, por ocasião do Colóquio 'O Sagrado e as Culturas,' promovido pelo Serviço ACARTE"--Verso t.p.   DDC 704.9/482/09469074469425 20
1. Christian art and symbolism - Modern period, 1500- - Portugal - Exhibitions. 2. Art, Portuguese - Exhibitions. 3. Art, Modern - 20th century - Portugal - Exhibitions. I. Nadal, Emília, 1938-. II. Centro de Arte Moderna (Fundação Calouste Gulbenkian).
N7963.A1 I4 1989

IMAGERY (PSYCHOLOGY) - CONGRESSES.
Rank Prize Funds' International Symposium (1986 : Royal Society) Images and understanding . Cambridge , New York , 1990. xiii, 401 p. :   ISBN 0-521-34177-9   DDC 152.1/4 19
QP474 .R36 1986   **NYPL [JFF 90-2299]**

IMAGES AND IDOLS. see IDOLS AND IMAGES.

Images and understanding . Rank Prize Funds' International Symposium (1986 : Royal Society) Cambridge , New York , 1990. xiii, 401 p. :   ISBN 0-521-34177-9   DDC 152.1/4 19
QP474 .R36 1986   **NYPL [JFF 90-2299]**

Images des loisirs : Musée national Fernand Léger, Biot-Alpes-Maritimes, 30 juin-2 octobre 1989 / [catalogue rédigé par Jean Lacambre]. Paris : Editions de la Réunion des musées nationaux, 1989. 183 p. : ill. (some col.) ; 21 cm. Includes index.   ISBN 2-7118-2269-9
1. Leisure in art - Exhibitions. I. Lacambre, Jean. II. Musée national Fernand Léger (France). III. Réunion des musées nationaux (France).
           NYPL [3-MAMZ 91-6590]

Images du patrimoine.
(no 26) Canton de Sierck-les-Bains, Moselle /. [Metz] , c1987. 72 p. :   ISBN 2-9501474-1-0   DDC 709/.44/3825 20
N6849.S53 C35 1987

(no 34) Châteaux de Haut-Léon . Saint-Brice-en Coglès , c1987. 32 p. :   ISBN 2-86934-006-0
           NYPL [3-MQWF+ 90-5362]

(no 49) Canton de Cattenom . [Metz] , c1988. 79 p. :   ISBN 2-9501474-3-7   DDC 709/.44/3825 20
N6849.C36 C36 1988

(no 50) Canton de Longuyon . [Metz] , c1988. 80 p. :   ISBN 2-9501474-4-5   DDC 709/.44/3823 20
N6849.L74 C36 1988

(no 51) Marville . [Metz] , c1988. 80 p. :   ISBN 2-9501474-5-3   DDC 709/.44/381 20
N6851.M34 M37 1988

(no 54) Canton de Seurre . [Dijon] , c1988. 59 p. :   ISBN 2-904727-02-7; 2-904727-02-07   DDC 709/.44/42 20
N6849.S48 C36 1988

(no 58) Canton et dentelles d'Arlanc, Puy-de-Dôme /. Clermont-Ferrand , c1989. 56 p. :   ISBN 2-905554-03-7 :   DDC 709/.44/591 20
N6849.A69 C36 1989

(no 66) Laon, ville haute, Aisne /. Amiens , c1989. 64 p. :   ISBN 2-906340-06-5 :   DDC 720/.44/345 20
NA1051.L3 L36 1989

(no 68) Eraud, Dominique. Laval, Mayenne /. [Nantes] [1990] 138 p. :   ISBN 2-906344-24-9   DDC 709/.44/16 20
N6851.L36 E7 1990

(no 71) Eglise Saint-Germain . [Caen, France]

[1990] 16 p. : ISBN 2-908621-00-2 : DDC 726/.5/094423 20
NA5551.A674 E36 1990

(no 72) Manase, Viviane. Canton de Montreuil-Bellay /. [Nantes] [1990] 100 p. : ISBN 2-906344-00-00 : DDC 709/.44/18 20
N6849.M66 M35 1990

(no 76) Falaise, Calvados /. [Caen, France] [1990] 64 p. : ISBN 2-908621-01-0 : DDC 709/44/22 20
N6851.F35 F35 1990

Images for the end of the century . Kennard, Peter. London , c1990. 1 v. (unpaged) : ISBN 1-85172-032-4 (pb)
NYPL [MFX (Kennard) 91-4655]

Images interdites /. Frémion, Yves. Paris , c1989. 125 p. : ISBN 2-86738-423-0 :
MLCM 90/04283 (H)
NYPL [3-MAMZ 90-12310]

IMAGES, MENTAL. see IMAGERY (PSYCHOLOGY)

Images, objects, and ideas . Nemett, Barry. Fort Worth , c1991. p. cm. ISBN 0-03-021782-2 DDC 701/.1 20
N71 .N46 1991

Images of America . Baekeland, Frederick. Birmingham, Ala. , 1991. p. cm. ISBN 0-931394-31-7 : DDC 759.13/09/03407473 20
ND1460.U54 B34 1991

Images of Asia.
Dumarçay, Jacques. Borobudur /. Singapore , New York , 1992. p. cm. ISBN 0-19-588550-3 : DDC 726/.143/095982 20
NA6026.6.B6 D8513 1992

Fickle, Dorothy H. Images of the Buddha in Thailand /. Singapore , New York , 1989. ix, 86 p. : ISBN 0-19-588920-7 (U. S.) DDC 704.9/4894363/09593 20
NB1912.G38 F53 1989

Images of death in contemporary art : March 22-June 3, 1990, the Patrick and Beatrice Haggerty Museum of Art, Marquette University. Milwaukee, Wis. : The Museum, c1990. 56 p. : ill. (some col.) ; 28 cm. Essays by Curtis L. Carter, Kit Basquin, Peter Halley. Includes bibliographical references. ISBN 0-87462-902-X
1. Death in art - Exhibitions. 2. Art, Modern - 20th century - Themes, motives - Exhibitions. I. Carter, Curtis L. II. Basquin, Kit. III. Halley, Peter. IV. Patrick and Beatrice Haggerty Museum of Art.
NYPL [3-MAMZ 91-7063]

Images of faith . Lepovitz, Helena Waddy, 1945- Athens , c1991. xviii, 228 p. : ISBN 0-8203-1256-8 (alk. paper) DDC 760/.04482/094336 20
NK5435.G3 L4 1991
NYPL [3-MRY 91-4876]

Images of fin-de-siècle architecture and interior decoration /. Tahara, Keiichi, 1951- [Seikimatsu no kenchiku. English.] London , New York , 1988. 263 p. : ISBN 0-00-215354-8 : DDC 724.9/1 19
NA3485   *NYPL [3-MRX+ 91-3382]*

Images of our time . Postle, Bruce. Ridgwood, Vic. Australia , 1989. 159 p. : ISBN 0-670-90229-2   *NYPL [MFW+ 91-5034]*

Images of paradise in Islamic art / edited by Sheila S. Blair and Jonathan M. Bloom ; with contributions by Walter B. Denny, Gene R. Garthwaite, A. Kevin Reinhart. Hanover, N.H. : Hood Museum of Art, Dartmouth College, 1991. p. cm. An illustrated catalogue of an exhibition to open at the Hood Museum of Art and to travel to the Asia Society, and other locations. Includes bibliographical references (p.) and index. ISBN 0-944722-07-5 (hardcover) DDC 704.9/489723 20
1. Art, Islamic - Exhibitions. 2. Paradise (Islam) in art - Exhibitions. I. Blair, Sheila S. II. Bloom, Jonathan (Jonathan M.). III. Hood Museum of Art. IV. Asia Society.
N6263.D37 H664 1991

Images of penance, images of mercy . Wroth, William, 1938- Norman , c1991. xvii, 196 p. : ISBN 0-8061-2325-7 DDC 704.9/482 20
N7908.6 .W76 1991
NYPL [3-MAIH+ 91-6054]

Images of prehistory /. Fowler, P. J. Cambridge , New York , 1990. 223 p. : ISBN 0-521-35646-6

DDC 936.1/0022/2 20
GN805 .F69 1990

Images of reality, images of Arcadia . Russell, Margarita. Winterthur [Switzerland] , Washington, D.C. , c1989. 131 p. : ISBN 3-907798-01-5   *NYPL [MFX (Sharp) 91-4460]*

Images of the Buddha in Thailand /. Fickle, Dorothy H. Singapore , New York , 1989. ix, 86 p. : ISBN 0-19-588920-7 (U. S.) DDC 704.9/4894363/09593 20
NB1912.G38 F53 1989

Images of the French Revolution /. Hould, Claudette. Québec , c1989. 446 p. : ISBN 2-551-08407-5   *NYPL [MDZ+ 90-12786]*

Images of war : the artist's vision of World War II / selected and edited by Ken McCormick and Hamilton Darby Perry ; foreword by John Hersey.1st ed. New York : Orion Books, c1990. xvi, 453 p. : ill. (chiefly col.) ; 30 cm. Includes indexes. Includes bibliographical references (p. 445-447). ISBN 0-517-57065-3 : DDC 758/.994054 20
1. World War, 1939-1945 - Art and the war. I. McCormick, Ken, 1906-. II. Perry, Hamilton Darby. D810.A7 I43 1990
NYPL [3-MAMZ 91-3270]

Images of wood : aspects of the history of sculpture in 20th-century South Africa : Johannesburg Art Gallery, 1989 / Elizabeth Rankin ; biographies, Elizabeth Dell ; documentation of works, Julia Meintjes. [Johannesburg] : The Gallery, 1989. 188 p. : ill. ; 28 cm. Includes bibliographical references (p. 184) and index. ISBN 0-620-13867-X DDC 730/.968/07468221 20
1. Sculpture, South African - Exhibitions. 2. Wood-carving - South Africa - History - 20th century - Exhibitions. I. Rankin, Elizabeth Deane. II. Dell, Elizabeth. III. Meintjes, Julia. IV. Johannesburg Art Gallery.
NB1255.S6 I46 1989

Imaginación de la materia . Cabrera, Geles, 1930- [Mexico] [1988] 1 v. (unpaged) : DDC 730/.92 20
NB249.C33 A4 1988

Imago lignea : sculture lignee nel Trentino dal XIII al XVI secolo / a cura di Enrico Castelnuovo ; testi di Marco Bellabarba ... [et al.] ; schede di Andrea Bacchi, Serenella Castri, Silvia Spada ; fotografie di Mario Ronchetti-Scala, Firenze. Trento : Editrice Temi, c1989. 287 p. : ill. (some col.), 1 map ; 34 cm. (Storia dell'arte e della cultura) Illustrated lining papers. Includes index. Includes bibliographical references. ISBN 88-85114-07-5
1. Sculpture, Italian - Italy - Trentino-Alto Adige. 2. Sculpture, Medieval - Italy - Trentino-Alto Adige. 3. Sculpture, Renaissance - Italy - Trentino-Alto Adige. 4. Wood-carved figurines - Italy - Trentino-Alto Adige. 5. Christian art and symbolism - Medieval, 500-1500 - Italy - Trentino-Alto Adige. I. Bellabarba, Marco. II. Castelnuovo, Enrico. III. Bacchi, Andrea. IV. Castri, Serenella. V. Spada Pintarelli, Silvia. VI. Title: Sculture lignee nel Trentino dal XIII al XVI secolo. VII. Series.
NYPL [3-MGI+ 91-4470]

Imago lignea : sculture lignee nel Trentino dal XIII al XVI secolo / a cura di Enrico Castelnuovo ; testi di Marco Bellabarba ... [et al.] ; schede di Andrea Bacchi, Serenella Castri, Silvia Spada ; fotografie di Mario Ronchetti-Scale, Firenze. Trento, Italia : Temi, c1989. 287 p. : ill. (some col.) ; 34 cm. (Storia dell'arte e della cultura) Includes bibliographical references (p. 279-283) and index. ISBN 88-85114-07-5 : DDC 730/.945/38 20
1. Sculpture, Medieval - Italy - Trentino-Alto Adige. 2. Sculpture, Renaissance - Italy - Trentino-Alto Adige. 3. Polychromy - Italy - Trentino-Alto Adige. 4. Wood-carving, Medieval - Italy - Trentino-Alto Adige. 5. Wood-carving, Renaissance - Italy - Trentino-Alto Adige. 6. Wood-carving - Italy - Trentino-Alto Adige. 7. Christian art and symbolism - Medieval, 500-1500 - Italy - Trentino-Alto Adige. I. Castelnuovo, Enrico. II. Bellabarba, Marco. III. Series.
NB1255.I8 I45 1989

Imaná, Gil, 1933-
Gil Imaná : obra de 1948 a 1989 : exposición antológica, Casa de la Cultura Franz Tamayo, H. Municipalidad de La Paz, octubre-noviembre 1989, La Paz, Bolivia. [La Paz, Bolivia : La Casa, 1989?] 1 v. (unpaged) : col. ill. ; 27 cm.

DDC 759.984 20
1. Imaná, Gil, 1933- - Exhibitions. I. Casa de la Cultura Franz Tamayo. II. Title.
ND349.I43 A4 1989

IMANÁ, GIL, 1933- - EXHIBITIONS.
Imaná, Gil, 1933- Gil Imaná. [La Paz, Bolivia , 1989?] 1 v. (unpaged) : DDC 759.984 20
ND349.I43 A4 1989

IMCoS. Chartographēsē tou Hellēnikou paraliou kai nēsiōtikou chōrou. [Athēna] , c1989. 84 p. :
GA881 .C43 1989
NYPL [Map Div. 91-3879]

Imiela, Hans-Jürgen, 1927-
Fritz Steisslinger, 1891-1957 : Leben und Werk / Hans-Jürgen Imiela. Stuttgart : Theiss, c1990. 342 p. : ill. ; 30 cm. ISBN 3-8062-0840-9
1. Steisslinger, Fritz, 1891-1957. I. Title.
NYPL [3-MCK+ S8232 90-13357]

Fritz Steisslinger, 1891-1957, Leben und Werk / Hans-Jürgen Imiela ; [herausgegeben von Eberhard Steisslinger]. Stuttgart : Theiss, c1990. 342 p. : ill. (some col.) ; 30 cm. Includes bibliographical references (p. 334). Includes index. ISBN 3-8062-0840-9 : DDC 759.3 B 20
1. Steisslinger, Fritz, 1891-1957. 2. Painters - Germany - Biography. I. Steisslinger, Fritz, 1891-1957. II. Steisslinger, Eberhard. III. Title. IV. Title: Leben und Werk.
ND588.S7127 I45 1990

Imitation and inspiration : Japanese influence on Dutch art / edited by Stefan van Raay. [Amsterdam] : Art Unlimited Books, c1989. 179 p. : ill. (chiefly col.), map ; 22 cm. English translation and editing: Cees Tinke ... [et al.]. Translated from the Dutch; bibliographical references are in Japanese. Includes bibliographical references and index.
1. Art, Dutch - Japanese influences. 2. Art, Japanese - Influence. 3. Art - Netherlands - History. I. Raaij, Stefan van.   *NYPL [3-MAME+ 90-11986]*

IMITATION (IN ART)
Levin, Marianne, 1942- Plagiat, stöld, förebild, inspiration /. [Solna] , c1990. 138 p. : ISBN 91-7332-505-8 :
NK789 .L48 1990

IMITATION (IN ART) - CONGRESSES.
Retaining the original . Washington , Hanover , c1989. 180 p. :   *NYPL [3-MAS 90-13011]*

L'Immagine della ragione : la Casa del fascio di Giuseppe Terragni, 1932-1936 / fotografie, NODO ; testo, Thomas L. Schumacher ; [traduzione, Fabio Cani]. Como : NODO libri, [1989] 61 p. : ill. ; 29 cm. (Punto di vista. 1) Italian and English. ISBN 88-7185-000-9
1. Terragni, Giuseppe, 1904-. I. Schumacher, Thomas L.
IN PROCESS (ONLINE)
NYPL [3-MQZ (Terragni) 91-3997]

Immagini dal Veronese . Gabinetto nazionale delle stampe. Roma [1978] 127 p. :
ND623.V5 A4 1978
NYPL [MDG (Veronese) 80-1248]

Immagini del Mugello : la terra dei Medici / testi di Cristina Acidini Luchinat ... [et al.]. Firenze : Alinari, c1990. 246 p. : ill. ; 30 cm. ISBN 88-7292-117-1
1. Mugello Valley (Italy). 2. Mugello Valley (Italy) - Description and travel - Views. 3. Mugello Valley (Italy) - Social life and customs - Pictorial works. I. Acidini, Cristina.   *NYPL [MFW+ 91-7415]*

Immagini del post-moderno : il dibattito sulla società post-industriale e l'architettura / Daniel Bell ... [et al.] ; a cura di Claudio Aldegheri e Maurizio Sabini ; saggi introduttivi di Paolo Portoghesi e Maurizio Ferraris. Venezia : Cluva, c1983. 345 p. : ill. ; 22 cm. (Architettura/temi) Includes bibliographical references. ISBN 88-85067-09-3 DDC 724.9/1 19
1. Architecture, Postmodern. 2. Architecture, Modern - 20th century. I. Bell, Daniel. II. Aldegheri, Claudio. III. Sabini, Maurizio. IV. Series.
NA682.P67 I48 1983
NYPL [3-MQV 91-6389]

Immagini di architettura e design, 1958-1986 /. Savio, Giulio, 1923- Milano , c1987. 178 p. : ISBN 88-435-2183-7 DDC 720/.92/4 19
NA1123.S315 A4 1987
NYPL [3-MQZ (Savio) 90-13002]

Immagini scritte : calligrafia giapponese moderna : Istituto giapponese di cultura-Roma,

26 ottobre-9 novembre 1984 / organizzata da
The Yomiuri Shimbun [i.e. Shinbun], Nippon
Television Network Corporation, Japan
Foundation. [Tokyo] : Yomiuri Shimbun [i.e.
Shinbun], c1984. 171 p. : ill. (some col.) ; 30
cm. Translated from the English.   DDC
745.6/19956/074 20
1. Calligraphy, Japanese - History - 20th century -
Exhibitions. I. Japan Cultural Institute in Rome. II.
Yomiuri Shinbunsha. III. Nihon Terebi. IV. Kokusai
Kōryū Kikin.
NK3637.A2 I46 1984

L'immago espressa, Villa Palagonia . Tedesco,
Natale. Siracusa , c1986. 231 p. :   DDC
728.8/0945/823 20
NA7595.B298 T4 1986
NYPL [3-MQWB+ 90-11739]

Les Immatériaux. Paris : Centre Georges
Pompidou, c1985. 2 v. : ill (some col.), plans ;
30 cm. Published in conjunction with the exhibition
"Les immatériaux", presented by the Centre de Création
Industrielle, held Mar. 28-July 15, 1985 at the Grande
galerie of the Centre national d'art et de culture George
Pompidou. Cover title. Includes bibliographical
references. CONTENTS. - Epreuves d'écriture. --
Album et inventaire.   ISBN 2-85850-299-4 (Epreuves
d'écriture)
1. Conceptual art - France - Exhibitions.
NYPL [3-MAL+ 86-2657]

Immerwahr, Sara Anderson, 1914- Aegean
painting in the Bronze Age / Sara A.
Immerwahr. University Park : Pennsylvania
State University Press, c1990. xxiv, 240 p., [45]
p. of plates : ill. (some col.), maps ; 29 cm.
Includes index. Errata slip inserted. Includes
bibliographical references (p. [223]-230).   ISBN
0-271-00628-5 :   DDC 751.7/3/093918 19
1. Mural painting and decoration, Minoan - Themes,
motives. 2. Mural painting and decoration, Mycenean -
Themes, motives. I. Title.
ND2570 .I45 1990
NYPL [3-MLP 90-10401]

Immeubles de bureaux /. Bédarida, Marc. Paris ,
c1991. 119 p. :   ISBN 2-281-19052-8
NA6230 .B43 1991

'Imparaticci' = 'Samplers' : esercizi di ricamo
delle bambine europee ed americane dal
Seicento all'Ottocento : Firenze, Palazzo
Davanzati, 26 giugno-26 novembre 1986 /
introduzione di Maria Fossi Todorow ; catalogo
a cura di Marina Carmignani. [Firenze] : Centro
Di, c1986. 78, [1] p. : ill. (some col.) ; 23 cm.
(Centro Di cat. . 203) Bibliography: p. 78-[79].   ISBN
88-7038-120-X
1. Samplers - Europe - Exhibitions. 2. Samplers -
United States - Exhibitions. 3. Children's art - Europe -
Exhibitions. 4. Children's art - United States -
Exhibitions. I. Carmignani, Marina. II. Museo
dell'antica casa fiorentina (Italy). III. Title: 'Samplers' :
esercizi di ricamo delle bambine europee ed
americane ... IV. Series: Cat. (Centro Di) , 203.
NK9109 .I663 1986
NYPL [3-MOT 90-10855]

**Imperatorskiĭ khar'kovskiĭ universitet. Muzeĭ
iziashchnykh iskusstv.**
**[Ukazatel' proizvedeniĭ, khraniashchikhsia v
Muzee iziashchnykh isskustv pri
Imperatorskom khar'kovskom universitete]**
Ukazatel' proizvedeniĭ, khraniashchikhsia v
Muzeĭe iziashchnykh iskusstv pri
Imperatorskom khar'kovskom universitetie.
Khar'kov : V Univ. tip., 1870-1883. 3 v. ; 20
cm. Source: Purchase from Gennadiĭ Vasil'evich
Yudin. 1906. DLC Includes indexes. CONTENTS. -
Contents: 1. Skul'ptura -- 2. Zhivopis' -- 3. Graviŭry,
oforty, khromolitografii i proch.
1. Art - Ukraine - Kharkov - Catalogs. 2. Imperatorskiĭ
khar'kovskiĭ universitet. Muzeĭ iziashchnykh iskusstv -
Catalogs. I. Title.
N3315.52 .A58 1870

**IMPERATORSKIĬ KHAR'KOVSKIĬ
UNIVERSITET. MUZEĬ
IZIASHCHNYKH ISKUSSTV -
CATALOGS.**
Imperatorskiĭ khar'kovskiĭ universitet. Muzeĭ
iziashchnykh iskusstv. [Ukazatel' proizvedeniĭ,
khraniashchikhsia v Muzee iziashchnykh
isskustv pri Imperatorskom khar'kovskom
universitete]. Ukazatel' proizvedeniĭ,
khraniashchikhsia v Muzee iziashchnykh
iskusstv pri Imperatorskom khar'kovskom
universitetie. Khar'kov , 1870-1883. 3 v. ;
N3315.52 .A58 1870

**Imperatorskoe obshchestvo pooshchreniia
khudozhestv (Russia). Muzeĭ.** Sbornik
khudozhestvenno-promyshlennykh risunkov.
S.-Peterburg , 1889. [2] p., [60] plates in
portfolio :   *NYPL [Slav. Reserve 90-4456 no.
73 (Bates).]*

Imperial China /. Chan, Charis. San Francisco ,
1992. p. cm.   ISBN 0-8118-0018-0   DDC 720/.951
20
NA1543.5 .C4 1992

IMPERIAL COUNTY (CALIF.) - MAPS.
Thomas Bros. Maps. San Diego County street
guide & directory . [Irvine, CA] [c1987] 1
atlas (1 v. (various pagings)) :   ISBN
0-88130-257-0 :   DDC 912/.79498 19
G1528.S24P8 T46 1987
NYPL [Map Div. 90-11915]

Imperial War Museum (Great Britain)
Foot, M. R. D. (Michael Richard Daniel),
1919- Art and war . London , 1990. 240 p. :
ISBN 0-7472-0286-9   DDC 758/.994053 20
N8260 .F58 1990

Kennard, Peter. Images for the end of the
century . London , c1990. 1 v. (unpaged) :
ISBN 1-85172-032-4 (pb)
NYPL [MFX (Kennard) 91-4655]

Rosoman, Leonard. Leonard Rosoman .
London , 1989. [24] p. :   ISBN 0-901627-53-4
(pbk.) :   DDC 759.2 20
NYPL [3-MCV R815 90-10822]

**IMPERIAL WAR MUSEUM (GREAT
BRITAIN)**
Foot, M. R. D. (Michael Richard Daniel),
1919- Art and war . London , 1990. 240 p. :
ISBN 0-7472-0286-9   DDC 758/.994053 20
N8260 .F58 1990

Imperial wardrobe /. Dickinson, Gary. London ,
1990. 203 p. :   ISBN 1-87007-607-9 :   DDC
391.0220951 20
NYPL [3-MMR+ 91-4972]

Impey, O. R. (Oliver R.)
Ayers, John. Porcelain for palaces . [London] ,
c1990. 328 p. :   ISBN 0-903421-24-0
NYPL [3-MPFK 91-7595]

Kakiemon porcelain from the English country
house . London , 1989. 64 p. :   ISBN
0-903432-35-8   *NYPL [3-MPFK 91-4566]*

Metropolitan Museum of Art (New York, N.Y.)
Japanese art from the Gerry collection in the
Metropolitan Museum of Art . New York ,
c1989. 141 p. :   ISBN 0-87099-556-1   DDC
738/.0952/0747471 20
N7352 .F67 1989   *NYPL [3-MAG 89-28868]*

Implement yourself [sound recording]. New
York : New World/Countercurrents, p1990. 1
sound disc : digital, stereo. ; 4 3/4 in. Brief
record. CONTENTS. - You're the fool -- Cha-ha --
Little Italy (la passione) -- The faker -- Seven guys with
a reason -- Augie the rat -- Peace in the valley --
March 19th -- Indian Club bombardment -- Easy to
love.
1. Jazz - 1981-1990.
New World/Countercurrents NW398-2

**IMPLEMENTS, UTENSILS, ETC. - FRANCE -
NORMANDY.**
Fréal, Jacques. La Normandie /. [Paris] ,
c1980. 110 p. :   ISBN 2-7050-0260-X :   DDC
392/.36/009442 19
NA8203 .F693   *NYPL [3-MQWF 81-936]*

Important old master paintings . Piero Corsini
Gallery. New York, N.Y. , 1990. 99 p. :
NYPL [3-MC 90-13103]

Important old master paintings . Simon, Robert
Barry, 1952- New York, N.Y. [1989] 125 p. :
NYPL [3-MC 90-11623]

IMPRESA MARIANI.
Una Famiglia di architetti e costruttori a Roma,
1887-1987 /. Roma , 1987. xxiv, 75 p. :   ISBN
88-7813-027-3
NYPL [3-MQWB+ 90-9457]

A impressão da cultura /. Silva, José Antônio,
1951- Porto Alegre-RS , c1990. 104 p. :   ISBN
85-20-50026-9
NX456 .S53 1990

Impressionism / David Bomford ... [et al.] ; with
contributions by Raymond White and Louise
Williams. London : National Gallery in
association with Yale University Press, New
Haven, c1990. 227 p. : ill. (some col.) ; 28 cm.
(Art in the making) Catalog of an exhibition held at the
National Gallery, London, Nov. 28, 1990-Apr. 21,
1991. Bibliography: p. 213-227.   ISBN 0-300-05035-6
(cased) :   DDC 759.054074 20
1. Impressionism (Art) - France - Exhibitions. 2.
Painting, Modern - 19th century - France - Exhibitions.
3. Painting - Radiography - Exhibitions. 4. Painting -
Technique - Exhibitions. 5. Artists' materials -
Exhibitions. 6. Pigments - Exhibitions. I. Bomford,
David. II. National Gallery (Great Britain). III. Series.
ND192.I4   *NYPL [3-MCN 91-5511]*

Impressionism . Broude, Norma. New York ,
1991. p. cm.   ISBN 0-8478-1397-5   DDC 759.05/4
20
ND547.5.I4 B76 1991

Impressionism and European modernism .
Columbus Museum of Art. Columbus, Ohio ,
Seattle , 1991. p.   ISBN 0-295-97133-9 :   DDC
709/.03/407477157 20
N6447 .C65 1991

Impressionism and post impressionism : the
collector's passion / essay by Carole Calo ; with
an introduction by Barbara S. Nosanow ;
entries by Karyn Eiselonis ... [et al.]. Portland,
Me. : Portland Museum of Art, c1991. p. cm.
Catalog of an exhibition held at the Portland Museum
of Art, Jul. 30-Oct. 13, 1991.   DDC
709/.03/4407474191 20
1. Art, French - Exhibitions. 2. Impressionism (Art) -
France - Exhibitions. 3. Art, Modern - 19th century -
France - Exhibitions. 4. Post-impressionism (Art) -
France - Exhibitions. 5. Art, Modern - 20th century -
France - Exhibitions. 6. Art, American - Exhibitions. 7.
Impressionism (Art) - United States - Exhibitions. 8.
Art, Modern - 19th century - United States -
Exhibitions. 9. Post-impressionism (Art) - United
States - Exhibitions. 10. Art, Modern - 20th century -
United States - Exhibitions. 11. Art - Private
collections - United States - Exhibitions. 12. Art -
Collectors and collecting - United States - Exhibitions.
13. Calo, Carole Gold. I. Portland Museum of Art.
N6847.5.I4 I43 1991

IMPRESSIONISM (ART) - AUSTRALIA.
Astbury, Leigh, 1950- Sunlight and shadow .
Sydney , 1989. 232 p. :   ISBN 1-86256-295-4
NYPL [3-MCY+ 90-882]

IMPRESSIONISM (ART) - CATALOGS.
Stiftung Langmatt Sidney and Jenny Brown.
Sammlungskataloge. Baden , c1990- v. :   ISBN
3-85545-044-7 (Bd. 1)
NYPL [3-MAX+ (Brown) 91-1053]

**IMPRESSIONISM (ART) - DICTIONARIES
AND ENCYCLOPEDIAS.**
Denvir, Bernard, 1917- The Thames and
Hudson encyclopaedia of Impressionism /.
London , New York, N.Y. , 1990. 240 p. :
ISBN 0-500-20239-7 :
NYPL [MBK 90-12515]

**IMPRESSIONISM (ART) - EUROPE -
EXHIBITIONS.**
Impressionismo in Europa . Bologna , c1990.
170 p. :   ISBN 88-7779-126-8
NYPL [3-MAVZ (Prague) 91-6701]

IMPRESSIONISM (ART) - EXHIBITIONS.
Impressionismo e postimpressionismo . Lugano ,
Milano , c1990. 111 p. :   ISBN 88-435-3137-9
*NYPL [3-MAX (Thyssen-Bornemisza)
91-6804]*

Landschaft im Licht . Köln , Zürich , c1990.
519 p. :   DDC 759.05/4/074435514 20
ND192.I4 L27 1990
NYPL [3-MC+ 91-5272]

IMPRESSIONISM (ART) - FRANCE.
Broude, Norma. Impressionism . New York ,
1991. p. cm.   ISBN 0-8478-1397-5   DDC 759.05/4
20
ND547.5.I4 B76 1991

Bumpus, Judith. Impressionist gardens /.
Oxford , 1990. 80 p. :   ISBN 0-7148-2660-X :
DDC 759.054 20
ND192.I4   *NYPL [3-MCN+ 90-13280]*

Clayson, Hollis, 1946- Painted love . New
Haven , c1991. p. cm.   ISBN 0-300-04730-4
DDC 760/.0449306742/094436109034 20
N6847.5.I4 C58 1991

Distel, Anne. Les collectionneurs des
impressionnistes . [Paris] , c1989. 283 p. :
ISBN 2-85047-042-2
NYPL [MAVC+ 91-6788]

The Impressionists' river . New York, NY ,

1991. p. cm.   ISBN 0-87663-620-2   DDC
759.4/09/034 20
ND547.5.I4 I5 1991

Lévêque, Jean Jacques. Les années
impressionnistes, 1870-1889 /. Courbevoie,
Paris , c1990. 660 p. :   ISBN 2-86770-042-6
IN PROCESS (ONLINE)
    NYPL [3-MAMI+ 91-4871]

Lurie, Patty, 1944- A guide to the impressionist
landscape . Boston , c1990. 135 p. :   ISBN
0-8212-1796-8 DDC 758/.144/094409034 20
ND1355.5 .L8 1990
    NYPL [3-MCN 91-2248]

Madeleine-Perdrillat, Alain, 1949- [Seurat.
English.] Seurat /. New York , 1990. 215 p. :
ISBN 0-8478-1286-3 DDC 759.4 20
ND553.S5 M3313 1990
    NYPL [3-MCO+ S49 91-5347]

Morisot, Berthe, 1841-1895. [Correspondence
de Berthe Morisot avec sa famille et ses amis.
English.] The correspondence of Berthe Morisot
with her family and her friends . New York ,
1957. 187 p. :
ND553.M88 A313
    NYPL [3-MCO M86 90-11559]

Sefrioui, Anne. Impressionist fans /. New
York , 1991. p. cm.   ISBN 0-86565-129-9 DDC
759.4/09/034 20
N6847.5.I4 S44 1991

**IMPRESSIONISM (ART) - FRANCE -
AUVERS-SUR-OISE - EXHIBITIONS.**
Van Gogh et les peintres d'Auvers-sur-Oise .
[Paris] , 1954. xl, 100 p., xxxii p. of plates :
N6847.5.I4 V36 1954

**IMPRESSIONISM (ART) - FRANCE -
CATALOGS.**
Mráz, Bohumír. Aquarelles et dessins
impressionnistes . [Gennevilliers?] , 1987. 206
p. :   ISBN 2-86901-027-3
    NYPL [3-MBH+ 89-28607]

**IMPRESSIONISM (ART) - FRANCE -
EXHIBITIONS.**
Boudin, Eugène, 1824-1898. Boudin . Salem,
Mass. , 1991. p.   DDC 759.4 20
ND553.B73 A4 1991

Fossier, François. Il fiore dell'impressionismo
=. Milano , c1990. 388 p. :
NE647.6.I4 F67 1990

Impressionism /. London , c1990. 227 p. :
ISBN 0-300-05035-6 (cased) :   DDC 759.054074
20
ND192.I4   *NYPL [3-MCN 91-5511]*

Impressionism and post impressionism .
Portland, Me. , c1991. p. cm.   DDC
709/.03/4407474191 20
N6847.5.I4 I43 1991

The passionate eye . [Zurich?] , Zurich , c1990.
244 p. :   ISBN 0-8478-1215-4
    NYPL [3-MAX (Bührle) 90-12982]

**IMPRESSIONISM (ART) - FRANCE -
JUVENILE LITERATURE.**
Waldron, Ann. Claude Monet /. New York ,
1991. p. cm.   ISBN 0-8109-3620-8 (cloth) DDC
759.4 B 20
ND553.M7 W24 1991

**IMPRESSIONISM (ART) - GERMANY -
CATALOGS.**
Pfalzgalerie Kaiserslautern. Graphische
Sammlung. Graphik des deutschen
Impressionismus . Kaiserslautern , 1985. 91 p. :
DDC 769/.074/0343 s 769.943/074/0343 19
NE55.G4 K346 1985 vol. 1 NE651.6.I4
    NYPL [MDE 91-4007]

**IMPRESSIONISM (ART) - RUSSIAN S.F.S.R.
- EXHIBITIONS.**
Russische Malerei im 19. Jahrhundert .
[Zürich , 1989] 321 p. :   DDC 759.7/074/49457
20
ND687 .R744 1989
    NYPL [3-MCY 90-12884]

**IMPRESSIONISM (ART) - UNITED
STATES - CONGRESSES.**
American art around 1900 . Washington ,
Hanover [N.H.] , 1990. 136 p. :   ISBN
0-89468-143-5 *NYPL [3-MAMT 91-7570]*

**IMPRESSIONISM (ART) - UNITED
STATES - EXHIBITIONS.**
Gerdts, William H. American Impressionism .
[Lugano-Castagnola] [Einsiedeln, Switzerland] ,

c1990. 161 p. :   DDC 759.13/09/03407449478 20
ND210.5.I4 G474 1990a

Gerdts, William H. Masterworks of American
impressionism /. Lugano-Castagnola,
Switzerland : Einsiedeln, Switzerland : 163 p. :
ISBN 0-8109-3614-3 DDC 759.13/074/49478 20
ND210.5.I4 G476 1991
    NYPL [3-MCW+ 91-7414]

Hiesinger, Ulrich W., 1943- Impressionism in
America . Munich , New York, NY , c1991.
255 p. :   ISBN 3-7913-1142-5
    NYPL [3-MCW+ 91-7730]

Impressionism and post impressionism .
Portland, Me. , c1991. p. cm.   DDC
709/.03/4407474191 20
N6847.5.I4 I43 1991

Pennsylvania Academy of the Fine Arts. Light,
air, and color . Philadelphia, Pa. , c1990. 91 p. :
ISBN 0-943836-13-1 DDC 759.13/074/74811 20
ND212.5.I45 P4 1990
    NYPL [3-MCW 91-7196]

Ten American painters /. New York , c1990.
187 p. :   ISBN 0-945936-07-9
    NYPL [3-MCW 90-11805]

Impressionism in America . Hiesinger, Ulrich W.,
1943- Munich , New York, NY , c1991. 255
p. :   ISBN 3-7913-1142-5
    NYPL [3-MCW+ 91-7730]

Impressionismo e postimpressionismo : Collezione
Thyssen-Bornemisza / catalogo a cura di Sarah
Whitfield. Lugano : Fondazione
Thyssen-Bornemisza ; Milano : Electa, c1990.
111 p. : ill. (some col.) ; 28 cm. Italian and
French; exhibition held at the Villa Favorita,
Castagnola, Lugano, April 1-July 8, 1990.   ISBN
88-435-3137-9
  *1. Sammlung Thyssen-Bornemisza - Exhibitions. 2.
Impressionism (Art) - Exhibitions. I. Whitfield, Sarah.
II. Villa favorita (Lugano, Switzerland).*
    *NYPL [3-MAX (Thyssen-Bornemisza)
91-6804]*

Impressionismo in Europa : origini, sviluppi,
influenze : capolavori dalle collezioni della
Galleria Nazionale di Praga / a cura di Franca
Varignana ; con scritti di Jiří Kotalík ... [et al.].
Bologna : Nuova Alfa, c1990. 170 p. : ill. (some
col.) ; 29 cm. Catalog of an exhibition held at San
Giorgio in Poggiale, Bologna, 24 Mar.-24 June 1990. At
head of title: Istituto per i beni culturali della Regione
Emilia-Romagna; Cassa di risparmio in Bologna,
Collezione d'arte e di storia. Includes bibliographical
references.   ISBN 88-7779-126-8
  *1. Národní galerie v Praze - Exhibitions. 2.
Impressionism (Art) - Europe - Exhibitions. 3. Art,
Modern - 19th century - Europe - Exhibitions. 4. Art,
Modern - 20th century - Europe - Exhibitions. I.
Varignana, Franca. II. Národní galerie v Praze. III. S.
Giorgio in Poggiale (Church : Bologna, Italy).*
    NYPL [3-MAVZ (Prague) 91-6701]

Impressionist and modern . Whistler, Catherine.
Oxford , 1990. 128 p. :   ISBN 0-907849-97-0
(pbk.)   *NYPL [3-MAX (Gross) 90-11583]*

Impressionist fans /. Sefrioui, Anne. New York ,
1991. p. cm.   ISBN 0-86565-129-9 DDC
759.4/09/034 20
N6847.5.I4 S44 1991

Impressionist gardens /. Bumpus, Judith.
Oxford , 1990. 80 p. :   ISBN 0-7148-2660-X :
DDC 759.054 20
ND192.I4   *NYPL [3-MCN+ 90-13280]*

Impressionist landscape. Lurie, Patty, 1944- A
guide to the impressionist landscape . Boston ,
c1990. 135 p. :   ISBN 0-8212-1796-8 DDC
758/.144/094409034 20
ND1355.5 .L8 1990
    NYPL [3-MCN 91-2248]

**IMPRESSIONISTS. see IMPRESSIONISM
(ART)**

The Impressionists' river : glorious views of the
Seine. New York, NY : Universe, 1991. p. cm.
ISBN 0-87663-620-2 DDC 759.4/09/034 20
  *1. Impressionism (Art) - France. 2. Painting, French. 3.
Painting, Modern - 19th century - France. 4. Seine
River (France) in art.*
ND547.5.I4 I5 1991

Impressions Gallery of Photography. Johnston,
Frances Benjamin, 1864-1952. Frances
Benjamin Johnston . York [1984] [20] p. :

ISBN 0-906361-45-1 (pbk.)
TR820.5 M544 1984
    NYPL [MFX (Johnston) 91-3499]

Imprimerie Bénard.
Plakate aus der Druckerei Benard, Sammlung
des Musée de la Vie Wallone, Lüttich =.
Köln , 1980. 92 p. :
    NYPL [3-MDW 90-4651]

IMPRIMERIE BÉNARD - EXHIBITIONS.
Plakate aus der Druckerei Benard, Sammlung
des Musée de la Vie Wallone, Lüttich =.
Köln , 1980. 92 p. :
    NYPL [3-MDW 90-4651]

In Freiheit zu sich selbst. Hülsmann, Boda. Paula
Modersohn-Becker . Stuttgart , c1988. 75 p. :
ISBN 3-87838-586-2
    NYPL [3-MCK M68 90-4525]

In Medusa's gaze : still life paintings in upstate
New York museums / essay by Norman
Bryson ; catalogue by Bernard Barryte.
Rochester, NY : Memorial Art Gallery of the
University of Rochester, c1991. p. cm.
"Organized by Memorial Art Gallery of the University
of Rochester, 1991." Exhibition held at various
institutions between Dec. 7, 1991 and May 2, 1993.
Includes bibliographical references and index.   ISBN
0-918098-05-X   DDC 758/.4/074747 20
  *1. Still-life painting - Exhibitions. 2. Art museums -
New York (State) - Exhibitions. I. Bryson, Norman,
1949-. II. Barryte, Bernard. III. University of Rochester.
Memorial Art Gallery.*
ND1390 .I5 1991

In other words : Wort und Schrift in Bildern der
Konzeptuellen Kunst : [Ausstellung] 10.
September-15. Oktober 1989, Museum am
Ostwall, Dortmund /. Nancy Dyer ... [et al. ;
Ausstellung und Katalog, Anna Meseure].
[Stuttgart] : Edition Cantz, [1989] 107 p. : ill.
(some col.) ; 29 cm. Includes bibliographical
references.   ISBN 3-89322-159-X
  *1. Conceptual art - Exhibitions. I. Dwyer, Nancy. II.
Meseure, Anna. III. Museum am Ostwall (Dortmund,
Germany).*   *NYPL [3-MAL 90-8164]*

In/progetto : appunti ed esercizi da un corso di
progettazione architettonica / A. Cuomo ... [et
al.] ; 2 cura di Alberto Cuomo. Napoli :
C.L.E.A.N, 1985. 128 p. : ill. (some col.),
plans ; 31 cm.
  *1. Architecture, Modern - 20th century - Italy. I.
Cuomo, Alberto. II. Title.*
    NYPL [3-MQWB+ 90-10577]

In pursuit of the unicorn /. Bradley, Josephine.
Corte Madera, Calif. , 1980. [111]p. :   ISBN
0-917556-06-2 *NYPL [3-MAMZ 91-6657]*

In search of van Gogh /. Wilkie, Kenneth, 1942-
[Van Gogh assignment.] Rocklin, CA , 1991. p.
cm.   ISBN 1-559-58101-8 :   DDC 759.9492 B 20
ND653.G7 W54 1991

**In the context of the art world (1976 : Center
for Experimental Art and Communication)**
Świdziński, Jan. Quotations on contextual art /.
[Eindhoven , New York (U. S.A.) , 1988?] 190
p. ;   ISBN 90-71638-04-9 DDC 701 20
N71 .S95 1988   *NYPL [3-MA 91-4598]*

In the footsteps of Le Corbusier /. Sulle tracce di
Le Corbusier. English. New York , 1991. 268
p. :   ISBN 0-8478-1219-7 (pbk.) :   DDC 720/.92 20
NA1053.J4 S913 1991

In the mountains of Japan . Hunter, Sam, 1923-
New York, NY [1988?] 288 p. :   ISBN
0-89659-949-3 DDC 735/.23/00740952136 19
NB198 .H86 1988
    NYPL [3-MGI+ 90-11775]

In the romantic style . Chase, Linda. New York,
N.Y. , 1990. 160 p. :   ISBN 0-500-23592-9
    NYPL [3-MLO 90-11995]

In the stream of stars : the Soviet/American
space art book / edited by William K.
Hartmann ... [et al.] ; with a historical
perspective by Ray Bradbury. New York :
Workman Pub., 1990. 183 p. : col. ill. ; 26 x 28
cm. "With the cooperation of the International
Association for the Astronomical Arts, the Planetary
Society, the U. S.S.R. Union of Artists."   ISBN
0-89480-705-6 (paper)   DDC 758/.96294 20
  *1. Outer space in art. 2. Art, Soviet. I. Hartmann,
William K. II. International Association for the
Astronomical Arts. III. Planetary Society. IV. Soi͡uz*

khudozhnikov SSSR.
N8234.O8 I5 1990
       NYPL [3-MAMZ 91-5459]

In the Vernacular : interviews at Yale with
sculptors of culture / edited by Melissa E.
Biggs. Jefferson, N.C. : McFarland, 1991. p.
cm. Includes index. ISBN 0-89950-645-3 (lib. bdg. :
alk. paper) DDC 700/.92/273 20
*1. Artists - United States - Interviews. 2. Arts,
Modern - 20th century - United States. I. Biggs,
Melissa E., 1967-. II. Yale vernacular.*
NX504 .I526 1991

In the Victorian style /. Delehanty, Randolph.
San Francisco , c1991. p. cm. ISBN
0-87701-750-6 (hc) : DDC 720/.9794/6109034
20
NA7238.S35 D4 1991

In the watercolor tradition . Mellon Bank.
Pittsburgh, Pa. , 1990. 78 p. : ISBN
0-88039-046-8 : DDC 759.2/074/74886 20
ND1928 .M45 1990
       NYPL [3-MBO 91-6675]

**In tribute to Madame de Pompadour and the
court of Louis XV /.** Lincoln, Paul. Cambridge ,
1985. 1 v. (unpaged) :
       NYPL [MEMZ 91-2442]

In unnachahmlicher Treue : Photographie im 19.
Jahrhundert, ihre Geschichte in den
deutschsprachigen Ländern : eine Ausstellung
der Josef-Haubrich-Kunsthalle Köln in
Zusammenarbeit mit dem Foto-Historama
Agfa-Gevaert Leverkusen vom 8. September bis
21. Oktober 1979 / [Katalog, Heinz Langholz,
Ferdinand von den Ecker, Christoph Müller].
Köln : Museen der Stadt Köln, 1979. 370 p. :
ill. (some col.) ; 28 cm. Includes bibliographical
references and index.
*1. Photography - Germany - History - Exhibitions. I.
Langholz, Heinz. II. Ecker, Ferdinand van den. III.
Müller, Christoph. IV. Cologne. Kunsthalle. V.
Foto-Historama Agfa-Gevaert Leverkusen.*
TR6.G3 C644   *NYPL [MFW 81-577]*

In vivo /. Danuser, Hans, 1953- Baden , c1989. 1
v. : ISBN 3-906700-19-4
       NYPL [MFX+ (Danuser) 91-4457]

In what style should we build? : the German
debate on architectural style / Heinrich
Hübsch ... [et al.] ; introduction and translation
by Wolfgang Herrmann. Santa Monica, Calif. :
Getty Center for the History of Art and the
Humanities, 1991. p. cm. (Texts & documents)
Includes bibliographical references (p.) and index.
   ISBN 0-89236-199-9 : DDC 720/.1 20
*1. Architecture. 2. Architecture - Composition,
proportion, etc. 3. Architectural design. I. Hübsch,
Heinrich, 1795-1863. II. Herrmann, Wolfgang, 1899-.
III. Series.*
NA2500 .I5 1991

In your face . Marlette, Doug, 1949- Boston ,
1991. p. cm. ISBN 0-395-60236-X DDC
741.5/092 20
NC1429.M4215 A2 1991

Inability to endure or deny the world . Sultan,
Terrie, 1952- Washington, D.C. , c1990. 65 p. :
ISBN 0-88675-036-9 : DDC 760/.092 20
ND237.M74 A4 1990
       NYPL [3-MCX+ M877 91-4930]

Incontri internazionale d'arte (Firm) Open
mind . Milano , c1989. 318 p. :
       NYPL [3-MAMZ 90-11011]

Incontri internazionali d'arte (Firm) Merz,
Mario. Mario Merz at MOCA. [Milan] [c1989]
126 p. : ISBN 0-914357-17-4 (Museum of
Contemporary Art) DDC 709/.2 20
N6923.M43 M4 1989
       NYPL [3-MGO (Merz) 91-6017]

L'incoronazione della Vergine del Botticelli .
Botticelli, Sandro, 1444 or 5-1510. Firenze ,
1990. 141 p. :
IN PROCESS (ONLINE)
       NYPL [3-MCF B75 90-11619]

The incredible cross-section book /. Biesty,
Stephen. New York , 1992. p. cm. ISBN
0-679-81411-6 DDC 741.6/42/092 20
NC975.5.B5 A4 1992

INCUNABULA.
Vanderwielen, Betty. An index of woodcuts and
engravings in incunabula and early printed
books (to 1600) in the Library of the Institute
of Cistercian Studies /. Kalamazoo, Mich. ,

1988. viii, 284 leaves ; ISBN 0-918720-92-3
   DDC 769.94/09/03107477417 20
NE1052 .V36 1988

INCUNABULA - PORTUGAL - CATALOGS.
Pacheco, José, 1954- A divina arte negra e o
livro português . Lisboa [1988?] 282 p. :
NE1163 .P33 1988
       NYPL [MDOH 90-12803]

INDEPENDENCE (PSYCHOLOGY) see
AUTONOMY (PSYCHOLOGY)

Independent Curators Incorporated.
Barnes, Lucinda. Imágenes líricas =. Long
Beach , c1990. 119 p. : ISBN 0-936270-30-6
       NYPL [3-MAML+ 91-5035]

Sollins, Susan. Eternal metaphors . New York,
N.Y. , c1989. 72 p. : ISBN 0-916365-28-X
       NYPL [3-MAMC 90-11056]

Stein, Donna. Contemporary illustrated books .
New York, N.Y. , c1989. 72 p. : ISBN
0-916365-00-X *NYPL [MDTT+ 91-6216]*

Team spirit /. New York, N.Y. , c1990. 84 p. :
ISBN 0-916365-30-1
       NYPL [3-MAL 91-6734]

The Independent Group : postwar Britain and the
aesthetics of plenty / edited by David Robbins.
Cambridge, Mass. : MIT Press, c1990. 256 p. :
ill. (some col.) ; 25 x 31 cm. Exhibition organized
by the Hood Museum of Art, Dartmouth College ... [et
al.] held between February 1, 1990 and August 18,
1991 at various locations. Includes bibliographical
references (p. 250-255). ISBN 0-262-18139-8 DDC
709/.41/074 20
*1. Independent Group (Association : Great Britain) -
Exhibitions. 2. Art, Modern - 20th century - Great
Britain - Exhibitions. I. Robbins, David, 1937-. II. Hood
Museum of Art. III. Title: Postwar Britain and the
aesthetics of plenty.*
N6768.5.I53 I53 1990
       NYPL [3-MAMR+ 90-11745]

**INDEPENDENT GROUP (ASSOCIATION :
GREAT BRITAIN) - EXHIBITIONS.**
The Independent Group . Cambridge, Mass. ,
c1990. 256 p. : ISBN 0-262-18139-8 DDC
709/.41/074 20
N6768.5.I53 I53 1990
       NYPL [3-MAMR+ 90-11745]

**An index of woodcuts and engravings in
incunabula and early printed books (to 1600)
in the Library of the Institute of Cistercian
Studies /.** Vanderwielen, Betty. Kalamazoo,
Mich. , 1988. viii, 284 leaves ; ISBN
0-918720-92-3 DDC 769.94/09/03107477417 20
NE1052 .V36 1988

**Index to Architecture series, Bibliography, no.
A-1 to A-154 (June 1978-December 1979).**
Vance Bibliographies (Firm) Monticello, Ill. ,
1980. 38 p. ;
Z5941 .V34 1980 NA25   *NYPL [*XMC-359]*

India, a pageant of prints / edited by Pauline
Rohatagi and Pheroza Godrej. Bombay : Marg
Publications, c1989. xii, 240 p. : ill. (some
col.) ; 33 cm. Includes bibliographical references.
   ISBN 81-85026-08-4 : DDC 769/.49954 20
*1. Prints, British. 2. Prints - 18th century - Great
Britain. 3. Prints - 19th century - Great Britain. 4. India
in art. I. Rohatagi, Pauline. II. Godrej, Pheroza.*
NE954.3.G7 I5 1989
       NYPL [MDZ+ 91-6181]

INDIA - ANTIQUITIES.
Bhattacharyya, Benoytosh, 1897-1964. The
Indian Buddhist iconography. Calcutta [1968]
xxxiii, 478 p.   *NYPL [3-MAF 75-368]*

Soundara Rajah, K.V., 1925- Secularism in
Indian art /. New Delhi , c1988. viii, 109 p. :
ISBN 81-7017-245-4
       NYPL [3-MAE 89-28260]

India - Archaeology. see **India - Antiquities.**

India. Census Commissioner. Census of India,
1981. Series 1, India. Delhi , 1983- v. in :
DDC 304.6/0954/021 19
HA4581.5 1981g
       NYPL [JLM 88-578 & Map Div. 90-54]

INDIA - CENSUS, 1981.
Census of India, 1981. Series 1, India. Delhi ,
1983- v. in : DDC 304.6/0954/021 19
HA4581.5 1981g
       NYPL [JLM 88-578 & Map Div. 90-54]

INDIA - CIVILIZATION.
Srivastava, A. L., 1936- Śilpa-śrī, studies in

Indian art and culture /. Delhi , 1990. xvi, 226
p., 85 leaves of plates : ISBN 81-85067-29-5 :
DDC 709/.54 20
N7302 .S75 1990   *NYPL [3-MAF 91-6395]*

India. Dept. of Tourism. Bawa, Manmohan Singh.
Himalayan trekking maps /. [Bombay?] [New
Delhi, India , 1985]. 1 atlas (unpaged) :
       NYPL [Map Div. 90-11639]

**INDIA - DESCRIPTION AND TRAVEL - 1981-
- GUIDE-BOOKS.**
Tamilnad Printers & Traders Private Ltd. The
city atlas of India . Madras, India , 1985. 1
atlas (232 p.) : DDC 912/.54 19
G2284.A1 T3 1985
       NYPL [Map Div. 91-6606]

India - Government. see **India - Politics and
government.**

INDIA IN ART.
India, a pageant of prints /. Bombay , c1989.
xii, 240 p. : ISBN 81-85026-08-4 : DDC
769/.49954 20
NE954.3.G7 I5 1989
       NYPL [MDZ+ 91-6181]

Potabenko, S. I. Vision of India in the works of
Russian and Soviet artists /. New Delhi ,
c1989. viii, 57 p., [64] p. of plates : ISBN
81-207-0955-1 :
IN PROCESS (ONLINE)
       NYPL [3-MAMY 90-11293]

India. Office of the Registrar General. Census of
India, 1981. Series 1, India. Delhi , 1983- v.
in : DDC 304.6/0954/021 19
HA4581.5 1981g
       NYPL [JLM 88-578 & Map Div. 90-54]

**INDIA - POLITICS AND GOVERNMENT -
20TH CENTURY.**
Josh, Sohan Singh, 1898- Hindustan Gadar
Party . New Delhi , 1977. 1 v. ;
DS480.45 .J66   *NYPL [JLK 80-148]*

Josh, Sohan Singh, 1898- Hindustan Gadar
Party . New Delhi , 1977-1978. 2 v. ;
DS480.45 .J66   *NYPL [JLL 79-458]*

**INDIA - POLITICS AND GOVERNMENT -
1947- - CARICATURES AND CARTOONS.**
Laxman, R. K. The eloquent brush /.
[Bombay] , c1988. 303 p. :
       NYPL [3-MEM+ (Laxman) 89-25506]

INDIA - SCHEDULED TRIBES - MAPS.
Raza, Moonis. An atlas of tribal India . New
Delhi , 1990. xxv, 472 p. : ISBN 81-7022-286-9 :
       NYPL [Map Div. 91-4975]

**INDIA - SCHEDULED TRIBES -
STATISTICS.**
Raza, Moonis. An atlas of tribal India . New
Delhi , 1990. xxv, 472 p. : ISBN 81-7022-286-9 :
       NYPL [Map Div. 91-4975]

Indian art. Victoria and Albert Museum. London,
1952. [32] p.   *NYPL [3-MAF 90-5981]*

The Indian Buddhist iconography. Bhattacharyya,
Benoytosh, 1897-1964. Calcutta [1968] xxxiii,
478 p.   *NYPL [3-MAF 75-368]*

**Indian images: photographs of North American
Indians, 1847-1928, from the Smithsonian
Institution, National Anthropological Archives.**
Scherer, Joanna Cohan. Washington, 1970. 31
p. : DDC 779/.9/9701   *NYPL [MFW 90-11184]*
E77.5 .N3

Indian miniature painting series 2. New Delhi :
Lalit Kalā Akademi, 1986. 1 portfolio ([4] p., 8
leaves of col. ; 11.); 40 an. (Lalit Kalā series .
portfolio no. 28) Title from portfolio cover. Text: Usha
Bhatia. On spine of binder's case: Vol. 2.
*1. Miniature painting, Indic - Catalogs. 2. Illumination
of books and manuscripts, Indic - Catalogs. I. Bhatia,
Usha. II. Series.*   *NYPL [3-MAF+ 87-3545]*

Indian painting for British patrons, 1770-1860 :
27 February to 28 March 1991. London :
Hazlitt, Gooden & Fox, c1991. 1 v. (unpaged) :
ill. (some col.) ; 25 cm. Includes index. ISBN
1-87327-701-6
*1. Painting, Indic - Exhibitions. I. Hazlitt, Gooden &
Fox.*   *NYPL [3-MAF 91-5920]*

Indian temple architecture. Encyclopaedia of
Indian temple architecture . New Delhi ,
Philadelphia , 1983- v. : ISBN 0-8122-7840-2 (U.
S. : v. 1, pt. 1) DDC 726/.14/0954 19
NA6001 .E53 1983
       NYPL [3-MQWS 87-1248]

INDIANA COUNTY (PA.) - MAPS.
Indiana County, Pennsylvania, land atlas & plat book . Rockford, Ill. , Indiana, Pa. , c1991. 1 atlas (83 p.) :   ***NYPL [Map Div. 91-8057]***

Indiana County, Pennsylvania, land atlas & plat book : 1991. 5th ed. Rockford, Ill. : Rockford Map Publishers ; Indiana, Pa. : Distributed by Indiana County 4-H Clubs, c1991. 1 atlas (83 p.) : maps ; 28 cm. Cover title. Includes index.
1. Real property - Pennsylvania - Indiana County - Maps. 2. Indiana County (Pa.) - Maps. I. Rockford Map Publishers. II. Title: Land atlas and plat book, Indiana County, Pennsylvania.
NYPL [Map Div. 91-8057]

Indiana, Gary. Dickson, Jane. Jane Dickson life under neon . Philadelphia, PA , c1989. 12 p. :
NYPL [3-MCX D568 91-4639]

Indiana, Robert, 1928- Weinhardt, Carl J. Robert Indiana /. New York , 1990. 232 p. :   ISBN 0-8109-1116-7
NYPL [3-MCX I39 90-13194]

INDIANA, ROBERT, 1928-
Weinhardt, Carl J. Robert Indiana /. New York , 1990. 232 p. :   ISBN 0-8109-1116-7
NYPL [3-MCX I39 90-13194]

Indiana University, Bloomington. School of Fine Arts. Gallery. Photo-derived . Bloomington, Ind. , 1989. [16] p. :   ***NYPL [MFW 91-6987]***

Indiana. University. Museum of Art. Echo Press . Bloomington , c1990. 95 p. :
NYPL [MDF+ 91-3853]

Indianapolis Museum of Art. Day, Holliday T. Power . Indianapolis, Ind. , 1991. p. cm.   ISBN 0-253-31658-8   DDC 709/.73/07477252 20
N72.P6 D38 1991

INDIANS, AMERICAN. see INDIANS.

INDIANS - ANTIQUITIES - CONGRESSES.
International Congress of Americanists, 40th, Rome and Genoa, 1972. Atti del XL Congresso internazionale degli americanisti. Genova [1973-76] 4 v.   ***NYPL [HBC 74-2090]***

INDIANS - CONGRESSES.
International Congress of Americanists, 40th, Rome and Genoa, 1972. Atti del XL Congresso internazionale degli americanisti. Genova [1973-76] 4 v.   ***NYPL [HBC 74-2090]***

INDIANS - ETHNOLOGY. see INDIANS; INDIANS OF NORTH AMERICA; INDIANS OF SOUTH AMERICA.

INDIANS, MEXICAN. see INDIANS OF MEXICO.

INDIANS, NORTH AMERICAN. see INDIANS OF NORTH AMERICA.

INDIANS OF CENTRAL AMERICA - ANTIQUITIES.
Schezen, Roberto. Visions of ancient America /. New York , 1990. 216 p. :   ISBN 0-8478-1178-6 : DDC 779/.997201 20
F1219 .S38 1990
NYPL [MFX (Schezen) 91-3399]

INDIANS OF CENTRAL AMERICA - ANTIQUITIES - PICTORIAL WORKS.
Schezen, Roberto. Visions of ancient America /. New York , 1990. 216 p. :   ISBN 0-8478-1178-6 : DDC 779/.997201 20
F1219 .S38 1990
NYPL [MFX (Schezen) 91-3399]

INDIANS OF CENTRAL AMERICA - GUATEMALA - PORTRAITS.
Namuth, Hans. Los Todos Santeros . Berlin , c1989. 127 p. :   ISBN 3-88940-026-4
NYPL [MFX (Namuth) 90-13468]

INDIANS OF MEXICO - ANTIQUITIES.
Schezen, Roberto. Visions of ancient America /. New York , 1990. 216 p. :   ISBN 0-8478-1178-6 : DDC 779/.997201 20
F1219 .S38 1990
NYPL [MFX (Schezen) 91-3399]

Spranz, Bodo. Die Pyramiden von Totimehuacán, Puebla <Mexico>. Wiesbaden, 1970. viii, 64 p.   ***NYPL [HTC 74-1117 Bd. 2]***

INDIANS OF MEXICO - ANTIQUITIES - PICTORIAL WORKS.
Schezen, Roberto. Visions of ancient America /. New York , 1990. 216 p. :   ISBN 0-8478-1178-6 : DDC 779/.997201 20
F1219 .S38 1990
NYPL [MFX (Schezen) 91-3399]

INDIANS OF MEXICO - ART - BIBLIOGRAPHY.
Kendall, Aubyn. The art of pre-Columbian Mexico. Austin, 1973. x, 115 p.   DDC 016.709/72
Z1208.M4 K46   ***NYPL [JFD 90-11458]***

INDIANS OF MEXICO - ART - EXHIBITIONS.
Mexico . New York , Boston , c1990. xv, 712 p. :   ISBN 0-87099-595-2   DDC 709/.72/0747471 20
N6550 .M48 1990
NYPL [3-MAM+ 91-3897]

INDIANS OF MEXICO - HISTORY.
Berichte über begonnene und geplante Arbeiten. Wiesbaden, 1968. 210 p.
NYPL [HTC 74-1117 Bd. 1]

INDIANS OF MEXICO - TRIBES. See individual tribes, e. g. Mixtec Indians. For list of tribes, see under: **INDIANS OF MEXICO.**

INDIANS OF NORTH AMERICA - ART - EXHIBITIONS.
Archuleta, Margaret, 1950- Shared visions . Phoenix, Ariz. , 1991. 110 p. :   ISBN 0-934351-21-X :   DDC 704/.0397/0904 20
N6538.A4 A7 1991

INDIANS OF NORTH AMERICA - BEADWORK. see BEADWORK.

INDIANS OF NORTH AMERICA - ETHNOLOGY. see INDIANS OF NORTH AMERICA.

INDIANS OF NORTH AMERICA - NEW YORK (STATE) - PORTRAITS - EXHIBITIONS.
Tucker, Toba. Toba Tucker . East Hampton, N.Y. , c1987. 23 p. :   ISBN 0-933793-07-3   DDC 779/.2/092 20
E99.S38 T83 1987   ***NYPL [MFW 91-6717]***

INDIANS OF NORTH AMERICA - PICTORIAL WORKS - EXHIBITIONS.
Scherer, Joanna Cohan. Indian images: photographs of North American Indians, 1847-1928, from the Smithsonian Institution, National Anthropological Archives. Washington, 1970. 31 p. :   DDC 779/.9/9701
E77.5 .N3   ***NYPL [MFW 90-11184]***

INDIANS OF NORTH AMERICA - PICTORIAL WORKS - JUVENILE LITERATURE.
Sufrin, Mark. George Catlin . New York : Toronto : p. cm.   ISBN 0-689-31608-9   DDC 759.13 B 92 20
ND237.C35 S8 1991

INDIANS OF NORTH AMERICA - PORTRAITS.
Hathaway, Nancy, 1946- Native American portraits, 1862-1918 . San Francisco , c1990. 115, [1] p. :   ISBN 0-87701-766-2
E89 .H38 1990   ***NYPL [MFW 91-3605]***

INDIANS OF NORTH AMERICA - SOUTH DAKOTA - ARTS.
Huseboe, Arthur R., 1931- An illustrated history of the arts in South Dakota /. Sioux Falls, S.D. , 1989. xiii, 396 p. :   ISBN 0-931170-44-3 :   DDC 700/.9783 20
NX510.S8 H87 1989

INDIANS OF NORTH AMERICA - TRIBES. See individual tribes, e.g. Apache Indians. For list of tribes, see under: **INDIANS OF NORTH AMERICA.**

INDIANS OF NORTH AMERICA - UNITED STATES. see INDIANS OF NORTH AMERICA.

INDIANS OF NORTH AMERICA - UTAH - ANTIQUITIES.
Castleton, Kenneth Bitner, 1903- Petroglyphs and pictographs of Utah /. Salt Lake City , 1978-1979. 2 v. :   DDC 709/.01/1309792 19
E78.U55 C37   ***NYPL [HBC 81-457]***

INDIANS OF NORTH AMERICA - UTAH - ART.
Castleton, Kenneth Bitner, 1903- Petroglyphs and pictographs of Utah /. Salt Lake City , 1978-1979. 2 v. :   DDC 709/.01/1309792 19
E78.U55 C37   ***NYPL [HBC 81-457]***

INDIANS OF SOUTH AMERICA - ETHNOLOGY. see INDIANS OF SOUTH AMERICA.

INDIANS OF SOUTH AMERICA - PERU - POTTERY.
La Cerámica tradicional del Perú /. Lima , 1989. 228 p. :   ISBN 84-89291-21-7
Nk4077 .C47 1989

INDIANS OF SOUTH AMERICA - TRIBES. See individual tribes, e.g. Carib Indians. For list of tribes, see under: **INDIANS OF SOUTH AMERICA.**

INDIANS OF SOUTH AMERICA - VENEZUELA - SOCIAL LIFE AND CUSTOMS - PICTORIAL WORKS.
Segall, Thea. [Fotosecuencia /] Caracas, Venezuela , 1988. 3 v. :   ISBN 980-615-106-2 (v. 1)   ***NYPL [MFX+ (Segall) 90-13452]***

INDIANS OF THE UNITED STATES. see INDIANS OF NORTH AMERICA.

INDIANS, SOUTH AMERICAN. see INDIANS OF SOUTH AMERICA.

INDIANS, TREATMENT OF - DOMINICAN REPUBLIC.
Peña Batlle, Manuel Arturo. La rebelión del bahoruco. Santo Domingo, 1970. 257,[5] p.
NYPL [HBC 76-2412]

INDIC ART. see ART, INDIC.

INDIC ARTS. see ARTS, INDIC.

INDIC PAINTING. see PAINTING, INDIC.

INDIC SCULPTURE. see SCULPTURE, INDIC.

INDIGENOUS ARCHITECTURE. see VERNACULAR ARCHITECTURE.

Indigenous architecture worldwide . Wodehouse, Lawrence. Detroit , c1980. x, 392 p. ;   ISBN 0-8103-1450-9 :   DDC 016.72
Z5943.V47 W62 NA208
NYPL [3-MAC 91-7863]

Individualités : artisti francesi d'oggi / [curatore della mostra e del catalogo, Geneviève Bréerette]. Milano : Electa, c1984. 107 p. : chiefly ill. (some col.), ports. ; 24 cm. Catalog of an exhibition held at the Galleria nazionale d'arte moderna, Rome, from May 29-July 22, 1984. Includes bibliographical references.
1. Art, French - Exhibitions. 2. Art, Modern - 20th century - France - Exhibitions. I. Bréerette, Geneviève. II. Galleria nazionale d'arte moderna (Italy).
NYPL [3-MAMI 90-12643]

Individuum und Gruppe . Schwalm, Hans-Jürgen, 1955- Essen , c1990. 230 p., [36] p. of plates :   ISBN 3-89206-329-X
N6490 .S3335 1990

INDONESIA - KINGS AND RULERS - ART PATRONAGE - EXHIBITIONS.
Jessup, Helen Ibbitson. Court arts of Indonesia /. New York , c1990. 288 p. :   ISBN 0-8109-3165-6
IN PROCESS (ONLINE)
NYPL [3-MAF+ 91-6099]

INDONESIAN ART. see ART, INDONESIAN.

Indonesian primitive art /. Hersey, Irwin. Singapore , New York , 1991. p. cm.   ISBN 0-19-588553-8 :   DDC 730/.089/9922 20
N7326 .H47 1991

INDUSTRIAL ARCHAEOLOGY - AUSTRIA - VIENNA.
Lehne, Andreas. Wiener Warenhäuser, 1865-1914 /. Wien , 1990. 195 p. :   ISBN 3-7005-4488-X
NA6227.D45 L44 1990

Industrial architecture in Europe.
Industriearchitektur in Europa =. Hannover , c1990. p. :   ISBN 3-87870-350-3   DDC 725/.4/09409048 20
NA6403.E85 I53 1990

Industrial atlas of Texas. University of Texas. Bureau of Business Research. 1965 industrial atlas of Texas. Austin, 1965. 20, 20 p.
G1371.G1 A32 1965
NYPL [Map Div. 90-6571]

INDUSTRIAL DESIGN. see DESIGN, INDUSTRIAL.

INDUSTRIAL DESIGN COORDINATION.
Myerson, Jeremy. Design . London , c1990. 255 p. :   ISBN 0-904866-77-7
NYPL [3-MNF 91-6321]

INDUSTRIAL DESIGN - HANDBOOKS, MANUALS, ETC.

Industrial design - Handbooks, manuals, etc. (cont.)

Powell, Dick. Presentation techniques .
London , 1990. 160 p. : ISBN 0-356-17584-7 :
DDC 745.2 19
TS171 *NYPL [3-MDW 90-11572]*

**INDUSTRIAL DESIGN - HISTORY - 20TH
CENTURY - EXHIBITIONS.**
La Coppia =. Milano , c1989. 205 p. : DDC
745.4/442 20
NK1390 .C66 1989
NYPL [3-MNF 90-11125]

Industriearchitektur in Europa = Industrial
architecture in Europe / herausgegeben von
Helmut C. Schulitz im Auftrage der Deutschen
Messe AG, Hannover ; [Übersetzungen,
Deborah L. van der Horst]. Hannover :
Vincentz, c1990. 128 p. : ill. (some col.) ; 25
cm. English and German. At head of title:
Constructa-Preis '90. Includes bibliographical references.
ISBN 3-87870-350-3 DDC 725/.4/09409048 20
*1. Architecture, Industrial - Europe. 2. Architecture,
Modern - 20th century - Europe. I. Schulitz, Helmut C.
II. Deutsche Messe AG. III. Title: Industrial
architecture in Europe. IV. Title: Constructa-Preis '90.*
NA6403.E85 I53 1990

**INDUSTRY AND ART. see ART AND
INDUSTRY.**

INDUSTRY IN ART.
Wadsworth, Edward, 1889-1949. A genius of
industrial England . [Bradford] , c1990. 128 p. :
ISBN 0-9505532-7-1
NYPL [3-MCV W12 91-6333]

Inextinguishable. Nielsen, Carl, 1865-1931.
[Concertos, violin, orchestra, op. 33.] Concerto
for violin & orchestra, op. 33 ; Symphony no.
4, op. 29 . Oslo, Norway , p1989. 1 sound
disc :
Norsk IDCD 5

**The influence of Persian art on Gauguin, Matisse,
and Kandinsky /.** Daftari, Fereshteh. New
York , 1991. p. cm. ISBN 0-8153-0715-2 (alk.
paper) DDC 709/.2/24 20
N7280 .D34 1991

**The influence of photography on American
landscape painting [microform] .** Cock,
Elizabeth M., 1925- 1967. 2 v. (xiii, 247
leaves) : *NYPL [*ZM-71]*

Information art . McCarty, Cara. New York ,
c1990. 46 p. : ISBN 0-87070-310-2
NYPL [3-MAMZ+ 91-5558]

Information Design, Inc. Notes on architecture.
Los Altos, Calif. , c1990. 46 p. : ISBN
1-560-52057-4 : DDC 720 20
NA2540 .N67 1990

Information on artists : a study of artists'
work-related human and social service needs in
ten U. S. locations / [report prepared by the
Research Center for Arts and Culture,
Columbia University ; Joan Jeffri, editor]. New
York, NY : Columbia University, Research
Center for Arts and Culture, c1989. 2 v.
(various pagings) ; 30 cm. Includes bibliographical
references. CONTENTS. - v. 1. Boston. Cape Cod.
Chicago. Dallas. Los Angeles -- v. 2. Minneapolis/St.
Paul. New York. Philadelphia. San Francisco. Western
Massachusetts. Actor's Equity. DDC
331.7/617/00973 20
*1. Artists - Information services - United States. I.
Jeffri, Joan. II. Columbia University. Research Center
for Arts and Culture.*
N58 .I54 1989

Information sources in cartography / editors,
C.R. Perkins, R.B. Parry. London [England] ;
New York : Bowker-Saur, c1990. xiii, 540 p. ;
23 cm. (Guides to information sources) Includes
bibliographical references and indexes. ISBN
0-408-02458-5 (U. S.) DDC 016.526 20
*1. Cartography - Bibliography. I. Perkins, C.R. II.
Parry, Robert B. III. Series: Guides to information
sources (London, England).*
Z6021 .I53 1990 GA105.3
NYPL [Map Div. 91-2555]

Informazioni di base : situazione urbanistica
mondiale e italiana / a cura di Bruno F.
Lapadula. Roma : Bulzoni, [1978?] 99 p., [1] :
ill. ; 24 cm. (Rome (City). Università. Istituto di
Urbanistica. Quaderni. [n.] 4 4) Bibliography: p.
99-[100]
*1. City planning - Addresses, essays, lectures. 2. City
planning - Italy - Addresses, essays, lectures. I.
Lapadula, Bruno F. II. Series.*
HT166 .I545 *NYPL [JLL 80-69 n.4]*

**Informe sobre los trabajos iniciados y
proyectados.** Berichte über begonnene und
geplante Arbeiten. Wiesbaden, 1968. 210 p.
NYPL [HTC 74-1117 Bd. 1]

INFRARED PHOTOGRAPHY.
American infrared survey . Akron, Ohio ,
c1982. [82] p. : ISBN 0-9609812-0-9 (pbk.) :
DDC 779/.092/2 19
TR755 .A44 1982 *NYPL [MFW 90-13460]*

Ingamells, John. The Wallace Collection / John
Ingamells. London : Scala, 1990. 132 p. : col.
ill. ; 29 cm. Includes index. ISBN 1-87024-843-0
*1. Wallace Collection (London, England). 2. Art -
England - London. I. Wallace Collection (London,
England). II. Title.*
NYPL [3-MAVZ (London) 91-6835]

Ingberman, Jeanette, 1952- Durham, Jimmie.
Jimmie Durham . New York , c1990. 37 p. :
NYPL [3-MGO (Durham) 90-10679]

**Ingeborg Strobl, oder, Mit den kleinen Wölfen
heulen.** Strobl, Ingeborg, 1949- St. Gallen ,
1989. 1 v. (unpaged) : ISBN 3-909090-01-X
NYPL [MEMZ 91-3982]

Ingersoll, Richard Joseph. Le Corbusier,
1887-1965. Le Corbusier . New York, NY ,
c1990. 37 p. : ISBN 1-87827-122-9
NYPL [3-MCO J42 91-4349]

INGHAM COUNTY (MICH.) - MAPS.
Rockford Map Publishers. Ingham County,
Michigan, land atlas & plat book . Rockford,
Ill. , Mason, Mich. , 1976, c1967. 1 atlas (36
p.) : *NYPL [Map Div. 91-1167]*

**Ingham County, Michigan, land atlas & plat
book .** Rockford Map Publishers. Rockford,
Ill. , Mason, Mich. , 1976, c1967. 1 atlas (36
p.) : *NYPL [Map Div. 91-1167]*

Un Inglese a Roma, 1864-1877 : la raccolta
Parker nell'Archivio fotografico comunale.
Roma : Artemide, c1989. 239 p. : ill. ; 28 x 29
cm. Includes bibliographical references.
*1. Parker, John Henry, 1806-1884 - Archives -
Catalogs. 2. Archivio fotografico comunale (Rome,
Italy) - Catalogs. 3. Rome (Italy) - Description -
1870-1945 - Views. 4. Rome (Italy) - Antiquities -
Pictorial works. I. Archivio fotografico comunale
(Rome, Italy).* *NYPL [MFX (Parker) 91-3346]*

Ingres /. Picon, Gaëtan. [Ingres. English.]
Geneva, Switzerland , New York , 1991. 119
p. : ISBN 0-8478-1351-7 DDC 759.4 20
ND553.I5 P513 1991

Ingres and other parables. Baldessari, John, 1931-
[London] 1971 [i.e. 1972] 22 p. ISBN
0-902063-10-3
N6512 .B26 *NYPL [3-MCX+ B176 81-385]*

Ingres, Jean-Auguste-Dominique, 1780-1867.
J.A.D. Ingres 1780-1867 : Zeichnungen und
Ölstudien aus dem Musée Ingres, Montauban /
[Ausstellung, Katalog, Christine
Ekelhart-Reinwetter]. Wien : Selbstverlag der
Albertina, [1991] 297 p. : ill. ; 31 cm. Catalog of
an exhibition held at the Tiroler Landesmuseum
Ferdinandeum, Innsbruck, 23-Feb. 24, 1991 and at
the Graphische Sammlung Albertina, Vienna, Mar.
15-Apr. 28, 1991. ISBN 3-900656-14-2
*1. Ingres, Jean-Auguste-Dominique, 1780-1867 -
Exhibitions. I. Tiroler Landesmuseum Ferdinandeum. II.
Graphische Sammlung Albertina. III. Title.*
NYPL [3-MCO+ I55 91-6971]

**INGRES, JEAN-AUGUSTE-DOMINIQUE,
1780-1867 - CRITICISM AND
INTERPRETATION.**
Picon, Gaëtan. [Ingres. English.] Ingres /.
Geneva, Switzerland , New York , 1991. 119
p. : ISBN 0-8478-1351-7 DDC 759.4 20
ND553.I5 P513 1991

**INGRES, JEAN-AUGUSTE-DOMINIQUE,
1780-1867 - EXHIBITIONS.**
Ingres, Jean-Auguste-Dominique, 1780-1867.
J.A.D. Ingres 1780-1867 . Wien [1991] 297
p. : ISBN 3-900656-14-2
NYPL [3-MCO+ I55 91-6971]

Iniciação às artes plásticas no Brasil /. Battistoni
Filho, Duílio, 1937- Campinas, SP, Brasil
[1990] 97 p. : ISBN 85-308-0098-2 DDC 709/.81
20
N6650 .B38 1990

Iñiguez, Diego Angulo. see Angulo Iñiguez,
Diego.

Une initiation à l'art . Théron, Michel.
Montpellier , 1987. 183 p. : ISBN 2-86626-819-9
NYPL [3-MAB+ 90-2744]

INK DRAWING. see PEN DRAWING.

**INK PAINTING - CHINA - BEIJING -
CATALOGS.**
Hall, Dickson. Chinese paintings in the Palace
Museum, Beijing, 4th-14th century /. Hong
Kong , 1989. viii, 175 p., [12] p. of plates :
ISBN 962-04-0691-5 : DDC 759.951/074/51156
20
ND2068 .H35 1989
NYPL [3-MAG 91-5448]

**INK PAINTING, CHINESE - 20TH
CENTURY - EXHIBITIONS.**
Cahill, James, 1926- New dimensions in
Chinese ink painting . Middlebury, Vt. , c1991.
p. cm. ISBN 0-9625262-3-1 DDC
759.951/074/7435 20
ND2068 .C33 1991

INK PAINTING, CHINESE - CATALOGS.
Hall, Dickson. Chinese paintings in the Palace
Museum, Beijing, 4th-14th century /. Hong
Kong , 1989. viii, 175 p., [12] p. of plates :
ISBN 962-04-0691-5 : DDC 759.951/074/51156
20
ND2068 .H35 1989
NYPL [3-MAG 91-5448]

**INK PAINTING - PRIVATE COLLECTIONS -
UNITED STATES - EXHIBITIONS.**
Cahill, James, 1926- New dimensions in
Chinese ink painting . Middlebury, Vt. , c1991.
p. cm. ISBN 0-9625262-3-1 DDC
759.951/074/7435 20
ND2068 .C33 1991

Inkarnationen . Abakanowicz, Magdalena.
Zürich , c1988. 67 p. :
MLCM 90-03313 (N)
NYPL [3-MGO (Abakanowicz) 90-10621]

Inkunabeln der Lithographie . Stift Göttweig
(Steinaweg, Austria). Graphisches Kabinett.
Furth/NÖ [1982] 113 p. : DDC
769.94/074/03612 19
NE2275.A9 S747 1982
NYPL [MDP 91-4330]

**INLAND NAVIGATION - MAPS. see
NAUTICAL CHARTS.**

The inner harmony of the Japanese house /.
Ueda, Atsushi, 1930- [Nihonjin to sumai.
English.] Tokyo ; New York : 199 p. : ISBN
0-87011-934-6 : DDC 728/.0952 20
NA7451 .U3313 1990
NYPL [3-MQWS 90-11554]

Inner natures . Doll, Nancy, 1947- Santa Barbara,
Calif. , 1990. 40 p. : ISBN 0-89951-080-9 DDC
759.14/074/79491 20
ND212 .D65 1990

Innere Mongolei. Beuys, Joseph. Joseph Beuys .
Hannover [1990] 267 p. : DDC 759.3 20
N6888.B463 A4 1990

Innere Visionen . Lichtenberg, Christian. Baden ,
c1988. ca. 65 p. : *NYPL [MFW 91-6669]*

Innes, Jocasta. Scandinavian painted decor /
Jocasta Innes ; photography by David George.
New York : Rizzoli, 1990. 256 p. : col. ill. ; 29
cm. Includes index. Includes bibliographical references
(p. 249). ISBN 0-8478-1235-9 DDC 729/.4/0948 20
*1. Mural painting and decoration - Scandinavia. 2.
Painted woodwork - Scandinavia. 3. Decoration and
ornament - Scandinavia - Themes, motives. 4. Mural
painting and decoration - Baltic States. 5. Painted
woodwork - Baltic States. 6. Decoration and ornament -
Baltic States - Themes, motives. I. Seamark, Roger. II.
Title.*
ND2770 .I55 1990 NYPL [3-MLP 91-3275]

**INNOCENTI, BRUNO, 1906-1986 -
CATALOGS.**
Cappugi, Luana. Bruno Innocenti . Firenze ,
1991. 79 p., [51] p. of plates : ISBN
88-22-23837-0
NYPL [3-MCF I57 91-5735]

**INNOVATIONS, AGRICULTURAL. see
AGRICULTURAL INNOVATIONS.**

Inquietud sin tregua. Silva Herzog, Jesús, 1893-
México, 1965. 367 p. *NYPL [HTW 78-3108]*

Inrō : Gürtelschmuck des Japaners : aus
Beständen des Linden-Museum Stuttgart.
Pforzheim : Schmuckmuseum Pforzheim, [1988]
[62] p. : chiefly ill. (some col.) ; 23 cm.

Bibliography: p. [62].
1. Linden-Museum Stuttgart - Catalogs. 2. Inro - Germany (West) - Catalogs. 3. Lacquer and lacquering - Catalogs. I. Linden-Museum Stuttgart.
NYPL [3-MNX 90-12396]

INRO - GERMANY (WEST) - CATALOGS.
Inrō . Pforzheim [1988] [62] p. :
NYPL [3-MNX 90-12396]

INSANITY AND ART. see ART AND MENTAL ILLNESS.

INSECTS IN ART - JUVENILE LITERATURE.
Ames, Lee J. Draw 50 creepy crawlies /. New York , c1991. p. cm. ISBN 0-385-41189-8 DDC 743/.6 20
NC783 .A44 1991

Inside Christie's /. Herbert, John, 1924- London , 1990. 407 p., [16] p. of plates : ISBN 0-340-43043-5 : DDC 381/.1 19
NYPL [3-MAZ 90-10748]

Inside story.
Macdonald, Fiona. A medieval cathedral /. New York , 1991. p. cm. ISBN 0-87226-350-9 DDC 726/.6/0940902 20
NA4830 .M34 1991

Ryan, Christopher, 1952- The Eiffel Tower /. Mankato, MN, U. S.A. , c1991. p. cm. ISBN 1-560-65026-5 : DDC 725/.97/0944361 20
NA2930 .R93 1991

Inside story (Mankato, Minn.)
Ryan, Christopher, 1952- The Eiffel Tower /. Mankato, MN, U. S.A. , c1991. p. cm. ISBN 1-560-65026-5 : DDC 725/.97/0944361 20
NA2930 .R93 1991

Inside story (Peter Bedrick Books)
Macdonald, Fiona. A medieval cathedral /. New York , 1991. p. cm. ISBN 0-87226-350-9 DDC 726/.6/0940902 20
NA4830 .M34 1991

Inside Texas . Brandimarte, Cynthia. Ft. Worth, Tex. , 1991. p. cm. ISBN 0-87565-092-9 DDC 747.2164 20
NK2003.5 .B7 1991

Insight into contemporary Soviet photography, 1968-1988. Un Regard sur la photographie soviétique contemporaine, 1968-1988 =. Paris, France , 1988. 156 p. :
NYPL [MFW 91-7483]

Insigne accademia di San Luca, Rome. see Accademia nazionale di San Luca.

L'Insistenza dello sguardo : fotografie italiane, 1839-1989 / a cura di Paolo Costantini ... [et al.]. Firenze : Alinari, c1989. 316 p. : ill. (some col.) ; 25 x 29 cm. Italian and English. Catalog of an exhibition held at the Palazzo Fortuny, Venice, Mar. 25-July 2, 1989. Includes bibliographical references. ISBN 88-7292-141-4
1. Photography - Italy - History - Exhibitions. I. Costantini, Paolo, 1959-. II. Museo Fortuny.
IN PROCESS   **NYPL [MFW+ 91-7442]**

Inspirationists. see Amana Society.

Installation, Klangraum, Musik : Leo Brunschwiler, Ulrich Gasser, Martin Gasser : [Ausstellung], Kunstverein St. Gallen / [Redaktion, Rudolf Hanhart]. [St. Gallen] : Der Kunstverein, [1983] [29] p. : ill., music, ports. ; 15 x 22 cm. Exhibition held Apr. 16-May 15, 1983.
1. Brunschwiler, Leo, 1955- - Exhibitions. 2. Gasser, Ulrich, 1950- - Exhibitions. 3. Gasser, Martin, 1955- - Exhibitions. I. Hanhart, Rudolf. II. Kunstverein St. Gallen.
NYPL [3-MAL 90-12516]

INSTALLATIONS (ART)
L'Exposition imaginaire . 's-Gravenhage , 1989. 391 p. : ISBN 90-12-06105-9 :
N4396 .E96 1989 **NYPL [3-MAV 91-5887]**

INSTALLATIONS (ART) - CALIFORNIA - EXHIBITIONS.
Knode, Marilu. Third Newport biennial . Newport Beach, Calif. , 1991. p. cm. ISBN 0-917493-19-2 DDC 709/.794/07479496 20
N6530.C2 K64 1991

INSTALLATIONS (ART) - GERMANY - EXHIBITIONS.
Ganz tief unten] [Germany , 1989?] 1 v. (unpaged) :
N6868 .G34 1989

INSTALLATIONS (ART) - UNITED STATES - EXHIBITIONS.

Alfredo Jaar . Richmond, VA , c1991. p. cm.
ISBN 0-917046-32-3 DDC 709/.2 20
N6537.J26 A4 1991

Alvin Lucier . Middletown, Conn. , c1988. 23 p. ; ISBN 0-929687-01-9 (pbk.)
NYPL [3-MGO+ (Lucier) 89-21332]

Auping, Michael. Jenny Holzer . Buffalo, N.Y. , 1991. p. cm. ISBN 0-914782-80-0 DDC 709/.2 20
N6537.H577 A4 1991

Instant design . Jones, Terry. London , 1990. [120] p. : ISBN 1-85454-838-7 (pbk.) : DDC 741.6 20
NC997   **NYPL [3-MDW 90-10937]**

The Instant national locator guide. San Francisco, Calif. : Creighton-Morgan Pub. Group, c1991. 1 v. (various pagings) : maps ; 28 cm.
1. Telephone - United States - Area codes - Directories. 2. Telephone - United States - Area codes - Maps. 3. Zip code - United States - Directories. 4. Zip code - United States - Maps. 5. Cities and towns - United States - Directories. 6. Cities and towns - United States - Maps. **NYPL [Map Div. 91-7663]**

Institut Català del Sòl (Spain) Realitzacions de la Direcció General d'Arquitectura i Habitatge i de l'Institut Català del Sòl 1981-1987. Barcelona [1988?] 2 cases (101 fasc.) : DDC 728/.314/0946709048 20
NA7860 .R35 1988

L'Institut de France /. Bibal, François. [Paris?] , c1988. 164 p. : ISBN 2-905547-05-7
NYPL [MFX+ (Bibal) 90-1062]

INSTITUT DE FRANCE - PICTORIAL WORKS.
Bibal, François. L'Institut de France /. [Paris?] , c1988. 164 p. : ISBN 2-905547-05-7
NYPL [MFX+ (Bibal) 90-1062]

Institut de recherche et d'histoire des textes (France) Iconographie médiévale . Paris , 1990. 207 p. : ISBN 2-222-04344-1 : DDC 709/.02 20
N5970 .I26 1990

Institut d'Estudis Andorrans. Atlas d'Andorra. [Andorra] : Institut d'Estudios Andorrans, 1980- 1 atlas : col. ill., col. maps ; 32 x 47 cm. CONTENTS. - Territori [&] Institucions -- Llengua -- Història -- Geografia física -- Vegetació [&] fauna -- Població [&] Societat -- Comunicacions [&] Transports -- Indústries -- Agricultura [&] ramaderia -- Sector terciari, Turisme [&] Endegament -- Geografia urbana -- Geografia política -- Parròquies [&] aspectes locals. DDC 912/.4679 19
1. Andorra - Maps. I. Title.
G1970 .I5 1980 **NYPL [Map Div. 90-57]**

Institut d'Estudis Metropolitans de Barcelona. Cities . [Barcelona] , 1988. 5 v. (xxix, 1673 p.) : ISBN 84-404-2436-1 (set)
NYPL [Map Div. 91-162]

Institut français d'Amérique latine (Mexico) Angelina Beloff . México, D.F. : Guanajuato, Gto. : 95 p. : ISBN 968-292-336-0 DDC 760/.092 20
N6999.B425 A4 1989

Institut français d'architecture.
Arcachon, la ville d'hiver /. Liège , 1988. 238 p. : ISBN 2-87009-372-1
NA1051.A73 A73 1988

Le Nouvel Amiens /. Liège , 1989. 471 p. : ISBN 2-87009-368-3
NA9198.A42 N68 1989

Loyer, François. Henri Sauvage . Bruxelles , 1987. 159 p. : ISBN 2-87009-304-7 (pbk.)
NYPL [3-MQZ (Savage) 90-12030]

Institut für Auslandsbeziehungen.
Höch, Hannah, 1889- Colagens, Hannah Höch, 1889-1978 /. Lisboa , 1989. 134 p. :
N6888.H6 A4 1989a

Kollwitz, Käthe, 1867-1945. Käthe Kollwitz . Stuttgart , 1990. 113 p. : DDC 709/.2 20
N6888.K62 A4 1990a

Institut für kultur und Ästhetik. Schriften.
(Bd.2) Eingreifendes Fotografieren . Berlin , 1979. 240 p. :
TR820.5 .E38   **NYPL [MFW 81-506]**

Institut für Moderne Kunst Nürnberg. Hoehme, Gerhard, 1920- Gerhard Hoehme, Bilder .

Düsseldorf , 1979. 200 p. :
N6888.H63 A4 1979
NYPL [3-MCK H6931 81-779]

Institut für Auslandbeziehungen. Grieshaber, Helmut A. P., 1909- HAP Grieshaber, Farbholzschnitte . Stuttgart , c1983. 43 p., 73 leaves of plates :
NYPL [MDG (Grieshaber) 90-13133]

Institut für Denkmalpflege in der DDR.
Drachenberg, Erhard. Die mittelalterliche Glasmalerei in Erfurt. Berlin, Wien, 1976- v in. ISBN 3-205-00581-3 (v. 2, pt. 1)
NYPL [MRY+ 77-1943 Bd.1, T.1-2]

Institut für Denkmalpflege (Lower Saxony, Germany) Das Rathaus in Duderstadt /. Hameln , c1989. 304 p. : ISBN 3-87585-096-3
NYPL [3-MQWD+ 91-5449]

Institut iazyka, literatury i istorii im. G. Ibragimova. Iskusstvo, rozhdennoe Oktiabrem . Kazan´ , 1989. 119 p. ;
N6999.U76 I8 1989

Institut istorii, iazyka i literatury im. G. TSadasy. Drevniaia i srednevekovaia arkhitektura Dagestana . Makhachkala , 1989. 184, [4] p. :
NA1492.8 .D7 1989

Institut national haïtien de la culture et des arts. Grubair, Hélène. Musée du Panthéon national haïtien. [Port-au-Prince] [1984] 3 v. : DDC 069/.097294 19
AM101.H1466 G78 1984
NYPL [3-MAV 86-3034]

Institut néerlandais, Paris. Berge, Mària van. Wenzel Hollar, 1607-1677 . Paris , 1979. 77 p., [15] leaves of plates :
NE642.H7 A4 1979
NYPL [3-MCZ H737 81-151]

Institut néerlandais (Paris, France)
Eloge de la navigation hollandaise au XVIIe siécle . Paris , 1989. xix, 181 p., [50] of plates : **NYPL [3-MAME 91-7020]**

Fondation Custodia. Le héraut du dix-septième siècle . Paris , 1985. xi, 153 p., 80 p. of plates :
NE670.G74 A4 1985

Quimper, France. Musée des beaux-arts. Tableaux flamands et hollandais du Musée des beaux-arts de Quimper. Paris , Quimper , 1987. xxxiv, 101 p. : ISBN 2-906739-10-3 DDC 759.9492/074/44361 20
ND636 .Q5 1987

Institut suisse pour l'étude de l'art, Zurich. see Schweizerisches Institut für Kunstwissenschaft.

Institut za izkustvoznanie (Bŭlgarska akademiia na naukite). Sektsiia "Izkustva na zhiznenata sreda." Sŭvremenni dekorativno-prilozhni izkustva v Bŭlgariia /. Sofiia , 1989. 262 p. :
NK1019 .S95 1989

Institut zhivopisi, skul´ptury i arkhitektury imeni I.E. Repina.
Russkoe i sovetskoe iskusstvo . Leningrad , 1989. 79 p. ;
N6987 .R877 1989

Voprosy izucheniia otechestvennogo iskusstva . Leningrad , 1989. 83 p. :
N6984 .V6 1989

Institute of Arts, Detroit. see Detroit. Institute of Arts.

Institute of Contemporary Art (Boston, Mass.)
Between spring and summer . Tacoma, Wash. , Boston, Mass. , c1990. x, 206 p. : ISBN 0-910663-49-1
N6988.5.C62 B48 1990
NYPL [3-MAM 90-12998]

Sussman, Elisabeth, 1939- El corazón sangrante =. Boston, Mass. , Seattle, Wash. , c1991. p. ISBN 0-910663-50-5 (paperback) DDC 704.9/46 20
N8217.H53 S87 1991

Institute of Contemporary Art, Los Angeles. see Los Angeles Institute of Contemporary Art.

Institute of Contemporary Art, Philadelphia. see Pennsylvania. University. Institute of Contemporary Art.

Institute of Contemporary Arts, London. see London. Institute of Contemporary Arts.

Institute of Contemporary Arts (London, England) Kabakov, Il´īa Iosifovich, 1933- Ilya Kabakov . London [1989] 72 p. : ISBN 0-905263-47-2 (pbk.)
NYPL [3-MGO (Kabakov) 90-12888]

Institute of Social and Economic Research (Eastern Caribbean) see Mona, Jamaica. University of the West Indies. Institute of Social and Economic Research.

Instituto Boliviano de Cultura. Conservaci´on de los monumentos virreinales de Bolivia. La Paz , 1987. 32 p. : *NYPL [3-MQWM+ 89-26926]*

Instituto Brasileiro de Desenvolvimento. Centro João Vinte e Três. see Centro João Vinte e Três.

Instituto Cultural Cabañas (Guadalajara, Mexico) Anguiano, Raúl, 1915- Raúl Anguiano . Guadalajara [1985] iii, 124 p. : DDC 709/.2 20
N6559.A54 A4 1985

Instituto de Arte Americano-Mario J. Buschiazzo. Exposición barroco latinoamericano. [Buenos Aires, Argentina] [between 1983 and 1989] 116 p. : DDC 724/.16 20
NA702.2 .E97 1983

Instituto de Conservación y Restauración de Bienes Culturales. Inventario artístico de Cáceres y su provincia /. Madrid , 1989- v. <1-2 > : ISBN 84-7483-610-7 (obra completa) DDC 709/.46/28 20
N7109.C15 I58 1989

Instituto de Conservación y Restauración de Bienes Culturales (Spain) Intervenciones en el patrimonio arquitectónico (1980-1985) /. [Madrid] [1990] 465 p. : ISBN 84-7483-661-1 DDC 720/.28/8094609048 20
NA1301 .I57 1990

Instituto de Cooperación Iberoamericana. Orfebreria hispanoamericana, siglos XVI-XIX . Madrid , 1986. 123 p. :
NYPL [3-MNO+ 90-8754]

instituto de la Juventud (Spain) Konstruktioner, seks skulptører . København , 1989. 1 v. (unpaged) :
NB808 .K66 1989

Instituto di corrispondenza archeologica. see Deutsches Archäologisches Institut.

Instituto do Emprego e Formação Profissional (Portugal). Delegação Regional do Norte. Núcleo de Apoio ao Artesanato. Artesanato da região norte . Porto , 1989. 406 p. : ISBN 972-90030-0-9 DDC 745/.09469 20
NK1003 .A83 1989

Instituto Dominicano de Cultura Hispánica. Arte contemporáneo dominicano . [Santo Domingo, Dominican Republic?] [1987?] [72] p. ;
N6615.D6 A77 1987

Instituto Geográfico "Agustín Codazzi." Subdirección Agrológica. Suelos y bosques de Colombia. Bogotá : Ministerio de Hacienda y Crédito Público, Instituto Geográfico "Agustín Codazzi", Subdirección Agrológica, 1988. 1 atlas (133 p.) : ill. (some col.), maps ; 60 cm. Includes bibliographical references (p. 15).
1. Soils - Colombia - Maps. 2. Forests and forestry - Colombia - Maps. 3. Colombia - Maps. I. Title.
NYPL [Map Div. 91-13234]

Instituto Geográfico "Agustín Codazzi." Subdirección de Investigación y Divulgación Geográfica. Atlas básico de Colombia / Ministerio de Hacienda y Crédito Público, Instituto Geográfico "Agustín Codazzi", Subdirección de Investigación y Divulgación Geográfica. 5a. ed. [Bogotá] : El Instituto, 1986. 1 atlas (217 p. (some folded)) : col. ill., col. maps ; 34 cm. DDC 912/.861 19
1. Colombia - Maps. 2. Colombia - Economic conditions - 1971- - Maps. 3. Colombia - Social conditions - Maps. I. Title.
G1730 .I53 1986   NYPL [Map Div. 87-697]

Atlas básico de Colombia / Ministerio de Hacienda y Crédito Público, Instituto Geográfico "Agustín Codazzi", Subdirección de Investigación y Divulgación Geográfica. 6a ed. [Bogotá] : El Instituto, 1989. 1 atlas (446 p. (some folded)) : col. ill., col. maps ; 34 cm. Accompanied by: 3D glasses (in pocket). Errata sheet inserted.
1. Colombia - Maps. 2. Colombia - Economic

conditions - 1971- - Maps. 3. Colombia - Social conditions - Maps. I. Title.
NYPL [Map Div. 91-6225]

Instituto Geográfico e Cadastral (Portugal) Selecções do Reader's Digest (Firm) Atlas de Portugal . Lisboa , 1988. 1 atlas (159 p.) : DDC 912.469 20
G1975 .S4 1988   NYPL [Map Div. 91-80]

Instituto Geográfico Nacional (Honduras) Instituto Geográfico Nacional (Honduras). Sección Diccionario Geográfico. Nombres geográficos de Honduras /. [Tegucigalpa] [1976?- v. :
F1502 .I57 1976a   NYPL [Map Div. 91-81]

Instituto Geográfico Nacional (Honduras). Sección Diccionario Geográfico. Nombres geográficos de Honduras / Ministerio de Comunicaciones, Obras Públicas y Transporte, Instituto Geográfico Nacional, Departamento Geográfico, Sección Diccionario Geográfico. Ed. provisional. [Tegucigalpa] : La Sección, [1976?- v. : ill. ; 21 x 35 cm. Vols. 10-11 have cover title. Vols. 7 and 8 have title: Diccionario geográfico de Honduras. Vols. 9-11 have imprint: Ministerio de Communicaciones, Obras Públicas y Transporte, Instituto Geográfico Nacional. CONTENTS. - v. 1. Indice, Depto. de Atlántida.--v. 2. Indice, Depto. de Cortés.--v. 3. Indice, Depto. de Copán.--v. 4. Indice, Depto. de Comayagua.--v. 5. Indice, Depto. de Choluteca.--v. 6. Indice, Depto. de Islas de la Bahía.--v. 7. Indice, Departamento Francisco Morazán.--v. 8. Indice, Departamento de Colón.--v. 9. Indice, Depto. de Gracias a Dios.--v. 10. Indice, Depto. de Intibuca.--v. 11. Indice, Depto. de La Paz.
1. Honduras - Gazetteers. I. Instituto Geográfico Nacional (Honduras). II. Title. III. Title: Diccionario geográfico de Honduras.
F1502 .I57 1976a   NYPL [Map Div. 91-81]

Instituto Hidrográfico de la Armada. Atlas hidrográfico de Chile / Instituto Hidrográfico de la Armada. 1. ed. [Valparaíso] : El Instituto, 1974. 37, [14], [212] p. : col. maps ; 32 x 44 cm. "Preparado por Raúl Herrera Aldana." Includes index. DDC 623.89/2
1. Hydrography - Chile - Maps. 2. Nautical charts - Chile. I. Aldana, Raúl Herrera. II. Title.
G1751.C3 I5 1974
NYPL [Map Div. 91-6470]

Instituto Nacional de Antropología e Historia (Mexico). Dirección de Estudios Históricos. En tiempos de la posmodernidad. [Mexico City] . 116 p. : ISBN 968-8405-58-2
N6555 .E5 1989

Instituto Nacional de Bellas Artes (Mexico) Angelina Beloff . México, D.F. : Guanajuato, Gto. : 95 p. : ISBN 968-292-336-0 DDC 760/.092 20
N6999.B425 A4 1989

Belkin, Arnold. Arnold Belkin . [Mexico City] , c1989. 206 p., [8] folded leaves of plates : ISBN 968-292-434-0
NYPL [3-MCZ B432 91-4574]

Rivera, Diego, 1886-1957. Diego Rivera . [Mexico City, Mexico] , 1988. 387 p. : ISBN 968-292-277-1 DDC 759.972 20
ND259.R5 A4 1988

Rivera, Diego, 1887-1957. Diego Rivera . [Mexico City, Mexico] , 1989. 339 p. : ISBN 968-290-640-7 DDC 760/.092 20
N6559.R55 A4 1989

Los Zapatas de Diego Rivera /. Ciudad de México , Cuernavaca, Morelos , 1989. 117 p., [2] folded leaves of plates : ISBN 968-292-333-6 DDC 760/.092 20
N6559.R58 Z37 1989
NYPL [3-MCZ R62 91-4245]

Instituto Nacional de Bellas Artes (Mexico). Departamento de Artes Plásticas. Artes decorativas modernas del Japón . México , 1964. [14] p. :   *NYPL [3-MNE 91-833]*

Instituto Sabogal de Arte. Centenario del nacimiento de José Sabogal, 1888-19 marzo-1988 /. Lima, Perú , 1989 (Miraflores : Librería Editorial "Minerva") 68 p. :
N6719.S23 C46 1989

INSTRUCTION. see **EDUCATION.**

INSURRECTIONS. see **REVOLUTIONS.**

INTAGLIO PRINTING - EXHIBITIONS. Hansen, Trudy V. Intaglio printing in the 1980s . [New Brunswick, N.J.] , c1990. v, 45

p. :
IN PROCESS (ONLINE)
NYPL [MDE 91-3493]

Intaglio printing in the 1980s . Hansen, Trudy V. [New Brunswick, N.J.] , c1990. v, 45 p. :
IN PROCESS (ONLINE)
NYPL [MDE 91-3493]

INTAGLIOS - ITALY. Donati, Valentino. Pietre dure e medaglie del Rinascimento . Ferrara [1989]. 291 p. :
NYPL [3-MGW+ 91-7173]

Intar Latin American Gallery. Trejo, Ruben, 1937- Ruben Trejo, recent works. NYC [i.e. New York City] (420 W. 42nd St., New York 10036) , c1990. 12 p. : DDC 709/.2 20
N6537.T675 A4 1990

Intarsiatori savonesi dell'Ottocento /. Bottaro, Silvia. Savona , c1989. 181 p. : DDC 745.51 20
NK9924.I8 B67 1989
NYPL [3-MOC 90-13408]

Integração das artes : Memorial da América Latina. São Paulo : Fundação Memorial da América Latina, 1990. 113 p. : ill. (some col.) ; 31 cm.
1. Art, Brazilian. 2. Art, Modern - 20th century - Brazil. I. Fundação Memorial da América Latina.
N6655 .I58 1990

Integración latino americana a través de sus artistas y sus museos. Integración latinoamericana, 1986-1987 . [Bogotá, Colombia] [Roldanillo, Colombia] [between 1986 and 1990] 57 p. :
NE502 .I58 1986

Integración latinoamericana, 1986-1987 : exposición itinerante / Ministerio de Relaciones Exteriores de Colombia [y] Museo Rayo. [Bogotá, Colombia] : El Ministerio ; [Roldanillo, Colombia] : El Museo, [between 1986 and 1990] 57 p. : ill. (some col.) ; 21 x 24 cm. Cover title: Integración latino americana a través de sus artistas y sus museos. Exhibition catalog.
1. Prints, Latin American - Exhibitions. 2. Prints - 20th century - Latin America - Exhibitions. I. Colombia. Ministerio de Relaciones Exteriores. II. Museo Rayo. III. Title: Integración latino americana a través de sus artistas y sus museos.
NE502 .I58 1986

INTEGRATED CIRCUITS - DESIGN AND CONSTRUCTION - EXHIBITIONS. McCarty, Cara. Information art . New York , c1990. 46 p. : ISBN 0-87070-310-2
NYPL [3-MAMZ+ 91-5558]

Inter Nationes. Art today in the Federal Republic of Germany /. Bonn , c1988. 114 p. :
NYPL [3-MAMG+ 90-12546]

INTERCULTURAL COMMUNICATION - UNITED STATES. Lippard, Lucy R. Mixed blessings . New York , c1990. viii, 278 p., [40] p. of plates : ISBN 0-394-57759-0; 0-06-797296-6 DDC 704/.0693/0973 20
N6537.5 .L5 1990
NYPL [3-MAMT 91-2488]

Interfoto (Agency) Contes de la ville quotidienne / Interfoto. Genève : Editions "Que faire?", c1987. 123 p. : ill. ; 24 x 26 cm.
1. Geneva (Switzerland) - Description - Views. I. Title.
NYPL [MFW 90-13469]

Intergenerational arts in the nursing home . Clark, Patch. New York , 1991. p. cm. ISBN 0-313-25965-8 (alk. paper) DDC 362.1/6 20
NX180.A35 C5 1991

INTERIOR ARCHITECTURE. Blackwell, Lewis. International interiors 2 . London , c1990. 256 p. : ISBN 1-558-59013-7
NYPL [3-MLO+ 90-12789]

The Elements of style . New York , c1991. p. cm. ISBN 0-671-73981-6 DDC 721 20
NA2850 .E44 1991

Malnar, Joy Monice. The interior dimension . New York, N.Y. , c1992. p. cm. ISBN 0-442-23739-1 DDC 729 20
NA2850 .M35 1992

INTERIOR ARCHITECTURE - AUSTRALIA - HISTORY. Lane, Terence, 1946- Australians at home . Melbourne , New York , 1990. xiii, 449 p. : ISBN 0-19-553128-0 DDC 747.2994 20
NK2090.A1 L36 1990

INTERIOR ARCHITECTURE - AUSTRIA - VIENNA.
Miller, Dwight C. (Dwight Cameron), 1923- Marcantonio Franceschini and the Liechtensteins . Cambridge , New York , 1991. xx, 296 p., [16] p. of plates :   ISBN 0-521-36503-1   DDC 759.5 B 20
ND623.F78125 A3 1990
NYPL   [3-MCF F813 91-7475]

INTERIOR ARCHITECTURE - ENGLAND.
Pawley, Martin. Eva Jiricna, design in exile /. London , 1990. 112 p. :   ISBN 1-87218-016-7
NYPL   [3-MQZ (Jiricna) 91-5084]

INTERIOR ARCHITECTURE - ENGLAND - CONGRESSES.
The Fashioning and functioning of the British country house /. Washington, D.C. , Hanover [N.H.] , 1989. 417 p. :   ISBN 0-89468-128-1
NYPL   [3-MRG 90-12992]

INTERIOR ARCHITECTURE - EUROPE.
Tahara, Keiichi, 1951- [Seikimatsu no kenchiku. English.] Images of fin-de-siècle architecture and interior decoration /. London , New York , 1988. 263 p. :   ISBN 0-00-215354-8 :   DDC 724.9/1 19
NA3485   NYPL   [3-MRX+ 91-3382]

INTERIOR ARCHITECTURE - FRANCE.
Feray, Jean. Architecture intérieure et décoration en France, des origines à 1875 /. Paris , c1988. 399 p. :   ISBN 2-7013-0752-X   DDC 729/.0944 20
NA2850 .F4 1988
NYPL   [3-MLF+ 90-12087]

INTERIOR ARCHITECTURE - FRANCE - HISTORY - 20TH CENTURY.
Goguel, Solange. René Herbst /. Paris , c1990. 363 p. :   ISBN 2-903370-56-7   DDC 720/.92 20
NK2049.Z9 H4734 1990

INTERIOR ARCHITECTURE - HISTORY - 20TH CENTURY.
Dru, Line, 1957- [Cafés. English.] Cafes /. New York, NY , c1989. 118 p. :   ISBN 0-910413-66-5
NYPL   [3-MLO 90-10718]
Fitoussi, Brigitte, 1956- [Boutiques. English.] Showrooms /. New York, NY , 1989. 118 p. :   ISBN 0-910413-67-3
NYPL   [3-MLO 90-10719]

INTERIOR ARCHITECTURE - ILLINOIS - CHICAGO.
Vinci, John. The Trading Room . Chicago, IL , c1989. 72 p. :   ISBN 0-86559-082-6   DDC 725/.25 20
NA6253.C4 C438 1989
NYPL   [3-MQWO 90-12029]

INTERIOR ARCHITECTURE - ILLINOIS - CHICAGO - AWARDS.
5 years of interior architecture awards /. Chicago, Ill. , c1985. 104 p. :   DDC 729/.09773/1109048 20
NA2850 .A14 1985

INTERIOR ARCHITECTURE - JUVENILE LITERATURE.
Biesty, Stephen. The incredible cross-section book /. New York , 1992. p. cm.   ISBN 0-679-81411-6   DDC 741.6/42/092 20
NC975.5.B5 A4 1992

INTERIOR ARCHITECTURE - NEBRASKA - LINCOLN.
A Harmony of the arts . Lincoln , c1990. x, 119 p. :   ISBN 0-8032-2887-2 (alk. paper)   DDC 725/.11/09782293 19
NA4413.L56 H37 1990
NYPL   [3-MQWO 90-11994]

INTERIOR ARCHITECTURE - ROME.
Roman art in the private sphere . Ann Arbor , c1991. 156 p. :   ISBN 0-472-10196-X (alk. paper)   DDC 747.2937 20
N5760 .R66 1991

INTERIOR ARCHITECTURE - STANDARDS - HANDBOOKS, MANUALS, ETC.
De Chiara, Joseph, 1929- Time-saver standards for interior design and space planning /. New York , c1991. p. cm.   ISBN 0-07-016299-9   DDC 729 20
NK2110 .D35 1991

INTERIOR ARCHITECTURE - SWEDEN - HISTORY - 18TH CENTURY.
Groth, Håkan. Neo-classicism in the North . New York , 1990. 224 p. :   ISBN 0-8478-1273-1

DDC 728/.37/09485 20
NK1461.A1 G76 1990
NYPL   [3-MLO 91-3368]

INTERIOR ARCHITECTURE - UNITED STATES.
The Elements of style . New York , c1991. p. cm.   ISBN 0-671-73981-6   DDC 721 20
NA2850 .E44 1991
Kemp, Jim. American vernacular . Washington, D.C. , 1990, c1987. 256 p. :   ISBN 1-558-35074-8 :
NYPL   [3-MQWO 91-6742]

INTERIOR ARCHITECTURE - UNITED STATES - AWARDS.
5 years of interior architecture awards /. Chicago, Ill. , c1985. 104 p. :   DDC 729/.09773/1109048 20
NA2850 .A14 1985

INTERIOR DECORATION.
Bedroom decorating. Minnetonka, MN , 1991. p. cm.   ISBN 0-86573-351-1 :   DDC 747.7/7 20
NK2117.B4 B424 1991
Chambers, Karen S. Trompe l'oeil at home . New York , c1991. p.   ISBN 0-8478-1420-3   DDC 751.7/3 20
N7430.5 .C48 1991
Harling, Robert. The House & garden book of living rooms /. New York , 1991. p. cm.   ISBN 0-86565-125-6   DDC 747.7/5 20
NK2117.L5 H37 1991
Kilmer, Rosemary. Designing interiors /. Fort Worth, TX , 1992. p. cm.   ISBN 0-03-032233-2   DDC 729 20
NK2110 .K45 1992
Le Più belle case al mare di AD /. Milano , 1989. 157 p. :
NK2195.V34 P58 1989

INTERIOR DECORATION ACCESSORIES.
Moss, Charlotte. A passion for detail /. New York , c1991. p. cm.   ISBN 0-385-26760-6 :   DDC 747/.9 20
NK2115.5.A25 M67 1991

INTERIOR DECORATION - AUSTRALIA - HISTORY.
Lane, Terence, 1946- Australians at home . Melbourne , New York , 1990. xiii, 449 p. :   ISBN 0-19-553128-0   DDC 747.2994 20
NK2090.A1 L36 1990

INTERIOR DECORATION - AUSTRIA - VIENNA.
Miller, Dwight C. (Dwight Cameron), 1923- Marcantonio Franceschini and the Liechtensteins . Cambridge , New York , 1991. xx, 296 p., [16] p. of plates :   ISBN 0-521-36503-1   DDC 759.5 B 20
ND623.F78125 A3 1990
NYPL   [3-MCF F813 91-7475]

INTERIOR DECORATION - CALIFORNIA.
Harris, Bill, 1933- Great homes of California /. New York , 1990. 160 p. :   ISBN 0-517-62377-3   DDC 728.8/09794 20
NA7511.3.C2 H3 1990

INTERIOR DECORATION - DATA PROCESSING.
Burden, Ernest E., 1934- Perspective grid sourcebook . New York , 1991. p. cm.   ISBN 0-442-21132-5   DDC 720/.28/40285 20
NA2728 .B87 1991

INTERIOR DECORATION - DESIGN.
Sutherland, Martha, 1927- Graphic fundamentals . New York, N.Y. , 1991. p. cm.   ISBN 0-8306-3480-0 :   DDC 720/.28/4 20
NA2708 .S88 1991

INTERIOR DECORATION - DICTIONARIES.
Jones, Frederic H. (Frederic Hicks), 1944- A concise dictionary of interior design /. Los Altos, Calif. , c1990. 215 p. :   ISBN 1-560-52067-1   DDC 729/.03 20
NK1704 .J6 1991

INTERIOR DECORATION - EAST (U. S.) - HISTORY - 20TH CENTURY.
Crouch, Elizabeth G., 1942- Showcase of interior design /. Grand Rapids, Mich. , 1991. p. cm.   ISBN 0-9624596-2-3:   DDC 729/.025/74 20
NK2004 .C76 1991

INTERIOR DECORATION - ENGLAND.
Hussey, Christopher, 1899- English country houses /. London , 1988. 3 v. :   ISBN

1-85149-029-9 (set : pbk.)
NYPL   [3-MRG 90-12887]
Pawley, Martin. Eva Jiricna, design in exile /. London , 1990. 112 p. :   ISBN 1-87218-016-7
NYPL   [3-MQZ (Jiriena) 91-5084]

INTERIOR DECORATION - ESTIMATES - UNITED STATES.
Sampson, Carol A. Estimating for interior designers . New York , 1991. p. cm.   ISBN 0-8230-1600-5   DDC 729/.029/9 20
NK2116.2 .S26 1991

INTERIOR DECORATION - EUROPE - HISTORY.
Calloway, Stephen. Royal style . Boston , 1991. p.   ISBN 0-316-12509-1 :   DDC 745/.094 20
NK925 .C35 1991

INTERIOR DECORATION - FRANCE.
Feray, Jean. Architecture intérieure et décoration en France, des origines à 1875 /. Paris , c1988. 399 p. :   ISBN 2-7013-0752-X   DDC 729/.0944 20
NA2850 .F4 1988
NYPL   [3-MLF+ 90-12087]

INTERIOR DECORATION - FRANCE - HISTORY.
Ladd, Mary-Sargent. The Frenchwoman's bedroom /. New York , c1991. p. cm.   ISBN 0-385-26558-1 :   DDC 747.7/7 20
NK2117.B4 L33 1991

INTERIOR DECORATION - FRANCE - HISTORY - 19TH CENTURY.
Percier,Charles, 1764-1838. [Recueil de décorations intérieures. English.] Empire stylebook of interior design . New York , 1991. p. cm.   ISBN 0-486-26754-7   DDC 747.24/09/034 20
NK1449.A1 P4713 1991

INTERIOR DECORATION - FRANCE - HISTORY - 20TH CENTURY.
Couvrat Desvergnes, Thierry, 1945- Paul Dupré-Lafon, décorateur des millionnaires /. Paris, France , c1990. 206, [2] p. :   ISBN 2-901151-45-0 (Editions de l'Amateur)   DDC 747.24 20
NK2049.Z9 D8633 1990
Goguel, Solange. René Herbst /. Paris , c1990. 363 p. :   ISBN 2-903370-56-7   DDC 720/.92 20
NK2049.Z9 H4734 1990

INTERIOR DECORATION - FRANCE - VERSAILLES - HISTORY - 17TH CENTURY.
Pérouse de Montclos, Jean-Marie. [Versailles. English.] Versailles /. New York , 1991. p. cm.   ISBN 0-500-59228-8   DDC 725/.17/0944366 20
NA7736.V5 P4713 1991

INTERIOR DECORATION - GERMANY - HISTORY - 19TH CENTURY.
Rammert-Götz, Michaela. Richard Riemerschmid, Möbel und Innenräume von 1895-1900 /. München , c1987. 185 p. ;   ISBN 3-88073-253-1
NK2554.R54 R36 1987
NYPL   [3-MOF 90-11037]

INTERIOR DECORATION - GERMANY - HISTORY - 20TH CENTURY.
Schink, Arnold. Mies van der Rohe . Stuttgart , c1990. 379 p. :   ISBN 3-7828-4004-6
NA1088.M65 S34 1990

INTERIOR DECORATION - GREAT BRITAIN - HISTORY - 19TH CENTURY.
Wilhide, Elizabeth. William Morris . New York , 1991. p. cm.   ISBN 0-8109-3623-2 (cloth)   DDC 745.4/492 20
NK2043.Z9 M648 1991

INTERIOR DECORATION - HANDBOOKS, MANUALS, ETC.
Garey, Carol Cooper. House beautiful decorating style /. New York , 1991. p. cm.   ISBN 0-688-09734-0 :   DDC 747.213 20
NK2115 .G25 1991

INTERIOR DECORATION - HISTORY - 20TH CENTURY.
Dampierre, Florence de. The decorator /. New York , 1989. 255 p. :   ISBN 0-08-478118-2   DDC 729/.092/2 B 20
NK2115.8 .D36 1989
NYPL   [3-MLO+ 91-3369]
Glancey, Jonathan. The new moderns /. New York , c1990. 191 p. :   ISBN 0-517-57662-7 :

DDC 728/.09/045 20
NA680 .G57 1990
NYPL [3-MLO+ 91-4945]

**INTERIOR DECORATION - HISTORY -
20TH CENTURY - THEMES, MOTIVES.**
Bullivant, Lucy. International interior design /.
New York , 1991. p. cm. ISBN 1-558-59235-0
DDC 725/.09/048 20
NK1980 .B84 1991

**INTERIOR DECORATION - ITALY -
BOLOGNA - HISTORY - 17TH
CENTURY.**
Feinblatt, Ebria. Seventeenth-century Bolognese
ceiling decorators /. Santa Barbara, Calif. ,
1991. p. cm. ISBN 0-931832-89-6 : DDC
729/.4/09454109032 20
ND2757.B54 F45 1991

**INTERIOR DECORATION - JUVENILE
LITERATURE.**
Sherrow, Victoria. Dream rooms, decorating
with flair /. Mahwah, N.J. , c1991. 114 p. :
ISBN 0-8167-2293-5 (lib. bdg.) : DDC 747.7/7
20
NK2115 .S48 1991

INTERIOR DECORATION - MANAGEMENT.
Stasiowski, Frank, 1948- Project management
for the design professional /. New York , 1991.
p. cm. ISBN 0-8230-4413-0 DDC 720/.68 20
NA1996 .S74 1991

INTERIOR DECORATION RENDERING.
Porter, Tom. Design drawing techniques . New
York : Toronto : p. cm. ISBN 0-684-19045-1
DDC 720/.28/4 20
NA2714 .P67 1991

**INTERIOR DECORATION RENDERING -
CATALOGS.**
Fuhring, Peter. Design into art . London , New
York , 1989. 2 v. (792 p.) : ISBN 0-85667-354-4
(London) ***NYPL [MLD+ 89-23146]***

INTERIOR DECORATION - ROME.
Roman art in the private sphere . Ann Arbor ,
c1991. 156 p. : ISBN 0-472-10196-X (alk. paper)
DDC 747.2937 20
N5760 .R66 1991

**INTERIOR DECORATION - SOUTHERN
STATES.**
Gammon, Mitzi. The south /. New York ,
1991. p. cm. ISBN 0-553-07550-0 DDC
728/.37/0975 20
NA7211 .G35 1991

**INTERIOR DECORATION - STANDARDS -
HANDBOOKS, MANUALS, ETC.**
De Chiara, Joseph, 1929- Time-saver standards
for interior design and space planning /. New
York , c1991. p. cm. ISBN 0-07-016299-9 DDC
729 20
NK2110 .D35 1991

**INTERIOR DECORATION - SWEDEN -
HISTORY - 18TH CENTURY.**
Groth, Håkan. Neo-classicism in the North .
New York , 1990. 224 p. : ISBN 0-8478-1273-1
DDC 728/.37/09485 20
NK1461.A1 G76 1990
NYPL [3-MLO 91-3368]

**INTERIOR DECORATION - TEXAS -
HISTORY - 19TH CENTURY.**
Brandimarte, Cynthia. Inside Texas . Ft. Worth,
Tex. , 1991. p. cm. ISBN 0-87565-092-9 DDC
747.2164 20
NK2003.5 .B7 1991

**INTERIOR DECORATION - TEXAS -
HISTORY - 20TH CENTURY.**
Brandimarte, Cynthia. Inside Texas . Ft. Worth,
Tex. , 1991. p. cm. ISBN 0-87565-092-9 DDC
747.2164 20
NK2003.5 .B7 1991

**INTERIOR DECORATION - TEXAS -
HUMAN FACTORS.**
Brandimarte, Cynthia. Inside Texas . Ft. Worth,
Tex. , 1991. p. cm. ISBN 0-87565-092-9 DDC
747.2164 20
NK2003.5 .B7 1991

INTERIOR DECORATION - THAILAND.
Nangs [Bangkok? , 1980 (Krung Thēp : Siwaph
156 p. :
NK2078.7.A1 N36 1980

**INTERIOR DECORATION - THEMES,
MOTIVES.**
Harle, Lesley. Designer china . New York ,
1991. p. cm. ISBN 0-688-10923-3 DDC 738.1/5

20
NK4605 .H36 1991

**INTERIOR DECORATION - UNITED
STATES.**
Bowman, Irving. A portfolio of interiors . [New
York] [1941?] 17, 17 leaves :
NYPL [3-MLO+ 90-2451]

Gross, Steve. Old houses /. New York , 1991.
p. cm. ISBN 1-556-70184-5 : DDC 728/.0973 20
NA7205 .G764 1991

Wilson, José. Decoration U. S.A. New York
[c1965] 278 p. DDC 747.213
NK2002 .W53   ***NYPL [3-MLO+ 91-6753]***

**INTERIOR DECORATION - UNITED
STATES - HISTORY - 19TH CENTURY.**
Creating a dignified past . Savage, Md. , c1991.
ix, 129 p. : ISBN 0-8476-7690-0
NYPL [3-MLF 91-6907]

**INTERIOR DECORATION - UNITED
STATES - HISTORY - 20TH CENTURY.**
Hampton, Mark. Legendary decorators of the
twentieth century /. New York , 1992. p. cm.
ISBN 0-385-26361-9 : DDC 747.213/09/04 20
NK2004 .H36 1992

Slavin, Maeve. Davis Allen . New York ,
c1990. 136 p. : ISBN 0-8478-1255-3 DDC
729/.092 20
NK2004.3.A45 S5 1990
NYPL [3-MLO 91-3724]

Spectre, Jay. Point of view . Boston , c1991. p.
cm. ISBN 0-8212-1849-2 : DDC 729/.092 20
NK2004.3.S68 A2 1991

INTERIOR DECORATORS - BIOGRAPHY.
Dampierre, Florence de. The decorator /. New
York , 1989. 255 p. : ISBN 0-08-478118-2 DDC
729/.092/2 B 20
NK2115.8 .D36 1989
NYPL [3-MLO+ 91-3369]

**INTERIOR DECORATORS - UNITED
STATES - BIOGRAPHY.**
Hampton, Mark. Legendary decorators of the
twentieth century /. New York , 1992. p. cm.
ISBN 0-385-26361-9 : DDC 747.213/09/04 20
NK2004 .H36 1992

INTERIOR DESIGN - UNITED STATES.
Kemp, Jim. American vernacular . Washington,
D.C. , 1990, c1987. 256 p. : ISBN
1-558-35074-8 :
NYPL [3-MQWO 91-6742]

The interior dimension . Malnar, Joy Monice.
New York, N.Y. , c1992. p. cm. ISBN
0-442-23739-1 DDC 729 20
NA2850 .M35 1992

INTERIOR WALLS.
Kaufman, Donald. Color atmospheres . New
York , 1991. p. cm. ISBN 0-517-57660-0 : DDC
728 20
NK2115.5.C6 K38 1991

**INTERIORS (DECORATION) see INTERIOR
DECORATION.**

International Academy of Architecture. Sofia,
Bulgaria : Centre of Pub. Activity of IAA,
[1989?] 68 p. : ill. ; 23 cm. Cover title. DDC
720/.601 20
1. International Academy of Architecture.
NA10 .I48 1989

**INTERNATIONAL ACADEMY OF
ARCHITECTURE.**
International Academy of Architecture. Sofia,
Bulgaria [1989?] 68 p. : DDC 720/.601 20
NA10 .I48 1989

International antiques price guide. Miller, Martin.
[International antiques price guide.] Miller's
International antiques price guide /. New York,
N.Y., U. S.A. , c1990. 632 p. :
NYPL [MAVC+ 91-5384]

International Art Fair Zürich. Forum
Internationale Kunstmesse Zürich (1984) Forum
Internationale Kunstmesse Zürich =. Zürich
[1984] [124] leaves :
NYPL [3-MAL+ 90-11547]

**International Association for the Astronomical
Arts.** In the stream of stars . New York ,
1990. 183 p. : ISBN 0-89480-705-6 (paper) :
DDC 758/.96294 20
N8234.O8 I5 1990
NYPL [3-MAMZ 91-5459]

International Center of Photography.
Ray, Man, 1890-1976. Man Ray in fashion /.
New York City , 1990. 95 p. : ISBN
0-933642-14-8
NYPL [MFX (Ray) 91-3335]

Salgado, Sebastião, 1944- An uncertain grace /.
New York, c1990. 155, [1] p. : ISBN
0-89381-421-0 (Hardcover)
NYPL [MFX+ (Salgado) 91-3484]

**International Commission for the History of
Towns.**
Latina /. Roma , 1990. 94 p. :
NYPL [Map Div. 91-5807]

Petrucci, Giulia. San Martino al Cimino
(Viterbo, III) /. Roma , 1987 [i.e. 1988] 73 p. :
ISBN 88-7597-033-5 (pbk.)
NYPL [Map Div. 88-1082]

**International Committee of Historical Sciences.
International Commission for the History of
Towns. see International Commission for the
History of Towns.**

**International Congress of Americanists, 40th,
Rome and Genoa, 1972.** Atti del XL
Congresso internazionale degli americanisti,
Roma-Genova, 3-10 settembre 1972. Genova,
Tilgher [1973-76] 4 v. illus. 25 cm. English,
French, German, Italian, Portuguese, or Spanish.
Includes bibliographies.
*1. Indians - Congresses. 2. Indians - Antiquities -
Congresses. 3. America - Antiquities - Congresses. I.
Title.*   ***NYPL [HBC 74-2090]***

International corporate design systems / edited
by David E. Cater. New York : Direction Book
Co., 1989- 127 p. : chiefly ill. (some col.) ; 29
cm. ISBN 0-88108-069-1
1. Logotype. 2. Corporate image. I. Carter, David E.
NYPL [3-MDW 91-1143]

**International Council of Museums. Comité
National Belge.** Le musée et son public.
[Bruxelles, 1968?] 250 p.
NYPL [3-MAV 90-5745]

International dictionary of art and artists / with
a foreword by Cecil Gould ; editor, James
Vinson. Chicago : St. James Press, c1990. 2 v. :
ill. ; 29 cm. Includes bibliographical references and
indexes. CONTENTS. - v. [1] Artists -- v. [2] Art.
ISBN 1-558-62000-1 (v. [1])
*1. Artists - Biography - Dictionaries. I. Vinson, James,
1933-.*   ***NYPL [MAO 90-11519]***

**The international dictionary of artists who
painted Malta /.** De Piro, Nicholas, 1941-
Valletta, Malta , 1988. 207 p. : ISBN
1-87168-400-5 DDC 758/.994585 20
N8213 .D4 1988

International furniture design for the '90s /
edited by Lois Lambert. New York, N.Y. : PBC
International, 1991. p. cm. Includes index. ISBN
0-86636-136-7 : DDC 749.2/0499 20
*1. Furniture design - History - 20th century. I.
Lambert, Lois.*
NK2395 .I57 1991

International interior design /. Bullivant, Lucy.
New York , 1991. p. cm. ISBN 1-558-59235-0
DDC 725/.09/048 20
NK1980 .B84 1991

International interiors two. Blackwell, Lewis.
International interiors 2 . London , c1990. 256
p. : ISBN 1-558-59013-7
NYPL [3-MLO+ 90-12789]

International interiors 2 . Blackwell, Lewis.
London , c1990. 256 p. : ISBN 1-558-59013-7
NYPL [3-MLO+ 90-12789]

International Silver Co. International Silver
Company. Catalogue of International Silver
Co. . New York, U. S.A. [1915?] 160 p. :
NK7241.5.I58 A4 1915

International Silver Company.
Catalogue of International Silver Co. : makers
of all grades of silver plated ware and cut glass.
New York, U. S.A. : The Company, Export
Dept., [1915?] 160 p. : ill. ; 31 cm. English and
Spanish. Cover title: International Silver Co. Includes
index. "Catalogue no. 102-I."
*1. International Silver Company - Catalogs. 2.
Silver-plated ware - Connecticut - Catalogs. 3. Cut
glass - Connecticut - Catalogs. I. Title. II. Title:
International Silver Co. III. Title: Catalog of
International Silver Co. IV. Title: Catalogue of
International Silver Company.*
NK7241.5.I58 A4 1915

INTERNATIONAL SILVER COMPANY - CATALOGS.
International Silver Company. Catalogue of
International Silver Co. . New York, U. S.A.
[1915?] 160 p. :
NK7241.5.I58 A4 1915

INTERNATIONAL STYLE (ARCHITECTURE)
Pearson, Paul David, 1936- Alvar Aalto and the
International style /. London , 1989, c1978.
240 p. : ISBN 0-7134-6300-7 (pbk) : DDC
720/.92/4 19
NA1455.F53A2
NYPL [3-MQZ+ (Aalto) 90-10795]

Wodehouse, Lawrence. The roots of
international style architecture /. West
Cornwall, CT , 1991. p. cm. ISBN 0-933951-46-9
(alk. paper) : DDC 724/.6 20
NA682.I58 W6 1991

INTERNATIONAL STYLE (ARCHITECTURE) - GERMANY - STUTTGART.
Pommer, Richard. Weissenhof 1927 and the
modern movement in architecture /. Chicago ,
1991. xxii, 304 p., [115] p. of plates : ISBN
0-226-67515-7 (alk. paper) DDC
728/.0943/47309042 20
NA7351.S7 P6 1991
NYPL [3-MQWD 91-4874]

INTERNATIONAL STYLE (ARCHITECTURE) - ISRAEL - EXHIBITIONS.
Turner, Judith. White city . [Tel Aviv] , 1984.
88 p. : *NYPL [MFX (Turner) 86-728]*

**International Symposium on the Art of Oceania
(3rd : 1984 : New York, N.Y.)** Art and
identity in Oceania /. Honolulu , c1990. viii,
315 p., [8] p. of plates : ISBN 0-8248-1304-9 :
DDC 700/.995 20
N7399.7 .A78 1990
NYPL [3-MADF 91-5014]

**Internationale Commissie voor
Stedengeschiedenis. see International
Commission for the History of Towns.**

**Internationale Kommission für Städtegeschichte.
see International Commission for the
History of Towns.**

**Internationale Kulturtage (10th : 1989 :
Mannheim, Germany)** Ungarische Avantgarde
in der Malerei der achtziger Jahre .
[Mannheim] [Budapest] , c1989. 55 p. : ISBN
3-927224-01-4
ND520 .U54 1989

Internationale Kunstmesse Zürich. Forum
Internationale Kunstmesse Zürich (1984) Forum
Internationale Kunstmesse Zürich =. Zürich
[1984] [124] leaves :
NYPL [3-MAL+ 90-11547]

INTERNATIONALE SITUATIONNISTE.
Ohrt, Roberto. Phantom Avantgarde . Hamburg
[München] , 1990. 333 p., [16] p. of plates :
ISBN 3-89401-168-8
NX542 .O38 1990

Plant, Sadie, 1964- The most radical gesture .
London , New York, NY , 1992. p. cm. ISBN
0-415-06221-7 DDC 700/.1/03 20
NX542 .P5 1992

**Internationale Tage (1990 : Ingelheim am Rhein,
Germany)** Biedermeier in Wien 1815-1848 .
Mainz , c1990. 251 p. : ISBN 3-8053-1128-1
NX548.V53 B54 1990

**Internationaler Exlibriskongress (23rd : 1990 :
Mönchengladbach, Germany)**
Schutt-Kehm, Elke M., 1954- Albrecht Dürer
und die Frühzeit der Exlibriskunst .
Wiesbaden , c1990. 39 p. : ISBN 3-922835-18-X
NYPL [MDVF 91-7231]

Thoms, Klaus. Das Exlibris von heute
1988-1990 . Wiesbaden , c1990. 286 p. : ISBN
3-922835-20-1 *NYPL [MDVF 91-7229]*

**Internationaler Kongress Europäisches
Kunsthandwerk 1988, Stuttgart .**
Internationaler Kongress Europäisches
Kunsthandwerk 1988 : Stuttgart, Germany)
Frankfurt , 1988. 56 p. ; ISBN 3-87864-176-1
NYPL [3-MNC+ 90-12554]

**Internationaler Kongress Europäisches
Kunsthandwerk (1988 : Stuttgart, Germany)**
Internationaler Kongress Europäisches
Kunsthandwerk 1988, Stuttgart :
Bestandsaufnahme, Kunsthandwerk /
vollständige Fassung der Referate von Reinhart

Chr. Bartholomäi ... [et al.]. Frankfurt :
Bundesverband Kunsthandwerk, 1988. 56 p. ;
30 cm. Includes bibliographical references. ISBN
3-87864-176-1
*1. Decorative arts - Europe - Congresses. I.
Bartholomäi, Reinhart Chr. II. Title. III. Title:
Bestandsaufnahme, Kunsthandwerk.*
NYPL [3-MNC+ 90-12554]

Internationaler Pianisten Wettweberb "Busoni".
Concorso pianistico internazionale "Busoni"
[sound recording] =. Pontelambro (Co), Italy ,
p1988. 6 sound discs :
Nuova era 6716-DM--6721 DM

**Internationaler Pianisten Wettweberb "Ferruccio
Busoni" Bozen.** Concorso pianistico
internazionale "Busoni" [sound recording] =.
Pontelambro (Co), Italy , p1988. 6 sound discs :
Nuova era 6716-DM--6721 DM

Internationales Design Zentrum Berlin.
Raymond Loewy, pioneer of American
industrial design /. Munich , c1990. 262 p. :
ISBN 3-7913-1066-6
NYPL [3-MNF+ 90-11648]

INTEROR DECORATION FIRMS - EAST (U. S.)
Crouch, Elizabeth G., 1942- Showcase of
interior design /. Grand Rapids, Mich. , 1991.
p. cm. ISBN 0-9624596-2-3: DDC 729/.025/74 20
NK2004 .C76 1991

Interpretations . Cleveland Museum of Art.
Cleveland, OH , 1991. p. cm. ISBN
0-940717-11-5 DDC 708.71/32 20
N552 .A84 1991

Interpretations & innovations. Quilt National
(1989 : Athens, Ohio) New quilts . West
Chester, Pa. , c1989. 96 p. : ISBN 0-88740-157-0
DDC 746.9/7/097307477197 20
NK9112 .Q5 1989
NYPL [3-MOT 90-11613]

Interpretations in art.
Crone, Rainer, 1942- Paul Klee . New York ,
c1991. p. cm. ISBN 0-231-07034-6 (alk. paper) :
DDC 759.9494 20
ND588.K5 C76 1991

Interpreting contemporary art / edited by
Stephen Bann and William Allen. London :
Reaktion, 1991. xix, 22 p. : ill. ; 24 cm. Includes
bibliography and index. ISBN 0-948462-15-9 (cased) :
DDC 709.047 20
N6490 *NYPL [MA 91-6285]*
I. Bann, Stephen. II. Allen, William, 1967-.

**Interrelationships between the Buddhist art of
China and the art of India and Central Asia
from 618-755 A.D.** /. Rhie, Marylin M.
Napoli , 1988. 44 p., xxxii p. of plates : DDC
704.9/48943/095109021 20
N8193.C6 R48 1988

**Intervenciones en el patrimonio arquitectónico
(1980-1985)** / [coordinador de la edición,
Alberto Humanes Bustamante]. [Madrid] :
Ministerio de Cultura, Dirección General de
Bellas Artes y Archivos, Instituto de
Conservación y Restauración de Bienes
Culturales, [1990] 465 p. : ill. (some col.) ; 31
cm. Includes bibliographical references and indexes.
ISBN 84-7483-661-1 DDC 720/.28/8094609048
20
*1. Architecture - Spain - Conservation and restoration.
2. Buildings - Spain - Remodeling for other use. 3.
Architecture and history - Spain. I. Humanes
Bustamante, Alberto. II. Instituto de Conservación y
Restauración de Bienes Culturales (Spain).*
NA1301 .I57 1990

Interventi classensi .
(11) Fifteenth century Italian woodcuts from
the Biblioteca Classense in Ravenna. Ravenna ,
c1989. 13 p., [46] p. of plates :
NYPL [MDOH 90-11354]

Interversa Gesellschaft für Beteiligungen.
Reitkunst in Bild und Schrift des 16.-19.
Jahrhunderts /. Hamburg [1982] 44 p. :
Z6240 .R44 1982 SF309
NYPL [MDZ 87-5069]

INTIFADA, 1987-
Occupation and resistance . New York, N.Y. ,
c1990. 80 p. : ISBN 0-932075-30-4
IN PROCESS (ONLINE)
NYPL [3-MAMT 91-7487]

Intimidades . Ivelić, Milan. Santiago, Chile

[1989] 119 p. : ISBN 956-25-3018-2
IN PROCESS (ONLINE)
NYPL [3-MAM+ 90-13346]

Into the darkness laughing . Chaplin, Patrice.
London , 1990. 151 p., [8] p. of plates : ISBN
1-85381-235-8
NYPL [3-MCF M69 91-4515]

Introducing Michelangelo /. Richmond, Robin.
Boston , 1992. p. cm. ISBN 0-316-74440-9 :
DDC 709/.2 B 20
N6923.B9 R52 1992

An introduction to modern welfare economics /.
Johansson, Per-Olov, 1949- Cambridge , New
York , 1991. p. cm. ISBN 0-521-35616-4 (hard)
DDC 330.15/56 20
NB846 .J64 1991

**An introduction to the history of maps and
mapmaking.** R. V. Tooley Ltd. London , 1980.
68 p. : *NYPL [Map Div. 91-4077]*

Inventaire des dessins /. Musée Rodin. [Paris] ,
c1984- v. : ISBN 2-901428-10-X (v. 3) DDC
741.944 19
NC248.R58 A4 1984
NYPL [MCO R69 88-2276]

**Inventaire général des monuments et des
richesses artistiques de la France.**
Pyrénées-Atlantiques . Paris , 1989. 719 p. :
ISBN 2-11-080952-3 : DDC 709/.44/79 20
N6849.P92 P97 1989

**Inventaire général des monuments et des
richesses artistiques de la France. Région
d'Auvergne.** Canton et dentelles d'Arlanc,
Puy-de-Dôme /. Clermont-Ferrand , c1989. 56
p. : ISBN 2-905554-03-7 : DDC 709/.44/591 20
N6849.A69 C36 1989

**Inventaire général des monuments et des
richesses artistiques de la France. Région de
Bourgogne.** Canton de Seurre . [Dijon] ,
c1988. 59 p. : ISBN 2-904727-02-7; 2-904727-02-07
DDC 709/.44/42 20
N6849.S48 C36 1988

**Inventaire général des monuments et des
richesses artistiques de la France. Région de
Lorraine.**
Canton de Cattenom . [Metz] , c1988. 79 p. :
ISBN 2-9501474-3-7 DDC 709/.44/3825 20
N6849.C36 C36 1988

Canton de Longuyon . [Metz] , c1988. 80 p. :
ISBN 2-9501474-4-5 DDC 709/.44/3823 20
N6849.L74 C36 1988

Canton de Sierck-les-Bains, Moselle /. [Metz] ,
c1987. 72 p. : ISBN 2-9501474-1-0 DDC
709/.44/3825 20
N6849.S53 C35 1987

Marville . [Metz] , c1988. 80 p. : ISBN
2-9501474-5-3 DDC 709/.44/381 20
N6851.M34 M37 1988

**Inventaire général des monuments et des
richesses artistiques de la France. Région de
Picardie.** Laon, ville haute, Aisne /. Amiens ,
c1989. 64 p. : ISBN 2-906340-06-5 : DDC
720/.44/345 20
NA1051.L3 L36 1989

**Inventaire général des monuments et des
richesses artistiques de la France. Région des
Pays de la Loire.**
Eraud, Dominique. Laval, Mayenne /. [Nantes]
[1990] 138 p. : ISBN 2-906344-24-9 DDC
709/.44/16 20
N6851.L36 E7 1990

Manase, Viviane. Canton de Montreuil-Bellay /.
[Nantes] [1990] 100 p. : ISBN 2-906344-00-00 :
DDC 709/.44/18 20
N6849.M66 M35 1990

**Inventaire général des monuments et des
richesses artistiques de la France. Service
régional (Basse-Normandie, France)** Falaise,
Calvados /. [Caen, France] [1990] 64 p. :
ISBN 2-908621-01-0 : DDC 709/44/22 20
N6851.F35 F35 1990

Inventario . López-Chaves Meléndez, Juan M.
(Juan Manuel) [Pontevedra] , 1988- v. <1 > :
ISBN 84-86845-09-02 (v. 1)
NA7775 .L6 1988

Inventario artístico de Cáceres y su provincia /
[Ministerio de Cultura, Instituto de
Conservación y Restauración de Bienes
Culturales]. Madrid : El Instituto, 1989- v.

<1-2 > : ill. ; 18 cm. CONTENTS. - t. 1. Partidos
judiciales de Alcántara y Cáceres, y Comarca de la
Vera de Cáceres -- t. 2. Partidos judiciales de
Garrovillas, Montánchez y Trujillo   ISBN
84-7483-610-7 (obra completa)   DDC 709/.46/28
20
1. Art - Spain - Cáceres (Province). 2. Cáceres (Spain :
Province) - Antiquities. I. Instituto de Conservación y
Restauración de Bienes Culturales.
N7109.C15 I58 1989

Inventario artístico de Soria y su provincia /.
Manrique Mayor, María Angeles. Madrid ,
1989. 2 v. : ISBN 84-7483-539-9 (obra completa)
NYPL [3-MAI 90-13098]

Inventario artístico de Toledo / [dirigido por
Matilde Revuelta Tubino]. Madrid : Centro
Nacional de Información Artística,
Arqueológica y Etnológica, 1983- v. : ill. ; 18
cm. Vol. 2 published by Ministerio de Cultura,
Instituto de Conservación y Restauración de Bienes
Culturales. Vol. 1-2 have running title: Inventario del
patrimonio artístico de España. Includes bibliographical
references. CONTENTS. - t. 1. [without special title] --
t. 2. La catedral primada (2 v.)   ISBN 84-7483-328-0
(set)
1. Art, Spanish - Spain - Toledo. 2. Christian art and
sybolism - Spain - Toledo. I. Revuelta Tubino, Matilde.
II. Title: Inventario del patrimonio artístico de España.
NYPL [3-MAML 86-2086]

Inventário artístico do Algarve . Lameira,
Francisco I. C. Faro , 1989-<1990. v. <1-3
> :
NB1255.P8 L3 1989

Inventario del patrimonio artístico de España.
Inventario artístico de Toledo /. Madrid , 1983-
v. : ISBN 84-7483-328-0 (set)
NYPL [3-MAML 86-2086]

Inventario general de pinturas. Museo del Prado.
Museo del Prado . Madrid , 1990- v. : ISBN
84-239-4310-0 (obra completa)
NYPL [3-MAVZ+ (Madrid) 91-5374]

**INVENTIONS - CARICATURES AND
CARTOONS - JUVENILE LITERATURE.**
Goldberg, Rube, 1883-1970. The best of Rube
Goldberg /. Englewood Cliffs, N.J. [1979] xiii,
130 p. : ISBN 0-13-074807-2 : DDC 741.5/973
NC1429.G46 A4 1979
NYPL [3-MEM (Goldberg) 81-1046]

**Investigating artistic environments in the ancient
Near East /** edited by Ann C. Gunter.
Washington, D.C.: Arthur M. Sackler Gallery,
Smithsonian Institution, c1990. xii, 153 p. : ill. ;
26 cm. Essays presented at a symposium held in April
1988 at the Arthur M. Sackler Gallery. Includes
bibliographies. ISBN 0-299-97070-1 (alk. paper) :
DDC 709/.35 20
1. Art, Ancient - Middle East - Congresses. 2. Art -
Middle East - Congresses. 3. Middle East -
Antiquities - Congresses. I. Gunter, Ann Clyburn,
1951-. II. Arthur M. Sackler Gallery (Smithsonian
Institution).
N7265 .I58 1990   **NYPL [3-MAE 90-12590]**

**Investigation (University of Pennsylvania.
Institute of Contemporary Art) .**
(20) Hajamadi, Fariba, 1957- Fariba Hajamadi .
[Philadelphia] , c1988. 1 folded sheet (7 p.) :
ISBN 0-88454-045-6
NYPL [3-MCX H152 90-12728]

Invisible twenty-one artists visible. Long Beach,
Calif. : Long Beach Museum of Art, 1972. 59
p. : chiefly ill. ; 22 cm. Catalogue of an exhibition
held March 26 through April 23, 1972.
1. Women artists - California - Exhibitions. 2. Art,
Modern - 20th century - California - Exhibitions. 3.
Art, American - Exhibitions. I. Long Beach Museum of
Art.   **NYPL [3-MAMT 90-5889]**

The invitational--artists of northeast Ohio .
Hinson, Tom E. [Cleveland] , c1991. vii, 64 p. :
ISBN 0-940717-07-7 : DDC
709/.771/307477132 20
N6530.O3 H56 1991

Ion Tuculesco, 1910-1962. Ţuculescu, Ion,
1910-1962. Bucureşti , 1966. 91 p. :
MLCS 91/01748 (N)
NYPL [3-MCZ T895 91-7236]

Ionas, Ioannis. La maison rurale de Chypre
(XVIIIe-XXe siècle) : aspects et techniques de
construction / par Ioannis Ionas. Nicosie :
Centre de recherche scientifique de Chypre,
1988. 238 p. : ill. (some col.) ; 31 cm.
(Publications du Centre de recherche scientifique de

Chypre . 12) Includes bibliographical references (p.
225-228) and indexes.   ISBN 996-308-012-X DDC
728/.095645 20
1. Farmhouses - Cyprus. 2. Housing, Rural - Cyprus. 3.
Vernacular architecture - Cyprus. I. Title. II. Series.
NA8210.C93 I57 1988

Ionel Jianu şi opera lui : un om, o viaţă, un
destin / realizatori, Ion Manea ... [et al.]. Los
Angeles, Calif. : American Romanian Academy
of Arts and Sciences, c1990. 361 p. : ill. ; 24
cm. Half title: Un om, o viaţă, un destin. Includes
bibliographical references (p. 358-361).   ISBN
0-912131-11-X
1. Jianu, Ionel - Criticism andinterpretation. I. Manea,
Ion. II. Title: Un om, o viaţă, un destin. III. Title: Om,
o viaţă, un destin.
N7483.J53 I56 1990

Ionescu, Adrian-Silvan. Artă şi document : arta
documentaristă în România secolului al XIX-lea
/ Adrian-Silvan Ionescu ; [diapozitive color,
Alexandru Comănescu, Sorin Comănescu ;
fotografii alb-negru, Alexandru Comănescu,
Adrian-Silvan Ionescu]. Bucureşti : Editura
Meridiane, 1990. 318 p., [48] p. of plates : ill.
(some col.) ; 17 cm. (Curente şi sinteze. 53)
Summary in English. Includes bibliographical references
(p. 305-[312]) and index.   ISBN 973-330-072-1 :
1. Romania in art. 2. Exoticism in art - Europe. 3. Art,
European. 4. Art, Modern - 19th century - Europe. 5.
Exoticism in art - Romania. 6. Art, Romanian. 7. Art,
Modern - 19th century - Romania. I. Title.
N8214.5.R6 I55 1990

Ionescu, Alexandra. Contemporary Romanian
painting : 1973, Corcoran Gallery of Art ...
Minnesota Museum of Art ... Akron Art
Institute ... / [the organization of the exhibition
and compilation of the catalogue, Alexandra
Ionescu]. [s.l. : s.n., 1973] [59] p. : ill. (some
col.) ; 22 cm. "Exhibition arranged by the Office for
the Organization of Exhibitions of Bucharest, under the
Council for Culture and Socialist Education."   DDC
759.9498/074/013
1. Painting, Romanian - Exhibitions. 2. Painting,
Modern - 20th century - Romania - Exhibitions. I.
Corcoran Gallery of Art. II. Minnesota Museum of Art.
III. Akron Art Institute. IV. Conciliul Culturii şi
Educaţiei Socialiste. Oficiul pentru Organizarea
Expoziţiilor. V. Title.
ND928 .I66   **NYPL [3-MCY 90-12375]**

Ionescu, Alexandru. Bucuresti, ghidul străzilor /
[elaborare, Alexandru Ionescu, Constantin
Kiriac ; coordonare cartografie, Ştefan Pandele,
Mircea Vlad]. [Bucharest] : Sport-Turism, 1982.
1 atlas (132, 138 p.) : col maps ; 20 cm. Three
folded col. maps inserted. Includes index.   DDC
912/.4982 19
1. Bucharest - Maps. I. Kiriac, Constantin. II. Title.
G2039 .B816 1982
NYPL [Map Div. 84-1514]

Iotta Communications. Open mind . Milano ,
c1989. 318 p. :   **NYPL [3-MAMZ 90-11011]**

Iotti, Nilde. Santa Maria sopra Minerva /.
Roma , c1990. 303 p. : ISBN 88-7060-223-0
NYPL [3-MRBD+ 91-7451]

Iparművészeti Múzeum (Hungary)
Képes kárpitok az Iparművészeti Múzeum
gyűjteményében = Tapestries in the collection
of the Museum of Applied Arts / [a katalógust
írta, László Emőke]. Budapest : A Múzeum,
1987-1989. 2 v. : ill. (some col.) ; 30 cm. Cover
title. Hungarian and English. Vol. 1 issued in portfolio.
Includes bibliographical references.
1. Iparművészeti Múzeum (Hungary) - Catalogs. 2.
Tapestry - Hungary - Budapest - Catalogs. I. László,
Emőke. II. Title. III. Title: Tapestries in the collection
of the Museum of Applied Arts.
NYPL [3-MOR+ 91-2510]

**IPARMŰVÉSZETI MÚZEUM (HUNGARY) -
CATALOGS.**
Iparművészeti Múzeum (Hungary) Képes
kárpitok az Iparművészeti Múzeum
gyűjteményében =. Budapest , 1987-1989. 2
v. :   **NYPL [3-MOR+ 91-2510]**

Ipoustéguy /. Gaudibert, Pierre. Paris , c1989.
204 p. : ISBN 2-7022-0246-2
NYPL [3-MGO+ (Ipoustéguy) 91-3898]

Ipoustéguy, Jean, 1920- Gaudibert, Pierre.
Ipoustéguy /. Paris , c1989. 204 p. : ISBN
2-7022-0246-2
NYPL [3-MGO+ (Ipoustéguy) 91-3898]

IPOUSTÉGUY, JEAN, 1920-
Gaudibert, Pierre. Ipoustéguy /. Paris , c1989.
204 p. : ISBN 2-7022-0246-2
NYPL [3-MGO+ (Ipoustéguy) 91-3898]

Ippa's kastelengids voor België /. Remoortere,
Julien van. Tielt , 1988. 431 p. : ISBN
90-209-1647-5
NA7725 .R46 1988

Ira Spanierman Gallery.
Kaelin, Charles Salis, 1858-1929. Dialogues
with nature . New York , c1990. 41 p., [30] p.
of plates : ISBN 0-945936-09-5
NYPL [3-MCX K118 90-13101]

Ten American painters /. New York , c1990.
187 p. : ISBN 0-945936-07-9
NYPL [3-MCW 90-11805]

Twachtman, John Henry, 1853-1902. John
Henry Twachtman, 1853-1902. New York
[1968] [24] p. :
NYPL [3-MCX T96 91-1183]

Irak. see Iraq.

IRAN - ANTIQUITIES.
Brentjes, Burchard. Steppenreiter und
Handelsherren . Leipzig , 1990. 132 p. : ISBN
3-363-00459-1 :
N5899.P36 B74 1990

Iran - Archaeology. see Iran - Antiquities.

**IRANIAN ILLUMINATION OF BOOKS AND
MANUSCRIPTS. see ILLUMINATION
OF BOOKS AND MANUSCRIPTS,
IRANIAN.**

**IRANIAN PAINTING. see PAINTING,
IRANIAN.**

IRAQ - MAPS.
(1959) Sousa, Ahmed. al-ʻIrāq fī al-Khawāriṭ
al-qadīmah. Baghdād, 1959. 22 p.
NYPL [Map-Div. 85-3120]

Irasuto patān-shū "erements." Elements =.
[Tokyo] , 1989. 12 v. : ISBN 4-87210-018-2 (v.
1) : DDC 745.4 20
NK1530 .E44 1989

Ireland, and artist's year. Bewick, Pauline, 1935-
Pauline Bewick's Ireland . London , 1990. 192
p. : ISBN 0-413-64320-4 (cased) : DDC
914.1504824 20
DA978   **NYPL [3-MCV B572 91-4511]**

IRELAND - ANTIQUITIES.
Horn, Walter William, 1908- The forgotten
hermitage of Skellig Michael /. Berkeley ,
c1990. xi, 111 p. : ISBN 0-520-06410-0 (alk.
paper) DDC 941.9/6 19
BX2602.S54 H67 1989
NYPL [3-MRBB+ 91-3376]

Ireland - Archaeology. see Ireland - Antiquities.

IRELAND - CULTURAL POLICY.
Kennedy, Brian P. Dreams and responsibilities .
[Dublin, Ireland] [1990?] xiii, 292 p. : ISBN
0-906627-32-X DDC 700/.1/03 20
NX750.I7 K4 1990   **NYPL [JFE 91-2989]**

**IRELAND - DESCRIPTION AND TRAVEL -
1981-**

**IRELAND - DESCRIPTION AND TRAVEL -
1981- VIEWS.**
Bewick, Pauline, 1935- Pauline Bewick's
Ireland . London , 1990. 192 p. : ISBN
0-413-64320-4 (cased) : DDC 914.1504824 20
DA978   **NYPL [3-MCV B572 91-4511]**

Bewick, Pauline, 1935- Pauline Bewick's
Ireland . London , 1990. 192 p. : ISBN
0-413-64320-4 (cased) : DDC 914.1504824 20
DA978   **NYPL [3-MCV B572 91-4511]**

**IRELAND - DESCRIPTION AND TRAVEL -
1981- - VIEWS - EXHIBITIONS.**
Doherty, Willie, 1959- Willie Doherty,
unknown depths. Cardiff , c1990. [39] p. :
ISBN 1-87277-101-7
NYPL [MFX (Doherty) 90-13467]

IRELAND - GAZETTEERS.
Gasaitéar na hÉireann . Baile Átha Cliath ,
1989. xxxiv, 283 p. : ISBN 0-7076-0076-6
NYPL [Map Div. 91-3800]

Ireland. Placenames Branch. Gasaitéar na
hÉireann . Baile Atha Cliath , 1989. xxxiv, 283
p. : ISBN 0-7076-0076-6
NYPL [Map Div. 91-3800]

İrez, Feryal. XIX. yüzyıl Osmanlı saray mobilyası
/ Feryal İrez. Ankara : Atatürk Kültür Merkezi,

1988. 110 p., [83] p. of plates : ill. ; 25 cm.
(Atatürk Kültür Merkezi yayını . 23)
"89.06.4.0143.4"--P. 3 of cover. Includes bibliographical
references (p. [95]-99) and index. ISBN
975-16-0039-1
1. Furniture - Europe - History - 19th century. 2.
House furnishings - Turkey - Istanbul - History - 19th
century. 3. Palaces - Turkey - Istanbul. I. Title. II. Title:
19. yüzyıl Osmanlı saray mobilyası.
NK2525 .I7 1988

Iriarte, María Cristina. Núñez Borda, Luis,
1872-1970. L. Núñez Borda, el pintor de
Bogotá /. [Bogotá, Colombia?] 1988 (Bogotá,
Colombia : Litográficos de Escala) 116 p. :
ISBN 958-9082-41-6 DDC 759.9861 20
ND379.N85 A4 1988

Iride, schedule d'arte, Firenze '82 : [mostra] Villa
Romana, Comune di Firenze / a cura di Katalin
Burmeister e Alessandro Vezzosi ; interventi di
Renato Barilli ... [et al] ; testo storico-critico di
Alessandro Vezzosi. Firenze : Vallecchi, c1982.
107 p. : ill. ; 31 x 16 cm. Catalogue of an
exhibition sponsored jointly by the Comune di Firenze
and by the Villa Romana, seat of the German Institute
in Florence. Includes index.
1. Art, Italian - Italy - Florence - Exhibitions. 2. Art,
Modern - 20th century - Italy - Florence - Exhibitions.
I. Barilli, Renato. II. Vezzosi, Alessandro. III.
Burmeister, Katalin. IV. Villa Romana.
NYPL [3-MAMC+ 90-5983]

Irigoyen, Adriana. Nueva arquitectura Argentina :
pluralidad y coincidencia / Adriana Irigoyen,
Ramón Gutiérrez ; [traducción, Brian J. Mallet].
Bogotá, Colombia : [Escala], 1990. 221 p. : ill.
(some col.) ; 23 x 24 cm. (Colección SomoSur . t.
8) Spanish and English. ISBN 958-9082-52-1
1. Architecture - Argentina. I. Title.
IN PROCESS (ONLINE)
NYPL [3-MQWN 91-5871]

IRIS (PLANT) IN ART - EXHIBITIONS.
Irises and five masterpieces. [Australia] [1989]
1 v. (unpaged) : ISBN 0-9598384-1-4
NYPL [MAX (Bond) 91-6719]

Irises and five masterpieces. [Australia] : Bond
Corporation, [1989] 1 v. (unpaged) : col. ill. ;
28 cm. Catalog of an exhibition held at the Australian
National Gallery, June 29-July 9, 1989, and at 4 other
Australian locations through Sept. 1989. ISBN
0-9598384-1-4
1. Bond, Alan - Art collections - Exhibitions. 2. Iris
(Plant) in art - Exhibitions. 3. Art - Private collections -
Australia - Exhibitions. 4. Art, Modern - 19th century -
Exhibitions. I. Australian National Gallery.
NYPL [MAX (Bond) 91-6719]

Irish Architectural Archive.
The Architecture of Richard Morrison
(1767-1849) and William Vitruvius Morrison
(1794-1838). Dublin , 1989. xiii, 189 p. : ISBN
0-9515536-0-7
NYPL [3-MQZ (Morrison) 91-6143]

FitzGerald, Desmond. Vanishing country houses
of Ireland /. [Dublin] [Leixlip] , 1988. vi, 161
p. : ISBN 0-948018-04-6
NYPL [3-MRGF 89-17124]

IRISH ART. see ART, IRISH.

Irish art of the eighties. A new tradition .
Dublin , 1990. 139 p. : ISBN 0-907660-37-1 :
DDC 709.415 20
NYPL [3-MAMR 91-5078]

**Irish decorative arts from the collections of the
National Museum of Ireland.** National Museum
of Ireland. Irish decorative arts, 1550-1928 /.
[Dublin] 1990. 94 p. : ISBN 0-901777-21-8
NYPL [3-MNE 90-13211]

Irish decorative arts, 1550-1928 /. National
Museum of Ireland. [Dublin] 1990. 94 p. :
ISBN 0-901777-21-8
NYPL [3-MNE 90-13211]

Irish Georgian Society. FitzGerald, Desmond.
Vanishing country houses of Ireland /. [Dublin]
[Leixlip] , 1988. vi, 161 p. : ISBN 0-948018-04-6
NYPL [3-MRGF 89-17124]

Irkutsk . Soviet Union. Glavnoe upravlenie
geodezii i kartografii. Moskva , 1977. [14] p. :
NYPL [Map Div. 91-1089]

IRKUTSK (R.S.F.S.R.) - MAPS.
Soviet Union. Glavnoe upravlenie geodezii i
kartografii. Irkutsk . Moskva , 1977. [14] p. :
NYPL [Map Div. 91-1089]

Irmgard Hatzack, Leben und Werk . Aichelburg,

Wolf. München , 1988. 19 p., [26] p. of plates :
ISBN 3-88356-057-X DDC 730/.92 20
NB933.H38 A87 1988
NYPL [3-MGO (Hatzack) 90-10824]

Irmscher, Reinhard. Bönitz, Helmut, 1914-
Helmut Bönitz /. [Göttingen] , c1990. 119 p. :
N6888.B6165 A4 1990

IRON AGE - ARMENIA.
Frühe Bergvölker in Armenien und im
Kaukasus . Berlin , 1984. 84 p. :
NYPL [3-MAE 90-10823]

IRON AGE - CAUCASUS.
Frühe Bergvölker in Armenien und im
Kaukasus . Berlin , 1984. 84 p. :
NYPL [3-MAE 90-10823]

IRON AGE - ITALY, SOUTHERN.
Yntema, Douwe Geert. The matt-painted
pottery of Southern Italy . Galatina , 1990. 370
p. : ISBN 88-7786-428-0
NYPL [3-MPGD 91-5545]

**IRON AND STEEL BUILDING. see
BUILDING, IRON AND STEEL.**

**IRON AND STEEL WORKERS - BRAZIL -
PICTORIAL WORKS.**
Gente do aço /. [Rio de Janeiro, RJ], c1989.
147 p. : ISBN 85-7083-026-2 NYPL [MFX+
(Stewart-Granger) 91-7436]

**IRON AND STEEL WORKERS - FRANCE -
PICTORIAL WORKS.**
Bonnet, Serge, 1924- Automne, hiver de
l'homme du fer /. [Nancy] [Metz] , c1986. 102
p. : ISBN 2-86480-255-4
HD8039.I52 F823 1986
NYPL [MFW+ 89-20431]

**IRON MINERS - FRANCE - PICTORIAL
WORKS.**
Bonnet, Serge, 1924- Automne, hiver de
l'homme du fer /. [Nancy] [Metz] , c1986. 102
p. : ISBN 2-86480-255-4
HD8039.I52 F823 1986
NYPL [MFW+ 89-20431]

IRONWORK - EUROPE - HISTORY.
Zimelli, Umberto. [Ferro battuto. English.]
Decorative ironwork /. [London] , 1987. 154
p. : ISBN 0-304-32158-3 (pbk.) : DDC 739/.474 19
NK8242 NYPL [3-MNK 91-5042]

IRONWORK - EXHIBITIONS.
Made of iron. [Houston, 1966?] 288 p. DDC
739.4
NK8201 .H6 NYPL [3-MNK 90-5660]

**IRONWORK - PRIVATE COLLECTIONS -
BERLIN (GERMANY) - EXHIBITIONS.**
Aus einem Guss . Berlin , c1988. 248 p. :
ISBN 3-87584-203-0 DDC
730/.0943/074431554 20
NK8250.A3 P784 1988
NYPL [3-MNK 91-3716]

**IRONWORK - PRUSSIA (GERMANY) -
HISTORY - 19TH CENTURY -
EXHIBITIONS.**
Aus einem Guss . Berlin , c1988. 248 p. :
ISBN 3-87584-203-0 DDC
730/.0943/074431554 20
NK8250.A3 P784 1988
NYPL [3-MNK 91-3716]

IROQUOIS COUNTY, ILL. - MAPS.
(1990) Rockford Map Publishers. Iroquois
County, Illinois, land atlas & plat book .
Rockford, Ill. [c1990] 1 atlas (69 p.) :
NYPL [Map Div. 90-12846]

**Iroquois County, Illinois, land atlas & plat
book** . Rockford Map Publishers. Rockford, Ill.
[c1990] 1 atlas (69 p.) :
NYPL [Map Div. 90-12846]

Irvin, Albert, 1922-
Albert Irvin : paintings 1960-1989. Edinburgh :
Talbot Rice Art Gallery ; London : Serpentine
Gallery, [1989] 64 p. : ill. (chiefly col.) ; 22 x
28 cm. Catalog of an exhibition held at the Talbot
Rice Art Gallery, University of Edinburgh, Nov.
17-Dec. 16, 1989, and at 3 other locations through June
16, 1990. Includes bibliographical references (p. 63).
ISBN 1-87081-460-6
1. Irvin, Albert, 1922- - Exhibitions. I. Talbot Rice Art
Center. II. Serpentine Gallery.
NYPL [3-MCV I721 91-5056]

IRVIN, ALBERT, 1922- - EXHIBITIONS.
Irvin, Albert, 1922- Albert Irvin . Edinburgh ,
London [1989] 64 p. : ISBN 1-87081-460-6
NYPL [3-MCV I721 91-5056]

**IRVING, FLORENCE - ART COLLECTIONS -
EXHIBITIONS.**
Metropolitan Museum of Art (New York, N.Y.)
East Asian lacquer . New York , 1991. p. cm.
ISBN 0-87099-622-3 DDC
745.7/26/09510747471 20
NK9900.7.E15 M47 1991

**IRVING, HERBERT - ART COLLECTIONS -
EXHIBITIONS.**
Metropolitan Museum of Art (New York, N.Y.)
East Asian lacquer . New York , 1991. p. cm.
ISBN 0-87099-622-3 DDC
745.7/26/09510747471 20
NK9900.7.E15 M47 1991

Irving Ramsey Wiles, 1861-1948 . Wiles, Irving
Ramsay, 1861-1948. [New York] , c1967. ca.
50 p. : NYPL [3-MCX W669 91-879]

Is no. MacLennan, Alastair, 1943- Alastair
MacLennan . Bristol : Derry : 157 p. : ISBN
0-907738-20-6
NYPL [3-MCV+ M1645 90-12067]

Isaac Simpson's world . Scott, Geraldine Tidd.
Falmouth, Me. , c1990. xxiii, 183 p. : ISBN
0-933858-09-4 DDC 779/.99741 20
TR652 .S36 1990
NYPL [MFX (Simpson) 91-4040]

Isaacs, Charles. The Strange and the sublime .
Bethlehem, Pa. , c1989. 32 p. :
NYPL [MFW 91-3497]

Isaacs, Reginald R., 1911- Gropius : an illustrated
biography of the creator of the Bauhaus / by
Reginald Isaacs.1st English-language ed.
Boston : Little, Brown, c1991. xix, 344 p. : ill. ;
29 cm. "A Bulfinch Press book." Includes
bibliographical references (p. 333) and index. ISBN
0-8212-1753-4 : DDC 720/.92 B 20
1. Gropius, Walter, 1883-1969. 2. Architects -
Germany - Biography. I. Title.
NA1088.G85 I79 1991
NYPL [3-MQZ (Gropius) 91-5539]

Isaacson, Philip M., 1924- A short walk around
the Pyramids and through the world of art / by
Philip M. Isaacson ; with photographs by the
author. New York : Knopf, 1992. p. cm.
Introduces tangible and abstract components of art, and
the many forms art can take including sculpture,
pottery, painting, photographs, and even furniture and
cities. ISBN 0-679-81523-6 DDC 700 20
1. Art - Juvenile literature. I. Title.
N7440 .I8 1992

Isabel Bishop, etchings and aquatints . Bishop,
Isabel, 1902- New York, NY (20 W. 57th St.,
New York 10019) , 1985. 60 p. : DDC 769.92/4
19
NE2012.B55 A4 1985
NYPL [MDG (Bishop) 90-12809]

Isabelle Rouault . Rouault, Isabelle. Paris [1984]
[39] p. :
MLCS 86/4499 (N)
NYPL [3-MCO R853 90-721]

Isabelle Rouault. Rouault, Isabelle. [Washington,
D.C. , 1990] ii, 49 p. :
NYPL [3-MCO R853 91-7596]

The Isamu Noguchi Garden Museum /. Noguchi,
Isamu, 1904- New York , 1987. 284 p. : ISBN
0-8109-1374-7 DDC 730/.92/4 19
NB237.N6 A4 1987
NYPL [3-MGO (Noguchi) 90-10783]

**ISAMU NOGUCHI GARDEN MUSEUM -
CATALOGS.**
Noguchi, Isamu, 1904- The Isamu Noguchi
Garden Museum /. New York , 1987. 284 p. :
ISBN 0-8109-1374-7 DDC 730/.92/4 19
NB237.N6 A4 1987
NYPL [3-MGO (Noguchi) 90-10783]

L'Isauro e la foglia : Pesaro e suoi castelli nei
disegni di Romolo Liverani / scritti di Mario
Omicciolo ... [et al.] ; grafica di Dante
Piermattei. Provincia di Pesaro e
Urbino :bAmministrazione Provinciale di Pesaro
e Urbino, 1986. 428 p. : ill. (some col.) ; 24
cm.
1. Liverani, Romolo, 1809-1872. 2. Castles - Italy -
Pesaro. 3. Pesaro (Italy) - Buildings, structures, etc. I.
Liverani, Romolo, 1809-1872. II. Omiccioli, Mario. III.

Title: Pesaro e suoi castelli nei disegni di Romolo Liverani. **NYPL [3-MCF L782 90-10784]**

Iseli, Rolf, 1934-
Rolf Iseli / textes par Erika Billeter ... [et al.].
Bern : Benteli, c1990. 178 p. : ill. ; 29 cm.
French and German. "Musée cantonal des beaux-arts,
Lausanne, 23 novembre 1990-13 janvier 1991"--T.p.
verso.
*1. Iseli, Rolf, 1934- - Exhibitions. I. Billeter, Erika,
1927-. II. Musée cantonal des beaux-arts Lausanne. III.
Title.* **NYPL [3-MCZ I78 91-6919]**

ISELI, ROLF, 1934- - EXHIBITIONS.
Iseli, Rolf, 1934- Rolf Iseli /. Bern , c1990. 178
p. : **NYPL [3-MCZ I78 91-6919]**

**İSHAN (TURKEY) - BUILDINGS,
STRUCTURES, ETC.**
Kadiroğlu, Mine, 1944- The architecture of the
Georgian Church at İshan /. Frankfurt am
Main , New York , 1991. p. cm. ISBN
3-631-42828-6 DDC 726/.5/095662 20
NA5871.I84 K33 1991

ISIS (EGYPTIAN DEITY) - ART.
Eingartner, Johannes. Isis und ihre Dienerinnen
in der Kunst der römischen Kaiserzeit /.
Leiden , New York , 1991. 197 p., [97] p. of
plates : ISBN 90-04-09312-5 DDC 733/.5 20
NB115 .E37 1990

**Isis und ihre Dienerinnen in der Kunst der
römischen Kaiserzeit /.** Eingartner, Johannes.
Leiden , New York , 1991. 197 p., [97] p. of
plates : ISBN 90-04-09312-5 DDC 733/.5 20
NB115 .E37 1990

**Iskusstvo i massy v sovremennom burzhuaznom
obshchestve /** redaktor-sostavitel′ D.V.
Zhitomirskiĭ. Izd. 2., dop. Moskva : "Sov.
kompozitor", 1989. 319 p. ; 20 cm. On verso t.p.:
Vsesoi͡uznyĭ nauchno-issledovatel′skiĭ institut
iskusstvoznaniia͡ Ministerstva kul′tury SSSR. Includes
bibliographical references and index. ISBN
5-85285-074-8 :
*1. Art, Modern - 20th century. 2. Popular culture. I.
Zhitomirskiĭ, D. (Daniėl). II. Vsesoi͡uznyĭ
nauchno-issledovatel′skiĭ institut iskusstvoznaniia͡.*
NX458 .I84 1989

Iskusstvo, rozhdennoe Oktia͡brem : o tvorchestve
narodnogo khudozhnika Tatarii B. Urmanche /
[redaktsionnaia͡ kollegiia͡ D.K. Valeeva
(otvetstvennyĭ redaktor i sostavitel′), F.V.
Akhmetova, R.G. Shageeva]. Kazan :
Akademiia͡ nauk SSSR, Kazanskiĭ filial, In-t
ia͡zyka, lit-ry i istorii im. G. Ibragimova, 1989.
119 p. ; 21 cm. Includes bibliographical references
(p. 113-117).
*1. Urmanche, Baki Idrisovich - Criticism and
interpretation. I. Valeeva, D. K. II. Akhmetova, F. V.
III. Shageeva, R. G. IV. Institut ia͡zyka, literatury i
istorii im. G. Ibragimova.*
N6999.U76 I8 1989

**Iskusstvo v khudozhestvennoĭ zhizni
sotsialisticheskogo obshchestva /** otvetstvennyĭ
redaktor V.N. Dmitrievskiĭ ; [avtory, L.K.
Bubennikova ... et al.]. Moskva : "Nauka", 1990.
173 p. ; 22 cm. "Nauchnoe izdanie"--Colophon. At
head of title: Akademiia͡ nauk SSSR. Vsesoi͡uznyĭ
nauchno-issledovatel′skiĭ institut iskusstvoznaniia͡
Ministerstva kul′tury SSSR. Includes bibliographical
references. ISBN 5-02-012744-2 :
*I. Dmitrievskiĭ, Vitaliĭ Nikolaevich. II. Bubennikova, L.
K. III. Vsesoi͡uznyĭ nauchno-issledovatel′skiĭ institut
iskusstvoznaniia͡.*
NX556.A1 I85 1990

Isla Estrada, Juan Antonio. Querétaro, ciudad
barroca /. Querétaro, Qro. [Mexico] , c1988.
228, [8] p. : ISBN 968-614-033-6 DDC
709/.72/45 20
N6557.Q47 Q47 1988

Islam and Muslim art /. Papadopoulo, Alexandre.
[Islam et l'art musulman. English.] New York ,
1979, c1976. 631 p. : ISBN 0-8109-0641-4 :
DDC 709/.1/7671
N6260 .P3613 1979 **NYPL [MAF+ 80-470]**

**ISLAMIC ARCHITECTURE. see
ARCHITECTURE, ISLAMIC.**

Islamic art /. Brend, Barbara, 1940- Cambridge,
Mass. , 1991. p. cm. ISBN 0-674-46865-1: DDC
709/.17/671 20
N6250 B76 1991

Islamic art . World Seminar on "Common
Principles, Forms and Themes of Islamic Art"

(1983 : Istanbul, Turkey) Damascus , 1989.
289, 165 p. : ISBN 92-9063-354-9
NYPL [3-MAF 91-3423]

ISLAMIC ART. see ART, ISLAMIC.

Islamic art & patronage : treasures from Kuwait
/ edited by Esin Atıl. New York : Rizzoli,
c1990. 313 p. : ill. (some col.), map ; 31 cm.
"Published on the occasion of the exhibition Islamic Art
and Patronage: Treasures from Kuwait, a loan exhibition
from the al-Sabah Collection, Kuwait, organized by the
Trust for Museums Exhibitions, Washington, D.C."--T.p.
verso. Includes bibliographical references (p. 309-310)
and index. ISBN 0-8478-1366-5 DDC
709/.17/67107473 20
*1. Sabah, Nasir - Art collections - Exhibitions. 2. Sabah,
Hussah - Art collections - Exhibitions. 3. Art, Islamic -
Exhibitions. 4. Art - Private collections - Kuwait -
Exhibitions. I. Atıl, Esin. II. Trust for Museum
Exhibitions. III. Title: Islamic art and patronage.*
N6263.W3 A785 1990
NYPL [3-MAF+ 91-5747]

Islamic art and patronage. Islamic art &
patronage . New York , c1990. 313 p. : ISBN
0-8478-1366-5 DDC 709/.17/67107473 20
N6263.W3 A785 1991
NYPL [3-MAF+ 91-5747]

ISLAMIC ART AND SYMBOLISM.
Bloom, Jonathan (Jonathan M.) Minaret,
symbol of Islam /. Oxford [England] , c1989.
216 p. : ISBN 0-19-728013-7 DDC 726/.2 20
NA4670 .B55 1989
NYPL [3-MQT 90-12010]

Islamic art in the Keir collection / B.W.
Robinson ... [et al.] ; edited by B.W. Robinson ;
with a foreword by Basil Gray. London ;
Boston : Faber and Faber, 1988. xviii, 316 p.,
[60] p. of plates : ill. (some col.) ; 29 cm. At
head of title: The Keir collection. Includes
bibliographical references and index. ISBN
0-571-13753-9 DDC 745/.0917/67107442176 20
*1. Decorative arts, Islamic - Catalogs. 2. Illumination of
books and manuscripts, Islamic - Catalogs. I. Robinson,
B. W. (Basil William).*
NK720 .I84 1988 **NYPL [3-MAF 91-3908]**

**ISLAMIC CITIES AND TOWNS. see CITIES
AND TOWNS, ISLAMIC.**

**ISLAMIC COUNTRIES - HISTORICAL
GEOGRAPHY - MAPS.**
Majīd, 'Abd al-Mun'im. al-Aṭlas al-tārīkhī
lil-'ālam al-Islāmī fī al-'uṣūr al-Wusṭá.
[al-Qāhirah] 1967. 13, 36p.
G1786.S1 M3 1967
NYPL [Map-Div. 85-3121]

**ISLAMIC DECORATION AND ORNAMENT.
see DECORATION AND ORNAMENT,
ISLAMIC.**

**ISLAMIC POTTERY. see POTTERY,
ISLAMIC.**

**ISLAMIC SYMBOLISM. see ISLAMIC ART
AND SYMBOLISM.**

ISLAMIC WOMEN. see WOMEN, MUSLIM.

Islamische Kunst /. Enderlein, Volkmar.
Dresden , 1990. 324 p. : ISBN 3-364-00195-2
DDC 709/.17/671 20
N6260 .E64 1990

Islammagomedov, A. I. Drevnia͡ia͡ i
srednevekovaia͡ arkhitektura Dagestana .
Makhachkala , 1989. 184, [4] p. :
NA1492.8 .D7 1989

**ISLANDS OF THE AEGEAN -
ANTIQUITIES - EXHIBITIONS.**
New York (City). Metropolitan Museum of Art.
Greek art of the Aegean Islands . New York ,
c1979. 238 p. : ISBN 0-87099-216-3
N5640 .N48 1979 **NYPL [MAH 80-2168]**

**ISLANDS OF THE PACIFIC - HANDBOOKS,
MANUALS, ETC.**
Motteler, Lee S. Pacific Island names .
Honolulu , 1986. 91 p. : ISBN 0-930897-12-9
(pbk.) DDC 912/.9 19
DU18 .M68 1986 **NYPL [Map Div. 88-67]**

ISLANDS OF THE PACIFIC - MAPS.
(1986) Motteler, Lee S. Pacific Island names .
Honolulu , 1986. 91 p. : ISBN 0-930897-12-9
(pbk.) DDC 912/.9 19
DU18 .M68 1986 **NYPL [Map Div. 88-67]**

**ISLANDS - PACIFIC OCEAN. see ISLANDS
OF THE PACIFIC.**

Íslenzk list.
Jóhannes Sveinsson Kjarval, 1885-1972.
Jóhannes Sveinsson Kjarval /. Reykjavík , 1950.
99 p. : DDC 759.94912 20
ND753.K43 A4 1950

Ismaël de la Serna, silent builder-- /. Barotte,
René. [New York, N.Y. , 196-?] 31 p. :
NYPL [3-MCQ L111 90-6381]

Isolated incidents /. Mahr, Mari. London ,
c1989. [8] p., [27] p. of plates : ISBN
0-907879-21-7
NYPL [MFX+ (Mahr) 89-21465]

Isozaki, Arata.
Arata Isozaki . Los Angeles , New York , 1991.
304 p. : ISBN 0-8478-1318-5 DDC 720/.92 20
NA1559.I79 A4 1991
NYPL [3-MQZ (Isozaki) 91-7248]

ISOZAKI, ARATA - EXHIBITIONS.
Arata Isozaki . Los Angeles , New York , 1991.
304 p. : ISBN 0-8478-1318-5 DDC 720/.92 20
NA1559.I79 A4 1991
NYPL [3-MQZ (Isozaki) 91-7248]

Israel. Agaf ha-medidot. Karṭa (Firm) Atlas of
Israel . Tel-Aviv ; New York : [168] 80 p. :
ISBN 0-02-905950-X : DDC 912/.5694 19
G2235 .K3 1985
NYPL [*P-*PXLB++ 86-3877]

Israel builds. [Jerusalem : Ministry of Housing,
State of Israel, 1964] 1 v. (unpaged) : ill.,
plans ; 27 cm. Cover title.
*1. Homesites - Israel. 2. City planning - Israel -
History - 20th century. I. Israel. Misrad ha-shikun.*
NA9051 .I77 1964

Israel builds. Israel. Misrad ha-shikun. Agaf
le-tikhnun fisi. [Tel Aviv, 1967?] [96] p. DDC
720/.95694
NA7419.I8 A54

**Israel. Housing, Ministry of. see Israel. Misrad
ha-shikun.**

ISRAEL - MAPS.
(1985) Karṭa (Firm) Atlas of Israel . Tel-Aviv ;
New York : [168] 80 p. : ISBN 0-02-905950-X :
DDC 912/.5694 19
G2235 .K3 1985
NYPL [*P-*PXLB++ 86-3877]

ISRAEL, MARGARET, 1929-1987.
Slivka, Rose. Margaret Ponce Israel . N.Y.,
N.Y. , c1990. 18 p. :
NYPL [3-MGO (Israel) 91-7038]

**Israel. Ministry of Housing. see Israel. Misrad
ha-shikun.**

Israel. Misrad ha-shikun.
Israel builds. [Jerusalem , 1964] 1 v.
(unpaged) :
NA9051 .I77 1964

Israel. Misrad ha-shikun. Agaf le-tikhnun fisi.
Israel builds; new trends in planning of housing.
[Tel Aviv, Ministry of Housing, Division of
Physical Planning, 1967?] [96] p. illus., plans.
27 cm. Cover title. CONTENTS. - New towns and
housing, 1948-1967, by S. Shaked. -- From the dwelling
unit to the regional unit, by H. Mertens. -- Projects, by
Y. Drexler. DDC 720/.95694
*1. Architecture, Domestic - Israel. 2. Architecture,
Domestic - Designs and plans. I. Title.*
NA7419.I8 A54

**Israel. Misrad ha-shikun. Division of Physical
Planning. see Israel. Misrad ha-shikun. Agaf
le-tikhnun fisi.**

Israel motor atlas. Karṭa (Firm) Carta's Israel
motor atlas =. Jerusalem , c1980. 1 atlas (73
[i.e. 78] p.) : ISBN 965-220-011-5 DDC
912/.5694 19
G2236.P2 K3 1980
NYPL [Map Div. 90-9721]

ISRAEL - ROAD MAPS.
(1980) Karṭa (Firm) Carta's Israel motor atlas
=. Jerusalem , c1980. 1 atlas (73 [i.e. 78] p.) :
ISBN 965-220-011-5 DDC 912/.5694 19
G2236.P2 K3 1980
NYPL [Map Div. 90-9721]

Israel (State) see Israel.

**ISRAELI PAINTING. see PAINTING,
ISRAELI.**

ISRAELITES. see JEWS.

Issa, Ahmed Mohammed. World Seminar on
"Common Principles, Forms and Themes of

Islamic Art" (1983 : Istanbul, Turkey) Islamic art . Damascus , 1989. 289, 165 p. : ISBN 92-9063-354-9   *NYPL [3-MAF 91-3423]*

Issari, Mohammad Ali. Cinema in Iran, 1900-1979 / by M. Ali Issari. Metuchen, N.J. : Scarecrow Press, 1989. ix, 446 : ill. ; 22 cm. Filmography: p. 264-337. Includes bibliographical references (p. 251-255) and index. ISBN 0-8108-2142-7 DDC 791.43/0955 19
1. Motion pictures - Iran - History. I. Title.
PN1993.5.I846 I87 1989
                      NYPL [MLF 90-12713]

Issermann, Dominique. Anne Rohart / von Dominique Issermann. München : Schirmer/Mosel, c1987. [1] p., 29 leaves of plates : ill. ; 35 cm. ISBN 3-88814-215-6
I. Title.   *NYPL [MFX+ (Issermann) 91-7940]*

Issues & debates.
Art in history/history in art . Santa Monica, CA [Chicago, Ill.] , 1991. p. cm. ISBN 0-89236-201-4 :   DDC 701/.03/0949209032 20
N72.S6 A746 1991

Issues in abstract expressionism . Gibson, Ann Eden, 1944- Ann Arbor, Mich. , c1990. xvi, 430 p. : ISBN 0-8357-1944-8 (alk. paper) DDC 709.747/1/09044 20
N6535.N5 G53 1989
                      NYPL [3-MAMT 90-11594]

ISTANBUL (TURKEY) - BUILDINGS, STRUCTURES, ETC.
Cantay, Tanju. XVI.-XVII. yüzyıllarda Süleymaniye Camii ve bağlı yapıları /. Beyoğlu, İstanbul , 1989. 56, 32 p., [2] leaves of plates : ISBN 975-7622-05-2
NA5870.S93 C36 1989

Eyice, Semavi. Fotoğraflarla Fatih anıtları /. Fatih [Istanbul, Turkey] [1989?] 126 p. :
NA1370 .E88 1989

Necipoğlu, Gülru. Architecture, ceremonial, and power . New York, N.Y. , Cambridge, Mass. , 1991. p. cm. ISBN 0-262-14050-0 DDC 725/.17/0949618 20
NA1370 .N43 1991

Istituto di corrispondenza archeologica. see Deutsches Archäologisches Institut.

Istituto di storia dell'arte (Fondazione "Giorgio Cini") Bellotto, Bernardo, 1721-1780. Bernardo Bellotto . Milano , c1990. 172 p. : ISBN 88-435-3242-1
ND623.B43 A4 1990

Istituto di studi etruschi e italici. Pellegrini, Enrico. La Necropoli di Poggio Buco . Firenze , 1989. 154 p., lxxxvii p. of plates : ISBN 88-22-23683-1
                      NYPL [3-MPEK+ 91-3375]

Monumenti etruschi. see Monumenti etruschi.

Istituto geografico De Agostini. William Collins Sons and Co. Collins road atlas Italy /. Glasgow , 1990, c1989. 1 atlas (128 p.) :
                      NYPL [Map Div. 91-2596]

Istituto nazionale per la grafica (Italy) Ruggieri, Ugo. Disegni veneti e lombardi dal XVI al XVIII secolo dalle collezioni del Gabinetto dei disegni e delle stampe /. Roma , 1989. 226 p. : ISBN 88-7597-101-3
                      NYPL [3-MBH 90-12366]

Istituto statale d'arte per il mosaico "Gino Severini" (Ravenna, Italy) Seminario di studi "Metodologia e prassi della conservazione musiva" (2nd : 1986 : Ravenna, Italy) Metodologia e prassi della conservazione musiva. Volume secondo . Ravenna , c1989. 109 p. :   *NYPL [3-MRXZ 91-6525]*

Istituto universitario di magistero "Suor Orsola Benincasa". Cassiano dal Pozzo . Roma , c1989. 260 p. :   *NYPL [3-MAVC 90-12003]*

Istoki iskusstva Udmurtii : sbornik nauchnykh trudov / [redaktsionnaiā kollegiiā M.G. Atamanov ... V.V. Lozhkin (otvetstvennyĭ redaktor) ... et al.]. Izhevsk : Ural'skoe otd-nie Akademii nauk SSSR, Udmurtskiĭ in-t istorii, iāzyka i lit-ry, 1989. 116 p., [8] p. of plates : ill. ; 21 cm. Includes bibliographical references.
1. Arts, Udmurt - Sources. I. Atamanov, M. G. II. Lozhkin, V. V. (Veniamin Vasil'evich). III. Udmurtskiĭ institut istorii, iāzyka i literatury.
NX556.A3 U3538 1989

Istoriā arkhitektury : ob"ekt, predmet i metod issledovaniiā : sbornik nauchnykh trudov / pod

obshcheĭ redaktsieĭ A.A. Voronova. Moskva : TSNIIP gradostroitel'stva, 1988. 114 p. ; 22 cm. At head of title: Gosudarstvennyĭ komitet po arkhitekture i gradostroitel'stvu pri Gosstroe SSSR. TSentral'nyĭ nauchno-issledovatel'skiĭ i proektnyĭ institut po gradostroitel'stvu Goskomarkhitektury. Errata slip inserted. Includes bibliographical references.
1. Architecture - History. I. Voronov, A. A., kand. arkhit. II. TSentral'nyĭ nauchno-issledovatel'skiĭ i proektnyĭ institut po gradostroitel'stvu Goskomarkhitektury (Soviet Union).
NA200 .I88 1988

István Tar (1910-1971) retrospective. Tar, István. Tar István (1910-1971) bemlékkiállítása . Budapest , 1972. [96] p. :
                      NYPL [3-MGO (Tar) 90-6462]

It is an irrevocable action. Fisher, Joel. Ein unwiderruflicher Schritt =. [s.l. , 1975?] (Mönchengladbach : H. Schlechtriem) 48 p. :
N6537.F48 A58
                      NYPL [3-MCX F532 81-643]

ITALIAN AMERICAN WOMEN.
Italian-American women artists . [San Francisco, Calif. , 1979] [19] p. :
                      NYPL [3-MAMT 90-12524]

Italian-American women artists : first annual show : painting, sculpture, prints : [exhibition] June 6-September 16, Museo Italo Americano, San Francisco, CA. [San Francisco, Calif. : The Museum, 1979] [19] p. : ill. ; 22 cm.
1. Art, American - Exhibitions. 2. Art, Modern - 20th century - United States - Exhibitions. 3. Women artists - United States - Exhibitions. 4. Italian American women. I. Museo Italo Americano (San Francisco, Calif.).   *NYPL [3-MAMT 90-12524]*

ITALIAN ART. see ART, ITALIAN.

Italian art and the southern European tradition / [editor, Andreas C. Papadakis]. London : Academy Editions ; New York : St. Martin's Press, 1989. 80 p. : ill. (chiefly col.) ; 28 cm. (Art & design profile . 13) Cover title: Italian art now : the southern European tradition : Chia, Clemente, Cucchi, Paladino. "Art & Design Profile 13 is published as part of Art & Design, Vol. 5 1/2-1989"--T.p. verso.
ISBN 0-312-03123-8 (pbk.).
1. Art, Modern - 20th century - Italy. I. Papadakēs, A. II. Title: Italian art now. III. Series.
                      NYPL [3-MAMC 91-6693]

Italian art now. Italian art and the southern European tradition /. London , New York , 1989. 80 p. : ISBN 0-312-03123-8 (pbk.)
                      NYPL [3-MAMC 91-6693]

ITALIAN ARTS. see ARTS, ITALIAN.

ITALIAN DRAWING. see DRAWING, ITALIAN.

Italian fifteenth- to seventeenth-century drawings /. Forlani Tempesti, Anna. New York , Princeton , 1991. p. cm. ISBN 0-87099-606-1 DDC 741.945/074/7471 20
NC255 .F6 1991

The Italian furniture / coordinated by Fumio Shimizu, David Palterer. Tokyo, Japan : Graphic-sha Pub. Co., c1991. 273 p. : ill. ; 31 cm. English and Japanese. ISBN 4-7661-0609-1
1. Furniture - Italy - History - 20th century. 2. Furniture designers - Italy - Biography. I. Shimizu, Fumio, 1950-. II. Palterer, David.
                      NYPL [3-MOF+ 91-5637]

Italian old master drawings from the collection of Jeffrey E. Horvitz /. Wolk-Simon, Linda, 1958- Gainesville, Fla. , 1991. v, 175 p. : ISBN 0-9629384-0-8 (alk. paper) DDC 741.945/074/73 20
NC255 .W6 1991

ITALIAN PAINTING. see PAINTING, ITALIAN.

Italian painting before 1400 : National Gallery, London, 29 November 1989-28 February 1990 / David Bomford ... [et al.] ; with contributions from Jo Kirby. [London] : National Gallery Publications, c1989 x, 225 p. : ill. (some col.) ; 28 cm. (Art in the making) Includes bibliographical references (p. 211-221) and index. ISBN 0-947645-67-5 DDC 759.5/09/02207442132 20
1. Panel painting, Italian - Exhibitions. 2. Panel painting, Medieval - Italy - Exhibitions. 3. National Gallery (Great Britain) - Exhibitions. I. Bomford, David. II. National Gallery (Great Britain). III. Series.
ND613 .I87 1989

Italian painting before 1400 : National Gallery,

London, 29 November 1989-28 February 1990 / David Bomford ... [et al.] ; with contributions from Jo Kirby. London : The Gallery, c1989. x, 225 p. : ill. (some col.) ; 27 cm. (Art in the making) All paintings are in collection of the National Gallery, London. Includes index. Includes bibliographical references (p. 210-221). ISBN 0-947645-67-5 (pbk) DDC 759.5 19
1. National Gallery (Great Britain) - Exhibitions. 2. Painting, Italian - Conservation and restoration - Exhibitions. 3. Painting, Medieval - Italy - Conservation and restoration - Exhibitions. 4. Painting, Medieval - Italy - Exhibitions. 5. Artists' materials - Exhibitions. I. Bomford, David. II. Kirby, Jo. III. National Gallery (Great Britain). IV. Series.
                      NYPL [3-MCE 91-3327]

ITALIAN POSTERS. see POSTERS, ITALIAN.

ITALIAN POTTERY. see POTTERY, ITALIAN.

The Italian presence in American art, 1860-1920 / edited by Irma B. Jaffe. New York : Fordham University Press ; Roma : Istituto della enciclopedia italiana, 1991. p. cm. Includes bibliographical references. ISBN 0-8232-1342-0 : DDC 709/.73/09034 20
1. Art, American - Italian influences. 2. Art, Modern - 19th century - United States. 3. Art, Modern - 20th century - United States. I. Jaffe, Irma B.
N6510 .I8 1991

ITALIAN QUESTION, 1849-1870. see ITALY - HISTORY - 1849-1870.

The Italian Renaissance frames /. Newbery, Timothy J. New York , c1990. 111 p. : ISBN 0-87099-587-1 DDC 749/.7/09450747471 20
NK9752.A1 N49 1990
                      NYPL [3-MNE 90-11624]

The Italian Renaissance interior, 1400-1600 /. Thornton, Peter, 1926- New York , 1991. p. cm. ISBN 0-8109-3459-0 DDC 747.25/09/024 20
NK959 .T47 1991

Italian Renaissance maiolica from Southern collections /. Ladis, Andrew, 1949- [Athens] , c1989. 118 p. : ISBN 0-915977-03-6 : DDC 738.3/0945/07475 20
NK4315 .L3 1989
                      NYPL [3-MPGD 91-4567]

ITALIAN SCULPTURE. see SCULPTURE, ITALIAN.

ITALIAN STILL-LIFE PAINTING. see STILL-LIFE PAINTING, ITALIAN.

Italian Tile Center. Tunick, Susan. Ceramic ornament in the New York subway system /. New York, N.Y. , Italy [1989?] [14] p. :
                      NYPL [3-MRXZ+ 90-10715]

Italian Touring Club. see Touring club italiano.

Italian tradition in American art. Hollander, John. Landscape painting, 1960-1990 . Charleston, S.C. , 1990. 70 p. :
                      NYPL [3-MCW 91-4635]

ITALIAN WIT AND HUMOR, PICTORIAL.
Chiappori, Alfredo, 1943- Storie d'Italia . Milano , 1978. 174 p. : DDC 945.081/02/07
DG552 .C47
                      NYPL [3-MEM (Chiappori) 90-4348]

Italia's Cup (3rd : 1989 : Milan, Italy) La Coppia =. Milano , c1989. 205 p. : DDC 745.4/442 20
NK1390 .C66 1989
                      NYPL [3-MNF 90-11125]

Italienische Architektur /. Hetzer, Theodor, 1890-1946. Stuttgart , c1990. 472 p. : ISBN 3-87838-905-1 DDC 720/.945/09024 20
NA1115 .H48 1990

Italienische Druckgraphik der Gegenwart . Albrecht-Dürer-Gesellschaft. Nürnberg [1976] [129] p. :
NE659 .A5 1976   *NYPL [MDBF 80-380]*

Italienische Renaissancekunst im Kaiser Wilhelm Museum Krefeld /. Kaiser Wilhelm Museum Krefeld. [Krefeld] , 1987. 154, [2] p. : ISBN 3-926530-30-8
                      NYPL [3-MAVZ (Krefeld) 90-12394]

Italienische Skulpturen . Schlegel, Ursula. Berlin , c1989. 27 p., [52] p. of plates : ISBN 3-7861-1579-6   *NYPL [3-MGI 90-12655]*

Italy. Hürlimann, Martin, 1897- London [1953] xiii, 248 p.   *NYPL [3-MQWB+ 90-11464]*

ITALY - ANTIQUITIES.
Carta archeologica del Veneto /. Modena
[1988]- 4 v. : *NYPL [Map Div. 90-2171]*

Cichorius, Conrad, 1863- Trajan's Column .
Gloucester, UK , Wolfboro, N.H., USA , 1988.
xviii, 339 p. [94] p. of plates : ISBN
0-86299-467-5 : DDC 937/.07 19
DG59.D3 C63 1988
NYPL [3-MGH 91-6949]

Portogruaro: Museo nazionale concordiese.
[Bologna, 1973, c1971] 113 p.
N2510.P66 *NYPL [3-MAVZ (Portogruaro, Italy) 90-6420]*

ITALY - ANTIQUITIES - CATALOGS.
Le Ciste prenestine /. [Roma] , 1979- v. :
DG70.P33 C57 1979
NYPL [3-MGR+ 83-2202]

Corpus speculorum Etruscorum. France. Roma ,
c1988- v. : ISBN 88-7062-645-8
NYPL [3-MAE+ 89-23865]

ITALY - ANTIQUITIES - EXHIBITIONS.
Cateni, Gabriele. Die Etrusker--Volterra .
Solingen , 1986. 90 p. :
NYPL [3-MAE 90-12646]

Civiche raccolte numismatiche di Milano. Gli
Etruschi e Cerveteri . Milano , c1980. 267 p. :
DDC 937/.5 19
DG70.C12 E88 1980
NYPL [3-MPEK 89-13643]

Italy - Archaeology. see Italy - Antiquities.

Italy - Archives. see Archives - Italy.

Italy. Centro di studio per l'archeologia etrusco-
italica. see Centro di studio per l'archeologia
etrusco-italica.

ITALY - CIVILIZATION - 1945-
Neorealismo e fotografia . Udine , 1987. 186
p. : ISBN 88-85893-01-5
NYPL [MFW+ 91-4966]

**ITALY - COLONIES - HISTORY -
PICTORIAL WORKS.**
Colonialismo e fotografia . Messina [1989?]
354 p. :
IN PROCESS (ONLINE)
NYPL [MFW 91-8015]

Italy. Consiglio nazionale delle ricerche. Centro
di studio per l'archeologia etrusco-italica. see
Centro di studio per l'archeologia etrusco-
italica.

**ITALY - DESCRIPTION AND TRAVEL - 1801-
1860.**
Galassi, Peter. Corot in Italy . New Haven,
Conn. , c1991. viii, 258 p. : ISBN 0-300-04957-9
DDC 759.4 20
ND553.C8 G245 1991
NYPL [3-MCO+ C82 91-7307]

**ITALY - DESCRIPTION AND TRAVEL - 1975-
- VIEWS.**
A Day in the life of Italy . San Francisco,
Calif. , 1990. 220 p. : ISBN 0-00-215729-2 :
DDC 945/.0022/2 20
DG420 .D35 1990 *NYPL [MFW+ 91-3408]*

**ITALY - DESCRIPTION AND TRAVEL -
VIEWS.**
Hürlimann, Martin, 1897- Italy. London [1953]
xiii, 248 p. *NYPL [3-MQWB+ 90-11464]*

Snelson, Kenneth, 1927- Full circle . New
York, N.Y. , 1990. 95 p. : ISBN 0-89381-438-5
NYPL [MFX (Snelson) 91-3355]

Italy fifties. Roth, Sanford, 1906-1962. Italy
'50s . San Francisco, St. Paul, Minn. , 1990.
xii, 138 p. : ISBN 0-916515-72-9 : DDC 779/.092
20
TR654 .R6794 1990
NYPL [MFX (ROTH) 91-3432]

Italy - Government. see Italy - Politics and
government.

**ITALY - HISTORY - 1849-1870 -
CARICATURES AND CARTOONS.**
Chiappori, Alfredo, 1943- Storie d'Italia .
Milano , 1978. 174 p. : DDC 945.081/02/07
DG552 .C47
NYPL [3-MEM (Chiappori) 90-4348]

ITALY IN ART.
Galassi, Peter. Corot in Italy . New Haven,
Conn. , c1991. viii, 258 p. : ISBN 0-300-04957-9

DDC 759.4 20
ND553.C8 G245 1991
NYPL [3-MCO+ C82 91-7307]

ITALY - MAPS.
(1990) William Collins Sons and Co. Collins
road atlas Italy /. Glasgow , 1990, c1989. 1
atlas (128 p.) : *NYPL [Map Div. 91-2596]*

ITALY - MAPS - TO 1800.
Ventura, António. Gli stati italiani di Piri
Re'is . [Cavallino] [1991?] 1 atlas ([15] p., 13
leaves of plates) : *NYPL [Map Div. 91-6616]*

Italy, new tendencies. New York, N.Y. : Galeria
Bonino, [1966] [16] p. : chiefly ill., ports. ; 26
cm. Title from cover. Catalog of an exhibition of works
by Bonalumi, Castellani, Ceroli, Grisi, Scheggi and
Tacchi held Oct. 11-Nov. 5, 1966.
*1. Art, Italian - Exhibitions. 2. Art, Modern - 20th
century - Italy - Exhibitions. I. Galeria Bonino (New
York, N.Y.).* *NYPL [3-MAMC 90-6953]*

**ITALY. PARLAMENTO. CAMERA DEI
DEPUTATI. BIBLIOTECA.**
Santa Maria sopra Minerva /. Roma , c1990.
303 p. : ISBN 88-7060-223-0
NYPL [3-MRBD+ 91-7451]

**ITALY - POLITICS AND GOVERNMENT -
1268-1559.**
Starn, Randolph. Arts of power . Berkeley ,
c1992. p. cm. ISBN 0-520-07383-5 (cloth) DDC
725/.17/0945 20
NA6815 .S787 1992

**ITALY - SOCIAL LIFE AND CUSTOMS -
PICTORIAL WORKS.**
A Day in the life of Italy /. San Francisco,
Calif. , 1990. 220 p. : ISBN 0-00-215729-2 :
DDC 945/.0022/2 20
DG420 .D35 1990 *NYPL [MFW+ 91-3408]*

Italy. Soprintendenza speciale alla Galeria
nazionale d'arte moderna e contemporanea.
Dottori, Gerardo, 1884- Gerardo Dottori,
1884-1977 . Roma , c1979. 71 p. :
MLCM 80/99 *NYPL [3-MCF D725 91-878]*

Italy. Soprintendenza ai beni artistici e storici
per le province di Firenze e Pistoia. Ufficio
restauri. La Compagnia della Santissima
Annunziata . Firenze , c1989. 61 p. : ISBN
88-7038-178-1 *NYPL [3-MLP 90-10711]*

Italy. Soprintendenza archeologica di Roma.
Museo nazionale romano. Museo nazionale
romano. Roma , 1979- v. in : DDC
709/.38/07405632 19
N2934 .A85
NYPL [MAVZ (Rome) 81-1402]

Italy. Soprintendenza archeologica per l'Etruria
meridionale. Un Artista etrusco e il suo
mondo . Roma , 1988. 112 p., [8] p. of plates :
ISBN 88-7813-131-8
NYPL [3-MPEK 90-12767]

Italy. Soprintendenza per i beni AA.AA.AA.SS.
dell'Umbria. Testa, Giusi. La Cattedrale di
Orvieto . [Roma] , c1990. 249, [2] p. : ISBN
88-24-00040-1 DDC 726/.6/0945652 20
NA5621.O426 T4 1990

Italy. Soprintendenza per i beni ambientali,
architettonici, artistici, e storici di Arezzo.
Centauro, Giuseppe. Dipinti murali di Piero
della Francesca . Milano , c1990. 317 p. :
ISBN 88-435-3147-6
NYPL [3-MCF F81 91-7303]

Italy. Soprintendenza per i beni artistici e storici
di Modena e Reggio. Galleria, museo e
medagliere estense (Modena, Italy) La Galleria
estense . Modena [1990] 197 p. : ISBN
88-7686-154-8 :
NYPL [3-MAVZ+ (Modena) 91-4947]

Italy. Soprintendenza per i beni artistici e storici
di Roma. L'Arte per i papi e per i principi
nella campagna romana . Roma , c1990. 2 v. :
ISBN 88-7140-015-1 (v. 1) :
ND1432.I8 A77 1990
NYPL [3-MCE 91-3418]

Italy. Soprintendenza per i beni culturali e
ambientali di Palermo. Pietro Novelli e il suo
ambiente /. Palermo , c1990. 550 p. : ISBN
88-7804-048-7
NYPL [3-MCF N9385 91-3641]

Italy. Soprintendenza speciale alla Galleria
nazionale d'arte moderna e contemporanea.
Il Palazzo del Quirinale . Roma , 1989. 2 v. :
NYPL [3-MQWB+ 90-12794]

ITALY, SOUTHERN - ANTIQUITIES.
Yntema, Douwe Geert. The matt-painted
pottery of Southern Italy . Galatina , 1990. 370
p. : ISBN 88-7786-428-0
NYPL [3-MPGD 91-5545]

Italy, Southern - Archaeology. see Italy,
Southern - Antiquities.

**ITALY, SOUTHERN - DESCRIPTION AND
TRAVEL - VIEWS - EXHIBITIONS.**
Zanotti-Bianco, Umberto. Il sud di Umberto
Zanotti-Bianco . Venezia , c1981. 117 p. :
NYPL [MFX (Zanotti-Bianco) 90-7053]

Italy '50s . Roth, Sanford, 1906-1962. San
Francisco , St. Paul, Minn. , 1990. xii, 138 p. :
ISBN 0-916515-72-9 : DDC 779/.092 20
TR654 .R6794 1990
NYPL [MFX (ROTH) 91-3432]

Itinerari apuani di architettura moderna /.
Giorgieri, Pietro. Firenze , 1989. 263 p. :
NYPL [3-MQWB 90-11118]

Itinerari d'arte e di cultura. Luoghi.
Il Vittoriano . Roma, Italy , c1986. 188 p. :
ISBN 88-7621-298-1 : DDC 725/.94/0945632
20
NA9355.R7 V5 1986
NYPL [3-MQWB 90-13008]

Itinerari d'arte e di cultura. Musei.
Bon, Caterina. Il Collegio del Cambio /. Roma ,
1987. 61 p., [8] p. of plates :
NYPL [3-MAVZ (Perugia) 90-12513]

Itinerari dei musei, gallerie e monumenti
d'Italia .
(n. 23) Franzoi, Umberto. Il Palazzo ducale di
Venezia /. Roma , 1987. 170 p., [24] p. of
plates (2 folded) :
NYPL [3-MQWB 90-10853]

Itinerari di architettura moderna . Suppressa,
Alessandro. Firenze [1990] 335 p. : DDC
720/.945/520904 20
NA1119.T8 S86 1990

Itinerari d'immagini .
(30) Campione, Adele. Il cappello da donna =.
Milano , 1989. 143 p. : ISBN 88-7143-086-7
NYPL [3-MMV 91-7599]

(32) Bordignon Elestici, Letizia. Gli ombrelli
=. Milano , 1990. 143 p. : ISBN 88-7143-093-X
NYPL [3-MMW 91-4277]

Itinerari storico-artistico-naturalistici .
(5) Testimonianze Liberty a Genova /.
Genova , c1986. 46 p. : ISBN 88-7058-218-3
NYPL [3-MAMC 90-11119]

Itò, Toyoo, 1941-
Roulet, Sophie. Toyo Ito, l'architecture de
l'éphémère /. Paris , c1991. 164 p. : ISBN
2-281-15122-0 DDC 720/.92 20
NA1559.I84 R68 1991

**ITŌ, TOYOO, 1941- - CRITICISM AND
INTERPRETATION.**
Roulet, Sophie. Toyo Ito, l'architecture de
l'éphémère /. Paris , c1991. 164 p. : ISBN
2-281-15122-0 DDC 720/.92 20
NA1559.I84 R68 1991

Itoh, Ikutarō. The Radiance of jade and the
clarity of water . Chicago, IL , New York
[1991] p. cm. ISBN 0-86559-096-6 (Art Institute of
Chicago) DDC 738/.09519/07473 20
NK4168.6.A1 R34 1991

It's a cat's life /. Sipress, David. New York,
N.Y., U.S.A. , c1992. p. cm. ISBN
0-453-26758-7 DDC 741.5/973 20
NC1429.S532 A4 1992

Itsell, Mary K. United States. Dept. of State.
Treasures of State . New York , 1991. p. cm.
ISBN 0-8109-3911-8 (cloth) DDC
709/.73/074753 20
N6505 .U48 1991

IVAM Centre Julio González.
Arte abstracto, arte concreto . [Valencia?] ,
c1990. 439 p. : ISBN 84-7890-151-5
N6494.A2 A78 1990
Baldessari, John, 1931- Nipor ésas =. [Madrid]
[1989] 92 p. : ISBN 84-7506-254-7 (pbk.)
NYPL [MFX (Baldessari) 89-28407]
Gris, Juan, 1887-1927. Juan Gris . [Valencia,
Spain] [Paris, France] [1990] 150 p. : ISBN
2-85850-595-0
NC287.G76 A4 1990

Hamilton, Richard, 1922- Richard Hamilton .
Hannover [1990] 153 p. :   DDC 708.3/5954 s
709/.2 20
N5070.H3 K4 1990/5 N6797.H3

Ivan Chermayeff . Chermayeff, Ivan. New York ,
1991. 64 p. :   ISBN 0-8109-2476-5
       NYPL [3-MCX++ C517 91-5325]

Ivanhoë Fortier . Fortier, Ivanhoë, 1931-
Montréal , 1980. 22 p. :   ISBN 2-551-03707-7
       NYPL [3-MGO (Fortier) 90-6907]

The Iveagh Bequest, Kenwood /. Bryant, Julius.
[London] , 1990. 84 p. :   ISBN 1-85074-278-2
       NYPL [3-MQWK 90-11057]

**IVEAGH BEQUEST, KENWOOD (LONDON,
ENGLAND)**
Bryant, Julius. The Iveagh Bequest, Kenwood /.
[London] , 1990. 84 p. :   ISBN 1-85074-278-2
       NYPL [3-MQWK 90-11057]

Ivelić, Milan. Intimidades : 20 artistas visuales
chilenos / Milan Ivelić, Luisa Ulibarri ; diseño,
Ignacio Armstrong Cox ; fotografía, Alfredo
Gildemeister Meier ; montaje, Alfredo Rojas
Bouey.1a ed. Santiago, Chile : Editorial La
Puerta Abierta, [1989] 119 p. : ill. (some col.) ;
30 cm. ISBN 956-25-3018-2
1. Art, Chilean. I. Ulibarri, Luisa. II. Title.
IN PROCESS (ONLINE)
       NYPL [3-MAM+ 90-13346]

Ives, Colta Feller. Metropolitan Museum of Art
(New York, N.Y.) French drawings & prints of
the eighteenth century . [New York , 1972]
[19] p., [4] p. of plates :
       NYPL [3-MBH 91-409]

Ivica Propadalo . Bužančić, Vlado. Zagreb , 1990.
151 p. :   ISBN 86-343-0618-6
NC312.Y83 P762 1990

Ivon Hitchens /. Khoroche, Peter. London ,
1990. viii, 277 p. :   ISBN 0-233-98607-3 :   DDC
759.2 20   *NYPL [3-MCV H674 91-5928]*

IVORIES.
Krzyszkowska, O. (Olga) Ivory and related
materials . London , 1990. xv, 109 p., [70] p. of
plates :   ISBN 0-900587-62-8
       NYPL [3-MNW 91-7005]

IVORY.
Krzyszkowska, O. (Olga) Ivory and related
materials . London , 1990. xv, 109 p., [70] p. of
plates :   ISBN 0-900587-62-8
       NYPL [3-MNW 91-7005]

Ivory and related materials . Krzyszkowska, O.
(Olga) London , 1990. xv, 109 p., [70] p. of
plates :   ISBN 0-900587-62-8
       NYPL [3-MNW 91-7005]

IVORY CARVING.
Krzyszkowska, O. (Olga) Ivory and related
materials . London , 1990. xv, 109 p., [70] p. of
plates :   ISBN 0-900587-62-8
       NYPL [3-MNW 91-7005]

**IVORY CARVING - DENMARK - HISTORY -
17TH CENTURY.**
Paulsen, Åshild. Magnus Berg, 1666-1739 .
Oslo , c1989. 348 p. :   ISBN 82-09-10580-9 :
NK5998.B47 P38 1989

**IVORY CARVING - NORWAY - HISTORY -
17TH CENTURY.**
Paulsen, Åshild. Magnus Berg, 1666-1739 .
Oslo , c1989. 348 p. :   ISBN 82-09-10580-9 :
NK5998.B47 P38 1989

Ivory, Lesley Anne.
Christmas cats / Lesley Anne Ivory. New
York : Crown, 1991. p. cm.   ISBN
0-517-58549-9 :   DDC 759.13 20
*1. Ivory, Lesley Anne. 2. Cats in art. 3. Christmas in
art. I. Title.*
ND237.I94 A4 1991

Glorious cats : the paintings of Lesley Anne
Ivory. Miniature ed. New York : Crown, 1992.
p. cm.   ISBN 0-517-58692-4 :   DDC 759.13 20
1. Ivory, Lesley Anne. 2. Cats in art. I. Title.
ND237.I94 A4 1992

IVORY, LESLEY ANNE.
Ivory, Lesley Anne. Christmas cats /. New
York , 1991. p. cm.   ISBN 0-517-58549-9 :   DDC
759.13 20
ND237.I94 A4 1991

Ivory, Lesley Anne. Glorious cats . New York ,
1992. p. cm.   ISBN 0-517-58692-4 :   DDC 759.13

20
ND237.I94 A4 1992

Ivy, Judy Crosby, 1945- Constable and the
critics, 1802-1837 / Judy Crosby Ivy.
Woodbridge, Suffolk ; Rochester, NY, USA :
Boydell in association with the Suffolk Records
Society, 1991. xv, 255 p. : ill. ; 25 cm. Includes
bibliographical references and index.   ISBN
0-85115-293-7 (acid-free paper) :   DDC 759.2 20
*1. Constable, John, 1776-1837 - Criticism and
interpretation. 2. Constable, John, 1776-1837 - Catalogs.
I. Title.*
ND497.C7 I9 1991

Iwaki, Nobuyoshi.
Nobuyoshi Iwaki, private exhibition. [s.l. : s.n.,
1978] (Tokyo : Mainichi Printing Company) 31
p. : chiefly ill. ; 29 cm. Cover title. Catalog of an
exhibition held at Gallery 5610, Oct. 13-22, 1978. Part
of illustrative matter inserted.
*1. Iwaki, Nobuyoshi - Exhibitions. I. Gallery 5610. II.
Title.*
NB1059.I95 A4 1978
       NYPL [3-MGO (Iwaki) 81-791]

IWAKI, NOBUYOSHI - EXHIBITIONS.
Iwaki, Nobuyoshi. Nobuyoshi Iwaki, private
exhibition. [s.l. , 1978] (Tokyo : Mainichi
Printing Company) 31 p. :
NB1059.I95 A4 1978
       NYPL [3-MGO (Iwaki) 81-791]

Izquierdo, María, 1906-
Maria Izquierdo. Mexico : Centro Cultural/Arte
Contemporáneo, 1988. 415 p. : ill. (some col.),
ports. ; 29 cm. Exhibition presented by the Centro
Cultural/Arte Contemporáneo between November 1988
and February 1989. Bibliography: p. 383-405.   ISBN
968-619-110-0
*1. Izquierdo, María, 1906- - Exhibitions. 2. Painting,
Mexican - Exhibitions. I. Centro Cultural/Arte
Contemporáneo (Mexico). II. Title.*
       NYPL [3-MCZ I99 90-12875]

**IZQUIERDO, MARÍA, 1906- -
EXHIBITIONS.**
Izquierdo, María, 1906- Maria Izquierdo.
Mexico , 1988. 415 p. :   ISBN 968-619-110-0
       NYPL [3-MCZ I99 90-12875]

Izzo, Antonia. Elaborati urbanistici . Milano
[1987?] 10 pamphlets in portfolio :
       NYPL [3-MQWB 90-11014]

J.A.D. Ingres 1780-1867 . Ingres,
Jean-Auguste-Dominique, 1780-1867. Wien
[1991] 297 p. :   ISBN 3-900656-14-2
       NYPL [3-MCO+ I55 91-6971]

J. Alden Weir . Cummings, Hildegard. Storrs ,
c1991. p. cm.   ISBN 0-918386-43-8   DDC 759.13
20
ND237.W4 A4 1991

J.B. Kléber architecte, 1784-1793 . Kléber,
Jean-Baptiste, 1753-1800. [Colmar, France ,
1986] 96 p., xii p. of plates :
       NYPL [3-MQZ (Kléber) 91-5546]

J. I. Linazasoro /. Linazasoro, José Ignacio.
Barcelona , c1989. 96 p. :   ISBN 84-252-1388-6
       NYPL [3-MQZ (Linazasoro) 90-11075]

J.J. Henner. Henner, Jean-Jacques, 1829-1905.
Mulhouse [Steinbrunn-le-Haut] [1989-] v. ` <1
> :   ISBN 2-86339-059-7 (v. 1) :   DDC 759.4 20
ND553.H4 A3 1989

J.J. Reilly : a stereoscopic odyssey, 1838-1894 /
edited by Peter E. Palmquist. Yuba City,
Calif. : Community Memorial Museum, 1989.
48 p. : ill. ; 26 cm. "Edition limited to 500
copies"--T.p. verso. Catalog of an exhibition. Includes
bibliographical references.
*1. Reilly, John James, 1838-1894 - Exhibitions. 2.
Photography, Stereoscopic - Exhibitions. 3. Stereoscopic
views - Exhibitions. 4. California - Description and
travel - Views - Exhibitions. I. Palmquist, Peter E. II.
Reilly, John James, 1838-1894. III. Community
Memorial Museum (Yuba City, Calif.).*
       NYPL [MFX (Reilly) 91-3601]

J. J. Tissot . Misfeldt, Willard E. Alexandria,
Va. , 1991. p. cm.   ISBN 0-88397-097-X   DDC
769.92 20
NE650.T56 M57 1991

J. Obiols. Obiols i Palau, Josep, 1894-1967. Josep
Obiols . [Barcelona] [1990?] 231 p. :   ISBN
84-7609-348-9
N7113.O25 A4 1990

J. Paul Getty Museum.
Greek vases in the J. Paul Getty Museum.

Malibu, Calif. , 1983- v. :   ISBN 0-89236-058-5 (v.
1 : pbk.)   DDC 738.3/0938/074019493 19
NK4623.M37 G7 1983
       NYPL [3-MPEK 86-4692]

The J. Paul Getty Museum handbook of the
collections. Rev. ed. Malibu, Calif. : The
Museum, 1991. p. cm.   ISBN 0-89236-189-1
(pbk.) :   DDC 708.194/93 20
*1. J. Paul Getty Museum - Catalogs. 2. Art -
California - Malibu - Catalogs. I. Title.*
N582.M25 A627 1991

Marble . Malibu, Calif. , 1990. 299 p. :   ISBN
0-89236-174-3 :   DDC 733 20
       NYPL [3-MGH 91-6655]

Smith, Graham, 1942- Disciples of light .
Malibu [Calif.] , 1990. 170 p. :   ISBN
0-89236-158-1   DDC 779/.074 20
TR654 .S555 1990   NYPL [MFW 91-3475]

Vincennes and Sèvres porcelain : catalogue of
the collections / Adrian Sassoon. Malibu,
Calif. : J. Paul Getty Museum, 1991. p. cm.
Includes bibliographical references and index.   ISBN
0-89236-173-5 :   DDC 738.2/0944/363 20
*1. Vincennes porcelain - Catalogs. 2. Sèvres porcelain -
Catalogs. 3. Porcelain - California - Malibu - Catalogs.
4. J. Paul Getty Museum - Catalogs. I. Sassoon, Adrian,
1961-. II. Title.*
NK4399.V55 J2 1991

J. PAUL GETTY MUSEUM - CATALOGS.
J. Paul Getty Museum. The J. Paul Getty
Museum handbook of the collections. Malibu,
Calif. , 1991. p. cm.   ISBN 0-89236-189-1 (pbk.) :
DDC 708.194/93 20
N582.M25 A627 1991

J. Paul Getty Museum. Vincennes and Sèvres
porcelain . Malibu, Calif. , 1991. p. cm.
0-89236-173-5 :   DDC 738.2/0944/363 20
NK4399.V55 J2 1991

Smith, Graham, 1942- Disciples of light .
Malibu [Calif.] , 1990. 170 p. :   ISBN
0-89236-158-1   DDC 779/.074 20
TR654 .S63 1990   NYPL [MFW 91-3475]

J. Paul Getty Museum. Dept. of Antiquities.
Marble . Malibu, Calif. , 1990. 299 p. :   ISBN
0-89236-174-3 :   DDC 733 20
NB1210.M3 M28 1990
       NYPL [3-MGH 91-6655]

Small bronze sculpture from the ancient world .
Malibu, Calif. , 1990. 284 p. :   ISBN
0-89236-176-X (paper) :   DDC 730/.093 20
NK7907 .S63 1990   NYPL [3-MGR 91-6336]

**J. Paul Getty Museum. Dept. of Antiquities
Conservation.**
Marble . Malibu, Calif. , 1990. 299 p. :   ISBN
0-89236-174-3 :   DDC 733 20
NB1210.M3 M28 1990
       NYPL [3-MGH 91-6655]

Small bronze sculpture from the ancient world .
Malibu, Calif. , 1990. 284 p. :   ISBN
0-89236-176-X (paper) :   DDC 730/.093 20
NK7907 .S63 1990   NYPL [3-MGR 91-6336]

**The J. Paul Getty Museum handbook of the
collections.** J. Paul Getty Museum. Malibu,
Calif. , 1991. p. cm.   ISBN 0-89236-189-1 (pbk.) :
DDC 708.194/93 20
N582.M25 A627 1991

**The J. Russell Young School of Expression Class
song ; The J. Russell Young School of
Expression Hymn [sound recording].** [New
York] : Columbia Broadcasting System, [194-] 1
sound disc : analog, 78 rpm. ; 12 in. Brief record.
CONTENTS. - Hymn -- Class song.
*1. Humorous songs. I. Young, John Russell, 1882-1967.
II. Title: J. Russell Young School of Expression Hymn.*
NCP 4246

J. Russell Young School of Expression Hymn.
The J. Russell Young School of Expression
Class song ; The J. Russell Young School of
Expression Hymn [sound recording]. [New
York] [194-] 1 sound disc :
NCP 4246

J.S. Sirén, 1889-1961, architect. Sirén, J. S.
(Johan Sigfrid), 1889-1961. J.S. Sirén,
1889-1961, arkkitehti /. Helsinki , 1989. 108
p. :   ISBN 951-9229-58-2   DDC 720/.92 20
NA1455.F53 S5537 1989

J.S. Sirén, 1889-1961, arkkitehti /. Sirén, J. S.
(Johan Sigfrid), 1889-1961. Helsinki , 1989. 108

p. :   ISBN 951-9229-58-2   DDC 720/.92 20
NA1455.F53 S5537 1989

J. Segrelles. Montagud, Bernardo. José Segrelles
Albert . Alzira , 1985. 239 p. :   ISBN
84-398-3281-8
ND813.S388 M65 1985

J. Terruella /. Manzano, Rafael, 1917- Barcelona,
c1989. 110 p. :   ISBN 84-86147-93-X
     NYPL [3-MCQ+ T278 90-11998]

**J. W. Morrice; James Wilson Morrice,
1865-1924.** Morrice, James Wilson, 1865-1924.
[Montreal, 1965] 83 p.
ND249.M6 A48
     NYPL [3-MCZ M87 90-6260]

Jaan Koorti päevaraamat /. Kirme, Kaalu.
Tallinn , 1989. 320 p., [48] p. of plates :
N6999.K588 K5 1989

Jaar, Alfredo.
Alfredo Jaar . Richmond, VA , c1991. p. cm.
   ISBN 0-917046-32-3   DDC 709/.2 20
N6537.J26 A4 1991

JAAR, ALFREDO - EXHIBITIONS.
Alfredo Jaar . Richmond, VA , c1991. p. cm.
   ISBN 0-917046-32-3   DDC 709/.2 20
N6537.J26 A4 1991

Jaca Book (Firm) Pintura boliviana del siglo XX
/. La Paz, Bolivia , 1989. 317 p. :   DDC
759.984/074 20
ND345 .P56 1989

Jacek Malczewski /. Ławniczakowa, Agnieszka.
Warszawa , 1976. 132 p. :
ND955.P63 M337
     NYPL [3-MCZ M243 79-1313]

Jack B. Yeats . Yeats, Jack Butler, 1871-1957.
Bristol : London : 111 p. :   ISBN 0-85488-091-7
(Arnolfini)   DDC 759.2/915 20
ND497.Y42 A4 1991

Jack B. Yeats . Yeats, Jack Butler, 1871-1957.
Bristol : London : 111 p. :   ISBN 0-907738-29-X
(Arnolfini Gallery)
     NYPL [3-MCV Y41 91-6477]

Jack Bush [motion picture] / produced by
Cinema Productions for the National Film
Board of Canada ; producer, Rudy Buttignol ;
director, Murray Battle. New York, NY :
National Film Board of Canada, 1979. 1 film
reel (56 min., 50 sec.) : sd., col. ; 16 mm.
Cataloged from contributor's data. Camera, Mark
Irwin ; editor, Peter Maynard. Senior high school
through college students and adults. Issued also as
videorecording. Presents an introduction to the life and
works of Canadian abstract painter Jack Bush.   DDC
759.971 11
*1. Bush, Jack, 1909-. 2. Painters - Canada - Biography.
3. Painting, Abstract - Canada. I. Cinema Productions
(Firm). II. National Film Board of Canada.*
ND249

Jack Bush [videorecording] / produced by
Cinema Productions for the National Film
Board of Canada ; producer, Rudy Buttignol ;
director, Murray Battle. New York, NY :
National Film Board of Canada, 1979. 1
videocassette (56 min., 50 sec.) : sd., col.
Cataloged from contributor's data. Camera, Mark
Irwin ; editor, Peter Maynard. Senior high school
through college students and adults. Issued as U-matic
3/4 in. or Beta 1/2 in. or VHS 1/2 in. Issued also as
motion picture. Presents an introduction to the life and
works of Canadian abstract painter Jack Bush.   DDC
759.971 11
*1. Bush, Jack, 1909-. 2. Painters - Canada - Biography.
3. Painting, Abstract - Canada. I. Cinema Productions
(Firm). II. National Film Board of Canada.*
ND249

Jack, Kenneth.
Kenneth Jack : World War II paintings and
drawings. Bowen Hills, Brisbane, Qld. :
Boolarong Publications, 1990. 104 p. : ill. ; 27
cm.   ISBN 0-86439-096-3
*1. Jack, Kenneth. 2. World War, 1939-1945 - Art and
the war. I. Title.*   *NYPL [3-MCZ J113 91-4265]*

Klepac, Lou. Kenneth Jack /. Sydney [1988?]
164 p. :   ISBN 1-86256-320-9
     NYPL [3-MCZ + J113 89-17049]

JACK, KENNETH.
Jack, Kenneth. Kenneth Jack . Bowen Hills,
Brisbane, Qld. , 1990. 104 p. :   ISBN
0-86439-096-3
     NYPL [3-MCZ J113 91-4265]

Klepac, Lou. Kenneth Jack /. Sydney [1988?]
164 p. :   ISBN 1-86256-320-9
     NYPL [3-MCZ + J113 89-17049]

Jack Shadbolt /. Watson, Scott. Vancouver ,
c1990. 243 p. :   ISBN 0-88894-613-9 :   DDC
759.11 20
     NYPL [3-MCZ+ S524 91-4468]

Jack Whitten /. Wright, Beryl J. Newark, N.J. ,
1990. 40 p. :   ISBN 0-932828-23-X :   DDC 759.13
20
ND237.W6234 A4 1990

**JACKSON, BILLY MORROW - CRITICISM
AND INTERPRETATION.**
Wooden, Howard E. Billy Morrow Jackson .
Urbana , c1990. 147 p. :   ISBN 0-252-01735-8
(alk. paper)   DDC 760/.092 20
N6537.J29 W6 1990
     NYPL [3-MCX+ J129 91-3992]

Jackson, Cath. Visibly Vera : cartoons / by Cath
Jackson. London : Women's Press, 1986. [62]
p. : chiefly ill. ; 15 x 23 cm.   ISBN 0-7043-4029-1
(pbk.) :   DDC 741.5/942 19
1. English wit and humor, Pictorial. I. Title.
NC1479 NC1479
     NYPL [3-MEM (Jackson) 90-10991]

**Jackson, Christine E. (Christine Elisabeth),
1936-** Bird etchings : the illustrators and their
books, 1655-1855 / Christine E. Jackson.
Ithaca : Cornell University Press, 1985. 292 p.,
[4] leaves of plates : ill. (some col.) ; 27 cm.
Includes indexes. Bibliography: p. 267-279.   ISBN
0-8014-1695-7 (alk paper)   DDC 598/.022/2 19
1. Etching, British. 2. Birds in art. I. Title.
NE2043 .J33 1985   *NYPL [MDZ 85-4087]*

JACKSON COUNTY, ILL. - MAPS.
(1990) Rockford Map Publishers. Jackson
County, Illinois, land atlas & plat book .
Rockford, Ill. , Murphysboro, Ill. , c1990. 1
atlas (37 p.) :   *NYPL [Map Div. 91-4670]*

Jackson County, Illinois, land atlas & plat book .
Rockford Map Publishers. Rockford, Ill. ,
Murphysboro, Ill. , c1990. 1 atlas (37 p.) :
     NYPL [Map Div. 91-4670]

JACKSON COUNTY, WIS. - MAPS.
(1991) Rockford Map Publishers. Jackson
County, Wisconsin, land atlas & plat book .
Rockford, Ill. , c1991. 1 atlas (81 p.) :
     NYPL [Map Div. 91-7461]

**Jackson County, Wisconsin, land atlas & plat
book .** Rockford Map Publishers. Rockford,
Ill. , c1991. 1 atlas (81 p.) :
     NYPL [Map Div. 91-7461]

Jackson, Olga. Architecture/Colorado. George
Thorson, editor. DeVon Carlson, jury
consultant. [Denver, Colorado Chapter of the
American Institute of Architects, c1966] 96 p.
illus., maps. 23 x 10 cm. Cover title: Mountains,
mines & mansions; an architectural guide to Colorado.
*1. Architecture - Colorado. I. American Institute of
Architects. Colorado Chapter. II. Title. III. Title:
Mountains, mines and mansions.*
     NYPL [3-MQWO 91-225]

Jackson Pollock . Cernuschi, Claude, 1961- New
York, NY , c1992. p.   ISBN 0-06-430978-9
(cloth) :   DDC 759.13 20
ND237.P73 C47 1992

Jackson Pollock. Pollock, Jackson, 1912-1956.
New York, 1969. 60 p.   DDC 759.13
N6537.P57 M3

Jackson Pollock . Pollock, Jackson, 1912-1956.
London , c1989. [61] p. :   ISBN 0-947564-26-8
     NYPL [3-MCX P777 90-12889]

Jackson-Stops, Gervase.
The country house in perspective / Gervase
Jackson-Stops ; illustrations by Brian Delf,
Peter Morter, Mel Wright. London : Pavilion,
1990. 160 p. : ill. (some col.), plans ; 32 cm.
Includes index. At head of title: The National Trust.
Bibliography: p. 155.   ISBN 1-85145-383-0 :   DDC
728.8 20
*1. Country homes - England. I. National Trust
(London, England). II. Title.*
NA7620   *NYPL [3-MRGF+ 91-6514]*
The Fashioning and functioning of the British
country house /. Washington, D.C. , Hanover
[N.H.] , 1989. 417 p. :   ISBN 0-89468-128-1
     NYPL [3-MRG 90-12992]

Jacob, John P. The Metamorphic medium .
[Oberlin, Ohio] , c1989. ix, 46 p. :
     NYPL [MFW 90-11187]

Jacob, Julius, 1842-1929.
Der Berliner Maler Julius Jacob : 1842-1929 :
Ausstellung vom 12. Mai bis 29. Juli 1979 /
Berlin Museum ; [Katalog, Irmgard Wirth].
[Berlin] : Berlin-Museum, [1979] 16, [40] p. :
chiefly ill. (some col.) ; 24 cm.
*1. Jacob, Julius, 1842-1929 - Exhibitions. 2. Berlin in
art - Exhibitions. I. Wirth, Irmgard. II. Berlin. Berlin
Museum. III. Title.*
ND588.J27 A4 1979
     NYPL [3-MCK J158 81-436]

JACOB, JULIUS, 1842-1929 - EXHIBITIONS.
Jacob, Julius, 1842-1929. Der Berliner Maler
Julius Jacob . [Berlin] [1979] 16, [40] p. :
ND588.J27 A4 1979
     NYPL [3-MCK J158 81-436]

Jacob Lawrence . Wheat, Ellen Harkins.
Hampton, Va. , 1991. p. cm.   ISBN
0-9616982-4-1 :   DDC 759.13 20
ND237.L29 W48 1991

Jacob, Mary Jane.
Kubota, Shigeko, 1937- Shigeko Kubota video
sculpture /. Astoria, N.Y. , Bellevue , c1991. 96
p. :   ISBN 0-295-97131-2   DDC 700/.92 20
N7359.K83 A4 1991

Merz, Mario. Mario Merz at MOCA. [Milan]
[c1989] 126 p. :   ISBN 0-914357-17-4 (Museum of
Contemporary Art)   DDC 709/.2 20
N6923.M43 A4 1989
     NYPL [3-MGO (Merz) 91-6017]

Jacob, Max, 1876-1944.
Max Jacob et les artistes de son temps .
Orléans [1989] 240 p. :
     NYPL [3-MCO J15 91-6271]

JACOB, MAX, 1876-1944 - EXHIBITIONS.
Max Jacob et les artistes de son temps .
Orléans [1989] 240 p. :
     NYPL [3-MCO J15 91-6271]

**JACOB, MAX, 1876-1944 - FRIENDS AND
ASSOCIATES - EXHIBITIONS.**
Max Jacob et les artistes de son temps .
Orléans [1989] 240 p. :
     NYPL [3-MCO J15 91-6271]

JACOB ROTHBERGER (FIRM) - HISTORY.
Lehne, Andreas. Wiener Warenhäuser,
1865-1914 /. Wien , 1990. 195 p. :   ISBN
3-7005-4488-X
NA6227.D45 L44 1990

**Jacob van Ruisdael and the perception of
landscape /.** Walford, E. John, 1945- New
Haven, CT , 1992. p. cm.   ISBN 0-300-04994-3
   DDC 759.9492 20
ND653.R95 W35 1991

Jacobi, Walter. Bildersturm in der Provinz : die
NS-Aktion "Entartete Kunst" 1937 in Südbaden
/ Walter Jacobi.1. Aufl. Freiburg : Dreisam,
1988. 64 p. : ill. ; 25 cm. Includes bibliographical
references.   ISBN 3-89125-272-2
*1. Art, German - Germany (West) -
Baden-Württemberg. 2. Art, Modern - 20th century -
Germany, West - Baden-Württemberg. I. Title.*
     NYPL [3-MAMG 90-12384]

**JACOBS, RAINER - ART COLLECTIONS -
EXHIBITIONS.**
Rückriem, Ulrich. Ulrich Rückriem, Multiples
und Druckgraphik 1969-1985 . Freiburg , 1986.
62 p. :   *NYPL [3-MGO (Rückriem) 89-2488]*

Jacobs, Stephen Paul. The CAD design studio :
3D modeling as a fundamental design skill /
Stephen Paul Jacobs ; models and illustrations
with the assistance of David Pedersen. New
York : McGraw-Hill, c1991. vi, 120 p. : ill. ; 24
cm. Includes bibliographical references and index.
   ISBN 0-07-032227-9   DDC 721/.0285 20
*1. Architectural design - Data processing. 2. Computer
aided design. I. Title.*
NA2728 .J33 1991

Jacobsen, Arne, 1902-1971.
Arne Jacobsen : architecte et designer danois
1902-1971 : [exposition] 16 novembre 1987-31
janvier 1988, Musée des arts décoratifs, Paris.
Paris : Le Musée, c1987. 79 p. : ill. ; 31 cm.
   ISBN 2-901422-05-5
*1. Jacobsen, Arne, 1902-1971 - Exhibitions. I. Musée
des arts décoratifs (France). II. Title.*
     NYPL [3-MQZ+ (Jacobsen) 90-11627]

JACOBSEN, ARNE, 1902-1971 - EXHIBITIONS.
Jacobsen, Arne, 1902-1971. Arne Jacobsen . Paris , c1987. 79 p. : ISBN 2-901422-05-5
NYPL [3-MQZ+ (Jacobsen) 90-11627]

Jacobsen, Bent Karl. Den Åbne dør, polsk nutidskunst, 1989. [Copenhagen , 1989] 56 p. : ISBN 87-88944-07-7
N7255.P6 A36 1989

Jacobus, John M. Hunter, Sam, 1923- Modern art . New York , 1992. p. cm. ISBN 0-8109-3609-7 DDC 709/.04 20
N6447 .H86 1992

Hunter, Sam, 1923- Modern art . Englewood Cliffs, N.J. , New York , 1992. p. cm. ISBN 0-13-596073-8 (pbk.) DDC 709/.04 20
N6447 .H86 1992b

Jacopo Barozzi da Vignola, 1528-1550 . Orazi, Anna Maria. Roma , c1982. 557 p. : DDC 720/.92/4 19
NA1123.V53 O7 1982
NYPL [3-MQZ (Vignola) 84-1736]

Jacopo della Quercia /. Beck, James H. New York , 1991. p. cm. ISBN 0-231-07200-7 DDC 730/.92 B 20
NB623.O4 B39 1991

JACOPO, DELLA QUERCIA, 1372?-1436.
Beck, James H. Jacopo della Quercia /. New York , 1991. p. cm. ISBN 0-231-07200-7 DDC 730/.92 B 20
NB623.O4 B39 1991

JACOPO, DELLA QUERCIA, 1372?-1436 - CATALOGUES RAISONNÉS.
Beck, James H. Jacopo della Quercia /. New York , 1991. p. cm. ISBN 0-231-07200-7 DDC 730/.92 B 20
NB623.O4 B39 1991

Jacopo Sansovino a Vittorio Veneto . Sansovino, Iacopo, 1486-1570. [Treviso] , 1989. 67 p. : ISBN 88-85066-55-0
NYPL [3-MGO (Sansovino) 91-3693]

Jacopo Tintoretto e la Scuola grande di San Rocco /. Valcanover, Francesco. Venezia , c1983. 127, [1] p. : ISBN 88-7666-019-4
NYPL [3-MCF T59 91-7049]

Jacot-Guillarmod /. Reymond, Armande. Neuchâtel , c1990. 126 p. : ISBN 2-88380-002-2
NYPL [3-MGO+ (Jacot-Guillarmod) 91-5155]

JACOT-GUILLARMOD, ROBERT, 1918-
Reymond, Armande. Jacot-Guillarmod /. Neuchâtel , c1990. 126 p. : ISBN 2-88380-002-2
NYPL [3-MGO+ (Jacot-Guillarmod) 91-5155]

Jacques Hachuel collection. Modern masterpieces from the collection of Jacques Hachuel . [New York, N.Y.] [1990?] 123 p. : ISBN 84-86022-41-X
NYPL [3-MAX (Hachuel) 91-3852]

Jacques Lipchitz. Lipchitz, Jacques, 1891- [Tel Aviv, 1971] 1 v.
NYPL [3-MGO (Lipchitz) 90-6039]

Jacques Lipchitz, a life in sculpture /. Wilkinson, Alan G., 1941- Toronto, Canada , c1989. xi, 196 p. : ISBN 0-919777-76-7 DDC 730/.92 20
NB553.L55 A4 1989
NYPL [3-MGO+ (Lipchitz) 91-6396]

Jacques Lipchitz, sculptures and drawings, 1911-1970 . Lipchitz, Jacques, 1891- [Tel Aviv , 1971] 1 v. :
NYPL [3-MGO (Lipchitz) 90-6039]

Jacques-Louis David. Lévêque, Jean Jacques. La vie et l'œuvre de Jacques-Louis David /. Courbevoie (Paris) , c1989. 239 p. : ISBN 2-86770-036-1
NYPL [3-MCO D25 90-13274]

Jacques-Louis David, 1748-1825 . David, Jacques-Louis, 1748-1825. Paris :Ministère de la culture, de la communication, des grands travaux et du Bicentenaire, Editions de la Réunion des musées nationaux, c1989. 655 p. : ISBN 2-7118-2258-3 DDC 759.4 20
N6853.D315 A4 1989

Jacques Pajak. Pajak, Jacques. Berne [196-?] 1 v. (unpaged) : *NYPL [3-MCO P149 90-6924]*

Jacques Petit /. Petit, Jacques, 1925- Paris ,

c1990. 147 p. :
NYPL [3-MCO+ P489 91-3769]

Jacques Ripault /. Ripault, Jacques, 1953- Paris , 1990. 1 v. (unpaged) : ISBN 2-907687-05-0 : DDC 720/.22/22 20
NA2707.R56 A4 1990

Jacques Villon, l'œuvre gravé . Villon, Jacques, 1875-1963. [Gravelines] [1989] 171 p. : DDC 769.92 20
NE2049.5.V54 A4 1989

Jade /. Keverne, Roger. New York , 1991. p. cm. ISBN 0-442-30847-7 DDC 730 20
NK5750 .K47 1991

JADE ART OBJECTS.
Keverne, Roger. Jade /. New York , 1991. p. cm. ISBN 0-442-30847-7 DDC 730 20
NK5750 .K47 1991

JADE ART OBJECTS - CHINA - EXHIBITIONS.
Magic, art and order . Palm Springs, Calif. , c1990. 155 p. : *NYPL [3-MNW+ 90-13208]*

Jade in Chinese culture. Magic, art and order . Palm Springs, Calif. , c1990. 155 p. :
NYPL [3-MNW+ 90-13208]

JADES. see JADE ART OBJECTS.

Jäcklein, Klaus. Los popolocas de Tepexi (Puebla) : un estudio etnohistórico / Klaus Jäcklein. 1. Aufl. Wiesbaden : Steiner, 1978. xv, 316 p. : ill. ; 29 cm. (Mexiko-Projekt der Deutschen Forschungsgemeinschaft . [Bd.] 15) Added t. p. in German: Die Popoloca von Tepexi (Puebla); eine ethnohistorische Studie. Bibliography: p. 289-316. ISBN 3-515-02888-9
1. Popoloca Indians. 2. Tepexi de Rodriguez, Mexico - History. I. Title. II. Title: Die Popoloca von Tepexi (Puebla). III. Series.
F1203 .D46 vol. 15 F1221.P6
NYPL [HTC 74-1117 [Bd.] 15]

Jaeger, Heino, 1938- Heino Jaeger : Gemälde, Zeichnungen, Radierungen / herausgegeben von Ralf Busch ; mit Beiträgen von Ralf Busch ... [et al.]. Hamburg : Christians, 1988. 99 p. : ill. (some col.) ; 31 cm. (Veröffentlichung des Hamburger Museums für Archäologie und die Geschichte Harburgs (Helms-Museum). Nr. 53) ISBN 3-7672-1072-X DDC 760/.092 20
1. Jaeger, Heino, 1938-. I. Busch, Ralf. II. Title. III. Title: Gemälde, Zeichnungen, Radierungen. IV. Series.
NC251.J265 A4 1988
NYPL [3-MCK+ J221 91-4186]

JAEGER, HEINO, 1938-
Jaeger, Heino, 1938- Heino Jaeger . Hamburg , 1988. 99 p. : ISBN 3-7672-1072-X DDC 760/.092 20
NC251.J265 A4 1988
NYPL [3-MCK+ J221 91-4186]

Jähnig, Bernhart. Kleiner Atlas zur deutschen Territorialgeschichte / von Bernhart Jähnig, Ludwig Biewer. Bonn : Kulturstiftung der deutschen Vertriebenen, 1990 192 p. : maps ; 32 cm. One folded map in pocket. ISBN 3-88557-057-2
1. Germany - Historical geography - Maps. I. Title.
NYPL [Map Div. 91-67]

JAÉN (SPAIN : PROVINCE) - ANTIQUITIES - CATALOGS.
Bazzana, Andrés. La céramique islamique du Musée archéologique provincial de Jaén (Espagne) /. Madrid , Paris , 1985. 78 p. : DDC 738.3/0946/83 20
DP302.J1 B38 1985
NYPL [3-MPG+ 91-5911]

Jaenisch, Hans, 1907-
Hans Jaenisch. [Berlin : Galerie Nierendorf, 1987] [20] p. : ill. (some col.) ; 26 cm. Cover title. "Ausstellung zum 80. Geburtstag, vom 23. März bis zum 9. Mai 1987"--Verso cover. Catalog of an exhibition held at the Galerie Nierendorf, Berlin. Price-list: [2] p., inserted.
1. Jaenisch, Hans, 1907- Exhibitions. I. Galerie Nierendorf. *NYPL [3-MCK J225 90-5359]*

JAENISCH, HANS, 1907- - EXHIBITIONS.
Jaenisch, Hans, 1907- Hans Jaenisch. [Berlin , 1987] [20] p. :
NYPL [3-MCK J225 90-5359]

Jaffe, Irma B. The Italian presence in American art, 1860-1920 /. New York , Roma , 1991. p. cm. ISBN 0-8232-1342-0 : DDC 709/.73/09034 20
N6510 .I8 1991

Jaffé, Patricia. Women engravers / Patricia Jaffe. Camden Town, London : Virago, 1990. 128 p. : ill. ; 28 cm. "First published in Great Britain by Virago Press 1988"--T.p. verso. Includes bibliographical references (p. 127-128). ISBN 1-85381-188-2 : DDC 769.941/082 20
1. Women wood-engravers - Great Britain - Biography. 2. Wood-engraving, British. 3. Wood-engraving - 20th century - Great Britain. I. Title.
NE1143 .J34 1990

Jaffee, David. Meet your neighbors . Sturbridge, Mass. , Amherst, Mass. , 1992. p. cm. ISBN 0-87023-771-3 (cloth) : DDC 757/.0974/0747443 20
ND1311.5 .M44 1992

Jaffee, Maggie. Small, Deborah, 1948- 1492 . New York, N.Y. , 1991. p. cm. ISBN 0-85345-836-7 : DDC 700/.92 20
N7433.4.S43 A4 1991

Jaffrennou, Michel. Breule, l'aimée verte; roman hypergraphique. Vaduz, Centre international de création kladologique, 1968. 1 v. (unpaged) illus. 21 cm.
1. Jaffrennou, Michel. I. Title.
NYPL [MDG (Jaffrennou) 91-1292]

JAFFRENNOU, MICHEL.
Jaffrennou, Michel. Breule, l'aimée verte. Vaduz, 1968. 1 v. (unpaged)
NYPL [MDG (Jaffrennou) 91-1292]

Jagodič, Stane. Stane Jagodič / Lev Menaše ... [et al. ; translation, Alenka Goričan]. Zagreb : Globus, 1989. 399 p. : chiefly ill. (some col.), ports. ; 31 cm. Includes list of artist's exhibitions. Includes bibliographical references (p. 393-399) ISBN 86-343-0514-7
1. Jagodič, Stane. 2. Artists - Yugoslavia - Biography. I. Menaše, Lev. II. Title.
NYPL [3-MCZ+ J247 90-11068]

JAGODIČ, STANE.
Jagodič, Stane. Stane Jagodič /. Zagreb , 1989. 399 p. : ISBN 86-343-0514-7
NYPL [3-MCZ+ J247 90-11068]

Jaguer, Edouard. Joseph Cornell / Edouard Jaguer. [Paris] : Filipacchi, c1989. 93 p. : ill. (some col.), ports. ; 31 cm. Bibliography: p. 92. ISBN 2-85018-249-4
1. Cornell, Joseph. I. Cornell, Joseph. II. Title.
NYPL [3-MCX+ C795 90-11997]

Jahangir, Burhanuddin Khan. Jaẏanula Ābedinera jijñāsā / Borahānauddina Khāna Jāhāṅgira. 1st ed. Ḍhākā : Muktadhārā, 1990. 82 p., [14] p. of plates : ill. ; 22 cm. In Bengali. Critical analysis on the works of Zainul Abedin, Bangladeshi painter. Includes bibliographical references.
1. Abedin, Zainul - Criticism and interpretation. 2. Social problems in art. I. Title.
N7310.8.B25 J344 1990

Jahn, Fred.
Amerikanische Zeichnungen in den achtziger Jahren . München , c1990. 190 p. : DDC 741.973/09/04807443551 20
NC108 .A55 1990

Richter, Gerhard, 1932- Gerhard Richter, Atlas /. München , c1989. 232 p. :
NYPL [3-MCK+ R528 91-3384]

Jahn, Hans, 1884- Berlin : der Kern der Reichshauptstadt in seiner geschichtlichen Entwicklung von 1650-1920 / [Text, Hans Jahn ; Zeichnungnen u. Ausstattung, Bruno Böttger]. [Berlin] : Die Reichshauptstadt, [1920?] 25 p. : ill. (some col), maps, plans ; 22 x 30 cm. Loose folded map inserted.
1. Berlin (Germany) - History. 2. Berlin (Germany) - Historical geography - Maps. I. Title.
NYPL [Map Div. 91-6615]

Jahn, Helmut, 1940- Airports / Helmut Jahn ; edited by Werner Blaser ; [translation into English by Cynthia Baer and Leslie Koechlin]. Basel ; Boston : Birkhäuser, c1991. p. cm. Introd. in English; text in German. Includes index. ISBN 0-8176-2613-1 (U. S.) DDC 725/.39 20
1. Airport terminals. 2. Airports - Terminals. I. Blaser, Werner, 1924-. II. Title.
NA6300 .J34 1991

Jahn, Johannes, 1892- Haubenreisser, Wolfgang. Wörterbuch der Kunst /. Stuttgart , c1989. ix, 932 p. : ISBN 3-520-16511-2 : DDC 703 20
N33 .H35 1989

Jahrhunderthalle Hoechst (Frankfurt am Main, Germany)

Höchster Porzellan des 18. Jahrhunderts aus Privatbesitz . Hoechst (Frankfurt am Main) , c1984. 183 p. :   **NYPL** *[3-MPGK 90-10661]*

Die Pioniere der Photographie 1840-1900 . Weingarten , c1989. 125 p. :   ISBN 3-8170-2501-7   **NYPL** *[MFW 90-8398]*

Jaipur brassware in Government Central Museum, Jaipur. Government Central Museum (Jaipur, India) Jaipur , 1955. 61 p. :   **NYPL** *[3-MNK 90-7182]*

Jakob, Volker. Menschen im Silberspiegel : die Anfänge der Fotografie in Westfalen / Volker Jakob in Zusammenarbeit mit Cäcilia Jansen und Angela Schöppner ; Fotos, Josef Klem. Greven : Eggenkamp, 1989. 168 p. : ill. ; 24 cm. (Aus westfälischen Bildsammlungen. Bd. 1) ISBN 3-923166-30-3
1. Photography - Portraits. I. Title. II. Series.
IN PROCESS (ONLINE)
- NYPL *[MFW 91-2653]*

Jakubowski-Zalonis, Susanne. Architektur und Städtebau des Islam /. Stuttgart , 1985- v. ;   ISBN 3-8167-0105-1   DDC 016.72/0917/671 19
Z5943.I84 A73 1984 NA380
NYPL *[3-MQT 91-826]*

Jamaican song and story. Jekyll, Walter. (ed) New York [1966] xv, 288 p.   **NYPL** *[JMD 74-129]*

James Abbott McNeill Whistler--pastels /. Whistler, James McNeill, 1834-1903. New York , 1991. p. cm.   ISBN 0-8076-1266-9 :   DDC 741.973 20
NC139.W45 A4 1991

James Brooks, Giorgio Cavallon : paintings of the seventies : [exhibition] November 14-December 31, 1979, Gruenebaum Gallery, Ltd. / introduction and essays by Carter Ratcliff. New York : The Gallery, 1979. 24 p. : col. ill., ports. ; 22 x 26 cm. Bibliography: p. 11, 20.
1. Brooks, James, 1906- - Exhibitions. 2. Cavallon, Giorgio, 1904- - Exhibitions. I. Brooks, James, 1906-. II. Cavallon, Giorgio, 1904-. III. Ratcliff, Carter. IV. Gruenebaum Gallery (New York, N.Y.).
NYPL *[3-MCW 91-284]*

James Brown . Brown, James. Paris , 1989. 32 p. :   ISBN 2-85587-173-5
NYPL *[3-MGO+ (Brown) 90-10558]*

James Brown . Brown, James, 1951- Paris , c1990. 42 p. :   ISBN 2-85587-184-0
NYPL *[3-MCX+ B8765 90-13074]*

James, Bruce. Grace Cossington Smith / Bruce James. Roseville, NSW, Australia : Craftsman House, 1990. 189 p. : ill. ; 34 cm.   ISBN 0-947131-35-3
1. Smith, Grace Cossington. I. Title.
NYPL *[3-MCZ+ S6485 90-13355]*

James Ensor. Hoozee, Robert. [James Ensor, tekeningen en prenten. French.] James Ensor, dessins et estampes /. Antwerpen , Paris , c1987. 271 p. :   ISBN 90-6153-177-2 (Fonds Mercator)   DDC 760/.092 20
N6973.E5 A4 1987

James Ensor, dessins et estampes /. Hoozee, Robert. [James Ensor, tekeningen en prenten. French.] Antwerpen , Paris , c1987. 271 p. :   ISBN 90-6153-177-2 (Fonds Mercator)   DDC 760/.092 20
N6973.E5 A4 1987

James, Fred. New international atlas of the world /. Chicago , c1943. 224, lxiv p. :
NYPL *[Map Div. 91-4958]*

James, Henry, 1843-1916.
The painter's eye : notes and essays on the pictorial arts / by Henry James ; selected and edited with an introduction by John L. Sweeney ; with a foreword by Susan M. Griffin. Madison, Wis. : University of Wisconsin Press, c1989. viii, 276 p. : port. ; 22 cm. Reprint. Originally published: London : R. Hart-Davis, 1956. Includes bibliographical references.   ISBN 0-299-12280-8 :   DDC 759.05 20
1. Art, Modern - 19th century. I. Sweeney, John L. II. Title.
N6450 .J36 1989   **NYPL** *[3-MAL 90-10758]*

JAMES, HENRY, 1843-1916 - CRITICISM AND INTERPRETATION.
Honour, Hugh. The Venetian hours of Henry James, Whistler, Sargent /. Boston , c1991. p.   ISBN 0-8212-1861-1   DDC 700 20
NX653.V46 H66 1991

James, Henry, 1843-1916 - Interpretation and criticism. see James, Henry, 1843-1916 - Criticism and interpretation.

James Henry Cafferty, N.A. (1819-1869) /. Cafferty, James H., 1819-1869. New York , c1986. 55 p. :   **NYPL** *[3-MCX C129 91-6656]*

James, John, 1959- (ill) Macdonald, Fiona. A medieval cathedral /. New York , 1991. p. cm.   ISBN 0-87226-350-9   DDC 726/.6/0940902 20
NA4830 .M34 1991

James McNeill Whistler at the Hunterian Art Gallery : an illustrated guide. [Glasgow] : The Gallery, [1990]. 56 p. : ill. (some col.) ; 24 cm. Guide prepared by Martin Hopkinson. Includes bibliographical references (p. 56).   ISBN 0-904254-11-9
1. Whistler, James McNeill, 1834-1903 - Exhibitions. I. Whistler, James McNeill, 1834-1903. II. Hopkinson, Martin J. III. Hunterian Art Gallery (University of Glasgow).   **NYPL** *[3-MCX W57 91-6660]*

James, Peter. Centuries of darkness . London , 1991. xxii, 434 p., [8] p. of plates :   ISBN 0-224-02647-X :   DDC 930 20
CB311   **NYPL** *[JFE 91-4489]*

James Reineking . Reineking, James, 1937- Lüdenscheid , 1989. 58 p. :
NYPL *[3-MGO+ (Reineking) 89-11776]*

James Rosenquist . Rosenquist, James, 1933- [Mount Kisco, N.Y.] , 1989. 48 p. :   ISBN 0-9625185-0-6
NYPL *[3-MCX+ R797 90-12772]*

James Sprunt studies in history and political science.
(57) Mixon, Wayne. Southern writers and the New South movement, 1865-1913 /. Chapel Hill , c1980. x, 169 p. ;   ISBN 0-8078-5057-8
PS261 .M5   **NYPL** *[IAA 74-813 no.57]*

James Turrell . Adcock, Craig E. Berkeley , c1990. xxiv, 272 p., [32] p. of plates :   ISBN 0-520-06728-2 (alk. paper)   DDC 709/.2 20
N6537.T78 A84 1990
NYPL *[3-MCX+ T941 91-5229]*

James Wyeth . Wyeth, James, 1946- [Omaha?] c1975 (Omaha : Barnhart Press) [64] p. :
NYPL *[3-MCX W980 90-7181]*

Jamharat al-khaṭṭāṭīn al-Baghdādiyīn . A'ẓami, Walīd. A'ẓamiyah, Baghdād, al-'Irāq , 1989. 2 v. (800 p.) :
NK3630.6.I72 A93 1989

Jamieson, Doug. Draw from your head : a step-by-step system for drawing the human figure / Doug Jamieson. New York : Watson-Guptil Publications, 1991. p. cm. Includes bibliographical references and index.   ISBN 0-8230-1374-X   DDC 743/.49 20
1. Anatomy, Artistic. 2. Human figure in art. 3. Drawing - Technique. I. Title.
NC760 .J34 1991

Jan Brueghel the elder . Brod Gallery (London, England) London , c1979. 122 p. :   DDC 759.9493 19
ND673.B72 A4 1979
NYPL *[3-MCH+ B88-90-12668]*

Jan Gerrit Wyers, 1888-1973 /. Oko, Andrew, 1946- Regina, Sask. , c1989. 132 p. :   ISBN 0-920922-57-0   DDC 759.11 20
NYPL *[3-MCH W961 91-6979]*

Jan Groth, tegn : festskrift, 1938, 13.XI, 1988 / redigert av Inger-Margrethe Lunde & Steinar Wiik = Jan Groth, signs : festschrift, 1938, 13.XI, 1988 / edited by Inger-Margrethe Lunde & Steinar Wiik. Oslo : Biblioscandia & Signum, 1988. 84 p. : ill. ; 30 x 30 cm. Norwegian and English.   ISBN 82-7418-154-9
1. Groth, Jan, 1938-. 2. Tapestry - Norway - History - 20th century. I. Groth, Jan, 1938-. II. Lunde, Inger-Margrethe. III. Wiik, Steinar.
NK3060.A3 G7635 1988

Jan Sawka . Sawka, Jan, 1946- [New Paltz, N.Y.] [1989?] p. :   DDC 709/.2 20
N6537.S333 A4 1989

Jan Verkade, Hollandse volgeling van Gauguin /. Boyle-Turner, Caroline. Zwolle , Amsterdam , c1989. 190 p. :   ISBN 90-6630-171-6
NYPL *[3-MCH+ V52 89-28467]*

Jandl, H. Ward. Yesterday's houses of tomorrow : innovative American homes 1850 to 1950 / H. Ward Jandl, John A. Burns, Michael Auer. Washington, DC : Preservation Press, 1991. p. cm. Includes bibliographical references and

index.   ISBN 0-89133-186-7   DDC 728/.0973/09034 20
1. Architecture, Domestic - United States. 2. Architecture, Modern - 19th century - United States. 3. Architecture, Modern - 20th century - United States. I. Burns, John A. II. Auer, Michael. III. Title.
NA7207 .J36 1991

Jane Dickson life under neon . Dickson, Jane. Philadelphia, PA , c1989. 12 p. :
NYPL *[3-MCX D568 91-4639]*

Jane Voorhees Zimmerli Art Museum. Hansen, Trudy V. Intaglio printing in the 1980s . [New Brunswick, N.J.] , c1990. v, 45 p. :
IN PROCESS (ONLINE)
NYPL *[MDE 91-3493]*

Meech-Pekarik, Julia. Japonisme comes to America . New York , 1990. 256 p. :   ISBN 0-8109-3501-5   DDC 760/.0973/07474942 20
N6510 .M44 1990   **NYPL** *[MDBV 90-11897]*

Jane Vorhees Zimmerli Art Museum. Outside Cuba . [New Brunswick, N.J.] , Miami, Fla. , 1989. 366 p. :   ISBN 0-935501-13-4
NYPL *[3-MAM 90-12497]*

Janeček, Ota. Hlaváček, Luboš. Ota Janeček /. Praha , 1989. 213 p. :   ISBN 80-207-0082-X :
ND534.5.J27 H58 1989

JANEČEK, OTA - CRITICISM AND INTERPRETATION. Hlaváček, Luboš. Ota Janeček /. Praha , 1989. 213 p. :   ISBN 80-207-0082-X :
ND534.5.J27 H58 1989

Janet Marqusee Fine Arts Ltd. Simkhovitch, Simka, 1893-1949. Simka Simkhovitch, 1893-1949 . New York, N.Y. , c1987. [32] p. :
NYPL *[3-MCX S589 91-7026]*

Janis, Eugenia Parry.
The Kiss of Apollo . San Francisco , c1991. 105 p. :   ISBN 0-938491-66-0 :   DDC 779/.973 20
TR658.3 .K57 1991   **NYPL** *[MFW 91-6782]*

Women photographers /. New York , 1990. 263 p. :   ISBN 0-8109-3950-9   DDC 779/.082 20
TR650 .W65 1990   **NYPL** *[MFW 90-13676]*

Janis Gallery, New York. see Sidney Janis Gallery.

Janis (Sidney) Gallery. see Sidney Janis Gallery.

Janneau, Guillaume, 1887- Le meuble d'ébénisterie / par Guillaume Janneau. Paris : Editions de l'amateur, c1989. 236 p. : ill. ; 22 cm. At head of title: Le mobilier français. Bibliography: p. 235.   ISBN 2-85917-083-9
1. Furniture - France. 2. Cabinet-work - France. I. Title. II. Title: Le mobilier français.
NYPL *[3-MOI 91-6666]*

Jannis Kounellis /. Kounellis, Jannis, 1946- Paris , 1989. 31 p. :   ISBN 2-85587-177-8
NYPL *[3-MCZ+ K865 90-11632]*

János Megyik . Megyik, János, 1938- Wien [1988] 39 p. :   ISBN 3-900776-02-8   DDC 709.2 20
N6822.5.M48 A4 1988
NYPL *[3-MGO+ (Megyik) 90-11666]*

Jansen, Guido. Museum Boymans-Van Beuningen. Rubens en zijn tijd . Rotterdam , 1990. 176 p. :   ISBN 90-6918-063-4
ND673.R9 A4 1990

Janson, Anthony F.
Janson, H. W. (Horst Woldemar), 1913- A basic history of art /. Englewood Cliffs, N.J. , New York , 1991. p. cm.   ISBN 0-13-062878-6   DDC 709 20
N5300 .J29 1991

Janson, H. W. (Horst Woldemar), 1913- History of art for young people /. New York , 1992. p. cm.   ISBN 0-8109-3405-1   DDC 709 20
N5300 .J33 1992

Janson, H. W. (Horst Woldemar), 1913-
A basic history of art / H.W. Janson and Anthony F. Janson. 4th ed. Englewood Cliffs, N.J. : Prentice Hall ; New York : Abrams, 1991. p. cm. Includes bibliographical references and index.   ISBN 0-13-062878-6   DDC 709 20
1. Art - History. I. Janson, Anthony F. II. Title.
N5300 .J29 1991

History of art for young people / H.W. Janson and Anthony F. Janson. 4th ed. New York : Abrams, 1992. p. cm. Includes bibliographical

references and index. Surveys the history of art, including painting, sculpture, architecture, and photography, from cave paintings to modern art. ISBN 0-8109-3405-1 DDC 709 20
1. Art - History. I. Janson, Anthony F. II. Title.
N5300 .J33 1992

Janson, Horst Woldemar, 1913- The Romantics to Rodin . Los Angeles, Calif. , New York , c1980. 368 p. : ISBN 0-8076-0953-4 (Brazilier) DDC 730/.944
NB547 .R65   ***NYPL [MGI 80-2189]***

Janssen, Hans. Serra, Richard, 1939- Richard Serra . Bern [1990] 282 p. : ISBN 3-7165-0703-2
    NYPL [3-MCX S487 91-4458]

Janssen, Horst, 1929-
Frauenbildnisse, 1947-1988 / Horst Janssen ; zusammengetragen und herausgegeben von Dierk Lemcke. Hamburg : Verlag St. Gertrude, c1988. 1 v. (unpaged) : 390 ill. (chiefly col.) ; 36 cm. Includes index. ISBN 3-923848-22-6 DDC 760/.092 20
1. Janssen, Horst, 1929- - Catalogs. 2. Women in art - Catalogs. I. Lemcke, Dierk. II. Title.
N6888.J37 A4 1988 <fol.>

Landschaften 1942-1989 / Horst Janssen ; zusammengetragen und herausgegeben von Dierk Lemcke. Hamburg : Verlag St. Gertrude, c1989. 1 v. (unpaged) : 529 ill. (chiefly col.) ; 36 cm. Includes index. ISBN 3-923848-24-2 DDC 760/.092 20
1. Janssen, Horst, 1929- - Catalogs. I. Lemcke, Dierk. II. Title.
N6888.J37 A4 1989a
    NYPL [MDG+ (Janssen) 91-6183]

Schack, Gerhard, 1929- Horst Janssen . München , c1989. 1 v. (unpaged) : ISBN 3-7913-1042-9 DDC 760/.092 20
N6888.J37 A4 1989

JANSSEN, HORST, 1929-
Schack, Gerhard, 1929- Horst Janssen . München , c1989. 1 v. (unpaged) : ISBN 3-7913-1042-9 DDC 760/.092 20
N6888.J37 A4 1989

JANSSEN, HORST, 1929- - CATALOGS.
Janssen, Horst, 1929- Frauenbildnisse, 1947-1988 /. Hamburg , c1988. 1 v. (unpaged) : ISBN 3-923848-22-6 DDC 760/.092 20
N6888.J37 A4 1988 <fol.>

Janssen, Horst, 1929- Landschaften 1942-1989 /. Hamburg , c1989. 1 v. (unpaged) : ISBN 3-923848-24-2 DDC 760/.092 20
N6888.J37 A4 1989a
    NYPL [MDG+ (Janssen) 91-6183]

Janssens, Jacques.
[James Ensor. English]
Ensor / by Jacques Janssens. 1st ed. New York : Crown Publishers, c1990. p. cm. (Crown art library) Translation of: James Ensor. Includes bibliographical references. ISBN 0-517-53284-0 : DDC 760/.092 20
1. Ensor, James, 1860-1949 - Criticism and interpretation. 2. Red 2 FC09. I. Title. II. Series.
N6973.E5 J3613 1990

Janszoon, Willem. see **Blaeu, Willem Janszoon, 1571-1638.**

Januarius Zick . Strasser, Josef. München , c1987. iii, 85 p., [20] p. of plates : ISBN 3-88073-265-5 DDC 759.3 19
ND588.Z47 S78 1987
    NYPL [3-MCK Z64 91-5652]

Japan : the shaping of Daimyo culture, 1185-1868 / edited by Yoshiaki Shimizu. New York : G. Brazilier, c1988. xi, 402 p. : col. ill., plates ; 30 cm. Catalog of an exhibition held at the National Gallery of Art, Washington, Oct. 30, 1988 to Jan. 23, 1989. Bibliography: p. 394-402. ISBN 0-8076-1214-6 DDC 952/.00740153 19
1. Daimyo - Exhibitions. 2. Art, Japanese - Kamakura-Momoyama periods, 1185-1600 - Exhibitions. 3. Art, Japanese - Edo period, 1600-1868 - Exhibitions. 4. Material culture - Japan - Exhibitions. 5. Japan - Civilization - 1185-1600 - Exhibitions. 6. Japan - Civilization - 1600-1868 - Exhibitions. I. Shimizu, Yoshiaki, 1936-. II. National Gallery of Art (U. S.).
DS827.D34 J37 1988
    NYPL [3-MAG+ 89-864]

Japan. Agency for Cultural Affairs. see **Japan. Bunkachō.**

JAPAN - ANTIQUITIES - EXHIBITIONS.
The Rise of a great tradition . New York [1990?] 112 p. : ISBN 0-913304-30-1
    NYPL [3-MPFK+ 91-5067]

Japan - Archaeology. see **Japan - Antiquities.**

Japan. Bunkachō. The Rise of a great tradition . New York [1990?] 112 p. : ISBN 0-913304-30-1
    NYPL [3-MPFK+ 91-5067]

JAPAN - CIVILIZATION - 1185-1600.
Hennig, Karl. Der Karesansui-Garten als Ausdruck der Kultur der Muromachi-Zeit /. Hamburg , 1982. vi, 412 p. :
    NYPL [3-MSK 90-6887]

JAPAN - CIVILIZATION - 1185-1600 - EXHIBITIONS.
Japan . New York , c1988. xi, 402 p. : ISBN 0-8076-1214-6 DDC 952/.00740153 19
DS827.D34 J37 1988
    NYPL [3-MAG+ 89-864]

JAPAN - CIVILIZATION - 1600-1868 - EXHIBITIONS.
Japan . New York , c1988. xi, 402 p. : ISBN 0-8076-1214-6 DDC 952/.00740153 19
DS827.D34 J37 1988
    NYPL [3-MAG+ 89-864]

Vos, Ken. Assignment Japan . The Hague , 1989. 107 p. : ISBN 90-12-06415-5
    NYPL [3-MAG+ 90-12025]

JAPAN - CIVILIZATION - DUTCH INFLUENCES - EXHIBITIONS.
Vos, Ken. Assignment Japan . The Hague , 1989. 107 p. : ISBN 90-12-06415-5
    NYPL [3-MAG+ 90-12025]

Japan. Cultural Affairs Agency. see **Japan. Bunkachō.**

Japan Cultural Institute in Rome.
Immagini scritte . [Tokyo] , c1984. 171 p. : DDC 745.6/19956/074 20
NK3637.A2 I46 1984

Pittura etrusca al Museo di Villa Giulia /. Roma , 1989. 208 p. : ISBN 88-7813-219-5 : DDC 751.7/3/0937507445632 20
ND2565 .P58 1989   ***NYPL [3-MCD 91-3776]***

Japan Foundation. see **Kokusai Kōryū Kikin.**

JAPAN - HISTORY.
Kennedy, Alan. Japanese costume . Paris, France , New York, N.Y. , 1990. 153, [3] p. : ISBN 2-87660-083-8 DDC 391/.00952 20
GT1560 .K42 1990
    NYPL [3-MMR+ 91-4466]

JAPAN - HISTORY - ALLIED OCCUPATION, 1945-1952 - COLLECTIBLES - CATALOGS.
Florence, Gene, 1944- The collector's encyclopedia of Occupied Japan collectibles . Paducah, KY , c1990. 127 p. : ISBN 0-89145-401-2 : DDC 738/.0952/075 20
NK1071 .F583 1990

The Japan idea . Hosley, William. Hartford, Conn. , 1990. 211 p. : ISBN 0-918333-07-5
    NYPL [3-MAMT+ 91-3289]

JAPAN IN ART.
Mason, Tim, 1934- Helen Hyde /. Washington , c1991. 120 p. : ISBN 1-560-98009-5 (pbk.) DDC 769.92 20
NE539.H9 M37 1991
    NYPL [MDG (Hyde) 91-7232]

JAPAN - KINGS AND RULERS - ART PATRONAGE - EXHIBITIONS.
Courtly splendor . Boston [1990] 173 p. : ISBN 0-87846-328-3
    NYPL [3-MAG+ 91-3336]

JAPAN - MAPS.
(1990) Kokudo Chiriin. The national atlas of Japan /. Tokyo , c1990. 218 p. :
    NYPL [Map Div. 91-6364]

JAPAN - SOCIAL LIFE AND CUSTOMS.
Bosslet, Klaus. Ästhetik und Gestaltung in der japanischen Architektur . Düsseldorf , c1990. viii, 154 p. : ISBN 3-8041-1247-1 :
NA7451 .B67 1990

Kennedy, Alan. Japanese costume . Paris, France , New York, N.Y. , 1990. 153, [3] p. : ISBN 2-87660-083-8 DDC 391/.00952 20
GT1560 .K42 1990
    NYPL [3-MMR+ 91-4466]

Japan Society (New York, N.Y.) The Rise of a great tradition . New York [1990?] 112 p. : ISBN 0-913304-30-1
    NYPL [3-MPFK+ 91-5067]

JAPANESE AMERICAN SCULPTORS - BIOGRAPHY.
Ashton, Dore. Noguchi east and west /. New York , 1992. p. cm. ISBN 0-394-58804-5 DDC 709/.2 B 20
NB237.N6 A8 1992

JAPANESE ART. see **ART, JAPANESE.**

Japanese art from the Gerry collection in the Metropolitan Museum of Art /. Metropolitan Museum of Art (New York, N.Y.) New York , c1989. 141 p. : ISBN 0-87099-556-1 DDC 738/.0952/0747471 20
N7352 .F67 1989   ***NYPL [3-MAG 89-28868]***

JAPANESE BRONZES. see **BRONZES, JAPANESE.**

Japanese ceramics. Klein, Adalbert, 1913- [Japanische Keramik von der Jōmon-Zeit bis zur Gegenwart. English.] A connoisseur's guide to Japanese ceramics /. London , c1987. 275 p. :   ***NYPL [3-MPFK+ 90-11010]***

Japanese collections in the Freer Gallery of Art. Cort, Louise Allison, 1944- Seto and Mino ceramics /. Washington, D.C. , Honolulu, Hawaii , 1992. p. cm. ISBN 0-08-248143-1 : DDC 738/.0952/16 20
NK4168.S4 C67 1992

Japanese costume . Kennedy, Alan. Paris, France , New York, N.Y. , 1990. 153, [3] p. : ISBN 2-87660-083-8 DDC 391/.00952 20
GT1560 .K42 1990
    NYPL [3-MMR+ 91-4466]

Japanese floral stencil designs / edited by James Spero. New York : Dover, 1991. 94 p. : all ill. ; 31 cm. (Dover pictorial archive series) ISBN 0-486-26655-9 : DDC 746.6 20
1. Decoration and ornament - Plant forms - Japan - Themes, motives. 2. Stencil work - Japan. I. Spero, James.
NK1484.A1 J37 1991

Japanese flower arrangement . Allen, Ellen G. (Ellen Gordon), 1897- Rutland, Vt. , 1963, cc1962. 86 p. :   ***NYPL [3-MLT 90-5857]***

JAPANESE FLOWER ARRANGEMENT. see **FLOWER ARRANGEMENT, JAPANESE.**

JAPANESE PAINTING. see **PAINTING, JAPANESE.**

JAPANESE PAPER FOLDING. see **ORIGAMI.**

JAPANESE - PICTORIAL WORKS.
Tsuchida, Hiromi, 1939- Zokushin /. Yokohama-shi , c1976. 232 p. :
    NYPL [MFX (Tsuchida) 90-6214]

JAPANESE POETRY.
Hosoda, Eishi, 1756-1829. The thirty-six immortal women poets . New York , 1991. p. cm. ISBN 0-8076-1256-1 DDC 769.92 20
NE1325.H69 A4 1991

JAPANESE PORCELAIN. see **PORCELAIN, JAPANESE.**

JAPANESE POTTERY. see **POTTERY, JAPANESE.**

Japanese style. Kyoto, Japan : Kyoto Shoin ; Tokyo, Japan : Distributed by Nippon Shuppan Hanbai, c1989. 2 v. in 6 : chiefly col. ill. ; 29 cm. (The Best in international textile design) CONTENTS. - [1] Textile dyeing patterns (4 v.) -- [2] Textile design patterns (2 v.). ISBN 4-7636-8059-5 (v. 1) DDC 745.4/4952 20
1. Textile fabrics - Japan - Themes, motives. 2. Resist-dyed textiles - Japan - Themes, motives. I. Kyōto Shoin. II. Series.
NK8984.A1 J37 1989

Japanische Plakate heute : 250 Beispiele von 25 Künstlern : Ausstellung 27. Januar bis 8. April 1979, Kunstgewerbemuseum der Stadt Zürich. Mailand : Electa, c1979. 165 p. : ill. (some col.) ; 24 cm. (Wegleitung. Nr. 324) Concept and catalog by Gian Carlo Calza. Translated by Barbara von Münchhausen.
1. Posters, Japanese - Exhibitions. 2. Posters - 20th century - Japan - Exhibitions. I. Calza, Gian Carlo. II. Kunstgewerbemuseum Zürich.
    NYPL [3-MDW 90-4437]

Japanisches Kulturinstitut (Cologne, Germany) Worte in Bewegung . [Tokyo] , c1984. 187 p. :

DDC 745.6/19956/074 20
NK3637.A2 W67 1984

Japanska konstskatter från Tokyo Fuji Art Museum / [katalogredaktör, Jan Wirgin ; katalogtext, Helena Ewenfält]. Stockholm : Östasiatiska museet, 1990. 78 p.: col. ill. ; 23 x 25 cm. (Östasiatiska museets utställningskatalog, 0585-3257 . nr 49)
1. Decorative arts - Japan - Exhibitions. 2. Tōkyō Fuji Bijutsukan - Exhibitions. I. Wirgin, Jan. II. Ewenfält, Helena. III. Tōkyō Fuji Bijutsukan. IV. Östasiatiska museet. V. Series.
NK1071 .J37 1990

Japón y Occidente . Gutiérrez, Fernando G. Sevilla , 1990. 245 p. : ISBN 84-86080-27-4 DDC 709/.52 20
N7350 .G88 1990

Japonisme comes to America . Meech-Pekarik, Julia. New York , 1990. 256 p. : ISBN 0-8109-3501-5 DDC 760/.0973/07474942 20
N6510 .M44 1990 **NYPL [MDBV 90-11897]**

Japonisme in Vienna. Verborgene Impressionen =. [Wien] , c1990. 445 p. : ISBN 3-900688-13-3 (Katalogausgabe) **NYPL [3-MAM 91-3678]**

Japonismus in Wien. Verborgene Impressionen =. [Wien] , c1990. 445 p. : ISBN 3-900688-13-3 (Katalogausgabe) **NYPL [3-MAM 91-3678]**

Jaramillo, Carmen María. Serrano, Eduardo. Roberto Páramo . Bogotá , 1989. 190 p. : ISBN 958-9058-01-9
NYPL [3-MCZ P234 90-12088]

Jardín Borda (Cuernavaca, Mexico) Los Zapatas de Diego Rivera /. Ciudad de México , Cuernavaca, Morelos , 1989. 117 p., [2] folded leaves of plates : ISBN 968-292-333-6 DDC 760/.092 20
N6559.R58 Z37 1989
NYPL [3-MCZ R62 91-4245]

Jargstorf, Sibylle. Glass in jewelry : hidden artistry in glass / Sibylle Jargstorf. West Chester, Pa. : Schiffer, c1991. 174 p. : col. ill. ; 28 cm. Includes bibliographical references and index. ISBN 0-88740-295-X DDC 748.8 20
1. Glass jewelry. I. Title.
NK5440.J48 J37 1991

Jasbar, Gerald. Steingewordene Träume . Ulm , c1990. 111 p. :
NA5559 .S68 1990

Jason /. Kiefer, Anselm, 1945- Dublin , c1990. 1 v. (unpaged) : ISBN 0-907660-36-3
MLCM 90/06234 (N)
NYPL [3-MGO (Kiefer) 91-5151]

Jasper Morrison . Morrison, Jasper, 1959- London , 1990. 82 p. : ISBN 1-85454-435-7 (pbk) : DDC 749.22 20
NYPL [3-MOF 90-11539]

Jassenjawsky, Igor. Von Eisenstein bis Tarkowsky . München , c1990. 159 p. : ISBN 3-7913-1068-2
NX556.A1 V6 1990

Jászai, Géza, 1931-
Barockskulptur . Münster , 1979. 163 p. :
NB193 .B37 **NYPL [3-MGI 81-434]**

Das Werk des Bildhauers Gerhard Gröninger, 1582-1652 / Géza Jászai. Münster : Landschaftsverband Westfalen-Lippe : Westfälisches Landesmuseum Münster, 1989. 207 p. : chiefly ill. ; 23 cm. (Bildhefte des Westfälischen Landesmuseums für Kunst und Kulturgeschichte . Nr. 28) Includes bibliographical references. ISBN 3-88789-090-6
1. Gröninger, Gerhard, 1582-1652. 2. Sculpture, German - Germany (West) - Münster. 3. Sculpture, Baroque - Germany (West) - Münster. 4. Church decoration and ornament - Germany (West) - Münster. I. Title. II. Series.
NYPL [3-MGO (Gröninger) 91-6968]

Javacheff, Christo. see Christo, 1935-

Javault, Patrick. Boudaille, Georges. L'art abstrait /. [Paris] , c1990. 264, [8] p. : ISBN 2-7079-0024-9 DDC 709/.04/052 20
N6494.A2 B68 1990

Jawlensky, Alexej von, 1864-1941.
Alexej Jawlensky, vom Abbild zum Urbild : Ausstellung, Galerie im Ganserhaus , 15. September bis 28. Oktober 1979 / Arbeitskreis 68, Künstlergemeinschaft Wasserburg am Inn e.V., in zusammenarbeit mit den Bayerischen Staatsgemäldesammlungen ; [Katalog, Gottlieb

Leinz]. Wasserburg am Inn : Der Arbeitskreis, 1979. 107 p. : ill. (some col.) ; 24 cm. Bibliography: p. 107.
1. Jawlensky, Alexej von, 1864-1941 - Exhibitions. I. Leinz, Gottlieb. II. Galerie im Ganserhaus. III. Arbeitskreis Achtundsechzig. IV. Bavaria. Bayerische Staatsgemäldesammlungen. V. Title.
N6999.J38 A4 1979
NYPL [3-MCZ J41 81-398]

JAWLENSKY, ALEXEJ VON, 1864-1941 - EXHIBITIONS.
Jawlensky, Alexej von, 1864-1941. Alexej Jawlensky, vom Abbild zum Urbild . Wasserburg am Inn , 1979. 107 p. :
N6999.J38 A4 1979
NYPL [3-MCZ J41 81-398]

Jaworska, Władysława. Puget, Catherine. Gauguin et ses amis à Pont-Aven /. Douarnenez , 1989. 113 p. : ISBN 2-903708-22-3
IN PROCESS (ONLINE)
NYPL [3-MAMI 91-6154]

Jaxa, Piotr. L'esprit de Genève : 100 photographies / Piotr Jaxa. Lausanne : Editions 24 heurei, c1988. 150 p. : Col. ill. ; 25 x 33 cm. Includes bibliographical references. ISBN 2-8265-1051-7
1. Geneva (Switzerland) - Description - Views. I. Title.
NYPL [MFX+ (Jaxa) 89-17890]

Jay Connaway, fifty years of his works, 1919-1969. Connaway, Jay Hall, 1893-1970. [Binghamton, c1969] 60 p. DDC 759.13
ND237.C677 A47 **NYPL [3-MCX C752.N5]**

Jay DeFeo . Stich, Sidra. Berkeley, Calif. , 1989. 89 p. :
IN PROCESS (ONLINE)
NYPL [3-MCX+ D313 90-11686]

Jay, Paul.
Musée Nicéphore Niépce. Niépce, premiers outils, premiers résultats . Ville de Chalon-sur-Saône [France] , 1978. 59 p. :
NYPL [MFX (Niépce) 90-5757]

Niépce, genèse d'une invention / Paul Jay. Chalon-sur-Saône [France] : Société des amis du Musée Nicéphore Niépce, 1988. 360 p. : ill. (some col.) ; 29 cm. Includes bibliographical references (p. 352-355) ISBN 2-907284-12-6 DDC 770/.92 20
1. Niépce, Nicéphore, 1765-1833 - Museums. 2. Niépce, Nicéphore, 1765-1833 - Archives. 3. Photography - History - Museums. I. Title.
TR6.F82 C475 1988
NYPL [MFX (Niépce) 91-3594]

Jaya Appasamy. see Appasamy, Jaya, 1918-

Jayadeva, 12th cent.
GITAGOVINDA - ILLUSTRATIONS.
Vatsyayan, Kapila. Mewari Gita-Govinda /. New Delhi , c1987. xi, 276 p. :
ND1337.I5 V38 1987
NYPL [3-MAF+ 91-4471]

Jayakar, Pupul.
The earth mother / Pupul Jayakar ; [foreword by Stella Kramrisch]. Rev., updated ed. New Delhi, India ; New York, N.Y., U. S. A. : Penguin Books, 1989. 229 p., [32] p. of plates : ill. ; 21 cm. Revision of: The earthen drum. On ritual arts of rural India. Includes bibliographical references (p. [195]-207) and index. ISBN 0-14-012352-0 : DDC 704.9/4894/0954 20
1. Folk art - India. 2. Arts, Indic. 3. Rites and ceremonies - India. 4. Mother-goddesses in art. I. Title.
NX576.A1 J38 1989
NYPL [3-MAF 91-3706]

The earth mother : legends, goddesses, and ritual arts of India / by Pupul Jayakar.1st Harper & Row ed. San Francisco, Calif. : Harper & Row, c1990. xxx, 248 p., [32] p. of plates : ill. ; 21 cm. Rev. and updated ed. of: The earthen drum. 1980. "Reprinted by arrangement with Penguin Books India, Ltd."--T.p. verso. Includes bibliographical references (p. 221-230) and index. ISBN 0-06-250405-3 : DDC 700/.954 20
1. Art, Indic. 2. Mother-goddesses in art. 3. Art and society - India. I. Jayakar, Pupul. Earthen drum. II. Title.
N8191.I4 J39 1990 **NYPL [3-MAF 91-5051]**

Earthen drum. Jayakar, Pupul. The earth mother : legends, goddesses, and ritual arts of India / by Pupul Jayakar.1st Harper & Row ed. San Francisco, Calif. , c1990. xxx, 248 p., [32] p. of plates : ISBN 0-06-250405-3 : DDC

700/.954 20
N8191.I4 J39 1990 **NYPL [3-MAF 91-5051]**

Jayanula Ābedinera jijñāsā /. Jahangir, Burhanuddin Khan. Ḍhākā , 1990. 82 p., [14] p. of plates :
N7310.8.B25 J344 1990

Jayasinghe, Gamini, 1940- Bandaranayake, Senake. The rock and wall paintings of Sri Lanka /. Colombo , c1986. 300 p. : ISBN 955-9029-00-2 : DDC 751.7/3/095493 19
ND2830.A1 B36 1986
NYPL [3-MAF+ 90-11751]

JAZZ.
Barbecue strut [sound recording]. Chantenay-Villedieu , p1986. 1 sound disc :
NATO 907

Tango subversivo [sound recording]. Aachen , p1984. 1 sound disc :
Nabel Nbl 8413

West End Avenue [sound recording]. Aachen , p1989. 1 sound disc :
Nabel 4633

JAZZ - 1981-1990.
Implement yourself [sound recording]. New York , p1990. 1 sound disc :
New World/Countercurrents NW398-2

UIT [sound recording]. Italy , 1986. 1 sound disc :
Nato 994

JAZZ BAND MUSIC. see BIG BAND MUSIC.

JAZZ MUSIC - WEST INDIES.
Gilbert, Will G. Rumbamuziek [microform]. s-Gravenhage [1947?] 119 p.
NYPL [Sc Micro R-5903 no.2]

JAZZ SONGS. see JAZZ VOCALS.

JAZZ VOCALS.
Carmen sings Monk [sound recording]. New York , p1990. 1 sound disc :
Novus 3086-2-N

J.B. Speed Art Museum. Hall, Michael D. Michael Hall, sculpture, 1964-1970 . [Louisville, Ky. , 1970] [16] p. :
NYPL [3-MGO (Hall) 91-7024]

Je regarde Manet /. Bacherich, Martine. Paris , c1990. 160 p. : ISBN 2-87660-074-9 : DDC 759.4 20
ND553.M3 B24 1990

Jean Charlot . Charlot, Jean, 1898- Honolulu, Hawaii , 1991. p. cm. DDC 760/.092 20
N6853.C4733 A4 1991

Jean Cocteau . Cocteau, Jean, 1889-1963. Köln , c1989. 418 p. : ISBN 3-7701-2380-8
NYPL [3-MCO C66 89-21295]

Jean Cocteau and the illustrated book /. Emboden, William A. [Northridge, Calif.] , 1990. 29 p. :
NYPL [MDG+ (Cocteau) 90-11895]

Jean Cocteau & the illustrated book. Emboden, William A. Jean Cocteau and the illustrated book /. [Northridge, Calif.] , 1990. 29 p. :
NYPL [MDG+ (Cocteau) 90-11895]

Jean Dubuffet: paintings. Dubuffet, Jean, 1901- London, 1966. 63 p.
ND553.D772 A9
NYPL [3-MCO D82 90-5661]

Jean-Emile Laboureur, gravures et lithographies individuelles. Laboureur, Sylvain. Catalogue complet de l'œuvre de Jean-Emile Laboureur /. Neuchâtel, Suisse , c1989-c1990. 2 v. : ISBN 2-8258-0026-0 (v. 1)
NYPL [MDG (Laboureur) 90-1276]

Jean-Emile Laboureur, 1877-1943 . Laboureur, Jean Émile, 1877-1943. New York , c1977. 62 p. :
NE650.L3 A48
NYPL [MDG (Laboureur) 77-1287]

Jean Fautrier /. Cabanne, Pierre. Paris , c1988. 167 p. : ISBN 2-7291-0346-5 DDC 759.4 20
ND553.F36 A4 1988

Jean-Francis Auburtin, 1866-1930 . Auburtin, Jean-Francis, 1866-1930. Paris [1990?] 158 p. : ISBN 2-905118-27-X
NYPL [3-MCO A897 91-7473]

Jean-Jacques Henner. Henner, Jean-Jacques, 1829-1905. J.J. Henner. Mulhouse [Steinbrunn-le-Haut] [1989-] v. <1 > : ISBN

2-86339-059-7 (v. 1) : DDC 759.4 20
ND553.H4 A3 1989

Jean Lecoultre /. Thévoz, Michel. Genève ,
c1989. 159 p. : ISBN 2-605-00147-4 DDC
759.9494 20
ND853.L435 T4 1989
     NYPL [3-MCZ L468 91-6815]

Jean-Marie Poumeyrol . Poumeyrol, Jean-Marie,
1946- [Paris] , c1991. 79 p. : ISBN
2-85956-910-3 : DDC 759.4 20
ND553.P7 A4 1991

Jean-Michel Basquiat . Basquiat, Jean Michel.
Hannover , 1989. [122] p. : ***NYPL [3-MAW
(Hanover) 73-2900 1989/4]***

Jean-Michel Basquiat . Basquiat, Jean Michel.
New York, NY , c1989. 153 p. : ISBN
0-922678-03-0 DDC 760/.092 20
N6608.B276 A4 1989
     NYPL [3-MCX+ B317 91-3366]

Jean Michel Basquiat drawings /. Basquiat, Jean
Michel. Boston , c1990. p. ISBN 0-8212-1887-5 :
DDC 741.973 20
NC179.B37 A4 1990

Jean-Pierre Pincemin /. Rose, Barbara.
[Aubusson] [Paris] [1986] 79 p. : ISBN
2-7291-0207-4 :
MLCM 89/01361 (N)
     NYPL [3-MCO P643 90-12613]

Jean-Pierre Raynaud . Raynaud, Jean Pierre,
1939- Houston, Tex. , c1991. 135 p. : ISBN
0-939594-23-4 : DDC 709/.2 20
N6853.R33 A4 1991
     NYPL [3-MGO (Raynaud) 91-7980]

Jean, Raymond, 1925- L'Artiste, témoin de son
temps (?) . Aix-en-Provence , 1990. xiv, 168
p. ; ISBN 2-85399-238-1 : DDC 700/.942 20
NX543 .A83 1990

Jeanne Bardey et Rodin /. Thiolier, Hubert.
[Bron, France] [1990] 270 p. : ISBN
2-9504835-3-4 DDC 709/.2 B 20
NB553.B23 T48 1990

Jeanneau, Hubert. Vitou, Elisabeth. Gabriel
Guévrékian, 1900-1970 . Paris , c1987. 150 p. :
ISBN 2-86649-003-7 : DDC 720/.92/4 19
NA1053.G77 V5 1987
     NYPL [3-MQZ (Guévrékian) 91-4588]

Jeannin, Pierre. see **Clébert, Jean Paul.**

Jedd Garet . Garet, Jedd, 1955- New York
[1981] [43] p. :
     NYPL [3-MCX G229 91-849]

Jedlicka, Gotthard, 1899-1965. Albert Durer /
par Gothard Jedlicka. Paris : Rieder, 1928. 64
p., 60 p. of plates : ill. ; 20 cm. (Maitres de l'art
ancien) Bibliography: p. [57]
I. Title. ***NYPL [3-MCK D85 90-8674]***

Jeff Wall, 1990 /. Dufour, Gary, 1954-
[Vancouver , 1990] 119 p. : ISBN 0-920095-83-6
DDC 779/.092/4 19
     NYPL [MFX (Wall) 90-11194]

Jefferies, Richard, 1848-1887. Hanscomb, Brian.
Sun, sea & earth /. Andoversford,
Gloucestershire , 1989. [21] p. : ISBN
1-85428-004-X DDC 769.92 20
NE642.H34 A4 1989

Jeffers, Wendy. Spencer, Niles, 1893-1952. Niles
Spencer . New York, N.Y. , c1990. 26 p. :
     NYPL [3-MCX S745 91-6441]

JEFFERSON COUNTY, WIS. - MAPS.
(1990) Rockford Map Publishers. Jefferson
County, Wisconsin, land atlas & plat book.
Rockford, Ill. , Jefferson, Wis. [c1990] 1 atlas
(71 p.) : ***NYPL [Map Div. 91-4671]***

**Jefferson County, Wisconsin, land atlas & plat
book.** Rockford Map Publishers. Rockford, Ill. ,
Jefferson, Wis. [c1990] 1 atlas (71 p.) :
     NYPL [Map Div. 91-4671]

Jeffrey Smart . McDonald, John, 1961- Roseville,
NSW, Australia , c1990. 168 p. : ISBN
976-8097-01-9
     NYPL [3-MCZ+ S644 91-6381]

Jeffri, Joan. Information on artists. New York,
NY , c1989. 2 v. (various pagings) ; DDC
331.7/617/00973 20
N58 .I54 1989

Jeg. Portrett av jeg /. Oslo , c1990. 131 p. :
ISBN 82-504-1793-3
N7073.E36 P67 1990

Jegodzienski, Harald, 1952-
Harald Jegodzienski : keramische plastieken =
Keramische Plastiken : [tentoonstelling]
Museum Boymans-van Beuningen, Rotterdam,
16-12-89 - 28-1-90 ; Oberhessisches Museum,
Giessen, 11-5 - 24-6-90. Rotterdam : Het
Museum, [1989] 48 p. : ill., port. ; 27 cm. Dutch
and German. ISBN 90-6918-051-0
*1. Jegodzienski, Harald, 1952- - Exhibitions. I.
Oberhessisches Museum. II. Museum Boymans-Van
Beuningen. III. Title.*
   NYPL [3-MGO (Jegodzienski) 90-11665]

**JEGODZIENSKI, HARALD, 1952- -
EXHIBITIONS.**
Jegodzienski, Harald, 1952- Harald
Jegodzienski . Rotterdam [1989] 48 p. : ISBN
90-6918-051-0
   NYPL [3-MGO (Jegodzienski) 90-11665]

Jehl, Gerhard. Tafelmaier, Walter, 1935-
Architekturmalerei an Fassaden . Stuttgart ,
1988. 159 p. : ISBN 3-421-02937-7
     NYPL [3-MRX 90-12633]

Jeiter, Michael. Stolz, Georg. Franken.
[München] [1989] 371 p. : ISBN 3-422-03012-3
DDC 709/.43/32 20
N6874.F7 S76 1989

Jekyll, Walter. (ed) Jamaican song and story;
Annancy stories, digging sings, ring tunes, and
dancing tunes. With new introductory essays by
Philip Sherlock, Louise Bennett and Rex
Nettleford. New York, Dover Publications
[1966] xv, 288 p. 22 cm. Includes unacc. melodies.
"An unabridged and unaltered republication of the work
first published ... in 1907."
*1. Folklore - Jamaica. 2. Folk-songs, English - Jamaica.
3. Folk music - Jamaica. I. Title.*
     NYPL [JMD 74-129]

Jemima . Blackburn, Jemima, 1823-1909.
Edinburgh , 1988. 207 p. : ISBN 0-86241-186-6
   NYPL [3-MCV B628 90-12435]

Jencks, Charles.
The language of post-modern architecture /
Charles Jencks. 6th rev. ed. New York :
Rizzoli, 1991. p. cm. Includes bibliographical
references. ISBN 0-8478-1359-2 DDC 724/.6 20
1. Architecture, Postmodern. I. Title.
NA682.P67 J38 1991

The new moderns from late to neo-modernism
/ Charles Jencks. London : Academy Editions,
1990. 300 p. : ill. (some col.) ; 32 cm. Includes
bibliographical references and index. ISBN
0-85670-968-9
1. Architecture, Modern - 20th century. I. Title.
     NYPL [3-MQV+ 90-13384]

Jenkins, David.
Financial Times Print Works, London, 1988 :
architects: Nicholas Grimshaw and Partners /
text and drawings, David Jenkins ; photographs,
Jo Reid and John Peck. London : Architecture
and Design Technology Press ; New York :
Van Nostrand Reinhold, 1991. ca. 60 p. : ill.
(some col.), plans ; 30 cm. (Architecture in detail .
05) Includes bibliographical references. ISBN
1-85454-255-9 (pbk.). DDC 725.4 20
*1. Grimshaw, Nicholas. 2. Financial Times Print Works
(London, England). 3. Nicholas Grimshaw and Partners.
I. Title. II. Series.*
NA6400
     NYPL [3-MQZ+ (Grimshaw) 91-6989]

Mound stand, Lord's Cricket Ground, London,
1987 : architects: Michael Hopkins and Partners
/ text, David Jenkins ; photographs, Dave
Bower. London : Architecture Design and
Technology Press ; New York : Van Nostrand
Reinhold, 1991. 1 v. (ca. 58 p.) : ill. (some
col.), plans ; 30 cm. (Architecture in detail . 01)
Includes bibliographical references. ISBN
1-85454-558-2 (pbk.) : DDC 725.827 20
*1. Michael Hopkins and Partners. 2. Lord's Cricket
Ground (London, England). 3. Recreation centers -
Great Britain. 4. Sports facilities - Great Britain. I.
Title. II. Series.*
NA6800
     NYPL [3-MQZ+ (Hopkins) 91-6983]

Jenkins, Nicholas, 1961- Kirstein, Lincoln, 1907-
By with to & from . New York , 1991. p. cm.
ISBN 0-374-18765-7 : DDC 700/.9/04 20
NX456 .K56 1991

Jenkins, Patrick. Animation : how to draw your
own flipbooks, and other fun ways to make
cartoons move / by Patrick Jenkins. Reading,

Mass. : Addison Wesley Pub. Co., c1991. p.
cm. Includes instructions for creating drawings that
give the illusion of various kinds of movement and
special effects. Also describes several early motion
picture devices. ISBN 0-201-56757-1 : DDC
741.5/8 20
*1. Animated films - Technique - Juvenile literature. I.
Title.*
NC1765 .J46 1991

Jenkins, Susan, 1947- The American quilt story :
the how-to and heritage of a craft tradition :
step-by-step directions for 30 antique quilts /
by Susan Jenkins and Linda Seward. Emmaus,
Pa. : Rodale Press ; New York : Distributed by
St. Martin's Press, c1991. p. cm. "First published
as Quilts, the American story, in 1991 by HarperCollins
Publishers, London"--T.p. verso. Includes bibliographical
references (p.) and index. ISBN 0-87857-992-3
(hardcover) : DDC 746.9/7 20
*1. Quilts - United States - History. I. Seward, Linda. II.
Title.*
NK9112 .J4 1991

Jenkins, Suzy Logan. Carter, Cheryl G. North
American schools of the arts . [Washington,
D.C.] [c1990] vii, 172 p. : DDC 700/.71/273 20
NX303 .C37 1990

Jenks, Bill. Early American pattern glass,
1850-1910 : major collectible table settings with
prices / Bill Jenks, Jerry Luna. Radnor, Pa. :
Wallace-Homestead Book Co., c1990. xv, 602
p. : ill. ; 27 cm. Includes bibliographical references.
ISBN 0-87069-545-2 : DDC 748.2913/075 20
*1. Pattern glass - United States - History - 19th
century - Collectios and collecting - Catalogs. 2. Pattern
glass - United States - History - 20th century -
Collectors and collecting - Catalogs. I. Luna, Jerry. II.
Title.*
NK5439.P36 E18 1990
     NYPL [3-MPW 90-11097]

Jenny, Christine. Minkoff, Gérald. Gérald
Minkoff, Muriel Olesen . [Solothurn] , 1988. 48
p. : ISBN 3-906663-14-0
     NYPL [3-MCZ + M6435 90-132]

Jenny Holzer . Auping, Michael. Buffalo, N.Y. ,
1991. p. cm. ISBN 0-914782-80-0 DDC 709/.2 20
N6537.H577 A4 1991

Jensen, Jens Christian.
Kunsthalle zu Kiel. Otto Dix, Zeichnungen aus
dem Nachlass, 1911-1942 . Kiel [1980?] [71]
p. : ***NYPL [3-MCK+ D619 90-5743]***

Schmaltz, K. L., 1932- K-L Schmaltz . [Kiel ,
1979] [33] leaves :
N6888.S366 A4 1979
     NYPL [3-MGO (Schmaltz) 81-963]

Zorn, Anders, 1860-1920. Anders Zorn,
1860-1920 . [München] , 1989. 237 p. : ISBN
3-923701-36-5
     NYPL [3-MCZ Z89 90-11754]

Zorn, Anders, 1860-1920. Anders Zorn,
1860-1920 . [Munich] [1990?] 237 p. : ISBN
3-923701-36-5 DDC 760/.092 20
N7093.Z6 A4 1990

Jensen, Jens Christian, 1928-
Antes, Horst, 1936- Horst Antes . Kiel , c1990.
84 p. : ISBN 3-923701-41-1
     NYPL [3-MCK+ A62 91-6789]

Lüpertz, Markus, 1941- Markus Lüpertz .
[Kiel] , c1988. 56 p. : ISBN 3-923701-31-4
     NYPL [3-MCK+ L997 90-10786]

Jensen, Jon. Gammon, Mitzi. The south /. New
York , 1991. p. cm. ISBN 0-553-07550-0 DDC
728/.37/0975 20
NA7211 .G35 1991

Jensen, Ludvig Irgens.
[Instrumental music. Selections]
Passacaglia ; Partita sinfonica ; Sonata in B♭
major for violin & piano [sound recording] /
Ludvig Irgens Jensen. [Norway] : NIM,
p1988. 1 sound disc : digital ; 4 3/4 in. The
1st and 2nd works for orchestra. Oslo Philharmonic
Orchestra ; Ole Kristian Ruud, conductor ; Stig
Nilsson, violin ; Jens Harald Bratlie, piano. Recorded
1986 in the Oslo Concert Hall (1st-2nd works) and
1987 in the studios of the Norwegian Broadcasting
Corp. (3rd work). Eds. recorded: Norsk
mussikkforlag and the Norwegian Music Information
Centre. Compact disc. Durations: 21:00; 19:00; 28:00.
*1. Orchestral music. 2. Suites (Orchestra). 3. Sonatas
(Violin and piano). I. Title: Partita sinfonica.*
NIM CDN 31003

Jenssen Pharmaceutica. Open mind . Milano ,
c1989. 318 p. : *NYPL [3-MAMZ 90-11011]*

Jentsch, Ralph. Franken, Franz Hermann. Hans
Meid . Stuttgart-Bad Cannstatt , c1987. 462 p. :
ISBN 3-922608-58-2
NYPL [3-MCK+ M4978 90-11755]

Jeřábek, Jaroslav. Vondrušková, Alena. Tradice
lidové tvorby . V Praze , 1988. 191 p. :
NK1035.C92 B649 1988

Jerome C. Krause & Tom Uttech : visions from
the north woods : Milwaukee Art Center,
February 18-March 27,1977. [Milwaukee : The
Center, 1977?] 22 p. : ill. ; 26 cm. Includes
bibliographical references.
*1. Krause, Jerome C., 1943- - Exhibitions. 2. Uttech,
Tom, 1942- - Exhibitions. 3. Romanticism in art -
United States - Exhibitions. 4. Painting, Modern - 20th
century - United States - Exhibitions. I. Krause, Jerome
C., 1943-. II. Uttech, Tom, 1942-. III. Milwaukee. Art
Center.* *NYPL [3-MCW 91-549]*

Jerrehian, Aram, 1934- Oriental rug primer :
buying and understanding new Oriental rugs /
by Aram K. Jerrehian, Jr.Updated and rev.
Philadelphia, Pa. : Running Press, c1990. 221
p. : ill. (some col.) ; 26 cm. Includes bibliographical
references and index. ISBN 0-89471-739-1 (pbk.) :
DDC 746.7/5/095 20
1. Rugs, Oriental - Handbooks, manuals, etc. I. Title.
NK2808 .J47 1990 *NYPL [MOP 91-3455]*

Jersey City Museum. Contemporary woodblock
prints . [Jersey City, N.J.] , c1989. 16 p. :
NYPL [MDO 91-4747]

JERSEY CITY (N.J.) - MAPS.
Atlas of Hudson County, New Jersey.
Philadelphia, Pa. , 1908-1909. 2 atlases :
NYPL [Map Div. 91-4092]

**JERUSALEM - HISTORY - LATIN
KINGDOM, 1099-1244.**
Pringle, Denys. The churches of the Crusader
Kingdom of Jerusalem . Cambridge , New
York , 1992- p. cm. ISBN 0-521-39036-2 (v. 1)
DDC 726/.5/0956909021 20
NA5989.6 .P75 1992

Jerusalem, holy business as usual. Katz, Shemuel,
1926- Tel Aviv [1970] 1 v. (unpaged)
*NYPL [*PXLL (Jerusalem) 90-1882]*

**JERUSALEM - SOCIAL LIFE AND
CUSTOMS - CARICATURES AND
CARTOONS.**
Katz, Shemuel, 1926- Jerusalem, holy business
as usual. Tel Aviv [1970] 1 v. (unpaged)
*NYPL [*PXLL (Jerusalem) 90-1882]*

Jessel, Hans, 1956- Friesenhaustüren / Hans
Jessel. Hamburg : Ellert & Richter, c1990. 56
p. : chiefly col. ill. ; 29 cm. (Die Weisse Reihe)
Includes bibliographical references (p. 56). ISBN
3-89234-159-1
*1. Architecture, Domestic - Germany - Friesland. 2.
Doors - Germany - Friesland. 3. Architecture -
Germany - Friesland - Details. I. Series: Weisse Reihe
(Hamburg, Germany). II. Title.*
NA7350.F84 J4 1990

Jessup, Helen Ibbitson. Court arts of Indonesia /
Helen Ibbitson Jessup. 1st ed. New York : Asia
Society Galleries in association with H.N.
Abrams, c1990. 288 p. : ill. (some col.), maps ;
30 cm. Catalog of an exhibition held at the Asia
Society Galleries, New York, Sept. 19-Dec. 16, 1990
and at three other U. S. locations through Jan. 5, 1992.
Includes bibliographical references (p. 275-280) and
index. ISBN 0-8109-3165-6
*1. Art, Indonesian - Exhibitions. 2. Indonesia - Kings
and rulers - Art patronage - Exhibitions. I. Asia
Society. Galleries. II. Title.*
IN PROCESS (ONLINE)
NYPL [3-MAF+ 91-6099]

**JESUITS - MISSIONS - CANADA -
PICTORIAL WORKS.**
Pomedli, Michael. William Kurelek's Huronia
mission paintings /. Lewiston, N.Y. , 1991. p.
cm. ISBN 0-7734-9731-5 DDC 759.11 20
ND249.K85 P66 1991

JESUS CHRIST - ART.
Christus in der bildenden Kunst . München ,
c1989. 150 p. : ISBN 3-466-36334-9
N8050 .C44 1989

Greenstein, Jack Matthew. Mantegna and
painting as historical narrative /. Chicago ,
1992. p. cm. ISBN 0-226-30707-7 DDC 759.5 20
ND623.M3 G7 1992

Gross, Friedrich. Jesus, Luther und der Papst
im Bilderkampf 1871 bis 1918 . Marburg ,
c1989. 588 p. : ISBN 3-922561-37-3
ND566 .G75 1989

**Jesus Christ - Cross. see Jesus Christ -
Crucifixion.**

JESUS CHRIST - CRUCIFIXION - ART.
Das Panorama in Altötting . München , 1990.
112 p., 1 folded leaf of plate : ISBN
3-87490-544-6 *NYPL [3-MBO+ 91-3683]*

Pattis, Erich. Christus Dominator . Innsbruck
[1964] 287 p. :
MLCM 87/381 (N) *NYPL [3-MAI 91-292]*

Raw, Barbara Catherine. Anglo-Saxon
crucifixion iconography and the art of the
monastic revival /. Cambridge [England] , New
York , 1990. xii, 296 p., 16 p. of plates ; ISBN
0-521-36370-5 DDC 704.9/4853/0942 20
N6763 .R38 1990
NYPL [3-MAMZ 90-11590]

Jesus Christ in art. see Jesus Christ - Art.

JESUS CHRIST - NATIVITY - ART.
Stichel, Rainer. Die Geburt Christi in der
russischen Ikonenmalerei . Stuttgart , 1990. 176
p., 92 p. of plates : ISBN 3-515-04273-3 DDC
755/.53/0947 20
N8189.S62 R9773 1990

Stichel, Rainer. Die Geburt Christi in der
russischen Ikonenmalerei . Stuttgart , 1990. 176
p., 92 p. of plates : ISBN 3-515-04273-3
NYPL [3-MAIH+ 91-4218]

**JESUS CHRIST - NATIVITY - ART -
EXHIBITIONS.**
Autour de la Nativité dans la peinture des
collections angevines . [Angers] [1989] 200 p. :
ISBN 2-905608-01-3 :
ND1432.F8 A98 1989

**Jesus Christ - Passion - Art. see Jesus Christ -
Art.**

**Jesus Christ - Pictures, illustrations, etc. see
Jesus Christ - Art.**

JESUS CHRIST - RESURRECTION - ART.
Sheingorn, Pamela. The Easter sepulchre in
England /. Kalamazoo, MI , 1987. 426 p., [36]
p. of plates : ISBN 0-918720-79-6 (hardbound)
DDC 730/.942/0902 20
NB1912.J47 S48 1987

Jesús F. Contreras, 1866-1902 . Contreras, Jesús
F. (Jesús Fructuoso), 1866-1902. [Mexico
City] , c1990. 129 p. : DDC 730/.92 20
NB259.C65 A4 1990

Jesús Gallardo. Gallardo, Jesús, 1931- Cuaderno
de dibujos /. Guanajuato, Gto. [i.e. Guanajuato,
Mexico] , 1989. 112 p. : ISBN 968-617-017-0
DDC 741.972 20
NC146.G35 A4 1989

**Jesus, Luther und der Papst im Bilderkampf
1871 bis 1918 .** Gross, Friedrich. Marburg ,
c1989. 588 p. : ISBN 3-922561-37-3
ND566 .G75 1989

Jesús Reyes Ferreira. Reyes Ferreira, Jesús.
[Mexico?] , 1978 (México : Fernando
Fernández Ediciones) 1 v. (unpaged) : DDC
759.972 20
ND259.R46 A4 1987a

**Jesús Reyes Ferreira, pintor mexicano y
universal.** Reyes Ferreira, Jesús. Jesús Reyes
Ferreira. [Mexico?] , 1978 (México : Fernando
Fernández Ediciones) 1 v. (unpaged) : DDC
759.972 20
ND259.R46 A4 1987a

Jetelová, Magdalena, 1946-
Magdalena Jetelová : Skulpturen : 18. März-25.
April 1990, Städtische Galerie Göppingen /
[Ausstellung und Katalog, Werner Meyer].
[Göppingen] : Die Galerie, c1990. 56 p. : ill.
(some col.) ; 31 cm. Includes bibliographical
references (p. 53-55). ISBN 3-927791-02-4
*1. Jetelová, Magdalena, 1946- - Exhibitions. I. Meyer,
Werner. II. Städtische Galerie Göppingen. III. Title.*
NYPL [3-MGO+ (Jetelová) 91-5434]

**JETELOVÁ, MAGDALENA, 1946- -
EXHIBITIONS.**
Jetelová, Magdalena, 1946- Magdalena
Jetelová. [Göppingen] , c1990. 56 p. : ISBN
3-927791-02-4
NYPL [3-MGO+ (Jetelová) 91-5434]

**Jewelers' circular/keystone sterling flatware
pattern index.** 2nd ed., 4th revision. Radnor,
PA : Jewelers' Circular-Keystone, c1989. xxxvi,
154 p. : ill. ; 20 x 31 cm. Includes indexes. ISBN
0-931744-12-1 : DDC 739.2/383 19
*1. Silver flatware - United States - Patterns. I. Jewelers'
circular/keystone. II. Title: Sterling flatware pattern
index.*
TS735 .J453 1989 *NYPL [3-MNO 91-3650]*

Jewelers' circular/keystone. Jewelers'
circular/keystone sterling flatware pattern
index. Radnor, PA , c1989. xxxvi, 154 p. :
ISBN 0-931744-12-1 : DDC 739.2/383 19
TS735 .J453 1989 *NYPL [3-MNO 91-3650]*

Jewell, Linda L. Peter Walker . New York ,
1990. 71 p. : ISBN 0-8478-1069-0
NYPL [3-MSCC 91-5205]

Jewellery : makers, motifs, history, techniques /
Diana Scarisbrick ... [et al.]. London : Thames
and Hudson, 1989. 192 p. : col. ill. ; 27 cm. "A
Quarto book." ISBN 0-500-01465-5
1. Jewelry - History. I. Scarisbrick, Diana.
NYPL [MNR 89-20158]

Jewellery in studio. Houston, John, 1935-
Caroline Broadhead . London , 1990. 64 p. :
ISBN 0-947792-48-1 (pbk.) : DDC 739.27092 20
NYPL [3-MNR 90-12744]

JEWELRY, ANCIENT.
Études sur l'orfèvrerie antique =.
Louvain-la-Neuve , 1980. viii, 154 p. :
NYPL [3-MNR 83-1678]

JEWELRY, ANCIENT - CATALOGS.
Museum für Kunst und Gewerbe Hamburg.
Antiker Gold- und Silberschmuck . Mainz am
Rhein , c1968. x, 246 p. :
NK7307 .H6 *NYPL [3-MNR 90-7024]*

JEWELRY, ANCIENT - MIDDLE EAST.
Musche, Brigitte. Vorderasiatischer Schmuck
von den Anfängen bis zur Zeit der
Achaemeniden (ca. 10,000-330 v. Chr.) /.
Leiden , New York , 1992. p. cm. ISBN
90-04-09491-1 DDC 739.27/09394 20
NK7307 .M8 1992

JEWELRY, ANCIENT - SPAIN.
Nicolini, Gérard. Techniques des ors antiques .
[Paris] , 1990. 2 v. : ISBN 2-7084-0405-9 (set)
DDC 739.27/09366/09014 20
NK7162.A1 N53 1990

JEWELRY - DENMARK - HISTORY.
Thage, Jacob. Danske smykker =.
[Copenhagen] , 1990. 191 p. : ISBN
87-7512-366-5 :
NK7358.A1 T48 1990

JEWELRY - DESIGN.
Houston, John, 1935- Caroline Broadhead .
London , 1990. 64 p. : ISBN 0-947792-48-1
(pbk.) : DDC 739.27092 20
NYPL [3-MNR 90-12744]

The jewelry design source book / Patricia
Bayer ... [et al]. New York : Van Nostrand
Reinhold, c1989. 191 p. : ill. (some col.) ; 27
cm. ISBN 0-442-23828-2 :
I. Bayer, Patricia. *NYPL [3-MNR 91-4492]*

**JEWELRY - EUROPE - HISTORY - 19TH
CENTURY - EXHIBITIONS.**
Becker, Ingeborg, 1947- Schmuckkunst im
Jugendstil /. Berlin , c1988. 95 p. : ISBN
3-496-01064-9 *NYPL [3-MNR 90-12395]*

**JEWELRY - EUROPE - HISTORY - 20TH
CENTURY - EXHIBITIONS.**
Becker, Ingeborg, 1947- Schmuckkunst im
Jugendstil /. Berlin , c1988. 95 p. : ISBN
3-496-01064-9 *NYPL [3-MNR 90-12395]*

JEWELRY - EXHIBITIONS.
Le Bijou 1900 . Bruxelles , 1965. 102 p., [26]
of plates : *NYPL [3-MNR 90-6082]*

**JEWELRY - FRANCE - HISTORY - 19TH
CENTURY - EXHIBITIONS.**
L'Art de Cartier . [Paris] , 1989. 177 p. : ISBN
2-905028-27-0 DDC 739.27/092/2 20
NK7398.C37 A4 1989

**JEWELRY - FRANCE - HISTORY - 20TH
CENTURY - EXHIBITIONS.**
L'Art de Cartier . [Paris] , 1989. 177 p. : ISBN
2-905028-27-0 DDC 739.27/092/2 20
NK7398.C37 A4 1989

**JEWELRY - AGERMANY (EAST) -
HISTORY - 20TH CENTURY.**
Schumann, Rainer, 1941- Rainer Schumann .

[Leipzig] [1987?] [44] p. :
MLCS 88/01806 (N)
NYPL [3-MNR 90-12730]

**JEWELRY - GERMANY - HISTORY - 20TH
CENTURY - CATALOGS.**
Rudolph, Monika, 1956- Naum Slutzky .
Stuttgart [1990] 273 p. : ISBN 3-925369-06-6
NK7198.S58 A4 1990

**JEWELRY - GERMANY (WEST) - HISTORY -
20TH CENTURY - EXHIBITIONS.**
Zeitgenössische Schmuckkunst aus der
Bundesrepublik Deutschland . Stuttgart , c1989.
87 p. : **NYPL [3-MNR 91-4285]**

JEWELRY - HISTORY.
Bennett, David. Understanding jewellery /.
Woodbridge , c1989. 386 p. : ISBN
1-85149-075-2 : DDC 739.2709 20
NK7306 **NYPL [MNR 90-11502]**

Jewellery . London , 1989. 192 p. : ISBN
0-500-01465-5 **NYPL [MNR 89-20158]**

Jewelry, 7000 years . New York [1991] p. cm.
ISBN 0-8109-8103-3 DDC 739.27/09 20
NK7306 .J494 1991

JEWELRY - HISTORY - 19TH CENTURY.
Gere, Charlotte. Artists' jewellery . Woodbridge
[England] , c1989. 244 p. : ISBN 1-85149-024-8
NYPL [MNR 89-11557]

JEWELRY - HISTORY - 20TH CENTURY.
Gere, Charlotte. Artists' jewellery . Woodbridge
[England] , c1989. 244 p. : ISBN 1-85149-024-8
NYPL [MNR 89-11557]

JEWELRY - HUNGARY.
Baloghné Horváth, Terézia. [Népi ékszerek.
English.] Hungarian folk jewelry /. Budapest ,
1983. 66 p., [56] p. of plates : ISBN
963-13-1762-5 DDC 739.27/09439 19
GT2252.H9 B3513 1983
NYPL [3-MNR 90-11105]

**JEWELRY - ITALY - HISTORY - 20TH
CENTURY - EXHIBITIONS.**
Oro d'autore . [Arezzo] [1988] 135 p. :
NYPL [3-MNR 91-6356]

Oro d'autore . Arezzo [1989] 147 p. :
NYPL [3-MNR 91-6510]

JEWELRY MAKING - EXHIBITIONS.
Wie gerät Gerät schmuck? /. Zürich [1989?]
126 p. : ISBN 3-907065-36-0
IN PROCESS (ONLINE)
NYPL [3-MNR 91-5889]

JEWELRY - MIDDLE EAST.
Musche, Brigitte. Vorderasiatischer Schmuck
von den Anfängen bis zur Zeit der
Achaemeniden (ca. 10,000-330 v. Chr.) /.
Leiden , New York , 1992. p. cm. ISBN
90-04-09491-1 DDC 739.27/09394 20
NK7307 .M8 1992

JEWELRY - NEW YORK (N.Y.) - CATALOGS.
Metropolitan Museum of Art (New York, N.Y.)
Metropolitan jewelry . New York , Boston ,
1991. p. cm. ISBN 0-87099-616-9 DDC
739.27/074/7471 20
NK7302.N5 M486 1991

Jewelry of the stars . Ball, Joanne Dubbs. West
Chester, Pa. , c1991. 192 p. : ISBN
0-88740-294-1 DDC 739.27/092 20
NK7398.J67 B35 1991

JEWELRY - POLAND - EXHIBITIONS.
Polonia, gioielli, ornamenti e arredi . [Arezzo ,
1989] xxxi, 197 p. :
NYPL [3-MNO+ 90-13368]

**JEWELRY - POLAND - HISTORY - 20TH
CENTURY - EXHIBITIONS.**
Oro d'autore . Arezzo [1989] 147 p. :
NYPL [3-MNR 91-6510]

JEWELRY - PRICES.
Cailles, Françoise. Le prix des bijoux, 1986,
1987, 1988 /. Courbevoie, Paris , c1989. 373
p. : ISBN 2-86770-035-3
NYPL [3-MNR+ 91-8]

**JEWELRY - PRIVATE COLLECTIONS -
ITALY - EXHIBITIONS.**
Il Tesoro dell'architettura . Firenze [1990] 149
p. : DDC 739.27/09/0480744551 20
NK7310 .T47 1990

**JEWELRY - RUSSIAN S.F.S.R. - MOSCOW -
EXHIBITIONS.**
Gosudarstvennyĭ istoricheskiĭ muzeĭ (Moscow,

R.S.F.S.R.) Meraviglie sconosciute dal Museo
storico di Mosca . Milano , c1989. 198 p. :
NYPL [3-MNR+ 91-4646]

Jewelry, seven thousand years. Jewelry, 7000
years . New York [1991] p. cm. ISBN
0-8109-8103-3 DDC 739.27/09 20
NK7306 .J494 1991

JEWELRY - SPAIN.
Nicolini, Gérard. Techniques des ors antiques .
[Paris] , 1990. 2 v. : ISBN 2-7084-0405-9 (set)
DDC 739.27/09366/09014 20
NK7162.A1 N53 1990

Nicolini, Gérard. Techniques des ors antiques .
[Paris] , 1990. 2 v. : ISBN 2-7084-0405-9 (set)
DDC 739.27/09366/09014 20
NK7162.A1 N53 1990

**JEWELRY - SWITZERLAND - HISTORY -
20TH CENTURY - CATALOGS.**
Schobinger, Bernhard. Devon, Karbon, Perm .
[Zürich?] c1988. [64] p. :
NYPL [3-MNR+ 89-28258]

**JEWELRY - UNITED STATES - HISTORY -
20TH CENTURY - EXHIBITIONS.**
Norton, Deborah. Albert Paley . Washington,
D.C. , 1991. p. cm. ISBN 0-295-97152-5 DDC
739.27/092 20
NK7398.P35 A4 1991

JEWELRY, VICTORIAN.
Dawes, Ginny Redington. Victorian jewelry .
New York , 1991. p. cm. ISBN 1-558-59135-4
DDC 739.27/09/034 20
NK7309.85 V53.D38 1991

Jewelry, 7000 years : an international history and
illustrated survey from the collections of the
British Museum / edited by Hugh Tait. New
York : Abradale Press, [1991] p. cm. Previously
published: New York : H.N. Abrams, 1987. Includes
bibliographical references and index. ISBN
0-8109-8103-3 DDC 739.27/09 20
*1. Jewelry - History. 2. British Museum. I. Tait, Hugh.
II. British Museum. III. Title: Jewelry, seven thousand
years.*
NK7306 .J494 1991

JEWELS. see GEMS; JEWELRY.

Jewett Arts Center (Wellesley, Mass.) Chinese
art: symbols and images. [Wellesley, Mass.,
c1967] 63 p. DDC 709/.51
N7342 .L58 **NYPL [3-MAG 90-6432]**

**Jewish Museum, Jewish Theological Seminary of
America. see Jewish Theological Seminary of
America. Jewish Museum.**

Jewish Museum (New York, N.Y.)
Painting a place in America . New York ,
Bloomington , 1991. p. cm. ISBN 0-253-33121-8
(cloth) DDC 704/.0392407471/090410747471
20
N6538.J4 P35 1991

Turner, Judith. White city . [Tel Aviv] , 1984.
88 p. : **NYPL [MFX (Turner) 86-728]**

**Jewish Theological Seminary of America. Jewish
Museum.** Ben-Zion. Ben-Zion 1933-1959 .
New York [1959] xxxii p. :
NYPL [3-MCZ B470 90-12696]

JEWISH WAY OF LIFE IN ART.
Oppenheim, Moritz, d. 1882. Bilder aus dem
altjüdischen Familienleben /. Frankfurt am
Main [188-?] Portfolio ([14] leaves of plates) :
NYPL [*PVP 84-1266]

JEWS - AUSTRIA - DIRECTORIES.
Mokotoff, Gary. Where once we walked .
Teaneck, N.J. , c1991. xxviii, 514 p. : ISBN
0-9626373-1-9 (acid-free paper) : DDC
914.7/0003 20
DS135.E83 M65 1991
NYPL [*PWA 91-4243]

**JEWS - CUSTOMS. see JEWS - SOCIAL LIFE
AND CUSTOMS.**

**JEWS - EUROPE, EASTERN -
DIRECTORIES.**
Mokotoff, Gary. Where once we walked .
Teaneck, N.J. , c1991. xxviii, 514 p. : ISBN
0-9626373-1-9 (acid-free paper) : DDC
914.7/0003 20
DS135.E83 M65 1991
NYPL [*PWA 91-4243]

JEWS - GERMANY - DIRECTORIES.
Mokotoff, Gary. Where once we walked .
Teaneck, N.J. , c1991. xxviii, 514 p. : ISBN

0-9626373-1-9 (acid-free paper) : DDC
914.7/0003 20
DS135.E83 M65 1991
NYPL [*PWA 91-4243]

JEWS IN ART.
Michaelson, Menachem. Zvi Ribak . Studio
City, CA , 1991. p. ISBN 0-88734-615-4 : DDC
759.95694 20
N7279.R53 M53 1991

Revel-Neher, Elisabeth. The image of the Jew
in Byzantine art /. Oxford, England , New
York , 1991. p. cm. ISBN 0-08-040655-6 (HC) :
DDC 704.9/499495004924 20
N6250 .R44 1991

**JEWS, RUSSIAN - SOCIAL LIFE AND
CUSTOMS - JUVENILE LITERATURE.**
Bober, Natalie. Marc Chagall . Philadelphia ,
1991. p. cm. ISBN 0-8276-0379-7 DDC 759.7 B
20
N6999.C46 B6 1991

**JEWS - SOCIAL CUSTOMS. see JEWS -
SOCIAL LIFE AND CUSTOMS.**

**JEWS - SOCIAL LIFE AND CUSTOMS -
PICTORIAL WORKS.**
Oppenheim, Moritz, d. 1882. Bilder aus dem
altjüdischen Familienleben /. Frankfurt am
Main [188-?] Portfolio ([14] leaves of plates) :
NYPL [*PVP 84-1266]

Jezler, Peter. Der spätgotische Kirchenbau in der
Zürcher Landschaft : die Geschichte eines
"Baubooms" am Ende des Mittelalters :
Festschrift zum Jubiläum "500 Jahre Kirche
Pfäffikon" / Peter Jezler. Wetzikon : Buchverlag
der Druckerei Wetzikon, c1988. 144 p. : ill.
(some col.) ; 23 cm. "Eine Publikation der
Reformierten Kirchgemeinde Pfäffikon und der
Antiquarischen Gesellschaft Pfäffikon." Published on the
occasion of an exhibition held Sept. 3-Oct. 30, 1988,
Heimatmuseum Pfäffikon. Includes bibliographical
references (p. 139-144). ISBN 3-85981-150-9 : DDC
726/.5/094945707449457 20
*1. Church architecture - Switzerland - Zurich
(Canton) - Exhibitions. 2. Architecture, Gothic -
Switzerland - Zurich (Canton) - Exhibitions. I.
Reformierte Kirchgemeinde Pfäffikon. II. Antiquarische
Gesellschaft Pfäffikon. III. Title.*
NA5849.Z87 J49 1988
NYPL [3-MRBB 91-3251]

**JIANU, IONEL - CRITICISM
ANDINTERPRETATION.**
Ionel Jianu și opera lui . Los Angeles, Calif. ,
c1990. 361 p. : ISBN 0-912131-11-X
N7483.J53 I56 1990

Jim Dine . Dine, Jim, 1935- [Munich] , c1969. 28
p. : **NYPL [3-MCX D58 90-6937]**

Jim Dine . Dine, Jim, 1935- London , 1988. 67 p.
(some folded) :
NYPL [MDG+ (Dine) 90-10861]

Jim Dine . Rogers-Lafferty, Sarah. Cincinnati ,
c1988. 119 p. : ISBN 0-917562-50-X DDC
741.973 20
NC139.D56 A4 1988

Jim Dine, drawings . Dine, Jim, 1935- New
York , 1990. 1 v. (unpaged) : ISBN
1-89828-304-9
MLCM 90/00383 (N)
NYPL [3-MCX+ D58 90-12022]

Jim Dine prints, 1977-1985 /. D'Oench, Ellen.
New York , c1986. 182 p. : ISBN
0-06-431501-0 : DDC 769/.92/4 19
NE539.D5 A4 1986
NYPL [MDG (Dine) 86-1962]

Jiménez, María Paz, 1909-1975.
María Paz Jiménez (1909-1975). 1a ed. [San
Sebastián] : Sociedad Guipuzcoana de Ediciones
y Publicaciones : Obra Cultural de la Caja de
Ahorros Municipal de San Sebastián, 1989. 181
p. : ill. (some col.) ; 28 cm. (Colección Antologías.
38) Catalog of an exhibition held at the Museo de San
Telmo, San Sebastián. Includes bibliographical
references (p. 179). ISBN 84-7173-143-6
*1. Jiménez, María Paz, 1909-1975 - Exhibitions. I.
Museo de San Telmo. II. Series: Colección "Antologías"
(San Sebastián, Spain) , 38. III. Title.*
MLCM 90/01366 (N)
NYPL [3-MCQ J58 91-5339]

**JIMÉNEZ, MARÍA PAZ, 1909-1975 -
EXHIBITIONS.**
Jiménez, María Paz, 1909-1975. María Paz
Jiménez (1909-1975). [San Sebastián] , 1989.

181 p. : ISBN 84-7173-143-6
MLCM 90/01366 (N)
            NYPL [3-MCQ J58 91-5339]

Jimeno, Oswaldo, 1928- La magia del muro :
Gaudí-Wright / Oswaldo Jimeno. Lima, Peru :
Eunafev, 1973. 151 p. : ill. ; 21 cm. Includes
bibliographical references and index.
*1. Gaudí, Antoni, 1852-1926. 2. Wright, Frank Lloyd,
1867-1959. 3. Architecture, Modern - 20th century -
History and criticism. I. Title.*
            NYPL [3-MQV 91-819]

Jimmie Durham . Durham, Jimmie. New York ,
c1990. 37 p. :
            NYPL [3-MGO (Durham) 90-10679]

Jindřich Štyrský . Štyrský, Jindřich, 1899-1942.
V Praze , 1946. 8 p., [4] p. of plates :
            NYPL [MCZ S936 89-19257]

Jiří Sopko /. Kroutvor, Josef. Praha , 1990. 117
p. : ISBN 80-207-0042-0 :
ND534.5.S644 K76 1990

Jiricna, Eva, 1939-
Pawley, Martin. Eva Jiricna, design in exile /.
London , 1990. 112 p. : ISBN 1-87218-016-7
            NYPL [3-MQZ (Jiriena) 91-5084]

JIRICNA, EVA, 1939-
Manser, José. Joseph shops . London , Van
Nostrand Reinhold, 1991. [60] p. : ISBN
1-85454-445-4 (pbk.) : DDC 747.8521 20
NK2195.S89   *NYPL [3-MLT+ 91-6982]*

**JIRICNA, EVA, 1939- - CRITICISM AND
INTERPRETATION.**
Pawley, Martin. Eva Jiricna, design in exile /.
London , 1990. 112 p. : ISBN 1-87218-016-7
            NYPL [3-MQZ (Jiriena) 91-5084]

**JIRICNA KERR AND ASSOCIATES -
CRITICISM AND INTERPRETATION.**
Pawley, Martin. Eva Jiricna, design in exile /.
London , 1990. 112 p. : ISBN 1-87218-016-7
            NYPL [3-MQZ (Jiriena) 91-5084]

Joachim Ringelnatz. Ringelnatz, Joachim,
1883-1934. Ringelnatz der Maler . Hamburg
[1983] 80 p. :
ND588.R553 A4 1983
            NYPL [3-MCK R5815 84-824]

Joan Miró /. Danoff, I. Michael. [Milwaukee] ,
1977. 15 p. :   *NYPL [3-MCQ M67 91-401]*

Joan Miró . Miró, Joan, 1893- Genève , 1979.
[120] p. : DDC 741.64/092/4 19
NC987.5.M57 A4 1979
            NYPL [MDG (Miró) 81-676]

Joan Miró . Miró, Joan, 1893- Paris , c1990. 63
p. : ISBN 2-85587-185-9
            NYPL [MDG+ (Miró) 91-4765]

Joan Miró . Miró, Joan, 1893- Saint-Paul , c19.
205 p. : ISBN 2-900923-01-87 DDC 759.6 20
N7113.M54 A4 1990

Joan Miro, Skulpturen /. Miró, Joan, 1893-
München , c1990. 246, [1] p. : ISBN
3-7774-5300-5 DDC 730/.92 20
NB813.M5 A4 1990

Joan Mitchell, new paintings . Mitchell, Joan,
1926- New York, N.Y. [1976] [12] p. :
            NYPL [3-MCX M68 91-1156]

Joan Personette . Personette, Joan, 1914-
Washington, D.C. , 1990. [8] p., 38 p. of
plates : ISBN 0-940979-15-2 DDC 709/.2 20
N6537.P414 A4 1990
            NYPL [3-MCX P467 91-4636]

João Câmara . Câmara Filho, João, 1944-
[Berlin] , 1988. 78 p. :
            NYPL [3-MCZ+ C171 90-13212]

Jobe, Brock. Layton Art Collection. American
furniture with related decorative arts,
1660-1830 /. New York , c1991. p. ISBN
1-555-95068-X : DDC 749.213/074/77595 20
NK2406 .L38 1991

Jochimsen, Margarethe.
Bach, Elvira, 1951- Elvira Bach /. München ,
c1990. 103 p. :   *NYPL [3-MCK+ B118 91-3385]*

Sander, Ernemann F., 1925- Ernemann F.
Sander, Skulpturen und Zeichnungen . Bonn ,
c1985. 76 p. :
MLCM 87/63 (N)
            NYPL [3-MGO (Sander) 90-10662]

Jockel, Nils. Alles Plastik : 100 Jahre
Kunst(stoff)gewerbe im Alltag / Nils Jockel

unter Mitarbeit von Eberhard Hempel.
[Hamburg] : Museum für Kunst und Gewerbe
Hamburg : Museumspädagogischer Dienst
Hamburg, 1985. 36 p. : ill. ; 23 cm. Bibliography:
p. 29.
*1. Plastics as art material - History. 2. Decorative arts.
I. Hempel, Eberhard. II. Museum für Kunst und
Gewerbe Hamburg. III. Museumspädagogischer Dienst
Hamburg. IV. Title.*   *NYPL [3-MGF 86-364]*

Joe Overstreet . Overstreet, Joe. New York,
N.Y. , c1989. 39 p. :   *NYPL [3-MCX+ 096]*

Joedicke, Jürgen.
Architektur im Umbruch. Joedicke, Jürgen.
Architekturgeschichte des 20. Jahrhunderts :
von 1950 bis zur Gegenwart / Jürgen
Joedicke. Stuttgart , c1990. 256 p. : ISBN
3-7828-0459-7 DDC 724/.6 20
NA680 .J574 1990

Architekturgeschichte des 20. Jahrhunderts :
von 1950 bis zur Gegenwart / Jürgen Joedicke.
Stuttgart : K. Krämer, c1990. 256 p. : ill. ; 20
cm. (Archpaper-Edition Krämer) Rev. ed. of:
Architektur im Umbruch. Überarb. Neuaufl. 1980.
Includes bibliographical references (p. 252) and index.
    ISBN 3-7828-0459-7 DDC 724/.6 20
*1. Architecture, Modern - 20th century. I. Joedicke,
Jürgen. Architektur im Umbruch. II. Title. III. Title:
Architekturgeschichte des zwanzigsten Jahrhunderts.*
NA680 .J574 1990

Vogt-Göknil, Ulya. Osmanische Türkei /.
Fribourg , c1965. 192 p. :
            NYPL [3-MQT 90-6997]

Joel Shapiro . Shapiro, Joel. Des Moines, Ia. ,
1990. 80 p. : ISBN 1-87900-300-7
            NYPL [3-MGO (Shapiro) 91-7050]

Jörg Krichbaum . Krichbaum, Jörg, 1945-
Recklinghausen [1989?] 110 p. :
            NYPL [MFX+ (Krichbaum) 90-2137]

Jõesaar, Ernst, 1905-
Ernst Jõesaar : sulptuur, maal, joonistus / tekst
Eevi End, Sten Karling. Stockholm :
Välis-Eesti, 1975. 25 p. [132] p. of plates :
chiefly ill. ; 21 cm.
*1. Jõesaar, Ernst, 1905- - Catalogs. I. End, Eevi. II.
Karling, Sten Ingvar, 1906-. III. Title.*
NB955.F53 J642 1975

JÕESAAR, ERNST, 1905- - CATALOGS.
Jõesaar, Ernst, 1905- Ernst Jõesaar .
Stockholm , 1975. 25 p. [132] p. of plates :
NB955.F53 J642 1975

Joffroy, Pascale. Claude Vasconi, 1980-1990 /
Pascale Joffroy. Paris : Electa Moniteur, c1990.
166 p. : ill. (some col.) ; 24 cm. "Monographies
d'architecture"--Jacket. ISBN 2-86653-084-5 DDC
720/.92 20
*1. Vasconi, Claude, 1940- - Themes, motives. 2.
Architecture, Modern - 20th century - France -
Themes, motives. I. Vasconi, Claude, 1940-. II. Title.*
NA1053.V37 J64 1990

**Johann Adam Andreas, Fürst Liechtenstein, 1656-
1712.**
Miller, Dwight C. (Dwight Cameron), 1923-
Marcantonio Franceschini and the
Liechtensteins . Cambridge , New York , 1991.
xx, 296 p., [16] p. of plates : ISBN
0-521-36503-1 DDC 759.5 B 20
ND623.F78125 A3 1990
            NYPL [3-MCF F813 91-7475]

**JOHANN ADAM ANDREAS, FÜRST
LIECHTENSTEIN, 1656-1712 - ART
PATRONAGE.**
Miller, Dwight C. (Dwight Cameron), 1923-
Marcantonio Franceschini and the
Liechtensteins . Cambridge , New York , 1991.
xx, 296 p., [16] p. of plates : ISBN
0-521-36503-1 DDC 759.5 B 20
ND623.F78125 A3 1990
            NYPL [3-MCF F813 91-7475]

**JOHANN ADAM ANDREAS, FÜRST
LIECHTENSTEIN, 1656-1712 -
CORRESPONDENCE.**
Miller, Dwight C. (Dwight Cameron), 1923-
Marcantonio Franceschini and the
Liechtensteins . Cambridge , New York , 1991.
xx, 296 p., [16] p. of plates : ISBN
0-521-36503-1 DDC 759.5 B 20
ND623.F78125 A3 1990
            NYPL [3-MCF F813 91-7475]

**Johann Bucker Karte des Rheins von Duisburg
bis Arnheim aus dem Jahre 1713** . Bucker,

Johann. Düsseldorf , 1984. 1 atlas (14 leaves) :
DDC 912/.43 19
G1797.22.R5 B7 1984
            NYPL [Map Div. 90-1]

Johann Gottfried Schadow /. Krenzlin, Ulrike.
Stuttgart , c1990. 197 p. : ISBN 3-421-02997-0
DDC 730/.92 B 20
NB588.S35 K7 1990

Johann Gottfried Schadow /. Krenzlin, Ulrike.
Stuttgart , c1990. 197 p. : ISBN 3-421-02997-0
            NYPL [3-MGO+ (Schadow) 91-3892]

Johann Heinrich Schönfeld. Schönfeld, Johann
Heinrich, 1609-1682 or 3. [Ulm, 1967] 112 p.
DDC 760/.0924
ND588.S2853 U4
            NYPL [3-MCK S365 91-1295]

Johann Heinrich Tischbein d.Ä. (1722-1789) :
Neue Galerie, Staatliche und Städtische
Kunstsammlungen Kassel : Ausstellung 25.
November 1989-11. Februar 1990 /
[Ausstellung und Katalog, Marianne Heinz,
Erich Herzog]. Kassel : Staatliche
Kunstsammlungen Kassel und Stadtsparkasse
Kassel, [1989] 204 p. : ill., (some col.) ; 21 x 22
cm. Includes bibliographical references (p. 199-201)
    ISBN 3-925272-20-8
*1. Tischbein, Johann Heinrich, 1722-1789 - Exhibitions.
I. Tischbein, Johann Heinrich, 1722-1789. II. Heinz,
Marianne. III. Heinz, Erich. IV. Staatliche
Kunstsammlungen Kassel. Neue Galerie.*
            NYPL [3-MCK T598 90-10764]

**Johann Joachim Winckelmann in den
ostslawischen Ländern** /. Husar, Irene.
Stendal , 1979. 98 p. ; DDC 709/.2/4 19
N7483.W5 H8 1979
            NYPL [3-MAB 90-12523]

Johannes, Dieter. Grimm, Günter. Kunst der
Ptolemäer- und Römerzeit im Ägyptischen
Museum Kairo /. Mainz [1975] 34 p, 118 p.,
[6] leaves of plates :
N5888.A1 G74   *NYPL [3-MAH 90-5474]*

Johannes Dörflinger . Dörflinger, Johannes, 1941-
Stuttgart , c1989. [37] p. :
            NYPL [3-MCK+ D663 89-25787]

Johannes Molzahn . Molzahn, Johannes,
1892-1965. München , 1985. 72 p. : ISBN
3-7954-0635-8
            NYPL [3-MCK M731 91-6581]

Jóhannes Sveinsson Kjarval /. Jóhannes
Sveinsson Kjarval, 1885-1972. Reykjavík , 1950.
99 p. : DDC 759.94912 20
ND753.K43 A4 1950

Jóhannes Sveinsson Kjarval, 1885-1972.
Jóhannes Sveinsson Kjarval / inngangsorð eftir
Halldór Kiljan Laxness. Reykjavík : Helgafell,
1950. 99 p. : ill. (some col.) ; 31 cm. (Íslenzk
list) Introductory essay in English and Icelandic.
    DDC 759.94912 20
*1. Jóhannes Sveinsson Kjarval, 1885-1972 - Catalogs. I.
Title. II. Series.*
ND753.K43 A4 1950

**JÓHANNES SVEINSSON KJARVAL, 1885-
1972 - CATALOGS.**
Jóhannes Sveinsson Kjarval, 1885-1972.
Jóhannes Sveinsson Kjarval /. Reykjavík , 1950.
99 p. : DDC 759.94912 20
ND753.K43 A4 1950

**Johannes-Wüsten-Symposium (1976 : Görlitz,
Dresden, Germany)** Protokollband
Johannes-Wüsten-Symposium, Görlitz, 1976, 2.
Oktober / veranstaltet vom Rat der Stadt
Görlitz und den Städtischen Kunstsammlungen
Görlitz im Rahmen der
Johannes-Wüsten-Ehrung der Stadt Görlitz vom
2. bis 4. Oktober 1976. Görlitz : Der Rat, 1978.
109 p. : ill. ; 23 cm. (Schriftenreihe des Ratsarchivs
der Stadt Görlitz . 9) Includes bibliographies.
*1. Wüsten, Johannes, 1896-1943. 2. Artists - Germany -
Biography. I. Wüsten, Johannes, 1896-1943. II. Görlitz
(Germany). Rat. III. Städtische Kunstsammlungen
Görlitz. IV. Title.*
NX550.Z9 W875 1976
            NYPL [3-MCK W953 90-13398]

Johannesburg Art Gallery.
Images of wood . [Johannesburg] , 1989. 188
p. : ISBN 0-620-13867-X DDC 730/.968/07468221
20
NB1255.S6 I46 1989

The Neglected tradition . Johannesburg , c1988.
155 p. : ISBN 0-620-13184-5 DDC

704/.03968/0090407468221 20
N7392 .N44 1988

Johannesen, Ole Rønning, 1922-
Lillehammermalerne / av Ole Rønning
Johannesen. Espa : Lokalhistorisk forlag, 1990.
125 p. : ill. (some col.) ; 27 cm. Summary in
English. Includes bibliographical references (p. 125).
ISBN 82-7404-036-8
*1. Painting, Norwegian - Norway - Lillehammer. 2.
Painting, Modern - 19th century - Norway -
Lillehammer. 3. Painting, Modern - 20th century -
Norway - Lillehammer. 4. Painters - Norway -
Lillehammer - Biography. 5. Lillehammer (Norway) in
art. I. Title.*
ND771.L55 J64 1990

Johansson, Per-Olov, 1949- An introduction to
modern welfare economics / Per-Olov
Johansson. Cambridge ; New York : Cambridge
University Press, 1991. p. cm. Includes
bibliographical references. ISBN 0-521-35616-4 (hard)
DDC 330.15/56 20
1. Welfare economics. I. Title.
NB846 .J64 1991

John and Mable Ringling Museum of Art.
Lemieux, Annette. Annette Lemieux, the
appearance of sound . Sarasota, Fla. , c1989. 16
p. : ISBN 0-916758-27-3
NYPL [3-MCX+ L554 90-8047]

Stearns, Thomas. Thomas Stearns,
constructions . Sarasota, Fla. , 1968. [8] p. :
NYPL [3-MGO (Stearns) 91-5207]

This is not a photograph . Sarasota, Fla. ,
c1987. 1 v. (various pagings) : ISBN
0-916758-23-0 DDC 779/.09/04507474 20
TR645.S372 J647 1987
NYPL [MFW 88-3001]

**The John and Sara Lindsey series in
architectural studies .**
(no. 1) George, Mary Carolyn Hollers. O'Neil
Ford, architect . College Station , c1992. p.
cm. ISBN 0-89096-433-5 DDC 720/.92 20
NA737.O5 G46 1992

**JOHN B. PUTNAM, JR., MEMORIAL
COLLECTION (PRINCETON, N.J.)**
The Sculpture of Princeton University .
[Princeton, N.J. , c1982] [32] p. :
NYPL [3-MGI 91-4577]

John Baldessari /. Bruggen, Coosje van. New
York , 1990. 256 p. : ISBN 0-8478-1182-4 :
DDC 709/.2 20
N6537.B17 B78 1990
NYPL [3-MCX+ B176 90-11225]

John Bartholomew and Son. The Times atlas of
the world /. New York , c1990. xlvii, 225 p.,
[123] p. of plates : ISBN 0-8129-1874-6
NYPL [Map Div. 90-11947]

John Carter Brown Library. The mapping of the
Great Lakes in the seventeenth century. .
Providence, R. I, 1989. xix, [3], 85 p. incl.
maps : *NYPL [Map Div. 90-65]*

John Chamberlain, new sculpture . Chamberlain,
John, 1927- New York , c1991. 17 p., [15]
leaves of plates : ISBN 1-87828-314-6
NYPL [MGO (Chamberlain) 91-5999]

John Coburn, paintings. Amadio, Nadine.
Coburn . Roseville, NSW , 1988. 205 p. :
ISBN 0-947131-20-5
NYPL [3-MCZ+ C657 89-20391]

John Constable . Rhyne, Charles. Portland,
Oregon , 1990. xi, 206 p. ; ISBN 0-9627197-0-6
NYPL [3-MCV C75 90-11734]

John Constable /. Walker, John, 1906 Dec. 24-
New York , 1991. p. cm. ISBN 0-8109-3171-0
(cloth) DDC 759.2 20
ND497.C7 W34 1991

John Constable, R.A (1776-1837) . Constable,
John, 1776-1837. New York, NY [1988] 201
p. : DDC 760/.092 20
N6797.C63 A4 1988
NYPL [3-MCV C75 90-13632]

John Coplans . Coplans, John. Frankfurt am
Main [1990] 60 p. :
NYPL [MFX (Coplans) 91-7947]

**John Frederick Amelung, early American
glassmaker /** Dwight P. Lanmon ... [et al.].
Corning : Corning Museum of Glass Press ;
London ; 243 p., [4] p. of plates : ill. (some
col.), facsims. ; 29 cm. Revised version of the 1976
issue of the Journal of glass studies, issued by the

Corning Museum of Glass. Includes bibliographical
references (p. 126-128) ISBN 0-87290-075-4 (alk.
paper) DDC 748.2913 19
*1. Amelung, John Frederick, 1741 or 2-1798. 2.
Glassware - United States - History - 18th century. 3.
Glass manufacture - United States. I. Lanmon, Dwight
P. II. Corning Museum of Glass.*
NK5198.A44 A4 1988
NYPL [3-MPW 91-6798]

John Golding . Golding, John. New Haven,
Conn. , 1989. 39 p. : ISBN 0-930606-60-4
NYPL [3-MCV G618 90-12734]

John Hejduk . Hejduk, John, 1929- Berlin ,
c1988. [43] p. :
NYPL [3-MCX H458 91-7235]

John Henry Twachtman, 1853-1902. Twachtman,
John Henry, 1853-1902. New York [1968] [24]
p. : *NYPL [3-MCX T96 91-1183]*

John Hoyland /. Gooding, Mel. Hatfield, Herts ,
1990. 39 p., 80 leaves of plates : ISBN
0-85331-564-7
NYPL [3-MCV+ H867 91-6325]

John Kacere. Brach, Paul, 1924- Kacere /.
[Paris] , c1989. 169 p. : ISBN 2-85018-313-X
NYPL [3-MCX+ K115 90-2574]

John La Farge, watercolors and drawings /.
Yarnall, James L. Yonkers, N.Y. , c1990. 143
p. : ISBN 0-943651-24-7 : DDC 759.13 20
N6537.L28 A4 1990

John Marin . Marin, John, 1870-1953. New
York , c1990. 32 p. : DDC 741.973 20
NC139.M27 A4 1990

John Marin's New York. Marin, John,
1870-1953. New York , c1981. [88] p. :
NYPL [3-MAMY 91-762]

John McQueen . McQueen, John, 1943-
Washington, D.C. , 1991. p. ISBN 0-295-97153-3
DDC 746.41/2/092 20
NK3649.55.U64 M372 1991

John Michael Kohler Arts Center.
Religious visionaries. Sheboygan, Wis. , 1991. p.
cm. ISBN 0-932718-31-0 DDC
704.9/482/097307477569 20
N7904 .R44 1991

Structure and surface . Sheboygan, Wis. ,
c1990. vii, 32 p. : ISBN 0-932718-28-0 DDC
709/.73/07477569 20
N6512 .S78 1990
NYPL [3-MAMT 90-13004]

John Moores Liverpool exhibition sixteen. The
John Moores Liverpool exhibition 16 . [Great
Britain] , 1989. 1 v. : ISBN 0-901534-95-1 DDC
759.2/09/04807442753 20
N6768 .J645 1989

The John Moores Liverpool exhibition 16 :
Walker Art Gallery, Liverpool, 20 October
1989-14 January 1990. [Great Britain] :
National Museums & Galleries on Merseyside,
1989. 1 v. : ill. (some col.) ; 24 cm. ISBN
0-901534-95-1 DDC 759.2/09/04807442753 20
*1. Painting, English - Exhibitions. 2. Painting, Modern -
20th century - England - Exhibitions. I. Moores, John.
II. Walker Art Gallery. III. National Museums and
Galleries on Merseyside. IV. Title: John Moores
Liverpool exhibition sixteen.*
N6768 .J645 1989

John O'Brien, marine painter. Laurette, Patrick
Condon. John O'Brien, 1831-1891 /. Halifax,
N.S. , c1984. 128 p. :
ND249.O37 L38 1984
NYPL [3-MCZ+ O128 90-9675]

John O'Brien, 1831-1891 /. Laurette, Patrick
Condon. Halifax, N.S. , c1984. 128 p. :
ND249.O37 L38 1984
NYPL [3-MCZ+ O128 90-9675]

John Paul Jones /. Jones, John Paul, 1924- Los
Angeles , c1983. 48 p. :
NYPL [3-MCX J775 85-3055]

John Ruskin and Switzerland /. Hayman, John,
1935- Waterloo, Ont. ; Canada , c1990. ix, 141
p. : ISBN 0-88920-966-9 DDC 759.2 20
NC242.R8 A4 1990

John Ruskin, the last chapter . Measham,
Donald. Sheffield (England) , 1989. 60 p. :
ISBN 0-86321-104-6
NYPL [3-MCV R45 90-11132]

John Safer. Safer, John. Dallas, 1971. [24] p.

DDC 730/.92/4
ND237.S16 V3

John Soane and the Bank of England /.
Schumann-Bacia, Eva, 1950- [Bank von
England und ihr Architekt John Soane.
English.] New York , 1991. p. cm. ISBN
1-87827-131-8 : DDC 725/.24/092 20
NA6245.G72 L63713 1991

John Weber Gallery. De Europa . New York
[1972] [52] p. : *NYPL [3-MAL 91-639]*

John Williams, photographs /. Williams, John
(John Frank) Sydney, N.S.W. , 1989. 112 p. ;
ISBN 0-7305-6188-7
NYPL [MFX (Williams) 91-2387]

Johnová, Helena, 1884-1962. Lidový malovaný
nábytek v českých zemích : z muzejních sbírek
/ Helena Johnová, Jitka Staňková, Ludvík
Baran.1. vyd. V Praze : Panorama, 1989. 196
p. : col. ill. ; 26 cm. (Poklady uměleckých sbírek .
sv. 2) Summary in German. Includes bibliographical
references (p. 182-184) and index. ISBN
80-7038-034-9 :
*1. Country painted furniture - Czechoslovakia - Themes,
motives. I. Staňková, Jitka. II. Baran, Ludvík. III. Title.
IV. Series.*
NK2635.C9 J64 1989

Johns, Elizabeth, 1937- American genre
painting : the politics of everyday life /
Elizabeth Johns. New Haven : Yale University
Press, c1991. p. cm. Includes bibliographical
references and index. ISBN 0-300-05019-4 DDC
754/.0973/09034 20
*1. Genre painting, American. 2. Genre painting - 19th
century - United States. 3. United States in art. I. Title.*
ND1451.5 .J64 1991

Johnson, Anthony. Cerwinske, Laura. Russian
imperial style /. New York , c1990. 223 p. :
ISBN 0-13-784810-2 : DDC 745/.0947 20
NK975 .C45 1990
NYPL [3-MLF+ 91-3951]

Johnson, Cathy (Cathy A.) Creating textures in
watercolor : a guide to painting 83 textures
from grass to glass to tree bark to fur / Cathy
Johnson.1st ed. Cincinnati, Ohio : North Light
Books, c1992. p. cm. Includes index. ISBN
0-89134-417-9 (hrdcvr) : DDC 751.42/2 20
*1. Watercolor painting - Technique. 2. Texture (Art) -
Technique. I. Title.*
ND2422 .J64 1992

Johnson, Dale T. American portrait miniatures in
the Manney collection / Dale T. Johnson ;
[with an essay on materials and techniques by
Carol Aiken]. New York : Metropolitan
Museum on Art : Distributed by Harry
N.Abrams,Inc., New York, 1990. 271 p. : ill.
(some col.) ; 29 cm. Exhibition catalog. Includes
index. Includes bibliographical references (p. 249-252).
ISBN 0-87099-597-9 DDC 757/.7/09730747471
20
*1. Manney, Richard - Art collections - Exhibitions. 2.
Manney, Gloria - Art collections - Exhibitions. 3.
Metropolitan Museum of Art (New York, N.Y.) -
Exhibitions. 4. Portrait miniatures, American -
Exhibitions. 5. Portrait miniatures - Private collections -
New York (N.Y.) - Exhibitions. I. Aiken, Carol. II.
Metropolitan Museum of Art (New York, N.Y.). III.
Title.*
ND1337.U5 J64 1990
NYPL [3-MCW 91-4980]

Johnson, Donald Leslie. Frank Lloyd Wright
versus America : the 1930s / Donald Leslie
Johnson. Cambridge, Mass. : MIT Press, c1990.
xi, 436 p. : ill. ; 20 x 26 cm. Includes
bibliographical references (p. [403]-411) and index.
ISBN 0-262-10044-4 DDC 720/.92 B 20
*1. Wright, Frank Lloyd, 1867-1959. 2. Architects -
United States - Biography. I. Title.*
NA737.W7 J6 1990
NYPL [3-MQZ (Wright) 91-4307]

Johnson, Frances. Collecting antique linens, lace,
and needlework / Frances Johnson. Radnor,
Pa. : Wallace-Homestead Book Co., c1991. p.
cm. Includes bibliographical references and index.
ISBN 0-87069-634-3 (hc) : DDC 746/.075 20
*1. Household linens - Collectors and collecting. 2. Lace
and lace making - Collectors and collecting. 3.
Needlework - Collectors and collecting. I. Title.*
NK8904 .J64 1991

Johnson, J. Stewart. Eileen Gray, designer / J.
Stewart Johnson. London : Debrett's Peerage
for Museum of Modern Art, c1979. 67 p. : ill. ;

27 cm. Prepared to accompany exhibition held at the Museum of Modern Art and the Victoria and Albert Museum. Includes bibliographical references. ISBN 0-87070-307-2 :
1. Gray, Eileen, 1879-1976. 2. Designers - Ireland - Biography. I. Gray, Eileen, 1879-1976. II. New York (City). Museum of Modern Art. III. Victoria and Albert Museum, South Kensington. IV. Title.
NK1535.G68 J63   **NYPL [MOI 80-2273]**

Johnson, Lee, art historian. Delacroix, Eugène, 1798-1863. [Letters. Selections.] Eugène Delacroix, further correspondence, 1817-1863 /. Oxford , New York , 1991. p. cm. ISBN 0-19-817395-4 DDC 759.4 B 20
ND553.D33 A3 1991

Johnson, Linda L., 1961- Howard Ben Tré : contemporary sculpture / Linda L. Johnson. Washington, D.C. : Phillips Collection, 1989. 48 p. : ill. (some col.) ; 28 cm. "Exhibition schedule: The Phillips Collection, Washington, D.C., December 16, 1989-February 25, 1990; Carnegie-Mellon Art Gallery, Pittsburgh, Pennsylvania, April 14-May 27, 1990; Laumeier Sculpture Park, St. Louis, Missouri, June 16-August 25, 1990; DeCordova and Dana Museum and Park, Lincoln, Massachusetts, November 16, 1990-January 27, 1991"--T.p. verso. Includes bibliographical references (p. 46). ISBN 0-943044-14-6 : DDC 730/.92 20
1. Ben Tré, Howard, 1949- - Exhibitions. I. Ben Tré, Howard, 1949-. II. Phillips Collection. III. Title.
NB237.B434 J64 1989
NYPL [3-MGO (Ben Tré) 91-6438]

Johnson, Michael, 1938-
Michael Johnson : paintings, 1968-1988 / Michael Johnson. [Sydney] : Art Gallery of New South Wales, [1989?] [36] leaves : col. ill (some folded) ; 30 cm. Catalog of an exhibition at the Art Gallery of New South Wales, Feb. 8-April 2, 1989. Cover title. Includes bibliographical references.
1. Johnson, Michael, 1938- - Exhibitions. I. Art Gallery of New South Wales. II. Title.
NYPL [3-MCZ+ J675 89-23194]

JOHNSON, MICHAEL, 1938- - EXHIBITIONS.
Johnson, Michael, 1938- Michael Johnson . [Sydney] [1989?] [36] leaves :
NYPL [3-MCZ+ J675 89-23194]

Johnson, Robert Flynn.
Bukovnik, Gary, 1947- Flowers . New York , 1990. 119 p. : ISBN 0-8109-3105-2 DDC 760/.092 20
N6537.B835 A4 1990
NYPL [3-MCX B924 90-11081]

Thiebaud, Wayne. Ties, pies, cities, and other things /. San Francisco , c1991. p. cm. ISBN 0-938491-56-3 (paper) : DDC 769.92 20
NE539.T5 A4 1991

Johnson, Uwe, 1934- Szymanski, Rolf. Rolf Szymanski . Stuttgart , c1989. 175 p. : ISBN 3-7757-0266-0 DDC 730/.92 20
NB588.S98 A4 1989
NYPL [3-MGO+ (Szymanski) 91-6925]

JOHNSON, WILLIAM H., 1901-1970.
Powell, Richard J., 1953- Homecoming . Washington, D.C. [1991] p. ISBN 0-8478-1421-1 : DDC 759.13 20
ND237.J73 P69 1991

JOHNSON, WILLIAM H., 1901-1970 - JUVENILE LITERATURE.
Everett, Gwen. Li'l Sis and Uncle Willie . Washington, DC , New York , c1991. p. cm. ISBN 0-8478-1462-9 DDC 759.13 B 20
ND237.J73 E94 1991

Johnston, Frances Benjamin, 1864-1952.
Frances Benjamin Johnston : what a woman can do with a camera. York : Impressions Gallery of Photography, [1984] [20] p. : ill. ; 21 cm. Catalog of a touring exhibition of material selected from the Prints and Photographs Division, Library of Congress, Washington, D.C., and first shown at the Impressions Gallery of Photography, York, July 13-August 25, 1984. Catalog written by Frances Middlestorb. Includes bibliographical references (p. [8]). ISBN 0-906361-45-1 (pbk.)
1. Johnston, Frances Benjamin, 1864-1952 - Exhibitions. 2. Library of Congress. Prints and Photographs Division - Exhibitions. 3. Photography, Documentary - Exhibitions. I. Middlestorb, Frances. II. Impressions Gallery of Photography. III. Title.
TR820.5 M544 1984
NYPL [MFX (Johnston) 91-3499]

JOHNSTON, FRANCES BENJAMIN, 1864-1952 - EXHIBITIONS.
Johnston, Frances Benjamin, 1864-1952. Frances Benjamin Johnston . York [1984] [20] p. : ISBN 0-906361-45-1 (pbk.)
TR820.5 M544 1984
NYPL [MFX (Johnston) 91-3499]

JOHNSTON, HENRIETTA - EXHIBITIONS.
Henrietta Johnston . Winston-Salem, N.C. , c1991. p. DDC 741.973 20
NC139.J6 H4 1991

Johnston, Shirley. Schezen, Roberto. Palm Beach houses /. New York , 1991. 324 p. : ISBN 0-8478-1313-4 DDC 728.8/09759/32 20
NA7238.P235 S34 1991

Johnston, William R. Lovett, Jennifer Gordon. Empires restored, Elysium revisited . Williamstown, Mass. , 1991. p. cm. ISBN 0-931102-30-8 (pbk.) DDC 759.2 20
ND497.A4 A4 1991

Joie de vivre . National Gallery of Art (U. S.) New York, NY , 1991. p. cm. ISBN 0-87663-608-3 DDC 759.4/074/753 20
ND547 .N38 1991

Joking aside! Shutki v storonu! English. Joking aside! Time to laugh seriously /. Moscow , Chicago, Ill. , c1990. 111 p. : ISBN 5-01-001979-5 DDC 741.5/947/09048 20
NC1576 .S48 1990

Joking aside! Time to laugh seriously /. Shutki v storonu! English. Moscow , Chicago, Ill. , c1990. 111 p. : ISBN 5-01-001979-5 DDC 741.5/947/09048 20
NC1576 .S48 1990

Jolicoeur, Nicole.
Charcot, deux concepts de nature. 1988. De humani corporis fabrica. Montréal, Québec, Canada , 1988, c1985-c1986. 3 v. in 1 case : DDC 700/.92/271428 20
N7433.35.C2 D4 1988
NYPL [MEMZ 90-11163]

Jolig, K. Niederlandische Einflüsse in der deutschen Kartographie besonders des 18. Jahrhunderts / von K. Jolig. Amsterdam : Meridian Pub. Co., 1980. 82 p. ; 23 cm. Reprint. Originally published: Leipzig, 1903. ISBN 90-6041-143-9
1. Cartography - Germany - History. I. Title.
NYPL [Map Div. 90-7139]

Jolles, Claudia. Artisti russi contemporanei . Prato , c1990. 208 p. : ISBN 88-85191-01-0
NYPL [3-MAM 90-10469]

Jolliffe, John. Haydon, Benjamin Robert, 1786-1846. Neglected genius . London , 1990. xii, 260 p. : ISBN 0-09-173546-7 : DDC 759.2 20
NYPL [3-MCV H41 90-11598]

Jolly, David C.
Antique maps, sea charts, city views, celestial charts & battle plans : price guide and collectors' handbook for 1983 / compiled and edited by David C. Jolly. Brookline, Mass. : D.C. Jolly, 1983. viii, 279 p. : ill., maps ; 24 cm. Spine title: Antique map prices--1983. Includes bibliographies. ISBN 0-911775-00-5 DDC 912/.075 19
1. Maps, Early - Collectors and collecting. 2. Maps, Early - Prices. I. Title. II. Title: Antique map prices--1983.
GA197.3 .J64 1983
NYPL [Map Div. 84-417]

Maps in British periodicals / compiled by David C. Jolly. 1st ed. Brookline, Mass. : D.C. Jolly, 1990-1991. 2 v. : map ; 24 cm. Includes indexes. CONTENTS. - pt. 1. Major monthlies before 1800 -- pt. 2. Annuals, scientific periodicals & miscellaneous magazines, mostly before 1800. ISBN 0-911775-51-X (v. 1) DDC 016.912 20
1. Maps - Bibliography - Catalogs. 2. British periodicals - Bibliography - Catalogs. I. Title.
Z6028 .J64 1990 GA300
NYPL [Map Div. 90-47]

Joly, Raymond, 1911-
Joly, Raymond, 1911- Raymond Joly, un médailleur d'aujourd'hui. Paris, 1967. 133 p. DDC 709/.2/4
N6853.J64 G64
NYPL [3-MGP (Joly) 90-7101]

Raymond Joly, un médailleur d'aujourd'hui. Monnaie de Paris. [Janvier-mars 1967. Catalogue par Yvonne Goldenberg.] Paris,

Monnaie de Paris, 1967. 133 p. illus., col. plates. 21 x 27 cm. Cover title. DDC 709/.2/4
1. Joly, Raymond, 1911- - Exhibitions. I. Goldenberg, Yvonne. II. Joly, Raymond, 1911-. III. Musée de la monnaie (France).
N6853.J64 G64
NYPL [3-MGP (Joly) 90-7101]

JOLY, RAYMOND, 1911- - EXHIBITIONS.
Joly, Raymond, 1911- Raymond Joly, un médailleur d'aujourd'hui. Paris, 1967. 133 p. DDC 709/.2/4
N6853.J64 G64
NYPL [3-MGP (Joly) 90-7101]

Jonah Jones, John Petts, Kyffin Williams : [exhibition catalog]. [London, England] : Arts Council of Great Britain, Welsh Committee, 1961. 14 p., [8] p. of plates : ill. ; 23 cm.
1. Art, Welsh - Exhibitions. 2. Art, Modern - 20th century - Wales - Exhibitions. I. Arts Council of Great Britain. Welsh Committee.
MLCM 87/7416 (N)
NYPL [3-MAMR 91-226]

Jonathan Shahn . Kennedy Galleries. New York , c1972. [12] p. :
NYPL [3-MGO (Shahn) 91-417]

Jones, Allen, 1937- Das graphische Werk. [Köln] Verlag Galerie Der Spiegel [1969?] [74] p. illus. 23 cm. Introduction also in English.
1. Jones, Allen, 1937-. I. Title.
NE642.J6 A46
NYPL [MDG (Jones, A.) 90-6297]

JONES, ALLEN, 1937-
Jones, Allen, 1937- Das graphische Werk. [Köln, 1969?] [74] p.
NE642.J6 A46
NYPL [MDG (Jones, A.) 90-6297]

Jones, Barri. An atlas of Roman Britain / Barri Jones and David Mattingly. Oxford ; Cambridge, Mass., USA : Basil Blackwell, 1990. vii, 341 p. : ill., maps ; 29 cm. (Blackwell reference) ISBN 0-631-13791-2 : DDC 911.41 20
1. Great Britain - History - Roman period, 55 A.D.-449 A.D. - Maps. 2. Great Britain - Antiquities, Roman - Maps. I. Mattingly, David, 1958-. II. Title.
NYPL [Map Div. 90-10987]

Jones, David Michael, 1895-1974.
David Jones : paintings, drawings, inscriptions, prints / [exhibition organized by Caroline Collier]. London : South Bank Centre, c1989. 48 p. : ill. (some col.), ports. ; 30 cm. Catalog of exhibition held at the City Museum and Art Gallery, Bristol, and three other institutions between March 4 and August 20, 1989. Bibliography: p. 47. ISBN 1-85332-040-4 (pbk.)
1. Jones, David Michael, 1895-1974 - Exhibitions. I. Collier, Caroline. II. Bristol City Art Gallery. III. Title.
NYPL [3-MCV+ J765 89-19109]

JONES, DAVID MICHAEL, 1895-1974 - EXHIBITIONS.
Jones, David Michael, 1895-1974. David Jones . London , c1989. 48 p. : ISBN 1-85332-040-4 (pbk.)
NYPL [3-MCV+ J765 89-19109]

Jones-Davies, Marie Thérèse. Le Monde animal au temps de la Renaissance /. Paris , 1990. 259 p. : ISBN 2-86433-036-9 : DDC 700 20
NX650.A55 M66 1990

Jones, Eleanor L. Broun, Elizabeth. Albert Pinkham Ryder /. Washington , c1989. viii, 344 p. : ISBN 0-87474-328-1 (alk. paper) DDC 759.13 19
ND237.R8 A4 1989
NYPL [3-MCX R99 90-12872]

Jones, Frederic H. (Frederic Hicks), 1944-
A concise dictionary of architecture / Frederic H. Jones. Los Altos, Calif. : Crisp Publications, 1991. p. cm. (The Concise dictionary series) ISBN 1-560-52066-3 : DDC 720/.3 20
1. Architecture - Dictionaries. I. Title. II. Series.
NA31 .J6 1991

A concise dictionary of interior design / Frederic H. Jones. Los Altos, Calif. : Crisp Publications, c1990. 215 p. ; 24 cm. (The Concise dictionary series) ISBN 1-560-52067-1 DDC 729/.03 20
1. Interior decoration - Dictionaries. 2. Architecture - Dictionaries. I. Title. II. Series.
NK1704 .J6 1991

Jones, John Paul, 1924-
John Paul Jones : a survey exhibition,

1950-1983 : Los Angeles Municipal Art Gallery, January 24-February 19, 1984. Los Angeles : Los Angeles Municipal Art Gallery, c1983. 48 p. : ill. (some col.), ports. ; 24 cm. Catalogue essay by Susan C. Larsen. Errata slip inserted. Bibliography: p. 43-44.
1. Jones, John Paul, 1924- - Exhibitions. I. Larsen, Susan C. II. Los Angeles. Municipal Art Gallery. III. Title.   **NYPL [3-MCX J775 85-3055]**

JONES, JOHN PAUL, 1924- - EXHIBITIONS.
Jones, John Paul, 1924- John Paul Jones . Los Angeles , c1983. 48 p. :
           NYPL [3-MCX J775 85-3055]

Jones, Lois Mailou.
The world of Lois Mailou Jones : Meridian House International, Washington, D.C., January 28-March 18, 1990. Washington, D.C. (1630 Crescent Place, NW, Washington) : Meridian House International, c1990. x, 38 p. : ill. (some col.) ; 21 x 22 cm. "Prepared in coordination with an exhibition at Meridian House International"--P. [2] of cover. Includes bibliographical references (p. 35-38). DDC 759.13 20
1. Jones, Lois Mailou - Exhibitions. I. Meridian House International. II. Title.
ND237.J76 A4 1990

JONES, LOIS MAILOU - EXHIBITIONS.
Jones, Lois Mailou. The world of Lois Mailou Jones . Washington, D.C. (1630 Crescent Place, NW, Washington) , c1990. x, 38 p. : DDC 759.13 20
ND237.J76 A4 1990

Lois Mailou Jones . Washington, DC [1988?] 29 p. : DDC 759.13 20
N6537.J68 A4 1988

Jones, Mark, 1951- Fake? . London , 1990. 312 p. : ISBN 0-7141-1703-X
N8790 .F3 1990b

Jones, Michael Owen. Woodworking traditions in Lindsborg, Kansas : an overview with recommendations for documentation, presentation, and development / prepared by Michael Owen Jones. [Los Angeles : Folklore and Mythology Center, University of California, 1989] 66 leaves : ill. ; 28 cm. Cover title. "June 1989." Includes bibliographical references (leaves 56-59). DDC 730/.09781/55 20
1. Woodwork - Kansas - Lindsborg - Themes, motives. I. Title.
NK9612 .J66 1989

Jones, Olive R. The Parks Canada glass glossary for the description of containers, tableware, flat glass, and closures / Olive Jones and Catherine Sullivan ; with contributions by George L. Miller ... [et al.]. Rev. ed. Ottawa, Ont. : National Historic Parks and Sites, Canadian Parks Service, Environment Canada, 1989. 184 p. : ill. ; 28 cm. (Studies in archaeology, architecture, and history, 0821-1027) Includes bibliographical references (p. 173-178) and index. ISBN 0-660-13245-1 DDC 748.2/014 20
1. Glassware - Terminology. I. Sullivan, Catherine. II. Parks Canada. National Historic Parks and Sites Branch. III. Title. IV. Title: Glass glossary. V. Series.
NK5104 .J66 1989

Jones, Owen, 1809-1874.
The complete "Chinese ornament" : all 100 color plates / by Owen Jones. New York : Dover, 1990. 100 p. of plates : all col. ill. ; 32 cm. (Dover pictorial archive series) "An unaltered republication of the plates from the work originally published by S. & T. Gilbert, London, in 1867 under the title: Examples of Chinese ornament selected from objects in the South Kensington Museum and other collections"--T.p. verso. ISBN 0-486-26259-6 : DDC 745.4/4951 20
1. Decoration and ornament - China - Themes, motives. I. Jones, Owen, 1809-1874. Examples of Chinese ornament selected from objects in the South Kensington Museum and other collections. II. Title.
NK1483.A1 J64 1990
        NYPL [3-MLF+ 91-3685]

Examples of Chinese ornament selected from objects in the South Kensington Museum and other collections. Jones, Owen, 1809-1874. The complete "Chinese ornament" : all 100 color plates / by Owen Jones. New York , 1990. 100 p. of plates : ISBN 0-486-26259-6 : DDC 745.4/4951 20
NK1483.A1 J64 1990
        NYPL [3-MLF+ 91-3685]

Jones, Philippe Roberts- see **Roberts-Jones, Philippe.**

Jones, Stephen, 1954- Calloway, Stephen. Royal style . Boston , 1991. p. ISBN 0-316-12509-1 : DDC 745/.094 20
NK925 .C35 1991

Jones, Terry. Instant design : a manual of graphic techniques / by Terry Jones. London : Architecture Design and Technology, 1990. [120] p. : ill. (some col.) ; 21 cm. (ADT DesignFile) "Wink." Includes bibliography ISBN 1-85454-838-7 (pbk.) : DDC 741.6 20
I. Title. II. Title: Wink.
NC997   **NYPL [3-MDW 90-10937]**

JONESBORO (TENN.) - BUILDINGS, STRUCURES, ETC.
Tennessee State Planning Commission. Upper East Tennessee Office. Historic district plan, Jonesborough, Tennessee /. Johnson City, Tenn. , Springfield, Va. , 1972. 115 p. :
        NYPL [3-MQWO 90-6607]

Jonge, Lia de. Nicolaas Bastert : Vechtschilder, 1854-1939 / Lia de Jonge. Alphen aan den Rijn : Repro-Holland, in samenwerking met Oudheidkundig Genootschap Niftarlake, 1990. 120 p. : ill. (some col.) ; 29 cm. Includes bibliographical references (p. 116-117) and index. ISBN 90-6471-238-7 :
1. Bastert, Nicolaas, 1854-1939. 2. Painters - Netherlands - Biography. I. Bastert, Nicolaas, 1854-1939. II. Title.
ND653.B36 J66 1990

Jongh, Ludolf de, 1616-1679.
Fleischer, Roland E. Ludolf de Jongh (1616-1679) . Doornspijk, The Netherlands , c1989. 100 p., [93] p. of plates : ISBN 90-70288-53-2 DDC 759.9492 20
ND653.J4 F54 1989
        NYPL [3-MCH J763 91-6586]

JONGH, LUDOLF DE, 1616-1679 - CRITICISM AND INTERPRETATION.
Fleischer, Roland E. Ludolf de Jongh (1616-1679) . Doornspijk, The Netherlands , c1989. 100 p., [93] p. of plates : ISBN 90-70288-53-2 DDC 759.9492 20
ND653.J4 F54 1989
        NYPL [3-MCH J763 91-6586]

Jonkanski, Dirk. Baudenkmale in Niedersachsen /. Hannover , c1990. 356 p. : ISBN 3-87706-322-5 DDC 720/.943/59 20
NA1081 .B38 1990

Jonke, Gert, 1946- Neue Möbel, Holzwerkstätten aus Südkävnten . Wien , 1981. [28] p. :
        NYPL [3-MOF 89-11605]

Jonovic, Donald J., 1943- Danco, Léon A., 1923- Someday, it'll all be-- whos's? /. Cleveland , c1990. vi, 196 p. : ISBN 0-915607-09-3 (Jamieson) : DDC 741.5/973 20
NC1429.D2344 A4 1990

Joosten, Ellen. Rijksmuseum Kröller-Müller. Cent dessins du Musée Kröller-Müller. Bruxelles, c1971. [viii], 100, [xvi] p. : DDC 741.9/074/04582
NC17.N4 O8773   **NYPL [3-MBH 90-6298]**

Joostens, Paul, 1889-1960.
Paul Joostens : tekeningen en collages : schenking galerij Ronny Van de Velde en Co : [tentoonstelling] Koninklijk Museum voor Schone Kunsten, Antwerpen, 5 juli-24 augustus 1986 / [redactie, J.F. Buyck, D. Cardyn-Oomen]. [Brussel] : Ministerie van de Vlaamse Gemeenschap, [1986] 59 p. : chiefly ill. ; 21 cm. Includes bibliographical references.
1. Joostens, Paul, 1889-1960 - Exhibitions. I. Buyck, Jean. II. Cardyn-Oomen, Dorine. III. Koninklijk Museum voor Schone Kunsten (Belgium). IV. Title.
        NYPL [3-MCH J815 90-8180]

JOOSTENS, PAUL, 1889-1960 - EXHIBITIONS.
Joostens, Paul, 1889-1960. Paul Joostens . [Brussel] [1986] 59 p. :
        NYPL [3-MCH J815 90-8180]

Joppien, Rüdiger, 1946- Treskow, Elisabeth, 1898- Elisabeth Treskow, Goldschmiedekunst des 20. Jahrhunderts . Köln [1990] 168 p. : DDC 739.2/272 20
NK7198.T734 A4 1990

Jordaens, Jacob, 1593-1678.
Rubenshuis (Antwerp, Belgium) Tekeningen van Jacob Jordaens, 1593-1678. [Antwerp, 1966] 133 p.   **NYPL [3-MCH J82 91-564]**

JORDAENS, JACOB, 1593-1678 - EXHIBITIONS.
Rubenshuis (Antwerp, Belgium) Tekeningen van Jacob Jordaens, 1593-1678. [Antwerp, 1966] 133 p.   **NYPL [3-MCH J82 91-564]**

Jordan Art Gallery (Boston, Mass.)
First exhibition of oil and water colors by English painters /. Boston , 1897. 49 p., [5] leaves of plates :   **NYPL [3-MCT 90-5919]**

Paintings from the Salon and the Champs de Mars, Paris, 1897 /. Boston , 1897-8 [i.e. 1897] 45 p., [5] leaves of plates :
        NYPL [3-MCN 90-5918]

Jordán, Olga Lucía. Panesso, Fausto, 1953- Arte y parte . [Bogotá, Colombia?] [1990- v. <1 >:
N6675 .P35 1990

Jordan-Volpe Gallery. Hiesinger, Ulrich W., 1943- Impressionism in America . Munich , New York, NY , c1991. 255 p. : ISBN 3-7913-1142-5   **NYPL [3-MCW+ 91-7730]**

Jörg, C. J. A. Chinese export porcelain . Hong Kong , 1989. 303 p. : ISBN 962-215-094-2
        NYPL [3-MPFF 91-5164]

Jorge Dahm . Dahm, Jorge. [Santiago, Chile] [1990?] 1 v. (unpaged) : DDC 759.983 20
ND369.D35 A4 1990

Jornadas sobre Criterios de Intervención en el Patrimonio Arquitectónico (1987 : Madrid, Spain) Monumentos y proyecto : Jornadas sobre Criterios de Intervención en el Patrimonio Arquitectónico : [celebradas en Madrid del 19 al 23 de octubre de 1987]. Madrid : Ministerio de Cultura, Instituto de Conservación y Restauración de Bienes Culturales, [1990] 407 p. : ill. (some col.) ; 33 cm. Includes bibliographical references (p. 402-407). ISBN 84-7483-642-5
1. Architecture - Spain - Conservation and restoration - Congresses.
NA109.S7 J68 1987

Jos Albert /. Roberts-Jones, Philippe. Bruxelles [1986] 154 p. : DDC 759.9493 20
ND673.A35 R6 1986

José Caballero . Caballero, José, 1916- [Sevilla] [1988?] 1 v. (unpaged) : DDC 769.92 20
NE702.C3 A4 1988

José Chávez Morado . Chávez Morado, José, 1909- Guanajuato, Gto. , 1988. 215 p. : ISBN 968-617-012-X
        NYPL [3-MCZ C51 90-11331]

José Cúneo . Pereda, Raquel. Montevideo [1988] xiii, 196 p. : DDC 759.9895 B 20
ND429.C8 P47 1988

José María Sicilia . Sicilia, José María, 1954- London , 1990. 44 p. : ISBN 1-87071-503-9 (pbk.) DDC 760.092 20
        NYPL [3-MCQ S566 91-5914]

José Pérez Jiménez, 1887-1967 /. Pérez Jiménez, José, 1887-1967. [[Badajoz] [1989] 279 p. ISBN 84-7796-975-2
        NYPL [3-MCQ P413 90-12327]

José Sabogal, 1888-marzo-1988. Centenario del nacimiento de José Sabogal, 1888-19 marzo-1988 /. Lima, Perú , 1989 (Miraflores : Librería Editorial "Minerva") 68 p. :
N6719.S23 C46 1989

José Segrelles Albert . Montagud, Bernardo. Alzira , 1985. 239 p. : ISBN 84-398-3281-8
ND813.S388 M65 1985

Josef Albers . Feeney, Kelly, 1961- Alexandria, Va. , 1991. p. cm. ISBN 0-88397-100-3 DDC 760/.092 20
NC251.A36 A4 1991

Josef Bramer /. Bäumer, Angelica. [Wien] [1990] 89 p. : ISBN 3-203-51094-4 DDC 759.36 20
ND511.5.B69 A4 1990

Josef Doerr /. Meuser, Bernhard. Speyer am Rhein , 1989. 96 p. : ISBN 3-87637-040-X DDC 709/. 20
N6888.D634 M4 1989

Josef-Haubrich-Kunsthalle. see Cologne. Kunsthalle.

Josef-Haubrich-Kunsthalle Köln.
Baukhage, Gerd, 1911- Gerd Baukhage . [Köln

[1989] 114 p. :
MLCM 90/03723 (N)
NYPL [3-MCK B339 91-2508]

Nay, E. W. (Ernst Wilhelm), 1902-1968. E.W.
Nay, Retrospektive /. Köln , c1990. 210 p. :
ISBN 3-7701-2726-9
NYPL [3-MCK+ N331 91-5930]

Schober, Helmut, 1947- Helmut Schober .
München , c1989. 153 p. :   ISBN 3-7913-1013-5
NYPL [3-MCK+ S3627 89-26518]

Josef Herman . Davies, Peter. Bristol [England] ,
1990. 136 p. :   ISBN 1-87297-150-4
NYPL [3-MCZ H545 91-5532]

Josef Hoffmann. Rochowanski, L. W. (Leopold
Wolfgang), 1885- Wien [c1950] 67 p.
NA1038.H6 R6
NYPL [3-MQZ (Hoffmann) 90-6083]

Josef Lebovic Gallery. Masterpieces of Australian
photography . Paddington, Sydney, Australia ,
c1989. 200 p. :   **NYPL [MFW+ 91-3430]**

Josef Müller-Brockmann . Müller-Brockmann,
Josef, 1914- [Zurich , 1988?] 35 p. :
**NYPL [3-MDWS (Müller-Brockmann)
91-5922]**

Josef Neuhaus, Plastiken und Reliefs . Neuhaus,
Josef, 1923- Neuss , 1988. 77 p. :
NYPL [3-MGO (Neuhaus) 89-25259]

Josef Pillhofer . Pillhofer, Josef, 1921- Düsseldorf
[1989?] [76] p. :
NB511.5.P5 A4 1989

Josef Sudek . Sudek, Josef, 1896-1976. New
York, N.Y. , c1990. 159 p. :   ISBN
0-89381-386-9
NYPL [MFX+ (Sudek) 90-9102]

Josef Wopfner 1843-1927 /. Holz, Irmgard.
Rosenheim , c1989. 255 p. :   ISBN 3-475-52594-1
NYPL [3-MCK+ W915 90-12081]

Josef Wopfner, 1843-1927 /. Holz, Irmgard.
Rosenheim , c1989. 255 p. :   ISBN
3-475-52594-1 :   DDC 759.3 20
ND588.W76 A4 1989

**JOSEFF, EUGENE, 1905-1948 - THEMES,
MOTIVES.**
Ball, Joanne Dubbs. Jewelry of the stars . West
Chester, Pa. , c1991. 192 p. :   ISBN
0-88740-294-1   DDC 739.27/092 20
NK7398.J67 B35 1991

Josef,Schulz, 1893-1973. Rohrmoser, Albin. Der
Maler Josef Schulz . Salzburg , c1986. 144 p. :
NYPL [3-MCK S3868 90-11496]

Josep Obiols . Obiols i Palau, Josep, 1894-1967.
[Barcelona] [1990?] 231 p. :   ISBN
84-7609-348-9
N7113.O25 A4 1990

Josep Obiols . Obiols, Josep. [Barcelona] , 1990.
231 p. :   **NYPL [3-MCQ O17 90-13284]**

Josep Puig i Cadafalch . Puig i Cadafalch, Josep,
1869-1957. Barcelona , 1989. 193 p. :   ISBN
84-7664-239-3
IN PROCESS (ONLINE)   **NYPL [3-MQZ+
(Puig i Cadafalch) 91-4264]**

**Josep Puig i Cadafalch : architecture between the
house and the city.** Puig i Cadafalch, Josep,
1869-1957. Josep Puig i Cadafalch . Barcelona ,
1989. 193 p. :   ISBN 84-7664-239-3
IN PROCESS (ONLINE)   **NYPL [3-MQZ+
(Puig i Cadafalch) 91-4264]**

Josep Royo . Royo, Josep. Barcelona , 1972. 1 v.
(unpaged) :   **NYPL [3-MON 90-6888]**

Joseph Beuys : der erweiterte Kunstbegriff /
[Hrsg. Matthias Bleyl].1. Aufl. Darmstadt : G.
Büchner, c1989. 179 p. : ill. ; 26 cm. Includes
bibliographical references.   ISBN 3-925376-30-5 (trade
ed.)
*1. Beuys, Joseph. 2. Beuys, Joseph - Catalogs. 3.
Hessisches Landesmuseum (Darmstadt, Germany) -
Catalogs. I. Beuys, Joseph. II. Bleyl, Matthias. III.
Hessisches Landesmuseum (Darmstadt, Germany).*
NYPL [3-MGO (Beuys) 91-6704]

Joseph Beuys . Beuys, Joseph. München , c1990.
228 p. :
MLCM 91/01681 (N)
NYPL [3-MCK+ B569 91-6473]

Joseph Beuys . Beuys, Joseph. Stuttgart , c1990.
135 p. :   ISBN 3-7757-0313-6
NYPL [3-MCK+ B569 91-3920]

Joseph Beuys . Beuys, Joseph. Hannover [1990]

267 p. :   DDC 759.3 20
N6888.B463 A4 1990

Joseph Beuys /. Stachelhaus, Heiner. [Joseph
Beuys. English.] New York , 1991. 223 p. :
ISBN 1-558-59107-9   DDC 709/.2 B 20
N6888.B463 S7413 1991
NYPL [3-MCK B569 91-6313]

**Joseph Beuys im Gespräch mit Knut Fischer und
Walter Smerling.** Beuys, Joseph. Köln , c1989.
75 p. :   ISBN 3-462-01970-8
NYPL [3-MGO (Beuys) 90-2524]

Joseph Cornell /. Jaguer, Edouard. [Paris] ,
c1989. 93 p. :   ISBN 2-85018-249-4
NYPL [3-MCX+ C795 90-11997]

Joseph Cornell and the ballet /. Starr, Sandra
Leonard. New York , c1983. viii, 87 p. :   DDC
709/.2/4 19
N6537.C66 A4 1983
NYPL [MCX C795 84-702]

Joseph Crawhall, 1861-1913 . Hamilton, Vivien.
London , 1990. xiii, 177 p. :   ISBN
0-7195-4827-6 :   DDC 759.2/911 20
ND1942.C89 A4 1990

Joseph Deutschmann 1717-1787 . Vogl, Hubert.
Weissenhorn in Bayern , c1989. 223 p., 3 leaves
of plates :   ISBN 3-87437-223-5   DDC 730/.92 20
NB588.D434 V63 1989
NYPL [3-MGO (Deutschmann) 90-6255]

**Joseph Fassbender, Malerei zurischen Figuration
und Abstraktion** /. Fassbender, Joseph,
1903-1974. Köln , 1988. 171 p. :   ISBN
3-87909-203-6
NYPL [3-MCK+ F249 89-11746]

Joseph Kaspar Sattler . Hollweck, Ludwig.
Pfaffenhofen , c1988. 156 p. :   ISBN
3-7787-2090-2
IN PROCESS (ONLINE)
NYPL [MDG (Sattler) 90-5109]

Joseph Mallord William Turner /. Walker, John,
1906 Dec. 24- New York , 1983. 128 p. :
ISBN 0-8109-5331-5 (EP)   DDC 759.2 19
ND497.T8 W34 1982
NYPL [3-MCV+ T94 91-3927]

Joseph, Peter T. (Peter Thomas), 1950- Castle,
Wendell, 1932- Angel chairs . New York ,
1991. 111 p. :   ISBN 0-9628849-0-1   DDC 749.213
20
NK2439.C3 A4 1991

Joseph Raffael : the California years, 1969-1978 :
[exhibition] organized by Thomas H. Garver for
the San Francisco Museum of Modern Art,
January 20-March 5, 1978. [San Francisco] :
The Museum, c1978. 64 p. : ill. ; 25 x 31 cm.
Includes a catalog of the exhibition, which was also
held at other museums, Mar. 27, 1978-Mar. 4, 1979.
Bibliography: p.
*1. Raffael, Joseph, 1933- - Exhibitions. I. Raffael,
Joseph, 1933-. II. Garver, Thomas H. III. San
Francisco. Museum of Modern Art.*
N6537.R23 A4 1978
NYPL [3-MCX+ R136 79-2011]

JOSEPH, SAINT - ART.
Lara Roche, Carlos, 1932- San José en el arte
colonial guatemalteco /. Guatemala, C.A. ,
1989. 161 p. :
N6576 .L37 1989

Joseph shops . Manser, José. London , Van
Nostrand Reinhold, 1991. [60] p. :   ISBN
1-85454-445-4 (pbk.) :   DDC 747.8521 20
NK2195.S89   **NYPL [3-MLT+ 91-6982]**

Josephs, Wilfred, 1927-
[Doubles]
Piano music [sound recording] / Wilfred
Josephs. [S.l.] : Novello, p1989. 1 sound
disc : digital ; 4 3/4 in. Heidi Hendrickx and
Levente Kende, pianos (1st work), and Yonty
Solomon, piano (2nd work). Eds. recorded: Orpheus
Publications. Analog recording. Issued also as analog
disc (NVL 104) and cassette (NVLC 104). Compact
disc. CONTENTS. - Doubles : op. 85 (25:30) --
Fourteen studies, op. 53 (32:06).
1. Piano music (Pianos (2)). 2. Piano music.
Novello NVLCD 104

Josh, Sohan Singh, 1898-
Hindustan Gadar Party : a short history / by
Sohan Singh Josh. New Delhi : People's Pub.
House, 1977-1978. 2 v. ; 22 cm. Continuation of
the author's Tragedy of the Komagataramu. Includes
bibliographical references.
1. Hindustan Gadar Party - History. 2. East Indians -

North America - Politics and government. 3. India -
Politics and government - 20th century. I. Title.
DS480.45 .J66   **NYPL [JLL 79-458]**

Hindustan Gadar Party : a short history / by
Sohan Singh Josh. New Delhi : People's Pub.
House, 1977. 1 v. ; 22 cm. Continuation of
the author's Tragedy of the Komagatamaru. Includes
bibliographies and indexes.
*1. Hindustan Gadar Party - History. 2. East Indians in
North America - Politics and government. 3. India -
Politics and government - 20th century.*
DS480.45 .J66   **NYPL [JLK 80-148]**

Joslyn Art Museum. Wyeth, James, 1946- James
Wyeth . [Omaha?] c1975 (Omaha : Barnhart
Press) [64] p. :
NYPL [3-MCX W980 90-7181]

**Joslyn Memorial Art Museum, Omaha. see
Joslyn Art Museum.**

Jotamario. El Espíritu erótico /. Bogotá , 1990.
207 p. :   DDC 704.9/428/098610904 20
N8217.E6 E87 1990

Joubert, Caroline. Symbolique & botanique .
Caen [1987] 30, [68] p. :
NYPL [3-MBT 90-12364]

Journal des dames et des modes. Parisian fashion,
from the "Journal des dames et des modes," vol.
1, 1912-1913 /. New York , c1979. [12] p.,
[93] p. of plates :   ISBN 0-8478-0253-1 :   DDC
391/.2/0944361
GT887 .P3   **NYPL [MML 81-188]**

Journal impersonal, 1968-1972 /. Moucha,
Miloslav, 1942- Paris [between 1972 and 1974]
1 v. (unpaged) :   **NYPL [MEMZ 91-567]**

**JOURNALISTIC PHOTOGRAPHY. see
PHOTOGRAPHY, JOURNALISTIC.**

Jové, Angel.
Angel Jové : capiscar la fior de la mà morta /
Angel Jové ; [organització, Generalitat de
Catalunya, Departament de Cultura, Direcció
General de Promoció Cultural, Arts Plàstiques ;
traducció i correcció de textos, Josep-Lluís
Sotorra, Margarita Hernández]. [Barcelona] :
Generalitat de Catalunya, Departament de
Cultura, [1991?] 229 p. : col. ill. ; 31 cm.
Catalan, with English and Spanish translations. At head
of title: Centre d'Art Santa Mònica, Barcelona, 30
gener-3 març 1990. Includes bibliographical references
(p. 199-[200]).
*1. Jové, Angel - Exhibitions. I. Centre d'Art Santa
Mònica (Barcelona, Spain). II. Catalonia (Spain).
Direcció General de Promoció Cultural. Arts Plàstiques.
III. Title. IV. Title: Capiscar la fior de la mà morta.*
N7113.J68 A4 1991

JOVÉ, ANGEL - EXHIBITIONS.
Jové, Angel. Angel Jové . [Barcelona] [1991?]
229 p. :
N7113.J68 A4 1991

Joy of painting series twenty-one, Bob Ross.
Ross, Bob, 1942- The Joy of painting series
XXI, Bob Ross /. Sterling, VA , c1990. 78 p. :
ISBN 0-924639-20-2   DDC 751.45/436 20
ND1500 .R645 1990

The Joy of painting series XXI, Bob Ross /.
Ross, Bob, 1942- Sterling, VA , c1990. 78 p. :
ISBN 0-924639-20-2   DDC 751.45/436 20
ND1500 .R645 1990

Joy of painting series 21, Bob Ross. Ross, Bob,
1942- The Joy of painting series XXI, Bob Ross
/. Sterling, VA , c1990. 78 p. :   ISBN
0-924639-20-2   DDC 751.45/436 20
ND1500 .R645 1990

Joy of painting (Television program)
Ross, Bob, 1942- The Joy of painting series
XXI, Bob Ross /. Sterling, VA , c1990. 78 p. :
ISBN 0-924639-20-2   DDC 751.45/436 20
ND1500 .R645 1990

Ross, Bob, 1942- The joy of painting, volume
twenty with Bob Ross. Sterling, Va. , c1990. 79
p. :   ISBN 0-924639-17-2   DDC 751.45/436 20
ND1342 .N65 1990

**The joy of painting, volume twenty with Bob
Ross.** Ross, Bob, 1942- Sterling, Va. , c1990. 79
p. :   ISBN 0-924639-17-2   DDC 751.45/436 20
ND1342 .N65 1990

Joy, Steve, 1952-
Steve Joy : new paintings 1989-90 : October 10
to November 10, 1990 / introduction by
William Zimmer. New York, NY : Ruth Siegel
Gallery, c1990. [24] p. : ill. (chiefly col.) ; 28

cm.
1. Joy, Steve, 1952- - Exhibitions. I. Zimmer, William,
1946-. II. Ruth Siegel Gallery. III. Title.
NYPL [3-MCV J885 91-7332]

JOY, STEVE, 1952- - EXHIBITIONS.
Joy, Steve, 1952- Steve Joy . New York, NY ,
c1990. [24] p. :
NYPL [3-MCV J885 91-7332]

Joyce, David. Garden styles . London , c1989.
192 p. : ISBN 1-87130-778-3
NYPL [3-MSC 90-8787]

**József Attila Tudományegyetem. I. sz.--Magyar
Irodalomtörténeti Tanszék.** Erdély és a
Részek térképe és helységnévtára . Szeged ,
1987 ([Budapest] : Franklin Nyomda) 1 atlas
(41, 214 p., [9] p. of plates) : ISBN
963-481-771-8 : DDC 912/.4984 19
G2037.T7 E7 1987
NYPL [Map Div. 91-145]

Juan Gris . Gris, Juan, 1887-1927. [Valencia,
Spain] [Paris, France] [1990] 150 p. : ISBN
2-85850-595-0
NC287.G76 A4 1990

Juca Martins. Martins, Juca, 1949- Rio de
Janeiro , c1990. [15] p., [46] leaves of plates :
ISBN 85-7222-000-11
NYPL [MFX (Martins) 91-3427]

Judd, Donald, 1928-
Donald Judd : Staatliche Kunsthalle
Baden-Baden, 27. August bis 15. Oktober 1989
/ [herausgegeben von Jochen Poetter].
Baden-Baden : Die Kunsthalle, 1989. 215 p. :
ill. (chiefly col.) ; 29 cm. German and English.
Includes bibliographical references (p. 197-215). ISBN
3-89322-168-9
1. Judd, Donald, 1928- - Exhibitions. I. Poetter, Jochen.
II. Staatliche Kunsthalle Baden-Baden. III. Title.
NYPL [3-MGO (Judd) 90-12983]

Donald Judd : [Ausstellung], Staatliche
Kunsthalle Baden-Baden, 27. August bis 15.
Oktober 1989 / [herausgegeben von Jochen
Poetter ; Katalog-Redaktion, Jochen Poetter,
Mitarbeit, Rosemarie E. Pahlke ; Fotografien,
Philipp Schönborn ; Übersetzungen, Andrew
Bird ... et al.]. Stuttgart-Bad Cannstatt : Ed.
Cantz, [1989] 215 p. : ill. (chiefly col.) ; 30 cm.
German and English. "Buchhandelsausgabe"--Colophon.
Includes bibliographical references (p. 197-215). ISBN
3-89322-168-9 : DDC 709/.2 20
1. Judd, Donald, 1928- - Exhibitions. I. Poetter, Jochen.
II. Pahlke, Rosemarie E. III. Staatliche Kunsthalle
Baden-Baden. IV. Title.
NB237.J76 A4 1989

JUDD, DONALD, 1928- - EXHIBITIONS.
Judd, Donald, 1928- Donald Judd .
Baden-Baden , 1989. 215 p. : ISBN
3-89322-168-9
NYPL [3-MGO (Judd) 90-12983]

Judd, Donald, 1928- Donald Judd .
Stuttgart-Bad Cannstatt [1989] 215 p. : ISBN
3-89322-168-9 : DDC 709/.2 20
NB237.J76 A4 1989

Judging dolls . Seeley, Mildred. Livonia, Mich.
(30595 8 Mile Rd., Livonia 46152-1798)
[c1991] 166 p. : DDC 688.7/221/075 20
NK4893 .S384 1991

Judith Clancy . Clancy, Judith S. [Paris] , c1986.
71 p. : ISBN 2-901414-19-2
NYPL [3-MCX C587 88-2596]

Judrin, Claudie. Musée Rodin. Inventaire des
dessins /. [Paris] , c1984- v. : ISBN
2-901428-10-X (v. 3) DDC 741.944 19
NC248.R58 A4 1984
NYPL [MCO R69 88-2276]

Judson, J. Richard (Jay Richard) Book
illustrations and title-pages / J. Richard Judson,
Carl van de Velde. Brussels : Arcade Press ;
Philadelphia, PA : Distribution, Heyden, 1977.
2 v. (552 p., unpaged p. of plates) : 294 ill. ; 27
cm. (Corpus Rubenianum Ludwig Burchard . pt. 21)
"Published jointly by Harvey Miller Publishers and
Heyden & Son Ltd"--T.p. verso. Includes bibliographical
references and indexes. ISBN 2-8005-0124-3
I. Velde, C. van de (Carl). II. Title. III. Series.
ND673.R9 C63 pt. 21 1977 NC984.5.R8

Juego de espejos. Jurado, María Cristina. Zañartu
/. Santiago , 1989. 64 p. :
NYPL [3-MCZ+ Z449 90-12332]

Juego y deporte en la pintura de Goya /. Mestre
Sancho, Juan Antonio. [Valencia] [1990?] 294

p. : ISBN 84-7890-087-X DDC 760/.092 20
N7113.G68 A4 1990a

Jürgen Partenheimer, Linolschnitte und Bücher .
Partenheimer, Jürgen. Reutlingen , 1988. 139
p. : ISBN 90-71584-09-7 DDC 769.92 20
NE1336.P36 A4 1988
NYPL [MDG (Partenheimer) 90-13141]

Jugend im Sozialismus : Ausstellung anlässlich
des 70. Jahrestages der Grossen Sozialistischen
Oktoberrevolution / [Herausgeber], Akademie
der Künste der UdSSR, Akademie der Künste
der DDR. Berlin : Akademie der Künste der
DDR, [1987] 83 p. : ill. ; 27 cm. Catalog of an
exhibition held Nov. 6-Dec. 20, 1987 in Berlin.
1. Art, German - Germany (East) - Exhibitions. 2. Art,
Modern - 20th century - Germany (East) - Exhibitions.
3. Art, Russian - Russian S.F.S.R. - Exhibitions. 4. Art,
Modern - 20th century - Russian S.F.S.R. - Exhibitions.
5. Youth in art - Exhibitions. I. Akademiîa khudozhestv
SSSR.
N6889 .J75 1987 NYPL [3-MAMZ 91-4201]

Jugendliche im Gefängnis : Bilder einer Aktion :
Kinder und Jugendliche malen für Amnesty
International / herausgegeben von Amnesty
International. Köln ; DuMont, 1987. 95 p. : ill.
(some col.) ; 21 X 30 cm. ISBN 3-7701-2138-4
1. Children's drawings. 2. Juvenile corrections - Art.
NYPL [3-MATC+ 89-25803]

Jugendstil . Landesmuseum Mainz. Mainz ,
c1990. 396 p. : ISBN 3-8053-1141-9
NK5109.85.A7 L35 1990

JUGENDSTIL. see ART NOUVEAU.

Jugendwerke vom Schillerplatz / herausgegeben
von Gustav Peichl. Wien : Akademie der
bildenden Künste zu Wien, c1988. 280 p. : ill. ;
25 cm. (Wiener Akademie-Reihe . Bd. 22)
Introduction inserted. Katalog of an exhibition held at
the Akademie der bildenden Künste zu Wien, May
3-June 2, 1988.
1. Akademie der Bildenden Künste in Wien -
Exhibitions. 2. Art, Modern - 17th-18th centuries -
Austria - Exhibitions. 3. Art, Modern - 19th century -
Austria - Exhibitions. 4. Art, Modern - 20th century -
Austria - Exhibitions. 5. Art, Austrian - Exhibitions. I.
Peichl, Gustav. II. Akademie der bildenden Künste in
Wien. III. Series. *NYPL [3-MAMG 90-9782]*

Jugoslavenski leksikografski zavod. Jugoslavija,
auto atlas / urednik Branko Šoštarić ; izradba
karata Biserka Cerovečki ... [et al.]. Zagreb :
Jugoslavenski leksikografski zavod, 1972. [104]
p. : col. ill., col. maps : 24 cm. Scale of principal
maps: 1:500,000. Polyglot text. Includes index.
1. Yugoslavia - Road maps. I. Šoštarić, Branko. II.
Title. *NYPL [Map Div. 90-4942]*

Jugoslavija. see Yugoslavia.

Jugoslavija, auto atlas /. Jugoslavenski
leksikografski zavod. Zagreb , 1972. [104] p. :
NYPL [Map Div. 90-4942]

Juhl, Finn, 1912- Hiort, Esbjørn. Arkitekten Finn
Juhl . København , 1990. 143, [1] p. : ISBN
87-7407-093-2 :
N7023.J84 H5 1990

JUHL, FINN, 1912-
Hiort, Esbjørn. Arkitekten Finn Juhl .
København , 1990. 143, [1] p. : ISBN
87-7407-093-2 :
N7023.J84 H5 1990

Jujol /. Solà-Morales Rubío, Ignasi de, 1942-
Barcelona , c1990. 127 p. : ISBN 84-343-0597-6
NYPL [3-MQZ+ (Jujol) 90-10921]

JUJOL, JOSEP MARÍA, 1879-1949.
Solà-Morales Rubío, Ignasi de, 1942- Jujol /.
Barcelona , c1990. 127 p. : ISBN 84-343-0597-6
NYPL [3-MQZ+ (Jujol) 90-10921]

Jules Olitski /. Olitski, Jules, 1922- [New York] ,
c1990. 5 v. : *NYPL [3-MCX O47 91-6724]*

Jules Olitski, spray paintings of the 1960s :
[exhibition] October 5-28, 1989, André
Emmerich Gallery. Olitski, Jules, 1922- New
York, NY , c1989. [32] p. :
NYPL [3-MCX+ O47 91-5567]

Julia Codesido, 1883-1979 /. Moll, Eduardo,
1929- [Lima, Peru?] 1990 (Lima : Editorial
Navarrete) 127 p. : DDC 759.985 20
ND419.C62 A4 1990

Julia Wachtel / [edited by Thomas Fredrickson].
Chicago : Museum of Contemporary Art,
c1991. p. cm. "This catalogue was produced in
conjunction with the exhibition OPTIONS 41: Julia

Wachtel, March 23 through April 13, 1991 at the
Museum of Contemporary Art, Chicago. Includes
bibliographical references. ISBN 0-933856-33-4
DDC 759.13 20
1. Wachtel, Julia, 1956- - Exhibitions. I. Wachtel, Julia,
1956-. II. Fredrickson, Thomas. III. Museum of
Contemporary Art (Chicago, Ill.).
ND237.W24 A4 1991

Julian, John. (ed) Spilt image. [Melbourne] 1969.
1 v. (unpaged) DDC 779
TR654 .S6 NYPL [MFW 90-6798]

Julian Schnabel /. Schnabel, Julian, 1951- Prato ,
c1989. 159 p. : ISBN 88-85191-00-2
NYPL [3-MCX S358 90-4741]

Julien, Edouard.
[Lautrec. English]
Toulouse-Lautrec / by Edouard Julien ;
[translated by Helen C. Slonim]. New York :
Crown Publishers, 1991. p. cm. (Crown art
library) Translation of: Lautrec. Includes index.
ISBN 0-517-03718-1 : DDC 759.4 20
1. Toulouse-Lautrec, Henri de, 1864-1901 - Criticism
and interpretation. I. Title. II. Series.
ND553.T7 J8413 1991

Julier, Guy. New Spanish design / Guy Julier.
London : Thames and Hudson, c1991. 191 p. :
ill. (some col.) ; 26 cm. Includes bibliographical
references (p. 185-186) and index. ISBN
0-500-23599-6
1. Design - Spain - History - 20th century. 2. Design,
Industrial - Spain - History - 20th century. I. Title.
NYPL [3-MNF 91-5804]

Julio E. Payró /. Alva Negri, Tomás. Buenos
Aires , c1976. 68 p. :
N6639.P38 A94 1976

Julio González. González, Julio, 1876-1942.
Sculpture, drawings, collages. [Chicago, 1969] 1
v.(unpaged)
NYPL [3-MGO (González) 90-6908]

Júlio Resende /. Resende, Júlio, 1917- Lisboa ,
1989. 122 p. : DDC 759.69 20
ND833.R46 A4 1989

**June Leaf, a survey of paintings, sculpture, and
works on paper, 1948-1991 /.** Leaf, June, 1929-
Washington, D.C. , 1991. 48 p. : ISBN
0-937237-01-9 (pbk.) DDC 709/.2 20
N6537.L398 A4 1991

Jung-kwang. The mad monk : paintings of
unlimited action / by Jung-kwang ; with an
introd. by Lewis R. Lancaster ; [photography of
original art work by Hyun-kuk Chon]. Berkeley,
Calif. : Lancaster-Miller Publishers, 1979. 60
p. : ill. ; 21 cm. (Lancaster-Miller art series) ISBN
0-89581-017-4 :
1. Jung-kwang. I. Title.
ND2073.6.Z8 J862 1979
NYPL [3-MAG 81-933]

JUNG-KWANG.
Jung-kwang. The mad monk . Berkeley, Calif. ,
1979. 60 p. : ISBN 0-89581-017-4 :
ND2073.6.Z8 J862 1979
NYPL [3-MAG 81-933]

**JUNG, RICHARD, 1911-1986 - ART
COLLECTIONS - EXHIBITIONS.**
Zeichnungen des 16. bis 18. Jahrhunderts .
[Stuttgart , 1989?] 207 p. :
IN PROCESS (ONLINE)
NYPL [3-MBH 90-12017]

Junge Berliner Künstler : Ausstellung mit
Werken von Stipendiaten der
Karl-Hofer-Gesellschaft, Christine Baetcke ... :
BASF-Feierabendhaus, Ludwigshafen 8. März
bis 4. April 1987 / [Koordination, Günter
Dorn, Thomas Siedhoff]. Ludwigshafen : BASF
Aktiengesellschaft, c1987. 103 p. : col. ill. ; 27
cm.
1. Art, Modern - 20th century - Berlin (Germany) -
Exhibitions. I. Baetcke, Christine. II. Siedhoff, Thomas.
III. Dorn, Günter. IV. Karl-Hofer-Gesellschaft (Berlin,
Germany).
IN PROCESS (ONLINE)
NYPL [3-MAMG 90-12473]

Der junge Kokoschka . Schweiger, Werner J.,
1949- Wien , c1983. 272 p. : ISBN
3-85447-035-5 DDC 760/.092/4 B 19
N6811.5.K56 S39 1983
NYPL [3-MCZ+ K79 91-4016]

**JUNGE RHEINLAND (ASSOCIATION) -
EXHIBITIONS.**
Am Anfang, Das Junge Rheinland .

Düsseldorf , c1985. 351 p. : ISBN 3-546-47771-5
DDC 700/.943/55 19
NX550.D87 A5 1985
NYPL [3-MAMG+ 85-2357]

Illustrierte Bücher und Mappenwerke des
Jungen Rheinlands . Düsseldorf , 1985. ii, 56
p., xvii leaves of plates :
NYPL [MDTT 88-673]

Jungo. Jungo, Jean-Pierre, 1920- [Lausanne ,
1990] 119 p. : DDC 760/.092 20
N7153.J86 A4 1990

Jungo, Jean-Pierre, 1920-
Jungo. [Lausanne : Diffusion Payot, 1990] 119
p. : ill. (some col.) ; 26 cm. Prepared by Pernette
Rickli-Gos. DDC 760/.092 20
*1. Jungo, Jean-Pierre, 1920- - Catalogs. I. Rickli-Gos,
Pernette. II. Title.*
N7153.J86 A4 1990

JUNGO, JEAN-PIERRE, 1920- - CATALOGS.
Jungo, Jean-Pierre, 1920- Jungo. [Lausanne ,
1990] 119 p. : DDC 760/.092 20
N7153.J86 A4 1990

Junta de Andalucia, Consejería de Obras
Públicos y Transportes. Vázquez Consuegra,
Guillermo. Sevilla, cien edificios /. [Sevilla?] ,
1988. 398 p. : ISBN 89-87001-08-4
NYPL [3-MQWH+ 89-25523]

Jurado, María Cristina.
Zañartu / texto de María Cristina Juardo ;
reproducción período 1946-1988 ; proyectó la
edición, Hernán Garfías. Santiago : Editorial
Los Andes, 1989. 64 p. : ill. (some col.) ; 32
cm. Caption title: Juego de espejos. Issued in
conjunction with the exhibition Paysage au corps in the
Galería Praxis, Santiago, Chile.
*1. Zañartu, Enrique, 1921- - Exhibitions. I. Zañartu,
Enrique, 1921-. II. Garfías, Hernán. III. Galería Praxis
(Santiago, Chile). IV. Title. V. Title: Juego de espejos.*
NYPL [3-MCZ+ Z449 90-12332]

Zañartu / texto de María Cristina Jurado ;
reproducción período, 1946-1988. Santiago de
Chile : Editorial Los Andes, 1989. 64 p. : ill.
(some col.) ; 32 cm. (Serie Maestros del siglo XX)
Spine title: Enrique Zañartu. DDC 759.983 20
*1. Zañartu, Enrique, 1921- - Catalogs. I. Zañartu,
Enrique, 1921-. II. Title. III. Title: Enrique Zañartu. IV.
Series.*
ND369.D38 A4 1989

Juraj Najdhart--život i djelo /.
Karlić-Kapetanović, Jelica. Sarajevo , 1990. 383
p. : ISBN 86-21-00357-0
NA1453.N4 K3 1990

Jurgeit, Fritzi. Le Ciste prenestine /. [Roma] ,
1979- v. :
DG70.P33 C57 1979
NYPL [3-MGR+ 83-2202]

Jürgen Partenheimer . Hofmann, Werner, 1928-
Hamburg , c1990. 1 v. (unpaged) :
N6888.P24 A4 1990

Juries on trial . Anthony, Kathryn H. New
York , 19. p. cm. ISBN 0-442-00235-1 DDC
729/079 20
NA2750 .A64 1991

Jurkowski, Józef. Pasierb, Janusz St. The Shrine
of the Black Madonna at Częstochowa /.
Warsaw [1989] 223, [1] p. : ISBN
83-223-2501-0
NYPL [3-MAIH+ 90-12436]

Jurkuvienė, Teresė. Liaudies kūrybos palikimas
dabarties kultūroje . Kaunas , 1989. 220 p. :
ISBN 5-430-00541-X :
NX180.S6 L5 1989

JURY - BIOGRAPHY - HISTORY AND
CRITICISM.
Anthony, Kathryn H. Juries on trial . New
York , 19. p. cm. ISBN 0-442-00235-1 DDC
729/079 20
NA2750 .A64 1991

Jusepe de Ribera, grabador, 1591-1652 . Ribera,
José de, 1588?-1652. [Valencia] , c1989. 113
p. : ISBN 84-7664-196-6 DDC 769.92 20
NE2062.5.R52 A4 1989
NYPL [MDG (Ribera) 91-3604]

Jussim, Estelle. Pfahl, John, 1939- A distanced
land . [Albuquerque] , 1990. xvi, 204 p. : ISBN
0-8263-1214-4 DDC 779/.36/092 20
TR647 .P494 1990
NYPL [MFX (Pfahl) 91-7438]

Just for nice . Machmer, Richard S. [Reading,

PA] (940 Centre Ave., Reading 19601) , c1991.
88 p. : DDC 730/.09748/107474816 20
NK9710.P4 M33 1991

Justin O'Brien, image and icon /. France,
Christine, 1939- Seaforth, NSW, Australia ,
1987. 125 p. : ISBN 0-947131-04-3 DDC 759.994
19
ND1105.O27 A4 1987
NYPL [3-MCZ+ O129 89-1698]

Jutikkala, Eino Kaarlo Ilmari, 1907-
Scandinavian atlas of historic towns. Odense ,
1977- portfolios : ISBN 87-7492-216-5 (no. 1)
NYPL [Map Div. 82-813]

Jüttner, Werner. Oellers, Adam C. Barthel Gilles,
1891-1977 . Recklinghausen , c1987. 326 p. :
ISBN 3-7647-0387-3
ND588.G46 O45 1987
NYPL [3-MCK G475 91-4613]

JUVENILE CORRECTIONS - ART.
Jugendliche im Gefängnis . Köln , 1987. 95 p. :
ISBN 3-7701-2138-4
NYPL [3-MATC+ 89-25803]

JUVENILE LITERATURE. see CHILDREN'S
LITERATURE.